RECEIVED
20 JUL 2006

Moreton Morrell Site

THE ROYAL HORTICULTURAL SOCIETY

ENCYCLOPEDIA *of* PLANTS AND FLOWERS

Editor-in-chief
CHRISTOPHER BRICKELL

DORLING KINDERSLEY

LONDON, NEW YORK, MUNICH, MELBOURNE, DELHI

FIRST EDITION

Senior Editor Jane Aspden
Editors Liza Bruml, Joanna Chisholm, Roger Smoothy, Jo Weeks
Additional editorial assistance from Jane Birdsell, Lynn Bresler, Jenny Engelmann, Kate Grant, Shona Grimbly, Susanna Longley, Andrew Mikolajski, Diana Miller, Celia Van Oss, Anthony Whitehorn

Senior Art Editor Ina Stradins
Designer Amanda Lunn

FOURTH EDITION 2006

Senior Editor Helen Fewster
Project Editors Jane Simmonds, Monica Byles, Joanna Chisholm, Candida Frith-Macdonald

Senior Art Editor Sue Megginson
Project Art Editor Rachael Smith
Designer Alison Shackelton
DTP Project Manager Louise Waller
Picture Research Lucy Claxton, Richard Dabb, Mel Watson

Managing Editor Anna Kruger
Managing Art Editor Alison Donovan

Photographers Claire Austin, Clive Boursnell, Deni Bown, Jonathan Buckley, Andrew Butler, Eric Crichton, Christine M. Douglas, John Fielding, Neil Fletcher, Nancy Gardiner, John Glover, Jerry Harpur, Sunniva Harte, Neil Holmes, Jacqui Hurst, Andrew Lawson, Andrew de Lory, Martin Page, Howard Rice, Roger Smith, Matthew Ward, Steve Wooster
Illustrators Vanessa Luff, Amanda Lunn, Eric Thomas, Janos Marffy

Advisors and consultants In addition to the contributors listed on the Contents page, Dorling Kindersley would like to thank Barry Ambrose, John Bond, Tony Clements, Steven Davis, Sheila Ecklin, Barbara Ellis, the late Thomas Everett, Jim Gardiner, Ralph Gould, David Kerly, David Pycraft, Piers Trehane, Dr Simon Thornton-Wood, Adrian Whiteley, and the staff of the Royal Horticultural Society at Vincent Square and Wisley Garden.

Copyright © 1989, 1994, 1999, 2006 Dorling Kindersley Limited, London
First edition published in Great Britain in 1989 by Dorling Kindersley Limited,

Reprinted and updated 1990, 2/1990, 3/1990, 4/1990, 1991, 2/1991
Second edition revised and expanded, published in Great Britain in 1994 by Dorling Kindersley Limited. Reprinted 1995, 1996, 1997
Third edition revised and expanded, published in Great Britain in 1999 by Dorling Kindersley Limited

This revised edition published in Great Britain in 2006 by Dorling Kindersley Limited
80 Strand, London WC2R ORL
A Penguin Company

All rights reserved. No part of this book may be reproduced, stored in a retrieval system, or transmitted in any form or by any means, electronic, mechanical, photocopying, recording or otherwise, without the prior permission of the copyright owner.

A CIP catalogue record for this book is available from the British Library

ISBN 13: 978-1-4053-1454-1
ISBN 10: 1-4053-1454-0

Colour reproduction by Colourscan, Singapore
Printed and bound in Germany by Mohndruck GmbH, Gütersloh

Discover more at
www.dk.com

WARWICKSHIRE COLLEGE
LIBRARY
Class No: 635.9
Acc No: 00529819

Preface

It is now 17 years since the first edition of *The Royal Horticultural Society Gardeners' Encyclopedia of Plants & Flowers* was published. During that time the book has sold well over 2,000,000 copies worldwide and has become established as one of the most popular and respected reference guides to garden plants. One of the main reasons for its success is the way the plants are arranged in the photographic section – by plant type, size, season of interest and colour. Another reason lies in the accuracy of its horticultural information.

Last year, with the publishers Dorling Kindersley, we took the decision to produce a fourth revised edition of the book. This has allowed us to make further improvements to the text, such as updating all the plant names, and to add 20 pages of colour photographs of the latest cultivars and hybrids, many of which have received the RHS Award of Garden Merit (AGM) following extensive trials at the RHS Garden, Wisley.

One of the primary aims of this Encyclopedia is to assist gardeners in their choice of plants and so in this revised edition a new section called "Colour in the Garden" accompanies the Plant Selector, which was extended in the last revision. This attractive new feature demonstrates the spectrum of colour possible using key garden plants through the seasons. Used in conjunction with the illustrated Plant Catalogue, both these sections will be an invaluable help to the reader, not only in choosing the right plant for the right place, but also in picking the best colours for the particular times of the year.

All the additions and improvements have been made to ensure that this book, now published in its fourth edition, continues to fulfil the Society's commitment to make the very best of gardening information available to all who seek it – I commend it to you. On behalf of the RHS, I would like to thank the Editor-in-Chief, Christopher Brickell, the other contributors, and the publisher for their continuing support in the publication of this book.

Sir Richard Carew Pole
President, The Royal Horticultural Society
London, December 2005

Contributors

Susyn Andrews	*Hollies*
Larry Barlow (with W.B. Wade)	*Chrysanthemums*
Kenneth A. Beckett (with David Pycraft)	*Shrubs, Climbers, Bromeliads* *The Plant Selector*
John Brookes (with Linden Hawthorne)	*Creating a Garden*
Eric Catterall (with Richard Gilbert)	*Begonias*
Allen J. Coombes	*Plant Origins and Names, Trees, Shrubs, Glossary of Terms*
Philip Damp (with Roger Aylett)	*Dahlias*
Kate Donald	*Peonies, Daffodils*
Kath Dryden	*Rock plants*
Raymond Evison	*Clematis*
Diana Grenfell	*Hostas*
Peter Harkness	*Roses*
Linden Hawthorne	*Chapter introductions in Plant Catalogue*
Terry Hewitt	*Cacti and other Succulents*
David Hitchcock	*Carnations and Pinks*
Hazel Key	*Pelargoniums*
Sidney Linnegar	*Irises*
Brian Mathew	*Irises, Bulbs*
Victoria Matthews	*Climbers, Lilies, Tulips*
David McClintock	*Grasses, Bamboos, Rushes and Sedges*
Diana Miller (with Richard Gilbert)	*Perennials* *African violets*
John Paton	*Perennials*
Charles Puddle	*Camellias*
Wilma Rittershausen (with Sabina Knees)	*Orchids*
Peter Q. Rose (with Hazel Key)	*Ivies*
Keith Rushforth	*Conifers*
A.D. Schilling	*Rhododendrons and Azaleas*
Arthur Smith	*Gladioli*
Philip Swindells (with Peter Barnes) (with Kath Dryden and Jack Wemyss-Cooke) (with Peter Robinson)	 *Ferns* *Primulas* *Water plants and Water lilies*
John Thirkell	*Delphiniums*
Alan Toogood	*Annuals and Biennials*
Major General Patrick Turpin (with David Small)	*Heathers*
Michael Upward	*Perennials*
John Wright (with Nancy Darnley)	*Fuchsias*

Contents

How to Use this Book

The Royal Horticultural Society Encyclopedia of Plants and Flowers is the ideal reference when planning a garden, selecting plants or identifying specimens; it provides a wealth of information on the appearance and cultivation of thousands of individual plants.

The Encyclopedia is divided into several sections. Plant Names and Origins explains the international system for classifying and naming plants, while Colour in the Garden offers advice on how you can make the most of colour in your garden throughout the year. The Plant Selector is designed to help you select suitable species and varieties, while the heart of the book – the Plant Catalogue and the Plant Dictionary – provide detailed photographs, descriptions and cultivation information.

Size categories

Within most groups in the Plant Catalogue, plants are arranged by size (then subsequently by season of interest). Size categories range from large to small, but are defined differently from group to group. Sizes are based on plant heights. The specific height ranges for large, medium, and small can be found in the introductory section for the relevant plant group.

The colour order

Within each group, plants are arranged by the colour of their main feature. Colours are arranged in the same order: from white through reds, purples and blues to greens, yellows and oranges.

Variegated plants are categorized by the colour of their foliage variegation (i.e. white or yellow); succulents are arranged by the colour of their flowers, if produced.

The symbols

- Prefers sun
- Prefers partial shade
- Tolerates full shade
- Prefers well-drained soil
- Prefers moist soil
- Prefers wet soil
- pH Needs acid soil
- Toxic plant
- Award of Garden Merit

- ❄ Half hardy : can withstand temperatures down to 0°C (32°F)
- ❄❄ Frost hardy : can withstand temperatures down to -5°C (23°F)
- ❄❄❄ Fully hardy : can withstand temperatures down to -15°C (5°F)

The Plant Selector

The Plant Selector recommends plants for a particular site, soil or purpose, making it easy to find one to suit your needs. The list is divided into 23 useful categories, ranging from plants for hedges and windbreaks to those suitable for containers. Cross-references to the Plant Catalogue lead you to a photograph and description of the plant you choose.

Photographic reference
Garden themes and uses are illustrated, together with photographs of selected plants.

Top choices
Recommended plants are arranged by group, then listed alphabetically.

The Plant Catalogue

This section brings together plant portraits and descriptions in a colourful catalogue that is divided into groups: Trees (including conifers), Shrubs, Roses, Climbers, Perennials (including grasses, bamboos, rushes, sedges and ferns), Annuals and Biennials, Rock plants, Bulbs, Water plants, and Cacti and other succulents.

Each group is introduced by a short section providing valuable information for growing and designing with plants in the group. This is followed by a catalogue of plants arranged by size, season of interest and colour. Also included are a number of feature panels on plants of special interest, such as camellias, hollies and African violets.

Catalogue page

If you know a plant but cannot recall its name, have a specimen that you want to identify, or simply wish to choose plants for your garden based on their size or colouring, the Plant Catalogue will provide the answer.

Colour boxes
These show the colour range of plants featured on each page. (See also chart, left.)

Page headings
The headings on each page reflect the way in which each plant group is subdivided – usually by size and main season of interest. (See also Size categories, left.)

Plant portraits
Colour photographs assist in the identification and selection of plants.

Plant names
The botanical name is given for each plant, and where appropriate, their common names are also listed (in brackets).

Captions
Captions describe the plants in detail and draw attention to any special uses they may have.

Size and shape
For most plants the approximate height (H) and spread (S) are given at the end of each caption. (The 'height' of a trailing plant is the length of its stems, either hanging or spreading.) For Trees, Conifers and Shrubs a scale drawing shows the size and shape of each plant at maturity.

Award of Garden Merit
This symbol indicates that the plant has received the RHS Award of Garden Merit.

Cultivation and hardiness
Symbols show the plant's preferred growing conditions and hardiness. For frost tender plants the minimum temperature required for its cultivation is stated. However, the climatic and soil conditions of your particular site should also be taken into account as they may affect a plant's growth. (See also key, left.)

Cotoneaster simonsii
Deciduous or semi-evergreen, upright shrub, suitable for hedging. Has oval, glossy, dark green leaves, shallowly cup-shaped, white flowers in early summer and long-lasting, orange-red fruits in autumn.

Toxic plants
This symbol indicates that the plant can be toxic. Details are given in the genus introductions in the Plant Dictionary.

Group opener

Each new group begins with a stunning close-up photograph featuring one of the plants in the group.

Design advice

Group openers are followed by more detailed descriptions of the characteristics of plants in the group, together with ideas for how to use these plants to best effect in the garden.

Tabs

Colour-coded tabs make it easy to find each plant group.

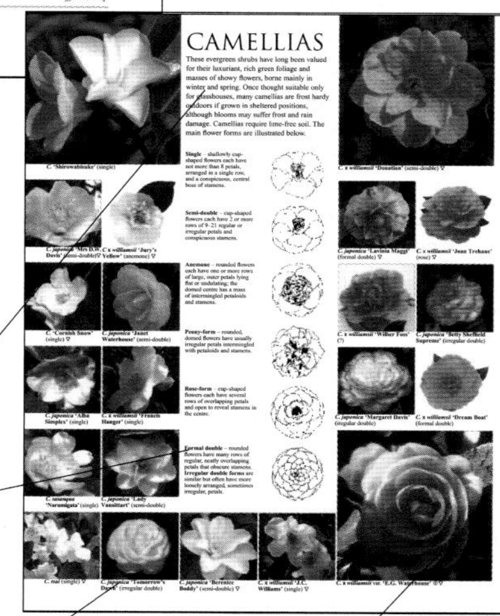

Feature panels

Plant types or genera of special interest to the gardener are presented in separate feature panels within the appropriate group.

Key characteristics
The introduction outlines the features of that type of plant and gives guidance on cultivation and planting.

Flower forms
Detailed descriptions of forms and horticultural classifications within a genus are given where appropriate and often supported by line drawings.

Plant names
The botanical name is given and the Group or classification where appropriate. Plant descriptions appear in the Plant Dictionary.

Plant portraits
Close-up photographs of individual flowers or plants allow quick identification or selection.

The Plant Dictionary

The Plant Dictionary contains entries for every genus in the Encyclopedia and includes over 4,000 recommended plants not featured in the Plant Catalogue. It also functions as the index to the Plant Catalogue.

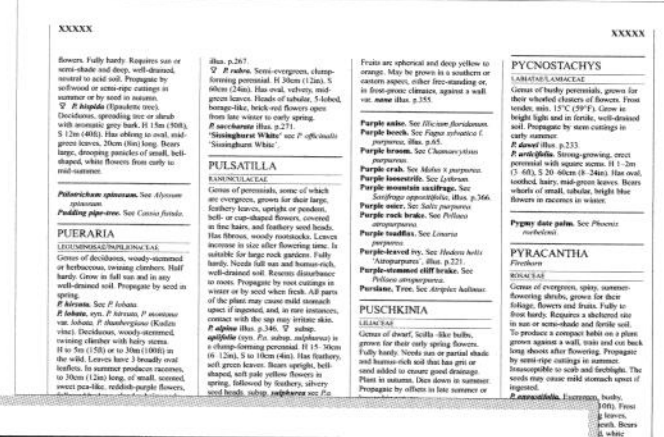

Genus names
The genus name is followed by common names, where appropriate, and family names.

Genus entries
A concise introduction covers the distinctive characteristics and hardiness range of plants in the genus, as well as advice on siting, cultivation, propagation, and, if relevant, pruning, pests and diseases, and toxicity.

Synonyms
Synonyms cross-refer to the correct botanical name.

Illustrated plants
Descriptions for illustrated plants appear in the Plant Catalogue, unless part of a feature panel (see below left).

Plant names
Botanical names, synonyms and common names are given as appropriate. The genus name is abbreviated; specific epithets (e.g. *sagittifolia*) are abbreviated only if previously given in full.

Plant descriptions
Key characteristics of the plant are described. Hardiness and cultivation needs are included only if specific to the plant. Cultivar entries run on from the species entry, with the binomial omitted.

SAGITTARIA
Arrowhead
ALISMATACEAE

Genus of deciduous, perennial, submerged and marginal water plants, grown for their foliage and flowers. Fully hardy to frost tender, min. 5°C (41°F). Some species are suitable for pools, others for aquariums. All require full sun. Remove fading foliage as necessary. Propagate by division in spring or summer or by breaking off turions (scaly, young shoots) in spring.

S. japonica. See *S. sagittifolia* 'Flore Pleno'.
S. latifolia illus. p.446.
S. sagittifolia (Common arrowhead). Deciduous, perennial, marginal water plant. H 45cm (18in), S 30cm (12in). Fully hardy. Upright, mid-green leaves are acutely arrow-shaped. In summer produces 3-petalled, white flowers with dark purple centres. May be grown in up to 23cm (9in) depth of water. **'Flore Pleno'** (syn. *S. japonica*; Japanese arrowhead) has double flowers.

Saguaro. See *Carnegiea gigantea*, illus. p.456.
St Augustine grass. See *Stenotaphrum secundatum*.

Cross-references
Common name and synonym cross-references are listed alphabetically.

Abbreviations

cv(s)	cultivar(s)	illus.	illustrated	subsp.	subspecies
f.	forma	min.	minimum	subspp.	subspecies (pl.)
H	height (or length of trailing stems)	p(p).	page(s)	syn.	synonym(s)
		pl.	plural	var.	varietas
		S	spread		

The RHS Award of Garden Merit

The Royal Horticultural Society's Award of Garden Merit (AGM) recognizes plants of outstanding excellence for garden decoration or use, whether grown in the open or under glass. Besides being the highest accolade the Society can give to a plant, the AGM is of practical value for ordinary gardeners, helping them in making a choice from the many thousands of plants currently available. The AGM means that plants satisfy the following criteria:

- Excellent for garden use
- Not particularly susceptible to pests and diseases
- Do not require specialist care other than the provision of suitable growing conditions

Plant Names and Origins

People have always given names to plants, but once they began to travel extensively they discovered that the same plant was often called by a different name in various parts of the world. To overcome this problem, a common naming system was devised.

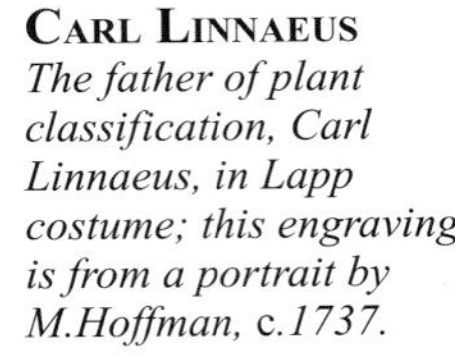

Carl Linnaeus
The father of plant classification, Carl Linnaeus, in Lapp costume; this engraving is from a portrait by M.Hoffman, c.*1737.*

The binomial system

Greek and Roman scholars laid the foundations of our method of naming plants, and their practice of observing and describing nature in detail was continued in the monasteries and universities of Europe, where classical Latin remained the common language. However, the binomial system in use today was established largely under the influence of the famous eighteenth-century Swedish botanist, Carl Linnaeus (1707–78). In his definitive works *Genera plantarum* and *Species plantarum*, Linnaeus classified each plant by using two words in Latin form, instead of adopting the descriptive phrases that had been in common usage among the botanists and herbalists of his day. The first word was the name of the genus (e.g. *Ilex*) and the second the specific epithet (e.g. *aquifolium*). Together they provided a name by which a particular plant (species) could be universally known (*Ilex aquifolium*, English or common holly). Other species in the same genus were then given different epithets (*Ilex crenata*, *Ilex pernyi*, *Ilex serrata* and so on).

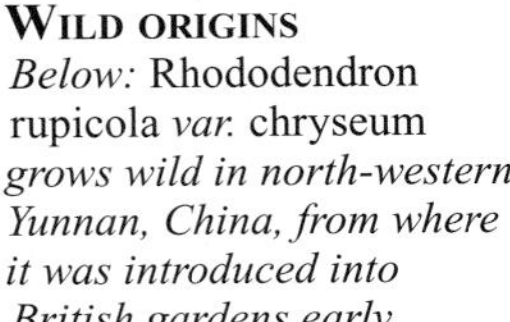

Wild origins
Below: Rhododendron rupicola *var.* chryseum *grows wild in north-western Yunnan, China, from where it was introduced into British gardens early in the nineteenth century.*

The meaning of plant names

A greater appreciation of botanical names may be gained by knowing something of their meaning. A name may be commemorative: the *Fuchsia* is a tribute to Leonhart Fuchs, a German physician and herbalist. It may tell us where a plant comes from, as with *Parrotia persica* (of Persia, now Iran). A plant may bear the name of the collector who introduced it: *Primula forrestii* was brought into cultivation by George Forrest. Or the name may tell us something about its physical character: *Pelargonium* derives from the Greek word *pelargos* (a stork), an appropriate description of the fruits of these plants, which resemble storks' bills; *quinquefolia*, the epithet of *Parthenocissus quinquefolia*, means with foliage made up of five leaflets, from the Latin *quinque* ('five') and *folium* ('leaf').

Common names

Although many have familiar common names, plants are usually listed under their botanical names. There are a number of reasons for this. Many plants either do not possess a common name, or they share a common name with others. Even more confusingly, the same common name may be used in different regions to describe different plants: in Scotland 'plane' refers to *Acer pseudoplatanus* (sycamore), in England to the London plane (*Platanus* × *hispanica*), while in North America the native plane (*Platanus occidentalis*) may be called plane or sycamore. Unlike botanical names, which bring related plants together by grouping them in a genus (all true hollies belong to the genus *Ilex*), with common names the same word is often used for quite unrelated plants, such as sea holly (*Eryngium*), hollyhock (*Alcea*) and summer holly (*Arctostaphylos diversifolia*), none of which is related to the true holly. Conversely, one plant may have several common names: heartsease, love-in-idleness and Johnny-jump-up are all charming titles for *Viola tricolor*.

Even greater confusion arises when a vernacular common name is in Malay, Chinese or Arabic. In botany, as in other scientific disciplines, the universal use of Latin has therefore been found to be a convenient and precise basis for the naming of plants.

International codes

Since its instigation the Linnaean system of plant classification has been developed by scientists so that the entire plant kingdom is divided into a multi-branched 'family tree' (see p.13). International co-operation has been essential to ensure that the system is reliable for scientific, commercial and horticultural use. To this end, there are now rules laid down in the *International Code of Nomenclature for Cultivated Plants* (1995) and the *International Code of Botanical Nomenclature* (1994).

Plant introductions

Just as the origins of plant names may be traced to Classical civilization, so can the first plant introductions. The Roman Empire at its peak covered a vast area, from western Europe to Asia, and as the Romans travelled they brought with them plants they used for food or ornament, such as the Spanish chestnut, peach, fig and many herbs. During the thirteenth century, returning Crusaders brought the Damask rose from Damascus. Centuries later, cultivated plants such as Persian lilac and the apricot were brought home from the sophisticated Turkish and Moorish gardens along the shores of the Mediterranean.

Plant hunting became more systematic when intrepid private collectors such as the two John Tradescants (father and son) made trips specifically to look for plants on the eastern coasts of North America, particularly Virginia. As the world was mapped and colonized in the eighteenth century, an explosion of botanical interest brought many plants from the New World, notably the western coasts of the American continent, South Africa, Australia, and New Zealand. In the twentieth century, the greatest rewards for the determined plant collector were to be found in the diverse flora of eastern Asia. Although not an easy region for Westerners to explore, thousands of plants, particularly trees and shrubs, were introduced from China, the Himalayan region and Japan.

Genetics and hybridization

Natural mutations in plants have been observed for centuries but only in the twentieth century has plant breeding developed into a science used throughout the world. Although Thomas Knight carried out some pioneering plant-breeding experiments in the nineteenth century, and the word 'hybrid' was used by Darwin, it was not until Gregor Mendel's work with sweet peas in 1899 that the process was understood and could therefore be exploited commercially.

Once the mysteries of recessive genes and chromosomes were revealed, it became clear that plants could be bred to be more vigorous and produce more flowers, as well as be altered in other ways. Today, breeders can produce hybrids of a certain shape, colour and habit. One result of this is that certain successful plant 'cultivars' (**culti**vated **var**ieties) have to be protected (see Coded cultivar names, p.12).

Understanding botanical divisions

The plant kingdom may be broadly divided into vascular plants and non-vascular plants. Vascular plants are of most interest to the gardener and have specialized conducting tissue that enables them to grow in a wider range of habitats and reach a larger size than the non-vascular plants such as algae, mosses

Plant Hunters

A desire to see the world was the original incentive for the earliest botanists but, as interest in new and rare plants developed, private collectors began to bring back plants with them. These exotic novelties proved extremely popular, especially in fashionable gardens, and fuelled the demand for further new plants for garden adornment. To encourage this new market, commercial and scientific organizations began to sponsor the plant hunters. David Douglas was employed in 1824 by the Royal Horticultural Society to travel to America's west coast, where he gathered vast quantities of seed from hitherto unknown species including the Douglas fir. Access to China was restricted until 1842, but in the following year Robert Fortune began an expedition, again sponsored by the Royal Horticultural Society, that was to yield many ornamental garden plants. In his wake went French botanist-missionaries Father Jean Pierre Armand David, who discovered the lovely *Davidia* tree and after whom *Buddleja davidii* is named, and Father Jean Marie Delavay, who found the blue poppy (*Meconopsis betonicifolia*). Japan was also the source of hundreds of garden plants – many being introduced to Europe by the German plant hunter Philipp von Siebold in the nineteenth century.

The golden age of plant hunting was the early twentieth century. E.H. Wilson, one of the most famous plant hunters (see above right), discovered *Magnolia wilsonii* in 1904 and, in the same period, George Forrest introduced many rhododendrons and other plants from China and Tibet. In the 1920s and 1930s, Frank Kingdon Ward collected unusual primulas, rhododendrons, lilies and gentians from the Himalayas.

Today, plant-hunting expeditions are still sponsored and new plants introduced, although in smaller quantities than before. However, the impetus for plant discovery has shifted from garden adornment and novelty to plant conservation and breeding.

Magnolia wilsonii

Ernest Henry Wilson
Above: E.H. Wilson, who collected in Asia for the English nursery Messrs Veitch and for the Arnold Arboretum, in Boston, USA, discovered more than 900 new plants species and varieties, including Magnolia Wilsonii.

Cotoneaster lancasteri

Recent finds
Roy Lancaster (above) is a modern-day plant hunter who has introduced many new species to Britain. Among them are Hypericum lancasteri *and* Cotoneaster lancasteri *(left), both from China.*

Gentiana sino-ornata
George Forrest had a special interest in gentians, collecting hundreds of specimens during his trips to China. He first discovered this plant in 1904, during a hazardous expedition high in the mountain ranges of north-western Yunnan.

Rose hybrids
To create a new hybrid that inherits the best features of both parents, roses are pollinated manually.

and liverworts. Vascular plants are classified into many groups, mainly according to the way they bear their seeds. For example conifers, part of the Gymnosperm group, are distinct because they bear their naked seeds in cone-like fruits. The basic division within these groups is the family.

The family

Plants are grouped in particular families according to the structure of their flowers, fruits and other organs. This means that families may consist of clearly related and specialized plants such as the orchids (family Orchidaceae) and the bromeliads (family Bromeliaceae), or embrace plants as diverse (in terms of what they offer the gardener) as those in the family Rosaceae: *Alchemilla*, *Cotoneaster*, *Crataegus*, *Geum*, *Malus*, *Prunus*, *Pyracantha*, *Sorbus* and *Spiraea*.

The genus and its species

A family may contain one genus (for example, *Eucryphia* is the only genus in the family Eucryphiaceae) or many (the daisy family Compositae has over 1,000 genera). Each genus comprises related plants, such as oaks (genus *Quercus*), maples (genus *Acer*) and lilies (genus *Lilium*), with several features in common. A genus may contain one or many species. Thus a reference to a member of the genus *Lilium* could be to any of the lilies, but one to *Lilium candidum* would denote one particular lily (in this case the Madonna lily). Certain genera form separate horticultural groups within families. An example of this would be the heaths or heathers (including *Calluna*, *Daboecia* and *Erica*) within the family Ericaceae, which also includes *Kalmia*, *Rhododendron* and *Vaccinium* (see visual key, opposite).

A species is a group of plants that consistently and naturally reproduces itself, generating a plant population that shares similar characteristics and which is distinguishable from other natural populations.

Subspecies, varieties and forms

In the wild, even plants of the same species can exhibit slight differences, and on the basis of these are often split into three botanically recognized but occasionally overlapping subdivisions. The subspecies (subsp.) is a distinct variant, usually as a result of the plant's particular geographical distribution; the variety (botanical *varietas*, abbreviated to 'var.') differs slightly in its botanical structure; and the form (*forma*, f.) has only minor variations, such as habit or colour of leaf, flower or fruit.

Cultivars

Many plants grown in today's gardens may be adequately described by their botanical names, but numerous variants exist in cultivation which differ slightly from the wild form of the species. These forms may be of considerable horticultural interest, for their variegated leaves or other characters. They may be found as individuals in the wild and introduced to cultivation, be selected from a batch of seedlings, or occur as a mutation; all are known as cultivars – a contraction of 'cultivated varieties'. To come true to type, many cultivars need to be propagated vegetatively (cuttings, grafting or division) or grown annually from specially selected seed.

Cultivars named since 1959 must be given vernacular names, which are printed in Roman type within quotes (e.g. *Phygelius aequalis* 'Yellow Trumpet'); this distinguishes them from wild varieties, which are described by a Latin name in italic type.

Hybrids

Sexual crosses between botanically distinct species or genera are known as hybrids and are indicated by a multiplication sign. If the cross is between species in different genera, the result is called an intergeneric hybrid and, when two (occasionally three or more) genera are concerned, the name given is a condensed form of the names of the genera involved: × *Cupressocyparis* covers hybrids between all species of *Chamaecyparis* and *Cupressus*. If more than three genera are involved, then the hybrids are called after a person and given the ending -ara. Thus × *Potinara*, covering hybrids of *Brassavola*, *Cattleya*, *Laelia* and *Sophronitis*, commemorates M. Potin of the French orchid society. Most common, however, are hybrids between species in the same genus. These are known as interspecific hybrids and are given a collective name similar to a species name but preceded by a multiplication sign; for example *Epimedium* × *rubrum* covers hybrids between *E. alpinum* and *E. grandiflorum*.

When one plant is grafted onto another, a new plant may occasionally arise at the point of grafting, which contains the tissues of both parents. For naming purposes, these graft chimaeras or graft hybrids are treated in the same way as sexual hybrids, except that they are denoted by a plus sign, as in +*Laburnocytisus adamii*, which is a graft hybrid between species of *Laburnum* and *Chamaecytisus*.

Cultivars of hybrids should be listed under a botanical name if one is available or, if the parentage is complex or obscure, by giving the generic name followed solely by the cultivar name (e.g. *Rosa* 'Buff Beauty').

Name changes

It is often confusing and frustrating to come across name changes in new publications. Long-established names disappear, only to be replaced by unfamiliar ones. But there are good reasons for such changes: a plant may originally have been incorrectly identified; the same plant may already have been given a different, earlier name; a name may be found to apply to two different plants; or new scientific knowledge may cause a plant's classification to be changed. In this Encyclopedia, numerous synonyms have been given in order to minimize the problems of identifying or purchasing renamed plants.

Davidia involucrata
This lovely tree from China is named after its discoverer Father Jean Pierre Armand David. It has several common names including Dove tree, Ghost tree and Pocket handkerchief tree.

Coded cultivar names

When plant breeders raise a new cultivar, it is given a code name to ensure its formal identification; this may be different to the name under which the plant is sold. For example, the rose selling under the name Casino also has the code name 'Macca'; in this book, both names are cited, and styled thus: *Rosa* Casino ('Macca'). To safeguard their ownership of the cultivar, plant breeders may apply for Plant Breeder's Rights (PBR), which are granted using the code name.

Visual Key to Plant Classification

In horticulture, as in other areas of botany, plants are classified according to a hierarchical system (taxonomy) and named primarily on the basis of Linnaeus's binomial approach (genus followed by species epithet).

For a better understanding of this system, part of the family Ericaceae has been set out below, showing all levels from family through genera and species down to cultivars, Groups and hybrids.

FAMILY
A group of several genera that share a set of underlying natural characteristics. Family names usually end in -aceae. Family limits are often controversial.

Ericaceae

GENUS (PL. GENERA)
A group of one or more plants that share a range of distinctive characteristics. Several (rarely one) genera are classified into one family. Each genus contains one or more species and its name is printed in italic type with an initial capital letter.

Daboecia

Calluna

Erica

Vaccinium

Kalmia

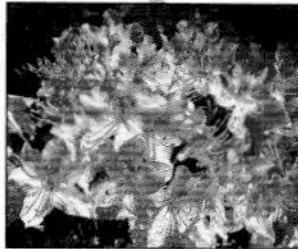
Rhododendron

SPECIES
A group of plants that breeds naturally to produce offspring with similar characteristics; these keep it distinct from other populations in nature. Each species has a two-part name printed in italic type.

Daboecia cantabrica

Daboecia azorica

Erica arborea

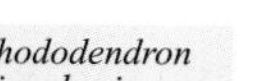
Rhododendron cinnabarinum

Rhododendron yakushimanum

HYBRID
Sexual crosses between species within a genus give rise to interspecific hybrids (see also box below).

Daboecia × *scotica*

FORMA
A minor variant of a species, often differing in flower colour or habit from others in the species. Indicated by 'f.' *in Roman type and an epithet printed in italic type.*

Daboecia cantabrica f. *alba*

VARIETAS
A minor species subdivision, differing slightly in botanical structure. Indicated by 'var.' *(short for varietas) in Roman type and an epithet in italic type.*

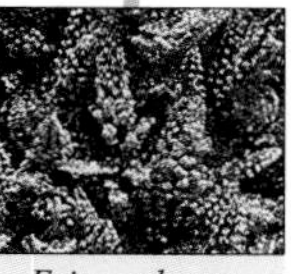
Erica arborea var. *alpina*

SUBSPECIES
A naturally occurring, distinct variant of a species, differing in one or more characteristic. Indicated by 'subsp.' *in Roman type and an epithet in italic type.*

Rhododendron cinnabarinum subsp. *xanthocodon*

GROUP (CULTIVAR GROUP)
An assemblage of cultivars with similar characteristics within a genus, species or hybrid. They may be designated with a name in a modern language or in some cases be in Latin form.

Rhododendron cinnabarinum Concatenans Group

Rhododendron cinnabarinum Purpurellum Group

CULTIVAR
Selected or artificially raised, distinct variant of a species, subspecies, varietas, forma or hybrid. Indicated by a vernacular name printed in Roman type within single quotation marks.

Daboecia cantabrica 'Alba Globosa'

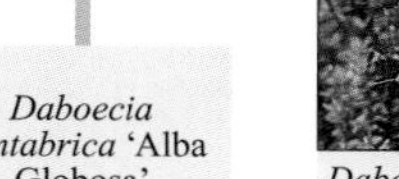

Daboecia × *scotica* 'William Buchanan'

Daboecia × *scotica* 'Jack Drake'

Daboecia × *scotica* 'Silverwells'

Rhododendron cinnabarinum 'Copper'

Rhododendron cinnabarinum 'Amber'

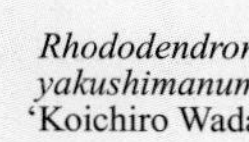
Rhododendron yakushimanum 'Koichiro Wada'

Rhododendron 'Ken Janeck'

HYBRIDS

A graft hybrid is a non-sexual plant created through the merging of plant tissue at the point of graft between a rootstock and its scion. For example, when *Laburnum* and *Chamaecytisus* species are combined they form +*Laburnocytisus adamii*.

Laburnum anagyroides + *Chamaecytisus purpureus* = +*Laburnocytisus adamii*

A more common type of hybrid is a sexual cross between botanically distinct species or genera. If the resulting hybrids are fertile, several generations of plants may be produced, all sharing characters of both parents. Here two species of viburnum have cross-fertilized to create *Viburnum* × *bodnantense*.

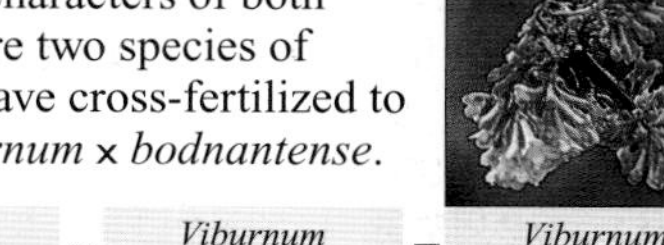
Viburnum farreri × *Viburnum grandiflorum* = *Viburnum* × *bodnantense*

Colour in the Garden

Colour through the Seasons

The most successful gardens are those that provide interest throughout the year. Since no individual plant is at its peak for all twelve months, its impact in a group planting will alter as the year progresses. For example, a tree that is spectacular in spring when covered in blossom may fade into the background during the rest of the year. The appearance of the planting as a whole will therefore change with the seasons. However, there are no set times at which seasons begin or end; that depends on the climate and the region you live in, as well as the particular site and situation of your garden. In mild years, flower buds can open up to two weeks earlier than in other years, while severe droughts or early frosts can mean an untimely end to summer blooms.

When selecting plants, remember to take into account seasonal variations in their appearance, so you can try to ensure that each grouping sustains year-round interest. A planting of summer-flowering perennials alone may look dull in spring, autumn and winter. Consider all the merits of each plant – its size, habit, leaf form, colour, bark and texture – not merely the flower colour. These are the long-term qualities of a plant, which will be on display long after its main season of interest has passed.

Ideally, try to provide a succession of "feature" plants against a relatively unchanging background of shrubs and trees. In this way, when the eye-catching flowers of one plant in the bed are over, another will have begun to blossom. Alternatively, you might wish to plan this seasonal succession in the garden as a whole, rather than just one border. In this way, the focal point will move around the garden and highlight different areas. Consider, also, planting up a few containers to add add interest to existing planting schemes.

Spring

With the arrival of spring, the garden is soon awash with colour. Some is provided by spring-flowering trees and shrubs, such as flowering cherries and magnolias, and by myriad rock plants, but most of the colour comes from an abundance of flowering bulbs and corms, including snowdrops, crocuses and daffodils . As these die down, they are followed by camellias, forsythias, azaleas and rhododendrons and the fresh green of young leaves,

Late spring
Fresh green foliage and the lovely reddish-purple leaves of the berberis are a fitting backdrop for the dramatic heads of the purple allium in this late spring border in shades of lilac and pink.

Late summer
In this glorious perennial planting, swathes of repeated colour draw the eye, with grasses and sword-shaped leaves adding structure. The cool blues of eryngium and agapanthus contrast beautifully with hot orange crocosmias.

with scented viburnum and lilac flowers appearing in succession through late spring.

Summer to autumn

In early summer, more colour is added by a profusion of perennials and biennials, often lasting until autumn. Shrub interest diminishes as the season progresses, which is when the annuals make their contribution, brightening up the heavy green face of summer. Annual flowers, although often extremely bright, last for only short periods, so it is necessary to sow seeds and transplant seedlings successively to maintain the display. Self-seeding annuals will emerge year after year in a random way, often providing short explosions of colour in unexpected places. The wealth of interesting plants that bloom in late summer, including clematis, repeat-flowering roses, as well as annuals and herbaceous perennials, creates a pitfall of its own: be selective otherwise the effect might be overwhelming.

As summer fades, the greenery starts to flare into the fiery colours of autumn, the intensity of the colours and their duration depending on the weather. In your planting include trees or shrubs with spectacular autumn leaves, such as acers; they can make the garden as handsome in this season as in any other. Late-flowering perennials, such as Michaelmas daisies and chrysanthemums, brighten up the garden until the arrival of the first frosts and, when the browned leaves fall, return us to the winter landscape.

Winter

During winter, flower interest in the garden is likely to be minimal, and it is then that the bold shapes and foliage colour provided by evergreens, such as conifers, holly and ivy, come into their own. Less obviously, the colours and textures of twigs, branches, bark and berries of deciduous trees and shrubs also have roles to play in providing visual interest. The branches of the elegant willow, for instance, can look quite brilliant in winter sunlight; silver birches are especially attractive, graceful, open trees with lovely, white bark that glistens on even the greyest day. The shapes of deciduous as well as evergreen plants play an important part at this time, whether silhouetted against a clear, winter sky or bearing a cloak of snow.

Autumn
As the days shorten, the glowing yellow berries of Sorbus *'Joseph Rock' and the wonderful golds of perennial grasses introduce brightness, while late-flowering helenium and deep-purple aconitum inject colour.*

Winter
Low winter sun lights up the skeletons of deciduous trees and catches the tops of the lush green spikes of the dwarf pine, Pinus mugo. *At the foot of the conifers, carpets of magenta* Erica carnea *add vibrant colour.*

Combining Colour

Everyone interprets the moods that colours create in different ways, and many people change their minds according to the weather, the time of day or their emotional state. Individuals with perfectly normal colour vision perceive colours differently, and colour blindness is a surprisingly common phenomenon.

Colour choice is first and foremost about personal preferences. Although there are some fundamental design rules on how to use colour, including the avoidance of such obvious clashes as hot orange with delicate pink, they really constitute only a broad guide for the use of flat planes of basic colour. Often they have little to do with the realities of a garden – the textures of living plants, the changing light, the varying hues of a colour range, the season of the year and the location.

The intricacies of colour perception

The key to perceiving colour is light. Soft colours look wonderful in the early morning, in the evening and in dull or damp weather. In the Mediterranean sunshine, these colours would look blanched, and strong colours, which may be overpowering in a soft light, come into their own. Happily nature has ensured that plants with strong-coloured flowers are usually native to sunny regions.

The damp light of a temperate climate is quite unlike humid, tropical light or clear, desert light; sharp, winter light is quite distinct from the hazy light of a summer noon, and both differ from misty, autumnal and dusky, evening lights. All have different effects on colours, altering our perception of them and transforming the mood of the garden. If you are only going to be using your garden at one time of day, for example the evening, bear this in mind when choosing your plants: white flowers can take on a luminous quality in fading light but dark blue ones will be invisible.

Apart from climatic conditions, other factors determine how we notice colour. The sea, for example, can alter colour perception, reflecting light for some distance inland. A background building or fence will also influence colour tones by reflecting or absorbing light: whether shiny or matt, made of glass, stone, brick or timber, it will influence our view of the colours of plants grown in front of it. Colours themselves affect each other too. The many shades of green modify any colours placed in front of them, as do the mousy-brown colours of a wintry landscape. The individual colour masses in a group influence each other, as well as affecting the whole planting. A largely white planting with a touch of purple will create one mood; but what about the reverse – a largely purple planting with a touch of white? The mood of one will be bright and sharp, the other sombre and tranquil.

Pastels
Soft colours harmonize in this delicate planting with Geranium *'Johnson's Blue' in the foreground, enhanced by white* Rosa *'Iceberg' and red valerian.*

Considering the character of the site

In the days before the introduction of foreign species and mass hybridization, there was an indigenous range of colours in every area. To help design a harmonious garden you might keep to this spirit of planting by analyzing the location of the garden; the particular flavour of a place is dictated by its climate and the shapes and colours of its natural plant forms.

The background colour may be a dark, coniferous green with the grey of granite or it may be deciduous green with mellower sandstone or limestone. In chalky areas, indigenous vegetation might include a proportion of grey foliage with the darker greens of yew or box. Although there are some bright-coloured flowers in the temperate zones, the really brilliantly coloured flowers originate in hotter climates, where the intensity of the sun accentuates them. Thus the nearer the equator you go, the brighter the indigenous flowers.

Seasonal colour associations

As well as geographical factors, there is a natural progression of dominant colours through the seasons. Pale spring colours transmute into the blues of early summer; hotter pinks of mid-summer are transformed into yellows and bronzes in autumn, before turning into the browns of winter. When choosing plants for individual plant groups it is wise to avoid certain colours against these seasonal backdrops, in case they introduce a jarring note. For example, refrain from setting soft pink against spring green, using purple in the middle of summer or planting bright blue in autumn.

Even within the walls of a town garden with a backdrop of bricks and mortar, the seasons will still influence your colour choices. In temperate zones, for a natural look, try whites and pale lemon in spring; pinks, blues and greys in mid-summer; in late summer a little red but mainly yellows; and in autumn some bronze and purple.

Colour preferences

There remain, of course, more personal preferences for certain colour combinations. Strong colours are stimulating and work well in bright light and brilliant sunshine and also in a modern setting. Softer colours, such as shades of grey, soft pastel blues and pinks, are more restful. Plants in muted shades can be combined to produce subtle effects or you can introduce patches of vivid colour to draw the eye and create impact.

Making your personal mark

Your individual style and feelings about the moods that different colours create will be the final factors affecting the colours in your garden, just as they are in the decoration of your home. If the garden is small, the result of linking the colours with those in the room adjacent to it will have a dramatic effect on both room and garden. Where room and garden meet, avoid startling clashes such as pink roses against orange-red brick or curtains. Conversely, where the garden is larger, gradually change the colours in it so that, although those of the flowers nearest the house still link with the interior, those at the bottom of the garden work with the backdrop of the fence, hedge or countryside beyond.

Colour may be used to enhance perspective, too: hotter ranges of colour (reds, oranges and pinks) look better closer to the house, while cool colours (blues and whites) introduced at a distance from it will increase the sense of space.

Exotic touch
The luxuriant pink-tinged leaves of Canna *'Durban' act as a focal point and are beautifully set off by the underplanting of orange* Lantana.

Shades of green
The bright yellow of Bowles' golden sedge (Carex elata 'Aurea') *complements the two hostas perfectly, in shape, form and colour.*

SPRING

Tulipa 'Red Riding Hood' p.427

Photinia* × *fraseri 'Birmingham' p.113

Camellia japonica 'Mathotiana' p.125

Chaenomeles* × *superba 'Nicoline' p.152

SUMMER

Pelargonium Multibloom Series p.340

Dianthus 'Nina' p.291

Ismelia carinata 'Monarch Court Jesters' p.341

Rosa ALEC'S RED ('Cored') p.188

AUTUMN

Parthenocissus tricuspidata p.216

Cotoneaster horizontalis p.168

Crocosmia 'Bressingham Blaze' p.413

Euonymus hamiltonianus subsp. ***sieboldianus*** 'Red Elf' p.143

WINTER/ALL YEAR

Hippeastrum aulicum p.441

Sempervivum tectorum p.401

Hamamelis* × *intermedia 'Diane' p.121

Cornus alba 'Sibirica' p.146

SPRING

Cytisus* × *praecox 'Allgold' p.153

Forsythia* × *intermedia 'Spectabilis' p.131

Narcissus 'Pipit' p.434

SUMMER

Coreopsis lanceolata p.305

Rosa **GRAHAM THOMAS** ('Ausmas') p.185

Lysimachia punctata p.261

AUTUMN

Sorbus 'Joseph Rock' p.78

Rudbeckia 'Herbstonne' p.232

Helianthus* × *multiflorus 'Loddon Gold' p.232

Aster 'Linosyris' p.270

WINTER/ALL YEAR

Mahonia* × *media 'Charity' p.121

Corylus avellana 'Contorta' p.121

Acacia baileyana p.93

Eranthis hyemalis p.457

SPRING

Fritillaria imperialis p.408

Erysimum* × *allionii 'Orange Bedder' p.352

Clivia miniata p.435

SUMMER

Calceolaria 'Walter Shrimpton' p.398

Crocosmia 'Star of the East' p.415

Alstroemeria aurea p.415

AUTUMN

Dahlia 'Hamari Gold' p.422

Pyracantha 'Golden Charmer' p.145

Kniphofia rooperi p.271

Helenium 'Moerheim Beauty' p.271

WINTER/ALL YEAR

Hakonechloa macra 'Aureola' p.321

Viola × wittrockiana Universal Series p.351

Codiaeum variegatum var. ***pictum*** p.173

SPRING

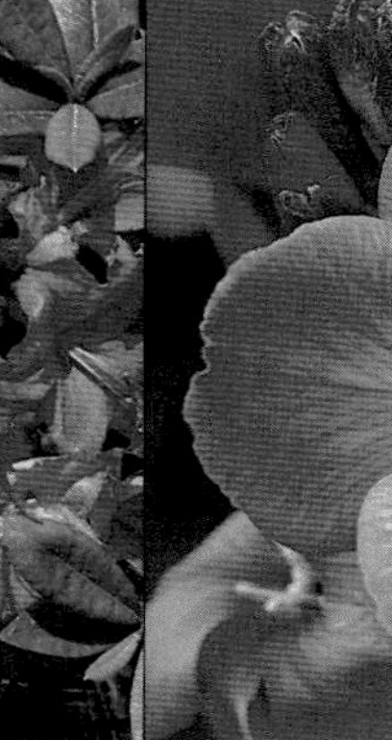

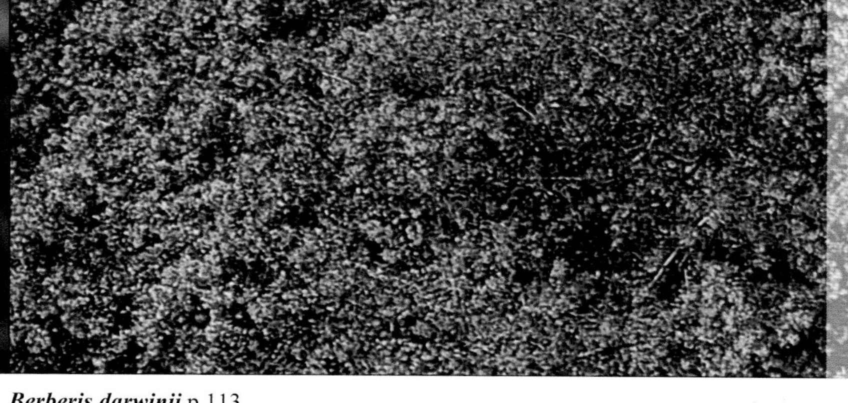

Rhododendron 'Gloria Mundi' p.130

Erysimum cheiri 'Fire King' p.353

Berberis darwinii p.113

SUMMER

Thunbergia alata p.214

Dahlia 'Dandy' p.353

Hemerocallis fulva 'Flore Pleno' p.265

AUTUMN

Nerine sarniensis p.440

Acer palmatum 'Sango-kaku' p.120

Calendula officinalis 'Fiesta Gitana' p.351

WINTER/ALL YEAR

Canarina canariensis p.217

Leonotis leonurus p.145

Nertera granadensis p.399

Calluna vulgaris 'Boskoop' p.175

SPRING

Aquilegia alpina p.360

Anemone blanda 'Atrocaerulea' p.449

Sollya heterophylla p.202

Hepatica nobilis var. ***japonica*** p.381

SUMMER

Allium caeruleum p.438

Veronica austriaca subsp. ***teucrium*** p.370

Ipomoea tricolor 'Heavenly Blue' p.213

Nigella damascena Persian Jewels Series p.345

AUTUMN

Gentiana sino-ornata p.399

Tweedia caerulea p.213

Ceanothus 'Autumnal Blue' p.144

Hebe 'Autumn Glory' p.163

WINTER/ALL YEAR

Viola × wittrockiana 'True Blue' p.345

Abies concolor 'Argentea' p.97

Pycnostachys dawei p.233

Lachenalia orchioides var. ***glaucina*** p.441

Myosotis alpestris p.382

Muscari latifolium p.429

Cardamine pentaphyllos p.278

Eryngium bourgatii p.296

Phlox divaricata subsp. ***laphamii*** p.368

Heliotropium arborescens p.163

Clematis 'Jackmanii' p.211

Campanula lactiflora 'Pritchard's Variety' p.226

Crocus speciosus 'Oxonian' p.445

Aster 'Professor Anton Kippenburg' p.270

Petrea volubilis p.202

Browallia speciosa p.274

Phormium 'Bronze Baby' p.314

Iris unguicularis subsp. ***cretenis*** p.236

CHOOSING COLOUR THROUGH THE SEASONS

SPRING

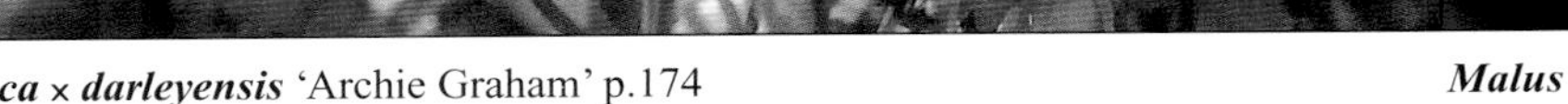

Erica* × *darleyensis 'Archie Graham' p.174

Malus 'Royalty' p.85

Magnolia 'Ricki' p.71

SUMMER

Syringa vulgaris 'Président Grévy' p.116

Passiflora caerulea p.212

Bougainvillea glabra 'Variegata' p.207

Fuchsia 'Leonora' p.160

AUTUMN

Eupatorium purpureum p.231

Billardiera longiflora p.216

Sedum spectabile 'Brilliant' p.306

Colchicum 'Waterlily' p.455

WINTER/ALL YEAR

Begonia 'Merry Christmas' p.307

Tradescantia pallida 'Purpurea' p.315

Ajuga reptans 'Atropurpurea' p.315

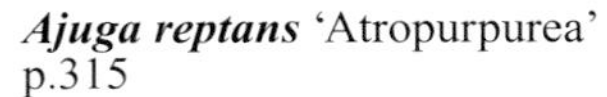

Helleborus* × *hybridus p.314

Ribes sanguineum 'Brocklebankii' p.151

Chionodoxa forbesii 'Pink Giant' p.443

Arenaria purpurascens p.377

Rosa LOVELY LADY ('Dicjubell') p.186

Papaver somniferum 'Peony Flowered' p.333

Rosa 'Felicia' p181

Astilbe 'Venus' p.246

Nerine bowdenii p.440

Echinacea purpurea 'Robert Bloom' p.246

Anemone huphensis 'September Charm' p.231

Schizostylis coccinea 'Sunrise' p.306

Helleborus* × *sternii p.313

Cyclamen coum p.456

Bauhinia variegata p.93

Erica carnea 'December Red' p.175

SPRING

Narcissus 'Thalia' p.432

Deutzia gracilis p.149

Sanguinaria canadensis p.375

Prunus avium 'Plena' p.72

SUMMER

Exochorda* × *macrantha 'The Bride' p.131

Trachelospermum jasminoides p.203

Leucanthemum* × *superbum 'Elizabeth' p.242

AUTUMN

Arbutus unedo p.89

Anemone* × *hybrida 'Honorine Jobert' p.231

Gaultheria cuneata p.372

Zephyranthes candida p.453

WINTER/ALL YEAR

Skimmia japonica 'Fructu Albo' p.169

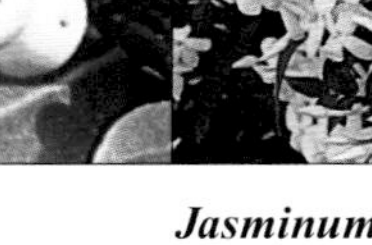

Jasminum polyanthum p.217

Viburnum tinus p.145

Trillium grandiflorum p.276

Euonymus fortunei 'Silver Queen' p.147

Cerastium tomentosum p.373

Lavatera trimestris 'Mont Blanc' p.330

Philadelphus 'Boule d'Argent' p.133

Helichrysum petiolare p.171

Populus maximowiczii p.60

Eryngium* × *tripartitum p.259

Lithops marmorata p.485

Tanacetum argenteum p.372

Cyclamen hederifolium f. ***albiflorum*** p.453

Ranunculus calandrinioides p.372

Rubus biflorus p.145

Galanthus nivalis 'Sandersii' p.456

Plant Selector

HOW TO USE THIS SECTION

The following lists suggest plants that are suitable for growing in particular situations, or that have special uses or characteristics. For each category the list is broadly subdivided into plant groups, following the arrangement of The Plant Catalogue, pp.56–496. Plants listed here that are featured in this Catalogue are followed by page numbers. Refer to The Plant Dictionary for a whole genus or a plant not followed by a page number. If a plant is listed for a particular purpose (acid soil, coastal sites, shade, etc.) it should thrive there happily in normal growing conditions, even if the situation is not the plant's naturally preferred location. Bear in mind, however, that plants are not always consistent in their growing habits and much of their success depends on climate, location, aspect, care and available nutrients.

Plants for Sandy Soil

Sandy soils are often termed 'light' or 'hungry' soils. They are usually well-drained, but dry out rapidly during drier summer periods and hold only low reserves of plant foods. Many plants have adapted to such soils by developing deeply penetrating root systems. Their leaves are also modified to reduce moisture loss: small and reflexed, evergreen and glossy, or densely covered with fine grey or silver hairs. Once established, they will usually grow steadily with little attention. To improve moisture retention, incorporate some organic matter when planting in autumn; little watering is then needed and plants can establish well before summer.

Trees
Acacia dealbata, p.79
Agonis flexuosa, p.86
Amelanchier lamarckii, p.112
Betula ermanii, p.68
Betula pendula 'Dalecarlica', p.69
Castanea sativa
Celtis australis, p.63
Cercis siliquastrum, p.84
Crataegus laevigata 'Paul's Scarlet', p.87
Genista aetnensis, p.89
Nothofagus obliqua, p.64
Phoenix canariensis
Quercus ilex
Robinia pseudoacacia 'Frisia', p.77

A GARDEN ON SANDY GRAVEL
Alliums and lavenders thrive on light, sandy soils and are ideal for gravel gardens in dry areas.

Conifers
Abies grandis, p.100
Cupressocyparis × *leylandii* and cvs
Juniperus
Larix decidua
Pinus pinaster, p.99
Pinus radiata, p.100
Pseudotsuga menziesii var. *glauca*, p.98
Thuja occidentalis and cvs

Shrubs
Artemisia arborescens 'Faith Raven', p.171
Berberis empetrifolia, p.153
Boronia megastigma, p.152
Brachyglottis Dunedin Hybrids 'Sunshine', p.136
Calluna vulgaris and cvs
Caragana arborescens 'Lorbergii'
Ceanothus thyrsiflorus and forms
Chamelaucium uncinatum, pp.145, 146
Chorizema ilicifolium, p.153
Cistus
Convolvulus cneorum, p.154
Cotoneaster lacteus, p.121
Elaeagnus pungens 'Maculata', p.123
Enkianthus cernuus f. *rubens*, p.127
Erica arborea var. *alpina*, p.174
Erica cinerea and cvs
Gaultheria mucronata 'Mulberry Wine', p.170
Gaultheria mucronata 'Wintertime', p.169
Genista tinctoria, p.153
× *Halimiocistus sahucii*, p.155
Halimium 'Susan', p.165
Hippophäe rhamnoides, p.120
Hypericum 'Hidcote', p.166
Lavandula
Leucospermum reflexum, p.127
Olearia nummulariifolia, p.132
Perovskia 'Blue Spire', p.164
Phlomis fruticosa, p.166
Robinia hispida, p.137
Rosa pimpinellifolia, p.180
Rosmarinus officinalis and cvs
Salvia fulgens, p.162
Santolina pinnata subsp. *neapolitana* 'Sulphurea', p.165
Spartium junceum, p.143
Tamarix ramosissima, p.117
Teucrium fruticans 'Azureum'
Yucca gloriosa, p.133

Climbers
Clianthus puniceus, p.200
Eccremocarpus scaber, p.215
Kennedia rubicunda, p.200
Lapageria rosea, p.206
Petrea volubilis, p.202
Solanum wendlandii, p.212
Streptosolen jamesonii, p.218
Tropaeolum tricolorum, p.201
Vitis vinifera 'Purpurea', p.216

Perennials
Acanthus spinosus, p.255
Achillea 'Moonshine', p.303
Aphelandra squarrosa 'Louisae', p.262
Artemisia absinthium 'Lambrook Silver'
Artemisia ludoviciana var. *albula*, p.274
Asphodeline
Baptisia australis, p.258
Billbergia nutans, p.273
Centranthus ruber, p.247
Cryptanthus zonatus
Echinops sphaerocephalus, p.224
Eryngium × *tripartitum*, p.259
Gaillardia × *grandiflora* cvs
Gazania rigens var. *uniflora*, p.304
Limonium latifolium 'Blue Cloud', p.296
Nepeta × *faassenii*, p.296
Oenothera fruticosa 'Fyrverkeri', p.303
Origanum vulgare 'Aureum', p.302
PELARGONIUMS, pp.248–9
Phlomis russeliana, p.261
Platycodon grandiflorus, p.294
Romneya coulteri, p.224
Ruellia devosiana, p.287
Sansevieria trifasciata 'Laurentii', p.275
Solidago 'Goldenmosa', p.261
Strelitzia reginae, p.275
Verbascum

Annuals and biennials
Antirrhinum majus and cvs
Brachyscome iberidifolia, p.346
Bracteantha bracteata Monstrosum Series, p.352
Cleome hassleriana and cvs
Coreopsis tinctoria, p.348
Eschscholzia californica, p.351
Impatiens walleriana Novette Series, p.339
Limnanthes douglasii, p.348
Limonium sinuatum, p.344
Linaria maroccana 'Fairy Lights', p.342
Mentzelia lindleyi, p.348
Papaver rhoeas Shirley Series, pp.334, 340
Portulaca grandiflora Series and cvs
Psylliostachys suworowii, p.342
Schizanthus
Senecio cineraria 'Silver Dust', p.346
Tagetes
Tanacetum parthenium, p.331
Verbena × *hybrida* Series and cvs
Xanthophthalmum segetum, p.349

Rock plants
Acaena caesiiglauca, p.402
Achillea × *kellereri*, p.387
Aethionema 'Warley Rose', p.388
Andromeda polifolia 'Compacta', p.359
Arenaria montana, p.386
Armeria juniperifolia, p.377
Cytisus × *beanii*, p.361
Dianthus deltoides
Gaultheria procumbens, p.399
Gypsophila repens
Helianthemum
Maianthemum canadense, p.395
Petrorhagia saxifraga, p.387
Phlox bifida, p.393
Saponaria ocymoides, p.390
Sedum
Sempervivum
Tanacetum argenteum, p.372
Vaccinium vitis-idaea subsp. *minus*, p.378

Bulbs, corms and tubers
Allium
Babiana rubrocyanea, p.447
Crocus
Freesia
Ipheion uniflorum 'Froyle Mill', p.447
IRISES (bulbous species), pp.234–5
Ixia
Muscari
Narcissus tazetta and Div.8 hybrids
Nerine bowdenii, p.440
Ornithogalum
Romulea bulbocodium, p.447
Scilla
Zephyranthes

Cacti and other succulents (all)

STATELY SPIRES
Admired for its grand appearance and long flowering season, Verbascum 'Gainsborough' *is an undemanding plant for a dry border in a gravel or cottage garden.*

Plants for Clay Soils

Clay soil is usually wet, glutinous and heavy in winter, and during drier summers sometimes shrinks and cracks, damaging plant roots. Whether establishing a new garden on clay or renovating an older one, always choose plants that will tolerate and grow satisfactorily in clay soil. Prepare the soil thoroughly, digging in the autumn, then leaving roughly dug over winter to benefit from the weathering effects of frost and winter rains. Dig in coarse organic matter, and work in grit or sharp sand to ensure the soil is well drained. Plant in early spring, at the beginning of the growing season, to avoid losses over winter.

Trees
Alnus glutinosa
Castanospermum australe
Drimys winteri, p.74
Fraxinus
Juglans nigra, p.63
Melaleuca viridiflora var. *rubriflora*
Oxydendrum arboreum, p.74
Populus
Pterocarya fraxinifolia
Quercus palustris, p.65
Quercus robur
Salix x *sepulcralis* var. *chrysocoma*, p.70
Salix babylonica var. *pekinensis* 'Tortuosa', p.81

Conifers
Cryptomeria
Metasequoia
Taxodium distichum, p.100

Shrubs
Aronia arbutifolia, p.126
Calycanthus floridus
Clethra alnifolia
Cornus alba 'Sibirica', p.146
Kalmia latifolia, p.137
Ledum groenlandicum, p.150

WATERSIDE PLANTING
Imposing Gunnera manicata, *and willow, are moisture-lovers and will flourish in rich, moist clay, especially at the edges of ponds, in bog gardens and by slow-moving streams.*

Magnolia virginiana
Salix caprea
Salix purpurea
Sambucus racemosa
Tetrapanax papyrifer, p.122
Viburnum lentago
Viburnum opulus and cvs

Climbers
Celastrus scandens
Humulus lupulus 'Aureus', p.202
Rosa filipes 'Kiftsgate', p.192
Vitis coignetiae, p.216

Ferns
Matteuccia struthiopteris, p.324
Onoclea sensibilis, p.324
Osmunda regalis, p.324
Polystichum setiferum Groups, pp.323, 325
Thelypteris palustris, p.324
Woodwardia radicans

Perennials
Aruncus dioicus, p.224
Cyperus papyrus, p.319
Darmera peltata, p.240
Filipendula ulmaria 'Aurea', p.302
Gunnera manicata, p.226
Helonias bullata
Houttuynia cordata 'Chameleon', p.463
Iris laevigata, p.235
Lythrum
Mimulus guttatus
Primula florindae, p.281
Primula japonica
Scrophularia auriculata 'Variegata'
Trollius

Water plants
Butomus umbellatus, p.464
Caltha palustris, p.467
Lysichiton americanus, p.467
Pontederia cordata, p.464
Ranunculus lingua, p.467
Sagittaria latifolia, p.462
Thalia dealbata

Plants requiring Neutral to Acid Soil

Some plants, notably camellias, rhododendrons and most heathers, grow naturally in regions such as open woodland, hillsides or moorland where the soil is neutral to acid, and are intolerant of alkaline soils such as chalk or limestone. These are often termed 'lime-haters' or 'acid-lovers'. Before planting, ensure that the soil is suitable for lime-hating plants, and work in some acidic planting compost or humus. After planting, keep woody plants well mulched. In drier regions, check water needs regularly.

Trees
Arbutus menziesii
Arbutus unedo, p.89
CAMELLIAS, pp.124–5
Embothrium coccineum, p.89
Eucryphia (most) most
Michelia doltsopa, p.79
Nyssa sinensis, p.78
Nyssa sylvatica, p.67
Oxydendrum arboreum, p.74
Pterostyrax hispida
Stewartia
Styrax japonicus, p.73

Conifers
Abies
Picea (most)
Pinus densiflora
Pinus pumila
Pseudolarix amabilis, p.103
Pseudotsuga
Sciadopitys verticillata, p.102
Tsuga heterophylla

Shrubs
Amelanchier lamarckii, p.112
Andromeda polifolia 'Compacta', p.359
Arctostaphylos (some)
Boronia megastigma, p.152
CAMELLIAS, pp.124–5
Chamaedaphne calyculata
Crinodendron hookerianum, p.138
Cyrilla racemiflora
Desfontainia spinosa, p.139
Enkianthus some
Epacris impressa, p.151
Fothergilla major, p.123
Gardenia augusta
Gaultheria
Hamamelis
HEATHERS, pp.174–5, most
Kalmia
Ledum groenlandicum, p.150
Leiophyllum buxifolium
Leucothöe
Lyonia ligustrinum
Menziesia ciliicalyx var. *purpurea*, p.151
Philesia magellanica
Pieris
Pimelea ferruginea, p.158
Protea
RHODODENDRONS, pp.128–9, most
Styrax officinalis, p.114
Telopea speciosissima, p.138
Vaccinium, most
Zenobia pulverulenta, p.134

Climbers
Agapetes (several)
Allamanda cathartica
Asteranthera ovata
Berberidopsis corallina, p.207
Mitraria coccinea, p.201

Perennials
Adiantum some
Blechnum
Cryptogramma crispa, p.325
Cypripedium reginae, p.308
Dianella tasmanica, p.259
Drosera
Lilium speciosum var. *rubrum*, p.416
Lilium superbum, p.417
Nepenthes
Sarracenia flava, p.302
Smilacina racemosa, p.233
Tolmiea menziesii
Trillium
Uvularia

Rock plants
Arctostaphylos
Cassiope
Cornus canadensis, p.386
Corydalis cashmeriana
Cyananthus
Epigaea
Galax urceolata, p.363
Gaultheria
Gentiana sino-ornata, p.399
Leucothöe keiskei
Linnaea borealis, p.387
Lithodora diffusa cvs
Mitchella repens
Ourisia
Phlox adsurgens
Phlox stolonifera
Phyllodoce
Pieris nana
Shortia

SPRING COLOUR
*Acid-loving azaleas (*Rhododendron *family), backed by magnolias, provide a dazzling technicolour display in spring and will thrive in a well-drained position.*

Plants for Chalk and Limestone

Chalk and limestone regions are rich in wildflowers and wildlife, and where there is a reasonable depth of topsoil above chalk or limestone a wide range of attractive garden plants can be grown. Often, there are only a few centimetres of chalky soil above bedrock and here there is an increased risk of drought in summer. It may be necessary to excavate planting holes and to incorporate organic matter to increase humus levels. On well-drained chalk, plant in autumn or spring; on limestone soils other than well-drained chalk soils, defer planting until spring. Keep all young woody plants well mulched.

Trees
Acer negundo 'Variegatum', p.75
Aesculus x *carnea* 'Briotii, p.60
Catalpa bignonioides, p.74
Cercis siliquastrum, p.84
Crataegus
Fagus sylvatica, p.64
Fraxinus ornus, p.72
Gleditsia triacanthos 'Sunburst', p.73
Ilex aquifolium cvs, pp.94–5
Laurus nobilis
Malus
Morus nigra
Phillyrea latifolia
Prunus avium 'Plena', p.72
Robinia pseudoacacia 'Frisia', p.77
Sorbus aria and cvs
Tilia tomentosa

Conifers
Calocedrus decurrens, p.102
Cedrus libani, p.99
Chamaecyparis lawsoniana and cvs
Cupressocyparis x *leylandii* and cvs
Cupressus glabra
Ginkgo biloba, p.99
Juniperus
Picea omorika, p.99
Pinus nigra
Taxus baccata and cvs
Thuja orientalis and cvs
Thuja plicata and cvs

Shrubs
Abutilon 'Kentish Belle', p.167
Aucuba japonica 'Crotonifolia', p.148
Azara microphylla, p.121
Berberis darwinii, p.113
Buddleja davidii and cvs
Carpenteria californica, p.134
Ceanothus impressus, p.141
Choisya ternata, p.123
Cistus
Cornus mas 'Variegata', p.115
Cotoneaster, some
Deutzia
Forsythia suspensa, p.127
Fremontodendron 'California Glory', p.119
Fuchsia 'Riccartonii', p.160
Hebe 'Great Orme', p.159
Hypericum 'Hidcote', p.166
LILACS, p.116
Malus sargentii, p.112
Malus sieboldii, p.126
Nerium oleander, p.117
Paeonia ludlowii, p.239
Philadelphus
Phlomis fruticosa, p.166
Photinia x *fraseri* 'Red Robin'
Potentilla (all shrubby species)
ROSES (most), pp.180–5, some
Rosmarinus officinalis 'Miss Jessopp's Upright'
Sambucus nigra 'Guincho Purple'
Spartium junceum, p.147
Spiraea nipponica 'Snowmound', p.139
Viburnum tinus, p.143
Vitex agnus-castus
Weigela florida 'Variegata'
Yucca aloifolia, p.149

Climbers
Actinidia kolomikta, p.205
Campsis radicans
Celastrus orbiculatus
CLEMATIS, pp.208–9, some
Eccremocarpus scaber, p.215
IVIES, p.219
Jasminum officinale f. *affine*, p.204
Lonicera, some
Parthenocissus henryana
Passiflora caerulea, p.212
Rosa 'Albéric Barbier', p.192
Rosa 'Albertine', p.193
Rosa banksiae 'Lutea', p.194
Solanum crispum 'Glasnevin', p.212
Trachelospermum jasminoides, p.203
Wisteria sinensis, p.213

Ferns
Asplenium scolopendrium, p.325
Asplenium trichomanes, p.325
Dryopteris filix-mas, p.322
Polypodium vulgare 'Cornubiense', p.324

Perennials
Acanthus spinosus, p.255
Achillea
Aster novae-angliae and cvs
Aster novi-belgii and cvs
Bergenia
Doronicum
Eryngium, some
Gypsophila paniculata cvs

BRIGHT YELLOW
Achillea 'Moonshine' is a robust perennial that thrives in chalk or limestone soils and will withstand periods of drought. Throughout summer, the bright yellow flowers attract bees and butterflies.

Helenium
IRISES (most), pp.234–5, some
Rudbeckia 'Goldquelle', p.227
Salvia nemorosa
Scabiosa caucasica 'Clive Greaves', p.295
Sidalcea
Verbascum
Veronica spicata

Annuals and biennials
Ageratum houstonianum and cvs
Calendula officinalis and Series and cvs
Callistephus chinensis Series and cvs
Calomeria amaranthoides, p.342
Erysimum cheiri and Series and cvs
Gomphrena globosa, p.343
Lavatera trimestris 'Silver Cup', p.336
Limonium sinuatum, p.334
Lobularia maritima
Lunaria annua, p.337
Matthiola
Salvia viridis, p.343
Tagetes
Ursinia anthemoides, p.350
Xeranthemum annuum
Zinnia

Rock plants
Aethionema
Alyssum
Androsace lanuginosa, p.389
Aster alpinus, p.393
Campanula (most rock garden species), some
Dianthus (most rock garden species)
Draba
Erysimum helveticum, p.385
Gypsophila repens
Helianthemum
Lathyrus vernus, p.278
Leontopodium alpinum, p.358
Linum arboreum, p.370
Origanum dictamnus
Papaver burseri
Penstemon pinifolius, p.366
Rhodanthemum hosmariense, p.358
Saponaria ocymoides, p.390
Saxifraga (most)
Thymus caespititius, p.387
Veronica (all rock garden species), some

Bulbs, corms and tubers
Babiana
Chionodoxa
Colchicum
Crinum × *powellii*, p.410
Crocus
Cyclamen hederifolium, p.454
DAFFODILS, pp.432–34
GLADIOLI, p.411
Hermodactylus tuberosus, p.430
Leucocoryne ixioides, p.429
Lilium regale, p.416
Muscari
Pancratium illyricum, p.435
Scilla
TULIPS, pp.426–28
Zephyranthes

LILACS AND DEUTZIA
An exquisitely scented lilac, here combined with deutzia and paeonies, grows in the shelter of a wall. Lilacs prefer the alkaline nature of chalk soils, providing they are deep and well-drained.

Plants for Coastal Sites

In coastal regions, salt from sea spray is carried a considerable distance inland on the wind, causing problems for many plants. Some, however, show tolerance of higher levels of salt; these frequently have hard-surfaced or high-gloss leaves with low absorbency levels, or leaves covered with fine hairs that prevent salt reaching the surface. Coastal gardens are often exposed, so protect plants with hedges or wattle hurdles. Prepare sandy soil by incorporating organic matter and garden loam, to encourage deep root penetration, and use dense ground-cover plants to stabilize the sand and keep root areas cool.

Trees
Acer pseudoplatanus and cvs
Agonis flexuosa, p.86
Alnus incana, p.62
Arbutus unedo, p.89
Castanea sativa
Cordyline australis
Crataegus laevigata 'Paul's Scarlet', p.87
Crataegus x *lavallei* 'Carrierei'
Eucalyptus coccifera, p.68
Eucalyptus globulus
Eucalpytus gunnii, p.68
Ficus macrophylla
Fraxinus excelsior
Ilex aquifolium cvs, pp.94–5
Laurus nobilis
Melaleuca viridiflora var. *rubriflora*
Melia azedarach, p.72
Populus alba, p.60
Quercus ilex
Salix alba
Schefflera actinophylla, p.80
Schinus molle
Sorbus aria 'Lutescens', p.74
Tabebuia chrysotricha, p.93
Thevetia peruviana, p.89
Tipuana tipu

Conifers
Cupressocyparis x *leylandii*
Cupressus macrocarpa
Juniperus conferta
Pinus contorta var. *latifolia*, p.102
Pinus nigra subsp. *nigra*, p.100
Pinus radiata, p.100

Shrubs
Acacia verticillata
Atriplex halimus
Baccharis halimifolia
Berberis darwinii, p.113
Brachyglottis Dunedin Hybrids 'Sunshine', p.166
Buddleja globosa, p.119
Bupleurum fruticosum, p.142
Cassinia leptophylla subsp. *fulvida*
Chamaerops humilis, p.172
Choisya ternata, p.123
Cistus ladanifer, p.155
Colutea arborescens, p.142
Corokia x *virgata*
Cytisus x *spachianus*
Duranta erecta, p.146
Elaeagnus x *ebbingei*
Elaeagnus pungens 'Maculata', p.123
Erica arborea var. *alpina*, p.174
Erica cinerea 'Eden Valley', p.175
Erica vagans 'Lyonesse', p.174
Escallonia rubra 'Crimson Spire'
Euonymus japonicus
Euphorbia characias subspp., p.152
Fabiana imbricata 'Prostrata'
Felicia amelloides 'Santa Anita', p.164
Fuchsia magellanica, p.160
Fuchsia 'Riccartonii', p.160
Garrya elliptica 'James Roof'
Genista hispanica, p.166
Griselinia littoralis
Halimium lasianthum subsp. *formosum*, p.165
Hebe x *franciscana* 'Blue Gem'
Hebe salicifolia
Hebe 'White Gem', p.154
Helichrysum italicum
Hibiscus rosa-sinensis
Hippophäe rhamnoides, p.120
Hydrangea macrophylla and cvs
Lavandula 'Hidcote', p.163
Lavatera 'Rosea', p.137
Leptospermum scoparium 'Red Damask', p.127
Leycesteria formosa
Lonicera pileata, p.172
Lycium barbarum
Malvaviscus arboreus, p.117
Nerium oleander, p.117
Olearia x *haastii*, p.135
Olearia macrodonta
Ozothamnus ledifolius, p.156
Parahebe perfoliata, p.296
Phillyrea latifolia
Phlomis fruticosa, p.166
Pittosporum tobira
Pyracantha coccinea 'Lalandei'
Rhamnus alaternus 'Argenteovariegata'
Rosa pimpinellifolia
Rosa rugosa, p.183
Rosmarinus officinalis, p.163
Sambucus racemosa and cvs
Santolina chamaecyparissus
Spartium junceum, p.143
Tamarix ramosissima, p.117
Ulex europaeus 'Flore Pleno'
Viburnum tinus, p.145
Yucca gloriosa, p.133

Climbers
Antigonon leptopus, p.205
Bougainvillea glabra, p.212
Eccremocarpus scaber, p.215
Ercilla volubilis
Euonymus fortunei 'Coloratus'
Fallopia baldschuanica, p.215
Ficus pumila
Hedera canariensis var. *algeriensis*
Muehlenbeckia complexa
Pandorea jasminoides, p.204
Pyrostegia venusta, p.216
Schisandra rubriflora, p.207
Solandra maxima, p.202
Tripterygium regelii
Tropaeolum tuberosum var. *lineamaculatum* 'Ken Aslet', p.214
Wisteria sinensis, p.213

Silver and Grey
Left: The tough, spiny leaves of the sea holly (Eryngium) *can contend with sun, salty air and strong winds. Lavenders, native to rocky Mediterranean hillsides, are another good choice for coastal gardens.*

Grasses (including bamboos)
Cortaderia selloana 'Sunningdale Silver', p.318
Pseudosasa japonica, p.320

Perennials
Anaphalis margaritacea, p.241
Anchusa azurea 'Loddon Royalist', p.260
Anthurium andraeanum, p.272
Argyranthemum frutescens, p.242
Artemisia absinthium 'Lambrook Silver'
Carpobrotus edulis
Centaurea hypoleuca 'John Coutts', p.289
Centranthus ruber, p.247
Crambe maritima, p.286
Echinacea purpurea
Erigeron 'Charity', p.288
Eryngium variifolium, p.296
Euphorbia griffithii 'Fireglow', p.266
Geranium sanguineum, p.366
IRISES, pp.234–5, some
Kniphofia, some
Lampranthus aurantiacus, p.484
Myosotidium hortensia, p.297
Osteospermum jucundum, p.289
Peperomia obtusifolia 'Variegata', p.317
Pericallis × *hybrida*
Phormium tenax
Pilea cadierei, p.312
Romneya coulteri,
Senecio cineraria 'Silver Dust', p.346
Stachys byzantina, p.316
Tradescantia fluminensis

Annuals and biennials
Antirrhinum majus and cvs
Bassia scoparia f. *trichophylla*, p.347
Calendula officinalis Series and cvs
Clarkia amoena and Series
Coreopsis tinctoria, p.348
Cynoglossum amabile 'Firmament', p.346
Dahlia 'Coltness Gem', p.341
Dianthus chinensis Series
Dorotheanthus bellidiformis
Echium
Eschscholzia californica, p.350
Gilia capitata, p.345
Impatiens walleriana Novette Series, p.339
Lavatera trimestris cvs
Limnanthes douglasii, p.348
Matthiola
Portulaca grandiflora Series and cvs
Rhodanthe chlorocephala subsp. *rosea*, p.333
Tagetes

Rock plants
Achillea clavennae, p.385
Aethionema grandiflorum, p.364
Armeria maritima 'Vindictive', p.392
Aubrieta deltoidea 'Argenteovariegata', p.380
Dianthus deltoides
Draba aizoides
Epilobium glabellum of gardens, p.363
Iberis sempervirens, p.358
Origanum laevigatum, p.366
Oxalis enneaphylla
Parahebe catarractae, p.368
Phlox subulata 'Marjorie', p.390
Pulsatilla vulgaris, p.360
Saxifraga paniculata
Sedum spathulifolium 'Cape Blanco', p.403
Sempervivum arachnoideum, p.401
Silene schafta, p.391
Thlaspi cepaeifolium subsp. *rotundifolium*, p.377
Viola cornuta, p.361

COASTAL RETREAT
In this cliff-side garden the striking blue heads of the agapanthus and tough, sword-shaped phormium leaves add height and structure. Both plants are ideal for exposed, coastal sites with mild winters.

Bulbs, corms and tubers
Amaryllis
Agapanthus
Crinum
Crocosmia 'Lucifer', p.413
Crocus
DAFFODILS, pp.432–34
Eucharis × *grandiflora*, p.441
Freesia
Galtonia candicans, p.409
Hippeastrum
HYACINTHS, p.447
Hymenocallis
Nerine
Scilla
Sprekelia formosissima, p.429
TULIPS, pp.426–28
Veltheimia bracteata, p.441
Zantedeschia aethiopica

Trees and Shrubs for Exposed Sites

In cold, inland gardens, particularly those exposed to strong winter winds, only the hardiest plants thrive without the protection of a windbreak. Where providing one is not practical, it is essential to establish a basic framework of trees, shrubs and conifers that are fully hardy. Carefully positioned within the garden, in groups, they provide sheltered situations where less hardy plants can be grown, while still retaining a degree of openness if desired.

Trees
Acer platanoides and cvs
Acer pseudoplatanus
Betula utilis var. *jacquemontii*, p.79
Crataegus laevigata 'Paul's Scarlet', p.87
Crataegus x *lavallei* 'Carrierei'
Fagus sylvatica and cvs
Fraxinus excelsior 'Jaspidea'
Fraxinus ornus, p.72
Laburnum x *watereri* 'Vossii', p.88
Populus tremula
Sorbus aria 'Lutescens', p.74
Sorbus aucuparia 'Fructu Luteo'
Sorbus commixta 'Embley'
Sorbus scalaris
Sorbus vilmorinii, p.90
Tilia cordata

Conifers
Chamaecyparis nootkatensis
Chamaecyparis obtusa and cvs
Chamaecyparis pisifera and cvs
Juniperus communis 'Hibernica', p.107
Juniperus x *pfitzeriana* and cvs
Picea breweriana, p.101
Pinus nigra subsp. *nigra*, p.100
Pinus sylvestris
Taxus baccata and cvs
Thuja occidentalis and cvs
Tsuga canadensis, p.103

Shrubs
Amorpha canescens
Berberis darwinii, p.113
Berberis 'Rubrostilla', p.168
Berberis x *stenophylla*, p.131
Buddleja davidii 'Royal Red', p.117
Cornus alba 'Sibirica', p.146
Corylus maxima 'Purpurea', p.118
Cotinus coggygria 'Flame', p.120
Cotoneaster lacteus, p.121
Cotoneaster simonsii, p.144
Euonymus europaeus 'Red Cascade', p.143
Ledum groenlandicum, p.150
LILACS, p.116
Mahonia aquifolium, p.153
Philadelphus 'Beauclerk', p.131
Philadelphus 'Belle Etoile', p.132
Prunus laurocerasus 'Otto Luyken', p.150
Pyracantha x *watereri*, p.132
Rubus thibetanus, p.145
Salix purpurea
Sambucus nigra 'Guincho Purple'
Spiraea x *vanhouttei*, p.150
Ulex europaeus 'Flore Pleno'
Viburnum opulus 'Xanthocarpum'

Ground cover
Arctostaphylos uva-ursi, p.400
Calluna vulgaris and cvs
Cotoneaster 'Gnom'
Hedera hibernica, p.219
Juniperus horizontalis 'Wiltonii'
Lonicera pileata, p.172
Symphoricarpos x *chenaultii* 'Hancock'

MAXIMUM EXPOSURE
Evergreen Arctostaphylos x media *is ideal for windswept sites and bears large, shiny red berries in autumn.*

Climbers and Shrubs for Sunless Walls

Against cold, sunless walls, it is essential to choose climbers that grow naturally in shade or semi-shade. These provide reliable and effective foliage cover, and some have attractive flowers. Climbing roses also may flower reasonably well in sunless situations and, together with shade-tolerant shrubs, add colour to shaded walls and wallside borders. Shade-growing plants prefer moist, leafy, woodland-type soils; when planting, enrich the soil well with organic matter, such as leaf mould.

COOL SHADE
Non-variegated forms of ivy (Hedera) *provide good foliage cover for a sunless wall.*

Climbers
Akebia quinata, p.202
Berberidopsis corallina, p.207
Celastrus scandens
Clematis alpina 'Frances Rivis', p.209
Ercilla volubilis
Euonymus fortunei 'Coloratus'
Euonymus fortunei 'Silver Queen', p.147
Hedera colchica 'Dentata Variegata'
Hedera colchica 'Sulphur Heart', p.219
Hedera helix cvs
Hedera hibernica, p.219
Hydrangea petiolaris, p.204
Lapageria rosea and forms, p.206
Lonicera japonica 'Halliana', p.213
Lonicera periclymenum and cvs
Lonicera tragophylla
Parthenocissus henryana
Parthenocissus quinquefolia (rough surfaces)
Parthenocissus tricuspidata and cvs
Pileostegia viburnoides, p.204
Schisandra rubriflora, p.207
Schizophragma hydrangeoides
Schizophragma integrifolium, p.204

Shrubs
Azara microphylla, p.121
Camellia japonica cvs
Camellia x *williamsii* cvs
Chaenomeles speciosa 'Moerloosei', p.126
Chaenomeles x *superba* 'Rowallane', p.151
Choisya ternata, p.123
Cotoneaster horizontalis, p.168
Cotoneaster lacteus, p.121
Crinodendron hookerianum, p.138
Drimys winteri, p.74
Eucryphia x *nymansensis* 'Nymansay', p.77
x *Fatshedera lizei*, p.148
Fatsia japonica
Forsythia suspensa, p.127
Garrya elliptica 'James Roof'
Itea ilicifolia, p.142
Jasminum nudiflorum, p.147
Mahonia japonica, p.147
Mahonia x *media* 'Charity', p.121
Muehlenbeckia complexa
Osmanthus decorus
Pyracantha 'Orange Glow'
Pyracantha x *watereri*, p.132
Ribes laurifolium, p.171
Rosa 'Albéric Barbier', p.192
Rosa 'Félicité Perpétue', p.192
Rosa 'Gloire de Dijon', p.192
Rosa 'Golden Showers', p.195
Rosa 'Maigold', p.195
Rosa 'Madame Alfred Carrière', p.192
Rosa 'Madame Grégoire Staechelin', p.193

Rabbit-resistant Plants

Rabbits can be a serious problem in gardens, entering through gaps in hedges or fences or by tunnelling, then causing damage to a wide range of ornamental plants. Various deterrents are available, but where rabbits are persistent it is best to remove plants they like; replace these with ones they dislike because of their smell, taste, leaf texture or thorns. Even these, however, may be damaged in severe winters or when producing new shoots in spring.

Trees and shrubs
Arbutus unedo, p.89
Aucuba japonica 'Crotonifolia', p.149
Berberis, some
Betula
Buddleja davidii cvs
Buxus sempervirens
Ceanothus some
Choisya ternata and cvs
Cytisus some
Daphne mezereum, p.170
Deutzia scabra, p.132
Elaeagnus pungens 'Maculata', p.123
Escallonia some
Eucalyptus
Euphorbia characias subsp. *wulfenii*, p.152
Fatsia japonica
Fuchsia (some)
Gaultheria shallon, p.158
Hippophäe rhamnoides, p.120
Hydrangea
Kalmia latifolia, p.137
Laburnum x *watereri* 'Vossii', p.88
Laurus nobilis
Olearia x *haastii*, p.135
Philadelphus
Prunus (ornamental cherries) some
RHODODENDRONS, pp.128–30, most
Rhus typhina 'Dissecta', p.120
Ribes sanguineum and cvs
ROSES (spiny species only) pp.180–4
Rosmarinus officinalis and cvs
Ruscus aculeatus
Sambucus
Skimmia japonica and cvs
Symphoricarpos albus var. *laevigatus*
Syringa vulgaris and cvs
Viburnum opulus 'Compactum', p.168
Viburnum tinus, p.145
Yucca

Climbers
Clematis some
Lonicera some

Grasses (including bamboos)
Cortaderia selloana and cvs
Pseudosasa japonica, p.320

Perennials
Acanthus spinosus, p.255
Aconitum
Agapanthus, some
Anaphalis margaritacea, p.241
Anemone x *hybrida* 'Honorine Jobert', p.231
Aquilegia
Aster novae-angliae and cvs
Aster novi-belgii and cvs
Bergenia 'Silberlicht', p.276
Chelidonium majus 'Flore Pleno', p.240
DAYLILIES, p.263, some
Digitalis some
Doronicum
Eryngium agavifolium
Euphorbia myrsinites, p.383
Euphorbia polychroma, p.285
Geranium 'Johnson's Blue', p.295
Helianthus x *multiflorus* 'Loddon Gold', p.232
Helleborus argutifolius, p.316
Helleborus foetidus, p.317
IRISES, pp.234–5, some
Kniphofia caulescens, p.271
Lamium maculatum, p.277
Lychnis chalcedonica, p.266
Lupinus, some
Miscanthus sinensis 'Zebrinus', p.318
Nepeta x *faassenii*, p.296
PEONIES, pp.238–9
Persicaria bistorta 'Superba', p.245
Phormium tenax 'Dazzler', p.272
Primula vulgaris, p.281
Pulmonaria some
Sedum spectabile 'Brilliant', p.296
Tanacetum parthenium, p.331
Verbena rigida, p.294
Viola odorata

Ground cover
Ajuga reptans 'Atropurpurea', p.315
Alchemilla mollis, p.302
Bergenia cordifolia 'Purpurea', p.277
Brunnera macrophylla
Convallaria majalis, p.276
Gaultheria mucronata and cvs
Hypericum calycinum, p.166
Lamium galeobdolon subsp. *montanum* 'Florentinum'
Liriope muscari, p.206
Phalaris arundinaria var. *picta*, p.318
Saxifraga x *urbium*
Stachys byzantina 'Silver Carpet'
Symphoricarpos x *chenaultii* 'Hancock'
Vinca

Annuals and biennials
Antirrhinum, some
Eschscholzia
Impatiens some
Nicotiana alata, p.241
Papaver somniferum
Tagetes erecta
Tagetes patula
Zinnia elegans

Bulbs, corms and tubers
Chionodoxa luciliae, p.449
Colchicum
Crocosmia
Cyclamen
DAFFODILS, pp.432–34
DAHLIAS, pp.420–421
Fritillaria
Galanthus nivalis
Muscari
TULIPS, pp.426–28

RABBIT RESISTOR
The woolly grey leaves of Stachys byzantina*, growing here with a tree lupin, should escape the attentions of hungry rabbits.*

FORMAL STRUCTURE
In this mature garden, high yew hedges form green walls, providing shelter as well as excellent structure. Twin box hedges give a formal edge to the beds of cottage-garden plants.

Plants for Hedges and Windbreaks

Plants for hedging are often selected for their ornamental qualities, but there are also other aspects to consider. Boundary hedges may provide visual privacy, or screen unsightly buildings; they may also be bushy or thorny to keep out animals or intruders. Make sure that plants for screening will grow to the required height, choosing conifers or evergreen shrubs for year-round effect. In exposed situations, trees and larger conifers may be used as windbreaks; two or three staggered rows are usually much more effective than a single, close-planted one.

Trees
Alnus cordata, p.62
Arbutus unedo, p.89
Carpinus betulus
Carpinus betulus 'Fastigiata', p.96
Crataegus monogyna
Fagus sylvatica, p.64
Ilex aquifolium, p.94
Ilex aquifolium 'Argentea Marginata', p.94
Laurus nobilis
Melaleuca viridiflora var. *rubriflora*
Metrosideros excelsus, p.79
Nothofagus dombeyi, p.64
Nothofagus obliqua, p.64
Olea europaea
Populus x *canadensis* 'Robusta', p.61
Prunus lusitanica
Syzygium paniculatum, p.77
Umbellularia californica, p.70
Zelkova serrata, p.67

Conifers
Abies grandis, p.100
Cedrus deodara
Cephalotaxus harringtonii
Chamaecyparis lawsoniana
Cupressocyparis x *leylandii*
Cupressus macrocarpa
Juniperus communis
Larix decidua
Picea omorika, p.99
Pinus nigra
Pinus radiata, p.100
Pseudotsuga menziesii var. *glauca*, p.98
Taxus baccata
Thuja plicata
Tsuga canadensis, p.103

Shrubs
Berberis darwinii, p.113
Buxus sempervirens 'Suffruticosa', p.173
Choisya ternata, p.123
Codiaeum variegatum var. *pictum*, p.173
Cotoneaster simonsii, p.144
Dodonaea viscosa 'Purpurea', p.147
Duranta erecta, p.146
Elaeagnus x *ebbingei*
Escallonia 'Langleyensis', p.138
Euonymus japonicus 'Macrophyllus'
Griselinia littoralis
Hibiscus rosa-sinensis
Hippophäe rhamnoides, p.120
Hydrangea macrophylla cvs
Lavandula cvs
Leptospermum scoparium cvs
Ligustrum ovalifolium, p.122
Lonicera nitida
Photinia x *fraseri* 'Birmingham', p.113
Pittosporum tenuifolium, p.123
Prunus laurocerasus
Prunus lusitanica
Pyracantha x *watereri*, p.132
Rosmarinus officinalis and cvs
Tamarix ramosissima, p.117

Roses
Rosa californica
Rosa 'Céleste', p.181
Rosa 'Felicia', p.181
Rosa 'Frühlingsmorgen'
Rosa gallica var. *officinalis*
Rosa gallica 'Versicolor', p.183
Rosa glauca, p.182
Rosa 'Great Maiden's Blush', p.181
Rosa 'Marguerite Hilling', p.182
Rosa moyesii 'Geranium', p.183
Rosa 'Nevada', p.181
Rosa 'Penelope', p.180
Rosa 'Président de Sèze'
Rosa rugosa, p.183
Rosa 'Tuscany Superb'

Grasses (including bamboos)
Arundo donax
Cortaderia selloana 'Sunningdale Silver', p.318
Fargesia nitida
Phyllostachys bambusoides, p.320
Pseudosasa japonica, p.320
Semiarundinaria fastuosa, p.320
Stipa gigantea, p.319

Perennials
Echinops bannaticus, p.226
Eupatorium purpureum, p.231
Filipendula camtschatica
Helianthus atrorubens 'Monarch'
Macleaya microcarpa 'Kelway's Coral Plume', p.225
Phormium tenax
Rudbeckia 'Goldquelle', p.227

Architectural Plants

In gardens, plants that stand out, immediately drawing the eye with their strong, distinctive appearance, are termed 'architectural' plants. Whether by chance or design, such plants give character and substance, and help form the basic framework of a garden. Most are trees, conifers and shrubs, which provide a permanent effect throughout the year. They impress by shape, as in strongly vertical, conical or fastigiate forms of conifer, or with striking foliage – the immense leaf size of gunneras or the sword-like leaves of phormiums. In established gardens, areas attracting little attention may be improved by introducing plants with good architectural qualities.

Trees
Cordyline
Dracaena draco, p.96
Eucalyptus (many)
Jacaranda mimosifolia, p.75
Kalopanax septemlobus, p.76
MAGNOLIAS, p.71, some
Paulownia tomentosa, p.73
Phoenix canariensis
Salix (several)
Trachycarpus fortunei, p.80
Trochodendron aralioides, p.80
Washingtonia

Conifers
Abies
Araucaria
Calocedrus decurrens, p.102
Cedrus
Juniperus x *pfitzeriana* 'William Pfitzer', p.107
Metasequoia glyptostroboides, p.98
Picea
Pseudolarix amabilis, p.103
Sciadopitys verticillata, p.102
Sequoia sempervirens
Sequoiadendron giganteum, p.98
Taxodium distichum, p.100
Tsuga heterophylla

Shrubs
Aesculus parviflora, p.115
Brachyglottis repanda, p.123
Cycas revoluta, p.148
Daphniphyllum macropodum, p.113
Eriobotrya japonica
Fatsia japonica
Fatsia japonica 'Variegata', p.147
Mahonia (most)
Parkinsonia aculeata
Protea
Rhus typhina
Rhus typhina 'Dissecta', p.120
Yucca

Climbers
Epipremnum aureum 'Marble Queen', p.217
Hedera colchica 'Dentata', p.219
Monstera deliciosa, p.218
Schizophragma hydrangeoides
Schizophragma integrifolium, p.204
Vitis coignetiae, p.216

Ferns
Asplenium scolopendrium Marginatum Group, p.325
Blechnum tabulare
Cyathea australis, p.96
Dicksonia antarctica, p.322
Matteuccia struthiopteris, p.324
Platycerium bifurcatum, p.322
Polystichum munitum, p.328
Woodwardia radicans

Grasses (including bamboos)
Chusquea culeou, p.320
Cortaderia selloana 'Sunningdale Silver', p.318

Perennials
Acanthus spinosus, p.255
Angelica archangelica, p.226
Berkheya macrocephala, p.266
Crambe cordifolia, p.224
Cynara cardunculus, p.226
Darmera peltata, p.240
Echinops bannaticus, p.226
Echium wildpretii
Ensete ventricosum, p.233
Euphorbia characias subsp. *characias*, p.152
Gunnera manicata, p.226
Heliconia
Hosta (many)
Kniphofia caulescens, p.271
Ligularia (most)
Macleaya
Meconopsis (most), several
Phormium tenax and cvs
Puya chilensis, p.273
Rheum palmatum 'Atrosanguineum'
Rodgersia
Strelitzia reginae, p.275
Veratrum nigrum, p.226
Verbascum olympicum, p.227

Annuals and biennials
Alcea rosea, p.333
Amaranthus tricolor cvs
Calomeria amaranthoides, p.342
Helianthus annuus and cvs
Onopordum acanthium, p.334
Silybum marianum, p.334
Verbascum densiflorum

Bulbs, corms and tubers
Arisaema (most)
Arum creticum, p.431
Begonia rex and hybrids
Cardiocrinum giganteum, p.410
Dracunculus vulgaris, p.413
GLADIOLI, p.411 most
Sauromatum venosum, p.429
Zantedeschia aethiopica

Water plants
Colocasia esculenta and cvs
Eichhornia crassipes, p.464
Lysichiton americanus, p.467
Nelumbo nucifera and cvs
Orontium aquaticum, p.467
Pontederia cordata, p.464
Sagittaria
Thalia dealbata

Cacti and other succulents
Most of the larger species, especially:
Aeonium tabuliforme, p.494
Agave americana 'Striata', p.473
Aloe (most)
Carnegiea gigantea, p.472
Cereus (most)
Cyphostemma juttae, p.475
Euphorbia candelabrum
Opuntia (most)

Striking shapes
Statuesque spiky plants with lance-shaped leaves such as yuccas, cordylines and phormiums make superb focal points and add structure and form to the garden as well as an exotic touch.

Plants for Quick Cover

In new gardens there are often steep banks or large spaces impractical to turf or plant, and in older gardens areas may become neglected or there may be little time for maintenance. Such problems may be resolved by using plants that have good ground-covering qualities – rapid, dense, low, and leafy or twiggy growth that helps to suppress weeds permanently. Always select plants that are suitable for the soil conditions and, in large areas, use vigorous ones such as ivy (*Hedera*), which may be spaced to give good cover in two or three seasons.

Conifers
Juniperus conferta
Juniperus sabina var. *tamariscifolia*, p.106

Shrubs
Ceanothus thyrsiflorus var. *repens*, p.164
Cotoneaster conspicuus
Cotoneaster 'Gnom'
Cotoneaster 'Skogholm'
Gaultheria shallon, p.158
Hypericum calycinum, p.166
Lantana camara
Rosa GROUSE ('Korimro'), p.185
Rosa PINK BELLS ('Poulbells'), p.186
Rubus tricolor
Stephanandra incisa 'Crispa'
Symphoricarpos x *chenaultii* 'Hancock'

Climbers
Hedera canariensis var. *algeriensis* 'Ravensholst'
Hedera colchica 'Dentata', p.219
Hedera helix (small cvs)
Hedera hibernica, p.219
Hydrangea petiolaris, p.204
Lonicera japonica cvs
Pueraria lobata
Trachelospermum asiaticum
Trachelospermum jasminoides, p.203

Ferns
Dryopteris dilatata
Polystichum aculeatum
Polystichum setiferum Groups, pp.323, 325

Perennials
Aegopodium podagraria 'Variegatum', p.286
Alchemilla mollis, p.302
Anthemis punctata subsp. *cupaniana*, p.286
Asarum europaeum, p.402
Campanula portenschlagiana, p.394
Cerastium tomentosum, p.373
Chelidonium majus 'Flore Pleno', p.240
Duchesnea indica
Euphorbia amygdaloides var. *robbiae*, p.279
Geranium macrorrhizum, p.289
Geranium × *oxonianum* 'Claridge Druce'
Glechoma hederacea 'Variegata', p.312
Heterocentron elegans, p.294
Lamium maculatum and cvs
Osteospermum jucundum, p.289
Phalaris arundinacea var. *picta*, p.318
Prunella grandiflora 'Pink Loveliness'
Pulmonaria (most), some
Stachys byzantina, p.316
Symphytum × *uplandicum* 'Variegatum', p.240

CARPETING CRANESBILLS
Geranium x magnificum *is one of several hardy cranesbills that grow rapidly, providing good ground cover. The violet-blue flowers make an attractive contrast with the red flowers of* Rosa moyesii.

Annuals and biennials
Lathyrus odoratus 'Bijou', p.336
Portulaca grandiflora Series and cvs
Sanvitalia procumbens, p.348
Tropaeolum majus Series and cvs

Rock plants
Acaena anserinifolia of gardens
Arabis caucasica and cvs
Aubrieta
Campanula poscharskyana, p.393
Helianthemum
Persicaria affinis and cvs
Persicaria vacciniifolia, p.399
Phlox douglasii cvs
Phlox subulata
Phuopsis stylosa, p.364
Saxifraga stolonifera
Tiarella cordifolia, p.359
Waldsteinia

Ground-cover Plants for Shade

An area that is shaded for some or most of the day may be regarded by some gardeners as a problem space, when in fact it should be viewed as a fortunate opportunity to experiment with a different, and often equally exciting, range of plants from those more suited to sunny positions. The following ground-cover plants may be planted in any depth of shade, given reasonably fertile soil conditions.

Shrubs
Cotoneaster conspicuus
Cotoneaster 'Gnom'
Cotoneaster 'Herbstfeuer'
Daphne laureola subsp. *philippi*, p.152
Epigaea asiatica
Euonymus fortunei 'Kewensis'
Gaultheria shallon, p.158
Hypericum calycinum, p.166
Leucothöe fontanesiana
Lonicera pileata, p.172
Mahonia aquifolium, p.153
Mahonia repens
Pachysandra terminalis, p.400
Paxistima canbyi
Prunus laurocerasus 'Otto Luyken', p.150
Rubus tricolor
Ruscus hypoglossum, p.172
Sarcococca confusa
Sarcococca humilis, p.170
Vinca difformis
Vinca minor, p.172

Climbers
Asteranthera ovata
Berberidopsis corallina, p.207
Epipremnum aureum 'Marble Queen', p.217
Ficus pumila
Hedera colchica 'Dentata', p.219
Hedera helix 'Green Ripple', p.219
Hedera helix 'Ivalace', p.219
Hedera hibernica, p.221
Hydrangea petiolaris, p.204
Rhoicissus capensis
Rhoicissus rhomboidea
Schizophragma hydrangeoides

Ferns
Adiantum venustum, p.325
Athyrium filix-femina
Blechnum penna-marina
Blechnum spicant
Polypodium vulgare, p.325
Polystichum setiferum Groups, pp.323, 325

Perennials
Acanthus spinosus, p.255
Ajuga pyramidalis
Ajuga reptans 'Atropurpurea', p.315
Alchemilla mollis, p.302
Anemone apennina
Arisarum proboscideum
Asarum caudatum
Asarum europaeum, p.402
Aspidistra elatior
Astrantia maxima, p.287
Bergenia cordifolia 'Purpurea', p.277
Brunnera macrophylla
Campanula portenschlagiana, p.394
Campanula poscharskyana, p.393
Ceratostigma plumbaginoides, p.372
Chelidonium majus 'Flore Pleno', p.240
Convallaria majalis, p.276
Dicentra formosa
Dicentra spectabilis, p.247
Duchesnea indica
Elatostema repens, p.315
Epimedium perralderianum
Euphorbia amygdaloides var. *robbiae*, p.279
Fittonia argyroneura, p.312
Galax urceolata, p.363
Galium odoratum, p.285
Geranium macrorrhizum, p.289
Geranium nodosum, p.278
Geranium renardii, p.287
Geranium sanguineum, p.366
Geranium wallichianum 'Buxton's Variety', p.297
Glechoma hederacea 'Variegata', p.312
HOSTAS (some), pp.298–9
Hypsela reniformis
Iris foetidissima
Lamium maculatum, p.277
Liriope muscari, p.306
Luzula sylvatica 'Marginata'
Maianthemum bifolium
Meehania urticifolia
Omphalodes cappadocica, p.361
Pachyphragma macrophyllum, p.275
Persicaria affinis 'Donald Lowndes', p.388
Persicaria campanulata, p.267
Phalaris arundinacea var. *picta*, p.318
Plectranthus oertendahlii
Pulmonaria saccharata, p.279
Saxifraga x *geum*, p.359
Symphytum grandiflorum of gardens
Tellima grandiflora Rubra Group, p.314
Tiarella cordifolia, p.359
Tolmiea menziesii
Tradescantia fluminensis 'Variegata', p.312
Vancouveria hexandra, p.359
Viola riviniana 'Purpurea', p.381
Waldsteinia ternata, p.397

Rock plants
Asarina procumbens, p.396
Cardamine trifolia, p.374
Cornus canadensis, p.386
Homogyne alpina
Mitchella repens
Prunella grandiflora, p.393
Saxifraga stolonifera
Saxifraga x *urbium*
Tiarella cordifolia, p.359

BRIGHT EDGING
The dead nettle (Lamium maculatum *'Album') is an excellent plant for ground cover. Its white flowers combine with the pink of* Geranium maculatum *to brighten the fringe of a wooded area.*

Ground-cover Plants for Sun

Many plants grow naturally in dry, sunny conditions. Some have developed foliage characteristics to minimize moisture loss from their leaves; others are densely branched, keeping the soil surface shaded and cool. Most have extensive root systems that penetrate deeply to find moisture. These plants are adapted to well-drained soils; in poorly drained situations, they may not survive prolonged wet conditions. Although adapted to poorer, dry soils, young plants may have been grown in richer composts and well watered, so when planting incorporate organic matter, such as leaf mould or coir, and check water needs until well established.

Conifers
Juniperus communis 'Prostrata'
Juniperus horizontalis 'Wiltonii'
Juniperus sabina var. *tamariscifolia*, p.106
Juniperus squamata 'Blue Carpet'
Juniperus squamata 'Blue Star'
Microbiota decussata, p.106
Picea abies 'Inversa'

Shrubs
Arctostaphylos nevadensis
Arctostaphylos nummularia
Arctostaphylos uva-ursi, p.400
Berberis wilsoniae
Brachyglottis Dunedin Hybrids 'Sunshine', p.166
Calluna vulgaris 'White Lawn'
Ceanothus thyrsiflorus var. *repens*, p.164
Cotoneaster cochleatus of gardens
Cotoneaster 'Skogholm'
Cytisus x *beanii*, p.361
Cytisus scoparius subsp. *maritimus*
Ephedra gerardiana
Erica carnea 'Springwood White', p.174
Euonymus fortunei 'Emerald Gaiety'
Euonymus fortunei 'Kewensis'
Gaultheria myrsinoides
Genista hispanica, p.166
x *Halimiocistus sahucii*, p.155
Hebe pinguifolia 'Pagei', p.363
Hebe 'Youngii'
Hypericum calycinum, p.166
Lantana montevidensis, p.163
Leiophyllum buxifolium
Leptospermum rupestre, p.156
Potentilla fruticosa 'Abbotswood', p.154
Rosa GROUSE ('Korimro'), p.185
Rosa 'Nozomi', p.185
Rosa PINK BELLS ('Poulbells'), p.186
Rosmarinus officinalis 'Prostratus'
Salix repens, p.152
Santolina chamaecyparissus
Stephanandra incisa 'Crispa'
Symphoricarpos x *chenaultii* 'Hancock'
Ulex europaeus 'Flore Pleno'
Vinca minor and cvs
Vinca major 'Variegata', p.171

Climbers
Anredera cordifolia
Campsis radicans
Clematis armandii, p.208
Clematis rehderiana, p.209
Clematis tangutica, p.209
Decumaria sinensis
Hardenbergia comptoniana, p.202
Hedera canariensis var. *algeriensis* 'Ravensholst'
Hedera colchica 'Dentata Variegata'
Hedera hibernica, p.219
Hibbertia scandens
Kennedia rubicunda, p.200
Lathyrus latifolius, p.207
Lonicera japonica 'Halliana', p.213
Parthenocissus tricuspidata, p.216
Pueraria lobata
Pyrostegia venusta, p.216
Trachelospermum asiaticum
Vitis coignetiae, p.216

Perennials
Alchemilla mollis, p.302
Anthemis punctata subsp. *cupaniana*, p.286
Artemisia alba 'Canescens'
Centaurea montana, p.294
Darmera peltata, p.240
Euphorbia polychroma, p.285
Geranium sanguineum, p.366
Heterocentron elegans, p.294
Liriope muscari, p.306
Lysimachia punctata, p.261
Nepeta x *faassenii*, p.296
Origanum vulgare 'Aureum', p.302
Osteospermum jucundum, p.289
Phlomis russeliana, p.261
Rheum palmatum 'Atrosanguineum', p.225
Stachys byzantina, p.316
Veronica prostrata and cvs
Waldsteinia ternata, p.397

Annuals and biennials
Any of spreading habit, such as *Tropaeolum*

Rock plants
Acaena microphylla, p.401
Antennaria dioica var. *rosea*, p.378
Arabis alpina subsp. *caucasica* 'Variegata', p.374
Armeria maritima 'Vindictive', p.392
Aubrieta cvs
Aurinia saxatilis, p.362
Campanula portenschlagiana, p.394
Campanula poscharskyana, p.393
Dianthus gratianopolitanus, p.389
Dryas octopetala, p.387
Helianthemum 'Ben More', p.366
Hypericum olympicum
Iberis sempervirens, p.358
Lithodora diffusa 'Heavenly Blue', p.369
Nierembergia repens, p.386
Persicaria affinis and cvs
Phlox douglasii 'Crackerjack', p.391
Phuopsis stylosa, p.364
Thymus serpyllum
Veronica prostrata 'Kapitan', p.369

NATURAL SPREADERS
Mat-forming nasturtiums (Tropaeolum) *make ideal, summer-flowering cover for sunny sites.*

Plants for Dry Shade

Dry, shady conditions persist under evergreen trees throughout the year. Under the summer leaf canopy of deciduous trees, too, very little moisture penetrates, except during prolonged rainfall. A few early-flowering bulbs, such as bluebells (*Hyacinthoides non-scripta*), and small woodland plants grow naturally in deciduous woodlands, dying down as the trees resume growth in spring. In gardens, dry shade occurs under larger, low-branched trees or where eaves extend over borders. Planting should be done in the autumn so that roots are well established by the following spring. Feed regularly and monitor water needs until the plants are established.

Trees and conifers
Ilex aquifolium, p.94
Taxus baccata 'Adpressa'
Taxus cuspidata, p.105
Tsuga canadensis, p.103

Shrubs
Aucuba japonica 'Crotonifolia', p.149
Buxus sempervirens
Choisya ternata, p.123
Cotoneaster horizontalis, p.168
Daphne laureola and forms
Elaeagnus x *ebbingei*
Euonymus japonicus
Fatsia japonica
Gaultheria shallon, p.158
Hedera colchica var. *algeriensis* 'Ravensholst', p.219
Hedera helix
Hedera hibernica, p.219
Hypericum calycinum, p.166
Hypericum x *inodorum* 'Elstead', p.166
Hypericum x *moserianum*
Lonicera pileata, p.172
Mahonia aquifolium, p.153
Osmanthus decorus
Osmanthus delavayi, p.112
Pachysandra terminalis, p.400
Prunus laurocerasus 'Otto Luyken', p.150
Prunus laurocerasus 'Zabeliana', p.150
Prunus lusitanica
Rubus tricolor
Ruscus aculeatus
Ruscus hypoglossum, p.172
Sambucus nigra 'Guincho Purple'
Sarcococca humilis, p.170
Symphoricarpos albus var. *laevigatus*
Vaccinium angustifolium var. *laevifolium*, p.168
Viburnum rhytidophyllum, p.114
Viburnum tinus, p.145
Vinca major
Vinca minor, p.172

Climbers
Berberidopsis corallina, p.207
Celastrus orbiculatus
Cissus striata
Epipremnum aureum 'Marble Queen', p.217
Euonymus fortunei 'Emerald Gaiety'
Hedera canariensis var. *algeriensis*
Lapageria rosea, p.206
Lonicera japonica 'Halliana', p.213
Lonicera periclymenum and cvs
Philodendron scandens, p.218

Ferns
Asplenium ceterach, p.323
Asplenium scolopendrium, p.325
Cyrtomium falcatum, p.323
Davallia canariensis
Dryopteris affinis
Nephrolepis exaltata, p.324
Polypodium vulgare, p.325
Polystichum aculeatum
Pteris cretica, p.323

Perennials
Acanthus spinosus, p.255
Achimenes
Ajuga reptans cvs
Alchemilla mollis, p.302
Chelidonium majus 'Flore Pleno', p.240
Chirita
Corydalis lutea, p.367
Digitalis purpurea
Doronicum x *excelsum* 'Harpur Crewe'
Epimedium grandiflorum and cvs
Epimedium pinnatum subsp. *colchicum*
Euphorbia amygdaloides var. *robbiae*, p.279
Geranium macrorrhizum, p.289
Geranium phaeum, p.240
Iris foetidissima
Kohleria digitaliflora, p.246
Lamium maculatum, p.277
Lunaria rediviva
Luzula sylvatica 'Marginata'
Pachysandra terminalis, p.400
Polygonatum x *hybridum*, p.240
Scopolia carniolica, p.279
Sedum spathulifolium, p.401
Streptocarpus saxorum, p.294
Symphytum 'Goldsmith'
Symphytum ibericum
Tellima grandiflora
Tolmiea menziesii
Tradescantia zebrina 'Quadricolor'
Viola riviniana 'Purpurea', p.381

Bulbs, corms and tubers
Clivia miniata, p.435
Colchicum autumnale, p.453
Haemanthus albiflos
Hyacinthoides hispanica, p.430
Hyacinthoides x *massartiana*, p.430
Hyacinthoides non-scripta, p.430

GREEN FRONDS
The elegant, slightly frilled fronds of the evergreen Hart's tongue fern, Asplenium scolopendrium, *add a welcome splash of bright green to dry, shady areas of the garden. This fern grows best in alkaline soils.*

Plants for Moist Shade

In areas with high rainfall, the soil in parts of the garden that receive little or no sun may be cool and moist throughout the year. Low-lying gardens with a high water table or drainage problems may have shady, permanently moist areas. Similar conditions occur along the margins of natural streams, or when an artificial bog is created beside a garden pond. Take advantage of these situations to grow plants such as broad-leaved hostas, ferns and taller moisture-loving primulas. Plant in spring, enriching lighter soils with organic material. During extended dry periods, keep a check on moisture levels.

Fresh, cool greens
Ferns and large-leaved hostas, seen here with blue Corydalis flexuosa, *will flourish in moist shade.*

Shrubs
Anopterus glandulosus, p.112
Cassiope lycopodioides, p.375
Clethra arborea
Crataegus laevigata 'Punicea'
Cyathodes colensoi, p.372
Danäe racemosa
Gaultheria procumbens, p.399
Kalmia latifolia, p.137
Ledum groenlandicum, p.150
Leucothöe fontanesiana
Lindera benzoin, p.127
Lyonia ligustrina
Neillia thibetica, p.136
Paeonia lutea var. *ludlowii*, p.239
Paeonia rockii, p.238
Paxistima canbyi
Pieris formosa var. *forrestii* 'Wakehurst', p.138
Pittosporum eugenioides
Prunus laurocerasus
RHODODENDRONS, pp.128–30, most
Salix magnifica
Sarcococca ruscifolia
Skimmia japonica, p.171
Viburnum 'Pragense', p.135
Xanthorhiza simplicissima

Climbers
Akebia quinata, p.202, some
Asteranthera ovata
Decumaria sinensis, p.202
Dioscorea discolor, p.217
Humulus lupulus 'Aureus', p.202
Hydrangea petiolaris, p.204
Lonicera tragophylla
Macleania insignis
Mikania scandens
Passiflora coccinea, p.201
Pileostegia viburnoides, p.204
Schizophragma integrifolium, p.204
Smilax china
Thunbergia mysorensis, p.203
Trachelospermum jasminoides, p.203

Ferns
Athyrium nipponicum, p.325
Blechnum tabulare
Cyathea australis, p.96
Cyathea medullaris
Dicksonia antarctica, p.322
Dryopteris goldieana
Lygodium japonicum
Matteuccia struthiopteris, p.324
Onoclea sensibilis, p.324
Osmunda claytoniana
Polystichum munitum, p.322
Selaginella martensii, p.323
Woodwardia radicans

Perennials
Actaea pachypoda, p.267
Ajuga reptans 'Atropurpurea', p.315
Anemone × *hybrida* cvs
Anemonella thalictroides, p.376
Anthurium scherzerianum, p.314
Aruncus dioicus, p.224
Asarum europaeum, p.402
Begonia rex and hybrids
Bergenia
Brunnera macrophylla
Calathea zebrina, p.274
Cardamine pentaphyllos, p.278
Cimicifuga racemosa
Convallaria majalis, p.276
Cortusa matthioli, p.366
Cyathodes colensoi, p.372
Darmera peltata, p.240
Deinanthe caerulea
Dichorisandra reginae, p.258
Digitalis × *mertonensis*
Epigaea gaultherioides, p.376
Galax urceolata, p.363
Geranium nodosum, p.278
Hacquetia epipactis, p.383
Hedyotis michauxii, p.395
Helleborus × *ballardiae* 'December Dawn'
Helleborus × *hybridus*, p.314
HOSTAS, pp.298–9
Isopyrum thalictroides
Jeffersonia diphylla, p.359
Kirengeshoma palmata, p.271
Lamium galeobdolon subsp. *montanum* 'Florentinum'
Lamium maculatum, p.277
Lathraea clandestina, p.279
Lithophragma parviflorum, p.358
Maianthemum canadense, p.375
Maranta leuconeura 'Erythroneura', p.315
Mitella breweri, p.396
Omphalodes cappadocica, p.361
Ourisia caespitosa, p.386
Pachysandra terminalis, p.400
Periscaria campanulata, p.267
Polygonatum × *hybridum*, p.240
Pratia pedunculata, p.395
PRIMULAS (many), pp.280–1
Prunella grandiflora, p.393
Pulmonaria, some
Ranzania japonica
Ruellia devosiana, p.287
Tiarella cordifolia, p.359
Trillium grandiflorum, p.276
Uvularia grandiflora, p.284
Vancouveria hexandra, p.359
Xanthosoma sagittifolium, p.274

Bulbs, corms and tubers
Arisaema
Arisarum proboscideum
Arum italicum 'Marmoratum', p.450
Camassia leichtlinii, p.409
Galanthus elwesii, p.455
Galanthus nivalis and cvs
Galanthus plicatus subsp. *plicatus*
Leucojum aestivum, p.408
Leucojum vernum, p.442
Narcissus cyclamineus, p.434

Shrubs preferring Wall Protection

Walls can provide favourable growing conditions for shrubs, mostly evergreen, that are only moderately frost hardy. Some winter-flowering shrubs also flower more reliably and freely when given wall protection. The best wall-side situations are warm and sunny, and give good shelter from the cold winds of winter and early spring. The warmth from heat loss through house walls, and the well-drained conditions near the base of such walls, also assist the survival of less hardy shrubs.

Abelia floribunda
Abutilon megapotamicum
Acacia podalyriifolia, p.130
Acacia pravissima, p.93
Acca sellowiana, p.138
Aloysia triphylla, p.139
Artemisia arborescens, p.171
Azara serrata, p.131
Buddleja asiatica
Buddleja crispa, p.139
Callistemon citrinus 'Splendens', p.139
Cantua buxifolia, p.151
Carpenteria californica, p.134
Ceanothus impressus, p.141
Chaenomeles speciosa 'Moerloosei', p.126
Chimonanthus praecox
Coronilla valentina subsp. *glauca*, p.153
Cytisus x *spachianus*
Daphne odora 'Aureomarginata', p.170
Dendromecon rigida, p.143
Drimys winteri, p.74
Elsholtzia stauntonii, p.169
Escallonia 'Iveyi', p.114
Fabiana imbricata f. *violacea*, p.141
Fremontodendron 'California Glory', p.119
Fremontodendron 'Pacific Sunset'
Garrya elliptica, p.121
Itea ilicifolia, p.142
Jasminum mesnyi, p.203
Lagerstroemia indica, p.87
Leptospermum scoparium 'Red Damask', p.127
Lonicera fragrantissima
Luma apiculata, p.115
Melianthus major
Myrtus communis, p.123
Olearia x *scilloniensis*
Osteomeles schwerinae, p.134
Piptanthus nepalensis, p.142
Robinia hispida, p.137
Rosa banksiae 'Lutea', p.194
Rosa 'Mermaid', p.194
Rosmarinus officinalis, p.163
Salvia involucrata 'Bethellii', p.231
Solanum crispum 'Glasnevin', p.212
Tibouchina urvilleana, p.118
Vestia foetida

Plants for Paving and Wall Crevices

In mountainous regions, many alpine plants grow in deep cracks and crevices in the rock. Some are clump-forming or trailing in habit; others, such as saxifrages and sempervivums, grow as rosettes extending by means of runners. If laying irregularly shaped paving, leave crevices for small plants, but restrict planting to little-used areas where the plants can survive. When building stone retaining walls, tilt rock slabs slightly backwards to create deep pockets, planting as the wall is being constructed. Most wall plants thrive in sunny situations, but ramondas and most small ferns prefer cool, moist shade.

Annuals and biennials (not walls)
Ageratum houstonianum (small cvs)
Ionopsidium acaule
Limnanthes douglasii, p.348
Lobelia erinus cvs
Lobularia maritima
Malcolmia maritima, p.335
Nemophila maculata, p.331
Nemophila menziesii, p.345
Portulaca grandiflora Series and cvs

Rock plants
Acaena microphylla, p.401
Acantholimon glumaceum (wall), p.389
Achillea x *kellereri*, p.387
Achillea x *lewisii* 'King Edward'
Aethionema 'Warley Rose', p.388
Alyssum montanum
Androsace sarmentosa
Antennaria dioica
Armeria maritima 'Vindictive', p.392
Artemisia pedemontana
Artemisia schmidtiana
Asplenium ceterach, p.323
Aubrieta
Aurinia saxatilis 'Citrina', p.361
Campanula cochleariifolia, p.395
Campanula poscharskyana, p.393
Cassiope 'Edinburgh', p.358
Chamaemelum nobile
Chiastophyllum oppositifolium (wall), p.361
Cyananthus microphyllus, p.395
Cymbalaria muralis
Dianthus deltoides
Draba aizoides
Dryas octopetala, p.387
Erigeron karvinskianus, p.389
Erinus alpinus, p.378
Gypsophila repens and cvs
Haberlea rhodopensis 'Virginalis', p.385
Helianthemum
Hypericum olympicum
Lithodora diffusa 'Heavenly Blue', p.369
Mazus reptans, p.380
Mentha requienii
Nierembergia repens, p.386
Parahebe lyallii
Phlox douglasii cvs
Physoplexis comosa (wall), p.392
Ramonda myconi (wall only), p.394
Saxifraga cotyledon, p.364
Sedum spathulifolium 'Cape Blanco', p.403
Sempervivum montanum, p.402
Thymus serpyllum and cvs
Vitaliana primuliflora, p.384

FLORAL COVERING
Spreading Aubrieta, *with masses of flowers tumbling over a wall, is perfect for growing in crevices.*

Plants for Containers

Containers full of plants can brighten patios, courtyards and balconies. These situations are often sheltered and sunny, so use large containers which retain more moisture than small ones. Small trees, conifers or shrubs in small groups, together with perennials, will give long-term interest in shape and foliage, with periods of flowering. For colourful displays, plant spring-flowering bulbs, followed by petunias and tagetes, which will flower throughout the summer.

Trees
Acer negundo
Cordyline australis and cvs
Crataegus laevigata and cvs
Eucalyptus (when young)
Ficus (most)
Ilex aquifolium and cvs
Jacaranda mimosifolia, p.75
Laurus nobilis
Malus (small species and cvs)
Melia azederach, p.72
Olea europaea
Phoenix canariensis
Prunus (small species and cvs)
Sorbus (small species and cvs)
Washingtonia

Conifers
All the small species and cvs of:
Abies
Chamaecyparis
Juniperus
Picea
Pinus
Thuja
Thujopsis dolabrata

Shrubs
Buxus sempervirens and cvs
Catharanthus roseus, p.156
Erica
FUCHSIAS, pp.160–1
Hebe
HYDRANGEAS, p.140
Lavandula
Myrtus communis, p.126
Pittosporum
RHODODENDRONS (most), pp.128–30, most
ROSES (most), pp.180–4, some
Santolina
Senecio (shrubby species)
Spiraea
Viburnum tinus, p.145

Climbers
Cissus antarctica, p.218
CLEMATIS (small cvs), pp.208–9, some

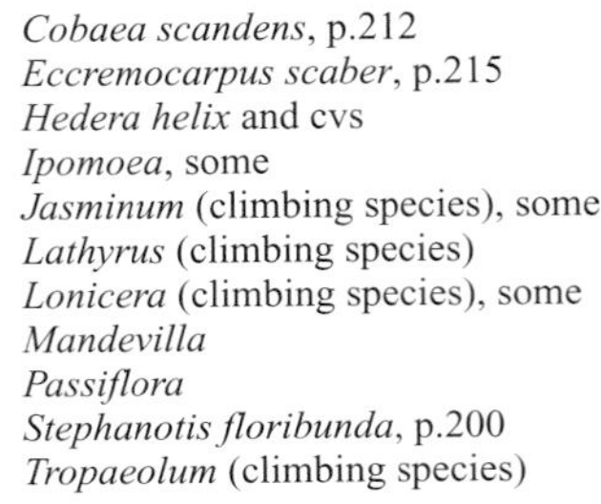

Cobaea scandens, p.212
Eccremocarpus scaber, p.215
Hedera helix and cvs
Ipomoea, some
Jasminum (climbing species), some
Lathyrus (climbing species)
Lonicera (climbing species), some
Mandevilla
Passiflora
Stephanotis floribunda, p.200
Tropaeolum (climbing species)

Ferns
Adiantum (most)
Asplenium scolopendrium Marginatum Group, p.325
Athyrium niponicum, p.324
Polypodium vulgare 'Cornubiense', p.324
Polystichum setiferum Divisilobum Group, p.323

Perennials
Agapanthus
Bergenia
DAYLILIES, p.263
Geranium, some
Geum
HOSTAS, pp.298–9
Phormium
PRIMULAS (tall species and cvs), pp.280–1
Pulmonaria, some
Rudbeckia fulgida var. *sullivantii* 'Goldsturm', p.262
Salvia (many)
Stachys, some
Verbena, some

Annuals and biennials
Ageratum
Bassia scoparia f. *trichophylla*, p.347
Browallia speciosa, p.274
Calendula officinalis Series and cvs
Callistephus chinensis Series and cvs
Lobelia erinus cvs
Nemesia strumosa and Series
Petunia
Salpiglossis sinuata Series and cvs
Solenostemon scutellarioides Series and cvs, pp.336, 341
Tagetes
Viola x *wittrockiana* hybrids

Rock plants
All rock plants are suitable, the following being particularly recommended:
Campanula (many), some
Dianthus (many)
Geranium (several), some
Hebe
Helianthemum
Iberis sempervirens, p.358
Penstemon (many), some
Periscaria affinis
Phlox (several)
Primula auricula and hybrids
Saponaria ocymoides, p.390
Saxifraga (many)
Silene schafta, p.391

Springtime tulips
Terracotta containers planted in late autumn with single and double tulips make an elegant and colourful arrangement. Once the flowers have faded, replace the pots with containers of summer-flowering annuals to prolong the display.

Bulbs, corms and tubers
All bulbous plants are suitable, the following being particularly recommended:
CROCUSES, pp.444–5
DAFFODILS, pp.432–34
HYACINTHS, p.447
irises (bulbous species), pp.234–5
LILIES (most), pp.416–7
TULIPS, pp.426–428
Zantedeschia aethiopica 'Crowborough', p.409 🏆

Water plants
Watertight containers are ideal for the following:
Acorus calamus 'Argenteostriatus', p.463
Aponogeton distachyos, p.463
Azolla filiculoides, p.464
Eichhornia crassipes, p.462
Menyanthes trifoliata, p.462
Nelumbo nucifera and cvs
Pontederia cordata, p.464 🏆
Thalia dealbata
WATER LILIES (small cvs), p.466

Trailing Plants for Walls or Baskets

Many plants grow naturally in crevices, their trailing stems covering large areas of vertical rock. In gardens, trailing alpines may be planted in pockets of earth in dry stone walls. If a garden has retaining walls, climbers or low-growing conifers, trailing from the top, can soften brickwork. Smaller trailing plants, such as tender perennials or annuals, are ideal for hanging baskets. After planting, baskets may be set on large, inverted pots on a patio or old tree stump, the plants forming a conical mound of tumbling stems and flowers.

Conifers
Juniperus conferta
Juniperus horizontalis and cvs
Juniperus squamata 'Blue Carpet'
Microbiota decussata, p.106

Shrubs
Arctostaphylos uva-ursi, p.400
Ceanothus thyrsiflorus var. *repens*, p.164
Chorizema ilicifolium, p.153
Cotoneaster microphyllus
Euonymus fortunei 'Coloratus'
Fuchsia procumbens, p.161
Genista lydia, p.371
Hebe pinguifolia 'Pagei', p.363
Helichrysum petiolare, p.171
Lantana montevidensis, p.163
Leptospermum rupestre, p.156
Loiseleuria procumbens, p.389
Nematanthus strigillosus
Salix lindleyana
Salix repens, p.152

Perennials
Achimenes 'Peach Blossom'
Aeschynanthus speciosus, p.305
Aporocactus flagelliformis, p.479
Campanula isophylla
Carpobrotus edulis
Columnea (most)
Convolvulus sabatius, p.368
Cyanotis kewensis
Elatostema repens, p.315
Episcia cupreata, p.313
Episcia dianthiflora, p.311
Glechoma hederacea 'Variegata', p.312
Hedera colchica 'Dentata Variegata'
Hedera colchica 'Sulphur Heart'
Lampranthus spectabilis, p.479
Lotus berthelotii, p.293
Pelargonium peltatum
Peperomia scandens
Plectranthus verticillatus
Ruellia devosiana, p.287
Sarmienta repens
Tradescantia fluminensis and cvs
Tradescantia zebrina, p.313
Tropaeolum polyphyllum, p.305
Verbena peruviana
Verbena 'Sissinghurst', p.292

Annuals and biennials
Calceolaria integrifolia
Limnanthes douglasii, p.348
Lobelia erinus cvs
Nemophila maculata, p.331
Nolana paradoxa
Petunia Cascade Series
Petunia Jamboree Series
Petunia Surfinia Series
Portulaca grandiflora Series and cvs
Sanvitalia procumbens, p.348
Tropaeolum majus Series and cvs

Rock plants
Acaena 'Blue Haze'
Androsace lanuginosa, p.389
Arabis caucasica
Campanula cochleariifolia, p.395
Cymbalaria muralis
Cytisus × *beanii*, p.361
Euphorbia myrsinites, p.383
Gypsophila repens
Iberis sempervirens, p.358
Lithodora diffusa cvs
Lysimachia nummularia, p.398
Oenothera macrocarpa, p.397
Othonna cheirifolia, p.370
Parahebe catarractae, p.368
Parochetus communis, p.396
Persicaria vacciniifolia, p.399
Phlox subulata
Pterocephalus perennis, p.392
Saxifraga stolonifera

SUMMER DISPLAY
Colourful, trailing plants are ideal for vibrant summer displays in hanging baskets and wall-mounted containers. In this exuberant planting, magenta petunias are combined with yellow bidens, a compact fuchsia and pink pelargoniums.

Plants with Aromatic Foliage

The leaves of many plants contain essential aromatic oils, used in medicine or cooking. For gardeners, their value lies in the pleasant, pungent aromas released naturally or when bruised. Those of culinary value, such as rosemary, are often grown in herb gardens. Low-growing thymes may be planted next to paths or between paving stones to give off scent when trodden underfoot. The fragrance from trees may be best appreciated as it drifts through the garden on the wind.

Trees
Agonis flexuosa, p.86
Atherosperma moschatum
Eucalyptus
Juglans regia, p.62
Laurus nobilis
Phellodendron chinense, p.77
Populus balsamifera
Populus trichocarpa
Sassafras albidum, p.64
Umbellularia californica, p.70

Conifers
Calocedrus decurrens, p.102
Chamaecyparis
Cupressus
Juniperus
Pseudotsuga menziesii
Thuja (most)

Shrubs
Aloysia triphylla, p.139
Artemisia abrotanum, p.172
Boronia megastigma, p.152
Caryopteris × *clandonensis* 'Arthur Simmonds', p.164
Choisya ternata, p.123
Cistus laurifolius
Elsholtzia stauntonii, p.169
Gaultheria procumbens, p.399
Helichrysum italicum
Hyssopus officinalis, p.164
Lavandula (most)
Lindera
Myrtus communis, p.126
PELARGONIUMS (scented-leaved forms), pp.248–9
Perovskia 'Blue Spire', p.164
Phlomis fruticosa, p.166
Prostanthera
Rhododendron cinnabarinum subsp. *xanthocodon*, p.129
Rhododendron rubiginosum
Ribes sanguineum 'Brocklebankii', p.151
Rosa rubiginosa, p.181
Rosmarinus officinalis, p.163
Salvia officinalis cvs
Santolina chamaecyparissus
Zanthoxylum piperitum, p.141

Perennials
Artemisia absinthium 'Lambrook Silver'
Chamaemelum nobile
Galium odoratum, p.285
Geranium macrorrhizum, p.289
Houttuynia cordata 'Chameleon', p.463
Kaempferia pulchra, p.293
Mentha, some
Monarda didyma
Myrrhis odorata, p.242
Origanum vulgare
Perovskia atriplicifolia
Tanacetum parthenium, p.331

Rock plants
Mentha requienii
Origanum laevigatum, p.366
Satureja montana
Thymus

Scented seating
A stylish bench makes the perfect resting place when surrounded by aromatic herbs such as lavender, thyme and marjoram.

Plants with Fragrant Flowers

Fragrance is released from the flowers of numerous plants. It can be strong, pervading the air around the plant, or apparent only when you are close to individual blooms. Some plants release scent continually, but with others it is more noticeable at night. A sunny, sheltered patio is an ideal situation for small fragrant plants. Position large scented shrubs close to paths, and train fragrant climbers around doorways. Hyacinths in pots bring welcome early spring fragrance indoors.

Trees
Acacia dealbata, p.79
Aesculus hippocastanum, p.60
Bauhinia variegata, p.93
Clethra arborea
Crataegus monogyna
Drimys winteri, p.74
Eucryphia lucida, p.86
Fraxinus ornus, p.72
Genista aetnensis, p.89
Laburnum × *watereri* 'Vossii', p.88
MAGNOLIAS, p.71
Malus coronaria 'Charlottae'
Malus hupehensis, p.70
Malus 'Profusion', p.73
Pittosporum tenuifolium, p.123
Pittosporum undulatum
Plumeria rubra, p.92
Prunus mume 'Beni-chidori', p.126
Prunus padus 'Grandiflora', p.72
Prunus × *yedoensis*, p.83
Pterostyrax hispida
Robinia pseudoacacia
Styrax japonicus, p.73
Styrax obassia
Tilia × *euchlora*
Tilia 'Petiolaris', p.64
Virgilia oroboides

Shrubs
Abelia grandiflora, p.117
Abeliophyllum distichum
Azara microphylla, p.121
Berberis × *stenophylla*, p.131
Boronia megastigma, p.152
Brugmansia arborea
Buddleja asiatica
Buddleja davidii and cvs
Camellia sasanqua 'Narumigata', p.124
Chimonanthus praecox
Choisya ternata, p.123
Clerodendrum bungei, p.144
Clerodendrum trichotomum, p.143
Clethra delavayi, p.117
Colletia hystrix, p.143
Coronilla valentina subsp. *glauca*, p.153
Corylopsis pauciflora, p.127
Cytisus battandieri, p.119
Daphne (many), most
Deutzia × *elegantissima* cvs
Edgeworthia chrysantha
Elaeagnus × *ebbingei* 'Limelight', p.149
Erica arborea
Erica lusitanica
Fothergilla major, p.123
Gardenia augusta 'Veitchii', p.154
Hamamelis mollis
Heliotropium arborescens, p.163
Itea ilicifolia, p.142
Lavandula 'Hidcote', p.163
Lavandula stoechas, p.163
Ligustrum lucidum 'Excelsum Superbum', p.123
LILACS (most), p.116
Lonicera fragrantissima
Lupinus arboreus, p.165
MAGNOLIAS, p.71
Osmanthus
Philadelphus (many)
Pittosporum tobira
ROSES (many), pp.180–4, some
Sarcococca
Viburnum (many), some

Climbers
Clematis montana 'Elizabeth'
Hoya carnosa, p.204
Jasminum (many), most
Lathyrus odoratus and cvs
Lonicera (many), some
Mandevilla laxa
ROSES (many), pp.180–4, some
Stephanotis floribunda, p.200
Trachelospermum
Wattakaka sinensis
Wisteria

Perennials
Anemone sylvestris, p.276
CARNATIONS and PINKS (most), pp.290–1
Clematis heracleifolia 'Wyevale', p.209
Convallaria majalis, p.276
Cosmos atrosanguineus, p.253
Crambe cordifolia, p.224
Galium odoratum, p.285
Hedychium gardnerianum, p.232
Hemerocallis lilioasphodelus, p.263
Hesperis matronalis, p.241
HOSTAS (some), pp.298–9
Iris graminea
Iris unguicularis
Meehania urticifolia
Mirabilis jalapa, p.247
Myrrhis odorata, p.242
Nicotiana sylvestris, p.224
Petasites fragrans
Primula elatior, p.281
Primula veris, p.281
Tulbaghia natalensis
Verbena × *hybrida* Series and cvs
Viola odorata

Annuals and biennials
Amberboa moschata, p.347
Antirrhinum majus Series
Argemone mexicana, p.347
Dianthus barbatus Roundabout Series, p.338
Erysimum cheiri Series and cvs
Exacum affine, p.393
Iberis amara, p.330
Lathyrus odoratus and cvs
Limnanthes douglasii, p.348
Matthiola incana
Mentzelia lindleyi, p.348
Nicotiana alata, p.251
Primula Primrose Group
Reseda odorata, p.331
Scabiosa atropurpurea
Verbena × *hybrida* (most)

Rock plants
Alyssum montanum
Dianthus (most)
Erysimum helveticum, p.385
Papaver croceum
Primula auricula
Viola odorata

Bulbs, corms and tubers
Amaryllis belladonna, p.424
Arisaema candidissimum, p.451
Chlidanthus fragrans, p.452
Crinum bulbispermum
Crinum × *powellii*, p.410
Crocus angustifolius
Crocus longiflorus
Cyclamen persicum, p.456
Cyclamen repandum
Eucharis × *grandiflora*, p.441
Freesia (most)
Hyacinthus orientalis and cvs
Hymenocallis
LILIES (several), pp.416–7
Muscari armeniacum, p.449
Narcissus jonquilla and Div.7 hybrids
Narcissus tazetta and Div.8 hybrids
Ornithogalum arabicum, p.436
Polianthes tuberosa

Orchids
Cattleya J.A.Carbone, p.309
Coelogyne flaccida, p.308

Cacti
Epiphyllum laui, p.477

Water plants
Aponogeton distachyos, p.465
Nymphaea 'Blue Beauty', p.466
Nymphaea 'James Brydon', p.466
Nymphaea odorata 'Sulphurea Grandiflora'

INTERMINGLING FRAGRANCE
A cascade of climbing roses, underplanted with Lilium regale *and masses of lavender looks beautiful and gives off a delicious scent.*

Decorative Fruits or Seed Heads

As winter approaches, dull corners of the garden or featureless borders can be brightened with the colourful fruits or berries of berberis, cotoneasters, viburnums and other ornamental free-fruiting shrubs. On pergolas and trellis, *Celastrus orbiculatus* and *Clematis orientalis* provide late-season interest with trailing skeins of yellow fruits and feathery seeds. Wall-trained pyracanthas will colour drab winter walls with yellow, orange or scarlet fruits. Hollies (*Ilex*) also provide berried material for winter decoration. The dried seed heads of many plants are used in flower arrangements, to give a contrast in form and texture.

LATE-SEASON SCULPTURE
The huge, spiky seed heads of Allium cristophii *complement the dried brown seed pods of* Nigella damascena, *adding form and texture to this herbaceous border as winter approaches.*

Trees
Annona reticulata
Arbutus
Cornus kousa
Cotoneaster frigidus
Crataegus (most)
HOLLIES (most), pp.94–5, most
Koelreuteria paniculata, p.88
MAGNOLIAS, p.71, some
Malus (most)
Photinia davidiana, p.90
Schinus molle
Sorbus (most)

Conifers
Abies (some)
Cedrus (some)
Picea (some)
Pinus (some)

Shrubs
Aucuba japonica, p.148
Berberis (most), some
Callicarpa bodinieri var. *giraldii*, p.144
Chaenomeles
x *Citrofortunella microcarpa*, p.147
Cotoneaster (most), some
Cyphomandra betacea, p.121
Decaisnea fargesii, p.118
Euonymus (many), some
Gaultheria mucronata and cvs
Hippophäe rhamnoides, p.120
Hypericum x *inodorum* 'Elstead', p.166
Leycesteria formosa
Poncirus trifoliata
Pyracantha
ROSES (most), pp.180–4, some
Sambucus racemosa
Sarcococca hookeriana var. *digyna*, p.170
Shepherdia argentea
Skimmia (some)
Symphoricarpos
Symplocos paniculata, p.134
Vaccinium vitis-idaea
Viburnum (several), some

Climbers
Actinidia deliciosa
Akebia, some
Billardiera longiflora, p.216
Cardiospermum halicacabum
Celastrus orbiculatus
Clematis orientalis
Holboellia coriacea
ROSES (several), pp.180–4, some
Trichosanthes cucumerina var. *anguina*
Tropaeolum speciosum, p.206

Perennials
Actaea
Clintonia borealis
Disporum hookeri
Duchesnea indica
Iris foetidissima
Ophiopogon
Physalis alkekengi
Phytolacca
Podophyllum
Smilacina racemosa, p.233

Annuals and biennials
Briza maxima
Capsicum annuum 'Holiday Cheer'
Coix lacryma-jobi, p.320
Lagurus ovatus, p.318
Lunaria annua, p.337
Martynia annua, p.332
Nicandra physalodes
Nigella damascena and cvs
Pulsatilla vulgaris, p.360
Solanum capsicastrum
Zea mays

Rock plants
Acaena microphylla, p.401
Cornus canadensis, p.386
Dryas octopetala, p.387
Gaultheria (most)
Maianthemum
Margyricarpus pinnatus
Mitchella repens
Nertera granadensis, p.347
Pulsatilla (most)

Bulbs, corms and tubers
Allium cristophii, p.437
Arisaema triphyllum, p.430
Arum italicum 'Marmoratum', p.450
Cardiocrinum giganteum, p.410

Water plants
Nelumbo
Nuphar lutea, p.467
Thalia dealbata

Flowers for Cutting

With careful selection, flowers can be cut from the garden at most times of the year, from the Christmas rose (*Helleborus niger*) in mid-winter to *Nerine bowdenii* in autumn. In small gardens, integrate plants for cutting into the general scheme, and leave some blooms for display; or plant away from the house so that the cutting is less noticeable. Feed regularly to counteract the weakening effects of cutting plants.

Shrubs
Calluna vulgaris (tall cvs)
Camellia japonica cvs
Erica
Forsythia
Hamamelis mollis
LILACS, p.116
Lonicera fragrantissima
Philadelphus
ROSES (some), pp.180–4, some
Salix caprea
Turraea obtusifolia, p.138

Perennials
Alstroemeria Ligtu Hybrids, p.439
Anaphalis
Anchusa azurea
Anemone × *hybrida* cvs
Astrantia major, p.287
CARNATIONS and PINKS, pp.290–1
Cattleya (most)
CHRYSANTHEMUMS, pp.268–9
Cymbidium (most)
DELPHINIUMS (most), p.230
Helleborus niger, p.313
Phalaenopsis (most)
Phlox paniculata cvs
Rudbeckia (most)
Strelitzia reginae, p.275

Annuals and biennials
Amaranthus caudatus, p.338
Amberboa moschata, p.347
Callistephus chinensis Series and cvs
Centaurea cyanus and cvs
Clarkia
Eustoma grandiflorum, p.331
Gaillardia pulchella 'Lollipops', p.350
Gypsophila elegans, p.330
Lathyrus odoratus and cvs
Malope trifida, p.336
Matthiola cvs
Moluccella laevis, p.347
Rhodanthe chlorocephala subsp. *rosea*, p.333
Xeranthemum annuum
Zinnia elegans Series and cvs (tall hybrids)

Bulbs, corms and tubers
Allium (tall species)
Alstroemeria (tall species and cvs)
DAFFODILS (tall species and cvs), pp.432–34
DAHLIAS, pp.420–21
GLADIOLI (most), p.411
LILIES (some), pp.416–7
Nerine bowdenii, p.440
Ornithogalum thyrsoides, p.436
Polianthes tuberosa
TULIPS (tall cvs), pp.426–28
Zantedeschia aethiopica

Cutting garden
In this well-tended plot, garden favourites such as dahlias and sweet peas are specially grown for cutting.

Trees

Trees

Trees are the most permanent elements in any planting scheme. Fortunately there is a wealth of ornamental trees in cultivation to suit the individual climate and growing conditions in your garden.

What are trees?

Tree are long-lived, deciduous or evergreen, perennial, woody plants that have a lifespan ranging from decades to several centuries. Most have a single stem, with a crown of branches above a clear trunk, although many species produce multiple stems, either naturally or as a result of pruning and training. Trees are diverse in size, ranging from dwarf conifers at 1m (3ft) tall, to forest giants at 90m (300ft) or more in height. They are equally variable in shape, from narrowly conical, through columnar to rounded and spreading, offering strong design elements within the garden. Most conifers are evergreen and cone-bearing.

Choosing trees

Since a tree is probably the most expensive of garden plants and usually the most prominent, selection and siting are the most important decisions – even more so in a small garden with room for only one or two specimens. If it is to thrive, you must consider whether a tree is suitable for your garden's climate, soil type and degree of exposure. It is then vital to research the tree's final height and spread, and site it where it will have room to mature unimpeded by and not interfering with walls, pipes, drains or cables.

Designing with trees

Trees make a strong visual impact in a planting scheme by virtue of their size alone; they can also contribute to the garden's structure. For example, several trees can be planted to form enclosures or define spaces; they can be used in pairs to frame a view, or in rows to form an avenue or an arch. In exposed or very large gardens, a row of trees can provide wind protection to an area five times its own height. In smaller gardens, trees that tolerate clipping, notably hornbeam (*Carpinus betulus*), beech (*Fagus sylvatica*) and yew (*Taxus baccata*), are ideal for a wind- and noise-filtering hedge that also affords a degree of privacy.

When a tree is grown singly as a specimen plant, it can create an interesting focal point, which is especially effective if it can be viewed from several angles. The tree's shape and ornamental qualities also influence the style of the garden. The neat, crisp outlines of the narrowly columnar *Juniperus chinensis* 'Obelisk', for example, or the flame-shaped *Carpinus betulus* 'Fastigiata' would suit a formal garden design, whereas the rounded, relaxed

Fruit for colour
In autumn, the rowans *(Sorbus)* offer berries of many colours, among them the creamy yellow fruits of *S.* 'Joseph Rock' (left), the pearly white fruits of *S. cashmiriana* and the rich scarlets of *S. aucuparia*. Many also have splendid autumn foliage.

Conifers on display
Above: The extraordinary and exciting diversity of size, form, texture and colour to be found in dwarf

All-round interest
Right: Cherries *(Prunus)* often have more than one season of interest and are among the most valuable

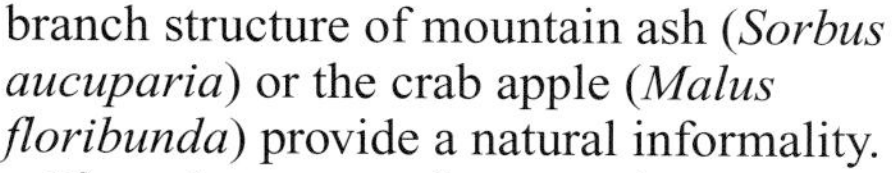

SPRING BENEFITS
Above: With the glorious *Malus* 'Katherine', a profusion of large double flowers in spring gives rise to tiny, red-flushed, yellow fruits in autumn.

SUMMER PROMISE
Left: *Acer shirasawanum* 'Aureum' is noted for its elegant habit, compact size and vibrant leaf colour – the verdant greens of late spring and summer turning into peerless autumn brilliance.

ATTRACTIVE BARK
Below: Many eucalyptus, such as this *Eucalyptus pauciflora subsp. niphophila*, are renowned for their beautiful, peeling and flaking bark.

branch structure of mountain ash (*Sorbus aucuparia*) or the crab apple (*Malus floribunda*) provide a natural informality.

If you have room for several trees, you can develop a woodland-style garden, in the shelter of which shade-loving plants can be established. In an oriental-style garden, Japanese maples (*Acer* species) and Japanese cherries such as *Prunus* 'Shirofugen' are ideal. Many small trees are suitable for growing in containers and can then be used to decorate patios, courtyards and roof terraces.

MAINTAINING YEAR-ROUND INTEREST

Broadleaved evergreens, such as hollies (*Ilex*) and *Quercus coccifera*, provide an invaluable green backdrop throughout the year, while conifers can provide a useful contrast in shape and texture: many have a strong conical outline; others, such as *Picea breweriana*, weep gracefully. Dwarf conifers range from the neat, rounded domes of *Pinus mugo* 'Gnom' to the spreading *Juniperus* × *pfitzeriana*.

Broadleaved, deciduous trees offer a seasonally changing palette of leaf colour, from the fresh, lemon-yellows and lime-greens of spring to the ruddy brilliance of autumn. The form of their foliage is infinitely variable: why not try interesting textural contrasts such as the delicate false acacia (*Robinia pseudoacacia*) with the architectural *Catalpa bignonioides*.

Although most flowering and fruiting trees bloom in spring, some produce a welcome burst of colour at other times. *Maackia amurensis*, many eucryphias and Arbutus unedo bear their flowers in late summer and autumn, while *Magnolia campbellii* and *Prunus* × *subhirtella* 'Autumnalis' brighten dark winter days.

SIZE CATEGORIES USED WITHIN THIS GROUP		
LARGE OVER 15M (50FT)	MEDIUM 10–15M (30–50FT)	SMALL UP TO 10M (30FT)

WHITE–YELLOW

Aesculus hippocastanum
(Horse-chestnut)
Vigorous, deciduous, spreading tree. Has large leaves with 5 or 7 leaflets and spires of white flowers, flushed pink and yellow in centres, in spring. Spiny fruits contain glossy, brown nuts in autumn.

100ft 30m
75ft 22.5m
0

***Aesculus* × *carnea* 'Briotii'**
Deciduous, round-headed tree. Leaves, consisting of 5 or 7 leaflets, are glossy, dark green. Panicles of red flowers are borne in late spring.

Acer macrophyllum
(Oregon maple)
Deciduous, round-headed tree with large, deeply lobed, dark green leaves that turn yellow and orange in autumn. Yellowish-green flowers in spring are followed by pale green fruits.

100ft 30m
75ft 22.5m
0

WHITE

Populus maximowiczii
Fast-growing, deciduous, conical tree. Oval, heart-shaped, bright green leaves have green-veined, white undersides and turn yellow in autumn. Bears long, pendent seed heads surrounded by silky, white hairs in late summer.

100ft 30m
75ft 22.5m
0

Aesculus chinensis
(Chinese horse-chestnut)
Slow-growing, deciduous, spreading tree. Leaves are glossy, dark green with 7 leaflets. Slender spires of white flowers are produced in mid-summer.

Populus alba
(Abele, White poplar)
Deciduous, spreading tree with wavy-margined or lobed leaves, dark green above, white beneath, turning yellow in autumn.

WHITE–PURPLE

***Castanea sativa* 'Albomarginata'**
Deciduous, spreading tree. Has glossy, white-edged, dark green leaves that turn yellow in autumn. Spikes of creamy-yellow flowers in summer are followed by edible fruits in autumn.

100ft 30m
75ft 22.5m 0

Liriodendron tulipifera
(Tulip tree)
Vigorous, deciduous, spreading tree. Deep green leaves, with a cut-off or notched tip and lobed sides, turn yellow in autumn. In mid-summer, has tulip-shaped, orange-marked, greenish-white flowers.

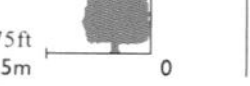

100ft 30m
75ft 22.5m 0

Prunus serotina
(Black cherry, Wild rum cherry)
Deciduous, spreading tree. Spikes of fragrant, white flowers appear in early summer followed by red fruits that turn black in autumn. Glossy, dark green leaves become yellow in autumn.

100ft 30m
75ft 22.5m 0

Brachychiton acerifolius
(Illawarra flame tree)
Deciduous tree with clusters of bright scarlet flowers in late winter, spring or summer before 3–7-lobed, lustrous leaves develop.
Min. 7–10°C (45–50°F).

100ft 30m
75ft 22.5m 0

Fagus sylvatica* f. *atropunicea
(Copper beech, Purple beech)
Deciduous, round-headed tree with oval, wavy-margined, purple leaves. In autumn, leaves turn a rich coppery colour.

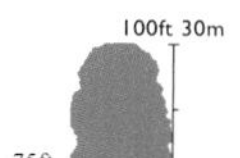

100ft 30m
75ft 22.5m 0

PURPLE–GREEN

***Acer platanoides* 'Crimson King'**
Vigorous, deciduous, spreading tree. Leaves are large, lobed and deep reddish-purple, turning orange in autumn. Tiny, red-tinged, deep yellow flowers are carried in mid-spring.

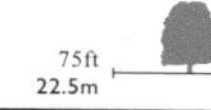

100ft 30m
75ft 22.5m 0

Populus × canescens
(Grey poplar)
Vigorous, deciduous, spreading tree with slightly lobed leaves, grey when young, glossy, dark green in summer and yellow in autumn.
Usually bears greyish-red catkins in spring.

100ft 30m
75ft 22.5m 0

***Populus × canadensis* 'Robusta'**
Fast-growing, deciduous, conical tree with upright branches. Broadly oval, bronze, young leaves mature to glossy, dark green. Bears long, red catkins in spring.

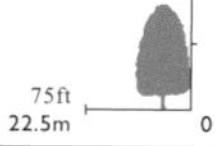

100ft 30m
75ft 22.5m 0

GREEN

***Populus* x *canadensis* 'Serotina de Selys'**
Fast-growing, deciduous, upright tree. Has broadly oval, grey-green leaves, pale green when young, and red catkins in spring.

Quercus macranthera
(Caucasian oak)
Deciduous, spreading, stout-branched, handsome tree with large, deeply lobed, dark green leaves.

Alnus incana (Grey alder)
Deciduous, conical tree useful for cold, wet areas and poor soils. Yellow-brown catkins are carried in late winter and early spring, followed by oval, dark green leaves.

Fagus sylvatica* f. *pendula
(Weeping beech)
Deciduous, weeping tree with oval, wavy-edged, mid-green leaves that in autumn take on rich hues of yellow and orange-brown.

Quercus robur* f. *fastigiata
Deciduous, upright, columnar tree of dense habit carrying lobed, dark green leaves.

Alnus cordata (Italian alder)
Fast-growing, deciduous, conical tree. Yellow, male catkins appear in late winter and early spring, followed by heart-shaped, glossy, deep green leaves. Has persistent, round, woody fruits in autumn.

***Populus nigra* 'Italica'**
(Lombardy poplar)
Very fast-growing, deciduous, narrowly columnar tree with erect branches, diamond-shaped, bright green leaves and red catkins in mid-spring.

Quercus canariensis
(Algerian oak, Mirbeck's oak)
Deciduous or semi-evergreen tree, narrow when young, broadening with age. Large, shallowly lobed, rich green leaves become yellowish-brown in autumn, often persisting into late winter.

Acer cappadocicum* subsp. *lobelii
(Lobel's maple)
Deciduous tree of narrow, upright habit, well-suited for growing in restricted space. Has wavy-edged, lobed leaves that turn yellow in autumn.

Juglans regia (Walnut)
Deciduous tree with a spreading head. Leaves, usually with 5 or 7 leaflets, are aromatic, bronze-purple when young, glossy, mid-green when mature. Produces edible nuts.

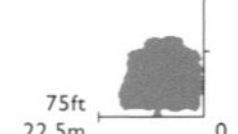

Tilia oliveri
Deciduous, spreading, open tree with pointed, heart-shaped leaves, bright green above and silvery-white beneath. Produces small, fragrant, greenish-yellow flowers in summer, followed by winged fruits.

100ft 30m
75ft 22.5m
0

Juglans nigra (Black walnut)
Fast-growing, deciduous, handsome, spreading tree with large, aromatic leaves of many pointed, glossy, dark green leaflets. Produces edible nuts in autumn.

100ft 30m
75ft 22.5m
0

Quercus muehlenbergii
Deciduous, round-headed tree with sharply toothed, bright green leaves.

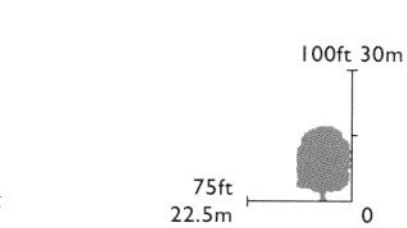

Celtis australis (Nettle tree)
Deciduous, spreading tree. Has oval, pointed, sharply toothed, dark green leaves and small, purple-black fruits.

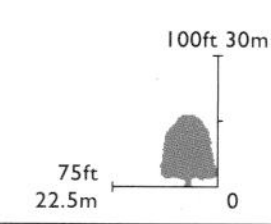

Platanus* × *hispanica
(London plane)
Vigorous, deciduous, spreading tree with ornamental, flaking bark. Has large, sharply lobed, bright green leaves. Spherical fruit clusters hang from shoots in autumn.

Nothofagus* × *alpina
(Rauli, Southern beech)
Fast-growing, deciduous, conical tree. Leaves, with many impressed veins, are dark green, turning orange and red in autumn.

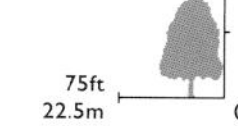

GREEN

Sassafras albidum
Deciduous, upright, later spreading tree. Aromatic, glossy, dark green leaves vary from oval to deeply lobed and turn yellow or red in autumn. Has insignificant, yellowish-green flowers in spring.

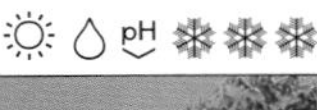

Juglans ailantifolia* var. *cordiformis
Deciduous, spreading tree with large, aromatic leaves consisting of many glossy, bright green leaflets. Long, yellow-green, male catkins are borne in early summer. In autumn has edible nuts.

Quercus nigra (Water oak)
Deciduous, spreading tree with glossy, bright green foliage retained until well into winter.

Nothofagus obliqua
(Roblé, Southern beech)
Fast-growing, deciduous, elegant tree with slender, arching branches. Has deep green leaves that turn orange and red in autumn.

Firmiana simplex
(Chinese parasol tree)
Robust, deciduous tree with large, lobed leaves, small, showy, lemon-yellow flowers and papery, leaf-like fruits. Min. 2°C (36°F).

***Tilia* 'Petiolaris'**
(Pendent silver lime)
Deciduous, spreading tree with pendent branches. Pointed, heart-shaped leaves, dark green above, silver beneath, shimmer in the breeze. Has fragrant, creamy-yellow flowers in late summer.

***Quercus petraea* 'Columna'**
Deciduous, upright, slender tree with large, wavy-edged, leathery, dark green leaves, tinged bronze when young.

Quercus castaneifolia
Deciduous, spreading tree with sharply toothed leaves, glossy, dark green above, grey beneath.

Fagus sylvatica (Common beech)
Deciduous, spreading tree with oval, wavy-edged leaves. These are pale green when young, mid- to dark green when mature, and turn rich yellow and orange-brown in autumn, when nuts are produced.

GREEN

Quercus frainetto (Hungarian oak)
Fast-growing, deciduous, spreading tree with a large, domed head and handsome, large, deeply lobed, dark green leaves.

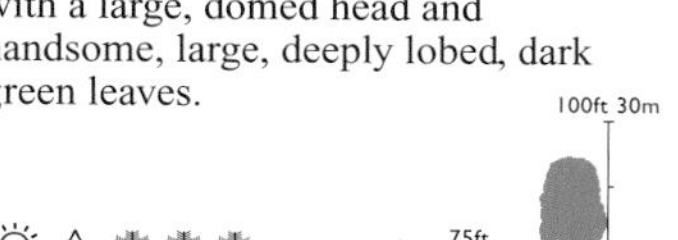

Quercus palustris (Pin oak)
Fast-growing, deciduous, spreading tree with slender branches, pendulous at the tips. Deeply lobed, glossy, bright green leaves turn scarlet or red-brown in autumn.

Carya ovata (Shag-bark hickory)
Deciduous tree with flaking, grey bark. Has dark green leaves, usually consisting of 5 slender leaflets, that turn golden-yellow in autumn.

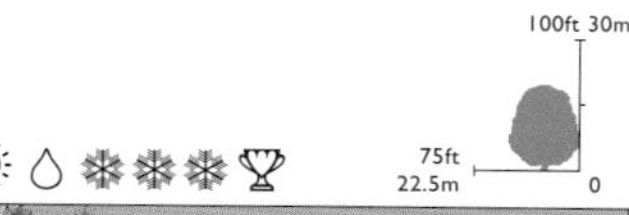

***Populus alba* 'Raket'**
Deciduous, upright, narrow tree. Leaves, often lobed, are dark green with white undersides. In autumn, foliage turns yellow.

Quercus laurifolia
Deciduous, round-headed tree with narrow, glossy, bright green leaves, bronze-tinged when young, that are retained until late in the year.

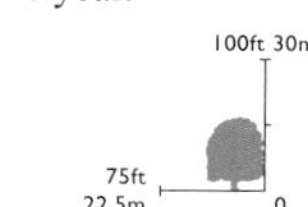

GREEN–YELLOW

Quercus rubra (Red oak)
Fast-growing, deciduous, spreading tree. Attractively lobed leaves, often large, are deep green becoming reddish- or yellowish-brown in autumn.

100ft 30m
75ft 22.5m
0

***Liriodendron tulipifera* 'Aureomarginatum'**
Vigorous, deciduous tree. Deep green leaves have yellow margins, cut-off or notched tips and lobed sides. Bears cup-shaped, greenish-white flowers, splashed orange, in summer on mature trees.

pH
100ft 30m
75ft 22.5m
0

Pterocarya × rehderiana
Very fast-growing, deciduous, spreading tree. Has glossy, bright green leaves consisting of narrow, paired leaflets that turn yellow in autumn and long catkins of winged fruits in late summer and autumn.

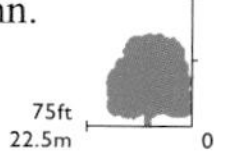

PINK–RED

Chorisia speciosa (Floss silk tree)
Fast-growing, deciduous tree, the trunk and branches studded with thick, conical thorns. Pink to burgundy flowers appear as indented, light green leaves fall. Min. 15°C (59°F).

Liquidambar styraciflua (Sweet gum)
Deciduous, conical to spreading tree. Shoots develop corky ridges. Lobed, glossy, dark green leaves turn brilliant orange, red and purple in autumn.

Quercus ellipsoidalis
Deciduous, spreading tree with deeply lobed, glossy, dark green leaves that turn dark purplish-red, then red in autumn.

Acer pseudoplatanus* f. *erythrocarpum
Vigorous, deciduous, spreading tree with lobed, deep green leaves. Wings of young autumn fruits are bright red.

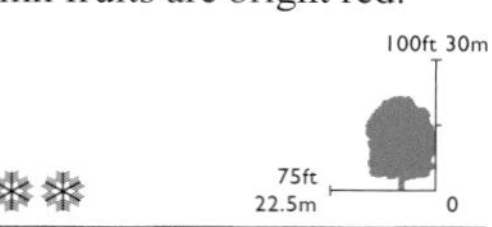

***Acer rubrum* 'Scanlon'**
Deciduous, upright tree. Has lobed, dark green foliage that in autumn becomes bright red, particularly on acid or neutral soil. Clusters of small, red flowers decorate bare branches in spring.

Quercus coccinea (Scarlet oak)
Deciduous, round-headed tree. Glossy, dark green leaves have deeply cut lobes ending in slender teeth. In autumn, they turn bright red, usually persisting for several weeks on the tree.

***Acer rubrum* 'Schlesingeri'**
Deciduous, round-headed tree. In early autumn, dark green leaves turn deep red. Tiny, red flowers appear on bare wood in spring.

Acer rubrum (Red maple)
Deciduous, round-headed tree. Dark green leaves turn bright red in autumn, producing best colour on acid or neutral soil. In spring, bare branches are covered with tiny, red flowers.

Cercidiphyllum japonicum
(Katsura)
Fast-growing, deciduous, spreading tree. Leaves, bronze when young, turn rich green, then yellow to purple in autumn, especially on acid soil. Fallen leaves smell of burnt toffee.

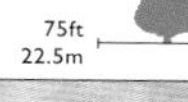

Spathodea campanulata (African tulip tree, Flame-of-the-forest)
Evergreen, showy tree. Leaves have 9–19 deep green leaflets. Clusters of tulip-shaped, scarlet or orange-red flowers appear intermittently.
Min. 16–18°C (6–14°F).

100ft 30m
75ft 22.5m
0

Quercus phellos
(Willow oak)
Deciduous, spreading tree of elegant habit. Narrow, willow-like, pale green leaves turn yellow then brown in autumn.

100ft 30m
75ft 22.5m
0

Zelkova serrata
Deciduous, spreading tree with sharply toothed, finely pointed, dark green leaves that turn yellow or orange in autumn.

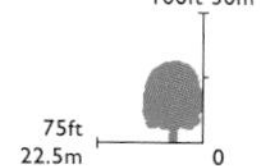

Nyssa sylvatica
(Black gum, Tupelo)
Deciduous, broadly conical tree with oval, glossy, dark to mid-green leaves that turn brilliant yellow, orange and red in autumn.

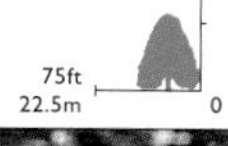

Prunus avium
(Gean, Wild cherry)
Deciduous, spreading tree with red-banded bark. Has sprays of white flowers in spring, deep red fruits and dark green leaves that turn red and yellow in autumn.

100ft 30m
75ft 22.5m
0

Quercus alba
(American white oak)
Deciduous, spreading tree. Deeply lobed, glossy, dark green leaves turn reddish-purple in autumn.

***Acer platanoides* 'Palmatifidum'**
Vigorous, deciduous, spreading tree. Deeply divided, pale green leaves with slender lobes turn yellow or reddish-orange in autumn. Tiny, yellow flowers appear in mid-spring.

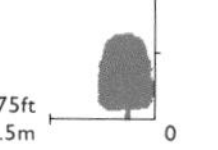

***Sophora japonica* 'Violacea'**
Fast-growing, deciduous, round-headed tree. Large sprays of pea-like, white flowers, tinged with lilac-pink, appear in late summer and early autumn.

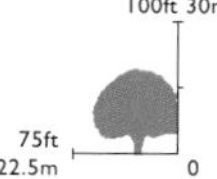

WHITE–GREEN

Eucalyptus dalrympleana (Mountain gum)
Vigorous, evergreen tree. Creamy-white, young bark becomes pinkish-grey, then peels. Leaves are long, narrow and pendent. Clusters of white flowers appear in late summer and autumn.

Betula papyrifera (Canoe birch, Paper birch)
Vigorous, deciduous, open-branched, round-headed tree with peeling, shiny, white bark, yellowish catkins in spring and oval, coarsely serrated leaves that turn clear yellow in autumn.

Betula ermanii
Deciduous, open-branched, elegant tree that has peeling, pinkish-white bark, distinctively marked with large lenticels. Oval, glossy, green leaves give excellent autumn colour.

Eucalyptus gunnii (Cider gum)
Evergreen, conical tree with peeling, cream, pinkish and brown bark. Leaves are silver-blue when young, blue-green when mature. Clusters of white flowers, with numerous stamens, appear in mid-summer.

***Ficus elastica* 'Doescheri'** (Rubber plant)
Strong-growing, evergreen, upright then spreading tree with oblong to oval, leathery, lustrous, deep green leaves, patterned with grey-green, yellow and white. Min. 10°C (50°F).

GREEN

Ficus benghalensis (Banyan)
Evergreen, wide-spreading tree with trunk-like prop roots. Has oval, leathery leaves, rich green with pale veins, to 20cm (8in) long, and small, fig-like, brown fruits. Min. 15–18°C (59–64°F).

Eucalyptus coccifera (Tasmanian snow gum)
Evergreen tree with peeling, blue-grey and white bark and aromatic, pointed, grey-green leaves. Bears clusters of white flowers, with numerous stamens, in summer.

Archontophoenix alexandrae (Alexandra palm, Northern bungalow palm)
Evergreen palm with feather-shaped, arching leaves. Mature trees bear sprays of small, white or cream flowers. Min. 15°C (59°F).

Quercus* × *turneri
Semi-evergreen, rounded, dense tree. Lobed, leathery, dark green leaves fall just before new foliage appears in spring.

Nothofagus dombeyi
Evergreen, loosely conical tree of elegant habit with shoots that droop at the tips. Leaves are sharply toothed, gloss y and dark green.

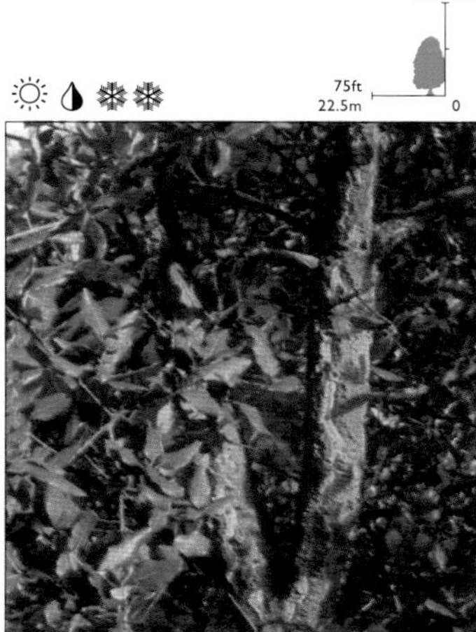

Quercus suber (Cork oak)
Evergreen, round-headed tree with thick, corky bark. Oval, leathery leaves are glossy, dark green above and greyish beneath.

***Betula pendula* 'Tristis'**
(Weeping birch)
Deciduous, slender, elegant tree with a strongly weeping habit and white bark. Oval, bright green leaves, with toothed margins, provide excellent golden colour in autumn.

Washingtonia robusta
(Thread palm)
Fast-growing, evergreen palm with large, fan-shaped leaves and, in summer, tiny, creamy-white flowers in large, long-stalked sprays. Black berries appear in winter-spring. Min. 10°C (50°F).

Macadamia integrifolia
(Macadamia nut, Queensland nut)
Evergreen, spreading tree with edible, brown nuts in autumn. Has whorls of leathery, semi-glossy leaves and panicles of small, creamy-yellow flowers in spring.
Min. 10–13°C (50–55°F).

Syagrus romanzoffiana
(Queen palm)
Majestic, evergreen palm. Has feather-shaped leaves with lustrous, green leaflets. Mature trees carry clusters of yellow flowers in summer. Min. 18°C (64°F).

Quercus* × *hispanica
'Lucombeana' (Lucombe oak)
Semi-evergreen, spreading tree with toothed leaves, glossy, dark green above, grey beneath.

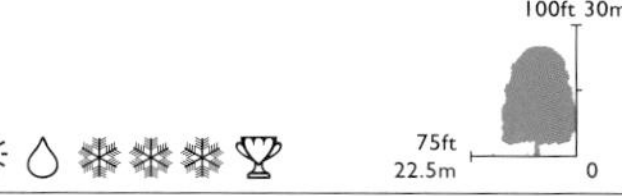

GREEN

Betula albosinensis
(White Chinese birch)
Deciduous, open-branched, elegant tree with serrated, oval to lance-shaped, pale green leaves. Peeling bark is honey-coloured or reddish-maroon with a grey bloom.

Nothofagus betuloides
Evergreen, columnar tree with dense growth of oval, glossy, dark green leaves on bronze-red shoots.

YELLOW

Umbellularia californica
(Californian laurel)
Evergreen, spreading tree with aromatic, leathery, glossy, dark green leaves and creamy-yellow flowers in late spring. Pungent leaves may cause nausea and headache when crushed.

100ft 30m
75ft 22.5m
0

Salix alba var. ***vitellina***
(Golden willow)
Deciduous, spreading tree, usually cut back hard to promote growth of strong, young shoots that are bright orange-yellow in winter. Lance-shaped, mid-green leaves appear in spring.

100ft 30m
75ft 22.5m
0

Salix* × *sepulcralis var. ***chrysocoma*** (Golden weeping willow)
Deciduous tree with slender, yellow shoots falling to the ground as a curtain. Yellow-green, young leaves mature to mid-green.

100ft 30m
75ft 22.5m
0

TREES medium SPRING INTEREST

WHITE

Malus hupehensis (Hupeh crab)
Vigorous, deciduous, spreading tree. Has deep green leaves, large, fragrant, white flowers, pink in bud, from mid- to late spring, followed by small, red-tinged, yellow crab apples in late summer and autumn.

50ft 15m
50ft 15m
0

Salix daphnoides (Violet willow)
Fast-growing, deciduous, spreading tree. Has lance-shaped, glossy, dark green leaves, silver, male catkins in spring and purple shoots with bluish-white bloom in winter.

Malus baccata var. ***mandschurica***
Vigorous, deciduous, spreading tree with dark green leaves and a profusion of white flowers in clusters in mid-spring, followed by long-lasting, small, red or yellow crab apples.

MAGNOLIAS

A mature magnolia in full bloom makes a spectacular sight in spring. Most magnolias are elegant in habit and though slow-growing, eventually form imposing trees and shrubs that are valuable as focal points or as single specimens in lawns. Some, like *Magnolia stellata*, may be grown in the smallest of gardens.

The flowers are generally saucer- or goblet-shaped and often have a subtle fragrance. Colours range from pure white or white flushed or stained with pink or purple, to pink and rich wine-purple. The genus includes some evergreen, summer-flowering species. These, and cultivars that are not fully hardy, are good for planting against a sunny wall. Some magnolias prefer acid or neutral soil, but most tolerate any soil provided it is humus-rich. Plenty of organic matter should be dug into the soil before planting.

***M.* × *soulangeana* 'Lennei Alba'** ♀

***M.* 'Heaven Scent'** ♀

***M.* 'Norman Gould'**

M.* × *wieseneri

***M.* 'Manchu Fan'**

***M.* × *loebneri* 'Leonard Messel'** ♀

***M.* × *veitchii* 'Peter Veitch'**

***M.* × *soulangeana* 'Etienne Soulange-Bodin'** ♀

***M.* 'Pegasus'**

***M. grandiflora* 'Ferruginea'**

M. campbellii subsp. ***mollicomata***

M. salicifolia ♀

M. denudata ♀

M. fraseri

***M.* × *soulangeana* 'Rustica Rubra'** ♀

***M. liliiflora* 'Nigra'** ♀

M. campbellii

M. wilsonii ♀

***M. stellata* 'Waterlily'** ♀

***M. campbellii* 'Darjeeling'**

M. sprengeri

M. obovata ♀

***M. sprengeri* 'Wakehurst'**

***M.* 'Ricki'**

***M. campbellii* 'Charles Raffill'**

WHITE

***Pyrus calleryana* 'Chanticleer'**
Deciduous, conical tree with glossy leaves that turn purplish in autumn. Sprays of small, white flowers appear in spring. Resists fireblight.

Prunus mahaleb
Deciduous, round-headed, bushy tree that bears a profusion of fragrant, cup-shaped, white flowers from mid- to late spring. Rounded, glossy, dark green leaves turn yellow in autumn.

Halesia monticola
(Silver bell, Snowdrop tree)
Fast-growing, deciduous, conical or spreading tree. Masses of pendent, bell-shaped, white flowers appear in late spring before leaves, followed by 4-winged fruits in autumn.

Cornus nuttallii
(Mountain dogwood, Pacific dogwood)
Deciduous, conical tree. Large, white bracts, surrounding tiny flowers, appear in late spring. Has oval, dark green leaves.

***Prunus avium* 'Plena'**
Deciduous, spreading tree with reddish-brown bark and masses of double, pure white flowers in spring. Dark green foliage turns red in autumn.

Fraxinus ornus (Manna ash)
Deciduous, round-headed tree. Has deep green leaves with 5–9 leaflets. Panicles of scented, creamy-white flowers appear in late spring and early summer.

WHITE–PINK

Prunus padus (Bird cherry)
Deciduous, spreading tree, conical when young. Bears fragrant, white flowers in pendent spikes during late spring, followed by small, black fruits in late summer. Dark green leaves turn yellow in autumn.

Melia azedarach
(Bead tree, Persian lilac)
Deciduous, spreading tree. Has dark green leaves with many leaflets and fragrant, star-shaped, pinkish-lilac flowers in spring, followed by pale orange-yellow fruits in autumn.

Prunus jamasakura
(Hill cherry)
Deciduous, spreading tree bearing cup-shaped, white or pink flowers from mid- to late spring. Oval leaves, bronze when young, mature to deep green.

PINK–YELLOW

***Prunus* 'Kanzan'**
Deciduous, vase-shaped tree. Large, double, pink to purple flowers are borne profusely from mid- to late spring amid bronze, young leaves that mature to dark green.

Paulownia tomentosa
(Foxglove tree, Princess tree)
Deciduous, spreading tree. Has large, lobed, mid-green leaves and terminal sprays of fragrant, foxglove-like, pinkish-lilac flowers in spring.

***Malus* 'Profusion'**
Deciduous, spreading tree. Dark green foliage is purple when young. Cup-shaped, deep purplish-pink flowers are freely borne in late spring, followed by small, reddish-purple crab apples in late summer and autumn.

***Gleditsia triacanthos* 'Sunburst'**
Deciduous, spreading tree with fern-like, glossy foliage that is golden-yellow when young, deep green in summer.

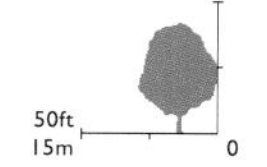

WHITE

Styrax japonicus
Deciduous, spreading tree bearing in early summer a profusion of pendent, fragrant, bell-shaped, white flowers amid glossy, dark green foliage.

Ostrya virginiana (American hop hornbeam, Ironwood)
Deciduous, conical tree with dark brown bark and deep green leaves, yellow in autumn. Has yellowish catkins in spring, followed by greenish-white fruit clusters.

Davidia involucrata
(Dove tree, Ghost tree, Pocket handkerchief tree)
Deciduous, conical tree with heart-shaped, vivid green leaves, felted beneath. Large, white bracts appear on mature trees from late spring.

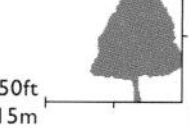

□ WHITE

Oxydendrum arboreum
(Sorrel tree)
Deciduous, spreading tree with glossy, dark green foliage that turns bright red in autumn. Sprays of white flowers appear in late summer and autumn.

Catalpa speciosa
Deciduous, spreading tree. Heads of large, white flowers marked with yellow and purple are borne in mid-summer among glossy, mid-green leaves.

Drimys winteri (Winter's bark)
Evergreen, conical, sometimes shrubby tree with long, glossy, pale or dark green leaves, usually bluish-white beneath. Bears clusters of fragrant, star-shaped, white flowers in early summer.

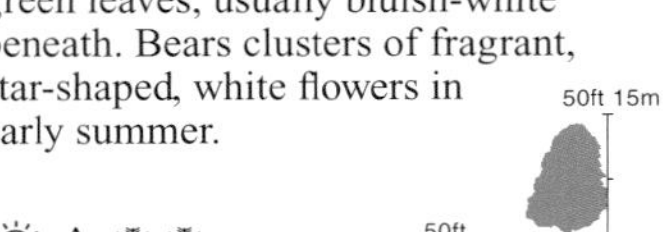

***Quercus cerris* 'Argenteovariegata'**
Deciduous, spreading tree. Strongly toothed or lobed, glossy, dark green leaves are edged with creamy-white.

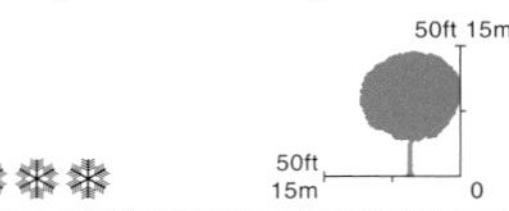

Sorbus vestita
Deciduous, broadly conical tree. Has very large, veined, grey-green leaves, white-haired when young. Heads of pink-stamened, white flowers in late spring or early summer are followed by russet or yellowish-red fruits.

Stewartia pseudocamellia
Deciduous, spreading tree with ornamental, peeling bark. Bears white flowers in mid-summer. Foliage is mid-green, turning orange and red in autumn.

Catalpa bignonioides
(Indian bean tree)
Deciduous, spreading tree. Large, light green leaves are purplish when young. White flowers marked with yellow and purple appear in summer, followed by long, cylindrical, pendent pods.

Cornus macrophylla
Deciduous, spreading tree. Clusters of small, creamy-white flowers appear in summer. Glossy, bright green leaves are large, pointed and oval.

***Sorbus aria* 'Lutescens'**
Deciduous, spreading tree, upright when young. Young foliage is silvery, maturing to grey-green. White flowers in late spring and early summer are followed by orange-red fruits in autumn.

WHITE–PINK

***Acer pseudoplatanus* 'Simon Louis Frères'**
Deciduous, spreading tree. Young leaves are marked with creamy-white and pink; older foliage is pale green with white markings.

***Acer negundo* 'Variegatum'**
Fast-growing, deciduous, spreading tree. Has pinkish- then white-margined, bright green leaves with 3 or 5 leaflets. Inconspicuous, greenish-yellow flowers appear in late spring.

***Aesculus indica* 'Sydney Pearce'**
Deciduous, spreading tree with glossy, dark green leaves, bronze when young and orange or yellow in autumn. Pinkish-white flowers, marked red and yellow, appear from early to mid-summer.

PURPLE–GREEN

Jacaranda mimosifolia
Fast-growing, deciduous, rounded tree with fern-like leaves of many tiny, bright green leaflets. Has trusses of vivid blue to blue-purple flowers in spring and early summer. Min. 7°C (45°F).

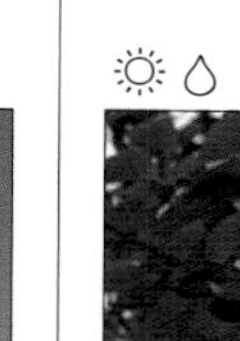

Broussonetia papyrifera
(Paper mulberry)
Deciduous, round-headed tree. Dull green leaves are large, broadly oval, toothed and sometimes lobed. In early summer, small globes of purple flowers appear on female plants.

***Sorbus thibetica* 'John Mitchell'**
Strong-growing, deciduous, conical tree with dark green leaves, silvery beneath. Has white flowers in spring and brown fruits in late summer.

Hovenia dulcis (Raisin-tree)
Deciduous, spreading tree with large, glossy, dark green leaves. In summer it may bear small, greenish-yellow flowers, the stalks of which become red, fleshy and edible.

Toona sinensis
Deciduous, spreading tree with shaggy bark when old. Dark green leaves with many leaflets turn yellow in autumn. Bears fragrant, white flowers in mid-summer. Shoots are onion-scented.

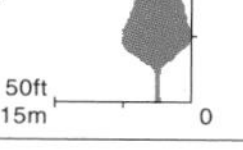

***Populus tremula* 'Pendula'**
(Weeping aspen)
Vigorous, deciduous, weeping tree. Leaves, reddish when young, grey-green in summer and yellow in autumn, tremble in the wind. Has purplish catkins in late winter and spring.

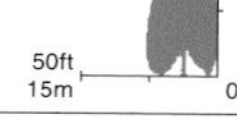

GREEN

Quercus marilandica
(Black Jack oak)
Deciduous, spreading tree. Large leaves, 3-lobed at the apex, are glossy, dark green above, paler beneath, and turn yellow, red or brown in autumn.

Fraxinus velutina
(Arizona ash)
Deciduous, spreading tree. Leaves vary but usually consist of 3 or 5 narrow, velvety, grey-green leaflets.

Quercus garryana
(Oregon oak)
Slow-growing, deciduous, spreading tree with deeply lobed, glossy, bright green leaves.

***Tilia cordata* 'Rancho'**
Deciduous, conical, dense tree, spreading when young. Has small, oval, glossy, dark green leaves, and clusters of small, fragrant, cup-shaped, yellowish flowers are borne in mid-summer.

Meliosma veitchiorum
Deciduous, spreading tree with stout, grey shoots and large, dark green, red-stalked leaves with 9 or 11 leaflets. Small, fragrant, white flowers in late spring are followed by violet fruits in autumn.

Gleditsia japonica
Deciduous, conical tree with a trunk armed with spines. Shoots are purplish when young. Fern-like leaves consist of many small, mid-green leaflets.

Emmenopterys henryi
Deciduous, spreading tree. Large, pointed, dark green leaves are bronze-purple when young. Clusters of white flowers (some bearing a large, white bract) are rarely produced except in hot summers.

Idesia polycarpa
Deciduous, spreading tree with large, heart-shaped, glossy, dark green leaves on long stalks. Small, fragrant, yellow-green flowers in mid-summer are followed in autumn, on female plants, by red fruits hanging in clusters.

Kalopanax septemlobus
Deciduous, spreading tree with spiny stems, large, 5–7-lobed, glossy, dark green leaves and umbels of small, white flowers, then black fruits in autumn.

Quercus macrocarpa (Bur oak)
Slow-growing, deciduous, spreading tree. Large, oblong-oval, lobed, glossy, dark green leaves turn yellow or brown in autumn.

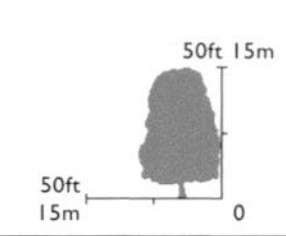

Quercus ithaburensis* subsp. *macrolepis
Deciduous or semi-evergreen, spreading tree. Has grey-green leaves with angular lobes.

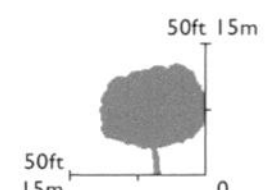

***Quercus rubra* 'Aurea'**
Slow-growing, deciduous, spreading tree. Large, lobed leaves are clear yellow when young, becoming green by mid-summer. Produces best colour in an open but sheltered position.

GREEN–YELLOW

Phellodendron chinense
Deciduous, spreading tree. Aromatic leaves, with 7–13 oblong leaflets, are dark green, turning yellow in autumn. Pendent racemes of greenish flowers in early summer are followed on female trees by berry-like, black fruits.

***Robinia pseudoacacia* 'Frisia'**
Deciduous, spreading tree with luxuriant leaves divided into oval leaflets, golden-yellow when young, greenish-yellow in summer and orange-yellow in autumn.

***Ulmus minor* 'Dicksonii'** (Cornish golden elm, Dickson's golden elm)
Slow-growing, deciduous, conical tree of dense habit. Carries small, broadly oval, bright golden-yellow leaves.

WHITE–RED

***Eucryphia × nymansensis* 'Nymansay'**
Evergreen, columnar tree. Some of the leathery, glossy, dark green leaves are simple, others consist of 3 (rarely 5) leaflets. Clusters of large, white flowers open in late summer or early autumn.

Syzygium paniculatum
(Australian brush cherry)
Evergreen tree with glossy leaves, coppery when young. Has creamy-white flowers, with reddish sepals, and fragrant, rose-purple fruits. Min. 10°C (50°F)

***Acer davidii* 'Madeline Spitta'**
Deciduous tree with upright branches that are striped green and white. Glossy, dark green foliage turns orange in autumn after the appearance of winged, green fruits that ripen reddish-brown.

***Sorbus hupehensis* 'Rosea'**
Deciduous, spreading tree with leaves of 4–8 pairs of blue-green leaflets turning orange-red in late autumn. White flowers in spring are followed by long-lasting, pink fruits.

Sorbus commixta
Vigorous, deciduous, spreading tree. Leaves have 6–8 pairs of glossy, deep green leaflets that turn orange and red in autumn. White flowers in spring are followed by bright red fruits.

Sorbus aucuparia
(Mountain ash, Rowan)
Deciduous, spreading tree. Leaves have mid-green leaflets that turn red or yellow in autumn. Bears white flowers in spring and red fruits in autumn.

***Acer rubrum* 'Columnare'**
Deciduous, slender, upright tree with lobed, dark green foliage becoming a fiery column of red and yellow in autumn.

RED–YELLOW

Acer rufinerve (Snake-bark maple)
Deciduous tree with arching branches striped green and white. In autumn, lobed, dark green leaves turn brilliant red and orange.

Stewartia monadelpha
Deciduous, spreading tree with peeling bark and glossy, dark green leaves that turn orange and red in autumn. Small, violet-anthered, white flowers appear in mid-summer, followed by small fruits.

***Acer saccharum* 'Temple's Upright'**
Deciduous, columnar tree. In autumn, large, lobed leaves turn brilliant orange and red.

Aesculus flava (Sweet buckeye, Yellow buckeye)
Deciduous, spreading tree. Glossy, dark green leaves, with 5 or 7 oval leaflets, redden in autumn. Has yellow flowers in late spring and early summer followed by round fruits (chestnuts).

Acer henryi
Deciduous, spreading tree. Dark green leaves with 3 oval, toothed leaflets turn bright orange and red in autumn.

Parrotia persica (Persian ironwood)
Deciduous, spreading, short-trunked tree with flaking, grey and fawn bark. Rich green leaves turn yellow, orange and red-purple in autumn. Small, red flowers are borne on bare wood in early spring.

Nyssa sinensis
Deciduous, spreading tree. Has long, narrow, pointed leaves that are purplish when young, dark green when mature and brilliant scarlet in autumn.

Acer capillipes (Snake-bark maple)
Deciduous, spreading tree. Has lobed, bright green leaves that turn brilliant red and orange in autumn. Older branches are striped green and white.

Quercus* × *heterophylla (Bartram's oak)
Deciduous, spreading tree with toothed, glossy, bright green leaves that turn orange-red and yellow in autumn.

***Sorbus* 'Joseph Rock'**
Deciduous, upright tree. Bright green leaves composed of many leaflets turn orange, red and purple in autumn. White flowers in late spring are followed by large clusters of small, yellow berries in late summer and autumn.

Cladrastis kentukea (Yellow wood)
Deciduous, round-headed tree. Leaves of 7 or 9 rounded-oval leaflets are dark green, turning yellow in autumn. Clusters of fragrant, pea-like, yellow-marked, white flowers appear in early summer.

WHITE–YELLOW

Betula utilis* var. *jacquemontii
(West Himalayan birch)
Deciduous, open-branched, elegant tree with bright white bark. Oval, serrated, mid-green leaves turn clear yellow in autumn.

Michelia doltsopa
Evergreen, rounded tree with oval, glossy, dark green leaves, paler beneath. Strongly scented, magnolia-like flowers, with white to pale yellow petals, appear in winter-spring.

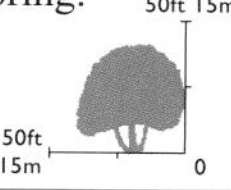

Acacia dealbata
(Mimosa, Silver wattle)
Fast-growing, evergreen, spreading tree. Has feathery, blue-green leaves with many leaflets. Racemes of globular, fragrant, bright yellow flower heads are borne in winter-spring.

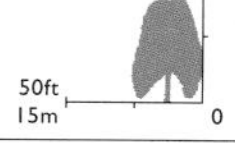

RED

Arbutus × andrachnoides
Evergreen, bushy, spreading tree with peeling, reddish-brown bark and glossy, dark green foliage. Clusters of small, white flowers in autumn to spring are followed by small, strawberry-like, orange or red fruits.

Metrosideros excelsa
(New Zealand Christmas tree, Pohutukawa)
Evergreen, wide-spreading tree. Oval, grey-green leaves are white felted beneath. Bears showy tufts of crimson stamens in winter. Min. 5°C (41°F).

WHITE–GREEN

***Ficus benjamina* 'Variegata'**
Evergreen, dense, round-headed, weeping tree, often with aerial roots. Has slender, pointed, lustrous leaves that are rich green with white variegation. Min. 15–18°C (59–64°F).

Trochodendron aralioides
Evergreen, broadly conical tree with glossy, dark green foliage. In late spring and early summer bears clusters of unusual, petal-less, wheel-like, green flowers.

Schefflera actinophylla
(Queensland umbrella tree)
Evergreen, upright tree with large, spreading leaves of 5–16 leaflets. Has large sprays of small, dull red flowers in summer or autumn. Min. 16°C (61°F).

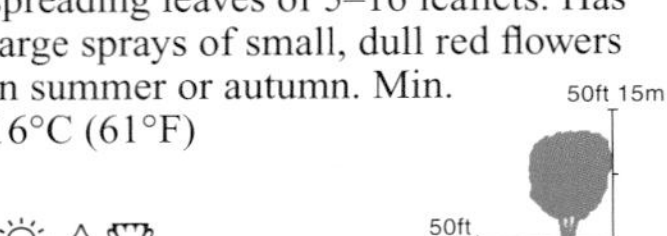

Acer pensylvanicum
(Snake-bark maple)
Deciduous, upright tree. Shoots are boldly striped green and white. Large, lobed, mid-green leaves turn bright yellow in autumn.

Eucalyptus pauciflora
(White Sally)
Evergreen, spreading tree with peeling, white, young bark and red, young shoots. In summer, white flower clusters appear amid glossy, bright grey-green foliage.

Trachycarpus fortunei
(Chusan palm, Windmill palm)
Evergreen palm with unbranched stem and a head of large, deeply divided, fan-like, mid-green leaves. Sprays of fragrant, creamy-yellow flowers appear in early summer.

Eucalyptus pauciflora* subsp. *niphophila (Snow gum)
Evergreen, spreading tree. Has patchwork-like, flaking bark, red-rimmed, grey-green leaves and white flowers in summer.

Quercus myrsinifolia
Evergreen, rounded tree with narrow, pointed, glossy, dark green leaves, reddish-purple when young.

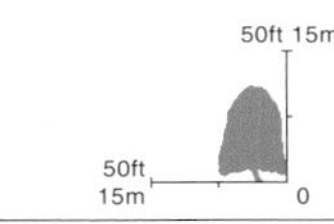

Prunus maackii
Deciduous, spreading tree with peeling, yellowish-brown bark. Produces spikes of small, white flowers in mid-spring and pointed, dark green leaves that turn yellow in autumn.

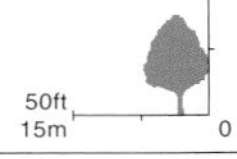

GREEN–ORANGE

Jubaea chilensis
(Chilean wine palm, Coquito)
Slow-growing, evergreen palm with a massive trunk and large, silvery-green leaves. Has small, maroon and yellow flowers in spring and woody, yellow fruits in autumn.

Livistona chinensis (Chinese fan palm, Chinese fountain palm)
Slow-growing, evergreen palm with a stout trunk. Has fan-shaped, glossy leaves, 1–3m (3–10ft) across. Mature trees bear loose clusters of berry-like, black fruits in autumn. Min. 7°C (45°F).

Quercus agrifolia
(Californian live oak)
Evergreen, spreading tree bearing rigid, spiny-toothed, glossy, dark green leaves.

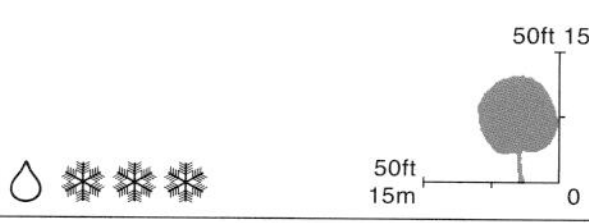

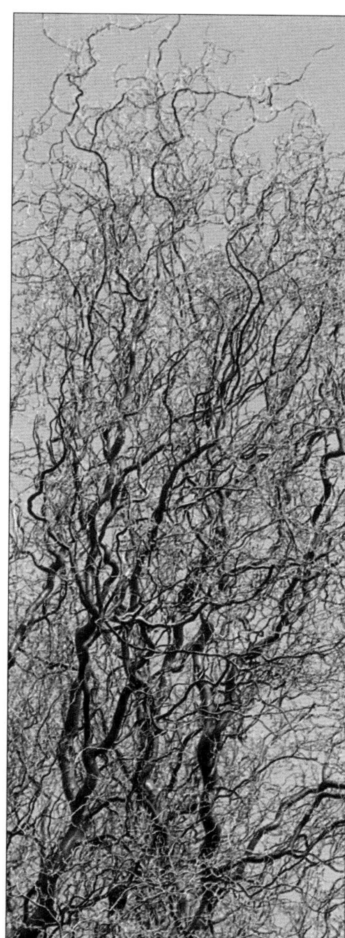

Salix babylonica var. ***pekinensis* 'Tortuosa'** (Dragon's-claw willow)
Fast-growing, deciduous, spreading tree with curiously twisted shoots and contorted, narrow, tapering, bright green leaves.

Corynocarpus laevigatus
Evergreen, upright tree, spreading with age. Has leathery leaves and clusters of small, greenish flowers in spring-summer. Plum-like, orange fruits appear in winter. Min. 7–10°C (45–50°F).

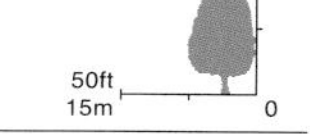

WHITE

Mespilus germanica (Medlar)
Deciduous, spreading tree or shrub. Has dark green leaves that turn orange-brown in autumn, white flowers in spring-summer and brown fruits in autumn, edible when half rotten.

Amelanchier laevis
Deciduous, spreading tree or large shrub. Oval, bronze, young leaves turn dark green in summer, red and orange in autumn. Sprays of white flowers in spring are followed by rounded, fleshy, red fruits.

Crataegus laciniata
Deciduous, spreading tree with deeply lobed, hairy, dark green leaves. A profusion of white flowers in late spring or early summer is followed by red fruits tinged with yellow.

***Cornus florida* 'White Cloud'**
Deciduous, spreading tree. Massed flower heads, comprising large, white bracts around tiny flowers, appear in spring. Oval, pointed, dark green leaves turn red and purple in autumn.

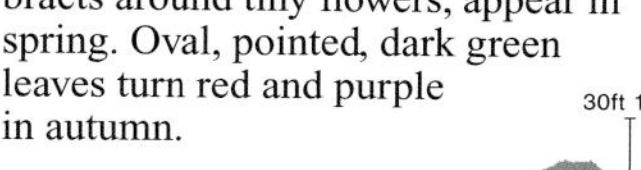

Aesculus californica
(California buckeye)
Deciduous, spreading, sometimes shrubby tree. Dense heads of fragrant, sometimes pink-tinged, white flowers appear in spring and early summer. Small, dark green leaves have 5–7 leaflets.

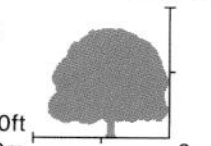

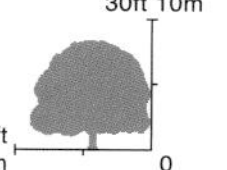

□ WHITE

***Prunus* 'Shogetsu'**
Deciduous, round-topped tree. In late spring, pink buds open to large, double, white flowers that hang in clusters from long stalks. Mid-green leaves turn orange and red in autumn.

***Cornus* 'Porlock'**
Deciduous, spreading tree. Creamy-white bracts around tiny flowers turn to deep pink in summer. These are often followed by heavy crops of strawberry-like fruits in autumn.

30ft 10m
30ft
10m
0

Prunus incisa (Fuji cherry)
Deciduous, spreading tree. White or pale pink flowers appear in early spring. Sharply toothed, dark green leaves are reddish when young, orange-red in autumn.

***Prunus* 'Taihaku'** (Great white cherry)
Vigorous, deciduous, spreading tree. Very large, single, pure white flowers are borne in mid-spring among bronze-red, young leaves that mature to dark green.

***Prunus* 'Ukon'**
Vigorous, deciduous, spreading tree. Semi-double, pale greenish-white flowers open from pink buds in mid-spring amid pale bronze, young foliage that later turns dark green.

***Prunus* 'Shirotae'**
Deciduous, spreading tree with slightly arching branches. Large, fragrant, single or semi-double, pure white flowers appear in mid-spring. Foliage turns orange-red in autumn.

Prunus* × *yedoensis
(Yoshino cherry)
Deciduous, round-headed tree with spreading, arching branches and dark green foliage. Sprays of pink buds open to white or pale pink flowers in early spring.

***Prunus* 'Spire'**
Deciduous, vase-shaped tree, conical when young. Soft pink flowers appear profusely from early to mid-spring. Dark green leaves, bronze when young, turn brilliant orange-red in autumn.

***Prunus* 'Hokusai'**
Deciduous, spreading tree. Oval, bronze, young leaves mature to dark green, then turn orange and red in autumn. Semi-double, pale pink flowers are borne in mid-spring.

***Prunus pendula* 'Stellata'**
Deciduous, spreading tree. Pink flowers with narrow, pointed petals, red in bud, open from early to mid-spring. Dark green leaves turn yellow in autumn.

***Prunus* 'Pandora'**
Deciduous tree, upright when young, later spreading. Massed, pale pink flowers appear in early spring. Leaves are bronze when young, dark green in summer and often orange and red in autumn.

Malus* × *arnoldiana
Deciduous, low, spreading tree with arching branches. In mid- to late spring red buds open to fragrant, pink flowers that fade to white. Bears small, red-flushed, yellow crab apples in autumn. Leaves are oval.

Prunus sargentii (Sargent cherry)
Deciduous, spreading tree. Oval, dark green leaves are red when young, turning brilliant orange-red in early autumn. Clusters of blush-pink flowers appear in mid-spring.

***Prunus* 'Shirofugen'**
Deciduous, spreading tree with bronze-red leaves turning orange-red in autumn. Pale pink buds open to fragrant, double, white blooms that turn pink before they fade in late spring.

***Prunus* 'Pink Perfection'**
Deciduous, upright tree that bears double, pale pink flowers in late spring. Oval leaves are bronze when young, dark green in summer.

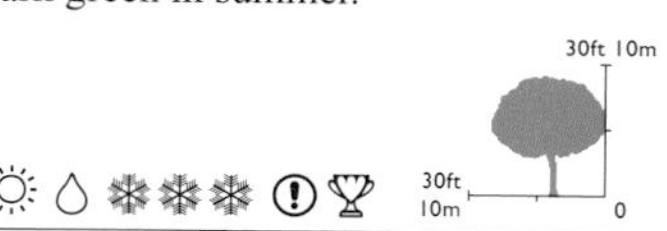

PINK

***Prunus* 'Accolade'**
Deciduous, spreading tree with clusters of deep pink buds opening to semi-double, pale pink flowers in early spring. Toothed, mid-green leaves turn orange-red in autumn.

***Prunus × subhirtella* 'Pendula Rubra'**
Deciduous, weeping tree that bears deep pink flowers in spring before oval, dark green leaves appear; these turn yellow in autumn.

30ft 10m
30ft 10m 0

***Malus* 'Magdeburgensis'**
Deciduous, spreading tree with dark green foliage. Dense clusters of large, semi-double, deep pink flowers appear in late spring, occasionally followed by small, yellow crab apples in autumn.

30ft 10m
30ft 10m 0

***Cercis siliquastrum* (Judas tree)**
Deciduous, spreading, bushy tree. Clusters of pea-like, bright pink flowers appear in mid-spring, before or with heart-shaped leaves, followed by long, purplish-red pods in late summer.

30ft 10m
30ft 10m 0

***Prunus persica* 'Prince Charming'**
Deciduous, upright, bushy-headed tree with narrow, bright green leaves. Double, deep rose-pink flowers are produced in mid-spring.

30ft 10m
30ft 10m 0

***Prunus* 'Kiku-shidare-zakura'**
Deciduous, weeping tree. Has double, bright pink flowers that cover pendent branches from mid- to late spring.

Malus floribunda
Deciduous, spreading, dense-headed tree with pale pink flowers, red in bud, appearing from mid- to late spring, followed by tiny, pea-shaped, yellow crab apples in autumn.

Dombeya × cayeuxii
(Pink snowball)
Evergreen, bushy tree with rounded, toothed, hairy leaves to 20cm (8in) long. Pink flowers appear in pendent, ball-like clusters in winter or spring. Min. 10–13°C (50–55°F).

30ft 10m
30ft 10m 0

***Prunus* 'Yae-murasaki'**
Deciduous, spreading tree with bright green leaves, bronze when young, orange-red in autumn. Semi-double, deep pink flowers are produced in mid-spring.

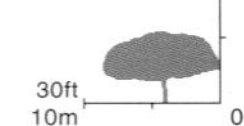

RED–YELLOW

Malus **'Royalty'**
Deciduous, spreading tree with glossy, purple foliage. Crimson-purple flowers appear from mid- to late spring, followed by dark red crab apples in autumn.

Acer pseudoplatanus **'Brilliantissimum'**
Slow-growing, deciduous, spreading tree. Lobed leaves are salmon-pink when young, then turn yellow and finally dark green in summer.

Malus **'Lemoinei'**
Deciduous, spreading tree. Oval leaves are deep reddish-purple when young, later becoming tinged with bronze. Wine-red flowers in late spring are followed by dark reddish-purple crab apples in autumn.

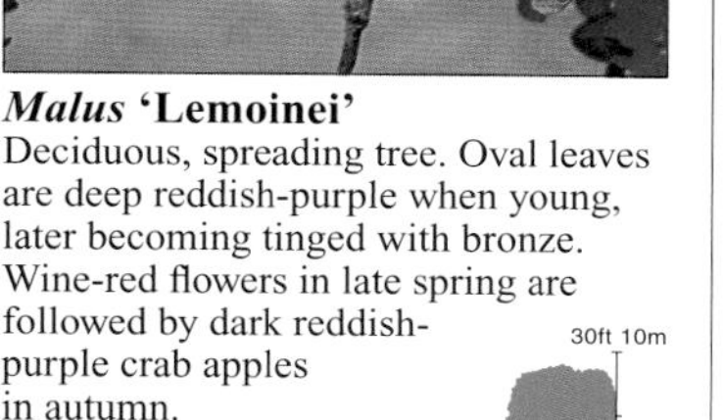

Michelia figo
Evergreen tree or rounded shrub. Has oval, glossy, rich green leaves and banana-scented, creamy-yellow flowers, edged maroon, in spring-summer. Min. 5°C (41°F).

Aesculus* × *neglecta **'Erythroblastos'**
Deciduous, spreading tree. Leaves with 5 leaflets emerge bright pink, turn yellow, then dark green, and finally orange and yellow in autumn. May bear panicles of flowers in summer.

Sophora tetraptera
Semi-evergreen, spreading tree or large shrub with dark green leaves composed of many tiny leaflets. Clusters of golden-yellow flowers appear in late spring.

WHITE

Cornus alternifolia **'Argentea'**
Deciduous, spreading tree, grown for its attractive, narrowly oval, white-variegated leaves. Has small heads of white flowers in spring.

Acer crataegifolium **'Veitchii'**
Deciduous, bushy tree with branches streaked with green and white. Small, pointed, dark green leaves, blotched with white and paler green, turn deep pink and reddish-purple in autumn.

Cornus controversa **'Variegata'**
(Wedding-cake tree)
Deciduous tree with layered branches. Clusters of small, white flowers appear in summer. Leaves are bright green with broad, creamy-white margins and turn yellow in autumn.

WHITE

Crataegus flava
(Yellow haw)
Deciduous, spreading tree. Has small, dark green leaves and white flowers in late spring and early summer, followed by greenish-yellow fruits.

Agonis flexuosa
(Peppermint tree, Willow myrtle)
Evergreen, weeping tree. Aromatic, lance-shaped, leathery leaves are bronze-red when young. In spring-summer, mature trees bear masses of small, white flowers. Min. 10°C (50°F).

Eucryphia glutinosa
Deciduous, upright or spreading tree. Glossy, dark green leaves, consisting of 3–5 leaflets, turn orange-red in autumn. Large, fragrant, white flowers appear from mid- to late summer.

Hoheria angustifolia
Evergreen, columnar tree with narrow, dark green leaves. Shallowly cup-shaped, white flowers are borne from mid- to late summer.

Hoheria lyallii
Deciduous, spreading tree with deeply toothed, grey-green leaves. Clusters of white flowers are borne in mid-summer.

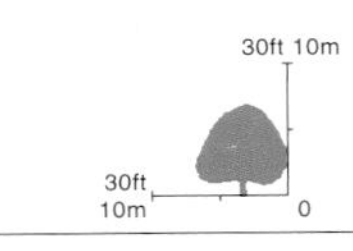

Eucryphia lucida
Evergreen, upright, bushy tree with narrow, glossy, dark green leaves and fragrant, white flowers in early or mid-summer.

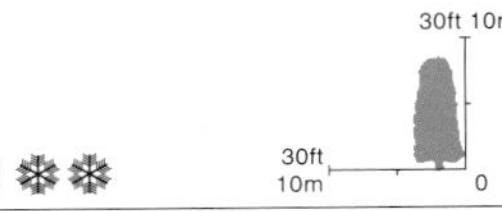

WHITE–PINK

Maackia amurensis
Deciduous, spreading tree with deep green leaves consisting of 7–11 leaflets. Dense, upright spikes of white flowers appear from mid- to late summer.

Albizia julibrissin (Silk tree)
Deciduous, spreading tree. Large leaves are light to mid-green and divided into many leaflets. Clusters of brush-like, clear pink flowers appear in late summer or autumn.

***Cornus florida* 'Spring Song'**
Deciduous, spreading tree. Pink bracts, surrounding tiny flowers, appear in spring-summer. Leaves are oval, pointed and dark green, turning red and purple in autumn.

PINK–PURPLE

Lagerstroemia indica
(Crape myrtle)
Deciduous, rounded tree or large shrub. Has trusses of flowers with strongly waved, pink, white or purple petals in summer and early autumn.

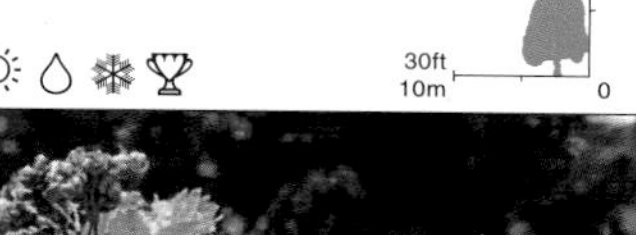

Malus yunnanensis* var. *veitchii
Deciduous, upright tree with lobed, heart-shaped leaves, covered with grey down beneath. Bears white, sometimes pink-tinged, flowers in late spring and a mass of small, red-flushed, brown crab apples in late summer and autumn.

***Crataegus laevigata* 'Paul's Scarlet'**
Deciduous, spreading tree. Has toothed, glossy, dark green leaves and a profusion of double, red flowers in late spring and early summer.

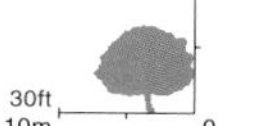

***Aesculus pavia* 'Atrosanguinea'**
Deciduous, round-headed, sometimes shrubby tree. In summer, panicles of deep red flowers appear among glossy, dark green leaves, which have 5 narrow leaflets.

***Cercis canadensis* 'Forest Pansy'**
Deciduous, spreading tree or shrub. In mid-spring has flowers that are magenta in bud, opening to pale pink, before heart-shaped, reddish-purple leaves appear.

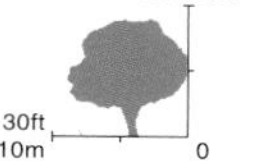

PURPLE–GREEN

***Prunus cerasifera* 'Nigra'**
Deciduous, round-headed tree with deep purple leaves, red when young. Pink flowers are borne in profusion from early to mid-spring.

Ehretia dicksonii
Deciduous, spreading tree with stout, ridged branches and large, dark green leaves. Large, flattish heads of small, fragrant, white flowers are borne in mid-summer.

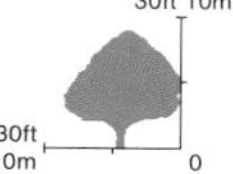

***Pyrus salicifolia* 'Pendula'**
Deciduous, weeping, mound-shaped tree with white flowers in mid-spring and narrow, grey leaves.

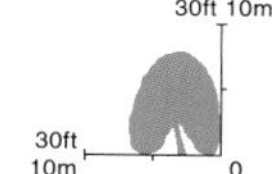

GREEN

Pseudopanax ferox
Evergreen, upright tree with long, narrow, rigid, sharply toothed leaves that are dark bronze-green overlaid white or grey.

***Ulmus glabra* 'Camperdownii'**
Deciduous, strongly weeping tree with sinuous branches. Leaves are very large, rough and dull green.

Juglans microcarpa
(Little walnut, Texan walnut)
Deciduous, bushy-headed tree with large, aromatic leaves of many narrow, pointed leaflets that turn yellow in autumn.

***Cydonia oblonga* 'Vranja'**
Deciduous, spreading tree. Pale green leaves, grey-felted beneath, mature to dark green and set off large, white or pale pink flowers in late spring and, later, very fragrant, golden-yellow fruits.

***Betula pendula* 'Youngii'**
(Young's weeping birch)
Deciduous, weeping tree forming a mushroom-shaped dome of thread-like branchlets. Has triangular, serrated leaves and smooth, white bark that is fissured black at maturity.

GREEN–YELLOW

Acer carpinifolium
(Hornbeam maple)
Deciduous tree of elegant habit, often with several main stems. Prominent-veined, hornbeam-like leaves turn golden-brown in autumn.

***Acer shirasawanum* 'Aureum'**
Deciduous, bushy tree or large shrub. Has rounded, many-lobed, pale yellow leaves.

***Morus alba* 'Laciniata'**
Deciduous, spreading tree. Has rounded, deeply lobed, glossy leaves that turn yellow in autumn and bears edible, pink, red or purple fruits in summer.

Koelreuteria paniculata
(Golden-rain tree, Pride of India)
Deciduous, spreading tree with mid-green leaves, turning yellow in autumn. Bears sprays of yellow flowers in summer, followed by inflated, bronze-pink fruits.

***Laburnum x watereri* 'Vossii'**
(Voss's laburnum)
Deciduous, spreading tree. Leaves, consisting of 3 leaflets, are glossy, deep green. Pendent chains of large, yellow flowers are borne in late spring and early summer.

YELLOW–ORANGE

Genista aetnensis
(Mount Etna broom)
Almost leafless, rounded tree with many slender, bright green branches and a profusion of fragrant, pea-like, golden-yellow flowers in mid-summer.

Paraserianthes lophantha
Fast-growing, deciduous, spreading tree. Has fern-like, dark green leaves comprising many leaflets. Creamy-yellow flower spikes appear in spring-summer.

Thevetia peruviana
(Yellow oleander)
Evergreen, erect tree with narrow, lance-shaped, rich green leaves and funnel-shaped, yellow or orange-yellow flowers from winter to summer. Min. 16–18°C (61–4°F)

Laburnum alpinum
(Scotch laburnum)
Deciduous, spreading tree. Leaves consist of 3 leaflets and are glossy, dark green. Long, slender chains of bright yellow flowers appear in late spring or early summer.

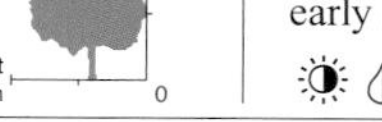

Embothrium coccineum
(Chilean firebush)
Evergreen or semi-evergreen, upright, suckering tree with lance-shaped, glossy, deep green leaves. Clusters of brilliant orange-red flowers are borne in late spring and early summer.

WHITE–RED

Sorbus cashmiriana
Deciduous, spreading tree with leaves consisting of 6–9 pairs of rich green leaflets. Pink-flushed, white flowers in early summer are followed by large, white fruits in autumn.

***Cornus florida* 'Welchii'**
Deciduous, spreading tree. Bears white bracts, surrounding tiny flowers, in spring. Dark green leaves, edged with white and pink, turn red and purple in autumn.

Arbutus unedo (Strawberry tree)
Evergreen, spreading tree or shrub with rough, brown bark and glossy, deep green leaves. Pendent, urn-shaped, white flowers appear in autumn-winter as previous season's strawberry-like, red fruits ripen.

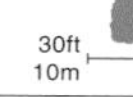

■ RED

Sorbus vilmorinii
Deciduous, spreading, arching, elegant tree. Leaves of 9–14 pairs of dark green leaflets become orange- or bronze-red in autumn. Has white blooms in late spring and small, deep pink fruits in autumn.

Crataegus macrosperma* var. *acutiloba
Deciduous, spreading tree with broad, sharply toothed, dark green leaves. White flowers with red anthers in late spring are followed by bright red fruits in autumn.

Photinia davidiana
Evergreen, spreading tree or large shrub with narrow, glossy, dark green leaves, older ones turning red in autumn. Sprays of white flowers in early summer are followed by clusters of bright red fruits in autumn.

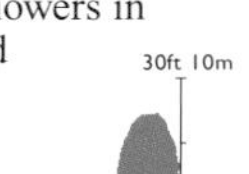

***Malus* 'Cowichan'**
Deciduous, spreading tree. Has dark green foliage, reddish-purple when young. Pink flowers appear in mid-spring, followed by reddish-purple crab apples.

***Malus* 'Veitch's Scarlet'**
Deciduous, spreading tree with dark green foliage. Carries white flowers in late spring and crimson-flushed, scarlet crab apples in autumn.

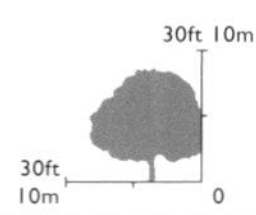

Acer palmatum* var. *coreanum
Deciduous, bushy-headed tree or large shrub. Leaves are deeply lobed and mid-green, turning brilliant red in autumn. Small, reddish-purple flowers are borne in spring.

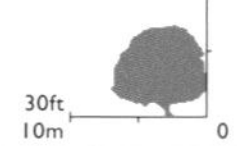

***Acer japonicum* 'Aconitifolium'**
Deciduous, bushy tree or large shrub. Deeply divided, mid-green leaves turn red in autumn. Reddish-purple flowers appear in mid-spring.

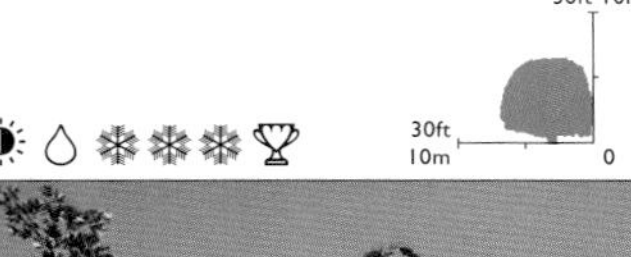

***Acer japonicum* 'Vitifolium'**
Vigorous, deciduous, bushy tree or large shrub with large, rounded, lobed, mid-green leaves that turn brilliant red, orange and purple in autumn.

Crataegus pedicellata
Deciduous, spreading tree with sharply toothed, lobed, dark green leaves that turn orange and red in autumn. White flowers with red anthers in late spring are followed by bright red fruits in autumn.

***Malus* 'John Downie'**
Deciduous tree, narrow and upright when young, conical when mature. White flowers, borne amid bright green foliage in late spring, are followed by large, edible, red-flushed, orange crab apples in autumn.

Rhus trichocarpa
Deciduous, spreading tree. Large, ash-like leaves with 13–17 leaflets are pinkish when young, dark green in summer and purple-red to orange in autumn. Bears pendent, bristly, yellow fruits.

Malus prunifolia
Deciduous, spreading tree. Has dark green leaves and fragrant, white flowers in mid-spring. In autumn bears long-lasting, small, red or occasionally yellowish crab apples.

Acer tataricum* subsp. *ginnala
(Amur maple)
Deciduous, spreading tree or large shrub. Clusters of fragrant, creamy-white flowers are borne in early summer amid dainty, bright green leaves that turn red in autumn.

RED

Acer triflorum
Slow-growing, deciduous, spreading tree with peeling, grey-brown bark. Leaves, composed of 3 leaflets, are dark green, turning brilliant orange-red in autumn. Clusters of tiny, yellow-green flowers appear in late spring.

***Malus × zumi* 'Calocarpa'**
Deciduous, spreading tree. Dark green leaves are sometimes deeply lobed. White flowers in late spring are followed by dense clusters of long-lasting, cherry-like, red crab apples in autumn.

***Cornus* 'Eddie's White Wonder'**
Deciduous, spreading tree or shrub. Large, white bracts, surrounding insignificant flowers, appear in late spring. Oval leaves are mid-green, turning red and purple in autumn.

***Malus* 'Marshall Oyama'**
Deciduous, upright tree with dark green leaves. Pink-flushed, white flowers borne in late spring are followed by a profusion of large, rounded, crimson and yellow crab apples in autumn.

ORANGE–YELLOW

***Malus* 'Professor Sprenger'**
Deciduous, rounded, dense tree. Dark green leaves turn yellow in late autumn. White flowers, pink in bud, open from mid- to late spring and are followed by orange-red crab apples in autumn.

Plumeria rubra (Frangipani)
Deciduous, spreading tree or large shrub, sparingly branched. Has fragrant flowers, in shades of yellow, orange, pink, red and white, in summer-autumn. Min. 13°C (55°F).

Tecoma stans
(Yellow bells, Yellow elder)
Evergreen, rounded, upright tree or large shrub. Leaves have 5–13 leaflets. Has funnel-shaped, yellow flowers from spring to autumn. Min. 13°C (55°F).

YELLOW

Picrasma quassioides (Quassia)
Deciduous, spreading tree with glossy, bright green leaves, composed of 9–13 leaflets, that turn brilliant yellow, orange and red in autumn.

***Malus* 'Golden Hornet'**
Deciduous, spreading tree with dark green foliage and open cup-shaped, white flowers in late spring. In autumn, branches are weighed down by a profusion of golden-yellow crab apples.

WHITE–PINK

***Bauhinia variegata* 'Candida'**
Deciduous tree, rounded when young, spreading with age. Has broadly oval, deeply notched leaves and fragrant, pure white flowers, 10cm (4in) across, in winter-spring or sometimes later. Min. 15–18°C (59–64°F).

Bauhinia variegata
Deciduous, rounded tree with broadly oval, deeply notched leaves. Fragrant, magenta to lavender flowers, to 10cm (4in) across, appear in winter-spring, sometimes later. Min. 15–18°C (59–64°F).

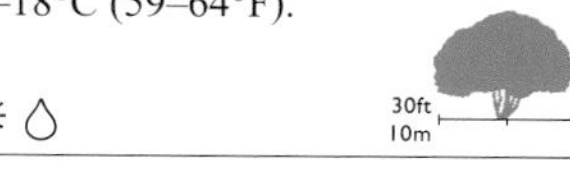

YELLOW

Acacia pravissima (Ovens wattle)
Evergreen, spreading, arching tree or shrub. Has triangular, spine-tipped, silver-grey phyllodes (flat, leaf-like stalks) and small heads of bright yellow flowers in late winter or early spring.

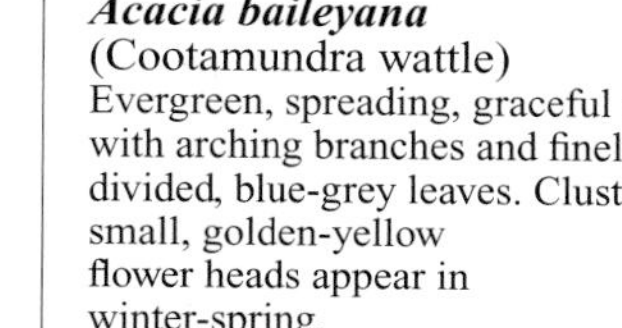

Acacia baileyana
(Cootamundra wattle)
Evergreen, spreading, graceful tree with arching branches and finely divided, blue-grey leaves. Clusters of small, golden-yellow flower heads appear in winter-spring.

Tabebuia chrysotricha
(Golden trumpet tree)
Deciduous, round-headed tree with dark green leaves, divided into 3–5 oval leaflets, and rich yellow flowers, 7cm (3in) long, borne in late winter or early spring. Min. 16–18°C (61–4°F).

Hollies

I. fargesii var. ***brevifolia*** ①

The common holly, *Ilex aquifolium*, is one of the best-known evergreen trees, but many other hollies, including lesser-known *Ilex* cultivars, make attractive garden plants. In size they range from tall, specimen trees to small shrubs useful in the rock garden or for growing in containers. Hollies respond well to pruning and many may be clipped to form good hedges. Leaves of different species and cultivars may be smooth-edged or spiny and vary in colour, several having gold, yellow, cream, white or grey variegation. Small, often white, male and female flowers, borne on separate plants during summer, are followed by attractive, red, yellow or black berries. In almost all cases hollies are unisexual, that is the berries are borne only on female plants, so to obtain fruits it is usually necessary to grow plants of both sexes.

I. aquifolium ① 🏆

I. ciliospinosa ①

I. pernyi ①

I. crenata var. ***paludosa*** ①

I. × ***altaclerensis*** **'Balearica'** ①

I. × ***altaclerensis*** **'Camelliifolia'** ① 🏆

I. aquifolium **'Argentea Marginata'** ① 🏆

I. macrocarpa ①

I. × ***koehneana*** ①

I. × ***altaclerensis*** **'N.F. Barnes'** ①

I. verticillata ①

I. aquifolium **'Silver Milkmaid'** ① 🏆

I. crenata f. **'Latifolia'** ①

I. cornuta **'Burfordii'** ①

I. fargesii ①

I. aquifolium **'Pyramidalis'** ① 🏆

I. opaca ①

I. × ***aquipernyi*** ①

I. aquifolium **'Argentea Marginata Pendula'** ①

I. aquifolium **'Silver Queen'** ① 🏆

I. crenata **'Convexa'** ① 🏆

I. × ***altaclerensis*** **'Belgica'** ①

I. × ***meserveae*** **'Blue Princess'** ① 🏆

I. × ***altaclerensis*** **'Belgica Aurea'** ① 🏆

I. aquifolium **'Golden Milkboy'** ①

I. aquifolium 'Madame Briot' ⓘ🏆

I. aquifolium 'Aurifodina' ⓘ

I. aquifolium 'Amber' 🏆

I. aquifolium 'Pyramidalis Aureomarginata' ⓘ

I. aquifolium 'Crispa Aureopicta' ⓘ

I. aquifolium 'Ovata Aurea' ⓘ

I. crenata 'Variegata' ⓘ

I. aquifolium 'Watereriana' ⓘ

I. serrata f. *leucocarpa* ⓘ

I. × altaclerensis 'Camelliifolia Variegata' ⓘ

I. purpurea ⓘ

I. aquifolium 'Golden van Tol'

I. pedunculosa ⓘ

I. aquifolium 'Ferox Argentea'

WHITE–PURPLE

***Pittosporum crassifolium* 'Variegatum'**

Evergreen, bushy-headed, dense tree or shrub with grey-green leaves edged with white. Clusters of small, fragrant, deep reddish-purple flowers appear in spring.

***Pittosporum eugenioides* 'Variegatum'**

Evergreen, columnar tree. Wavy-edged, glossy, dark green leaves have white margins. Honey-scented, pale yellow flowers are borne in spring.

Acer laxiflorum

Deciduous, spreading tree with arching branches streaked white and green. In late summer has pale red, winged fruits. Pointed, red-stalked, dark green leaves turn orange in autumn.

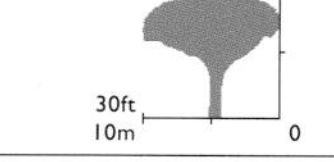

Grevillea banksii

Evergreen, loosely branched tree or tall shrub. Has leaves divided into 5–11 slender leaflets, silky-downy beneath. Spider-like, red flowers appear in dense heads intermittently throughout the year. Min. 10°C (50°F).

***Dracaena marginata* 'Tricolor'**

Slow-growing, evergreen, upright tree or shrub with narrow, strap-shaped, cream-striped, rich green leaves, prominently edged with red. Min. 13°C (55°F).

***Cordyline australis* 'Atropurpurea'**

Slow-growing, evergreen tree with purple to purplish-green leaves. Has terminal sprays of white flowers in summer and small, globular, white fruits in autumn. Min. 5°C (41°F).

GREY–GREEN

Leucadendron argenteum (Silver tree)
Evergreen, conical to columnar tree, spreading with age. Leaves are covered with long, silky, white hairs. Has insignificant flowers set in silvery bracts in autumn-winter. Min. 7°C (45°F).

Butia capitata (Jelly palm)
Slow-growing, evergreen palm. Feather-shaped leaves, composed of many leathery leaflets, are strongly arching to recurved, 2m (6ft) or more long. Min. 5°C (41°F).

***Carpinus betulus* 'Fastigiata'**
Deciduous, erect tree, with a very distinctive, flame-like outline, that becomes more open with age. Oval, prominently veined, dark green leaves turn yellow and orange in autumn.

Cyathea australis (Australian tree fern)
Evergreen, upright tree fern with a robust, almost black trunk. Finely divided leaves, 2–4m (6–12ft) long, are light green, bluish beneath. Min. 13°C (55°F).

Eucalyptus perriniana (Spinning gum)
Fast-growing, evergreen, spreading tree with rounded, grey-blue, young leaves joined around stems. Leaves on mature trees are long and pendulous. White flowers appear in late summer.

Meryta sinclairii (Puka, Pukanui)
Evergreen, round-headed tree with large, glossy, deep green leaves. Greenish flowers appear sporadically in spring to autumn, followed by berry-like, black fruits. Min. 5°C (41°F).

Pittosporum dallii
Evergreen, rounded, dense tree or shrub. Has purplish stems and sharply toothed, deep green leaves. Clusters of small, fragrant, shallowly cup-shaped, white flowers are borne in summer.

Beaucarnea recurvata (Elephant's foot, Pony-tail)
Slow-growing, evergreen tree or shrub with a sparsely branched stem. Recurving leaves, 1m (3ft) long, persist after turning brown. Min. 7°C (45°F).

Dracaena draco (Dragon tree)
Slow-growing, evergreen tree, eventually with a wide-branched head. Has stiff, lance-shaped, grey- or blue-green leaves. Mature trees bear clusters of orange berries, usually from mid- to late summer. Min. 13°C (55°F).

Lithocarpus henryi
Slow-growing, evergreen, broadly conical tree with glossy, pale green leaves that are long, narrow and pointed.

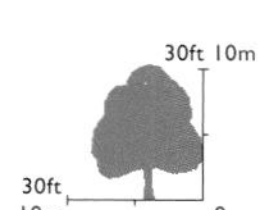

Dypsis lutescens (Golden-feather palm, Yellow palm)
Evergreen, suckering palm, forming clumps of robust, cane-like stems. Has long, arching leaves of slender, yellowish-green leaflets. Min. 16°C (61°F).

Acer griseum (Paper-bark maple)
Deciduous, spreading tree with striking, peeling, orange-brown bark. Dark green leaves have 3 leaflets and turn red and orange in autumn.

BLUE–GREEN

***Abies concolor* 'Argentea'**
Conical conifer with silvery foliage that contrasts well with dark grey bark. Oblong to ovoid, pale blue or green cones are 8–12cm (3–5in) long.

100ft 30m
75ft 22.5m
0

Pinus* × *holfordiana
(Holford pine)
Broadly conical, open conifer with large cones, brown when ripe. Pendent, glaucous blue-green leaves are held in 5s.

100ft 30m
75ft 22.5m
0

Cupressus cashmeriana
(Kashmir cypress)
Handsome, broadly conical conifer, spreading with age, with aromatic foliage borne in pendent, flat, glaucous blue sprays. Bears small, globose, dark brown, mature cones.

100ft 30m
75ft 22.5m
0

× *Cupressocyparis leylandii* 'Haggerston Grey'
Vigorous, upright, columnar conifer, tapering at the apex. Has smooth bark, becoming stringy with age, flat sprays of pointed, grey-green leaves, and dark brown female cones. A popular screening plant.

100ft 30m
75ft 22.5m
0

Cedrus atlantica* f. *glauca
(Blue Atlas cedar)
Conical conifer with silvery-blue foliage that is very bright, especially in spring. Erect, cylindrical cones are produced in autumn. Is widely planted as a specimen tree.

100ft 30m
75ft 22.5m
0

Pinus peuce (Macedonian pine)
Upright conifer, forming a slender pyramid. Has dense, grey-green foliage and cylindrical, green cones with white resin that ripen brown in autumn. Is an attractive tree that grows consistently well in all sites.

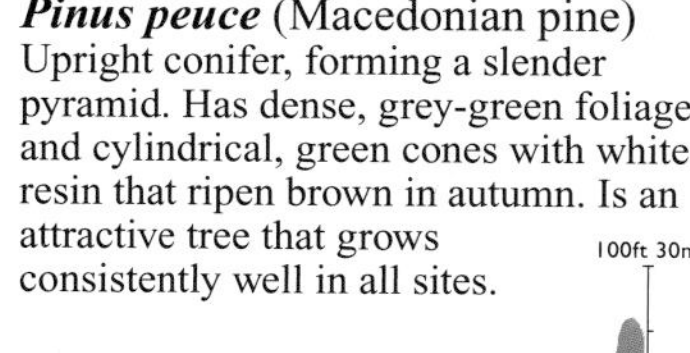

100ft 30m
75ft 22.5m
0

GREEN

***Chamaecyparis lawsoniana* 'Intertexta'**
Elegant, weeping conifer with aromatic, grey-green foliage carried in lax, pendulous sprays. Old trees become columnar with some splayed branches.

Pseudotsuga menziesii* var. *glauca
(Blue Douglas fir)
Fast-growing, conical conifer with thick, grooved, corky, grey-brown bark, aromatic, glaucous blue-green leaves, and sharply pointed buds. Cones have projecting, 3-pronged bracts.

Metasequoia glyptostroboides
(Dawn redwood)
Fast-growing, deciduous, upright conifer with fibrous, reddish bark. Soft, blue-green leaves turn yellow, pink and red in autumn. Cones are globose to ovoid, 2cm (¾in) long.

Pinus strobus (Eastern white pine, Weymouth pine)
Conifer with an open, sparse, whorled crown. Has grey-green foliage and cylindrical cones. Smooth, grey bark becomes fissured with age. Does not tolerate pollution.

Pinus coulteri
(Big-cone pine, Coulter pine)
Fast-growing conifer with large, broadly ovoid, prickly cones, each 1–2kg (2–4½lb). Grey-green leaves in crowded clusters are sparsely set on branches. Grows in all soils, even heavy clays.

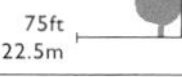

Abies veitchii
(Veitch fir)
Upright conifer with dark green leaves, silvery beneath, and cylindrical, violet-blue cones.

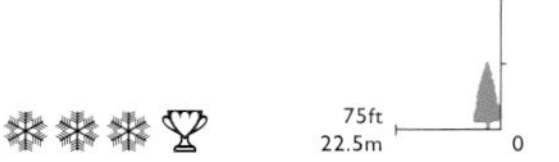

Sequoiadendron giganteum
(Big tree, Giant redwood, Wellingtonia)
Very fast-growing, conical conifer. Has thick, fibrous, red-brown bark and sharp, bluish-green leaves. Is one of the world's largest trees when mature.

Cedrus libani (Cedar of Lebanon)
Spreading conifer, usually with several arching stems. Branches carry flat layers of dark grey-green foliage and oblong to ovoid, greyish-pink cones, 8–15cm (3–6in) long.

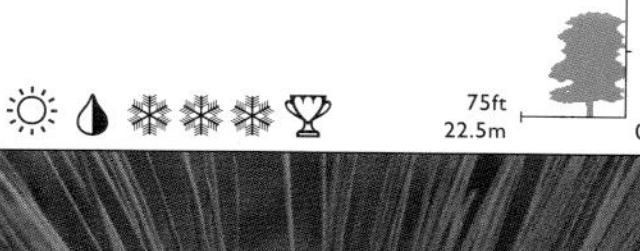

Pinus muricata (Bishop pine)
Fast-growing, often flat-topped conifer. Leaves are blue- or grey-green and held in pairs. Ovoid cones, 7–9cm (3–3½ in) long, rarely open. Does particularly well in a poor, sandy soil.

Picea omorika (Serbian spruce)
Narrow, conical conifer, resembling a church spire, with dark green leaves that are white below. Branches are pendulous and arch out at tips. Violet-purple cones age to glossy brown. Grows steadily in all soils.

 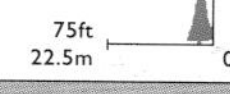

Araucaria araucana
(Chile pine, Monkey puzzle)
Open, spreading conifer with grey bark, wrinkled like elephant hide. Has flattened and sharp, glossy, dark green leaves and 15cm (6in) long cones. Makes a fine specimen tree.

 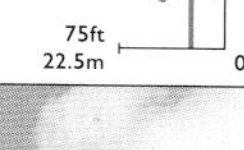

Pinus ponderosa
(Western yellow pine)
Conical or upright conifer, grown for its distinctive, deeply fissured bark, with smooth, brown plates, and bold greyish-green foliage. Bears ovoid, purplish-brown cones.

Pinus jeffreyi
(Black pine, Jeffrey pine)
Upright, narrow-crowned conifer with stout, grey-green leaves, 12–26cm (5–10in) long. Bark is black with fine, deep fissures and shoots have an attractive, greyish bloom.

Pinus wallichiana
(Bhutan pine, Himalayan pine)
Conical conifer with long, drooping, blue-green leaves in 5s. Has smooth bark, grey-green on young trees, later fissured and dark, and cylindrical cones.

 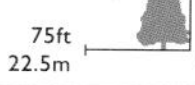

Pinus pinaster
(Cluster pine, Maritime pine)
Vigorous, domed conifer with a long, branchless trunk. Has grey-green leaves and whorls of rich brown cones. Purple-brown bark is deeply fissured. Is well-suited to a dry, sandy soil.

Ginkgo biloba (Maidenhair tree)
Long-lived, deciduous conifer, upright when young, spreading with age. Has fan-shaped, 12cm (5in) long, bright green leaves. Bears fruits, with edible kernels, in late summer and autumn, if male and female plants are grown together.

 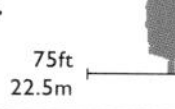

GREEN

Pinus nigra subsp. ***nigra***
(Austrian pine)
Broadly crowned conifer, with well-spaced branches, often with several stems. Paired, dark green leaves are densely tufted. Tolerates an exposed site.

100ft 30m 75ft 22.5m 0

Pinus radiata (Monterey pine)
Very fast-growing conifer, conical when young, domed when mature. Black bark contrasts well with soft, bright green leaves. Makes an excellent windbreak.

100ft 30m 75ft 22.5m 0

Pinus heldreichii (Bosnian pine)
Dense, conical conifer with dark green leaves held in pairs. Ovoid cones, 5–10cm (2–4in) long, are cobalt-blue in their second summer, brown when ripe.

100ft 30m 75ft 22.5m 0

Abies grandis (Giant fir, Grand fir)
Very vigorous, narrow, conical conifer, with a neat habit. Mid-green leaves have an orange aroma when crushed. Cones, 7–8cm (3in) long, ripen red-brown. Makes a useful specimen tree.

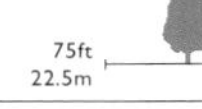

100ft 30m 75ft 22.5m 0

Picea abies
(Common spruce, Norway spruce)
Fast-growing, pyramidal conifer with dark green leaves. Narrow, pendulous, glossy, brown cones are 10–20cm (4–8in) long. Much used as a Christmas tree but less useful as an ornamental.

100ft 30m 75ft 22.5m 0

× ***Cupressocyparis leylandii***
'Harlequin'
(Variegated Leyland cypress)
Fast-growing, columnar conifer with a conical tip. Grey-green foliage, with patches of clear ivory-white, is held in plume-like sprays.

100ft 30m 75ft 22.5m 0

GREEN–ORANGE

× ***Cupressocyparis leylandii***
'Castlewellan'
Upright, vigorous conifer, slightly slower-growing than the species, grown for its bronze-yellow foliage.

100ft 30m 75ft 22.5m 0

Picea orientalis **'Skylands'**
Dense, upright, graceful conifer that retains the gold coloration of short, glossy leaves throughout the year. Narrowly oblong cones are dark purple, males turning brick-red in spring.

100ft 30m 75ft 22.5m 0

Taxodium distichum
(Bald cypress, Swamp cypress)
Deciduous, broadly conical conifer with small, globose to ovoid cones. Yew-like, fresh green leaves turn rich brown in late autumn. Grows in a very wet site, producing special breathing roots.

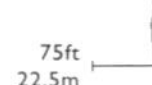

100ft 30m 75ft 22.5m 0

BLUE–GREEN

***Picea pungens* 'Koster'**
Upright conifer with whorled branches. Has scaly, grey bark and attractive, needle-like, silvery-blue leaves, which fade to green with age. Tends to suffer from aphid attack.

***Picea glauca* 'Coerulea'**
Dense, upright, conical conifer with needle-like, blue-green to silver leaves and ovoid, light brown cones.

***Juniperus chinensis* 'Keteleeri'**
Dense, regular, slender, columnar conifer with scale-like, aromatic, greyish-green leaves and peeling, brown bark. Makes a reliable, free-fruiting form for formal use.

Picea breweriana
(Brewer's spruce)
Upright conifer with level branches and completely pendulous branchlets, to 2m (6ft) long. Leaves are stout and blue-green. Bears oblong, purplish cones, 6–8cm (2½–3in) long.

Picea engelmannii (Engelmann spruce, Mountain spruce)
Broadly conical conifer. Leaves encircle shoots and are prickly or soft, lush, glaucous or bluish-green. Bears small, cylindrical cones. Is good for a very poor site.

Abies forrestii (Forrest fir)
Conical conifer with an open, whorled habit and smooth, silvery-grey bark. Shoots are red-brown, with spherical, white buds. Has dark green leaves, silvery-white beneath, and ovoid-cylindrical, violet-blue cones.

***Tsuga mertensiana* 'Glauca'**
Slow-growing, dwarf or medium-sized, columnar-conical conifer with red-brown shoots bearing spirally arranged, needle-like, flattened, glaucous, silver-grey leaves. Cones are yellow-green to purple, ripening to dark brown.

***Chamaecyparis lawsoniana* 'Pembury Blue'**
Magnificent, conical conifer with aromatic, bright blue-grey foliage held in pendulous sprays.

Pinus parviflora
(Japanese white pine)
Slow-growing, conical or spreading conifer with fine, bluish foliage and purplish-brown bark. Leaves are held in 5s. Bears ovoid cones, 5–10cm (2–4in) long.

GREEN

Fitzroya cupressoides
(Patagonian cypress)
Vase-shaped to sprawling conifer with red-brown bark that peels in long strips. White-lined, dark green leaves are held in open, pendulous, wiry sprays.

Podocarpus salignus
Upright conifer. Leaves are willow-like, 5–11cm (2–4in) long, and glossy above. Attractive, fibrous, red-brown bark peels in strips.

Pinus thunbergii
(Japanese black pine)
Rounded conifer, conical when young, with dark green leaves and grey-brown cones, 4–6cm (1½–2½in) long. Buds are covered with a silky cobweb of white hairs. Tolerates sea spray well.

Pinus rigida (Northern pitch pine)
Conical conifer, often with sucker shoots from trunk. Twisted, dark green leaves are borne in 3s. Ovoid to globose, red-brown cones, 3–8cm (1¼–3in) long, persist, open, on the tree.

Austrocedrus chilensis
(Chilean incense cedar)
Conical conifer with flattened, feathery sprays of 4-ranked, small, dark green leaves, white beneath.

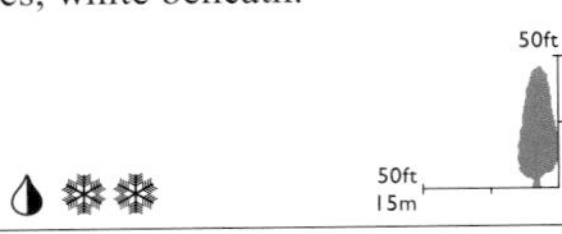

Cunninghamia lanceolata
(Chinese fir)
Upright conifer, mop-headed on a dry site, with distinctive, thick and deeply furrowed, red-brown bark. Glossy, green leaves are sharply pointed and lance-shaped.

Phyllocladus trichomanoides
Slow-growing conifer, conical when young, developing a more rounded top with age. Leaf-like, deep green, modified shoots, 10–15cm (4–6in) long, have 5–10 lobed segments.

Sciadopitys verticillata
(Japanese umbrella pine)
Conical conifer with reddish-brown bark. Deep green leaves, yellowish beneath, are whorled at the ends of shoots, like umbrella spokes. Ovoid cones ripen over 2 years.

Calocedrus decurrens
(Incense cedar)
Upright conifer with short, horizontal branches and flaky, grey bark, brown beneath. Has flat sprays of aromatic, dark green leaves. Resists honey fungus.

Pinus cembra (Arolla pine)
Dense, conical conifer with dark green or bluish-green leaves grouped in 5s. Ovoid, bluish or purplish cones, 6–8cm (2½– 3in) long, ripen brown.

Pinus contorta var. ***latifolia***
(Lodgepole pine)
Conical conifer with bright green leaves, 6–9cm (2½–4in) long. Small, oval cones remain closed on the tree. Is suitable for a wet or coastal site.

Pseudolarix amabilis
(Golden larch)
Deciduous, open-crowned conifer, slow-growing when young. Has clusters of linear, fresh green leaves, 2.5–6cm (1–2½in) long, which gradually turn bright orange-gold in autumn.

***Chamaecyparis lawsoniana* 'Green Pillar'**
Conical conifer with upright branches. Aromatic foliage is bright green and becomes tinged with gold in spring. Is suitable for hedging as requires little clipping.

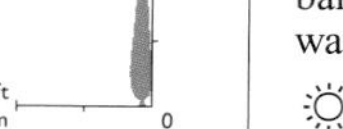

Pinus banksiana (Jack pine)
Slender, conical, scrubby-looking conifer with fresh green leaves in twisted, divergent pairs. Curved cones, 3–6cm (1¼–2½in) long, point forward along shoots.

Chamaecyparis thyoides
(White cypress)
Upright conifer with aromatic, green or blue-grey leaves in rather erratic, fan-shaped sprays on very fine shoots. Cones are small, round and glaucous blue-grey.

Pinus contorta
(Beach pine, Shore pine)
Dense, conical or domed conifer. Has paired, bright green leaves and conical to ovoid cones, 3–8cm (1¼–3in) long. Is well-suited to a windy, barren site and tolerates waterlogged ground.

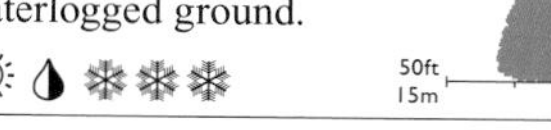

Picea morrisonicola
(Taiwan spruce)
Upright, conical conifer, becoming columnar with age. Needle-like, deep green leaves are pressed down on slender, pale brown shoots. Cones are cylindrical and 5–7cm (2–3in) long.

Tsuga canadensis (Canada hemlock, Eastern hemlock)
Broadly conical conifer, often with several stems. Grey shoots have 2-ranked, dark green leaves, often inverted to show silver lines beneath. Cones are ovoid and light brown.

Pinus halepensis (Aleppo pine)
Conical, open-crowned conifer with an open growth of bright green leaves, 6–11cm (2½–4½in) long, and ovoid, glossy, brown cones. Young trees retain glaucous, juvenile needles for several years.

Torreya californica
(California nutmeg)
Upright conifer with very prickly, glossy, dark green leaves, yellowish-green beneath, similar to those of yew. Fruits are olive-like.

***Chamaecyparis lawsoniana* 'Lanei Aurea'**
Upright conifer that forms a neat column of aromatic, golden-yellow-tipped foliage.

Pinus virginiana
(Scrub pine, Virginia pine)
Conifer of untidy habit. Grey- to yellow-green leaves are 4–7cm (1½–3in) long. Young shoots have a pinkish-white bloom. Bears oblong to conical, red-brown cones, 6cm (2½in) long.

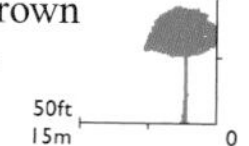

GREEN

***Picea mariana* 'Doumetii'**
Densely branched, globose or broadly conical conifer with short, needle-like, silvered, dark green leaves and pendulous, ovoid, purplish cones.

Pinus aristata (Bristle-cone pine)
Slow-growing, bushy conifer. Leaves are in bundles of 5, very dense and blue-white to grey-green, flecked with white resin. Ovoid cones, 4–10cm (1½–4in) long, have bristly prickles. Is the oldest-known living plant, over 4,000 years old.

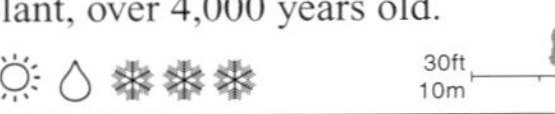

Juniperus recurva
(Drooping juniper, Himalayan weeping juniper)
Slow-growing, conical conifer with aromatic, incurved, grey- or blue-green leaves and fleshy, black berries. Smooth bark flakes in thin sheets.

***Juniperus chinensis* 'Robust Green'**
Slow-growing, column-like, conical conifer, making only 7–8cm (3in) a year, with aromatic, green foliage and small, grey-green juniper berries.

***Chamaecyparis lawsoniana* 'Columnaris'**
Narrow, upright conifer that forms a neat column of aromatic, blue-grey foliage. Will tolerate poor soil and some clipping. Is an effective, small, specimen tree.

***Pinus sylvestris* 'Fastigiata'**
Upright conifer with erect branches forming a narrow, obelisk shape. Has flaky, red-brown bark, blue-green foliage and conical cones. Suffers wind-damage in an exposed site.

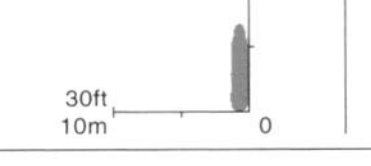

Pinus bungeana (Lace-bark pine)
Slow-growing, bushy conifer with dark green foliage, planted for its exquisite, grey-green bark that flakes to reveal creamy-yellow patches, darkening to red or purple.

***Juniperus chinensis* 'Obelisk'**
Slender, irregularly columnar conifer. Has ascending branches and long, prickly, needle-like, aromatic, dark green leaves. Tolerates a wide range of soils and conditions but is particularly suited to a hot, dry site.

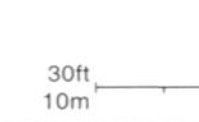

Pinus cembroides
(Mexican stone pine, Pinyon)
Slow-growing, bushy conifer, rarely more than 6–7m (20–22ft) high. Scaly bark is a striking silver-grey or greyish-brown. Leaves, in 2s and 3s, are sparse and dark green to grey-green.

Abies koreana (Korean fir)
Broadly conical conifer. Produces cylindrical, violet-blue cones when less than 1m (3ft) tall. Leaves are dark green above, silver beneath.

***Cryptomeria japonica* 'Cristata'**
Conical conifer with twisted, curved shoots and soft, fibrous bark. Foliage is bright green, ageing brown.

***Thujopsis dolabrata* 'Variegata'**
Slow-growing, broadly conical, bushy conifer. Stout, hatchet-shaped leaves have irregular, creamy patches above and are silvery beneath.

***Cryptomeria japonica* 'Pyramidata'**
Narrowly columnar or obelisk-shaped conifer. Foliage is blue-green when young, maturing to dark green.

Pinus pinea
(Stone pine, Umbrella pine)
Conifer with a rounded crown on a short trunk. Leaves are dark green, but blue-green, juvenile foliage is retained on young trees. Broadly ovoid cones ripen shiny brown; seeds are edible.

Taxus cuspidata (Japanese yew)
Evergreen, spreading conifer. Leaves are dark green above, yellowish-green beneath, sometimes becoming tinged red-brown in cold weather. Tolerates very dry and shady conditions.

***Cedrus deodara* 'Aurea'**
Slow-growing, upright conifer with pendent branch tips and golden-yellow leaves when young in spring-summer. Foliage matures to yellowish-green. Makes a dramatic, small garden evergreen.

***Chamaecyparis obtusa* 'Crippsii'**
Attractive, small-garden, conical conifer, grown for its flattened sprays of aromatic, bright golden foliage. Bark is stringy and red-brown. Cones are round, 1cm (½in) across, and brown.

***Cupressus macrocarpa* 'Goldcrest'**
Fast-growing, conical conifer with aromatic, golden-yellow foliage held in plume-like sprays that are useful in flower arrangements. Dislikes clipping.

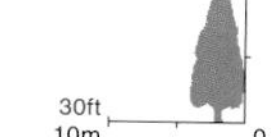

Dwarf conifers

Picea pungens
'Montgomery'

Dwarf conifers are valuable plants, especially for the small garden, requiring little attention and providing year-round interest. They can be planted as features in their own right, displaying their varied shapes, habits and often striking colours, or, in the rock garden, for example, to provide scale or act as a foil for other plants such as bulbs. Several species and cultivars are spreading and good for ground cover.

Most conifers are suited to a wide range of growing conditions, although *Cedrus* and *Juniperus* do not tolerate shade and *Juniperus* and *Pinus* are best for dry, sandy soils. Most *Abies*, *Taxus*, *Thuja* and *Tsuga* are particularly tolerant of shade. Some species may be clipped to form a low hedge but new growth seldom occurs from wood more than 3 or 4 years old.

Thuja occidentalis
'Hetz Midget'

Juniperus squamata
'Holger' ♀

Abies lasiocarpa var.
arizonica **'Compacta'** ♀

Picea × mariorika
'Gnom'

Thuja occidentalis
'Caespitosa' ①

Juniperus procumbens
'Nana' ♀

Abies lasiocarpa
'Roger Watson'

Pinus sylvestris
'Doone Valley'

Juniperus × pfitzeriana
'Glauca'

Microbiota decussata ♀

Juniperus horizontalis
'Turquoise Spreader'

Picea mariana
'Nana' ♀

Abies concolor
'Compacta' ♀

Juniperus scopulorum
'Springbank'

Juniperus sabina **'Mas'**

Abies balsamea **'Nana'**

Podocarpus nivalis

Juniperus virginiana
'Grey Owl' ♀

Juniperus squamata
'Chinese Silver'

Juniperus scopulorum
'Skyrocket'

Abies cephalonica
'Meyer's Dwarf'

Juniperus sabina
'Cupressifolia'

Juniperus horizontalis
'Douglasii'

Juniperus squamata
'Blue Star' ♀

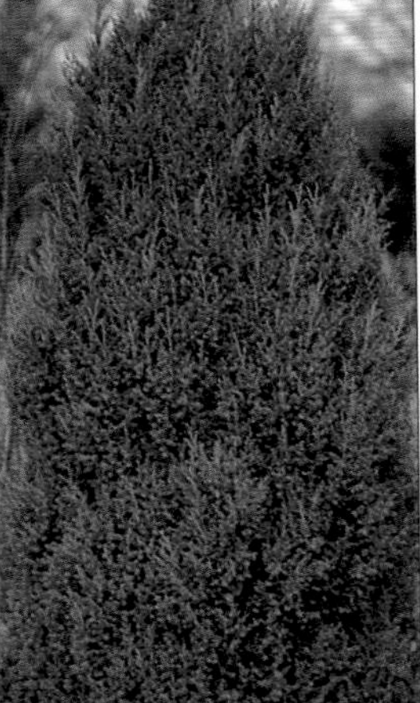

Juniperus chinensis
'Stricta'

Juniperus procumbens

Pseudotsuga menziesii
'Fretsii'

Juniperus recurva
'Densa'

Juniperus sabina var. *tamariscifolia*

Picea abies **'Gregoryana'**

Thuja occidentalis **'Filiformis'** ①

Picea abies **'Ohlendorffii'**

Chamaecyparis obtusa **'Intermedia'** ①

Juniperus communis **'Hibernica'** 🏆

Juniperus chinensis **'Expansa Variegata'**

Thuja plicata **'Collyer's Gold'** ①

Picea abies **'Reflexa'**

Juniperus × *pfitzeriana* **'Wilhelm Pfitzer'** 🏆

Cedrus libani **'Sargentii'**

Juniperus × *pfitzeriana* **'Aurea'**

Chamaecyparis obtusa **'Tetragona Aurea'**

Abies nordmanniana **'Golden Spreader'** 🏆

Pinus sylvestris **'Watereri'**

Pinus heldreichii **'Smidtii'** 🏆

Pinus heldreichii **'Compact Gem'**

Juniperus chinensis **'Plumosa Aurea'** 🏆

Taxus baccata **Aurea Group** ①

Tsuga canadensis **'Aurea'**

Pseudotsuga menziesii **'Oudemansii'**

Platycladus orientalis **'Semperaurea'** ①

Cryptomeria japonica **'Spiralis'**

Taxus baccata **'Dovastonii Aurea'** ① 🏆

Thuja plicata **'Stoneham Gold'** 🏆

Chamaecyparis lawsoniana **'Gnome'** ①

Chamaecyparis obtusa **'Nana Pyramidalis'** ①

Juniperus chinensis **'Blue and Gold'**

Chamaecyparis pisifera **'Filifera Aurea'** ① 🏆

Cryptomeria japonica **'Elegans Compacta'** 🏆

Chamaecyparis lawsoniana **'Minima'** ①

Picea glauca var. *albertiana* **'Conica'** 🏆

Platycladus orientalis **'Aurea Nana'** ① 🏆

Cryptomeria japonica **'Sekkan-sugi'**

Pinus sylvestris **'Aurea'** ① 🏆

Pinus sylvestris **'Gold Coin'**

Shrubs

Shrubs

Shrubs can form the backbone of your garden design, and with their variety of foliage, flowers, fruits and stems they also provide interest through the seasons.

What are shrubs?

Shrub are woody-stemmed, deciduous or evergreen plants that branch freely at or near ground level. Some shrubs grow to more than 6m (20ft) in height, although most species and cultivars attain less than half this size. There is some overlap between shrubs and other plant groups because larger shrubs, such as certain lilacs (*Syringa* species and cultivars), can be grown on a single stem and may equally

Colourful underplanting
Above: The flowering stems of *Exochorda* x *macrantha* 'The Bride' arch gracefully above forget-me-nots *(Myosotis sylvatica),* daisies *(Bellis perennis)* and *Tulipa* 'Couleur Cardinal'.

Eye-catching impact
Above right: In a glorious scheme, the golds of senecio, *Hypericum* 'Hidcote' and violas are set against greys of santolina and *Stachys byzantina*.

Contrasting foliage
Right: The golden leaves of *Choisya ternata* Sundance ('Lich') provide a glowing contrast with those of *Cotinus coggygria* 'Royal Purple' and *Berberis thunbergii* 'Rose Glow'.

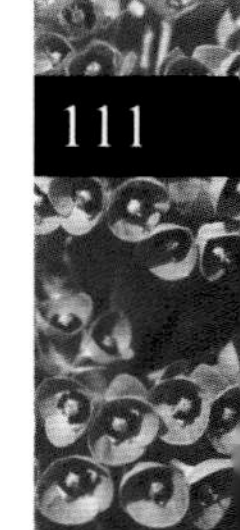

well be classified as trees, while others, called sub-shrubs, are woody only at the base. In these, as in ceratostigma and fuchsias, softer top growth dies back annually with the onset of winter frosts, and so they are commonly treated as herbaceous perennials in cold climates. Some shrubs, such as *Jasminum nudiflorum*, can be wall trained, and many are grown like this because it is the neatest way to manage their sprawling growth. They also benefit from the warmth and shelter a wall provides, giving them some frost protection and helping their wood to ripen and so improve flowering.

Shrubs in tubs
Left: In this planting of elegant simplicity, the pink flowers of a standard fuchsia are echoed by an underplanting of pastel busy lizzies *(Impatiens)*. After a prolonged display, the container can be moved under glass for protection during winter.

Choosing shrubs

When selecting a shrub, as with all garden plants, it is essential to match its hardiness and cultural requirements to the conditions in your garden. It is also vital to consider the shrub's final dimensions and to site it with sufficient room to mature. If you frequently have to prune a shrub to restrict its size, not only does this make unnecessary work but it may also weaken that shrub's resistance to disease.

Designing with shrubs

Whatever the size or style of your garden, the permanent woody structure of shrubs can form a key element in its framework. Many shrubs can be used formally or informally to create hedges, enclosures or screens. These range in size from small, domed forms, as in *Buxus microphylla* 'Green Pillow', to almost tree-like rhododendrons and amelanchiers.

The low, spreading, prostrate or mat-forming shrubs, such as *Juniperus procumbens* or *Dryas octopetala*, or the tiered branch structure of shrubs such as *Viburnum plicatum* 'Mariesii' and *Cornus alternifolia*, provide strong horizontal lines in a composition. These can be planted so they lead the eye to contrasting rounded forms, found in many hebes or *Choisya ternata* and its variants, or to the strong verticals of *Eucryphia* x *nymansensis* 'Nymansay' or *Pittosporum tenuifolium*, which may also be used to make a focal point.

Certain shrubs are ideal for topiary, but they must be able to tolerate close regular clipping and preferably have small leaves that permit fine surface texture and detailed shaping. Suitable shrubs include box (*Buxus*), yew (*Taxus*) and *Lonicera nitida*.

The gracefully arching or weeping shrubs, among them *Kerria japonica* 'Pleniflora', *Forsythia suspensa*, *Kolkwitzia amabilis* and *Malus* x *arnoldiana* can be used to link other elements in a border.

Shrubs can be planted alone, or in a mixed border as a backdrop to the more transient bulbs, annuals and perennials. Compact shrubs such as bay are ideal for containers.

Maintaining year-round interest

For autumn interest, pyracanthas, cotoneasters and *Skimmia japonica* have brilliantly coloured fruits, while most species of euonymus, disanthus and enkianthus offer vibrant foliage. In winter, the fragrant flowers of witch hazel (*Hamamelis*) and *Lonicera* x *purpusii*, and the coloured stems of *Cornus alba* 'Sibirica' lift the spirits, while the swags of *Garrya elliptica* come into their own in the soft, golden winter sun.

Size categories used within this group		
Large	**Medium**	**Small**
over 3m (10ft)	1.5m–3m (5–10ft)	up to 1.5m (5ft)

Autumn colour
Top: *Hamamelis* x *intermedia* 'Diane', which bears its spidery, deep red flowers from mid- to late winter, gives added ornamental value with its vibrant autumn colour.

Winter interest
Above: The vivid red berries of a female *Skimmia japonica*, produced where plants of both sexes are grown together, persist well into winter and are at their most perfect when rimed with frost.

□ WHITE

Osmanthus delavayi
Evergreen, rounded, bushy shrub with arching branches. Has small, glossy, dark green leaves and a profusion of very fragrant, tubular, white flowers from mid- to late spring.

Pieris japonica
Evergreen, rounded, bushy, dense shrub with glossy, dark green foliage that is bronze when young. Produces drooping racemes of white flowers during spring.

Amelanchier lamarckii
Deciduous, spreading shrub. Young leaves unfold bronze as abundant sprays of star-shaped, white flowers open from mid- to late spring. Foliage matures to dark green, then turns brilliant red and orange in autumn.

Osmanthus* × *burkwoodii
Evergreen, rounded, dense shrub. Glossy foliage is dark green and sets off a profusion of small, very fragrant, white flowers from mid- to late spring.

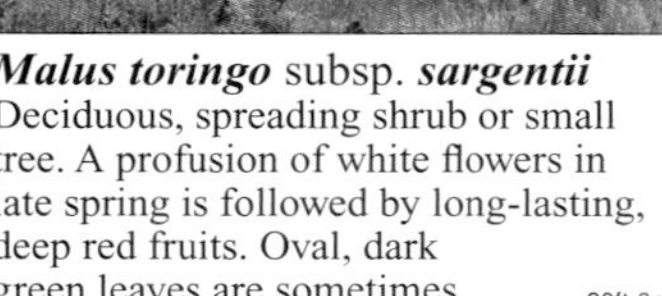

Malus toringo subsp. ***sargentii***
Deciduous, spreading shrub or small tree. A profusion of white flowers in late spring is followed by long-lasting, deep red fruits. Oval, dark green leaves are sometimes lobed.

Anopterus glandulosus
Evergreen, bushy shrub or, occasionally, small tree. Has narrow, glossy, dark green leaves, amid which clusters of cup-shaped, white or pink flowers appear from mid- to late spring.

Dipelta yunnanensis
Deciduous, arching shrub with peeling bark and glossy leaves. In late spring produces tubular, creamy-white flowers, marked orange inside.

***Viburnum plicatum* 'Mariesii'**
Deciduous, bushy, spreading shrub with tiered branches clothed in dark green leaves, which turn reddish-purple in autumn. Large, rounded heads of flowers with white bracts appear in late spring and early summer.

Staphylea pinnata (Bladder nut)
Deciduous, upright shrub that in late spring carries clusters of white flowers, tinted pink with age, followed by bladder-like, green fruits. Foliage is divided and bright green.

Dipelta floribunda
Vigorous, deciduous, upright, tree-like shrub with peeling, pale brown bark. Fragrant, pale pink flowers, marked yellow inside, open in late spring and early summer. Has pointed, mid-green leaves.

Enkianthus campanulatus
Deciduous, bushy, spreading shrub with red shoots and tufts of dull green leaves that turn bright red in autumn. Small, bell-shaped, red-veined, creamy-yellow flowers appear in late spring.

Viburnum* × *carlcephalum
Deciduous, rounded, bushy shrub. In late spring large, rounded heads of pink buds open to fragrant, white flowers. These are borne amid dark green foliage that often turns red in autumn.

***Staphylea holocarpa* 'Rosea'**
Deciduous, upright shrub or spreading, small tree. From mid- to late spring bears pink flowers, followed by bladder-like, pale green fruits. Bronze, young leaves mature to blue-green.

***Photinia* × *fraseri* 'Birmingham'**
Evergreen, upright, bushy, dense shrub with glossy, dark green leaves that are bright purple-red when young. Broad heads of small, white flowers are carried in late spring.

Daphniphyllum macropodum
Evergreen, bushy, dense shrub with stout shoots and dark green leaves. Small flowers, green on female plants, purplish on male plants, appear in late spring.

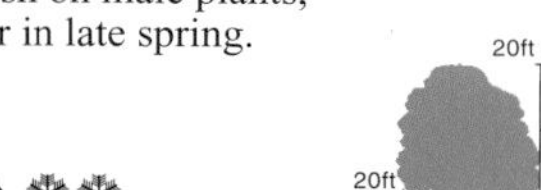

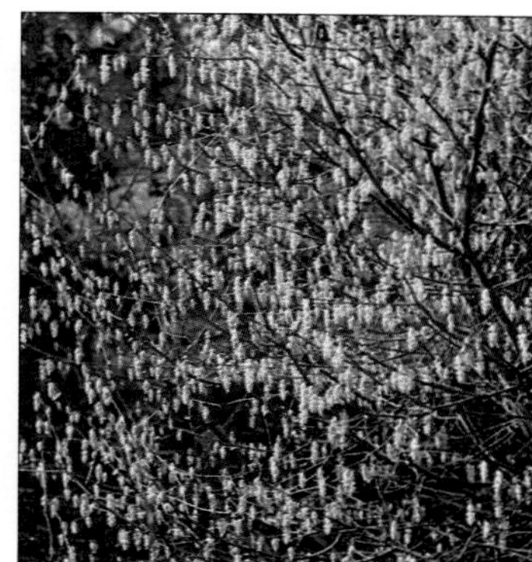

Corylopsis glabrescens
Deciduous, open shrub. Oval leaves, with bristle-like teeth along margins, are dark green above, blue-green beneath. Drooping spikes of fragrant, bell-shaped, pale yellow flowers appear in mid-spring on bare branches.

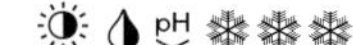

Berberis darwinii
(Darwin's barberry)
Vigorous, evergreen, arching shrub. Has small, glossy, dark green leaves and a profusion of rounded, deep orange-yellow flowers from mid- to late spring, followed by bluish berries.

□ WHITE

Escallonia leucantha
Evergreen, upright shrub. Narrow, oval, glossy, dark green leaves set off large racemes of small, shallowly cup-shaped, white flowers in mid-summer.

Olearia virgata
Evergreen, arching, graceful shrub with very narrow, dark grey-green leaves. Produces an abundance of small, star-shaped, white flower heads in early summer, arranged in small clusters along stems.

Viburnum rhytidophyllum
Vigorous, evergreen, open shrub with long, narrow, deep green leaves. Dense heads of small, creamy-white flowers in late spring and early summer are succeeded by red fruits that mature to black.

Styrax officinalis
Deciduous, loose to dense shrub or small tree. Fragrant, bell-shaped, white flowers appear in early summer among oval, dark green leaves with greyish-white undersides.

Sparrmannia africana
(African hemp)
Evergreen, erect shrub or small tree. Has large, shallowly lobed leaves and clusters of white flowers, with yellow and red-purple stamens, in late spring and summer.
Min. 7°C (45°F).

Ligustrum sinense
Deciduous or semi-ever green, bushy, upright shrub with oval, pale green leaves. Large panicles of fragrant, tubular, white flowers are borne in mid-summer, followed by small, purplish-black fruits.

***Buddleja davidii* 'Peace'**
Vigorous, deciduous, arching shrub. Long, pointed, dark green leaves, white-felted beneath, set off long plumes of fragrant, white flowers from mid-summer to autumn.

***Escallonia* 'Iveyi'**
Evergreen, upright shrub. Glossy, dark green foliage sets off large racemes of fragrant, tubular, pure white flowers, with short lobes, borne from mid- to late summer.

Xanthoceras sorbifolium
Deciduous, upright shrub or small tree with bright green leaves divided into many slender leaflets. In late spring and early summer produces spikes of white flowers with red patches inside at the base of the petals.

Brugmansia* × *candida
Semi-evergreen, rounded shrub or small tree. Has downy, oval leaves and strongly scented, pendulous, white flowers, sometimes cream or pinkish, in summer-autumn.
Min. 10°C (50°F).

Luma apiculata
Strong-growing, evergreen shrub with peeling, golden-brown and grey-white bark and cup-shaped flowers amid aromatic leaves in summer-autumn.

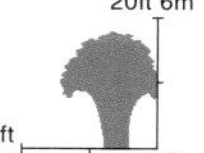
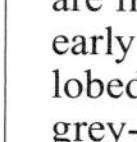
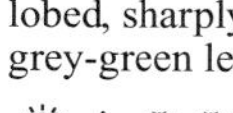

Abutilon vitifolium* var. *album
Fast-growing, deciduous, upright shrub. Large, bowl-shaped, white blooms, pink-tinged when young, are freely borne in late spring and early summer amid deeply lobed, sharply toothed, grey-green leaves.

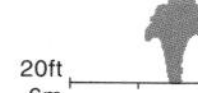

Abelia triflora
Vigorous, deciduous, upright shrub with pointed, deep green leaves. Small, extremely fragrant, white flowers, tinged pale pink, appear in mid-summer.

Chionanthus virginicus
(Fringe tree)
Deciduous, bushy shrub or small tree. Has large, glossy, dark green leaves that turn yellow in autumn. Drooping sprays of fragrant, white flowers appear in early summer.

***Cornus mas* 'Variegata'**
Deciduous, bushy, dense shrub or small tree. Small, star-shaped, yellow flowers appear on bare branches in early spring before white-edged, dark green leaves develop.

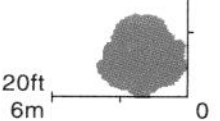

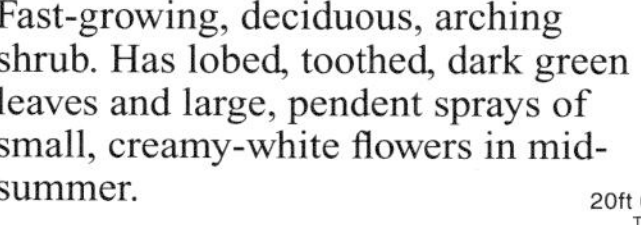
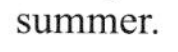

Holodiscus discolor
Fast-growing, deciduous, arching shrub. Has lobed, toothed, dark green leaves and large, pendent sprays of small, creamy-white flowers in mid-summer.

Aesculus parviflora
(Bottlebrush buckeye)
Deciduous, open shrub. Leaves are bronze when young, dark green in summer and yellow in autumn. Panicles of red-centred, white flowers appear from mid- to late summer.

***S. vulgaris* 'Madame Florent Stepman'**

Lilacs

The heady scent of the lilac (*Syringa*) epitomizes early summer. The abundant flowers are excellent for cutting. Apart from the classic lilacs and mauves, colours include white, pink, cream and rich red-purple; double forms are also available. Most lilacs grown in gardens are vigorous shrubs derived from *S. vulgaris*. They may eventually become tree-like and are best planted at the back of a shrub border or in groups in a wild garden; they may also be used as an informal hedge. Where space is restricted choose smaller-growing species, some of which may be grown in containers. Spent flower heads are best removed, with care taken not to damage the new shoots that form below the flowers. Otherwise little pruning is required, though older, straggly plants may be rejuvenated by hard pruning in winter.

***S. meyeri* 'Palibin'** 🏆

***S. vulgaris* 'Jan van Tol'**

***S. vulgaris* 'Madame Lemoine'** 🏆

***S. vulgaris* 'Mrs Edward Harding'** 🏆

***S. vulgaris* 'Monge'**

***S. vulgaris* 'Charles Joly'** 🏆

S.* × *persica 🏆

***S.* × *hyacinthiflora* 'Cora Brandt'**

***S.* × *chinensis* 'Alba'**

***S. vulgaris* 'Masséna'**

***S. vulgaris* 'Paul Thirion'**

***S. vulgaris* 'Président Grévy'**

***S. pubescens* subsp. *microphylla* 'Superba'**

S. yunnanensis

***S. vulgaris* 'Maréchal Foch'**

***S. vulgaris* 'Congo'**

***S. vulgaris* 'Madame Antoine Buchner'** 🏆

***S.* × *hyacinthiflora* 'Esther Staley'** 🏆

***S. vulgaris* 'Michel Buchner'**

***S. vulgaris* 'Madame F. Morel'**

***S. vulgaris* 'Decaisne'**

***S.* × *hyacinthiflora* 'Clarke's Giant'**

***S.* × *hyacinthiflora* 'Blue Hyacinth'**

***S. vulgaris* 'Primrose'**

WHITE–PINK

Clethra delavayi
Deciduous, open shrub with lance-shaped, toothed, rich green leaves. Dense, spreading clusters of pink buds opening to scented, white flowers appear in mid-summer.

Tamarix ramosissima
Deciduous, arching, graceful shrub or small tree with tiny, narrow, blue-green leaves. In late summer and early autumn bears large, upright plumes of small, pink flowers.

Abelia × grandiflora
Vigorous, semi-evergreen, arching shrub. Has glossy, dark green foliage and an abundance of fragrant, pink-tinged, white flowers from mid-summer to mid-autumn.

Nerium oleander (Oleander)
Evergreen, upright, bushy shrub with leathery, deep green leaves. Clusters of salver-form, pink, white, red, apricot or yellow flowers appear from spring to autumn, often on dark red stalks. Min. 10°C (50°F).

***Kolkwitzia amabilis* 'Pink Cloud'**
Deciduous, arching shrub that bears a mass of bell-shaped, pink flowers amid small, oval, mid-green leaves in late spring and early summer.

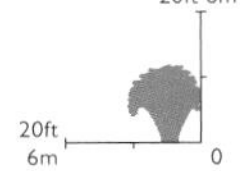

RED–PURPLE

***Buddleja davidii* 'Royal Red'**
Vigorous, deciduous, arching shrub. Has long, pointed, dark green leaves, with white-felted undersides, and plumes of fragrant, rich purple-red flowers from mid-summer to autumn.

Acer palmatum* f. *atropurpureum
Deciduous, bushy-headed shrub or small tree with lobed, reddish-purple foliage that turns brilliant red in autumn. Small, reddish-purple flowers are borne in mid-spring.

***Buddleja davidii* 'Harlequin'**
Vigorous, deciduous, arching shrub. Leaves are long, pointed and dark green with creamy-white margins. Plumes of fragrant, red-purple flowers appear from mid-summer to autumn.

Buddleja colvilei
Deciduous, arching shrub, often tree-like with age. Large, white-centred, deep pink to purplish-red flowers are borne in drooping racemes amid dark green foliage during early summer.

Malvaviscus arboreus
(Sleepy mallow)
Vigorous, evergreen, rounded shrub. Serrated, bright green leaves are soft-haired. Has bright red flowers with protruding stamens in summer-autumn.
Min. 13–16°C (55–61°F).

***Cotinus coggygria* 'Notcutt's Variety'**
Deciduous, bushy shrub with deep reddish-purple foliage. Long-lasting, purplish-pink plumes of massed, small flowers are produced in late summer.

RED–PURPLE

***Acer palmatum* var. *heptalobum* 'Rubrum'**
Deciduous, bushy-headed shrub or small tree. Large leaves are red when young, bronze in summer and brilliant red, orange or yellow in autumn. Has small, reddish-purple flowers in mid-spring.

Buddleja alternifolia
Deciduous, arching shrub that can be trained as a weeping tree. Has slender, pendent shoots and narrow, grey-green leaves. Neat clusters of fragrant, lilac-purple flowers appear in early summer.

***Prunus spinosa* 'Purpurea'**
Deciduous, dense, spiny shrub or small tree. Bright red, young leaves become deep reddish-purple. Bears saucer-shaped, pale pink flowers from early to mid-spring, followed by blue-bloomed, black fruits.

Tibouchina urvilleana
(Glory bush)
Evergreen, slender-branched shrub. Velvet-haired leaves are prominently veined. Has satiny, blue-purple flowers in clusters from summer to early winter. Min. 7°C (45°F).

***Corylus maxima* 'Purpurea'**
Vigorous, deciduous, open shrub or small tree with deep purple leaves and purplish catkins, with yellow anthers, that hang from bare branches in late winter. Edible nuts mature in autumn.

***Acer palmatum* var. *heptalobum* 'Lutescens'**
Deciduous, bushy-headed shrub or small tree. Large, lobed leaves become clear yellow in autumn. In mid-spring produces small, reddish-purple flowers, followed by winged fruits.

GREEN–YELLOW

Decaisnea fargesii
Deciduous, semi-arching, open shrub with blue-bloomed shoots and large, deep green leaves of paired leaflets. Racemes of greenish flowers in early summer are followed by pendent, sausage-shaped, bluish fruits.

Elaeagnus angustifolia (Oleaster)
Deciduous, bushy shrub or spreading, small tree. Has narrow, silvery-grey leaves and small, fragrant, creamy-yellow flowers, with spreading lobes, in early summer, followed by small, oval, yellow fruits.

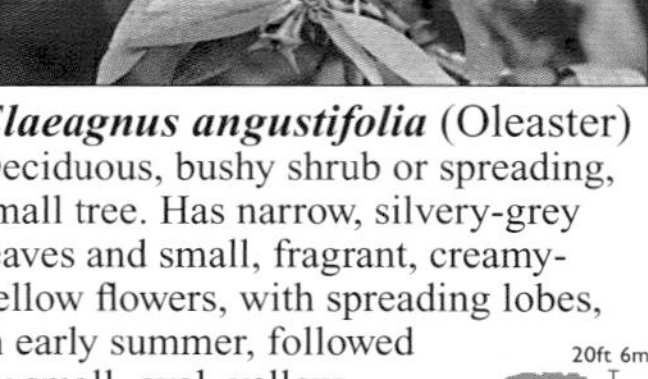

Paliurus spina-christi
(Christ's thorn, Jerusalem thorn)
Deciduous, bushy shrub with slender, thorny shoots. Has oval, glossy, bright green leaves, tiny, y ellow flowers in summer and curious, woody, winged fruits in autumn.

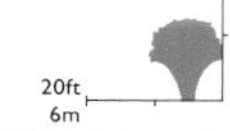

***Brugmansia* × *candida* 'Grand Marnier'**
Evergreen, robust shrub with large, oval to elliptic leaves. Pendent, flared, trumpet-shaped, apricot flowers open from an inflated calyx in summer. Min. 7–10°C (45–50°F).

Brugmansia sanguinea
Semi-evergreen, erect to rounded shrub or small tree with lobed, young leaves. Has large, trumpet-shaped, yellow and orange-red flowers from late summer to winter. Min. 10°C (50°F).

Crotalaria agatiflora (Canary-bird bush)
Evergreen, loose, somewhat spreading shrub with grey-green leaves. Racemes of greenish-yellow flowers appear in summer and also intermittently during the year. Min. 15°C (59°F).

Cytisus battandieri (Moroccan broom, Pineapple broom)
Semi-evergreen, open shrub. Leaves have 3 silver-grey leaflets. Pineapple-scented, yellow flowers appear in summer.

Caesalpinia gilliesii
Deciduous, open shrub or small tree. Has finely divided, dark green leaves and bears short racemes of yellow flowers with long, red stamens from mid- to late summer.

Genista cinerea
Deciduous, arching shrub that produces an abundance of fragrant, pea-like, yellow blooms from early to mid-summer. Has silky, young shoots and narrow, grey-green leaves.

Buddleja globosa
Deciduous or semi-evergreen, open shrub with dark green foliage. Dense, rounded clusters of orange-yellow flowers are carried in early summer.

***Fremontodendron* 'California Glory'**
Very vigorous, evergreen or semi-evergreen, upright shrub. Has rounded, lobed, dark green leaves and large, bright yellow flowers from late spring to mid-autumn.

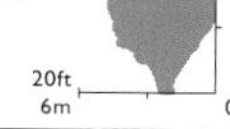

RED–YELLOW

***Cotoneaster* 'Cornubia'**
Vigorous, semi-evergreen, arching shrub. Clusters of white flowers, produced in early summer amid dark green foliage, are followed by large, pendent clusters of decorative, bright red fruits.

20ft 6m

***Rhus typhina* 'Dissecta'**
Deciduous, spreading, open shrub or small tree with velvety shoots. Fern-like, dark green leaves turn brilliant orange-red in autumn, when deep red fruit clusters are also borne.

20ft 6m

***Cotinus* 'Flame'**
Deciduous, bushy, tree-like shrub with dark green leaves that turn brilliant orange-red in autumn. From late summer, showy, plume-like, purplish-pink flower heads appear above the foliage.

20ft 6m

Hippophäe rhamnoides
(Sea buckthorn)
Deciduous, bushy, arching shrub or small tree with narrow, silvery leaves. Tiny, yellow flowers borne in mid-spring are followed in autumn by bright orange berries on female plants.

20ft 6m

Acer palmatum* var. *heptalobum
Deciduous, bushy-headed shrub or small tree with large, lobed, mid-green leaves that turn brilliant red, orange or yellow in autumn. Bears small, reddish-purple flowers in mid-spring.

20ft 6m

***Hamamelis vernalis* 'Sandra'**
Deciduous, upright, open shrub. Bears small, fragrant, spidery, deep yellow blooms in late winter and early spring. Oval leaves are purple when young, mid-green in summer, purple, red, orange and yellow in autumn.

20ft 6m

Euonymus myrianthus
Evergreen, bushy shrub with pointed, leathery, mid-green leaves. Dense clusters of small, greenish-yellow flowers in summer are followed by yellow fruits that open to show orange-red seeds.

20ft 6m

***Acer palmatum* 'Sango-kaku'**
(Coral-bark maple)
Deciduous, bushy-headed shrub or tree. Has coral-pink, young shoots in winter. Palmate, orange-yellow leaves turn green, then in autumn pink, then yellow.

20ft 6m

***Pyracantha atalantioides* 'Aurea'**
Vigorous, evergreen, upright, spiny shrub, arching with age. Has narrowly oval, glossy, dark green leaves and white flowers in early summer, followed by large clusters of small, yellow berries in early autumn.

20ft 6m

YELLOW

***Mahonia* × *media* 'Charity'**
Evergreen, upright, dense shrub with large leaves composed of many spiny, dark green leaflets. Slender, upright, later spreading spikes of fragrant, yellow flowers are borne from early autumn to early spring.

20ft 6m | 20ft 6m | 0

***Mahonia* × *media* 'Buckland'**
Evergreen, upright, dense shrub. Has large leaves with many spiny, dark green leaflets. Clustered, upright then spreading, long, branched spikes of fragrant, yellow flowers appear from late autumn to early spring.

20ft 6m | 20ft 6m | 0

Hamamelis virginiana
(Virginian witch hazel)
Deciduous, open, upright shrub. Small, fragrant, spidery, yellow flowers with 4 narrow petals open in autumn as leaves fall. Broadly oval leaves turn yellow in autumn.

20ft 6m | 20ft 6m | 0

RED

Cotoneaster lacteus
Evergreen, arching shrub suitable for hedging. Oval, dark green leaves set off shallowly cup-shaped, white flowers from early to mid-summer. Long-lasting, red fruits are carried in large clusters in autumn-winter.

20ft 6m | 20ft 6m | 0

***Hamamelis* × *intermedia* 'Diane'**
Deciduous, open, spreading shrub that produces fragrant, spidery, deep red flowers on bare branches from mid- to late winter. Broadly oval, mid-green leaves turn yellow and red in autumn.

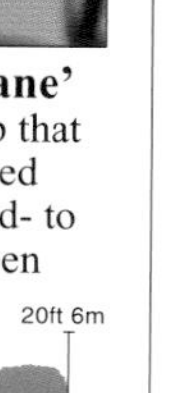

20ft 6m | 20ft 6m | 0

Cyphomandra betacea
(Tree tomato)
Evergreen, sparingly branched shrub or small tree, upright when young, with large, heart-shaped, rich green leaves. Has edible, tomato-like, red fruits from summer to winter. Min. 10°C (50°F).

20ft 6m | 20ft 6m | 0

GREEN–YELLOW

Garrya elliptica (Silk-tassel bush)
Evergreen, bushy, dense shrub with leathery, wavy-edged, dark green leaves. Grey-green catkins, longer on male than female plants, are borne from mid-winter to early spring.

20ft 6m | 20ft 6m | 0

Azara microphylla
Elegant, evergreen shrub or small tree. Has tiny, glossy, dark green leaves and small clusters of vanilla-scented, deep yellow flowers in late winter and early spring.

20ft 6m | 20ft 6m | 0

***Corylus avellana* 'Contorta'**
Deciduous, bushy shrub with curiously twisted shoots and broad, sharply toothed, mid-green leaves. In late winter, bare branches are covered with pendent, pale yellow catkins.

20ft 6m | 20ft 6m | 0

YELLOW

***Hamamelis* × *intermedia* 'Arnold Promise'**
Deciduous, open, spreading shrub. Large, fragrant, spidery, yellow flowers with 4 narrow, crimped petals appear from mid- to late winter. Broadly oval, green leaves turn yellow in autumn.

***Hamamelis japonica* 'Sulphurea'**
Deciduous, upright, open shrub. In mid-winter, fragrant, spidery, pale yellow flowers with 4 narrow, crimped petals are borne on leafless branches. Broadly oval, dark green leaves turn yellow in autumn.

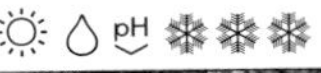

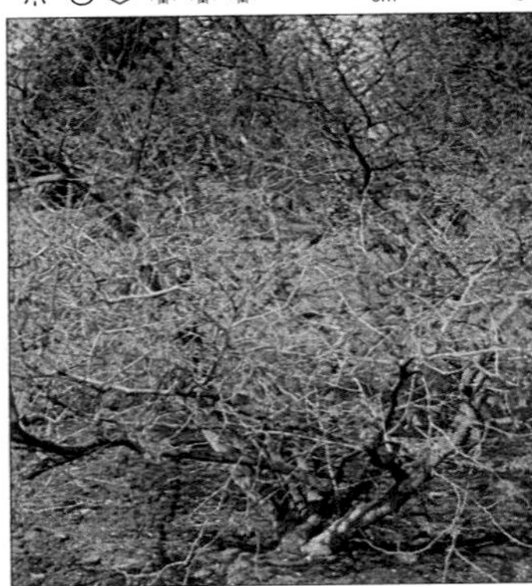

***Hamamelis mollis* 'Coombe Wood'**
Deciduous, open, spreading shrub. From mid- to late winter bears very fragrant, spidery, golden-yellow flowers with 4 narrow petals. Broadly oval, mid-green leaves turn yellow in autumn.

SHRUBS large ALL YEAR INTEREST

WHITE–GREEN

***Dracaena fragrans* Deremensis Group 'Warneckei'**
Slow-growing, evergreen shrub. Erect to arching, lance-shaped leaves are banded grey-green and cream. Min. 15–18°C (59–64°F).

Ligustrum ovalifolium
Vigorous, evergreen or semi-evergreen, upright, dense shrub with glossy, mid-green leaves. Dense racemes of small, rather unpleasantly scented, tubular, white flowers appear in mid-summer, followed by black fruits.

***Prunus lusitanica* 'Variegata'**
Slow-growing, evergreen, bushy shrub with reddish-purple shoots. Has oval, glossy, dark green, white-edged leaves. Fragrant, shallowly cup-shaped, creamy-white flowers in summer are followed by purple fruits.

Prunus lusitanica* subsp. *azorica
Evergreen, bushy shrub with reddish-purple shoots and bright green leaves, red when young. Bears spikes of small, fragrant, white flowers in summer, followed by purple fruits.

Tetrapanax papyrifer (Rice-paper plant)
Evergreen, upright, suckering shrub. Long-stalked, circular leaves are deeply lobed. Has bold sprays of small, creamy-white flowers in summer and black berries in autumn-winter.

***Griselinia littoralis* 'Variegata'**
Evergreen, upright shrub of dense, bushy habit. Leathery leaves are grey-green, marked with bright green and creamy-white. Bears inconspicuous, yellow-green flowers in late spring.

***Pittosporum* 'Garnettii'**
Evergreen, columnar or conical shrub of dense, bushy habit. Rounded, grey-green leaves, irregularly edged creamy-white, become tinged with deep pink in cold areas. May bear small, greenish-purple flowers in spring-summer.

***Polyscias guilfoylei* 'Victoriae'** (Lace aralia)
Slow-growing, evergreen, rounded shrub or small tree with leaves that are divided into several oval to rounded, serrated, white-margined, deep green leaflets. Min. 15–18°C (59–64°F).

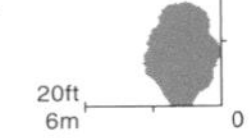

GREEN–YELLOW

Schefflera elegantissima (False aralia)
Evergreen, upright, open shrub. Large leaves have 7–10 coarsely toothed, lustrous, grey-green, sometimes bronze-tinted, leaflets. Min. 13°C (55°F).

20ft 6m / 20ft 6m 0

***Ligustrum lucidum* 'Excelsum Superbum'**
Evergreen, upright shrub or small tree. Large, glossy, bright green leaves are marked with pale green and yellow-edged. Small, tubular, white flowers open in late summer and early autumn.

20ft 6m / 20ft 6m 0

Brachyglottis repanda (Pukapuka, Rangiora)
Evergreen, bushy shrub or tree, upright when young, with robust, downy, white stems. Has veined leaves, white beneath, and fragrant, white flower heads in summer. Min. 3°C (37°F).

20ft 6m / 20ft 6m 0

***Osmanthus heterophyllus* 'Aureomarginatus'**
Evergreen, upright shrub. Sharply toothed, holly-like, glossy, bright green leaves have yellow margins. Small, fragrant, white flowers are produced in autumn.

20ft 6m / 20ft 6m 0

Pittosporum tenuifolium
Evergreen, columnar, later rounded shrub or small tree with purple shoots and wavy-edged, oval, glossy, mid-green leaves. Bears honey-scented, purple flowers in late spring.

20ft 6m / 20ft 6m 0

***Elaeagnus pungens* 'Maculata'**
Evergreen, bushy, slightly spiny shrub. Glossy, dark green leaves are marked with a central, deep yellow patch. Very fragrant, urn-shaped, creamy-white flowers open from mid- to late autumn.

20ft 6m / 20ft 6m 0

WHITE

Pieris floribunda
(Fetterbush, Mountain fetterbush)
Evergreen, bushy, dense, leafy shrub with oval, glossy, dark green leaves. Greenish-white flower buds appear in winter, opening to urn-shaped, white blooms from early to mid-spring.

10ft 3m / 10ft 3m 0

Enkianthus perulatus
Deciduous, bushy, dense shrub. Dark green leaves turn bright red in autumn. A profusion of small, pendent, urn-shaped, white flowers is borne in mid-spring.

10ft 3m / 10ft 3m 0

Fothergilla major
Deciduous, upright shrub with glossy, dark green leaves, slightly bluish-white beneath, that turn red, orange and yellow in autumn. Tufts of fragrant, white flowers appear in late spring.

10ft 3m / 10ft 3m 0

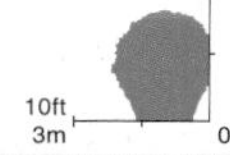

***Pieris japonica* 'Scarlett O'Hara'**
Evergreen, rounded, bushy, dense shrub. Young foliage and shoots are bronze-red, leaves becoming glossy, dark green. Produces sprays of white flowers in spring.

10ft 3m / 10ft 3m 0

Choisya ternata
(Mexican orange blossom)
Evergreen, rounded, dense shrub with aromatic, glossy, bright green leaves composed of 3 leaflets. Clusters of fragrant, white blooms open in late spring and often again in autumn.

10ft 3m / 10ft 3m 0

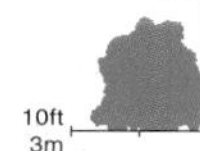

CAMELLIAS

These evergreen shrubs and small trees have long been valued for their luxuriant, rich green foliage and masses of showy flowers, in shades of white, pink, red and yellow, borne mainly in winter and spring. Once thought suitable only for glasshouses, many camellias are frost hardy outdoors if grown in sheltered positions, although blooms may suffer frost and rain damage. Camellias require lime-free soil. The main flower forms are illustrated below.

***C.* 'Shiroiwabisuke'** (single)

***C. japonica* 'Mrs D.W. Davis'** (s-db)♀

***C* × *williamsii* 'Jury's Yellow'** (anemone) ♀

***C.* 'Cornish Snow'** (single) ♀

***C. japonica* 'Janet Waterhouse'** (semi-double)

***C. japonica* 'Alba Simplex'** (single)

***C.* × *williamsii* 'Francis Hanger'** (single)

***C. sasanqua* 'Narumigata'** (single)

***C. japonica* 'Lady Vansittart'** (semi-double)

Single – shallowly cup-shaped flowers each have not more than 8 petals, arranged in a single row, and a conspicuous, central boss of stamens.

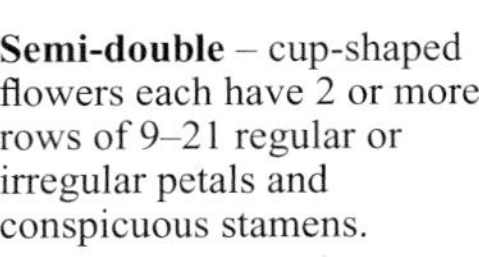

Semi-double – cup-shaped flowers each have 2 or more rows of 9–21 regular or irregular petals and conspicuous stamens.

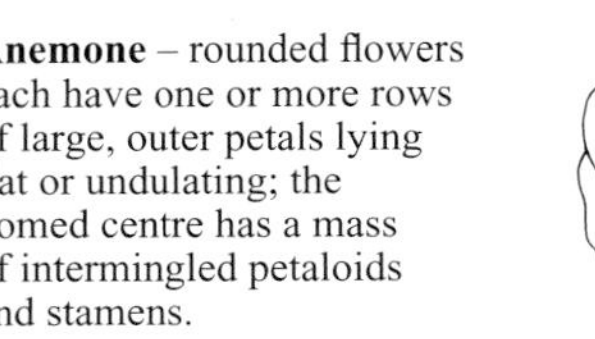

Anemone – rounded flowers each have one or more rows of large, outer petals lying flat or undulating; the domed centre has a mass of intermingled petaloids and stamens.

Peony-form – rounded, domed flowers have usually irregular petals intermingled with petaloids and stamens.

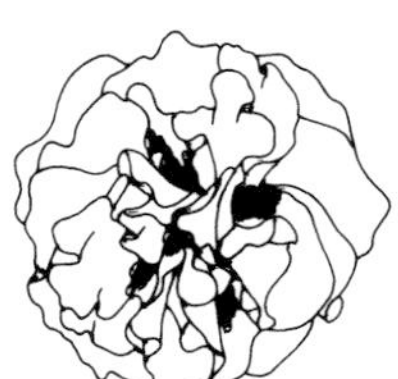

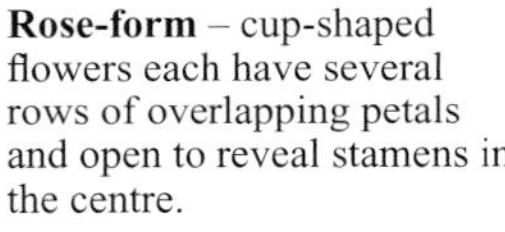

Rose-form – cup-shaped flowers each have several rows of overlapping petals and open to reveal stamens in the centre.

Formal double – rounded flowers have many rows of regular, neatly overlapping petals that obscure stamens. **Irregular double forms** are similar but often have more loosely arranged, sometimes irregular, petals.

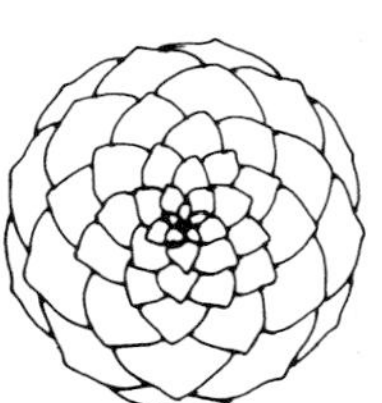

***C.* × *williamsii* 'Donation'** (semi-double) ♀

***C. japonica* 'Lavinia Maggi'** (formal double) ♀

***C.* × *williamsii* 'Joan Trehane'** (rose) ♀

***C.* × *williamsii* 'Wilber Foss'** (single)

***C. japonica* 'Betty Sheffield Supreme'** (irregular double)

***C. japonica* 'Margaret Davis'** (irregular double)

***C.* × *williamsii* 'Dream Boat'** (formal double)

C. tsaii (single) ♀

***C. japonica* 'Tomorrow's Dawn'** (irregular double)

***C. japonica* 'Berenice Boddy'** (semi-double) ♀

***C.* × *williamsii* 'J.C. Williams'** (single) ♀

***C.* × *williamsii* 'E.G. Waterhouse'** (double) ⓘ♀

C. saluenensis (single)

***C. reticulata* 'Mandalay Queen'** (semi-double) 🏆

***C.* 'Doctor Clifford Parks'** (variable) 🏆

***C. japonica* 'Guilio Nuccio'** (semi-double) 🏆

***C. × williamsii* 'Brigadoon'** (semi-double) 🏆

***C. reticulata* 'Arch of Triumph'** (peony) 🏆

***C.* 'Satan's Robe'** (semi-double) 🏆

***C. japonica* 'R.L. Wheeler'** (variable) 🏆

***C. japonica* 'Apollo'** (semi-double)

***C. × williamsii* 'Saint Ewe'** (single) 🏆

***C. japonica* 'Jupiter'** (single) 🏆

***C. × williamsii* 'George Blandford'** (semi-double) 🏆

***C. japonica* 'Julia Drayton'** (variable)

***C.* 'Inspiration'** (semi-double) 🏆

***C.* 'Leonard Messel'** (semi-double) 🏆

***C. japonica* 'Mathotiana'** (formal double)

***C. × williamsii* 'Golden Spangles'** (single)

***C. japonica* 'Elegans'** (anemone) 🏆

***C.* 'Innovation'** (peony)

***C. reticulata* 'Houye Diechi'** (semi-double)

***C. japonica* 'Adolphe Audusson'** (semi-double) 🏆

***C.* 'Francie L.'** (semi-double)

***C. japonica* 'Gloire de Nantes'** (semi-double) 🏆

***C.* 'Black Lace'** (formal double)

***C. japonica* 'Alexander Hunter'** (single) 🏆

***C. × williamsii* 'Water Lily'** (formal double) 🏆

***C.* 'William Hertrich'** (semi-double)

***C.* 'Anticipation'** (peony) 🏆

***C. japonica* 'Bob's Tinsie'** (anemone) 🏆

***C. japonica* 'Coquettii'** (variable)

WHITE–PINK

Aronia arbutifolia
(Red chokeberry)
Deciduous shrub, upright when young, later arching. Clusters of small, white flowers with red anthers appear in late spring, followed by red berries. Dark green foliage turns red in autumn.

Myrtus communis
(Common myrtle)
Evergreen, bushy shrub with aromatic, glossy, dark green foliage. Fragrant, white flowers are borne from mid-spring to early summer, followed by purple-black berries.

Malus toringo
Deciduous, spreading shrub with arching branches. Bears white or pale to deep pink flowers in mid-spring followed by small, red or yellow fruits. Dark green leaves, often lobed, turn red or yellow in autumn.

***Prunus mume* 'Omoi-no-mama'**
Deciduous, spreading shrub with fragrant, semi-double, occasionally single, pink-flushed, white flowers wreathing young growths in early spring, before oval, toothed leaves appear.

***Viburnum plicatum* 'Pink Beauty'**
Deciduous, bushy shrub. Dark green leaves become reddish-purple in autumn. In late spring and early summer bears white, later pink, blooms, followed by red, then black, fruits.

***Chaenomeles speciosa* 'Moerloosei'**
Vigorous, deciduous, bushy shrub. Has glossy, dark green leaves and pink-flushed, white flowers in early spring, followed by greenish-yellow fruits.

PINK–RED

Cotoneaster divaricatus
Deciduous, bushy, spreading shrub. Leaves are glossy, dark green, turning red in autumn. Shallowly cup-shaped, pink-flushed, white flowers in late spring and early summer are followed by deep red fruits.

***Ribes sanguineum* 'Pulborough Scarlet'**
Deciduous, upright shrub that in spring bears pendent, tubular, deep red flowers amid aromatic, dark green leaves, with 3–5 lobes, sometimes followed by black fruits with a white bloom.

***Prunus mume* 'Beni-chidori'**
Deciduous, spreading shrub with fragrant, single, carmine flowers in early spring before pointed, dark green leaves appear.

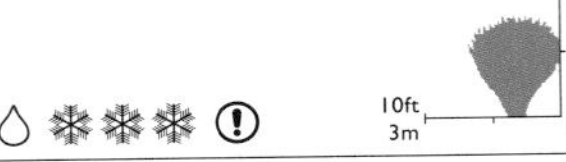

***Acer palmatum* 'Corallinum'**
Very slow-growing, deciduous, bushy-headed shrub or small tree. Lobed, bright reddish-pink, young foliage becomes mid-green, then brilliant red, orange or yellow in autumn. Reddish-purple flowers appear in mid-spring.

Banksia coccinea
Evergreen, dense shrub with toothed, dark green leaves, grey-green beneath. Flower heads comprising clusters of bright red flowers with prominent styles and stigmas are borne in late winter and spring. Min. 10°C (50°F).

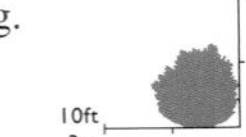

Enkianthus cernuus* f. *rubens
Deciduous, bushy shrub with dense clusters of dull green leaves that turn deep reddish-purple in autumn. Small, bell-shaped, deep red flowers appear in late spring.

Leucospermum reflexum
Evergreen, erect shrub with ascending branchlets. Has small, blue-grey or grey-green leaves. Slender, tubular, crimson flowers with long styles are carried in tight, rounded heads in spring-summer.
Min. 10°C (50°F).

Telopea truncata
(Tasmanian waratah)
Evergreen, upright shrub, bushy with age. Has deep green leaves and dense, rounded heads of small, tubular, crimson flowers in late spring and summer.

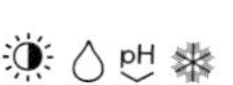

Greyia sutherlandii
Deciduous or semi-evergreen, rounded shrub. Coarsely serrated, leathery leaves turn red in autumn. Spikes of small, bright red flowers appear in spring with new foliage.
Min. 7–10°C (45–50°F).

***Leptospermum scoparium* 'Red Damask'**
Evergreen, upright, bushy shrub. Narrow, aromatic, dark green leaves set off sprays of double, dark red flowers in late spring and summer.

Berberis thunbergii* f. *atropurpurea
Deciduous, arching, dense shrub. Reddish-purple foliage turns bright red in autumn. Globose to cup-shaped, red-tinged, pale yellow flowers in mid-spring are followed by red fruits.

Corylopsis pauciflora
Deciduous, bushy, dense shrub. Oval, bright green leaves, bronze when young, have bristle-like teeth. Bears fragrant, tubular to bell-shaped, pale yellow flowers from early to mid-spring.

Berberis gagnepainii* var. *lanceifolia
Evergreen, bushy, dense shrub. Massed, globose to cup-shaped, yellow flowers appear among long, narrow, pointed, dark green leaves in late spring. Forms blue-bloomed, black berries.

Lindera benzoin
(Benjamin, Spice bush)
Deciduous, bushy shrub with aromatic, bright green leaves that turn yellow in autumn. Tiny, greenish-yellow flowers in mid-spring are followed by red berries on female plants.

***Kerria japonica* 'Pleniflora'**
Vigorous, deciduous, graceful shrub. Double, golden-yellow flowers are borne along green shoots from mid- to late-spring. Leaves are narrowly oval, sharply toothed and bright green.

Forsythia suspensa
Deciduous, arching, graceful shrub with slender shoots. Nodding, narrowly trumpet-shaped, bright yellow flowers open from early to mid-spring, before mid-green leaves appear.

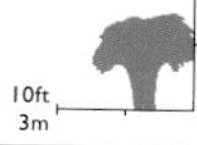

Rhododendrons

R. **'Ptarmigan'**
(rhododendron) ① 🏆

Rhododendrons and azaleas both belong to the huge genus *Rhododendron*, one of the largest in the plant kingdom. Azalea is the common name used for all the deciduous species and hybrids and many of the dwarf, small-leaved evergreens. In stature the genus ranges from alpine shrubs only a few inches high to tall, spreading trees, in the wild reaching 24m (80ft).

Rhododendrons require well-drained, acid soil rich in organic matter. Most prefer cool, woodland conditions although many dwarf forms thrive in more open sites. Many grow well in containers, in which it is often easier to provide suitable growing conditions. Once established, they require little attention apart from an annual mulch and occasional feeding, and provide a colourful display for years.

R. falconeri
(rhododendron) ① 🏆

R. cubittii
(rhododendron) ①

R. rex subsp. ***fictolacteum***
(rhododendron) ① 🏆

R. sinogrande
(rhododendron) ① 🏆

R. **'Loderi King George'**
(rhododendron) ① 🏆

R. **'Polar Bear'**
(rhododendron) ① 🏆

R. sutchuenense
(rhododendron) ①

R. souliei
(rhododendron) ①

R. leucaspis
(rhododendron) ①

R. **'Fragrantissimum'**
(rhododendron) ① 🏆

R. **'Beauty of Littleworth'**
(rhododendron) ①

R. yakushimanum
(rhododendron) ①

R. calophytum
(rhododendron) ① 🏆

R. **'Olive'**
(rhododendron) ①

R. auriculatum
(rhododendron) ①

R. **'Palestrina'**
(azalea) ① 🏆

R. argyrophyllum
(rhododendron) ①

R. **'Percy Wiseman'**
(rhododendron) ① 🏆

***R.* 'Susan'** (rhododendron) ① 🏆

***R.* 'Seta'** (rhododendron) ①

***R.* 'Mrs G. W. Leak'** (rhododendron) ①

***R.* 'Hinode-giri'** (azalea) ① 🏆

***R.* 'Vuyk's Scarlet'** (azalea) ① 🏆

***R.* 'Hinomayo'** (azalea) ① 🏆

R. calostrotum (rhododendron) ①

R. arboreum (rhododendron) ①

***R.* 'Irohayama'** (azalea) ① 🏆

R. orbiculare (rhododendron) ① 🏆

***R.* 'Corneille'** (azalea) ① 🏆

R. kaempferi (azalea) ①

***R.* 'Homebush'** (azalea) ① 🏆

R. racemosum (rhododendron) ① 🏆

***R.* 'Pink Pearl'** (rhododendron) ①

***R.* 'Kirin'** (azalea) ①

***R.* Nobleanum Group** (rhododendron) ①

R. williamsianum (rhododendron) ① 🏆

***R.* 'May Day'** (rhododendron) ① 🏆

***R.* 'Hatsugiri'** (azalea) ①

***R.* 'Azuma-kagami'** (azalea) ①

R. oreotrephes (rhododendron) ①

***R.* 'Strawberry Ice'** (azalea) ① 🏆

R. thomsonii (rhododendron) ①

***R.* 'John Cairns'** (azalea) ①

R. cinnabarinum (rhododendron) ①

R. rex subsp. ***arizelum*** (rhododendron) ①

R. wardii (rhododendron) ①

R. lutescens (rhododendron) ①

***R.* 'Crest'** (rhododendron) ①🏆

R. luteum (azalea) ①🏆

***R.* 'Queen Elizabeth II'** (rhododendron) ①🏆

***R.* 'Narcissiflorum'** (azalea) ①🏆

***R.* 'Frome'** (azalea) ①

***R.* 'Fabia'** (rhododendron) ①🏆

***R.* 'Yellow Hammer'** (rhododendron) ①🏆

***R.* 'Curlew'** (rhododendron) ①🏆

***R.* 'Goldkrone'** (rhododendron) ①🏆

***R.* 'Gloria Mundi'** (azalea) ①

***R.* 'George Reynolds'** (azalea) ①

***R.* 'Blue Peter'** (rhododendron) ①🏆

R. maccabeanum (rhododendron) ①🏆

R. hippophaeoides (rhododendron) ①

R. augustinii (rhododendron) ①

***R.* 'Freya'** (azalea) ①

***R.* 'Medway'** (azalea) ①🏆

R. cinnabarinum subsp. ***xanthocodon*** (rhodo.) ①🏆

***R.* 'Glory of Littleworth'** (azalea × rhododendron) ①

***R.* 'Moonshine Crescent'** (rhododendron) ①🏆

R. laetum (rhododendron) ①

***R.* 'Blue Diamond'** (rhododendron) ①

YELLOW–ORANGE

Azara serrata
Evergreen, upright shrub with glossy, bright green foliage and rounded bunches of fragrant, yellow flowers in late spring or early summer.

10ft 3m

***Forsythia* × *intermedia* 'Beatrix Farrand'**
Vigorous, deciduous, bushy, arching shrub with stout shoots. A profusion of large, deep yellow flowers appears from early to mid-spring before oval, coarsely toothed, mid-green leaves emerge.

10ft 3m

***Forsythia* × *intermedia* 'Spectabilis'**
Vigorous, deciduous, spreading shrub with stout growths. A profusion of large, deep yellow flowers is borne from early to mid-spring before sharply toothed, dark green leaves appear.

10ft 3m

Berberis* × *stenophylla
Evergreen, arching shrub with slender shoots and narrow, spine-tipped, deep green leaves, blue-grey beneath. Massed, golden-yellow flowers appear from mid- to late spring followed by small, blue-black fruits.

10ft 3m

***Berberis* × *lologensis* 'Stapehill'**
Vigorous, evergreen, arching shrub. Glossy, dark green foliage sets off profuse racemes of globose to cup-shaped, orange flowers from mid- to late spring.

10ft 3m

***Berberis linearifolia* 'Orange King'**
Evergreen, upright, stiff-branched shrub with narrow, rigid, dark green leaves. Bears large, globose to cup-shaped, deep orange flowers in late spring.

10ft 3m

WHITE

***Carissa macrocarpa* 'Tuttlei'**
Evergreen, compact and spreading shrub with thorny stems and leathery leaves. Has fragrant flowers in spring-summer and edible, plum-like, red fruits in autumn. Min. 13°C (55°F).

10ft 3m

***Philadelphus* 'Beauclerk'**
Deciduous, slightly arching shrub. Large, fragrant flowers, white with a small, central, pale purple blotch, are produced from early to mid-summer. Leaves are dark green.

10ft 3m

***Exochorda* × *macrantha* 'The Bride'**
Deciduous, arching, dense shrub that forms a mound of pendent branches. Large, white flowers are produced in abundance amid dark green foliage in late spring and early summer.

10ft 3m

□ WHITE

Deutzia scabra
Deciduous, upright shrub with narrowly oval, dark green leaves that, from early to mid-summer, set off dense, upright clusters of 5-petalled, white blooms.

***Philadelphus* 'Belle Etoile'**
Deciduous, arching shrub. Very fragrant, white flowers, each with a pale purple mark at the base, are borne profusely among mid-green foliage in late spring and early summer.

Pyracantha* × *watereri
Evergreen, upright, dense, spiny shrub with glossy, dark green foliage. Shallowly cup-shaped, white flowers in early summer are succeeded by bright red berries in autumn.

Spiraea canescens
Deciduous shrub with upright shoots arching at the top. Small heads of white flowers are borne in profusion amid narrowly oval, grey-green leaves from early to mid-summer.

***Deutzia* × *magnifica* 'Staphyleoides'**
Vigorous, deciduous, upright shrub. Large, 5-petalled, pure white blooms, borne in dense clusters in early summer, have recurved petals. Leaves are bright green.

Aronia melanocarpa
(Black chokeberry)
Deciduous, bushy shrub. White flowers appear in late spring and early summer, followed by black fruits. Has glossy, dark green leaves that turn red in autumn.

Fallugia paradoxa
(Apache plume)
Deciduous, bushy shrub that bears white flowers in mid-summer, followed by silky, pink- and red-tinged, green fruits. Dark green leaves are finely cut and feathery.

***Rubus* 'Benenden'**
Deciduous, arching, thornless shrub with peeling bark. Large, rose-like, pure white flowers are borne among lobed, deep green leaves in late spring and early summer.

Olearia nummulariifolia
Evergreen, rounded shrub with stiff, upright shoots densely covered with small, very thick, mid- to dark green leaves. Small, fragrant, white flowers appear in mid-summer.

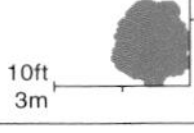

Sorbaria sorbifolia
Deciduous, upright shrub that forms thickets by suckering. Mid-green leaves consist of many sharply toothed leaflets. Large panicles of small, white flowers appear in summer.

10ft 3m

10ft 3m 0

Prinsepia uniflora
Deciduous, arching, spiny shrub. From late spring to summer bears small, fragrant, white flowers amid narrow, glossy, dark green leaves followed by cherry-like, deep red fruits. Grows best in hot sun.

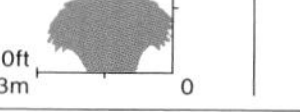

Yucca gloriosa (Spanish dagger)
Evergreen shrub with a stout stem crowned with a tuft of long, pointed, deep green leaves, blue-green when young. Bears very long panicles of bell-shaped, white flowers in summer-autumn.

10ft 3m

10ft 3m 0

***Philadelphus* 'Boule d'Argent'**
Deciduous, bushy, arching shrub with dark green foliage that sets off clusters of slightly fragrant, semi-double to double, pure white flowers from early to mid-summer.

10ft 3m

10ft 3m 0

Eucryphia milliganii
Evergreen, upright, narrow shrub. Has tiny, dark green leaves, bluish-white beneath, and small, white flowers, borne in mid-summer.

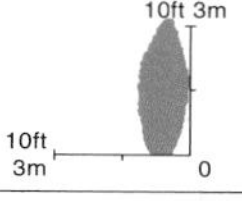

***Philadelphus* 'Dame Blanche'**
Deciduous, bushy, compact shrub with dark, peeling bark. Dark green foliage sets off slightly fragrant, semi-double to loosely double, pure white flowers borne in profusion from early to mid-summer.

10ft 3m

10ft 3m 0

Escallonia virgata
Deciduous, spreading, graceful shrub with arching shoots and small, glossy, dark green leaves. Bears racemes of small, open cup-shaped, white flowers from early to mid-summer.

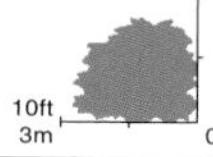

☐ WHITE

Osteomeles schweriniae
Evergreen, arching shrub with long, slender shoots. Leaves, consisting of many small leaflets, are dark green. Clusters of small, white flowers in early summer are followed by red, later blue-black, fruits.

Carpenteria californica
Evergreen, bushy shrub. Glossy, dark green foliage sets off fragrant, yellow-centred, white flowers borne during summer.

Styrax wilsonii
Deciduous, bushy shrub with slender shoots that produce an abundance of yellow-centred, white flowers in early summer. Leaves are small and deep green.

***Philadelphus* 'Lemoinei'**
Deciduous, upright, slightly arching shrub that produces profuse racemes of small, extremely fragrant, white flowers from early to mid-summer.

Symplocos paniculata
(Sapphire berry)
Deciduous, bushy shrub or small tree. Panicles of small, fragrant, white flowers in late spring and early summer are followed by small, metallic-blue berries. Has dark green leaves.

Ozothamnus rosmarinifolius
Evergreen, upright, dense shrub with woolly, white shoots and narrow, dark green leaves. Clusters of fragrant, white flower heads open in early summer.

Clethra barbinervis
Deciduous, upright shrub with peeling bark. Has oval, toothed, dark green leaves that turn red and yellow in autumn. Racemes of fragrant, white flowers are borne in late summer and early autumn.

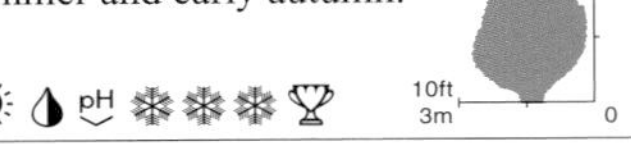

Ceanothus incanus
Evergreen, bushy shrub. Has spreading, spiny shoots, broad, grey-green leaves and large racemes of white flowers in late spring and early summer.

Zenobia pulverulenta
Deciduous or semi-evergreen, slightly arching shrub, often with bluish-white-bloomed shoots. Glossy leaves have a bluish-white reverse when young. Bears fragrant, bell-shaped, white flowers from early to mid-summer.

***Cornus alba* 'Elegantissima'**
Vigorous, deciduous shrub. Young shoots are bright red in winter. Has white-edged, grey-green leaves and small, creamy-white flowers in late spring and early summer followed by white fruits.

***Viburnum dilatatum* 'Catskill'**
Deciduous, low, spreading shrub with sharply toothed, dark green leaves that turn yellow, orange and red in autumn. Flat heads of creamy-white flowers in late spring and early summer are followed by bright red fruits.

Olearia* × *haastii
Evergreen, bushy, dense shrub, good for hedging. Has small, oval, glossy, dark green leaves and is covered with heads of fragrant, daisy-like, white flowers from mid- to late summer.

***Philadelphus coronarius* 'Variegatus'**
Deciduous, bushy shrub with racemes of very fragrant, creamy-white flowers in late spring and early summer and mid-green leaves broadly edged with white.

***Spiraea nipponica* 'Snowmound'**
Deciduous, spreading shrub with stout, arching, reddish branches. Small, narrow, dark green leaves set off profuse, dense clusters of small, white flowers in early summer.

Eriogonum giganteum
(St Catherine's lace)
Evergreen, rounded shrub with oblong to oval, woolly, white leaves. Small, white flowers are carried in branching clusters to 30cm (12in) or more wide in summer. Min. 5°C (41°F).

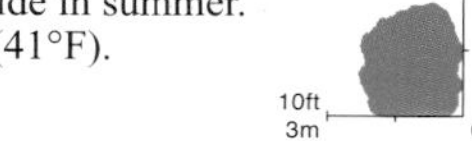

***Viburnum* 'Pragense'**
Evergreen, rounded, bushy shrub that has dark green foliage and domed heads of white flowers opening from pink buds in late spring and early summer.

Leptospermum polygalifolium
Evergreen, arching, graceful shrub with small, glossy, bright green leaves. Bears an abundance of small, pink-tinged, white flowers in mid-summer.

Philadelphus delavayi* f. *melanocalyx
Deciduous, upright shrub, grown for its extremely fragrant flowers, with pure white petals and deep purple sepals, opening from early to mid-summer. Leaves are dark green.

***Hibiscus syriacus* 'Red Heart'**
Deciduous, upright shrub that bears large, white flowers, with conspicuous red centres, from late summer to mid-autumn. Oval leaves are lobed and deep green.

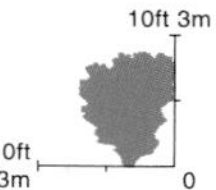

WHITE–PINK

Lonicera xylosteum
(Fly honeysuckle)
Deciduous, upright, bushy, dense shrub. Creamy-white flowers are produced amid grey-green leaves in late spring and early summer and are followed by red berries.

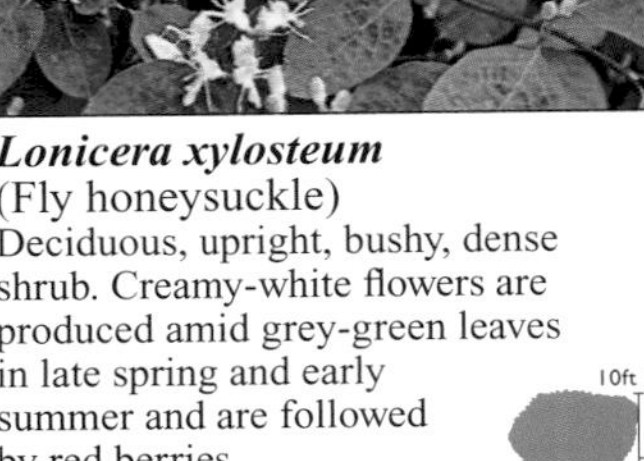

Stephanandra tanakae
Deciduous, arching shrub with orange-brown shoots and sharply toothed, mid-green leaves that turn orange and yellow in autumn. Small, yellow-green buds open to white flowers from early to mid-summer.

***Acer palmatum* 'Butterfly'**
Slow-growing, deciduous, mounded shrub or small tree with lobed, grey-green leaves edged with cream and pink. In mid-spring bears small, reddish-purple flowers.

Lonicera tatarica
Deciduous, bushy shrub. Tubular to trumpet-shaped, 5-lobed, white, pink or red flowers cover dark green foliage in late spring and early summer and are succeeded by red berries.

***Escallonia* 'Donard Seedling'**
Vigorous, evergreen, arching shrub with small, glossy, dark green leaves. Masses of pink flower buds open to white blooms, flushed with pale pink, from early to mid-summer.

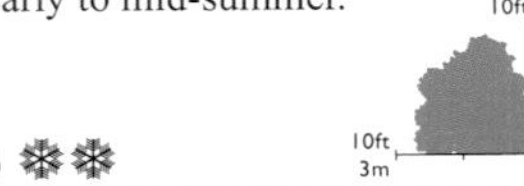

PINK

***Deutzia longifolia* 'Veitchii'**
Deciduous, arching shrub with narrow, pointed leaves and large clusters of 5-petalled, deep pink flowers from early to mid-summer.

Protea neriifolia
Evergreen, bushy, upright shrub with narrow leaves. Flower heads, about 13cm (5in) long, are red, pink or white, the bracts tipped with tufts of black hair, and appear in spring-summer. Min. 5–7°C (41–5°F).

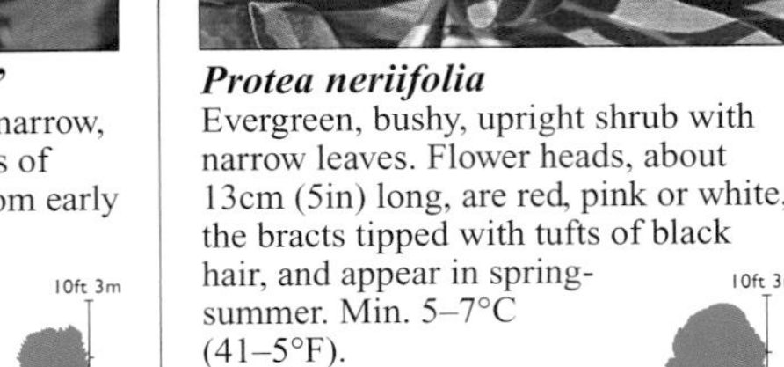

Neillia thibetica
Deciduous, arching shrub. Slender spikes of rose-pink flowers are borne profusely in late spring and early summer. Leaves are sharply toothed.

***Escallonia* 'Apple Blossom'**
Evergreen, bushy, dense shrub. From early to mid-summer apple-blossom-pink flowers are borne in profusion amid glossy, dark green leaves.

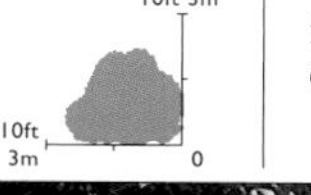

Robinia hispida (Rose acacia)
Deciduous shrub of loose habit with brittle, bristly stems that carry dark green leaves composed of 7–13 leaflets. Pendent racemes of deep rose-pink blooms open in late spring and early summer.

Indigofera heterantha
Deciduous, slightly arching shrub. Has greyish-green leaves consisting of many small leaflets and spikes of small, purplish-pink flowers from early summer to early autumn.

***Lavatera × clementii* 'Rosea'**
Semi-evergreen, erect shrub that produces abundant clusters of hollyhock-like, deep pink flowers throughout summer. Has lobed, sage-green leaves.

Kalmia latifolia (Calico bush)
Evergreen, bushy, dense shrub. In early summer large clusters of pink flowers open from distinctively crimped buds amid glossy, rich green foliage.

Medinilla magnifica
Evergreen, upright shrub, with sparingly produced, 4-angled, robust stems and boldly veined leaves. Pink to coral-red flowers hang in long trusses beneath large, pink bracts in spring-summer. Min. 16–18°C (61–4°F).

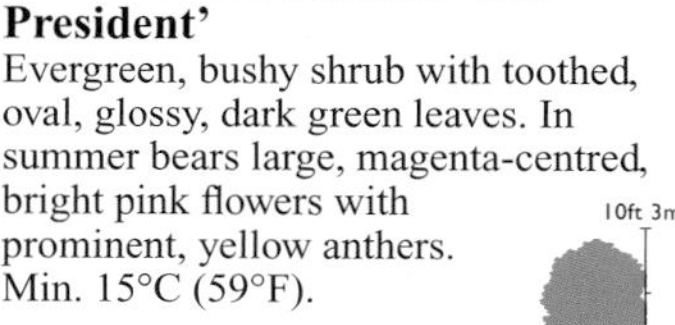

***Hibiscus rosa-sinensis* 'The President'**
Evergreen, bushy shrub with toothed, oval, glossy, dark green leaves. In summer bears large, magenta-centred, bright pink flowers with prominent, yellow anthers. Min. 15°C (59°F).

***Hibiscus syriacus* 'Woodbridge'**
Deciduous, upright shrub. From late summer to mid-autumn large, reddish-pink flowers, with deeper-coloured centres, appear amid lobed, dark green leaves.

Lavatera assurgentiflora
Semi-evergreen shrub with twisted, grey stems. Clusters of hollyhock-like, darkly veined, deep cerise blooms open in mid-summer. Palmate, mid-green leaves are white-haired beneath.

PINK–RED

Melaleuca elliptica
(Granite bottlebrush)
Evergreen, rounded shrub with long, leathery, usually greyish-green leaves. Flowers, consisting of a brush of red stamens, are borne in dense, terminal spikes in spring-summer.

Cestrum elegans
Vigorous, evergreen, arching shrub. Nodding shoots carry downy, deep green foliage. Dense racemes of tubular, purplish-red flowers in late spring and summer are followed by deep red fruits.

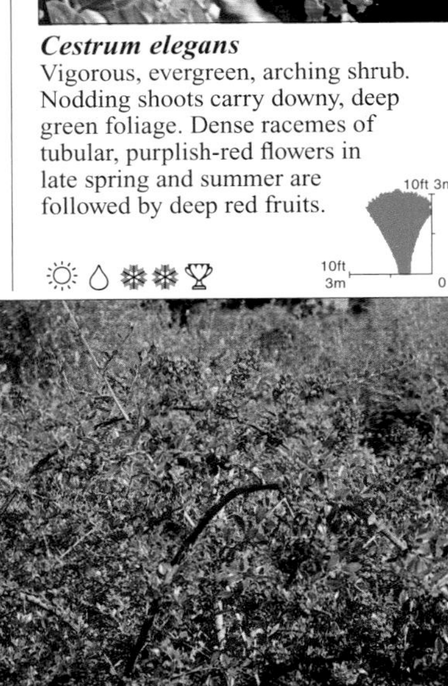

***Escallonia* 'Langleyensis'**
Evergreen or semi-evergreen, arching shrub with small, glossy, bright green leaves and an abundance of rose-pink flowers from early to mid-summer.

RED

***Pieris formosa* var. *forrestii* 'Wakehurst'**
Evergreen, bushy, dense shrub. Young leaves are brilliant red in early summer, becoming pink, creamy-yellow and finally dark green. Bears urn-shaped, white flowers in spring-summer.

Calycanthus occidentalis
(California allspice)
Deciduous, bushy shrub. Leaves are large, aromatic and dark green. Fragrant, purplish-red flowers with many strap-shaped petals appear during summer.

Crinodendron hookerianum
(Lantern tree)
Evergreen, stiff-branched shrub. In late spring and early summer, lantern-like, red flowers hang from shoots clothed with narrow, dark green leaves.

Lonicera ledebourii
Deciduous, bushy shrub. Red-tinged, orange-yellow flowers are borne amid dark green foliage in late spring and early summer and are followed by black berries. As these ripen, deep red bracts enlarge around them.

Bauhinia galpinii
Semi-evergreen or evergreen, spreading shrub, occasionally semi-climbing. Has 2-lobed leaves and, in summer, fragrant, bright brick-red flowers. Min. 5°C (41°F).

Telopea speciosissima (Waratah)
Evergreen, erect, fairly bushy shrub with coarsely serrated leaves. Has tubular, red flowers in dense, globose heads, surrounded by bright red bracts, in spring-summer.

RED

Erythrina crista-galli
(Cockspur coral-tree)
Deciduous, mainly upright shrub or small tree. Leaves have 3 oval leaflets. Has leafy racemes of crimson flowers in summer-autumn. Dies back to ground level in winter in cold areas.

Desfontainia spinosa
Evergreen, bushy, dense shrub with spiny, holly-like, glossy, dark green leaves. Long, tubular, drooping, red flowers, tipped with yellow, are borne from mid-summer to late autumn.

Callistemon rigidus
Evergreen, bushy, slightly arching shrub with long, narrow, sharply pointed, dark green leaves and dense spikes of deep red flowers in late spring and early summer.

Erythrina* × *bidwillii
Deciduous, upright shrub with pale to mid-green leaves divided into 3 leaflets, up to 10cm (4in) long. Bright red flowers are carried in racemes in late summer or autumn.

***Callistemon citrinus* 'Splendens'**
Evergreen, arching shrub with broad, lemon-scented, grey-green leaves that are bronze-red when young. In early summer bright red flowers are borne in bottlebrush-like spikes.

Rhus glabra (Smooth sumach)
Deciduous, bushy shrub with bluish-white-bloomed, reddish-purple stems. Deep blue-green leaves turn red in autumn. Bears panicles of greenish-red flower heads in summer followed by red fruits on female plants.

RED–PURPLE

Acca sellowiana (Pineapple guava)
Evergreen, bushy shrub or tree. Dark green leaves have white undersides. In mid-summer bears large, dark red flowers with white-edged petals, followed by edible, red-tinged, green fruits.

***Acer palmatum* 'Bloodgood'**
Deciduous, bushy-headed shrub or small tree with deep reddish-purple leaves that turn brilliant red in autumn. Small, reddish-purple flowers in mid-spring are often followed by decorative, winged, red fruits.

Acalypha wilkesiana
(Copperleaf, Jacob's coat)
Evergreen, bushy shrub. Oval, serrated leaves are 10cm (4in) or more long, rich copper-green, variably splashed with shades of red.
Min.16°C (61°F).

Aloysia triphylla (Lemon verbena)
Deciduous, bushy shrub. Leaves are pale green and lemon-scented. Racemes of tiny, lilac-tinged, white flowers appear in early summer.

Buddleja crispa
Deciduous, upright, bushy shrub that, from mid- to late summer, bears racemes of small, fragrant, lilac flowers with white eyes. Has woolly, white shoots and oval, greyish-green leaves.

***Hibiscus sinosyriacus* 'Lilac Queen'**
Deciduous, spreading, open shrub. From late summer to mid-autumn produces large, pale lilac flowers with red centres. Broad, lobed leaves are dark green.

HYDRANGEAS

H. paniculata 'Unique' ① 🏆

Valued for their late summer flowers, hydrangeas are versatile shrubs that thrive in a variety of situations. Larger-growing species, some of which may become tree-like with age, are suited to light woodland, while the range of cultivars, mostly of *H. macrophylla*, make excellent border plants. Some may also be grown in containers. Colours range from white through pink, red and purple to blue. The truest blue is obtained only on acid soil. Lacecap hydrangeas have a central corymb of small, fertile flowers surrounded by showy, coloured bracts; mopheads (or hortensias) have domed heads of sterile bracts only. *H. paniculata* cultivars bear larger though fewer cone-shaped flower heads if pruned hard in spring. Hydrangea flower heads persist for many months, and may be dried for winter decoration indoors.

H. villosa ① 🏆

H. quercifolia ① 🏆

H. paniculata 'Praecox' ①

H. arborescens 'Annabelle' ① 🏆

H. paniculata 'Brussels Lace' ①

H. macrophylla 'Lilacina' ① 🏆

H. macrophylla 'Lanarth White' ① 🏆

H. heteromalla 'Bretschneideri' ①

H. involucrata 'Hortensis' ① 🏆

H. paniculata 'Floribunda' ①

H. macrophylla 'Mariesii Perfecta' ① 🏆

H. arborescens 'Grandiflora' ① 🏆

H. macrophylla 'Générale Vicomtesse de Vibraye' ① 🏆

H. paniculata PINK DIAMOND ① 🏆

H. macrophylla 'Veitchii' ① 🏆

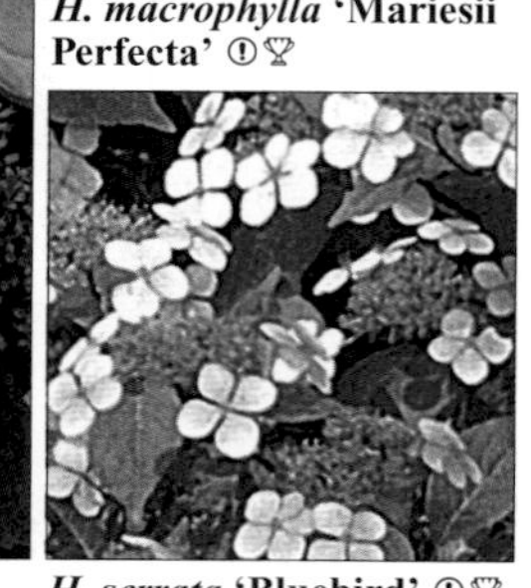

H. serrata 'Bluebird' ① 🏆

H. macrophylla 'Altona' ① 🏆

H. macrophylla 'Hamburg' ①

H. serrata ①

H. macrophylla 'Blue Bonnet' ①

PURPLE

Prostanthera ovalifolia
Evergreen, bushy, rounded shrub with tiny, sweetly aromatic, oval, thick-textured leaves. Cup-shaped, 2-lipped, purple flowers appear in short, leafy racemes in spring-summer.
Min. 5°C (41°F).

Melaleuca nesophila
(Western tea-myrtle)
Evergreen, bushy shrub or small tree with oval, grey-green leaves. Flowers, consisting of a brush of lavender to rose-pink stamens, are borne in rounded, terminal heads in summer.

***Abutilon* × *suntense* 'Violetta'**
Fast-growing, deciduous, upright, arching shrub that carries an abundance of large, bowl-shaped, deep violet flowers in late spring and early summer. Vine-like leaves are sharply toothed and dark green.

Prostanthera rotundifolia
(Round-leaved mint-bush)
Evergreen, bushy, rounded shrub with tiny, sweetly aromatic, deep green leaves and short, leafy racemes of bell-shaped, lavender to purple-blue flowers in late spring or summer.

***Solanum rantonnetii* 'Royal Robe'**
Evergreen, loosely rounded shrub with smooth, bright green leaves. In summer has clusters of rich purple-blue flowers that open almost flat.
Min. 7°C (45°F).

Sophora davidii
Deciduous, bushy shrub with arching shoots. Produces short racemes of small, pea-like, purple and white flowers in late spring and early summer. Grey-green leaves have many leaflets.

PURPLE–BLUE

Fabiana imbricata* f. *violacea
Evergreen, upright shrub with shoots that are densely covered with tiny, heath-like, deep green leaves. Tubular, lilac flowers are borne profusely in early summer.

***Hibiscus syriacus* 'Oiseau Bleu'**
Deciduous, upright shrub that carries large, red-centred, lilac-blue flowers from late summer to mid-autumn. Has lobed, deep green leaves.

Ceanothus impressus
Evergreen, bushy shrub. Spreading growth is covered with small, crinkled, dark green leaves. Deep blue flowers appear in small clusters from mid-spring to early summer.

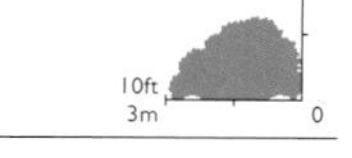

GREEN

Eleutherococcus sieboldianus
Deciduous, bushy, elegant shrub. Has glossy, bright green leaves, divided into 5 leaflets, and is armed with spines. Clusters of small, greenish flowers appear in early summer.

Zanthoxylum piperitum
(Japan pepper)
Deciduous, bushy, spiny shrub or small tree with aromatic, glossy, dark green leaves composed of many leaflets. Small, red fruits follow tiny, greenish-yellow, spring flowers.

***Ptelea trifoliata* 'Aurea'**
Deciduous, bushy, dense shrub or low tree. Leaves, consisting of 3 leaflets, are bright yellow when young, maturing to pale green. Bears racemes of greenish flowers in summer, followed by winged, green fruits.

GREEN–YELLOW

Itea ilicifolia
Evergreen, bushy shrub with arching shoots and oval, sharply toothed, glossy, dark green leaves. Long, catkin-like racemes of small, greenish flowers appear in late summer and early autumn.

Callistemon pallidus
Evergreen, arching shrub. Grey-green foliage is pink-tinged when young and in early summer is covered with dense spikes of creamy-yellow flowers that resemble bottlebrushes.

***Physocarpus opulifolius* 'Dart's Gold'**
Deciduous, compact shrub with peeling bark and oval, lobed, golden-yellow leaves. Produces clusters of shallowly cup-shaped, white or pale pink flowers in late spring.

***Cornus alba* 'Spaethii'**
Vigorous, deciduous shrub with bright red, young shoots in winter. Bright green leaves are yellow-edged. Bears small, creamy-white flowers in late spring and early summer, followed by rounded, white fruits.

Bupleurum fruticosum
(Shrubby hare's ear)
Evergreen, bushy shrub with slender shoots. From mid-summer to early autumn rounded heads of small, yellow flowers are borne amid glossy, dark bluish-green foliage.

Colutea arborescens
(Bladder senna)
Fast-growing, deciduous, open shrub. Has pale green leaves with many leaflets, pea-like, yellow flowers throughout summer and bladder-like seed pods in late summer and autumn.

Piptanthus nepalensis
Deciduous or semi-evergreen, open shrub with leaves consisting of 3 large, dark blue-green leaflets. Racemes of pea-like, bright yellow flowers appear in spring-summer.

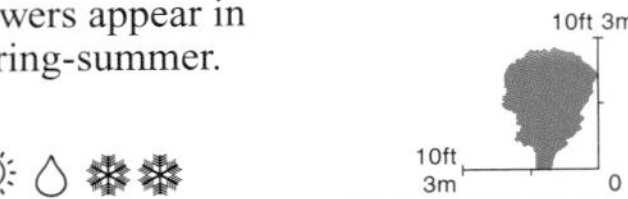

Hibbertia cuneiformis
Evergreen, upright, bushy shrub with small, oval leaves, serrated at tips. Has small clusters of bright yellow flowers, with spreading petals, in spring-summer.
Min. 5–7°C (41–5°F).

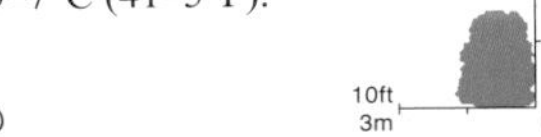

Jasminum humile
(Yellow jasmine)
Evergreen, bushy shrub that bears bright yellow flowers on long, slender, green shoots from early spring to late autumn. Leaves, with 5 or 7 leaflets, are bright green.

YELLOW–ORANGE

Colutea × media
Vigorous, deciduous, open shrub. Grey-green leaves have many leaflets. Racemes of yellow flowers, tinged with copper-orange, appear in summer, followed by bladder-like, papery, red-tinged seed pods.

Senna corymbosa
Vigorous, evergreen or semi-evergreen shrub. Leaves have 4–6 oval, bright green leaflets; sprays of bowl-shaped, rich yellow flowers appear in late summer. Min. 7°C (45°F).

Spartium junceum
(Spanish broom)
Deciduous, almost leafless, upright shrub that arches with age. Fragrant, pea-like, golden-yellow flowers appear from early summer to early autumn on dark green shoots.

Dendromecon rigida
Vigorous, evergreen, upright shrub, best grown against a wall. Large, fragrant, golden-yellow flowers appear amid grey-green foliage from spring to autumn.

Senna didymobotrya (Golden wonder)
Evergreen, rounded, sometimes spreading shrub with leaves of several leaflets. Spikes of rich yellow flowers open from glossy, blackish-brown buds throughout the year. Min. 13°C (55°F).

***Abutilon pictum* 'Thompsonii'**
Robust, evergreen, upright shrub with 3–5-lobed, serrated, rich green, heavily yellow-mottled leaves. Yellow-orange flowers with crimson veins are borne from summer to autumn. Min. 5–7°C (41–5°F).

WHITE–RED

Colletia hystrix
Almost leafless, arching, stoutly branched shrub armed with rigid, grey-green spines. Pink flower buds open in late summer to fragrant, tubular, white blooms that last into autumn.

Clerodendrum trichotomum
Deciduous, upright, bushy-headed, tree-like shrub. Clusters of deep pink and greenish-white buds open to fragrant, white flowers above large leaves from late summer to mid-autumn, followed by decorative, blue berries.

Viburnum farreri
Deciduous, upright shrub. In late autumn and during mild periods in winter and early spring bears fragrant, white or pale pink flowers. Dark green foliage is bronze when young.

Calliandra haematocephala
[pink form]
Evergreen, spreading shrub. Leaves have 16–24 narrowly oval leaflets. Flower heads consist of many pink-stamened florets from late autumn to spring. Min. 7°C (45°F).

***Euonymus hamiltonianus* subsp. *sieboldianus* 'Red Elf'**
Deciduous, upright shrub with mid- to dark green foliage. Decorative, deep pink fruits, borne in profusion after tiny, green flowers in early summer, open in autumn to reveal red seeds.

***Euonymus europaeus* 'Red Cascade'**
Deciduous, bushy shrub or small tree with narrowly oval, mid-green leaves that redden in autumn as red fruits open to show orange seeds. Has inconspicuous, greenish flowers in early summer.

RED

Viburnum betulifolium
Deciduous, upright, arching shrub. Bright green leaves are slightly glossy beneath. Heads of small, white flowers in early summer are succeeded by profuse nodding clusters of decorative, bright red fruits in autumn-winter.

Euonymus alatus (Winged spindle)
Deciduous, bushy, dense shrub with shoots that develop corky wings. Dark green leaves turn brilliant red in autumn. Inconspicuous, greenish flowers in summer are followed by small, purple-red fruits.

Euonymus latifolius
Deciduous, open shrub. Mid-green foliage turns brilliant red in late autumn. At the same time large, deep red fruits with prominent wings open to reveal orange seeds.

Nymania capensis
Evergreen, more or less rounded, rigidly branched shrub or small tree. In spring has flowers with upright, pink to rose-purple petals. Bears papery, inflated, red fruits in autumn. Min. 7–10°C (45–50°F).

***Cornus alba* 'Kesselringii'**
Vigorous, deciduous shrub with deep purplish stems. Dark green leaves become flushed reddish-purple in autumn. Creamy-white flowers in late spring and early summer are followed by white fruits.

PURPLE–BLUE

Callicarpa bodinieri* var. *giraldii
Deciduous, bushy shrub. Leaves are pale green, often bronze-tinged when young. Tiny, lilac flowers in mid-summer are followed by small, violet berries.

Clerodendrum bungei
Evergreen or deciduous, upright, suckering shrub or sub-shrub with heart-shaped, coarsely serrated leaves. Has domed clusters of small, fragrant, red-purple to deep pink flowers in late summer and early autumn.

***Ceanothus* 'Autumnal Blue'**
Fast-growing, evergreen, bushy shrub. Has glossy, bright green foliage and large panicles of pale to mid-blue flowers from late spring to autumn.

ORANGE

***Berberis × carminea* 'Barbarossa'**
Semi-evergreen, arching shrub. Has narrowly oval, dark green leaves and racemes of rounded, yellow flowers in late spring and early summer, followed by globose, orange-scarlet fruits.

Zanthoxylum simulans
Deciduous, bushy shrub or small tree with stout spines. Aromatic, glossy, bright green leaves consist of 5 leaflets. Tiny, yellowish-green flowers in late spring and early summer are followed by orange-red fruits.

Cotoneaster simonsii
Deciduous or semi-evergreen, upright shrub, suitable for hedging. Has oval, glossy, dark green leaves, shallowly cup-shaped, white flowers in early summer and long-lasting, orange-red fruits in autumn.

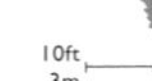

ORANGE–YELLOW

Colquhounia coccinea
Evergreen or semi-evergreen, open shrub. Has aromatic, sage-green leaves and whorls of scarlet or orange flowers in late summer and autumn.

Leonotis leonurus (Lion's ear)
Semi-evergreen, sparingly branched, erect shrub. Has lance-shaped leaves and whorls of tubular, bright orange flowers in late autumn and early winter.

***Pyracantha* 'Golden Charmer'**
Evergreen, bushy, arching, spiny shrub with glossy, bright green leaves. Flattish clusters of white flowers in early summer are succeeded by large, bright orange berries in early autumn.

Cotoneaster sternianus
Evergreen or semi-evergreen, arching shrub. Leaves are grey-green, white beneath. Pink-tinged, white flowers in early summer are followed by orange-red fruits.

***Pyracantha* 'Golden Dome'**
Evergreen, rounded, very dense, spiny shrub. Dark green foliage sets off white flowers borne in early summer. These are followed by orange-yellow berries in early autumn.

WHITE

Rubus biflorus
Deciduous, upright shrub with chalky-white, young shoots in winter. Leaves, consisting of 5–7 oval leaflets, are dark green above, white beneath. White flowers in late spring and early summer are followed by edible, yellow fruits.

Rubus thibetanus
Deciduous, arching shrub with white-bloomed, brownish-purple, young shoots in winter and fern-like, glossy, dark green foliage, white beneath. Small, pink flowers from mid- to late summer are followed by black fruits.

Viburnum foetens
Deciduous, bushy shrub that has aromatic, dark green leaves. Dense clusters of pink buds open to very fragrant, white flowers from mid-winter to early spring.

Viburnum tinus (Laurustinus)
Evergreen, bushy, dense shrub with oval, dark green leaves. Freely produced flat heads of small, white blooms open from pink buds during late winter and spring.

Chamelaucium uncinatum [white form] (Geraldton waxflower)
Evergreen, wiry-stemmed, bushy shrub. Each needle-like leaf has a tiny, hooked tip. Flowers ranging from deep rose-purple to pink, lavender or white appear in late winter or spring. Min. 5°C (41°F).

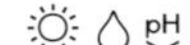

Calliandra haematocephala [white form]
Evergreen, spreading shrub. Leaves have 16–24 leaflets. Flower heads comprising many white-stamened florets appear from late autumn to spring. Min. 7°C (45°F).

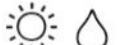

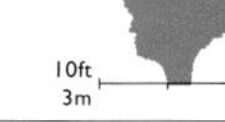

WHITE–PINK

Dombeya burgessiae
Evergreen shrub with rounded, 3-lobed, downy leaves and dense clusters of fragrant, white flowers, with pink to red veins, in autumn-winter. Min. 5°C (41°F).

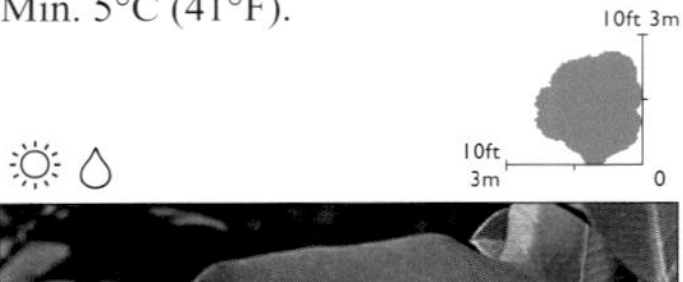

Chamelaucium uncinatum [pink form] (Geraldton waxflower)
Evergreen, wiry-stemmed, bushy shrub. Each needle-like leaf has a tiny, hooked tip. Flowers ranging from deep rose-purple to pink, lavender or white appear in late winter or spring. Min. 5°C (41°F).

Acokanthera oblongifolia (Wintersweet)
Evergreen, rounded shrub. Has fragrant, white or pinkish flowers in late winter and spring and poisonous, black fruits in autumn. Min. 10°C (50°F).

Viburnum × _bodnantense_ 'Dawn'
Deciduous, upright shrub with oval, bronze, young leaves that mature to dark green. Racemes of deep pink buds open to fragrant, pink flowers during mild periods from late autumn to early spring.

Daphne bholua
Evergreen, occasionally deciduous, upright shrub with leathery, dark green foliage. Terminal clusters of richly fragrant, purplish-pink and white flowers are borne in winter.

Euphorbia pulcherrima (Poinsettia)
Evergreen, sparingly branched shrub. Has small, greenish-red flowers surrounded by bright red, pink, yellow or white bracts from late autumn to spring. Min. 15°C (59°F).

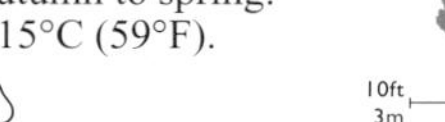

RED–PURPLE

Cornus alba 'Sibirica'
Deciduous, upright shrub with scarlet, young shoots in winter. Has dark green foliage and heads of creamy-white flowers in late spring and early summer, succeeded by rounded, white fruits.

Ardisia crenata (Coralberry, Spiceberry)
Evergreen, upright, open shrub. Has fragrant, star-shaped, white flowers in early summer, followed by long-lasting, bright red fruits. Min. 10°C (50°F).

Iochroma cyanea
Evergreen, semi-upright, slender-branched shrub. Tubular, deep purple-blue flowers, with flared mouths, appear in dense clusters from late autumn to early summer. Min. 7–10°C (45–50°F).

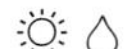

YELLOW

Stachyurus praecox
Deciduous, spreading, open shrub with purplish-red shoots. Drooping spikes of pale greenish-yellow flowers open in late winter and early spring, before pointed, deep green leaves appear.

Duranta erecta (Pigeon berry, Skyflower)
Fast-growing, usually evergreen, bushy shrub. Has spikes of lilac-blue flowers, mainly in summer, followed by yellow fruits. Min. 10°C (50°F).

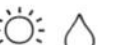

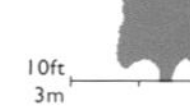

YELLOW

Mahonia japonica
Evergreen, upright shrub with deep green leaves consisting of many spiny leaflets. Long, spreading sprays of fragrant, yellow flowers appear from late autumn to spring, succeeded by purple-blue fruits.

Jasminum nudiflorum
(Winter jasmine)
Deciduous, arching shrub with oval, dark green leaves. Bright yellow flowers appear on slender, leafless, green shoots in winter and early spring.

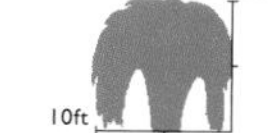

× ***Citrofortunella microcarpa***
(Calamondin)
Evergreen, bushy shrub with leathery, leaves. Intermittently has tiny, fragrant flowers followed by orange-yellow fruits. Min. 5–10°C (41–50°F).

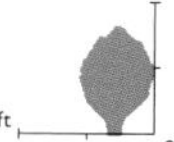

WHITE–PURPLE

***Euonymus japonicus* 'Latifolius Albomarginatus'**
Evergreen, upright, bushy and dense shrub with oval, dark green leaves broadly edged with white. Produces clusters of insignificant, greenish-white flowers in late spring.

***Fatsia japonica* 'Variegata'**
Evergreen, rounded, bushy and dense shrub with palmate, glossy, dark green leaves, variegated marginally with creamy-white, and large sprays of small, white flowers in autumn.

***Euonymus fortunei* 'Silver Queen'**
Evergreen, bushy, sometimes scandent shrub with a dense growth of dark green leaves, broadly edged with white. Produces insignificant, greenish-white flowers in spring.

***Nandina domestica* 'Firepower'**
Evergreen or semi-evergreen, elegant, bamboo-like, dwarf shrub. Leaves have dark green leaflets, purplish-red when young and in autumn-winter. Bears small, white flowers in summer followed in warm areas by orange-red fruits.

Dracaena sanderiana
(Ribbon plant)
Evergreen, upright shrub with seldom branching, cane-like stems. Lance-shaped leaves, 15–25cm (6–10in) long, are pale to grey-green, with bold, creamy-white edges. Min. 13°C (55°F).

***Dodonaea viscosa* 'Purpurea'**
Evergreen, bushy shrub or tree. Firm-textured leaves are flushed copper-purple. Has clusters of small, reddish or purplish seed capsules in late summer or autumn. Makes a good hedge in a windy site. Min. 5°C (41°F).

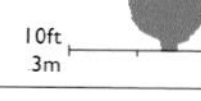

GREEN

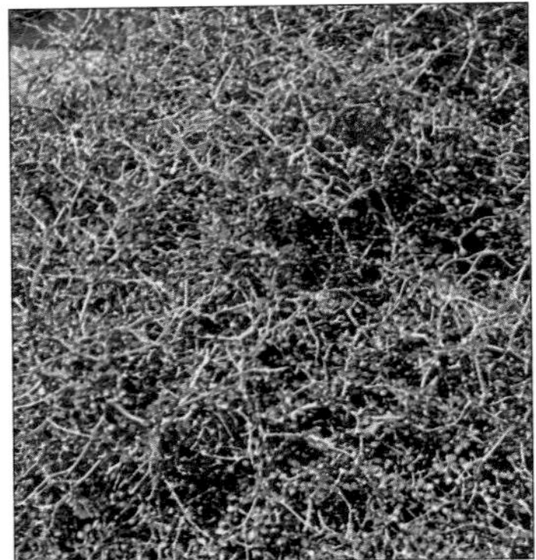

Corokia cotoneaster (Wire-netting bush)
Evergreen, bushy, open shrub with interlacing shoots. Has small, spoon-shaped, dark green leaves, fragrant, yellow flowers in late spring and red fruits in autumn.

Encephalartos ferox
Slow-growing, evergreen, palm-like plant, almost trunkless for many years. Feather-shaped leaves, 60–180cm (2–6ft) long, have many serrated and spine-tipped, leathery, greyish leaflets. Min. 10–13°C (50–55°F).

Cycas revoluta (Japanese sago palm)
Slow-growing, evergreen, palm-like plant that may produce several trunks. Leaves have spine-tipped leaflets with rolled margins. Bears tight clusters of reddish fruits in autumn. Min. 13°C (55°F).

Aucuba japonica
Evergreen, dense, bushy shrub with stout, green shoots and glossy, dark green leaves. Small, purplish flowers in mid-spring are followed on female plants by rounded to egg-shaped, bright red berries.

Arctostaphylos patula
Evergreen, rounded shrub with reddish-brown bark and bright grey-green foliage. Urn-shaped, white or pale pink flowers appear from mid- to late spring, followed by brown fruits.

Rhapis excelsa (Bamboo palm, Slender lady palm)
Evergreen fan palm, eventually forming clumps. Leaves are 20–30cm (8–12in) long, composed of 20 or more narrow, glossy, deep green lobes in fan formation. Min. 15°C (59°F).

***Buxus sempervirens* 'Handsworthensis'**
Vigorous, evergreen, bushy, upright shrub or small tree. Has broad, very dark green leaves. A dense habit makes it ideal for hedging or screening.

× *Fatshedera lizei* (Tree ivy)
Evergreen, loose-branched shrub that forms a mound of deeply lobed, glossy, deep green leaves. May also be trained as a climber. Sprays of small, white flowers appear in autumn.

Ficus deltoidea (Mistletoe fig)
Slow-growing, evergreen, bushy shrub with bright green leaves, red-brown-tinted beneath. Bears small, greenish-white fruits that mature to dull yellow. Min. 15–18°C (59–64°F).

Philodendron bipinnatifidum
Evergreen, unbranched shrub. Glossy leaves, to 60cm (2ft) or more long, are divided into many finger-like lobes. Occasionally produces greenish-white spathes. Min. 15–18°C (59–64°F).

Polyscias filicifolia (Fern-leaf aralia)
Evergreen, erect, sparingly branched shrub. Leaves are 30cm (12in) long and are divided into many small, serrated, bright green leaflets. Min. 15–18°C (59–64°F).

Chamaedorea elegans (Dwarf mountain palm, Parlour palm)
Evergreen, slender palm, suckering with age. Feather-shaped leaves of many glossy leaflets are 60–100cm (2–3ft) long. Min. 18°C (64°F).

GREEN–YELLOW

Portulacaria afra (Elephant bush)
Semi-evergreen, upright shrub with horizontal branches and tiny, fleshy, bright green leaves. Clusters of pale pink flowers appear in late spring and summer. Min. 7–10°C (45–50°F).

Buxus balearica
(Balearic box)
Evergreen, tree-like shrub suitable for hedging in mild areas. Has broadly oval, bright green leaves.

Yucca aloifolia (Spanish bayonet)
Slow-growing, evergreen shrub or small tree with few branches. Has sword-shaped, deep green leaves, 50–75cm (20–30in) long, and large panicles of purple-tinted, white flowers in summer-autumn. Min. 7°C (45°F).

***Elaeagnus* × *ebbingei* 'Limelight'**
Evergreen, bushy, dense shrub with glossy, dark green leaves, silver beneath, centrally marked yellow and pale green. Bears small, fragrant, white flowers in autumn.

***Ligustrum* 'Vicaryi'**
Semi-evergreen, bushy, dense shrub with broad, oval, golden-yellow leaves. Dense racemes of small, white flowers appear in mid-summer.

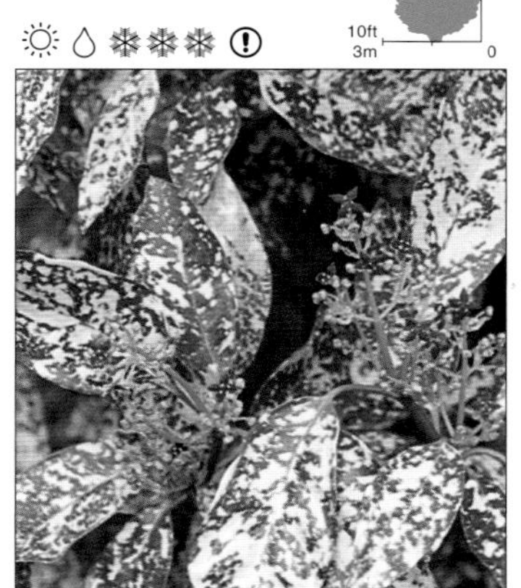

***Aucuba japonica* 'Crotonifolia'**
Evergreen, bushy, dense shrub with stout, green shoots. Large, glossy, dark green leaves are heavily mottled yellow. Small, purplish flowers in mid-spring are followed by bright red berries.

WHITE

***Salix hastata* 'Wehrhahnii'**
Deciduous, upright-branched shrub with deep purple stems that contrast with silver-grey catkins borne in early spring before foliage appears. Stems later turn yellow. Has oval, bright green leaves.

Deutzia gracilis
Deciduous, upright or spreading shrub. Massed, 5-petalled, pure white flowers are borne in upright clusters amid bright green foliage in late spring and early summer.

***Prunus glandulosa* 'Alba Plena'**
Deciduous, open shrub, with narrowly oval, mid-green leaves, bearing racemes of double, white flowers in late spring.

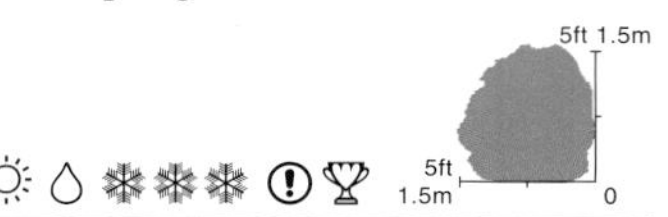

□ WHITE

Ledum groenlandicum
(Labrador tea)
Evergreen, bushy shrub. Foliage is dark green and aromatic. Rounded heads of small, white flowers are carried from mid-spring to early summer.

Azorina vidalii
Evergreen sub-shrub with erect stems. Has coarsely serrated, glossy, dark green leaves and racemes of bell-shaped, white or pink flowers in spring and summer. Min. 5°C (41°F).

Spiraea* × *vanhouttei
(Bridal wreath)
Deciduous, compact shrub with slender, arching shoots. In late spring and early summer abundant, small, dense clusters of white flowers appear amid diamond-shaped, dark green leaves.

***Prunus laurocerasus* 'Zabeliana'**
Evergreen, wide-spreading, open shrub. Leaves are very narrow and glossy, dark green. Spikes of white flowers in late spring are followed by cherry-like, red, then black, fruits.

***Prunus laurocerasus* 'Otto Luyken'**
Evergreen, very dense shrub. Has upright, narrow, glossy, dark green leaves, spikes of white flowers in late spring, followed by cherry-like, red, then black, fruits.

 WHITE–PINK

***Gaultheria* × *wisleyensis* 'Wisley Pearl'**
Evergreen, bushy, dense shrub with oval, deeply veined, dark green leaves. Bears small, white flowers in late spring and early summer, then purplish-red fruits.

Deutzia* × *rosea
Deciduous, bushy, dense shrub. In late spring and early summer produces massed, broad clusters of 5-petalled, pale pink flowers. Leaves are oval and dark green.

Prunus* × *cistena
Slow-growing, deciduous, upright shrub with deep reddish-purple leaves, red when young. Small, pinkish-white flowers from mid- to late spring may be followed by purple fruits.

Viburnum* × *juddii
Deciduous, rounded, bushy shrub with dark green foliage. Rounded heads of very fragrant, pink-tinged, white flowers open from pink buds from mid- to late spring.

Viburnum carlesii
Deciduous, bushy, dense shrub with dark green leaves that redden in autumn. Rounded heads of very fragrant, white and pink flowers, pink in bud, appear from mid- to late spring, followed by decorative, black fruits.

***Daphne* × *burkwoodii* 'Somerset'**
Semi-evergreen, upright shrub that bears dense clusters of very fragrant, white and pink flowers in late spring and sometimes again in autumn. Leaves are lance-shaped and pale to mid-green.

Daphne retusa
Evergreen, densely branched, rounded shrub clothed with leathery, glossy leaves notched at the tips. In late spring and early summer, deep purple buds open to very fragrant, pink-flushed, white flowers borne in terminal clusters.

5ft 1.5m

Menziesia ciliicalyx* var. *purpurea
Deciduous, bushy shrub with bright green foliage and racemes of nodding, purplish-pink blooms in late spring and early summer.

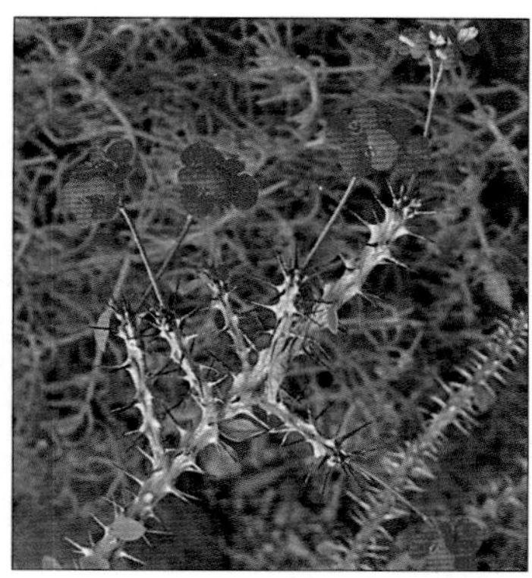

***Euphorbia milii* (Crown of thorns)**
Fairly slow-growing, mainly evergreen, spiny, semi-succulent shrub. Clusters of tiny, yellowish flowers, enclosed by 2 bright red bracts, open intermittently during the year. Min. 8°C (46°F).

***Chaenomeles × superba* 'Rowallane'**
Deciduous, low, spreading shrub. Has glossy, dark green foliage and bears a profusion of large, red flowers during spring.

Prunus tenella
Deciduous, bushy shrub with upright shoots and narrowly oval, glossy leaves. Shallowly cup-shaped, bright pink flowers appear from mid- to late spring.

5ft 1.5m

***Ribes sanguineum* 'Brocklebankii'**
Deciduous, spreading shrub. Has aromatic, pale yellow leaves and pendent clusters of small, pale pink flowers in spring, followed by white-bloomed, black fruits.

***Epacris impressa* (Australian heath)**
Evergreen, usually erect, fairly open, heath-like shrub with short, red-tipped leaves. Tubular, pink or red flowers appear in late winter and spring. Min. 5°C (41°F).

Cantua buxifolia
Evergreen, arching, bushy shrub. Has grey-green foliage and drooping clusters of bright red and magenta flowers from mid- to late spring.

RED–GREEN

***Chaenomeles* × *superba* 'Nicoline'**
Deciduous, bushy, dense shrub. Has glossy, dark green leaves and a profusion of large, scarlet flowers in spring, followed by yellow fruits.

Salix lanata (Woolly willow)
Deciduous, bushy, dense shrub with stout, woolly, grey shoots and broad, silver-grey leaves. Large, yellowishgreen catkins appear in late spring with foliage.

Boronia megastigma
Evergreen, well branched, wirystemmed shrub. Small leaves have 3–5 narrow leaflets. Fragrant, bowl-shaped, brownish-purple and yellow flowers hang from leaf axils in late winter and spring. Min. 7–10°C (45–50°F).

Euphorbia characias* subsp. *characias
Evergreen, upright shrub with clusters of narrow, grey-green leaves. During spring and early summer, bears dense spikes of pale yellowish-green flowers with deep purple centres.

***Arctostaphylos* 'Emerald Carpet'**
Evergreen shrub that, with a low, dense growth of oval, bright green leaves and purple stems, makes excellent ground cover. Bears small, urn-shaped, white flowers in spring.

Daphne laureola **subsp.** ***philippi***
Evergreen, dwarf shrub with oval, dark green leaves. Slightly fragrant, tubular, pale green flowers with short, spreading lobes appear in late winter and early spring, followed by black fruits.

GREEN–YELLOW

Euphorbia characias* subsp. *wulfenii
Evergreen, upright shrub. Stems are biennial, producing clustered, greygreen leaves one year and spikes of yellow-green blooms the following spring.

Salix repens (Creeping willow)
Deciduous, prostrate or semi-upright and bushy shrub. Silky, grey catkins become yellow from mid- to late spring, before small, narrowly oval leaves, which are grey-green above, silvery beneath, appear.

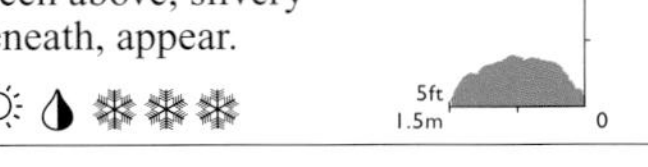

***Cytisus* × *praecox* 'Warminster'** (Warminster broom)
Deciduous, densely branched shrub. From mid- to late spring, pea-like, creamy-yellow flowers appear in profusion amid tiny, silky, grey-green leaves with 3 leaflets.

YELLOW

Mahonia aquifolium
(Oregon grape)
Evergreen, open shrub. Leaves, with glossy, bright green leaflets, often turn red or purple in winter. Bunches of small, yellow flowers in spring are followed by blue-black berries.

***Caragana arborescens* 'Nana'**
Deciduous, bushy, dwarf shrub with mid-green leaves consisting of many oval leaflets. Pea-like, yellow flowers are borne in late spring.

Pachystachys lutea
(Lollipop plant)
Evergreen, loose, more or less rounded shrub, often grown annually from cuttings. Has tubular, white flowers in tight, golden-bracted spikes in spring-summer.

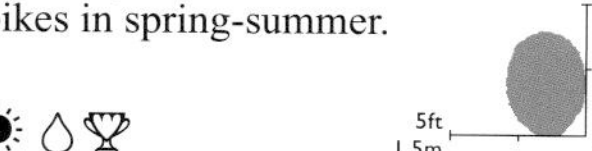

***Cytisus* × *praecox* 'Allgold'**
Deciduous, densely branched shrub with silky, grey-green leaves, divided into 3 leaflets, and a profusion of pealike, yellow flowers from mid- to late spring.

Ulex europaeus (Gorse)
Leafless or almost leafless, bushy shrub with year-round, dark green shoots and spines that make it appear evergreen. Bears massed, fragrant, pea-like, yellow flowers in spring.

Berberis empetrifolia
Evergreen, arching, prickly shrub with narrow, grey-green leaves, globose, golden-yellow flowers in late spring and black fruits in autumn.

Coronilla valentina* subsp. *glauca
Evergreen, bushy, dense shrub. Has blue-grey leaves with 5 or 7 leaflets. Fragrant, pea-like, yellow flowers are borne from mid-spring to early summer.

Acacia pulchella
(Western prickly Moses)
Semi-evergreen or deciduous shrub of diffuse habit, with spiny twigs and rich green foliage. Tiny, deep yellow flowers appear in dense, globular heads in spring.
Min. 5–7°C (41–5°F).

YELLOW–ORANGE

Genista tinctoria
(Dyers' greenweed)
Deciduous, spreading, dwarf shrub that bears dense spires of pea-like, golden-yellow flowers in spring and summer. Leaves are narrow and dark green.

Chorizema ilicifolium
(Holly flame pea)
Evergreen, sprawling or upright shrub, with spiny-toothed, leathery leaves. Has spikes of bicoloured, orange and pinkish-red flowers in spring-summer.
Min. 7°C (45°F).

Nematanthus gregarius
Evergreen, prostrate or slightly ascending shrub with fleshy, glossy leaves. Inflated, orange and yellow flowers appear mainly from spring to autumn.
Min. 13–15°C (55–9°F).

□ WHITE

Deutzia monbeigii
Deciduous, arching, elegant shrub. Clusters of small, 5-petalled, white flowers appear in profusion among small, dark green leaves from early to mid-summer.

***Hebe* 'White Gem'**
Evergreen, rounded shrub that produces a dense mound of small, glossy leaves covered in early summer with tight racemes of small, white flowers.

Rhodotypos scandens
Deciduous, upright or slightly arching shrub. In late spring and early summer, amid sharply toothed leaves, bears shallowly cupped, white flowers, followed by small, pea-shaped, black fruits.

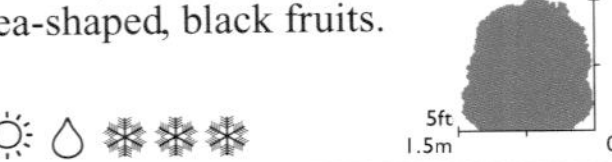

Olearia phlogopappa* var. *subrepanda
Evergreen, upright, compact shrub. Heads of daisy-like, white flowers are borne profusely from mid-spring to early summer amid narrow, toothed, grey-green leaves.

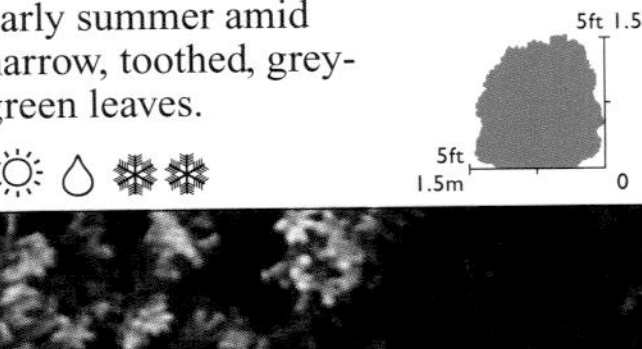

Cuphea hyssopifolia
(False heather)
Evergreen, rounded, dense shrub with tiny, narrowly lance-shaped, deep green leaves. Rose-purple to lilac or white flowers appear in summer-autumn.

Westringia fruticosa
(Australian rosemary)
Evergreen, rounded, compact shrub. Crowded leaves, in whorls of 4, are white-felted beneath. White to palest blue flowers open in spring-summer.
Min. 5–7°C (41–5°F).

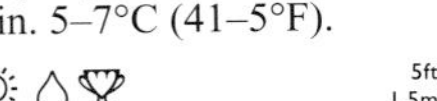

***Gardenia augusta* 'Veitchii'**
Fairly slow-growing, evergreen, leafy shrub with oval, glossy leaves up to 10cm (4in) long and fragrant, double, white flowers from summer to winter.
Min. 15°C (59°F).

***Philadelphus* 'Manteau d'Hermine'**
Deciduous, bushy, compact shrub. Clusters of fragrant, double, creamy-white flowers appear amid small, pale to mid-green leaves from early to mid-summer.

***Potentilla fruticosa* 'Abbotswood'**
Deciduous, bushy shrub. Large, pure white flowers are borne amid dark blue-green leaves, divided into 5 narrowly oval leaflets, throughout summer-autumn.

***Potentilla fruticosa* 'Manchu'**
Deciduous, mound-forming shrub with reddish-pink, prostrate shoots. Pure white flowers are borne amid divided, silvery-grey leaves from late spring to early autumn.

Convolvulus cneorum
Evergreen, rounded, bushy, dense shrub. Pink-tinged buds opening to white flowers with yellow centres are borne from late spring to late summer among narrow, silky, silvery-green leaves.

Halimium umbellatum
Evergreen, upright shrub. Narrow, glossy, dark green leaves are white beneath. White flowers, centrally blotched with yellow, are produced in early summer from reddish buds.

***Potentilla fruticosa* 'Farrer's White'**
Deciduous, bushy shrub with divided, grey-green leaves. Bears an abundance of white flowers during summer-autumn.

× *Halimiocistus sahucii*
Evergreen, bushy, dense shrub with narrow, dark green leaves that set off an abundance of pure white flowers in late spring and early summer.

Cistus salviifolius
Evergreen, bushy, dense shrub with slightly wrinkled, grey-green foliage. White flowers, with central, yellow blotches, appear in profusion during early summer.

Cistus monspeliensis
Evergreen, bushy shrub with narrow, wrinkled, dark green leaves and small, white flowers freely borne from early to mid-summer.

Cistus* × *hybridus
Evergreen, bushy, dense shrub. Has wrinkled, wavy-edged, dark green leaves and massed white flowers, with central, yellow blotches, carried in late spring and early summer.

Cistus* × *cyprius
Evergreen, bushy shrub with sticky shoots and narrow, glossy, dark green leaves. In early summer bears large, white flowers, with a red blotch at each petal base, that appear in succession for some weeks but last only a day.

***Cistus* × *aguilarii* 'Maculatus'**
Evergreen, bushy shrub with narrow, wavy-edged, slightly sticky, rich green leaves. Large, white flowers, with a central, deep red and yellow pattern, appear from early to mid-summer.

Cistus ladanifer
Evergreen, open, upright shrub. Leaves are narrow, dark green and sticky. Bears large, white flowers, with red markings around the central tuft of stamens, in profusion in early summer.

□ WHITE

Leptospermum rupestre
Evergreen, semi-prostrate, widely arching shrub with reddish shoots and small, dark green leaves that turn bronze-purple in winter. Small, open cup-shaped, white flowers, red-flushed in bud, appear in early summer.

Yucca whipplei
Evergreen, virtually stemless shrub that forms a dense tuft of slender, pointed, blue-green leaves. Very long panicles of fragrant, greenish-white flowers are produced in late spring and early summer.

Vaccinium corymbosum (Highbush blueberry)
Deciduous, upright, slightly arching shrub. Small, white or pinkish flowers in late spring and early summer are followed by sweet, edible, blue-black berries. Foliage turns red in autumn.

***Yucca flaccida* 'Ivory'**
Evergreen, very short-stemmed shrub that produces tufts of narrow, dark green leaves and long panicles of bell-shaped, white flowers from mid- to late summer.

Catharanthus roseus (Rose periwinkle)
Evergreen, spreading shrub, becoming untidy with age. Has white to rose-pink flowers in spring to autumn, also in winter in warm areas.
Min. 5–7°C (41–5°F).

Rhaphiolepis umbellata
Evergreen, bushy shrub with rounded, leathery, dark green leaves and clusters of fragrant, white flowers in early summer.

***Weigela florida* 'Variegata'**
Deciduous, bushy, dense shrub. Carries a profusion of funnel-shaped, pink flowers in late spring and early summer and has mid-green leaves broadly edged with creamy-white.

Ozothamnus ledifolius
Evergreen, dense shrub. Yellow shoots are covered with small, aromatic leaves, glossy, dark green above, yellow beneath. Small, white flower heads are borne in early summer.

WHITE

Lomatia silaifolia
Evergreen, bushy shrub. Spikes of creamy-white flowers, each with 4 narrow, twisted petals, are borne amid deeply divided, dark green leaves from mid- to late summer.

Cassinia leptophylla **subsp. *vauvilliersii***
Evergreen, upright shrub. Whitish shoots are covered with tiny, dark green leaves and heads of small, white flowers from mid- to late summer.

Viburnum acerifolium
Deciduous, upright-branched shrub with bright green leaves that turn orange, red and purple in autumn. Decorative, red fruits, which turn purple-black, follow heads of creamy-white flowers in early summer.

Eriogonum arborescens
Evergreen, sparingly branched shrub. Small leaves have recurved edges and woolly, white undersides. Leafy umbels of small, white or pink flowers appear from spring to autumn. Min. 5°C (41°F).

Hebe recurva
Evergreen, open, spreading shrub. Leaves are narrow, curved and blue-grey. Small spikes of white flowers appear from mid- to late summer.

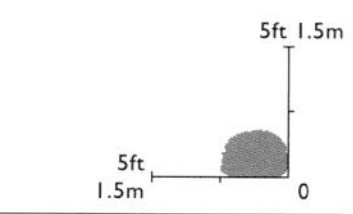

WHITE–PINK

Hebe albicans
Evergreen shrub that forms a dense mound of blue-grey foliage covered with small, tight clusters of white flowers from early to mid-summer.

***Deutzia* 'Mont Rose'**
Deciduous, bushy shrub that produces clusters of pink or pinkish-purple flowers, in early summer, with yellow anthers and occasionally white markings. Leaves are sharply toothed and dark green.

***Potentilla fruticosa* 'Daydawn'**
Deciduous, bushy, rather arching shrub. Creamy-yellow flowers, flushed with orange-pink, appear among divided, mid-green leaves from early summer to mid-autumn.

Protea cynaroides **(King protea)**
Evergreen, bushy, rounded shrub. Water lily-shaped flower heads, 13–20cm (5–8in) wide, with silky-haired, petal-like, pink to red bracts, appear in spring-summer. Leaves are oval and mid- to dark green. Min. 5–7°C (41–5°F).

***Abelia* 'Edward Goucher'**
Deciduous or semi-evergreen, arching shrub. Oval, bright green leaves are bronze when young. Bears a profusion of lilac-pink flowers from mid-summer to autumn.

PINK

Abelia schumannii
Deciduous, arching shrub. Pointed, mid-green leaves are bronze when young. Yellow-blotched, rose-purple and white flowers appear from mid-summer to mid-autumn.

Myoporum parvifolium
Evergreen, spreading to prostrate shrub with semi-succulent leaves. In summer has clusters of small, honey-scented flowers, white or pink with purple spots, and tiny, purple fruits in autumn. Min. 2–5°C (36–41°F).

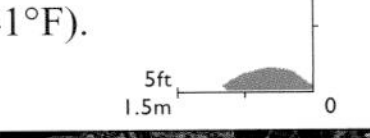

Cistus × skanbergii
Evergreen, bushy shrub. A profusion of pale pink flowers appears amid narrow, grey-green leaves from early to mid-summer.

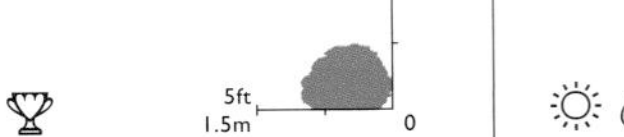

Pimelea ferruginea
Evergreen, dense, rounded shrub with tiny, recurved, deep green leaves. Small, tubular, rich pink flowers appear in dense heads in spring or early summer. Min. 7°C (45°F).

Gaultheria shallon (Shallon)
Evergreen, bushy shrub. Red shoots carry broad, sharply pointed, dark green leaves. Racemes of urn-shaped, pink flowers in late spring and early summer are followed by purple berries.

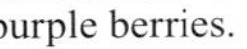

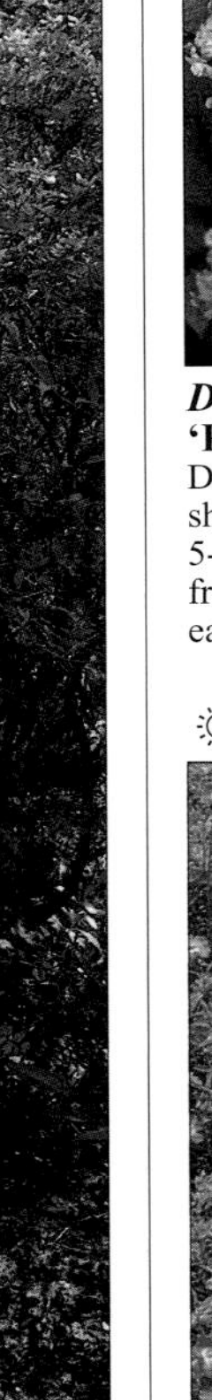

Indigofera dielsiana
Deciduous, upright, open shrub. Dark green leaves consist of 7–11 oval leaflets. Slender, erect spikes of pale pink flowers are borne from early summer to early autumn.

***Deutzia × elegantissima* 'Rosealind'**
Deciduous, rounded, bushy, dense shrub that produces clusters of 5-petalled, deep pink flowers from late spring to early summer.

Phlomis italica
Evergreen, upright shrub. In mid-summer, whorls of lilac-pink flowers are borne at the ends of shoots amid narrow, woolly, grey-green leaves.

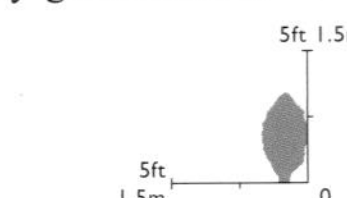

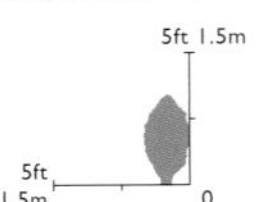

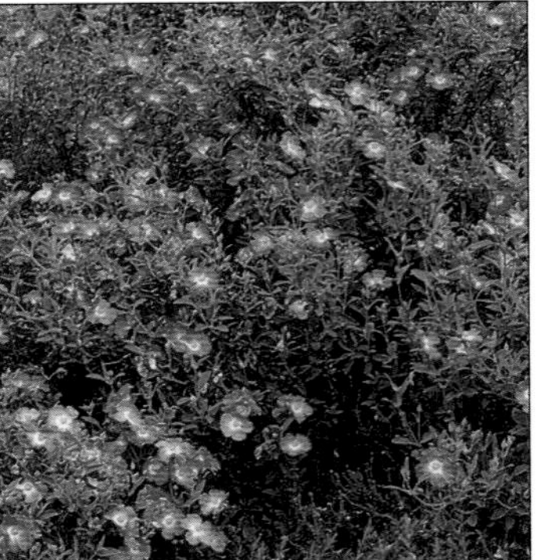

***Cistus* 'Peggy Sammons'**
Evergreen, bushy shrub with oval, grey-green leaves. Saucer-shaped, pale purplish-pink flowers are produced freely during early summer.

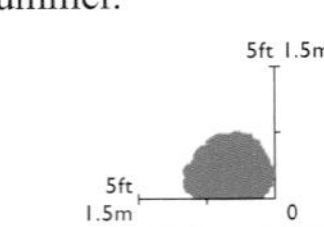

***Weigela florida* 'Foliis Purpureis'**
Deciduous, low, bushy shrub that bears funnel-shaped flowers, deep pink outside, pale pink to white inside, in late spring and early summer. Leaves are dull purple or purplish-green.

***Spiraea japonica* 'Little Princess'**
Slow-growing, deciduous, mound-forming shrub that produces copious small heads of rose-pink blooms from mid- to late summer. Small, dark green leaves are bronze when young.

***Spiraea japonica* 'Goldflame'**
Deciduous, upright, slightly arching shrub with orange-red, young leaves turning to bright yellow and finally pale green. Bears heads of deep rose-pink flowers from mid- to late summer.

***Ceanothus* 'Perle Rose'**
Deciduous, bushy shrub that from mid-summer to early autumn bears dense racemes of bright carmine-pink flowers amid broad, oval, mid-green leaves.

***Hebe* 'Great Orme'**
Evergreen, rounded, open shrub. Has deep purplish shoots and glossy, dark green foliage. Slender spikes of deep pink flowers that fade to white are produced from mid-summer to mid-autumn.

Justicia carnea (King's crown)
Evergreen, sparingly branched shrub with velvety-haired leaves. Has spikes of pink to rose-purple flowers in summer-autumn. Min. 10–15°C (50–59°F).

Penstemon isophyllus
Slightly untidy, deciduous shrub or sub-shrub that, from mid- to late summer, carries long sprays of large, white- and red-throated, deep pink flowers above spear-shaped, glossy, mid-green leaves.

Pentas lanceolata
(Egyptian star, Star-cluster)
Mainly evergreen, loosely rounded shrub with hairy, bright greeen leaves. In summer-autumn produces dense clusters of pink, lilac, red or white flowers. Min. 10–15°C (50–59°F).

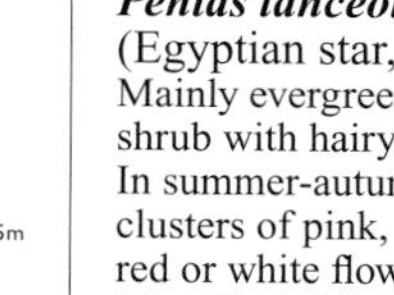

***Spiraea japonica* 'Anthony Waterer'**
Deciduous, upright, compact shrub. Red, young foliage matures to dark green. Heads of crimson-pink blooms appear from mid- to late summer.

Fuchsias

F. 'Bicentennial'

With their vivid blooms and long flowering season (usually throughout the summer and into autumn), fuchsias make outstanding shrubs for the greenhouse and for the garden. Single to double flowers often have flared or elegantly recurved sepals. In mild areas fuchsias may be grown outside all year. In cool climates most are best grown in a greenhouse or as summer bedding; some are frost hardy. Fuchsias raised from cuttings are sparingly branched and often become straggly unless pruned from an early age by pinching out the growing tips. To produce standard plants, the leader shoot is left, supported, but side shoots are pinched back to one pair of leaves. When the stem has reached the required height and has produced 2 or 3 pairs of leaves above this, it is then pinched out and the plant is left to develop naturally.

F. 'Lady Thumb' ♀

F. 'Harry Gray'

F. 'Annabel' ♀

F. arborescens

F. 'Swingtime' ♀

F. 'Nellie Nuttall' ♀

F. 'Golden Dawn'

F. 'Other Fellow'

F. 'Pink Galore'

F. 'Heidi Weiss'

F. 'Peppermint Stick'

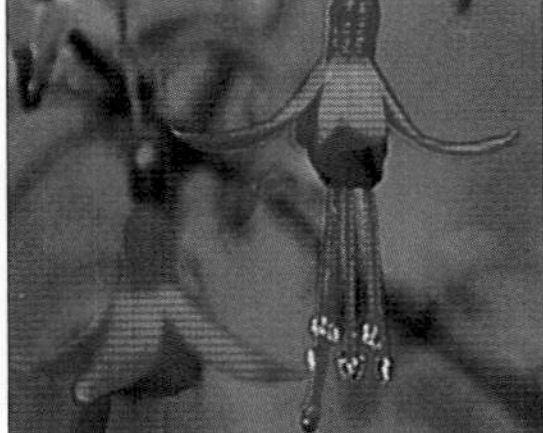
F. 'Riccartonii' ♀

F. 'Rufus' ♀

F. 'Leonora'

F. 'Dollar Princess' ♀

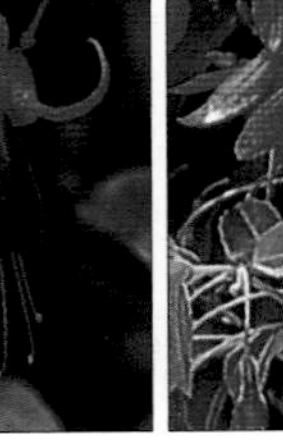
F. 'Gruss aus dem Bodethal'

F. 'Tom Thumb' ♀

F. 'Golden Marinka' ♀

F. magellanica

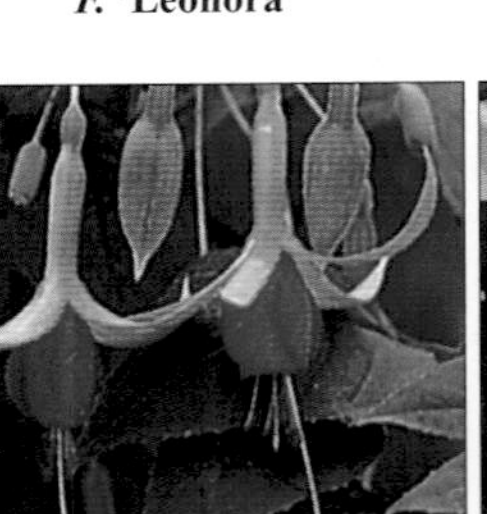
F. 'Jack Shahan' ♀

F. 'Ballet Girl' ♀

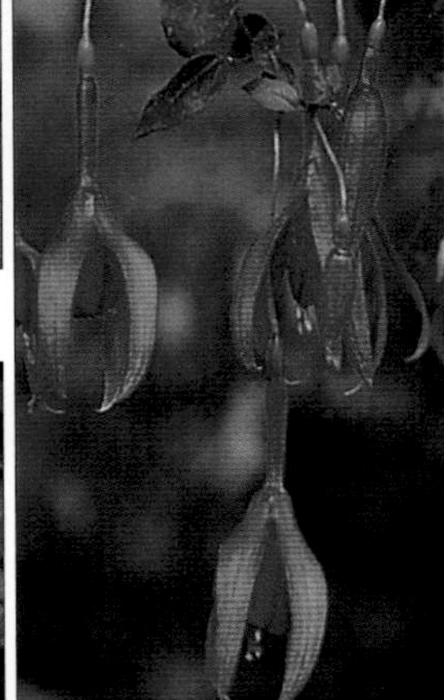
F. 'Red Spider'

F. 'Autumnale' ♀

F. 'Mrs Popple' ♀

F. × ***bacillaris***

F. **'Thalia'** ♡

F. **'Tom West'**

F. **'Celia Smedley'** ♡

F. **'Cascade'** ♡

F. **'Estelle Marie'**

F. ***boliviana*** var. ***alba***

F. **'La Campanella'**

F. **'Love's Reward'** ♡

F. **'Mrs Lovell Swisher'** ♡

F. **'Rose of Castile'** ♡

F. ***procumbens***

F. **'Lye's Unique'** ♡

F. ***fulgens*** ♡

F. **'Coralle'**

PINK–RED

Cistus creticus
Evergreen, bushy shrub. Pink or purplish-pink flowers, each with a central, yellow blotch, appear amid grey-green leaves from early to mid-summer.

5ft 1.5m

***Escallonia rubra* 'Woodside'**
Evergreen, bushy, dense shrub. Has small, glossy, dark green leaves and short racemes of small, tubular, crimson flowers in summer-autumn.

5ft 1.5m

Kalmia angustifolia f. ***rubra***
(Sheep laurel)
Evergreen, bushy, mound-forming shrub with oval, dark green leaves and clusters of small, deep red flowers in early summer.

5ft 1.5m

Sutherlandia frutescens
Evergreen, upright shrub. Has leaves of 13–21 grey-haired, deep green leaflets; bright red flowers in late spring and summer are followed by pale green, later red-flushed, inflated seed pods. Min. 10°C (50°F).

5ft 1.5m

Crossandra nilotica
Evergreen, upright to spreading, leafy shrub with oval, pointed, rich green leaves. Small, tubular, apricot to pale brick-red flowers with spreading petals are carried in short spikes from spring to autumn. Min. 15°C (59°F).

5ft 1.5m

Ixora coccinea
Evergreen, rounded shrub with glossy, dark green leaves to 10cm (4in) long. Small, tubular, red, pink, orange or yellow flowers appear in dense heads in summer. Min. 13–16°C (55–61°F).

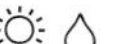

5ft 1.5m

■ RED

***Potentilla fruticosa* 'Red Ace'**
Deciduous, spreading, bushy, dense shrub. Bright vermilion flowers, pale yellow on the backs of petals, are produced among mid-green leaves from late spring to mid-autumn but fade quickly in full sun.

Salvia microphylla* var. *neurepia
Evergreen, well-branched, upright shrub with pale to mid-green leaves. Has tubular, bright red flowers from purple-tinted, green calyces in late summer and autumn.

Justicia brandegeeana
(Shrimp plant)
Evergreen, rounded shrub intermittently, but mainly in summer, producing white flowers surrounded by shrimp-pink bracts. Min. 10–15°C (50–59°F).

***Grevillea* 'Robyn Gordon'**
Evergreen, sprawling shrub with leathery, dark green leaves. At intervals from early spring to late summer, arching stems bear racemes of crimson flowers with protruding, recurved styles. Min. 5–10°C (41–50°F).

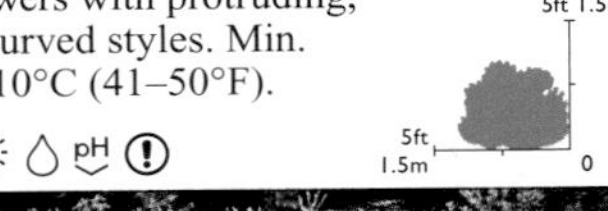

***Acer palmatum* 'Chitoseyama'**
Deciduous, arching, mound-forming shrub or small tree with lobed, mid-green foliage that gradually turns brilliant red from late summer to autumn. Produces small, reddish-purple flowers in mid-spring.

Phygelius aequalis
Evergreen or semi-evergreen, upright sub-shrub. Clusters of tubular, pale red flowers with yellow throats appear from mid-summer to early autumn. Leaves are oval and dark green.

Salvia fulgens
Evergreen, upright sub-shrub. Oval leaves are white and woolly beneath, hairy above. Racemes of tubular, 2-lipped, scarlet flowers appear in late summer.

***Acer palmatum* 'Dissectum Atropurpureum'**
Deciduous shrub that forms a mound of deeply divided, bronze-red or purple foliage, which turns brilliant red, orange or yellow in autumn. Has small, reddish-purple flowers in mid-spring.

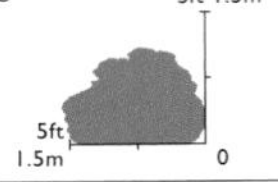

***Hebe hulkeana* 'Lilac Hint'**
Evergreen, upright, open-branched shrub with toothed, glossy, pale green leaves. Aprofusion of small, pale lilac flowers appears in large racemes in late spring and early summer.

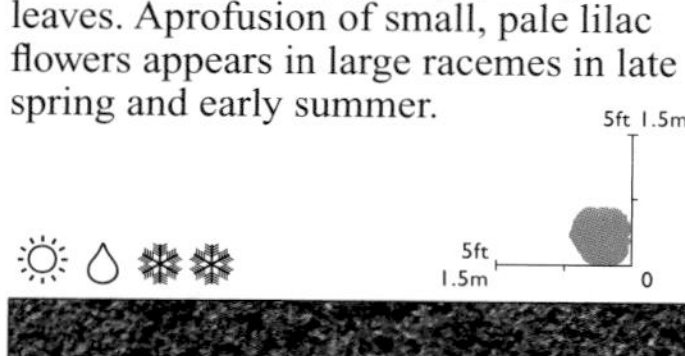

Desmodium elegans
Deciduous, upright sub-shrub. Mid-green leaves consist of 3 large leaflets. Large racemes of pale lilac to deep pink flowers appear from late summer to mid-autumn.

Heliotropium arborescens
Evergreen, bushy shrub. Semi-glossy, dark green leaves are finely wrinkled. Purple to lavender flowers are borne in dense, flat clusters from late spring to winter. Min. 7°C (45°F).

Lavandula stoechas
(French lavender)
Evergreen, bushy, dense shrub. Heads of tiny, fragrant, deep purple flowers, topped by rose-purple bracts, appear in late spring and summer. Mature leaves are silver-grey and aromatic.

Rosmarinus officinalis (Rosemary)
Evergreen, bushy, dense shrub with aromatic, narrow leaves. Small, purplish-blue to blue flowers appear from mid-spring to early summer and sometimes in autumn. Used as a culinary herb.

***Hebe* 'E.A. Bowles'**
Evergreen, rounded, bushy shrub with narrow, glossy, pale green leaves and slender spikes of lilac flowers produced from mid-summer to late autumn.

Polygala × dalmaisiana
Evergreen, erect shrub with small, greyish-green leaves. White-veined, rich purple flowers appear from late spring to autumn. Min. 7°C (45°F).

***Hebe* 'Autumn Glory'**
Evergreen shrub that forms a mound of purplish-red shoots and rounded, deep green leaves, over which dense racemes of deep purple-blue flowers appear from mid-summer to early winter.

Lantana montevidensis
Evergreen, trailing or mat-forming shrub with serrated leaves. Has heads of rose-purple flowers, each with a yellow eye, intermittently all year but mainly in summer. Min. 10–13°C (50–55°F).

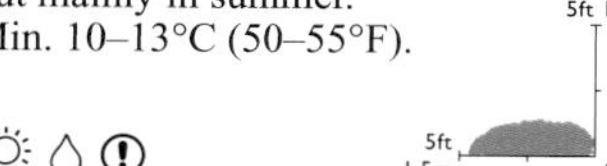

***Brunfelsia pauciflora* 'Macrantha'**
Evergreen, spreading shrub with leathery leaves. Blue-purple flowers, ageing to white in about 3 days, appear from winter to summer. Min. 10–13°C (50–55°F).

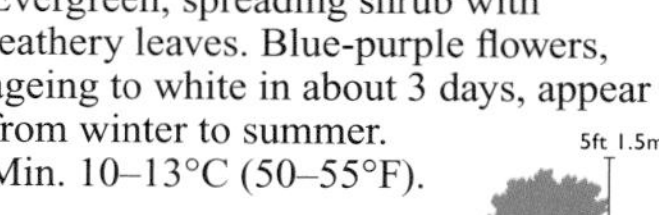

***Lavandula* 'Hidcote'**
Evergreen, bushy shrub with dense spikes of fragrant, deep purple flowers from mid- to late summer and narrow, aromatic, silver-grey leaves.

PURPLE–BLUE

***Hebe* 'Purple Queen'**
Evergreen, bushy, compact shrub with glossy, deep green leaves that are purple-tinged when young. Dense racemes of deep purple flowers appear from early summer to mid-autumn.

Hyssopus officinalis (Hyssop)
Semi-evergreen or deciduous, bushy shrub with aromatic, narrowly oval, deep green leaves. Small, blue flowers appear from mid-summer to early autumn. Sometimes used as a culinary herb.

***Hebe* 'Bowles' Variety'**
Evergreen, rounded shrub with ovate-oblong, slightly glossy, mid-green leaves. In summer, bears mauve-blue flowers in compact, tapered, terminal racemes.

Ceanothus thyrsiflorus* var. *repens (Creeping blue blossom)
Evergreen, dense shrub that forms a mound of broad, glossy, dark green leaves. Racemes of blue flowers are borne in late spring and early summer.

***Ceanothus* 'Gloire de Versailles'**
Vigorous, deciduous, bushy shrub. Has broad, oval, mid-green leaves and large racemes of pale blue flowers from mid-summer to early autumn.

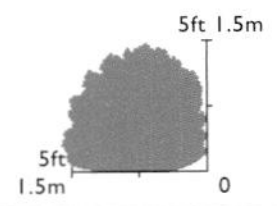

***Felicia amelloides* 'Santa Anita'**
Evergreen, bushy, spreading shrub. Blue flower heads, with bright yellow centres, are borne on long stalks from late spring to autumn among round to oval, bright green leaves.

***Caryopteris × clandonensis* 'Arthur Simmonds'**
Deciduous, bushy sub-shrub. Masses of blue to purplish-blue flowers appear amid narrowly oval, irregularly toothed, grey-green leaves from late summer to autumn.

***Perovskia* 'Blue Spire'**
Deciduous, upright sub-shrub with grey-white stems. Profuse spikes of violet-blue flowers appear from late summer to mid-autumn above aromatic, deeply cut, grey-green leaves.

GREEN–YELLOW

***Symphoricarpos orbiculatus* 'Foliis Variegatis'**
Deciduous, bushy, dense shrub with bright green leaves edged with yellow. Occasionally bears white or pink flowers in summer-autumn.

***Justicia brandegeeana* 'Chartreuse'**
Evergreen, arching shrub producing white flowers surrounded by pale yellow-green bracts mainly in summer but also intermittently during the year. Min. 10–15°C (50–59°F).

Weigela middendorffiana
Deciduous, bushy, arching shrub. From mid-spring to early summer funnel-shaped, sulphur-yellow flowers, spotted with orange inside, are borne amid bright green foliage.

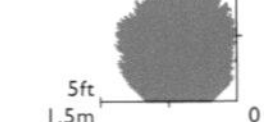

***Potentilla fruticosa* 'Vilmoriniana'**
Deciduous, upright shrub that bears pale yellow or creamy-white flowers from late spring to mid-autumn. Leaves are silver-grey and divided into narrow leaflets.

***Santolina pinnata* subsp. *neapolitana* 'Sulphurea'**
Evergreen, rounded, bushy shrub with aromatic, deeply cut, feathery, grey-green foliage. Produces heads of pale primrose-yellow flowers in mid-summer.

***Lupinus arboreus* (Tree lupin)**
Fast-growing, semi-evergreen, sprawling shrub that in early summer usually bears short spikes of fragrant, clear yellow flowers above hairy, pale green leaves composed of 6–9 leaflets.

***Phygelius aequalis* 'Yellow Trumpet'**
Evergreen or semi-evergreen, upright sub-shrub. Bears clusters of pendent, tubular, pale creamy-yellow flowers from mid-summer to early autumn.

***Potentilla fruticosa* 'Elizabeth'**
Deciduous, bushy, dense shrub with small, deeply divided leaves and large, bright yellow flowers that appear from late spring to mid-autumn.

Grevillea juniperina* f. *sulphurea
Evergreen, rounded, bushy shrub with almost needle-like leaves, recurved and dark green above, silky-haired beneath. Has clusters of small, spidery, pale yellow flowers in spring-summer.

***Potentilla fruticosa* 'Friedrichsenii'**
Vigorous, deciduous, upright shrub. From late spring to mid-autumn pale yellow flowers are produced amid grey-green leaves.

***Halimium* 'Susan'**
Evergreen, spreading shrub with narrow, oval, grey-green leaves. Numerous single or semi-double, bright yellow flowers with central, deep purple-red markings are borne in small clusters along branches in summer.

Halimium lasianthum* subsp. *formosum
Evergreen, spreading, bushy shrub. Has grey-green foliage and golden-yellow flowers, with central, deep red blotches, borne in late spring and early summer.

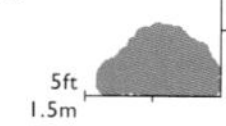

YELLOW

Phlomis fruticosa
(Jerusalem sage)
Evergreen, spreading shrub with upright shoots. Whorls of deep golden-yellow flowers are produced amid sage-like, grey-green foliage from early to mid-summer.

***Berberis thunbergii* 'Aurea'**
Deciduous, bushy, spiny shrub with small, golden-yellow leaves. Racemes of small, red-tinged, pale yellow flowers in mid-spring are followed by red berries in autumn.

Cytisus nigricans
Deciduous, upright shrub with dark green leaves composed of 3 leaflets. Has a long-lasting display of tall, slender spires of yellow flowers during summer.

Genista hispanica (Spanish gorse)
Deciduous, bushy, very spiny shrub with few leaves. Bears dense clusters of golden-yellow flowers profusely in late spring and early summer.

***Brachyglottis* Dunedin Hybrids 'Sunshine'**
Evergreen, bushy shrub that forms a mound of silvery-grey, young leaves, later turning dark green. Bears bright yellow flower heads on felted shoots from early to mid-summer.

Hypercium calycinum
(Aaron's beard, Rose of Sharon)
Evergreen or semi-evergreen dwarf shrub that makes good ground cover. Has large, bright yellow flowers from mid-summer to mid-autumn and dark green leaves.

***Hypericum* 'Hidcote'**
Evergreen or semi-evergreen, bushy, dense shrub. Bears an abundance of large, golden-yellow flowers from mid-summer to early autumn amid narrowly oval, dark green leaves.

***Hypericum × inodorum* 'Elstead'**
Deciduous or semi-evergreen, upright shrub. Abundant, small, yellow flowers borne from mid-summer to early autumn are followed by ornamental, orange-red fruits. Dark green leaves are aromatic when crushed.

Hypericum kouytchense
Deciduous or semi-evergreen, arching shrub. Golden-yellow flowers with conspicuous stamens are borne among foliage from mid-summer to early autumn and followed by decorative, bronze-red fruit capsules.

Reinwardtia indica (Yellow flax)
Evergreen, upright sub-shrub, branching from the base. Has greyish-green leaves and small clusters of yellow flowers mainly in summer but also during the year.
Min. 10°C (50°F).

Euryops pectinatus
Evergreen, upright shrub. Deeply cut, grey-green leaves set off large heads of daisy-like, bright yellow flowers, borne in late spring and early summer and often again in winter.
Min. 5–7°C (41–5°F).

Brachyglottis monroi
Evergreen, bushy, dense shrub that makes an excellent windbreak in mild, coastal areas. Has small, wavy-edged, dark green leaves with white undersides. Bears heads of bright yellow flowers in mid-summer.

Grindelia chiloensis
Mainly evergreen, bushy shrub with sticky stems. Sticky, lance-shaped, serrated leaves are up to 12cm (5in) long. Has large, daisy-like, yellow flower heads in summer.

Cytisus scoparius* f. *andreanus
Deciduous, arching shrub with narrow, dark green leaves that are divided into 3 leaflets. Bears a profusion of bright yellow-and-red flowers along elegant, green branchlets in late spring and early summer.

***Abutilon* 'Kentish Belle'**
Semi-evergreen, arching shrub with purple shoots and deeply lobed, purple-veined, dark green leaves. Bears large, pendent, bell-shaped, orange-yellow and red flowers in summer-autumn.

Mimulus aurantiacus
Evergreen, domed to rounded shrub with sticky, lance-shaped, glossy, rich green leaves. Has tubular, orange, yellow or red-purple flowers from late spring to autumn.

Isoplexis canariensis
Evergreen, rounded, sparingly branched shrub. Bears foxglove-like, yellow to red- or brownish-orange flowers in dense, upright spikes, to 30cm (12in) tall, in summer.
Min. 7°C (45°F).

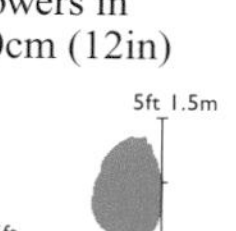

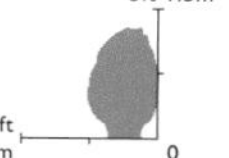

***Potentilla fruticosa* 'Sunset'**
Deciduous shrub, bushy at first, later arching. Deep orange flowers, fading in hot sun, appear from early summer to mid-autumn. Mid-green leaves are divided into narrowly oval leaflets.

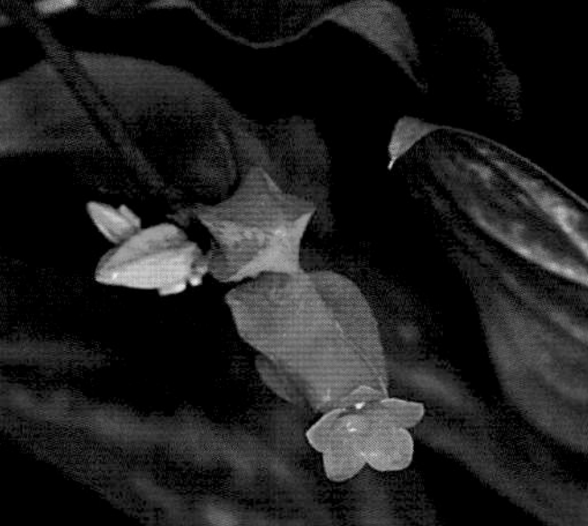

Juanulloa mexicana
Evergreen, upright, sparingly branched shrub. Leaves are felted beneath. Has orange flowers, each with a ribbed calyx, in short, nodding clusters in summer. Min. 13–15°C (55–9°F).

***Lantana* 'Spreading Sunset'**
Evergreen, rounded to spreading shrub with finely wrinkled, deep green leaves. Has tiny, tubular flowers in a range of colours, carried in dense, rounded heads from spring to autumn. Min. 10–13°C (50–55°F).

ORANGE

Cuphea ignea (Cigar flower)
Evergreen, spreading, bushy sub-shrub with bright green leaves. From spring to autumn has tubular, dark orange-red flowers, each with a dark band and white ring at the mouth. Min. 2°C (36°F).

Cuphea cyanea
Evergreen, rounded sub-shrub with narrowly oval, sticky-haired leaves. Tubular flowers, orange-red, yellow and violet-blue, are carried in summer.

Justicia spicigera
Evergreen, well-branched shrub with spikes of tubular, orange or red flowers in summer and occasionally other seasons. Min. 10–15°C (50–59°F).

SHRUBS small AUTUMN INTEREST

WHITE–RED

Turraea obtusifolia
Evergreen, rounded, bushy, arching shrub with oval to lance-shaped leaves. Bears fragrant, white flowers from autumn to spring, followed by orange-yellow fruits like tiny, peeled tangerines. Min. 13°C (55°F).

Calliandra eriophylla
(Fairy duster)
Evergreen, stiff, dense shrub. Leaves have numerous tiny leaflets. From late spring to autumn has pompons of tiny, pink-anthered, white florets, followed by brown seed pods. Min. 13°C (55°F).

***Berberis* 'Rubrostilla'**
Deciduous, arching shrub. Globose to cup-shaped, pale yellow flowers, appearing in early summer, are followed by a profusion of large, coral-red fruits. Grey-green leaves turn brilliant red in late autumn.

Cotoneaster horizontalis
(Wall-spray)
Deciduous, stiff-branched, spreading shrub. Glossy, dark green leaves redden in late autumn. Bears pinkish-white flowers from late spring to early summer, followed by red fruits.

***Viburnum opulus* 'Compactum'**
Deciduous, dense shrub. Has deep green leaves, red in autumn, and profuse white flowers in spring and early summer, followed by bunches of bright red berries.

Vaccinium angustifolium* var. *laevifolium (Low-bush blueberry)
Deciduous, bushy shrub with bright green leaves that redden in autumn. Edible, blue fruits follow white, sometimes pinkish, spring flowers.

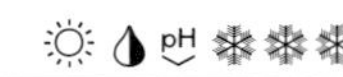

RED

Bouvardia ternifolia
(Scarlet trompetilla)
Mainly evergreen, bushy, upright shrub with leaves in whorls of 3. Has tubular, bright scarlet flowers from summer to early winter. Min. 7–10°C (45–50°F).

***Vaccinium corymbosum* 'Pioneer'**
Deciduous, upright, slightly arching shrub. Dark green leaves turn bright red in autumn. Small, white or pinkish flowers in late spring are followed by sweet, edible, blue-black berries.

Vaccinium parvifolium
Deciduous, upright shrub. Has small, dark green leaves that become bright red in autumn. Edible, bright red fruits are produced after small, pinkish-white flowers borne in late spring and early summer.

PURPLE–YELLOW

Elsholtzia stauntonii (Mint bush)
Deciduous, open sub-shrub. Sharply toothed, mint-scented, dark green leaves turn red in autumn. Slender spires of pale purplish flowers appear during late summer and autumn.

Ceratostigma willmottianum
Deciduous, open shrub. Has leaves that turn red in late autumn and bright, rich blue flowers from late summer until well into autumn.

Coriaria terminalis* var. *xanthocarpa
Deciduous, arching sub-shrub. Leaves have oval leaflets and turn red in autumn. Greenish flowers in late spring are followed by decorative, succulent, yellow fruits in late summer and autumn.

WHITE

***Skimmia japonica* 'Fructo Albo'**
Evergreen, bushy, dense, dwarf shrub. Has aromatic, dark green leaves and dense clusters of small, white flowers from mid- to late spring, succeeded by white berries.

***Gaultheria mucronata* 'Wintertime'**
Evergreen, bushy, dense shrub. Has prickly, glossy, dark green leaves and white flowers in late spring and early summer, followed by large, long-lasting, white berries.

Lonicera* × *purpusii
Semi-evergreen, bushy, dense shrub with oval, dark green leaves. Small clusters of fragrant, short-tubed, white flowers, with spreading petal lobes and yellow anthers, appear in winter and early spring.

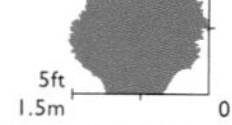

WHITE–PINK

Sarcococca humilis
Evergreen, low, clump-forming shrub. Tiny, fragrant, white flowers with pink anthers appear amid glossy, dark green foliage in late winter and are followed by spherical, black fruits.

Sarcococca hookeriana* var. *digyna
Evergreen, clump-forming, suckering, dense shrub with narrow, bright green leaves. Tiny, fragrant, white flowers, with pink anthers, open in winter and are followed by spherical, black fruits.

***Gaultheria mucronata* 'Mulberry Wine'**
Evergreen, bushy, dense shrub with large, globose, magenta berries that mature to deep purple. These follow white flowers borne in spring-summer. Leaves are glossy, dark green.

***Daphne odora* 'Aureomarginata'**
Evergreen, bushy shrub with glossy, dark green leaves narrowly edged with yellow. Clusters of very fragrant, deep purplish-pink and white flowers appear from mid-winter to early spring.

***Daphne mezereum* (Mezereon)**
Deciduous, upright shrub. Very fragrant, purple or pink blooms clothe the bare stems in late winter and early spring, followed by red fruits. Mature leaves are narrowly oval and dull grey-green.

RED

***Skimmia japonica* 'Rubella'**
Evergreen, upright, dense shrub with aromatic, red-rimmed, bright green foliage. Deep red flower buds in autumn and winter open to dense clusters of small, white flowers in spring.

Correa pulchella
Evergreen, fairly bushy, slender-stemmed shrub with oval leaves. Small, pendent, tubular, rose-red flowers appear from summer to winter, sometimes at other seasons.

***Skimmia japonica* subsp. *reevesiana* 'Robert Fortune'**
Evergreen, bushy, rather weak-growing shrub with aromatic leaves. Small, white flowers in spring are followed by crimson berries.

RED–GREEN

Skimmia japonica
Evergreen, bushy, dense shrub. Has aromatic, mid- to dark green leaves and dense clusters of small, white flowers from mid- to late spring, followed on female plants by bright red fruits if plants of both sexes are grown.

5ft 1.5m

Ribes laurifolium
Evergreen, spreading shrub. Has leathery, deep green leaves and pendent racemes of greenish-yellow flowers in late winter and early spring. Produces edible, black berries on female plants if plants of both sexes are grown.

5ft 1.5m

WHITE–GREEN

Viburnum davidii
Evergreen shrub that forms a dome of dark green foliage, over which heads of small, white flowers appear in late spring. If plants of both sexes are grown, female plants bear decorative, metallic-blue fruits.

5ft 1.5m

Breynia disticha (Snow bush)
Evergreen, well-branched shrub with slender stems. Leaves are green with white marbling. Tiny, greenish flowers, borne intermittently, have no petals. Min. 13°C (55°F).

5ft 1.5m

***Coprosma × kirkii* 'Variegata'**
Evergreen, densely branched shrub, prostrate when young, later semi-erect. White-margined leaves are borne singly or in small clusters. Tiny, translucent, white fruits appear in autumn on female plants if both sexes are grown.

5ft 1.5m

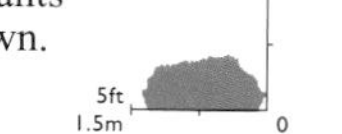

***Vinca major* 'Variegata'**
Evergreen, prostrate, arching, spreading sub-shrub. Has bright green leaves broadly edged with creamy-white and large, bright blue flowers borne from late spring to early autumn.

5ft 1.5m

***Pandanus tectorius* 'Veitchii'**
(Veitch's screw pine)
Evergreen, upright, arching shrub with rosettes of long, light green leaves that have spiny, white to cream margins. Min. 13–16°C (55–61°F).

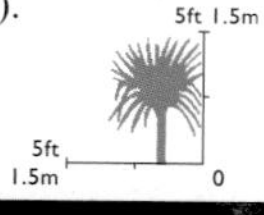

5ft 1.5m

Helichrysum petiolare
Evergreen shrub forming mounds of silver-green shoots and grey-felted leaves. Has creamy-yellow flower heads in summer. Usually grown as an annual for ground cover and edging.

5ft 1.5m

Leucophyta brownii
Evergreen, intricately branched shrub with velvety, grey branches and tiny, scale-like leaves. Clusters of flower heads, silver in bud, yellowish when expanded, appear in summer. Min. 7–10°C (45–50°F).

5ft 1.5m

Artemisia arborescens
Evergreen, upright shrub, grown for its finely cut, silvery-white foliage. Heads of small, bright yellow flowers are borne in summer and early autumn.

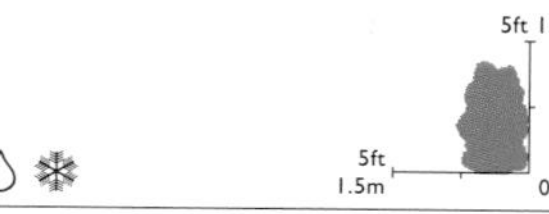

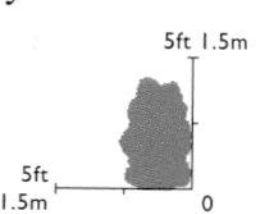

5ft 1.5m

GREEN

Ballota acetabulosa
Evergreen sub-shrub that forms a mound of rounded, grey-green leaves, felted beneath. Whorls of small, pink flowers open from mid- to late summer.

Vaccinium glaucoalbum
Evergreen shrub with deep green leaves that, when young, are pale green above, bluish-white beneath. Pink-tinged, white flowers in late spring and early summer are followed by white-bloomed, blue-black fruits.

Hebe cupressoides
Evergreen, upright, dense shrub with cypress-like, grey-green foliage. On mature plants tiny, pale lilac flowers are borne from early to mid-summer.

Ruscus hypoglossum
Evergreen, clump-forming shrub with arching shoots. Pointed, glossy, bright green 'leaves'are actually flattened shoots that bear tiny, yellow flowers in spring, followed by large, bright red berries.

Vinca minor (Lesser periwinkle)
Evergreen, prostrate, spreading sub-shrub that forms extensive mats of small, glossy, dark green leaves. Bears small, purple, blue or white flowers, mainly from mid-spring to early summer.

Mimosa pudica
(Humble plant, Sensitive plant)
Short-lived, evergreen shrub with prickly stems; needs support. Fern-like leaves fold when touched. Has minute, pale mauve-pink flowers in summer-autumn. Min. 13–16°C (55–61°F).

Eurya emarginata
Slow-growing, evergreen, densely branched, rounded shrub with small, leathery, deep green leaves. Small, greenish-white flowers in late spring or summer are followed by tiny, purple-black berries.

Lonicera pileata
Evergreen, low, spreading, dense shrub with narrow, dark green leaves and tiny, short-tubed, creamy-white flowers in late spring, followed by violet-purple berries. Makes good ground cover.

Chamaerops humilis (Dwarf fan palm, European fan palm)
Slow-growing, evergreen palm, suckering with age. Fan-shaped leaves, 60–90cm (2–3ft) across, have green to grey-green lobes. Has tiny, yellow flowers in summer.

Artemisia abrotanum (Lad's love, Old man, Southernwood)
Deciduous or semi-evergreen, moderately bushy shrub. Aromatic, grey-green leaves have many very slender lobes. Has clusters of small, yellowish flower heads in late summer.

***Buxus microphylla* 'Green Pillow'**
Evergreen, compact, dwarf shrub, forming a dense, rounded mass of small, oval, dark green leaves. Bears insignificant flowers in late spring or early summer.

Sabal minor (Dwarf palmetto)
Evergreen, suckering fan palm with stems mainly underground. Has leaves of 20–30 green or grey-green lobes. Erect sprays of small, white flowers are followed by shiny, black berries. Min. 5°C (41°F).

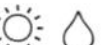

GREEN–YELLOW

***Buxus sempervirens* 'Suffruticosa'**
Evergreen, dwarf shrub that forms a tight, dense mass of oval, bright green leaves. Bears insignificant flowers in late spring or early summer. Trimmed to about 15cm (6in) is used for edging.

5ft 1.5m / 5ft 1.5m / 0

***Salvia officinalis* 'Icterina'**
Evergreen or semi-evergreen, bushy shrub used as a culinary herb. Has aromatic, grey-green leaves variegated with pale green and yellow. Occasionally bears small spikes of tubular, 2-lipped, purplish flowers.

5ft 1.5m / 5ft 1.5m / 0

Sanchezia speciosa
Evergreen, erect, soft-stemmed shrub. Glossy leaves have yellow- or white-banded main veins. Tubular, yellow flowers appear in axils of red bracts, in summer. Min. 15–18°C (59–64°F).

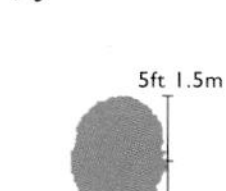

5ft 1.5m / 5ft 1.5m / 0

***Ruta graveolens* 'Jackman's Blue'**
Evergreen, bushy, compact sub-shrub. Has aromatic, finely divided, blue foliage. In summer, clusters of small, mustard-yellow flowers are borne.

5ft 1.5m / 5ft 1.5m / 0

***Euonymus fortunei* 'Emerald 'n' Gold'**
Evergreen, bushy shrub with bright green leaves, margined with bright yellow and tinged with pink in winter.

5ft 1.5m / 5ft 1.5m / 0

***Leucothöe fontanesiana* 'Rainbow'**
Evergreen, arching shrub with sharply toothed, leathery, dark green leaves that age from pink- to cream-variegated. Racemes of white flowers open below shoots in spring.

5ft 1.5m / 8ft 2.5m / 0

YELLOW–ORANGE

***Lonicera nitida* 'Baggesen's Gold'**
Evergreen, bushy shrub with long, arching shoots covered with tiny, bright yellow leaves. Insignificant, yellowish-green flowers in mid-spring are occasionally followed by mauve fruits.

5ft 1.5m / 5ft 1.5m / 0

Codiaeum variegatum* var. *pictum
(Croton)
Evergreen, erect, sparingly branched shrub. Leathery, glossy leaves vary greatly in size and shape, and are variegated with red, pink, orange or yellow. Min. 10–13°C (50–55°F).

5ft 1.5m / 5ft 1.5m / 0

***Pittosporum tenuifolium* 'Tom Thumb'**
Evergreen, rounded, dense shrub with pale green, young leaves that contrast with deep reddish-brown, older foliage. Bears cup-shaped, purplish flowers in summer.

5ft 1.5m / 5ft 1.5m / 0

E. carnea **'Golden Starlet'** ♀ (all year)

HEATHERS

As a group, heathers (or heaths) are remarkable in that species and cultivars are available to provide interest at all times of the year. Several are grown for their golden foliage, which often turns a deep burnt orange in winter, while others flower for a long period during summer, autumn or winter. Flowers are in a variety of hues, and are occasionally bicoloured; those with double flowers may be dried for winter decoration. In habit heathers vary from tree-heaths of up to 6m (20ft) to dwarf, prostrate forms, many of which are excellent for providing ground cover.

There are three genera: *Calluna*, *Daboecia* and *Erica*. All *Calluna* and *Daboecia* cultivars and most *Erica* species must be grown in acid soil but otherwise heathers require little attention. Main seasons of interest are given for each plant.

E. cinerea **'Eden Valley'** ♀ (sum)

C. v. **'Kinlochruel'** ♀ (sum-aut)

E. × *darleyensis* **'White Perfection'** ♀ (win-spr)

C. vulgaris **'My Dream'** ♀ (sum-aut)

C. vulgaris **'County Wicklow'** ♀ (sum-aut)

C. vulgaris **'Spring Cream'** ♀ (spr-aut)

E. × *veitchii* **'Exeter'** ♀ (win-spr)

E. × *darleyensis* **'White Glow'** (win-spr)

C. vulgaris **'Elsie Purnell'** ♀ (sum-aut)

E. mackaiana **'Plena'** (sum)

D. cantabrica **'Snowdrift'** ♀ (spr-aut)

E. tetralix **'Alba Mollis'** ♀ (sum-aut)

E. × *veitchii* **'Pink Joy'** (win-spr)

C. vulgaris **'Anthony Davis'** ♀ (sum-aut)

E. cinerea **'Hookstone White'** (sum)

E. arborea var. *alpina* ♀ (win-spr)

E. carnea **'Springwood White'** ♀ (win-spr)

E. × *darleyensis* **'Archie Graham'** (win-spr)

E. perspicua (aut-win)

E. canaliculata ♀ (win-spr)

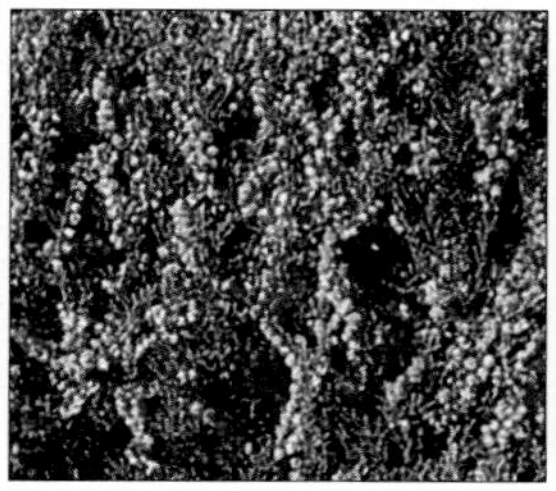

E. ciliaris **'David McClintock'** (sum)

C. vulgaris **'J.H. Hamilton'** ♀ (sum-aut)

E. × *williamsii* **'P.D. Williams'** ♀ (sum)

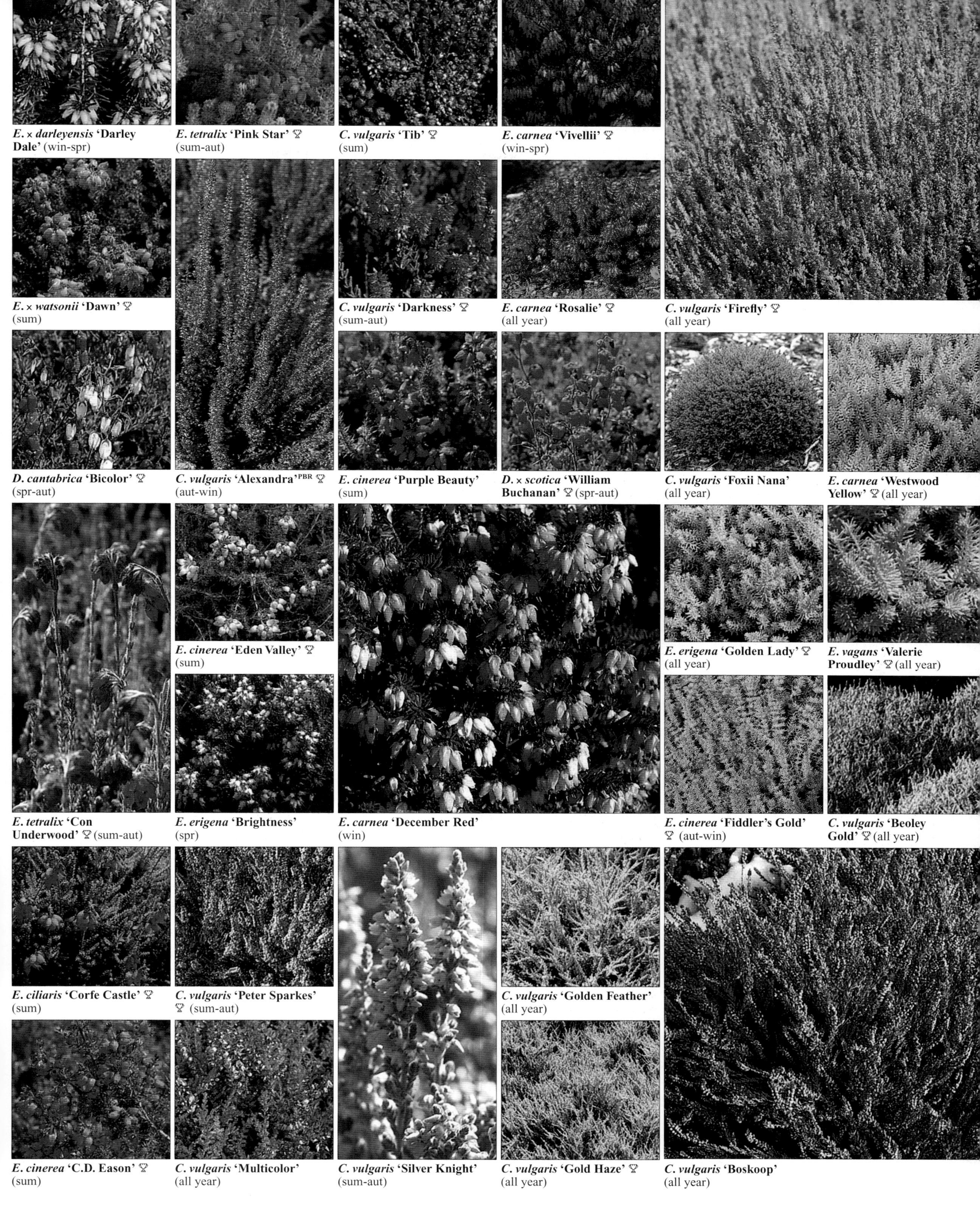

E. × *darleyensis* **'Darley Dale'** (win-spr)

E. tetralix **'Pink Star'** 🏆 (sum-aut)

C. vulgaris **'Tib'** 🏆 (sum)

E. carnea **'Vivellii'** 🏆 (win-spr)

E. × *watsonii* **'Dawn'** 🏆 (sum)

C. vulgaris **'Darkness'** 🏆 (sum-aut)

E. carnea **'Rosalie'** 🏆 (all year)

C. vulgaris **'Firefly'** 🏆 (all year)

D. cantabrica **'Bicolor'** 🏆 (spr-aut)

C. vulgaris **'Alexandra'**PBR 🏆 (aut-win)

E. cinerea **'Purple Beauty'** (sum)

D. × *scotica* **'William Buchanan'** 🏆 (spr-aut)

C. vulgaris **'Foxii Nana'** (all year)

E. carnea **'Westwood Yellow'** 🏆 (all year)

E. cinerea **'Eden Valley'** 🏆 (sum)

E. erigena **'Golden Lady'** 🏆 (all year)

E. vagans **'Valerie Proudley'** 🏆 (all year)

E. tetralix **'Con Underwood'** 🏆 (sum-aut)

E. erigena **'Brightness'** (spr)

E. carnea **'December Red'** (win)

E. cinerea **'Fiddler's Gold'** 🏆 (aut-win)

C. vulgaris **'Beoley Gold'** 🏆 (all year)

E. ciliaris **'Corfe Castle'** 🏆 (sum)

C. vulgaris **'Peter Sparkes'** 🏆 (sum-aut)

C. vulgaris **'Golden Feather'** (all year)

E. cinerea **'C.D. Eason'** 🏆 (sum)

C. vulgaris **'Multicolor'** (all year)

C. vulgaris **'Silver Knight'** (sum-aut)

C. vulgaris **'Gold Haze'** 🏆 (all year)

C. vulgaris **'Boskoop'** (all year)

Roses

Roses

These most romantic of flowers are unsurpassed in beauty and fragrance by any other single group of plants. Roses are cultivated and prized by many, and for some they are an almost indispensable element in the modern garden.

Growing roses

With some 150 species and thousands of cultivars, both ancient and modern, there are members of the genus *Rosa* to suit an enormous number of garden situations. They come from a wide range of habitats throughout the northern hemisphere and, with few exceptions, most roses in cultivation are very hardy. Given attention to their cultivation needs, they will repay the gardener with a profusion of blooms.

All roses do well when grown in open, sunny sites in fertile, humus-rich, moist but well-drained soil. However, avoid planting in soil that has grown roses before as roses may be affected by soil sickness, which is caused by a build-up of harmful soil organisms.

Roses can be grown among bulbs, perennials and other shrubs in a mixed border provided that their fellow plants do not compete directly for moisture and nutrients. Choose companions that are shallow-rooted, such as the many herbaceous geraniums and pinks (*Dianthus* cultivars), or space plants at a sufficient distance to allow for mulching and feeding around the rose's root zone.

Maintaining year-round interest

As a group, roses have a long flowering season, from the early summer blooms of 'Frühlingsmorgen' through the main flourish in mid-summer to the first frosts, thanks to the repeat-flowering roses. Some also have attractive fruits (hips) that prolong the season, notably the tomato-like hips of the Rugosas, the flask-shaped, vibrant scarlet fruits of *R. moyesii* and the rounded, black hips of *R. pimpinellifolia*. Regular dead-heading extends the season because it redirects the expenditure of energy from seed formation into flower production.

Ornamental features

Roses embrace almost every shade of the spectrum, excluding true blue, and some have a strong fragrance, which can range from the heady, sweet scent of the Damasks to that of musk or spice. A few roses have ornamental thorns, notably *R. sericea* subsp. *omeiensis* f. *pteracantha*, with its large triangular thorns that glow blood-red when backlit.

Foliage can also make an impact: the soft grey-purple leaves of R. *glauca* and the blue-green of the Alba roses are both perfect foils to crimson and purple flowers.

Relaxed informality
Above: In this informal planting, the profuse blooms of the gracefully arching shrub *Rosa* 'Cerise Bouquet' are complemented by the rounded, pink heads of *Allium cristophii* and the vivid spires of foxgloves *(Digitalis purpurea)*.

Formal dressing
Right: Here, a sturdy arch clothed with clematis and a vigorous, free-flowering rambler lends height to the scheme and forms a perfect frame to draw the eye to an elegant focal point.

Roses range in size from the tiny Miniature bushes such as *R*. 'Rouletii', which at 20cm (8in) high are perfect for containers and window boxes, to the most rampant of ramblers, such as *R*. 'Bobbie James', which can achieve 10m (30ft) or more in height when scrambling through large trees. Using taller cultivars of dense, thorny shrub roses, such as the Rugosa roses, you can create divisions within the garden. These may take the form of large impenetrable boundary hedges that give privacy and security or they can form garden compartments defined by low hedging or edging.

Climbing and rambling roses are extremely versatile, and can be trained on a wall to act as a colourful backdrop, or on trellis to form a screen. Like all climbers, they are invaluable for lending height when grown on pergolas and arches, and can make a focal point if grown on free-standing structures such as tripods and pyramids. Many are also available trained as weeping standards.

The ground-cover roses are ideal for clothing sunny and inaccessible banks, since most require little regular pruning.

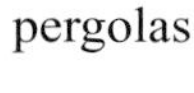

SUMMER BEDFELLOWS
Above: Alliums and bearded irises are perfect companions to roses in a mid-summer border. As a bonus, *Crambe cordifolia* adds its subtle topnotes to the fragrance of the roses.

POTTED ROSES
Right: Small bush roses, notably the miniatures and patio roses, are ideal for container planting. Alternatively, use trailing ground-cover roses in hanging baskets.

Foliage textures range from glossy to matt, from delicately fern-like to robustly wrinkled, as in *R. rugosa*.

DESIGNING WITH ROSES

Roses can be used for a variety of design functions in the garden since they have a diversity of habit that includes the mound-forming, sometimes stem-rooting, ground-cover roses, the densely thorny Gallicas and the open, gracefully arching Chinas and Damasks. Many are versatile enough to be used in more than one way.

A rose garden laid out in a formal style is perhaps the most traditional way to use roses, and geometrically ordered beds are particularly suited to the neatly upright growth of many bush roses. Roses can be used equally well as specimens, although the selection of a single favourite is difficult with so many to choose from.

CONTAINER-GROWING

Smaller roses, especially the Miniature bush roses, are ideal for containers. The smallest such as BABY MASQUERADE ('Tanba') – are suitable for window boxes, while trailing or spreading cultivars are perfect for baskets.

□ WHITE

***R.* 'Madame Hardy'**
Vigorous, upright Damask rose with plentiful, leathery, matt leaves. Richly fragrant, quartered-rosette, fully double flowers, 10cm (4in) across, white with green eyes, are borne in summer.
H 1.5m (5ft), S 1.2m (4ft).

***R.* 'Boule de Neige'**
Upright Bourbon rose with arching stems and very fragrant, cupped to rosette, fully double flowers. White flowers, sometimes tinged with pink, 8cm (3in) across, appear in summer-autumn. Leaves are glossy and dark green. H 1.5m (5ft), S 1.2m (4ft).

***R. pimpinellifolia* 'Plena'**
Dense, spreading, prickly species rose with cupped, double, creamy-white flowers, 4cm (1½in) across, in early summer. Has small, fern-like, dark green leaves and blackish hips. H 1m (3ft), S 1.2m (4ft).

***R.* 'Penelope'**
Dense, bushy shrub rose, with plentiful, dark green foliage, that bears many scented, cupped, double, pink-cream flowers, 8cm (3in) across, in clusters in summer-autumn. H and S 1m (3ft), more if lightly pruned.

Categories of Rose

Grown for the extraordinary beauty of their flowers, roses have been in cultivation for some hundreds of years. They have been widely hybridized, producing a vast number of shrubs suitable for growing as specimen plants, in the border, as hedges and as climbers for training on walls, pergolas and pillars. Roses are classified into three main groups:

Species
Species, or wild, roses and **species hybrids**, which share most of the characteristics of the parent species, bear flowers generally in one flush in summer and hips in autumn.

Old Garden roses
Alba – large, freely branching roses with clusters of flowers in mid-summer and abundant, greyish-green foliage.
Bourbon – open, remontant shrub roses that may be trained to climb. Flowers are borne, often 3 to a cluster, in summer-autumn.
China – remontant shrubs with flowers borne singly or in clusters in summer-autumn; provide shelter.
Damask – open shrubs bearing loose clusters of usually very fragrant flowers mainly in summer.
Gallica – fairly dense shrubs producing richly coloured flowers, often 3 to a cluster, in the summer months.
Hybrid Perpetual – vigorous, remontant shrubs with flowers borne singly or in 3s in summer-autumn.
Moss – often lax shrubs with a furry, moss-like growth on stems and calyx, and flowers in summer.
Noisette – remontant climbing roses that bear large clusters of flowers, with a slight spicy fragrance, in summer-autumn; provide shelter.
Portland – upright, rather dense, remontant shrubs bearing loose clusters of flowers in summer-autumn.
Provence (Centifolia) – lax, thorny shrubs bearing scented flowers in summer.
Sempervirens – semi-evergreen climbing roses that bear numerous flowers in late summer.
Tea – remontant shrubs and climbers with elegant, pointed buds that open to loose flowers with a spicy fragrance; provide shelter.

Modern Garden roses
Shrub – a diverse group, illustrated here with the Old Garden roses because of their similar characteristics. Most are remontant and are larger than bush roses, with flowers borne singly or in sprays in summer and/or autumn.
Large-flowered bush (Hybrid Tea) – remontant shrubs with large flowers borne in summer-autumn.
Cluster-flowered bush (Floribunda) – remontant shrubs with usually large sprays of flowers in summer-autumn.
Dwarf clustered-flowered bush (Patio) – neat, remontant shrubs with sprays of flowers borne in summer-autumn.
Miniature bush – very small, remontant shrubs with sprays of tiny flowers in summer-autumn.
Polyantha – tough, compact, remontant shrubs with many small flowers in summer-autumn.
Ground cover – trailing and spreading roses, some flowering in summer only, others remontant, flowering in summer-autumn.
Climbing – vigorous climbing roses, diverse in growth and flower, some flowering in summer only, others remontant, flowering in summer-autumn.
Rambler – vigorous climbing roses with flexible stems that bear clusters of flowers mostly in summer.

Flower shapes

With the mass hybridization that has occurred in recent years, roses have been developed to produce plants with a wide variety of characteristics, in particular different forms of flower, often with a strong fragrance. These flower types, illustrated below, give a general indication of the shape of the flower at its perfect state (which in some cases may be before it has opened fully). Growing conditions may affect the form of the flower. Flowers may be single (4–7 petals), semi-double (8–14 petals), double (15–30 petals) or fully double (over 30 petals).

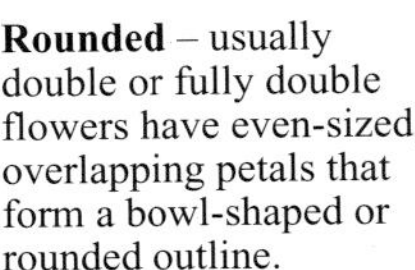

Flat – open, usually single or semi-double flowers have petals that are almost flat.

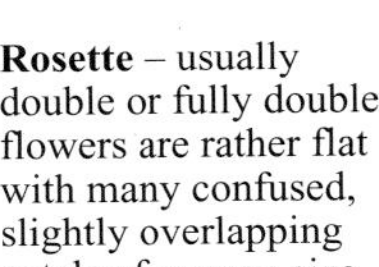

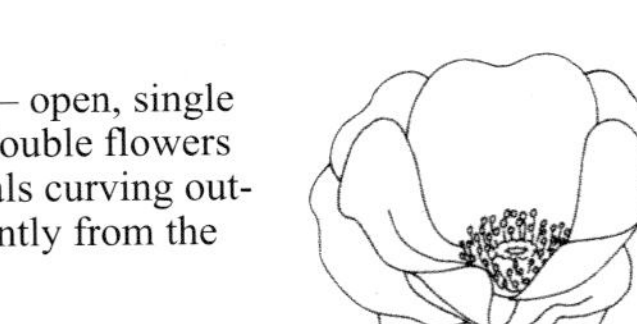

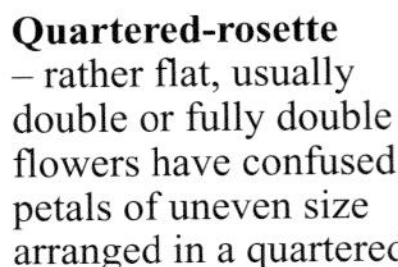

Cupped – open, single to fully double flowers have petals curving outwards gently from the centre.

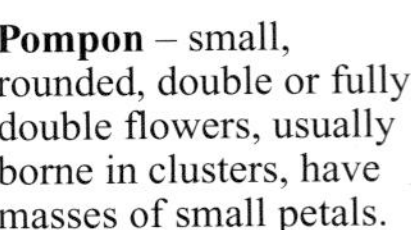

Pointed – elegant, 'Hybrid Tea' shape; semi-double to fully double flowers have high, tight centres.

Urn-shaped – classic, curved, flat-topped, semi-double to fully double flowers are of 'Hybrid Tea' type.

Rounded – usually double or fully double flowers have even-sized, overlapping petals that form a bowl-shaped or rounded outline.

Rosette – usually double or fully double flowers are rather flat with many confused, slightly overlapping petals of uneven size.

Quartered-rosette – rather flat, usually double or fully double flowers have confused petals of uneven size arranged in a quartered pattern.

Pompon – small, rounded, double or fully double flowers, usually borne in clusters, have masses of small petals.

WHITE–PINK

***R.* 'Dupontii'** (Snowbush rose)
Upright, bushy shrub rose with abundant, greyish foliage. Bears many clusters of fragrant, flat, single, white flowers, tinged with blush-pink, 6cm (2½in) across, in mid-summer. H and S 2.2m (7ft).

***R.* 'Nevada'**
Dense, arching shrub rose with abundant, light green leaves. Scented, flat, semi-double, creamy-white flowers, 10cm (4in) across, are borne freely in summer and more sparsely in autumn. H and S 2.2m (7ft).

***R.* Pearl Drift ('Leggab')**
Bushy, spreading shrub rose that produces clusters of lightly scented, cupped, double, blush-pink flowers, 10cm (4in) across, in summer-autumn. Leaves are plentiful and glossy. H 1m (3ft), S 1.2m (4ft).

PINK

***R.* 'Fantin-Latour'**
Vigorous, shrubby Provence rose. Flowers appear in summer and are fragrant, cupped to flat, fully double, blush-pink, with neat, green button eyes, and 10cm (4in) across. Has broad, dark green leaves. H 1.5m (5ft), S 1.2m (4ft).

***R.* 'Conrad Ferdinand Meyer'**
Vigorous, arching shrub rose with cupped, fully double, pink flowers, 7cm (3in) across, that are richly fragrant and borne in large numbers in summer, fewer in autumn. Foliage is leathery and prone to rust. H 2.5m (8ft), S 1.2m (4ft).

***R.* 'Great Maiden's Blush'**
Vigorous, upright Alba rose. Very fragrant, rosette, fully double, pinkish-white flowers, 8cm (3in) across, appear in mid-summer. H 2m (6ft), S 1.3m (4½ft).

***R.* 'Céleste'**
Vigorous, spreading, bushy Alba rose. Fragrant, cupped, double, light pink flowers, 8cm (3in) across, appear in summer. Makes a good hedge. H 1.5m (5ft), S 1.2m (4ft).

***R.* 'Felicia'**
Vigorous shrub rose with abundant, healthy, greyish-green foliage. Scented, cupped, double flowers, 8cm (3in) across, are light pink, tinged with apricot, and are borne in summer-autumn. H 1.5m (5ft), S 2.2m (7ft).

R. rubiginosa
(Eglantine, Sweet briar)
Vigorous, arching, thorny species rose that has distinctive, apple-scented foliage. Bears cupped, single, pink flowers, 2.5cm (1in) across, in mid-summer and red hips in autumn. H and S 2.4m (8ft).

PINK

R. Rosy Cushion ('Interall')
Dense, spreading shrub rose with plentiful, glossy, dark green leaves. Bears clusters of scented, cupped, semi-double flowers, 6cm (2½in) across, that are pink with ivory centres, in summer-autumn. H 1m (3ft), S 1.2m (4ft).

R. glauca
Vigorous, arching species rose, grown for its fine, greyish-purple leaves and red stems. Flat, single, cerise-pink flowers, 4cm (1½in) across, with pale centres and gold stamens, appear in early summer, followed by red hips in autumn. H 2m (6ft), S 1.5m (5ft).

R. Marguerite Hilling
Dense, arching shrub rose. Many scented, flat, semi-double, rose-pink flowers, 10cm (4in) across, are borne in summer and a few in autumn. Has light green foliage. H and S 2.2m (7ft).

R. 'Reine Victoria'
Lax Bourbon rose with slender stems and light green leaves. Sweetly scented, rosette, double flowers, 8cm (3in) across, in shades of pink, are borne in summer-autumn. Grows well on a pillar. H 2m (6ft), S 1.2m (4ft).

R. 'Complicata'
Very vigorous Gallica rose, with thorny, arching growth, useful as a large hedge. Slightly fragrant, cupped, single flowers, 11cm (4½in) across, are pink with pale centres and appear in mid-summer. H 2.2m (7ft), S 2.5m (8ft).

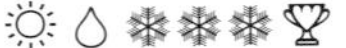

R. 'Königin von Dänemark'
Vigorous, rather open Alba rose. Heavily scented, quartered-rosette, fully double, warm-pink flowers, 8cm (3in) across and with green button eyes, appear in mid-summer. H 1.5m (5ft), S 1.2m (4ft).

R. Bonica ('Meidomonac')
Vigorous, spreading shrub rose bearing large sprays of slightly fragrant, cup-shaped, fully double, rose-pink flowers, 7cm (3in) across, in summer-autumn. Foliage is glossy and plentiful. H 1m (3ft), S 1.1m (3½ft).

R. 'Pink Grootendorst'
Upright, bushy shrub rose with plentiful, small leaves. Rosette, double flowers, 5cm (2in) across, have serrated, clear pink petals. Blooms are carried in sprays in summer-autumn. H 2m (6ft), S 1.5m (5ft).

R. Constance Spry ('Austance')
Shrub rose of arching habit that will climb if supported. Cupped, fully double, pink flowers, 12cm (5in) across, with a spicy scent, are borne freely in summer. Leaves are large and plentiful. H 2m (6ft), S 1.5m (5ft).

R. 'Mrs John Laing'
Bushy Hybrid Perpetual rose with plentiful, light green foliage. Produces many richly fragrant, rounded, fully double, pink flowers, 12cm (5in) across, in summer and a few in autumn. H 1m (3ft), S 80cm (2½ft).

***R.* × *odorata* 'Pallida'** (Old blush china, Parson's pink china)
Bushy China rose that may be trained as a climber on a sheltered wall. Cupped, double, pink flowers, 6cm (2½in) across, are produced freely from summer to late autumn. H 1m (3ft), S 80cm (2½ft) or more.

***R. gallica* 'Versicolor'**
(Rosa mundi)
Neat, bushy Gallica rose. In summer produces striking, slightly scented, flat, semi-double flowers, 5cm (2in) across, very pale blush-pink with crimson stripes. H 75cm (2½ft), S 1m (3ft).

***R.* × *odorata* 'Mutabilis'**
Open species rose with coppery young foliage. In summer-autumn bears shallowly cup-shaped, single, buff-yellow flowers, 6cm (2½in) across, that age to coppery-pink or -crimson. H and S 1m (3ft), to 2m (6ft) against a wall.

***R. moyesii* 'Geranium'**
Vigorous, arching species rose. Flat, single flowers, 5cm (2in) across, are dusky scarlet with yellow stamens and are borne on branches in summer. Has small, dark green leaves and in autumn large, red hips. H 3m (10ft), S 2.5m (8ft).

R. 'Madame Isaac Pereire'
Vigorous, arching Bourbon rose. Fragrant, cupped to quartered-rosette, fully double flowers, 15cm (6in) across, are deep purplish-pink and are produced freely in summer-autumn. H 2.2m (7ft), S 2m (6ft).

R. rugosa
(Hedgehog rose, Japanese rose)
Vigorous, dense species rose with wrinkled leaves and large, red hips. Cupped, single, white or purplish-red flowers, 9cm (3½in) across, appear in good succession in summer-autumn. H and S 1–2m (3–6ft).

R. 'Roseraie de l'Haÿ'
Vigorous, dense shrub rose. Bears many strongly scented, cupped to flat, double, reddish-purple flowers, 11cm (4½in) across, in summer-autumn. Leaves are abundant and disease-resistant. H 2.2m (7ft), S 2m (6ft).

R. 'Henri Martin'
Vigorous, upright Moss rose. Rosette, double, purplish-crimson flowers, 9cm (3½in) across, appear in summer and have a light scent and some furry, green 'mossing' of the calyces underneath. H 1.5m (5ft), S 1m (3ft).

RED–PURPLE

***R.* 'Empereur du Maroc'**
Compact, shrubby Hybrid Perpetual rose. Fragrant, quartered-rosette, fully double flowers, 8cm (3in) across, are rich purplish-crimson and are borne freely in summer and more sparsely in autumn. H 1.2 m (4ft), S 1m (3ft).

***R.* CARDINAL HUME ('Harregale')**
Bushy, spreading shrub rose. Cupped, fully double, reddish-purple flowers, 7.5cm (3in) across, are borne in dense clusters in summer-autumn and have a musky scent. H and S 1m (3ft).

***R.* 'Cardinal de Richelieu'**
Vigorous, compact Gallica rose that bears plentiful, dark green foliage and fragrant, rounded, fully double, deep burgundy-purple flowers, 8cm (3in) across, in summer. H 1.2m (4ft), S 1m (3ft).

***R.* 'Belle de Crécy'**
Gallica rose of rather lax growth and few thorns. Rosette, fully double flowers, 8cm (3in) across, are pink, tinged greyish-purple with green eyes, have a rich, spicy fragrance and are produced in summer. H 1.2 m (4ft), S 1m (3ft).

***R.* 'William Lobb'**
Moss rose with strong, arching, prickly stems that will climb if supported. In summer bears rosette, double, deep purplish-crimson flowers, 9cm (3½in) across, that fade to lilac-grey. H and S 2m (6ft).

***R.* 'Tour de Malakoff'**
Provence rose of open habit. Scented, rosette, double flowers, 12cm (5in) across, are magenta with violet veins, fading to greyish-purple, and appear in summer. H 2m (6ft), S 1.5m (5ft).

YELLOW

R. primula **(Incense rose)**
Lax, arching species rose that bears scented, cupped, single, primrose-yellow flowers, 4cm (1½in) across, in late spring. Foliage is plentiful, aromatic and fern-like. May die back in hard winters. H and S 2m (6ft).

***R. foetida* 'Persiana'**
Upright, arching species rose with cupped, double, yellow flowers, 2.5cm (1in) across, in early summer. Glossy leaves are prone to blackspot. Prune spent branches only and shelter from cold winds. H and S 1.5m (5ft).

R. ecae
Erect, wiry species rose. Cupped, single, bright yellow flowers, 2cm (¾in) across, with a musky scent, are borne close to reddish stems in late spring. Foliage is fern-like and graceful. Needs shelter. H 1.5m (5ft), S 1.2m (4ft).

YELLOW

***R. xanthina* 'Canary Bird'**
Vigorous, dense, arching species hybrid with small, fern-like leaves. Cupped, single, yellow flowers, 5cm (2in) across, with a musky scent, appear in late spring and sparsely in autumn. May die back in hard winters. H and S 2.1m (7ft).

***R.* Graham Thomas ('Ausmas')**
Vigorous, arching shrub rose, lax in habit, with glossy, bright green leaves. In summer-autumn bears cupped, fully double, yellow flowers, 11cm (4½in) across, with some scent. H 1.2m (4ft), S 1.5m (5ft).

WHITE–PINK

***R.* Iceberg ('Korbin')**
Cluster-flowered bush rose. Produces many sprays of cupped, fully double, white flowers, 7cm (3in) across, in summer-autumn. Has abundant, glossy leaves. H 75cm (30in), S 65cm (26in), more if not pruned hard.

***R.* Margaret Merril ('Harkuly')**
Upright, cluster-flowered bush rose. Very fragrant, double, blush-white or white flowers, are well-formed, urn-shaped and 10cm (4in) across, and are borne singly or in clusters in summer-autumn. H 1m (3ft), S 60cm (2ft).

***R.* Grouse ('Korimro')**
Trailing, ground-cover rose with very abundant, glossy foliage and flat, single, blush-pink flowers, 4cm (1½in) across, borne close to stems in summer-autumn. Has a pleasant fragrance. H 45cm (1½ft), S 3m (10ft).

***R.* 'Elizabeth Harkness'**
Neat, upright, large-flowered bush rose with abundant, dark green foliage. Fragrant, pointed, fully double flowers, 12cm (5in) across, are pale creamy-pink, tinted buff, and are borne in summer-autumn. H 80cm (30in), S 60cm (24in).

***R.* 'The Fairy'**
Dense, cushion-forming, dwarf cluster-flowered bush rose with abundant, small, glossy leaves. Rosette, double, pink flowers, 2.5cm (1in) across, are borne freely in late summer and autumn. H and S 60cm (2ft).

***R.* 'Nozomi'**
Creeping, ground-cover rose bearing flat, single, blush-pink and white flowers, 2.5cm (1in) across, close to stems in summer. Has small, dark green leaves. May be used for a container. H 45cm (1½ft), S 1.2m (4ft).

PINK

***R.* Pink Bells ('Poulbells')**
Very dense, spreading, ground-cover rose with abundant, small, dark green leaves and many pompon, fully double, pink flowers, 2.5cm (1in) across, borne in clusters in summer. H 75cm (2½ft), S 1.2m (4ft).

***R.* 'Queen Elizabeth'**
Upright, cluster-flowered bush rose that bears long-stemmed, rounded, fully double, pink flowers, 10cm (4in) across, singly or in clusters, in summer-autumn. Leaves are large and leathery. H 1.5m (5ft), S 75cm (2½ft), more if not pruned hard.

***R.* 'Iced Ginger'**
Upright, cluster-flowered bush rose with sparse, reddish foliage. Pointed, fully double, buff to copper-pink flowers, 11cm (4½in) across, are borne singly or in clusters in summer-autumn. H 90cm (36in), S 70cm (28in).

***R.* 'Alpine Sunset'**
Compact, large-flowered bush rose with fragrant, rounded, fully double, peach-yellow flowers, 20cm (8in) across, appearing on short stems in summer-autumn. Has large, semi-glossy leaves. May die back in hard winters. H and S 60cm (2ft).

***R.* Sexy Rexy ('Macrexy')**
Compact, bushy, cluster-flowered bush rose. Bears clusters of slightly fragrant, cupped, camellia-like, fully double, pink flowers, 8cm (3in) across, in summer-autumn. Leaves are dark green. H and S 60cm (2ft).

***R.* Peek-a-boo ('Dicgrow')**
Dense, cushion-forming, dwarf cluster-flowered bush rose with sprays of urn-shaped, double, apricot-pink flowers, 4cm (1½in) across, from summer to early winter. Leaves are narrow and dark green. H and S 45cm (18in).

***R.* Rosemary Harkness ('Harrowbond')**
Vigorous, large-flowered bush rose with abundant, glossy leaves. Bears fragrant, pointed, double flowers, 10cm (4in) across, in salmon-pink and orange, singly or in clusters in summer-autumn. H 1m (3ft), S 75cm (2½ft).

***R.* Lovely Lady ('Dicjubell')**
Dense, rounded, large-flowered bush rose. Slightly scented, pointed, fully double, rose-pink flowers, 10cm (4in) across, are produced freely in summer-autumn. H 80cm (30in), S 70cm (28in).

***R.* 'Blessings'**
Upright, large-flowered bush rose with slightly fragrant, salmon-pink flowers that are urn-shaped and fully double, 10cm (4in) across, and are borne singly or in clusters in summer-autumn. Has large, dark green leaves. H 1m (3ft), S 75cm (2½ft).

PINK

R. ANISLEY DICKSON ('Dickimono')
Vigorous, cluster-flowered bush rose. Carries large clusters of slightly fragrant, pointed, double, salmon-pink flowers, 8cm (3in) across, in summer-autumn. H 1m (3ft), S 75cm (2½ft).

R. PAUL SHIRVILLE ('Harqueterwife')
Spreading, large-flowered bush rose. Bears fragrant, pointed, fully double, rosy salmon-pink flowers, 9cm (3½in) across, in summer-autumn. Leaves are glossy, reddish and abundant. H and S 75cm (30in).

R. 'Silver Jubilee'
Dense, upright, large-flowered bush rose. Bears slightly scented, pointed, fully double, soft salmon-pink flowers, 12cm (5in) across, very freely in summer-autumn. Foliage is abundant and glossy. H 1.1m (3½ft), S 75cm (2½ft).

R. KEEPSAKE ('Kormalda')
Neat, bushy, large-flowered bush rose with plentiful, glossy leaves. Slightly scented, rounded, fully double, pink flowers, 12cm (5in) across, are freely produced in summer-autumn. H 75cm (30in), S 60cm (24in).

R. DOUBLE DELIGHT ('Andeli')
Large-flowered bush rose of upright, uneven growth. Fragrant, rounded, fully double flowers, 12cm (5in) across, are creamy-white, edged with red, and are borne in summer-autumn. H 1m (3ft), S 60cm (2ft).

PINK–RED

R. ESCAPADE ('Harpade')
Dense, cluster-flowered bush rose. Fragrant, cupped, semi-double, rose-violet flowers, 8cm (3in) across, with white eyes, are borne in sprays in summer-autumn. Foliage is light green and glossy. H 75cm (30in), S 60cm (24in).

R. ANNA FORD ('Harpiccolo')
Dwarf cluster-flowered bush rose. Has urn-shaped (opening flat), double, orange-red flowers, 4cm (1½in) across, borne in summer-autumn, and many small, dark green leaves. H 45cm (18in), S 38cm (15in).

R. TRUMPETER ('Mactru')
Neat, bushy, cluster-flowered bush rose with many cupped, fully double, bright red flowers, 6cm (2½in) across, in summer-autumn. Leaves are deep green and semi-glossy. H 60cm (24in), S 50cm (20in).

RED

***R.* Royal William ('Korzaun')**
Vigorous, large-flowered bush rose with large, dark green leaves. Slightly scented, pointed, fully double, deep crimson flowers, 12cm (5in) across, are carried on long stems in summer-autumn. H 1m (3ft), S 75cm (2½ft).

***R.* 'Precious Platinum'**
Vigorous, large-flowered bush rose with abundant, glossy leaves. Bears slightly scented, rounded, fully double, deep crimson-scarlet flowers, 10cm (4in) across, in summer-autumn. H 1m (3ft), S 60cm (2ft).

***R.* Alexander ('Harlex')**
Vigorous, upright, large-flowered bush rose with abundant, dark green foliage. Slightly scented, pointed, double, bright red flowers, 12cm (5in) across, are borne on long stems in summer-autumn. H 1.5m (5ft), S 75cm (2½ft).

***R.* Wee Jock ('Cocabest')**
Dense, bushy, dwarf cluster-flowered bush rose. Bears rosette, fully double, crimson flowers, 4cm (1½in) across, in summer-autumn. Plentiful leaves are small and dark green. H and S 45cm (18in).

***R.* The Times Rose ('Korpeahn')**
Spreading, cluster-flowered bush rose. Slightly scented, cupped, double, deep crimson flowers, 8cm (3in) across, are borne in wide clusters in summer-autumn. Foliage is dark green and plentiful. H 60cm (24in), S 75cm (30in).

***R.* Alec's Red ('Cored')**
Vigorous, large-flowered bush rose bearing strongly fragrant, deep cherry-red flowers that are pointed and fully double, 15cm (6in) across, in summer-autumn. H 1m (3ft), S 60cm (2ft).

YELLOW

***R.* Champagne Cocktail ('Horflash')**
Upright, cluster-flowered bush rose. Fragrant, cupped, double, yellow-pink flowers, 9cm (3½in) across, opening wide, are borne in summer-autumn. H 1m (3ft), S 60cm (2ft).

***R.* Peace ('Madame A. Meilland')**
Vigorous, shrubby, large-flowered bush rose with scented, pointed to rounded, fully double flowers, 15cm (6in) across, borne freely in clusters in summer-autumn. Has abundant, large, glossy foliage. H 1.2m (4ft), S 1m (3ft).

***R.* Golden Penny ('Rugul')**
Compact, dense, dwarf cluster-flowered bush rose with cupped to flat, double, yellow flowers, 5cm (2in) across, that are borne in summer-autumn, and rich green leaves. H 30cm (12in), S 40cm (16in).

***R.* 'Grandpa Dickson'**
Neat, upright, large-flowered bush rose with sparse, pale, glossy foliage. Bears many slightly scented, pointed, fully double, light yellow flowers, 18cm (7in) across, in summer-autumn. H 80cm (30in), S 60cm (24in).

***R.* Simba ('Korbelma')**
Upright, large-flowered bush rose with lightly fragrant, urn-shaped, fully double, yellow flowers, 9cm (3½in) across, borne freely in summer-autumn. Leaves are large and dark green. H 75cm (30in), S 60cm (24in).

***R.* Mountbatten ('Harmantelle')**
Shrubby, cluster-flowered bush rose with disease-resistant foliage. Bears scented, rounded, fully double, yellow flowers, 10cm (4in) across, singly or in clusters, in summer-autumn. H 1.2m (4ft), S 75cm (2½ft).

***R.* 'Korresia'**
Bushy, upright, cluster-flowered bush rose. Bears open sprays of strongly scented, urn-shaped, double flowers, 8cm (3in) across, with waved, yellow petals, in summer-autumn. H 75cm (30in), S 60cm (24in).

***R.* Bright Smile ('Dicdance')**
Low, bushy, cluster-flowered bush rose with bright, glossy leaves. Bears clusters of slightly scented, flat, semi-double, yellow flowers, 8cm (3in) across, in summer-autumn. H and S 45cm (18in).

***R.* Freedom ('Dicjem')**
Neat, large-flowered bush rose, with many shoots and abundant, glossy foliage. Bears many lightly scented, rounded, double, bright yellow flowers, 9cm (3½in) across, in summer-autumn. H 75cm (30in), S 60cm (24in).

***R.* 'Glenfiddich'**
Upright, cluster-flowered bush rose. Slightly fragrant, urn-shaped, double, amber-yellow flowers, 10cm (4in) across, are borne singly or in clusters in summer-autumn. H 75cm (30in), S 60cm (24in).

***R.* Amber Queen ('Harroony')**
Spreading, cluster-flowered bush rose. Amber flowers are fragrant, rounded and fully double, 8cm (3in) across, and are borne in summer-autumn. Has abundant, reddish foliage. H and S 50cm (20in).

YELLOW–ORANGE

***R.* Pot o' Gold ('Dicdivine')**
Large-flowered bush rose of neat, even growth. Fragrant, rounded, fully double, golden-yellow flowers, 9cm (3½in) across, are carried singly or in wide sprays in summer-autumn. H 75cm (30in), S 60cm (24in).

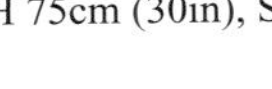

***R.* 'Southampton'**
Upright, cluster-flowered bush rose. Bears fragrant, pointed, double, apricot flowers, 8cm (3in) across, singly or in clusters in summer-autumn. Foliage is glossy and disease-resistant. H 1m (3ft), S 60cm (2ft).

***R.* Anne Harkness ('Harkaramel')**
Upright, cluster-flowered bush rose. Urn-shaped, double, amber flowers, 8cm (3in) across, are borne in sprays of many blooms in late summer and autumn. H 1.2m (4ft), S 60cm (2ft).

***R.* Sweet Magic ('Dicmagic')**
Bushy, dwarf cluster-flowered bush rose. Bears sprays of lightly fragrant, urn-shaped, double, pink-flushed, golden-orange flowers, 4cm (1½in) across, in summer-autumn. H 38cm (15in), S 30cm (12in).

***R.* 'Doris Tysterman'**
Vigorous, upright, large-flowered bush rose with lightly scented, pointed, fully double, orange-red flowers, 10cm (4in) across, borne in summer-autumn. Leaves are large, glossy and dark green. H 1.2m (4ft), S 75cm (2½ft).

***R.* Remember Me ('Cocdestin')**
Vigorous, dense, large-flowered bush rose with pointed, fully double, copper-orange flowers, 9cm (3½in) across, freely borne in summer-autumn. Leaves are abundant and glossy. H 1m (3ft), S 75cm (2½ft).

***R.* Troika ('Poumidor')**
Vigorous, dense, large-flowered bush rose with semi-glossy leaves. Fragrant, pointed, double flowers, 15cm (6in) across, are orange-red, tinged with pink, and are borne in summer-autumn. H 1m (3ft), S 75cm (2½ft).

***R.* Piccadilly ('Macar')**
Vigorous, bushy, large-flowered bush rose with pointed, double, red and yellow flowers, 12cm (5in) across, produced freely singly or in clusters in summer-autumn. Abundant foliage is reddish and glossy. H 1m (3ft), S 60cm (2ft).

***R.* 'Just Joey'**
Branching, open, large-flowered bush rose with leathery, dark green foliage. Bears rounded, fully double flowers, 12cm (5in) across, with waved, copper-pink petals and some scent, in summer-autumn. H 75cm (30in), S 60cm (24in).

WHITE–PINK

***R.* Snowball (‘Macangeli’)**
Compact, creeping, miniature bush rose with pompon, fully double, white flowers, 2.5cm (1in) across, that are borne in summer-autumn. Leaves are small, glossy and plentiful. H 20cm (8in), S 30cm (12in).

***R.* ‘Stacey Sue’**
Spreading, miniature bush rose with plentiful, dark green foliage and rosette, fully double, pink flowers, 2.5cm (1in) across, that are borne freely in summer-autumn. H and S 38cm (15in).

***R.* Baby Masquerade (‘Tanba’)**
Dense, miniature bush rose with plentiful, leathery foliage and clusters of rosette, double, yellow-pink flowers, 2.5cm (1in) across, in summer-autumn. H and S 40cm (16in), more if not pruned.

***R.* Angela Rippon (‘Ocaru’)**
Miniature bush rose with slightly fragrant, urn-shaped, fully double, salmon-pink flowers, 4cm (1½in) across, in summer-autumn, and many small, dark green leaves. H 45cm (18in), S 30cm (12in).

***R.* ‘Hula Girl’**
Wide, bushy, miniature bush rose with glossy, dark green foliage. Slightly scented, urn-shaped, fully double, salmon-orange flowers, 2.5cm (1in) across, are produced freely in summer-autumn. H 45cm (18in), S 40cm (16in).

RED

***R.* Sheri Anne (‘Morsherry’)**
Upright, miniature bush rose with glossy, leathery foliage. Slightly scented, rosette, double, light red flowers, 2.5cm (1in) across, are borne in summer-autumn. H 45cm (18in), S 30 cm (12in).

***R.* ‘Fire Princess’**
Upright, miniature bush rose with small, glossy leaves. Bears sprays of rosette, fully double, scarlet flowers, 4cm (1½in) across, in summer-autumn. H 45cm (18in), S 30cm (12in).

***R.* Red Ace (‘Amruda’)**
Compact, miniature bush rose with rosette, double, dark red flowers, 4cm (1½in) across, borne in summer-autumn. H 35cm (14in), S 30cm (12in).

RED–ORANGE

R. Orange Sunblaze ('Meijikitar')
Compact, miniature bush rose. Rosette, fully double, bright orange-red flowers, 4cm (1½in) across, are freely produced in summer-autumn. Has plentiful, dark green leaves. H and S 30cm (12in).

R. 'Rise 'n' Shine'
Bushy, upright, miniature bush rose with dark green leaves that bears rosette, fully double, yellow flowers, 2.5cm (1in) across, in summer-autumn. H 40cm (16in), S 25cm (10in).

R. Colibre '79 ('Meidanover')
Upright, rather open, miniature bush rose. Urn-shaped, double, red-veined, orange flowers, 4cm (1½in) across, are borne in summer-autumn. H 38cm (15in), S 25cm (10in).

ROSES climbing

WHITE

R. 'Albéric Barbier'
Vigorous, semi-evergreen rambler rose. Slightly fragrant, rosette, fully double, creamy-white flowers, 8cm (3in) across, appear in clusters in summer. Leaves are small and bright green. Tolerates a north-facing wall. H to 5m (15ft), S 3m (10ft).

R. 'Paul's Lemon Pillar'
Stiff, upright climbing rose with large leaves and scented, pointed to rounded, fully double, lemon-white flowers, 15cm (6in) across, that appear in summer. Prefers a sunny, sheltered wall. H 5m (15ft), S 3m (10ft).

R. filipes 'Kiftsgate'
Rampant climbing rose with abundant, glossy, light green foliage. Cupped to flat, single, creamy-white flowers, 2.5cm (1in) across, appear in late summer in spectacular clusters. Use to grow up a tree or in a wild garden. H and S 10m (30ft) or more.

R. 'Félicité Perpétue'
Sempervirens climbing rose with long, slender stems. Clusters of rosette, fully double, blush-pink to white flowers, 4cm (1½in) across, appear in midsummer. Small leaves are semievergreen. Prune spent wood only. H 5m (15ft), S 4m (12ft).

R. 'Madame Alfred Carrière'
Noisette climbing rose with slender, smooth stems. Very fragrant, rounded, double flowers are creamy-white, tinged pink, 4cm (1½in) across, and are borne in summer-autumn. H to 5.5m (18ft), S 3m (10ft).

R. 'Gloire de Dijon'
Stiffly branched Noisette or climbing Tea rose. Fragrant, quartered-rosette, fully double, creamy-buff flowers, 10cm (4in) across, are borne in summer-autumn. H 4m (12ft), S 2.5m (8ft).

R. 'New Dawn'
Vigorous, very hardy climbing rose. Fragrant, cupped, double, pale pearl-pink flowers, 8cm (3in) across, are borne in clusters in summer-autumn. Tolerates a north-facing wall. H and S 5m (15ft).

R. Breath of Life ('Harquanne')
Stiff, upright climbing rose with large, lightly scented, rounded, fully double, pinkish-apricot flowers, 10cm (4in) across, borne in summer-autumn. Leaves are semi-glossy. H 2.8m (9ft), S 2.2m (7ft).

R. 'Albertine'
Vigorous rambler rose with arching, thorny, reddish stems. Scented, cup-shaped, fully double, salmon-pink flowers, 8cm (3in) across, are borne in abundant clusters in summer. Is prone to mildew in a dry site. H to 5m (15ft), S 3m (10ft).

R. Handel ('Macha')
Stiff, upright climbing rose. Slightly scented, urn-shaped, double flowers, 8cm (3in) across, are cream, edged with pinkish-red, and produced in clusters in summer-autumn. Has glossy, dark green foliage. H 3m (10ft), S 2.2m (7ft).

R. 'Chaplin's Pink Companion'
Vigorous climbing rose with glossy, dark green foliage and slightly scented, rounded, double, light pink flowers, 5cm (2in) across, borne freely in large clusters in summer. H and S 3m (10ft).

R. 'Madame Grégoire Staechelin'
Vigorous, arching climbing rose with large clusters of blooms in summer. Bears rounded to cupped, fully double flowers, 13cm (5in) across, with ruffled, clear pink petals, shaded carmine. H to 6m (20ft), S to 4m (12ft).

R. 'Pink Perpétué'
Stiffly branched climbing rose that may be pruned to grow as a shrub. Bears clusters of cupped to rosette, double, deep pink flowers, 8cm (3in) across, in summer-autumn. Leathery foliage is plentiful. H 2.8m (9ft), S 2.5m (8ft).

R. 'Zéphirine Drouhin'
(Thornless rose)
Lax, arching Bourbon rose that will climb if supported. Bears fragrant, cupped, double, deep pink flowers, 8cm (3in) across, in summer-autumn. Is prone to mildew. May be grown as a hedge. H to 2.5m (8ft), S to 2m (6ft).

R. 'Rosy Mantle'
Stiff, open-branched climbing rose. Very fragrant, pointed, fully double, rose-pink flowers, 10cm (4in) across, are borne in summer-autumn. Dark green foliage is rather sparse. H 2.5m (8ft), S 2m (6ft).

WHITE–PINK

***R.* 'Rambling Rector'**
Rampant rambler rose. Clusters of scented, cupped to flat, semi-double, creamy-white flowers, 4cm (1½in) across, with golden stamens, appear in summer, followed by red hips. Arching stems are covered in greyish-green foliage. H and S 6m (20ft).

***R.* HIGH HOPES ('Haryup')**
Vigorous, upright and arching, long-stemmed climbing rose. Scented, urn-shaped to rounded, double, light pink flowers, 8cm (3in) across, are freely borne in summer-autumn. Has purplish green foliage. Good for high walls and pergolas. H 4m (12ft), S 2.2m (7ft).

***R.* CITY GIRL ('Harzorba')**
Vigorous, free-branching climbing rose. Abundant, glossy, dark green leaves are borne on arching stems. Scented, semi-double, saucer-shaped, salmon-pink flowers, 11cm (4½in) across, appear in summer-autumn. H and S 2.2m (7ft).

***R.* 'Compassion'**
Upright, free-branching climbing rose with glossy, dark leaves on reddish stems. Fragrant, rounded, double, pink-tinted, salmon-apricot flowers, 10cm (4in) across, are borne in summer-autumn. H 3m (10ft), S 2.5m (8ft).

***R.* 'Aloha'**
Strong-growing, bushy climbing rose. Fragrant, cupped, fully double, rose- and salmon-pink flowers, 9cm (3½in) across, appear in summer-autumn. Leaves are leathery and dark green. May be grown as a shrub. H and S 2.5m (8ft).

RED

***R.* 'Danse du Feu'**
Vigorous, stiffly branched climbing rose with abundant, glossy foliage. Bears rounded, double, scarlet flowers, 8cm (3in) across, in summer-autumn. H and S 2.5m (8ft).

***R.* 'Dortmund'**
Upright climbing rose that may be pruned to make a shrub. Flat, single, red flowers, 10cm (4in) across, with white eyes and a slight scent, are borne freely in clusters in summer-autumn. Has healthy, dark green foliage. H 3m (10ft), S 1.8m (6ft).

***R.* DUBLIN BAY ('Macdub')**
Dense, shrubby climbing rose that may be pruned to grow as a shrub. Bears clusters of cupped, double, bright crimson flowers, 10cm (4in) across, in summer-autumn. Foliage is glossy, dark green and plentiful. H and S 2.2m (7ft).

***R.* 'Sympathie'**
Vigorous, free-branching climbing rose. Slightly scented, cupped, fully double, bright deep red flowers, 8cm (3in) across, are borne in summer-autumn, usually in clusters. Has plentiful, glossy, dark green foliage. H 3m (10ft), S 2.5m (8ft).

RED–YELLOW

***R.* 'Guinée'**
Vigorous, stiffly branched climbing rose. Fragrant, cupped, fully double, blackish-red to maroon flowers, 11cm (4½in) across, are borne in summer. Leaves are large and leathery. H 5m (15ft), S 2.2m (7ft).

***R.* 'Emily Gray'**
Semi-evergreen rambler rose with long, lax stems. Small trusses of slightly fragrant, cupped, fully double, butter-yellow flowers, 5cm (2in) across, appear in summer. Leaves are lustrous, dark green. Is prone to mildew. H 5m (15ft), S 3m (10ft).

***R.* 'Veilchenblau'**
Vigorous rambler rose. Rosette, double, violet flowers, streaked white, 2.5cm (1in) across, have a fruity scent and appear in clusters in summer. H 4m (12ft), S 2.2m (7ft).

***R.* Casino ('Macca')**
Upright, free-branching climbing rose. Sparse, dark green leaves appear on stiffly arching stems. Rounded, double, fragrant, yellow flowers, 9cm (3½in) across, are borne in summer-autumn. H 3m (10ft), S 2.2m (7ft).

***R.* 'Mermaid'**
Slow-growing climbing rose that produces flat, single, primrose-yellow flowers, 12cm (5in) across, in summer-autumn. Has stiff, reddish stems, large, hooked thorns and glossy, dark green leaves. Prefers a sunny, sheltered wall. H and S to 6m (20ft).

***R.* 'Golden Showers'**
Stiff, upright climbing rose that may be pruned to grow as a shrub. In summer-autumn produces many fragrant, pointed, double, yellow flowers, 10cm (4in) across, that open flat. H 2m (6ft), S 2.2m (7ft) or more.

YELLOW

***R.* Laura Ford ('Chewarvel')**
Upright, stiffly branching climbing rose with small, dark, glossy leaves. Sprays of scented, urn-shaped to flat, yellow flowers, 4.5cm (1¾in) across, appear in summer-autumn. Good for pillars. H 2.2m (7ft), S 1.2m (4ft).

***R. banksiae* 'Lutea'**
(Yellow banksian)
Vigorous climbing rose bearing clusters of many scentless, rosette, fully double, yellow flowers, 2cm (¾in) across, in late spring. Needs a sunny, sheltered wall and pruning of spent wood only. H and S to 10m (30ft).

***R.* 'Maigold'**
Vigorous climbing rose with prickly, arching stems that may be pruned to grow as shrub. Fragrant, cupped, semi-double, bronze-yellow flowers, 10cm (4in) across, are borne freely in early summer and sparsely in autumn. H and S 2.5m (8ft).

Climbers

Climbers

One of the most versatile of plant groups, climbers are able to spread fast and trail decoratively over or through other plants and buildings, as well as across the ground, offering enormous scope for imaginative design.

What are climbers?

Most climbers are woody, evergreen or deciduous plants, while a few are herbaceous perennials or annuals that die back with the onset of winter. They have one of several methods of climbing. They can be self-clinging or twining (with or without tendrils), or scandent, scrambling species that do not cling. It is important to identify the type, since this dictates which method of support is most appropriate.

Self-clingers such as Virginia creeper (*Parthenocissus quinquefolia*) climb by means of adhesive pads or, as in the case of ivies (*Hedera*) and the Swiss cheese plant (*Monstera deliciosa*), by aerial roots which attach themselves to any surface offering purchase such as tree trunks, cliff faces, walls and stout fences. In contrast, twiners such as wisteria draw themselves up by encircling their support, while passion flowers (*Passiflora*) secure their stems with coiling tendrils. Both these types require the support of tree branches, or a system of wires, mesh or trellis if they are wall-trained. Self-clinging and twining climbers need initial guidance to the support but are self-supporting once established.

Scandent, scrambling plants such as winter jasmine (*Jasminum nudiflorum*) attach themselves loosely, if at all, by threading long, flexible stems through those of a host plant or by mounding their new stems over those made in previous seasons. Their stems must be tied in to their support throughout their life, but in more naturalistic plantings they can be allowed to cascade over walls or tumble down banks as they do in the wild.

Wisteria arch
A sturdy arch forms the ideal support for training climbers, such as *Wisteria sinensis,* since it displays the pendent flowers to perfection. When grown around a window, as shown here, the subtle scent of the fragrant flowers can be appreciated both indoors and out.

Ornamental features

Climbing plants provide a range of foliage forms, from the fine-textured, divided leaves of *Tropaeolum speciosum* to the sculptural, heart-shaped ones of *Actinidia deliciosa*. Leaf surfaces alone provide limitless possibilities for interesting textural contrasts, from the softly downy *Vitis vinifera* to the highly glossy ivies (*Hedera* cultivars). The colour range includes the golden-hued *Humulus lupulus* 'Aureus' to the deep green of many jasmines, as well as the intense purple tints of plants such as *Vitis vinifera* 'Purpurea'. Many have such attractive foliage that they make beautiful specimens in their own right – among them *Actinidia kolomikta*, with its green leaves splashed with cream and pink, or the subtle, silver-veined *Parthenocissus henryana*. Some, most notably species of parthenocissus and vitis, reserve their particularly brilliant foliage displays until the autumn. In winter, the architectural forms of twiners such as wisteria come into their own.

Climbers bear some of the most beautiful flowers – as shown by the intricate blooms of the passifloras and the elegant chains of wisteria – and many, especially the honeysuckles (*Lonicera*), sweet peas (*Lathyrus odoratus*) and jasmines, have fragrances that pervade the air over some distance. The flower colours of climbers span the spectrum from the creamy whites of *Schizophragma*

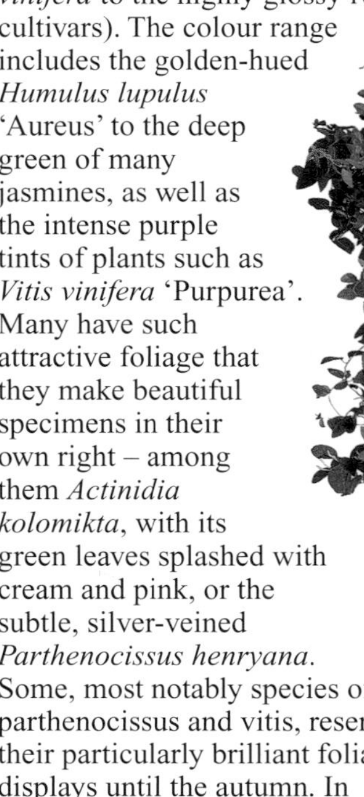

Fragrant pot
Graceful climbers such as this honeysuckle *(Lonicera)* lend elegance and fragrance to a patio. For stability, plant in a terracotta or stoneware container in a heavy, loam-based compost.

integrifolium* and *Hydrangea petiolaris* to the vivid magentas of bougainvillea and sombre, chocolate-maroon of *Rhodochiton atrosanguineus*. With many climbers their season is further prolonged by decorative, silky seed heads, as in clematis, or striking berries, notably the oblong, purple fruits of *Billardiera longiflora* and the orange-yellow fruits of *Celastrus orbiculatus* that split when ripe to reveal bright red seeds.

Designing with climbers

Growing climbers vertically to create a backdrop to other, lower, foreground plantings is one of the most obvious ways of providing height in a design, although climbers can be used in a variety of other imaginative ways. Grown on free-standing supports,they can form living screens to provide privacy and wind-filtering shelter, or visual and physical barriers between areas in the garden. If grown through trees or on pillars and pyramids, climbers can form a splendid focal point, and on arches they can provide a frame for a vista. On pergolas, climbers act as a shade-forming element, linking different parts of the garden, and if you use a scented plant to clothe an arbour, it can provide both fragrance and seclusion for quiet contemplation.

When covering walls or buildings, climbers can complement the warmth of brick or stone walls or soften their hard lines, while the most vigorous are indispensable for camouflaging unsightly garden structures. If unsupported, many climbers trail along the ground and, when pegged at the nodes, will root to develop a dense carpet of ground cover. Such a strongly horizontal design element draws the eye into a scheme.

Some climbers look very effective when scrambling through other plants, which must be matched carefully for vigour and pruning requirements. This extends their season of interest if they flower before or after the host plant, but you can achieve attractive associations of colour and texture when they flower simultaneously.

Spectacular flowers
Above: This passion flower *(Passiflora caerulea* 'Constance Elliot') produces exquisite blooms. To display them attractively, support these plants against trellis or wires fitted to a wall or fence.

Pretty climber
Left: Here, the self-clinging *Hydrangea petiolaris* clothes a wall, forming a superb backdrop for foreground plantings while framing a view to the garden beyond.

Autumn display
Below: The tendril-climbing ornamental vine, *Vitis coignetiae*, is perfect for wall-training and equally suited to pergolas and arches. Reaching some 15m (50ft) in height, its splendid autumn colour is spectacular *en masse*.

WHITE–PINK

Beaumontia grandiflora
(Herald's trumpet)
Vigorous, evergreen, woody-stemmed, twining climber with rich green leaves that are hairy beneath. Has large, fragrant, white flowers from late spring to summer. H 8m (25ft). Min. 7–10°C (45–50°F).

Decumaria sinensis
Evergreen, woody-stemmed, root climber with oval, often toothed leaves, 2.5–8cm (1–3in) long. Conical clusters of small, honey-scented, cream flowers are produced in late spring and early summer. H to 2m (6ft) or more.

Stephanotis floribunda
(Madagascar jasmine, Wax flower)
Moderately vigorous, evergreen, woody-stemmed, twining climber with leathery, glossy leaves. Scented, waxy, white flowers appear in small clusters from spring to autumn. H 5m (15ft) or more. Min. 13–16°C (55–61°F).

Clianthus puniceus f. ***albus***
Evergreen or semi-evergreen, woody-stemmed, scrambling climber, grown for its drooping clusters of claw-like, creamy-white flowers that open in spring and early summer. Mid-green leaves consist of many small leaflets. H 4m (12ft).

Ercilla volubilis
Evergreen, root climber with oval to heart-shaped, mid-green leaves, 2.5–5cm (1–2in) long. Spikes of petalless flowers, each consisting of 5 greenish or purple sepals and 6–8 white stamens, are borne in spring. H to 10m (30ft) or more.

PINK–RED

Mandevilla splendens
Evergreen, woody-stemmed, twining climber. Has lustrous leaves and trumpet-shaped, rose-pink flowers, with yellow centres, appearing in late spring or early summer. H 3m (10ft). Min. 7–10°C (45–50°F).

Clianthus puniceus (Parrot's bill)
Evergreen or semi-evergreen, woody-stemmed, scrambling climber with leaves composed of many leaflets. In spring and early summer bears drooping clusters of unusual, claw-like, brilliant red flowers. H 4m (12ft).

Distictis buccinatoria
(Mexican blood flower)
Vigorous, evergreen, woody-stemmed, tendril climber. Has trumpet-shaped, rose-crimson flowers, orange-yellow within, from early spring to summer. H to 5m (15ft) or more. Min. 5°C (41°F).

Kennedia rubicunda
(Dusky coral pea)
Fast-growing, evergreen, woody-stemmed, twining climber with leaves divided into 3 leaflets. Coral-red flowers are borne in small trusses in spring-summer. H to 3m (10ft). Min. 5–7°C (41–5°F).

Agapetes serpens
Evergreen, arching to pendulous, scandent shrub, best grown with support as a perennial climber. Has small, lance-shaped, lustrous leaves and pendent flowers, rose-red with darker veins, in spring. H 2–3m (6–10ft). Min. 5°C (41°F).

Akebia quinata (Chocolate vine)
Woody-stemmed, twining climber, semi-evergreen in mild winters or warm areas, with leaves of 5 leaflets. Vanilla-scented, brownish-purple flowers appear in late spring, followed by sausage-shaped, purplish fruits. H 10m (30ft) or more.

Passiflora coccinea
(Red passion flower)
Vigorous, evergreen, woody-stemmed, tendril climber with rounded, oblong leaves. Has bright deep scarlet flowers, with red, pink and white crowns, from spring to autumn. H 3–4m (10–12ft). Min. 15°C (59°F).

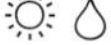

Mitraria coccinea
Evergreen, woody-stemmed, scrambling climber with oval, toothed leaves. Small, tubular, orange-red flowers are borne singly in leaf axils during late spring to summer. H to 2m (6ft).

Hoya macgillivrayi
Strong-growing, twining climber with thick stems and lustrous, dark green leaves. From spring to summer, bears large, cup-shaped, red-purple, purple or brownish-red flowers, with dark red, occasionally white-centred coronas. H 5–8m (15–25ft). Min. 7°C (45°F).

Clytostoma callistegioides
Fast-growing, evergreen, woody-stemmed, tendril climber. Each leaf has 2 oval leaflets and a tendril. Small, nodding clusters of purple-veined, lavender flowers, fading to pale pink, are borne in spring-summer. H to 5m (15ft). Min. 10–13°C (50–55°F).

Tropaeolum tricolorum
Herbaceous climber with delicate stems, small tubers and 5–7-lobed leaves. Small, orange or yellow flowers with black-tipped, reddish- orange calyces are borne from early spring to early summer. H to 1m (3ft). Min. 5°C (41°F).

Manettia luteorubra
(Brazilian firecracker)
Fast-growing, evergreen, semi-woody-stemmed, twining climber with glossy leaves. Has small, funnel-shaped, red flowers, with yellow tips, in spring-summer. H 2m (6ft). Min. 5°C (41°F).

Akebia × pentaphylla
Mainly deciduous, woody-stemmed, twining climber. Mid-green leaves, bronze-tinted when young, have 3 or 5 oval leaflets. Pendent racemes of small, 3-petalled, purple flowers (female at base, male at apex) are borne in spring. H to 10m (30ft).

Holboellia coriacea
Evergreen, twining climber with glossy, green leaves. Clusters of tiny, mauve, male flowers and, lower down stems, larger, purple-tinged, green-white female flowers are borne in spring, followed by sausage-shaped, purple fruits. H to 7m (22ft) or more.

PURPLE–BLUE

Ipomoea indica
(Blue dawn flower)
Vigorous, perennial climber with evergreen, mid-green leaves. From late spring to autumn bears abundant, funnel-shaped, rich purple-blue to blue flowers, often maturing to purplish-red. H 6m (20ft) or more. Min. 7°C (45°F).

Hardenbergia comptoniana
Evergreen, woody-stemmed, twining climber with leaves of 3 or 5 lance-shaped leaflets. Has racemes of pea-like, deep purple-blue flowers in spring. H to 2.5m (8ft).

Petrea volubilis
Strong-growing, evergreen, woody-stemmed, twining climber with elliptic, rough-textured leaves and deep violet and lilac-blue flowers carried in simple or branched spikes from late winter to late summer. H 6m (20ft) or more. Min. 13–15°C (55–9°F).

***Hardenbergia violacea* 'Happy Wanderer'**
Evergreen, woody-stemmed, twining climber. In spring, bears pendent panicles of deep mauve-purple flowers, with yellow marks on upper petals. H to 3m (10ft). Min. 7°C (45°F).

Solanum seaforthianum
(Italian jasmine, St Vincent lilac)
Evergreen, scrambling climber with nodding clusters of star-shaped, blue, purple, pink, or white flowers, with yellow stamens, from spring to autumn, followed by scarlet berries. H 2–3m (6–10ft). Min. 7°C (45°F).

Sollya heterophylla
Evergreen, woody-based, twining climber with narrowly lance-shaped to oval leaves, 2–6cm (¾-2½in) long. Nodding clusters of 4–9 broadly bell-shaped, sky-blue flowers are carried from spring to autumn. H to 3m (10ft).

GREEN–YELLOW

Strongylodon macrobotrys
(Jade vine)
Fast-growing, evergreen, woody-stemmed, twining climber with claw-like, luminous, blue-green flowers in long, pendent spikes in winter-spring. Leaves have 3 oval, glossy leaflets. H to 20m (70ft). Min. 18°C (64°F).

***Humulus lupulus* 'Aureus'**
Herbaceous, twining climber with rough, hairy stems and toothed, yellowish leaves divided into 3 or 5 lobes. Greenish, female flower spikes are borne in pendent clusters in autumn. H to 6m (20ft).

***Tecoma capensis* 'Aurea'**
Erect, scrambling, evergreen shrub or climber with lustrous, mid- to dark green leaves. Racemes, to 15cm (6in) long, of slender, tubular, yellow flowers, to 5cm (2in) long, are borne mainly in summer. Min. 5°C (41°F).

Gelsemium sempervirens
Moderately vigorous, evergreen, twining climber with pointed, lustrous leaves. Clusters of fragrant, funnel-shaped, pale to deep yellow flowers are borne from late spring to late summer. H to 6m (20ft).

Solandra maxima (Copa de oro, Golden-chalice vine)
Strong-growing, evergreen, woody-stemmed, scrambling climber with glossy leaves. In spring-summer bears fragrant, pale yellow, later golden flowers. H 7–10m (23–30ft) or more. Min. 13–16°C (55–61°F).

YELLOW

Thunbergia mysorensis
Evergreen, woody-stemmed, twining climber. Has narrow leaves and pendent spikes of flowers with yellow tubes and recurved, reddish-brown lobes from spring to autumn. H 6m (20ft). Min. 15°C (59°F).

Jasminum mesnyi
(Primrose jasmine)
Evergreen or semi-evergreen, woody-stemmed, scrambling climber. Leaves are divided into 3 leaflets; semi-double, pale yellow flowers appear in spring. H to 3m (10ft).

WHITE

***Bougainvillea glabra* 'Snow White'**
Vigorous, evergreen or semi-evergreen, woody-stemmed, scrambling climber with rounded-oval leaves. In summer has clusters of white floral bracts with green veins. H to 5m (15ft). Min. 7–10°C (45–50°F).

***Solanum laxum* 'Album'**
Semi-evergreen, woody-stemmed, scrambling climber. Oval to lance-shaped leaves are sometimes lobed or divided into leaflets. Has star-shaped, white flowers, 2–2.5cm (¾–1in) across, in summer-autumn. H to 6m (20ft).

Trachelospermum jasminoides
(Confederate jasmine, Star jasmine)
Evergreen, woody-stemmed, twining climber with oval leaves up to 10cm (4in) long. Has very fragrant, white flowers in summer, then pairs of pods, up to 15cm (6in) long. H to 9m (28ft).

***Wisteria sinensis* 'Alba'**
Vigorous, deciduous, woody-stemmed, twining climber. Leaves are 25–30cm (10–12in) long with 11 leaflets. Has strongly scented, pea-like, white flowers in racemes, 20–30cm (8–12in) long, in early summer. H to 30m (100ft).

Araujia sericifera
(Cruel plant)
Evergreen, woody-stemmed, twining climber with leaves that are white-downy beneath. Has scented, white flowers, often striped pale maroon inside, from late summer to autumn. H to 7m (23ft).

***Wisteria floribunda* 'Alba'**
Deciduous, woody-stemmed, twining climber with leaves of 11–19 oval leaflets. Scented, pea-like, white flowers are carried in drooping racemes, up to 60cm (2ft) long, in early summer. H to 9m (28ft).

WHITE

Hydrangea petiolaris
(Climbing hydrangea)
Deciduous, woody-stemmed, root climber. Has toothed leaves and lacy heads of small, white flowers in summer, only sparingly borne on young plants. H to 15m (50ft).

Clerodendrum thomsoniae
Vigorous, evergreen, woody-stemmed, scandent shrub with oval, rich green leaves. Flowers with crimson petals and bell-shaped, pure white calyces appear in clusters in summer. H 3m (10ft) or more. Min. 16°C (61°F).

Pileostegia viburnoides
Slow-growing, evergreen, woody-stemmed, root climber. Tiny, white or cream flowers, with many prominent stamens, are borne in heads from late summer to autumn. H to 6m (20ft).

Schizophragma integrifolium
Deciduous, woody-stemmed, root climber with oval or heart-shaped leaves. In summer, white flowers are borne in flat heads up to 30cm (12in) across, marginal sterile flowers each having a large, white bract. H to 12m (40ft).

WHITE–PINK

Hoya lanceolata subsp. ***bella***
Evergreen, woody-stemmed, trailing shrub with narrowly oval, pointed leaves. In summer bears tiny, star-shaped, white flowers, with red centres, in pendulous, flattened clusters. H 45cm (18in). Min. 10–12°C (50–54°F).

Hoya australis
Moderately vigorous, evergreen, woody-stemmed, twining, root climber with fleshy, rich green leaves. Has trusses of 20–50 fragrant, star-shaped flowers, white with red-purple markings, in summer. H to 5m (15ft). Min. 15°C (59°F).

Pandorea jasminoides
(Bower vine)
Evergreen, woody-stemmed, twining climber with leaves of 5–9 leaflets. Has clusters of funnel-shaped, white flowers, with pink-flushed throats, from late winter to summer. H 5m (15ft). Min. 5°C (41°F).

Hoya carnosa (Wax plant)
Fairly vigorous, evergreen, woody-stemmed, twining, root climber. Scented, star-shaped flowers, white, fading to pink, with deep pink centres, are borne in dense trusses in summer-autumn. H to 5m (15ft) or more. Min. 5–7°C (41–5°F).

Jasminum officinale f. ***affine***
Semi-evergreen or deciduous, woody-stemmed, twining climber with leaves comprising 7 or 9 leaflets. Clusters of fragrant, 4- or 5-lobed flowers, white inside and pink outside, are borne in summer-autumn. H to 12m (40ft).

Lathyrus odoratus
'Mrs Bernard Jones'
Vigorous, annual, tendril climber with mid-green leaves. Produces large, strongly scented, wavy-edged, sugar-pink flowers, suffused white at the margins from summer to early autumn. H 2m (6ft).

Actinidia kolomikta
Deciduous, woody-stemmed, twining climber with 8–16cm (3–6in) long leaves, the upper sections often creamy-white and pink. Has small, cup-shaped, white flowers in summer, male and female on separate plants. H 4m (12ft).

***Mandevilla* x *amoena* 'Alice du Pont'**
Vigorous, evergreen, woody-stemmed, twining climber with oval, impressed leaves. Has large clusters of trumpet-shaped, glowing pink flowers in summer. H 3m (10ft). Min. 7–10°C (45–50°F).

Lathyrus grandiflorus
(Everlasting pea)
Herbaceous, tendril climber with unwinged stems and neat racemes of pink-purple and red flowers in summer. H to 1.5m (5ft).

***Lonicera* x *heckrottii* 'Gold Flame'**
Deciduous, woody-stemmed, twining climber that needs support. Leaves are oblong or oval, bluish beneath, upper ones joined into shallow cups. Scented, orange-throated, pink flowers appear in clusters in summer. H to 5m (15ft).

***Lathyrus odoratus* 'Charles Unwin'**
Vigorous, annual, tendril climber with oval, mid-green leaves. Produces large, scented, wavy-margined, soft salmon-pink flowers with cream keels, paling to salmon-tinted cream at the margins in summer and early autumn. H 2m (6ft).

Antigonon leptopus (Coral vine)
Fast-growing, evergreen, woody-stemmed, tendril climber with crinkly, pale green leaves. Has dense trusses of bright pink, sometimes red or white, flowers mainly in summer but all year in tropical conditions. H 6m (20ft). Min. 15°C (59°F).

Lophospermum erubescens
Evergreen, soft-stemmed, scandent, perennial climber, sometimes woody-stemmed, often grown as an annual. Stems and leaves are downy. Rose-pink flowers, 7cm (2¾in) long, are borne in summer-autumn. H to 3m (10ft) or more. Min. 5°C (41°F).

Ipomoea horsfalliae
Strong-growing, evergreen, woody-stemmed, twining climber. Leaves have 5–7 radiating lobes or leaflets; stalked clusters of deep rose-pink or rose-purple flowers, 6cm (2½in) long, appear from summer to winter. H 2–3m (6–10ft). Min. 7–10°C (45–50°F).

PINK–RED

Lonicera sempervirens
(Coral honeysuckle)
Evergreen or deciduous, woody-stemmed, twining climber with oval leaves, upper ones united and saucer-like. Has salmon-red to orange flowers, yellow inside, in whorls on shoot tips in summer. H to 4m (12ft).

***Bougainvillea* 'Miss Manila'**
Vigorous, mainly evergreen, woody-stemmed, scrambling climber with rounded-oval leaves. Bears clusters of pink floral bracts in summer. H to 5m (15ft). Min. 7–10°C (45–50°F).

***Bougainvillea* 'Dania'**
Vigorous, mainly evergreen, woody-stemmed, scrambling climber. Has rounded-oval, mid-green leaves and bears clusters of deep pink floral bracts in summer. H to 5m (15ft). Min. 7–10°C (45–50°F).

Lapageria rosea
(Chilean bellflower, Copihue)
Evergreen, woody-stemmed, twining climber with oblong to oval, leathery leaves. Has pendent, fleshy, pink to red flowers, 7–9cm (2¾–3½in) long, with paler flecks, from summer to late autumn. H to 5m (15ft).

Ipomoea lobata
Deciduous or semi-evergreen, twining climber with 3-lobed leaves, usually grown as an annual. One-sided racemes of small, tubular, dark red flowers fade to orange, then creamy-yellow, in summer. H to 5m (15ft).

Ipomoea quamoclit (Cypress vine)
Annual, twining climber with oval, bright green leaves cut into many thread-like segments. Slender, tubular, orange or scarlet flowers are carried in summer-autumn. H 2–4m (6–12ft).

***Lathyrus odoratus* 'Barry Dare'**
Vigorous, annual, tendril climber with ovate, mid-green leaves and large, sweetly-scented, bright orange-red, pea-flowers from summer to autumn. H 2m (6ft).

***Lonicera* × *brownii* 'Dropmore Scarlet'**
Deciduous, woody-stemmed, twining climber with oval, blue-green leaves. Small, fragrant, red flowers with orange throats are borne throughout summer. H to 4m (12ft).

Tropaeolum speciosum
(Flame creeper, Flame nasturtium)
Herbaceous, twining climber with a creeping rhizome and lobed, blue-green leaves. Bears scarlet flowers in summer, followed by bright blue fruits surrounded by deep red calyces. Roots should be in shade. H to 3m (10ft).

Quisqualis indica
(Rangoon creeper)
Fairly fast-growing, deciduous or semi-evergreen, scandent shrub, often grown as an annual. From late spring to late summer has fragrant flowers, varying from orange to red, sometimes pink. H 3–5m (10–15ft). Min. 10°C (50°F).

Rhodochiton atrosanguineus
Evergreen, leaf-stalk climber, usually grown as an annual, with toothed leaves. Has tubular, blackish-purple flowers, with bell-shaped, red-purple calyces, from late spring to late autumn. H to 3m (10ft). Min. 5°C (41°F).

Aristolochia littoralis
(Calico flower)
Fast-growing, evergreen, woody-stemmed, twining climber with heart-to kidney-shaped leaves. Heart-shaped, 12cm (5in) wide flowers, maroon with white marbling, are carried in summer. H to 7m (23ft). Min. 13°C (55°F).

Lathyrus latifolius
(Everlasting pea, Perennial pea)
Herbaceous, tendril climber with winged stems. Leaves have broad stipules and a pair of leaflets. Has small racemes of pink-purple flowers in summer and early autumn. H 2m (6ft) or more.

Schisandra rubriflora
Deciduous, woody-stemmed, twining climber with leathery, toothed leaves, paler beneath. Has small, crimson flowers in spring or early summer and drooping, red fruits in late summer. H to 6m (20ft).

Berberidopsis corallina
(Coral plant)
Evergreen, woody-stemmed, twining climber with oval to heart-shaped, leathery leaves edged with small spines. Bears pendent clusters of globular, deep red flowers in summer to early autumn. H 4.5m (14ft).

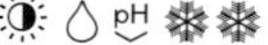

Lablab purpureus (Australian pea, Hyacinth bean, Lablab)
Deciduous, woody-stemmed, twining climber, often grown as an annual. Purple, pinkish or white flowers in summer are followed by long pods with edible seeds. H 10m (30ft). Min. 5°C (41°F).

***Bougainvillea glabra* 'Variegata'**
Vigorous, mainly evergreen, woody-stemmed, scrambling climber. Rounded-oval, dark green leaves are edged with creamy-white. Has many bright purple floral bracts in summer. H to 5m (15ft). Min. 7–10°C (45–50°F).

Clematis

C. Arctic Queen 'Evitwo'PBR ♀
(2, early large-fl.)

Among the climbers, clematis are unsurpassed in their long period of flowering (with species flowering in almost every month of the year), the variety of flower shapes and colours, and their tolerance of almost any aspect and climate. Some spring-flowering species and cultivars are vigorous and excellent for rapidly covering buildings, old trees and pergolas. Other, less rampant cultivars display often large, exquisite blooms from early summer to autumn in almost every colour. Flower colours may vary according to your climatic conditions; generally speaking, the warmer the climate, the darker the flowers are likely to be.

Clematis look attractive when trained on walls or trellises and when grown in association with other climbers, trees or shrubs, treating them as hosts. Less vigorous cultivars may also be left unsupported to scramble at ground level, where their flowers will be clearly visible.

The various types of clematis (see the Plant Dictionary) may be divided into 3 groups, each of which has different pruning requirements. Incorrect pruning may result in cutting out the stems that will produce flowers in the current season, so the following guidelines should be followed closely.

C. armandii
(1, early)

C. Alabast™ 'Poulala'(N) ♀ (2)

C. *florida* Pistachio™ 'Evirida'(N) (3, late large-fl.)

C. Gazelle™ 'Evipo014'(N)
(3, late small-fl.)

C. montana
(1, Montana)

Group 2
Early, large-flowered cultivars
Flowers are produced on short, current season's stems, so prune before new growth starts, in early spring. Remove dead or damaged stems and cut back all others to where strong, leaf-axil buds are visible. (These buds will produce the first crop of flowers.)

Current season's stems each have one flower and are 15–45cm (6–18in) long

Discarded previous season's old flower stem

Discarded previous season's leaves

Group 1
Early-flowering species, Alpina, Macropetala and Montana types
Flower stems are produced direct from the previous season's ripened stems. Prune after flowering to allow new growth to be produced and ripened for the next season. Remove dead or damaged stems and cut back other shoots that have outgrown their allotted space.

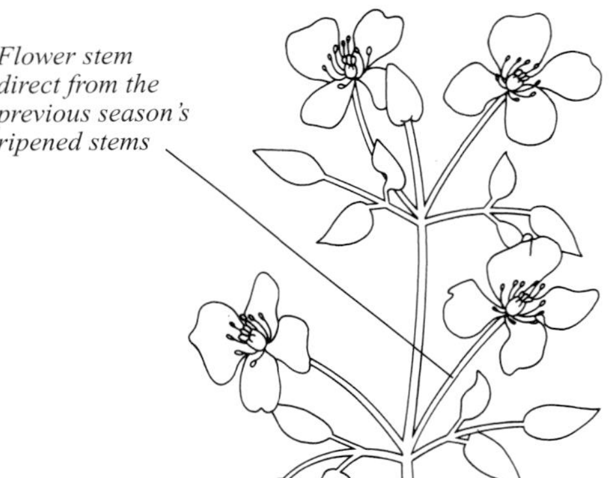

Group 3
Late, large-flowered cultivars, Late-flowering species, Small-flowered cultivars and Herbaceous types
Flowers are produced on the current season's growth only, so prune before new growth commences, in early spring. Remove all of the previous season's stems down to a pair of strong, leaf-axil buds, 15–30cm (6–12in) above the soil.

Flowering stems on current season's growth only

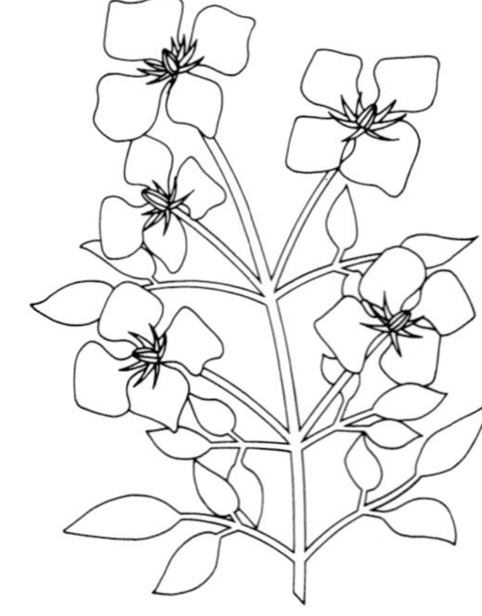

C. 'Henryi' ♀
(2, early large-fl.)

C. Hyde Hall™ 'Evipo009'(N)
(2, early large-fl.)

C. Ice Blue™ 'Evipo003'(N)
(2, early large-fl.)

C. Chantilly™ 'Evipo021'(N)
(2, early large-fl.)

C. florida var. *sieboldiana* (3, small-fl.)

C. 'Huldine' ♀ (3, late large-fl.)

C. viticella 'Purpurea Plena Elegans' ♀ (3, late-fl.)

C. Royal Velvet 'Evifour'[PBR] (2, early large-fl.)

C. 'Madame Julia Correvon' ♀ (3, late-fl.)

C. 'Markham's Pink' ♀ (1, Macrop.)

C. 'Abundance' ♀ (3, late-fl.)

C. 'Mrs George Jackman' ♀ (2, early large-fl.)

C. Peppermint™ 'Evipo005'[(N)] (3, large-fl.)

C. montana var. *rubens* ♀ (1, Montana)

C. 'Star of India' (3, late large-fl.)

C. Vino™ 'Poulvo'[(N)] (2, early large-fl.)

C. recta (3, herbaceous)

C. Viennetta™ 'Evipo006'[(N)] (3, large-fl.)

C. 'Lincoln Star' (2, early large-fl.)

C. 'Ernest Markham' ♀ (3, late large-fl.)

C. flammula (3, late-fl.)

C. 'Nelly Moser' ♀ (2, early large-fl.)

C. 'Duchess of Albany' (3, small-fl.)

C. 'Gravetye Beauty' (3, small-fl.)

C. rehderiana ♀ (3, late-fl.)

C. cirrhosa (1, early-fl.)

C. montana 'Tetrarose' ♀ (1, Montana)

C. 'Hagley Hybrid' (3, late large-fl.)

C. 'Bill MacKenzie' ♀ (3, late-fl.)

C. tangutica (3, late-fl.)

C. Blue Moon 'Evirin'[(N)] (3, late large-fl.)

C. Josephine 'Evijohill'[PBR] ♀ (2, early large-fl.)

C. Rosemoor™ 'Evipo002'[(N)] (2, early large-fl.)

C. Bourbon™ **'Evipo018'**(N)
(2, early large-fl.)

C. Anna Louise **'Evithree'**PBR 🏆
(2, early large-fl.)

C. Medley™ **'Evipo012'**(N)
(3, late small-fl.)

C. Confetti™ **'Evipo036'**(N)
(3, late small-fl.)

C. Cassis™ **'Evipo020'**(N)
(3, late large-fl.)

C. integrifolia
(3, herbaceous)

C. Avant-garde™ **'Evipo017'**(N)
(3, mid-season small-fl.)

C. **'The President'** 🏆
(2, early large-fl.)

C. Victor Hugo™
'Evipo007'(N) (3, late large-fl.)

C. Parisienne™ **'Evipo012'**(N)
(2, early medium-fl.)

C. Savannah™ **'Evipo015'**(N)
(3, late small-fl.)

C. Galore™ **'Evipo032'**(N)
(3, late small-fl.)

C. Chinook™ **'Evipo013'**(N)
(3, late small-fl.)

C. Crystal Fountain™ **'Evipo038'**(N)
(2, early large-fl.)

C. **'Elsa Spath'**
(2, early large-fl.)

C. **'Vyvyan Pennell'**
(2, early large-fl)

C. BONANZA™ 'Evipo031'(N)
(3, early to mid-season, large-fl.)

C. HARLOW CARR™ 'Evipo004'(N)
(3, herbaceous large-fl.)

C. WISLEY™ 'Evipo001'(N)
(3, mid-season, large-fl.)

C. FRANZISKA MARIA™ 'Evipo008'(N) (3, large-fl.)

C. *macropetala*
(1, Macropetala)

C. CEZANNE™ 'Evipo023'(N)
(2, mid-season, large-fl.)

C. ANGELIQUE™ 'Evipo033'(N)
(2, mid- to late, large-fl.)

C. 'Frances Rivis'
(1, Alpina)

C. 'Perle d'Azur'
(3, late large-fl.)

C. PETIT FAUCON™ 'Evisix'(N) ♀
(3, small-fl.)

C. 'Etoile Violette' ♀
(3, late-fl.)

C. *heracleifolia* 'Wyevale'
(3, herbaceous)

C. 'H. F. Young'
(2, early large-fl.)

C. CLAIR DE LUNE 'Evirin'PBR
(2, early large-fl.)

C. 'Lasurstern' ♀
(2, early large-fl.)

C. 'Ascotiensis'
(3, late large-fl.)

C. 'Jackmanii' ♀
(3, late large-fl.)

■ PURPLE

Bougainvillea glabra
Vigorous, evergreen or semi-evergreen, woody-stemmed, scrambling climber with rounded-oval leaves. Clusters of floral bracts, in shades of cyclamen-purple, appear in summer. H to 5m (15ft). Min. 7–10°C (45–50°F).

***Lathyrus odoratus* 'Lady Diana'**
Moderately fast-growing, slender, annual, tendril climber with oval, mid-green leaves. Fragrant, pale violet-blue flowers are borne from summer to early autumn. H 2m (6ft).

***Solanum crispum* 'Glasnevin'**
Vigorous, evergreen or semi-evergreen, woody-stemmed, scrambling climber with oval leaves. Has clusters of lilac to purple flowers, 2.5cm (1in) across, in summer. H to 6m (20ft).

***Passiflora × caponii* 'John Innes'**
Strong-growing, evergreen, woody-stemmed, tendril climber with 3-lobed leaves. Has bowl-shaped, nodding, white flowers, flushed claret-purple, with purple-banded, white crowns, in summer-autumn. H 8m (25ft). Min. 7–10°C (45–50°F).

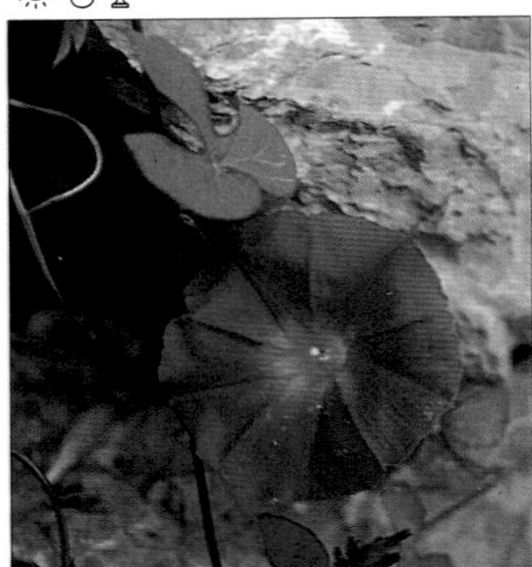

Ipomoea hederacea
(Morning glory)
Annual, twining climber with heart-shaped or 3-lobed, mid- to bright green leaves. Has funnel-shaped, red, purple, pink or blue flowers in summer to early autumn. H 3–4m (10–12ft).

Codonopsis convolvulacea
Herbaceous, twining climber with 5cm (2in) long, oval or lance-shaped leaves. Widely bell- to saucer-shaped, bluish-violet flowers, 2.5–5cm (1–2in) across, are borne in summer. H to 2m (6ft).

Cobaea scandens
(Cup-and-saucer vine)
Evergreen or deciduous, woody-stemmed, tendril climber, grown as an annual. From late summer to first frosts has flowers that open yellow-green and age to purple. H 4–5m (12–15ft). Min. 4°C (39°F).

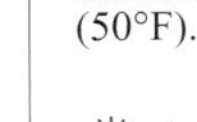

Solanum wendlandii
Robust, mainly evergreen, prickly-stemmed, scrambling climber with oblong, variably lobed leaves. Lavender flowers appear in late summer and autumn. H 3–6m (10–20ft). Min. 10°C (50°F).

Passiflora caerulea (Blue passion flower, Common passion flower)
Fast-growing, evergreen or semi-evergreen, woody-stemmed, tendril climber. Has white flowers, sometimes pink-flushed, with blue- or purple-banded crowns, in summer-autumn. H 10m (30ft).

PURPLE–BLUE

Passiflora quadrangularis (Giant granadilla)
Strong-growing, evergreen, woody-stemmed climber with angled, winged stems. White, pink, red or pale violet flowers, the crowns banded white and deep purple, appear mainly in summer. H 5–8m (15–25ft). Min. 10°C (50°F).

Wisteria × formosa
Deciduous, woody-stemmed, twining climber with leaves of 9–15 narrowly oval leaflets. Scented, pea-like, mauve and pale lilac flowers are carried in early summer in drooping racemes, 25cm (10in) long, followed by velvety pods. H to 25m (80ft) or more.

Wisteria sinensis (Chinese wisteria)
Vigorous, deciduous, woody-stemmed, twining climber. Has leaves of 11 leaflets and fragrant, lilac or pale violet flowers, in racemes 20–30cm (8–12in) long, in early summer, followed by velvety pods. H to 30m (100ft).

***Ipomoea tricolor* 'Heavenly Blue'**
Fast-growing, annual, twining climber with heart-shaped leaves and large, funnel-shaped, sky-blue flowers borne from summer to early autumn. H to 3m (10ft).

Plumbago auriculata (Cape leadwort)
Fast-growing, evergreen, woody-stemmed, scrambling climber. Trusses of sky-blue flowers are carried from summer to early winter. H 3–6m (10–20ft). Min. 7°C (45°F).

Tweedia caerulea
Herbaceous, twining climber with white-haired stems. Small, fleshy, pale blue flowers, maturing purple, appear in summer and early autumn; has green fruits to 15cm (6in) long. H to 1m (3ft). Min. 5°C (41°F).

YELLOW

Lonicera × americana
Very free-flowering, deciduous, woody-stemmed, twining climber. Leaves are oval, upper ones united and saucer-like. Has clusters of strongly fragrant, yellow flowers, flushed with red-purple, in summer. H to 7m (23ft).

***Lonicera japonica* 'Halliana'**
Evergreen or semi-evergreen, woody-stemmed, twining climber with soft-haired stems and oval, sometimes lobed, bright green leaves. Very fragrant, white flowers, ageing to pale yellow, are borne in summer and autumn. H to 10m (30ft).

***Lonicera periclymenum* 'Graham Thomas'**
Deciduous, woody-stemmed, twining climber. Oval or oblong leaves are bluish beneath; fragrant, white flowers ageing to yellow, are borne in summer. H to 7m (23ft).

YELLOW–ORANGE

***Allamanda cathartica* 'Hendersonii'**
Fast-growing, evergreen, woody-stemmed, scrambling climber. Has lance-shaped leaves in whorls and trumpet-shaped, rich bright yellow flowers in summer-autumn. H to 5m (15ft). Min. 13–15°C (55–9°F).

Thunbergia alata
(Black-eyed Susan)
Moderately fast-growing, annual, twining climber. Has toothed, oval to heart-shaped leaves and rounded, rather flat, small flowers, orange-yellow with very dark brown centres, from early summer to early autumn. H 3m (10ft).

Thladiantha dubia
Fast-growing, herbaceous or deciduous, tendril climber. Oval to heart-shaped, mid-green leaves, 10cm (4in) long, are hairy beneath; bell-shaped, yellow flowers are carried in summer. H 3m (10ft).

Stigmaphyllon ciliatum
Fast-growing, evergreen, woody-stemmed, twining climber with heart-shaped, pale green leaves fringed with hairs. Bright yellow flowers with ruffled petals appear in spring-summer. H 5m (15ft) or more. Min. 15–18°C (59–64°F).

Macfadyena unguis-cati
(Cat's claw)
Fast-growing, evergreen, woody-stemmed, tendril climber. Leaves have 2 leaflets and a tendril. Has yellow flowers, 10cm (4in) long, in late spring or early summer. H 8–10m (25–30ft). Min. 5°C (41°F).

***Tropaeolum tuberosum* var. *lineamaculatum* 'Ken Aslet'**
Herbaceous climber with yellowish, red-streaked tubers and blue-green leaves. From mid-summer to autumn has flowers with red sepals and orange petals. In cool areas, lift and store tubers in winter. H to 2.5m (8ft).

ORANGE

Bomarea caldasii
Herbaceous, twining climber with rounded clusters of 5–40 tubular to funnel-shaped, orange-red flowers, spotted crimson within, in summer. H 3–4m (10–12ft).

Eccremocarpus scaber
(Chilean glory flower, Glory vine)
Evergreen, sub-shrubby, tendril climber, often grown as an annual. In summer has racemes of small, orange-red flowers, followed by inflated fruit pods containing many winged seeds. H 2–3m (6–10ft).

Senecio confusus
(Mexican flame vine)
Evergreen, woody-stemmed, twining climber bearing clusters of daisy-like, orange-yellow flower heads, ageing to orange-red, mainly in summer. H to 3m (10ft) or more. Min. 7–10°C (45–50°F).

Lonicera* × *tellmanniana
Deciduous, woody-stemmed, twining climber with oval leaves; upper ones are joined and resemble saucers. Bright yellowish-orange flowers are carried in clusters at the ends of shoots in late spring and summer. H to 5m (15ft).

Thunbergia gregorii
Evergreen, woody-stemmed, twining climber, usually grown as an annual. Triangular-oval leaves have winged stalks. Glowing orange flowers are carried in summer. H to 3m (10ft). Min. 10°C (50°F).

Mutisia decurrens
Evergreen, tendril climber with narrowly oblong leaves, 7–13cm (2¾–5in) long. Flower heads, 10–13cm (4–5in) across with red or orange ray flowers, are produced in summer. Proves difficult to establish, but is worthwhile. H to 3m (10ft).

WHITE–RED

Fallopia baldschuanica (Mile-a-minute plant, Russian vine)
Vigorous, deciduous, woody-stemmed, twining climber with drooping panicles of pink or white flowers in summer-autumn. H 12m (40ft) or more.

***Campsis* × *tagliabuana* 'Madame Galen'**
Deciduous, woody-stemmed, root climber with leaves of 7 or more narrowly oval, toothed leaflets. Trumpet-shaped, orange-red flowers are borne in pendent clusters from late summer to autumn. H to 10m (30ft).

Passiflora manicata
Fast-growing, evergreen, woody-stemmed, tendril climber with slender, angular stems and 3-lobed leaves. Red flowers, with deep purple and white crowns, appear in summer-autumn. H 3–5m (10–15ft). Min. 7°C (45°F).

RED–PURPLE

Parthenocissus tricuspidata
(Boston ivy, Japanese ivy)
Vigorous, deciduous, woody-stemmed, tendril climber. Has spectacular, crimson, autumn leaf colour and dull blue berries. Will cover large expanses of wall. H to 20m (70ft).

***Parthenocissus tricuspidata* 'Lowii'**
Vigorous, deciduous, woody-stemmed, tendril climber with deeply cut and crinkled, 3–7-lobed leaves that turn crimson in autumn. Has insignificant flowers, followed by dull blue berries. H to 20m (70ft).

Vitis coignetiae
(Crimson glory vine)
Vigorous, deciduous, woody-stemmed, tendril climber. Large leaves, brown-haired beneath, are brightly coloured in autumn. Has tiny, pale green flowers in summer, followed by purplish-bloomed, black berries. H to 15m (50ft).

Parthenocissus thomsonii
Deciduous, woody-stemmed, tendril climber. Has glossy, green leaves with 5 leaflets that turn red-purple in autumn, and black berries. Provide some shade for best autumn colour. H to 10m (30ft).

***Vitis vinifera* 'Purpurea'**
Deciduous, woody-stemmed, tendril climber with toothed, 3- or 5-lobed, purplish leaves, white-haired when young. Has tiny, pale green flowers in summer and tiny, green or purple berries. H to 7m (23ft).

***Parthenocissus tricuspidata* 'Veitchii'**
Vigorous, deciduous, woody-stemmed, tendril climber. Has spectacular, red-purple, autumn leaf colour and dull blue berries. Greenish flowers are insignificant. H to 20m (70ft).

PURPLE–ORANGE

Billardiera longiflora
Evergreen, woody-stemmed, twining climber with narrow leaves. Small, bell-shaped, sometimes purple-tinged, green-yellow flowers are produced singly in leaf axils in summer, followed by purple-blue fruits in autumn. H to 2m (6ft).

Tropaeolum tuberosum
Herbaceous, tuberous-rooted, leaf-stalk climber. Greyish-green leaves have 3–5 lobes; from mid-summer to late autumn has cup-shaped flowers with orange-yellow petals, orange-red sepals and a long spur. H 2–3m (6–10ft).

Pyrostegia venusta (Flame flower, Flame vine, Golden shower)
Fast-growing, evergreen, woody-stemmed, tendril climber with clusters of tubular, golden-orange flowers from autumn to spring. H 10m (30ft) or more. Min. 13–15°C (55–9°F).

WHITE–ORANGE

Jasminum polyanthum
Evergreen, woody-stemmed, twining climber. Dark green leaves have 5 or 7 leaflets. Large clusters of fragrant, 5-lobed, white flowers, sometimes reddish on the outside, are carried from late summer to winter. H 3m (10ft) or more.

Agapetes variegata var. ***macrantha***
Evergreen or semi-evergreen, loose, scandent shrub that may be trained against supports. Has lance-shaped leaves and narrowly urn-shaped, white or pinkish-white flowers, patterned in red, in winter. H 1–2m (3–6ft). Min. 15–18°C (59–64°F).

Canarina canariensis
(Canary Island bellflower)
Herbaceous, tuberous, scrambling climber with triangular, serrated leaves. Has waxy, orange flowers with red veins from late autumn to spring. H 2–3m (6–10ft). Min. 7°C (45°F).

WHITE–GREEN

Asparagus scandens
Evergreen, scrambling climber with lax stems and short, curved, leaf-like shoots in whorls of 3. Tiny, nodding, white flowers appear in clusters of 2–3 in summer, followed by red berries. H 1m (3ft) or more. Min. 10°C (50°F).

***Senecio macroglossus* 'Variegatus'**
Evergreen, woody-stemmed, twining climber with triangular, fleshy leaves, bordered in white to cream, and, mainly in winter, daisy-like, cream flower heads. H 3m (10ft). Min. 7°C (45°F), but best at 10°C (50°F).

***Epipremnum aureum* 'Marble Queen'**
Fairly fast-growing, evergreen, woody-stemmed, root climber. Leaves are streaked and marbled with white. Is less robust than the species. H 3–10m (10–30ft). Min. 15–18°C (59–64°F).

***Epipremnum pictum* 'Argyraeum'** (Silver vine)
Slow-growing, evergreen, woody-stemmed, root climber. Heart-shaped leaves are dark green with silver markings. H 2–3m (6–10ft) or more. Min. 15–18°C (59–64°F).

***Syngonium podophyllum* 'Trileaf Wonder'**
Evergreen, woody-stemmed, root climber with tufted stems and arrow-head-shaped leaves when young. Mature leaves have 3 glossy leaflets with pale green or silvery-grey veins. H 2m (6ft) or more. Min. 18°C (64°F).

Dioscorea discolor
(Ornamental yam)
Evergreen, woody-stemmed, twining climber. Heart-shaped, olive-green leaves are 12–15cm (5–6in) long, marbled silver, paler green and brown, and are red beneath. H to 2m (6ft). Min. 5°C (41°F).

GREEN–ORANGE

Syngonium podophyllum
Evergreen, woody-stemmed, root climber with tufted stems and arrowhead-shaped leaves when young. Mature plants have leaves of 7–9 glossy leaflets up to 30cm (12in) long. H 2m (6ft). Min. 16–18°C (61–4°F).

Philodendron melanochrysum
Robust, fairly slow-growing, evergreen, woody-based, root climber. Heart-shaped leaves, to 75cm (30in) long, are lustrous, deep olive green with a coppery sheen and have pale veins. H 3m (10ft) or more. Min. 15–18°C (59–64°F).

Gynura aurantiaca (Velvet plant)
Evergreen, woody-based, soft-stemmed, semi-scrambling climber or lax shrub with purple-haired stems and leaves. Clusters of daisy-like, orange-yellow flower heads are borne in winter. H 2–3m (6–10ft), less as a shrub. Min. 16°C (61°F).

Tetrastigma voinierianum
(Chestnut vine)
Strong-growing, evergreen, woody-stemmed, tendril climber. Young stems and leaves are rust-coloured and hairy; mature leaves turn lustrous, deep green above. H 10m (30ft) or more. Min. 15–18°C (59–64°F).

Cissus antarctica (Kangaroo vine)
Moderately vigorous, evergreen, woody-stemmed, tendril climber. Oval, pointed, coarsely serrated leaves are lustrous, rich green. H to 5m (15ft). Min. 7°C (45°F).

Monstera deliciosa
(Swiss-cheese plant)
Robust, evergreen, woody-stemmed, root climber with large-lobed, holed leaves, 40–90cm (16–36in) long. Mature plants bear cream spathes, followed by scented, edible fruits. H to 6m (20ft). Min. 15–18°C (59–64°F).

Philodendron scandens
(Heart leaf)
Fairly fast-growing, evergreen, woody-based, root climber. Rich green leaves are 10–15cm (4–6in) long when young, to 30cm (12in) long on mature plants. H 4m (12ft) or more. Min. 15–18°C (59–64°F).

Cissus rhombifolia (Grape ivy)
Moderately vigorous, evergreen, woody-stemmed, tendril climber with lustrous leaves divided into 3 coarsely toothed leaflets. H 3m (10ft) or more. Min. 7°C (45°F).

Streptosolen jamesonii
(Marmalade bush)
Evergreen or semi-evergreen, loosely scrambling shrub. Has oval, finely corrugated leaves and, mainly in spring-summer, many bright orange flowers. H 2–3m (6–10ft). Min. 7°C (45°F).

H. helix **'Erecta'** ① 🏆

IVIES

Ivies (*Hedera*) are evergreen, climbing and trailing plants suitable for growing up walls and fences or as ground cover. Plants take a year or so to establish but thereafter growth is rapid. There is a large number of cultivars available, of which the non-variegated forms are shade tolerant. With height and access to light, the typical, ivy-shaped leaves may become less lobed. Not all ivies are fully hardy. Ivies show two distinct stages of growth. In the creeping or climbing juvenile stage, ivies have lobed leaves and minutely hairy yount shoots. In the adult stage, they produce aerial bushes with entire, usually broadly ovate leaves and, in autumn, spherical umbels of tiny, five-lobed, yellowish green, bisexual flowers. These are followed by spherical, black, sometimes orange or yellow fruits, a valuable winter food source for birds.

H. helix **'Little Diamond'** ①

H. colchica **'Dentata'** ① 🏆

H. helix **'Telecurl'** ①

H. helix **'Parsley Crested'** ①

H. helix **'Oro di Bogliasco'** ①

H. helix **'Glacier'** ① 🏆

H. helix **'Pittsburgh'** ①

H. helix **'Ivalace'** ① 🏆

H. helix **'Adam'** ① 🏆

H. helix **'Anna Marie'** ①

H. helix **'Eva'** ①

H. hibernica ①

H. nepalensis **'Suzanne'** ①

H. colchica **'Sulphur Heart'** ① 🏆

H. helix **'Nigra'** ①

H. helix **'Angularis Aurea'** ① 🏆

H. canariensis **'Ravensholst'** ① 🏆

H. pastuchovii var. *cypria*

H. helix **'Buttercup'** ① 🏆

H. helix **'Goldchild'** ① 🏆

H. helix **'Green Ripple'** ①

H. helix **'Merion Beauty'** ①

H. helix f. *poetarum* ①

H. helix **'Atropurpurea'** ①

H. helix **'Glymii'** ①

H. helix **'Heise'** ①

Perennials

Perennials

One of the largest and most versatile of plant groups, perennials offer a seasonally changing diversity of colour, fragrance, form and texture and a wealth of plants to suit every size and style of garden.

What are perennials?

Perennials are non-woody plants that live for two or more years and, when mature, produce flowers annually. In gardens, the term is also applied to woody-based sub-shrubs, like lavender or artemisia, and often encompasses the grasses and ferns. Although some perennials are evergreen, most are herbaceous and die back each autumn. While this leaves borders bare in winter, many gardeners value this characteristic because it reflects the turning of the seasons: the new growth heralds spring and anticipates the glories of the forthcoming summer.

Seed heads
Above: The sculptural forms of biennial teasels *(Dipsacus fullonum)* add height and contrast to perennials in high summer, while the seed heads that follow ensure interest well into winter.

Summer border
Right: In this mixed border, drifts of *Alstroemeria* Ligtu Hybrids lead the eye to a strong focal point formed by the architectural spikes of verbascum, which are cleverly echoed by the purple spires of *Salvia* x superba in the foreground.

Choosing perennials

All successful plantings reflect the care taken in selecting plants that suit the climate, aspect, soil type, and light levels in the garden, and this is especially true when designing with perennials. A plant that is struggling in unsuitable conditions will not fulfil its intended purpose if it fails to flower or grow well enough to fill its allotted space. The best results are usually gained by grouping plants with similar cultivation needs. Most ferns, for example, grow well in shady borders in moist, humus-rich soil, as do bamboos such as the black-stemmed *Phyllostachys nigra*, which thrive in similar soil conditions. When perennials are massed together in borders, it is vital to consider their eventual height and spread if the vigorous are not to swamp more delicate specimens.

Ornamental features

The form of perennial flowers includes strong contrasts, from the vertical spires of delphiniums or verbascums to the more horizontal shapes provided by the dense, flat flower heads of achillea. Those with arching flowers include *Polygonatum x hybridum*.

As foliage is such a large textural mass it

Contrasting foliage
Left: In damp, dappled shade, elegant contrasts of foliage form and texture create an atmosphere of lush abundance, but it is important to choose plants that thrive in similar conditions.

Colour and mood
Below: Use colour to influence the mood of a planting scheme. While red, yellow and orange suggest warmth and vitality, soft pastels and cool blues provide an air of restful charm.

Winter impact
Bottom: The strong verticals provided by the silky plumes of pampas grass *(Cortaderia selloana)* take on an added beauty when rimed by winter frost.

has great impact on a border design. Fortunately leaf forms of perennials span a vast range: from the boldly pleated foliage of veratrum to the delicate, pinnate leaves of *Polemonium caeruleum* and *Matteuccia struthiopteris*. Textural contrasts also abound: from silky *Stachys byzantina* to the glossy foliage of *Acanthus mollis*.

Designing with perennials

The traditional herbaceous border – a long rectangle flanked by smooth turf and backed by a wall or well-tended hedge – has long been used to display perennials. Its width – often 3m (10ft) or more – allows for banked effects from front to back so that small plants are not obscured by taller neighbours. While only the largest of gardens have space for such effects, the principles can be adapted to more modest plantings.

Patio planting
Pleasing arrangements of complementary colours and differing textures can be created in containers, as shown here with purple *Heuchera micrantha* var. *diversifolia* 'Palace Purple', *Houttuynia cordata* 'Chameleon' and *Tolmiea menziesii*.

Size categories used within this group		
LARGE over 1.2m (4ft)	MEDIUM 60cm–1.2m (2–4ft)	SMALL up to 60cm (2ft)

Low, ground-covering perennials such as *Cerastium tomentosum* and *Tiarella cordifolia* are ideal for the front of a border and, for greatest impact, small and medium-sized plants are best massed in odd-numbered groups. Superb effects can then be created by using single large specimens as focal points, especially those of architectural form such as *Cynara cardunculus*, *Rheum palmatum*, *Rodgersia aesculifolia* or a tall grass such as *Stipa gigantea*. Introduce variety of shape and texture by combining the rounded form of *Sedum spectabile* with the upright spires of *Kniphofia*, or the lacy foliage of dicentras with the bolder outlines of hostas.

The disadvantage of planting only herbaceous perennials is that when they fade in autumn, just bare earth will show until new growth emerges. A border mixed with shrubs to provide structure, however, and annuals, biennials and bulbs, will prolong interest.

□ WHITE

Epilobium angustifolium* f. *album
(White rosebay)
Vigorous, upright perennial bearing sprays of pure white flowers along wand-like stems in late summer. Leaves are small and lance-shaped. May spread rapidly. H 1.2–1.5m (4–5ft), S 50cm (20in) or more.

Nicotiana sylvestris
(Flowering tobacco)
Branching perennial, often grown as an annual, carrying panicles of fragrant, tubular, white flowers at the ends of stems in late summer. Has long, rough, mid-green leaves. H 1.5m (5ft), S 75cm (2½ft).

Romneya coulteri
(Tree poppy)
Vigorous, bushy, sub-shrubby perennial, grown for its large, fragrant, white flowers, with prominent centres of golden stamens, that appear in late summer. Has deeply divided, grey leaves. H and S 2m (6ft).

Crambe cordifolia
Robust perennial with clouds of small, fragrant, white flowers borne in branching sprays in summer above mounds of large, crinkled and lobed, dark green leaves. H to 2m (6ft), S 1.2m (4ft).

Eryngium eburneum
Evergreen, arching perennial bearing heads of thistle-like, green flowers with white stamens on branched stems in late summer. Has arching, spiny, grass-like leaves. H 1.5–2m (5–6ft), S 60cm (2ft).

Echinops sphaerocephalus
Massive, bushy perennial with deeply cut, mid-green leaves, pale grey beneath, and grey stems bearing round, greyish-white flower heads in late summer. H 2m (6ft), S 1m (3ft).

Eremurus himalaicus
Upright perennial with strap-shaped, basal leaves. In early summer has huge, dense racemes of open cup-shaped, pure white blooms with long stamens. Cover crowns in winter with compost or bracken. Needs staking. H 2–2.5m (6–8ft), S 1m (3ft).

Sanguisorba canadensis
(Canadian burnet)
Clump-forming perennial. In late summer bears slightly pendent spikes of bottlebrush-like, white flowers on stems that arise from toothed, divided, mid-green leaves. H 1.2–2m (4–6ft), S 60cm (2ft).

Aruncus dioicus
(Goat's beard)
Hummock-forming perennial carrying large leaves with lance-shaped leaflets on tall stems and above them, in mid-summer, branching plumes of tiny, creamy-white flowers. H 2m (6ft), S 1.2m (4ft).

WHITE–PINK

Artemisia lactiflora
(White mugwort)
Vigorous, erect perennial. Many sprays of creamy-white buds open to off-white flowers in summer. Dark green leaves are jagged-toothed. Needs staking and is best as a foil to stronger colours. H 1.2–1.5m (4–5ft), S 50cm (20in).

Alpinia zerumbet
(Shell flower, Shell ginger)
Evergreen, clump-forming perennial. Has racemes of white flowers, with yellow lips and pink- or red-marked throats, mainly in summer. H 3m (10ft), S 1m (3ft). Min. 18°C (64°F).

***Campanula lactiflora* 'Loddon Anna'**
Upright, branching perennial with narrowly oval leaves. In summer, slender stems bear racemes of large, nodding, bell-shaped, soft dusty-pink flowers. Needs staking on a windy site. H 1.2m (4ft), S 60cm (2ft).

***Macleaya microcarpa* 'Kelway's Coral Plume'**
Clump-forming perennial that in summer produces branching spikes of rich pink-buff flowers. Large, rounded, lobed leaves are grey-green above, grey-white beneath. H 2–2.5m (6–8ft), S 1–1.2m (3–4ft).

Eremurus robustus
Upright perennial with strap-like leaves that die back during summer as huge racemes of cup-shaped, pink blooms appear. Cover crowns in winter with compost or bracken. Needs staking. H 2.2m (7ft), S 1m (3ft).

PINK–RED

Lavatera cachemiriana
Semi-evergreen, woody-based perennial or sub-shrub with wiry stems bearing panicles of trumpet-shaped, silky, clear pink flowers in summer. Has ivy-shaped, downy, mid-green leaves. H 1.5–2m (5–6ft), S 1m (3ft).

Filipendula rubra
Vigorous, upright perennial with large, jagged leaves and feathery plumes of tiny, soft pink flowers on tall, branching stems in mid-summer. Will rapidly colonize a boggy site. H 2–2.5m, (6–8ft), S 1.2m (4ft).

***Rheum palmatum* 'Atrosanguineum'**
Clump-forming perennial with very large, lobed, deeply cut leaves that are deep red-purple when young. Bears large, fluffy panicles of crimson flowers in early summer. H and S 2m (6ft).

PURPLE–BLUE

Veratrum nigrum
(Black false hellebore)
Erect, stately perennial that from late summer onwards bears long spikes of chocolate-purple flowers at the ends of stout, upright stems. Stems are clothed with ribbed, oval to narrowly oval leaves. H 2m (6ft), S 60cm (2ft).

Verbena bonariensis
Perennial with a basal clump of dark green leaves. Upright, wiry stems carry tufts of tiny, purplish-blue flowers in summer-autumn. H 1.5m (5ft), S 60cm (2ft).

Cynara cardunculus (Cardoon)
Stately perennial with large clumps of arching, pointed, divided, silver-grey leaves, above which rise large, thistle-like, blue-purple flower heads borne singly on stout, grey stems in summer. Flower heads dry well. H 2m (6ft), S 1m (3ft).

***Campanula lactiflora* 'Prichard's Variety'**
Upright perennial with slender stems carrying branching heads of large, nodding, bell-shaped, violet-blue flowers from early summer to late autumn. May need staking. H 1.2–1.5m (4–5ft), S 60cm (2ft).

Echinops bannaticus
Upright perennial with narrow, deeply cut leaves and globose, pale to mid-blue heads of flowers, borne on branching stems in late summer. Flower heads dry well. H 1.2–1.5m (4–5ft), S 75cm (2½ft).

***Galega* 'Lady Wilson'**
Vigorous, upright perennial with spikes of small, pea-like, blue and pinkish-white flowers in summer above bold leaves divided into oval leaflets. Needs staking. H to 1.5m (5ft), S 1m (3ft).

GREEN–YELLOW

Gunnera manicata
Architectural perennial with rounded, prickly-edged leaves, to 1.5m (5ft) across. Has conical, light green flower spikes in early summer, followed by orange-brown seed pods. Needs mulch cover for crowns in winter and a sheltered site. H 2m (6ft), S 2.2m (7ft).

Angelica archangelica (Angelica)
Upright perennial, usually grown as a biennial, with deeply divided, bright green leaves and white or green flowers in late summer. Stems have culinary usage and when crystallized may be used for confectionery decoration. H 2m (6ft), S 1m (3ft).

Ferula communis (Giant fennel)
Upright perennial. Large, cow-parsley-like umbels of yellow flowers are borne from late spring to summer on the tops of stems that arise from a mound of finely cut, mid-green foliage. H 2–2.3m (6–7ft), S 1–1.2m (3–4ft).

YELLOW

Verbascum olympicum
Semi-evergreen, rosette-forming biennial or short-lived perennial. Branching stems, arising from felt-like, grey foliage at the plant base, bear sprays of 5-lobed, bright golden flowers from mid-summer onwards. H 2m (6ft), S 1m (3ft).

Ligularia przewalskii
Loosely clump-forming perennial with stems clothed in deeply cut, round, dark green leaves. Narrow spires of small, daisy-like, yellow flower heads appear from mid- to late summer. H 1.2–2m (4–6ft), S 1m (3ft).

***Rudbeckia laciniata* 'Goldquelle'**
Erect perennial. In late summer and autumn, daisy-like, double, bright yellow flower heads with green centres are borne singly on stout stems. Has deeply divided, mid-green foliage. H 1.5–2m (5–6ft), S 60–75 cm (2–2½ft).

Inula magnifica
Robust, clump-forming, upright perennial with a mass of lance-shaped to elliptic, rough leaves. Leafy stems bear terminal heads of large, daisy-like, yellow flower heads in late summer. Needs staking. H 1.8m (6ft), S 1m (3ft).

Ligularia stenocephala
Loosely clump-forming perennial with jagged-edged, round, mid-green leaves. Large heads of daisy-like, yellow-orange flowers open on purplish stems from mid- to late summer. H 1.2m (4ft) or more, S 60cm (2ft).

ORANGE

***Heliopsis helianthoides* subsp. *scabra* 'Light of Loddon'**
Upright perennial bearing dahlia-like, double, bright orange flower heads on strong stems in late summer. Dark green leaves are coarse and serrated. H 1.2–1.5m (4–5ft), S 60cm (2ft).

Hedychium densiflorum
Clump-forming, rhizomatous perennial bearing a profusion of short-lived, fragrant, orange or yellow flowers in dense spikes during late summer. Broadly lance-shaped leaves are glossy, mid-green. H 1.2–2m (4–6ft), S 60cm (2ft).

Heliconia psittacorum
(Parrot's flower, Parrot's plantain)
Tufted perennial with long-stalked, lance-shaped leaves. In summer, mature plants carry green-tipped, orange flowers with narrow, glossy, orange-red bracts. H to 2m (6ft), S 1m (3ft). Min. 18°C (64°F).

D. **'Ailsa'** ①

DELPHINIUMS

Delphiniums are among the most attractive of the tall perennials, with their showy spires of flowers making a spectacular display in the summer herbaceous border. In addition to the classic blues, hybrids are available in a broad range of colours, from white through the pastel shades of dusky-pink and lilac to the richer mauves and violet-purples. Grow tall delphiniums in a mixed border or island bed, and dwarf ones in a rock garden. Except for dwarf vaarieties, stake plants securely to support the heavy flower spikes. In growth, water all plants freely, applying a balanced liquid fertilizer every 2–3 weeks. Dead-head by cutting spent flower spikes back to small, flowering sideshoots. Cut all growth to ground level after it has withered in autumn. Delphiniums need protection from slugs and snails.

***D.* 'Sungleam'** ① 🏆

***D.* 'Sandpiper'** ① 🏆

***D.* 'Butterball'** ①

***D.* 'Sunkissed'** ① 🏆

***D.* 'Foxhill Nina'** ①

***D.* 'Conspicuous'** ① 🏆

***D.* 'Shimmer'** ①

***D.* 'Claire'** ① 🏆

***D.* 'Dunsden Green'** ①

***D.* 'Kennington Classic'** ①

***D.* 'Olive Poppleton'** ① 🏆

***D.* 'Emily Hawkins'** ① 🏆

***D.* 'Langdon's Royal Flush'** ① 🏆

D. 'Pink Ruffles' (!)

D. 'Fanfare' (!)

D. 'Gemini' (!)

D. 'Lucia Sahin' (!) 🏆

D. 'Ann Woodfield' (!)

D. 'Cliveden Beauty' (!)

D. 'Gertrude Sahin' (!)

D. 'Spindrift' (!) 🏆

D. 'Clifford Lass'

D. 'Strawberry Fair' (!)

D. 'Gillian Dallas' (!) 🏆

D. 'Lord Butler' 🏆

D. 'Clifford Sky' (!) 🏆

D. 'Gordon Forsyth' (!)

D. 'Michael Ayres' (!) 🏆

D. 'Mighty Atom' (!)

D. 'Min' (!) 🏆

D. 'Anne Kenrick' (!)

D. 'Langdon's Blue Lagoon' (!) 🏆

D. Blue Fountains Group (!)

D. 'Crown Jewel' ⓣ

D. 'Alice Artindale' ⓣ

D. 'Blue Dawn' ⓣ🏆

D. 'Joan Edwards' ⓣ

D. 'Tiger Eye' ⓣ

D. 'Gemma' ⓣ

D. 'Franjo Sahin' ⓣ

D. 'Blue Nile' ⓣ🏆

D. 'Tiddles' ⓣ🏆

D. 'Galileo' ⓣ🏆

D. 'Holly Cookland Wilkins' ⓣ

D. 'Can-can' ⓣ🏆

D. 'Fenella' ⓣ🏆

D. 'Loch Leven' ⓣ🏆

D. 'Giotto' ⓣ🏆

D. 'Bruce' ⓣ🏆

D. 'Chelsea Star' ⓣ

D. 'Nobility' ⓣ

D. 'Dora Larkan' ⓣ

D. Black Knight Group ⓣ

D. grandiflorum 'Blue Butterfly' ⓣ

WHITE–PINK

Cimicifuga simplex
Upright perennial with arching spikes of tiny, slightly fragrant, star-shaped, white flowers in autumn. Leaves are glossy and divided. Needs staking. H 1.2–1.5m (4–5ft), S 60cm (2ft).

***Anemone* × *hybrida* 'Honorine Jobert'**
Vigorous, branching perennial. Slightly cupped, white flowers with contrasting yellow stamens are carried on wiry stems in late summer and early autumn above deeply divided, dark green leaves. H 1.5m (5ft), S 60cm (2ft).

***Anemone hupehensis* 'September Charm'**
Vigorous, branching perennial. In late summer and early autumn bears slightly cupped, clear pink flowers on wiry stems. Leaves are deeply divided and dark green. H 75cm (30in), S 50cm (20in).

PINK–PURPLE

Eupatorium purpureum
(Joe Pye weed)
Stately, upright perennial with terminal heads of tubular, pinkish-purple flowers borne in late summer and early autumn. Coarse, oval leaves are arranged in whorls along purplish stems. H to 2.2m (7ft), S to 1m (3ft).

***Salvia involucrata* 'Bethellii'**
Sub-shrubby perennial that produces long racemes of large, cerise-crimson blooms, with pink bracts, in late summer and autumn. Leaves are oval to heart-shaped. H 1.2–1.5m (4–5ft), S 1m (3ft).

***Anemone hupehensis* var. *japonica* 'Bressingham Glow'**
Vigorous, branching perennial with slightly cupped, rose-purple flowers borne on wiry stems in late summer and early autumn over clumps of deeply divided, dark green leaves. H 1.2–1.5m (4–5ft), S 60cm (2ft).

GREEN–YELLOW

Gomphocarpus physocarpus
Deciduous, erect, hairy sub-shrub with lance-shaped leaves, 10cm (4in) long. Has umbels of 5-horned, creamy-white flowers in summer, followed by large, inflated, globose seed pods with soft bristles. H to 2m (6ft), S to 60cm (2ft).

***Helianthus* × *multiflorus* 'Loddon Gold'**
Upright perennial bearing showy, large, vivid deep yellow flower heads with rounded, double centres in late summer and early autumn. Needs staking and may spread quickly. H 1.5m (5ft), S 60cm (2ft).

Hedychium gardnerianum
Upright, rhizomatous perennial. In late summer and early autumn has many spikes of short-lived, fragrant, lemon-yellow and red flowers. Lance-shaped leaves are greyish-green, most markedly when young. H 1.5–2m (5–6ft), S 75cm (2½ft). Min. 5°C (41°F).

***Rudbeckia* 'Herbstsonne'**
Erect perennial bearing daisy-like, yellow flower heads, with conical, green centres, that are carried singly on tall stems in late summer and autumn. Mid-green leaves are shallowly lobed. H 1.5–2.3m (5–7ft), S 60–75cm (2–2½ft).

Helianthus* × *multiflorus
Upright perennial. Has large, yellow flower heads, with double centres surrounded by larger, rayed segments, that are borne in late summer and early autumn. Needs staking and may spread rapidly. H 1.5m (5ft), S 60cm (2ft).

PINK–PURPLE

***Musa ornata* (Flowering banana)**
Evergreen, palm-like, suckering perennial with oblong, waxy, bluish-green leaves to 2m (6ft) long. In summer has erect, yellow-orange flowers with pinkish bracts and greenish-yellow fruits. H to 3m (10ft), S 2.2m (7ft). Min. 18°C (64°F).

Strelitzia nicolai
Evergreen, palm-like perennial with a stout trunk. Has leaves, 1.5m (5ft) or more long, on very long stalks and intermittently bears beak-like, white and pale blue flowers in boat-shaped, dark purple bracts. H 8m (25ft), S 5m (15ft). Min. 5–10°C (41–50°F).

Calathea sanderiana
Evergreen, clump-forming perennial. Broadly oval, leathery, glossy leaves, to 60cm (2ft) long, are dark green with pink to white lines above, and purple beneath. Intermittently has short spikes of white to mauve flowers. H 1.2–1.5m (4–5ft), S 1m (3ft). Min. 15°C (59°F).

Doryanthes palmeri
Evergreen perennial with a rosette of arching, ribbed leaves, to 2m (6ft) long. Intermittently bears panicles of small, red-bracted, orange-red flowers, white within. Flowers are often replaced by bulbils. H 2–2.5m (6–8ft), S 2.5m (8ft). Min. 10°C (50°F).

***Phormium tenax* Purpureum Group**
Evergreen, upright perennial with bold, stiff, pointed leaves that are rich reddish-purple to dark copper. In summer, panicles of reddish flowers appear on purplish-blue stems. H 2–2.5m (6–8ft), S 1m (3ft).

BLUE–GREEN

Pycnostachys dawei
Strong-growing, bushy perennial with toothed, oblong leaves, 12–30cm (5–12in) long, that are reddish below. Has compact spikes of tubular, 2-lipped, bright blue flowers in winter-spring. H 1.2–1.5m (4–5ft), S 30–90cm (1–3ft). Min. 15°C (59°F).

Musa basjoo
(Japanese banana)
Evergreen, palm-like, suckering perennial with arching leaves to 1m (3ft) long. Has drooping, pale yellow flowers with brownish bracts in summer followed by green fruits. H 3–5m (10–15ft), S 2–2.5m (6–8ft).

Ensete ventricosum
Evergreen, palm-like perennial with small, banana-like fruits. Has 6m (20ft) long leaves with reddish midribs and, intermittently, reddish-green flowers with dark red bracts. H 6m (20ft), S 3m (10ft) or more. Min. 10°C (50°F).

WHITE

***Ranunculus aconitifolius* 'Flore Pleno'**
Clump-forming perennial with deeply divided, dark green leaves. Double, pure white flowers are borne on strong, branched stems in spring-summer. H 60–75cm (24–30in), S 50cm (20in).

Ranunculus aconitifolius
Vigorous, clump-forming perennial with deeply divided, dark green leaves. Single, white flowers, about 3cm (1in) across, are borne in spring and early summer. H and S 1m (3ft).

Smilacina racemosa
(False spikenard)
Arching perennial. Has oval, light green leaves terminating in feathery sprays of white flowers that appear from spring to mid-summer and are followed by fleshy, reddish fruits. H 75–90cm (30–36in), S 45cm (18in).

IRISES

These beautiful flowers were named after Iris, the Greek goddess of the rainbow, as the shades of their colouring and markings are reminiscent of those of the rainbow. Their flowers often have "beards" (short hairs) or crests along the centres of the falls. The genus is classified into many divisions, some of which are used horticulturally for irises with similar characteristics or cultural requirements. Of these, the easiest to grow are the bearded, crested, Xiphium and dwarf Reticulata groups. Siberian and Japanese types are excellent in a bog garden or by water, but also tolerate drier conditions. Others, such as Juno, Oncocyclus and Regelia irises, may be less easy to cultivate, though their flowers are among the most beautiful. Full details of all groups and guidance on their cultivation are given in the Plant Dictionary.

I. confusa
(crested) ① ♀

I. japonica
(Evansia) ① ♀

***I. sanguinea* 'Snow Queen'**
(beardless) ①

I. iberica
(Oncocyclus) ①

***I.* 'Champagne Elegance'**
(bearded) ①

I. magnifica
(Juno) ① ♀

***I.* 'Wisley White'**
(Siberian) ①

***I.* 'Dreaming Yellow'**
(Siberian) ① ♀

***I. ensata* 'Rose Queen'**
(bearded) ① ♀

***I.* 'Sweet Musette'**
(bearded) ①

***I.* 'Ringo'**
(bearded) ①

***I.* 'Geisha Gown'**
(Japanese) ①

***I. laevigata* 'Snowdrift'**
(beardless) ①

***I.* 'Frost and Flame'**
(bearded) ①

***I.* 'Anniversary'**
(Siberian) ①

***I. ensata* 'Moonlight Waves'**
(beardless) ①

***I.* 'Making Eyes'**
(bearded) ①

***I. ensata* hybrid**
(Japanese) ①

I. germanica
'Florentina' (b.ded) ①

I. orientalis
(beardless) ① ♀

***I.* 'English Cottage'**
(bearded) ①

***I.* 'Lady Mohr'**
(bearded) ①

***I.* 'Ballyhoo'**
(bearded) ①

***I.* 'Ruban Bleu'**
(bearded) ①

I. bucharica
(Juno) (!) 🏆

I. 'Mary McIlroy'
(bearded) (!)

I. 'Bumblebee Deelight'
(bearded) (!)

I. variegata
(bearded) (!) 🏆

I. 'Early Light'
(bearded) (!) 🏆

I. winogradowii
(Reticulata) (!) 🏆

I. 'Butter and Sugar'
(Siberian) (!) 🏆

I. innominata
(beardless) (!)

I. forrestii
(bearded) (!) 🏆

I. danfordiae
(Reticulata) (!)

I. 'Ola Kala'
(bearded) (!)

I. 'Eyebright'
(bearded) (!) 🏆

I. 'Supreme Sultan'
(bearded) (!)

I. 'Langport Storm'
(bearded) (!)

I. 'Autumn Leaves'
(bearded) (!)

I. 'Peach Frost'
(bearded) (!) 🏆

I. pseudacorus
(beardless) (!) 🏆

I. fulva
(beardless) (!)

I. 'Saturday Night Live'
(bearded) (!)

I. 'Flamenco'
(bearded) (!) 🏆

I. 'Sun Miracle'
(bearded) (!) 🏆

I. 'Bronze Queen'
(Xiphium) (!)

I. 'Blue Eyed Brunette'
(bearded) (!) 🏆

I. 'Joette'
(bearded) (!)

I. 'Carnaby'
(bearded) (!)

I. 'Kent Pride'
(bearded) (!)

I. × ***fulvala***
(beardless) ① ♀

I. **'Stepping Out'** ① ♀
(bearded)

I. **'Krasnia'**
(bearded) ①

I. ***unguicularis*** subsp. ***cretensis***
(beardless) ①

I. **'Sapphire Star'**
(Japanese) ①

I. **'Paradise Bird'**
(bearded) ① ♀

I. **'Oriental Eyes'**
(beardless) ①

I. ***cristata***
(Evansia) ① ♀

I. **'Ruffled Velvet'**
(Siberian) ① ♀

I. **'Annabel Jane'**
(bearded) ①

I. **'Bold Print'**
(bearded) ①

I. **'Rippling Rose'**
(bearded) ①

I. ***versicolor*** **'Kermesina'**
(beardless) ①

I. **'Jesse's Song'**
(bearded) ①

I. **'Conjuration'**
(bearded) ①

I. **'Flight of Butterflies'**
(Siberian) ①

I. **'Magic Man'**
(bearded) ①

I. **'Change of Pace'**
(bearded) ①

I. ***xiphium*** **'Wedgwood'**
(Xiphium) ①

I. **'Raspberry Candy'**
(beardless) ①

I. **'Lady of Quality'**
(Siberian) ①

***I.* 'Katharine Hodgkin'** (Reticulata) ① 🏆

***I.* 'Mary Frances'** (bearded) ①

***I.* 'Morwenna'** 🏆 (bearded) ①

I. sintenisii 🏆 (Reticulata) ①

***I.* 'Rare Treat'** (bearded) ①

I. hoogiana (Regelia) ① 🏆

I. laevigata (Japanese) ① 🏆

I. douglasiana (Pacific Coast) ① 🏆

***I.* 'Perry's Blue'** (beardless) ①

***I. pallida* 'Variegata'** (bearded) ① 🏆

I. setosa (beardless) ① 🏆

***I. reticulata* 'Cantab'** (Reticulata) ①

***I.* 'Harmony'** (Reticulata) ①

I. missouriensis (Pacific Coast) ① 🏆

***I.* 'Lavender Royal'** (Pacific Coast) ①

I. rosenbachiana (Juno) ①

***I. histrioides* 'Major'** (Reticulata) ①

***I. sibirica* 'Soft Blue'** (Siberian) ① 🏆

***I.* 'Autumn Circus'** (bearded) ①

***I.* 'Blue Rhythm'** (bearded) ①

***I.* 'Electric Rays'** (Japanese) ①

***I.* 'Tropic Night'** (Siberian) ①

***I. ensata* 'Galatea'** (Japanese) ①

I. tenax (Pacific Coast) ①

I. lazica 🏆 (beardless) ①

***I.* 'Titan's Glory'** (bearded) ①

***I.* 'Joyce'** (Reticulata) ①

***I.* 'Mountain Lake'** (Siberian) ①

I. tectorum (Evansia) ①

I. versicolor (beardless) ① 🏆

I. chrysographes (Siberian) ① 🏆

***I.* 'Matinata'** (bearded) ①

I. latifolia (Xiphium) ① 🏆

P. emodi (single) ①

Peonies

Peonies (*Paeonia* species and cultivars) are valued for their showy blooms, filling the border with subtle whites, pinks and reds in late spring and early to mid-summer. Peony flowers vary from single to double or anemone form (with broad, outer petals and a mass of petaloids in the centre) and may be scented. The flowers are good for cutting. Peony foliage is also striking, often tinged bronze when young and rich red in autumn. Besides the wide variety of border hybrids available, there are many attractive species as well as several tree peonies (cultivars of *P. suffruticosa*), open shrubs often over 2m (6ft) high.

Peonies are long-lived plants that should, if possible, be left undisturbed, as they resent transplanting. If it is necessary to lift and divide the clumps, do so in autumn or early spring.

P. 'Sarah Bernhardt' (double) ①🏆

P. obovata var. ***alba*** (single) ①🏆

***P. suffruticosa* 'Godaishu'** (double) ①

P. 'Duchesse de Nemours' (double) ①🏆

***P. suffruticosa* 'Hana-kisoi'** (double) ①

P. 'Ballerina' (double) ①

P. 'White Wings' (single) ①

P. rockii (semi-double) ①🏆

P. 'Alice Harding' (double) ①

***P. suffruticosa* 'Reine Elizabeth'** (double) ①

P. 'Bowl of Beauty' (anemone) ①🏆

P. mascula subsp. ***mascula*** (single) ①

***P. officinalis* 'Alba Plena'** (double) ①

P. 'Whitleyi Major' (single) ①🏆

P. 'Shirley Temple' (double) ①

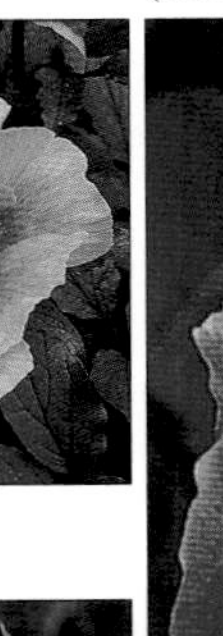

P. cambessedesii (single) ①🏆

P. 'Globe of Light' (anemone) ①

P. 'Krinkled White' (single) ①

P. 'Mother of Pearl' (single) ①

P. 'Kelway's Supreme' (double) ①

***P. suffruticosa* 'Kamada-nishiki'** (double) ①

P. veitchii (single) ①

P. 'Magic Orb' (double) ①

P. suffruticosa **'Cardinal Vaughan'** (semi-double) ①

P. tenuifolia (single) ①

P. **'Chocolate Soldier'** (semi-double) ①

P. wittmanniana (single) ①

P. **'L'Espérance'** (single) ①

P. peregrina **'Otto Froebel'** (single) ① 🏆

P. **'Souvenir de Maxime Cornu'** (double) ①

P. **'Laura Dessert'** (double) ① 🏆

P. delavayi var. ***angustiloba*** f. ***trollioides*** (single) ①

P. **'Kelway's Gorgeous'** (single) ①

P. officinalis **'China Rose'** (single) ①

P. mlokosewitschii (single) ① 🏆

P. **'Silver Flare'** (single) ①

P. **'Instituteur Doriat'** (anemone) ①

P. **'America'** ①

P. × *smouthii* (single) ① 🏆

P. **'Defender'** (single) ①

P. **'Argosy'** (single) ①

P. peregrina ①

P. suffruticosa **'Hana-daijin'** (double) ①

P. officinalis **'Rubra Plena'** (double) ① 🏆

P. **'Sir Edward Elgar'** (single) ①

P. **'Knighthood'** (double) ①

P. officinalis **'Crimson Globe'** ①

P. ludlowii (single) ① 🏆

WHITE–BLUE

Polygonatum* × *hybridum
(Solomon's seal)
Arching, leafy perennial with fleshy rhizomes. In late spring, clusters of small, pendent, tubular, greenish-white flowers are produced in axils of neat, oval leaves. H 1.2m (4ft), S 1m (3ft).

Geranium phaeum
(Mourning widow)
Clump-forming perennial with lobed, soft green leaves and maroon-purple flowers, with reflexed petals, borne on rather lax stems in late spring. H 75cm (30in), S 45cm (18in).

Darmera peltata (Umbrella plant)
Spreading perennial with large, rounded leaves. Has clusters of white or pale pink flowers in spring on white-haired stems before foliage appears. H 1–1.2m (3–4ft), S 60cm (2ft).

Symphytum caucasicum
Clump-forming perennial carrying clusters of pendent, azure-blue flowers in spring above rough, hairy, mid-green foliage. Is best suited to a wild garden. H and S 60–90cm (24–36in).

***Tanacetum coccineum* 'Eileen May Robinson'**
Upright perennial with slightly aromatic, feathery leaves. Daisy-like, pink flowers with yellow centres are produced on strong stems in summer. H 75cm (30in), S 45cm (18in).

BLUE–YELLOW

***Symphytum* × *uplandicum* 'Variegatum'**
Perennial with large, hairy, grey-green leaves that have broad, cream margins. In late spring and early summer, pink or blue buds open to tubular, blue or purplish-blue flowers. H 1m (3ft), S 60cm (2ft).

***Doronicum columnae* 'Miss Mason'**
Clump-forming, rhizomatous perennial with heart-shaped leaves. Slender stems bear daisy-like, bright yellow flower heads, 8cm (3in) across, held well above the foliage, in mid- and late spring. H and S 60cm (24in).

***Chelidonium majus* 'Flore Pleno'**
Upright perennial with divided, bright green leaves and many cup-shaped, double, yellow flowers borne on branching sprays in late spring and early summer. Seeds freely and is best in a wild garden. H 60–90cm (24–30in), S 30cm (12in).

Aciphylla aurea (Golden Spaniard)
Evergreen, rosette-forming perennial with long, bayonet-like, yellow-green leaves. Bears spikes of golden flowers up to 2m (6ft) tall from late spring to early summer. H and S in leaf 60–75cm (24–30in).

Asphodeline lutea
(Yellow asphodel)
Neat, clump-forming perennial that bears dense spikes of star-shaped, yellow flowers amid narrow, greygreen leaves in late spring. H 1–1.2m (3–4ft), S 60cm–1m (2–3ft).

□ WHITE

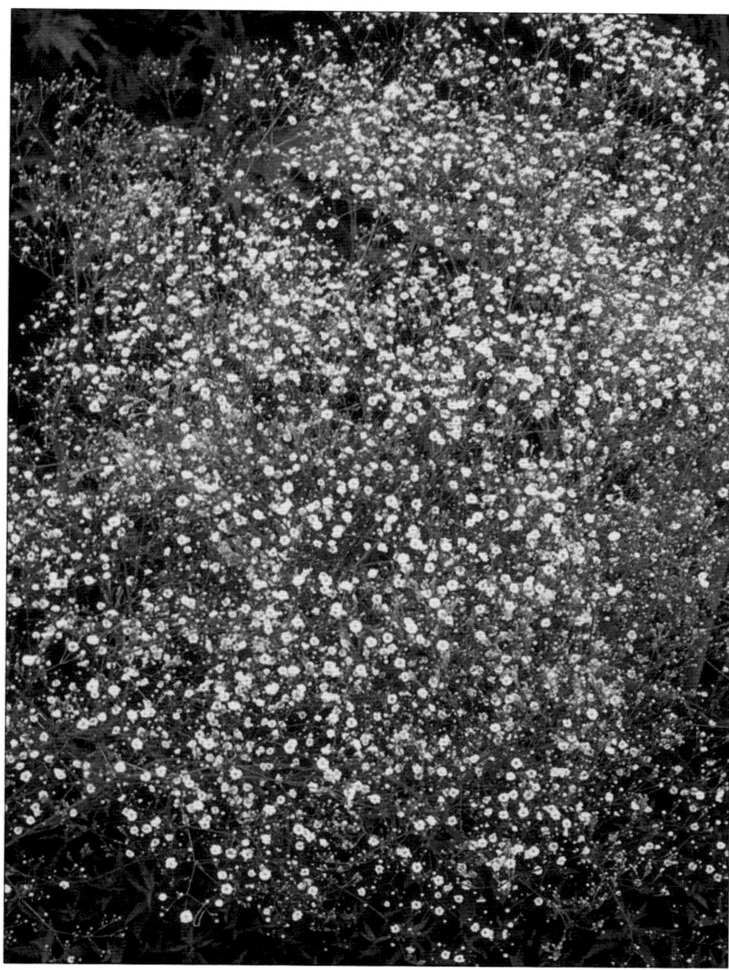

***Gypsophila paniculata* 'Bristol Fairy'**
Perennial with small, dark green leaves and wiry, branching stems bearing panicles of tiny, double, white flowers in summer. H 60–75cm (2–2½ft), S 1m (3ft).

***Achillea ptarmica* 'The Pearl'**
Upright perennial with large heads of small, pompon-like, white flowers in summer and tapering, glossy, dark green leaves. May spread rapidly. H and S 75cm (30in).

Nicotiana alata
Rosette-forming perennial, often grown as an annual, that in late summer bears clusters of tubular, creamy-white flowers, pale brownish-violet externally, which are fragrant at night. Has oval, mid-green leaves. H 75cm (30in), S 30cm (12in).

Libertia grandiflora
(New Zealand satin flower)
Loosely clump-forming, rhizomatous perennial. In early summer produces spikes of white flowers above grass-like, dark green leaves that turn brown at the tips. Has decorative seed pods in autumn. H 75cm (30in), S 60cm (24in).

Hesperis matronalis
(Dame's violet, Sweet rocket)
Upright perennial with long spikes of many 4-petalled, white or violet flowers borne in summer. Flowers have a strong fragrance in the evening. Leaves are smooth and narrowly oval. H 75cm (30in), S 60cm (24in).

Asphodelus albus (White asphodel)
Upright perennial with clusters of star-shaped, white flowers borne in late spring and early summer. Has narrow, basal tufts of mid-green leaves. H 1m (3ft), S 45cm (1½ft).

Anaphalis margaritacea
(Pearl everlasting)
Bushy perennial that has lance-shaped, grey-green or silvery-grey leaves with white margins and many heads of small, white flowers on erect stems in late summer. Flower heads dry well. H 60–75cm (24–30in), S 60cm (24in).

Dicentra spectabilis* f. *alba
Leafy perennial forming a hummock of fern-like, deeply cut, light green foliage with arching sprays of pendent, heart-shaped, pure white flowers in late spring and summer. H 60–75cm (24–30in), S 60cm (24in).

□ WHITE

Eupatorium rugosum (Hardy age, Mist flower, White snakeroot)
Erect perennial with nettle-like, grey-green leaves. In late summer bears dense, flat, white flower heads. H 1.2m (4ft), S 45cm (1½ft).

Dictamnus albus
(Burning bush)
Upright perennial bearing, in early summer, spikes of fragrant, star-shaped, white flowers with long stamens. Light green leaves are divided into oval leaflets. Dislikes disturbance. H 1m (3ft), S 60cm (2ft).

Myrrhis odorata (Sweet Cicely)
Graceful perennial that resembles cow parsley. Has aromatic, fern-like, mid-green foliage and fragrant, bright creamy-white flowers in early summer. H 60–90cm (24–36in), S 60cm (24in).

***Thalictrum aquilegiifolium* 'White Cloud'**
Perennial with divided, greyish-green leaves. In summer produces terminal sprays of delicate, fluffy, white flowers. H 1–1.2m (3–4ft), S 30cm (1ft).

***Leucanthemum × superbum* 'Elizabeth'**
Robust perennial with large, daisy-like, single, pure white flower heads borne singly in summer. Divide and replant every 2 years. H 1m (3ft), S 60cm (2ft).

Argyranthemum frutescens
(Marguerite)
Evergreen, woody-based, bushy perennial that bears many daisy-like, white, yellow or pink flower heads throughout summer. Attractive leaves are fresh green. H and S 1m (3ft).

Rodgersia podophylla
Clump-forming, rhizomatous perennial with large, many-veined leaves that are bronze when young and later become mid-green, then copper-tinted. Panicles of creamy-white flowers are borne well above foliage in summer. H 1.2m (4ft), S 1m (3ft).

Rodgersia sambucifolia
Clump-forming, rhizomatous perennial with emerald-green, sometimes bronze-tinged leaves composed of large leaflets. Sprays of creamy-white flowers appear above foliage in summer. H 1–1.2m (3–4ft), S 1m (3ft).

***Aruncus dioicus* 'Kneiffii'**
Hummock-forming perennial that has deeply cut, feathery leaves with lanceshaped leaflets on elegant stems and bears branching plumes of tiny, star-shaped, creamy-white flowers in midsummer. H 90cm (3ft), S 50cm (20in).

Rodgersia aesculifolia
Clump-forming, rhizomatous perennial that is excellent for a bog garden or pool side. In mid-summer, plumes of fragrant, pinkish-white flowers rise from crinkled, bronze foliage like that of a horse-chestnut tree. H and S 1m (3ft).

***Papaver orientale* 'Perry's White'**
Hairy-leaved perennial with deep, fleshy roots. Satiny, white flowers with purple centres appear on strong stems in early summer. May need support. H 80cm (32in), S 60cm (24in).

***Leucantheum × superbum* 'Wirral Pride'**
Robust, clump-forming perennial with glossy, dark green, slightly toothed leaves. Bears numerous, solitary, white double flower heads with yellowish anemone centres from early summer to autumn. H to 1m (3ft), S 60cm (24in).

Lysimachia clethroides
Vigorous, clump-forming, spreading perennial carrying spikes of small, white flowers above mid-green foliage in late summer. H 1m (3ft), S 60cm–1m (2–3ft).

Morina longifolia
Evergreen perennial that produces rosettes of large, spiny, thistle-like, rich green leaves. Whorls of hooded, tubular, white flowers, flushed pink within, are borne well above foliage in mid-summer. H 60–75cm (2–2½ft), S 30cm (1ft).

Gillenia trifoliata
Upright perennial with many wiry, branching stems carrying clusters of dainty, white flowers with reddish-brown calyces in summer. Leaves are dark green and lance-shaped. Needs staking. Thrives in most situations. H 1–1.2m (3–4ft), S 60cm (2ft).

Veronicastrum virginicum* f. *album
Upright perennial. In late summer, spires of small, white flowers, with pink-flushed bases and pink anthers, crown stems clothed with whorls of narrow, dark green leaves. H 1.2m (4ft), S 45cm (1½ft).

Valeriana officinalis
(Cat's valerian, Common valerian)
Clump-forming, fleshy perennial that bears spikes of white to deep pink flowers in summer. Leaves are deeply toothed and mid-green. Has the disadvantage of attracting cats. H 1–1.2m (3–4ft), S 1m (3ft).

Phlox

P. paniculata 'Fujiyama' ♀

Border phlox (cultivars of *Phlox maculata* and *P. paniculata*) are an elegant and stately mainstay of the herbaceous border in mid- to late summer. Their dome-shaped or conical panicles of flowers, often delicately scented, are produced in white, pink, red and purple, many with contrasting eyes. Some cultivars have strikingly variegated foliage.

Phlox thrive in sun or partial shade and in humus-rich, well-drained soil. Taller varieties may need staking. For larger flowers, reduce the number of stems in spring, when the plant is about a quarter of its eventual height, by pinching out the weakest shoots. To prolong flowering, cut back the central part of the flower head as the blooms fade to encourage sideshoots to flower. Once the plants have finished flowering in autumn, cut back to the ground.

P. paniculata 'Norah Leigh'

P. 'Junior Bouquet'

P. paniculata 'White Admiral' ♀

P. paniculata 'Mia Ruys'

P. maculata 'Alpha' ♀

P. maculata 'Omega' ♀

P. paniculata 'Mother of Pearl' ♀

P. paniculata 'Windsor' ♀

P. paniculata 'Sandringham'

P. paniculata 'Harlequin'

P. paniculata 'Balmoral'

P. paniculata 'Graf Zeppelin'

P. paniculata 'Prince of Orange' ♀

P. paniculata 'Le Mahdi' ♀

P. paniculata 'Eva Cullum'

P. paniculata 'Brigadier' ♀

P. paniculata 'Eventide' ♀

P. paniculata 'Amethyst'

P. paniculata 'Hampton Court'

PINK

***Linaria purpurea* 'Canon J. Went'**
Upright perennial bearing spikes of snapdragon-like, pink blooms with orange-tinged throats from mid- to late summer. Has narrow, grey-green leaves. H 60cm–1m (2–3ft), S 60cm (2ft).

***Geranium* × *oxonianum* 'Winscombe'**
Semi-evergreen, carpeting perennial with dense, dainty, lobed leaves and cup-shaped, deep pink flowers, which fade to pale pink, borne throughout summer. H 60–75cm (24–30in), S 45cm (18in).

Malva moschata
Bushy, branching perennial producing successive spikes of saucer-shaped, rose-pink flowers during early summer. Narrow, lobed, divided leaves are slightly scented. H 60cm–1m (2–3ft), S 60cm (2ft).

Dictamnus albus* var. *purpureus
Upright perennial. In early summer bears stiff spikes of fragrant, star-shaped, purplish-pink, sometimes paler, flowers with long stamens. Has light green leaves divided into oval leaflets. Dislikes disturbance. H 1m (3ft), S 60cm (2ft).

***Persicaria bistorta* 'Superba'**
Vigorous, clump-forming perennial that from early to late summer produces spikes of soft pink flowers above oval leaves. H 60–75cm (24–30in), S 60cm (24in).

***Monarda* 'Croftway Pink'**
Clump-forming perennial carrying whorls of hooded, soft pink blooms throughout summer above neat mounds of aromatic foliage. H 1m (3ft), S 45cm (1½ft).

***Argyranthemum* 'Mary Wootton'**
Evergreen, woody-based, bushy perennial bearing daisy-like, pink flower heads throughout summer. Has attractive, fern-like, divided, pale green foliage. H and S to 1m (3ft).

***Sidalcea* 'Oberon'**
Upright perennial with rounded, deeply cut leaves divided into narrowly oblong segments. In summer, produces racemes of shallowly cup-shaped, clear pink flowers. H 60cm (24in), S 45cm (18in).

PINK

***Astilbe* 'Venus'**
Leafy perennial bearing feathery, tapering plumes of tiny, pale pink flowers in summer. Foliage is broad and divided into leaflets; flowers remain on the plant, dried and brown, well into winter. Prefers humus-rich soil. H and S to 1m (3ft).

***Lupinus* 'The Chatelaine'**
Clump-forming perennial carrying spikes of pink-and-white flowers above divided, mid-green foliage in early summer. H 1.2m (4ft), S 45cm (1½ft).

***Physostegia virginiana* 'Variegata'**
Erect perennial. In late summer produces spikes of tubular, purplish-pink blooms that can be placed into position. Toothed, mid-green leaves are white-variegated. H 1–1.2m (3–4ft), S 60cm (2ft).

Rehmannia elata
Straggling perennial bearing foxglove-like, yellow-throated, rose-purple flowers in leaf axils of notched, stem-clasping, soft leaves from early to mid-summer. H 1m (3ft), S 45cm (1½ft). Min. 1°C(34°F).

***Astilbe* 'Straussenfeder'**
Leafy perennial with handsome, divided foliage and arching, feathery, tapering plumes of tiny, coral-pink flowers in summer. Dry, brown flowers remain on the plant well into winter. Prefers humus-rich soil. H and S to 1m (3ft).

***Echinacea purpurea* 'Robert Bloom'**
Upright perennial. Has lance-shaped, dark green leaves and large, daisy-like, deep crimson-pink flower heads, with conical, brown centres, borne singly on strong stems in summer. Needs humus-rich soil. H 1.2m (4ft), S 50cm (20in).

Centaurea pulcherrima
Upright perennial with deeply cut, silvery leaves. Rose-pink flower heads, with thistle-like centres paler than surrounding star-shaped ray petals, are borne singly on slender stems in summer. H 75cm (2½ft), S 60cm (2ft).

Kohleria digitaliflora
Erect, bushy, rhizomatous perennial with white-haired stems. Has scalloped, hairy leaves and clusters of tubular, hairy, pink-and-white flowers, with purple-spotted, green lobes, in summer-autumn. H 60cm (24in) or more, S 45cm (18in). Min. 15°C (59°F).

PINK

Dicentra spectabilis (Bleeding heart, Dutchman's trousers)
Leafy perennial forming a hummock of fern-like, mid-green foliage, above which rise arching stems of pendent, heart-shaped, pinkish-red and white flowers in late spring and summer. H 75cm (30in), S 50cm (20in).

***Lythrum salicaria* 'Feuerkerze'**
Clump-forming perennial for a waterside or bog garden. Bears spikes of intense rose-red blooms from mid-to late summer. Small, lance-shaped leaves are borne on flower stems. H 1m (3ft), S 45cm (1½ft).

Mirabilis jalapa (Four o'clock flower, Marvel of Peru)
Bushy, tuberous perennial. Fragrant, trumpet-shaped, crimson, pink, white or yellow flowers, opening in evening, cover mid-green foliage in summer. H 60cm–1.2m (2–4ft), S 60–75cm (2–2½ft).

***Lythrum virgatum* 'The Rocket'**
Clump-forming perennial that carries slender spikes of rose-red flowers above mid-green foliage during summer. Good for a waterside or bog garden. H 1m (3ft), S 45cm (1½ft).

Geranium psilostemon
Clump-forming perennial that has broad, deeply cut leaves with good autumn colour and many cup-shaped, single, black-centred, magenta flowers in mid-summer. H and S 1.2m (4ft).

RED

***Lupinus* 'The Page'**
Clump-forming perennial bearing spikes of intense, deep red flowers above palmate, divided, basal mid-green leaves from early to mid-summer. H 90–100cm (36–39in), S 75cm (30in).

Filipendula purpurea
Upright perennial with deeply divided leaves. Produces large, terminal heads of masses of tiny, rich reddish-purple flowers in summer. Makes a good waterside plant. H 1.2m (4ft), S 60cm (2ft).

Centranthus ruber (Red valerian)
Perennial forming spreading colonies of fleshy leaves. Branching heads of small, star-shaped, deep reddish-pink or white flowers are borne above foliage from late spring to autumn. Thrives in poor, exposed sites. H 60–90cm (24–36in), S 45–60cm (18–24in) or more.

PELARGONIUMS

P. **'Lady Plymouth'** (scented-leaved) ① ♕

Pelargoniums, with their colourful flowers, grow happily in containers or beds and flower almost continuously in warm climates or under glass. To flower well, they need warmth, sunshine (without too much humidity) and well-drained soil.

Zonal – common geranium, with rounded leaves, clearly marked with a darker "zone" and single to double flowers.
Regal – shrubby plants with deeply serrated leaves and exotic, trumpet-shaped flowers prone to weather damage.
Ivy-leaved – trailing plants, ideal for hanging baskets, with lobed, somewhat fleshy leaves and single to double flowers.
Scented-leaved, and species – plants with small, often irregularly star-shaped flowers; scented-leaved forms are grown for their fragrant leaves.
Unique – tall-growing sub-shrubs with regal-like, brightly coloured flowers that are borne continuously through the season. Leaves, which may be scented, vary in shape.

P. **'Dale Queen'** (zonal) ①

P. **'Rica'** (zonal) ①

P. **'Fragrans'** (scented-leaved) ①

P. **'Mauritania'** (zonal) ①

P. **'Golden Lilac Mist'** (zonal) ①

P. **'Apple Blossom Rosebud'** (zonal) ① ♕

P. **'Timothy Clifford'** (zonal) ①

P. **'Ivalo'** (scented-leaved) ①

P. acetosum (species) ①

P. **'Fraiche Beauté'** (zonal) ①

P. **'Fair Ellen'** (scented-leaved) ①

P. **'Autumn Festival'** (regal) ①

P. **'Cherry Blossom'** (zonal) ①

P. **'Brookside Primrose'** (zonal) ①

P. **'Buttefly Lorelei'** (zonal) ①

P. **'Mr Henry Cox'** (zonal) ① ♕

P. **'Francis Parrett'** (zonal) ① ♕

P. **'Bird Dancer'** (zonal) ① ♕

P. **'The Boar'** (species) ① ♕

P. **'Lachsball'** (zonal) ①

P. **'Lachskönigin'** (ivy-leaved) ①

P. **'Mr Everaarts'** (zonal) ①

P. **'Schöne Helena'** (zonal) ①

P. **'Lesley Judd'** (regal) ①

P. **'Alberta'** (zonal) ①

P. **'Clorinda'** (scented-leaved) ①

P. 'Amethyst' (ivy-leaved) ⓘ🏆

P. 'Purple Unique' (unique) ⓘ

P. 'Mini Cascade' (ivy-leaved) ⓘ

P. 'Gustav Emich' (zonal) ⓘ

P. 'Voodoo' (unique) ⓘ🏆

P. 'Manx Maid' (regal) ⓘ

P. 'Royal Oak' (scented-leaved) ⓘ🏆

P. 'Bredon' (regal) ⓘ🏆

P. 'Purple Emperor' (regal) ⓘ

P. 'Rouletta' (ivy-leaved) ⓘ

P. 'Friesdorf' (zonal) ⓘ

P. 'Mrs Pollock' (zonal) ⓘ

P. 'Coddenham' (zonal) ⓘ

P. 'Tavira' (ivy-leaved) ⓘ🏆

P. 'Happy Thought' (zonal) ⓘ🏆

P. 'Polka' (zonal) ⓘ

P. 'Prince of Orange' (scented-leaved) ⓘ

P. 'Splendide' (species) ⓘ

P. 'Rollisson's Unique' (zonal) ⓘ

P. 'Orange Ricard' (zonal) ⓘ

P. 'L'Elégante' (ivy-leaved) ⓘ🏆

P. 'Paton's Unique' (zonal) ⓘ🏆

P. 'Madame Fournier' (zonal) ⓘ

P. 'Dolly Varden' (zonal) ⓘ🏆

P. *crispum* 'Variegatum' (scented-leaved) ⓘ🏆

P. 'Mabel Grey' (scented-leaved) ⓘ🏆

P. *capitatum* (scented-leaved) ⓘ

P. 'Tip Top Duet' (regal) ⓘ🏆

P. 'Caligula' (zonal) ⓘ

P. 'Flower of Spring' (zonal) ⓘ🏆

P. 'Mrs Quilter' (zonal) ⓘ🏆

P. *tomentosum* (scented-leaved) ⓘ🏆

PENSTEMONS

Valued by gardeners for their long racemes of foxglove-like flowers, penstemons are elegant and reliable border perennials. Numerous cultivars are available, in colours that include white, pastel and deep pink, warm cherry-red, clear blue and dusky purple. Many penstemon flowers have contrasting white throats or are streaked with other colours. Penstemons flower prolifically in summer, but the display can be prolonged provided the plants are regularly dead-headed. Some taller cultivars may benefit from being staked. Penstemons thrive in well-drained soil, preferably with full sun as some are not fully hardy. Where winters are severe, plants should be overwintered in a cold frame. Plants are more likely to survive frost if they are grown in a sheltered spot in free-draining soil.

P. fruticosus var. ***scouleri*** f. ***albus*** ♀

P. 'Alice Hindley' ♀

P. 'Hopleys Variegated'

P. 'White Bedder' ♀

P. 'Mother of Pearl'

P. 'Madame Golding'

P. 'Beech Park' ♀

P. 'Kilimanjaro'

P. 'Apple Blossom' ♀

P. 'Husker Red'

P. 'Margery Fish' ♀

P. cardwellii

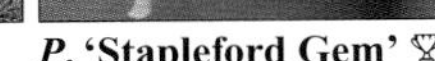

P. 'Stapleford Gem' ♀

P. 'Stromboli'

P. 'Osprey' ♀

P. 'Evelyn' ♀

P. 'Flamingo'

P. glaber

P. isophyllus ♀

P. 'Pennington Gem' ♀

P. 'Sour Grapes' ♀

P. heterophyllus

P. 'Rubicundus' ♀

P. 'Burgundy'

P. 'Raven' ♀

P. 'Schoenholzeri' ♀

P. 'Hidcote Pink' ♀

P. 'Cherry Ripe' ♀

P. 'Countess of Dalkeith'

P. 'Blackbird'

P. 'Connie's Pink' ♀

P. 'Port Wine' ♀

P. 'Chester Scarlet' ♀

P. 'King George V'

P. 'Pensham Just Jayne'

P. 'Rich Ruby'

P. 'Old Candy Pink'

P. *barbatus*

P. 'Torquay Gem'

P. 'Geoff Hamilton'

P. *kunthii*

P. 'Modesty'

P. *hartwegii* ♀

P. 'Andenken an Friedrich Hahn' ♀

P. 'George Home' ♀

P. 'Southgate Gem'

P. 'Maurice Gibbs' ♀

P. 'Red Emperor'

■ RED

***Helenium* 'Bruno'**
Erect, bushy perennial with stout stems and lance-shaped leaves. Sprays of deep bronze-red flower heads are produced from late summer to autumn. H 1.2m (4ft), S 75cm (2½ft).

***Persicaria amplexicaulis* 'Firetail'**
Clump-forming perennial that carries slender spikes of bright red flowers above heart-shaped leaves in summer-autumn. H and S 1–1.2m (3–4ft).

Lychnis chalcedonica
(Jerusalem cross, Maltese cross)
Neat, clump-forming perennial that bears flat heads of small, vermilion flowers at the tips of stout stems in early summer. Foliage is mid-green. H 1–1.2m (3–4ft), S 30–45cm (1–1½ft).

***Lobelia* 'Cherry Ripe'**
Clump-forming perennial bearing spikes of cerise-scarlet flowers from mid- to late summer. Leaves, usually fresh green, are often tinged red-bronze. H 1m (3ft), S 23cm (9in).

***Astilbe* 'Montgomery'**
Leafy perennial bearing feathery, tapering plumes of tiny, deep salmon-red flowers in summer. Foliage is broad and divided into leaflets; flowers, brown when dried, remain on the plant well into winter. Prefers humus-rich soil. H 75cm (2½ft), S to 1m (3ft).

Knautia macedonica
Upright perennial with deeply divided leaves and many rather lax, branching stems bearing double, almost globular, bright crimson flower heads in summer. Needs staking. H 75cm (30in), S 60cm (24in).

Cosmos atrosanguineus
(Chocolate cosmos)
Upright, tuberous perennial with chocolate-scented, maroon-crimson flower heads in late summer. In warm sites tubers may overwinter if protected. H 60cm (24in) or more, S 45cm (18in).

***Lobelia* 'Queen Victoria'**
Clump-forming perennial. From late summer to mid-autumn spikes of blazing red flowers on branching stems arise from basal, deep red-purple foliage. H 1m (3ft), S 30cm (1ft).

Ruellia graecizans
Evergreen, bushy sub-shrub with wide-spreading stems. Oval, pointed leaves are 10cm (4in) long. Intermittently bears clusters of small, tubular, scarlet flowers on stalks to 10cm (4in) long. H and S 60cm (24in) or more. Min. 15°C (59°F).

RED

Hedysarum coronarium
(French honeysuckle)
Spreading, shrubby perennial or biennial. Spikes of pea-like, bright red flowers are produced in summer above divided, mid-green leaves. H and S 1m (3ft).

Russelia equisetiformis
(Coral plant)
Evergreen, branching, bushy sub-shrub with rush-like stems and tiny leaves. Showy, pendent clusters of tubular, scarlet flowers appear in summer-autumn. H to 1m (3ft) or more, S 60cm (2ft). Min. 15°C (59°F).

Anigozanthos manglesii
(Red-and-green kangaroo paw)
Vigorous, bushy perennial that bears racemes of large, tubular, woolly, red-and-green flowers in spring and early summer. Has long, narrow, grey-green leaves. May suffer from ink disease. H 1m (3ft), S 45cm (1½ft).

***Monarda* 'Cambridge Scarlet'**
Clump-forming perennial that throughout summer bears whorls of hooded, rich red flowers above neat mounds of aromatic, hairy foliage. H 1m (3ft), S 45cm (1½ft).

***Papaver orientale* 'Allegro'**
Hairy-leaved perennial with very deep, fleshy roots. Papery, bright scarlet flowers are borne in summer on strong stems. H 60–75cm (24–30in), S 45cm (18in).

Columnea* × *banksii
Evergreen, trailing perennial with oval, fleshy leaves, glossy above, purplish-red below. Tubular, hooded, brilliant red flowers, to 8cm (3in) long, appear from spring to winter. Makes a useful plant for a hanging basket. H 1m (3ft), S indefinite. Min. 15°C (59°F).

RED–PURPLE

Kohleria eriantha
Robust, bushy, rhizomatous perennial with reddish-haired stems. Oval leaves, to 13cm (5in) long, are edged with red hairs. Has tubular, red flowers, with yellow-spotted lobes, in nodding clusters in summer. H and S 1m (3ft) or more. Min. 15°C (59°F).

***Papaver orientale* 'Beauty of Livermere'**
Hairy-leaved perennial with deep, fleshy roots. Large, solitary, cup-shaped, crimson-scarlet flowers, with a black mark at the base of each petal, are borne from late spring to mid-summer. H 1–1.2m (3–4ft), S 1m (3ft).

***Achillea* 'Fanal'**
Herbaceous perennial with slightly greyish-green, fern-like leaves that forms spreading, drought-resistant clumps. In early summer bears flat-topped, bold crimson flowerheads that atttract bees and butterflies. H 75cm (30in), S 60cm (24in).

Acanthus hungaricus
Perennial with long, deeply cut, basal, dark green leaves. Spikes of white or pink-flushed flowers, set in spiny, red-purple bracts, are carried in summer. H 60cm–1m (2–3ft), S 1m (3ft).

Linaria triornithophora
(Three birds toadflax)
Upright perennial that from early to late summer produces spikes of snapdragon-like, purple and yellow flowers above narrow, grey-green leaves. H 1m (3ft), S 60cm (2ft).

Monarda fistulosa
Clump-forming perennial that produces small heads of lilac-purple flowers from mid- to late summer. H 1.2m (4ft), S 45cm (1½ft).

***Campanula glomerata* 'Superba'**
Vigorous, clump-forming perennial with dense, rounded heads of large, bell-shaped, purple flowers borne in summer. Bears oval leaves in basal rosettes and on flower stems. Must be divided and replanted regularly. H 75cm (2½ft), S 1m (3ft) or more.

Acanthus spinosus
Stately perennial that has very large, arching, deeply cut and spiny-pointed, glossy, dark green leaves. Spires of funnel-shaped, soft mauve and white flowers are borne freely in summer. H 1.2m (4ft), S 60cm (2ft) or more.

***Geranium sylvaticum* 'Mayflower'**
Upright perennial with a basal clump of deeply lobed leaves, above which rise branching stems of cup-shaped, violet-blue flowers in early summer. H 1m (3ft), S 60cm (2ft).

Thalictrum aquilegiifolium
Clump-forming perennial with a mass of finely divided, grey-green leaves, resembling those of maidenhair fern. Bunched heads of fluffy, lilac-purple flowers are borne on strong stems in summer. H 1–1.2m (3–4ft), S 45cm (1½ft).

***Veronica spicata* 'Romiley Purple'**
Clump-forming perennial that in summer freely produces large spikes of purple flowers above whorled, mid-green leaves. H 1–1.2m (3–4ft), S 30–60cm (1–2ft).

Aquilegia

Aquilegias, commonly known as columbines, are among the most popular of all hardy perennials. Often considered the ideal cottage garden plant, they thrive in moist, but well-drained, sunny sites and are suitable for growing in borders, rock gardens, dappled shade, and also as fillers between summer-flowering shrubs. Most are graceful, elegant plants with divided foliage surmounted in late spring and summer by a succession of delicate, bell-shaped, usually spurred flowers that vary in colour from light to dark blue, purple to almost black, dark red to pink as well as orange, yellow and white. Many are bicoloured and some have neatly doubled flowers. Aquilegias are normally raised from seed, which is freely produced, and once established, they tend to self-seed, although most will not come true to type.

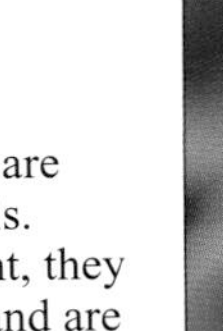

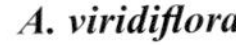

A. viridiflora

***A. vulgaris* 'Nivea'** ♀

A. 'Florida' ♀

***A. chrysantha* 'Yellow Queen'**

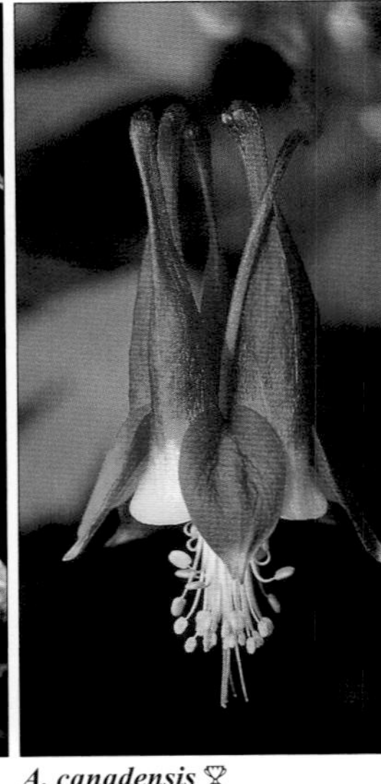

A. canadensis ♀

A. 'Bluebird' (Songbird Series) ♀

***A. flabellata alba* 'White Jewel' (Jewel Series)**

A. 'Dove' (Songbird Series) ♀

A. 'Cardinal' (Songbird Series)

A. chrysantha

A. vulgaris* var. *alba

A. fragrans

A. 'Goldfinch'

A. longissima ♀

A. 'Robin' (Songbird Series)

A. triternata

A. Biedermeier Group

A. 'Mrs Scott Elliot'

A. karelinei

A. 'Nuthatch'

A. vulgaris var. *stellata* 'Black Barlow'

A. 'Dragonfly'

A. coerulea ♡

A. vulgaris 'William Guiness'

A. alpina

A. flabellata Jewel Series

A. 'Winky Red-White'

A. 'Bunting' (Songbird Series) ♡

A. atrata

A. flabellata var. *pumila* ♡

A. 'Sunburst Ruby'

A. vulgaris 'Ruby Port'

A. rockii

A. flabellata 'Ministar'

A. bertolonii ♡

■ PURPLE

Campanula trachelium
(Nettle-leaved bellflower)
Upright perennial with rough, serrated, oval, pointed, basal leaves. Wide, bell-shaped, blue or purple-blue flowers are spaced along erect stems in summer. H 60cm–1m (2–3ft), S 30cm (1ft).

☼ ◊ ❄❄❄

Dichorisandra reginae
Evergreen, erect, clump-forming perennial. Glossy, often silver-banded and flecked leaves are purple-red beneath. Has small spikes of densely set, purple-blue flowers in summer-autumn. H 60–75cm (24–30in), S to 30cm (12in). Min. 20°C (68°F).

***Echinops ritro* 'Veitch's Blue'**
Upright perennial with round, thistle-like, purplish-blue heads of flowers carried in late summer on silvery stems. Sharply divided leaves have pale down beneath. H 1.2m (4ft), S 75cm (2½ft).

☼ ◊ ❄❄❄

Galega orientalis
Vigorous, upright but compact perennial that in summer bears spikes of pea-like, blue-tinged, violet flowers above delicate leaves divided into oval leaflets. Needs staking. Spreads freely. H 1.2m (4ft), S 60cm (2ft).

☼ ◊ ❄❄❄

***Salvia × superba* 'Mainacht'**
Neat, clump-forming perennial with narrow, wrinkled, mid-green leaves. In late spring and summer bears stiff racemes of violet-blue flowers. H 1m (3ft), S 45cm (1½ft).

☼ ◊ ❄❄❄ 🏆

***Campanula trachelium* 'Bernice'**
Upright perennial that has wide, bell-shaped, double, purple-violet flowers carried along erect stems in summer. Leaves are mostly basal and are rough, serrated, oval and pointed. H 75cm (30in), S 30cm (12in).

☼ ◊ ❄❄❄

***Aconitum × cammarum* 'Bicolor'**
Compact, tuberous perennial with violet-blue and white flowers borne in summer along upright stems. Has deeply cut, divided, glossy, dark green leaves and poisonous roots. H 1.2m (4ft), S 50cm (20in).

Baptisia australis
(False indigo)
Upright perennial bearing spikes of pea-like, violet-blue flowers in summer. Bright green leaves are divided into oval leaflets. Dark grey seed pods may be used for winter decoration. H 75cm (30in), S 60cm (24in).

☼ ◊ ❄❄❄ 🏆

Dianella tasmanica
Upright perennial with nodding, star-shaped, bright blue or purple-blue flowers carried in branching sprays in summer, followed by deep blue berries in autumn. Has untidy, evergreen, strap-shaped leaves. H 1.2m (4ft), S 50cm (20in).

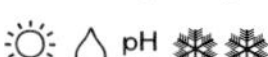

Eryngium alpinum
Upright perennial with basal rosettes of heart-shaped, deeply toothed, glossy foliage, above which rise stout stems bearing, in summer, heads of conical, purplish-blue flower heads, surrounded by blue bracts and soft spines. H 75cm–1m (2½–3ft), S 60cm (2ft).

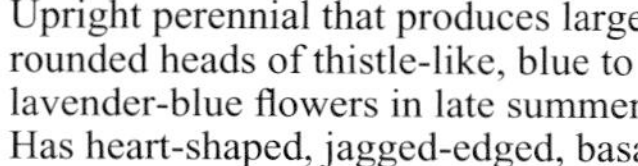

Eryngium* × *oliverianum
Upright perennial that produces large, rounded heads of thistle-like, blue to lavender-blue flowers in late summer. Has heart-shaped, jagged-edged, basal, mid-green leaves. H 60cm–1m (2–3ft), S 45–60cm (1½–2ft).

Eryngium* × *tripartitum
Perennial with wiry stems above a basal rosette of coarsely toothed, grey-green leaves. Conical, metallic-blue flower heads on blue stems are borne in summer-autumn and may be dried for winter decoration. H 1–1.2m (3–4ft), S 50cm (20in).

***Campanula persicifolia* 'Telham Beauty'**
Perennial with basal rosettes of narrow, bright green leaves. In summer, large, nodding, cup-shaped, light blue flowers are borne on slender spikes. H 1m (3ft), S 30cm (1ft).

Cichorium intybus (Chicory)
Clump-forming perennial with basal rosettes of light green leaves and daisy-like, bright blue flower heads borne along upper parts of willowy stems in summer. Flowers are at their best before noon. H 1.2m (4ft), S 45cm (1½ft).

Meconopsis grandis (Blue poppy)
Erect perennial with oblong, slightly toothed, hairy, mid-green leaves produced in rosettes at the base. Stout stems bear slightly nodding, cup-shaped, deep blue flowers in early summer. Divide every 2–3 years. H 1–1.5m (3–5ft), S 30cm (1ft).

Meconopsis betonicifolia
(Blue poppy)
Clump-forming perennial that bears blue flowers in late spring and early summer. Oblong, mid-green leaves are produced in basal rosettes and in decreasing size up flowering stems. H 1–1.2m (3–4ft), S 45cm (1½ft).

***Agapanthus* 'Blue Giant'**
Clump-forming perennial bearing rounded heads of open, bell-shaped rich blue flowers in mid- to late summer. Protect crowns in winter with mulch. H 1.2m (4ft), S 60cm (24in).

BLUE

Agapanthus praecox subsp. ***orientalis***
Perennial with large, dense umbels of sky-blue flowers borne on strong stems in late summer over clumps of broad, almost evergreen, dark green leaves. Makes a good plant for pots. H 1m (3ft), S 60cm (2ft).

Nepeta sibirica
Erect, leafy perennial that bears long, whorled cymes of blue to lavender-blue flowers in mid- and late summer. Leaves are dark green and aromatic. H 90cm (36in), S 45cm (18in).

***Anchusa azurea* 'Loddon Royalist'**
Upright perennial that bears flat, single, deep blue flowers on branching spikes in early summer. Most of the lance-shaped, coarse, hairy leaves are at the base of plant. Needs staking. H 1.2m (4ft), S 60cm (2ft).

GREEN–YELLOW

Euphorbia schillingii
Robust, clump-forming perennial that produces long-lasting, yellow cyathia and rounded, greenish-yellow bracts from mid-summer to mid-autumn. Stems are erect and leaves are dark green with pale green or white veins. H 1m (3ft), S 30cm (1ft).

Euphorbia sikkimensis
Spreading, upright perennial bearing yellow cyathia cupped by pale to greenish-yellow involucres in mid- to late summer. Young shoots are bright pink and the leaves deep green. H 1.2m (4ft), S 45cm (1½ft).

Anigozanthos flavidus
(Yellow kangaroo paw)
Bushy perennial with racemes of large, woolly, tubular, yellowish-green flowers, with reddish anthers, borne in spring-summer. Narrow leaves, to 60cm (2ft) long, are mid-green. H 1.2m (4ft), S 45cm (1½ft).

***Verbascum* 'Gainsborough'**
Semi-evergreen, rosette-forming, short-lived perennial bearing branched racemes of 5-lobed, pale sulphur-yellow flowers throughout summer above oval, mid-green leaves borne on flower stems. H 60cm–1.2m (2–4ft), S 30–60cm (1–2ft).

Thalictrum lucidum
Perennial with glossy leaves composed of numerous leaflets. Strong stems bear loose panicles of fluffy, greenish-yellow flowers in summer. H 1–1.2m (3–4ft), S 50cm (20in).

***Argyranthemum* 'Jamaica Primrose'**
Evergreen, woody-based perennial with fern-like, pale green leaves. Daisy-like, single, soft yellow flower heads are borne in summer. Take stem cuttings in early autumn. H and S to 1m (3ft).

Aconitum lycoctonum subsp. ***vulparia*** (Wolf's bane)
Upright, fibrous perennial that has hooded, straw-yellow flowers in summer. Leaves are dark green and deeply divided. Needs staking. H 1–1.2m (3–4ft), S 30–60cm (1–2ft).

Gentiana lutea
(Great yellow gentian)
Erect, unbranched perennial with oval, stalkless leaves to 30cm (1ft) long. In summer has dense whorls of tubular, yellow flowers in axils of greenish bracts. H 1–1.2m (3–4ft), S 60cm (2ft).

Phlomis russeliana
Evergreen perennial, forming excellent ground cover, with large, rough, heart-shaped leaves. Stout flower stems bear whorls of hooded, butter-yellow flowers in summer. H 1m (3ft), S 60cm (2ft) or more.

***Anthemis tinctoria* 'E.C. Buxton'**
Clump-forming perennial with a mass of daisy-like, lemon-yellow flower heads borne singly in summer on slim stems. Cut back hard after flowering to promote a good rosette of crinkled leaves for winter. H and S 1m (3ft).

Lysimachia punctata
(Garden loosestrife)
Clump-forming perennial that in summer produces spikes of bright yellow flowers above mid-green leaves. H 60–75cm (24–30in), S 60cm (24in).

***Solidago* 'Goldenmosa'**
Clump-forming perennial. Sprays of tufted, mimosa-like, yellow flower heads are carried in late summer and autumn above lance-shaped, toothed, hairy, yellowish-green leaves. H 1m (3ft), S 60cm (2ft).

***Achillea* 'Schwellenberg'**
Low-growing, spreading perennial with branched stems and grey-green foliage. Silvery buds are followed by lemon-yellow flower heads from early summer to early autumn. H 45cm (18in), S 60cm (24in).

YELLOW

Thermopsis rhombifolia
Upright perennial bearing spikes of bright yellow flowers above divided, mid-green leaves in summer. H 60cm–1m (2–3ft), S 60cm (2ft).

Inula hookeri
Clump-forming perennial with lance-shaped to elliptic, hairy leaves and a mass of slightly scented, daisy-like, greenish-yellow flower heads borne in summer. H 75cm (30in), S 45cm (18in).

***Aphelandra squarrosa* 'Louisae'**
Evergreen, erect perennial. Long, oval, glossy, slightly wrinkled, dark green leaves have white veins and midribs. Bears dense spikes of golden-yellow flowers from axils of yellow bracts in late summer to autumn. H to 1m (3ft), S 60cm (2ft). Min. 13°C (55°F).

***Solidago* 'Laurin'**
Compact perennial bearing spikes of deep yellow flowers in late summer. Foliage is mid-green. H 60–75cm (24–30in), S 45 cm (18in).

***Rudbeckia fulgida* var. *sullivantii* 'Goldsturm'**
Erect perennial. In late summer and autumn, daisy-like, golden flower heads with conical, black centres are borne at the ends of strong stems. Has narrow, rough, mid-green leaves. H 75cm (30in), S 30cm (12in) or more.

Verbascum nigrum
Semi-evergreen, clump-forming perennial bearing narrow spikes of small, 5-lobed, purple-centred, yellow flowers during summer and autumn. Oblong, mid-green leaves are downy beneath. H 60cm–1m (2–3ft), S 60cm (2ft).

***Achillea* 'Coronation Gold'**
Upright perennial with feathery, silvery leaves. Bears large, flat heads of small, golden flower heads in summer that dry well for winter decoration. Should be divided and replanted every third year. H 1m (3ft), S 60cm (2ft).

Inula royleana
Upright, clump-forming perennial with dark green stems and ovate, hairy leaves. Bears solitary, orange-yellow flower heads, 10–12cm (4–5in) across, from mid-summer to early autumn. H 45–60cm (18–24in), S 45cm (18in).

DAYLILIES

H. **'Joan Senior'**

Although they belong to the lily family (Liliaceae), daylilies (*Hemerocallis*) are not true lilies; their common name comes from the lily-like flowers that generally last only a day. Daylilies range in size from compact plants that grow only to 30–38cm (12–15in) tall, to large plants that may reach 1.5m (5ft). Modern cultivars are available in a wide range of colours, from creamy-white, through shades of yellow, orange, red, pink and purple, to almost black; some flowers have differently coloured bands on the petals. The flower forms are usually classified as single, double, or spider. Some species and a few cultivars are strongly fragrant. Most daylilies flower for four to six weeks; they thrive in almost any soil, except poorly drained clay, in sun or shade, but bloom best if they are in sun for at least half the day.

H. **'Siloam Ethel Smith'**

H. **'Gentle Shepherd'**

H. **'Siloam Baby Talk'**

H. **'Michele Coe'**

H. **'Millie Schlumpf'**

H. **'Always Afternoon'**

H. **'Pink Damask'** ♔

H. **'Siloam Virginia Henson'**

H. **'Little Grapette'**

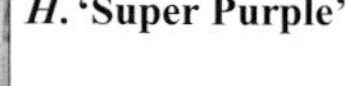

H. **'Super Purple'**

H. **'Jolyene Nichole'**

H. **'Summer Wine'**

H. **'Night Beacon'**

H. **'Prairie Blue Eyes'**

H. 'Marion Vaughn' ♀

H. 'Eenie Weenie'

H. 'Bonanza'

H. 'Burning Daylight' ♀

H. *aurantiaca*

H. 'Brocaded Gown'

H. 'Hyperion'

H. 'Solano Bulls Eye'

H. 'Golden Prize'

H. 'Ruffled Apricot'

H. 'Chicago Sunrise'

H. 'Corky' ♀

H. 'Lark Song'

H. *dumortieri*

H. *lilioasphodelus* ♀

H. 'Lady Fingers'

H. *fulva*

H. 'Cat's Cradle'

H. *citrina*

H. 'Betty Woods'

H. 'Cream Drop'

H. 'Golden Chimes' ♀

H. 'Mauna Loa'

H. 'Missenden' ♀

H. 'Berlin Red' ♀

H. 'Stafford'

H. 'Frans Hals' ♀

H. 'Real Wind'

H. *fulva* 'Flore Pleno'

H. 'Crimson Pirate'

H. 'Neyron Rose' ♀

H. 'Custard Candy'

H. 'Rose Emily'

H. 'Chorus Line'

H. 'Scarlet Oak'

H. 'Little Wine Cup'

H. 'Cherry Cheeks'

H. 'Scarlet Orbit'

H. 'Strawberry Candy'

H. 'Ed Murray'

YELLOW

Berkheya macrocephala
Upright perennial bearing large, daisy-like, yellow flower heads on branched, spiny-leaved stems throughout summer. Prefers rich soil and a warm, sheltered position. H and S 1m (3ft).

***Achillea filipendulina* 'Gold Plate'**
Upright perennial with stout, leafy stems carrying broad, flat, terminal heads of yellow flowers in summer, above filigree foliage. Flowers retain colour if dried. Divide plants regularly. H 1.2m (4ft) or more, S 60cm (2ft).

***Heliopsis* 'Ballet Dancer'**
Upright perennial flowering freely in late summer and bearing double, yellow flower heads with frilled petals. Dark green leaves are coarse and serrated. H 1–1.2m (3–4ft), S 60cm (2ft).

YELLOW–ORANGE

***Kniphofia* 'Royal Standard'**
Upright perennial with grass-like, basal tufts of leaves and terminal spikes of scarlet buds, opening to lemon-yellow flowers, borne on erect stems in late summer. Protect crowns with winter mulch. H 1–1.2m (3–4ft), S 60cm (2ft).

Sphaeralcea ambigua
Branching, shrubby perennial. Broadly funnel-shaped, orange-coral blooms are produced singly in leaf axils from summer until the onset of cold weather. Leaves are soft, hairy and mid-green. H and S 75–90cm (30–36in).

Kniphofia thomsonii* var. *snowdenii
Upright perennial with grass-like, basal foliage. In summer bears coral-pink flowers, with yellowish interiors, spaced widely along terminal spikes. Protect crowns with winter mulch. H 1m (3ft), S 50cm (20in).

Asclepias tuberosa
(Butterfly weed)
Erect, tuberous perennial with long, lance-shaped leaves. Small, 5-horned, bright orange-red flowers are borne in summer and followed by narrow, pointed pods, to 15cm (6in) long. H to 75cm (30in), S 45cm (18in).

***Euphorbia griffithii* 'Fireglow'**
Bushy perennial that bears orange-red flowers in terminal umbels in early summer. Leaves are lance-shaped, mid-green and have pale red midribs. H to 1m (3ft), S 50cm (20in).

WHITE–PINK

Actaea pachypoda
(Doll's eyes, White baneberry)
Compact, clump-forming perennial with spikes of small, fluffy, white flowers in summer and clusters of white berries, borne on stiff, fleshy scarlet stalks, in autumn. H 1m (3ft), S 50cm (20in).

Persicaria campanulata
Compact, mat-forming perennial bearing elegant, branching heads of bell-shaped, pink or white flowers from mid-summer to early autumn. Has oval leaves, brown-felted beneath. H and S 1m (3ft).

Chelone obliqua (Turtle-head)
Upright perennial that bears terminal spikes of hooded, lilac-pink flowers in late summer and autumn. Leaves are dark green and lance-shaped. H 1m (3ft), S 50cm (20in).

Tricyrtis formosana
Upright, rhizomatous perennial. In early autumn bears spurred flowers, heavily spotted with purplish-pink and with yellow-tinged throats. Glossy, dark green leaves clasp stems. H 60cm–1m (2–3ft), S 45cm (1½ft).

***Anemone hupehensis* 'Hadspen Abundance'**
Erect, branching perennial that bears pink flowers with rounded, dark reddish-pink outer tepals from summer to autumn. Leaves are dark green and deeply divided, with toothed leaflets. H 60cm–1.2m (2–4ft), S 45cm (1½ft).

***Chrysanthemum* 'Clara Curtis'**
Bushy perennial producing many clusters of flat, daisy-like, clear pink flower heads throughout summer and autumn. Divide plants every other spring. H 75cm (30in), S 45cm (18in).

CHRYSANTHEMUMS

Florists' chrysanthemum hybrids are grouped according to their differing flower forms, flowering season (early, mid- or late autumn), and habit (see also *Chrysanthemum* in the Plant Dictionary). The best groups for garden decoration are the sprays, pompons, and early reflexed chrysanthemums. The dwarf charms, forming a dense, dome-shaped mass of flowers, look most attractive displayed in pots. Most groups have only one large flower per stem, although the sprays, charms and pompons have several. The flower forms are described below.

C. **'Lemon Rynoon'**
(incurved, early)

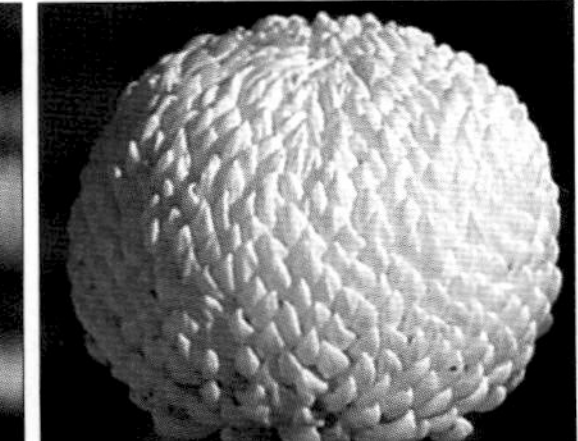

C. **'Pennine Oriel'**
(spray, anemone, early)

C. **'Alison Kirk'**
(incurved, early)

C. **'Bill Wade'**
(intermediate, early)

C. **'Lundy'**
(reflexed, late)

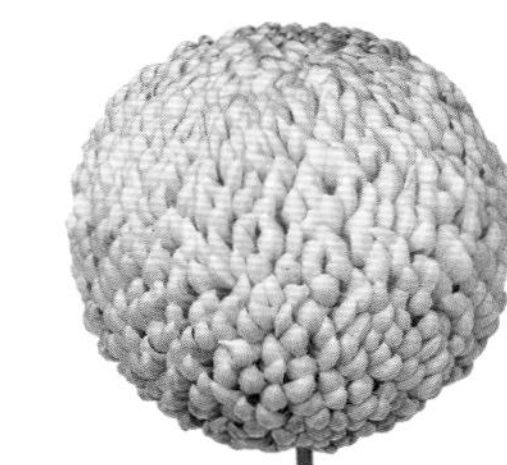

C. **'John Wingfield'**
(reflexed, late)

C. **'Fairweather'**
(incurved, late)

Incurved – fully double, dense, spherical flowers have incurved petals arising from the base of the flower and closing tightly over the crown.

Fully reflexed – fully double flowers have curved, pointed petals reflexing outwards and downwards from the crown, back to touch the stem.

Reflexed – fully double flowers are similar to those of fully reflexed forms except that the petals are less strongly reflexed and form an umbrella-like or spiky outline.

Intermediate – fully double, roughly spherical flowers have loosely incurving petals, which may close at the crown or may reflex for the bottom half of each flower.

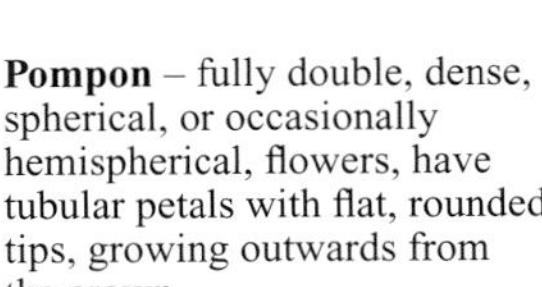

Anemone-centred – single flowers each have a central, dome-shaped disc, up to half the diameter of the bloom, and up to 5 rows of flat, or occasionally spoon-shaped, ray petals at right angles to the stem.

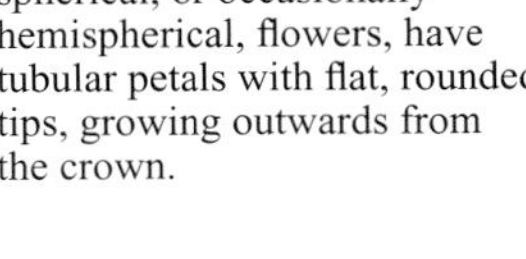

Single – flowers each have about 5 rows of flat petals, borne at right angles to the stem, that may incurve or reflex at the tips; the prominent, central disc is golden throughout or has a small, green centre.

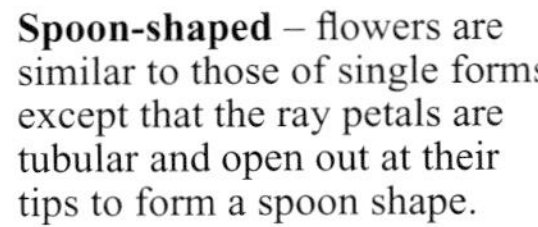

Pompon – fully double, dense, spherical, or occasionally hemispherical, flowers, have tubular petals with flat, rounded tips, growing outwards from the crown.

Spoon-shaped – flowers are similar to those of single forms except that the ray petals are tubular and open out at their tips to form a spoon shape.

Spider-form – double flower heads with long, thin ray-florets; the outer ray-florets are more or less pendent, the inner ones curling upwards.

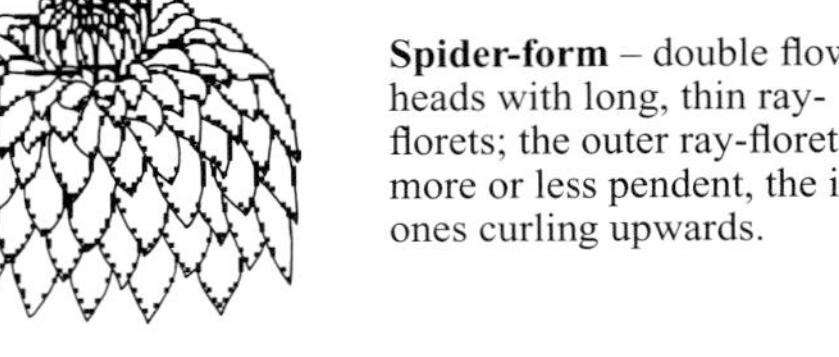

Quill-shaped – double flower heads with tubular ray-florets that open out at their tips to form spoon shapes.

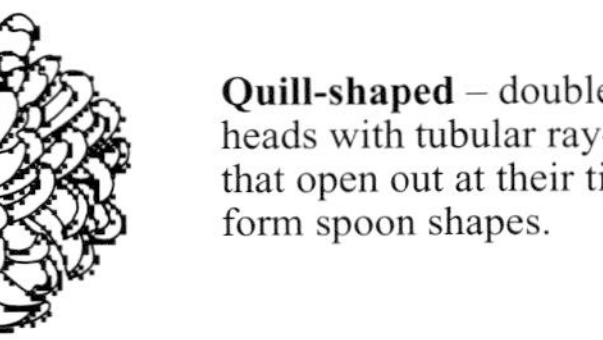

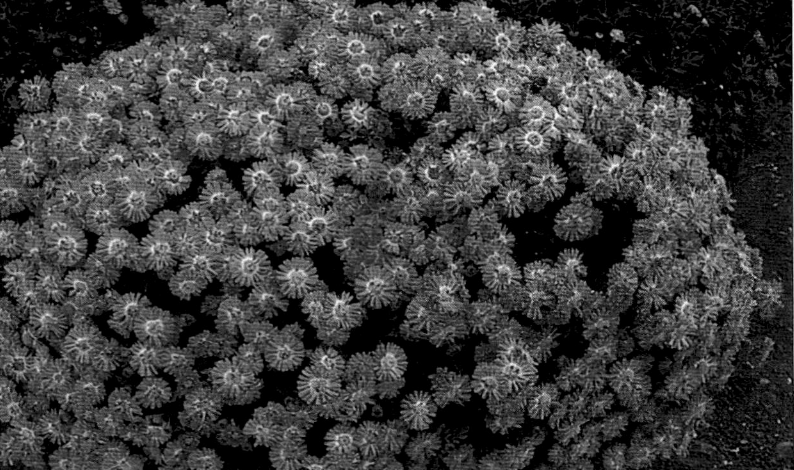

C. **'Ringdove'**
(charm, late)

C. **'Brietner'**
(reflexed, early)

C. **'Woking Rose'**
(intermediate, late)

C. **'Keith Luxford'**
(incurved, late)

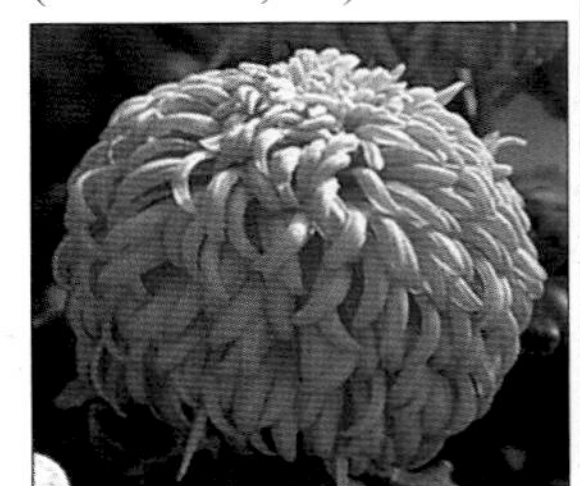

C. **'Marian Gosling'**
(reflexed, early)

C. **'Enbee Wedding'**
(spray, single, early) ♀

C. 'Talbot Jo'
(spray, single, early)

C. 'Robeam'
(spray, reflexed, late) ♀

C. 'Wendy'
(spray, reflexed, early) ♀

C. 'Salmon Fairie'
(pompon, late) ♀

C. 'Primrose West Bromwich' (reflexed, mid)

C. 'Majestic'
(reflexed, late)

C. 'Bronze Hedgerow'
(single, late)

C. 'Bronze Fairie'
(pompon, early) ♀

C. 'Yvonne Arnaud'
(reflexed, early) ♀

C. 'Green Satin'
(intermediate, late)

C. 'Golden Gigantic'
(incurved, late)

C. 'Gigantic'
(incurved, late)

C. 'Pennine Alfie'
(spray, spoon-shaped, early) ♀

C. 'George Griffiths'
(reflexed early) ♀

C. 'Marion'
(spray, reflexed, early)

C. 'Salmon Margaret'
(spray, reflexed, early) ♀

C. 'Maria'
(pompon, early)

C. 'Primrose John Hughes'
(incurved, late)

C. 'Golden Chalice'
(charm, late)

C. 'Autumn Days'
(intermediate, early)

C. 'Idris'
(incurved, late)

C. 'Nancye Furneaux'
(reflexed, late)

C. 'Roy Coopland'
(intermediate, late) ♀

C. 'Beacon'
(intermediate, late) ♀

C. 'Yellow Brietner'
(reflexed, early)

C. 'Yellow John Hughes'
(incurved, late) ♀

C. 'Oracle'
(intermediate, early)

C. 'Peach Brietner'
(reflexed, early)

C. 'Rytorch'
(spray, single, late)

MICHAELMAS DAISIES

A. ericoides **'White Heather'**

Michaelmas daisies (*Aster* species and cultivars, mostly of *A. novae-angliae* and *A. novi-belgii*) are invaluable border plants as they flower later than most other perennials and continue the display until late autumn. The daisy-like, single or double flowers, usually with yellow centres, range in colour from white, through pink and red, to purple and blue and are excellent for cutting. For larger flowers pinch out or cut back weaker shoots in spring; pinch out the top 2.5–5cm (1–2in) of the remaining shoots to produce bushier plants that will bear a greater quantity of smaller flowers. Tall cultivars may need staking. Michaelmas daisies thrive in sun or partial shade in well-drained soil. Many are susceptible to mildew; in areas where this is a problem treat plants regularly with a fungicide or choose resistant varieties.

A. novi-belgii **'Professor Anton Kippenburg'**

A. thomsonii **'Nanus'**

A. novi-belgii **'Kristina'**

A. novi-belgii **'Sandford White Swan'**

A. novi-belgii **'Orlando'**

A. novi-belgii **'Royal Ruby'**

A. amellus **'King George'** ♀

A. × frikartii **'Wunder von Stäfa'** ♀

A. ericoides **'Golden Spray'** ♀

A. novi-belgii **'Freda Ballard'**

A. novae-angliae **'Andenken an Alma Pötschke'**

A. × frikartii **'Mönch'** ♀

A. novae-angliae **'Herbstschnee'**

A. novi-belgii **'Apple Blossom'**

A. novi-belgii **'Royal Velvet'**

A. amellus **'Nocturne'**

A. novi-belgii **'Marie Ballard'**

A. cordifolius **'Silver Spray'**

A. novae-angliae **'Harrington's Pink'** ♀

A. lateriflorus var. ***horizontalis*** ♀

A. novi-belgii **'Patricia Ballard'**

A. novi-belgii **'Peace'**

A. linosyris

A. novi-belgii **'Fellowship'**

A. novi-belgii **'Lassie'**

A. novae-angliae **'Barr's Pink'**

A. novi-belgii **'Carnival'**

A. novi-belgii **'Chequers'**

PURPLE–YELLOW

Strobilanthes atropurpureus
Upright, branching perennial with oval, toothed leaves. Spikes of numerous, violet-blue to purple flowers appear in summer-autumn. H to 1.2m (4ft), S to 60cm (2ft).

Gentiana asclepiadea
(Willow gentian)

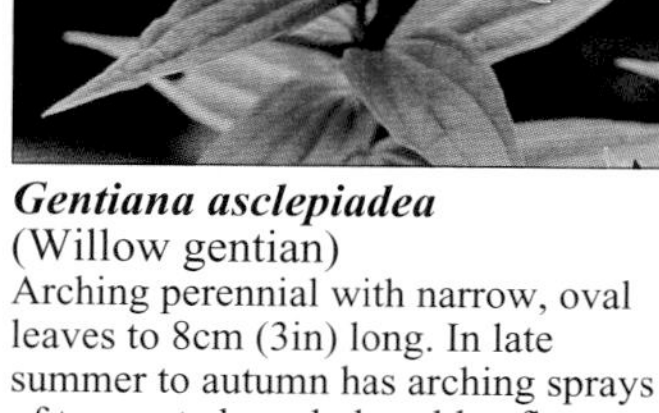

Arching perennial with narrow, oval leaves to 8cm (3in) long. In late summer to autumn has arching sprays of trumpet-shaped, deep blue flowers, spotted and striped inside. H to 90cm (36in), S to 60cm (24in).

***Kniphofia* 'Percy's Pride'**
Upright perennial with large, terminal spikes of creamy flowers, tinged green and yellow, borne on erect stems in autumn. Protect crowns with winter mulch. H 1m (3ft), S 50cm (20in).

YELLOW–ORANGE

Kirengeshoma palmata
Upright perennial with rounded, lobed, bright green leaves, above which strong stems bearing clusters of narrowly funnel-shaped, creamy yellow flowers appear in late summer to autumn. H 1m (3ft), S 60cm (2ft).

Kniphofia rooperi
Robust, evergreen perennial with arching, linear, dark green leaves. From early to late autumn, produces broadly ellipsoid racemes of orange-red flowers, becoming orange-yellow. H 1.2m (4ft), S 60cm (2ft).

***Helenium* 'Wyndley'**
Bushy perennial with branching stems bearing sprays of daisy-like, orange-yellow flower heads for a long period in late summer and autumn. Foliage is dark green. Needs regular division in spring or autumn. H 80cm (30in), S 50cm (20in).

Kniphofia caulescens
Stately, evergreen, upright perennial with basal tufts of narrow, blue-green leaves and smooth, stout stems bearing terminal spikes of reddish-salmon flowers in autumn. H 1.2m (4ft), S 60cm (2ft).

***Helenium* 'Moerheim Beauty'**
Upright perennial with strong, branching stems bearing sprays of daisy-like, rich reddish-orange flower heads in early autumn above dark green foliage. Needs regular division in spring or autumn. H 1m (3ft), S 60cm (2ft).

WHITE–PINK

***Ctenanthe oppenheimiana* 'Tricolor'**
Robust, evergreen, bushy perennial. Has leathery, lance-shaped leaves, over 30cm (12in) long, splashed with large, cream blotches, and, intermittently, spikes of 3-petalled, white flowers. H and S 1m (3ft). Min 15°C (59°F).

Anthurium crystallinum
(Crystal anthurium)
Evergreen, erect, tufted perennial. Long, velvety, dark green leaves are distinctively pale green- to white-veined. Has long-lasting, red-tinged, green spathes. H to 75cm (30in), S to 60cm (24in). Min. 15°C (59°F).

***Plectranthus forsteri* 'Marginatus'**
Evergreen, bushy perennial. Oval leaves, to 6cm (2½in) long, are greyish-green with scalloped, white margins. Irregularly has tubular, white to pale mauve flowers. H and S 60cm (24in) or more. Min. 10°C (50°F).

Hypoestes phyllostachya
(Freckle face, Polka-dot plant)
Evergreen, bush perennial or sub-shrub. Dark green leaves are covered with irregular, pink spots. Bears small, tubular, lavender flowers intermittently. H and S 75cm (30in). Min. 10°C (50°F).

***Dieffenbachia seguine* 'Exotica'**
Evergreen, tufted perennial, sometimes woody at the base. Broadly lance-shaped leaves, to 45cm (18in) long, are blotched with creamy-white. H and S 1m (3ft) or more. Min. 15°C (59°F).

***Caladium bicolor* 'Pink Beauty'**
Tufted, tuberous perennial. Has long-stalked, triangular, pink-mottled, green leaves, to 45cm (18in) long, with darker pink veins. White spathes appear in summer. H and S 90cm (3ft). Min. 19°C (66°F).

RED

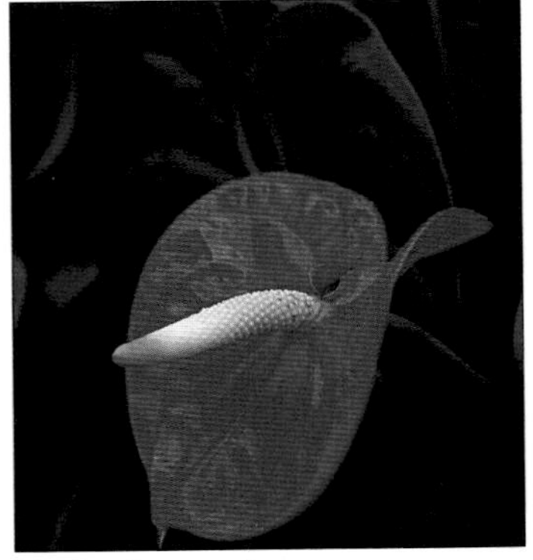

Anthurium andraeanum
(Tail flower)
Evergreen, erect perennial. Long-stalked, oval leaves, with a heart-shaped base, are 20cm (8in) long. Has long-lasting, bright red spathes with yellow spadices. H 60–75cm (24–30in), S 50cm (20in). Min. 15°C (59°F).

Nepenthes × hookeriana
Evergreen, epiphytic, insectivorous perennial with oval, leathery leaves to 30cm (12in) long and pendent, pale green pitchers, with reddish-purple markings and a spurred lid, to 13cm (5in) long. H 60–75cm (24–30in). Min. 18°C (64°F).

***Phormium* 'Dazzler'**
Evergreen, upright perennial with tufts of bold, stiff, pointed leaves in tones of yellow, salmon-pink, orange-red and bronze. Bluish-purple stems carry panicles of reddish flowers in summer. H 2–2.5m (6–8ft) in flower, S 1m (3ft).

Bromeliads

Bromelia balansae

Bromeliads, or plants that belong to the family Bromeliaceae, are distinguished by their bold, usually rosetted foliage and showy flowers in shades of white, red or purple, borne in dense, cylindrical or conical inflorescences in summer. The flowers are followed by ovoid yellow fruits containing large brown seeds.

Many bromeliads are epiphytes, or air plants (absorbing their food through moisture in the atmosphere and not from the host on which they grow), and are suitable for growing outdoors only in tropical regions, in a shady site or desert garden. In cooler climates, however, bromeliads make attractive indoor plants or for a warm greenhouse. Follow instructions for watering with care.

Neoregelia concentrica

Tillandsia cyanea 🏆

Tillandsia lindenii 🏆

***Cryptanthus zonatus* 'Zebrinus'**

Aechmea fasciata 🏆

Billbergia nutans

***Cryptanthus* 'Pink Starlight'** 🏆

Aechmea recurvata

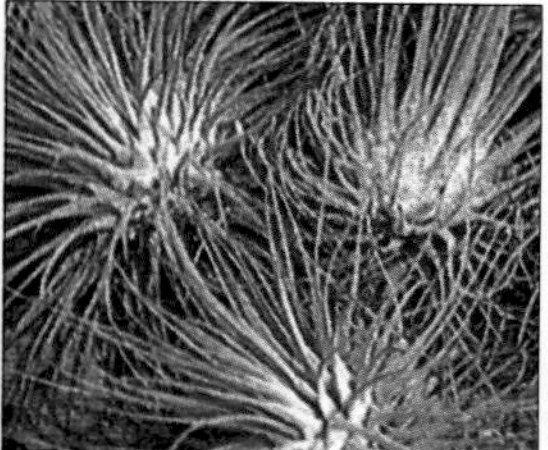

Tillandsia argentea 🏆

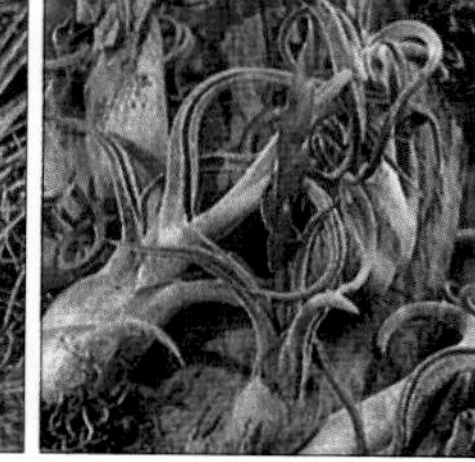

Tillandsia caput-medusae

***Ananas bracteatus* 'Tricolor'** 🏆

Aechmea distichantha

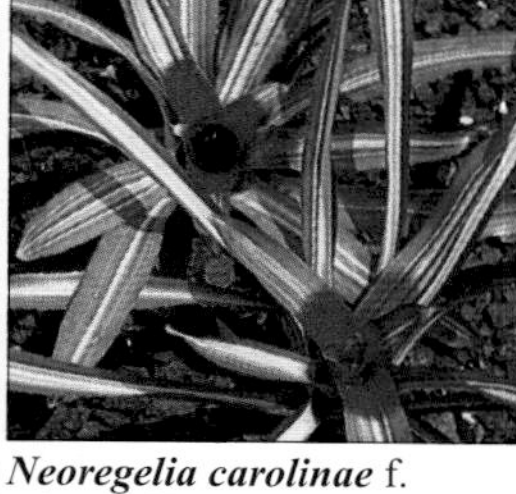

Neoregelia carolinae* f. *tricolor 🏆

Guzmania monostachia 🏆

Dyckia remotiflora

Cryptanthus bivittatus 🏆

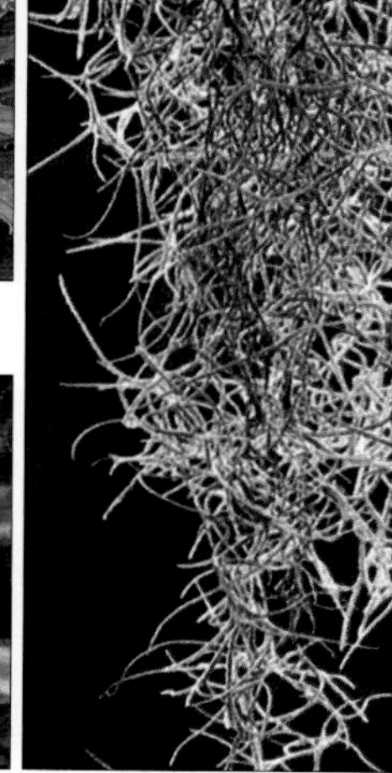

Tillandsia usneoides

***Aechmea* Foster's Favorite Group** 🏆

Puya alpestris

Tillandsia stricta

Vriesea splendens 🏆

Guzmania lingulata 🏆

Tillandsia fasciculata

Puya chilensis

PURPLE–GREEN

Browallia speciosa (Bush violet)
Bushy perennial, usually grown as an annual, propagated by seed each year. Has oval leaves to 10cm (4in) long and showy, violet-blue flowers with white eyes, the season depending when sown. H 60–75cm (24–30in), S 45cm (18in). Min. 10–15°C (50–59°F).

Artemisia ludoviciana
Bushy perennial, grown for its aromatic, lance-shaped leaves which are silvery-grey and woolly on both surfaces and have jagged margins. Bears slender plumes of tiny, greyish-white flower heads in summer. H 1.2m (4ft), S 60cm (2ft).

Aciphylla squarrosa
(Bayonet plant)
Evergreen, clump-forming perennial with tufts of pointed, divided leaves. In summer bears spiky, yellow flowers in compound umbels with male and female flowers often mixed. H and S 1–1.2m (3–4ft).

Asparagus densiflorus
Evergreen, trailing perennial with clusters of narrow, bright green, leaf-like stems. In summer has pink-tinged, white flowers, followed by red berries. Suits a hanging basket. H to 1m (3ft), S 50cm (20in). Min. 10°C (50°F).

Alocasia cuprea
Evergreen, tufted perennial. Oval leaves are 30cm (12in) long, with a metallic sheen and darker, impressed veins above, purple below; leaf stalks arise from the lower surface. Purplish spathes appear intermittently. H and S to 1m (3ft). Min. 15°C (59°F).

Xanthosoma sagittifolium
Spreading, tufted perennial with thick stems. Broadly arrow-shaped leaves, 60cm (2ft) or more long, on long leaf stalks, are green with a greyish bloom. Has green spathes intermittently during the year. H to 2m (6ft) in flower, S 2m (6ft) or more. Min. 15°C (59°F).

***Columnea microphylla* 'Variegata'**
Evergreen, trailing perennial. Has rounded leaves narrowly bordered with cream and tubular, hooded, scarlet flowers, with yellow throats, in winter-spring. H 1m (3ft) or more, S indefinite. Min. 15°C (59°F).

Calathea zebrina (Zebra plant)
Robust, evergreen, clump-forming perennial with long-stalked, velvety, dark green leaves, to 60cm (2ft) long (less if pot-grown), with paler veins, margins and midribs. Has short spikes of white to pale purple flowers. H and S to 90cm (3ft). Min. 15°C (59°F).

GREEN–ORANGE

***Asparagus densiflorus* 'Myersii'**
(Foxtail fern)
Evergreen, erect perennial with spikes of tight, feathery clusters of leaf-like stems and pinkish-white flowers in summer, then red berries. H to 1m (3ft), S 50cm (20in). Min. 10°C (50°F).

***Dieffenbachia seguine* 'Rudolph Roehrs'**
Evergreen, tufted perennial, sometimes woody at the base. Leaves, to 45cm (18in) long, are yellowish-green or white with green midribs and margins. H and S 1m (3ft). Min. 15°C (59°F).

***Sansevieria trifasciata* 'Laurentii'**
Evergreen, stemless perennial with a rosette of about 5 stiff, erect, lance-shaped and pointed leaves with yellow margins. Occasionally has pale green flowers. Propagate by division to avoid reversion. H 45cm–1.2m (1½–4ft), S 10cm (4in). Min. 10–15°C (50–59°F).

Globba winitii
Evergreen, clump-forming perennial with lance-shaped leaves to 20cm (8in) long. Intermittently has pendent racemes of tubular, yellow flowers with large, reddish-purple, reflexed bracts. H 1m (3ft), S 30cm (1ft). Min. 18°C (64°F).

***Peristrophe hyssopifolia* 'Aureovariegata'**
Evergreen, bushy perennial. Small leaves are broadly lance-shaped with long, pointed tips and central, creamy-yellow blotches. Has tubular, rose-pink flowers in winter. H to 60cm (2ft) or more, S 1.2m (4ft). Min. 15°C (59°F).

Strelitzia reginae
(Bird-of-paradise flower)
Evergreen, clump-forming perennial with long-stalked, bluish-green leaves. Has beak-like, orange-and-blue flowers in boat-shaped, red-edged bracts mainly in spring. H over 1m (3ft), S 75cm (2½ft). Min. 5–10°C (41–50°F).

WHITE

***Epimedium × youngianum* 'Niveum'**
Compact, ground-cover perennial with heart-shaped, serrated, bronze-tinted leaflets that turn green in late spring, when small, cup-shaped, snow-white flowers are borne. H 15–30cm (6–12in), S 30cm (12in).

***Lamium maculatum* 'White Nancy'**
Semi-evergreen, mat-forming perennial with white-variegated, mid-green foliage and spikes of hooded, white flowers in late spring and summer. H 15cm (6in), S 1m (3ft).

***Pulmonaria officinalis* 'Sissinghurst White'**
Semi-evergreen, clump-forming perennial that bears funnel-shaped, white flowers in spring above long, elliptic, mid-green, paler spotted leaves. H 30cm (12in), S 45–60cm (18–24in).

Pachyphragma macrophyllum
Creeping, mat-forming perennial with rosettes of rounded, long-stalked, glossy, bright green leaves, each to 10cm (4in) long. Bears many racemes of tiny, white flowers in spring. H to 30cm (12in), S indefinite.

Trillium cernuum
Clump-forming perennial with nodding, maroon-centred, white flowers borne in spring beneath luxuriant, 3-parted, mid-green leaves. H 30–45cm (12–18in), S 30cm (12in).

***Lamium maculatum* 'Album'**
Semi-evergreen, mat-forming perennial that has dark green leaves with central, white stripes. Bears clusters of hooded, white flowers in spring-summer. H 20cm (8in), S 1m (3ft).

□ WHITE

Convallaria majalis
(Lily-of-the-valley)
Low-growing, rhizomatous perennial with narrowly oval, mid- to dark green leaves and sprays of small, very fragrant, pendulous, bell-shaped, white flowers. Likes humus-rich soil. H 15cm (6in), S indefinite.

Trillium ovatum
Clump-forming perennial with white flowers, later turning pink, that are carried singly in spring just above red-stalked, 3-parted, dark green foliage. H 25–38cm (10–15in), S 20cm (8in).

Adonis brevistyla
Clump-forming perennial. Buttercup-like flowers, borne singly at tips of stems in early spring, are white, tinged blue outside. Has finely cut, mid-green leaves. H and S 15–23cm (6–9in).

Trillium chloropetalum
Clump-forming perennial with reddish-green stems carrying 3-parted, grey-marbled, dark green leaves. Flowers vary from purplish-pink to white and appear above foliage in spring. H and S 30–45cm (12–18in).

Trillium grandiflorum
(Wake-robin)
Clump-forming perennial. Large, pure white flowers that turn pink with age are borne singly in spring just above large, 3-parted, dark green leaves. H 38cm (15in), S 30cm (12in).

Podophyllum hexandrum
(Himalayan May apple)
Perennial with pairs of 3-lobed, brown-mottled leaves followed by white or pink flowers in spring and fleshy, red fruits in summer. H 30–45cm (12–18in), S 30cm (12in).

Epimedium pubigerum
Evergreen, carpeting perennial, grown for its dense, smooth, heart-shaped, divided foliage and clusters of cup-shaped, creamy-white or pink flowers in spring. H and S 45cm (18in).

Anemone sylvestris
(Snowdrop windflower)
Carpeting perennial that may be invasive. Fragrant, semi-pendent, white flowers with yellow centres are borne in spring and early summer. Has divided, mid-green leaves. H and S 30cm (12in).

***Bergenia* 'Silberlicht'**
Evergreen, clump-forming perennial that has flat, oval, mid-green leaves with toothed margins. Clusters of white flowers, sometimes suffused with pink, are borne on erect stems in spring. H 30cm (12in), S 50cm (20in).

PINK

Bergenia ciliata
Evergreen, clump-forming perennial with attractive, large, rounded, hairy leaves. In spring bears clusters of white flowers that age to pink. Leaves are often damaged by frost, although fresh ones will appear in spring. H 30cm (12in), S 50cm (20in).

***Geranium macrorrhizum* 'Ingwersen's Variety'**
Compact, carpeting perennial, useful as weed-suppressing ground cover. Small, soft rose-pink flowers appear in late spring and early summer. Aromatic leaves turn bronze- and scarlet-tinted in autumn. H 30cm (12in), S 60cm (24in).

Heloniopsis orientalis
Clump-forming perennial with basal rosettes of narrowly lance-shaped leaves, above which rise nodding, rose-pink flowers in spring. H and S 30cm (12in).

***Bergenia cordifolia* 'Purpurea'**
Evergreen, clump-forming perennial, useful for ground cover, with large, rounded, purple-tinged, deep green leaves. Clusters of bell-shaped, rose-pink flowers are carried on red stems from late winter to early spring. H and S 50cm (20in).

***Epimedium grandiflorum* 'Rose Queen'**
Carpeting perennial with dense, heart-shaped, divided leaves, tinged with copper, and wiry stems bearing clusters of cup-shaped, spurred, deep pink flowers in spring. H and S 30cm (12in).

Lamium maculatum
Semi-evergreen, mat-forming perennial with mauve-tinged, often pink-flushed leaves that have central, silvery stripes. Clusters of hooded, mauve-pink flowers are borne in mid-spring. H 15cm (6in), S 90cm (36in).

RED

Epimedium × rubrum
Carpeting perennial with dense, heart-shaped, divided leaves that are dark brownish-red in spring, when clusters of cup-shaped, crimson flowers with yellow spurs appear. H 30cm (12in), S 20cm (8in).

Trillium erectum
(Birthroot, Squawroot)
Clump-forming perennial with 3-lobed, mid-green leaves and bright maroon-purple flowers in spring. H 30–45cm (12–18in), S 30cm (12in).

Trillium sessile
(Toadshade, Wake-robin)
Clump-forming perennial that in spring bears red-brown flowers, nestling in a collar of 3-lobed leaves, marked white, pale green or bronze. H 30–38cm (12–15in), S 30–45cm (12–18in).

■ PURPLE

***Anemone nemorosa* 'Allenii'**
Carpeting perennial with many large, cup-shaped, single, rich lavender-blue flowers appearing in spring over deeply divided, mid-green leaves. H 15cm (6in), S 30cm (12in) or more.

Glaucidium palmatum
Leafy perennial that has large, lobed leaves and, in spring, large, delicate, cup-shaped, lavender flowers. A woodland plant, it requires humus-rich soil and a sheltered position. H and S 50cm (20in).

Geranium nodosum
Clump-forming perennial with lobed, glossy leaves and delicate, cup-shaped, lilac or lilac-pink flowers borne in spring-summer. Thrives in deep shade. H and S 45cm (18in).

Lathyrus vernus
Clump-forming perennial bearing in spring small, pea-like, bright purple and blue flowers veined with red, several on each slender stem. Leaves are soft and fern-like. Proves difficult to transplant successfully. H and S 30cm (12in).

***Anemone nemorosa* 'Robinsoniana'**
Carpeting perennial with flat, star-shaped, lavender-blue flowers, pale creamy-grey beneath, borne singly on maroon stems. Leaves are deeply divided into lance-shaped segments. H 15cm (6in), S 30cm (12in).

Cardamine pentaphyllos
Upright perennial spreading by fleshy, horizontal rootstocks. Produces clusters of large, white or pale purple flowers in spring. H 30–60cm (12–24in), S 45–60cm (18–24in).

Pulmonaria saccharata
Semi-evergreen, clump-forming perennial. In spring bears funnel-shaped flowers, opening pink and turning to blue. Long, elliptic leaves are variably spotted with creamy-white. H 30cm (12in), S 60cm (24in).

Lamium orvala
Clump-forming perennial that forms a mound of mid-green leaves, sometimes with central white stripes. Clusters of pink or purple-pink flowers open in late spring to early summer. H and S 30cm (12in).

Scopolia carniolica
Clump-forming perennial that carries spikes of nodding, purple-brown flowers, yellow inside, in early spring. H and S 60cm (24in).

Lathraea clandestina (Toothwort)
Spreading perennial that grows as a parasite on willow or poplar roots. Fleshy, underground stems have colourless scales instead of leaves. Bears bunches of hooded, purple flowers from late winter to early spring. H 10cm (4in), S indefinite.

***Pulmonaria* 'Mawson's Blue'**
Clump-forming perennial that in early spring bears clusters of funnel-shaped, blue flowers, tinged red with age, above narrow leaves. H and S 23cm (9in).

Mertensia virginica
Elegant perennial with rich blue flowers, hanging in clusters in spring. Leaves are soft blue-green. Dies down in summer. Crowns are prone to slug damage. H 30–60cm (12–24in), S 30–45cm (12–18in).

***Brunnera macrophylla* 'Dawson's White'**
Ground-cover perennial with heart-shaped leaves, marked creamy-white. In spring bears delicate sprays of small, bright blue flowers. Shelter from wind to prevent leaf damage. H 45cm (18in), S 60cm (24in).

Meconopsis quintuplinervia
(Harebell poppy)
Mat-forming perennial. Lavender-blue flowers, deepening to purple at the bases, are carried singly on hairy stems in late spring and early summer above a dense mat of large, mid-green leaves. H 30–45cm (12–18in), S 30cm (12in).

Euphorbia amygdaloides* var. *robbiae
Evergreen, spreading perennial with rosettes of dark green leaves, useful as ground cover even in poor, dry soil and semi-shade. Bears open, rounded heads of lime-green flowers in spring. H 45–60cm (18–24in), S 60cm (24in).

Euphorbia seguieriana
Bushy perennial with large, terminal clusters of yellowish-green flowers in late spring and narrow, lance-shaped, glaucous leaves on slender stems. H and S 45cm (18in).

Euphorbia cyparissias
Rounded, leafy perennial with a mass of slender, grey-green leaves and umbels of small, bright lime-green flowers in late spring. May be invasive. H and S 30cm (12in).

PRIMULAS

There are primulas to suit almost every kind of garden situation, ranging from boggy areas and the margins of ponds, to woodland and scree, but most have particular needs and care should be taken with their cultivation. Among the various botanical groups, Candelabra and Auricula primulas are the most widely known. Auriculas are evergreen with leathery leaves, and have beautiful markings and colourings. Candelabras, which prefer moist soil, are deciduous with flowers arranged in rings up sturdy stems. (For fuller details see the Plant Dictionary.)

P. japonica **'Postford White'** 🏆

P. nana

P. sieboldii **'Wine Lady'**

P. vulgaris subsp. ***sibthorpii***

P. chionantha subsp. ***melanops***

P. vulgaris **'Gigha White'**

P. denticulata var. ***alba***

P. petiolaris

P. farinosa

P. malacoides

P. **'Craddock White'**

P. allionii 🏆

P. warshenewskiana

P. rosea 🏆

P. vulgaris **'Alba Plena'**

P. pulverulenta **'Bartley'** 🏆

P. × ***scapeosa***

P. malacoides

P. sinensis

P. clusiana

P. **'Charisma Red'**

P. beesiana

P. frondosa

P. modesta var. faurieae

P. marginata 'Linda Pope' (Auricula) ♀

P. sonchifolia

P. denticulata

P. clarkei

P. secundiflora

P. poissonii

P. reidii var. williamsii

P. marginata 'Prichard's Variety' ♀

P. marginata ♀

P. Joker Series 'Cherry'

P. hirsuta

P. vulgaris 'Lilacina Plena'

P. whitei 'Sheriff's Variety'

P. 'Charisma Blue'

P. × pubescens 'Mrs J.H. Wilson' (Auricula)

P. 'Janet'

P. sieboldii ♀

P. gracilipes

P. 'Adrian' (Auricula)

P. polyneura

P. vulgaris 🏆

P. palinuri

P. **'Margaret Martin'** (Auricula)

P. veris

P. kewensis 🏆

P. elatior 🏆

P. aureata

P. verticillata

P. chungensis

P. **'Chloë'** (Auricula)

P. alpicola var. *alpicola*

P. sikkimensis 🏆

P. **'Moonstone'** (Auricula)

P. forrestii

P. **'Blairside Yellow'** (Auricula)

P. florindae 🏆

P. prolifera 🏆

P. **Gold-laced Group**

P. Grand Burgundy Series 'Yellow Eye'

P. bulleyana

P. vialii ♀

P. Crescendo Series

P. Wanda Supreme Series

P. 'Inverewe' ♀

P. japonica 'Miller's Crimson' ♀

P. 'Miss Indigo'

P. pulverulenta

P. 'Mark' (Auricula)

P. Joker Series 'Red and Gold'

P. 'Janie Hill' (Auricula)

P. 'Blossom' (Auricula)

P. 'Trouble' (Auricula)

P. 'Matthew Yates' (Auricula)

YELLOW

***Valeriana phu* 'Aurea'**
Perennial with rosettes of lemon- to butter-yellow young foliage that turns mid-green by summer, when heads of insignificant, white flowers appear. H 38cm (15in), S 30–38cm (12–15in).

Petasites japonicus
Spreading, invasive perennial that in early spring produces dense cones of small, daisy-like, yellowish-white flowers before large, light green leaves appear. H 60cm (2ft), S 1.5m (5ft).

Cardamine enneaphyllos
Lax perennial spreading by fleshy, horizontal rootstocks. In spring, nodding, pale yellow or white flowers open at the ends of shoots arising from deeply divided leaves. H 30–60cm (12–24in), S 45–60cm (18–24in).

***Epimedium* × *versicolor* 'Neosulphureum'**
Carpeting perennial with dense, heart-shaped, divided leaves, tinted reddish-purple in spring when it bears cup-shaped, pale yellow flowers in small, pendent clusters on wiry stems. H and S 30cm (12in).

***Trollius* × *cultorum* 'Alabaster'**
Clump-forming perennial producing rounded, yellowish-white flowers in spring. These emerge from a basal mass of rounded, deeply divided, mid-green leaves. H 60cm (24in), S 45cm (18in).

Anemone* × *lipsiensis
Prostrate, carpeting perennial that in spring has many single, pale yellow flowers with bright yellow stamens. Leaves are deeply cut with long leaflets. H 15cm (6in), S 30cm (12in).

Uvularia grandiflora
(Bellwort, Merry-bells)
Clump-forming perennial. Clusters of long, bell-shaped, yellow flowers hang gracefully from slender stems in spring. H 45–60cm (18–24in), S 30cm (12in).

Anemone ranunculoides
Spreading perennial for damp woodland, bearing buttercup-like, single, deep yellow flowers in spring. Divided leaves have short stalks. H and S 20cm (8in).

YELLOW–ORANGE

Trollius europaeus (Globeflower)
Clump-forming perennial that in spring bears rounded, lemon- to mid-yellow flowers above deeply divided, mid-green leaves. H 60cm (24in), S 45cm (18in).

Euphorbia polychroma
Rounded, bushy perennial with mid-green leaves and heads of bright yellow flowers carried for several weeks in spring. H and S 50cm (20in).

Adonis vernalis
Clump-forming perennial that in early spring produces buttercup-like, greenish-yellow blooms singly at the tips of stems. Mid-green leaves are delicately dissected. H and S 23–30cm (9–12in).

Adonis amurensis
Clump-forming perennial that in late winter and early spring bears buttercup-like, golden blooms singly at the tips of stems. Mid-green foliage is finely cut. H 30cm (12in), S 23–30cm (9–12in).

Meconopsis cambrica
(Welsh poppy)
Spreading perennial that in late spring carries lemon-yellow or rich orange blooms. Double forms are available. Has deeply divided, fern-like foliage. H 30–45cm (12–18in), S 30cm (12in).

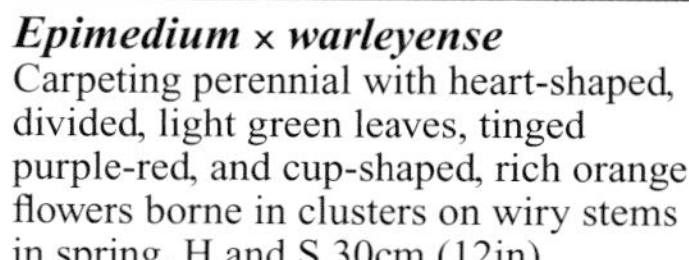

Epimedium* × *warleyense
Carpeting perennial with heart-shaped, divided, light green leaves, tinged purple-red, and cup-shaped, rich orange flowers borne in clusters on wiry stems in spring. H and S 30cm (12in).

WHITE

Campanula alliariifolia
Mound-forming perennial with heart-shaped leaves, above which rise nodding, bell-shaped, creamy-white flowers borne along arching, wiry stems throughout summer. H 60cm (24in), S 50cm (20in).

Galium odoratum (Woodruff)
Carpeting perennial that bears whorls of star-shaped, white flowers above neat, whorled leaves in summer. All parts of plant are aromatic. H 15cm (6in), S 30cm (12in) or more.

Anemone rivularis
Perennial with stiff, free-branching stems bearing delicate, cup-shaped, white flowers in summer above deeply divided, dark green leaves. H 60cm (24in), S 30cm (12in).

Anemone narcissiflora
Leafy perennial that in late spring and early summer produces cup-shaped, single, white flowers with a blue or purplish-pink stain on reverse of petals. Leaves are dark green and deeply divided. H to 60cm (24in), S 50cm (20in).

***Leucanthemum* × *superbum* 'Esther Read'**
Robust perennial with large, daisy-like, double, white flower heads borne singly on strong stems in summer. H and S 45cm (18in).

□ WHITE

Anthemis punctata subsp. ***cupaniana***
Evergreen, carpeting perennial with dense, finely cut, silvery foliage that turns green in winter. Small, daisy-like, white flower heads with yellow centres are borne singly on short stems in early summer. H and S 30cm (12in).

Anthericum liliago
(St Bernard's lily)
Upright perennial that in early summer bears tall racemes of trumpet-shaped, white flowers above clumps of long, narrow, grey-green leaves. H 45–60cm (18–24in), S 30cm (12in).

Anaphalis nepalensis var. ***monocephala***
Dwarf, leafy perennial that has woolly, silvery stems and lance-shaped leaves. Carries dense, terminal clusters of white flower heads in late summer. H 20–30cm (8–12in), S 15cm (6in).

***Mentha suaveolens* 'Variegata'**
(Variegated apple mint)
Spreading perennial with soft, woolly, mid-green leaves, splashed with white and cream, that smell of apples. Seldom produces flowers. H 30–45cm (12–18in), S 60cm (24in).

Crambe maritima (Sea kale)
Robust perennial with a mound of wide, curved, lobed, silvery-green leaves. Bears large heads of small, fragrant, white flowers, opening into branching sprays in summer. H and S 60cm (24in).

***Aegopodium podagraria* 'Variegatum'** (Variegated Bishop's weed, Variegated gout weed)
Vigorous, spreading perennial, superb for ground cover, with lobed, creamy-white-variegated leaves. Insignificant, white flowers borne in summer are best removed. H 10cm (4in), S indefinite.

***Astilbe* 'Irrlicht'**
Leafy perennial bearing tapering, feathery plumes of tiny, white flowers in summer. Foliage is dark green and flowers remain on the plant, dried and brown, well into winter. Prefers humus-rich soil. H 45–60cm (1½–2ft), S to 1m (3ft).

***Heuchera cylindrica* 'Greenfinch'**
Evergreen, clump-forming perennial with rosettes of lobed, heart-shaped leaves and, in summer, graceful spikes of small, bell-shaped, pale green or greenish-white flowers. H 45–60cm (18–24in), S 50cm (20in).

***Tradescantia* Andersoniana Group 'Osprey'**
Clump-forming perennial with narrow, lance-shaped leaves, 15–30cm (6–12in) long. Has clusters of white flowers with purple-blue stamens, surrounded by 2 leaf-like bracts, in summer. H to 60cm (24in), S 45cm (18in).

***Geranium clarkei* 'Kashmir White'**
Carpeting, rhizomatous perennial with divided leaves and loose clusters of cup-shaped flowers, white with pale lilac-pink veins, borne for a long period in summer. H and S 45–60cm (18–24in).

Streptocarpus caulescens
Erect perennial with small, narrow to oval, fleshy, dark green leaves. Stalked clusters of small, tubular, violet-striped, violet or white flowers are carried in leaf axils intermittently. H and S to 45cm (18in) or more. Min. 10–15°C (50–59°F).

WHITE

Geranium renardii
Compact, clump-forming perennial with lobed, circular, sage-green leaves and purple-veined, white flowers, borne in early summer. H and S 30cm (12in).

Diplarrhena moraea
Clump-forming perennial with fans of long, strap-shaped leaves and clusters of iris-like, white flowers, with centres of yellow and purple, borne on wiry stems in early summer. H 45cm (18in), S 23cm (9in).

***Osteospermum* 'Whirlygig'**
Evergreen, clump-forming, semi-woody perennial of lax habit that bears bluish-white flower heads singly, but in great profusion, during summer. Leaves are grey-green. H 60cm (24in), S 30–45cm (12–18in).

WHITE–PINK

Ruellia devosiana
Evergreen, bushy sub-shrub with spreading, purplish branches. Leaves are broadly lance-shaped, dark green with paler veins above and purple below. Has mauve-tinged, white flowers in spring-summer. H and S to 45cm (18in) or more. Min. 15°C (59°F).

Astrantia major* subsp. *involucrata
Clump-forming perennial very similar to A. major (below) but with longer bracts surrounding centres of flower heads. H 60cm (24in), S 45cm (18in).

***Heuchera micrantha* var. *diversifolia* 'Palace Purple'**
Clump-forming perennial with persistent, heart-shaped, deep purple leaves and sprays of small, white flowers in summer. Cut leaves last well in water. H and S 45cm (18in).

Astrantia major (Masterwort)
Clump-forming perennial producing greenish-white, sometimes pink-tinged flower heads throughout summer-autumn above a dense mass of divided, mid-green leaves. H 60cm (24in), S 45cm (18in).

Melittis melissophyllum
(Bastard balm)
Erect perennial that in early summer bears white flowers with purple lower lips in axils of rough, oval, mid-green leaves. H and S 30cm (12in).

Astrantia maxima
Clump-forming perennial that bears rose-pink flower heads during summer-autumn. H 60cm (24in), S 30cm (12in).

PINK

Mimulus naiandinus
Spreading perennial, with hairy leaves, that in summer bears snapdragon-like, rose-pink flowers tipped with creamy-yellow and spotted deep pink. H 23cm (9in), S 25cm (10in).

***Dicentra* 'Spring Morning'**
Neat, leafy perennial with small, heart-shaped, pink flowers hanging in arching sprays in late spring and summer. Attractive, fern-like foliage is grey-green and finely cut. H and S 30cm (12in).

***Dicentra* 'Stuart Boothman'**
Tufted perennial with oval, finely cut, deep grey-green leaves. In spring-summer, produces arching sprays of heart-shaped, carmine flowers. H 30cm (12in), S 40cm (16in).

***Diascia* 'Blackthorn Apricot'**
Mat-forming perennial with narrowly heart-shaped, tapering leaves. From summer to autumn, produces loose racemes of apricot-pink flowers with small, narrow 'windows' and almost straight, downward-pointing spurs. H 25cm (10in), S to 50cm (20in).

× *Heucherella tiarelloides*
Evergreen, ground-cover perennial that has dense clusters of leaves and feathery sprays of tiny, bell-shaped, pink flowers in early summer. H and S 45cm (18in).

× *Heucherella alba* 'Bridget Bloom'
Evergreen, clump-forming perennial with dense, bright green leaves and, in early summer, many feathery sprays of tiny, bell-shaped, rose-pink flowers, which continue intermittently until autumn. H 45cm (18in), S 30cm (12in).

***Erigeron* 'Charity'**
Clump-forming perennial with a mass of daisy-like, light pink flower heads with greenish-yellow centres borne for a long period in summer. May need some support. H and S to 60cm (24in).

Geranium endressii
Semi-evergreen, compact, carpeting perennial with small, lobed leaves and cup-shaped, rose-pink flowers borne throughout summer. H 45cm (18in), S 60cm (24in).

***Geranium* × *oxonianum* 'Wargrave Pink'**
Semi-evergreen, carpeting perennial with dense, dainty, lobed, basal leaves acting as weed-suppressing ground cover. Cup-shaped, bright salmon-pink flowers are borne throughout summer. H 45cm (18in), S 60cm (24in).

Osteospermum jucundum
Evergreen, neat, clump-forming perennial with mid-green leaves. In late summer, soft pink flower heads, mostly dark-eyed, are borne singly but in great abundance. H and S 30cm (12in).

Erodium manescaui
Mound-forming perennial with divided, ferny, blue-green leaves. Produces loose clusters of single, deep pink, darker blotched flowers throughout summer. H 45cm (18in), S 60cm (24in).

Mimulus lewisii
Upright perennial with downy, sticky, grey leaves that provide an excellent foil for snapdragon-like, deep rose-pink flowers borne singly in summer. Tolerates dry soil. H 60cm (24in), S 45cm (18in).

Lychnis flos-jovis
Clump-forming perennial with rounded clusters of deep rose-pink flowers, opening in mid-summer, that are set off by grey foliage. H and S 45cm (18in).

***Centaurea hypoleuca* 'John Coutts'**
Upright perennial. Deep rose-red flower heads, with thistle-like centres encircled by star-shaped ray petals, are borne on slender stems in summer. Deeply divided leaves are white-grey beneath. H 60cm (24in), S 45cm (18in).

Incarvillea mairei
Compact, clump-forming perennial that has short stems bearing several trumpet-shaped, purplish-pink flowers in early summer. Leaves are divided into oval leaflets. Protect crowns with winter mulch. H and S 30cm (12in).

Geranium macrorrhizum
Semi-evergreen, carpeting perennial bearing magenta flowers in early summer. Rounded, divided, aromatic leaves make good, weed-proof ground cover and assume bright tints in autumn. H 30–38cm (12–15in), S 60cm (24in).

Persicaria macrophylla
Compact perennial carrying neat spikes of rich rose-pink blooms above narrow, lance-shaped, glaucous leaves in late summer. H 45–60cm (18–24in), S 30cm (12in).

Liatris spicata
Clump-forming perennial. In late summer bears spikes of crowded, rose-purple flower heads on stiff stems that arise from basal tufts of grassy, mid-green foliage. H 60cm (24in), S 30cm (12in).

***Physostegia virginiana* 'Vivid'**
(Obedient plant)
Erect, compact perennial that in late summer and early autumn bears spikes of tubular, dark lilac-pink flowers that can be placed in postion. Has toothed, mid-green leaves. H and S 30–60cm (12–24in).

Carnations & pinks

Although perhaps best known for providing excellent, long-lasting cut flowers, carnations and pinks (*Dianthus* cultivars) are highly ornamental border subjects, valued for their usually fragrant ("clove-scented") blooms, produced over a long period in summer, and their distinctive, silvery- or grey-green foliage. Shorter-growing cultivars – the old-fashioned and modern pinks – are excellent edging plants. Many of the flowers are attractively marked or have fringed petals. Carnations and pinks need an open, sunny position, preferably in alkaline soil. All except the perpetual-flowering carnations are frost hardy. The myriad of carnation and pinks cultivars are divided into the following groups:

Border carnations – plants are of upright habit and flower prolifically once in mid-summer; each stem bears 5 or more flowers. Picotee forms (with petals outlined in a darker, contrasting colour) are available.

Perpetual-flowering carnations – similar in habit to border carnations, they are usually grown for cut flowers and bloom year-round under glass. Plants are normally disbudded, leaving one flower per stem, but spray forms have up to 5 flowers per stem.

Malmaison carnations – these produce intensely fragrant flowers sporadically throughout the year under glass.

Old-fashioned pinks – these have a low, spreading habit and form neat cushions of foliage; masses of fragrant flowers are produced in mid-summer. Good for border edging and cutting.

Modern pinks – usually more vigorous than old-fashioned pinks, they are repeat-flowering with 2 or 3 main flushes of flowers in summer.

Alpine pinks – in early summer, these plants form cushions of small, scented flowers. Good for edging, in a rockery, raised bed, trough, or alpine house.

***D.* 'Mrs Sinkins'**
(old-fashioned pink)

***D.* 'Haytor'**
(modern pink)

***D.* 'Musgrave's Pink'**
(old-fashioned pink)

***D.* 'Eva Humphries'**
(border carnation)

***D.* 'White Ladies'**
(old-fashioned pink)

***D.* 'Fair Folly'**
(modern pink)

***D.* 'Alice'**
(modern pink)

***D.* Pierrot**
(perpetual-fl. carnation)

***D.* 'Dad's Favourite'**
(old-fashioned pink)

***D.* 'Emile Paré'**
(old-fashioned pink)

***D.* 'Doris'**
(modern pink) 🏆

***D.* 'Becky Robinson'**
(modern pink) 🏆

***D.* 'Truly Yours'**
(perpetual-fl. carnation) 🏆

***D.* 'Duchess of Westminster'**
(Malmaison carnation)

***D.* 'Gran's Favourite'**
(old-fashioned pink) 🏆

***D.* 'Monica Wyatt'**
(modern pink) 🏆

***D.* 'London Brocade'**
(modern pink)

D. **'Prudence'**
(old-fashioned pink)

D. **'Forest Treasure'**
(border carnation)

D. **'Houndspool Ruby'**
(modern pink) ♀

D. **'Christopher'**
(modern pink)

D. **'London Delight'**
(modern pink)

D. **'Sandra Neal'**
(border)

D. **'Aldridge Yellow'**
(border carnation)

D. **'Lavender Clove'**
(border carnation)

D. **'Laced Monarch'**
(modern pink) ♀

D. **'Nina'**
(perpetual-flowering carnation)

D. **'Raggio di Sole'**
(perpetual-fl. carnation)

D. **'Valencia'**
(perpetual-fl. carnation)

D. **'Albisola'**
(perpetual-fl. carnation)

D. **'Christine Hough'**
(border carnation)

D. **'Pink Jewel'**
(alpine pink)

D. **'Golden Cross'**
(border carnation) ♀

D. **'Happiness'**
(border carnation)

D. **'Bookham Fancy'**
(border carnation)

D. **'Clara'**
(perpetual-flowering carnation)

D. **'Crompton Princess'**
(perpetual-fl. carnation)

D. **'Cream Sue'**
(perpetual-fl. carnation)

PINK

***Achimenes* 'Little Beauty'**
Bushy perennial with oval, toothed leaves. Large, funnel-shaped, deep pink flowers with yellow eyes are carried in summer. H 25cm (10in), S 30cm (12in). Min. 10°C (50°F).

Incarvillea delavayi
Clump-forming perennial with deeply divided leaves and erect stems bearing several trumpet-shaped, pinkish-red flowers in early summer. Has attractive seed pods. H 45–60cm (18–24in), S 30cm (12in).

***Sinningia* 'Red Flicker'**
Short-stemmed, tuberous perennial with rosettes of oval, velvety leaves, to 20cm (8in) long. In summer has fleshy, nodding, funnel-shaped, pinkish-red flowers, pouched on lower sides. H to 30cm (12in), S 45cm (18in). Min. 15°C (59°F).

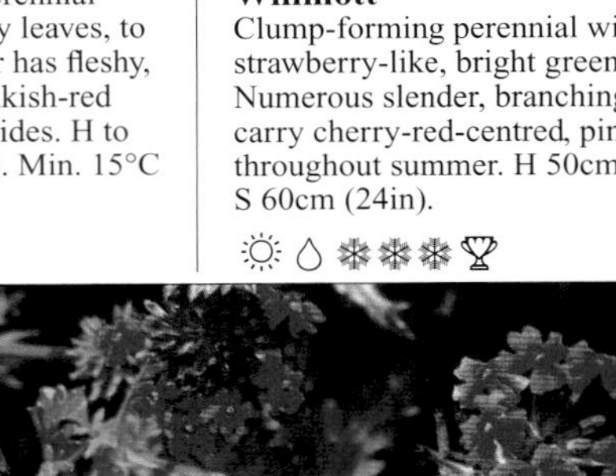

***Potentilla nepalensis* 'Miss Willmott'**
Clump-forming perennial with palmate, strawberry-like, bright green leaves. Numerous slender, branching stems carry cherry-red-centred, pink flowers throughout summer. H 50cm (20in), S 60cm (24in).

***Verbena* 'Sissinghurst'**
Mat-forming perennial that throughout summer bears heads of brilliant pink flowers above mid-green foliage. Is excellent for edging a path or growing in a tub. H 15–20cm (6–8in), S 45cm (18in).

RED

***Lychnis viscaria* 'Splendens Plena'**
Clump-forming perennial bearing spikes of double, magenta flowers in early summer. Stems and large, oval to lance-shaped, basal leaves are covered in sticky hairs. H 30–45cm (12–18in), S 23cm (9in) or more.

***Astilbe* 'Fanal'**
Leafy perennial with strong stems. In summer bears neat, tapering, feathery panicles of tiny, crimson-red flowers that turn brown and keep their shape in winter. Broad leaves are divided into leaflets. Prefers humus-rich soil. H 60cm (24in), S to 90cm (36in).

Lychnis coronaria
Clump-forming perennial, often grown as a biennial. From mid-to late summer, brilliant rose-crimson flowers are borne in panicles on branched, grey stems that rise from neat, grey leaves. H 45–60cm (18–24in), S 45cm (18in).

***Sinningia* 'Switzerland'**
Short-stemmed, tuberous perennial with rosettes of oval, velvety leaves, to 20cm (8in) long. In summer has large, fleshy, trumpet-shaped, bright scarlet flowers with ruffled, white borders. H to 30cm (12in), S 45cm (18in). Min. 15°C (59°F).

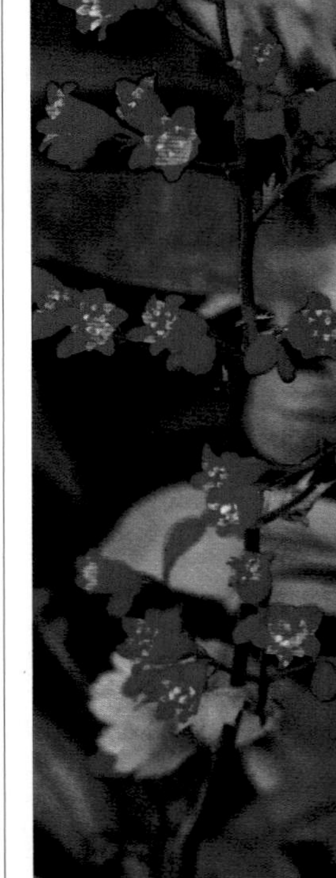

***Heuchera* 'Red Spangles'**
Evergreen perennial forming clumps of heart-shaped, purplish-green leaves. Bears spikes of small, bell-shaped, crimson-scarlet flowers in summer. H and S 30cm (12in).

RED

Lotus berthelotii (Coral gem)
Semi-evergreen, straggling perennial suitable for a hanging basket or large pan in an alpine house. Has hairy, silvery branches and leaves, and clusters of pea-like, scarlet flowers in summer. H 30cm (12in), S indefinite. Min. 5°C (41°F).

Columnea crassifolia
Evergreen, shrubby perennial with fleshy, lance-shaped leaves. Erect, tubular, hairy, scarlet flowers, about 8cm (3in) long, each with a yellow throat, are carried from spring to autumn. H and S to 45cm (18in). Min. 15°C (59°F).

Potentilla atrosanguinea
Clump-forming perennial with hairy, palmate, strawberry-like leaves. Loose clusters of dark red flowers are borne throughout summer. H 45cm (18in), S 60cm (24in).

***Smithiantha* 'Orange King'**
Strong-growing, erect, rhizomatous perennial. Large, scalloped, velvety leaves are emerald-green with dark red-marked veins. In summer-autumn has tubular, orange-red flowers, red-spotted within and with yellow lips. H and S to 60cm (24in). Min. 15°C (59°F).

***Gaillardia* × *grandiflora* 'Dazzler'**
Upright, rather open perennial bearing large, terminal, daisy-like, yellow-tipped, red flower heads for a long period in summer. Leaves are soft and divided. Needs staking and may be short-lived. H 60cm (24in), S 50cm (20in).

***Mimulus* 'Royal Velvet'**
Compact perennial, often grown as an annual, producing in summer many large, snapdragon-like, mahogany-red flowers with mahogany-speckled, gold throats. Leaves are mid-green. H 30cm (12in), S 23cm (9in).

PURPLE

Polemonium carneum
Clump-forming perennial that carries clusters of cup-shaped, pink or lilac-pink flowers in early summer. Foliage is finely divided. H and S 45cm (18in).

Kaempferia pulchra
Tufted, rhizomatous perennial with horizontal, aromatic, dark green leaves, variegated with paler green above. Short spikes of lilac-pink flowers appear from the centre of tufts in summer. H 15cm (6in), S 30cm (12in). Min. 18°C (64°F).

Tulbaghia violacea
Vigorous, semi-evergreen, clump-forming perennial that in summer-autumn carries umbels of lilac-purple or lilac-pink flowers above a mass of narrow, glaucous, blue-grey leaves. H 45–60cm (18–24in), S 30cm (12in).

■ PURPLE

Streptocarpus saxorum
(False African violet)
Evergreen, rounded, woody-based perennial with small, oval, hairy leaves in whorls. Lilac flowers with white tubes arise from leaf axils in summer-autumn. H and S 30cm (12in) or more. Min. 10–15°C (50–59°F).

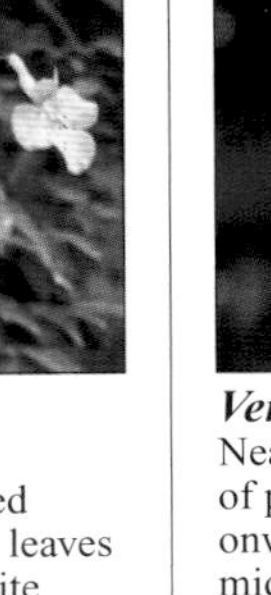

Verbena rigida
Neat, compact perennial bearing heads of pale violet flowers from mid-summer onwards. Has lance-shaped, rough, mid-green leaves borne on flower stems. H 45–60cm (18–24in), S 30cm (12in).

Heterocentron elegans
Evergreen, mat-forming perennial with dense, creeping, mid-green foliage. Massed, bright deep purple flowers open in summer-autumn and, under glass, in winter. H 5cm (2in), S indefinite. Min. 5°C (41°F).

Polemonium pulcherrimum
Vigorous perennial with bright green leaves divided into leaflets. Tubular, purple-blue flowers with throats of yellow or white are borne in summer. H 50cm (20in), S 30cm (12in).

***Tradescantia* Andersoniana Group 'Purple Dome'**
Clump-forming perennial with narrow, lance-shaped leaves, 15–30cm (6–12in) long. Has clusters of rich purple flowers, surrounded by 2 leaf-like bracts, in summer. H to 60cm (24in), S 45cm (18in).

Centaurea montana
Spreading perennial with many rather lax stems carrying, in early summer, one or more large, purple, blue, white or pink flower heads with thistle-like centres encircled by star-shaped ray petals. H 50cm (20in), S 60cm (24in).

***Erigeron* 'Serenity'**
Clump-forming perennial. Many daisy-like, violet flower heads, with yellow centres, are borne in early and mid-summer. Needs some support. H and S to 60cm (24in).

Platycodon grandiflorus
(Balloon flower)
Neat, clump-forming perennial that in summer has clusters of large, balloon-like buds opening to bell-shaped, blue or purplish flowers. Stems are clothed with bluish-green leaves. H 45–60cm (18–24in), S 30–45cm (12–18in).

***Stachys macrantha* 'Superba'**
Clump-forming perennial with heart-shaped, soft, wrinkled, mid-green leaves, from which arise stout stems producing whorls of hooded, purple-violet flowers in summer. H 30–45cm (12–18in), S 30–60cm (12–24in).

Geranium* × *magnificum
Clump-forming perennial with hairy, deeply lobed leaves and cup-shaped, prominently veined, violet-blue flowers borne in small clusters in summer. H 45cm (18in), S 60cm (24in).

***Geranium* 'Johnson's Blue'**
Vigorous, clump-forming perennial with many divided leaves and cup-shaped, deep lavender-blue flowers borne throughout summer. H 30cm (12in), S 60cm (24in).

Geranium himalayense
Clump-forming perennial with large, cup-shaped, violet-blue flowers borne on long stalks in summer over dense tufts of neatly cut leaves. H 30cm (12in), S 60cm (24in).

***Scabiosa caucasica* 'Clive Greaves'**
Clump-forming perennial that throughout summer has violet-blue flower heads with pincushion-like centres. Basal, mid-green leaves are lance-shaped and slightly lobed on the stems. H and S 45–60cm (18–24in).

Polemonium caeruleum
(Jacob's ladder)
Clump-forming perennial. Clusters of cup-shaped, lavender-blue flowers with orange-yellow stamens open in summer amid finely divided foliage. H and S 45–60cm (18–24in).

***Geranium pratense* 'Mrs Kendall Clark'**
Clump-forming perennial with hairy stems and deeply divided leaves. In early and mid-summer, bears erect, saucer-shaped, pearl-grey or violet-blue flowers with white or pale pink veins. H 60–90cm (24–36in), S 60cm (24in).

Stokesia laevis
Perennial with overwintering, evergreen rosettes. In summer, cornflower-like, lavender- or purple-blue flower heads are borne freely. Leaves are narrow and mid-green. H and S 30–45cm (12–18in).

***Catananche caerulea* 'Major'**
Perennial forming clumps of grassy, grey-green leaves, above which rise wiry, branching stems each carrying a daisy-like, lavender-blue flower head in summer. Propagate regularly by root cuttings. H 45–60cm (18–24in), S 30cm (24in).

PURPLE

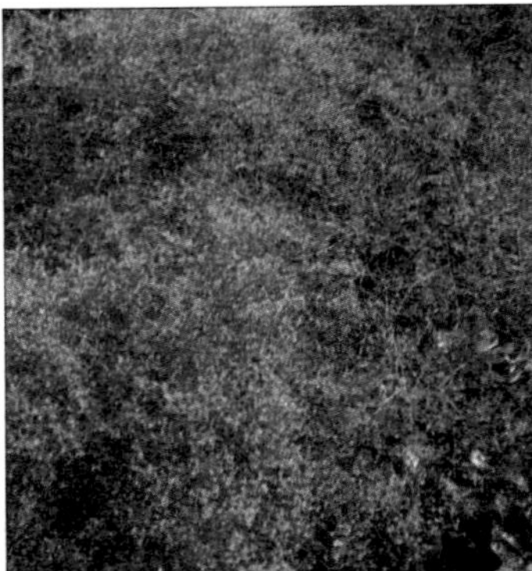

***Limonium latifolium* 'Blue Cloud'**
Clump-forming perennial. In late summer carries diffuse clusters of bluish-mauve flowers that can be dried for indoor decoration. Has large, leathery, dark green leaves. H 30cm (12in), S 45cm (18in).

***Campanula* 'Burghaltii'**
Mound-forming perennial with long, pendent, funnel-shaped, pale lavender flowers displayed on erect, wiry stems in summer. Leaves are oval, soft and leathery. May need staking. H 60cm (24in), S 30cm (12in).

Eryngium bourgatii
Clump-forming perennial that, from mid- to late summer, carries heads of thistle-like, blue-green, then lilac-blue, flowers on branched, wiry stems well above deeply cut, basal, grey-green leaves. H 45–60cm (18–24in), S 30cm (12in).

Anemonopsis macrophylla
(False anemone)
Clump-forming perennial with waxy, nodding, purplish-blue flowers, borne on slender, branching stems in summer above fern-like leaves. H 45–60cm (18–24in), S 50cm (20in).

Nepeta* × *faassenii (Catmint)
Bushy, clump-forming perennial, useful for edging. Forms mounds of small, greyish-green leaves, from which loose spikes of tubular, soft lavender-blue flowers appear in early summer. H and S 45cm (18in).

BLUE

Amsonia orientalis
Neat, clump-forming perennial. In summer, heads of small, star-shaped, grey-blue flowers open on tops of wiry stems clothed with green, sometimes greyish, leaves. H 45–60cm (18–24in), 30–45cm (12–18in).

Parahebe perfoliata
(Digger's speedwell)
Evergreen sub-shrub with willowy stems clasped by leathery, glaucous leaves. Elegant, long, branching sprays of blue flowers are borne in summer. H 45–60cm (18–24in), S 45cm (18in).

Eryngium variifolium
Evergreen, rosette-forming perennial with stiff stems that, in late summer, bear heads of thistle-like, grey-blue flowers, each with a collar of white bracts. Jagged-edged leaves are mid-green, marbled with white. H 45cm (18in), S 25cm (10in).

Veronica gentianoides
Mat-forming perennial with spikes of very pale blue flowers opening in early summer on tops of stems that arise from glossy, basal leaves. H and S 45cm (18in).

Amsonia tabernaemontana
Clump-forming perennial with willowy stems bearing drooping clusters of small, tubular, pale blue flowers in summer. Leaves are small and narrow. H 45–60cm (18–24in), S 30cm (12in).

Myosotidium hortensia
(Chatham Island forget-me-not)
Evergreen, clump-forming perennial bearing large clusters of forget-me-not-like, blue flowers in summer above a basal mound of large, ribbed, glossy leaves. H 45–60cm (18–24in), S 60cm (24in).

Linum narbonense
Clump-forming, short-lived perennial, best renewed frequently from seed. Has lance-shaped, greyish-green leaves and heads of somewhat cup-shaped, pale to deep blue flowers in spring-summer. H 30–60cm (12–24in), S 30cm (12in).

Veronica peduncularis
Mat-forming perennial with ovate to lance-shaped, glossy, purple-tinged, mid-green leaves. Bears abundant, saucer-shaped, deep blue flowers, with small, white eyes, over a long period from early spring to summer. H to 10cm (4in), S 60cm (24in) or more.

***Geranium wallichianum* 'Buxton's Variety'**
Spreading perennial with luxuriant, white-flecked leaves and large, white-centred, blue or blue-purple flowers from mid-summer to autumn. H 30–45cm (12–18in), S 90cm (36in).

Veronica spicata* subsp. *incana
Mat-forming perennial, densely covered with silver hairs, with linear to lance-shaped leaves. In summer, bears spikes of small, star-shaped, clear blue flowers. H and S 30cm (12in).

***Campanula isophylla* Kristal Hybrids 'Stella Blue'**
Compact, free-flowering perennial with strong stems and small, heart-shaped, toothed, light green leaves. Large, upright, saucer-shaped, pale blue flowers are produced in mid-summer. H 15–20cm (6–8in), S to 30cm (12in).

***Salvia patens* 'Cambridge Blue'**
Erect, branching perennial with ovate, mid-green leaves. From mid-summer to mid-autumn, produces loose terminal racemes of paired, pale blue flowers, 5cm (2in) long, with wide open mouths. H 45–60cm (18–24in), S 45cm (18in).

H. sieboldii **'Paxton's Original'** 🏆

HOSTAS

Their luxuriant foliage and attractive habit have made hostas, or plantain lilies, increasingly sought after as plants for every garden, large or small. Native to the East, they add an exotic touch to any waterside or damp, shady corner. Hostas vary in size from plants a few centimetres high to vigorous forms that will make a clump of up to 1.5m (5ft) across. Their elegant leaves are diverse in shape, texture, and coloration, with subtle variegations and shadings. Many hostas produce decorative flower spikes, which rise gracefully above the foliage in mid-summer.

Suitable for a range of situations from containers to borders and pool sides, hostas are essentially shade- and moisture-loving plants, preferring rich, well-drained soils. Leaves must be protected from slugs to avoid damage.

***H.* 'Ground Master'**

***H.* 'Fragrant Bouquet'**

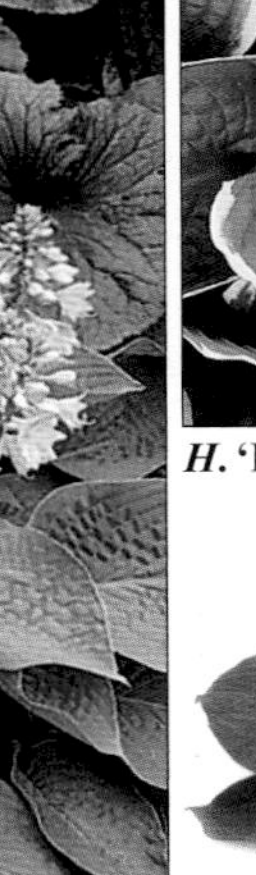

H. sieboldiana

***H.* 'Francee'** 🏆

***H.* 'Regal Splendor'**

***H.* 'Big Daddy'**

***H.* 'Krossa Regal'** 🏆

***H.* 'Inniswood'**

H. gracillima

H. undulata var. ***albomarginata***

***H.* 'Shade Fanfare'** 🏆

***H.* 'Snowden'**

H. sieboldiana var. ***elegans*** 🏆

***H.* 'Green Fountain'**

H. tokudama f. ***aureonebulosa***

***H.* 'Ginko Craig'**

H. undulata var. ***univittata*** 🏆

***H.* 'Blue Mouse Ears'**

***H.* 'Dream Weaver'**

H. tokudama

H. tardiflora

H. 'Love Pat' ♀

H. 'Blue Cadet'

H. 'Antioch'

H. 'Halcyon' ♀

H. 'Blue Wedgwood'

H. 'Hadspen Blue'

H. 'American Halo'

H. 'Torchlight'

H. ventricosa ♀

H. 'Candy Hearts'

H. venusta 'Suzuki Thumbnail'

H. 'Buckshaw Blue'

H. 'August Moon'

H. 'Blue Angel' ♀

H. 'Devon Green'

H. 'Striptease'

H. *plantaginea*

H. *montana* 'Aureomarginata'

H. 'Tall Boy'

H. 'Revolution'

H. *sieboldiana* 'Frances Williams' ♀

H. 'Honeybells' ♀

H. 'Great Expectations'

H. *nigrescens*

H. 'Royal Standard' ♀

H. *ventricosa* 'Variegata'

H. 'Moonlight'

H. *venusta* ♀

H. *tokudama* 'Flavocircinalis'

H. *fortunei* f. *aureomarginata* ♀

H. 'Allan P. McConnell'

H. 'Yellow River'

H. 'Grand Tiara'

H. 'So Sweet'

H. fortunei var. *albopicta* ♀

H. sieboldii f. *kabitan*

H. 'Gold Standard'

H. 'Cherry Berry'

H. 'Sea Thunder'

H. 'Brim Cup'

H. 'Morning Light'

H. 'Birchwood Parky's Gold'

H. 'Fire and Ice'

H. 'Whirlwind'

H. tokudama f. *aureonebulosa*

H. 'Zounds'

H. 'Wide Brim' ♀

H. 'Stiletto'

H. 'Golden Tiara' ♀

H. 'Piedmont Gold'

H. 'Golden Prayers'

H. 'Sum and Substance' ♀

GREEN–YELLOW

Artemisia pontica
(Roman wormwood)
Vigorous, upright perennial with aromatic, feathery, silver-green foliage and tall spikes of small, greyish flower heads in summer. May spread. H 60cm (24in), S 20cm (8in).

Alchemilla mollis (Lady's mantle)
Clump-forming, ground-cover perennial that has rounded, pale green leaves with crinkled edges. Bears small sprays of tiny, bright greenish-yellow flowers, with conspicuous outer calyces, in mid-summer that may be dried. H and S 50cm (20in).

Alchemilla conjuncta
Clump-forming perennial that has neat, wavy, star-shaped leaves with pale margins. In mid-summer, bears loose clusters of tiny, greenish-yellow flowers, with conspicuous, outer calyces, which may be dried for winter decoration. H and S 30cm (12in).

Sarracenia flava
(Trumpets, Yellow pitcher plant)
Erect perennial with red-marked, yellow-green pitchers (modified leaves) that have hooded tops. From late spring to early summer bears nodding, yellow or greenish-yellow flowers. H and S 45cm (18in). Min. 5°C (41°F).

***Persicaria virginiana* 'Painter's Palette'**
Mounded perennial grown for its attractive leaves, which are green with central, brown zones, ivory-yellow splashes and stripes and an overall deep pink tinge. Seldom flowers in cultivation. H and S 60cm (24in).

***Origanum vulgare* 'Aureum'**
Woody-based perennial forming a dense mat of aromatic, golden-yellow, young leaves that turn pale yellow-green in mid-summer. Occasionally bears tiny, mauve flowers in summer H in leaf 8cm (3in), S indefinite.

YELLOW

Sisyrinchium striatum
Semi-evergreen perennial that forms tufts of long, narrow, grey-green leaves. Bears slender spikes of purple-striped, straw-yellow flowers in summer. Self seeds freely. H 45–60cm (18–24in), S 30cm (12in).

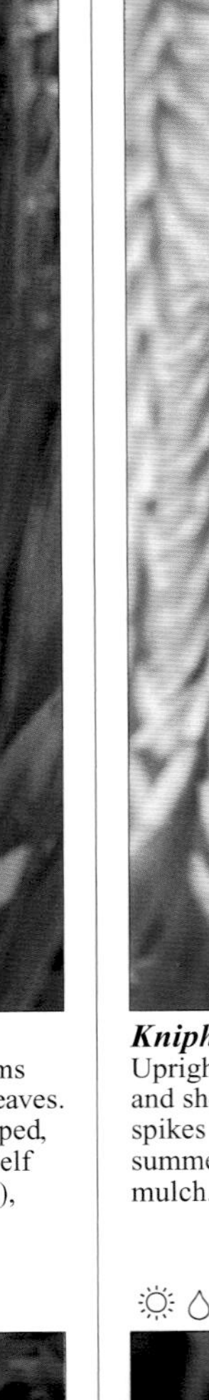

***Kniphofia* 'Little Maid'**
Upright perennial with grass-like leaves and short, erect stems bearing terminal spikes of pale creamy-yellow flowers in summer. Protect crowns with winter mulch. H 60cm (24in), S 45cm (18in).

***Filipendula ulmaria* 'Aurea'**
Leafy perennial, grown for its divided foliage, which is bright golden-yellow in spring and pale green in summer. Clusters of creamy-white flowers are carried in branching heads in mid-summer. H and S 30cm (12in).

***Osteospermum* 'Buttermilk'**
Evergreen, upright, semi-woody perennial. Daisy-like, pale yellow flower heads, with dark eyes, are borne singly amid grey-green foliage from mid-summer to autumn. H 60cm (24in), S 30cm (12in).

***Stachys byzantina* 'Primrose Heron'**
Evergreen, mat-forming perennial with woolly, yellowish-grey leaves, to 10cm (4in) long. Erect stems bear interrupted spikes of pink-purple flowers from early summer to early autumn. H 45cm (18in), S 60cm (24in).

***Achillea* 'Moonshine'**
Upright perennial that bears flat heads of bright yellow flowers throughout summer above a mass of small, feathery, grey-green leaves. Divide plants regularly in spring. H 60cm (24in), S 50cm (20in).

***Barbarea vulgaris* 'Variegata'**
Perennial with rosettes of long, toothed, glossy leaves, blotched with cream, above which rise branching heads of small, silvery-yellow flowers in early summer. H 25–45cm (10–18in), S to 23cm (9in).

Gaillardia aristata (Blanket flower)
Upright, rather open perennial that has large, terminal, daisy-like, single flower heads, yellow with red centres, over summer, and aromatic, divided leaves. Needs staking and may be short-lived. H 60cm (24in), S 50cm (20in).

***Achillea* 'Taygetea'**
Perennial with erect stems bearing flat heads of lemon-yellow flowers throughout summer above clumps of feathery, grey leaves. Divide and replant every third year. H 60cm (24in), S 50cm (20in).

***Potentilla recta* 'Warrenii'**
Clump-forming perennial with lobed, mid-green leaves. Rich golden-yellow flowers are borne on open, branched stems throughout summer. H 50cm (20in), S 60cm (24in).

× *Solidaster luteus*
Clump-forming perennial. From mid-summer onwards, slender stems carry dense heads of bright creamy-yellow flowers above narrow, mid-green leaves. H 60cm (24in), S 75cm (30in).

***Helichrysum* 'Schwefellicht'**
Clump-forming perennial that bears silver-grey leaves and a mass of ever-lasting, fluffy, sulphur-yellow flower heads from mid- to late summer. H 40–60cm (16–24in), S 30cm (12in).

***Oenothera fruticosa* 'Fyrverkeri'**
Clump-forming perennial that from mid- to late summer bears spikes of fragrant, cup-shaped flowers. Has reddish stems and glossy, mid-green foliage. H and S 30–38cm (12–15in).

YELLOW

***Ranunculus constantinopolitanus* 'Plenus'**
Clump-forming perennial with divided, toothed leaves sometimes spotted grey and white. Neat, pompon-like, double, yellow flowers appear in early summer. H 50cm (20in), S 30cm (12in).

Mimulus luteus (Yellow musk)
Spreading perennial. Throughout summer, snapdragon-like, occasionally red-spotted, yellow flowers are freely produced above hairy, mid-green foliage. H and S 30cm (12in).

Meconopsis integrifolia
(Lampshade poppy)
Rosette-forming biennial or short-lived perennial carrying spikes of large, pale yellow flowers in late spring and early summer. Has large, pale green leaves. H 45–60cm (18–24in), S 60cm (24in).

***Geum* 'Lady Stratheden'**
Clump-forming perennial with lobed leaves and cup-shaped, double, bright yellow flowers with prominent, green stamens borne on slender, branching stems for a long period in summer. H 45–60cm (18–24in), S 45cm (18in).

Potentilla megalantha
Clump-forming perennial with large, palmate, hairy, soft green leaves. Large, rich yellow flowers are produced in summer. H 20cm (8in), S 15cm (6in).

Buphthalmum salicifolium
(Yellow ox-eye)
Spreading perennial that carries daisy-like, deep yellow flower heads singly on willowy stems throughout summer. May need staking. Divide regularly; spreads on rich soil. H 60cm (24in), S 90cm (36in).

Gazania rigens* var. *uniflora
Mat-forming perennial, grown as an annual in all except mildest areas. Yellow or orange-yellow flower heads, sometimes with central white spots, are borne singly in early summer above rosettes of narrow, silver-backed leaves. H 23cm (9in), S 20–30cm (8–12in).

***Potentilla* 'Yellow Queen'**
Clump-forming perennial with strawberry-like, dark green leaves and bright yellow flowers in mid-summer. H to 60cm (24in) or more, S 45cm (18in).

***Ranunculus acris* 'Flore Pleno'**
(Double meadow buttercup)
Clump-forming perennial. Wiry stems with lobed and cut leaves act as a foil for rosetted, double, golden-yellow flowers in late spring and early summer. H and S 45–60cm (18–24in).

YELLOW

***Sedum aizoon* 'Aurantiacum'**
Erect perennial with red stems carrying fleshy, toothed, dark green leaves. In summer produces gently rounded heads of dark yellow flowers followed by red seed capsules. H and S 45cm (18in).

Tropaeolum polyphyllum
Prostrate perennial with spurred, short, trumpet-shaped, rich yellow flowers, borne singly in summer above trailing, grey-green leaves and stems. May spread widely once established but is good on a bank. H 5–8cm (2–3in), S 30cm (12in) or more.

Coreopsis lanceolata
Bushy perennial that in summer freely produces daisy-like, bright yellow flower heads on branching stems. Lance-shaped leaves are borne on flower stems. Propagate by seed or division. H 45cm (18in), S 30cm (12in).

Hieracium lanatum
Clump-forming perennial that produces mounds of broad, downy, grey leaves, above which dandelion-like, yellow flower heads appear on wiry stems in summer. H 30–45cm (12–18in), S 30cm (12in).

Coreopsis verticillata
Bushy perennial with finely divided, dark green foliage and many tiny, star-shaped, golden flower heads borne throughout summer. Divide and replant in spring. H 40–60cm (16–24in), S 30cm (12in).

Impatiens repens
Evergreen, creeping perennial with rooting stems. Has small, oval to rounded leaves and, in summer, yellow flowers, each with a large, hairy spur. H to 5cm (2in), S indefinite. Min. 10°C (50°F).

Eriophyllum lanatum
Perennial forming low cushions of divided, silvery leaves. Daisy-like, yellow flower heads are produced freely in summer, usually singly, on grey stems. H and S 30cm (12in).

Inula ensifolia
Clump-forming perennial with small, lance-shaped to elliptic leaves, bearing many daisy-like, yellow flower heads, singly on wiry stalks, in late summer. H and S 30cm (12in).

***Calceolaria* 'John Innes'**
Vigorous, evergreen, clump-forming perennial that in spring-summer produces large, pouch-like, reddish-brown-spotted, deep yellow flowers, several to each stem. Has broadly oval, basal, mid-green leaves. H 15–20cm (6–8in), S 25–30cm (10–12in).

ORANGE

Aeschynanthus speciosus
Evergreen, trailing perennial with waxy, narrowly oval leaves usually carried in whorls. Erect, tubular, bright orange-red flowers are borne in large clusters in summer. H and S 30–60cm (12–24in). Min. 18°C (64°F).

Geum coccineum
Clump-forming perennial with irregularly lobed leaves, above which in summer rise slender, branching, hairy stems bearing single, orange flowers with prominent, yellow stamens. H and S 30cm (12in).

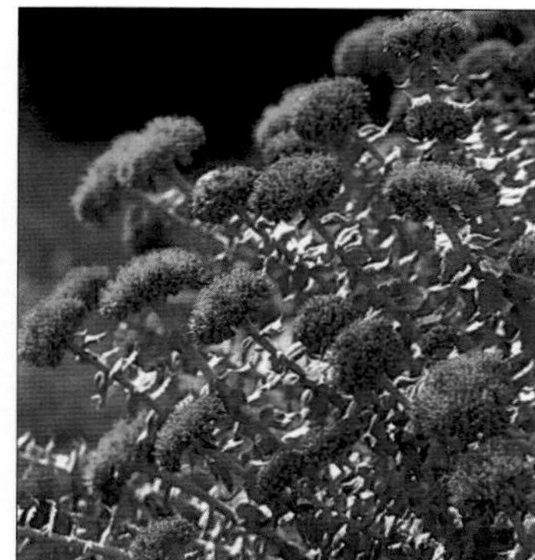

Rhodiola heterodonta
Clump-forming perennial with heads of yellow or red, sometimes greenish flowers from spring to early summer. Stems bear toothed, blue-green leaves. H 45cm (18in), S 25cm (10in).

WHITE–PINK

Tricyrtis hirta* var. *alba
Upright, rhizomatous perennial that bears clusters of large, bell-shaped, spurred, white flowers, occasionally purple-spotted, in upper leaf axils of hairy, stem-clasping, dark green leaves during late summer and early autumn. H 45–60cm (18–24in), S 45cm (18in).

***Sedum spectabile* 'Brilliant'**
(Ice-plant)
Clump-forming perennial that from late summer to autumn produces flat heads of bright rose-pink flowers. These are borne over a mass of fleshy, grey-green leaves and attract butterflies. H and S 30–45cm (12–18in).

***Schizostylis coccinea* 'Sunrise'**
Clump-forming, rhizomatous perennial that in early autumn produces spikes of large, shallowly cup-shaped, pink flowers above grassy, mid-green foliage. H 60cm (24in), S 23–30cm (9–12in).

RED–YELLOW

***Schizostylis coccinea* 'Major'**
Rhizomatous perennial with long, narrow, grass-like leaves. Gladiolus-like spikes of cup-shaped, bright crimson flowers appear in autumn. H 60cm (24in) or more, S 30cm (12in) or more.

Liriope muscari
Evergreen, spreading perennial that in autumn carries spikes of thickly clustered, rounded-bell-shaped, lavender or purple-blue flowers among narrow, glossy, dark green leaves. H 30cm (12in), S 45cm (18in).

Cautleya spicata
Upright perennial that in summer and early autumn bears spikes of light orange or soft yellow flowers in maroon-red bracts. Has handsome, long, mid-green leaves. Needs a sheltered site and rich, deep soil. H 60cm (24in), S 50cm (20in).

Chirita lavandulacea
Evergreen, erect perennial with downy, pale green leaves to 20cm (8in) long. In leaf axils has clusters of lavender-blue flowers with white tubes. May be sown in succession to flower from spring to autumn. H and S 60cm (24in). Min. 15°C (59°F).

Senecio pulcher
Perennial with leathery, hairy, dark green leaves. In summer-autumn produces handsome, daisy-like, yellow-centred, bright purplish-pink flower heads. H 45–60cm (18–24in), S 50cm (20in).

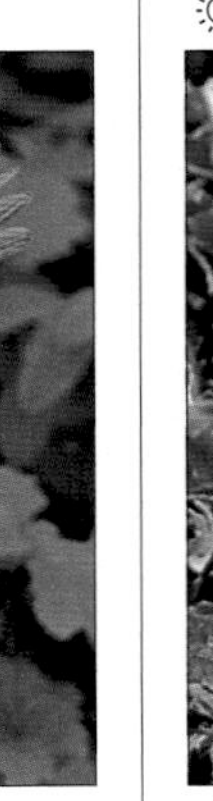

Arctotheca calendula
(Cape dandelion)
Carpeting perennial. Leaves are woolly below, rough-haired above. Heads of daisy-like, bright yellow flowers, with darker yellow centres, appear from late spring to autumn. H 30cm (12in), S indefinite. Min. 5°C (41°F).

BEGONIAS

B. dregei

The genus *Begonia* is one of the most versatile, providing interest throughout the year. Semperflorens begonias are excellent for summer bedding, while the Rex-cultorum group has distinctive and handsome foliage, borne with a vast variety of decorative shades and textures. Other begonias, such as the Tuberhybrida cultivars with their large and showy blooms, are grown mainly for their flowers. Many make attractive house plants, or make a good display in hanging baskets.

The majority of begonias are suitable for permanent outdoor cultivation only in relatively humid, tropical and subtropical regions, where they are grown in a bed or border. Begonias may be fibrous-rooted, rhizomatous, or tuberous, the tubers becoming dormant in winter.

B. **'Can-can'**

B. scharffii

***B.* 'Billie Langdon'**

***B.* 'Orpha C. Fox'**

B. masoniana 🏆

***B.* 'Tiger Paws'** 🏆

***B.* 'Apricot Cascade'**

***B.* 'Weltoniensis'**

B. olsoniae

***B.* 'Helen Lewis'**

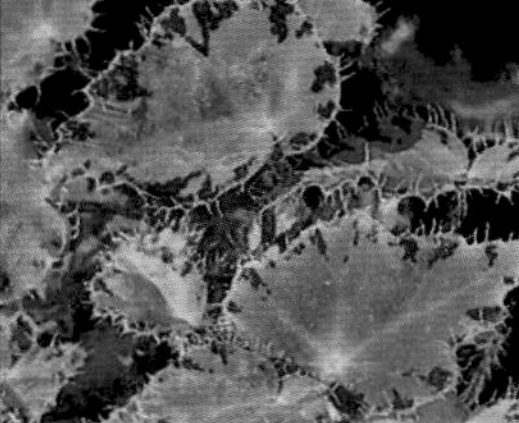

B. bowerae

***B.* 'Oliver Twist'**

B. albopicta

***B.* 'Ingramii'**

***B.* 'Duartei'**

***B. manicata* 'Crispa'**

B. prismatocarpa

B. sutherlandii 🏆

B. serratipetala

***B.* 'Thurstonii'** 🏆

***B. pustulata* 'Argentea'**

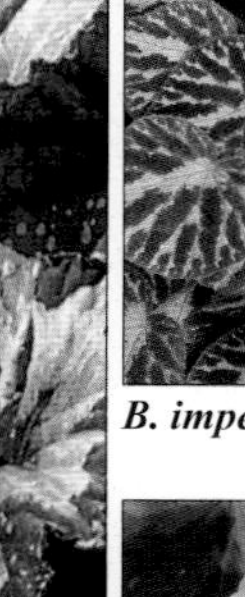

***B.* 'Merry Christmas'** 🏆

B. imperialis

***B.* 'Orange Rubra'** 🏆

***B.* 'City of Ballarat'**

***B.* 'Roy Hartley'**

Coelogyne cristata [e]

ORCHIDS

Flamboyant, exotic, even seductive, orchids are prized for their unusual flowers. Their aura of mystique and many popular misconceptions may have discouraged gardeners from growing these beautiful plants, but their cultivation is not always difficult and some will thrive happily indoors as house plants.

There are two main groups. Terrestrials [t] grow in a wide range of habitats in the wild; many are at least frost hardy. Epiphytes [e], the more showy of the two and mostly native to the tropics, cling to tree branches or rocks, obtaining nourishment through their leaves and aerial roots. They need special composts and in cool climates must be grown under glass (see also 'Orchids' in Plant Dictionary).

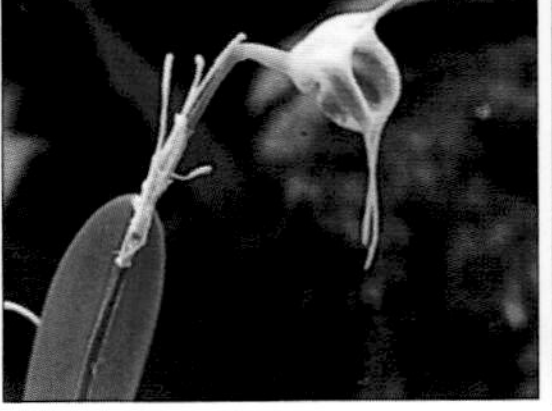
Masdevallia infracta [e]

Lemboglossum rossii [e]

Cypripedium acaule [t]

Masdevallia tovarensis [e] 🏆

Dendrobium infundibulum [e] 🏆

Coelogyne flaccida [e]

Angraecum sesquipedale [e] 🏆

Calanthe vestita [t]

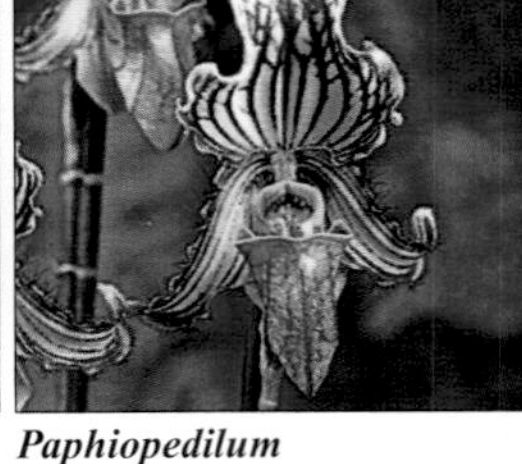
Paphiopedilum fairrieanum [t] ①

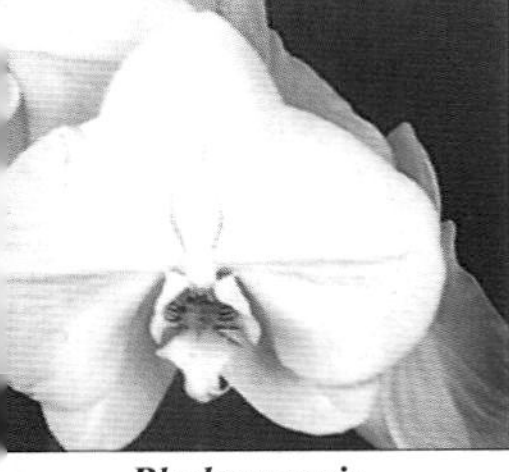
Phalaenopsis Allegria [e]

Odontoglossum Royal Occasion [e]

Paphiopedilum Freckles [t] ①

Dendrobium momozono 'Oriental Paradise' [e]

Cypripedium reginae [t]

Paphiopedilum niveum [t] ①

Coelogyne nitida [e] 🏆

Cymbidium Portelet Bay [e] ①

Lemboglossum cervantesii [e]

Paphiopedilum callosum [t] ①

Oncidium ornithorrhynchum [e] 🏆

Spiranthes cernua [t]

Odontoglossum crispum [e]

Miltoniopsis Robert Strauss 'Ardingly' [e]

Cymbidium Strathbraan [e] ①

Paphiopedilum bellatulum [t] ①

Brassavola nodosa [e]

Paphiopedilum appletonianum [t] ①

Lemboglossum bictoniense [e] 🏆

Dendrobium nobile **[e] 🏆**

× *Laeliocattleya* Rojo 'Mont Millais' [e]

Cymbidium **Pontac 'Mont Millais' [e] (!)**

Ophrys tenthredinifera **[t]**

Calypso bulbosa **[t]**

× *Odontioda* Mount Bingham [e]

Cymbidium **Strath Kanaid [e] (!)**

Lemboglossum cordatum **[e]**

× *Brassolaeliocattleya* Hetherington Horace 'Coronation' [e]

Pleione bulbocodioides **[t]**

Masdevallia coccinea **[e] 🏆**

× *Vuylstekeara* Cambria 'Lensing's Favorite' [e]

× *Odontioda* Pacific Gold × *Odontoglossum cordatum* [e]

× *Wilsonara* Hambuhren Stern 'Cheam' [e]

Laelia anceps **[e]**

Bletilla striata **[t]**

Cattleya **J.A. Carbone [e]**

Epidendrum ibaguense **[e]**

Rossioglossum grande **[e] 🏆**

× *Brassocattleya* Mount Adams [e]

Dendrobium momozono **Trizac 'Princess' [e]**

× *Sophrolaeliocattleya* Trizac 'Purple Emperor' [e]

Phalaenopsis **Lady Jersey × Lippeglut [e]**

× *Brassolaeliocattleya* St Helier [e]

Miltoniopsis **Anjou 'St Patrick' [e]**

Cymbidium **Strathdon 'Cooksbridge Noel' [e] (!) 🏆**

× *Odontocidium* Tiger Butter × *Wilsonara* Wigg's 'Kay' [e]

× *Odontocidium* Artur Elle 'Colombian' [e]

Cattleya bowringiana **[e] 🏆**

Odontoglossum **Le Nez Point [e]**

Phaius tankervilleae **[t]**

Paphiopedilum **Lyric 'Glendora' [t] (!)**

Paphiopedilum **Maudiae [t] (!) 🏆**

Phalaenopsis cornu-cervi [e]

Cymbidium devonianum [e] ①

Paphiopedilum sukhakulii [t] ① 🏆

Gomesa planifolia [e]

Paphiopedilum **Buckhurst 'Mont Millais'** [t] ①

Miltonia candida [e]

Zygopetalum mackaii [e]

Paphiopedilum haynaldianum [t] ①

Odontoglossum **Eric Young** [e]

× *Aliceara* **Dark Warrior** [e]

Zygopetalum **Perrenoudii** [e]

Coelogyne speciosa [e]

Cymbidium **King's Loch 'Cooksbridge'** [e] ① 🏆

Masdevallia wagneriana [e]

× *Odontocidium* **Tigersun 'Orbec'** [e]

Gongora quinquenervis [e]

Orchis morio [t]

Ophrys fusca [t]

Phalaenopsis **Lundy** [e]

Oncidium tigrinum [e]

Bulbophyllum careyanum [e]

Cymbidium hookerianum [e] ①

Cymbidium **Caithness Ice 'Trinity'** [e] ①

Cymbidium elegans [e] ①

Ophrys lutea [t]

Miltonia clowesii [e]

Vanda **Rothschildiana** [e] 🏆

Cymbidium tracyanum [e] ①

Cypripedium macranthos [t]

Epidendrum difforme [e]

Cypripedium calceolus [t]

Maxillaria porphyrostele [e]

× *Potinara* Cherub 'Spring Daffodil' [e]

Laelia cinnabarina [e]

Dendrobium chrysotoxum [e]

Lycaste cruenta [e]

Psychopsis papilio [e]

× ***Odontocidium*** **Tiger Hambuhren** [e]

Oncidium flexuosum [e]

Ada aurantiaca [e]

Cypripedium pubescens [t]

× ***Sophrolaeliocattleya*** **Hazel Boyd 'Apricot Glow'** [e]

Paphiopedilum venustum [t] ①

Cymbidium **Christmas Angel 'Cooksbridge Sunburst'** [e] ①

× ***Odontioda*** × ***Odontoglossum*** **Buttercrisp** [e]

☐ WHITE

Spathiphyllum **'Mauna Loa'**
Robust, evergreen, tufted perennial with rhizomes. Has long, lance-shaped, glossy leaves. Irregularly bears fleshy, white spadices of fragrant flowers enclosed in large, oval, white spathes. H and S 45–60cm (18–24in). Min. 15°C (59°F).

◑ 💧 ① 🏆

Episcia dianthiflora
(Lace flower)
Evergreen perennial with creeping, prostrate stems. Has thick, velvety leaves with brownish midribs and, intermittently, pure white flowers with fringed petals. H 10cm (4in), S indefinite. Min. 15°C (59°F).

◑ 💧

Hemigraphis repanda
Evergreen, prostrate perennial with spreading, rooting stems. Lance-shaped, toothed, purple-tinged leaves, 5cm (2in) long, are darker purple below. Has tiny, tubular, white flowers intermittently. H to 15cm (6in), S indefinite. Min. 15°C (59°F).

◑ 💧

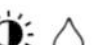

□ WHITE

Spathiphyllum wallisii
(Peace lily, White sails)
Evergreen, tufted, rhizomatous perennial. Has clusters of long, lance-shaped leaves. Fleshy, white spadices of fragrant flowers in white spathes are irregularly produced. H and S 30cm (12in) or more. Min. 15°C (59°F).

Pilea cadierei (Aluminium plant)
Evergreen, bushy perennial with broadly oval leaves, each with a sharply pointed tip and raised, silvery patches that appear quilted. Has insignificant, greenish flowers. H and S 30cm (12in). Min. 10°C (50°F).

***Tradescantia fluminensis* 'Variegata'**
Evergreen, trailing perennial with rooting stems and leaves, irregularly striped creamy-white. Intermittently has clusters of white flowers. H 30cm (12in), S indefinite. Min. 15°C (59°F).

***Fittonia albivenis* Argyroneura Group** (Silver net-leaf)
Evergreen, creeping perennial with small, oval, white-veined, olive-green leaves. Remove flowers if they form. H to 15cm (6in), S indefinite. Min. 15°C (59°F).

***Tradescantia fluminensis* 'Albovittata'**
Strong-growing, evergreen perennial with trailing, rooting stems. Bluish-green leaves have broad, white stripes. Bears small, white flowers. H 30cm (12in), S indefinite. Min. 15°C (59°F).

***Glechoma hederacea* 'Variegata'**
(Variegated ground ivy)
Evergreen, carpeting perennial that has small, heart-shaped leaves, with white marbling, on trailing stems. Bears insignificant flowers in summer. Spreads rapidly but is useful for a container. H 15cm (6in), S indefinite.

Helleborus × hybridus
(Lenten rose) [white form]
Evergreen, clump-forming perennial with dense, divided foliage, above which rise nodding, cup-shaped, white, pink or purple flowers, sometimes darker spotted, in winter or early spring. H and S 45cm (18in).

***Aglaonema commutatum* 'Treubii'**
Evergreen, erect, tufted perennial. Lance-shaped leaves, to 30cm (12in) long, are marked with pale green or silver. Occasionally has greenish-white spathes. H and S to 45cm (18in). Min. 15°C (59°F).

Peperomia caperata
(Emerald ripple)
Evergreen, bushy perennial with pinkish leaf stalks. Has oval, fleshy, wrinkled, dark green leaves, to 5cm (2in) long, with sunken veins; spikes of white flowers appear irregularly. H and S to 15cm (6in). Min. 10°C (50°F).

WHITE–PINK

***Chlorophytum comosum* 'Vittatum'**
Evergreen, tufted, rosette-forming perennial. Long, narrow, lance-shaped, creamy-white leaves have green stripes and margins. Irregularly has small, star-shaped, white flowers on thin stems. H and S 30cm (12in). Min. 5°C (41°F).

***Aspidistra elatior* 'Variegata'**
Evergreen, rhizomatous perennial with upright, narrow, glossy, dark green leaves which are longitudinally cream-striped. Occasionally has inconspicuous, cream to purple flowers near soil level. H 60cm (24in), S 45cm (18in). Min. 5–10°C (41–50°F).

***Oplismenus africanus* 'Variegatus'**
Evergreen, creeping, perennial grass with wiry, rooting stems. White-striped leaves, with wavy margins, are often tinged pink. Bears inconspicuous flowers intermittently. H 20cm (8in) or more, S indefinite. Min. 12°C (54°F).

Helleborus niger (Christmas rose)
Evergreen, clump-forming perennial with divided, deep green leaves and cup-shaped, nodding, white flowers, with golden stamens, borne in winter or early spring. H and S 30cm (12in).

Helleborus* × *sternii
Evergreen, clump-forming perennial with divided leaves and cup-shaped, often pink-tinged, pale green flowers borne in terminal clusters in winter and early spring. H and S 45cm (18in).

Helleborus* × *hybridus
(Lenten rose) [pink form]
Evergreen, clump-forming perennial with dense, divided foliage, above which rise nodding, cup-shaped, white, pink or purple flowers, sometimes darker spotted, in winter or early spring. H and S 45cm (18in).

PINK–RED

***Streptocarpus* 'Nicola'**
Evergreen, stemless perennial with a rosette of strap-shaped, wrinkled leaves. Funnel-shaped, rose-pink flowers are produced intermittently in small clusters. H 25cm (10in), S 50cm (20in). Min. 10–15°C (50–59°F).

Tradescantia zebrina
(Silver inch plant)
Evergreen, trailing or mat-forming perennial. Bluish-green leaves, purple-tinged beneath, have 2 broad, silver bands. Has pink or violet-blue flowers intermittently during the year. H 15cm (6in), S indefinite. Min. 15°C (59°F).

Episcia cupreata (Flame violet)
Evergreen, creeping perennial. Has small, downy, wrinkled leaves, usually silver-veined or -banded, and, intermittently, scarlet flowers marked yellow within. H 10cm (4in), S indefinite. Min. 15°C (59°F).

African violets

African violet is the common name for the genus *Saintpaulia*, although it is often applied to the numerous cultivars derived from *S. ionantha*. These low-growing, rosetted, evergreen perennials may be grown as summer bedding in warm, humid climates but also make attractive indoor pot plants, flowering freely throughout the year if kept in a suitable draught-free, light, humid position. A wide range of attractive flower colours and forms is available. Their leaves are somewhat succulent, and usually hairy.

S. 'Ice Maiden'

S. 'Porcelain'

S. 'Colorado'

S. 'Garden News'

S. 'Starry Trail'

S. 'Rococo Anna'

S. 'Pip Squeek'

S. 'Delft'

S. 'Zoja'

S. 'Bright Eyes'

RED–PURPLE

Anthurium scherzerianum
(Flamingo flower)
Evergreen, tufted perennial with erect, leathery, dark green leaves to 20cm (8in) long. Has large, long-lasting, bright red spathes and fleshy, orange to yellow spadices. H and S 30–60cm (12–24in). Min. 15°C (59°F).

Gerbera jamesonii
(Barberton daisy)
Evergreen, upright perennial with daisy-like, variably coloured flower heads, borne intermittently on long stems, and basal rosettes of large, jagged leaves. Flowers are excellent for cutting. H 60cm (24in), S 45cm (18in).

***Tellima grandiflora* Rubra Group**
Semi-evergreen, clump-forming perennial with a mass of hairy, basal, reddish-purple leaves, underlaid dark green. In late spring, erect stems bear spikes of bell-shaped, pinkish-cream flowers. H and S 60cm (24in).

Helleborus × hybridus
(Lenten rose)[purple form]
Evergreen, clump-forming perennial with dense, divided foliage, above which rise nodding, cup-shaped, white, pink or purple flowers, sometimes darker spotted, in winter or early spring. H and S 45cm (18in).

***Phormium* 'Bronze Baby'**
Evergreen, upright perennial with tufts of bold, stiff, pointed, wine-red leaves. Panicles of reddish flowers are occasionally produced on purplish stems during summer. H and S 45–60cm (18–24in).

***Fittonia albivenis* Verschaffeltii Group** (Painted net-leaf)
Evergreen, creeping perennial with small, oval, red-veined, olive-green leaves. Flowers are best removed if they form. H to 15cm (6in), S indefinite. Min. 15°C (59°F).

PURPLE

***Ophiopogon planiscapus* 'Nigrescens'**
Evergreen, spreading, clump-forming perennial, grown for its distinctive, grass-like, black leaves. Racemes of lilac flowers in summer are followed by black fruits. H 23cm (9in), S 30cm (12in).

***Tradescantia pallida* 'Purpurea'**
Evergreen, creeping perennial with dark purple stems and slightly fleshy leaves. Has pink or pink-and-white flowers in summer. H 30–40cm (12–16in), S 30cm (12in) or more. Min. 15°C (59°F).

***Ajuga reptans* 'Atropurpurea'**
Evergreen, ground-cover perennial, spreading freely by runners, with small rosettes of glossy, deep bronze-purple leaves. Short spikes of blue flowers appear in spring. H 15cm (6in), S 90cm (36in).

Elatostema repens
(Watermelon begonia)
Evergreen, creeping perennial with rooting stems. Broadly oval, olive-green leaves have purplish-brown edges and paler green centres. Flowers are insignificant. H 10cm (4in), S indefinite. Min. 15°C (59°F).

Tradescantia sillamontana,
Evergreen, erect perennial. Oval, stem-clasping leaves are densely covered with white, woolly hairs. Has clusters of small, bright purplish-pink flowers in summer. H and S to 30cm (12in). Min. 10–15°C (50–59°F).

Tetranema roseum (Mexican foxglove, Mexican violet)
Short-stemmed perennial with crowded, stalkless leaves, bluish-green beneath. Intermittently, has nodding, purple flowers with paler throats. H to 20cm (8in), S 30cm (12in). Min. 13°C (55°F).

***Ajuga reptans* 'Multicolor'**
Evergreen, mat-forming perennial. Dark green leaves, marked with cream and pink, make good ground cover. Spikes of small, blue flowers appear in spring. H 12cm (5in), S 45cm (18in).

***Streptocarpus* 'Constant Nymph'**
Evergreen, stemless perennial with a rosette of strap-shaped, wrinkled leaves. Funnel-shaped, purplish-blue flowers, darker veined and yellow-throated, are intermittently produced in small clusters. H 25cm (10in), S 50cm (20in). Min. 10–15°C (50–59°F).

PURPLE–GREEN

Cyanotis somaliensis
(Pussy ears)
Evergreen, creeping perennial. Small, narrow, glossy, dark green leaves with white hairs surround stems. Has purplish-blue flowers in leaf axils in winter-spring. H 5cm (2in), S indefinite. Min. 10–15°C (50–59°F).

***Maranta leuconeura* 'Erythroneura'**
(Herringbone plant)
Evergreen perennial. Oblong leaves have veins marked red, with paler yellowish-green midribs, and are upright at night, flat by day. H and S to 30cm (12in). Min. 15°C (59°F).

***Sansevieria trifasciata* 'Hahnii'**
Evergreen, stemless perennial with a rosette of about 5 stiff, erect, broadly lance-shaped and pointed leaves, banded horizontally with pale green or white. Occasionally has small, pale green flowers. H 15–30cm (6–12in), S 10cm (4in). Min. 15°C (59°F).

GREEN

Calathea makoyana
(Peacock plant)
Evergreen, clump-forming perennial. Horizontal leaves, 30cm (12in) long, are dark and light green above, reddish-purple below. Has short spikes of white flowers intermittently. H to 60cm (2ft), S to 1.2m (4ft). Min. 15°C (59°F).

Aglaonema pictum
Evergreen, erect, tufted perennial. Oval leaves, to 15cm (6in) long, are irregularly marked with greyish-white or grey-green. Has creamy-white spathes in summer. H and S to 60cm (24in). Min. 15°C (59°F).

***Aglaonema* 'Silver King'**
Evergreen, erect, tufted perennial. Broadly lance-shaped, mid-green leaves, to 30cm (12in) long, are marked with dark and light green. Has greenish-white spathes in summer. H and S to 45cm (18in). Min. 15°C (59°F).

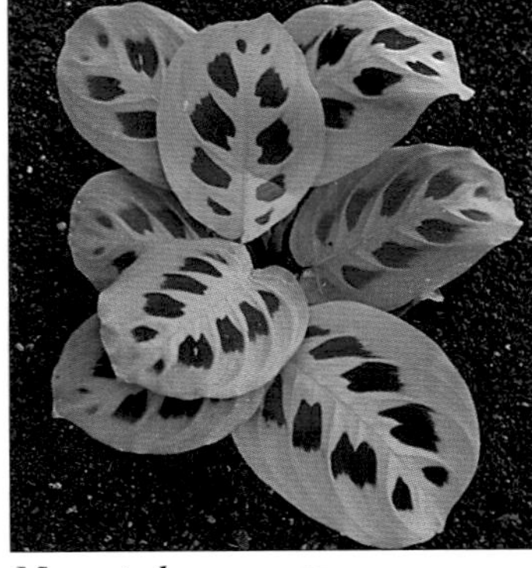

***Maranta leuconeura* 'Kerchoviana'** (Rabbit tracks)
Evergreen perennial that intermittently bears white to mauve flowers. Oblong leaves with dark brown blotches become greener with age and are upright at night, flat by day. H and S to 30cm (12in). Min. 15°C (59°F).

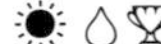

Welwitschia mirabilis
Evergreen perennial with a short, woody trunk. Has 2 strap-shaped leaves, to 2.5m (8ft) long, with tips splitting to form many tendril-like strips. Bears small, reddish-brown cones. H to 30cm (12in), S indefinite. Min. 10°C (50°F).

Peperomia marmorata
(Silver heart)
Evergreen, bushy perennial with insignificant flowers. Has oval, long-pointed, fleshy, dull green leaves, marked with greyish-white and quilted above, reddish below. H and S to 20cm (8in). Min. 10°C (50°F).

Stachys byzantina
(Bunnies' ears, Lamb's tongue)
Evergreen, mat-forming perennial with woolly, grey foliage that is excellent for a border front or as ground cover. Bears mauve-pink flowers in summer. H 30–38cm (12–15in), S 60cm (24in).

Ophiopogon japonicus
Evergreen, clump or mat-forming perennial with grass-like, glossy, dark green foliage. Spikes of lilac flowers in late summer are followed by blue-black berries. H 30cm (12in), S indefinite.

Helleborus argutifolius
Clump-forming perennial with evergreen, divided, spiny, dark green leaves and cup-shaped, pale green flowers borne in large clusters in winter-spring. H 60cm (24in), S 45cm (18in).

Soleirolia soleirolii (Baby's tears, Mind-your-own-business)
Usually evergreen, invasive, prostrate perennial with small, round, vivid green leaves that form a carpet. May choke other plants if not controlled. H 5cm (2in), S indefinite.

Callisia repens
Evergreen, creeping perennial with rooting stems and densely packed leaves, sometimes white-banded and often purplish beneath. Rarely, has inconspicuous, white flowers in winter. H 10cm (4in), S indefinite. Min. 15°C (59°F).

GREEN

Drosera spatulata
Evergreen, insectivorous perennial with rosettes of spoon-shaped leaves that have sensitive, red, glandular hairs. Has many small, pink or white flowers on leafless stems in summer. H and S to 8cm (3in). Min. 5–10°C (41–50°F).

Peperomia glabella (Wax privet)
Evergreen perennial with wide-spreading, red stems. Has broadly oval, fleshy, glossy, bright green leaves, to 5cm (2in) long, and insignificant flowers. H to 15cm (6in), S 30cm (12in). Min. 10°C (50°F).

Helleborus viridis
(Green hellebore)
Clump-forming perennial with deciduous, divided, dark green leaves. Bears cup-shaped, green flowers in late winter or early spring. H and S 30cm (12in).

Drosera capensis (Cape sundew)
Evergreen, insectivorous perennial. Rosettes of narrow leaves have sensitive, red, glandular hairs. Many small, purple flowers are borne on leafless stems in summer. H and S to 15cm (6in). Min. 5–10°C (41–50°F).

***Peperomia obtusifolia* 'Variegata'**
Evergreen, bushy perennial with spade-shaped, fleshy leaves, to 20cm (8in) long, that have irregular, yellowish-green to creamy-white margins and usually greyish centres. Flowers are insignificant. H and S to 15cm (6in). Min. 10°C (50°F).

Pilea nummulariifolia
(Creeping Charlie)
Evergreen, mat-forming perennial with creeping, rooting, reddish stems. Rounded, pale green leaves, 2cm (¾in) wide, have a ridged surface. Flowers are insignificant. H to 5cm (2in), S 30cm (12in). Min. 10°C (50°F).

GREEN–YELLOW

***Iresine herbstii* 'Aureoreticulata'**
Evergreen, bushy perennial with red stems and inconspicuous flowers. Rounded, mid-green leaves, 10cm (4in) long, have yellow or red veins and notched tips. H to 60cm (24in), S 45cm (18in). Min. 10–15°C (50–59°F).

Dionaea muscipula
(Venus flytrap)
Evergreen, insectivorous perennial with rosettes of 6 or more spreading, hinged leaves, pink-flushed inside, edged with stiff bristles. Clusters of tiny, white flowers are carried in summer. H 10cm (4in), S 30cm (12in). Min. 5°C (41°F).

Helleborus foetidus
(Stinking hellebore)
Evergreen, clump-forming perennial with deeply divided, dark green leaves and, in late winter and early spring, panicles of cup-shaped, red-margined, pale green flowers. H and S 45cm (18in).

***Sansevieria trifasciata* 'Golden Hahnii'**
Evergreen, stemless perennial with a rosette of about 5 stiff, erect, broadly lance-shaped leaves with wide, yellow borders. Sometimes bears small, pale green flowers. H 15–30cm (6–12in), S 10cm (4in). Min. 15°C (59°F).

Nautilocalyx lynchii
Robust, evergreen, erect, bushy perennial. Broadly lance-shaped, slightly wrinkled leaves are glossy, greenish-red above, reddish beneath. In summer has tubular, red-haired, pale yellow flowers with red calyces. H and S to 60cm (24in). Min. 15°C (59°F).

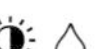

WHITE–GREEN

***Cortaderia selloana* 'Silver Comet'**
Evergreen, clump-forming, perennial grass with very narrow, sharp-edged, recurved leaves, 1m (3ft) long, that have silver margins. Carries plume-like panicles of spikelets from late summer. H 1.2–1.5m (4–5ft), S 1m (3ft).

Phalaris arundinacea* var. *picta
(Gardener's garters)
Evergreen, spreading, perennial grass with broad, white-striped leaves. Produces narrow panicles of spikelets in summer. Can be invasive. H 1m (3ft), S indefinite.

***Holcus mollis* 'Albovariegatus'**
(Variegated creeping soft grass)
Evergreen, spreading, perennial grass with white-striped leaves and hairy nodes. In summer carries purplish-white flower spikes. H 30–45cm (12–18in), S indefinite.

Pleioblastus variegatus
(Dwarf white-stripe bamboo)
Evergreen, slow-spreading bamboo with narrow, slightly downy, white-striped leaves. Stems are branched near the base. H 80cm (30in), S indefinite.

Arundo donax* var. *versicolor
Herbaceous, rhizomatous, perennial grass with strong stems bearing broad, creamy-white-striped leaves. May bear dense, erect panicles of whitish-yellow spikelets in late summer. H 2.5–3m (8–10ft), S 60cm (2ft).

Sasa veitchii
Evergreen, slow-spreading bamboo. Leaves, 25cm (10in) long, soon develop white edges. Stems, often purple, produce a single branch at each node. White powder appears beneath nodes. H to 1.5m (5ft), S indefinite.

Lagurus ovatus (Hare's-tail grass)
Tuft-forming, annual grass that in early summer bears dense, egg-shaped, soft panicles of white flower spikes, with golden stamens, lasting well into autumn. Leaves are long, narrow and flat. Self seeds readily. H 45cm (18in), S 15cm (6in).

***Cortaderia selloana* 'Sunningdale Silver'**
Evergreen, clump-forming, perennial grass with narrow, sharp-edged, recurved leaves, 1.5m (5ft) long. Bears long-lasting, feathery panicles of creamy-white spikelets in late summer. H 2.1m (7ft), S 1.2m (4ft).

***Glyceria maxima* 'Variegata'**
Herbaceous, spreading, perennial grass with cream-striped leaves, often tinged pink at the base. Bears open panicles of greenish spikelets in summer. H 80cm (30in), S indefinite.

***Miscanthus sinensis* 'Zebrinus'**
Herbaceous, clump-forming, perennial grass. Leaves, hairy beneath, have transverse, yellowish-white ring markings. May carry awned, hairy, white spikelets in fan-shaped panicles in autumn. H 1.2m (4ft), S 45cm (1½ft).

***Schoenoplectus lacustris* subsp. *tabernaemontani* 'Zebrinus'**
Evergreen, spreading, perennial sedge with leafless stems, striped horizontally with white, and brown spikelets in summer. Withstands brackish water. H 1.5m (5ft), S indefinite.

Luzula nivea
(Snowy woodrush)
Evergreen, slow-spreading, perennial rush with fairly dense clusters of shining, white flower spikes in early summer. Leaves are edged with white hairs. H 60cm (24in), S 45–60cm (18–24in).

Hordeum jubatum
(Foxtail barley, Squirrel tail grass)
Tufted, short-lived perennial or annual grass. In summer to early autumn has flat, arching, feathery, plume-like flower spikes with silky awns. H 30–60cm (12–24in), S 30cm (12in).

Pennisetum villosum
(Feather-top)
Herbaceous, tuft-forming, perennial grass with long-haired stems. In autumn has panicles of creamy-pink spikelets, fading to pale brown, with very long, bearded bristles. H to 1m (3ft), S 50cm (20in).

Stipa gigantea (Golden oats)
Evergreen, tuft-forming, perennial grass with narrow leaves, 45cm (18in) or more long. In summer carries elegant, open panicles of silvery spikelets, with long awns and dangling, golden anthers, which persist well into winter. H 2.5m (8ft), S 1m (3ft).

Cyperus papyrus
(Paper reed, Papyrus)
Evergreen, clump-forming, perennial sedge with stout, triangular, leafless stems, carrying in summer huge umbels of spikelets with up to 100 rays. Grows in water. H to 3–5m (10–15ft), S 1m (3ft). Min 7–10°C (45–50°F).

Helictotrichon sempervirens
(Blue oat grass)
Evergreen, tufted, perennial grass with stiff, silvery-blue leaves up to 30cm (12in) or more long. Produces erect panicles of straw-coloured flower spikes in summer. H 1m (3ft), S 60cm (2ft).

Bambusa multiplex
(Hedge bamboo)
Evergreen, clump-forming bamboo with narrow leaves, 10–15cm (4–6in) long. Useful for hedges and wind-breaks. H to 15m (50ft), S indefinite.

Bouteloua gracilis
(Blue grama, Mosquito grass)
Semi-evergreen, tuft-forming, narrow-leaved, perennial grass. In summer bears comb-like flower spikes, 4cm (1½in) long, held at right-angles to stems. H 50cm (20in), S 20cm (8in).

***Melica altissima* 'Atropurpurea'**
Evergreen, tuft-forming, perennial grass with broad leaves, short-haired beneath. Purple spikelets in narrow panicles, 10cm (4in) long, hang from the tops of stems during summer. H and S 60cm (24in).

GREEN

Yushania anceps
(Anceps bamboo)
Evergreen, spreading bamboo with erect, later arching, stems bearing several branches at each node. H 2–3m (6–10ft), S indefinite.

Phyllostachys nigra* var. *henonis
Evergreen, clump-forming bamboo with bristled auricles on culm sheaths and a profusion of leaves. H 10m (30ft), S 2–3m (6–10ft).

Pseudosasa japonica
(Arrow bamboo, Metake)
Evergreen, clump-forming bamboo that may run. Has long-persistent, roughly pubescent, brown sheaths and broad leaves, 35cm (14in) long. H 5m (15ft), S indefinite.

Semiarundinaria fastuosa
(Narihira bamboo)
Evergreen, clump-forming bamboo with 15cm (6in) long leaves and short, tufted branches at each node. Culm sheaths open to reveal polished, purplish interiors. H 6m (20ft), S indefinite.

***Juncus effusus* 'Spiralis'**
(Corkscrew rush)
Evergreen, tuft-forming, perennial rush with leafless stems that twist and curl and are often prostrate. Fairly dense, greenish-brown flower panicles form in summer. H 1m (3ft), S 60cm (2ft).

Phyllostachys bambusoides
(Timber bamboo)
Evergreen, clump-forming bamboo with stout, erect, green stems. Bears leaf sheaths with prominent bristles, and large, broad leaves. H 6–8m (20–25ft), S indefinite.

Shibataea kumasasa
Evergreen, clump-forming bamboo with stubby, side branches on greenish-brown stems. Leaves are broad, 5–10cm (2–4in) long. H 1–1.5m (3–5ft), S 30cm (1ft).

Chusquea culeou
(Chilean bamboo)
Slow-growing, evergreen, clump-forming bamboo. Bears long-lasting culm sheaths, shining white when young, at the swollen nodes of stout, solid stems. H to 5m (15ft), S 2.5m (8ft) or more.

Coix lacryma-jobi (Job's tears)
Tuft-forming, annual grass with broad leaves and insignificant spikelets followed by hard, bead-like, green fruits turning shiny, greyish-mauve in autumn. H 45cm–90cm (18–36in), S 10–15cm (4–6in).

Panicum capillare
(Old-witch grass)
Tuft-forming, annual grass with broad leaves and hairy stems. Top half of each stem carries a dense panicle of numerous, minute, greenish-brown spikelets on delicate stalks in summer. H 60cm–1m (2–3ft), S 30cm (1ft).

Cyperus involucratus
Evergreen, tuft-forming, perennial sedge with leaf-like bracts forming a whorl beneath the clustered flower spikes in summer. H to 1m (3ft), S 30cm (1ft). Min. 4–7°C (39–45°F).

Phyllostachys flexuosa
(Zigzag bamboo)
Evergreen, clump-forming bamboo with slender, markedly zigzag stems that turn black with age. Leaf sheaths have no bristles. Leaves stay fresh green all winter. H 6–8m (20–25ft), S indefinite.

***Miscanthus sinensis* 'Gracillimus'**
Herbaceous, clump-forming, perennial grass with very narrow leaves, hairy beneath, often turning bronze. May bear fan-shaped panicles of awned, hairy, white spikelets in early autumn. H 1.2m (4ft), S 45cm (1½ft).

***Spartina pectinata* 'Aureomarginata'**
Herbaceous, spreading, rhizomatous grass with long, arching, yellow-striped leaves, which turn orange-brown in late autumn to winter. H to 2m (6ft), S indefinite.

Pleioblastus auricomus
Evergreen, slow-spreading bamboo with purple stems and broad, softly downy, bright yellow leaves with green stripes. H 1.5m (5ft), S indefinite.

***Alopecurus pratensis* 'Aureovariegatus'**
(Golden foxtail)
Herbaceous, tuft-forming, perennial grass with yellow or yellowish-green-streaked leaves and dense flower spikes in summer. H and S 23–30cm (9–12in).

Carex pendula
(Pendulous sedge)
Evergreen, tuft-forming, graceful, perennial sedge with narrow, green leaves, 45cm (18in) long. Solid, triangular stems freely produce pendent, greenish-brown flower spikes in summer. H 1m (3ft), S 30cm (1ft).

***Carex hachijoensis* 'Evergold'**
Evergreen, tuft-forming, perennial sedge with narrow, yellow-striped leaves, 20cm (8in) long. Solid, triangular stems may carry insignificant flower spikes in summer. H 20cm (8in), S 15–20cm (6–8in).

Phyllostachys viridiglaucescens
Evergreen, clump-forming bamboo with greenish-brown stems that arch at the base. Has white powder beneath nodes. H 6–8m (20–25ft), S indefinite.

***Carex elata* 'Aurea'**
(Bowles' golden sedge)
Evergreen, tuft-forming, perennial sedge with golden-yellow leaves. Solid, triangular stems bear blackish-brown flower spikes in summer. H to 40cm (16in), S 15cm (6in).

***Hakonechloa macra* 'Aureola'**
Slow-growing, herbaceous, shortly rhizomatous grass with purple stems and green-striped, yellow leaves that age to reddish-brown. Open panicles of reddish-brown flower spikes appear in early autumn and last into winter. H 40cm (16in), S 45–60cm (18–24in).

GREEN

***Phlebodium aureum* 'Mandaianum'**
Evergreen fern with creeping rhizomes. Has arching, deeply lobed, glaucous fronds with attractive, orange-yellow sporangia on reverses; pinnae are deeply cut and wavy. H 1–1.5m (3–5ft), S 60cm (2ft). Min. 5°C (41°F).

Dryopteris filix-mas (Male fern)
Deciduous or semi-evergreen fern with 'shuttlecocks' of elegantly arching, upright, broadly lance-shaped, mid-green fronds that arise from crowns of large, upright, brown-scaled rhizomes. H 1.2m (4ft), S 1m (3ft).

Dicksonia antarctica
(Australian tree fern)
Evergreen, tree-like fern. Stout trunks are covered with brown fibres and crowned by spreading, somewhat arching, broadly lance-shaped, much-divided, palm-like fronds. H 10m (30ft) or more, S 4m (12ft).

Polystichum munitum
(Giant holly fern)
Evergreen fern with erect, leathery, lance-shaped, dark green fronds that consist of small, spiny-margined pinnae. H 1.2m (4ft), S 30cm (1ft).

Polypodium glycyrrhiza
(Liquorice fern)
Deciduous fern. Has oblong-triangular to narrowly oval, divided, mid-green fronds, with lance-shaped to oblong pinnae, that arise from a liquorice-scented rootstock. H and S 45cm (18in).

Platycerium bifurcatum
(Common stag's-horn fern)
Evergreen, epiphytic fern with broad, plate-like sterile fronds and long, arching or pendent, forked, grey-green fertile fronds bearing velvety, brownish spore patches beneath. H and S 1m (3ft). Min. 5°C (41°F).

***Polystichum setiferum* 'Pulcherrimum Bevis'**
Evergreen or semi-evergreen fern with broadly lance-shaped, daintily cut, sharp-edged fronds that are yellowish-green in spring and mature to a glossy, rich dark green. H 60cm (24in), S 75cm (30in).

Blechnum penna-marina
Fast-growing, evergreen, carpeting fern. Has narrow, ladder-like, dark green fronds, red-tinged when young. Outer, sterile fronds are spreading; inner, fertile ones erect. H 15–30cm (6–12in), S 30–45cm (12–18in).

Microlepia speluncae
Large, terrestrial fern with a spreading rhizome and triangular, divided, softly hairy fronds, consisting of triangular to lance-shaped pinnae. H to 1.2m (4ft), S to 2m (6ft). Min. 5–10°C (41–50°F).

Polypodium scouleri
Evergreen, creeping fern with triangular to oval, leathery, divided fronds that arise from a spreading rootstock. H and S 30–40cm (12–16in).

***Pteris cretica* 'Wimsettii'**
Evergreen or semi-evergreen fern with broadly ovate fronds divided into narrow pinnae, each with an incised margin and crested tip. H 45cm (18in), S 30cm (12in). Min. 5°C (41°F).

Adiantum aleuticum
Semi-evergreen fern with a short rootstock. Has glossy, dark brown or blackish stems and dainty, divided, finger-like fronds, with blue-green pinnae, that are more crowded than those of *A. pedatum*. Grows well in alkaline soils. H and S to 45cm (18in).

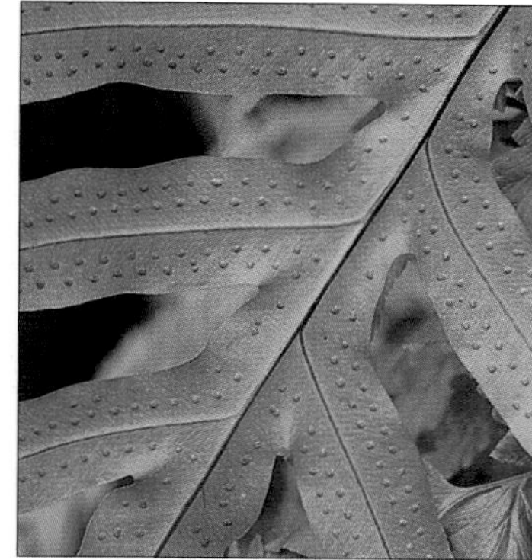

Phlebodium aureum
Evergreen fern with creeping, golden-scaled rhizomes. Has arching, deeply lobed, mid-green or glaucous fronds with attractive, orange-yellow sporangia on reverses. H 90cm–1.5m (3–5ft), S 60cm (2ft). Min. 5°C (41°F).

Selaginella martensii
Evergreen, moss-like perennial with dense, much-branched, frond-like sprays of glossy, rich green foliage. H and S 23cm (9in). Min. 5°C (41°F).

Asplenium ceterach
(Rusty-back fern)
Semi-evergreen fern with lance-shaped, leathery, dark green fronds divided into alternate, bluntly rounded lobes. Backs of young fronds are covered with silvery scales that mature to reddish-brown. H and S 15cm (6in).

Cyrtomium falcatum
(Fishtail fern, Holly fern)
Evergreen fern. Fronds are lance-shaped and have holly-like, glossy, dark green pinnae; young fronds are often covered with whitish or brown scales. H 30–60cm (12–24in), S 30–45cm (12–18in).

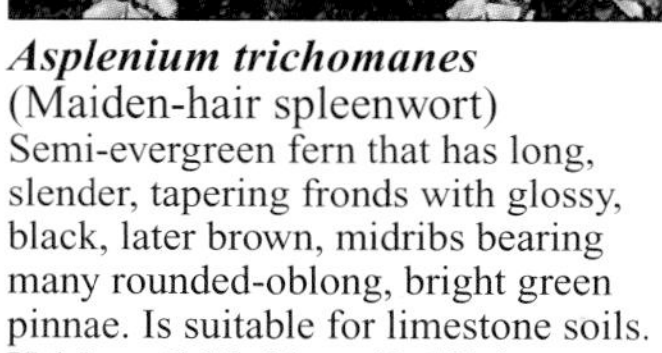

Asplenium trichomanes
(Maiden-hair spleenwort)
Semi-evergreen fern that has long, slender, tapering fronds with glossy, black, later brown, midribs bearing many rounded-oblong, bright green pinnae. Is suitable for limestone soils. H 15cm, S 15–30cm (6–12in).

Polystichum setiferum
Divisilobum Group
Evergreen or semi-evergreen fern. Broadly lance-shaped or oval, soft-textured, much-divided, spreading fronds are clothed with white scales as they unfurl. H 60cm (24in), S 45cm (18in).

GREEN

Thelypteris palustris
(Marsh buckler fern, Marsh fern)
Deciduous fern. Has strong, erect, lance-shaped, pale green fronds, with widely separated, deeply cut pinnae, produced from wiry, creeping, blackish rhizomes. Grows well beside a pool or stream. H 75cm (30in), S 30cm (12in).

Nephrolepis exaltata
(Sword fern)
Evergreen fern. Has erect, sometimes spreading, lance-shaped, divided, pale green fronds borne on wiry stems. H and S 90cm (36in) or more. Min. 5°C (41°F).

***Polypodium vulgare* 'Cornubiense'**
Evergreen fern with narrow, lance-shaped, divided, fresh green fronds; segments are further sub-divided to give an overall lacy effect. H and S 25–30cm (10–12in).

Osmunda regalis (Royal fern)
Deciduous fern with elegant, broadly oval to oblong, divided, bright green fronds, pinkish when young. Mature plants bear tassel-like, rust-brown fertile flower spikes at ends of taller fronds. H 2m (6ft), S 1m (3ft).

Onoclea sensibilis
(Sensitive fern)
Deciduous, creeping fern with handsome, arching, almost triangular, divided, fresh pale green fronds, often suffused pinkish-brown in spring. In autumn, fronds turn an attractive yellowish-brown. H and S 45cm (18in).

Selaginella kraussiana
Evergreen, trailing, more or less prostrate, moss-like perennial with bright green foliage. H 1cm (½in), S indefinite. Min. 5°C (41°F).

Adiantum pedatum
(Northern maidenhair fern)
Semi-evergreen fern with a stout, creeping rootstock. Dainty, divided, finger-like, mid-green fronds are produced on glossy, dark brown or blackish stems. H and S to 45cm (18in).

Matteuccia struthiopteris
(Ostrich-feather fern, Ostrich fern)
Deciduous, rhizomatous fern. Lance-shaped, erect, divided fronds are arranged like a shuttlecock; outermost, fresh green sterile fronds surround denser, dark brown fertile fronds. H 1m (3ft), S 45cm (1½ft).

***Polystichum setiferum* Plumosodivisilobum Group**
Evergreen fern that produces a "shuttlecock" of lance-shaped, divided fronds with segments narrowed towards the frond tips; lower pinnae often overlap. H 1.2m (4ft), S 1m (3ft).

Polypodium vulgare
(Common polypody, Polypody)
Evergreen fern with narrow, lance-shaped, divided, herring-bone-like, mid-green fronds, arising from creeping rhizomes covered with copper-brown scales. Suits a rock garden. H and S 25–30cm (10–12in).

Asplenium scolopendrium
(Hart's-tongue fern)
Evergreen fern with stocky rhizomes and tongue-shaped, leathery, bright green fronds. Is good in alkaline soils. H 45–75cm (18–30in), S to 45cm (18in).

Asplenium nidus
(Bird's-nest fern)
Evergreen fern. Produces broadly lance-shaped, glossy, bright green fronds in a shuttlecock-like arrangement. H 60cm–1.2m (2–4ft), S 30–60cm (1–2ft). Min. 5°C (41°F).

***Asplenium scolopendrium* Marginatum Group**
Evergreen fern with stocky, upright rhizomes and lobed, slightly frilled, tongue-shaped fronds that are leathery and bright green. Is good in alkaline soils. H and S 30cm (12in) or more.

Athyrium niponicum
(Painted fern)
Deciduous fern. Broad, triangular, divided, purple-tinged, greyish-green fronds arise from a scaly, creeping, brownish or reddish rootstock. H and S 30cm (12in).

Cryptogramma crispa
(Parsley fern)
Deciduous fern with broadly oval to triangular, finely divided, bright pale green fronds that resemble parsley. In autumn, fronds turn bright rusty-brown and persist during winter. H 15–23cm (6–9in), S 15–30cm (6–12in).

Adiantum venustum
Deciduous fern. Bears delicate, pale green fronds, tinged brown when young, consisting of many small, triangular pinnae, on glossy stems. H 23cm (9in), S 30cm (12in).

Annuals & Biennials

Annuals and Biennials

The rapid growth and relatively low cost of annuals and biennials make them ideal for providing immediate colour in new gardens until more permanent plantings of trees, shrubs and perennials are established, which can take several seasons. They are invaluable as bedding plants to fill gaps in a more formal scheme and maintain colour and interest. With such a diversity of shape, size and habit, they are also suitable for a range of informal designs from cottage garden plantings to a wildflower meadow.

What are annuals and biennials?

Annuals are plants that grow, bloom, set seed and die in a single growing season. Biennials complete their life cycle in two seasons: most are sown in summer and make leafy growth in the first year, then flower, set seed and die in the next.

Growing annuals and biennials

Hardy annuals withstand some frost and so can be sown *in situ* in early autumn or spring. Half-hardy and frost-tender annuals are sown under glass between late winter and early spring and are planted out when all danger of frost has passed. Gardeners often use other types of plants in the same way as annuals, in particular frost-tender perennials, such as pelargoniums or busy lizzies (*Impatiens*), which grow vigorously and flower freely in their first year from seed. Like annuals, such frost-tender perennials are cleared away at the end of the season.

Ornamental features

Annuals and biennials are available in an enormous range of sizes and habits, from the lowest hummock-forming cultivars of *Ageratum houstonianum* and trailing nasturtiums (*Tropaeolum majus*) to the tall spires of foxgloves (*Digitalis purpurea*) or the grandeur of the Scotch thistle (*Onopordum acanthium*). They include climbers such as *Tropaeolum peregrinum* and fragrant sweet peas (*Lathyrus odoratus*), as well as a number grown primarily for foliage effects, for instance the feathery leaved *Bassia scoparia* f. *trichophylla* or *Senecio cineraria* with its bright, ash-grey foliage. The flower range, in all colours and tones, is also huge, and presents a bewildering choice. Colours extend from the opalescent whites of *Lavatera trimestris* 'Mont Blanc' to the vibrant scarlets of pelargoniums, the bright orange of *Escholzia californica* or the intense magentas and purples of petunias, as well as the more subtle pastel shades of plants such as *Anoda cristata*.

Multi-purpose marigolds
Above: Forming a strong edging in a potager, the edible flowers of marigolds *(Calendula officinalis)* attract beneficial insects such as hoverflies to prey on any aphid pests.

Early season scents
Right: Self-sown Dame's violet *(Hesperis matronalis)* and poached egg plant *(Limnanthes douglasii)* add scents and a natural informality.

Maintaining year-round colour

The long and prolific season of annuals and biennials has traditionally been exploited in formal beds devoted entirely to achieving brilliant, seasonally changing displays. Spring displays of primulas and forget-me-nots (*Myosotis*) are sometimes used as a carpet beneath spring bulbs, then lifted to make way for a summer scheme juxtaposing, for example, the exotic foliage of *Ricinus communis* with swathes of hot colour provided by zinnias or pelargoniums. As summer fades, the entire display may be replaced with winter-flowering pansies (*Viola* x *wittrockiana*) or spring wallflowers (*Erysimum cheiri*).

This potential for year-round colour can also be employed in more domestic situations, albeit scaled down to suit modest plots. While the uniformity of habit and colour of many modern annuals are perfect where formality or complex patternwork is needed, they are equally adaptable to more informal plantings. Sinuous drifts of graduated height suggest a cottage-garden style, while yet more naturalistic effects are possible by using cornfield annuals like corncockle (*Agrostemma githago*), cornflower (*Centaurea cyanus*) or field poppy (*Papaver rhoeas*).

If there is room, annuals and biennials can be grown in a border for cutting, especially stocks (*Matthiola incana*), *Cleome hassleriana* and china asters (*Callistephus*) for fresh displays, and everlastings such as *Bracteantha bracteata* and *Limonium sinuatum* for dried arrangements. In a mixed border annuals and biennials are invaluable, whether used to add textural qualities or colour highlights among more permanent plants, or as fillers to mask gaps left by the foliage of herbaceous perennials that dies back after flowering.

Summer harmonies
Above: Opium poppies *(Papaver somniferum)* and foxgloves *(Digitalis purpurea)* are used here to add subtle colour to a mixed border.

Annuals in pots
Right: Use annuals in pots to bring summer-long colour to patio plantings. Here, these vivid nasturtiums *(Tropaeolum majus)* will flower continuously, well into early autumn.

Wildflower gardens
Below: Sown *en masse*, corn marigolds *(Xanthophthalmum segetum)*, field poppies *(Papaver rhoeas)* and cornflowers *(Centaurea cyanus)* look entirely natural.

Planting in containers

Annuals and biennials are perfect for containers and can create eye-catching features in pots, tubs and hanging baskets. Use them alone in compositions in which trailers, such as the ivy-leaved pelargoniums or cascading lobelias, surround mound-forming verbenas or busy lizzies, and link them with the airy foliage of brachyscome or felicia. Or add colour to permanent plantings of dwarf conifers, such as *Juniperus communis* 'Compressa', or trailing evergreen ivy (*Hedera* cultivars).

□ WHITE

Digitalis purpurea* f. *albiflora
Slow-growing, short-lived perennial, grown as a biennial. Has a rosette of large, pointed-oval leaves and erect stems carrying tubular, white flowers in summer. H 1–1.5m (3–5ft), S 30–45cm (1–1½ft).

Iberis amara
Fast-growing, erect, bushy annual with lance-shaped, mid-green leaves. Has flattish heads of small, scented, 4-petalled, white flowers in summer. H 30cm (12in), S 15cm (6in).

Omphalodes linifolia
(Venus's navelwort)
Fairly fast-growing, slender, erect annual with lance-shaped, grey-green leaves. Tiny, slightly scented, rounded, white flowers, rarely tinged blue, are carried in summer. H 15–30cm (6–12in), S 15cm (6in).

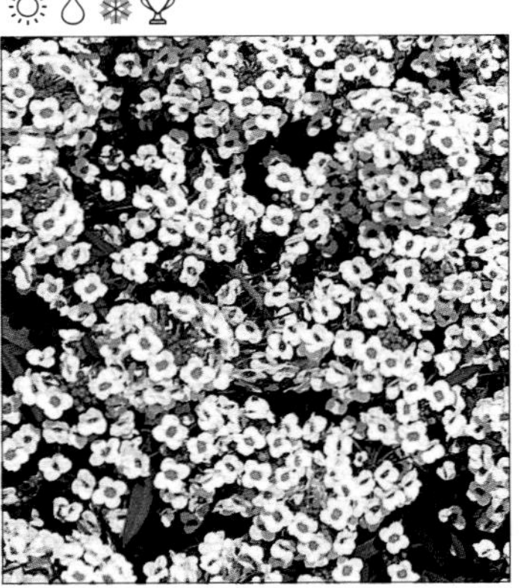

***Lobularia maritima* 'Carpet of Snow'**
Ground-hugging, mound-forming annual with narrow leaves and heads of tiny, 4-petalled, white flowers in summer and early autumn. Useful in paving cracks and along path edges. H to 10cm (4in), S 20–30cm (8–12in).

***Matthiola* 'Giant Imperial'**
Fast-growing, erect, bushy biennial, grown as an annual. Has lance-shaped, greyish-green leaves and long spikes of highly scented, white to creamy-yellow flowers in summer. Produces excellent flowers for cutting. H to 60cm (24in), S 30cm (12in).

Gypsophila elegans
Fast-growing, erect, bushy annual. Has lance-shaped, greyish-green leaves and clouds of tiny, white flowers in branching heads from summer to early autumn. H 60cm (24in), S 30cm (12in) or more.

***Lavatera trimestris* 'Mont Blanc'**
Moderately fast-growing, erect, branching annual with oval, lobed leaves. Shallowly trumpet-shaped, brilliant white flowers appear from summer to early autumn. H to 60cm (24in), S 45cm (18in).

***Petunia* Recoverer Series [white]**
Moderately fast-growing, branching, bushy perennial, grown as an annual. Has oval, mid- to deep green leaves and large, flared, trumpet-shaped, white flowers in summer-autumn. H 15–30cm (6–12in), S 30cm (12in).

Dimorphotheca pluvialis
(Rain daisy)
Branching annual with oval, hairy, deep green leaves. In summer has small, daisy-like flower heads, the rays purple beneath and white above, with brownish-purple centres. H 20–30cm (8–12in), S 15cm (6in).

Nemophila maculata
(Five-spot baby)
Fast-growing, spreading annual with lobed leaves. Small, bowl-shaped, white flowers with purple-tipped petals are carried in summer. H and S 15cm (6in).

Tanacetum parthenium
(Feverfew)
Moderately fast-growing, short-lived, bushy perennial, grown as an annual. Has aromatic leaves and small, white flower heads in summer and early autumn. H and S 20–45cm (8–18in).

Euphorbia marginata (Snow-in-summer, Snow-on-the-mountain)
Moderately fast-growing, upright, bushy annual. Has pointed-oval, bright green leaves; upper leaves are white-margined. Broad, petal-like, white bracts surround tiny flowers in summer. H 60cm (24in), S 30cm (12in).

***Nicotiana × sanderae* Saratoga Series** [white]
Slow-growing, bushy annual with ovate mid-green leaves. In summer and early autumn produces a long display of sparkling, white, long-tubed, salverform flowers. H and S 30cm (12in).

Reseda odorata (Mignonette)
Moderately fast-growing, erect, branching annual with oval leaves. Conical heads of small, very fragrant, somewhat star-shaped, white flowers with orange-brown stamens are carried in summer and early autumn.
H 30–60cm (12–24in), S 30cm (12in).

***Viola × wittrockiana* Floral Dance Series** [white]
Bushy perennial, grown as an annual or biennial. Has oval, mid-green leaves and rounded, 5-petalled, white flowers in winter. H 15–20cm (6–8in), S 20cm (8in).

Eustoma grandiflorum
Slow-growing, upright annual with lance-shaped, deep green leaves. Poppy-like, pink, purple, blue or white flowers, 5cm (2in) wide, are carried in summer. H 60cm (24in), S 30cm (12in). Min. 4–7°C (39–45°F).

WHITE–PINK

Hibiscus trionum (Flower-of-the-hour)
Fairly fast-growing, upright annual with oval, serrated leaves. Trumpet-shaped, creamy-white or pale yellow flowers, with purplish-brown centres, are borne from late summer to early autumn. H 60cm (24in), S 30cm (12in).

***Zea mays* 'Gracillima Variegata'**
Fairly fast-growing, erect annual with lance-shaped leaves, striped green and creamy-white. Has tassel-like, silvery flower heads, followed by large, bright yellow seed heads (cobs). H 90cm (3ft), S 30–45cm (1–1½ft).

Impatiens balsamina (Balsam)
Fairly fast-growing, erect, compact, bushy annual with lance-shaped leaves. Small, cup-shaped, spurred, pink or white flowers are borne in summer and early autumn. H to 75cm (30in), S 45cm (18in).

Martynia annua (Unicorn plant)
Fairly fast-growing, upright annual with long-stalked leaves. Has foxglove-like, lobed, creamy-white flowers marked red, pink and yellow in summer, followed by horned, green, then brown, fruits. H 60cm (24in), S 30cm (12in).

***Ismelia carinata* 'Monarch Court Jesters'**
Fast-growing, erect, branching annual. Has feathery, grey-green leaves and, in summer, daisy-like, zoned flower heads, to 8cm (3in) wide, in various colour combinations. H 60cm (24in), S 30cm (12in).

***Lathyrus odoratus* 'Knee Hi'**
Fast-growing annual with oval, divided, mid-green leaves and large, fragrant flowers, in shades of pink, red, blue or white, that are borne in summer or early autumn. H and S 90cm (3ft).

Crepis rubra
Fairly fast-growing, rosette-forming annual with lance-shaped, serrated leaves. In summer bears dandelion-like, pink, occasionally red or white flower heads. H 30cm (12in), S 15cm (6in).

Silene coeli-rosa
Moderately fast-growing, erect annual with lance-shaped, greyish-green leaves. Has 5-petalled, pinkish-purple flowers with white centres in summer. H 45cm (18in), S 15cm (6in).

Rhodanthe chlorocephala subsp. ***rosea***
Moderately fast-growing, erect annual. Lance-shaped leaves are greyish-green; small, daisy-like, papery, semi-double, pink flower heads appear in summer. Flowers dry well. H 30cm (12in), S 15cm (6in).

***Matthiola* 'Giant Excelsior'**
Fast-growing, erect, bushy biennial, grown as an annual. Lance-shaped leaves are greyish-green; long spikes of highly scented flowers in shades of pink, red, pale blue or white appear in summer. H to 75cm (30in), S 30cm (12in).

***Antirrhinum majus* Coronette Series**
Erect, bushy, compact perennial, grown as an annual, with lance-shaped leaves. Spikes of tubular, 2-lipped flowers in a wide range of colours are produced from spring to autumn. H 60cm (24in), S 30cm (12in).

***Primula* 'Dreamer'** (Primrose Group)
Rosette-forming perennial, normally grown as a biennial, with oval leaves. In spring, has flat flowers in cream, apricot, pink or rose-pink; all bicolours have darker eyes and yellow centres. H 8–10cm (3–4in), S 15–20cm (6–8in).

Rhodanthe manglesii
Moderately fast-growing, erect annual. Has pointed-oval, greyish-green leaves and daisy-like, papery, red, pink or white flower heads, in summer and early autumn. Flowers dry well. H 30cm (12in), S 15cm (6in).

***Papaver somniferum* 'Peony Flowered'**
Fast-growing, erect annual with lobed, pale greyish-green leaves. Has large, rounded, often cup-shaped, double flowers in a mixture of colours – red, pink, purple or white – in summer. H 75cm (30in), S 30cm (12in).

***Matthiola* Brompton Group**
Fast-growing, erect, bushy biennial, grown as an annual. Lance-shaped leaves are greyish-green; long spikes of highly scented flowers in shades of pink, red, purple, yellow or white are borne in summer. H 45cm (18in), S 30cm (12in).

***Pelargonium* Orbit Series** [salmon]
Slow-growing, evergreen, branching, bushy perennial, grown as an annual, with lobed leaves, zoned with bronze or red. Has large, rounded heads of salmon-pink flowers in summer-autumn. H and S 30–60cm (12–24in).

Alcea rosea (Hollyhock)
Biennial with tall, erect stems and lobed, rough-textured leaves. Spikes of single flowers, in a range of colours including pink, yellow and cream, appear in summer and early autumn. H 1.5–2m (5–6ft), S to 60cm (2ft).

***Salvia splendens* Cleopatra Series** [salmon]
Slow-growing, bushy perennial, grown as an annual. Oval, serrated leaves are fresh green; dense racemes of tubular, salmon-pink flowers are carried in summer and early autumn. H to 30cm (12in), S 20–30cm (8–12in).

***Impatiens walleriana* Swirl Series**
Subshrubby perennial, usually grown as an annual, with light green to red-flushed stems and leaves. In summer, bears flattened, slender-spurred, pink-and-orange flowers margined in rose-red. H 15–20cm (6–8in), S to 60cm (24in). Min. 10°C (50°F).

PINK

***Petunia* Aladdin Series**
Fairly fast-growing, branching, bushy perennial, grown as an annual. Has oval leaves and in summer-autumn produces flowers in a range of colours, including strong shades of red and salmon-pink. H to 30cm (12in), S 30–90cm (12–36in).

***Papaver rhoeas* Shirley Series**
[double]
Fast-growing, slender, erect annual with lobed, light green leaves. In summer has rounded, often cup-shaped, double flowers, in shades of red, pink or white, including bicolours. H 60cm (24in), S 30cm (12in).

***Cleome hassleriana* 'Colour Fountain'**
Fast-growing, bushy annual with hairy stems and divided leaves. In summer has heads of narrow-petalled flowers, with long, protruding stamens, in shades of pink, purple or white. H 1–1.2m (3–4ft), S 45–60cm (1½–2ft).

***Lobularia maritima* 'Rosie O'Day'**
Fast growing, compact annual with lance-shaped, mid-green leaves. In summer bears rounded, compact heads of small, sweet-scented flowers, which open white but become red-purple. H to 15cm (6in) S to 25cm (10in).

***Zinnia elegans* Dreamland Series**
[pink]
Moderately fast-growing, sturdy, erect annual with ovate, mid-green leaves. In summer and autumn produces large, daisy-like, semi-double, deep dusky-pink flower heads. H and S 30cm (12in).

***Schizanthus* Dwarf Bouquet**
[mixed]
Moderately fast-growing, erect annual with fern-like, mid-green leaves. Bears massed, 2-lipped, open-faced flowers in a range of colours from pink to red, purple, yellow or white in summer and autumn. H and S 20–25cm (8–10in).

Centaurea cyanus [tall, rose]
(Cornflower)
Fast-growing, erect, branching annual with lance-shaped, grey-green leaves. Branching heads of daisy-like, rose-pink flower heads are carried in summer and early autumn. H to 90cm (3ft), S 30cm (1ft).

Limonium sinuatum
Fairly slow-growing, bushy, upright perennial, grown as an annual. Has lance-shaped, lobed, deep green leaves and, in summer and early autumn, tiny, blue, pink or white flowers borne in clusters on winged stems. H 45cm (18in), S 30cm (12in).

***Eschscholzia californica* Ballerina Series**
Fast-growing, slender, erect annual. Has feathery, bluish-green leaves and cup-shaped, 4-petalled, frilled, double flowers, in shades of red, yellow, pink or orange, in summer-autumn. H 30cm (12in), S 15cm (6in).

Onopordum acanthium
(Cotton thistle, Scotch thistle)
Slow-growing, erect, branching biennial. Large, lobed, spiny leaves are hairy and bright silvery-grey; winged, branching flower stems bear deep purplish-pink flower heads in summer. H 1.8m (6ft), S 90cm (3ft).

Silybum marianum
(Blessed Mary's thistle)
Biennial with a basal rosette of deeply lobed, very spiny, heavily white-marbled, deep green leaves. Has thistle-like, dark purplish-pink flower heads on erect stems in summer and early autumn. H 1.2m (4ft), S 60cm (2ft).

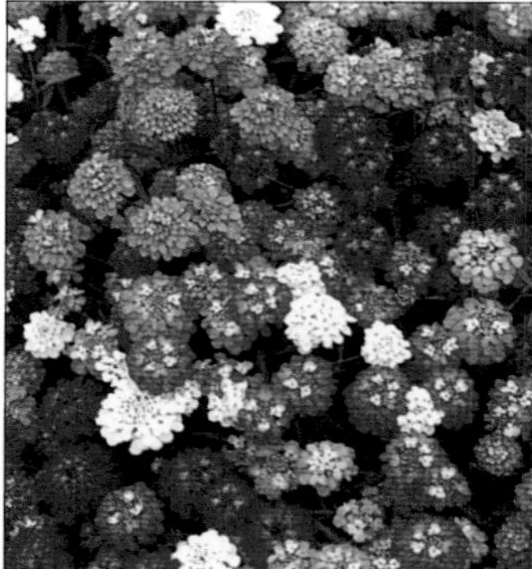

***Iberis umbellata* Fairy Series**
Fast-growing, upright, bushy annual with lance-shaped, mid-green leaves. Heads of small, 4-petalled flowers, in shades of pink, red, purple or white, are carried in summer and early autumn. H and S 20cm (8in).

***Petunia* Primetime Series**
Moderately fast-growing perennial, grown as an annual. In summer-autumn, bears flowers in a very wide range of colours, including white, blue, pink or red, some with dark veins or central stars, or picotee margins. H to 35cm (14in), S 30–90cm (12–36in).

***Agrostemma githago* 'Milas'**
Fast-growing, slender, upright, thin-stemmed annual. Has lance-shaped leaves and 5-petalled, purplish-pink flowers, 8cm (3in) wide, in summer. H 60–90cm (2–3ft), S 30cm (1ft).

Malcolmia maritima
(Virginian stock)
Fast-growing, slim, erect annual with oval, greyish-green leaves. Carries tiny, fragrant, 4-petalled, pink, red or white flowers from spring to autumn. Sow in succession for a long flowering season. H 20cm (8in), S 5–8cm (2–3in).

***Matthiola* Brompton Group**
[pink]
Fast-growing, erect, bushy biennial, grown as an annual, with lance-shaped, greyish-green leaves. Long spikes of highly scented, pink flowers are carried in summer. H 45cm (18in), S 30cm (12in).

***Lunaria annua* 'Variegata'**
Fast-growing, erect biennial with pointed-oval, serrated, white-variegated leaves. Heads of small, scented, 4-petalled, deep purplish-pink flowers are borne in spring and early summer followed by rounded, silvery seed pods. H 75cm (30in), S 30cm (12in).

***Silene armeria* 'Electra'**
Moderately fast-growing, erect annual with oval, greyish-green leaves. Heads of 5-petalled, bright rose-pink flowers are carried in summer and early autumn. H 30cm (12in), S 15cm (6in).

PINK

***Clarkia amoena* 'Sybil Sherwood'**
Erect annual with lance-shaped, sometimes toothed leaves. Single, fluted, salmon-pink flowers, fading to white at the margins, are borne at the tips of long, leafy shoots in summer. H to 45cm (18in), S 30cm (12in).

Brassica oleracea forms (Ornamental cabbage)
Moderately fast-growing, evergreen, rounded biennial, grown as an annual. Has heads of large, often crinkled leaves, in combinations of red/green, white/pink, pink/green. Do not allow to flower. H and S 30–45cm (12–18in).

Solenostemon scutellarioides
Fast-growing, bushy perennial, grown as an annual. Leaves are a mixture of colours, including pink, red, green or yellow. Flower spikes should be removed. H to 45cm (18in), S 30cm (12in) or more. Min. 10°C (50°F).

Malope trifida
Moderately fast-growing, erect, branching annual with rounded, lobed leaves. Flared, trumpet-shaped, reddish-purple flowers, to 8cm (3in) wide and with deep pink veins, are carried in summer and early autumn. H 90cm (3ft), S 30cm (1ft).

***Lavatera trimestris* 'Silver Cup'**
Moderately fast-growing, erect, branching annual with oval, lobed leaves. Shallowly trumpet-shaped, rose-pink flowers are carried in summer and early autumn. H 60cm (24in), S 45cm (18in).

***Dianthus chinensis* Baby Doll Series**
Neat, bushy annual or biennial, grown as an annual. Light or mid-green leaves are lance-shaped; small, single, zoned flowers in various colours are carried in summer and early autumn. H 15cm (6in), S 15–30cm (6–12in).

***Lathyrus odoratus* 'Bijou'**
Fast-growing annual with oval, divided, mid-green leaves and large, fragrant flowers, in shades of pink, red or blue, that are carried in summer or early autumn. H and S 45cm (18in).

***Clarkia* 'Brilliant'**
Fast-growing, erect, bushy annual with oval leaves. Large, rosette-like, double, bright reddish-pink flowers are carried in long spikes in summer and early autumn. H to 60cm (24in), S 30cm (12in).

***Callistephus chinensis* Milady Super Series** [rose]
Moderately fast-growing, erect, bushy annual with oval, toothed leaves. Has large, daisy-like, double, rose-pink flower heads in summer and early autumn. H 25–30cm (10–12in), S 30–45cm (12–18in).

***Matthiola* Ten-week Group** [dwarf]
Fast-growing, erect, bushy biennial, grown as an annual. Lance-shaped leaves are greyish-green; long spikes of highly scented, single to double flowers, in shades of pink, red or white, appear in summer. H and S 30cm (12in).

Lunaria annua (Honesty)
Fast-growing, erect biennial with pointed-oval, serrated leaves. Heads of scented, 4-petalled, white to deep purple flowers in spring and early summer are followed by rounded, silvery seed pods. H 75cm (30in), S 30cm (12in).

***Silene coeli-rosa* 'Rose Angel'**
Moderately fast-growing, slim, erect annual. Has lance-shaped, greyish-green leaves and 5-petalled, deep rose-pink flowers in summer. H 30cm (12in), S 15cm (6in).

***Dorotheanthus bellidiformis* 'Magic Carpet'**
Carpeting annual with succulent, lance-shaped, pale green leaves. Daisy-like flower heads, in bright shades of red, pink, yellow or white, open only in summer sunshine. H 15cm (6in), S 30cm (12in).

***Petunia* Resisto Series** [rose-pink]
Moderately fast-growing, branching, bushy perennial, grown as an annual. Has oval leaves and rain-resistant, flared, trumpet-shaped, rose-pink flowers in summer-autumn. H 15–30cm (6–12in), S 30cm (12in).

***Antirrhinum majus* Princess Series** [white, with purple eye]
Erect perennial, grown as an annual, branching from the base. Has lance-shaped leaves and spikes of tubular, 2-lipped, white and pinkish-purple flowers borne from spring to autumn. H and S 45cm (18in).

Xeranthemum annuum [double]
Erect annual with lance-shaped, silvery leaves and branching heads of daisy-like, papery, double flower heads in shades of pink, mauve, purple or white, in summer. Produces good dried flowers. H 60cm (24in), S 45cm (18in).

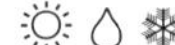

***Cosmos bipinnatus* Sensation Series**
Moderately fast-growing, bushy, erect annual. Has feathery, mid-green leaves and daisy-like flower heads, to 10cm (4in) wide, in shades of red, pink or white, from early summer to early autumn. H 90cm (3ft), S 60cm (2ft).

***Impatiens balsamina* Tom Thumb Series**
Dwarf, sparsely branched, slightly hairy annual with toothed leaves. From summer to early autumn, bears double, pink, scarlet, violet or white flowers. H to 30cm (12in), S 45cm (18in). Min. 5°C (41°F).

PINK–RED

***Phlox drummondii* 'Chanal'**
Erect to spreading, but compact, bushy, hairy annual with very variable, stem-clasping leaves. In late spring, bears cymes of double, almost rose-like, pink flowers. H 10–45cm (4–18in), S to 25cm (10in) or more.

***Impatiens* New Guinea Group 'Mimas'**
Subshrubby hybrid perennial, grown as an annual. Opposite or whorled, mid-green, toothed leaves often have central yellowish-green marks. Bears large, red open-faced flowers in spring-autumn. H 30cm (12in), S 35–40cm (14–16in).

***Verbena × hybrida* 'Showtime'**
Fairly slow-growing, bushy perennial, grown as an annual. Has lance-shaped, serrated, mid- to deep green leaves and clusters of small, tubular flowers, in a range of colours, in summer-autumn. H 20cm (8in), S 30cm (12in).

***Portulaca grandiflora* Sundance Hybrids**
Slow-growing, semi-trailing annual with lance-shaped, succulent, bright green leaves. Cup-shaped flowers, with conspicuous stamens, appear in a mixture of colours in summer and early autumn. H to 20cm (8in), S 15cm (6in).

Amaranthus caudatus
(Love-lies-bleeding, Tassel flower)
Bushy annual with oval, pale green leaves. Pendulous panicles of tassel-like, red flowers, 45cm (18in) long, are carried in summer-autumn. H to 1.2m (4ft), S 45cm (1½ft).

***Dianthus barbatus* Roundabout Series** [dwarf]
Slow-growing, upright, bushy biennial with lance-shaped leaves. In early summer has flat heads of zoned and eyed flowers in shades of pink, red or white. H 15cm (6in), S 20–30cm (8–12in).

***Petunia* Picotee Series 'Picotee Rose'**
Fairly fast-growing, compact perennial, grown as an annual, with oval leaves. In summer-autumn, has large, deep rose-pink flowers with white margins. H to 20cm (8in), S 45cm (18in).

***Nicotiana × sanderae* Saratoga Series** [deep rose]
Slow-growing, bushy annual with ovate mid-green leaves. In summer and early autumn produces a long display of sparkling, long-tubed, salverform, deep rose-coloured flowers. H and S 30cm (12in).

***Petunia* 'Mirage Velvet'**
Branching, bushy perennial, grown as an annual, with oval, dark green leaves. Large, flared, trumpet-shaped, rich red flowers, with almost black centres, appear in summer-autumn. H 25cm (10in), S 30cm (12in).

***Phlox drummondii* 'Sternenzauber'**
Moderately fast-growing, slim, erect annual. Lance-shaped leaves are pale green; heads of star-shaped flowers in a bright mixture of colours, some with contrasting centres, are carried in summer. H 15cm (6in), S 10cm (4in).

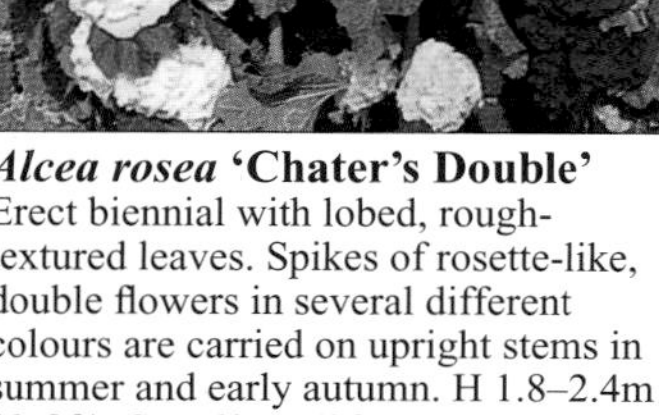

***Alcea rosea* 'Chater's Double'**
Erect biennial with lobed, rough-textured leaves. Spikes of rosette-like, double flowers in several different colours are carried on upright stems in summer and early autumn. H 1.8–2.4m (6–8ft), S to 60cm (2ft).

***Viola* × *wittrockiana* Imperial Series 'Imperial Frosty Rose'**
Erect, bushy perennial, grown as an annual or biennial, with oval leaves. In summer, bears large, unusual, rose-purple flowers fading to pink and white. H 16–23cm (6–9in), S 23–30cm (9–12in).

***Impatiens walleriana* Expo Series**
(Busy lizzie)
Fast-growing, evergreen, bushy perennial usually grown as an annual. Has pointed, ovate leaves and from late spring to autumn bears spurred, flat-faced, red, pink or white flowers. H 10–15cm (4–6in), S 15–30cm (6–12in).

***Impatiens* Confection Series**
(Busy lizzie)
Fast-growing, evergreen, bushy perennial, grown as an annual. Has fresh green leaves and small, flat, spurred, double or semi-double flowers, in shades of red or pink, from spring to autumn. H and S 20–30cm (8–12in).

***Salvia splendens* Vista Series**
[red]
Slow-growing, bushy perennial grown as an annual, with dark green, ovate, toothed leaves. Produces long-tubed, 2-lipped, bright scarlet flowers in dense, terminal spikes during summer and autumn. H and S 30cm (12in).

***Bellis perennis* Pomponette Series**
Slow-growing, carpeting perennial, grown as a biennial. Has oval leaves and small, daisy-like, double flower heads, in red, pink or white, in spring. H and S 10–15cm (4–6in).

***Dianthus chinensis* 'Fire Carpet'**
Slow-growing, bushy annual or biennial, grown as an annual. Lance-shaped leaves are light or mid-green. Small, rounded, single, bright red flowers are carried in summer and early autumn. H 20cm (8in), S 15–30cm (6–12in).

***Linum grandiflorum* 'Rubrum'**
Fairly fast-growing, slim, erect annual. Lance-shaped leaves are grey-green; small, rounded, flattish, deep red flowers are carried in summer. H 45cm (18in), S 15cm (6in).

***Phlox drummondii* Buttons Series**
Moderately fast-growing, compact, upright annual with mid-green, stem-clasping leaves. Bears numerous, flat-faced flowers in a range of colours from deep red to pink and white from spring to autumn. H and S 15–25cm (6–10in).

RED

Zinnia elegans **Dreamland Series** [scarlet]
Moderately fast-growing, sturdy, erect annual with ovate, mid-green leaves. In summer and autumn produces large, daisy-like, semi-double, bright scarlet flower heads. H and S 30cm (12in).

Salvia splendens **'Scarlet King'**
Slow-growing, compact, bushy perennial, usually grown as an annual, with oval, toothed, dark green leaves. Produces long-tubed, bright scarlet flowers in dense, terminal spikes in early summer. H to 25cm (10in), S 23–35cm (9–14in).

Pelargonium **Multibloom Series**
Erect, bushy, evergreen perennials, grown as annuals. Abundant flowers in white or shades of pink or red are borne in clusters over a long period throughout summer. H 25–30cm (10–12in), S 30cm (12in). Min. 2°C (36°F).

Petunia **Carpet Series**
Moderately fast-growing, compact, spreading perennial, grown as an annual, with oval leaves. In summer-autumn, bears flowers in a colour range that includes strong reds and oranges. H 20–25cm (8–10in), S 30–90cm (12–36in).

Papaver rhoeas **Shirley Series** [single]
Fast-growing, slender, erect annual with lobed, light green leaves. Rounded, often cup-shaped, single flowers, in shades of red, pink, salmon or white, appear in summer. H 60cm (24in), S 30cm (12in).

Nemesia strumosa **Carnival Series**
Fairly fast-growing, bushy annual with serrated, pale green leaves. In summer has small, somewhat trumpet-shaped flowers in a range of colours, including yellow, red, orange, purple and white. H 20–30cm (8–12in), S 15cm (6in).

Verbena* × *hybrida **Quartz Series** [mixed]
Compact, bushy perennials, grown as annuals, with lance-shaped, toothed, mid- to dark green leaves, and rounded heads of pink, red, maroon or purple flowers with white "eyes" in summer to autumn. H 20cm (8in) S 30cm (12in).

Petunia **Picotee Series** [red]
Fairly fast-growing, branching, bushy perennial, grown as an annual, with oval leaves. Has flared, somewhat trumpet-shaped, red flowers, edged with white, in summer-autumn.
H 15–30cm (6–12in), S 30cm (12in).

Primula **Pacific Series** [dwarf]
Rosette-forming perennial, normally grown as a biennial, with lance-shaped leaves. Has heads of large, fragrant, flat flowers in shades of blue, yellow, red, pink or white in spring. H 10–15cm (4–6in), S 20cm (8in).

***Zinnia elegans* 'Red Sun'**
Moderately fast-growing, upright annual with ovate, mid-green leaves. In summer and autumn produces semi- to fully double, daisy-like, deep bright red flower heads. H and S 30–40cm (12–16in).

Alonsoa warscewiczii
(Mask flower)
Perennial, grown as an annual, with slender, branching, red stems carrying oval, toothed, deep green leaves. Spurred, bright scarlet flowers are produced during summer-autumn. H 30–60cm (12–24in), S 30cm (12in).

***Salpiglossis sinuata* Casino Series**
Erect, compact annual with slender, freely branching stems. From summer to autumn, has broadly funnel-shaped, 5-lobed flowers in blue, purple, red, yellow or orange, often heavily veined. H to 60cm (24in), S to 30cm (12in).

***Dahlia* 'Coltness Gem'**
Well-branched, erect, bushy, tuberous perennial, grown as an annual. Has deeply lobed leaves and daisy-like, single flower heads in many colours throughout summer until autumn frosts. H and S 45cm (18in).

***Ismelia carinata* 'Monarch Court Jesters'**
Fast-growing, erect, branching annual. In summer has feathery, grey-green leaves and daisy-like, zoned flower heads, to 8cm (3in) wide, in various colour combinations. H 60cm (24in), S 30cm (12in).

***Viola* × *wittrockiana* Floral Dance Series**
Fairly fast-growing, bushy perennial, grown as an annual or biennial. Has oval, mid-green leaves and rounded, 5-petalled flowers in a wide range of colours in winter. H 15–20cm (6–8in), S 20cm (8in).

***Tagetes* 'Cinnabar'**
Fast-growing, bushy annual with aromatic, very feathery, deep green leaves. Heads of rounded, daisy-like, single, rich rust-red flowers, yellow-red beneath, are carried in summer and early autumn. H and S 30cm (12in).

***Solenostemon scutellarioides* 'Brightness'**
Fast-growing, bushy perennial, grown as an annual. Has rust-red leaves, edged with green. Flower spikes should be removed. H to 45cm (18in), S 30cm (12in) or more. Min 10°C (50°F).

RED

Amaranthus hypochondriacus
(Prince's feather)
Bushy annual with upright, sometimes flattened panicles, 15cm (6in) or more long, of dark red flowers in summer-autumn. Leaves are heavily suffused purple. H to 1.2m (4ft), S 45cm (1½ft).

***Ricinus communis* 'Impala'**
Fast-growing, evergreen, erect shrub, usually grown as an annual. Has deeply lobed, bronze leaves to 30cm (12in) wide and clusters of small, red flowers in summer, followed by globular, prickly, red seed heads. H 1.5m (5ft), S 90cm (3ft).

Calomeria amaranthoides
(Incense plant)
Erect, branching biennial with a strong fragrance of incense. Has lance-shaped leaves and heads of tiny, pink, brownish-red or crimson flowers in summer-autumn. H to 1.8m (6ft), S 90cm (3ft). Min. 4°C (39°F).

PURPLE

Trachelium caeruleum
(Throatwort)
Moderately fast-growing, erect perennial, grown as an annual. Has oval, serrated leaves and clustered heads of small, tubular, lilac-blue or white flowers in summer. H 60–90cm (2–3ft), S 30cm (1ft).

Psylliostachys suworowii
(Statice)
Fairly slow-growing, erect, branching annual with lance-shaped leaves. Bears branching spikes of small, tubular, pink to purple flowers in summer and early autumn. Flowers are good for drying. H 45cm (18in), S 30cm (12in).

Salvia sclarea* var. *turkestanica
Moderately fast-growing, erect biennial, grown as an annual. Has aromatic, oval, hairy leaves and panicles of tubular, white and lavender-purple flowers with prominent, lavender-purple bracts in summer. H 75cm (30in), S 30cm (12in).

***Linaria maroccana* 'Fairy Lights'**
Fast-growing, erect, bushy annual with lance-shaped, pale green leaves. Tiny, snapdragon-like flowers, in shades of red, pink, purple, yellow or white, are borne in summer. H 20cm (8in), S 15cm (6in).

Schizanthus pinnatus
Moderately fast-growing, upright, bushy annual with feathery, light green leaves. In summer-autumn has rounded, lobed, multicoloured flowers in shades of pink, purple, white or yellow. H 30cm–1.2m (1–4ft), S 30cm (1ft). Min. 5°C (41°F).

PURPLE

Exacum affine (Persian violet)
Evergreen, bushy biennial, usually grown as an annual. Has oval, glossy leaves and masses of tiny, scented, saucer-shaped, purple flowers, with yellow stamens, in summer and early autumn. H and S 20–30cm (8–12in). Min. 7–10°C (45–50°F).

Collinsia grandiflora
Moderately fast-growing, slender-stemmed annual. Upper leaves are lance-shaped; lower are oval. Whorls of pale purple flowers, with purplish-blue lips, are carried in spring-summer. H and S 15–30cm (6–12in).

***Campanula medium* 'Bells of Holland'**
Slow-growing, evergreen, clump-forming, erect biennial with lance-shaped, toothed leaves. In spring and early summer has bell-shaped flowers in blue, lilac, pink or white. H to 60cm (24in), S 30cm (12in).

Echium vulgare [dwarf]
Moderately fast-growing, erect, bushy annual or biennial with lance-shaped, dark green leaves. Spikes of tubular flowers, in shades of white, pink, blue or purple, appear in summer. H 30cm (12in), S 20cm (8in).

***Nierembergia caerulea* 'Purple Robe'**
Moderately fast-growing, rounded, branching perennial, grown as an annual, with narrow, lance-shaped leaves. Has cup-shaped, dark bluish-purple flowers in summer and early autumn. H and S 15–20cm (6–8in).

Salvia viridis
Moderately fast-growing, upright, branching annual with oval leaves. Tubular, lipped flowers, enclosed by purple, pink or white bracts, are carried in spikes at tops of stems in summer and early autumn. H 45cm (18in), S 20cm (8in).

Orychophragmus violaceus
Moderately fast-growing, upright annual or biennial with branching flower stems and pointed-oval, pale green leaves. Heads of 4-petalled, purple-blue flowers are carried in spring. H 30–60cm (12–24in), S 30cm (12in).

***Callistephus chinensis* Ostrich Plume Series**
Fast-growing, bushy annual with long, branching stems. From late summer to late autumn, produces spreading, feathery, reflexed, double flower heads, mainly in pinks and crimsons. H to 60cm (2ft), S 30cm (1ft).

Gomphrena globosa
(Globe amaranth)
Moderately fast-growing, upright, bushy annual with oval, hairy leaves. Has oval, clover-like flower heads in pink, yellow, orange, purple or white in summer and early autumn. H 30cm (12in), S 20cm (8in).

***Petunia* Daddy Series 'Sugar Daddy'**
Fairly fast-growing, branching, bushy, perennial, grown as an annual, with oval leaves. In early summer to autumn, has large, purple flowers with dark veins. H to 35cm (14in), S 30–90cm (12–36in).

***Salvia splendens* Cleopatra Series** [violet]
Slow-growing, bushy perennial, grown as an annual. Oval, serrated leaves are dark green; dense racemes of tubular, deep violet-purple flowers are carried in summer and early autumn. H to 30cm (12in), S 20–30cm (8–12in).

***Cerinthe major* 'Purpurascens'**
Annual of lax habit with oval to spoon-shaped leaves, to 6cm (2½in) long. Bears terminal sprays of nodding, tubular, pale to mid-yellow flowers, with violet-tinged tips. Bracts around flowers are strongly suffused purple. H and S 60cm (2ft).

PURPLE–BLUE

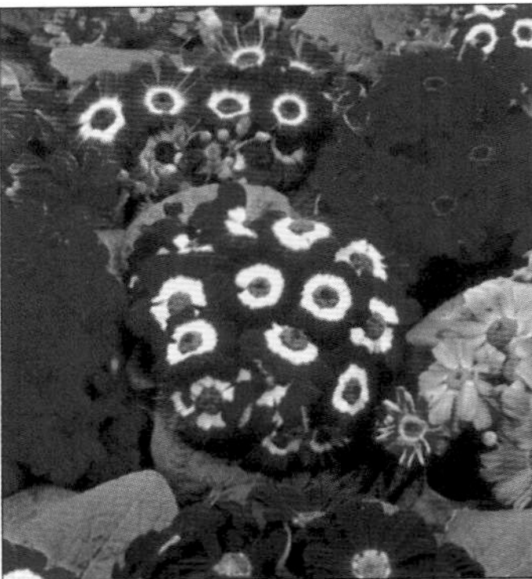

***Pericallis* × *hybrida* 'Spring Glory'** (Cineraria)
Slow-growing, evergreen, mound- or dome-shaped perennial, grown as a biennial, with large, oval, serrated leaves. Bears heads of large flowers in a mixture of colours in spring. H 20cm (8in), S 30cm (12in). Min. 5°C (41°F).

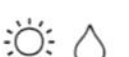

***Callistephus chinensis* Milady Super Series** [blue]
Moderately fast-growing, erect, bushy annual with oval, toothed leaves. Has large, daisy-like, double, purplish-blue flower heads in summer and early autumn. H 25–30cm (10–12in), S 30–45cm (12–18in).

***Petunia* Resisto Series** [blue]
Moderately fast-growing, branching, bushy perennial, grown as an annual. Has oval leaves and rain-resistant, flared, trumpet-shaped, intense blue flowers in summer-autumn. H 15–30cm (6–12in), S 30cm (12in).

***Lobelia erinus* 'Sapphire'**
Slow-growing, pendulous, spreading annual or occasionally perennial. Oval to lance-shaped leaves are pale green; small, sapphire-blue flowers with white centres are produced continuously in summer and early autumn. H 20cm (8in), S 15cm (6in).

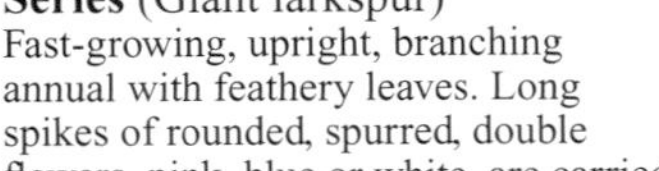

***Consolida ajacis* Giant Imperial Series** (Giant larkspur)
Fast-growing, upright, branching annual with feathery leaves. Long spikes of rounded, spurred, double flowers, pink, blue or white, are carried in summer. H 1.2 m (4ft), S 30cm (1ft).

***Convolvulus tricolor* 'Blue Flash'**
Moderately fast-growing, upright, bushy annual with oval to lance-shaped leaves. Has small, saucer-shaped, intense blue flowers with cream and yellow centres in summer. H 20–30cm (8–12in), S 20cm (8in).

***Viola* × *wittrockiana* Joker Series**
Bushy, spreading perennial, usually grown as an annual or biennial. Large, rounded, 5-petalled, purplish-blue flowers, with black and white 'faces' and yellow eyes, appear in summer. H and S 15cm (6in).

***Salvia farinacea* 'Victoria'**
Moderately fast-growing perennial, grown as an annual, with many erect stems. Has oval or lance-shaped leaves and spikes of tubular, violet-blue flowers in summer. H 45cm (18in), S 30cm (12in).

***Primula* Super Giants Series** [blue]
Rosette-forming perennial, usually grown as a biennial, with lance-shaped leaves. Heads of large, fragrant, flat, blue flowers appear in spring. H and S to 30cm (12in).

Torenia fournieri
(Wishbone flower)
Moderately fast-growing, erect, branching annual with serrated, light green leaves. Dark blue-purple flowers, paler and yellow within, are carried in summer and early autumn. H 30cm (12in), S 20cm (8in). Min. 5°C (41°F).

Gilia capitata
Erect, branching annual. Has very feathery, mid-green leaves and tiny, dense, rounded heads of soft lavender-blue flowers in summer and early autumn. Is good for cut flowers. H 45cm (18in), S 20cm (8in).

***Ageratum houstonianum* 'Blue Mink'**
Moderately fast-growing, hummock-forming annual. Has pointed-oval leaves and clusters of feathery, brush-like, pastel blue flower heads in summer-autumn. Is a useful edging plant. H and S 20–30cm (8–12in).

***Nigella damascena* 'Miss Jekyll'**
Fast-growing, slender, erect annual. Feathery leaves are bright green; small, rounded, many-petalled, semi-double, blue flowers are carried in summer, followed by inflated seed pods which can be cut and dried. H 45cm (18in), S 20cm (8in).

***Nigella damascena* Persian Jewels Series**
Fast-growing, erect annual with feathery leaves. Small, semi-double flowers, in shades of blue, pink or white, appear in summer, followed by inflated seed pods which can be cut and dried. H 45cm (18in), S 20cm (8in).

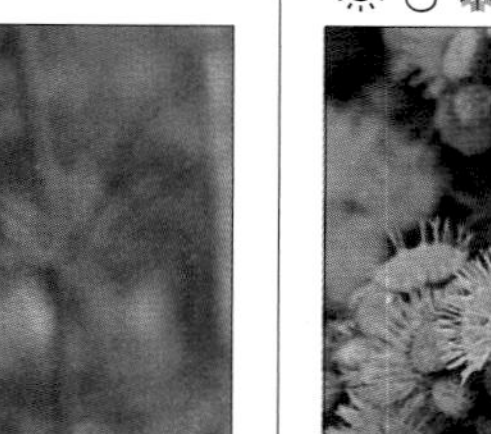

***Ageratum houstonianum* 'Blue Danube'**
Moderately fast-growing, hummock-forming annual with pointed-oval leaves. Has clusters of feathery, brush-like, lavender-blue flower heads in summer-autumn. Makes a useful edging plant. H and S 15cm (6in).

Sedum caeruleum
Moderately fast-growing annual with branching flower stems. Oval, light green leaves become red-tinged when clusters of small, star-shaped, light blue flowers with white centres are borne in summer. H and S 10–15cm (4–6in).

Nemophila menziesii
(Baby blue-eyes)
Fast-growing, spreading annual with serrated, grey-green leaves. Small, bowl-shaped, blue flowers with white centres are carried in summer. H 20cm (8in), S 15cm (6in).

***Viola* × *wittrockiana* 'True Blue'**
Erect, bushy perennial, grown as an annual or biennial, with spreading stems and oval leaves. In winter or summer, bears large, clear sky-blue flowers each with a small, yellow eye. H 16–23cm (6–9in), S 23–30cm (9–12in).

BLUE

Centaurea cyanus [tall, blue] (Cornflower)
Fast-growing, erect, branching annual. Has lance-shaped, grey-green leaves and branching heads of daisy-like, blue flowers in summer and early autumn. H to 90cm (3ft), S 30cm (1ft).

Brachyscome iberidifolia (Swan River daisy)
Moderately fast-growing, thin-stemmed, bushy annual with deeply cut leaves. Has small, fragrant, daisy-like flowers, usually blue but also pink, mauve, purple or white, in summer and early autumn. H and S to 45cm (18in).

Felicia bergeriana (Kingfisher daisy)
Fairly fast-growing, mat-forming annual. Has lance-shaped, hairy, grey-green leaves. Small, daisy-like, blue flower heads with yellow centres open only in sunshine in summer and early autumn. H and S 15cm (6in).

***Myosotis sylvatica* 'Blue Ball'**
Slow-growing, bushy, compact perennial, often grown as a biennial. Has lance-shaped leaves and, in spring and early summer, spikes of tiny, 5-lobed, deep blue flowers. H to 20cm (8in), S 15cm (6in).

***Cynoglossum amabile* 'Firmament'**
Slow-growing, upright, bushy annual or biennial with lance-shaped, hairy, grey-green leaves. Pendulous, tubular, pure sky-blue flowers are carried in summer. H 45cm (18in), S 30cm (12in).

Commelina coelestis (Day flower)
Fairly fast-growing, upright perennial, usually grown as an annual, with lance-shaped, mid-green leaves. Small, 3-petalled, bright pure blue flowers are freely produced from late summer to mid-autumn. H to 45cm (18in), S 30cm (12in).

Phacelia campanularia (California bluebell)
Moderately fast-growing, branching, bushy annual with oval, serrated, deep green leaves. Bell-shaped, pure blue flowers, 2.5cm (1in) wide, are carried in summer and early autumn. H 20cm (8in), S 15cm (6in).

***Anchusa capensis* 'Blue Angel'**
Bushy biennial, grown as an annual. Has lance-shaped, bristly leaves. Heads of shallowly bowl-shaped, brilliant blue flowers are borne in summer. H and S 20cm (8in).

Borago officinalis (Borage)
Spreading, clump-forming, annual herb. Has oval, crinkled, rough-haired leaves and sprays of star-shaped, blue flowers in summer and early autumn. Young leaves are sometimes used as a coolant in drinks. Self seeds prolifically. H 90cm (3ft), S 30cm (1ft).

BLUE–GREEN

***Lobelia erinus* 'Crystal Palace'**
Slow-growing, spreading, compact, bushy annual or occasionally perennial. Bronzed leaves are oval to lance-shaped; small, deep blue flowers are produced continuously in summer and early autumn. H 10–20cm (4–8in), S 10–15cm (4–6in).

***Senecio cineraria* 'Silver Dust'**
Moderately fast-growing, evergreen, bushy sub-shrub, usually grown as an annual, with deeply lobed, silver leaves. Small, daisy-like, yellow flower heads appear in summer but are best removed. H and S 30cm (12in).

Nicotiana langsdorffii
Fairly slow-growing, erect, branching perennial, grown as an annual, with oval to lance-shaped leaves. Slightly pendent, bell-shaped, pale green to yellow-green flowers appear in summer. H 1–1.5m (3–5ft), S 30cm (1ft).

GREEN–YELLOW

Moluccella laevis
(Bells of Ireland, Shell flower)
Fairly fast-growing, erect, branching annual. Rounded leaves are pale green; spikes of small, tubular, white flowers, each surrounded by a conspicuous, pale green calyx, appear in summer. H 60cm (24in), S 20cm (8in).

***Zinnia elegans* 'Envy'**
Moderately fast-growing, sturdy, erect annual. Has oval to lance-shaped, pale or mid-green leaves and large, daisy-like, double, green flower heads in summer and early autumn. H 60cm (24in), S 30cm (12in).

Bassia scoparia* f. *trichophylla
(Burning bush, Summer cypress)
Moderately fast-growing, erect, very bushy annual. Narrow, lance-shaped, light green leaves, 5–8cm (2–3in) long, turn red in autumn. Has insignificant flowers. H 90cm (3ft), S 60cm (2ft).

Ricinus communis
(Castor-oil plant)
Fast-growing, evergreen, erect shrub, usually grown as an annual. Has large, deeply lobed, mid-green leaves and heads of green and red flowers in summer, followed by globular, prickly seed pods. H 1.5m (5ft), S 90cm (3ft).

Amberboa moschata
(Sweet sultan)
Fast-growing, upright, slender-stemmed annual with lance-shaped, greyish-green leaves. Has large, fragrant, cornflower-like flower heads, in a range of colours, in summer and early autumn. H 45cm (18in), S 20cm (8in).

Platystemon californicus
(Cream cups)
Moderately fast-growing, upright, compact annual with lance-shaped, greyish-green leaves. Saucer-shaped, cream or pale yellow flowers, about 2.5cm (1in) across, appear in summer. H 30cm (12in), S 10cm (4in).

YELLOW

Smyrnium perfoliatum
Slow-growing, upright biennial. Upper leaves, rounded and yellow-green, encircle stems which bear heads of yellowish-green flowers in summer. H 60cm–1m (2–3ft), S 60cm (2ft).

Argemone mexicana
(Devil's fig, Prickly poppy)
Spreading perennial, grown as an annual, with leaves divided into white-marked, greyish-green leaflets. In summer has fragrant, poppy-like, yellow or orange flowers, 8cm (3in) wide. H to 60cm (24in), S 30cm (12in).

Glaucium flavum
(Horned poppy)
Slow-growing, erect biennial with oval, lobed, light greyish-green leaves. Poppy-like, vivid yellow flowers, 8cm (3in) wide, appear in summer and early autumn. H 30–60cm (12–24in), S 45cm (18in).

YELLOW

***Viola* × *wittrockiana* 'Clear Sky Primrose'**
Erect, bushy perennial, grown as an annual or biennial, with spreading stems and oval leaves. In winter, produces primrose-yellow flowers brushed in canary yellow. H 16–23cm (6–9in), S 23–30cm (9–12in).

Limnanthes douglasii (Meadow foam, Poached-egg flower)
Fast-growing, slender, erect annual. Feathery leaves are glossy, light green; slightly fragrant, cup-shaped, white flowers with yellow centres are carried from early to late summer. H 15cm (6in), S 10cm (4in).

Eschscholzia caespitosa
Fast-growing, slender, erect annual with feathery, bluish-green leaves. Cup-shaped, 4-petalled, yellow flowers, 2.5cm (1in) wide, appear in summer and early autumn. H and S 15cm (6in).

***Antirrhinum majus* Chimes Series** [yellow]
Erect perennial usually grown as an annual, with branching shoots and mid- to dark green, lance-shaped leaves. During summer and autumn produces racemes of bright yellow, 2-liped flowers. H 30cm (12in), S 20cm (8in).

***Helianthus annuus* 'Music Box'**
Fast-growing, free-flowering, many-branched, hairy-stemmed annual. Bears daisy-like flower heads, 10–12cm (4–5in) across, with ray-florets ranging from creamy-yellow to dark red, and black disc-florets, in summer. H 70cm (28in), S to 60cm (24in).

Lindheimera texana (Star daisy)
Moderately fast-growing, erect, branching annual with hairy stems and oval, serrated, hairy leaves. Daisy-like, yellow flower heads appear in late summer and early autumn. H 30–60cm (12–24in), S 30cm (12in).

***Viola* × *wittrockiana* 'Super Chalon Giants'**
Fairly fast-growing, bushy perennial, grown as an annual or biennial. Has oval, serrated leaves and, in summer-autumn, 5-petalled, ruffled and waved, bicoloured flowers. H 15–20cm (6–8in), S 20cm (8in).

***Calendula officinalis* 'Daisy May'**
Fast-growing, bushy annual with aromatic, lance-shaped, mid-green leaves and numerous, semi-double, yellow flower heads from late spring to autumn. H and S 30–40cm (12–16in).

Mentzelia lindleyi
Fairly fast-growing, bushy annual with fleshy stems and lance-shaped, serrated leaves. Has fragrant, cup-shaped, deep yellow flowers, with conspicuous stamens, in summer. H 45cm (18in), S 20cm (8in).

***Tagetes* 'Gold Coins'** [Erecta Group]
Fast-growing, erect, bushy annual. Has aromatic, feathery, glossy, deep green leaves and large, daisy-like, double flower heads in shades of yellow and orange in summer and early autumn. H 90cm (3ft), S 30–45cm (1–1½ft).

Sanvitalia procumbens
(Creeping zinnia)
Moderately fast-growing, prostrate annual with pointed-oval leaves. Daisy-like, yellow flower heads, 2.5cm (1in) wide, with black centres, are borne in summer. H 15cm (6in), S 30cm (12in).

Coreopsis tinctoria (Tick-seed)
Fast-growing, erect, bushy annual with lance-shaped leaves. Large, daisy-like, bright yellow flower heads with red centres are carried in summer and early autumn. H 60–90cm (2–3ft), S 20cm (8in).

***Viola* × *wittrockiana* Panola Series** [yellow]
Bushy perennial, grown as an annual. Has ovate, sparingly toothed, mid-green leaves and produces a long display of large, 5-petalled, bright yellow, black-centred flowers in summer. H 12–15cm (5–6in), S 15–20cm (6–8in).

***Viola* × *wittrockiana* Crystal Bowl Series** [yellow]
Bushy, spreading perennial, usually grown as an annual or biennial, with oval, mid-green leaves. Large, rounded, 5-petalled, yellow flowers are carried in summer. H and S 15cm (6in).

Xanthophthalmum segetum
Moderately fast-growing, erect annual with lance-shaped, grey-green leaves. Daisy-like, single flower heads, to 8cm (3in) wide, in shades of yellow, are carried in summer and early autumn. Is excellent for cut flowers. H 45cm (18in), S 30cm (12in).

Cladanthus arabicus
Moderately fast-growing, hummock-forming annual with aromatic, feathery, light green leaves. Has fragrant, daisy-like, single, deep yellow flower heads, 5cm (2in) wide, in summer and early autumn. H 60cm (24in), S 30cm (12in).

***Antirrhinum majus* Sonnet Series**
Erect, bushy, early flowering perennial, grown as an annual, branching from the base, with lance-shaped leaves. From spring to autumn, freely produces 2-lipped flowers in bronze, pink, carmine-red, crimson, burgundy, white and yellow. H and S 45cm (18in).

***Coreopsis* 'Sunray'**
Spreading, clump-forming perennial, grown as an annual by sowing under glass in early spring. Has lance-shaped, serrated leaves and daisy-like, double, bright yellow flower heads in summer. H 45cm (18in), S 30–45cm (12–18in).

Helianthus annuus
Fast-growing, erect annual with oval, serrated, mid-green leaves. Daisy-like, yellow flower heads to 30cm (12in) or more wide, with brown or purplish centres, appear in summer. H 1–3m (3–10ft), S 30–45cm (1–1½ft).

***Helianthus annuus* 'Teddy Bear'**
Fast-growing, compact, hairy-stemmed annual with toothed, roughly hairy leaves. Produces daisy-like, double, deep yellow flower heads, to 13cm (5in) across, in summer. H 90cm (36in), S to 60cm (24in).

YELLOW

***Zinnia elegans* Dreamland Series** [yellow]
Moderately fast-growing, sturdy, erect annual with ovate, mid-green leaves. In summer and autumn produces large, daisy-like, semi-double, deep bright yellow flower heads. H and S 30cm (12in).

Ursinia anthemoides
Moderately fast-growing, bushy annual with feathery, pale green leaves. Small, daisy-like, purple-centred flower heads with orange-yellow rays, purple beneath, appear in summer and early autumn. H 30cm (12in), S 20cm (8in).

***Gaillardia pulchella* 'Lollipops'**
Moderately fast-growing, upright annual with lance-shaped, hairy, greyish-green leaves. Daisy-like, double, red-and-yellow flower heads, 5cm (2in) wide, are carried in summer. H and S 30cm (12in).

***Calceolaria* 'Bright Bikinis'**
Compact, bushy annual or biennial. Has oval, slightly hairy, mid-green leaves, and heads of small, rounded, pouched flowers in shades of yellow, orange or red in summer. H and S 20cm (8in). Min. 5°C (41°F).

***Tagetes* Boy-o Boy Series**
Compact, bushy annual with divided, mid-green leaves. Produces double, crested flower heads in a range of gold and bright orange shades from late spring to summer. H and S 20–30cm (8–12in).

***Tagetes* 'Naughty Marietta'**
Fast-growing, bushy annual with aromatic, deeply cut, deep green leaves. Heads of daisy-like, bicoloured flowers, deep yellow and maroon, are carried in summer and early autumn. H and S 30cm (12in).

***Calendula officinalis* Pacific Beauty Series 'Lemon Queen'**
Fast-growing, erect annual with softly hairy, aromatic leaves. Daisy-like, double, lemon-yellow flower heads, with red-brown disc-florets, are borne from summer to autumn. H to 45cm (18in), S 30–45cm (12–18in).

***Viola × wittrockiana* Forerunner Series**
Erect, bushy perennials, grown as annuals or biennials, with oval leaves. In winter and spring, bears medium-sized flowers in a range of bright, single colours and bicolours. H 16–23cm (6–9in), S 23–30cm (9–12in).

Eschscholzia californica [mixed]
Fast-growing, slender, erect annual. Feathery leaves are bluish-green; cup-shaped, 4-petalled, single flowers, in shades of red, orange, yellow or cream, are borne in summer-autumn. H 30cm (12in), S 15cm (6in).

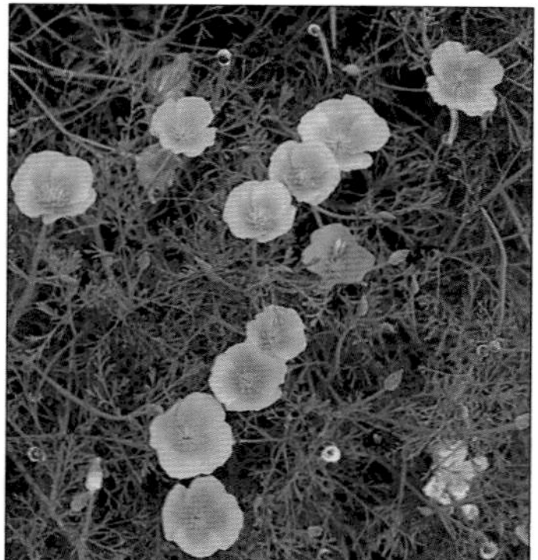

Eschscholzia californica
Fast-growing, slender, erect annual with feathery, bluish-green leaves. Cup-shaped, 4-petalled, vivid orange-yellow flowers are borne in summer-autumn. H 30cm (12in), S 15cm (6in).

***Eschscholzia californica* Thai Silk Series**
Fast-growing, compact, slender, erect annual with feathery, bluish-green leaves. In summer-autumn, produces single or semi-double, fluted, bronze-tinged flowers in red, pink or orange. H 20–25cm (8–10in), S 15cm (6in).

***Tropaeolum* Alaska Series**
Fast-growing, bushy annual with rounded, variegated leaves. Spurred, trumpet-shaped flowers, in shades of red or yellow, appear in summer and early autumn. H and S 30cm (12in).

***Primula* 'Yellow Dream'**
(Polyanthus)
Rosette-forming perennial, usually grown as a biennial, with ovate, toothed leaves. Produces large, fragrant bright yellow flower heads with slightly darker yellow centres in late winter and spring. H and S 15–23cm (6–9in).

***Nemesia strumosa* Carnival Series**
Compact, dwarf, branched annuals with lance-shaped, mid-green leaves. In mid- and late summer produce racemes of purple-veined, red, orange, pink, white, bronze-yellow, or yellow, 2-lipped flowers. H and S 15–23cm (6–9in).

***Viola* × *wittrockiana* Universal Series** [apricot]
Bushy, spreading perennial, usually grown as a biennial. Large, rounded, 5-petalled, deep apricot flowers are borne in winter-spring. H and S 15–20cm (6–8in).

***Calceolaria* 'Sunshine'**
Evergreen, compact, bushy perennial, grown as an annual. Has oval, mid-green leaves and heads of small, rounded, pouched, bright golden-yellow flowers in late spring and summer. H and S 20cm (8in).

***Calendula officinalis* 'Fiesta Gitana'**
Fast-growing, bushy annual with strongly aromatic, lance-shaped, pale green leaves. Daisy-like, double flower heads, ranging from cream to orange in colour, are carried from spring to autumn. H and S 30cm (12in).

ORANGE

***Rudbeckia hirta* 'Marmalade'**
Moderately fast-growing, erect, branching perennial, grown as an annual, with lance-shaped leaves. In summer-autumn bears daisy-like, deep golden-orange flower heads, 8cm (3in) wide, with black centres. H 45cm (18in), S 30cm (12in).

***Rudbeckia hirta* 'Goldilocks'**
Moderately fast-growing, erect, branching perennial, grown as an annual. Has lance-shaped leaves and daisy-like, double or semi-double, golden-orange flower heads, 8cm (3in) across, in summer-autumn. H 60cm (24in), S 30cm (12in).

***Tagetes* 'Tangerine Gem'**
Fast-growing, bushy annual with aromatic, feathery leaves. Small, single, deep orange flower heads appear in summer and early autumn. H 20cm (8in), S 30cm (12in).

***Rudbeckia hirta* 'Toto Gold'**
Upright, strong-stemmed biennial or short-lived perennial, often grown as an annual, with ovate to lance-shaped, mid-green leaves. Has large, daisy-like, bright yellow flower heads with very dark brown centres in summer and early autumn. H and S to 45cm (18in).

***Tithonia rotundifolia* 'Torch'**
Slow-growing, erect annual with rounded, lobed leaves. Has daisy-like, bright orange or scarlet flower heads, 5–8 cm (2–3in) wide, in summer and early autumn. H 90cm (3ft), S 30cm (1ft).

***Tagetes* Antigua Series** [mixed] (African marigold)
Compact annuals, producing orange, lemon-yellow, golden-yellow, or primrose-yellow flowers from late spring to early autumn. H to 30cm (12in), S to 45cm (18in).

***Tagetes* Boy Series**
Compact annual that bears double, crested flower heads in a range of colours, including shades of golden-yellow, yellow, orange or reddish-brown, with deep orange or yellow crests, in late spring and early summer. H to 15cm (6in), S to 30cm (12in).

***Erysimum × allionii* 'Orange Bedder'**
Slow-growing, short-lived, evergreen, bushy perennial, grown as a biennial. Has lance-shaped, mid-green leaves. Heads of scented, 4-petalled, brilliant orange flowers appear in spring. H and S 30cm (12in).

***Bracteantha bracteata* Monstrosum Series**
Moderately fast-growing, erect, branching annual. Has daisy-like, papery, double flower heads, in pink, red, orange, yellow or white, in summer and early autumn. Flowers dry well. H 90cm (3ft), S 30cm (1ft).

***Zinnia haageana* 'Orange Star'**
Dwarf, bushy annual with daisy-like, broad-petalled, orange flower heads, borne in summer. Is mildew-resistant and good for ground cover. H to 25cm (10in), S to 30cm (12in).

***Tropaeolum* Jewel Series**
Fast-growing, bushy annual with rounded leaves. Spurred, trumpet-shaped flowers, in shades of red, yellow or orange, are held well above leaves from early summer to early autumn. H and S 30cm (12in).

***Calendula officinalis* 'Geisha Girl'**
Fast-growing, bushy annual with strongly aromatic, lance-shaped, pale green leaves. Heads of double, orange flowers with incurved petals are borne from late spring to autumn. H 60cm (24in), S 30–60cm (12–24in).

***Erysimum cheiri* 'Fire King'**
Moderately fast-growing, evergreen, bushy perennial, grown as a biennial. Lance-shaped leaves are mid- to deep green; heads of 4-petalled, reddish-orange flowers are carried in spring. H 38cm (15in), S 30–38cm (12–15in).

Emilia coccinea (Tassel flower)
Moderately fast-growing, upright annual with lance-shaped, greyish-green leaves and double, red or yellow flower heads in summer. H 30–60cm (12–24in), S 30cm (12in) or more.

***Solanum pseudocapsicum* 'Balloon'**
Evergreen, bushy shrub, grown as an annual. Has lance-shaped leaves and, in summer, small, star-shaped, white flowers. Large, cream fruits turn orange in winter. H 30cm (12in), S 30–45cm (12–18in). Min. 5°C (41°F).

***Solanum pseudocapsicum* 'Red Giant'**
Fairly slow-growing, evergreen, bushy shrub, usually grown as an annual. Has lance-shaped, deep green leaves, small, white flowers in summer and large, round, orange-red fruits in winter. H and S 30cm (12in). Min. 5°C (41°F).

***Clarkia amoena* Princess Series** [salmon]
Fast-growing annual with slender, upright stems and lance-shaped, mid-green leaves. Spikes of frilled, salmon-pink flowers are carried in summer. H and S 30cm (12in).

***Sanvitalia procumbens* 'Mandarin Orange'**
Moderately fast-growing, prostrate annual. Has pointed-oval, mid-green leaves and daisy-like, orange flower heads, 2.5cm (1in) wide, in summer. H 15cm (6in), S 30cm (12in).

***Dahlia* 'Dandy'**
Well-branched, erect, bushy, tuberous perennial, grown as an annual. Has pointed-oval, serrated leaves and heads of daisy-like flowers, with contrasting central collars of quilled petals, in shades of red, yellow or orange in summer. H and S 60cm (2ft).

***Celosia argentea* 'Fairy Fountains'**
Moderately fast-growing, erect, bushy perennial, grown as an annual. Has pointed-oval leaves and conical, feathery flower heads, to 15cm (6in) tall, in a wide range of colours in summer-autumn. H and S 30cm (12in).

Rock Plants

Rock Plants

Noted for their natural charm and simple, clear-coloured, abundant flowers, in spring and early summer, rock plants are suited to almost every situation, from the tiniest trough to the grandest rock garden.

What are rock plants?

The term rock plants includes bulbs and mat- and cushion-forming perennials (many of which are evergreen) as well as dwarf, evergreen, coniferous and deciduous trees and shrubs. They may be true alpines or simply plants of small stature that are suitable for rock garden plantings. While many of the alpines have specialized needs, the latter group includes many species and cultivars, such as aubrieta and *Aurinia saxatilis*, that are undemanding in cultivation and thrive in any well-drained site of suitable aspect.

True alpines grow at high altitudes above the tree-line, on scree slopes, in rock crevices or in short turf, while sub-alpine plants live below the tree-line on rocky slopes or in high pastures or meadow land. Most alpines are compact in habit and frequently deep-rooting, usually with small leaves that are leathery, fleshy or covered in fine hair. These adaptations help them survive the drying, high-velocity winds, brilliant, burning sun and extreme temperature fluctuations of their natural mountain habitat.

Most rock plants grow in areas characterized by stony soils with rapid drainage, and so cannot withstand the combination of constant wetness at the roots and winter cold that is experienced in lower-altitude gardens. Such species also dislike warm, humid summers. In the wild, high-growing species are insulated from winter cold by a blanket of snow, beneath which they remain dormant at temperatures around 0°C (32°F) until spring. Those environments that mimic conditions in the wild, such as rock gardens, scree beds, troughs, raised beds, and open frames, are therefore best for cultivating rock plants, which must have sharp drainage and, usually, protection from excessive winter moisture.

Woodland plants
Above: Natives of mountain woodland, such as the trilliums seen here, generally need moist, neutral to acid soil and are perfectly at home in a bed in dappled shade.

Planning a rock garden
Right: Siting a rock garden on a gentle slope assists rapid drainage, while carefully placed rocks form a niche where penetrating roots can be kept cool and moist during the summer.

Designing with rock plants

One of the major attractions of this group is their diminutive size, which can satisfy the gardener's hunger for diversity because many different plants can be grown in a relatively confined space. In a rock garden – as in larger-scale plantings – small shrubs, such as the highly fragrant *Daphne cneorum* and D. *retusa* or the catkin-bearing *Salix bockii* and *S. apoda*, can be used to form the structural framework of a design. Miniature conifers, such as *Juniperus communis* 'Compressa', can create vertical emphasis and year-round colour, in contrast to plants of rounded habit, such as the evergreen *Hebe cupressoides* 'Boughton Dome'.

This structure can then be filled in with mat- and cushion-forming plants, such as sandworts (*Arenaria*) or *Dianthus deltoides*, at the feet of taller, feathery-leaved pulsatillas or the airy *Linum narbonense*. There are also tight, dome-forming saxifrages, rosette-forming sedums and fleshy-leaved sempervivums, whose

Container planting
Troughs are ideal for creating landscapes in miniature but to provide perfect drainage they must be filled with gritty compost. Here, the flowers of alpine poppies, campanulas and lewisias lend colour to the neat, lime-encrusted rosettes of high-alpine saxifrages.

surfaces contrast perfectly with the white-haired leaves of edelweiss (*Leontopodium*) or the silky, silver leaves of the celmisias.

Maintaining year-round interest

Evergreen and structural plantings are more important in rock gardens than in other styles of garden because most alpines bloom in one burst between spring and early summer. The season can be extended, however, by planting early spring bulbs, such as alpine narcissus or crocuses, by using later-flowering rock plants such as helianthemums, phlox or veronicas, and by planting the autumn-flowering cyclamen, or the berry-bearing gaultherias.

Miniature landscapes

In courtyards or tiny gardens, or where the soil in the open garden is too heavy or drainage is inadequate, rock plants can be grown in troughs or raised beds to create landscapes in miniature. The latter also bring small plants closer to eye level and are ideal for gardeners of reduced mobility.

Dry stone walls are also potential planting sites for many crevice-lovers, such as lewisias or ramonda, while the tops of the walls are ideal planting positions for cascading specimens, such as *Saxifraga* 'Tumbling Waters'.

Size categories used within this group		
LARGE over 15cm (6in)	—	SMALL up to 15cm (6in)

Rock plants for edging
Above: Robust, low-growing mat-formers such as aubrieta and mossy saxifrages make excellent edging plants at the front of a rock garden.

A perfect partnership
Left: In an open site in full sun, dwarf shrubs and conifers provide a permanent, structural framework for the profuse spring and early summer flowers that are typical of alpine plants.

□ WHITE

Leontopodium alpinum
(Edelweiss)
Short-lived perennial with lance-shaped, woolly leaves. Small, silvery-white flower heads, in spring or early summer, are surrounded by petal-like, felted bracts in a star shape. Dislikes wet. H and S 15–20cm (6–8in).

Lithophragma parviflorum
Clump-forming, tuberous perennial that has small, open clusters of campion-like, white or pink flowers in spring above a basal cluster of deeply toothed, kidney-shaped leaves. Lies dormant in summer. H 15–20cm (6–8in), S to 20cm (8in).

Iberis sempervirens
Evergreen, spreading sub-shrub, with narrow, oblong, dark green leaves, bearing dense, rounded heads of white flowers in late spring and early summer. Trim after flowering. H 15–30cm (6–12in), S 45–60cm (18–24in).

Pulsatilla alpina
(Alpine anemone)
Tufted perennial with feathery leaves. Has upright, or nodding, cup-shaped, white, sometimes blue- or pink-flushed flowers singly in spring and early summer, then feathery seed heads. H 15–30cm (6–12in), S to 10cm (4in).

Saxifraga granulata (Fair maids of France, Meadow saxifrage)
Clump-forming perennial that loses its kidney-shaped, crumpled, glossy leaves in summer. Sticky stems carry loose panicles of rounded, white flowers in late spring. H 23–38cm (9–15in), S to 15cm (6in) or more.

Rhodanthemum hosmariense
Evergreen, shrubby perennial with finely cut, bright silvery-green leaves that clothe lax, woody stems. From late spring to early autumn, white flower heads are borne singly above foliage. H 15cm (6in) or more, S 30cm (12in).

***Andromeda polifolia* 'Alba'**
Evergreen, open, twiggy shrub bearing terminal clusters of pitcher-shaped, white flowers in spring and early summer. Glossy, dark green leaves are leathery and lance-shaped. H 45cm (18in), S 60cm (24in).

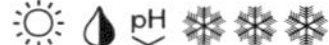

***Cassiope* 'Muirhead'**
Evergreen, loose, bushy shrub with scale-like, dark green leaves on upright branches. In spring, these bear tiny, virtually stemless, bell-shaped, white flowers along their length. H and S 20cm (8in).

***Cassiope* 'Edinburgh'**
Evergreen, dwarf shrub with tiny, dark green leaves tightly pressed to upright stems. In spring, many small, bell-shaped, white flowers are borne singly in leaf axils. H and S 20cm (8in).

WHITE

Saxifraga hirsuta
Evergreen, mound-forming perennial with rosettes of round, hairy leaves and loose panicles of tiny, star-shaped, white flowers, often yellow-spotted at the base of petals, in late spring and early summer. H 15–20cm (6–8in), S 20cm (8in).

Jeffersonia diphylla
Slow-growing, tufted perennial with distinctive, 2-lobed, light to mid-green leaves. Bears solitary cup-shaped, white flowers with prominent, yellow stamens in late spring. Do not disturb roots. H 15–23cm (6–9in), S to 23cm (9in).

Daphne blagayana
Evergreen, prostrate shrub with trailing branches each bearing a terminal cluster of oval, leathery leaves and, in early spring, dense clusters of fragrant, tubular, white flowers. Likes humus-rich soil. H 30–40cm (12–16in), S 60–80cm (24–32in) or more.

Tiarella cordifolia (Foamflower)
Vigorous, evergreen, spreading perennial. Lobed, pale green leaves sometimes have darker marks; veins turn bronze-red in winter. Bears many spikes of profuse white flowers in late spring and early summer. H 15–20cm (6–8in), S to 30cm (12in) or more.

***Saxifraga* 'Tumbling Waters'**
Slow-growing, evergreen, mal-forming perennial with a tight rosette of narrow, lime-encrusted leaves. After several years produces arching sprays of white flowers in conical heads; main rosette then dies but small offsets survive. H to 60cm (24in), S to 20cm (8in).

Daphne alpina
Compact and upright deciduous shrub with softly hairy, oval, grey-green leaves. In late spring produces terminal clusters of small, white flowers that are sweetly scented. These are followed by spherical, orange-red fruits. H and S to 60cm (24in).

WHITE–PINK

Dodecatheon meadia* f. *album
Clump-forming perennial with basal rosettes of oval, pale green leaves. In spring, strong stems bear several white flowers with dark centres and reflexed petals. Lies dormant in summer. H 20cm (8in), S 15cm (6in).

Saxifraga* × *geum
Evergreen, mat-forming perennial with shallow-rooted rosettes of spoon-shaped, hairy leaves. In summer, star-shaped, pink-spotted, white flowers, deep pink in bud, are borne on loose panicles on slender stems. H 15–20cm (6–8in), S 30cm (12in).

Andromeda polifolia
Evergreen, open, twiggy shrub with narrow, leathery, glossy, mid-green leaves. Bears terminal clusters of pitcher-shaped, pink flowers in spring and early summer. H 30–45cm (12–18in), S 60cm (24in).

***Andromeda polifolia* 'Compacta'**
Evergreen, compact, twiggy shrub that bears delicate, terminal clusters of pitcher-shaped, coral-pink flowers, with white undertones, in spring and early summer. Leaves are lance-shaped and glossy, dark green. H 15–23cm (6–9in), S 30cm (12in).

Dodecatheon hendersonii
Clump-forming perennial with a flat rosette of kidney-shaped leaves, above which deep pink flowers with reflexed petals appear in late spring. Needs a dry, dormant summer period. H 30cm (12in), S 8cm (3in).

***Phyllodoce* × *intermedia* 'Drummondii'**
Evergreen, bushy, dwarf shrub with narrow, heath-like, glossy leaves. From late spring to early summer bears terminal clusters of pitcher-shaped, rich pink flowers on slender, red stalks. H and S 23cm (9in).

PINK–PURPLE

Daphne cneorum
Evergreen, low-growing shrub with trailing branches clothed in small, oval, leathery, dark green leaves. Fragrant, deep rose pink flowers are borne in terminal clusters in late spring. Prefers humus-rich soil. H 23cm (9in), S to 2m (6ft).

***Dodecatheon* 'Red Wings'**
Clump-forming perennial with a basal cluster of oblong, soft, pale green leaves. In late spring and early summer bears small, loose clusters of deep magenta flowers, with reflexed petals, on strong stems. Lies dormant in summer. H 20cm (8in), S 10cm (4in).

Phyllodoce empetriformis
Evergreen, mat-forming shrub with fine narrow, heath-like leaves and terminal clusters of bell-shaped, purplish-pink flowers in late spring and early summer. H 15–23cm (6–9in), S 20cm (8in).

Phyllodoce caerulea
Evergreen, dwarf shrub with fine, narrow, heath-like leaves. Bears bell-shaped, purple to purplish-pink flowers, singly or in clusters, in late spring and summer. H and S to 30cm (12in).

Pulsatilla vulgaris (Pasque flower)
Tufted perennial with feathery, light green leaves. In spring bears nodding, cup-shaped flowers, in shades of purple, red, pink or white, with bright yellow centres. Flower stems rapidly elongate as feathery seeds mature. H and S 15–23cm (6–9in).

PURPLE–BLUE

Erinacea anthyllis
(Hedgehog broom)
Slow growing, evergreen sub-shrub with hard, blue-green spines. Pea-like, soft lavender flowers appear in axils of spines in late spring to early summer. H and S 15–25cm (6–10in).

Pulsatilla halleri
Tufted perennial, intensely hairy in all parts, that in spring bears nodding, later erect, cup-shaped flowers in shades of purple. Has feathery leaves and seed heads. H 15–38cm (6–15in), S 15–20cm (6–8in).

Aquilegia alpina
(Alpine columbine)
Short-lived, upright perennial with spurred, clear blue or violet-blue flowers on slender stems in spring and early summer. Has basal rosettes of rounded, finely divided leaves. Needs rich soil. H 45cm (18in), S 15cm (6in).

BLUE

Viola cornuta (Horned violet)
Rhizomatous perennial with oval, toothed leaves and flat-faced, rather angular, spurred, pale to deep purplish-blue, occasionally white flowers in spring and much of summer. H 12–20cm (8in), S to 20cm (8in) or more.

Omphalodes verna
Semi-evergreen, clump-forming perennial that in spring bears long, loose sprays of flat, bright blue flowers with white eyes. Leaves are oval and mid-green. H and S 20cm (8in) or more.

Omphalodes cappadocica
Spreading perennial with creeping underground stems and many loose sprays of flat, bright blue flowers in spring-summer above tufts of oval, hairy, basal leaves. H 15–20cm (6–8in), S 25cm (10in) or more.

GREY–YELLOW

Salix helvetica
Deciduous, spreading, much-branched, dwarf shrub that has small, oval, glossy leaves, white-haired beneath. In spring bears short-stalked, silky, grey, then yellow catkins. H 60cm (24in), S 30cm (12in).

Betula nana (Arctic birch)
Deciduous, bushy, dwarf shrub with small, toothed leaves that turn bright yellow in autumn. Has tiny, yellowish-brown catkins in spring. H 30cm (12in), S 45cm (18in).

Corydalis cheilanthifolia
Evergreen perennial with fleshy roots. Produces spreading rosettes of fern-like, near-prostrate, sometimes bronze-tinted, mid-green leaves. Has dense spikes of short-spurred, yellow flowers in late spring and early summer. H 20–30cm (8–12in), S 15–20cm (6–8in).

Corydalis wilsonii
Evergreen perennial with a fleshy rootstock. Forms rosettes of near-prostrate, divided, bluish-green leaves. Loose racemes of spurred, green-tipped, yellow flowers are produced in spring. H and S 10–25cm (4–10in).

***Aurinia saxatilis* 'Citrina'**
Evergreen, clump-forming perennial with oval, hairy, grey-green leaves. Bears racemes of many, small, pale lemon-yellow flowers in late spring and early summer. H 23cm (9in), S 30cm (12in).

***Aurinia saxatilis* 'Variegata'**
Evergreen perennial that bears racemes of many small, yellow flowers in spring above a mat of large, oval, soft grey-green leaves with cream margins.
H 23cm (9in), S 30cm (12in).

Chiastophyllum oppositifolium
Evergreen, trailing perennial with large, oblong, serrated, succulent leaves. In late spring and early summer bears many tiny, yellow flowers in arching sprays. H 15–20cm (6–8in), S 15cm (6in).

Cytisus* × *beanii
Deciduous, low-growing shrub with arching sprays of pea-like, golden-yellow flowers that appear in late spring and early summer on previous year's wood. Leaves, divided into 3 leaflets, are small, linear and hairy. H 15–40cm (6–16in), S 30–75cm (12–30in).

YELLOW–ORANGE

Hylomecon japonica
Vigorous, spreading perennial with large, cup-shaped, bright yellow flowers that are borne singly on slender stems in spring. Soft, dark green leaves are divided into 4 unequal lobes. H to 30cm (12in), S 20cm (8in).

***Erysimum* 'Moonlight'**
Mat-forming, evergreen perennial with narrowly oval leaves. In early summer, produces clusters of pale, sulphur-yellow flowers on short, leafy stems. Prefers an open site and gritty soil. H 25cm (10in), S 45cm (18in).

Aurinia saxatilis (Gold dust)
Evergreen perennial forming low clumps of oval, hairy, grey-green leaves. Has substantial spikes of small, chrome-yellow flowers in spring. H 23cm (9in), S 30cm (12in).

***Erysimum* 'Bredon'**
Semi-evergreen, rounded, woody perennial clothed in oval, dark green leaves. In late spring bears dense spikes of flat, bright mustard-yellow flowers. H 30–45cm (12–18in), S 45cm (18in).

***Erysimum* × *kewense* 'Harpur Crewe'**
Evergreen, shrubby perennial with stiff stems and narrow leaves. Fragrant, double, deep yellow flowers open in succession from late spring to mid-summer. Grows best in poor soil and a sheltered site. H and S 30cm (12in).

***Berberis* × *stenophylla* 'Corallina Compacta'**
Evergreen, neat, dwarf shrub with spiny stems clothed in small, narrowly oval leaves. In late spring bears many tiny, bright orange flowers. Is slow-growing and difficult to propagate. H and S to 25cm (10in).

WHITE

Parnassia palustris
(Grass of Parnassus)
Perennial with low, basal tufts of heart-shaped, pale to mid-green leaves. Bears saucer-shaped, white flowers, with dark green or purplish-green veins, on erect stems in late spring and early summer. H 20cm (8in), S 6cm (2½in) or more.

Armeria pseudarmeria
Evergreen, clump-forming perennial with large, spherical heads of white flowers occasionally suffused pink; these are borne in summer on stiff stems above long, narrow, glaucous leaves. H and S 30cm (12in).

Celmisia walkeri
Evergreen, loose, spreading perennial with long, oval or lance-shaped leaves, glossy, green above and hairy, white beneath. Has large, daisy-like, white flower heads in summer. H 23cm (9in), S to 2m (6ft).

Helianthemum apenninum
Evergreen, spreading, much-branched shrub that bears saucer-shaped, pure white flowers in mid-summer. Stems and small, linear leaves are covered in white down. H and S 45cm (18in).

Galax urceolata
Evergreen, clump-forming perennial. Large, round, leathery, mid-green leaves on slender stems turn bronze in autumn-winter. Has dense spikes of small, white flowers in late spring and early summer. H 15–20cm (6–8in), S to 30cm (12in).

***Hebe pinguifolia* 'Pagei'**
Evergreen, semi-prostrate shrub with small, oblong, slightly cupped, intensely glaucous leaves. Bears short spikes of small, white flowers in late spring or early summer. Is excellent for ground or rock cover. H 15–30cm (6–12in), S 60cm–1m (24–36in).

Saxifraga cuneifolia
Evergreen, carpeting perennial with neat rosettes of rounded leaves. In late spring and early summer bears panicles of tiny, white flowers, frequently with yellow, pink or red spots, on slender stems. H 15–20cm (6–8in), S 30cm (12in) or more.

***Diascia* 'Ice Cracker'**
Mat-forming perennial with narrowly ovate, mid to dark green leaves. From summer to autumn produces upright racemes of 2-lipped, hooded, shallowly bell-shaped, spurred, white flowers, touched pink at the base. H 30cm (12in), S 15–20cm (6–8in).

Corydalis ochroleuca
Evergreen, clump-forming perennial with fleshy, fibrous roots and much divided, basal, grey-green leaves. Bears slender, yellow-tipped, creamy-white flowers in late spring and summer. H and S 20–30cm (8–12in).

Chamaecytisus purpureus* f. *albus
Deciduous, low-growing shrub with semi-erect stems clothed in leaves, divided into 3 leaflets. A profusion of pea-like, white flowers appear in early summer on previous year's wood. H 45cm (18in), S 60cm (24in).

***Helianthemum* 'Wisley White'**
Evergreen, spreading shrub, with oblong, grey-green leaves, bearing saucer-shaped, white flowers for a long period in summer. H 23cm (9in), S 30cm (12in) or more.

Hebe vernicosa
Evergreen, bushy, compact shrub with small, oval, glossy, dark green leaves densely packed on stems. In early and mid-summer, spikes of small, 4-lobed, white flowers are freely produced. H 60cm (2ft), S 1.2m (4ft).

WHITE–PINK

***Diascia* 'Salmon Supreme'**
Mat-forming perennial with heart-shaped leaves. Dense spikes of pretty, pale-apricot flowers with very small, deeply concave "windows" are produced over a long period, from summer through to autumn. H 15cm (6in), S to 50cm (20in).

Aethionema grandiflorum
(Persian stone cress)
Short-lived, evergreen or semi-evergreen, lax shrub. Bears tiny, pale to deep rose-pink flowers in loose sprays in spring-summer. Blue-green leaves are narrow and lance-shaped. H 30cm (12in), S 23cm (9in).

Onosma alborosea
Semi-evergreen, clump-forming perennial covered in fine hairs, which may irritate skin. Clusters of long, pendent, tubular flowers, borne for a long period in summer, open white and then turn pink. H 15–30cm (6–12in), S 20cm (8in).

***Saxifraga* 'Southside Seedling'**
Evergreen, mat-forming perennial, with large, pale green rosettes of leaves, dying after flowering. In late spring and early summer bears arching panicles of open cup-shaped, white flowers, strongly red-banded within. H and S to 30cm (12in).

Rhodothamnus chamaecistus
Evergreen, low-growing, dwarf shrub with narrow, oval leaves, edged with bristles. In late spring and early summer bears cup-shaped, rose- to lilac-pink flowers, with dark stamens, in leaf axils. H 15–20cm (6–8in), S to 25cm (10in).

PINK

Anthyllis montana
Rounded, bushy or somewhat spreading perennial with loose branches and finely cut foliage. Heads of clover-like, pale pink flowers with red markings are borne in late spring and early summer. H and S 30cm (12in).

Phuopsis stylosa
Low-growing perennial with whorls of pungent, pale green leaves and rounded heads of small, tubular, pink flowers in summer. Is good grown over a bank or large rock. H 30cm (12in), S 30cm (12in) or more.

***Lewisia* 'George Henley'**
Evergreen, clump-forming perennial with rosettes of narrow, fleshy, dark green leaves. Bears dense sprays of open cup-shaped, deep pink flowers, with magenta veins, from late spring to late summer. H 15cm (6in) or more, S 10cm (4in).

***Origanum* 'Kent Beauty'**
Prostrate perennial with trailing stems clothed in aromatic, rounded-oval leaves. In summer bears short spikes of tubular, pale pink flowers with darker bracts. Is suitable for a wall or ledge. H 15–20cm (6–8in), S 30cm (12in).

***Helianthemum* 'Rhodanthe Carneum'**
Evergreen, lax shrub with saucer-shaped, soft, pale pink flowers with orange centres borne for a long period in summer. Has oblong, grey-green leaves. H and S 30cm (12in) or more.

Oxalis tetraphylla
Tuft-forming, tuberous perennial with brown-marked, basal leaves, usually divided into 4 leaflets. Produces loose sprays of widely funnel-shaped, deep pink flowers in late spring and summer. Needs a sheltered site. H 15–30cm (6–10in), S 10–15cm (4–6in).

***Astilbe* 'Perkeo'**
Erect, compact perennial bearing small plumes of tiny, salmon-pink flowers from mid- to late summer on fine stems. Has stiff, deeply cut, crinkled leaves. H 15–20cm (6–8in), S 10cm (4in).

***Diascia cordata* of gardens**
Prostrate perennial with stems clothed in heart-shaped, pale green leaves. Bears terminal clusters of spurred, flat-faced, bright pink flowers in summer and early autumn. H 15–20cm (6–8in), S 20cm (8in).

Diascia rigescens
Trailing perennial with semi-erect stems covered in heart-shaped, mid-green leaves. Spurred, flat-faced, salmon-pink flowers are borne along stem length in summer and early autumn. H 23cm (9in), S to 30cm (12in).

Crassula sarcocaulis
Evergreen or, in severe climates, semi-evergreen, bushy sub-shrub with tiny, oval, succulent leaves. Bears terminal clusters of tiny, red buds opening to pale pink flowers in summer. H and S 30cm (12in).

Ononis fruticosa
(Shrubby restharrow)
Deciduous shrub that in summer bears pendent clusters of large, pea-like, purplish-pink blooms with darker streaks. Leaves are divided into 3 serrated leaflets, which are hairy when young. H and S 30–60cm (12–24in).

Geranium orientalitibeticum
Perennial spreading by tuberous, underground runners. Has cup-shaped, pink flowers, with white centres, in summer. Leaves are deeply cut and marbled in shades of green. May be invasive. H in flower 15–25cm (6–10in), S indefinite.

PINK

Cortusa matthioli
Clump-forming perennial with a basal rosette of rounded, dull green leaves and, in late spring and early summer, one-sided racemes of small, pendent, bell-shaped, reddish- or pinkish-purple flowers. H 15–20cm (6–10in), S 10cm (4in).

Geranium sanguineum
(Bloody cranesbill)
Hummock-forming, spreading perennial with many cup-shaped, deep magenta-pink flowers borne in summer above round, deeply divided, dark green leaves. Makes good ground cover. H to 25cm (10in), S 30cm (12in) or more.

Origanum laevigatum
Deciduous, mat-forming sub-shrub with small, aromatic, dark green leaves, branching, red stems and a profusion of tiny, tubular, cerise-pink flowers, surrounded by red-purple bracts, in summer. H 23–30cm (9–12in), S 20cm (8in) or more.

***Lewisia* Cotyledon Hybrids**
Evergreen, clump-forming perennials with rosettes of large, thick, toothed leaves. In early summer bear clusters of flowers, in various shades of pink to purple, on erect stems. Is good for a rock crevice or an alpine house. H to 30cm (12in), S 15cm (6in) or more.

Dianthus carthusianorum
Evergreen perennial carrying rounded, upward-facing, cherry-red or deep pink flowers on slender stems in summer above small tufts of grass-like leaves. H 20cm (8in), S 6cm (2½in).

RED

Penstemon newberryi* f. *humilior
Evergreen, mat-forming shrub with arching branches clothed in small, leathery, dark green leaves. Bears short sprays of tubular, lipped, cherry-red to deep pink flowers in early summer. H 15–20cm (6–8in), S 30cm (12in).

***Helianthemum* 'Ben More'**
Evergreen, spreading, twiggy shrub that bears a succession of saucer-shaped, reddish-orange flowers in loose, terminal clusters in late spring and summer. Has small, glossy, dark green leaves. H 23–30cm (9–12in), S 30cm (12in).

***Helianthemum* 'Raspberry Ripple'**
Evergreen, spreading shrub with saucer-shaped, red-centred, white flowers that are borne in mid-summer. Has small, linear, grey-green leaves. H 15–23cm (6–9in), S 23–30cm (9–12in).

Penstemon pinifolius
Evergreen, bushy shrub with branched stems clothed in fine, dark green leaves. In summer, very narrow, tubular, orange-red flowers are borne in loose, terminal spikes. H 10–20cm (4–8in), S 15cm (6in).

***Helianthemum* 'Fire Dragon'**
Evergreen, spreading shrub with saucer-shaped, orange-scarlet flowers in late spring and summer. Leaves are linear and grey-green. H 23–30cm (9–12in), S 45cm (18in).

■ RED

Zauschneria californica subsp. ***cana* 'Dublin'**
Clump-forming, woody-based perennial with lance-shaped, grey-green leaves. From late summer to early autumn bears terminal clusters of tubular, deep orange-scarlet flowers. H 30cm (12in), S 45cm (18in).

Punica granatum var. ***nana***
(Dwarf pomegranate)
Slow-growing, deciduous, rounded shrub that, in summer, bears funnel-shaped, red flowers with somewhat crumpled petals, followed by small, rounded, orange-red fruits. H and S 30–90cm (12–36in).

Delphinium nudicaule
Short-lived, upright perennial with erect stems bearing deeply divided, basal leaves and, in summer, spikes of hooded, red or occasionally yellow flowers, with contrasting stamens. H 20cm (8in), S 5–10cm (2–4in).

■ PURPLE

Calceolaria arachnoidea
Evergreen, clump-forming perennial with a basal rosette of wrinkled leaves, covered in white down. Upright stems carry spikes of many pouch-shaped, dull purple flowers in summer. Is best treated as a biennial. H 25cm (10in), S 12cm (5in).

Erodium cheilanthifolium
Compact, mound-forming perennial with pink flowers, veined and marked with purple-red, borne on stiff stems in late spring and summer. Greyish-green leaves are crinkled and deeply cut. H 15–20cm (6–8in), S 20cm (8in) or more.

Scabiosa lucida
Clump-forming perennial with tufts of oval leaves and rounded heads of pale lilac to deep mauve flowers, borne on erect stems in summer. H 20cm (8in), S 15cm (6in).

Penstemon serrulatus
Semi-evergreen sub-shrub, deciduous in severe climates, that has small, elliptic, dark green leaves and tubular, blue to purple flowers borne in loose spikes in summer. Soil should not be too dry. H 60cm (24in), S 30cm (12in).

Erigeron alpinus
(Alpine fleabane)
Clump-forming perennial of variable size that bears daisy-like, lilac-pink flower heads on erect stems in summer. Leaves are long, oval and hairy. Suits a sunny border, bank or large rock garden. H 25cm (10in), S 20cm (8in).

Semiaquilegia ecalcarata
Short-lived, upright perennial with narrow, lobed leaves. In summer each slender stem bears several pendent, open bell-shaped, dusky-pink to purple flowers, with no spurs. H 20cm (8in), S 6cm (2½in).

PURPLE–BLUE

Parahebe catarractae
Evergreen sub-shrub with oval, toothed, mid-green leaves and, in summer, loose sprays of small, open funnel-shaped, white flowers, heavily zoned and veined pinkish-purple. H and S 30cm (12in).

Wulfenia amherstiana
Evergreen perennial with rosettes of narrowly spoon-shaped, toothed leaves. Erect stems bear loose clusters of small, tubular, purple or pinkish-purple flowers in summer. H 15–30cm (6–12in), S to 30cm (12in).

***Phlox divaricata* subsp. *laphamii* 'Chatahoochee'**
Short-lived, clump-forming perennial that has saucer-shaped, red-eyed, bright lavender flowers throughout summer-autumn. Narrow, pointed leaves are dark reddish-purple when young. H 15–20cm (6–8in), S 30cm (12in).

Campanula barbata
(Bearded bellflower)
Evergreen perennial with a basal rosette of oval, hairy, grey-green leaves. In summer bears one-sided racemes of bell-shaped, white to lavender-blue flowers. Is short lived but sets seed freely. H 20cm (8in), S 12cm (5in).

Phlox divaricata* subsp. *laphamii
Semi-evergreen, creeping perennial with oval leaves and upright stems bearing loose clusters of saucer-shaped, pale to deep violet-blue flowers in summer. H 30cm (12in) or more, S 20cm (8in).

Convolvulus sabatius
Trailing perennial with slender stems clothed in small, oval leaves and open trumpet-shaped, vibrant blue-purple flowers in summer and early autumn. Shelter in a rock crevice in a cold site. H 15–20cm (6–8in), S 30cm (12in).

Sisyrinchium graminoides
Semi-evergreen, erect perennial with tufts of grass-like leaves. Small, iris-like, pale to dark purplish-blue flowers with yellow bases are borne in terminal clusters in late spring and early summer. H to 30cm (12in), S 8cm (3in).

Lithodora oleifolia
Evergreen shrub with oval, pointed, silky, mid-green leaves. Curving stems carry loose sprays of several small, funnel-shaped, light blue flowers in early summer. H 15–20cm (6–8in), S to 1m (3ft).

Linum perenne
Upright perennial with slender stems, clothed in grass-like leaves, that bear terminal clusters of open funnel-shaped, clear blue flowers in succession throughout summer. H 30cm (12in), S to 15cm (6in).

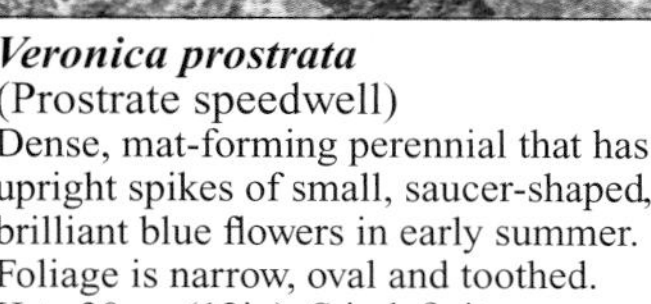

Veronica prostrata
(Prostrate speedwell)
Dense, mat-forming perennial that has upright spikes of small, saucer-shaped, brilliant blue flowers in early summer. Foliage is narrow, oval and toothed. H to 30cm (12in), S indefinite.

Moltkia suffruticosa
Deciduous, upright sub-shrub. In summer bears clusters of funnel-shaped, bright blue flowers, pink in bud, on hairy stems. Leaves are long, pointed and hairy. H 15–40cm (6–16in), S 30cm (12in).

***Veronica prostrata* 'Trehane'**
Dense, mat-forming perennial bearing upright spikes of small, saucer-shaped, deep violet-blue flowers in early summer above narrow, toothed, yellow or yellowish-green leaves. H in flower 15–20cm (6–8in), S indefinite.

***Veronica prostrata* 'Kapitan'**
Dense, mat-forming perennial bearing erect spikes of small, saucer-shaped, bright deep blue flowers in early summer. Foliage is narrow, oval and toothed. H to 30cm (12in), S indefinite.

Mertensia echioides
Clump-forming perennial with basal rosettes of long, oval, hairy, blue-green leaves. Slender stems carry many open funnel-shaped, dark blue flowers in summer. H 15–23cm (6–9in), S 15cm (6in).

Phyteuma scheuchzeri
Tufted perennial with narrow, dark green leaves and terminal heads of spiky, blue flowers that are borne in summer. Seeds freely; dislikes winter wet. H 15–20cm (6–8in), S 10cm (4in).

Symphyandra wanneri
Clump-forming perennial with branching stems and hairy, oval leaves. In summer bears pendent, bell-shaped, blue to violet-blue flowers in loose, terminal spikes. H 15–23cm (6–9in), S 25cm (10in).

***Lithodora diffusa* 'Heavenly Blue'**
Evergreen, prostrate shrub with trailing stems bearing pointed, oblong, hairy leaves and, in summer, many open funnel-shaped, deep blue flowers in leaf axils. Trim stems hard after flowering. H 15–30cm (6–12in), S to 45cm (18in).

BLUE–YELLOW

Veronica austriaca subsp. ***teucrium***
Spreading perennial with narrow spikes of small, flat, outward-facing, bright blue flowers in summer. Leaves are small, divided, hairy and greyish-green. H and S 25–60cm (10–24in).

Erodium chrysanthum
Mound-forming perennial, grown for its dense, silvery stems and finely cut, fern-like leaves. Has small sprays of cup-shaped, sulphur- or creamy-yellow flowers in late spring and summer. H and S 23cm (9in).

Hypericum olympicum f. ***uniflorum* 'Citrinum'**
Deciduous, dense, rounded sub-shrub with tufts of upright stems, clothed in small, oval, grey-green leaves. Bears terminal clusters of lemon-yellow flowers throughout summer. H and S 15–30cm (6–12in).

YELLOW

***Verbascum* 'Letitia'**
Evergreen, stiff-branched shrub with toothed, grey leaves. Bears outward-facing, 5-lobed, bright yellow flowers with reddish-orange centres continuously from late spring to mid-autumn. Hates winter wet; is good in an alpine house. H and S to 25cm (10in).

***Helianthemum* 'Wisley Primrose'**
Fast-growing, evergreen, compact shrub with saucer-shaped, soft pale yellow flowers in summer. Has oblong, grey-green leaves. H 23cm (9in), S 30cm (12in) or more.

Linum arboreum
Evergreen, compact shrub with blue-green leaves. In summer has a succession of funnel-shaped, bright yellow flowers opening in sunny weather and borne in terminal clusters. H to 30cm (12in), S 30cm (12in).

Othonna cheirifolia
Evergreen shrub with narrow, somewhat fleshy, grey leaves. In early summer bears daisy-like, yellow flower heads singly on upright stems. Needs a warm, sheltered site. H 20–30cm (8–12in), S 30cm (12in) or more.

Euryops acraeus
Evergreen, dome-shaped shrub with stems clothed in toothed, silvery-blue leaves. Bears solitary daisy-like, bright yellow flower heads in late spring and early summer. H and S 30cm (12in).

Eriogonum umbellatum
Evergreen, prostrate to upright perennial with mats of green leaves, white and woolly beneath. In summer carries heads of tiny, yellow flowers that later turn copper. Dwarf forms are available. H 8–30cm (3–12in), S 15–30cm (6–12in).

□ YELLOW

Corydalis lutea
Evergreen, clump-forming perennial with fleshy, fibrous roots, semi-erect, basal, grey-green leaves. Bears racemes of slender, yellow flowers, with short spurs, in late spring and summer. H and S 20–30cm (8–12in).

Verbascum dumulosum
Evergreen, mat-forming, shrubby perennial with hairy, grey or grey-green leaves. In late spring and early summer bears a succession of 5-lobed, bright yellow flowers in short racemes. Dislikes winter wet. H 15cm (6in) or more, S 23–30cm (9–12in) or more.

Chrysogonum virginianum
Mat-forming perennial with daisy-like, yellow flower heads borne on short stems in summer-autumn and oval, toothed, mid-green leaves. Although plant spreads by underground runners, it is not invasive. H 15–20cm (6–8in), S 10–15cm (4–6in) or more.

Sedum rupestre
(Reflexed stonecrop)
Evergreen perennial with loose mats of rooting stems bearing narrow, fleshy leaves. Carries flat, terminal heads of tiny, bright yellow flowers in summer. Makes good ground cover. H 15–20cm (6–8in), S indefinite.

Ranunculus gramineus
Erect, slender perennial with grass-like, blue-green leaves. Bears several cup-shaped, bright yellow flowers in late spring and early summer. Prefers rich soil. Seedlings will vary in height and flower size. H 40–50cm (16–20in), S 8–10cm (3–4in).

□ YELLOW–ORANGE

Ononis natrix
(Large yellow restharrow)
Deciduous, compact, erect shrub with pea-like, red-streaked, yellow flowers in pendent clusters in summer. Hairy leaves are divided into 3 leaflets. H and S 30cm (12in) or more.

Genista lydia
Deciduous, domed shrub with slender, arching branches and blue-green leaves. Massed terminal clusters of pea-like, bright yellow flowers appear in late spring and early summer. Will trail over a large rock or wall. H 45–60cm (18–24in), S 60cm (24in) or more.

Crepis aurea
Clump-forming perennial with a basal cluster of oblong, light green leaves. In summer produces dandelion-like, orange flower heads, singly, on stems covered with black and white hairs. H 10–30cm (4–12in), S 15cm (6in).

WHITE–BLUE

Gaultheria cuneata
Evergreen, compact shrub with stiff stems clothed in leathery, oval leaves. In summer bears nodding, urn-shaped, white flowers, in leaf axils, followed by white berries in autumn. H and S 30cm (12in).

Ceratostigma plumbaginoides
Bushy perennial that bears small, terminal clusters of single, brilliant blue flowers on reddish, branched stems in late summer and autumn. Oval leaves turn rich red in autumn. H 45cm (18in), S 20cm (8in).

Sorbus reducta
Deciduous shrub forming a low thicket of upright branches. Small, grey-green leaves, divided into leaflets, turn bronze-red in late autumn. In early summer bears loose clusters of flat, white flowers, followed by pink berries. H and S to 30cm (12in) or more.

Gentiana septemfida
Evergreen perennial with many upright, then arching stems clothed with oval leaves. Bears heads of trumpet-shaped, mid-blue flowers in summer-autumn. Likes humus-rich soil but tolerates reasonably drained, heavy clay. H 15–20cm (6–8in), S 30cm (12in).

WHITE–GREY

Ranunculus calandrinioides
Clump-forming perennial that loses its long, oval, blue-green leaves in summer; in a reasonable winter will bear a succession of cup-shaped, pink-flushed, white flowers for many weeks. Needs very sharp drainage. H and S to 20cm (8in).

Cyathodes colensoi
Evergreen, low-growing shrub with stiff stems clothed in tiny, grey-green leaves. Bears clusters of small, tubular, white flowers in spring at the ends of new growth. Red or white berries in late summer are rare in cultivation. H and S 30cm (12in).

Celmisia semicordata
Evergreen perennial with sword-like, silver leaves in large clumps and, in summer, daisy-like, white flower heads borne singly on hairy stems. H and S 30cm (12in).

Tanacetum argenteum
Mat-forming perennial, usually evergreen, grown for its finely cut, bright silver leaves. Has a profusion of small, daisy-like, white flower heads in summer. H in flower 15–23cm (6–9in), S 20cm (8in).

GREY–GREEN

Tanacetum densum subsp. ***amani***
Clump-forming perennial retaining fern-like, hairy, grey leaves in winter in mild climates. Bears daisy-like, yellow flower heads with woolly bracts in summer. Dislikes winter wet. H and S 20cm (8in).

Ozothamnus coralloides
Evergreen, upright shrub with grey stems clothed in neat, dark green leaves, marked silver. Occasionally bears fluffy, yellow flower heads. Suits a cold frame or an alpine house. Hates winter wet. H 15–23cm (6–9in), S 15cm (6in).

Salix* × *boydii
Very slow-growing, deciduous, upright shrub forming a gnarled, branched bush. Has oval, rough-textured leaves; catkins are rarely produced. Will tolerate light shade. H to 15–23cm (6–9in), S to 30cm (12in).

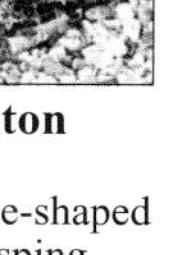

***Hebe cupressoides* 'Boughton Dome'**
Slow-growing, evergreen, dome-shaped shrub with scale-like, stem-clasping, dark grey-green leaves. Has terminal clusters of small, 4-lobed, blue-tinged, white flowers in summer. H 30cm (12in), S to 60cm (24in).

Ozothamnus selago
Evergreen, upright shrub with stiff stems covered in scale-like leaves. Intermittently bears fluffy, creamy-white flower heads. Makes a good foil for spring bulbs. H and S 15–23cm (6–9in).

Ballota pseudodictamnus
Evergreen, mound-forming sub-shrub with rounded, grey-green leaves and stems covered with woolly, white hairs. In summer bears whorls of small, pink flowers with conspicuous, enlarged, pale green calyces. H 60cm (2ft), S 90cm (3ft).

WHITE

Cerastium tomentosum
(Snow-in-summer)
Very vigorous, ground-cover perennial, only suitable for a hot, dry bank, with prostrate stems covered by tiny, grey leaves. In late spring and summer bears star-shaped, white flowers above foliage. H 8cm (3in), S indefinite.

Androsace pyrenaica
Evergreen perennial with small rosettes of tiny, hairy leaves, tightly packed to form hard cushions. Minute, stemless, single, white flowers appear in spring. H 4cm (1½in), S to 10cm (4in).

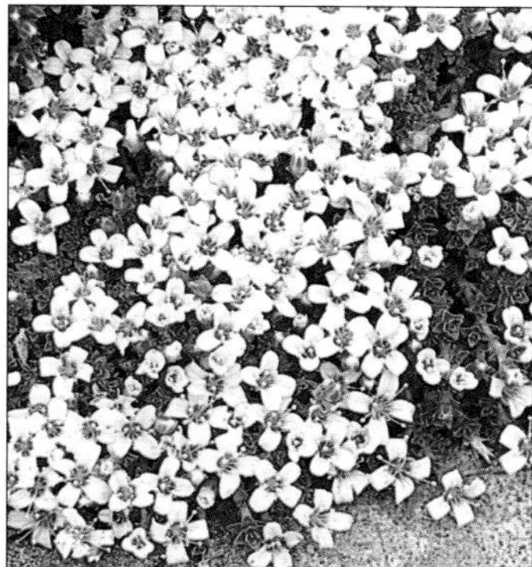

Arenaria tetraquetra
Evergreen perennial that forms a grey-green cushion of small leaves. Stemless, star-shaped, white flowers appear in late spring. Is well-suited a trough or an alpine house. H 2.5cm (1in), S 15cm (6in) or more.

□ WHITE

Cardamine trifolia
Ground-cover perennial with creeping stems clothed in rounded, toothed, 3-parted leaves. In late spring and early summer bears loose heads of open cup-shaped, white flowers on bare stems. H 10–15cm (4–6in), S 30cm (12in).

Androsace vandellii
Evergreen, dense, cushion-forming perennial with narrow, grey leaves and a profusion of stemless, white flowers in spring. Needs careful cultivation with a deep collar of grit under the cushion. H 2.5cm (1in), S to 10cm (4in).

Arabis alpina subsp. ***caucasica* 'Variegata'**
Evergreen, mat-forming perennial with rosettes of oval, cream-splashed, mid-green leaves. Bears bunches of single, sometimes pink-flushed, white flowers from early spring to summer. H and S 15cm (6in).

Saxifraga scardica
Slow-growing, evergreen perennial with hard cushions composed of blue-green rosettes of leaves. In spring bears small clusters of upward-facing, cup-shaped, white flowers. Does best in an alpine house or sheltered scree. H 2.5cm (1in), S 8cm (3in).

Weldenia candida
Perennial with rosettes of strap-shaped, wavy-margined leaves, growing from tuberous roots. Bears a succession of upright, cup-shaped, pure white flowers in late spring and early summer. H and S 8–15cm (3–6in).

Arenaria balearica
Prostrate perennial that is evergreen in all but the most severe winters. Will form a green film over a wet, porous rock face. Minute, white flowers stud mats of foliage in late spring and early summer. H less than 1cm (½in), S indefinite.

Dicentra cucullaria
(Dutchman's breeches)
Compact perennial with fern-like foliage and arching stems each bearing a few small, yellow-tipped, white flowers, like tiny, inflated trousers, in spring. Lies dormant in summer. H 15cm (6in), S to 30cm (12in).

Maianthemum canadense
Vigorous, ground-cover, rhizomatous perennial with large, upright, oval, wavy-edged, glossy leaves. Slender stems bear sprays of small, white flowers in late spring and early summer followed by red berries. H 10cm (4in), S indefinite.

Saxifraga burseriana
Slow-growing, evergreen perennial with hard cushions of spiky, grey-green leaves. In spring bears open cup-shaped, white flowers on short stems. H 2.5–5cm (1–2in), S to 10cm (4in).

Androsace villosa
Evergreen, mat-forming perennial with very hairy rosettes of tiny leaves. Bears umbels of small, white flowers, with yellow centres that turn red, in spring. H 2.5cm (1in), S 20cm (8in).

Sanguinaria canadensis
(Bloodroot)
Rhizomatous perennial with fleshy, underground stems that exude red sap when cut. In spring bears white flowers, sometimes pink-flushed or slate-blue on reverses, as blue-grey leaves unfurl. H 10–15cm (4–6in), S 30cm (12in).

Pulsatilla vernalis
Tufted perennial with rosettes of feathery leaves. Densely hairy, brown flower buds appear in late winter and open in early spring to somewhat nodding, open cup-shaped, pearl-white flowers. Buds dislike winter wet. H 5–10cm (2–4in), S 10cm (4in).

Salix apoda
Slow-growing, deciduous, prostrate shrub. In early spring, male forms bear fat, silky, silver catkins with orange to pale yellow stamens and bracts. Oval, leathery leaves are hairy when young, becoming dark green later. H to 15cm (6in), S 30–60cm (12–24in).

Ranunculus alpestris
(Alpine buttercup)
Short-lived, evergreen, clump-forming perennial that bears cup-shaped, white flowers on erect stems from late spring to mid-summer. Glossy, dark green leaves are rounded and serrated. H 2.5–12cm (1–5in), S 10cm (4in).

Cassiope lycopodioides
Evergreen, prostrate, mat-forming shrub with slender stems densely set with minute, scale-like, dark green leaves. In spring, short, reddish stems carry tiny, bell-shaped, white flowers, in red calyces, singly in leaf axils. H 8cm (3in), S 30cm (12in).

***Ranunculus ficaria* 'Albus'**
Mat-forming perennial bearing in early spring cup-shaped, single, creamy-white flowers with glossy petals. Leaves are heart-shaped and dark green. Can spread rapidly; is good for a wild garden. H 5cm (2in), S 20cm (8in).

WHITE–PINK

Cassiope mertensiana
Evergreen, dwarf shrub with scale-like, dark green leaves tightly pressed to stems. In early spring carries bell-shaped, creamy-white flowers, with green or red calyces, in leaf axils. H 15cm (6in), S 20cm (8in).

Scoliopus bigelowii
Compact perennial with basal, veined leaves, sometimes marked brown. In early spring bears flowers with purple inner petals and greenish-white outer petals with deep purple lines. H 8–10cm (3–4in), S 10–15cm.

Gypsophila cerastioides
Prostrate perennial with a profusion of small, saucer-shaped, purple-veined, white flowers borne in late spring and early summer above mats of rounded, velvety, mid-green foliage. H 2cm (¾in), S to 10cm (4in) or more.

Paraquilegia anemonoides
Tufted perennial with fern-like, blue-green leaves. In spring, pale lavender-blue buds open to pendent, cup-shaped, almost white flowers borne singly on arching stems. May be difficult to establish. H and S 10–15cm (4–6in).

Corydalis popovii
Tuberous perennial with leaves divided into 3–6 bluish-green leaflets. In spring bears loose racemes of deep red-purple and white flowers, each with a long spur. Keep dry when dormant. H and S 10–15cm (4–6in).

Leptinella atrata* subsp. *luteola
Evergreen, mat-forming perennial that in late spring and early summer bears blackish-red flower heads with creamy-yellow stamens. Leaves are small, finely cut and dark green. Needs adequate moisture; best in an alpine house. H 2.5cm (1in), S to 25cm (10in).

Anemonella thalictroides
Perennial with delicate, fern-like leaves growing from a cluster of small tubers. From spring to early summer bears small, cup-shaped, white or pink flowers, singly on finely branched stems. Needs humus-rich soil. H 10cm (4in), S 4cm (1½in) or more.

Lewisia tweedyi
Evergreen, rosetted perennial with large, fleshy leaves and stout, branched stems that bear open cup-shaped, many-petalled, white to pink flowers in spring. Best grown in an alpine house. H 15cm (6in), S 12–15cm (5–6in).

Shortia galacifolia (Oconee bells)
Evergreen, clump-forming, dwarf perennial with round, toothed, leathery, glossy leaves. In late spring bears cup- to trumpet-shaped, often pink-flushed, white flowers with deeply serrated petals. H to 15cm (6in), S 15–23cm (6–9in).

Daphne jasminea
Evergreen, compact shrub. Bears small, white flowers, pink-flushed externally, in late spring and early summer and again in autumn. Brittle stems are clothed in grey-green leaves. Suits an alpine house or a dry wall. H 8–10cm (3–4in), S to 30cm (12in).

Epigaea gaultherioides
Evergreen, prostrate sub-shrub with cup-shaped, shell-pink flowers borne in terminal clusters in spring. Hairy stems carry heart-shaped, dark green leaves. Is difficult to grow and propagate. H to 10cm (4in), S to 25cm (10in) or more.

Trillium rivale
Perennial with oval leaves, divided into 3 leaflets. In spring bears open cup-shaped, white or pale pink flowers with dark-spotted, heart-shaped petals, singly on upright, later arching stems. H to 15cm (6in), S 10cm (4in).

Saxifraga **×** ***irvingii*** **'Jenkinsiae'**
Slow-growing perennial with very tight, grey-green cushions of foliage. Carries a profusion of open cup-shaped, lilac-pink flowers on slender stems in early spring. H 8–10cm (3–4in), S to 15cm (6in).

Androsace carnea
Evergreen, cushion-forming perennial that has small rosettes of pointed leaves with hairy margins. In spring, 2 or more stems rise above each rosette, bearing tiny, single, pink flowers. Suits a trough. H and S 5cm (2in).

Thlaspi cepaeifolium subsp. ***rotundifolium***
Clump-forming perennial with dense tufts of round leaves and small, open cup-shaped, pale to deep purplish- or lilac-pink flowers in spring. Needs cool conditions. May be short-lived. H 5–8cm (2–3in), S 10cm (4in).

Arenaria purpurascens
Evergreen, mat-forming perennial with sharp-pointed, glossy leaves, above which rise many small clusters of star-shaped, pale to deep purplish-pink flowers in early spring. H 1cm (½in), S to 15cm (6in).

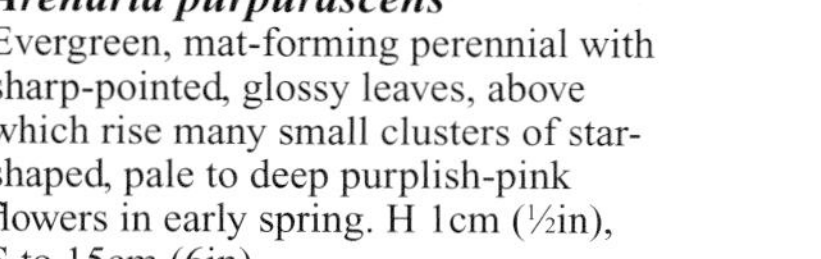

Oxalis acetosella var. ***subpurpurascens***
Creeping, rhizomatous perennial forming mats of 3-lobed leaves. Cup-shaped, soft pink flowers, each 1cm (½in) across, with 5 darker-veined petals, are produced in spring. H 5cm (2in), S indefinite.

Silene acaulis (Moss campion)
Evergreen, cushion-forming perennial with minute, bright green leaves studded with tiny, stemless, 5-petalled, pink flowers in spring. May be difficult to bring into flower; prefers a cool climate. H to 2.5cm (1in), S 15cm (6in).

Armeria juniperifolia
Evergreen, cushion-forming perennial composed of loose rosettes of sharp-pointed, mid- to grey-green leaves. Pale pink flowers are borne in spherical umbels in late spring and early summer. H 5–8cm (2–3in), S 15cm (6in).

Arabis **×** ***arendsii*** **'Rosabella'**
Evergreen, mat-forming perennial with a profusion of single, deep pink flowers in spring and early summer and large rosettes of small, oval, soft green leaves. H 15cm (6in), S 30cm (12in).

PINK

Oxalis adenophylla
Mat-forming, fibrous-rooted, tuberous perennial with grey-green leaves divided into narrow, wavy lobes. In spring bears rounded, purplish-pink flowers, each 2.5–4cm (1–1½in) across, with darker purple eyes. H to 5cm (2in), S 8–10cm (3–4in).

Shortia soldanelloides
Evergreen, mat-forming perennial with rounded, toothed leaves and small, pendent, bell-shaped and fringed, deep pink flowers in late spring. H 5–10cm (2–4in), S 10–15cm (4–6in).

Saxifraga oppositifolia
(Purple mountain saxifrage)
Evergreen, prostrate perennial with clusters of tiny, white-flecked leaves. Has open cup-shaped, dark purple, purplish-pink or, rarely, white flowers in early spring. Likes an open position. H 2.5–5cm (1–2in), S 15cm (6in).

Erinus alpinus
Semi-evergreen, short-lived perennial with rosettes of soft, mid-green leaves covered, in late spring and summer, with small, purple, pink or white flowers. Self seeds freely. H and S 5–8cm (2–3in).

***Daphne petraea* 'Grandiflora'**
Slow-growing, evergreen, compact shrub that bears terminal clusters of fragrant, rich pink flowers in late spring and tiny, glossy leaves. Suits an alpine house, a sheltered, humus-rich rock garden or a trough. H to 15cm (6in), S to 25cm (10in).

Claytonia megarhiza* var. *nivalis
Evergreen perennial with a rosette of spoon-shaped, succulent leaves. Bears small heads of tiny, deep pink flowers in spring. Grows best in a deep pot of gritty compost in an alpine house. H 1cm (½in), S 8cm (3in).

Antennaria dioica* var. *rosea
Semi-evergreen perennial forming a spreading mat of tiny, oval, woolly leaves. Bears fluffy, rose-pink flower heads in small, terminal clusters in late spring and early summer. Is good as ground cover with small bulbs. H 2.5cm (1in), S to 40cm (16in).

Daphne arbuscula
Evergreen, prostrate shrub. In late spring bears many very fragrant, tubular, deep pink flowers in terminal clusters. Narrow, leathery, dark green leaves are crowded at the ends of the branches. Likes humus-rich soil. H 10–15cm (4–6in), S 50cm (20in).

Vaccinium vitis-idaea* subsp. *minus
Evergreen, mat-forming sub-shrub with tiny, oval, leathery leaves. In late spring produces small, erect racemes of many tiny, bell-shaped, deep pink or deep pink-and-white flowers. H 5–8cm (2–3in), S 10–15cm (4–6in).

PINK–RED

***Anagallis tenella* 'Studland'**
Short-lived perennial that forms prostrate mats of tiny, bright green leaves studded in spring with honey-scented, star-shaped, bright pink flowers. H 1cm (½in), S 15cm (6in) or more.

Androsace carnea subsp. ***laggeri***
Evergreen, cushion-forming perennial composed of small, tight rosettes of pointed leaves. Cup-shaped, deep pink flowers are borne in small clusters above cushions in spring. H and S 5cm (2in).

***Corydalis solida* 'George Baker'**
Tuberous perennial with fern-like, divided leaves and dense racemes of spurred, rich deep rose-red flowers in spring. H and S 10–15cm (4–6in).

Saxifraga frederici-augustii subsp. ***grisebachii* 'Wisley Variety'**
Evergreen perennial with rosettes of lime-encrusted leaves. Crosier-shaped stems with pale pink to bright red hairs, bear dense racemes of dark red flowers in spring. H 10cm (4in), S 15cm (6in).

Saxifraga sempervivum
Evergreen, hummock-forming perennial with tight rosettes of tufted, silvery-green leaves. Crosier-shaped flower stems, covered in silvery hairs and emerging from rosettes, bear racemes of dark red flowers in early spring. H and S 10–15cm (4–6in).

Leptinella atrata
Evergreen, mat-forming perennial with small, finely cut, greyish-green leaves and blackish-red flower heads in late spring and early summer. Is uncommon and not easy to grow successfully. H 2.5cm (1in), S to 25cm (10in).

PURPLE

Corydalis diphylla
Tuberous perennial with semi-erect, basal leaves, divided into narrow leaflets, and loose racemes of purple-lipped flowers with white spurs in spring. Protect tubers from excess moisture in summer. H 10–15cm (4–6in), S 8–10cm (3–4in).

Polygonatum hookeri
Slow-growing, dense, rhizomatous perennial that bears loose spikes of several small, bell-shaped, lilac-pink flowers in late spring and early summer. Leaves are tiny and lance-shaped. Suits a peat bed. H to 5cm (2in), S to 30cm (12in).

***Aubrieta* 'Joy'**
Vigorous, evergreen, trailing perennial that forms mounds of soft green leaves. In spring bears double, pale mauve flowers on short stems. H 10cm (4in), S 20cm (8in).

PURPLE

***Aubrieta deltoidea* 'Argenteovariegata'**
Evergreen, compact perennial, grown for its trailing, green leaves which are heavily splashed with creamy-white. Produces pinkish-lavender flowers in spring. H 5cm (2in), S 15cm (6in).

Mazus reptans
Prostrate perennial that has tubular, purple or purplish-pink flowers, with protruding, white lips, spotted red and yellow, borne singly on short stems in spring. Narrow, toothed leaves are in pairs along stem. H to 5cm (2in), S 30cm (12in) or more.

Soldanella villosa
Evergreen, clump-forming perennial with round, leathery, hairy-stalked leaves and nodding, bell-shaped, fringed, purplish-lavender flowers borne on erect stems in early spring. Dislikes winter wet. H 10cm (4in), S 10–15cm (4–6in).

***Aubrieta* 'Hartswood Purple'**
Vigorous, evergreen, mound-forming perennial that carries many short spikes of large, single, violet-purple flowers in spring above small, soft green leaves. H 10cm (4in), S 30cm (12in).

Soldanella alpina
(Alpine snowbell)
Evergreen, clump-forming perennial with tufts of leaves and short, bell-shaped, fringed, pinkish-lavender or purplish-pink flowers in early spring. Is difficult to flower well. H to 8cm (3in), S 8–10cm (3–4in).

Saxifraga stribrnyi
Evergreen, mound-forming perennial with small, lime-encrusted rosettes of leaves. Crosier-shaped stems, covered in pinkish-buff hairs, bear racemes of deep maroon-red flowers above leaves in late spring and early summer. H 8cm (3in), S 10–12cm (4–5in).

***Aubrieta* 'J.S. Baker'**
Evergreen perennial with single, purple flowers in spring borne above mounds of small, soft green leaves. H 10cm (4in), S 20cm (8in).

Polygala chamaebuxus* var. *grandiflora
Evergreen, woody-based perennial with terminal clusters of pea-like, reddish-purple and yellow flowers in late spring and early summer. Leaves are small, oval, leathery and dark green. H to 15cm (6in), S to 30cm (12in).

Viola calcarata
Clump-forming perennial, with oval leaves, that bears flat, outward-facing, single, white, lavender or purple flowers for a long period from late spring to summer. Prefers rich soil. H 10–15cm (4–6in), S to 20cm (8in).

***Aubrieta* 'Cobalt Violet'**
Evergreen, mound-forming perennial with single, blue-violet flowers carried in short, terminal spikes in spring above a mat of small, soft green leaves. H 10cm (4in), S 20cm (8in).

Viola tricolor
(Heartsease, Wild pansy)
Short-lived perennial or annual with neat, flat-faced flowers in combinations of white, yellow and shades of purple from spring to autumn. Self seeds profusely. H 5–15cm (2–6in), S 5–15cm (2–6in) or more.

***Viola riviniana* 'Purpurea'**
Clump-forming perennial with tiny, flat-faced, purple flowers in spring-summer. Leaves are kidney-shaped and dark purple-green. Is invasive but suits a bank, woodland or wild garden. H 2.5–5cm (1–2in), S indefinite.

Viola pedata (Bird's-foot violet)
Clump-forming perennial with finely divided foliage and yellow-centred, pale violet, rarely white flowers borne singly on slender stems in late spring and early summer. Needs sharp drainage; grow in an alpine house. H 5cm (2in) S 8cm (3in).

Mertensia maritima
Prostrate perennial with oval, fleshy, bright silver-blue or silver-grey leaves. Stout stems carry clusters of pendent, funnel-shaped, sky-blue flowers in spring. Is prone to slug damage. Needs very sharp drainage. H 10–15cm (4–6in), S 12cm (5in).

Hepatica nobilis* var. *japonica
Slow-growing perennial with leathery, lobed leaves, semi-evergreen in all but very cold or arid climates. Bears slightly cupped, lilac-mauve, pink or white flowers in spring. H to 8cm (3in), S to 12cm (5in).

Jeffersonia dubia
Tufted perennial with 2-lobed, blue-green leaves, sometimes flushed pink when unfolding. Bears cup-shaped, pale lilac to purplish blue flowers singly in spring. H 10–15cm (4–6in), S to 23cm (9in).

Jancaea heldreichii
Perennial with rosettes of thick, hairy, silver-green leaves, above which rise slender stems bearing clusters of tiny, lavender-blue flowers in late spring. Is rare and difficult to grow and is best in an alpine house. H and S to 8cm (3in).

Synthyris stellata
Evergreen, mounded, rhizomatous perennial that bears dense spikes of small, violet-blue flowers in spring above rounded, deeply toothed leaves. Tolerates sun if soil remains moist. H 10–15cm (4–6in), S 15cm (6in).

BLUE

Myosotis alpestris
(Alpine forget-me-not)
Short-lived, clump-forming perennial producing dense clusters of tiny, bright blue flowers with creamy-yellow eyes in late spring and early summer, just above tufts of hairy leaves. Prefers gritty soil. H and S 10–15cm (4–6in).

Anchusa cespitosa
Evergreen, mound-forming perennial with rosettes of lance-shaped, dark green leaves. In spring, stemless, white-centred, blue flowers appear in centres of rosettes. Old plants do not flower well; take early summer cuttings. H 2.5–5cm (1–2in), S to 23cm (9in).

Gentiana verna (Spring gentian)
Evergreen perennial, often short-lived, with small rosettes of oval, dark green leaves. In early spring, tubular, bright blue flowers with white throats are held upright on short stems. H and S to 5cm (2in).

BLUE–GREEN

Gentiana acaulis
(Stemless gentian)
Evergreen, clump-forming perennial with narrowly oval, glossy leaves. Has trumpet-shaped, deep blue flowers, with green-spotted throats, on short stems in spring and often in autumn. H in leaf 2cm (¾in), S to 10cm (4in) or more.

***Viola tricolor* 'Bowles' Black'**
Clump-forming perennial with flat-faced, very dark violet, almost black, flowers, borne continuously from spring to autumn. Oval leaves are sometimes lobed and toothed. Is short-lived; treat as biennial. H 5–15cm (2–6in), S 5–8cm (2–3in).

Salix reticulata
(Net-veined willow)
Deciduous, spreading, mat-forming shrub. Carries plump, reddish-brown, then yellow catkins on male plants in spring and rounded, slightly crinkled leaves. Likes cool, peaty soil. H 5–8cm (2–3in), S 20cm (8in) or more.

GREEN–YELLOW

Mandragora officinarum
Rosetted, fleshy-rooted perennial with coarse, wavy-edged leaves. Bears funnel-shaped, yellowish- or purplish-white flowers in spring, followed by large, tomato-like, shiny yellow fruits. H 5cm (2in), S 30cm (12in).

Hacquetia epipactis
Clump-forming perennial spreading by short rhizomes. In late winter and early spring bears yellow or yellow-green flower heads, encircled by apple-green bracts, before rounded, 3-parted leaves appear. H 6cm (2½in), S 15–23cm (6–9in).

Euphorbia myrsinites
Evergreen, prostrate perennial with terminal clusters of bright yellow-green flowers in spring. Woody stems are clothed in small, pointed, fleshy, grey leaves. Is good on a wall or ledge. H 5–8cm (2–3in), S to 20cm (8in) or more.

YELLOW

***Saxifraga* × *boydii* 'Hindhead Seedling'**
Evergreen perennial that forms a hard dome of small, tufted, spiny, blue-green leaves. In spring bears upward-facing, open, cup-shaped, pale yellow flowers, 2 or 3 to each short stem. H 2.5cm (1in), S 8cm (3in).

***Saxifraga* × *apiculata* 'Gregor Mendel'**
Evergreen perennial with a tight cushion of bright green foliage. Bears clusters of open, cup-shaped, pale yellow flowers in early spring. H 10–15cm (4–6in), S 15cm (6in) or more.

***Saxifraga* 'Elizabethae'**
Evergreen, cushion-forming perennial, composed of densely packed, tiny rosettes of spiny leaves. In spring, tight upward-facing, bright yellow flowers are carried on tops of red-based stems. H 2.5cm (1in), S 10–15cm (4–6in).

Viola aetolica
Clump-forming perennial bearing flat-faced, yellow flowers singly on upright stems in late spring and early summer. Leaves are oval and mid-green. H 5–8cm (2–3in), S 15cm (6in).

Draba rigida
Evergreen perennial with tight hummocks of minute, dark green leaves. Tiny clusters of bright yellow flowers on fine stems cover hummocks in spring. Suits a rough, scree garden or alpine house. Dislikes winter wet. H 4cm (1½in), S 6cm (2½in).

Draba longisiliqua
Semi-evergreen, cushion-forming perennial composed of firm rosettes of tiny, silver leaves. Bears sprays of small, yellow flowers on long stalks in spring. Needs plenty of water in growth; is best grown in an alpine house. H 5–8cm (2–3in), S 15cm (6in).

Saxifraga sancta
Evergreen, mat-forming perennial with tufts of bright green leaves. Bears short racemes of upward-facing, open cup-shaped, bright yellow flowers in spring. H 5cm (2in), S 15cm (6in).

Dionysia aretioides
Evergreen perennial forming cushions of soft, hairy, greyish-green leaves that are covered in early spring by scented, stemless, round, bright yellow flowers. H 5–10cm (2–4in), S 15–30cm (6–12in).

YELLOW

Draba mollissima
Semi-evergreen, cushion-forming perennial with clusters of tiny, yellow flowers on slender stems in spring. Minute leaves form a soft green dome, which should be packed beneath with small stones. Grow in an alpine house. H 4cm (1½in), S 15cm (6in) or more.

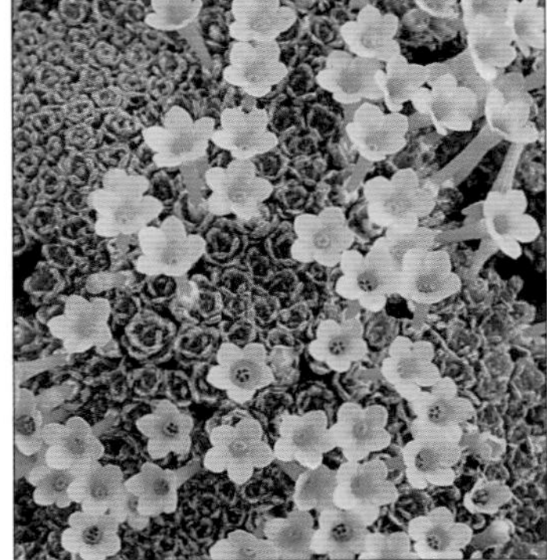

Dionysia tapetodes
Evergreen, prostrate perennial producing a tight mat of tiny, grey-green leaves. Bears small, upward-facing, yellow flowers in early spring. H 1cm (½in), S to 15cm (6in).

Morisia monanthos
Prostrate perennial with flat rosettes of divided, leathery, dark green leaves. Bears stemless, flat, bright yellow flowers in late spring and early summer. Needs very sharp drainage. H 2.5cm (1in), S to 8cm (3in).

***Ranunculus ficaria* 'Flore Pleno'**
Mat-forming perrennial with heart-shaped, dark green leaves and, in early spring, double, bright yellow flowers with glossy petals. May spread rapidly. Is good for a wild garden. H 2.5–5cm (1–2in), S 20cm (8in).

Vitaliana primuliflora
Evergreen, prostrate perennial with a mat of rosetted, mid-green leaves that are covered in spring with many small clusters of stemless, tubular, bright yellow flowers. H 2.5cm (1in), S 20cm (8in).

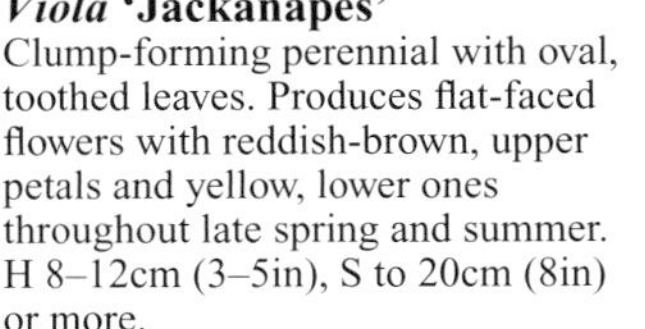

***Viola* 'Jackanapes'**
Clump-forming perennial with oval, toothed leaves. Produces flat-faced flowers with reddish-brown, upper petals and yellow, lower ones throughout late spring and summer. H 8–12cm (3–5in), S to 20cm (8in) or more.

YELLOW

Trollius pumilus
Tufted perennial with leaves divided into 5 segments, each further lobed. Carries solitary cup-shaped, bright yellow flowers in late spring and early summer. H 15cm (6in), S 15cm (6in) or more.

Erysimum helveticum
Semi-evergreen, clump-forming perennial with closely-packed tufts of long, narrow leaves and many fragrant, bright yellow flowers borne in flat heads in late spring and early summer. H 10cm (4in), S 15cm (6in).

***Ranunculus ficaria* 'Aurantiacus'**
Mat-forming perennial bearing in early spring cup-shaped, single, orange flowers with glossy petals. Leaves are heart-shaped and mid-green. May spread rapidly. Is good for a wild garden. H 5cm (2in), S 20cm (8in).

WHITE

Silene alpestris
Perennial with branching stems and narrow leaves. Bears small, rounded, fringed, white, occasionally pink-flushed flowers in late spring and early summer. Self seeds freely. H 10–15cm (4–6in), S 20cm (8in).

***Phlox stolonifera* 'Ariane'**
Evergreen, low-growing perennial with flowering side shoots that bear heads of open, saucer-shaped, white blooms in early summer. Has oval, pale green leaves. Cut back flowered shoots by half after flowering. H to 15cm (6in), S 30cm (12in).

Achillea clavennae
Semi-evergreen, carpeting perennial that bears loose clusters of white flower heads with gold centres from summer to mid-autumn. Leaves are narrowly oval, many-lobed and covered with fine, white hairs. Dislikes winter wet. H 15cm (6in), S 23cm (9in) or more.

***Haberlea rhodopensis* 'Virginalis'**
Evergreen perennial with small, arching sprays of funnel-shaped, pure white flowers borne in late spring and early summer above neat rosettes of oval, toothed, dark green leaves. H and S in flower 10–15cm (4–6in).

Potentilla alba
Vigorous mat-forming perennial bearing loose sprays of flat, single, white flowers in summer. Leaves are divided into oval leaflets and are silvery beneath. H 5–8cm (2–3in), S 8cm (3in).

Cyananthus lobatus* f. *albus
Prostrate perennial with branched stems clothed in small, wedge-shaped, dull green leaves. Bears funnel-shaped, single, white flowers with spreading lobes in late summer. H 8cm (3in), S 30cm (12in).

***Campanula carpatica* 'Bressingham White'**
Clump-forming perennial bearing open cup-shaped, white flowers, singly on unbranched stems, in summer. Has abundant, rounded, bright green leaves. H 10–15cm (4–6in), S 15cm (6in).

Lewisia rediviva [white form]
(Bitter root)
Tufted, rosetted perennial with clusters of fine, narrow leaves that are summer-deciduous. Bears large, white flowers that open in bright weather in late spring and early summer. H 1–4cm (½–1½in), S to 5cm (2in).

□ WHITE

Arenaria montana
Prostrate perennial that forms loose mats of small, narrowly oval leaves and bears large, round, white flowers in summer. Suits a wall or rock crevice. Must have adequate moisture. H 5cm (2in), S 12cm (5in).

Epilobium chlorifolium* var. *kaikourense
Clump-forming, woody-based perennial with deciduous but persistent, oval, hairy, bronze and dark green leaves. In summer has short spikes of funnel-shaped, white to pink flowers. H 10cm (4in), S 15cm (6in).

Gentiana saxosa
Evergreen, hummock-forming perennial clothed in small, spoon-shaped, fleshy, dark green leaves. Produces small, upturned, bell-shaped, white flowers in early summer. Is a short-lived scree plant. H 5cm (2in), S 15cm (6in).

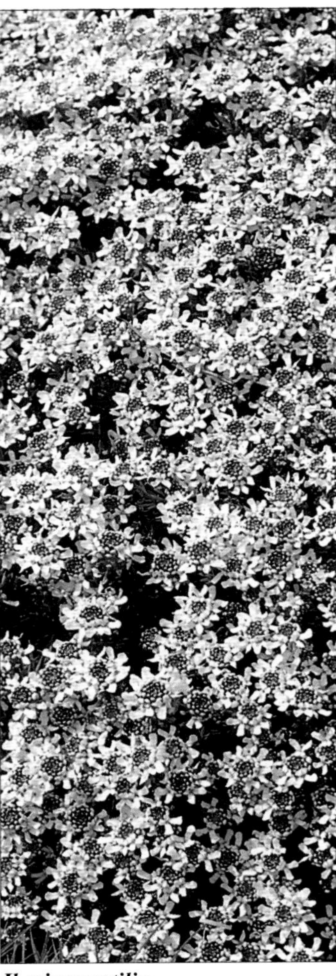

Iberis saxatilis
Evergreen, dwarf sub-shrub that in late spring and early summer produces large heads of numerous small, white flowers, which become tinged violet with age. Glossy, dark leaves are linear and cylindrical. Trim after flowering. H 8–12cm (3–5in), S 30cm (12in).

Cornus canadensis
(Creeping dogwood)
Ground-cover perennial with whorls of oval leaves. In late spring and early summer bears green, sometimes purple-tinged flowers, within white bracts, followed by red berries. H 10–15cm (4–6in), S 30cm (12in) or more.

Celmisia ramulosa
Evergreen, shrubby perennial with small, hairy, grey-green leaves. Daisy-like, white flower heads are borne singly on short stems in late spring and early summer. H and S 10cm (4in).

Ourisia caespitosa
Evergreen, prostrate perennial with creeping rootstocks and stems bearing tiny, oval leaves and many outward-facing, open cup-shaped, white flowers in late spring and early summer. H 2.5cm (1in), S 10cm (4in).

Nierembergia repens
Mat-forming perennial with upright, open bell-shaped, yellow-centred, white flowers, occasionally flushed pink with age, borne for a long period in summer. Leaves are small, oval and light green. Is useful for cracks in paving. H 5cm (2in), S 20cm (8in) or more.

Anacyclus pyrethrum* var. *depressus
Short-lived, prostrate perennial that has white flower heads, with red reverses to ray petals, in summer. Flowers close in dull light. Stems are clothed in fine leaves. Dislikes wet. H 2.5–5cm (1–2in) or more, S 10cm (4in).

Petrocosmea kerrii
Evergreen perennial with compact rosettes of oval, pointed, hairy, rich green leaves. In summer bears clusters of short, outward-facing, tubular, open-mouthed white flowers. Suits an alpine house. H to 8cm (3in), S 12–15cm (5–6in). Min. 2–5°C (36–41°F)

WHITE–PINK

Dryas octopetala
Evergreen, prostrate perennial forming mats of oval, lobed, leathery, dark green leaves on stout stems. In late spring and early summer, cup-shaped, creamy-white flowers are borne just above foliage, followed by attractive, feathery seeds. H 6cm (2½in), S indefinite.

Achillea* × *kellereri
Semi-evergreen perennial that bears daisy-like, white flower heads in loose clusters in summer. Leaves are feathery and grey-green. Is good for a wall or bank. Dislikes winter wet and must have perfect drainage. H 15cm (6in), S 23cm (9in) or more.

Carlina acaulis (Alpine thistle)
Clump-forming perennial that in summer-autumn bears large, stemless, thistle-like, single, off-white or pale brown flower heads, with papery bracts, on rosettes of long, spiny-margined, deeply-cut leaves. H 8–10cm (3–4in), S 15–23cm (6–9in).

Linnaea borealis (Twin flower)
Evergreen, mat-forming, sub-shrubby perennial with rooting stems bearing small, oval leaves, above which in summer rise thread-like stems bearing pairs of small, fragrant, tubular, pale pink and white flowers. H 2cm (¾in), S 30cm (12in) or more.

Dianthus pavonius
Evergreen, prostrate perennial with comparatively large, rounded, pale to deep pink flowers, buff on reverses, borne on short stems in summer above low mats of spiky leaves. H 5cm (2in), S 8cm (3in).

***Gypsophila repens* 'Dorothy Teacher'**
Semi-evergreen, prostrate perennial. Sprays of small, rounded, white flowers, which age to deep pink, cover mats of narrow, bluish-green leaves in summer. trim stems after flowering. H 2.5–5cm (1–2in), S 30cm (12in) or more.

PINK

Petrorhagia saxifraga
(Tunic flower)
Mat-forming perennial with tufts of grass-like leaves. In summer bears a profusion of small, pale pink flowers, veined deeper pink, on slender stems. Grows best on poor soil and self-seeds easily. H 10cm (4in), S 15cm (6in).

Convolvulus althaeoides
Vigorous perennial with long, trailing stems clothed in heart-shaped, cut, mid-green leaves, overlaid silver. Bears large, open trumpet-shaped pink flowers in summer. May be invasive in a mild climate. H 5cm (2in), S indefinite.

Thymus cilicicus
Compact, cushion-forming, aromatic sub-shrub with upright stems covered in small, prominently veined, dark-green leaves. In early summer, bears lilac or mauve flowers in dense rounded heads. H 15cm (6in), S 20cm (8in).

PINK

Geranium sanguineum var. ***striatum***
Hummock-forming, spreading perennial that has cup-shaped, pink flowers, with darker veins, borne singly in summer above round, deeply divided, dark green leaves. H 10–15cm (4–6in), S 30cm (12in) or more.

Ourisia microphylla
Semi-evergreen, mat-forming perennial, with neat, scale-like, pale green leaves, bearing a profusion of small, pink flowers in late spring and early summer. Is difficult to grow in an arid climate. H 5–10cm (2–4in), S 15cm (6in).

Asperula suberosa
Clump-forming perennial with a mound of loose stems bearing tiny, hairy, grey leaves and, in early summer, many tubular, pale pink flowers. 2Dislikes winter wet but needs moist soil in summer. Is best in an alpine house. H 8cm (3in), S to 30cm (12in).

Erodium corsicum
Compact, clump-forming perennial that has soft, grey-green leaves with wavy margins. Bears flat-faced, pink flowers, with darker veins, on stiff, slender stems in late spring and summer. Is best in an alpine house as dislikes winter wet. H 8cm (3in), S 15cm (6in).

Saponaria × olivana
Compact perennial with a firm cushion of narrow leaves. Flowering stems, produced around edges of the cushion, bear flat, single, pale pink flowers in summer. Needs very sharp drainage. H 8cm (3in), S 10cm (4in).

Rhodohypoxis **'Margaret Rose'**
Perennial with a tuber-like rootstock and an erect, basal tuft of narrowly lance-shaped, hairy leaves. Bears a succession of upright, flattish, pale pink flowers on slender stems in spring and early summer. H 5–10cm (2–4in), S 2.5–5cm (1–2in).

Aethionema **'Warley Rose'**
Short-lived, evergreen or semi-evergreen, compact sub-shrub with tiny, linear, bluish-green leaves. Bears racemes of small, pink flowers on short stems in profusion in spring-summer. H and S 15cm (6in).

Phlox adsurgens **'Wagon Wheel'**
Evergreen, prostrate perennial forming wide mats of woody stems, clothed in oval leaves. Bears heads of wheel-shaped, pink flowers with narrow petals in summer. Needs humus-rich soil. H 10cm (4in), S 30cm (12in).

Persicaria affinis **'Donald Lowndes'**
Evergreen, mat-forming perennial that has stout, branching, spreading stems clothed with pointed leaves. In summer bears dense spikes of small, red flowers, which become paler with age. H 8–15cm (3–6in), S to 15cm (6in).

Geranium dalmaticum
Prostrate, spreading perennial with outward-facing, almost flat, shell-pink flowers borne in summer above divided, dark green leaves. Will grow taller in partial shade and is evergreen in all but severest winters. H 8–10cm (3–4in) or more, S 12–20cm (5–8in).

Erigeron karvinskianus
Spreading perennial with lax stems bearing narrow, lance-shaped, hairy leaves and, in summer-autumn, daisy-like flower heads that open white, turn pink and fade to purple. H 10–15cm (4–6in), S indefinite.

Aethionema armenum
Short-lived, evergreen or semi-evergreen, dense sub-shrub with narrow, blue-green leaves. Carries loose sprays of tiny, pale to deep pink flowers in summer. H and S 15cm (6in).

Androsace lanuginosa
Evergreen, trailing perennial with loose stems, covered in silky hairs, carrying deep green leaves and, in summer, clusters of small, flat, lilac-pink or pale pink flowers with dark pink or yellow eyes. H 4cm (1½in), S to 18cm (7in).

***Dianthus* 'Little Jock'**
Evergreen, compact, clump-forming perennial with spiky, silvery-green foliage. In summer produces strongly fragrant, rounded, semi-double, pink flowers, with darker eyes, above foliage. H and S 10cm (4in).

Dianthus gratianopolitanus
(Cheddar pink)
Evergreen perennial with loose mats of narrow, grey-green leaves. In summer, produces very fragrant, flat, pale pink flowers on slender stems. H to 15cm (6in), S to 30cm (12in).

Loiseleuria procumbens
(Alpine azalea, Trailing azalea)
Evergreen, prostrate shrub with small, oval leaves, hairy and beige beneath. Has terminal clusters of open funnel-shaped, rose-pink to white flowers in early summer. H to 8cm (3in), S 10–15cm (4–6in).

Acantholimon glumaceum
Evergreen, cushion-forming perennial with hard, spiny, dark green leaves and short spikes of small, star-shaped, pink flowers in summer. H 10cm (4in), S 20cm (8in).

PINK

***Dianthus* 'Pike's Pink'**
Evergreen, compact, cushion-forming perennial, with spiky, grey-green foliage, that bears fragrant, rounded, double, pink flowers in summer. H and S 10cm (4in).

Saponaria caespitosa
Mat-forming perennial with small, lance-shaped leaves. Tiny, flat, single, pink to purple flowers are borne in small heads in summer. Needs very sharp drainage. H 8cm (3in), S 10cm (4in).

Oxalis depressa
Tuberous perennial with 3-lobed leaves and short-stemmed, widely funnel-shaped, bright rose-pink flowers, 2cm (3/4in) across, in summer. Needs a sheltered site or cool greenhouse. H 5cm (2in), S 8–10cm (3–4in).

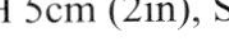

Androsace villosa* var. *jacquemontii
Evergreen, mat-forming perennial with small rosettes of hairy, grey-green leaves. Bears tiny, pinkish-purple flowers on red stems in late spring and early summer. Suits an alpine house. H 1–4cm (1/2–1 1/2in), S 20cm (8in).

Dianthus microlepis
Evergreen perennial with tiny tufts of minute, fine, grass-like leaves, above which rise numerous small, rounded, pink flowers in early summer. Is best suited to a trough. H 5cm (2in), S 20cm (8in).

Saponaria ocymoides
(Tumbling Ted)
Perennial with compact or loose, sprawling mats of hairy, oval leaves, above which a profusion of tiny, flat, pale pink to crimson flowers is carried in summer. Is excellent on a dry bank. H 2.5–8cm (1–3in), S 40cm (16in).

Dianthus myrtinervius
Evergreen, spreading perennial with numerous small, rounded, pink flowers that appear in summer above tiny, grass-like leaves. H 5cm (2in), S 20cm (8in).

***Dianthus* 'La Bourboule'**
Evergreen perennial with small clumps of tufted, spiky foliage. Bears a profusion of strongly fragrant, small, single, pink flowers in summer. H 5cm (2in), S 8cm (3in).

Dianthus alpinus (Alpine pink)
Evergreen, compact perennial that bears comparatively large, rounded, rose-pink to crimson flowers, singly in summer, above mats of narrow, dark green foliage. Likes humus-rich soil. H 5cm (2in), S 8cm (3in).

***Phlox subulata* 'Marjorie'**
Evergreen, mound-forming perennial with fine leaves and a profusion of flat, star-shaped, bright rose-pink flowers in early summer. Trim after flowering. H 10cm (4in), S 20cm (8in).

***Dianthus* 'Annabelle'**
Evergreen, compact, clump-forming perennial with spiky, grey-green foliage. In summer bears fragrant, rounded, semi-double, cerise-pink flowers, singly on slender stems. H and S 10cm (4in).

***Phlox* 'Camla'**
Evergreen mound-forming perennial with wiry, arching stems and fine leaves. Has a profusion of open saucer-shaped, rich pink flowers in early summer. Trim after flowering. Needs humus-rich soil. H 12cm (5in), S 30cm (12in).

***Geranium cinereum* 'Ballerina'**
Spreading, rosetted perennial that bears cup-shaped, purplish-pink flowers, with deep purple veins, on lax stems in late spring and summer. Basal leaves are round, deeply divided and soft. H 10cm (4in), S 30cm (12in).

Teucrium polium
Deciduous, dome-shaped sub-shrub that has much-branched, woolly, white or yellowish stems and leaves with scalloped margins. Bears yellowish-white or pinkish-purple flowers in flat heads in summer. Requires very sharp drainage. H and S 15cm (6in).

Lewisia rediviva [pink form] (Bitter root)
Tufted, rosetted perennial. Clusters of narrow leaves are summer-deciduous. Large, many-petalled, pink flowers open on bright days in late spring and early summer. Suits an alpine house. H 1–4cm (½–1½in), S to 5cm (2in).

***Phlox douglasii* 'Crackerjack'**
Evergreen, compact, mound-forming perennial. Has a profusion of saucer-shaped, bright crimson or magenta flowers in early summer. Leaves are lance-shaped and mid-green. Cut back after flowering. H to 8cm (3in), S 20cm (8in).

Silene schafta
Spreading perennial with tufts of narrow, oval leaves. Bears sprays of 5-petalled, rose-magenta flowers from late spring to late autumn. H 10–15cm (4–6in), S 8–10cm (3–4in).

Geranium cinereum* var. *subcaulescens
Spreading perennial with round, deeply divided, soft leaves. In summer bears brilliant purple-magenta flowers, with striking, black eyes and stamens, on lax stems. H 10cm (4in), S 30cm (12in).

PINK

***Rhodohypoxis* 'Albrighton'**
Perennial with tuber-like rootstock and an erect, basal tuft of narrowly lance-shaped, hairy leaves. Bears a succession of erect, deep pink flowers singly on slender stems in spring and early summer. H 5–10cm (2–4in), S 2.5–5cm (1–2in).

***Armeria maritima* 'Vindictive'**
Evergreen, clump-forming perennial with grass-like, dark blue-green leaves, above which rise stiff stems bearing spherical heads of small, deep rose-pink flowers for a long period in summer. H 10cm (4in), S 15cm (6in).

***Dianthus deltoides* 'Leuchtfunk'**
Evergreen, mat-forming perennial. Many small, flat, upward-facing, brilliant cerise flowers are borne singly above tiny, oblong, pointed leaves. H 10–15cm (4–6in), S 20cm (8in).

RED–PURPLE

***Rhodohypoxis* 'Douglas'**
Perennial with a tuber-like rootstock and an erect, basal tuft of narrowly lance-shaped, hairy leaves. Bears a succession of upright, flattish, rich deep red flowers singly on slender stems in spring and early summer. H 5–10cm (2–4in), S 2.5–5cm (1–2in).

Penstemon hirsutus* var. *pygmaeus
Short-lived, evergreen, compact sub-shrub that bears tubular, lipped, hairy, purple- or blue-flushed, white flowers in summer. Has tightly packed, dark green leaves and is suitable for a trough. H and S 8cm (3in).

Pterocephalus perennis
Semi-evergreen, mat-forming perennial with crinkled, hairy leaves. Bears tight, rounded heads of tubular, pinkish-lavender flowers, singly on short stems in summer, followed by feathery seed heads. H 5cm (2in), S 10cm (4in).

PURPLE

***Phlox douglasii* 'Boothman's Variety'**
Evergreen, mound-forming perennial with lance-shaped leaves and masses of pale lavender-blue flowers, with violet-blue markings around eyes, in early summer. Cut back after flowering. H to 5cm (2in), S 20cm (8in).

Physoplexis comosa
Tufted perennial with deeply cut leaves and round heads of bottle-shaped, violet-blue, rarely white, flowers in summer. Suits crevices but dislikes winter wet. H 8cm (3in), S 10cm (4in).

Globularia meridionalis
Evergreen, dome-shaped sub-shrub. In summer, globular, fluffy, lavender to lavender-purple flower heads are borne singly just above glossy leaves. H to 10cm (4in), S to 20cm (8in).

Thymus leucotrichus
Evergreen, aromatic, mound-forming sub-shrub with fine, twiggy stems and narrow leaves fringed with white hairs. Bears dense heads of small, pinkish-purple flowers with purple bracts in summer. H 10–12cm (4–5in), S 15cm (6in).

***Phlox* 'Emerald Cushion'**
Evergreen perennial with emerald-green mounds of fine leaves, studded in late spring and early summer with large, saucer-shaped, bright violet-blue flowers. Trim after flowering. H 8cm (3in), S 15cm (6in).

Phlox bifida (Sand phlox)
Evergreen, mound-forming perennial with lance-shaped leaves. Bears a profusion of small heads of star-shaped, lilac or white flowers with deeply cleft petals in summer. Cut back stems by half after flowering. H 10–15cm (4–6in), S 15cm (6in).

***Viola* 'Nellie Britton'**
Clump-forming perennial with small, oval, toothed leaves and flat-faced, lavender-pink flowers borne from late spring to late summer. Soil should not be too dry. H 8–15cm (3–6in), S to 20cm (8in).

Thymus herba-barona
(Caraway thyme)
Evergreen sub-shrub with a loose mat of tiny, caraway-scented, dark green leaves. In summer, small, lilac flowers are borne in terminal clusters. H in flower 5–10cm (2–4in), S to 20cm (8in).

Campanula poscharskyana
Rampant, spreading perennial with bell-shaped, violet flowers borne on leafy stems in summer. Leaves are round with serrated edges. Vigorous runners make it suitable for a bank or a wild garden. H 10–15cm (4–6in), S indefinite.

Aster alpinus
Clump-forming, spreading perennial with lance-shaped, dark green leaves. Bears daisy-like, purplish-blue or pinkish-purple flower heads, with yellow centres, from mid- to late summer. H 15cm (6in), S 30–45cm (12–18in).

Edraianthus serpyllifolius
Evergreen, prostrate perennial with tight mats of tiny leaves and small, bell-shaped, deep violet flowers, borne on short stems in early summer. Is uncommon and seldom sets seed in gardens. H 1cm (½in), S to 5cm (2in).

***Campanula carpatica* 'Jewel'**
Low-growing, compact and clump-forming perennial with mid-green, toothed leaves on branching stems. Bright, purple-blue, upturned, bell-shaped flowers are produced over several months in summer. H and S 10–15cm (4–6in).

PURPLE

Prunella grandiflora
(Large self-heal)
Semi-evergreen, spreading, mat-forming perennial with basal rosettes of leaves. In mid-summer bears short spikes of funnel-shaped, purple flowers in whorls. H 10–15cm (4–6in), S 30cm (12in).

***Campanula* 'Birch Hybrid'**
Vigorous, evergreen perennial with tough, arching, prostrate stems and ivy-shaped, bright green leaves. Bears many open bell-shaped, deep violet flowers in summer. H 10cm (4in), S 30cm (12in) or more.

Campanula portenschlagiana
Vigorous, evergreen, prostrate perennial with dense mats of small, ivy-shaped leaves and large clusters of erect, open bell-shaped, violet flowers in summer. H 15cm (6in), S indefinite.

Ramonda myconi
Evergreen, rosette-forming perennial with hairy, crinkled leaves and, in late spring and early summer, flat, blue-mauve, pink or white flowers, borne on branched stems. H 8cm (3in), S to 10cm (4in).

***Viola* 'Huntercombe Purple'**
Perennial forming wide clumps of neat, oval, toothed leaves. Has a profusion of flat-faced, rich violet flowers from spring to late summer. Divide clumps every 3 years. H 10–15cm (4–6in), S 15–30cm (6–12in) or more.

Pinguicula grandiflora
Clump-forming perennial with a basal rosette of sticky, oval, pale green leaves. In summer bears spurred, open funnel-shaped, violet-blue to purple flowers singly on upright, slender stems. H 12–15cm (5–6in), S 5cm (2in).

***Campanula* 'G.F. Wilson'**
Neat, mound-forming perennial with large, upturned, bell-shaped, violet flowers in summer. Has rounded, pale yellow-green leaves. H 8–10cm (3–4in), S 12–15cm (5–6in).

Edraianthus pumilio
Short-lived perennial with low tufts of fine, grass-like leaves. In early summer, upturned, bell-shaped, pale to deep lavender flowers, on very short stems, appear amid foliage. H 2.5cm (1in), S 8cm (3in).

Cyananthus microphyllus
Mat-forming perennial with very fine, red stems clothed in tiny leaves. Bears funnel-shaped, violet-blue flowers at the end of each stem in late summer. Likes humus-rich soil. H 2cm (¾in), S 20cm (8in).

Sisyrinchium idahoense
Semi-evergreen, upright, clump-forming perennial that for a long period in summer and early autumn has many flowering stems carrying tiny tufts of iris-like, blue to violet-blue flowers. Foliage is grass-like. Self seeds readily. H to 12cm (5in), S 10cm (4in).

Globularia cordifolia
Evergreen, mat-forming, dwarf shrub with creeping, woody stems clothed in tiny, oval leaves. Bears stemless, round, fluffy, blue to pale lavender-blue flower heads in summer. H 2.5–5cm (1–2in), S to 20cm (8in).

Aquilegia jonesii
Compact perennial that bears short-spurred, violet-blue flowers in summer, a few to each slender stem. Has small rosettes of finely divided, blue-grey or grey-green leaves. Is uncommon, suitable for an alpine house only. H 2.5cm (1in), S to 5cm (2in).

Campanula cochleariifolia
(Fairy thimbles)
Spreading perennial. Runners produce mats of rosetted, tiny, round leaves. Bears small clusters of white, lavender or pale blue flowers in summer on many thin stems above foliage. H 8cm (3in), S indefinite.

Townsendia grandiflora
Short-lived, evergreen perennial with basal rosettes of small, spoon-shaped leaves. Upright stems carry solitary daisy-like, violet or violet-blue flower heads in late spring and early summer. H to 15cm (6in), S 10cm (4in).

Pratia pedunculata
Vigorous, evergreen, creeping perennial with small leaves and a profusion of star-shaped, pale to mid-blue or occasionally purplish-blue flowers borne in summer. Makes good ground cover in a moist site. H 1cm (½in), S indefinite.

Trachelium asperuloides
Mat-forming perennial with thread-like stems clothed in minute, mid-green leaves, above which rise many tiny, upright, tubular, pale blue flowers in summer. Do not remove old stems in winter. H 8cm (3in), S to 15cm (6in).

Hedyotis michauxii
(Creeping bluets)
Vigorous perennial with rooting stems. Produces mats of mid-green foliage studded with star-shaped, violet-blue flowers in late spring and early summer. H 8cm (3in), S 30cm (12in).

Eritrichium nanum
Clump-forming perennial with tufts of hairy, grey-green leaves. Bears small, stemless, flat, pale blue flowers in late spring and early summer. Requires sharp drainage. Is only suitable for an alpine house. H 2cm (¾in), S 2.5cm (1in).

BLUE

Parochetus communis (Shamrock pea)
Evergreen, prostrate perennial with clover-like leaves and pea-like, brilliant blue flowers that are borne almost continuously. Grows best in an alpine house. H 2.5–5cm (1–2in), S indefinite.

***Polygala calcarea* 'Bulley's Form'**
Evergreen, prostrate perennial with rosettes of small, narrowly oval leaves and loose heads of deep blue flowers in late spring and early summer. Likes humus-rich soil. Suits a trough. H 2.5cm (1in), S 8–10cm (3–4in).

Polygala calcarea
Evergreen, prostrate, occasionally upright, perennial. Has small, narrowly oval leaves and pale to dark blue flowers in late spring and early summer. Likes humus-rich soil. Suits a trough. May be difficult to establish. H 2.5cm (1in), S to 15cm (6in).

GREEN–YELLOW

Gunnera magellanica
Mat-forming perennial, grown for its rounded, toothed leaves, often bronze-tinged when young, on short, creeping stems. Small, green, unisexual flowers, with reddish-bracts, are borne on male and female plants. Likes peaty soil. H 2.5cm (1in), S to 30cm (12in).

Mitella breweri
Neat, clump-forming, rhizomatous perennial with slender, hairy stems bearing small, pendent, tubular, greenish-white flowers, with flared mouths, in summer. Has lobed, kidney-shaped, basal leaves. H and S 15cm (6in).

Sedum acre (Biting stonecrop, Common stonecrop)
Evergreen, mat-forming perennial with dense, spreading shoots and tiny, fleshy, pale green leaves. Bears flat, terminal heads of tiny, yellow summer flowers. Is invasive but easily controlled. H 2.5–5cm (1–2in), S indefinite.

YELLOW

Asarina procumbens
Semi-evergreen perennial with trailing stems bearing soft, hairy leaves and tubular, pale cream flowers, with yellow palates, throughout summer. Dislikes winter wet. Self seeds freely. H 1–2.5cm (½–1in), S 23–30cm (9–12in).

Papaver fauriei
Short-lived, clump-forming perennial with basal rosettes of finely cut, hairy, soft grey leaves. Bears pendent, open cup-shaped, pale yellow flowers in summer. Dislikes winter wet. H and S 5–10cm (2–4in).

Polygala chamaebuxus
Evergreen, woody-based perennial with tiny, hard, dark green leaves. In late spring and early summer bears many racemes of small, pea-like, white-and-yellow flowers, sometimes marked brown. Needs humus-rich soil. H 5cm (2in), S 20cm (8in).

***Sedum acre* 'Aureum'**
Evergreen, mat-forming perennial with spreading shoots, yellow-tipped in spring and early summer, clothed in tiny, fleshy, yellow leaves. Has flat heads of tiny, yellow flowers in summer. Is invasive but easy to control. H 2.5–5cm (1–2in), S to 23cm (9in).

Waldsteinia ternata
Semi-evergreen perennial with loose, spreading mats of toothed, 3-parted leaves. Bears saucer-shaped, yellow flowers in late spring and early summer. Is good on a bank. H 10cm (4in), S 20–30cm (8–12in).

***Linum flavum* 'Compactum'**
Shrubby perennial with narrow leaves and terminal clusters of many upward-facing, open funnel-shaped, single, bright yellow flowers in summer. Provide a sunny, sheltered position and protection from winter wet. H and S 15cm (6in).

Scutellaria orientalis
Rhizomatous perennial with hairy, grey, rooting stems. Has terminal spikes of tubular, yellow flowers, with brownish-purple lips, in summer. Leaves are toothed and oval. May be invasive in a small space. H 5–10cm (2–4in), S to 23cm (9in).

Oenothera macrocarpa
Spreading perennial with stout stems and oval leaves. Throughout summer bears a succession of wide, bell-shaped, yellow flowers, sometimes spotted red, that open at sundown. H to 10cm (4in), S to 40cm (16in) or more.

Potentilla eriocarpa
Clump-forming perennial with tufts of oval, dark green leaves divided into leaflets. Flat, single, pale yellow flowers are borne throughout summer just above leaves. H 5–8cm (2–3in), S 10–15cm (4–6in).

Calceolaria tenella
Vigorous, evergreen, prostrate perennial with creeping, reddish stems and oval, mid-green leaves, above which rise small spikes of pouch-shaped, red-spotted, yellow flowers in summer. H 10cm (4in), S indefinite.

YELLOW

Genista sagittalis
Deciduous, semi-prostrate shrub with winged stems bearing a few oval, dark green leaves. Pea-like, yellow flowers appear in dense, terminal clusters in early summer, followed by hairy seed pods. H 8cm (3in), S 30cm (12in) or more.

Cytisus ardoinoi
Deciduous, hummock-forming, dwarf shrub with arching stems. In late spring and early summer, pea-like, bright yellow flowers are produced in pairs in leaf axils. Leaves are divided into 3 leaflets. H 10cm (4in), S 15cm (6in).

Potentilla aurea
Rounded perennial, with a woody base, that in late summer bears loose sprays of flat, single, yellow flowers with slightly darker eyes. Leaves are divided into oval, slightly silvered leaflets. H 10cm (4in), S 20cm (8in).

YELLOW–ORANGE

***Lysimachia nummularia* 'Aurea'**
(Golden creeping Jenny)
Prostrate perennial. Creeping, rooting stems bear pairs of round, soft yellow leaves, which later turn greenish-yellow or green in dense shade. Has bright yellow flowers in leaf axils in summer. H 2.5–5cm (1–2in), S indefinite.

***Hypericum empetrifolium* var. *prostratum* of gardens**
Evergreen, prostrate shrub with angled branches and bright green leaves that have curled margins. Bears flat heads of small, bright yellow flowers in summer. Needs winter protection. H 2cm (¾in), S 30cm (12in).

Hippocrepis comosa
(Horseshoe vetch)
Vigorous perennial with prostrate, rooting stems bearing open spikes of pea-like, yellow flowers in summer and leaves divided into leaflets. Self seeds freely and may spread rapidly. H 5–8cm (2–3in), S indefinite.

***Calceolaria* 'Walter Shrimpton'**
Evergreen, mound-forming perennial with glossy, dark green leaves. In early summer bears short spikes of many pouch-shaped, bronze-yellow flowers, spotted rich brown, with white bands across centres. H 10cm (4in), S 23cm (9in).

Alstroemeria hookeri
Tuberous perennial with narrow leaves and loose heads of widely flared, orange-suffused, pink flowers in summer; upper petals are spotted and blotched red and yellow. H 10–15cm (4–6in), S 45–60cm (18–24in).

PINK–BLUE

Persicaria vacciniifolia
Evergreen, perennial with woody, red stems. Leaves are tinged red in autumn. Bears deep pink or rose-red flowers in late summer and autumn. H 10–15cm (4–6in), S to 30cm (12in).

Gaultheria procumbens
Vigorous, evergreen sub-shrub with prostrate stems carrying clusters of oval, leathery leaves that turn red in winter. In summer, solitary bell-shaped, pink-flushed, white flowers appear in leaf axils, followed by scarlet berries. H 5–15cm (2–6in), S indefinite.

***Gentiana* × *macaulayi* 'Wells's Variety'**
Evergreen, prostrate perennial with trumpet-shaped, mid-blue flowers in late summer and autumn. Spreading stems are clothed in narrow, mid-green leaves. Soil should be quite moist. H in flower 5cm (2in), S 20cm (8in).

BLUE–ORANGE

Gentiana sino-ornata
Evergreen, prostrate, spreading perennial that, in autumn, bears trumpet-shaped, rich blue flowers singly at the ends of stems. Leaves are narrow. Lift and divide every 3 years. Needs moist soil. H in flower 5cm (2in), S to 30cm (12in).

Oxalis lobata
Clump-forming perennial with woolly-coated tubers. Mid-green leaves have up to 5 rounded lobes. Produces racemes of widely funnel-shaped, bright yellow flowers, 1–2cm (½–¾in) across, in late summer and autumn. H 5cm (2in), S 8–10cm (3–4in).

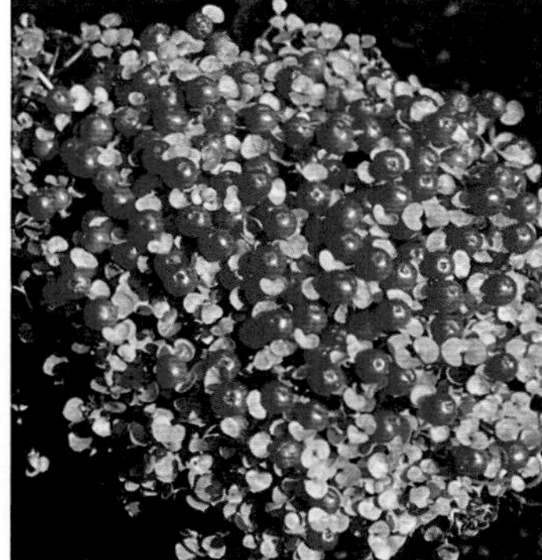

Nertera granadensis (Bead plant)
Prostrate perennial with dense mats of tiny, bright green leaves. In early summer bears minute, greenish-white flowers, then many shiny, orange berries. Needs ample moisture in summer. H to 1cm (½in), S 10cm (4in).

WHITE–RED

***Arabis procurrens* 'Variegata'**
Evergreen, mat-forming perennial with small, oval, green leaves, splashed with cream. Bears small, white flowers in spring and early summer. May revert to type, with plain green leaves. H 2cm (¾in), S 30cm (12in).

***Arctostaphylos uva-ursi* 'Point Reyes'**
Evergreen, prostrate shrub with long shoots and glossy leaves. In late spring and early summer bears terminal clusters of urn-shaped, pale pink to white flowers, followed by red berries. H 10cm (4in), S 50cm (20in).

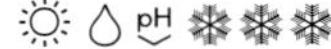

Pachysandra terminalis
Evergreen, creeping perennial that has smooth leaves clustered at the ends of short stems. Bears spikes of tiny, white flowers, sometimes flushed purple, in early summer. Makes excellent ground cover in a moist or dry site. H 10cm (4in), S 20cm (8in).

Sedum lydium
Evergreen, mat-forming perennial with reddish stems and narrow, fleshy, often red-flushed leaves. Bears flat-topped, terminal clusters of tiny, white flowers in summer. H 5cm (2in), S to 15cm (6in).

Jovibarba hirta
Evergreen, mat-forming perennial with rosettes of hairy, mid-green leaves, often suffused red, and terminal clusters of star-shaped, pale yellow flowers in summer. Dislikes winter wet. H 8–15cm (3–6in), S 10cm (4in).

Arctostaphylos uva-ursi
Evergreen, low-growing shrub with arching, intertwining stems clothed in small, oval, bright green leaves. Bears urn-shaped, pinkish-white flowers in summer followed by scarlet berries. H 10cm (4in), S 50cm (20in).

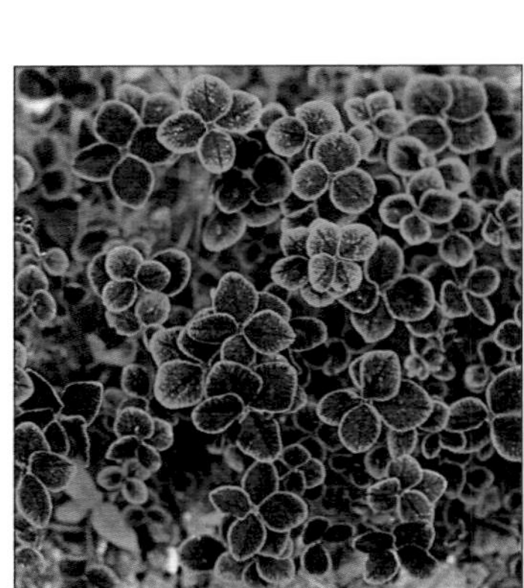

Sedum obtusatum
Evergreen, prostrate perennial with small, fat, succulent leaves that turn bronze-red in summer. Loose, flat sprays of tiny, bright yellow flowers are borne in summer. Dislikes summer wet. H 5cm (2in), S 10–15cm (4–6in).

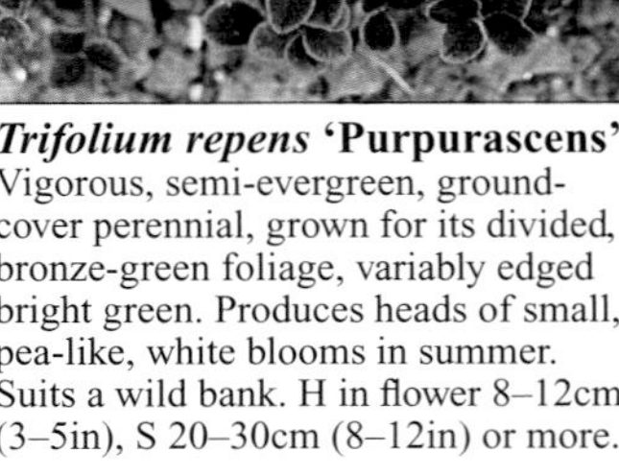

***Trifolium repens* 'Purpurascens'**
Vigorous, semi-evergreen, ground-cover perennial, grown for its divided, bronze-green foliage, variably edged bright green. Produces heads of small, pea-like, white blooms in summer. Suits a wild bank. H in flower 8–12cm (3–5in), S 20–30cm (8–12in) or more.

Acaena microphylla
Compact, mat-forming perennial, usually evergreen, with leaves divided into tiny leaflets, bronze-tinged when young. Heads of small flowers with spiny, dull red bracts are borne in summer and develop into decorative burs. H 5cm (2in), S 15cm (6in).

Raoulia hookeri var. ***albo-sericea***
Evergreen, prostrate perennial with tiny rosettes of silver leaves. Flower heads appear briefly in summer as fragrant, yellow fluff. Is best in poor, gritty humus in an alpine house. Dislikes winter wet. H to 1cm (½in), S 25cm (10in).

***Artemisia schmidtiana* 'Nana'**
Prostrate perennial with fern-like, silver foliage. Has insignificant sprays of daisy-like, yellow flowers in summer. Is suitable for a wall or bank. H 8cm (3in), S 20cm (8in).

Sempervivum tectorum (Common houseleek, Roof houseleek)
Vigorous, evergreen perennial with purple-tipped leaves, sometimes suffused deep red. In summer has clusters of star-shaped, reddish-purple flowers on stems 30cm (12in) tall. H 10–15cm (4–6in), S to 20cm (8in).

Sempervivum arachnoideum
(Cobweb houseleek)
Evergreen, mat-forming perennial. Rosettes of oval, fleshy leaves with red tips are covered in a web of white hairs. Bears loose clusters of star-shaped, rose-red flowers in summer. H 5–12cm (2–5in), S to 10cm (4in) or more.

Sedum spathulifolium
Evergreen, mat-forming perennial with rosettes of fleshy, green or silver leaves, usually strongly suffused bronze-red, and small clusters of tiny, yellow flowers borne just above foliage in summer. Tolerates shade. H 5cm (2in), S indefinite.

Leucogenes grandiceps
Evergreen, dense, woody-based perennial with neat rosettes of downy, silver leaves. Yellow flower heads, within woolly, white bracts, are borne singly in spring or early summer. H and S 10–15cm (4–6in).

Sempervivum ciliosum
Evergreen, mat-forming perennial with rosettes of hairy, grey-green leaves and, in summer, heads of small, star-shaped, yellow flowers. Dislikes winter wet; is best grown in an alpine house. H 8–10cm (3–4in), S 10cm (4in).

GREEN

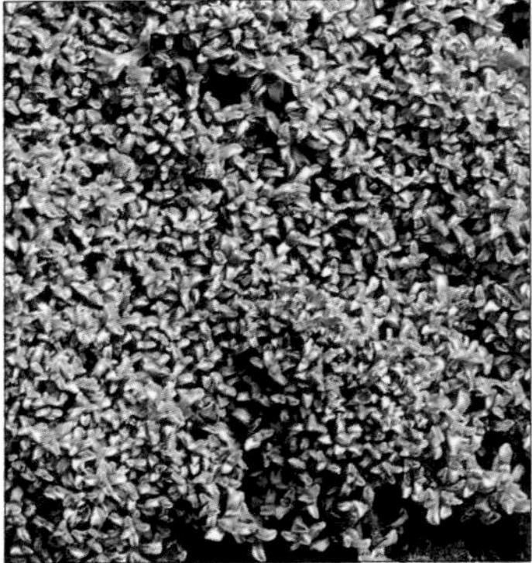

Raoulia australis
Evergreen, carpeting perennial forming a hard mat of grey-green leaves. Bears tiny, fluffy, sulphur-yellow flower heads in summer. H to 1cm (½in), S 25cm (10in).

Acaena caesiiglauca
Vigorous, ground-cover perennial, usually evergreen. Has hairy, glaucous blue leaves divided into leaflets. Heads of small flowers with spiny, brownish-green bracts, borne in summer, develop into brownish-red burs. H 5cm (2in), S 75cm (30in) or more.

Sempervivum montanum
Evergreen, mat-forming perennial with dark green rosettes of fleshy, hairy leaves. Star-shaped, wine-red flowers are borne in terminal clusters in summer. Is a variable plant that hybridizes freely. H 10–15cm (3–6in), S 10cm (4in).

Azorella trifurcata
Evergreen perennial forming tight, hard cushions of tiny, leathery, oval leaves in rosettes. Bears many small, stalkless umbels of yellow flowers in summer. H to 10cm (4in), S 15cm (6in).

Asarum europaeum (Asarabacca)
Vigorous, evergreen, prostrate, rhizomatous perennial with large, kidney-shaped, leathery, glossy leaves that hide tiny, brown flowers appearing in spring. H 15cm (6in), S indefinite.

Sagina boydii
Evergreen perennial with hard cushions of minute, stiff, bottle-green leaves in small rosettes. Bears insignificant flowers in summer. Is difficult and slow-growing. H 1cm (½in), S to 20cm (8in).

GREEN–YELLOW

Sempervivum giuseppii
Vigorous, evergreen, prostrate perennial. Leaves are hairy, especially in spring, and have dark spots at tips. Produces terminal clusters of star-shaped, deep pink or red flowers in summer. H in flower 8–10cm (3–4in), S 10cm (4in).

Bolax gummifera
Very slow-growing, evergreen perennial with neat rosettes of small, blue-green leaves forming extremely hard cushions. Insignificant, yellow flowers are rarely produced. Grows well on tufa. H 2.5cm (1in), S 10cm (4in).

Plantago nivalis
Evergreen perennial with neat rosettes of thick, silver-haired, green leaves. Bears spikes of insignificant, dull grey flowers in summer. Dislikes winter wet. H in leaf 2.5cm (1in), S 5cm (2in).

Raoulia haastii
Evergreen perennial forming low, irregular hummocks of minute leaves that are apple-green in spring, dark green in autumn and chocolate-brown in winter. Occasionally has small, fluffy, yellow flower heads in summer. H to 1cm (½in), S 25cm (10in).

Paronychia kapela **subsp. *serpyllifolia***
Evergreen, very compact, mat-forming perennial with minute, silver leaves. Inconspicuous flowers, borne in summer, are surrounded by papery, silver bracts. Is good for covering tufa. H to 1cm (½in), S 20cm (8in).

YELLOW

***Sedum kamtschaticum* 'Variegatum'**
Semi-evergreen, prostrate perennial with fleshy, cream-edged leaves. Has fleshy stems and leaf buds in winter and loose, terminal clusters of orange-flushed, yellow flowers in early autumn. H 5–8cm (2–3in), S 20cm (8in).

***Sedum spathulifolium* 'Cape Blanco'**
Evergreen perennial with rosettes of fleshy leaves, frequently suffused purple. Tiny, yellow flowers appear above foliage in summer. Tolerates shade. H 5cm (2in), S indefinite.

Saxifraga exarata **subsp. *moschata* 'Cloth of Gold'**
Evergreen hummock-forming perennial with small, soft rosettes of bright golden foliage; produces best colour in shade. Has star-shaped, white flowers on slender stems in summer. H 10–15cm (4–6in), S 15cm (6in).

Bulbs

Bulbs

Bulbous plants are found throughout the world in habitats as varied as woodland and scrub, meadows, the sides of rivers and streams and on rocky hills and mountains. They provide some of the loveliest of flowers in the plant kingdom.

What are bulbs?

The term bulb can be used to describe all swollen, underground, food-storage organs, and includes true bulbs as well as corms, rhizomes and tubers. True bulbs have fleshy scales – modified leaves or leaf bases – that are tightly overlapping and can be enclosed in a papery tunic, as in the narcissus, or be naked and loosely arranged, as in the lily. Corms are compressed and enlarged stem bases, usually enclosed in a fibrous or papery tunic, as in the crocus. Each corm lasts one year, and is replaced by a new one after flowering. Tubers, seen in plants such as cyclamen or dahlia, are solid, underground sections of modified stem or root and they seldom possess scales or tunics. Rhizomes are modified stems that creep at or just below soil level; they may be thin and wiry, as in lily-of-the-valley, (*Convallaria*), or swollen and fleshy, as in bearded irises.

Although a few bulbs are evergreen, most grow and bloom during a fairly short season, then die back to below ground level. Although they are then described as dormant, bulbs are far from quiescent, as they are ripening and developing the following year's flowers. This is why the siting of bulbs is often crucial to their continued success. Those bulbs that originated in dry, summer climates usually need warm, dry conditions when dormant to aid ripening and flower formation, while those bulbs from woodland or other damp, shaded habitats require a cool and slightly moist position. Since their leaves produce the food store for the following year, it is vital to leave bulb foliage in place until it has died down naturally.

Designing with bulbs

There are bulbs to suit almost every garden site and design, from the tiny *Iris danfordiae* or the autumn daffodil (*Sternbergia lutea*) for the rock garden, to the carpeting erythroniums or the towering *Cardiocrinum giganteum* for the dappled shade of woodland gardens.

Bulbs are extremely versatile when used to define a garden style. The strongly upright habit and sculptural flower forms of many hybrid tulips, the precise formation of the dahlias or the flamboyant spires of gladioli are ideal in formal beds. Amaryllis, lilies and agapanthus, often grown in containers to add

Container combination
Left: Planting two different tulip bulbs together can highlight the beauty of both. Site the container where it can be appreciated at close quarters.

Naturalized bulbs
Above: Short turf sprinkled with naturalized early crocuses (here, cultivars of *Crocus chrysanthus*) confirm the onset of spring.

Summer colour
Right: From mid-summer to early autumn, the robust, vibrantly coloured flower spikes of cormous perennial *Crocosmia* 'Lucifer' lend height and arching grace to the mixed border.

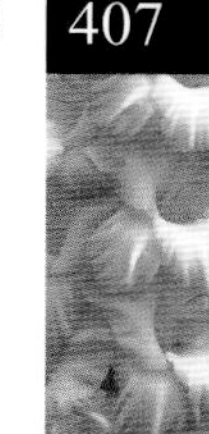

Spring beauty
Left: As spring eases into summer, the crown imperials (*Fritillaria imperialis*) raise their majestic heads above a carpet of late-flowering narcissi and grape hyacinths.

Autumn highlights
Below: Autumn-flowering colchicums here providing a startling finale to the season next to the scarlet-flowered *Stachys coccinea*.

formal elegance to patio plantings, are equally at home among perennials and roses. Many bulbs thrive in pots, whether indoors or outside.

Bulbs can be planted in informal groups in a border with annuals, shrubs and perennials for year-round interest. In a woodland setting, drifts of lily-of-the-valley (*Convallaria majalis*) and erythroniums look natural, while short turf spangled with crocuses or snake's-head fritillaries (*Fritillaria meleagris*) mimics their wild habitat to perfection.

Maintaining year-round interest

Most bulbs have a distinct flowering season, yet with careful planning it is possible to extend or enhance this period of interest.

The first snowdrops (*Galanthus*) and early narcissus mark the onset of spring, and begin the gardening year. Most bulbs bloom in spring and early summer, producing splashes of colour before the summer-flowering shrubs and perennials reach their peak. The combination of certain genera, notably narcissus and tulip, can provide constant colour from spring to summer. Summer-flowering species such as *Galtonia candicans* and many alliums offer colourful highlights, then as summer draws to an end, the crinums, nerines and crocosmias are at their best, and often continue to bloom into autumn.

The autumn-flowering crocuses, colchicums and cyclamen give their best displays with the onset of autumn rains, when much else in the garden is fading quietly. Some bulbs, for example *Arum italicum* 'Marmoratum' or *Cyclamen hederifolium*, have pretty marbled foliage that persists through winter. These, and early-flowering bulbs such as winter aconites (*Eranthis*), *Anemone blanda* and dwarf narcissus brighten the garden before most shrubs come into leaf. Grape hyacinths, chionodoxas, scillas and dwarf irises can create complementary carpets of blue beneath flowering shrubs such as forsythia and witch hazel (*Hamamelis*).

Many bulbs, notably lilies, also offer an intense fragrance and are ideal mixed with other highly scented plants such as roses.

Size categories used within this group		
Large	**Medium**	**Small**
over 60cm (2ft)	23cm–60cm (9in–2ft)	up to 23cm (9in)

□ WHITE

Leucojum aestivum
(Summer snowflake)
Spring-flowering bulb with long, strap-shaped, semi-erect, basal leaves. Bears heads of pendent, long-stalked, bell-shaped, green-tipped, white flowers on leafless stems. H 50cm–1m (1½–3ft), S 10–12cm (4–5in).

Fritillaria raddeana
Robust, spring-flowering bulb with lance-shaped leaves in whorls on lower half of stem. Has a head of up to 20 widely conical, pale or greenish-yellow flowers, 3–4cm (1¼–1½in) long, topped by a 'crown' of small leaves. H to 1m (3ft), S 15–23cm (6–9in).

Fritillaria verticillata
Spring-flowering bulb with slender leaves in whorls up stem, which bears a loose spike of 1–15 bell-shaped, white flowers, 2–4cm (¾–1½in) long and chequered green or brown. H to 1m (3ft), S 8–10cm (3–4in).

PURPLE–ORANGE

Fritillaria persica
Spring-flowering bulb with narrow, lance-shaped, grey-green leaves along stem. Produces a spike of 10–20 or more narrow, bell-shaped, blackish- or brownish-purple flowers, 1.5–2cm (⅝–¾in) long. H to 1.5m (5ft), S 10cm (4in).

Fritillaria recurva
(Scarlet fritillary)
Spring-flowering bulb with whorls of narrow, lance-shaped, grey-green leaves. Bears a spike of up to 10 narrow, yellow-chequered, orange or red flowers with flared tips. H to 1m (3ft), S 8–10cm (3–4in).

Fritillaria imperialis
(Crown imperial)
Spring-flowering bulb with glossy, pale green leaves carried in whorls on leafy stems. Has up to 5 widely bell-shaped, orange flowers crowned by small, leaf-like bracts. H to 1.5m (5ft), S 23–30cm (9–12in).

□ WHITE

***Crinum* × *powellii* 'Album'**
Late summer- or autumn-flowering bulb, with a long neck, producing a group of semi-erect, strap-shaped leaves. Leafless flower stems carry heads of fragrant, widely funnel-shaped, white flowers. H to 1m (3ft), S 60cm (2ft).

Hymenocallis* × *macrostephana
Evergreen, spring- or summer-flowering bulb with strap-shaped, semi-erect, basal leaves. Bears fragrant, white or cream- to greenish-yellow flowers, 15–20cm (6–8in) wide. H 80cm (32in), S 30–45cm (12–18in). Min. 15°C (59°F).

Eucomis pallidiflora (Giant pineapple flower, Giant pineapple lily)
Summer-flowering bulb with sword-shaped, crinkly edged, semi-erect, basal leaves. Bears a dense spike of star-shaped, greenish-white flowers, topped with a cluster of leaf-like bracts. H to 75cm (30in), S 30–60cm (12–24in).

***Zantedeschia aethiopica* 'Green Goddess'**
Robust, summer-flowering tuber with arrow-shaped, semi-erect, basal, deep green leaves. Bears a succession of green spathes each with a large, central, green-splashed, white area. H 45cm–1m (1½–3ft), S 45–60cm (1½–2ft).

Galtonia candicans
(Summer hyacinth)
Late summer- or autumn-flowering bulb with widely strap-shaped, fleshy, semi-erect, basal, grey-green leaves. Leafless stem has a spike of up to 30 pendent, short-tubed, white flowers. H 1–1.2m (3–4ft), S 18–23cm (7–9in).

***Zantedeschia aethiopica* 'Crowborough'**
Early to mid-summer-flowering tuber with arrow-shaped, semi-erect, basal, deep green leaves. Produces a succession of arum-like, white spathes, each with a yellow spadix. H 45cm–1m (1½–3ft), S 35–45cm.

Camassia leichtlinii
Tuft-forming bulb with long, narrow, erect, basal leaves. Each leafless stem bears a dense spike of 6-petalled, star-shaped, bluish-violet or white flowers, 4–8in (1½–3in) across, in summer. H 1–1.5m (3–5ft), S 20–30cm (8–12in).

***Camassia leichtlinii* 'Semiplena'**
Tuft-forming bulb with long, narrow, erect, basal leaves. Each leafless stem carries a dense spike of narrow-petalled, double, creamy-white flowers, 4–8cm (1½–3in) across, in summer. H 1–1.5m (3–5ft), S 20–30cm (8–12in).

WHITE–PINK

Crinum moorei
Summer-flowering bulb with a long neck, up to 1m (3ft) tall, and strap-shaped, semi-erect, grey-green leaves grouped at neck top. Leafless flower stems bear heads of long-tubed, funnel-shaped, white to deep pink flowers. H 50–70cm (20–28in), S 60cm (24in).

Nectaroscordum siculum **subsp. *bulgaricum***
Late spring- to early summer-flowering bulb with pendent, bell-shaped, white flowers, flushed purple-red and green. In seed, stalks bend upwards, holding dry seed pods erect. H to 1.2m (4ft), S 30–45cm (1–1½ft).

Cardiocrinum giganteum
(Giant lily)
Stout, leafy-stemmed bulb. In summer has long spikes of fragrant, slightly pendent, cream flowers, 15cm (6in) long, with purple-red streaks inside, then brown seed pods. H to 3m (10ft), S 75cm–1.1m (2½–3½ft).

Eucomis comosa
Clump-forming bulb with strap-shaped, wavy-margined leaves, spotted purple beneath. Purple-spotted stem bears a spike of white or greenish-white, sometimes pink-tinted flowers, with purple ovaries. H to 70cm (28in), S 30–60cm (12–24in).

Nomocharis pardanthina
Summer-flowering bulb with stems bearing whorls of lance-shaped leaves and up to 15 outward-facing, white or pale pink flowers, each with purple blotches and a dark purple eye. H to 1m (3ft), S 12–15cm (5–6in).

Crinum × powellii
Late summer- or autumn-flowering bulb with a long neck producing a group of strap-shaped, semi-erect leaves. Leafless flower stems bear heads of fragrant, widely funnel-shaped, pink flowers. H to 1m (3ft), S 60cm (2ft).

Gladioli

The genus has about 180 species of cormous perennials, with over 10,000 hybrids and cultvars developed for garden cultivation, exhibiting and cutting. Gladioli are prized for their showy spikes of usually open, funnel-shaped flowers, borne mainly from spring to early autumn. Gladiolus hybrids are divided into the Grandiflorus Group, with long, densely packed flower spikes, categorized as miniature, small, medium-sized, large or giant according to the width of the lowest flowers, and the Primulinus and Nanus Groups, with loose spikes of small flowers. Plant gladioli in clumps in a mixed border, or in rows for cutting. In frost-prone areas, grow gladioli by a sheltered, sunny wall; winter-flowering South African gladioli require a cool greenhouse. (See also the Plant Dictionary.)

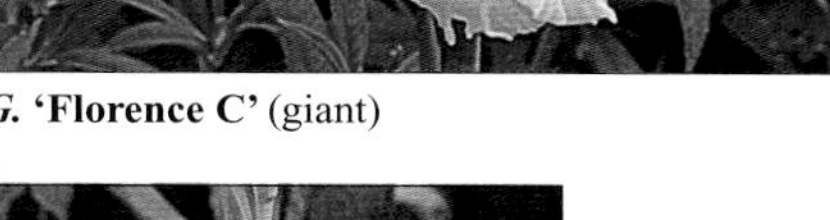

G. **'Florence C'** (giant)

G. ***communis*** subsp. ***byzantinus*** 🏆

G. **'Rose Supreme'** (giant)

G. **'Amanda Mahy'** (Nanus Group)

G. **'Renegade'** (Grandiflorus)

G. **'Drama'** (large)

G. **'Deliverance'** (Grandiflorus)

G. **'White Ice'** (medium)

G. **'Halley'** (Nanus Group)

G. **'Anna Leorah'** (large)

G. **'Pink Lady'** (large)

G. **'Peter Pears'** (large)

G. **'Esta Bonita'** (giant)

G. **'The Bride'** (Nanus Group) 🏆

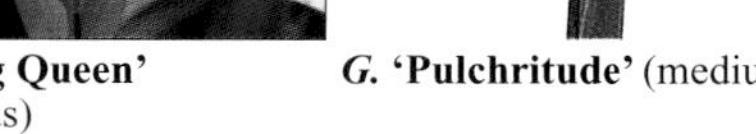

G. **'Dancing Queen'** (Grandiflorus)

G. **'Pulchritude'** (medium)

G. **'Miss America'** (medium)

G. **'Tesoro'** (medium)

G. **'Green Woodpecker'** (medium)

PINK–RED

Notholirion campanulatum
Early summer-flowering bulb with long, narrow leaves in a basal tuft. Leafy stem bears a spike of 10–40 pendent, funnel-shaped flowers, each 4–5cm (1½–2in) long, with green-tipped, deep rose-purple petals. H to 1m (3ft), S 8–10cm (3–4in).

Watsonia borbonica
Very robust, summer-flowering corm with narrowly sword-shaped leaves both at base and on stem. Produces a loose, branched spike of rich pink flowers, with 6 spreading, pointed, rose-red lobes. H 1–1.5m (3–5ft), S 45–60cm (1½–2ft).

Gladiolus italicus
Early summer-flowering corm with a fan of erect, sword-shaped leaves from the basal part of stem. Carries a loose spike of up to 20 pinkish-purple flowers, 4–5cm (1½–2in) long. H to 1m (3ft), S 10–15cm (4–6in).

Dierama pulcherrimum
Upright, summer-flowering corm with long, narrow, strap-like, evergreen leaves, above which rise elegant, arching, wiry stems bearing funnel-shaped, deep pink flowers. Prefers deep, rich soil. H 1.5m (5ft), S 30cm (1ft).

Gladiolus communis subsp. ***byzantinus***
Early summer-flowering corm with a dense spike of up to 20 deep purplish-red or purplish-pink flowers, 4–6cm (1½–2½in) long. Produces a fan of sword-shaped, erect, basal leaves. H to 70cm (28in), S 10–15cm (4–6in).

Phaedranassa carmioli
Spring- and summer-flowering bulb with upright, elliptic or lance-shaped, basal leaves. Bears a head of 6–10 pendent, pinkish-red flowers, with green bases and yellow-edged, green lobes at each apex. H 50–70cm (20–28in), S 30–45cm (12–18in).

Watsonia pillansii
Summer-flowering corm with long, sword-shaped, erect leaves, some basal and some on stem. Stem carries a dense, branched spike of tubular, orange-red flowers, each 6–8cm (2½–3in) long, with 6 short lobes. H to 1m (3ft), S 30–45cm (1–1½ft).

***Alstroemeria* MARGARET (‘Stacova’)**
Mid- to late summer-flowering tuber with narrow, lance-shaped, twisted, bright green leaves. Stout, leafy stems bear widely flared, funnel-shaped, deep red flowers. H 1m (3ft), S 60cm–1m (2–3ft).

RED

Dracunculus vulgaris (Dragon's arum)
Spring- and summer-flowering tuber with deeply divided leaves at apex of thick, blotched stem. A blackish-maroon spadix protrudes from a deep maroon spathe, 35cm (14in) long. H to 1m (3ft), S 45–60cm (1½–2ft).

***Gloriosa superba* 'Rothschildiana'** (Glory lily)
Deciduous, summer-flowering, tuberous, tendril climber. Upper leaf axils each bear a large flower that has 6 reflexed, red petals with scalloped, yellow edges. H to 2m (6ft), S 30–45cm (1–1½ft). Min. 8°C (46°F).

***Crocosmia* 'Bressingham Blaze'**
Clump-forming, late summer-flowering corm with sword-shaped, pleated, basal, erect leaves. Branched stem bears widely funnel-shaped, fiery-red flowers. H 75cm (30in), S 15–20cm (6–8in).

***Crocosmia* 'Lucifer'**
Robust, clump-forming corm with sword-shaped, erect, basal, bright green leaves. Bears funnel-shaped, deep rich red flowers in dense, branching spikes in mid-summer. H to 1m (3ft), S 20–25cm (8–10in).

***Canna* 'Assaut'**
Summer-flowering, rhizomatous perennial with stout, leafy stems bearing wide, purple-green leaves. Has a spike of scarlet flowers surrounded by purple bracts. H to 1.2m (4ft), S 45–60cm (1½–2ft).

Crocosmia masoniorum
Robust, clump-forming corm with erect, basal, deep green leaves, pleated lengthways. Erect, branched stem has a horizontal, upper part, which carries upright, reddish-orange flowers in summer-autumn. H to 1.5m (5ft), S 30–45cm (1–1½ft).

RED–PURPLE

Scadoxus multiflorus* subsp. *katherinae (Blood flower)
Very robust, clump-forming bulb with lance-shaped, wavy-edged leaves. Bears an umbel of up to 200 red flowers in summer. H to 1.2m (4ft), S 30–45cm (1–1½ft). Min. 10°C (50°F).

Allium rosenbachianum
Summer-flowering bulb with ridged stems and grey-green strap-like, basal leaves. Carries 50 or more star-shaped, deep purple flowers in a spherical umbel, 10cm (4in) across. Good for drying. H 1m (3ft), S 10cm (4in).

Dierama pendulum (Angel's fishing rod)
Clump-forming, late summer-flowering corm with arching, basal leaves. Bears pendulous, loose racemes of bell-shaped, pinkish-purple flowers, 2.5cm (1in) long. H to 1.5m (5ft), S 15–20cm (6–8in).

PURPLE–BLUE

Allium giganteum
Robust, summer-flowering bulb with long, wide, semi-erect, basal leaves. Produces a stout stem with a dense, spherical umbel, 12cm (5in) across, of 50 or more star-shaped, purple flowers. H to 2m (6ft), S 30–35cm (12–14in).

Allium × hollandicum
Summer-flowering bulb with mid-green, basal leaves dying away by flowering time. Carries numerous star-shaped, purplish-pink flowers in a dense, spherical umbel, 10cm (4in) across. H 1m (3ft), S 10cm (4in).

Dichelostemma congestum
Early summer-flowering bulb with semi-erect, basal leaves dying away when a dense head of funnel-shaped, purple flowers, each 1.5–2cm (⅝–¾in) long, appears. H to 1m (3ft), S 8–10cm (3–4ft).

Aristea major
Robust, evergreen, clump-forming rhizome with sword-shaped, erect leaves, to 2.5cm (1in) across, and dense spikes of purple-blue flowers on short stalks in summer. H to 1m (3ft), S 45–60cm (1½–2ft).

Neomarica caerulea
Summer-flowering rhizome with sword-shaped, semi-erect leaves in basal fans. Stems each bear a leaf-like bract and a succession of iris-like, blue flowers, with white, yellow and brown central marks. H to 1m (3ft), S 1–1.5m (3–5ft). Min. 10°C (50°F).

GREEN–YELLOW

Dietes bicolor
Evergreen, tuft-forming, summer-flowering rhizome with tough, long and narrow, erect, basal leaves. Branching stems each bear a succession of flattish, iris-like, pale to mid-yellow flowers; each large petal has a brown patch. H to 1m (3ft), S 30–60cm (1–2ft).

Galtonia viridiflora
Clump-forming, summer-flowering bulb with widely strap-shaped, fleshy, semi-erect, basal, grey-green leaves. Leafless stem bears a spike of up to 30 pendent, short-tubed, funnel-shaped, pale green flowers. H 1–1.2m (3–4ft), S 18–23cm (7–9in).

Arisaema consanguineum
Summer-flowering tuber with robust, spotted stems and erect, umbrella-like leaves with narrow leaflets. Produces purplish-white- or white-striped, green spathes, 15–20cm (6–8in) long, and bright red berries. H to 1m (3ft), S 30–45cm (1–1½ft).

Fritillaria chitralensis
Spring- to early summer-flowering bulb with ovate, mid- to light green leaves and open umbels of 4 or 5 conical, pendent, bright yellow flowers. Similar to *F. imperialis*. H 50–80cm (20–32in), S 10cm (4in).

Moraea ramosissima
Late spring- to early summer-flowering corm with numerous, semi-erect, narrowly linear, channelled, basal leaves. Bears yellow flowers, with deeper yellow marks on the inner petals, on many-branched stems. H 50–120cm (20–48in), S 10cm (4in).

Zantedeschia elliottiana
(Golden arum lily)
Summer-flowering tuber with heart-shaped, semi-erect, basal leaves with transparent marks. Bears a 15cm (6in) long, yellow spathe surrounding a yellow spadix. H 60cm–1m (2–3ft), S 45–60cm (1½–2ft). Min. 10°C (50°F).

YELLOW–ORANGE

***Crocosmia* 'Golden Fleece'**
Clump-forming, late summer-flowering corm with sword-shaped, erect, basal, grey-green leaves. Flowers are funnel-shaped and clear golden-yellow. H 60–75cm (24–30in), S 15–20cm (6–8in).

Moraea huttonii
Summer-flowering corm with long, narrow, semi-erect, basal leaves. Tough stem bears a succession of iris-like, yellow flowers, 5–7cm (2–3in) across, with brown marks near the centre. H 75cm–1m (2½–3ft), S 15–25cm (6–10in).

***Crocosmia* 'Star of the East'**
Late summer-flowering corm with sword-shaped, erect, basal, mid-green leaves. Bears horizontal-facing, funnel-shaped, clear orange flowers, each with a paler orange centre, on branched stems. H 70cm (28in), S 8cm (3in).

ORANGE

Alstroemeria aurea
Summer-flowering, tuberous perennial with narrow, lance-shaped, twisted leaves and loose heads of orange flowers, tipped with green and streaked dark red. H to 1m (3ft), S 60cm–1m (2–3ft).

Littonia modesta
Deciduous, summer-flowering, tuberous, scandent climber with slender stems and lance-shaped leaves with tendrils at apex. Leaf axils bear bell-shaped, pendent, orange flowers, 4–5cm (1½–2in) across. H 1–2m (3–6ft), S 10–15cm (4–6in). Min. 16°C (61°F).

Canna iridiflora
Very robust, spring- or summer-flowering, rhizomatous perennial with broad, oblong leaves and spikes of pendent, long-tubed, reddish-pink or orange flowers, each 10–15cm (4–6in) long, with reflexed petals. H 3m (10ft), S 45–60cm (1½–2ft).

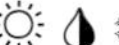

L. 'Olivia'

Lilies

Lilies (*Lilium* species and cultivars) bring elegance to the summer border. Their flamboyant flowers are variously shaped, some nodding, some upright or trumpet-shaped, others in the distinctive turkscap form (with recurving petals), and are borne usually several per stem. Many have a distinctive, powerful fragrance, although a few species are unpleasantly scented. Most widely grown are the many hybrids, available in dazzling colours from white, pink, and red to rich shades of yellow and orange, but among the species are several that have been undeservedly neglected. Lily flowers are often attractively spotted with a darker or contrasting colour, or have conspicuous stamens or pollen. Lilies thrive in sun and well-drained soil. Once established, they are best left undisturbed, as the bulbs are easily damaged.

L.* × *testaceum 🏆

***L.* Olympic Group**

L. duchartrei

L. auratum* var. *platyphyllum 🏆

***L.* 'Mont Blanc'**

***L.* 'Lime Star'**

***L.* 'Casa Blanca'** 🏆

***L.* 'Black Magic'**

***L.* 'Sterling Star'**

L. martagon* var. *album 🏆

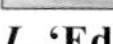

***L.* 'Ed'**

***L.* 'Bright Star'**

***L.* 'Royal Gold'**

L. regale 🏆

***L.* 'Arena'**

L. candidum 🏆

L. longiflorum 🏆

***L.* Imperial Gold Group**

***L.* 'Mona Lisa'**

L. 'Pink Tiger'

L. 'Star Gazer'

L. rubellum

L. 'Cover Girl'

L. mackliniae 🏆

L. speciosum var. *rubrum*

L. 'Rosita'

L. lankongense

L. 'Bronwen North'

L. 'Magic Pink'

L. 'Angela North'

L. 'Montreux'

L. 'Lollypop'

L. 'Côte d'Azur'

L. 'Journey's End'

L. martagon 🏆

L. 'Corsage'

L. 'Black Beauty'

L. 'Eros'

L. nepalense

L. Pink Perfection Group 🏆

L. × *dalhansonii*

L. Golden Splendor Group ♀

L. monadelphum ♀

L. 'Roma'

L. 'Gran Cru' ♀

L. canadense

L. superbum ♀

L. 'California Gold'

L. 'Destiny'

L. 'Connecticut King'

L. rosthornii

L. 'Limelight'

L. wigginsii

L. Golden Clarion Group

L. medeoloides

L. leichtlinii

L. pyrenaicum ♀

L. 'Luxor'

L. 'Amber Gold'

L. 'Rosemary North' ♀

L. 'Brocade'

L. **'Orange Pixie'**

L. ***pyrenaicum*** var. ***rubrum***

L. ***davidii*** var. ***willmottiae***

L. **'Brushmarks'**

L. ***lancifolium*** var. ***splendens***

L. ***tsingtauense***

L. ***bulbiferum*** var. ***croceum*** 🏆

L. **'Enchantment'** 🏆

L. ***pardalinum***

L. **'Red Carpet'**

L. ***hansonii*** 🏆

L. **'Apollo'**

L. **'Karen North'** 🏆

L. **'Lady Bowes Lyon'**

L. ***pomponium***

L. **'Crimson Pixie'**

L. **'Harmony'**

L. ***chalcedonicum*** 🏆

L. **'Gran Paradiso'**

DAHLIAS

The variety of border hybrids offers a dazzling display of colour and form to every gardener, and no special skills are required to cultivate or propagate them. In colour the flowers range from deep reds, crimsons, purples, hues of mauve, and vibrant pinks to whites, apricots, oranges, bronzes, and brilliant scarlets, in size from the tiny pompons of 52mm (2in) to huge exhibition blooms greater than 254mm (10in) across.

Dahlias are excellent for providing cut flowers and will bloom vigorously throughout summer until the first frosts – provided with the right conditions a single plant may produce up to 100 blooms. Their various flower types (shown below) form the basis of the recognized groups.

D. **'White Ballet'** 🏆
(collerette)

Decorative – fully double flowers have broad, flat petals that incurve slightly at their margins and usually reflex to the stem.

Ball – flattened to spherical, fully double flowers have densely packed, almost tubular petals.

Single – each flower usually has 8–10 broad petals surrounding an open, central disc.

Pompon – flattened to spherical, fully double flowers are no more than 52mm (2in) across – a miniature form of ball flowers.

D. **'Klondike'**
(cactus)

D. **'White Alva's'** 🏆
(cactus)

Anemone – fully double flowers each have one or more rings of flattened ray petals surrounding a dense group of shorter, tubular petals, usually longer than disc petals found in single dahlias.

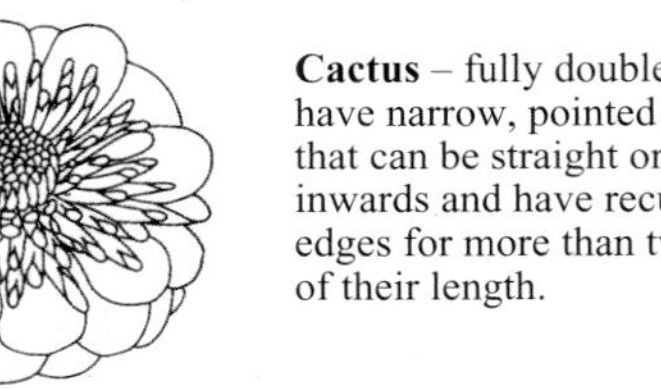

Cactus – fully double flowers have narrow, pointed petals that can be straight or curl inwards and have recurved edges for more than two-thirds of their length.

D. **'Trelyn Kiwi'**
(semi-cactus)

D. **'White Klankstad'**
(cactus)

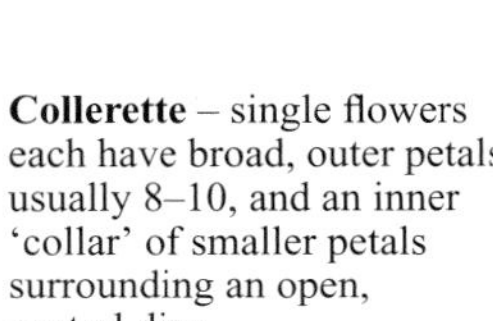

Collerette – single flowers each have broad, outer petals, usually 8–10, and an inner 'collar' of smaller petals surrounding an open, central disc.

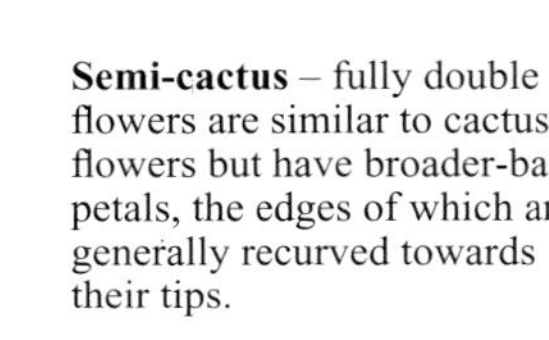

Semi-cactus – fully double flowers are similar to cactus flowers but have broader-based petals, the edges of which are generally recurved towards their tips.

D. **'Small World'** 🏆
(pompon)

Water-lily – fully double flowers have large, generally sparse ray petals, which are flat or with slightly incurved or recurved margins, giving the flower a flat appearance.

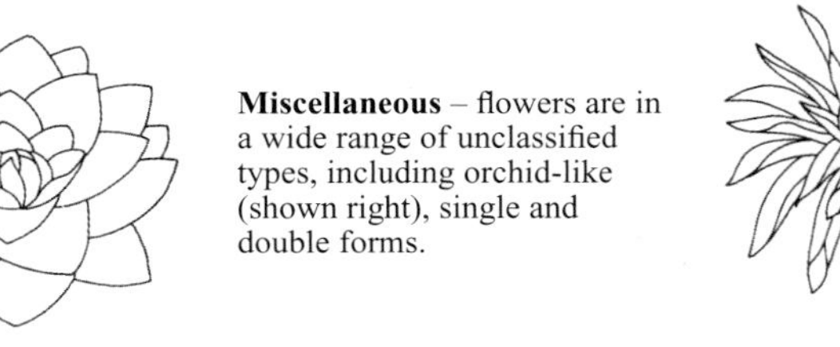

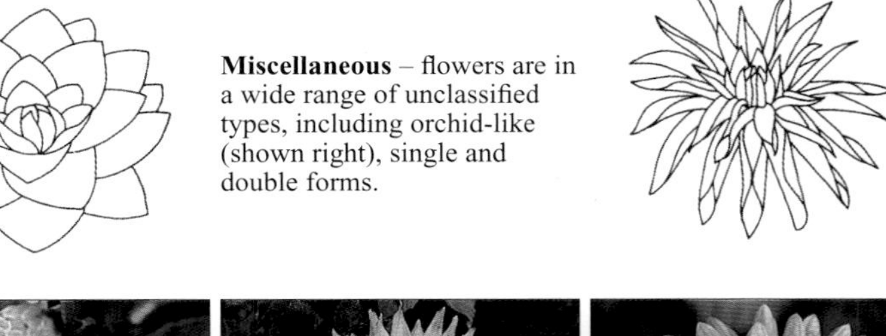

Miscellaneous – flowers are in a wide range of unclassified types, including orchid-like (shown right), single and double forms.

D. **'Jura'**
(semi-cactus)

D. **'Fusion'** 🏆
(decorative)

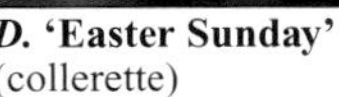

D. **'Easter Sunday'**
(collerette)

D. **'Rhonda'**
(pompon)

D. **'Pearl of Heemstede'** 🏆
(water-lily)

D. **'Sir Alf Ramsey'**
(decorative)

D. **'Vicky Crutchfield'**
(water-lily)

D. **'Dancing Queen'**
(semi-cactus)

D. **'Mary Richards'**
(decorative)

D. **'Candy Cupid'** ♀ (ball)

D. **'Onesta'** (water-lily)

D. **'Cottesmore'** (water-lily)

D. **'Cherokee Beauty'** (decorative)

D. **'Berwick Wood'** (decorative)

D. **'Marston Lilac'** ♀ (decorative)

D. **'Mermaid of Zennor'** (single)

D. **'Pontiac'** (cactus)

D. **'Pink Jupiter'** (semi-cactus)

D. **'Hayley Jayne'** (semi-cactus)

D. **'Ryecroft Gem'** (decorative)

D. **'Noreen'** (pompon)

D. **'Deborah's Kiwi'** (cactus)

D. **'Brian's Dream'** (decorative)

D. **'Sascha'** ♀ (water-lily)

D. **'NZ's Robert'** (water-lily)

D. **'Gay Princess'** (decorative)

D. **'Aranka'** (collerette)

D. **'Pink Shirley Alliance'** (cactus)

D. **'Jaldec Joker'** ♀ (semi-cactus)

D. **'Currant Cream'** (ball)

D. **'Mi-Wong'** (pompon)

D. **'Lavender Athalie'** (cactus)

D. **'Wootton Cupid'** (ball) ♀

D. coccinea (single)

D. **'Pink Symbol'** (semi-cactus)

D. **'Fascination'** ♀ (miscellaneous)

D. **'Whale's Rhonda'** (pompon)

D. **'Jim Branigan'** (semi-cactus)

D. **'Moor Place'** (pompon)

D. **'Hillcrest Jessica'** (dec.)

D. 'Preston Park' ♀ (single)

D. 'Zorro' ♀ (decorative)

D. 'Tui Ruth' (semi-cactus)

D. 'Comet' (anemone)

D. 'Chimborazo' (collerette)

D. 'Hillcrest Royal' ♀ (cactus)

D. 'Bishop of Llandaff' ♀ (miscellaneous)

D. 'Julie One' (orchid)

D. 'Yelno Enchanted' (water-lily)

D. 'Giraffe' (orchid)

D. 'Kaiserwalzer' (collerette)

D. 'Demi Schneider' (collerette)

D. 'Weston Pirate' ♀ (cactus)

D. 'Yelno Firelight' (water-lily)

D. 'Jescot Julie' (miscellaneous)

D. 'Charlie Dimmock' (water-lily)

D. 'Black Narcissus' (s.-c.)

D. 'Hexton Copper' (ball)

D. 'Marie Schnugg' (semi-cactus)

D. 'Biddenham Sunset' (decorative)

D. 'Hamari Gold' ♀ (decorative)

D. 'Akita' (miscellaneous)

D. 'Onslow Renown' (semi-cactus)

D. 'Cherwell Skylark' ♀ (semi-cactus)

D. 'Gwyneth' (water-lily)

D. 'Oosterbeck Remembered' (semi-cactus)

D. 'Orange Berger's Record' (semi-cactus)

D. 'Kathryn's Cupid' 🏆 (ball)

D. 'Barry Williams' (decorative)

D. 'Smokey O' (semi-cactus)

D. 'Gilwood Terry G' (semi-cactus)

D. 'Mum's Lipstick' (decorative)

D. 'Lakeland Sunset' 🏆 (cactus)

D. 'So Dainty' 🏆 (semi-cactus)

D. 'Grenidor Pastelle' (semi-cactus)

D. 'Shirley Alliance' (cactus)

D. 'East Anglian' (decorative)

D. 'Appetiser' (semi-cactus)

D. 'Avoca Cree' (semi-cactus)

D. 'Moonfire' 🏆 (semi-cactus)

D. 'Avoca Kiowa' (semi-cactus)

D. 'Jean Fairs' 🏆 (miscellaneous)

D. 'Yellow Hammer' 🏆 (single)

D. 'Bicentenary' (decorative)

D. 'Wanda's Capella' (decorative)

D. 'Hamari Accord' 🏆 (semi-cactus)

D. 'Harvest Inflammation' 🏆 (single)

D. 'Clair de Lune' 🏆 (collerette)

D. 'Butterball' (decorative)

D. 'Jeanette Carter' 🏆 (decorative)

D. 'Swanvale' (decorative)

D. 'Geerlings' Moonlight' (semi-cac.)

D. 'Kenora Superb' (semi-cactus)

D. 'Dutch Triumph' (water-lily)

D. 'Hamari Katrina' (semi-cactus)

D. 'Hillcrest Ultra' (decorative)

D. 'Gateshead Festival' (decorative)

D. 'Wootton Impact' 🏆 (semi-cactus)

D. 'Trengrove Millennium' (decorative)

D. 'Davenport Sunlight' (semi-cactus)

D. 'Mark Hardwick' (decorative)

D. 'Honka' 🏆 (orchid)

WHITE–PURPLE

***Amaryllis belladonna* 'Hathor'**
Autumn-flowering bulb with a stout, purple stem bearing fragrant, pure white flowers, 10cm (4in) long, with yellow throats. Strap-shaped, semi-erect, basal leaves appear in late winter or spring. H 50–80cm (20–32in), S 30–45cm (12–18in).

x *Amarcrinum memoria-corsii*
Evergreen, clump-forming bulb with wide, semi-erect, basal leaves. Stout stems carry fragrant, rose-pink flowers in loose heads in late summer and autumn. H and S to 1m (3ft).

Amaryllis belladonna
(Belladonna lily)
Autumn-flowering bulb with a stout, purple stem bearing fragrant, funnel-shaped, pink flowers, 10cm (4in) long. Forms strap-shaped, semi-erect, basal leaves after flowering. H 50–80cm (20–32in), S 30–45cm (12–18in).

x *Amarygia parkeri*
Early autumn-flowering bulb. Stout stem carries a large head of funnel-shaped, deep rose flowers with yellow and white throats. Produces strap-shaped, semi-erect, basal leaves after flowering. H to 1m (3ft), S 60cm–1m (2–3ft).

Gladiolus papilio
Clump-forming, summer- or autumn-flowering corm with stolons. Bears up to 10 yellow or white flowers, suffused violet, with hooded, upper petals and darker yellow patches on lower petals. H to 1m (3ft), S 15cm (6in).

WHITE

Erythronium oregonum
Clump-forming, spring-flowering tuber with 2 semi-erect, mottled, basal leaves. Has up to 3 pendent, white flowers, with yellow eyes and often brown rings near centre; petals reflex as flowers open. Increases rapidly by offsets. H to 35cm (14in), S 12cm (5in).

Allium neapolitanum
Spring-flowering bulb with narrow, semi-erect leaves on the lower quarter of flower stems. Stems each develop an umbel, 5–10cm (2–4in) across, of up to 40 white flowers. H 20–50cm (8–20in), S 10–12cm (4–5in).

Calochortus venustus
Late spring-flowering bulb with 1 or 2 narrow, erect leaves near the base of the branched stem. Bears 1–4 white, yellow, purple or red flowers, with a dark red, yellow-margined blotch on each large petal. H 20–60cm (8–24in), S 5–10cm (2–4in).

□ WHITE

***Erythronium californicum* 'White Beauty'**
Vigorous, clump-forming tuber with basal, mottled leaves. In spring has a loose spike of 1–10 reflexed, white flowers, each with a brown ring near the centre. Spreads rapidly. H 20–30cm (8–12in), S 10–12cm (4–5in).

Calochortus albus
(Fairy lantern, Globe lily)
Spring-flowering bulb with long, narrow, erect, grey-green leaves near the base of the loosely branched stem. Each branch carries a pendent, globose, white or pink flower. H 20–50cm (8–20in), S 5–10cm (2–4in).

Pamianthe peruviana
Evergreen, spring-flowering bulb with a stem-like neck and semi-erect leaves with drooping tips. Stem has a head of 2–4 fragrant, white flowers, each with a bell-shaped cup and 6 spreading petals. H 50cm (20in), S 45–60cm (18–24in). Min. 12°C (54°F).

▥ PINK

Erythronium hendersonii
Spring-flowering tuber with 2 semi-erect, basal, brown- and green-mottled leaves. Flower stem carries up to 10 lavender or lavender-pink flowers, with reflexed petals and deep purple, central eyes. H 20–30cm (8–12in), S 10–12cm (4–5in).

Allium unifolium
Late spring-flowering bulb with one semi-erect, basal, grey-green leaf. Each flower stem carries a domed umbel, 5cm (2in) across, of up to 30 purplish-pink flowers. H to 30cm (12in), S 8–10cm (3–4in).

TULIPS

Tulips are excellent in the rock garden, in formal bedding, as elegant cut flowers and for containers. Their bold flowers are generally simple in outline and held upright, often with bright, strong colours. Many of the species deserve to be more widely grown alongside the large variety of hybrids now available. *Tulipa* is classified in 15 divisions, described below.

Div.1 Single early – cup-shaped, single flowers, often opening wide in sun, are borne from early to mid-spring.
Div.2 Double early – long-lasting, double flowers open wide in early and mid-spring.
Div.3 Triumph – sturdy stems bear rather conical, single flowers, becoming more rounded, in mid- and late spring.
Div.4 Darwin hybrids – large, single flowers are borne on strong stems from mid- to late spring.
Div.5 Single late – single flowers, usually with pointed petals, are borne in late spring and very early summer.
Div.6 Lily-flowered – strong stems bear narrow-waisted, single flowers, with long, pointed, often reflexed petals, in late spring.
Div.7 Fringed – flowers are similar to those in Div.6, but have fringed petals.
Div.8 Viridiflora – variable, single flowers, with partly greenish petals, are borne in late spring.
Div.9 Rembrandt – flowers are similar to those in Div.6, but have striped or feathered patterns caused by virus, and appear in late spring.
Div.10 Parrot – has large, variable, single flowers, with frilled or fringed and usually twisted petals, in late spring.
Div.11 Double late (peony-flowered) – usually bowl-shaped, double flowers appear in late spring.
Div.12 Kaufmanniana hybrids – single flowers are usually bicoloured, open flat in the sun and appear in early spring. Leaves are usually mottled or striped.
Div.13 Fosteriana hybrids – large, single flowers open wide in the sun from early to mid-spring. Leaves are often mottled or striped.
Div.14 Greigii hybrids – large, single flowers appear in mid- and late spring. Mottled or striped leaves are often wavy-edged.
Div.15 Miscellaneous – a diverse category of other species and their cultivars and hybrids. Flowers appear in spring and early summer.

T. **'Spring Green'** (Div.8) ① 🏆

T. **'Don Quichotte'** (Div.3) ① 🏆

T. **'Page Polka'** (Div.3) ①

T. **'Peer Gynt'** (Div.3) ①

T. turkestanica (Div.15) ① 🏆

T. **'White Triumphator'** (Div.6) ① 🏆

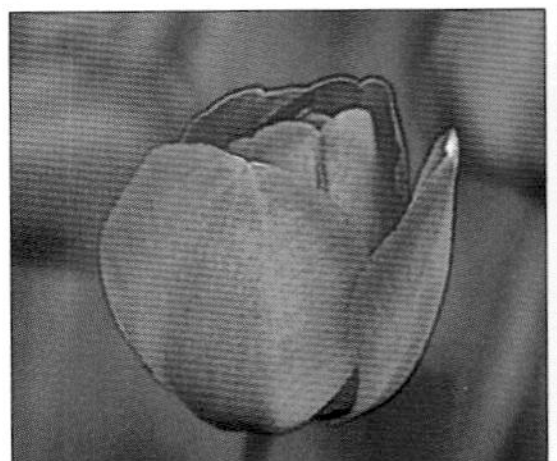

T. **'Gordon Cooper'** (Div.4) ①

T. **'Dreamland'** (Div.5) ① 🏆

T. **'White Dream'** (Div.3) ①

T. **'Diana'** (Div.1) ①

T. **'China Pink'** (Div.6) ① 🏆

T. biflora (Div.15) ①

T. **'Groenland'** (Div.8) ①

T. **'Angélique'** (Div.11) ① 🏆

T. saxatilis (Div.15) ①

T. **'Purissima'** (Div.13) ① 🏆

T. **'Carnaval de Nice'** (Div.11) ① 🏆

T. **'Menton'** (Div.5) ①

T. **'Attila'** (Div.3) ①

T. **'White Parrot'** (Div.10) ①

T. **'Fancy Frills'** (Div.10) ① 🏆

T. **'New Design'** (Div.3) ①

T. **'Ballade'** (Div.6) ① 🏆

T. **'Bird of Paradise'** (Div.10) ①

T. clusiana (Div.15) ①

T. hageri (Div.15) ①

***T.* 'Margot Fonteyn'** (Div.3) ①

***T.* 'Estella Rijnveld'** (Div.10) ①

***T.* 'Ad Rem'** (Div.4) ①

***T.* 'Red Riding Hood'** (Div.14) ①🏆

***T.* 'Queen of Sheba'** (Div.6) ①🏆

***T.* 'Fringed Beauty'** (Div.7) ①

***T.* 'Union Jack'** (Div.5) ①🏆

***T.* 'Bing Crosby'** (Div.3) ①

***T.* 'Balalaika'** (Div.5) ①

T. acuminata (Div.15) ①

***T.* 'Glück'** (Div.12) ①

***T.* 'Garden Party'** (Div.3) ①

***T.* 'Juan'** (Div.13) ①🏆

***T.* 'Cape Cod'** (Div.14) ①

***T.* 'Keizerskroon'** (Div.1) ①🏆

***T.* 'Madame Lefèber'** (Div.13) ①

***T.* 'Kingsblood'** (Div.5) ①🏆

***T.* 'Apeldoorn's Elite'** (Div.4) ①🏆

T. sprengeri (Div.15)①🏆

***T.* 'Uncle Tom'** (Div.11) ①

***T.* 'Lustige Witwe'** (Div.3) ①

***T.* 'Flaming Parrot'** (Div.10) ①

T. batalinii (Div.15) ①🏆

T. linifolia (Div.15)①🏆

***T. praestans* 'Unicum'** (Div.15)①

T. marjolletii (Div.15) ①

***T.* 'West Point'** (Div.6) ①🏆

T. urumiensis (Div.15) ①🏆

T. 'Golden Apeldoorn' (Div.4) ①

T. 'Golden Artist' (Div.8) ①

T. 'Prinses Irene' (Div.1) ①♀

T. whittallii (Div.15) ①

T. kaufmanniana (Div.15) ①

T. 'Maja' (Div.7) ①

T. 'Giuseppe Verdi' (Div.12) ①

T. praestans 'Van Tubergen's Variety' (Div.15) ①

T. 'Dreaming Maid' (Div.3) ①

T. tarda (Div.15) ①♀

T. 'Fringed Elegance' ①

T. violacea (Div.15) ①

T. humilis (Div.15) ①

T. sylvestris (Div.15) ①

T. 'Yokohama' (Div.1) ①

T. 'Dreamboat' (Div.14) ①

T. 'Blue Parrot' (Div.10) ①

T. 'Queen of Night' (Div.5) ①

T. clusiana var. chrysantha (Div.15) ①♀

T. 'Artist' (Div.8) ①♀

T. 'Shakespeare' (Div.12) ①

T. 'Bellona' (Div.1) ①♀

T. 'Candela' (Div.13) ①

T. 'Dillenburg' (Div.5) ①

T. orphanidea (Div.15) ①

T. 'Greuze' (Div.5) ①

RED–PURPLE

Anemone pavonina
Leafy tuber with cup-shaped, single, dark-centred, scarlet, purple or blue flowers rising above divided, frilly leaves in early spring. H 40cm (16in), S 20cm (8in).

Sprekelia formosissima
(Aztec lily, Jacobean lily)
Clump-forming, spring-flowering bulb with semi-erect, basal leaves. Stem bears a deep red flower, 12cm (5in) wide, that has 6 narrow petals with green-striped bases. H 15–35cm (6–14in), S 12–15cm (5–6in).

Sauromatum venosum
(Monarch-of-the-East, Voodoo lily)
Early spring-flowering tuber. Bears a large, acrid, purple-spotted spathe, then a lobed leaf on a long, spotted stalk. H 30–45cm (12–18in), S 30–35cm (12–14in). Min. 5–7°C (41–5°F).

Fritillaria meleagris
(Snake's-head fritillary)
Spring-flowering bulb with slender stems producing scattered, narrow, grey-green leaves. Has solitary bell-shaped, prominently chequered flowers, in shades of pinkish-purple or white. H to 30cm (12in), S 5–8cm (2–3in).

Fritillaria pyrenaica
Spring-flowering bulb with scattered, lance-shaped leaves, often rather narrow. Develops 1, or rarely 2, broadly bell-shaped flowers with flared-tipped, chequered, deep brownish- or blackish-purple petals. H 15–30cm (6–12in), S 5–8cm (2–3in).

PURPLE

Muscari latifolium
Spring-flowering bulb with one strap-shaped, semi-erect, basal, grey-green leaf. Has a dense spike of tiny, bell-shaped, blackish-violet to -blue flowers with constricted mouths; upper ones are paler and smaller. H to 25cm (10in), S 5–8cm (2–3in).

Fritillaria camschatcensis
(Black sarana)
Spring-flowering bulb. Stout stems carry lance-shaped, glossy leaves, mostly in whorls. Bears up to 8 deep blackish-purple or brown flowers. Needs humus-rich soil. H 15–60cm (6–24in), S 8–10cm (3–4in).

Leucocoryne ixioides
(Glory-of-the-sun)
Spring-flowering bulb with long, narrow, semi-erect, basal leaves that are withered by flowering time. Wiry, slender flower stem has a loose head of up to 10 lilac-blue flowers. H 30–40cm (12–16in), S 8–10cm (3–4in).

BLUE

Hyacinthoides* × *massartiana
(Spanish bluebell)
Spring-flowering bulb with strap-shaped, glossy leaves and pendent, bell-shaped, blue, white or pink flowers. H to 30cm (12in), S 10–15cm (4–6in).

Hyacinthoides non-scripta
(English bluebell)
Tuft-forming, spring-flowering bulb with strap-shaped leaves. An erect stem, arching at the apex, bears fragrant, blue, pink or white flowers. H 20–40cm (8–16in), S 8–10cm (3–4in).

Ixiolirion tataricum
Spring- to early summer-flowering bulb with long, narrow, semi-erect leaves on the lower part of stem. Has a loose cluster of blue flowers with a darker, central line along each petal. H to 40cm (16in), S 8–10cm (3–4in).

GREEN

Fritillaria acmopetala
Spring-flowering bulb with slender stems that bear narrowly lance-shaped, scattered leaves, and 1 or 2 broadly bell-shaped, green flowers, with brown-stained petals flaring outwards at the tips. H 15–40cm (6–16in), S 5–8cm (2–3in).

Fritillaria pontica
Spring-flowering bulb with stems carrying lance-shaped, grey-green leaves, the topmost in a whorl of 3. Has solitary broadly bell-shaped, green flowers, 3–4.5cm (1¼–1¾in) long, often suffused brown. H 15–45cm (6–18in), S 5–8cm (2–3in).

Arisaema triphyllum
(Jack-in-the-pulpit)
Summer-flowering tuber with 3-lobed, erect leaves. Produces green or purple spathes, hooded at tips, followed by bright red berries. H 40–50cm (16–20in), S 30–45cm (12–18in).

Ixia viridiflora
Spring- to early summer-flowering corm with very narrow, erect leaves mostly at stem base. Carries a spike of flattish, jade-green flowers, 2.5–5cm (1–2in) across, with purple-black eyes. H 30–60cm (12–24in), S 2.5–5cm (1–2in).

Hermodactylus tuberosus
(Widow iris)
Spring-flowering perennial with finger-like tubers. Long, narrow, grey-green leaves are square in cross-section. Has a fragrant, yellowish-green flower with large, blackish-brown-tipped petals. H 20–40cm (8–16in), S 5–8cm (2–3in).

Fritillaria cirrhosa
Spring-flowering bulb with slender stems and narrow, whorled leaves; upper leaves have tendril-like tips. Produces up to 4 widely bell-shaped flowers, purple or yellowish-green with dark purple chequered patterns. H to 60cm (24in), S 5–8cm (2–3in).

Fritillaria pallidiflora
Robust, spring-flowering bulb with broadly lance-shaped, grey-green leaves, scattered or in pairs on stem. Has 1–5 widely bell-shaped, yellow to greenish-yellow flowers, usually faintly chequered brownish-red within. H 15–70cm (6–28in), S 8–10cm (3–4in).

Arum creticum
Spring-flowering tuber that bears white or yellow spathes, each bottle-shaped at the base, slightly reflexed at the apex and with a protruding, yellow spadix. Has arrow-shaped, semi-erect, deep green leaves in autumn. H 30–50cm (12–20in), S 20–30cm (8–12in).

☼ ◊ ❄❄

Ferraria crispa
Spring-flowering corm with leafy stem bearing a succession of upward-facing, brown or yellowish-brown flowers, 4–5cm (1½–2in) across, with 6 wavy-edged, spreading petals that are conspicuously lined and blotched. H 20–40cm (8–16in), S 8–10cm (3–4in).

☼ ◊ ❄

***Gladiolus* 'Christabel'**
Spring-flowering corm with a wiry stem producing a loose spike of fragrant, widely funnel-shaped, primrose-yellow flowers, 6–8cm (2½–3in) across, with purple-brown-veined, upper petals. H to 45cm (18in), S 8–10cm (3–4in).

***Erythronium* 'Pagoda'**
Robust, spring-flowering tuber with 2 semi-erect, basal, faintly mottled, glossy leaves. Flower stem produces up to 10 pendent, pale yellow flowers with reflexed petals. H 25–35cm (10–14in), S 15–20cm (6–8in).

Calochortus luteus
(Yellow mariposa)
Late spring-flowering bulb with long, narrow, erect leaves near the base of the loosely branched stem. Each branch bears a 3-petalled, yellow flower with central, brown blotches. H 20–45cm (8–18in), S 5–10cm (2–4in).

☼ ◊ ❄❄

Daffodils

N. cantabricus (Div.13) ①

Narcissus graces the garden early in the year with its diverse flowers, from the tiny Cyclamineus daffodil, with its swept-back petals, to the stately trumpet daffodil. Many daffodils may be naturalized, forming a golden carpet in grass or a wild garden, but dwarf forms are best in rock gardens or troughs.

The genus is classified in 13 divisions. Their flower forms are illustrated below, with the exception of Div.12, miscellaneous, and Div.13, mostly wild species. Both have varying flowers, including hoop-petticoat forms, produced between autumn and early summer.

***N.* 'Portrush'** (Div.3) ①

N. poeticus var. ***recurvus*** (Div.13) ①🏆

Div.1 Trumpet – usually solitary flowers each have a trumpet that is as long as, or longer, than the petals. Early to late spring-flowering.

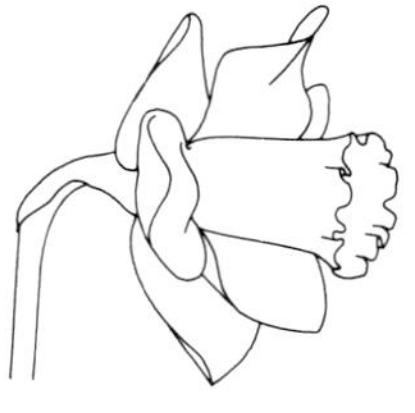

Div.2 Large-cupped – solitary flowers each have a cup at least one-third the length of, but shorter than, the petals. Spring-flowering.

***N.* 'Trousseau'** (Div.1) ①

N. rupicola subsp. ***watieri*** (Div.13) ①

Div.3 Small-cupped – flowers are often borne singly; each has a cup not more than one-third the length of the petals. Spring- or early summer-flowering.

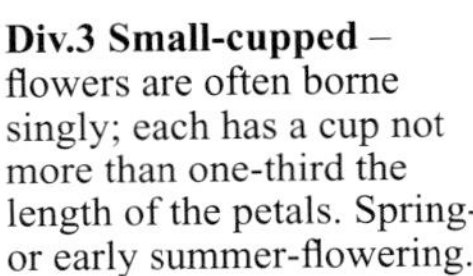

Div.4 Double – most have solitary large, fully or semi-double flowers with the cup and petals, or just the cup, replaced by petaloid structures. Some have smaller flowers in clusters of 4 or more. Spring- or early summer-flowering.

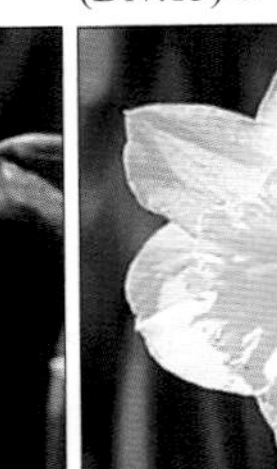

***N.* 'Cheerfulness'** (Div.4) ①🏆

***N.* 'Ice Follies'** (Div.2) ①🏆

Div.5 Triandrus – nodding flowers, with short, sometimes straight-sided cups and narrow, reflexed petals, are borne 2–6 per stem. Spring-flowering.

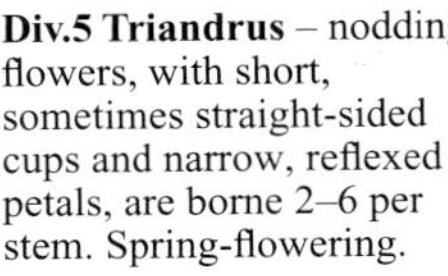

Div.6 Cyclamineus – flowers are borne usually 1 or 2 per stem with cups that are sometimes flanged and often longer than those of Div.5. Petals are narrow, pointed and reflexed. Early to mid-spring flowering.

Div.7 Jonquil – sweetly scented flowers are borne usually 2 or more per stem. Cups are short, sometimes flanged; petals are often flat, fairly broad and rounded. Spring-flowering.

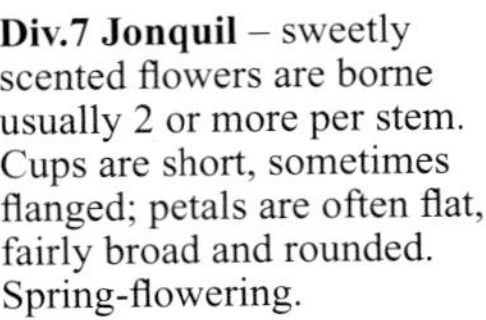

Div.8 Tazetta – flowers are borne in clusters of either 12 or more small, fragrant flowers per stem or 3 or 4 large ones. Cups are small and often straight-sided, petals broad and mostly pointed. Late autumn- to mid-spring-flowering.

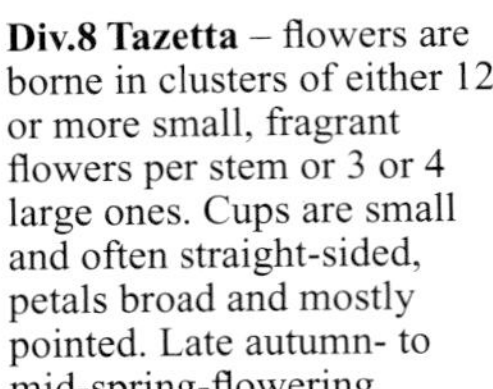

Div.9 Poeticus – flowers each have a small, coloured cup and glistening white petals. They are borne usually 1 but sometimes 2 per stem and may be sweetly fragrant. Late spring- or early summer-flowering.

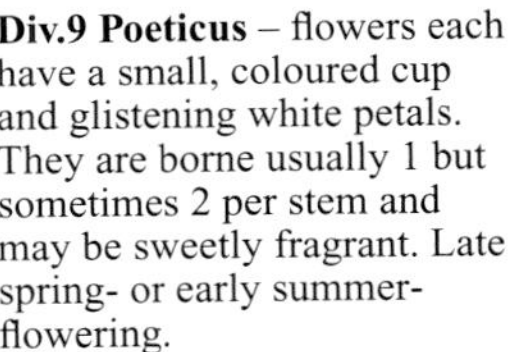

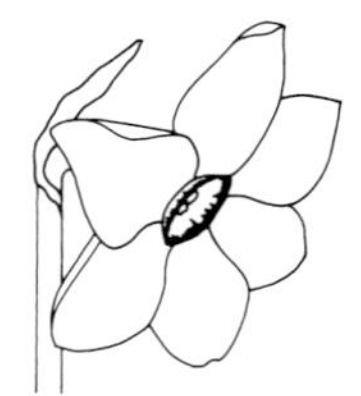

Div.10 Bulbocodium – flowers usually borne singly on very short stems, with insignificant petals and large, widely flaring cups. Winter- to spring-flowering.

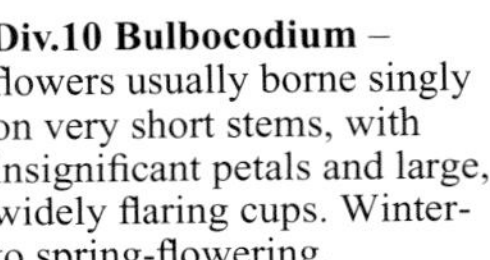

Div.11 Split-cupped – usually solitary flowers that have cups split for more than half their length. Spring-flowering.

(a) Collar – wide cup segments lie back on the petals.

(b) Papillon – narrower cup segments have tips arranged at the margin of the petals.

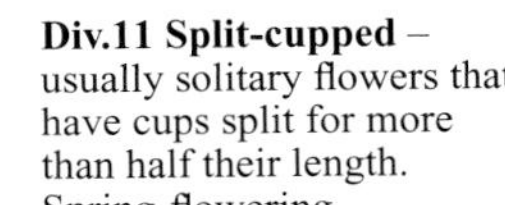

***N.* 'Thalia'** (Div.5) ①

***N.* 'Irene Copeland'** (Div.4) ①

***N.* 'Aircastle'** (Div.3) ①

***N.* 'Canisp'** (Div.2) ①

***N.* 'Passionale'** (Div.2) ①🏆

N. 'Rainbow' (Div.2) ⓘ♀

N. 'Dove Wings' (Div.6) ⓘ♀

N. 'Jack Snipe' (Div.6) ⓘ♀

N. 'February Silver' (Div.6) ⓘ

N. 'Silver Chimes' (Div.8) ⓘ

N. 'Honeybird' (Div.1) ⓘ

N. triandrus (Div.13) ⓘ♀

N. 'Satin Pink' (Div.2) ⓘ

N. 'Woodland Star' (Div.3)

N. 'Rockall' (Div.3) ⓘ

N. 'Avalanche' (Div.8) ⓘ♀

N. 'Binkie' (Div.2) ⓘ

N. 'Actaea' (Div.9) ⓘ♀

N. 'Bridal Crown' (Div.4) ⓘ♀

N. 'Panache' (Div.1) ⓘ

N. 'Empress of Ireland' (Div.1) ⓘ♀

N. 'Kilworth' (Div.2) ⓘ

N. 'Acropolis' (Div.4) ⓘ

N. 'Canaliculatus' (Div.8) ⓘ

N. 'Cool Crystal' (Div.3) ⓘ

N. romieuxii (Div.13) ⓘ♀

N. 'Cantabile' (Div.9) ⓘ♀

N. 'Broadway Star' (Div.11b) ⓘ

N. poeticus var. *recurvus* (Div.13) ⓘ♀

N. 'Cassata' (Div.11a) ⓘ

N. 'Merlin' (Div.3) ⓘ♀

N. 'Bravoure' (Div.1) ⓘ♀

N. 'Minnow' (Div.8) ⓘ♀

N. 'Spellbinder' (Div.1) ⓘ♀

N. pseudonarcissus (Div.13) ⓘ♕

N. 'Rip van Winkle' (Div.4) ⓘ

N. 'Sweetness' (Div.7) ⓘ♕

N. 'Ambergate' (Div.2) ⓘ

N. rupicola (Div.13) ⓘ

N. 'February Gold' (Div.6) ⓘ♕

N. 'Stratosphere' (Div.7) ⓘ♕

N. 'Suzy' (Div.7) ⓘ♕

N. 'Liberty Bells' (Div.5) ⓘ

N. jonquilla (Div.13) ⓘ♕

N. bulbocodium (Div.13) ⓘ♕

N. cyclamineus (Div.13) ⓘ♕

N. 'Jetfire' (Div.6) ⓘ♕

N. 'Home Fires' (Div.2) ⓘ

N. minor (Div.13) ⓘ♕

N. 'Pipit' (Div.7) ⓘ♕

N. 'Pencrebar' (Div.4) ⓘ

N. 'Golden Ducat' (Div.4) ⓘ

N. 'Tahiti' (Div.4) ⓘ♕

N. 'Hawera' (Div.5) ⓘ♕

N. 'Fortune' (Div.2) ⓘ

N. 'Tête-à-Tête' (Div.12) ⓘ♕

N. 'Bartley' (Div.6) ⓘ

N. 'Shining Light' (Div.2) ⓘ

N. 'Scarlet Gem' (Div.8) ⓘ

N. 'Charity May' (Div.6) ⓘ♕

N. × ***odorus*** **'Rugulosus'** (Div.7) ⓘ♕

N. 'Jumblie' (Div.12) ⓘ♕

N. 'Kingscourt' (Div.1) ⓘ♕

N. 'Grand Soleil d'Or' (Div.8) ⓘ

N. 'Altruist' (Div.3) ⓘ

ORANGE

Stenomesson variegatum
Clump-forming bulb. Bears reddish-yellow, pink or white flowers, with 6 green lobes at the apex, in winter or spring. H 30–60cm (12–24in), S 30cm (12in). Min. 10°C (50°F).

Stenomesson miniatum
Late spring-flowering bulb with strap-shaped, semi-erect, basal leaves. Bears a head of red or orange flowers, 2–4cm (¾–1½in) long, with yellow anthers. H 20–30cm (8–12in), S 10–15cm (4–6in). Min. 5°C (41°F).

Clivia miniata
Evergreen, tuft-forming rhizome with strap-shaped, semi-erect, basal, dark green leaves, 40–60cm (16–24in) long. Stems each produce a head of 10–20 orange or red flowers in spring or summer. H 40cm (16in), S 30–60cm (12–24in). Min. 10°C (50°F).

WHITE

Crinum asiaticum
Clump-forming bulb with strap-shaped, semi-erect, basal, dark green leaves, 1m (3ft) long. Leafless flower stems produce heads of long-tubed, white flowers, with narrow petals, in spring or summer. H 45–60cm (1½–2ft), S 60cm–1m (2–3ft). Min. 16°C (61°F).

Ornithogalum narbonense
Clump-forming, late spring- to summer-flowering bulb with long, narrow, semi-erect, basal, grey-green leaves. Leafless stem produces a spike of star-shaped, white flowers, 2cm (¾in) wide. H 30–40cm (12–16in), S 10–15cm (4–6in).

Pancratium illyricum
Summer-flowering bulb with strap-shaped, semi-erect, basal, greyish-green leaves. Leafless stem has a head of 5–12 fragrant, 6-petalled, white flowers, 8cm (3in) across. H to 45cm (18in), S 25–30cm (10–12in).

Triteleia hyacinthina
Late spring- to early summer-flowering corm with long, narrow, semi-erect or spreading, basal leaves. Heads of white, sometimes purple-tinged flowers are borne on wiry stems. H 30–50cm (12–20in), S 8–10cm (3–4in).

Arisaema sikokianum
Early summer-flowering tuber with erect leaves divided into 3–5 leaflets. Produces deep brownish-purple and white spathes, 15cm (6in) long, with club-like, white spadices protruding from the mouths. H 30–50cm (12–20in), S 30–45cm (12–18in).

WHITE

Ornithogalum thyrsoides (Chincherinchee)
Summer-flowering bulb with strap-shaped, semi-erect, basal leaves. Bears a dense, conical spike of cup-shaped, white flowers, 2–3cm (¾–1¼in) across. H 30–45cm (12–18in), S 10–15cm (4–6in).

Zigadenus fremontii
Clump-forming, early summer-flowering bulb with long, strap-shaped, semi-erect, basal leaves. Stem produces a spike of star-shaped, pale creamy-green flowers with darker green nectaries on petal bases. H 30–50cm (12–20in), S 10–15cm (4–6in).

Hymenocallis narcissiflora (Peruvian daffodil)
Spring- or summer-flowering bulb with semi-erect, basal leaves, dying down in winter. Bears a loose head of 2–5 fragrant, white flowers. H to 60cm (24in), S 30–45cm (12–18in).

WHITE–RED

Ornithogalum arabicum
Early summer-flowering bulb with strap-shaped, semi-erect leaves in a basal cluster. Has a flattish head of up to 15 scented, white or creamy-white flowers, 4–5cm (1½–2in) across, with black ovaries in centres. H 30–45cm (12–18in), S 10–15cm (4–6in).

Allium cernuum
Clump-forming, summer-flowering bulb with narrow, semi-erect, basal leaves. Each stem produces up to 30 cup-shaped, pink or white flowers in a loose, nodding umbel, 2–4cm (¾–1½in) across. H 30–70cm (12–28in), S 8–12cm (3–5in).

Allium senescens subsp. ***montanum***
Vigorous, clump-forming, summer-flowering bulb with strap-shaped, often twisted, grey-green leaves. Has dense umbels, 2cm (¾in) across, of up to 30 long-lasting, cup-shaped, pink flowers. H 45cm (18in), S 60cm (24in).

Alstroemeria pelegrina
Summer-flowering tuber with narrow, lance-shaped leaves. Each leafy stem has 1–3 white flowers, stained pinkish-mauve and spotted yellow and brownish-purple. H 30–60cm (1–2ft), S 60cm–1m (2–3ft).

Tritonia disticha subsp. ***rubrolucens***
Late summer-flowering corm with narrowly sword-shaped, erect leaves in a flattish, basal fan. Has pink flowers in a loose, one-sided spike. H 30–50cm (12–20in), S 8–10cm (3–4in).

Lycoris radiata (Red spider lily)
Late summer-flowering bulb with a head of 5 or 6 bright rose-red flowers with narrow, wavy-margined, reflexed petals and conspicuous anthers. Has strap-shaped, semi-erect, basal leaves after flowering time. H 30–40cm (12–16in), S 10–15cm (4–6in).

RED–PURPLE

Rhodophiala advena
Clump-forming, spring- to summer-flowering bulb with basal, grey-green leaves. Leafless stem carries a head of 2–8 narrowly funnel-shaped, red flowers, 5cm (2in) long. H to 40cm (16in), S 15–20cm (6–8in).

Ranunculus var. **asiaticus** (Persian buttercup)
Early summer-flowering perennial with claw-like tubers and long-stalked leaves both at base and on stem. Has single or double flowers in red, white, pink, yellow or orange. H 45–55cm (18–22in), S 10cm (4in).

Allium schubertii
Early summer-flowering bulb with widely strap-shaped, semi-erect, basal leaves. Bears large umbels of 40 or more star-shaped, pink or purple flowers on very unequal stalks, then brown seed capsules. H 30–60cm (12–24in), S 15–20cm (6–8in).

PURPLE

Allium cristophii
Summer-flowering bulb with semi-erect, hairy, grey leaves that droop at tips. Has a large, spherical umbel of 50 or more star-shaped, purplish-violet flowers, which dry well. H 15–40cm (6–16in), S 15–20cm (6–8in).

Patersonia umbrosa
Evergreen, clump-forming, spring- and early summer-flowering rhizome with erect, basal leaves. Tough flower stems each carry a succession of iris-like, purple-blue flowers, 3–4cm (1¼–1½in) across. H 30–45cm (12–18in), S 30–60cm (12–24in).

Gloxinia perennis
Late summer- to autumn-flowering rhizome with heart-shaped, toothed, hairy leaves on spotted stems. Has bell-shaped, lavender-blue flowers, with rounded lobes and purple-blotched throats. H to 60cm (24in), S 30–35cm (12–14in). Min. 10°C (50°F).

BLUE

Allium caeruleum
Clump-forming, summer-flowering bulb with narrow, erect leaves on the lower third of slender flower stems, which bear 30–50 star-shaped, blue flowers in a dense, spherical umbel, 3–4cm (1¼–1½in) across. H 20–80cm (8–32in), S 10–15cm (4–6in).

Triteleia laxa
Early summer-flowering corm with narrow, semi-erect, basal leaves. Stem carries a large, loose umbel of funnel-shaped, deep to pale purple-blue flowers, 2–5cm (¾–2in) long, mostly held upright. H 10–50cm (4–20in), S 8–10cm (3–4in).

GREEN–YELLOW

Arisaema griffithii
Summer-flowering tuber with large, erect leaves above a green or purple spathe, 20–25cm (8–10in) long, strongly netted with paler veins and expanded like a cobra's hood. Protect in winter or lift for frost-free storage. H to 60cm (24in), S 45–60cm (18–24in).

Arisaema jacquemontii
Summer-flowering tuber with 1 or 2 erect leaves, divided into wavy-edged leaflets. Produces slender, white-lined, green spathes that are hooded at tips and drawn out into long points. H 30–50cm (12–20in), S 30–38cm (12–15in).

Eucomis bicolor
Summer-flowering bulb with wavy-edged, semi-erect, basal leaves. Stem, often spotted purple, bears a spike of green or greenish-white flowers, with 6 purple-edged petals, topped by a cluster of leaf-like bracts. H 30–50cm (12–20in), S 30–60cm (12–24in).

Allium flavum
Clump-forming, summer-flowering bulb. Leaves are linear and semi-erect on lower half of slender flower stem. Produces a loose umbel of up to 60 small, bell-shaped, yellow flowers on thin, arching stalks. H 10–35cm (4–14in), S 5–8cm (2–3in).

Cyrtanthus mackenii* var. *cooperi
Clump-forming, summer-flowering bulb with long, narrow, semi-erect, basal leaves. Leafless stems each carry a head of up to 10 fragrant, tubular, cream or yellow flowers, 5cm (2in) long and slightly curved. H 30–40cm (12–16in), S 8–10cm (3–4in).

Calochortus barbatus
Summer-flowering bulb with narrow, erect leaves near the base of the loosely branched stem. Each branch bears a pendent, yellow or greenish-yellow flower that is hairy inside. H 30–60cm (12–24in), S 5–10cm (2–4in).

Ranunculus asiaticusv var. ***flavus***
(Persian buttercup)
Early summer-flowering perennial with claw-like tubers and long-stalked, palmate leaves at base and on stem. Has single or double flowers in yellow, white, pink, red or orange. H 45–55cm (18–22in), S 8–10cm (3–4in).

Cypella herbertii
Summer-flowering bulb with a fan of narrow, sword-shaped, erect, basal leaves. Branched flower stem carries a succession of short-lived, iris-like, orange-yellow flowers, each spotted purple in the centre. H 30–50cm (12–20in), S 8–10cm (3–4in).

***Alstroemeria* 'Parigo Charm'**
Summer-flowering tuber with narrow, twisted, mid- to grey-green leaves and umbels of salmon-pink flowers. The inner tepals are primrose-yellow, marked carmine-red. H 1m (3ft), S 60cm (24in).

Polianthes geminiflora
Summer-flowering tuber with narrowly strap-shaped, semi-erect leaves in a basal tuft. Stems each carry long spikes of downward-curving, tubular, red or orange flowers in pairs. H 20–40cm (8–16in), S 10–15cm (4–6in).

***Alstroemeria* Ligtu Hybrids**
Summer-flowering tuber with narrow, twisted leaves and heads of widely flared flowers in shades of pink, yellow or orange, often spotted or streaked with contrasting colours. H 45–60cm (1½–2ft), S 60cm–1m (2–3ft).

Sandersonia aurantiaca
(Chinese-lantern lily)
Deciduous, summer-flowering, tuberous climber with a slender stem bearing scattered, lance-shaped leaves, some tendril-tipped. Orange flowers are produced in axils of upper leaves.
H 60cm (24in), S 25–30cm (10–12in).

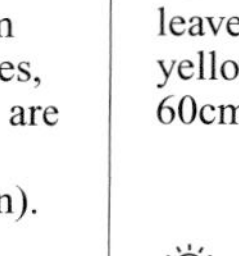

***Crocosmia* 'Jackanapes'**
Clump-forming, late summer-flowering corm with sword-shaped, erect, basal leaves. Produces striking bicoloured, yellow and orange-red flowers. H 40–60cm (16–24in), S 15–20cm (6–8in).

Tigridia pavonia
(Peacock flower, Tiger flower)
Summer-flowering bulb with sword-shaped, pleated, erect leaves near stem base. A succession of short-lived flowers vary from white to orange, red or yellow, often with contrasting spots.
H to 45cm (18in), S 12–15cm (4–6in).

WHITE–PINK

Nerine bowdenii* f. *alba
Autumn-flowering bulb with a stout stem and strap-shaped, semi-erect, basal leaves. Produces a head of 5–10 white, often pink-flushed flowers; petals widen slightly towards wavy-margined, recurved tips. H 45–60cm (18–24in), S 12–15cm (5–6in).

Nerine undulata
Autumn-flowering bulb with narrowly strap-shaped, semi-erect, basal leaves. Flower stem carries a head of pink flowers with very narrow petals crinkled for their whole length. H 30–45cm (12–18in), S 10–12cm (4–5in).

***Nerine* 'Orion'**
Autumn-flowering bulb with strap-shaped, semi-erect, basal leaves. Stout, leafless stem bears a head of pale pink flowers with very wavy-margined petals that have recurved tips. H 30–50cm (12–20in), S 20–25cm (8–10in).

Nerine bowdenii
Autumn-flowering bulb with a stout stem and strap-shaped, semi-erect, basal leaves. Carries a head of 5–10 glistening, pink flowers with petals that widen slightly towards wavy-margined, recurved tips. H 45–60cm (18–24in), S 12–15cm (5–6in).

Scilla scilloides
Late summer- and autumn-flowering bulb with 2–4 narrowly strap-shaped, semi-erect, basal leaves. Stem bears a slender, dense spike of up to 30 flattish, pink flowers, 0.5–1cm (¼–½in) across. H to 30cm (12in), S 5cm (2in).

PINK–ORANGE

Zephyranthes grandiflora
Late summer- to early autumn-flowering bulb with narrowly strap-shaped, semi-erect, basal leaves. Each stem bears a funnel-shaped, pink flower, held almost erect. H 20–30cm (8–12in), S 8–10cm (3–4in).

***Nerine* 'Brian Doe'**
Autumn-flowering bulb with strap-shaped, semi-erect, basal leaves. Stout, leafless stem bears a head of salmon flowers with 6 reflexed, wavy-margined petals. H 30–50cm (12–20in), S 20–25cm (8–10in).

***Nerine sarniensis* (Guernsey lily)**
Autumn-flowering bulb with strap-shaped, semi-erect, basal leaves. Leafless stem carries a spherical head of up to 20 deep orange-pink flowers, 6–8cm (2½–3in) across, with wavy-margined petals. H 45–60cm (18–24in), S 12–15cm (5–6in).

WHITE–RED

Eucharis amazonica
Evergreen, clump-forming bulb with strap-shaped, semi-erect, basal leaves. Bears a head of up to 6 fragrant, slightly pendent, white flowers at almost any season. H 40–60cm (16–24in), S 60cm–1m (2–3ft). Min. 15°C (59°F).

***Hippeastrum* 'Apple Blossom'**
Winter- to spring-flowering bulb with strap-shaped, semi-erect, basal leaves produced as, or just after, flowers form. Stout stem has a head of 2–6 white flowers, becoming pink at petal tips. H 30–50cm (12–20in), S 30cm (12in). Min. 13°C (55°F).

***Hippeastrum* 'Striped'**
Winter- to spring-flowering bulb with strap-shaped, semi-erect, basal leaves produced with or just after flowers. Stout stem has a head of 2–6 widely funnel-shaped flowers, striped white and red. H 50cm (20in), S 30cm (12in). Min. 13°C (55°F).

Veltheimia bracteata
Clump-forming, winter-flowering bulb with semi-erect, strap-shaped, basal, glossy leaves and dense spikes of pendent, tubular, pink, red or yellowish-red flowers. H 30–45cm (12–18in), S 25–38cm (10–15in). Min. 10°C (50°F).

***Hippeastrum* 'Red Lion'**
Tuft-forming, winter- and spring-flowering bulb with a stout stem bearing a head of 2–6 dark red flowers with yellow anthers. Strap-shaped leaves appear with or just after flowers. H 30–50cm (12–20in), S 30cm (12in). Min. 13°C (55°F).

Hippeastrum aulicum
Winter- and spring-flowering bulb with a basal cluster of strap-shaped, semi-erect leaves. Stout stem bears two red flowers with green-striped petals and green throats. H 30–50cm (12–20in), S 30cm (12in). Min. 13–15°C (55–59°F).

RED–YELLOW

***Hippeastrum* 'Orange Sovereign'**
Winter- to spring-flowering bulb with strap-shaped, semi-erect, basal, grey-green leaves produced as, or just after, flowers form. Stout stem carries a head of 2–6 rich orange-red flowers. H 30–50cm (12–20in), S 30cm (12in). Min. 13°C (55°F).

Lachenalia orchioides* var. *glaucina
Late winter- and early spring-flowering bulb with 2 strap-shaped, semi-erect, basal leaves, usually spotted purple. Has a spike of fragrant, whitish-blue or pale lilac flowers. H to 30cm (12in), S 5–8cm (2–3in).

***Freesia* 'Oberon'**
Winter- and spring-flowering corm with narrow, erect, basal leaves. Produces yellow flowers, 4–5cm (1½–2in) long, light blood-red inside; the throats are lemon-yellow with small, red veins. H to 40cm (16in), S 4–6cm (1½–2½in).

□ WHITE

***Anemone blanda* 'White Splendour'**
Knobbly tuber with semi-erect leaves that have 3 deeply toothed lobes. Bears upright, flattish, white flowers, 4–5cm (1½–2in) across, with 9–14 narrow petals, in early spring. H 5–10cm (2–4in), S 10–15cm (4–6in).

***Puschkinia scilloides* var. *libanotica* 'Alba'**
Spring-flowering bulb with usually 2 strap-shaped, semi-erect, basal leaves. Produces a dense spike of star-shaped, white flowers, 1.5–2cm (⅝–¾in) across. H 15cm (6in), S 2.5–5cm (1–2in).

Ornithogalum balansae
Spring-flowering bulb with 2 almost prostrate, inversely lance-shaped, mid-green basal leaves. Has a broad head of 2–5 flowers, glistening white inside, bright green outside, that open wide. H 5–15cm (2–6in), S 5–8cm (2–3in).

Leucojum vernum
(Spring snowflake)
Spring-flowering bulb with strap-shaped, semi-erect, basal leaves. Leafless stem carries 1 or 2 pendent, bell-shaped flowers, 1.5–2cm (⅝–¾in) long, with 6 green-tipped, white petals. H 10–15cm (4–6in), S 8–10cm (3–4in).

Sternbergia candida
Spring-flowering bulb. Strap-shaped, semi-erect, basal, greyish-green leaves appear together with a fragrant, funnel-shaped, white flower, 4–5cm (1½–2in) long, borne on a leafless stem. H 10–20cm (4–8in), S 8–10cm (3–4in).

Ornithogalum montanum
Clump-forming, spring-flowering bulb with strap-shaped, semi-erect, basal, grey-green leaves. Leafless stem produces a head of star-shaped, white flowers, 3–4cm (1¼–1½in) across, striped green outside. H and S 10–15cm (4–6in).

Ornithogalum lanceolatum
Spring-flowering, dwarf bulb with a flattish rosette of prostrate, lance-shaped, basal leaves. Carries a head of flattish, star-shaped, white flowers, 3–4cm (1¼–1½in) across, broadly striped green outside. H 5–10cm (2–4in), S 10–15cm (4–6in).

WHITE–PINK

Erythronium californicum
Clump-forming, spring-flowering tuber. Has 2 semi-erect, basal, mottled leaves. Up to 3 white or creamy-white flowers, sometimes red-brown externally, have reflexed petals, yellow eyes and often brown rings near centres. H 15–35cm (6–14in), S 10–12cm (4–5in).

Allium akaka
Spring-flowering bulb with 1–3 broad, prostrate and basal, grey-green leaves and an almost stemless, spherical umbel, 5–7cm (2–3in) across of 30–40 star-shaped, white to pinkish-white flowers with red centres. H 15–20cm (6–8in), S 12–15cm (5–6in).

Allium karataviense
Late spring-flowering bulb with narrowly elliptic to elliptic, prostrate, basal, greyish-purple leaves. Stem bears 50 or more star-shaped, pale purplish-pink flowers in a spherical umbel, 15cm (6in) or more across. H to 20cm (8in), S 25–30cm (10–12in).

PINK

***Chionodoxa* 'Pink Giant'**
Early spring-flowering bulb with 2 narrow, semi-erect, basal leaves. Leafless stem produces a spike of 5–10 flattish, white-eyed, pink flowers, 2–2.5cm (¾–1in) across. H 10–25cm (4–10in), S 2.5–5cm (1–2in).

Cyclamen libanoticum
Spring-flowering tuber with ivy-shaped, dull green leaves with lighter patterns and purplish-green undersides. Has musty-scented, clear pink flowers, each with deep carmine marks at the mouth. Grows best in an alpine house. H to 10cm (4in), S 10–15cm (4–6in).

Anemone tschaernjaewii
Spring-flowering tuber with 3-palmate, oval, mid-green leaves, the leaflets shallowly lobed. Has 5-petalled, saucer-shaped, purple-centred, white or pink flowers, 2–4.5cm (¾–1¾in) across. Needs warm, dry, summer dormancy. H 5–10cm (2–4in), S 5–8cm (2–3in).

C. 'Eyecatcher'

CROCUSES

Crocus (*Crocus* species and cultivars) are versatile and reliable dwarf bulbous plants. Most flower in late winter or early spring; a few flower in autumn. Colours range from white through pinkish-lilac to rich purples, creams and yellows, many attractively striped or feathered with other colours. Their usually goblet-shaped flowers, sometimes produced before the leaves, open wide in full sun, in some cases to reveal contrasting centres or conspicuous stamens. Most crocuses are also fragrant. Plant in rock gardens in association with other early-flowering dwarf bulbs or perennials, or *en masse* in drifts or beneath deciduous trees and shrubs, where they will rapidly colonize large areas. To promote vigour, feed once the flowers have faded. If naturalized in grass, delay mowing until the leaves have died down.

C. minimus

C. vernus subsp. *albiflorus*

C. sieberi 'Bowles' White' 🏆

C. tommasinianus f. *albus*

C. goulimyi 🏆

C. imperati 'De Jager'

C. malyi 🏆

C. boryi

C. hadriaticus 🏆

C. sieberi subsp. *sublimis* f. *tricolor* 🏆

C. etruscus 'Zwanenburg'

C. 'Snow Bunting' 🏆

C. kotschyanus 🏆

C. dalmaticus

C. medius 🏆

C. nudiflorus

C. 'Blue Bird'

C. laevigatus 🏆

C. pulchellus 🏆

C. 'Blue Pearl' 🏆

C. banaticus 🏆

C. etruscus 🏆

C. longiflorus ♀

C. baytopiorum

C. sieberi 'Hubert Edelsten' ♀

C. speciosus 'Conqueror'

C. vernus 'Queen of the Blues'

C. biflorus

C. 'Advance'

C. vernus

C. tommasinianus 'Ruby Giant'

C. vernus 'Prinses Juliana'

C. vernus 'Pickwick'

C. 'Dorothy'

C. cvijicii

C. 'Ladykiller' ♀

C. tommasinianus 'Whitewell Purple'

C. speciosus ♀

C. vernus 'Purpureus Grandiflorus'

C. cartwrightianus ♀

C. 'Cream Beauty' ♀

C. vernus 'Remembrance'

C. speciosus 'Oxonian'

C. gargaricus

C. 'E.A. Bowles' ♀

PINK

Erythronium dens-canis
(Dog's-tooth violet)
Spring-flowering tuber with 2 basal, mottled leaves. Stem has a pendent, pink, purple or white flower, with bands of brown, purple and yellow near the centre and reflexed petals. H 15–25cm (6–10in), S 8–10cm (3–4in).

Allium acuminatum
Spring-flowering bulb with 2–4 long, narrow, semi-erect, basal leaves. Stem bears an umbel, 5cm (2in) across, of up to 30 small, purplish-pink flowers. H 10–30cm (4–12in), S 5–8cm (2–3in).

Allium oreophilum
Spring- and summer-flowering, dwarf bulb with 2 narrow, semi-erect, basal leaves. Has loose, domed umbels of up to 10 widely bell-shaped, deep rose-pink flowers, 1.5–2cm (⅝–¾in) across. H 5–10cm (2–4in), S 8–10cm (3–4in).

***Anemone blanda* 'Radar'**
Knobbly tuber with semi-erect, deep green leaves with 3 deeply toothed lobes. In early spring, stems each bear an upright, flattish, white-centred, deep reddish-carmine flower with 9–14 narrow petals. H 5–10cm (2–4in), S 10–15cm (4–6in).

RED–PURPLE

Anemone × fulgens
Spring- or early summer-flowering tuber with deeply divided, semi-erect, basal leaves. Stout stems each carry an upright, bright red flower, 5–7cm (2–3in) across, with 10–15 petals. H 10–30cm (4–12in), S 8–10cm (3–4in).

Sparaxis tricolor
Spring-flowering corm with erect, lance-shaped leaves in a basal fan. Stem produces a loose spike of up to 5 flattish, orange, red, purple, pink or white flowers, 5–6cm (2–2½in) across, with black or red centres. H 10–30cm (4–12in), S 8–12cm (3–5in).

Bulbocodium vernum
Spring-flowering corm with stemless, widely funnel-shaped, reddish-purple flowers. Narrow, semi-erect, basal leaves appear with flowers but do not elongate until later. Dies down in summer. H 3–4cm (1¼–1½in), S 3–5cm (1¼–2in).

Babiana rubrocyanea (Winecups)
Spring-flowering corm with lance-shaped, erect, folded leaves in a basal fan. Carries short spikes of 5–10 flowers, each with 6 petals, purple-blue at the top and red at the base. H 15–20cm (6–8in), S 5–8cm (2–3in). Min. 10°C (50°F).

☼ ◊

***Ipheion uniflorum* 'Froyle Mill'**
Spring-flowering bulb with narrow, semi-erect, basal, pale green leaves that smell of onions if crushed. Each leafless stem carries a star-shaped, violet-blue flower, 3–4cm (1¼–1½in) across. H 10–15cm (4–6in), S 5–8cm (2–3in).

◐ ◊ ❄❄ 🏆

Romulea bulbocodium
Spring-flowering corm with long, semi-erect, thread-like leaves in a basal tuft. Slender flower stems each carry 1–6 upward-facing flowers, usually pale lilac-purple with yellow or white centres. H 5–10cm (2–4in). S 2.5–5cm (1–2in).

☼ ◊ ❄❄

Hyacinths

Grown for their sweet, penetrating scent, hyacinths (*Hyacinthus*) are deservedly popular spring bulbs. The most widely offered for sale are showy cultivars derived from *H. orientalis*, available in white, shades of pink, lilac, blue, purple, yellow and salmon-orange. In the garden they are most effective planted *en masse* in blocks of a single colour, or in containers near the house where their fragrance can be appreciated. They are also excellent for growing in bowls indoors; the bulbs may later be planted out. Specially treated bulbs for indoor culture are available that flower in mid-winter. (For details see the Plant Dictionary.) These forced bulbs may afterwards be planted outdoors in a sheltered spot, where they should flower again in later years. Feed the bulbs well after the flower spikes have faded.

***H. orientalis* 'Delft Blue'** ① 🏆

***H. orientalis* 'White Pearl'** ①

***H. orientalis* 'Lady Derby'** ①

***H. orientalis* 'Ostara'** ① 🏆

***H. orientalis* 'Queen of the Pinks'** ① 🏆

***H. orientalis* 'Jan Bos'** ①

***H. orientalis* 'Blue Jacket'** ① 🏆

***H. orientalis* 'City of Haarlem'** ① 🏆

***H. orientalis* 'Distinction'** ①

***H. orientalis* 'Violet Pearl'** ①

***H. orientalis* 'Princess Maria Christina'** ①

PURPLE–BLUE

Gynandriris sisyrinchium
Spring-flowering corm with 1 or 2 semi-erect, narrow, basal leaves. Wiry stems each carry a succession of lavender- to violet-blue flowers, 3–4cm (1¼–1½in) across, with white or orange patches on the 3 larger petals. H 10–20cm (4–8in), S 8–10cm (3–4in).

***Muscari comosum* 'Plumosum'**
(Feather grape hyacinth)
Spring-flowering bulb with up to 5 strap-shaped, semi-erect, basal, grey-green leaves. Sterile flowers are replaced by a fluffy mass of purple threads. H to 25cm (10in), S 10–12cm (4–5in).

Puschkinia scilloides* var. *libanotica (Striped squill)
Spring-flowering bulb with usually 2 strap-shaped, semi-erect, basal leaves. Carries a dense spike of star-shaped, pale blue flowers with a darker blue stripe down each petal centre. H 15cm (6in), S 2.5–5cm (1–2in).

Hyacinthella leucophaea
Spring-flowering bulb with 2 narrowly strap-shaped, semi-erect, basal leaves and a thin, wiry, leafless flower stem. Carries a short spike of tiny, bell-shaped, very pale blue, almost white flowers. H 10cm (4in), S 2.5–5cm (1–2in).

Brimeura amethystina
Late spring-flowering bulb with very narrow, semi-erect, basal leaves. Each leafless stem bears a spike of up to 15 pendent, tubular, blue flowers. H 10–25cm (4–10in), S 2.5–5cm (1–2in).

Bellevalia hyacinthoides
Spring-flowering bulb with prostrate, narrow leaves in a basal cluster. Bears a dense spike of up to 20 bell-shaped, pale lavender-blue, almost white flowers with darker, central veins. H 5–15cm (2–6in), S 5cm (2in).

Scilla mischtschenkoana
Early spring-flowering bulb with 2 or 3 strap-shaped, semi-erect, basal, mid-green leaves. Stems elongate as cup-shaped or flattish, pale blue flowers, with darker blue veins, open. H 5–10cm (2–4in), S 5cm (2in).

Tecophilaea cyanocrocus* var. *leichtlinii
Spring-flowering corm with 1 or 2 narrowly lance-shaped, semi-erect, basal leaves and solitary upward-facing, widely funnel-shaped, pale blue flowers with large, white centres. H 8–10cm (3–4in), S 5–8cm (2–3in).

***Scilla siberica* 'Atrocoerulea'**
Early spring-flowering bulb with 2–4 strap-shaped, semi-erect, basal, glossy leaves, widening towards tips. Bell-shaped, deep rich blue flowers, 1–1.5cm (½–⅝in) long, are borne in a short spike. H 10–15cm (4–6in), S 5cm (2in).

Muscari aucheri
Spring-flowering bulb with 2 strap-shaped, greyish-green leaves. Bears small, almost spherical, bright blue flowers with white-rimmed mouths; upper flowers are often paler.
H 5–15cm (2–6in), S 5–8cm (2–3in).

☼ ◊ ❄❄❄ 🏆

Chionodoxa luciliae
Early spring-flowering bulb with 2 somewhat curved, semi-erect, basal leaves. Leafless stem bears 1–3 upward-facing, blue flowers with white eyes. H 5–10cm (2–4in), S 2.5–5cm (1–2in).

☼ ◊ ❄❄❄ 🏆

Chionodoxa siehei
Early spring-flowering bulb with 2 semi-erect, narrow, basal leaves. Bears a spike of 5–10 outward-facing, rich blue-lilac flowers with white eyes. H 10–25cm (4–10in), S 2.5–5cm (1–2in).

☼ ◊ ❄❄❄ 🏆

Tecophilaea cyanocrocus
(Chilean blue crocus)
Spring-flowering corm with 1 or 2 lance-shaped, semi-erect, basal leaves. Carries upward-facing, funnel-shaped, deep gentian-blue flowers, 4–5cm (1½–2in) across, with white throats. H 8–10cm (3–4in), S 5–8cm (2–3in).

☼ ◊ ❄❄❄ 🏆

Muscari armeniacum
Spring-flowering bulb with 3–6 long, narrow, semi-erect, basal leaves. Carries a dense spike of small, fragrant, bell-shaped, deep blue flowers with constricted mouths that have a rim of small, paler blue or white 'teeth'.
H 15–20cm (6–8in), S 8–10cm (3–4in).

☼ ◊ ❄❄❄ 🏆

Muscari neglectum
Spring-flowering bulb. Bears 4–6 often prostrate leaves from autumn to early summer. Has small, ovoid, deep blue or blackish-blue flowers with white-rimmed mouths. Increases rapidly.
H 10–20cm (4–8in), S 8–10cm (3–4in).

☼ ◊ ❄❄❄

***Anemone blanda* 'Atrocaerulea'**
Knobbly tuber with semi-erect, dark green leaves that have 3 deeply toothed lobes. In early spring, stems each bear an upright, flattish, bright blue flower, 4–5cm (1½–2in) across, with 9–14 narrow petals. H 5–10cm (2–4in), S 10–15cm (4–6in).

◐ ◊ ❄❄❄ ⓘ

× *Chionoscilla allenii*
Early spring-flowering bulb with 2 narrow, semi-erect, basal, dark green leaves and flattish, star-shaped, deep blue flowers, 1–2cm (½–¾in) across, in a loose spike. H 10–15cm (4–6in), S 2.5–5cm (1–2in).

☼ ◊ ❄❄❄

GREEN–YELLOW

Ledebouria socialis
Evergreen, spring-flowering bulb with lance-shaped, semi-erect, basal, dark-spotted, grey or green leaves. Produces a short spike of bell-shaped, purplish-green flowers. H 5–10cm (2–4in), S 8–10cm (3–4in).

Muscari macrocarpum
Spring-flowering bulb with 3–5 semi-erect, basal, greyish-green leaves. Carries a dense spike of fragrant, brown-rimmed, bright yellow flowers. Upper flowers may initially be brownish-purple. H 10–20cm (4–8in), S 10–15cm (4–6in).

***Arum italicum* 'Marmoratum'**
Late spring-flowering tuber. Produces semi-erect leaves, with cream or white veins, in autumn, followed by pale green or creamy-white spathes, then red berries in autumn. Is good for flower arrangements. H 15–25cm (6–10in), S 20–30cm (8–12in).

YELLOW–ORANGE

Calochortus amabilis (Golden fairy lantern, Golden globe tulip)
Spring-flowering bulb with one long, narrow, erect leaf, near the base of the loosely branched stem. A fringed, deep yellow, sometimes green-tinged flower hangs from each branch. H 10–30cm (4–12in), S 5–10cm (2–4in).

Colchicum luteum
Spring-flowering corm with wineglass-shaped, yellow flowers – the only known yellow *Colchicum*. Semi-erect, basal leaves are short at flowering time but later expand. H 5–10cm (2–4in), S 5–8cm (2–3in).

Erythronium americanum
Spring-flowering tuber with 2 semierect, basal leaves, mottled green and brown, and a pendent, yellow flower, often bronze outside, with petals reflexing in sunlight. Forms clumps by stolons. H 5–25cm (2–10in), S 5–8cm (2–3in).

Fritillaria pudica
(Yellow fritillary)
Spring-flowering bulb with stems bearing scattered, narrowly lance-shaped, grey-green leaves. Has 1 or 2 deep yellow, sometimes red-tinged flowers, 1–2.5cm (½–1in) long. H 5–20cm (2–8in), S 5cm (2in).

Dipcadi serotinum
Spring-flowering bulb with 2–5 very narrow, semi-erect, basal leaves. Leafless stem has a loose spike of nodding, tubular, brown or dull orange flowers, 1–1.5cm (½–⅝in) long. H 10–30cm (4–12in), S 5–8cm (2–3in).

WHITE–PINK

Lloydia serotina
Early summer-flowering bulb with wiry stems bearing scattered, threadlike, semi-erect leaves near stem base. Carries 1 or 2 bell-shaped, white flowers, 1–1.5cm (½–⅝in) long, with purple or purple-red veins. H 5–15cm (2–6in), S 2.5–5cm (1–2in).

Arisaema candidissimum
Early summer-flowering tuber with large, cowl-like, pink-striped, white spathes, enclosing tiny, fragrant flowers on spadices, followed by broad, 3-palmate, semi-erect leaves, 30cm (12in) long. H 10–15cm (4–6in), S 30–45cm (12–18in).

Albuca humilis
Summer-flowering, dwarf bulb with very narrow, basal, dark green leaves. Carries a loose head of 1–3 cup-shaped, white flowers, 1cm (½in) long, striped green, later reddish, outside. H 5–10cm (2–4in), S 5–8cm (2–3in).

Allium schoenoprasum (Chives)
Clump-forming, summer-flowering bulb with narrow, hollow, erect, dark green leaves at base. Stems each carry up to 20 tiny, bell-shaped, pale purple or pink flowers in a dense umbel up to 5cm (2in) across. H 12–25cm (5–10in), S 5–10cm (2–4in).

Cyclamen purpurascens
Summer- and autumn-flowering tuber with rounded, silver-patterned leaves. Bears very fragrant, lilac-pink to reddish-purple flowers. H to 10cm (4in), S 10–15cm (4–6in).

RED

Hippeastrum striatum
Spring- and summer-flowering bulb with strap-shaped, semi-erect, basal, bright green leaves. Funnel-shaped flowers have pointed, scarlet petals with central, green stripes. H 30cm (12in), S 20–25cm (8–10in). Min. 15°C (59°F).

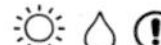

Cyrtanthus brachyscyphus
Clump-forming, summer-flowering bulb with strap-shaped, semi-erect, basal, bright green leaves. Leafless stem bears a head of 6–12 tubular, orange- or brilliant red flowers with 6 lobes. H 20–30cm (8–12in), S 10–15cm (4–6in).

Haemanthus coccineus (Blood lily)
Summer-flowering bulb with 2 elliptic leaves, hairy beneath, that lie flat on the ground. Spotted stem, forming before leaves, bears a cluster of tiny, red flowers with prominent stamens, within fleshy, red or pink bracts. H to 30cm (12in), S 20–30cm (8–12in). Min. 10°C (50°F).

PURPLE

Allium narcissiflorum
Clump-forming, summer-flowering bulb with very narrow, erect, grey-green leaves on the lower part of the flower stem. Has an umbel of up to 15 bell-shaped, pinkish-purple flowers. H 15–30cm (6–12in), S 8–10cm (3–4in).

Allium cyathophorum* var. *farreri
Clump-forming, summer-flowering bulb with tufts of narrow, erect, basal leaves. Each stem bears a small, loose umbel, 1.5–4cm (⅝–1½in) wide, of up to 30 bell-shaped, dark reddish-purple flowers with sharply pointed petals. H 15–30cm (6–12in), S 10–15cm (4–6in).

Roscoea humeana
Summer-flowering tuber. Erect, broadly lance-shaped, rich green leaves form a stem-like sheath at base. Has up to 10 long-tubed, purple flowers, each with a hooded, upper petal, a wide, pendent lip and 2 narrower petals. H 15– 25cm (6–10in), S 15–20cm (6–8in).

BLUE–YELLOW

Scilla peruviana
Early summer-flowering bulb with a basal cluster of up to 10 lance-shaped, semi-erect leaves. Stem bears a broadly conical head of up to 50 flattish, violet-blue flowers, 1.5–3cm (⅝–1¼in) across. H 10–25cm (4–10in), S 15–20cm (6–8in).

Chlidanthus fragrans
Summer-flowering bulb with narrow, semi-erect leaves in a basal tuft. Leafless stem carries a head of 3–5 fragrant, funnel-shaped, yellow flowers, 4–7cm (1½–2¾in) long. H 10–30cm (4–12in), S 8–10cm (3–4in).

Roscoea cautleyoides
Summer-flowering tuber. Erect, lance-shaped leaves form a stem-like sheath at base. Has up to 5 long-tubed, yellow flowers, each with a hooded, upper petal, a broad, 2-lobed, lower lip and 2 narrower petals. H 15–25cm (6–10in), S 10–15cm (4–6in).

Allium moly
Clump-forming, summer-flowering bulb with 1–3 broad, semi-erect, basal, grey-green leaves. Stems each bear up to 40 star-shaped, yellow flowers in a fairly dense umbel, 4–8cm (1½–3in) across. H 10–35cm (4–14in), S 10–12cm (4–5in).

Calochortus monophyllus
Summer-flowering bulb with an erect, branched stem with 1–3 slender leaves and one long, narrow basal leaf. Bears cup-shaped, deep yellow flowers, often with a reddish mark on the claws. Petals are fringed and densely bearded. H 8–20cm (3–8in), S 5cm (2in).

Hypoxis angustifolia
Summer-flowering corm with slender, hairy, semi-erect, basal leaves. Stems each carry 3–7 star-shaped, yellow flowers, 1.5–2cm (⅝–¾in) across. H 10–20cm (4–8in), S 5–8cm (2–3in).

☐ WHITE

Cyclamen hederifolium* f. *albiflorum
Autumn-flowering tuber. Pure white flowers, with reflexed petals, appear before or with leaves, which vary but are often ivy-shaped with silvery-green patterns. H to 10cm (4in), S 10–15cm (4–6in).

***Colchicum speciosum* 'Album'**
Vigorous, autumn-flowering corm with large, semi-erect, basal leaves in late winter or spring. Cup-shaped, white flowers successfully withstand bad weather. H and S 15–20cm (6–8in).

Leucojum autumnale
(Autumn snowflake)
Autumn-flowering bulb with thread-like, erect, basal leaves appearing with, or just after, flowers. Slender stems each produce a head of 14 bell-shaped, white flowers, tinged pink at bases. H 10–15cm (4–6in), S 2.5–5cm (1–2in).

WHITE–PINK

Zephyranthes candida
Autumn-flowering bulb with narrow, erect, basal leaves forming rush-like tufts. Each leafless stem carries crocus-like, white flowers, to 6cm (2½in) across. H 15–25cm (6–10in), S 5–8cm (2–3in).

Cyclamen africanum
Autumn-flowering tuber with ivy-shaped, deep green leaves with lighter patterns. Bears pendent, white or pink flowers, with reflexed petals and darker stains around mouths, as or just before leaves appear. H to 10cm (4in), S 10–15cm (4–6in).

Cyclamen mirabile
Autumn-flowering tuber with pale pink flowers with toothed petals and dark purple-stained mouths. Heart-shaped, patterned leaves, purplish-green beneath, are minutely toothed on margins. H to 10cm (4in), S 5–8cm (2–3in).

Habranthus robustus
Late summer- to early autumn-flowering bulb with narrowly strap-shaped, semi-erect, basal leaves. Leafless flower stems each bear a funnel-shaped, pink flower inclined at an angle. H 20–30cm (8–12in), S 8–10cm (3–4in).

Colchicum autumnale
(Autumn crocus, Meadow saffron)
Autumn-flowering corm with up to 8 long-tubed, wineglass-shaped, purple, pink or white flowers, followed by 3–5 large, strap-shaped, semi-erect, basal, glossy leaves in spring. H and S 10–15cm (4–6in).

Colchicum byzantinum
Robust, autumn-flowering corm with up to 20 large, funnel-shaped, pale purplish-pink flowers, 10–15cm (4–6in) long. In spring produces very broad, semi-erect, basal leaves, ribbed lengthways. H and S 15–20cm (6–8in).

PINK

Cyclamen graecum
Autumn-flowering tuber with heart-shaped, toothed, velvety, dark green leaves, patterned silver or light green. Flowers are pink or white, with purple stains around mouths. Grows best in an alpine house. H to 10cm (4in), S 10–15cm (4–6in).

Cyclamen rohlfsianum
Autumn-flowering tuber with coarsely toothed leaves, zoned with light and dark green patterns, and pale pink-lilac flowers, stained darker at mouths. H to 10cm (4in), S 10–15cm (4–6in).

Cyclamen cilicium
Autumn-flowering tuber with broadly heart-shaped leaves that have light and dark green zones. Has white or pink flowers, each with a dark purple stain at the mouth, just before or with leaves. H to 10cm (4in), S 5–10cm (2–4in).

Colchicum cilicicum
Autumn-flowering corm with large, cup-shaped, pale pink to deep rose-purple flowers, sometimes slightly chequered. Very broad, semi-erect, basal leaves, ribbed lengthways, appear soon after flowers have faded. H and S 15–20cm (6–8in).

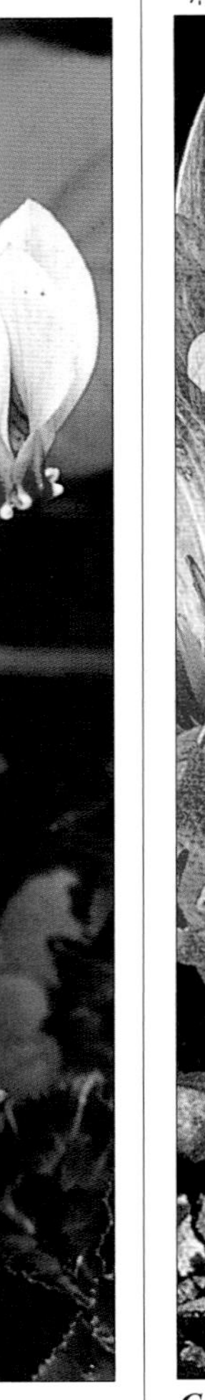

Cyclamen hederifolium
Autumn-flowering tuber. Pale to deep pink flowers, stained darker at mouths, appear before or with foliage. Leaves vary but are often ivy-shaped with silvery-green patterns. H to 10cm (4in), S 10–15cm (4–6in).

Colchicum bivonae
Autumn-flowering corm with large, funnel-shaped, pinkish-purple flowers, strongly chequered darker purple and with purple anthers. Produces 8–10 erect leaves in spring. H 10–15cm (4–6in), S 15–20cm (6–8in).

PINK–PURPLE

Colchicum agrippinum
Early autumn-flowering corm. Narrow, slightly waved, semi-erect, basal leaves develop in spring. Bears erect, funnel-shaped, bright purplish-pink flowers with a darker chequered pattern and pointed petals. H 10–15cm (4–6in), S 8–10cm (3–4in).

***Colchicum* 'Waterlily'**
Autumn-flowering corm with rather broad, semi-erect, basal leaves in winter or spring. Tightly double flowers have 20–40 pinkish-lilac petals. H 10–15cm (4–6in), S 15–20cm (6–8in).

Merendera montana
Autumn-flowering corm with narrowly strap-shaped, semi-erect, basal leaves, produced just after upright, broad-petalled, funnel-shaped, rose- or purple-lilac flowers appear. H to 5cm (2in), S 5–8cm (2–3in).

PURPLE–YELLOW

Biarum tenuifolium
Late summer- or autumn-flowering tuber producing clusters of acrid, narrow, erect, basal leaves after stemless, upright and often twisted, blackish-purple spathes appear. H to 20cm (8in), S 8–10cm (3–4in).

Arum pictum
Autumn-flowering tuber. Arrow-shaped, semi-erect, glossy leaves, with cream veins, appear at the same time as a cowl-like, deep purple-brown spathe and dark purple spadix. H 15–25cm (6–10in), S 15–20cm (6–8in).

Sternbergia lutea
Autumn-flowering bulb with strap-shaped, semi-erect, basal, deep green leaves appearing together with a funnel-shaped, bright yellow flower, 2.5–6cm (1–2½in) long, on a leafless stem. H 2.5–15cm (l–6in), S 8–10cm (3–4in).

WHITE

***Galanthus nivalis* 'Flore Pleno'**
(Double common snowdrop)
Late winter- and early spring-flowering bulb with semi-erect, basal, grey-green leaves. Bears rosetted, many-petalled, double, white flowers, some inner petals having a green mark at the apex. H 10–15cm (4–6in), S 5–8cm (2–3in).

***Galanthus nivalis* 'Pusey Green Tip'**
Late winter- and early spring-flowering bulb with narrowly strap-shaped, semierect, basal, grey-green leaves. Each stem bears a white flower with many mostly green-tipped petals. H 10–15cm (4–6in), S 5–8cm (2–3in).

Galanthus gracilis
Late winter- and early spring-flowering bulb with slightly twisted, strap-shaped, semi-erect, basal, grey-green leaves. Bears white flowers with 3 inner petals, each marked with a green blotch at the apex and base. H 10–15cm (4–6in), S 5–8cm (2–3in).

Galanthus rizehensis
Late winter- and early spring-flowering bulb with very narrow, strap-shaped, semi-erect, basal, dark green leaves. Produces white flowers, 1.5–2cm (5/8–3/4in) long, with a green patch at the apex of each inner petal. H 10–20cm (4–8in), S 5cm (2in).

Galanthus elwesii
Late winter- and early spring-flowering bulb with semi-erect, basal, grey-green leaves that widen gradually towards tips. Each inner petal of the white flowers bears green marks at the apex and base, which may merge. H 10–30cm (4–12in), S 5–8cm (2–3in).

***Galanthus* 'Atkinsii'**
Vigorous, late winter- and early spring-flowering bulb with strap-shaped, semi-erect, basal, grey-green leaves. Each stem carries a slender, white flower with a green mark at the apex of each inner petal. H 10–25cm (4–10in), S 5–9cm (2–3½in).

WARWICKSHIRE COLLEGE LIBRARY

WHITE

Galanthus nivalis 'Sandersii'
Late winter- and early spring-flowering bulb with narrowly strap-shaped, semi-erect, basal, grey-green leaves. Flowers, 1.5–2cm (⅝–¾in) long, are white with yellow patches at the apex of each inner petal. H 10cm (4in), S 2.5–5cm (1–2in).

Galanthus ikariae
Late winter- and early spring-flowering bulb with strap-shaped, semi-erect, basal, glossy, bright green leaves. Produces one white flower, 1.5–2.5cm (⅝–1in) long, marked with a green patch at the apex of each inner petal. H 10–25cm (4–10in), S 5–8cm (2–3in).

Galanthus nivalis 'Scharlockii'
Vigorous, late winter- and early spring-flowering bulb with semi-erect, basal, grey-green leaves. Has white flowers, with green marks at the apex of inner petals, overtopped by 2 narrow spathes that resemble donkeys' ears. H 10–15cm (4–6in), S 5–8cm (2–3in).

Galanthus plicatus subsp. ***byzantinus***
Late winter- and early spring-flowering bulb. Semi-erect, basal, deep green leaves have a grey bloom and reflexed margins. White flowers have green marks at bases and tips of inner petals. H 10–20cm (4–8in), S 5–8cm (2–3in).

Cyclamen coum f. ***albissimum***
Winter-flowering tuber with rounded, deep green leaves, sometimes silver-patterned. Carries white flowers, each with a maroon mark at the mouth. H to 10cm (4in), S 5–10cm (2–4in).

PINK

Cyclamen persicum
Winter- or spring-flowering tuber with heart-shaped leaves, marked light and dark green and silver. Bears fragrant, slender, white or pink flowers, 3–4cm (1¼–1½in) long and stained carmine at mouths. H 10–20cm (4–8in), S 10–15cm (4–6in). Min. 5–7°C (41–5°F).

Cyclamen persicum 'Pearl Wave'
Winter- and spring-flowering tuber with heart-shaped leaves, marked light and dark green and silver. Produces fragrant, slender, deep pink flowers, with 5–6cm (2–2½in) long, frilly-edged petals. H 10–20cm (4–8in), S 10–15cm (4–6in). Min. 5–7°C (41–5°F).

Cyclamen coum
Winter-flowering tuber with rounded leaves, plain deep green or silver-patterned. Produces bright carmine flowers with dark stains at mouths. H to 10cm (4in), S 5–10cm (2–4in).

■ RED

***Cyclamen persicum* 'Esmeralda'**
Winter-flowering tuber with heart-shaped, silver-patterned leaves and broad-petalled, carmine-red flowers. H 10–20cm (4–8in), S 15–20cm (6–8in). Min. 5–7°C (41–5°F).

***Cyclamen persicum* 'Renown'**
Winter- and spring-flowering tuber with heart-shaped, bright silver-green leaves, each with a central, dark green mark. Carries fragrant, slender, scarlet flowers, 5–6cm (2–2½in) long. H 10–20cm (4–8in), S 10–15cm (4–6in). Min. 5–7°C (41–5°F).

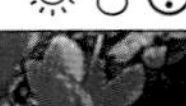

***Cyclamen persicum* Kaori Series**
Winter-flowering tuber with neat, heart-shaped, silver-marbled leaves. Produces fragrant flowers, 4cm (1½in) long, in a wide range of colours. H 10–20cm (4–8in), S 10–15cm (4–6in). Min. 5–7°C (41–5°F).

□ YELLOW

Lachenalia aloides* var. *quadricolor
Winter- to spring-flowering bulb with 2 strap-shaped, semi-erect, basal leaves. Has a spike of 10–20 purplish-red buds opening to greenish-yellow or -orange flowers. H 15–25cm (6–10in), S 5–8cm (2–3in).

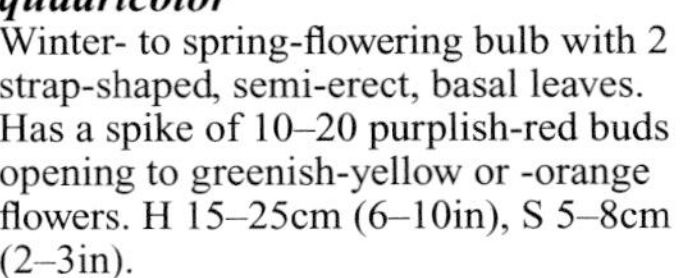

***Lachenalia aloides* 'Nelsonii'**
Winter- to spring-flowering bulb with 2 strap-shaped, purple-spotted, semi-erect, basal leaves. Has a spike of 10–20 pendent, tubular, green-tinged, bright yellow flowers, 3cm (1¼in) long. H 15–25cm (6–10in), S 5–8cm (2–3in).

Eranthis hyemalis
(Winter aconite)
Clump-forming tuber. Bears stalkless, cup-shaped, yellow flowers, 2–2.5cm (¾–1in) across, from late winter to early spring. Adissected, leaf-like bract forms a ruff beneath each bloom. H 5–10cm (2–4in), S 8–10cm (3–4in).

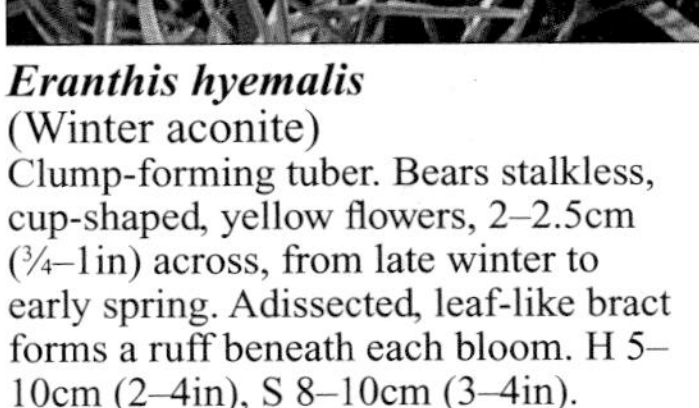

Water Plants

Water Plants

The sound- and light-reflecting qualities of water have long been used to bring vitality to garden designs. For many, still or moving water is the soul of the garden and it also greatly extends the range of plants that can be grown.

What are water plants?

The broad definition of water plants includes all plants that grow rooted, submerged or floating in water. They may be further sub-divided into deep-water aquatics, surface- or free-floating, marginal, bog, or moisture-loving plants, depending on the depth of water that is required for them to thrive.

Why cultivate water plants?

Water plants differ from other plant groups in that they are seldom grown for ornament alone. Nearly all are important for the creation of the healthy ecosystem that is essential if you wish to maintain a water feature's beauty. To do this you need to introduce a balanced range of water plants to regulate the light, oxygen and nutrient levels, thus producing conditions in which plants and animals alike can thrive.

Submerged plants, such as lagarosiphon act as 'oxygenators', providing the dissolved oxygen that is vital for all pond life. They also remove excess nutrients from the water and help keep it clear by controlling algal growth, which causes cloudy, green water and blocks out the light necessary for healthy, aquatic plant and pond life. Surface-floaters, such as the water hyacinth (*Eichhornia crassipes*), also reduce dissolved nutrients by absorbing them through their slender roots. Apart from being very attractive in themselves, deep-water plants, such as *Nuphar* and water lilies (*Nymphaea*), with their roots at the pond bottom and flowers and foliage floating at the surface, provide shelter for pond life and also shade out algal growth.

Ornamental water features

Whether tiny or large, formal or informal, every garden has room for a water feature and its associated plants. In restricted spaces, aquatics such as the dwarf water lily *Nymphaea tetragona* 'Helvola' or slender water irises (*Iris laevigata*) can be grown, while in larger areas *Typha latifolia* will look effective. In a sunken or raised formal pool,using those plants with an architectural outline, such as *Pontederia cordata* or *Zantedeschia aethiopica*, can provide an elegant focal point and emphasize the formal style. The advantage

Formal feature
Above: This formal, split-level pool not only makes an elegant focal point within the garden, but also cleverly provides different water depths to accommodate the needs of various water plants, from deep-water perennials like water lilies to shallow-water marginals such as *Houttuynia cordata*.

Marginal planting
Below: The curving edges of an informal pool offer perfect conditions for marginals such as *Pontederia cordata* and *Sagittaria latifolia*, which root in wet mud and in water up to 15cm (6in) deep. Not only do marginals disguise and soften muddy margins but they provide invaluable shelter for wildlife.

of an informal pond is that it offers great versatility: its sinuous margins are longer than straight-sided ponds of similar size, and its sloping banks can provide a range of planting depths, greatly increasing your choice of marginal plants.

Attracting wildlife

Informal ponds, with their sloping and possibly boggy banks, are particularly good for encouraging a range of beneficial wildlife into the garden. This lends an extra dimension of interest and also benefits both gardener and plants, because many amphibians, birds and small mammals actively prey on garden pests and will help to keep your plants healthy.

Water lilies
Water lilies *(Nymphaea),* which need still water to thrive, perform a dual function: they are incomparably ornamental and their floating leaves shade out algal growth and provide shelter for fish and their fry.

Marginal plants, which have their roots and bases underwater and their top growth visible above the water surface, provide the shelter needed by fish and amphibians in the shallows as well as cover for insects and visiting birds. The floating leaves of water lilies, too, are particularly effective at shading fish and amphibians from the sun, especially where water is shallow and heats up quickly. In winter, water that is more than 60cm (24in) deep will help creatures escape freezes.

Designing with water plants

A water feature should be designed following the same principles that apply to other plant groups, using contrasting and complementary colours, textures and forms. Water plants can offer a wide succession of interest if you choose those that provide diversity in foliage, flower colour and shape, and seed heads.

To accommodate a range of water plants, however, it is essential to provide differing depths of water. Deep-water plants, such as Cape pondweed (*Aponogeton distachyos*) with its very fragrant white flowers at the water surface, and the floating water soldier (*Stratiotes aloides*) with its spiky, aloe-like leaves, require a depth of about 1m (3ft). Water lilies (*Nymphaea*), with their pristine flowers in colours ranging from pure white to deepest red, need to root at depths of 15–100cm (6in–3ft), depending on the species or cultivar.

Marginal plants, which thrive in conditions ranging from pure mud to water that is 30–45cm (1–1½ft) deep, are the most diverse of aquatics. They are invaluable for disguising edges of artificial and natural ponds, for creating interesting reflections and for providing wildlife cover. Marginals have a range of habits: from bog bean (*Menyanthes trifoliata*), with its dainty clusters of white flowers in spring and glossy leaves that spill out across the water surface, to the flowering rush (*Butomus umbellatus*), with its upright stems bearing umbels of small pink flowers, and the substantial skunk cabbages (*Lysichiton*), with their large arum-like blooms and handsome foliage.

In a bog garden, saturated soil provides perfect conditions for many bog natives and moisture-lovers, including the robust candelabra primulas, the globeflower (*Trollius europaeus*), with its deeply divided foliage, and the elegant, architectural fern *Matteuccia struthiopteris*.

Stream-side planting
Above right: The damp soil of a stream bank makes an ideal home for moisture-loving perennials like the candelabra primulas, while water crowfoot *(Ranunculus aquatilis),* which thrives in fast-moving water, is a good choice for planting in the stream bed.

Contrasting foliage
Right: A lush profusion of foliage makes a strong design statement if plants of contrasting form are set side by side. Here, the horizontal, flat shapes of water lilies bring into high relief the vertical heart-shaped foliage of *Pontederia cordata.*

□ WHITE

Menyanthes trifoliata
(Bog bean, Buckbean)
Deciduous, perennial, marginal water plant that has 3-parted, mid-green leaves and fringed, white flowers borne in spring. H 23cm (9in), S 30cm (12in).

Alisma plantago-aquatica
(Water plantain)
Deciduous, perennial, marginal water plant with upright, oval, bright green leaves that emerge well above water. Bears loose, conical panicles of small, pinkish to white flowers in summer. H 75cm (30in), S 45cm (18in).

Lysichiton camtschatcensis
Vigorous, deciduous, perennial, marginal water or bog plant. Pure white spathes, surrounding spikes of small, insignificant flowers, are borne in spring, before oblong to oval, bright green leaves emerge. H 75cm (30in), S 60cm (24in).

Hydrocharis morsus-ranae
(Frogbit)
Deciduous, perennial, floating water plant with rosettes of kidney-shaped, olive-green leaves and small, white flowers during summer. S 10cm (4in), but young plantlets remain attached to form a mass up to 1m (3ft) across.

Calla palustris (Bog arum)
Deciduous or semi-evergreen, perennial, spreading, marginal water plant with heart-shaped, glossy, mid- to dark green leaves. In spring produces large, white spathes usually followed by red or orange fruits. H 25cm (10in), S 30cm (12in).

Sagittaria latifolia
(American arrowhead, Duck potato)
Deciduous, perennial, marginal water plant with curved, soft green leaves and sprays of white flowers in summer. H 1.5m (5ft), S 60cm (2ft).

WHITE

Saururus cernuus (Lizard's tail, Swamp lily, Water dragon)
Deciduous, perennial, marginal water or bog plant. Has clumps of heart-shaped, mid-green leaves and racemes of creamy flowers in summer. H 23cm (9in), S 30cm (12in).

Aponogeton distachyos
(Cape pondweed, Water hawthorn)
Deciduous, perennial, deep-water plant with floating, oblong, mid- to dark green leaves, often splashed with purple. Very fragrant, 'forked', white flowers with black stamens are borne throughout summer. S 1.2m (4ft).

Caltha leptosepala
Deciduous, perennial, marginal water plant with heart-shaped, dark green leaves and buttercup-like, white flowers produced in spring. H and S 30cm (12in).

Hottonia palustris (Water violet)
Deciduous, perennial, submerged water plant. Dense whorls of much-divided, light green leaves form a spreading mass of foliage. Lilac or whitish flowers appear above water surface in summer. S indefinite.

Acorus calamus
'Argenteostriatus'
Semi-evergreen, perennial, marginal water plant. Sword-like, tangerine-scented, mid-green leaves have cream variegation and are flushed rose-pink in spring. H 75cm (30in), S 60cm (24in).

***Acorus gramineus* 'Variegatus'**
Semi-evergreen, perennial, marginal or submerged water plant. Narrow, stiff, grass-like leaves are dark green with cream variegation. H 25cm (10in), S 15cm (6in).

WHITE–PINK

Stratiotes aloides (Water soldier)
Semi-evergreen, perennial, submerged, free-floating water plant. Spiny, olive-green leaves are arranged in rosettes. Produces cup-shaped, white, sometimes pink-tinged flowers in summer. Increases by producing small water buds. S 30cm (12in).

***Houttuynia cordata* 'Chameleon'**
Vigorous, deciduous, perennial, ground-cover, marginal water plant. Aromatic, leathery leaves are splashed yellow and red. Has small sprays of white flowers in summer. Needs some sun to enhance variegation. H 10cm (4in), S indefinite.

Nelumbo nucifera (Sacred lotus)
Vigorous, deciduous, perennial, marginal water plant. Sturdy stems carry very large, plate-like, blue-green leaves and, in summer, large, vivid rose-pink flowers, maturing to flesh-pink. H 1–1.5m (3–5ft) above water surface, S 1.2m (4ft). Min. 7°C (45°F).

PINK–BLUE

Butomus umbellatus
(Flowering rush)
Deciduous, perennial, rush-like, marginal water plant with narrow, twisted, mid-green leaves and umbels of pink to rose-red flowers in summer. H 1m (3ft), S 45cm (1½ft).

Azolla filiculoides
(Fairy moss, Water fern)
Deciduous, perennial, floating water fern with divided fronds that vary from red to purple in full sun and from pale green to blue-green in shade. Helps reduce algae. Is invasive. S indefinite.

Pontederia cordata
(Pickerel weed)
Deciduous, perennial, marginal water plant. In late summer, dense spikes of blue flowers emerge between lance-shaped, glossy, dark green leaves. H 75cm (30in), S 45cm (18in).

BLUE–GREEN

***Myosotis scorpioides* 'Mermaid'**
Deciduous, perennial, marginal water plant for mud or very shallow water. Narrow, mid-green leaves form sprawling mounds. Bears small, blue, forget-me-not flowers throughout summer. H 15cm (6in), S 30cm (12in).

Eichhornia crassipes
(Water hyacinth)
Evergreen or semi-evergreen, perennial water plant, with glossy leaves, floating on air-filled leaf stalks. Bears spikes of blue-and-lilac flowers in summer. May be invasive in warm conditions. S 23cm (9in). Min. 1°C (34°F).

Veronica beccabunga (Brooklime)
Usually evergreen, marginal water plant with creeping, hollow, fleshy stems and rounded, mid-green leaves. Bears blue flowers with white centres from late spring to late summer. Grow in wet soil or water to 12cm (5in) deep. H 10cm (4in), S indefinite.

Typha latifolia
Deciduous, perennial, marginal water plant with large clumps of mid-green foliage. Produces spikes of beige flowers in late summer, followed by decorative, cylindrical, dark brown seed heads. Is invasive. H to 2.5m (8ft), S 60cm (2ft).

Myriophyllum aquaticum
(Parrot feather)
Deciduous, perennial, partially or completely submerged water plant. Spreading, finely divided, blue-green foliage turns reddish in autumn if it surfaces. Is invasive. S indefinite.

Potamogeton crispus
(Curled pondweed)
Deciduous, perennial, submerged water plant that produces spreading colonies of seaweed-like, bronze-or mid-green foliage. Insignificant, reddish flowers are borne in summer. Prefers cool water. S indefinite.

GREEN

Pistia stratiotes (Water lettuce)
Deciduous, perennial, floating water plant for a pool or aquarium, evergreen in tropical conditions. Hairy, soft green foliage is lettuce-like in arrangement. Produces tiny, greenish flowers at varying times. H and S 10cm (4in). Min. 10–15°C (50–59°F).

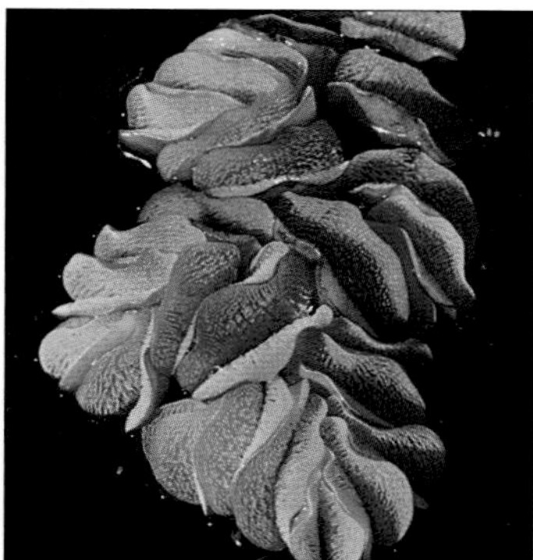

Salvinia auriculata
Deciduous, perennial, floating water plant, evergreen in tropical conditions, that forms spreading colonies. Has rounded, pale to mid-green leaves, sometimes suffused purplish-brown, in pairs on branching stems. S indefinite. Min. 10–15°C (50–59°F).

Trapa natans
(Jesuit's nut, Water chestnut)
Annual, floating water plant with diamond-shaped, mid-green leaves, often marked purple, arranged in neat rosettes. Bears white flowers in summer. S 23cm (9in).

Lagarosiphon major,
Semi-evergreen, perennial, spreading, submerged water plant that forms dense, underwater swards of foliage. Ascending stems are covered in narrow, reflexed, dark green leaves. Bears insignificant flowers in summer. S indefinite.

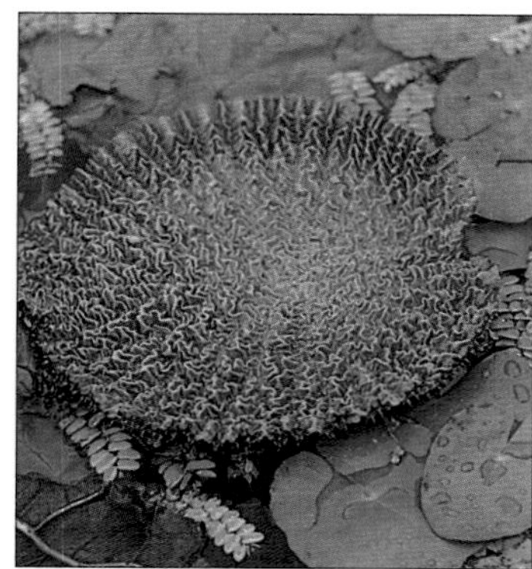

Euryale ferox
Annual, deep-water plant. Has floating, rounded, spiny, olive-green leaves with rich purple undersides and bears small, violet-purple flowers in summer. Is suitable only for a tropical pool. S 1.5m (5ft). Min. 5°C (41°F).

Typha minima
Deciduous, perennial, marginal water plant with grass-like leaves. Spikes of rust-brown flowers in late summer are succeeded by decorative, cylindrical seed heads. H 45–60cm (18–24in), S 30cm (12in).

GREEN–YELLOW

Sparganium erectum,
(Branched bur reed)
Vigorous, deciduous or semi-evergreen, perennial, marginal water plant with narrow, mid-green leaves. Bears small, greenish-brown burs in summer. H 1m (3ft), S 60cm (2ft).

Myriophyllum verticillatum
(Whorled water milfoil)
Deciduous, perennial, spreading, submerged water plant, overwintering by club-shaped winter buds. Slender stems are covered with whorls of finely divided, olive-green leaves. S indefinite.

Hydrocleys nymphoides
(Water poppy)
Deciduous, perennial, deep-water plant, evergreen in tropical conditions, with floating, oval, mid-green leaves. Poppy-like, yellow flowers are held above foliage during summer. S to 60cm (2ft). Min. 1°C (34°F).

WATER LILIES

The serene beauty of a water lily (*Nymphaea*) adds a focal point and colour to any water garden. The submerged aquatic perennials occur worldwide and are cultivated for their showy, sometimes fragrant flowers and floating leaves. The mostly white, yellow, pink, red or, in the non-hardy species, blue flowers are borne in summer. Neat, small-leaved plants grow in only 8cm (3in) of water, but more vigorous plants may need up to 1m (3ft). The large, plate-like leaves provide shelter for fish and help to reduce the spread of algae. Water lilies make few demands, although they prefer an open, sunny site and still water.

***N.* 'Virginia'**

***N.* 'Escarboucle' 🏆**

***N.* 'Gladstoneana' 🏆**

***N. tetragona* 'Alba'**

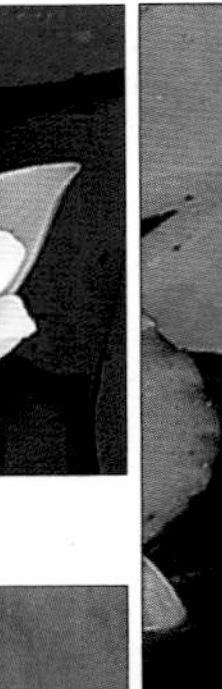

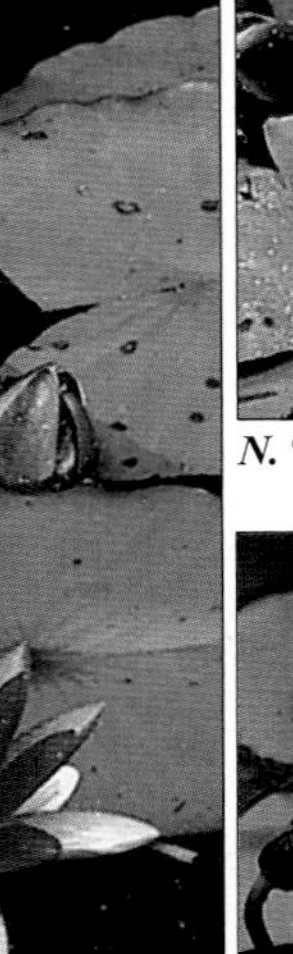

***N.* 'Attraction'**

***N.* 'James Brydon' 🏆**

***N.* Laydekeri Group 'Fulgens'**

***N.* 'Blue Beauty'**

***N.* Marliacea Group 'Albida'**

***N.* 'Rose Arey'**

***N.* 'Firecrest'**

***N.* 'Helvola'**

***N.* Marliacea Group 'Chromatella' 🏆**

***N.* 'General Pershing'**

***N.* 'American Star'**

***N.* 'Lucidia'**

***N.* 'Froebelii'**

***N.* 'Sunrise'**

YELLOW

Lysichiton americanus
(Yellow skunk cabbage)
Vigorous, deciduous, perennial, marginal water or bog plant. In spring, before large, fresh green leaves appear, produces showy, bright yellow spathes. H 1m (3ft), S 75cm (2½ft).

***Caltha palustris* 'Flore Pleno'**
Deciduous, perennial, marginal water plant with rounded, dark green leaves. Bears clusters of double, bright golden-yellow flowers in spring. H and S 25cm (10in).

Nymphoides peltata
(Fringed water lily, Water fringe)
Deciduous, perennial, deep-water plant with floating, small, round, mid-green leaves, often spotted and splashed with brown. Produces small, fringed, yellow flowers throughout summer. S 60cm (24in).

Caltha palustris
(Kingcup, Marsh marigold)
Deciduous, perennial, marginal water plant that has rounded, dark green leaves and bears clusters of cup-shaped, bright golden-yellow flowers in spring. H 60cm (24in), S 45cm (18in).

Ranunculus lingua
Deciduous, perennial, marginal water plant with stout stems and lance-shaped, glaucous leaves. Clusters of yellow flowers are borne in late spring. H 90cm (3ft), S 45cm (1½ft).

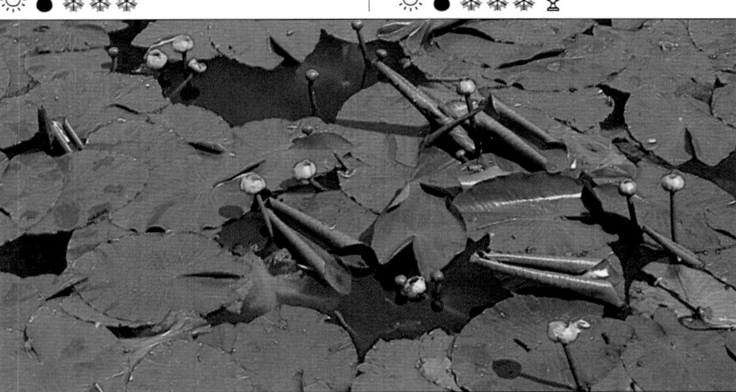

Nuphar lutea
(Brandy bottle, Yellow water lily)
Vigorous, deciduous, perennial, deep-water plant for a large pool. Mid-green leaves are leathery. Small, sickly-smelling, bottle-shaped, yellow flowers open in summer and are followed by decorative seed heads. S 1.5m (5ft).

Orontium aquaticum
(Golden club)
Deciduous, perennial, deep-water plant or, less suitably, marginal water plant. In spring, pencil-like, gold-and-white flower spikes emerge from floating, oblong, blue-grey or blue-green leaves. S 60cm (24in).

Cacti & Succulents

Cacti and other Succulents

The world's harshest climates have imposed evolutionary pressures on the plant life that survives in them, and these have resulted in a group of plants unrivalled in the strangeness and diversity of their forms.

What are cacti and succulents?

Succulents are plants in which the leaves, stems or roots have become adapted for water storage, enabling them to sustain life during seasons of drought. Cacti differ from other succulents in that they have areoles, which are cushion-like growths on their stems.

Since their leaves are primary sites of water loss, many succulents either drop them during periods of drought, or do without them altogether. Their surfaces have also developed to conserve moisture and be protected from harsh light and extreme heat, and range from the waxy, blue-grey-bloomed leaves of pachyphytum and the leathery gasterias to the densely hairy *Oreocereus celsianus* or fiercely spiny echinocactus. Spines, which are prized by gardeners as an ornamental feature, in fact protect plants from predators and also condense droplets of atmospheric moisture which then fall onto the roots.

Choosing succulents

In order to grow succulents successfully it is important to understand and imitate their natural environments as closely as possible. The most familiar cacti and other succulents are native to arid desert and semi-desert conditions, but some originate from cold, high-alpine habitats – the sempervivums for instance – while others, such as the epiphyllums, come from sub-tropical and tropical rainforests.

Gardeners who live in frost-free, dry climates can therefore grow desert cacti and other succulents outside, in large, architectural compositions in a border. In such areas, rainfall is often highly seasonal, but when it does occur it stimulates spectacular floral displays.

In frost-free, humid regions, conditions are perfect for the rainforest cacti and other succulents such as selenicereus, schlumbergera and epiphyllums. These need a little shade, and can be planted where they will cascade from the branches of a host tree. Meanwhile their flowers, which are often nocturnal and sometimes highly fragrant, may scent the air over some distance.

In cooler, frost-prone regions, tender species must be grown indoors or in a greenhouse or conservatory. Most need a minimum temperature of 10–15°C (50–59°F) while some tropical species require at least 20°C (68°F). Borders in open ground or raised beds provide a home for such hardy genera as sempervivum, jovibarba, sedum and some of the euphorbias. Most require sharp drainage and grow well with true alpines, which have similar drainage, light and moisture needs.

Displaying small succulents
Here, neat architectural forms of ribbed parodias and astrophytums provide strong contrasts with the more globose mammillarias.

Hanging beauty
Left: Rainforest cacti such as aporocactus and epiphyllums and their hybrids often flower along the length of trailing stems. Here, × *Aporophyllum* 'Sussex Pink' is shown to perfection in a hanging basket.

Designing with succulents

Succulent textures and shapes range from the tight cushions of fleshy, rosetted leaves of the echeverias, through the spiny, cylindrical, branching desert cacti cereus and cleistocactus to the gracefully pendent, rainforest tree-clingers (epiphytes) rhipsalis and schlumbergera. There are also globose and ribbed forms, as in mammillaria, haageocereus and the very small, pebble-like lithops.

Such a distinctive range has many decorative uses. The majestic, highly sculptural globes, cylinders and branching, candelabra-shaped types, for example, offer scope for exciting designs when contrasted with the basal-rosetted aloes, agaves and yuccas, with their spiky leaves.

Growing in containers

Most cacti and other succulents adapt successfully to container cultivation, and impressive displays can be created to decorate outdoor patios and terraces during the warmer months. In frost-prone climates they should be moved under glass for the winter. The most important rule for effective compositions of different species in containers is to group

Glorious flowers
Above: The brilliant, hot shades of the summer-flowering *Echinopsis 'Glorious'*, which are typical of many cactus flowers, add vibrant colour to a display of sculptural forms.

In a natural setting
Left: In their native hot, dry climates, cacti and other succulents can achieve spectacular dimensions, as here, where the rosettes of agaves are used as a foil to the living, columnar sculptures of the saguaro cactus *(Carnegiea gigantea)* and pad-forming opuntias.

Greenhouse cultivation
Below: Although there are hardy species, in cool temperate climates most cacti and other succulents need protection from frost, cold and damp. The greenhouse and the home provide the ideal conditions for the cultivation and display of their many and varied forms.

plants of similar growth rates and cultivation needs together, so that they will thrive without outgrowing their allotted space and overwhelming their companions.

Many cacti and other succulents, such as the jade tree (*Crassula ovata*), *Aeonium arboreum* and many agaves, make splendid specimens when grown alone in attractive containers. These, along with plants such as sansevieria, *Senecio rowleyanus* or *Ceropegia linearis* subsp. *woodii*, are often so long-lived, easily propagated and extraordinarily tolerant of neglect that specimens and their offspring have been passed from generation to generation between families and friends.

Be careful where you site cacti with spines because they are capable of inflicting injury. They must be placed well away from eye-level and out of reach of small children and pets.

Size categories used within this group		
Large over 1m (3ft)	**Medium** 23cm–1m (9in–3ft)	**Small** up to 23cm (9in)

□ WHITE

Selenicereus grandiflorus
(Queen-of-the-night)
Climbing, perennial cactus. Has 7-ribbed, 1–2cm (½–¾in) wide, green stems with yellow spines. White flowers, 18–30cm (7–12in) across, open at night in summer. H 3m (10ft), S indefinite. Min. 5°C (41°F).

Cereus uruguayanus
Columnar, perennial cactus. Has a branching, silvery-blue stem and golden spines on 4–8 indented ribs. Bears cup-shaped, white flowers, 10cm (4in) across, at night in summer, and pear-shaped, red fruits. H 5m (15ft), S 4m (12ft). Min. 7°C (45°F).

Browningia hertlingiana
Slow-growing, columnar, perennial cactus with a silvery-blue stem, golden spines and tufted areoles. Nocturnal, white flowers appear in summer, only on plants over 1m (3ft) high. H 8m (25ft), S 4m (12ft). Min. 7°C (45°F).

Echinopsis lageniformis
Columnar, perennial cactus with 4–8-ribbed stems branching at base. Areoles each produce up to 6 spines. Scented, funnel-shaped, white flowers open at night in summer. H to 5m (15ft), S 1m (3ft). Min. 10°C (50°F).

Myrtillocactus geometrizans
(Blue candle)
Columnar, perennial cactus with a branched, 5- or 6-ribbed, blue-green stem. Bears short, black spines, on plants over 30cm (1ft) tall, and white flowers at night in summer. H to 4m (12ft), S 2m (6ft). Min. 12°C (54°F).

Pachypodium lamerei
Tree-like, perennial succulent with a spiny, pale green stem crowned by linear leaves. Has fragrant, trumpet-shaped, creamy-white flowers in summer, on plants over 1.5m (5ft) tall. Stems branch after flowering. H 6m (20ft), S 2m (6ft). Min. 11°C (52°F).

Cereus validus
Columnar, perennial cactus with a branching, blue-green stem bearing dark spines on 4–7 prominent ribs. Has 25cm (10in) long, cup-shaped, white flowers at night in summer, followed by red fruits. H 7m (22ft), S 3m (10ft). Min. 7°C (45°F).

Carnegiea gigantea (Saguaro)
Very slow-growing, perennial cactus with a thick, 12–24-ribbed, spiny, green stem. Tends to branch and bears short, funnel-shaped, fleshy, white flowers at stem tips in summer, only when over 4m (12ft) high. H to 12m (40ft), S 3m (10ft). Min. 7°C (45°F).

Pachycereus marginatus (Organ-pipe cactus)
Columnar, perennial cactus with a 5- or 6-ribbed, branching, shiny stem. Areoles bear minute spines. Produces funnel-shaped, white flowers in summer. H 7m (22ft), S 3m (10ft). Min. 11°C (52°F).

Agave parviflora
Basal-rosetted, perennial succulent. Has narrow, white-marked, dark green leaves with white fibres peeling from edges. Produces white flowers in summer. H 1.5m (5ft), S 50cm (20in). Min. 5°C (41°F).

Stetsonia coryne
Tree-like, perennial cactus with a short, swollen trunk bearing 8- or 9-ribbed, blue-green stems. Black spines fade with age to white with black tips. Funnel-shaped, white flowers appear at night in summer. H 8m (25ft), S 4m (12ft). Min. 10°C (50°F).

Crassula ovata (Friendship tree, Jade tree, Money tree)
Perennial succulent with a swollen stem crowned by glossy, green leaves, at times red-edged. Bears 5-petalled, white flowers in autumn-winter. H 4m (12ft), S 2m (6ft). Min. 5°C (41°F).

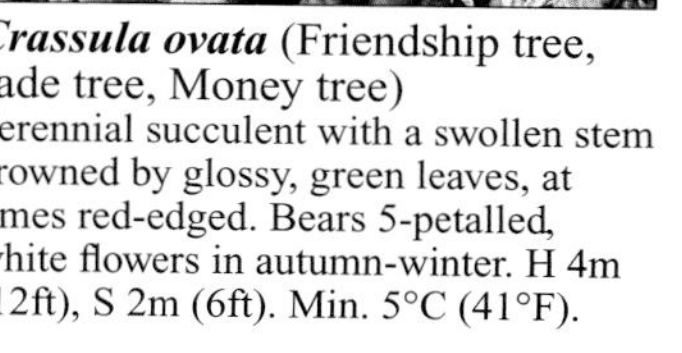

Echinopsis spachiana (Torch cactus)
Clump-forming, perennial cactus with glossy, green stems bearing 10–15 ribs and pale golden spines. Fragrant, funnel-shaped, white flowers open at night in summer. H and S 2m (6ft). Min. 8°C (46°F).

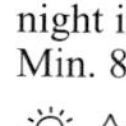

Espostoa lanata (Cotton ball, Peruvian old-man cactus)
Very slow-growing, columnar, perennial cactus with a branching, woolly, green stem. Foul-smelling, white flowers appear in summer, only on plants over 1m (3ft) high. H to 4m (12ft), S 2m (6ft). Min. 10°C (50°F).

Pereskia aculeata (Barbados gooseberry, Lemon vine)
Fast-growing, deciduous, climbing cactus with broad, glossy leaves. Orange-centred, creamy-white flowers appear in autumn, only on plants over 1m (3ft) high. H to 10m (30ft), S 5m (15ft). Min. 5°C (41°F).

***Agave americana* 'Striata'**
Basal-rosetted, perennial succulent. Has sharply pointed, sword-shaped, blue-green leaves with yellow edges. Stem carries white flowers, each 9cm (3½in) long, in spring-summer. Offsets freely. H and S 2m (6ft).

WHITE–PINK

Haageocereus versicolor
Columnar, perennial cactus. Dense, radial spines, golden, red or brown, at times form coloured bands around a longer, central spine up the green stem. Long-tubed, white flowers appear near crown of plant in summer. H to 2m (6ft), S 1m (3ft). Min. 11°C (52°F).

Crassula arborescens
(Silver jade plant)
Perennial succulent with a thick, robust stem crowned by branches bearing rounded, silvery-blue leaves, often with red edges. Has 5-petalled, pink flowers in autumn-winter. H 4m (12ft), S 2m (6ft). Min. 7°C (45°F).

Pereskia grandifolia
(Rose cactus)
Deciduous, bushy, perennial cactus with black spines. Single rose-like, pink flowers form in summer-autumn only on plants over 30cm (1ft) high. H 5m (15ft), S 3m (10ft). Min. 10°C (50°F).

Adenium obesum
Tree-like, perennial succulent with a fleshy, tapering, green trunk and stems crowned by oval, glossy, green leaves, dull green beneath. Carries funnel-shaped, pink to pinkish-red flowers, white inside, in summer. H 2m (6ft), S 50cm (20in). Min. 15°C (59°F).

Pachycereus schottii
Columnar, perennial cactus, branching with age. Olive- to dark green stem, covered with small, white spines, bears 4–15 ribs. Funnel-shaped, pink flowers are produced at night in summer. H 7m (22ft), S 2m (6ft). Min. 10°C (50°F).

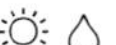

Pilosocereus leucocephalus
Columnar, perennial cactus with a 10–12-ribbed stem and white-haired crown. Bears tubular, pink flowers, with cream anthers, at night in summer, on plants over 1.5m (5ft) tall. H to 6m (20ft), S 1m (3ft). Min. 11°C (52°F).

***Aloe arborescens* 'Variegata'**
Evergreen, bushy, succulent-leaved shrub. Each stem is crowned by rosettes of long, slender, blue-green leaves with toothed edges and cream stripes. Produces numerous spikes of red flowers in late winter and spring. H and S 2m (6ft). Min. 7°C (45°F).

Aloe ferox
Evergreen, succulent tree with a woody stem crowned by a dense rosette of sword-shaped, blue-green leaves that have spined margins. Carries an erect spike of bell-shaped, orange-scarlet flowers in spring. H to 3m (10ft), S 1.5–2m (5–6ft). Min. 7°C (45°F).

Cyphostemma juttae
Perennial succulent. Swollen stem has peeling bark and deciduous, scandent branches with broad leaves. Bears inconspicuous, yellow-green flowers in summer. Green fruits turn yellow or red. H and S 2m (6ft). Min. 10°C (50°F).

***Pedilanthus tithymaloides* 'Variegata'** (Redbird flower)
Bushy, perennial succulent with stems angled at each node. Leaves have white or pink marks. Stem tips carry small, greenish flowers in red to yellowish-green bracts in summer. H to 3m (10ft), S 30cm (1ft). Min. 10°C (50°F).

Aloe ciliaris
Climbing, perennial succulent with a slender stem crowned by a rosette of narrow, green leaves. Has white teeth where leaf base joins stem. Bears bell-shaped, scarlet flowers, with yellow and green mouths, in spring. H 5m (15ft), S 30cm (1ft). Min. 7°C (45°F).

Neobuxbaumia euphorbioides
Columnar, perennial cactus. Has grey-green to dark green stems, 10cm (4in) across, with 8–10 ribs and 1 or 2 black spines per areole. Funnel-shaped, wine-red flowers appear in summer. H to 3m (10ft), S 1m (3ft). Min. 15°C (59°F).

Cleistocactus strausii
(Silver torch)
Fast-growing, columnar, perennial cactus with 8cm (3in) wide stems and short, dense, white spines. Tubular, red flowers appear in spring on plants over 60cm (2ft) high. H 3m (10ft), S 1–2m (3–6ft). Min. 5°C (41°F).

GREEN–YELLOW

Cephalocereus senilis
(Old-man cactus)
Very slow-growing, columnar, perennial cactus with a green stem covered in long, white hairs, masking short, white spines. Is unlikely to flower in cultivation. H 15m (50ft), S 15cm (6in). Min. 5°C (41°F).

***Furcraea foetida* 'Mediopicta'**
Basal-rosetted, perennial succulent with broad, sword-shaped, green leaves, striped with creamy-white, to 2.5m (8ft) long. Has bell-shaped, green flowers, with white interiors, in summer. H 3m (10ft), S 5m (15ft). Min. 6°C (43°F).

Bowiea volubilis
Bulbous succulent with climbing, much-branched, slender stems and no proper leaves. Produces small, star-shaped, green flowers at tips of stems in summer. Provide support. H 1–2m (3–6ft), S 45–60cm (1½–2ft). Min. 10°C (50°F).

Kalanchoe beharensis
Bushy, perennial succulent with triangular to lance-shaped, olive-green leaves, covered with fine, brown hairs. Bell-shaped, yellow flowers appear in late winter, only on plants over 2m (6ft) high. H and S to 4m (12ft). Min. 10°C (50°F).

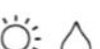

Pachycereus pringlei
Slow-growing, columnar, perennial cactus with a branched, bluish-green stem that has 10–15 ribs. Large areoles each have 15–25 black-tipped, white spines. Is unlikely to flower in cultivation. H 11m (35ft), S 3m (10ft). Min. 10°C (50°F).

Echinocactus grusonii (Golden barrel cactus, Mother-in-law's seat)
Slow-growing, hemispherical, perennial cactus. Spined, green stem has 30 ribs. Woolly crown bears a ring of straw-coloured flowers in summer, only on stems over 38cm (15in) wide. H and S to 2m (6ft). Min. 11°C (52°F).

Ferocactus cylindraceus
Slow-growing, columnar, perennial cactus, spherical when young. Green, 10–20-ribbed stem has large, hooked, red or yellow spines. Funnel-shaped, yellow flowers form in summer on plants over 25cm (10in) across. H 3m (10ft), S 80cm (32in). Min. 5°C (41°F).

Opuntia robusta
Bushy, perennial cactus. Silvery-blue stem has flattened, oval segments with either no spines or 8–12 white ones, to 5cm (2in) long, per areole. Saucer-shaped, yellow flowers, 7cm (3in) across, appear in spring-summer. H and S 5m (15ft). Min. 5°C (41°F).

□ WHITE

Gymnocalycium gibbosum
Spherical to columnar, perennial cactus that has a dark green stem with 12–19 rounded ribs, pale yellow spines, darkening with age, and white flowers, to 7cm (3in) long, in summer. H 30cm (12in), S 20cm (8in). Min. 5°C (41°F).

Echinopsis candicans
Clump-forming, branching, perennial cactus with up to 11 ribs. Areoles each have 10–15 radial spines and 4 central ones. Fragrant, funnel-shaped, white flowers open at night in summer. H 1m (3ft), S indefinite. Min. 8°C (46°F).

Echinopsis oxygona
Spherical to columnar, perennial cactus with a 13–15-ribbed, green stem and long spines. Has 10cm (4in) wide, tubular, white to lavender flowers, to 20cm (8in) long, in spring-summer. H and S 30cm (12in). Min. 5°C (41°F).

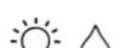

Agave victoriae-reginae
(Royal agave)
Very slow-growing, domed, perennial succulent with a basal rosette of spineless, white-striped and -edged leaves. Has cream flowers on a 4m (12ft) tall stem in spring-summer after 20–30 years. H and S 60cm (2ft). Min. 5°C (41°F).

Rhipsalis cereuscula
(Coral cactus)
Pendent, perennial cactus with 4- or 5-angled or cylindrical, green stems and branches, to 3cm (1¼in) long in whorls. Bell-shaped, white flowers on stem tips in winter-spring. H 60cm (24in), S 50cm (20in). Min. 10°C (50°F).

Epiphyllum laui
Bushy, perennial cactus, usually with strap-shaped, red-tinged, glossy stems, which may also be spiny, cylindrical or 4-angled. Has fragrant, white flowers, with brown sepals, in spring-summer. H 30cm (12in), S 50cm (20in). Min. 10°C (50°F).

Epiphyllum anguliger
(Fishbone cactus)
Erect, then pendent, perennial cactus. Has strap-shaped, flattened, green stems with indented margins. Produces tubular, 10cm (4in) wide, white flowers in summer. H 1m (3ft), S 40cm (16in). Min. 11°C (52°F).

Lepismium warmingianum
Erect, then pendent, perennial cactus with slender, notched, cylindrical, green branches, sometimes tinged red or brown, with 2–4 angles. Has green-white flowers in winter-spring, followed by violet berries. H 1m (3ft), S 50cm (20in). Min. 11°C (52°F).

Rhipsalis floccosa
Pendent, perennial cactus with cylindrical, green stems, to 1cm (½in) across, branching less than many other *Rhipsalis* species. Has masses of very pale pink flowers in early summer, then pinkish-white berries. H 1m (3ft), S 50cm (20in). Min. 10°C (50°F).

WHITE–PINK

Senecio rowleyanus
(String-of-beads)
Pendent, perennial succulent. Very slender, green stems bear cylindrical, green leaves. Has heads of fragrant, tubular, white flowers from spring to autumn. Suits a hanging pot. H 1m (3ft), S indefinite. Min. 5°C (41°F).

Ceropegia linearis **subsp. *woodii***
(Heart vine, Rosary vine, String-of-hearts)
Semi-evergreen, trailing, succulent sub-shrub with tuberous roots. Leaves redden in sun. Has hairy, pinkish-green flowers from spring to autumn. H 1m (3ft), S indefinite. Min. 7°C (45°F).

***Kalanchoe fedtschenkoi* 'Variegata'**
Bushy, perennial succulent. Blue-green and cream leaves also colour red. Bears a new plantlet in each leaf notch. Has brownish-pink flowers in late winter. H and S to 1m (3ft). Min. 10°C (50°F).

Echinocereus schmollii
(Lamb's-tail cactus)
Erect to prostrate, tuberous cactus with 8–10-ribbed, purplish-green stems and mostly white spines. Has pinkish-purple flowers in spring-summer. H and S 30cm (12in). Min. 8°C (46°F).

PINK

***Senecio articulatus* 'Variegatus'**
Deciduous, spreading, perennial succulent with grey-marked stems. Has cream- and pink-marked, blue-green leaves in summer and yellow flower heads from autumn to spring. H 60cm (2ft), S indefinite. Min. 10°C (50°F).

Hesperaloe parviflora
Basal-rosetted, perennial succulent, often with peeling, white fibres at leaf edges. Flower stems each bear a raceme of bell-shaped, pink to red flowers in summer-autumn. H 1m (3ft) or more, S 2m (6ft). Min. 3°C (37°F).

***Discocactus phyllanthoides* 'Deutsche Kaiserin'**
Pendent, epiphytic, perennial cactus with flattened, toothed, glossy, green stems, each 5cm (2in) across. Stem margins each bear pink flowers, to 10cm (4in) across, in spring. H 60cm (2ft), S 1m (3ft). Min. 10°C (50°F).

Oreocereus celsianus
(Old man of the Andes)
Slow-growing, perennial cactus. Has heavy and wispy spines. Mature plants bear pink flowers in summer. H 1m (3ft), S 30cm (1ft). Min. 10°C (50°F).

Kalanchoe daigremontiana
(Mexican hat plant)
Erect, perennial succulent with a stem bearing fleshy, boat-shaped, toothed leaves. Produces a plantlet in each leaf notch. Umbels of pink flowers appear at stem tops in winter. H to 1m (3ft), S 30cm (1ft). Min. 7°C (45°F).

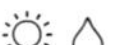

Echinocereus reichenbachii **var. *baileyi***
Columnar, perennial cactus with a slightly branched stem bearing 12–23 ribs and yellowish-white, 3cm (1¼in) long spines. Produces pink flowers with darker bases in spring. H 30cm (12in), S 20cm (8in). Min. 7°C (45°F).

***Kalanchoe* 'Wendy'**

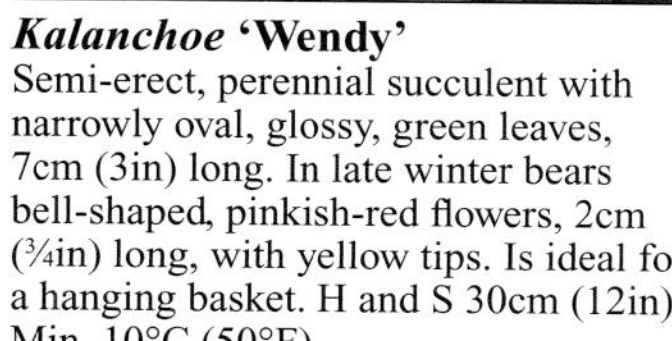

Semi-erect, perennial succulent with narrowly oval, glossy, green leaves, 7cm (3in) long. In late winter bears bell-shaped, pinkish-red flowers, 2cm (¾in) long, with yellow tips. Is ideal for a hanging basket. H and S 30cm (12in). Min. 10°C (50°F).

Aporocactus flagelliformis
(Rat's-tail cactus)
Pendent, perennial cactus with pencil-thick, green stems bearing short, golden spines. Has double, cerise flowers along stems in spring. Is good for a hanging basket. H 1m (3ft), S indefinite.

***Discocactus* 'Gloria'**
Erect, then pendent, perennial cactus. Strap-shaped, flattened, green stems have toothed edges. Produces pinkish-red flowers, 10cm (4in) across, in spring. H 30cm (1ft), S 1m (3ft). Min. 10°C (50°F).

***Discocactus* 'M.A. Jeans'**
Erect, then pendent, perennial cactus. Strap-shaped, flattened, green stems have shallowly toothed edges. In spring has deep pink flowers, 8cm (3in) across, with white anthers. H 30cm (12in), S 50cm (20in). Min. 10°C (50°F).

Echinocereus pentalophus
Clump-forming, perennial cactus with spined, green stems, 3–4cm (1¼–1½in) wide, that have 4–8 ribs, later rounded. Has trumpet-shaped, bright pink flowers, paler at base, to 12cm (5in) across, in spring. H 60cm (2ft), S 1m (3ft). Min. 5°C (41°F).

Lampranthus spectabilis
Spreading, perennial succulent with erect stems and narrow, cylindrical, grey-green leaves. In summer produces daisy-like flowers, cerise with yellow centres or golden-yellow throughout. H 30cm (1ft), S indefinite. Min. 5°C (41°F).

PINK–RED

Kalanchoe blossfeldiana
Bushy, perennial succulent with oval to oblong, toothed, glossy, green leaves. Produces clusters of yellow, orange, pink, red or purple flowers, year-round. Makes an excellent house plant. H and S 30cm (1ft). Min. 10°C (50°F).

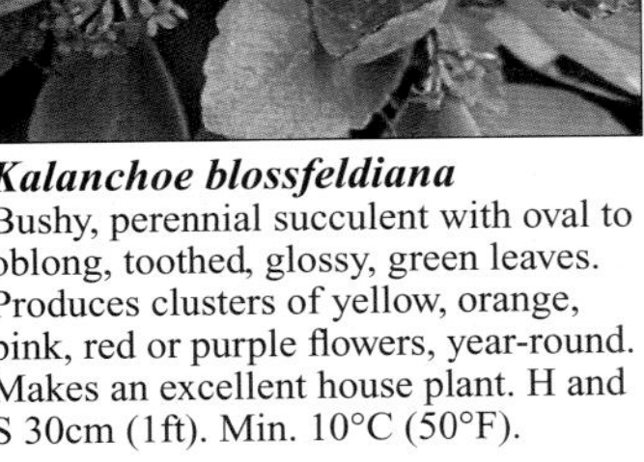

Oroya peruviana
Spherical, perennial cactus with a much-ribbed stem covered in yellow spines, 1.5cm (⅝in) long, with darker bases. Pink flowers, with yellow bases, open in spring-summer. H 25cm (10in), S 20cm (8in). Min. 10°C (50°F).

***Kalanchoe* 'Tessa'**
Prostrate to pendent, perennial succulent with narrowly oval, green leaves, 3cm (1¼in) long. Bears tubular, orange-red flowers, 2cm (¾in) long, in late winter. H 30cm (1ft), S 60cm (2ft). Min. 10°C (50°F).

***Gymnocalycium mihanovichii* 'Red Head'**
Perennial cactus with a red stem, 8 angular ribs and curved spines. Must be grafted on to any fast-growing stock as it contains no chlorophyll. Has pink flowers in spring-summer. H and S as per graft stock. Min. 10°C (50°F).

Ferocactus hamatacanthus
Slow-growing, spherical to columnar, perennial cactus with a 13-ribbed stem that bears hooked, red spines, to 12cm (5in) long. Has yellow blooms in summer, then spherical, red fruits. H and S 60cm (2ft). Min. 5°C (41°F).

Aloe variegata
(Partridge-breasted aloe)
Humped, perennial succulent. Has triangular, white-marked, dark green leaves with pronounced keels beneath. Bears a spike of pinkish-red flowers in spring. Is a good house plant. H 30cm (12in), S 10cm (4in). Min. 7°C (45°F).

Echeveria pulvinata (Plush plant)
Bushy, perennial succulent with brown-haired stems each crowned by a rosette of thick, rounded, green leaves that become red-edged in autumn. Leaves have short, white hairs. Bears red flowers in spring. H 30cm (12in), S 50cm (20in). Min. 5°C (41°F).

Dudleya pulverulenta
Basal-rosetted, perennial succulent with strap-shaped, pointed, silvery-grey leaves. Bears masses of star-shaped, red flowers in spring-summer. H 60cm (2ft), S 30cm (1ft). Min. 7°C (45°F).

Crassula perfoliata* var. *minor
(Aeroplane propeller)
Bushy, perennial succulent that branches freely. Long leaves each twist like a propeller. Has large clusters of fragrant, red flowers in late summer. H and S 1m (3ft). Min. 7°C (45°F).

Mammillaria hahniana (Old-lady cactus, Old-woman cactus)
Spherical to columnar, perennial cactus with a green stem bearing long, woolly, white hairs. Carries cerise flowers in spring and spherical, red fruits in autumn. H 40cm (16in), S 15cm (6in). Min. 5°C (41°F).

Opuntia erinacea
Bushy, perennial cactus with a green stem of 15cm (6in) long, flattened segments. Areoles bear 6–15 flattened, 20cm (8in) long, hair-like spines. Has masses of saucer-shaped, red or yellow flowers in summer. H 50cm (20in), S 2m (6ft). Min. 5°C (41°F).

Beschorneria yuccoides
Clump-forming, perennial succulent with a basal rosette of up to 20 rough, greyish-green leaves, to 1m (3ft) long and 5cm (2in) across. Produces pendent, tubular, bright red flowers in summer in spikes over 2m (6ft) tall. H 1m (3ft), S 3m (10ft).

Tylecodon reticulatus
(Barbed-wire plant)
Deciduous, bushy, succulent shrub. Swollen branches bear cylindrical leaves in winter. Has tubular, green-yellow flowers on a woody stem in autumn. H and S 30cm (1ft). Min. 7°C (45°F).

Mammillaria geminispina
Clump-forming, perennial cactus. Has a spherical, green stem densely covered with short, white, radial spines and very long, white, central spines. Has red flowers, 1–2cm ($\frac{1}{2}$–$\frac{3}{4}$in) across, in spring. H 25cm (10in), S 50cm (20in). Min. 5°C (41°F).

Agave filifera (Thread agave)
Basal-rosetted, perennial succulent with narrow, green leaves, each spined at the tip. White leaf margins gradually break away, leaving long, white fibres. Carries yellow-green flowers on a 2.5m (8ft) tall stem in summer. Offsets freely. H 1m (3ft), S 2m (6ft).

YELLOW

Aloe vera
Clump-forming, perennial succulent with basal rosettes of tapering, thick leaves, mottled green, later grey-green. Flower stems carry bell-shaped, yellow flowers in summer. Propagate by offsets as plant is sterile. H 60cm (2ft), S indefinite. Min. 10°C (50°F).

Astrophytum myriostigma (Bishop's cap, Bishop's mitre)
Slow-growing, spherical to slightly elongated, perennial cactus. A fleshy stem has 4–6 ribs and is flecked with tiny tufts of white spines. Bears yellow flowers in summer. H 30cm (12in), S 20cm (8in). Min. 5°C (41°F).

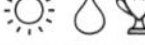

× ***Pachyveria glauca***
Clump-forming, perennial succulent with a dense, basal rosette of fleshy, incurved, oval, silvery-blue leaves, to 6cm (2½in) long, with darker marks. Bears star-shaped, yellow flowers, each with a red tip, in spring. H and S 30cm (12in). Min. 7°C (45°F).

Aeonium haworthii (Pinwheel)
Bushy, perennial succulent. Freely branching stems bear rosettes, 12cm (5in) across, of blue-green leaves, often with red margins. Has a terminal spike of star-shaped, pink-tinged, pale yellow flowers in spring. H 60cm (2ft), S 1m (3ft). Min. 5°C (41°F).

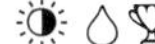

Agave parryi
Basal-rosetted, perennial succulent with stiff, broad, grey-green leaves, each to 30cm (12in) long with a solitary dark spine at its pointed tip. Flower stem, to 4m (12ft) long, bears creamy-yellow flowers in summer. H 50cm (20in), S 1m (3ft). Min. 5°C (41°F).

Leuchtenbergia principis
Basal-rosetted, perennial cactus with narrow, angular, dull grey-green tubercles, each 10cm (4in) long and crowned by papery spines to 10cm (4in) long. Crown bears yellow flowers, to 7cm (3in) across, in summer. H and S 30cm (12in). Min. 6°C (43°F).

Copiapoa cinerea
Very slow-growing, clump-forming, perennial cactus. Blue-green stem bears up to 25 ribs and black spines. Has a woolly, white-grey crown and, on plants over 10cm (4in) across, yellow flowers in spring-summer. H 50cm (20in), S 2m (6ft). Min. 10°C (50°F).

Opuntia microdasys var. ***albispina***
Bushy, perennial cactus with green, flattened, oval segments. Spineless areoles, with slender, barbed, white hairs, are set in diagonal rows. Funnel-shaped, yellow flowers appear in summer. H 60cm (2ft), S 30cm (1ft). Min. 10°C (50°F).

Dioscorea elephantipes
(Elephant's foot)
Very slow-growing, deciduous, perennial succulent with a domed, woody trunk, annual, climbing stems and yellow flowers in autumn. H 50cm (20in), S 1m (3ft). Min. 10°C (50°F).

Kalanchoe tomentosa
(Panda plant, Pussy ears)
Bushy, perennial succulent with thick, oval, grey leaves, covered with velvety bristles and often edged with brown at tips. Has yellowish-purple flowers in winter. H 50cm (20in), S 30cm (12in). Min. 10°C (50°F).

Thelocactus setispinus
Slow-growing, perennial cactus with a 13-ribbed stem and yellow or white spines. Fragrant, yellow flowers with red throats appear in summer, only on plants over 5cm (2in) across. H and S 30cm (12in). Min. 7°C (45°F).

Echinopsis marsoneri
Columnar, perennial cactus with a 20–25-ribbed, bluish- to dark green stem that has yellow, radial spines with longer, darker, central ones. In summer produces yellow flowers, 7cm (3in) across, with red throats. H 30cm (12in), S 15cm (6in). Min. 5°C (41°F).

Agave attenuata
Perennial succulent with a thick stem crowned by a rosette of sword-shaped, spineless, pale green leaves. Arching flower stem, to 1.5m (5ft) long, is densely covered with yellow flowers in spring-summer. H 1m (3ft), S 2m (6ft). Min. 5°C (41°F).

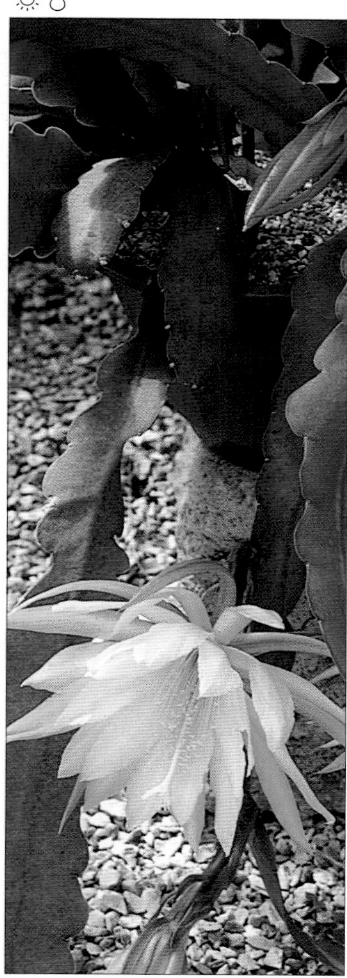

***Discocactus* 'Jennifer Ann'**
Erect, then pendent, perennial cactus. Has strap-shaped, flattened, green stems with toothed margins. Bears yellow flowers, 15cm (6in) across, in spring. H 30cm (12in), S 50cm (20in). Min. 10°C (50°F).

YELLOW–ORANGE

Parodia chrysacanthion
Spherical, perennial cactus with a much-ribbed, green stem densely covered with bristle-like, golden spines, each 1–2cm (½–¾in) long. Crown bears yellow flowers in spring and, often, pale yellow wool. H and S 30cm (1ft). Min. 10°C (50°F).

***Aeonium* 'Zwartkop'**
Bushy, perennial succulent with stems each crowned by a rosette, to 15cm (6in) across, of narrow, purple leaves. Bears golden pyramids of flowers in spring on 2–3-year-old stems, which then die. H 60cm (2ft), S 1m (3ft). Min. 5°C (41°F).

Aloe striata
Basal-rosetted, perennial succulent. Has broad, blue-green leaves, with white margins and marks, that become suffused red in full sun. Has a panicle of reddish-orange flowers in spring. Makes a good house plant. H and S 1m (3ft). Min. 7°C (45°F).

Hatiora salicornioides
(Bottle plant, Drunkard's dream)
Bushy, perennial, epiphytic cactus with freely branching, 3cm (1¼in) long stems. Has joints with expanded tips and terminal, bell-shaped, golden-yellow flowers in spring. H and S 30cm (1ft). Min. 11°C (52°F).

Cotyledon orbiculata* var. *oblonga
Evergreen, upright, succulent sub-shrub with a swollen stem bearing oval, green leaves, densely coated in white wax, with flat, wavy tips. Each 70cm (28in) long flower stem bears a bell-shaped, orange flower in autumn. H and S 50cm (20in). Min. 7°C (45°F).

Parodia leninghausii
(Golden ball cactus)
Clump-forming, perennial cactus. Woolly crown always slopes towards sun. In summer, on plants over 10cm (4in) tall, yellow blooms open flat. H 1m (3ft), S 30cm (1ft). Min. 10°C (50°F).

Opuntia tunicata
Mounded, perennial cactus. Cylindrical, green stem segments are covered with 5cm (2in) long, golden spines, enclosed in a silver papery sheath. Bears shallowly saucer-shaped, yellow flowers in spring-summer. H 60cm (2ft), S 1m (3ft). Min. 10°C (50°F).

Kalanchoe delagoensis
Erect, perennial succulent with long, almost cylindrical, grey-green leaves with reddish-brown mottling and flattened, notched tips that form plantlets. Bears an umbel of orange-yellow flowers in late winter. H to 1m (3ft), S 30cm (1ft). Min. 8°C (46°F).

Lampranthus aurantiacus
Erect, then prostrate, sparse-branching perennial succulent with short, cylindrical, tapering, grey-green leaves. Masses of daisy-like, bright orange flowers, 5cm (2in) wide, open in summer sun. H 50cm (20in), S 70cm (28in). Min. 5°C (41°F).

□ WHITE

Mammillaria plumosa
Clump-forming, perennial cactus. Has a spherical, green stem completely covered with feathery, white spines. Carries cream flowers in mid-winter. Is difficult to grow. Add calcium to soil. H 12cm (5in), S 40cm (16in). Min. 10°C (50°F).

Gibbaeum velutinum
Clump-forming, perennial succulent with paired, finger-like, velvety, bluish grey-green leaves, to 6cm (2½in) long. Produces daisy-like, pink, lilac or white flowers, 5cm (2in) across, in spring. H 8cm (3in), S 30cm (12in). Min. 5°C (41°F).

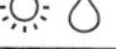

Haworthia truncata
Clump-forming, perennial succulent with a basal fan of broad, erect, rough, blue-grey leaves with pale grey lines and flat ends. Produces small, tubular, white flowers, with spreading petals, from spring to autumn. H 2cm (¾in), S 10cm (4in). Min. 10°C (50°F).

Lithops marmorata
Egg-shaped, perennial succulent, divided into 2 unequal-sized, swollen, pale grey leaves with dark grey marks on convex, upper surfaces. Bears a white flower in late summer or early autumn. H 2–3cm (¾–1¼in), S 5cm (2in). Min. 5°C (41°F).

Lithops karasmontana
Egg-shaped, perennial succulent, divided into 2 unequal-sized, grey leaves, that have pink, upper surfaces with sunken, darker pink marks. Bears a white flower in late summer or early autumn. H to 4cm (1½in), S 5cm (2in). Min. 5°C (41°F).

Adromischus maculatus
Clump-forming, perennial succulent with rounded, glossy, green leaves with purple marks. Leaf tips are often wavy. Carries tubular, purplish-white flowers, on a 30cm (12in) tall stem, in summer. H 6cm (2½in), S 10–15cm (4–6in). Min. 7°C (45°F).

Echinocereus leucanthus
Clump-forming, tuberous cactus with spined, 6- or 7-ribbed, prostrate stems. In spring bears often terminal, dark-throated, white flowers, softly streaked purple, with green stigmas. H 20cm (8in), S 30cm (12in). Min. 8°C (46°F).

Trichodiadema mirabile
Bushy to prostrate, perennial succulent with cylindrical, dark green leaves tipped with dark brown bristles and covered in papillae. Stem tip bears white flowers, 4cm (1½in) across, from spring to autumn. H 15cm (6in), S 30cm (12in). Min. 5°C (41°F).

Haworthia attenuata
Clump-forming, perennial succulent with a basal rosette of triangular, 3cm (1¼in) long, dark green leaves, that have pronounced white dots. Has tubular, white flowers, with spreading petals, from spring to autumn. H 7cm (3in), S 25cm (10in). Min. 5°C (41°F).

□ WHITE

Crassula socialis
Spreading, perennial succulent with short, dense rosettes, to 1cm (½in) across, of fleshy, triangular, green leaves. Produces clusters of star-shaped, white flowers on 3cm (1¼in) tall stems in spring. H 5cm (2in), S indefinite. Min. 5°C (41°F).

Strombocactus disciformis
Very slow-growing, hemispherical, perennial cactus with a grey-green to brown stem set with a spiral of blunt tubercles. Woolly crown has bristle-like spines, which soon fall off, and cream flowers in summer. H 3cm (1¼in), S 10cm (4in). Min. 5°C (41°F).

Mammillaria schiedeana
Clump-forming, perennial cactus. Green stem is covered with short, feathery, yellow spines that turn white. Produces cream flowers and narrow, red seed pods in late summer. H 10cm (4in), S 30cm (12in). Min. 10°C (50°F).

Eriosyce villosa
Clump-forming, perennial cactus with a branched, green to dark grey-green stem. Has dense, sometimes curved, grey spines, 3cm (1¼in) long. Produces tubular, pink or white flowers in spring or autumn. H 15cm (6in), S 10cm (4in). Min. 8°C (46°F).

Oophytum nanus
Clump-forming, perennial succulent with 2 united, very fleshy, bright green leaves. Has daisy-like, white flowers, 1cm (½in) across, in autumn. Is covered in a dry, paper-like sheath, except in spring. H 2cm (¾in), S 1cm (½in). Min. 5°C (41°F).

Haworthia arachnoidea
Slow-growing, clump-forming, perennial succulent with a basal rosette of triangular leaves. Bears soft, white teeth along leaf margins. Has white flowers from spring to autumn. H 5cm (2in), S 10cm (4in). Min. 6°C (43°F).

Lithops lesliei* var. *albinica
Egg-shaped, perennial succulent, divided into 2 unequal-sized leaves; convex, pale green, upper surfaces have dark green and yellow marks. Bears a white flower in late summer or early autumn. H 2–3cm (¾–1¼in), S 5cm (2in). Min. 5°C (41°F).

Conophytum truncatum
Slow-growing, clump-forming, perennial succulent with pea-shaped, dark spotted, blue-green leaves, each with a sunken fissure at the tip. Produces cream flowers, 1.5cm (⅝in) across, in autumn. H 1.5cm (⅝in), S 15cm (6in). Min. 4°C (39°F).

Mammillaria elongata
(Lace cactus)
Clump-forming, perennial cactus. Has a columnar, green stem, 3cm (1¼in) across, densely covered with yellow, golden or brown spines. Bears cream flowers in summer. Offsets freely. H 15cm (6in), S 30cm (12in). Min. 5°C (41°F).

WHITE–PINK

Mammillaria bocasana
(Powder-puff cactus)
Clump-forming, perennial cactus. Long, white hairs cover a hemispherical stem. Has cream or rose-pink flowers in summer and red seed pods the following spring-summer. H 10cm (4in), S 30cm (12in). Min. 5°C (41°F).

Eriosyce napina
Flattened spherical, perennial cactus with very short, grey spines pressed flat against a greenish-brown stem. Produces white, pink, carmine or brown flowers, 5cm (2in) across, from crown in summer. H 2cm (¾in), S 3.5cm (1½in). Min. 8°C (46°F).

Lophophora williamsii
(Dumpling cactus, Mescal button)
Very slow-growing, clump-forming, perennial cactus with an 8-ribbed, blue-green stem. Masses of pink flowers appear in summer on plants over 3cm (1¼in) high. H 5cm (2in), S 8cm (3in). Min. 10°C (50°F).

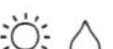

Crassula multicava
Bushy, perennial succulent with oval, grey-green leaves, 8cm (3in) across. Carries numerous clusters of small, star-shaped, pink flowers on elongated stems in spring, followed by small plantlets. H 15cm (6in), S 1m (3ft). Min. 7°C (45°F).

Oscularia deltoides
Spreading, perennial succulent. Has chunky, triangular, blue-green leaves, to 1cm (½in) long, with small-toothed, often reddened leaf margins. Fragrant, pink flowers, 1–2cm (½–¾in) wide, appear in early summer. H 15cm (6in), S 1m (3ft). Min. 7°C (45°F).

Epithelantha micromeris
Slow-growing, spherical, perennial cactus with a green stem completely obscured by close-set areoles bearing tiny, white spines. Bears funnel-shaped, pale pinkish-red flowers, 0.5cm (¼in) across, on a woolly crown in summer. H and S 4cm (1½in). Min. 10°C (50°F).

PINK

Parodia rutilans
Columnar, perennial cactus. Areoles each have about 15 radial spines and 2 upward- or downward-pointing, central spines. Has cream-centred, pink flowers in summer. H 10cm (4in), S 5cm (2in). Min. 10°C (50°F).

Echeveria elegans
Clump-forming, perennial succulent with a basal rosette of broad, fleshy, pale silvery-blue leaves, edged with red, and yellow-tipped, pink flowers in summer. Keep dry in winter. Makes a good bedding plant. H 5cm (2in), S 50cm (20in). Min. 5°C (41°F).

Escobaria vivipara
Spherical, perennial cactus with a green stem densely covered with grey spines. Bears funnel-shaped, pink flowers, 3.5cm (1½in) across, in summer. Is much more difficult to grow than many other species in this genus. H and S 5cm (2in). Min. 5°C (41°F).

PINK

***Schlumbergera* 'Gold Charm'**
Erect, then pendent, perennial cactus. Has flattened, oblong, green stem segments with toothed margins. Yellow flowers in early autumn turn pinkish-orange in winter. H 15cm (6in), S 30cm (12in). Min. 10°C (50°F).

Mammillaria sempervivi
Slow-growing, spherical, perennial cactus. Has a dark green stem with short, white spines. Has white wool between short, angular tubercles on plants over 4cm (1½in) high. Bears cerise flowers in spring. H and S 7cm (3in). Min. 5°C (41°F).

Melocactus intortus
(Melon cactus)
Flattened spherical, perennial cactus. Has an 18–20-ribbed stem with yellow-brown spines. Crown matures to a white column with brown spines. Bears pink flowers in summer. H 20cm (8in), S 25cm (10in). Min. 15°C (59°F).

Ariocarpus fissuratus
Very slow-growing, flattened spherical, perennial cactus. Grey stem is covered with rough, triangular tubercles each producing a tuft of wool. Has 4cm (1½in) wide, pink-red flowers in autumn. H 10cm (4in), S 15cm (6in). Min. 5°C (41°F).

Stenocactus obvallatus
Spherical, perennial cactus with wavy-margined ribs. White areoles each bear 5–12 greyish-brown spines. In spring, has pale yellow to pale pink flowers, with a purplish-red stripe on each petal. H and S 8cm (3in). Min. 7°C (45°F).

Aptenia cordifolia
Fast-growing, prostrate, perennial succulent with oval, glossy, green leaves and, in summer, daisy-like, bright pink flowers. Is ideal for ground cover. H 5cm (2in), S indefinite. Min. 7°C (45°F).

Hatiora rosea
Bushy, perennial cactus with slender, 3- or 4-angled, bristly, green stem segments, usually tinged purple, to 5cm (2in) long. Has masses of bell-shaped, pink flowers, to 4cm (1½in) across, in spring. H and S 10cm (4in). Min. 10°C (50°F).

Conophytum concordans
Clump-forming, perennial succulent with 2 fleshy, grey-green leaves that are broad, erect and united for most of their length but have distinctly divided, upper lobes. Pale pink flowers appear in late summer. H 2.5cm (1in), S 1cm (½in). Min. 5°C (41°F).

Thelocactus bicolor
Spherical to columnar, perennial cactus with an 8–13-ribbed stem. Areoles each have 4 usually flattened, yellow, central spines, or bicoloured yellow and red, and numerous shorter, radial spines. Flowers are purple-pink. H and S 20cm (8in). Min. 7°C (45°F).

Rebutia minuscula
Clump-forming, perennial cactus with a tuberculate, dark green stem. Areoles each produce 15–20 brown spines, to 0.5cm (¼in) long. Has trumpet-shaped, deep pink to violet flowers, to 2cm (¾in) across, in spring. H 5cm (2in), S 15cm (6in). Min. 5°C (41°F).

PINK

Mammillaria crinita
(Rose pincushion)
Clump-forming, perennial cactus with a spherical, green stem that has hooked spines and bears a ring of deep pink to purple flowers in spring. H 15cm (6in), S 30cm (12in). Min. 10°C (50°F).

Echinopsis backebergii
Clump-forming, almost spherical, perennial cactus with a 10–15-ribbed, spined, dark green stem. Has funnel-shaped, pink, red or purple flowers, with paler throats, in summer. H 10cm (4in), S 15cm (6in). Min. 5°C (41°F).

Echinopsis pentlandii
Clump-forming or solitary, variable, perennial cactus with a 10–20-ribbed stem and 6–20 spined aeroles. Has white, pink, purple or orange flowers, with paler throats, in summer. H 8cm (3in), S 10cm (4in). Min. 5°C (41°F).

PINK–RED

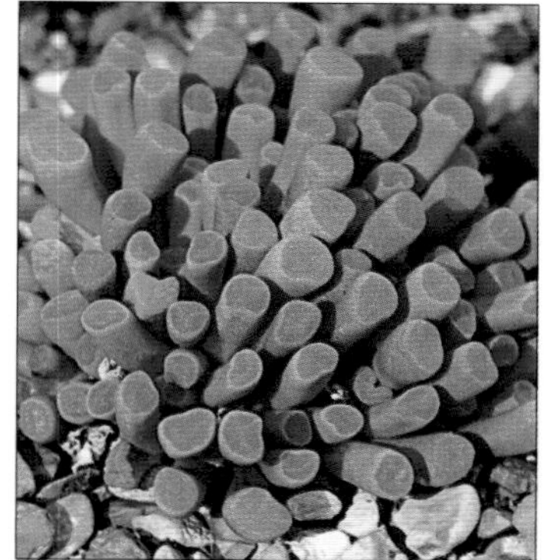

Frithia pulchra
Basal-rosetted, perennial succulent with erect, rough, grey leaves, cylindrical with flattened tips. Produces masses of stemless, daisy-like, bright pink flowers, with paler centres, in summer. H 3cm (1¼in), S 6cm (2½in). Min. 10°C (50°F).

Graptopetalum bellum
Basal-rosetted, perennial succulent with triangular to oval, grey leaves, 5cm (2in) long. Has clusters of deep pink to red flowers, 2cm (¾in) across, in spring-summer. H 3cm (1¼in), S 15cm (6in). Min. 10°C (50°F).

Crassula schmidtii
Carpeting, perennial succulent with dense rosettes of linear, dark green leaves, pitted and marked, each 3–4cm (1¼–1½in) long. Bears masses of star-shaped, bright pinkish-red flowers in clusters in winter. H 10cm (4in), S 30cm (12in). Min. 7°C (45°F).

Argyroderma pearsonii
Prostrate, egg-shaped, perennial succulent. A united pair of very fleshy, silvery-grey leaves has a deep fissure in which a red flower, 3cm (1¼in) across, appears in summer. H 3cm (1¼in), S 5cm (2in). Min. 5°C (41°F).

Echeveria secunda
Clump-forming, perennial succulent with short stems each crowned by a rosette of broad, fleshy, light green to grey leaves, reddened near tips. Bears cup-shaped, red-and-yellow flowers in spring-summer. H 4cm (1½in), S 30cm (12in). Min. 5°C (41°F).

Schlumbergera truncata
(Crab cactus, Lobster cactus)
Erect, then pendent, perennial cactus. Oblong stem segments have toothed margins. Bears purple-red flowers in early autumn and winter. H 15cm (6in), S 30cm (12in). Min. 10°C (50°F).

■ RED

Cephalophyllum alstonii
(Red spike)
Prostrate, perennial succulent with cylindrical, grey-green leaves, to 7cm (3in) long. Carries daisy-like, dark red flowers, 8cm (3in) across, in summer. H 10cm (4in), S 1m (3ft). Min. 5°C (41°F).

Rebutia steinbachii subsp. ***tiraquensis***
Variable, perennial cactus with a green stem. Elongated areoles bear spines of gold or bicoloured red and white. Has dark pink- or orange-red flowers in spring. H 15cm (6in), S 10cm (4in). Min. 10°C (50°F).

Cotyledon ladismithensis
Evergreen, freely branching, later prostrate, succulent sub-shrub with fleshy, green leaves, swollen and blunt at tips and covered with short, golden-brown hairs. Clusters of tubular, brownish-red flowers appear in autumn. H and S 20cm (8in). Min. 5°C (41°F).

Parodia microsperma
Clump-forming, perennial cactus. Has a much-ribbed, green stem densely covered with brown, radial spines and red, central spines, some of which are hooked. Bears blood-red, occasionally yellow flowers in spring. H 8cm (3in), S 30cm (12in). Min. 10°C (50°F).

Rebutia marsoneri
Clump-forming, perennial cactus with a tuberculate, dark green stem. Bears prominent, white areoles with very short, white spines. Trumpet-shaped, bright red flowers, to 5cm (2in) across, appear at stem base in spring. H 5cm (2in), S 20cm (8in). Min. 5°C (41°C).

Opuntia verschaffeltii
Clump-forming, perennial cactus with cylindrical, usually spineless stems, to 25cm (10in) long. Stem tips each bear short-lived, cylindrical leaves from spring to autumn. Has orange-red flowers in spring. H 15cm (6in), S 1–2m (3–6ft). Min. 5°C (41°F).

Parodia nivosa
Ovoid, perennial cactus that has a much-ribbed, green stem with stiff, white spines, each 1–2cm (½–¾in) long. Has a white, woolly crown and bright red flowers, to 5cm (2in) across, in summer. H to 15cm (6in), S 10cm (4in). Min. 10°C (50°F).

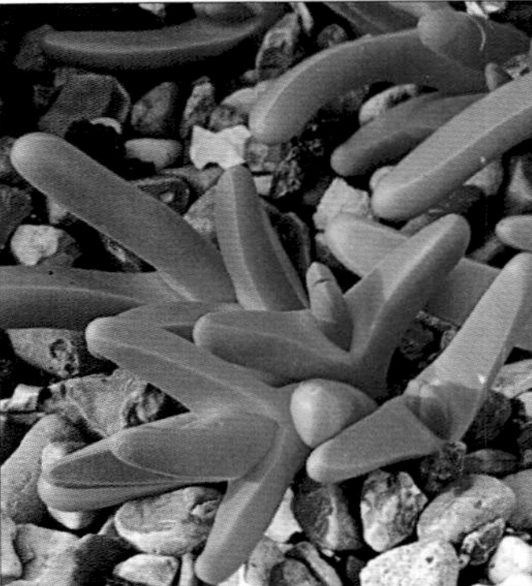

Argyroderma fissum
Clump-forming, perennial succulent with finger-shaped, fleshy leaves, 5–10cm (2–4in) long and often reddish at the tip. Has light red flowers between leaves in summer. H 15cm (6in), S 10cm (4in). Min. 5°C (41°F).

Echeveria agavoides
Basal-rosetted, perennial succulent with tapering, light green leaves, often red-margined. Carries cup-shaped, red flowers, 1cm (½in) long, in summer. H 15cm (6in), S 30cm (12in). Min. 5°C (41°F).

RED

Rebutia spegazziniana
Clump-forming, perennial cactus with a spherical, spined, green stem, to 4cm (1½in) across, becoming columnar with age. Bears masses of slender-tubed, orange-red flowers at base in late spring. H 10cm (4in), S 20cm (8in). Min. 5°C (41°F).

Echinopsis chamaecereus
(Peanut cactus)
Clump-forming, perennial cactus with spined stems, initially erect, then prostrate. Has funnel-shaped, orange-red flowers in late spring. H 10cm (4in), S indefinite. Min. 3°C (37°F).

Hatiora gaertneri (Easter cactus)
Bushy, perennial cactus with flat, oblong, glossy, green stem segments, each to 5cm (2in) long, often tinged red at edges. Segment ends each bear orange-red flowers in spring. H 15cm (6in), S 20cm (13in). Min. 13°C (55°F).

Parodia haselbergii subsp. ***haselbergii*** (Scarlet ball cactus)
Slow-growing, perennial cactus with a stem covered in white spines. Slightly sunken crown bears red flowers, with yellow stigmas, in spring. H 10cm (4in), S 25cm (10in). Min. 10°C (50°F).

Pachyphytum oviferum
(Moonstones, Sugared-almond plum)
Clump-forming, perennial succulent with a basal rosette of oval, pinkish-blue leaves. Stem bears 10–15 bell-shaped flowers, with powder-blue calyces and orange-red petals, in spring. H 10cm (4in), S 30cm (12in). Min. 10°C (50°F).

Echinocereus triglochidiatus var. ***paucispinus***
Clump-forming, perennial cactus with a 10cm (4in) wide, dark green stem that has 6 or 7 ribs, and 4–6 spines, 3–4cm (1¼–1½in) long, per areole. Has orange-red flowers in spring. H 20cm (8in), S 50cm (20in). Min. 5°C (41°C).

PURPLE

***Schlumbergera* 'Bristol Beauty'**
Erect, then pendent, perennial cactus with flattened, green stem segments with toothed margins. Bears reddish-purple flowers, with silvery-white tubes, in early autumn and winter. H 15cm (6in), S 30cm (12in). Min. 10°C (50°F).

Neolloydia conoidea
Clump-forming, perennial cactus. Has a columnar, blue-green stem densely covered with white, radial spines and longer, black, central spines. Bears funnel-shaped, purple-violet flowers in summer. H 10cm (4in), S 15cm (6in). Min. 10°C (50°F).

Caralluma joannis
Clump-forming, perennial succulent with blue-grey stems and rudimentary leaves on stem angles. Bears clusters of star-shaped, purple flowers, with short, fine hairs on petal tips, in late summer near stem tips. H 20cm (8in), S 1m (3ft). Min. 11°C (52°F).

PURPLE

Argyroderma delaetii
Prostrate, egg-shaped, perennial succulent with 2 very fleshy, silvery-green leaves between which daisy-like, pink-purple flowers, 5cm (2in) across, appear in late summer. H 3cm (1½in), S 5cm (2in). Min. 5°C (41°F).

Stenocactus coptonogonus
Spherical, perennial cactus. White areoles each have 3–5 flat, upward-curving, pale brownish-red spines. Bears purple to white flowers, with pink-purple or violet-purple stripes, in spring. H 10cm (4in), S 16cm (6in). Min. 7°C (45°F).

Huernia macrocarpa
Clump-forming, perennial succulent with finger-shaped, 4- or 5-sided, green stems. Produces short-lived, deciduous leaves and, in autumn, bell-shaped, white-haired, dark purple flowers with recurved petal tips. H and S 10cm (4in). Min. 8°C (46°F).

Orbea variegata (Star flower)
Clump-forming, branching, perennial succulent with 4-angled, indented stems. Flowers, variable in colour and blotched yellow, purple- or red-brown, appear in summer-autumn. H to 10cm (4in), S indefinite. Min. 11°C (52°F).

Stapelia grandiflora
Clump-forming, perennial succulent with 4-angled, hairy, toothed, green stems. In summer-autumn carries star-shaped, purple-brown flowers, to 10cm (4in) across, ridged with white or purple hairs. H to 20cm (8in), S indefinite. Min. 11°C (52°F).

GREEN–YELLOW

Duvalia corderoyi
Clump-forming, perennial succulent. Has a prostrate, leafless stem with 6 often purple, indistinct ribs. Bears star-shaped, dull green flowers, 1cm (½in) across and covered in purple hairs, in summer-autumn. H 5cm (2in), S 60cm (24in). Min. 10°C (50°F).

Crassula deceptor
Slow-growing, clump-forming, perennial succulent with branching stems surrounded by fleshy, grey leaves set in 4 rows. Each leaf has minute lines around raised dots. Bears insignificant flowers in spring. H and S 10cm (4in). Min. 5°C (41°F).

Stapelia gigantea
Clump-forming, perennial succulent. In summer-autumn bears star-shaped, red-marked, yellow-brown flowers, 30cm (12in) across, with white-haired, recurved edges. H to 20cm (8in), S indefinite. Min. 11°C (52°F).

Sclerocactus scheeri
Spherical to columnar, perennial cactus. Stem bears spines and, in spring, funnel-shaped, straw-coloured flowers. Lowest and longest spines are darker and hooked. H 10cm (4in), S 6cm (2½in). Min. 7–10°C (45–50°F).

Frailea pygmaea
Columnar, perennial cactus with a much-ribbed, dark green stem bearing white to light brown spines. Buds, which rarely open to flattish, yellow flowers in summer, become tufts of spherical, spiny seed pods. H to 5cm (2in), S 2cm (¾in). Min. 5°C (41°F).

Maihuenia poeppigii
Slow-growing, clump-forming, perennial cactus. Has a cylindrical, branched, spiny, green-brown stem. Most branches produce a spike of cylindrical, green leaves at the tip, with a funnel-shaped, yellow flower in summer. H 6cm (2½in), S 30cm (12in).

Aloinopsis schooneesii
Dwarf, mounded, perennial succulent with tuberous roots and fleshy, almost spherical, blue-green leaves arranged tightly in tufts. Produces flattish, yellow flowers in winter-spring. H 3cm (1½in), S to 7cm (3in). Min. 7°C (45°F).

Astrophytum ornatum
Elongated, spherical, perennial cactus with a very fleshy, 8-ribbed stem. Crown of each rib bears 5–11cm (2–4½in) long spines on each raised areole. Has yellow flowers, 8cm (3in) across, in summer. H 15cm (6in), S 12cm (5in). Min. 5°C (41°F).

Aichryson × domesticum* 'Variegatum'** ***(Cloud grass)
Prostrate, perennial succulent with stems crowned by rosettes of hairy, cream-marked, green leaves, sometimes pure cream. Has star-shaped, yellow flowers in spring. H 15cm (6in), S 40cm (16in). Min. 5°C (41°F).

Parodia mammulosa
Spherical, perennial cactus. Green stem has about 20 ribs and straight, stiff, yellow-brown to white spines, to 1cm (½in) long. Woolly crown produces masses of golden flowers in summer. H and S 10cm (4in). Min. 10°C (50°F).

Gymnocalycium andreae
Clump-forming, spherical, perennial cactus with a glossy, dark green stem bearing 8 rounded ribs and up to 8 pale yellow-white spines per areole. Has 5cm (2in) wide, yellow flowers in spring-summer. H 6cm (2½in), S 10cm (4in). Min. 10°C (50°F).

Euphorbia obesa
(Gingham golf ball)
Spherical, perennial succulent. Spineless, dark green stem, often chequered light green, has 8 low ribs. Crown bears rounded heads of cupped, yellow flowers in summer. H 12cm (5in), S 15cm (6in). Min. 10°C (50°F).

YELLOW

Rhombophyllum rhomboideum
Clump-forming, perennial succulent. Linear, glossy, grey-green leaves have expanded middles and white margins. Stems, 2–5cm (¾–2in) long, bear 3–7 yellow flowers, to 4cm (1½in) across, in summer. H 5cm (2in), S 15cm (6in). Min. 5°C (41°F).

Schwantesia ruedebuschii
Mat-forming, perennial succulent with cylindrical, bluish-green leaves, 3–5cm (1–2in) long, with expanded tips. Leaf edges each produce 3–7 minute, blue teeth with brown tips. Has yellow flowers in summer. H 5cm (2in), S 20cm (8in). Min. 5°C (41°F).

Pleiospilos compactus
Clump-forming, perennial succulent with 1 or 2 pairs of thick, grey leaves, to 8cm (3in) long. Bears coconut-scented, yellow flowers in early autumn. H 10cm (4in), S 30cm (12in). Min. 5°C (41°F).

Lithops pseudotruncatella subsp. ***dendritica***
Egg-shaped, perennial succulent, divided into 2 unequal-sized, grey leaves with dark green and red marks on upper surfaces. Has a yellow flower in summer or autumn. H 2–3cm (¾–1¼in), S 4cm (1½in). Min. 5°C (41°F).

Aeonium tabuliforme
Prostrate, almost stemless, short-lived, perennial succulent with a basal rosette, to 30cm (12in) across, like a flat, bright green plate. Has star-shaped, yellow flowers in spring, then dies. Propagate from seed. H 5cm (2in), S 30cm (12in). Min. 5°C (41°F).

Lithops schwantesii
Egg-shaped, perennial succulent, divided into 2 unequal-sized leaves with blue or red marks on upper surface. Has a yellow flower in late summer or autumn. H 2–3cm (¾–1¼in), S 3cm (1¼in). Min. 5°C (41°F).

Lithops dorotheae
Egg-shaped, perennial succulent, divided into 2 unequal-sized leaves, pale pink-yellow to green with darker areas and red marks on upper surfaces. Produces a daisy-like, yellow flower in summer or autumn. H 2–3cm (¾–1¼in), S 5cm (2in). Min. 5°C (41°F).

Mammillaria microhelia
Columnar, perennial cactus with a 5cm (2in) wide, green stem bearing cream or brown spines, discolouring with age. Has 1.5cm (⅝in) wide, yellow or pink flowers in spring. Offsets slowly with age. H 20cm (8in), S 40cm (16in). Min. 5°C (41°F).

Opuntia humifusa
Prostrate, perennial cactus. Each areole bears up to 3 spines, 3cm (1¼in) long. Has flat, rounded to oval, purple-tinged, dark green stem segments, 7–18cm (3–7in) long. Bears 8cm (3in) wide, yellow flowers in spring-summer. Keep dry in winter. H 15cm (6in), S 1m (3ft).

Agave utahensis
Basal-rosetted, perennial succulent with rigid, blue-grey leaves, each with spines up margins and a long, dark spine at tip. Flower stem, to 1.5m (5ft) long, carries yellow flowers in summer. H 23cm (9in) or more, S 2m (6ft).

Graptopetalum paraguayense
(Mother-of-pearl plant)
Clump-forming, perennial succulent with a basal rosette, 15cm (6in) across, of grey-green leaves, often tinged pink. Bears star-shaped, yellow-and-red flowers in summer. H 10cm (4in), S 1m (3ft). Min. 5°C (41°F).

Coryphantha cornifera
Spherical to columnar, perennial cactus with angular tubercles, each bearing a curved, dark, central spine and shorter, radial spines. Has funnel-shaped, yellow flowers in summer. H 15cm (6in), S 10cm (4in). Min. 5°C (41°F).

Parodia erinacea
(Colombian ball cactus)
Slow-growing, flattened spherical, perennial cactus with a glossy stem, up to 20 wart-like ribs, bearing yellow-white spines, and yellow blooms in summer. H 8cm (3in), S 9cm (3½in). Min. 10°C (50°F).

Fenestraria rhopalophylla* subsp. *aurantiaca
(Baby's toes)
Clump-forming, perennial succulent with a basal rosette of glossy leaves. Has yellow flowers in late summer and autumn. H 5cm (2in), S 30cm (12in). Min. 6°C (43°F).

Conophytum bilobum
Slow-growing, clump-forming, perennial succulent with 2-lobed, fleshy, green leaves, each 4cm (1½in) long and 2cm (¾in) wide. Has a flared, yellow flower, 3cm (1¼in) across, in autumn. H 4cm (1½in), S 15cm (6in). Min. 4°C (39°F).

Titanopsis calcarea
Clump-forming, perennial succulent with a basal rosette of very fleshy, triangular, blue-grey leaves covered in wart-like, grey-white and beige tubercles. Has yellow flowers from autumn to spring. H 3cm (1¼in), S 10cm (4in). Min. 8°C (46°F).

Faucaria tigrina (Tiger-jaws)
Clump-forming, stemless, perennial succulent. Fleshy, green leaves, 5cm (2in) long, have 9 or 10 teeth along each margin. Bears daisy-like, yellow flowers, 5cm (2in) across, in autumn. H 10cm (4in), S 50cm (20in). Min. 6°C (43°F).

Glottiphyllum nelii
Clump-forming, perennial succulent with semi-cylindrical, fleshy, green leaves, to 5cm (2in) long. Carries daisy-like, golden-yellow flowers, 4cm (1½in) across, in spring-summer. H 5cm (2in), S 30cm (12in). Min. 5°C (41°F).

Echinopsis aurea
Columnar, perennial cactus. Has narrow, much-ribbed, green stems covered with pale, radial spines often surrounded by 1–3 very stout, central spines, to 2.5cm (1in) long. Produces yellow flowers in summer. H and S 10cm (4in). Min. 5°C (41°F).

Pleiospilos bolusii
(Living rock, Mimicry plant)
Clump-forming, perennial succulent with 1 or 2 pairs of grey leaves, often wider than long and narrowing at incurved tips. Has golden-yellow flowers in early autumn. H 10cm (4in), S 20cm (8in). Min. 5°C (41°F).

YELLOW–ORANGE

Rebutia arenacea
Spherical, perennial cactus. Has a brown-green stem with white spines on spirally arranged tubercles. Has golden-yellow blooms, to 3cm (1¼in) across, in spring. H 5cm (2in), S 6cm (2½in). Min. 10°C (50°F).

Gasteria bicolor* var. *liliputana
Perennial succulent that forms rosettes of dark green leaves blotched with white. Flower stems, to 15cm (6in) long, bear spikes of bell-shaped, orange-green flowers in spring. H 7cm (3in), S 10cm (4in). Min. 5°C (41°F).

Pachyphytum compactum
Clump-forming, perennial succulent with a basal rosette of green leaves, each narrowing to a blunt point, with angular, paler edges. Stems each bear 3–10 flowers with green to pink calyces and orange petals in spring. H 15cm (6in), S indefinite. Min. 5°C (41°F).

Conophytum notabile
Slow-growing, spherical, perennial succulent forming clumps of 2-lobed, very fleshy, grey-green leaves, often with a red spot on edge of fissure between the lobes. Carries copper-orange flowers in autumn. H 3cm (1¼in). S indefinite. Min. 4°C (39°F).

Malephora crocea
Erect or spreading, perennial succulent with semi-cylindrical, blue-green leaves on short shoots. Carries solitary daisy-like, orange-yellow flowers, reddened on outsides, in spring-summer. H 20cm (8in), S 1m (3ft). Min. 5°C (41°F).

Matucana aurantiaca
Spherical, perennial cactus with a 15–17-ribbed stem. Elongated areoles each bear up to 30 spines. Has orange-yellow flowers in summer. H 12cm (5in), S 40cm (16in). Min. 10°C (50°F).

Aloe aristata
(Lace aloe, Torch plant)
Clump-forming, perennial succulent that has a basal rosette of pointed, dark green leaves with white spots and soft-toothed edges. Has orange flowers in spring. Offsets freely. H 10cm (4in), S 30cm (12in). Min. 7°C (45°F).

Rebutia aureiflora
Clump-forming, perennial cactus with a dark green stem, often tinged violet-red, that has stiff, radial spines and longer, soft, central spines. Has masses of yellow, violet or red flowers in late spring. H 10cm (4in), S 20cm (8in). Min. 5°C (41°F).

Gasteria carinata* var. *verrucosa
Clump-forming, perennial succulent with stiff, dark green leaves, with raised, white dots and incurved edges. Has spikes of bell-shaped, orange-green flowers in spring. H 10cm (4in), S 30cm (12in). Min. 5°C (41°F).

Rebutia fiebrigii
Clump-forming, perennial cactus. Has a dark green stem densely covered with soft, white spines, to 0.5cm (¼in) long. Bears bright orange flowers, 2–3cm (¾–1¼in) across, in late spring. H 10cm (4in), S 15cm (6in). Min. 5°C (41°F).

PLANT DICTIONARY

including common names

A complete listing of more than 8,000 plants, suitable for growing in temperate gardens worldwide. Includes full descriptions of the characteristics and cultivation of over 4,000 plants not already described in the Plant Catalogue.

Aaron's beard. See *Hypericum calycinum*, illus. p.166.
Abele. See *Populus alba*, illus. p.60.

ABELIA
CAPRIFOLIACEAE

Genus of deciduous, semi-evergreen or evergreen shrubs, grown for their foliage and freely borne flowers. Fully to half hardy, but in cold areas does best against a south- or west-facing wall. Requires a sheltered, sunny position and fertile, well-drained soil. Remove dead wood in late spring and prune out older branches after flowering to restrict growth, if required. Propagate by softwood cuttings in summer.
***A.* 'Edward Goucher'** illus. p.157.
♀ ***A. floribunda.*** Evergreen, arching shrub. H 3m (10ft), S 4m (12ft). Half hardy. Has oval, glossy, dark green leaves and, in early summer, drooping, tubular, bright red flowers.
♀ ***A.* x *grandiflora*** illus. p.117. **'Francis Mason'** is a vigorous, semi-evergreen, arching shrub. H 2m (6ft), S 3m (10ft). Frost hardy. Has coppery-yellow, young shoots and oval, yellowish-green leaves, darker in centres. Bears a profusion of fragrant, bell-shaped, white flowers, tinged with pink, from mid-summer to mid-autumn.
♀ ***A. schumannii*** illus. p.158.
A. triflora illus. p.115.

ABELIOPHYLLUM
OLEACEAE

Genus of one species of deciduous shrub, grown for its winter flowers. Fully hardy, but in cold areas grow against a south- or west-facing wall. Requires plenty of sun and fertile, well-drained soil. Thin out excess older shoots after flowering each year to encourage vigorous, young growth. Propagate by softwood cuttings in summer.
A. distichum. Deciduous, open shrub. H and S 1.2m (4ft). In late winter produces fragrant, star-shaped, white flowers, tinged with pink, on bare stems; flowers may be damaged by hard frosts. Leaves are oval and dark green.

ABIES
Silver fir
PINACEAE

Genus of tall conifers with whorled branches. Spirally arranged leaves are needle-like, flattened, usually soft and often have silvery bands beneath. Bears erect cones that ripen in their first autumn to release seeds and scales. See also CONIFERS.
A. alba. Fast-growing, conical conifer. H 15–25m (50–80ft), S 5–8m (15–25ft). Fully hardy. Has silvery-grey bark and dull green leaves, silvery beneath. Cylindrical cones, 10–15cm (4–6in) long, ripen to red-brown.
A. amabilis (Pacific fir). Conical conifer. H 15m (50ft), S 4–5m (12–15ft). Fully hardy. Dense, notched, square-tipped, glossy, dark green leaves, banded with white beneath, are borne on hairy, grey shoots. Oblong, violet-blue cones are 9–15cm (3½–6in) long. **'Spreading Star'**, H 50cm (20in), S 4–5m (12–15ft), is a procumbent form suitable for ground cover.
A. balsamea (Balsam fir).
♀ f. ***hudsonia***, syn. Hudsonia Group, is a dense, dwarf conifer of flattened to globose habit. H and S 60cm–1m (2–3ft). Fully hardy. Has smooth, grey bark and grey-green leaves that are semi-spirally arranged. **Hudsonia Group** see *A.b.* f. *hudsonia*. **'Nana'** (illus. p.106) is another dwarf form that makes a dense, globose mound with spirally arranged leaves.
A. cephalonica (Greek fir). Upright conifer with a conical crown; old trees have massive, spreading, erect branches. H 20–30m (70–100ft), S 5–10m (15–30ft). Fully hardy. Sharp, stiff, glossy, deep green leaves are whitish-green beneath. Cylindrical, tapered cones, 10–15cm (4–6in) long, are brown when ripe. **'Meyer's Dwarf'** (syn. *A.c.* 'Nana'; illus. p.106), H 50cm (20in), S 1.5m (5ft), has short leaves and forms a spreading, flat-topped mound.
♀ ***A. concolor*** (White fir). Upright conifer. H 15–30m (50–100ft), S 5–8m (15–25ft). Fully hardy. Has widely spreading, blue-green or grey leaves and cylindrical, green or pale blue cones, 8–12cm (3–5in) long. **'Argentea'**, syn. *A.c.* 'Candicans' illus. p.93. ♀ **'Compacta'**, syn. *A.c.* 'Glauca Compacta' (illus. p.106), H to 2m (6ft), S 2–3m (6–10ft), is a cultivar with steel-blue foliage.
A. delavayi (Delavay's fir). Upright conifer producing tiered, spreading branches. H 10–15m (30–50ft), S 4–6m (12–20ft). Fully hardy. Has maroon shoots and curved, bright deep green leaves, spirally arranged, with vivid silver bands beneath and rolled margins. Cones are narrowly cylindrical, 6–15cm (2½–6in) long, and violet-blue.
A. forrestii illus. p.101.
A. grandis illus. p.100.
A. homolepis (Nikko fir). Conifer that is conical when young, later columnar. H 15m (50ft), S 6m (20ft). Fully hardy. Pink-grey bark peels in fine flakes. Has pale green leaves, silver beneath, and cylindrical, violet-blue cones, 8–12cm (3–5in) long. Tolerates urban conditions.
A. koreana illus. p.105.
A. lasiocarpa (Subalpine fir). Narrowly conical conifer. H 10–15m (30–50ft), S 3–4m (10–12ft). Fully hardy. Has grey or blue-green leaves and cylindrical, violet-blue cones, 6–10cm (2½–4in) long. ♀ var. ***arizonica* 'Compacta'** (illus. p.106), H 4–5m (12–15ft), S 1.5–2m (5–6ft), is a slow-growing, ovoid to conical tree with corky bark and blue foliage. **'Roger Watson'** (illus. p.106), H and S 75cm (2½ft), is dwarf and conical, with silvery-grey leaves.
♀ ***A. nordmanniana*** (Caucasian fir). Columnar, dense conifer. H 15–25m (50–80ft), S 5m (15ft). Fully hardy. Luxuriant foliage is rich green. Cylindrical cones, 10–15cm (4–6in) long, are green-brown, ripening to brown. ♀ **'Golden Spreader'** (illus. p.107), H and S 1m (3ft), is a dwarf form with a spreading habit and bright golden-yellow leaves.
♀ ***A. procera*** (Noble fir). Narrowly conical conifer. H 15m (50ft), S 5m (15ft). Fully hardy. Has attractive, smooth, silvery-grey bark and grey-green or bright blue-grey leaves. Produces stoutly cylindrical, green cones, 15–25cm (6–10in) long, that ripen to brown.
A. veitchii illus. p.98.

ABUTILON
MALVACEAE

Genus of evergreen, semi-evergreen or deciduous shrubs, perennials and annuals, grown for their flowers and foliage. Frost hardy to frost tender, min. 5–7°C (41–5°F). Needs full sun or partial shade and fertile, well-drained soil. Water containerized specimens freely when in full growth, less at other times. In the growing season, young plants may need tip pruning to promote bushy growth. Mature specimens may have previous season's stems cut back hard annually in early spring. Tie lax-growing species to a support if necessary. Propagate by seed in spring or by softwood, greenwood or semi-ripe cuttings in summer. Whitefly and red spider mite may be troublesome.
***A.* 'Ashford Red'.** Strong-growing, evergreen, erect to spreading shrub. H and S 2–3m (6–10ft). Half hardy. Has maple- to heart-shaped, serrated, pale to mid-green leaves. Pendent, bell-shaped, crimson flowers are carried from spring to autumn.
***A.* 'Golden Fleece'.** Strong-growing, evergreen, rounded shrub. H and S 2–3m (6–10ft). Half hardy. Has maple- to heart-shaped, serrated, rich green leaves. Pendent, bell-shaped, yellow flowers are carried from spring to autumn.
♀ ***A.* 'Kentish Belle'** illus. p.167.
♀ ***A. megapotamicum.*** Evergreen shrub with long, slender branches normally trained against a wall. H and S to 3m (10ft). Half hardy. Pendent, bell-shaped, yellow-and-red flowers appear from late spring to autumn. Leaves are oval, with heart-shaped bases, and dark green.
A. pictum, syn. *A. striatum* of gardens. **'Thompsonii'** illus. p.143.
A. striatum of gardens. See *A. pictum*.
A.* x *suntense. Fast-growing, deciduous, upright, arching shrub. H 5m (15ft), S 3m (10ft). Frost hardy. Has oval, lobed, toothed, dark green leaves. Produces an abundance of large, bowl-shaped, pale to deep purple, occasionally white, flowers from late spring to early summer. **'Violetta'** illus. p.141.
A. vitifolium. Fast-growing, deciduous, upright shrub. H 4m (12ft), S 2.5m (8ft). Frost hardy. Masses of large, bowl-shaped, purplish-blue flowers are produced in late spring and early summer. Has oval, lobed, sharply toothed, grey-green leaves. var. ***album*** illus. p.115.

ACACIA
Mimosa
LEGUMINOSAE/MIMOSACEAE

Genus of evergreen, semi-evergreen or deciduous trees and shrubs, grown for their tiny flowers, composed of massed

stamens, and for their foliage. Many species have phyllodes instead of true leaves. Frost hardy to frost tender, min. 5–7°C (41–5°F). Requires full sun and well-drained soil. Propagate by seed in spring. Red spider mite and mealy bug may be problematic.
♀ ***A. baileyana*** illus. p.93.
♀ ***A. dealbata*** illus. p.79.
A. juniperina. See *A. ulicifolia*.
A. longifolia (Sydney golden wattle). Evergreen, spreading tree. H and S 6m (20ft). Frost hardy. Has narrowly oblong, dark green phyllodes. Bears cylindrical clusters of golden-yellow flowers in early spring.
A. podalyriifolia (Mount Morgan wattle, Queensland silver wattle). Evergreen, arching shrub. H 3–5m (10–15ft), S 3–4m (10–12ft). Half hardy. Has blue-green phyllodes and produces racemes of bright yellow flowers in spring.
♀ ***A. pravissima*** illus. p.93.
A. pulchella illus. p.153.
A. ulicifolia, syn. *A. juniperina*. Evergreen, bushy shrub. H 1m (3ft), S 1.5m (5ft). Frost hardy. Has very narrow, cylindrical, spine-like, rich green phyllodes and, in mid-spring, globular clusters of pale yellow flowers.
A. verticillata (Prickly Moses). Evergreen, spreading tree or bushy shrub. H and S 9m (28ft). Half hardy. Has needle-like, dark green phyllodes and, in spring, dense, bottle brush-like spikes of bright yellow flowers.

Acacia
False. See *Robinia pseudoacacia*.
Rose. See *Robinia hispida*, illus. p.137.

ACAENA
ROSACEAE

Genus of mainly summer-flowering sub-shrubs and perennials, evergreen in all but the severest winters, grown for their leaves and coloured burs and as ground cover. Has tight, rounded heads of small flowers. Is good for a rock garden, but some species may be invasive. Fully to frost hardy. Needs sun or partial shade and well-drained soil. Propagate by division in early spring or by seed in autumn.
A. anserinifolia of gardens. See *A. novae-zelandiae*.
A. buchananii. Vigorous, evergreen, prostrate perennial. H 2cm (¾in), S 75cm (30in) or more. Fully hardy. Bears glaucous leaves composed of 11–17 oval, toothed leaflets. Globose, green flower heads are borne in summer and develop into spiny, yellow-green burs.
A. caerulea. See *A. caesiiglauca*.
A. caesiiglauca, syn. *A. caerulea*, illus. p.402.
♀ ***A. microphylla*** illus. p.401.
A. novae-zelandiae, syn. *A. anserinifolia* of gardens. Vigorous, evergreen, prostrate sub-shrub. H 10cm (4in), S 75cm (30in) or more. Fully hardy. Has brown-green leaves, divided into 9–13 oval, toothed leaflets. In summer, red-spined, brownish burs develop from spherical heads of greenish-brown flowers.
***A.* 'Pewter'.** See *A. saccaticupula* 'Blue Haze'.
***A. saccaticupula* 'Blue Haze'**, syn. *A.* 'Pewter'. Vigorous, evergreen, prostrate perennial. H 10cm (4in), S 75cm (30in) or more. Fully hardy. Leaves are divided into 9–15 oval, toothed, steel-blue leaflets. Produces spherical, brownish-red flower heads that develop in autumn to dark red burs with pinkish-red spines.

ACALYPHA
EUPHORBIACEAE

Genus of evergreen shrubs and perennials, grown for their flowers and foliage. Frost tender, min. 10–13°C (50–55°F), but best at min. 16°C (61°F). Needs partial shade and humus-rich, well-drained soil. Water containerized plants freely when in full growth, much less at other times and in low temperatures. Stem tips may be removed in growing season to promote branching of young plants. Propagate by softwood, greenwood or semi-ripe cuttings in summer. Red spider mite, whitefly and mealy bug may be troublesome.
♀ ***A. hispida*** (Red-hot cat's tail). Evergreen, upright, soft-stemmed shrub. H 2m (6ft) or more, S 1–2m (3–6ft). Has oval, toothed, lustrous, deep green leaves. Tiny, crimson flowers hang in long, dense, catkin-like spikes, intermittently year-round. May be grown as a short-lived cordon.
A. wilkesiana illus. p.139.

ACANTHOLIMON
PLUMBAGINACEAE

Genus of evergreen perennials, grown for their flowers and tight cushions of spiny leaves. Is suitable for rock gardens and walls. Fully hardy. Prefers sun and well-drained soil. Dislikes damp winters. Seed is rarely set in cultivation. Propagate by softwood cuttings in late spring.
A. glumaceum illus. p.389.
A. venustum. Evergreen, cushion-forming perennial. H and S 10cm (4in). Small spikes of star-shaped, pink flowers, on 3cm (1¼ in) stems, are produced from late spring to early summer amid rosetted, spear-shaped, spiny, blue-green leaves that are edged with silver. Needs a very hot, well-drained site. Makes an excellent alpine house plant.

Acanthopanax. See *Eleutherococcus* except for:
A. ricinifolius for which see *Kalopanax septemlobus*.

ACANTHUS
Bear's breeches
ACANTHACEAE

Genus of perennials, some of which are semi-evergreen, grown for their large, deeply cut leaves and their spikes of flowers. Fully hardy. Prefers full sun, warm conditions and well-drained soil, but will tolerate shade. Protect crowns in first winter after planting. Long, thong-like roots make plants difficult to eradicate if wrongly placed. Propagate by seed or division in early autumn or spring or by root cuttings in winter.
A. balcanicus. See *A. hungaricus*.
A. dioscoridis. Upright, architectural perennial. H to 1m (3ft), S 45cm (18in). Has oval, deeply cut, rigid, basal leaves and hairy stems. Dense spikes of small, funnel-shaped, purple-and-white flowers are produced in summer.
A. hungaricus, syn. *A. balcanicus*, *A. longifolius*, illus. p.255.
A. longifolius. See *A. hungaricus*.
A. mollis. Semi-evergreen, stately, upright perennial. H 1.2m (4ft), S 45cm (18in). Has long, oval, deeply cut, bright green leaves and, in summer, produces many spikes of funnel-shaped, mauve-and-white flowers.
♀ ***A. spinosus*** illus. p.255.

ACCA,
syn. FEIJOA
MYRTACEAE

Genus of evergreen, opposite-leaved shrubs, grown for their shallowly cup-shaped flowers. Frost hardy. Needs a sheltered, sunny site and light, well-drained soil. Propagate by seed sown as soon as ripe or by semi-ripe cuttings in summer.
A. sellowiana illus. p.139.

ACER
Maple
ACERACEAE

Genus of deciduous or evergreen trees and shrubs, grown for their foliage, which often colours brilliantly in autumn and, in some cases, for their ornamental bark or stems. Small, but often attractive flowers are followed by 2-winged fruits. Fully to frost hardy. Requires sun or semi-shade and fertile, moist but well-drained soil. Many acers produce their best autumn colour on neutral to acid soil. Propagate species by seed as soon as ripe or in autumn; cultivars by various grafting methods in late winter or early spring, or by budding in summer. Leaf-eating caterpillars or aphids sometimes infest plants, and maple tar spot may affect *A. platanoides* and *A. pseudoplatanus*.
A. buergerianum (Trident maple). Deciduous, spreading tree. H 10m (30ft) or more, S 8m (25ft). Fully hardy. Has 3-lobed, glossy, dark green leaves, usually providing an attractive, long-lasting display of red, orange and purple in autumn.
♀ ***A. capillipes*** illus. p.78.
A. cappadocicum (Cappadocian maple). Deciduous, spreading tree. H 20m (70ft), S 15m (50ft). Fully hardy. Has 5-lobed, bright green leaves that turn yellow in autumn.
♀ **'Aureum'** has bright yellow, young leaves that turn light green in summer and assume yellow autumn tints.
A. carpinifolium illus. p.88.
A. circinatum (Vine maple). Deciduous, spreading, bushy tree or shrub. H 5m (15ft) or more, S 6m (20ft). Fully hardy. Rounded, 7–9-lobed, mid-green leaves turn brilliant orange and red in autumn. Bears clusters of small, purple-and-white flowers in spring.
A. cissifolium. Deciduous, spreading tree. H 8m (25ft), S 12m (40ft). Fully hardy. Leaves consist of 3 oval, toothed leaflets, bronze-tinged when young, dark green in summer, turning red and yellow in autumn. Does best in semi-shade and on neutral to acid soil. subsp. ***henryi*** see *A. henryi*.
A. crataegifolium (Hawthorn maple). Deciduous, arching tree. H and S 10m (30ft). Fully hardy. Branches are streaked green and white. Small, oval, mid-green leaves turn orange in autumn. **'Veitchii'** illus. p.85.
A. davidii (Père David's maple, Snake-bark maple). Deciduous tree with upright branches. Fully hardy. H and S 15m (50ft). Branches are striped green and white. Oval, glossy, dark green leaves often turn yellow or orange in autumn. subsp. ***grosseri*** see *A. grosseri*. **'Madeline Spitta'** illus. p.77.
A. ginnala. See *A. tataricum* subsp. *ginnala*.
A. giraldii. Deciduous, spreading tree. H and S 10m (30ft). Frost hardy. Shoots have a blue-grey bloom. Large, sycamore-like, shallowly lobed leaves, with long, pink stalks, are dark green above, blue-white beneath.
A. grandidentatum. See *A. saccharum* subsp. *grandidentatum*.
♀ ***A. griseum*** illus. p.96.
♀ ***A. grosseri***, syn. *A. davidii* subsp. *grosseri* (Snake-bark maple). Deciduous, upright and spreading tree. H and S 10m (30ft). Fully hardy. Has white-striped trunk and branches. Broadly oval, deeply lobed, bright green leaves turn red in autumn.
A. henryi, syn. *A. cissifolium* subsp. *henryi*, illus. p.78.
A. japonicum (Full-moon maple, Japanese maple). Deciduous, bushy tree or shrub. H and S 10m (30ft). Fully hardy. Rounded, lobed leaves are mid-green, turning red in autumn. Clusters of small, reddish-purple flowers open in mid-spring. Shelter from strong winds. ♀ **'Aconitifolium'** illus. p.91. **'Aureum'** see *A. shirasawanum* 'Aureum'. ♀ **'Vitifolium'** illus. p.91.
A. laxiflorum, syn. *A. pectinatum* subsp. *laxiflorum*, illus. p.95.
A. lobelii. syn. *A. cappadocicum* subsp. *lobelii*, illus. p.62.
A. macrophyllum illus. p.60.
A. maximowiczianum, syn. *A. nikoense* (Nikko maple). Slow-growing, deciduous, round-headed tree. H and S 12m (40ft). Fully hardy. Leaves have 3 oval, bluish-green leaflets that turn brilliant red and yellow in autumn.
A. monspessulanum (Montpelier maple). Deciduous, usually compact, round-headed tree or shrub. H and S 12m (40ft). Fully hardy. Small, 3-lobed, glossy, dark green leaves remain on tree until late autumn.
A. negundo (Ash-leaved maple, Box elder). Fast-growing, deciduous, spreading tree. H 15m (50ft), S 8m (25ft). Fully hardy. Bright green leaves have 3–5 oval leaflets. Clusters of inconspicuous, greenish-yellow flowers are borne in late spring. **'Variegatum'** illus. p.75. var. ***violaceum*** has purplish branchlets covered in a glaucous bloom and prominent clusters of tassel-like, purplish-pink flowers.
A. nikoense. See *A. maximowiczianum*.
A. opalus (Italian maple). Deciduous, round-headed tree. H and S 15m (50ft). Fully hardy. Clusters of small, yellow flowers emerge from early to mid-spring, before foliage. Leaves are broad, 5-lobed and dark green, turning yellow in autumn.
A. palmatum (Japanese maple). Deciduous, bushy-headed shrub or tree. H and S 6m (20ft) or more. Fully hardy. Palmate, deeply lobed, mid-

green leaves turn brilliant orange, red or yellow in autumn. Clusters of small, reddish-purple flowers are borne in mid-spring. f. ***atropurpureum*** illus. p.117. ♀ **'Bloodgood'** illus. p.139. **'Butterfly'** illus. p.136. ♀ **'Chitoseyama'** illus. p.162. **'Corallinum'** illus. p.126. var. ***coreanum*** illus. p.90. **'Dissectum Atropurpureum'** see *A.p.* 'Ornatum'. var. ***heptalobum*** illus. p.120. var. ***heptalobum*** **'Lutescens'** illus. p.118. var. ***heptalobum*** **'Rubrum'** illus. p.118. **'Ornatum'**, syn. *A.p.* 'Dissectum Atropurpureum', illus. p.162. ♀ **'Osakazuki'** has large leaves, with 7 lobes, that turn brilliant scarlet in autumn. ♀ **'Sango-kaku'** (syn. *A.p.* 'Senkaki') illus. p.120.
A. pectinatum subsp. ***laxiflorum.*** See *A. laxiflorum*.
♀ ***A. pensylvanicum*** (Snake-bark maple) illus. p.80. **'Erythrocladum'** is a deciduous, upright tree. H 10m (30ft), S 6m (20ft). Fully hardy. Has brilliant candy-pink, young shoots in winter and large, boldly lobed, mid-green leaves that turn bright yellow in autumn.
♀ ***A. platanoides*** (Norway maple). Vigorous, deciduous, spreading tree. H 25m (80ft), S 15m (50ft). Fully hardy. Has large, broad, sharply lobed, bright green leaves that turn yellow or orange in autumn and clusters of yellow flowers borne in mid-spring before the leaves appear. **'Columnare'**, H 12m (40ft), S 8m (25ft), is dense and columnar. ♀ **'Crimson King'** illus. p.61. **'Drummondii'** has leaves broadly edged with creamy-white. **'Emerald Queen'** is upright when young. **'Globosum'**, H 8m (25ft), S 10m (30ft), has a dense, round crown. **'Lorbergii'** see *A.p.* 'Palmatifidum'. **'Palmatifidum'** (syn. *A.p.* 'Lorbergii') illus. p.67. **'Royal Red'** has deep reddish-purple leaves. Those of ♀ **'Schwedleri'** are bright red when young, maturing to purplish-green in summer and turn orange-red in autumn. **'Summershade'** has dark green leaves.
A. pseudoplatanus (Sycamore). Fast-growing, deciduous, spreading tree. H 30m (100ft), S 15m (50ft). Fully hardy. Has broadly 5-lobed, dark green leaves. Makes a fine specimen tree and is good for an exposed position. ♀ **'Brilliantissimum'** illus. p.85. f. ***erythrocarpum*** illus. p.66. **'Simon-Louis Frères'** illus. p.75.
A. rubrum (Red maple) illus. p.66. **'Columnare'** illus. p.77. **'Franksred'** see *A.r.* RED SUNSET. ♀ **'October Glory'** is a deciduous, spreading tree. H 20m (70ft), S 12m (40ft). Fully hardy. Has 3- or 5-lobed, glossy, dark green leaves that become intense red in autumn, particularly on neutral to acid soil. In spring, bare branches are covered with clusters of tiny, red flowers. **RED SUNSET ('Franksred')** has dense growth that also turns brilliant red in autumn. **'Scanlon'** and **'Schlesingeri'** illus. p.66.
♀ ***A. rufinerve*** (Snake-bark maple) illus. p.78. **'Hatsuyuki'** (syn. *A.r.* f. *albolimbatum*) is a deciduous, arching tree. H 10m (30ft), S 8m (25ft). Fully hardy. Branches are striped green and white. Has 3-lobed, mid-green leaves, mottled and edged with white, that turn orange and red in autumn.
A. saccharinum (Silver maple). Fast-growing, deciduous, spreading tree. H 25m (80ft), S 15m (50ft). Fully hardy. Deeply lobed, mid-green leaves, with silver undersides, turn yellow in autumn. f. ***laciniatum*** **'Wieri'** (syn. *A.s.* 'Laciniatum Wieri') has pendent, lower branches and deeply lobed leaves.
A. saccharum (Sugar maple). subsp. ***grandidentatum*** (syn. *A. grandidentatum*) is a deciduous, spreading tree. H and S 10m (30ft) or more. Fully hardy. Broad 3- or 5-lobed, bright green leaves turn bright orange-red in early autumn. **'Green Mountain'**, H 20m (70ft), S 12m (40ft), is upright. Large, 5-lobed leaves turn brilliant scarlet in autumn. **'Temple's Upright'** illus. p.78.
♀ ***A. shirasawanum*** **'Aureum',** syn. *A. japonicum* 'Aureum', illus. p.88.
A. tataricum subsp. ***ginnala,*** syn. *A. ginnala*, illus. p.91.
♀ ***A. triflorum*** illus. p.92.
A. velutinum. Deciduous, spreading tree. H 20m (70ft), S 15m (50ft). Fully hardy. Produces large, sycamore-like, lobed, dark green leaves, with undersides covered with pale brown down. var. ***vanvolxemii*** (Van Volxem's maple) has even larger leaves, slightly glaucous and smooth beneath.

ACHILLEA

ASTERACEAE/COMPOSITAE

Genus of mainly upright perennials, some of which are semi-evergreen, suitable for borders and rock gardens. Has fern-like foliage and large, usually plate-like, flower heads mainly in summer. Flower heads may be dried for winter decoration. Fully hardy. Tolerates most soils but does best in a sunny, well-drained site. Tall species and cultivars need staking. Propagate by division in early spring or autumn or by softwood cuttings in early summer. Contact with foliage may aggravate skin allergies.
A. aegyptica of gardens. See *A.* 'Taygetea'.
A. argentea. See *Tanacetum argenteum*.
A. argentea of gardens. See *A. clavennae*.
***A.* 'The Beacon'.** See. *A.* 'Fanal'
A. clavennae, syn. *A. argentea* of gardens, illus. p.385.
A. clypeolata. Semi-evergreen, upright perennial. H 45cm (18in), S 30cm (12in). Has divided, hairy, silver leaves and dense, flat heads of small, yellow flowers in summer. Divide plants regularly in spring.
♀ ***A.* 'Coronation Gold'** illus. p.262.
***A.* 'Fanal'** syn. *A.* 'The Beacon' illus. p.254.
♀ ***A. filipendulina*** **'Gold Plate'** illus. p.266.
A.* × *kellereri illus. p.387.
♀ ***A.* × *lewisii*** **'King Edward'.** Semi-evergreen, rounded, compact, woody-based perennial. H 10cm (4in), S 23cm (9in) or more. Has feathery, soft, grey-green leaves. Bears compact heads of minute, buff-yellow flower heads in summer. Is suitable for a rock garden, wall or bank.
A. millefolium (Yarrow). **'Fire King'** is a vigorous, upright perennial. H and S 60cm (24in). Has a mass of feathery, dark green leaves and flat heads of rich red flowers in summer.
♀ ***A.* 'Moonshine'** illus. p.303.
♀ ***A. ptarmica*** **'The Pearl'** illus. p.241.
***A.* 'Schwellenburg'** illus. p.261.
***A.* 'Taygetea'**, syn. *A. aegyptica* of gardens, illus. p.303.

ACHIMENES

Hot-water plant

GESNERIACEAE

Genus of erect or trailing perennials with small rhizomes and showy flowers. Frost tender, min. 10°C (50°F). Prefers bright light, but not direct sunlight, and well-drained soil. Use tepid water for watering pot-grown plants. Allow plants to dry out after flowering and store rhizomes in a frost-free place over winter. Propagate by division of rhizomes or by seed, if available, in spring or by stem cuttings in summer.
A. antirrhina. Erect perennial. H and S 35cm (14in) or more. Has oval, toothed leaves, to 5cm (2in) or more long and of unequal size in each opposite pair. In summer bears funnel-shaped, red-orange flowers, to 4cm (1½in) long, with yellow throats.
***A.* 'Brilliant'.** Erect, compact perennial. H and S 30cm (12in). Has oval, toothed leaves and, in summer, large, funnel-shaped, scarlet flowers.
A. coccinea. See *A. erecta*.
A. erecta, syn. *A. coccinea, A. pulchella.* Erect, bushy, branching perennial. H and S 45cm (18in). Has narrowly oval, toothed leaves, often arranged in whorls of 3. Tubular, scarlet flowers with yellow eyes are produced in summer.
A. grandiflora. Erect perennial. H and S to 60cm (24in). Oval, toothed leaves are often reddish below. In summer has tubular, dark pink to purple flowers with white eyes.
***A.* 'Little Beauty'** illus. p.292.
♀ ***A.* 'Paul Arnold'.** Erect, compact, free-flowering perennial. H and S 30cm (12in). Has oval, toothed leaves. Bears large, funnel-shaped, purple flowers in summer.
***A.* 'Peach Blossom'.** Trailing perennial. H and S to 25cm (10in). Has oval, toothed leaves, and large, funnel-shaped, peach-coloured flowers in summer.
A. pulchella. See *A. erecta*.

Achnatherum calamagrostis. See *Stipa calamagrostis*.
Acidanthera bicolor var. ***murieliae.*** See *Gladiolus callianthus*.
Acidanthera murieliae. See *Gladiolus callianthus*.

ACIPHYLLA

UMBELLIFERAE/APIACEAE

Genus of evergreen perennials, grown mainly for the architectural value of their spiky foliage but also for their flowers, which are produced more freely on male plants. Frost hardy. Requires sun and well-drained soil. Protect neck of plant from winter wet with a deep layer of stone chippings. Propagate by seed when fresh, in late summer, or in early spring.
A. aurea illus. p.240.
A. scott-thomsonii (Giant Spaniard). Evergreen, rosette-forming perennial. H to 4.5m (14ft), S 60cm–1m (2–3ft). Much-dissected, spiny foliage is bronze when young, maturing to silver-grey. Prickly spikes of tiny, creamy-yellow flowers are rarely produced. Prefers a moist but well-drained site.
A. squarrosa illus. p.274.

Acis. See *Leucojum*.

ACOKANTHERA

APOCYNACEAE

Genus of evergreen shrubs and trees, grown for their flowers and overall appearance. Frost tender, min. 10°C (50°F). Requires full light and good drainage. Water containerized plants moderately, less when not in full growth. Propagate by seed in spring or autumn or by semi-ripe cuttings in summer. The sap and small, plum-like fruits that follow the flowers are highly toxic if ingested.
A. oblongifolia, syn. *A. spectabilis, Carissa spectabilis*, illus. p.146.
A. spectabilis. See *A. oblongifolia*.

Aconite. See *Aconitum*.
Winter. See *Eranthis hyemalis*, illus. p.457.

ACONITUM

Aconite, Monkshood, Wolf's bane

RANUNCULACEAE

Genus of perennials with poisonous, tuberous or fibrous roots and upright, sometimes scandent, stems, bearing curious, hooded flowers in summer. Leaves are mostly rounded in outline. Is good when grown in rock gardens and bo rders. Fully hardy. Prefers a position in sun, but tolerates some shade and this may enhance flower colour. Requires fertile, well-drained soil. Propagate by division in autumn, every 2–3 years, or by seed in autumn. Contact with the foliage may irritate skin; all parts are highly toxic if ingested.
A. anthora. Compact, tuberous perennial. H 60cm (24in), S 50cm (20in). Has erect, leafy stems that bear several hooded, yellow flowers in summer. Leaves are divided and dark green.
A.* × *bicolor. See *A.* × *cammarum* 'Bicolor'.
♀ ***A.* 'Bressingham Spire'.** Compact, upright, tuberous perennial. H 1m (3ft), S 50cm (20in). Very erect spikes of hooded, violet-blue flowers are produced in summer. Bears deeply divided leaves that are glossy and dark green.
♀ ***A.* × *cammarum*** **'Bicolor',** syn. *A.* × *bicolor*, illus. p.258.
♀ ***A. carmichaelii*** **'Arends',** syn. *A.c.* 'Arendsii'. Erect, tuberous perennial. H 1.5m (5ft), S 30cm (1ft). Has divided, rich green leaves and, in autumn, spikes of hooded, rich deep blue flowers. Upright stems may need staking, particularly if planted in a shady site.
A. hemsleyanum, syn. *A. volubile* of gardens. Wiry, scandent, fibrous perennial. H 2–2.5m (6–8ft), S 1–1.2m (3–4ft). Hooded, lilac flowers are produced in drooping clusters in late summer. Leaves are divided and mid-green. Is best grown where it can scramble through a shrub or be supported.

***A.* 'Ivorine'.** Upright, tuberous perennial. H 1.5m (5ft), S 50cm (20in). Bears hooded, creamy-white flowers in erect spikes in early summer. Strong stems bear deeply divided, glossy, green leaves.
A. lycoctonum subsp. ***vulparia,*** syn. *A. orientale* of gardens, *A. vulparia,* illus. p.261.
A. napellus (Helmet flower, Monkshood). Upright, tuberous perennial. H 1.5m (5ft), S 30cm (1ft). Bears tall, slender spires of hooded, light indigo-blue flowers in late summer and deeply cut, mid-green leaves. subsp. ***vulgare* 'Albidum'** (syn. *A.n.* 'Albiflorus') has white flowers.
***A.* 'Newry Blue'.** Upright, tuberous perennial. H 1.2m (4ft), S 50cm (20in). Produces hooded, dark blue flowers on erect stems in summer and has deeply divided, glossy, dark green leaves.
A. orientale of gardens. See *A. lycoctonum* subsp. *vulparia*.
♀ ***A.* 'Spark's Variety'.** Upright, tuberous perennial. H 1.2m (4ft), S 50cm (20in). Bears violet-blue flowers on branching stems in summer and has deeply divided, glossy, dark green leaves.
A. volubile of gardens. See *A. hemsleyanum*.
A. vulparia. See *A. lycoctonum* subsp. *vulparia*.

ACORUS

ARACEAE

Genus of semi-evergreen, perennial, marginal and submerged water plants, grown for their frequently aromatic foliage. Fully to frost hardy. Needs an open, sunny position. *A. calamus* requires up to 25cm (10in) depth of water. Tidy up fading foliage in autumn and lift and divide plants every 3 or 4 years, in spring, as clumps become congested.
***A. calamus* 'Argenteostriatus'**, syn. *A.c.* 'Variegatus', illus. p.463.
A. gramineus var. ***pusillus.*** Semi-evergreen, perennial, marginal water plant or submerged aquarium plant. Frost hardy. H and S 10cm (4in). Has narrow, grass-like, stiff leaves. Rarely, insignificant, greenish flower spikes are produced in summer. **'Variegatus'** illus. p.463.

ACRADENIA

RUTACEAE

Genus of evergreen shrubs, grown for their foliage and flowers. Half hardy. Requires a sheltered position in sun or semi-shade and fertile, well-drained soil. Does best planted against a south- or west-facing wall. Propagate by semi-ripe cuttings in summer.
A. frankliniae. Evergreen, upright, stiffly branched shrub. H and S 2m (6ft). Has aromatic, dark green leaves with 3 narrowly lance-shaped leaflets and, from late spring to early summer, bears small clusters of star-shaped, white flowers.

Acroclinium. See *Rhodanthe.*
A. roseum. See *Rhodanthe chlorocephala* subsp. *rosea*

ACTAEA

Baneberry

RANUNCULACEAE

Genus of clump-forming perennials, grown for their colourful, poisonous berries. Fully hardy. Likes woodland conditions – moist, peaty soil and shade. Propagate by division in spring or by seed in autumn. The berries are highly toxic if ingested.
A. alba. See *A. pachypoda.*
A. alba of gardens. See *A. rubra* f. *neglecta*.
A. erythrocarpa of gardens. See *A. rubra*.
♀ ***A. pachypoda***, syn. *A. alba*, illus. p.267.
Actaea racemosa. See *Cimicifuga racemosa*.
♀ ***A. rubra***, syn. *A. erythrocarpa* of gardens (Red baneberry). Clump-forming perennial. H 50cm (20in), S 30cm (12in). Small, fluffy, white flowers are followed in autumn by clusters of poisonous, rounded, scarlet berries, borne above oval, divided, bright green leaves. f. ***neglecta*** (syn. *A. alba* of gardens) has white berries.
Actaea simplex. See *Cimicifuga simplex*.

ACTINIDIA

ACTINIDIACEAE

Genus of mainly deciduous, woody-stemmed, twining climbers. Fully hardy to frost tender, min. 10°C (50°F). Grows in partial shade but needs sun for fruit to form and ripen. Grow in any well-drained soil that does not dry out. Prune in winter if necessary. Propagate by seed in spring or autumn, by semi-ripe cuttings in mid-summer or by layering in winter.
A. chinensis of gardens. See *A. deliciosa*.
A. deliciosa, syn. *A. chinensis* of gardens (Chinese gooseberry, Kiwi fruit). Vigorous, mainly deciduous, woody-stemmed, twining climber. H 9–10m (28–30ft). Frost hardy. Heart-shaped leaves are 13–20cm (5–8in) long. In summer bears clusters of cup-shaped, white flowers that later turn yellowish, followed by edible, hairy, brown fruits. To obtain fruits, both male and female plants must usually be grown.
♀ ***A. kolomikta*** illus. p.205.
A. polygama (Silver vine). Mainly deciduous, woody-stemmed, twining climber. H 4–6m (12–20ft). Frost hardy. Heart-shaped leaves, 7–13cm (3–5in) long, are bronze when young and sometimes have creamy upper sections. In summer has scented, cup-shaped, white flowers, usually arranged in groups of 3 male, female or bisexual, followed by edible but not very palatable, egg-shaped, bright yellow fruits.

ADA

SEE ALSO ORCHIDS.
A. aurantiaca illus. p.311. Evergreen, epiphytic orchid for a cool greenhouse. H 23cm (9in). Bears sprays of tubular, orange flowers, 2.5cm (1in) long, in early spring. Has narrowly oval leaves, 10cm (4in) long. Needs shade in summer.

Adam's needle. See *Yucca filamentosa*.

ADANSONIA

Baobab

BOMBACACEAE

Genus of deciduous or semi-evergreen, mainly spring-flowering trees, grown for their characteristically swollen trunks, their foliage and for shade. Has flowers only on large, mature specimens. Frost tender, min. 13–16°C (55–61°F). Requires full light and sharply drained soil. Allow soil of containerized specimens almost to dry out between waterings. Propagate by seed sown in spring. Pot specimens under glass are susceptible to red spider mite.
A. digitata. Slow-growing, semi-evergreen, rounded tree. H and S 15m (50ft) or more. Has palmate leaves of 5–7 lustrous, green leaflets. Produces fragrant, pendent, long-stalked, white flowers, with 5 reflexed petals, in spring, followed by edible, sausage-shaped, brown fruits.

ADENIUM

Desert rose

APOCYNACEAE

Genus of perennial succulents with fleshy, swollen trunks. Frost tender, min. 15°C (59°F). Needs sun or partial shade and well-drained soil; plants are very prone to rotting. Propagate by seed sown in spring or summer. The milky sap that exudes from broken stems may irritate skin and cause severe discomfort if ingested.
A. obesum illus. p.474.

ADENOCARPUS

LEGUMINOSAE/PAPILIONACEAE

Genus of deciduous or semi-evergreen shrubs, grown for their profuse, broom-like, yellow flowers, which are produced in spring or early summer. Frost to half hardy. Requires a site in full sun and well-drained soil. Does best grown against a south- or west-facing wall. Propagate by seed sown in autumn.
A. viscosus. Semi-evergreen, arching shrub. H and S 1m (3ft). Frost hardy. Grey-green leaves with 3 narrowly lance-shaped leaflets densely cover shoots. Produces dense, terminal racemes of orange-yellow flowers in late spring.

ADENOPHORA

Gland bellflower

CAMPANULACEAE

Genus of summer-flowering, fleshy-rooted perennials. Fully hardy. Requires a site in full sun and rich, well-drained but not over-dry soil. May sometimes become invasive but resents disturbance. Propagate by basal cuttings taken in early spring or by seed sown in autumn.
A. potaninii. Rosette-forming perennial. H 45cm (18in) or more, S 60cm (24in). Arching sprays of bell-shaped, pale bluish-lavender flowers are produced in late summer. Has oval to lance-shaped, basal, mid-green leaves.

Adhatoda duvernoia. See *Justicia adhatoda*.

ADIANTUM

ADIANTACEAE/PTERIDACEAE

Genus of deciduous, semi-evergreen or evergreen ferns. Fully hardy to frost tender, min. 7–13°C (45–55°F). Prefers semi-shade and moist, neutral to acid soil (*A. aleuticum* prefers alkaline soil). Remove fading fronds regularly. Propagate by spores in summer.
♀ ***A. aleuticum***, syn. *A. pedatum* var. *aleuticum*, illus. p.323.
A. capillus-veneris (Maidenhair fern). Semi-evergreen or evergreen fern. H and S 30cm (12in). Half hardy. Has dainty, triangular to oval, segmented, arching, light green fronds borne on black stems.
A. cuneatum. See *A. raddianum*.
♀ ***A. pedatum*** illus. p.324. var. ***aleuticum.*** See *A. aleuticum*.
♀ ***A. raddianum***, syn. *A. cuneatum* (Delta maidenhair). Semi-evergreen or evergreen fern. H and S 30cm (12in). Frost tender, min. 7°C (45°F). Triangular, divided, pale green segments are borne on finely dissected fronds that have purplish-black stems. ♀ **'Fritz-Lüthi'** has bright green fronds. **'Grandiceps'** (Tassel maidenhair) has elegant, tasselled fronds.
A. tenerum. Semi-evergreen or evergreen fern. H 30cm–1m (1–3ft), S 60cm–1m (2–3ft). Frost tender, min. 13°C (55°F). Broadly lance-shaped, much-divided, spreading, mid-green fronds consist of rounded or diamond-shaped pinnae.
♀ ***A. venustum*** illus. p.325

ADLUMIA

PAPAVERACEAE/FUMARIACEAE

Genus of one species of herbaceous, biennial, leaf-stalk climber, grown for its leaves and flowers. Frost hardy. Grow in semi-shade in any soil. Propagate by seed in spring.
A. cirrhosa. See *A. fungosa*.
A. fungosa, syn. *A. cirrhosa* (Allegheny vine, Climbing fumitory). Herbaceous, biennial, leaf-stalk climber. H 3–4m (10–12ft). Delicate leaves have numerous leaflets. Tiny, tubular, spurred, white or purplish flowers are carried in drooping panicles in summer.

ADONIS

RANUNCULACEAE

Genus of spring-flowering perennials, grown for their foliage and flowers. Fully hardy. Some thrive in semi-shade; others need an open, well-drained site. Propagate by seed when fresh, in late summer, or by division after flowering.
A. amurensis illus. p.285.
A. brevistyla illus. p.276.
A. vernalis illus. p.285.

ADROMISCHUS

CRASSULACEAE

Genus of perennial succulents and evergreen sub-shrubs with rounded, thin or fat leaves. Frost tender, min. 7°C (45°F). Needs partial shade and very well-drained soil. Propagate by

leaf or stem cuttings in spring or summer.
A. cooperi, syn. *Cotyledon cooperi, Echeveria cooperi.* Freely branching perennial succulent. H 10cm (4in), S to 15cm (6in). Has greyish-brown stems and inversely lance-shaped, glossy, grey-green leaves, to 5cm (2in) long, often purple-marked above. In summer, produces tubular, green-and-red flowers, with white-margined, pink or purple lobes, on a stem 25cm (10in) or more long.
A. maculatus illus. p.485.

AECHMEA

BROMELIACEAE

Genus of evergreen, rosette-forming, epiphytic perennials, cultivated for their foliage, flowers and fruits. Frost tender, min. 10–15°C (50–59°F). May be grown in full light or a semi-shaded site. Provide a rooting medium of equal parts humus-rich soil and either sphagnum moss or bark or plastic chips used for orchid culture. Using soft water, water moderately in summer, sparingly at all other times, and keep cup-like, rosette centres filled with water from spring through to autumn. Propagate by offsets in late spring.
A. distichantha illus. p.273. Evergreen, basal-rosetted, epiphytic perennial. H and S to 1m (3ft). Forms dense rosettes of narrowly oblong, round-tipped, arching leaves that are dull green above, grey and scaly beneath. Has panicles of small, tubular, purple or blue flowers among white-felted, pink bracts, usually in summer.
♀ ***A. fasciata***, syn. *Billbergia rhodocyanea* (Silver vase plant, Urn plant; illus. p.273). Evergreen, tubular-rosetted, epiphytic perennial. H 40–60cm (16–24in), S 30–50cm (12–20in). Has loose rosettes of broadly oblong, round-tipped, incurved, arching leaves with dense, grey scales and silver cross-banding. Bears dense, pyramidal panicles of tubular, blue-purple flowers among pink bracts, just above foliage, from spring to autumn.
♀ ***A. Foster's Favorite Group*** (Lacquered wine-cup; illus. p.273). Evergreen, basal-rosetted, epiphytic perennial. H and S 30–60cm (12–24in). Has loose rosettes of strap-shaped, arching, lustrous, wine-red leaves. Drooping spikes of small, tubular, deep purple-blue flowers are borne in summer, followed later by pear-shaped, red fruits.
A. fulgens (Coral berry). Evergreen, basal-rosetted, epiphytic perennial. H and S 40–75cm (16–30in). Forms loose rosettes of broadly oblong, arching, glossy, mid-green leaves with grey scales beneath and rounded or pointed tips. In summer produces, above foliage, erect panicles of small, tubular, violet-purple flowers that turn red with age. These are succeeded by small, rounded to ovoid, red fruits on red stalks.
♀ ***A. nudicaulis.*** Evergreen, basal-rosetted, epiphytic perennial. H and S 40–75cm (16–30in). Produces loose rosettes of a few broadly strap-shaped, arching, olive-green leaves with spiny edges and usually banded with grey scales beneath. Spikes of small, tubular, yellow flowers open above large, red bracts in summer.
A. recurvata illus. p.273. Evergreen, basal-rosetted, epiphytic perennial. H and S 15–20cm (6–8in). Narrowly triangular, tapered, spiny-edged, arching, red-flushed, mid-green leaves are produced in dense rosettes. In summer bears a short, dense spike of tubular, red-and-white flowers, with red bracts, just above leaves.

AEGOPODIUM

Bishop's weed, Gout weed, Ground elder

UMBELLIFERAE/APIACEAE

Genus of invasive, rhizomatous perennials, most of which are weeds although *A. podagraria* 'Variegatum' provides excellent ground cover. Fully hardy. Tolerates sun or shade and any well-drained soil. Propagate by division of rhizomes in spring or autumn.
***A. podagraria* 'Variegatum'** illus. p.286.

AEONIUM

CRASSULACEAE

Genus of perennial succulents, some of which are short-lived, and evergreen, succulent shrubs, grown for their rosettes of bright green or blue-green, occasionally purple, leaves. Frost tender, min. 5°C (41°F). Prefers partial shade and very well-drained soil. Most species grow from autumn to spring and are semi-dormant in mid-summer. Propagate by seed in summer or, for branching species, by stem cuttings in spring or summer.
♀ ***A. arboreum.*** Bushy, perennial succulent. H to 60cm (2ft), S 1m (3ft). Branched stems are each crowned by a rosette, up to 15cm (6in) across, of broadly lance-shaped, glossy, bright green leaves. In spring produces cones of small, star-shaped, golden flowers on 2–3-year-old stems, which then die back. **'Schwarzkopf'** see *A.* 'Zwartkop'.
♀ ***A. haworthii*** illus. p.482.
♀ ***A. tabuliforme*** illus. p.494.
♀ ***A. 'Zwartkop'***, syn. *A. arboreum* 'Schwarzkopf', illus. p.484.

Aeroplane propeller. See *Crassula perfoliata* var. *minor*, illus. p.480.

AESCHYNANTHUS

GESNERIACEAE

Genus of evergreen, climbing, trailing or creeping perennials, useful for growing in hanging baskets. Frost tender, min. 15–18°C (59–64°F). Needs a fairly humid atmosphere and a position out of direct sun. Water sparingly in low temperatures. Propagate by tip cuttings in spring or summer.
***A.* 'Black Pagoda'.** Semi-trailing perennial. H 60cm (24in), S to 45cm (18in). Has elliptic leaves, to 10cm (4in) long, pale green with dark brown marbling above, and purple beneath. Bears terminal clusters of deep burnt-orange flowers, with green calyces, from summer to winter.
A. marmoratus, syn. *A. zebrinus.* Evergreen, trailing perennial. H and S to 60cm (24in). Oval, waxy leaves are dark green, veined yellowish-green above, purplish below. Produces tubular, greenish flowers, with dark brown markings, borne in terminal clusters in summer.
♀ ***A. pulcher*** (Lipstick plant, Royal red bugler). Evergreen, climbing or trailing perennial. H and S indefinite. Produces thick, oval leaves and small, tubular, hooded, bright red flowers, with yellow throats, borne in terminal clusters from summer to winter.
♀ ***A. speciosus***, syn. *A. splendens*, illus. p.305.
A. splendens. See *A. speciosus.*
A. zebrinus. See *A. marmoratus.*

AESCULUS

Buckeye, Horse-chestnut

HIPPOCASTANACEAE

Genus of deciduous trees and shrubs, grown for their bold, divided leaves and conspicuous, upright panicles or clusters of flowers, followed by fruits (horse-chestnuts) sometimes with spiny outer casings. Fully to frost hardy. Requires sun or semi-shade and fertile, well-drained soil. Propagate species by sowing seed in autumn, cultivars by budding in late summer or by grafting in late winter. Leaf spot may affect young foliage, and coral spot fungus may attack damaged wood. All parts of these plants may cause mild stomach upset if ingested.
A. californica illus. p.81.
A.* × *carnea (Red horse-chestnut). ♀ **'Briotii'** illus. p.60.
A. chinensis illus. p.60.
♀ ***A. flava***, syn. *A. octandra*, illus. p.78.
A. glabra (Ohio buckeye). Deciduous, round-headed, sometimes shrubby tree. H and S 10m (30ft). Fully hardy. Leaves, usually composed of 5 narrowly oval leaflets, are dark green. Bears 4-petalled, greenish-yellow flowers in upright clusters in late spring and early summer.
♀ ***A. hippocastanum*** (Horse-chestnut) illus. p.60. ♀ **'Baumannii'** is a vigorous, deciduous, spreading tree. H 30m (100ft), S 15m (50ft). Fully hardy. Large, dark green leaves, consisting of 5 or 7 narrowly oval leaflets, turn yellow in autumn. Has large panicles of long-lasting, double, yellow- or red-marked, white flowers from mid- to late spring.
♀ ***A. indica*** (Indian horse-chestnut). Deciduous, spreading, elegant tree. H 20m (70ft), S 12m (40ft). Frost hardy. Glossy, dark green leaves with usually 7 narrowly oval leaflets are bronze when young, orange or yellow in autumn. Upright panicles of 4-petalled, pink-tinged, white flowers, marked with red or yellow, appear in mid-summer. ♀ **'Sydney Pearce'** illus. p.75.
A.* × *neglecta (Sunrise horse-chestnut). ♀ **'Erythroblastos'** illus. p.85.
A. octandra. See *A. flava.*
♀ ***A. parviflora*** illus. p.115.
♀ ***A. pavia*** (Red buckeye). Deciduous, round-headed, sometimes shrubby tree. H 5m (15ft), S 3m (10ft). Fully hardy. Glossy, dark green leaves consist of 5 narrowly oval leaflets. Has panicles of 4-petalled, red flowers in early summer. **'Atrosanguinea'** illus. p.87.
A. turbinata (Japanese horse-chestnut). Deciduous, spreading, stout-branched tree. H 20m (70ft), S 12m (40ft). Fully hardy. Large, dark green leaves consist of 5 or 7 narrowly oval leaflets. Panicles of creamy-white flowers appear in late spring and early summer.

AETHIONEMA

BRASSICACEAE/CRUCIFERAE

Genus of short-lived, evergreen or semi-evergreen shrubs, sub-shrubs and perennials, grown for their prolific flowers. Fully hardy. Needs sun and well-drained soil. Propagate by softwood cuttings in spring or by seed in autumn. Most species self seed readily.
A. armenum illus. p.389.
♀ ***A. grandiflorum***, syn. *A. pulchellum*, illus. p.364.
A. iberideum. Evergreen or semi-evergreen, rounded, compact shrub. H and S 15cm (6in). Bears small, lance-shaped, grey-green leaves and, in summer, 2cm (¾in) stems each bear a raceme of small, saucer-shaped, white flowers.
A. pulchellum. See *A. grandiflorum.*
♀ ***A.* 'Warley Rose'** illus. p.388.
***A.* 'Warley Ruber'.** Evergreen or semi-evergreen, rounded, compact sub-shrub. H and S 15cm (6in). Has tiny, linear, bluish-green leaves. Racemes of small, deep rose-pink flowers appear on 2–3cm (¾–1¼in) stems in spring-summer.

African daisy. See *Arctotis venusta*; *Dimorphotheca*
African fountain grass. See *Pennisetum setaceum.*
African hemp. See *Sparrmannia africana*, illus. p.114.
African lily. See *Agapanthus africanus.*
African marigold. See *Tagetes erecta.*
African red alder. See *Cunonia capensis.*
African tulip tree. See *Spathodea campanulata*, illus. p.67.
African violet. See *Saintpaulia.*
False. See *Streptocarpus saxorum*, illus. p.294.

AGAPANTHUS

LILIACEAE/ALLIACEAE

Genus of clump-forming perennials, some of which are evergreen, with erect stems that carry large umbels of bell- to tubular-bell-shaped or trumpet-shaped flowers, usually blue and often fading to purple with age. Leaves are strap-shaped. Narrow-leaved forms are frost hardy, broad-leaved ones half hardy. Grow in full sun and in moist but well-drained soil. Protect crowns in winter with ash or mulch. Plants increase slowly but may be propagated by division in spring; may also be raised from seed in autumn or spring. Named cultivars will not come true from seed.
♀ ***A. africanus*** (African lily). Evergreen, clump-forming perennial. H 1m (3ft), S 50cm (20in). Half hardy. In late summer has rounded umbels of deep blue flowers on upright stems, above broad, dark green leaves.
***A.* 'Alice Gloucester'.** Clump-forming perennial. H 1m (3ft), S 50cm (20in). Frost hardy. Produces large, dense, rounded umbels of white flowers in summer, above narrow, mid-green leaves.
***A.* 'Ben Hope'.** Clump-forming perennial. H 1–1.2m (3–4ft), S 50cm (20in). Frost hardy. Erect stems support dense, rounded umbels of deep blue flowers in late summer and early autumn, borne over narrow, greyish-green leaves.

A. 'Blue Giant' illus. p.259.
A. campanulatus. Clump-forming perennial. H 60cm–1.2m (2–4ft), S 50cm (20in). Frost hardy. Rounded umbels of blue flowers are borne on strong stems in summer, above narrow, greyish-green leaves.
***A.* 'Cherry Holley'.** Clump-forming perennial. H 1m (3ft), S 50cm (20in). Frost hardy. Rounded umbels of dark blue flowers, carried in summer above narrow leaves, do not fade to purple with age.
***A.* 'Dorothy Palmer'.** Clump-forming perennial. H 1m (3ft), S 50cm (20in). Frost hardy. Rounded umbels of rich blue flowers, fading to reddish-mauve, are borne on erect stems above narrow, greyish-green leaves in late summer.
A. inapertus. Clump-forming perennial. H 1.5m (5ft), S 60cm (2ft). Frost hardy. Pendent, narrowly tubular, blue flowers are borne on very erect stems, above narrow, bluish-green leaves, in late summer and autumn.
***A.* 'Lilliput'.** Compact, clump-forming perennial. H 80cm (32in), S 50cm (20in). Frost hardy. Has small, rounded umbels of dark blue flowers that are produced in summer. Leaves are narrow and mid-green.
♀ ***A.* 'Loch Hope'.** Clump-forming perennial. H 1–1.2m (3–4ft), S 50cm (20in). Frost hardy. Bears large, rounded umbels of deep blue flowers in late summer and early autumn, above narrow, greyish-green leaves.
A. orientalis. See *A. praecox* subsp. *orientalis*.
A. praecox subsp. ***orientalis,*** syn. *A. orientalis*, illus. p.260.

AGAPETES,
syn. PENTAPTERYGIUM

ERICACEAE

Genus of evergreen or deciduous, scandent shrubs and semi-scrambling climbers, grown for their flowers. Frost tender, min. 5–18°C (41–64°F). Provide full light or partial shade and a humus-rich, well-drained but not dry, neutral to acid soil. Water potted specimens freely when in full growth, but moderately at other times. Overlong stems may be cut back to promote branching, but they are best tied to supports. Propagate by seed sown in spring or by semi-ripe cuttings taken in late summer.
♀ ***A.* 'Ludgvan Cross'.** Evergreen, scandent shrub with arching or pendulous stems. H and S 2–3m (6–10ft). Min. 5°C (41°F). Lance-shaped leaves are dark green. Urn-shaped, red flowers with darker patterns are produced in spring.
A. macrantha. See *A. variegata* var. *macrantha*.
A. rugosa. See *A. variegata* var. *rugosa*.
♀ ***A. serpens*** illus. p.201.
A. variegata var. ***macrantha,*** syn. *A.macrantha*, illus. p.217. var. ***rugosa*** (syn. *A. rugosa*) is an evergreen, loose shrub with arching or spreading stems. H and S to 3m (10ft). Min. 5°C (41°F). Leaves are lance-shaped, wrinkled and bright green. In spring, clusters of pendent, urn-shaped, white flowers, patterned with purple-red, are borne from leaf axils.

AGASTACHE
Mexican giant hyssop

LABIATAE/LAMIACEAE

Genus of summer-flowering perennials with aromatic leaves. Half hardy. Needs full sun and fertile, well-drained soil. Plants are short-lived and should be propagated each year by softwood or semi-ripe cuttings taken in late summer.
A. mexicana, syn. *Brittonastrum mexicanum, Cedronella mexicana.* Upright perennial with aromatic leaves. H to 1m (3ft), S to 30cm (1ft). In summer bears whorls of small, tubular flowers in shades of pink to crimson. Leaves are oval, pointed, toothed and mid-green.

Agathaea. See *Felicia.*

AGATHOSMA

RUTACEAE

Genus of evergreen shrubs, grown for their flowers and overall appearance. Frost tender, min. 5–7°C (41–5°F). Needs full light and well-drained, acid soil. Water containerized specimens moderately, less when not in full growth. Propagate by semi-ripe cuttings in late summer.
A. pulchella, syn. *Barosma pulchella.* Evergreen, rounded, wiry, aromatic shrub. H and S to 1m (3ft). Has a dense mass of small, oval, leathery leaves. Small, 5-petalled, purple flowers are freely produced in terminal clusters in spring-summer.

AGAVE

AGAVACEAE

Genus of rosetted, perennial succulents with sword-shaped, sharp-toothed leaves. Small species, to 30cm (1ft) high, flower only after 5–10 years; tall species, to 5m (15ft) high, may take 20–40 years to flower. The majority of species that have hard, blue-grey leaves are half hardy; grey-green- or green-leaved species are usually frost tender, requiring min. 5°C (41°F). Agave needs full sun and well-drained soil. Propagate by seed or offsets in spring or summer.
♀ ***A. americana*** (Century plant). Basal-rosetted, perennial succulent. H 1–2m (3–6ft), S 2–3m (6–10ft) or more. Half hardy. Has sharply pointed, toothed leaves, to 1.5–2m (5–6ft) long. Branched flower stem, to 8m (25ft) long, bears dense, tapering spikes of bell-shaped, white to pale creamy-yellow flowers, each 9cm (3½in) long, in spring-summer. Offsets freely.
♀ **'Mediopicta'**, H and S 2m (6ft), has central, yellow stripes along leaves. **'Striata'** illus. p.473.
A. attenuata illus. p.483.
♀ ***A. filifera*** illus. p.481.
A. parryi illus. p.482.
♀ ***A. parviflora*** illus. p.473.
A. utahensis illus. p.494.
♀ ***A. victoriae-reginae*** illus. p.477.

Agave
Royal. See *Agave victoriae-reginae*, illus. p.477.
Thread. See *Agave filifera*, illus. p.481.

Ageratina ligustrina. See *Eupatorium ligustrinum*.

AGERATUM
Floss flower

COMPOSITAE/ASTERACEAE

Genus of annuals and biennials. Half hardy. Grow in sun and in fertile, well-drained soil, which should not be allowed to dry out otherwise growth and flowering will be poor. Plants must be dead-headed regularly to ensure continuous flowering. Propagate by seed sown outdoors in late spring.
A. houstonianum. Moderately fast-growing, hummock-forming annual. Tall cultivars, H and S 30cm (12in); medium, H and S 20cm (8in); dwarf, H and S 15cm (6in). All have oval, mid-green leaves and clusters of feathery, brush-like flower heads throughout summer and into autumn. Is useful for bedding. ♀ **'Blue Danube'** (dwarf) and **'Blue Mink'** (tall) illus. p.345. **Hawaii Series** includes uniform, compact plants, with deep to pale blue or white flower heads.
♀ **'Pacific'** (medium) is neat, with tight clusters of deep violet-blue flower heads. **'Swing Pink'** (dwarf) has attractive, pink flower heads.

AGLAONEMA
Chinese evergreen

ARACEAE

Genus of evergreen, erect, tufted perennials, grown mainly for their foliage. Frost tender, most species requiring min. 15°C (59°F). Tolerates shade, although the variegated forms need more light, and prefers moist but well-drained soil. Water moderately when in full growth, less in winter. Propagate by division or stem cuttings in summer. Mealy bug may be a problem.
A. commutatum. Evergreen, erect, tufted perennial. H and S to 45cm (18in) or more. Broadly lance-shaped leaves are 30cm (12in) long and dark green with irregular, greyish-white patches along lateral veins. Has greenish-white spathes produced in summer. **'Malay Beauty'** (syn. *A.c.* 'Pewter') bears very dark green leaves mottled greenish-white and cream. **'Pewter'** see *A.c.* 'Malay Beauty'.**'Treubii'** illus. p.312.
A. pictum illus. p.316.
***A.* 'Silver King'** illus. p.316.

AGONIS
Willow myrtle

MYRTACEAE

Genus of evergreen, mainly spring-flowering shrubs and trees, grown for their foliage, flowers and graceful appearance. Frost tender, min. 10°C (50°F). Needs full light and well-drained but moisture-retentive soil. Water containerized specimens moderately, scarcely at all in winter. Pruning is tolerated when necessary. Propagate by seed in spring or by semi-ripe cuttings in summer.
A. flexuosa illus. p.86.

AGROSTEMMA
Corn cockle

CARYOPHYLLACEAE

Genus of summer-flowering annuals. Fully hardy. Grow in sun; flowers best in very well-drained soil that is not very fertile. Support with sticks and dead-head to prolong flowering. Propagate by seed sown *in situ* in spring or early autumn. Seeds may cause severe discomfort if ingested.
A. coeli-rosa. See *Silene coeli-rosa*.
A. githago. Fast-growing, erect annual with thin stems. H 60cm–1m (2–3ft), S 30cm (1ft). Has lance-shaped, mid-green leaves and, in summer, 5-petalled, open trumpet-shaped, pink flowers, 8cm (3in) wide. Seeds are tiny, rounded, dark brown and poisonous. **'Milas'** illus. p.335.

AICHRYSON

CRASSULACEAE

Genus of annual and perennial succulents, often shrub-like, grown for their fleshy, spoon-shaped to rounded, hairy leaves. Most species are short-lived, dying after flowering. Frost tender, min. 5°C (41°F). Needs full sun or partial shade and very well-drained soil. Propagate by seed or stem cuttings in spring or summer.
♀ ***A.* × *aizoides* 'Variegatum'**, syn. *A.* × *domesticum* 'Variegatum', illus. p.493.
***A.* × *domesticum* 'Variegatum'.** See *A.* × *aizoides* 'Variegatum'

AILANTHUS

SIMAROUBACEAE

Genus of deciduous trees, grown for their foliage and 3–5-winged fruits; they can be particularly useful as they are extremely tolerant of urban pollution. Fully hardy. Needs sun or semi-shade and deep, fertile, well-drained soil. To grow as shrubs, cut back hard in spring, after which vigorous shoots bearing very large leaves are produced. Propagate by seed sown in autumn or by suckers or root cuttings taken in winter. Male flowers are unpleasantly scented; the pollen may cause an allergic reaction.
♀ ***A. altissima,*** syn. *A. glandulosa* (Tree of heaven). Fast-growing, deciduous, spreading tree. H 25m (80ft), S 15m (50ft). Large, dark green leaves consist of 15–30 paired, oval leaflets. Large clusters of small, green flowers in mid-summer are followed by attractive, winged, green, then reddish-brown fruits.
A. glandulosa. See *A. altissima.*

AJUGA

LABIATAE/LAMIACEAE

Genus of annuals and perennials, some of which are semi-evergreen or evergreen and excellent as ground cover. Fully hardy. Tolerates sun or shade and any soil, but grows more vigorously in moist conditions. Propagate by division in spring.
A. pyramidalis (Pyramidal bugle). Semi-evergreen perennial. H 15cm (6in), S 45cm (18in). Forms a creeping carpet of oblong to spoon-shaped, deep green leaves, above which appear spikes of whorled, 2-lipped, blue

flowers in spring. **'Metallica Crispa'** has crisp, curled leaves, with a metallic-bronze lustre, and dark blue flowers.
***A. reptans* 'Atropurpurea'** illus. p.315. **'Jungle Beauty'** is a semi-evergreen, mat-forming perennial. H 38cm (15in), S 60cm (24in). Has large, oval, toothed or slightly lobed, dark green leaves, sometimes suffused purple, and, in spring, spikes of whorled, 2-lipped, blue flowers. **'Multicolor'** (syn. *A.r.* 'Rainbow') illus. p.315. **'Rainbow'** see *A.r.* 'Multicolor'.

AKEBIA

LARDIZABALACEAE

Genus of deciduous or semi-evergreen, woody-stemmed, twining climbers, grown for their leaves and flowers. Individual plants seldom produce fruits; cross-pollination between 2 individuals is required for fruit formation. Frost hardy. Prefers a position in full sun and any good, well-drained soil. Tolerates an east- or north-facing position. Dislikes disturbance. May be propagated in a number of ways: by seed sown in autumn or spring; by semi-ripe cuttings taken in summer; or by layering in winter.
A. lobata. See *A. trifoliata*.
A. × pentaphylla illus. p.201.
A. quinata illus. p.201.
A. trifoliata, syn. *A. lobata*. Deciduous, woody-stemmed, twining climber. H to 10m (30ft) or more. Mid-green leaves, bronze-tinted when young, have 3 oval leaflets; drooping racemes of 3-petalled, purple flowers appear in spring, followed by sausage-shaped, purplish fruits.

ALANGIUM

ALANGIACEAE

Genus of deciduous or evergreen trees and shrubs, grown for their foliage and flowers. Frost hardy. Needs full sun and any fertile, well-drained soil. Propagate by sowing seed in spring or by taking softwood cuttings in summer.
A. platanifolium. Deciduous, upright, tree-like shrub. H 3m (10ft), S 2m (6ft). Produces maple-like, 3-lobed, mid-green leaves. Fragrant, tubular, white flowers are borne from early to mid-summer.

Albany bottlebrush. See *Callistemon speciosus*.

ALBIZIA

LEGUMINOSAE/MIMOSACEAE

Genus of deciduous or semi-evergreen trees, grown for their feathery foliage and unusual flower heads, composed of numerous stamens and resembling bottlebrushes. Half hardy, so it is best grown against a south- or west-facing wall; in cold areas do not risk planting out until late spring. Requires full sun and well-drained soil. *A. julibrissin* may be grown as a summer bedding plant for its foliage. Propagate by seed in autumn.
A. distachya. See *Paraserianthes lophantha*.
A. julibrissin. illus. p.86.
A. lophantha. See *Paraserianthes lophantha*.

ALBUCA

HYACINTHACEAE/LILIACEAE

Genus of spring- or summer-flowering bulbs. Half hardy to frost tender, min. 10°C (50°F). Needs an open, sunny position and well-drained soil. Dies down in spring or late summer after flowering. Propagate by seed in spring or by offsets when dormant.
A. canadensis, syn. *A. major, A. minor.* Spring-flowering bulb. H 15cm (6in), S 8–10cm (3–4in). Half hardy. Has 3–6 narrowly lance-shaped, erect, basal leaves. Produces a loose spike of tubular, yellow flowers, 1.5–2cm (⅝–¾in) long, with a green stripe on each petal.
A. humilis illus. p.451.
A. major. See *A. canadensis*.
A. minor. See *A. canadensis*.

ALCEA
Hollyhock

MALVACEAE

Genus of biennials and short-lived perennials, grown for their tall spikes of flowers. Fully hardy. Needs full sun and well-drained soil. Propagate by seed in late summer or spring. Rust may be a problem.
A. rosea, syn. *Althaea rosea* (biennial), illus. p.333. **Chater's Double Group** (biennial), illus. p.339. **'Majorette'** is an erect biennial, grown as an annual. H 60cm (24in), S to 30cm (12in). Rounded, lobed, pale green leaves have a rough texture. Spikes of rosette-like, double flowers, in several different colours, are produced during summer and early autumn. **'Summer Carnival'** (annual or biennial), H 1.8–2.4m (6–8ft), S to 60cm (2ft), has double flowers in mixed colours.

ALCHEMILLA
Lady's mantle

ROSACEAE

Genus of perennials that produce sprays of tiny, greenish-yellow flowers, with conspicuous outer calyces, in summer. Some are good for ground cover. Fully hardy. Grow in sun or partial shade, in all but boggy soils. Propagate by seed or division in spring or autumn.
A. alpina (Alpine lady's mantle). Mound-forming perennial. H 15cm (6in), S 60cm (24in) or more. Rounded, lobed, pale green leaves are covered in silky hairs. Bears upright spikes of tiny, greenish-yellow flowers, with conspicuous, green, outer calyces, in summer. Is suitable for ground cover and a dry bank.
A. conjuncta illus. p.302.
♀ ***A. mollis*** illus. p.302.

Alder. See *Alnus*.
  African red. See *Cunonia capensis*.
  Black. See *Alnus glutinosa*.
  Common. See *Alnus glutinosa*.
  Grey. See *Alnus incana*, illus. p.62.
  Italian. See *Alnus cordata*, illus. p.62.
  Witch. See *Fothergilla gardenii*.
Aleppo pine. See *Pinus halepensis*, illus. p.103.
Alexandra palm. See *Archontophoenix alexandrae*, illus. p.68.
Alexandrian laurel. See *Danäe racemosa*.
Algerian iris. See *Iris unguicularis*.
Algerian oak. See *Quercus canariensis*, illus. p.62.
Algerian winter iris. See *Iris unguicularis*.

× ALICEARA

ORCHIDACEAE

See also ORCHIDS.
×*A.* Dark Warrior illus. p.310. Evergreen, epiphytic orchid for a cool greenhouse. H 25cm (10in). Produces sprays of wispy, mauve-brown, cream-yellow or green flowers, 4cm (1½in) across; flowering season varies. Leaves, 10cm (4in) long, are narrowly oval. Grow in semi-shade in summer.

ALISMA

ALISMATACEAE

Genus of deciduous, perennial, marginal water plants, grown for their foliage and flowers. Fully to frost hardy. Requires an open, sunny position in mud or up to 25cm (10in) depth of water. Tidy up fading foliage in autumn and remove dying flower spikes before ripening seeds are dispersed. May be propagated by division in spring or by seed in late summer. Contact with sap may irritate skin; all parts may cause mild stomach upset if ingested.
A. natans. See *Luronium natans*.
A. plantago-aquatica illus. p.462.
A. ranunculoides. See *Baldellia ranunculoides*.

ALLAMANDA,
syn. ALLEMANDA

APOCYNACEAE

Genus of evergreen, woody-stemmed, scrambling climbers, grown for their trumpet-shaped flowers. Frost tender, min. 13–15°C (55–9°F). Prefers partial shade in summer and humus-rich, well-drained, neutral to acid soil. Water regularly, less when not in full growth. Stems must be tied to supports. Prune previous season's growth back to 1 or 2 nodes in spring. Propagate by softwood cuttings in spring or summer. Whitefly and red spider mite may be troublesome. Contact with sap may irritate skin; all parts may cause mild stomach upset if ingested.
A. cathartica (Golden trumpet).
♀ **'Hendersonii'** illus. p.214.

Allegheny vine. See *Adlumia fungosa*.
Allemanda. See *Allamanda*.

ALLIUM
Onion

LILIACEAE/ALLIACEAE

Genus of perennials, some of which are edible, with bulbs, rhizomes or fibrous rootstocks. Nearly all have narrow, basal leaves smelling of onions when crushed, and most have small flowers packed together in a dense, spherical or shuttlecock-shaped umbel. Dried umbels of tall border species are good for winter decoration. Fully to frost hardy. Requires an open, sunny situation and well-drained soil; is best left undisturbed to form clumps. Plant in autumn. Propagate by seed in autumn or by division of clumps – spring-flowering varieties in late summer and summer-flowering ones in spring. Contact with the bulbs may irritate skin or aggravate skin allergies.
A. acuminatum, syn. *A. murrayanum*, illus. p.446.
A. aflatunense of gardens. See *A. hollandicum*.
A. akaka illus. p.443.
A. albopilosum. See *A. cristophii*.
A. azureum. See *A. caeruleum*.
A. beesianum. Clump-forming, late summer-flowering bulb. H 20–30cm (8–12in), S 5–10cm (2–4in). Fully hardy. Has linear, grey-green leaves and, in late summer, pendent heads of bell-shaped, blue flowers.
♀ ***A. caeruleum***, syn. *A. azureum*, illus. p.438.
A. campanulatum. Clump-forming, summer-flowering bulb. H 10–30cm (4–12in), S 5–10cm (2–4in). Frost hardy. Linear, semi-erect, basal leaves die away before flowering time. Bears a domed umbel, 2.5–7cm (1–3in) wide, of up to 30 small, star-shaped, pale pink or white flowers.
♀ ***A. carinatum*** subsp. ***pulchellum,*** syn. *A. pulchellum.* Clump-forming, summer-flowering bulb. H 30–60cm (12–24in), S 8–10cm (3–4in). Fully hardy. Linear, semi-erect leaves sheathe lower two-thirds of stem. Has an umbel of pendent, cup-shaped, purple flowers.
A. cernuum illus. p.436.
A. christophii. See *A. cristophii*.
A. cowanii. See *A. neapolitanum*.
♀ ***A. cristophii***, syn. *A. albopilosum, A. christophii*, illus. p.437.
♀ ***A. cyaneum.*** Tuft-forming, summer-flowering bulb. H 10–30cm (4–12in), S 5–8cm (2–3in). Fully hardy. Leaves are thread-like and erect. Stems each bear a small, dense umbel of 5 or more pendent, cup-shaped, blue or violet-blue flowers, 0.5cm (¼in) long.
A. cyathophorum var. ***farreri*** illus. p.452.
♀ ***A. flavum*** illus. p.438.
♀ ***A. giganteum*** illus. p.414.
♀ ***A. hollandicum***, syn. *A. aflatunense* of gardens, illus. p.414.
A. kansuense. See *A. sikkimense*.
♀ ***A. karataviense*** illus. p.443.
A. macranthum. Tuft-forming, summer-flowering bulb. H 20–30cm (8–12in), S 10–12cm (4–5in). Fully hardy. Has linear leaves on lower part of flower stem, which bears a loose umbel of up to 20 bell-shaped, deep purple flowers, each 1cm (½in) long, on slender stalks.
A. mairei. Clump-forming, late summer- to autumn-flowering bulb. H 10–20cm (4–8in), S 10–12cm (4–5in). Fully hardy. Leaves are erect, thread-like and basal. Wiry stems, each carry a small, shuttlecock-shaped umbel of up to 20 upright, bell-shaped, pink flowers, each 1cm (½in) long.
A. moly illus. p.452.
A. murrayanum. See *A. acuminatum*.
A. murrayanum of gardens. See *A. unifolium*.
A. narcissiflorum, syn. *A.pedemontanum* of gardens, illus. p.452.
A. neapolitanum, syn. *A. cowanii*, illus. p.424.
A. oreophilum, syn. *A. ostrowskianum*, illus. p.446.
A. ostrowskianum. See *A. oreophilum*.
A. pedemontanum of gardens. See *A. narcissiflorum*.
A. pulchellum. See *A. carinatum* subsp. *pulchellum*.

A. rosenbachianum illus. p.413.
A. schoenoprasum illus. p.451.
A. schubertii illus. p.437.
A. senescens var. ***calcareum.*** See *A. s.* subsp. *montanum*. subsp. ***montanum*** (syn. *A.s.* var. *calcareum*) illus. p.436.
A. sikkimense, syn. *A. kansuense.* Tuft-forming, summer-flowering bulb. H 10–25cm (4–10in), S 5–10cm (2–4in). Fully hardy. Leaves are linear, erect and basal. Up to 15 bell-shaped, blue flowers, 0.5–1cm (¼–½in) long, are borne in a small, pendent umbel.
A. sphaerocephalon. Clump-forming, summer-flowering bulb. H to 60cm (24in), S 8–10cm (3–4in). Fully hardy. Has linear, semi-erect leaves on basal third of slender, wiry stems and a very dense umbel, 2–4cm (¾–1½in) across, of up to 40 small, bell-shaped, pinkish-purple flowers.
A. stipitatum Summer-flowering bulb. H to 1–1.5m (3–4ft), S 15–20cm (6–8in). Frost hardy. Stout stems with strap-like, semi-erect, basal leaves carry 50 or more star-shaped, purplish-pink flowers in a spherical umbel, 8–12cm (3–5in) across.
♀ ***A. unifolium,*** syn. *A. murrayanum* of gardens illus. p.425.

Allspice
California. See *Calycanthus occidentalis*, illus. p.138.
Carolina. See *Calycanthus floridus*.
Almond. See *Prunus dulcis*.
Indian. See *Terminalia catappa*.
Tropical. See *Terminalia catappa*.

ALNUS
Alder

BETULACEAE

Genus of deciduous trees and shrubs, grown mainly for their ability to thrive in wet situations. Flowers are borne in catkins in late winter or early spring, the males conspicuous and attractive, the females forming persistent, woody, cone-like fruits. Fully hardy. Most do best in sun and any moist or even waterlogged soil, but *A. cordata* will also grow well on poor, dry soils. Propagate species by seed sown in autumn, cultivars by budding in late summer or by hardwood cuttings taken in early winter.
♀ ***A. cordata*** illus. p.62.
A. glutinosa (Black alder, Common alder). **'Aurea'** is a slow-growing, deciduous, conical tree. H to 25m (80ft), S 10m (30ft). Has rounded leaves, bright yellow until mid-summer, later becoming pale green. Produces yellow-brown catkins in early spring. Is useful grown in a boggy area.
♀ **'Imperialis'**, H 10m (30ft), S 4m (12ft), is slow-growing and has deeply cut, lobed leaves.
A. incana (Grey alder) illus. p.62. **'Aurea'** is a deciduous, conical tree. H 20m (70ft), S 8m (25ft). Has reddish-yellow or orange shoots in winter and broadly oval, yellow leaves. Reddish-yellow or orange catkins are borne in late winter and early spring. Is useful for cold, wet areas and poor soils. **'Ramulis Coccineis'** has red, winter shoots and buds, and orange catkins.

ALOCASIA

ARACEAE

Genus of evergreen perennials with underground rhizomes, grown for their attractive foliage. Produces tiny flowers on a spadix enclosed in a leaf-like spathe. Frost tender, min. 15°C (59°F). Needs high humidity, partial shade and well-drained soil. Propagate by seed, stem cuttings or division of rhizomes in spring. Contact with sap may irritate skin; all parts may cause mild stomach upset if ingested.
A. cuprea illus. p.274.
A. longiloba, syn. *A. lowii* var. *picta*, *A.l.* var. *veitchii, A. veitchii.* Evergreen, tufted perennial. H 1m (3ft) or more, S 75cm (30in). Narrow leaves, triangular with arrow-shaped bases, are 45cm (18in) long and green with greyish midribs, veins and margins, purple below. Greenish spathes.
A. lowii. var. ***picta.*** See *A. longiloba.*
A.l. var. ***veitchii.*** See *A. longiloba.*
A. macrorrhiza (Giant elephant's ear, Taro). Evergreen, tufted perennial with a thick, trunk-like stem. H to 3m (10ft) or more, S 2m (6ft). Broad, arrow-shaped, glossy, green leaves, to 1m (3ft) long, are carried on stalks 1m (3ft) long. Has yellowish-green spathes to 20cm (8in) high.
A. veitchii. See *A. longiloba.*

ALOE

LILIACEAE/ALOACEAE

Genus of evergreen, rosetted trees, shrubs, perennials and scandent climbers with succulent foliage and tubular to bell-shaped flowers. Frost tender, min. 7–10°C (45–50°F). Tree aloes and shrubs with a spread over 30cm (1ft) prefer full sun; most smaller species prefer partial shade. Needs very well-drained soil. Propagate by seed, stem cuttings or offsets in spring or summer.
A. arborescens. Evergreen, bushy, succulent-leaved shrub. H and S 2m (6ft). Stems are crowned by rosettes of widely spreading, long, slender, curved, dull blue-green leaves with toothed margins. Long flower stems produce masses of tubular to bell-shaped, red flowers in late winter and spring. ♀ **'Variegata'** illus. p.475.
♀ ***A. aristata*** (Lace aloe) illus. p.496.
A. barbadensis. See *A. vera.*
♀ ***A. brevifolia.*** Basal-rosetted, perennial succulent, producing many offsets. H 15cm (6in), S 30cm (12in). Has broadly sword-shaped, fleshy, blue-green leaves with a few teeth along edges. In spring, flower stems, 50cm (20in) long, carry narrowly bell-shaped, bright red flowers.
A. ciliaris illus. p.475.
A. ferox illus. p.475.
A. humilis. Rosetted, perennial succulent. H 10cm (4in), S 30cm (12in). Has a dense, basal rosette of narrowly sword-shaped, spine-edged, fleshy, blue-green leaves, often erect, with incurving tips. Produces flower stems 30cm (12in) long, each bearing a spike of narrowly bell-shaped, orange flowers in spring. Offsets freely.
A. punctata. See *A. variegata.*
A. striata illus. p.484.
♀ ***A. variegata***, syn. *A. punctata* (Partridge-breasted aloe) illus. p.480.
♀ ***A. vera***, syn. *A. barbadensis*, illus. p.482.

Aloe
Lace. See *Aloe aristata*, illus. p.496.
Partridge-breasted. See *Aloe variegata*, illus. p.480.

ALOINOPSIS

AIZOACEAE

Genus of dwarf, tuberous, perennial succulents with daisy-like flowers from late summer to early spring. Frost tender, min. 7°C (45°F). Requires a sunny site and very well-drained soil. Is very susceptible to overwatering. Propagate by seed in summer.
A. schooneesii illus. p.493.

ALONSOA

SCROPHULARIACEAE

Genus of perennials, grown as annuals. May be used for cut flowers. Half hardy. Grow in sun and in rich, well-drained soil. Flowering may be poor outdoors in a wet summer. Young plants should have growing shoots pinched out to encourage bushy growth. Propagate by seed sown outdoors in late spring. Aphids may be troublesome, particularly under glass.
A. warscewiczii illus. p.341.

ALOPECURUS

GRAMINEAE/POACEAE

See also GRASSES, BAMBOOS, RUSHES and SEDGES.
A. pratensis **'Aureovariegatus'**, syn. *A.p.* 'Aureomarginatus', illus. p.321.

ALOYSIA

VERBENACEAE

Genus of deciduous or evergreen, summer-flowering shrubs, grown for their aromatic foliage and sprays of tiny flowers. Frost to half hardy; in cold areas plant against a south- or west-facing wall or raise afresh each year. Needs full sun and well-drained soil. Cut out any dead wood in early summer. Propagate by softwood cuttings in summer.
♀ ***A. triphylla***, syn. *Lippia citriodora*, illus. p.139.

Alpine anemone. See *Pulsatilla alpina*, illus. p.358.
Alpine avens. See *Geum montanum*.
Alpine azalea. See *Loiseleuria procumbens*, illus. p.389.
Alpine buttercup. See *Ranunculus alpestris*, illus. p.375.
Alpine catchfly. See *Lychnis alpina*.
Alpine cinquefoil. See *Potentilla crantzii*.
Alpine coltsfoot. See *Homogyne alpina*.
Alpine columbine. See *Aquilegia alpina*, illus. p.360.
Alpine fleabane. See *Erigeron alpinus*, illus. p.367.
Alpine forget-me-not. See *Myosotis alpestris*, illus. p.382.
Alpine heath. See *Erica carnea*.
Alpine lady's mantle. See *Alchemilla alpina*.
Alpine mouse-ear. See *Cerastium alpinum*.
Alpine penny-cress. See *Thlaspi alpinum*.
Alpine pink. See *Dianthus alpinus*, illus. p.390.
Alpine poppy. See *Papaver burseri*.
Alpine snowbell. See *Soldanella alpina*, illus. p.380.
Alpine thistle. See *Carlina acaulis*, illus. p.387.
Alpine toadflax. See *Linaria alpina*.
Alpine totara. See *Podocarpus nivalis*, illus. p.106.
Alsophila. See *Cyathea*.

ALPINIA

ZINGIBERACEAE

Genus of mainly evergreen perennials with fleshy rhizomes, grown for their flowers. Frost tender, min. 18°C (64°F). Needs well-drained soil with plenty of humus, partial shade and a moist atmosphere. Is not easy to grow successfully in containers. Propagate by division in late spring or early summer. Red spider mite may be a problem.
A. calcarata (Indian ginger). Evergreen, upright, clump-forming perennial. H and S to 1m (3ft). Has stalkless, aromatic, lance-shaped leaves, to 30cm (1ft) long. At any time of year may bear horizontal spikes of whitish flowers, with 2.5cm (1in) long, yellow lips marked reddish-purple.
A. nutans of gardens. See *A. zerumbet.*
A. speciosa. See *A. zerumbet.*
A. zerumbet, syn. *A. nutans* of gardens, *A. speciosa*, illus. p.225.

Alsobia dianthiflora. See *Episcia dianthiflora*.
Alsophila. See *Cyathea*.

ALSTROEMERIA

ALSTROEMERIACEAE

Genus of mostly summer-flowering, tuberous perennials with showy, multicoloured flowers. Flowers are good for cutting as they last well. Frost hardy, but in very cold winters protect by covering dormant tubers with dry bracken or loose peat. Needs sun and well-drained soil. Propagate by seed or division in early spring. Contact with foliage may aggravate skin allergies.
A. aurantiaca. See *A. aurea*.
A. aurea, syn. *A. aurantiaca*, illus. p.415.
A. hookeri illus. p.398.
A. **Ligtu Hybrids** illus. p.439.
A. **MARGARET ('Stacova')** illus. p.412
A. **'Parigo Charm'** illus. p.439
A. pelegrina illus. p.436.
A. **'Stacova'.** See *A.* MARGARET.
A. **'Walter Fleming'.** Summer-flowering, tuberous perennial. H to 1m (3ft), S 60cm–1m (2–3ft). Each leafy stem produces narrowly lance-shaped, twisted leaves and widely funnel-shaped, deep yellow flowers, 5–6cm (2–2½in) across, flushed purple with reddish-purple spots.

ALTERNANTHERA

AMARANTHACEAE

Genus of bushy perennials, grown for their attractive, coloured foliage. Is useful for carpeting or bedding. Frost tender, min. 15–18°C (59–64°F). Needs sun or partial shade and moist but well-drained soil. Propagate by tip cuttings or division in spring.
A. amoena. See *A. ficoidea* var. *amoena*.

A. ficoidea (Parrot leaf). var. *amoena* (syn. *A. amoena*) is a mat-forming perennial. H 5cm (2in), S indefinite. Has narrowly oval, green leaves, marked red, yellow and orange, with wavy margins. **'Versicolor'** (syn. *A. versicolor*) is an erect form, H and S to 30cm (12in), with rounded to spoon-shaped leaves shaded brown, red and yellow.
A. versicolor. See *A. ficoidea* 'Versicolor'.

Althaea rosea. See *Alcea rosea*.
Alum root. See *Heuchera*.
Aluminium plant. See *Pilea cadierei*, illus. p.312.

ALYSSOIDES

CRUCIFERAE/BRASSICACEAE

Genus of one species of short-lived, evergreen sub-shrub, grown for its flowers and swollen fruits. It is particularly suitable for dry banks and rock gardens. Frost hardy. Needs sun and well-drained soil. Propagate by seed sown in autumn.
A. utriculata. Evergreen, rounded sub-shrub. H and S 30cm (12in). Has oval, glossy, dark green leaves. Loose sprays of small, bright yellow flowers, which are produced in spring, are followed later by balloon-like, buff seed pods.

ALYSSUM

CRUCIFERAE/BRASSICACEAE

Genus of perennials, some of which are evergreen, and annuals, grown for their flowers. Fully hardy. Requires a sunny site and well-drained soil. Cut back lightly after flowering. Propagate either by softwood cuttings taken in late spring or by seed sown in autumn.
A. maritimum. See *Lobularia maritima*.
A. montanum. Evergreen, prostrate perennial. H and S 15cm (6in). Leaves are small, oval, hairy and grey. Flower stems, 15cm (6in) long, each bear an open, spherical raceme carrying small, highly fragrant, soft yellow flowers in summer. Is a good plant for a rock garden.
A. saxatile. See *Aurinia saxatilis*.
A. spinosum, syn. *Ptilotrichum spinosum*. Semi-evergreen, rounded, compact shrub. H 20cm (8in) or more, S 30cm (12in). Intricate branches bear spines and narrowly oval to linear, silver leaves. Spherical heads of tiny, 4-petalled, white to purple-pink flowers appear in early summer.
A. wulfenianum. Prostrate perennial. H 2cm (¾in), S 20cm (8in). Loose heads of small, bright yellow flowers appear in summer above small, oval, grey leaves.

Alyssum, Sweet. See *Lobularia maritima*.
Amaranth, Globe. See *Gomphrena globosa*, illus. p.343.

AMARANTHUS

AMARANTHACEAE

Genus of annuals, grown for their dense panicles of tiny flowers or their colourful foliage. Half hardy. Grow in a sunny position in rich or fertile, well-drained soil. Propagate from seed sown outdoors in late spring. Aphids may be a problem.
A. caudatus illus. p.338.
A. hypochondriacus illus. p.342.
***A. tricolor* 'Joseph's Coat'.** Bushy annual. H to 1m (3ft), S 45cm (1½ft) or more. Has oval, scarlet, green and yellow leaves, to 20cm (8in) long, and produces small panicles of tiny, red flowers in summer. Leaves of **'Molten Fire'** are crimson, bronze and purple.

× AMARCRINUM

AMARYLLIDACEAE

Hybrid genus (*Amaryllis* × *Crinum*) of one robust, evergreen bulb, grown for its large, funnel-shaped flowers. Frost hardy. Needs a sunny position and well-drained soil. Plant with neck just covered by soil. Propagate by division in spring.
×***A. memoria-corsii***, syn. × *Crinodonna corsii*, illus. p.424.

× AMARYGIA

AMARYLLIDACEAE

Hybrid genus (*Amaryllis* × *Brunsvigia*) of stout, autumn-flowering bulbs, which are cultivated for their large, showy flowers. Frost hardy. Needs full sun and, preferably, the shelter of a wall. Plant bulbs just beneath the surface of well-drained soil. Propagate by division in spring.
×***A. parkeri***, syn. × *Brunsdonna parkeri*, illus. p.424.

AMARYLLIS

AMARYLLIDACEAE

Genus of autumn-flowering bulbs, grown for their funnel-shaped flowers. Frost hardy, but in cool areas should be grown against a south-facing wall for protection. Grow in a sheltered, sunny situation down, or in late summer, before growth recommences.
A. belladonna and **'Hathor'** illus. p.424.

Amaryllis, Blue. See *Worsleya*.

AMBERBOA

Sweet sultan

COMPOSITAE/ASTERACEAE

Genus of erect annuals or biennials, grown for their attractive, cornflower-like flower heads, which are borne from spring to autumn. Fully hardy. Needs full sun and moderately fertile, well-drained soil. Dead-head to prolong flowering. Propagate by seed in spring or autumn.
A. moschata, syn. *Centaurea moschata*, illus. p.347.

AMELANCHIER

Juneberry, Serviceberry, Shadbush

ROSACEAE

Genus of deciduous, spring-flowering trees and shrubs, grown primarily for their profuse flowers and their foliage, which is frequently brightly coloured in autumn. Fully hardy. Requires sun or semi-shade and well-drained but not too dry, preferably neutral to acid soil. Propagate in autumn by seed, in late autumn to early spring by layering or, in the case of suckering species, by division. Fireblight may sometimes be troublesome.
A. alnifolia. Deciduous, upright, suckering shrub. H 4m (12ft) or more, S 3m (10ft) or more. Leaves are oval to rounded and dark green. Erect spikes of star-shaped, creamy-white flowers are borne in late spring, followed by small, edible, juicy, rounded, purple-black fruits.
A. arborea. Deciduous, spreading, sometimes shrubby, tree. H 10m (30ft), S 12m (40ft). Clusters of star-shaped, white flowers appear in mid-spring as oval, white-haired, young leaves unfold. Foliage matures to dark green, turning to red or yellow in autumn. Rounded fruits are small, dry and reddish-purple.
A. asiatica. Deciduous, spreading tree or shrub of elegant habit. H 8m (25ft), S 10m (30ft). Leaves are oval and dark green, usually woolly when young and turning yellow or red in autumn. Star-shaped, white flowers are borne profusely in late spring, followed by edible, juicy, rounded, blackcurrant-like fruits.
A. canadensis. Deciduous, upright, dense shrub. H 6m (20ft), S 3m (10ft). Star-shaped, white flowers are borne from mid- to late spring amid unfolding, oval, white-haired leaves that mature to dark green and turn orange-red in autumn. Fruits are edible, rounded, blackish-purple, sweet and juicy.
A. laevis illus. p.81.
♀ ***A. lamarckii*** illus. p.112.

American arbor-vitae. See *Thuja occidentalis*.
American arrowhead. See *Sagittaria latifolia*, illus. p.462.
American aspen. See *Populus tremuloides*.
American beech. See *Fagus grandifolia*.
American bittersweet. See *Celastrus scandens*.
American chestnut. See *Castanea dentata*.
American elder. See *Sambucus canadensis*.
American holly. See *Ilex opaca*, illus. p.94.
American hop hornbeam. See *Ostrya virginiana*, illus. p.73.
American hornbeam. See *Carpinus caroliniana*.
American lime. See *Tilia americana*.
American lotus. See *Nelumbo lutea*.
American mountain ash. See *Sorbus americana*.
American spatterdock. See *Nuphar advena*.
American white elm. See *Ulmus americana*.
American white oak. See *Quercus alba*, illus. p.67.
Amomyrtus luma. See *Luma apiculata*.
***Amomyrtus luma* 'Glanleam Gold'.** See *Luma apiculata* 'Glanleam Gold'.

AMORPHA

LEGUMINOSAE/PAPILIONACEAE

Genus of deciduous shrubs and sub-shrubs, grown for their flowers and foliage. Is a useful plant for cold, dry, exposed positions. Fully hardy. Requires full sun and well-drained soil. May be propagated by softwood cuttings taken in summer or by seed sown in autumn.
A. canescens (Lead plant). Deciduous, open sub-shrub. H 1m (3ft), S 1.5m (5ft). Dense spikes of tiny, pea-like, purple flowers, with orange anthers, are produced in late summer and early autumn, amid oval, grey-haired leaves divided into 21–41 narrowly oval leaflets.

AMORPHOPHALLUS

ARACEAE

Genus of tuberous perennials, cultivated for their huge and dramatic, but foul-smelling, spathes, which surround tiny flowers on stout spadices. Frost tender, min. 10°C (50°F). Requires partial shade and humus-rich soil kept continuously moist during the growing season. Keep tubers dry in winter. Propagate by seed sown in spring or by offsets in spring or summer.
A. konjac, syn. *A. rivieri*. Summer-flowering, tuberous perennial. H to 40cm (16in), S 60cm–1m (2–3ft). Has a flattish, wavy-edged, dark reddish-brown spathe, to 40cm (16in) long, from which protrudes an erect, dark brown spadix. Brownish-green-mottled, pale green stem, 1m (3ft) long, bears one large, deeply lobed leaf after flowering.
A. rivieri. See *A. konjac*.

AMPELOPSIS

VITACEAE

Genus of deciduous, woody-stemmed, tendril climbers, some of which are twining, grown for their leaves. Frost hardy. Grow in a sheltered position, in sun or partial shade in any soil. Needs plenty of room as grows quickly and can cover a large area. Propagate by greenwood or semi-ripe cuttings in mid-summer.
A. aconitifolia, syn. *Vitis aconitifolia*. Fast-growing, deciduous, woody-stemmed, twining, tendril climber. H to 12m (40ft). Rounded leaves have 3 or 5 toothed, lobed, dark green leaflets; inconspicuous, greenish flowers appear in late summer, followed later by orange berries.
A. brevipedunculata var. ***maximowiczii,*** syn. *A. glandulosa* var. *brevipedunculata, A. heterophylla, Vitis heterophylla*. Vigorous, deciduous, woody-stemmed, twining, tendril climber with hairy young stems. H to 5m (15ft) or more. Has dark green leaves that vary in size and shape and are almost hairless beneath. Inconspicuous, greenish flowers are produced in summer, followed by bright blue berries.
A. glandulosa var. ***brevipedunculata.*** See *A. brevipedunculata* var. *maximowiczii*.
A. heterophylla. See *A. brevipedunculata* var. *maximowiczii*.
A. sempervirens. See *Cissus striata*.
A. veitchii. See *Parthenocissus tricuspidata* 'Veitchii'.

AMSONIA
Blue star

APOCYNACEAE

Genus of slow-growing, clump-forming, summer-flowering perennials. Fully hardy. Grow in full sun and in well-drained soil. Is best left undisturbed for some years. May be propagated by division in spring, by softwood cuttings in summer or by seed in autumn. Contact with the milky sap may irritate skin.
A. orientalis, syn. *Rhazya orientalis*, illus. p.296.
A. tabernaemontana illus. p.297.

Amur cork tree. See *Phellodendron amurense*.
Amur grape. See *Vitis amurensis*.
Amur maple. See *Acer tataricum* subsp. *ginnala*, illus. p.91.
Amur silver grass. See *Miscanthus sacchariflorus*.
Anacharis densa. See *Egeria densa*.

ANACYCLUS
COMPOSITAE/ASTERACEAE

Genus of summer-flowering, prostrate perennials with stems radiating from a central rootstock. Frost hardy. Needs full sun and well-drained soil. Propagate by softwood cuttings in spring or by seed in autumn.
A. depressus. See *A. pyrethrum* var. *depressus*.
A. pyrethrum var. ***depressus,*** syn. *A. depressus*, illus. p.386.

ANAGALLIS
PRIMULACEAE

Genus of annuals and creeping perennials, grown for their flowers. Fully to frost hardy. Plant in an open, sunny site in fertile, moist soil. Propagate by seed or division in spring. Raise *A. tenella* by soft tip cuttings in spring or early summer.
A. tenella (Bog pimpernel). **'Studland'** illus. p.379.

ANANAS
BROMELIACEAE

Genus of evergreen, rosette-forming perennials, grown for their foliage and edible fruits (pineapples). Frost tender, min. 13–15°C (55–9°F). Prefers full light, but tolerates some shade. Needs fertile, well-drained soil. Water moderately during growing season, sparingly at other times. Propagate by suckers or cuttings of 'leafy' fruit tops in spring or summer.
A. bracteatus (Red pineapple, Wild pineapple). ***'Striatus'*** See 'Tricolor'. ♀ **'Tricolor'** (syn. *A.b.* 'Striatus', *A.b.* var. *tricolor*; illus. p.273) is an evergreen, basal-rosetted perennial. H and S 1m (3ft). Forms dense rosettes of strap-shaped, spiny-edged, arching, deep green leaves, longitudinally yellow-striped and often with marginal, red spines. Dense spikes of small, tubular, lavender-violet flowers, with prominent, reddish-pink bracts, appear usually in summer. These are followed by brownish-orange-red fruits that are 15cm (6in) or more long.
A. comosus **'Variegatus',** syn. *A.c.* var. *variegatus.* Evergreen, basal-rosetted perennial. H and S 60cm (24in) or more. Produces very narrowly strap-shaped, channelled, rigid, grey-green leaves that are suffused pink, have cream margins, are grey-scaled beneath and sometimes have spiny edges. Produces tubular, purple-blue flowers with inconspicuous, green bracts; fruits are the edible pineapples grown commercially, but are much smaller on pot-grown plants.

ANAPHALIS
Pearl everlasting

ASTERACEAE/COMPOSITAE

Genus of perennials with heads of small, papery flowers, used dried for winter decoration. Fully hardy. Prefers sun but will grow in semi-shade. Soil should be well-drained but not too dry. Propagate by seed in autumn or by division in winter or spring.
A. margaritacea illus. p.241.
A. nepalensis var. ***monocephala,*** syn. *A. nubigena*, illus. p.286.
A. nubigena. See *A. nepalensis* var. *monocephala*.

Anceps bamboo. See *Yushania anceps*, illus. p.320.

ANCHUSA
BORAGINACEAE

Genus of annuals, biennials and perennials, some of which are evergreen, with usually blue flowers. Fully to frost hardy. Needs sun and well-drained soil; resents too much winter wet. Tall, perennial species may need to be staked and allowed room to spread. Propagate perennials by root cuttings in winter, annuals and biennials by seed in autumn or spring.
A. azurea, syn. *A. italica.* **'Little John'** is a clump-forming perennial. H 50cm (20in), S 60cm (24in). Fully hardy. Mainly basal leaves are narrowly oval and hairy. Bears branching racemes of large, open cup-shaped, dark blue flowers in early summer. ♀ **'Loddon Royalist'** illus. p.260. **'Opal'**, H 1.2m (4ft), has paler blue flowers.
A. caespitosa. See *A. cespitosa.*
A. capensis **'Blue Angel'** illus. p.346. **'Blue Bird'** is a bushy biennial, grown as an annual. H to 45cm (18in), S 20cm (8in). Frost hardy. Has lance-shaped, bristly, mid-green leaves and, in summer, heads of shallowly bowl-shaped, sky-blue flowers.
A. cespitosa, syn. *A. caespitosa*, illus. p.382.
A. italica. See *A. azurea*.

Ancistrocactus megarhizus. See *Sclerocactus scheeri*.
Ancistrocactus scheeri. See *Sclerocactus scheeri*.
Ancistrocactus uncinatus. See *Sclerocactus uncinatus*.

ANDROMEDA
ERICACEAE

Genus of evergreen shrubs with an open, twiggy habit. Fully hardy. Needs full light and humus-rich, moist, acid soil. Propagate by semi-ripe cuttings taken in late summer or by seed sown in spring.
A. polifolia illus. p.359. **'Alba'** illus. p.358. ♀ **'Compacta'** illus. p.359.

ANDROSACE
PRIMULACEAE

Genus of annuals and evergreen perennials, usually compact cushion-forming and often with soft, hairy leaves. Many species are suitable for cold greenhouses and troughs with winter cover. Fully to frost hardy. Needs sun and very well-drained soil; some species prefer acid soil. Resents wet foliage in winter. Propagate by tip cuttings in summer or by seed in autumn. Is prone to botrytis and attack by aphids.
A. carnea illus. p.377.
♀ subsp ***laggeri*** illus. p.379.
A. chamaejasme. Evergreen, basal-rosetted, variable perennial with easily rooted stolons. H 3–6cm (1¼–2½in), S to 15cm (6in). Fully hardy. Has open, hairy rosettes of oval leaves. In spring bears clusters of 2–8 flattish, white flowers, each with a yellow eye that sometimes turns red with age.
A. cylindrica. Evergreen, basal-rosetted perennial. H 1–2cm (½–¾in), S 10cm (4in). Fully hardy. Leaves are linear and glossy. Flower stems each carry up to 10 small, flattish, white flowers, each with a yellow-green eye, in early spring. Is suitable for a cold greenhouse.
A. hedraeantha. Evergreen, tight cushion-forming perennial. H 1–2cm (½–¾in), S to 10cm (4in). Fully hardy. Bears loose rosettes of narrowly oval, glossy leaves. Umbels of 5–10 flattish, yellow-throated, pink flowers are produced in spring. Is best in a cold greenhouse.
A. hirtella. Evergreen, tight cushion-forming perennial. H 1cm (½in), S to 10cm (4in). Fully hardy. Produces rosettes of small, thick, linear to oblong, hairy leaves. Almond-scented, flattish, white flowers are borne in spring on very short stems, 1 or 2 per rosette.
A. imbricata. See *A. vandellii*.
♀ ***A. lanuginosa*** illus. p.389.
A. pyrenaica illus. p.373.
A. sarmentosa. Evergreen, mat-forming perennial, spreading by runners. H 4–10cm (1½–4in), S 30cm (12in). Fully hardy. Has open rosettes of small, narrowly elliptic, hairy leaves. Large clusters of flattish, yellow-eyed, bright pink flowers open in spring. Is a good rock plant in all but extremely wet areas.
♀ ***A. sempervivoides.*** Evergreen, mat-forming, rosetted perennial with stolons. H 1–7cm (½–3in), S 30cm (12in). Fully hardy. Has leathery, oblong or spoon-shaped leaves. In spring produces small heads of 4–10 flattish, pink flowers, with yellow, then red, eyes. Is a good rock plant.
A. vandellii, syn. *A. imbricata*, illus. p.374.
A. villosa illus. p.375. var. ***jacquemontii*** illus. p.390.

ANEMANTHELE
GRAMINAE/POACEAE

See also GRASSES, BAMBOOS, RUSHES and SEDGES
A. lessoniana (New Zealand Wind Grass, Pheasant's Tail Grass) Evergreen, tuft-forming perennial grass. H 1.5m (5ft) S 1.2m (4ft). Frost hardy. Brownish-green leaves, 30cm (1ft) long, turn soft orange in late summer. Has pendent, open panicles of purplish-green flowers spikes in autumn.

ANEMONE
Windflower

RANUNCULACEAE

Genus of spring-, summer- and autumn-flowering perennials, sometimes tuberous or rhizomatous, with mainly rounded, shallowly cup-shaped flowers. Leaves are rounded to oval, often divided into 3–15 leaflets. Fully to frost hardy. Most species thrive in full light or semi-shade in humus-rich, well-drained soil. Propagate by division in spring, by seed sown in late summer, when fresh, or by root cuttings in winter. Contact with the sap may irritate skin.
♀ ***A. apennina*** (Apennine anemone). Spreading, spring-flowering, rhizomatous perennial. H and S 15–20cm (6–8in). Fully hardy. Fern-like leaves have 3 deeply toothed lobes. Each stem carries a large, upright, flattish, blue, white or pink flower, with 10–20 narrow petals.
♀ ***A. blanda.*** Spreading, early spring-flowering perennial with a knobbly tuber. H 5–10cm (2–4in), S 10–15cm (4–6in). Fully hardy. Leaves are broadly oval and semi-erect, with 3 deeply toothed lobes. Each stem bears an upright, flattish, blue, white or pink flower, 4–5cm (1½–2in) across, with 9–14 narrow petals. **'Atrocaerulea'** illus. p.449. **'Ingramii'** bears purple-backed, deep blue flowers. ♀ **'Radar'** illus. p.446. ♀ **'White Splendour'** illus. p.442.
A. coronaria. Spring-flowering perennial with a misshapen tuber. H 5–25cm (2–10in), S 10–15cm (4–6in). Frost hardy. Produces parsley-like, divided, semi-erect leaves. Each stiff stem carries a large, 5–8-petalled, shallowly cup-shaped flower in shades of red, pink, blue or purple. Garden groups include **De Caen Group** and **Saint Bridgid Group**, which have larger flowers varying in colour from white through red to blue.
A. × fulgens illus. p.446.
A. hepatica. See *Hepatica nobilis*.
♀ ***A. hupehensis*** **'Hadspen Abundance'** illus. p.267. var. ***japonica*** **'Bressingham Glow'** (syn. *A. × hybrida* 'Bressingham Glow'; semi-double) illus. p.231.
♀ var. ***japonica*** **'Prinz Heinrich'** (syn. *A. × hybrida* 'Prince Henry') has single, deep pink flowers on slender stems. ♀ **'September Charm'** see *A. × hybrida* 'September Charm'.
A. × hybrida, syn. *A. japonica* of gardens (Japanese anemone). Group of vigorous, branching, perennials. H 1.5m (5ft), S 60cm (2ft). Fully hardy. Bears shallowly cup-shaped, single, semi-double or double flowers in late

summer and early autumn. Leaves are deeply divided and dark green. **'Bressingham Glow'** see *A. hupehensis* var. *japonica* 'Bressingham Glow'. ♀ **'Elegans'** (syn. *A.* × *h.* 'Max Vogel') has semi-double, pinkish-mauve flowers on wiry stems. ♀ **'Honorine Jobert'** (single) illus. p.231. **'Max Vogel'** see *A.* × *h.* 'Elegans'. **'Prince Henry'** see *A. hupehensis* var. *japonica* 'Prinz Heinrich'. ♀ **'September Charm'** (syn. *A. hupehensis* 'September Charm', single) illus. p.231.
***A.* × *intermedia*.** See *A.* × *lipsiensis*.
A. japonica of gardens. See *A.* × *hybrida*.
A.* × *lipsiensis, syn. *A.* × *intermedia*, *A.* × *seemannii*, illus. p.284.
A. narcissiflora illus. p.285.
♀ ***A. nemorosa*** (Wood anemone). Vigorous, carpeting, rhizomatous perennial. H 15cm (6in), S 30cm (12in). Fully hardy. Produces masses of star-shaped, single, white flowers, with prominent, yellow stamens, in spring and early summer, above deeply cut, mid-green leaves. Likes woodland conditions. ♀ **'Allenii'** and ♀ **'Robinsoniana'** illus. p.278. ♀ **'Vestal'** has anemone-centred, double, white flowers. **'Wilks' Giant'** (syn. *A.n.* 'Wilk's Giant') has larger, single, white flowers.
A. pavonina illus. p.429.
♀ ***A. ranunculoides*** illus. p.284. **'Pleniflora'** (syn *A.r.* 'Flore Pleno') is a spreading, rhizomatous perennial. H and S 20cm (8in). Fully hardy. Bears buttercup-like, double, yellow flowers in spring. Leaves are divided. Likes damp, woodland conditions.
A. rivularis illus. p.285.
***A.* × *seemannii*.** See *A.* × *lipsiensis*.
A. sylvestris illus. p.276. **'Macrantha'** is a clump-forming perennial that can be invasive. H and S 30cm (12in). Fully hardy. Large, fragrant, semi-pendent, shallowly cup-shaped, white flowers are produced in spring and early summer. Leaves are divided and mid-green.
A. tschaernjaewii illus. p.443.
***A. vitifolia*.** Branching, clump-forming perennial. H 1.2m (4ft), S 50cm (20in). Fully hardy. In summer bears open cup-shaped, occasionally pink-flushed, white flowers with yellow stamens. Vine-like leaves are woolly beneath.

Anemone
Alpine. See *Pulsatilla alpina*, illus. p.358.
Apennine. See *Anemone apennina*.
False. See *Anemonopsis*.
Japanese. See *Anemone* × *hybrida*, illus. p.231.
Wood. See *Anemone nemorosa*.

ANEMONELLA

RANUNCULACEAE

Genus of one species of tuberous perennial, grown for its flowers. Fully hardy. Needs shade and humus-rich, moist soil. Propagate by seed when fresh or by division every 3–5 years in autumn.
A. thalictroides illus. p.376. **'Oscar Schoaf'** (syn. *A.t.* 'Schoaf's Double') is a slow-growing, tuberous perennial. H 10cm (4in), S 4cm (1½in) or more. Has delicate, fern-like leaves. From spring to early summer bears small, cup-shaped, double, strawberry-pink flowers, singly on finely branched, slender stems.

ANEMONOPSIS

False anemone

RANUNCULACEAE

Genus of one species of perennial, related to *Anemone*. Fully hardy. Likes a sheltered, semi-shaded position and humus-rich, moist but well-drained soil. Propagate by division in spring or by seed sown in late summer, when fresh.
A. macrophylla illus. p.296.

ANEMOPAEGMA

BIGNONIACEAE

Genus of evergreen, tendril climbers, grown for their flowers. Frost tender, min. 13–15°C (55–9°F). Needs partial shade in summer and humus-rich, well-drained soil. Water regularly and freely when in full growth, less at other times. Provide support and in summer thin out stems at intervals; shorten all growths by half in spring. Propagate by softwood or semi-ripe cuttings in spring or summer.
***A. chamberlaynei*.** Fast-growing, evergreen, tendril climber. H to 6m (20ft). Leaves have 2 pointed, oval leaflets and a 3-hooked tendril. Foxglove-like, primrose-yellow flowers are carried in pairs from upper leaf axils in summer.

ANGELICA

UMBELLIFERAE/APIACEAE

Genus of summer-flowering, often short-lived perennials, some of which have culinary and medicinal uses. Fully hardy. Grows in sun or shade and in any well-drained soil. Remove seed heads when produced, otherwise plants may die. Propagate by seed when ripe.
A. archangelica (Angelica) illus. p.226.

Angelica. See *Angelica archangelica*, illus. p.226.
Angelica tree, Japanese. See *Aralia elata*.
Angel's fishing rod. See *Dierama*.
Angel's tears. See *Billbergia* × *windii*; *Narcissus triandrus*, illus. p.433.
Angels' trumpets. See *Brugmansia*.
Angels' wings. See *Caladium bicolor*.
Angelwing begonia. See *Begonia coccinea*.
Angled Solomon's seal. See *Polygonatum odoratum*.

ANGRAECUM

ORCHIDACEAE

See also ORCHIDS.
A. sesquipedale (Star-of-Bethlehem orchid; illus. p.308). Evergreen, epiphytic orchid for an intermediate greenhouse. H 30cm (12in) or more. Waxy, apple-white flowers, 8cm (3in) across, each with a 30cm (12in) long spur, are borne, usually 2 to a stem, in winter. Has narrowly oval, semi-rigid, horizontal leaves, 15cm (6in) long. Needs shade in summer.

ANGULOA

ORCHIDACEAE

See also ORCHIDS.
A. clowesii (Cradle orchid). Deciduous, epiphytic orchid for a cool greenhouse. H 60cm (24in). Fragrant, erect, cup-shaped, lemon-yellow flowers, 10cm (4in) long, each with a loosely hinged, yellow lip, are produced singly in early summer. Broadly oval, ribbed leaves are 45cm (18in) long. Grow in semi-shade in summer.

ANIGOZANTHOS

Kangaroo paw

HAEMODORACEAE

Genus of perennials, with thick rootstocks and fans of sword-shaped leaves, grown for their curious flowers. Half hardy. Needs an open, sunny position and does best in well-drained, peaty or leafy, acid soil. Propagate by division in spring or by seed when fresh, in late summer.
A. flavidus illus. p.260.
♀ ***A. manglesii*** illus. p.254.
***A. rufus*.** Tufted perennial. H 1m (3ft), S 60cm (2ft). Panicles of 2-lipped, rich burgundy flowers, covered with purple hairs, appear in spring. Has long, sword-shaped, stiff, mid-green leaves.

Anise
Chinese. See *Illicium anisatum*.
Purple. See *Illicium floridanum*.

ANISODONTEA

MALVACEAE

Genus of evergreen shrubs and perennials, grown for their flowers. Frost tender, min. 3–5°C (37–41°F). Needs full light and well-drained soil. Water containerized plants freely when in full growth, very little at other times. In growing season, young plants may need tip pruning to promote a bushy habit. Propagate by seed in spring or by greenwood or semi-ripe cuttings in late summer.
A. capensis, syn. *Malvastrum capensis*. Evergreen, erect, bushy shrub. H to 1m (3ft), S 60cm (2ft) or more. Each oval leaf has 3–5 deep lobes. Bowl-shaped, 5-petalled, rose-magenta flowers, with darker veins, appear from spring to autumn.

ANNONA

Cherimoya, Custard apple, Sweet sop

ANNONACEAE

Genus of deciduous or evergreen shrubs and trees, grown for their edible fruits and ornamental appearance. Frost tender, min. 15°C (59°F), preferably higher. Needs full light or partial shade and fertile, moisture-retentive but well-drained soil. Water containerized specimens moderately when in full growth, sparingly in winter. Propagate by seed in spring or by semi-ripe cuttings in late summer. Red spider mite may be a nuisance.
A. reticulata (Bullock's heart, Custard apple). Mainly deciduous, rounded tree. H 6m (20ft) or more, S 3–5m (10–15ft). Has oblong to lance-shaped, 13–25cm (5–10in) long leaves. Cup-shaped, olive-green flowers, often flushed purple, appear in summer, followed by edible, heart-shaped, red-flushed, greenish-brown fruits, each 13cm (5in) long.

Annual phlox. See *Phlox drummondii*.
***Anoiganthus breviflorus*.** See *Cyrtanthus breviflorus*.
***Anoiganthus luteus*.** See *Cyrtanthus breviflorus*.

ANOMATHECA

IRIDACEAE

Genus of upright, summer-flowering corms, grown for their trumpet- to funnel-shaped, red flowers, followed by egg-shaped seed pods that split to reveal red seeds. Frost hardy. Plant 5cm (2in) deep in an open, sunny situation and in well-drained soil. In cold areas, lift corms and store dry for winter. Propagate by seed in spring.
***A. cruenta*.** See *A. laxa*.
♀ ***A. laxa***, syn. *A. cruenta*, *Lapeirousia cruenta*, *L. laxa*. Upright, summer-flowering corm. H 10–30cm (4–12in), S 5–8cm (2–3in). Narrowly sword-shaped, erect, mid-green basal leaves form a flat fan. In early summer each stem bears a loose spike of up to 6 long-tubed, red flowers, 2.5cm (1in) across. Lower petals have basal, darker red spots.

ANOPTERUS

ESCALLONIACEAE

Genus of evergreen shrubs or small trees, grown for their foliage and flowers. Half hardy. Needs shade or semi-shade and moist but well-drained, lime-free soil. Propagate by semi-ripe cuttings in summer.
A. glandulosus illus. p.112.

ANREDERA

Madeira vine, Mignonette vine

BASELLACEAE

Genus of evergreen, tuberous, twining climbers, grown for their luxuriant foliage and small, scented flowers. Frost tender, min. 7°C (45°F). If grown in cool areas will die down in winter. Requires a position in full light and well-drained soil. Water moderately in growing season, but sparingly at other times. Provide support. Cut back the previous season's growth by half or to just above ground level in spring. Propagate by tubers, produced at stem bases, in spring or by softwood cuttings in summer.
A. cordifolia, syn. *Boussingaultia baselloides* of gardens. Fast-growing, evergreen, tuberous, twining climber. H to 6m (20ft). Has oval to lance-shaped, fleshy leaves and tiny, fragrant, white flowers borne in clusters from upper leaf axils in summer.

Antarctic beech. See *Nothofagus antarctica*.

ANTENNARIA

Cat's ears

COMPOSITAE/ASTERACEAE

Genus of evergreen or semi-evergreen perennials, grown for their almost stemless flower heads and mats of often woolly leaves. Makes good ground cover. Fully hardy. Needs sun and well-

drained soil. Propagate by seed or division in spring.
A. dioica. Semi-evergreen, mat-forming, dense perennial. H 2.5cm (1in), S 25cm (10in). Leaves are tiny, oval, usually woolly and greenish-white. Short stems carry fluffy, white or pale pink flower heads in late spring and early summer. Is good when grown in a rock garden. Compact **'Nyewoods'** has very deep rose-pink flowers. **'Rosea'** see *A.d.* var. *rosea*. ♡ var. ***rosea*** (syn. *A.d.* 'Rosea') illus. p.378.

ANTHEMIS
Dog's fennel

COMPOSITAE/ASTERACEAE

Genus of carpeting and clump-forming perennials, some of which are evergreen, grown for their daisy-like flower heads and fern-like foliage. Fully to frost hardy. Prefers a position in sun and well-drained soil. May need staking for support. Cut to ground level after flowering to produce good leaf rosettes in winter. Propagate by division in spring or, for some species, by basal cuttings in late summer, autumn or spring.
A. nobilis. See *Chamaemelum nobile*.
♡ ***A. punctata*** subsp. ***cupaniana*** illus. p.286.
A. sancti-johannis. Evergreen, spreading, bushy perennial. H and S 60cm (24in). Frost hardy. In summer bears many daisy-like, bright orange flower heads among fern-like, shaggy, mid-green leaves.
A. tinctoria. Evergreen, clump-forming perennial. H and S 1m (3ft). Fully hardy. Produces a mass of daisy-like, yellow flower heads in mid-summer, borne singly above a basal clump of fern-like, crinkled, mid-green leaves. Propagate by basal cuttings in spring or late summer. **'E.C. Buxton'** illus. p.261.

ANTHERICUM
Spider plant

LILIACEAE/ANTHERICACEAE

Genus of upright perennials with saucer- or trumpet-shaped flowers rising in spike-like racemes from clumps of leaves. Fully hardy. Likes a sunny site and fertile, well-drained soil that does not dry out in summer. Propagate by division in spring or by seed in autumn.
A. graminifolium. See *A. ramosum*.
A. liliago illus. p.286.
A. ramosum, syn. *A. graminifolium*. Upright perennial. H 1m (3ft), S 30cm (1ft). Erect racemes of small, saucer-shaped, white flowers are borne in summer above a clump of grass-like, greyish-green leaves.

Antholyza paniculata. See *Crocosmia paniculata*.

ANTHURIUM

ARACEAE

Genus of evergreen, erect, climbing or trailing perennials, some grown for their foliage and others for their bright flower spathes. Frost tender, min. 15°C (59°F). Prefers bright light in winter and indirect sun in summer; needs a fairly moist atmosphere and moist, but not waterlogged, peaty soil. Propagate by division in spring. If ingested, all parts may cause mild stomach disorder; contact with sap may irritate skin.
♡ ***A. andraeanum*** illus. p.272.
♡ ***A. crystallinum*** (Crystal anthurium) illus. p.272.
♡ ***A. scherzerianum*** illus. p.314. **'Rothschildianum'** is an evergreen, erect, short-stemmed perennial. H and S 30cm (12in). Produces upright, oblong leaves, to 20cm (8in) long. Intermittently bears a long-lasting, red spathe, spotted with white, that surrounds a yellow spadix.
A. veitchii (Queen anthurium). Evergreen, erect, short-stemmed perennial. H 1m (3ft) or more, S to 1m (3ft). Glossy, corrugated leaves, to 1m (3ft) long, are oval, with heart-shaped bases on 60cm–1m (2–3ft) long leaf stalks. Intermittently bears a long-lasting, leathery, green to white spathe that surrounds a cream spadix.

Anthurium
Crystal. See *Anthurium crystallinum*, illus. p.272.
Queen. See *Anthurium veitchii*.

ANTHYLLIS

LEGUMINOSAE/PAPILIONACEAE

Genus of rounded, bushy perennials, grown for their flowers and finely divided leaves. Frost hardy. Needs sun and well-drained soil. Propagate by softwood cuttings in summer or by seed in autumn.
A. hermanniae. Rounded, bushy perennial. H and S to 60cm (24in). Spiny, tangled stems bear simple or 3-parted, bright green leaves. Has small, pea-like, yellow flowers in summer. Is good for a rock garden.
A. montana illus. p.364.
♡ **'Rubra'** is a rounded or spreading, woody-based perennial. H and S 30cm (12in). Divided leaves consist of 17–41 narrowly oval leaflets. Heads of clover-like, bright pink flowers are borne in late spring and early summer. Is good for a rock garden.

ANTIGONON
Coral vine

POLYGONACEAE

Genus of evergreen, woody-stemmed, tendril climbers, grown for their foliage and profuse clusters of small flowers. Frost tender, min. 15°C (59°F). Grow in full light and any fertile, well-drained soil. Water freely in growing season, sparingly at other times. Needs tropical conditions to flower well. Provide support. Thin out congested growth in early spring. Propagate by seed in spring or by softwood cuttings in summer.
A. leptopus illus. p.205.

ANTIRRHINUM
Snapdragon

SCROPHULARIACEAE

Genus of perennials and semi-evergreen sub-shrubs, usually grown as annuals, flowering from spring to autumn. Fully to half hardy. Needs sun and rich, well-drained soil. Dead-head to prolong flowering season. Propagate by seed sown outdoors in late spring or by stem cuttings in early autumn or spring. Rust disease may be a problem with *A. majus*, but rust-resistant cultivars are available.
A. asarina. See *Asarina procumbens*.
A. majus. Erect perennial that branches from the base. Cultivars are grown as annuals and are grouped according to size and flower type: tall, H 60cm–1m (2–3ft), S 30–45cm (12–18in); intermediate, H and S 45cm (18in); dwarf, H 20–30cm (8–12in), S 30cm (12in); regular tubular-shaped (hyacinth-like) flowers; penstemon, trumpet-shaped flowers; double; and irregular tubular-shaped flowers. Half hardy. All have lance-shaped leaves and, from spring to autumn, carry spikes of usually 2-lipped, sometimes double, flowers in a variety of colours, including white, pink, red, purple, yellow and orange. **Bells Series** (dwarf, regular) is early-flowering, with long-lasting flowers in purple, purple and white, red, rose-pink, pink, bronze, yellow, or white. ♡ **Bells Series 'Pink Bells'** has pink flowers. **Chimes Series** (dwarf, regular) is very compact, producing flowers in a wide colour range including several bicolours. **Chimes Series 'Chimes Yellow'** illus. p.348. ♡ **Coronette Series** (tall, regular) illus. p.333. **'Floral Showers'** (dwarf, regular) is early-flowering, bearing flowers in up to 10 colours, including some bicolours; tolerates wet weather. ♡ **Kim Series** (intermediate, regular) has flowers in scarlet, deep rose, deep orange, primrose-yellow and white as well as orange bicolour. **Madame Butterfly Series** (tall, peloric) is available in a mixture of colours. **Princess Series** (intermediate, peloric) has flowers in a mixture of colours (white with purple eye, illus. p.337). **Rocket Series** (tall, regular) is vigorous, with flowers in a broad colour range; they are excellent for cut flowers. ♡ **Sonnet Series** (intermediate, regular) illus. p.349. **'Trumpet Serenade'** (dwarf, penstemon) has bicoloured flowers in a mixture of pastel shades.

Apache plume. See *Fallugia paradoxa*, illus. p.132.
Apennine anemone. See *Anemone apennina*.

APHELANDRA

ACANTHACEAE

Genus of evergreen shrubs and perennials with showy flowers. Frost tender, min. 13°C (55°F). Grows best in bright light but out of direct sun in summer. Use soft water and keep soil moist but not waterlogged. Benefits from feeding when flower spikes are forming. Propagate by seed or tip cuttings from young stems in spring.
A. squarrosa (Zebra plant). **'Dania'** is an evergreen, compact perennial. H 1m (3ft), S slightly less. Oval, glossy, dark green leaves, with white veins and mid-ribs, are nearly 30cm (1ft) long. Has dense, 4-sided spikes, to 15cm (6in) long, of 2-lipped, bright yellow flowers in axils of yellow bracts in autumn.
♡ **'Louisae'** illus. p.262.

APHYLLANTHES

LILIACEAE/APHYLLANTHACEAE

Genus of one species of summer-flowering perennial. Frost hardy, but shelter from cold wind. Grow in a sunny, warm, sheltered corner, preferably in an alpine house, and in well-drained, sandy, peaty soil. Resents disturbance. Propagate by seed in autumn or spring.
A. monspeliensis. Tuft-forming perennial. H 15–20cm (6–8in), S 5cm (2in). Star-shaped, pale to deep blue flowers are borne singly or in small groups at tops of wiry, glaucous green stems from early to mid-summer. Leaves are reduced to red-brown sheaths surrounding stems.

APONOGETON

APONOGETONACEAE

Genus of deciduous, perennial, deep-water plants, grown for their floating foliage and often heavily scented flowers. Frost hardy to frost tender, min. 16°C (61°F). Requires an open, sunny position. Tidy fading foliage in autumn. Propagate by division in spring or by seed while still fresh.
A. distachyos illus. p.463.

APOROCACTUS

CACTACEAE

Genus of perennial cacti, grown for their pendent, slender, fleshy stems and bright flowers. Is suitable for hanging baskets. Half hardy to frost tender, min. 5°C (41°F). Needs partial shade and very well-drained soil. Occasional light watering in winter will stop stems dying back from the tips. Propagate by stem cuttings in spring or summer.
A. flagelliformis illus. p.479.

Apple
Custard. See *Annona*.
Elephant. See *Dillenia indica*.
May. See *Podophyllum peltatum*.
Pitch. See *Clusia major*.
Apple mint. See *Mentha suaveolens*.
Apple of Peru. See *Nicandra physalodes*.
Apricot, Japanese. See *Prunus mume*.

APTENIA

AIZOACEAE

Genus of fast-growing, perennial succulents, with trailing, freely branching stems, that make good ground cover. Frost tender, min. 7°C (45°F). Requires full sun and very well-drained soil. Keep dry in winter. Propagate by seed or stem cuttings in spring or summer.
A. cordifolia, syn. *Mesembryanthemum cordifolium*, illus. p.488. **'Variegata'** is a fast-growing, prostrate, perennial succulent. H 5cm (2in), S indefinite. Has oval, glossy, bright green leaves, with creamy-white margins, and small, daisy-like, bright pink flowers in summer.

AQUILEGIA
Columbine

RANUNCULACEAE

Genus of graceful, clump-forming, short-lived perennials, grown for their mainly bell-shaped, spurred flowers in spring and summer. Is suitable for rock gardens. Fully to frost hardy. Prefers an open, sunny site and well-drained soil. Propagate species by seed in autumn or spring. Selected forms only occasionally come true from seed (e.g. *A. vulgaris* 'Nora Barlow') as they cross freely; they should be widely segregated. Is prone to aphid attack. Contact with sap may irritate skin.

A. akitensis. See *A. flabellata*.

A. alpina (Alpine columbine) illus. p.257, p.360. Upright, hardy, short-lived perennial. H 45cm (18in) S 15cm (6in). Spurred, clear blue or violet-blue flowers appear in spring and early summer on slender stems above rounded, finely divided leaves.

A. atrata (Black columbine) illus. p.257. Clump-forming, hardy perennial H 60–70 cm (24–28in) S 30cm (12in). Bell-shaped, fluted, deep purple-violet flowers with spreading sepals and short 1cm long, strongly hooked spurs appear in early summer above mid-green, glaucous-backed leaves divided into 9 segments.

♀ ***A. bertolonii*** syn. ***A. reuteri*** illus. p.257. Clump-forming, compact, hardy perennial. H 10–30cm (4–12in) S 8–20cm (3–8in). Bell-shaped, blue-violet flowers with spreading sepals and short, 1cm, long curved spurs appear in late spring and early summer above dark green leaves divided into 9 segments.

***A.* Biedermeier Group** illus. p.257. Short-stemmed, compact, hardy perennials. H 30–35cm (12–14in). S 20–30cm (8–12in). More or less upward-facing, open-bell-shaped flowers in colours varying from purple-blue to lilac, red, pink or white are produced from late spring to mid-summer above the bluish-green divided foliage.

♀ ***A.* 'Bluebird' (Songbird Series)** illus. p.256. Clump-forming. Compact, hardy perennial H 60–70cm (24–28in), S 35–40 cm (14–16in).Open bell-shaped very large, fluted flowers with white petals, soft, pale violet blue sepals and long, slightly curved spurs appear in late spring and early summer above fern-like, divided, mid-green leaves.

♀ ***A.* 'Bunting' (Songbird Series)** illus. p.257. Clump-forming, compact, hardy perennial. H 60cm (24in), S 30–35cm (12–14in). Open bell-shaped, fluted flowers with white, blue flushed petals, violet-blue sepals and long spurs are produced in late spring and early summer above fern-like, divided, mid-green leaves.

♀ ***A. canadensis*** (Canadian columbine) illus. p.256. Clump-forming, leafy perennial. H 60cm (24in), S 30cm (12in). Fully hardy. In early summer bears semi-pendent, bell-shaped flowers, with yellow sepals and red spurs, several per slender stem, above fern-like, dark green foliage.

***A.* 'Cardinal' (Songbird Series)** illus. p.256. Clump-forming, compact, hardy perennial H 50cm (20in), S 30–35cm (12–14in). Open bell-shaped, fluted flowers with white petals, deep red-pink at the base, dark red sepals and long, curved spurs are produced in late spring and early summer above fern-like, divided, mid-green leaves.

A. chrysantha. Vigorous, clump-forming perennial. H 1.2m (4ft), S 60cm (2ft). Fully hardy. Bears semi-pendent, bell-shaped, from pale to bright yellow flowers, with long spurs, several per stem, in early summer. Has fern-like, divided, mid-green leaves. **'Yellow Queen'** (illus. p.256) has golden-yellow flowers.

♀ ***A. coerulea*** Rocky mountain columbine. ♀ illus. p.257. Upright, hardy perennial. H 60–80cm (24–32in), S 30–40cm (12–16in). More-or-less upward-facing flowers, with open-spreading white sepals, pale to deep sky-blue petals and long spurs are borne from late spring to mid-summer above mid-green, divided leaves.

♀ ***A.* 'Dove' (Songbird Series)** illus. p.256. Clump-forming, compact, hardy perennial H 75cm (30in), S 35–40cm (14–16in). Open bell-shaped, fluted, large flowers with white petals, sepals and long spurs are produced in late spring and early summer above fern-like, divided, light green leaves.

***A.* 'Dragonfly'** illus. p.257. Upright, hardy perennial. H 60cm (24in) S 30cm (12in) Bell-shaped, upright to semi-horizontally-placed, fluted, large flowers with yellow, basally red-flushed petals and purplish-red sepals and spurs are produced from late spring to mid-summer above fern-like, mid-green, divided leaves.

♀ ***A. flabellata***, syn. *A. akitensis.* Clump-forming perennial. H 25cm (10in), S 10cm (4in). Fully hardy. Bell-shaped, soft blue flowers, each with fluted petals and a short spur, are produced in summer. Rounded, finely divided leaves form an open, basal rosette. Needs semi-shade and moist soil. var. ***alba* 'White Jewel' (Jewel Series,** illus. p.256) has white flowers. The flowers of **Jewel Series** (illus. p.257) vary from blue to pink or white. **'Ministar'** (illus. p.257) has slightly nodding blooms with contrasting purple-blue, spreading sepals and white, blue-based petals. **'Nana Alba'** see *A.f.* var. *pumila* f. *alba.* ♀ var. ***pumila*** (illus. p.257) grows to 10cm (4in) and has deep blue and white petals. ♀ var. ***pumila*** f. ***alba*** (syn. *A.f.* 'Nana Alba'), H 10cm (4in), is compact and has white flowers.

♀ ***A.* 'Florida' (State Series)** illus. p.256. Clump-forming, upright, hardy perennial. H 60cm (24in) S 30cm (12in). Open, bell-shaped, fluted flowers with mid-yellow petals, creamy-yellow, spreading sepals and long spurs are produced during late spring and early summer above fern-like, divided, light green leaves.

A. fragrans illus. p.256. Upright, hardy perennial. H 15–40cm (6–16in) S 15–20cm (6–8in). Nodding, bell-shaped, fragrant flowers with creamy-white petals and bluish-or pinkish-white sepals and spurs to 2cm (¾in.) long are produced in midsummer above finely divided bluish-green leaves.

***A.* 'Goldfinch' (Songbird Series)** illus. p.256. Clump-forming, compact, hardy perennial. H 60–70cm (24–28in), S 35cm (14in). Open bell-shaped, fluted flowers with bright yellow petals, sepals and long spurs appear in late spring and early summer above fern-like, divided, mid-green leaves.

A. jonesii illus. p.395.

A. karelinii illus. p.257. Clump-forming, hardy perennial. H 20–80cm (8–32in) S 12–30cm (5–12in) . Nodding, bell-shaped flowers with violet to wine-purple petals, spreading sepals and short, hooked spurs are produced above the light green, slightly glaucous leaves in early summer.

♀ ***A. longissima*** illus. p.256. Clump-forming, leafy perennial. H 60cm (24in), S 50cm (20in). Fully hardy. Bell-shaped, pale yellow flowers, with very long, bright yellow spurs, are borne, several per stem, in early summer, above fern-like, divided, mid-green leaves.

***A.* 'Mrs Scott Elliott'.** See *A.* Mrs Scott Elliott Hybrids.

***A.* Mrs Scott Elliott Hybrids,** syn. *A.* 'Mrs Scott Elliott' illus. p.257. Clump-forming, leafy perennial. H 1m (3ft), S 50cm (20in). Fully hardy. Bell-shaped flowers of various colours, often bicoloured, have long spurs and appear in early summer on branching, wiry stems. Has fern-like, divided, bluish-green leaves.

***A.* 'Nuthatch' (Songbird Series)** illus. p.257. Clump-forming, compact, hardy perennial. H 60–70cm (24–28in), S 30cm (12in). Open, bell-shaped, fluted flowers with white, pink-based petals, deep pink sepals and long spurs appear in late spring and early summer above fern-like divided, mid-green leaves.

***A.* 'Robin' (Songbird Series)** illus. p.256. Clump-forming, compact, hardy perennial. H 60cm (24in) S 30cm (12in). Open bell-shaped, fluted flowers with white petals, pink-flushed at the base, dusky pink spreading sepals and long spurs are produced in late spring and early summer above fern-like, divided, pale mid-green leaves.

A. rockii illus. p.257. Upright, hardy perennial. H 50–80cm (20–32in) S 30–35cm (12–14in). Nodding to semi-erect, narrowly bell-shaped, deep purple flowers with spreading sepals and curved spurs to 2cm (¾in.) long are borne above the mid-green, divided leaves, which are glaucous beneath, in late spring and early summer.

A. scopulorum. Clump-forming perennial. H 6cm (2½in), S 9cm (3½in). Frost hardy. In summer produces bell-shaped, fluted, pale blue, or rarely pink, flowers, each with a cream centre and very long spurs. Leaves are divided into 9 oval, glaucous leaflets.

***A.* 'Sunburst Ruby'** illus. p.257. Clump-forming, hardy perennial. H 60cm (24in) S 30cm (12in). Semi-double to double, deep ruby-red, semi-upright flowers are borne above golden, fern-like, divided leaves in late spring and early summer.

A. triternata illus. p.256. Upright, hardy perennial. H 20–60cm (8–24in) S 20–30cm (8–12in). Narrowly bell-shaped, nodding flowers with short, yellow, sometimes red-flushed petals, red sepals and 2.5cm (1in) long spurs are produced in early summer above the 3-parted , mid-green leaves.

A. viridiflora illus. p.256. Upright, short-lived, hardy perennial. H 20–50cm (8–20in) S 10–20cm (4–8in).In late spring and early summer produces fragrant, nodding, bell-shaped flowers with purple, chocolate-brown or sometimes yellow-green petals with contrasting green sepals and 2cm (¾in.) long spurs above the 3-parted, mid-green leaves.

A. vulgaris (Granny's bonnets). Clump-forming, leafy perennial. H 1m (3ft), S 50cm (20in). Fully hardy. Many funnel-shaped, short-spurred flowers, in shades of pink, crimson, purple and white, are borne, several per long stem, in early summer. Leaves are grey-green, rounded and divided into leaflets. var. ***alba*** (illus. p.256) has white flowers. 'Magpie' see 'William Guiness'.**'Munstead White'** see 'Nivea'. ♀ **'Nivea'** syn. 'Munstead White' (illus. p.256) has grey-green leaves and glistening white flowers. ♀ var. ***stellata* 'Nora Barlow'** bears double red flowers, pale green at the tips. var. ***stellata* 'Black Barlow'** (illus. p.257) has spurless, deep purple-black, double flowers. var. ***stellata* 'Ruby Port'** (illus. p.257) has spurless, deep ruby-red double flowers. **'William Guiness'** syn. 'Magpie' (illus. p.257) has nodding, deep blue-purple flowers with the tips of the petals white.

***A.* 'Winky Red-White' (Winky Series)** illus. p.257. Clump-forming, compact, hardy perennial. H 35–50cm (14–20in) S 30cm (12in). Double or semi-double flowers with a mix of red and white petals are produced in late spring and early summer above fern-like, divided, pale mid-green leaves.

ARABIS

CRUCIFERAE/BRASSICACEAE

Genus of robust, evergreen perennials. Makes excellent ground cover in a rock garden. Fully to frost hardy. Needs sun and well-drained soil. Propagate by softwood cuttings in summer or by seed in autumn.

A. albida. See *A. alpina* subsp. *caucasica*.

A. alpina subsp. ***caucasica***, syn. *A. albida, A. caucasica.* Evergreen, mat-forming perennial. H 15cm (6in), S 50cm (20in). Fully hardy. Bears loose rosettes of obovate, toothed, mid-green leaves and, in late spring and summer, fragrant, 4-petalled, white, occasionally pink, flowers. Is excellent on a dry bank. Trim back after flowering. ♀ **'Flore Pleno'** (syn. *A. caucasica* 'Plena') has double, white flowers. **'Variegata'** (syn. *A. caucasica* 'Variegata') illus. p.374.

***A.* × *arendsii* 'Rosabella',** syn. *A. caucasica* 'Rosabella', illus. p.377.

A. blepharophylla. Short-lived, evergreen, mat-forming perennial. H 12cm (5in), S 20cm (8in). Fully hardy, but dislikes winter wet. Has oval, toothed, dark green leaves, with hairy, grey margins, borne in loose rosettes. Fragrant, 4-petalled, bright pink to white flowers are produced in spring.

A. caucasica. See *A. alpina* subsp. *caucasica*.**'Plena'** see *A. alpina* subsp. *caucasica* 'Flore Pleno'. **'Rosabella'** see *A.* × *arendsii* 'Rosabella'. **'Variegata'** see *A. alpina* subsp. *caucasica* 'Variegata'.

***A. ferdinandi-coburgi* 'Variegata'.** See *A. procurrens* 'Variegata'.

♀ ***A. procurrens* 'Variegata',** syn. *A. ferdinandi-coburgi* 'Variegata', illus. p.400.

Aralia

ARALIACEAE

Genus of deciduous trees, shrubs and perennials, grown for their bold leaves and small, but profusely borne flowers. Fully hardy. Requires sun or semi-shade, some shelter and fertile, well-drained soil. Propagate those listed below by seed in autumn or by suckers or root cuttings in late winter.

♀ ***A. elata*** (Japanese angelica tree). Deciduous tree or suckering shrub with sparse, stout, prickly stems. H and S 10m (30ft). Has large, dark green leaves with numerous oval, paired leaflets. Billowing heads of tiny, white flowers, forming a large panicle, 30–60cm (12–24in) long, are borne in late summer and autumn. **'Albomarginata'** see *A.e.* 'Variegata'. **'Aureovariegata'** has leaflets broadly edged with yellow. Leaflets of ♀ **'Variegata'** (syn. *A.e.* 'Albomarginata') have creamy-white margins.

A. elegantissima. See *Schefflera elegantissima.*

A. japonica. See *Fatsia japonica.*

A. sieboldii. See *Fatsia japonica.*

Aralia

False. See *Schefflera elegantissima*, illus. p.123.

Fern-leaf. See *Polyscias filicifolia*, illus. p.148.

Japanese. See *Fatsia japonica.*

Lace. See *Polyscias guilfoylei* 'Victoriae', illus. p.122.

Araucaria

ARAUCARIACEAE

See also CONIFERS.

A. araucana illus. p.99.

A. excelsa of gardens. See *A. heterophylla.*

♀ ***A. heterophylla***, syn. *A. excelsa* of gardens (Norfolk Island pine). Upright conifer. H 30m (100ft), S 5–8m (15–25ft). Half hardy. Has spirally set, needle-like, incurved, fresh green leaves. Cones are seldom produced in cultivation. Is often grown as a shade-tolerant house plant.

Araujia

ASCLEPIADACEAE

Genus of evergreen, twining climbers with woody stems that exude milky juice when cut. Half hardy. Needs sun and fertile, well-drained soil. Propagate by seed in spring or by stem cuttings in late summer or early autumn.

A. sericifera illus. p.203.

Arbor-vitae

American. See *Thuja occidentalis.*

Chinese. See *Platycladus orientalis.*

Arbutus

ERICACEAE

Genus of evergreen trees and shrubs, grown for their leaves, clusters of small, urn-shaped flowers, ornamental bark and strawberry-like fruits, which are edible but insipid. Frost hardy, but must be protected from strong, cold winds when young. Prefers a position in full sun and needs fertile, well-drained soil; *A. menziesii* requires acid soil. May be propagated by semi-ripe cuttings in late summer or by seed sown in autumn.

A. andrachne (Grecian strawberry tree). Evergreen, spreading tree or shrub. H and S 6m (20ft). Has oval, glossy, dark green leaves and peeling, reddish-brown bark. Panicles of urn-shaped, white flowers in late spring, are followed by orange-red fruits. Prefers a sheltered position.

♀ ***A. × andrachnoides*** illus. p.79.

♀ ***A. menziesii*** (Madroña Madroñe). Evergreen, spreading tree. H and S 15m (50ft). Has smooth, peeling, reddish bark and oval, dark green leaves. Large, upright, terminal panicles of urn-shaped, white flowers in early summer are followed by orange or red fruits.

♀ ***A. unedo*** illus. p.89.

Arbutus, Trailing. See *Epigaea repens.*

Archontophoenix
King palm

PALMAE/ARECACEAE

Genus of evergreen palms, grown for their majestic appearance. Frost tender, min. 15°C (59°F). Needs full light or partial shade and humus-rich, well-drained soil. Water containerized specimens moderately, much less when temperatures are low. Propagate by seed in spring at not less than 24°C (75°F). Red spider mite may be troublesome.

A. alexandrae illus. p.68.

♀ ***A. cunninghamiana*** (Illawarra palm, Piccabeen palm). Evergreen palm. H 15–20m (50–70ft), S 2–5m (6–15ft). Has long, arching, feather-shaped leaves. Mature trees produce large clusters of small, lavender or lilac flowers in summer, followed by large, egg-shaped, red fruits.

Arcterica nana. See *Pieris nana.*

Arctic birch. See *Betula nana*, illus. p.361.

Arctostaphylos
Manzanita

ERICACEAE

Genus of evergreen trees and shrubs, grown for their foliage, flowers and fruits. Some species are also grown for their bark, others for ground cover. Fully hardy to frost tender, min. 7°C (45°F). Provide shelter from strong winds. Does best in full sun and well-drained, acid soil. Propagate by semi-ripe cuttings in summer or by seed in autumn.

A. alpina, syn. *Arctous alpinus.* Deciduous, creeping shrub. H 5cm (2in), S to 12cm (5in). Has drooping, terminal clusters of tiny, urn-shaped, pink-flushed, white flowers in late spring, followed by rounded, purple-black berries. Leaves are oval, toothed, glossy and bright green.

A. diversifolia, syn. *Comarostaphylis diversifolia* (Summer holly). Evergreen, upright shrub or tree. H 5m (15ft), S 3m (10ft). Half hardy. Leaves are oblong, glossy and dark green. Terminal racemes of fragrant, urn-shaped, white flowers appear from early to mid-spring, followed by spherical, red fruits.

***A.* 'Emerald Carpet'** illus. p.152.

***A. hookeri* 'Monterey Carpet'**, syn. *A. uva-ursi* subsp. *hookeri* 'Monterey Carpet'. Evergreen, open shrub. H 10–15cm (4–6in), S 40cm (16in) or more. Half hardy. Has hairy branchlets bearing glossy, pale green leaves and, in early summer, urn-shaped, white flowers, sometimes flushed pink, that are followed by globose, red fruits.

A. manzanita. Evergreen, upright shrub. H and S 2m (6ft) or more. Frost hardy. Has peeling, reddish-brown bark and oval, leathery, grey-green leaves. From early to mid-spring produces small, urn-shaped, deep pink flowers.

A. nevadensis (Pine-mat manzanita). Evergreen, prostrate shrub. H 10cm (4in), S 1m (3ft). Frost hardy. Has small, oval leaves. In summer, pendent, urn-shaped, white flowers are borne in clusters in leaf axils, followed by globose, brownish-red fruits. Is useful as ground cover.

A. nummularia. Evergreen, erect to prostrate shrub. H 30cm (1ft) or more, S 1m (3ft). Frost hardy. Leaves are small, rounded, leathery and toothed. Pendent, urn-shaped, white flowers are borne in clusters from leaf axils in summer, followed by globose, green fruits. Makes good ground cover.

A. patula illus. p.148.

A. stanfordiana (Stanford manzanita). Evergreen, erect shrub. H and S 1.5m (5ft). Half hardy. Bark is smooth and reddish-brown. Has narrowly oval, glossy, bright green leaves. Bears drooping clusters of urn-shaped, pink flowers from early to mid-spring.

A. uva-ursi illus. p.400. subsp. ***hookeri* 'Monterey Carpet'** see *A. hookeri* 'Monterey Carpet'. **'Point Reyes'** illus. p.400. **'Vancouver Jade'** is an evergreen, trailing, sometimes arching shrub. H 10cm (4in), S 50cm (20in). Fully hardy. Has small, oval, bright green leaves and bears urn-shaped, white flowers in summer.

Arctotheca

COMPOSITAE/ASTERACEAE

Genus of creeping perennials. Frost tender, min. 5°C (41°F). Needs bright light and fertile, well-drained soil; dislikes humid conditions. Propagate by seed or division in spring.

A. calendula, syn. *Cryptostemma calendulaceum*, illus. p.306.

Arctotis,
syn. × Venidioarctotis

COMPOSITAE/ASTERACEAE

Genus of annuals and perennials, grown for their flower heads and foliage. Half hardy to frost tender, min. 1–5°C (34–41°F). Requires full sun and leafy loam with sharp sand added. Propagate by seed in autumn or spring or by stem cuttings year-round.

***A.* Harlequin Hybrids**, syn. *A. × hybrida*, *× Venidioarctotis.* Fairly slow-growing, upright, branching perennial, usually grown as an annual. H and S 45cm (18in). Half hardy. Lance-shaped, lobed leaves are greyish-green above, white below. In summer has large, daisy-like flower heads in many shades, including yellow, orange, bronze, purple, pink, cream and red. **'Bacchus'** has purple flower heads; **'China Rose'** deep pink; **'Sunshine'** yellow; **'Tangerine'** orange-yellow; and **'Torch'** bronze.

A. × hybrida. See *A.* Harlequin Hybrids.

A. stoechadifolia. See *A. venusta.*

A. venusta, syn. *A. stoechadifolia* (African daisy). Compact perennial, often grown as an annual. H 50cm (20in) or more, S 40cm (16in). Half hardy. Daisy-like, creamy-white flower heads with blue centres are borne singly throughout summer and into autumn. Chrysanthemum-like leaves are dark green above, grey beneath.

Arctous alpinus. See *Arctostaphylos alpina.*

Ardisia

MYRSINACEAE

Genus of evergreen shrubs and trees, grown for their fruits and foliage. Half hardy to frost tender, min. 10°C (50°F). Needs partial shade and humus-rich, well-drained but not dry soil. Water potted plants freely when in full growth, moderately at other times. Cut back old plants in early spring if required. Propagate by seed in spring or by semi-ripe cuttings in summer.

A. crenata, syn. *A. crenulata*, illus. p.146.

A. crenulata. See *A. crenata.*

Areca lutescens. See *Dypsis lutescens.*

Arecastrum romanozoffianum. See *Syagrus romanozoffiana.*

Aregelia carolinae. See *Neoregelia carolinae.*

Arenaria
Sandwort

CARYOPHYLLACEAE

Genus of spring- and summer-flowering annuals and perennials, some of which are evergreen. Fully to frost hardy. Most need sun and well-drained, sandy soil. Propagate by division or softwood cuttings in early summer or by seed in autumn or spring.

A. balearica illus. p.374.

♀ ***A. montana*** illus. p.386.

A. purpurascens illus. p.377.

A. tetraquetra illus. p.373.

Argemone

PAPAVERACEAE

Genus of robust perennials, most of which are best treated as annuals. Fully to half hardy. Grow in sun and in very well-drained soil without supports. Dead-head plants to prolong the flowering season. Propagate by seed sown outdoors in late spring.

A. mexicana illus. p.347.

Argyranthemum

COMPOSITAE/ASTERACEAE

Genus of evergreen sub-shrubs, grown for their daisy-like flowers. Frost to half hardy. Needs full sun and moderately fertile, well-drained soil. Propagate by semi-ripe cuttings in summer or root greenwood cuttings in spring.

A. frutescens, syn. *Chrysanthemum frutescens* (Marguerite), illus. p.242.

♀ ***A.* 'Jamaica Primrose'**, syn. *Chrysanthemum frutescens* 'Jamaica Primrose', illus. p.261.

A. 'Mary Wootton', syn. *Chrysanthemum frutescens* 'Mary Wootton', illus. p.245.

ARGYREIA

CONVOLVULACEAE

Genus of evergreen, twining climbers, closely allied to *Ipomoea* and grown for their showy flowers. Frost tender, min. 13°C (55°F). Needs full light and fertile, well-drained soil. Water freely when in full growth, sparingly at other times. Support is needed. Thin out previous season's growth in spring. Propagate by seed in spring or by softwood or greenwood cuttings in summer. Red spider mite and whitefly may be troublesome.
A. nervosa, syn. *A. speciosa* (Woolly morning glory). Evergreen, twining climber. H 8–10m (25–30ft). Oval, silver-backed leaves are 18–27cm (7–11in) long. Clusters of funnel-shaped, lavender-blue flowers with darker bases and white downy in bud, appear in summer-autumn.
A. speciosa. See *A. nervosa*.

Argyrocytisus battandieri. See *Cytisus battandieri*.

ARGYRODERMA

AIZOACEAE

Genus of perennial succulents, grown for their very fleshy, grey-green leaves united in a prostrate, egg shape. In summer, daisy-like flowers appear in central split between leaves. Frost tender, min. 5°C (41°F). Needs full sun and very well-drained soil. Over-watering causes leaves to split or plant to rot. Propagate by seed in summer.
A. aureum. See *A. delaetii*.
A. blandum. See *A. delaetii*.
A. brevipes. See *A. fissum*.
A. delaetii, syn. *A. aureum, A. blandum*, illus. p.492.
A. fissum, syn. *A. brevipes*, illus. p.490.
A. pearsonii, syn. *A. schlechteri*, illus. p.489.
A. schlechteri. See *A. pearsonii*.

ARIOCARPUS
Living rock

CACTACEAE

Genus of extremely slow-growing, perennial cacti with large, swollen roots. Produces flattened, spherical, green stems with angular tubercles and tufts of wool. Frost tender, min. 5°C (41°F). Prefers full sun and extremely well-drained, lime-rich soil. Is very prone to rotting. Propagate by seed in spring or summer.
A. fissuratus illus. p.488.

ARISAEMA

ARACEAE

Genus of tuberous perennials, grown for their large, curious, hooded spathes, each enclosing a pencil-shaped spadix. Forms spikes of fleshy, red fruits in autumn, before dying down. Fully to half hardy. Needs sun or partial shade and moist but well-drained humus-rich soil. Plant tubers 15cm (6in) deep in spring. Propagate by seed in autumn or spring or by offsets in spring.
A. atrorubens. See *A. triphyllum*.
♀ ***A. candidissimum*** illus. p.451.
A. consanguineum illus. p.414.
A. griffithii illus. p.438.
A. jacquemontii illus. p.438.
A. ringens. Early spring-flowering, tuberous perennial. H 25–30cm (10–12in), S 30–45cm (12–18in). Half hardy. Bears 2 erect leaves, each with 3 long-pointed lobes, and a widely hooded, green spathe, enclosing the spadix, that has paler green stripes and is edged with dark brown-purple.
A. sikokianum illus. p.435.
A. tortuosum. Summer-flowering, tuberous perennial. H 30cm–1m (1–3ft), S 30–45cm (1–1½ft). Half hardy. Each dark green-mottled, pale green stem bears 2–3 erect leaves, divided into several oval leaflets. A hooded, green or purple spathe, with a protruding, S-shaped spadix, overtops leaves. Produces spikes of attractive, fleshy, red fruits in autumn.
A. triphyllum, syn. *A. atrorubens*, illus. p.430.

ARISARUM

ARACEAE

Genus of tuberous perennials, grown mainly for their curious, hooded spathes enclosing spadices with minute flowers. Frost hardy. Needs partial shade and humus-rich, well-drained soil. Propagate in autumn by division of an established clump of tubers, which produce offsets freely.
A. proboscideum (Mouse plant). Clump-forming, spring-flowering, tuberous perennial. H to 10cm (4in), S 20–30cm (8–12in). Leaves are arrow-shaped and prostrate. Produces a spadix of minute flowers concealed in a hooded, dark brown spathe that is drawn out into a tail up to 15cm (6in) long – a mouse-like effect.

ARISTEA

IRIDACEAE

Genus of evergreen, clump-forming, rhizomatous perennials, grown for their spikes of blue flowers in spring or summer. Half hardy. Prefers a sunny position and well-drained soil. Established plants cannot be moved satisfactorily. Propagate by seed in autumn or spring.
A. ecklonii. Evergreen, clump-forming, rhizomatous perennial. H 30–60cm (12–24in), S 20–40cm (8–16in). Has long, sword-shaped, tough leaves, overtopped in summer by loosely branched spikes of saucer-shaped, blue flowers, produced in long succession.
A. major, syn. *A. thyrsiflora*, illus. p.414.
A. thyrsiflora. See *A. major*.

ARISTOLOCHIA
Birthwort

ARISTOLOCHIACEAE

Genus of evergreen or deciduous, woody-stemmed, twining and scrambling climbers, grown for their foliage and flowers. Frost hardy to frost tender, min. 10–13°C (50–55°F). Requires partial shade in summer and well-drained soil. Water regularly, less when not in full growth. Provide support. Cut back previous season's growth to 2 or 3 nodes in spring. Propagate by seed in spring or by semi-ripe cuttings in summer. Red spider mite and whitefly may be a nuisance.
A. elegans. See *A. littoralis*.
A. gigas. See *A. grandiflora*.
A. grandiflora, syn. *A. gigas* (Pelican flower, Swan flower). Fast-growing, evergreen, woody-stemmed, twining climber. H 7m (22ft) or more. Frost tender. Leaves are broadly oval, 15–25cm (6–10in) long. In summer bears large, unpleasant-smelling, tubular, purple-veined, white flowers, each with a long tail and expanding at the mouth into a heart-shaped lip.
A. griffithii, syn. *Isotrema griffithii*. Moderately vigorous, evergreen, woody-stemmed, twining climber. H 5–6m (15–20ft). Half hardy; deciduous in cold winters. Has heart-shaped leaves and tubular, dark red flowers, each with an expanded, spreading lip, in summer.
♀ ***A. littoralis***, syn. *A. elegans*, illus. p.207.

ARISTOTELIA

ELAEOCARPACEAE

Genus of evergreen shrubs and deciduous trees, grown for their foliage. Needs separate male and female plants in order to obtain fruits. Frost hardy, but in most areas protect by growing against other shrubs or a south- or west-facing wall. Needs sun or semi-shade and fertile, well-drained soil. Propagate by semi-ripe cuttings in summer.
A. chilensis, syn. *A. macqui*. Evergreen, spreading shrub. H 3m (10ft), S 5m (15ft). Leaves are oval, glossy and deep green. Tiny, star-shaped, green flowers are borne in summer, followed by small, spherical, black fruits.
A. macqui. See *A. chilensis*.

Arizona ash. See *Fraxinus velutina*, illus. p.76.
Arizona cypress. See *Cupressus arizonica* var. *glabra*.
Armand pine. See *Pinus armandii*.
Armenian oak. See *Quercus pontica*.

ARMERIA

PLUMBAGINACEAE

Genus of evergreen perennials and, occasionally, sub-shrubs, grown for their tuft-like clumps or rosettes of leaves and their flower heads. Fully to frost hardy. Requires sun and well-drained soil. Propagate by semi-ripe cuttings in summer or by seed in autumn.
***A.* 'Bees Ruby'**, syn. *A. pseudarmeria* 'Bees Ruby'. Evergreen, clump-forming, dwarf sub-shrub. H and S 30cm (12in). Fully hardy. Round heads of many small, ruby-red flowers are produced in summer on stiff stems above narrow, grass-like, dark green leaves.
A. caespitosa. See *A. juniperifolia*.
♀ ***A. juniperifolia***, syn. *A. caespitosa*, illus. p.377. ♀ **'Bevans Variety'** is an evergreen, densely cushioned sub-shrub. H 5–8cm (2–3in), S 15cm (6in). Fully hardy. Has narrow, pointed, mid- to grey-green leaves in loose rosettes. Round heads of small, deep pink flowers are borne in late spring and early summer.
A. latifolia. See *A. pseudarmeria*.
A. maritima (Sea pink, Thrift). Evergreen, clump-forming perennial or dwarf sub-shrub. H 10cm (4in), S 15cm (6in). Fully hardy. Leaves are narrow, grass-like and dark green. Stiff stems carry round heads of many small, white to pink flowers in summer. Makes a good edging plant.
♀ **'Vindictive'** illus. p.392.
A. pseudarmeria, syn. *A. latifolia*, illus. p.362. **'Bees Ruby'** see *A.* 'Bees Ruby'.

ARNEBIA

BORAGINACEAE

Genus of perennials with hairy leaves, suitable for rock gardens and banks. Fully hardy. Needs sun and gritty, well-drained soil. Propagate by seed in autumn, by root cuttings in winter or by division in spring.
A. echioides. See *A. pulchra*.
A. pulchra, syn. *A. echioides, Echioides longiflorum, Macrotomia echioides* (Prophet flower). Clump-forming perennial. H 23–30cm (9–12in), S 25cm (10in). Leaves are lance-shaped to narrowly oval, hairy and light green. In summer produces loose racemes of tubular, bright yellow flowers, each with 5 spreading lobes and fading, dark spots at petal bases.

ARNICA

COMPOSITAE/ASTERACEAE

Genus of rhizomatous perennials, grown for their large, daisy-like flower heads. Is suitable for large rock gardens. Fully hardy. Prefers sun and humus-rich, well-drained soil. Propagate by division or seed in spring. All parts may cause severe discomfort if ingested, and contact wit h sap may aggravate skin allergies.
A. montana. Tufted, rhizomatous perennial. H 30cm (12in), S 15cm (6in). Bears narrowly oval to oval, hairy, grey-green leaves and, in summer, solitary daisy-like, golden flower heads, 5cm (2in) wide. Prefers acid soil.

Arolla pine. See *Pinus cembra*, illus. p.102.

ARONIA
Chokeberry

ROSACEAE

Genus of deciduous shrubs, cultivated for their flowers, fruits and colourful autumn foliage. Fully hardy. Needs sun (for autumn colour at its best) or semi-shade and fertile, well-drained soil. May be propagated in several ways: by softwood or semi-ripe cuttings taken in summer; by seed sown in autumn; or by division from early autumn to spring.
A. arbutifolia illus. p.126.
A. melanocarpa illus. p.132.
A. × prunifolia. Deciduous, upright shrub. H 3m (10ft), S 2.5m (8ft). Oval, glossy, dark green leaves redden in autumn. Produces star-shaped, white flowers in late spring and early summer, followed by spherical, purplish-black fruits.

ARRHENATHERUM

GRAMINEAE/POACEAE

See also GRASSES, BAMBOOS, RUSHES and SEDGES.
A. elatius (False oat grass). subsp. **bulbosum 'Variegatum'** is a loosely tuft-forming, herbaceous, perennial grass. H 50cm (20in), S 20cm (8in). Fully hardy. Has a basal stem swelling, hairless, grey-green leaves, with white margins, and open panicles of brownish spikelets in summer.

Arrow bamboo. See *Pseudosasa japonica*, illus. p.320.
Arrowhead. See *Sagittaria*.
American. See *Sagittaria latifolia*, illus. p.462.
Common. See *Sagittaria sagittifolia*.
Japanese. See *Sagittaria sagittifolia* 'Flore Pleno'.
Arrowroot
East Indian. See *Tacca leontopetaloides*.
South Sea. See *Tacca leontopetaloides*.

ARTEMISIA

Wormwood

COMPOSITAE/ASTERACEAE

Genus of perennials and spreading, dwarf sub-shrubs and shrubs, some of which are evergreen or semi-evergreen, grown mainly for their fern-like, silvery foliage that is sometimes aromatic. Fully to half hardy. Prefers an open, sunny, well-drained site; dwarf types benefit from a winter protection of sharp grit or gravel. Trim lightly in spring. Propagate by division in spring or autumn or by softwood or semi-ripe cuttings in summer.
♀ ***A. abrotanum*** illus. p.172.
♀ ***A. absinthium* 'Lambrook Silver'.** Evergreen, bushy perennial, woody at base. H 80cm (32in), S 50cm (20in). Frost hardy. Has a mass of finely divided, aromatic, silvery-grey leaves. Produces tiny, insignificant, grey flower heads, borne in long panicles, in summer. Needs protection in an exposed site.
♀ ***A. alba* 'Canescens',** syn. *A. canescens, A. splendens.* Semi-evergreen, bushy perennial. H 50cm (20in), S 30cm (12in). Fully hardy. Has delicate, finely cut, curling, silvery-grey leaves. In summer, insignificant, yellow flower heads are borne on erect, silver stems. Makes good ground cover.
A. arborescens illus. p.171. **'Brass Band'** see *A.* 'Powis Castle'.**'Faith Raven'** is an evergreen, upright shrub. H 1.2m (4ft), S 1m (3ft). Differs from the species only in that it is frost hardy. Has finely cut, aromatic, silvery-white foliage and, in summer and early autumn, rounded heads of small, bright yellow flowers.
A. assoana. See *A. caucasica*.
A. canescens. See *A. alba* 'Canescens'.
♀ ***A. caucasica***, syn. *A. assoana, A. lanata, A. pedemontana.* Evergreen or semi-evergreen, prostrate perennial. H and S 30cm (12in). Fully hardy. Fern-like foliage is densely covered with silvery-white hairs. Small clusters of small, rounded, yellow flower heads are borne in summer. Suits a rock garden or wall.
♀ ***A. frigida.*** Semi-evergreen, mat-forming perennial with a woody base. H 30cm (12in) in flower, S 30cm (12in) or more. Fully hardy. Bears small, fern-like, aromatic, silky, grey-white leaves, divided into many linear lobes. In summer produces narrow panicles of small, rounded, yellow flower heads.
♀ ***A. lactiflora*** illus. p.225.
A. lanata. See *A. caucasica*.
A. ludoviciana illus. p.274. ♀ **'Silver Queen'** is a semi-evergreen, clump-forming perennial. H 75cm (30in), S 60cm (24in) or more. Fully hardy. Has large, lance-shaped, downy, silvery-white leaves, which become greener with age. From mid-summer to autumn bears densely white-woolly panicles of brownish-yellow flower heads.
A. pedemontana. See *A. caucasica*.
A. pontica illus. p.302.
♀ ***A.* 'Powis Castle',** syn. *A. arborescens* 'Brass Band'. Vigorous, evergreen sub-shrub. H 1m (3ft), S 1.2m (4ft). Frost hardy. Has abundant, finely cut, aromatic, silvery-grey foliage and sprays of insignificant, yellowish-grey flower heads in summer.
♀ ***A. schmidtiana.*** Semi-evergreen, hummock-forming perennial with creeping stems. H 8–30cm (3–12in), S 60cm (24in). Frost hardy. Has fern-like, very finely and deeply cut, silver leaves and, in summer, produces short racemes of small, rounded, pale yellow flower heads. Is good for a large rock garden, wall or bank. Needs sandy, peaty soil. ♀ **'Nana'** illus. p.401.
A. splendens. See *A. alba* 'Canescens'.
A. stelleriana. Evergreen, rounded, rhizomatous perennial with a woody base. H 30–60cm (1–2ft), S 60cm–1m (2–3ft). Fully hardy. White-haired, silver leaves are deeply lobed or toothed. Bears slender sprays of small, yellow flower heads in summer. Needs light soil. **'Boughton Silver'** (syn. *A.s.* 'Mori', *A.s.* 'Silver Brocade'), S 1m (3ft), is vigorous and arching in habit. **'Mori'** see *A.s.* 'Boughton Silver'.**'Silver Brocade'** see *A.s.* 'Boughton Silver'.

ARTHROPODIUM

LILIACEAE/ANTHERICACEAE

Genus of tufted perennials, grown for their flowers. Half hardy. Prefers a position against a sunny, sheltered wall in fertile soil. Propagate by division in spring or by seed in spring or autumn.
A. cirratum, syn. *A. cirrhatum* (Rienga lily, Rock lily). Branching perennial. H 1m (3ft), S 30cm (1ft). Bears sprays of nodding, shallowly cup-shaped, white flowers on wiry stems in early summer. Has a basal tuft of narrowly sword-shaped leaves and fleshy roots.
A. cirrhatum. See *A. cirratum*.

ARUM

Cuckoo pint,Lords and ladies

ARACEAE

Genus of tuberous perennials, grown for their leaves and spathes, each enclosing a pencil-shaped spadix of tiny flowers. Fully to half hardy. Requires sun or partial shade and moist but well-drained soil. Propagate by seed in autumn or by division in early autumn.
A. creticum illus. p.431.
A. dioscoridis. Spring-flowering, tuberous perennial. H 20–35cm (8–14in), S 30–45cm (12–18in). Frost hardy. Has a sail-like, green or purple spathe, blotched dark purple, surrounding a blackish-purple spadix. Arrow-shaped, semi-erect leaves appear in autumn. Needs a sheltered, sunny site.
A. dracunculus. See *Dracunculus vulgaris*.
♀ ***A. italicum* 'Marmoratum',** syn. *A.i.* 'Pictum', illus. p.450.
A. pictum illus. p.455.

Arum
Bog. See *Calla palustris*, illus. p.462.
Dragon's. See *Dracunculus vulgaris*, illus. p.413.
Pink. See *Zantedeschia rehmannii*.
Arum lily. See *Zantedeschia aethiopica*.

ARUNCUS

ROSACEAE

Genus of perennials, grown for their hummocks of broad, fern-like leaves and their plumes of white flowers in summer. Fully hardy. Thrives in full light and any well-drained soil. Propagate by seed in autumn or by division in spring or autumn.
♀ ***A. dioicus***, syn. *A. sylvester, Spiraea aruncus*, illus. p.224. **'Kneiffii'** illus. p.242.
A. sylvester. See *A. dioicus*.

Arundinaria anceps. See *Yushania anceps*.
Arundinaria auricoma. See *Pleioblastus auricomus*.
Arundinaria falconeri. See *Himalayacalamus falconeri*.
Arundinaria fastuosa. See *Semiarundinaria fastuosa*.
Arundinaria fortunei. See *Pleioblastus variegatus*.
Arundinaria japonica. See *Pseudosasa japonica*.
Arundinaria jaunsarensis. See *Yushania anceps*.
Arundinaria murieliae. See *Fargesia murieliae*.
Arundinaria nitida. See *Fargesia nitida*.

ARUNDO

GRAMINEAE/POACEAE

See also GRASSES, BAMBOOS, RUSHES and SEDGES.
A. donax (Giant reed). Herbaceous, rhizomatous, perennial grass. H to 6m (20ft), S 1m (3ft). Half hardy. Has thick stems that bear broad, floppy, blue-green leaves. Produces dense, erect panicles of whitish-yellow spikelets in summer. Can be grown in moist soil. var. ***versicolor*** (syn. *A.d* 'Variegata') illus. p.318.
'Variegata' see *A.d.* var. ***versicolor***

Asarabacca. See *Asarum europaeum*, illus. p.402.

ASARINA

SCROPHULARIACEAE

Genus of evergreen climbers and perennials, often with scandent stems, grown for their flowers. Is herbaceous in cold climates. Frost hardy to frost tender, min. 5°C (41°F). Grow in a position with full light and in any well-drained soil. Propagate by seed in spring.
A. barclayana. See *Maurandya barclayana*.
A. erubescens. See *Lophospermum erubescens*.
A. procumbens, syn. *Antirrhinum asarina*, illus. p.396.

ASARUM,

syn. HEXASTYLIS
Wild ginge r

ARISTOLOCHIACEAE

Genus of rhizomatous perennials, some of which are evergreen, with pitcher-shaped flowers carried under kidney- or heart-shaped leaves. Makes good ground cover, although leaves may become damaged in severe weather. Fully hardy. Prefers shade and humus-rich, moist but well-drained soil. Propagate by division in spring. Self seeds readily.
A. caudatum. Evergreen, prostrate, rhizomatous perennial. H 8cm (3in), S 25cm (10in) or more. Heart-shaped, leathery, glossy, dark green leaves, 5–10cm (2–4in) across, conceal small, pitcher-shaped, reddish-brown or brownish-purple flowers, with tail-like lobes, in early summer.
A. europaeum (Asarabacca) illus. p.402.
A. hartwegii. Evergreen, prostrate, rhizomatous perennial. H 8cm (3in), S 25cm (10in) or more. Pitcher-shaped, very dark brown, almost black, flowers, with tail-like lobes, appear in early summer beneath heart-shaped, silver-marked, mid-green leaves, 5–10cm (2–4in) wide.
A. shuttleworthii. Evergreen, prostrate, rhizomatous perennial. H 8cm (3in), S 25cm (10in) or more. Has broadly heart-shaped, usually silver-marked, mid-green leaves, 8cm (3in) across. Bears pitcher-shaped, dark brown flowers, mottled violet inside, in early summer.

ASCLEPIAS

Silk weed

ASCLEPIADACEAE

Genus of tuberous perennials or sub-shrubs, some of which are evergreen, grown for their flowers. Stems exude milky, white latex when cut. Fully hardy to frost tender, min. 5–10°C (41–50°F). Fully to half hardy species prefer a position in sun and a humus-rich, well-drained soil. Propagate by division or seed in spring. Frost tender species require sun and a moist atmosphere; cut back during periods of growth. Water very sparingly in low temperatures. Propagate by tip cuttings or seed in spring. Contact with the milky sap may irritate skin.
A. curassavica (Blood flower). Evergreen, bushy, tuberous sub-shrub. H and S 1m (3ft). Frost tender. Has narrowly oval leaves to 15cm (6in) long. Umbels of small, but showy, 5-horned, orange-red flowers with yellow centres appear in summer-autumn and are followed by narrowly ovoid, pointed fruits, 8cm (3in) long, with silky seeds.
A. hallii. Upright, tuberous perennial. H to 1m (3ft), S 60cm (2ft). Fully

hardy. Has oblong leaves, to 13cm (5in) long. Umbels of small, 5-horned, dark pink flowers are carried in summer; tightly packed silky seeds are enclosed in narrowly ovoid fruits, to 15cm (6in) long.
A. physocarpa. See *Gomphocarpus physocarpus*.
A. syriaca. Upright, tuberous perennial. H and S 1m (3ft) or more. Fully hardy. Bears oval leaves to 20cm (8in) long. Produces umbels of small, 5-horned, purplish-pink flowers carried on drooping flower stalks in summer, followed by narrowly ovoid fruits, to 15cm (6in) long and filled with silky seeds.
A. tuberosa illus. p.266.

Ash. See *Fraxinus*.
Arizona. See *Fraxinus velutina*, illus. p.76.
Blueberry. See *Elaeocarpus cynaneus*.
Claret. See *Fraxinus angustifolia* 'Raywood'.
Common. See *Fraxinus excelsior*.
Green. See *Fraxinus pennsylvanica*.
Manna. See *Fraxinus ornus*, illus. p.72.
Mountain. See *Sorbus aucuparia*, illus. p.77.
Narrow-leaved. See *Fraxinus angustifolia*.
Red. See *Fraxinus pennsylvanica*.
White. See *Fraxinus americana*.
Ash-leaved maple. See *Acer negundo*.
Asian chain fern. See *Woodwardia unigemmata*.

ASIMINA
ANNONACEAE

Genus of deciduous or evergreen shrubs and trees, grown for their foliage and flowers. Fully hardy. Prefers full sun and fertile, deep, moist but well-drained soil. Propagate by seed in autumn or by layering or root cuttings in winter.
A. triloba (Pawpaw). Deciduous, open shrub. H and S 4m (12ft). Large, oval, mid-green leaves emerge in late spring or early summer, just after, or at the same time as, 6-petalled, purplish-brown flowers. Later it produces small, globular, brownish fruits.

ASPARAGUS
LILIACEAE/ASPARAGACEAE

Genus of perennials and scrambling climbers and shrubs, some of which are evergreen, grown for their foliage. Fully hardy to frost tender, min. 10°C (50°F). Grow in partial shade or bright light, but not direct sun, in any fertile, well-drained soil. Propagate by seed or division in spring.
A. densiflorus illus. p.274. ♀ **'Myersii'** (syn. *A. meyeri*, *A.* 'Myers') illus. p.275.
A. meyeri. See *A. densiflorus* 'Myersii'.
***A.* 'Myers'.** See *A. densiflorus* 'Myersii'.
A. scandens illus. p.217.

Aspen. See *Populus tremula*.
American. See *Populus tremuloides*.
Quaking. See *Populus tremuloides*.
Weeping. See *Populus tremula* 'Pendula', illus. p.75.

ASPERULA
RUBIACEAE

Genus of annuals and perennials; some species make good alpine house plants. Fully to frost hardy. Most species need sun and well-drained soil with moisture at roots. Dislikes winter wet on crown. Propagate by softwood cuttings or seed in early summer.
A. athoa of gardens. See *A. suberosa*.
A. odorata. See *Galium odoratum*.
A. suberosa, syn. *A. athoa* of gardens, illus. p.388.

Asphodel. See *Asphodelus aestivus*.
White. See *Asphodelus albus*, illus. p.241.
Yellow. See *Asphodeline lutea*, illus. p.240.

ASPHODELINE
LILIACEAE/ASPHODELACEAE

Genus of perennials with thick, fleshy roots. Frost to half hardy. Requires sun and not over-rich soil. Propagate by division in early spring, taking care not to damage roots, or by seed in autumn or spring.
A. liburnica. Neat, clump-forming perennial. H 25–60cm (10–24in), S 30cm (12in). Frost hardy. In spring produces racemes of shallowly cup-shaped, yellow flowers on slender stems above linear, grey-green leaves.
A. lutea illus. p.240.

ASPHODELUS
LILIACEAE/ASPHODELACEAE

Genus of spring- or summer-flowering annuals and perennials. Frost to half hardy. Requires sun; most prefer fertile, well-drained soil. *A. albus* prefers light, well-drained soil. Propagate by division in spring or by seed in autumn.
A. acaulis. Prostrate perennial. H 5cm (2in), S 23cm (9in). Half hardy. In spring or early summer, stemless, funnel-shaped, flesh-pink flowers appear in the centre of each cluster of grass-like, mid-green leaves. Is suitable for an alpine house.
A. aestivus, syn. *A. microcarpus* (Asphodel). Upright perennial. H 1m (3ft), S 30cm (1ft). Frost hardy. Dense panicles of star-shaped, white flowers are borne in late spring. Has basal rosettes of upright, then spreading, grass-like, channelled, leathery, mid-green leaves.
A. albus illus. p.241.
A. microcarpus. See *A. aestivus*.

ASPIDISTRA
LILIACEAE/CONVALLARIACEAE

Genus of evergreen, rhizomatous perennials that spread slowly, grown mainly for their glossy foliage. Frost tender, min. 5–10°C (41–50°F). Very tolerant, but is best grown in a cool, shady position away from direct sunlight and in well-drained soil. Water frequently when in full growth, less at other times. Propagate by division of rhizomes in spring.
♀ ***A. elatior*** (Cast-iron plant). Evergreen, rhizomatous perennial. H 60cm (24in), S 45cm (18in). Has upright, narrow, pointed-oval leaves, to 60cm (24in) long; inconspicuous, cream to purple flowers are occasionally produced on short stalks near soil level. ♀ **'Variegata'** illus. p.313.

ASPLENIUM
ASPLENIACEAE

Genus of evergreen or semi-evergreen ferns. Fully hardy to frost tender, min. 5°C (41°F). Plants described prefer partial shade, but *A. trichomanes* tolerates full sun. Grow in any moist soil, although containerized plants should be grown in a compost including chopped sphagnum moss or coarse peat. Remove fading fronds regularly. Propagate by spores or bulbils, if produced, in late summer.
♀ ***A. bulbiferum*** (Hen-and-chicken fern, Mother spleenwort). Semi-evergreen or evergreen fern. H 15–30cm (6–12in), S 30cm (12in). Frost tender. Lance-shaped, finely divided, dark green fronds produce bulbils from which young plants develop.
A. ceterach, syn. *Ceterach officinarum* illus. p.323.
♀ ***A. nidus*** illus. p.325.
♀ ***A. scolopendrium***, syn. *Phyllitis scolopendrium, Scolopendrium vulgare*, illus. p.325. **Marginatum Group** (syn. *Phyllitis scolopendrium* 'Marginatum') illus. p.325.
♀ ***A. trichomanes*** illus. p.323.

ASTELIA
ASTELIACEAE

Genus of clump-forming perennials, grown mainly for their foliage. Frost to half hardy. Prefers full sun or semi-shade and fertile soil that does not dry out readily. Propagate by division in spring.
A. nervosa. Clump-forming perennial. H 60cm (2ft), S 1.5m (5ft). Frost hardy. Has long, sword-shaped, arching, silvery-grey leaves, above which, in summer, rise graceful, branching panicles of small, star-shaped, pale brown flowers.

ASTER
Michaelmas daisy
COMPOSITAE/ASTERACEAE

Genus of perennials and deciduous or evergreen sub-shrubs with daisy-like flower heads borne in summer-autumn. Fully to half hardy. Prefers sun or partial shade and fertile, well-drained soil, with adequate moisture all summer. Tall asters require staking. Propagate by softwood cuttings in spring or by division in spring or autumn. Spray modern forms of *A. novi-belgii* against mildew and insect attack. Other species may suffer too. See also feature panel p.270.
A. acris. See *A. sedifolius*.
A. albescens, syn. *Microglossa albescens*. Deciduous, upright, slender-stemmed sub-shrub. H 1m (3ft), S 1.5m (5ft). Frost hardy. Has narrowly lance-shaped, grey-green leaves and flattish sprays of lavender-blue flower heads, with yellow centres, in mid-summer.
♀ ***A. alpinus*** illus. p.393. **'Dark Beauty'** see *A.a.* 'Dunkle Schöne'.**'Dunkle Schöne'** (syn. *A.a.* 'Dark Beauty') is a clump-forming perennial. H 25cm (10in), S 45cm (18in). Fully hardy. Leaves are lance-shaped and dark green. Deep purple flower heads are borne from mid- to late summer. Is suitable for a rock garden.
♀ ***A. amellus*** **'King George'** illus. p.270. Bushy perennial. H and S 50cm (20in). Fully hardy. In autumn, carries many large, terminal, daisy-like, deep blue-violet flower heads with yellow centres. Leaves are oval and rough. **'Mauve Beauty'** bears clusters of large, violet flower heads, with yellow centres, in autumn. Leaves are lance-shaped, coarse and mid-green. **'Nocturne'** (illus. p.270), H 75cm (30in), has deep lilac flower heads with yellow centres. **'Rudolph Goethe'** with large, violet-blue flower heads, **'Sonia'** with pink flower heads and ♀ **'Veilchenkönigin'** (syn. *A.a.* 'Violet Queen') with deep violet flower heads are other good cultivars. **'Violet Queen'** see *A.a.* 'Veilchenkönigin'.
A. capensis. See *Felicia amelloides*.
A. cordifolius **'Silver Spray'** illus. p.270. Bushy perennial. H 1.2m (4ft), S 1m (3ft). Fully hardy. Dense, arching stems carry sprays of small, pink-tinged, white flower heads in autumn. Mid-green leaves are lance-shaped. Needs staking.
A. diffusus. See *A. lateriflorus*.
♀ ***A. ericoides*** **'Golden Spray'** illus. p.270. Bushy perennial. H 1m (3ft), S 30cm (1ft). Fully hardy. Produces daisy-like, pink-tinged, white flower heads, with bold, golden-yellow centres, from late summer to late autumn. Has small, lance-shaped, mid-green leaves and slender, freely branched stems. **'White Heather'** (illus. p.270) has long-lasting, neat, white flower heads in late autumn and wiry stems that may need support.
♀ ***A.* × *frikartii*** **'Mönch'** illus. p.270. Bushy perennial. H 75cm (30in), S 45cm (18in). Fully hardy. Bears daisy-like, single, soft lavender-blue flower heads with yellowish-green centres continuously from mid-summer to late autumn. Leaves are oval and rough. May need staking. ♀ **'Wunder von Stäfa'** (illus. p.270) is similar but has lavender flowers.
A. lateriflorus, syn. *A. diffusus*. Branching perennial. H 60cm (24in), S 50cm (20in). Fully hardy. Bears sprays of tiny, mauve flower heads, with pinkish-brown centres, in autumn. Lance-shaped leaves are small and dark green. ♀ var. ***horizontalis*** (illus. p.270) has flowers heads that are sometimes tinged pink, with darker pink centres.
A. linosyris (Goldilocks; illus. p.270). Upright, unbranched perennial. H 60cm (24in), S 30cm (12in). Fully hardy. Bears numerous small, dense, single, golden-yellow flower heads in late summer-autumn. Leaves are narrowly lance-shaped.
A. novae-angliae **'Andenken an Alma Pötschke'**, syn. *A.n.-a.* 'Alma Pöstchke' illus. p.270. Vigorous, upright perennial. H 75cm (30in), S to 60cm (24in). Fully hardy. In autumn produces clusters of single, pink flower heads on stiff stems. Has lance-shaped, rough leaves. May need staking. **'Autumn Snow'** see *A.n.-a* 'Herbstschnee'.**'Barr's Pink'** (illus. p.270) bears semi-double, bright rose-pink flower heads in summer-autumn. ♀ **'Harrington's Pink'** (illus. p.270), H 1.2–1.5m (4–5ft), has single, clear

pink flower heads with yellow centres. Those of **'Herbstschnee'** (syn. *A.n.-a.* 'Autumn Snow'; illus. p.270), H 75cm–1.1m (2½–3½ft), are white with yellow centres.
***A. novi-belgii* 'Apple Blossom'** illus. p.270. Vigorous, spreading perennial. H 90cm (36in), S 60–75cm (24–30in). Fully hardy. Panicles of single, pale soft pink flowers are borne in autumn amid lance-shaped, mid-green leaves. **'Carnival'** (illus. p.270), H 75cm (30in), S to 45cm (18in), bears double, cerise-red flower heads with yellow centres. Leaves are dark green. Is prone to mildew. **'Chequers'** (illus. p.270), H 90cm (36in), S 60–75cm (24–30in), has single, purple flowers. **'Climax'**, H 1.5m (5ft), S 60cm (2ft), bears single, light blue flowers. Is mildew-resistant. The flower heads of **'Fellowship'** (illus. p.270), H 1.2m (4ft), S 50cm (20in), are large, double and clear, deep pink; those of **'Freda Ballard'** (illus. p.270) are semi-double and rich rose-red. **'Kristina'** (illus. p.270), H 30cm (12in), S 45cm (18in), has large, semi-double, white flower heads with yellow centres. **'Lassie'** (illus. p.270), H 1.2m (4ft), S 75cm (30in), produces large, single, clear pink flowers. **'Little Pink Beauty'**, H 45cm (18in), S 50cm (20in), is a good dwarf semi-double, pink cultivar. **'Marie Ballard'** (illus. p.270), H to 1m (3ft), S to 45cm (18in), has double, mid-blue flowers. Is prone to mildew. **'Orlando'** (illus. p.270), H 1m (3ft), S to 45cm (18in), has large, single, bright pink flower heads with golden centres. Leaves are dark green. Mildew may be a problem. **'Patricia Ballard'** (illus. p.270), H 1.2m (4ft), S 75cm (30in), produces semi-double, pink flowers. Large, single flowers of **'Peace'** (illus. p.270) are mauve; **'Professor Anton Kippenburg'** (illus. p.270) H 30cm (12in), S to 45cm (18in), are clear blue with yellow centres, and those of **'Raspberry Ripple'**, H 75cm (30in), S 60cm (24in), are smaller and reddish-violet. **'Royal Ruby'** (illus. p.270), H and S to 45cm (18in), bears semi-double, rich red flower heads with yellow centres. Is prone to mildew. **'Royal Velvet'** (illus. p.270), H 1.2m (4ft), S 75cm (30in), has single deep violet flowers. **'Sandford White Swan'** (illus. p.270), H 90cm (36in), S 60cm (24in), bears white flower heads.
♀ ***A. pilosus* var. *demotus*,** syn. *A. tradescantii* of gardens. Erect perennial. H 1.2m (4ft), S 50cm (20in). Fully hardy. Has lance-shaped, mid-green leaves. In autumn, clusters of small, white flower heads appear on wiry, leafy stems and provide a good foil to bright, autumn leaf colours.
***A. sedifolius*,** syn. *A. acris.* Bushy perennial. H 1m (3ft), S 60cm (2ft). Fully hardy. Produces clusters of almost star-shaped, lavender-blue flower heads, with yellow centres, in autumn. Has small, narrowly oval, bright green leaves. **'Nanus'**, H and S 50cm (20in), makes a compact dome of blooms.
A. thomsonii. Upright perennial. H 1m (3ft), S 50cm (20in). Fully hardy. Produces long-petalled, pale lilac flower heads, freely in autumn. Leaves are slightly heart-shaped. **'Nanus'** (illus. p.270) is more compact, H 45cm (18in), S 23cm (9in).
A. tongolensis. Mat-forming perennial. H 50cm (20in), S 30cm (12in). Fully hardy. Large, lavender-blue flower heads, with orange centres, are borne singly in early summer. Has lance-shaped, hairy, dark green leaves.
A. tradescantii of gardens. See *A. pilosus* var. *demotus*.

Aster, China. See *Callistephus*.

Asteranthera

GESNERIACEAE

Genus of one species of evergreen, root climber. May be grown up mossy tree-trunks, trained against walls or used as ground cover. Frost hardy. Needs a dampish, semi-shaded position and neutral to slightly acid soil. Propagate by tip cuttings in summer or by stem cuttings in late summer or early autumn.
A. ovata. Evergreen, root climber with stems covered in white hairs. H to 4m (12ft). Has small, oblong, toothed leaves. Tubular, reddish-pink flowers, 5–6cm (2–2½in) long, often with yellow-striped, lower lips, appear singly or in pairs in leaf axils in summer.

Astilbe

SAXIFRAGACEAE

Genus of summer-flowering perennials, grown for their panicles of flowers that remain handsome even when dried brown in winter. Is suitable for borders and rock gardens. Fully hardy. Needs partial shade in most species, and a rich, moist soil. Leave undisturbed if possible, and give an annual spring mulch of well-rotted compost. Propagate species by seed sown in autumn, others by division in spring or autumn.
***A.* 'Bressingham Beauty'.** Leafy, clump-forming perennial. H and S to 1m (3ft). In summer bears feathery, tapering panicles of small, star-shaped, rich pink flowers on strong stems. Broad leaves are divided into oblong to oval, toothed leaflets.
♀ ***A. chinensis* var. *pumila*.** Clump-forming perennial. H 30cm (12in), S 20cm (8in). Lower two-thirds of flower stem bears deeply dissected, coarse, toothed, hairy, dark green leaves. Dense, fluffy spikes of tiny, star-shaped, deep raspberry-red flowers appear in summer. Is good for a shaded, moist rock garden.
***A.* × *crispa* 'Perkeo'.** See *A.* 'Perkeo'.
♀ ***A.* 'Fanal'** illus. p.292.
***A.* 'Gnom',** syn. *A. simplicifolia* 'Gnom'. Arching, clump-forming, slender-stemmed perennial. H 15cm (6in), S 10cm (4in). Has oval, deeply lobed or cut, crimped, reddish-green leaves in a basal rosette. Produces dense racemes of tiny, star-shaped, pink flowers in summer. Is good for a shaded, moist rock garden or peat bed. Self seeds in damp places but will not come true.
***A.* 'Granat'.** Clump-forming, leafy perennial. H 60cm (2ft), S to 1m (3ft). Produces pyramidal trusses of tiny, star-shaped, deep red flowers in summer above broad, bronze-flushed, rich green leaves, which are divided into oblong to oval, toothed leaflets.
***A.* 'Irrlicht'** illus. p.286.
***A.* 'Montgomery'** illus. p.253.
***A.* 'Ostrich Plume'.** See *A.* 'Straussenfeder'.
♀ ***A.* 'Perkeo',** syn. *A.* × *crispa* 'Perkeo', illus. p.365.
***A. simplicifolia* 'Gnom'.** See *A.* 'Gnom'.
♀ ***A.* 'Sprite'.** Clump-forming, dwarf, leafy perennial. H 50cm (20in), S to 1m (3ft). Has feathery, tapering panicles of tiny, star-shaped, shell-pink flowers in summer, borne above broad leaves divided into narrowly oval, toothed leaflets.
♀ ***A.* 'Straussenfeder',** syn *A.* 'Ostrich Plume', illus. p.246.
***A.* 'Venus'** illus. p.246.

Astrantia

Masterwort

UMBELLIFERAE/APIACEAE

Genus of perennials, widely used in flower arrangements. Fully hardy. Needs sun or semi-shade and well-drained soil. Propagate by division in spring or by seed when fresh, in late summer.
A. major illus. p.287. subsp. ***carinthiaca*** see *A.m.* subsp. *involucrata*.**'Hadspen Blood'** has dark red bracts and flowers. subsp. ***involucrata*** (syn. *A.m.* subsp. *carinthiaca*) illus. p.287.
♀ ***A. maxima*** illus. p.287.

Astrophytum

CACTACEAE

Genus of slow-growing, perennial cacti, grown for their freely produced, flattish, yellow flowers, some with red centres. Frost tender, min. 5°C (41°F). Prefers sun and very well-drained, lime-rich soil. Allow to dry completely in winter. Is prone to rot if wet. Propagate by seed sown in spring or summer.
***A. asterias*,** syn. *Echinocactus asterias* (Sea urchin, Silver dollar cactus). Slow-growing, slightly domed, perennial cactus. H 8–10cm (3–4in), S 10cm (4in). Spineless stem has about 8 low ribs bearing small, tufted areoles. Produces bright yellow flowers, to 6cm (2½in) across, in summer.
♀ ***A. myriostigma*,** syn. *Echinocactus myriostigma*, illus. p.482.
***A. ornatum*,** syn. *Echinocactus ornatus*, illus. p.493.

Asystasia bella. See *Mackaya bella*.
Atamasco lily. See *Zephyranthes atamasco*.

Atherosperma

MONIMIACEAE

Genus of evergreen trees, grown for their foliage and flowers in summer. Frost tender, min. 3–5°C (37–41°F). Needs full light or partial shade and well-drained soil. Water containerized specimens moderately, less in winter. Pruning is tolerated if necessary. Propagation is by seed sown in spring or by semi-ripe cuttings taken in summer.
A. moschatum (Australian sassafras, Tasmanian sassafras). Evergreen, spreading tree, conical when young. H 15–25m (50–80ft), S 5–10m (15–30ft). Has lance-shaped, nutmeg-scented, glossy leaves, slightly toothed and covered with white down beneath. Produces small, saucer-shaped, creamy-white flowers in summer.

Athrotaxis

TAXODIACEAE

Genus of conifers with awl-shaped leaves that clasp stems. See also CONIFERS.
A. selaginoides (King William pine). Irregularly conical conifer. H 15m (50ft) or more, S 5m (15ft). Half hardy. Has tiny, thick-textured, loosely overlapping, dark green leaves and insignificant, globular cones.

Athyrium

ATHYRIACEAE/WOODSIACEAE

Genus of deciduous or, occasionally, semi-evergreen ferns. Fully hardy to frost tender, min. 5°C (41°F). Needs shade and humus-rich, moist soil. Remove fading fronds regularly. Propagate by spores in late summer or by division in autumn or winter.
♀ ***A. filix-femina*** (Lady fern). Deciduous fern. H 60cm–1.2m (2–4ft), S 30cm–1m (1–3ft). Fully hardy. Dainty, lance-shaped, much-divided, arching fronds are pale green. Has very variable frond dissection.
A. goeringianum. See *A. niponicum*.
***A. niponicum*,** syn. *A. goeringianum, A. nipponicum*, illus. p.325.
A. nipponicum. See *A. niponicum*.
♀ ***A. otophorum.*** Semi-evergreen fern. H and S to 75cm (30in). Fully hardy (borderline). Has arching, broadly ovate, mid-green or purple- tinged, divided fronds, 45–75cm (18–30in) long. Stalk and midrib are a contrasting deep wine-purple.

Atlas cedar. See *Cedrus atlantica*

Atriplex

CHENOPODIACEAE

Genus of annuals, perennials and evergreen or semi-evergreen shrubs, grown for their foliage. Grows well by the coast. Fully to half hardy. Needs full sun and well-drained soil. Propagate by softwood cuttings taken in summer or by seed sown in autumn.
A. halimus (Tree purslane). Semi-evergreen, bushy shrub. H 2m (6ft), S 3m (10ft). Frost hardy. Oval leaves are silvery-grey. Produces flowers very rarely.
A. hortensis* var. *rubra (Red mountain spinach, Red orach). Fast-growing, erect annual. H 1.2m (4ft), S 30cm (1ft). Half hardy. Triangular, deep red leaves, to 15cm (6in) long, are edible. Bears insignificant flowers in summer.

Aubrieta

CRUCIFERAE/BRASSICACEAE

Genus of evergreen, trailing and mound-forming perennials. Is useful on dry banks, walls and in rock gardens. Fully hardy. Thrives in sun and in any well-drained soil. To maintain a compact shape, cut back hard after flowering. Propagate by greenwood cuttings in summer or by semi-ripe cuttings in late summer or autumn.
***A.* 'Carnival'.** See *A.* 'Hartswood Purple'.
***A.* 'Cobalt Violet'** illus. p.381.

A. deltoidea **'Argenteovariegata'** illus. p.380.
♀ ***A.* 'Doctor Mules'.** Vigorous, evergreen, mound-forming perennial. H 5–8cm (2–3in), S 30cm (12in). Has rounded, toothed, soft green leaves and, in spring, large, single, rich purple flowers on short spikes.
***A.* 'Gurgedyke'.** Evergreen, mound-forming perennial. H 10cm (4in), S 20cm (8in). Bears rounded, toothed, soft green leaves. Produces 4-petalled, deep purple flowers in spring.
***A.* 'Hartswood Purple',** syn. *A.* 'Carnival', illus. p.380.
***A.* 'Joy'** illus. p.379.
***A.* 'J.S. Baker'** illus. p.380.

AUCUBA

CORNACEAE/AUCUBACEAE

Genus of evergreen shrubs, grown for their foliage and fruits. To obtain fruits, grow both male and female plants. Makes good house plants when kept in a cool, shaded position. Fully to frost hardy. Tolerates full sun through to dense shade. Grow in any but water-logged soil. To restrict growth, cut old shoots back hard in spring. Propagate by semi-ripe cuttings taken in summer.
A. japonica illus. p.148.
♀ **'Crotonifolia'** (male) illus. p.149. **'Gold Dust'** is an evergreen, bushy, dense, female shrub. H and S 2.5m (8ft). Frost hardy. Has stout, green shoots and oval, glossy, gold-speckled, dark green leaves. Small, star-shaped, purple flowers in mid-spring are followed by egg-shaped, bright red fruits. Bright green leaves of **'Picturata'** (male) each have a central, golden blotch. Some plants of **'Crotonifolia'** and **'Picturata'** are known to be female and have produced fruits.

August lily. See *Hosta plantaginea*, illus. p.300.

AURINIA

BRASSICACEAE/CRUCIFERAE

Genus of evergreen perennials, grown for their grey-green foliage and showy flower sprays. Is suitable for rock gardens, walls and banks. Fully hardy. Needs sun and well-drained soil. Propagate by softwood or greenwood cuttings in early summer or by seed in autumn.
♀ ***A. saxatilis***, syn. *Alyssum saxatile*, illus. p.362. ♀ **'Citrina'** illus. p.361. **'Dudley Nevill'** is an evergreen, clump-forming perennial. H 23cm (9in), S 30cm (12in). Has oval, hairy, grey-green leaves and, in late spring and early summer, produces racemes of many small, 4-petalled, buff-yellow flowers. **'Variegata'** illus. p.361.

Australian banyan. See *Ficus macrophylla*.
Australian brush cherry. See *Syzygium paniculatum*, illus. p.77.
Australian cabbage palm. See *Livistona australis*.
Australian firewheel tree. See *Stenocarpus sinuatus*.
Australian heath. See *Epacris impressa*, illus. p.151.
Australian pea. See *Lablab purpureus*, illus. p.207.
Australian rosemary. See *Westringia fruticosa*, illus. p.154.
Australian sarsparilla. See *Hardenbergia violacea*.
Australian sassafras. See *Atherosperma moschatum*.
Australian tree fern. See *Cyathea australis*, illus. p.96; *Dicksonia antarctica*, illus. p.322.
Australian violet. See *Viola hederacea*.
Austrian pine. See *Pinus nigra* subsp. *nigra*, illus. p.100.

AUSTROCEDRUS

CUPRESSACEAE

Genus of conifers with flattish sprays of scale-like leaves. See also CONIFERS.
A. chilensis, syn. *Libocedrus chilensis*, illus. p.102.

Austrocylindropuntia cylindrica. See *Opuntia cylindrica*
Austrocylindropuntia verschaffeltii. See *Opuntia verschaffeltii*
Autograph tree. See *Clusia major*.
Autumn crocus. See *Colchicum autumnale*, illus. p.453; *Crocus nudiflorus,* illus. p.444
Autumn snowdrop. See *Galanthus reginae-olgae*.
Autumn snowflake. See *Leucojum autumnale*, illus. p.453.
Avena candida. See *Helictotrichon sempervirens*.
Avena sempervirens. See *Helicto-trichon sempervirens*.
Avens. See *Geum*.
 Alpine. See *Geum montanum*.
 Mountain. See *Dryas*.
Azalea. See *Rhododendron*.
 Alpine. See *Loiseleuria procumbens*, illus. p.389.
 Flame. See *Rhododendron calendulaceum*.
 Trailing. See *Loiseleuria procumbens*, illus. p.389.

AZARA

FLACOURTIACEAE

Genus of evergreen shrubs and trees, grown for their foliage and also for their yellow flowers that are composed of a mass of stamens. Frost to half hardy; in cold climates, plants are best grown situated against a south- or west-facing wall for added protection. Grows in sun or shade, and in fertile, well-drained soil. Propagate by semi- ripe cuttings in summer.
A. lanceolata. Evergreen, bushy shrub or spreading tree. H and S 6m (20ft). Frost hardy. Has narrowly oval, sharply toothed, bright green leaves. Small, rounded clusters of pale yellow flowers are carried in late spring or early summer.
A. microphylla illus. p.121.
A. serrata illus. p.131.

AZOLLA

AZOLLACEAE

Genus of deciduous, perennial, floating water ferns, grown for their decorative foliage and also to control algal growth by reducing light in water beneath. Frost to half hardy. Grows in sun or shade. If not kept in check, may be invasive; reduce spread by removing portions with a net. Propagate by redistributing clusters of plantlets when they appear.
A. caroliniana. See *A. filiculoides*.
A. filiculoides, syn *A. caroliniana*, illus. p.464.

AZORELLA

UMBELLIFERAE/APIACEAE

Genus of evergreen, tufted or spreading perennials, grown for their flowers and neat, rosetted foliage. Is useful as alpine house plants. Fully hardy. Thrives in full light and well-drained soil. Propagate by division in spring.
A. nivalis. See *A. trifurcata*.
A. trifurcata, syn. *A. nivalis*, illus. p.402.

AZORINA

CAMPANULACEAE

Genus of one species of erect evergreen shrub with bell-shaped flowers. Frost tender, min. 5°C (41°F). Needs full light and fertile, moist but well-drained soil. Propagate by seed in spring or take softwood or semi-ripe cuttings in summer.
Azorina vidalii, syn. *Campanula vidalii*, illus. p.150.

Azureocereus hertlingianus. See *Browningia hertlingiana*.
Aztec lily. See *Sprekelia formosissima*, illus. p.429.
Aztec marigold. See *Tagetes erecta*.

B

Babiana

IRIDACEAE

Genus of spring- and early summer-flowering corms, valued for their brightly coloured flowers, which are somewhat like freesias. Frost tender, min. 10°C (50°F). Requires a position in sun and well-drained soil. Propagate in autumn by seed or natural division of corms.
B. disticha. See *B. plicata*.
B. plicata, syn. *B. disticha*. Spring-flowering corm. H 10–20cm (4–8in), S 5–8cm (2–3in). Has a fan of lance-shaped, erect, basal leaves and short spikes of funnel-shaped, violet-blue flowers, 4–5cm (1½–2in) long, with yellow-patched petals.
B. rubrocyanea illus. p.447.
♀ ***B. stricta.*** Spring-flowering corm. H 10–20cm (4–8in), S 5–8cm (2–3in). Produces a fan of narrowly lance-shaped, erect, basal leaves and short spikes of up to 10 funnel-shaped, purple, blue, cream or pale yellow flowers, 2.5–4cm (1–1½in) long and sometimes red-centred.

Baby blue-eyes. See *Nemophila menziesii*, illus. p.345.
Baby rubber plant. See *Peperomia clusiifolia*.
Baby's tears. See *Soleirolia*.
Baby's toes. See *Fenestraria rhopodophylla* subsp. *aurantiaca*, illus. p.495.

Baccharis

COMPOSITAE/ASTERACEAE

Genus of evergreen or deciduous, mainly autumn-flowering shrubs, grown for their foliage and fruits. Is useful for exposed, coastal gardens and dry soil. Fully hardy. Requires a position in full sun and well-drained soil. Propagate by softwood cuttings in summer.
B. halimifolia (Bush groundsel). Vigorous, deciduous, bushy shrub. H and S 4m (12ft). Has grey-green, sharply toothed, oval leaves. Large clusters of tiny, white flower heads in mid-autumn are followed by fluffy, white heads of tiny fruits.

Bahia lanata. See *Eriophyllum lanatum*.
Bald cypress. See *Taxodium distichum*, illus. p.100.

Baldellia

ALISMATACEAE

Genus of deciduous or evergreen, perennial, bog plants and submerged water plants, grown for their foliage. Frost hardy. Prefers a position in sun, but tolerates shade. Remove fading foliage and excess growth as required. Propagate by division in spring or summer.
B. ranunculoides, syn. *Alisma ranunculoides, Echinodorus ranunculoides*. Deciduous, perennial, bog plant or submerged water plant. H 23cm (9in), S 15cm (6in). Has lance-shaped, mid-green leaves and, in summer, umbels of small, 3-parted, pink or white flowers with basal, yellow marks.

Baldmoney. See *Meum athamanticum*.
Balearic box. See *Buxus balearica*, illus. p.149.
Balkan blue grass. See *Sesleria heufleriana*.
Balloon flower. See *Platycodon*.
Balloon vine. See *Cardiospermum halicacabum*.

Ballota

LABIATEA/LAMIACEAE

Genus of perennials and evergreen or deciduous sub-shrubs, grown for their foliage and flowers. Frost hardy. Requires very well-drained soil and full sun. Cut back in spring before growth starts. Propagate by semi-ripe cuttings in summer.
B. acetabulosa illus. p.172.
♀ ***B. pseudodictamnus*** illus. p.373.

Balm
Bastard. See *Melittis*.
Bee. See *Monarda didyma*.
Balm of Gilead. See *Populus × jackii*.
Balsam. See *Impatiens balsamina*, illus. p.332.
Balsam fir. See *Abies balsamea*.
Balsam poplar. See *Populus balsamifera*.
Bamboo. See Grasses, Bamboos, Rushes and Sedges.
Anceps. See *Yushania anceps*, illus. p.320.
Arrow. See *Pseudosasa japonica*, illus. p.320.
Black. See *Phyllostachys nigra*.
Chilean. See *Chusquea culeou*, illus. p.320.
Dwarf white-stripe. See *Pleioblastus variegatus*, illus. p.318.
Fishpole. See *Phyllostachys aurea*.
Golden. See *Phyllostachys aurea*.
Golden-groove. See *Phyllostachys aureosulcata*.
Heavenly. See *Nandina domestica*.
Hedge. See *Bambusa multiplex*, illus. p.319.
Muriel. See *Fargesia murieliae*.
Narihira. See *Semiarundinaria fastuosa*, illus. p.320.
Sacred. See *Nandina domestica*.
Timber. See *Phyllostachys bambusoides*, illus. p.320.
Zigzag. See *Phyllostachys flexuosa*, illus. p.320.
Bamboo palm. See *Rhapis excelsa*, illus. p.148.

Bambusa

GRAMINEAE/POACEAE

See also GRASSES, BAMBOOS, RUSHES and SEDGES.
B. glaucescens. See *B. multiplex*.
B. multiplex, syn. *B. glaucescens*, illus. p.319.

Banana. See *Musa*.
Flowering. See *Musa ornata*, illus. p.232.
Japanese. See *Musa basjoo*, illus. p.233.
Scarlet. See *Musa coccinea*.
Banana passion fruit. See *Passiflora antioquiensis*.
Baneberry. See *Actaea*.
Red. See *Actaea rubra*.
White. See *Actaea pachypoda*, illus. p.267.

Banksia

PROTEACEAE

Genus of evergreen shrubs and trees, grown for their flowers and foliage. Frost tender, min. 7–10°C (45–50°F). Requires full light and sharply drained, sandy soil that contains little phosphates or nitrates. Water containerized plants moderately when in full growth, sparingly at other times. Freely ventilate plants grown under glass. Propagate by seed in spring.
B. baxteri. Evergreen, spreading, open shrub. H and S 2–3m (6–10ft). Leathery, mid-green leaves are strap-shaped, cut from the midrib into triangular, sharply pointed lobes. Produces dense, spherical heads of small, tubular, yellow flowers in summer.
B. coccinea illus. p.126.
B. ericifolia (Heath banksia). Evergreen, irregularly rounded, wiry, freely branching shrub. H and S to 3m (10ft). Has small, needle-like leaves and dense, upright, bottlebrush-like spikes, each 10–15cm (4–6in) long, of small, tubular, bronze-red or yellow flowers in late winter and spring.
B. serrata. Evergreen, bushy, upright shrub or tree. H 3–10m (10–30ft), S 1.5–3m (5–10ft). Oblong to lance-shaped, saw-toothed, leathery leaves are mid- to deep green. Small, tubular, reddish-budded, cream flowers appear in dense, upright, bottlebrush-like spikes, each 10–15cm (4–6in) long, from spring to late summer.

Banksia
Heath. See *Banksia ericifolia*.
Yellow. See *Rosa banksiae* 'Lutea', illus. p.195.
Banksian rose. See *Rosa banksiae*.
Banyan. See *Ficus benghalensis*, illus. p.68.
Australian. See *Ficus macrophylla*.
Baobab. See *Adansonia*.

Baptisia

LEGUMINOSAE/PAPILIONACEAE

Genus of summer-flowering perennials, grown for their flowers. Fully hardy. Requires full sun and deep, well-drained, preferably neutral to acid soil. Is best not disturbed once planted. Propagate by division in early spring or by seed in autumn.
♀ ***B. australis*** illus. p.258.

Barbacenia elegans. See *Vellozia elegans*.
Barbados gooseberry. See *Pereskia aculeata*, illus. p.473.
Barbados pride. See *Caesalpinia pulcherrima*.

Barbarea

CRUCIFERAE/BRASSICACEAE

Genus of summer-flowering perennials, biennials and annuals. Most species are weeds or winter salad plants, but the variegated form of *B. vulgaris* is grown for decorative purposes. Fully hardy. Grows in a sunny or shady position and in any well-drained but not very dry soil. Propagate by seed or division in spring.
B. vulgaris (Winter cress, Yellow rocket). **'Variegata'** illus. p.303.

Barbed-wire plant. See *Tylecodon reticulatus*, illus. p.481.
Barberry. See *Berberis*.
Darwin's. See *Berberis darwinii*, illus. p.113.
Barberton daisy. See *Gerbera jamesonii*, illus. p.314.

Barleria

ACANTHACEAE

Genus of evergreen shrubs and perennials, grown for their flowers. Frost tender, min. 7–18°C (45–64°F). Needs full light or partial shade and fertile soil. Water potted plants well when in full growth, moderately at other times. In the growing season, prune tips of young plants to encourage branching. For a more compact habit, shorten long stems after flowering. May be propagated by seed in spring or by greenwood or semi-ripe cuttings in summer.
B. cristata (Philippine violet). Evergreen, semi-erect shrub. H and S 60cm–1.2m (2–4ft). Min. 15–18°C (59–64°F). Has elliptic, coarsely haired leaves. Tubular, light violet flowers, sometimes pale pink or white, are produced from upper leaf axils in summer.
B. obtusa. Evergreen, erect, spreading shrub. H and S to 1m (3ft). Min. 7–10°C (45–50°F). Leaves are elliptic. Tubular, mauve flowers are produced from upper leaf axils during winter-spring.

Barley, Foxtail. See *Hordeum jubatum*, illus. p.319.
Barosma pulchella. See *Agathosma pulchella*.
Barrel cactus. See *Ferocactus*.
Barrenwort. See *Epimedium*.
Bartonia aurea. See *Mentzelia lindleyi*.
Bartlettina sordida. See *Eupatorium sordidum*.
Bartram's oak. See *Quercus × heterophylla*, illus. p.78.
Basket grass. See *Oplismenus africanus*.

Bassia, syn. Kochia

CHENOPODIACEAE

Genus of annuals and perennials, grown for their habit, the feathery effect of their leaves and their autumn tints. Half hardy. Does best in sun and in fertile, well-drained soil. May require support in very windy areas. Propagate by seed sown under glass in early to mid-spring, or outdoors in late spring.
B. scoparia f. ***trichophylla*** illus. p.347.

Basswood. See *Tilia americana*.
Bastard balm. See *Melittis*.
Bat flower. See *Tacca chantrierei*.

Bauera

CUNONIACEAE

Genus of evergreen shrubs, grown mainly for their flowers. Frost tender, min. 3–5°C (37–41°F). Needs full sun and humus-rich, well-drained, neutral to acid soil. Water potted plants moderately, less when not in full growth. Remove straggly stems after flowering. May be propagated by seed sown in spring or by semi-ripe cuttings taken in late summer.
B. rubioides. Evergreen, bushy, wiry-stemmed shrub, usually of spreading habit. H and S 30–60cm (1–2ft). Leaves each have 3 oval to lance-shaped, glossy leaflets. Bowl-shaped, pink or white flowers appear in early spring and summer.

Bauhinia

LEGUMINOSAE/PAPILIONACEAE

Genus of evergreen, semi-evergreen or deciduous trees, shrubs and scandent climbers, grown for their flowers. Frost tender, min. 5–18°C (41–64°F). Requires full light and fertile, well-drained soil. Water containerized specimens freely when in full growth, less in winter. Thin out congested growth after flowering. Propagate by seed in spring.
B. galpinii, syn. *B. punctata*, illus. p.138.
B. punctata. See *B. galpinii*.
B. variegata and **'Candida'** illus. p.93.

Bay
Bull. See *Magnolia grandiflora*.
Loblolly. See *Gordonia lasianthus*.
Sweet. See *Laurus nobilis; Magnolia virginiana*.
Bay laurel. See *Laurus nobilis*.
Bay tree. See *Laurus*.
Bay willow. See *Salix pentandra*.
Bayonet plant. See *Aciphylla squarrosa*, illus. p.274.
Bayonet, Spanish. See *Yucca aloifolia*, illus. p.149.
Beach pine. See *Pinus contorta*, illus. p.103.
Bead plant. See *Nertera granadensis*, illus. p.399.
Bead tree. See *Melia azedarach*, illus. p.72.
Bean
Black. See *Kennedia nigricans*.
Bog. See *Menyanthes trifoliata*, illus. p.462.
Hyacinth. See *Lablab purpureus*, illus. p.207.
Bean tree
Black. See *Castanospermum*.
Indian. See *Catalpa bignonioides*, illus. p.74.
Bear grass. See *Dasylirion*.
Bear's breeches. See *Acanthus*.
Bearded bellflower. See *Campanula barbata*, illus. p.368.

Beaucarnea

AGAVACEAE/DRACAENACEAE

Genus of evergreen shrubs and trees, grown mainly for their intriguing, overall appearance. Frost tender, min. 7°C (45°F). Needs full light and sharply drained, fertile soil; drought conditions are tolerated. Water potted specimens moderately; allow compost almost to dry out between waterings. Propagate by seed or suckers in spring or by stem-tip cuttings in summer.
♀ ***B. recurvata***, syn. *Nolina recurvata, N. tuberculata*, illus. p.96.

Beaumontia

APOCYNACEAE

Genus of evergreen, woody-stemmed, twining climbers, grown for their large, fragrant flowers and handsome leaves. Frost tender, min. 7–10°C (45–50°F). Requires fertile, well-drained soil and full light. Water freely in growing season, sparingly otherwise. Provide support. Thin out previous season's growth after flowering. Propagate by semi-ripe cuttings in late summer.
B. grandiflora illus. p.200.

Beauty bush. See *Kolkwitzia amabilis*.
Bedstraw. See *Galium*.
Bee balm. See *Monarda didyma*.
Beech. See *Fagus*.
American. See *Fagus grandifolia*.
Antarctic. See *Nothofagus antarctica*.
Common. See *Fagus sylvatica*, illus. p.64.
Copper. See *Fagus sylvatica* f. *atropunicea*, illus. p.61.
Oriental. See *Fagus orientalis*.
Purple. See *Fagus sylvatica* f. *atropunicea*, illus. p.61.
Silver. See *Nothofagus menziesii*.
Southern. See *Nothofagus*.
Weeping. See *Fagus sylvatica* f. *pendula*, illus. p.62.
Beech fern. See *Phegopteris connectilis*.
Beefsteak plant. See *Iresine herbstii*.

Begonia

BEGONIACEAE

Genus of evergreen or deciduous shrubs and small, tree-like plants, perennials and annuals, grown for their colourful flowers and/or ornamental leaves. Prefers slightly acidic soil. Is susceptible to powdery mildew and botrytis from late spring to early autumn. Commonly cultivated begonias are divided into the following groupings, each with varying cultivation requirements. See also feature panel p.307.

Cane-stemmed begonias
Evergreen, woody perennials, many known as 'Angelwings', with usually erect, cane-like stems bearing regularly spaced, swollen nodes and flowers in large, pendulous panicles. Encourage branching by pinching out growing tips. New growth develops from base of plant. Frost tender, min. 10°C (50°F). Grow under glass in good light but not direct sun (poor light reduces quantity of flowers) and in free-draining, loam-based compost. Stake tall plants. Propagate in spring by seed or tip cuttings.

Rex-cultorum begonias
Mostly evergreen, rhizomatous perennials of variable habit derived from crosses of *B. rex* and related species. They are grown for their brilliantly coloured, oval to lance-shaped leaves, 8–30cm (3–12in) long, that are sometimes spirally twisted. Frost tender, min. 13–15°C (55–9°F), but preferably 21–4°C (70–75°F), with 40–75% relative humidity. Grow under glass in cool climates, in partial shade and in well-drained soil; water only sparingly. Do not allow water to remain on the leaves, otherwise they become susceptible to botrytis. Propagate in spring by seed, leaf cuttings or division of rhizomes.

Rhizomatous begonias
Variable, mostly evergreen, rhizomatous perennials, grown for their foliage and small, single flowers. Smooth, crested or puckered, green or brown leaves, 8–30cm (3–12in) long, often marked silver, are sometimes spirally twisted. Creeping cultivars are more freely branched than erect ones and are useful for hanging baskets. Frost tender, min. 13–15°C (55–9°F), but preferably 19°C (66°F), with 40–75% relative humidity. Grow under glass in cool climates, in partial shade and in well-drained soil; water only sparingly. Do not allow water to remain on the leaves, otherwise they become susceptible to botrytis. Propagate in spring by seed, leaf cuttings or division of rhizomes.

Semperflorens begonias
Evergreen, bushy perennials, derived from *B. cucullata* var. *hookeri*, *B. schmidtiana* and other species, often grown as half-hardy bedding annuals. Stems are soft, succulent and branch freely, bearing generally rounded, green, bronze or variegated leaves, 5cm (2in) long. Flowers are single or double. Pinch out growing tips to produce bushy plants. Frost tender, min. 10–15°C (50–59°F). Requires sun or partial shade and well-drained soil. Propagate in spring by seed or stem cuttings.

Shrub-like begonias
Evergreen, multi-stemmed, bushy perennials, usually freely branched with flexible, erect or pendent stems, often hairy. Leaves may be hairy or glabrous and up to 15cm (6in) across, 10–30cm (4–12in) long. Single flowers are pink, cream or white. Frost tender, min. 7°C (45°F) with 55% relative humidity. Grow under glass in good light and moist but well-drained soil. Propagate in spring by seed or stem cuttings.

Tuberous begonias (including the Tuberhybrida, Multiflora and Pendula begonias)
Mostly upright, bushy, tuberous, winter-dormant perennials grown for their foliage and flowers. Tuberhybrida begonias, H and S 75cm (30in), vary from pendent to erect, with sparsely branched, succulent stems and oval, pointed, glossy, bright to dark green leaves, 20cm (8in) long. Most are summer flowering and mainly double-flowered. Multiflora cultivars, H and S 30cm (12in), are more bushy and have 8cm (3in) long leaves and single, semi-double or double, flowers, each 4–5cm (1½–2in) across, in summer; tolerates full sun. Pendula cultivars, H to 1m (3ft), have long, thin, trailing stems; leaves are 6–8cm (2½–3in) long. Masses of single or double flowers are borne in summer. Frost tender, min. 5–7°C (41–5°F). Outdoors, grow in dappled shade and moist conditions; under glass, plant in cool shade with 65–70% relative humidity. Tubers are dormant in winter. Start into growth in spring for mid-summer to early autumn flowering. Remove all flower buds until stems show at least 3 pairs of leaves; with large-flowered types allow only central male bud to flower, so remove flanking buds. Plants may require staking. Propagate in spring by seed, stem or basal cuttings or division of tubers.

Winter-flowering begonias
Evergreen, low-growing, very compact perennials, with succulent, thin stems, that are often included in the tuberous group. Two main groups are recognized: the single-flowered, usually pink or white, Lorraine, Cheimantha or Christmas begonias; and the single, semi-double or double, Elatior and Rieger begonias that occur in a wide range of colours. Leaves are green or bronze, 5cm (2in) long. Flowers are borne mainly from late autumn to mid-spring. Frost tender, min. 18°C (64°F) with 40% relative humidity. Indirect sun and moist soil are preferred. Cut back old stems to 10cm (4in) after flowering. Propagate in spring by seed or stem cuttings.

B. albopicta illus. p.307. Fast-growing, evergreen, cane-stemmed begonia. H to 1m (3ft), S 30cm (1ft). Freely branched, green stems turn brown-green when mature. Narrowly oval to lance-chaped, wavy-edged, green leaves are silver-spotted. Has clusters of single, green-white flowers in summer-autumn.
B. angularis. See *B. stipulacea*.
***B.* 'Apricot Cascade'** illus. p.307. Pendent Tuberhybrida begonia. H and S 60cm (2ft). Has emerald-green leaves and, from early summer to mid-autumn, double, orange-apricot flowers. Other cascades are **'Bridal Cascade'** (pink-edged, white petals), **'Crimson Cascade'**, **'Gold Cascade'** and **'Orange Cascade'**.
***B.* 'Beatrice Haddrell'.** Evergreen, creeping, rhizomatous begonia. H 20–30cm (8–12in), S 25–30cm (10–12in). Oval leaves are deeply cleft, 8–15cm (3–6in) long, and dark green with paler veins. Produces single, pink flowers, above foliage, in winter and early spring.
***B.* 'Bethlehem Star'.** Evergreen, creeping, rhizomatous begonia. H 20–30cm (8–12in), S 25–30cm (10–12in). Oval, slightly indented, almost black leaves, less than 8cm (3in) long, each have a central, creamy-green star. Bears masses of single, pale pink flowers, with darker pink spots, from late winter to early spring.
***B.* 'Billie Langdon'** illus. p.307. Upright Tuberhybrida begonia. H 60cm (2ft), S 45cm (18in). In summer has masses of heavily veined, double, white flowers, each 18cm (7in) across, with a perfect rose-bud centre.
***B.* 'Bokit'.** Evergreen, erect, rhizomatous begonia. H 20–30cm (8–12in), S 25–35cm (10–14in). Has oval, spirally twisted, yellow-green leaves with brown tiger stripes. Bears masses of single, white flowers, flecked with

pink, in winter.
B. bowerae (Eyelash begonia; illus. p.307). Evergreen, creeping, rhizomatous begonia. H 25–30cm (10–12in), S 20–25cm (8–10in). Has oval, bright green leaves, 2.5cm (1in) long, with chocolate marks and bristles around edges. Bears single, pink-tinted, white flowers freely in winter.
***B.* 'Bridal Cascade'.** See *B.* 'Apricot Cascade'.
***B.* 'Can-can'** illus. p.307. Upright Tuberhybrida begonia. H 1m (3ft), S 45cm (18in). Has double, yellow flowers, each 20cm (8in) wide, with rough-edged, red petals, in summer. Produces few side shoots.
***B.* 'City of Ballarat'** illus. p.307. Vigorous, upright Tuberhybrida begonia. H 60cm (2ft), S 45cm (18in). Leaves are rich dark green. Carries double, glowing orange flowers, each 18cm (7in) across, with broad petals and a formal centre, in summer.
B. coccinea (Angelwing begonia). Evergreen, cane-stemmed begonia. H 1.2m (4ft), S 30cm (1ft). Produces narrowly oval, glossy, green leaves, buff-coloured beneath, and, in spring, profuse, single, pink or coral-red flowers.
♀ ***B.* 'Cocktail Series'.** Semperflorens begonia. H and S 20–30cm (8–12in). Produces rounded, wavy, green-bronze leaves and pink, red or white flowers from summer until autumn frosts.
***B.* 'Corallina de Lucerna'.** See *B.* 'Lucerna'.
***B.* 'Crimson Cascade'.** See *B.* 'Apricot Cascade'.
***B.* 'Curly Merry Christmas'.** Rex-cultorum begonia. H 25cm (10in), S 30cm (12in). Is a sport of *B.* 'Merry Christmas' with spirally twisted leaves.
B. dichroa. Evergreen, cane-stemmed begonia. H 35cm (14in), S 25cm (10in). Oval leaves are mid-green, 12cm (5in) long; occasionally new leaves bear silver spots. Produces small, single, orange flowers, each with a white ovary, in summer.
B. disticha. See *B. stipulacea*.
♀ ***B. dregei*** (Mapleleaf begonia; illus. p.307). Semi-tuberous begonia. H 75cm (30in), S 35cm (14in). Has small, maple-like, lobed, purple-veined, bronze leaves, with red beneath and occasionally silver-speckled when young. Profuse, pendent, single, white flowers are borne in summer. Needs winter rest.
***B.* 'Duartei'** illus. p.307. Rex-cultorum begonia. H and S 45–60cm (18–24in). Has spirally twisted, red-haired, very dark green leaves, over 15cm (6in) long, with silver-grey streaks and almost black edges. Is difficult to grow to maturity.
B.* × *erythrophylla. See *B.* 'Erythrophylla'.
***B.* 'Erythrophylla',** syn. *B.* × *erythrophylla, B.* 'Feastii'. Evergreen, creeping, rhizomatous begonia. H 20cm (8in), S 23–30cm (9–12in). Thick, mid-green leaves, 8–15cm (3–6in) long, are almost rounded, with leaf stalks attached to centre of red undersides; slightly wavy margins have white hairs. Produces single, light pink flowers well above foliage, in early spring.
***B.* 'Feastii'.** See *B.* 'Erythrophylla'.
***B.* 'Flamboyant'.** Upright Tuberhybrida begonia. H 17cm (7in), S 15cm (6in). Leaves are slender and bright green. Has single, scarlet flowers in profusion in summer.
B. foliosa. Evergreen, shrub-like begonia. H 30–50cm (12–20in), S 30–35cm (12–14in). Bears erect, then arching stems and oval, toothed, dark green leaves, 1cm (½in) long. Has very small, single, white flowers in spring and autumn. Is susceptible to whitefly.
♀ ***B. fuchsioides*** (Fuchsia begonia). Evergreen, shrub-like begonia. H to 1.2m (4ft), S 30cm (1ft). Oval, toothed leaves are numerous and dark green, 4cm (1½in) long. Pendent, single, bright red flowers are borne in winter.
***B.* 'Gloire de Lorraine'** (Christmas begonia, Lorraine begonia). Evergreen, winter-flowering, Cheimantha begonia. H 30cm (12in), S 30–35cm (12–14in). Is well-branched with rounded, bright green leaves and single, white to pale pink flowers. Male flowers are sterile, female, highly infertile.
***B.* 'Gold Cascade'.** See *B.* 'Apricot Cascade'.
B. gracilis var. ***martiana*,** syn. *B. martiana.* Tuberous begonia. H 60–75cm (24–30in), S 40cm (16in). Has small, oval to lance-shaped, lobed, pale green or brown-green leaves with tapering tips and large, fragrant, single, pink flowers, 2.5cm (1in) across, in summer.
B. haageana. See *B. scharffii*.
***B.* 'Helen Lewis'** illus. p.307. Rex-cultorum begonia. H and S 45–60cm (18–24in). Has an erect rhizome and silky, deep royal purple leaves, 15–20cm (6–8in) long, with silver bands. Slightly hairy, single, cream flowers are produced in early summer.
B. imperialis illus. p.307. Rhizomatous begonia. H 13cm (5in), S 23cm (9in). Ovate, toothed, light green leaves, 10cm (4in) long, have puckered edges and silver-green splashes on the main veins. Produces sprays of sparse white flowers, to 1.5cm (½in) across, in winter.
***B.* 'Ingramii'** illus. p.307. Evergreen, shrub-like begonia. H 70cm (28in), S 45cm (18in). Produces elliptic, toothed, bright green leaves, 8cm (3in) long, and, intermittently from spring to autumn, masses of single, pink flowers on spreading branches.
***B.* 'Iron Cross'.** See *B. masoniana.*
***B.* 'Krefeld'.** Evergreen, winter-flowering, Rieger begonia. H 25cm (10in), S 30cm (12in). Is semi-tuberous with succulent stems, oval, mid-green leaves and masses of single, vivid orange or bright crimson flowers. Is very susceptible to botrytis and mildew at base of stems, so water by pot immersion.
***B.* 'Lucerna',** syn. *B.* 'Corallina de Lucerna'. Vigorous, evergreen, cane-stemmed begonia. H 2–2.2m (6–7ft), S 45–60cm (1½–2ft). Has oval, silver-spotted, bronze-green leaves, 25–35cm (10–14in) long, with tapered tips and, year-round, large panicles of single, deep pink flowers; male flowers remain almost closed.
***B.* 'Mac's Gold'.** Evergreen, creeping, rhizomatous begonia. H and S 20–25cm (8–10in). Star-shaped, lobed, yellow leaves, 8–15cm (3–6in) long, have chocolate-brown marks. Has single, pink flowers intermittently in spring-summer but in moderate quantity.
***B.* 'Madame Richard Galle'.** Upright Tuberhybrida begonia. H 25cm (10in), S 20cm (8in). Has masses of small, double, soft apricot flowers in summer.
B. manicata. Evergreen, erect, rhizomatous begonia. H 60cm (24in), S 30–40cm (12–16in). Bears large, oval, brown-mottled, green leaves and, below each leaf base, a collar of stiff, red hairs around leaf stalk. Produces single, pale pink flowers in very early spring. Propagate by plantlets during growing season. **'Crispa'** (syn. *B.m.* 'Cristata'; illus. p.307) has deeper pink flowers and light green leaves with crested margins. **'Cristata'** see *B.m.* 'Crispa'.
B. martiana. See *B. gracilis* var. *martiana.*
♀ ***B. masoniana*,** syn. *B.* 'Iron Cross' (Iron cross begonia; illus. p.307). Evergreen, creeping, rhizomatous begonia. H 45–60cm (18–24in), S 30–45cm (12–18in). Bears oval, toothed, rough, bright green leaves, 15cm (6in) long, with tapering tips and cross-shaped, black or dark brown centres. Has single, pink-flushed, white flowers during summer.
B. mazae. Evergreen, trailing, rhizomatous begonia. H to 23cm (9in), S indefinite. Bears rounded, red-veined, bronze-green leaves and in early spring fragrant, single, red-spotted, pink flowers. Is good for a hanging basket.
♀ ***B.* 'Merry Christmas'** (syn. *B.* 'Ruhrtal'; illus. p.307). Rex-cultorum begonia. H and S 25–30cm (10–12in). Has satiny, red leaves, 15–20cm (6–8in) long, each with an outer, broad band of emerald-green and a deep velvet-red centre, sometimes edged with grey.
♀ ***B. metallica*** (Metal-leaf begonia). Evergreen, shrub-like begonia. H 50cm–1.2m (20in–4ft), S 45cm (18in). Bears white-haired stems and oval, toothed, silver-haired, bronze-green leaves, 18cm (7in) long, with dark green veins, red beneath. Has single, pink flowers, with red bristles, in summer-autumn.
***B.* 'OliverTwist'** illus. p.307. Evergreen, creeping, rhizomatous begonia. H 45–60cm (18–24in), S 25–45cm (10–18in). Oval leaves are pale to mid-green, to 30cm (12in) long, with heavily crested edges. Has single, pink flowers in early spring.
B. olsoniae illus. p.307. Evergreen, compact, shrub-like begonia. H 23–30cm (9–12in), S 30cm (12in). Rounded, satiny, bronze-green leaves have cream veins. Bears single, very pale pink flowers, year-round, on arching, 30cm (12in) long stems.
***B.* 'Orange Cascade'.** See *B.* 'Apricot Cascade'.
♀ ***B.* 'Orange Rubra'** illus. p.307. Slow-growing, evergreen, cane-stemmed begonia. H 50cm (20in), S 45cm (18in). Oval leaves are light green. Produces abundant clusters of single, orange flowers all year.
***B.* 'Organdy'.** Weather-resistant Semperflorens begonia. H and S 15cm (6in). Has rounded, waxy, green-bronze leaves and pink, red or white flowers throughout summer until autumn frosts.
***B.* 'Orpha C. Fox'** illus. p.307. Evergreen, cane-stemmed begonia. H 1m (3ft), S 30cm (1ft). Oval, silver-spotted, olive-green leaves, 15cm (6in) long, are maroon beneath. Produces large clusters of single, bright pink flowers year-round.
B. paulensis. Evergreen, creeping, rhizomatous begonia. H and S 25–30cm (10–12in). Erect stems bear rounded, mid-green leaves, 15cm (6in) long, with 'seersucker' surfaces criss-crossed with a spider's web of veins. Produces single, cream-white flowers, with wine-coloured hairs, in late spring.
***B.* 'Président Carnot'.** Vigorous, evergreen, cane-stemmed begonia. H to 2.2m (7ft), S 45cm (1½ft). Erect stems bear 28cm (11in) long, 'angelwing', green leaves, with lighter spots. Produces large panicles of single, pink flowers, each 4cm (1½in) across, year-round.
***B.* 'Princess of Hanover'.** Rex-cultorum begonia. H and S 25–30cm (10–12in). Has spirally twisted, deep green leaves, 20cm (8in) long, with bands of silver edged with ruby-red; entire leaf surfaces are covered with fine, pink hairs.
B. prismatocarpa illus. p.307. Evergreen, creeping, rhizomatous begonia. H 15–20cm (6–8in), S 20–25cm (8–10in). Leaves are oval, lobed, light green and less than 8cm (3in) long. Produces single, bright yellow flowers year-round. Needs 60–65% relative humidity.
B. pustulata. Evergreen, creeping, rhizomatous begonia. H 15–20cm (6–8in), S 20–25cm (8–10in). Bears oval, fine-haired, dark green leaves, with small blisters or pustules, and single, rose-pink flowers in summer. Prefers min. 22–4°C (72–5°F) and 70–75% relative humidity. **'Argentea'** (syn. *B.* 'Silver'; illus. p.307) has silver-splashed leaves and creamy-white flowers.
***B.* 'Red Ascot'.** Semperflorens begonia. H and S 15cm (6in). Has rounded, emerald-green leaves and masses of crimson-red flowers in summer.
B. rex. Rhizomatous begonia, the parent of the Rex-cultorum begonias. H 25cm (10in), S 30cm (12in). Has 20–25cm (8–10in) long, heart-shaped, deep green leaves, with a metallic sheen zoned silvery-white above. Produces pink flowers in winter.
***B.* 'Roy Hartley'** illus. p.307. Upright Tuberhybrida begonia. H 60cm (2ft), S 45cm (18in). In summer, bears double, salmon-coloured flowers, with soft pink tinge. Colour depth depends on light intensity. Has few side shoots.
***B.* 'Ruhrtal'.** See *B.* 'Merry Christmas'.
***B. scharffii*,** syn. *B. haageana* illus. p.307. Evergreen, shrub-like begonia. H 60cm–1.2m (2–4ft), S 60cm (2ft). Stems are often covered with white hairs. Has oval, fine-haired, dark metallic-green leaves, 28cm (11in) long, with very tapered tips and reddish-green undersides. Produces single, pinkish-white flowers, each with a pink beard, from autumn to summer.
***B.* 'Scherzo'.** Evergreen, creeping, rhizomatous begonia. H 25–30cm (10–12in), S 30–35cm (12–14in). Oval leaves are small, highly serrated and yellow with black marks. Bears single, white flowers in early spring.
B. serratipetala illus. p.307. Evergreen, trailing, shrub-like begonia. H and S 45cm (18in). Obliquely oval leaves are highly serrated and bronze-green,

with raised, deep pink spots. Produces mostly female, single, deep pink flowers intermittently throughout the year. Prefers 60% relative humidity, but with fairly dry roots.
***B.* 'Silver'.** See *B. pustulata* 'Argentea'.
***B.* 'Silver Helen Teupel'.** Rex-cultorum begonia. H and S 30–35cm (12–14in). Has long, deeply cut, silver leaves, each with a glowing pink centre, giving a feathered effect.
B. stipulacea, syn. *B. angularis, B.disticha, B. zebrina.* Evergreen, cane-stemmed begonia. H 60cm–1.2m (2–4ft), S 30cm (1ft). Bears well-branched, angular stems and oval, wavy-edged, 20cm (8in) long, grey-green leaves, with silver-grey veins, pale green beneath. Single, white flowers are produced in winter-spring.
***B.* 'Sugar Candy'.** Tuberhybrida begonia. H 60cm (24in), S 45cm (18in). Leaves are mid-green. Produces double, clear pink flowers in summer.
♀ ***B. sutherlandii*** illus. p.307. Trailing, tuberous begonia. H 1m (3ft), S indefinite. Slender stems carry small, lance-shaped, lobed, bright green leaves, with red veins, and, in summer, loose clusters of single, orange flowers in profusion. In late autumn, leaves and stems collapse prior to winter dormancy. Makes an excellent hanging-basket plant. Is particularly susceptible to mildew.
♀ ***B.* 'Thurstonii'** illus. p.307. Evergreen, shrub-like begonia. H to 1.2m (4ft), S 45cm (1½ft). Has rounded to oval, smooth, glossy, bronze-green leaves, with dark red veins, and, in summer, bears single, pink flowers.
♀ ***B.* 'Tiger Paws'** illus. p.307. Evergreen, creeping, rhizomatous begonia. H 15cm (6in), S 25–30cm (10–12in). Small, rounded, striking bright green leaves, with yellow and brown splashes, have bristly, white hairs on the margins. Many clusters of small, white flowers are carried well above the foliage in spring.
B. versicolor. Evergreen, creeping, rhizomatous begonia. H 15cm (6in), S 15–30cm (6–12in). Produces broadly oval or oblong, velvety leaves, 8cm (3in) long, in shades of mahogany, apple-green and maroon, and, in spring-summer, single, salmon-pink flowers. Provide min. 16–19°C (61–6°F) with 65–70% relative humidity.
B.* x *weltoniensis. See *B.* 'Weltoniensis'.
***B.* 'Weltoniensis',** syn. *B.* x *weltoniensis.* (Mapleleaf begonia; illus. p.307). Semi-tuberous begonia with a shrub-like habit. H 30–50cm (12–20in), S 30cm (12in). Has small, oval, long-pointed, toothed, dark green leaves. Heads of 5–8 single, pink or white flowers appear from leaf axils in summer.
B. xanthina. Evergreen, bushy, creeping, rhizomatous begonia. H 25–30cm (10–12in), S 30–35cm (12–14in). Bears oval, dark green leaves, 15–23cm (6–9in) long, with yellow veins, purple and hairy beneath. Pendent, single, orange-yellow flowers are borne in summer. Provide min. 21–4°C (70–75°F) with 75% relative humidity.
B. zebrina. See *B. stipulacea.*

Begonia
Angelwing. See *Begonia coccinea.*
Christmas. See *Begonia* 'Gloire de Lorraine'.
Eyelash. See *Begonia bowerae*, illus. p.307.
Fuchsia. See *Begonia fuchsioides.*
Iron cross. See *Begonia masoniana*, illus. p.307.
Lorraine. See *Begonia* 'Gloire de Lorraine'.
Mapleleaf. See *Begonia dregei; Begonia* 'Weltoniensis', illus. p.307.
Metal-leaf. See *Begonia metallica.*
Watermelon. See *Elatostema repens*, illus. p.315.

BELAMCANDA

IRIDACEAE

Genus of summer-flowering bulbs, grown for their iris-like flowers. Frost hardy, but protect in cold winters. Needs sun and well-drained, humus-rich soil. Propagate by seed in spring.
B. chinensis. Summer-flowering bulb. H 45cm–1m (1½–3ft), S 15–25cm (6–10in). Carries a fan of sword-shaped, semi-erect leaves. A loosely branched stem bears a succession of flattish, orange-red flowers, 4–5cm (1½–2in) across, with darker blotches. Seeds are shiny and black.

Bell
Canterbury. See *Campanula medium.*
Silver. See *Halesia.*
Spring. See *Olsynium douglasii.*
Bell heather. See *Erica cinerea.*
Belladonna lily. See *Amaryllis belladonna*, illus. p.424.

BELLEVALIA

LILIACEAE/HYACINTHACEAE

Genus of spring-flowering bulbs, similar to *Muscari*, but with longer, more tubular flowers. Some species have ornamental value, but most are uninteresting horticulturally. Frost hardy. Needs an open, sunny position and well-drained soil that dries out in summer. Propagate by seed, preferably in autumn.
B. hyacinthoides, syn. *Strangweja spicata*, illus. p.448.
B. paradoxa of gardens. See *B. pycnantha.*
B. pycnantha, syn. *B. paradoxa* of gardens, *Muscari paradoxum* of gardens, *M. pycnantha.* Spring-flowering bulb. H to 40cm (16in), S 5–8cm (2–3in). Has strap-shaped, semi-erect, basal, greyish-green leaves. Tubular, deep dusky-blue flowers, 0.5cm (¼in) long and with yellow tips, appear in a dense, conical spike.

Bellflower. See *Campanula.*
Bearded. See *Campanula barbata*, illus. p.368.
Canary Island. See *Canarina canariensis*, illus.p.217.
Chilean. See *Lapageria rosea*, illus. p.206.
Chimney. See *Campanula pyramidalis.*
Gland. See *Adenophora.*
Nettle-leaved. See *Campanula trachelium*, illus. p.258.
Bell-flowered cherry. See *Prunus campanulata.*

BELLIS
Daisy

COMPOSITAE/ASTERACEAE

Genus of perennials, some grown as biennials for spring bedding. Fully hardy. Grow in sun or semi-shade and in fertile, very well-drained soil. Dead-head regularly. Propagate by seed in early summer or by division after flowering.
B. perennis (Common daisy). Stoloniferous, carpeting perennial. Cultivars are grown as biennials. H and S 15–20cm (6–8in). All have inversely lance-shaped to spoon-shaped, mid-green leaves and semi-double to fully double flower heads in spring. Large-flowered (flower heads to 8cm/3in) wide) and miniature-flowered (flower heads to 2½cm/1in) wide) cultivars are available. **Habanera Series** cultivars bear long-petalled, pink, white or red flower heads, to 6cm (2.5in) across, in early summer.
♀ **Pomponette Series** (illus. p.339) cultivars bear double, pink, white or red flower heads, to 4cm (1½in) across, with quilled petals. **Roggli Series** cultivars flower early and prolifically, with semi-double, red, rose-pink, salmon-pink or white flower heads, to 3cm (1¼in) across. ♀ **Tasso Series** cultivars have double, pink, white or red flower heads, to 6cm (2½in) across, with quilled petals.

Bells
Fairy. See *Disporum.*
Temple. See *Smithiantha cinnabarina.*
Yellow. See *Tecoma stans*, illus. p.92.
Bells of Ireland. See *Moluccella laevis*, illus. p.347.
Bellwort. See *Uvularia grandiflora*, illus. p.284.
Beloperone guttata. See *Justicia brandegeeana.*
Benjamin. See *Lindera benzoin*, illus. p.127.
Bentham's cornel. See *Cornus capitata.*

BERBERIDOPSIS

FLACOURTIACEAE

Genus of one species of evergreen, woody-stemmed, twining climber. Frost hardy. Dislikes strong winds and strong sun and is best grown in a north or west aspect. Soil, preferably lime-free, should be moist but well-drained. Cut out dead growth in spring; train to required shape. Propagate by seed in spring or by stem cuttings or layering in late summer or autumn.
B. corallina illus. p.207.

BERBERIS
Barberry

BERBERIDACEAE

Genus of deciduous, semi-evergreen or evergreen, spiny shrubs, grown mainly for their rounded to cup-shaped flowers, with usually yellow sepals and petals, and for their fruits. The evergreens are also cultivated for their leaves, the deciduous shrubs for their colourful autumn foliage. Fully to frost hardy. Requires sun or semi-shade and any but waterlogged soil. Propagate species by seed in autumn, deciduous hybrids and cultivars by softwood or semi-ripe cuttings in summer, evergreen hybrids and cultivars by semi-ripe cuttings in summer. All parts may cause mild stomach upset if ingested; contact with the spines may irritate skin.
B. aggregata. Deciduous, bushy shrub. H and S 1.5m (5ft). Fully hardy. Oblong to oval, mid-green leaves redden in autumn. Dense clusters of pale yellow flowers appear in late spring or early summer and are followed by egg-shaped, white-bloomed, red fruits.
B. buxifolia. Semi-evergreen or deciduous, arching shrub. H 2.5m (8ft), S 3m (10ft). Fully hardy. Has oblong to oval, spine-tipped, leathery, dark green leaves. Deep orange-yellow flowers appear from early to mid-spring and are followed by spherical, black fruits with a white bloom.
B. calliantha. Evergreen, bushy shrub. H and S 1–1.5m (3–5ft). Fully hardy. Has oblong, sharply spiny, glossy, green leaves, white beneath, and large, pale yellow flowers in late spring, followed by egg-shaped, black fruits with a white bloom.
B. candidula. Evergreen, bushy, compact shrub. H and S 1m (3ft). Fully hardy. Leaves are narrowly oblong, glossy, dark green, white beneath. Has bright yellow flowers in late spring, then egg-shaped, blue-purple fruits.
***B.* x *carminea* 'Barbarossa'** illus. p.144. **'Pirate King'** is a deciduous, arching shrub. H 2m (6ft), S 3m (10ft). Fully hardy. Bears oblong, dark green leaves. In late spring and early summer produces clusters of yellow flowers, followed by spherical, pale red fruits.
***B.* 'Chenault'.** See *B.* 'Chenaultii'.
***B.* 'Chenaultii',** syn. *B.* 'Chenault'. Evergreen, bushy shrub. H 1.5m (5ft), S 2m (6ft). Fully hardy. Narrowly oblong, wavy-edged, glossy, dark green leaves set off golden-yellow flowers in late spring and early summer. Bears egg-shaped, blue-black fruits.
B. coxii. Evergreen, bushy, dense shrub. H 2m (6ft), S 3m (10ft). Fully hardy. Produces narrowly oval, glossy, dark green leaves with white undersides and, in late spring, yellow flowers. Egg-shaped, blue-black fruits have a grey-blue bloom.
♀ ***B. darwinii*** illus. p.113.
B. empetrifolia illus. p.153.
B. gagnepainii var. ***lanceifolia*** illus. p.127.
B. jamesiana. Vigorous, deciduous, arching shrub. H and S 4m (12ft). Fully hardy. Yellow flowers in late spring are followed by pendent racemes of spherical, red berries. Oval, dark green leaves redden in autumn.
B. julianae. Dense, bushy, evergreen shrub. H 2.5m (8ft), S 3m (10ft). Fully hardy. Has glossy, dark green leaves yellow flowers in late spring and early summer, and egg-shaped, blue-black fruits in autumn.
***B. linearifolia* 'Orange King'** illus. p.131.
B.* x *lologensis. Vigorous, evergreen, arching shrub. H 3m (10ft), S 5m (15ft). Fully hardy. Has broadly oblong, glossy, dark green leaves. Profuse clusters of orange flowers are borne from mid- to late spring. **'Stapehill'** illus. p.131.
***B.* x *ottawensis* 'Purpurea'.** See *B.* x *o.* f. *purpurea* 'Superba'.

♀ *B.* × *o.* f. *purpurea* **'Superba'** (syn. *B.* × *o.* 'Purpurea') is a deciduous, arching shrub. H and S 2.5m (8ft). Fully hardy. Produces rounded to oval, deep reddish-purple leaves. Bears small, red-tinged, yellow flowers in late spring, then egg-shaped, red fruits in autumn.
***B.* 'Park Jewel'.** See *B.* 'Parkjuweel'.
***B.* 'Parkjuweel',** syn. *B.* 'Park Jewel'. Semi-evergreen, bushy, rounded shrub. H and S 1m (3ft). Fully hardy. Leaves are oval, glossy and bright green; some turn red in autumn. Flowers are of little value.
B. polyantha of gardens. See *B. prattii*.
B. prattii, syn. *B. polyantha* of gardens. Deciduous, bushy shrub. H and S 3m (10ft). Fully hardy. Has oblong, glossy, dark green leaves. Large clusters of small, yellow flowers in late summer are followed by a profusion of long-lasting, egg-shaped, coral-pink fruits.
***B.* × *rubrostilla*.** See *B.* 'Rubrostilla'.
***B.* 'Rubrostilla',** syn. *B.* × *rubrostilla*, illus. p.168.
***B. sargentiana*.** Evergreen, bushy shrub. H and S 2m (6ft). Fully hardy. Leaves are oblong, glossy, bright green. Yellow flowers produced in late spring and early summer are succeeded by egg-shaped, blue-black fruits.
♀ ***B.* × *stenophylla*** illus. p.131.
♀ **'Corallina Compacta'** illus. p.362.
♀ ***B. thunbergii*.** Deciduous, arching, dense shrub. H 2m (6ft), S 3m (10ft). Fully hardy. Broadly oval, pale to mid-green leaves turn brilliant orange-red in autumn. Small, red-tinged, pale yellow flowers appear in mid-spring, followed by egg-shaped, bright red fruits.
f. ***atropurpurea*** illus. p.127.
♀ **'Atropurpurea Nana'** (syn. *B.t.* 'Crimson Pygmy'), H and S 60cm (24in), bears reddish-purple foliage. **'Aurea'** illus. p.166. **'Crimson Pygmy'** see *B.t.* 'Atropurpurea Nana'. Upright branches of **'Erecta'** spread with age. ♀ **'Golden Ring'** has purple leaves narrowly margined with golden-yellow, turning red in autumn, and produces red fruit. ♀ **'Rose Glow'** has reddish-purple leaves marbled with pink and white.
***B. verruculosa*.** Slow-growing, evergreen, bushy shrub. H and S 1.5m (5ft). Fully hardy. Glossy, dark green leaves have blue-white undersides. Clusters of small, cup-shaped, bright yellow flowers in late spring and early summer are followed by blue-black fruits.
***B. wilsoniae*.** Deciduous or semi-evergreen, bushy shrub. H 1m (3ft), S 1.5m (5ft). Fully hardy. Narrowly oblong, grey-green leaves turn bright orange-red in autumn. In late spring and early summer has yellow flowers, then showy, spherical, coral-red fruits.

BERCHEMIA
RHAMNACEAE

Genus of deciduous, twining climbers, grown for their leaves and fruit. Is useful for covering walls, fences and tree stumps. Fully hardy. Grow in sun or shade, in any we ll-drained soil. Propagate by seed in autumn or spring, by semi-ripe cuttings in summer or by layering or root cuttings in winter.
***B. racemosa* 'Variegata'.** Deciduous, twining climber. H 5m (15ft) or more. Has heart-shaped, green leaves, 3–8cm (1¼–3in) long and paler beneath, that are variegated creamy-white. Small, bell-shaped, greenish-white flowers in summer are followed by rounded, green fruits that turn red, then black.

Bergamot. See *Monarda*.

BERGENIA,
syn. MEGASEA
SAXIFRAGACEAE

Genus of evergreen perennials with thick, usually large, rounded to oval or spoon-shaped, leathery leaves, with indented veins, that make ideal ground cover. Fully to frost hardy. Tolerates sun or shade and any well-drained soil, but leaf colour is best on poor soil and in full sun. Propagate by division in spring after flowering.
***B.* 'Abendglut',** syn. *B.* 'Evening Glow'. Evergreen, clump-forming perennial. H 23cm (9in), S 30cm (12in). Fully hardy. Bears rosettes of oval, crinkled, short-stemmed, maroon leaves, from which arise racemes of open cup-shaped, semi-double, deep magenta flowers in spring.
♀ ***B.* 'Ballawley'.** Evergreen, clump-forming perennial. H and S 60cm (24in). Fully hardy. Large, rounded to oval, flat, deep green leaves turn red in winter. Racemes of cup-shaped, bright crimson flowers are borne on red stems in spring. Shelter from cold winds.
***B. beesiana*.** See *B. purpurascens*.
B. ciliata illus. p.277.
***B. cordifolia*.** Evergreen, clump-forming perennial. H 45cm (18in), S 60cm (24in). Fully hardy. Leaves are rounded, puckered and crinkle-edged. Produces racemes of open cup-shaped, light pink flowers in spring.
♀ **'Purpurea'** illus. p.277.
***B. crassifolia*.** Evergreen, clump-forming perennial. H 30cm (12in), S 45cm (18in). Fully hardy. Has oval- or spoon-shaped, fleshy, flat leaves that turn mahogany in winter. Bears spikes of open cup-shaped, lavender-pink flowers in spring.
***B.* 'Evening Glow'.** See *B.* 'Abendglut'.
♀ ***B.* 'Morgenröte',** syn. *B.* 'Morning Red'. Evergreen, clump-forming perennial. H 45cm (18in), S 30cm (12in). Fully hardy. Leaves are rounded, crinkled and deep green. Spikes of open cup-shaped, deep carmine flowers in spring are often followed by a second crop in summer.
***B.* 'Morning Red'.** See *B.* 'Morgenröte'.
♀ ***B. purpurascens***, syn. *B. beesiana*. Evergreen, clump-forming perennial. H 45cm (18in), S 30cm (12in). Fully hardy. Oval to spoon-shaped, flat, dark green leaves turn beetroot-red in late autumn. In spring bears racemes of open cup-shaped, rich red flowers.
♀ ***B.* × *schmidtii*.** Evergreen, clump-forming perennial. H 30cm (12in), S 60cm (24in). Fully hardy. Oval, flat leaves have toothed margins. Sprays of open cup-shaped, soft pink flowers are borne in early spring on short stems.
♀ ***B.* 'Silberlicht',** syn. *B.* 'Silver Light', illus. p.276.
***B.* 'Silver Light'.** See *B.* 'Silberlicht'.
***B. stracheyi*.** Evergreen, clump-forming perennial. H 23cm (9in), S 30cm (12in). Fully hardy. Small, rounded, flat leaves form neat rosettes, among which nestle heads of open cup-shaped, white or pink flowers in spring.
***B.* 'Sunningdale'.** Evergreen, clump-forming perennial. H 60cm (24in), S 30cm (12in). Fully hardy. Rounded, slightly crinkled, deep green leaves are mahogany beneath. Bears racemes of open cup-shaped, lilac-carmine flowers on red stalks in spring.

BERKHEYA
COMPOSITAE/ASTERACEAE

Genus of summer-flowering perennials. Frost to half hardy, but, except in mild areas, grow most species against a south- or west-facing wall. Needs full sun and fertile, well-drained soil. Sow seed in autumn or divide in spring.
B. macrocephala illus. p.266.

Berlin poplar. See *Populus berolinensis*.
Bermuda lily. See *Lilium longiflorum*, illus. p.416.
Berry bladderfern. See *Cystopteris bulbifera*.

BERTOLONIA
MELASTOMATACEAE

Genus of evergreen perennials, grown for their foliage. Frost tender, min. 15°C (59°F) but preferably warmer. Requires a fairly shaded position and high humidity, although soil should not be waterlogged. Propagate by tip or leaf cuttings in spring or summer.
***B. marmorata*.** Evergreen, rosette-forming perennial. H 15cm (6in) or more in flower, S 45cm (18in). Broadly oval, slightly fleshy leaves have heart-shaped bases, silvery midribs and puckered surfaces, and are reddish-purple below, velvety green above. Intermittently produces spikes of saucer-shaped, pinkish-purple flowers.

BERZELIA
BRUNIACEAE

Genus of evergreen, heather-like, summer-flowering shrubs, grown for their flowers. Frost tender, min. 7°C (45°F). Requires full sun and well-drained, neutral to acid soil. Water containerized plants moderately, less when not in full growth. Plants may be cut back lightly after flowering. Propagate by seed in spring or by semi-ripe cuttings in late summer.
***B. lanuginosa*.** Evergreen, erect shrub with soft-haired, young shoots. H and S to 1m (3ft). Has small, heather-like leaves. Compact, spherical heads of tiny, creamy-white flowers are carried in dense, terminal clusters in summer.

BESCHORNERIA
AGAVACEAE

Genus of perennial succulents with narrowly lance-shaped leaves forming erect, almost stemless, basal rosettes. Half hardy. Needs full sun and very well-drained soil. Propagate by seed or division in spring or summer.
♀ ***B. yuccoides*** illus. p.481.

Besom heath. See *Erica scoparia*.

BESSERA
LILIACEAE/ALLIACEAE

Genus of summer-flowering bulbs, grown for their striking, brightly coloured flowers. Half hardy. Needs an open, sunny situation and well-drained soil. Propagate by seed in spring.
B. elegans (Coral drops). Summer-flowering bulb. H to 60cm (24in), S 8–10cm (3–4in). Has long, narrow, erect, basal leaves. Each leafless stem bears pendent, bell-shaped, bright red flowers on long, slender stalks.

***Betonica officinalis*.** See *Stachys officinalis*.
Betony. See *Stachys officinalis*.

BETULA
Birch
BETULACEAE

Genus of deciduous trees and shrubs, grown for their bark and autumn colour. Fully hardy. Needs sun and moist but well-drained soil; some species prefer acid soil. Transplant young trees in autumn. Propagate by grafting in late winter or by softwood cuttings in early summer.
♀ ***B. albosinensis*** illus. p.70.
B. alleghaniensis, syn. *B. lutea* (Yellow birch). Deciduous, upright, open tree, often multi-stemmed. H 12m (40ft) or more, S 3m (10ft). Smooth, glossy, golden-brown bark peels in thin shreds. Oval, mid- to pale green leaves rapidly turn gold in autumn. Bears yellow-green catkins in spring.
B. ermanii illus. p.68.
***B. jacquemontii*.** See *B. utilis* var. *jacquemontii*.
***B.* 'Jermyns'.** See *B. utilis* var. *jacquemontii* 'Jermyns'.
***B. lutea*.** See *B. alleghaniensis*.
B. maximowicziana (Monarch birch). Fast-growing, deciduous, broad-headed tree. H 18m (60ft), S 3m (10ft). Has orange-brown or pink bark, and racemes of yellowish catkins in spring. Large, oval, mid-green leaves turn bright butter-yellow in autumn.
B. nana illus. p.361.
B. papyrifera illus. p.68.
♀ ***B. pendula*** (Silver birch). Deciduous, broadly columnar or conical, graceful tree. H 25m (80ft) or more, S 10m (30ft). Has slender, drooping shoots and silver-white bark that becomes black and rugged at base of trunk with age. Yellow-brown catkins appear in spring. Oval, bright green leaves turn yellow in autumn.
'Dalecarlica' has a more upright habit, with pendant, shorter shoots at the end of the branches, and much more deeply cut leaves. ♀ **'Laciniata'** has a narrow crown. ♀ **'Tristis'** illus. p.69.
'Youngii' illus. p.88.
***B. platyphylla* var. *szechuanica*.** See *B. szechuanica*.
B. szechuanica, syn. *B. platyphylla* var. *szechuanica* (Szechuan birch). Vigorous, deciduous, open tree with stiff branches. H 14m (46ft), S 2.5m (8ft). Bark is strikingly chalky-white when mature. Has triangular to oval, serrated, leathery, deep green leaves that turn brilliant gold in autumn. Bears yellow-green catkins in spring.
B. utilis (Himalayan birch). Deciduous, upright, open tree. H 18m (60ft), S 10m

(30ft). Paper-thin, peeling bark varies from creamy-white to dark copper-brown. Yellow-brown catkins are borne in spring. Oval, mid-green leaves, hairy beneath when young, turn golden-yellow in autumn. var. ***jacquemontii*** (syn *B. jacquemontii*) illus. p.79. 🏆 var. ***jacquemontii* 'Jermyns'** (syn. *B.* 'Jermyns'), H 15m (50ft), S 10m (30ft), has bright white bark and very long, elegant, yellow, male catkins.

Bhutan pine. See *Pinus wallichiana*, illus. p.99.

Biarum

ARACEAE

Genus of mainly autumn-flowering, tuberous perennials with tiny flowers carried on a pencil-shaped spadix, enclosed within a tubular spathe. Upper part of spathe is hooded or flattened out and showy. Frost hardy, but during cold, wet winters protect in a cold frame or greenhouse. Needs a sunny position and well-drained soil. Dry out tubers when dormant in summer. Propagate in autumn by seed or offsets.

B. eximium. Early autumn-flowering, tuberous perennial. H and S 8–10cm (3–4in). Lance-shaped, semi-erect, basal leaves follow stemless, tubular, velvety, blackish-maroon spathe, up to 15cm (6in) long and often lying flat on ground. Upper part is flattened out. Spadix is upright and black.

B. tenuifolium illus. p.455.

Bidens atrosanguinea. See *Cosmos atrosanguineus*.

Big tree. See *Sequoiadendron giganteum*, illus. p.98.

Big-cone pine. See *Pinus coulteri*, illus. p.98.

Bignonia

BIGNONIACEAE

Genus of one species of evergreen, tendril climber. Frost hardy; in cool areas may lose its leaves in winter. Needs sun and fertile soil to flower well. If necessary, prune in spring. Propagate by stem cuttings in summer or autumn or by layering in winter.

B. capensis. See *Tecoma capensis*.

B. capreolata, syn. *Doxantha capreolata* (Cross vine, Trumpet flower). Evergreen, tendril climber. H 10m (30ft) or more. Each leaf has 2 narrowly oblong leaflets and a branched tendril. In summer, funnel-shaped, reddish-orange flowers appear in clusters in leaf axils. Pea-pod-shaped fruits, to 15cm (6in) long, are produced in autumn.

B. grandiflora. See *Campsis grandiflora*.

B. jasminoides. See *Pandorea jasminoides*.

B. pandorana. See *Pandorea pandorana*.

B. radicans. See *Campsis radicans*.

B. stans. See *Tecoma stans*.

Bilberry. See *Vaccinium myrtillus*.

Bilderdykia. See *Fallopia*.

Billardiera

PITTOSPORACEAE

Genus of evergreen, woody-stemmed, twining climbers, grown mainly for their fruits. Half hardy. Grow in any well-drained soil, in a sheltered position and partial shade. Propagate by seed in spring or stem cuttings in summer or autumn.

🏆 ***B. longiflora*** illus. p.216.

Billbergia

BROMELIACEAE

Genus of evergreen, rosette-forming perennials, grown for their flowers and foliage. Frost tender, min. 5–7°C (41–5°F). Requires semi-shade and well-drained soil, ideally adding sphagnum moss or plastic chips used for orchid culture. Water moderately when in full growth, sparingly at other times. Propagate by division or offsets after flowering or in late spring.

B. nutans (Queen's tears; illus. p.273). Evergreen, clump-forming, tubular-rosetted perennial. H and S to 40cm (16in). Strap-shaped leaves are usually dark green. In spring, pendent clusters of tubular, purple-blue-edged, lime-green flowers emerge from pink bracts.

B. rhodocyanea. See *Aechmea fasciata*.

🏆 ***B. × windii*** (Angel's tears). Evergreen, clump-forming, tubular-rosetted perennial. H and S to 40cm (16in). Is similar to *B. nutans*, but produces broader, spreading, grey-green leaves and larger bracts. Flowers intermittently from spring to autumn.

Biota orientalis. See *Platycladus orientalis*.

Birch. See *Betula*.
- **Arctic.** See *Betula nana*, illus. p.361.
- **Canoe.** See *Betula papyrifera*, illus. p.68.
- **Himalayan.** See *Betula utilis*.
- **Monarch.** See *Betula maximowicziana*.
- **Paper.** See *Betula papyrifera*, illus. p.68.
- **Silver.** See *Betula pendula*.
- **Szechuan.** See *Betula szechuanica*.
- **Weeping.** See *Betula pendula* 'Tristis', illus. p.69.
- **West Himalayan.** See *Betula utilis* var. *jacquemontii*, illus. p.79.
- **White Chinese.** See *Betula albosinensis*, illus. p.70.
- **Yellow.** See *Betula alleghaniensis*.
- **Young's weeping.** See *Betula pendula* 'Youngii', illus. p.88.

Bird cherry. See *Prunus padus*, illus. p.72.
- **Virginian.** See *Prunus virginiana*.

Bird's-eye primrose. See *Primula farinosa*, illus. p.280.

Bird's-foot ivy. See *Hedera helix* 'Pedata'.

Bird's-foot violet. See *Viola pedata*, illus. p.381.

Bird's-nest bromeliad. See *Nidularium innocentii*.

Bird's-nest fern. See *Asplenium nidus*, illus. p.325.

Bird-catcher tree. See *Pisonia umbellifera*.

Bird-of-paradise flower. See *Strelitzia*.

Birthroot. See *Trillium erectum*, illus. p.277.

Birthwort. See *Aristolochia*.

Bishop pine. See *Pinus muricata*, illus. p.99.

Bishop's cap. See *Astrophytum myriostigma*, illus. p.482.

Bishop's mitre. See *Astrophytum myriostigma*, illus. p.482.

Bishop's weed, Variegated. See *Aegopodium podagraria* 'Variegatum', illus. p.286.

Bistort. See *Persicaria bistorta*.

Biting stonecrop. See *Sedum acre*, illus. p.396.

Bitter cress. See *Cardamine*.

Bitter orange, Japanese. See *Poncirus trifoliata*.

Bitter root. See *Lewisia rediviva*, illus. pp.385 and 391.

Bitternut. See *Carya cordiformis*.

Bitternut hickory. See *Carya cordiformis*.

Bittersweet
- **American.** See *Celastrus scandens*.
- **Oriental.** See *Celastrus orbiculatus*.

Black alder. See *Alnus glutinosa*.

Black bamboo. See *Phyllostachys nigra*.

Black bean. See *Kennedia nigricans*.

Black bean tree. See *Castanospermum*.

Black cherry. See *Prunus serotina*, illus. p.61.

Black chokeberry. See *Aronia melanocarpa*, illus. p.132.

Black cottonwood. See *Populus trichocarpa*.

Black false hellebore. See *Veratrum nigrum*, illus. p.226.

Black gum. See *Nyssa sylvatica*, illus. p.67.

Black huckleberry. See *Gaylussacia baccata*.

Black Jack oak. See *Quercus marilandica*, illus. p.76.

Black mulberry. See *Morus nigra*.

Black oak. See *Quercus velutina*.

Black pine. See *Pinus jeffreyi*, illus. p.99; *Pinus nigra*.
- **Japanese.** See *Pinus thunbergii*, illus. p.102.

Black poplar. See *Populus nigra*.

Black sarana. See *Fritillaria camschatcensis*, illus. p.429.

Black spruce. See *Picea mariana*.

Black tree fern. See *Cyathea medullaris*.

Black walnut. See *Juglans nigra*, illus. p.63.

Black willow. See *Salix gracilistyla* 'Melanostachys'.

Blackberry. See *Rubus*.

Blackboy. See *Xanthorrhoea*.

Black-eyed Susan. See *Rudbeckia fulgida; Thunbergia alata*, illus. p.214.

Blackthorn. See *Prunus spinosa*.

Bladder cherry. See *Physalis alkekengi*.

Bladder nut. See *Staphylea*.

Bladder senna. See *Colutea arborescens*, illus. p.142.

Blanket flower. See *Gaillardia*.

Blechnum

BLECHNACEAE

Genus of evergreen or semi-evergreen ferns. Fully hardy to frost tender, min. 5°C (41°F). Most species prefer semi-shade. Requires moist, neutral to acid soil. Remove fading fronds regularly. Propagate *B. penna-marina* by division in spring, other species by spores in late summer.

B. alpinum. See *B. penna-marina*.

B. chilense of gardens. See *B. tabulare*.

🏆 ***B. penna-marina***, syn. *B. alpinum*, illus. p.322.

🏆 ***B. spicant*** (Hard fern). Evergreen fern. H 30–75cm (12–30in), S 30–45cm (12–18in). Fully hardy. Bears narrowly lance-shaped, indented, leathery, spreading, dark green fronds. Prefers shade and peaty or leafy soil.

🏆 ***B. tabulare***, syn. *B. chilense* of gardens. Evergreen or semi-evergreen fern. H 30cm–1m (1–3ft), S 30–60cm (1–2ft). Half hardy. Outer, mid-green, sterile fronds are broadly lance-shaped, heavily indented and arranged symmetrically. Inner fertile fronds are brown and fringed.

Bleeding heart. See *Dicentra spectabilis*, illus. p.247.

Blessed Mary's thistle. See *Silybum marianum*, illus. p.334.

Bletilla

ORCHIDACEAE

See also ORCHIDS.

B. hyacinthina. See *B. striata*.

B. striata, syn. *B. hyacinthina* illus. p.309. Deciduous, terrestrial orchid. H to 60cm (24in). Half hardy. In late spring or early summer bears magenta or white flowers, 3cm (1¼in) long, and broadly lance-shaped leaves, 50cm (20in) long. Needs shade in summer.

Blood flower. See *Asclepias curassavica; Scadoxus multiflorus* supsp. *katherinae*, illus.p.413.
- **Mexican.** See *Distictis buccinatoria*, illus. p.200.

Blood leaf. See *Iresine lindenii*.

Blood lily. See *Haemanthus coccineus*, illus. p.451.

Bloodroot. See *Sanguinaria canadensis*, illus. p.375.

Bloody cranesbill. See *Geranium sanguineum*, illus. p.366.

Bloomeria

LILIACEAE/ALLIACEAE

Genus of onion-like, spring-flowering bulbs, with spherical flower heads on leafless stems, which die down in summer. Frost hardy. Needs a sheltered, sunny situation and well-drained soil. Propagate by seed in autumn or by division in late summer or autumn.

B. crocea. Late spring-flowering bulb. H to 30cm (12in), S to 10cm (4in). Long, narrow, semi-erect, basal leaves die at flowering time. Each leafless stem carries a loose, spherical head, 10–15cm (4–6in) across, of star-shaped, dark-striped, yellow flowers.

Blue amaryllis. See *Worsleya*.

Blue Atlas cedar. See *Cedrus atlantica* f. *glauca*, illus. p.97.

Blue candle. See *Myrtillocactus geometrizans*, illus. p.472.

Blue cupidone. See *Catananche*.

Blue dawn flower. See *Ipomoea indica*, illus. p.202.

Blue Douglas fir. See *Pseudotsuga menziesii* var. *glauca*, illus. p.98.

Blue fescue. See *Festuca glauca*.

Blue flag. See *Iris versicolor*, illus. p.237.

Blue grama. See *Bouteloua gracilis*, illus. p.319.

Blue gum. See *Eucalyptus globulus*.

Blue holly. See *Ilex × meserveae*.
Blue lace flower. See *Trachymene coerulea*.
Blue marguerite. See *Felicia amelloides*.
Blue oat grass. See *Helictotrichon sempervirens*, illus. p.319.
Blue passion flower. See *Passiflora caerulea*, illus. p.212.
Blue poppy. See *Meconopsis betonicifolia*, illus. p.259; *M. grandis*, illus. p.259.
Blue potato bush. See *Solanum rantonnetii*.
Blue star. See *Amsonia*.
Blue trumpet vine. See *Thunbergia grandiflora*.
Bluebell. See *Hyacinthoides*.
California. See *Phacelia campanularia*, illus. p.346.
English. See *Hyacinthoides non-scripta*, illus. p.430.
New Zealand. See *Wahlenbergia albomarginata*.
Spanish. See *Hyacinthoides × massartiana*, illus. p.430.
Bluebell creeper. See *Sollya*.
Blueberry
Highbush. See *Vaccinium corymbosum*, illus. p.156.
Low-bush. See *Vaccinium angustifolium* var. *laevifolium*, illus. p.168.
Blueberry ash. See *Elaeocarpus cyaneus*.
Bluebottle. See *Centaurea cyanus*.
Blue-flowered torch. See *Tillandsia lindenii*, illus. p.273.
Bluets, Creeping. See *Hedyotis michauxii*, illus. p.395.
Blushing bromeliad. See *Neoregelia carolinae; Nidularium fulgens*.
Blushing philodendron. See *Philodendron erubescens*.
Bo. See *Ficus religiosa*.
Boat lily. See *Tradescantia spathacea*.
Bocconia cordata. See *Macleaya cordata*.

BOENNINGHAUSENIA

RUTACEAE

Genus of one species of deciduous sub-shrub, usually with soft, herbaceous stems, grown for its foliage and flowers. Frost hardy, although cut to ground level in winter. Needs full sun and fertile, well-drained but not too dry soil. Propagate by softwood cuttings in summer or by seed in autumn.
B. albiflora. Deciduous, bushy sub-shrub. H and S 1m (3ft). Has pungent, mid-green leaves, divided into oval leaflets. Loose panicles of small, cup-shaped, white flowers appear from mid-summer to early autumn.

Bog arum. See *Calla palustris*, illus. p.462.
Bog bean. See *Menyanthes trifoliata*, illus. p.462.
Bog pimpernel. See *Anagallis tenella*.
Bog sage. See *Salvia uliginosa*.

BOLAX

UMBELLIFERAE/APIACEAE

Genus of evergreen, hummock- and cushion-forming perennials, often included in *Azorella*. Is grown for its symmetrical rosettes of small, thick, tough leaves. Flowers only rarely in cultivation. Is suitable for gritty screes, troughs and alpine houses. Fully hardy. Needs sun and humus-rich, well-drained soil. Propagate by rooting rosettes in summer.
B. gummifera illus. p.403.

BOMAREA

ALSTROEMERIACEAE

Genus of herbaceous or evergreen, tuberous-rooted, scrambling and twining climbers, grown for their tubular or bell-shaped flowers. Half hardy to frost tender, min. 5°C (41°F). Grow in any well-drained soil and in full light. Water regularly in growing season, sparingly when dormant. Provide support. Cut out old flowering stems at ground level when leaves turn yellow. Propagate by seed or division in early spring.
B. andimarcana, syn. *B. pubigera* of gardens. Evergreen, scrambling climber with straight, slender stems. H 2–3m (6–10ft). Frost tender. Has lance-shaped leaves, white and hairy beneath. Bears nodding, tubular, green-tipped, pale yellow flowers, suffused pink, from early summer to autumn.
♀ ***B. caldasii***, syn. *B. kalbreyeri* of gardens, illus. p.215.
B. kalbreyeri of gardens. See *B. caldasii*.
B. pubigera of gardens. See *B. andimarcana*.

Bonin Isles juniper. See *Juniperus procumbens*, illus. p.106.
Borage. See *Borago*.

BORAGO

Borage

BORAGINACEAE

Genus of annuals and perennials, grown for culinary use as well as for their flowers. Fully hardy. Requires sun and fertile, well-drained soil. For culinary use gather only young leaves. Propagate by seed sown outdoors in spring. Some species will self seed prolifically and may become invasive.
B. officinalis illus. p.346.

BORONIA

RUTACEAE

Genus of evergreen shrubs, grown primarily for their flowers. Frost tender, min. 7–10°C (45–50°F). Requires full light and sandy, neutral to acid soil. Water potted specimens moderately, less when not in full growth. For a compact habit, shorten long stems after flowering. Propagate by seed in spring or by semi-ripe cuttings in late summer. Red spider mite may be a problem.
B. megastigma illus. p.152.

Bosnian pine. See *Pinus heldreichii*, illus. p.100.
Boston ivy. See *Parthenocissus tricuspidata*, illus. p.216.
Bottle, Brandy. See *Nuphar lutea*, illus. p.476.
Bottle plant. See *Hatiora salicornioides*, illus. p.484.
Bottlebrush. See *Callistemon*.
Albany. See *Callistemon speciosus*.
Granite. See *Melaleuca elliptica*, illus. p.138.
Bottlebrush buckeye. See *Aesculus parviflora*, illus. p.115.

BOUGAINVILLEA

NYCTAGINACEAE

Genus of deciduous or evergreen, woody-stemmed, scrambling climbers, grown for their showy floral bracts. Frost tender, min. 7–10°C (45–50°F). Grow in fertile, well-drained soil and in full light. Water moderately in the growing season; keep containerized plants almost dry when dormant. Tie to a support. Cut back previous season's lateral growths in spring, leaving 2–3cm (¾–1¼in) long spurs. Propagate by semi-ripe cuttings in summer or by hardwood cuttings when dormant. Whitefly and mealy bug may attack.
B. × buttiana. Vigorous, evergreen, woody-stemmed, scrambling climber. H 8–12m (25–40ft). Has ovate, mid-green leaves, to 8cm (3in) long, lighter below. Bears large clusters of strongly waved, golden-yellow, purple or red floral bracts from summer to autumn. **'California Gold'** see *B. × b.* 'Enid Lancaster'.**'Crimson Lake'** see *B. × b.* 'Mrs Butt'. Floral bracts of **'Enid Lancaster'** (syn. *B. × b.* 'California Gold', *B. × b.* 'Golden Glow') are orange-yellow. **'Golden Glow'** see *B. × b.* 'Enid Lancaster'. Bracts of ♀ **'Mrs Butt'** (syn. *B. × b.*'Crimson Lake') are crimson-magenta; those of **'Scarlet Queen'** are scarlet.
***B.* 'Dania'** illus. p.206.
♀ ***B. glabra*** illus. p.212. **'Sanderiana'** illus. p.207. **'Snow White'** illus. p.203.
***B.* 'Miss Manila',** syn. *B.* 'Tango', illus. p.206.
B. spectabilis. Strong-growing, mainly evergreen, woody-stemmed, scrambling climber; stems usually have a few spines. H to 7m (22ft). Has elliptic to oval leaves and, in summer, large trusses of red-purple floral bracts.
***B.* 'Tango'.** See *B.* 'Miss Manila'.

Boussingaultia baselloides of gardens. See *Anredera cordifolia*.

BOUTELOUA

GRAMINEAE/POACEAE

See also GRASSES, BAMBOOS, RUSHES and SEDGES.
B. gracilis, syn. *B. oligostachya*, illus. p.319.
B. oligostachya. See *B. gracilis*.

BOUVARDIA

RUBIACEAE

Genus of deciduous, semi-evergreen or evergreen shrubs and perennials, grown for their flowers. Frost tender, min. 7–10°C (45–50°F), but 13–15°C (55–9°F) for winter-flowering species. Prefers full light and fertile, well-drained soil. Water freely when in full growth, moderately at other times. Cut back stems by half to three-quarters after flowering. Propagate by softwood cuttings in spring or by greenwood or semi-ripe cuttings in summer. Whitefly and mealy bug may be troublesome.
B. humboldtii. See *B. longiflora*.
B. longiflora, syn. *B. humboldtii*. Semi-evergreen, spreading shrub. H and S 1m (3ft) or more. Min. 13–15°C (55–9°F) until flowering ceases, then 7°C (45°F). Has lance-shaped leaves, and terminal clusters of fragrant, white flowers, with slender tubes and 4 petal lobes, from summer to early winter.
B. ternifolia, syn. *B. triphylla*, illus. p.169.
B. triphylla. See *B. ternifolia*.

Bower vine. See *Pandorea jasminoides*, illus. p.204.

BOWIEA

LILIACEAE/HYACINTHACEAE

Genus of summer-flowering, bulbous succulents with scrambling, branched, green stems that produce no proper leaves. Frost tender, min. 10°C (50°F). Needs sun and well-drained soil; plant with half of bulb above soil level. Support with sticks or canes. Propagate by seed, sown under glass in winter or spring. May produce offsets.
B. volubilis illus. p.476.

Bowles' golden sedge. See *Carex elata* 'Aurea', illus. p.321.

BOYKINIA

SAXIFRAGACEAE

Genus of mound-forming perennials. Fully hardy. Most species require shade and humus-rich, moist but well-drained, acid soil. Propagate by division in spring or by seed in autumn.
B. aconitifolia. Mound-forming perennial. H 1m (3ft), S 15cm (6in). Has rounded to kidney-shaped, lobed leaves. In summer, flower stems carry very small, bell-shaped, white flowers.
B. jamesii, syn. *Telesonix jamesii*. Mound-forming, rhizomatous perennial. H and S 15cm (6in). Each woody stem bears a rosette of kidney-shaped leaves with lacerated edges. In early summer bears open bell-shaped, frilled, pink flowers with green centres.

Box. See *Buxus*.
Balearic. See *Buxus balearica*, illus. p.149.
Brisbane. See *Lophostemon confertus*.
Christmas. See *Sarcococca*.
Common. See *Buxus sempervirens*.
Himalayan. See *Buxus wallichiana*.
Small-leaved. See *Buxus microphylla*.
Sweet. See *Sarcococca*.
Victorian. See *Pittosporum undulatum*.
Box elder. See *Acer negundo*.
Box-leaved holly. See *Ilex crenata*.
Bracelet honey myrtle. See *Melaleuca armillaris*.
Brachychilum horsfieldii. See *Hedychium horsfieldii*.

BRACHYCHITON

STERCULIACEAE

Genus of evergreen or deciduous, mainly spring-and summer-flowering trees, grown for their flowers and overall appearance. Frost tender, min. 7–10°C (45–50°F). Needs full light and humus-rich, well-drained, preferably acid soil. Water containerized plants moderately, much less in winter. Prune if needed. Propagate by seed in spring. Red spider mite may be a nuisance.
B. acerifolius, syn. *Sterculia acerifolia*, illus. p.61.
B. populneus, syn. *Sterculia*

diversifolia (Kurrajong). Evergreen, conical tree, pyramidal when young. H and S 15–20m (50–70ft). Pointed or 3–5-lobed, glossy, deep green leaves are chartreuse when young. In spring-summer has panicles of saucer-shaped, cream or greenish-white flowers with red, purple or yellow throats.

Brachyglottis

COMPOSITAE/ASTERACEAE

Genus of evergreen shrubs and trees, grown for their bold foliage and daisy-like flower heads. Fully hardy to frost tender, min. 3°C (37°F). Needs full light or partial shade and well-drained soil. Water containerized plants freely in summer, moderately at other times. Take semi-ripe cuttings in late summer.
B. compacta, syn. *Senecio compactus.* Evergreen, bushy, dense shrub. H 1m (3ft), S 2m (6ft). Frost hardy. Bears small, oval, white-edged, dark green leaves, white below, and daisy-like, bright yellow flowers in clustered heads from mid- to late summer. Felt-like, white hairs cover the shoots.
***B.* Dunedin Group,** syn. *Senecio* Dunedin Hybrids*, S. greyi* of gardens, *S. laxifolius* of gardens. Spreading, bushy, mound-forming shrubs. H 1.5m (5ft), S 2m (6ft) or more. Fully hardy. Leaves are obovate to elliptic, often wavy-margined, white-hairy, later hairless, and mid- to dark green. Loose, terminal panicles of bright yellow flower heads, with conspicuous ray florets, are produced from summer to autumn. ♀ **'Sunshine'** (syn. *Senecio* 'Sunshine') illus. p.166.
B. laxifolia, syn. *Senecio laxifolius.* Evergreen, bushy, spreading shrub. H 1m (3ft), S 2m (6ft). Frost hardy. Oval, grey-white leaves become dark green. Has large clusters of daisy-like, golden-yellow flower heads in summer.
♀ ***B. monroi***, syn. *Senecio monroi*, illus. p.167.
B. repanda illus. p.123.
B. rotundifolia, syn. *Senecio reinholdii, S. rotundifolius.* Evergreen, rounded, dense shrub. H and S 1m (3ft). Frost hardy. Has rounded, leathery, glossy leaves, dark green above, white-felted below, and tiny, yellow flower heads from early to mid-summer. Withstands salt winds in mild coastal areas.

Brachyscome

COMPOSITAE/ASTERACEAE

Genus of annuals and perennials, grown for their daisy-like flower heads and very variable, often finely divided foliage. Fully hardy. Requires sun, a sheltered position and rich, well-drained soil. Pinch out growing shoots of young plants to encourage a bushy habit. Propagate by seed sown under glass in spring or outdoors in late spring.
B. iberidifolia illus. p.346.

Bracteantha. See *Xerochrysum.*
Brake
Cretan. See *Pteris cretica.*
Purple rock. See *Pellaea atropurpurea.*
Purple-stemmed cliff. See *Pellaea atropurpurea.*
Snow. See *Pteris ensiformis.*
Bramble. See *Rubus.*
Branched bur reed. See *Sparganium erectum*, illus. p.465.
Brandy bottle. See *Nuphar lutea*, illus. p.467.
Brasiliopuntia brasiliensis. See *Opuntia brasiliensis.*
Brass buttons. See *Cotula coronopifolia.*
Brassaia. See *Schefflera.*

Brassavola

ORCHIDACEAE

See also ORCHIDS.
B. nodosa (Lady-of-the-night; illus. p.308). Evergreen, epiphytic orchid for an intermediate greenhouse. H 23cm (9in). Narrow-petalled, pale green flowers, 5cm (2in) across and each with a white lip, are produced, 1–3 to a stem, in spring; they are fragrant at night. Leaves, 8–10cm (3–4in) long, are thick and cylindrical. Is best grown on a bark slab. Provide good light in summer.

Brassica

CRUCIFERAE/BRASSICACEAE

Genus of annuals and evergreen biennials and perennials. Most are edible vegetables, e.g. cabbages and kales, but forms of *B. oleracea* are grown for their ornamental foliage. Fully hardy. Grow in sun and in fertile, well-drained soil. Lime-rich soil is recommended, though not essential. Propagate by seed sown outdoors in spring or under glass in early spring. Is susceptible to club root.
B. oleracea forms illus. p.336.

× Brassocattleya

ORCHIDACEAE

See also ORCHIDS.
× ***B. Mount Adams*** illus. p.309. Evergreen, epiphytic orchid for an intermediate greenhouse. H 45cm (18in). Intermittently produces lavender-pink flowers, to 15cm (6in) across, each with a darker lip marked yellow and red, up to 4 per stem. Has oval, stiff leaves, 10–15cm (4–6in) long. Needs good light in summer.

× Brassolaelio-cattleya

ORCHIDACEAE

See also ORCHIDS.
× ***B. Hetherington Horace*** **'Coronation'** illus. p.309. Evergreen, epiphytic orchid for an intermediate greenhouse. H 45cm (18in). Bears stiff, oval leaves, 10–15cm (4–6in) long, and fragrant, light pink flowers, 10cm (4in) across, each with a deep pink-yellow lip, up to 4 to a stem, mainly in spring. Provide good light in summer.
× ***B. St Helier*** illus. p.309. Evergreen, epiphytic orchid for an intermediate greenhouse. H 45cm (18in). Produces oval, stiff leaves, 10–15cm (4–6in) long. Pinkish-purple flowers, to 10cm (4in) across, each with a yellow-marked, rich red lip, are borne 1–4 to a stem, mainly in spring. Grow in good light in summer.

Bravoa geminiflora. See *Polianthes geminiflora.*
Brazilian firecracker. See *Manettia luteo-rubra*, illus. p.201.
Breath of heaven. See *Diosma ericoides.*
Brewer's spruce. See *Picea breweriana*, illus. p.101.

Breynia

EUPHORBIACEAE

Genus of evergreen shrubs and trees, grown for their foliage. Frost tender, min. 13°C (55°F). Needs full light or partial shade and fertile, well-drained soil. Water containerized plants freely when in full growth, moderately at other times. Large bushes should be cut back hard after flowering. Propagate by greenwood or semi-ripe cuttings in summer. Whitefly, red spider mite and mealy bug may be troublesome.
B. disticha, syn. *B. nivosa, Phyllanthus nivosus*, illus. p.171. **'Roseopicta'** is an evergreen, rounded, well-branched shrub with slender stems. H and S to 1m (3ft). Has broadly oval, green leaves variably bordered and splashed with white and flushed pink. Insignificant, petalless flowers are borne in spring-summer.
B. nivosa. See *B. disticha.*

Briar, Sweet. See *Rosa rubiginosa*, illus. p.181.
Bridal bouquet. See *Porana paniculata.*
Bridal wreath. See *Francoa appendiculata; Spiraea* 'Arguta'*; Spiraea* × *vanhouttei*, illus. p.150.
Bridgesia. See *Ercilla.*

Briggsia

GESNERIACEAE

Genus of evergreen perennials, grown for their rosettes of hairy leaves. Frost tender, min. 2–5°C (36–41°F). Needs shade and peaty soil with plenty of moisture in summer and good air circulation in winter. Protect against damp in winter. Propagate by seed in spring.
B. muscicola. Evergreen, basal-rosetted perennial. H 8–10cm (3–4in), S 23cm (9in). Leaves are oval, silver-haired and pale green. Arching flower stems bear loose clusters of tubular, pale yellow flowers, with protruding tips, in early summer. Is best grown in an alpine house.

Brimeura

LILIACEAE/HYACINTHACEAE

Genus of spring-flowering bulbs, similar to miniature bluebells, cultivated for their attractive flowers. Is suitable for rock gardens and shrub borders. Frost hardy. Requires partial shade and prefers humus-rich, well-drained soil. Propagate by sowing seed in autumn or by division in late summer.
♀ ***B. amethystina***, syn. *Hyacinthus amethystinus*, illus. p.448.

Brisbane box. See *Lophostemon confertus.*
Bristle club-rush. See *Isolepis setaceus.*
Bristle-cone pine. See *Pinus aristata*, illus. p.104.
Bristle-pointed iris. See *Iris setosa.*
Brittle bladderfern. See *Cystopteris fragilis.*
Brittonastrum mexicanum. See *Agastache mexicana.*

Briza

Quaking grass

GRAMINEAE/POACEAE

See also GRASSES, BAMBOOS, RUSHES and SEDGES.
B. maxima (Greater quaking grass). Robust, tuft-forming, annual grass. H to 50cm (20in), S 8–10cm (3–4in). Fully hardy. Mid-green leaves are mainly basal. Produces loose panicles of up to 10 pendent, purplish-green spikelets, in early summer, that dry particularly well for winter decoration. Self seeds readily.
B. media (Common quaking grass). Evergreen, tuft-forming, rhizomatous, perennial grass. H 30–60cm (12–24in), S 8–10cm (3–4in). Fully hardy. Mid-green leaves are mainly basal. In summer produces open panicles of up to 30 pendent, purplish-brown spikelets that dry well for winter decoration.

Broad bucklerfern. See *Dryopteris dilatata.*
Broadleaf. See *Griselinia littoralis.*
Broad-leaved lime. See *Tilia platyphyllos.*

Brodiaea

LILIACEAE/ALLIACEAE

Genus of mainly spring-flowering bulbs with colourful flowers produced in loose heads on leafless stems. Frost hardy. Needs a sheltered, sunny situation and light, well-drained soil. Dies down in summer. Propagate in autumn by seed or in late summer and autumn by freely produced offsets.
B. capitata. See *Dichelostemma pulchellum.*
B. congesta. See *Dichelostemma congestum.*
B. coronaria, syn. *B. grandiflora.* Late spring- to early summer-flowering bulb. H 10–25cm (4–10in), S 8–10cm (3–4in). Long, narrow, semi-erect, basal leaves die down by flowering time. Leafless stems each carry a loose head of erect, funnel-shaped, violet-blue flowers on long, slender stalks.
B. grandiflora. See *B. coronaria.*
B. hyacinthina. See *Triteleia hyacinthina.*
B. ida-maia. See *Dichelostemma ida-maia.*
B. ixioides. See *Triteleia ixioides.*
B. lactea. See *Triteleia hyacinthina.*
B. laxa. See *Triteleia laxa.*
B. lutea. See *Triteleia ixioides.*
B. peduncularis. See *Triteleia peduncularis.*
B. pulchella. See *Dichelostemma pulchellum.*

Bromelia

BROMELIACEAE

Genus of evergreen, rosette-forming perennials, grown for their overall appearance. Frost tender, min. 5–7°C (41–45°F). Needs full light and well-drained soil. Water moderately in summer, sparingly at other times. Propagate by suckers in spring.
B. balansae (Heart of flame; illus. p.273). Evergreen, clump-forming, basal-rosetted perennial. H 1m (3ft),

S 1.5m (5ft). Produces narrowly strap-shaped, arching, mid- to grey-green leaves with large, hooked spines. Club-shaped panicles of tubular, red- or violet-purple flowers, with long, bright red bracts, are borne in spring-summer or sometimes later.

Bromeliad. See feature panel p.273.
Bird's-nest. See *Nidularium innocentii.*
Blushing. See *Neoregelia carolinae; Nidularium fulgens.*
Bromeliads, King of the. See *Vriesea hieroglyphica.*
Brompton stock. See *Matthiola incana.*

BROMUS

GRAMINEAE/POACEAE

See also GRASSES, BAMBOOS, RUSHES and SEDGES.
B. ramosus (Hairy brome grass). Evergreen, tuft-forming, perennial grass. H to 2m (6ft), S 30cm (1ft). Fully hardy. Mid-green leaves are lax and hairy. Produces long, arching panicles of nodding, grey-green spikelets in summer. Prefers shade.

Bronvaux medlar. See + *Crataegomespilus dardarii.*
Broom. See *Cytisus; Genista.*
Butcher's. See *Ruscus aculeatus.*
Climbing butcher's. See *Semele androgyna.*
Common. See *Cytisus scoparius.*
Hedgehog. See *Erinacea anthyllis*, illus. p.360.
Moroccan. See *Cytisus battandieri*, illus. p.119.
Mount Etna. See *Genista aetnensis*, illus. p.89.
Pineapple. See *Cytisus battandieri*, illus. p.119.
Pink. See *Notospartium carmichaeliae.*
Purple. See *Chamaecytisus purpureus.*
Spanish. See *Spartium junceum*, illus. p.143.
Warminster. See *Cytisus × praecox* 'Warminster', illus. p.152.

BROUSSONETIA

MORACEAE

Genus of deciduous trees and shrubs, grown for their foliage and unusual flowers. Male and female flowers are produced on different plants. Frost hardy. Requires a position in full sun and well-drained soil. Propagate by softwood cuttings in summer or by seed in autumn.
B. papyrifera illus. p.75.

BROWALLIA

SOLANACEAE

Genus of shrubby perennials, usually grown as annuals, with showy, open trumpet-shaped flowers. Frost tender, min. 4–15°C (39–59°F). Grows best in sun or partial shade and in fertile, well-drained soil that should not dry out completely. Feed when flowering if pot-grown and pinch out young shoots to encourage bushiness. Propagate by seed in spring; for winter flowers, sow in late summer.
B. americana, syn. *B. elata.* Moderately fast-growing, bushy perennial, usually grown as an annual. H 30cm (12in), S 15cm (6in). Min. 4°C (39°F). Has oval, mid-green leaves and, in summer, trumpet-shaped, blue flowers, 4cm (1½ in) wide.
B. elata. See *B. americana.*
B. speciosa illus. p.274.

BROWNINGIA

syn. AZUREOCEREUS

CACTACEAE

Genus of slow-growing, eventually tree-like, perennial cacti. Spiny, silvery- or green-blue stems, with up to 20 or more ribs, are crowned by stiff, erect, green-blue branches. Frost tender, min. 7°C (45°F). Requires a position in full sun and very well-drained soil. Propagate by seed in spring or summer.
B. hertlingiana, syn. *Azureocereus hertlingianus*, illus. p.472.

Bruckenthalia spiculifolia. See *Erica spiculifolia.*

BRUGMANSIA

Angels' trumpets

SOLANACEAE

Genus of evergreen or semi-evergreen shrubs, trees and annuals, cultivated for their flowers borne mainly in summer-autumn. Frost hardy to frost tender, min. 7–10°C (45–50°F). Prefers full light and fertile, well-drained soil. Water containerized specimens freely in full growth, moderately at other times. May be pruned hard in early spring. Propagate by seed sown in spring or by greenwood or semi-ripe cuttings in early summer or later. Whitefly and red spider mite may be troublesome. All parts are highly toxic if ingested.
B. arborea, syn. *B. versicolor* of gardens. Evergreen or semi-evergreen, rounded, robust shrub. H and S to 3m (10ft). Frost tender. Bears narrowly oval leaves, each 20cm (8in) or more long. Bears strongly fragrant, pendent, trumpet-shaped, white flowers, each 16–20cm (6–8in) long with a spathe-like calyx, in summer-autumn.
B. aurea. Evergreen, rounded shrub or tree. H and S 6–11m (20–35ft). Frost tender. Has oval leaves, 15cm (6in) long, and, in summer-autumn, pendent, trumpet-shaped, white or yellow flowers, 15–25cm (6–10in) long.
B. × candida illus. p.115. ♀ **'Grand Marnier'** (syn. *B.*'Grand Marnier') illus. p.119.
***B.* 'Grand Marnier'.** See *B. × candida* 'Grand Marnier'.
B. rosei of gardens. See *B. sanguinea.*
B. sanguinea, syn. *B. rosei* of gardens, illus. p.119.
B. versicolor of gardens. See *B. arborea.*

BRUNFELSIA

SOLANACEAE

Genus of evergreen shrubs, grown for their flowers. Frost tender, min. 10–13°C (50–55°F), but 15–18°C (59–64°F) for good winter flowering. Needs semi-shade and humus-rich, well-drained soil. Water containerized plants moderately, much less in low temperatures. Remove stem tips to promote branching in growing season. Propagate by semi-ripe cuttings in summer. Mealy bug and whitefly may be a problem.
B. calycina. See *B. pauciflora.*
B. eximia. See *B. pauciflora.*
♀ ***B. pauciflora***, syn. *B. calycina, B. eximia* (Yesterday-today-and-tomorrow). Evergreen, spreading shrub. H and S 60cm (2ft) or more. Bears oblong to lance-shaped, leathery, glossy leaves. Blue-purple flowers, each with a tubular base and 5 overlapping, wavy-edged petals, are carried from winter to summer. **'Macrantha'** illus. p.163.

BRUNNERA

BORAGINACEAE

Genus of spring-flowering perennials. Fully hardy. Prefers light shade and moist soil. Propagate by division in spring or autumn or by seed in autumn.
♀ ***B. macrophylla*** (Siberian bugloss). Clump-forming perennial. H 45cm (18in), S 60cm (24in). Delicate sprays of small, star-shaped, forget-me-not-like, bright blue flowers in early spring are followed by heart-shaped, rough, long-stalked leaves. Makes good ground cover. **'Dawson's White'** (syn. *B.m.* 'Variegata') illus. p.279.

× *Brunsdonna parkeri.* See × *Amarygia parkeri.*

BRUNSVIGIA

AMARYLLIDACEAE

Genus of autumn-flowering bulbs with heads of showy flowers. Half hardy. Requires sun and well-drained soil. Water in autumn to encourage bulbs into growth and continue watering until summer, when the leaves will die away and dormant bulbs should be kept fairly dry and warm. Propagate by seed sown in autumn or by offsets in late summer.
B. josephinae (Josephine's lily). Autumn-flowering bulb. H to 45cm (18in), S 45–60cm (18–24in). Bears a stout, leafless stem with a spherical head of 20–30 funnel-shaped, red flowers, 7–9cm (3–3½in) long, with recurved petal tips. Semi-erect, oblong leaves appear after flowering.

Brush-box tree. See *Lophostemon confertus.*
Bryophyllum. See *Kalanchoe.*
Buckbean. See *Menyanthes trifoliata*, illus. p.462.
Buckeye. See *Aesculus.*
Bottlebrush. See *Aesculus parviflora*, illus. p.115.
California. See *Aesculus californica*, illus. p.81.
Ohio. See *Aesculus glabra.*
Red. See *Aesculus pavia.*
Sweet. See *Aesculus flava*, illus. p.78.
Yellow. See *Aesculus flava*, illus. p.78.
Buckthorn. See *Rhamnus.*
Italian. See *Rhamnus alaternus.*
Sea. See *Hippophäe rhamnoides*, illus. p.120.
Buckwheat, Wild. See *Eriogonum.*

BUDDLEJA

BUDDLEJACEAE

Genus of deciduous, semi-evergreen or evergreen shrubs and trees, grown for their clusters of small, often fragrant flowers. Fully to half hardy. Requires full sun and fertile, well-drained soil. *B. crispa, B. davidii, B. fallowiana, B.* 'Lochinch' and *B. × weyeriana* should be cut back hard in spring. Prune *B. alternifolia* by removing shoots that have flowered. Other species may be cut back lightly after flowering. Propagate by semi-ripe cuttings in summer.
♀ ***B. alternifolia*** illus. p.118.
♀ ***B. asiatica.*** Evergreen, arching shrub. H and S 3m (10ft). Half hardy. Long plumes of very fragrant, tubular, white flowers appear amid long, narrow, dark green leaves in late winter and early spring. Grow against a south- or west-facing wall.
B. colvilei illus. p.117. **'Kewensis'** is a deciduous, arching shrub, often tree-like with age. H and S 5m (15ft). Frost hardy. Has lance-shaped, dark green leaves. Large, tubular, white-throated, deep red flowers hang in drooping clusters in early summer.
B. crispa illus. p.139.
B. davidii (Butterfly bush). ♀ **'Black Knight'** is a vigorous, deciduous, arching shrub. H and S 5m (15ft). Fully hardy. Leaves are long, lance-shaped and dark green with white-felted undersides. Dense clusters of fragrant, tubular, dark violet-purple flowers are borne from mid-summer to autumn. Flowers of ♀ **'Empire Blue'** are rich violet-blue. **'Harlequin'** illus. p.117. **'Peace'** illus. p.114. **'Pink Pearl'** produces pale lilac-pink flowers. ♀ **'Royal Red'** illus. p.117.
B. fallowiana. Deciduous, arching shrub. H 2m (6ft), S 3m (10ft). Frost hardy. Shoots and lance-shaped leaves, when young, are covered with white hairs; foliage then becomes dark grey-green. Has fragrant, tubular, lavender-purple flowers in late summer and early autumn. Is often damaged in very severe winters; grow against a wall in cold areas. ♀ var. ***alba*** has white flowers.
♀ ***B. globosa*** illus. p.119.
♀ ***B.* 'Lochinch'.** Deciduous, arching shrub. H and S 3m (10ft). Frost hardy. Long plumes of fragrant, tubular, lilac-blue flowers are borne above lance-shaped, grey-green leaves in late summer and autumn.
♀ ***B. madagascariensis***, syn. *Nicodemia madagascariensis.* Evergreen, arching shrub. H and S 4m (12ft) or more. Half hardy. Has narrowly lance-shaped, dark green leaves, white beneath, and, in late winter and spring, long clusters of tubular, orange-yellow flowers. Grow against a south-or west-facing wall.
B. × weyeriana. Deciduous, arching shrub. H and S 4m (12ft). Fully hardy. Bears lance-shaped, dark green leaves, and loose, rounded clusters of tubular, orange-yellow flowers, often tinged purple, from mid-summer to autumn.

Buffalo berry. See *Shepherdia argentea.*
Buffalo currant. See *Ribes odoratum.*
Bugbane. See *Cimicifuga.*

Bugle, Pyramidal. See *Ajuga pyramidalis*.
Bugler, Royal red. See *Aeschynanthus pulcher*.
Bugloss, Siberian. See *Brunnera macrophylla*.

BULBOCODIUM

LILIACEAE/COLCHICACEAE

Genus of spring-flowering corms, related to *Colchicum* and with funnel-shaped flowers. Is particularly suitable for rock gardens and cool greenhouses. Fully hardy. Requires an open, sunny site and well-drained soil. Propagate by seed sown in autumn or by division in late summer and early autumn.
B. vernum illus. p.446.

BULBOPHYLLUM

ORCHIDACEAE

See also ORCHIDS.
B. careyanum illus. p.310. Evergreen, epiphytic orchid for an intermediate greenhouse. H 8cm (3in). Oval leaves are 8–10cm (3–4in) long. In spring produces tight sprays of many slightly fragrant, brown flowers, 0.5cm (¼in) across. Grows best in a hanging basket. Needs semi-shade in summer.

Bull bay. See *Magnolia grandiflora*.
Bullock's heart. See *Annona reticulata*.
Bunch-flowered daffodil. See *Narcissus tazetta*.
Bunnies' ears. See *Stachys byzantina*, illus. p.316.
Bunny ears. See *Opuntia microdasys*.

BUPHTHALMUM

COMPOSITAE/ASTERACEAE

Genus of summer-flowering perennials. Fully hardy. Requires full sun; grows well in any but rich soil. Propagate by seed in spring or autumn or by division in autumn. Needs frequent division to curb invasiveness.
B. salicifolium illus. p.304.
B. speciosum. See *Telekia speciosa*.

BUPLEURUM

UMBELLIFERAE/APIACEAE

Genus of perennials and evergreen shrubs, grown for their foliage and flowers. Grows well in coastal gardens. Frost hardy. Needs full sun and well-drained soil. Propagate by semi-ripe cuttings in summer.
B. fruticosum illus. p.142.

Bur oak. See *Quercus macrocarpa*, illus. p.76.
Bur reed. See *Sparganium*.
Burnet. See *Sanguisorba*.
Canadian. See *Sanguisorba canadensis*, illus. p.224.
Great. See *Sanguisorba officinalis*.
Burnet rose. See *Rosa spinosissima*.
Burning bush. See *Dictamnus albus* var. *albus*, illus p.242; *Bassia scoparia* f. *trichophylla*, illus. p.347.
Burro's tail. See *Sedum morganianum*.
Bush groundsel. See *Baccharis halimifolia*.
Bush violet. See *Browallia speciosa*, illus. p.274.
Busy lizzie. See *Impatiens walleriana* cvs.
Butcher's broom. See *Ruscus aculeatus*.

BUTIA
Yatay palm

ARECACEAE/PALMAE

Genus of evergreen palms, grown for their overall appearance. Frost hardy to frost tender, min. 5°C (41°F). Grow in any fertile, well-drained soil and in full light or partial shade. Water regularly, less in winter. Propagate by seed in spring at not less than 24°C (75°F). Red spider mite may be a problem.
B. capitata, syn. *Cocos capitata*, illus. p.96.

BUTOMUS

BUTOMACEAE

Genus of one species of deciduous, perennial, rush-like, marginal water plant, grown for its fragrant, cup-shaped flowers. Fully hardy. Requires an open, sunny situation in up to 25cm (10in) depth of water. Propagate by division in spring or by seed in spring or late summer.
♀ ***B. umbellatus*** illus. p.464.

Butter tree. See *Tylecodon paniculatus*.
Buttercup. See *Ranunculus*.
Alpine. See *Ranunculus alpestris*, illus. p.375.
Double meadow. See *Ranunculus acris* 'Flore Pleno', illus. p.304.
Giant. See *Ranunculus lyallii*.
Meadow. See *Ranunculus acris*.
Persian. See *Ranunculus asiaticus*, illus. pp.437 and 439.
Butterfly bush. See *Buddleja davidii*.
Butterfly flower. See *Schizanthus*.
Butterfly orchid. See *Psychopsis papilio*, illus. p.311.
Butterfly weed. See *Asclepias tuberosa*, illus. p.266.
Butternut. See *Juglans cinerea*.
Button-fern. See *Pellaea rotundifolia*.
Buttons, Brass. See *Cotula coronopifolia*.

BUXUS
Box

BUXACEAE

Genus of evergreen shrubs and trees, grown for their foliage and habit. Is excellent for edging, hedging and topiary work. Flowers are insignificant. Fully to frost hardy. Requires sun or semi-shade and any but waterlogged soil. Trim hedges in summer. Promote new growth by cutting back stems to 30cm (12in) or less in late spring. Propagate by semi-ripe cuttings in summer. Contact with box sap may irritate skin.
♀ ***B. balearica*** illus. p.149.
B. microphylla (Small-leaved box). Evergreen, bushy shrub. H 1m (3ft), S 1.5m (5ft). Fully hardy. Forms a dense, rounded mass of small, oblong, dark green leaves. **'Green Pillow'** illus. p.172.
♀ ***B. sempervirens*** (Common box). Evergreen, bushy shrub or tree. H and S 5m (15ft). Fully hardy. Produces leaves that are oblong, glossy and dark green. Is useful for hedging and screening. **'Handsworthensis'** illus. p.148. ♀ **'Suffruticosa'** illus. p.173.
B. wallichiana (Himalayan box). Slow-growing, evergreen, bushy, open shrub. H and S 2m (6ft). Frost hardy. Produces long, narrow, glossy, bright gree leaves

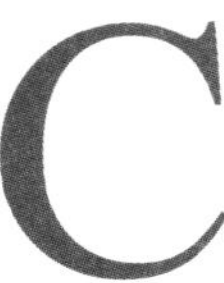

Cabbage
Ornamental. See *Brassica oleracea* forms, illus. p.336.
Yellow skunk. See *Lysichiton americanus*, illus. p.467.

Cabbage palm
Australian. See *Livistona australis*.
New Zealand. See *Cordyline australis*.

CABOMBA

CABOMBACEAE

Genus of deciduous or semi-evergreen, perennial, submerged water plants with finely divided foliage. Is suitable for aquariums. Frost tender, min. 5°C (41°F). Prefers partial shade. Propagate by stem cuttings in spring or summer.
C. caroliniana (Fanwort, Fish grass, Washington grass). Deciduous or semi-evergreen, perennial, submerged water plant. S indefinite. Forms dense, spreading hummocks of fan-shaped, coarsely cut, bright green leaves. Is used as an oxygenating plant.

Cactus
Barrel. See *Ferocactus*.
Chain. See *Rhipsalis paradoxa*.
Christmas. See *Schlumbergera* × *buckleyi*.
Colombian ball. See *Parodia erinacea*, illus. p.495.
Coral. See *Rhipsalis cereuscula*, illus. p.477.
Crab. See *Schlumbergera truncata*, illus. p.489.
Dumpling. See *Lophophora williamsii*, illus. p.487.
Easter. See *Hatiora gaertneri*, illus. p.491.
Fishbone. See *Epiphyllum anguliger*, illus. p.477.
Golden ball. See *Parodia leninghausii*, illus. p.484.
Golden barrel. See *Echinocactus grusonii*, illus. p.476.
Lace. See *Mammillaria elongata*, illus. p.486.
Lamb's-tail. See *Echinocereus schmollii*, illus. p.478.
Lobster. See *Schlumbergera truncata*, illus. p.489.
Melon. See *Melocactus intortus*, illus. p.488.
Mistletoe. See *Rhipsalis*.
Old-lady. See *Mammillaria hahniana*, illus. p.481.
Old-man. See *Cephalocereus senilis*, illus. p.476.
Old-woman. See *Mammillaria hahniana*, illus. p.481.
Orchid. See *Epiphyllum*.
Organ-pipe. See *Pachycereus marginatus*, illus. p.473.
Peanut. See *Echinopsis chamaecereus*, illus. p.491.
Peruvian old-man. See *Espostoa lanata*, illus. p.473.
Pincushion. See *Mammillaria*.
Powder-puff. See *Mammillaria bocasana*, illus. p.487.
Rat's-tail. See *Aporocactus flagelliformis*, illus. p.479.
Red orchid. See *Nopalxochia ackermannii*.
Rose. See *Pereskia grandifolia*, illus. p.474
Scarlet ball. See *Parodia haselbergii* subsp. *haselbergii*, illus p.491.
Silver ball. See *Parodia scopa*.
Silver dollar. See *Astrophytum asterias*.
Strap. See *Epiphyllum*.
Strawberry. See *Mammillaria prolifera*.
Torch. See *Echinopsis spachiana*, illus. p.473.

CAESALPINIA

LEGUMINOSAE/CAESALPINIACEAE

Genus of deciduous or evergreen shrubs, trees and scrambling climbers, grown for their foliage and flowers. Frost hardy to frost tender, min. 5–10°C (41–50°F). Needs full sun and fertile, well-drained soil. Propagate by softwood cuttings in summer or by seed in autumn or spring.
C. gilliesii, syn. *Poinciana gilliesii*, illus. p.119.
C. pulcherrima, syn. *Poinciana pulcherrima* (Barbados pride). Evergreen shrub or tree of erect to spreading habit. H and S 3–6m (10–20ft). Frost tender, min. 5°C (41°F). Has fern-like leaves composed of many small, mid-green leaflets. In summer bears cup-shaped, yellow flowers, 3cm (1¼in) wide, with very long, red anthers, in short, dense, erect racemes.

CALADIUM

ARACEAE

Genus of perennials with tubers from which arise long-stalked, ornamental leaves. Frost tender, min. 18–19°C (64–6°F). Requires partial shade and moist, humus-rich soil. After leaves die down, store tubers in a frost-free, dark place. Propagate by separating small tubers when planting in spring. Contact with all parts may irritate skin, and may cause mild stomach upset if ingested.
C. bicolor (Angels' wings). **'Candidum'** is a tufted perennial. H and S to 90cm (36in). Triangular, green-veined, white leaves, to 45cm (18in) long, have arrow-shaped bases and long leaf stalks. Intermittently bears white spathes; small flowers clustered on spadix sometimes produce whitish berries. **'John Peed'** has purple stems and waxy, green leaves with metallic orange-red centres and scarlet veins. **'Pink Beauty'** illus. p.272. **'Pink Cloud'** has large, dark green leaves with mottled pink centres, and pink to white areas along the veins.

Calamondin. See × *Citrofortunella microcarpa*, illus. p.147.
Calandrinia megarhiza. See *Claytonia megarhiza*.

CALANTHE

ORCHIDACEAE

See also ORCHIDS.
C. vestita illus. p.308. Deciduous, terrestrial orchid. H 60cm (24in). Frost tender, min. 18°C (64°F). In winter bears sprays of many white flowers, 4cm (1½in) across, each with a large, red-marked lip. Has broadly oval, ribbed, soft leaves, 30cm (12in) long. In summer requires semi-shade and regular feeding.

CALATHEA

MARANTACEAE

Genus of evergreen perennials with brightly coloured and patterned leaves. Frost tender, min. 15°C (59°F). Prefers a shaded, humid position, without fluctuations of temperature, in humus-rich, well-drained soil. Water with soft water, sparingly in low temperatures, but do not allow to dry out completely. Propagate by division in spring.
C. lindeniana. Evergreen, clump-forming perennial. H 1m (3ft), S 60cm (2ft). Lance-shaped, long-stalked, more or less upright leaves, over 30cm (1ft) long, are dark green, with paler green, feathered midribs above and marked with reddish-purple below. Intermittently bears short, erect spikes of 3-petalled, pale yellow flowers.
***C. majestica* 'Roseolineata',** syn. *C. ornata* 'Roseolineata'. Evergreen, clump-forming, stemless perennial. H to 2m (6ft), S to 1.5m (5ft). Narrowly oval, leathery leaves, to 60cm (2ft) long, are dark green, with close-set, fine, pink stripes along the lateral veins and reddish-purple below. Intermittently bears short, erect spikes of 3-petalled, white to mauve flowers. **'Sanderiana'** see *C. sanderiana*.
♀ ***C. makoyana*** illus. p.316.
C. oppenheimiana. See *Ctenanthe oppenheimiana*.
***C. ornata* 'Roseolineata'.** See *C. majestica* 'Roseolineata'.
C. sanderiana, syn. *C. majestica* 'Sanderiana', illus. p.232.
♀ ***C. zebrina*** illus. p.274.

CALCEOLARIA

SCROPHULARIACEAE

Genus of annuals, biennials and evergreen perennials, sub-shrubs and scandent climbers, some of which are grown as annuals. Fully hardy to frost tender, min. 5–7°C (41–5°F). Most prefer sun but some like a shady, cool site and moist but well-drained soil, incorporating sharp sand and compost, and dislike wet conditions in winter. Propagate by softwood cuttings in late spring or summer or by seed in autumn.
C. acutifolia. See *C. polyrrhiza*.
***C.* Anytime Series.** Compact, bushy annuals or biennials. H 20cm (8in), S 15cm (6in). Half hardy. Has oval, slightly hairy, mid-green leaves and, in spring-summer, heads of 5cm (2in) long, rounded, pouched flowers in red and yellow shades, including bicolours.
C. arachnoidea illus. p.367.
***C.* 'Bright Bikinis'** illus. p.350.
C. darwinii. See *C. uniflora* var. *darwinii*.
C. fothergillii. Evergreen, clump-forming, short-lived perennial. H and S 12cm (5in). Frost hardy. Has a rosette of rounded, light green leaves with hairy edges and, in summer, solitary pouch-shaped, sulphur-yellow flowers with crimson spots. Is good for a sheltered rock ledge or trough or in an alpine house. Needs gritty, peaty soil. Is prone to aphid attack.
♀ ***C. integrifolia.*** Evergreen, upright sub-shrub, sometimes grown as an annual. H to 1.2m (4ft), S 60cm (2ft). Half hardy. In summer bears crowded clusters of pouch-shaped, yellow to red-brown flowers above oblong to elliptic, mid-green leaves, sometimes rust-coloured beneath.♀ **'Sunshine'** illus. p.351.
***C.* 'John Innes'** illus. p.305.
***C.* 'Monarch'.** Group of bushy annuals or biennials. H and S 30cm (12in). Half hardy. Has oval, lightly hairy, mid-green leaves and, in spring-summer, bears heads of large, rounded, pouched flowers, 5cm (2in) long, in a wide range of colours.
C. pavonii. Robust, evergreen, scandent climber. H 2m (6ft) or more. Frost tender, min. 7°C (45°F). Has oval, serrated, soft-haired leaves with winged stalks. Pouched, yellow flowers with brown marks appear in large trusses from late summer to winter.
C. polyrrhiza, syn. *C. acutifolia*. Evergreen, prostrate perennial. H 2.5cm (1in), S 15cm (6in). Frost hardy. Has rounded, hairy, mid-green leaves along flower stem, which bears pouch-shaped, purple-spotted, yellow flowers in summer. Is good for a shady rock garden. May also be propagated by division in autumn or spring.
C. tenella illus. p.397.
***C. uniflora* var. *darwinii*,** syn. *C. darwinii*. Evergreen, clump-forming, short-lived perennial. H 8cm (3in), S 10cm (4in). Fully hardy. Bears rounded, wrinkled, glossy, dark green leaves. In late spring, flower stems carry pendent, pouch-shaped, yellow flowers with dark brown spots on lower lips and central, white bands. Is difficult to grow. Needs a sheltered, sunny site in moist, gritty, peaty soil. Is prone to attack by aphids.
***C.* 'Walter Shrimpton'** illus. p.398.

CALENDULA
Marigold

COMPOSITAE/ASTERACEAE

Genus of annuals and evergreen shrubs. Annuals are fully hardy; shrubs are frost tender, min. 4°C (39°F). Grow in sun or partial shade and in any well-drained soil. Dead-head regularly to prolong flowering. Propagate annuals by seed sown outdoors in spring or autumn, shrubs by stem cuttings in summer. Annuals may self-seed. Cucumber mosaic virus and powdery mildew may cause problems.
C. officinalis (Pot marigold). Fast-growing, bushy annual. Tall cultivars, H and S 60cm (24in); dwarf forms, H and S 30cm (12in). All have lance-shaped, strongly aromatic, pale green leaves. Daisy-like, single or double flower heads in a wide range of yellow and orange shades are produced from spring to autumn. **'Daisy May'** illus. p.348.♀ **'Fiesta Gitana'** illus. p.351. **'Geisha Girl'** (tall) illus. p.353. **Pacific Beauty Series 'Lemon Queen'** illus. p.350.

Calico bush. See *Kalmia latifolia*, illus. p.137.
Calico flower. See *Aristolochia littoralis*, illus. p.207.
California allspice. See *Calycanthus occidentalis*, illus. p.138.
California bluebell. See *Phacelia campanularia*, illus. p.346.
California buckeye. See *Aesculus californica*, illus. p.81.
California nutmeg. See *Torreya californica*, illus. p.103.

California poppy. See *Eschscholzia.*
Californian laurel. See *Umbellularia californica*, illus. p.70.
Californian live oak. See *Quercus agrifolia*, illus. p.81.
Californian pepper-tree. See *Schinus molle*.

CALLA

ARACEAE

Genus of one species of deciduous or semi-evergreen, perennial, spreading, marginal water plant, grown for its foliage and showy spathes that surround insignificant flower clusters. Fully hardy. Requires a sunny position, in mud or in water to 25cm (10in) deep. Propagate by division in spring or by seed in late summer. Contact with the foliage may aggravate skin allergies.
C. palustris illus. p.462.

Callery pear. See *Pyrus calleryana*.

CALLIANDRA

MIMOSACEAE/LEGUMINOSAE

Genus of evergreen trees, shrubs and scandent semi-climbers, grown for their flowers and overall appearance. Frost tender, min. 7–18°C (45–64°F). Requires full light or partial shade and well-drained soil. Water containerized plants freely when in full growth, much less when temperatures are low. To restrict growth, cut back stems by one-half to two-thirds after flowering. Propagate by seed sown indoors in spring. Whitefly and mealy bug may be troublesome.
C. eriophylla illus. p.168.
C. haematocephala [pink form] illus. p.143, [white form] illus. p.145.

CALLIANTHEMUM

RANUNCULACEAE

Genus of perennials, grown for their daisy-like flowers and thick, dissected leaves. Is excellent for rock gardens and alpine houses. Fully hardy. Needs sun and moist but well-drained soil. Propagate by seed when fresh.
C. coriandrifolium, syn. *C. rutifolium*. Prostrate perennial with upright flower stems. H 8cm (3in), S 20cm (8in). Leaves, forming open rosettes, are long-stalked, very dissected and blue-green. In spring has short-stemmed, many-petalled, white flowers with yellow centres. Is susceptible to slugs.
C. rutifolium. See *C. coriandrifolium*.

CALLICARPA

VERBENACEAE

Genus of deciduous, summer-flowering shrubs, grown for their small but striking, clustered fruits. Fully hardy. Does best in full sun and fertile, well-drained soil. Propagate by softwood cuttings in summer.
C. bodinieri. Deciduous, bushy shrub. H 3m (10ft), S 2.5m (8ft). Has oval, dark green leaves. Tiny, star-shaped, lilac flowers in mid-summer are followed by dense clusters of spherical, violet fruits. var. ***giraldii*** illus. p.144.

CALLISIA

COMMELINACEAE

Genus of evergreen, prostrate perennials, grown for their ornamental foliage and trailing habit. Frost tender, min. 10–15°C (50–59°F). Grow in full light, but out of direct sunlight, in fertile, well-drained soil. Propagate by tip cuttings in spring, either annually or when plants become straggly.
C. navicularis, syn. *Tradescantia navicularis*. Evergreen, low-growing perennial with creeping, rooting shoots, 50cm (20in) or more long. H 5–8cm (2–3in), S indefinite. Has 2 rows of oval, keeled leaves, 2.5cm (1in) long, sheathing the stem, and stalkless clusters of small, 3-petalled, pinkish-purple flowers in leaf axils in summer-autumn.
C. repens illus. p.316.

CALLISTEMON
Bottlebrush

MYRTACEAE

Genus of evergreen shrubs, usually with narrow, pointed leaves, grown for their clustered flowers, which, with their profusion of long stamens, resemble bottlebrushes. Fully hardy to frost tender, min. 5°C (41°F); in cool areas, grow half hardy and tender species against a south-or west-facing wall or in a cool greenhouse. Requires full sun and fertile, well-drained soil. Propagate by semi-ripe cuttings in summer or by seed in autumn or spring.
🏆 ***C. citrinus* 'Splendens'** illus. p.139.
C. pallidus illus. p.142.
C. paludosus. See *C. sieberi*.
C. pityoides. Evergreen, compact, upright shrub. H 1.5m (5ft), S 1m (3ft). Fully hardy. Is densely covered with sharply pointed, dark green leaves, and has short spikes of yellow flowers in mid- and late summer.
C. rigidus illus. p.139.
C. sieberi, syn. *C. paludosus*. Evergreen, bushy, dense shrub. H 1.5m (5ft), S 1m (3ft). Frost hardy. Has short, narrowly lance-shaped, rigid, mid-green leaves and, from mid- to late summer, small clusters of pale yellow flowers.
C. speciosus (Albany bottlebrush). Evergreen, bushy shrub. H and S 3m (10ft). Half hardy. Produces long, narrow, grey-green leaves. Cylindrical clusters of bright red flowers appear in late spring and early summer.
C. subulatus. Evergreen, arching shrub. H and S 1.5m (5ft). Fully hardy. Leaves are narrowly oblong and bright green. Dense spikes of crimson flowers are produced in summer.
C. viminalis. Evergreen, arching shrub. H and S 5m (15ft). Half hardy. Narrowly oblong, bronze, young leaves mature to dark green. Bears clusters of bright red flowers in summer.

CALLISTEPHUS
China aster

COMPOSITAE/ASTERACEAE

Genus of one species of annual. Half hardy. Requires sun, a sheltered position and fertile, well-drained soil. Tall cultivars need support; all should be dead-headed. Propagate by seed sown under glass in spring; seed may also be sown outdoors in mid-spring. Wilt disease, virus diseases, foot rot, root rot and aphids may be a problem.
C. chinensis. Moderately fast-growing, erect, bushy annual. Tall cultivars, H 60cm (24in), S 45cm (18in); intermediate, H 45cm (18in), S 30cm (12in); dwarf, H 25–30cm (10–12in), S 30–45cm (12–18in); very dwarf, H 20cm (8in), S 30cm (12in). All have oval, toothed, mid-green leaves and flower in summer and early autumn. Different forms are available in a wide colour range, including pink, red, blue and white. **Duchesse Series** (tall) has incurved, chrysanthemum-like flower heads. 🏆 **Milady Super Series** (dwarf) has incurved, fully double flower heads available either in mixed or single colours (blue, illus. p.344; rose, illus. p.336). **Ostrich Plume Series** (tall) illus. p.343. **Pompon Series** (tall) has small, double flower heads. **Princess Series** (tall) has double flower heads with quilled petals.

CALLUNA

ERICACEAE

See also HEATHERS.
C. vulgaris (Ling, Scotch heather). Evergreen, bushy shrub. H to 60cm (24in), S 45cm (18in). Fully hardy. Slightly fleshy, linear leaves, in opposite and overlapping pairs, may range in colour from bright green to many shades of grey, yellow, orange and red. Spikes of bell- to urn-shaped, single or double flowers are produced from mid-summer to late autumn. Unlike *Erica*, most of the flower colour derives from the sepals. The following cultivars are H 45cm (18in), have mid-green leaves and bear single flowers in late summer and early autumn, unless otherwise stated.
'Alba Plena', H 30–45cm (12–18in), bears double, white flowers.
🏆 **'Alexandra'PBR** (illus. p.175), H 30cm (12in), S 40cm (16in), has an upright habit, dark green foliage, and deep crimson buds until early winter.
🏆 **'Alicia'PBR**, H 30cm (12in), S 40cm (16in), has white buds until early winter, and a neat, compact habit.
🏆 **'Allegro'**, H 60cm (24in), is compact in habit and produces purple-red flowers. **'Alportii'**, H 60–90cm (24–36in), has purple-red flowers.
🏆 **'Anette'PBR**, H 35cm (14in), S 40cm (16in), has clear pink buds until early winter. 🏆 **'Annemarie'**, H 50cm (20in), S 60cm (24in), has outstanding, double, rose-pink flowers, ideal for cutting. 🏆 **'Anthony Davis'** (illus. p.174) has grey leaves and white flowers. 🏆 **'Beoley Gold'** (illus. p.175), S 50cm (20in), has golden foliage and white flowers. **'Beoley Silver'**, H 40cm (16in), has silver foliage and white flowers. **'Blazeaway'**, H 35cm (14in), S 60cm (24in), has gold foliage in summer that turns orange, then fiery red in winter. **'Bonfire Brilliance'**, H 30cm (12in), has bright, flame-coloured foliage and mauve-pink flowers. **'Boskoop'** (illus. p.175), H 30cm (12in), is compact with golden foliage that turns deep orange in winter and lilac-pink flowers. 🏆 **'County Wicklow'** (illus. p.174), H 30cm (12in), S 35cm (14in), is compact with double, shell-pink flowers. 🏆 **'Dark Beauty'**, H 20cm (8in), S 35cm (14in), is neat and compact, and bears bright, semi-double, crimson flowers.
🏆 **'Darkness'** (illus. p.175), H 40cm (16in), S 35cm (14in), is compact with crimson flowers. 🏆 **'Elsie Purnell'** (illus. p.174) is a spreading cultivar with greyish-green leaves and double, pale pink flowers. **'Finale'** bears dark pink flowers from late autumn to early winter. 🏆 **'Firefly'** (illus. p.175), S 50cm (20in), with deep mauve flowers, has foliage that is terracotta in summer, brick-red in winter. **'Foxii Nana'** (illus. p.175), H 15cm (6in), forms low mounds of bright green foliage and produces a few mauve-pink flowers. **'Fred J. Chapple'** has bright pink- and coral-tipped foliage in spring; mauve-pink flowers are borne on long stems. 🏆 **'Gold Haze'** (illus. p.175) has bright golden foliage and white flowers. **'Golden Feather'** (illus. p.175) has bright yellow foliage, turning orange in winter, and mauve-pink flowers. **'Hammondii Aureifolia'**, H 30cm (12in), S 40cm (16in), has white flowers. Foliage is light green, tipped yellow in spring and early summer. **'H. E. Beale'**, H 50cm (20in), is one of the best double-flowered heathers, with pale pink flowers on long stems. 🏆 **'J. H. Hamilton'** (illus. p.174), H 20cm (8in), S 40cm (16in), is compact with double, salmon-pink flowers. 🏆 **'Joy Vanstone'** has golden foliage, turning to orange and bronze, and mauve-pink flowers. 🏆 **'Kerstin'**, H 30cm (12in), produces mauve flowers and has downy, deep lilac-grey foliage in winter, tipped pale yellow and red in spring. 🏆 **'Kinlochruel'** (illus. p.174), H 30cm (12in), S 35cm (14in), bears an abundance of large, double, white flowers. **'Loch Turret'**, H 30cm (12in), has emerald-green foliage and produces white flowers in early summer.
🏆 **'Mair's Variety'**, an old cultivar, has white flowers on long spikes.
'Marleen' is unusual in that its long-lasting, dark mauve flower buds, borne from early to late autumn, do not open fully. 🏆 **'Mullion' H** 25cm (10in), S 50cm (20in), is a spreading cultivar with rich mauve-pink flowers.
'Multicolor' (illus. p.175), H 20cm (8in), is compact with foliage in shades of yellow, orange, red and green year-round; flowers are mauve-pink. 🏆 **'My Dream'** (syn. *C.v.* 'Snowball'; illus. p.174), H 50cm (20in), produces double, white flowers that are borne on long, tapering stems. 🏆 **'Peter Sparkes'** (illus. p.175), H 50cm (20in), S 55cm (22in), bears double, deep pink flowers. 🏆 **'Robert Chapman'** (illus. p.175) is a spreading cultivar and grown mainly for its foliage, which is golden-yellow in summer, turning orange and brilliant red in winter; flowers are mauve-pink. **'Ruth Sparkes'**, H 25cm (10in), has golden foliage and white flowers. **'Silver Knight'** (illus. p.175), H 30cm (12in), is of upright habit with grey leaves and mauve-pink flowers. 🏆 **'Silver Queen'** (illus. p.174), H 40cm (16in), S 55cm (22in), is a spreading cultivar with dark mauve-pink flowers. 🏆 **'Sir John Charrington'** has bright-coloured foliage, varying from golden-yellow in summer to orange and red in winter, and dark mauve-pink flowers. 🏆 **'Sister Anne'**, H 15cm (6in), has grey leaves

and pale mauve-pink flowers. **'Snowball'** see *C.v.* 'My Dream'. ♀ **'Spring Cream'** (illus. p.174) has bright green leaves, which have cream tips in spring, and white flowers. **'Spring Torch'**, H 40cm (16in), S 60cm (24in), has mauve flowers with cream, orange and red tips in spring. ♀ **'Sunset'**, H 25cm (10in), has brightly coloured foliage, changing from golden-yellow in spring to orange in summer and fiery red in winter; flowers are mauve-pink. ♀ **'Tib'** (illus. p.175), H 30cm (12in), S 40cm (16in), is the earliest-flowering double cultivar, producing small, double, deep pink flowers in early summer. ♀ **'White Lawn'**, H 10cm (4in), is a creeping cultivar with bright green foliage and white flowers on long stems; is suitable for a rock garden. ♀ **'Wickwar Flame'** is primarily a foliage plant with leaves in shades of yellow, orange and flame that are particularly effective in winter; flowers are mauve-pink.

CALOCEDRUS

CUPRESSACEAE

See also CONIFERS.
♀ ***C. decurrens***, syn. *Libocedrus decurrens*, illus. p.102.

Calocephalus brownii. See *Leucophyta brownii.*

CALOCHONE

RUBIACEAE

Genus of evergreen, scrambling climbers, grown for their showy flowers. Frost tender, min. 18°C (64°F). Requires full light and humus-rich, well-drained soil. Water regularly, less in cold weather. Needs tying to a support. Thin out crowded stems after flowering. Propagate by semi-ripe cuttings in summer.
C. redingii. Moderately vigorous, evergreen, scrambling climber. H 3–5m (10–15ft). Has oval, pointed, hairy leaves, 7–12cm (3–5in) long. Trusses of primrose-shaped, red to orange-pink flowers appear in winter.

CALOCHORTUS

Cat's ears, Fairy lantern, Mariposa tulip

LILIACEAE

Genus of bulbs, grown for their spring and summer flowers. Frost hardy. Needs a sheltered, sunny position and well-drained soil. In cold, damp climates, cover or lift spring-flowering species when dormant (in summer), or grow in cold frames or cold houses. After flowering, remove bulbils formed in leaf axils for propagation. Propagate by seed or bulbils – spring-flowering species in autumn, summer-flowering species in spring.
C. albus illus. p.425.
C. amabilis illus. p.450.
C. barbatus, syn. *Cyclobothra lutea*, illus. p.438.
C. luteus illus. p.431.
C. monophyllus illus. p.452.
C. splendens. Late spring-flowering bulb. H 20–60cm (8–24in), S 5–10cm (2–4in). Bears 1 or 2 linear, erect leaves near base of branched stem and 1–4 upward-facing, saucer-shaped, pale purple flowers, 5–7cm (2–3in) across, with a darker blotch at the base of each of the 3 large petals.
C. superbus. Late spring-flowering bulb. H 20–60cm (8–24in), S 5–10cm (2–4in). Is similar to *C. splendens*, but flowers are white, cream or pale lilac, with a brown mark near the base of each of the 3 large petals.
C. venustus illus. p.424.
C. vestae. Late spring-flowering bulb. H 20–60cm (8–24in), S 5–10cm (2–4in). Is similar to *C. splendens*, but flowers are white or purple, with a rust-brown mark near the base of each of the 3 large petals.
C. weedii. Summer-flowering bulb. H 30–60cm (12–24in), S 5–10cm (2–4in). Has a linear, erect leaf near base of stem. Carries usually 2 upright, saucer-shaped flowers, 4–5cm (1½–2in) across, that are orange-yellow with brown lines and flecks and hairy inside.

CALODENDRUM

RUTACEAE

Genus of evergreen trees, grown for their flowers that are produced mainly in spring-summer. Frost tender, min. 7–10°C (45–50°F). Needs full light and fertile, well-drained but moisture-retentive soil. Water containerized specimens freely when in full growth, less at other times. Tolerates some pruning. Propagate by seed in spring or by semi-ripe cuttings in summer.
C. capense (Cape chestnut). Fairly fast-growing, evergreen, rounded tree. H and S to 15m (50ft) or more. Has oval leaves patterned with translucent dots. Terminal panicles of 5-petalled, light pink to deep mauve flowers appear from spring to early summer.

CALOMERIA, syn. HUMEA

COMPOSITAE/ASTERACEAE

Genus of perennials and evergreen shrubs. Only *C. amaranthoides* is cultivated, usually as a biennial. Frost tender, min. 4°C (39°F). Needs sun and fertile, well-drained soil. Propagate by seed sown under glass in mid-summer.
C. amaranthoides, syn. *C. elegans*, illus. p.342.
C. elegans. See *C. amaranthoides.*

Calonyction aculeatum. See *Ipomoea alba.*

CALOSCORDUM

LILIACEAE/ALLIACEAE

Genus of one species of summer-flowering bulb, related and similar to *Allium*. Is suitable for a rock garden. Frost hardy. Needs an open, sunny situation and well-drained soil. Lies dormant in winter. Propagate in early spring by seed or division before growth starts.
C. neriniflorum, syn. *Nothoscordum neriniflorum.* Clump-forming bulb. H 10–25cm (4–10in), S 8–10cm (3–4in). Thread-like, semi-erect, basal leaves die down at flowering time. Each leafless stem produces a loose head of 10–20 small, funnel-shaped, pinkish-red flowers in late summer.

CALOTHAMNUS

MYRTACEAE

Genus of evergreen, summer-flowering shrubs, grown for their flowers and overall appearance. Thrives in a dryish, airy environment. Frost tender, min. 5°C (41°F). Requires full sun and well-drained, sandy soil. Water containerized plants moderately when in full growth, less at other times. Propagate by seed or semi-ripe cuttings in summer.
C. quadrifidus (Common net bush). Erect to spreading, evergreen shrub. H 2–4m (6–12ft), S 2–5m (6–15ft). Has linear, greyish to dark green or grey leaves. Irregular, axillary, one-sided spikes of rich red, feathery flowers, 2.5cm (1in) long, are produced from late spring to autumn, often forming clusters, 20cm (8in) or more across, around the stems.

CALTHA

RANUNCULACEAE

Genus of deciduous, perennial, marginal water plants, bog plants and rock garden plants, grown for their attractive flowers. Fully hardy. Most prefer an open, sunny position. Smaller growing species are suitable for rock gardens, troughs and alpine houses and require moist but well-drained soil; larger species are best in marginal conditions. Propagate species by seed in autumn or by division in autumn or early spring, selected forms by division in autumn or early spring.
C. leptosepala illus. p.463.
♀ ***C. palustris*** illus. p.467. var. ***alba*** (syn. *C.p.* 'Alba') is a compact, deciduous, perennial, marginal water plant. H 22cm (9in), S 30cm (12in). Has rounded, glossy, dark green leaves, and bears solitary, white flowers with yellow stamens in early spring, often before the foliage develops. ♀ **'Flore Pleno'** illus. p.467.

CALYCANTHUS

CALYCANTHACEAE

Genus of deciduous, summer-flowering shrubs, grown for their purplish-or brownish-red flowers with strap-shaped petals. Fully hardy. Requires sun or light shade and fertile, deep, moist but well-drained soil. Propagate by softwood cuttings in summer or by seed in autumn.
C. floridus (Carolina allspice). Deciduous, bushy shrub. H and S 2m (6ft). Has oval, aromatic, dark green leaves and, from early to mid-summer, fragrant, brownish-red flowers with masses of spreading petals.
C. occidentalis (California allspice) illus. p.138.

CALYPSO

ORCHIDACEAE

See also ORCHIDS.
C. bulbosa illus. p.309. Deciduous, terrestrial orchid. H 5–20cm (2–8in). Fully hardy. Corm-like stem produces a single, oval, pleated leaf, 3–10cm (1¼–4in) long. Purplish-pink flowers, 1.5–2cm (⅝–¾in) long, with hairy, purple-blotched, white or pale pink lips, are produced singly in late spring or early summer. Requires a damp, semi-shaded position with a mulch of leaf mould.

CAMASSIA

LILIACEAE/HYACINTHACEAE

Genus of summer-flowering bulbs, suitable for borders and pond margins. Frost hardy. Requires sun or partial shade and deep, moist soil. Plant bulbs in autumn, 10cm (4in) deep. Lies dormant in autumn-winter. Propagate by seed in autumn or by division in late summer. If seed is not required, cut off stems after flowering.
C. esculenta. See *C. quamash.*
♀ ***C. leichtlinii*** illus. p.409. **'Semiplena'** illus. p.409.
C. quamash, syn. *C. esculenta* (Common camassia, Quamash). Clump-forming, summer-flowering bulb. H 20–80cm (8–32in), S 20–30cm (8–12in). Produces long, narrow, erect, basal leaves. Leafless stems each bear a dense spike of star-shaped, blue, violet or white flowers, to 7cm (3in) across.

Camassia, Common. See *Camassia quamash.*

CAMELLIA

THEACEAE

Genus of evergreen shrubs and trees, grown for their flowers and foliage. Flowers are classified according to the following types: single, semi-double, anemone-form, peony-form, rose-form, formal double and irregular double. See feature panel pp.124–5 for illustrations and descriptions. Grows well against walls and in containers. Fully hardy to frost tender, min. 7–10°C (45–50°F). Most forms prefer a sheltered position and semi-shade. Well-drained, neutral to acid soil is essential. Prune to shape after flowering. Propagate by semi-ripe or hardwood cuttings from mid-summer to early winter or by grafting in late winter or early spring. Aphids, thrips and scale insects may cause problems under glass.
'Anticipation'. See *C.* × *williamsii* ♀'Anticipation'
♀ ***C.* 'Black Lace'** illus. p.125. Slow-growing, dense, upright shrub. H 1.5–2.5m (5–8ft), S 1–2.5m (3–8ft). Fully hardy. Has ovate, dark green leaves, 8cm (3in) long, and large, formal double, deep velvet-red flowers from early to late spring.
C. chrysantha. See *C. nitidissima.*
♀ ***C.* 'Cornish Snow'** illus. p.124. Fast-growing, evergreen, upright, bushy shrub. H 3m (10ft), S 1.5m (5ft). Frost hardy. Has lance-shaped leaves, bronze when young, maturing to dark green. In early spring bears a profusion of small, cup-shaped, single, white flowers.
C. cuspidata. Evergreen, upright shrub becoming bushy with age. H 3m (10ft), S 1.5m (5ft). Frost hardy. Has small, lance-shaped leaves, bronze when young, maturing to purplish-green. Small, cup-shaped, single, pure white flowers are freely produced from leaf axils in early spring.
♀ ***C.* 'Dr Clifford Parks'** illus. p.125. Evergreen, spreading shrub. H 4m (12ft), S 2.5m (8ft). Frost hardy. In mid-spring has large, flame-red flowers, often semi-double, peony- and anemone-form on the same plant.

Leaves are large, oval and dark green.
♀ ***C.* 'Francie L.'** illus. p.125. Vigorous shrub with long, fan-shaped branches. H 5m (15ft), S 6m (20ft). Fully hardy (if trained on a wall). Leaves are lance-shaped and dark green, 6–10cm (2½–4in) long. Has large, semi-double, salmon-red to deep rose-red flowers from late winter to late spring.
C. granthamiana. Evergreen, open shrub. H to 3m (10ft), S 2m (6ft). Half hardy. Oval, leathery leaves are crinkly and glossy, deep green. In late autumn bears large, saucer-shaped, single, white flowers, to 18cm (7in) across, with up to 8 broad petals.
C. hiemalis. Evergreen, upright, bushy shrub. H 2–3m (6–10ft), S 1.5m (5ft). Frost hardy. Has small, lance-shaped leaves and fragrant, single, cup-shaped, semi- or irregular double, white, pink or red flowers borne in late autumn and winter. Is good for hedging.
C. hongkongensis. Evergreen, bushy shrub or tree. H to 3m (10ft), S 2m (6ft). Half hardy. Lance-shaped leaves, 10cm (4in) long, are dark red when young, maturing to dark green. Bears cup-shaped, single, deep crimson flowers, velvety beneath, in late spring.
***C.* 'Innovation'** illus. p.125. Evergreen, open, spreading shrub. H 5m (15ft), S 3m (10ft). Frost hardy. Has large, oval, leathery leaves and, in spring, produces large, peony-form, lavender-shaded, claret-red flowers with twisted petals.
♀ ***C.* 'Inspiration'** illus. p.125. Evergreen, upright shrub. H 4m (12ft), S 2m (6ft). Frost hardy. Leaves are oval and leathery. Saucer-shaped, semi-double, phlox-pink flowers are freely produced in spring.
C. japonica (Common camellia). Evergreen shrub that is very variable in habit, foliage and floral form. H 10m (30ft), S 8m (25ft). Frost hardy. Numerous cultivars are available; they are spring-flowering unless otherwise stated.
♀ **'Adolphe Audusson'** (illus. p.125) is a very reliable, old cultivar that is suitable for all areas and will withstand lower temperatures than most other variants. Produces large, saucer-shaped, semi-double, dark red flowers with prominent, yellow stamens. Leaves are broadly lance-shaped and dark green.
'Alba Simplex' (illus. p.124) is bushy in habit with broadly lance-shaped, mid-to yellow-green leaves and cup-shaped, single, white flowers in early spring.
♀ **'Alexander Hunter'** (illus. p.125), an upright, compact shrub, has flattish, single, deep crimson flowers, with some petaloids, and lance-shaped, dark green leaves.
'Althaeiflora' (illus. p.125) has a vigorous, bushy habit, large, peony-form, dark red flowers and broadly oval, very dark green leaves.
'Apollo' (syn. *C.j.* 'Paul's Apollo'; illus. p.125) is a vigorous, branching shrub that produces semi-double, red flowers sometimes blotched with white. Leaves are glossy, dark green.
♀ **'Berenice Boddy'** (illus. p.124) is a vigorous shrub that bears semi-double, light pink flowers amid lance-shaped, dark green leaves.
'Betty Sheffield Supreme' (illus. p.124) is upright in habit with lance-shaped, mid-green leaves. Irregular double flowers have white petals bordered with shades of rose-pink.
♀ **'Bob's Tinsie'** (illus. p.125) has a dense, upright habit, and bears miniature, anemone-form, brilliant red flowers from early to late spring.
♀ **'Coquettii'** (syn. *C.j.* 'Glen 40'; illus. p.125) is a slow-growing, erect shrub. In early and mid-spring, bears profuse, medium to large, deep red flowers, sometimes formal double, sometimes peony-form.
'Donckelaeri' see *C.j.* 'Masayoshi'.
♀ **'Elegans'** (illus. p.125) has a spreading habit and anemone-form, deep rose-pink flowers with central petaloids often variegated white. Leaves are broadly lance-shaped and dark green.
'Glen 40' see *C.j.* 'Coquettii'.
♀ **'Gloire de Nantes'** (illus. p.125) is an upright shrub, becoming bushy with age, that bears flattish to cup-shaped, semi-double, bright rose-pink flowers over a long period. Has oval to lance-shaped, glossy, dark green leaves.
♀ **'Guilio Nuccio'** (illus. p.125) is an upright, free-flowering cultivar that spreads with age. Produces large, cup-shaped, semi-double, rose-red flowers with wavy petals and often a confused centre of petaloids and golden stamens. Dark green leaves are lance-shaped and occasionally have 'fish-tail' tips.
♀ **'Hagoromo'** (syn. *C.j.* 'Magnoliiflora') has a bushy habit and flattish to cup-shaped, semi-double, blush-pink flowers. Twisted, light green leaves point downwards.
'Janet Waterhouse' (illus. p.124) is strong-growing and has semi-double, white flowers with golden anthers borne amid dark green foliage.
'Julia Drayton' (illus. p.125) has an upright habit and large, crimson flowers varying from formal double to rose-form. Dark green leaves are oval to lance-shaped and slightly twisted.
♀ **'Jupiter'** (illus. p.125) is an upright shrub that bears lance-shaped, dark green leaves and large, saucer-shaped, single, pinkish-red flowers with golden stamens.
'Kumasaka' (syn. *C.j.* 'Lady Marion') has an upright habit with narrowly lance-shaped, mid-green leaves. Produces formal double, or occasionally peony-form, deep rose-pink flowers.
'Lady Marion' see *C.j.* 'Kumasaka'.
'Lady Vansittart' (illus. p.124) is upright, with unusual, holly-like, twisted, mid-green foliage. Saucer-shaped, semi-double, white flowers are flushed rose-pink; flower colour is variable and often self-coloured mutations appear.
♀ **'Lavinia Maggi'** (illus. p.124) has an upright habit and formal double, white flowers striped with pink and carmine. Sometimes sports red flowers.
'Magnoliiflora' see *C.j.* 'Hagoromo'.
'Margaret Davis' (illus. p.124) is a spreading cultivar, with oval to lance-shaped, dark green leaves. Has irregular double blooms with ruffled, creamy-white petals, often lined with pink. Edges of each petal are bright rose-red.
♀ **'Masayoshi'** (syn. *C.j.* 'Donckelaeri') is slow-growing, bushy and pendulous with saucer-shaped, semi-double, red flowers, often white-marbled. Has lance-shaped, dark green leaves.
♀ **'Mathotiana'** (illus. p.125) is of spreading habit. Very large, formal double, velvety, dark crimson flowers become purplish with age and in warm climates often have rose-form centres. Leaves are lance-shaped to oval, slightly twisted and dark green.
'Mrs D.W. Davis' (illus. p.124) is a dense, spreading cultivar that bears very large, pendulous, cup-shaped, semi-double, delicate pink flowers that are backed by oval to lance-shaped, dark green leaves.
'Paul's Apollo' see *C.j.* 'Apollo'.
♀ **'R.L. Wheeler'** (illus. p.125) has a robust, upright growth, large, broadly oval, leathery, very dark green leaves and very large, flattish, anemone-form to semi-double, rose-pink flowers, with distinctive rings of golden stamens, often including some petaloids.
♀ **'Rubescens Major'** (illus. p.125) is an upright cultivar, becoming bushy with age, with oval to lance-shaped, dark green leaves. Bears formal double, crimson-veined, rose-red flowers.
'Sieboldii' see *C.j.* 'Tricolor'.
'Tomorrow Park Hill', one of the best of many mutations of 'Tomorrow', is of vigorous, upright habit. Has lance-shaped, mid-green leaves and bears irregular double flowers with deep pink, outer petals gradually fading to soft pink centres that are often variegated with white.
'Tomorrow's Dawn' (illus. p.124) is similar to 'Tomorrow Park Hill', but produces pale pink flowers, each with a white border and frequently red-streaked.
♀ **'Tricolor'** (syn. *C.j.* 'Sieboldii') has bright green, crinkled, holly-like leaves, and bears medium, single or semi-double, red flowers, striped pink and white, in early spring.
♀ ***C.* 'Leonard Messel'** illus. p.125. Evergreen, open shrub. H 4m (12ft), S 2.5m (8ft). Frost hardy. Has large, oval, leathery, dark green leaves. In spring bears a profusion of large, flattish to cup-shaped, semi-double, rose-pink flowers.
C.* × *maliflora. Evergreen, upright, bushy shrub. H 2m (6ft), S 1m (3ft). Frost hardy. Has small, lance-shaped, thin-textured, light green leaves and, in spring, produces flattish to cup-shaped, semi-double, pale pink-or white-centred flowers with rose-pink margins.
C. nitidissima, syn. *C. chrysantha.* Fast-growing, evergreen, open shrub or tree. H 6m (20ft) or more, S 3m (10ft). Half hardy. Has large, oval, leathery, veined leaves. Small, stalked, cup-shaped, single, clear yellow flowers are produced from leaf axils in spring.
C. oleifera. Evergreen, bushy shrub. H 2m (6ft), S 1.5m (5ft). Frost hardy. Leaves are oval and dull green. Has cup-shaped, single, sometimes pinkish, white flowers in early spring.
C. reticulata. Evergreen, open, tree-like shrub. H 10m (30ft) or more, S 5m (15ft). Half hardy. Has large, oval, leathery leaves; large, saucer-shaped, single, rose-pink and salmon-red flowers are borne in spring. Needs shelter. **'Arch of Triumph'** (illus. p.125) bears very large, loose peony-form, orange-tinted, crimson-pink flowers. **'Butterfly Wings'** see *C.r.* 'Houye Diechi'. **'Captain Rawes'** (illus. p.125) has a profusion of large, semi-double, carmine-rose blooms. **'Houye Diechi'** (syn. *C.r.* 'Butterfly Wings'; illus. p.125) produces very large, flattish to cup-shaped, semi-double, rose-pink flowers with wavy, central petals. **'Mandalay Queen'** (illus. p.125) has large, semi-double, deep rose-pink flowers. **'Robert Fortune'** see *C.r* 'Songzilin'. **'Songzilin'** (syn. *C.r.* 'Robert Fortune') is upright and has large, formal double, deep red flowers.
C. rosiflora. Evergreen, spreading shrub. H and S 1m (3ft). Frost hardy. Leaves are oval and dark green. In spring bears small, saucer-shaped, single, rose-pink flowers.
C. saluenensis illus. p.124. Fast-growing, evergreen, bushy shrub. H to 4m (12ft), S to 2.5m (8ft). Half hardy. Has lance-shaped, stiff, dull green leaves. Cup-shaped, single, white to rose-red flowers are freely produced in early spring. Some forms may withstand lower temperatures.
C. sasanqua. Fast-growing, evergreen, dense, upright shrub. H 3m (10ft), S 1.5m (5ft). Frost hardy. Has lance-shaped, glossy, bright green leaves. In autumn bears a profusion of fragrant, flattish to cup-shaped, single, rarely semi-double, white flowers; they may occasionally be pink or red. Does best in a hot, sunny site. **'Narumigata'** (illus. p.124) has large, cup-shaped, single, white flowers, sometimes pink-flushed. **'Shishigashira'** has small, semi-double to rose-form double, pinkish-red flowers.
***C.* 'Satan's Robe'** illus. p.125. Vigorous, erect shrub. H 3–5m (10–15ft), S 2–3m (6–10ft). Frost hardy. Leaves are broadly elliptic, glossy and dark green, 12–16cm (5–6in) long. From early to late spring, produces large, semi-double, bright carmine-red flowers, with yellow stamens.
***C.* 'Shiro-wabisuke'** illus. p.124. Slow-growing, compact shrub. H 2.5m (8ft), S 1.5m (5ft). Fully hardy. Has narrow, mid-green leaves. From mid-winter to early spring produces small, single, bell-shaped, white flowers.
C. tsaii illus. p.124. Evergreen, bushy shrub. H 4m (12ft), S 3m (10ft). Half hardy. Small, lance-shaped, light green leaves turn bronze with age. Small, cup-shaped, single, white flowers are freely produced in spring.
C.* × *vernalis. Fast-growing, evergreen, upright shrub. H to 3m (10ft), S 1.5m (5ft). Frost hardy. Has lance-shaped, bright green leaves and, in late winter, fragrant, flattish to cup-shaped, single, white, pink or red flowers. Some forms produce irregular double flowers.
***C.* 'William Hertrich'** illus. p.125. Strong-growing, evergreen, open shrub. H 5m (15ft), S 3m (10ft). Half hardy. Is free-flowering with large, flattish to cup-shaped, semi-double blooms of a bright cherry-red in spring. Petal formation is very irregular, and petals often form a confused centre with only a few golden stamens. Leaves are large, oval and deep green.
C.* × *williamsii ♀ **'Anticipation'** illus. p.125. Robust, evergreen, upright shrub. H 3m (10ft), S 1.5m (5ft). Frost hardy. Has lance-shaped, dark green leaves. Large, peony-form, deep rose-

pink blooms are freely produced in spring. **'Bow Bells'** illus. p.124. Evergreen, upright, spreading shrub. H 4m (12ft), S 2.5m (8ft). Fully hardy. Has small, lance-shaped, mid-green leaves and, in early spring, masses of cup-shaped, single, rose-pink flowers with deeper pink centres and veins. ♀ **'Brigadoon'** (illus. p.124) is a bushy shrub, bearing semi-double, rose-pink flowers with broad, down-curving petals. ♀ **'Donation'** (illus. p.124) is a compact, upright plant that is very floriferous, with large, cup-shaped, semi-double, pink flowers. **'Dream Boat'** (illus. p.124) has a spreading habit, and bears medium, formal double, pale purplish-pink flowers, with incurved petals, in mid-spring. **'E. G. Waterhouse'** (illus. p.124) is an upright, free-flowering cultivar bearing formal double, pink flowers among pale green foliage.
'Elizabeth de Rothschild' is vigorous and upright; cup-shaped, semi-double, rose-pink flowers appear among glossy foliage. **'Francis Hanger'** (illus. p.124) has an upright habit and carries single, white flowers with gold stamens.
♀ **'George Blandford'** (illus. p.125) is spreading and bears semi-double, bright crimson-pink flowers in early spring. **'Golden Spangles'** (illus. p.125) is a cup-shaped, single, deep pink cultivar with unusual, variegated foliage, yellowish in centres of leaves with dark green margins.
♀ **'J. C. Williams'** (illus. p.124) is of pendulous habit when mature and bears cup-shaped, single, pink flowers from early winter to late spring. ♀ **'Joan Trehane'** (illus. p.124) has strong, upright growth and large, rose-form double, rose-pink flowers. ♀ **'Jury's Yellow'** (illus. p.124) is narrow and erect, bearing medium, anemone-form, white flowers, with centres of yellow petaloids. ♀ **'Saint Ewe'** (illus. p.124) has glossy, light green foliage and funnel-shaped, single, deep pink flowers. ♀ **'Water Lily'** (illus. p.125) is an upright, compact cultivar with dark green leaves that bears formal double, mid-pink flowers with incurving petals in mid-to late spring.

Camellia, Common. See *Camellia japonica*.

CAMPANULA
Bellflower

CAMPANULACEAE

Genus of spring- and summer-flowering annuals, biennials and perennials, some of which are evergreen. Fully to half hardy. Grows in sun or shade, but delicate flower colours are preserved best in shade. Most forms prefer moist but well-drained soil. Propagate by softwood or basal cuttings in summer or by seed or division in autumn or spring. Is prone to slug attack, and rust may be a problem in autumn.
C. alliariifolia illus. p.285.
C. armena. See *Symphyandra armena*.
C. barbata illus. p.368.
♀ ***C. betulifolia.*** Prostrate, slender-stemmed perennial. H 2cm (¾in), S 30cm (12in). Fully hardy. In summer, long, branching flower stems each carry a cluster of open bell-shaped, single, white to pink flowers, deep pink outside. Leaves are wedge-shaped.
♀ ***C.* 'Birch Hybrid'** illus. p.394.
C.* × *burghaltii. See *C.* 'Burghaltii'.
♀ ***C.* 'Burghaltii'**, syn. *C.* × *burghaltii*, illus. p.296.
♀ ***C. carpatica.*** Clump-forming perennial. H 8–10cm (3–4in), S to 30cm (12in). Fully hardy. Leafy, branching stems bear rounded to oval, toothed leaves and, in summer, broadly bell-shaped, blue or white flowers. **'Bressingham White'** illus. p.385. **'Jewel'** has deep violet flowers. Flowers of **'Turbinata'** (syn. *C.c.* var. *turbinata*) are pale lavender.
♀ ***C. cochleariifolia***, syn. *C. pusilla*, illus. p.395.
♀ ***C. garganica.*** Spreading perennial. H 5cm (2in), S 30cm (12in). Fully hardy. Has small, ivy-shaped leaves along stems. Clusters of star-shaped, single, pale lavender flowers are produced from leaf axils in summer. Makes an excellent wall or bank plant.
♀ **'W.H. Paine'** has bright lavender-blue flowers, each with a white eye.
♀ ***C.* 'G.F. Wilson'** illus. p.394.
♀ ***C. glomerata* 'Superba'** illus. p.255.
C.* × *haylodgensis. See *C.* × *haylodgensis* 'Plena'.
***C.* × *haylodgensis* 'Plena'**, syn. *C.* × *haylodgensis*. Spreading perennial. H 5cm (2in), S 20cm (8in). Fully hardy. Has small, heart-shaped leaves and, in summer, bears pompon-like, double, deep lavender-blue flowers. Is suitable for a rock garden or wall.
♀ ***C. isophylla.*** Evergreen, dwarf, trailing perennial. H 10cm (4in), S 30cm (12in). Half hardy. In summer, star-shaped, blue or white flowers are borne above small, heart-shaped, toothed leaves. Is ideal for a hanging basket. **Kristal Hybrids 'Stella Blue'** illus. p.297.
♀ ***C.* 'Joe Elliott'.** Mound-forming perennial. H 8cm (3in), S 12cm (5in). Fully hardy. In summer, large, funnel-shaped, mid-lavender-blue flowers almost obscure small, heart-shaped, downy, grey-green leaves. Is good for an alpine house, trough or rock garden. Needs well-drained, alkaline soil. Protect from winter wet. Is prone to slug attack.
C. lactiflora. Upright, branching perennial. H 1.2m (4ft), S 60cm (2ft). Fully hardy. In summer, slender stems bear racemes of large, nodding, bell-shaped, blue, occasionally pink or white flowers. Leaves are narrowly oval. Needs staking on a windy site.
♀ **'Loddon Anna'** illus. p.225.
♀ **'Prichard's Variety'** illus. p.226.
***C. latifolia* 'Brantwood'.** Clump-forming, spreading perennial. H 1.2m (4ft), S 60cm (2ft). Fully hardy. Strong stems are clothed with bell-shaped, rich violet-purple flowers in summer. Oval leaves are rough-textured.
C. latiloba. Rosette-forming perennial. H 1m (3ft), S 45cm (1½ft). Fully hardy. Leaves are oval. Widely cup-shaped flowers, in shades of blue, occasionally white, are borne in summer. ♀ **'Percy Piper'** has lavender flowers.
C. medium (Canterbury bell). Slow-growing, evergreen, erect, clump-forming biennial. Tall cultivars, H 1m (3ft), S 30cm (1ft); dwarf, H 60cm (2ft), S 30cm (1ft). Fully hardy. All have lance-shaped, toothed, fresh green leaves. Bell-shaped, single or double flowers, white or in shades of blue and pink, are produced in spring and early summer. **'Bells of Holland'** illus. p.343.
C. morettiana. Tuft-forming perennial. H 2.5cm (1in), S 7cm (3in). Frost hardy. Leaves are ivy-shaped with fine hairs. Arching flower stems each carry a solitary erect, bell-shaped, violet-blue flower in late spring and early summer. Needs gritty, alkaline soil and a dry but not arid winter climate. Red spider mite may be troublesome.
C. pendula. See *Symphyandra pendula*.
C. persicifolia. Rosette-forming, spreading perennial. H 1m (3ft), S 30cm (1ft). Fully hardy. In summer, nodding, bell-shaped, papery, white or blue flowers are borne above narrowly lance-shaped, bright green leaves.
♀ **'Fleur de Neige'** has double, white flowers. **'Pride of Exmouth'** bears double, powder-blue flowers. **'Telham Beauty'** illus. p.259.
♀ ***C. portenschlagiana*** illus. p.394.
C. poscharskyana illus. p.393.
C. pulla. Often short-lived perennial that spreads by underground runners. H 2.5cm (1in), S 10cm (4in). Fully hardy. Tiny, rounded leaves form 1cm (½in) wide rosettes, each bearing a flower stem with a solitary pendent, bell-shaped, deep violet flower from late spring to early summer. Is good for a scree or rock garden. Needs gritty, alkaline soil that is not too dry. Slugs may prove troublesome.
C. pusilla. See *C. cochleariifolia*.
C. pyramidalis (Chimney bellflower). Erect, branching biennial. H 2m (6ft), S 60cm (2ft). Half hardy. Produces long racemes of star-shaped, blue or white flowers in summer. Leaves are heart-shaped. Needs staking.
♀ ***C. raineri.*** Perennial that spreads by underground runners. H 4cm (1½in), S 8cm (3in). Frost hardy. Leaves are oval, toothed and grey-green. Flower stems each carry a large, upturned, bell-shaped, pale lavender flower in summer. Is suitable for an alpine house or trough that is protected from winter wet. Requires semi-shade.
C. trachelium and **'Bernice'** illus. p.258.
C. vidalii. See *Azorina vidalii*.
C. wanneri. See *Symphyandra wanneri*.
C. zoysii. Tuft-forming perennial. H 5cm (2in), S 10cm (4in). Frost hardy. Has tiny, rounded, glossy green leaves. In summer, flower stems each bear a bottle-shaped, lavender flower held horizontally. Needs gritty, alkaline soil. Is difficult to grow and flower well, dislikes winter wet and is prone to slug attack.

Campernelle jonquil. See *Narcissus* × *odorus*.
Campion. See *Silene*.
Double sea. See *Silene uniflora* 'Robin Whitebreast'.
Moss. See *Silene acaulis*, illus. p.377.

CAMPSIS

BIGNONIACEAE

Genus of deciduous, woody-stemmed, root climbers, grown for their flowers. Frost hardy; in cooler areas needs protection of a sunny wall. Grow in sun in fertile, well-drained soil, and water regularly in summer. Prune in spring. Propagate by semi-ripe cuttings in summer or by layering in winter.
C. chinensis. See *C. grandiflora*.
C. grandiflora, syn. *Bignonia grandiflora, Campsis chinensis, Tecoma grandiflora* (Chinese trumpet creeper, Chinese trumpet vine). Deciduous, woody-stemmed, root climber. H 7–10m (22–30ft). Leaves have 7 or 9 oval, toothed leaflets, hairless beneath. Drooping clusters of trumpet-shaped, deep orange or red flowers, 5–8cm (2–3in) long, are produced in late summer and autumn, abundantly in warm areas.
C. radicans, syn. *Bignonia radicans, Tecoma radicans* (Trumpet creeper, Trumpet honeysuckle, Trumpet vine). Deciduous, woody-stemmed, root climber. H to 12m (40ft). Leaves of 7–11 oval, toothed leaflets are downy beneath. Small clusters of trumpet-shaped, orange, scarlet or yellow flowers, 6–8cm (2½–3in) long, open in late summer and early autumn.
♀ ***C.* × *tagliabuana* 'Madame Galen'** illus. p.215.

Canada hemlock. See *Tsuga canadensis*, illus. p.103.
Canada lily. See *Lilium canadense*.
Canada moonseed. See *Menispermum canadense*.
Canada wild rice. See *Zizania aquatica*.
Canadian burnet. See *Sanguisorba canadensis*, illus. p.224.
Canadian columbine. See *Aquilegia canadensis*.
Canadian poplar. See *Populus* × *canadensis*.

CANARINA

CAMPANULACEAE

Genus of herbaceous, tuberous, scrambling climbers, grown for their flowers. Frost tender, min. 7°C (45°F). Grow in full light and in any fertile, well-drained soil. Water moderately from early autumn to late spring, then keep dry. Needs tying to a support. Remove dead stems when dormant. Propagate by basal cuttings or seed sown in spring or autumn.
C. campanula. See *C. canariensis*.
♀ ***C. canariensis***, syn. *C. campanula*, illus. p.217.

Canary creeper. See *Tropaeolum peregrinum*.
Canary Island bellflower. See *Canarina canariensis*, illus. p.217.
Canary Island date palm. See *Phoenix canariensis*.
Canary-bird bush. See *Crotalaria agatiflora*, illus. p.119.
Candle plant. See *Senecio articulatus*.
Candle, Blue. See *Myrtillocactus geometrizans*, illus. p.472.
Candollea cuneiformis. See *Hibbertia cuneiformis*.
Candytuft. See *Iberis*.
Cane, Dumb. See *Dieffenbachia*.

CANNA

CANNACEAE

Genus of robust, showy, rhizomatous perennials, grown for their striking flowers and ornamental foliage. Is generally used for summer-bedding displays and container growing. Half hardy to frost tender, min. 5–15°C (41–59°F). Requires a warm, sunny position and humus-rich, moist soil. If grown under glass or for summer bedding, encourage into growth in spring at 16°C (61°F) and store rhizomes in slightly damp soil or peat in winter. Propagate in spring by division or in winter by seed sown at 20°C (68°F) or more.

***C.* 'Assault'.** See *C.*'Assaut'.

***C.* 'Assaut',** syn. *C.*'Assault', illus. p.413.

***C.* 'Black Knight'.** Rhizomatous perennial. H 1.8m (6ft), S 45–60cm (1½–2ft). Half hardy. Stout stems bear broadly lance-shaped, bronze-green leaves. From mid-summer to early autumn has large racemes of gladiolus-like, very dark red flowers, 7cm (3in) across, with wavy petals.

C. iridiflora illus. p.415.

***C.* 'Lucifer'.** Rhizomatous perennial. H 1m (3ft), S 45–60cm (1½–2ft). Half hardy. Has broadly lance-shaped, mid-green leaves, and profuse racemes of iris-like, yellow-edged, red flowers from mid-summer to early autumn.

Canoe birch. See *Betula papyrifera*, illus. p.68.

Canterbury bell. See *Campanula medium*.

CANTUA

POLEMONIACEAE

Genus of evergreen shrubs, grown for their showy flowers in spring. Only one species is in general cultivation. Half hardy; is best grown against a south- or west-facing wall. Requires full sun and fertile, well-drained soil. Propagate by semi-ripe cuttings in summer.

***C. buxifolia*,** syn. *C. dependens*, illus. p.151.

C. dependens. See *C. buxifolia*.

Cape blue water lily. See *Nymphaea capensis*.

Cape chestnut. See *Calodendrum capense*.

Cape dandelion. See *Arctotheca calendula*, illus. p.306.

Cape grape. See *Rhoicissus capensis*.

Cape honey suckle. See *Tecoma capensis*.

Cape jasmine. See *Gardenia augusta*.

Cape leadwort. See *Plumbago auriculata*, illus. p.213.

Cape marigold. See *Dimorphotheca*.

Cape myrtle. See *Myrsine africana*.

Cape pondweed. See *Aponogeton distachyos*, illus. p.463.

Cape primrose. See *Streptocarpus rexii*.

Cape sundew. See *Drosera capensis*, illus. p.317.

Cappadocian maple. See *Acer cappadocicum*.

CAPSICUM

SOLANACEAE

Genus of evergreen shrubs, sub-shrubs and short-lived perennials, usually grown as annuals. Some species produce edible fruits (e.g. sweet peppers), others small, ornamental ones. Frost tender, min. 4°C (39°F). Grow in sun and in fertile, well-drained soil. Spray flowers with water to encourage fruit to set. Propagate by seed sown under glass in spring. Red spider mite may cause problems.

C. annuum (Ornamental pepper). **'Holiday Cheer'** is a moderately fast-growing, evergreen, bushy perennial, grown as an annual. H and S 20–30cm (8–12in). Has oval, mid-green leaves. Bears small, star-shaped, white flowers in summer and, in autumn-winter, spherical, green fruits maturing to red.

CARAGANA

LEGUMINOSAE/PAPILIONACEAE

Genus of deciduous shrubs, grown for their foliage and flowers. Fully hardy. Needs full sun and fertile but not over-rich, well-drained soil. Propagate species by softwood cuttings in summer or by seed in autumn, cultivars by softwood or semi-ripe cuttings or budding in summer or by grafting in winter.

C. arborescens. Fast-growing, deciduous, upright shrub. H 6m (20ft), S 4m (12ft). Has spine-tipped, dark green leaves, each composed of 8–12 oblong leaflets. Produces clusters of pea-like, yellow flowers in late spring. Arching **'Lorbergii'**, H 3m (10ft), S 2.5m (8ft), has very narrow leaflets and smaller flowers and is often grown as a tree by top-grafting. **'Nana'** illus. p.153. **'Walker'**, H 30cm (1ft), S 2–3m (6–10ft), is prostrate but is usually top-grafted to form a weeping tree, H 2m (6ft), S 75cm (2½ft).

***C. frutex* 'Globosa'.** Slow-growing, deciduous, upright shrub. H and S 30cm (1ft). Mid-green leaves each have 4 oblong leaflets. Pea-like, bright yellow flowers are borne only rarely in late spring.

CARALLUMA

ASCLEPIADACEAE

Genus of perennial succulents with 4–6-ribbed, finger-like, blue-grey or blue-green to purple stems. Frost tender, min. 11°C (52°F). Needs sun and extremely well-drained soil. Water sparingly, only in the growing season. May be difficult to grow. Propagate by seed or stem cuttings in summer.

***C. europaea*,** syn. *Stapelia europaea*. Clump-forming, perennial succulent. H 20cm (8in), S 1m (3ft). Rough, 4-angled, erect to procumbent, grey stems often arch over and root. Has clusters of small, star-shaped, yellow and brownish-purple flowers near stem crown from mid- to late summer, then twin-horned, grey seed pods. Flowers smell faintly of rotten meat. Is one of the easier species to grow.

C. joannis illus. p.491.

Caraway thyme. See *Thymus herba-barona*, illus. p.393.

CARDAMINE

Bitter cress

CRUCIFERAE/BRASSICACEAE

Genus of spring-flowering annuals and perennials. Some are weeds, but others are suitable for informal and woodland gardens. Fully hardy. Requires sun or semi-shade and moist soil. Propagate by seed or division in autumn.

***C. enneaphyllos*,** syn. *Dentaria enneaphyllos*, illus. p.284.

***C. pentaphyllos*,** syn. *Dentaria pentaphyllos*, illus. p.278.

C. pratensis (Cuckoo flower, Lady's smock). **'Flore Pleno'** is a neat, clump-forming perennial. H 45cm (18in), S 30cm (12in). Bears dense sheaves of double, lilac flowers in spring. Mid-green leaves are divided into rounded leaflets. May also be propagated by leaf-tip cuttings in mid-summer. Prefers moist or wet conditions.

C. trifolia illus. p.374.

Cardinal climber. See *Ipomoea × multifida*.

Cardinal flower. See *Lobelia cardinalis*.

Cardinal's guard. See *Pachystachys coccinea*.

CARDIOCRINUM

LILIACEAE

Genus of summer-flowering, lily-like bulbs, grown for their spectacular flowers. Frost hardy. Needs partial shade and deep, humus-rich, moist soil. Plant bulbs just below soil surface, in autumn. Water well in summer and mulch with humus. Provide a deep mulch in winter. After flowering, main bulb dies, but produces offsets. To produce flowers in up to 5 years, propagate by offsets in autumn; may also be propagated by seed in autumn or winter and will then flower in 7 years.

C. giganteum (Giant lily) illus. p.410. var. ***yunnanense*** is a stout, leafy-stemmed bulb. H 1.5–2m (5–6ft), S 75cm–1m (2½–3ft). Has bold, heart-shaped, bronze-green leaves. Fragrant, pendent, trumpet-shaped, cream flowers, 15cm (6in) long, with purple-red streaks inside, are borne in long spikes in summer and are followed by decorative seed heads.

CARDIOSPERMUM

SAPINDACEAE

Genus of herbaceous or deciduous, shrubby climbers, grown mainly for their attractive fruits. Is useful for covering bushes or trellises. Frost tender, min. 5°C (41°F). Grow in full light and any soil. Propagate by seed in spring.

C. halicacabum (Balloon vine, Heart pea, Heart seed, Winter cherry). Deciduous, shrubby, scandent, perennial climber, usually grown as an annual or biennial. H to 3m (10ft). Has toothed leaves of 2 oblong leaflets. Inconspicuous, whitish flowers are produced in summer, followed by downy, spherical, inflated, 3-angled, straw-coloured fruits containing black seeds, each with a heart-shaped, white spot.

Cardoon. See *Cynara cardunculus*, illus. p.226.

CAREX

CYPERACEAE

See also GRASSES, BAMBOOS, RUSHES and SEDGES.

C. buchananii (Leatherleaf sedge). Evergreen, tuft-forming, perennial sedge. H to 60cm (24in), S 20cm (8in). Fully hardy. Very narrow, copper-coloured leaves turn red towards base. Solid, triangular stems bear insignificant, brown spikelets in summer.

***C. elata*,** syn. *C. stricta* (Tufted sedge). Evergreen, tuft-forming, perennial sedge. H to 1m (3ft), S 15cm (6in). Fully hardy. Leaves are somewhat glaucous. Solid, triangular stems bear blackish-brown spikelets in summer. ♀ **'Aurea'** illus. p.321.

C. grayi (Mace sedge). Evergreen, tuft-forming, perennial sedge. H to 60cm (24in), S 20cm (8in). Fully hardy. Has bright green leaves. Large, female spikelets, borne in summer, mature to pointed, knobbly, greenish-brown fruits.

♀ ***C. hachijoensis* 'Evergold',** syn. *C. oshimensis* 'Evergold', illus. p.321.

C. morrowii of gardens. See *C. oshimensis*.

***C. oshimensis*,** syn. *C. morrowii* of gardens. Evergreen, tuft-forming, perennial sedge. H 20–50cm (8–20in), S 20–25cm (8–10in). Fully hardy. Has narrow, mid-green leaves. Solid, triangular stems bear insignificant spikelets in summer. **'Evergold'** see *hachijoensis* 'Evergold'.

C. pendula illus. p.321.

C. riparia (Greater pond sedge). **'Variegata'** is a vigorous, evergreen, perennial sedge. H 60cm–1m (2–3ft), S indefinite. Fully hardy. Has broad, white-striped, mid-green leaves and solid, triangular stems that bear narrow, bristle-tipped, dark brown spikelets in summer.

C. stricta. See *C. elata*.

Caricature plant. See *Graptophyllum pictum*.

CARISSA

APOCYNACEAE

Genus of evergreen, spring- to summer-flowering shrubs, grown for their flowers and overall appearance. Frost tender, min. 10–13°C (50–55°F). Needs partial shade and well-drained soil. Water containerized specimens moderately, less when temperatures are low. Propagate by seed when ripe or in spring or by semi-ripe cuttings in summer. The seeds are poisonous.

C. grandiflora. See *C. macrocarpa*.

***C. macrocarpa*,** syn. *C. grandiflora* (Natal plum). **'Tuttlei'** illus. p.131.

C. spectabilis. See *Acokanthera oblongifolia*.

CARLINA
Thistle

COMPOSITAE/ASTERACEAE

Genus of annuals, biennials and perennials, grown for their ornamental flower heads. Fully hardy. Requires a sunny position and well-drained soil. Propagate by seed: annuals in spring, perennials in autumn.
C. acaulis (Alpine thistle) illus. p.387.

CARMICHAELIA

LEGUMINOSAE/PAPILIONACEAE

Genus of deciduous, usually leafless shrubs, grown for their profusion of tiny flowers in summer. Flattened, green shoots assume function of leaves. Frost to half hardy. Needs full sun and well-drained soil. Cut out dead wood in spring. Propagate by semi-ripe cuttings in summer or by seed in autumn or spring.
C. arborea. Deciduous, upright shrub. H 2m (6ft), S 1.5m (5ft). Frost hardy. Small clusters of pea-like, pale lilac flowers appear from early to mid-summer. May need staking when mature.
C. enysii. Deciduous, mound-forming, dense shrub. H and S 30cm (1ft). Frost hardy. Shoots are rigid. Pea-like, violet flowers are borne in mid-summer. Is best grown in a rock garden.

Carnation. See *Dianthus*.

CARNEGIEA

CACTACEAE

Genus of one species of very slow-growing, perennial cactus with thick, 12–24-ribbed, spiny stems. Is unlikely to flower or branch at less than 4m (12ft) high. Frost tender, min. 7°C (45°F). Requires full sun and very well-drained soil. Propagate by seed in spring or summer.
C. gigantea illus. p.472.

Carolina allspice. See *Calycanthus floridus*.
Carolina hemlock. See *Tsuga caroliniana*.
Carolina jasmine. See *Gelsemium sempervirens*, illus. p.202.

CARPENTERIA

HYDRANGEACEAE

Genus of one species of evergreen, summer-flowering shrub, cultivated for its flowers and foliage. Frost hardy. Grows well against a south- or west-facing wall. Prefers full sun and fairly moist but well-drained soil. Propagate by greenwood cuttings in summer or by seed in autumn.
♀ ***C. californica*** illus. p.134.

CARPINUS
Hornbeam

CORYLACEAE

Genus of deciduous trees, grown for their foliage, autumn colour and clusters of small, winged nuts. Fully hardy. Needs sun or semi-shade and fertile, well-drained soil. Propagate species by seed in autumn, cultivars by budding in late summer.
♀ ***C. betulus*** (Common hornbeam). Deciduous, round-headed tree. H 25m (80ft), S 20m (70ft). Has a fluted trunk and oval, prominently veined, dark green leaves that turn yellow and orange in autumn. Bears green catkins from late spring to autumn, when clusters of winged nuts appear.
♀ **'Fastigiata'** (syn. *C.b.* 'Pyramidalis'; illus. p.96).
'Pyramidalis' see *C.b* 'Fastigiata'.
C. caroliniana (American hornbeam). Deciduous, spreading tree with branches that droop at tips. H and S 10m (30ft). Has a fluted, grey trunk, green catkins in spring and oval, bright green leaves that turn orange and red in autumn, when clusters of winged nuts appear.
C. tschonoskii. Deciduous, rounded tree of elegant habit, with branches drooping at tips. H and S 12m (40ft). Has oval, sharply toothed, glossy, dark green leaves. Green catkins are carried in spring and clusters of small, winged nuts appear in autumn.
♀ ***C. turczaninowii.*** Deciduous, spreading tree of graceful habit. H 12m (40ft), S 10m (30ft). Green catkins are borne in spring. Produces clusters of small, winged nuts in autumn, when small, oval, glossy, deep green leaves turn orange.

CARPOBROTUS

AIZOACEAE

Genus of mat-forming, perennial succulents with triangular, fleshy, dark green leaves and daisy-like flowers. Is excellent for binding sandy soils. Half hardy to frost tender, min. 5°C (41°F). Needs full sun and well-drained soil. Propagate by seed or stem cuttings in spring or summer.
C. edulis (Hottentot fig, Kaffir fig). Carpeting, perennial succulent. H 15cm (6in), S indefinite. Frost tender. Prostrate, rooting branches bear leaves 1.5cm (⅝in) thick and 12cm (5in) long. Yellow, purple or pink flowers, 12cm (5in) across, open in spring-summer from about noon in sun. Bears edible, fig-like, brownish fruits in late summer and autumn.

CARRIEREA

FLACOURTIACEAE

Genus of deciduous trees. Only *C. calycina,* grown for its flowers, is in general cultivation. Frost hardy. Requries full sun and fertile, well-drained soil. Propagate by softwood cuttings in summer.
C. calycina. Deciduous, spreading tree. H 8m (25ft), S 10m (30ft). Oval, glossy, mid-green leaves set off upright clusters of cup-shaped, creamy-white or greenish-white flowers borne in early summer.

CARYA
Hickory

JUGLANDACEAE

Genus of deciduous trees, grown for their stately habit, divided leaves, autumn colour and, in some cases, edible nuts. Has insignificant flowers in spring. Fully hardy. Requires sun or semi-shade and deep, fertile soil. Plant young seedlings in a permanent position during their first year since older plants resent transplanting. Propagate by seed in autumn.
C. cordiformis (Bitternut, Bitternut hickory). Vigorous, deciduous, spreading tree. H 25m (80ft), S 15m (50ft). Bark is smooth at first, later fissured. Bright yellow, winter leaf buds develop into large, dark green leaves, with usually 7 oval to oblong leaflets; these turn yellow in autumn. Nuts are pear-shaped or rounded, 2–4cm (¾–1½in) long, each with a bitter kernel.
C. glabra (Pignut, Pignut hickory). Deciduous, spreading tree. H 25m (80ft), S 20m (70ft). Dark green leaves, with usually 5 narrowly oval leaflets, turn bright yellow and orange in autumn. Pear-shaped or rounded nuts, 2–4cm (¾–1½in) long, each have a bitter kernel.
C. ovata illus. p.65.

CARYOPTERIS

VERBENACEAE

Genus of deciduous sub-shrubs, grown for their foliage and small, but freely produced, blue flowers. Frost hardy. Prefers full sun and light, well-drained soil. Cut back hard in spring. Propagate species by greenwood or semi-ripe cuttings in summer or by seed in autumn; propagate cultivars by cuttings only, in summer.
***C. × clandonensis* 'Arthur Simmonds'** illus. p.164. ♀ **'Heavenly Blue'** is a deciduous, bushy sub-shrub. H and S 1m (3ft). Forms an upright, compact mass of lance-shaped, grey-green leaves. Dense clusters of tubular, blue to purplish-blue flowers, with prominent stamens, are borne from late summer to autumn.
C. incana, syn. *C. mastacanthus.* Deciduous, bushy sub-shrub. H and S 1.2m (4ft). Bears tubular, violet-blue flowers, with prominent stamens, amid lance-shaped, grey-green leaves from late summer to early autumn.
C. mastacanthus. See *C. incana*.

Caspian locust. See *Gleditsia caspica*.

CASSIA

LEGUMINOSAE/CAESALPINIACEAE

Genus of annuals, perennials and evergreen or deciduous trees and shrubs, grown for their flowers mainly produced from winter to summer. Fully hardy to frost tender, min. 7–18°C (45–64°F). Needs full light and fertile, well-drained soil. Water containerized specimens freely when in full growth, moderately to sparingly in winter. Pruning is tolerated, severe if need be, but trees are best left to grow naturally. Propagate by seed in spring.
C. artemisioides. See *Senna artemisioides*.
C. corymbosa. See *Senna corymbosa*. var. ***plurijuga*** of gardens. See *Senna × floribunda*.
C. didymobotrya. See *Senna didymobotrya*.
C. fistula (Golden shower, Indian laburnum, Pudding pipe-tree). Fast-growing, almost deciduous, ovoid tree. H 8–10m (25–30ft), S 4–6m (12–20ft). Frost tender, min. 16°C (61°F). Has 30–45cm (12–18in) long leaves, each with 4–8 pairs of oval leaflets, coppery when young. In spring produces racemes of small, fragrant, 5-petalled, cup-shaped, bright yellow flowers. Cylindrical, dark brown pods, to 60cm (24in) long, yield cassia pulp.
C. × floribunda. See *Senna × floribunda*.
C. siamea. See *Senna siamea*.

Cassia
Silver. See *Senna artemisioides*.
Wormwood. See *Senna artemisioides*.

CASSINIA

COMPOSITAE/ASTERACEAE

Genus of evergreen shrubs, grown for their foliage and flowers. Frost hardy, but avoid cold, exposed positions. Needs full sun and fertile, well-drained soil. Propagate by softwood cuttings in summer.
C. fulvida. See *C. leptophylla* subsp. *fulvida*.
C. leptophylla subsp. ***fulvida***, syn. *C. fulvida.* Evergreen, bushy shrub. H and S 2m (6ft). Has yellow shoots, small, oblong, dark green leaves and, in mid-summer, clustered heads of minute, white flowers. Is useful as a coastal hedging plant.
subsp. ***vauvilliersii*** (syn. *C. vauvilliersii*) illus. p.157.
C. vauvilliersii. See *C. leptophylla* subsp. *vauvilliersii*.

CASSIOPE

ERICACEAE

Genus of evergreen, spring-flowering shrubs, suitable for peat beds and walls and for rock gardens. Fully hardy. Needs a sheltered, shaded or semi-shaded site and moist, peaty, acid soil. Propagate by semi-ripe or greenwood cuttings in summer or by seed in autumn or spring.
♀ ***C.* 'Edinburgh'** illus. p.358.
C. fastigiata. Evergreen, upright, loose shrub. H 30cm (12in), S 15–20cm (6–8in). In spring, bell-shaped, creamy-white flowers, resting in green or red calyces, are borne on short stalks in leaf axils. Leaves are tiny and scale-like. Needs semi-shade.
♀ ***C. lycopodioides*** illus. p.375.
C. mertensiana illus. p.376.
♀ ***C.* 'Muirhead'** illus. p.358.
C. selaginoides. Evergreen, spreading shrub. H 25cm (10in), S 15cm (6in). Stem is hidden by dense, scale-like, mid-green leaves. Bears solitary relatively large, pendent, bell-shaped, white flowers in spring. Needs a shaded site.
C. tetragona. Evergreen, upright shrub. H 10–25cm (4–10in), S 10–15cm (4–6in). Dense, scale-like, dark green leaves conceal branched stems. In spring, leaf axils bear solitary pendent, bell-shaped, white flowers in red calyces. Needs a semi-shaded site.
C. wardii. Evergreen, upright to spreading, loose shrub. H 15cm (6in), S 20cm (8in). Semi-upright stems are densely clothed with scale-like, dark green leaves that give them a squared appearance. Bell-shaped, white flowers, set close to stems, open in spring. Needs shade in all but cool areas. May also be propagated by division of runners in spring.

CASTANEA
Chestnut

FAGACEAE

Genus of deciduous, summer-flowering trees and shrubs, grown for their foliage, stately habit, flowers and edible fruits (chestnuts). Fully hardy. Requires sun or semi-shade; does particularly well in hot, dry areas. Needs fertile, well-drained soil; grows poorly on shallow, chalky soil. Propagate species by seed in autumn, cultivars by budding in summer or by grafting in late winter.
C. dentata (American chestnut). Deciduous, spreading tree with rough bark. H 30m (100ft), S 15m (50ft). Oblong, toothed, dull green leaves turn orange-yellow in autumn. Has catkins of greenish-white flowers in summer, followed by typical spiny 'chestnut' fruits.
♀ ***C. sativa*** (Spanish chestnut, Sweet chestnut). Deciduous, spreading tree. H 30m (100ft), S 15m (50ft). Bark becomes spirally ridged with age. Oblong, glossy, dark green leaves turn yellow in autumn. Spikes of small, creamy-yellow flowers in summer are followed by edible fruits in rounded, spiny husks. ♀ **'Albomarginata'** illus. p.61.

CASTANOPSIS

FAGACEAE

Genus of evergreen shrubs and trees, grown for their habit and foliage. Flowers are insignificant. Frost hardy. Needs a sheltered position in sun or semi-shade and fertile, well-drained but not too dry, acid soil. Propagate by seed when ripe, in autumn.
C. cuspidata. Evergreen, bushy, spreading shrub or tree with drooping shoots. H and S 8m (25ft) or more. Bears long, oval, slender-tipped, leathery leaves, glossy, dark green above, bronze beneath.

CASTANOSPERMUM
Black bean tree, Moreton Bay chestnut

LEGUMINOSAE/PAPILIONACEAE

Genus of one species of evergreen tree, grown for its overall ornamental appearance and for shade. Frost tender, min. 10–15°C (50–59°F). Requires full light and fertile, moisture-retentive but well-drained soil. Water containerized specimens freely when in full growth, moderately at other times. Propagate by seed in spring.
C. australe. Strong-growing, evergreen, rounded tree. H 15m (50ft) or more, S 8m (25ft) or more. Has 45cm (18in) long leaves of 8–17 oval leaflets. Racemes of large, pea-like, yellow flowers, that age to orange and red, are produced in autumn, but only on mature trees, and are succeeded by cylindrical, reddish-brown pods, each 25cm (10in) long, containing large, chestnut-like seeds.

Cast-iron plant. See *Aspidistra elatior*.
Castor-oil plant. See *Ricinus communis*, illus. p.347.
Catalina ironwood. See *Lyonothamnus floribundus*.

CATALPA

BIGNONIACEAE

Genus of deciduous, summer-flowering trees and shrubs, extremely resistant to urban pollution, grown for their foliage and bell- or trumpet-shaped flowers with frilly lobes. Trees are best grown as isolated specimens. Fully hardy. Prefers full sun and does best in hot summers. Needs deep, fertile, well-drained but not too dry soil. Propagate species by seed in autumn, cultivars by softwood cuttings in summer or by budding in late summer.
♀ ***C. bignonioides*** (Indian bean tree) illus. p.74. ♀ **'Aurea'** is a deciduous, spreading tree. H and S 10m (30ft). Has broadly oval, bright yellow leaves, bronze when young. Bell-shaped, white flowers, marked with yellow and purple, appear in summer, followed by long, pendent, cylindrical pods, often persisting after leaf fall.
♀ ***C. × erubescens*** **'Purpurea'.** Deciduous, spreading tree. H and S 15m (50ft). Broadly oval or 3-lobed, very dark purple, young leaves mature to dark green. Fragrant, bell-shaped, white flowers, marked with yellow and purple, appear from mid- to late summer.
C. ovata. Deciduous, spreading tree. H and S 10m (30ft). Bears 3-lobed, purplish leaves when young, maturing to pale green. Has large clusters of bell-shaped, white flowers, spotted with red and yellow, from mid-to late summer.
C. speciosa illus. p.74.

CATANANCHE
Blue cupidone

COMPOSITAE/ASTERACEAE

Genus of perennials with daisy-like flower heads that may be successfully dried for winter flower arrangements. Fully hardy. Needs sun and light, well-drained soil. Propagate by seed in spring or by root cuttings in winter.
♀ ***C. caerulea*** **'Major'** illus. p.295.

CATHARANTHUS

APOCYNACEAE

Genus of evergreen shrubs, grown for their flowers. *C. roseus* is often grown annually from seed or cuttings and used as a summer bedding plant in cool climates. Frost tender, min. 5–7°C (41–5°F). Needs full light and well-drained soil. Water potted specimens moderately, less when temperatures are low. Prune long or straggly stems in early spring to promote a more bushy habit. Propagate by seed in spring or by greenwood or semi-ripe cuttings in summer.
♀ ***C. roseus***, syn. *Vinca rosea*, illus. p.156.

Cat's claw. See *Macfadyena unguis-cati*, illus. p.214.
Cat's ears. See *Antennaria; Calochortus*.
Cat's tail, Red-hot. See *Acalypha hispida*.
Cat's valerian. See *Valeriana officinalis*, illus. p.243.
Cat's whiskers. See *Tacca chantrierei*.
Catalina ironwood. See *Lyonothamnus floribundus*.

Catchfly. See *Silene*.
Alpine. See *Lychnis alpina*.
Nodding. See *Silene pendula*.
Catmint. See *Nepeta*.

CATTLEYA

ORCHIDACEAE

See also ORCHIDS.
C. bowringiana illus. p.309. Evergreen, epiphytic orchid for a cool greenhouse. H 45cm (18in). In autumn bears large heads of rose-purple-lipped, magenta flowers, 8cm (3in) across. Has oval, stiff leaves, 8–10cm (3–4in) long. Grow in semi-shade during summer and do not spray from overhead.
C. **J.A. Carbone** illus. p.309. Evergreen, epiphytic orchid for an intermediate greenhouse. H 45cm (18in). Large heads of fragrant, pinkish-mauve flowers, 10cm (4in) across and each with a yellow-marked, deep pink lip, open in early summer. Has oval, stiff leaves, 10–15cm (4–6in) long. Avoid spraying from overhead.

Caucasian elm. See *Zelkova carpinifolia*.
Caucasian fir. See *Abies nordmanniana*, illus. p.107.
Caucasian lime. See *Tilia × euchlora*.
Caucasian oak. See *Quercus macranthera*, illus. p.62.
Caucasian spruce. See *Picea orientalis*.
Caucasian whortleberry. See *Vaccinium arctostaphylos*.
Caucasian wing nut. See *Pterocarya fraxinifolia*.

CAUTLEYA

ZINGIBERACEAE

Genus of summer-and autumn-flowering perennials. Frost hardy. Grow in a sunny, wind-free position and in deep, rich, moist but well-drained soil. Propagate by seed or division in spring.
C. spicata illus. p.306.

CAYRATIA

VITACEAE

Genus of deciduous, woody-stemmed, tendril climbers, gown for their leaves and autumn colour. Tendril tips have sucker-like pads that cling to supports. Insignifiant greenish flowers appear in summer. Half-hardy. Grow in shade or semi-shade and well-drained soil. Propagate by softwood or greenwood cuttings in summer or by hardwood cuttings in early spring. The berries may cause mild stomach upset if ingested.
Cayratia thomsonii, syn. *Parthenocissus thomsonii*, illus. p.216.

CEANOTHUS

RHAMNACEAE

Genus of evergreen or deciduous shrubs and small trees, grown for their small but densely clustered, mainly blue flowers. Frost to half hardy; in cold areas plant against a south-or west-facing wall. Needs a sheltered site in full sun and light, well-drained soil. Cut dead wood from evergreens in spring and trim their side-shoots after flowering. Cut back shoots of deciduous species to basal framework in early spring. Propagate by semi-ripe cuttings in summer.
♀ ***C. arboreus*** **'Trewithen Blue'.** Vigorous, evergreen, bushy, spreading shrub. H 6m (20ft), S 8m (25ft) or more. Frost hardy. In spring and early summer, large, pyramidal clusters of rich blue flowers are borne amid broadly oval to rounded, dark green leaves.
♀ ***C.*** **'Autumnal Blue'** illus. p.144.
♀ ***C.*** **'Blue Mound'.** Evergreen, bushy, dense shrub. H 1.5m (5ft), S 2m (6ft). Frost hardy. Forms a mound of oblong, glossy, dark green leaves, covered, in late spring, with rounded clusters of deep blue flowers.
♀ ***C.*** **'Burkwoodii'.** Evergreen, bushy, dense shrub. H 1.5m (5ft), S 2m (6ft). Frost hardy. Has oval, glossy, dark green leaves, downy and grey beneath. Produces dense panicles of bright blue flowers from mid-summer to mid-autumn.
C. **'Burtonensis'.** Evergreen, bushy, spreading shrub. H 2m (6ft) or more, S 4m (12ft). Frost hardy. Has small, rounded, almost spherical, crinkled leaves that are lustrous and dark green. Small, deep blue flowers appear in clusters, 2cm (¾in) wide, from mid-spring to early summer.
♀ ***C.*** **'Cascade'.** Vigorous, evergreen, arching shrub. H and S 4m (12ft). Frost hardy. Leaves are narrowly oblong, glossy and dark green. Large panicles of powder-blue flowers open in late spring and early summer.
C. **'Delight'.** Fast-growing, evergreen, bushy shrub. H 3m (10ft), S 5m (15ft). Frost hardy. Bears oblong, glossy, deep green leaves. Long clusters of rich blue flowers appear in late spring.
C. × delileanus **'Gloire de Versailles'.** See *C.* 'Gloire de Versailles'.
C. dentatus. Evergreen, bushy, dense shrub. H 1.5m (5ft), S 2m (6ft). Frost hardy. Produces small, oblong, glossy, dark green leaves and is covered, in late spring, with rounded clusters of bright blue flowers.
C. dentatus of gardens. See *C. × lobbianus*.
♀ ***C.*** **'Gloire de Versailles',** syn. *C. × delileanus* **'Gloire de Versailles'**, illus. p.164.
C. gloriosus. Evergreen, prostrate shrub. H 30cm (1ft), S 2m (6ft). Frost hardy. Leaves are oval and dark green. Rounded clusters of deep blue or purplish-blue flowers appear from mid- to late spring. May suffer from chlorosis on chalky soils.
C. impressus illus. p.141.
C. incanus illus. p.134.
♀ ***C.*** **'Italian Skies'.** Evergreen, bushy, spreading shrub. H 1.5m (5ft), S 3m (10ft). Frost hardy. Has small, oval, glossy, dark green leaves. Produces dense, conical clusters of bright blue flowers during late spring.
C. × lobbianus, syn. *C. dentatus* of gardens. Evergreen, bushy, dense shrub. H and S 2m (6ft). Frost hardy. Rounded clusters of bright deep blue flowers are borne in late spring and early summer amid oval, dark green leaves.
C. **'Marie Simon'.** Deciduous, bushy shrub. H and S 1.5m (5ft). Frost hardy. Has broadly oval, mid-green leaves. Conical clusters of soft pink flowers are carried in profusion from mid-summer to early autumn.

C. papillosus. Evergreen, arching shrub. H 3m (10ft), S 5m (15ft). Frost hardy. Leaves are narrowly oblong, glossy, dark green and sticky. Produces dense racemes of blue or purplish-blue flowers during late spring.
***C.* 'Perle Rose'** illus. p.159.
C. rigidus (Monterey ceanothus). Evergreen, bushy shrub of dense, spreading habit. H 1.2m (4ft), S 2.5m (8ft). Frost hardy. Bears oblong to rounded, glossy, dark green leaves and, from mid-spring to early summer, produces rounded clusters of deep purplish-blue flowers.
♀ ***C.* 'Southmead'.** Evergreen, bushy, dense shrub. H and S 1.5m (5ft). Frost hardy. Has small, oblong, glossy, dark green leaves. Deep blue flowers are produced in rounded clusters in late spring and early summer.
C. thyrsiflorus. Evergreen, bushy shrub or spreading tree. H and S 6m (20ft). Frost hardy. Has broadly oval, glossy, mid-green leaves and, in late spring and early summer, bears rounded clusters of pale blue flowers. ♀ var. ***repens*** illus. p.164.
C.* × *veitchianus. Vigorous, evergreen, bushy shrub. H and S 3m (10ft). Frost hardy. Dense, oblong clusters of deep blue flowers are borne in late spring and early summer amid oblong, glossy, dark green leaves.

Ceanothus, Monterey. See *Ceanothus rigidus.*
Cedar. See *Cedrus.*
Atlas. See *Cedrus atlantica.*
Blue Atlas. See *Cedrus atlantica* f. *glauca*, illus. p.97.
Chilean incense. See *Austrocedrus chilensis*, illus. p.102.
Eastern white. See *Thuja occidentalis.*
Incense. See *Calocedrus decurrens*, illus. p.102.
Japanese. See *Cryptomeria japonica.*
Pencil. See *Juniperus virginiana.*
Western red. See *Thuja plicata.*
White. See *Thuja occidentalis.*
Cedar of Goa. See *Cupressus lusitanica.*
Cedar of Lebanon. See *Cedrus libani*, illus. p.99.
Cedrela sinensis. See *Toona sinensis.*
Cedronella mexicana. See *Agastache mexicana.*

CEDRUS
Cedar

PINACEAE

See also CONIFERS.
C. atlantica, syn. *C. libani* subsp. *atlantica* (Atlas cedar). Conifer that is conical when young, broadening with age. H 15–25m (50–80ft), S 5–10m (15–30ft). Fully hardy. Leaves are spirally arranged, needle-like, dull green or bright blue-grey. Has ovoid cones, males pale brown, females pale green, ripening to brown. f. ***fastigiata*** (syn. *C.a.* Fastigiata Group), S 4–5m (12–15ft), has a narrower, more upright habit. ♀ f. ***glauca*** (syn. *C.a.* Glauca Group) illus. p.97.
♀ ***C. deodara*** (Deodar). Fast-growing conifer, densely conical with weeping tips when young, broader when mature. H 15–25m (50–80ft), S 5–10m (15–30ft). Fully hardy. Has spirally arranged, needle-like, grey-green leaves and barrel-shaped, glaucous cones, 8–12cm (3–5in) long, ripening to brown. ♀ **'Aurea'** illus. p.105.
♀ ***C. libani*** (Cedar of Lebanon; illus. p.99). Open conifer with tiered, arching branches. H 25m (80ft), S 15m (50ft). Fully hardy. Spirally arranged, needle-like, grey-green foliage is produced in dense, flat layers. Has greyish-pink cones. subsp. ***atlantica*** see *C. atlantica.* **'Comte de Dijon'**, H 1–2m (3–6ft), S 60cm–1.2m (2–4ft), is a dwarf form that grows only 5cm (2in) a year. **'Sargentii'** (illus. p.107), H and S 1–1.5m (3–5ft), has horizontal, then weeping branches and makes a bush that is rounded in shape.

CEIBA

BOMBACACEAE

Genus of evergreen, semi-evergreen or deciduous trees, grown for their overall appearance and for shade. Frost tender, min. 15°C (59°F). Requires full light or light shade and fertile, moisture-retentive but well-drained soil. Water potted specimens freely while in full growth, less at other times. Pruning is tolerated if necessary. Propagate by seed in spring or by semi-ripe cuttings in summer.
C. pentandra (Kapok, Silk cotton tree). Fast-growing, semi-evergreen tree with a spine-covered trunk. H and S 25m (80ft) or more. Hand-shaped leaves have 5–9 elliptic leaflets, red when young, becoming mid-green. Bears clusters of 5-petalled, white, yellow or pink flowers in summer, followed by woody, brownish seed pods containing silky kapok fibre.
C. speciosa. See *Chorisia speciosa.*

Celandine. See *Chelidonium.*
Greater. See *Chelidonium.*
Lesser. See *Ranunculus ficaria.*
Celandine crocus. See *Crocus korolkowii.*

CELASTRUS

CELASTRACEAE

Genus of deciduous shrubs and twining climbers, grown for their attractive fruits. Most species bear male and female flowers on separate plants, so both sexes must be grown to obtain fruits; hermaphrodite forms of *C. orbiculatus* are available. Fully to frost hardy. Grow in any soil and in full or partial shade. Likes regular feeding. Prune in spring to cut out old wood and maintain shape. Propagate by seed in autumn or spring or by semi-ripe cuttings in summer.
C. articulatus. See *C. orbiculatus.*
C. orbiculatus, syn. *C. articulatus* (Oriental bittersweet, Staff vine). Vigorous, deciduous, twining climber. H to 14m (46ft). Frost hardy. Has small, rounded, toothed leaves. Clusters of 2–4 small, green flowers are produced in summer; tiny, long-lasting, spherical fruits begin green, turn black in autumn, then split and show yellow insides and red seeds.
C. scandens (American bittersweet, Staff tree). Deciduous, twining climber. H to 10m (30ft). Frost hardy. Oval leaves are 5–10cm (2–4in) long. Tiny, greenish flowers are borne in small clusters in leaf axils in summer. Long-lasting, spherical fruits are produced in bunches, 5–8cm (2–3in) long; each fruit splits to show an orange interior and scarlet seeds.

CELMISIA

COMPOSITAE/ASTERACEAE

Genus of evergreen, late spring- and summer-flowering perennials, grown for their foliage and daisy-like flower heads. Is suitable for rock gardens and peat beds, but may be difficult to grow in hot, dry climates. Frost hardy. Needs a sheltered, sunny site and humus-rich, moist but well-drained, sandy, acid soil. Propagate by division in early summer or by seed when fresh.
C. bellidioides. Evergreen, mat-forming perennial. H 2cm (¾in), S to 15cm (6in). Dark green leaves are rounded and leathery. Bears almost stemless, 1cm (½in) wide, daisy-like, white flower heads in early summer.
C. coriacea of gardens. See *C. semicordata.*
C. ramulosa illus. p.386.
C. semicordata, syn. *C. coriacea* of gardens, illus. p.372.
C. traversii. Slow-growing, evergreen, clump-forming perennial. H 15cm (6in), S 20cm (8in). Sword-shaped, dark green leaves have reddish-brown margins and cream undersides. In summer carries 6–7cm (2½–3in) wide, daisy-like, white flower heads. Is difficult to establish.
C. walkeri, syn. *C. webbiana*, illus. p.362.
C. webbiana. See *C. walkeri.*

CELOSIA

AMARANTHACEAE

Genus of erect perennials, grown as annuals. Half hardy. Grows best in a sunny, sheltered position and in fertile, well-drained soil. Propagate by seed sown under glass in spring.
C. argentea. Moderately fast-growing, erect, bushy perennial, grown as an annual. H 30–60cm (12–24in), S to 45cm (18in). Has oval to lance-shaped, pale to mid-green leaves and, in summer, silvery-white, pyramid-shaped, feathery flower heads, to 10cm (4in) long. Cultivars are available in red, orange, yellow and cream. Dwarf cultivars, H 30cm (12in), include **'Fairy Fountains',** illus. p.353, and **Olympia Series**, which has crested, coral-like heads of tightly clustered flowers, 8–12cm (3–5in) across, in colours such as golden yellow, scarlet, light red, deep cerise and purple.

CELTIS
Hackberry, Nettle tree

ULMACEAE

Genus of deciduous trees, with inconspicuous flowers in spring, grown for their foliage and small fruits. Fully hardy. Needs full sun (doing best in hot summers) and fertile, well-drained soil. Propagate by seed in autumn.
C. australis illus. p.63.
C. occidentalis (Common hackberry). Deciduous, spreading tree. H and S 20m (70ft). Oval, sharply toothed, glossy, bright green leaves turn yellow in autumn, when they are accompanied by globose, yellowish-red, then red-purple fruits.
C. sinensis. Deciduous, rounded tree. H and S 10m (30ft). Has oval, glossy, dark green leaves, with fine teeth, and small, globose, orange fruits.

CENTAUREA
Knapweed

COMPOSITAE/ASTERACEAE

Genus of annuals and perennials, grown for their flower heads that each have a thistle-like centre surrounded by a ring of slender ray petals. Fully hardy. Requires sun; grows in any well-drained soil, even poor soil. Propagate by seed or division in autumn or spring.
C. cyanus (Bluebottle, Cornflower). Fast-growing, upright, branching annual. H 30cm–1m (1–3ft), S 30cm (1ft). Has lance-shaped, grey-green leaves and, in summer and early autumn, branching stems with usually double, daisy-like flower heads in shades of blue, pink, red, purple or white. Flowers are excellent for cutting. Tall (blue, illus. p.346; rose, illus. p.334) and dwarf cultivars are available. **Baby Series** (dwarf), H to 30cm (1ft), has blue, white or pink flower heads.
C. dealbata. Erect perennial. H 1m (3ft), S 60cm (2ft). Lilac-purple flower heads are borne freely in summer, one or more to each stem. Has narrowly oval, finely cut, light green leaves. **'Steenbergii'**, H 60cm (2ft), has carmine-lilac flowers.
***C. hypoleuca* 'John Coutts'** illus. p.289.
C. macrocephala. Robust, clump-forming perennial. H 1m (3ft), S 60cm (2ft). In summer, stout stems bear large, yellow flower heads, enclosed in papery, silvery-brown bracts. Mid-green leaves are narrowly oval and deeply cut.
C. montana illus. p.294.
C. moschata. See *Amberboa moschata.*
C. pulcherrima illus. p.246.

CENTRADENIA

MELASTOMATACEAE

Genus of evergreen perennials and shrubs, grown for their flowers and foliage. Frost tender, min. 13°C (55°F). Needs light shade and fertile, well-drained soil. Water containerized plants freely when in full growth, moderately at other times. Tip prune young plants to promote a bushy habit; old plants become straggly unless trimmed each spring. Propagate from early spring to early summer by seed or by softwood or greenwood cuttings. If grown as pot plants, propagate annually.
C. floribunda. Evergreen, loosely rounded, soft-stemmed shrub. H and S to 60cm (24in). Lance-shaped leaves are prominently veined, glossy, green above, bluish-green beneath. Large, terminal clusters of 4-petalled, pink or white flowers develop from pink buds in late winter and spring.

CENTRANTHUS

VALERIANACEAE

Genus of late spring-to autumn-flowering perennials. Fully hardy. Requires sun. Thrives in an exposed position and in poor, alkaline soil.

Propagate by seed in autumn or spring.
C. ruber illus. p.247.

Century plant. See *Agave americana.*

CEPHALARIA

DIPSACACEAE

Genus of coarse, summer-flowering perennials, best suited to large borders and wild gardens. Fully hardy. Prefers sun and well-drained soil. Propagate by division in spring or by seed in autumn.
C. gigantea, syn. *C. tatarica* (Giant scabious, Yellow scabious). Robust, branching perennial. H 2m (6ft), S 1.2m (4ft). In early summer, wiry stems bear pincushion-like heads of primrose-yellow flowers well above lance-shaped, deeply cut, dark green leaves.
C. tatarica. See *C. gigantea.*

CEPHALOCEREUS

CACTACEAE

Genus of slow-growing, columnar, perennial cacti with 20–30-ribbed, green stems. Frost tender, min. 5°C (41°F). Prefers full sun and extremely well-drained, lime-rich soil. Is prone to rot if overwatered. Propagate by seed in spring or summer.
C. senilis illus. p.476.

CEPHALOPHYLLUM

AIZOACEAE

Genus of clump-forming, bushy, perennial succulents with semi-cylindrical to cylindrical, green leaves. Flowers are borne after 1 or 2 years. Frost tender, min. 5°C (41°F). Requires sun and well-drained soil. Propagate by seed in spring or summer.
C. alstonii illus. p.490.
C. pillansii. Clump-forming, perennial succulent. H 8cm (3in), S 60cm (24in). Leaves are cylindrical, 6cm (2½in) long, dark green and covered in darker dots. Short flower stems produce daisy-like, red-centred, yellow flowers, 6cm (2½in) across, from spring to autumn.

CEPHALOTAXUS

CEPHALOTAXACEAE

See also CONIFERS.
C. harringtonii (Cow's-tail pine, Plum yew). Bushy, spreading conifer. H 5m (15ft), S 3m (10ft). Frost hardy. Needle-like, flattened leaves are glossy, dark green, greyish beneath, radiating around erect shoots. Bears ovoid, fleshy, green fruits that ripen to brown.

CERASTIUM

CAROPHYLLACEAE

Genus of annuals and perennials with star-shaped flowers. Some species are useful as ground cover. Fully hardy. Needs sun and well-drained soil. Propagate by division in spring.
C. alpinum (Alpine mouse-ear). Prostrate perennial. H 8cm (3in), S 40cm (16in). Tiny, oval, grey leaves cover stems. Flower stems carry solitary 1cm (½in) wide, star-shaped, white flowers throughout summer.
C. tomentosum illus. p.373.

CERATOPHYLLUM

CERATOPHYLLACEAE

Genus of deciduous, perennial, submerged water plants, grown for their foliage. Is suitable for pools and cold-water aquariums. Fully to half hardy. Prefers an open, sunny position, but tolerates shade better than most submerged plants. Propagation occurs naturally when scaly, young shoots or winter buds separate from main plants. Alternatively, take stem cuttings in the growing season.
C. demersum (Hornwort). Deciduous, perennial, spreading, submerged water plant that occasionally floats. S indefinite. Fully hardy. Has small, dark green leaves with 3 linear lobes. Is best suited to a cool-water pool.

CERATOPTERIS

PARKERIACEAE

Genus of deciduous or semi-evergreen, perennial, floating water ferns, grown for their attractive foliage. Is suitable for aquariums. Frost tender, min. 10°C (50°F). Prefers a sunny position. Remove fading fronds regularly. Propagate in summer by division or by buds that develop on the leaves.
C. thalictroides (Water fern). Semi-evergreen, perennial, spreading, floating water fern that sometimes roots and becomes submerged. S indefinite. Lance-or heart-shaped, soft green fronds are wavy-edged.

CERATOSTIGMA

PLUMBAGINACEAE

Genus of deciduous, semi-evergreen or evergreen shrubs and perennials, grown for their blue flowers and autumn colour. Fully hardy to frost tender, min. 10°C (50°F). Requires a sunny position, with well-drained soil. Cut out old, dead wood from shrubs in spring. Propagate shrubs by softwood cuttings in summer, perennials by division in spring.
C. griffithii. Evergreen or semi-evergreen, bushy, dense shrub. H 1m (3ft), S 1.5m (5ft). Half hardy. Spoon-shaped, bristly, purple-edged, dull green leaves redden in autumn. Clusters of tubular, bright blue flowers, with spreading petal lobes, appear in late summer and autumn.
♀ ***C. plumbaginoides*** illus. p.372.
♀ ***C. willmottianum*** illus. p.169.

CERCIDIPHYLLUM

CERCIDIPHYLLACEAE

Genus of deciduous trees, grown for their foliage and often spectacular autumn colour. Fully hardy. Late frosts may damage young foliage, but do not usually cause lasting harm. Requires sun or semi-shade and fertile, moist but well-drained soil. Propagate by seed in autumn.
♀ ***C. japonicum*** illus. p.67.

CERCIS

Judas tree, Redbud

LEGUMINOSAE/PAPILIONACEAE

Genus of deciduous shrubs and trees with sometimes shrubby growth, cultivated for their foliage and small, pea-like flowers, borne profusely in spring. Fully hardy. Requires a position in full sun with deep, fertile, well-drained soil. Plant out as young specimens. Resents transplanting. Propagate species by seed sown in autumn, cultivars by budding in summer.
C. canadensis (Eastern redbud). Deciduous, spreading tree or shrub. H and S 10m (30ft). Heart-shaped, dark green leaves turn yellow in autumn. Pea-like flowers are magenta in bud, opening to pale pink in mid-spring before leaves emerge. ♀ **'Forest Pansy'** illus. p.87.
♀ ***C. siliquastrum*** illus. p.84.

CEREUS

CACTACEAE

Genus of columnar, perennial cacti with spiny stems, most having 4–10 pronounced ribs. Cup-shaped flowers usually open at night. Frost tender, min. 7°C (45°F). Needs full sun and very well-drained soil. Propagate in spring by seed or, for branching species, by stem cuttings.
C. forbesii. See *C. validus.*
C. peruvianus of gardens. See *C. uruguayanus.*
C. spachianus. See *Echinopsis spachiana.*
C. uruguayanus, syn. *C. peruvianus* of gardens., illus. p.472. **'Monstrosus'** is a columnar, perennial cactus. H 5m (15ft), S 4m (12ft). Swollen, occasionally fan-shaped, silvery-blue stems bear golden spines on 4–8 (or more) uneven ribs. Is unlikely to flower in cultivation.
C. validus, syn. *C. forbesii*, illus. p.472.

Cereus, Night-blooming. See *Hylocereus undatus.*

CERINTHE

BORAGINACEAE

Genus of annuals, biennials, and perennials with somewhat fleshy stems and leaves. Fully to frost hardy. Requires a site in full sun, with dry to moist, but well-drained soil. Propagate by seed sown in autumn or spring.
***C. major* 'Purpurascens'** illus. p.343.

CEROPEGIA

ASCLEPIADACEAE

Genus of semi-evergreen, succulent shrubs and sub-shrubs, most with slender, climbing or pendent stems, grown for their unusual flowers. Frost tender, min. 7–11°C (45–52°F). Needs partial shade and very well-drained soil. Propagate by seed or stem cuttings in spring or summer. *C. woodii* is often used as grafting stock for difficult asclepiads.
C. distincta subsp. ***haygarthii.*** See *C. haygarthii.*
C. haygarthii, syn. *C. distincta* subsp. *haygarthii.* Semi-evergreen, climbing, succulent sub-shrub. H 2m (6ft) or more, S indefinite. Min. 11°C (52°F). Bears oval or rounded, dark green leaves, 1–2cm (½–¾in) long. In summer, produces masses of small, white or pinkish-white flowers, each with a pitcher-shaped tube, widening towards the top and then united at the tip by purplish-spotted petals that form a short stem ending in 5 'knobs' edged with fine hairs. The whole resembles an insect hovering over a flower.
♀ ***C. linearis*** subsp. ***woodii,*** syn. *C. woodii*, illus. p.478.
C. sandersoniae. See *C. sandersonii.*
C. sandersonii, syn. *C. sandersoniae* (Fountain flower, Parachute plant). Semi-evergreen, scrambling, succulent sub-shrub. H 2m (6ft), S indefinite. Min. 11°C (52°F). Leaves are triangular to oval, fleshy and 2cm (¾in) long. In summer-autumn has tubular, green flowers, 5cm (2in) long, with paler green to white marks; the petals are flared widely at tips to form 'parachutes'.
C. woodii. See *C. linearis* subsp. *woodii.*

CESTRUM

SOLANACEAE

Genus of deciduous or evergreen shrubs and semi-scrambling climbers, grown for their showy flowers. Foliage has an unpleasant scent. Frost hardy to frost tender, min. 7–10°C (45–50°F); in cold areas grow frost hardy species against a south-or west-facing wall or in a greenhouse. Requires a sheltered, sunny position and fertile, well-drained soil. Water containerized specimens freely when in full growth, moderately at other times. Support is needed for scrambling species. Propagate frost hardy species by softwood cuttings in summer, tender species by seed in spring or by semi-ripe cuttings in summer.
C. aurantiacum. Mainly evergreen semi-scrambler that remains a rounded shrub if cut back annually. H and S to 2m (6ft). Frost tender, min. 7–10°C (45–50°F); is deciduous at low temperatures. Bears oval, bright green leaves. Tubular, bright orange flowers are carried in large, terminal trusses in summer and may be followed by spherical, white fruits. Prune annually, cutting out old stems to near base after flowering.
C. elegans, syn. *C. purpureum* of gardens, illus. p.138.
♀ ***C.* 'Newellii'.** Evergreen, arching shrub. H and S 3m (10ft). Frost hardy. Bears clusters of tubular, crimson flowers in late spring and summer. Leaves are large, broadly lance-shaped and dark green.
♀ ***C. parqui.*** Deciduous, open shrub. H and S 2m (6ft). Frost hardy. Large clusters of tubular, yellowish-green flowers, fragrant at night, are borne in profusion in summer amid narrowly lance-shaped, mid-green leaves.
C. purpureum of gardens. See *C. elegans.*

Ceterach officinarum. See *Asplenium ceterach.*

CHAENOMELES

Flowering quince, Japonica

ROSACEAE

Genus of deciduous, usually thorny, spring-flowering shrubs, grown for their showy flowers and fragrant fruits, produced in autumn and used for preserves. Fully hardy. Prefers sun and

well-drained soil. On wall-trained shrubs cut back side-shoots after flowering to 2 or 3 buds and shorten shoots growing away from wall during growing season. Propagate species by softwood or greenwood cuttings in summer or by seed in autumn, cultivars by cuttings only in summer. Fireblight and, on chalk soils, chlorosis are common problems.
C. cathayensis. Deciduous, spreading, open shrub with thorns. H and S 3m (10ft) or more. Produces long, narrow, pointed, mid-green leaves. Small, 5-petalled, pink-flushed, white flowers appear from early to mid-spring, followed by large, egg-shaped, yellow-green fruits.
C. japonica (Japanese quince, Japonica). Deciduous, bushy, spreading shrub with thorns. H 1m (3ft), S 2m (6ft). Has oval, mid-green leaves and, in spring, a profusion of 5-petalled, red or orange-red flowers, then spherical, yellow fruits.
C. speciosa. Vigorous, deciduous, bushy shrub with thorns. H 2.5m (8ft), S 5m (15ft). Leaves are oval, glossy and dark green. Clustered, 5-petalled, red flowers are borne from early to mid-spring, and are followed by spherical, greenish-yellow fruits.
♀ **'Moerloosei'** illus. p.126. Flowers of **'Nivalis'** are pure white. **'Simonii'**, H 1m (3ft), S 2m (6ft), bears masses of semi-double, deep red flowers.
♀ ***C. x superba*** **'Crimson and Gold'.** Deciduous, bushy, dense shrub with thorns. H 1m (3ft), S 2m (6ft). Has oval, glossy, dark green leaves. Bears masses of 5-petalled, deep red flowers, with conspicuous, golden-yellow anthers, in spring, followed by round, yellow fruits. Flowers of **'Etna'**, H 1.5m (5ft), S 3m (10ft), are scarlet.
♀ **'Knap Hill Scarlet'**, H 1.5m (5ft), S 3m (10ft), produces large, brilliant red flowers. ♀ **'Nicoline'** illus. p.152.
♀ **'Rowallane'** illus. p.151.

Chain cactus. See *Rhipsalis paradoxa.*
Chain fern. See *Woodwardia radicans.*
Asian. See *Woodwardia unigemmata.*

CHAMAEBATIARIA

ROSACEAE

Genus of one species of deciduous shrub, grown for its foliage and summer flowers. Frost hardy. Needs a sheltered, sunny position and well-drained soil. Propagate by semi-ripe cuttings in summer.
C. millefolium. Deciduous, upright, open shrub. H and S 1m (3ft). Has finely divided, aromatic, grey-green leaves. Shallowly cup-shaped, white flowers, with yellow stamens, are borne in terminal, branching panicles from mid- to late summer.

Chamaecereus silvestrii. See *Echinopsis chamaecereus.*

CHAMAECYPARIS

False Cypress

CUPRESSACEAE

Contact with the foliage may aggravate skin allergies. See also CONIFERS.
C. lawsoniana (Lawson cypress). Upright, columnar conifer with branches drooping at tips. H 15–25m (50–80ft), S 3–4m (10–12ft). Fully hardy. Bears flattened sprays of scale-like, aromatic, dark green leaves and globular cones, the males brick-red, the females insignificant and green.
'Columnaris' illus. p.104.
♀ **'Ellwoodii'**, H 3m (10ft), S 1.5m (5ft), is erect with incurved, blue-grey leaves. ♀ **'Fletcheri'**, H 5–12m (15–40ft), S 2–3m (6–10ft), has grey leaves that are incurved. **'Gnome'** (illus. p.107), H and S 50cm (20in), is a dwarf, bun-shaped form with blue foliage. **'Green Pillar'** illus. p.103.
♀ **'Intertexta'** illus. p.98.
♀ **'Kilmacurragh'**, H 10–15m (30–50ft), S 1m (3ft), has very bright green foliage. ♀ **'Lanei Aurea'** illus. p.103.
'Minima' (illus. p.107), H and S 1m (3ft), is dwarf and globular, and has light green foliage. ♀ **'Pembury Blue'** illus. p.101. **'Tamariscifolia'** (syn. *C.l.* Tamariscifolia Group), H 3m (10ft), S 4m (12ft), is a dwarf, spreading form. **'Triomf van Boskoop'**, H 20m (70ft), is broadly columnar, with grey-blue foliage.
♀ **'Wisselii'**, H 15m (50ft), S 2–3m (6–10ft), is fast-growing, with erect branches and blue-green leaves.
C. nootkatensis (Nootka cypress). Almost geometrically conical conifer. H 15m (50ft), S 6m (20ft). Fully hardy. Bears long, pendent sprays of scale-like, aromatic, grey-green leaves and globular, hooked, dark blue and green cones that ripen to brown. ♀ **'Pendula'** has a gaunt crown of arching, weeping foliage.
C. obtusa (Hinoki cypress). Conical conifer. H 15–20m (50–70ft), S 5m (15ft). Fully hardy. Has stringy, red-brown bark and scale-like, aromatic, dark green leaves with bright silver lines at sides and incurving tips. Small, rounded cones ripen to yellow-brown.
'Coralliformis', H to 50cm (20in), S 1m (3ft), is dwarf, with thread-like shoots. ♀ **'Crippsii'** illus. p.105.
'Intermedia' (illus. p.107), H to 30cm (12in), S 40cm (16in), is a globular, open, dwarf shrub with downward-spreading, light green foliage.
'Kosteri', H 1–2m (3–6ft), S 2–3m (6–10ft), forms a sprawling bush with twisted, lustrous foliage. Extremely slow-growing ♀ **'Nana'**, eventual H 1m (3ft), S 1.5–2m (5–6ft), makes a flat-topped bush. ♀ **'Nana Aurea'** (illus. p.107), H and S 2m (6ft), is a form with golden-yellow leaves.
♀ **'Nana Gracilis'**, H 2m (6ft), S 1.5–2m (5–6ft), is a form with glossy foliage. **'Nana Pyramidalis'** (illus. p.107), H and S to 60cm (2ft), is a slow-growing, dense, conical, dwarf cultivar with horizontal, cup-shaped leaves. **'Tetragona Aurea'**, H 10m (30ft), S 2–3m (6–10ft), produces golden- or bronze-yellow leaves.
C. pisifera (Sawara cypress). Conical conifer with horizontal branches. H 15m (50ft), S 5m (15ft). Fully hardy. Has ridged, peeling, red-brown bark, scale-like, aromatic, fresh green leaves, white at sides and beneath, and angular, yellow-brown cones. ♀ **'Boulevard'** has silver-blue foliage. **'Filifera'** has whip-like, hanging shoots and dark green foliage. ♀ **'Filifera Aurea'** (illus. p.107), H 12m (40ft), S 3–5m (10–15ft), also has whip-like shoots, but with golden-yellow leaves.
'Filifera Nana', H 60cm (2ft), S 1m (3ft), is a dwarf form with whip-like branches. **'Nana'**, H and S 50cm (20in), is also dwarf, with dark bluish-green foliage. **'Plumosa'** is broadly conical to columnar, with yellowish-grey-green leaves. **'Plumosa Rogersii'**, H 2m (6ft), S 1m (3ft), has yellow foliage. Slow-growing **'Squarrosa'**, H to 20m (70ft), has a broad crown and soft, blue-grey foliage.
C. thyoides illus. p.103. **'Andelyensis'** is a slow-growing, conical, dwarf conifer. H 3m (10ft), S 1m (3ft). Fully hardy. Has wedge-shaped tufts of scale-like, aromatic, blue-green leaves. Globular cones are glaucous blue-grey.

CHAMAECYTISUS

LEGUMINOSAE/PAPILIONACEAE

Genus of evergreen and deciduous trees, shrubs and sub-shrubs, grown for their pea-like flowers. Fully to half hardy. Best in full sun and moderately fertile, well-drained soil. Propagate by seed in autumn or spring or by semi-ripe cuttings in summer.
C. albus, syn *Cytisus albus*, *Cytisus leucanthus.* Deciduous, spreading shrub. H 30cm (1ft), S 1m (3ft). Fully hardy. Has oval leaves, each with 3 tiny leaflets and, from early to mid-summer, creamy-white flowers borne in dense clusters.
C. demissus, syn. *C. hirsutus* var. *demissus, Cytisus demissus.* Slow-growing, deciduous, prostrate shrub. H 8cm (3in), S 20–30cm (8–12in). Fully hardy. Densely hairy stems bear tiny, bright green leaves with 3-palmate, obovate leaflets. Produces axillary clusters of 2–4 bright yellow flowers, each with a brown keel, in early summer. Is good for a rock garden or trough.
C. hirsutus var. ***demissus.*** See *C. demissus*.
C. purpureus, syn. *Cytisus purpureus* (Purple broom). Deciduous, arching shrub. H 45cm (18in), S 60cm (24in). Fully hardy. Semi-erect stems are clothed with leaves of 3-palmate, obovate leaflets. Clusters of 2–3 pale lilac to purple flowers open in early summer on previous year's wood. Is good for a bank or sunny border. f. ***albus*** illus. p.363.
C. supinus, syn. *Cytisus supinus.* Deciduous, bushy, rounded shrub. H and S 1m (3ft). Fully hardy. Dense, terminal heads of large, yellow flowers are borne from mid-summer to autumn amid grey-green leaves with 3-palmate, oblong-elliptic leaflets.

CHAMAEDAPHNE

ERICACEAE

Genus of one species of evergreen shrub, grown for its white flowers. Fully hardy. Needs sun or semi-shade and moist, peaty, acid soil. Propagate by semi-ripe cuttings in summer.
C. calyculata (Leatherleaf). Evergreen, arching, open shrub. H 75cm (2½ft), S 1m (3ft). Leaves are small, oblong, leathery and dark green. Leafy racemes of small, urn-shaped flowers appear on slender branches in mid- to late spring.

CHAMAEDOREA

ARECACEAE/PALMAE

Genus of evergreen palms, grown for their overall appearance. Frost tender,min. 18°C (64°F). Needs shade or semi-shade and humus-rich, well-drained soil. Water containerized plants moderately, less when temperatures are low. Propagate by seed in spring at not less than 25°C (77°F). Red spider mite may be troublesome.
♀ ***C. elegans***, syn. *Neanthe bella*, illus. p.148.

CHAMAEMELUM

COMPOSITAE/ASTERACEAE

Genus of evergreen perennials, suitable as ground cover or for a lawn. Flowers may be used to make tea. Fully hardy. Needs sun and well-drained soil. Propagate by division in spring or by seed in autumn.
C. nobile, syn. *Anthemis nobilis* (Chamomile). Evergreen, mat-forming, invasive perennial. H 10cm (4in), S 45cm (18in). Has finely divided, aromatic leaves and daisy-like heads of white flowers, with yellow centres, borne in late spring or summer.
'Treneague' is a non-flowering, less invasive cultivar that, requiring less mowing, is better for a lawn.

Chamaenerion. See *Epilobium.*
Chamaepericlymenum canadense. See *Cornus canadensis*.

CHAMAEROPS

ARECACEAE/PALMAE

Genus of evergreen palms, cultivated for their overall appearance. Half hardy to frost tender, min. 7°C (45°F). Needs full light and fertile, well-drained soil. Water containerized plants moderately, less when not in full growth. Propagate by seed in spring at not less than 22°C (72°F) or by suckers in late spring. Red spider mite may be a nuisance.
♀ ***C. humilis*** illus. p.172.

Chamaespartium sagittale. See *Genista sagittalis.*
Chamaespartium sagittale subsp. ***delphinense.*** See *Genista delphinensis.*

CHAMELAUCIUM

MYRTACEAE

Genus of evergreen shrubs, grown for their flowers and overall appearance. Frost tender, min. 5°C (41°F), but best at 7–10°C (45–50°F). Requires full sun and well-drained, sandy, neutral to acid soil. Water containerized specimens moderately, sparingly when not in full growth. To maintain a more compact habit, cut back flowered stems by half when the last bloom falls. Propagate by seed in spring or by semi-ripe cuttings in summer.
C. uncinatum [pink form] illus. p.146, [white form] illus. p.145.

Chamomile. See *Chamaemelum nobile.*
Channelled heath. See *Erica canaliculata*, illus. p.174.

CHASMANTHE

IRIDACEAE

Genus of corms, grown for their showy flowers. Frost to half hardy. Requires a site in full sun or partial shade and well-drained soil, with plenty of water in growing season (late winter and early spring). Reduce watering in summer-autumn. Propagate by division in autumn.

C. aethiopica. Spring-and early summer-flowering corm. H to 80cm (32in), S 12–18cm (5–7in). Frost hardy. Has narrowly sword-shaped, erect, basal leaves in a flat fan. Produces a spike of scarlet flowers, all facing one way, with yellow tubes, 5–6cm (2–2½in) long, and hooded, upper lips.

C. floribunda. Summer-flowering corm. H to 80cm (32in), S 12–18cm (5–7in). Half hardy. Is similar to *C. aethiopica,* but the leaves are much wider, and the longer, orange or scarlet flowers do not all face in the same direction.

Chaste tree. See *Vitex agnus-castus.*
Chatham Island forget-me-not. See *Myosotidium.*
Cheddar pink. See *Dianthus gratianopolitanus*, illus. p.389.

CHEILANTHES

ADIANTACEAE

Genus of evergreen ferns. Half hardy. Needs full light and humus-rich, well-drained soil. Do not overwater containerized plants or splash water on fronds. Remove fading foliage regularly. Propagate by spores in summer.

C. lanosa of gardens. See *C. tomentosa.*

C. tomentosa, syn. *C. lanosa* of gardens. Evergreen fern. H and S 15–23cm (6–9in). Leaves are triangular or lance-shaped and have much divided, soft green fronds on hairy, black stems.

Cheiranthus. See *Erysimum.*

CHEIRIDOPSIS

AIZOACEAE

Genus of clump-forming, perennial succulents with pairs of semi-cylindrical leaves. Frost tender, min. 5°C (41°F). Needs sun and well-drained soil. Water in autumn to encourage flowers. Propagate by seed or stem cuttings in spring or summer.

C. candidissima. See *C. denticulata.*

C. denticulata, syn. *C. candidissima.* Clump-forming, perennial succulent. H 10cm (4in), S 20cm (8in). Has semi-cylindrical, slender, fleshy, blue-grey leaves, each 10cm (4in) long with a flat top, joined in pairs for almost half their length. Bears daisy-like, shiny, white flowers, to 6cm (2½in) across, in spring.

C. purpurata. See *C. purpurea.*

C. purpurea, syn. *C. purpurata.* Carpeting, perennial succulent. H 10cm (4in), S 30cm (12in). Has semi-cylindrical, thick, short, glaucous green leaves, each with a flat top. In early spring produces daisy-like, purple-pink flowers, 4cm (1½in) across.

CHELIDONIUM

Celandine, Greater Celandine

PAPAVERACEAE

Genus of one species of perennial that rapidly forms ground cover. Fully hardy. Grows in sun or shade and in any but very wet soil. Propagate by seed or division in autumn. Contact with the sap may cause skin blisters.

***C. majus* 'Flore Pleno'** illus. p.240.

CHELONE

Turtle-Head

SCROPHULARIACEAE

Genus of summer- and autumn-flowering perennials. Fully hardy. Needs semi-shade and moist soil. Propagate by soft-tip cuttings in summer or by division or seed in autumn or spring.

C. barbata. See *Penstemon barbatus.*

C. obliqua illus. p.267.

Cherimoya. See *Annona.*
Cherry. See *Prunus.*
Australian brush. See *Syzygium paniculatum*, illus. p.77.
Bell-flowered. See *Prunus campanulata.*
Bird. See *Prunus padus*, illus. p.72.
Black. See *Prunus serotina*, illus. p.61.
Bladder. See *Physalis alkekengi.*
Cornelian. See *Cornus mas.*
Downy. See *Prunus tomentosa.*
Fuji. See *Prunus incisa*, illus. p.82.
Great white. See *Prunus* 'Taihaku', illus. p.82.
Higan. See *Prunus × subhirtella.*
Hill. See *Prunus jamasakura*, illus. p.72.
Jerusalem. See *Solanum pseudocapsicum.*
Pin. See *Prunus pensylvanica.*
Rosebud. See *Prunus × subhirtella.*
Sargent. See *Prunus sargentii*, illus. p.83.
Taiwan. See *Prunus campanulata.*
Virginian bird. See *Prunus virginiana.*
Wild. See *Prunus avium*, illus. p.67.
Wild rum. See *Prunus serotina*, illus. p.61.
Winter. See *Cardiospermum halicacabum; Physalis alkekengi; Solanum capsicastrum.*
Yoshino. See *Prunus × yedoensis*, illus. p.83.
Cherry laurel. See *Prunus laurocerasus.*
Cherry plum. See *Prunus cerasifera.*
Chestnut. See *Castanea.*
American. See *Castanea dentata.*
Cape. See *Calodendrum capense.*
Moreton Bay. See *Castanospermum.*
Spanish. See *Castanea sativa.*
Sweet. See *Castanea sativa.*
Water. See *Trapa natans*, illus. p.465.
Chestnut vine. See *Tetrastigma voinierianum*, illus. p.218.

CHIASTOPHYLLUM

CRASSULACEAE

Genus of one species of evergreen perennial, grown for its succulent leaves and attractive sprays of small, yellow flowers. Thrives in rock crevices. Fully hardy. Needs shade and well-drained soil that is not too dry. Propagate by side-shoot cuttings in early summer or by seed in autumn.

♀ ***C. oppositifolium***, syn. *Cotyledon simplicifolia*, illus. p.361.

Chicory. See *Cichorium.*
Chile pine. See *Araucaria araucana*, illus. p.99.
Chilean bamboo. See *Chusquea culeou*, illus. p.320.
Chilean bellflower. See *Lapageria rosea*, illus. p.206.
Chilean blue crocus. See *Tecophilaea cyanocrocus*, illus. p.449.
Chilean firebush. See *Embothrium coccineum*, illus. p.89.
Chilean glory flower. See *Eccremocarpus scaber*, illus. p.215.
Chilean hazel. See *Gevuina avellana.*
Chilean incense cedar. See *Austrocedrus chilensis*, illus. p.102.
Chilean jasmine. See *Mandevilla laxa.*
Chilean laurel. See *Laurelia sempervirens.*
Chilean wine palm. See *Jubaea chilensis*, illus. p.81.
Chimney bellflower. See *Campanula pyramidalis.*

CHIMONANTHUS

CALYCANTHACEAE

Genus of deciduous or evergreen, winter-flowering shrubs, grown for their flowers. Frost hardy, but in cold areas reduce susceptibility of flowers to frost by training plants against a south- or west-facing wall. Needs full sun and fertile, well-drained soil. Propagate species by seed when ripe, in late spring and early summer, cultivars by softwood cuttings in summer.

C. fragrans. See *C. praecox.*

C. praecox, syn. *C. fragrans* (Wintersweet). Deciduous, bushy shrub. H 2.5m (8ft) or more, S 3m (10ft). Has oval, rough, glossy, dark green leaves. Bears very fragrant, many-petalled, cup-shaped, yellow flowers, with purple centres, on bare branches in mild periods during winter. ♀ **'Luteus'** (syn. *C.p.* var. *concolor, C.p.* 'Concolor', *C.p.* var. *luteus*) has pure yellow flowers.

China aster. See *Callistephus.*
Chincherinchee. See *Ornithogalum thyrsoides*, illus. p.436.
Chinese anise. See *Illicium anisatum.*
Chinese arbor-vitae. See *Platycladus orientalis.*
Chinese box thorn. See *Lycium barbarum.*
Chinese elm. See *Ulmus parvifolia.*
Chinese evergreen. See *Aglaonema.*
Chinese fan palm. See *Livistona chinensis*, illus. p.81.
Chinese fir. See *Cunninghamia lanceolata*, illus. p.102.
Chinese fountain grass. See *Pennisetum alopecuroides.*
Chinese fountain palm. See *Livistona chinensis*, illus. p.81.
Chinese fringe tree. See *Chionanthus retusus.*
Chinese gooseberry. See *Actinidia deliciosa.*
Chinese hat plant. See *Holmskioldia sanguinea.*
Chinese horse-chestnut. See *Aesculus chinensis*, illus. p.60.
Chinese juniper. See *Juniperus chinensis.*
Chinese lantern. See *Physalis.*
Chinese necklace poplar. See *Populus lasiocarpa.*
Chinese parasol tree. See *Firmiana simplex*, illus. p.64.
Chinese persimmon. See *Diospyros kaki.*
Chinese privet. See *Ligustrum lucidum.*
Chinese tallow tree. See *Sapium sebiferum.*
Chinese thuja. See *Platycladus orientalis.*
Chinese trumpet creeper. See *Campsis grandiflora.*
Chinese trumpet vine. See *Campsis grandiflora.*
Chinese tulip tree. See *Liriodendron chinense.*
Chinese walnut. See *Juglans cathayensis.*
Chinese wing nut. See *Pterocarya stenoptera.*
Chinese wisteria. See *Wisteria sinensis*, illus. p.213.
Chinese witch hazel. See *Hamamelis mollis.*
Chinese-lantern lily. See *Sandersonia aurantiaca*, illus. p.439.

CHIONANTHUS

OLEACEAE

Genus of deciduous shrubs, grown for their profuse, white flowers. Flowers more freely in areas with hot summers. Fully hardy. Prefers full sun and fertile, well-drained but not too dry soil. Propagate by seed in autumn.

C. retusus (Chinese fringe tree). Deciduous, often tree-like, arching shrub. H and S 3m (10ft). From early to mid-summer, star-shaped, pure white flowers appear in large clusters amid oval, bright green leaves.

C. virginicus illus. p.115.

CHIONOCHLOA

GRAMINEAE/POACEAE

See also GRASSES, BAMBOOS, RUSHES and SEDGES.

C. conspicua (Hunangemoho grass). Evergreen, tussock-forming, perennial grass. H 1.2–1.5m (4–5ft), S 1m (3ft). Fully hardy. Very long, mid-green leaves are tinged reddish-brown. Has stout, arching stems with long, loose, open panicles of cream spikelets in summer.

CHIONODOXA

Glory-of-the-snow

LILIACEAE/HYACINTHACEAE

Genus of spring-flowering bulbs, related to *Scilla*. Is suitable for rock gardens and for naturalizing under shrubs, in sun or partial shade. Fully hardy. Requires well-drained soil, top dressed with leaf mould or mature garden compost in autumn. Propagate by seed in autumn or by division in late summer or autumn.

C. forbesii. See *C. siehei.*

C. gigantea. See *C. luciliae.*

♀ ***C. luciliae***, syn. *C. gigantea*, illus. p.449.

C. luciliae of gardens. See *C. siehei.*

***C.* 'Pink Giant'** illus. p.443.

♀ ***C. sardensis.*** Early spring-flowering bulb. H 10–20cm (4–8in), S 2.5–5cm (1–2in). Has 2 narrowly lance-shaped,

semi-erect, basal leaves. Leafless stem produces 4–15 flattish, slightly pendent or outward-facing, deep rich blue flowers, 1.5–2cm (⅝–¾in) across and without, or with an indistinct, white eye.
♀ ***C. siehei.*** syn *C. forbesii*, *C. luciliae* of gardens, *C. tmolusii,* illus. p.449
C. tmolusii. See *C. siehei*.

× CHIONOSCILLA

LILIACEAE/HYACINTHACEAE

Hybrid genus (*Chionodoxa* × *Scilla*) of spring-flowering bulbs, suitable for rock gardens. Fully hardy. Needs full sun or partial shade and humus-rich, well-drained soil. Propagate by division in late summer or autumn.
× ***C. allenii*** illus. p.449.

CHIRITA

GESNERIACEAE

Genus of evergreen perennials or sub-shrubs, grown for their flowers. Frost tender, min. 15°C (59°F). Requires well-drained soil, a fairly humid atmosphere and a light position out of direct sunlight. Propagate by tip cuttings in summer or, if available, seed in late winter or spring.
C. lavandulacea illus. p.306.
♀ ***C. sinensis.*** Evergreen, stemless, rosetted perennial. H to 15cm (6in), S 25cm (10in) or more. Has oval, almost fleshy leaves, the corrugated, hairy surfaces usually patterned with silver marks. In spring-summer, clusters of tubular, lavender flowers are held above leaves.

Chives. See *Allium schoenoprasum*, illus. p.452.

CHLIDANTHUS

AMARYLLIDACEAE

Genus of one species of summer-flowering bulb, grown for its showy, funnel-shaped flowers. Half hardy. Needs a sunny site and well-drained soil. Plant in the open in spring and after flowering, if necessary, lift and dry off for winter. Propagate by offsets in spring.
C. fragrans illus. p.452.

CHLOROGALUM

LILIACEAE/HYACINTHACEAE

Genus of summer-flowering bulbs, grown more for botanical interest than for floral display. Frost hardy, but in cold areas plant in a sheltered site. Requires sun and well-drained soil. Propagate by seed in autumn or spring.
C. pomeridianum. Summer-flowering bulb. H to 2.5m (8ft), S 15–20cm (6–8in). Semi-erect, basal leaves are long, narrow and grey-green, with wavy margins. Carries a large, loosely branched head of small, saucer-shaped, white flowers, with a central, green or purple stripe on each petal, that open after midday.

CHLOROPHYTUM

LILIACEAE/ANTHERICACEAE

Genus of evergreen, stemless perennials with short rhizomes, grown for their foliage. Frost tender, min. 5°C (41°F). Grow in a light position, away from direct sun, in fertile, well-drained soil. Water freely in growing season but sparingly at other times if pot-grown. Propagate by seed, division or plantlets (produced on flower stems of some species) at any time except winter.
C. capense. Evergreen, tufted perennial. H 30cm (12in), S indefinite. Forms rosettes of lance- or strap-shaped, bright green leaves, to 60cm (24in) long. Tiny, white flowers in racemes, to 60cm (24in) long, are borne in summer. Does not produce plantlets.
C. capense of gardens. See *C. comosum.*
C. comosum, syn. *C. capense* of gardens. (Spider plant). Evergreen, tufted perennial. H 30cm (12in), S indefinite. Very narrow leaves, to 45cm (18in) long, spread from a rosette. Racemes of many small, star-shaped, white flowers are carried on thin stems, 60cm (24in) or more long,at any time. Small rosettes of leaves may appear on flower stems, forming plantlets. ♀ **'Vittatum'** illus. p.313.

Chocolate cosmos. See *Cosmos atrosanguineus*, illus. p.253.
Chocolate vine. See *Akebia quinata*, illus. p.201.

CHOISYA

RUTACEAE

Genus of evergreen shrubs, grown for their foliage and flowers. Frost to half hardy; in most areas needs some shelter. Requires full sun and fertile, well-drained soil. Propagate by semi-ripe cuttings in late summer.
♀ ***C. ternata*** (Mexican orange blossom) illus. p.123. ♀ **SUNDANCE** (**'Lich'**) is an evergreen, rounded, dense shrub. H and S 2.5m (8ft). Frost hardy. Aromatic, glossy, bright yellow leaves each consist of 3 oblong leaflets. Fragrant, star-shaped, white flowers are produced in clusters in late spring and often again in autumn.

Chokeberry. See *Aronia.*
Black. See *Aronia melanocarpa*, illus. p.132.
Red. See *Aronia arbutifolia*, illus. p.126.

CHORDOSPARTIUM

LEGUMINOSAE/PAPILIONACEAE

Genus of one species of deciduous, almost leafless shrub, grown for its habit and flowers. Slender, green shoots assume function of leaves. Frost hardy. Requires a sheltered, sunny position and fertile, well-drained soil. Propagate by seed in autumn.
C. stevensonii. Deciduous, almost leafless, arching shrub. H 3m (10ft), S 2m (6ft). Produces small, pea-like, purplish-pink flowers in cylindrical racemes in mid-summer.

CHORISIA

BOMBACACEAE

Genus of deciduous trees, usually with spine-covered trunks, grown mainly for their flowers in autumn and winter and their overall appearance. Frost tender, min. 15°C (59°F). Needs full light and well-drained soil. Water containerized specimens freely when in full growth, very little when leafless. Pruning is tolerated if necessary. Propagate by seed in spring. Red spider mite may be troublesome.***C. speciosa,*** syn *Ceiba speciosa*, illus. p.66.

CHORIZEMA

LEGUMINOSAE/PAPILIONACEAE

Genus of evergreen sub-shrubs, shrubs and scandent climbers, grown mainly for their flowers. Frost tender, min. 7°C (45°F). Requires full light and humus-rich, well-drained, sandy soil, preferably neutral to acid. Water potted plants moderately, less when not in full growth. Tie climbers to supports, or grow in hanging baskets. Propagate by seed in spring or by semi-ripe cuttings in summer.
C. ilicifolium illus. p.153.

Christ's thorn. See *Paliurus spina-christi*, illus. p.118.
Christmas begonia. See *Begonia* 'Gloire de Lorraine'.
Christmas berry. See *Heteromeles salicifolia.*
Christmas box. See *Sarcococca.*
Christmas cactus. See *Schlumbergera × buckleyi.*
Christmas fern. See *Polystichum acrostichoides.*
Christmas rose. See *Helleborus.*
Christmas tree, New Zealand. See *Metrosideros excelsus*, illus. p.79.
Chrysalidocarpus lutescens. See *Dypsis lutescens.*

CHRYSANTHEMUM

COMPOSITAE/ASTERACEAE

Genus of annuals, perennials, some of which are evergreen, and evergreen sub-shrubs, grown for their flowers. Each flower head is referred to horticulturally as a flower, even though it does in fact comprise a large number of individual flowers or florets; this horticultural usage has been followed in the descriptions below. Leaves are usually deeply lobed or cut, often feathery, oval to lance-shaped. Florists' chrysanthemums (nowadays considered to belong to the genus *Dendranthema*) comprise the vast majority of chrysanthemums now cultivated and are perennials grown for garden decoration, cutting and exhibition. Annuals are fully to half hardy. Florists' chrysanthemums are fully hardy to frost tender, min. 10°C (50°F); those that are half hardy or frost tender should be lifted and stored in a frost-free place over winter. Other perennial chrysanthemums are fully to half hardy. Provide a sunny site and reasonably fertile, well-drained soil. If grown for exhibition will require regular feeding. Pinch out growing tips to encourage lateral growths on which flowers will be borne, and stake tall plants with canes. Propagate annuals by seed sown in position in spring; thin out, but do not transplant. Propagate hardy perennials by division in autumn, after flowering, or in early spring. Florists' chrysanthemums should be propagated from basal softwood cuttings in spring. Spray regularly to control aphids, capsids, froghoppers, earwigs, mildew and white rust.

Florists' chrysanthemums
Florists' chrysanthemums are grouped according to their widely varying flower forms, approximate flowering season (early, mid- or late autumn) and habit. They are divided into disbudded and non-disbudded types. For descriptions and illustrations of flower forms see feature panel pp.268–9.

Disbudded types – single, anemone-centred, incurved, intermediate and reflexed – are so called because all buds, except the one that is to flower, are removed from each stem. To produce exhibition flowers, incurved, intermediate and reflexed chrysanthemums may be restricted to only 2 blooms per plant by removing all except the 2 most vigorous lateral growths. In gardens, allow 4 or 5 blooms per plant to develop. Single and anemone-centred flowers should be reduced to 4–8 blooms per plant for exhibition, according to their vigour, and 10 or more for garden decoration or cutting.

Non-disbudded types – charm, pompon and spray chrysanthemums – have several flowers per stem.
Charm chrysanthemums are dwarf plants that produce hundreds of star-shaped, single flowers, 2.5cm (1in) across, densely covering each plant to form a hemispherical to almost spherical head. For exhibition, finish growing in at least 30cm (12in) pots. Plants for indoor decoration are grown in smaller pots and have correspondingly smaller, though equally dense, heads of blooms.
Pompon chrysanthemums are also dwarf. Each plant has 50 or more dense, spherical or occasionally hemispherical, fully double flowers that have tubular petals (for illustrations see p.269). They are excellent for growing in borders.
Spray chrysanthemums have a variety of flower forms: single, anemone-centred, intermediate, reflexed, pompon, spoon-shaped (in which each straight, tubular floret opens out like a spoon at its tip), quill-shaped and spider-form. Each plant should be allowed to develop 4 or 5 stems with at least 5 flowers per stem. Grow late-flowering sprays on up to 3 stems per plant. With controlled day length, to regulate flowering dates for exhibition purposes, late sprays should be allowed to develop at least 12 flowers per stem; without day length control, 6 or 7 flowers per stem.

Those most suitable for garden decoration are sprays, pompons and early reflexed chrysanthemums. All are suitable for cutting, except for charms. Late-flowering chrysanthemums are only suitable for growing under glass as flowers need protection from poor weather; they should be grown in pots and placed in a greenhouse in early autumn, when the flower buds have developed. Intermediate cultivars are also less suitable for garden decoration as florets may collect and retain rain and thus become damaged. Those cultivars suitable for exhibition are noted below. Measurements of flowers given are the greatest normally achieved and may vary considerably depending on growing conditions.

***C.* 'Alison Kirk'** illus. p.268. Incurved florists' chrysanthemum. H 1.2m (4ft), S 30–60cm (1–2ft). Half hardy. Produces white flowers, to 12–15cm (5–6in) across, in early autumn. Is more suitable for exhibition than for garden use.
C. alpinum. See *Leucanthemopsis alpina.*
♀ ***C.* 'Amber Yvonne Arnaud'.** Reflexed florists' chrysanthemum. H 1.2m (4ft), S 60–75cm (2–2½ft). Half hardy. Is a sport of *C.* **'Yvonne Arnaud'** with fully reflexed, amber flowers in early autumn.
***C.* 'Autumn Days'** illus. p.269. Intermediate florists' chrysanthemum. H 1.1–1.2m (3½–4ft), S to 75cm (2½ft).Half hardy. Bears loosely incurving, bronze flowers, 12cm (5in) across, in early autumn.
♀ ***C.* 'Beacon'** illus. p.269. Intermediate florists' chrysanthemum. H 1.2m (4ft), S 60cm (2ft). Frost tender. Bears red, sometimes bronze, flowers, to 18cm (7in) wide, in late autumn. Is good for exhibition.
***C.* 'Bill Wade'** illus. p.268. Intermediate florists' chrysanthemum. H 1.35m (4½ft), S 60cm (2ft). Half hardy. Loosely incurving, white flowers, 18–20cm (7–8in) across, are produced in early autumn. Is more suitable for exhibition than for garden use.
♀ ***C.* 'Brietner'** illus. p.268. Reflexed florists' chrysanthemum. H 1.1–1.2m (3½–4ft), S 75cm (2½ft). Half hardy. Fully reflexed, pink flowers, to 12cm (5in) wide, appear in early autumn.
♀ ***C.* 'Bronze Fairie'** illus. p.269. Pompon florists' chrysanthemum. H 30–60cm (1–2ft), S 60cm (2ft). Fully hardy. Has bronze flowers, 4cm (1½in) across, in early autumn.
***C.* 'Bronze Hedgerow'** illus. p.269. Single florists' chrysanthemum. H 1.5m (5ft), S 75cm–1m (2½–3ft). Frost tender. Produces bronze flowers, 12cm (5in) across, in late autumn.
***C.* 'Bronze Yvonne Arnaud'** illus. p.269. Reflexed florists' chrysanthemum. H 1.2m (4ft), S 60–75cm (2–2½ft). Half hardy. Is a sport of *C.* **'Yvonne Arnaud'** with fully reflexed, bronze flowers in early autumn.
***C.* 'Buff Margaret'** illus. p.269. Spray florists' chrysanthemum. H 1.2m (4ft), S to 75cm (2½ft). Fully hardy. Has reflexed, pale bronze flowers, to 9cm (3½in) wide, in early autumn.
C. carinatum. See *Ismelia carinata.*
***C.* 'Chessington'.** Intermediate florists' chrysanthemum. H 2–2.2m (6–7ft), S 75cm (2½ft). Half hardy. Produces fairly tightly incurving, white flowers, 18–20cm (7–8in) across, in early autumn. Is more suitable for exhibition than for garden use.
***C.* 'Christina'.** Intermediate florists' chrysanthemum. H 1.35–1.5m (4½–5ft), S 60–75cm (2–2½ft). Half hardy. Bears loosely incurving, white flowers, to 14cm (5½in) wide, in early autumn. Is suitable for exhibition.
***C.* 'Claire Louise'.** Reflexed florists' chrysanthemum. H 1.2–1.35m (4–4½ft), S 75cm (2½ft). Half hardy. Produces fully reflexed, bronze flowers, to 15cm (6in) across, in early autumn. Is ideal for exhibition.
***C.* 'Clara Curtis',** syn. *C. rubellum* 'Clara Curtis', illus. p.267.
C. coccineum. See *Tanacetum coccineum.*
C. coronarium. See *Xanthophthalmum coronarium.*
C. densum. See *Tanacetum densum* subsp. *amani.*
***C.* 'Elsie Prosser'** illus. p.268. Fully reflexed florists' chrysanthemum. H 1.3–1.5m (4½–5ft), S 30cm (1ft). Frost tender. Bears pink flowers, 25cm (10in) wide, in late autumn. Is good for exhibition.
♀ ***C.* 'Enbee Wedding'** illus. p.268. Spray florists' chrysanthemum. H 1.2m (4ft), S 75cm (2½ft). Fully hardy. Has single, light pink flowers, to 8cm (3in) wide, in early autumn. Is good for exhibition.
***C.* 'Fairweather'** illus. p.268.Incurved florists' chrysanthemum. H 1.1m (3½ft), S 60cm (2ft). Frost tender. Bears pale purplish-pink flowers, 14cm (5½in) wide, in late autumn. Is good for exhibition.
***C.* 'Fiona Lynn'.** Reflexed florists'chrysanthemum. H 1.5m (5ft), S 75cm (2½ft). Fully reflexed, pink flowers, to18–20cm (7–8in) across, appear in early autumn. Is ideal for exhibition.
C. frutescens. See *Argyranthemum frutescens.* **'Jamaica Primrose'** see *A.* 'Jamaica Primrose'.**'Mary Wootton'** see *A.*'Mary Wootton'.
♀ ***C.* 'George Griffiths'** illus. p.269. Reflexed florists' chrysanthemum. H 1.2–1.35m (4–4½ft), S 75cm (2½ft). Half hardy. Produces fully reflexed, deep red flowers, to 14cm (5½in) wide, in early autumn. Is excellent for exhibition.
***C.* 'Gigantic'** illus. p.269. Tightly incurved or loosely reflexed florists' chrysanthemum, its form depending on the amount of warmth provided. H 1.3m (4½ft), S 30cm (1ft). Frost tender. Has salmon-pink flowers, 25–27cm (10–11in) wide, in late autumn. Is good for exhibition.
***C.* 'Ginger Nut'.** Intermediate florists' chrysanthemum. H 1.2m (4ft), S 60–75cm (2–2½ft). Half hardy. Bears tightly incurving, light bronze flowers, to 14cm (5½in) across, occasionally closing at top to form a true incurved flower, in early autumn. Is good for exhibition.
***C.* 'Golden Chalice'** illus. p.269. Charm florists' chrysanthemum. H and S 1m (3ft). Frost tender. Bears single, yellow flowers, 2.5cm (1in) wide, in late autumn. Is good for exhibition.
***C.* 'Golden Gigantic'** illus. p.269. Tightly incurved or loosely reflexed florists' chrysanthemum. H 1.3m (4½ft), S 30cm (1ft). Frost tender. Produces large, gold flowers, 25–27cm (10–11in) wide, in late autumn. Is good for exhibition.
***C.* 'Golden Woolman's Glory'** illus. p.269. Single florists' chrysanthemum. H 1.5m (5ft), S 1m (3ft). Frost tender. Golden flowers, to 18cm (7in) across, appear in late autumn. Is excellent for exhibition.
***C.* 'Green Satin'** illus. p.269. Intermediate florists' chrysanthemum. H 1.2m (4ft), S 60cm (2ft). Frost tender. Produces loosely incurving, green flowers, to 12cm (5in) wide, in late autumn.
C. haradjanii. See *Tanacetum haradjanii.*
C. hosmariense. See *Rhodanthemum hosmariense.*
***C.* 'Idris'** illus. p.269. Incurved florists'chrysanthemum. H 1.3m (4½ft), S 45cm (1½ft). Frost tender.Has salmon-pink flowers, 21–25cm (8–10in) wide, in late autumn.
***C.* 'John Wingfield'** illus. p.268. Reflexed florists' chrysanthemum. H 1.5m (5ft), S 45–60cm (1½–2ft). Frost tender. Produces white, often pink-flushed, flowers, 12cm (5in) wide, in late autumn. Is good for exhibition.
***C.* 'Keith Luxford'** illus. p.268. Incurved florists' chrysanthemum. H 1.5m (5ft), S 45cm (1½ft). Frost tender. Bears pink flowers, 21–25cm (8–10in) wide, in late autumn. Is good for exhibition.
***C.* 'Lundy'** illus. p.268. Fully reflexed florists' chrysanthemum. H 1.5m (5ft), S 45cm (1½ft). Frost tender. Bears white flowers, 21–25cm (8–10in) wide, often broader than they are deep, in late autumn. Is good for exhibition.
♀ ***C.* 'Madeleine'** illus. p.268. Spray florists' chrysanthemum. H 1.2m (4ft), S 75cm (2½ft). Fully hardy. Has reflexed, pink flowers, to 8cm (3in) across, in early autumn. Is good for exhibition.
***C.* 'Majestic'** illus. p.269. Fully reflexed florists' chrysanthemum. H 1.3m (4½ft), S 45cm (1½ft). Frost tender. Has light bronze flowers, 21–25cm (8–10in) wide, in late autumn. Is good for exhibition.
***C.* 'Maria'** illus. p.269. Pompon florists' chrysanthemum. H 45cm (1½ft), S 30–60cm (1–2ft). Fully hardy. Bears masses of pink flowers, to 4cm (1½in) across, in early autumn.
***C.* 'Marian Gosling'** illus. p.268. Reflexed florists' chrysanthemum. H 1.2–1.35m (4–4½ft), S 60cm (2ft). Half hardy. Fully reflexed, pale pink flowers, to 14cm (5½in) wide, appear in early autumn. Is good for exhibition.
***C.* 'Marion'** illus. p.269. Spray florists' chrysanthemum. H 1.2m (4ft), S 75cm (2½ft). Fully hardy. Produces reflexed, pale yellow flowers, to 8cm (3in) wide, from late summer.
***C.* 'Mason's Bronze'.** Single florists' chrysanthemum. H 1.35–1.5m (4½–5ft), S to 1m (3ft). Frost tender. Has bronze flowers, to 12cm (5in) wide, in late autumn. Is excellent for exhibition.
C. maximum of gardens. See *Leucanthemum × superbum.*
***C.* 'Nancye Furneaux'** illus. p.269. Reflexed florists' chrysanthemum. H 1.5m (5ft), S 45cm (1½ ft). Frost tender. Has yellow flowers, 21–25cm (8–10in) wide, in late autumn. Is good for exhibition.
***C.* 'Oracle'** illus. p.269. Intermediate florists' chrysanthemum. H 1.2m (4ft), S 60–75cm (2–2½ft). Half hardy. Produces loosely incurving, pale bronze flowers, to 12cm (5in) wide, in early autumn. Is useful for exhibition.
C. parthenium. See *Tanacetum parthenium.*
***C.* 'Peach Brietner'** illus. p.269. Reflexed florists' chrysanthemum. H 1.1–1.2m (3½–4ft), S 75cm (2½ft). Half hardy. Is a sport of *C.* 'Brietner' with fully reflexed, peach-coloured flowers.
♀ ***C.* 'Pennine Alfie'** illus. p.269. Spray florists' chrysanthemum. H 1.2m (4ft), S 60–75cm (2–2½ft). Fully hardy. Spoon-shaped , pale bronze flowers, to 6–8cm (2½–3in) wide, appear in early autumn. Is suitable for exhibition.
♀ ***C.* 'Pennine Flute'** illus. p.268. Quill-shaped florists' chrysanthemum. H 1.2m (4ft), S 60–75cm (2–2½ft). Fully hardy. Is similar to *C.* 'Pennine Alfie', but has pink flowers.
♀ ***C.* 'Pennine Oriel'** illus. p.268. Spray florists' chrysanthemum. H 1.2m (4ft), S 60–75cm (2–2½ft). Fully hardy. Anemone-centred, white flowers, to 9cm (3½in) across, are produced in early autumn. Is very good for exhibition.
***C.* 'Peter Rowe'.** Incurved florists' chrysanthemum. H 1.35m (4½ft), S 60–75cm (2–2½ft). Half hardy. Produces yellow flowers, to 14cm (5½in) across, in early autumn. Is ideal for exhibition.
***C.* 'Primrose Fairweather'.** Incurved florists' chrysanthemum. H 1–1.1m (3–3½ft), S to 75cm (2½ft). Half hardy. Produces pale yellow flowers, to 14–15cm (5½–6in) wide, in late autumn. Is good for exhibition.
***C.* 'Primrose John Hughes'** illus. p.269. Perfectly incurved florists' chrysanthemum. H 1.2m (4ft), S 60–75cm (2–2½ft). Frost tender. Bears primrose-yellow flowers, 12–14cm (5–5½in) wide, in late autumn. Is good for exhibition.
***C.* 'Primrose West Bromwich'** illus. p.269. Reflexed florists' chrysanthemum. H 2.2m (7ft), S 45–60cm (1½–2ft). Fully reflexed, pale yellow flowers, to 18cm (7in) or more wide, appear in mid-autumn. Use only for exhibition.
♀ ***C.* 'Purple Pennine Wine'** illus. p.269. Spray florists' chrysanthemum. H 1.2m (4ft), S 60–75cm (2–2½ft). Half hardy. Bears reflexed, purplish-red flowers, to 8cm (3in) wide, in early autumn. Is very good for exhibition.
***C.* 'Ringdove'** illus. p.268. Charm florists' chrysanthemum. H and S 1m (3ft). Frost tender. Has masses of pink flowers, 2.5cm (1in) across, in late autumn. Is excellent for exhibition.
♀ ***C.* 'Robeam'** illus. p.269. Spray florists' chrysanthemum. H 1.5m (5ft), S 75–100cm (2½–3ft). Frost tender. Produces reflexed, yellow flowers, to 8cm (3in) wide, in late autumn. Is good for exhibition.
***C.* 'Rose Yvonne Arnaud'** illus. p.269. Reflexed florists' chrysanthemum. H 1.2m (4ft), S 60–75cm (2–2½ft). Half hardy. Is a sport of *C.* 'Yvonne Arnaud', producing fully reflexed, red flowers in early autumn.

♀ *C.* **'Roy Coopland'** illus. p.269. Intermediate to loosely incurved florists' chrysanthemum. H 1.3m (4½ft), S 60cm (2ft). Frost tender. Produces bronze flowers, 15cm (6in) wide, in late autumn. Is good for exhibition.
***C. rubellum* 'Clara Curtis'.** See *C.* 'Clara Curtis'.
♀ *C.* **'Salmon Fairie'** illus. p.269. Pompon florists' chrysanthemum. H 30–60cm (1–2ft), S 60cm (2ft). Fully hardy. Is similar to *C.* 'Bronze Fairie', but has salmon flowers.
♀ *C.* **'Salmon Margaret'** illus. p.269. Spray florists' chrysanthemum. H 1.2m (4ft), S to 75cm (2½ft). Is similar to *C.* 'Buff Margaret', but has salmon flowers.
C. segetum. See *Xanthophthalmum segetum.*
C. **'Senkyo Emiaki'** illus. p.268. Spider-form florists' chrysanthemum. H 30–60cm (1–2ft), S to 60cm (2ft). Frost tender. Bears light pink flowers, 15cm (6in) wide, in early autumn. Is good for exhibition.
C. serotinum. See *Leucanthemella serotina.*
C. × superbum. See *Leucanthemum × superbum.*
C. tricolor. See *Ismelia carinata.*
C. uliginosum. See *Leucanthemella serotina.*
C. **'Venice'.** Reflexed florists' chrysanthemum. H 1.2m (4ft), S 60–75cm (2–2½ft). Half hardy. Reflexed, pink flowers, to 15cm (6in) wide, are produced in early autumn. Is good for exhibition.
♀ *C.* **'Wendy'** illus. p.269. Spray florists' chrysanthemum. H 1.2m (4ft), S 60–75cm (2–2½ft). Fully hardy. Produces reflexed, pale bronze flowers, to 8cm (3in) wide, in early autumn. Is excellent for exhibition.
C. **'Woking Rose'** illus. p.268. Intermediate florists' chrysanthemum. H 1.5m (5ft), S 45cm (1½ft). Frost tender. Has rose-pink flowers, to 21cm (8in) wide, in late autumn. Is good for exhibition.
C. **'Yellow Brietner'** illus. p.269. Reflexed florists' chrysanthemum. H 1.1–1.2m (3½–4ft), S 75cm (2½ft). Half hardy. Is a sport of *C.* 'Brietner' with fully reflexed, yellow flowers in early autumn.
♀ *C.* **'Yellow John Hughes'** illus. p.269. Incurved florists' chrysanthemum. H 1.2m (4ft), S 60–75cm (2–2½ft). Frost tender. Yellow flowers, to 12–14cm (5–5½in) wide, appear in late autumn. Is excellent for exhibition.
♀ *C.* **'Yvonne Arnaud'** illus. p.269. Reflexed florists' chrysanthemum. H 1.2m (4ft), S 60–75cm (2–2½ft). Half hardy. Fully reflexed, purple flowers, to 12cm (5in) wide, are produced in early autumn.

CHRYSOGONUM

COMPOSITAE/ASTERACEAE

Genus of one species of summer- to autumn-flowering perennial. Suits a rock garden. Fully hardy. Needs partial shade and moist but well-drained, peaty, sandy soil. Propagate by division in spring or by seed when fresh.
C. virginianum illus. p.371.

Chusan palm. See *Trachycarpus fortunei*, illus. p.80.

CHUSQUEA

GRAMINEAE/POACEAE

See also GRASSES, BAMBOOS, RUSHES and SEDGES.
♀ ***C. culeou*** illus. p.320.

CICERBITA, syn. MULGEDIUM

COMPOSITAE/ASTERACEAE

Genus of perennials, grown for their attractive flower heads. Fully hardy. Requires shade and damp but well-drained soil. Propagate by division in spring or by seed in autumn. Some species may be invasive.
C. alpina, syn. *Lactuca alpina* (Mountain sow thistle). Branching, upright perennial. H to 2m (6ft), S 60cm (2ft). Mid-green leaves are lobed, with a large, terminal lobe. Elongated panicles of thistle-like, pale blue flower heads are produced in summer.
C. bourgaei, syn. *Lactuca bourgaei.* Rampant, erect perennial. H to 2m (6ft), S 60cm (2ft). Leaves are oblong to lance-shaped, toothed and light green. Many-branched panicles of thistle-like, mauve-blue or purplish-blue flower heads appear in summer.

CICHORIUM
Chicory

COMPOSITAE/ASTERACEAE

Genus of annuals, biennials and perennials, grown mainly as ornamental plants (*C. intybus* has edible leaves). Fully hardy. Needs full sun and well-drained soil. Propagate by seed in autumn or spring. Contact with all parts of the plants may irritate skin or aggravate skin allergies.
C. intybus illus. p.259.

Cider gum. See *Eucalyptus gunnii*, illus. p.68.
Cigar flower. See *Cuphea ignea*, illus. p.168.

CIMICIFUGA
Bugbane

RANUNCULACEAE

Genus of perennials, grown for their flowers, which have an unusual, slightly unpleasant smell. Fully hardy. Grow in light shade and moist soil. Needs staking. Propagate by seed when fresh or by division in spring. Sometimes included in the closely related genus *Actaea*, which has fleshy, berry-like, fruits, whereas the pods of *Cimicifuga* are dry and not fleshy.
♀ ***C. racemosa,*** syn. *Actaea racemosa.* Clump-forming perennial. H 30–150cm (1–5ft), S 60cm (2ft). Spikes of bottlebrush-like, pure white flowers are borne in mid-summer above broadly oval, divided, fresh green leaves. var. ***cordifolia,*** see *C. cordifolia.*
C. cordifolia, syn. *C. rubifolia. C. racemosa* var. *cordifolia.* Clump-forming perennial. H 1.5m (5ft), S 60cm (2ft). Feathery plumes of star-shaped, creamy-white flowers are produced in mid-summer above broadly oval to lance-shaped, dissected, light green leaves.
C. rubifolia, see *C. cordifolia.*
C. simplex, syn. *Actaea simplex,* illus. p.231. ♀ **'Elstead'** is an upright perennial. H 1.2m (4ft), S 60cm (2ft). Purple stems bear arching racemes of fragrant, bottlebrush-like, white flowers in autumn. Has broadly oval to lance-shaped, divided, glossy leaves. **'Prichard's Giant'**, H 2.2m (7ft), has large, much-divided leaves and produces white flowers on arching panicles.

Cineraria cruentus of gardens. See *Pericallis × hybrida.*
Cineraria × hybridus. See *Pericallis × hybrida.*
Cineraria. See *Pericallis × hybrida.*

CINNAMOMUM

LAURACEAE

Genus of evergreen trees, grown for their foliage and to provide shade. Frost tender, min. 10°C (50°F). Requires full light or partial shade and fertile, moisture-retentive but well-drained soil. Water containerized specimens freely when in full growth but less at other times. May be pruned if necessary. Propagate by seed in spring or by semi-ripe cuttings in summer.
C. camphora. Moderately fast-growing, evergreen, rounded tree. H and S 12m (40ft) or more. Oval, lustrous, rich green leaves, tinted blue-grey beneath, reddish or coppery when young, are camphor-scented when bruised. Has insignificant flowers in spring.

Cinnamon fern. See *Osmunda cinnamomea.*
Cinquefoil, Alpine. See *Potentilla crantzii.*

CIONURA

ASCLEPIADACEAE

Genus of one species of deciduous, twining climber, grown for its flowers. Half hardy. Grow in any soil and in full sun. Prune after flowering. Propagate by seed in spring or by stem cuttings in late summer or early autumn. Contact with the latex exuded by cut leaves and stems may irritate skin or cause blisters, and may cause severe discomfort if ingested.
C. erecta, syn. *Marsdenia erecta.* Deciduous, twining climber. H 3m (10ft) or more. Heart-shaped, greyish-green leaves are 3–6cm (1¼–2½in) long. In summer, clusters of fragrant, white flowers, with 5 spreading petals, are borne in leaf axils, followed by 7cm (3in) long fruits, containing many silky seeds, in autumn.

CIRSIUM

COMPOSITAE/ASTERACEAE

Genus of annuals, biennials and perennials. Most species are not cultivated – indeed some are pernicious weeds – but *C. rivulare* has decorative flower heads. Fully hardy. Tolerates sun or shade and any but wet soil. Propagate by division in spring or by seed in autumn.
***C. rivulare* 'Atropurpureum'.** Erect perennial. H 1.2m (4ft), S 60cm (2ft). Heads of pincushion-like, deep crimson flowers are borne on erect stems in summer. Leaves are narrowly oval to oblong or lance-shaped and deeply cut, with weakly spiny margins.

CISSUS

VITACEAE

Genus of evergreen, woody-stemmed, mainly tendril climbers, grown for their attractive foliage. Bears insignificant, greenish flowers, mainly in summer. Half hardy to frost tender, min. 7–18°C (45–64°F). Provide fertile, well-drained soil, with semi-shade in summer. Water regularly, less in cold weather. Needs tying to supports. Thin out crowded stems in spring. Propagate by semi-ripe cuttings in summer.
♀ ***C. antarctica*** illus. p.218.
C. bainesii. See *Cyphostemma bainesii.*
C. discolor (Rex begonia vine). Moderately vigorous, evergreen, tendril climber with slender, woody stems. H to 3m (10ft). Frost tender, min. 18°C (64°F). Has oval, pointed leaves, 10–15cm (4–6in) long, that are deep green with silver bands above, maroon beneath.
C. hypoglauca. Evergreen, woody-stemmed, scrambling climber. H 2–3m (6–10ft). Frost tender, min. 7°C (45°F). Leaves are divided into 4 or 5 oval leaflets that are pale green above and blue-grey beneath.
C. juttae. See *Cyphostemma juttae.*
♀ ***C. rhombifolia***, syn. *Rhoicissus rhombifolia, R. rhomboidea*, illus. p.218.
C. striata, syn. *Ampelopsis sempervirens, Parthenocissus striata, Vitis striata* (Ivy of Uruguay, Miniature grape ivy). Fast-growing, evergreen, woody-stemmed, tendril climber. H 10m (30ft) or more. Half hardy. Has leaves of 3–5 oval, serrated, lustrous, green leaflets. Mature plants may produce pea-shaped, glossy, black berries in autumn.
C. voinieriana. See *Tetrastigma voinierianum.*

CISTUS
Rock rose

CISTACEAE

Genus of evergreen shrubs, grown for their succession of freely borne, short-lived, showy flowers. Is good in coastal areas, withstanding sea winds well. Frost to half hardy; in cold areas needs shelter. Does best in full sun and light, well-drained soil. Resents being transplanted. Cut out any dead wood in spring, but do not prune hard. Propagate species by softwood or greenwood cuttings in summer or by seed in autumn, hybrids and cultivars by cuttings only in summer.
♀ ***C. × aguilarii* 'Maculatus'** illus. p.155.
C. albidus. Evergreen, bushy shrub. H and S 1m (3ft). Half hardy. Leaves are oblong and white-felted. Saucer-shaped, pale rose-pink flowers, each with a central, yellow blotch, open in early summer.
C. algarvensis. See *Halimium ocymoides.*
C. × corbariensis. See *C. × hybridus.*
C. creticus, syn. *C. incanus* subsp.

creticus, illus. p.161.
♀ ***C.* × *cyprius*** illus. p.155.
C.* × *dansereaui, syn. *C.* × *lusitanicus* of gardens. Evergreen, bushy, compact shrub. H and S 1m (3ft). Frost hardy. Leaves are narrowly oblong and dark green. Saucer-shaped, white flowers, each with a central, deep red blotch, appear from early to mid-summer.
C.* × *hybridus, syn. *C.* × *corbariensis*, illus. p.155.
C. incanus subsp. ***creticus.*** See *C. creticus*.
♀ ***C. ladanifer***, syn. *C. ladaniferus*, illus. p.155.
C. ladaniferus. See *C. ladanifer*.
♀ ***C. laurifolius.*** Evergreen, bushy, dense shrub. H and S 2m (6ft). Frost hardy. Has oval, aromatic, dark green leaves and, in summer, saucer-shaped, white flowers, each with a central, yellow blotch.
C.* × *lusitanicus of gardens. See *C.* × *dansereaui*.
C. monspeliensis illus. p.155.
C. parviflorus. Evergreen, bushy, dense shrub. H and S 1m (3ft). Frost hardy. Small, saucer-shaped, pale pink flowers appear among oval, grey-green leaves in early summer.
♀ ***C.* 'Peggy Sammons'** illus. p.158.
♀ ***C.* × *purpureus.*** Evergreen, bushy, rounded shrub. H and S 1m (3ft). Frost hardy. Produces saucer-shaped, deep purplish-pink flowers, each blotched with deep red, from early to mid-summer. Leaves are narrowly lance-shaped and grey-green.
C. revolii of gardens. See × *Halimiocistus sahucii*.
C. salviifolius illus. p.155.
***C.* 'Silver Pink'.** Evergreen, bushy shrub. H 60cm (2ft), S 1m (3ft). Frost hardy. Oval, dark green leaves set off large, saucer-shaped, clear pink flowers, each with conspicuous, yellow stamens, from early to mid-summer.
♀ ***C.* × *skanbergii*** illus. p.158.

× CITROFORTUNELLA

RUTACEAE

Hybrid genus (*Citrus* × *Fortunella*) of evergreen shrubs and trees, grown for their flowers, fruits and overall appearance. Frost tender, min. 5–10°C (41–50°F). Requires full light and fertile, well-drained but not dry soil. Water containerized specimens freely when in full growth, moderately at other times. Propagate by seed when ripe or by greenwood or semi-ripe cuttings in summer. Whitefly, red spider mite, mealy bug, lime-induced and magnesium-deficiency chlorosis may be troublesome.
♀ × ***C. microcarpa***, syn. × *C. mitis, Citrus mitis*, illus. p.147.
× ***C. mitis.*** See × *C. microcarpa*.

Citrus mitis. See × *Citrofortunella microcarpa*.

CLADANTHUS

COMPOSITAE/ASTERACEAE

Genus of one species of annual, grown for its fragrant foliage and daisy-like flower heads. Fully hardy. Grow in sun and in reasonably fertile, very well-drained soil. Dead-head to prolong flowering. Propagate by seed sown outdoors in mid-spring.
C. arabicus illus. p.349.

CLADRASTIS

LEGUMINOSAE/PAPILIONACEAE

Genus of deciduous, summer-flowering trees, grown for their pendent, wisteria-like flower clusters and autumn foliage. Fully hardy. Requires full sun and fertile, well-drained soil. Propagate by seed in autumn or by root cuttings in late winter. The wood is brittle: old trees are prone to damage by strong winds.
C. kentukea, syn. *C. lutea*, illus. p.78.
C. lutea. See *C. kentukea*.

Claret ash. See *Fraxinus angustifolia* 'Raywood'.

CLARKIA, syn. GODETIA

ONAGRACEAE

Genus of annuals, grown for their flowers, which are good for cutting. Fully hardy. Grow in sun and in reasonably fertile, well-drained soil. Avoid rich soil as this encourages vegetative growth at the expense of flowers. Propagate by seed sown outdoors in spring, or in early autumn in mild areas. Botrytis may be troublesome.
C. amoena. Fast-growing annual with upright, thin stems. H to 60cm (24in), S 30cm (12in). Has lance-shaped, mid-green leaves. Spikes of 5-petalled, single or double flowers, in shades of lilac to pink, are produced in summer. Tall forms, H 60cm (24in), have double flowers in shades of pink or red. **Grace Series,** intermediate, H to 50cm (20in), has single, lavender-pink, red, salmon-pink or pink flowers with contrasting centres. **Princess Series,** dwarf, H 30cm (12in), has frilled flowers in shades of pink, including salmon (illus. p.353). **Satin Series,** dwarf, H to 20cm (8in), has single flowers in various colours, many with white margins or contrasting centres. **'Sybil Sherwood'** illus. p.336.
***C.* 'Brilliant'** illus. p.336.

CLAYTONIA

PORTULACACEAE

Genus of mainly evergreen perennials with succulent leaves; is related to *Lewisia*. Grows best in alpine houses. Fully hardy. Tolerates sun or shade and prefers well-drained soil. Propagate by seed or division in autumn. May be difficult to grow.
C. megarhiza, syn. *Calandrinia megarhiza*. Evergreen, basal-rosetted perennial with a long tap root. H 1cm (½in), S 8cm (3in). Leaves are spoon-shaped and fleshy. Bears small heads of tiny, bowl-shaped, white flowers in spring. Prefers sun and gritty soil. Is prone to aphid attack. var. ***nivalis*** illus. p.378.
C. virginica (Spring beauty). Clump-forming perennial with flat, black tubers. H 10cm (4in), S 20cm (8in) or more. Narrowly spoon-shaped leaves, reddish when young, later turn green and glossy. Branched stems bear cup-shaped, white or pink flowers, striped deep pink, in early spring. Needs shade.

CLEISTOCACTUS, syn. BORZICACTUS

CACTACEAE

Genus of columnar, perennial cacti with branched, cylindrical, much-ribbed stems with spines. Is one of the faster-growing cacti, some reaching 2m (6ft) in 5 years or less. Tubular flowers contain plenty of nectar and are pollinated by hummingbirds. Frost tender, min. 5°C (41°F). Needs full sun and very well-drained soil. Propagate by seed or stem cuttings in spring or summer.
C. baumannii. Erect, then prostrate, perennial cactus. H 1m (3ft) or more, S 5m (15ft). Thick stems produce long, uneven, variable-coloured spines. Has S-shaped, tubular, bright orange-red flowers in spring-summer.
C. celsianus. See *Oreocereus celsianus*.
C. smaragdiflorus. Erect, then prostrate, perennial cactus. H 1.5m (5ft), S 6m (20ft). Is similar to *C. baumannii*, but has straight, tubular flowers with green-tipped petals.
♀ ***C. strausii*** illus. p.475.
C. trollii. See *Oreocereus trollii*.

CLEMATIS

Old man's beard, Travellers' joy

RANUNCULACEAE

Genus of evergreen or deciduous, mainly twining climbers and herbaceous perennials, cultivated for their mass of flowers, often followed by decorative seed heads, and grown on walls and trellises and together with trees, shrubs and other host plants. Only early-flowering species are evergreen, although some later-flowering species are semi-evergreen. Most species have nodding, bell-shaped flowers, with 4 petals (botanically known as perianth segments), or flattish flowers, each usually with 4–6 generally pointed petals. Large-flowered cultivars also bear flattish flowers, but with 4–10 petals. Flower colour may vary according to climatic conditions: in general, the warmer the climate, the darker the flower colour. Fully to half hardy. May be grown in partial shade or full sun, but prefers rich, well-drained soil with roots shaded. Propagate cultivars in early summer by softwood or semi-ripe cuttings or layering, species from seed sown in autumn. Aphids, mildew and clematis wilt may cause problems.

Clematis may be divided into groups according to their approximate flowering seasons, habit and pruning needs. See also feature panel pp.208–11.

Group 1
Early-flowering species preferring a sheltered, sunny site with well-drained soil. Small, single flowers, either bell-shaped or open-bell-shaped, 2–5cm (¾–2in) long, or saucer-shaped, 4–5cm (1½–2in) across, are borne on the previous season's ripened shoots in spring or, occasionally, in late winter. Leaves are evergreen and glossy, or deciduous, and usually divided into 3 lance-shaped, 12cm (5in) long leaflets or into 3 fern-like, 5cm (2in) long leaflets. Fully to half hardy.
C. alpina, C. macropetala **and their cultivars** tolerate cold, exposed positions. Small, bell-shaped to open bell-shaped, single, semi-double, or double flowers, 3–7cm (1¼–3in) across, are borne on the previous season's ripened shoots in spring, occasionally also on the current season's shoots in summer. Deciduous, pale to mid-green leaves are divided into 3–5 lance-shaped to broadly oblong, toothed leaflets, 3cm (1¼in) long. Fully hardy.
C. montana **and its cultivars** are vigorous, deciduous climbers, suitable for growing over large buildings and trees. Small, flat to saucer-shaped, usually single flowers, 5–7cm (2–3in) across, are borne on the previous season's ripened shoots in late spring. Leaves are mid- to purplish-green and divided into 3 lance-shaped to broadly oval, serrated leaflets, 8cm (3in) long with pointed tips. Fully hardy.

Prune all group 1 clematis after flowering to allow new growth to be produced and ripened for the following season. Remove dead or damaged stems and cut back other shoots that have outgrown their allotted space. This will encourage production of new growth to bear flowers in the following season.

Group 2
Early- to mid-season, large-flowered cultivars bearing mostly saucer-shaped, single, semi-double, or fully double flowers, 10–20cm (4–8in) across, that are borne on the previous season's ripened shoots, in late spring and early summer, and on new shoots in mid- and late summer. Generally the second flush of flowers on semi-double and double forms produces single flowers. Deciduous, pale to mid-green leaves are usually 10–15cm (4–6in) long and divided into 3 ovate or lance-shaped leaflets, or are simple and ovate, and to 10cm (4in) long. Fully to frost hardy.

Prune before new growth starts, in early spring. Remove any dead or damaged stems and cut back all remaining shoots to where strong buds are visible. These buds provide a framework of second-year shoots which, in turn, produce sideshoots that flower in late spring and early summer. The flowers may then be removed. Young shoots bear more flowers later in the summer.

Group 3
Late, large-flowered cultivars producing outward-facing, usually saucer-shaped, single flowers, 7–15cm (3–6in) across, borne on new shoots in summer or early autumn. Leaves are deciduous and similar to those of early cultivars (group 2), described above. Fully hardy.
Late-flowering species and **small-flowered cultivars** that bear small, single or double flowers on the current

season's shoots in summer-autumn. Flowers vary in shape and may be star-shaped, tubular, bell-shaped, flattish or resembling nodding lanterns; they vary in size from 1cm (½in) to 10cm (4in) across. Have generally deciduous, pale to dark green or grey-green leaves divided into 3 lance-shaped to broadly oval leaflets, each 1cm (½in) long, or hairy and/or toothed leaves divided into 5 or more lance-shaped to broadly oval leaflets, each 1–10cm (½–4in) long. Fully to half hardy.

Herbaceous species and cultivars producing single flowers that are either saucer-shaped, 1–2cm (½–¾in) wide, or bell-shaped or tubular, 1–4cm (½–1½in) long, and are produced on the current season's shoots in summer. Mid- to dark green or grey-green leaves are simple and lance-shaped to elliptic, 2.5–15cm (1–6in) long, or are divided into 3–5 lance-shaped to ovate, serrated leaflets, each 10–15cm (4–6in) long with a pointed tip. Fully to frost hardy.

Prune all group 3 clematis before new growth begins, in early spring. Cut back all the previous season's stems to a pair of strong buds, 15–20cm (6–8in) above soil level.

***C.* 'Abundance'**, syn. *C. viticella* 'Abundance' illus. p.209. Late-flowering clematis (group 3). H 2–3m (6–10ft), S 1m (3ft). Fully hardy. Produces flattish, deep purplish-red flowers, 5cm (2in) across, with cream anthers, in summer.

♀ ***C.* ALABAST ('Poulala')** illus. p.208. Vigorous, long flowering, large-flowered clematis (group 2). H 3m (10ft) S 1m (3ft). Fully hardy. Freely produces creamy-green, rounded, large flowers 12–15cm (5–6in) across, with creamy-yellow anthers, in late spring and again from mid- to late summer.

♀ ***C.* 'Alionushka'.** Semi-herbaceous, non-clinging clematis (group 3). H 1–1.2m (3–4ft), S 1m (3ft). Fully hardy. In mid-summer to early autumn, produces single, rich mauvish-pink flowers, 6–8cm (2½–3in) wide, with a satin sheen when young, with deep ridges on the reverse and crumpled edges; the petal tips recurve and twist as they age.

♀ ***C. alpina.*** Alpina clematis (group 1). H 2–3m (6–10ft), S 1.5m (5ft). Fully hardy. Has lantern-shaped, single, blue flowers, 4–7cm (1½–3in) long, in spring and, occasionally, summer. Forms attractive, fluffy, silvery seed heads in summer. Is ideal for a north-facing or very exposed site.

'Columbine'. See *C.* 'Columbine'.

'Constance'. See *C.* 'Constance'.

'Frances Rivis'. See *C.*'Frances Rivis'.

'Frankie'. See *C.* 'Frankie'

***C.* ANGELIQUE™ ('Evipo033'(N))** illus. p.211. Compact, mid-to late season clematis (group 2). H 90cm–1.2m (3–4ft) S 1m (3ft). Fully hardy. Produces an abundance of lilac-blue, brown-anthered flowers 10cm (4in) across, from early summer to late autumn.

♀ ***C.* ANNA LOUISE ('Evithree')** illus. p.210. Compact, early, large-flowered clematis (group 2). H 1–1.2m (3–4ft), S 1m (3ft). Fully hardy. Freely produces single flowers with violet petals with a contrasting red-purple central bar, and striking brown anthers, in late spring to early summer, and again in late summer to early autumn.

♀ ***C.* ARCTIC QUEEN ('Evitwo')** illus. p.208. Early, large-flowered clematis (group 2). H 3m (10ft), S 1m (3ft). Fully hardy. From early summer to early autumn, freely produces double, clear creamy-white flowers, 10–18cm (4–7in) across, with yellow anthers.

C. armandii illus. p.208. Strong-growing, evergreen, early-flowering clematis (group 1). H 3–5m (10–15ft), S 2–3m (6–10ft). Frost hardy. Bears scented, flattish, single, white flowers, 4cm (1½in) across, in early spring. Needs a sheltered, south- or south-west-facing site.

***C.* 'Ascotiensis'** illus. p.211. Vigorous, late, large-flowered clematis (group 3). H 3–4m (10–12ft), S 1m (3ft). Frost hardy. Single, bright violet-blue flowers, 9–12cm (3½–5in) across, with pointed petals and brownish-green anthers, are produced in summer.

***C.* AVANT-GARDE™ ('Evipo017'(N))** illus. p.210. Vigorous, mid-season clematis (group 3). H 3m (10ft) S 1m (3ft). Fully hardy. Free-flowering climber, producing deep red flowers to 5cm (2in) across, with central pom-poms of pink, petaloid stamens, in abundance from mid-summer to autumn.

***C.* 'Bees Jubilee'.** Compact, early, large-flowered clematis (group 2). H 2.5m (8ft), S 1m (3ft). Frost hardy. In early summer bears a profusion of single, deep pink flowers, 10–12cm (4–5in) across with brown anthers and a central, rose-madder stripe on each petal. Prefers partial shade.

♀ ***C.* 'Bill MacKenzie'** illus. p.209. Vigorous, late-flowering clematis (group 3). H 7m (22ft), S 3–4m (10–12ft). Fully hardy. Has dark green leaves. Flowers are yellow and 6–7cm (2½–3in) wide. Is best pruned with shears.

***C.* BLUE MOON ('Evirin')** illus. p.209. Compact, free-flowering, early, large-flowered clematis (group 2). H 2.5–3m (8–10ft), S 1m (3ft). Fully hardy. Bears single, white flowers, 15–18cm (6–7in) wide, suffused with pale lilac becoming darker at the wavy petal edges, in late spring to early summer. In late summer to early autumn, flowers are slightly smaller and darker.

***C.* BONANZA™ ('Evipo031'(N))** illus. p.211. Vigorous, mid-season clematis (group 3). H 3m (10ft) S 1m (3ft). Fully hardy. Free-flowering climber producing blue-purple blooms to 7cm (3in) across, with pale yellow anthers, from mid-summer to autumn.

***C.* BOURBON™ ('Evipo018'(N))** illus. p.210. Compact, mid-season clematis (group 2). H 1.2–2m (4–6ft) S 1m (3ft). Fully hardy. Produces an abundance of vibrant, red, yellow-centred flowers, 8cm (3in) across, from early to mid-summer.

C. calycina. See *C. cirrhosa*.

***C.* 'Carnaby'.** Compact, early, large-flowered clematis (group 2). H 2.5m (8ft), S 1m (3ft). Frost hardy. In early summer has a profusion of single, deep pink flowers, 8–10cm (3–4in) across, with a darker stripe on each petal and red anthers. Prefers partial shade.

***C.* CASSIS™ ('Evipo020'(N))** illus. p.210. Vigorous, long-flowering clematis (group3). H 2–3m (6–10ft). Fully hardy. Free-flowering climber with fully double, plum red, rosetted flowers, 8cm (3in) across, borne from early summer to early autumn.

***C.* CEZANNE™ ('Evipo023'(N))** illus. p.211. Compact, long-flowering clematis (group 2). H 90cm–1.2m (3–4ft) S 1m (3ft). Fully hardy. Free-flowering climber producing sky-blue flowers, 10cm (4in) across, with broad overlapping sepals and yellow anthers, blooming from early summer to late autumn.

***C.* CHANTILLY™ ('Evipo021'(N))** illus. p.208. Compact, long-flowering clematis (group 2). H 90cm–1.2m (3–4ft) S 1m (3ft). Fully hardy. Free-flowering climber producing single, occasionally semi-double, pale pink flowers, to 10cm (4in) across, the sepals with a pronounced, deeper pink central bar, in abundance from early summer to late autumn.

***C.* 'Charissima'.** Free-flowering, early, large-flowered clematis (group 2). H 2.5–3m (8–10ft), S 1m (3ft). Fully hardy. In late spring to early summer, produces single flowers, 15–18cm (6–7in) across, with pointed, cerise-pink petals, a deeper pink bar and veins throughout the flower, and dark maroon anthers.

***C.* CHINOOK™ ('Evipo013'(N))** illus. p.210. Low growing, scandent, non-clinging clematis (group 3). H 1m (3ft) S 60cm (2ft). Fully hardy. Produces numerous, nodding, mid-violet-blue flowers 12cm (5in) across, with twisted sepals, each with a prominent, central boss of yellow stamens, from mid-summer to early autumn.

C. cirrhosa, syn. *C. calycina* illus. p.209. Evergreen, early-flowering clematis (group 1). H 2–3m (6–10ft), S 1–2m (3–6ft). Frost hardy. Produces bell-shaped, cream flowers, 3cm (1¼in) across and spotted red inside, in late winter and early spring during frost-free weather.

***C.* CLAIR DE LUNE™ ('Evirin'(N))** illus. p.211. Vigorous, large-flowered clematis (group 2). H 2.5–3m (8–10ft) S 1–1.5m (3–5ft). Fully hardy. Produces an abundance of large, blue-purple flowers, to 12cm (5in) across, with paler central bands on the sepals and dark anthers, from late spring to early summer and again from late summer to early autumn.

***C.* 'Columbine' (Atragene Group),** syn. *C. alpina* 'Columbine'. Deciduous, early-flowering climber. H 2–4m (6–12ft). In early and mid-spring produces soft lavender-blue, nodding, bell-shaped flowers 4–5cm (2in) across with creamy-white or green staminodes, sometimes blooming again in summer.

♀ ***C.* 'Comtesse de Bouchaud'.** Strong-growing, late, large-flowered clematis (group 3). H 2–3m (6–10ft), S 1m (3ft). Fully hardy. In summer has masses of single, bright mauve-pink flowers, 8–10cm (3–4in) across, with yellow anthers.

***C.* CONFETTI™ ('Evipo036'(N))** illus. p.210. Vigorous, mid-season clematis (group 3). H 3m (10ft) S 1m (3ft). Fully hardy. Free flowering climber with nodding, pink flowers produced from mid-summer to autumn.

♀ ***C.* 'Constance' (Atragene Group),** syn. *C. alpina* 'Constance'. Deciduous, early-flowering climber. H 2–4m (6–12ft) S 1m (3ft). Semi-double, nodding, rich purple-pink or reddish-pink, bell-like flowers, 2.5–6cm (1–2½in) across, with purple or creamy-white staminodes, are produced from early to mid-spring and occasionally again in summer.

***C.* CRYSTAL FOUNTAIN™ ('Evipo038'(N))** illus. p.210. Compact, large-flowered clematis (group 2), H 1.5–2m (4–6ft) S 1m (3ft). Fully hardy. Produces an abundance of double, deep lilac-blue flowers to 10cm (4in) across, with a central boss of narrow staminodes, from late spring to early summer and again in early autumn.

♀ ***C.* 'Daniel Deronda'.** Vigorous, early, large-flowered clematis (group 2). H 3m (10ft), S 1m (3ft). Frost hardy. Has double and semi-double, deep purple-blue flowers, 10–14cm (4–5½in) across, with cream anthers, then single flowers in late summer.

***C.* 'Doctor Ruppel'.** Early, large-flowered clematis (group 2). H 2.5m (8ft), S 1m (3ft). Fully hardy. Single flowers, 10–15cm (4–6in) across, with deep rose-pink petals with darker central bands and light chocolate anthers, are freely produced throughout summer.

***C.* 'Duchess of Albany'** illus. p.209. Vigorous, small-flowered clematis (group 3). H 2.5m (8ft), S 1m (3ft). Frost hardy. In summer and early autumn has masses of small, tulip-like, single, soft pink flowers, 6cm (2½in) long, with brown anthers and a deeper pink stripe inside each petal.

***C.* 'Duchess of Edinburgh'.** Early, large-flowered clematis (group 2). H 2–3m (6–10ft), S 1m (3ft). Frost hardy. In summer produces double, white flowers, 8–10cm (3–4in) across, with yellow anthers and green, outer petals. May be weak-growing.

♀ ***C.* × *durandii.*** Semi-herbaceous, late-flowering clematis (group 3). H 1–2m (3–6ft), S 45cm–1.5m (1½–5ft). Frost hardy. In summer has flattish, single, deep blue flowers, 6–8cm (2½–3in) across, with 4 petals and yellow anthers. Leaves are elliptic.

***C.* 'Elsa Spath'** illus. p.210. Early, large-flowered clematis (group 2). H 2–3m (6–10ft), S 1m (3ft). Frost hardy. Bears masses of single, 12cm (5in) wide flowers, with overlapping, rich mauve-blue petals and red anthers, throughout summer.

♀ ***C.* 'Ernest Markham'** illus. p.209. Vigorous, late, large-flowered clematis (group 3). H 3–4m (10–12ft), S 1m (3ft). Fully hardy. In summer bears 10cm (4in) wide, single flowers with blunt-tipped, vivid magenta petals and chocolate anthers. Thrives in full sun.

♀ ***C.* 'Etoile Violette'**, syn. *C. viticella* 'Etoile Violette' illus. p.211. Vigorous, late-flowering clematis (group 3). H 3–5m (10–15ft), S 1.5m (5ft). Fully hardy. Produces masses of flattish, single, violet-purple flowers, 4–6cm (1½–2½in) wide, with yellow anthers, in summer.

***C.* 'Evifour'.** See *C.* ROYAL VELVET.

***C.* Evijohill.** PRB See *C.* 'JOSEPHINE'

C. **'Evione'.** See *C.* SUGAR CANDY

C. **'Evipo001'.(N)** See *C.* WISLEY™
C. **'Evipo002'.(N)** See *C.* ROSEMOOR™
C. **'Evipo003'.(N)** See *C.* ICE BLUE™
C. **'Evipo004'.(N)** See *C.* HARLOW CARR™
C. **'Evipo005'.(N)** See *C.* PEPPERMINT™
C. **'Evipo006'.(N)** See *C.* VIENETTA™
C. **'Evipo007'.(N)** See *C.* VICTOR HUGO™
C. **'Evipo008'.(N)** See *C.* FRANZISKA MARIA™
C. **'Evipo009'.(N)** See *C.* HYDE HALL™
C. **'Evipo012'.(N) PRB** See *C.* PARISIENNE™
C. **'Evipo013'.(N)** See *C.* CHINOOK™
C. **'Evipo014'.(N)** See *C.* GAZELLE™
C. **'Evipo015'.(N)** See *C.* SAVANNAH™
C. **'Evipo017'.(N)** See *C.* AVANT-GARDE™
C. **'Evipo018'.(N)** See *C.* BOURBON™
C. **'Evipo019'.(N)** See *C.* MEDLEY™
C. **'Evipo020'.(N)** See *C.* CASSIS™
C. **'Evipo021'.(N)** See *C.* CHANTILLY™
C. **'Evipo023'.(N)** See *C.* CEZANNE™
C. **'Evipo031'.(N)** See *C.* BONANZA™
C. **'Evipo032'.(N)** See *C.* GALORE™
C. **'Evipo033'.(N)** See *C.* ANGELIQUE™
C. **'Evipo036'.(N)** See *C.* CONFETTI™
C. **'Evipo038'.(N)** See *C.* CRYSTAL FOUNTAIN™
C. **'Evirida'**. See *C. florida* PISTACHIO
C. **'Evirin'**. See *C.* CLAIR DE LUNE™
***C.* 'Evirin'**. See *C.* BLUE MOON.
***C.* 'Evisix'**. See *C.* PETIT FAUCON.
***C.* 'Evithree'**. See *C.* ANNA LOUISE.
***C.* 'Evitwo'**. See *C.* ARCTIC QUEEN.
C. flammula illus. p.209. Vigorous, late-flowering clematis; may be semi-evergreen (group 3). H 3–5m (10–15ft), S 2m (6ft). Frost hardy. Produces masses of almond-scented, flattish, single, white flowers, 2cm (¾in) across, in summer and early autumn.
C. florida*.**'Bicolor', see *C.f.* var. *sieboldiana*. **PISTACHIO ('Evirida')** illus. p.208. Vigorous, long-flowering clematis (group 3). H 3m (10ft) S 1m (3ft). Fully hardy. From early summer to late autumn produces an abundance of creamy-white, rounded flowers 6–9cm (2½–3½in) across, each with a central cluster of pinkish-grey anthers and green styles. 'Sieboldii', see *C.f.* var. *sieboldiana*. **var. *sieboldiana syn. *C.f.* 'Bicolor', *C.f.* 'Sieboldii', illus. p.209. Weak-growing, small-flowered clematis (group 3). H 2–3m (6–10ft), S 1m (3ft). Frost hardy. In summer has passion-flower-like, single blooms, each 8cm (3in) wide with creamy-white petals and a domed boss of petal-like, rich purple stamens. Needs a sheltered aspect.
🏆 ***C.* 'Frances Rivis' (Atragene Group),** syn. *C. alpina* 'Francis'. Deciduous, early-flowering climber. H 2–4m (6–12ft) S 1m (3ft). In early and mid-spring produces an abundance of deep blue, nodding, bell-shaped flowers 5–8cm (2–3in) across, with white staminodes.
🏆 ***C.* 'Frankie' (Atragene Group)** syn. *C. alpina* 'Frankie'. Deciduous, early-flowering climber. H 2.2–4m (7–12ft) S 1m (3ft). In early and mid-spring produces nodding, bell-shaped, mid-blue to deep mauve-blue flowers to 2.5–6cm (1–2½in) across, with creamy-white, blue-tipped staminodes.
***C.* FRANZISKA MARIA™ ('Evipo008'(N))** illus. p.211. Compact, very long-flowering clematis (group 2). Fully hardy. Free-flowering climber producing fully double, deep blue-purple flowers 10–15cm (4–6in) across, with yellow anthers, from early summer to early autumn.
***C.* GALORE™ ('Evipo032'(N))** illus. p.210. Vigorous, mid-season, small-flowered clematis (group 3). H 3m (10ft) S 1m (3ft). Fully hardy. From mid-summer to autumn produces numerous, deep purple flowers to 7cm (3in) across, with contrasting yellow anthers.
***C.* GAZELLE™ ('Evipo014'(N))** illus. p.208. Low growing, scandent, non-clinging clematis (group 3). H 1m (3ft) S 60cm (2ft). Fully hardy. Produces numerous nodding, slightly scented, white flowers to 6cm (2½in) across, with twisted sepals and yellow stamens, from mid-summer to early autumn.
***C.* 'Général Sikorski'.** Early, large-flowered clematis (group 2). H 3m (10ft), S 1m (3ft). Frost hardy. Has numerous 10cm (4in) wide, single flowers, with large, overlapping, blue petals and cream anthers, in summer.
🏆 ***C.* 'Gipsy Queen'.** Vigorous, late, large-flowered clematis (group 3). H 3m (10ft), S 1m (3ft). Fully hardy. Bears single, 10cm (4in) wide flowers, with velvety, violet-purple petals and red anthers, in summer.
***C.* 'Gravetye Beauty'** illus. p.209. Vigorous, small-flowered clematis (group 3). H 2.5m (8ft), S 1m (3ft). Frost hardy. In summer and early autumn has masses of small, tulip-like, single, bright red flowers, 6cm (2½in) long, with brown anthers. Is similar to *C.* 'Duchess of Albany', but flowers are more open.
***C.* 'Guernsey Cream'.** Early, large-flowered clematis (group 2). H 2.5m (8ft), S 1m (3ft). Fully hardy. Bears single flowers, 12cm (5in) across, with creamy yellow petals and anthers, in early summer. Flowers are smaller and creamy white in late summer. Fades in full sun.
***C.* 'Hagley Hybrid'** illus. p.209. Vigorous, late, large-flowered clematis (group 3). H 2.5m (8ft), S 1m (3ft). Fully hardy. Produces 8–10cm (3–4in) wide, single flowers with boat-shaped, rose-mauve petals and red anthers, in summer. Prefers partial shade.
***C.* HARLOW CARR™ ('Evipo004'(N))** illus. p.211. Scandent, herbaceous clematis (group 3). H 2–3m (6–10ft) S 1m (3ft). Fully hardy. From early to late summer produces semi-pendent, dark violet-blue, open flowers to 7cm (3in) across, each with 4 twisted petals, dark brown anthers and white filaments.
🏆 ***C.* 'Henryi'** illus. p.208. Vigorous, early, large-flowered clematis (group 2). H 3m (10ft), S 1m (3ft). Frost hardy. Has 12cm (5in) wide, single flowers, with white petals and dark chocolate anthers, in summer.
***C. heracleifolia* var. *davidiana*.** Herbaceous clematis (group 3). H 1m (3ft), S 75cm (2½ft). Fully hardy. In summer, thick stems bear axillary clusters of scented, tubular, single, pale blue flowers, 2–3cm (¾–1¼in) long, with reflexed petal tips. 🏆 **'Wyevale'** (illus. p.211) has strongly scented, dark blue flowers.
***C.* 'H.F. Young'** illus. p.211. Compact, early, large-flowered clematis (group 2). H 2.5m (8ft), S 1m (3ft). Frost hardy. Bears 10cm (4in) wide, single flowers, with violet-tinged, blue petals and cream anthers, in summer. Is ideal for a container or patio garden.
🏆 ***C.* 'Huldine'** illus. p.209. Very vigorous, late, large-flowered clematis (group 3). H 3–4m (10–12ft), S 2m (6ft). Fully hardy. In summer has 6cm (2½in) wide, single, white flowers, mauve beneath and with cream anthers. Is ideal for an archway or pergola.
***C.* HYDE HALL™ ('Evipo009'(N))** illus. p.208. Vigorous, large-flowered clematis (group 2). H 2–2.5m (6–8ft) S 1m (3ft). Fully hardy. Flowers prolifically from early to mid-summer producing large, creamy-white blooms, 12–18cm (5–7in) across, sometimes tinged pink or green, with chocolate-brown anthers.
***C.* ICE BLUE™ ('Evipo003'(N))** illus. p.208. Early, large-flowered clematis (group 2). H 2–2.5m (6–8ft) S 1m (3ft). Fully hardy. In late spring and early summer produces an abundance of very large, ice-blue flowers 15–20cm (6–8in) across, repeat-flowering during late summer and early autumn.
C. integrifolia illus. p.210. Herbaceous clematis (group 3). H and S 75cm (30in). Fully hardy. Leaves are narrowly lance-shaped. In summer bears bell-shaped, single, deep blue flowers, 3cm (1¼in) long with cream anthers, followed by attractive, grey-brown seed heads.
🏆 ***C.* 'Jackmanii'** illus. p.211. Vigorous, late, large-flowered clematis (group 3). H 3m (10ft), S 1m (3ft). Fully hardy. Bears masses of velvety, single, dark purple flowers, fading to violet, 8–10cm (3–4in) across, with light brown anthers, in mid-summer.
***C.* 'Jackmanii Superba'.** Vigorous, late, large-flowered clematis (group 3). Is similar to *C.* 'Jackmanii', but has more rounded, darker flowers.
🏆 ***C.* 'John Huxtable'.** Late, large-flowered clematis (group 3). H 2–3m (6–10ft), S 1m (3ft). Fully hardy. Bears masses of 8cm (3in) wide, single, white flowers, with cream anthers, in mid-summer.
***C.* 'JOSEPHINE' (Evijohill) PRB** illus. p.209. Early, large-flowered clematis (group 2). H 2.5m (8ft), S 1m (3ft). Fully hardy. From early summer to early autumn, bears double flowers, 12cm (5in) across, with almost bronze, green-tinged petals with a darker central bar; the petals become lilac in mid-summer, with a pink bar. Best colour in sun.
***C.* x *jouiniana*.** Sprawling, sub-shrubby, late-flowering clematis (group 3). H 1m (3ft), S 3m (10ft). Frost hardy. Has coarse foliage and, in summer, masses of tubular, single, soft lavender or off-white flowers, 2cm (¾in) wide, with reflexed petal tips. Is non-clinging. 🏆 **'Praecox'** has slightly darker flowers, 2 weeks earlier.
***C.* 'Kathleen Wheeler'.** Early, large-flowered clematis (group 2). H 2.5–3m (8–10ft), S 1m (3ft). Frost hardy. Has single, plum-mauve flowers, 12–14cm (5–5½in) across with yellow anthers, in early summer.
🏆 ***C.* 'Lasurstern'** illus. p.211. Vigorous, early, large-flowered clematis (group 2). H 2–3m (6–10ft), S 1m (3ft). Frost hardy. In summer bears single, blue flowers, 10–12cm (4–5in) across, with overlapping, wavy-edged petals and cream anthers.
***C.* 'Lincoln Star'** illus. p.209. Early, large-flowered clematis (group 2). H 2–3m (6–10ft), S 1m (3ft). Frost hardy. Has 10–12cm (4–5in) wide, single, raspberry-pink flowers, with red anthers, in early summer. Early flowers are darker than late ones, which have very pale pink petal edges. Prefers partial shade.
C. macropetala illus. p.211. Macropetala clematis (group 1). H 3m (10ft), S 1.5m (5ft). Fully hardy. During late spring and summer has masses of semi-double, mauve-blue flowers, 5cm (2in) long and lightening in colour towards the centre, followed by fluffy, silvery seed heads. 🏆 **'Markham's Pink'** illus. p.209 has pink flowers.
***C.* 'Madame Edouard André'.** Late, large-flowered clematis (group 3). H 2.5m (8ft), S 1m (3ft). Fully hardy. Freely produces single, deep red flowers, 8–10cm (3–4in) across, with silver undersides, pointed petals, and yellow anthers, in mid-summer.
🏆 ***C.* 'Madame Julia Correvon',** syn. *C. viticella* 'Madame Julia Correvon' illus. p.209. Late-flowering clematis (group 3). H 2.5–3.5m (8–11ft), S 1m (3ft). Fully hardy. Has flattish, single, wine-red flowers, 5–7cm (2–3in) wide, with twisted petals, in summer.
***C.* 'Madame Le Coultre'.** See *C.* 'Marie Boisselot'.
🏆 ***C.* 'Marie Boisselot',** syn. *C.* 'Madame Le Coultre'. Vigorous, early, large-flowered clematis (group 2). H 3m (10ft), S 1m (3ft). Frost hardy. Bears single flowers, 12cm (5in) across, with overlapping, white petals and cream anthers, in summer.
***C.* MEDLEY™ ('Evipo012'(N))** illus. p.210. Low-growing, scandent, non-clinging clematis (group 3). H 1m (3ft) S 60cm (2ft). Fully hardy. From mid-summer to autumn produces light pink, nodding, slightly scented flowers, 4–5cm (1½–2in) across, with twisted sepals that open to reveal a boss of yellow stamens in the centre.
🏆 ***C.* 'Miss Bateman'.** Compact, early, large-flowered clematis (group 2). H 2.5m (8ft), S 1m (3ft). Frost hardy. Masses of single, white flowers, 8–10cm (3–4in) across with red anthers, are produced in summer. Is good for a container or patio garden.
C. montana illus. p.208. Vigorous, Montana clematis (group 1). H 7–12m (22–40ft), S 2–3m (6–10ft). Fully hardy. In late spring bears masses of single, white flowers, 4–5cm (1½–2in) across, with yellow anthers. **'Broughton Star'**, H 4–5m (12–15ft), bears semi-double to fully double, cup-shaped, dusty pink flowers, with slightly darker veins. **'Elizabeth'**, H 10–12m (30–40ft), has scented, soft pink flowers with widely spaced petals. Flowers of var. ***rubens*** (illus. p.209) are pale pink. 🏆 **'Tetrarose'** (illus. p.209), H 7–8m (22–25ft), has coarse, 8cm (3in) long leaflets and 6–7cm (2½–3in) wide, deep satin-pink flowers.

♀ ***C.* 'Mrs Cholmondeley'.** Early, large-flowered clematis (group 2). H 2–3m (6–10ft), S 1m (3ft). Frost hardy. In summer has single, light bluish-lavender flowers, 10–12cm (4–5in) across with widely spaced petals and light chocolate anthers.
♀ ***C.* 'Mrs George Jackman'** illus. p.209. Early, large-flowered clematis (group 2). H 2–3m (6–10ft), S 1m (3ft). Frost hardy. Bears 10cm (4in) wide, semi-double flowers, with creamy-white petals and light brown anthers, in early summer.
***C.* 'Mrs N. Thompson'.** Compact, early, large-flowered clematis (group 2). H 2.5m (8ft), S 1m (3ft). Frost hardy. Produces masses of 8–10cm (3–4in) wide, single, magenta flowers, with a central, slightly darker stripe on each bluish-purple-edged petal and red anthers, in summer. Is good for a container or patio garden.
♀ ***C.* 'Nelly Moser'** illus. p.209. Early, large-flowered clematis (group 2). H 3.5m (11ft), S 1m (3ft). Frost hardy. In early summer has 12–16cm (5–6½in) wide, single, rose-mauve flowers, with reddish-purple anthers and, on each petal, a carmine stripe that fades in strong sun. Prefers a shaded, east-, west- or north-facing situation.
♀ ***C.* 'Niobe'.** Early, large-flowered clematis (group 2). H 2–3m (6–10ft), S 1m (3ft). Frost hardy. Throughout summer produces masses of single, rich deep red flowers, 10–14cm (4–5½in) across with yellow anthers.
C. orientalis. Late-flowering clematis (group 3). H 3–4m (10–12ft), S 1.5m (5ft). Fully hardy. Leaves are grey- to dark green. In summer lantern-shaped, single, greenish-yellow flowers, 3cm (1¼in) wide with recurved petal tips, are followed by feathery seed heads.
***C.* PARISIENNE™ ('Evipo019'[(N)])** illus. p.210. Compact, medium-flowered clematis (group 2). H 90–120cm (3–4ft) S.60cm (2ft). Fully hardy. Produces an abundance of pale violet flowers, 7–10cm (3–4in) across, with wavy-edged sepals and attractive red anthers, from early summer to late autumn.
***C.* PEPPERMINT™ ('Evipo005'[(N)])** illus. p.209. Vigorous, medium-flowered clematis (group 3). H 2–3m (6–10ft) S 1m (3ft). Fully hardy. From early summer to late autumn produces numerous creamy-white, rosetted flowers, 7–10cm (3–4in) across, with 6 large, outer sepals, which drop as the tight, inner rosette of smaller sepals expand. The late season's flowers are greenish-white.
***C.* 'Perle d'Azur'** illus. p.211. Late, large-flowered clematis (group 3). H 3m (10ft), S 1m (3ft). Fully hardy. Single, azure-blue flowers, 8cm (3in) across, with recurved petal tips and creamy-green anthers, open in summer.
♀ ***C.* PETIT FAUCON ('Evisix')** illus. p.211. Vigorous, scandent, non-clinging clematis (group 3). H 1–1.5m (3–5ft) S 60cm (2ft). Fully hardy. From summer to early autumn produces broadly bell-shaped, nodding to semi-pendent, deep blue-violet flowers 5–8cm (2–3in) across, with violet filaments and orange-yellow anthers.
C. **'Poulala'**. See *C.* ALABAST
C. **'Poulvo'**. See *C.* VINO
***C.* 'Purpurea Plena Elegans'.** See *C. viticella* 'Purpurea Plena Elegans'.
***C.* 'Ramona'.** Early, large-flowered clematis (group 2). H 3m (10ft), S 1m (3ft). Frost hardy. Has coarse, dark green leaves offset, in summer, by single, pale blue flowers, 10–12cm (4–5in) across with red anthers. Prefers a south-or south-west-facing position.
C. recta illus. p.209. Clump-forming, herbaceous clematis (group3). H 1–2m (3–6ft), S 50cm (20in). Fully hardy. Leaves are dark or grey-green. Bears masses of sweetly scented, flattish, single, white flowers, 2cm (¾in) across, in mid-summer.
♀ ***C. rehderiana*** illus. p.209. Vigorous, late-flowering clematis (group 3). H 6–7m (20–22ft), S 2–3m (6–10ft). Frost hardy. Bears loose clusters of fragrant, tubular, single, yellow flowers, 1–2cm (½–¾in) long, in late summer and early autumn. Leaves are coarse-textured.
***C.* 'Rhapsody'.** Compact, early, large-flowered clematis (group 2). H 2.5m (8ft), S 1m (3ft). Fully hardy. From early summer to early autumn, bears single, sapphire-blue flowers, 10–13cm (4–5in) across, with splayed, creamy-yellow anthers. Colour deepens with age.
♀ ***C.* 'Richard Pennell'.** Early, large-flowered clematis (group 2). H 2–3m (6–10ft), S 1m (3ft). Frost hardy. Produces 10–12cm (4–5in) wide, single flowers, with rich purple-blue petals and golden-yellow anthers, in summer.
***C.* 'Rouge Cardinal'.** Early, large-flowered clematis (group 3). H 2–3m (6–10ft), S 1m (3ft). Frost hardy. In summer has single, velvety, crimson flowers, 8–10cm (3–4in) across, with red anthers.
***C.* ROSEMOOR™ ('Evipo002'[(N)])** illus. p.209. Vigorous, large-flowered, long-flowering clematis (group 2). H 2–2.5m (6–8ft) S 1m (3ft). Fully hardy. From early summer to autumn deep red flowers, 12–15cm (5–6in) across, with contrasting yellow anthers, are produced in abundance.
***C.* ROYAL VELVET ('Evifour')** illus. p.209. Early, large-flowered clematis (group 2). H 2–2.5m (6–8ft), S 1m (3ft). Fully hardy. In early and mid-summer, bears single flowers, 10–15cm (4–6in) wide, with bluish, rich velvet-purple petals, with darker central bands, and red anthers.
***C.* SAVANNAH™ ('Evipo015'[(N)])** illus. p.210. Low-growing, scandent, non-clinging clematis (group 3). H 1m (3ft) S 60cm (2ft). Fully hardy. From mid-summer to autumn produces dark pink, nodding flowers, to 6cm (2½in) across, with twisted sepals that open to reveal clusters of yellow stamens in the centre.
***C.* 'Souvenir du Capitaine Thuilleaux'.** Compact, early, large-flowered clematis (group 2). H 2.5m (8ft), S 1m (3ft). Frost hardy. In early summer bears 8–10cm (3–4in) wide, single flowers, with red anthers and deep pink-striped, cream-pink petals. Is ideal for a container or patio garden.
***C.* 'Star of India'** illus. p.209. Vigorous, late, large-flowered clematis (group 3). H 3m (10ft), S 1m (3ft). Fully hardy. Bears masses of 8–10cm (3–4in) wide, single, deep purple-blue flowers, with light brown anthers, in mid-summer; each petal has a deep carmine-red stripe.
***C.* SUGAR CANDY ('Evione').** Vigorous, early, large-flowered clematis (group 2). H 3m (10ft) S 1m (3ft). Fully hardy. Produces an abundance of pinkish-mauve to light purple flowers, 10–18cm (4–6in) across, with darker, central bars on the sepals and yellow anthers.
C. tangutica illus. p.209. Vigorous, late-flowering clematis (group 3). H 5–6m (15–20ft), S 2–3m (6–10ft). Fully hardy. Has lantern-shaped, single, yellow flowers, 4cm (1½in) long, throughout summer and early autumn, followed by fluffy, silvery seed heads.
♀ ***C.* 'The President'** illus. p.210. Early, large-flowered clematis (group 2). H 2–3m (6–10ft), S 1m (3ft). Frost hardy. In early summer bears masses of single, rich purple flowers, silver beneath, 10cm (4in) wide, with red anthers.
***C.* VICTOR HUGO™ ('Evipo007'[(N)])** illus. p.210. Vigorous, scandent, non-clinging clematis (group 3). H 2.5–3m (8–10ft) S 1m (3ft). Fully hardy. Produces an abundance of red-violet flowers, 8cm (3in) across, with dark, violet-tipped stamens, from early summer until autumn.
***C.* VIENETTA™ ('Evipo006'[(N)])** illus. p.209. Vigorous, medium-flowered clematis (group 3). H 2–3m (6–10ft) S 1m (3ft). Fully hardy. Between early summer and autumn produces unusual, passion-flower-like, rounded blooms with 6 creamy-white, regularly placed sepals, surrounding a ring of purple, modified stamens and a dark centre. In autumn the outer sepals develop a greenish hue.
***C.* 'Ville de Lyon'.** Late, large-flowered clematis (group 3). H 2–3m (6–10ft), S 1m (3ft). Fully hardy. In mid-summer has single, bright carmine-red flowers, 8–10cm (3–4in) across, with darker petal edges and yellow anthers. Lower foliage tends to become scorched by late summer.
***C.* VINO ('Poulvo')** illus. p.209. Vigorous, early, large-flowered clematis (group 2). H 3m (10ft) S 1m (3ft). Fully hardy. Produces numerous, deep petunia-red flowers, 10–18cm (4–7in) across, with contrasting, white to cream filaments and yellow anthers, in late spring and again in late summer and early autumn.
C. viticella. Late-flowering clematis (group 3). H 2–3m (6–10ft), S 1m (3ft). Fully hardy. Produces nodding, open bell-shaped, single, purple-mauve flowers, 3.5cm (1½in) long, in summer. **'Abundance'** see *C.* 'Abundance'. **'Etoile Violette'** see *C.* 'Etoile Violette'.**'Madame Julia Correvon'** see *C.* 'Madame Julia Correvon'.
♀ **'Purpurea Plena Elegans'** (syn *C.* 'Purpurea Plena Elegans'; illus. p.209) bears abundant, double flowers, with many purplish-mauve sepals, occasionally green outer sepals, and no anthers, from mid-summer to late autumn.
***C.* 'Vyvyan Pennell'** illus. p.210. Early, large-flowered clematis (group 2). H 2–3m (6–10ft), S 1m (3ft). Frost hardy. Has double, lilac flowers, 10–12cm (4–5in) wide with a central, lavender-blue rosette of petals and golden-yellow anthers, in early summer, then single, blue-mauve flowers.
***C.* 'W.E. Gladstone'.** Vigorous, early, large-flowered clematis (group 2). H 3–4m (10–12ft), S 1m (3ft). Frost hardy. Produces single, lavender flowers, 15cm (6in) wide with red anthers, in summer.
***C.* 'William Kennett'.** Early, large-flowered clematis (group 2). H 2–3m (6–10ft), S 1m (3ft). Frost hardy. In summer has masses of single flowers, 10–12cm (4–5in) across, with red anthers and tough, lavender-blue petals each bearing a central, darker stripe that fades as the flower matures.
***C.* WISLEY™ ('Evipo001'[(N)])** illus. p.211. Strong growing, mid-season large-flowered clematis (group3). H 2.5–3m (8–10ft) S 1m (3ft). Fully hardy. From mid-summer to early autumn produces numerous, slightly nodding, violet-blue, yellow-anthered flowers,10–12cm (4–5in) across.

CLEOME
Spider flower

CAPPARACEAE

Genus of annuals and a few evergreen shrubs, grown for their unusual, spidery flowers. Half hardy to frost tender, min. 4°C (39°F). Grow in sun and in fertile, well-drained soil. Remove dead flowers. Propagate by seed sown outdoors in late spring. Aphids may be a problem.
C. hassleriana, syn. *C. spinosa*. Fast-growing, bushy annual. H to 1.2m (4ft), S 45cm (1½ft). Half hardy. Has hairy, spiny stems and mid-green leaves divided into lance-shaped leaflets. Large, rounded heads of narrow-petalled, pink-flushed, white flowers, with long, protruding stamens, appear in summer. **'Colour Fountain'** illus. p.334. **'Rose Queen'** has rose-pink flowers.
C. spinosa. See *C. hassleriana*.

CLERODENDRUM

VERBENACEAE

Genus of evergreen or deciduous, small trees, shrubs, sub-shrubs and woody-stemmed, twining climbers, grown for their showy flowers. Fully hardy to frost tender, min. 10–16°C (50–61°F). Needs humus-rich, well-drained soil and full sun, with partial shade in summer. Water freely in growing season, less at other times. Stems require support. Thin out crowded growth in spring. Propagate by seed in spring, by softwood cuttings in late spring or by semi-ripe cuttings in summer. Whitefly, red spider mite and mealy bug may be a problem.
C. bungei illus. p.144.
♀ ***C. chinense* var. *chinense*,** syn. ***C. c.*** 'Pleniflorum', *C. fragrans* 'Pleniflorum', *C. philippinum*. Evergreen or deciduous, bushy shrub. H and S to 2.5m (8ft). Frost tender, min. 10°C (50°F). Leaves are broadly oval, coarsely and shallowly toothed and downy. Fragrant, double, pink or white flowers are borne in domed, terminal clusters in summer.
C. fallax. See *C. speciosissimum*.
***C. fragrans* 'Pleniflorum'.** See *C. chinense* var. *chinense*.
C. philippinum. See *C. chinense* 'var. *chinense*'.

C. speciosissimum, syn. *C. fallax.* Evergreen, erect to spreading, sparingly branched shrub. H and S to 3m (10ft). Frost tender, min. 15°C (59°F). Bears broadly heart-shaped, wavy-edged leaves, each to 30cm (1ft) across, on long stalks and, from late spring to autumn, tubular, scarlet flowers, with spreading petal lobes, in 30cm (1ft) long, terminal clusters. Makes a good pot plant.
♀ ***C. splendens.*** Vigorous, evergreen, woody-stemmed, twining climber. H 3m (10ft) or more. Frost tender, min. 15°C (59°F). Has oval to elliptic, rich green leaves. Clusters of 5-petalled, tubular, scarlet flowers, 2.5cm (1in) wide, are produced in summer.
♀ ***C. thomsoniae*** illus. p.204.
C. trichotomum illus. p.143.

CLETHRA

CLETHRACEAE

Genus of deciduous or evergreen shrubs and trees, grown for their fragrant, white flowers. Fully to half hardy. Needs semi-shade and moist, peaty, acid soil. Propagate by softwood cuttings in summer or by seed in autumn.
C. alnifolia (Sweet pepper-bush). Deciduous, bushy shrub. H and S 2.5m (8ft). Fully hardy. Has oval, toothed, mid-green leaves and, in late summer and early autumn, slender spires of small, bell-shaped flowers.
C. arborea (Lily-of-the-valley tree). Evergreen, bushy, dense shrub or tree. H 8m (25ft), S 6m (20ft). Half hardy. Bears long, nodding clusters of small, strongly fragrant, bell-shaped flowers among oval, toothed, rich green leaves from late summer to mid-autumn.
♀ ***C. barbinervis*** illus. p.134.
C. delavayi illus. p.117.

CLEYERA

THEACEAE

Genus of evergreen, summer-flowering shrubs and trees, grown for their foliage and flowers. Frost to half hardy. Requires a sheltered position in sun or semi-shade and moist, acid soil. Propagate by semi-ripe cuttings in summer.
***C. fortunei* 'Variegata'.** See *C. japonica* 'Tricolor'.
C. japonica. Evergreen, bushy shrub. H and S 3m (10ft). Frost hardy. Small, fragrant, bowl-shaped, creamy-white flowers are borne in summer amid narrowly oblong to oval-oblong, glossy, dark green leaves. Occasionally has small, spherical, red fruits, ripening to black. **'Tricolor'** (syn. *C. fortunei* 'Variegata', *Eurya japonica* 'Variegata' of gardens), H and S 2m (6ft), is half hardy and produces pink-flushed, young leaves, later green edged with creamy-white.

CLIANTHUS

LEGUMINOSAE/PAPILIONACEAE

Genus of evergreen or semi-evergreen, woody-stemmed, scrambling climbers, grown for their attractive flowers. Half hardy to frost tender, min. 7°C (45°F). Grow outdoors in warm areas in well-drained soil and full sun. In cooler areas needs to be under glass. In spring prune out growing tips to give a bushier habit and cut out any dead wood. Propagate by seed in spring or stem cuttings in late summer.
♀ ***C. puniceus*** and ♀ f. ***albus*** illus. p.200.

Climbing butcher's broom. See *Semele androgyna.*
Climbing dahlia. See *Hidalgoa.*
Climbing fumitory. See *Adlumia fungosa.*
Climbing hydrangea. See *Hydrangea petiolaris*, illus. p.204.

CLINTONIA

LILIACEAE/CONVALLARIACEAE

Genus of late spring- or summer-flowering, rhizomatous perennials. Fully hardy. Prefers shade and moist but well-drained, peaty, neutral to acid soil. Propagate by division in spring or by seed in autumn.
C. andrewsiana. Clump-forming, rhizomatous perennial. H 60cm (24in), S 30cm (12in). In early summer produces clusters of small, bell-shaped, pinkish-purple flowers at tops of stems, above sparse, broadly oval, glossy, rich green leaves. Bears globose, blue fruits in autumn.
C. borealis. Clump-forming, rhizomatous perennial. H and S 30cm (12in). Is similar to *C. andrewsiana*, but has nodding, yellowish-green flowers and small, globose, blackish fruits.
C. uniflora (Queencup). Spreading, rhizomatous perennial. H 15cm (6in), S 30cm (12in). Has oval, glossy, green leaves. Slender stems bear solitary star-shaped, white flowers in late spring, then large, globose, blue-black fruits.

CLITORIA

LEGUMINOSAE/PAPILIONACEAE

Genus of perennials and evergreen shrubs and twining climbers, grown for their large, pea-like flowers. Frost tender, min. 15°C (59°F). Grow in full light and in any fertile, well-drained soil. Water moderately, less when not in full growth. Provide support for stems. Thin out crowded stems in spring. Propagate by seed in spring or by softwood cuttings in summer. Whitefly and red spider mite may be a problem.
C. ternatea. Evergreen, twining climber with slender stems. H 3–5m (10–15ft). Leaves are divided into 3 or 5 oval leaflets. Clear bright blue flowers, 7–12cm (3–5in) wide, are carried in summer.

CLIVIA

AMARYLLIDACEAE

Genus of robust, evergreen, rhizomatous perennials, cultivated for their funnel-shaped flowers. Suits borders and large containers. Frost tender, min. 10°C (50°F). Needs partial shade and well-drained soil. Water well in summer, less in winter. Propagate by seed in winter or spring or by division in spring or summer after flowering. Mealy bugs may cause problems. All parts of *C. miniata* may cause mild stomach upset if ingested, and the sap may irritate skin.
♀ ***C. miniata*** illus. p.435.
C. nobilis. Evergreen, spring- or summer-flowering, rhizomatous perennial. H 30–40cm (12–16in), S 30–60cm (12–24in). Has strap-shaped, semi-erect, basal leaves, 40–60cm (16–24in) long. Each leafless stem bears a dense, semi-pendent head of over 20 narrowly funnel-shaped, red flowers, with green tips and yellow margins to petals.

Cloth-of-gold crocus. See *Crocus angustifolius.*
Cloud grass. See *Aichryson × domesticum* 'Variegatum', illus. p.493.
Clover. See *Trifolium.*
Club, Devil's. See *Oplopanax horridus.*
Club-rush.
Bristle. See *Isolepsis setaceus.*
Round-headed. See *Scirpoides holoschoenus.*

CLUSIA

CLUSIACEAE

Genus of evergreen, mainly summer-flowering climbers, shrubs and trees, grown for their foliage and flowers. Frost tender, min. 16–18°C (61–4°F). Needs partial shade and well-drained soil. Water potted specimens moderately, very little when temperatures are low. Pruning is tolerated if necessary. Propagate by layering in spring or by semi-ripe cuttings in summer. Whitefly and red spider mite may be a problem.
C. major, syn. *C. rosea* (Autograph tree, Copey, Fat pork tree, Pitch apple). Slow-growing, evergreen, rounded tree or shrub. H and S to 15m (50ft). Bears oval, lustrous, deep green leaves. Cup-shaped, pink flowers, 5cm (2in) wide, are produced in summer, followed by globose, greenish fruits that yield a sticky resin.
C. rosea. See. *C. major*

Cluster pine. See *Pinus pinaster*, illus. p.99.
Clustered ivy. See *Hedera helix* 'Conglomerata'.

CLYTOSTOMA

BIGNONIACEAE

Genus of evergreen, woody-stemmed, tendril climbers, grown for their flowers. Frost tender, min. 10–13°C (50–55°F). Grow in well-drained soil, with partial shade in summer. Water freely in summer, less at other times. Provide support for stems. Thin out congested growth after flowering or in spring. Propagate by semi-ripe cuttings in summer.
C. callistegioides, syn. *Pandorea lindleyana*, illus. p.201.

Coast redwood. See *Sequoia sempervirens.*

COBAEA

COBAEACEAE/POLEMONIACEAE

Genus of evergreen or deciduous, woody-stemmed, tendril climbers. Only one species, *C. scandens*, is generally cultivated. Frost tender, min. 4°C (39°F). Grow outdoors in warm areas in full light and in any well-drained soil. In cool regions may be grown under glass or treated as an annual. Propagate by seed in spring.
♀ ***C. scandens*** illus. p.212.
♀ f. ***alba*** is an evergreen, woody-stemmed, tendril climber. H 4–5m (12–15ft). Has long-stalked, bell-shaped, green, then white flowers from late summer until first frosts. Leaves have 4 or 6 oval leaflets.

Cobnut. See *Corylus avellana.*
Cobweb houseleek. See *Sempervivum arachnoideum*, illus. p.401.
Cock's foot. See *Dactylis glomerata.*
Cockle, Corn. See *Agrostemma.*
Cockspur coral-tree. See *Erythrina crista-galli*, illus. p.139.
Cockspur thorn. See *Crataegus crus-galli.*
Cocos capitata. See *Butia capitata.*

CODIAEUM

EUPHORBIACEAE

Genus of evergreen shrubs, grown for their foliage. Frost tender, min. 10–13°C (50–55°F). Prefers partial shade and fertile, moist but well-drained soil. Remove tips from young plants to promote a branched habit. Propagate by greenwood cuttings from firm stem tips in spring or summer. Mealy bug and soft scale may be a nuisance. Contact with the foliage may aggravate skin allergies.
C. variegatum var. ***pictum*** illus. p.173.

CODONOPSIS

CAMPANULACEAE

Genus of perennials and mostly herbaceous, twining climbers, grown for their bell- or saucer-shaped flowers. Fully to frost hardy. Requires a position in semi-shade, with light, well-drained soil. Train over supports or leave to scramble through other, larger plants. Propagate by seed sown in autumn or spring.
C. clematidea. Herbaceous, twining climber. H to 1.5m (5ft). Frost hardy. Has small, oval, mid-green leaves. In summer produces nodding, bell-shaped

flowers, 2.5cm (1in) long; they are white, tinged with blue, and marked inside with darker veining and 2 purple rings.
♀ ***C. convolvulacea*** illus. p.212.
C. ovata. Upright perennial with scarcely twining stems. H to 30cm (12in). Frost hardy. Has small, oval leaves and, in summer, small, bell-shaped, pale blue flowers, often with darker veins.

Coelogyne

ORCHIDACEAE

See also ORCHIDS.
C. cristata illus. p.308. Evergreen, epiphytic orchid for a cool greenhouse. H 15cm (6in). In winter produces sprays of crisp, white flowers, 5cm (2in) across, and marked orange on each lip. Narrowly oval leaves are 8–10cm (3–4in) long. Needs a position in good light in summer.
C. flaccida illus. p.308. Evergreen, epiphytic orchid for a cool greenhouse. H 15cm (6in). During spring bears drooping spikes of fragrant, star-shaped, light buff flowers, 4cm (1½in) across, with yellow and brown marks on each lip. Has narrowly oval, semi-rigid leaves, 8–10cm (3–4in) long. Grow in semi-shade in summer.
C. nitida, syn. *C. ochracea* illus. p.308. Evergreen, epiphytic orchid for a cool greenhouse. H 12cm (5in). In spring produces sprays of very fragrant, white flowers, 2.5cm (1in) across and with a yellow mark on each lip. Narrowly oval, semi-rigid leaves are 8–10cm (3–4in) long. Requires semi-shade in summer.
C. ochracea. See *C. nitida*.
C. speciosa illus. p.310. Vigorous, evergreen, epiphytic orchid for an intermediate greenhouse. H 25cm (10in). In summer, produces pendent, light green flowers, 6cm (2½in) across, with brown-and white-marked lips, that open in succession along stems. Has broadly oval leaves, 23–5cm (9–10in) long. Grow in good light in summer.

Coffee, Wild. See *Polyscias guilfoylei*.
Coffee tree, Kentucky. See *Gymnocladus dioica*.

Coix

GRAMINEAE/POACEAE

See also GRASSES, BAMBOOS, RUSHES and SEDGES.
C. lacryma-jobi illus. p.320.

Colchicum

COLCHICACEAE/LILIACEAE

Genus of spring- and autumn-flowering corms, grown for their mainly goblet-shaped blooms, up to 20cm (8in) long, most of which emerge before leaves. Each corm bears 2–7 narrowly strap-shaped to broadly elliptic, basal leaves. Fully to frost hardy. Needs an open, sunny situation and well-drained soil. Propagate by seed or division in autumn. All parts are highly toxic if ingested and, if in contact with skin, may cause irritation.
♀ ***C. agrippinum*** illus. p.455.
C. autumnale illus. p.453.
'Alboplenum' is an autumn-flowering corm. H and S 10–15cm (4–6in). Fully hardy. In spring has 3–5 large, semi-erect, basal, glossy, green leaves. Produces a bunch of up to 8 long-tubed, rounded, double, white flowers with 15–30 narrow petals.
C. 'Beaconsfield'. Robust, autumn-flowering corm. H and S 15–20cm (6–8in). Fully hardy. Bears large, goblet-shaped, rich pinkish-purple flowers, faintly chequered and white in centres. Large, semi-erect, basal leaves appear in spring.
C. bivonae, syn. *C. bowlesianum, C. sibthorpii*, illus. p.454.
C. bowlesianum. See *C. bivonae*.
♀ ***C. byzantinum*** illus. p.453.
C. cilicicum illus. p.454.
C. 'Lilac Wonder'. Vigorous, autumn-flowering corm. H and S 15–20cm (6–8in). Fully hardy. Produces goblet-shaped, deep lilac-pink flowers, 15–20cm (6–8in) long. Broad, semi-erect, basal leaves appear in spring.
C. luteum illus. p.450
C. sibthorpii. See *C. bivonae*.
♀ ***C. speciosum.*** Vigorous, autumn-flowering corm. H and S 15–20cm (6–8in). Fully hardy. Bears goblet-shaped, pale to deep pinkish-purple flowers, 15–20cm (6–8in) long, often with white throats. Large, semi-erect, basal leaves develop in winter or spring.
♀ **'Album'** illus. p.453.
C. 'The Giant'. Robust, autumn-flowering corm. H and S 15–20cm (6–8in). Fully hardy. Produces up to 5 funnel-shaped, deep mauve-pink flowers, each 15–20cm (6–8in) long and fading to white in the centre. Broad, semi-erect, basal leaves form in winter or spring.
C. variegatum. Autumn-flowering corm. H 10–15cm (4–6in), S 8–10cm (3–4in). Frost hardy. Bears widely funnel-shaped, reddish-purple flowers with strong chequered patterns. More or less horizontal, basal leaves with wavy margins appear in spring. Needs a hot, sunny site.
♀ ***C.* 'Waterlily'** illus. p.455.

Coleonema

RUTACEAE

Genus of evergreen, heath-like shrubs, grown for their flowers and overall appearance. Frost tender, min. 3–5°C (37–41°F). Requires a position in full sun and well-drained, neutral to acid soil. Water potted plants moderately when in full growth, sparingly at other times. For a more compact habit, clip after flowering. Propagate by seed sown in spring or by semi-ripe cuttings in late summer.
C. pulchrum. Evergreen, spreading to domed shrub with wiry stems. H 60cm–1.2m (2–4ft), S 1–1.5m (3–5ft). Has soft, needle-like, bright green leaves. Carries 5-petalled, pale pink to red flowers in spring-summer.

Coleus. See *Solenostemon* except for: ***C. thyrsoideus*** for which see *Plectranthus thyrsoideus*.
Coleus, Prostrate. See *Plectranthus oertendahlii*.

Colletia

RHAMNACEAE

Genus of deciduous, usually leafless shrubs, grown for their curious, spiny shoots and profuse, small flowers. Shoots assume function of leaves. Frost hardy. Requires a sheltered, sunny site and well-drained soil. Propagate by semi-ripe cuttings in late summer.
C. armata. See *C. hystrix*.
C. cruciata. See *C. paradoxa*.
C. hystrix, syn. *C. armata*, illus. p.143.
'Rosea' is a deciduous, stoutly branched shrub. H 2.5m (8ft), S 5m (15ft). Shoots have rigid, grey-green spines. Bears fragrant, tubular, pink flowers in late summer and early autumn.
C. paradoxa, syn. *C. cruciata*. Deciduous, arching shrub with stiff branches. H 3m (10ft), S 5m (15ft). Has stout, flattened, blue-green spines. Fragrant, tubular, white flowers are borne in late summer and early autumn.

Collinsia

SCROPHULARIACEAE

Genus of spring- to summer-flowering annuals. Fully hardy. Grow in partial shade and in fertile, well-drained soil. Support with thin sticks. Propagate by seed sown outdoors in spring or early autumn.
C. grandiflora illus. p.343.

Colocasia

ARACEAE

Genus of deciduous or evergreen, perennial, marginal water plants, grown for their foliage. Has edible tubers, known as 'taros', for which it is widely cultivated. Is suitable for the edges of frost-free pools; may also be grown in wet soil in pots. Frost tender, min. 1°C (34°F); with min. 25°C (77°F) is evergreen. Grows in sun or light shade and in mud or shallow water. Propagate by division in spring. All parts may cause mild stomach upset if ingested without cooking, and contact with the sap may irritate the skin.
C. antiquorum. See *C. esculenta*.
♀ ***C. esculenta***, syn. *C. antiquorum*.
'Fontanesii' is a deciduous, perennial, marginal water plant. H 1.1m (3½ft), S 60cm (2ft). Has large, bold, oval, mid-green leaves with dark green veins and margins and blackish-violet leaf stalks and spathe tubes. **'Illustris'** has brownish-purple leaf stalks and dark green leaf blades with purple spots.

Colombian ball cactus. See *Parodia erinacea*, illus. p.495.
Colorado spruce. See *Picea pungens*.

Colquhounia

LABIATAE/LAMIACEAE

Genus of evergreen or semi-evergreen shrubs, grown for their flowers in late summer and autumn. Frost hardy, but is cut to ground level in cold winters. Needs a sheltered, sunny position and well-drained soil. Propagate by softwood cuttings in summer.
C. coccinea illus. p.145.

Coltsfoot, Alpine. See *Homogyne alpina*.
Columbine. See *Aquilegia*.
Alpine. See *Aquilegia alpina*, illus. p.360.
Canadian. See *Aquilegia canadensis*.

Columnea

GESNERIACEAE

Genus of evergreen, creeping or trailing perennials or sub-shrubs, grown for their showy flowers. Trailing species are useful for hanging baskets. Frost tender, min. 15°C (59°F). Needs bright but indirect light, a fairly humid atmosphere and moist soil, except in winter. Propagate by tip cuttings after flowering.
♀ ***C. × banksii*** illus. p.254.
C. crassifolia illus. p.293.
C. gloriosa (Goldfish plant). Evergreen, trailing perennial with more or less unbranched stems. H or S to 90cm (3ft). Oval leaves have reddish hairs. Has tubular, hooded, scarlet flowers, to 8cm (3in) long with yellow throats, in winter-spring.
C. microphylla. Evergreen perennial, sparsely branched on each trailing stem. H or S 1m (3ft) or more. Has small, rounded leaves with brown hairs. Hooded, tubular, scarlet flowers, to 8cm (3in) long with yellow throats, are produced in winter-spring.
'Variegata' illus. p.274.

Colutea

LEGUMINOSAE/PAPILIONACEAE

Genus of deciduous, summer-flowering shrubs, grown for their foliage, pea-like flowers and bladder-shaped seed pods. Fully hardy. Grow in full sun and any but waterlogged soil. Propagate by softwood cuttings in summer or by seed in autumn. Seeds may cause mild stomach upset if ingested.
C. arborescens illus. p.142.
C. × media illus. p.143.
C. orientalis. Deciduous, bushy shrub. H and S 2m (6ft). Has blue-grey leaves consisting of 7 or 9 oval leaflets. Clusters of yellow-marked, coppery-red flowers produced in summer are followed by inflated, green, then pale brown seed pods.

Comarostaphylis diversifolia. See *Arctostaphylos diversifolia*.

Combretum

COMBRETACEAE

Genus of evergreen trees, shrubs and scandent to twining climbers, grown for their small, showy flowers. Frost tender, min. 16°C (61°F). Provide humus-rich, well-drained soil, with partial shade in summer. Water freely in summer, less at other times. Support for stems is necessary. Thin out and spur back congested growth after flowering. Propagate by semi-ripe cuttings in summer. Red spider mite may be a problem.
C. grandiflorum. Moderately vigorous, evergreen, scandent to twining climber. H to 6m (20ft). Has oblong to elliptic, pointed leaves, 10–20cm (4–8in) long. Tubular, bright red flowers with long stamens are borne in summer in one-sided spikes, 10–13cm (4–5in) long.

Comfrey. See *Symphytum*.
Russian. See *Symphytum* × *uplandicum*.

Commelina

COMMELINACEAE

Genus of perennials, usually grown as annuals. Half hardy. Grow in a sunny, sheltered position and in fertile, well-drained soil. Crowns should be lifted before the frosts and overwintered in slightly moist, frost-free conditions. Propagate by seed sown under glass or by division of the crown in spring.
C. coelestis, syn. *C. tuberosa* Coelestis Group, illus. p.346.
***C. tuberosa* Coelestis Group.** See *C. coelestis*.

Common alder. See *Alnus glutinosa*.
Common arrowhead. See *Sagittaria sagittifolia*.
Common ash. See *Fraxinus excelsior*.
Common beech. See *Fagus sylvatica*, illus. p.64.
Common box. See *Buxus sempervirens*.
Common broom. See *Cytisus scoparius*.
Common camassia. See *Camassia quamash*.
Common camellia. See *Camellia japonica*.
Common devil's claw. See *Proboscidea louisianica*.
Common elder. See *Sambucus nigra*.
Common English ivy. See *Hedera helix*.
Common gardenia. See *Gardenia augusta*.
Common German flag. See *Iris germanica*.
Common hackberry. See *Celtis occidentalis*.
Common hawthorn. See *Crataegus monogyna*.
Common holly. See *Ilex aquifolium*, illus. p.94.
Common honeysuckle. See *Lonicera periclymenum*.
Common hop. See *Humulus lupulus*.
Common hornbeam. See *Carpinus betulus*.
Common houseleek. See *Sempervivum tectorum*, illus. p.401.
Common jasmine. See *Jasminum officinale*.
Common juniper. See *Juniperus communis*.
Common laburnum. See *Laburnum anagyroides*.
Common lime. See *Tilia* × *europaea*.
Common morning glory. See *Ipomoea purpurea*.
Common moss rose. See *Rosa* × *centifolia* 'Muscosa'.
Common myrtle. See *Myrtus communis*, illus. p.126.
Common net bush. See *Calothamnus quadrifidus*.
Common oak. See *Quercus robur*.
Common passion flower. See *Passiflora caerulea*, illus. p.212.
Common pear. See *Pyrus communis*.
Common pitcher plant. See *Sarracenia purpurea*.
Common polypody. See *Polypodium vulgare*, illus. p.325.
Common quaking grass. See *Briza media*.
Common rue. See *Ruta graveolens*.
Common snowdrop. See *Galanthus nivalis*.
Common spruce. See *Picea abies*, illus. p.100.
Common stag's-horn fern. See *Platycerium bifurcatum*, illus. p.322.
Common stonecrop. See *Sedum acre*, illus. p.396.
Common unicorn plant. See *Proboscidea louisianica*.
Common valerian. See *Valeriana officinalis*, illus. p.243.
Compass plant. See *Silphium laciniatum*.

Conandron

GESNERIACEAE

Genus of one species of tuberous perennial, grown for its fleshy leaves and drooping flower clusters. Frost hardy. Grow in alpine houses. Needs shade and humus-rich, well-drained soil. Keep containerized plants moist in summer, dry when dormant in winter. Propagate by division or seed in spring.
C. ramondioides. Hummock-forming, tuberous perennial. H 30cm (12in), S 20cm (8in). Bears broadly oval, fleshy, wrinkled, mid-green leaves with toothed edges. In mid-summer, each flower stem carries 5–25 tubular flowers, usually lilac, but white, purple or pink forms also occur.

Coneflower. See *Echinacea; Rudbeckia*.
Confederate jasmine. See *Trachelospermum jasminoides*, illus. p.203.
Confederate rose. See *Hibiscus mutabilis*.

Conifers

Group of trees and shrubs distinguished botanically from others by producing seeds exposed or uncovered on the scales of fruits. Most conifers are evergreen, have needle-like leaves and bear woody fruits (cones). All genera in the Cupressaceae family, however, have needle-like juvenile leaves and, excepting many junipers and some other selected forms, scale-like adult leaves. Conifers described in this book are evergreen unless otherwise stated.
Conifers are excellent garden plants. Most provide year-round foliage, which may be green, blue, grey, bronze, gold or silver. They range in height from trees 30m (100ft) or more tall to dwarf shrubs that grow less than 5cm (2in) every 10 years. Tall conifers may be planted as specimen trees or to provide shelter, screening or hedging. Dwarf conifers make good features in their own right as well as in groups; they also associate well with heathers, add variety to rock gardens and provide excellent ground cover. They may also be grown in containers.

Hardiness

Nearly all conifers described in this book are fully hardy. Some, such as *Picea sitchensis*, *P. omorika* and *Pinus contorta*, thrive in the coldest, most windswept sites. *Araucaria, Cupressus* and *Pinus* are good for coastal conditions. *Athrotaxis, Austrocedrus, Cephalotaxus, Podocarpus* and certain species noted in other genera are frost to half hardy and flourish only in mild localities. Elsewhere they need a very sheltered position or may be grown indoors as dwarf plants.

Frost may damage new growth of several genera, especially *Abies, Larix, Picea* and *Pseudotsuga*, and severe cold, dry spells in winter may temporarily harm mature foliage.

Position and soil

× *Cupressocyparis*, *Cupressus*, *Larix* and *Pinus* need full sun. *Cedrus*, *Juniperus* and *Pseudolarix* do not tolerate shade. All other conifers will thrive in sun or shade, and most *Abies* and all *Cephalotaxus*, *Podocarpus*, *Taxus*, *Thuja*, *Torreya* and *Tsuga* will grow in deep shade once established.

Conifers grow well on most soils, but certain genera and species will not do well on soils over chalk or limestone. In this book such conifers are: *Abies, Pseudolarix*, *Pseudotsuga* and *Tsuga*; also *Picea*, except *P. likiangensis*, *P. omorika* and *P. pungens*; and *Pinus*, except *P. aristata*, *P. armandii*, *P. cembroides*, *P. halepensis*, *P. heldreichii*, *P. nigra*, *P. peuce* and *P. wallichiana*.

Certain conifers tolerate extreme conditions. *Abies alba*, *A. homolepis, A. nordmanniana, Cryptomeria, Cunninghamia, Metasequoia, Pinus coulteri, P. peuce, P. ponderosa, Sciadopitys, Sequoia, Sequoiadendron and Taxodium* will grow on heavy clay soils. *Picea omorika*, *P. sitchensis, Pinus contorta, Sciadopitys verticillata* and *Thuja plicata* are all happy on wet soil, and *Metasequoia* and *Taxodium* thrive in waterlogged conditions. *Cupressus*, *Juniperus* and *Pinus* grow well on dry, sandy soil.

Pruning

If a conifer produces more than one leader, remove all but one. Bear in mind when trimming hedges that most conifers will not make new growth when cut back into old wood or from branches that have turned brown. This does not, however, apply to *Cephalotaxus*, *Cryptomeria*, *Cunninghamia*, *Sequoia*, *Taxus* and *Torreya*, and these conifers may be kept to a reasonable size in the garden by cutting back the main stem, which will later coppice (make new growth). Young specimens of *Araucaria*, *Ginkgo*, *Metasequoia* and *Taxodium* will sometimes do the same.

Propagation

Seed is the easiest method of propagation, but forms selected for leaf colour (other than blue in some species) do not come true. Sow in autumn or spring. All genera apart from *Abies*, *Cedrus*, *Picea* (except young plants or dwarf forms), *Pinus*, *Pseudolarix*, *Pseudotsuga* and *Tsuga* (except young plants or dwarf forms) may be raised fairly easily from cuttings: current growth from autumn to spring for evergreens, softwood cuttings in summer for deciduous conifers. Tall-growing forms of Pinaceae (*Abies*, *Cedrus*, *Picea*, *Pinus*, *Pseudolarix*, *Pseudotsuga* and *Tsuga*) are usually propagated by grafting in late summer, winter or early spring. Layering may be possible for some dwarf conifers.

Pests and diseases

Honey fungus attacks many conifers, especially young plants. Most resistant to the disease are *Abies*, *Calocedrus*, *Larix*, *Pseudotsuga* and *Taxus*. Green spruce aphid may be a problem on *Picea*, and conifer spinning mite may defoliate *Abies*, *Picea* and some *Pinus*.

Conifers are illustrated on pp.97–105, dwarf forms on pp.106–7. See also *Abies*, *Araucaria*, *Athrotaxis*, *Austrocedrus*, *Calocedrus*, *Cedrus*, *Cephalotaxus*, *Chamaecyparis*, *Cryptomeria*, *Cunninghamia*, × *Cupressocyparis*, *Cupressus*, *Fitzroya*, *Ginkgo*, *Juniperus*, *Larix*, *Metasequoia*, *Microbiota*, *Phyllocladus*, *Picea*, *Pinus*, *Podocarpus*, *Pseudolarix*, *Pseudotsuga*, *Saxegothaea*, *Sciadopitys*, *Sequoia*, *Sequoiadendron*, *Taxodium*, *Taxus*, *Thuja*, *Thujopsis*, *Torreya* and *Tsuga*.

Conophytum

AIZOACEAE

Genus of slow-growing, clump-forming, perennial succulents with spherical or 2-eared leaves that grow for only 2 months each year, after flowering. In early summer, old leaves gradually shrivel to papery sheaths from which new leaves and flowers emerge in late summer. Frost tender, min. 4°C (39°F) if dry. Needs full sun and well-drained soil. Keep dry in winter. Propagate by seed from spring to autumn or by division in late summer.
🏆 ***C. bilobum*** illus. p.495.
C. concordans, syn. *Ophthalmophyllum villetii*, illus. p.488.
C. longum, syn. *Ophthalmophyllum herri*, *O. longum*. Clump forming, perennial succulent. H 3cm (1¼in), S 1.5cm (⅝in). Has 2 almost united, cylindrical, very fleshy, erect, grey-green to brown leaves. In late summer bears daisy-like, white to pink flowers 2cm (¾in) across.
C. notabile illus. p.496.
🏆 ***C. truncatum*** illus. p.486.

Consolida
Larkspur

RANUNCULACEAE

Genus of annuals, providing excellent cut flowers. Fully hardy. Needs sun and fertile, well-drained soil. Support stems of tall-growing plants with sticks. Propagate by seed sown outdoors in spring, or in early autumn in mild areas. Protect young plants from slugs and snails. The seeds are poisonous.
C. ajacis, syn. *C. ambigua, Delphinium consolida*. Fast-growing, upright, branching annual. Giant forms, H to 1.2m (4ft), S 30cm (1ft); dwarf, H and S 30cm (1ft). All have feathery, mid-green leaves and, throughout summer, spikes of rounded, spurred flowers. **Dwarf Hyacinth Series** has spikes of tubular flowers in shades of pink, mauve, blue or white. **Giant Imperial Series** illus. p.344.
C. ambigua. See *C. ajacis*.

Convallaria
Lily-of-the-valley

LILIACEAE/CONVALLARIACEAE

Genus of spring-flowering, rhizomatous perennials. Fully hardy. Prefers partial shade and does best in humus-rich, moist soil. Propagate by division after flowering or in autumn. The seeds of *C. majalis* may cause mild stomach upset if ingested.
♀ ***C. majalis*** illus. p.276. **'Flore Pleno'** is a low-growing, rhizomatous perennial. H 23–30cm (9–12in), S indefinite. Sprays of small, very fragrant, pendent, bell-shaped flowers that are double and white open in spring. Narrowly oval leaves are mid-to dark green. **'Fortin's Giant'**, H 45cm (18in), has larger flowers and leaves that appear a little earlier.

Convolvulus

CONVOLVULACEAE

Genus of dwarf, bushy and climbing annuals, perennials and evergreen shrubs and sub-shrubs. Fully hardy to frost tender, min 2°C (36°F). Grow in sun and in poor to fertile, well-drained soil. Dead-head to prolong flowering. Propagate by seed sown outdoors in mid-spring for hardy plants or under glass in spring for tender plants, perennials and sub-shrubs by softwood cuttings in late spring or summer.
C. althaeoides illus. p.387.
♀ ***C. cneorum*** illus. p.154.
C. mauritanicus. See *C. sabatius*.
C. minor. See *C. tricolor*.
C. purpureus. See *Ipomoea purpurea*.
♀ ***C. sabatius***, syn. *C. mauritanicus*, illus. p.368.
C. tricolor, syn. *C. minor.* Moderately fast-growing, upright, bushy or climbing annual. H 20–30cm (8–12in), S 20cm (8in). Fully hardy. Has oval to lance-shaped, mid-green leaves. In summer bears saucer-shaped, blue or white flowers, 2.5cm (1in) wide, with yellowish-white throats. Tall, climbing forms, H to 3m (10ft), are half hardy and have flowers to 10cm (4in) wide. **'Blue Flash'** (bushy) illus. p.344. **'Flying Saucers'** (climber) has blue-and-white-striped flowers.

Copiapoa

CACTACEAE

Genus of slow-growing, perennial cacti with funnel-shaped, yellow flowers. Many species have large tap roots. Frost tender, min. 8–10°C (46–50°F). Needs partial shade and very well-drained soil. Propagate by seed or grafting in spring or summer.
C. cinerea illus. p.482.
C. coquimbana. Clump-forming, spherical, then columnar, perennial cactus. H to 30cm (1ft), S 1m (3ft). Min. 8°C (46°F). Dark grey-green stem has 10–17 ribs. Areoles each bear 8–10 dark brown radial spines and 1 or 2 stouter central spines. Yellow flowers, 3cm (1¼in) across, appear in summer. Is slow to form clumps.
C. echinoides. Flattened spherical, perennial cactus, ribbed like a sea-urchin. H 15cm (6in), S 10cm (4in). Min. 10°C (50°F). Solitary grey-green stem bears dark brown spines, 3cm (1¼in) long, which soon fade to grey. In summer produces pale yellow flowers, 4cm (1½in) across.
C. marginata. Clump-forming, perennial cactus. H 60cm (2ft), S 30cm (1ft). min. 10°C (50°F). Grey-green stem bears very close-set areoles with dark-tipped, pale brown spines, to 3cm (1¼in) long. Has yellow flowers, 2–5cm (¾–2in) across, in spring-summer.

Cootamundra wattle. See *Acacia baileyana*, illus. p.93.
Copa de oro. See *Solandra maxima*, illus. p.202.
Copey. See *Clusia major*.
Copihue. See *Lapageria rosea*, illus. p.206.
Copper beech. See *Fagus sylvatica* f. *atropunicea*, illus. p.61.
Copperleaf. See *Acalypha wilkesiana*, illus. p.139.

Coprosma

RUBIACEAE

Genus of evergreen shrubs and trees, grown for their foliage and fruits. Separate male and female plants are needed to obtain fruits. Half hardy to frost tender, min. 2–5°C (36–41°F). Prefers full light and well-drained soil. Water containerized specimens freely in summer, moderately at other times. Propagate by seed in spring or by semi-ripe cuttings in late summer.
C. baueri of gardens. See *C. repens*.
C. baueriana. See *C. repens*.
C. × kirkii. Evergreen, prostrate, then semi-erect, densely branched shrub. H to 1m (3ft), S 1.2–2m (4–6ft). Half hardy. Narrowly oblong to lance-shaped, leathery, glossy leaves are borne singly or in small clusters. In late spring has insignificant flowers, followed on female plants by tiny, egg-shaped, translucent, white fruits with red speckles. **'Variegata'** illus. p.171.
C. repens, syn. *C. baueri* of gardens, *C. baueriana.* Evergreen, spreading, then erect shrub. H and S to 2m (6ft). Frost tender, min. 2°C (36°F). Has broadly oval, leathery, lustrous, rich green leaves. Carries insignificant flowers in late spring, followed on female plants by egg-shaped, orange-red fruits from late summer to autumn. Leaves of ♀ **'Picturata'** each have a central, cream blotch.

Coquito. See *Jubaea chilensis*, illus. p.81.
Coral berry. See *Aechmea fulgens*.
Coral bush. See *Templetonia retusa*.
Coral cactus. See *Rhipsalis cereuscula*, illus. p.477.
Coral drops. See *Bessera elegans*.
Coral gem. See *Lotus berthelotii*, illus. p.293.
Coral honeysuckle. See *Lonicera sempervirens*, illus. p.206.
Coral pea. See *Hardenbergia violacea*.
Coral plant. See *Berberidopsis corallina*, illus. p.207; *Russelia equisetiformis*, illus. p.254.
Coral tree
Flame. See *Erythrina coralloides*.
Naked. See *Erythrina coralloides*.
Coral vine. See *Antigonon*.
Coral-bark maple. See *Acer palmatum* 'Sango-kaku', illus. p.120
Coralberry. See *Ardisia crenata*, illus. p.146; *Symphoricarpos orbiculatus*.
Coral-tree, Cockspur. See *Erythrina crista-galli*, illus. p.139.

Cordyline

AGAVACEAE

Genus of evergreen shrubs and trees, grown primarily for their foliage, although some also have decorative flowers. Half hardy to frost tender, min. 5–16°C (41–61°F). Provide fertile, well-drained soil and full light or partial shade. Water potted plants moderately, less in winter. Propagate by seed or suckers in spring or by stem cuttings in summer. Red spider mite may be a nuisance.
♀ ***C. australis***, syn. *Dracaena australis* (New Zealand cabbage palm). Slow-growing, evergreen, sparsely branched tree. H 15m (50ft) or more, S 5m (15ft) or more. Half hardy. Each stem is crowned by a rosette of strap-shaped, 30cm–1m (1–3ft) long leaves. Has small, scented, white flowers in large, open panicles in summer and, in autumn, globose, white fruits. **'Atropurpurea'** illus. p.95. Long, sword-shaped leaves of **'Veitchii'** have red bases and midribs.
C. fruticosa, syn. *C. terminalis* (Good-luck plant, Ti tree). Slow-growing, evergreen, upright shrub, sparingly branched and suckering. H 2–4m (6–12ft), S 1–2m (3–6ft). Frost tender, min. 13°C (55°F). Broadly lance-shaped, glossy, deep green leaves are 30–60cm (1–2ft) long. Produces branched panicles of small, white, purplish or reddish flowers in summer. Foliage of ♀ **'Baptisii'** is deep green with pink and yellow stripes and spots. **'Imperialis'** has red- or pink-marked, deep green leaves.
C. indivisa, syn. *Dracaena indivisa.* Slow-growing, evergreen, erect tree or shrub. H 3m (10ft) or more, S 2m (6ft). Half hardy. Bears lance-shaped, 60cm–2m (2–6ft) long, green leaves, orange-brown veined above, blue-grey tinted beneath. In summer tiny, star-shaped, white flowers in dense clusters, 60cm (2ft) or more long, are followed by tiny, spherical, blue-purple fruits.
C. terminalis. See *C. fruticosa*.

Coreopsis
Tickseed

COMPOSITAE/ASTERACEAE

Genus of annuals and perennials, grown for their daisy-like flower heads. Fully to frost hardy. Needs full sun and fertile, well-drained soil. Propagate annuals by seed in spring; *C. lanceolata* by seed or division in spring; *C. auriculata* 'Superba', *C.* 'Goldfink' and *C. grandiflora* 'Badengold' by softwood cuttings or division in spring or summer; and *C. verticillata* by division in spring.
C. auriculata **'Superba'.** Bushy perennial. H and S 45cm (18in). Fully hardy. Daisy-like, rich yellow flower heads, with central, purple blotches, are borne in summer. Oval to lance-shaped leaves are lobed and light green. Some plants grown as *C. auriculata* are the closely related annual *C. basalis*.
***C.* 'Goldfink'.** Short-lived, dwarf, bushy perennial. H and S 30cm (12in). Fully hardy. Sprays of daisy-like, deep yellow flower heads appear in summer above narrowly oval, deep green leaves.
C. grandiflora **'Badengold'.** Short-lived, erect perennial with lax stems. H 75cm (30in), S 60cm (24in). Fully hardy. Bears large, daisy-like, rich buttercup-yellow flower heads in summer and broadly lance-shaped, divided, bright green leaves.
C. lanceolata illus. p.305.
***C.* 'Sunray'** illus. p.349.
C. tinctoria illus. p.349. **'Golden Crown'** is a fast-growing, upright, bushy annual. H 60cm (24in), S 20cm (8in). Fully hardy. Has lance-shaped, deep green leaves and, in summer and early autumn, large, daisy-like, deep yellow flower heads with brown centres.
C. verticillata illus. p.305.

Coriaria

CORIARIACEAE

Genus of deciduous, spring- or summer-flowering shrubs and sub-shrubs, grown for their habit, foliage and fruits. Frost to half hardy. Needs full sun and fertile, well-drained soil. Propagate by softwood cuttings in summer or by seed in autumn. The leaves and fruits of some species may cause severe stomach upset if ingested; in other species, the fruits are edible, although the seeds are thought to be poisonous.
C. terminalis. Deciduous, arching sub-shrub. H 1m (3ft), S 2m (6ft). Frost hardy. Broadly lance-shaped, fern-like, mid-green leaves turn red in autumn. Minute, green flowers in late spring are succeeded by small, spherical, black fruits. var. ***xanthocarpa*** illus. p.169.

Cork oak. See *Quercus suber*, illus. p.69
Cork tree, Amur. See *Phellodendron amurense*.
Corkscrew rush. See *Juncus effusus* f. *spiralis*, illus. p.320.
Corn
Indian. See *Zea*.
Sweet. See *Zea mays*.
Corn cockle. See *Agrostemma*.
Corn plant. See *Dracaena fragrans*.
Corn poppy. See *Papaver rhoeas*.
Cornel, Bentham's. See *Cornus capitata*.
Cornelian cherry. See *Cornus mas*.
Cornflower. See *Centaurea cyanus*.
Cornish elm. See *Ulmus minor* 'Cornubiensis'.
Cornish golden elm. See *Ulmus minor* 'Dicksonii', illus. p.77.
Cornish heath. See *Erica vagans*.

Cornus
Dogwood

CORNACEAE

Genus of deciduous shrubs and deciduous or evergreen trees, grown for their flowers, foliage or brightly coloured winter stems. Fully to half hardy. Needs sun or semi-shade and fertile, well-drained soil. Those grown for winter stem colour do best in full sun. *C. florida, C. kousa* and *C. nuttallii* dislike shallow, chalky soil. *C. canadensis* prefers acid soil. Plants grown for their stems should be cut back almost to ground level each year in early spring. Propagate *C. alba* and

C. stolonifera 'Flaviramea' by softwood cuttings in summer or by hardwood cuttings in autumn or winter; variegated forms of *C. alternifolia* and *C. controversa* by grafting in winter; *C. canadensis* by division in spring or autumn; *C. capitata, C. florida* and *C. kousa* by seed in autumn or by softwood cuttings in summer; *C. nuttallii* by seed in autumn; all others described here by softwood cuttings in summer. The fruits of some species may cause mild stomach upset if ingested; contact with the leaf hairs may irritate skin.
C. alba (Red-barked dogwood). Vigorous, deciduous, upright, then spreading shrub. H and S 3m (10ft). Fully hardy. Young shoots are bright red in winter. Has oval, dark green leaves, often red or orange in autumn. Bears flattened heads of star-shaped, creamy-white flowers in late spring and early summer, followed by spherical, sometimes blue-tinted, white fruits. ♀ **'Elegantissima'** illus. p.134. **'Gouchaultii'** has pink-flushed leaves broadly edged with yellow. **'Kesselringii'** illus. p.144. ♀ **'Sibirica'** illus. p.146. ♀ **'Spaethii'** illus. p.142.
C. alternifolia. Deciduous, spreading tree or bushy shrub, with tiered branches. H and S 6m (20ft). Fully hardy. Oval, bright green leaves, which each taper to a point, often turn red in autumn. Clusters of tiny, star-shaped, creamy-white flowers in early summer are followed by small, rounded, blue-black fruits. ♀ **'Argentea'** illus. p.85.
♀ ***C. canadensis***, syn. *Chamaepericlymenum canadense*, illus. p.386.
C. capitata, syn. *Dendrobenthamia capitata* (Bentham's cornel). Evergreen or semi-evergreen, spreading tree. H and S up to 12m (40ft). Frost to half hardy. Pale yellow bracts, surrounding insignificant flowers, appear in early summer, followed by large, strawberry-like, red fruits. Has oval, grey-green leaves. Is good for mild coastal areas.
C. controversa. Deciduous tree with layered branches. H and S 15m (50ft). Fully hardy. Clusters of small, star-shaped, white flowers appear in summer. Leaves are oval, pointed and bright green, turning purple in autumn. ♀ **'Variegata'** illus. p.85.
♀ ***C.* 'Eddie's White Wonder'** illus. p.92.
C. florida (Flowering dogwood). Deciduous, spreading tree. H 6m (20ft), S 8m (25ft). Fully hardy. In late spring bears white or pinkish-white bracts surrounding tiny, insignificant flowers. Oval, pointed, dark green leaves turn red and purple in autumn. **'Apple Blossom'** has pale pink bracts. f. ***rubra*** bears pink or red bracts. **'Spring Song'** illus. p.86. **'Welchii'** illus. p.89. **'White Cloud'** illus. p.81.
C. kousa. Deciduous, vase-shaped tree or shrub. H 7m (22ft), S 5m (15ft). Fully hardy. Flower heads of large, white bracts, surrounding insignificant flowers, appear in early summer, followed, after a hot summer, by strawberry-like fruits. Oval, glossy, dark green leaves turn bright red-purple in autumn. ♀ var. ***chinensis*** has larger flower heads and more narrowly pointed bracts.
C. macrophylla illus. p.74.
C. mas (Cornelian cherry). Deciduous, spreading, open shrub or tree. H and S 5m (15ft). Fully hardy. Oval, dark green leaves change to reddish-purple in autumn. Produces small, star-shaped, yellow flowers on bare shoots in late winter and early spring, then edible, oblong, bright red fruits. **'Aureoelegantissima'** (syn. *C.m.* 'Elegantissima'), H 2m (6ft), S 3m (10ft). has pink-tinged leaves edged with yellow. **'Elegantissima'** see *C.m.* 'Aureoelegantissima'.
♀ **'Variegata'** illus. p.115.
♀ ***C.* 'Norman Hadden'.** Deciduous, spreading tree. H and S 8m (25ft). Fully hardy. Creamy-white bracts around tiny flowers turn to deep pink in summer. These are often followed by strawberry-like fruits in autumn.
C. nuttallii illus. p.72
♀ ***C.* 'Porlock'** illus. p.82.
♀ ***C. stolonifera* 'Flaviramea'.** Vigorous, deciduous, spreading shrub with creeping, underground stems. H 2m (6ft), S 4m (12ft). Fully hardy. Has bright greenish-yellow, young shoots in winter and oval, dark green leaves. Small, star-shaped, white flowers appear in late spring and early summer, and are followed by spherical, white fruits.

COROKIA

ESCALLONIACEAE

Genus of evergreen shrubs, grown for their habit, foliage, flowers and fruits. Is good in mild, coastal areas, where it is very wind-tolerant. Frost to half hardy; in cold areas protect from strong winds. Needs full sun and fertile, well-drained soil. Propagate by softwood cuttings in summer.
C. buddlejoides. Evergreen, upright shrub. H 3m (10ft), S 2m (6ft). Half hardy. Has slender, grey shoots and narrowly oblong, glossy, dark green leaves. Produces panicles of star-shaped, yellow flowers in late spring, followed by spherical, blackish-red fruits.
C. cotoneaster illus. p.148.
C. × virgata. Evergreen, upright, dense shrub. H and S 3m (10ft). Frost hardy. Leaves are oblong and glossy, dark green above, white beneath. Produces star-shaped, yellow flowers in mid-spring, then egg-shaped, bright orange fruits. Makes a good hedge, especially in coastal areas.

CORONILLA

LEGUMINOSAE/PAPILIONACEAE

Genus of deciduous or evergreen shrubs and perennials, grown for their foliage and flowers. Fully to half hardy; in cold areas grow half hardy species against a south- or west-facing wall. Requires full sun and light, well-drained soil. Propagate by softwood cuttings in summer.
C. glauca. See *C. valentina* subsp. *glauca*.
♀ ***C. valentina*** subsp. ***glauca,*** syn. *C. glauca*, illus. p.153.

CORREA

RUTACEAE

Genus of evergreen shrubs, grown for their flowers. Half hardy to frost tender, min. 3–5°C (37–41°F). Prefers full light or partial shade and fertile, well-drained, neutral to acid soil. Water potted specimens moderately, less when not in flower. Propagate by seed in spring or by semi-ripe cuttings in late summer.
♀ ***C. backhouseana.*** Evergreen, rounded, well-branched shrub. H and S 2m (6ft). Half hardy. Leaves are oval to elliptic and dark green, with dense, pale buff down beneath. Tubular, pale yellow-green to white flowers appear in spring and intermittently until autumn.
C. × harrisii. See *C.* 'Mannii'.
***C.* 'Harrisii'.** See *C.* 'Mannii'.
♀ ***C.* 'Mannii',** syn. *C. × harrisii, C.* 'Harrisii'. Evergreen, bushy, slender-stemmed shrub. H and S 2m (6ft). Frost tender. Has narrowly oval leaves with short hairs beneath. Tubular, scarlet flowers are carried in summer-autumn, sometimes in other seasons.
♀ ***C. pulchella*** illus. p.170.
C. reflexa, syn. *C. speciosa.* Evergreen, bushy, slender-stemmed shrub. H and S to 2m (6ft). Frost tender. Oval leaves have thick down beneath. Bears tubular, greenish-yellow to crimson or rose flowers, with greenish-white petal tips, in summer-autumn, sometimes in other seasons.
C. speciosa. See *C. reflexa*.

Corsican heath. See *Erica terminalis*.
Corsican mint. See *Mentha requienii*.
Corsican pine. See *Pinus nigra* subsp. *laricio*.

CORTADERIA

GRAMINEAE/POACEAE

See also GRASSES, BAMBOOS, RUSHES and SEDGES.
C. selloana (Pampas grass). Evergreen, clump-forming, stately, perennial grass. H to 2.5m (8ft), S 1.2m (4ft). Frost hardy. Has narrow, very sharp-edged, outward-curving leaves, 1.5m (5ft) long. In late summer, erect, plume-like, silvery panicles, up to 60cm (2ft) long, are borne above mid-green leaves. Male and female flowers are produced on separate plants; females, with long, silky hairs, are more decorative.
♀ **'Aureolineata'** (syn. *C.s.* 'Gold Band'), H to 2.2m (7ft), is compact, and has leaves with rich yellow margins ageing to dark golden-yellow. **'Gold Band'** see *C.s.* 'Aureolineata'.**'Silver Comet'** and ♀ **'Sunningdale Silver'** illus. p.318.

CORTUSA

PRIMULACEAE

Genus of clump-forming, spring- and summer-flowering perennials, related to *Primula*, with one-sided racemes of bell-shaped flowers. Fully hardy. Is not suited to hot, dry climates as needs shade and humus-rich, moist soil. Propagate by seed when fresh or by division in autumn.
C. matthioli illus. p.366.

CORYDALIS

PAPAVERACEAE

Genus of spring- and summer-flowering annuals and tuberous or fibrous-rooted perennials, some of which are evergreen, grown for their tubular, spurred, 2-lipped flowers or for their fern-like leaves. Fully to frost hardy. Needs full sun or partial shade and well-drained soil; some require humus-rich soil and cool growing conditions. Propagate by seed in autumn or by division when dormant: autumn for spring-flowering species, spring for summer-flowering species.
C. ambigua of gardens. See *C. fumariifolia*.
C. bulbosa of gardens. See *C. cava*.
C. cashmeriana. Tuft-forming, fibrous-rooted perennial. H 10–25cm (4–10in), S 8–10cm (3–4in). Fully hardy. Has divided, semi-erect, basal leaves and, in summer, dense spikes of 2-lipped, brilliant blue flowers. Needs cool, partially shaded, humus-rich, neutral to acid soil. Is good for a rock garden. Dies down in winter.
C. cava, syn. *C. bulbosa* of gardens. Spring-flowering, tuberous perennial. H 10–20cm (4–8in), S 8–10cm (3–4in). Fully hardy. Leaves are semi-erect, basal and much divided. Carries dense spikes of tubular, dull purple flowers. Dies down in summer.
C. cheilanthifolia illus. p.361.
C. diphylla illus. p.379.
C. fumariifolia, syn. *C. ambigua* of gardens. Tuberous perennial, flowering from spring to early summer. H to 15cm (6in), S to 10cm (4in). Fully hardy. Stem bears much-divided leaves and a short spike of 2-lipped, azure blue or purplish-blue flowers, with flattened, triangular spurs. Dies down in summer.
C. halleri. See *C. solida*.
C. lutea, syn. *Pseudofumaria lutea*, illus. p.371.
C. nobilis. Perennial with long, fleshy, fibrous roots. H and S 20–35cm (8–14in). Fully hardy. Bears much-divided leaves on lower part of flower stems, each of which carries a dense spike of long-spurred, pale yellow flowers, with lips tipped green or brown, in early summer.
C. ochroleuca, syn. *Pseudofumaria ochroleuca*, illus. p.363.
C. popovii illus. p.376.
C. solida, syn. *C. halleri.* Tuft-forming, tuberous perennial. H 10–20cm (4–8in), S 8–12cm (3–5in). Fully hardy. Leaves alternate on flower stems, each of which carries a dense spike of dull purplish-red flowers in spring. Dies down in summer. ♀ **'George Baker'** (syn. *C.s.* 'G.P. Baker') illus. p.379.
C. wilsonii illus. p.361.

CORYLOPSIS

HAMAMELIDACEAE

Genus of deciduous shrubs and trees, grown for their fragrant, yellow flowers, which are produced before hazel-like leaves emerge. Fully hardy, but late frosts may damage flowers. Prefers semi-shade and fertile, moist but well-drained, acid soil. Propagate by softwood cuttings in summer or by seed in autumn.
C. glabrescens illus. p.113.

♀ ***C. pauciflora*** illus. p.127.
♀ ***C. sinensis***, syn. *C. willmottiae.* Vigorous, deciduous, spreading, open shrub. H and S 4m (12ft). Leaves are bright green above, blue-green beneath. Clusters of bell-shaped, pale yellow flowers open from early to mid-spring. **'Spring Purple'** has deep plum-purple, young leaves.
C. spicata. Deciduous, spreading, open shrub. H 2m (6ft), S 3m (10ft). Bristle-toothed leaves are dull, pale green above, blue-green beneath. Drooping clusters of bell-shaped, pale yellow flowers are borne in mid-spring.
C. willmottiae. See *C. sinensis.*

CORYLUS
Hazel

CORYLACEAE

Genus of deciduous trees and shrubs, grown for their habit, catkins and often edible fruits (nuts). Fully hardy. Prefers sun or semi-shade and fertile, well-drained soil. Cut out suckers as they arise. Propagate species by seed in autumn, cultivars by grafting in late summer or by suckers or layering in late autumn to early spring. Mildew may cause defoliation; other fungi and insects may spoil nuts.
C. avellana (Cobnut). ♀ **'Contorta'** illus. p.121.
♀ ***C. colurna*** (Turkish hazel). Deciduous, conical tree. H 20m (70ft), S 7m (22ft). Has broadly oval, strongly toothed, almost lobed, dark green leaves. Long, yellow catkins are borne in late winter. Clusters of nuts are set in fringed husks.
C. maxima (Filbert). Vigorous, deciduous, bushy, open shrub or tree. H 6m (20ft), S 5m (15ft). Bears oval, toothed, mid-green leaves, long, yellow catkins in late winter and edible, egg-shaped, brown nuts. ♀ **'Purpurea'** illus. p.118.

CORYNOCARPUS

CORYNOCARPACEAE

Genus of evergreen trees, grown for their foliage and overall appearance. Frost tender, min. 7–10°C (45–50°F). Needs full light or partial shade and fertile, moisture-retentive but well-drained soil. Water containerized specimens moderately, less when temperatures are low. Pruning is tolerated if necessary. Propagate by seed when ripe or by semi-ripe cuttings in summer.
C. laevigatus illus. p.81.

CORYPHANTHA

CACTACEAE

Genus of perennial cacti with roughly spherical, spiny, green stems. Stems have elongated areoles in grooves running along upper sides of tubercles; many species only show this groove on very old plants. Funnel-shaped flowers are produced in summer, followed by cylindrical, green seed pods. Frost tender, min. 5°C (41°F). Needs a site in full sun with very well-drained soil. Propagate by seed in spring or summer.
C. cornifera, syn. *C. radians*, illus. p.495.
C. radians. See *C. cornifera.*
C. vivipara. See *Escobaria vivipara.*

COSMOS

COMPOSITAE/ASTERACEAE

Genus of summer- and early autumn-flowering annuals and tuberous perennials. Fully hardy to frost tender, min. 5°C (41°F). Needs sun and does best in moist but well-drained soil. In mild areas, tubers of half hardy *C. atrosanguineus* may be overwintered in ground if protected with a deep mulch. Propagate half-hardy species by basal cuttings in spring, annuals by seed in autumn or spring.
C. atrosanguineus, syn. *Bidens atrosanguinea*, illus. p.253.
C. bipinnatus. Upright, bushy annual. H to 1.5m (5ft), S 45cm (1½ft). Half hardy. Has feathery, mid-green leaves, and, throughout summer, produces solitary, bowl- or saucer-shaped flower heads in white, pink, or crimson, with yellow centres. **'Candy Stripe'**, H to 90cm (3ft), has white flower heads, edged and flecked with crimson. **'Sea Shells'**, H to 90cm (3ft), produces carmine-red, pink, or white flower heads with tubular florets. **Sensation Series** illus. p.337.
***C. sulphureus* Ladybird Series.** Group of upright, bushy annuals. H 30–40cm (12–16in), S 20cm (8in). Frost tender. Has feathery, mid-green leaves, and in summer produces clusters of semi-double, bowl-shaped flower heads in yellow, orange, or scarlet, with black centres.

Cosmos, Chocolate. See *Cosmos atrosanguineus*, illus. p.253.

COSTUS

ZINGIBERACEAE

Genus of mostly clump-forming, rhizomatous perennials, grown for their showy, solitary or paired, tubular flowers with basal bracts. Frost tender, min. 18°C (64°F). Grow in a humid atmosphere, out of direct sunlight, in humus-rich soil. Propagate by division in spring. Pot-grown plants may be attacked by red spider mite.
C. speciosus (Malay ginger). Clump-forming, rhizomatous perennial. H 2m (6ft) or more, S 1m (3ft). Has narrowly oval, downy leaves, to 25cm (10in) long. Reddish bracts are spine-tipped, each surrounding one white or pink-flushed flower, to 10cm (4in) wide with a broad, yellow-centred lip; flowers are produced intermittently throughout the year.

COTINUS

ANACARDIACEAE

Genus of deciduous shrubs and trees, grown for their foliage, flower heads and autumn colour. Individual flowers are inconspicuous. Fully hardy. Requires a position in full sun or semi-shade, with fertile but not over-rich soil. Purple-leaved forms need full sun to bring out their best colours. Propagate species by softwood or greenwood cuttings in summer or by seed in autumn, cultivars by cuttings only in summer.
C. americanus. See *C. obovatus.*
♀ ***C. coggygria***, syn. *Rhus cotinus* (Smoke tree, Venetian sumach). Deciduous, bushy shrub. H and S 5m (15ft). Leaves are rounded or oval and light green, becoming yellow or red in autumn. From late summer, as insignificant fruits develop, masses of tiny flower stalks form showy, pale fawn, later grey, plume-like clusters. **'Flame'** see *C.* 'Flame'.**'Notcutt's Variety'** illus. p.117. ♀ **'Royal Purple'** has deep pink plumes and deep purplish-red leaves.
♀ ***C.* 'Flame',** syn. *C. coggygria* 'Flame', illus. p.120
♀ ***C. obovatus***, syn. *C. americanus, Rhus cotinoides.* Vigorous, deciduous, bushy shrub or tree. H 10m (30ft), S 8m (25ft). Has large, oval leaves that are bronze-pink when young, maturing to mid-green and turning orange, red and purple in autumn.

COTONEASTER

ROSACEAE

Genus of deciduous, semi-evergreen or evergreen shrubs and trees, grown for their foliage, flowers and fruits. Some species make fine specimen plants; others may be used for hedging or ground cover. Fully to frost hardy. Deciduous species and cultivars prefer full sun, but evergreens do well in either sun or semi-shade. All resent waterlogged soil and are particularly useful for dry sites. Propagate species by cuttings in summer or by seed in autumn, hybrids and cultivars by cuttings only, in summer. Take semi-ripe cuttings for evergreens and semi-evergreens, softwood cuttings for deciduous plants. Fireblight is a common problem. The seeds may cause mild stomach upset if ingested.
♀ ***C. adpressus.*** Deciduous, arching shrub. H 30cm (1ft), S 2m (6ft). Fully hardy. Rounded, wavy-edged, dark green leaves redden in autumn. Produces small, 5-petalled, pink flowers in early summer, then spherical, red fruits.
***C.* 'Autumn Fire'.** See *C.* 'Herbstfeuer'.
C. bullatus* 'Firebird',** syn. *C.* 'Firebird'. Deciduous, bushy, open shrub. H and S 3m (10ft). Fully hardy. Large, oval, deeply veined, dark green leaves redden in autumn. Small, 5-petalled, white flowers in early summer are followed by masses of spherical, bright red fruits. var. ***macrophyllus see *C. rehderi.*
♀ ***C. cashmiriensis***, syn. *C. cochleatus* of gardens, *C. microphyllus* var. *cochleatus* of gardens. Evergreen, prostrate shrub. H to 45cm (1½ft), S 2m (6ft). Has small, oval, notched, dark green leaves. Small, white flowers are produced in late spring, followed by spherical, red fruits.
C. cochleatus of gardens. See *C. cashmiriensis.*
C. congestus. Evergreen, prostrate shrub. H 20cm (8in), S 2m (6ft). Fully hardy. Forms dense mounds of oval, dull green leaves. Produces small, 5-petalled, pinkish-white flowers in early summer, followed by spherical, bright red fruits. Is excellent for a rock garden.
C. conspicuus, syn. *C.c.* var. *decorus.* Evergreen, prostrate, arching shrub. H 30cm (1ft), S 2–3m (6–10ft). Fully hardy. Leaves are oblong, glossy, very dark green. Small, 5-petalled, white flowers in late spring are succeeded by large, spherical, scarlet or orange-red fruits.
***C.* 'Coral Beauty'.** Evergreen, arching, dense shrub. H 1m (3ft), S 2m (6ft). Fully hardy. Has small, oval, glossy, dark green leaves and, in early summer, produces small, 5-petalled, white flowers. Fruits are spherical and bright orange-red.
♀ ***C.* 'Cornubia'** illus. p.120.
C. dielsianus. Deciduous, arching shrub. H and S 2.5m (8ft). Fully hardy. Slender shoots are clothed in oval, dark green leaves. Produces small, 5-petalled, pink flowers in early summer, followed by spherical, glossy, red fruits.
C. divaricatus illus. p.126.
***C.* 'Exburiensis'.** Evergreen or semi-evergreen, arching shrub. H and S 5m (15ft). Frost hardy. Has narrowly lance-shaped, bright green leaves, small, 5-petalled, white flowers, in early summer, and spherical, yellow fruits, sometimes tinged pink later.
***C.* 'Firebird'.** See *C. bullatus* 'Firebird'.
C. franchetii. Evergreen or semi-evergreen, arching shrub. H and S 3m (10ft). Fully hardy. Oval, grey-green leaves are white beneath. Bears small, 5-petalled, pink-tinged, white flowers in early summer, then a profusion of oblong, bright orange-red fruits. var. ***sternianus*** see *C. sternianus.*
C. frigidus (Tree cotoneaster). Vigorous, deciduous tree, upright when young, arching when mature. H and S 10m (30ft). Fully hardy. Has large, broadly oval, wavy-edged, dull green leaves and broad heads of small, 5-petalled, white flowers borne in early summer, followed by large clusters of long-lasting, small, spherical, bright red fruits.
C. glaucophyllus. Evergreen, arching, open shrub. H and S 3m (10ft). Fully hardy. Leaves are oval, dark green, bluish-white beneath. Produces small, 5-petalled, white flowers in mid-summer, followed by small, spherical, deep red fruits in autumn. var. ***serotinus*** see *C. serotinus.*
***C.* 'Gnom',** syn. *C.* 'Gnome', *C. salicifolius* 'Gnom'. Evergreen, prostrate shrub. H 20cm (8in), S 2m (6ft). Fully hardy. Bears narrowly lance-shaped, dark green leaves, small, 5-petalled, white flowers, in early summer, and clusters of small, spherical, red fruits. Makes good ground cover.
***C.* 'Gnome'.** See *C.* 'Gnom'.
***C.* 'Herbstfeuer',** syn. *C.* 'Autumn Fire'. Evergreen, prostrate or arching shrub. H 30cm (1ft), S 2m (6ft). Fully hardy. Has lance-shaped, bright green leaves. Small, 5-petalled, white flowers in early summer are followed by spherical, bright red fruits. May be grown as ground cover or as a weeping standard.
♀ ***C. horizontalis*** illus. p.168.
C. hupehensis. Deciduous, arching shrub. H 2m (6ft), S 3m (10ft). Fully hardy. Oval, bright green leaves become yellow in autumn. Masses of small, 5-petalled, white flowers in late spring are succeeded by large, spherical, bright red fruits.
***C.* 'Hybridus Pendulus'.** Evergreen, prostrate shrub, almost always grown

as a weeping standard. H 2m (6ft), S 1.5m (5ft). Frost hardy. Has oblong, dark green leaves. Small, 5-petalled, white flowers in early summer are followed by spherical, deep red fruits.
♀ ***C. lacteus*** illus. p.121.
C. linearifolius, syn. *C. microphyllus* var. *thymifolius* of gardens. Evergreen, prostrate shrub. H 60cm (2ft), S 2m (6ft). Fully hardy. Rigid branches bear tiny, narrow, blunt-ended, glossy leaves. Produces small, white flowers in late spring, followed by spherical red fruits.
C. microphyllus. Evergreen, spreading, dense shrub. H 1m (3ft), S 2m (6ft). Fully hardy. Rigid shoots are clothed in small, oval, dark green leaves. Small, 5-petalled, white flowers in late spring are followed by spherical, red fruits. var. ***cochleatus*** of gardens see *C. cashmiriensis*. var. ***thymifolius*** of gardens see *C. linearifolius*.
C. prostratus of gardens. See *C. rotundifolius*.
C. rehderi, syn. *C. bullatus* var. *macrophyllus*. Deciduous, bushy, open shrub. H 5m (15ft), S 3m (10ft). Fully hardy. Very large, oval, deeply veined, dark green leaves change to red in autumn. Clusters of small, 5-petalled, pink flowers appear in late spring and early summer, succeeded by spherical, bright red fruits.
♀ ***C. 'Rothschildianus'.*** Evergreen or semi-evergreen, arching shrub. H and S 5m (15ft). Frost hardy. Has narrowly oval, bright green leaves, small, 5-petalled, white flowers, in early summer, and large clusters of spherical, golden-yellow fruits.
C. rotundifolius, syn. *C. prostratus* of gardens. Evergreen, arching shrub. H 1.5m (5ft), S 2.5m (8ft). Fully hardy. Has small, oval, glossy, dark green leaves. Produces small, 5-petalled, white flowers in early summer, followed by spherical, deep red fruits.
C. salicifolius. Vigorous, evergreen, arching shrub. H and S 5m (15ft). Fully hardy. Has narrowly lance-shaped, dark green leaves. Small, 5-petalled, white flowers, in early summer, are followed by clusters of small, spherical, red fruits. **'Gnom'** see *C.* 'Gnom'.
C. serotinus, syn. *C. glaucophyllus* var. *serotinus*. Evergreen, arching, open shrub. H and S 6m (20ft). Fully hardy. Has oval, dark green leaves. Small white flowers are borne from mid- to late summer and the fruits last until spring.
♀ ***C. simonsii*** illus. p.144
C. 'Skogholm', syn. *C.* 'Skogsholmen'. Evergreen, arching, wide-spreading shrub. H 60cm (2ft), S 3m (10ft). Fully hardy. Leaves are small, oval and glossy, dark green. Bears small, 5-petalled, white flowers during early summer, then rather sparse, spherical, red fruits. Makes good ground cover.
C. 'Skogsholmen'. See *C.* 'Skogholm'.
♀ ***C. sternianus***, syn. *C. franchetii* var. *sternianus*, illus. p.145.
♀ ***C. × watereri* 'John Waterer'.** Vigorous, evergreen or semi-evergreen, arching shrub. H and S 5m (15ft). Frost hardy. Has lance-shaped, dark green leaves. Bears small, 5-petalled, white flowers, in early summer, and produces a profusion of spherical, red fruits in large clusters.

Cotoneaster, Tree. See *Cotoneaster frigidus*.
Cotton ball. See *Espostoa lanata*, illus. p.473.
Cotton lavender. See *Santolina chamaecyparissus*.
Cotton rose. See *Hibiscus mutabilis*.
Cotton thistle. See *Onopordum acanthium*, illus. p.334.
Cotton tree, Silk. See *Ceiba pentandra*.
Cottonwood. See *Populus deltoides*.
Black. See *Populus trichocarpa*.
Eastern. See *Populus deltoides*.

COTULA

COMPOSITAE/ASTERACEAE

Genus of perennials and a few marginal water plants, most of which are evergreen, grown for their neat foliage and button-like flower heads. Many species are useful for cracks in paving stones, but may be invasive. Fully to frost hardy. Most need a position in full sun, with well-drained soil that is not too dry. Propagate by division in spring.
C. atrata. See *Leptinella atrata*.
C. coronopifolia (Brass buttons). Short-lived, deciduous, perennial, marginal water plant. H 15cm (6in), S 30cm (12in). Frost hardy. Has fleshy stems, small, lance-shaped, mid-green leaves and, in summer, button-like, yellow flower heads.

COTYLEDON

CRASSULACEAE

Genus of evergreen, succulent shrubs and sub-shrubs, grown for their diverse foliage that ranges from large, oval, grey leaves to small, cylindrical, mid-green leaves. Frost tender, min. 5–7°C (41–5°F). Likes a sunny or partially shaded site and very well-drained soil. Propagate by seed or stem cuttings in spring or summer.
C. cooperi. See *Adromischus cooperi*.
C. ladismithensis illus. p.490.
C. orbiculata. Evergreen, upright, succulent shrub. H and S 50cm (20in) or more. min. 7°C (45°F). Swollen stem bears thin, oval, mid-green leaves, densely coated in white wax and sometimes red-edged. Flower stems, to 70cm (28in) long, have pendent, tubular, orange flowers in autumn. var. ***oblonga*** (syn. *C. undulata*) illus. p.484.
C. paniculata. See *Tylecodon paniculatus*.
C. reticulata. See *Tylecodon reticulatus*.
C. simplicifolia. See *Chiastophyllum oppositifolium*.
C. undulata. See *C. orbiculata* var. *oblonga*.
C. wallichii. See *Tylecodon wallichii*.

Coulter pine. See *Pinus coulteri*, illus. p.98.
Cow's-tail pine. See *Cephalotaxus harringtonii*.
Cowslip. See *Primula veris*, illus. p.281.
Giant. See *Primula florindae*, illus. p.281.
Crab
Purple. See *Malus × purpurea*.
Siberian. See *Malus baccata*.
Crab apple. See *Malus*.
Crab cactus. See *Schlumbergera truncata*, illus. p.489.
Crack willow. See *Salix fragilis*.
Cradle orchid. See *Anguloa clowesii*.

CRAMBE

BRASSICACEAE/CRUCIFERAE

Genus of annuals and perennials, grown for their bold leaves and large sprays of white flowers in summer. Leaf shoots of *C. maritima* (Sea kale) are eaten as a spring vegetable. Fully hardy. Will grow in any well-drained soil; prefers an open position in full sun but tolerates some shade. Propagate by division in spring or by seed in autumn or spring.
♀ ***C. cordifolia*** illus. p.224.
♀ ***C. maritima*** illus. p.286.

Cranesbill. See *Geranium*.
Bloody. See *Geranium sanguineum*, illus. p.366.
Meadow. See *Geranium pratense*.
Crape myrtle. See *Lagerstroemia indica*, illus. p.87.

CRASPEDIA

COMPOSITAE/ASTERACEAE

Genus of basal-rosetted, summer-flowering perennials, some of which are best treated as annuals. Half hardy to frost tender, min. 5°C (41°F). Needs a site in sun and well-drained soil. Propagate by seed sown when very fresh in summer.
C. incana. Basal-rosetted perennial. H 20–30cm (8–12in), S 10cm (4in). Frost tender. Has narrowly oval, basal leaves, with dense, woolly, white hairs beneath, and smaller leaves on flower stem. In summer, many domed heads of 3–10 tiny, tubular, yellow flowers are produced in large, terminal clusters.

CRASSULA

CRASSULACEAE

Genus of perennial succulents and evergreen, succulent shrubs and sub-shrubs, ranging from 2cm (¾in) high, very succulent-leaved species to 5m (15ft) shrubby ones. Most are easy to grow. Frost hardy to frost tender, min. 5–7°C (41–5°F). Most prefer full sun; others like partial shade. Needs very well-drained soil and a little water in winter. Propagate by seed or stem cuttings in spring or autumn.
C. arborescens illus. p.474.
C. argentea of gardens. See *C. ovata*.
C. coccinea, syn. *Rochea coccinea*. Evergreen, erect, succulent shrub. H to 60cm (24in), S 30cm (12in) or more. Alternate pairs of fleshy, oval to oblong-oval, hairy-margined, dull green leaves, each united at the base, are arranged at right angles in 4 rows up the woody, green stems. Produces umbels of tubular, bright red flowers in summer or autumn.
C. cooperi. See *C. exilis* subsp. *cooperi*.
C. deceptor, syn. *C. deceptrix*, illus. p.492.
C. deceptrix. See *C. deceptor*.
C. exilis subsp. ***cooperi,*** syn. *C. cooperi*. Carpeting, perennial succulent. H 2cm (¾in), S 30cm (12in). Frost tender, min. 7°C (45°F). Has small, spoon- to lance-shaped, light green leaves, pitted with darker green or blackish-green marks. Produces clusters of minute, 5-petalled, white to pale pink flowers in winter.
C. falcata. See *C. perfoliata* var. *minor*.
C. lactea. Prostrate to semi-erect, perennial succulent. H 20cm (8in), S 1m (3ft). Frost tender, min. 5°C (41°F). Leaves are triangular-oval, glossy and dark green. In winter produces masses of small, 5-petalled, white flowers in terminal clusters. Likes partial shade
C. lycopodioides. See *C. muscosa*.
C. muscosa, syn. *C. lycopodioides*. Dense, bushy, woody-based, perennial succulent. H 15cm (6in), S 30cm (12in). Frost tender, min. 5°C (41°F). Bears small, scale-like, neatly overlapping, mid-green leaves arranged in 4 rows around erect stems. In spring, produces tiny, 5-petalled, greenish-yellow flowers. Likes partial shade.
C. multicava illus. p.487.
♀ ***C. ovata***, syn. *C. argentea* of gardens, *C. portulacea*, illus. p.473.
C. perfoliata var. ***minor,*** syn. *C. falcata* (Aeroplane propellor), illus. p.480.
C. portulacea. See *C. ovata*.
C. sarcocaulis illus. p.365.
C. schmidtii illus. p.489.
C. socialis illus. p.486.

+ CRATAEGOMESPILUS

ROSACEAE

Group of grafted, hybrid, deciduous trees *(Crataegus and Mespilus)*, grown for their flowers, foliage and fruits. Fully hardy. Requires sun or semi-shade and fertile, well-drained soil. Propagate by grafting in late summer.
+ *C. dardarii* (Bronvaux medlar). **'Jules d'Asnières'** is a deciduous, spreading tree. H and S 6m (20ft). Has drooping branches and spiny shoots. Variable, oval or deeply lobed, dark green leaves, grey when young, turn orange and yellow in autumn. Clusters of saucer-shaped, white, sometimes rose-tinted, flowers in late spring or early summer are followed by small, rounded, red-brown fruits.

CRATAEGUS

Hawthorn, Thorn

ROSACEAE

Genus of deciduous, or more rarely semi-evergreen, spiny, often spreading trees and shrubs, grown for their clustered, 5-petalled, occasionally double flowers in spring-summer, ornamental fruits and, in some cases, autumn colour. Fully hardy. Prefers full sun but is suitable for most sites and may be grown in any but very wet soil. Is useful for growing in polluted urban areas, exposed sites and coastal gardens. Propagate species by seed in autumn, cultivars by budding in late summer. Fireblight is sometimes a problem. The seeds may cause mild stomach upset if ingested.
C. cordata. See *C. phaenopyrum*.
C. crus-galli (Cockspur thorn). Deciduous, flat-topped tree. H 8m (25ft), S 10m (30ft). Has shoots armed with long, curved thorns and oval, glossy, dark green leaves that turn bright crimson in autumn. Clusters of white flowers, with pink anthers, in late spring are followed by long-lasting, rounded, bright red fruits.

C. crus-galli of gardens. See *C. persimilis* 'Prunifolia'.
C. ellwangeriana. Deciduous, spreading tree. H and S 6m (20ft). Broadly oval, dark green leaves are shallowly toothed and lobed. Bears clusters of white flowers, with pink anthers, in late spring, followed by rounded, glossy, crimson fruits.
C. flava illus. p.86.
C. laciniata, syn. *C. orientalis*, illus. p.81.
C. laevigata, syn. *C. oxyacantha* of gardens (Hawthorn, May). ♀ **'Paul's Scarlet'** illus. p.87. **'Punicea'** is a deciduous, spreading tree. H and S 6m (20ft). In late spring and early summer, oval, lobed, toothed, glossy, dark green leaves set off clusters of crimson flowers, which are followed by rounded, red fruits.
♀ ***C. × lavallei* 'Carrierei'.** Vigorous, deciduous, spreading tree. H 7m (22ft), S 10m (30ft). Oval, glossy, dark green leaves turn red in late autumn. Has clusters of white flowers in late spring, followed by long-lasting, rounded, orange-red fruits.
C. macrosperma var. ***acutiloba*** illus. p.90.
C. mollis. Deciduous, spreading tree. H 10m (30ft), S 12m (40ft). Large, broadly oval, lobed, dark green leaves have white-haired undersides when young. Bears heads of large, white flowers in late spring, followed by short-lived, rounded, red fruits.
C. monogyna (Common hawthorn). Deciduous, round-headed tree. H 10m (30ft), S 8m (25ft). Has broadly oval, deeply lobed, glossy, dark green leaves. Clusters of fragrant, white flowers are borne from late spring to early summer, followed by rounded, red fruits. Makes a dense hedge. **'Biflora'** (Glastonbury thorn) has flowers and leaves in mild winters as well as in spring.
C. orientalis. See *C. laciniata*.
C. oxyacantha of gardens. See *C. laevigata*.
C. pedicellata illus. p.91.
♀ ***C. persimilis* 'Prunifolia'**, syn. *C. crus-galli* of gardens, *C. × prunifolia.* Deciduous, spreading, thorny tree. H 8m (25ft), S 10m (30ft). Oval, glossy, dark green leaves turn red or orange in autumn. Has clusters of white flowers, with pink anthers, in early summer, then rounded, dark red fruits.
C. phaenopyrum, syn. *C. cordata* (Washington thorn). Deciduous, round-headed tree. H and S 10m (30ft). Broadly oval leaves are sharply lobed, glossy and dark green. Clusters of white flowers, with pink anthers, are produced from early to mid-summer, followed by rounded, glossy, red fruits that last through winter.
C. × prunifolia. See *C. persimilis* 'Prunifolia'.
C. tanacetifolia (Tansy-leaved thorn). Deciduous, upright, usually thornless tree. H 10m (30ft), S 8m (25ft). Has oval to diamond-shaped, deeply cut, grey-green leaves, clusters of fragrant, white flowers, with red anthers, in mid-summer and small, apple-shaped, yellow fruits.

Cream cups. See *Platystemon californicus*, illus. p.347.
Creeper
Canary. See *Tropaeolum peregrinum*.
Flame. See *Tropaeolum speciosum*, illus. p.206.
Rangoon. See *Quisqualis indica*, illus. p.207.
Snow. See *Porana paniculata*.
Trumpet. See *Campsis radicans*.
Virginia. See *Parthenocissus quinquefolia*.
Creeping blue blossom. See *Ceanothus thyrsiflorus* var. *repens*, illus. p.164.
Creeping bluets. See *Hedyotis michauxii*, illus. p.395.
Creeping Charlie. See *Pilea nummulariifolia*, illus. p.317.
Creeping dogwood. See *Cornus canadensis*, illus. p.386.
Creeping fig. See *Ficus pumila*.
Creeping juniper. See *Juniperus horizontalis*.
Creeping phlox. See *Phlox stolonifera*.
Creeping soft grass. See *Holcus mollis*.
Creeping willow. See *Salix repens*, illus. p.152.
Creeping zinnia. See *Sanvitalia procumbens*, illus. p.348.

CREMANTHODIUM

COMPOSITAE/ASTERACEAE

Genus of basal-rosetted perennials, grown for their pendent, half-closed, daisy-like flower heads. Is often very difficult to grow in all but very cool areas with snow cover. Dislikes winter wet. Fully to frost hardy. Needs shade and humus-rich, moist but well-drained soil. Propagate by seed when fresh.
C. reniforme. Basal-rosetted perennial. H and S 20cm (8in). Fully hardy. Leaves are large and kidney-shaped. Stout stems each carry a large, daisy-like, yellow flower head in summer.

CREPIS

Hawk's beard

COMPOSITAE/ASTERACEAE

Genus of summer-flowering annuals, biennials and perennials, some of which are evergreen, with long tap roots and leaves in flat rosettes. Many species are persistent weeds, but some are grown for their many-petalled, dandelion-like flower heads. Fully hardy. Tolerates sun or shade and prefers well-drained soil. Propagate annuals and biennials by seed in autumn, perennials by root cuttings (not from tap root) in late winter, although most species self-seed freely.
C. aurea illus. p.371.
♀ ***C. incana*** (Pink dandelion). Basal-rosetted perennial. H 20cm (8in), S 10cm (4in). Bears oblong, divided, hairy, greyish-green leaves. Uneven discs of ragged, pink flower heads are produced on stiff stems in summer. Is good for a sunny rock garden or border.
C. rubra illus. p.332.

Cress
Bitter. See *Cardamine*.
Persian stone. See *Aethionema grandiflorum*, illus. p.364.
Violet. See *Ionopsidium acaule*.
Winter. See *Barbarea vulgaris*.
Crested moss rose. See *Rosa × centifolia* 'Cristata'.
Cretan brake. See *Pteris cretica*.
Cretan dittany. See *Origanum dictamnus*.
Cricket-bat willow. See *Salix alba* var. *caerulea*.
Crimean lime. See *Tilia × euchlora*.
Crimson glory vine. See *Vitis coignetiae*, illus. p.216.

CRINODENDRON

ELAEOCARPACEAE

Genus of evergreen shrubs and trees, grown for their flowers and foliage. Frost to half hardy. Requires shade or semi-shade, with plant base in cool shade. Soil should be fertile, moist but well-drained, and acid. Propagate by softwood cuttings in summer or by seed in autumn.
♀ ***C. hookerianum***, syn. *Tricuspidaria lanceolata*, illus. p.138.

× ***Crinodonna corsii.*** See × *Amarcrinum memoria-corsii*.

CRINUM

AMARYLLIDACEAE

Genus of robust bulbs, grown for their often fragrant, funnel-shaped flowers. Frost hardy to frost tender, min. 16°C (61°F). Needs full sun, shelter and rich, well-drained soil. Propagate by offsets in spring or by seed when fresh or in spring. All parts may cause severe discomfort if ingested; contact with the sap may irritate skin.
C. americanum. Tuft-forming, spring- and summer-flowering bulb. H 40–75cm (16–30in), S 60cm (24in). Half hardy. Has 6–10 strap-shaped, semi-erect, basal leaves. Leafless stem bears a head of up to 6 fragrant, long-tubed, white flowers with narrow petals.
C. asiaticum illus. p.435.
C. bulbispermum, syn. *C. longifolium*. Summer-flowering bulb. H to 1m (3ft), S 60cm (2ft). Half hardy. Leafless flower stem has a head of fragrant, long-tubed, white or pinkish-red flowers with darker red stripes. Bears long, strap-shaped, semi-erect leaves grouped in a tuft on a short stalk.
C. longifolium. See *C. bulbispermum*.
C. macowanii. Autumn-flowering bulb. H and S 60cm (2ft) or more. Half hardy. Is similar to *C. bulbispermum*, but leaves are wavy-edged.
C. moorei illus. p.410.
♀ ***C. × powellii*** illus. p.410.
♀ **'Album'** illus. p.409.

CROCOSMIA

Montbretia

IRIDACEAE

Genus of corms, grown for their brightly coloured flowers produced mainly in summer. Forms dense clumps of sword-shaped, erect leaves. Frost hardy. Requires well-drained soil and an open, sunny site. In very cold areas, plant in a sheltered position or lift and store corms over winter. Propagate by division as growth commences in spring.
C. aurea. Tuft-forming, summer-flowering corm. H 50–75cm (20–30in), S 15–20cm (6–8in). Erect, basal leaves are long, narrow and sword-shaped. Carries a loosely branched spike of tubular, orange or yellow flowers, each 3–5cm (1–2in) long and with 6 spreading petals.
***C.* 'Bressingham Blaze'** illus. p.413.
***C.* 'Citronella'** of gardens. See *C.* 'Golden Fleece'.
***C.* 'Emily McKenzie'.** Compact, late summer-flowering corm. H to 60cm (24in), S 15–20cm (6–8in). Leaves are erect, basal and sword-shaped. Bears a dense spike of widely funnel-shaped, deep orange flowers, each with a dark mahogany throat.
***C.* 'Golden Fleece'**, syn. *C.* 'Citronella' of gardens, illus. p.415.
***C.* 'Jackanapes'** illus. p.439.
♀ ***C.* 'Lucifer'** illus. p.413
♀ ***C. masoniorum***, syn. *C. masonorum*, illus. p.413.
C. masonorum. See *C. masoniorum*.
C. paniculata, syn. *Antholyza paniculata, Curtonus paniculatus.* Summer-flowering corm. H to 1.5m (5ft), S 30–45cm (1–1½ft). Has sword-shaped, erect, basal leaves, pleated lengthways. Carries long-tubed, orange flowers on branched stems, which are strongly zig-zag in shape.
♀ ***C.* 'Star of the East'** illus. p.415.

CROCUS

IRIDACEAE

Genus of mainly spring- or autumn-flowering corms with funnel-shaped to rounded, long-tubed flowers. Has long, very narrow, semi-erect, basal leaves, each with a white line along centre, usually 1–5 per corm. Some autumn-flowering species have no leaves at flowering time, these appearing in winter or spring. Most species are less than 10cm (4in) tall when in flower and have a spread of 2.5–8cm (1–3in). Is ideal for rock gardens and for slight forcing in bowls for an early indoor display. Fully to frost hardy. Most require well-drained soil and a sunny situation; *C. banaticus* prefers moist soil and semi-shade. Plant 5–6cm (2–2½in) deep, in late summer or early autumn. Propagate in early autumn by seed or division if clumps of corms have formed. See also feature panel pp.444–5.
***C.* 'Advance'** illus. p.445. Late winter- to mid-spring-flowering corm. Fully hardy. Funnel-shaped flowers are buttercup yellow inside and paler yellow outside, suffused violet-bronze.
C. aerius of gardens. See *C. biflorus* subsp. *pulchricolor*.
C. ancyrensis. Spring-flowering corm. Frost hardy. Produces up to 7 fragrant, bright orange-yellow flowers, 5–6cm (2–2½in) long.
♀ ***C. angustifolius***, syn. *C. susianus* (Cloth-of-gold crocus). Spring-flowering corm. Fully hardy. Fragrant flowers are bright golden-yellow, striped or stained bronze outside.
C. aureus. See *C. flavus*.
C. balansae. See *C. olivieri* subsp. *balansae*.
♀ ***C. banaticus***, syn. *C. iridiflorus* illus.

p.445. Autumn-flowering corm. Fully hardy. Usually has one long-tubed, pale violet flower; outer 3 petals are much larger than inner 3. Very narrow, semi-erect, basal leaves, each with a paler line along the centre, appear in spring.
C. baytopiorum illus. p.445. Spring-flowering corm. Frost hardy. Each corm bears 1 or 2 rounded, clear torquoise-blue, slightly darker-veined flowers.
C. biflorus illus. p.445. Early spring-flowering corm. Fully hardy. Has narrow, semi-erect, basal leaves, each with a white line along the centre. Bears fragrant, white or purplish-white flowers, with yellow throats, vertically striped purple outside. subsp. ***alexandri*** has fragrant, deep violet flowers, with white insides. subsp. ***pulchricolor*** (syn. *C. aerius* of gardens) has rich deep blue flowers with golden-yellow centres.
***C.* 'Blue Bird'** illus. p.444. Late winter- to mid-spring-flowering corm. Fully hardy. Funnel-shaped flowers are white inside with deep yellow throats and violet margined with white outside.
♀ ***C.* 'Blue Pearl'** illus. p.444. Early spring-flowering corm. Fully hardy. Produces narrow, semi-erect, basal leaves, with white lines along the centres. Fragrant, long-tubed, funnel-shaped, soft lavender-blue flowers, bluish-white within, have golden-yellow throats.
C. boryi illus. p.444. Autumn-flowering corm. Frost hardy. Flowers are ivory-white, sometimes veined or flushed with mauve outside.
C. cancellatus. Autumn-flowering corm. Frost hardy. Slender flowers are pale blue, slightly striped outside. Leaves form after flowering, in spring.
♀ ***C. cartwrightianus*** illus. p.445. Autumn-flowering corm. Frost hardy. Produces leaves at same time as strongly veined, violet or white flowers, each 4–6cm (1½–2½in) across and with 3 long, bright red stigmas, similar to those of *C. sativus.*
♀ ***C. chrysanthus.*** Spring-flowering corm. Fully hardy. Scented flowers are orange-yellow throughout with deeper orange-red stigmas.
♀ ***C.* 'Cream Beauty'** illus. p.445. Spring-flowering corm. Fully hardy. Scented rich cream flowers, with deep yellow throats, are stained purplish-brown outside at base. Bears very narrow, semi-erect, basal, dark green leaves, each with a white, central line.
C. cvijicii illus. p.445. Spring-flowering corm. Fully hardy. Usually has one funnel-shaped, yellow flower. Produces very narrow, semi-erect, basal leaves, each with a white line along the centre, which scarcely show at flowering time.
C. dalmaticus illus. p.444. Spring-flowering corm. Fully hardy. Very narrow, semi-erect leaves have central, white lines. Bears 1–3 purple-veined, pale violet flowers, with yellow centres, overlaid with silver or yellow outside.
***C.* 'Dorothy'** illus. p.445. Spring-flowering corm. Fully hardy. Scented flowers are pale lemon-yellow.
***C.* 'Dutch Yellow'.** See *C.* 'Golden Yellow'.
♀ ***C.* 'E.A. Bowles'** illus. p.445. Early spring-flowering corm. Fully hardy. Has scented, funnel-shaped, deep yellow flowers, stained bronze near base on outside. Has narrow, semi-erect leaves, each with a central white line. Increases well by offsets.
♀ ***C. etruscus*** illus. p.445. Spring-flowering corm. Frost hardy. Has very narrow, semi-erect, basal, dark green leaves with central, white lines. Bears long-tubed, funnel-shaped, pale purple-blue flowers, washed silver outside, with violet veining. **'Zwanenburg'** (illus. p.444) has pale purple-blue flowers, washed with biscuit-brown and flecked violet outside.
***C.* 'Eyecatcher'** illus. p.444. Late winter- to mid-spring-flowering corm. Fully hardy. Produces funnel-shaped, grey-white, yellow-throated flowers with white-edged, deep purple outer segments.
♀ ***C. flavus***, syn. *C. aureus.* Spring-flowering corm. Fully hardy. Fragrant flowers are bright yellow or orange-yellow throughout; often several flowers are produced together or in quick succession.
C. gargaricus illus. p.445. Spring-flowering corm. Frost hardy. Bears yellow flowers, 4–5cm (1½–2in) long. Increases by stolons. Tolerates slightly damper conditions than most crocuses.
♀ ***C.* 'Golden Yellow',** syn. *C.* 'Dutch Yellow', *C.* × *luteus* 'Golden Yellow'. Very vigorous, clump-forming, spring-flowering corm. Fully hardy. Bears yellow flowers, 8–10cm (3–4in) long and faintly striped outside at bases. Naturalizes well in grass.
♀ ***C. goulimyi*** illus. p.444. Autumn-flowering corm. Frost hardy. Usually has one long-tubed, pale lilac to pinkish-lilac flower, with a white throat and 3 inner petals usually paler than the 3 outer ones. Leaves and flowers appear together. Needs a warm site.
♀ ***C. hadriaticus*** illus. p.444. Autumn-flowering corm. Frost hardy. Leaves appear with the white flowers, which usually have yellow throats and may be lilac-feathered at the base.
♀ ***C. imperati.*** Strikingly bicoloured, spring-flowering corm. Frost hardy. Develops 1 or 2 scented, purple flowers, 6–8cm (2½–3in) long, fawn with purple striping outside and with yellow throats. In **'De Jager'** (illus. p.444) flowers are rich violet-purple inside and biscuit-coloured with violet feathering outside.
C. iridiflorus. See *C. banaticus.*
C. korolkowii (Celandine crocus). Spring-flowering corm. Fully hardy. Produces up to 20 narrow leaves. Carries fragrant, yellow flowers that are speckled or stained brown or purple outside. When open in sun, petals have glossy surfaces.
♀ ***C. kotschyanus***, syn. *C. zonatus* illus. p.444. Autumn-flowering corm. Fully hardy. Pinkish-lilac or purplish-blue flowers have yellow centres and white anthers. Narrow, semi-erect, basal leaves, with white lines along centres, appear in winter-spring. var. ***leucopharynx*** has pale lilac-blue flowers with white centres and white anthers. Leaves appear in winter-spring.
♀ ***C.* 'Ladykiller'** illus. p.445. Late winter- to mid-spring-flowering corm. Fully hardy. Has funnel-shaped flowers, white or pale lilac within and deep violet-purple with white margins outside.
♀ ***C. laevigatus*** illus. p.444. Very variable corm, flowering intermittently for a month or more in autumn or winter depending on the form. Frost hardy. Fragrant flowers appear with leaves and are usually lilac-purple with bold stripes on outside; inside each has a yellow eye and cream-white anthers.
♀ ***C. longiflorus.*** illus. p.445. Autumn-flowering corm. Frost hardy. Produces fragrant, slender, purple flowers, which are striped darker purple outside, at the same time as leaves. Flowers have yellow centres and anthers and red stigmas.
***C.* × *luteus* 'Golden Yellow'.** See *C.* 'Golden Yellow'.
♀ ***C. malyi*** illus. p.444. Spring-flowering corm. Fully hardy. Has 1 or 2 funnel-shaped, white flowers with yellow throats, brown or purple tubes and showy, bright orange stigmas. Leaves are very narrow, semi-erect and basal with central, white lines.
♀ ***C. medius*** illus. p.444. Autumn-flowering corm. Frost hardy. Has 1 or 2 funnel-shaped, uniform rich purple flowers, with yellow anthers and red stigmas cut into many thread-like branches. Linear, basal leaves appear in winter-spring, after flowering.
C. minimus illus. p.444. Late spring-flowering corm. Frost hardy. Has very narrow, semi-erect, basal, dark green leaves that have central, white lines. Bears 1 or 2 flowers, purple inside and stained darker violet or sometimes darker striped on outside.
C. niveus. Autumn-flowering corm. Frost hardy. Produces 1 or 2 white or pale lavender flowers, 10–15cm (4–6in) long, with conspicuous, yellow throats. Leaves appear with flowers or just afterwards. Needs a warm, sunny site.
C. nudiflorus (Autumn crocus; illus. p.444). Autumn-flowering corm. Fully hardy. Has linear, basal leaves in winter-spring. Usually bears one slender, long-tubed, rich purple flower, with a frilly, bright orange or yellow stigma. Naturalizes in grass.
C. olivieri. Spring-flowering corm. Frost hardy. Bears rounded, bright orange flowers. Flowers of subsp. ***balansae*** (syn. *C. balansae*) are stained or striped bronze-brown outside.
♀ ***C. pulchellus*** illus. p.444. Autumn-flowering corm. Fully hardy. Bears long-tubed, pale lilac-blue flowers with darker veins, conspicuous, yellow throats and white anthers. Leaves are very narrow, semi-erect and basal, with white lines along centres.
C. salzmannii. See *C. serotinus* subsp. *salzmannii.*
C. sativus, syn. *C.s.* var. *cashmirianus* (Saffron crocus). Autumn-flowering corm. Frost hardy. Leaves appear with saucer-shaped, dark-veined, purple flowers, 5–7cm (2–3in) across, each with 3 long, bright red stigmas that yield saffron.
C. serotinus subsp. ***salzmannii,*** syn. *C. salzmannii.* Autumn-flowering corm. Frost hardy. Lilac-blue flowers, to 10cm (4in) long, sometimes with yellow throats, appear with leaves.
♀ ***C. sieberi.*** Spring-flowering corm. Fully hardy. Has white flowers with yellow throats and purple staining outside, either in horizontal bands or vertical stripes. **'Albus'** see *C.s.* 'Bowles' White'. subsp. ***atticus*** has pale lilac to violet-blue flowers with frilly, orange stigmas. ♀ **'Bowles' White'** (syn. *C.s.* 'Albus'; illus. p.444) produces pure white flowers with large, deep yellow areas in throats.
♀ **'Hubert Edelsten'** has yellow-throated, pale lilac flowers, the outer segments of which are white, tipped, centrally marked and feathered with rich purple. ♀ subsp. ***sublimis*** f. ***tricolor*** (illus. p.444) has unusual flowers, divided into 3 distinct bands of lilac, white and golden yellow.
♀ ***C.* 'Snow Bunting'** illus. p.444. Spring-flowering corm. Fully hardy. Fragrant long-tubed, funnel-shaped, white flowers have mustard-yellow centres and orange stigmas. Very narrow, semi-erect, basal leaves are dark green with white, central lines.
♀ ***C. speciosus*** illus. p.445. Autumn-flowering corm. Fully hardy. Produces lilac-blue to deep purple-blue flowers, usually with a network of darker veins and a much-divided, orange stigma. Leaves appear in winter-spring. **'Conqueror'** (illus. p.445) has large, deep sky-blue flowers. **'Oxonian'** (illus. p.445) produces dark violet-blue flowers with prominent darker veining externally.
C. susianus. See *C. angustifolius.*
♀ ***C. tommasinianus.*** Spring-flowering corm. H to 10cm (4in), S 2.5–8cm (1–3in). Fully hardy. Bears slender, long-tubed, funnel-shaped flowers, varying in colour from lilac or purple to violet, sometimes with darker tips to petals and occasionally silver outside. Naturalizes well. f. ***albus*** (illus. p.444) has white flowers. **'Ruby Giant'** (illus. p.445) bears clusters of large rich reddish-purple flowers. **'Whitewell Purple'** (illus. p.445) has slender, reddish-purple flowers.
♀ ***C. tournefortii.*** Autumn-flowering corm. Frost hardy. Leaves appear at same time as 1 or 2 pale lilac-blue flowers that open flattish to reveal a much-divided, orange stigma and white anthers. Requires a warm, sunny site.
C. vernus (Dutch crocus, Spring crocus; illus. p.445). Spring-flowering corm. H to 10cm (4in), S 2.5–8cm (1–3in). Fully hardy. Variable in colour from white to purple or violet and often striped and feathered. Stigmas are large, frilly and orange or yellow. Is suitable for naturalizing. subsp. ***albiflorus*** (illus. p.444) has small, white flowers sometimes slightly marked or striped purple. **'Jeanne d'Arc'** has white flowers with a deep purple base. **'Pickwick'** (illus. p.445) has pale, greyish-white flowers, with dark violet stripes and purplish bases. **'Prinses Juliana'** (illus. p.445) has mid-purple flowers with darker veins. **'Purpureus Grandiflorus'** (illus. p.445) has shiny, violet-purple flowers. **'Queen of the Blues'** (illus. p.445) has rich blue flowers that have higher margins and a darker base. **'Remembrance'** (illus. p.445). has shiny, violet flowers. **'Vanguard'**, a very early cultivar, has bluish-lilac flowers, paler and silvered outside.
♀ ***C.* 'Zephyr'.** Autumn-flowering corm. Fully hardy. Bears very pale silver-blue flowers, veined darker, each with a conspicuous, yellow throat and

white anthers.
C. zonatus. See *C. kotschyanus.*
♀ ***C.* 'Zwanenburg Bronze'.** Spring-flowering corm. H to 10cm (4in), S 2.5–8cm (1–3in). Fully hardy. Has bicoloured flowers, rich yellow inside, stained bronze outside.

Crocus
Autumn. See *Colchicum autumnale*, illus. p.453; *Crocus nudiflorus*, illus. p.444.
Celandine. See *Crocus korolkowii*.
Chilean blue. See *Tecophilaea cyanocrocus*, illus. p.449.
Cloth-of-gold. See *Crocus angustifolius*.
Dutch. See *Crocus vernus*, illus. p.445.
Saffron. See *Crocus sativus*.
Spring. See *Crocus vernus*, illus. p.445.
Cross vine. See *Bignonia capreolata*.

CROSSANDRA

ACANTHACEAE

Genus of evergreen perennials, sub-shrubs and shrubs, grown mainly for their flowers. Frost tender, min. 15°C (59°F). Needs partial shade or full light and humus-rich, well-drained soil. Water potted plants freely when in full growth, moderately at other times. For a strong branch system, cut back flowered growth by at least half in late winter. Propagate by seed in spring or by greenwood cuttings in late spring or summer. Whitefly may be troublesome.
♀ ***C. infundibuliformis***, syn. *C. undulifolia*. Evergreen, erect to spreading, soft-stemmed shrub or sub-shrub. H to 1m (3ft), S 60cm (2ft). Has oval to lance-shaped, glossy, deep green leaves and, in summer-autumn or earlier, fan-shaped, salmon-red flowers in conical spikes, each 10cm (4in) long.
C. nilotica illus. p.161.
C. undulifolia. See *C. infundibuliformis*.

Cross-leaved heath. See *Erica tetralix*.

CROTALARIA

LEGUMINOSAE/PAPILIONACEAE

Genus of evergreen shrubs, perennials and annuals, grown mainly for their flowers. Frost tender, min. 10–15°C (50–59°F). Requires full light and well-drained soil. Water containerized specimens freely when in full growth, less at other times. For a more compact habit, cut back old stems by half after flowering. Propagate by seed in spring or by semi-ripe cuttings in summer. Red spider mite may be troublesome.
C. agatiflora illus. p.119.

Croton. See *Codiaeum variegatum* var. *pictum*, illus. p.173.
Crowfoot, Water. See *Ranunculus aquatilis*.
Crown imperial. See *Fritillaria imperialis*, illus. p.408.
Crown of thorns. See *Euphorbia milii*, illus. p.151.
Crucianella stylosa. See *Phuopsis stylosa*.
Cruel plant. See *Araujia sericifera*, illus. p.203.
Crusaders' spears. See *Urginea maritima*.

CRYPTANTHUS

BROMELIACEAE

Genus of evergreen, rosette-forming perennials, grown for their attractive foliage. Frost tender, min. 10–13°C (50–55°F). Needs semi-shade and well-drained soil, preferably mixed with sphagnum moss. Water moderately during the growing season, sparingly at other times. Propagate by offsets or suckers in late spring.
C. acaulis (Green earth star). Evergreen, clump-forming, basal-rosetted perennial. H to 10cm (4in), S 15–30cm (6–12in). Loose, flat rosettes of lance-shaped to narrowly triangular, wavy, mid-green leaves have serrated edges. A cluster of fragrant, tubular, white flowers appears from each rosette centre, usually in summer. **'Ruber'** has red-flushed foliage.
♀ ***C. bivittatus*** illus. p.273. Evergreen, clump-forming, basal-rosetted perennial. H to 15cm (6in), S 25–38cm (10–15in). Loose, flat rosettes of broadly lance-shaped, wavy, mid- to yellowish-green leaves have finely toothed margins and are striped lengthways with 2 coppery-fawn to buff bands. Small clusters of tubular, white flowers appear from centre of each rosette, usually in summer.
C. bromelioides (Rainbow star). Evergreen, spreading, basal-rosetted perennial. H 20cm (8in) or more, S 35cm (14in) or more. Strap-shaped, wavy, finely toothed, arching, mid- to bright green leaves are produced in dense rosettes. Occasionally bears clusters of tubular, white flowers in centre of each rosette, usually in summer. ♀ **'Tricolor'** has carmine-suffused, white-striped foliage.
♀ ***C.* 'Pink Starlight'** illus. p.273. Vigorous, evergreen, spreading, basal-rosetted perennial. H 20cm (8in) or more, S 35cm (14in) or more. Strap-shaped, wavy, finely toothed, arching, green leaves are striped yellowish-green, and heavily suffused deep pink. Clusters of tubular, white flowers occasionally appear from each rosette centre in summer.
♀ ***C. zonatus.*** Evergreen, basal-rosetted perennial. H 10–15cm (4–6in), S 30–40cm (12–16in). Forms loose, flat rosettes of strap-shaped, wavy, finely toothed, sepia-green leaves, cross-banded with grey-buff and with greyish-white scales beneath. A cluster of tubular, white flowers opens in each rosette, usually in summer. **'Zebrinus'** (illus. p.273) has silver-banded foliage.

× CRYPTBERGIA

BROMELIACEAE

Hybrid genus *(Cryptanthus × Billbergia)* of evergreen, rosette-forming perennials, grown for their foliage. Frost tender, min. 8–10°C (46–50°F). Needs semi-shade and fertile, well-drained soil. Water moderately during growing season, sparingly in winter. Propagate by suckers or offsets in spring.
× *C.* 'Rubra'. Evergreen, clump-forming, basal-rosetted perennial. H and S 15–30cm (6–12in). Loose rosettes comprise strap-shaped, pointed, bronze-red leaves. Rarely, small, tubular, white flowers are produced in rosette centres in summer.

CRYPTOCORYNE

ARACEAE

Genus of semi-evergreen, perennial, submerged water plants and marsh plants, grown for their foliage. Is suitable for tropical aquariums. Frost tender, min. 10°C (50°F). Needs sun and rich soil. Remove fading foliage, and divide plants periodically. Propagate by division in spring or summer.
C. beckettii* var. *ciliata. See *C. ciliata.*
C. ciliata, syn. *C. beckettii* var. *ciliata.* Semi-evergreen, perennial, submerged water plant. S 15cm (6in). Lance-shaped, deep green leaves have paler midribs. Small, hooded, fringed, purplish spathes appear intermittently at base of plant.
C. spiralis. Semi-evergreen, perennial, submerged water plant. S 15cm (6in). Small, hooded, purplish spathes are borne intermittently among lance-shaped, purplish-green leaves.

CRYPTOGRAMMA

ADIANTACEAE/CRYPTOGRAMMACEAE

Genus of deciduous or semi-evergreen ferns. Fully to frost hardy. Needs partial shade and moist but well-drained, neutral or acid soil. Remove fading fronds. Propagate by spores in late summer.
C. crispa illus. p.325.

CRYPTOMERIA

TAXODIACEAE

See also CONIFERS.
♀ ***C. japonica*** (Japanese cedar). Fast-growing, columnar to conical, open conifer. H 15–20m (50–70ft), S 5–8m (15–25ft). Fully hardy. Has soft, fibrous, red-brown bark, needle-like, incurved, mid- to dark green leaves, spirally arranged, and globular, brown cones. ♀ **'Bandai-sugi'**, H and S 2m (6ft), makes an irregularly rounded shrub with foliage that turns bronze in winter. **'Cristata'** illus. p.105.
♀ **'Elegans Compacta'** (illus. p.107), H 2–5m (6–15ft), S 2m (6ft), is a dwarf form. **'Pyramidata'** illus. p.105. **'Sekkan-sugi'** (illus. p.107), H 10m (30ft), S 3–4m (10–12ft), has semi-pendulous branches and light golden-cream foliage. **'Spiralis'** (illus. p.107), H and S 2–3m (6–10ft), forms a tree or dense shrub with spirally twisted foliage and is very slow-growing.
♀ **'Vilmoriniana'**, H and S 1m (3ft), forms a globular mound of yellow-green foliage that turns bronze in winter.

CRYPTOSTEGIA

ASCLEPIADACEAE

Genus of evergreen, twining climbers, grown for their flowers. Frost tender, min. 15°C (59°F). Provide fertile, well-drained soil and full light. Water regularly, less when not in full growth. Stems require support. Spur back previous season's old flowering stems in spring. Propagate by seed in spring or by softwood cuttings in summer.
C. grandiflora (Rubber vine). Strong-growing, evergreen, twining climber. H 10m (30ft) or more. Has thick-textured, oval, glossy leaves. Funnel-shaped, reddish to lilac-purple flowers appear in summer. Stems yield a poisonous latex that may cause severe discomfort if ingested.

Cryptostemma calendulaceum. See *Arctotheca calendula*.
Crystal anthurium. See *Anthurium crystallinum*, illus. p.272.

CTENANTHE

MARANTACEAE

Genus of evergreen, bushy perennials, grown for their ornamental foliage. Frost tender, min. 15°C (59°F). Requires a humid atmosphere, even temperature and partial shade. Prefers moist but well-drained soil and soft water; do not allow to dry completely. Propagate by division in spring.
♀ ***C. lubbersiana.*** Evergreen, clump-forming, bushy perennial. H and S to 75cm (30in) or more. Long-stalked, lance-shaped, sharply pointed leaves are 25cm (10in) long, green above, irregularly marked and striped with pale yellowish-green, and pale greenish-yellow below. Intermittently bears dense, one-sided spikes of many small, 3-petalled, white flowers.
C. oppenheimiana, syn. *Calathea oppenheimiana.* Robust, evergreen, bushy perennial. H and S 1m (3ft) or more. Lance-shaped, leathery leaves are over 30cm (1ft) long, red below, dark green above with pale green or white bands along veins on either side of midribs. Dense, one-sided spikes of many small, 3-petalled, white flowers are produced intermittently.
♀ **'Tricolor'** illus. p.272.

Cuban royal palm. See *Roystonea regia*.
Cuckoo flower. See *Cardamine pratensis*.
Cuckoo pint. See *Arum*.
Cucumber tree. See *Magnolia acuminata*.
Cudrania tricuspidata. See *Maclura tricuspidata*.

CUNNINGHAMIA

TAXODIACEAE

See also CONIFERS.
C. lanceolata illus. p.102.

CUNONIA

CUNONIACEAE

Genus of evergreen, summer-flowering trees, grown for their foliage, flowers and overall appearance. Frost tender, min. 10°C (50°F). Requires full light and well-drained soil. Water potted plants moderately, less in winter. Pruning is tolerated. Propagate by seed in spring or by semi-ripe cuttings in summer.
C. capensis (African red alder). Moderately fast-growing, evergreen, rounded tree. H and S 10–15m (30–50ft), more in rich soil. Has lustrous, dark green leaves, divided into pairs of lance-shaped, serrated leaflets. Tiny, long-stamened, white flowers appear in dense, bottlebrush-like spikes, each 10–13cm (4–5in) long, in late summer.

Cup-and-saucer vine. See *Cobaea scandens*, illus. p.212.

CUPHEA

LYTHRACEAE

Genus of annuals, perennials and evergreen shrubs and sub-shrubs, grown for their flowers. Half hardy to frost tender, min. 2–7°C (36–45°F). Prefers full sun and fertile, well-drained soil. Water freely when in full growth, moderately at other times. Remove flowered shoots after flowering to maintain a bushy habit. Propagate by seed in spring or by greenwood cuttings in spring or summer. Red spider mite may be troublesome.
C. cyanea illus. p.168.
🏆 ***C. hyssopifolia*** illus. p.154.
🏆 ***C. ignea***, syn. *C. platycentra*, illus. p.168.
C. platycentra. See *C. ignea*.

Cupid peperomia. See *Peperomia scandens*.
Cupidone, Blue. See *Catananche*.

× CUPRESSOCYPARIS

CUPRESSACEAE

Contact with the foliage may aggravate skin allergies. See also CONIFERS.
× ***C. leylandii*** **'Castlewellan'** illus. p.100. **'Haggerston Grey'** illus.p.97. **'Harlequin'** illus. p.100. **'Leighton Green'** is a very fast-growing, columnar conifer with a conical tip. H 25–35m (80–120ft), S 4–5m (12–15ft). Fully hardy. Bears flattened sprays of paired, scale-like, rich green leaves and globular, glossy, dark brown cones. 🏆 **'Robinson's Gold'**, H 15–20m (50–70ft), has bright golden leaves.

CUPRESSUS

Cypress

CUPRESSACEAE

See also CONIFERS.
C. arizonica **var.** ***glabra***, syn. *C. glabra* (Arizona cypress, Smooth cypress). Conical conifer. H 10–15m (30–50ft), S 3–5m (10–15ft). Fully hardy. Has smooth, flaking, reddish-purple bark and upright, spirally arranged sprays of scale-like, aromatic, glaucous blue-grey leaves that are flecked with white resin. Globular cones are chocolate-brown.
🏆 ***C. cashmeriana***, syn. *C. torulosa* 'Cashmeriana', illus. p.97.
C. glabra. See *C. arizonica* var. *glabra*.
C. lusitanica (Cedar of Goa, Mexican cypress). Conical conifer. H 20m (70ft), S 5–8m (15–25ft). Fully hardy. Has fissured bark and spreading, spirally arranged sprays of scale-like, aromatic, grey-green leaves. Bears small, globular cones that are glaucous blue when young, ripening to glossy brown.
C. macrocarpa (Monterey cypress). Fast-growing, evergreen conifer, columnar when young, often wide-spreading with age. H 20m (70ft), S 6–25m (20–80ft). Fully hardy. Bark is shallowly fissured. Scale-like, aromatic, bright to dark green leaves are borne in plume-like sprays. Globular cones are glossy and brown. 🏆 **'Goldcrest'** illus. p.105.
C. torulosa **'Cashmeriana'.** See *C. cashmeriana*.

Curled pondweed. See *Potamogeton crispus*, illus. p.464.
Currant. See *Ribes*.
Buffalo. See *Ribes odoratum*.
Flowering. See *Ribes sanguineum*.
Fuchsia-flowered. See *Ribes speciosum*.
Indian. See *Symphoricarpos orbiculatus*.
Curry plant. See *Helichrysum italicum*.
Curtonus paniculatus. See *Crocosmia paniculata*.
Cushion bush. See *Leucophyta*.
Custard apple. See *Annona*.

CYANANTHUS

CAMPANULACEAE

Genus of late summer-flowering perennials, suitable for rock gardens, walls and troughs. Fully hardy. Needs partial shade and humus-rich, moist but well-drained soil. Propagate by softwood cuttings in spring or by seed in autumn.
🏆 ***C. lobatus.*** Prostrate perennial. H 2cm (¾in), S 20cm (8in). Branched stems are clothed in small, wedge-shaped, dull green leaves. In late summer, each stem carries a funnel-shaped, blue flower. f. ***albus*** illus. p.385.
🏆 ***C. microphyllus*** illus. p.395.

CYANOTIS

COMMELINACEAE

Genus of evergreen, creeping perennials, grown for their foliage.Frost tender, min. 10–15°C (50–59°F). Prefers a position in sun or partial shade, with humus-rich, well-drained soil. Propagate by tip cuttings from spring to autumn.
🏆 ***C. kewensis*** (Teddy-bear vine). Evergreen perennial forming rosettes with trailing stems. H 5cm (2in), S 30cm (12in). Clasping the stem are 2 rows of overlapping, oval leaves, to 5cm (2in) long, dark green above, purple with velvety, brown hairs below. Stalkless clusters of 3-petalled, purplish-pink flowers are produced in axils of leaf-like bracts almost all year round.
🏆 ***C. somaliensis*** illus. p.315.

CYATHEA,

syn. ALSOPHILA, SPHAEROPTERIS

CYATHEACEAE

Genus of evergreen tree ferns, grown for their foliage and overall appearance. Frost tender, min. 10–13°C (50–55°F). Needs a humid atmosphere, sun or partial shade and humus-rich, moisture-retentive but well-drained soil. Water potted plants freely in summer, moderately at other times. Propagate by spores in spring.
C. australis syn. *Alsophila australis* illus. p.96.
C. medullaris (Black tree fern, Mamaku). Evergreen, upright tree fern with a slender, black trunk. H 7–16m (22–52ft), S 6–12m (20–40ft). Has arching fronds, each to 7m (22ft) long, divided into small, oblong, glossy, dark green leaflets, paler beneath.

CYATHODES

EPACRIDACEAE

Genus of evergreen, heath-like shrubs, suitable for rock gardens and peat beds. Frost hardy to frost tender, min. 7°C (45°F). Needs a sheltered, shaded site and gritty, moist, peaty soil. Propagate in summer by seed or semi-ripe cuttings.
C. colensoi, syn. *Leucopogon colensoi*, illus. p.372.

CYBISTAX

BIGNONIACEAE

Genus of deciduous trees, grown for their spring flowers and for shade.Frost tender, min. 16–18°C (61–4°F). Needs full light and fertile, moisture-retentive but well-drained soil. Will not bloom when confined to a container.Young plants may be pruned to shape when leafless; otherwise pruning is not required. Propagate by seed or air-layering in spring or by semi-ripe cuttings in summer.
C. donnell-smithii, syn. *Tabebuia donnell-smithii.* Fairly fast-growing, deciduous, rounded tree. H and S 10m (30ft) or more. Leaves have 5–7 oval, 5–20cm (2–8in) long leaflets. Bell-shaped, 5-lobed, bright yellow flowers appear in spring before the leaves, often in great profusion.

CYCAS

CYCADACEAE

Genus of slow-growing, evergreen, woody-stemmed perennials, grown for their palm-like appearance. Frost tender, min. 10–13°C (50–55°F). Prefers a position in full light and humus-rich, well-drained soil. Water potted specimens moderately, less when not in full growth. Propagate in spring by seed or suckers taken from mature plants.
🏆 ***C. revoluta*** illus. p.148.

CYCLAMEN

PRIMULACEAE

Genus of tuberous perennials, some of which are occasionally evergreen, grown for their pendent flowers, each with 5 reflexed petals and a mouth often stained with a darker colour.Fully hardy to frost tender, min. 5–7°C (41–5°F). Grow in sun or partial shade, and in humus-rich, well-drained soil. If grown in containers, in summer dry off tubers of all except *C. purpurascens* (which is evergreen and flowers in summer); repot in autumn and water to restart growth. Propagate by seed in late summer or autumn. *C. persicum* and its cultivars are susceptible to black root rot. All parts may cause severe discomfort if ingested.
C. africanum illus. p.453.
C. alpinum, syn *C. trochopteranthum*. Spring-flowering, tuberous perennial. H 10cm (4in), S 5–10cm (2–4in). Fully hardy. Bears rounded or heart-shaped leaves, zoned with silver. Produces musty-scented, pale carmine or white flowers, stained dark carmine at mouths; petals are twisted and propeller-shaped.
C. caucasicum. See *C. coum* subsp. *caucasicum*.
🏆 ***C. cilicium*** illus. p.454.
🏆 ***C. coum*** and f. ***albissimum*** (syn. *C.c.* 'Album') illus. p.456. subsp. ***caucasicum*** (syn. *C. caucasicum*) is a winter-flowering, tuberous perennial. H to 10cm (4in), S 5–10cm (2–4in). Frost hardy. Has heart-shaped, silver-patterned leaves and produces a succession of bright carmine flowers, each with a dark stain at the mouth.
C. creticum. Spring-flowering, tuberous perennial. H to 10cm (4in), S 5–10cm (2–4in). Frost hardy. Produces heart-shaped, dark green leaves, sometimes silver-patterned, and fragrant, white flowers.
C. cyprium. Autumn-flowering, tuberous perennial. H to 10cm (4in), S 5–10cm (2–4in). Frost hardy. Heart-shaped, toothed, dark green leaves, patterned with lighter green, appear with or just after fragrant, white flowers, each with carmine marks around the mouth.
C. europaeum. See *C. purpurascens*.
C. fatrense. See *C. purpurascens*.
C. graecum illus. p.454.
🏆 ***C. hederifolium***, syn. *C. neapolitanum*, illus. p.454. f. ***albiflorum*** illus. p.453.
C. libanoticum illus. p.443.
🏆 ***C. mirabile*** illus. p.453.
C. neapolitanum. See *C. hederifolium*.
C. persicum illus. p.456. **'Esmeralda'** illus. p.457. **Halios Series** is a late summer- or autumn-flowering, tuberous perennial. H 30cm (12in), S 18cm (7in). Frost tender. Blunt-toothed, heart-shaped, dark green leaves have silver marbling. Produces a succession of white, pink, scarlet, lilac or purple flowers. **Kaori Series** illus. p.457. **'Pearl Wave'** illus. p.456. **'Renown'** illus. p.457. **'Scentsation'**, H 15cm (6in), bears strongly scented flowers in pink, carmine-red or crimson from early winter to early spring.
🏆 ***C. pseudibericum.*** Spring-flowering, tuberous perennial. H to 10cm (4in), S 10–15cm (4–6in). Frost hardy. Has heart-shaped, toothed leaves patterned with silvery- and dark green zones. Flowers are deep carmine-purple with darker, basal stains and white-rimmed mouths.
🏆 ***C. purpurascens***, syn. *C. europaeum, C. fatrense*, illus. p.451.
🏆 ***C. repandum.*** Spring-flowering, tuberous perennial. H to 10cm (4in), S 10–15cm (4–6in). Frost hardy. Has heart-shaped, jagged-toothed, dark green leaves with lighter patterns. Bears fragrant, slender, reddish-purple flowers.
C. rohlfsianum illus. p.454.
C. trochopteranthum. See *C. alpinum*.

Cyclobothra lutea. See *Calochortus barbatus*.

Cydonia

ROSACEAE

Genus of one species of deciduous, spring-flowering tree, grown for its flowers and fruits, which are used as a flavouring and for preserves. Fully hardy, but grow against a south- or west-facing wall in cold areas. Requires sun and fertile, well-drained soil. Propagate species by seed in autumn, cultivars by softwood cuttings in summer. Mildew, brown rot and fireblight are sometimes a problem.
C. oblonga (Quince). **'Lusitanica'** is a deciduous, spreading tree. H and S 5m (15ft). Broadly oval, dark green leaves are grey-felted beneath. Has a profusion of large, 5-petalled, pale pink flowers in late spring, followed by fragrant, pear-shaped, deep yellow fruits.
♀ **'Vranja'** illus. p.88.
C. sinensis. See *Pseudocydonia sinensis*.

Cylindropuntia tunicata. See *Opuntia tunicata*.

Cymbalaria

SCROPHULARIACEAE

Genus of annuals, biennials and short-lived perennials, related to *Linaria*, grown for their tiny flowers on slender stems. Is good for rock gardens, walls and banks, but may be invasive. Fully hardy. Needs shade and moist soil. Propagate by seed in autumn. Self-seeds readily.
C. muralis (Ivy-leaved toadflax, Kenilworth ivy). Spreading perennial. H 5cm (2in), S 12cm (5in). Bears small, ivy-shaped, pale green leaves and, in summer, masses of tiny, tubular, spurred, sometimes purple-tinted, white flowers.

Cymbidium

ORCHIDACEAE

Contact with the foliage may aggravate skin allergies. See also ORCHIDS.
***C.* Caithness Ice 'Trinity'** illus. p.310. Evergreen, epiphytic orchid for a cool greenhouse. H 75cm (30in). Sprays of green flowers, 10cm (4in) across, each with a red-marked, white lip, are borne in early spring. Has narrowly oval leaves, to 60cm (24in) long. Needs a position in semi-shade in summer.
***C.* Christmas Angel 'Cooksbridge Sunburst'** illus. p.311. Evergreen, epiphytic orchid for a cool greenhouse. H 75cm (30in). In winter produces sprays of yellow flowers, 10cm (4in) across and with red-spotted lips. Narrowly oval leaves are up to 60cm (24in) long. Grow in semi-shade in summer.
C. devonianum illus. p.310. Evergreen, epiphytic orchid for a cool greenhouse. H 60cm (24in). In early summer bears pendent spikes of 2.5cm (1in) wide, olive-green flowers overlaid with purple and with purple lips. Has broadly oval, semi-rigid leaves, to 30cm (12in) long. Needs semi-shade in summer.
C. elegans, syn. *Cyperorchis elegans* illus. p.310. Evergreen, epiphytic orchid for a cool greenhouse. H 75cm (30in). Dense, pendent sprays of fragrant, tubular, yellow flowers, 4cm (1½in) across, appear in early summer. Has narrowly oval leaves, to 60cm (24in) long. Requires semi-shade in summer.
C. grandiflorum. See *C. hookerianum*.
C. hookerianum, syn. *C. grandiflorum* illus. p.310. Evergreen, epiphytic orchid for a cool greenhouse. H 75cm (30in). In winter produces sprays of deep green flowers, 8cm (3in) across, each with a hairy, brown-spotted, creamy-white lip. Narrowly oval leaves are up to 60cm (24in) long. Grow in semi-shade in summer.
♀ ***C.* King's Loch 'Cooksbridge'** illus. p.310. Evergreen, epiphytic orchid for a cool greenhouse. H 60cm (24in). Sprays of green flowers, 5cm (2in) across and each with a purple-marked, white lip, open in spring. Leaves are narrowly oval and up to 60cm (24in) long. Provide semi-shade in summer.
***C.* Pontac 'Mont Millais'** illus. p.309. Evergreen, epiphytic orchid for a cool greenhouse. H 75cm (30in). Bears sprays of 8cm (3in) wide, rich deep red flowers, edged and marked with white, in spring. Has narrowly oval leaves, to 60cm (24in) long. Grow in semi-shade in summer.
***C.* Portelet Bay** illus. p.308. Evergreen, epiphytic orchid for a cool greenhouse. H 75cm (30in). Red-lipped, white flowers, 10cm (4in) across, are borne in sprays in spring. Has narrowly oval leaves, to 60cm (24in) long. Provide semi-shade in summer.
***C.* Strath Kanaid** illus. p.309. Evergreen, epiphytic orchid for a cool greenhouse. H 60cm (24in). In spring bears arching spikes of deep red flowers, 5cm (2in) across. Lips are white, marked deep red. Narrowly oval leaves are up to 60cm (24in) long. Requires semi-shade in summer.
***C.* Strathbraan** illus. p.308. Evergreen, epiphytic orchid for a cool greenhouse. H 60cm (24in). In spring produces slightly arching spikes of off-white flowers, 5cm (2in) across, with red marks on each lip. Leaves are narrowly oval, to 60cm (24in) long. Requires semi-shade in summer.
♀ ***C.* Strathdon 'Cooksbridge Noel'** illus. p.309. Evergreen, epiphytic orchid for a cool greenhouse. H 1m (3ft). Sprays of rich pink flowers, 5cm (2in) across, with red-spotted, yellow-tinged lips, appear in winter. Has narrowly oval leaves, up to 60cm (24in) long. Needs semi-shade in summer.
C. tracyanum illus. p.310. Evergreen, epiphytic orchid for a cool greenhouse. H 75cm (30in). In autumn produces long spikes of fragrant, olive-green flowers, 8cm (3in) across, overlaid with reddish dots and dashes. Has narrowly oval leaves, to 60cm (24in) long. Grow in semi-shade in summer.

Cynara

COMPOSITAE/ASTERACEAE

Genus of architectural perennials, grown for their large heads of flowers. The plant described is grown both as a vegetable and as a decorative border plant. Frost hardy. Requires sun and fertile, well-drained soil. Propagate by seed or division in spring.
♀ ***C. cardunculus*** illus. p.226.

Cynoglossum

Hound's tongue

BORAGINACEAE

Genus of annuals, biennials and perennials, grown for their long flowering period from late spring to early autumn. Fully hardy. Needs sun and fertile but not over-rich soil. Propagate by division in spring or by seed in autumn or spring.
***C. amabile* 'Firmament'** illus. p.346.

Cypella

IRIDACEAE

Genus of summer-flowering bulbs, grown for their short-lived, iris-like flowers that have 3 large, spreading outer petals and 3 small, incurved inner ones. Half hardy; may survive outdoors in cool areas if planted near a sunny wall. Needs full sun and well-drained soil. Lift bulbs when dormant; partially dry off in winter. Propagate by seed in spring.
C. herbertii illus. p.439.

Cyperorchis elegans. See *Cymbidium elegans*.

Cyperus

CYPERACEAE

See also GRASSES, BAMBOOS, RUSHES and SEDGES.
C. albostriatus, syn. *C. diffusus* of gardens, *C. elegans* of gardens. Evergreen, perennial sedge. H 60cm (24in), S indefinite. Frost tender, min. 7°C (45°F). Stem has prominently veined, mid-green leaves and up to 8 leaf-like, green bracts surrounding a well-branched umbel of brown spikelets, produced in summer. **'Variegatus'** has white-striped leaves and bracts.
C. alternifolius of gardens. See *C. involucratus*.
C. diffusus of gardens. See *C. albostriatus*.
C. elegans of gardens. See *C. albostriatus*.
C. flabelliformis. See *C. involucratus*.
♀ ***C. involucratus***, syn. *C. alternifolius* of gardens, *C. flabelliformis*, illus. p.320.
C. isocladus of gardens. See *C. papyrus* 'Nanus'.
C. longus (Galingale). Deciduous, spreading, perennial sedge. H 1.5m (5ft), S indefinite. Fully hardy. Bears rough-edged, glossy, dark green leaves and, in summer, attractive umbels of narrow, flattened, milk-chocolate-coloured spikelets that keep their colour well. Tolerates its roots in water.
♀ ***C. papyrus*** illus. p.319. ♀ **'Nanus'** (syn. *C. isocladus* of gardens) is an evergreen, spreading, perennial sedge with a red rhizome; it is a dwarf variant of the species, sometimes considered distinct, and is often grown under misapplied names. H 80cm (32in), S indefinite. Frost tender, min. 7–10°C (45–50°F). Triangular, leafless stems bear umbels of brown spikelets on 8–10cm (3–4in) stalks in summer.

Cyphomandra

SOLANACEAE

Genus of evergreen shrubs and trees, grown for their fruits and foliage. Frost tender, min. 10°C (50°F). Grow in full light or partial shade and in well-drained soil. Water containerized specimens freely when in growth, sparingly at other times, when some leaves may fall. Tip prune at intervals while young to promote branching. Propagate by seed in spring. Whitefly and red spider mite may cause problems.
C. betacea, syn. *C. crassicaulis*, illus. p.121.
C. crassicaulis. See *C. betacea*.

Cyphostemma

VITACEAE

Genus of deciduous, perennial succulents with very thick, fleshy, almost woody caudices and branches. Leaf undersides often exude droplets of resin. Frost tender, min. 10°C (50°F). Needs full sun and very well-drained soil. Keep dry in winter. Is difficult to grow. Propagate by seed in spring.
C. bainesii, syn. *Cissus bainesii*. Deciduous, perennial succulent. H and S 60cm (24in). Has a thick, swollen, bottle-shaped trunk, often unbranched, covered in peeling, papery, yellow bark. Fleshy, silvery-green leaves, with deeply serrated edges, are divided into 3 oval leaflets, silver-haired when young. Bears tiny, cup-shaped, yellow-green flowers in summer, then grape-like, red fruits.
C. juttae, syn. *Cissus juttae*, illus. p.475.

Cypress. See *Cupressus*.
- **Arizona.** See *Cupressus arizonica* var. *glabra*.
- **Bald.** See *Taxodium distichum*, illus. p.100.
- **False.** See *Chamaecyparis*.
- **Hinoki.** See *Chamaecyparis obtusa*.
- **Kashmir.** See *Cupressus cashmeriana*, illus. p.97.
- **Lawson.** See *Chamaecyparis lawsoniana*.
- **Mexican.** See *Cupressus lusitanica*.
- **Monterey.** See *Cupressus macrocarpa*.
- **Nootka.** See *Chamaecyparis nootkatensis*.
- **Patagonian.** See *Fitzroya cupressoides*, illus. p.102.
- **Sawara.** See *Chamaecyparis pisifera*.
- **Smooth.** See *Cupressus arizonica* var. *glabra*.
- **Summer.** See *Bassia scoparia* f. *trichophylla*, illus. p.347.
- **Swamp.** See *Taxodium distichum*, illus. p.100.
- **Variegated Leyland.** See × *Cupressocyparis leylandii* 'Harlequin', illus. p.100.
- **White.** See *Chamaecyparis thyoides*, illus. p.103.

Cypress vine. See *Ipomoea quamoclit*, illus. p.206.

CYPRIPEDIUM
Slipper orchid

ORCHIDACEAE

See also ORCHIDS.
C. acaule (Moccasin flower; illus. p.308). Deciduous, terrestrial orchid. H to 40cm (16in). Fully hardy. Yellowish-green or purple flowers, 4–6cm (1½–2½in) long, each with a pouched, pink or white lip, are borne singly in spring-summer. Leaves are broadly lance-shaped, pleated and 10–30cm (4–12in) long. Does best in partial shade.
C. calceolus (Lady's slipper orchid, Yellow lady's slipper orchid; illus. p.310). Deciduous, terrestrial orchid. H 75cm (30in). Fully hardy. In spring-summer bears paired or solitary yellow-pouched, purple flowers, 3–7cm (1¼–3in) long. Broadly lance-shaped leaves, 5–20cm (2–8in) long, are arranged in a spiral up stem. Stems and leaves are slightly hairy. Prefers partial shade. var. ***pubescens*** see *C. pubescens*.
C. macranthon. See *C. macranthos*.
C. macranthos, syn. *C. macranthon* illus. p.310. Deciduous, terrestrial orchid. H 50cm (20in). Fully hardy. Pouched, violet or purplish-red flowers, 4–6cm (1½–2½in) long, usually borne singly, open in spring-summer. Stems and oval leaves, 4–7cm (1½–3in) long, are slightly hairy. Prefers partial shade.
C. pubescens, syn. *C. calceolus* var. *pubescens* illus. p.311. Deciduous, terrestrial orchid. H 75cm (30in). Fully hardy. Has large, purple-marked, greenish-yellow flowers, 8–10cm (3–4in) long, in spring-summer. Large, broadly lance-shaped leaves, 15–20cm (6–8in) long, are arranged in a spiral up stem. Stems and leaves are hairy. Prefers partial shade.
C. reginae (Showy lady's slipper orchid; illus. p.308). Deciduous, terrestrial orchid. H to 1m (3ft). Fully hardy. In spring-summer, white flowers, 2–5cm (¾–2in) long, each with a pouched, white-streaked, pink lip, are borne singly or in groups of 2 or 3. Stem and oval leaves, 10–25cm (4–10in) long, are hairy. Does best in partial shade.

Cyprus turpentine. See *Pistacia terebinthus*.

CYRILLA

CYRILLACEAE

Genus of one very variable species of deciduous or evergreen shrub, grown for its flowers in late summer and autumn. Fully to half hardy. Prefers full sun and needs peaty, acid soil. Propagate by semi-ripe cuttings in summer.
C. racemiflora (Leatherwood). Deciduous or evergreen, bushy shrub. H and S 1.2m (4ft). Oblong, glossy, dark green leaves redden in autumn. Slender spires of small, 5-petalled, white flowers are borne in late summer and autumn.

CYRTANTHUS

AMARYLLIDACEAE

Genus of bulbs with brightly coloured flowers, usually in summer. Frost hardy to frost tender, min. 15°C (59°F). Requires full sun and free-draining, light soil. In frost-free areas may flower for much of the year. Plant in spring. Water freely in the growing season. Propagate by seed or offsets in spring.
C. brachyscyphus, syn. *C. parviflorus*, illus. p.451.
C. breviflorus, syn. *Anoiganthus breviflorus, A. luteus.* Clump-forming summer-flowering bulb. H 20–30cm (8–12in), S 8–10cm (3–4in). Frost hardy. Has narrowly strap-shaped, semi-erect, basal leaves. Leafless flower stem bears up to 6 funnel-shaped, yellow flowers, 2–3cm (¾–1¼in) long. Prefers a warm, sheltered situation.
♀ ***C. elatus***, syn. *C. purpureus, Vallota speciosa.* Clump-forming, summer-flowering bulb. H 30–50cm (12–20in), S 12–15cm (5–6in). Half hardy. Bears widely strap-shaped, semi-erect, basal, bright green leaves. Stout stem produces a head of up to 5 widely funnel-shaped, scarlet flowers, 8–10cm (3–4in) long. Makes an excellent house plant.
C. mackenii. Clump-forming, summer-flowering bulb. H 30–40cm (12–16in), S 8–10cm (3–4in). Half hardy. Bears strap-shaped, semi-erect, basal leaves. Leafless stems each carry an umbel of up to 10 fragrant, tubular, white flowers, 5cm (2in) long and slightly curved. var. ***cooperi*** illus. p.438.
C. obliquus. Clump-forming, summer-flowering bulb. H 20–60cm (8–24in), S 12–15cm (5–6in). Half hardy. Bears widely strap-shaped, semi-erect, basal, greyish-green leaves, twisted lengthways. Carries a head of up to 12 pendent, tubular, red-and-yellow flowers, each 7cm (3in) long.
C. parviflorus. See *C. brachyscyphus*.
C. purpureus. See *C. elatus*.
C. sanguineus. Clump-forming, summer-flowering bulb. H 30–50cm (12–20in), S 12–15cm (5–6in). Half hardy. Has strap-shaped, semi-erect, basal, bright green leaves. Stout stem bears 1 or 2 long-tubed, scarlet flowers, 8–10cm (3–4in) long.

CYRTOMIUM

DRYOPTERIDACEAE

Genus of evergreen ferns. Fully to half hardy. Does best in semi-shade and humus-rich, moist soil. Remove fading fronds. Propagate by division in spring or summer or by spores in summer.
♀ ***C. falcatum*** illus. p.323.
♀ ***C. fortunei***, syn. *Phanerophlebia fortunei.* Evergreen fern. H 60cm (24in). Fully hardy. S 40cm (16in). Has erect, dull, pale green fronds, 30–60cm (12–24in) long, with broadly sickle-shaped pinnae, 2.5–5cm (1–2in) long.

CYSTOPTERIS

WOODSIACEAE

Genus of deciduous ferns, suitable for rock gardens. Fully hardy. Does best in semi-shade and in soil that is never allowed to dry out. Remove fronds as they fade. Propagate by division in spring, by spores in summer or by bulbils when available.
C. bulbifera (Berry bladder fern). Deciduous fern. H 15cm (6in), S 23cm (9in). Broadly lance-shaped, much-divided, dainty, pale green fronds produce tiny bulbils along their length. Propagate by bulbils as soon as mature.
C. dickieana. Deciduous fern. H 15cm (6in), S 23cm (9in). Has broadly lance-shaped, divided, delicate, pale green fronds, with oblong, blunt, indented pinnae, that arch downwards.
C. fragilis (Brittle bladder fern). Deciduous fern. H 15cm (6in), S 23cm (9in). Broadly lance-shaped, pale green fronds are delicate and much divided into oblong, pointed, indented pinnae.

CYTISUS
Broom

LEGUMINOSAE/PAPILIONACEAE

Genus of deciduous or evergreen shrubs, grown for their abundant, pea-like flowers. Fully to half hardy. Prefers full sun and fertile, but not over-rich, well-drained soil. Resents being transplanted. Propagate species by semi-ripe cuttings in summer or by seed in autumn, hybrids and cultivars by semi-ripe cuttings in late summer. All parts, especially the seeds, may cause mild stomach upset if ingested.
C. albus. See *Chamaecytisus albus*.
C. ardoinii. See *C. ardoinoi*.
♀ ***C. ardoinoi***, syn. *C. ardoinii*, illus. p.398.
♀ ***C. battandieri***, syn. *Argyrocytisus battandieri*, illus. p.119.
♀ ***C. × beanii*** illus. p.361.
C. canariensis of gardens. See *C. × spachianus*.
C. demissus. See *Chamaecytisus demissus*.
C. 'Firefly'. Deciduous, bushy shrub with slender, arching shoots. H and S 1.5–2m (5–6ft). Fully hardy. Small, mid-green leaves are oblong and have 3 tiny leaflets. Produces masses of yellow flowers, marked with red, from late spring to early summer.
♀ ***C. × kewensis.*** Deciduous, arching shrub. H 30cm (1ft), S to 2m (6ft). Fully hardy. Has leaves, each composed of 3 tiny leaflets, along downy stems. In late spring bears creamy-white flowers. Is good for a bank or large rock garden.
C. leucanthus. See *Chamaecytisus albus*.
C. nigricans, syn. *Lembotropis nigricans*, illus. p.166.
♀ ***C. × praecox 'Allgold'*** illus. p.153.
♀ ***'Warminster'*** illus. p.152.
C. purpureus. See *Chamaecytisus purpureus*.
C. racemosus of gardens. See *C. × spachianus*.
C. scoparius (Common broom).
♀ f. ***andreanus*** illus. p.167. subsp. ***maritimus*** (syn. *C.s.* var. *prostratus*) is a deciduous, prostrate shrub forming dense mounds of interlocking shoots. H 20cm (8in), S 1.2–2m (4–6ft). Fully hardy. Small, grey-green leaves usually have 3 oblong leaflets, but may be reduced to a single leaflet. Has masses of golden-yellow flowers in late spring and early summer. var. ***prostratus*** see *C.s.* subsp. *maritimus*.
♀ ***C. × spachianus***, syn. *C. canariensis* of gardens, *C. racemosus* of gardens, *Genista fragrans* of gardens, *G. × spachiana.* Vigorous, evergreen, arching shrub. H and S 3m (10ft). Half hardy. Has dark green leaves with 3 oval leaflets. Produces long, slender clusters of fragrant, golden-yellow flowers in winter and early spring. Is often grown as a houseplant.
C. supinus. See *Chamaecytisus supinus*.
C. 'Windlesham Ruby'. Deciduous, bushy shrub with slender, arching shoots. H and S 1.5–2m (5–6ft). Fully hardy. Small, mid-green leaves have 3 oblong leaflets. Large, rich red flowers are borne in profusion in late spring and early summer.
♀ ***C. 'Zeelandia'.*** Deciduous, bushy shrub with slender, arching shoots. H and S 1.5–2m (5–6ft). Fully hardy. Small, mid-green leaves have 3 oblong leaflets. Has masses of bicoloured, creamy-white and lilac-pink flowers from late spring to early summer.

Daboecia

ERICACEAE

See also HEATHERS.

D. azorica. Evergreen, compact shrub. H to 15cm (6in), S to 60cm (24in). Half hardy. Lance-shaped leaves are dark green above, silver-grey beneath. Urn- to bell-shaped flowers are vivid red and open in late spring or early summer.

D. cantabrica (St Dabeoc's heath). Evergreen, straggling shrub. H to 45cm (18in), S 60cm (24in). Frost hardy; top growth may be damaged by frost and cold winds, but plants respond well to hard pruning and produce new growth from base. Leaves are lance-shaped to oval, dark green above, silver-grey beneath. Bears bell- to urn-shaped, single or double, white, purple or mauve flowers from late spring to mid-autumn. ♀ **'Bicolor'** (illus. p.175) bears white, purple and striped flowers on the same plant. **'Praegerae'**, H 35cm (14in), has glowing deep pink flowers. **'Snowdrift'** (illus. p.174) has bright green foliage and long racemes of large, white flowers. subsp. ***scotica*** see *D.* × *scotica*.

D.* × *scotica, syn. *D. cantabrica* subsp. *scotica*. Evergreen, compact shrub. H to 15cm (6in), S to 60cm (2ft). Frost hardy. Lance-shaped to oval leaves are dark green above, silver-grey beneath. Bears bell- to urn-shaped, white, purple or mauve flowers from late spring to mid-autumn. ♀ **'Jack Drake'**, H 20cm (8in), has small, dark green leaves and ruby-coloured flowers. ♀ **'Silverwells'** has small, bright green leaves and large, white flowers. ♀ **'William Buchanan'** (illus. p.174), H 45cm (18in), is a vigorous cultivar with dark green leaves and deep purple flowers.

Dactylis

GRAMINEAE/POACEAE

See also GRASSES, BAMBOOS, RUSHES and SEDGES.

D. glomerata (Cock's-foot, Orchard grass). **'Variegata'** is an evergreen, tuft-forming, perennial grass. H 1m (3ft), S 20–25cm (8–10in). Fully hardy. Silver-striped, grey-green leaves arise from tufted rootstock. In summer bears panicles of densely clustered, awned, purplish-green spikelets.

Dactylorhiza

ORCHIDACEAE

See also ORCHIDS.

♀ ***D. elata***, syn. *Orchis elata*. Deciduous, terrestrial orchid. H 1.1m (3½ft). Frost hardy. Spikes of pink or purple flowers, 1–2cm (½–¾in) long, open in spring-summer. Lance-shaped leaves, 15–25cm (6–10in) long, are spotted with brownish-purple and arranged spirally on stem. Requires shade outdoors; keep pot plants semi-shaded in summer.

♀ ***D. foliosa***, syn. *D. maderensis*, *Orchis maderensis*. Deciduous, terrestrial orchid. H 70cm (28in). Frost hardy. Spikes of bright purple or pink flowers, 1–2cm (½–¾in) long, are borne in spring-summer. Has lance-shaped or triangular leaves, 10–20cm (4–8in) long, arranged spirally on stem. Cultivate as for *D. elata*.

D. maderensis. See *D. foliosa*.

Daffodil. See *Narcissus*.
- **Bunch-flowered.** See *Narcissus tazetta*.
- **Hoop-petticoat.** See *Narcissus bulbocodium*.
- **Peruvian.** See *Hymenocallis narcissiflora*, illus. p.436.
- **Poet's.** See *Narcissus poeticus*.
- **Polyanthus.** See *Narcissus tazetta*.
- **Queen Anne's double.** See *Narcissus* 'Eystettensis'.
- **Sea.** See *Pancratium maritimum*.
- **Tenby.** See *Narcissus obvallaris*.
- **Wild.** See *Narcissus pseudonarcissus*, illus. p.434.

Dahlia

COMPOSITAE/ASTERACEAE

Genus of bushy, summer- and autumn-flowering, tuberous perennials, grown as bedding plants or for their flower heads, which are good for cutting or exhibition. Dwarf forms are used for mass-planting and are also suitable for containers. Half hardy. Needs a sunny position and well-drained soil. All apart from dwarf forms require staking. After flowering, lift tubers and store in a frost-free place; replant once all frost danger has passed. In frost-free areas, plants may be left in ground as normal herbaceous perennials, but they benefit from regular propagation to maintain vigour. Propagate dwarf forms by seed sown under glass in late winter, others in spring by seed, basal shoot cuttings or division of tubers. Dahlias may be subject to attack by aphids, red spider mite and thrips. In recent years, powdery mildew has become a problem in certain areas, and spraying is essential. Dahlias also succumb quickly to virus infection. See also feature panel pp.420–23.

Border dahlias

Prolific and long-flowering, various species of *Dahlia* have been hybridized and, with constant breeding and selection, have developed into many forms and have a wide colour range (although there is no blue). Shoots may be stopped, or pinched out, to promote vigorous growth and a bushy shape. Spread measurements depend on the amount of stopping carried out and the time at which it is done: early stopping encourages a broader shape, stopping later in the growing season results in a taller plant with much less spread, even in the same cultivar. Leaves are generally mid-green and divided into oval leaflets, some with rounded tips and some with toothed margins. Each flower head is referred to horticulturally as a flower, even though it does in fact comprise a large number of individual flowers. This horticultural usage has been followed in the descriptions below. All forms with flower heads to 150mm (6in) across are suitable for cutting; those suitable for exhibition are so noted.

Groups and flower sizes

Dahlias are divided into groups, according to the size and type of their flower heads, although the latter may vary in colour and shape depending on soil and weather conditions. The groups are: (1) single; (2) anemone; (3) collerette; (4) water-lily; (5) decorative; (6) ball; (7) pompon; (8) cactus; (9) semi-cactus; (10) miscellaneous; (11) fimbriated; (12) single orchid; (13) double orchid. For illustrations and descriptions see p.420. Certain groups have been subdivided; flower sizes are as follows:

Groups 4, 5, 8 and 9

A – giant-flowered; usually over 250mm (10in) in diameter.
B – large-flowered; usually 200–250mm (8–10in) in diameter.
C – medium-flowered; usually 150–200mm (6–8in) in diameter.
D – small-flowered; usually 100–150mm (4–6in) in diameter.
E – miniature-flowered; usually not exceeding 100mm (4in) in diameter.

Group 6

A – small ball dahlias; usually 100–150mm (4–6in) in diameter.
B – miniature ball dahlias; usually 50–100mm (2–4in) in diameter.

Group 7

Pompon dahlias; not exceeding 50mm (2in) in diameter.

***D.* 'Akita'** illus. p.422. Miscellaneous dahlia. H 1.2m (4ft), S 60cm (2ft). In summer and autumn produces dark crimson to red flowers, to 13cm (5in) across, with yellow centres. The reverses of the petals are tipped white.

***D.* 'Appetiser'** illus. p.423. Small-flowered semi-cactus dahlia. H 1.2m (4ft), S 60cm (2ft). Produces yellow-and-pink flowers in summer-autumn.

***D.* 'Aranka'** illus. p.421. Collerette dahlia. H 1.2m (4ft), S 60cm (2ft). Produces flowers, 7–10cm (3–4in) across, with white-tipped, dark pink outer petals, white inner petals and yellow centres, in summer-autumn.

***D.* 'Avoca Cree'** illus. p.423. Small-flowered semi-cactus dahlia. H 1.5m (5ft), S 60cm (2ft). Produces masses of bright orange flowers in summer and autumn. Is good for cutting.

***D.* 'Avoca Kiowa'** illus. p.423. Small-flowered semi-cactus dahlia. H 1.2m (4ft) S 60cm (2ft). Produces masses of lavender-tipped, pale yellow flowers in summer-autumn. Is good for cutting.

***D.* 'Barry Williams'** illus. p.423. Medium-flowered decorative dahlia. H 1.2m (4ft), S 60cm (2ft). Bears pink-and-yellow flowers in summer-autumn.

***D.* 'Berwick Wood'** illus. p.421. Medium-flowered decorative dahlia. H 1.3m (4½ft), S 60cm (2ft). In summer and autumn produces dark-centred, purple flowers on strong stems.

***D.* 'Bicentenary'** illus. p.423. Medium-flowered decorative dahlia. H 1.2m (4ft), S 60cm (2ft). In summer and autumn produces dark orange flowers, fading to pale orange at the tips. Is good for cutting.

***D.* 'Biddenham Sunset'** illus. p.422. Small-flowered decorative dahlia. H 1.1m (3½ft), S 60cm (2ft). Orange-red flowers are borne in mid-summer and autumn.

♀ ***D.* 'Bishop of Llandaff'** illus. p.422. Miscellaneous dahlia. H 1m (3ft), S 45cm (18in). Has bronze-green leaves and single, open-centred, dark red flowers, 78mm (3in) across, in summer-autumn. It is excellent as a bedding plant.

***D.* 'Black Narcissus'** illus. p.422. Medium-flowered semi-cactus dahlia. H 1.5m (5ft), S 60cm (2ft). Produces intensely dark red blooms in summer-autumn.

***D.* 'Brian's Dream'** illus. p.421. Miniature-flowered decorative dahlia. H 1–1.2m (3–4ft), S 60cm (2ft). Produces creamy-white flowers with the tips of the petals suffused purplish-pink, in summer and autumn.

***D.* 'Butterball'** illus. p.423. Miniature-flowered decorative dahlia. H 60cm (2ft), S 30cm (1ft). Produces bright yellow flowers in early summer.

♀ ***D.* 'Candy Cupid'** illus. p.421. Miniature ball dahlia. H 1.1m (3½ft), S 60cm (2ft). In summer and autumn bears lavender-pink flowers that are good for exhibition.

***D.* 'Charlie Dimmock'** illus. p.422. Small-flowered water-lily dahlia. H 1.6m (5½ft) S 60cm (2ft). Produces apricot flowers on a pale yellow ground, during summer and autumn.

***D.* 'Cherokee Beauty'** illus. p.421. Giant-flowered decorative dahlia. H 1.3m (4½ft), S 60–80cm (24–32in). In summer-autumn has pink flowers.

♀ ***D.* 'Cherwell Skylark'** illus. p.422. Small-flowered semi-cactus dahlia. H 1m (3ft), S 50–60cm (20–24in). Bears orange-flushed, salmon-pink blooms in summer and autumn.

***D.* 'Chimborazo'** illus. p.422. Collerette dahlia. H 1.1m (3½ft), S 60cm (2ft). Leaves are glossy, dark green. Has 102mm (4in) wide flowers, with red, outer petals and yellow, inner petals, in summer-autumn. Flowers are good for exhibition.

♀ ***D.* 'Clair de Lune'** illus. p.423. Collerette dahlia. H 1.1m (3½ft), S 60cm (2ft). Has 102mm (4in) wide flowers, with lemon-yellow, outer petals and paler yellow, inner petals, in summer-autumn. Is good for exhibition.

D. coccinea illus. p.421. Tuberous-rooted herbaceous perennial. H 2–3m (6–10ft), S 1–2m (3–6ft). From summer to late autumn produces sprays of single, yellow, orange-red, maroon or purple-red flowers, 5–8cm (2–3in) across. Is a parent of many garden dahlias.

***D.* 'Coltness Gem'** illus. p.341.

***D.* 'Comet'** illus. p.422. Anemone dahlia. H 1.1m (3½ft), S 60cm (2ft). Leaves are glossy, dark green. Dark red flowers, 10–15cm (4–6in) across, are produced in summer-autumn.

***D.* 'Cottesmore'** illus. p.421. Medium-flowered water-lily dahlia. H 1.1m (3½ft), S 60cm (2ft). Produces purplish-pink flowers, with yellow shading at the petal bases, in summer and autumn.

***D.* 'Currant Cream'** illus. p.421. Small ball dahlia. H 1.2m (4ft), S 60cm (2ft). In summer and autumn produces dark pink flowers with the pink-and-white petal bases. Is good for cutting.

***D.* 'Dancing Queen'** illus. p.420. Small-flowered semi-cactus dahlia. H 1.1m (3½ft), S 60cm (2ft). In summer and autumn produces pink flowers, with deeper pink centres. Petals are primrose-yellow at the bases.

***D.* 'Dandy'** illus. p.353.
***D.* 'Davenport Sunlight'** illus. p.423. Medium-flowered semi-cactus dahlia. H 1.2m (4ft), S 60cm (2ft). Has bright yellow flowers in summer and autumn. Is good for exhibition.
***D.* 'Deborah's Kiwi'** illus. p.421. Small-flowered cactus dahlia. H 1.1m (3½ft), S 60cm (2ft). Produces pink flowers, with white bases to the petals, during summer and autumn.
***D.* 'Demi Schneider'** illus. p.422. Collerette dahlia. H 1.5m (5ft), S 60cm (2ft). In summer and autumn produces single, red flowers, to 14cm (5½in) across, with yellow centres.
***D.* 'Dutch Triumph'** illus. p.423. Large-flowered water-lily dahlia. H 1.1m (3½ft), S 60cm (2ft). Bears yellow-pink flowers in summer-autumn.
***D.* 'East Anglian'** illus. p.423. Small-flowered decorative dahlia. H 1m (3ft), S 60cm (2ft). Has orange-yellow flowers in summer-autumn.
***D.* 'Easter Sunday'** illus. p.420. Collerette dahlia. H 1m (3ft), S 60cm (2ft). Leaves are glossy, dark green. Produces 102mm (4in) wide flowers, with white, inner and outer petals and dark yellow centres, in summer-autumn. Is good for exhibition.
♀ ***D.* 'Fascination'** illus. p.421. Dwarf miscellaneous dahlia. H 45cm (18in), S 30cm (12in). Has single, light purple flowers, 78mm (3in) across, in summer-autumn. Is useful for bedding.
♀ ***D.* 'Fusion'** illus. p.420. Small-flowered decorative dahlia. H 1m (3ft), S 60cm (2ft). In summer and autumn produces white flowers, the outer petals flushed pale pink, the inner petals veined purple-violet. Has bronze-tinged, very dark green foliage. Is good for cutting.
***D.* 'Gateshead Festival'**, syn. *D.* 'Peach Melba' illus. p.423. Small-flowered decorative dahlia. H 1.2m (4ft), S 60cm (2ft). In summer-autumn, bears peach to orange flowers with lemon-yellow petal bases. Is good for exhibition.
***D.* 'Gay Princess'** illus. p.421. Small-flowered decorative dahlia. H 1.2m (4ft), S 60cm (2ft). Produces lilac-lavender flowers in summer-autumn.
***D.* 'Geerling's Moonlight'** illus. p.423. Medium-flowered semi-cactus dahlia. H 1.3m (4½ft), S 60cm (2ft). Produces brilliant yellow flowers in summer and autumn.
***D.* 'Gilwood Terry G'** illus. p.423. Small-flowered semi-cactus dahlia. H 1.3m (4½ft), S 1–1.2m (3–4ft). Flowers have bronze-tinted, orange outer petals and yellow inner petals, borne in summer-autumn. Is excellent for cutting.
***D.* 'Giraffe'** illus. p.422. Double orchid dahlia. H 1m (3ft), S 60cm (2ft). In summer and autumn has spotted, yellow-bronze flowers, to 8cm (3in) across. Is good for cutting.
***D.* 'Grenidor Pastelle'** illus. p.423. Medium-flowered semi-cactus dahlia. H 1.3m (4½ft), S 60cm (2ft). Bears salmon-pink flowers, with cream petal bases, in summer-autumn. Is good for exhibition.
***D.* 'Gwyneth'** illus. p.422. Small-flowered water-lily dahlia. H 1.8m (6ft), S 60cm (2ft). Bears bronze-tinted, orange flowers in summer-autumn. Is good for cutting.
♀ ***D.* 'Hamari Accord'** illus. p.423. Large-flowered semi-cactus dahlia. H 1.2m (4ft), S 60cm (2ft). Has clear yellow flowers held well above the foliage on strong stems in summer-autumn. Is good for exhibition.
♀ ***D.* 'Hamari Gold'** illus. p.422. Giant-flowered decorative dahlia. H 1.1m (3½ft), S 60cm (2ft). Has golden orange-bronze flowers in summer-autumn. Is suitable for exhibition.
***D.* 'Hamari Katrina'** illus. p.423. Large-flowered semi-cactus dahlia. H 1.2m (4ft), S 60cm (2ft). Bears deep butter-yellow flowers in summer-autumn. Is good for exhibition.
♀ ***D.* 'Harvest Inflammation'** illus. p.423. Single dahlia. H 55cm (22in), S 40cm (16in). In summer and autumn produces orange flowers, 5cm (2in) across, suffused orange-red, with the central disc orange-yellow.
***D.* 'Hayley Jayne'** illus. p.421. Small-flowered semi-cactus dahlia. H 1.1m (3½ft), S 60cm (2ft). Produces flowers that are white at base with purple-red tips, in summer and autumn. Is good for exhibition.
***D.* 'Hexton Copper'** illus. p.422. Small ball dahlia. H 1.1m (3½ft), S 60cm (2ft). In summer-autumn has orange flowers.
***D.* 'Hillcrest Jessica'** illus. p.421. Large-flowered decorative dahlia. H 1.25m (4ft), S 60cm (2ft). Bears red-purple flowers in summer and autumn.
♀ ***D.* 'Hillcrest Royal'** illus. p.422. Medium-flowered cactus dahlia. H 1.1m (3½ft), S 60cm (2ft). In summer-autumn has rich purple flowers, with incurving petals, held on strong stems.
***D.* 'Hillcreat Ultra'** illus. p.423. Small-flowered decorative dahlia. H 1.2m (4ft), S 60cm (2ft). Produces flowers, with pink outer petals and lemon-yellow inner petals, in summer and autumn.
♀ ***D.* 'Honka'** illus. p.423. Single orchid dahlia. H 1–1.2m (3–4ft), S 60cm (2ft). Has masses of star-shaped, bright yellow flowers, 5cm (2in) across, with darker yellow discs, in summer and autumn. Is good for cutting.
♀ ***D.* 'Jaldec Joker'** illus. p.421. Small-flowered semi-cactus dahlia. H 1.1m (3½ft), S 60cm (2ft). In summer and autumn has bright orange-red flowers, shading to yellow at the bases. Petals are tipped white.
♀ ***D.* 'Jean Fairs'** illus. p.423. Miscellaneous dahlia. H 1.3m (4½ft), S 60cm (2ft). In summer and autumn produces semi-double, orange-yellow flowers, to 10cm (4in) across, the yellow outer petals strongly flushed orange, the inner petals orange-red.
♀ ***D.* 'Jeanette Carter'** illus. p.423. Miniature-flowered decorative dahlia. H 1.1m (3½ft), S 60cm (2ft). Bears yellow flowers, sometimes flushed pink in the centres, in summer-autumn.
***D.* 'Jescot Julie'** illus. p.422. Double orchid dahlia. H 60cm (24in), S 45cm (18in). Has sparse, mid-green foliage and orange-purple flowers, 78mm (3in) across, with purple-backed petals, in summer-autumn.
***D.* 'Jim Branigan'** illus. p.421. Large-flowered semi-cactus dahlia. H 1.3m (4½ft), S 60cm (2ft). Bright red flowers are held well above the foliage in summer-autumn. Is good for exhibition.
***D.* 'Julie One'** illus. p.422. Double orchid dahlia. H 1.2m (4ft), S 60cm (2ft). In summer and autumn produces bronze-purple flowers, 8cm (3in) across. Is good for cutting.
***D.* 'Jura'** illus. p.420. Small-flowered semi-cactus dahlia. H 1.2m (4ft), S 60cm (2ft). In summer and autumn produces purple-tipped, white flowers.
***D.* 'Kaiser Waltzer'**. See *D.* 'Kaiserwaltzer'.
***D.* 'Kaiserwaltzer'**, syn. *D.* 'Kaiser Waltzer' illus. p.422. Collerette dahlia. H 1.1m (3½ft), S 60cm (2ft). Produces flowers, 10cm (4in) across, with large, red outer petals and narrower, yellow inner petals, in summer and autumn. Is good as a border plant.
♀ ***D.* 'Kathryn's Cupid'** illus. p.423. Miniature ball dahlia. H 1.2m (4ft), S 60cm (2ft). In summer-autumn, produces peach flowers that are good for exhibition.
♀ ***D.* 'Kenora Sunset'.** Medium-flowered semi-cactus dahlia. H 1.2m (4ft), S 60cm (2ft). Produces bicoloured, brilliant red and yellow blooms in summer and autumn.
***D.*'Kenora Superb'** illus. p.423. Giant-flowered semi-cactus dahlia. H 1.2m (4ft), S 60cm (2ft). Produces bright orange-and-yellow flowers in summer-autumn.
***D.* 'Klondike'** (syn. D. 'Klondyke'; illus. p.420). Large-flowered semi-cactus dahlia. H 1.2m (4ft), S 60cm (2ft). Produces white flowers in summer and autumn.
***D.* 'Klondyke'**. See *D.* 'Klondike'.
♀ ***D.* 'Lakeland Sunset'** illus. p.423. Small-flowered cactus dahlia. H 1.65m (5½ft), S 60cm (2ft). Produces yellow-orange flowers, with brighter yellow centres, in late summer and autumn. Is good for cutting.
***D.* 'Lavender Athalie'** illus. p.421. Small-flowered cactus dahlia. H 1.2m (4ft), S 60cm (2ft). Is a sport of *D.* 'Athalie'. Bears soft lilac-lavender flowers in summer-autumn.
***D.* 'Marie Schnugg'** illus. p.422. Single orchid dahlia. H 1.1m (3½ft), S 60cm (2ft). Bears star-like, red flowers, 5–7cm (2–3in) across, in summer and autumn. Is good as a border plant as well as for cutting. (12in). Produces dark foliage before yellow-red flowers, 5–7cm (2–3in)
***D.* 'Mark Hardwick'** illus. p.423. Giant-flowered decorative dahlia. H 1.1m (3½ft), S 60cm (2ft). Compact plant bearing bright, deep yellow flowers, on strong stems, in summer-autumn. Is good for exhibition.
♀ ***D.* 'Marston Lilac'** illus. p.421. Miniature-flowered decorative dahlia. H 1.4m (4½ft), S 60cm (2ft). Has very compact, deep lilac flowers in summer and autumn.
***D.* 'Mary Richards'** illus. p.420. Small-flowered decorative dahlia. H 1.2m (4ft), S 60cm (2ft). In summer and autumn produces white flowers strongly suffused lavender-pink.
***D.* 'Mermaid of Zennor'** illus. p.421. Single dahlia. H 75cm (30in), S 60cm (2ft). In summer-autumn produces lavender flowers, 2.5cm (1in) across, above delicate foliage. Is good as a border plant.
***D.* 'Mi Wong'** illus. p.421. Pompon dahlia. H 1.1m (3½ft), S 60cm (2ft). Bears white flowers, suffused pink, in summer-autumn. Is good for exhibition.
♀ ***D.* 'Moonfire'** illus. p.423. Dwarf, single dahlia. H 45cm (18in), S 30cm (12in). Produces dark foliage before yellow-red flowers, 5–7cm (2–3in) across, appear in summer-autumn. Is very good as a container plant and in a border.
***D.* 'Moor Place'** illus. p.421. Pompon dahlia. H 1m (3ft), S 60cm (2ft). Leaves are glossy, dark green. Has red-purple flowers in summer-autumn. Is a good exhibition cultivar.
***D.* 'Mum's Lipstick'** illus. p.423. Fimbriated cactus dahlia. H 1–1.2m (3–4ft), S 60cm (2ft). Bears red-tipped, yellow flowers, 7–10cm (3–4in) across, in summer-autumn.
***D.* 'Noreen'** illus. p.421. Pompon dahlia. H 1m (3ft), S 60cm (2ft). In summer-autumn produces dark pinkish-purple flowers Is good for exhibition.
***D.* 'NZ's Robert'** illus. p.421. Miniature water-lily dahlia. H 50cm (20in), S 30cm (12in). Produces red-pink flowers, with greeny-yellow discs, in summer and autumn. Is a good container plant.
***D.* 'Onesta'** illus. p.421. Small-flowered water-lily dahlia. H 1.2m (4ft), S 60cm (2ft). Produces masses of flowers, with dark pink inner petals fading to pale pink outer petals, in summer-autumn. Is good for cutting.
***D.* 'Onslow Renown'** illus. p.422. Large-flowered semi-cactus dahlia. H 1.2m (4ft), S 60cm (2ft). Bears yellowish-orange flowers in summer and autumn.
***D.* 'Oosterbeck Remembered'** illus. p.422. Small-flowered semi-cactus dahlia. H 1.2m (4ft), S 60cm (2ft). Bears dark orange flowers, with bright yellow inner petals, in summer-autumn. Is good for cutting.
***D.* 'Orange Berger's Record'** illus. p.422. Medium-flowered semi-cactus dahlia. H 1.2m (4ft), S 60cm (2ft). Bears yellowish-orange flowers in summer-autumn.
***D.* 'Peach Melba'.** See *D.* 'Gateshead Festival'.
♀ ***D.* 'Pearl of Heemstede'** illus. p.420. Small-flowered water-lily dahlia. H 1m (3ft), S 45cm (18in). Produces pale silvery-pink flowers on long, thin stems in summer-autumn. Is very very free-flowering.
***D.* 'Pink Jupiter'** illus. p.421. Giant-flowered semi-cactus dahlia. H 1.3m (4½ft), S 60cm (2ft). In summer-autumn produces deep pinkish-mauve flowers. Is good for exhibition.
***D.* 'Pink Shirley Alliance'** illus. p.421. Small-flowered cactus dahlia. H 1.2m (4ft), S 60cm (2ft). Has soft lilac-pink flowers in summer-autumn.
***D.* 'Pink Symbol'** illus. p.421. Medium-flowered semi-cactus dahlia. H 1–1.2m (3–4ft), S 60cm (2ft). Bears pink flowers in summer-autumn. Is good for exhibition.
***D.* 'Pontiac'** illus. p.421. Small-flowered cactus dahlia. H 1m (3ft), S 60cm (2ft). Leaves are glossy, dark green. Bears dark pinkish-purple flowers in summer-autumn.
♀ ***D.* 'Preston Park'** illus. p.422. Dwarf single dahlia. H 45cm (18in), S 30cm (12in). Bedding plant with

nearly black foliage. In summer-autumn bears bright scarlet flowers, to 78mm (3in) across, with prominent yellow anthers in the centre, on short stems.
***D.* 'Rhonda'** illus. p.420. Pompon dahlia. H 1m (3ft), S 60cm (2ft). In summer-autumn produces whitish-lilac flowers. Is suitable for exhibition.
***D.* 'Ryecroft Gem'** illus. p.421. Miniature-flowered decorative dahlia. H 90cm (3ft), S 60cm (2ft). In summer-autumn produces violet-margined, lavender-pink flowers. Is good for exhibition.
♀ ***D.* 'Sascha'** illus. p.421. Small-flowered water-lily dahlia. H 1.8m (6ft), S 60cm (2ft). Bears bright purple-pink flowers, fading to paler purple-pink towards the margins, in summer-autumn.
***D.* 'Shandy'** illus. p.423. Small-flowered semi-cactus dahlia. H 1.1m (3½ft), S 60cm (2ft). Has pale orange-brown flowers in summer-autumn.
***D.* 'Shirley Alliance'** illus. p.423. Small-flowered cactus dahlia. H 1.3m (4½ft), S 60cm (2ft). In summer-autumn bears soft orange flowers with a gold base to each petal. Is good for exhibition.
***D.* 'Sir Alf Ramsey'** illus. p.420. Giant-flowered decorative dahlia. H 1.1m (3½ft), S 60cm (2ft). In summer and autumn bears lavender-pink flowers, with white petal bases.
♀ ***D.* 'Small World'** illus. p.420. Pompon dahlia. H 1m (3ft), S 60cm (2ft). Leaves are glossy, dark green. Has white flowers in summer-autumn. Is suitable for exhibition.
***D.* 'Smokey O'** illus. p.423. Medium-flowered semi-cactus dahlia. H 1–1.2m (3–4ft), S 60cm (2ft). Produces dark pink flowers in summer-autumn.
***D.* 'Swanvale'** illus. p.423. Small-flowered decorative dahlia. H 1.1m (3½ft), S 60cm (2ft). Bears yellow flowers in summer-autumn.
***D.* 'Trelyn Kiwi'** illus. p.420. Small-flowered semi-cactus dahlia. H 1.2m (4ft), S 60cm (2ft). Produces pink-flushed, white flowers, with darker pink central petals, in summer and autumn.
***D.* 'Trengrove Millennium'** illus. p.423. Medium-flowered decorative dahlia. H 1.2m (4ft), S 60cm (2ft). Produces yellow flowers in summer-autumn. Is suitable for exhibition.
***D.* 'Tui Ruth'** illus. p.422. Small-flowered semi-cactus dahlia. H 1.1m (3½ft), S 60cm (2ft). Bears pink-yellow flowers in summer-autumn.
***D.* 'Vicky Crutchfield'** illus. p.420. Small-flowered water-lily dahlia. H 1m (3ft), S 60cm (2ft). Bears pink flowers in summer-autumn. Is suitable for exhibition.
***D.* 'Wanda's Capella'** illus. p.423. Giant-flowered decorative dahlia. H 1.2m (4ft), S 60cm (2ft). Has bright yellow flowers in summer-autumn. Is good for exhibition.
♀ ***D.* 'Weston Pirate'** illus. p.422. Miniature-flowered cactus dahlia. H 1.3m (4½ft), S 50–60cm (20–24in). Produces prolific, semi-double, dark red flowers in summer-autumn. Is good for cutting.
***D.* 'Whale's Rhonda'** illus. p.421. Pompon dahlia. H 1m (3ft), S 60cm (2ft). Leaves are glossy, very dark green. In summer-autumn has bright purple flowers. Is good for exhibition.
♀ ***D.* 'White Alva's'** illus. p.420. Giant-flowered decorative dahlia. H 1.2m (4ft), S 60cm (2ft). Produces pure white flowers, held well above the foliage on strong stems, in summer-autumn. Is good for exhibition.
♀ ***D.* 'White Ballet'** illus. p.420. Small-flowered water-lily dahlia. H 1m (3ft), S 60cm (2ft). Produces pure white flowers in summer-autumn.
***D.* 'White Klankstad'** illus. p.420. Small-flowered cactus dahlia. H 1.1–1.2m (3½–4ft), S 60cm (2ft). Is a sport of *D.* 'Klankstad Kerkrade' with white flowers in summer-autumn.
♀ ***D.* 'Wootton Cupid'** illus. p.421. Miniature ball dahlia. H 1.1–1.2m (3½–4ft), S 60cm (2ft). Has pink flowers in summer-autumn. Is good for exhibition.
♀ ***D.* 'Wootton Impact'** illus. p.423. Medium-flowered semi-cactus dahlia. H 1.2m (4ft), S 60cm (2ft). Has flowers in shades of bronze, held well above the foliage on strong stems, in summer-autumn. Is good for exhibition.
♀ ***D.* 'Yellow Hammer'** illus. p.423. Dwarf, single dahlia. H 45cm (18in), S 30cm (12in). Has rich yellow flowers, 78mm (3in) across, in summer-autumn.
***D.* 'Yelno Enchanted'**, syn. *D.* 'Yelno Enchantment' illus. p.422. Small-flowered water-lily dahlia. H 1.2m (4ft), S 60cm (2ft). Bears pale pink flowers in summer-autumn. Is good for cutting.
***D.* 'Yelno Enchantment'.** See *D.* 'Yelno Enchanted'.
***D.* 'Yelno Firelight'** illus. p.422. Small-flowered water-lily dahlia. H 1.2m (4ft), S 60cm (2ft). In summer-autumn has red and yellow flowers, with a neat petal formation, held on strong stems.
♀ ***D.* 'Zorro'** illus. p.422. Giant-flowered decorative dahlia. H 1.2m (4ft), S 60cm (2ft). Produces bright blood-red flowers in summer-autumn, that are good for exhibition.

Dahlia, Climbing. See *Hidalgoa.*
Daimio oak. See *Quercus dentata.*

DAIS

THYMELAEACEAE

Genus of deciduous, summer-flowering shrubs, grown for their flowers and overall appearance. Frost tender, min. 5°C (41°F). Requires full sun and well-drained soil. Water containerized plants well when in full growth, less when leafless. Propagate by seed in spring or by semi-ripe cuttings in summer.
D. cotinifolia. Deciduous, bushy, neat shrub. H and S 2–3m (6–10ft). Has small, oval to oblong, lustrous leaves. In summer bears scented, star-shaped, rose-lilac flowers in flattened clusters, 8cm (3in) across. Bark yields fibres strong enough to be used as thread.

Daiswa polyphylla. See *Paris polyphylla.*
Daisy. See *Bellis.*
African. See *Arctotis stoechadifolia; Dimorphotheca.*
Barberton. See *Gerbera jamesonii*, illus. p.314.
Common. See *Bellis perennis.*
Kingfisher. See *Felicia bergeriana*, illus. p.346.
Livingstone. See *Dorotheanthus bellidiformis.*
Michaelmas. See *Aster.*
Rain. See *Dimorphotheca pluvialis*, illus. p.331.
Shasta. See *Leucanthemum* × *superbum.*
Star. See *Lindheimera texana*, illus. p.348.
Swan River. See *Brachyscome iberidifolia*, illus. p.346.
Daisy bush. See *Olearia.*
Dalmatian iris. See *Iris pallida.*
Dalmatian laburnum. See *Petteria ramentacea.*
Dalmatian toadflax. See *Linaria genistifolia* var. *dalmatica.*
Dame's violet. See *Hesperis matronalis*, illus. p.241.

DANÄE

LILIACEAE/RUSCACEAE

Genus of one species of evergreen shrub, with inconspicuous flowers, grown for its attractive, flattened, leaf-like shoots. Frost hardy. Grows in sun or shade and in moist soil. Propagate by seed in autumn or by division from autumn to spring.
D. racemosa (Alexandrian laurel). Evergreen, arching, dense shrub. H and S 1m (3ft). Has slender stems, lance-shaped, leaf-like, glossy, green shoots and pointed, glossy, bright green 'leaves'. Occasionally bears spherical, red berries.

Dancing-doll orchid. See *Oncidium flexuosum*, illus. p.311.
Dandelion.
Cape. See *Arctotheca calendula*, illus. p.306.
Pink. See *Crepis incana.*

DAPHNE

THYMELAEACEAE

Genus of evergreen, semi-evergreen or deciduous shrubs, grown for their usually fragrant, tubular flowers, each with 4 spreading lobes, and, in some species, for their foliage or fruits (seeds are poisonous). Dwarf species and cultivars are good for rock gardens. Fully to frost hardy. Most need full sun (although *D. alpina, D. arbuscula* and *D. blagayana* may be grown in semi-shade and *D. laureola* tolerates deep shade) and fertile, well-drained but not over-dry soil. Resents being transplanted. Propagate species by seed when fresh or by semi-ripe cuttings in summer, cultivars by cuttings only. Is susceptible to viruses that cause leaf mottling. All parts, including the seed, are highly toxic if ingested, and contact with the sap may irritate skin.
D. alpina illus. p.359. Deciduous, erect shrub. H 50cm (20in), S 40cm (16in). Fully hardy. Leaves are oval, downy and grey-green. Carries terminal clusters of fragrant, white flowers in late spring. Is suitable for a rock garden.
♀ ***D. arbuscula*** illus. p.378.
D. bholua illus. p.146.
D. blagayana illus. p.359.
***D.* × *burkwoodii* 'Somerset'** illus. p.150. **'Somerset Variegated'** is a semi-evergreen, upright shrub. H 1.5m (5ft), S 1m (3ft). Fully hardy. Bears dense clusters of very fragrant, white-throated, pink flowers in late spring, sometimes again in autumn. Narrowly oblong, grey-green leaves are edged with creamy-white or pale yellow.
D. cneorum illus. p.360. ♀ **'Eximia'** is an evergreen, prostrate shrub. H 10cm (4in), S to 50cm (20in) or more. Fully hardy. Has small, oval, leathery, dark green leaves and, in late spring, terminal clusters of fragrant, white flowers, crimson outside and often pink-flushed within.
D. collina. Evergreen, domed, compact shrub. H and S 50cm (20in). Frost hardy. Oval, dark green leaves densely cover upright branches. Has terminal clusters of small, fragrant, purple-rose flowers in late spring. Is good for a rock garden or shrubbery.
D. genkwa. Deciduous, upright, open shrub. H and S 1.5m (5ft). Fully hardy after a hot summer, otherwise frost hardy. Oval, dark green leaves are bronze when young. Large, faintly scented, lilac flowers are borne from mid- to late spring.
D. giraldii. Deciduous, upright shrub. H and S 60cm (2ft). Fully hardy. Clusters of fragrant, golden-yellow flowers are produced amid oblong, pale blue-green leaves in late spring and early summer and are followed by egg-shaped, red fruits.
D. jasminea illus. p.376.
D. laureola (Spurge laurel). Evergreen, bushy shrub. H 1m (3ft), S 1.5m (5ft). Fully hardy. Has oblong, dark green leaves. Slightly fragrant, pale green flowers are borne from late winter to early spring, followed by spherical, black fruits. subsp. ***philippi*** illus. p.152.
D. mezereum illus. p.170. f. ***alba*** is a deciduous, upright to spreading shrub. H and S 1.2m (4ft). Fully hardy. Bears very fragrant, white or creamy-white flowers that clothe bare stems in late winter and early spring. Has spherical, yellow fruits. Leaves are oblong and dull grey-green.
D. odora. Evergreen, bushy shrub. H and S 1.5m (5ft). Frost hardy. Has oval, glossy, dark green leaves and, from mid-winter to early spring, very fragrant, deep purplish-pink-and-white flowers. ♀ **'Aureomarginata'** illus. p.170.
***D. petraea* 'Grandiflora'** illus. p.378.
♀ ***D. retusa***, syn. *D. tangutica* Retusa Group, illus. p.151.
♀ ***D. tangutica.*** Evergreen, bushy shrub with stout shoots. H and S 1m (3ft). Fully hardy. Narrowly oval, leathery leaves are dark green. Bears clusters of fragrant, white-flushed, purple-pink flowers in mid- to late spring. **Retusa Group** see *D. retusa.*

DAPHNIPHYLLUM

DAPHNIPHYLLACEAE

Genus of evergreen trees and shrubs, grown for their habit and foliage. Male and female flowers are borne on separate plants. Frost hardy. Needs a sheltered position in sun or semi-shade and deep, fertile, well-drained but not too dry soil. Propagate by semi-ripe cuttings in summer.
D. himalaense subsp. ***macropodum.*** See *D. macropodum.*
D. macropodum, syn. *D. himalaense* subsp. *macropodum*, illus. p.113.

Darling pea. See *Swainsona galegifolia.*

DARMERA,
syn. PELTIPHYLLUM
Umbrella plant

SAXIFRAGACEAE

Genus of one species of perennial, grown for its unusual foliage. Makes fine marginal water plants. Fully hardy. Grows in sun or shade and requires moist soil. Propagate by division in spring or by seed in autumn or spring.
♀ ***D. peltata*** illus. p.240.

DARWINIA

MYRTACEAE

Genus of evergreen, spring-flowering shrubs, grown for their flowers and overall appearance. Frost tender, min. 7–10°C (45–50°F). Needs full light and moist, neutral to acid soil, not rich in nitrogen. Water moderately when in full growth, sparingly at other times. Propagate by seed in spring or by semi-ripe cuttings in late summer. Is difficult to root and to grow under glass.
D. citriodora. Evergreen, rounded, well-branched shrub. H and S 60cm–1.2m (2–4ft). Oblong to broadly lance-shaped, blue-green leaves are lemon-scented when bruised. In spring produces pendent, terminal heads of usually 4 small, tubular, yellow or red flowers, each surrounded by 2 red or yellowish bracts.

Darwin's barberry. See *Berberis darwinii*, illus. p.113.

DASYLIRION
Bear grass

DRACAENACEAE

Genus of evergreen, palm-like perennials, grown for their foliage and flowers. Male and female flowers are produced on separate plants. Frost tender, min. 10°C (50°F). Requires well-drained soil and a sunny position. Water freely when in full growth, sparingly at other times. Propagate by seed in spring.
D. texanum. Evergreen, palm-like perennial with a 75cm (30in) high trunk. H over 1m (3ft), S 3m (10ft). Has a rosette of narrow, drooping, green leaves, each 60–90cm (2–3ft) long, with yellowish prickles along margins. Stems, 5m (15ft) long, emerge from centre of plant carrying dense, narrow panicles of small, bell-shaped, whitish flowers in summer. Dry, 3-winged fruits appear in autumn.

Date plum. See *Diospyros lotus.*

DAVALLIA

DAVALLIACEAE

Genus of evergreen or semi-evergreen, often epiphytic ferns, best suited to growing in pots and hanging baskets. Half hardy to frost tender, min. 5°C (41°F). Requires semi-shade and very fibrous, moist, peaty soil. Remove fading fronds regularly. Propagate by division in spring or summer or by spores in summer.
♀ ***D. canariensis*** (Hare's-foot fern). Semi-evergreen fern. H and S 30cm (12in). Frost tender. Broadly lance-shaped, leathery, mid-green fronds, with numerous triangular pinnae, arise from a scaly, brown rootstock.
♀ ***D. mariesii*** (Squirrel's-foot fern). Evergreen fern. H 15cm (6in), S 23cm (9in). Half hardy. Broadly triangular, delicately divided, leathery, mid-green fronds arise from a creeping, scaly, brown rootstock.

DAVIDIA

CORNACEAE/DAVIDIACEAE

Genus of one species of deciduous, spring- and summer-flowering tree, grown for its habit and showy, white bracts surrounding insignificant flower heads. Fully hardy; needs shelter from strong winds. Requires sun or semi-shade and fertile, well-drained but preferably moist soil. Propagate by semi-ripe cuttings in spring or by seed when ripe in autumn.
♀ ***D. involucrata*** illus. p.73.

David's peach. See *Prunus davidiana.*
David's pine. See *Pinus armandii.*
Dawn flower, Blue. See *Ipomoea indica.*
Dawn redwood. See *Metasequoia glyptostroboides*, illus. p.98.
Day flower. See *Commelina coelestis*, illus. p.346.
Daylily. See *Hemerocallis.*
  Fulvous. See *Hemerocallis fulva.*
  Grass-leaved. See *Hemerocallis minor.*
  Tawny. See *Hemerocallis fulva.*
Deadnettle. See *Lamium.*

DECAISNEA

LARDIZABALACEAE

Genus of deciduous, summer-flowering shrubs, grown for their foliage, flowers and sausage-shaped fruits. Frost hardy. Requires a sheltered, sunny situation and fertile soil that is not too dry. Propagate by seed in autumn.
D. fargesii illus. p.118.

DECUMARIA

HYDRANGEACEAE

Genus of evergreen or deciduous, woody-stemmed, root climbers. Half hardy. Prefers sun and loamy, well-drained soil that does not dry out. Prune, if necessary, after flowering. Propagate by stem cuttings in late summer or early autumn.
D. sinensis illus. p.200.

DEINANTHE

HYDRANGEACEAE

Genus of slow-growing perennials with creeping, underground rootstocks. Is useful for rock gardens and peat beds. Fully hardy. Needs shaded, moist soil. Propagate by division in spring or by seed when fresh.
D. bifida. Slow-growing, mound-forming perennial. H 20cm (8in), S 10–20cm (4–8in). Nodding, star-shaped, white flowers are produced in summer amid rounded, crinkled leaves with 2-lobed, lacerated tips.
D. caerulea. Slow-growing, mound-forming perennial. H 20cm (8in), S to 15cm (6in). Stems, each carrying a cluster of nodding, bowl-shaped, pale violet-blue flowers, rise above 3–4 oval, toothed leaves in summer.

Delairea odorata. See *Senecio mikanioides.*
Delavay's fir. See *Abies delavayi.*

DELOSPERMA

AIZOACEAE

Genus of densely branched, trailing, perennial, sometimes shrubby succulents, some with tuberous roots. Frost tender, min. 5°C (41°F). Requires full sun and very well-drained soil. Propagate by seed or stem cuttings in spring or summer.
D. cooperi. Spreading, mat-forming, perennial succulent. H 5cm (2in), S indefinite. Has cylindrical, fleshy, light green leaves, 5cm (2in) long, and, in mid- to late summer, solitary, daisy-like, magenta flowers.

DELPHINIUM

RANUNCULACEAE

Genus of perennials, biennials, and annuals, grown for their spikes of irregularly cup-shaped, sometimes hooded, spurred flowers. Fully to half hardy. Needs an open, sunny position and fertile or rich, well-drained soil. Tall cultivars need staking and ample feeding and watering in spring and early summer. In spring remove thin growths from well-established plants, leaving 5–7 strong shoots. If flower spikes are removed after they fade, a second flush may be produced in late summer, provided plants are fed and watered well. Propagate species by seed in autumn or spring; Belladonna Group cultivars by division or basal cuttings of young shoots in spring; Elatum Group cultivars by cuttings only. All parts may cause severe discomfort if ingested, and contact with foliage may irritate skin. See also feature panel pp.228–30.

For ease of reference, delphinium cultivars have been grouped as follows:
Belladonna Group. Upright, branched perennials with palmately lobed leaves. H 1–1.2m (3–4ft), S to 45cm (18in). Fully hardy. Wiry stems bear loose, branched spikes, 30cm (12in) long, of elf cap-shaped, single flowers, 2cm (¾in) or more across, with spurs up to 3cm (1¼in) long, in early and late summer.
Elatum Group. Erect perennials with large, palmate leaves. H 1.5–2m (5–6ft), S 60–90cm (24–36in). Fully hardy. In summer, produce closely packed spikes, 40cm–1.2m (16in–4ft) long, of regularly spaced, semi-double, rarely fully double flowers, 8–10cm (3–4in) wide, in a range of colours from white to blue and purple, sometimes red-pink, usually with contrasting eyes.
Pacific Hybrids. Similar to Elatum Group cultivars, but grown as annuals or biennials. They produce short-lived, large, semi-double flowers on spikes in early and mid-summer.
***D.* 'Ailsa'** illus. p.228. Elatum Group herbaceous perennial. H 1.7m (5½ft). In early to mid-summer produces semi-double, off-white or very pale greyish-white flowers, 6–7.5cm (2½–3in) across, with white eyes, on spikes 70–90cm (28–36in) long.
***D.* 'Alice Artindale'** illus. p.230. Elatum Group herbaceous perennial. H 1.5m (5ft). Bears neat, button-like, fully double, bicolour, rosy-mauve and sky-blue flowers, to 3cm (1¼in) across, on narrow spikes, 50–60cm (20–24in) or more long, in early to mid-summer.
***D.* 'Ann Woodfield'** illus. p.229. Elatum Group herbaceous perennial. H 1.5m (5ft). In mid-summer produces semi-double, pale blue flowers, to 10cm (4in) across, suffused pale mauve, on tapering spikes to 1m (3ft) long.
***D.* 'Anne Kenrick'** illus. p.229. Elatum Group herbaceous perennial. H 1.5m (5ft). In mid-summer produces semi-double, pale blue flowers to 8cm (3in) across, with a pink suffusion towards the central white eye, borne on tapering spikes to 1m (3ft) long.
***D.* Black Knight Group** illus. p.230. Short-lived, Pacific Hybrids herbaceous perennial. H 1.5–1.7m (5–5½ft) Produces semi-double, purple to deep purple, black-eyed flowers, to 8cm (3in) across, on spikes, 60–100cm (2–3ft), in early to mid-summer.
♀ ***D.* 'Blue Dawn'** illus. p.230. Elatum Group herbaceous perennial. H 2.4m (8ft). In mid-summer bears pale blue flowers, to 7cm (3in) across, with dark brown eyes, on spikes to 1.25m (4ft) long.
***D.* Blue Fountains Group** illus. p.229. Short-lived, Pacific Hybrids herbaceous perennial. H 1.5m (5ft). In early to mid-summer produces variable, white-eyed, mid-blue flowers, to 7cm (3in) across, on spikes 70–100cm (2–3ft) long.
***D.* 'Blue Lagoon'.** See *D.* 'Langdon's Blue Lagoon'.
♀ ***D.* 'Blue Nile'** illus. p.230. Elatum Group herbaceous perennial. H 1.5–1.8m (5–6ft). In mid-summer has rich blue flowers, 6–7cm (2½–3in), with lightly blue-streaked, white eyes, on spikes to 85cm (34in) long.
♀ ***D.* 'Bruce'** illus. p.230. Elatum Group herbaceous perennial. H 1.7–2.2m (5½–7ft). In mid-summer, spikes to 1.2m (4ft) long bear deep violet-purple flowers, to 8cm (3in), silver-flushed towards centres and with dark brown eyes.
D. brunonianum. Upright herbaceous perennial. H and S to 20cm (8in). Fully hardy. Hairy stems bear rounded, 3- or 5-lobed leaves. In early summer, flower stems each produce a spike, to 15cm (6in) long, of hooded, single, pale blue to purple flowers, 4cm (1½in) wide, with short, black spurs. Is good for a rock garden.
***D.* 'Butterball'** illus. p.228. Elatum Group herbaceous perennial. H 1.5–1.7m (5–5½ft). In mid-summer bears cream-eyed, white flowers, to 8cm (3in), overlaid with very pale greenish-yellow, on spikes to 50cm (20in) long.
♀ ***D.* 'Can-can'** illus. p.230. Elatum Group herbaceous perennial. H 1.9m (6ft). In mid-summer, spikes to 75cm (30in) long bear fully double flowers, to 9cm (3½in) across, the outer sepals margined dark blue, the inner sepals purple-mauve with darker veining.
D. cardinale. Short-lived, upright herbaceous perennial. H 1–2m (3–6ft), S 60cm (2ft). Half hardy. In summer has single, scarlet flowers, 4cm (1½in)

wide, with yellow eyes, on spikes, 30–45cm (12–18in) long, above palmate, finely divided leaves.

***D.* 'Chelsea Star'** illus. p.230. Elatum Group herbaceous perennial. H 2m (6ft). Has rich deep violet flowers, 6–8cm (2½–3in) across, with white eyes, on spikes to 1.1m (3½ft) long in mid-summer.

D. chinense. See *D. grandiflorum*.

♀ ***D.* 'Claire'** illus. p.228. Elatum Group herbaceous perennial. H 1.4m (4½ft). In mid-summer, semi-double, pale mauve-pink flowers, to 5cm (2in) across, with cream to pale brown eyes, are borne on spikes to 55cm (22in) long.

***D.* 'Clifford Lass'** illus. p.229. Elatum Group herbaceous perennial. H 1.3m (4½ft). In mid-summer, spikes 80–100cm (32–36in) long bear semi-double, dusky-pink flowers, to 7.5cm (3in) across, with white-tipped, dark brown eyes.

♀ ***D.* 'Clifford Sky'** illus. p.228. Elatum Group herbaceous perennial. H 2m (6ft). In mid-summer bears semi-double, white-eyed, sky-blue flowers, to 7.5cm (3in) across, on spikes to 1m (3ft) long.

***D.*'Cliveden Beauty'** illus. p.229. Belladonna Group herbaceous perennial. H 1–1.2m (3–4ft). Produces sky-blue flowers, 2–3cm (¾–1in) across, on spikes 30cm (12in) long in early to mid-summer.

D. consolida. See *Consolida ajacis*.

♀ ***D.* 'Conspicuous'** illus. p.228. Elatum Group herbaceous perennial. H 1.5m (5ft). In mid-summer produces semi-double, pale mauve and blue flowers, 5–6cm (2–2½in) across, with prominent dark eyes, in dense spikes to 60cm (2ft) long.

***D.* 'Crown Jewel'** illus. p.230. Elatum Group herbaceous perennial. H 1.5m (5ft). Spikes, to 85cm (34in) long, bear semi-double, pale blue and mauve flowers, to 5cm (2in) across, with deep brown eyes, in mid-summer

***D.* 'Dora Larkan'** illus. p.230. Elatum Group herbaceous perennial. H 2m. (6ft). In mid-summer produces spikes, 60cm (2ft) long, of deep mid-blue flowers, to 6cm (2½in) across, with white eyes.

***D.* 'Dunsdon' Green'** illus. p.228. Elatum Group herbaceous perennial. H 1.3m (4½ft). Spikes, 60cm (2ft) long, of semi-double, lime-green-suffused, white flowers, to 5cm (2in) across, with small, green eyes, are produced in mid-summer.

♀ ***D.* 'Emily Hawkins'** illus. p.228. Elatum Group herbaceous perennial. H 2–2.2m (6–7ft). Semi-double, purple-mauve flowers, to 6cm (2½in) across, with light yellowish-brown eyes are borne in mid-summer on spikes to 80cm (32in) long.

***D.* 'Fanfare'** illus. p.229. Elatum Group herbaceous perennial. H 2–2.2m (6–7ft). In mid-summer bears pale blue to silvery-mauve flowers, 6–7cm (2½–3in) across, with white-and-violet eyes, on spikes 60–75cm (2–2½ft) long.

♀ ***D.* 'Fenella'** illus. p.230. Elatum Group herbaceous perennial. H 1–1.65m (3–5½ft). Bears purple-flushed, gentian-blue flowers, 5–6cm (2–2½in) across, with black eyes, on spikes to 1m (3ft) long in mid-summer.

***D.* 'Foxhill Nina'** illus. p.228. Elatum Group herbaceous perennial. H 1.2m (4ft). Bears semi-double, white-eyed, pale pink flowers, 5–6cm (2–2½in) across, on spikes, to 60cm (2ft) long, in mid-summer.

***D.* 'Franjo Sahin'** illus. p.230. Elatum Group herbaceous perennial. H 2m (6ft). In mid-summer, tapering spikes, to 1.1m (3½ft) long, produce semi-double, purplish–mauve flowers, to 10cm (4ft) across, with black eyes.

♀ ***D.* 'Galileo'** illus. p.230. Elatum Group herbaceous perennial. H 1.8m (6ft). In early and mid-summer, tapering spikes, to 80cm (32in) long, bear semi-double, violet-blue blooms, 7cm (3in) wide, paling slightly towards the centre, with brownish-black eyes.

***D.* 'Gemini'** illus. p.229. Elatum Group herbaceous perennial. H 1.8m (6ft). In mid-summer, produces spikes to 85cm (34in) long bearing semi-double, pale violet flowers, to 7.5cm (3in) across, edged reddish-violet with dark black-brown eyes, touched white near the centre.

***D.* 'Gemma'** illus. p.230. Elatum Group herbaceous perennial. H 2m (6ft). Semi-double, pale lavender flowers, to 7.5cm (3in) across, with white eyes, are borne in mid-summer on spikes to 1m long.

***D.* 'Gertrude Sahin'** illus. p.229. Elatum Group herbaceous perennial. H 1.7–1.9m (5½–6ft). In mid-summer produces mid- to light blue flowers, 7.5–9.5cm (3–3½in) across, with prominent white eyes, on spikes to 1m (3ft) long.

♀ ***D.* 'Gillian Dallas'** illus. p.229. Elatum Group herbaceous perennial. H 2.1m (6½ft). In mid-summer has spikes, to 90cm (3ft) long, of blue-violet flowers, to 8cm (3in) across, with white eyes and violet flecks.

♀ ***D.* 'Giotto'** illus. p.230. Elatum Group herbaceous perennial. H 1.7–2m (5½–6ft). In mid-summer, spikes to 80cm (32in) long bear semi-double flowers, to 7.5cm (3in) across, with deep purple inner sepals, dark blue outer sepals and light yellowish-brown eyes.

***D.* 'Gordon Forsyth'** illus. p.229. Elatum Group herbaceous perennial. H 2m (6ft). In mid-summer produces semi-double, amethyst-purple blooms, 6–7cm (2½–3in) across, with violet-flecked, black eyes, on spikes 60–70cm (24–28in) long.

D. grandiflorum, syn. *D. chinense.* **'Blue Butterfly'** (illus. p.230) is a short-lived, erect herbaceous perennial, usually grown as an annual. H 45cm (1½ft), S 30cm (1ft). Fully hardy. Has palmate, divided leaves. In summer produces loose, branching spikes, to 15cm (6in) long, of single, deep blue flowers, 3.5cm (1½in) wide. Is useful as a bedding plant.

***D.* 'Holly Cookland Wilkins'** illus. p.230. Elatum Group herbaceous perennial. H 1.5m (5ft). Produces tapering spikes. 1m (3ft) long. of semi-double, black-eyed, lavender flowers, to 7.5cm (3in) across, in mid-summer.

***D.* 'Joan Edwards'** illus. p.230. Elatum Group herbaceous perennial. H 1.5m (5ft). In mid-summer, tapering spikes, 80–90cm (32–36in) long, bear semi-double, vivid purplish-blue flowers, 5.5–7.5cm (2¼–3in) across, becoming paler and purple striated towards the central, prominent, white eye.

***D.* 'Kennington Classic'** illus. p.228. Elatum Group herbaceous perennial. H 1.5m (5ft). Semi-double, rich cream flowers, to 8cm (3in) across, with well-formed, yellow eyes are borne in mid-summer on spikes to 90cm (3ft) long.

♀ ***D.* 'Langdon's Blue Lagoon'**, syn. *D.* 'Blue Lagoon' illus. p.229. Elatum Group herbaceous perennial. H 2m (6ft). Tapering spikes, to 90cm long, bear semi-double, pale to mid-blue flowers, to 7cm (3in) across, which are paler towards the centre, with blue-specked, white eyes.

♀ ***D.* 'Langdon's Royal Flush'** illus. p.228. Elatum Group herbaceous perennial. H 2m (6ft). In mid-summer has semi-double, magenta-pink flowers, 5–6cm (2–2½in) across, on spikes to 85cm (34in) long; upper petals are a darker shade than lower ones.

♀ ***D.* 'Loch Leven'** illus. p.230. Elatum Group herbaceous perennial. H to 1.5m (5ft). Bears semi-double, mid-blue flowers, to 7.5cm (3in) across, with white eyes, on spikes to 1m (3ft) long in early to mid-summer.

♀ ***D.* 'Lord Butler'** illus. p.229. Elatum Group herbaceous perennial. H 1.5–1.7m (5–5½ft). Produces semi-double, mid-blue flowers, to 7.5cm (3in) across, lightly flushed with pale lilac and with blue-marked, white eyes, on spikes to 75cm (30in) long.

♀ ***D.* 'Lucia Sahin'** illus. p.229. Elatum Gro up herbaceous perennial. H 2m (6ft).In mid-summer, spikes to 90cm (36in) long bear semi-double, deep purple-pink flowers, to 7.5cm (3in) across, with dark brown eyes.

♀ ***D.* 'Michael Ayres'** illus. p.229. Elatum Group herbaceous perennial. H 1.8m (6ft). In early and mid-summer, semi-double, deep purple-blue flowers, to 6cm (2½in) across, with black-brown eyes, are borne on spikes to 80cm (32in) long.

***D.* 'Mighty Atom'** illus. p.229. Elatum Group herbaceous perennial. H 1.5–2m (5–6ft). In mid-summer has semi-double, mid-violet flowers, to 6cm (2½in) across, with violet-marked, yellowish-brown eyes, on spikes to 75cm (2½ft) long.

♀ ***D.* 'Min'** illus. p.229. Elatum Group herbaceous perennial. H 1.6–2m (5½–6ft). In mid-summer, tapering spikes, to 1m (3ft) long, bear semi-double, pale lavender flowers, to 9.5cm (3¾in) across, with deep lavender suffusions and veining, as well as dark brown eyes.

***D.* 'Nobility'** illus. p.230. Elatum Group herbaceous perennial. H 1.6m (5½ft). Semi-double, deep purple and dark mauve flowers, to 7.5cm (3in) across, with prominent white eyes, are borne in mid-summer on spikes to 1m (3ft) long.

D. nudicaule illus. p.367.

♀ ***D.* 'Olive Poppleton'** illus. p.228. Elatum Group herbaceous perennial. H 2–2.5m (6–8ft). Off-white flowers, 5–6cm (2–2½in) across, sometimes very faintly flushed pink and with fawn eyes, are borne on spikes to 1m (3ft) long in mid-summer.

***D.* 'Pink Ruffles'** illus. p.229. Elatum Group herbaceous perennial. H 1.5m (5ft). Fully double, shell-pink flowers, to 7.5cm (3in) across, are borne in mid-summer on spikes to 80cm (32in) long.

♀ ***D.* 'Sandpiper'** illus. p.228. Elatum Group herbaceous perennial. H 1–1.5m (3–4ft). In mid-summer has semi-double, white flowers, to 6cm (2½in) across, with dark creamy-brown eyes, on spikes to 75cm (2½ft) long.

***D.* 'Shimmer'** illus. p.228. Elatum Group herbaceous perennial. H 1.8m (6ft). In mid-summer produces semi-double, bright blue flowers, 5–7cm (2–3in) across, with prominent white eyes, on spikes to 80cm (32in) long.

♀ ***D.* 'Spindrift'** illus. p.229. Elatum Group herbaceous perennial. H 1.7–2m (5½–6ft). In early and mid-summer produces spikes, to 1m (3ft) long, of semi-double, pinkish-purple flowers, 5–7cm (2–3in) across, overlaid with pale blue and with creamy-white eyes; towards centres, the pinkish-purple becomes paler and the blue darker. Flower colour varies according to different types of soil; on acid soil, flowers are greenish.

***D.* 'Strawberry Fair'** illus. p.229. Elatum Group herbaceous perennial. H 1.7m (5½ft). Has semi-double, white-eyed, mulberry-pink flowers, 5–7cm (2–3in) across, on spikes to 78cm (31in) long in mid-summer .

♀ ***D.* 'Sungleam'** illus. p.228. Elatum Group herbaceous perennial. H 1.7–2m (5½–6ft). In mid-summer produces spikes, 40–75cm (16–30in) long, of semi-double, white flowers, 5–7cm (2–3in) across, overlaid with pale yellow and with yellow eyes.

♀ ***D.* 'Sunkissed'** illus. p.228. Elatum Group herbaceous perennial. H 1.7m (5½ft). In mid-summer, spikes to 80cm (32in) long bear semi-double, deep cream flowers, to 6.5cm (2¾in) across, with canary-yellow eyes.

D. tatsienense. Short-lived, upright herbaceous perennial. H 30cm (12in), S 5–10cm (2–4in). Fully hardy. Loose spikes, to 15cm (6in) long, of small-spurred, single, bright blue flowers, 2.5cm (1in) long, are borne in summer. Leaves are rounded to oval and deeply cut. Suits a rock garden. Requires soil that is gritty.

♀ ***D.* 'Tiddles'** illus. p.230. Elatum Group herbaceous perennial. H 1.8m (6ft). In mid-summer, semi-double to almost double, greyish-violet flowers, 5–6cm (2–2½in) across, with brown eyes, are borne on spikes to 90cm (3ft) long.

***D.* 'Tiger Eye'** illus. p.230. Elatum Group herbaceous perennial. H 1.7m (5½ft). In mid-summer, spikes 60–70cm (24–28in) long bear semi-double, light violet flowers, 5–6cm (2–2½in) across, with yellow-edged, brown eyes.

Delta maidenhair. See *Adiantum raddianum*.

Dendrobenthamia capitata. See *Cornus capitata*.

Dendrobium

ORCHIDACEAE

See also ORCHIDS.

D. aphyllum, syn. *D. pierardii*. Deciduous, epiphytic orchid for an intermediate greenhouse. H to 60cm (24in). In early spring produces pairs of soft pink flowers, 4cm (1½in) across and each with a large, cream lip. Has oval leaves, 5–8cm (2–3in) long. Requires semi-shade in summer. Is best grown hanging from a bark slab.
D. chrysotoxum illus. p.311. Deciduous, epiphytic orchid for an intermediate greenhouse. H 60cm (24in). Trusses of cup-shaped, deep yellow flowers, 2cm (¾in) across and with hairy, red-marked lips, are borne in spring. Oval leaves are 5–8cm (2–3in) long. Provide good light in summer.
D. infundibulum illus. p.308. Evergreen, epiphytic orchid for a cool greenhouse. H 30cm (12in). In spring, stems each produce up to 6 pure white flowers, 8cm (3in) wide and each with a yellow-marked lip. Has oval leaves, 5–8cm (2–3in) long. Grow in semi-shade in summer.
D. nobile illus. p.309. Deciduous, epiphytic orchid (often evergreen in cultivation) for a cool greenhouse. H 30cm (12in). Trusses of delicate, rose-pink flowers, 5cm (2in) across and each with a prominent, maroon lip, are borne along stems in spring. Oval leaves are 5–8cm (2–3in) long. Requires semi-shade in summer.
***D.* Oriental Paradise** illus. p.308. Evergreen, epiphytic orchid. H 60cm (24in). White flowers, 7cm (3in) across, with dark pink notches on th petals and yellow marks on the lips, are borne in pairs in spring. Oblong leaves are 10cm (4in) long. Requires semi-shade in summer.
D. pierardii. See *D. aphyllum*.

Dendrochilum

ORCHIDACEAE

See also ORCHIDS.

D. glumaceum (Silver chain). Evergreen, epiphytic orchid for a cool greenhouse. H 10cm (4in). Pendent sprays of fragrant, pointed, orange-lipped, creamy-white flowers, 1cm (½in) long, are produced in autumn. Narrowly oval leaves are 15cm (6in) long. Requires semi-shade in summer.

Dendromecon

PAPAVERACEAE

Genus of evergreen shrubs, grown for their foliage and showy flowers. Frost to half hardy. Plant against a south- or west-facing wall in cold areas. Requires full sun and very well-drained soil. Propagate by softwood cuttings in summer, by seed in autumn or spring or by root cuttings in winter.
D. rigida illus. p.143.

Dentaria enneaphyllos. See *Cardamine enneaphyllos*.
Dentaria pentaphyllos. See *Cardamine pentaphyllos*.
Deodar. See *Cedrus deodara*.
Deptford pink. See *Dianthus armeria*.

Deschampsia

GRAMINEAE/POACEAE

See also GRASSES, BAMBOOS, RUSHES and SEDGES.
D. cespitosa (Tufted hair grass). Evergreen, tuft-forming, perennial grass. H to 1m (3ft), S 25–30cm (10–12in). Fully hardy. Has dense, narrow, rough-edged, dark green leaves. In summer produces dainty, open panicles of minute, pale brown spikelets that last well into winter. Tolerates sun or shade.

Desert fan palm. See *Washingtonia filifera*.
Desert rose. See *Adenium*.

Desfontainia

DESFONTAINIACEAE/LOGANIACEAE

Genus of evergreen shrubs, grown for their foliage and showy, tubular flowers. Frost to half hardy. Provide shelter in cold areas. Needs some shade, particularly in dry regions, and moist, peaty, preferably acid soil. Propagate by semi-ripe cuttings in summer.
♀ ***D. spinosa*** illus. p.139.

Desmodium

LEGUMINOSAE/PAPILIONACEAE

Genus of perennials and deciduous shrubs and sub-shrubs, grown for their flowers. Fully to frost hardy. Needs full sun and well-drained soil. Propagate by softwood cuttings in late spring or by seed in autumn. May also be divided in spring.
♀ ***D. elegans***, syn. *D. tiliifolium*, illus. p.163.
D. tiliifolium. See *D. elegans*.

Deutzia

HYDRANGEACEAE

Genus of deciduous shrubs, grown for their profuse, 5-petalled flowers. Fully to frost hardy. Needs full sun and fertile, well-drained soil. Plants benefit from regular thinning out of old shoots after flowering. Propagate by softwood cuttings in summer.
***D. × elegantissima* 'Fasciculata'.** Deciduous, upright shrub. H 2m (6ft), S 1.5m (5ft). Fully hardy. From late spring to early summer produces large clusters of 5-petalled, pale pink flowers. Leaves are oval, toothed and mid-green. ♀ **'Rosealind'** illus. p.158.
D. gracilis illus. p.149.
***D.* 'Joconde'.** Deciduous, upright shrub. H and S 1.5m (5ft). Fully hardy. Bears 5-petalled, white flowers, striped purple outside, in early summer. Oval, mid-green leaves are long-pointed.
D. longifolia. Deciduous, arching shrub. H 2m (6ft), S 3m (10ft). Fully hardy. Large clusters of 5-petalled, deep pink flowers are produced from early to mid-summer. Narrowly lance-shaped leaves are grey-green.
♀ **'Veitchii'** illus. p.136.
D. × magnifica. Vigorous, deciduous, upright shrub. H 2.5m (8ft), S 2m (6ft). Fully hardy. Produces dense clusters of 5-petalled, pure white flowers in early summer. Leaves are narrowly oval and bright green. **'Staphyleoides'** illus. p.132.
D. monbeigii illus. p.154.
♀ ***D.* 'Mont Rose'** illus. p.157.
D. pulchra. Vigorous, deciduous, upright shrub. H 2.5m (8ft), S 2m (6ft). Frost hardy. Has peeling, orange-brown bark and lance-shaped, dark green leaves. Slender, pendulous panicles of 5-petalled, pink-tinged, white flowers appear in late spring and early summer.
D. × rosea illus. p.150.
D. scabra illus. p.132. **'Plena'** (syn. *D.s.* 'Flore Pleno') is a deciduous, upright shrub. H 3m (10ft), S 2m (6ft). Fully hardy. Narrowly oval, dark green leaves set off dense, upright clusters of double, white flowers, purplish-pink outside, from early to mid-summer.
♀ ***D. setchuenensis*** var. ***corymbiflora.*** Deciduous, upright shrub with peeling, pale brown bark when mature. H 2m (6ft), S 1.5m (5ft). Frost hardy. Small, 5-petalled, white flowers are borne in broad clusters in early and mid-summer. Produces lance-shaped, long-pointed, grey-green leaves.

Devil's club. See *Oplopanax horridus*.
Devil's fig. See *Argemone mexicana*, illus. p.347.

Dianella

Flax lily

LILIACEAE/PHORMIACEAE

Genus of evergreen, summer-flowering perennials. Frost to half hardy; is suitable outdoors only in mild areas and elsewhere requires a cold greenhouse or frame. Needs sun and well-drained, neutral to acid soil. Propagate by division or seed in spring.
D. caerulea. Evergreen, tuft-forming perennial. H 75cm (30in), S 30cm (12in). Half hardy. In summer has panicles of small, star-shaped, blue flowers, above grass-like leaves, followed by blue berries.
D. tasmanica illus. p.259.

Dianthus

Carnation, Pink

CARYOPHYLLACEAE

Genus of evergreen or semi-evergreen, mainly summer-flowering perennials, annuals and biennials, grown for their mass of flowers, often scented, some of which are excellent for cutting. Carnations and pinks (see below) are excellent for cut flowers and border decoration, the biennial *D. barbatus* (Sweet William) is suitable for bedding and smaller, tuft-forming species and cultivars are good for rock gardens. Fully to half hardy. Needs an open, sunny position and well-drained, slightly alkaline soil, except for *D. pavonius*, which prefers acid soil. Dead-heading of repeat-flowering types is beneficial. Tall forms of carnations and pinks have a loose habit and need staking. Propagate border carnations by layering in late summer, other named forms by softwood cuttings in early to mid-summer and species by seed at any time. Is susceptible to rust, red spider mite and virus infection through aphids, but many cultivars are available from virus-free stock.

Carnations and pinks have narrowly lance-shaped, silvery- or grey-green leaves, scattered up flower stems, which may coil outwards on carnations. They are divided into the following groups, all with self-coloured and bicoloured cultivars. See also feature panel pp.290–91.

Carnations

Border carnations are annuals or evergreen perennials that flower prolifically once in mid-summer and are good for border decoration and cutting. Each stem bears 5 or more often scented, semi-double or double flowers, to 8cm (3in) across; picotee forms (with petals outlined in a darker colour) are available. H 75cm–1.1m (2½–3½ft), S to 30cm (1ft). Frost hardy.
Perpetual-flowering carnations are evergreen perennials that flower year-round if grown in a greenhouse, but more prolifically in summer. They are normally grown for cut flowers: flower stems should be disbudded, leaving one terminal bud per stem. Fully double flowers, to 10cm (4in) across, are usually unscented and are often flecked or streaked. H 1–1.5m (3–5ft), S 30cm (1ft) or more. Half hardy.

Spray forms are not disbudded so have 5 or more flowers per stem, each 5–6cm (2–2½in) across. H 60cm–1m (2–3ft), S to 30cm (1ft).
Malmaison carnations are evergreen perennials, derived from *D.* 'Souvenir de la Malmaison'. Grown under glass, they bear large, double, scented flowers sporadically during the year. The flowers can reach up to 13cm (5in) across. They are mostly self-coloured, and tend to split their calyces. H 50–70cm (20–28in), S 40cm (16in). Half hardy.

Pinks

Evergreen, clump-forming perennials, grown for border decoration and cutting, that in summer produce a succession of basal shoots, each bearing 4–6 fragrant, single to fully double flowers, 3.5–6cm (1½–2½in) across. H 30–45cm (12–18in), S 23–30cm (9–12in) or more. Frost hardy.
Old-fashioned pinks have a low, spreading habit and produce masses of flowers in one flowering period in mid-summer. Mule types (a border carnation crossed with a Sweet William) and laced types (in which the central colour extends as a loop around each petal) are available.
Modern pinks, obtained by crossing an old-fashioned pink with a perpetual-flowering carnation, are more vigorous than old-fashioned pinks, and are repeat-flowering with two or three main flushes of flowers in summer.
Alpine pinks are evergreen species and cultivars forming neat mat or cushion plants. They will grow at the edge of a border or in a rock garden, trough or alpine house. In early summer, they bear single, semi-double or double, often scented flowers. Foliage is grey-green. H 8–10cm (3–4in), S 20cm (8in). Fully hardy.
***D.* 'A.J. MacSelf'.** See *D.* 'Dad's Favourite'.
***D.* 'Albisola'** illus. p.291. Perpetual-flowering carnation. Fully double flowers are clear tangerine-orange.

***D.* 'Aldridge Yellow'** illus. p.291. Border carnation. Semi-double flowers are clear yellow.

***D.* 'Alice'** illus. p.290. Modern pink. Has clove-scented, semi-double, ivory-white flowers, each with a bold, crimson eye.

♀ ***D. alpinus*** (Alpine pink) illus. p.390.

***D.* 'Annabelle'** illus. p.391.

D. armeria (Deptford pink). Evergreen, tuft-forming perennial, sometimes grown as an annual. H 30cm (12in), S 45cm (18in). Fully hardy. Has narrowly lance-shaped, dark green leaves. In summer, tall stems each carry small, 5-petalled, cerise-pink flowers in small bunches. Is good for a rock garden or bank.

D. barbatus (Sweet William). **Roundabout Series** (dwarf) illus. p.338.

♀ ***D.* 'Becky Robinson'** illus. p.290. Modern pink. Bears clove-scented, fully double, rose-pink flowers with ruby-red lacing. Is good for exhibition.

***D.* 'Bombardier'.** Evergreen, tuft-forming perennial. H and S 10cm (4in). Frost hardy. Has a basal tuft of linear, grey-green leaves and, in summer, small, double, scarlet flowers. Is good for a rock garden.

***D.* 'Bookham Fancy'** illus. p.291. Border carnation. Produces bright yellow flowers, margined and flecked carmine-purple, on short, stiff stems.

***D.* 'Bookham Perfume'.** Perennial border carnation. Has scented, semi-double, crimson flowers.

♀ ***D.* 'Bovey Belle'.** Modern pink. Has clove-scented, fully double, bright purple flowers that are excellent for cutting.

***D.* 'Brympton Red'.** Old-fashioned pink. Flowers are single, bright crimson with deeper shading.

D. caesius. See *D. gratianopolitanus*.

D. carthusianorum illus. p.366.

***D.* 'Charles Musgrave'.** See *D.* 'Musgrave's Pink'.

D. chinensis (Indian pink). Slow-growing, bushy annual. H and S 15–30cm (6–12in). Fully hardy. Lance-shaped leaves are pale or mid-green. Tubular, single or double flowers, 2.5cm (1in) or more wide and with open, spreading petals, in shades of pink, red or white, are produced in summer and early autumn. **Baby Doll Series** illus. p.336. **'Fire Carpet'** illus. p.339. **Heddewigii Group**, H 30cm (12in), has flowers in mixed colours.

***D.* 'Christine Hough'** illus. p.291. Perennial border carnation. Semi-double flowers are apricot, overlaid and streaked with rose-pink.

***D.* 'Christopher'** illus. p.291. Modern pink. Produces lightly scented, fully double, bright salmon-red flowers.

***D.* 'Clara'** illus. p.291. Perpetual-flowering carnation. Fully double flowers are yellow with salmon flecks.

***D.* 'Constance Finnis'.** See *D.* 'Fair Folly'.

***D.* 'Cream Sue'** illus. p.291. Perpetual-flowering carnation. Flowers are cream. Is a sport of *D.* 'Apricot Sue'.

***D.* 'Crompton Princess'** illus. p.291. Perpetual-flowering carnation. Flowers are pure white.

***D.* 'Dad's Favourite'**, syn. *D.* 'A.J. MacSelf' illus. p.290. Old-fashioned pink. Bears scented, semi-double, white flowers with chocolate-brown lacing.

♀ ***D. deltoides*** (Maiden pink). Evergreen, mat-forming, basal-tufted perennial. H 15cm (6in), S 30cm (12in). Fully hardy. In summer, small, 5-petalled, white, pink or cerise flowers are borne singly above tiny, lance-shaped leaves. Is good for a rock garden or bank. Trim back after flowering. **'Leuchtfunk'** (syn. *D.d.* 'Flashing Light') illus. p.392.

***D.* 'Denis'.** Modern pink. Strongly clove-scented, fully double, magenta flowers are freely produced.

♀ ***D.* 'Doris'** illus. p.290. Modern pink. Has compact growth and an abundance of fragrant, semi-double, pale pink flowers, each with a salmon-red ring towards base of flower. Is one of the most widely grown cultivars and provides excellent flowers for cutting.

***D.* 'Duchess of Westminster'** illus. p.291. Vigorous Malmaison carnation. Produces salmon-pink flowers with stronger calyces than most Malmaison carnations.

***D.* 'Emile Paré'** illus. p.290. Old-fashioned, mule pink. Has clusters of semi-double, salmon-pink flowers and, unusually for a pink, mid-green foliage.

***D.* 'Eva Humphries'** illus. p.290. Perennial border carnation. Has fragrant, semi-double flowers with white petals outlined in purple.

***D.* 'Fair Folly'**, syn. *D.* 'Constance Finnis' illus. p.290. Modern pink. Flowers are single and of variable colour, usually dusky-pink to dusky-purple with 2 white splashes on each petal.

***D.* 'Forest Treasure'** illus. p.291. Perennial border carnation. Has double, white flowers with reddish-purple splashes on each petal.

***D.* 'Freckles'.** Modern pink. A compact cultivar, it has fully double flowers that are red-speckled and dusky-pink.

♀ ***D.* 'Golden Cross'** illus. p.291. Border carnation. Produces bright yellow flowers on short, stiff stems.

♀ ***D.* 'Gran's Favourite'** illus. p.290. Old-fashioned pink. Bears fragrant, semi-double, white flowers with deep raspberry lacing.

♀ ***D. gratianopolitanus***, syn. *D. caesius*, illus. p.389.

***D.* 'Green Eyes'.** See *D.* 'Musgrave's Pink'.

D. haematocalyx. Evergreen, tuft-forming perennial. H 12cm (5in), S 10cm (4in). Fully hardy. Leaves are lance-shaped and usually glaucous. Bears 5-petalled, toothed, beige-backed, deep pink flowers on slender stems in summer. Suits a rock garden or scree.

***D.* 'Happiness'** illus. p.291. Perennial border carnation. Semi-double flowers are yellow, striped scarlet-orange.

***D.* 'Haytor'.** See *D.* 'Haytor White'.

♀ ***D.* 'Haytor White'**, syn. *D.* 'Haytor' illus. p.290. Modern pink. Fully double, white flowers, borne on strong stems, have a good scent. Is widely grown, especially to provide cut flowers.

***D.* 'Hidcote'.** Evergreen, tufted, compact perennial. H and S 10cm (4in). Fully hardy. Bears a basal tuft of linear, spiky, grey-green leaves and, in summer, double, red flowers. Suits a rock garden.

♀ ***D.* 'Houndspool Ruby'**, syn. *D.* 'Ruby', *D.* 'Ruby Doris' illus. p.291. Modern pink. Is a sport of *D.* 'Doris' with strongly scented, ruby-pink flowers that each have a deeper eye.

***D.* 'Ibiza'.** Perpetual-flowering, spray carnation. Fully double flowers are shell-pink.

***D.* 'Iceberg'.** Modern pink. Fragrant flowers are semi-double and pure white. Has a somewhat looser habit than *D.* 'White Haytor'.

♀ ***D.* 'Joy'.** Modern pink. Bears semi-double, pink flowers that are strongly scented and good for cutting.

***D.* 'Kobusa'.** See *D.* PIERROT.

***D.* 'La Bourbille'.** See *D.* 'La Bourboule'.

♀ ***D.* 'La Bourboule'**, syn. *D.* 'La Bourbille', illus. p.390.

***D.* 'Laced Monarch'** illus. p.291. Modern pink. Double flowers are pink, laced with maroon-red.

***D.* 'Laced Prudence'.** See *D.* 'Prudence'.

***D.* 'Lavender Clove'** illus. p.291. Vigorous border carnation. Bears lavender-grey flowers on long stems.

***D.* 'Little Jock'** illus. p.389.

***D.* 'London Brocade'** illus. p.290. Modern pink. Has clove-scented, crimson-laced, pink flowers.

***D.* 'London Delight'** illus p.291. Old-fashioned pink. Fragrant flowers are semi-double and lavender, laced with purple.

***D.* 'Manon'.** Perpetual-flowering carnation. Is one of the best deep pink cultivars with fully double flowers.

***D.* 'Mars'.** Evergreen, tuft-forming perennial. H and S 10cm (4in). Frost hardy. Has small, double, cherry-red flowers in summer. Bears a basal tuft of linear, grey-green leaves. Is good in a rock garden.

***D.* 'Master Stuart'.** Perennial border carnation. Has striking, semi-double flowers that are white with scarlet stripes.

D. microlepis illus. p.390.

♀ ***D.* 'Monica Wyatt'** illus. p.290. Modern pink. Very fragrant, fully double flowers are cyclamen-pink, each with a magenta eye. Is very free-flowering and provides excellent cut flowers.

D. monspessulanus. Evergreen, mat-forming perennial. H 30cm (12in), S 10–15cm (4–6in). Fully hardy. In summer, masses of strongly fragrant, 5-petalled, deeply fringed, pale lavender flowers rise on slender stems above short tufts of fine, grass-like leaves. Is good for a rock garden. Needs gritty soil.

***D.* 'Mrs Sinkins'** illus. p.290. Old-fashioned pink. Flowers are heavily scented, fringed, fully double and white.

***D.* 'Murcia'.** Perpetual-flowering carnation. Has fully double, deep golden-yellow flowers.

***D.* 'Musgrave's Pink'**, syn. *D.* 'Charles Musgrave', *D.* 'Green Eyes' illus. p.290. Old-fashioned pink. An old cultivar, it bears single, white flowers with green eyes.

D. myrtinervius illus. p.390.

D. neglectus. See *D. pavonius*.

***D.* 'Nina'** illus. p.291. Perpetual-flowering carnation. Is one of the best crimson cultivars. Fully double flowers have smooth-edged petals.

♀ ***D. pavonius***, syn. *D. neglectus*, illus. p.387.

***D.* PIERROT ('Kobusa')** illus. p.290. Perpetual-flowering carnation. Bears fully double, light rose-lavender flowers with purple-edged petals.

♀ ***D.* 'Pike's Pink'** illus. p.390.

***D.* 'Pink Calypso'.** See *D.* 'Truly Yours'.

***D.* 'Pink Jewel'** illus. p.291. Alpine pink. Has strongly scented, semi-double, pink flowers.

***D.* 'Prudence'**, syn. *D.* 'Laced Prudence' illus. p.291. Old-fashioned pink. Fragrant flowers are semi-double and pinkish-white with purple lacing. Has a spreading habit.

***D.* 'Raggio di Sole'** illus. p.291. Perpetual-flowering carnation. Fully double flowers are bright orange.

***D.* 'Red Barrow'.** Perpetual-flowering, spray carnation. Fully double, bright scarlet flowers are borne in abundance.

***D.* 'Ruby'.** See *D.* 'Houndspool Ruby'.

***D.* 'Ruby Doris'.** See *D.* 'Houndspool Ruby'.

***D.* 'Sam Barlow'.** Old-fashioned pink. Bears very fragrant, frilly, fully double, white flowers with chocolate-brown centres.

***D.* 'Sandra Neal'** illus. p.291. Border carnation. Fully double, golden-apricot flowers are flaked deep rose-pink.

***D.* 'Show Ideal'.** Modern pink. Flat-petalled, semi-double flowers are white with red eyes and are strongly scented. Is excellent for exhibition.

***D.* 'Sops-in-wine'.** Old-fashioned pink. Bears fragrant, single, maroon flowers with white markings.

D. superbus. Evergreen, mat-forming perennial. H to 20cm (8in), S 15cm (6in). Fully hardy. Has narrowly lance-shaped, pale green leaves. In summer, slender stems bear very fragrant, 5-petalled, deeply fringed, pink flowers with darker centres. Suits a rock garden.

***D.* 'Tigré'.** Perpetual-flowering carnation. Has fully double, yellow flowers with a uniform, pinkish-purple stripe and edging to each petal.

***D.* 'Tony'.** Perpetual-flowering, spray carnation. Fully double flowers are yellow with red stripes.

***D.* 'Truly Yours'**, syn. *D.* 'Pink Calypso' illus. p.290. Perpetual-flowering carnation. Fully double flowers are a good pink.

♀ ***D.* 'Valda Wyatt'.** Modern pink. Flowers are very fragrant, fully double and rose-lavender.

***D.* 'Valencia'** illus. p.291. Perpetual-flowering carnation. Has fully double, golden-orange flowers.

***D.* 'White Ladies'** illus. p.290. Old-fashioned pink. Bears very fragrant, fully double, white flowers with greenish centres.

♀ ***D.* 'Widecombe Fair'.** Modern pink. Semi-double flowers, borne on strong stems, are of unusual colouring – peach-apricot, opening to blush-pink.

DIAPENSIA

DIAPENSIACEAE

Genus of evergreen, spreading sub-shrubs, suitable for rock gardens and troughs. Fully hardy. Needs partial shade and peaty, sandy, acid soil. Is very difficult to grow in hot, dry climates at low altitudes. Propagate by seed in spring or by semi-ripe cuttings in summer.

D. lapponica. Evergreen, spreading sub-shrub. H and S 7cm (3in). Has tufts of small, rounded, leathery leaves.

Carries solitary tiny, bowl-shaped, white flowers in early summer.

Diascia

SCROPHULARIACEAE

Genus of summer- and autumn-flowering annuals and perennials, some of which are semi-evergreen, grown for their tubular, pink flowers. Is suitable for banks and borders. Frost hardy. Needs sun and humus-rich, well-drained soil that is not too dry. Cut back old stems in spring. Propagate by softwood cuttings in late spring, by semi-ripe cuttings in summer or by seed in autumn.
♀ ***D. barberae* 'Blackthorn Apricot'**, syn. *D.* 'Blackthorn Apricot', illus. p.288. ♀ **'Ruby Field'.** is a mat-forming perennial. H 8cm (3in), S 15cm (6in). Heart-shaped, pale green leaves clothe short, wiry stems. Produces tubular, wide-lipped, salmon-pink flowers throughout summer.
♀ ***D.* 'Blackthorn Apricot'.** See *D. barberae* 'Blackthorn Apricot'.
D. cordata of gardens illus. p.365.
***D.* 'Ice Cracker'** illus. p.353.
♀ ***D. rigescens*** illus. p.365.
♀ ***D.* 'Salmon Supreme'** illus. p.364.
♀ ***D. vigilis.*** Prostrate perennial. H 30–40cm (12–16in), S 60cm (24in). Leaves are small, rounded, toothed and pale green. Upright branchlets carry loose spikes of flattish, outward-facing, pale pink flowers in summer.

Dicentra

PAPAVERACEAE

Genus of perennials, grown for their elegant sprays of pendent flowers. Fully hardy. Most do best in semi-shade and humus-rich, moist but well-drained soil. Propagate by division when dormant in late winter, species also by seed in autumn. Contact with the foliage may aggravate skin allergies.
***D.* 'Adrian Bloom'.** Spreading, tuft-forming perennial. H 45cm (18in), S 30cm (12in). Produces sprays of pendent, heart-shaped, rich carmine-pink flowers above oval, grey-green leaves.
D. cucullaria illus. p.374.
D. eximia of gardens. See *D. formosa*.
D. formosa, syn. *D. eximia* of gardens. Spreading, tufted perennial. H 45cm (18in), S 30cm (12in). In spring-summer bears slender, arching sprays of pendent, heart-shaped, pink or dull red flowers above oval, finely cut, grey-green leaves.
D. peregrina. Tuft-forming perennial. H 8cm (3in), S to 5cm (2in). Locket-shaped, pink flowers appear in spring-summer above fern-like, blue-green leaves. Needs gritty soil. Is suitable for an alpine house.
♀ ***D. spectabilis*** illus. p.247. ♀ f. ***alba*** (syn. *D.s.* 'Alba') illus. p.241.
***D.* 'Spring Morning'** illus. p.288.
♀ ***D.* 'Stuart Boothman'** illus. p.288.

Dichelostemma

LILIACEAE/ALLIACEAE

Genus of summer-flowering bulbs, grown for their dense flower heads on leafless stems. Is related to *Brodiaea* and is similar to *Allium* in appearance. Frost hardy, but in cold areas grow in a sheltered position. Needs a sunny site and well-drained soil. Water freely in spring, but dry out after flowering. Propagate by seed in autumn or spring or by offsets in autumn before growth commences.
D. congestum, syn. *Brodiaea congesta*, illus. p.414.
D. ida-maia, syn. *Brodiaea ida-maia.* Early summer-flowering bulb. H to 1m (3ft), S 8–10cm (3–4in). Long, narrow leaves are semi-erect and basal. Leafless stem carries a dense head of 2–2.5cm (¾–1in) long flowers, each with a red tube and 6 green petals.
D. pulchellum, syn. *Brodiaea capitata, B. pulchella.* Early summer-flowering bulb. H 30–60cm (12–24in), S 8–10cm (3–4in). Long, narrow leaves are semi-erect and basal. Leafless stem produces a dense head of narrowly funnel-shaped, pale to deep violet flowers, 1–2cm (½–¾in) long, with violet bracts.

Dichorisandra

COMMELINACEAE

Genus of erect, clump-forming, evergreen perennials, grown for their ornamental foliage. Frost tender, min. 15–20°C (59–68°F). Prefers fertile, moist but well-drained soil, humid conditions and partial shade. Propagate by division in spring or by stem cuttings in summer.
D. reginae illus. p.258.

Dicksonia

DICKSONIACEAE

Genus of evergreen or semi-evergreen, tree-like ferns that resemble palms and that are sometimes used to provide height in fern plantings. Half hardy to frost tender, min. 5°C (41°F). Needs semi-shade and humus-rich, moist soil. Remove faded fronds regularly. Propagate by spores in summer.
♀ ***D. antarctica*** illus. p.322.
♀ ***D. fibrosa.*** Evergreen, tree-like fern (deciduous in cold climates). H to 6m (20ft), S to 4m (12ft). Half hardy. Stout trunks are crowned by a rosette of spreading, divided, lance-shaped, dark green fronds, to 2m (6ft) long.
♀ ***D. squarrosa.*** Evergreen, tree-like fern (deciduous in cold climates). H to 6m (20ft), S to 4m (12ft). Half hardy. Slender trunks are crowned by a rosette of spreading, divided, lance-shaped, mid-green fronds, to 2m (6ft) long, with blackish stalks and midribs.

Dickson's golden elm. See *Ulmus minor* 'Dicksonii', illus. p.77.

Dictamnus

RUTACEAE

Genus of summer-flowering perennials. Fully hardy. Requires full sun and fertile, well-drained soil. Resents disturbance. Propagate by seed sown in late summer when fresh. The foliage, roots and seeds of *D. albus* may cause mild stomach upset if ingested, and contact with the foliage may cause photodermatitis.
♀ ***D. albus*** var. ***albus*** illus. p.242.
♀ var. ***purpureus*** (syn. *D. fraxinella*) illus. p.245.
D. fraxinella. See *D. albus* var. *purpureus*.

Didiscus coeruleus. See *Trachymene coerulea*.

Didymochlaena

DRYOPTERIDACEAE/ASPIDIACEAE

Genus of one species of evergreen fern. Frost tender, min. 10°C (50°F). Has tufts of glossy, mid-green fronds, tinged with rose-pink or red when young. Requires partial shade, high humidity and moist, humus-rich soil. Propagate by spores as soon as ripe, or divide in spring.
D. lunulata. See *D. truncatula*.
D. truncatula, syn. *D. lunulata.* Evergreen fern. H and S to 1m (3ft). Has erect rhizomes and triangular, divided fronds, 60cm–1.5m (2–5ft) long, with simple, obliquely ovoid to diamond-shaped segments.

Dieffenbachia

Dumb cane, Leopard lily

ARACEAE

Genus of evergreen, tufted perennials, grown for their foliage. Frost tender, min. 15°C (59°F). Grow in fertile, well-drained soil and in partial shade. Propagate in spring or summer by stem cuttings or pieces of leafless stem placed horizontally in compost. Scale insect or red spider mite may be troublesome. All parts may cause severe discomfort if ingested, and contact with sap may irritate skin.
D. amoena of gardens. See *D. seguine* 'Amoena'.
***D.* 'Exotica'.** See. *D. seguine* 'Exotica'.
***D. maculata* 'Exotica'.** See *D. seguine* 'Exotica'.**'Rudolph Roehrs'** see *D. seguine* 'Rudolph Roehrs'.
***D.* 'Memoria'.** See *D. seguine* 'Memoria Corsii'.
D. seguine. Evergreen, tufted perennial. H and S 1m (3ft) or more. Broadly lance-shaped leaves, to 45cm (18in) long, are glossy and dark green. Insignificant, tiny, greenish-white flowers, clustered on the spadix, are surrounded by a narrow, leaf-like spathe that appears intermittently. **'Amoena'** (syn *D. amoena* of gardens) is robust, H to 2m (6ft), with creamy-white bars along lateral veins on the leaves. ♀ **'Exotica'** (syn. *D.* 'Exotica', *D. maculata* 'Exotica') illus. p.272. **'Memoria Corsii'** (syn. *D.* 'Memoria') has grey-green leaves, marked dark green and spotted white. **'Rudolph Roehrs'** (syn. *D. maculata* 'Rudolph Roehrs', *D.s.* 'Roehrs') illus. p.275.

Dierama

Angel's fishing rod, Wandflower

IRIDACEAE

Genus of evergreen, clump-forming, summer-flowering corms with pendent, funnel- or bell-shaped flowers on long, arching, wiry stems. Flourishes near pools. Frost to half hardy. Prefers a warm, sheltered, sunny site and well-drained soil that should be kept moist in summer when in growth. Dies down partially in winter. Propagate by division of corms in spring or by seed in autumn or spring. Resents disturbance, and divisions take a year or more to settle and start flowering again.
***D.* 'Blackbird'.** Evergreen, upright perennial. H 1.5m (5ft), S 30cm (1ft). Frost hardy. Produces cascades of nodding, funnel-shaped, violet-mauve flowers on wiry, pendulous stems in summer above grass-like leaves.
D. dracomontanum, syn. *D. pumilum* of gardens. Vigorous, evergreen, upright perennial. H 75cm (30in), S 30cm (12in). Frost hardy. In summer freely produces nodding, funnel-shaped flowers, in shades of pink and violet, on wiry stems. Leaves are grass-like.
D. ensifolium. See *D. pendulum*.
D. pendulum, syn. *D. ensifolium*, illus. p.413.
D. pulcherrimum illus. p.412.
D. pumilum of gardens. See *D. dracomontanum*.

Diervilla

CAPRIFOLIACEAE

Genus of deciduous, summer-flowering shrubs, grown for their overall appearance. Is similar to *Weigela*. Frost hardy. Tolerates partial shade or full light and moderately fertile, well-drained soil. For a more shapely shrub remove 2- and 3-year-old stems in winter or after flowering. Propagate by semi-ripe cuttings in late summer or by hardwood cuttings in autumn.
D. sessilifolia. Deciduous, spreading shrub. H and S 1–1.5m (3–5ft). Narrowly oval, pointed, serrated, green leaves are often copper-tinted when young. Has terminal and lateral clusters of tubular, pale yellow flowers in summer. To treat as an herbaceous perennial, cut back to ground level each spring and apply a mulch and a fertilizer.

Dietes

IRIDACEAE

Genus of evergreen, iris-like, rhizomatous perennials, grown for their attractive flowers in spring or summer. Half hardy. Needs sun or partial shade and humus-rich, well-drained soil that does not dry out excessively. Propagate by seed in autumn or spring or by division in spring (although divisions do not become re-established very readily).
D. bicolor illus. p.414.
D. iridioides, syn. *D. vegeta* of gardens. Evergreen, spring- and summer-flowering, rhizomatous perennial. H to 60cm (2ft), S 30–60cm (1–2ft). Bears sword-shaped, semi-erect, basal leaves in a spreading fan. Branching, wiry stems bear iris-like, white flowers, 6–8cm (2½–3in) across. Each of the 3 large petals has a central, yellow mark.
D. vegeta of gardens. See *D. iridioides*.

Digger's speedwell. See *Parahebe perfoliata*, illus. p.296.

Digitalis

Foxglove

SCROPHULARIACEAE

Genus of biennials and perennials, some of which are evergreen, grown for their flower spikes in summer. Fully to frost hardy. Species mentioned grow in most conditions, even dry, exposed sites, but do best in semi-shade and moist but well-drained soil. Propagate by seed in autumn. All parts may cause severe discomfort if ingested. Contact with foliage may irritate skin.

D. ambigua. See *D. grandiflora*.
D. canariensis. See *Isoplexis canariensis*.
D. eriostachya. See *D. lutea*.
🏆 ***D. ferruginea*** Perennial best treated as a biennial. H 1–1.2m (3–4ft), S 30cm (1ft). Fully hardy. Long, slender spikes bear funnel-shaped, orange-brown and white flowers in mid-summer above basal rosettes of oval, rough leaves.
🏆 ***D. grandiflora***, syn. *D. ambigua* (Yellow foxglove). Evergreen, clump-forming perennial. H 75cm (30in), S 30cm (12in). Fully hardy. Racemes of downward-pointing, tubular, creamy-yellow flowers appear in summer above a rosette of oval to oblong, smooth, strongly veined leaves.
D. lutea, syn. *D. eriostachya*. Upright perennial. H 75cm (30in), S 30cm (12in). Fully hardy. In summer, delicate spires of downward-pointing, narrowly tubular, creamy-yellow flowers are borne above a rosette of oval, smooth, mid-green leaves.
🏆 ***D. × mertonensis.*** Clump-forming perennial. H 75cm (30in), S 30cm (12in). Fully hardy. Produces spikes of downward-pointing, tubular, rose-mauve to coppery flowers in summer, above a rosette of oval, hairy, soft leaves. Divide after flowering.
D. purpurea. Upright, short-lived perennial, grown as a biennial. H 1–1.5m (3–5ft), S 60cm (2ft). Fully hardy. Has a rosette of oval, rough, deep green leaves and, in summer, tall spikes of tubular flowers in shades of pink, red, purple or white. 🏆 f. ***albiflora*** (syn. *D.p.* f. *alba*) illus. p.330.

Dillenia

DILLENIACEAE

Genus of evergreen or briefly deciduous, spring-flowering trees, grown for their flowers and foliage and for shade. Frost tender, min. 16°C (61°F). Needs moisture-retentive, fertile soil and full light. Water potted plants freely while in full growth, less in winter. Propagate by seed in spring.

D. indica (Elephant apple). Briefly deciduous, spreading tree. H and S 8–12m (25–40ft). Has oval, serrated, boldly parallel-veined, glossy leaves, each 30cm (1ft) long. Nodding, cup-shaped, white flowers, each 15–20cm (6–8in) wide, are produced in spring, followed by edible, globular, greenish fruits.

Dimorphotheca

African daisy, Cape marigold

COMPOSITAE/ASTERACEAE

Genus of annuals, perennials and evergreen sub-shrubs. Half hardy. Grow in sun and in fertile, very well-drained soil. Dead-head to prolong flowering. Propagate annuals by seed sown under glass in mid-spring, perennials by semi-ripe cuttings in summer. Is susceptible to botrytis in wet summers.

D. annua. See *D. pluvialis*.
D. barberae of gardens. See *Osteospermum jucundum*.
D. pluvialis, syn. *D. annua*, illus. p.331.

Dionaea

DROSERACEAE

Genus of evergreen, insectivorous, rosette-forming perennials. Frost tender, min. 5°C (41°F). Needs partial shade and a humid atmosphere; grow in a mixture of peat and moss, kept constantly moist. Propagate by seed or division in spring.

D. muscipula illus. p.317.

Dionysia

PRIMULACEAE

Genus of evergreen, cushion-forming perennials. Fully hardy. Grow in an alpine house in sun and very gritty, well-drained soil. Position deep collar of grit under cushion and ensure good ventilation at all times. Dislikes winter wet. Propagate by softwood cuttings in summer. Plants are susceptible to botrytis.

🏆 ***D. aretioides*** illus. p.383.
D. microphylla. Evergreen perennial. H 5cm (2in), S 15cm (6in). Rosettes of oval to rounded, often sharply pointed, grey-green leaves, with a mealy, yellow coating beneath, form tight cushions. Small, short-stemmed, 5-petalled, white-eyed, pale to deep violet-yellow flowers, with darker petal bases, appear in early spring.
D. tapetodes illus. p.384.

Dioon

ZAMIACEAE

Genus of evergreen shrubs, grown for their palm-like appearance. Frost tender, min. 13–18°C (55–64°F). Requires full sun and fertile, well-drained soil. Water containerized specimens moderately, less when not in full growth. Propagate by seed in spring.

🏆 ***D. edule*** (Virgin's palm). Very slow-growing, evergreen, palm-like shrub, eventually with a thick, upright trunk. H 2–4m (6–12ft), S 1.5–3m (5–10ft). Leaves are feather-like, 60cm–1.2m (2–4ft) long, with spine-tipped, deep blue-green leaflets.

Dioscorea

DIOSCOREACEAE

Genus of tuberous perennials, some of which are succulent, and herbaceous or evergreen, twining climbers, grown mainly for their decorative leaves. Insignificant flowers are generally yellow. Frost tender, min. 5–13°C (41–55°F). Prefers full sun or partial shade and fertile, well-drained soil. Propagate by division, or by cutting off sections of tuber in spring or autumn or by seed in spring.

D. discolor illus. p.217.
🏆 ***D. elephantipes***, syn. *Testudinaria elephantipes*, illus. p.483.

Diosma

RUTACEAE

Genus of evergreen, wiry-stemmed shrubs, grown for their flowers and overall appearance. Frost tender, min. 7°C (45°F). Needs full light and well-drained, neutral to acid soil. Water potted specimens moderately, less when not in full growth. To create a compact habit shorten flowered stems after flowering. Propagate by seed in spring or by semi-ripe cuttings in late summer.

D. ericoides (Breath of heaven). Fast-growing, evergreen, loosely rounded shrub. H and S 30–60cm (1–2ft). Aromatic, needle-like leaves are crowded on stems. In winter-spring carries a profusion of small, fragrant, 5-petalled, white flowers, sometimes tinted red.

Diosphaera. See *Trachelium*.

Diospyros

EBENACEAE

Genus of deciduous or evergreen trees and shrubs, grown for their foliage and fruits. Fully to frost hardy. Needs full sun and does best in hot summers. Requires fertile, well-drained soil. To obtain fruits, plants of both sexes should be grown. Propagate by seed in autumn.

D. kaki (Chinese persimmon, Kaki, Persimmon). Deciduous, spreading tree. H 10m (30ft), S 7m (22ft). Frost hardy. Oval, glossy, dark green leaves turn orange, red and purple in autumn. Tiny, yellowish-white flowers in summer are followed on female trees by large, edible, rounded, yellow or orange fruits.
D. lotus (Date plum). Deciduous, spreading tree. H 10m (30ft), S 6m (20ft). Fully hardy. Has oval, glossy, dark green leaves, tiny, red-tinged, green flowers from mid- to late summer and, on female trees, unpalatable, rounded, purple or yellow fruits.

Dipcadi

LILIACEAE/HYACINTHACEAE

Genus of spring-flowering bulbs, grown mainly for botanical interest. Frost hardy, but will not tolerate cold, wet winters, so is best grown in a cold frame or alpine house. Needs a warm, sunny situation and light, well-drained soil. Is dormant in summer. Propagate by seed in autumn.

D. serotinum illus. p.450.

Dipelta

CAPRIFOLIACEAE

Genus of deciduous shrubs, with bold, long-pointed leaves, grown for their showy, tubular flowers and peeling bark. After flowering, bracts beneath flowers enlarge and become papery and brown, surrounding the fruits. Fully hardy. Requires sun or semi- shade and fertile, well-drained soil. Benefits from the occasional removal of old shoots after flowering. Propagate by softwood cuttings in summer.

🏆 ***D. floribunda*** illus. p.113.
D. yunnanensis illus. p.112.

Diphylleia

BERBERIDACEAE

Genus of perennials with creeping rootstocks and umbrella-like leaves. Is best suited to woodland gardens. Fully hardy. Needs semi-shade and moist soil. Propagate by division in spring or by seed in autumn.

D. cymosa (Umbrella leaf). Rounded perennial. H 60cm (24in), S 30cm (12in). Has large, rounded, 2-lobed leaves. In spring bears loose heads of inconspicuous, white flowers followed by indigo-blue berries on red stalks.

Dipidax. See *Onixotis*.
Diplacus glutinosus. See *Mimulus aurantiacus*.
Dipladenia. See *Mandevilla*.

Diplarrhena

IRIDACEAE

Genus of one species of summer-flowering perennial. Half hardy. Needs sun and well-drained soil. Propagate by seed or division in spring.

D. moraea illus. p.287.

Dipsacus

Teasel

DIPSACACEAE

Genus of biennials or short-lived perennials grown for their flower heads, which are good for drying. Fully hardy. Requires sun or partial shade and any fertile soil, including heavy clay. Propagate by seed in autumn or spring.

D. fullonum. Prickly biennial. H 1.5–2m (5–6ft), S 30–80cm (12–32in). In the first year produces a basal rosette of toothed, dark green leaves covered in spiny pustules. Thistle-like, pinkish-purple or white flower heads, with stiff, prickly bracts, are borne terminally on upright stems with paired leaves in mid- and late summer of the second year.

Dipteronia

ACERACEAE

Genus of deciduous trees, grown for their foliage and fruits. Fully hardy. Needs full sun and fertile, well-drained soil. Propagate by softwood cuttings in summer or by seed in autumn.

D. sinensis. Deciduous, spreading, sometimes shrubby tree. H 10m (30ft), S 6m (20ft). Large, mid-green leaves have 7–11 oval to lance-shaped leaflets. Inconspicuous, greenish-white flowers in summer are followed by large clusters of winged, red fruits.

Disa

ORCHIDACEAE

See also ORCHIDS.

D. uniflora. Deciduous, terrestrial orchid. H 45–60cm (1½–2ft). Frost tender, min. 7–10°C (45–50°F). Has narrowly lance-shaped, glossy, dark green leaves, to 22cm (9in) long, that clasp stems. In early summer each stem bears up to 7 hooded, scarlet flowers, 8–10 cm (3–4in) long, that have darker veins and are suffused yellow. Is the parent of many hybrids cultivated commercially for cut flowers. Needs partial shade and continually moist soil. Raise from seed or propagate by division of offsets when dormant.

DISANTHUS

HAMAMELIDACEAE

Genus of one species of deciduous, autumn-flowering shrub, grown for its overall appearance and autumn colour. Frost hardy. Needs partial shade and humus-rich, moist but not wet, neutral to acid soil. Propagate by layering in spring or by seed when ripe or in spring.

♀ ***D. cercidifolius.*** Deciduous, rounded shrub. H and S to 3m (10ft). Bears broadly oval to almost circular, bluish-green leaves that turn yellow, orange, red or purple in autumn. Has small, dark red flowers in autumn as the leaves fall, or later.

DISCARIA

RHAMNACEAE

Genus of deciduous or almost leafless shrubs and trees, grown for their habit and flowers. Spiny, green shoots assume function of leaves. Frost hardy. Needs a sheltered, sunny site and fertile, well-drained soil. Propagate by softwood cuttings in summer.

D. toumatou (Wild Irishman). Deciduous or almost leafless, bushy shrub. H and S 2m (6ft). Shoots have sharp, rigid spines. Tiny, star-shaped, greenish-white flowers are borne in dense clusters in late spring.

Disk-leaved hebe. See *Hebe pinguifolia*.

DISCOCACTUS

CACTACEAE

Genus of epiphytic, perennial cacti with flattened, strap-shaped stems. Is closely related to *Epiphyllum*, with which it hybridizes. Spines are insignificant. Stems may die back after flowering. Frost tender, min. 10°C (50°F). Needs partial shade and rich, well-drained soil. Is easy to grow. Propagate by stem cuttings in spring or summer.

D. ackermannii, syn. *Epiphyllum ackermannii, Nopalxochia ackermannii* (Red orchid cactus). Erect, then pendent, epiphytic, perennial cactus. H 30cm (1ft), S 60cm (2ft). Has fleshy, toothed, green stems, to 7cm (3in) across and 40cm (16in) long; 15cm (6in) wide, funnel-shaped, red flowers in spring-summer along indented edges of stems.

***D.* 'Gloria'** illus. p.479.

***D.* 'Jennifer Ann'** illus. p.483.

***D.* 'M.A. Jeans'** illus. p.479.

***D. phyllanthoides* 'Deutsche Kaiserin'**, illus. p.478.

DISPORUM

Fairy bells

LILIACEAE/CONVALLARIACEAE

Genus of spring- or early summer-flowering perennials. Is best suited to woodland gardens. Fully hardy. Requires a cool, semi-shaded position and humus-rich soil. Propagate by division in spring or by seed in autumn.

D. hookeri. Clump-forming perennial. H 75cm (30in), S 30cm (12in). Leaves are narrowly oval and mid-green. Orange-red berries in autumn follow clusters of drooping, open bell-shaped, greenish-white flowers in spring.

***D. sessile* 'Variegatum'.** Rapidly spreading, clump-forming perennial. H 45cm (18in), S 30cm (12in). Solitary tubular-bell-shaped to bell-shaped, creamy-white flowers are produced in spring. Narrowly oval, pleated leaves are irregularly striped with white.

DISTICTIS

BIGNONIACEAE

Genus of evergreen, woody-stemmed, tendril climbers, grown for their colourful, trumpet-shaped flowers. Frost tender, min. 5–7°C (41–5°F). Well-drained soil is suitable with full light. Water freely in summer, less at other times. Support for stems is necessary. Thin out congested growth in spring. Propagate by softwood cuttings in early summer or by semi-ripe cuttings in late summer.

D. buccinatoria, syn. *Phaedranthus buccinatorius*, illus. p.200.

DISTYLIUM

HAMAMELIDACEAE

Genus of evergreen shrubs and trees, grown for their foliage and flowers. Frost hardy. Prefers a sheltered, partially shaded position and moist, peaty soil. Propagate by semi-ripe cuttings in summer.

D. racemosum. Evergreen, arching shrub. H 2m (6ft), S 3m (10ft). Leaves are oblong, leathery, glossy and dark green. Small flowers, with red calyces and purple anthers, are borne in late spring and early summer.

Dittany. See *Origanum*.
 Cretan. See *Origanum dictamnus*.

Dizygotheca elegantissima. See *Schefflera elegantissima*.

DOCYNIA

ROSACEAE

Genus of evergreen or semi-evergreen, spring-flowering trees, grown for their flowers and foliage; is related to *Cydonia*. Half hardy. Requires full light and well-drained soil. Other than shaping while young, pruning is not necessary. Propagate by seed in spring or autumn, by budding in summer or by grafting in winter. Is usually trouble-free, though caterpillars may be troublesome.

D. delavayi. Evergreen or semi-evergreen, spreading tree. H and S 8m (25ft) or more. Oval to lance-shaped leaves are white-felted beneath. In spring has fragrant, 5-petalled, white flowers, pink in bud, followed by ovoid, downy, yellow fruits in autumn.

DODECATHEON

Shooting stars

PRIMULACEAE

Genus of spring- and summer-flowering perennials, grown for their distinctive flowers, with reflexed petals and prominent stamens. Once fertilized, flowers turn skywards – hence their common name. Is dormant after flowering. Fully to frost hardy. Prefers sun or partial shade and moist but well-drained soil. Propagate by seed in autumn or by division in winter.

♀ ***D. dentatum.*** Clump-forming perennial. H 7cm (3in), S 25cm (10in). Fully hardy. Leaves are long, oval and toothed. In late spring, frail stems bear white flowers with prominent, dark stamens and reflexed petals. Prefers a partially shaded position.

♀ ***D. hendersonii***, syn. *D. latifolium*, illus. p.359.

D. latifolium. See *D. hendersonii*.

♀ ***D. meadia.*** Clump-forming perennial. H 20cm (8in), S 15cm (6in). Fully hardy. Leaves are oval and pale green. In spring, strong stems carry pale pink flowers, with reflexed petals, above foliage. Prefers a partially shaded position. ♀ f. ***album*** illus. p.359.

D. pauciflorum of gardens. See *D. pulchellum*.

♀ ***D. pulchellum***, syn. *D. pauciflorum* of gardens. Clump-forming perennial. H 15cm (6in), S 10cm (4in). Fully hardy. Is similar to *D. meadia*, but flowers are usually deep cerise.

***D.* 'Red Wings'** illus. p.360.

DODONAEA

SAPINDACEAE

Genus of evergreen trees and shrubs, grown mainly for their foliage and overall appearance. Half hardy to frost tender, min. 3–5°C (37–41°F). Prefers full sun and well-drained soil. Water potted plants freely when in full growth, less at other times. Cut back in late summer and in spring if needed, to maintain a balanced shape. Propagate by seed in spring or by semi-ripe cuttings in late summer.

***D. viscosa* 'Purpurea'** illus. p.147.

Dog's fennel. See *Anthemis*.

Dog's-tooth violet. See *Erythronium dens-canis*, illus. p.446.

Dogwood. See *Cornus*.
 Creeping. See *Cornus canadensis*, illus. p.386.
 Flowering. See *Cornus florida*.
 Mountain. See *Cornus nuttallii*, illus. p.72.
 Pacific. See *Cornus nuttallii*, illus. p.72.
 Red-barked. See *Cornus alba*.

Dolichos lablab. See *Lablab purpureus*.

Dolichos purpureus. See *Lablab purpureus*.

Doll's eyes. See *Actaea pachypoda*, illus. p.267.

DOMBEYA

STERCULIACEAE

Genus of evergreen shrubs and trees, grown for their flowers. Frost tender, min. 5–13°C (41–55°F). Needs full light or partial shade and fertile, well-drained soil. Water potted specimens freely when in full growth, less when temperatures are low. May be cut back after flowering. Propagate by seed in spring or by semi-ripe cuttings in summer. Whitefly and red spider mite may be a nuisance.

D. burgessiae, syn. *D. mastersii*, illus. p.146.

D. × cayeuxii illus. p.84.

D. mastersii. See *D. burgessiae*.

Dondia. See *Hacquetia*.

Donkey-tail. See *Sedum morganianum*.

DORONICUM

Leopard's bane

COMPOSITAE/ASTERACEAE

Genus of perennials, grown for their daisy-like flower heads, which are good for cutting. Fully hardy. Most prefer full light or shade and moist, well-drained soil. Propagate by division in autumn.

D. austriacum. Clump-forming perennial. H 45cm (18in), S 30cm (12in). Daisy-like, pure yellow flower heads are produced singly on slender stems in spring. Heart-shaped, bright green leaves are hairy and wavy-edged.

D. columnae, syn. *D. cordatum*. ♀ **'Miss Mason'** illus. p.240.

D. cordatum. See *D. columnae*.

***D. × excelsum* 'Harpur Crewe'**, syn. *D. plantagineum* 'Excelsum'. Elegant, clump-forming perennial. H 1m (3ft), S 60cm (2ft). Large, daisy-like, buttercup-yellow flower heads are borne, 3 or 4 to a stem, in spring. Leaves are heart-shaped and bright green. Is good for a dry, shaded site.

***D.* 'Frühlingspracht'**, syn *D.* 'Spring Beauty'. Clump-forming perennial. H 45cm (18in), S 30cm (12in). Produces daisy-like, double, bright yellow flower heads in spring. Bears heart-shaped, bright green leaves.

***D. plantagineum* 'Excelsum'.** See *D. × excelsum* 'Harpur Crewe'.

***D.* 'Spring Beauty'.** See *D.* 'Frühlingspracht'.

DOROTHEANTHUS

AIZOACEAE

Genus of succulent annuals, suitable for hot, dry places such as rock gardens, banks and gaps in paving. Half hardy. Needs sun and grows well in poor, very well-drained soil. Dead-head to prolong flowering. Propagate by seed sown under glass in early spring, or outdoors in mid- spring. Protect from slugs and snails.

D. bellidiformis, syn. *Mesembryanthemum criniflorum* (Ice-plant, Livingstone daisy). **'Magic Carpet'** illus. p.337.

Dorset heath. See *Erica ciliaris*.

DORYANTHES

LILIACEAE/DORYANTHACEAE

Genus of evergreen, rosette-forming perennials, grown for their flowers. Frost tender, min. 10°C (50°F). Needs a sunny position and humus-rich, well-drained soil. Propagate by mature bulbils, by seed in spring or by suckers after flowering.

D. palmeri illus. p.232.

Dorycnium hirsutum. See *Lotus hirsutus*.

Double common snowdrop. See *Galanthus nivalis* 'Flore Pleno', illus. p.455.

Double meadow buttercup. See *Ranunculus acris* 'Flore Pleno', illus. p.304.

Double sea campion. See *Silene*

uniflora 'Robin Whitebreast'.
Double soapwort. See *Saponaria officinalis* 'Rubra Plena'.
Douglas fir. See *Pseudotsuga menziesii*.
Douglasia vitaliana. See *Vitaliana primuliflora*.
Dove tree. See *Davidia involucrata*, illus. p.73.
Downy cherry. See *Prunus tomentosa*.
Doxantha. See *Macfadyena* except for: ***D. capreolata*** for which see *Bignonia capreolata*.

DRABA

CRUCIFERAE/BRASSICACEAE

Genus of spring-flowering annuals and evergreen or semi-evergreen, cushion- or mat-forming perennials with extensive root systems. Some species form soft, green cushions that in winter turn brown except at the tips, appearing almost dead. Is suitable for alpine houses. Fully to frost hardy. Needs sun and gritty, well-drained soil. Dislikes winter wet. Propagate by softwood cuttings of the rosettes in late spring or by seed in autumn.
D. aizoides (Yellow whitlow grass). Semi-evergreen, mat-forming perennial. H 2.5cm (1in), S 15cm (6in). Fully hardy. Has lance-shaped, stiff-bristled leaves in rosettes and, in spring, 4-petalled, bright yellow flowers. Suits a scree.
D. bryoides. See *D. rigida* var. *bryoides*.
D. hispanica. Semi-evergreen, cushion-forming perennial. H 5cm (2in), S 10cm (4in). Frost hardy. Leaves are oval, soft, fragile and pale green. Clusters of flat, 4-petalled, pale yellow flowers are borne in spring.
♀ ***D. longisiliqua*** illus. p.383.
D. mollissima illus. p.384.
D. polytricha. Semi-evergreen, cushion-forming perennial. H 6cm (2½in), S 15cm (6in). Fully hardy. Has minute, rounded leaves in neat, symmetrical rosettes. Frail stems carry flat, 4-petalled, golden-yellow flowers in spring. Is difficult to grow. Keep stones under cushion at all times. Remove dead rosettes at once.
D. rigida illus. p.383. var. ***bryoides*** (syn. *D. bryoides*) is an evergreen, tight hummock-forming perennial. H 4cm (1½in), S 6cm (2½in). Fully hardy. Leaves are tiny, rounded, hard and dark green. Produces small clusters of almost stemless, 4-petalled, bright yellow flowers that cover hummocks in spring. Also suited to a trough or scree.

DRACAENA

AGAVACEAE/DRACAENACEAE

Genus of evergreen trees and shrubs, grown for their foliage and overall appearance. Frost tender, min. 13–18°C (55–64°F). Needs full light or partial shade and well-drained soil. Water containerized plants moderately, much less in low temperatures. Rejuvenate leggy plants by cutting back to near soil level in spring. Propagate by seed or air-layering in spring or by tip or stem cuttings in summer. Mealy bug may be a nuisance.
D. australis. See *Cordyline australis*.
D. deremensis. See *D. fragrans* Deremensis Group. **'Souvenir de Schrijver'** see *D. fragrans* Deremenis Group 'Warneckei'. **'Warneckei'** see *D. fragrans* Deremensis Group 'Warneckei'.
♀ ***D. draco*** illus. p.96.
D. fragrans (Corn plant). **Deremensis Group**, syn. *D. deremensis*, is a slow-growing, evergreen, erect, sparsely branched shrub. H 2m (6ft) or more, S 1m (3ft) or more. Has lance-shaped, erect to arching, glossy, deep green leaves, to 45cm (18in) long. Mature plants may occasionally bear large panicles of small, red-and-white flowers in summer. ♀ **Deremensis Group 'Warneckei'** (syn. *D. deremensis* 'Souvenir de Schrijver', *D.d.* 'Warneckei') illus. p.122.
♀ **'Massangeana'**. Evergreen, erect, sparsely branched shrub. H 3–6m (10–20ft), S 1–3m (3–10ft). Has strap-shaped, arching leaves, to 60cm (2ft) long, with longitudinal bands of yellow and pale green. In early summer, fragrant, star-shaped, yellow flowers, rarely produced, are followed by rounded-oblong, orange-red fruits.
D. indivisa. See *Cordyline indivisa*.
♀ ***D. marginata*** (Madagascar dragon tree). Slow-growing, evergreen, erect shrub or tree. H 3m (10ft) or more, S 1–2m (3–6ft) or more. Leaves are narrowly strap-shaped and rich green with red margins. Flowers are rarely produced. ♀ **'Tricolor'** illus. p.95.
♀ ***D. sanderiana*** illus. p.147.

DRACOCEPHALUM

Dragon's head

LABIATAE/LAMIACEAE

Genus of summer-flowering annuals and perennials, suitable for rock gardens and borders. Fully hardy. Prefers sun and fertile, well-drained soil. Propagate by seed or division in spring or autumn or by basal cuttings of young growth in spring.
D. ruyschiana. Erect perennial. H 45–60cm (18–24in), S 30cm (12in). Freely bears whorled spikes of 2-lipped, violet-blue flowers from early to mid-summer. Mid-green leaves are linear to lance-shaped.
D. sibiricum. See *Nepeta sibirica*.

DRACUNCULUS

ARACEAE

Genus of robust, tuberous perennials that produce roughly triangular, foul-smelling spathes. Frost hardy, but in severe winters protect dormant tubers with a cloche or dead bracken. Needs sun and well-drained soil that dries out in summer. Propagate by freely borne offsets in late summer or by seed in autumn.
D. vulgaris, syn. *Arum dracunculus*, illus. p.413.

Dragon tree. See *Dracaena draco*, illus. p.96.
Madagascar. See *Dracaena marginata*.
Dragon's arum. See *Dracunculus vulgaris*, illus.p.413.
Dragon's head. See *Dracocephalum*.
Dragon's mouth. See *Horminum pyrenaicum*.
Dragon's-claw willow. See *Salix babylonica* var. *pekinensis* 'Tortuosa', illus. p.81.

DREGEA

ASCLEPIADACEAE

Genus of evergreen, woody-stemmed, twining climbers, grown for botanical interest. Frost hardy. Grow in sun and in any well-drained soil. Propagate by seed in spring or by stem cuttings in summer or autumn.
D. corrugata. See *D. sinensis*.
D. sinensis, syn. *D. corrugata, Wattakaka sinensis*. Evergreen, woody-stemmed, twining climber. H to 3m (10ft). Oval, mid-green leaves, heart-shaped at base, 3–10cm (1¼–4in) long, are greyish beneath. In summer has clusters of 10–25 small, fragrant, star-shaped flowers, white or cream with red dots and streaks, followed by pairs of slender pods, 5–7cm (2–3in) long.

Drejerella guttata. See *Justicia brandegeeana*.
Drepanostachyum falconeri. See *Himalayacalamus falconeri*.

DRIMYS

WINTERACEAE

Genus of evergreen trees and shrubs, grown for their foliage and star-shaped flowers. Frost hardy, but in cold areas grow against a south- or west-facing wall. Needs sun or semi-shade and fertile, moist but well-drained soil. Propagate by semi-ripe cuttings in summer or by seed in autumn.
D. aromatica. See *D. lanceolata*.
D. axillaris. See *Pseudowintera axillaris*.
D. colorata. See *Pseudowintera colorata*.
D. lanceolata, syn. *D. aromatica* (Mountain pepper). Evergreen, upright, dense shrub or tree. H 4m (12ft), S 2.5m (8ft). Has deep red shoots and oblong, dark green leaves. Produces clusters of star-shaped, white flowers in spring.
♀ ***D. winteri***, syn. *Wintera aromatica*, illus. p.74.

Drooping juniper. See *Juniperus recurva*, illus. p.104.
Drooping star-of-Bethlehem. See *Ornithogalum nutans*.
Dropwort. See *Filipendula vulgaris*.

DROSANTHEMUM

AIZOACEAE

Genus of erect or prostrate, succulent shrubs with slender stems and masses of flowers in summer. Leaves are finely covered in papillae. Frost tender, min. 5°C (41°F). Needs full sun and very well-drained soil. Propagate by seed or stem cuttings in spring or summer.
D. hispidum. Succulent shrub, with arching or spreading branches that root down. H 60cm (2ft), S 1m (3ft). Has cylindrical, light green leaves, 1.5–2.5cm (⅝–1in) long. In summer, masses of shiny, daisy-like, purple flowers, to 3cm (1¼in) across, are borne.
D. speciosum. Erect, shrubby succulent. H 60cm (2ft), S 1m (3ft). Has semi-cylindrical leaves, 1–2cm (½–¾in) long. Masses of daisy-like, green-centred, orange-red flowers, to 5cm (2in) across, appear in summer.

DROSERA

Sundew

DROSERACEAE

Genus of evergreen, insectivorous perennials. Fully hardy to frost tender, min. 5–10°C (41–50°F). Grow in sun, in a mixture of peat and moss that is not allowed to dry out. Propagate by seed or division in spring.
D. capensis illus. p.317.
D. spatulata illus. p.317.

Drumstick primula. See *Primula denticulata*, illus. p.281.
Drunkard's dream. See *Hatiora salicornioides*, illus. p.484.

DRYANDRA

PROTEACEAE

Genus of evergreen, spring- to summer-flowering shrubs and trees, grown for their flowers, foliage and overall appearance. Frost tender, min. 7°C (45°F). Needs full light and well-drained, sandy soil that contains few nitrates or phosphates. Is difficult to grow. Water containerized specimens moderately, much less in low temperatures. Plants under glass must be freely ventilated. Propagate by seed in spring.
D. formosa. Evergreen, bushy shrub. H 2–5m (6–15ft), S 1.5–3m (5–10ft). Strap-shaped leaves are divided into triangular, closely set lobes, creating a saw-blade effect. In spring carries small, scented, tubular, orange-yellow flowers in domed, terminal heads.

DRYAS

Mountain avens

ROSACEAE

Genus of evergreen, prostrate, woody-based perennials with oak-like leaves and cup-shaped flowers. Is useful on banks and walls, in rock gardens and as ground cover. Fully hardy. Prefers sun and gritty, well-drained, peaty soil. Propagate by seed when fresh or by semi-ripe cuttings in summer.
D. drummondii. Evergreen, prostrate, woody-based perennial. H 5cm (2in), S indefinite. Stout stems are clothed in small, oval, lobed, leathery, dark green leaves. Nodding, creamy-white flowers are borne in early summer but never fully open.
♀ ***D. octopetala*** illus. p.387.
♀ ***D. × suendermannii.*** Evergreen, prostrate, woody-based perennial. H 5cm (2in), S indefinite. Is similar to *D. drummondii*, but has slightly nodding, pale cream flowers that open horizontally.

DRYOPTERIS

DRYOPTERIDACEAE/ASPIDIACEAE

Genus of deciduous or semi-evergreen ferns, many of which form regular, shuttlecock-like crowns. Fully to half hardy. Requires shade and moist soil. Regularly remove fading fronds. Propagate by spores in summer or by division in autumn or winter.
♀ ***D. affinis***, syn. *D. borreri, D. pseudomas* (Golden male fern). Virtually evergreen fern. H and S to 1m (3ft). Fully hardy. Produces a

'shuttlecock' of lance-shaped, divided fronds, 20–80cm (8–32in) tall, from an erect rhizome. Fronds are pale green as they unfurl in spring, in contrast to the scaly, golden brown midribs; they mature to dark green and often remain green through winter. Distinguished from *D. filix-mas* by a dark spot where each pinna joins the midrib.

D. atrata of gardens. See *D. cycadina*.

D. austriaca. See *D. dilatata*.

D. borreri. See *D. affinis*.

D. carthusiana (Narrow buckler fern). Deciduous or semi-evergreen, creeping, rhizomatous fern. H 1m (3ft), S 45cm (18in). Fully hardy. Produces lance-shaped, much-divided, mid-green fronds with triangular to oval pinnae.

♀ ***D. cycadina***, syn. *D. atrata* of gardens, *D. hirtipes*. Deciduous fern. H 60cm (24in), S 45cm (18in). Fully hardy. Has an erect rhizome producing a 'shuttlecock' of lance-shaped, divided, bright green fronds, 45cm (18in) tall, with green midribs.

♀ ***D. dilatata***, syn. *D. austriaca* (Broad buckler fern). Deciduous or semi-evergreen fern. H 1m (3ft), S 45cm (18in). Fully hardy. Has much-divided, arching, mid-green fronds, with triangular to oval pinnae, on stout, dark brown stems.

♀ ***D. erythrosora*** (Japanese shield fern). Deciduous fern. H 45cm (18in), S 30cm (12in). Frost to half hardy. Broadly triangular, coppery-pink fronds, divided into triangular to oval pinnae, persist until mid-winter.

♀ ***D. filix-mas*** illus. p.322.

♀ **'Grandiceps Wills'** is a deciduous fern. H and S 90m (3ft). Fully hardy. Has 'shuttlecocks' of broadly lance-shaped, tasselled, elegantly arching, mid-green fronds, arising from crowns of large, upright, brown-scaled rhizomes. The tip of each frond has a heavy crest, and the pinnae are also finely crested.

D. goldieana (Giant wood fern). Deciduous fern. H 1m (3ft), S 60cm (2ft). Fully hardy. Has broadly oval, light green fronds divided into numerous oblong, indented pinnae.

D. hirtipes. See *D. cycadina*.

D. marginalis. Deciduous fern. H 60cm (24in), S 30cm (12in). Fully hardy. Fronds are lance-shaped, dark green and divided into numerous oblong, slightly indented pinnae.

D. pseudomas. See *D. affinis*.

D. sieboldii. Semi-evergreen, tufted fern. H and S 30–60cm (1–2ft). Fully or frost hardy. Produces long-stalked, erect or arching, yellowish-green fronds, 20–50cm (8–20in) long, with up to 6 pairs of narrowly lance-shaped pinnae, 15–30cm (6–12in) long.

♀ ***D. wallichiana*** (Wallich's wood fern). Deciduous fern. H 1–1.8m (3–6ft), S 75cm (30in). Fully hardy. Produces an erect rhizome and a 'shuttlecock' of lance-shaped, divided, dark green fronds, yellow-green when young, 1m (3ft) or more long. Midribs are covered with dark brown or black scales, providing attractive colour contrasts in spring.

DUCHESNEA

ROSACEAE

Genus of perennials, some of which are semi-evergreen, grown as ground cover as well as for their flowers. May be used in hanging baskets. Fully hardy. Grow in well-drained soil and in sun or partial shade. Propagate by division in spring, by rooting plantlets formed at ends of runners in summer or by seed in autumn.

D. indica, syn. *Fragaria indica*. Semi-evergreen, trailing perennial. H to 10cm (4in), S indefinite. Dark green leaves have 3 toothed leaflets like those of strawberries. Solitary, 5-petalled, bright yellow flowers, to 2.5cm (1in) wide and with leafy, green frills of sepals, appear from spring to early summer. Strawberry-like, tasteless, red fruits appear in late summer.

Duck potato. See *Sagittaria latifolia*, illus. p.462.

Duckweed. See *Wolffia*.

Least. See *Wolffia arrhiza*.

DUDLEYA

CRASSULACEAE

Genus of basal-rosetted, perennial succulents, closely related to *Echeveria*. Frost tender, min. 7°C (45°F). Requires full sun and very well-drained soil. Water sparingly when plants are semi-dormant in mid-summer. Propagate by seed or division in spring or summer.

D. brittonii. Basal-rosetted, perennial succulent. H 20–60cm (8–24in) or more when in flower, S 50cm (20in). Has narrowly lance-shaped, tapering, fleshy, silvery-white leaves. Masses of star-shaped, pale yellow flowers are produced in spring-summer.

D. pulverulenta illus. p.480.

Duke of Argyll's tea-tree. See *Lycium barbarum*.

Dumb cane. See *Dieffenbachia*.

Dumpling cactus. See *Lophophora williamsii*, illus. p.487.

DURANTA

VERBENACEAE

Genus of fast-growing, evergreen or partially deciduous trees and shrubs, grown for their flowers and overall appearance. Frost tender, min. 10–13°C (50–55°F). Needs full light and fertile, well-drained soil. Water potted plants freely when in full growth, moderately at other times. Prune as necessary to curb vigour. Propagate by seed in spring or by semi-ripe cuttings in summer. Whitefly may be troublesome.

D. erecta, syn. *D. plumieri, D. repens*, illus. p.146.

D. plumieri. See *D. erecta*.

D. repens. See *D. erecta*.

Durmast oak. See *Quercus petraea*.

Dusky coral pea. See *Kennedia rubicunda*, illus. p.201.

Dutch crocus. See *Crocus vernus*, illus. p.445.

Dutch elm. See *Ulmus × hollandica*.

Dutchman's breeches. See *Dicentra cucullaria*, illus. p.374.

Dutchman's trousers. See *Dicentra spectabilis*, illus. p.247.

DUVALIA

ASCLEPIADACEAE

Genus of clump-forming or carpeting, perennial succulents with short, thick, leafless stems; is closely related to *Stapelia*. Star-shaped flowers have thick, fleshy petals recurved at tips. Frost tender, min. 10°C (50°F), but best at 20°C (68°F). Requires partial shade and very well-drained soil. Propagate by seed or stem cuttings in spring or summer.

D. corderoyi illus. p.492.

Duvernoia adhatodoides. See *Justicia adhatoda*.

Dwarf bearded iris. See *Iris pumila*.

Dwarf fan palm. See *Chamaerops humilis*, illus. p.172.

Dwarf mountain palm. See *Chamaedorea elegans*, illus. p.148.

Dwarf palmetto. See *Sabal minor*, illus. p.172.

Dwarf pine. See *Pinus mugo*.

Dwarf pomegranate. See *Punica granatum* var. *nana*, illus. p.367.

Dwarf Siberian pine. See *Pinus pumila*.

Dwarf sumach. See *Rhus copallina*.

Dwarf white wood lily. See *Trillium nivale*.

Dwarf white-stripe bamboo. See *Pleioblastus variegatus*, illus. p.318.

Dwarf willow. See *Salix herbacea*.

DYCKIA

BROMELIACEAE

Genus of evergreen, rosette-forming perennials, grown for their overall appearance. Frost tender, min. 7–10°C (45–50°F). Requires full light and well-drained soil containing sharp sand or grit. Water moderately in summer, scarcely or not at all in winter, sparingly at other times. Propagate by offsets or division in spring.

D. remotiflora illus. p.273. Evergreen, basal-rosetted perennial. H and S 30–50cm (12–20in). Has dense rosettes of very narrowly triangular, pointed, thick-textured, arching, dull green leaves with hooked spines and grey scales beneath. Woolly spikes of tubular, orange-yellow flowers appear above foliage in summer-autumn.

Dyers's greenweed. See *Genista tinctoria*, illus. p.153.

DYPSIS

PALMAE/ARECACEAE

Genus of evergreen palms, grown for their elegant appearance. Frost tender, min. 16°C (61°F). Needs full light or partial shade and fertile, well-drained soil. Water potted specimens moderately, much less when temperatures are low. Propagate by seed in spring at not less than 26°C (79°F). Red spider mite may sometimes be a nuisance.

♀ ***D. lutescens***, syn. *Areca lutescens, Chrysalidocarpus lutescens*, illus. p.96.

East Indian arrowroot. See *Tacca leontopetaloides*.
Easter cactus. See *Hatiora gaertneri*, illus. p.491.
Easter lily. See *Lilium longiflorum*, illus. p.416.
Eastern cottonwood. See *Populus deltoides*.
Eastern hemlock. See *Tsuga canadensis*, illus. p.103.
Eastern redbud. See *Cercis canadensis*.
Eastern white cedar. See *Thuja occidentalis*.
Eastern white pine. See *Pinus strobus*, illus. p.98.
Eau-de-Cologne mint. See *Mentha* × *piperita* f. *citrata*.

ECCREMOCARPUS

BIGNONIACEAE

Genus of evergreen, sub-shrubby, tendril climbers grown for their attractive flowers, produced over a long season. One species only is commonly grown. Half hardy; in cold areas treat as an annual. Grow in full light and in any well-drained soil. Propagate by seed in early spring.
E. scaber illus. p.215.

ECHEVERIA

CRASSULACEAE

Genus of rosetted, perennial succulents with long-lasting flowers. Leaves take on their brightest colours from autumn to spring. Frost tender, min. 5–7°C (41–5°F). Needs sun, good ventilation and very well-drained soil. Propagate by seed, stem or leaf cuttings, division or offsets in spring or summer.
♀ ***E. agavoides*** illus. p.490.
E. cooperi. See *Adromischus cooperi*.
♀ ***E. derenbergii.*** Clump-forming, perennial succulent. H 4cm (1½in), S 30cm (12in). Min. 5°C (41°F). Produces a short-stemmed rosette of rounded, grey-green leaves. Flower stem, 8cm (3in) long, produces cup-shaped, yellow-and-red or orange flowers in spring. Offsets freely. Is often used as a parent in breeding.
♀ ***E. elegans*** illus. p.487.
E. gibbiflora. Rosetted, perennial succulent. H 10–25cm (4–10in), S 30cm (12in). Min. 7°C (45°F). Rosettes of spoon-shaped, pointed, grey-green leaves, often tinged red-brown, are stemless or borne on short stems. Cup-shaped, red flowers, yellow within, are borne on stems, 90cm (3ft) long, in autumn-winter. ♀ **'Metallica'** (syn. *E.g.* var. *metallica*) has white- or red-margined, purple-green leaves that mature to green-bronze.
♀ ***E. harmsii***, syn. *Oliveranthus elegans*. Bushy, perennial succulent. H 20cm (8in), S 30cm (12in). Min. 7°C (45°F). Erect stems are each crowned by a 6cm (2½in) wide rosette of short, narrowly lance-shaped, pale green leaves, covered in short hairs. In spring bears cup-shaped, orange-tipped, red flowers, yellow within.
♀ ***E. pulvinata*** illus. p.480.
E. secunda illus. p.489.
♀ ***E. setosa*** (Mexican firecracker). Basal-rosetted, perennial succulent. H 4cm (1½in), S 30cm (12in). Min. 7°C (45°F). Has long, narrow, mid-green leaves covered in short, thick, white hairs. Bears cup-shaped, red-and-yellow flowers in spring. Is prone to rotting: do not water foliage.

ECHINACEA

Coneflower

COMPOSITAE/ASTERACEAE

Genus of summer-flowering perennials. Fully hardy. Prefers sun and humus-rich, moist but well-drained soil. Propagate by division or root cuttings in spring.
E. purpurea, syn. *Rudbeckia purpurea*. **'Robert Bloom'** illus. p.246. **'White Lustre'** is a vigorous, upright perennial. H 1.2m (4ft), S 45cm (1½ft). Large, daisy-like, white flower heads, each with a prominent, central, orange-brown cone, are borne singly on strong stems in summer. Has lance-shaped, dark green leaves.

ECHINOCACTUS

CACTACEAE

Genus of slow-growing, hemispherical, perennial cacti. Frost tender, min. 11°C (52°F); lower temperatures cause yellow patches on *E. grusonii*. Requires full sun and very well-drained soil. Yellow-flowered species are easy to grow. Propagate by seed in spring.
E. asterias. See *Astrophytum asterias*.
E. chilensis. See *Neoporteria chilensis*.
E. eyriesii. See *Echinopsis eyriesii*.
E. grusonii illus. p.476.
E. ingens. See *E. platyacanthus*.
E. myriostigma. See *Astrophytum myriostigma*.
E. ornatus. See *Astrophytum ornatum*.
E. platyacanthus, syn. *E. ingens*. Slow-growing, hemispherical, perennial cactus. H 3m (10ft), S 2m (6ft). Grey-blue stem has a woolly crown and up to 50 ribs. Funnel-shaped, yellow flowers, 3cm (1¼in) across, appear in summer only on plants over 40cm (16in) in diameter.
E. scheeri. See *Sclerocactus scheeri*.
E. uncinatus. See *Sclerocactus uncinatus*.

ECHINOCEREUS

CACTACEAE

Genus of spherical to columnar, perennial cacti, freely branching with age, some with tuberous rootstocks. Buds, formed inside spiny stem, burst through skin, producing long-lasting flowers, with reflexed petal tips and prominent, green stigmas, followed by pear-shaped, spiny seed pods. Frost tender, min. 5–8°C (41–6°F); some species tolerate light frost if dry. Needs full sun and very well-drained soil. Propagate by seed or stem cuttings in spring or summer.
E. baileyi. See *E. reichenbachii* var. *baileyi*.
E. cinerascens. Clump-forming, perennial cactus. H 30cm (1ft), S 1m (3ft). Min. 5°C (41°F). Has 7cm (3in) wide stems, each with 5–12 ribs. Areoles each bear 8–15 yellowish-white spines. Mature plants produce masses of trumpet-shaped, bright pink or purple flowers, 12cm (5in) across and with paler petal bases, in spring.
E. leucanthus, syn. *Wilcoxia albiflora*, illus. p.485.
E. pectinatus. Columnar, perennial cactus. H 35cm (14in), S 20cm (8in). Min. 7°C (45°F). Has sparsely branched, green stems with 12–23 ribs and short, comb-like spines, often variably coloured. In spring produces trumpet-shaped, purple, pink or yellow flowers, 12cm (5in) across, with paler petal bases.
E. pentalophus, syn. *E. procumbens*, illus. p.479.
E. procumbens. See *E. pentalophus*.
♀ ***E. reichenbachii.*** Columnar, perennial cactus. H 35cm (14in), S 20cm (8in). Min. 7°C (45°F). Has a slightly branched, multicoloured stem with 12–23 ribs and comb-like spines, 1.5cm (⅝in) long. Carries trumpet-shaped, pink or purple flowers, 12cm (5in) across, with darker petal bases, in spring. var. ***baileyi*** (syn. *E. baileyi*) illus. p.478.
E. schmollii, syn. *Wilcoxia schmollii*, illus. p.478.
E. triglochidiatus. Clump-forming, perennial cactus. H 30cm (12in), S 15cm (6in). Min. 5°C (41°F). Has a short, thick, dark green stem with 3–5 spines, each to 2.5cm (1in) long, per areole. In spring bears funnel-shaped, bright red flowers, 7cm (3in) across, with prominent, red stamens and green stigmas. var. ***paucispinus*** illus. p.491.

Echinodorus ranunculoides. See *Baldellia ranunculoides*.
Echinofossulatus lamellosus See *Stenocactus crispatus*.
Echinofossulocactus. See *Stenocactus*.
Echinomastus macdowellii. See *Thelocactus macdowellii*.

ECHINOPS

Globe thistle

COMPOSITAE/ASTERACEAE

Genus of summer-flowering perennials, grown for their globe-like, spiky flower heads. Fully hardy. Does best in full sun and in poor soil. Propagate by division or seed in autumn or by root cuttings in winter.
E. bannaticus illus. p.226. ♀ **'Taplow Blue'** is an erect perennial, H 1.2m (4ft), S 1m (3ft). Wiry stems produce thistle-like, rounded heads of powder-blue flowers in summer. Narrowly oval leaves are divided and greyish-green.
E. ritro **'Veitch's Blue'** illus. p.258.
E. sphaerocephalus illus. p.224.

ECHINOPSIS

CACTACEAE

Genus of spherical to columnar, perennial cacti, mostly freely branching; it is sometimes held to include *Trichocereus*. Frost tender, min. 5–10°C (41–50°F). Requires full sun and well-drained soil. Tolerates long periods of neglect. Propagate by seed or offsets in spring or summer.
E. aurea, syn. *Lobivia aurea, L. cylindrica, Pseudolobivia aurea*. Clump-forming, perennial cactus. H 12cm (5in), S 20cm (8in). Green stem, with 14 or 15 ribs, is densely covered with white, radial spines and a longer, darker, central spine. Produces funnel-shaped to flattish, yellow flowers, 8cm (3in) across, in summer.
E. backebergii, syn. *Lobivia backebergii*, illus. p.489.
E. bridgesii. See *E. lageniformis*.
E. candicans, syn. *Trichocereus candicans*, illus. p.477.
♀ ***E. chamaecereus***, syn. *Chamaecereus silvestrii, Lobivia silvestrii*, illus. p.491.
E. cinnabarina, syn. *Lobivia cinnabarina*. Spherical, perennial cactus. H and S 15cm (6in). Glossy, dark green stem has about 20 warty ribs and mostly curved, dark spines. In summer bears funnel-shaped to flattish, carmine-red flowers, 8cm (3in) across.
♀ ***E. eyriesii***, syn. *Echinocactus eyriesii*. Flattened spherical, perennial cactus. H 30cm (12in), S 50cm (20in). Has slowly branching, mid-green stems with 11–18 ribs and very short spines. Tubular, white flowers appear in spring-summer.
E. lageniformis, syn. *E. bridgesii, Trichocereus bridgesii*, illus. p.472.
E. marsoneri syn. *Lobivia haageana* illus. p.483.
E. multiplex. See *E. oxygona*.
E. oxygona, syn. *E. multiplex*, illus. p.477.
E. pentlandii, syn. *Lobivia pentlandii*, illus. p.489.
E. rhodotricha. Spherical to columnar, perennial cactus. H 60cm (2ft), S 20cm (8in). Produces branching, dark green stems, 9cm (3½in) across, with 8–13 ribs. Curved, dark spines, 2cm (¾in) long, later turn pale. Has tubular, white to pink flowers in spring-summer.
E. spachiana, syn. *Cereus spachianus, Trichocereus spachianus*, illus. p.473.

Echioides longiflorum. See *Arnebia pulchra*.

ECHIUM

BORAGINACEAE

Genus of annuals and evergreen shrubs, biennials and perennials, grown for their flowers. Fully hardy to frost tender, min. 3°C (37°F). Needs full sun and fertile, well-drained soil. Water containerized specimens freely in summer, moderately at other times. Propagate by seed in spring or by greenwood or semi-ripe cuttings in summer. Whitefly may sometimes be troublesome. All parts may cause mild stomach upset if ingested; contact with the foliage may irritate skin.
E. bourgaeanum. See *E. wildpretii*.
E. vulgare [dwarf] illus. p.343.
♀ ***E. wildpretii***, syn. *E. bourgaeanum*. Evergreen, erect, unbranched biennial that dies after fruiting. H 2.5m (8ft) or more, S 60cm (2ft). Half hardy. Narrowly lance-shaped, silver-haired leaves, 30cm (1ft) long, form a dense rosette. Has compact spires, 1–1.5m (3–5ft) long, of small, funnel-shaped, red flowers in late spring and early summer.

Edelweiss. See *Leontopodium*.
New Zealand. See *Leucogenes*.
North Island. See *Leucogenes leontopodium*.

EDGEWORTHIA

THYMELAEACEAE

Genus of deciduous shrubs, grown for their flowers in late winter and early spring. Frost hardy, but flowers are susceptible to frost damage. Is best grown against a south- or west-facing wall in most areas. Requires full sun and well-drained soil. Dislikes being transplanted. Propagate by semi-ripe cuttings in summer or by seed in autumn.

E. chrysantha, syn. *E. papyrifera.* Deciduous, rounded, open shrub. H and S 1.5m (5ft). Very supple shoots produce terminal, rounded heads of fragrant, tubular, yellow flowers in late winter and early spring. Has oval, dark green leaves.

E. papyrifera. See *E. chrysantha.*

Edible prickly pear. See *Opuntia ficus-indica.*

EDRAIANTHUS

CAMPANULACEAE

Genus of short-lived perennials, some of which are evergreen, usually growing from central rootstocks. In winter, a small, resting bud is just visible from each rootstock. In spring, prostrate stems radiate to carry leaves and flowers. Is suitable for rock gardens, screes and troughs. Fully hardy. Needs sun and well-drained soil. Propagate by softwood cuttings from side shoots in early summer or by seed in autumn.

E. dalmaticus. Upright, then arching perennial. H 10cm (4in), S 15cm (6in). Bears narrowly lance-shaped, pale green leaves and, in early summer, terminal clusters of bell-shaped, violet-blue flowers, 2.5cm (1in) across.

♀ ***E. pumilio*** illus. p.394.

E. serpyllifolius, syn. *Wahlenbergia serpyllifolia.* **'Major'** is an evergreen, prostrate perennial. H 1cm (½in), S to 5cm (2in). Has tight mats of tiny, oval, dark green leaves. In early summer, bell-shaped, deep violet flowers, 1.5cm (⅝in) wide, are borne on very short stems. Needs a sheltered site. Seldom sets seed.

Edwardsia microphylla. See *Sophora microphylla.*

Eel grass. See *Vallisneria spiralis.*

EGERIA

HYDROCHARITACEAE

Genus of semi-evergreen or evergreen, perennial, floating or submerged water plants, grown for their foliage. Is similar to *Elodea*, but has more conspicuous flowers, held above water surface. In an aquarium, plants are useful for oxygenating water and provide a suitable depository for fish spawn. Frost tender, min. 1°C (34°F). Needs a sunny position. Thin regularly to keep under control. Propagate by stem cuttings in spring or summer.

E. densa, syn. *Anacharis densa, Elodea densa.* Semi-evergreen, perennial, spreading, submerged water plant. S indefinite. Forms a dense mass of whorled, small, lance-shaped, dark green leaves borne on long, wiry stems. Small, 3-parted, white flowers appear in summer.

Eglantine. See *Rosa rubiginosa*, illus. p.181.

Egyptian star. See *Pentas lanceolata*, illus. p.159.

EHRETIA

BORAGINACEAE

Genus of deciduous, summer-flowering trees, grown for their foliage and star-shaped flowers. Frost hardy, but is susceptible to frost damage when young. Requires sun or semi-shade and fertile, well-drained soil. Propagate by softwood cuttings in summer.

E. dicksonii illus. p.87.

EICHHORNIA

PONTEDERIACEAE

Genus of evergreen or semi-evergreen, perennial, floating and marginal water plants. Frost tender, min. 1°C (34°F). Needs an open, sunny position in warm water. Grows prolifically and requires regular thinning year-round. Propagate by detaching young plants as required.

E. crassipes, syn. *E. speciosa*, illus. p.464.

E. speciosa. See *E. crassipes.*

ELAEAGNUS

ELAEAGNACEAE

Genus of deciduous or evergreen shrubs and trees, grown for their foliage and small, usually very fragrant flowers, often followed by ornamental fruits. Evergreen species are good for providing shelter or for hedging, particularly in coastal areas. Fully to frost hardy. Most evergreen species thrive in sun or shade, but those with silver leaves and deciduous species prefer full sun. Needs fertile, well-drained soil. Trim hedges in late summer. Propagate species by seed in autumn, evergreen forms also by semi-ripe cuttings in summer, deciduous forms by softwood or semi-ripe cuttings in summer.

E. angustifolia illus. p.118.

E. × ebbingei. Evergreen, bushy, dense shrub. H and S 5m (15ft). Fully hardy. Has oblong to oval, glossy, dark green leaves, silvery beneath. Fragrant, bell-shaped, silvery-white flowers are borne from mid- to late autumn. Leaves of ♀ **'Gilt Edge'** have golden-yellow margins. **'Limelight'** illus. p.149.

E. macrophylla. Evergreen, bushy, dense shrub. H and S 3m (10ft). Frost hardy. Broadly oval leaves are silvery-grey when young, becoming glossy, dark green above, but remaining silvery-grey beneath, when mature. Fragrant, bell-shaped, creamy-yellow flowers, silvery outside, appear from mid- to late autumn, followed by egg-shaped, red fruits.

E. pungens **'Maculata'**, syn. *E. pungens* 'Aureovariegata', illus. p.123.

E. umbellata. Vigorous, deciduous, bushy shrub. H and S 5m (15ft). Fully hardy. Oblong, wavy-edged, bright green leaves are silvery when young. Has fragrant, bell-shaped, creamy-yellow flowers in late spring and early summer, then egg-shaped, red fruits.

ELAEOCARPUS

ELAEOCARPACEAE

Genus of evergreen, spring- and summer-flowering shrubs and trees, grown for their flowers and foliage. Half hardy to frost tender, min. 5°C (41°F). Requires full light or partial shade and fertile, well-drained but not dry soil. Water containerized specimens freely when in full growth, less in winter. Current season's growth may be cut back in winter. Propagate by seed in spring or by semi-ripe cuttings in summer. Red spider mite and whitefly may cause problems.

E. cyaneus, syn. *E. reticulatus* (Blueberry ash). Evergreen, rounded shrub or tree. H and S 3m (10ft), sometimes to 12m (40ft) or more. Frost tender. Bears elliptic to lance-shaped, toothed, lustrous leaves and, in summer, axillary racemes of bell-shaped, fringed, white flowers. Has globular, deep blue fruits in autumn.

E. reticulatus. See *E. cyaneus.*

ELATOSTEMA, syn. PELLIONIA

URTICACEAE

Genus of evergreen, creeping perennials and sub-shrubs with attractive foliage that often tends to lie flat, making useful ground cover. Frost tender, min. 15°C (59°F). Requires a humid atmosphere away from draughts, indirect light and moist soil. Propagate from stem cuttings in spring or summer.

E. pulchra, syn. *E. repens* var. *pulchra.* Evergreen, slightly fleshy perennial with rooting, creeping stems. H 8–10cm (3–4in), S 60cm (2ft) or more. Broadly oval leaves, 5cm (2in) long, are blackish-green with dark green veins above, purple below. Flowers are insignificant.

♀ ***E. repens***, syn. *Pellionia daveauana, P. repens*, (Watermelon begonia) illus. p.315. var. ***pulchra*** see *E. pulchra.*

Elder. See *Sambucus.*
- **American.** See *Sambucus canadensis.*
- **Box.** See *Acer negundo.*
- **Common.** See *Sambucus nigra.*
- **Golden.** See *Sambucus nigra* 'Aurea'.
- **Red-berried.** See *Sambucus racemosa.*
- **Yellow.** See *Tecoma stans*, illus. p.92.

ELEOCHARIS

CYPERACEAE

See also GRASSES, BAMBOOS, RUSHES and SEDGES.

E. acicularis (Needle spike-rush). Evergreen, spreading, rhizomatous, perennial sedge. H to 10cm (4in), S indefinite. Fully hardy. Basal, mid-green leaves are very narrow. Hairless, unbranched, square stems bear solitary minute, brown spikelets in summer.

Elephant apple. See *Dillenia indica.*

Elephant bush. See *Portulacaria afra*, illus. p.149.

Elephant's ear. See *Philodendron domesticum.*

Elephant's ear, Giant. See *Alocasia macrorrhiza.*

Elephant's ears. See *Hedera colchica* 'Dentata', illus. p.219.

Elephant's foot. See *Beaucarnea recurvata*, illus. p.96; *Dioscorea elephantipes*, illus. p.483.

ELEUTHEROCOCCUS, syn. ACANTHOPANAX

ARALIACEAE

Genus of deciduous shrubs and trees, grown for their foliage and fruits. Produces tiny, usually greenish-white flowers. Fully hardy. Prefers full sun and needs well-drained soil. Propagate by seed in spring or by root cuttings in late winter.

E. sieboldianus illus. p.141.

Elliottia paniculata. See *Tripetaleia paniculata.*

Elm. See *Ulmus.*
- **American white.** See *Ulmus americana.*
- **Caucasian.** See *Zelkova carpinifolia.*
- **Chinese.** See *Ulmus parvifolia.*
- **Cornish.** See *Ulmus minor* 'Cornubiensis'.
- **Cornish golden.** See *Ulmus minor* 'Dicksonii', illus. p.77.
- **Dickson's golden.** See *Ulmus minor* 'Dicksonii', illus. p.77.
- **Dutch.** See *Ulmus × hollandica.*
- **English.** See *Ulmus procera.*
- **Exeter.** See *Ulmus glabra* 'Exoniensis'.
- **Goodyer's.** See *Ulmus minor* subsp. *angustifolia.*
- **Huntingdon.** See *Ulmus × hollandica* 'Vegeta'.
- **Jersey.** See *Ulmus minor* 'Sarniensis'.
- **Siberian.** See *Ulmus pumila.*
- **Smooth-leaved.** See *Ulmus minor.*
- **Wheatley.** See *Ulmus minor* 'Sarniensis'.
- **White.** See *Ulmus americana.*
- **Wych.** See *Ulmus glabra.*

Elodea crispa of gardens. See *Lagarosiphon major.*

Elodea densa. See *Egeria densa.*

ELSHOLTZIA

LABIATAE/LAMIACEAE

Genus of perennials and deciduous shrubs and sub-shrubs, grown for their flowers, generally in autumn. Frost hardy. Needs full sun and fertile, well-drained soil. Cut back old shoots hard in early spring. Propagate by softwood cuttings in summer.

E. stauntonii illus. p.169.

Elymus arenarius. See *Leymus arenarius.*

EMBOTHRIUM

PROTEACEAE

Genus of evergreen or semi-evergreen trees, grown for their flowers. Frost hardy, but shelter from cold winds. Needs semi-shade and moist but well-drained, lime-free soil. Propagate by suckers in spring or autumn or by seed in autumn.

E. coccineum illus. p.89.

Emerald ripple. See *Peperomia caperata*, illus. p.312.

EMILIA,
syn. CACALIA

COMPOSITAE/ASTERACEAE

Genus of annuals and perennials with flower heads that are good for cutting. Is ideal for hot, dry areas and coastal soils. Half hardy. Requires sun and very well-drained soil. Propagate by seed sown under glass in spring, or outdoors in late spring.
E. coccinea, syn. *E. flammea, E. javanica* of gardens, illus. p.353.
E. flammea. See *E. coccinea.*
E. javanica of gardens. See *E. coccinea.*

EMMENOPTERYS

RUBIACEAE

Genus of deciduous trees, grown mainly for their foliage; flowers appear only rarely, during hot summers. Frost hardy, but young growths may be damaged by late frosts. Needs full sun and deep, fertile, well-drained soil. Propagate by softwood cuttings in summer.
E. henryi illus. p.76.

ENCEPHALARTOS

ZAMIACEAE

Genus of evergreen shrubs and trees, grown for their palm-like appearance. Frost tender, min. 10–13°C (50–55°F). Needs full light and well-drained soil. Water plotted plants moderately when in full growth, less at other times. Propagate by seed in spring.
E. ferox illus. p.148.
E. longifolius. Slow-growing, evergreen, palm-like tree, sometimes branched with age. H 3m (10ft) or more, S 1.5–2.5m (5–8ft). Has feather-shaped leaves, each 60cm–1.5m (2–5ft) long, divided into narrowly lance-shaped to oval, blue-green leaflets, usually with hook-tipped teeth. Cone-like, brownish flower heads appear intermittently.

ENCYCLIA

ORCHIDACEAE

SEE ALSO ORCHIDS.

E. cochleata. Evergreen, epiphytic orchid for a cool greenhouse. H 30cm (12in). Upright spikes of green flowers, 5cm (2in) long, with dark purple lips at the top and ribbon-like sepals and petals, are produced in summer and, on mature plants, intermittently throughout the year. Leaves are narrowly oval and 15cm (6in) long. Requires semi-shade in summer.
E. radiata. Evergreen, epiphytic orchid for a cool greenhouse. H 25cm (10in). Bears upright spikes of very fragrant, well-rounded, creamy-white flowers, 1cm (½in) across, with red-lined white lips, in summer. Narrowly oval leaves are 10–15cm (4–6in) long. Needs semi-shade in summer.

Endymion. See *Hyacinthoides.*
Engelmann spruce. See *Picea engelmannii*, illus. p.101.
English bluebell. See *Hyacinthoides non-scripta*, illus. p.430.
English elm. See *Ulmus procera.*
English iris. See *Iris latifolia*, illus. p.237.
English lavender. See *Lavandula × intermedia.*

ENKIANTHUS

ERICACEAE

Genus of deciduous or semi-evergreen, spring-flowering shrubs and trees, grown for their mass of small, bell- or urn-shaped flowers and their autumn colour. Fully to frost hardy. Needs sun or semi-shade and moist, peaty, acid soil. Propagate by semi-ripe cuttings in summer or by seed in autumn.
♀ ***E. campanulatus*** illus. p.113.
♀ ***E. cernuus*** f. ***rubens*** illus. p.127.
♀ ***E. perulatus*** illus. p.123.

ENSETE

MUSACEAE

Genus of evergreen perennials, grown for their foliage, which resembles that of bananas, and fruits. Has false stems made of overlapping leaf sheaths that die after flowering. Frost tender, min. 10°C (50°F). Grow in sun or partial shade and humus-rich soil. Propagate by seed in spring or by division year-round.
♀ ***E. ventricosum***, syn. *Musa arnoldiana, M. ensete*, illus. p.233.

EOMECON

PAPAVERACEAE

Genus of one species of perennial that spreads rapidly and deeply underground. Is suitable for large rock gardens. Fully hardy. Needs sun and well-drained soil. Propagate by seed or runners in spring.
E. chionantha (Snow poppy). Vigorous, spreading perennial. H to 40cm (16in), S indefinite. Leaves are large, palmate and grey. Erect stems each carry a long panicle of small, poppy-like, white flowers in summer.

EPACRIS

EPACRIDACEAE

Genus of evergreen, heath-like shrubs, grown for their flowers. Frost tender, min. 5°C (41°F). Needs full sun and humus-rich, well-drained, neutral to acid soil. Water potted plants moderately when in full growth, less at other times. Flowered stems may be shortened after flowering to maintain a neat habit. Propagate by seed in spring or semi-ripe cuttings in late summer.
E. impressa illus. p.151.

Epaulette tree. See *Pterostyrax hispida.*

EPHEDRA

EPHEDRACEAE

Genus of evergreen shrubs, grown for their habit and green shoots. Makes good ground cover in dry soil. Grow male and female plants together in order to obtain fruits. Fully hardy. Requires full sun and well-drained soil. Propagate by seed in autumn or by division in autumn or spring.
E. gerardiana. Evergreen, spreading shrub with slender, erect, rush-like, green shoots. H 60cm (2ft), S 2m (6ft). Leaves and flowers are inconspicuous. Bears small, spherical, red fruits.

EPIDENDRUM

ORCHIDACEAE

See also ORCHIDS.
E. difforme illus. p.310. Evergreen, epiphytic orchid for an intermediate greenhouse. H 23cm (9in). Large heads of semi-translucent, green flowers, 0.5cm (¼in) across, open in autumn. Has oval, rigid leaves, 2.5–5cm (1–2in) long. Requires shade in summer. Avoid spraying, which can cause spotting of leaves. Propagate by division in spring.
E. ibaguense, syn. *E. radicans* illus. p.309. Evergreen, epiphytic orchid for a cool greenhouse. H 2m (6ft) or more. Flowers more or less constantly, bearing a succession of feathery-lipped, deep red blooms, 0.5cm (¼in) across. Leaves, 2.5–5cm (1–2in) long, are oval and rigid. Grow in semi-shade during summer. Propagate by tip cuttings in spring.
E. radicans. See *E. ibaguense.*

EPIGAEA

ERICACEAE

Genus of evergreen, prostrate, spring-flowering sub-shrubs. Fully to frost hardy. Needs shade and humus-rich, moist, acid soil. Most are difficult to cultivate. Propagate by seed in spring or by softwood cuttings in early summer.
E. asiatica. Evergreen, creeping sub-shrub. H to 10cm (4in), S to 20cm (8in). Fully hardy. Stems and heart-shaped, deep green leaves are covered with brown hairs. Bears terminal clusters of 3–6 tiny, slightly fragrant, urn-shaped, white or pink flowers in spring.
E. gaultherioides, syn. *Orphanidesia gaultherioides*, illus. p.376.
E. repens (Mayflower, Trailing arbutus). Evergreen, creeping sub-shrub. H 10cm (4in), S 30cm (12in). Fully hardy. Hairy stems, bearing heart-shaped, leathery leaves, root at intervals. In spring produces terminal clusters of 4–6 cup-shaped, white flowers, sometimes flushed pink. Is relatively easy to grow.

EPILOBIUM,
syn. CHAMAENERION *Willow herb*

ONAGRACEAE

Genus of annuals, biennials, perennials and deciduous sub-shrubs, grown for their deep pink to white flowers in summer. Is useful on dry banks; many species are invasive. Fully to frost hardy. Tolerates sun or shade and prefers moist but well-drained soil. Propagate species by seed in autumn, selected forms by softwood cuttings from side-shoots in spring.
E. angustifolium f. ***album*** illus. p.224.
E. californicum. See *Zauschneria californica.*
E. canum. See *Zauschneria californica* subsp. *cana.*
E. chlorifolium var. ***kaikourense*** illus. p.386.
E. obcordatum. Clump-forming perennial. H 15cm (6in), S 10cm (4in). Frost hardy. Oval leaves are glossy green. Spikes of open cup-shaped, deep rose-pink flowers are borne in summer. Is good for a rock garden or alpine house. Needs a sheltered site and full sun. In cultivation may not retain character, especially in mild climates.
E. septentrionale. See *Zauschneria septentrionalis.*

EPIMEDIUM
Barrenwort

BERBERIDACEAE

Genus of spring-flowering perennials, some of which are evergreen. Flowers are cup-shaped with long or short spurs. Makes good ground cover. Fully hardy. Does best in partial shade and humus-rich, moist but well-drained soil. Cut back just before new growth appears in spring. Propagate by division in spring or autumn.
E. alpinum. Evergreen, clump-forming perennial. H 23cm (9in), S to 30cm (12in). Racemes of pendent, short-spurred flowers, with crimson sepals and yellow petals, appear in spring. Has finely toothed, glossy leaves divided into oval, angled, mid-green leaflets, bronze when young.
E. grandiflorum **'Crimson Beauty'** Clump-forming perennial. H and S 30cm (12in). Racemes of pendent, long-spurred, copper-crimson flowers are produced in spring at the same time as heart-shaped, copper-marked, light green leaves, divided into oval leaflets, which mature to mid-green. ♀ **'Rose Queen'** illus. p.277. f. ***violaceum*** has young leaves that are flushed bronze and produces purple-and-white flowers.
♀ ***E. × perralchicum.*** Evergreen, carpeting perennial. H 45cm (18in), S 30cm (12in). Short spires of pendent, yellow flowers, with short spurs, are borne on slender stems in spring. Leaves, divided into rounded to oval leaflets, are dark green.
E. perralderianum. Semi-evergreen, carpeting perennial. H 30cm (12in), S 45cm (18in). Clusters of small, pendent, short-spurred, bright yellow flowers are borne in spring. Has large, toothed, glossy, deep green leaves, divided into rounded to oval leaflets.
♀ ***E. pinnatum*** subsp. ***colchicum.*** Evergreen, carpeting perennial. H and S 30cm (12in). In spring, clusters of small, pendent, bright yellow flowers, with short spurs, are produced above dark green leaves, divided into rounded to oval leaflets, that are hairy when young.
E. pubigerum illus. p.276.
♀ ***E. × rubrum*** illus. p.277.
E. × versicolor. Clump-forming perennial. H and S 30cm (12in). Small, pendent clusters of yellow flowers, with long, red-tinged spurs, appear in spring. Heart-shaped, fresh green leaves are divided into oval leaflets that are tinted reddish-purple. **'Neosulphureum'** illus. p.284.
E. × warleyense illus. p.285.
♀ ***E. × youngianum*** **'Niveum'** illus. p.275.

EPIPHYLLUM
Orchid cactus, Strap cactus

CACTACEAE

Genus of perennial cacti with strap-shaped, flattened, green stems that have notched edges. Flowers are produced at notches. Frost tender, min. 5–11°C (41–52°F). Grow in sun or partial shade and in rich, well-drained soil. Propagate by stem cuttings in spring or summer.
E. ackermannii. See *Nopalxochia ackermannii*.
E. anguliger illus. p.477.
E. crenatum. Erect, then pendent, perennial cactus. H and S 3m (10ft). Min. 11°C (52°F). Has a flattened stem. Bears lightly perfumed, funnel-shaped, broad-petalled, white flowers, 20cm (8in) across, in spring-summer. Is often used as a parent for breeding.
E. laui illus. p.477.
E. oxypetalum. Erect, then pendent, perennial cactus. H 3m (10ft), S 1m (3ft). Min. 11°C (52°F). Produces freely branching, flattened stems, 12cm (5in) across. In spring-summer bears nocturnal, tubular, white flowers, 25cm (10in) long. Makes a good house plant.

EPIPREMNUM,
syn. POTHOS

ARACEAE

Genus of evergreen, woody-stemmed, root climbers, including *Pothos*, grown for their handsome leaves. Frost tender, min. 15–18°C (59–64°F). Grow in light shade away from direct sun; any well-drained, moisture-retentive soil is suitable. Water regularly, less in cold weather. Stems need good supports. Remove shoot tips to induce branching at any time. Propagate by leaf-bud or stem-tip cuttings in late spring or by layering in summer. All parts may cause severe discomfort if ingested, and contact with the sap of *E. aureum* may irritate skin.
***E. aureum* 'Marble Queen',** syn. *Scindapsus aureus* 'Marble Queen', illus. p.217.
***E. pictum* 'Argyraeum',** See *Scindapsus pictus* 'Argyraeus'.

EPISCIA

GESNERIACEAE

Genus of evergreen, low-growing and creeping perennials, grown for their ornamental leaves and colourful flowers. Is useful as ground cover or in hanging baskets. Frost tender, min. 15°C (59°F). Requires high humidity and a fairly shaded position in humus-rich, well-drained soil. Keep well watered, but avoid waterlogging. Propagate in summer by stem cuttings, division or removing rooted runners.
E. cupreata (Flame violet) illus. p.313. **'Metallica'** is an evergreen, creeping perennial. H 10cm (4in), S indefinite. Has oval, downy, wrinkled leaves, tinged pink to copper and with broad, silvery bands along midribs. Funnel-shaped, orange-red flowers, marked yellow within, are borne intermittently. **'Tropical Topaz'** has yellow flowers.
E. dianthiflora, syn. *Alsobia dianthiflora*, illus. p.311.
E. lilacina. Evergreen, low-growing perennial, with runners bearing plantlets. H 10cm (4in), S indefinite. Has oval, hairy, pale green leaves, to 8cm (3in) long. Funnel-shaped, white flowers, tinged mauve and with yellow eyes, are produced in small clusters from autumn to spring. Leaves of **'Cuprea'** are bronze-tinged.

EPITHELANTHA

CACTACEAE

Genus of very slow-growing, spherical, perennial cacti densely covered with very short spines. Frost tender, min. 10°C (50°F). Needs full sun and well-drained soil, and is prone to rot if overwatered. Is easier to cultivate if grafted. Propagate by seed or stem cuttings in spring or summer.
E. micromeris illus. p.487.

ERANTHEMUM

ACANTHACEAE

Genus of perennials and evergreen shrubs, grown for their flowers. Frost tender, min. 15–18°C (59–64°F). Requires full light or partial shade and fertile, well-drained soil. Water containerized plants freely when in full growth, moderately at other times. In spring or after flowering remove at least half of each spent flowering stem to encourage a bushier habit. Propagate by softwood cuttings in late spring. Whitefly may be a nuisance.
E. atropurpureum. See *Pseuderanthemum atropurpureum*.
E. nervosum. See *E. pulchellum*.
♀ ***E. pulchellum***, syn. *E. nervosum*. Evergreen, erect shrub. H 1–1.2m (3–4ft), S 60cm (2ft) or more. Produces elliptic to oval, prominently veined, deep green leaves. Blue flowers, each with a 3cm (1¼ in) long tube and rounded petal lobes, are produced in winter-spring.

ERANTHIS

RANUNCULACEAE

Genus of clump-forming perennials, with knobbly tubers, grown for their cup-shaped flowers surrounded by leaf-like ruffs of bracts. Fully to frost hardy. Prefers partial shade and humus-rich soil, well-drained but not drying out excessively. Dies down in summer. Propagate by seed in autumn or by division of clumps immediately after flowering while still in leaf. All parts may cause mild stomach upset if ingested, and contact with the sap may irritate skin.
♀ ***E. hyemalis*** illus. p.457.
♀ ***E. × tubergenii* 'Guinea Gold'.** Late winter- or early spring-flowering, tuberous perennial. H 8–10cm (3–4in), S 4–6cm (1½–2½in). Frost hardy. Stems each bear a stalkless, deep golden-yellow flower, 3–4cm (1¼–1½in) across, surrounded by a bronze-green bract, cut into narrow lobes. Rounded leaves are divided into finger-shaped lobes.

ERCILLA,
syn. BRIDGESIA

PHYTOLACCACEAE

Genus of evergreen, root climbers, grown for their neat, green leaves and green and purple flower spikes. Frost hardy. Grow in sun or partial shade and in any well-drained soil. Prune after flowering, if required. Propagate by stem cuttings in late summer or autumn.
E. spicata. See *E. volubilis*.
E. volubilis, syn. *E. spicata*, illus. p.200.

EREMURUS
Foxtail lily, King's spear

LILIACEAE/ASPHODELACEAE

Genus of perennials, with fleshy, finger-like roots, grown for their stately spires of shallowly cup-shaped flowers in summer. Fully to frost hardy. Requires a sunny, warm position and well-drained soil. Tends to come into growth very early, and young shoots may be frosted. Provide a covering of dry bracken in late winter to protect the crowns when shoots are first developing. Stake tall species and hybrids. Propagate by division in spring or early autumn or by seed in autumn.
E. himalaicus illus. p.224.
♀ ***E. robustus*** illus. p.225.
***E.* Shelford Hybrids.** Group of perennials of varying habit and flower colour. H 1.5m (5ft), S 60cm (2ft). Frost hardy. Long racemes of orange, buff, pink or white flowers are borne freely in mid-summer. Leaves are strap-shaped, in basal rosettes.
E. spectabilis. Erect perennial. H 1.2m (4ft), S 60cm (2ft). Frost hardy. Bears long racemes of pale yellow flowers, with brick-red anthers, in early summer. Leaves are strap-shaped, in basal rosettes.

ERIA

ORCHIDACEAE

See also ORCHIDS.
E. coronaria, syn. *Trichosma suavis*. Evergreen, epiphytic orchid for a cool greenhouse. H 23cm (9in). Sprays of fragrant, rounded, creamy-white flowers, 1cm (½in) across, each with a red- and yellow-marked lip, open in autumn. Has broadly oval, glossy leaves, 10cm (4in) long. Needs semi-shade in summer and moist compost year-round.

ERICA

ERICACEAE

See also HEATHERS.
E. arborea (Tree heath). Evergreen, upright, shrub-like tree heath. H 6m (20ft), S 1.5m (5ft). Frost hardy, but liable to damage from frost and cold winds. Has needle-like, bright green leaves in whorls of 3 or 4 and bears scented, bell-shaped, white flowers from late winter to late spring. May tolerate slightly alkaline soil.
♀ **'Albert's Gold'**, H 2m (6ft), retains its golden foliage year-round.
♀ var. ***alpina*** (illus. p.174) has vivid green foliage that contrasts well with compact racemes of white flowers. May be pruned hard to keep its shape and to encourage new growth.
♀ ***E. australis*** (Spanish heath, Spanish tree heath). Evergreen, shrub-like tree heath. H to 2.2m (7ft), S 1m (3ft). Frost hardy, but stems may be damaged by snow and frost. Has needle-like leaves in whorls of 4 and tubular to bell-shaped, white or purplish-pink flowers in spring. May tolerate slightly alkaline soil. ♀ **'Mr Robert'** has white flowers. ♀ **'Riverslea'** has bright purple-pink flowers, mostly in clusters of 4.
♀ ***E. canaliculata*** (Channelled heath; illus. p.174). Evergreen, erect shrub. H to 3m (10ft), S 1m (3ft). Half hardy. Dark green leaves are narrow and needle-like in whorls of 3. Cup-shaped, pearl-white flowers, sometimes rose-tinted, with dark brown, almost black anthers, are borne in winter (under glass) or early spring (in the open). Requires acid soil.
E. carnea, syn. *E. herbacea* (Alpine heath, Winter heath). Evergreen, spreading shrub. H to 30cm (12in), S to 45cm (18in) or more. Fully hardy. Produces whorls of needle-like, mid- to dark green leaves and bears tubular to bell-shaped flowers that are in shades of pink and red, occasionally white, from early winter to late spring. Tolerates limestone and some shade. Makes good ground cover. **'Altadena'** has golden foliage and pale pink flowers. ♀ **'Ann Sparkes'**, H 15cm (6in), has golden foliage, turning to bronze in winter, and rose-pink flowers. **'Bell's Extra Special'**, H 15cm (6in), S 40cm (16in), has a neat habit, with crimson flowers borne on distinctive, whisky-coloured foliage, flecked with tints of orange and gold. **'Cecilia M. Beale'**, H 15cm (6in), bears an abundance of white flowers from mid-winter to early spring. **'December Red'** (illus. p.175) has a spreading habit and vigorous growth. Deep rose-pink flowers are borne in winter.
♀ **'Foxhollow'**, a vigorous, spreading cultivar, has foliage that is golden-yellow in summer, with orange tips in spring, and a few pale pink flowers.
♀ **'Golden Starlet'** (illus. p.174), H 15cm (6in), S 40cm (16in), bears white flowers set on lime-green foliage that turns a glowing yellow in summer.
♀ **'Ice Princess'**, H 15cm (6in), S 35cm (14in), has white flowers held erect on bright green foliage.
♀ **'Isabell'**, H 15cm (6in), S 35cm (14in), has large, white flowers on bright green foliage, and an erect but spreading habit. **'King George'**, H 20cm (8in), has dark green foliage and deep rose-pink flowers from early winter to mid-spring. ♀ **'Loughrigg'**, H 15cm (6in), produces dark purplish-red flowers from late winter to spring. **'March Seedling'** has a spreading habit, dark green foliage and rich, rose-purple flowers. ♀ **'Myretoun Ruby'**, H 20cm (8in), is vigorous but compact with brilliant deep purple-red flowers in late winter and early spring.
♀ **'Nathalie'**, H 15cm (6in), S 40cm (16in), the deepest and brightest of the *E. carnea* cultivars, has purple flowers, neat, dark green foliage and a compact, upright habit. ♀ **'Pink Spangles'**, H 15cm (6in), is vigorous with flowers that have shell-pink sepals and deeper pink corollas. **'Pirbright Rose'** is very floriferous with bright pink flowers from early winter to early spring.
♀ **'R.B. Cooke'**, H 20cm (8in), bears clear pink flowers from early winter to early spring. ♀ **'Rosalie'** (illus. p.175), H 15cm (6in), S 35cm (14in), has bright pink flowers, bronze-green foliage and a low, upright but spreading habit. ♀ **'Springwood White'** (illus.

p.174), H 15cm (6in), the most vigorous white cultivar, is excellent as ground cover and bears large, white flowers, with brown anthers, from late winter to spring. ♀ **'Vivellii'** (illus. p.175), H 15cm (6in), has dark bronze-green foliage and bears deep purple-pink flowers from late winter to spring. ♀ **'Westwood Yellow'** (illus. p.175) is compact with golden-yellow foliage and deep pink flowers. **'Winter Sun'** see *E.c.* 'Wintersonne'.**'Wintersonne'** (syn. *E.c.* 'Winter Sun'), H 15cm (6in), S 35cm (14in), has magenta flowers and red-brown foliage.

E. ciliaris (Dorset heath). Evergreen, loose shrub. H to 30cm (12in), S 40cm (16in). Fully hardy, but may be damaged in severe weather. Has needle-like, dark green leaves in whorls of 3. Bears long racemes of bell-shaped, bright pink flowers in tiers of 3 or 4 in summer. Requires acid soil and prefers warm, moist conditions. **'Aurea'** has somewhat straggly growth with golden foliage and clear pink flowers. ♀ **'Corfe Castle'** (illus. p.175) produces salmon-pink flowers from summer to early autumn. **'David McClintock'** (illus. p.174) has light grey-green foliage and bears white flowers, with deep pink tips, from summer to early autumn. ♀ **'Mrs C.H. Gill'** has dark grey-green foliage and clear red flowers. **'White Wings'**, a sport of 'Mrs C.H. Gill', has dark grey-green foliage and white flowers.

E. cinerea (Bell heather). Evergreen, compact shrub. H 30cm (12in), S 45–60cm (18–24in). Fully hardy. Has needle-like, mid- to deep green leaves and bears bell-shaped flowers that are in shades of pink and dark red, occasionally white, from early summer to early autumn. Prefers a warm, dry position. Requires acid soil. **'Atropurpurea'** has deep purple flowers in long racemes. ♀ **'C.D. Eason'** (illus. p.175) has distinctive, dark green foliage and bright red flowers. **'Cevennes'** is upright in habit and bears a profusion of mauve flowers. ♀ **'C.G. Best'** has mid-green foliage and rose-pink flowers. **'Domino'** produces white flowers that contrast with dark brown stems and sepals and almost black stigmas. ♀ **'Eden Valley'** (illus. p.174), H 20cm (8in), bears white flowers with lavender-mauve tips. ♀ **'Fiddler's Gold'** (illus. p.175), H 25cm (10in), has golden-yellow foliage, deepening to red in winter, and lilac-pink flowers. ♀ **'Golden Hue'**, H 35cm (14in), has amethyst flowers set on pale yellow foliage, tipped orange in winter. **'Hookstone White'** (illus. p.174), H 35cm (14in), has bright green foliage and bears long racemes of large, white flowers. ♀ **'Lime Soda'**, H 35cm (14in), produces soft lavender flowers in profusion on attractive, lime-green foliage. ♀ **'Pentreath'** has rich purple flowers. ♀ **'Pink Ice'**, H 20cm (8in), is compact with soft pink flowers. ♀ **'P.S. Patrick'** is a vigorous cultivar with purple flowers and dark green foliage. **'Purple Beauty'** (illus. p.175) has purple flowers and dark foliage. ♀ **'Stephen Davis'**, H 25cm (10in), has brilliant, almost fluorescent, red flowers. ♀ **'Velvet Night'**, H 25cm (10in), produces very dark purple, almost black flowers. ♀ **'Windlebrooke'**, H 25cm (10in), is vigorous, with golden foliage, turning bright orange-red in winter, and mauve flowers.

E. × darleyensis. Evergreen, bushy shrub. H 45cm (18in), S 1m (3ft) or more. Fully hardy. Has needle-like, mid-green foliage, with cream, pink or red, young growth in late spring. Bell-shaped, white, pink or purple flowers are borne in racemes from early winter to late spring. Tolerates limestone. **'Archie Graham'** (illus. p.174), H 50cm (20in), is vigorous with mauve-pink flowers. ♀ **'Arthur Johnson'**, H 1m (3ft), has young foliage with cream and pink tips in spring and long racemes of mauve-pink flowers from mid-winter to spring.**'Darley Dale'** (illus. p.175) bears pale mauve flowers from mid-winter to spring. **'George Rendall'** carries deep pink flowers from early winter to early spring. ♀ **'Ghost Hills'** has cream-tipped foliage in spring and a profusion of pink flowers from mid-winter to spring. **'Jack H. Brummage'**, H 30cm (12in), has golden foliage, with yellow and orange tints, and mauve flowers. ♀ **'J.W. Porter'**, H 30cm (12in), has reddish, young shoots in spring and mauve-pink flowers from mid-winter to late spring. ♀ **'Kramer's Rote'** (syn. *E. × d.* 'Kramer's Red') has dark bronze-green foliage with deep purple-red flowers from late autumn to late spring. Spring foliage does not have cream or red tips. **'Molten Silver'** see *E. × d.* 'Silberschmelze'. **'Silberschmelze'** (syn. *E. × d.* 'Molten Silver') is vigorous and produces young shoots with creamy-pink tips in spring and white flowers. **'White Glow'** (illus. p.174), H 30cm (12in), bears white flowers. ♀ **'White Perfection'** (illus. p.174) has bright green foliage and white flowers.

E. erigena, syn. *E. hibernica, E. mediterranea.* Evergreen, upright shrub. H to 2.5m (8ft), S to 1m (3ft). Frost hardy; top growth may be damaged in severe weather, but plant recovers well from the base. Has needle-like, mid-green leaves and, usually, bell-shaped, mauve-pink flowers from early winter to late spring. Tolerates limestone. Flowers of some cultivars have a pronounced scent of honey. **'Brightness'** (illus. p.175), H 45cm (18in), has bronze-green foliage and mauve-pink flowers in spring. ♀ **'Golden Lady'** (illus. p.175), H 30cm (12in), has a neat, compact habit with year-round, golden foliage and white flowers in late spring. ♀ **'Irish Dusk'**, H 45cm (18in), has dark green foliage and salmon-pink flowers from mid-winter to early spring. **'Superba'**, H 2m (6ft), bears strongly scented, rose-pink flowers during spring. ♀ **'W.T. Rackliff'**, H 60cm (2ft), has dark green foliage and produces thick clusters of white flowers from late winter to late spring.

E. gracilis. Evergreen, compact shrub. H and S to 30cm (12in). Frost tender, min. 5°C (41°F). Has needle-like, mid-green leaves and clusters of small, bell-shaped, cerise flowers from early autumn to early spring. Is usually grown as a pot plant; may be planted outdoors in summer in a sheltered site.

E. herbacea. See *E. carnea.*

E. hibernica. See *E. erigena.*

E. × hiemalis. Evergreen, bushy shrub. H and S 30cm (12in). Half hardy. Has needle-like, mid-green foliage and racemes of tubular to bell-shaped, pink-tinged, white flowers from late autumn to mid-winter.

♀ ***E. lusitanica*** (Portuguese heath). Evergreen, upright, bushy, tree heath. H to 3m (10ft), S 1m (3ft). Frost hardy. Has feathery, bright green leaves and, from late autumn to late spring, bears tubular to bell-shaped flowers that are pink in bud but pure white when fully open. **'George Hunt'** has golden foliage; is frost hardy but needs a sheltered position.

E. mackaiana. See *E. mackayana.*

E. mackayana, syn. *E. mackaiana* (Mackay's heath). Evergreen, spreading shrub. H to 25cm (10in), S 40cm (16in). Fully hardy. Has needle-like, mid-green leaves and bears umbels of rounded, pink, mauve-pink or white flowers from mid-summer to early autumn. Likes damp, acid soil. **'Dr Ronald Gray'**, H 15cm (6in), has dark green foliage and pure white flowers. **'Plena'** (illus. p.174), H 15cm (6in), has double, deep-pink flowers, shading to white in centres.

E. mediterranea. See *E. erigena.*

E. pageana. Evergreen, bushy shrub. H to 60cm (2ft), S 30cm (1ft). Half hardy. Has needle-like, mid-green leaves and, from late spring to early summer, bell-shaped, rich yellow flowers.

E. perspicua Prince of Wales heath; illus. p.174. Variable, evergreen shrub. H to 2m (6ft), S 1m (3ft). Half hardy. Has overlapping, needle-like, grey-green leaves and, mainly from early autumn to winter, tubular flowers in white, pink-and-white, red-and-white, purple-and-white or red. Needs damp soil.

E. × praegeri. See *E. × stuartii.*

E. scoparia (Besom heath). Evergreen, bushy shrub. H to 3m (10ft), S 1m (3ft). Frost hardy. Has needle-like, dark green leaves. Clusters of rounded, bell-shaped, greenish-brown flowers appear in late spring and early summer. Requires acid soil. **'Minima'**, H 30cm (12in), has bright green foliage.

E. spiculifolia, syn. *Bruckenthalia spiculifolia* (Spike heath). Evergreen, heath-like shrub. H and S 15cm (6in). Tiny, needle-like, glossy, dark green leaves clothe stiff stems. Terminal clusters of tiny, pink flowers appear in summer.

E. stricta. See *E. terminalis.*

E. × stuartii, syn. *E. × praegeri.* Evergreen, compact shrub. H 15cm (6in), S 30cm (12in). Fully hardy. Has needle-like, dark green leaves. Numerous umbels of bell-shaped, pink flowers are produced in late spring and summer. Prefers moist, acid soil. ♀ **'Irish Lemon'** produces young foliage with lemon-yellow tips in spring and bright pink flowers. **'Irish Orange'** has orange-tipped young foliage and dark pink flowers.

♀ ***E. terminalis***, syn. *E. stricta* (Corsican heath). Evergreen, shrub-like tree heath with stiff, upright growth. H and S to 2.5m (8ft). Frost hardy. Has needle-like, mid-green foliage. Bell-shaped, mauve-pink flowers, borne from early summer to early autumn, turn russet as they fade in winter. Tolerates limestone.

E. tetralix (Cross-leaved heath). Evergreen, spreading shrub. H to 30cm (12in), S 45cm (18in). Fully hardy. Has needle-like, grey-green leaves in whorls of 4. Large umbels of bell-shaped, pink flowers appear from summer to early autumn. Requires acid, preferably moist soil. ♀ **'Alba Mollis'** (illus. p.174) has silver-grey foliage and bears white flowers from early summer to late autumn. ♀ **'Con Underwood'** (illus. p.175) has dark red flowers. **'Hookstone Pink'** has silver-grey foliage and bears rose-pink flowers from late spring to early autumn. ♀ **'Pink Star'** (illus. p.175) produces pink flowers held upright in a star-like pattern.

E. umbellata. Evergreen, bushy shrub. H and S 60cm (2ft). Frost hardy. Has needle-like, mid-green foliage and bell-shaped, mauve flowers, with chocolate-brown anthers, in late spring.

E. vagans (Cornish heath). Vigorous, evergreen, bushy shrub. H and S 75cm (30in). Fully hardy. Leaves are needle-like and mid-green. Rounded, bell-shaped, pink, mauve or white flowers appear from mid-summer to late autumn. Tolerates some limestone. Responds well to hard pruning. ♀ **'Birch Glow'**, H 45cm (18in), has bright green foliage and glowing rose-pink flowers. ♀ **'Lyonesse'**, H 45cm (18in), has dark green foliage and long, tapering spikes of white flowers with brown anthers. ♀ **'Mrs D.F. Maxwell'**, H 45cm (18in), has dark green foliage and glowing deep pink flowers. **'St Keverne'**, H 45cm (18in), is a neat, bushy shrub with rose-pink flowers; may be used for a low hedge. ♀ **'Valerie Proudley'** (illus. p.175), H 45cm (18in), has golden foliage year-round when grown in full light, and bears sparse, white flowers in late summer and autumn.

E. × veitchii. Evergreen, bushy, shrub-like tree heath. H to 2m (6ft), S 1m (3ft). Frost hardy. Has needle-like, mid-green leaves. Scented, tubular to bell-shaped, white flowers are produced in dense clusters from mid-winter to spring. ♀ **'Exeter'** (illus. p.174) has a profusion of white flowers, almost obscuring the foliage. ♀ **'Gold Tips'** is similar to 'Exeter', but young foliage has golden tips in spring. **'Pink Joy'** (illus. p.174) has pink flower buds that open to clear white.

E. verticillata. Evergreen, erect shrub. H to 60cm (2ft), S 30cm (1ft). Frost tender, min. 5–7°C (41–5°F). Has a very unusual and attractive arrangement of flowers tightly packed in whorls at intervals along an otherwise almost bare stem. Bears tubular, pale mauve-pink flowers, 1.5cm (½in) long, intermittently throughout the year.

E. × watsonii. Evergreen, compact shrub. H 30cm (12in), S 38cm (15in). Fully hardy. Needle-like, mid-green leaves often have bright-coloured tips in spring. Bears rounded, bell-shaped, pink flowers from mid- to late summer. **'Cherry Turpin'** has long racemes of pale pink flowers from mid-summer to mid-autumn. ♀ **'Dawn'** (illus. p.175) produces young foliage with orange-

yellow tips and bears deep mauve-pink flowers in compact clusters all summer.
E. × *williamsii*. Evergreen, spreading shrub. H 30cm (12in), S 60cm (24in). Fully hardy. Has needle-like, dark green leaves, with bright yellow tips when young in spring. Bears bell-shaped, mauve or pink flowers in mid-summer. Prefers acid soil. **'Gwavas'** has pale pink flowers on a neat, compact plant from mid-summer to autumn. ♀ **'P.D. Williams'** (illus. p.174), H 45cm (18in), has dark mauve-pink flowers; sometimes keeps its golden foliage tips all summer.

ERIGERON
Fleabane

COMPOSITAE/ASTERACEAE

Genus of mainly spring- and summer-flowering annuals, biennials and perennials, grown for their daisy-like flower heads. Is good for rock gardens or herbaceous borders. Fully to frost hardy. Prefers sun and well-drained soil but should not be allowed to dry out during growing season. Resents winter damp. Propagate by division in spring or early autumn or by seed in autumn, selected forms by softwood cuttings in early summer.
E. alpinus (Alpine fleabane) illus. p.367.
***E. aurantiacus*.** Clump-forming perennial. H 15cm (6in), S 30cm (12in). Fully hardy. Has long, oval, grey-green leaves and produces daisy-like, brilliant orange flower heads in summer. Propagate by seed or division in spring.
***E. aureus*.** Short-lived, clump-forming perennial. H 5–10cm (2–4in), S 15cm (6in). Fully hardy. Bears small, spoon-shaped to oval, hairy leaves. Slender stems each bear a relatively large, daisy-like, golden-yellow flower head in summer. Dislikes winter wet with no snow cover. Is excellent for a scree, trough or alpine house; is prone to aphid attack. ♀ **'Canary Bird'**, H to 10cm (4in), is longer lived, and bears bright canary-yellow flower heads.
***E.* 'Charity'** illus. p.288.
***E.* 'Darkest of All'.** See *E.* 'Dunkelste Aller'.
♀ ***E.* 'Dunkelste Aller',** syn. *E.* 'Darkest of All'. Clump-forming perennial. H 80cm (32in), S 60cm (24in) or more. Fully hardy. Produces a mass of daisy-like, deep purple flower heads, with yellow centres, in summer. Has narrowly oval, greyish-green leaves.
♀ ***E.* 'Foersters Liebling'.** Clump-forming perennial. H 80cm (32in), S 60cm (24in). Fully hardy. In summer daisy-like, semi-double, pink flower heads, with yellow centres, are borne above narrowly oval, greyish-green leaves.
***E. glaucus* 'Elstead Pink'.** Tufted perennial. H 30cm (12in), S 15cm (6in). Fully hardy. Daisy-like, dark lilac-pink flower heads appear throughout summer above oval, grey-green leaves.
♀ ***E. karvinskianus***, syn. *E. mucronatus*, illus. p.389.
***E. mucronatus*.** See *E. karvinskianus*.
***E.* 'Quakeress'.** Clump-forming perennial. H 80cm (32in), S 60cm (24in). Fully hardy. Produces a mass of daisy-like, delicate lilac-pink flower heads, with yellow centres, in summer. Narrowly oval leaves are greyish-green.
***E.* 'Serenity'** illus. p.294.

ERINACEA

LEGUMINOSAE/PAPILIONACEAE

Genus of one species of slow-growing, evergreen sub-shrub with hard, sharp, blue-green spines and pea-like flowers. In spring produces short-lived, soft leaves. Frost hardy. Needs a sheltered position with full sun and deep, gritty, well-drained soil. Propagate by seed when available or by softwood cuttings in late spring or summer.
♀ ***E. anthyllis***, syn. *E. pungens*, illus. p.360.
***E. pungens*.** See *E. anthyllis*.

ERINUS
Fairy foxglove

SCROPHULARIACEAE

Genus of short-lived, semi-evergreen perennials, suitable for rock gardens, walls and troughs. Fully hardy. Needs sun and well-drained soil. Propagate species by seed in autumn (but seedlings will vary considerably), selected forms by softwood cuttings in early summer. Self-seeds freely.
♀ ***E. alpinus*** illus. p.378. **'Dr Hähnle'** (syn. *E.a.* 'Dr Haenele') is a semi-evergreen, basal-rosetted perennial. H and S 5–8cm (2–3in). Small, flat, 2-lipped, deep pink flowers open in late spring and summer. Leaves are small, oval and mid-green.

ERIOBOTRYA

ROSACEAE

Genus of evergreen, autumn-flowering trees and shrubs, grown for their foliage, flowers and edible fruits. Frost hardy, but in cold areas grow against a south-or west-facing wall. Fruits, which ripen in spring, may be damaged by hard, winter frosts. Requires sunny, fertile, well-drained soil. Propagate by seed in autumn or spring.
♀ ***E. japonica*** (Loquat). Evergreen, bushy shrub or spreading tree. H and S 8m (25ft). Has stout shoots and large, oblong, prominently veined, glossy, dark green leaves. Fragrant, 5-petalled, white flowers are borne in large clusters in early autumn, followed by pear-shaped, orange-yellow fruits.

ERIOGONUM
Wild buckwheat

POLYGONACEAE

Genus of annuals, biennials and evergreen perennials, sub-shrubs and shrubs, grown for their rosetted, hairy, often silver or white leaves. Fully hardy to frost tender, min. 5°C (41°F). Needs full sun and well-drained, even poor soil. In cool, wet-winter areas protect shrubby species and hairy-leaved perennials. Water potted plants moderately in summer, less in spring and autumn, very little in winter. Remove flower heads after flowering unless seed is required. Propagate by seed in spring or autumn or by semi-ripe cuttings in summer. Divide perennial root clumps in spring.
E. arborescens illus. p.157.
***E. crocatum*.** Evergreen, sub-shrubby perennial. H to 20cm (8in), S 15cm (6in). Frost hardy. Oval, hairy leaves have woolly, white undersides. Heads of minute, sulphur-yellow flowers are borne in summer. Is a good alpine house plant.
E. giganteum illus. p.135.
***E. ovalifolium*.** Evergreen, domed perennial. H 30cm (12in), S 10cm (4in). Fully hardy. In summer carries tiny, bright yellow flowers in umbels above branched stems bearing tiny, spoon-shaped, hairy, grey leaves. Is excellent for an alpine house.
E. umbellatum illus. p.370.

ERIOPHYLLUM

COMPOSITAE/ASTERACEAE

Genus of summer-flowering perennials and evergreen sub-shrubs, with, usually, silvery foliage and attractive, daisy-like flower heads, suitable for rock gardens and front of borders. Frost hardy. Needs sun and well-drained soil. Propagate by division in spring or by seed in autumn.
E. lanatum, syn. *Bahia lanata*, illus. p.305.

ERIOSYCE

CACTACEAE

Genus of spherical to columnar, perennial cacti. Egg-shaped, red, brown or green seed pods are similar to those of *Wigginsia*. Frost tender, min. 8°C (46°F). Requires full sun and very well-drained soil. Propagate by seed in spring or summer.
E. chilensis, syn. *Echinocactus chilensis, Neoporteria chilensis.* Spherical, then columnar, perennial cactus. H 30cm (12in), S 10cm (4in). Pale green stem has a dense covering of stout, golden spines of varying lengths. Crown bears flattish, pink-orange or white flowers, to 5cm (2in) across, in summer.
***N. litoralis*.** See *N. subgibbosa*.
♀ ***E. napina***, syn. *Neochilenia mitis* of gardens, *Neoporteria mitis, Neoporteria napina* illus. p.487. Flattened spherical, perennial cactus. H 3cm (1¼in), S 5cm (2in). Has very short, black spines pressed flat against a chocolate-brown stem. In summer the crown produces flattish, yellow flowers, 5cm (2in) across.
E. kunzei, syn. ***Neoporteria nidus*.** Spherical to columnar, perennial cactus. H 10cm (4in), S 8cm (3in). Long, soft, grey spines completely encircle a dark greenish-brown stem. During spring or autumn the crown produces tubular, pink to cerise flowers that are 3–5cm (1¼–2in) long, with paler bases, and open only at the tips.
E. subgibbosa, syn. *Neoporteria subgibbosa, Neoporteria litoralis.* Spherical to columnar, perennial cactus. H 30cm (12in), S 10cm (4in). Light green to dark grey-green stem bears large, woolly areoles and stout, amber spines. In late summer, crown bears flattish, carmine-pink flowers, 4cm (1½in) across.
E. villosa, syn. *Neoporteria villosa* illus. p.486.

ERITRICHIUM

BORAGINACEAE

Genus of short-lived perennials with soft, grey-green leaves and forget-me-not-like flowers. Is suitable for rock gardens and alpine houses. Fully hardy. Needs sun and well-drained, peaty, sandy soil with a deep collar of grit; dislikes damp conditions. Is extremely difficult to grow. Propagate by seed when available or by softwood cuttings in summer.
***E. elongatum*.** Tuft-forming perennial. H 2cm (¾in), S 3cm (1¼in). Leaves are oval, hairy and grey-green. Short flower stems each carry small, rounded, flat, blue flowers in early summer.
E. nanum illus. p.395.

ERODIUM

GERANIACEAE

Genus of mound-forming perennials, suitable for rock gardens. Fully to half hardy. Needs sun and well-drained soil. Propagate by semi-ripe cuttings in summer or by seed when available.
***E. chamaedryoides*.** See *E. reichardii*.
E. cheilanthifolium, syn. *E. petraeum* subsp. *crispum*, illus. p.367.
E. chrysanthum illus. p.370.
E. corsicum illus. p.388.
E. foetidum, syn. *E. petraeum.* Compact, mound-forming perennial. H 15–20cm (6–8in), S 20cm (8in). Frost hardy. Produces saucer-shaped, single, red-veined, pink flowers in summer. Oval, grey leaves have deeply cut edges.
E. manescaui, syn. *E. manescavii*, illus. p.289.
***E. manescavii*.** See *E. manescaui*.
E. petraeum*.** See *E. foetidum*. subsp. ***crispum see *E. cheilanthifolium*.
E. reichardii, syn. *E. chamaedryoides.* Mound-forming perennial. H 2.5cm (1in), S 6–8cm (2½–3in). Half hardy. In summer saucer-shaped, single flowers, either white or pink with darker veins, are borne above tiny, oak-like leaves. Is good for a rock garden or trough.
***E. × variabile* 'Flore Pleno'.** Variable, cushion-forming or spreading perennial. H 10cm (4in), S 30cm (12in). Fully hardy. Has oval to narrowly oval, dark to grey-green leaves with scalloped edges and long stalks. From spring to autumn flower stems each bear 1 or 2 rounded, double, pink flowers with darker veins; outer petals are rounded, inner petals narrower. **'Ken Aslet'** has prostrate stems, mid-green leaves and single, deep pink flowers.

***Erpetion reniforme*.** See *Viola hederacea*.

ERYNGIUM
Sea holly

UMBELLIFERAE/APIACEAE

Genus of biennals and perennials, some of which are evergreen, grown for their flowers, foliage and habit. Fully to half hardy. Thrives in sun and fertile, well-drained soil. Propagate species by seed in autumn, selected forms by division in spring or by root cuttings in winter.
E. agavifolium, syn. *E. bromeliifolium* of gardens. Evergreen, clump-forming

perennial. H 1.5m (5ft), S 60cm (2ft). Half hardy. Forms rosettes of sword-shaped, sharply toothed, rich green leaves. Thistle-like, greenish-white flower heads are produced on branched stems in summer.

♀ ***E. alpinum*** illus. p.259.

E. amethystinum. Rosette-forming perennial. H and S 60cm (24in). Fully hardy. Oval leaves are divided, spiny and mid-green. Produces much-branched stems that, in summer, bear heads of small, thistle-like, blue flowers surrounded by spiky, darker blue bracts.

E. bourgatii illus. p.296.

E. bromeliifolium of gardens. See *E. agavifolium*.

E. eburneum, syn. *E. paniculatum*, illus. p.224.

♀ ***E. giganteum.*** Clump-forming biennial or short-lived perennial that dies after flowering. H 1–1.2m (3–4ft), S 75cm (2½ft). Fully hardy. Heart-shaped, basal leaves are mid-green. Large, rounded heads of thistle-like, blue flowers, surrounded by broad, spiny, silvery bracts, are produced in late summer.

♀ ***E.* × *oliverianum*** illus. p.259.

E. paniculatum. See *E. eburneum*.

♀ ***E.* × *tripartitum*** illus. p.259.

E. variifolium illus. p.296.

***E.* × *zabelii* 'Violetta'.** Upright perennial. H 75cm (30in), S 60cm (24in). Fully hardy. Has rounded, mid-green leaves divided into 3–5 segments. Loose heads of thistle-like, deep violet flowers, surrounded by narrow, spiny, silvery-blue bracts, appear in late summer.

ERYSIMUM

CRUCIFERAE/BRASSICACEAE

Genus of annuals, biennials, evergreen or semi-evergreen, short-lived perennials and sub-shrubs, grown for their flowers. Is closely related to *Cheiranthus* and is suitable for borders, banks and rock gardens. Fully to frost hardy. Needs sun and well-drained soil. Propagate by seed in spring or autumn or by softwood cuttings in summer.

♀ ***E.* × *allionii***, syn. *E.* × *marshallii* (Siberian wallflower). **'Orange Bedder'** illus. p.352.

♀ ***E.* 'Bowles' Mauve'**, syn. *Cheiranthus* 'Bowles' Mauve', *E.* 'E.A. Bowles'. Bushy perennial. H to 75cm (30in), S 45cm (18in). Half hardy. Narrowly lance-shaped, dark green leaves are 5cm (2in) long. Many clusters of small, rich mauve flowers, each with 4 spreading petals, are borne in spring and early summer.

♀ ***E.* 'Bredon'**, syn. *Cheiranthus* 'Bredon', illus. p.362.

E. cheiri, syn. *Cheiranthus cheiri*. Moderately fast-growing, evergreen, bushy perennial, grown as a biennial. H 25–80cm (10–32in), S 30–40cm (12–16in). Fully hardy. Has lance-shaped, mid- to deep green leaves. Heads of fragrant, 4-petalled flowers in many colours, including red, yellow, bronze, white and orange, are produced in spring. **Bedder Series** is dwarf and has golden-yellow, primrose-yellow, orange or scarlet-red flowers. **Fair Lady Series** bears flowers in pale pink, yellow and creamy white, with some reds. **'Fire King'** illus. p.353. Flowers of **'Ivory White'** are creamy white.

***E.* 'E.A. Bowles'.** See *E.* 'Bowles' Mauve'.

E. helveticum, syn. *E. pumilum*, illus. p.385.

♀ ***E.* × *kewense* 'Harpur Crewe'**, syn. *Cheiranthus cheiri* 'Harpur Crewe', illus. p.362.

E. linifolium. Short-lived, semi-evergreen, open, dome-shaped sub-shrub. H to 30cm (12in), S 20cm (8in) or more. Frost hardy. Leaves are narrowly lance-shaped and blue-grey. Tight heads of small, 4-petalled, pale violet flowers appear in early summer.

E.* × *marshallii. See *E.* × *allionii*.

***E.* 'Moonlight'**, syn. *Cheiranthus* 'Moonlight', illus. p.362. Evergreen, mat-forming perennial. H 5cm (2in), S 20cm (8in) or more. Fully hardy. Leaves are small and narrowly oval. Leafy stems each carry clusters of 4-petalled, pale yellow flowers, opening in succession during summer. Makes a good rock garden plant. Needs a sheltered, sunny site and poor, gritty soil.

E. pumilum. See *E. helveticum*.

ERYTHRINA

LEGUMINOSAE/PAPILIONACEAE

Genus of deciduous or semi-evergreen trees, shrubs and perennials, grown for their flowers from spring to autumn. Half hardy to frost tender, min. 5°C (41°F). Requires full light and well-drained soil. Water containerized plants moderately, very little in winter or when leafless. Propagate by seed in spring or by semi-ripe cuttings in summer. Red spider mite may be troublesome.

E. americana. See *E. coralloides*.

E.* × *bidwillii illus. p.139.

E. coralloides, syn. *E. americana* (Flame coral tree, Naked coral tree). Deciduous, untidily rounded shrub or tree with somewhat prickly stems. H and S 3–6m (10–20ft). Frost tender. Has leaves of 3 triangular leaflets, the largest central one 11cm (4½in) long. Racemes of pea-like, red flowers are borne on leafless stems in early spring and summer.

E. crista-galli illus. p.139.

ERYTHRONIUM

LILIACEAE

Genus of spring-flowering, tuberous perennials, grown for their pendent flowers and in some cases attractively mottled leaves. Fully to frost hardy. Requires partial shade and humus-rich, well-drained soil, where tubers will not become too hot and dry in summer while dormant. Prefers cool climates. Propagate by seed in autumn. Some species increase by offsets, which should be divided in late summer. Do not allow tubers to dry out before replanting, 15cm (6in) deep.

E. americanum illus. p.450.

♀ ***E. californicum*** illus. p.443.

♀ **'White Beauty'** illus. p.425.

♀ ***E. dens-canis*** illus. p.446.

E. grandiflorum. Spring-flowering, tuberous perennial. H 10–30cm (4–12in), S 5–8cm (2–3in). Fully hardy. Has 2 lance-shaped, semi-erect, basal, plain bright green leaves. Stem carries 1–3 pendent, bright yellow flowers with reflexed petals.

E. hendersonii illus. p.425.

E. oregonum illus. p.424.

♀ ***E.* 'Pagoda'** illus. p.431.

♀ ***E. revolutum.*** Spring-flowering, tuberous perennial. H 20–30cm (8–12in), S 15cm (6in). Frost hardy. Produces 2 lance-shaped, semi-erect, basal, brown-mottled, green leaves and a loose spike of 1–4 pendent, pale to deep pink flowers with reflexed petals.

♀ ***E. tuolumnense.*** Spring-flowering, tuberous perennial. H to 30cm (12in), S 12–15cm (5–6in). Frost hardy. Has 2 lance-shaped, semi-erect, basal, glossy, plain green leaves. Carries a spike of up to 10 pendent, bright yellow flowers with reflexed petals. Increases rapidly by offsets.

ESCALLONIA

ESCALLONIACEAE

Genus of evergreen, semi-evergreen or deciduous shrubs and trees, grown for their profuse, 5-petalled flowers and glossy foliage. Thrives in mild areas, where *Escallonia* is wind-resistant and ideal for hedging in coastal gardens. Frost hardy, but in cold areas protect from strong winds and grow against a south- or west-facing wall. Requires full sun and fertile, well-drained soil. Trim hedges and wall-trained plants after flowering. Propagate by softwood cuttings in summer.

♀ ***E.* 'Apple Blossom'** illus. p.137.

***E.* 'Donard Beauty'.** Evergreen, arching shrub with slender shoots. H and S 1.5m (5ft). Bears deep pink flowers from early to mid-summer among small, oval, dark green leaves.

***E.* 'Donard Seedling'** illus. p.136.

***E.* 'Edinensis'.** Vigorous, evergreen, arching shrub. H 2m (6ft), S 3m (10ft). Bears small, oblong, bright green leaves. Small, pink flowers are produced from early to mid-summer. Is one of the more hardy escallonias.

♀ ***E.* 'Iveyi'** illus. p.114.

♀ ***E.* 'Langleyensis'** illus. p.138.

E. leucantha illus. p.114.

♀ ***E. rubra* 'Crimson Spire'.** Very vigorous, evergreen, upright shrub. H and S 3m (10ft). Has oval, rich green leaves and, throughout summer, tubular, deep red flowers. **'Woodside'** illus. p.161.

E. virgata illus. p.133.

ESCHSCHOLZIA

California poppy

PAPAVERACEAE

Genus of annuals, grown for their bright, poppy-like flowers. Is suitable for rock gardens and gaps in paving. Fully hardy. Requires sun and grows well in poor, very well-drained soil. Dead-head regularly to ensure a long flowering period. Propagate by seed sown outdoors in spring or early autumn.

♀ ***E. caespitosa*** illus. p.348.

♀ ***E. californica*** illus. p.351, [mixed] illus. p.350. **Ballerina Series** illus. p.334. ♀ **Thai Silk Series** illus. p.351.

ESCOBARIA

CACTACEAE

Genus of mainly spherical to columnar perennial cacti. The stems are studded with tubercles (each with a furrow immediately above it) and very spiny, generally white aeroles. Frost tender, min. 5°C (41°F). Needs full sun and poor to moderately fertile, well-drained soil. Propagate by seed in spring or by offsets in summer.

E. vivipara, syn. *Coryphantha vivipara*, illus. p.487.

ESPOSTOA

CACTACEAE

Genus of columnar, perennial cacti, each with a 10–30-ribbed stem, eventually becoming bushy or tree-like with age. Most species are densely covered in woolly, white hairs masking short, sharp spines. Bears cup-shaped flowers, as well as extra wool down the side of stems facing the sun, only after about 30 years. Frost tender, min. 10°C (50°F). Needs full sun and very well-drained soil. Propagate by seed in spring or summer.

E. lanata illus. p.473.

Etruscan honeysuckle. See *Lonicera etrusca*.

EUCALYPTUS

Gum tree

MYRTACEAE

Genus of evergreen trees and shrubs, grown for their bark, flowers and aromatic foliage. Frost hardy to frost tender, min. 1–10°C (34–50°F). Needs full sun, shelter from strong, cold winds and fertile, well-drained soil. Plant smallest obtainable trees. Water potted plants moderately, less in winter. Attractive, young foliage of some species, normally lost with age, may be retained by cutting growth back hard in spring. Propagate by seed in spring or autumn.

E. camaldulensis (Murray red gum, River red gum). Fast-growing, evergreen, irregularly rounded tree. H 30m (100ft) or more, S 20m (70ft) or more. Frost tender, min. 3–5°C (37–41°F). Young bark is grey, brown and cream; leaves are lance-shaped, slender, green or blue-green. Has umbels of small, cream flowers in summer. Is a drought-resistant tree.

E. coccifera illus. p.68.

♀ ***E. dalrympleana*** illus. p.68.

E. ficifolia (Flowering gum). Moderately fast-growing, evergreen, rounded tree. H and S to 8m (25ft). Frost tender, min. 1–3°C (34–7°F). Has broadly lance-shaped, glossy, deep green leaves and, in spring-summer, large panicles of many-stamened, pale to deep red flowers. Is best in acid soil.

E. glaucescens (Tingiringi gum). Evergreen, spreading tree. H 12m (40ft), S 8m (25ft). Frost hardy. Young bark is white. Leaves are silvery-blue and rounded when young, long, narrow and blue-grey when mature. In autumn bears clusters of many-stamened, white flowers.

E. globulus (Blue gum, Tasmanian blue gum). Very fast-growing, evergreen,

spreading tree. H 30m (100ft), S 12m (40ft). Half hardy. Bark peels in ribbons. Large, oval to oblong, silvery-blue leaves are long, narrow and glossy, mid-green when mature. White flowers, consisting of tufts of stamens, appear in summer-autumn, often year-round.
♀ ***E. gunnii*** illus. p.68.
E. niphophila. See *E. pauciflora* subsp. *niphophila*.
E. pauciflora illus. p.80. ♀ subsp. ***niphophila*** (syn. *E. niphophila*) illus. p.80.
E. perriniana illus. p.96.
E. viminalis (Manna gum, Ribbon gum). Vigorous, evergreen, spreading tree. H 30m (100ft), S 15m (50ft). Frost tender, min. 5°C (41°F). Bark peels on upper trunk. Lance-shaped, dark green leaves become very long, narrow and pale green when mature. Bears clusters of stamened, white flowers in summer.

EUCHARIS

AMARYLLIDACEAE

Genus of evergreen bulbs, grown for their fragrant, white flowers that resemble large, white daffodils, with a cup and 6 spreading petals. Frost tender, min. 15°C (59°F). Prefers at least 50% relative humidity. Needs partial shade and humus-rich soil. Water freely in summer. Propagate by seed when ripe or by offsets in spring.
♀ ***E. amazonica***, syn. *E. grandiflora* of gardens, illus. p.441.
E. grandiflora of gardens. See *E. amazonica*.

EUCOMIS
Pineapple flower

LILIACEAE/HYACINTHACEAE

Genus of summer- and autumn-flowering bulbs, grown for their dense spikes of flowers, which are overtopped by a tuft of small, leaf-like bracts, as in a pineapple. Frost hardy, but in severe winters protect with dead bracken or loose, rough peat. Needs full sun and well-drained soil. Plant in spring and water freely in summer. Propagate by seed or division of clumps in spring.
♀ ***E. autumnalis***, syn. *E. undulata*. Late summer- to autumn-flowering bulb. H 20–30cm (8–12in), S 60–75cm (24–30in). Has strap-shaped, wavy-edged leaves in a semi-erect, basal tuft. Leafless stem bears small, star-shaped, pale green or white flowers in a dense spike, with cluster of leaf-like bracts at apex.
♀ ***E. bicolor*** illus. p.438.
E. comosa illus. p.410.
♀ ***E. pallidiflora*** illus. p.409.
E. undulata. See *E. autumnalis*.

EUCOMMIA

EUCOMMIACEAE

Genus of one species of deciduous tree, grown for its unusual foliage. Fully hardy. Needs full sun and fertile, well-drained soil. Propagate by softwood cuttings in summer.
E. ulmoides (Gutta-percha tree). Deciduous, spreading tree. H 12m (40ft), S 8m (25ft). Drooping, oval leaves are pointed and glossy, dark green; when pulled apart, leaf pieces stay joined by rubbery threads. Inconspicuous flowers appear in late spring before leaves.

EUCRYPHIA

EUCRYPHIACEAE

Genus of evergreen, semi-evergreen or deciduous trees and shrubs, grown for their foliage and often fragrant, white flowers. Frost hardy. Needs a sheltered, semi-shaded position in all but mild, wet areas, where it will withstand more exposure. Does best with roots in a cool, moist, shaded position and crown in sun. Requires fertile, well-drained, lime-free soil, except in the case of *E. cordifolia* and *E.* × *nymansensis*. Propagate by semi-ripe cuttings in late summer.
E. cordifolia (Ulmo). Evergreen, columnar tree. H 15m (50ft), S 8m (25ft). Has oblong, wavy-edged, dull green leaves, with grey down beneath. Large, rose-like, white flowers are borne in late summer and autumn.
♀ ***E. glutinosa*** illus. p.86.
E. lucida illus. p.86.
E. milliganii illus. p.133.
♀ ***E.* × *nymansensis* 'Nymansay'** illus. p.77.

Eugenia australis of gardens. See *Syzygium paniculatum*.
Eugenia paniculata. See *Syzygium paniculatum*.
Eugenia ugni. See *Ugni molinae*.
Euodia. See *Tetradium*.

EUONYMUS

CELASTRACEAE

Genus of evergreen or deciduous shrubs and trees, sometimes climbing, grown for their foliage, autumn colour and fruits. Fully to frost hardy. Needs sun or semi-shade and any well-drained soil, although, for evergreen species in full sun, soil should not be very dry. Propagate by semi-ripe cuttings in summer or by seed in autumn. *E. europaeus* and *E. japonicus* may be attacked by caterpillars; *E. japonicus* is susceptible to mildew. All parts may cause mild stomach upset if ingested.
♀ ***E. alatus*** illus. p.144.
♀ **'Compactus'** is a deciduous, bushy, dense shrub. H 1m (3ft), S 3m (10ft). Fully hardy. Shoots have corky wings. Oval, dark green leaves turn brilliant red in autumn. Bears inconspicuous, greenish-white flowers in summer, followed by small, 4-lobed, purple or red fruits.
E. cornutus var. ***quinquecornutus.*** Deciduous, spreading, open shrub. H 2m (6ft), S 3m (10ft). Frost hardy. Has narrowly lance-shaped, dark green leaves. Small, purplish-green flowers in summer are followed by showy, 5-horned, pink fruits that open to reveal orange-red seeds.
E. europaeus (Spindle tree). ♀ **'Red Cascade'** illus. p.143.
E. fortunei. Evergreen shrub, grown only as var. ***radicans*** and its cultivars, which are climbing or creeping and prostrate. H 5m (15ft) if supported, S indefinite. Fully hardy. Bears oval, dark green leaves and inconspicuous, greenish-white flowers from early to mid-summer. Makes good ground cover. Foliage of **'Coloratus'** turns reddish-purple in autumn-winter.
♀ **'Emerald Gaiety'**, H 1m (3ft), S 1.5m (5ft), is bushy, with rounded, white-edged, deep green leaves.
♀ **'Emerald 'n' Gold'** illus. p.173.
'Gold Tip' see *E.f.* 'Golden Prince'. Young, rounded leaves of **'Golden Prince'** (syn. *E.f.* 'Gold Tip') are edged bright yellow, ageing to creamy-white.
'Kewensis', H 10cm (4in) or more, has slender stems and tiny leaves, and forms dense mats of growth.
'Sarcoxie', H and S 1.2m (4ft), is vigorous, upright and bushy, with glossy, dark green leaves. **'Silver Queen'** illus. p.147. **'Sunspot'** bears deep green leaves, each marked in centre with golden-yellow.
E. hamiltonianus subsp. ***sieboldianus,*** syn. *E. yedoensis*. Deciduous, tree-like shrub. H and S 6m (20ft) or more. Fully hardy. Oval, mid-green leaves often turn pink and red in autumn. Tiny, green flowers in late spring and early summer are followed by 4-lobed, pink fruits. subsp. ***sieboldianus* 'Red Elf'** illus. p.143.
E. japonicus (Japanese spindle). **'Latifolius Albomarginatus'** (syn. *E.j.* 'Macrophyllus Albus') illus. p.147.
'Macrophyllus' is an evergreen, upright, dense shrub. H 4m (12ft), S 2m (6ft). Frost hardy. Has very large, oval, glossy, dark green leaves and, in summer, small, star-shaped, green flowers, sometimes succeeded by spherical, pink fruits with orange seeds. Is good for hedging, particularly in coastal areas. **'Macrophyllus Albus'** see *E.j.* 'Latifolius Albomarginatus'. Leaves of ♀ **'Ovatus Aureus'** are broadly edged with golden-yellow.
E. latifolius illus. p.144.
E. myrianthus illus. p.120.
E. oxyphyllus. Deciduous, upright shrub or tree. H and S 2.5m (8ft). Fully hardy. Oval, dull green leaves become purplish-red in autumn. Produces tiny, greenish-white flowers in late spring, followed by globose, 4- or 5-lobed, deep red fruits with orange-scarlet seeds.
♀ ***E. planipes***, syn. *E. sachalinensis* of gardens. Deciduous, upright, open shrub. H and S 3m (10ft). Fully hardy. Bears oval, mid-green leaves that turn to brilliant red in autumn, as large, 4- or 5-lobed, red fruits open to reveal bright orange seeds. Star-shaped, green flowers open in late spring.
E. sachalinensis of gardens. See *E. planipes*.
E. yedoensis. See *E. hamiltonianus* var. *sieboldianus*.

EUPATORIUM

COMPOSITAE/ASTERACEAE

Genus of perennials, sub-shrubs and shrubs, many of which are evergreen, grown mainly for their flowers, some also for their architectural foliage. Fully hardy to frost tender, min. 5–13°C (41–55°F). Requires full light or partial shade. Will grow in any conditions, although most species prefer moist but well-drained soil. Water containerized plants freely when in full growth, moderately at other times. Prune shrubs lightly after flowering or in spring. Propagate by seed in spring; shrubs and sub-shrubs may also be propagated by softwood or greenwood cuttings in summer, perennials by division in early spring or autumn. Red spider mite and whitefly may be troublesome.
E. ageratoides. See *E. rugosum*.
E. ianthinum. See *E. sordidum*.
♀ ***E. ligustrinum***, syn. *Ageratina ligustrina, E. micranthum, E. weinmannianum*. Evergreen, rounded shrub. H and S 2–4m (6–12ft). Half hardy. Has elliptic to lance-shaped, bright green leaves and, in autumn, fragrant, groundsel-like, white or pink flowers are produced in flattened clusters, 10–20cm (4–8in) wide.
E. micranthum. See *E. ligustrinum*.
E. purpureum illus. p.231.
E. rugosum, syn. *E. ageratoides, E. urticifolium*, illus. p.242.
E. sordidum, syn. *E. ianthinum, Bartlettina sordida*. Evergreen, rounded, robust-stemmed shrub. H and S 1–2m (3–6ft). Frost tender, min. 10–13°C (50–55°F). Oval, serrated, deep green leaves are red haired. Produces fragrant, pompon-like, violet-purple flower heads in flattened clusters, 10cm (4in) wide, mainly in winter.
E. urticifolium. See *E. rugosum*.
E. weinmannianum. See *E. ligustrinum*.

EUPHORBIA
Milkweed, Spurge

EUPHORBIACEAE

Genus of shrubs, succulents and perennials, some of which are semi-evergreen or evergreen, and annuals. Flower heads consist of cup-shaped bracts, in various colours and usually each containing several flowers lacking typical sepals and petals. Fully hardy to frost tender, min. 5–15°C (41–59°F). Does best in sun or partial shade and in moist but well-drained soil. Propagate by basal cuttings in spring or summer, by division in spring or early autumn or by seed in autumn or spring. All parts may cause severe discomfort if ingested; contact with their milky sap may irritate skin.
E. amygdaloides (Wood spurge). **'Purpurea'** is a semi-evergreen, erect perennial. H and S 30cm (1ft). Fully hardy. Stems and narrowly oval leaves are green, heavily suffused purple-red. Has flower heads of cup-shaped, yellow bracts in spring. Is susceptible to mildew. ♀ var. ***robbiae*** (syn. *E. robbiae*) illus. p.279.
E. biglandulosa. See *E. rigida*.
E. candelabrum. Deciduous, tree-like, perennial succulent. H 10m (30ft), S 5m (15ft). Frost tender, min. 10°C (50°F). Erect, 3–5-angled, deeply indented, glossy, dark green stems, often marbled white, branch and rebranch candelabra-like. Has short-lived, spear-shaped leaves. Rounded heads of small flowers, with cup-shaped, yellow bracts, are produced in spring.
E. characias subsp. ***characias*** and ♀ subsp. ***wulfenii*** illus. p.152.
E. cyparissias illus. p.279.
E. epithymoides. See *E. polychroma*.
♀ ***E. fulgens*** (Scarlet plume). Evergreen shrub of erect and arching habit. H 1–1.5m (3–5ft), S 60cm–1m (2–3ft). Frost tender, min. 5–7°C (41–5°F). Has elliptic to lance-shaped, mid- to deep green leaves, to 10cm (4in) long. From winter to spring, bears leafy, wand-like sprays of small

flowers, each cluster surrounded by 5 petal-like, bright scarlet bracts, 2–3cm (¾–1¼ in) across.
E. gorgonis (Gorgon's head). Deciduous, hemispherical, perennial succulent. H 8cm (3in), S 10cm (4in). Frost tender, min. 10°C (50°F). Has a much-ribbed, green main stem crowned by 3–5 rows of prostrate, 1cm (½in) wide stems that are gradually shed. In spring, crown also bears rounded heads of small, fragrant flowers with cup-shaped, yellow bracts.
E. griffithii **'Fireglow'** illus. p.266.
E. marginata illus. p.331.
♀ ***E. milii*** illus. p.151. ♀ var. ***splendens*** (syn. *E. splendens*) is a slow-growing, mainly evergreen, spreading, spiny, semi-succulent shrub. H to 2m (6ft), S to 1m (3ft). Frost tender, min. 5–7°C (41–5°F). Has oblong to oval leaves and, intermittently year-round but especially in spring, clusters of tiny flowers enclosed in large, petal-like, red bracts.
♀ ***E. myrsinites*** illus. p.383.
E. nicaeensis. Clump-forming perennial with a woody base. H 75cm (30in), S 45cm (18in). Fully hardy. Has narrowly oval, fleshy, grey-green leaves. Umbels of greenish-yellow flower heads with cup-shaped bracts are borne throughout summer.
♀ ***E. obesa*** illus. p.493.
♀ ***E. palustris.*** Bushy perennial. H and S 1m (3ft). Fully hardy. Clusters of yellow-green flower heads with cup-shaped bracts appear in spring above oblong to lance-shaped, yellowish-green leaves.
♀ ***E. polychroma***, syn. *E. epithymoides*, illus. p.285.
E. pulcherrima illus. p.146. **'Paul Mikkelson'** is a mainly evergreen, erect, freely branching shrub. H and S 3–4m (10–12ft). Frost tender, min. 5–7°C (41–5°F). Bears oval to lance-shaped, shallowly lobed leaves. From late autumn to spring, has flattened heads of small, greenish-white flowers with large, leaf-like, bright red bracts.
E. rigida, syn. *E. biglandulosa.* Evergreen, erect perennial. H and S 45cm (18in). Frost hardy. In early spring produces terminal heads of yellow flowers with cup-shaped bracts above oblong to oval, pointed, grey-green leaves.
E. robbiae. See *E. amygdaloides* var. *robbiae.*
♀ ***E. schillingii*** illus. p.260.
E. seguieriana illus. p.279.
♀ ***E. sikkimensis*** illus. p.260.
E. splendens. See *E. milii* var. *splendens.*

EUPTELEA

EUPTELEACEAE

Genus of deciduous trees, grown for their foliage. Fully to half hardy. Grows best in full sun and fertile, well-drained soil. Propagate by seed in autumn.
E. polyandra. Deciduous, bushy-headed tree. H 8m (25ft), S 6m (20ft). Fully hardy. Long-stalked, narrowly oval, pointed, sharply toothed leaves are glossy and bright green, turning red and yellow in autumn. Has inconspicuous flowers in spring before leaves emerge.

European fan palm. See *Chaemaerops humilis*, illus. p.172.
European larch. See *Larix decidua.*
European white lime. See *Tilia tomentosa.*

EURYA

THEACEAE

Genus of evergreen shrubs and trees, grown for their foliage. Insignificant flowers are produced from spring to summer. Half hardy to frost tender, min. 7°C (45°F). Tolerates partial shade or full light and needs fertile, well-drained soil. Water containerized specimens freely whc en in full growth, less at other times. Propagate by seed when ripe or in spring or by semi-ripe cuttings in late summer.
E. emarginata illus. p.172.
E. japonica. Evergreen, bushy shrub or small tree. H and S 10m (30ft). Frost hardy. Has elliptic to lance-shaped, bluntly toothed, leathery, dark green leaves. Inconspicuous, green flowers, borne from spring to summer, are followed on female plants by tiny, spherical, purple-black fruits. **'Variegata'** of gardens see *Cleyera japonica* 'Tricolor'.

EURYALE

NYMPHAEACEAE

Genus of one species of annual, deep-water plant, grown for its floating foliage; is suitable only for a tropical pool. Frost tender, min. 5°C (41°F). Needs full light, constant warmth and heavy feeding. Propagate by seed in spring.
E. ferox illus. p.465.

EURYOPS

COMPOSITAE/ASTERACEAE

Genus of evergreen shrubs and sub-shrubs, grown for their attractive leaves and showy, daisy-like flower heads. Is suitable for borders and rock gardens. Fully hardy to frost tender, min. 5–7°C (41–5°F). Needs sun and moist but well-drained soil. May not tolerate root disturbance. Propagate by softwood cuttings in summer.
♀ ***E. acraeus***, syn. *E. evansii* of gardens, illus. p.370.
E. evansii of gardens. See *E. acraeus.*
♀ ***E. pectinatus*** illus. p.166.

EUSTOMA

GENTIANACEAE

Genus of annuals and perennials with poppy-like flowers that are good for cutting. Makes good pot plants. Frost tender, min. 4–7°C (39–45°F). Needs sun and well-drained soil. Propagate by seed sown under glass in late winter.
E. grandiflorum, syn. *E. russellianum, Lisianthus russellianus*, illus. p.331. **Heidi Series** has flowers in shades of rose-pink, blue, white and bicolours.
E. russellianum. See *E. grandiflorum.*

Evening primrose. See *Oenothera.*
White. See *Oenothera speciosa.*
Everlasting flower. See *Xerochrysum bracteatum.*
Everlasting pea. See *Lathyrus grandiflorus*, illus. p.205; *Lathyrus latifolius*, illus. p.207; *Lathyrus sylvestris.*
Evodia. See *Tetradium.*

EXACUM

GENTIANACEAE

Genus of annuals, biennials and perennials, grown for their profusion of flowers, that are excellent as pot plants. Frost tender, min. 7–10°C (45–50°F). Grow in sun and in well-drained soil. Propagate by seed sown in early spring for flowering the same year or in late summer for the following year.
♀ ***E. affine*** illus. p.343.

Exeter elm. See *Ulmus glabra* 'Exoniensis'.

EXOCHORDA

ROSACEAE

Genus of deciduous shrubs, grown for their abundant, showy, white flowers. Fully hardy. Does best in full sun and fertile, well-drained soil. Improve vigour and flowering by thinning out old shoots after flowering. Propagate by softwood cuttings in summer or by seed in autumn. Chlorosis may be a problem on shallow, chalky soil.
E. giraldii. Deciduous, widely arching shrub. H and S 3m (10ft). Has pinkish-green, young growths and oblong leaves. Bears upright racemes of large, 5-petalled, white flowers in late spring.
♀ ***E. x macrantha*** **'The Bride'** illus. p.131.
E. racemosa. Deciduous, arching shrub. H and S 4m (12ft). Has upright clusters of 5-petalled, white flowers in late spring. Leaves are oblong and deep blue-green. Prefers acid soil.

Eyelash begonia. See *Begonia bowerae*, illus. p.307.

Fabiana

SOLANACEAE

Genus of evergreen shrubs, grown for their foliage and flowers. Frost hardy, but in cold areas plant in a sheltered position. Requires full sun and fertile, well-drained soil. Propagate by softwood cuttings in summer.
F. imbricata* 'Prostrata'.** Evergreen, mound-forming, very dense shrub. H 1m (3ft), S 2m (6ft). Shoots are densely covered with tiny, heath-like, deep green leaves. Bears a profusion of tubular, white flowers in early summer. 🏆 f. ***violacea, syn. *F.i.* 'Violacea', illus. p.141.

Fagus
Beech

FAGACEAE

Genus of deciduous trees, grown for their habit, foliage and autumn colour. Insignificant flowers appear in late spring and hairy fruits ripen in autumn to release edible, triangular nuts. Fully hardy. Requires sun or semi-shade; purple-leaved forms prefer full sun, yellow-leaved forms a little shade. Grows well in any but waterlogged soil. *F. sylvatica*, when used as hedging, should be trimmed in summer. Propagate species by seed sown in autumn, and selected forms by budding in late summer. Problems may be caused by bracket fungi, canker-causing fungi, aphids and beech coccus.
F. americana. See *F. grandifolia*.
F. grandifolia, syn. *F. americana* (American beech). Deciduous, spreading tree. H and S 10m (30ft). Oval, silky, pale green young leaves mature to dark green in summer, then turn golden-brown in autumn.
F. orientalis (Oriental beech). Deciduous, spreading tree. H 20m (70ft), S 15m (50ft). Has large, oval, wavy-edged, dark green leaves that turn yellow in autumn.
🏆 ***F. sylvatica*** (Common beech) illus. p.64. f. ***atropunicea*** (syn. *F. s.* f. *purpurea*) illus. p.61. . **'Aurea Pendula'** is a deciduous, slender tree with pendulous branches. H 30m (100ft), S 25m (80ft). Oval, wavy-edged leaves are bright yellow and become rich yellow and orange-brown in autumn. 🏆 **'Dawyck'**, S 7m (22ft), is columnar, with erect branches; pale green leaves mature to mid- to dark green, and turn rich yellow and orange-brown in autumn. 🏆 **'Dawyck Purple'** is similar, but has deep purple foliage. Leaves of f. ***laciniata*** are deeply cut. 🏆 f. ***pendula*** (syn. *F.s.* 'Pendula') illus. p.62. f. ***purpurea*** see *F.s.* f. *atropunicea*. **'Purpurea Pendula'**, H and S 3m (10ft), has stiff, weeping branches and blackish-purple foliage. Leaves of 🏆 **'Riversii'** are very dark purple. Those of **'Rohanii'** are deeply cut and reddish-purple. **'Zlatia'** produces yellow, young foliage that later becomes mid- to dark green.

Fair maids of France. See *Saxifraga granulata*, illus. p.358.
Fairy bells. See *Disporum*.
Fairy duster. See *Calliandra eriophylla*, illus. p.168.
Fairy foxglove. See *Erinus*.
Fairy lantern. See *Calochortus*.
Golden. See *Calochortus amabilis*, illus. p.450.
Fairy moss. See *Azolla filiculoides*, illus. p.464.
Fairy thimbles. See *Campanula cochleariifolia*, illus. p.395.

Fallopia,
syn. BILDERDYKIA, REYNOUTRIA

POLYGONACEAE

Genus of rhizomatous, climbing or scrambling, woody-based perennials that are good for training on pergolas and deciduous trees or for covering unsightly structures. Fully hardy. Grow in full sun or partial shade and moist but well-drained soil. Propagate by seed sown as soon as ripe or in spring or by semi-ripe cuttings in summer or hardwood cuttings in autumn.
F. aubertii, syn. *Polygonum aubertii* (Mile-a-minute plant, Russian vine). Vigorous, deciduous, woody-stemmed, twining climber. H to 12m (40ft) or more. Fully hardy. Leaves are broadly heart-shaped. Panicles of small, white or greenish flowers, ageing to pink, are carried in summer-autumn; they are followed by angled, pinkish-white fruits. Is often confused with *F. baldschuanica*.
F. aubertii of gardens. See *Fallopia baldschuanica*.
F. baldschuanica, syn. *F. aubertii* of gardens, *Polygonum baldschuanicum*, illus. p.215.

Fallugia

ROSACEAE

Genus of one species of deciduous shrub, grown for its flowers and showy fruit clusters. Frost hardy, but in cold areas protect in winter. Needs a hot, sunny position and well-drained soil. Propagate by softwood cuttings taken in summer or by seed sown in autumn.
F. paradoxa illus. p.132.

False acacia. See *Robinia pseudoacacia*.
False African violet. See *Streptocarpus saxorum*, illus. p.294.
False anemone. See *Anemonopsis*.
False aralia. See *Schefflera elegantissima*, illus. p.123.
False cypress. See *Chamaecyparis*.
False heather. See *Cuphea hyssopifolia*, illus. p.154.
False indigo. See *Baptisia australis*, illus. p.258.
False jasmine. See *Gelsemium sempervirens*, illus. p.202.
False oat grass. See *Arrhenatherum elatius*.
False spikenard. See *Smilacina racemosa*, illus. p.233.
Fanwort. See *Cabomba caroliniana*.

Farfugium

COMPOSITAE/ASTERACEAE

Genus of perennials, grown for their foliage and daisy-like flower heads. Frost hardy. Grow in sun or semi-shade and in moist but well-drained soil. Propagate by division in spring or by seed in autumn or spring.
F. japonicum, syn. *Ligularia tussilaginea*. Loosely clump-forming perennial. H and S 60cm (24in). Frost hardy. Has large, rounded, toothed, basal, mid-green leaves, above which rise woolly, branched stems bearing clusters of daisy-like, pale yellow flower heads in late summer.
🏆 **'Aureomaculatum'** (Leopard plant) has variegated, gold-and-white leaves and is half hardy.

Fargesia

GRAMINEAE/POACEAE

See also GRASSES, BAMBOOS, RUSHES and SEDGES.
🏆 ***F. murieliae***, syn. *Arundinaria murieliae, Fargesia spathacea* of gardens, *Sinarundinaria murieliae, Thamnocalamus murieliae, T. spathaceus* of gardens (Muriel bamboo). Evergreen, clump-forming bamboo. H 4m (12ft), S indefinite. Frost hardy. Has attractive, grey young culms with loose, light brown sheaths and broad, apple-green leaves, each very long, drawn-out at its tip. Flower spikes are unimportant.
F. nitida, syn. *Arundinaria nitida, Sinarundinaria nitida*. Evergreen, clump-forming bamboo. H 5m (15ft), S indefinite. Frost hardy. Has small, pointed, mid-green leaves on dark purple stalks and several branches at each node. Stems are often purple with close sheaths.
F. spathacea of gardens. See *F. murieliae*.

Fascicularia

BROMELIACEAE

Genus of evergreen, rosette-forming perennials, grown for their overall appearance. Half hardy. Prefers full light; any well-drained soil is suitable. Water moderately from spring to autumn, sparingly in winter. Propagate by offsets or division in spring.
F. andina. See *F. bicolor*.
F. bicolor, syn. *F. andina*. Evergreen, rosetted perennial forming congested hummocks. H to 45cm (18in), S to 60cm (24in). Has dense rosettes of linear, tapered, arching, mid- to deep green leaves. In summer produces a cluster of tubular, pale blue flowers, surrounded by bright red bracts, at the heart of each mature rosette. Is best grown at not less than 2°C (36°F).

Fat pork tree. See *Clusia major*.

× Fatshedera

ARALIACEAE

Hybrid genus (*Fatsia japonica* 'Moseri' × *Hedera helix* 'Hibernica') of one evergreen, autumn-flowering shrub, grown for its foliage. Is good trained against a wall or pillar or, if supported by canes, grown as a house plant. Frost hardy. Thrives in sun or shade and in fertile, well-drained soil. Propagate by semi-ripe cuttings in summer.
🏆 × ***F. lizei*** illus. p.148. 🏆 **'Variegata'** is an evergreen, mound-forming, loose-branched shrub. H 1.5m (5ft), or more if trained as a climber, S 3m (10ft). Has rounded, deeply lobed, glossy, deep green leaves, narrowly edged with creamy-white. From mid- to late autumn bears sprays of small, white flowers.

Fatsia

ARALIACEAE

Genus of one species of evergreen, autumn-flowering shrub, grown for its foliage, flowers and fruits. Is excellent for conservatories. Frost hardy, but in cold areas shelter from strong winds. Tolerates sun or shade and requires fertile, well-drained soil. May be propagated by semi-ripe cuttings taken in summer or by seed sown in autumn or spring.
🏆 ***F. japonica***, syn. *Aralia japonica, A. sieboldii* (Japanese aralia). Evergreen, rounded, dense shrub. H and S 3m (10ft). Has stout shoots and very large, rounded, deeply lobed, glossy, dark green leaves. In mid-autumn, produces dense clusters of tiny, white flowers, followed by rounded, black fruits.
🏆 **'Variegata'** illus. p.147.
F. papyrifera. See *Tetrapanax papyrifer*.

Faucaria

AIZOACEAE

Genus of clump-forming, stemless, perennial succulents with semi-cylindrical or 3-angled, fleshy, bright green leaves and yellow flowers that open in late afternoons in autumn. Buds and dead flowers may appear orange or red. Frost tender, min. 6°C (43°F). Needs full sun and well-drained soil. Keep dry in winter and water sparingly in spring. Propagate by seed or stem cuttings in spring or summer.
F. tigrina illus. p.495.

Feathergrape hyacinth. See *Muscari comosum* 'Plumosum', illus. p.448.
Feather-top. See *Pennisetum villosum*, illus. p.319.
Feijoa. See *Acca*.

Felicia,
syn. AGATHAEA

COMPOSITAE/ASTERACEAE

Genus of annuals, evergreen sub-shrubs and (rarely) shrubs, grown for their daisy-like, mainly blue flower heads. Fully hardy to frost tender, min. 5–7°C (41–5°F). Requires a position in full sun and well-drained soil. Water potted plants moderately, less when not in full growth; dislikes wet conditions, particularly in low temperatures. Cut off dead flowering stems and cut back straggly shoots regularly. Propagate by seed in spring or by greenwood cuttings in summer or early autumn.
F. amelloides, syn. *Aster capensis* (Blue marguerite). Bushy sub-shrub, grown as an annual. Bears deep green leaves, to 3cm (1¼in) long, and light to deep blue flowers from summer to autumn.
🏆 **'Santa Anita'** illus. p.164.
F. bergeriana illus. p.346.

Fenestraria

AIZOACEAE

Genus of clump-forming, perennial succulents with basal rosettes of fleshy leaves that have grey 'windows' in their flattened tips. Frost tender, min. 6°C (43°F). Needs sun and very well-drained soil. Keep bone dry in winter. Propagate by seed in spring or summer.

F. aurantiaca. See ***F. rhopalophylla*** subsp. ***aurantiaca.***

F. rhopalophylla subsp. ***rhopalophylla.*** Clump-forming, perennial succulent. H 5cm (2in), S 20cm (8in). Forms open cushions of erect, club-shaped, glossy, glaucous to mid-green leaves, each with a flattened tip. Bears daisy-like, white flowers on long stems in late summer and autumn. ♀ subsp. ***aurantiaca*** illus. p.495.

Fennel. See *Foeniculum vulgare*.
Dog's. See *Anthemis*.
Giant. See *Ferula*.
Fennel-leaved pondweed. See *Potamogeton pectinatus*.
Fern.
Asian chain. See *Woodwardia unigemmata*.
Beech. See *Phegopteris connectilis*.
Berry bladder. See *Cystopteris bulbifera*.
Bird's-nest. See *Asplenium nidus*, illus. p.325.
Brittle bladder. See *Cystopteris fragilis*.
Broad buckler. See *Dryopteris dilatata*.
Button. See *Pellaea rotundifolia*.
Chain. See *Woodwardia radicans*.
Christmas. See *Polystichum acrostichoides*.
Cinnamon. See *Osmunda cinnamomea*.
Common stag's-horn. See *Platycerium bifurcatum*, illus. p.322.
Fishtail. See *Cyrtomium falcatum*, illus. p.323.
Foxtail. See *Asparagus densiflorus* 'Myersii', illus. p.275.
Giant holly. See *Polystichum munitum*, illus. p.322.
Giant wood. See *Dryopteris goldieana*.
Golden male. See *Dryopteris affinis*.
Hard. See *Blechnum spicant*.
Hard shield. See *Polystichum aculeatum*.
Hare's-foot. See *Davallia canariensis*.
Hart's-tongue. See *Asplenium scolopendrium*, illus. p.325.
Hen-and-chicken. See *Asplenium bulbiferum*.
Holly. See *Cyrtomium falcatum*, illus. p.323.
Interrupted. See *Osmunda claytoniana*.
Japanese climbing. See *Lygodium japonicum*.
Japanese shield. See *Dryopteris erythrosora*.
Ladder. See *Nephrolepis cordifolia*.
Lady. See *Athyrium filix-femina*.
Liquorice. See *Polypodium glycyrrhiza*, illus. p.322.
Maidenhair. See *Adiantum capillus-veneris*.
Male. See *Dryopteris filix-mas*, illus. p.322.
Marsh. See *Thelypteris palustris*, illus. p.324.
Marsh buckler. See *Thelypteris palustris*, illus. p.324.
Mountain. See *Oreopteris limbosperma*.
Mountain buckler. See *Oreopteris limbosperma*.
Mountain wood. See *Oreopteris limbosperma*.
Narrow buckler. See *Dryopteris carthusiana*.
Northern maidenhair. See *Adiantum pedatum*, illus. p.324.
Oak. See *Gymnocarpium dryopteris*.
Ostrich. See *Matteuccia struthiopteris*, illus. p.324.
Ostrich-feather. See *Matteuccia struthiopteris*, illus. p.324.
Painted. See *Athyrium niponicum*, illus. p.325.
Parsley. See *Cryptogramma crispa*, illus. p.325.
Prickly shield. See *Polystichum aculeatum*.
Royal. See *Osmunda regalis*, illus. p.324.
Rusty-back. See *Asplenium ceterach*, illus. p.323.
Sensitive. See *Onoclea sensibilis*, illus. p.324.
Soft shield. See *Polystichum setiferum*.
Squirrel's-foot. See *Davallia mariesii*.
Stag's-horn. See *Platycerium*.
Sword. See *Nephrolepis cordifolia; Nephrolepis exaltata*, illus. p.324.
Wallich's wood. See *Dryopteris wallichiana*.
Water. See *Azolla filiculoides*, illus. p.464; *Ceratopteris thalictroides*.
Wintergreen. See *Polypodium cambricum*.
Fern-leaf aralia. See *Polyscias filicifolia*, illus. p.148.

Ferocactus

Barrel cactus

CACTACEAE

Genus of slow-growing, spherical, perennial cacti, becoming columnar after many years. Frost tender, min. 5°C (41°F). Needs full sun and very well-drained soil. Propagate by seed in spring or summer. Treat blackened areoles with systemic fungicide and ensure plants have good ventilation.

F. acanthodes of gardens. See *F. cylindraceus*.

F. chrysacanthus. Slow-growing, spherical, perennial cactus. H 1m (3ft), S 60cm (2ft). Green stem, with 15–20 ribs, is fairly densely covered with curved, yellow-white spines. In summer bears funnel-shaped, yellow, rarely red, flowers, 5cm (2in) across, only on plants 25cm (10in) or more in diameter.

F. cylindraceus, syn. *F. acanthodes* of gardens, illus. p.476.

F. hamatacanthus, syn. *Hamatocactus hamatacanthus*, illus. p.480.

F. latispinus. Slow-growing, flattened spherical, perennial cactus. H 20cm (8in), S 40cm (16in). Green stem, with 15–20 ribs, bears broad, hooked, red or yellow spines. Funnel-shaped, pale yellow or red flowers appear in summer on plants over 10cm (4in) wide.

F. setispinus. See *Thelocactus setispinus*.

F. wislizenii. Slow-growing, spherical, perennial cactus. H 2m (6ft), S 1m (3ft). Green stem, with up to 25 ribs, is covered in flattened, fish-hook, usually reddish-brown spines, to 5cm (2in) long. Funnel-shaped, orange or yellow flowers, 6cm (2½in) across, appear in late summer, on plants over 25cm (10in) wide, which should attain this size 10–15 years after raising from seed.

Ferraria

IRIDACEAE

Genus of spring-flowering corms, grown for their curious flowers with 3 large, outer petals and 3 small, inner ones, with very wavy edges. Is unpleasant-smelling to attract flies, which pollinate flowers. Half hardy. Requires full sun and well-drained soil. Plant in autumn, water during winter and dry off after flowering. Dies down in summer. Propagate by division in late summer or by seed in autumn.

F. crispa, syn. *F. undulata*, illus. p.431.

F. undulata. See *F. crispa*.

Ferula

Giant fennel

UMBELLIFERAE/APIACEAE

Genus of mainly summer-flowering perennials, grown for their bold, architectural form. Should not be confused with culinary fennel, *Foeniculum*. Frost hardy. Requires sun and well-drained soil. Propagate by seed when fresh, in late summer.

F. communis illus. p.226.

Fescue, Blue. See *Festuca glauca*.

Festuca

GRAMINEAE/POACEAE

See also GRASSES, BAMBOOS, RUSHES and SEDGES.

F. glauca, syn. *F. ovina* var. *glauca* (Blue fescue). Group of evergreen, tuft-forming, perennial grasses. H and S 10cm (4in). Fully hardy. Bears narrow leaves in various shades of blue-green to silvery-white. Produces unimportant panicles of spikelets in summer. Is good for bed edging. Divide every 2–3 years in spring.

F. ovina var. ***glauca.*** See *F. glauca*.

Fetterbush. See *Pieris floribunda*, illus. p.123.
Mountain. See *Pieris floribunda*, illus. p.123.
Feverfew. See *Tanacetum parthenium*, illus. p.331.

Ficus

MORACEAE

Genus of evergreen or deciduous trees, shrubs and scrambling or root climbers, grown for their foliage and for shade; a few species also for fruit. All bear insignificant clusters of flowers in spring or summer. Frost hardy to frost tender, min. 5–18°C (41–64°F). Prefers full light or partial shade and fertile, well-drained soil. Water potted specimens moderately, very little when temperatures are low. Propagate by seed in spring or by leaf-bud or stem-tip cuttings or air-layering in summer. Red spider mite may be a nuisance. The foliage may cause mild stomach upset if ingested; the sap may irritate skin or aggravate allergies.

F. benghalensis illus. p.68.

♀ ***F. benjamina*** (Weeping fig). Evergreen, weeping tree, often with aerial roots. H and S 18–20m (60–70ft). Frost tender, min. 10°C (50°F). Has slender, oval leaves, 7–13cm (3–5in) long, in lustrous, rich green. **'Variegata'** illus. p.80.

♀ ***F. deltoidea*** illus.p.148.

F. elastica (India rubber tree, Rubber plant). ♀ **'Decora'** is a strong-growing, evergreen, irregularly ovoid tree. H to 30m (100ft), S 15–20m (50–70ft). Frost tender, min. 10°C (50°F). Has broadly oval, leathery, lustrous, deep green leaves, pinkish-bronze when young. ♀ **'Doescheri'** illus. p.68. Leaves of **'Variegata'** are cream-edged, mottled with grey-green.

♀ ***F. lyrata*** (Fiddle-leaf fig). Evergreen, ovoid, robust-stemmed tree. H 15m (50ft) or more, S to 10m (30ft). Frost tender, min. 15–18°C (59–64°F). Fiddle-shaped leaves, 30cm (1ft) or more long, are lustrous, deep green.

F. macrophylla (Australian banyan, Moreton Bay fig). Evergreen, wide-spreading, dense tree with a buttressed trunk when mature. H 20–30m (70–100ft), S 30–40m (100–130ft). Frost tender, min. 15–18°C (59–64°F). Oval leaves, to 20cm (8in) long, are leathery, glossy, deep green.

♀ ***F. pumila***, syn. *F. repens* (Creeping fig). Evergreen, root climber. H 8m (25ft); 1.5m (5ft) as a pot-grown plant. Frost tender, min. 5°C (41°F). Bright green leaves are heart-shaped and 2–3cm (¾–1¼in) long when young, 3–8cm (1¼–3in) long, leathery and oval when mature. Unpalatable fruits are 6cm (2½in) long, orange at first, then flushed red-purple. Only reaches adult stage in very warm regions or under glass. Pinch out branch tips to encourage branching. The young leaves of **'Minima'** are shorter and narrower.

F. religiosa (Bo, Peepul, Sacred fig tree). Mainly evergreen, rounded to wide-spreading tree with prop roots from branches. H and S 20–30m (70–100ft). Frost tender, min. 15–18°C (59–64°F). Leaves, 10–15cm (4–6in) long, are broadly oval to almost triangular with long, thread-like tips, pink-flushed when expanding.

F. repens. See *F. pumila*.

♀ ***F. rubiginosa*** (Port Jackson fig, Rusty-leaved fig). Evergreen, dense-headed tree with a buttressed trunk. H and S 20–30m (70–100ft) or more. Frost tender, min. 15–18°C (59–64°F). Elliptic, blunt-pointed leaves, to 10cm (4in) long, are glossy, dark green above, usually with rust-coloured down beneath.

Fiddle-leaf fig. See *Ficus lyrata*.
Field poppy. See *Papaver rhoeas*.
Fig
Creeping. See *Ficus pumila*.
Devil's. See *Argemone mexicana*, illus. p.347.
Fiddle-leaf. See *Ficus lyrata*.
Hottentot. See *Carpobrotus edulis*.
Indian. See *Opuntia ficus-indica*.
Kaffir. See *Carpobrotus edulis*.
Mistletoe. See *Ficus deltoidea*, illus. p.148.

Moreton Bay. See *Ficus macrophylla*.
Port Jackson. See *Ficus rubiginosa*.
Rusty-leaved. See *Ficus rubiginosa*.
Weeping. See *Ficus benjamina*.
Fig tree, Sacred. See *Ficus religiosa*.
Figwort. See *Scrophularia*.
Water. See *Scrophularia auriculata*.
Filbert. See *Corylus maxima*.

FILIPENDULA
Meadowsweet

ROSACEAE

Genus of spring- and summer-flowering perennials. Fully hardy. Most grow in full sun or partial shade, in moist but well-drained, leafy soil; some species, e.g. *F. rubra*, will thrive in boggy sites. *F. vulgaris* needs a drier site, in full sun. Propagate by seed in autumn or by division in autumn or winter.

F. camtschatica, syn. *F. kamtschatica*. Clump-forming perennial. H to 1.5m (5ft), S 1m (3ft). In mid-summer, produces frothy, flat heads of scented, star-shaped, white or pale pink flowers above large, lance-shaped, divided and cut leaves.
F. hexapetala. See *F. vulgaris*. **'Flore Pleno'** see *F. vulgaris* 'Multiplex'.
F. kamtschatica. See *F. camtschatica*.
F. purpurea illus. p.247.
F. rubra illus. p.225.
F. ulmaria, syn. *Spiraea ulmaria*. **'Aurea'** illus. p.302.
F. vulgaris, syn. *F. hexapetala* (Dropwort). **'Multiplex'** (syn. *F. hexapetala* 'Flore Pleno') is an upright, rosette-forming perennial with fleshy, swollen roots. H 1m (3ft), S 45cm (1½ft). In summer produces flat panicles of rounded, double, white flowers, sometimes flushed pink, above fern-like, finely divided, toothed, hairless, dark green leaves.

Finger-leaved ivy. See *Hedera hibernica* 'Digitata'.
Fir
Balsam. See *Abies balsamea*.
Blue Douglas. See *Pseudotsuga menziesii* var. *glauca*, illus. p.98.
Caucasian. See *Abies nordmanniana*.
Chinese. See *Cunninghamia lanceolata*, illus. p.102.
Delavay's. See *Abies delavayi*.
Douglas. See *Pseudotsuga menziesii*.
Forrest. See *Abies forrestii*, illus. p.101.
Giant. See *Abies grandis*, illus. p.100.
Grand. See *Abies grandis*, illus. p.100.
Greek. See *Abies cephalonica*.
Korean. See *Abies koreana*, illus. p.105.
Nikko. See *Abies homolepis*.
Noble. See *Abies procera*.
Pacific. See *Abies amabilis*.
Silver. See *Abies*.
Subalpine. See *Abies lasiocarpa*.
Veitch. See *Abies veitchii*, illus. p.98.
White. See *Abies concolor*.
Fire lily. See *Lilium bulbiferum*.
Firebush, Chilean. See *Embothrium coccineum*, illus. p.89.
Firecracker
Brazilian. See *Manettia luteorubra*, illus. p.201.
Mexican. See *Echeveria setosa*.
Firecracker vine. See *Manettia cordifolia*.
Firethorn. See *Pyracantha*.
Firewheel tree, Australian. See *Stenocarpus sinuatus*.

FIRMIANA

STERCULIACEAE

Genus of mainly deciduous trees and shrubs, grown for their foliage and to provide shade. Half hardy, but to reach tree proportions needs min. 2–5°C (36–41°F). Requires well-drained but moisture-retentive, fertile soil and full light or partial shade. Water containerized specimens freely when in full growth, less in winter. Pruning is tolerated if necessary. Propagate by seed when ripe or in spring.

F. platanifolia. See *F. simplex*.
F. simplex, syn. *F. platanifolia*, *Sterculia platanifolia*, illus. p.64.

Fish grass. See *Cabomba caroliniana*.
Fishbone cactus. See *Epiphyllum anguliger*, illus. p.477.
Fishpole bamboo. See *Phyllostachys aurea*.
Fishtail fern. See *Cyrtomium falcatum*, illus. p.323.

FITTONIA

ACANTHACEAE

Genus of evergreen, creeping perennials, grown mainly for their foliage. Is useful as ground cover. Frost tender, min. 15°C (59°F). Needs a fairly humid atmosphere. Grow in a shaded position and in well-drained soil; keep well watered but avoid waterlogging, especially in winter. If it becomes too straggly, cut back in spring. Propagate in spring or summer, with extra heat, by division or stem cuttings.

♀ ***F. albivenis* Argyroneura Group**, syn. *F. argyroneura, F. verschaffeltii* var. *argyroneura*, illus. p.312. ♀ **Verschaffeltii Group** (syn. *F. verschaffeltii*) illus. p.314.
F. argyroneura. See *F. albivenis* Argyroneura Group.
F. verschaffeltii. See *F. albivenis* Verschaffeltii Group. var. ***argyroneura*** see *F. albivenis* Argyroneura Group.

FITZROYA

CUPRESSACEAE

See also CONIFERS.
F. cupressoides, syn. *F. patagonica*, illus. p.102.
F. patagonica. See *F. cupressoides*.

Five fingers. See *Pseudopanax arboreus; Syngonium auritum*.
Five-leaved ivy. See *Parthenocissus quinquefolia*.
Five-spot baby. See *Nemophila maculata*, illus. p.331.
Flag
Blue. See *Iris versicolor*, illus. p.237.
Common German. See *Iris germanica*.
Japanese. See *Iris ensata*.
Missouri. See *Iris missouriensis*, illus. p.237.
Myrtle. See *Acorus calamus*.
Siberian. See *Iris sibirica*.
Sweet. See *Acorus calamus*.
Wall. See *Iris tectorum*, illus. p.237.
Yellow. See *Iris pseudacorus*, illus. p.235.
Flaky juniper. See *Juniperus squamata*.
Flame azalea. See *Rhododendron calendulaceum*.
Flame coral tree. See *Erythrina coralloides*.
Flame creeper. See *Tropaeolum speciosum*, illus. p.206.
Flame flower. See *Pyrostegia venusta*, illus. p.216.
Flame nasturtium. See *Tropaeolum speciosum*, illus. p.206.
Flame tree, Illawarra. See *Brachychiton acerifolius*, illus. p.61.
Flame vine. See *Pyrostegia venusta*, illus. p.216.
Flame violet. See *Episcia cupreata*, illus. p.313.
Flame-of-the-forest. See *Spathodea campanulata*, illus. p.67.
Flaming Katy. See *Kalanchoe blossfeldiana*.
Flaming sword. See *Vriesea splendens*, illus. p.273.
Flamingo flower. See *Anthurium scherzerianum*, illus. p.314.
Flannel flower. See *Fremontodendron*.
Flax
Golden. See *Linum flavum*.
Holy. See *Santolina rosmarinifolia*.
Lily. See *Daniella*.
Mountain. See *Phormium cookianum*.
New Zealand. See *Phormium*.
Yellow. See *Linum flavum; Reinwardtia indica*, illus. p.166.
Floating water plantain. See *Luronium natans*.
Floss flower. See *Ageratum*.
Floss silk tree. See *Chorisia speciosa*, illus. p.66.
Flowering banana. See *Musa ornata*, illus. p.232.
Flowering currant. See *Ribes sanguineum*.
Flowering dogwood. See *Cornus florida*.
Flowering gum. See *Eucalyptus ficifolia*.
Flowering quince. See *Chaenomeles*.
Flowering raspberry. See *Rubus odoratus*.
Flowering rush. See *Butomus umbellatus*, illus. p.464.
Flowering tobacco. See *Nicotiana sylvestris*, illus. p.224.
Flower-of-the-hour. See *Hibiscus trionum*, illus. p.332.
Fly honeysuckle. See *Lonicera xylosteum*, illus. p.136.
Flytrap, Venus. See *Dionaea muscipula*, illus. p.317.
Foam of May. See *Spiraea* 'Arguta'.
Foam, Meadow. See *Limnanthes douglasii*, illus. p.348.
Foamflower. See *Tiarella*.

FOENICULUM

UMBELLIFERAE/APIACEAE

Genus of summer-flowering biennials and perennials, some of which are grown for their umbels of yellow flowers. Is also grown for its leaves, which are both decorative in borders and used for culinary flavouring. Fully to frost hardy. Grow in an open, sunny position and in fertile, well-drained soil. Remove flower heads after fading to prevent self seeding. Propagate by seed in autumn.

F. vulgare (Fennel). **'Purpureum'** is an erect, branching perennial. H 2m (6ft), S 45cm (1½ft). Fully hardy. Has very finely divided, hair-like, bronze leaves and, in summer, large, flat umbels of small, yellow flowers.

FONTINALIS
Water moss

SPHAGNACEAE/FONTINALACEAE

Genus of evergreen, perennial, submerged water plants, grown for their foliage, which provides dense cover for fish and a good site for the deposit of spawn. Fully hardy. Grows in sun or semi-shade in streams and other running water; tolerates still water if cool, but then does not grow to full size. Propagate by division in spring.

F. antipyretica (Water moss, Willow moss). Evergreen, perennial, submerged water plant. H 2.5cm (1in), S indefinite. Forms spreading colonies of moss-like, dark olive-green leaves.

Foothill penstemon. See *Penstemon heterophyllus*.
Forget-me-not. See *Myosotis*.
Alpine. See *Myosotis alpestris*, illus. p.382.
Chatham Island. See *Myosotidium*.
Water. See *Myosotis scorpioides*.
Forrest fir. See *Abies forrestii*, illus. p.101.

FORSYTHIA

OLEACEAE

Genus of deciduous, spring-flowering shrubs, grown for their usually profuse, yellow flowers, which are produced before the leaves emerge. *F. × intermedia* 'Beatrix Farrand' and *F. × i.* 'Lynwood' make attractive, flowering hedges. Fully hardy. Prefers a position in full sun and in fertile, well-drained soil. Thin out old shoots and trim hedges immediately after flowering. Propagate by softwood cuttings in summer or by hardwood cuttings in autumn or winter.

***F. × intermedia* 'Arnold Giant'.** Deciduous, bushy shrub. H 1.5m (5ft), S 2.5m (8ft). Has stout shoots and oblong, sharply toothed, mid-green leaves. Large, 4-lobed, deep yellow flowers are produced sparsely from early to mid-spring. **'Beatrix Farrand'** illus. p.131. **'Karl Sax'**, H 2.5m (8ft), is dense-growing, with an abundance of flowers. Some leaves turn red or purple in autumn. ♀ **'Lynwood'**, H 3m (10ft), is very free-flowering, vigorous and upright. **'Minigold'**, H and S 2m (6ft), has oblong, mid-green leaves, and produces masses of small, 4-lobed, yellow flowers from early to mid-spring. **'Spectabilis'** illus. p.130. **'Spring Glory'**, H 2m (6ft), S 1.5m (5ft), has clusters of large, 4-lobed, pale yellow flowers borne in mid-spring and oblong, toothed, bright green leaves.
F. ovata. Deciduous, bushy shrub. H and S 1.5m (5ft). Bears broadly oval, toothed, dark green leaves. Produces small, 4-lobed, bright yellow flowers in early spring. **'Tetragold'** has larger flowers.
F. suspensa illus. p.127.

Fothergilla

HAMAMELIDACEAE

Genus of deciduous, spring-flowering shrubs, grown for their autumn colour and fragrant flowers, each with a dense, bottlebrush-like cluster of stamens, which open before or as leaves emerge. Fully hardy. Grows in sun or semi-shade, but colours best in full sun. Requires moist, peaty, acid soil. Propagate by softwood cuttings taken in summer.

F. gardenii (Witch alder). Deciduous, bushy, dense shrub. H and S 1m (3ft). Produces dense clusters of tiny, fragrant, white flowers that appear from mid- to late spring, usually before broadly oval, dark blue-green leaves emerge. Leaves turn brilliant red in autumn.

♀ ***F. major***, syn. *F. monticola*, illus. p.123.

F. monticola. See *F. major*.

Fountain flower. See *Ceropegia sandersonii*.
Four o' clock flower. See *Mirabilis*.
Foxglove. See *Digitalis*.
Fairy. See *Erinus*.
Mexican. See *Tetranema roseum*, illus. p.315.
Yellow. See *Digitalis grandiflora*.
Foxglove tree. See *Paulownia tomentosa*, illus. p.73.
Foxtail, Golden. See *Alopecurus pratensis* 'Aureovariegatus', illus. p.321.
Foxtail barley. See *Hordeum jubatum*, illus. p.319.
Foxtail fern. See *Asparagus densiflorus* 'Myersii', illus. p.275.
Foxtail lily. See *Eremurus*.
Foxtail millet. See *Setaria italica*.
Fragaria indica. See *Duchesnea indica*.
Fragrant olive. See *Osmanthus fragrans*.
Fragrant snowbell. See *Styrax obassia*.

Frailea

CACTACEAE

Genus of spherical to columnar, perennial cacti with tuberculate ribs. Bears short spines, mostly bristle-like. In summer produces masses of buds, most of which develop into small, spherical, shiny pods without opening. Frost tender, min. 5°C (41°F). Needs partial shade and very well-drained soil. Is not well-adapted to long periods of drought. Propagate by seed in spring or summer.

F. pulcherrima. See *F. pygmaea*.

F. pygmaea, syn. *F. pulcherrima*, illus. p.493.

Francoa

SAXIFRAGACEAE

Genus of summer- and early autumn-flowering perennials. Frost hardy. Needs full sun and fertile, well-drained soil. Propagate by seed or division in spring.

F. appendiculata (Bridal wreath). Clump-forming perennial. H 60cm (24in), S 45cm (18in). Racemes of small, bell-shaped, pale pink flowers, spotted with deep pink at base, appear on graceful, erect stems from summer to early autumn, above oblong to oval, lobed, hairy, crinkled, dark green leaves.

F. sonchifolia. Clump-forming perennial. H 75cm (30in), S 45cm (18in). Bears racemes of cup-shaped, red-marked, pink flowers from summer to early autumn. Lobed leaves each have a large, terminal lobe.

Frangipani. See *Plumeria*.
Native Australian. See *Hymenosporum flavum*.

Franklinia

THEACEAE

Genus of one species of deciduous tree or shrub, grown for its flowers and autumn colour. Fully hardy, but thrives only during hot summers. Needs full sun and moist but well-drained, neutral to acid soil. Propagate by softwood cuttings in summer, by seed in autumn or by hardwood cuttings in early winter.

F. alatamaha. Deciduous, upright tree or shrub. H and S 5m (15ft) or more. Large, shallowly cup-shaped, white flowers with yellow stamens open in late summer and early autumn. Oblong, glossy, bright green leaves turn red in autumn.

Fraxinus

Ash

OLEACEAE

Genus of deciduous trees and shrubs, grown mainly for their foliage of paired leaflets; flowers are usually insignificant. Fully hardy. Requires a position in sun and fertile, well-drained but not too dry soil. Propagate species by seed in autumn, selected forms by budding in summer. Contact with lichens on the bark may aggravate skin allergies.

F. americana (White ash). Fast-growing, deciduous, spreading tree. H 25m (80ft), S 15m (50ft). Leaves are dark green, with 5–9 oval to lance-shaped leaflets, sometimes turning yellow or purple in autumn.

F. angustifolia subsp. ***oxycarpa***, syn. *F. oxycarpa* (Narrow-leaved ash). Deciduous, spreading, elegant tree. H 25m (80ft), S 12m (40ft). Leaves usually consist of 9–11 slender, lance-shaped, glossy, dark green leaflets that are golden-yellow in autumn. ♀ **'Raywood'** (Claret ash) is vigorous, H 20m (70ft), S 15m (50ft). Leaves have 5–7 narrowly oval leaflets that turn bright reddish-purple in autumn.

F. excelsior (Common ash). Vigorous, deciduous, spreading tree. H 30m (100ft), S 20m (70ft). Dark green leaves, with usually 9–11 oval leaflets, sometimes become yellow in autumn. Black leaf buds are conspicuous in winter. f. ***diversifolia*** has leaves that are simple or with only 3 leaflets. Leaves of ♀ **'Jaspidea'** are yellow in spring and turn golden in autumn; shoots are yellow in winter. ♀ **'Pendula'**, H 15m (50ft), S 8–10m (25–30ft), has branches weeping to the ground.

F. mariesii. See *F. sieboldiana*.

♀ ***F. ornus*** illus. p.72.

F. oxycarpa. See *F. angustifolia* subsp. *oxycarpa*.

F. pennsylvanica (Green ash, Red ash). Fast-growing, deciduous, spreading tree. H and S 20m (70ft). Leaves of usually 7 or 9 narrowly oval, dull green leaflets are often velvety beneath, like the shoots, and turn yellow in autumn. **'Patmore'** is disease-resistant, with long-lasting, glossy leaves, but does not bear fruit.

F. sieboldiana, syn. *F. mariesii*. Slow-growing, deciduous, compact-headed tree. H 6m (20ft), S 5m (15ft). Leaves consist of 3–5 oval, dark green leaflets, each on a purple stalk. Produces clusters of small, fragrant, star-shaped, creamy-white flowers in early summer, followed by narrowly oblong, purple fruits.

F. velutina illus. p.76.

Freckle face. See *Hypoestes phyllostachya*, illus. p.272.

Freesia

IRIDACEAE

Genus of winter- and spring-flowering corms, grown for their usually fragrant, funnel-shaped flowers, which are popular for cutting. Half hardy. Requires full sun and well-drained soil. Plant in autumn and water throughout winter. Support with twigs or small canes. Dry off corms after flowering. Plant specially prepared corms outdoors in spring for flowering in summer. Propagate by offsets in autumn or by seed in spring.

F. alba of gardens. See *F. caryophyllacea*.

F. armstrongii. See *F. corymbosa*.

F. caryophyllacea, syn. *F. alba* of gardens, *F. lactea*, *F. refracta* var. *alba*. Late winter- and spring-flowering corm. H 20–30cm (8–12in), S 4–6cm (1½–2½in). Has narrowly sword-shaped, erect leaves in a basal fan. Leafless stems bear loose spikes of very fragrant, white flowers, each 5–8cm (2–3in) long.

F. corymbosa, syn. *F. armstrongii*. Late winter-and spring-flowering corm. H to 30cm (12in), S 4–6cm (1½–2½in). Has narrowly sword-shaped, erect, basal leaves. Flower stem bends horizontally near the top and bears a spike of unscented, upright, pink flowers, 3–3.5cm (1¼–1½in) long, with yellow bases.

***F.* 'Golden Melody'.** Winter- and spring-flowering corm. H to 30cm (12in), S 4–6cm (1½–2½in). Is similar to *F. corymbosa*, but has larger, fragrant flowers, yellow throughout.

F. lactea. See *F. caryophyllacea*.

***F.* 'Oberon'** illus. p.441.

F. refracta var. ***alba.*** See *F. caryophyllacea*.

***F.* 'Romany'.** Winter- and spring-flowering corm. H to 30cm (12in), S 4–6in (1½–2½ in). Is similar to *F. corymbosa*, but has fragrant, double, pale mauve flowers.

***F.* 'White Swan'.** Winter- and spring-flowering corm. H to 30cm (12in), S 4–6cm (1½–2½in). Is similar to *F. corymbosa*, but has very fragrant, white flowers with cream throats.

Fremontia. See *Fremontodendron*.

Fremontodendron,

syn. FREMONTIA

Flannel flower

STERCULIACEAE

Genus of vigorous, evergreen or semi-evergreen shrubs, grown for their large, very showy flowers. Frost hardy, but in cold areas plant against a south- or west-facing wall. Needs full sun and light, not too rich, well-drained soil. In mild areas may be grown as a spreading shrub, but needs firm staking when young. Resents being transplanted. Propagate by semi-ripe cuttings in summer or by seed in autumn or spring. Contact with the foliage and shoots may irritate the skin.

♀ ***F.* 'California Glory'** illus. p.119.

F. californicum. Vigorous, evergreen or semi-evergreen, upright shrub. H 6m (20ft), S 4m (12ft), when grown against a wall. Large, saucer-shaped, bright yellow flowers are borne amid dark green leaves, each with 3 rounded lobes, from late spring to mid-autumn.

F. mexicanum. Vigorous, evergreen or semi-evergreen, upright shrub. H 6m (20ft), S 4m (12ft) when grown against a wall. Dark green leaves have 5 deep, rounded lobes. Bears a profusion of large, saucer-shaped, deep golden-yellow flowers from late spring to mid-autumn.

***F.* 'Pacific Sunset'.** Upright, evergreen shrub. H 5m (15ft), S 3–4m (10–12ft). Rounded, strongly lobed leaves are dark green. In summer produces saucer-shaped, bright yellow flowers, to 6cm (2½in) across, with long, slender-pointed lobes.

French honeysuckle. See *Hedysarum coronarium*, illus. p.254.
French lavender. See *Lavandula dentata; Lavandula stoechas*, illus. p.163.
French marigold. See *Tagetes patula*.
Friendship plant. See *Pilea involucrata*.
Friendship tree. See *Crassula ovata*, illus. p.473.
Fringe tree. See *Chionanthus virginicus*, illus. p.115.
Chinese. See *Chionanthus retusus*.
Fringecups. See *Tellima grandiflora*.
Fringed waterlily. See *Nymphoides peltata*, illus. p.467.

Frithia

AIZOACEAE

Genus of one species of rosette-forming, perennial succulent. Frost tender, min. 10°C (50°F). Needs sun and well-drained soil. Propagate by seed in spring or summer.

♀ ***F. pulchra*** illus. p.489.

Fritillaria

LILIACEAE

Genus of spring-flowering bulbs, grown for their pendent, mainly bell-shaped flowers on leafy stems. Fully to frost hardy; protect smaller, 5–15cm (2–6in) high species in cold frames or cold greenhouses. Needs full sun or partial shade and well-drained soil that dries out slightly in summer when bulbs are dormant but that does not become sunbaked. Grow *F. meleagris*, which is

good for naturalizing in grass, in moisture-retentive soil. Propagate by offsets in summer or by seed in autumn or winter.
♀ ***F. acmopetala*** illus. p.430.
F. bucharica. Spring-flowering bulb. H 10–35cm (4–14in), S 5cm (2in). Frost hardy. Stems each bear scattered, lance-shaped, grey-green leaves and a raceme of up to 10 cup-shaped, green-tinged, white flowers, 1.5–2cm (⅝–¾in) long.
F. camschatcensis illus. p.429.
F. chitralensis illus. p.414.
F. cirrhosa illus. p.430.
F. crassifolia. Spring-flowering bulb. H 10–20cm (4–8in), S 5cm (2in). Frost hardy. Has scattered, lance-shaped, grey leaves. Stems each produce 1–3 bell-shaped, green flowers, 2–2.5cm (¾–1in) long and chequered with brown.
F. delphinensis. See *F. tubiformis*.
F. imperialis illus. p.408. **'Lutea'** is a spring-flowering bulb. H to 1.5m (5ft), S 23–30cm (9–12in). Fully hardy. Leafy stems each bear lance-shaped, glossy, pale green leaves in whorls and a head of up to 5 widely bell-shaped, yellow flowers, 5cm (2in) long, crowned by small, leaf-like bracts. **'Rubra Maxima'** is very robust with red flowers.
F. meleagris illus. p.429.
♀ ***F. michailovskyi.*** Spring-flowering bulb. H 10–20cm (4–8in), S 5cm (2in). Frost hardy. Has lance-shaped, grey leaves scattered on stem. Bears 1–4 bell-shaped, 2–3cm (¾–1¼in) long flowers, coloured purplish-brown with upper third of petals bright yellow.
♀ ***F. pallidiflora*** illus. p.431.
F. persica illus. p.408. ♀ **'Adiyaman'** is a spring-flowering bulb. H to 1.5m (5ft), S 10cm (4in). Frost hardy. Has narrowly lance-shaped, grey leaves along stem. Produces a spike of 10–20 or more narrowly bell-shaped, deep blackish-purple flowers, 1.5–2cm (⅝–¾in) long.
F. pontica illus. p.430.
F. pudica illus. p.450.
♀ ***F. pyrenaica*** illus. p.429.
F. raddeana illus. p.408.
F. recurva illus. p.408.
F. sewerzowii, syn. *Korolkowia sewerzowii*. Spring-flowering bulb. H 15–25cm (6–10in), S 8–10cm (3–4in). Frost hardy. Stems bear scattered, broadly lance-shaped leaves. Produces a spike of up to 10 narrowly bell-shaped, green or metallic purplish-blue flowers, 2.5–3.5cm (1–1½in) long, with flared mouths.
F. tubiformis, syn. *F. delphinensis*. Spring-flowering bulb. H 15–35cm (6–14in), S 5–8cm (2–3in). Frost hardy. Stems carry scattered, narrowly lance-shaped, grey leaves and a solitary, broadly bell-shaped, purplish-pink flower, 3.5–5cm (1½–2in) long, conspicuously chequered and suffused grey outside.
F. verticillata illus. p.408.

Fritillary
Scarlet. See *Fritillaria recurva*, illus. p.408.
Snake's-head. See *Fritillaria meleagris*, illus. p.429.
Yellow. See *Fritillaria pudica*, illus. p.450.
Frogbit. See *Hydrocharis morsus-ranae*, illus. p.462.

FUCHSIA

ONAGRACEAE

Genus of deciduous or evergreen shrubs and trees, grown for their flowers, usually borne from early summer to early autumn. Frost hardy to frost tender, min. 5°C (41°F). If temperature remains above 4°C (39°F), deciduous plants are evergreen, but temperatures above 32°C (90°F) should be avoided. Prolonged low temperatures cause loss of top growth. If top growth dies in winter, cut back to ground level in spring. Needs a sheltered, partially shaded position, except where stated otherwise, and fertile, moist but well-drained soil. When grown as pot plants in a greenhouse, fuchsias also need high-nitrogen feeds and, when flowering, plenty of potash. Propagate by softwood cuttings in any season.

Tubular flowers are almost always pendulous and often bicoloured, with petals of one hue, and a tube and 4 sepals of another. Leaves are oval and mid-green unless otherwise stated. Spherical to cylindrical, usually blackish-purple fruits are edible, but mostly poor-flavoured. Upright types may be trained as compact bushes or standards or, with more difficulty, as pyramids. Lax or trailing plants are good for hanging baskets, but may be trained on trellises; if they are used for summer bedding they require staking. Heights given in descriptions below are of plants grown in frost-free conditions. See also feature panel pp.160–61.

♀ ***F.* 'Alice Hoffman'.** Deciduous, compact shrub. H and S 75cm (2½ft). Frost hardy. Has bronze foliage and small, semi-double flowers with rose-red tubes and sepals and rose-veined, white petals.
♀ ***F.* 'Annabel'** illus. p.160. Deciduous, upright shrub. H 1m (3ft), S 75cm (2½ft). Half hardy. Produces large, double, pink-tinged, creamy-white flowers amid pale green leaves. Makes an excellent standard.
***F.* 'Applause'.** Deciduous, lax, upright shrub. H 30–40cm (12–18in), S 45–60cm (18–24in). Half hardy. Bears very large, double flowers with short, thick, pale carmine tubes, very broad, carmine sepals with a pale central streak, and many, spreading, deep orange-red petals. Produces best colour in shade. Needs staking as a bush, but will trail with weights.
F. arborea. See *F. arborescens*.
F. arborescens, syn. *F. arborea* (Tree fuchsia; illus. p.160). Evergreen, upright tree. H 8m (25ft), S 2.5m (8ft). Frost tender. Foliage is mid- to dark green. Erect heads of tiny, pale mauve to pink flowers, borne year-round, are followed by black fruits with grey-blue bloom. May also be grown as a pot plant.
***F.* 'Auntie Jinks'.** Deciduous, trailing shrub. H 15–20cm (6–8in), S 20–40cm (8–16in). Half hardy. Bears small, single flowers with pink-red tubes, cerise-margined white sepals, and white-shaded purple petals.
♀ ***F.* 'Autumnale'**, syn. *F.* 'Burning Bush' illus. p.160. Deciduous, lax shrub, grown mainly for its foliage. H 2m (6ft), S 50cm (20in). Half hardy. Bears variegated red, gold and bronze leaves. Flowers have red tubes and sepals with reddish-purple petals. Is suitable for a hanging basket or for training as a weeping standard.
F. × bacillaris, syn. *F. parviflora* of gardens illus. p.161. Group of deciduous, lax shrubs. H and S 75cm (2½ft). Frost hardy. Small leaves are mid- to dark green. Bears minute, white, pink or crimson flowers (colour varying according to sun), sometimes followed by glossy, black fruits. Is suitable for a rock garden or hanging basket.
♀ ***F.* 'Ballet Girl'** illus. p.160. Deciduous, upright shrub. H 30–45cm (12–18in), S 45–75cm (18–30in). Half hardy. Produces large, double flowers with bright cerise tubes and sepals, and white petals with cerise veins at the base.
***F.* 'Bicentennial'** illus. p.160. Deciduous, lax shrub. H 30–45cm (12–18in), S 45–60cm (18–24in). Half hardy. Bears medium, double flowers with thin white tubes, orange sepals, and double corollas with magenta centres surrounded by orange petals.
F. boliviana. Fast-growing, deciduous, upright shrub. H 3m (10ft), S 1m (3ft). Frost tender. Has large, soft, grey-green leaves with reddish midribs. Long-tubed, scarlet flowers, bunched at ends of branches, are followed by pleasantly flavoured, black fruits. Needs a large pot and plenty of space to grow well. Resents being pinched back. Is very susceptible to whitefly. ♀ var. ***alba*** (syn. *F.b.* var. *luxurians* 'Alba', *F. corymbiflora* 'Alba'; illus. p.161) has flowers with white tubes and sepals and scarlet petals, followed by green fruits.
***F.* 'Bon Accorde'.** Vigorous, deciduous, upright shrub. H 1.5m (5ft), S 50cm (20in). Half hardy. Small, erect flowers have white tubes and sepals and pale purple petals.
***F.* 'Brookwood Belle'.** Deciduous, lax, bushy shrub with strong, short-jointed stems. H and S 45–60cm (18–24in). Frost hardy. Medium, double flowers have deep cerise tubes and sepals, and white petals flushed pink and veined deep rose-pink.
♀ ***F.* 'Brutus'.** Vigorous, deciduous, upright shrub. H 1.5m (5ft), S 1m (3ft). Frost hardy. Single or semi-double flowers have crimson-red tubes and sepals and deep purple petals.
***F.* 'Burning Bush'.** See *F.* 'Autumnale'.
***F.* 'Cascade'** illus. p.161. Deciduous, trailing shrub. H 2m (6ft), S indefinite. Half hardy. Bears red-tinged, white tubes and sepals and deep carmine petals. Is excellent grown in a hanging basket.
♀ ***F.* 'Celia Smedley'** illus. p.161. Vigorous, deciduous, upright shrub. H 1.5m (5ft), S 1m (3ft). Half hardy. Large, single or semi-double flowers have greenish-white tubes, pale pinkish-white sepals and currant-red petals. Is best when trained as a standard.
♀ ***F.* 'Checkerboard'.** Vigorous, deciduous, upright shrub with strong stems. H 75–90cm (30–36in), S 45–75cm (18–30in). Half hardy. Produces medium, single flowers with slightly recurved, long red tubes, red sepals turning white and white-based, dark red petals.
***F.* 'Cloverdale Pearl'.** Deciduous, upright shrub. H 1m (3ft), S 75cm (2½ft). Half hardy. Foliage is mid-green with crimson midribs. Flowers have pinkish-white tubes, pink-veined, white petals and green-tipped, pink sepals. Is readily trained as a standard.
***F.* 'Coquet Bell'.** Vigorous, deciduous, upright shrub. H 1.5m (5ft), S 1m (3ft). Half hardy. Has a profusion of single or semi-double flowers with pinkish-red tubes and sepals and red-veined, pale mauve petals.
***F.* 'Coralle'**, syn. *F.* 'Koralle' illus. p.161. Deciduous, upright shrub. H and S 1m (3ft). Frost tender. Foliage is velvety and deep green. Salmon-orange flowers, with long, narrow tubes and small sepals and petals, are bunched at branch ends. Is useful for summer bedding and as a specimen plant. Prefers sun.
***F. corymbiflora* 'Alba'.** See *F. boliviana* var. *alba*.
♀ ***F.* 'Dark Eyes'.** Deciduous, bushy, upright shrub. H 45–60cm (18–24in), S 60–75cm (24–30in). Half hardy. Bears medium, double flowers that hold their shape for a long period. The tubes and upturned sepals are deep red, and the petals deep violet-blue.
F. denticulata. Deciduous, straggling shrub. H 4m (12ft), S indefinite. Frost tender. Leaves are glossy, dark green above and reddish-green beneath. Flowers have long, crimson tubes, green-tipped, pale pink sepals and vermilion petals. With good cultivation under glass, flowers appear throughout autumn and winter.
♀ ***F.* 'Display'.** Deciduous, upright shrub. H 1m (3ft), S 75cm (2½ft). Frost hardy. Bears saucer-shaped flowers in shades of pink.
♀ ***F.* 'Dollar Princess'** illus. p.160. Deciduous, upright shrub. H 1m (3ft), S 75cm (2½ft). Frost hardy. Small, double flowers have cerise-red tubes and sepals and purple petals.
***F.* 'Estelle Marie'** illus. p.161. Deciduous, upright shrub. H 1m (3ft), S 50cm (20in). Half hardy. Flowers with white tubes, green-tipped, white sepals and mauve petals are borne above foliage. Is excellent for summer bedding.
♀ ***F.* 'Flash'.** Fast-growing, deciduous, stiffly erect shrub. H 2.5m (8ft), S 50cm (20in). Frost hardy. Produces small, red flowers amid small leaves.
***F.* 'Flirtation Waltz'.** Vigorous, deciduous, upright shrub. H 1m (3ft), S 75cm (2½ft). Half hardy. Has large, double flowers with petals in shades of pink, and white tubes and sepals.
♀ ***F. fulgens*** illus. p.161. Deciduous, upright shrub with tubers. H 2m (6ft), S 1m (3ft). Frost tender. Long-tubed, orange flowers hang in short clusters amid large, pale green leaves and are followed by edible but acidic, green fruits. Tubers may be stored dry for winter. May also be propagated by division of tubers in spring. Is highly susceptible to whitefly.
♀ ***F.* 'Garden News'.** Deciduous, upright shrub with strong stems. H and S 45–60cm (18–24in). Frost hardy (borderline). Medium, double flowers have short, thick, pink tubes, frost-pink sepals and magenta-rose petals becoming rose-pink at the base.
♀ ***F.* 'Genii'.** Deciduous, erect shrub.

H 1.5m (5ft), S 75cm (2½ft). Frost hardy. Has golden-green foliage. Produces small flowers with cerise-red tubes and sepals and reddish-purple petals. Makes a good standard.
***F.* 'Golden Dawn'** illus. p.160. Deciduous, upright shrub. H 1.5m (5ft), S 75cm (2½ft). Half hardy. Flowers are salmon-pink. Is good for training as a standard.
♀ ***F.* 'Golden Marinka'** illus. p.160. Deciduous, trailing shrub. H 2m (6ft), S indefinite. Half hardy. Has red flowers and variegated golden-yellow leaves with red veins. Is excellent for a hanging basket.
***F.* 'Gruss aus dem Bodethal'** illus. p.160. Deciduous, upright shrub. H 1m (3ft), S 75cm (2½ft). Half hardy. Small, single or semi-double, crimson flowers open almost black, becoming larger and paler with age.
***F.* 'Harry Gray'** illus. p.160. Deciduous, lax shrub. H 2m (6ft), S indefinite. Half hardy. Bears a profusion of double flowers with pale pink tubes, green-tipped, white sepals and white to pale pink petals. Is excellent in a hanging basket.
***F.* 'Heidi Weiss',** syn. *F.* 'White Ann' of gardens, *F.* 'White Heidi Ann' of gardens, illus. p.160. Deciduous, upright shrub. H 1m (3ft), S 75cm (2½ft). Half hardy. Has double flowers with red tubes and sepals and cerise-veined, white petals. Is good for training as a standard.
***F.* 'Hula Girl'.** Deciduous, trailing shrub. H 2m (6ft), S indefinite. Half hardy. Bears large, double flowers with deep rose-pink tubes and sepals and pink-flushed, white petals. Does best in a large hanging basket or when trained against a trellis.
♀ ***F.* 'Jack Shahan'** illus. p.160. Vigorous, deciduous, trailing shrub. H 2m (6ft), S indefinite. Half hardy. Has large, pale to deep pink flowers. Is excellent for a hanging basket or for training into a weeping standard or upright against a trellis.
***F.* 'Joy Patmore'.** Vigorous, deciduous, upright shrub. H 1.5m (5ft), S 1m (3ft). Half hardy. Flowers have white tubes, green-tipped, white sepals and cerise petals with white bases. Makes a good standard.
***F.* 'Koralle'.** See *F.* 'Coralle'.
♀ ***F.* 'La Campanella'** illus. p.161. Deciduous, trailing shrub. H 1.5m (5ft), S indefinite. Half hardy. Has small, semi-double flowers with white tubes, pink-flushed, white sepals and cerise-purple petals. Does best in a hanging basket or trained against a trellis.
♀ ***F.* 'Lady Thumb'** illus. p.160. Deciduous, upright, dwarf shrub. H and S 50cm (20in). Frost hardy. Has small, semi-double flowers with reddish-pink tubes and sepals and pink-veined, white petals. May be trained as a miniature standard.
♀ ***F.* 'Lena'.** Deciduous, lax shrub. H and S 1m (3ft). Frost hardy. Bears double flowers with pale pink sepals and tubes and pink-flushed, purple petals. Makes a good standard.
***F.* 'Leonora'** illus. p.160. Vigorous, deciduous, upright shrub. H 1.5m (5ft), S 1m (3ft). Half hardy. Flowers are pink with green-tipped sepals. Is good for training as a standard.
♀ ***F.* 'Love's Reward'** illus. p.161. Deciduous, upright, short-jointed shrub. H and S 30–45cm (12–18in). Half hardy. Small to medium, single flowers have white to pale pink tubes and sepals and violet-blue petals.
♀ ***F.* 'Lye's Unique'** illus. p.161. Vigorous, deciduous, upright shrub. H 1.5m (5ft), S 1m (3ft). Half hardy. Has small flowers with long, white tubes and sepals and orange-red petals. Is excellent for training as a large pyramid.
F. magellanica (Lady's eardrops; illus. p.160). Deciduous, upright shrub. H 3m (10ft), S 2m (6ft). Frost hardy. Small flowers with red tubes, long, red sepals and purple petals are followed by black fruits. **'Alba'** see *F. m.* var. *molinae.* var. ***molinae*** (syn. *F. m.* 'Alba') has very pale pink flowers. var. ***molinae* 'Enstone'** has gold and green, variegated foliage. var. ***molinae* 'Sharpitor'** produces cream and pale green, variegated leaves.
♀ ***F.* 'Margaret Brown'.** Deciduous, free-flowering, upright shrub. H and S 60–90cm (2–3ft). Has strong stems and light green foliage, and bears small, single, 2-tone pink flowers in summer.
♀ ***F.* 'Marinka'.** Deciduous, trailing shrub. H 2m (6ft), S indefinite. Half hardy. Red flowers with darker petals that are folded at outer edges are produced amid dark green leaves with crimson midribs. Foliage becomes discoloured in full sun or cold winds. Is excellent in a hanging basket.
♀ ***F.* 'Micky Goult'.** Vigorous, deciduous, upright shrub. H 1m (3ft), S 75cm (2½ft). Half hardy. Small flowers, with white tubes, pink-tinged, white sepals and pale purple petals, are produced amid pale green foliage.
♀ ***F.* 'Mieke Meursing'.** Deciduous, upright shrub. H 1m (3ft), S 75cm (2½ft). Half hardy. Single to semi-double flowers have red tubes and sepals and pale pink petals with cerise veins.
♀ ***F.* 'Mrs Lovell Swisher'** illus. p.161. Deciduous, upright shrub. H 45–60cm (18–24in), S 30–60cm (12–24in). Half hardy. Produces masses of small, single flowers with flesh-pink tubes, pinkish-white sepals and deep rose-pink petals.
♀ ***F.* 'Mrs Popple'** illus. p.160. Vigorous, deciduous, upright shrub. H 1.5m (5ft), S 75cm (2½ft). Frost hardy. Has flowers with red tubes, overhanging, red sepals and purple petals. In a sheltered area may be grown as a hedge.
***F.* 'Mrs Rundle'.** Vigorous, deciduous, lax shrub. H and S 75cm (2½ft). Frost tender. Produces large flowers with long, pink tubes, green-tipped, pink sepals and vermilion petals. Is good for training as a standard or growing in a large hanging basket.
***F.* 'Nancy Lou'.** Vigorous, deciduous, upright shrub. H and S 1m (3ft). Half hardy. Large, double flowers have pink tubes, upright, green-tipped, pink sepals and bright white petals.
♀ ***F.* 'Nellie Nuttall'** illus. p.160. Vigorous, deciduous, upright shrub. H 1m (3ft), S 75cm (2½ft). Half hardy. Flowers, with rose-red tubes and sepals and white petals, are borne well above foliage. Is especially suitable for summer bedding; is also good as a standard.
***F.* 'Other Fellow'** illus. p.160. Deciduous, upright shrub. H 1.5m (5ft), S 75cm (2½ft). Half hardy. Has small flowers with white tubes and sepals and pink petals.
***F.* 'Pacquesa'.** Vigorous, deciduous, upright shrub. H 1m (3ft), S 75cm (2½ft). Half hardy. Has flowers with deep red tubes and sepals and red-veined, white petals. Is good for training as a standard.
F. parviflora of gardens. See *F.* × *bacillaris*.
***F.* 'Peppermint Stick'** illus. p.160. Deciduous, upright shrub. H 1.5m (5ft), S 1m (3ft). Half hardy. Large, double flowers have carmine-red tubes and sepals and pink-splashed, purple petals. Makes a good standard.
♀ ***F.* 'Phyllis'.** Deciduous, upright shrub. H 2m (6ft), S 1m (3ft). Frost hardy. Single to semi-double flowers, with rose-red tubes and sepals and crimson petals, are followed by masses of black fruits. In a sheltered area may be grown as a hedge.
***F.* 'Pink Fantasia'.** Deciduous, stiff, upright shrub. H 30–40cm (12–18in), S 45–60cm (18–24in). Half hardy. Bears single, upward-looking flowers, in profusion, with white tubes and sepals blushed dark pink, and dark purple petals, veined pink, with white bases. Is excellent for borders or pots.
***F.* 'Pink Galore'** illus. p.160. Deciduous, trailing shrub. H 1.5m (5ft), S indefinite. Half hardy. Has large, double, pale pink flowers. Grows best in a large hanging basket or when trained against a trellis.
F. procumbens illus. p.161. Deciduous, prostrate shrub. H 10cm (4in), S indefinite. Half hardy. Produces tiny, erect, petalless, yellow-tubed flowers with purple sepals and bright blue pollen. Has small, dark green leaves and large, red fruits. Suits a rock garden as well as a hanging basket. Encourage flowering by root restriction or growing in poor, sandy soil.
***F.* 'Red Spider'** illus. p.160. Deciduous, trailing shrub. H 1.5m (5ft), S indefinite. Half hardy. Has long, red flowers with long, narrow, spreading sepals and darker petals. Is best in a large hanging basket or when trained against a trellis.
♀ ***F.* 'Riccartonii'** illus. p.160. Deciduous, stiff, upright shrub. H 2m (6ft), S 1.5m (5ft). Frost hardy, but, with good drainage and wind protection, is sometimes fully hardy. Has small flowers with red tubes, broad, overhanging, red sepals and purple petals. In a sheltered area may be grown as a hedge. Many plants sold under name of *F.* 'Riccartonii' are lax hybrids of *F. magellanica*.
***F.* 'Rose Fantasia'.** Deciduous, stiff, upright shrub. H 30–40cm (12–18in), S 45–60cm (18–24in). Half hardy. Produces single, upward-looking flowers, in profusion, with rose-pink tubes, dark rose-pink sepals with green tips and red-purple petals, veined rose-pink. Is excellent plant for either borders or pots.
♀ ***F.* 'Rose of Castile'** illus. p.161. Vigorous, deciduous, upright shrub. H 1.5m (5ft), S 1m (3ft). Frost hardy. Produces small flowers with white tubes, green-tipped, white sepals and purple-flushed, pink petals. Makes a good standard.
***F.* 'Rough Silk'.** Vigorous, deciduous, trailing shrub. H 2m (6ft), S indefinite. Half hardy. Bears large flowers with pink tubes, long, spreading, pink sepals and wine-red petals. Grows best in a large hanging basket or when trained against a trellis.
♀ ***F.* 'Royal Velvet'.** Vigorous, deciduous, upright shrub. H 1.5m (5ft), S 75cm (2½ft). Half hardy. Has large, double flowers with red tubes and sepals and deep purple petals, splashed deep pink. Is an excellent standard.
♀ ***F.* 'Rufus'** illus. p.160. Vigorous, deciduous, upright shrub. H 1.5m (5ft), S 75cm (2½ ft). Half hardy. Has a profusion of small, bright red flowers. Is easily trained as a standard.
***F.* 'Shelford'.** Deciduous, upright, short-jointed shrub. H 35–50cm (14–20in), S 45–60cm (18–24in). Half hardy. Bears masses of medium-sized, single flowers with slightly fluted, baby-pink tubes, long, narrow, baby-pink sepals and white petals with slight pink veining at the base. Suitable for all forms of training.
♀ ***F. splendens.*** Deciduous, upright shrub. H 2m (6ft), S 1m (3ft). Half hardy. Small flowers, with broad, orange tubes, pinched in their middles, and short, green sepals and petals, appear in spring amid pale green foliage. Is very susceptible to whitefly.
***F.* 'Strawberry Delight'.** Deciduous, lax shrub. H and S 1m (3ft). Half hardy. Leaves are yellowish-green and slightly bronzed. Large, double flowers have red tubes and sepals and pink-flushed, white petals. Is excellent as a standard or hanging basket plant.
♀ ***F.* 'Swingtime'** illus. p.160. Vigorous, deciduous, lax shrub. H and S 1m (3ft). Half hardy. Has large, double flowers with red tubes and sepals and red-veined, creamy-white petals. Makes a good standard or hanging basket plant.
***F.* 'Texas Longhorn'.** Deciduous, lax shrub. H and S 75cm (2½ft). Half hardy. Very large, double flowers have red tubes, long, spreading, red sepals and cerise-veined, white petals. Grow as a standard or in a hanging basket.
♀ ***F.* 'Thalia'** illus. p.161. Deciduous, upright shrub. H and S 1m (3ft). Frost tender. Foliage is dark maroon and velvety. Long, slender flowers, with long, red tubes, small, red sepals and small, orange-red petals, are bunched at ends of branches. Makes an excellent specimen plant in summer bedding schemes. Prefers full sun.
F. thymifolia. Deciduous, lax shrub. H and S 1m (3ft). Half hardy. Has pale green foliage and a few minute, greenish-white flowers that age to purplish-pink. Bears black fruits on female plants if pollen-bearing plants of this species or of *F.* × *bacillaris* are also grown.
♀ ***F.* 'Tom Thumb'** illus. p.160. Deciduous, upright shrub. H and S 50cm (20in). Frost hardy. Bears small flowers with red tubes and sepals and mauve-purple petals. May be trained as a miniature standard.
***F.* 'Tom West'** illus. p.161. Deciduous, upright, lax shrub. H and S 30–60cm (12–24in). Half hardy. Has green and cream variegated foliage and small, single flowers with red tubes and

sepals, and purple petals.
F. triphylla. Deciduous, upright shrub, sometimes confused with *F.* 'Thalia'. H and S 50cm (20in). Frost tender. Spikes of narrow, long-tubed, bright reddish-orange flowers, with small petals and sepals, are borne above dark bronze-green leaves that are purple beneath. Is very difficult to grow.
***F.* 'White Ann'** of gardens. See *F.* 'Heidi Weiss'.
***F.* 'White Heidi Ann'** of gardens. See *F.* 'Heidi Weiss'.

Fuchsia, Tree. See *Fuchsia arborescens*, illus. p.160.
Full moon maple. See *Acer japonicum*.

FURCRAEA

AGAVACEAE

Genus of perennial succulents with basal rosettes of sword-shaped, fleshy, toothed leaves; rosettes die after flowering. Resembles *Agave*, but has short-tubed flowers. Frost tender, min. 6°C (43°F). Requires a sunny position and well-drained soil. Propagate by bulbils, borne on lower stems, when developed.
F. foetida, syn. *F. gigantea.* Basal-rosetted, perennial succulent. H 3m (10ft), S 5m (15ft). Has broadly sword-shaped, fleshy, mid-green leaves, to 2.5m (8ft) long, with edges toothed only at the base. Flower stems, to 8m (25ft), bear scented, bell-shaped, green flowers, white within, in summer. **'Mediopicta'** (syn. *F.f.* var. *mediopicta, F.f.* 'Variegata') illus. p.476.
F. gigantea. See *F. foetida*.sepals, and purple petals.
F. gigantea. See *F. foetida*.

GAGEA

LILIACEAE

Genus of spring-flowering bulbs, grown for their clusters of funnel- or star-shaped, white or yellow flowers. Is suitable for rock gardens. Frost to half hardy. Prefers full light and well-drained soil that does not become too hot and dry. Dies down in summer. Propagate by division in spring or autumn or by seed in autumn.
G. graeca, syn. *Lloydia graeca*. Spring-flowering bulb. H 5–10cm (2–4in), S 3–5cm (1¼–2in). Half hardy. Thread-like, semi-erect leaves form at ground level and on wiry stems. Bears up to 5 widely funnel-shaped, purple-veined, white flowers, 1–1.5cm (½–⅝in) long.
G. peduncularis. Spring-flowering bulb. H 5–15cm (2–6in), S 2.5–5cm (1–2in). Frost hardy. Has thread-like, semi-erect leaves at base and on stem. Produces a loose head of flat, star-shaped, yellow flowers, each 1.5–3cm (⅝–1¼in) across, with green stripes outside.

GAILLARDIA
Blanket flower

COMPOSITAE/ASTERACEAE

Genus of summer-flowering annuals and perennials that tend to be short-lived. Fully to frost hardy. Requires sun and prefers well-drained soil. May need staking. Propagate species by seed in autumn or spring, selected forms by root cuttings in winter.
G. aristata illus. p.303.
♀ ***G. × grandiflora* 'Dazzler'** illus. p.293. **'Wirral Flame'** is a clump-forming, short-lived perennial. H 60cm (24in), S 50cm (20in). Fully hardy. Produces large, terminal, daisy-like, deep cardinal-red flower heads during summer. Leaves are lance-shaped, lobed and soft green.
G. pulchella. Moderately fast-growing, upright annual or short-lived perennial. H 45cm (18in), S 30cm (12in). Fully hardy. Has lance-shaped, hairy, greyish-green leaves and, in summer, daisy-like, double, crimson-zoned, yellow, pink or red flower heads.
'Lollipops' illus. p.350.

GALANTHUS
Snowdrop

AMARYLLIDACEAE

Genus of bulbs, grown for their pendent, white flowers, one on each slender stem between 2 basal leaves. Is easily recognized by its 3 large, outer petals and 3 small, inner ones forming a cup, which is green-marked. Fully to frost hardy. Needs a cool, partially shaded position and humus-rich, moist soil. Do not allow bulbs to dry out excessively. Propagate by division in spring after flowering or in late summer or autumn when bulbs are dormant. All parts may cause mild stomach upset if ingested; contact with the bulbs may irritate skin.
♀ ***G.* 'Atkinsii'** illus. p.455.
♀ ***G. elwesii*** illus. p.455.
G. gracilis, syn. *G. graecus* of gardens, illus. p.455.
G. graecus of gardens. See *G. gracilis*.
G. ikariae, illus. p.456.
♀ ***G. nivalis*** (Common snowdrop). Late winter- and early spring-flowering bulb. H 10–15cm (4–6in), S 5–8cm (2–3in). Fully hardy. Produces narrowly strap-shaped, semi-erect, basal, grey-green leaves. Flowers are 2–2.5cm (¾–1in) long with a green mark at the tip of each inner petal. ♀ **'Flore Pleno'** illus. p.455. **'Lutescens'** see *G.n.* 'Sandersii'.**'Pusey Green Tip'** illus. p.455. **'Sandersii'** (syn. *G.n.* 'Lutescens') illus. p.456. **'Scharlockii'** illus. p.456.
♀ ***G. plicatus*** subsp. ***plicatus.*** Late winter- and early spring-flowering bulb. H 10–20cm (4–8in), S 5–8cm (2–3in). Fully hardy. Bears broadly strap-shaped, semi-erect, basal, deep green leaves that have grey bands along the centres and reflexed margins. White flowers, 2–3cm (¾–1¼in) long, have a green patch at the tip of each inner petal. ♀ subsp. ***byzantinus*** illus. p.456.
G. reginae-olgae (Autumn snowdrop). Autumn-flowering bulb. H 10–20cm (4–8in), S 5cm (2in). Frost hardy. Has 1.5–2.5cm (⅝–1in) long flowers, with a green patch at the apex of each inner petal, before or just as narrowly strap-shaped, deep green leaves, each with a central, grey stripe, appear.
G. rizehensis illus. p.455.

GALAX

DIAPENSIACEAE

Genus of one species of evergreen perennial, grown for its foliage and for its flowers borne in late spring and summer. Is useful for underplanting shrubs. Fully hardy. Needs shade and moist, peaty, acid soil. Propagate by division of rooted runners in spring.
G. aphylla. See *G. urceolata*.
G. urceolata, syn. *G. aphylla*, illus. p.363.

GALEGA
Goat's rue

LEGUMINOSAE/PAPILIONACEAE

Genus of summer-flowering perennials. Fully hardy. Grow in an open, sunny position and in any well-drained soil. Requires staking. Propagate by seed in autumn or by division in winter.
***G.* 'Her Majesty'.** See *G.* 'His Majesty'.
***G.* 'His Majesty'**, syn. *G.* 'Her Majesty'. Vigorous, upright perennial. H to 1.5m (5ft), S 1m (3ft). In summer produces spikes of small, pea-like, clear lilac-mauve and white flowers. Bold, oblong to lance-shaped leaves consist of oval leaflets.
***G.* 'Lady Wilson'** illus. p.226.
G. orientalis illus. p.258.

Galingale. See *Cyperus longus*.

GALIUM
Bedstraw

RUBIACEAE

Genus of spring- and summer-flowering perennials, many of which are weeds; *G. odoratum* is cultivated as ground cover. Fully hardy. Grows well in partial shade, but tolerates sun and thrives in any well-drained soil. Propagate by division in early spring or autumn.
G. odoratum, syn. *Asperula odorata*, illus. p.285.

GALTONIA

LILIACEAE/HYACINTHACEAE

Genus of summer- and autumn-flowering bulbs, grown for their elegant spikes of pendent, funnel-shaped, white or green flowers. Frost hardy. Needs a sheltered, sunny site and fertile, well-drained soil that does not dry out in summer. Dies down in winter. May be lifted for replanting in spring. Propagate by seed in spring or by offsets in autumn or spring.
♀ ***G. candicans*** illus. p.409.
G. viridiflora illus. p.414.

Gandergoose. See *Orchis morio*, illus. p.310.
Garden loosestrife. See *Lysimachia punctata*, illus. p.261.
Gardener's garters. See *Phalaris arundinacea* var. *picta*, illus. p.318.

GARDENIA

RUBIACEAE

Genus of evergreen shrubs and trees, grown for their flowers and foliage. Frost tender, min. 15°C (59°F). Prefers partial shade and humus-rich, well-drained, neutral to acid soil. Water containerized specimens freely when in full growth, moderately at other times. After flowering, shorten strong shoots to maintain a shapely habit. Propagate by greenwood cuttings in spring or by semi-ripe cuttings in summer. Whitefly and mealy bug may cause problems.
♀ ***G. augusta***, syn. *G. florida, G. grandiflora, G. jasminoides* (Cape jasmine, Common gardenia). **'Veitchii'** illus. p.154.
G. capensis. See *Rothmannia capensis*.
G. florida. See *G. augusta*.
G. grandiflora. See *G. augusta*.
G. jasminoides. See *G. augusta*.
G. rothmannia. See *Rothmannia capensis*.
G. thunbergia. Evergreen, bushy shrub with white stems. H and S to 2m (6ft) or more. Has elliptic, glossy, deep green leaves. Fragrant, 7–9-petalled, white flowers, 6–10cm (2½–4in) wide, are borne in winter-spring.

Gardenia, Common. See *Gardenia augusta*.
Garland flower. See *Hedychium*.

GARRYA

GARRYACEAE

Genus of evergreen shrubs and trees, grown for their catkins in winter and spring, which are longer and more attractive on male plants. Frost hardy. Hard frosts may damage catkins. Requires a sheltered, sunny site and tolerates any poor soil. Is suitable for a south- or west-facing wall. Dislikes being transplanted. Propagate by semi-ripe cuttings in summer.
G. elliptica illus. p.121. ♀ **'James Roof'** is an evergreen, bushy, dense shrub. H and S 4m (12ft). Has oval, wavy-edged, leathery, dark green leaves. Very long, grey-green catkins, with yellow anthers, are borne from mid- or late winter to early spring.

GASTERIA

LILIACEAE/ALOACEAE

Genus of perennial succulents with thick, fleshy leaves, usually arranged in a fan, later becoming a tight rosette. Frost tender, min. 5°C (41°F). Is easy to grow, needing sun or partial shade and very well-drained soil. Propagate by seed, leaf cuttings or division in spring or summer.
G. bicolor var. ***bicolor***, syn. *G. caespitosa*. Fan-shaped, perennial succulent. H 15cm (6in), S 30cm (12in). Produces triangular, thick, dark green leaves, 15cm (6in) long, with horny borders. Upper leaf surfaces have numerous white or pale green dots, usually in diagonal rows. Bears spikes of bell-shaped, orange-green flowers in spring. var. ***liliputana***, syn. *G. liliputana*, illus. p.496.
G. caespitosa. See *G. bicolor* var. *bicolor*.
G. carinata var. ***verrucosa,*** syn. *G.verrucosa*, illus. p.496.
G. liliputana. See *G. bicolor* var. *liliputana*.
G. verrucosa. See *G. carinata* var. *verrucosa*.

× *Gaulnettya* 'Pink Pixie'. See *Gaultheria × wisleyensis* 'Pink Pixie'.
× *Gaulnettya* 'Wisley Pearl'. See *Gaultheria × wisleyensis* 'Wisley Pearl'.

GAULTHERIA

ERICACEAE

Genus of evergreen shrubs and sub-shrubs, grown for their foliage, flowers and fruits. Fully to half hardy. Grows best in shade or semi-shade and requires moist, peaty, acid soil. Will tolerate sun provided soil is permanently moist. Propagate by semi-ripe cuttings in summer or by seed in autumn; for *G. shallon* and *G. trichophylla* propagate by division in autumn or spring. All parts may cause mild stomach upset if ingested, except the fruits, which are edible.
♀ ***G. cuneata*** illus. p.372.
G. forrestii. Evergreen, rounded shrub. H and S 1.5m (5ft). Half hardy. Has oblong, glossy, dark green leaves and racemes of small, fragrant, rounded, white flowers, in spring, followed by rounded, blue fruits.
G. miqueliana. Evergreen, compact shrub. H and S 25cm (10in). Frost hardy. Has oval, leathery leaves clothing stiff stems. In late spring produces bell-shaped, pink-tinged, white flowers, up to 6 per stem, followed by rounded, white or pink fruits.
G. mucronata, syn. *Pernettya*

mucronata. Evergreen, bushy, dense shrub, spreading by underground stems. H and S 1.2m (4ft). Fully hardy. Oval, prickly, glossy, dark green leaves set off tiny, urn-shaped, white flowers in late spring and early summer. Has spherical, fleshy fruit varying in colour between cultivars. Sprays of fruit are good for indoor display. Fruits of **'Cherry Ripe'** (female) are large and bright cherry-red. **'Edward Balls'** (male) bears stout, upright, red shoots and sharply spined, bright green leaves. ♀ **'Mulberry Wine'** (female) illus. p.170. ♀ **'Wintertime'** (female) illus. p.169.
G. myrsinoides, syn. *G. prostrata, Pernettya prostrata.* Evergreen, spreading shrub. H 15–30cm (6–12in), S 30cm (12in) or more. Fully hardy. Bears oval, leathery, dark green leaves. Urn-shaped, white flowers are produced in early summer and are followed by large, rounded, blue-purple fruits. Is suitable for a rock garden or peat bed.
G. nummularioides. Evergreen, compact shrub. H 10–15cm (4–6in), S 20cm (8in). Frost hardy. Leaves are oval to heart-shaped and leathery. Egg-shaped, pink-flushed, white flowers are produced from the upper leaf axils in late spring or summer. Produces rounded, blue-black fruits, but only rarely.
♀ ***G. procumbens*** illus. p.399.
G. prostrata. See *G. myrsinoides.*
G. pumila, syn. *Pernettya pumila.* Evergreen, mat-forming, creeping shrub. H 5cm (2in), S 30–60cm (12–24in). Fully hardy. Prostrate branches bear tiny, bell-shaped, white flowers in early summer among tiny, rounded, leathery leaves. Rounded fruits are pink or white. Is good for a rock garden or peat bed.
G. shallon illus. p.158.
G. tasmanica, syn. *Pernettya tasmanica.* Evergreen, mat-forming shrub. H 5–8cm (2–3in), S 20cm (8in). Frost hardy. Has oval, toothed, leathery leaves with wavy edges. Bell-shaped, white flowers in early summer are followed by rounded, red fruits. Is good for a rock garden or peat bed.
G. trichophylla. Evergreen, compact shrub with creeping, underground stems. H 7–15cm (3–6in), S 20cm (8in). Frost hardy. Bell-shaped, pink flowers in early summer are followed by egg-shaped, blue fruits produced from leaf axils. Leaves are small and oval.
***G. × wisleyensis* 'Pink Pixie',** syn. × *Gaulnettya* 'Pink Pixie'. Evergreen, dense, bushy shrub. H and S 1m (3ft). Bears broadly oval, deeply veined, dark green leaves. Small, urn-shaped, pale pink flowers, produced in late spring and early summer, are followed by spherical, purplish-red fruits. **'Wisley Pearl'**, syn. × *Gaulnettya* 'Wisley Pearl', illus. p.150.

GAURA

ONAGRACEAE

Genus of summer-flowering annuals and perennials that are sometimes short-lived. Fully hardy. Prefers full sun and light, well-drained soil. Propagate by softwood or semi-ripe cuttings in summer or by seed in autumn or spring.
♀ ***G. lindheimeri.*** Bushy perennial. H 1.2m (4ft), S 1m (3ft). In summer produces racemes of tubular, pink-suffused, white flowers. Leaves are lance-shaped and mid-green.

Gay feather, Kansas. See *Liatris pycnostachya.*
Gay feathers. See *Liatris.*
Gean. See *Prunus avium*, illus. p.67.

GAYLUSSACIA
Huckleberry

ERICACEAE

Genus of deciduous occasionally evergreen shrubs, grown for their flowers, fruits and autumn colour. Fully hardy. Needs sun or semi-shade and moist, peaty, acid soil. Propagate by softwood cuttings in summer or by seed in autumn.
G. baccata (Black huckleberry). Deciduous, bushy shrub. H and S 1m (3ft). Oval, sticky, dark green leaves redden in autumn. Produces clusters of small, urn-shaped, dull red flowers in late spring, then edible, spherical, black fruits.

GAZANIA

COMPOSITAE/ASTERACEAE

Genus of evergreen perennials, often grown as annuals and useful for summer bedding, pots and tubs. Half hardy. Requires sun and sandy soil. Propagate by seed in spring or by heel cuttings in spring or summer.
***G.* Daybreak Series.** Carpeting perennial, grown as an annual. H and S 20cm (8in). Has lance-shaped leaves and, in summer, large, daisy-like flower heads in a mixture of orange, yellow, pink, bronze and white. Flowers remain open in dull weather.
G. pinnata. Mat-forming perennial. H 15cm (6in), S 30cm (12in). Daisy-like, orange-red flower heads, with central, black rings, appear singly in early summer above oval, finely cut, hairy, bluish-grey leaves.
♀ ***G. rigens*** var. ***uniflora,*** syn. *G. uniflora*, illus. p.304.
♀ ***G.* Talent Series.** Vigorous perennials. H and S to 25cm (10in). Have highly ornamental, mid-green leaves, to 15cm (6in) long, grey-felted on both surfaces. In summer produce solitary, yellow, orange, pink or brown flower heads on short stems just above the leaves.
G. uniflora. See *G. rigens* var. *uniflora.*

GELSEMIUM

LOGANIACEAE

Genus of evergreen, twining climbers, grown for their fragrant, jasmine-like flowers. Half hardy. In cool climates best grown under glass. Provide full light and fertile, well-drained soil. Water regularly, less in cold weather. Stems require support and should be thinned out after flowering or in spring. Propagate by seed in spring or by semi-ripe cuttings in summer.
♀ ***G. sempervirens*** illus. p.202.

GENISTA
Broom

LEGUMINOSAE/PAPILIONACEAE

Genus of deciduous, sometimes almost leafless, shrubs and trees, grown for their mass of small, pea-like flowers. Fully to half hardy. Does best in full sun and not over-rich, well-drained soil. Resents being transplanted. Propagate species by softwood or semi-ripe cuttings in summer or by seed in autumn, selected forms by softwood cuttings only in summer.
♀ ***G. aetnensis*** illus. p.89.
G. cinerea illus. p.119.
♀ ***G. delphinensis***, syn. *Chamaespartium sagittale* subsp. *delphinense, G. sagittalis* subsp. *delphinensis.* Deciduous, prostrate shrub. H 1cm (½in), S 20cm (8in). Frost hardy. Has tangled, winged branches, covered with minute, oval, dark green leaves. Masses of golden-yellow flowers are produced along stems in early summer. Suitable for a rock garden or wall.
G. fragrans of gardens. See *Cytisus × spachianus.*
G. hispanica illus. p.166.
♀ ***G. lydia*** illus. p.371.
G. monosperma. See *Retama monosperma.*
G. pilosa. Deciduous, domed shrub. H and S 30cm (12in). Fully hardy. Narrowly oval leaves are silky-haired beneath. Bright yellow flowers on short stalks are borne in leaf axils in summer. Is useful on a bank or as ground cover. Propagate by semi-ripe cuttings in summer.
G. sagittalis, syn. *Chamaespartium sagittale*, illus. p.398. subsp. ***delphinensis.*** See *G. delphinensis.*
G. × spachiana. See *Cytisus × spachianus.*
♀ ***G. tenera* 'Golden Shower'.** Vigorous, deciduous, arching shrub. H 3m (10ft), S 5m (15ft). Frost hardy. Narrowly oblong leaves are grey-green. Bears racemes of fragrant, golden-yellow flowers in early to mid-summer.
G. tinctoria illus. p.153. ♀ **'Royal Gold'** is a deciduous, upright shrub. H and S 1m (3ft). Fully hardy. Produces long, conical panicles of golden-yellow flowers in spring-summer and leaves that are narrowly lance-shaped and dark green.

Gentian. See *Gentiana.*
Great yellow. See *Gentiana lutea*, illus. p.361.
Spring. See *Gentiana verna*, illus. p.382.
Stemless. See *Gentiana acaulis*, illus. p.382.
Trumpet. See *Gentiana clusii.*
Willow. See *Gentiana asclepiadea*, illus. p.271.

GENTIANA
Gentian

GENTIANACEAE

Genus of annuals, biennials and perennials, some of which are semi-evergreen or evergreen, grown for their usually blue flowers. Is excellent for rock gardens and peat beds. Fully hardy. Prefers sun or semi-shade and humus-rich, well-drained, moist, neutral to acid soil. Some species grow naturally on limestone soils. Propagate by division or offshoots in spring or by seed in autumn. Divide autumn-flowering species and *G. clusii* every 3 years in early spring and replant in fresh soil.
♀ ***G. acaulis***, syn. *G. excisa, G. kochiana*, illus. p.382.
G. angustifolia. Evergreen, clump-forming perennial. H 10cm (4in), S 20cm (8in). Has rosettes of oblong, dull green leaves and, in summer, solitary, tubular, sky-blue flowers on 7cm (3in) stems. Tolerates alkaline soils.
♀ ***G. asclepiadea*** illus. p.271.
G. clusii (Trumpet gentian). Evergreen, clump-forming perennial. H 5cm (2in), S 15–23cm (6–9in). Has rosettes of oval, glossy, dark green leaves. Trumpet-shaped, azure-blue flowers,with green-spotted, paler throats, areborne on 2.5–10cm (1–4in) stems in early summer. Tolerates alkaline soils.
G. excisa. See *G. acaulis.*
G. gracilipes. Semi-evergreen, tufted perennial with arching stems. H 15cm (6in), S 20cm (8in). Forms a central rosette of long, strap-shaped, dark green leaves from which lax flower stems bearing tubular, dark purplish-blue flowers, greenish within, are produced in summer. Tolerates some shade.
G. kochiana. See *G. acaulis.*
G. lutea illus. p.261.
***G. × macaulayi* 'Wells's Variety',** syn. *G.* 'Wellsii', illus. p.399.
G. ornata. Semi-evergreen, clump-forming perennial with small, over-wintering rosettes. H 5cm (2in), S 10cm (4in). Forms a central rosette of grass-like leaves. In autumn, each stem tip carries an upright, bell-shaped, mid-blue flower, with a white throat and deep blue stripes shading to creamy-white outside. Requires acid soil and a moist atmosphere.
G. saxosa illus. p.386.
♀ ***G. septemfida*** illus. p.348.
♀ ***G. sino-ornata*** illus. p.399.
***G.* 'Susan Jane'.** Vigorous, semi-evergreen, spreading perennial with small, overwintering rosettes. H 5cm (2in), S 30cm (12in). Prostrate stems bear grass-like leaves. Large, trumpet-shaped, white-throated, deep blue flowers, greenish within, appear in autumn. Requires acid soil.
G. verna illus. p.382.
***G.* 'Wellsii'.** See *G. × macaulayi* 'Wells's Variety'.

Geraldton waxflower. See *Chamelaucium uncinatum*, illus. pp.145 and 146.

GERANIUM
Cranesbill

GERANIACEAE

Genus of perennials, some of which are semi-evergreen, grown for their flowers and often as ground cover. Compact species are suitable for rock gardens. Fully to half hardy. Most species prefer sun, but some do better in shade. Will grow in all but waterlogged soils. Propagate by semi-ripe cuttings in summer or by seed or division in autumn or spring. Cultivars should be propagated by division or cuttings only.

G. anemonifolium. See *G. palmatum.*
♀ ***G.* 'Ann Folkard'.** Spreading perennial. H 50cm (20in), S 1m (36in). Fully hardy. Has rounded, deeply cut, yellowish-green leaves and, in summer-autumn, masses of shallowly cup-shaped, rich magenta flowers with black veins.
G. armenum. See *G. psilostemon.*
G. cinereum. Semi-evergreen, rosetted perennial with spreading flowering stems. H 15cm (6in), S 30cm (12in). Fully hardy. Has cup-shaped flowers, either white to pale pink, strongly veined with purple, or pure white, on lax stems in late spring and summer. Basal leaves are rounded, deeply divided, soft and grey-green. Is good for a large rock garden. ♀ **'Ballerina'** illus. p.391. var. ***subcaulescens*** see *G. subcaulescens.*
***G. clarkei* 'Kashmir Purple',** syn. *G. pratense* 'Kashmir Purple'. Carpeting, rhizomatous perennial. H and S 45–60cm (18–24in). Fully hardy. Bears loose clusters of cup-shaped, deep purple flowers in summer. Rounded leaves are deeply divided and finely veined. ♀ **'KashmirWhite'** (syn. *G. pratense* 'Kashmir White') illus. p.286.
♀ ***G. dalmaticum*** illus. p.389.
♀ ***G. endressii*** illus. p.288. **'Wargrave Pink'** see *G.* × *oxonianum* 'Wargrave Pink'.
G. farreri. Rosetted perennial with a tap root. H 10cm (4in), S 10–15cm (4–6in) or more. Fully hardy. Outward-facing, flattish, very pale mauve-pink flowers set off blue-black anthers in early summer. Has kidney-shaped, matt green leaves. Both flower and leaf stems are red.
G. grandiflorum. See *G. himalayense.*
G. himalayense, syn. *G. grandiflorum, G. meeboldii*, illus. p.295.
G. ibericum. Clump-forming perennial. H and S 60cm (24in). Fully hardy. In summer produces sprays of 5-petalled, saucer-shaped, violet-blue flowers. Has heart-shaped, lobed or cut, hairy leaves.
G. incanum. Semi-evergreen, spreading, mounded perennial. H 30–38cm (12–15in), S 60cm–90cm (24–36in). Frost hardy. Shallowly cup-shaped flowers are variable, but usually deep pink, and borne singly in summer above aromatic, deeply divided, grey-green leaves with linear segments.
♀ ***G.* 'Johnson's Blue'** illus. p.295.
G. macrorrhizum illus. p.289.
♀ **'Ingwersen's Variety'** illus. p.277.
G. maculatum. Clump-forming perennial. H 75cm (30in), S 45cm (18in). Fully hardy. In spring bears heads of flattish, pinkish-lilac flowers above rounded, lobed or scalloped, mid-green leaves that turn fawn and red in autumn.
♀ ***G. maderense.*** Vigorous, semi-evergreen, bushy perennial with a woody base. H and S 1m (3ft). Half hardy. Produces large sprays of shallowly cup-shaped, deep magenta flowers in summer above palmate, finely cut, dark green leaves.
♀ ***G.* × *magnificum*** illus. p.295.
G. meeboldii. See *G. himalayense.*
G. nodosum illus. p.278.
G. orientalitibeticum, syn. *G. stapfianum* var. *roseum* of gardens, illus. p.365.
***G.* × *oxonianum* 'Claridge Druce'.** Vigorous, semi-evergreen, carpeting perennial. H and S 60–75cm (24–30in). Fully hardy. Bears clusters of cup-shaped, darker-veined, mauve-pink flowers throughout summer. Has dainty, rounded, lobed leaves. ♀ **'Wargrave Pink'** (syn. *G. endressii* 'Wargrave Pink') illus. p.289. **'Winscombe'** illus. p.245.
♀ ***G. palmatum***, syn. *G. anemonifolium.* Vigorous, semi-evergreen, bushy perennial with a woody base. H 45cm (18in), S 60cm (24in). Half hardy. Has palmate, deeply lobed, dark green leaves and, in late summer, large sprays of shallowly cup-shaped, purplish-red flowers.
G. phaeum illus. p.240.
G. pratense (Meadow cranesbill). Clump-forming perennial. H 75cm (30in), S 60cm (24in). Fully hardy. Bears 5-petalled, saucer-shaped, violet-blue flowers on branching stems in summer. Rounded, lobed to deeply divided, mid-green leaves become bronze in autumn. **'Kashmir Purple'** see *G. clarkei* 'Kashmir Purple'.**'Kashmir White'** see *G. clarkei* 'Kashmir White'. ♀ **'Mrs Kendall Clark'** illus. p.295.
♀ **'Plenum Violaceum'** is more compact than the species with double, deep violet flowers.
G. procurrens. Carpeting perennial. H 30cm (12in), S 60cm (24in). Fully hardy. Has rounded, lobed, glossy leaves and, in summer, clusters of saucer-shaped, deep rose-purple flowers.
♀ ***G. psilostemon***, syn. *G. armenum*, illus. p.247.
G. pylzowianum. Spreading perennial with underground runners and tiny tubers. H 12–25cm (5–10in), S 25cm (10in) or more. Fully hardy. Bears semi-circular, deeply cut, dark green leaves and, in late spring and summer, trumpet-shaped, green-centred, deep rose-pink flowers. May be invasive.
♀ ***G. renardii*** illus. p.287.
♀ ***G.* × *riversleaianum* 'Russell Prichard'.** Semi-evergreen, clump-forming perennial. H 30cm (1ft), S 1m (3ft). Frost hardy. Saucer-shaped, clear pink flowers are borne singly or in small clusters from early summer to autumn. Rounded leaves are lobed and grey-green.
G. sanguineum illus. p.366. ♀ var. ***striatum*** (syn. *G.s.* var. *lancastriense*) illus. p.388.
G. stapfianum var. ***roseum*** of gardens. See *G. orientalitibeticum.*
♀ ***G. subcaulescens***, syn. *G. cinereum* var. *subcaulescens*, illus. p.391.
♀ ***G. sylvaticum* 'Mayflower'** illus. p.255.
G. traversii var. ***elegans.*** Semi-evergreen, rosetted perennial with spreading stems. H 10cm (4in), S 25cm (10in). Frost hardy. Large, upward-facing, saucer-shaped, pale pink flowers, with darker veins, rise above rounded, lobed, grey-green leaves in summer. Is suitable for a sheltered ledge or rock garden. Protect from winter wet. Needs gritty soil.
♀ ***G. wallichianum* 'Buxton's Variety',** syn. *G.w.* 'Buxton's Blue', illus. p.297.
G. wlassovianum. Clump-forming perennial. H and S 60cm (24in). Fully hardy. Has velvety stems and rounded, lobed, dark green leaves. Saucer-shaped, deep purple flowers are borne singly or in small clusters in summer.

Geranium. See *Pelargonium.*
Peppermint. See *Pelargonium tomentosum*, illus. p.249.
Silver-leaved. See *Pelargonium* 'Flower of Spring', illus. p.249.
Strawberry. See *Saxifraga stolonifera* 'Tricolor'.

GERBERA

COMPOSITAE/ASTERACEAE

Genus of perennials, flowering from summer to winter depending on growing conditions. Half hardy. Grow in full sun and in light, sandy soil. Propagate by heel cuttings from side shoots in summer or by seed in autumn or early spring.
G. jamesonii illus. p.314.

German ivy. See *Senecio mikanioides.*
Germander
Shrubby. See *Teucrium fruticans.*
Tree. See *Teucrium fruticans.*

GEUM

Avens

ROSACEAE

Genus of summer-flowering perennials. Fully hardy. Does best in sun and prefers moist but well-drained soil. Propagate by division or by seed in autumn.
G.* × *borisii of gardens. See *G. coccineum.*
G. chiloense, syn. *G. coccineum* of gardens. Clump-forming perennial. H 40–60cm (16–24in), S 60cm (24in). Saucer-shaped, scarlet flowers are produced from early to late summer. Pinnate leaves are deeply lobed and toothed.
G. coccineum, syn. *G.* × *borisii* of gardens, illus. p.305.
G. coccineum of gardens. See *G. chiloense.*
♀ ***G.* 'Fire Opal'.** Clump-forming perennial. H 80cm (32in), S 45cm (18in). Rounded, double, bronze-scarlet flowers are borne in small clusters in summer above oblong to lance-shaped, lobed, fresh green leaves.
***G.* 'Goldball'.** See *G.* 'Lady Stratheden'.
♀ ***G.* 'Lady Stratheden',** syn. *G.* 'Goldball', illus. p.304.
***G.* 'Lionel Cox'.** Clump-forming perennial. H and S 30cm (12in). In early summer produces small clusters of 5-petalled, cup-shaped, shrimp-red flowers above oblong to lance-shaped, lobed, fresh green leaves.
♀ ***G. montanum*** (Alpine avens). Dense, clump-forming, rhizomatous perennial that spreads slowly. H 10cm (4in), S 23cm (9in). Shallowly cup-shaped, golden-yellow flowers in early summer are followed by fluffy, buff-coloured seed heads. Leaves are pinnate, each with a large, rounded, terminal lobe. Suitable for a rock garden.
♀ **'Mrs J. Bradshaw'.** Clump-forming perennial. H 80cm (32in), S 45cm (18in). Rounded, double, crimson flowers are borne in small sprays in summer. Fresh green leaves are oblong to lance-shaped and lobed.

GEVUINA

PROTEACEAE

Genus of evergreen trees, grown for their foliage and flowers in summer. Frost hardy. Needs semi-shade and fertile, moist but well-drained soil. Propagate by semi-ripe cuttings in late summer or by seed in autumn.
G. avellana (Chilean hazel). Evergreen, conical tree. H and S 10m (30ft). Has large, glossy, dark green leaves divided into numerous oval, toothed leaflets. Slender spires of spidery, white flowers in late summer are followed by cherry-like, red, then black fruits.

Ghost tree. See *Davidia involucrata*, illus. p.73.
Giant Burmese honeysuckle. See *Lonicera hildebrandiana.*
Giant buttercup. See *Ranunculus lyallii.*
Giant cowslip. See *Primula florindae*, illus. p.282.
Giant elephant's ear. See *Alocasia macrorrhiza.*
Giant fennel. See *Ferula.*
Giant fir. See *Abies grandis*, illus. p.100.
Giant granadilla. See *Passiflora quadrangularis*, illus. p.213.
Giant holly fern. See *Polystichum munitum*, illus. p.322.
Giant larkspur. See *Consolida ajacis Giant Imperial Series*, illus. p.344.
Giant lily. See *Cardiocrinum giganteum*, illus. p.410.
Giant pineapple flower. See *Eucomis pallidiflora*, illus. p.409.
Giant pineapple lily. See *Eucomis pallidiflora*, illus. p.409.
Giant redwood. See *Sequoiadendron giganteum*, illus. p.98.
Giant reed. See *Arundo donax.*
Giant scabious. See *Cephalaria gigantea.*
Giant Spaniard. See *Aciphylla scott-thomsonii.*
Giant wood fern. See *Dryopteris goldieana.*

GIBBAEUM

AIZOACEAE

Genus of clump-forming, perennial succulents with pairs of small, swollen leaves, often of unequal size. Frost tender, min. 5°C (41°F). Needs full sun and very well-drained soil. Water very lightly in early winter. Propagate by seed or stem cuttings in spring or summer.
G. petrense. Carpeting, perennial succulent. H 3cm (1¼in), S 30cm (12in) or more. Each branch carries 1 or 2 pairs of thick, triangular, pale grey-green leaves, 1cm (½in) long. Bears daisy-like, pink-red flowers, 1.5cm (⅝ in) across, in spring.
G. velutinum illus. p.485.

Gilia

POLEMONIACEAE

Genus of summer- and autumn-flowering annuals. Fully hardy. Grows best in sun and in fertile, very well-drained soil. Stems may need support, especially on windy sites. Propagate by seed sown outdoors in spring, or in early autumn for early flowering the following year.
G. achilleifolia. Fast-growing, upright, bushy annual. H 60cm (24in), S 20cm (8in). Finely divided, mid-green leaves are hairy and sticky. Heads of funnel-shaped, blue flowers, 2.5cm (1in) wide, are produced in summer.
G. capitata illus. p.345.

Gillenia

ROSACEAE

Genus of summer-flowering perennials. Fully hardy. Grow in sun or shade and any well-drained soil. Needs staking. Propagate by seed in autumn or spring.
♀ ***G. trifoliata*** illus. p.243.

Ginger
Indian. See *Alpinia calcarata.*
Malay. See *Costus speciosus.*
Shell. See *Alpinia zerumbet*, illus. p.225.
Spiral. See *Costus.*
Wild. See *Asarum.*
Gingerlily. See *Hedychium.*
Gingham golf ball. See *Euphorbia obesa*, illus. p.493.

Ginkgo

GINKGOACEAE

See also CONIFERS.
♀ ***G. biloba*** illus. p.99.

Gippsland fountain palm. See *Livistona australis.*

Gladiolus

IRIDACEAE

Genus of corms, each producing a spike of funnel-shaped flowers and a fan of erect, sword-shaped leaves on basal part of flower stem. Is suitable for cutting or for planting in mixed borders; most hybrids are also good for exhibition. Frost to half hardy. Needs a sunny and fertile, well-drained site. Plant 10–15cm (4–6in) deep and the same distance apart in spring. Water well in summer and support tall cultivars with canes. Lift half-hardy types in autumn, cut off stems and dry corms in a frost-free but cool place. Pot up spring-flowering species and cultivars in autumn and place in a cool greenhouse; after flowering, dry off corms during summer months and repot in autumn.
Propagate by seed or by removal of young cormlets from parent. Seed sown in early spring in a cool greenhouse will take 2–3 years to flower and may not breed true to type. Cormlets, removed after lifting, should be stored in frost-free conditions and then be planted out 5cm (2in) deep in spring; lift in winter as for mature corms. They will flower in 1–2 years.
While in store, corms may be attacked by various rots. Protect sound, healthy corms by dusting with a fungicide or soaking in a fungicide solution before drying; store in an airy, cool, frost-free place. Gladiolus scab causes blotches on leaves; gladiolus yellows shows as yellowing stripes on leaves, which then die; in both cases destroy affected corms. As a preventative measure, always plant healthy corms in a new site each year.See also feature panel p.411.

Gladiolus hybrids
Most hybrids are derived from *G.* × *hortulanus*. All have stiff leaves, 20–50cm (8–20in) long, ranging from pale willow-green or steely blue-green to almost bottle-green. Half hardy. All are good for flower arranging. They are divided into Grandiflorus, Primulinus, and Nanus Groups.
Grandiflorus Group produces long, densely packed spikes of funnel-shaped flowers, with ruffled, thick-textured petals or plain-edged, thin-textured ones. Giant-flowered hybrids have a bottom flower of over 14cm (5½in) across (flower head is 65–80cm (26–32in) long); large-flowered 11–14cm (4½–5½in) across (flower head 60cm–1m (24–36in) long); medium-flowered 9–11cm (3½–4½in) across (flower head 60–80cm (24–32in) long); small-flowered 6–9cm (2½–3½in) across (flower head 50–70cm (20–28in) long); and miniature-flowered 3.5–6cm (1½–2½in) across (flower head 40–60cm (16–24in) long).
Primulinus Group has fairly loose spikes of plain-edged, funnel-shaped flowers, 6–8cm (2½–3in) across, each with a strongly hooded, upper petal over the stigma and anthers. Flower heads are 30cm (12in) long.
Nanus Group produces 2 or 3 slender spikes, with loosely arranged flowers, 4–5cm (1½–2in) across. Flower heads are 22–35cm (9–14in) long.

***G.* 'Amanda Mahy'** illus. p.411. Nanus Group gladiolus. H 80cm (32in), S 8–10cm (3–4in). Produces spikes of up to 7 salmon-pink flowers, with lip tepals flecked violet and white, in early summer.
***G.* 'Amsterdam'.** Grandiflorus Group, giant-flowered gladiolus. H 1.7m (5½ft), S 30cm (1ft). Spikes of up to 27 slightly upward-facing, finely ruffled, white flowers are produced in late summer. Is good for exhibition.
***G.* 'Amy Beth'.** Grandiflorus Group, small-flowered gladiolus. H 1.2m (4ft), S 20–25cm (8–10in). Produces spikes of up to 22 heavily ruffled, lavender flowers, with thick, waxy, cream-lipped petals, in late summer.
***G.* 'Anna Leorah'** illus. p.411. Grandiflorus Group, large-flowered gladiolus. H 1.6m (5½ft), S 15cm (6in). In mid-summer bears spikes of up to 25 strongly ruffled, mid-pink flowers with large, white throats. Is good for exhibition.
***G.* 'Atlantis'.** Grandiflorus Group, medium-flowered gladiolus. H 1.5m (5ft), S 20–25cm (8–10in). Produces spikes of up to 20 lightly ruffled, deep violet-blue flowers with small, white throats, in late summer.
***G.* 'Beau Rivage'.** Grandiflorus Group, large-flowered gladiolus. H to 1.2m (4ft), S 30cm (1ft). Spikes of up to 15 ruffled, deep coral-pink flowers are produced in summer. Is good for exhibition.
***G.* 'Beauty of Holland'.** Grandiflorus Group, large-flowered gladiolus. H 1.7m (5½ft), S 15cm (6in). Produces spikes of up to 27 ruffled, pink-margined, white flowers in mid-summer. Is good for exhibition.
***G.* 'Black Lash'.** Grandiflorus Group, small-flowered gladiolus. H 1.35m (4½ft), S 15–20cm (6–8in). Bears spikes of up to 25 lightly ruffled, deep black-rose flowers, with pointed, slightly reflexed petals, from late summer to early autumn.
G. blandus. See *G. carneus.*
G. byzantinus. See *G. communis* subsp. *byzantinus.*
♀ ***G. callianthus***, syn. *Acidanthera bicolor* var. *murieliae, A. murieliae.* Late summer-flowering corm. H to 1m (3ft), S 10–15cm (4–6in). Half hardy. Has a loose spike of up to 10 fragrant flowers, each with a curved, 10cm (4in) long tube and 6 white petals, each with a deep purple blotch at the base.
G. cardinalis. Summer-flowering corm. H to 1.2m (4ft), S 10–15cm (4–6in). Half hardy. Arching stem bears a spike of up to 12 widely funnel-shaped flowers, each 8cm (3in) long and bright red with spear-shaped, white marks on lower 3 petals.
G. carneus, syn. *G. blandus.* Spring-flowering corm. H 20–40cm (8–16in), S 8–10cm (3–4in). Half hardy. Stem bears a loose spike of 3–12 widely funnel-shaped, white or pink flowers, 4–6cm (1½–2½in) long, marked on lower petals with darker red or yellow blotches.
***G.* 'Charmer'.** Grandiflorus Group, large-flowered gladiolus. H 1.7m (5½ft), S 15cm (6in). In early and mid-summer produces spikes of up to 27 strongly ruffled, almost translucent, light pink flowers. Is good for exhibition.
***G.* 'Christabel'** illus. p.431.
♀ ***G. communis*** subsp. ***byzantinus***, syn. *G. byzantinus*, illus. p.411.
***G.* 'Côte d'Azur'.** Grandiflorus Group, giant-flowered gladiolus. H 1.7m (5½ft), S 15cm (6in). Bears spikes of up to 23 ruffled, mid-blue flowers, with pale blue throats, in early summer. Is good for exhibition.
G. dalenii, syn. *G. natalensis, G. primulinus, G. psittacinus.* Vigorous, summer-flowering corm. H to 1.5m (5ft), S 10–15cm (4–6in). Half hardy. Produces up to 14 red, yellow-orange, yellow or greenish-yellow flowers, 8–12cm (3–5in) long, each with a hooded, upper petal and often flecked or streaked red.
***G.* 'Dancing Queen'** illus. p.411. Grandiflorus Group, large-flowered gladiolus. H 1.5m (5ft), S 12–15cm (5–6in). In mid- to late summer produces spikes of up to 20 white flowers, with feathered, dark red markings at the base of the lower petals.
***G.* 'Deliverance'** illus. p.411. Grandiflorus Group, large-flowered gladiolus. H.1.7m (5½ft), S 12–15cm (5–6in). In mid- to late summer produces spikes of 20 or more ruffled, coral-pink flowers, deeper peach-pink at the margins, with yellow-tinted, white throats.
***G.* 'Drama'** illus. p.411. Grandiflorus Group, large-flowered gladiolus. H 1.7m (5½ft), S 25–30cm (10–12in). In late summer produces spikes of up to 26 lightly ruffled, deep watermelon-pink flowers with red-marked, yellow throats. Is superb for exhibition.
***G.* 'Dutch Mountain'.** Grandiflorus Group, large-flowered gladiolus. H 1.7m (5½ft), S 15cm (6in). In mid-summer produces spikes of up to 25 slightly ruffled, white flowers with small green marks in the throats. Is good for exhibition.
***G.* 'Esta Bonita'** illus. p.411. Grandiflorus Group, giant-flowered gladiolus. H 1.7m (5½ft), S 30cm (1ft). Produces spikes of up to 24 apricot-orange flowers, slightly darker towards petal edges, in late summer. Is good for exhibition.
***G.* 'Firestorm'.** Grandiflorus Group, miniature-flowered gladiolus. H 1.1m (3½ft), S 8–10cm (3–4in). Spikes of up to 22 loosely spaced, ruffled, vivid scarlet flowers, with yellowish-white flecks on the outer tepals, are produced in early summer. Is good for exhibition.
***G.* 'Florence C'** illus. p.411. Grandiflorus Group, large-flowered gladiolus. H 1.7m (5½ft), S 15cm (6in). In late summer produces spikes of up to 26 strongly ruffled, white flowers.
***G.* 'Georgette'.** Grandiflorus Group, small-flowered gladiolus. H 1.2m (4ft), S 8–10cm (3–4in). Produces spikes of up to 22 slightly ruffled, yellow-suffused, orange flowers, with large lemon-yellow throats, in mid-summer. Is good for exhibition.
***G.* 'Green Isle'.** Grandiflorus Group, medium-flowered gladiolus. H 1.35m (4½ft), S 20–25cm (8–10in). Spikes carrying up to 22 slightly informal flowers, lime-green throughout with chiselled ruffling, are produced in late summer.
***G.* 'Green Woodpecker'** illus. p.411. Grandiflorus Group, medium-flowered gladiolus.H 1.5m (5ft), S 30cm (1ft). Has spikes of up to 25 uranium-green flowers, with wine-red throats, in late summer. Is very good for exhibition.
***G.* 'Halley'** illus. p.411. Nanus Group gladiolus. H 1m (3ft), S 8–10cm (3–4in). In early summer produces spikes carrying up to 7 white-flushed, pale yellow flowers, each with bright red marks in the throats.
***G.* 'Ice Cap'.** Grandiflorus Group, large-flowered gladiolus. H 1.7m (5½ft), S 25–30cm (10–12in). Produces spikes of up to 27 heavily ruffled, ice-white flowers from late summer to early autumn.
***G.* 'Inca Queen'.** Grandiflorus Group, large-flowered gladiolus. H 1.5m (5ft), S 20–25cm (8–10in). Bears spikes of up to 25 heavily ruffled, waxy, deep salmon-pink flowers, with lemon-yellow lip petals and throats, in late summer.
G. italicus, syn. *G. segetum*, illus. p.412.
***G.* 'Little Darling'.** Primulinus Group gladiolus. H 1.1m (3½ft), S 8–10cm (3–4in). Bears spikes of up to 16 loosely spaced, salmon-to rose-pink flowers, with lemon lip tepals, in mid-summer. Is good for exhibition.
***G.* 'Magistral'.** Grandiflorus Group, large-flowered gladiolus. H 1.8m (6ft), S 15cm (6in). Produces spikes of up to

24 ruffled, oyster-white flowers, with magenta lines, in mid-summer. Is good for exhibition.
***G.* 'Melodie'.** Grandiflorus Group, small-flowered gladiolus. H 1.2m (4ft), S 15–20cm (6–8in). Produces spikes of up to 17 salmon-rose flowers, with longitudinal, spear-like, red-orange marks in throats, in late summer.
***G.* 'Mi Mi'.** Grandiflorus Group, small-flowered gladiolus. H 1.3m (4½ft), S 8–10cm (3–4in). In mid-summer bears spikes of up to 24 strongly ruffled, deep lavender-pink flowers with white throats. Is good for exhibition.
***G.* 'Miss America'** illus. p.411. Grandiflorus Group, medium-flowered gladiolus. H 1.5m (5ft), S 30cm (1ft). In late summer produces spikes of up to 24 deep pink flowers that are heavily ruffled. Is excellent for exhibition.
G. natalensis. See *G. dalenii.*
G. papilio, syn. *G. purpureoauratus*, illus. p.424.
***G.* 'Parade'.** Grandiflorus Group, giant-flowered gladiolus. H 1.7m (5½ft), S 25–35cm (10–14in). Produces spikes of up to 27 finely ruffled, salmon-pink flowers, with small, cream throats, in early autumn. Is superb for exhibition.
***G.* 'Peace'.** Grandiflorus Group, giant-flowered gladiolus. H 1.7m (5½ft), S 15cm (6in). Bears spikes of up to 26 strongly ruffled, cream flowers, with pale lemon throats and pale pink margins, in mid-summer. Is good for exhibition.
***G.* 'Peter Pears'** illus. p.411. Grandiflorus Group, large-flowered gladiolus. H 1.7m (5½ft), S 35cm (14in). In late summer bears spikes of up to 26 apricot-salmon flowers with red throat marks. Is excellent for exhibition.
***G.* 'Pink Flare'.** Grandiflorus Group, small-flowered gladiolus. H 1.3m (4½ft), S 8–10cm (3–4in). Spikes of up to 25 ruffled, mid-pink flowers, each with a small, white throat, are produced in mid-summer. Is good for exhibition.
***G.* 'Pink Lady'** illus. p.411. Grandiflorus Group, large-flowered gladiolus. H 1.5m (5ft), S 25–30cm (10–12in). Has spikes of up to 25 lightly ruffled, deep rose-pink flowers, with large, white throats, in late summer and early autumn.
G. primulinus. See *G. dalenii.*
G. psittacinus. See *G. dalenii.*
***G.* 'Pulchritude'** illus. p.411. Grandiflorus Group, medium-flowered gladiolus. H 1.3m (4½ft), S 12cm (5in). Produces spikes of up to 27 ruffled, light lavender-pink flowers, deepening at the tepal margins, and with a magenta-red mark on each lip tepal, in mid-summer. Is good for exhibition.
G. purpureoauratus. See *G. papilio.*
***G.* 'Renegade'** illus. p.411. Grandiflorus Group, large-flowered gladiolus. H 1.5m (5ft), S 12–15cm (5–6in). In mid- to late summer produces spikes of 15–20 ruffled, deep red flowers.
***G.* 'Rose Supreme'** illus. p.411. Grandiflorus Group, giant-flowered gladiolus. H 1.7m (5½ft), S 25–30cm (10–12in). Spikes of up to 24 rose-pink flowers, flecked and streaked darker pink towards petal tips, and with cream throats, are produced in late summer.
***G.* 'Royal Dutch'.** Grandiflorus Group, large-flowered gladiolus. H 1.7m (5½ft), S 25–30cm (10–12in). Produces spikes of up to 27 flowers, each pale lavender blending into a white throat, from late summer to early autumn. Is very good for exhibition.
G. segetum. See *G. italicus.*
***G.* 'Stardust'.** Grandiflorus Group, miniature-flowered gladiolus. H 1.2m (4ft), S 8–10cm (3–4in). Has spikes of up to 21 ruffled, pale yellow flowers, with lighter yellow throats, in mid-summer. Is good for exhibition.
***G.* 'Tendresse'.** Grandiflorus Group, medium-flowered gladiolus. H 1.5m (5ft), S 20–25cm (8–10in). In late summer has spikes of up to 28 slightly ruffled, dark pink flowers, with small, cream throats marked with longitudinal, faint rose-pink 'spears'.
***G.* 'Tesoro'** illus. p.411. Grandiflorus Group, medium-flowered gladiolus. H 1.5m (5ft), S 20–25 cm (8–10in). Bears spikes of up to 26 silky flowers, slightly ruffled and glistening yellow, in early autumn. Is among the top exhibition gladioli.
♀ ***G.* 'The Bride'** illus. p.411. Nanus Group gladiolus. H 80cm (32in), S 8–10cm (3–4in). Produces spikes of up to 7 white flowers, with green-marked throats, in early summer.
***G.* 'Vaucluse'.** Grandiflorus Group, giant-flowered gladiolus. H 1.9m (6ft), S 15cm (6in). In late summer, bears spikes of up to 27 slightly ruffled, vermilion-red flowers with small, creamy-white throats. Is good for exhibition.
***G.* 'Victor Borge'.** Grandiflorus Group, large-flowered gladiolus. H 1.7m (5½ft), S 35cm (14in). Spikes of up to 22 vermilion-orange flowers, with pale cream throat marks, are produced in late summer.
***G.* 'White Ice'** illus. p.411. Grandiflorus Group, medium-flowered gladiolus. H 1.5m (5ft), S 12cm (5in). Produces spikes of up to 25 ruffled, white flowers in late summer. Is good for exhibition.
***G.* 'Zephyr'.** Grandiflorus Group, large-flowered gladiolus. H 1.7m (5½ft), S 15cm (6in). In mid-summer has spikes of up to 26 light lavender-pink flowers with small, ivory throats. Is good for exhibition.

Gladwin. See *Iris foetidissima.*
Gland bellflower. See *Adenophora.*
Glandulicactus uncinatus. See *Sclerocactus uncinatus.*
Glastonbury thorn. See *Crataegus monogyna* 'Biflora'.

GLAUCIDIUM

PAEONIACEAE/GLAUCIDIACEAE

Genus of one species of spring-flowering perennial. Is excellent in woodland gardens. Fully hardy. Needs a partially shaded, sheltered position and moist, peaty soil. Propagate by seed in autumn.
♀ ***G. palmatum*** illus. p.278.

GLAUCIUM

Horned poppy

PAPAVERACEAE

Genus of annuals, biennials and perennials, grown for their bright, poppy-like flowers. Fully hardy. Grow in sun and in fertile, well-drained soil. Propagate annuals by seed sown outdoors in spring; perennials by seed sown outdoors in spring or autumn; biennials by seed sown under glass in late spring or early summer. Roots are toxic if ingested.
G. flavum illus. p.347.

GLECHOMA

LABIATAE/LAMIACEAE

Genus of evergreen, summer-flowering perennials. Makes good ground cover, but may be invasive. Fully hardy. Tolerates sun or shade. Prefers moist but well-drained soil. Propagate by division in spring or autumn or by softwood cuttings in spring.
G. hederacea (Ground ivy). **'Variegata'** illus. p.312.

GLEDITSIA

LEGUMINOSAE/CAESALPINIACEAE

Genus of deciduous, usually spiny trees, grown for their foliage. Has inconspicuous flowers, often followed by large seed pods after hot summers. Fully hardy, but young plants may suffer frost damage. Requires plenty of sun and fertile, well-drained soil. Propagate species by seed in autumn, selected forms by budding in late summer.
G. caspica (Caspian locust). Deciduous, spreading tree. H 12m (40ft), S 10m (30ft). Trunk is armed with long, branched spines. Has fern-like, glossy, mid-green leaves.
G. japonica illus. p.76.
G. triacanthos (Honey locust). Deciduous, spreading tree. H 20m (70ft), S 15m (50ft). Trunk is very thorny. Fern-like, glossy, dark green leaves turn yellow in autumn. f. ***inermis*** is thornless. **'Shademaster'** is vigorous, with long-lasting leaves. **'Skyline'** is thornless, broadly conical and has golden-yellow foliage in autumn. ♀ **'Sunburst'** illus. p.73.

GLOBBA

ZINGIBERACEAE

Genus of evergreen, aromatic, clump-forming perennials, grown for their flowers. Frost tender, min. 18°C (64°F). Needs partial shade, high humidity and humus-rich, well-drained soil. Keep plants dry when dormant in winter. Propagate by division or seed in spring or by mature bulbils that fall off plants.
G. winitii illus. p.275.

Globe amaranth. See *Gomphrena globosa*, illus. p.343.
Globe lily. See *Calochortus albus*, illus. p.425.
Globe thistle. See *Echinops.*
Globeflower. See *Trollius.*

GLOBULARIA

GLOBULARIACEAE

Genus of mainly evergreen, summer-flowering shrubs and sub-shrubs, grown for their dome-shaped hummocks and usually blue or purple flower heads. Fully to frost hardy. Needs full sun and well-drained soil. Propagate by division in spring, by softwood or semi-ripe cuttings in summer or by seed in autumn.
G. bellidifolia. See *G. meridionalis.*
♀ ***G. cordifolia*** illus. p.395. subsp. ***bellidifolia*** see *G. meridionalis.*
G. meridionalis, syn. *G. bellidifolia, G. cordifolia* subsp. *bellidifolia, G. pygmaea*, illus. p.392.
G. pygmaea. See *G. meridionalis.*

GLORIOSA

LILIACEAE/COLCHICACEAE

Genus of deciduous, summer-flowering, tendril climbers with finger-like tubers. Frost tender, min. 8–10°C (46–50°F). Needs full sun and rich, well-drained soil. Water freely in summer and liquid feed every 2 weeks. Provide support. Dry off tubers in winter and keep cool but frost-free. Propagate by seed or division in spring. Highly toxic if ingested; handling tubers may irritate the skin.
G. rothschildiana. See *G. superba* 'Rothschildiana'.
♀ ***G. superba*** (Glory lily). Deciduous, tendril climber with tubers. H to 2m (6ft), S 30–45cm (1–1½ft). Min. 8°C (46°F). Slender stems bear scattered, broadly lance-shaped leaves. In summer, upper leaf axils carry large, yellow or red flowers, with 6 sharply reflexed, wavy-edged petals, changing to dark orange or deep red. Stamens are prominent. **'Rothschildiana'** (syn. *G. rothschildiana*) illus. p.413.
Glory bush. See *Tibouchina urvilleana*, illus. p.118.
Glory flower, Chilean. See *Eccremocarpus scaber*, illus. p.215.
Glory lily. See *Gloriosa superba.*
Glory vine. See *Eccremocarpus scaber*, illus. p.215.
Glory-of-the-snow. See *Chionodoxa.*
Glory-of-the-sun. See *Leucocoryne ixioides*, illus. p.429.

GLOTTIPHYLLUM

AIZOACEAE

Genus of clump-forming, perennial succulents with semi-cylindrical leaves often broader at tips. Frost tender, min. 5°C (41°F). Grow in full sun and poor, well-drained soil. Propagate by seed or stem cuttings in spring or summer.
G. difforme, syn. *G. semicylindricum.* Clump-forming, perennial succulent. H 8cm (3in), S 30cm (12in) or more. Has semi-cylindrical, bright green leaves, 6cm (2½in) long, with a tooth half-way along each margin. Short-stemmed, daisy-like, golden-yellow flowers, 4cm (1½in) across, appear in spring-summer.
G. nelii illus. p.495.
G. semicylindricum. See *G. difforme.*

GLOXINIA

GESNERIACEAE

Genus of late summer- to autumn-flowering, rhizomatous perennials. Frost tender, min. 10°C (50°F). Needs partial shade and humus-rich, well-drained soil. Dies down in late autumn or winter; then keep rhizomes nearly dry. Propagate by division or seed in spring or by stem or leaf cuttings in summer.
G. perennis illus. p.437.
G. speciosa. See *Sinningia speciosa*.

Gloxinia. See *Sinningia speciosa*.

GLYCERIA

POACEAE

See also GRASSES, BAMBOOS, RUSHES and SEDGES.
***G. aquatica* 'Variegata'.** See *G.maxima* 'Variegata'.
***G. maxima* 'Variegata',** syn. *G. aquatica* 'Variegata', illus. p.318.

GLYCYRRHIZA
Liquorice

LEGUMINOSAE/PAPILIONACEAE

Genus of summer-flowering perennials. Fully hardy. Needs sun and deep, rich, well-drained soil. Propagate by division in spring or seed in autumn or spring.
G. glabra. Upright perennial. H 1.2m (4ft), S 1m (3ft). Has pea-like, purple-blue and white flowers, borne in short spikes on erect stems in late summer, and large leaves divided into oval leaflets. Is grown commercially for production of liquorice.

Goat willow. See *Salix caprea*.
Goat's beard. See *Aruncus dioicus*, illus. p.224.
Goat's rue. See *Galega*.
Godetia. See *Clarkia*.
Gold dust. See *Aurinia saxatilis*, illus. p.362.
Golden arum lily. See *Zantedeschia elliottiana*, illus. p.414.
Golden ball cactus. See *Parodia leninghausii*, illus. p.484.
Golden bamboo. See *Phyllostachys aurea*.
Golden barrel cactus. See *Echinocactus grusonii*, illus. p.476.
Golden chain. See *Laburnum anagyroides*.
Golden creeping Jenny. See *Lysimachia nummularia* 'Aurea', illus. p.398.
Golden club. See *Orontium aquaticum*, illus. p.467.
Golden elder. See *Sambucus nigra* 'Aurea'.
Golden fairy lantern. See *Calochortus amabilis*, illus. p.450.
Golden flax. See *Linum flavum*.
Golden foxtail. See *Alopecurus pratensis* 'Aureovariegatus', illus. p.321.
Golden globe tulip. See *Calochortus amabilis*, illus. p.450.
Golden larch. See *Pseudolarix amabilis*, illus. p.103.
Golden male fern. See *Dryopteris affinis*.
Golden oak of Cyprus. See *Quercus alnifolia*.
Golden oats. See *Stipa gigantea*, illus. p.319.
Golden rod. See *Solidago*.
Golden shower. See *Cassia fistula; Pyrostegia venusta*, illus. p.216.
Golden Spaniard. See *Aciphylla aurea*, illus. p.240.
Golden spiderlily. See *Lycoris aurea*.
Golden top. See *Lamarckia aurea*.
Golden trumpet. See *Allamanda cathartica*.
Golden trumpet tree. See *Tabebuia chrysotricha*, illus. p.93.
Golden weeping willow. See *Salix × sepulcralis*, 'Chrysocoma' illus. p.70.
Golden willow. See *Salix alba* var. *vitellina*, illus. p.70.
Golden wonder. See *Senna didymobotrya*, illus. p.143.
Golden-chalice vine. See *Solandra maxima*, illus. p.202.
Golden-eyed grass. See *Sisyrinchium californicum*.
Golden-featherpalm. See *Dypsis lutescens*, illus. p.96.
Golden-groove bamboo. See *Phyllostachys aureosulcata*.
Golden-rain tree. See *Koelreuteria paniculata*, illus. p.88.
Golden-rayed lily of Japan. See *Lilium auratum*.
Goldfish plant. See *Columnea gloriosa*.
Goldilocks. See *Aster linosyris*, illus. p.270.
Golf ball, Gingham. See *Euphorbia obesa*, illus. p.493.

GOMESA

ORCHIDACEAE

See also ORCHIDS.
G. planifolia illus. p.310. Evergreen, epiphytic orchid for a cool greenhouse. H 23cm (9in). Sprays of star-shaped, pea-green flowers, 0.5cm (¼in) across, are produced in autumn. Narrowly oval leaves are 15cm (6in) long. Grow in semi-shade during summer.

GOMPHOCARPUS

ASCLEPIADACEAE

Genus of evergreen and deciduous sub-shrubs and perennials. Hooded, cup-shaped flowers are followed by seed pods that are usually inflated. Half hardy to frost tender, min. 5°C (41°F). Grows in sun or partial shade and in any well-drained soil. Propagate by seed or softwood cuttings in spring. Some species exude a milky sap, which may aggravate skin allergies.
G. physocarpus, syn. *Asclepias physocarpa*, illus. p.232.

GOMPHRENA

AMARANTHACEAE

Genus of annuals, biennials and perennials. Only one species, *G. globosa*, is usually cultivated; its flower heads are good for cutting and drying. Half hardy. Grows best in sun and in fertile, well-drained soil. Propagate by seed sown under glass in spring.
G. globosa (Globe amaranth) illus. p.343.

GONGORA

ORCHIDACEAE

See also ORCHIDS.
G. quinquenervis illus. p.310. Evergreen, epiphytic orchid for an intermediate greenhouse. H 25cm (10in). In summer, fragrant, brown, orange and yellow flowers, 1cm (½in) across, which resemble birds in flight, are produced in long, pendent spikes. Has oval, ribbed leaves, 12–15cm (5–6in) long. Is best grown in a hanging basket. Requires semi-shade in summer.

Good-luck plant. See *Cordyline fruticosa*.
Goodyer's elm. See *Ulmus minor* subsp. *angustifolia*.
Gooseberry
Barbados. See *Pereskia aculeata*, illus. p.473.
Chinese. See *Actinidia deliciosa*.

GORDONIA

THEACEAE

Genus of evergreen shrubs and trees, grown for their flowers and overall appearance. Half hardy, but best at min. 3°C (37°F). Prefers sun or partial shade and humus-rich, acid soil. Water potted plants moderately, less in winter. Propagate by semi-ripe cuttings in late summer or by seed when ripe, in autumn, or in spring.
G. axillaris. Evergreen, bushy shrub or tree. H and S 3–5m (10–15ft), sometimes much more. Has lance-shaped, leathery, glossy leaves, each with a blunt tip, and bears, from autumn to spring, saucer-shaped, white flowers.
G. lasianthus (Loblolly bay). Evergreen, upright tree. H to 20m (70ft), S to 10m (30ft). Lance-shaped to elliptic leaves are shallowly serrated. Has fragrant, saucer- to bowl-shaped, white flowers in summer. Needs sub-tropical summer warmth to grow and flower well.

Gorgon's head. See *Euphorbia gorgonis*.
Gorse. See *Ulex europaeus*, illus. p.153.
Gorse, Spanish. See *Genista hispanica*, illus. p.166.
Gourd, Snake. See *Trichosanthes cucumerina* var. *anguina*.
Gout weed. See *Aegopodium*.
Variegated. See *Aegopodium podagraria* 'Variegatum', illus. p.286.
Grama, Blue. See *Bouteloua gracilis*, illus. p.319.
Granadilla, Giant. See *Passiflora quadrangularis*, illus. p.213.
Grand fir. See *Abies grandis*, illus. p.100.
Granite bottlebrush. See *Melaleuca elliptica*, illus. p.138.
Granny's bonnets. See *Aquilegia vulgaris*.
Grape
Amur. See *Vitis amurensis*.
Cape. See *Rhoicissus capensis*.
Oregon. See *Mahonia aquifolium*, illus. p.153.
Grape hyacinth. See *Muscari*.
Grape ivy. See *Cissus rhombifolia*, illus. p.218.
Grape vine. See *Vitis vinifera*.

GRAPTOPETALUM

CRASSULACEAE

Genus of rosetted, perennial succulents very similar to *Echeveria*, with which it hybridizes. Frost tender, min. 5–10°C (41–50°F). Is easy to grow, needing sun or partial shade and very well-drained soil. Propagate by seed or by stem or leaf cuttings in spring or summer.
G. amethystinum. Clump-forming, prostrate, perennial succulent. H 40cm (16in), S 90cm (36in). Min. 10°C (50°F). Produces thick, rounded, blue-grey to red leaves, 7cm (3in) long, in terminal rosettes and star-shaped, yellow-and-red flowers, 1–2cm (½–¾in) across, in spring-summer.
♀ ***G. bellum***, syn. *Tacitus bellus*, illus. p.489.
G. paraguayense illus. p.494.

GRAPTOPHYLLUM

ACANTHACEAE

Genus of evergreen shrubs, grown mainly for their foliage. Frost tender, min. 16–18°C (61–4°F). Needs partial shade and fertile, well-drained soil. Water potted plants freely when in full growth, much less when temperatures are low. Young plants need tip pruning after flowering to promote branching; leggy specimens may be cut back hard after flowering or in spring. Propagate by greenwood or semi-ripe cuttings in spring or summer.
G. pictum (Caricature plant). Evergreen, erect, loose shrub. H to 2m (6ft), S 60cm (2ft) or more. Has oval, pointed, glossy, green leaves with central, yellow blotches. Bears short, terminal spikes of tubular, red to purple flowers in spring and early summer.

Grass
African fountain. See *Pennisetum setaceum*.
Amursilver. See *Miscanthus sacchariflorus*.
Balkan blue. See *Sesleria heufleriana*.
Basket. See *Oplismenus africanus*.
Bear. See *Dasylirion*.
Blue oat. See *Helictotrichon sempervirens*, illus. p.319.
Chinese fountain. See *Pennisetum alopecuroides*.
Cloud. See *Aichryson × domesticum* 'Variegatum', illus. p.493.
Common quaking. See *Brizia media*.
Creeping soft. See *Holcus mollis*.
Eel. See *Vallisneria spiralis*.
False oat. See *Arrhenatherum elatius*.
Fish. See *Cabomba caroliniana*.
Golden-eyed. See *Sisyrinchium californicum*.
Greater quaking. See *Briza maxima*.
Hairy brome. See *Bromus ramosus*.
Hare's-tail. See *Lagurus ovatus*, illus. p.318.
Hunangemoho. See *Chionochloa conspicua*.
Lyme. See *Leymus arenarius*.
Mosquito. See *Bouteloua gracilis*, illus. p.319.
Natal. See *Melinis repens*.
Old-witch. See *Panicum capillare*, illus. p.320.
Orchard. See *Dactylis glomerata*.
Pampas. See *Cortaderia selloana*.

Pheasant. See *Stipa arundinacea*.
Quaking. See *Briza*.
Ruby. See *Melinis repens*.
Scurvy. See *Oxalis enneaphylla*.
Squirrel tail. See *Hordeum jubatum*, illus. p.319.
St Augustine. See *Stenotaphrum secundatum*.
Tape. See *Vallisneria spiralis*.
Tufted hair. See *Deschampsia cespitosa*.
Variegated creeping soft. See *Holcus mollis* 'Albovariegatus', illus. p.318.
Variegated purple moor. See *Molinia caerulea* 'Variegata'.
Washington. See *Cabomba caroliniana*.
Yellow whitlow. See *Draba aizoides*.
Grass of Parnassus. See *Parnassia palustris*, illus. p.362.
Grass tree. See *Xanthorrhoea*.
Grass widow. See *Olsynium douglasii*.

Grasses, Bamboos, Rushes and Sedges

Group of evergreen or herbaceous, perennial and annual grasses or grass-like plants belonging to the Gramineae (including Bambusoideae), Juncaceae and Cyperaceae families. They are grown mainly as foliage plants, adding grace and contrast to borders and rock gardens, although several grasses have attractive flower heads in summer that may be dried for winter decoration. Dead foliage may be cut back on herbaceous perennials when dormant. Propagate species by seed in spring or autumn or by division in spring; selected forms by division only. Pests and diseases usually give little trouble. Grasses, bamboos, rushes and sedges are illustrated on pp.318–321.

Grasses (Gramineae)
Family of evergreen, semi-evergreen or herbaceous, sometimes creeping perennials, annuals and marginal water plants, usually with rhizomes or stolons, that form tufts, clumps or carpets. All have basal leaves and rounded flower stems that bear alternate, long, narrow leaves. Flowers are bisexual (males and females in same spikelet) and are arranged in panicles, racemes or spikes. Each flower head comprises spikelets, with one or more florets, that are covered with glumes (scales) from which awns (long, slender bristles) may grow. Fully hardy to frost tender, min. 5–12°C (41–54°F). Unless otherwise stated, grasses will tolerate a range of light conditions and flourish in any well-drained soil. Many genera, such as *Briza*, self-seed readily.
See also *Alopecurus*, *Anemanthele*, *Arrhenatherum*, *Arundo*, *Bouteloua*, *Briza*, *Bromus*, *Chionochloa*, *Coix*, *Cortaderia*, *Dactylis*, *Deschampsia*, *Festuca*, *Glyceria*, *Hakonechloa*, *Helictotrichon*, *Holcus*, *Hordeum*, *Lagurus*, *Lamarckia*, *Leymus*, *Melica*, *Melinis*, *Milium*, *Miscanthus*, *Molinia*, *Oplismenus*, *Panicum*, *Pennisetum*, *Phalaris*, *Sesleria*, *Setaria*, *Spartina*, *Stenotaphrum*, *Stipa*, *Zea* and *Zizania*.

Bamboos (Bambusoideae)
Sub-family of Gramineae, comprising evergreen, rhizomatous perennials, sometimes grown as hedging as well as for ornamentation. Most bamboos differ from other perennial grasses in that they have woody stems (culms). These are hollow (except in *Chusquea*), mostly greenish-brown and, due to their silica content, very strong, with a circumference of up to 15cm (6in) in some tropical species. Leaves are lance-shaped with cross veins that give a tessellated appearance, which may be obscured in the more tender species. Flowers are produced at varying intervals but are not decorative. After flowering, stems die down but few plants die completely. Fully to half hardy. Bamboos thrive in a sheltered, not too dry situation in sun or shade, unless otherwise stated.
See also *Bambusa*, *Chusquea*, *Fargesia*, *Himalayacalamus*, *Phyllostachys*, *Pleioblastus*, *Pseudosasa*, *Sasa*, *Semiarundinaria*, *Shibataea* and *Yushania*.

Rushes (Juncaceae)
Family of evergreen, tuft-forming or creeping, mostly rhizomatous annuals and perennials. All have either rounded, leafless stems or stems bearing long, narrow, basal leaves that are flat and hairless except *Luzula* (woodrushes) which has flat leaves, edged with white hairs. Rounded flower heads are generally unimportant. Fully to half hardy. Most rushes prefer sun or partial shade and a moist or wet situation, but *Luzula* prefers drier conditions.
See also *Isolepis*, *Juncus* and *Luzula*.

Sedges (Cyperaceae)
Family of evergreen, rhizomatous perennials that form dense tufts. Stems are triangular and bear long, narrow leaves, sometimes reduced to scales. Spikes or panicles of florets covered with glumes are produced and contain both male and female flowers, although some species of *Carex* have separate male and female flower heads on the same stem. Fully hardy to frost tender, min. 4–7°C (39–45°F). Grow in sun or partial shade. Some sedges grow naturally in water, but many may be grown in any well-drained soil.
See also *Carex*, *Cyperus*, *Eleocharis*, *Schoenoplectus* and *Scirpoides*.

Grass-leaved daylily. See *Hemerocallis minor*.
Great burnet. See *Sanguisorba officinalis*.
Great Solomon's seal. See *Polygonatum biflorum*.
Great white cherry. See *Prunus* 'Taihaku', illus. p.82.
Great yellow gentian. See *Gentiana lutea*, illus. p.261.
Greater celandine. See *Chelidonium*.
Greater periwinkle. See *Vinca major*.
Greater pond sedge. See *Carex riparia*.
Greater quaking grass. See *Briza maxima*.
Greater woodrush. See *Luzula sylvatica*.
Grecian strawberry tree. See *Arbutus andrachne*.
Greek fir. See *Abies cephalonica*.
Green ash. See *Fraxinus pennsylvanica*.
Green earth star. See *Cryptanthus acaulis*.
Green hellebore. See *Helleborus viridis*, illus. p.317.
Green-veined orchid. See *Orchis morio*, illus. p.310.
Greenweed, Dyers'. See *Genista tinctoria*, illus. p.153.

Grevillea

PROTEACEAE

Genus of evergreen shrubs and trees, grown for their flowers and foliage. Half hardy to frost tender, min. 5–10°C (41–50°F). Grow in full sun and well-drained, preferably acid soil. Water potted specimens moderately, very little in winter. Pruning is tolerated if necessary. Propagate by seed in spring or by semi-ripe cuttings in summer. All parts may aggravate skin allergies.
G. alpestris. See *G. alpina*.
G. alpina, *syn. G. alpestris.* Evergreen, rounded, wiry-stemmed shrub. H and S 30–60cm (1–2ft). Half hardy. Has narrowly oblong or oval leaves, dark green above, silky-haired beneath. Bears tubular, red flowers in small clusters in spring-summer.
G. banksii illus. p.95.
***G. juniperina* f. *sulphurea*,** syn. *G. sulphurea*, illus. p.165.
***G.* 'Poorinda Constance'.** Evergreen, bushy, rounded shrub. H and S to 2m (6ft). Half hardy. Has small, lance-shaped, mid- to deep green leaves with prickly toothed margins. Tubular, bright red flowers in conspicuous clusters are borne from spring to autumn, sometimes longer.
♀ ***G. robusta*** (Silky oak). Fast-growing, evergreen, upright to conical tree. H 30m (100ft), S to 15m (50ft). Frost tender, min. 5°C (41°F). Fern-like leaves are 15–25cm (6–10in) long. Mature specimens bear upturned bell-shaped, bright yellow or orange flowers in dense, one-sided spikes, 10cm (4in) or more long, in spring-summer.
***G.* 'Robyn Gordon'** illus. p.162.
♀ ***G. rosmarinifolia.*** Evergreen, rounded, well-branched shrub. H and S to 2m (6ft). Half hardy. Dark green leaves are needle-shaped with reflexed margins, silky-haired beneath. Has short, dense clusters of tubular, red, occasionally pink or white flowers in summer.
G. sulphurea. See *G. juniperina* f. *sulphurea*.

Grey alder. See *Alnus incana*, illus. p.62.
Grey poplar. See *Populus × canescens*, illus. p.61.

Greyia

GREYIACEAE

Genus of evergreen, semi-evergreen or deciduous, spring-flowering shrubs and trees, grown for their flowers and overall appearance. Frost tender, min. 7–10°C (45–50°F). Needs full light and well-drained soil. Water containerized specimens moderately, less when not in full growth. Remove or shorten flowered stems after flowering. Propagate by seed in spring or by semi-ripe cuttings in summer. Plants grown under glass need plenty of ventilation.
G. sutherlandii illus. p.127.

Grindelia

COMPOSITAE/ASTERACEAE

Genus of annuals, biennials, evergreen perennials and sub-shrubs, grown for their flower heads. Frost to half hardy, but in cold areas grow in a warm, sheltered site. Requires sun and well-drained soil. Water potted specimens moderately, less when not in full growth. Remove spent flowering stems either as they die or in following spring. Propagate by seed in spring or by semi-ripe cuttings in late summer.
G. chiloensis, syn. *G. speciosa*, illus. p.167.
G. speciosa. See *G. chiloensis*.

Griselinia

CORNACEAE/GRISELINIACEAE

Genus of evergreen shrubs and trees, with inconspicuous flowers, grown for their foliage. Thrives in mild, coastal areas where it is effective as a hedge or windbreak as it is very wind- and salt-resistant. Frost to half hardy; in cold areas provide shelter. Requires sun and fertile, well-drained soil. Restrict growth and trim hedges in early summer. Propagate by semi-ripe cuttings in summer.
♀ ***G. littoralis*** (Broadleaf). Fast-growing, evergreen, upright shrub of dense habit. H 6m (20ft), S 5m (15ft). Frost hardy. Bears oval, leathery leaves that are bright apple-green. Tiny, inconspicuous, yellow-green flowers are borne in late spring. **'Dixon's Cream'**, H 3m (10ft), S 2m (6ft), is slower-growing and has central, creamy-white leaf variegation. **'Variegata'** illus. p.122.
G. lucida. Fast-growing, evergreen, upright shrub. H 6m (20ft), S 5m (15ft). Half hardy. Is similar to *G. littoralis*, but has larger, glossy, dark green leaves.

Ground elder. See *Aegopodium*.
Ground ivy. See *Glechoma hederacea*.
Groundsel, Bush. See *Baccharis halimifolia*.
Guava, Pineapple. See *Acca sellowiana*, illus. p.139.
Guelder rose. See *Viburnum opulus*.
Guernsey lily. See *Nerine sarniensis*, illus. p.440.
Gum
Black. See *Nyssa sylvatica*, illus. p.67.
Blue. See *Eucalyptus globulus*.
Cider. See *Eucalyptus gunnii*, illus. p.68.
Flowering. See *Eucalyptus ficifolia*.
Manna. See *Eucalyptus viminalis*.
Mountain. See *Eucalyptus dalrympleana*, illus. p.68.
Murray red. See *Eucalyptus camaldulensis*.
Oriental sweet. See *Liquidambar orientalis*.
Ribbon. See *Eucalyptus viminalis*.
River red. See *Eucalyptus camaldulensis*.
Snow. See *Eucalyptus pauciflora* subsp. *niphophila*, illus. p.80.
Spinning. See *Eucalyptus perriniana*, illus. p.96.
Sweet. See *Liquidambar styraciflua*, illus. p.66.
Tasmanian blue. See *Eucalyptus globulus*.
Tasmanian snow. See *Eucalyptus*

coccifera, illus. p.68.
Tingiringi. See *Eucalyptus glaucescens*.
Gum tree. See *Eucalyptus.*

Gunnera

GUNNERACEAE/HALORAGIDACEAE

Genus of summer-flowering perennials, grown mainly for their foliage. Some are clump-forming with very large leaves; others are mat-forming with smaller leaves. Frost hardy, but shelter from wind in summer and cover with bracken or compost in winter. Some require sun while others do best in partial shade; all need moist soil. Propagate by seed in autumn or spring; small species by division in spring.
G. chilensis. See *G. tinctoria*.
G. magellanica illus. p.396.
♀ ***G. manicata*** illus. p.226.
G. scabra. See *G. tinctoria*.
G. tinctoria, syn. *G. chilensis, G. scabra.* Robust, rounded, clump-forming perennial. H and S 1.5m (5ft) or more. Has very large, rounded, puckered and lobed leaves, 45–60cm (1½–2ft) across. In early summer produces dense, conical clusters of tiny, dull reddish-green flowers.

Gutta-percha tree. See *Eucommia ulmoides*.

Guzmania

BROMELIACEAE

Genus of evergreen, rosette-forming, epiphytic perennials, grown for their overall appearance. Frost tender, min. 10–15°C (50–59°F). Needs semi-shade and a rooting medium of equal parts humus-rich soil and either sphagnum moss, or bark or plastic chips used for orchid culture. Using soft water, water moderately during growing season, sparingly at other times, and keep rosette centres filled with water from spring to autumn. Propagate by offsets in spring or summer.
♀ ***G. lingulata*** illus. p.273. Evergreen, basal-rosetted, epiphytic perennial. H and S 30–45cm (12–18in). Forms loose rosettes of broadly strap-shaped, arching, mid-green leaves. Bears a cluster of tubular, white to yellow flowers, surrounded by a rosette of bright red bracts, usually in summer. ♀ var. ***minor***, H and S 15cm (6in), has yellow-green leaves and red or yellow bracts.
♀ ***G. monostachia***, syn. *G. monostachya, G. tricolor* (Striped torch; illus. p.273). Evergreen, basal-rosetted, epiphytic perennial. H and S 30–40cm (12–16in). Has dense rosettes of strap-shaped, erect to arching, pale to yellowish-green leaves. In summer, elongated spikes of tubular, white flowers emerge from axils of oval bracts, the upper ones red, the lower ones green with purple-brown stripes.
G. monostachya. See *G. monostachia*.
♀ ***G. sanguinea.*** Evergreen, basal-rosetted, epiphytic perennial. H 20cm (8in), S 30–35cm (12–14in). Has dense, slightly flat rosettes of broadly strap-shaped, arching, mid- to deep green leaves. In summer, a compact cluster of tubular, yellow flowers, surrounded by red bracts, appears at the heart of each mature rosette.
G. tricolor. See *G. monostachia*.
G. vittata. Evergreen, basal-rosetted, epiphytic perennial. H and S 35–60cm (14–24in). Produces fairly loose rosettes of strap-shaped, erect, dark green leaves with pale green cross-bands and recurved tips. Stem bears a compact, egg-shaped head of small, tubular, white flowers in summer.

Gymnocalycium

CACTACEAE

Genus of perennial cacti with masses of funnel-shaped flowers in spring-summer. Crowns generally bear smooth, scaly buds. Frost tender, min. 5–10°C (41–50°F). Needs full sun or partial shade and very well-drained soil. Propagate by seed or offsets in spring or summer.
♀ ***G. andreae*** illus. p.493.
G. gibbosum illus. p.477.
***G. mihanovichii* 'Red Head',** syn. *G.m* 'Hibotan', *G.m.* 'Red Cap', illus. p.480.
♀ ***G. quehlianum.*** Flattened spherical, perennial cactus. H 5cm (2in), S 7cm (3in). Min. 5°C (41°F). Grey-blue to brown stem has 11 or so rounded ribs. Areoles each produce 5 curved spines. Has white flowers, 5cm (2in) across, with red throats, in spring-summer. Is easy to flower.
G. schickendantzii. Spherical, perennial cactus. H and S 10cm (4in). Min. 5°C (41°F). Dark green stem has 7–14 deeply indented ribs and long, red-tipped, grey-brown spines. Bears greenish-white to pale pink flowers, 5cm (2in) across, in summer.

Gymnocarpium

DRYOPTERIDACEAE/WOODSIACEAE

Genus of about 5 species of deciduous, rhizomatous, terrestrial ferns with triangular fronds, ideal for ground cover. Fully hardy. Grow in deep shade and preferably neutral to acid, leafy, moist soil. Propagate from spores when ripe, or divide in spring.
♀ ***G. dryopteris*** (Oak fern). Deciduous fern. H 20cm (8in), S indefinite. Bears distinctive, divided fronds, each with a leaf-blade 10–18cm (4–7in) long and across, on a stem 10cm (4in) long. Pinnae are triangular, with oblong to ovate, toothed and scalloped segments. Pale yellowish green when young, the fronds darken to vivid rich green as they mature.

Gymnocladus

LEGUMINOSAE/CAESALPINIACEAE

Genus of deciduous trees, grown for their foliage. Fully hardy. Needs full sun and deep, fertile, well-drained soil. Propagate by seed in autumn.
G. dioica (Kentucky coffee tree). Slow-growing, deciduous, spreading tree. H 20m (70ft), S 15m (50ft). Very large leaves, with 4–7 pairs of oval leaflets, are pinkish when young, dark green in summer, then yellow in autumn. Small, star-shaped, white flowers are borne in early summer.

Gynandriris

IRIDACEAE

Genus of iris-like, spring-flowering corms, grown mainly for botanical interest, with very short-lived blooms. Frost hardy. Dormant corms require warmth and dryness, so plant in a sunny site that dries out in summer. Needs well-drained soil, but with plenty of moisture in winter-spring. Propagate by seed or by removing cormlets from parent in autumn.
G. sisyrinchium illus. p.448.

Gynura

COMPOSITAE/ASTERACEAE

Genus of evergreen perennials, shrubs and semi-scrambling climbers, grown for their ornamental foliage or flower heads. Frost tender, min. 16°C (61°F). Needs light shade in summer and any fertile, well-drained soil. Water moderately throughout the year, less in cool conditions; do not overwater. Provide support for stems. Remove stem tips to encourage branching. Propagate by softwood or semi-ripe cuttings in spring or summer.
G. aurantiaca illus. p.218. ♀ **'Purple Passion'** (syn. *G. sarmentosa* of gardens) is an evergreen, erect, woody-based, soft-stemmed shrub or semi-scrambling climber. H 60cm (2ft) or more. Stems and lance-shaped, lobed, serrated leaves are covered with velvety, purple hairs. Leaves are purple-green above, deep red-purple beneath. In winter produces clusters of daisy-like, orange-yellow flower heads that become purplish as they mature.
G. sarmentosa of gardens. See *G. aurantiaca* 'Purple Passion'.

Gypsophila

CARYOPHYLLACEAE

Genus of spring- to autumn-flowering annuals and perennials, some of which are semi-evergreen. Fully hardy. Needs sun. Will grow in dry, sandy and stony soils, but does best in deep, well-drained soil. Resents being disturbed. Cut back after flowering for a second flush of flowers. Propagate *G. paniculata* cultivars by grafting in winter; others by softwood cuttings in summer or by seed in autumn or spring.
G. cerastioides illus. p.376.
G. elegans illus. p.330.
♀ ***G. paniculata* 'Bristol Fairy'** illus. p.241. **'Flamingo'** is a spreading, short-lived perennial. H 60–75cm (2–2½ft), S 1m (3ft). In summer bears panicles of numerous, small, rounded, double, pale pink flowers on wiry, branching stems. Has small, linear, mid-green leaves.
♀ ***G. repens.*** Semi-evergreen, prostrate perennial with much-branched rhizomes. H 2.5–5cm (1–2in) or more, S 30cm (12in) or more. In summer produces sprays of small, rounded, white, lilac or pink flowers on slender stems that bear narrowly oval, bluish-green leaves. Is excellent for a rock garden, wall or dry bank. May also be propagated by division in spring.
'Dorothy Teacher' illus. p.387.

HAAGEOCEREUS

CACTACEAE

Genus of perennial cacti with ribbed, densely spiny, columnar, green stems branching from the base. Frost tender, min. 11°C (52°F). Requires full sun and very well-drained soil. Propagate by seed or stem cuttings in spring or summer.
H. ambiguus. See *H. decumbens*.
H. chosicensis. See. *H. pseudomelanostele*.
H. decumbens, syn. *H. ambiguus, H. litoralis.* Prostrate, perennial cactus. H 30cm (1ft), S 1m (3ft). Stems, 6cm (2½in) across, with 20 or so ribs, have dark brown, central spines, 5cm (2in) long, and shorter, dense, golden, radial spines. Tubular, white flowers, 8cm (3in) across, are produced in summer near crowns, only on mature plants.
H. litoralis. See *H. decumbens*.
H. pseudomelanostele, syn. *H. chosicensis.* Upright, perennial cactus. H 1.5m (5ft), S 1m (3ft). Green stem, 10cm (4in) across, with 19 or so ribs, bears white, golden or red, central spines and shorter, dense, bristle-like, white, radial ones. Has tubular, white, lilac-white or pinkish-red flowers, 7cm (3in) long, near crown in summer.
H. versicolor illus. p.474.

HABERLEA

GESNERIACEAE

Genus of evergreen, rosetted perennials, grown for their elegant sprays of flowers. Is useful on walls. Fully hardy. Needs partially shaded, moist soil. Resents disturbance to roots. Propagate by seed in spring or by leaf cuttings or offsets in early summer.
H. ferdinandi-coburgii. Evergreen, dense, basal-rosetted perennial. H 10–15cm (4–6in), S 30cm (12in). Has oblong, toothed, dark green leaves, hairy below, almost glabrous above. Sprays of funnel-shaped, blue-violet flowers, each with a white throat, appear on long stems in late spring and early summer.
♀ ***H. rhodopensis.*** Evergreen, dense, basal-rosetted perennial. H 10cm (4in), S 15cm (6in) or more. Is similar to *H. ferdinandi-coburgii*, but leaves are soft-haired on both surfaces. **'Virginalis'** illus. p.385.

HABRANTHUS

AMARYLLIDACEAE

Genus of summer- and autumn-flowering bulbs with funnel-shaped flowers. Frost to half hardy. Needs a sheltered, sunny site and fertile soil, which is well supplied with moisture in growing season. Propagate by seed or offsets in spring.
H. andersonii. See *H. tubispathus*.
H. brachyandrus. Summer-flowering bulb. H to 30cm (12in), S 5–8cm (2–3in). Half hardy. Long, linear, semi-erect, narrow leaves form a basal cluster. Each flower stem bears a semi-erect, widely funnel-shaped, pinkish-red flower, 7–10cm (3–4in) long.
♀ ***H. robustus***, syn. *Zephyranthes robusta*, illus. p.453.
♀ ***H. tubispathus***, syn. *H. andersonii.* Summer-flowering bulb. H to 15cm (6in), S 5cm (2in). Frost hardy. Has linear, semi-erect, basal leaves and a succession of flower stems each bearing solitary 2.5–3.5cm (1–1½in) long, funnel-shaped flowers, yellow inside, copper-red outside.

Hackberry. See *Celtis*.
Common. See *Celtis occidentalis*.

HACQUETIA,
syn. DONDIA

UMBELLIFERAE/APIACEAE

Genus of one species of clump-forming, rhizomatous perennial that creeps slowly, grown for its yellow or yellow-green flower heads borne on leafless plants in late winter and early spring. Is good in rock gardens. Fully hardy. Prefers shade and humus-rich, moist soil. Resents disturbance to roots. Propagate by division in spring, by seed when fresh in autumn or by root cuttings in winter.
♀ ***H. epipactis*** illus. p.383.

HAEMANTHUS

AMARYLLIDACEAE

Genus of summer-flowering bulbs with dense heads of small, star-shaped flowers, often brightly coloured. Frost tender, min. 10°C (50°F). Prefers full sun or partial shade and well-drained soil or sandy compost. Liquid feed in the growing season. Leave undisturbed as long as possible before replanting. Propagate by offsets or seed before growth commences in early spring. All parts may cause mild stomach upset if ingested; contact with the sap may irritate skin.
♀ ***H. albiflos*** (Paintbrush). Summer-flowering bulb. H 5–30cm (2–12in), S 20–30cm (8–12in). Has 2–6 almost prostrate, broadly elliptic leaves with hairy edges. Flower stem, appearing between leaves, bears a brush-like head of up to 50 white flowers with very narrow petals and protruding stamens.
♀ ***H. coccineus*** illus. p.451.
H. katherinae. See *Scadoxus multiflorus* subsp. *katherinae*.
H. magnificus. See *Scadoxus puniceus*.
H. multiflorus. See *Scadoxus multiflorus*.
H. natalensis. See *Scadoxus puniceus*.
H. puniceus. See *Scadoxus puniceus*.
H. sanguineus. Summer-flowering bulb. H to 30cm (12in), S 20–30cm (8–12in). Bears 2 prostrate, elliptic, rough, dark green leaves, hairy beneath. Brownish-purple-spotted, green flower stem, forming before leaves, produces a dense head of small, narrow-petalled, red flowers, surrounded by whorls of narrow, leaf-like, red or pink bracts.

Hairy brome grass. See *Bromus ramosus*.

HAKEA

PROTEACEAE

Genus of evergreen shrubs and trees, grown for their often needle-like leaves and their flowers. Is very wind-resistant, except in cold areas. Frost hardy to frost tender, min. 5–7°C (41–5°F). Requires a position in full sun and fertile, well-drained soil. Water containerized specimens moderately in growing season, but only sparingly in winter. Propagate by semi-ripe cuttings in summer or by seed in autumn.
H. drupacea, syn. *H. suaveolens*. Evergreen, rounded shrub. H and S 2m (6ft) or more. Frost tender. Leaves are divided into cylindrical, needle-like leaflets or occasionally are undivided and lance-shaped. Small, fragrant, tubular, white flowers, carried in short, dense clusters, are produced from summer to winter.
H. lissosperma, syn. *H. sericea* of gardens. Evergreen, upright, densely branched shrub of pine-like appearance. H 5m (15ft), S 3m (10ft). Frost hardy. Bears long, slender, sharply pointed, grey-green leaves and produces, in late spring and early summer, clusters of small, spidery, white flowers.
H. sericea of gardens. See *H. lissosperma*.
H. suaveolens. See *H. drupacea*.

HAKONECHLOA

GRAMINEAE/POACEAE

See also GRASSES, BAMBOOS, RUSHES and SEDGES.
♀ ***H. macra* 'Aureola'** illus. p.321.

HALESIA
Silver bell, Snowdrop tree

STYRACACEAE

Genus of deciduous, spring-flowering trees and shrubs, grown for their showy, pendent, bell-shaped flowers and their curious, winged fruits. Fully hardy, but needs a sunny, sheltered position. Prefers moist but well-drained, neutral to acid soil. Propagate by softwood cuttings in summer or by seed in autumn.
H. carolina, syn. *H. tetraptera*. Deciduous, spreading tree or shrub. H 8m (25ft), S 10m (30ft). Oval leaves are mid-green. Masses of bell-shaped, white flowers, hanging from bare shoots, are produced in late spring, and are followed by 4-winged, green fruits.
H. monticola illus. p.72.
H. tetraptera. See *H. carolina*.

× HALIMIOCISTUS

CISTACEAE

Hybrid genus *(Cistus × Halimium)* of evergreen shrubs, grown for their flowers. Frost hardy, but in cold areas needs shelter. Requires full sun and well-drained soil. Propagate by semi-ripe cuttings in summer.
♀ **× *H. sahucii***, syn. *Cistus revolii* of gardens, illus. p.155.
♀ **× *H. wintonensis***, syn. *Halimium wintonense*. Evergreen, bushy shrub. H 60cm (2ft), S 1m (3ft). Saucer-shaped, white flowers, each with deep red bands and a yellow centre, open amid lance-shaped, grey-green leaves in late spring and early summer.

HALIMIUM

CISTACEAE

Genus of evergreen shrubs, grown for their showy flowers. Is good for coastal gardens. Frost hardy, but in cold areas needs shelter. Does best in full sun and light, well-drained soil. Propagate by semi-ripe cuttings in summer.
H. formosum. See *H. lasianthum* subsp. *formosum*.
♀ ***H. lasianthum.*** Evergreen, bushy, spreading shrub. H 1m (3ft), S 1.5m (5ft). Leaves are oval and grey-green. In late spring and early summer bears saucer-shaped, golden-yellow flowers, sometimes with small, central, red blotches. subsp. ***formosum*** (syn. *H. formosum*) illus. p.165.
♀ ***H. ocymoides***, syn. *Cistus algarvensis*. Evergreen, bushy shrub. H 60cm (2ft), S 1m (3ft). Narrowly oval leaves, covered in white hairs when young, mature to dark green. In early summer produces upright clusters of saucer-shaped, golden-yellow flowers, conspicuously blotched with black or purple. **'Susan'** see *H.* 'Susan'.
♀ ***H.* 'Susan'**, syn. *H. ocymoides* 'Susan', illus. p.165.
H. umbellatum, syn. *Helianthemum umbellatum*, illus. p.155.
H. wintonense. See × *Halimiocistus wintonensis*.

HAMAMELIS
Witch hazel

HAMAMELIDACEAE

Genus of deciduous, autumn- to early spring-flowering shrubs, grown for their autumn colour and fragrant, frost-resistant flowers, each with 4 narrowly strap-shaped petals. Fully hardy. Flourishes in sun or semi-shade and fertile, well-drained, peaty, acid soil, although tolerates good, deep soil over chalk. Propagate species by seed in autumn, selected forms by softwood cuttings in summer, by budding in late summer or by grafting in winter.
♀ ***H.* × *intermedia* 'Arnold Promise'** illus. p.122. ♀ **'Diane'** illus. p.121.
♀ **'Jelena'** is a deciduous, upright shrub. H and S 4m (12ft) or more. Broadly oval, glossy, bright green leaves turn bright orange or red in autumn. Bears masses of large, fragrant, orange flowers, along bare branches, from early to mid-winter.
♀ **'Pallida'** (syn. *H. mollis* 'Pallida'), S 3m (10ft), bears dense clusters of large, sulphur-yellow flowers.
H. japonica (Japanese witch hazel). Deciduous, upright, open shrub. H and S 4m (12ft). Broadly oval, glossy, mid-green leaves turn yellow in autumn. Fragrant, yellow flowers, with crinkled petals, are produced on bare branches from mid- to late winter. **'Sulphurea'** illus. p.122. **'Zuccariniana'** bears paler, lemon-yellow flowers in early spring and produces orange-yellow leaves in autumn.
♀ ***H. mollis*** (Chinese witch hazel). Deciduous, upright, open shrub. H and S 4m (12ft) or more. Broadly oval, mid-green leaves turn yellow in autumn. Produces extremely fragrant, yellow flowers, along bare branches, in mid- and late winter. **'Coombe Wood'** illus. p.122. ♀ **'Pallida'** see *H.* ×

intermedia 'Pallida'.
♀ ***H. vernalis* 'Sandra'** illus. p.120.
H. virginiana illus. p.121.

Hamatocactus hamatacanthus. See *Ferocactus hamatacanthus*.
Hamatocactus setispinus. See *Thelocactus setispinus*.
Hamatocactus uncinatus. See *Sclerocactus uncinatus*.
Hard fern. See *Blechnum spicant*.
Hard shield fern. See *Polystichum aculeatum*.

HARDENBERGIA

LEGUMINOSAE/PAPILIONACEAE

Genus of evergreen, woody-stemmed, twining climbers or sub-shrubs, grown for their curtains of leaves and racemes of pea-like flowers. Half hardy to frost tender, min. 7°C (45°F). Grows best in sun and in well-drained soil that does not dry out. Propagate by stem cuttings in late summer or autumn or by seed (soaked before sowing) in spring.
♀ ***H. comptoniana*** illus. p.202.
H. monophylla. See *H. violacea*.
♀ ***H. violacea***, syn. *H. monophylla* (Australian sarsparilla, Coral pea, Vine lilac). Evergreen, woody-stemmed, twining climber. H to 3m (10ft). Frost tender. Narrowly oval leaves are 2.5–12cm (1–5in) long. Violet, occasionally pink or white, flowers, with yellow blotches on upper petals, are borne in spring. Brownish pods, 3–4cm (1¼–1½in) long, are produced in autumn. **'Happy Wanderer'** illus. p.202.

Hardy age. See *Eupatorium rugosum*, illus. p.242.
Hare's ear, Shrubby. See *Bupleurum fruticosum*, illus. p.142.
Hare's-foot fern. See *Davallia canariensis*.
Hare's-tail grass. See *Lagurus ovatus*, illus. p.318.
Harebell poppy. See *Meconopsis quintuplinervia*, illus. p.279.
Harlequin flower. See *Sparaxis*.
Hart's-tongue fern. See *Asplenium scolopendrium*, illus. p.325.
Hat plant
Chinese. See *Holmskioldia sanguinea*.
Mandarin's. See *Holmskioldia sanguinea*.
Mexican. See *Kalanchoe daigremontiana*.

HATIORA

CACTACEAE

Genus of perennial, epiphytic cacti with short, jointed, cylindrical stems, each swollen at one end like a bottle. Frost tender, min. 10–13°C (50–55°F). Requires partial shade and very well-drained soil. Keep damp in summer; water a little in winter. Propagate by stem cuttings in spring or summer.
H. clavata. See *Rhipsalis gaertneri*.
♀ ***H. gaertneri***, syn. *Rhipsalidopsis gaertneri*, illus. p.491.
♀ ***H. rosea***, syn. *Rhipsalidopsis rosea*, illus. p.488.
♀ ***H. salicornioides***, syn. *Rhipsalis salicornioides*, illus. p.484.

Haw, Yellow. See *Crataegus flava*, illus. p.86.
Hawk's beard. See *Crepis*.
Hawkweed. See *Hieracium*.

HAWORTHIA

LILIACEAE/ALOACEAE

Genus of basal-rosetted, clump-forming, perennial succulents with triangular to rounded, green leaves. Roots tend to wither in winter or during long periods of drought. Frost tender, min. 5–10°C (41–50°F). Needs partial shade to stay green and grow quickly; if planted in full sun turns red or orange and grows slowly. Requires very well-drained soil. Keep dry in winter. Propagate by seed or division from spring to autumn.
H. arachnoidea, syn. *H. setata*, illus. p.486.
H. attenuata illus. p.485.
H. × cuspidata. Clump-forming, perennial succulent. H 5cm (2in), S 25cm (10in). Min. 5°C (41°F). Produces a basal rosette of smooth, rounded, fleshy, light green leaves covered with translucent marks. Tubular to bell-shaped, white flowers appear from spring to autumn on long, slender stems.
H. fasciata. Slow-growing, clump-forming, perennial succulent. H 15cm (6in), S 30cm (12in). Min. 5°C (41°F). Has raised, white dots, mostly in bands, on undersides of triangular, slightly incurved leaves, to 8cm (3in) long, which are arranged in a basal rosette. Bears tubular to bell-shaped, white flowers, on long, slender stems, from spring to autumn.
H. setata. See *H. arachnoidea*.
♀ ***H. truncata*** illus. p.485.

Hawthorn. See *Crataegus*.
Common. See *Crataegus monogyna*.
Indian. See *Rhaphiolepis indica*.
Water. See *Aponogeton distachyos*, illus. p.463.
Hawthorn maple. See *Acer crataegifolium*.
Hazel. See *Corylus*.
Chilean. See *Gevuina avellana*.
Chinese witch. See *Hamamelis mollis*.
Turkish. See *Corylus colurna*.
Virginian. See *Hamamelis virginiana*.
Witch. See *Hamamelis*.
Headache tree. See *Umbellularia*.
Heart leaf. See *Philodendron hederaceum*.
Heart of flame. See *Bromelia balansae*, illus. p.273.
Heart pea. See *Cardiospermum halicacabum*.
Heart seed. See *Cardiospermum halicacabum*.
Heart vine. See *Ceropegia linearis* subsp. *woodii*, illus. p.478.
Hearts-and-honey vine. See *Ipomoea × multifida*.
Heartsease. See *Viola tricolor*, illus. p.381.
Heath
Alpine. See *Erica carnea*.
Australian. See *Epacris impressa*, illus. p.151.
Besom. See *Erica scoparia*.
Channelled. See *Erica canaliculata*, illus. p.174.
Cornish. See *Erica vagans*.
Corsican. See *Erica terminalis*.
Cross-leaved. See *Erica tetralix*.
Dorset. See *Erica ciliaris*.
Mackay's. See *Erica mackayana*.
Portuguese. See *Erica lusitanica*.
Prince of Wales. See *Erica perspicua*, illus. p.174.
St Dabeoc's. See *Daboecia cantabrica*.
Spanish. See *Erica australis*.
Spanish tree. See *Erica australis*.
Spike. See *Erica spiculifolia*.
Tree. See *Erica arborea*.
Winter. See *Erica carnea*.
Heath banksia. See *Banksia ericifolia*.
Heather
Bell. See *Erica cinerea*.
False. See *Cuphea hyssopifolia*, illus. p.154.
Scotch. See *Calluna vulgaris*.

HEATHERS

ERICACEAE

Heathers (otherwise known as heaths) are evergreen, woody-stemmed shrubs, grown for their flowers and foliage, both of which may provide colour in the garden all year round. There are 3 genera: *Calluna*, *Daboecia* and *Erica*. *Calluna* has only one species, *C. vulgaris*, but it contains a large number of cultivars that flower mainly from mid-summer to late autumn. *Daboecia* has 2 species, both of which are summer-flowering. The largest genus is *Erica*, which, although broadly divided into 2 groups – winter-and summer-flowering species – has some species also flowering in spring and autumn. They vary in height from tree heaths, which may grow to 6m (20ft), to dwarf, prostrate plants that, if planted 30–45cm (12–18in) apart, soon spread to form a thick mat of ground cover.

Heathers are fully hardy to frost tender, min. 5–7°C (41–5°F). They prefer an open, sunny position and require humus-rich, well-drained soil. *Calluna* and *Daboecia* dislike limestone and must be grown in acid soil; some species of *Erica* tolerate slightly alkaline soil but all are better grown in acid soils. Prune lightly after flowering each year to keep plants bushy and compact. Propagate species by seed in spring or by softwood cuttings, division or layering in summer. Seed cannot be relied on to come true. All cultivars should be vegetatively propagated. Heathers are illustrated on pp.174–5.

Heavenly bamboo. See *Nandina domestica*.

HEBE

SCROPHULARIACEAE

Genus of evergreen shrubs, grown for their often dense spikes, panicles or racemes of flowers and their foliage. Grows well in coastal areas. Smaller species and cultivars are suitable for rock gardens. Fully to half hardy. Requires position in full sun and well-drained soil. Growth may be restricted, or leggy plants tidied, by cutting back in spring. Propagate by semi-ripe cuttings in summer.
♀ ***H. albicans*** illus. p.157. **'Cranleigh Gem'** is an evergreen, rounded shrub. H 60cm (2ft), S 1m (3ft). Frost hardy. Has dense spikes of small, 4-lobed, white flowers, with conspicuous, black anthers, amid narrowly oval, grey-green leaves in early summer.
♀ ***H.* 'Alicia Amherst'.** Fast-growing, evergreen, upright shrub. H and S 1.2m (4ft). Frost hardy. Has large, oblong, glossy, dark green leaves and, in late summer-autumn, large spikes of small, 4-lobed, deep violet-purple flowers.
***H.* 'Andersonii Variegata'.** See *H. × andersonii* 'Variegata'.
***H. × andersonii* 'Variegata'**, syn. *H.* 'Andersonii Variegata'. Evergreen, bushy shrub. H and S 2m (6ft). Half hardy. Leaves are oblong and dark green, each with a grey-green centre and creamy-white margins. Has dense spikes of small, 4-lobed, lilac flowers from mid-summer to autumn.
***H.* 'Autumn Glory'** illus. p.163.
***H.* 'Bowles' Variety'** illus. p.164.
H. brachysiphon. Evergreen, bushy, dense shrub. H and S 2m (6ft). Fully hardy. Has oblong, dark green leaves. Produces dense spikes of small, 4-lobed, white flowers in mid-summer. **'White Gem'** see *H.* 'White Gem'.
H. buchananii. Evergreen, dome-shaped shrub. H and S 15cm (6in) or more. Frost hardy. Very dark stems bear oval, bluish-green leaves. In summer produces clusters of small, 4-lobed white flowers at stem tips. **'Minor'**, H 5–10cm (2–4in), has smaller leaves.
H. canterburiensis, syn. *H.* 'Tom Marshall'. Evergreen, low growing, spreading shrub. H and S 30–90cm (1–3ft). Frost hardy. Small, oval, glossy, dark green leaves are densely packed on stems. In early summer, short racemes of small, white flowers are freely produced in leaf axils.
***H.* 'Carl Teschner'.** See *H.* 'Youngii'.
H. carnosula. Evergreen, prostrate shrub. H 15–30cm (6–12in), S 30cm (12in) or more. Frost hardy. Has small, oblong to oval, slightly convex, fleshy, glaucous leaves. Terminal clusters of many small, white flowers, with 4 pointed lobes, are borne in late spring or early summer.
H. cupressoides illus. p.172. **'Boughton Dome'** illus. p.373.
***H.* 'E.A. Bowles'** illus. p.163.
***H.* 'Eveline'**, syn. *H.* 'Gauntlettii'. Evergreen, upright shrub. H and S 1m (3ft). Frost hardy. Has long spikes of small, 4-lobed, pink flowers, each with a purplish tube, amid rich green, oblong leaves from late summer to late autumn.
***H.* 'Fairfieldii'.** Evergreen, upright shrub. H and S 60cm (2ft). Frost hardy. Oval, toothed, glossy, bright green leaves are red-margined. Large, open panicles of small, 4-lobed, pale lilac flowers are produced in late spring and early summer.
***H. × franciscana* 'Blue Gem'.** Evergreen, spreading shrub. H 60cm (2ft), S 1.2m (4ft). Frost hardy. Has oblong, densely arranged, mid-green leaves. Bears dense spikes of small, 4-lobed, violet-blue flowers from mid-summer until early winter.
***H.* 'Gauntlettii'.** See *H.* 'Eveline'.
♀ ***H.* 'Great Orme'** illus. p.159.
♀ ***H. hulkeana.*** Evergreen, upright, open shrub. H and S 1m (3ft). Frost hardy. Oval, toothed, glossy, dark

green leaves have red margins. Has masses of small, 4-lobed, pale lilac flowers in large, open panicles in late spring and early summer. **'Lilac Hint'** illus. p.163.
***H.* 'La Séduisante',** syn. *H.* 'Ruddigore', *H. speciosa* 'Ruddigore'. Evergreen, upright shrub. H and S 1m (3ft). Frost hardy. Oval, glossy, deep green leaves are purple beneath. Produces small, 4-lobed, deep purplish-red flowers in large spikes from late summer to late autumn.
♀ ***H. macrantha.*** Evergreen, bushy shrub. H 60cm (2ft), S 1m (3ft). Frost hardy. Has oval, toothed, fleshy, bright green leaves and produces racemes of large, 4-lobed, pure white flowers in early summer. May become bare at base.
♀ ***H.* 'Midsummer Beauty'.** Evergreen, rounded, open shrub. H 2m (6ft), S 1.5m (5ft). Frost hardy. Long, narrow, glossy, bright green leaves are reddish-purple beneath. Long spikes of small, 4-lobed, lilac flowers that fade to white are borne from mid-summer to late autumn.
H. ochracea. Evergreen, bushy, dense shrub. H and S 1m (3ft). Fully hardy. Slender shoots are densely covered with tiny, scale-like, ochre-tinged, olive-green leaves. Clusters of small, 4-lobed, white flowers appear in late spring and early summer.
H. pinguifolia (Disk-leaved hebe). ♀ **'Pagei'** illus. p.363.
***H.* 'Purple Queen'** illus. p.164.
♀ ***H. rakaiensis.*** Evergreen, rounded, compact shrub. H 1m (3ft), S 1.2m (4ft). Fully hardy. Produces small, dense spikes of small, 4-lobed, white flowers amid small, oblong, mid-green leaves from early to mid-summer.
H. recurva illus. p.157.
***H.* 'Ruddigore'.** See *H.* 'La Séduisante'.
H. salicifolia. Evergreen, upright shrub. H and S 2.5m (8ft). Frost hardy. Has long, narrow, pointed, pale green leaves and, in summer, produces slender spikes of small, 4-lobed, white or pale lilac flowers.
***H. speciosa* 'Ruddigore'.** See *H.* 'La Séduisante'.
***H.* 'Tom Marshall'.** See *H. canterburiensis.*
♀ ***H. vernicosa*** illus. p.363.
♀ ***H.* 'White Gem',** syn. *H. brachysiphon* 'White Gem', illus. p.154.
♀ ***H.* 'Youngii',** syn. *H.* 'Carl Teschner'. Evergreen, prostrate, becoming dome-shaped, shrub. H 15cm (6in), S 30cm (12in) or more. Frost hardy. Blackish-brown stems are covered in small, oval, glossy, dark green leaves. Bears short racemes of tiny, 4-lobed, white-throated, purple flowers in summer. Is excellent as a border plant.

Hebe, Disk-leaved. See *Hebe pinguifolia.*

HEDERA
Ivy

ARALIACEAE

Genus of evergreen, woody-stemmed, trailing perennials and self-clinging climbers with adventitious rootlets, used for covering walls and fences and as ground cover. Takes a year or so to become established, but thereafter growth is rapid. On the ground and while climbing, mostly bears roughly triangular, usually lobed leaves. Given extra height and access to light, leaves become less lobed and, in autumn, umbels of small, yellowish-green flowers are produced, followed by globose, black, occasionally yellow, fruits. Fully to half hardy. Ivies with green leaves are very shade tolerant and do well against a north-facing wall. Those with variegated or yellow leaves prefer more light, are usually less hardy and may sustain frost and wind damage in severe winters. All prefer well-drained, alkaline soil. Prune in spring to control height and spread, and to remove any damaged growth. Propagate in late summer by softwood cuttings or rooted layers. Red spider mite may be a problem when plants are grown against a south-facing wall or in dry conditions. All parts of ivy may cause severe discomfort if ingested; contact with the sap may aggravate skin allergies or irritate skin. See also feature panel p.219.
H. algeriensis. See *H. canariensis* of gardens.
H. canariensis of gardens, syn. *H. algeriensis*. Fast-growing, evergreen, self-clinging climber. H to 6m (20ft), S 5m (15ft). Half hardy; may be damaged in severe winters but soon recovers. Has oval to triangular, unlobed, glossy, mid-green leaves and reddish-purple stems. Is suitable for growing against a wall in a sheltered area. ♀ **'Gloire de Marengo'** has silver-variegated leaves.
♀ **'Ravensholst'** (illus. p.219) is vigorous with large leaves; makes good ground cover.
♀ ***H. colchica*** (Persian ivy). Evergreen, self-clinging climber or trailing perennial. H 10m (30ft), S 5m (15ft). Fully hardy. Has large, oval, unlobed, dark green leaves. Is suitable for growing against a wall. ♀ **'Dentata'** (Elephant's ears; illus. p.219) is more vigorous and has large, light green leaves that droop, hence its common name. Is good when grown against a wall or for ground cover. ♀ **'Dentata Variegata',** H 5m (15ft), has variegated, cream-yellow leaves; is useful to brighten a shady corner. **'Paddy's Pride'** see 'Sulphur Heart'. ♀ **'Sulphur Heart'** (syn. *H.c.* 'Paddy's Pride'; illus. p.219), H 5m (15ft), S 3m (10ft), has leaves variegated yellow and light green.
H. cypria, syn. *H. pastuchovii* var. *cypria* (illus p.219). Vigorous, evergreen, self-clinging climber. H 3m (10ft, S 2m (6ft). Fully hardy. Has shield-shaped, glossy, dark green leaves with prominent, grey-green veins. Should only be grown against a wall.
H. helix (Common English ivy). Vigorous, evergreen, self-clinging climber or trailing perennial. H 10m (30ft), S 5m (15ft). Fully hardy. Has 5-lobed, dark green leaves. Makes good ground and wall cover, but may be invasive; for a small garden, the more decorative cultivars are preferable. **'Adam'** (illus. p.219), H 1.2m (4ft), S 1m (3ft), is half hardy and has small, light green leaves variegated cream-yellow; may suffer leaf damage in winter, but will recover. ♀ **'Angularis Aurea'** (illus. p.219), H 4m (12ft), S 2.5m (8ft), has glossy, light green leaves, with bright yellow variegation; is not suitable as ground cover. **'Anna Marie'** (illus. p.219), H 1.2m (4ft), S 1m (3ft), is frost hardy and has light green leaves with cream variegation, mostly at margins; may suffer leaf damage in winter. **'Atropurpurea'** (syn. *H.h.* 'Purpurea'; Purple-leaved ivy; illus. p.219), H 4m (12ft), S 2.5m (8ft), has dark green leaves that turn deep purple in winter. var. ***baltica*** (syn. *H.h.* 'Baltica'), an exceptionally hardy cultivar, has small leaves and makes good ground cover in an exposed area. **'Buttercup'** (illus. p.219), H 2m (6ft), S 2.5m (8ft), is frost hardy and has light green leaves that turn rich butter-yellow in full sun. **'Caenwoodiana'** see *H.h.* 'Pedata'.♀ **'Congesta'**, H 45cm (1½ft), S 60cm (2ft), is a non-climbing, erect cultivar with spire-like shoots and small leaves; is suitable for a rock garden. **'Conglomerata'** (Clustered ivy), H and S 1m (3ft), will clamber over a low wall or grow in a rock garden; has small, curly, unlobed leaves. **'Cristata'** see *H.h.* 'Parsley Crested'.**'Curlylocks'** see *H.h.* 'Manda's Crested'.**'Deltoidea'** see *H. hibernica* 'Deltoidea'.**'Digitata'** see *H. hibernica* 'Digitata'. ♀ **'Erecta'** (illus. p.219), H 1m (3ft), S 1.2m (4ft), is a non-climbing, erect cultivar similar to *H.h.* 'Congesta'. **'Eva'** (illus. p.219), H 1.2m (4ft), S 1m (3ft), is frost hardy and has small, grey-green leaves with cream variegation; may suffer leaf damage in winter. ♀ **'Glacier'** (illus. p.219), H 3m (10ft), S 2m (6ft), is frost hardy and has silvery-grey-green leaves. **'Glymii'** (illus. p.219), H 2.5m (8ft), S 2m (6ft), has glossy, dark green leaves that turn deep purple in winter; is not suitable for ground cover. ♀ **'Goldchild'** (syn. *H.h.* 'Gold Harald'; illus. p.219), H 1m (3ft), is frost hardy and has small, 3- to 5-lobed, grey-green leaves with broad yellow margins. **'Gold Harald'** see *H.h.* 'Goldchild'. **'Goldheart'** see *H.h.* 'Oro di Bogliasco'. **'Gracilis'** see *H. hibernica* 'Gracilis'. **'Green Ripple'** (illus. p.219), H and S 1.2m (4ft), is frost hardy and has mid-green leaves with prominent, light green veins; is good for ground cover or for growing against a low wall. **'Hahn's Self-branching'** see *H.h.* 'Pittsburgh'.**'Heise'** (illus. p.219), H 30cm (1ft), S 60cm (2ft), is frost hardy and has small, grey-green leaves with cream variegation; is suitable as ground cover for a small, sheltered area. var. ***hibernica*** see *H. hibernica.* ♀ **'Ivalace'** (illus. p.219), H 1m (3ft), S 1.2m (4ft), is frost hardy and has curled and crimped, glossy leaves; is good for ground cover and for growing against a low wall. **'Jubiläum Goldherz'** see *H.h.* 'Oro di Bogliasco'.**'Jubilee Goldheart'** see *H.h.* 'Oro di Bogliasco'.**'Königers Auslese'** (syn. *H.h.* 'Sagittifolia' of gardens), H 1.2 m (4ft), S 1m (3ft), is frost hardy and has finger-like, deeply cut leaves; is not suitable for ground cover. **'Little Diamond'** (illus. p.219) is frost hardy, slow-growing and has entire, diamond-shaped, grey-green leaves, variegated creamy-white. **'Lobata Major'** see *H. hibernica* 'Lobata Major'. ♀ **'Manda's Crested'** (syn. *H.h.* 'Curlylocks'), H and S 2m (6ft), is frost hardy and has elegant, wavy-edged, mid-green leaves that turn a coppery shade in winter. **'Merion Beauty'** (illus. p.219), H 1.2m (4ft), S 1m (3ft), is frost hardy with delicately lobed leaves; is not suitable for ground cover. **'Nigra'** (illus. p.219), H and S 1.2m (4ft), has small, very dark green leaves that turn purple-black in winter. **'Oro di Bogliasco'** (syn. *H.h.* 'Goldheart', *H.h.* 'Jubiläum Goldherz', *H.h.* 'Jubilee Goldheart'; illus. p.219), H 6m (20ft), has dark green leaves with bright yellow centres; is slow to establish, then grows rapidly; is not suitable for ground cover. ♀ **'Parsley Crested'** (syn. *H.h.* 'Cristata'; illus. p.219), H 2m (6ft), S 1.2m (4ft), is frost hardy and has light green leaves, crested at margins; is not suitable for ground cover. **'Pedata'** (syn. *H.h.* 'Caenwoodiana'; Bird's-foot ivy), H 4m (12ft), S 3m (10ft), has grey-green leaves shaped like a bird's foot; is not suitable for ground cover. **'Pittsburgh'** (syn. *H.h.* 'Hahn's Self-branching'; illus. p.219), H 1m (3ft), S 1.2m (4ft), is frost hardy and has mid-green leaves; is suitable for growing against a low wall and for ground cover. edera H 3m (10ft), has large, 5-lobed, shiny, mid-green leaves. Is often grown as a "bush ivy", as it bears distinctive, orange-yellow fruit, even on comparatively young plants. **'Poetica'** see *H.h.* f. *poetarum*. **'Poetica Arborea'** see *H.h.* f. *poetarum*. **'Purpurea'** see *H.h.* 'Atropurpurea'. **'Sagittifolia'** of gardens see *H.h.* 'Königers Auslese'.**'Telecurl'** (illus. p.219), H and S 1m (3ft), is frost hardy and has elegantly twisted, light green leaves. **'Triton'**, H 45cm (1½ft), S 1m (3ft), is a non-climbing frost hardy cultivar that has leaves with deeply incised lobes that resemble whips; makes good ground cover. **'Woeneri'**, H 4m (12ft), S 3m (10ft), is a vigorous cultivar that has bluntly lobed, grey-green leaves, with lighter coloured veins, that turn purple in winter.
♀ ***H. hibernica***, syn. *H. helix* var. *hibernica* (Irish ivy). Vigorous, evergreen climber. H 5m (15ft), S 6m (20ft). Fully hardy. Has large, mid-green leaves. Is good for covering a large area, either on the ground or against a wall. ♀ **'Deltoidea'** (syn. *H. helix* 'Deltoidea'; Shield ivy, Sweetheart ivy; illus. p.219), H 5m (15ft), S 3m (10ft), has heart-shaped leaves; is suitable only for growing against a wall. **'Digitata'** (syn. *H. helix* 'Digitata'; Finger-leaved ivy), H 6m (20ft), has large leaves; is not suitable for ground cover. **'Gracilis'** (syn. *H. helix* 'Gracilis'), H 5m (15ft), has sharply lobed, dark green leaves that turn bronze-purple in winter; is not suitable for ground cover. **'Lobata Major'** (syn. *H. helix* 'Lobata Major';

illus. p.219), H 5m (15ft), is vigorous with large, 3-lobed leaves. **'Sulphurea'**, H and S 3m (10ft), has medium-sized leaves with sulphur-yellow variegation; is suitable for growing against a wall or for ground cover, and as a foil for brightly coloured plants.
H. nepalensis (Nepalese ivy). Evergreen, self-clinging climber. H 4m (12ft), S 2.5m (8ft). Half hardy; young growth may suffer damage from late frosts. Has oval to triangular, toothed, olive-green leaves and is suitable only for growing against a sheltered wall. **'Suzanne'** (illus. p.219), H 2m (6ft), is less vigorous that the species and has 5-lobed leaves with backward-pointing basal lobes.
H. pastuchovii. Moderately vigorous, evergreen, self-clinging climber. H 2.5m (8ft), S 2m (6ft). Fully hardy. Has shield-shaped, glossy, dark green leaves and should only be grown against a wall. var. ***cypria*** see *H. cypria*.
H. rhombea (Japanese ivy). Evergreen, self-clinging climber. H and S 1.2m (4ft). Frost hardy. Has small, fairly thick, diamond-shaped, unlobed, mid-green leaves. Is suitable only for growing against a low wall. **'Variegata'** has leaves with narrow, white margins.

Hedge bamboo. See *Bambusa multiplex*, illus. p.319.
Hedgehog broom. See *Erinacea anthyllis*, illus. p.360.
Hedgehog holly. See *Ilex aquifolium* 'Ferox'.
Hedgehog rose. See *Rosa rugosa*, illus. p.183.

HEDYCHIUM
Garland flower, Ginger lily

ZINGIBERACEAE

Genus of perennials with stout, fleshy rhizomes. Fragrant, showy flowers are short-lived, but borne profusely. Grow in sheltered borders and conservatories. Frost hardy to frost tender, min. 5°C (41°F). Needs sun and rich, moist soil. Propagate by division in spring; should not be divided when dormant.
H. coronarium (White ginger lily). Upright, rhizomatous perennial. H 1.5m (5ft), S 60cm–1m (2–3ft). Frost tender. Produces dense spikes of very fragrant, butterfly-like, white flowers with basal, yellow blotches in mid-summer. Lance-shaped, mid-green leaves are downy beneath.
H. densiflorum illus. p.227.
♀ ***H. gardnerianum*** illus. p.232.
H. horsfieldii, syn. *Brachychilum horsfieldii*. Clump-forming, tufted perennial. H and S to 1m (3ft). Has short-stalked, lance-shaped, leathery leaves, to 30cm (1ft) long. Produces showy, tubular, yellow-and-white flowers, to 8cm (3in) across, in summer, followed by orange fruits that open to reveal red seeds.

HEDYOTIS

RUBIACEAE

Genus of mat-forming, summer-flowering perennials. Fully hardy. Thrives in shady sites on moist, sandy leaf mould. Propagate by division in spring or by seed in autumn.
H. michauxii, syn. *Houstonia serpyllifolia*, illus. p.395.

HEDYSARUM

LEGUMINOSAE/PAPILIONACEAE

Genus of perennials, biennials and deciduous sub-shrubs. Fully hardy. Prefers sun and well-drained soil. Resents being disturbed. Propagate by seed in autumn or spring.
H. coronarium illus. p.254.

Heeria. See *Heterocentron*.
Heimerliodendron brunonianum. See *Pisonia umbellifera*.

HELENIUM
Sneezeweed

COMPOSITAE/ASTERACEAE

Genus of late summer- and autumn-flowering perennials, grown for their daisy-like flower heads, each with a prominent, central disc. Fully hardy. Needs a site in full sun and any well-drained soil. Propagate by division in spring or autumn. All parts may cause severe discomfort if ingested; contact with foliage may aggravate skin allergies.
***H.* 'Bressingham Gold'.** Erect, bushy perennial with stout stems clothed in lance-shaped, mid-green leaves. H 1m (3ft), S 60cm (2ft). Sprays of bright yellow flower heads are produced in late summer and autumn.
***H.*'Bruno'** illus. p.253. Erect, bushy perennial. H 1.2m (4ft), S 75cm (2½ft). Sprays of deep bronze-red flower heads are borne in late summer-autumn. Stout stems are clothed in lance-shaped leaves.
♀ ***H.* 'Butterpat'.** Compact perennial. H 1m (3ft), S 60cm (2ft). Has stout stems clothed in lance-shaped leaves. Bears sprays of rich deep yellow flower heads in late summer and autumn.
♀ ***H.* 'Moerheim Beauty'** illus. p.271.
***H.* 'Riverton Gem'.** Erect, bushy perennial. H 1.4m (4½ft), S 1m (3ft). Has sprays of red-and-gold flower heads in late summer-autumn. Stems are clothed in lance-shaped leaves.
***H.* 'Wyndley'** illus. p.271.

HELIANTHEMUM
Rock rose

CISTACEAE

Genus of evergreen, spring- to autumn-flowering shrubs and sub-shrubs, grown for their flowers. Is useful for rock gardens and dry banks. Fully to frost hardy. Needs full sun and well-drained soil. Cut back lightly after flowering. Propagate by semi-ripe cuttings in early summer.
H. apenninum illus. p.363.
***H.* 'Ben Hope'.** Evergreen, domed shrub. H 23–30cm (9–12in), S 45cm (18in). Fully hardy. Bears small, linear grey-green, leaves and saucer-shaped, carmine-red flowers in mid-summer.
***H.* 'Ben More'** illus. p.366.
***H.* 'Ben Nevis'.** Evergreen, hummock-forming, compact shrub. H and S 15–23cm (6–9in). Fully hardy. Has small, linear, dark green leaves and, in mid-summer, saucer-shaped, orange flowers with bronze centres.
♀ ***H.* 'Fire Dragon'** illus. p.366.
***H.* 'Golden Queen'.** Evergreen, domed, compact shrub. H 23cm (9in), S 30cm (12in). Fully hardy. Saucer-shaped, golden-yellow flowers appear amid small, linear, dark green leaves in mid-summer.
H. guttatum. See *Tuberaria guttata*.
♀ ***H.* 'Jubilee'.** Evergreen, domed, compact shrub. H 15–23cm (6–9in), S 23–30cm (9–12in). Fully hardy. Has small, linear, dark green leaves. Bears saucer-shaped, double, pale yellow flowers from spring to late summer.
♀ ***H. nummularium* 'Amy Baring'.** Evergreen, spreading shrub. H 10–15cm (4–6in), S 60cm (24in). Fully hardy. Small, oblong, light grey leaves are hairy beneath. In summer bears a succession of saucer-shaped, orange-centred, deep yellow flowers in loose, terminal clusters.
H. oelandicum subsp. ***alpestre.*** Evergreen, open, twiggy shrub. H 7–12cm (3–5in), S 15cm (6in) or more. Fully hardy. Produces terminal clusters of 3–6 saucer-shaped, bright yellow flowers from early to mid-summer. Leaves are tiny, oblong and mid-green. Is suitable for growing in a trough.
***H.* 'Raspberry Ripple'** illus. p.366.
♀ ***H.* 'Rhodanthe Carneum'**, syn. *H.* 'Wisley Pink', illus. p.365.
H. umbellatum. See *Halimium umbellatum*.
***H.* 'Wisley Pink'.** See 'Rhodanthe Carneum'.
♀ ***H.* 'Wisley Primrose'** illus. p.370.
***H.* 'Wisley White'** illus. p.363.

HELIANTHUS
Sunflower

COMPOSITAE/ASTERACEAE

Genus of summer- and autumn-flowering annuals and perennials, grown for their large, daisy-like, usually yellow flower heads. May be invasive. Fully hardy. All need sun and well-drained soil; some prefer moist conditions. Needs staking. Propagate by seed or division in autumn or spring. Contact with the foliage may aggravate skin allergies.
H. annuus illus. p.349. Fast-growing, upright annual. H 1–3m (3–10ft) or more; S 30–45cm (12–18in). Has large, oval, serrated, mid-green leaves. Very large, daisy-like, brown- or purplish-centred, yellow flower heads, 30cm (12in) or more wide, are produced in summer. Tall, intermediate and dwarf cultivars are available. **'Music Box'** (dwarf) illus p.348. **'Russian Giant'** (tall), H 3m (10ft) or more, has yellow flower heads with green-brown centres. **'Teddy Bear'** (dwarf) illus. p.349.
***H. atrorubens* 'Monarch'.** Erect perennial. H 2.2m (7ft), S 1m (3ft). Bears terminal, daisy-like, semi-double, golden-yellow flower heads on branching stems in late summer. Has lance-shaped, coarse, mid-green leaves. Replant each spring to keep in check.
H. debilis subsp. ***cucumerifolius*** **'Italian White'**. Erect perennial. H 1.2m (4ft), S 45–60cm (1½–2ft). In summer has large, black-centred, creamy-white flower heads. Purple-mottled stems bear coarsely hairy, sharply toothed, glossy, mid-green leaves.
H. × multiflorus illus. p.232.
♀ **'Capenoch Star'** is an erect perennial. H 1.2m (4ft), S 60cm (2ft). In summer, daisy-like, lemon-yellow flower heads are borne terminally on branching stems. Leaves are lance-shaped, coarse and mid-green.
♀ **'Loddon Gold'** illus. p.232.
H. orgyalis. See *H. salicifolius*.
H. salicifolius, syn. *H. orgyalis* (Willow-leaved sunflower). Upright perennial. H 2.2m (7ft), S 60cm (2ft). Bears small, daisy-like, yellow flower heads at ends of stout, branching stems in autumn. Has narrow, willow-like, drooping, deep green leaves.

HELICHRYSUM

COMPOSITAE/ASTERACEAE

Genus of summer- and autumn-flowering perennials, annuals and evergreen sub-shrubs and shrubs. When dried, flower heads are "everlasting". Fully hardy to frost tender, min. 5°C (41°F). Needs sun and well-drained soil. Propagate shrubs and sub-shrubs by heel or semi-ripe cuttings in summer; perennials by division or seed in spring; annuals by seed in spring.
H. angustifolium. See *H. italicum*.
H. bellidioides. Evergreen, prostrate shrub. H 5cm (2in), S 23cm (9in). Fully hardy. Has small, rounded, fleshy, dark green leaves and, in early summer, terminal clusters of daisy-like, white flower heads.
H. coralloides. See *Ozothamnus coralloides*.
♀ ***H. italicum***, syn. *H. angustifolium* (Curry plant). Evergreen, bushy sub-shrub. H 60cm (2ft), S 1m (3ft). Frost hardy. Has linear, aromatic, silvery-grey leaves. Broad clusters of small, oblong, bright yellow flower heads are produced on long, upright, white shoots during summer. subsp. ***serotinum*** (syn. *H. serotinum*), H and S 15cm (6in), is dome-shaped; stems and oval leaves are densely felted with white hairs. Dislikes winter wet and cold climates.
H. ledifolium. See *Ozothamnus ledifolius*.
H. marginatum of gardens. See *H. milfordiae*.
♀ ***H. milfordiae***, syn. *H. marginatum* of gardens. Evergreen, mat-forming, dense sub-shrub. H 5cm (2in), S 23cm (9in). Frost hardy. On sunny days in early summer, large, conical, red buds open into daisy-like, white flower heads with red-backed petals; they close in dull or wet weather. Has basal rosettes of oval, hairy, silver leaves. Prefers very gritty soil. Dislikes winter wet. Propagate in spring by rooting single rosettes.
♀ ***H. petiolare***, syn. *H. petiolatum* of gardens, illus. p.171. ♀ **'Limelight'** is an evergreen, mound-forming shrub. H to 50cm (20in), S 2m (6ft). Half hardy. Trailing, silver-green shoots bear oval to heart-shaped, bright lime-green leaves. In late summer and

autumn has daisy-like, off-white flower heads.
H. petiolatum of gardens. See *H. petiolare*.
H. rosmarinifolium. See *Ozothamnus rosmarinifolius*.
***H.* 'Schwefellicht'**, syn. *H.* 'Sulphur Light', illus. p.303.
H. selago. See. *Ozothamnus selago*.
H. serotinum. See *H. italicum* subsp. *serotinum*.
♀ ***H. splendidum.*** Evergreen, bushy, dense shrub. H and S 1.2m (4ft). Frost hardy. Woolly, white shoots are clothed in small, oblong, silvery-grey leaves. Small, oblong, bright yellow flower heads produced in clusters from mid-summer to autumn or sometimes into winter.
***H.* 'Sulphur Light'.** See *H.* 'Schwefellicht'.

HELICONIA
Lobster claws

HELICONIACEAE/MUSACEAE

Genus of tufted perennials, evergreen in warm climates, grown for their spikes of colourful flowers and for the attractive foliage on younger plants. Frost tender, min. 18°C (64°F). Needs partial shade and humus-rich, well-drained soil. Water generously in growing season, very sparingly when plants die down in winter. Propagate by seed or division of rootstock in spring.
H. metallica. Tufted perennial. H to 3m (10ft), S 1m (3ft). Oblong, long-stalked leaves, to 60cm (2ft) long, are velvety-green above with paler veins, sometimes purple below. In summer, mature plants bear erect stems with tubular, glossy, greenish-white-tipped, red flowers enclosed in narrow, boat-shaped, green bracts.
H. psittacorum illus. p.227.

HELICTOTRICHON

GRAMINEAE/POACEAE

See also GRASSES, BAMBOOS, RUSHES and SEDGES.
♀ ***H. sempervirens***, syn.. *Avena candida, A. sempervirens*, illus. p.319.

HELIOPSIS

COMPOSITAE/ASTERACEAE

Genus of summer-flowering perennials. Fully hardy. Requires sun and any well-drained soil. Propagate by seed or division in autumn or spring.
***H.* 'Ballet Dancer'** illus. p.266.
H. helianthoides* 'Incomparabilis'.** Upright perennial. H to 1.5m (5ft), S 60cm (2ft). Bears daisy-like, single, orange flower heads in late summer. Leaves are narrowly oval, coarsely toothed and mid-green. **'Patula'** bears flattish, semi-double, orange-yellow flower heads. subsp. ***scabra (syn. *H. scabra*) has very rough stems and leaves and double, orange-yellow flower heads. ♀ subsp. ***scabra* 'Light of Loddon'** (syn. *H.* 'Light of Loddon') illus. p.227.
***H.* 'Light of Loddon'.** See *H. helianthoides* subsp. *scabra* 'Light of Loddon'.
H. scabra. See *H. helianthoides* subsp. *scabra*.

Heliosperma alpestris. See *Silene alpestris*.
Heliotrope, Winter. See *Petasites fragrans*.

HELIOTROPIUM

BORAGINACEAE

Genus of annuals, evergreen sub-shrubs and shrubs, grown for their fragrant flowers. Frost hardy to frost tender, min. 5–7°C (41–5°F). Needs full sun and fertile, well-drained soil. Water potted plants freely when in full growth, moderately at other times. In spring, tip prune young plants to promote a bushy habit and cut leggy, older plants back hard. Propagate by seed in spring, by greenwood cuttings in summer or by semi-ripe cuttings in early autumn.
H. arborescens, syn. *H. peruvianum*, illus. p.163.
H. peruvianum. See *H. arborescens*.

Helipterum manglesii. See *Rhodanthe manglesii*.
Helipterum roseum. See *Rhodanthe chlorocephala* subsp. *rosea*.
Hellebore
Black false. See *Veratrum nigrum*, illus. p.226.
Green. See *Helleborus viridis*, illus. p.317.
Stinking. See *Helleborus foetidus*, illus. p.317.
White false. See *Veratrum album*.

HELLEBORUS
Christmas rose

RANUNCULACEAE

Genus of perennials, some of which are evergreen, grown for their winter and spring flowers. Most deciduous species retain their old leaves over winter. These should be cut off in early spring as flower buds develop. Is excellent in woodlands. Fully to half hardy. Prefers semi-shade and moisture-retentive, well-drained soil. Propagate by fresh seed or division in autumn or very early spring. Is prone to aphid attack in early summer. All parts may cause severe discomfort if ingested, and the sap may irritate skin on contact.
♀ ***H. argutifolius***, syn. *H. corsicus, H. lividus* subsp. *corsicus*, illus. p.316.
H. atrorubens of gardens. Clump-forming perennial. H and S 30cm (1ft). Fully hardy. Shallowly cup-shaped, deep purple flowers are borne in late winter. Has palmate, deeply divided, toothed, glossy, dark green leaves.
***H. × ballardiae* 'December Dawn'.** Clump-forming perennial with deep bluish-green leaves. H to 35cm (14in), S 30cm (12in). Fully hardy. From mid-winter to early spring bears saucer-shaped, white flowers, 6–8cm (2½–3in) across, flushed pinkish-purple, maturing to a dull metallic purple.
H. corsicus. See *H. argutifolius*.
H. cyclophyllus. Clump-forming perennial. H to 60cm (24in), S 45cm (18in). Fully hardy. In early spring produces shallowly cup-shaped, yellow-green flowers with prominent, yellowish-white stamens. Leaves are palmate, deeply divided, and bright green.

♀ ***H. foetidus*** illus. p.317.
H. × hybridus[white form] illus. p.312, [pink form] illus. p.313, [purple form] illus. p.314.
♀ ***H. lividus.*** Evergreen, clump-forming perennial. H and S 45cm (18in). Half hardy. Has 3-parted, mid-green leaves, marbled pale green, purplish-green below, with obliquely oval, slightly toothed or entire leaflets. Produces large clusters of cup-shaped, purple-suffused, yellow-green flowers in late winter. subsp. ***corsicus*** see *H. argutifolius*.
♀ ***H. niger*** illus. p.313.
H. purpurascens. Neat, clump-forming perennial. H and S 30cm (1ft). Fully hardy. Small, nodding, cup-shaped, pure deep purple or green flowers, splashed with deep purple on outside, are produced in early spring. Dark green leaves are palmate and deeply divided into narrowly lance-shaped, toothed segments.
H. × sternii illus. p.313.
H. viridis illus. p.317.

Helmet flower. See *Aconitum napellus*.

HELONIAS

LILIACEAE/MELIANTHACEAE

Genus of one species of spring-flowering perennial. Fully hardy. Is excellent when grown in bog gardens. Requires an open, sunny position and moist to wet soil. Propagate by division in spring or by seed in autumn.
H. bullata (Swamp pink). Rosetted, clump-forming perennial. H 38–45cm (15–18in), S 30cm (12in). Produces rosettes of strap-shaped, fresh green leaves, above which dense racemes of small, fragrant, star-shaped, pinkish-purple flowers are borne in spring.

HELONIOPSIS

LILIACEAE/MELANTHIACEAE

Genus of spring-flowering, rosette-forming perennials. Fully hardy. Grow in semi-shade and in moist soil. Propagate by division in autumn or by seed in autumn or spring.
H. orientalis illus. p.277.

HELWINGIA

HELWINGIACEAE

Genus of deciduous shrubs, bearing flowers and showy fruits directly on leaf surfaces, grown mainly for botanical interest. Requires separate male and female plants in order to produce fruits. Fully hardy. Needs sun or semi-shade and moist soil. Propagate by softwood cuttings in summer.
H. japonica. Deciduous, bushy, open shrub. H and S 1.5m (5ft). Oval, bright green leaves have bristle-like teeth. In early summer, tiny, star-shaped, green flowers appear at centre of each leaf and are followed by spherical, black fruits.

Helxine soleirolii. See *Soleirolia soleirolii*.

HEMEROCALLIS
Daylily

LILIACEAE/HEMEROCALLIDACEAE

Genus of perennials, some of which are semi-evergreen or evergreen. Flowers, borne in succession, each last for only a day. Fully hardy. Does best in full sun and fertile, moist soil. Propagate by division in autumn or spring. Cultivars raised from seed will not come true to type; species may come true if grown in isolation from other daylilies. Slug and snail control is essential in early spring when young foliage first appears. See also feature panel pp.263–5.
***H.* 'Always Afternoon'** illus. p.263. Robust, semi-evergreen, clump-forming perennial. H. 55cm (22in), S to 75cm (2½ft). In summer and again in autumn produces rounded, slightly ruffled, lavender-mauve flowers each with a dark purple band above the yellow-green throat.
H. aurantiaca illus. p.264. Robust, semi-evergreen perennial, spreading freely from underground runners. H 90cm (3ft), S 1m (3ft) or more. Produces numerous funnel-shaped, burnt-orange flowers, with yellowish midribs, over a long period in summer.
♀ ***H.* 'Berlin Red'** illus. p.265. Vigorous, deciduous or semi-evergreen, clump-forming perennial. H 70–90cm (28–36in), S 60cm (24in). In mid-summer produces open, rounded, rich velvety-red flowers with a blackish-red bloom at the margins and yellow midribs and throats.
***H.* 'Betty Woods'** illus. p.264. Robust, spreading evergreen, clump-forming perennial. H 65cm (26in), S 60cm (2ft). Large, peony-like, yellow flowers are borne in mid- and late summer.
***H.* 'Bonanza'** illus. p.264. Vigorous, deciduous or semi-evergreen, clump-forming perennial. H 1m (3ft), S 70cm (28in). Produces open, star-like, bright yellow flowers, with strongly red-marked centres, in mid-summer.
***H.* 'Brocaded Gown'** illus. p.264. Semi-evergreen, clump-forming perennial. H and S to 60cm (2ft). In summer has rounded, ruffled creamy-yellow flowers.
♀ ***H.* 'Burning Daylight'** illus. p.264. Robust, deciduous or semi-evergreen, clump-forming perennial. H 75cm (2½ft). S 60cm (2ft). Produces orange-brown flowers, with paler midribs and red marks around the throat bases, over a long period in summer.
***H.* 'Cat's Cradle'** illus. p.264. Semi-evergreen, clump-forming perennial. H 1m (3ft), S 75cm (2½ft). In summer produces large, spider-shaped, bright yellow flowers.
***H.* 'Cherry Cheeks'** illus. p.265. Vigorous, deciduous or semi-evergreen, clump-forming perennial. H 80cm (32in), S 50cm (20in). Produces bright cherry-red flowers, with white midribs, over a long period in summer.
***H.* 'Chicago Sunrise'** illus. p.264. Vigorous, clump-forming perennial. H 70cm (28in), S 85cm (34in). Very rounded, slightly ruffled, rich yellow flowers, with faint bronze bands and darker throats, are borne in summer.
***H.* 'Chorus Line'** illus. p.265. Extended-blooming, semi-evergreen, clump-forming perennial. H 50cm (20in), S 60cm (24in). Produces

remontant, triangular, slightly fragrant, bright pink flowers, with pink- and yellow-marked petals and dark green throats, from early to mid-summer.
H. citrina illus. p.264. Vigorous, coarse-growing, clump-forming perennial. H and S 75cm (2½ft). Many large, very fragrant, trumpet-shaped, rich lemon-yellow flowers open at night in mid-summer; each lasts only one day. ♀ ***H.* 'Corky'** illus. p.264. Clump-forming perennial. H and S 45cm (18in). Bears trumpet-shaped, lemon-yellow flowers, brown on outsides, in late spring and early summer. Flowers, borne prolifically, last only a day.
***H.* 'Cream Drop'** illus. p.264. Robust, deciduous or semi-evergreen, clump-forming perennial. H 60cm (2ft), S 45cm (18in). In mid-summer produces numerous, scented, well-formed, creamy-yellow flowers, with slightly ruffled margins.
***H.* 'Crimson Pirate'** illus. p.265. Vigorous, deciduous, clump-forming perennial. H 75cm (2½ft). S 50cm (20in). Produces open, star-shaped, bright crimson-red blooms, with paler midribs, in mid- and late summer.
***H.* 'Custard Candy'** illus. p.265. Vigorous, deciduous, clump-forming perennial. H 60cm (2ft), S 40cm (16in). In early and mid-summer produces an abundance of rounded, creamy-yellow flowers, each with a feathered band around the greenish-yellow eye.
H. dumortieri illus. p.264. Compact, clump-forming perennial. H 45cm (1½ft), S 60cm (2ft). In early summer produces fragrant, trumpet-shaped, brown-backed, golden-yellow flowers. Mid-green leaves are strap-shaped, stiff and coarse.
***H.* 'Ed Murray'** illus. p.265. Vigorous, free-flowering, deciduous or semi-evergreen, clump-forming perennial. H 65–70cm (26–28in), S 50cm (20in). Has rounded, ruffled, deep maroon-red flowers, with yellowish-green throats, in early and mid-summer.
***H.* 'Eenie Weenie'** illus. p.264. Clump-forming perennial. H and S 30cm (1ft). Bears an abundance of clear yellow flowers in early summer.
H. flava. See *H. lilioasphodelus*.
♀ ***H.* 'Frans Hals'** illus. p.265. Strong-growing, free-flowering, deciduous, clump-forming perennial. H 60cm (2ft), S 40cm (16in). In mid- and late summer bears open, star-like flowers, with yellow outer petals and three cinnamon-red inner petals with yellow midribs.
H. fulva (Fulvous daylily, Tawny daylily; illus p.264). Vigorous, clump-forming perennial. H 1m (3ft), S 75cm (2½ft). Trumpet-shaped, tawny-orange flowers appear from mid- to late summer above a mound of strap-shaped, light green leaves. **'Flore Pleno'** (illus. p.265), H 75cm (30in), has double flowers with dark red eyes. **'Kwanzo Variegated'** has leaves variably marked with white.
***H.* 'Gentle Shepherd'** illus. p.263. Semi-evergreen, clump-forming perennial. H 70cm (28in), S 60cm (24in). In early and mid-summer has ruffled, white flowers, with green throats.
♀ ***H.* 'Golden Chimes'** illus. p.265. Clump-forming perennial of graceful habit. H 75cm (2½ft), S 60cm (2ft). Bears small, delicate, trumpet-shaped, golden-yellow flowers, with a brown reverse, lasting only a day, from early to mid-summer.
***H.* 'Golden Prize'** illus. p.264. Vigorous, deciduous, clump-forming perennial. H 65–70cm (26–28in), S 40–50cm (16–20in). Produces large, rounded, golden-yellow flowers in mid- and late summer.
***H.* 'Hyperion'** illus. p.264. Clump-forming perennial. H and S 90cm (3ft). In mid-summer has very fragrant, lily-like, pale lemon-yellow flowers.
***H.* 'Joan Senior'** illus. p.263. Vigorous, semi-evergreen, clump-forming perennial. H 63cm (25in), S 1m (3ft). Open trumpet-shaped, almost pure white flowers are produced on well-branched stems from mid- to late summer.
***H.* 'Jolyene Nichole'** illus. p.263. Semi-evergreen, clump-forming perennial. H and S 50cm (20in). Bears rounded, ruffled, rose-pink flowers amid lush, blue-green leaves.
***H.* 'Lady Fingers'** illus. p.264. Semi-evergreen, clump-forming perennial with narrow leaves. H 80cm (32in), S 75cm (30in). In mid-summer bears spider-shaped, pale yellow-green flowers with green throats and spoon-shaped petals.
***H.* 'Lark Song'** illus. p.264. Vigorous, deciduous, clump-forming perennial. H 80–90cm (32–36in), S 60cm (2ft). Has fragrant, open bowl-shaped, bright pale yellow blooms, on blackish stems, in mid- and late summer.
♀ ***H. lilioasphodelus*** (syn. *H. flava*; illus. p.264). Robust, clump-forming, spreading perennial. H and S 60cm (2ft) or more. Very fragrant, delicate, lemon- to chrome-yellow flowers, lasting only 1 or 2 days, are borne in late spring and early summer. Strap-shaped leaves are mid-green.
***H.* 'Little Grapette'** illus. p.263. Free-flowering, deciduous, clump-forming perennial. H 45cm (18in), S 30cm (12in). Has lightly ruffled, wine-purple flowers, with yellow throats, in mid- and late summer.
***H.* 'Little Wine Cup'** illus. p.265. Vigorous, deciduous, clump-forming perennial. H 45cm (18in), S 30cm (12in). Produces masses of lightly ruffled, wine-red flowers, with paler midribs and yellow-green throats, in early and mid-summer.
♀ ***H.* 'Marion Vaughn'** illus. p.264. Clump-forming perennial. H 1m (3ft), S 60cm (2ft). Produces fragrant, trumpet-shaped, green-throated, pale lemon-yellow flowers, in late summer, each lasting only a day. Each petal has a raised, near-white midrib.
***H.* 'Mauna Loa'** illus. p.265. Vigorous, free-flowering, evergreen, clump-forming perennial. H 55cm (22in), S 1m (3ft). Produces rounded, bright tangerine-orange flowers, with chartreuse throats and contrasting black anthers, in mid- to late summer.
***H.* 'Michele Coe'** illus. p.263. Vigorous, evergreen or semi-evergreen, clump-forming perennial. H 70cm (28in), S 85cm (34in). In mid-summer has rounded, pale apricot flowers with light lavender-pink midribs.
***H.* 'Millie Schlumpf'** illus. p.263. Vigorous, free-flowering, evergreen, clump-forming perennial. H 50cm (20in), S 60cm (24in). Triangular to rounded, pale pink flowers, with deeper pink bands and green throats, are borne in early to mid-summer.
H. minor (Grass-leaved daylily). Compact, clump-forming perennial. H 40cm (16in), S 45cm (18in). In early summer, fragrant, trumpet-shaped, lemon-yellow flowers, with tawny-backed, outer petals, overtop narrowly strap-shaped, mid-green leaves that die back in early autumn.
♀ ***H.* 'Missenden'** illus. p.265. Vigorous, deciduous, clump-forming perennial. H 1.1m (3½ft), S 60–70cm (24–28in). In mid-summer has large, funnel-shaped, rich velvety-red flowers with a velvety, black sheen and yellow midribs.
♀ ***H.* 'Neyron Rose'** illus. p.265. Vigorous, deciduous, clump-forming perennial. H 1m (3ft), S 60–70cm (24–28in). In early and mid-summer has pink-suffused, orange-brown flowers, with white midribs.
***H.* 'Night Beacon'** illus. p.263. Evergreen, clump-forming perennial. H 70cm (28in), S 75cm (30in). In early and mid-summer produces rounded, very dark burgundy-black flowers, with black-purple bands, lemon-green throats and pearl-white midribs.
♀ ***H.* 'Pink Damask'** illus. p.263. Vigorous, deciduous, free-flowering, clump-forming perennial. H 1m (3ft), S 60–70cm (24–28in). Produces masses of rich salmon-pink flowers in summer.
***H.* 'Prairie Blue Eyes'** illus. p.263. Semi-evergreen, clump-forming perennial. H 80cm (32in), S 90cm (36in). In mid-summer produces lavender flowers, banded with blue-purple, that have green throats.
***H.* 'Real Wind'** illus. p.265. Vigorous, free-flowering, evergreen, clump-forming perennial with dense foliage. H 65cm (26in), S 1m (3ft). Produces triangular to round, pale buff to salmon-pink flowers, with bold rose-pink eyes, in mid- to late summer.
***H.* 'Rose Emily'** illus. p.265. Semi-evergreen, clump-forming perennial. H and S 45cm (18in). In mid-summer bears rounded, rose-pink flowers with ruffled margined petals and pale green throats.
***H.* 'Ruffled Apricot'** illus. p.264. Slow-growing, clump-forming perennial. Large, deep apricot flowers, with lavender-pink midribs, are ruffled at margins.
***H.* 'Scarlet Oak'** illus. p.265. Vigorous, semi-evergreen, clump-forming perennial. H 1.1m (3½ft), S 60–70cm (24–28in). In mid- and late summer has open rounded, scarlet flowers, with white midribs.
***H.* 'Scarlet Orbit'** illus. p.265. Semi-evergreen, clump-forming perennial. H 50cm (20in), S 65cm (26in). Scarlet flowers with green throats, open flat in mid-summer.
***H.* 'Siloam Baby Talk'** illus. p.263. Vigorous, free-flowering, deciduous, clump-forming perennial. H 35–40cm (14–16in), S 20–25cm (8–10in). Has rounded, ruffled-margined, creamy-pink flowers, with pale purple bands above bright green throats, in mid-summer
***H.* 'Siloam Ethel Smith'** illus. p.263. Evergreen, clump-forming perennial. H 50cm (20in), S 45cm (18in). In mid-summer bears masses of rounded, creamy-beige flowers, with triangular, red, yellow and olive-green eyes.
***H.* 'Siloam Virginia Henson'** illus. p.263. Clump-forming perennial. H 45cm (18in), S 65cm (26in). In early summer bears rounded, ruffled, creamy-pink flowers banded with rose-pink and with green throats.
***H.* 'Solano Bulls Eye'** illus. p.264. Vigorous, free-flowering, evergreen, clump-forming perennial. H 50cm (20in), S 75cm (30in). Produces round, bright yellow flowers, with deep brownish-purple eyes, over a long period from early to late summer.
***H.* 'Stafford'** illus. p.265. Vigorous, evergreen, clump-forming perennial. H 70cm (28in), S 1m (3ft). In mid-summer bears masses of star-shaped, scarlet flowers with yellow midribs and throats.
***H.* 'Strawberry Candy'** illus. p.265. Robust, deciduous or semi-evergreen, clump-forming perennial. H 75cm (30in), S 50cm (20in). In early and mid-summer bears bright apricot-pink flowers, with red picotee margins and ruby-red marks around yellowish throats.
***H.* 'Summer Wine'** illus. p.263. Strong-growing, deciduous, clump-forming perennial. H 60cm (2ft), S 45cm (18in). In early and mid-summer produces open, soft purple flowers, with yellowish-green throats and very pale purple to white midribs. Broad inner petals are slightly ruffled.
***H.* 'Super Purple'** illus. p.263. Clump-forming perennial. H 68cm (27in), S 65cm (26in). Bears rounded, ruffled, velvety, red-purple flowers, with lime-green throats, in mid-summer.

HEMIGRAPHIS

ACANTHACEAE

Genus of annuals and evergreen perennials, usually grown for their foliage. Frost tender, min. 15°C (59°F). Grows well in bright but not direct sunlight and in moist but well-drained soil. Water frequently during growing season, less in winter. Regularly cut back straggly stems to tidy. Propagate by stem cuttings in spring or summer.
H. repanda illus. p.311.

Hemlock
Canada. See *Tsuga canadensis*, illus. p.103.
Carolina. See *Tsuga caroliniana*.
Eastern. See *Tsuga canadensis*, illus. p.103.
Japanese. See *Tsuga diversifolia; Tsuga sieboldii*.
Mountain. See *Tsuga mertensiana*.
Northern Japanese. See *Tsuga diversifolia*.
Southern Japanese. See *Tsuga sieboldii*.
Western. See *Tsuga heterophylla*.
Hemp, African. See *Sparrmannia africana*, illus. p.114.
Hen-and-chicken fern. See *Asplenium bulbiferum*.

HEPATICA

RANUNCULACEAE

Genus of very variable perennials, some of which are semi-evergreen, flowers are produced in early spring before new leaves are properly formed. Fully hardy. Needs partial shade and deep, humus-rich, moist soil. Stout, much-branched rootstock resents disturbance. Propagate by seed when fresh or by division or removing side shoots in spring.
H. angulosa. See *H. transsilvanica*.
***H. x media* 'Ballardii'.** Slow-growing, dome-shaped perennial. H 10cm (4in), S 30cm (12in). Has rounded, 3-lobed, stalked, soft green leaves and, in early spring, shallowly cup-shaped, many-petalled, intense blue flowers. Fully double, coloured forms are also known. Propagate by division only.
♀ ***H. nobilis***, syn. *Anemone hepatica, H. triloba.* Slow-growing, semi-evergreen, dome-shaped perennial. H 8cm (3in), S 10–12cm (4–5in). Bears rounded, 3-lobed, fleshy, mid-green leaves. Shallowly cup-shaped, many-petalled flowers – white through pink to carmine, pale to deep blue or purple – are produced in early spring. Fully double, coloured forms are also known. Is excellent when grown in woodland or a rock garden. var. ***japonica*** illus. p.381.
♀ ***H. transsilvanica***, syn. *H. angulosa.* Semi-evergreen, spreading perennial. H 8cm (3in), S 20cm (8in). Shallowly cup-shaped, many-petalled flowers, varying from blue to white or pink, are produced in early spring amid rounded, 3-lobed, hairy, green leaves. Fully double, coloured forms are also known.
H. triloba. See *H. nobilis*.

Heptapleurum. See *Schefflera*.
Herald's trumpet. See *Beaumontia grandiflora*, illus. p.200.
Herb Paris. See *Paris*.
Herb, Willow. See *Epilobium*.

HERBERTIA

IRIDACEAE

Genus of spring-flowering bulbs, grown mainly for their iris-like flowers. Half hardy. Requires full sun and well-drained soil. Reduce watering when bulb dies down after flowering. Propagate by seed in autumn.
H. pulchella. Spring-flowering bulb. H 10–15cm (4–6in), S 3–5cm (1¼–2in). Leaves are narrowly lance-shaped, pleated, erect and basal. Bears a succession of upward-facing, violet-blue flowers, 5–6cm (2–2½in) wide and usually with dark-spotted centres.

HERMANNIA

STERCULIACEAE

Genus of evergreen sub-shrubs and shrubs, grown mainly for their flowers. Frost tender, min. 7°C (45°F). Prefers full light and fertile, well-drained soil. Water containerized plants freely when in full growth, moderately at other times. Tip prune young plants to produce well-branched specimens. Propagate by softwood or greenwood cuttings in late spring or summer.
H. candicans. See *H. incana*.
H. incana, syn. *H. candicans.* Evergreen, bushy sub-shrub. H and S 60cm (24in) or more. Oval to oblong leaves are covered with white down beneath. Produces small, nodding, bell-shaped, bright yellow flowers, carried in terminal clusters, to 15cm (6in) long, in spring–summer.

HERMODACTYLUS

IRIDACEAE

Genus of one species of spring-flowering tuber, with an elongated, finger-like rootstock, grown mainly for its attractive iris-like flowers. Fully hardy. Requires a hot, sunny site, where tubers will ripen well in summer, and well-drained soil. Grows particularly successfully on hot, chalky soils. Propagate by division in late summer.
H. tuberosus, syn. *Iris tuberosa*, illus. p.430.

Heropito. See *Pseudowintera axillaris*.
Herringbone plant. See *Maranta leuconeura* 'Erythroneura', illus. p.315.
Hers's maple. See *Acer davidii* subsp. *grosseri*.

HESPERALOE

AGAVACEAE

Genus of basal-rosetted, perennial succulents with very narrow, strap-shaped, grooved, dark green leaves, that often have peeling, white fibres at their margins. Is closly related to *Agave* and *Yucca*. Produces offsets freely at base. Frost tender, min. 3°C (37°F). Grows well in a sunny situation and in very well-drained soil. Propagate by seed or division in spring or summer.
H. parviflora, syn. *Yucca parviflora*, illus. p.478.

HESPERANTHA

IRIDACEAE

Genus of spring-flowering corms with spikes of small, funnel- or cup-shaped flowers. Half hardy. Needs full sun and well-drained soil. Plant in autumn, water through winter and dry off corms after flowering. Propagate by seed in autumn or spring.
H. buhrii. See *H. cucullata*.
H. cucullata, syn. *H. buhrii.* Spring-flowering corm. H 20–30cm (8–12in), S 3–5cm (1¼–2in). Has linear, erect leaves on lower part of branched stems, each of which produces a spike of up to 7 cup-shaped, white flowers, flushed pink or purple outside, that open only at evening.

HESPERIS

CRUCIFERAE/BRASSICACEAE

Genus of late spring- or summer-flowering annuals and perennials. Fully hardy. Requires a sunny site and well-drained soil. *H. matronalis* tolerates poor soil. Tends to become woody at base, so raise new stock from seed every few years. Propagate by basal cuttings in spring or by seed in autumn or spring.
H. matronalis illus. p.241.

HESPEROCALLIS

LILIACEAE/HYACINTHACEAE

Genus of spring- to summer-flowering bulbs. Half hardy. Needs a sunny, well-drained site. Is difficult to cultivate in all but warm, dry areas; in cool, damp climates, protect in a cool greenhouse. Requires ample water in spring, followed by a hot, dry period during its summer dormancy. Propagate by seed in autumn.
H. undulata. Spring- to summer-flowering bulb. H 20–50cm (8–20in), S 10–15cm (4–6in). Has a cluster of long, narrow, wavy-margined leaves, semi-erect or prostrate, at base. Stout stems each bear a spike of upward-facing, funnel-shaped, white flowers, with a central, green stripe along each of the 6 petals.

Hesperoyucca. See *Yucca*.

HETEROCENTRON, syn. HEERIA

MELASTOMATACEAE

Genus of evergreen, summer- and autumn-flowering perennials and shrubs. Frost tender, min. 5°C (41°F). Requires sun and well-drained soil. Propagate by softwood or stem-tip cuttings in late winter or early spring.
H. elegans, syn. *Schizocentron elegans*, illus. p.294.

HETEROMELES

ROSACEAE

Genus of one species of evergreen tree or large shrub, grown mainly for its showy clusters of holly-like fruits. Frost hardy. Requires fertile, well-drained soil in full sun, with protection from cold, drying winds in winter. Propagate by seed in autumn or by semi-ripe cuttings in summer.
H. arbutifolia. See *H. salicifolia*.
H. salicifolia, syn. *H. arbutifolia, Photinia arbutifolia* (Christmas berry, Toyon). Evergreen, bushy, spreading shrub or tree. H 6m (20ft), S 8m (25ft). Has oblong, sharply toothed, leathery, glossy, dark green leaves. Broad, flat heads of small, 5-petalled, white flowers, produced in late summer, are succeeded by large clusters of rounded, red fruits.

HEUCHERA

Alum root

SAXIFRAGACEAE

Genus of evergreen, summer-flowering perennials forming large clumps of leaves, that are often tinted bronze or purple. Makes good ground cover. Fully to frost hardy. Prefers semi-shaded position and moisture-retentive but well-drained soil. Propagate species by seed in autumn or by division in autumn or spring, and cultivars by division only, using young, outer portions of crown.
***H.* 'Coral Cloud'.** Evergreen, clump-forming perennial. H 45–75cm (18–30in), S 30–45cm (12–18in). Fully hardy. In early summer bears long, feathery sprays of small, pendent, bell-shaped, coral-red flowers. Leaves are rounded, lobed, toothed, glistening and dark green.
***H. cylindrica* 'Greenfinch'** illus. p.286.
***H.* 'Firebird'.** Evergreen, compact perennial. H 60cm (2ft), S 30cm (1ft). Fully hardy. In early summer bears long, feathery sprays of small, pendent, bell-shaped, crimson-scarlet flowers. Leaves are rounded, lobed, toothed and dark green.
***H. micrantha* var. *diversifolia* 'Palace Purple'** illus. p.287.
***H.* 'Pearl Drops'.** Evergreen, clump-forming perennial. H 60cm (2ft), S 30cm (1ft). Fully hardy. In early summer bears small, pendent, bell-shaped, white flowers tinged pink. Leaves are rounded, lobed, toothed and dark green.
***H.* 'Red Spangles'** illus. p.292.
♀ ***H.* 'Scintillation'.** Evergreen, clump-forming perennial. H 45–75cm (18–30in), S 30–45cm (12–18in). Fully hardy. In early summer produces long, feathery sprays of small, pendent, bell-shaped, deep pink flowers, each rimmed with coral-pink. Bears rounded, lobed, toothed and dark green leaves.

x HEUCHERELLA

SAXIFRAGACEAE

Hybrid genus *(Heuchera x Tiarella)* of evergreen, mainly late spring- and summer-flowering perennials. Fully hardy. Prefers semi-shade and needs fertile, well-drained soil. Propagate by basal cuttings in spring or by division in spring or autumn.
x *H. alba* 'Bridget Bloom' illus. p.288.
♀ **x *H. tiarelloides*** illus. p.288.

Hexastylis. See *Asarum*.
Hiba. See *Thujopsis dolabrata*.

HIBBERTIA, syn. CANDOLLEA

DILLENIACEAE

Genus of evergreen shrubs and twining climbers, grown for their flowers. Frost tender, min. 5–10°C (41–50°F). Grow in well-drained soil, in full light or semi-shade. Water freely in summer, less at other times. Provide stems with support. Thin out congested growth in spring. Propagate by semi-ripe cuttings in summer.
H. cuneiformis illus. p.142.
♀ ***H. scandens***, syn. *H. volubilis.* Vigorous, evergreen, twining climber. H 6m (20ft). Has 4–9cm (1½–3½in) long, oblong to lance-shaped, glossy, deep green leaves. Saucer-shaped, bright yellow flowers, 4cm (1½in) across, are produced mainly in summer.
H. volubilis. See *H. scandens*.

HIBISCUS

MALVACEAE

Genus of evergreen or deciduous shrubs, trees, perennials and annuals, grown for their flowers. Fully hardy to frost tender, min. 5–15°C (41–59°F). Needs full sun and humus-rich, well-drained soil. Water containerized specimens freely when in full growth, moderately at other times. Tip prune young plants to promote bushiness; cut old plants back hard in spring. Propagate by seed in spring; shrubs and trees by greenwood cuttings in late spring or by semi-ripe cuttings in

summer; and perennials by division in autumn or spring. Whitefly may cause problems.
H. mutabilis (Confederate rose, Cotton rose). Evergreen, erect to spreading shrub or tree. H and S 3–5m (10–15ft). Frost tender, min 5°C (41°F). Rounded leaves have 5–7 shallow lobes. In summer-autumn bears funnel-shaped, sometimes double, white or pink flowers, 7–10cm (3–4in) wide, that age from pink to deep red. In light frost dies back to ground level.
H. rosa-sinensis. Evergreen, rounded, leafy shrub. H and S 1.5–3m (5–10ft) or more. Frost tender, min. 10–13°C (50–55°F). Oval, glossy leaves are coarsely serrated. Produces funnel-shaped, bright crimson flowers, 10cm (4in) wide, mainly in summer but also in spring and autumn. Many colour selections are grown including **'The President'** illus. p.137.
♀ ***H. schizopetalus.*** Evergreen, upright, spreading, loose shrub. H to 3m (10ft), S 2m (6ft) or more. Frost tender, min. 10–13°C (50–55°F). Has oval, serrated leaves and, in summer, pendent, long-stalked flowers, 6cm (2½in) wide, with deeply fringed, reflexed, pink or red petals. May be trained as a climber.
***H. sinosyriacus* 'Lilac Queen'** illus. p.139.
***H. syriacus* 'Blue Bird'.** See *H.s.* 'Oiseau Bleu'. ♀ **'Diana'** is a deciduous, upright shrub. H 3m (10ft), S 2m (6ft). Fully hardy. Has oval, lobed, deep green leaves and very large, trumpet-shaped, pure white flowers, with wavy-edged petals, from late summer to mid-autumn. ♀ **'Oiseau Bleu'** (syn. *H.s.* 'Blue Bird') illus. p.141. ♀ **'Red Heart'** illus. p.135. ♀ **'Woodbridge'** illus. p.137.
H. trionum illus. p.332.

Hibiscus, Norfolk Island. See *Lagunaria patersonii.*
Hickory. See *Carya.*
Bitternut. See *Carya cordiformis.*
Pignut. See *Carya glabra.*
Shag-bark. See *Carya ovata*, illus. p.65.

HIDALGOA
Climbing dahlia

COMPOSITAE/ASTERACEAE

Genus of evergreen, leaf stalk climbers, grown for their single, dahlia-like flower heads. Frost tender, min. 10°C (50°F). Requires full light and humus-rich, well-drained soil. Water freely when in full growth, less at other times. Needs support. In spring thin out crowded stems or cut back all growth to ground level. Propagate by softwood cuttings in spring. Aphids, red spider mite and whitefly may be troublesome.
H. wercklei. Moderately vigorous, evergreen, leaf stalk climber. H 5m (15ft) or more. Oval leaves are divided into 3, 5 or more coarsely serrated leaflets. In summer bears dahlia-like, scarlet flower heads, yellowish in bud.

HIERACIUM
Hawkweed

COMPOSITAE/ASTERACEAE

Genus of perennials; most are weeds, but the species described is grown for its foliage. Fully hardy. Needs sun and poor, well-drained soil. Propagate by seed or division in autumn or spring.
H. lanatum illus. p.305.

Higan cherry. See *Prunus × subhirtella.*
Highbush blueberry. See *Vaccinium corymbosum*, illus. p.156.
Hill cherry. See *Prunus jamasakura*, illus. p.72.

HIMALAYACALAMUS

GRAMINEAE/POACEAE

See also GRASSES, BAMBOOS, RUSHES and SEDGES.
H. falconeri, syn. *Arundinaria falconeri, Drepanostachyum falconeri, Thamnocalamus falconeri.* Evergreen, clump-forming bamboo. H 5–10m (15–30ft), S 1m (3ft). Half hardy. Greenish-brown stems have a dark purple ring beneath each node. Has 10–15cm (4–6in) long, yellowish-green leaves, without visible tessellation, and unimportant flower spikes.

Himalayan birch. See *Betula utilis.*
Himalayan box. See *Buxus wallichiana.*
Himalayan holly. See *Ilex dipyrena.*
Himalayan honeysuckle. See *Leycesteria formosa.*
Himalayan lilac. See *Syringa emodi.*
Himalayan May apple. See *Podophyllum hexandrum*, illus. p.276.
Himalayan pine. See *Pinus wallichiana*, illus. p.99.
Himalayan weeping juniper. See *Juniperus recurva*, illus. p.104.
Hinoki cypress. See *Chamaecyparis obtusa.*

HIPPEASTRUM

AMARYLLIDACEAE

Genus of bulbs, grown for their huge, funnel-shaped flowers. Is often incorrectly cultivated as *Amaryllis.* Frost hardy to frost tender, min. 13–15°C (55–9°F). Requires a position in full sun or partial shade and well-drained soil. Plant large-flowered hybrids in autumn, half burying bulb; after the leaves die away, dry off bulb until following autumn. Smaller, summer-flowering species should be kept dry while dormant in winter. Propagate by seed in spring or by offsets in spring (summer-flowering species) or autumn (large-flowered hybrids). All parts may cause mild stomach upset if ingested.
H. advenum. See *Rhodophiala advena.*
***H.* 'Apple Blossom'** illus. p.441.
H. aulicum, syn. *H. morelianum*, illus. p.441.
♀ ***H.* 'Belinda'.** Winter- and spring-flowering bulb with a basal leaf cluster. H 30–50cm (12–20in), S 30cm (12in). Frost tender, min. 13°C (55°F). Is similar to *H. aulicum*, but flowers are deep velvety-red throughout, stained darker towards centres.
***H.* 'Bouquet'.** Winter- and spring-flowering bulb with a basal leaf cluster. H 30–50cm (12–20in), S 30cm (12in). Frost tender, min. 13°C (55°F). Is similar to *H. aulicum*, but has very wide, salmon-pink flowers, with deep red veins and red centres.
H. morelianum. See *H. aulicum.*
♀ ***H.* 'Orange Sovereign'** illus. p.441.
H. procerum. See *Worsleya rayneri.*
***H.* 'Red Lion'** illus. p.441.
H. reginae. Summer-flowering bulb. H to 50cm (20in), S 20–25cm (8–10in). Frost tender, min. 13°C (55°F). Flower stem produces a head of 2–4 scarlet flowers, each 10–15cm (4–6in) across and with a star-shaped, green mark in the throat. Long, strap-shaped, semi-erect leaves develop at base after flowering has finished.
H. rutilum. See *H. striatum.*
H. striatum, syn. *H. rutilum*, illus. p.451.
***H.* 'Striped'** illus. p.441.
H. vittatum. Vigorous, spring-flowering bulb. H 1m (3ft), S 30cm (1ft). Frost tender, min. 13°C (55°F). Leaves are broadly strap-shaped, semi-erect and basal. Stout, leafless stem precedes leaves and terminates in a head of 2–6 red-striped, white flowers, each 12–20cm (5–8in) across.
***H.* 'White Dazzler'.** Winter- and spring-flowering bulb with a basal leaf cluster. H 30–50cm (12–20in), S 30cm (12in). Frost tender, min. 13°C (55°F). Is similar to *H. aulicum*, but has pure white flowers.

HIPPOCREPIS
Vetch

LEGUMINOSAE/PAPILIONACEAE

Genus of annuals and perennials, grown for their pea-like flowers. Fully hardy. Requires full sun and well-drained soil. Propagate by seed in spring or autumn. Self-seeds readily. May be invasive.
H. comosa (Horseshoe vetch) illus. p.398. **'E.R. Janes'** is a vigorous, prostrate, woody-based perennial. H 5–8cm (2–3in), S 15cm (6in) or more. Rooting stems bear small, loose spikes of pea-like, yellow flowers from late spring to late summer. Leaves are divided, with 3–8 pairs of narrowly oval leaflets.

HIPPOPHÄE

ELAEAGNACEAE

Genus of deciduous shrubs and trees, with inconspicuous flowers, grown for their foliage and showy fruits. Separate male and female plants are required in order to obtain fruits. Is suitable for coastal areas, where it is wind-resistant and excellent when grown as hedging. Fully hardy. Needs a sunny position and is particularly useful for poor, dry or very sandy soil. Propagate by softwood cuttings in summer or by seed in autumn.
♀ ***H. rhamnoides*** illus. p.120.

Hoary willow. See *Salix elaeagnos.*

HOHERIA

MALVACEAE

Genus of deciduous, semi-evergreen or evergreen trees and shrubs, grown for their flowers produced mainly in summer. Frost hardy, but in cold areas grow against a south- or west-facing wall. Requires sun or semi-shade and fertile, well-drained soil. Propagate by semi-ripe cuttings in summer or by seed in autumn.
H. angustifolia illus. p.86.
♀ ***H.* 'Glory of Amlwch'.** Semi-evergreen, spreading tree. H 7m (22ft), S 6m (20ft). Has long, narrowly oval, glossy, bright green leaves and a profusion of large, 5-petalled, white flowers from mid- to late summer.
♀ ***H. lyallii*** illus. p.86.
H. populnea (Lace-bark). Evergreen, spreading tree. H 12m (40ft), S 10m (30ft). Bears narrowly oval, glossy, dark green leaves and produces dense clusters of 5-petalled, white flowers in late summer and early autumn. Bark on mature trees is pale brown and white and often flaky.
H. sexstylosa (Ribbonwood). Fast-growing, evergreen, upright tree or shrub. H 8m (25ft), S 6m (20ft). Glossy, pale green leaves are narrowly oval and sharply toothed. Star-shaped, 5-petalled, white flowers are borne in clusters from mid- to late summer.

HOLBOELLIA

LARDIZABALACEAE

Genus of evergreen, twining climbers, grown mainly for their fine foliage. Half hardy. Both male and female flowers are borne on the same plant. Grow in any well-drained soil, in a position in shade or full light. Propagate by stem cuttings in late summer or autumn.
H. coriacea illus. p.201.

HOLCUS

GRAMINEAE/POACEAE

See also GRASSES, BAMBOOS, RUSHES and SEDGES.
H. mollis (Creeping soft grass). **'Albovariegatus'** (syn. *H.m.* 'Variegatus') illus. p.318.

Holford pine. See *Pinus × holfordiana*, illus. p.97.
Holly. See *Ilex.*
American. See *Ilex opaca*, illus. p.94.
Blue. See *Ilex × meserveae.*
Box-leaved. See *Ilex crenata.*
Common. See *Ilex aquifolium*, illus. p.94.
Hedgehog. See *Ilex aquifolium* 'Ferox'.
Himalayan. See *Ilex dipyrena.*
Horned. See *Ilex cornuta.*
Japanese. See *Ilex crenata.*
Moonlight. See *Ilex aquifolium* 'Flavescens'.
Perry's weeping silver. See *Ilex aquifolium* 'Argentea Marginata Pendula', illus. p.94.
Sea. See *Eryngium.*
Silver hedgehog. See *Ilex aquifolium* 'Ferox Argentea', illus. p.95.

Silver-margined. See *Ilex aquifolium* 'Argentea Marginata', illus. p.94.
Summer. See *Arctostaphylos diversifolia*.
Tarajo. See *Ilex latifolia*.
Holly fern. See *Cyrtomium falcatum*, illus. p.323.
Holly-fern woodsia. See *Woodsia polystichoides*.
Holly flame pea. See *Chorizema ilicifolium*, illus. p.153.
Hollyhock. See *Alcea*.
Holm oak. See *Quercus ilex*.

HOLMSKIOLDIA

VERBENACEAE

Genus of evergreen shrubs or scrambling climbers. Frost tender, min. 16°C (61°F). Any fertile, well-drained soil is suitable in a position in full light. Water freely in growing season, less at other times. Requires tying to supports. Crowded growth should be thinned out in spring or after flowering has finished. Propagate by seed in spring or by softwood or semi-ripe cuttings in summer. Whitefly and red spider mite may be troublesome.

H. sanguinea (Chinese hat plant, Mandarin's hat plant). Evergreen, straggly shrub. H to 5m (15ft), S 2m (6ft). Leaves are 5–10cm (2–4in) long, oval and serrated. Produces showy, red or orange flowers, with saucer-shaped calyces and central, 5-lobed tubes, in autumn through to winter.

HOLODISCUS

ROSACEAE

Genus of deciduous shrubs, grown for their flowers in summer. Fully hardy. Needs sun or semi-shade and any but very dry soil. Propagate by softwood cuttings in summer.

H. discolor illus. p.115.

Holy flax. See *Santolina rosmarinifolia*.

HOMERIA

IRIDACEAE

Genus of spring- or summer-flowering corms with widely funnel-shaped, cup-shaped or flattish flowers. Half hardy. Needs a sunny site and well-drained soil. To produce flowers in spring, pot in autumn in a cool greenhouse, water until after flowering, then dry off for summer. To produce flowers in summer, plant in the open in spring. Propagate by seed, division or offsets in autumn. *H. collina* is toxic to livestock.

H. ochroleuca. Spring- or summer-flowering corm. H to 55cm (22in), S 5–8cm (2–3in). Slender, wiry stems each bear 1 or 2 long, narrow, semi-erect leaves on lower part of stem. Bears a succession of upright, cup-shaped to flattish, yellow flowers, each sometimes with a central, orange stain.

HOMOGYNE

COMPOSITAE/ASTERACEAE

Genus of evergreen perennials, useful for ground cover in rock gardens and woodland. Fully hardy. Needs shade and moist soil. Propagate by division in spring or by seed when fresh.

H. alpina (Alpine coltsfoot). Evergreen, mat-forming, rhizomatous perennial. H 8–15cm (3–6in), S 15cm (6in) or more. Has kidney-shaped, toothed, glossy leaves and, in summer, stems, 8–15cm (3–6in) or more long, each carry a daisy-like, rose-purple flower head.

Honesty. See *Lunaria*.
Honey locust. See *Gleditsia triacanthos*.
Honeybush. See *Melianthus major*.
Honeysuckle. See *Lonicera*.
Cape. See *Tecoma capensis*.
Common. See *Lonicera periclymenum*.
Coral. See *Lonicera sempervirens*, illus. p.206.
Etruscan. See *Lonicera etrusca*.
Fly. See *Lonicera xylosteum*, illus. p.136.
French. See *Hedysarum coronarium*, illus. p.254.
Giant Burmese. See *Lonicera hildebrandiana*.
Himalayan. See *Leycesteria formosa*.
Japanese. See *Lonicera japonica*.
Late Dutch. See *Lonicera periclymenum* 'Serotina'.
New Zealand. See *Knightia excelsa*.
Scarlet trumpet. See *Lonicera* × *brownii*.
Trumpet. See *Campsis radicans*.

HOODIA

ASCLEPIADACEAE

Genus of branching, perennial succulents with firm, erect, green stems, generally branching from the base. Frost tender, min. 10–15°C (50–59°F). Needs full sun and very well-drained soil. Is difficult to cultivate. Water sparingly at all times. Propagate by seed or grafting in spring or summer.

H. bainii. See *H. gordonii*.

H. gordonii, syn. *H. bainii*. Variable, erect, clump-forming, perennial succulent. H 80cm (32in), S 30cm (12in). Min 10°C (50°F). Green stem is covered with short, spine-tipped tubercles in distorted rows. Often branches into clumps. Produces 5-lobed, flesh-coloured to brownish flowers in late summer.

Hoop-petticoat daffodil. See *Narcissus bulbocodium*.
Hop. See *Humulus*.
Common. See *Humulus lupulus*.
Hop hornbeam. See *Ostrya carpinifolia*.
Hop tree. See *Ptelea trifoliata*.

HORDEUM

GRAMINEAE/POACEAE

See also GRASSES, BAMBOOS, RUSHES and SEDGES.

H. jubatum illus. p.319.

HORMINUM

LABIATAE/LAMIACEAE

Genus of one species of basal-rosetted perennial, suitable for rock gardens. Fully hardy. Needs sun and well-drained soil. Propagate by division in spring or by seed in autumn.

H. pyrenaicum (Dragon's mouth). Basal-rosetted perennial. H and S 20cm (8in). In summer carries whorls of nodding, short-stalked, funnel-shaped, blue-purple or white flowers above oval, leathery, dark green leaves, 8–10cm (3–4in) long.

Hornbeam. See *Carpinus*.
American. See *Carpinus caroliniana*.
American hop. See *Ostrya virginiana*, illus. p.73.
Common. See *Carpinus betulus*.
Hop. See *Ostrya carpinifolia*.
Hornbeam maple. See *Acer carpinifolium*, illus. p.88.
Horned holly. See *Ilex cornuta*.
Horned poppy. See *Glaucium*.
Horned tulip. See *Tulipa acuminata*, illus. p.427.
Horned violet. See *Viola cornuta*, illus. p.361.
Hornwort. See *Ceratophyllum demersum*.
Horse-chestnut. See *Aesculus*.
Chinese. See *Aesculus chinensis*, illus. p.60.
Indian. See *Aesculus indica*.
Japanese. See *Aesculus turbinata*.
Red. See *Aesculus* × *carnea*.
Sunrise. See *Aesculus* × *neglecta*.
Horseshoe vetch. See *Hippocrepis comosa*, illus. p.398.

HOSTA

Plantain lily

LILIACEAE/HOSTACEAE

Genus of perennials, grown mainly for their decorative foliage. Forms large clumps that are excellent for ground cover (heights given are those of foliage). Fully hardy. Most species prefer shade and rich, moist but well-drained, neutral soil. Propagate by division in early spring. Seed-raised plants (except of *H. ventricosa*) very rarely come true to type. Slug and snail control is essential. See also feature panel pp.298–301.

H. albomarginata. See *H. sieboldii* 'Paxton's Original'.

***H.* 'Allan P. McConnell'** illus. p.300. Clump-forming perennial. H 15–20cm (6–8in), S 30–45cm (12–18in). Has broadly to narrowly ovate, olive-green leaves with narrow, white margins. In mid-summer produces bell-shaped, purple flowers on scapes 35–40cm (14–16in) long.

***H.* 'American Halo'** illus. p.299. Robust, densely mounded, clump-forming perennial. H 55cm (22in), S 1.5m (5ft). Has large, broadly ovate, strongly veined, dark blue-green leaves, with heart-shaped bases and wide, irregular, yellow margins becoming ivory-white as they mature. In early and midsummer produces broadly funnel-shaped, pure white flowers on scapes 60cm (2ft) long.

***H.* 'Antioch'** illus. p.299. Robust, clump-forming perennial. H 50cm (20in), S 90cm (36in). Has broadly ovate, matt, dark green leaves irregularly margined grey-green and creamy-yellow, fading to white. In mid-summer bears funnel-shaped, lavender-blue flowers on scapes 90cm (36in) long.

***H.* 'August Moon'** illus. p.299. Vigorous, clump-forming perennial. H 50cm (20in), S 75cm (30in). Has rounded to heart-shaped, cupped, puckered, pale green leaves becoming golden-yellow with a faint glaucous bloom. In summer bears bell-shaped, greyish-white flowers on scapes 90cm (36in) long.

***H.* 'Big Daddy'** illus. p.298. Clump-forming perennial. H 60cm (2ft), S 1m (3ft). Has rounded to heart-shaped, cupped, deeply puckered, glaucous, grey-blue leaves. In early summer bears bell-shaped, greyish-white flowers on scapes 80cm (32in) long.

***H.* 'Birchwood Parky's Gold'**, syn. *H.* 'Golden', *H.* 'Golden Nakaiana' illus. p.301. Vigorous, clump-forming perennial. H 35–40cm (14–16in), S indefinite. Has heart-shaped, matt, yellow-green leaves becoming rich yellow with age. In mid-summer bears bell-shaped, pale lavender-blue flowers on scapes 70cm (28in) long.

♀ ***H.* 'Blue Angel'** illus. p.299. Slow-growing, clump-forming perennial. H 35cm (14in), S 60cm (24in). Has ovate to heart-shaped, wavy, glaucous, bluish-grey leaves. In mid-summer bears bell-shaped, greyish- or mauvish-white flowers on scapes 1m (3ft) long.

***H.* 'Blue Cadet'** illus. p.300. Clump-forming perennial H 35–40cm (14–16in), S 75cm (30in). Has small, broadly ovate leaves, blue-green above and glaucous beneath, with heart-shaped bases. Produces funnel-shaped, rich lavender flowers in long, dense racemes, 55cm (22in) long, from mid- to late summer.

***H.* 'Blue Moon'.** Slow-growing, compact, clump-forming perennial. H 12cm (5in), S 30cm (12in). Oval to rounded, greyish-blue leaves taper to a point. In mid-summer, dense clusters of trumpet-shaped, mauve flowers, on scapes 20–25cm (8–10in) long, are borne just above leaves. Is suitable for a rock garden. Prefers partial shade.

***H.* 'Blue Mouse Ears'** illus. p.298. Slow-growing, clump-forming perennial. H 15cm (6in), S 30cm (12in). Has very small, shallowly cupped, ovate, rich blue-green leaves, which in mature plants are almost round in shape. Produces clusters of bell-shaped, lavender-striped, rich violet flowers, on scapes 20cm (8in) long, in mid- and late summer.

***H.* 'Blue Wedgwood'** illus. p.299. Slow-growing, clump-forming perennial. H 30cm (1ft), S 45cm (1½ft). Has wedge-shaped, deeply quilted, blue leaves and, in summer, produces lavender flowers on scapes 40cm (16in) long.

***H.* 'Brim Cup'** illus. p.301. Slow-growing, clump-forming perennial. H 30cm (12in), S 35–40cm (14–16in). Erect, heart-shaped, slightly cupped and puckered, thick, dark green leaves are irregularly margined with cream fading to white. Bears pale lavender-blue flowers, on scapes 45cm (18in) long, in summer.

***H.* 'Buckshaw Blue'** illus. p.299. Slow-growing, clump-forming perennial. H 35cm (14in), S 60cm (24in). Has ovate to heart-shaped, concave, puckered, glaucous, deep blue-green leaves. In early summer bears bell-shaped, greyish-white flowers on scapes to 45cm (18in) long.

***H.* 'Candy Hearts'** illus. p.299. Vigorous, clump-forming perennial.

H 35–40cm (14–16in), S 55cm (22in). Has heart-shaped, pointed, greenish-grey-blue leaves. In summer bears bell-shaped, pale lavender-blue to off-white flowers on scapes to 50cm (20in) long.
***H.* 'Cherry Berry'** illus. p.301. Clump-forming perennial. H 30cm (12in), S 60cm (24in). Broadly lance-shaped, lustrous, creamy-yellow leaves turning ivory-white with age, irregularly margined mid- to dark green, with green streaks towards the midribs. In mid- to late summer bears funnel-shaped, rich violet flowers on scapes to 45cm (18in) long.
H. decorata. Stoloniferous perennial. H 30cm (12in), S 45cm (18in). Oval to rounded, dark green leaves have white margins. Dense racemes of trumpet-shaped, deep violet or sometimes white flowers, on scapes to 50cm (20in) long, are borne in mid-summer. f. ***normalis*** has plain green leaves.
***H.* 'Devon Green'** illus. p.299. Clump-forming perennial. H 45cm (18in), S 40cm (16in). Red-spotted leaf stalks bear lance-shaped, glossy, dark green leaves becoming broadly ovate to heart-shaped when mature. In mid-summer bears bell-shaped, greyish-lavender-blue flowers on scapes to 45cm (18in) long.
***H.* 'Dream Weaver'** illus. p.298. Vigorous, clump-forming perennial. H 45cm (18in), S 90cm (36in). Has large, broadly ovate, strongly-ribbed, chartreuse-green leaves, later ivory-white in the centre, with very broad,, dark blue-green margins, glaucous beneath. Produces funnel-shaped, lavender-striped, white flowers, on scapes to 70cm (28in) long, in mid- and late summer.
***H.* 'Fire and Ice'** illus. p.301. Upright, mounding, clump-forming perennial. H 20cm (8in), S 30cm (12in). Has small, narrowly ovate to ovate, ivory to white leaves, irregularly margined dark green, with twisted, acute tips. Produces narrowly funnel-shaped, pale lavender flowers, on 60cm (20in) scapes long, in mid- and late summer.
***H. fluctuans* 'Variegated'** see *H.* 'Sagae'.
H. fortunei. Group of vigorous, clump-forming, hybrid perennials. H 75cm–1m (2½–3ft), S 1m (3ft) or more. Leaves are oval to heart-shaped. ♀ var. ***albopicta*** (syn. *H.f.* 'Albopicta'; illus. p.301) has pale green leaves, with creamy-yellow centres, fading to dull green from mid-summer. Racemes of trumpet-shaped, pale violet flowers, on 75cm (30in) scapes long, open above foliage in early summer. ♀ f. ***aureomarginata*** (syn. *H.f.* 'Aureomarginata', *H.f.* 'Yellow Edge'; illus. p.300) has mid-green leaves with irregular, creamy-yellow edges. In mid-summer, trumpet-shaped, violet flowers, on 75cm (30in) scapes long, are carried in racemes above foliage. Mass planting produces effective results. Tolerates full sun. **'Yellow Edge'** see *H.f.* f. *aureomarginata*.
***H.* 'Fragrant Bouquet'** illus. p.298. Clump-forming perennial. H 45cm (18in), S 65cm (26in). Has oval to heart-shaped, slightly undulate, glossy, light green leaves with irregular, creamy-yellow margins. Racemes of fragrant, funnel-shaped, mauvish-white flowers, on 90cm (36in) scapes long, are produced in late summer. Tolerates some sun.
♀ ***H.* 'Francee'** illus. p.298. Vigorous, clump-forming perennial. H 55cm (22in), S 1m (3ft). Has oval to heart-shaped, slightly cupped and puckered, olive-green leaves with irregular, white margins. In summer, produces arching, leafy scapes bearing funnel-shaped, lavender-blue flowers on 70cm (28in) scapes long. Is late to emerge.
***H.* 'Ginko Craig'** illus. p.298. Low-growing, clump-forming perennial. H and S 30cm (1ft). Has small, narrow, dark green leaves irregularly margined white. In summer produces spikes of bell-shaped, deep mauve flowers on 55cm (22in) scapes long. Is a good edging plant.
***H.* 'Gold Standard'** illus. p.301. Vigorous, clump-forming perennial. H 75cm (2½ft), S 1m (3ft). Oval to heart-shaped leaves are pale green, turning to gold from mid-summer, with narrow, regular, dark green margins. Racemes of trumpet-shaped, violet flowers, on 1.1m (3½ft) scapes long, are produced above leaves in mid-summer. Prefers partial shade.
***H.* 'Golden'.** See *H.* 'Birchwood Parky's Gold'.
***H.* 'Golden Nakaiana'.** See *H.* 'Birchwood Parky's Gold'.
***H.* 'Golden Prayers'** illus. p.301. Upright, clump-forming perennial. H 15cm (6in), S 30cm (12in). Cupped leaves are puckered and bright golden-green. Flowers, on 45cm (18in) scapes long, are white suffused with pale lavender. Suits a rock garden.
♀ ***H.* 'Golden Tiara'** illus. p.301. Clump-forming perennial. H 15cm (6in), S 30cm (12in). Neat, broadly heart-shaped, dark green leaves have well-defined, chartreuse-yellow margins. In summer produces long spikes of lavender-purple flowers on 60cm (24in) scapes long.
H. gracillima illus. p.298. Clump-forming perennial. H 5cm (2in), S 18cm (7in). Has lance-shaped, wavy-margined, glossy, deep green leaves, paler beneath. In summer-autumn, produces purple-dotted scapes, on 25cm (10in) scapes long, of widely funnel-shaped, lavender-blue flowers, purple striped within.
***H.* 'Grand Tiara'** illus. p.300. Vigorous perennial forming a compact mound. H 30cm (12in), S 50cm (20in). Has ovate to heart-shaped, mid-green leaves with irregular, wide, yellow margins. In summer produces bell-shaped, sometimes remontant, deep purple flowers, on 80cm (32in) scapes long, each striped lavender-blue within.
***H.* 'Great Expectations'** illus. p.300. Clump-forming perennial. H 55cm (22in), S 85cm (34in). Green-margined, white leaf stalks bear heart-shaped, stiff, puckered, thick leaves that are glaucous, blue-green, and irregularly but widely splashed with yellow, fading to white in the centres. In early summer, bell-shaped, greyish-white flowers, on 70cm (28in) scapes long, are borne on leafy scapes.
***H.* 'Green Fountain'** illus. p.298. Clump-forming perennial. H 60cm (24in), S 45cm (18in). Red-dotted leaf stalks bear arching, lance-shaped, wavy-margined, glossy, mid-green leaves. Funnel-shaped, pale mauve flowers, on 60cm (24in) scapes long, are borne in summer.
***H.* 'Ground Master'** illus. p.298. Vigorous, stoloniferous, prostrate perennial. H 25cm (10in), S 55cm (22in). Has ovate to lance-shaped, matt, olive-green leaves with wavy, irregular, creamy margins, fading to white. Straight, leafy scapes of funnel-shaped, purple flowers, on 60cm (24in) scapes long, are borne in summer.
***H.* 'Hadspen Blue'** illus. p.299. Slow-growing, clump-forming perennial. H and S 30cm (12in). Smooth leaves are heart-shaped and deep glaucous blue. Produces short spikes of lavender flowers, on 35cm (14in) scapes long, in summer.
♀ ***H.* 'Halcyon'** illus. p.299. Robust, clump-forming perennial. H 30cm (1ft), S 1m (3ft). Has heart-shaped, tapering, greyish-blue leaves that fade to muddy-green in full sun; texture may be spoiled by heavy rain. Heavy clusters of trumpet-shaped, violet-mauve flowers, on 45cm (18in) scapes long, open just above foliage in mid-summer.
♀ ***H.* 'Honeybells'** illus. p.300. Clump-forming perennial. H 1m (3ft), S 60cm (2ft). Light green leaves are blunt at the tips and have wavy margins. In late summer bears fragrant, pale lilac flowers on 1.1m (3½ft) scapes long.
H. hypoleuca (White-backed hosta). Clump-forming perennial. H 45cm (1½ft), S 1m (3ft). Broadly oval leaves have widely spaced veins and are pale green above, striking white beneath. In late summer bears drooping racemes of trumpet-shaped, milky-violet flowers, on scapes 35cm (14in) long, with mauve-flecked, pale green bracts. Tolerates full sun.
***H.* 'Inniswood'** illus. p.298. Densely mounding, clump-forming perennial. H 60cm (24in), S 90cm (36in). Has large, broadly ovate to rounded, heart-shaped, seersuckered, rich golden-yellow leaves, with somewhat glaucous, dark green leaves that are glaucous beneath. In mid-summer produces funnel-shaped, pale lavender flowers on scapes 75cm (30in) long.
***H.* 'Kabitan'.** See *H. sieboldii* f. *Kabitan*.
H. kikutii. Clump-forming perennial. H 40cm (16in), S 60cm (2ft). Has oval to lance-shaped, deeply veined, dark green leaves. Racemes of bell-shaped, near-white flowers are borne in a tight bunch at the top of the raceme on conspicuously leaning scapes, 60cm (24in) long, in mid-summer. var. ***caput-avis*** is smaller, and the flower bud resembles a bird's head. **'Kifukurin'** has larger leaves, attractively margined cream.
♀ ***H.* 'Krossa Regal'** illus. p.298. Vase-shaped, clump-forming perennial. H and S 1m (3ft). Arching, deeply ribbed leaves are greyish-blue. Produces long spikes of pale lilac flowers, on scapes 1.4m (4½ft) long, in summer. Tolerates sun.
♀ ***H. lancifolia.*** Arching, clump-forming perennial. H 45cm (1½ft), S 75cm (2½ft). Has narrowly lance-shaped, thin-textured, glossy, mid-green leaves. Has racemes of trumpet-shaped, deep violet flowers, on scapes 65cm (26in) long, above foliage in late summer through to autumn.
♀ ***H.* 'Love Pat'** (illus p.299). Vigorous, clump-forming perennial. H and S to 60cm (2ft). Produces rounded, deeply puckered, deep glaucous blue leaves. Bears racemes of pale lilac flowers, on scapes 55cm (22in) long, during summer.
H. montana. Vigorous, clump-forming perennial. H 1.1m (3½ft), S 1m (3ft). Has oval, prominently veined, glossy, dark green leaves. Racemes of trumpet-shaped, pale violet flowers, on scapes 90cm (36in) long, open well above foliage in mid-summer. Slower-growing **'Aureomarginata'** (illus. p.300) has leaves irregularly edged with golden-yellow. Is always the first hosta to appear in spring.
***H.* 'Moonlight'** illus. p.300. Clump-forming perennial. H 50cm (20in), S 70cm (28in). Has pale yellow leaves that emerge olive-green, narrowly margined white. Produces funnel-shaped, violet-budded, pinkish-lavender flowers, on scapes 70cm (28in) long, in mid-summer. Requires full shade.
***H.* 'Morning Light'** illus. p.301. Clump-forming perennial forming upright mounds of foliage. H 45cm (18in), S 70cm (28in). Has ovate, long-pointed, rich ivory-yellow leaves, with irregular, dark green margins. Produces narrowly funnel-shaped, lavender flowers, on scapes to 70cm (28in) long, in mid-summer.
H. nigrescens illus. p.300. Vigorous, clump-forming perennial. H 70cm (28in), S 65cm (26in). In late summer has oval to heart-shaped, concave, puckered, glaucous grey-green leaves, and racemes of funnel-shaped, pearl-grey to white flowers, on undulating scapes 1.4m (4½ft) long.
***H.* 'Paxton's Original'.** See *H. sieboldii* 'Paxton's Original'.
***H.* 'Piedmont Gold'** illus. p.301. Slow-growing, clump-forming perennial. H 60cm (2ft), S 75cm (2½ft). Smooth leaves are bright yellowish-green with fluted margins. Racemes of white flowers, on scapes to 65cm (26in) long, are produced in summer. Is best in light shade.
H. plantaginea (August lily; illus. p.300). Lax, clump-forming perennial. H 60cm (2ft), S 1.2m (4ft). Leaves are oval and glossy, pale green. Rising well above these are scapes, to 65–75cm (26–30in) long, crowned in late summer and early autumn with fragrant, trumpet-shaped, white flowers that open in the evening. Prefers sunny conditions. ♀ **'Grandiflora'** (syn. *H.p.* var. *japonica*) has larger, longer-tubed flowers, to 13cm (5in) long. Prefers sun. var. ***japonica*** see *H.p.* 'Grandiflora'.
H. rectifolia. Upright, clump-forming perennial. H 1m (3ft), S 75cm (2½ft). Produces oval to lance-shaped, dark green leaves and racemes of large, trumpet-shaped, violet flowers, to 60–75cm (24–30in) long, from mid- to late summer.
***H.* 'Regal Splendor'** illus. p.298. Clump-forming perennial. H and S 1m (3ft). Arching, greyish-blue leaves are suffused white or yellow at the margins. Lilac flowers, on scapes 1.4m (4½ft) long, are produced in summer.
***H.* 'Revolution'** illus. p.300. Clump-forming perennial. H 50cm (20in),

S 1.1m (3½ft). Ivory-white leaf stalks, finely outlined dark green, bear broadly ovate, wavy, lustrous, green-flecked, ivory-cream leaves, margined and splashed dark green and overlaid with light olive-green. In mid-summer has narrowly funnel-shaped, lavender-blue flowers on scapes 50cm (20in) long.
♀ ***H.* 'Royal Standard'** illus. p.300. Upright, clump-forming perennial. H 60cm (2ft), S 1.2m (4ft). Broadly oval leaves are glossy, pale green. Pure white, slightly fragrant, trumpet-shaped flowers, to 1m (3ft) long, are carried well above foliage and open in the evening. Prefers sun.
♀ ***H.* 'Sagae',** syn. *H. fluctuans* 'Variegated'. Vigorous, clump-forming perennial. H and S 1m (3ft). Has undulate, heart-shaped, olive-green leaves, boldly margined creamy-white. Racemes of bell-shaped, near-white flowers are produced in mid- to late summer on leafy, glaucous, grey scapes 1.5m (5ft) long.
***H.* 'Sea Thunder'** illus. p.301. Vigorous, dense-mounding, clump-forming perennial. H 40–50cm (16–20in), S 1m (3ft). Has narrowly ovate to ovate, ivory-cream leaves, irregularly margined dark olive-green, often with intrusions of olive-green towards the centre. Produces broadly funnel-shaped, purple flowers, on scapes 90cm (36in) long, in late summer.
♀ ***H.* 'Shade Fanfare'** illus. p.298. Vigorous, clump-forming perennial. H 45cm (1½ft), S 75cm (2½ft). Heart-shaped leaves are pale green with cream margins. In summer has an abundance of lavender flowers on scapes 60cm (24in) long.
H. sieboldiana illus. p.298. Robust, clump-forming perennial. H 1m (3ft) or more, S 1.5m (5ft). Large, heart-shaped, deeply ribbed, puckered leaves are bluish-grey. Racemes of trumpet-shaped, very pale lilac flowers, on scapes 60cm (24in) long, open in early summer, just above foliage. Makes good ground cover. Tolerates sun, but leaves may then turn dull green. ♀ var. ***elegans*** (illus. p.298) has larger, bluer leaves and scapes 70cm (28in) long. ♀ **'Frances Williams'** (illus. p.300) has yellow-margined leaves, scapes 70cm (28in) long, is slower-growing and should not be grown in full sun.
***H. sieboldii* f. *kabitan*,** syn. *H.* 'Kabitan' illus. p.301. Clump-forming perennial, spreading by short runners. H to 30cm (1ft), S 60cm (2ft). Lance-shaped, thin-textured, glossy leaves are yellow-centred and have narrow, undulating, dark green margins. In early summer produces small, trumpet-shaped, pale violet flowers on scapes 30–40cm (12–16in) long. Is suitable for a shaded rock garden. Needs establishing in a pot for first few years. ♀ **'Paxton's Original'** (syn. *H. albomarginata, H.* 'Paxton's Original'; illus. p.298), H 45cm (1½ft), is vigorous, and has round-tipped, mid- to dark green leaves with irregular, white margins. Violet flowers appear in late summer and are followed by ovoid, glossy, dark green, then brown seed heads, which are useful for flower arrangements.
***H.* 'Snowden'** illus. p.298. Clump-forming perennial. H and S 1m (3ft) or more. Produces large, pointed, glaucous, blue leaves that age to sage-green. Long stems bear white tinged with green flowers, on scapes 1m (3ft) long, in summer.
***H.* 'So Sweet'** illus. p.300. Clump-forming perennial. H 35cm (14in), S 55cm (22in). Has ovate to lance-shaped, glossy, mid-green leaves margined creamy-white. In mid- and late summer lavender-blue buds open to fragrant, funnel-shaped, purple-striped, white flowers on scapes 60cm (24in) long.
***H.* 'Stiletto'** illus. p.301. Vigorous, clump-forming perennial. H 15cm (6in), S 20cm (8in). Has lance-shaped, rippled, mid-green leaves margined creamy-white. In summer produces funnel-shaped, purple-striped, lavender-blue flowers on scapes 30cm (12in) long.
***H.* 'Striptease'** illus. p.300. Densely mounding, clump-forming perennial. H 50cm (20in), S 1.2m (4ft). Has narrowly ovate to ovate leaves, dark green leaves, glaucous beneath, with chartreuse-green centres, sometimes white-flecked, later becoming ivory-yellow. Produces funnel-shaped, violet then lavender flowers on scapes, 70cm (28in) long, in mid-summer.
♀ ***H.* 'Sum and Substance'** illus. p.301. Vigorous, clump-forming perennial. H and S to 1m (3ft). Produces large, greenish-gold leaves that are thick in texture and, in mid-summer, pale lavender flowers on scapes 1m (3ft) long. Tolerates full sun.
***H.* 'Tall Boy'** illus. p.300. Clump-forming perennial. H and S 60cm (2ft). Has large, bright green leaves ending in long points. In summer an abundance of rich lilac flowers is produced on scapes 1.2m (4ft) long or more.
H. tardiflora illus. p.299. Slow-growing, clump-forming perennial. H 30cm (1ft), S 75cm (2½ft). Has narrowly lance-shaped, thick-textured, dark green leaves. Dense racemes of trumpet-shaped, lilac-purple flowers, on scapes 35cm (14in) long, open just above foliage from late summer to early autumn.
***H.* 'Thomas Hogg'.** See *H. undulata* var. *albomarginata*.
H. tokudama*,** syn. *H.* 'Tokudama' illus. p.299. Very slow-growing, clump-forming perennial. H 45cm (1½ft), S 75cm (2½ft). Produces cup-shaped, puckered, blue leaves. Racemes of trumpet-shaped, pale lilac-grey flowers, on scapes 40cm (16in) long, appear just above foliage in mid-summer. f. ***aureonebulosa (syn. *H.t.* 'Aureonebulosa', *H.t.* 'Variegata'; illus. p.301) has irregular, cloudy-yellow centres to leaves.
f. ***flavocircinalis*** (syn. *H.t.* 'Flavocircinalis'; illus. p.300), often mistaken for a juvenile *H. sieboldiana* 'Frances Williams', has heart-shaped leaves with wide, irregular, creamy-yellow margins. **'Variegata'** see *H.t.* f. *aureonebulosa*.
***H.* 'Tokudama'.** See *H. tokudama*.
***H.* 'Torchlight'** illus. p.299. Clump-forming perennial. H 35cm (14in), S 85cm (34in). Strongly red-streaked leaf stalks bear ovate, slightly folded, wavy, smooth, dark olive-green leaves lightly streaked chartreuse, with irregular, ivory margins. Bears funnel-shaped, rich lavender-blue flowers, on scapes 75cm (30in) long, in late summer.
♀ ***H. undulata* var. *undulata*,** syn. *H.* 'Undulata'. Clump-forming perennial. H to 1m (3ft), S 45cm (18in). Has lance-shaped to elliptic or narrowly ovate, slightly pointed, twisted, deeply channelled, mid-green leaves that are thin but leathery and strongly wavy-margined, with central, white or pale yellow-white markings. Produces funnel-shaped, mauve flowers, on arching leaf scapes 50–80cm (20–32in) long, in early and mid-summer. var. ***albomarginata*** (syn. *H.* 'Thomas Hogg', *H.* 'Undulata Albomarginata'; illus. p.298), H 55cm (22in), S 60cm (24in), has broadly oval, flat or slightly wavy-margined, dark green leaves, with irregular, cream or pale yellow margins. ♀ var. ***erromena*** (syn. *H.* 'Undulata Erromena'), H 45cm (1½ft), S 60cm (2ft), is robust and bears broadly oval, tapering, matt, mid-green leaves. ♀ var. ***univittata*** (syn. *H.* 'Undulata Univittata'; illus. p.298), H 45cm (1½ft), S 70cm (28in), has oval, twisted, matt, olive-green leaves that have narrow, cream centres.
***H.* 'Undulata'.** See *H. undulata* var. *undulata*.
***H.* 'Undulata Albomarginata'.** See *H. undulata* var. *albomarginata*.
***H.* 'Undulata Erromena'.** See *H. undulata* var. *erromena*.
***H.* 'Undulata Univittata'.** See *H. undulata* var. *univittataa*.
♀ ***H. ventricosa*** illus. p.299. Clump-forming perennial. H 70cm (28in), S 1m (3ft) or more. Has heart-shaped to oval, slightly wavy-margined, glossy, dark green leaves. Racemes of bell-shaped, deep purple flowers, on scapes 80cm–1m (32–36in) long, appear above foliage in late summer. Usually comes true from seed. **'Variegata'** (syn. *H.v.* 'Aureomarginata'; illus. p.300) has leaves with irregular, cream margins.
♀ ***H. venusta*** illus. p.300. Vigorous, mat-forming perennial. H 2.5cm (1in), S to 30cm (12in). Has oval to lance-shaped, mid- to dark green leaves and abundant racemes of trumpet-shaped, purple flowers, on scapes 25–35cm (10–14in) long, borne well above foliage in mid-summer. Is suitable for a rock garden. **'Suzuki Thumbnail'** (illus. p.299) has small leaves up to 5cm (2in) long by 2.5cm (1in) across.
***H.* 'Whirlwind'** illus. p.301. Clump-forming perennial. H 43cm (17in), S 85cm (34in). Has ovate to heart-shaped, folded, twisted and pointed, white to yellowish-green leaves, with wide dark green margins. Funnel-shaped, lavender-blue flowers, on scapes 60cm (24in) long, are produced in mid- and late summer.
♀ ***H.* 'Wide Brim'** illus. p.301. Vigorous, clump-forming perennial. H and S to 75cm (2½ft). Leaves are heavily puckered and dark blue-green, with wide, irregular, creamy-white margins. Produces white or very pale lavender flowers, on scapes 55cm (22in) long, in summer.
***H.* 'Yellow River'** illus. p.300. Clump-forming perennial. H 55cm (22in), S 1m (3ft). Has ovate to heart-shaped, pointed, thick, dark green leaves with irregular, yellow margins. Leafy scapes, 1m (3ft) long, of funnel-shaped, very pale lavender-blue flowers are produced in early summer.
***H.* 'Zounds'** illus. p.301. Slow-growing, clump-forming perennial. H and S to 1m (3ft). Large, bright gold leaves are heavily puckered and have melongic sheen. White or pale lavender flowers, on scapes 60cm (24in) long, are produced in early summer.

Hosta, White-backed. See *Hosta hypoleuca*.
Hottentot fig. See *Carpobrotus edulis*.

HOTTONIA

PRIMULACEAE

Genus of deciduous, perennial, submerged water plants, grown for their handsome foliage and delicate, primula-like flowers. Fully hardy. Needs sun and clear, cool water, still or running. Periodically thin overcrowded growth. Propagate by stem cuttings in spring or summer.
H. palustris illus. p.463.

Hot-waterplant. See *Achimenes*.
Hound's tongue. See *Cynoglossum*.
Houseleek. See *Sempervivum*.
Cobweb. See *Sempervivum arachnoideum*, illus. p.401.
Common. See *Sempervivum tectorum*, illus. p.401.
Roof. See *Sempervivum tectorum*, illus. p.401.
***Houstonia serpyllifolia*.** See *Hedyotis michauxii*.

HOUTTUYNIA

SAURURACEAE

Genus of one species of perennial or deciduous marginal water plant, with far-spreading rhizomes. Is suitable for ground cover, although invasive. Fully hardy. Prefers position in semi-shade and moist soil or shallow water, beside streams and ponds. Propagate by runners in spring.
***H. cordata* 'Chameleon',** syn. *H.c.* 'Variegata', illus. p.463. **'Flore Pleno'** (syn. *H.c.* 'Plena') is a spreading perennial. H 15–60cm (6–24in), S indefinite. Spikes of insignificant flowers, surrounded by 8 or more oval, white bracts, are produced above aromatic, fleshy, leathery, heart-shaped, pointed leaves, in spring. **'Plena'** see *H.c.* 'Flore Pleno'.**'Variegata'** see *H.c.* 'Chamaeleon'.

HOVENIA

RHAMNACEAE

Genus of one species of deciduous, summer-flowering tree, grown for its foliage. Fully hardy, but young, unripened growth is susceptible to frost damage. Does best in a position in full sun and requires fertile, well-drained soil. Propagate by softwood cuttings in summer or by seed in autumn.
H. dulcis illus. p.75.

HOWEA,
syn. HOWEIA, KENTIA

PALMAE/ARECACEAE

Genus of evergreen palms, grown for their ornamental appearance. Frost tender, min. 16–18°C (61–4°F). Needs partial shade and humus-rich, well-drained soil. Water containerized specimens freely in summer, minimally in winter and moderately at other times. Propagate by seed in spring at not less than 26°C (79°F). Is prone to red spider mite.

♀ ***H. forsteriana***, syn. *Kentia fosteriana* (Paradise palm, Sentry palm, Thatch-leaf palm). Evergreen, upright palm with a slender stem. H 10m (30ft), S 3–4m (10–12ft). Has spreading, feather-shaped leaves, 1.5–2.5m (5–8ft) long, made up of strap-shaped leaflets. Branching clusters of several spikes of small, greenish-brown flowers are produced in winter.

Howeia. See *Howea.*

HOYA

ASCLEPIADACEAE

Genus of evergreen, woody-stemmed, twining and/or root climbers and loose shrubs, grown for their flowers and foliage. Frost tender, min. 5–18°C (41–64°F). Grow in humus-rich, well-drained soil with semi-shade in summer. Water moderately when in full growth, sparingly at other times. Stems require support. Cut back and thin out crowded stems after flowering or in spring. Propagate by semi-ripe cuttings in summer.

H. australis, syn. *H. darwinii* of gardens, illus. p.204.

H. bella. See *H. lanceolata* subsp. *bella.*

♀ ***H. carnosa*** illus. p.204.

H. coronaria. Slow-growing, evergreen, woody-stemmed, twining and root climber. H 2–3m (6–10ft). Min. 16–18°C (61–4°F). Bears thick, leathery, oblong to oval leaves. In summer, bell-shaped, yellow to white flowers are borne, each spotted with red.

H. darwinii of gardens. See *H. australis.*

H. imperialis. Vigorous, evergreen, woody-stemmed, twining and root climber. H to 6m (20ft). Min. 16–18°C (61–4°F). Oval, leathery, leaves are covered with down and 10–23cm (4–9in) long. In summer, produces large, star-shaped, brown-purple to deep magenta flowers, each with a cream centre.

♀ ***H. lanceolata*** subsp. ***bella,*** syn. *H. bella*, illus. p.204.

H. macgillivrayi illus. p.201.

Huckleberry. See *Gaylussacia.*
Black. See *Gaylussacia baccata.*

HUERNIA

ASCLEPIADACEAE

Genus of clump-forming, perennial succulents with finger-like, usually 4-angled stems. Produces minute, short-lived, deciduous leaves on new growth. Frost tender, min. 8–11°C (46–52°F). Requires a position in sun or partial shade and extremely well-drained soil. Is one of easiest stapeliads to grow. Propagate by seed or stem cuttings in spring or summer.

H. macrocarpa, syn. *H.m.* var. *arabica*, illus p.492. var. ***arabica*** see *H. macrocarpa.*

H. pillansii. Deciduous, clump-forming, perennial succulent. H 5cm (2in), S 10cm (4in). Min. 11°C (52°F). Has a finger-like, light green stem that is densely covered with short tubercles with hair-like tips. Produces bell-shaped, creamy-red flowers, with red spots, at base of new growth, in summer through to autumn.

H. primulina. See *H. thuretii* var. *primulina.*

H. thuretii var. ***primulina,*** syn. *H. primulina.* Deciduous, clump-forming, perennial succulent. H 10cm (4in), S 15cm (6in). Min. 11°C (52°F). Stems are short, thick and grey-green. In summer through to autumn bell-shaped, dull yellow flowers, 2cm (¾in) across, with reflexed, blackish tips, are produced at base of new growth.

H. zebrina (Owl-eyes). Deciduous, clump-forming, perennial succulent. H 10cm (4in), S 15cm (6in). min. 11°C (52°F). Is similar to *H. thuretii* var. *primulina*, but produces pale yellow-green flowers with conspicuous bands of red-brown.

Humble plant. See *Mimosa pudica*, illus. p.172.

Humea. See *Calomeria.*

HUMULUS
Hop

CANNABACEAE

Genus of herbaceous, twining climbers. Is useful for concealing unsightly garden sheds or tree-stumps. Male and female flowers are produced on separate plants; female flower spikes become drooping clusters known as 'hops'. Fully hardy. Grow in a position in sun or semi-shade and in any well-drained soil. Propagate by tip cuttings in spring.

H. lupulus (Common hop). ♀ **'Aureus'** illus. p.202.

Hunangemoho grass. See *Chionochloa conspicua.*

Hungarian oak. See *Quercus frainetto*, illus. p.65.

HUNNEMANNIA

PAPAVERACEAE

Genus of poppy-like perennials, usually grown as annuals. Half hardy. Grow in sun and in poor to fertile, very well-drained soil. Dead-head plants regularly. Provide support, especially in windy areas. Propagate by seed sown under glass in early spring, or outdoors in mid-spring.

H. fumariifolia (Mexican tulip poppy). ♀ **'Sunlite'** is a fast-growing, upright perennial, grown as an annual. H 60cm (24in), S 20cm (8in). Has oblong, very divided, bluish-green leaves and, in summer and early autumn, poppy-like, semi-double, bright yellow flowers, to 8cm (3in) wide.

Huntingdon elm. See *Ulmus* × *hollandica* 'Vegeta'.

Huntsman's cup. See *Sarracenia purpurea.*

Hupeh crab. See *Malus hupehensis*, illus. p.70.

Hupeh rowan. See *Sorbus hupehensis.*

Hyacinth. See *Hyacinthus.*
Feather grape. See *Muscari comosum* 'Plumosum', illus. p.448.
Grape. See *Muscari.*
Summer. See *Galtonia candicans*, illus. p.409.
Tassel grape. See *Muscari comosum.*
Water. See *Eichhornia crassipes*, illus. p.464.

Hyacinth bean. See *Lablab purpureus*, illus. p.207.

HYACINTHELLA

LILIACEAE/HYACINTHACEAE

Genus of spring-flowering bulbs with short spikes of small, bell-shaped flowers, suitable for rock gardens and cold greenhouses. Frost hardy. Requires an open, sunny situation and well-drained soil, which partially dries out while bulbs are dormant in summer. Propagate by seed in autumn.

H. leucophaea illus. p.448.

HYACINTHOIDES,
syn. ENDYMION
Bluebell

LILIACEAE/HYACINTHACEAE

Genus of spring-flowering bulbs, grown for their bluebell flowers. Is suitable for growing in borders and for naturalizing in grass beneath trees and shrubs. Fully hardy. Requires partial shade and plenty of moisture. Prefers heavy soil. Plant bulbs in autumn 10–15cm (4–6in) deep. Propagate by division in late summer or by seed in autumn. All parts may irritate skin on contact, and may cause severe discomfort if ingested.

H. hispanica of gardens. See *H.* × *massartiana.*

♀ ***H. italica***, syn. *Scilla italica.* Spring-flowering bulb. H 15–20cm (6–8in), S 5–8cm (2–3in). Produces a basal cluster of narrowly strap-shaped, semi-erect leaves. Leafless stem produces a conical spike of many flattish, star-shaped, blue flowers, 1cm (½in) across.

H.* × *massartiana (*H. hispanica* × *H. non-scripta*), syn. *H. hispanica* of gardens, *Scilla campanulata, S. hispanica*, illus. p.430.

H. non-scripta, syn. *Scilla non-scripta, S. nutans*, illus. p.430.

HYACINTHUS
Hyacinth

LILIACEAE/HYACINTHACEAE

Genus of bulbs, grown for their dense spikes of fragrant, tubular flowers; is ideal for spring bedding displays and for pot cultivation indoors. Frost hardy. Needs an open, sunny situation or partial shade and well-drained soil. Plant in autumn. For winter flowers, force large-size, specially "treated" bulbs of *H. orientalis* cultivars by potting in early autumn, then keep cool and damp for several weeks to ensure adequate root systems develop. When shoot tips are visible, move into max. 10°C (50°F) at first, raising temperature as more shoot appears and giving as much light as possible. After forcing, keep in a cool place to finish growth, then plant out to recover. Propagate by offsets in late summer or early autumn. All parts may cause stomach upset if ingested; contact with the bulbs may aggravate skin allergies. See also feature panel p.447.

H. amethystinus. See *Brimeura amethystina.*

H. azureus. See *Muscari azureum.*

H. orientalis **'Amsterdam'.** Winter- or spring-flowering bulb. H 10–20cm (4–8in), S 6–10cm (2½–4in). Has strap-shaped, channelled, semi-erect, glossy, basal leaves that develop fully only after flowering. Flower stem carries a dense, cylindrical spike of fragrant, tubular, bright rose-red flowers, each with 6 recurving petals. ♀ **'Blue Jacket'** (illus. p.447) has very large spikes of navy-blue flowers with purple veining. ♀ **'City of Haarlem'** (illus. p.447) bears pale yellow flowers in a dense spike. ♀ **'Delft Blue'** (illus. p.447) has violet-flushed, soft blue flowers. **'Distinction'** (illus. p.447) produces slender, open spikes of reddish-purple flowers; those of **'Jan Bos'** (illus. p.447) are crimson. **'Lady Derby'** (illus. p.447) bears rose-pink flowers. ♀ **'L' Innocence'** has ivory-white flowers. ♀ **'Ostara'** (illus. p.447) has a large spike of blue flowers, with a dark stripe along each petal centre. ♀ **'Pink Pearl'** has a dense spike of carmine-pink flowers. Flowers of **'Princess Maria Christina'** (illus. p.447) are salmon-pink; those of **'Queen of the Pinks'** (illus. p.447) are soft pink. **'Violet Pearl'** (illus. p.447) produces spikes of violet flowers. **'White Pearl'** (illus. p.447) has pure white flowers.

HYDRANGEA

HYDRANGEACEAE

Genus of deciduous shrubs and deciduous or evergreen, root climbers, grown for their mainly domed or flattened flower heads. Each head usually consists of masses of small, inconspicuous, fertile flowers, surrounded by or mixed with much larger, sterile flowers bearing showy, petal-like sepals. However, in some forms, all or most of the flowers are sterile. Fully to frost hardy. Prefers a position in full sun or semi-shade and fertile, moist but well-drained soil. Requires more shade in dry areas. Propagate by softwood cuttings in summer. All parts of hydrangeas may cause mild stomach upset if ingested; contact with the foliage may aggravate skin allergies. See also feature panel p.140.

H. anomala subsp. ***petiolaris.*** See *H. petiolaris.*

♀ ***H. arborescens*** **'Annabelle'** illus. p.140. Deciduous, open shrub. H and S 2.5m (8ft). Fully hardy. Long-stalked, broadly oval leaves are glossy, dark green above, paler beneath. Very large, rounded heads of mainly sterile, white flowers are borne in summer. ♀ **'Grandiflora'** illus. p.140 has smaller flower heads but larger sterileflowers.

H. aspera **Villosa Group.** See *H.*

villosa. subsp. ***sargentiana*** see *H. sargentiana*.
H. bretschneideri. See *H. heteromalla* 'Bretschneideri'.
H. heteromalla. Deciduous, arching shrub. H 5m (15ft), S 3m (10ft). Fully hardy. Narrowly oval, dark green leaves turn yellow in autumn. Broad, flat, open heads of white flowers are borne in mid- and late summer, the outer ones ageing to deep pink. **'Bretschneideri'** (syn. *H. bretschneideri*) illus. p.140.
H. involucrata. Deciduous, spreading, open shrub. H 1m (3ft), S 2m (6ft). Frost hardy. Has broadly heart-shaped, bristly, mid-green leaves. During late summer and autumn bears heads of small, blue, inner flowers surrounded by large, pale blue to white, outer ones. ♀ **'Hortensis'** (illus. p.140) is smaller and has clusters of cream, pink and green flowers.
H. macrophylla. Deciduous, bushy shrub. H 1.5–2m (5–6ft), S 2–2.5m (6–8ft). Frost hardy. Has oval, toothed, glossy, light green leaves. In mid- to late summer, blue or purple flowers are produced in acid soils with a pH of up to about 5.5. In neutral or alkaline soils above this level, flowers are pink or red. White flowers are not affected by pH. Prune older shoots back to base in spring. Trim back winter-damaged shoots to new growth and remove spent flower heads in spring. Is divided into 2 groups: Hortensias, which have domed, dense heads of mainly sterile flowers; and Lacecaps, which have flat, open heads, each with fertile flowers in the centre and larger, sterile flowers on the outside that are green in bud. ♀ **'Altona'** (Hortensia; illus. p.140), H 1m (3ft), S 1.5m (5ft), has large heads of rich pink to deep purple-blue flowers. ♀ **'Ami Pasquier'** (Hortensia), H 60cm (2ft), S 1m (3ft), is compact, with deep crimson or blue-purple flowers. **'Blue Bonnet'** (Hortensia; illus. p.140), H 2m (6ft), S to 2.5m (8ft), produces heads of rich blue or lilac to pink flowers. **'Blue Wave'** see *H.m.* 'Mariesii Perfecta'. Flower heads of ♀ **'Générale Vicomtesse de Vibraye'** (Hortensia; illus. p.140), H and S 1.5m (5ft), are rounded and pale blue or pink. Foliage is light green. **'Hamburg'** (Hortensia; illus. p.140), H 1m (3ft), S 1.5m (5ft), is vigorous and has large, deep pink to deep blue flowers with serrated sepals. ♀ **'Lanarth White'** (Lacecap; illus. p.140), H and S 1.5m (5ft), has pink or blue fertile flowers edged with pure white sterile flowers. ♀ **'Madame Emile Mouillère'** (Hortensia) has white flowers, becoming pale pink, and prefers partial shade. ♀ **'Mariesii Lilacina'** (Lacecap; illus. p.140), H and S 2m (6ft), has deep, lilac, central flowers and pinkish-purple outer flowers. ♀ **'Mariesii Perfecta'** (syn. *H.m.* 'Blue Wave'; Lacecap; illus. p.140), H 2m (6ft), S to 2.5m (8ft), produces heads of rich blue or lilac to pink flowers. .subsp. ***serrata*** see *H. serrata*. subsp. ***serrata*** **'Preziosa'** see *H.* 'Preziosa'. ♀ **'Veitchii'** (Lacecap; illus. p.140) has lilac-blue flowers.
H. paniculata **'Brussels Lace'** illus. p.140. Deciduous, upright, open shrub. H and S to 3m (10ft). Fully hardy. Has large, pointed, dark green leaves. Bears delicate, open panicles of white flowers in late summer and early autumn. **'Floribunda'** (illus. p.140) has dense conical heads of small, fertile, central flowers surrounded by large, white ray flowers. ♀ **'Grandiflora'** has large, oval and dark green leaves. Large, conical panicles of mostly sterile, white flowers turn pink or red from late summer. Prune back hard in spring to obtain largest panicles. **'Interhydia'** see *H.p.* 'PINK DIAMOND'. Flower heads of ♀ **'PINK DIAMOND'** (**'Interhydia'**) (illus. p.140) turn pink with age. **'Praecox'** (illus. p.140) flowers from mid-summer. **'Tardiva'** has both fertile and sterile flowers from early to mid-autumn. ♀ **'Unique'** (illus. p.140) is similar to 'Grandiflora' but more vigorous and has larger flowers.
♀ ***H. petiolaris***, syn. *H. anomala* subsp. *petiolaris*, illus. p.204.
♀ ***H.*** **'Preziosa'**, syn. *H. macrophylla* subsp. *serrata* 'Preziosa', *H. serrata* 'Preziosa'. Deciduous, bushy shrub. H 1.5–2m (5–6ft), S 2–2.5m (6–8ft). Frost hardy. Has oval, toothed, light green leaves. Bears pink flowers, becoming deep crimson.
♀ ***H. quercifolia*** (Oak-leaved hydrangea; illus. p.140). Deciduous, bushy, mound-forming shrub. H and S 2m (6ft). Frost hardy. Deeply lobed, dark green leaves turn red and purple in autumn. Has white flower heads from mid-summer to mid-autumn.
♀ ***H. sargentiana***, syn. *H. aspera* subsp. *sargentiana*. Deciduous, upright, gaunt shrub. H 2.5m (8ft), S 2m (6ft). Frost hardy. Has peeling bark, stout shoots and very large, narrowly oval, bristly, dull green leaves with grey down beneath. In late summer to mid-autumn bears broad heads of flowers, the inner ones small and blue or deep purple, the outer ones larger and white, sometimes flushed purplish-pink.
H. serrata, syn. *H. macrophylla* subsp. *serrata* (illus p.140). Deciduous, bushy, dense shrub. H and S 1.2m (4ft). Frost hardy. Has slender stems and light green leaves. From mid- to late summer bears flat heads of pink, lilac or white inner and pink or blue outer flowers. ♀ **'Bluebird'** (illus. p.144) has pale pink, pale purple or blue flowers. **'Preziosa'** see *H.* 'Preziosa'.
♀ ***H. villosa*** (syn. *H. aspera* Villosa Group; illus. p.140). Deciduous, upright shrub. H and S 3m (10ft). Fully hardy. Has peeling bark and, from late summer to mid-autumn, heads of small, blue or purple, central flowers and larger, white, sometimes flushed purplish-pink, outer ones.

Hydrangea
Climbing. See *Hydrangea petiolaris*, illus. p.204.
Oak-leaved. See *Hydrangea quercifolia*, illus. p.140.

HYDROCHARIS

HYDROCHARITACEAE

Genus of one species of deciduous, perennial, floating water plant, grown for its foliage and flowers. Fully hardy. Requires an open, sunny position in still water. Propagate by detaching young plantlets as required.
H. morsus-ranae illus. p.462.

Hydrocleis. See *Hydrocleys*.

HYDROCLEYS, syn. HYDROCLEIS

LIMNOCHARITACEAE

Genus of deciduous or evergreen, annual or perennial, water plants, grown for their floating foliage and attractive flowers. Frost tender, min. 1°C (34°F). Is best grown in large aquariums and tropical pools with plenty of light. Propagate by seed when ripe or by tip cuttings year-round.
H. nymphoides illus. p.465.

HYGROPHILA

ACANTHACEAE

Genus of deciduous or evergreen, perennial, submerged water plants and marsh plants, grown for their foliage. Frost tender, min. 13°C (55°F). Remove fading leaves regularly. Propagate by stem cuttings in spring or summer.
H. polysperma. Deciduous, perennial, submerged water plant. S indefinite. Lance-shaped, pale green leaves are borne on woody stems. Given water above 16°C (61°F), is evergreen. Is suitable for a tropical aquarium.

HYLOCEREUS

CACTACEAE

Genus of fast-growing, perennial cacti with erect, slender, climbing stems that are jointed into sections, and many aerial roots. Makes successful grafting stock except in northern Europe. Frost tender, min. 11°C (52°F). Requires a position in sun or partial shade and very well-drained soil. Propagate by stem cuttings in spring or summer.
H. undatus (Night-blooming cereus, Queen-of-the-night). Fast-growing, climbing, perennial cactus. H 1m (3ft), S indefinite. Bears freely branching, 3-angled, weakly spined, dark green stems, 7cm (3in) wide and jointed into sections. In summer produces flattish, white flowers, 30cm (12in) across, that last only one night.

HYLOMECON

PAPAVERACEAE

Genus of one species of vigorous perennial, grown for its large, cup-shaped flowers. Is good for rock gardens, borders and woodlands but may be invasive. Fully hardy. Prefers partial shade and humus-rich, moist soil. Propagate by division in spring or by seed in autumn.
H. japonica illus. p.362.

Hylotelephium anacampseros. See *Sedum anacampseros*.
Hylotelephium cauticola. See *Sedum cauticola*.
Hylotelephium ewersii. See *Sedum ewersii*.
Hylotelephium populifolium. See *Sedum populifolium*.
Hylotelephium spectabile. See *Sedum spectabile*.
Hylotelephium sieboldii. See *Sedum sieboldii*
Hylotelephium tatarinowii. See *Sedum tatarinowii*.
Hymenanthera. See *Melicytus*.

HYMENOCALLIS

AMARYLLIDACEAE

Genus of bulbs, some of which are evergreen, grown for their fragrant flowers, somewhat like those of large daffodils. Half hardy to frost tender, min. 15°C (59°F). Needs a sheltered site, full sun or partial shade and well-drained soil. Plant in early summer, lifting for winter in cold districts. Alternatively, grow in a heated greenhouse; reduce water in winter, without drying out completely, then repot in spring. Propagate by offsets in spring or early summer.
H. calathina. See *H. narcissiflora*.
♀ ***H.* x *festalis.*** Spring- or summer-flowering bulb with a basal leaf cluster. H to 80cm (32in), S 30–45cm (12–18in). Frost tender. Bears strap-shaped, semi-erect leaves. Produces a head of 2–5 scented, white flowers, each 20cm (8in) across with a deep, central cup and 6 narrow, reflexed petals.
♀ ***H.* x *macrostephana*** illus. p.409.
H. narcissiflora, syn. *H. calathina, Ismene calathina*, illus. p.436.
H. speciosa. Evergreen, winter-flowering bulb. H and S 30–45cm (12–18in). Frost tender. Has broadly elliptic, semi-erect, basal leaves. Produces a head of 5–10 fragrant, white or green-white flowers, each 20–30cm (8–12in) wide with a funnel-shaped cup and 6 long, narrow petals.
♀ ***H.* 'Sulphur Queen'.** Spring- or summer-flowering bulb. H 60cm (24in), S 30–45cm (12–18in). Frost tender. Produces widely strap- or lance-3 shaped, semi-erect, basal leaves. Has a loose head of 2–5 fragrant, yellow-green flowers, each 16–20cm (6–8in) wide with a frilly-edged cup and 6 spreading petals.

HYMENOSPORUM

PITTOSPORACEAE

Genus of one species of evergreen shrub or tree, grown for its flowers and overall appearance. Frost tender, min. 5–7°C (41–5°F). Prefers full sun, though some shade is tolerated. Requires humus-rich, well-drained soil, ideally neutral to acid. Water containerized specimens freely when in full growth, less at other times. Propagate by seed when ripe, in autumn, or in spring or by semi-ripe cuttings in late summer.
H. flavum (Native Australian frangipani). Evergreen, erect shrub or tree, gradually spreading with age. H 10m (30ft) or more, S 5m (15ft) or more. Has oval to oblong, lustrous, rich green leaves. In spring-summer bears terminal panicles of very fragrant, tubular, 5-petalled, cream flowers that age to deep sulphur-yellow.

HYPERICUM

GUTTIFERAE/CLUSIACEAE

Genus of perennials and deciduous, semi-evergreen or evergreen sub-shrubs and shrubs, grown for their conspicuous, yellow flowers with prominent stamens. Fully to half hardy. Large species and cultivars need sun or semi-shade and fertile, not too dry soil. Smaller types, which are good in rock

gardens, do best in full sun and well-drained soil. Propagate species sub-shrubs and shrubs by softwood cuttings in summer or by seed in autumn, cultivars by softwood cuttings only in summer; perennials by seed or division in autumn or spring. Is generally trouble-free but *H.* × *inodorum* 'Elstead' is susceptible to rust, which produces orange spots on leaves, *H.* 'Hidcote' to a virus that makes leaves narrow and variegated.
H. balearicum. Evergreen, compact shrub. H and S to 60cm (2ft). Frost hardy. Small, oval, green leaves have wavy edges and rounded tips. Solitary, large, fragrant, shallowly cup-shaped, yellow flowers are produced at stem tips above foliage from early summer to autumn.
***H. beanii* 'Gold Cup'.** See *H.* × *cyathiflorum* 'Gold Cup'.
H. bellum. Semi-evergreen, arching, graceful shrub. H 1m (3ft), S 1.5m (5ft). Fully hardy. Cup-shaped, golden-yellow flowers are borne from mid-summer to early autumn. Shoots are red. Oval, wavy-edged, mid-green leaves redden in autumn.
H. calycinum illus. p.166.
H. cerastioides, syn. *H. rhodoppeum.* Vigorous, evergreen sub-shrub with upright and arching branches. H 15cm (6in) or more, S 40–50cm (16–20in). Fully hardy. Leaves are oval, hairy and soft greyish-green. In late spring and early summer produces masses of saucer-shaped, bright yellow flowers in terminal clusters. Cut back hard after flowering. Is suitable for a large rock garden.
H. coris. Evergreen, open, dome-shaped, occasionally prostrate, sub-shrub. H 15–30cm (6–12in), S 20cm (8in) or more. Frost hardy. Bears long-stemmed whorls of 3 or 4 pointed-oval leaves. Produces panicles of shallowly cup-shaped, bright yellow flowers, streaked red, in summer. Suits a sheltered rock garden.
***H.* × *cyathiflorum* 'Gold Cup'**, syn. *H. beanii* 'Gold Cup'. Semi-evergreen, arching shrub. H and S 1m (3ft). Frost hardy. Produces pinkish-brown shoots, oval, dark green leaves and, from mid-summer to early autumn, large, cup-shaped, golden-yellow flowers.
H. empetrifolium* subsp. *oliganthum. See *H.e.* var. *prostratum* of gardens. var. ***prostratum*** of gardens (syn. *H.e.* subsp. *oliganthum*) illus. p.398.
♡ ***H.* 'Hidcote'** illus. p.166.
***H.* × *inodorum* 'Elstead'** illus. p.166.
♡ ***H. kouytchense***, syn. *H. patulum* var. *grandiflorum*, illus. p.166.
♡ ***H.* × *moserianum.*** Deciduous, arching shrub. H 30cm (12in), S 60cm (24in). Frost hardy. Small, bowl-shaped, yellow flowers are produced above oval, dark green leaves from mid-summer to mid-autumn. **'Tricolor'** has leaves margined white and pink. Prefers a sheltered position.
♡ ***H. olympicum.*** Deciduous, upright, slightly spreading, dense sub-shrub. H 15–30cm (6–12in), S to 15cm (6in). Fully hardy. Tufts of upright stems are covered in small, oval, grey-green leaves. Produces terminal clusters of up to 5 cup-shaped, bright yellow flowers in summer. ♡ f. ***uniflorum* 'Citrinum'** (syn. *H.o.* 'Sulphureum') illus. p.370.
H. patulum. Evergreen or semi-evergreen, upright shrub. H and S 1m (3ft). Frost hardy. Large, cup-shaped, golden-yellow flowers open above oval, dark green leaves from mid-summer to mid-autumn. var. ***grandiflorum*** see *H. kouytchense*.
H. reptans. Deciduous, mat-forming shrub. H 5cm (2in), S 20cm (8in). Frost hardy. Oval, green leaves turn yellow or bright red in autumn. In summer produces flattish, golden-yellow flowers, crimson-flushed outside. Suits a rock garden.
H. rhodoppeum. See *H. cerastioides*.
♡ ***H.* 'Rowallane'.** Semi-evergreen, arching shrub. H and S 1.5m (5ft). Frost hardy, but is cut to ground level in severe winters. Bears large, bowl-shaped, deep golden-yellow flowers from mid-summer to mid- or late autumn. Oval leaves are rich green.

Hypocyrta radicans. See *Nematanthus gregarius*.
Hypocyrta strigillosa. See *Nematanthus strigillosus*.

HYPOESTES

ACANTHACEAE

Genus of mainly evergreen perennials, shrubs and sub-shrubs, grown for their flowers and foliage. Frost tender, min. 10°C (50°F). Grow in bright light and in well-drained soil. Water frequently in growing season, less in winter. Straggly stems should be cut back. Propagate by stem cuttings in spring or summer. *H. phyllostachya* may be treated as an annual and propagated by seed in spring.
H. aristata. Evergreen, bushy perennial or sub-shrub. H to 1m (3ft), S 60cm (2ft). Has oval, mid-green leaves to 8cm (3in) long. Small, tubular, deep pink to purple flowers are produced in terminal spikes in late winter.
♡ ***H. phyllostachya***, syn. *H. sanguinolenta* of gardens, illus. p.272.
H. sanguinolenta of gardens. See *H. phyllostachya*.

HYPOXIS

HYPOXIDACEAE

Genus of spring- or summer-flowering corms, grown for their flat, star-shaped flowers. Suits rock gardens. Frost to half hardy. Requires full sun and light, well-drained soil. Propagate by seed in autumn or spring.
H. angustifolia illus. p.452.
H. capensis, syn. *H. stellata, Spiloxene capensis.* Spring-flowering corm with a basal leaf cluster. H 10–20cm (4–8in), S 5–8cm (2–3in). Half hardy. Has very slender, narrowly lance-shaped, erect leaves. Stems each produce an upward-facing flower with pointed, white or yellow petals and a purple eye.
H. stellata. See *H. capensis*.

HYPSELA

CAMPANULACEAE

Genus of vigorous, creeping perennials, grown for their flowers and heart-shaped leaves. Good as ground cover, especially in rock gardens. Frost hardy. Needs shade and moist soil. Propagate by division in spring.
H. longiflora. See *H. reniformis*.
H. reniformis, syn. *H. longiflora.* Vigorous, creeping, stemless perennial. H 2cm (¾in), Sindefinite. Has tiny, heart-shaped, fleshy leaves and, in spring-summer, small, star-shaped, pink-and-white flowers.

Hyssop. See *Hyssopus officinalis*, illus. p.164.
Mexican giant. See *Agastache*.

HYSSOPUS

LABIATAE/LAMIACEAE

Genus of perennials and semi-evergreen or deciduous shrubs, grown for their flowers, which attract bees and butterflies, and for their aromatic foliage, which has culinary and medicinal uses. May be grown as a low hedge. Fully hardy. Requires full sun and fertile, well-drained soil. Cut back hard or, if grown as a hedge, trim lightly, in spring. Propagate by softwood cuttings in summer or by seed in autumn.
H. officinalis (Hyssop) illus. p.164. subsp. ***aristatus*** is a semi-evergreen or deciduous, upright, dense shrub. H 60cm (2ft), S 1m (3ft). Bears aromatic, narrowly lance-shaped leaves that are bright green. Produces densely clustered, small, 2-lipped, dark blue flowers from mid-summer through to early autumn.

I

Iberis

CRUCIFERAE/BRASSICACEAE

Genus of annuals, perennials, evergreen sub-shrubs and shrubs, grown for their flowers and excellent for rock gardens. Some species are short-lived, flowering themselves to death. Fully to half hardy. Requires sun and well-drained soil. Propagate by seed in spring, sub-shrubs and shrubs by semi-ripe cuttings in summer.

I. amara illus. p.330. **'Giant Hyacinth-flowered'** is a group of fast-growing, upright, bushy annuals. H 30cm (12in), S 15cm (6in). Fully hardy. Has lance-shaped, mid-green leaves and, in summer, flattish heads of large, scented, 4-petalled flowers in a variety of colours.

I. commutata. See *I. sempervirens*.

I. saxatilis illus. p.386.

🏆 ***I. sempervirens***, syn. *I. commutata*, illus. p.358. 🏆 **'Snowflake'** (syn. *I.s.* 'Schneeflocke') is an evergreen, spreading sub-shrub. H 15–30cm (6–12in), S 45–60cm (18–24in). Fully hardy. Leaves are narrowly oblong, glossy and dark green. Dense, semi-spherical heads of 4-petalled, white flowers are produced in late spring and early summer. Trim after flowering.

I. umbellata. Fast-growing, upright, bushy annual. H 15–30cm (6–12in), S 20cm (8in). Fully hardy. Has lance-shaped, mid-green leaves. Heads of small, 4-petalled, white or pale purple flowers, sometimes bicoloured, are carried in summer and early autumn. **Fairy Series** illus. p.334.

Iceland poppy. See *Papaver croceum*.

Ice-plant. See *Dorotheanthus bellidiformis; Sedum spectabile*.

Idesia

FLACOURTIACEAE

Genus of one species of deciduous, summer-flowering tree, grown for its foliage and fruits. Both male and female plants are required to obtain fruits. Fully hardy. Needs sun or semi-shade and fertile, moist but well-drained soil, preferably neutral to acid. Propagate by softwood cuttings in summer or by seed in autumn.

I. polycarpa illus. p.76.

Ilex

Holly

AQUIFOLIACEAE

Genus of evergreen or deciduous trees and shrubs, grown for their foliage and fruits (berries). Mainly spherical berries, ranging in colour from red through yellow to black, are produced in autumn, following insignificant, usually white, flowers borne in spring. Almost all plants are unisexual, and to obtain fruits on a female plant a male also needs to be grown. Fully to half hardy. All prefer well-drained soil. Grow in sun or shade, but deciduous plants and those with variegated foliage do best in sun or semi-shade. Hollies resent being transplanted, but respond well to hard pruning and pollarding, which should be carried out in late spring. Propagate by seed in spring or by semi-ripe cuttings from late summer to early winter. Holly leaf miner and holly aphid may cause problems. The berries may cause mild stomach upset if ingested. See also feature panel pp.94–5.

I. × altaclerensis. Group of vigorous, evergreen shrubs and trees. Frost hardy. Is resistant to pollution and coastal exposure.

'Balearica' (illus. p.94) is an erect, female tree. H 12m (40ft), S 5m (15ft). Has green to olive-green young branches. Large, broadly oval leaves are spiny- or smooth-edged and glossy, dark green. Freely produces large, bright red berries.

'Belgica' (illus. p.94) is an erect, dense, female tree. H 12m (40ft), S 5m (15ft). Young branches are green to yellowish-green. Has large, lance-shaped to oblong, spiny- or smooth-edged, glossy, mid-green leaves. Large, orange-red fruits are freely produced.

🏆 **'Belgica Aurea'** (syn. *I. × a.* 'Silver Sentinel', *I. perado* 'Aurea'; illus. p.94) is an upright, female tree. H 8m (25ft), S 3m (10ft). Young branches are green with yellow streaks. Has large, lance-shaped, mainly spineless, dark green leaves, mottled with grey-green and irregularly edged with yellow. Red berries are produced only rarely.

🏆 **'Camelliifolia'** (illus. p.94) is a narrow, pyramidal, female tree. H 14m (46ft), S 3m (10ft). Has purple young branches and large, oblong, mainly smooth-edged, glossy, dark green leaves. Reliably produces large, scarlet fruits; is an excellent specimen tree.

'Camelliifolia Variegata' illus. p.95. H 8m (25ft), S 3m (10ft). Is similar to *I. × a.* 'Camelliifolia', but leaves have broad, yellow margins.

🏆 **'Golden King'** is a bushy, female shrub. H 6m (20ft), S 5m (15ft). Young branches are green with a purplish flush. Has large, oblong to oval, sometimes slightly spiny, dark green leaves, each splashed with grey-green in the centre and with a bright yellow margin that turns to cream on older leaves. Is not a good fruiter, bearing only a few reddish-brown berries, but is excellent as a hedge or a specimen plant.

🏆 **'Hodginsii'** is a vigorous, dense, male tree. H 14m (46ft), S 10m (30ft). Shoots are purple; leaves are broadly oval, sparsely spiny and glossy, blackish-green.

🏆 **'Lawsoniana'** is a bushy, female shrub. H 6m (20ft), S 5m (15ft). Is similar to *I. × a.* 'Golden King', but has leaves splashed irregularly in the centre with gold and lighter green. Foliage tends to revert to plain green.

'N.F. Barnes' (illus. p.94) is a dense, female shrub. H 5.5m (18ft), S 4m (12ft). Has purple shoots and oval, mainly entire but spine-tipped, glossy, dark green leaves and red berries.

'Silver Sentinel' see *I. × a.* 'Belgica Aurea'.

'Wilsonii' is a vigorous, female tree. H 8m (25ft), S 5m (15ft). Has purplish-green young branches and large, oblong to oval, glossy, mid-green leaves with prominent veins and large spines. Freely produces large, scarlet fruits and makes a good hedging or specimen plant.

🏆 ***I. aquifolium*** (Common holly; illus. p.94). Evergreen, much-branched, erect shrub or tree. H 20m (70ft), S 6m (20ft). Frost hardy. Has variably shaped, wavy, sharply spined, glossy, dark green leaves and bright red berries.

🏆 **'Amber'** (illus. p.95) is a conical, female tree. H 6m (20ft), S 2.5m (8ft). Mid-green stems bear elliptic, usually entire, bright green leaves and abundant. amber-yellow berries.

🏆 **'Argentea Marginata'** (Silver-margined holly; illus. p.94) is a columnar, female tree. H 14m (46ft), S 5m (15ft). Young branches are green, streaked with cream. Broadly oval, spiny, dark green leaves, with wide, cream margins, are shrimp-pink when young. Bears an abundance of bright red berries. Is good for hedging.

'Argentea Marginata Pendula' (Perry's weeping silver holly; illus. p.94) is a slow-growing, weeping, female tree. H 6m (20ft), S 5m (15ft). Has purple young branches and broadly oval, spiny, dark green leaves, mottled with grey-green and broadly edged with cream. Bears red fruits. Is good as a specimen plant in a small garden.

'Atlas' is an erect, male shrub. H 5m (15ft), S 3m (10ft). Has green young branches and oval, spiny, glossy, dark green leaves. Is useful for landscaping and hedging.

'Aurea Regina' see *I.a.* 'Golden Queen'.

'Aurifodina' (illus. p.95) is an erect, dense, female shrub. H 6m (20ft), S 3m (10ft). Young branches are purplish. Oval, spiny leaves are olive-green with golden-yellow margins that turn tawny-yellow in winter. Produces a good crop of deep scarlet berries.

f. ***bacciflava*** (syn. *I.a.* 'Bacciflava') is a much-branched, usually erect shrub or tree. H 20m (70ft), S 6m (20ft). Has variably shaped, wavy, sharply spined, glossy, dark green leaves and yellow fruits.

'Crispa Aureopicta' (illus. p.95) is a male tree of open habit. H 10m (30ft), S 6m (20ft). Narrowly oval, twisted, sparsely spiny, blackish-green leaves are centrally blotched with golden-yellow. Foliage tends to revert to plain green.

'Ferox' (Hedgehog holly) is an open, male shrub. H 6m (20ft), S 4m (12ft). Has purple young branches and oval, dark green leaves with spines over entire leaf surface.

🏆 **'Ferox Argentea'** (Silver hedgehog holly; illus p.95) is similar to *I.a.* 'Ferox', but has leaves with cream margins.

'Flavescens' (Moonlight holly) is a columnar, female shrub. H 6m (20ft), S 5m (15ft). Young branches are purplish-red. Variably shaped leaves are dark green, with a yellowish flush when young that will last year-round when grown in good light. Produces plentiful, red berries.

'Golden Milkboy' (illus. p.94) is a dense, male shrub. H 6m (20ft), S 4m (12ft). Has purplish-green young branches and oval, very spiny, bright green leaves with heavily blotched, bright yellow centres. Leaves tend to revert to plain green.

🏆 **'Golden Queen'** (syn. *I.a.* 'Aurea Regina') is a dense tree that, despite its name, is male. H 10m (30ft), S 6m (20ft). Broadly oval, very spiny, mid-green leaves are edged with golden-yellow.

'Golden van Tol' (illus. p.95), a sport of *I.a.* 'J.C. van Tol', is an upright, female shrub. H 4m (12ft), S 3m (10ft). Young branches are purple. Oval, puckered, slightly spiny, dark green leaves have irregular, clear yellow margins. Produces a sparse crop of red fruits. Is good for hedging or as a specimen plant.

🏆 **'Handsworth New Silver'** is a dense, columnar, female shrub. H 8m (25ft), S 5m (15ft). Branches are purple. Oblong to oval, spiny, dark green leaves have broad, cream margins. Bears a profusion of bright red fruits. Is excellent as a hedge or specimen plant and is good for a small garden.

'Hascombensis' is a slow-growing, dense shrub of unknown sex. H 1.5m (5ft), S 1–1.2m (3–4ft). Has purplish-green young branches and small, oval, spiny, dark green leaves. Does not produce berries. Suits a rock garden.

🏆 **'J.C. van Tol'** is an open, female shrub that does not require cross-fertilization to produce fruits. H 6m (20ft), S 4m (12ft). Branches are dark purple when young. Oval, puckered, slightly spiny leaves are dark green. Produces a good crop of red berries. Is useful as a hedge or for a tub.

🏆 **'Madame Briot'** (illus. p.95) is a vigorous, bushy, female tree. H 10m (30ft), S 5m (15ft). Young branches are purplish-green. Leaves are large, broadly oval, spiny and dark green with bright golden borders. Bears scarlet berries.

'Ovata Aurea' (illus. p.95) is a dense, male shrub. H 5m (15ft), S 4m (12ft). Has reddish-brown young branches and oval, regularly spiny, dark green leaves with bright golden margins.

🏆 **'Pyramidalis'** (illus. p.94) is a dense, female tree that does not require cross-fertilization to produce fruits. H 6m (20ft), S 5m (15ft). Has green young branches and narrowly elliptic, slightly spiny, mid-green leaves. Produces masses of scarlet fruits. Is suitable for a small garden.

'Pyramidalis Aureomarginata' (illus. p.95) is an upright, female shrub. H 6m (20ft), S 5m (15ft). Young branches are green. Has narrowly elliptic, mid-green leaves with prominent, golden margins and spines on upper half. Bears a large crop of red berries.

🏆 **'Pyramidalis Fructu Luteo'** is a conical, female shrub that broadens with age. H 6m (20ft), S 4m (12ft). Branches are green when young. Has oval, often spineless, dark green leaves and bears yellow berries. Is excellent for a small garden.

'Scotica' is a large, stiff, compact, female shrub. H 6m (20ft), S 4m (12ft). Oval, usually spineless, glossy, very dark green leaves are slightly twisted. Bears red fruits.

'Silver King' see *I.a.* 'Silver Queen'.

'Silver Milkboy' see *I.a.* 'Silver Milkmaid'.

'Silver Milkmaid' (syn. *I.a.* 'Silver

Milkboy'; illus. p.94) is a dense, female shrub. H 5.5m (18ft), S 4m (12ft). Oval, wavy-edged, very spiny leaves are bronze when young, maturing to bright green, each with a central, creamy-white blotch, but tend to revert to plain green. Produces an abundance of scarlet berries. Makes a very attractive specimen plant.
♀ **'Silver Queen'** (syn. *I.a.* 'Silver King'; illus. p.94) is a dense shrub that, despite its name, is male. H 5m (15ft), S 4m (12ft). Has purple young branches. Oval, spiny leaves, pink when young, mature to very dark green, almost black, with broad, cream edging.
'Watereriana' (syn. *I.a.* 'Waterer's Gold'; illus. p.95) is a dense, male bush. H and S 5m (15ft). Young branches are green, streaked with yellow. Oval, spiny- or smooth-edged leaves are greyish-green, with broad, golden margins. Is best grown as a specimen plant.
'Waterer's Gold' see *I.a.* 'Watereriana'.

I. × aquipernyi illus. p.94. Evergreen, upright shrub. H 5m (15ft), S 3m (10ft). Frost hardy. Has small, oval, spiny, glossy, dark green leaves with long tips. Berries are large and red.

I. chinensis **of gardens.** See *I. purpurea*.

I. ciliospinosa illus. p.94. Evergreen, upright shrub or tree. H 6m (20ft), S 4m (12ft). Frost hardy. Has small, oval, weak-spined, dull green leaves and red berries.

I. cornuta (Horned holly). Evergreen, dense, rounded shrub. H 4m (12ft), S 5m (15ft). Frost hardy. Rectangular, dull green leaves are spiny except on older bushes. Produces large, red berries. **'Burfordii'** (illus. p.94) is female, S 2.5m (8ft), has glossy leaves with only a terminal spine and bears a profusion of fruits. **'Rotunda'**, H 2m (6ft), S 1.2m (4ft), is also female and produces a small crop of fruits; is useful for a tub or small garden.

I. crenata (Box-leaved holly, Japanese holly). Evergreen, spreading shrub or tree. H 5m (15ft), S 3m (10ft). Fully hardy. Has very small, oval, dark green leaves with rounded teeth. Bears glossy, black fruits. Is useful for landscaping or as hedging. **'Bullata'** see *I.c.* 'Convexa'. ♀ **'Convexa'** (syn. *I.c.* 'Bullata'; illus. p.94) is a dense, female shrub. H 2.5m (8ft), S 1.2–1.5m (4–5ft). Has purplish-green young branches and oval, puckered, glossy leaves. Bears glossy, black fruits. **'Helleri'** is a spreading, female shrub. H 1.2m (4ft), S 1–1.2m (3–4ft). Has green young branches and oval leaves with few spines. Has glossy, black fruits. Is much used for landscaping. f. ***latifolia*** (syn. *I.c.* 'Latifolia'; illus. p.94) is a spreading to erect, female shrub or tree. H 6m (20ft), S 3m (10ft). Young branches are green and broadly oval leaves have tiny teeth. Produces glossy, black berries. var. ***paludosa*** (illus. p.94) is a prostrate shrub or tree. H 15–30cm (6–12in), S indefinite. Has very small, oval, dark green leaves with rounded teeth. Bears glossy, black fruits. **'Variegata'** (illus. p.95) is an open, male shrub. H 4m (12ft), S 2.5m (8ft). Oval leaves are spotted or blotched with yellow, but tend to revert to plain green.

I. dipyrena (Himalayan holly). Evergreen, dense, upright tree. H 12m (40ft), S 8m (25ft). Frost hardy. Elliptic, dull green leaves are spiny when young, later smooth-edged. Bears large, red fruits.

I. fargesii illus. p.94. Evergreen, broadly conical tree or shrub. H 6m (20ft), S 5m (15ft). Frost hardy. Has green or purple shoots and oval, small-toothed, mid- to dark green leaves. Produces red berries. var. ***brevifolia*** (illus. p.94), H 4m (12ft), is dense and rounded.

I. georgei. Evergreen, compact shrub. H 5m (15ft), S 4m (12ft). Half hardy. Has small, lance-shaped or oval, weak-spined, glossy, dark green leaves with long tips. Berries are red.

I. glabra (Inkberry). Evergreen, dense, upright shrub. H 2.5m (8ft), S 2m (6ft). Fully hardy. Small, oblong to oval, dark green leaves are smooth-edged or may have slight teeth near tips. Produces black fruits.

I. insignis. See *I. kingiana*.

I. integra. Evergreen, dense, bushy shrub or tree. H 6m (20ft), S 5m (15ft). Frost hardy. Has oval, blunt-tipped, bright green leaves with smooth edges. Bears large, deep red berries.

I. **'Jermyns Dwarf'.** See *I. pernyi* 'Jermyns Dwarf'.

I. kingiana, syn. *I. insignis*. Evergreen, upright tree. H 6m (20ft), S 4m (12ft). Half hardy. Very large, oblong, leathery, dark green leaves have small spines. Berries are bright red.

I. × koehneana illus. p.94. Evergreen, conical shrub. H 6m (20ft), S 5m (15ft). Fully hardy. Young branches are green. Has very large, oblong, spiny, mid-green leaves and red fruits.

I. latifolia (Tarajo holly). Evergreen, upright shrub. H 6m (20ft), S 5m (15ft). Half hardy. Has stout, olive-green young branches, very large, oblong, dark green leaves with short spines and plentiful, red fruits.

I. macrocarpa illus. p.94. Deciduous, upright tree. H 10m (30ft), S 6m (20ft). Frost hardy. Has large, oval, saw-toothed, mid-green leaves and very large, black berries.

I. × meserveae (Blue holly). Group of vigorous, evergreen, dense shrubs. Fully hardy, but does not thrive in a maritime climate. Has oval, glossy, greenish-blue leaves. ♀ **'Blue Princess'** (illus. p.94), H 3m (10ft), S 1.2m (4ft), is female and has purplish-green young branches, small, oval, wavy, spiny leaves and an abundance of red fruits.

I. opaca (American holly; illus. p.94). Evergreen, erect tree. H 14m (46ft), S 1.2m (4ft). Fully hardy, but does not thrive in a maritime climate. Oval leaves are dull green above, yellow-green beneath and spiny- or smooth-edged. Has red fruits.

I. pedunculosa illus. p.95. Evergreen, upright shrub or tree. H 10m (30ft), S 6m (20ft). Fully hardy. Oval, dark green leaves are smooth-edged. Bright red berries are borne on very long stalks.

I. perado **'Aurea'.** See *I. × altaclerensis* 'Belgica Aurea'.

I. pernyi illus. p.94. Slow-growing, evergreen, stiff shrub. H 8m (25ft), S 4m (12ft). Fully hardy. Has pale green young branches and small, oblong, spiny, dark green leaves. Produces red berries. **'Jermyns Dwarf'** (syn. *I.* 'Jermyns Dwarf'), H 60cm (2ft), S 1.2m (4ft), is low-growing and female, with glossy, very spiny leaves.

I. purpurea, syn. *I. chinensis of gardens* illus. p.95. Evergreen, upright tree. H 12m (40ft), S 6m (20ft). Half hardy. Oval, thin-textured, glossy, dark green leaves have rounded teeth. Lavender flowers are followed by egg-shaped, glossy, scarlet fruits.

I. serrata. Deciduous, bushy shrub. H 4m (12ft), S 2.5m (8ft). Fully hardy. Small, oval, finely toothed, bright green leaves are downy when young. Pink flowers are followed by small, red fruits. f. ***leucocarpa*** (illus. p.95) bears white berries.

I. verticillata (Winterberry; illus. p.94). Deciduous, dense, suckering shrub. H 2m (6ft), S 1.2–1.5m (4–5ft). Fully hardy. Young branches are purplish-green. Produces oval or lance-shaped, saw-toothed, bright green leaves. Bears masses of long-lasting, red berries that remain on bare branches during winter.

I. yunnanensis. Evergreen, spreading to erect shrub. H 4m (12ft), S 2.5m (8ft). Frost hardy. Branches are downy. Small, oval leaves, with rounded teeth, are brownish-green when young, glossy, dark green in maturity. Produces red berries.

Illawarra flame tree. See *Brachychiton acerifolius*, illus. p.61.
Illawarra palm. See *Archontophoenix cunninghamiana*.

ILLICIUM

ILLICIACEAE

Genus of evergreen, spring- to early summer-flowering trees and shrubs, grown for their foliage and unusual flowers. Frost to half hardy. Does best in semi-shade or shade and moist, neutral to acid soil. Propagate by semi-ripe cuttings in summer.

I. anisatum (Chinese anise). Slow-growing, evergreen, conical tree or shrub. H and S 6m (20ft). Frost hardy. Produces oval, aromatic, glossy, dark green leaves. Star-shaped, greenish-yellow flowers, with numerous narrow petals, are carried in mid-spring.

I. floridanum (Purple anise). Evergreen, bushy shrub. H and S 2m (6ft). Half hardy. Lance-shaped, leathery, deep green leaves are very aromatic. Star-shaped, red or purplish-red flowers, with numerous, narrow petals, are produced in late spring and early summer.

Immortelle. See *Bracteantha bracteata; Xeranthemum*.

IMPATIENS

BALSAMINACEAE

Genus of annuals and mainly evergreen perennials and sub-shrubs, often with succulent but brittle stems. In cold climates some may be herbaceous. Fully hardy to frost tender, min. 10°C (50°F). Prefers sun or semi-shade and moist but not waterlogged soil. Propagate by seed or by stem cuttings in spring or summer. Red spider mite, aphids and whitefly may cause problems under glass.

I. balsamina illus. p.332. **'Blackberry Ice'** is a fast-growing, upright, bushy annual. H 70cm (28in), S 45cm (18in). Half hardy. Has lance-shaped, pale green leaves and, in summer and early autumn, large, double, purple flowers, splashed with white. **Tom Thumb Series** illus. p.337.

I. **Confection Series** illus. p.339.

I. **Expo Series 'Expo Pink'** illus. p.339.

I. **New Guinea Group 'Mimas'** illus p.338.

I. niamniamensis. Evergreen, bushy perennial. H to 90cm (3ft), S 30cm (1ft). Frost tender. Has reddish-green stems and oval, toothed leaves to 20cm (8in) long. Showy, 5-petalled, hooded, yellowish-green flowers, 2.5cm (1in) long and each with a long, orange, red, crimson or purple spur, appear in summer-autumn. **'Congo Cockatoo'** has red, green and yellow flowers.

I. oliveri. See *I. sodenii*.

♀ ***I. repens*** illus. p.305.

I. sodenii, syn. *I. oliveri*. Evergreen, strong-growing, bushy perennial. H 1.2m (4ft) or more, S 60cm (2ft). Frost tender. Narrowly oval, toothed leaves, in whorls of 4–10, are 15cm (6in) or more long. Almost flat, white or pale pink to mauve flowers, 5cm (2in) or more wide, are produced mainly in summer.

I. walleriana (Busy lizzie). Fast-growing, evergreen, bushy perennial,usually grown as an annual. H and S to 60cm (2ft). Half hardy. Has oval,fresh green leaves. Flattish, 5-petalled,spurred, bright red, pink, purple, violetor white flowers appear from springto autumn. ♀ **Super Elfin Series**, H and S 20cm (8in), has flattish flowers in mixed colours. **Super Elfin Series 'Lipstick'** illus. p.338. **Swirl Series** illus. p.333. Flowers of ♀ **Tempo Series**, H to 23cm (9in), include shades of violet, orange, pink and red, as well as bicolours and picotees.

INCARVILLEA

BIGNONIACEAE

Genus of late spring- or summer-flowering perennials, suitable for rock gardens and borders. Fully to frost hardy, but protect crowns with bracken or compost in winter. Requires sun and fertile, well-drained soil. Propagate by seed in autumn or spring.

I. delavayi illus. p.292.

I. mairei illus. p.289.

Incense cedar. See *Calocedrus decurrens*, illus. p.102.
Incense plant. See *Calomeria amaranthoides*, illus. p.342.
Incense rose. See *Rosa primula*, illus. p.184.
India rubber tree. See *Ficus elastica*.
Indian almond. See *Terminalia catappa*.
Indian bean tree. See *Catalpa bignonioides*, illus. p.74.
Indian corn. See *Zea*.
Indian currant. See *Symphoricarpos orbiculatus*.
Indian fig. See *Opuntia ficus-indica*.
Indian ginger. See *Alpinia calcarata*.

Indian hawthorn. See *Rhaphiolepis indica.*
Indian horse-chestnut. See *Aesculus indica.*
Indian laburnum. See *Cassia fistula.*
Indian pink. See *Dianthus chinensis.*
Indian plum. See *Oemleria cerasiformis.*
Indigo, False. See *Baptisia australis*, illus. p.258.

INDIGOFERA

LEGUMINOSAE/PAPILIONACEAE

Genus of perennials and deciduous shrubs, grown for their foliage and small, pea-like flowers. Fully to frost hardy; in cold areas, hard frosts may cut plants to ground, but they usually regrow from base in spring. Needs full sun and fertile, well-drained soil. Cut out dead wood in spring. Propagate by softwood cuttings in summer or by seed in autumn.
I. decora. Deciduous, bushy shrub. H 45cm (1½ft), S 1m (3ft). Frost hardy. Glossy, dark green leaves each have 7–13 oval leaflets. Long spikes of pink or white flowers appear from mid- to late summer.
I. dielsiana illus. p.158.
I. gerardiana. See *I. heterantha.*
♀ ***I. heterantha***, syn. *I. gerardiana*, illus. p.137.
I. pseudotinctoria. Deciduous, arching shrub. H 1m (3ft) or more, S 2m (6ft). Fully hardy. Each dark green leaf has usually 7–9 oval leaflets. Long, dense racemes of small, pale pink flowers are borne in mid-summer to early autumn.

Inkberry. See *Ilex glabra.*
Interrupted fern. See *Osmunda claytoniana.*

INULA

COMPOSITAE/ASTERACEAE

Genus of summer-flowering, clump-forming, sometimes rhizomatous perennials. Fully hardy. Most need sun and moist but well-drained soil. Propagate by seed or division in spring or autumn.
I. acaulis. Tuft-forming, rhizomatous perennial. H 5–10cm (2–4in), S 15cm (6in). Has lance-shaped to elliptic, hairy leaves. Solitary, almost stemless, daisy-like, golden-yellow flower heads are produced in summer. Is good for a rock garden.
I. ensifolia illus. p.305.
I. hookeri illus. p.262.
I. macrocephala of gardens. See *I. royleana.*
I. magnifica illus. p.227.
I. oculis-christi. Spreading, rhizomatous perennial. H 45cm (18in), S 60cm (24in). Stems each bear 2 or 3 daisy-like, yellow flower heads, which appear in summer. Has lance-shaped to elliptic, hairy, mid-green leaves.
I. royleana, syn. *I. macrocephala of gardens*, illus. p.262.

IOCHROMA

SOLANACEAE

Genus of evergreen shrubs, grown for their flowers. Frost tender, min. 7–10°C (45–50°F). Needs full light or partial shade and fertile, well-drained soil. Water potted plants freely when in full growth, moderately at other times. Tip prune young plants to stimulate a bushy habit. Cut back flowered stems by half in late winter. Propagate by greenwood or semi-ripe cuttings in summer. Whitefly and red spider mite are sometimes troublesome.
I. cyaneum, syn. *I. tubulosum*, illus. p.146.
I. tubulosum. See *I. cyaneum.*

IONOPSIDIUM

CRUCIFERAE/BRASSICACEAE

Genus of annuals. Only one species is usually cultivated, for rock gardens and as edging. Frost hardy. Grow in semi-shade and in fertile, well-drained soil. Propagate by seed sown outdoors in spring, early summer or early autumn.
♀ ***I. acaule*** (Violet cress). Fast-growing, upright annual. H 5–8cm (2–3in), S 2.5cm (1in). Rounded leaves are mid-green. Tiny, 4-petalled, lilac or white flowers, flushed with deep blue, are produced in summer and early autumn.

IPHEION

LILIACEAE/ALLIACEAE

Genus of bulbs that freely produce many star-shaped, blue, white or yellow flowers in spring and make excellent pot plants in cold greenhouses. Frost hardy. Prefers a sheltered situation in dappled sunlight and well-drained soil. Plant in autumn; after flowering, dies down for summer. Propagate by offsets in late summer or early autumn.
♀ ***I. uniflorum*** **'Froyle Mill'** illus. p.447. ♀ **'Wisley Blue'** is a spring-flowering bulb. H 10–15cm (4–6in), S 5–8cm (2–3in). Bears linear, semi-erect, basal, pale green leaves, which smell of onions if damaged. Leafless stems each produce an upward-facing, pale blue flower, 3–4cm (1¼–1½in) across.

IPOMOEA,
syn. MINA, PHARBITIS

CONVOLVULACEAE

Genus of mainly evergreen shrubs, perennials, annuals and soft- or woody-stemmed, twining climbers. Half hardy to frost tender, min. 7–10°C (45–50°F). Provide full light and humus-rich, well-drained soil. Water freely when in full growth, less at other times. Support is needed. Thin out or cut back congested growth in spring. Propagate by seed in spring or by softwood or semi-ripe cuttings in summer. Whitefly and red spider mite may cause problems. Seeds are highly toxic if ingested.
I. acuminata. See *I. indica.*
I. alba, syn. *Calonyction aculeatum, I. bona-nox* (Moon flower). Evergreen, soft-stemmed, twining climber with prickly stems that exude milky juice when cut. H 7m (22ft) or more. Frost tender, min. 10°C (50°F). Oval or sometimes 3-lobed leaves are 20cm (8in) long. Fragrant, tubular, white flowers, to 15cm (6in) long and expanded at the mouths to 15cm (6in) across, open at night in summer.
I. bona-nox. See *I. alba.*
I. coccinea, syn. *Quamoclit coccinea* (Red morning glory, Star ipomoea). Annual, twining climber. H to 3m (10ft). Frost tender, min. 10°C (50°F). Arrow- or heart-shaped leaves are long-pointed and often toothed. Fragrant, tubular, scarlet flowers, with yellow throats and expanded mouths, are produced in late summer and autumn.
I. hederacea illus. p.212.
♀ ***I. horsfalliae*** illus. p.205. **'Briggsii'** is a strong-growing, evergreen, woody-stemmed, twining climber. H 2–3m (6–10ft). Frost tender, min. 7–10°C (45–50°F). Has leaves with 5–7 radiating lobes or leaflets. Stalked clusters of funnel-shaped, deep rose-pink or rose-purple flowers are produced from summer to winter; flowers are larger and more richly coloured than those of the species.
I. imperialis. See *I. nil.*
♀ ***I. indica***, syn. *I. acuminata, I. learii*, illus. p.202.
I. learii. See *I. indica.*
I. lobata, syn. *I. versicolor, Quamoclit lobata*, illus. p.206.
I. × multifida, syn. *I. × sloteri* (Cardinal climber, Hearts-and-honey vine). Annual, twining climber. H 3m (10ft). Frost tender, min. 10°C (50°F). Triangular-oval leaves are divided into 7–15 segments. Tubular, wide-mouthed, crimson flowers with white eyes appear in summer.
I. nil, syn. *I. imperialis.* **'Early Call'** is a short-lived, soft-stemmed, perennial, twining climber with hairy stems, best grown as an annual. H to 4m (12ft). Half hardy. Leaves are heart-shaped or 3-lobed. From summer to early autumn bears large, funnel-shaped flowers in a range of colours, with white tubes. **'Scarlett O'Hara'** has deep red flowers.
I. purpurea, syn. *Convolvulus purpureus* (Common morning glory). Short-lived, soft-stemmed, perennial, twining climber, best grown as an annual, with hairy stems. H to 5m (15ft). Half hardy. Leaves are heart-shaped or 3-lobed. From summer to early autumn has funnel-shaped, deep purple to bluish-purple or reddish flowers with white throats and bristly sepals.
I. quamoclit, syn. *Quamoclit pennata*, illus. p.206.
I. rubrocaerulea **'Heavenly Blue'.** See *I. tricolor* 'Heavenly Blue'.
I. × sloteri. See *I. × multifida.*
♀ ***I. tricolor*** **'Heavenly Blue'**, syn. *I. rubrocaerulea* 'Heavenly Blue', illus. p.213.
I. tuberosa. See *Merremia tuberosa.*
I. versicolor. See *I. lobata.*

Ipomoea, Star. See *Ipomoea coccinea.*

IPOMOPSIS

POLEMONIACEAE

Genus of perennials and biennials, often grown as pot plants for greenhouses and conservatories. Half hardy. Grow in cool, airy conditions with bright light and in fertile, well-drained soil. Propagate by seed sown under glass in early spring or early summer.
I. aggregata. Slow-growing biennial with upright, slender, hairy stems. H to 1m (3ft), S 30cm (1ft). Mid-green leaves are divided into linear leaflets. Fragrant, trumpet-shaped flowers, borne in summer, are usually brilliant red, sometimes spotted yellow, but may be rose, yellow or white.

IRESINE

AMARANTHACEAE

Genus of perennials, grown for their colourful leaves. Frost tender, min. 10–15°C (50–59°F). Requires bright light to retain leaf colour and a good, loamy, well-drained soil. Pinch out tips in growing season to obtain bushy plants. Propagate by stem cuttings in spring.
I. herbstii (Beefsteak plant). Bushy perennial. H to 60cm (24in), S 45cm (18in). Has red stems and rounded, purplish-red leaves, notched at their tips and 10cm (4in) long, with paler or yellowish-red veins. Flowers are insignificant. **'Aureoreticulata'** illus. p.317.
♀ ***I. lindenii*** (Blood leaf). Bushy perennial. H 60cm (24in), S 45cm (18in). Has lance-shaped, dark red leaves, 5–10cm (2–4in) long. Flowers are insignificant.

IRIS

IRIDACEAE

Genus of upright, rhizomatous or bulbous (occasionally fleshy-rooted) perennials, some of which are evergreen, grown for their distinctive and colourful flowers. Each flower has 3 usually large 'falls' (pendent or semi-pendent petals), which in a number of species have conspicuous beards or crests; 3 generally smaller 'standards' (erect, horizontal or, occasionally, pendent petals); and a 3-branched style. In many irises the style branches are petal-like. Unless otherwise stated below, flower stems are unbranched. Green, then brown seed pods are ellipsoid to cylindrical and often ribbed. Irises are suitable for borders, rock gardens, woodlands, watersides, bog gardens, alpine houses, cold frames and containers. Species and cultivars described are fully hardy unless otherwise stated, but some groups may thrive only in the specific growing conditions mentioned below. Propagate species by division of rhizomes or offsets in late summer or by seed in autumn, named cultivars by division only. Botanically, irises are divided into a number of sub-genera and sections, and it is convenient, for horticultural purposes, to use some of these botanical names for groups of irises with similar characteristics and requiring comparable cultural treatment. All parts may cause severe discomfort if ingested; contact with the sap may irritate skin. See also feature panel pp.234–7.

Rhizomatous
These irises have rhizomes as rootstocks; leaves are sword-shaped and usually in a basal fan.

Bearded irises are rhizomatous and have 'beards', consisting of numerous often coloured hairs, along the centre of each fall. In some irises, the end of the beard is enlarged into the shape of a horn. The group covers the vast majority of irises, including many named cultivars, grown in gardens; all are derived from *I. pallida* and related species. Bearded irises thrive in full sun in fairly rich, well-drained, preferably slightly alkaline soil. Some are very tolerant and will grow and flower reasonably in partial shade in poorer soil. For horticultural purposes, various groupings of hybrid bearded irises are recognized, based mainly on the height of the plants in flower. These include **Miniature Dwarf**, H to 20cm (8in); **Standard Dwarf**, H 20–40cm (8–16in); **Intermediate**, H 40–70cm (16–28in); and **Standard Tall**, H 70cm (28in) or more (this last category may be further subdivided). In general, the shorter the iris, the earlier the flowering season (from early spring to early summer).

Oncocyclus irises are rhizomatous, with very large and often bizarrely coloured flowers, one to each stem, which have bearded falls. They require full sun, sharply drained but fairly rich soil and, after flowering, a dry period of dormancy in summer and early autumn. Difficult to cultivate successfully, they are best grown in an alpine house or covered frame in climates subject to summer rains.**Regelia** irises are closely related to Oncocyclus irises, differing in having bearded standards as well as falls and in having 2 flowers to each stem. They require similar conditions of cultivation, although a few species, such as *I. hoogiana*, have proved easier to grow than Oncocyclus irises. Hybrids between the 2 groups have been raised and are known as **Regeliocyclus** irises.

Beardless irises, also rhizomatous, lack hairs on the falls; most have very similar cultural requirements to bearded irises but some prefer heavier soil. Various groupings are recognized, of which the following are the most widely known. **Pacific Coast** irises, a group of Californian species and their hybrids, prefer acid to neutral soil and grow well in sun or partial shade, appreciating some humus in the soil; they are best grown from seed as they resent being moved. **Spuria** irises (*I. spuria* and its relatives) grow in sun or semi-shade and well-drained but moist soil. Anumber of species and hybrids prefers moist, waterside conditions; these include the well-known **Siberian** irises (*I. sibirica* and its relatives) and the **Japanese** water irises, such as *I. ensata* and *I. laevigata*, which may also be grown as border plants, but succeed best in open, sunny, humus-rich, moist sites.

Crested irises, also rhizomatous, have ridges, or cockscomb-like crests, instead of beards. They include the **Evansia** irises, with often widely spreading, creeping stolons. Most have very similar cultivation requirements to bearded irises but some prefer damp, humus-rich conditions; a few are half hardy to frost tender, min. 5°C (41°F).

Bulbous
These irisesare distinguished by having bulbs as storage organs, sometimes with thickened, fleshy roots, and leaves that are lance-shaped and channelled; 4-sided (more or less square in cross section); or almost cylindrical – unlike the flat and usually sword-shaped leaves of the rhizomatous irises. **Xiphium** irises include the commonly grown Spanish, English and Dutch irises, which are excellent both for garden decoration and as cut flowers. All are easy to cultivate in sunny, well-drained sites, preferring slightly alkaline conditions, but also growing well on acid soil. **Spanish** irises are derived from *I. xiphium*, which is variable in flower colour, from blue and violet to yellow and white, and produces its channelled leaves in autumn. **English** irises have been produced from *I. latifolia*, which varies from blue to violet (occasionally white) and produces its channelled leaves in spring. **Dutch** irises are hybrids of *I. xiphium* and the related pale to deep blue *I. latifolia*. They are extremely variable in flower colour.

Juno irises have bulbs with thickened, fleshy roots, channelled leaves and very small standards that are sometimes only bristle-like and usually horizontally placed. Although very beautiful in flower, they are mostly difficult to grow successfully, requiring the same cultivation conditions as Oncocyclus irises to thrive. Care must be taken not to damage the fleshy roots when transplanting or dividing clumps.

Reticulata irises include the dwarf, bulbous irises valuable for flowering early in the year. Unlike other bulbous irises, they have net-like bulb tunics and leaves that are 4-sided, or occasionally cylindrical. With few exceptions (not described here), Reticulata irises grow well in open, sunny, well-drained sites.

I. acutiloba. Rhizomatous Oncocyclus iris. H 8–25cm (3–10in), S 30–38cm (12–15in). Has narrowly sickle-shaped, mid-green leaves. In late spring produces solitary, strongly purple-violet- or brownish-purple-veined, white flowers, 5–7cm (2–3in) across, with a dark brown blaze around the beard of each fall.
***I.* 'Annabel Jane'** illus. p.236. Vigorous, rhizomatous, bearded iris (Standard Tall). H 1.2m (4ft), S indefinite. Well-branched stem bears 8–12 flowers, 15–25cm (6–10in) across, with pale lilac falls and paler standards. Flowers in early summer.
***I.* 'Anniversary'** illus. p.234. Rhizomatous, beardless Siberian iris. H 75cm (2½ft), S indefinite. In mid- and late spring bears 1–4 white flowers, 5–10cm (2–4in) across, with a yellow stripe in the throat of each fall. Grows well in moist soil or a bog garden.
I. aphylla. Rhizomatous, bearded iris. H 15–30cm (6–12in), S indefinite. Branched stem produces up to 5 pale to dark purple or blue-violet flowers, 6–7cm (2½–3in) across, in late spring and sometimes again in autumn if conditions suit.
♀ ***I. aucheri.*** Bulbous Juno iris. H 15–25cm (6–10in), S 15cm (6in). Has channelled, mid-green leaves packed closely together on stem, looking somewhat leek-like. In late spring bears up to 6 blue to white flowers, 6–7cm (2½–3in) across with yellow-ridged falls, in leaf axils.
I. aurea. See *I. crocea*.
***I.* 'Autumn Circus'** illus. p.237. Vigorous, rhizomatous, bearded iris (Standard Tall). H 80cm (32in), S indefinite. Well-branched stems bear scented, gently ruffled, white flowers, with violet-blue margins and violet-blue feathering and pencilling on the standards and falls, in late spring. Often blooms again in summer.
***I.* 'Autumn Leaves'** illus. p.235. Vigorous, rhizomatous, bearded iris (Standard Tall). H 80cm (32in), S indefinite. In mid-spring produces branched sprays of sweetly scented, caramel-coloured flowers, a blend of brown and purple, with orange-yellow beards.
I. bakeriana. Bulbous Reticulata iris. H 10cm (4in), S 5–6cm (2–2½in). In early spring bears a solitary, long-tubed, pale blue flower, 5–6cm (2–2½in) across, with each fall having a dark blue blotch at the tip and a spotted, deep blue centre. Has narrow, almost cylindrical leaves that are very short at flowering time but elongate later.
***I.* 'Ballyhoo'** illus. p.234. Robust, rhizomatous, bearded iris (Standard Tall). H 90–100cm (36–39in), S indefinite. In mid- to late spring produces large blooms with ruffled, lemon-white standards and veined, rosy-purple falls with yellow-tipped, white beards.
♀ ***I.* 'Banbury Beauty'.** Rhizomatous, beardless Pacific Coast iris. H 45cm (18in), S indefinite. In late spring and early summer, branched stem produces 2–10 light lavender flowers, 10–15cm (4–6in) across, with a purple zone on each fall.
♀ ***I.* 'Bibury'.** Rhizomatous, bearded iris (Standard Dwarf). H 30cm (12in), S indefinite. Has 2–4 cream flowers, 10cm (4in) wide, on a branched stem in late spring.
***I.* 'Blue Eyed Brunette'** illus. p.235. Rhizomatous, bearded iris (Standard Tall). H 1m (3ft), S indefinite. Well-branched stem produces 7–10 brown flowers, 10–15cm (4–6in) wide, with a blue blaze and a golden beard on each fall, in early summer.
***I.* 'Blue Rhythm'** illus. p.237. Vigorous, rhizomatous, bearded iris (Standard Tall). H 1.1m (3½ft), S indefinite. In early and mid-summer produces lemon-scented, well-formed, violet-blue flowers, the veins on the standards slightly paler than those on the broad falls, with their yellow-tipped, white beards.
***I.* 'Bold Print'** illus. p.236. Rhizomatous, bearded iris (Intermediate). H 55cm (22in), S indefinite. In late spring or early summer, branched stem bears up to 6 flowers, 13cm (5in) wide, with purple-edged, white standards and white falls that are each purple-stitched at the edge and have a bronze-tipped, white beard.
***I.* 'Bronze Queen'** illus. p.235. Bulbous Xiphium iris (Dutch). H to 80cm (32in), S 15cm (6in). In spring and early summer produces 1 or 2 golden-brown flowers, 8–10cm (3–4in) wide, flushed bronze and purple. Lance-shaped, channelled, mid-green leaves are scattered up flower stem.
♀ ***I.* 'Brown Lasso'.** Rhizomatous, bearded iris (Intermediate). H 55cm (22in), S indefinite. In early summer, sturdy, well-branched stem bears 6–10 flowers, 10–13cm (4–5in) across, with deep butterscotch standards and brown-edged, light violet falls.
♀ ***I. bucharica*** illus. p.235. Vigorous, bulbous Juno iris. H 20–40cm (8–16in), S 12cm (5in). In late spring produces 2–6 flowers, 6cm (2½in) across, golden-yellow to white with yellow falls, from leaf axils. Has narrowly lance-shaped, channelled, glossy, mid-green leaves scattered up flower stem. Is easier to grow than most Juno irises.
***I.* 'Bumblebee Deelight'** illus. p.235. Rhizomatous, bearded iris (Miniature Tall). H 45cm (18in), S indefinite. In late spring and early summer has flowers with yellow standards, yellow-margined, maroon falls and orange beards.
♀ ***I.* 'Butter and Sugar'** illus. p.235. Rhizomatous, beardless Siberian iris. H to 1m (3ft), S indefinite. From late spring to early summer produces large, yellow and white flowers.
***I.* 'Carnaby'** illus. p.235. Rhizomatous, bearded iris (Standard Tall). H to 1m (3ft), S indefinite. Well-branched stem bears 6–8 flowers, 15–18cm (6–7in) wide, with pale pink standards and deep rose-pink falls with orange beards, in early summer.
I. chamaeiris. See *I. lutescens*.
***I.* 'Champagne Elegance'** illus. p.234. Vigorous, rhizomatous, bearded iris (Standard Tall). H 85cm (34in), S indefinite. In early to mid- spring and again in summer produces scented, strongly ruffled flowers, with pink-washed, white standards and flaring, apricot-pink falls with darker veining and pale orange beards.
***I.* 'Change of Pace'** illus. p.236. Vigorous, rhizomatous, bearded iris (Standard Tall). H 90cm (36in), S indefinite. Large, scented flowers are produced from early to late spring, the ruffled, veined, delicate pink standards contrasting with the brilliant white falls, which are broadly margined and flecked deep rosy-violet.
♀ ***I. chrysographes*** illus. p.237. Rhizomatous, beardless Siberian iris. H 40cm (16in), S indefinite. From late spring to early summer, branched stem bears 1–4 deep red-purple or purple-black flowers, 5–10cm (2–4in) across, with gold etching down falls. Prefers moist conditions.
***I.* 'Clairette',** syn. *I. reticulata* 'Clairette'. Bulbous Reticulata iris. H 10–15cm (4–6in), S 4–6cm (1½–2½in). In early spring bears a solitary, fragrant, long-tubed, pale blue flower, 4–6cm (1½–2½in) wide, with white-flecked, deep violet falls. Narrow, squared leaves elongate after flowering time.
I. clarkei. Rhizomatous, beardless Siberian iris. H 60cm (2ft), S indefinite. From late spring to early summer, solid stem produces 2–3 branches each with 2 blue to red-purple flowers, 5–10cm (2–4in) across, with a violet-veined, white blaze on each fall. Prefers moist conditions.
I. colchica. See *I. graminea*.
♀ ***I. confusa*** illus. p.234. Evergreen or semi-evergreen, rhizomatous Crested iris. H 1m (3ft) or more, S indefinite.

Frost hardy. Bamboo-like, erect stem is crowned by a fan of broad leaves. In mid-spring, widely branched flower stem produces a long succession of up to 30 short-lived, white flowers, 4–5cm (1½–2in) across, with yellow or purple spots around the yellow crests. Prefers well-drained soil and the protection of a south-facing wall.

***I.* 'Conjuration'** illus. p.236. Rhizomatous, bearded iris (Standard Tall). H 90cm (3ft), S indefinite. In early summer bears 6–11 flowers with standards that are white at the margins, suffusing inwards to pale violet-blue, and white falls suffusing to deep amethyst-violet at the margins. The horned beard is white, tipped with yellow.

I. cretensis. See *I. unguicularis* subsp. *cretensis*.

🏆 ***I. cristata*** illus. p.236. Evansia iris with much-branched rhizomes. H 10cm (4in), S indefinite. Has neat fans of lance-shaped leaves. In early summer produces 1 or 2 virtually stemless, long-tubed, lilac, blue, lavender or white flowers, 3–4cm (1¼–1½in) across, with a white patch and orange crest on each fall. Prefers semi-shade and moist soil; is ideal for peat banks.

🏆 ***I. crocea***, syn. *I. aurea.* Rhizomatous, beardless Spuria iris. H 1–1.2m (3–4ft), S indefinite. Has long leaves. Strong, erect, sparsely branched stem produces terminal clusters of 2–10 golden-yellow flowers, 12–18cm (5–7in) across, with wavy-margined falls, in early summer. Resents being disturbed.

I. cuprea. See *I. fulva*.

***I.* 'Custom Design'.** Rhizomatous, beardless Spuria iris. H 1m (3ft), S indefinite. Strong, erect-branched stem produces 2–10 deep maroon-brown flowers, each 5–12cm (2–5in) wide, with a heavily veined, bright yellow blaze on each fall, from early to mid-summer.

I. danfordiae illus. p.235. Bulbous Reticulata iris. H 5–10cm (2–4in), S 5cm (2in). In early spring bears usually one yellow flower, 3–5cm (1¼–2in) across, with green spots on each fall. Standards are reduced to short bristles. Narrow, squared leaves are very short at flowering time but elongate later. Tends to produce masses of small bulblets and requires deeper planting than other Reticulata irises to maintain bulbs at flowering size.

🏆 ***I. douglasiana*** illus. p.237. Evergreen, rhizomatous, beardless Pacific Coast iris. H 25–70cm (10–28in), S indefinite. Leathery, dark green leaves are stained red-purple at base. Branched stem produces 1–3 lavender to purple, occasionally white, flowers, 7–12cm (3–5in) wide, with variable, central, yellowish zones on the falls, in late spring and early summer.

🏆 ***I.* 'Dreaming Spires'.** Rhizomatous, beardless Siberian iris. H 1m (3ft), S indefinite. From late spring to early summer, branched stem produces 1–4 flowers, 5–10cm (2–4in) wide, with lavender standards and royal-blue falls. Prefers moist soil.

🏆 ***I.* 'Dreaming Yellow'** illus. p.234. Rhizomatous, beardless Siberian iris. H 1m (3ft), S indefinite. From late spring to early summer, branched stem produces 1–4 flowers, 5–10cm (2–4in) across. Standards are white, falls creamy-yellow fading to white with age. Prefers moist soil.

🏆 ***I.* 'Early Light'** illus. p.235. Rhizomatous, bearded iris (Standard Tall). H 1m (3ft), S indefinite. In early summer, well-branched stem bears 8–10 ruffled, white flowers, 15–18cm (6–7in) wide, heavily flushed lemon-yellow on the standards; yellow-veined falls have broad margins flushed slightly deeper lemon-yellow and a yellow beard.

***I.* 'Electric Rays'** illus. p.237. Strong-growing, rhizomatous Japanese iris. H 1m (3ft), S indefinite. Ruffled, double, rich violet flowers, with white and intense, deep blue veining, are borne freely in early summer.

***I.* 'Elmohr'.** Rhizomatous, bearded iris. H 1m (3ft), S indefinite. In early summer, well-branched stem produces 2–5 strongly veined, red-purple flowers, 15–20cm (6–8in) across.

***I.* 'English Cottage'** illus. p.234. Robust, rhizomatous, bearded iris (Standard Tall). H 90–100cm (36–39in), S indefinite. In mid- to late spring and again in summer or early autumn produces large, white flowers with the margins of both standards and falls washed pale blue-violet. Has deeper veining at the base of the falls and yellow-tipped, white beards.

🏆 ***I. ensata***, syn. *I. kaempferi* (Japanese flag). Rhizomatous, beardless Japanese iris. H 60cm–1m (2–3ft), S indefinite. Branched stem produces 3–15 purple or red-purple flowers, 8–15cm (3–6in) across, with a yellow blaze on each fall, from early to mid-summer. May be distinguished from the related, smooth-leaved *I. laevigata* by the prominent midrib on the leaves. Has produced many hundreds of garden forms, some with double flowers, in shades of purple, pink, lavender and white, sometimes bicoloured. Prefers partial shade and thrives in a water or bog garden. **'Galatea'** (syn. *I.* 'Galatea'; illus. p.237), H 80cm (32in), has blue-purple flowers with a yellow blaze on each fall. **'Moonlight Waves'** (illus. p.234), H 90cm (36in), is strong-growing and produces large, open, spreading, white flowers, with lime-green blazes at the base of each petal. 🏆 **'Rose Queen'** (syn. *I. laevigata* 'Rose Queen'; illus. p.234), H 90–100cm (36–39in), is strong-growing and produces large, soft pink flowers, with deeper pink veining and a yellow blaze at the base of each fall. **[hybrid/cultivar]** (illus. p.234) bears double, rose-purple-veined, white flowers, with purple styles and a gold blaze on each fall.

I. extremorientalis. See *I. sanguinea*.

🏆 ***I.* 'Eyebright'** illus. p.235. Rhizomatous, bearded iris (Standard Dwarf). H 30cm (12in), S indefinite. In late spring produces 2–4 bright yellow flowers, 7–10cm (3–4in) wide, each with a brown zone on the falls surrounding the beard, on usually an unbranched stem.

***I.* 'Flamenco'** illus. p.235. Rhizomatous, bearded iris (Standard Tall). H 1m (3ft), S indefinite. In early summer, well-branched stem produces 6–9 flowers, 15cm (6in) wide, with gold standards, infused red, and white to yellow falls with red borders.

***I.* 'Flight of Butterflies'** illus. p.236. Elegant, rhizomatous, beardless Siberian iris. H 90cm (36in), S indefinite. From early to mid-summer produces delicate flowers with violet-blue standards and white falls veined deep violet-blue.

I. florentina. See *I. germanica* 'Florentina'.

🏆 ***I. foetidissima*** (Gladwin, Roast-beef plant, Stinking iris). Evergreen, rhizomatous, beardless iris. H 30cm–1m (1–3ft), S indefinite. Branched stem bears up to 9 yellow-tinged, dull purple or occasionally pure yellow flowers, 5–10cm (2–4in) wide, from early to mid-summer. Cylindrical seed pods open to reveal rounded, bright scarlet fruits throughout winter. Thrives in a bog or water garden, although tolerates drier conditions.

🏆 ***I. forrestii*** illus. p.235. Rhizomatous, beardless Siberian iris. H 15–40cm (6–16in), S indefinite. From late spring to early summer, unbranched stem produces 1 or 2 fragrant, yellow flowers, 5–6cm (2–2½in) across, with black lines on each fall and occasionally brownish-flushing on standards. Has linear, glossy, mid-green leaves, grey-green below. Prefers moist, lime-free soil.

I. fosteriana. Bulbous Juno iris. H 10–15cm (4–6in), S 6cm (2½in). In spring produces 1 or 2 long-tubed flowers, 4–5cm (1½–2in) wide, with downward-turned, rich purple standards, which are larger than those of most Juno irises, and creamy-yellow falls. Has narrowly lance-shaped, channelled, silver-edged, mid-green leaves scattered on flower stem. Is difficult to grow and is best in an alpine house or cold frame.

***I.* 'Frank Elder'.** Bulbous Reticulata iris. H 6–10cm (2½–4in), S 5–7cm (2–3in). Has a solitary, very pale blue flower, 6–7cm (2½–3in) wide, suffused pale yellow and veined and spotted darker blue, in early spring. Narrow, squared leaves are very short at flowering time but elongate later.

***I.* 'Frost and Flame'** illus. p.234. Strong-growing, rhizomatous, bearded iris (Standard Tall). H 90cm (36in), S indefinite. In early to mid-spring produces fragrant, glistening, white flowers with gently ruffled standards, rounded falls and bright orange beards.

I. fulva, syn. *I. cuprea* illus. p.235. Rhizomatous, beardless iris. H 45–80cm (18–32in), S indefinite. Frost hardy. In late spring or summer produces a slender, slightly branched stem with 4–6 (occasionally more) copper- or orange-red flowers, 5–7cm (2–3in) across, with 2 flowers per leaf axil. Thrives in a bog or water garden.

🏆 ***I.* × *fulvala***, syn. *I.* 'Fulvala' illus. p.236. Rhizomatous, beardless iris. H 45cm (18in), S indefinite. Frost hardy. In summer, zigzag stem produces 4–6 (occasionally more) velvety, deep red-purple flowers, 5–12cm (2–5in) across, with 2 flowers per leaf axil. Has a yellow blaze on each fall. Thrives in a bog or water garden.

***I.* 'Galatea'.** See *I. ensata* 'Galatea'.

***I.* 'Geisha Gown'** illus. p.234. Robust, rhizomatous, beardless Japanese iris. H 90cm (36in), S indefinite. In mid- and late spring produces large, delicate, double, white ruffled flowers with dark violet-blue veining and a central, deep purple-violet centre.

🏆 ***I. germanica*** (Common German flag). Rhizomatous, bearded iris. H to 60cm–1.2m (2–4ft), S indefinite. Sparsely branched stem produces up to 6 yellow-bearded, blue-purple or blue-violet flowers, 10–15cm (4–6in) wide, in late spring and early summer. 🏆 **'Florentina'** (syn. *I. florentina*; orris root; illus. p.234) has strongly scented, white flowers.

***I.* 'Golden Harvest'.** Bulbous Xiphium iris (Dutch). H to 80cm (32in), S 15cm (6in). Bears 1 or 2 deep rich yellow flowers, 6–8cm (2½–3in) wide, in spring and early summer. Has scattered, narrowly lance-shaped, channelled, mid-green leaves.

I. gracilipes. Clump-forming, rhizomatous Evansia iris with short stolons. H 15–20cm (6–8in), S indefinite. In late spring and early summer, slender, branched stem produces a succession of 4 or 5 lilac-blue flowers, each 3–4cm (1¼–1½in) across, with a violet-veined, white zone surrounding a yellow-and-white crest. Has narrow, grass-like leaves. Prefers semi-shade and peaty soil.

I. graeberiana. Bulbous Juno iris. H 15–35cm (6–14in), S 6–8cm (2½–3in). In late spring produces 4–6 bluish-lavender flowers, 6–8cm (2½–3in) across, with a white crest on each fall, from leaf axils. Lance-shaped, channelled leaves are white-margined, glossy, mid-green above, greyish-green below, and scattered up flower stem. Is easier to grow than most Juno irises.

🏆 ***I. graminea***, syn. *I. colchica.* Rhizomatous, beardless Spuria iris. H 20–40cm (8–16in), S indefinite. In late spring, narrowly lance-shaped leaves partially hide up to 10 plum-scented flowers, 5–12cm (2–5in) wide, with wine-purple standards and heavily veined, violet-blue falls, borne on flattened, angled stem. Resents being disturbed.

***I.* 'Harmony'** illus. p.237. Bulbous Reticulata iris. H 6–10cm (2½–4in), S 6–7cm (2½–3in). In early spring bears a solitary, fragrant, long-tubed, clear pale blue flower, 5–6cm (2–2½in) across, with white marks and a yellow ridge down each fall centre. Narrow, squared leaves are very short at flowering time but elongate later.

I. histrioides. Bulbous Reticulata iris. H 6–10cm (2½–4in), S 6–7cm (2½–3in). In early spring produces solitary flowers, 6–7cm (2½–3in) across, which vary from light to deep violet-blue. Each fall is lightly to strongly spotted with dark blue and has white marks and a yellow ridge down centre. Narrow, squared leaves are very short at flowering time but elongate later. **'Lady Beatrix Stanley'** has light blue flowers and heavily spotted falls. **'Major'** (illus. p.237) has darker blue-violet flowers.

🏆 ***I.* 'Holden Clough'.** Rhizomatous, beardless iris. H 50–70cm (20–28in), S indefinite. In early summer, branched stem bears 6–12 yellow flowers, each 5cm (2in) wide, with very heavy, burnt-sienna veining. Is excellent in a bog or water garden, but also grows well in any rich, well-drained soil.

♡ ***I. hoogiana*** illus. p.237. Regelia iris with stout rhizomes. H 40–60cm (16–24in), S indefinite. Produces 2 or 3 scented, delicately veined, lilac-blue flowers, 7–10cm (3–4in) across, in late spring and early summer. Is relatively easy to cultivate.

I. iberica illus. p.234. Rhizomatous Oncocyclus iris. H 15–20cm (6–8in), S indefinite. Has narrow, strongly curved, grey-green leaves. Bears solitary, bicoloured flowers, 10–12cm (4–5in) across, in late spring. Standards are white, pale yellow, or pale blue with slight brownish-purple veining; spoon-shaped falls are white or pale lilac, spotted and strongly veined brownish-purple. Grows best in a frame or alpine house.

I. innominata illus. p.235. Evergreen or semi-evergreen, rhizomatous, beardless Pacific Coast iris. H 16–25cm (6–10in), S indefinite. Stem bears 1 or 2 flowers, 6.5–7.5cm (2½–3in) across, from late spring to early summer. Varies greatly in colour from cream to yellow or orange and from lilac-pink to blue or purple; falls are often veined with maroon or brown.

♡ ***I. japonica*** illus. p.234. Vigorous, rhizomatous Evansia iris with slender stolons. H 45–80cm (18–32in), S indefinite. Frost hardy. Has fans of broadly lance-shaped, glossy leaves. In late spring produces branched flower stem with a long succession of flattish, frilled or ruffled, pale lavender or white flowers, 1–8cm (½–3in) across, marked violet around an orange crest on each fall. Prefers the protection of a sheltered, sunny wall.

***I.* 'Jesse's Song'** illus. p.236. Vigorous, rhizomatous, bearded iris (Standard Tall). H 90cm (36in), S indefinite. In early to mid-spring produces scented , ruffled, white flowers, the standards heavily suffused violet, the falls irregularly margined and speckled violet and the white beard tipped pale violet.

***I.* 'Joette'** illus. p.235. Rhizomatous, bearded iris (Intermediate). H 45cm (18in), S indefinite. In late spring or early summer, branched stems carry uniformly lavender-blue flowers with yellow beards. Is excellent in flower arrangements.

***I.* 'Joyce'** illus. p.237. Bulbous Reticulata iris. H 6–10cm (2½–4in), S 6–7cm (2½–3in). In early spring bears a solitary, fragrant, long-tubed, clear blue flower, 5–6cm (2–2½in) across, with white marks and a yellow ridge down each fall centre. Narrow, squared leaves are very short at flowering time but elongate later.

***I.* 'June Prom'.** Vigorous, rhizomatous, bearded iris (Intermediate). H 50cm (20in), S indefinite. In late spring or early summer, branched stem bears up to 6 pale blue flowers, 8–10cm (3–4in) wide, with a green tinge on each fall.

I. kaempferi. See *I. ensata*.

♡ ***I.* 'Katharine Hodgkin'** illus. p.237. Bulbous Reticulata iris. H 6–10cm (2½–4in), S 5–7cm (2–3in). Is similar to I. **'Frank Elder'**, but has yellower flowers, 6–7cm (2½–3in) wide, suffused pale blue, lined and dotted dark blue. Flowers in early spring.

***I.* 'Kent Pride'** illus. p.235. Strong-growing, rhizomatous, bearded iris (Standard Tall). H 90cm (36in), S indefinite. In mid-spring produces deep chestnut-brown and white flowers; the standards are faintly suffused yellow and the falls have a white central patch, yellow beards and yellow and brown veining, surrounded by chestnut-brown margins.

♡ ***I. kerneriana.*** Rhizomatous, beardless Spuria iris. H 25cm (10in), S indefinite. Has very narrow, grass-like leaves. Strong, erect-branched stem bears 2–4soft lemon- or creamy-yellow flowers, 5–12cm (2–5in) across, from each pair of bracts, in early summer. Resents being disturbed.

I. korolkowii. Regelia iris with stout rhizomes. H 40–60cm (16–24in), S indefinite. From late spring to early summer, each spathe encloses 2 or 3 delicately blackish-maroon- or olive-green-veined, creamy-white or light purple flowers, 6–8cm (2½–3in) across. Is best grown in a bulb frame.

***I.* 'Krasnia'** illus. p.236. Rhizomatous, bearded iris (Standard Tall). H 1m (3ft), S indefinite. In early summer, well-branched stem produces 8–12 flowers, 13–18cm (5–7in) wide, with purple standards and purple-maragined, white falls.

***I.* 'Lady Mohr'** illus. p.234. Rhizomatous, bearded Arilbred iris. H 75cm (30in), S indefinite. In early spring produces flowers with pearly-white standards and pale yellow falls veined and spotted brownish-purple around the chrome-yellow beards.

***I.* 'Lady of Quality'** illus. p.236. Rhizomatous, beardless Siberian iris. H to 1m (3ft), S indefinite. In mid- and late spring produces flowers with light blue-violet standards and lighter blue falls.

♡ ***I. laevigata*** illus. p.237. Rhizomatous, beardless Japanese iris. H 60–90cm (2–3ft) or more, S indefinite. Sparsely branched stem produces 2–4 blue, blue-purple or white flowers, 5–12cm (2–5in) across, from early to mid-summer. Is related to *I. ensata* but has smooth, not ridged leaves. Grows well in sun or semi-shade in moist conditions or in shallow water. **'Regal'** bears single, cyclamen-red flowers. **'Rose Queen'** see *I. ensata* 'Rose Queen'. Flowers of **'Snowdrift'** has single, white flowers marked yellow at the bases of the falls.

♡ **'Variegata'**, H 25cm (10in), has white-and-green-striped leaves and often flowers a second time in early autumn.

***I.* 'Langport Storm'** illus. p.235. Strong-growing, rhizomatous, bearded iris (Intermediate). H 45cm (18in), S indefinite. In mid-spring produces neat, smoky-chartreuse blooms, the falls overlaid with deep red-brown patches suffused and veined yellow, with cream beards.

♡ ***I. latifolia***, syn. *I. xiphioides* (English iris; illus. p.237). Bulbous Xiphium iris (English). H 80cm (32in), S 15cm (6in). In late spring and summer, 1 or 2 blue to deep violet flowers, 8–10cm (3–4in) wide, with a yellow stripe down centre of each very broad fall, are produced from the bracts. Lance-shaped, channelled, mid-green leaves are scattered up flower stem. **'Duchess of York'** bears purple flowers. Flowers of **'MontBlanc'** are pure white. **'Queen of the Blues'** has blue standards and purple-blue falls.

***I.* 'Lavender Royal'** illus. p.237. Rhizomatous, beardless Pacific Coast iris. H 45cm (18in), S indefinite. In late spring to early summer, branched stems carry lavender flowers with darker flushes.

♡ ***I. lazica*** illus. p.237. Evergreen, rhizomatous, beardless iris. H 15–25cm (6–10in), S indefinite. Has arching fans of broad, bright green leaves. In early spring produces stemless, long-tubed, lavender-blue flowers. Falls are white in the lower halves, spotted and veined lavender, each with a central yellow stripe. Thrives in slight shade in moist soil.

♡ ***I. lutescens***, syn. *I. chamaeiris*. Fast-growing, very variable, rhizomatous, bearded iris. H 5–30cm (2–12in), S indefinite. Branched stem produces 1or 2 yellow-bearded, violet, purple, yellow, white or bicoloured flowers, 6–8cm (2½–3in) across, in early summer. **'Nancy Lindsay'** has scented, yellow flowers.

***I.* 'Magic Man'** illus. p.236. Rhizomatous, bearded iris (Standard Tall). H 1m (3ft), S indefinite. In early summer, branched stems carry flowers that have light blue standards and velvety purple falls with light blue margins; beards are orange.

♡ ***I. magnifica*** illus. p.234. Bulbous Juno iris. H 30–60cm (12–24in), S 15cm (6in). In late spring produces 3–7 very pale lilac flowers, 6–8cm (2½–3in) across, with a central, yellow area on each fall, from leaf axils. Bears scattered, lance-shaped, channelled, glossy, mid-green leaves.

***I.* 'Making Eyes'** illus. p.234. Rhizomatous, bearded iris (Standard Dwarf). H 30–35cm (12–14in), S indefinite. In early spring produces neat flowers with pale lemon-white standards, narrow, white-margined, dark purple-violet falls and yellowish-white beards.

***I.* 'Margot Holmes'.** Rhizomatous, beardless Siberian iris. H 25cm (10in), S indefinite. Frost hardy. In early summer produces 2 or 3 purple-red flowers, 10–15cm (4–6in) across, with yellow veining on each fall.

***I.* 'Marhaba'.** Rhizomatous, bearded iris (Miniature Dwarf). H 15cm (6in), S indefinite. Bears 1, rarely 2 deep blue flowers, 5–8cm (2–3in) wide, in mid-spring.

***I.* 'Mary Frances'** illus. p.237. Rhizomatous, bearded iris (Standard Tall). H 1m (3ft), S indefinite. In early summer, well-branched stem bears 6–9, occasionally to 12 pink-lavender flowers, 15cm (6in) wide.

♡ ***I.* 'Mary McIlroy'** illus. p.235. Rhizomatous, bearded iris (Intermediate). H 40–50cm (16–20in), S indefinite. In early to mid-spring produces bright yellow blooms, the standards veined slightly deeper yellow, with darker veins on the falls and lemon-yellow beards.

***I.* 'Matinata'** illus. p.237. Rhizomatous, bearded iris (Standard Tall). H 1m (3ft), S indefinite. In early summer, well-branched stem produces 6–9, occasionally to 12 flowers, 15cm (6in) wide, that are dark purple-blue throughout.

♡ ***I. missouriensis***, syn. *I. tolmeiana* (Missouri flag; illus. p.237). Very variable, rhizomatous, beardless Pacific Coast iris. H to 75cm (2½ft), S indefinite. Branched stem produces 2 or 3 pale blue, lavender, lilac, blue or white flowers, 5–8cm (2–3in) wide, in each spathe, in late spring or early summer. Falls are veined and usually have a yellow blaze.

♡ ***I.* 'Morwenna'** illus. p.237. Robust, rhizomatous, bearded iris (Standard Tall). H 70–80cm (28–32in), S indefinite. In mid- to late spring produces ruffled, pale blue flowers, with both standards and falls feathered a slightly deeper blue, and with white beards.

***I.* 'Mountain Lake'** illus. p.237. Rhizomatous, beardless Siberian iris. H 1m (3ft), S indefinite. From late spring to early summer, branched stem produces 1–4 mid-blue flowers, 5–10cm (2–4in) across, with darker veining on falls. Prefers moist soil.

I. ochroleuca. See *I. orientalis*.

***I.* 'Ola Kala'** illus. p.235. Robust, rhizomatous, bearded iris (Standard Tall). H 1m (3ft), S indefinite. Produces neat, scented, rich deep yellow flowers; the falls have darker yellow bases and yellow beards.

***I.* 'Oriental Eyes'** illus. p.236. Vigorous, rhizomatous, beardless Japanese iris. H 1m (3ft), S indefinite. In early summer produces large, ruffled, strongly veined, purple violet flowers, with bright golden-yellow flares at the base of each petal.

♡ ***I. orientalis***, syn. *I. ochroleuca* illus. p.234. Rhizomatous, beardless Spuria iris. H to 90cm (3ft), S indefinite. In late spring each stem, usually with one branch, bears 3–5 white flowers, 8–10cm (3–4in) wide. Falls are white with yellow centres. Leaves are often present over winter.

I. orientalis of gardens. See *I. sanguinea*.

I. pallida (Dalmatian iris). Rhizomatous, bearded iris. H 70–90cm (28–36in) or more, S indefinite. In late spring and early summer produces 2–6 scented, lilac-blue flowers, 8–12cm (3–5in) across and with yellow beards, from silvery spathes on strong, branched stems. Leaves of

♡ **'Variegata'** (syn. *I.p.* 'Aurea Variegata'; illus. p.237) are striped green and yellow.

♡ ***I.* 'Paradise Bird'** illus. p.236. Rhizomatous, bearded iris (Standard Tall). H 85cm (34in), S indefinite. In early summer, well-branched stem produces 8–10 flowers, 14–15cm (5½–6in) wide, with magenta falls and paler standards.

***I.* 'Peach Frost'** illus. p.235. Rhizomatous, bearded iris (Standard Tall). H 1m (3ft), S indefinite. Well-branched stem bears 6–10 flowers, 15cm (6in) wide, in early summer. Standards are peach-pink, falls white with peach-pink margins and tangerine beards.

***I.* 'Perry's Blue'** illus. p.237. Robust, rhizomatous, beardless Siberian iris. H 1m (3ft), S indefinite. In late spring and early summer produces neat, pale purplish-blue flowers, with noticeably deeper blue veins. Slightly twisted standards and broad, rounded falls are white margined and creamy-white near the bases, and have dark yellow markings in the throats.

***I.* 'Piona'.** Rhizomatous, bearded iris (Intermediate). H 45cm (18in), S indefinite. In late spring and early summer, branched stem bears up to 6 deep violet flowers, 8–10cm (3–4in) wide, with golden beards. Mid-green leaves have purple bases.

♀ ***I.* 'Professor Blaauw'.** Bulbous Xiphium iris (Dutch). H 80cm (32in), S 15cm (6in). From spring to early summer produces 1 or 2 rich violet-blue flowers, 6–8cm (2½–3in) across. Narrowly lance-shaped, channelled, mid-green leaves are scattered up flower stem.

♀ ***I. pseudacorus*** (Yellow flag; illus. p.235). Robust, rhizomatous, beardless iris. H to 2m (6ft), S indefinite. Branched stem produces 4–12 golden-yellow flowers, 5–12cm (2–5in) wide, usually with brown or violet veining and a darker yellow patch on the falls, from early to mid-summer. Leaves are broad, ridged and greyish-green. Prefers semi-shade and thrives in a water garden. ♀ **'Variegata'** has yellow-and-green-striped foliage in spring, often turning green before flowering.

I. pumila (Dwarf bearded iris). Rhizomatous, bearded iris. H 10–15cm (4–6in), S indefinite. In mid-spring has a 1cm (½in) long flower stem bearing 2or 3 long-tubed flowers, 2.5–5cm (1–2in) wide, varying from violet-purple to white, yellow or blue, with yellow or blue beards on the falls. Prefers very well-drained, slightly alkaline soil.

***I.* 'Rare Treat'** illus. p.237. Robust, rhizomatous, bearded iris (Standard Tall). H 90cm (36in), S indefinite. In mid- to late spring produces ruffled, snow-white flowers, with both standards and falls margined deep purple-blue, and the bases of the falls and beards similarly coloured.

***I.* 'Raspberry Candy'** illus. p.236. Vigorous, rhizomatous, beardless Japanese iris. H 80–90cm (32–36in), S indefinite. In late spring and early summer produces large, open, white flowers strongly veined red-violet, with bright yellow blazes at the bases of the falls.

♀ ***I. reticulata.*** Bulbous Reticulata iris. H 10–15cm (4–6in), S 4–6cm (1½–2½in). In early spring bears a solitary, fragrant, long-tubed, deep violet-purple flower, 4–6cm (1½–2½in) wide, with a yellow ridge down each fall centre. Narrow, squared leaves elongate after flowering time. **'Cantab'** (illus. p.237) has clear pale blue flowers with a deep yellow ridge on each fall. **'Clairette'** see *I.* 'Clairette'. Flowers of **'J.S. Dijt'** are reddish-purple with an orange ridge on each fall. **'Violet Beauty'** see *I.* 'Violet Beauty'.

***I.* 'Ringo'** illus. p.234. Vigorous, rhizomatous, bearded iris (Standard Tall). H 90cm (36in), S indefinite. In late spring and early summer produces lightly ruffled flowers with white standards touched purple on the midribs and dark reddish-purple falls with narrow, white margins and orange beards.

***I.* 'Rippling Rose'** illus. p.236. Rhizomatous, bearded iris (Standard Tall). H 1m (3ft), S indefinite. In early summer, well-branched stem has 6–10 white flowers, 15cm (6in) wide, with purple marks and lemon-yellow beards.

I. rosenbachiana illus. p.237. Bulbous Juno iris. H 10–15cm (4–6in), S 6cm (2½in). In spring produces 1 or 2 long-tubed flowers, 4–5cm (1½–2in) wide, with small, downward-turned, rich purple standards and reddish-purple falls, each with a yellow ridge in the centre. Has lance-shaped, channelled, mid-green leaves in a basal tuft. Is difficult to grow and is best in an alpine house or cold frame.

***I.* 'Ruban Bleu'** illus. p.234. Strong-growing, rhizomatous, bearded iris (Standard Tall). H 85–90cm (32–36in), S indefinite. In late spring and early summer produces scented flowers with snow-white standards and slightly ruffled, dark blue-violet falls each with a large, white basal patch and orange beard.

♀ ***I.* 'Ruffled Velvet'** illus. p.236. Rhizomatous, beardless Siberian iris. H to 1m (3ft), S indefinite. In early summer produces 2 or 3 red-purple flowers marked with yellow.

***I.* 'Saffron Jewel'.** Rhizomatous, bearded iris (Intermediate). H 75cm (30in), S indefinite. In early summer, branched stem produces 2–5 flowers, 5–10cm (2–4in) across, with oyster falls, veined chartreuse, and paler standards. Falls each have a blue blaze and beard.

♀ ***I. sanguinea***, syn. *I. extremorientalis, I. orientalis* of gardens. Rhizomatous, beardless Siberian iris. H to 1m (3ft), S indefinite. From late spring to early summer, branched stem produces 2 or 3 deep purple or red-purple flowers, 5–10cm (2–4in) wide, from each set of bracts. Falls are red-purple with white throats finely veined purple. **'Snow Queen'** (illus. p.234) has pure white flowers with yellow-green marks at the bases of the falls.

***I.* 'Sapphire Star'** illus. p.236. Rhizomatous, beardless Japanese iris. H 1.2m (4ft), S indefinite. In summer, branched stem bears 3–5 white-veined, lavender flowers, 15–30cm (6–12in) wide, pencilled with a white halo around a yellow blaze on each fall. Prefers moist soil.

***I.* 'Saturday Night Live'** illus. p.235. Vigorous, rhizomatous, bearded iris (Standard Tall). H 90–95cm (36–38in), S indefinite. Has mildly scented, deep red-brown to burgundy-red flowers, with bronze-yellow beards and faint, light yellow veining near the bases of the falls, from mid-spring to early summer.

♀ ***I. setosa*** (Bristle-pointed iris; illus. p.237). Rhizomatous, beardless iris, very variable in stature. H 10–90cm (4–36in), S indefinite. Bears 2–13 deep blue or purple-blue flowers, 5–8cm (2–3in) across, from each spathe in late spring and early summer. Falls have paler blue or white marks; each standard is reduced to a bristle.

***I.* 'Shepherd's Delight'.** Rhizomatous, bearded iris (Standard Tall). H 1m (3ft), S indefinite. In early summer, well-branched stem produces 6–10 clear pink flowers, 15–18cm (6–7in) wide, with a yellow cast.

♀ ***I. sibirica*** (Siberian flag). Rhizomatous, beardless Siberian iris. H 50–120cm (20–48in), S indefinite. From late spring to early summer, branched stem bears 2 or 3 dark-veined, blue or blue-purple flowers, 5–10cm (2–4in) across, from each spathe. Prefers moist or boggy conditions.

♀ ***I. sintenisii*** illus. p.237. Rhizomatous, beardless Spuria iris. H 30cm (12in), S indefinite. Has linear, dark green leaves. In late spring produces 2 white flowers, densely veined blue-purple.

***I.* 'Soft Blue'** illus. p.237. Robust, rhizomatous, beardless Siberian iris. H 75cm (30in), S indefinite. In early to mid-spring produces pale blue flowers; the long, arching falls have yellow basal markings and darker blue veins.

***I.* 'Splash Down'.** Rhizomatous, beardless Siberian iris. H 1m (3ft), S indefinite. From late spring to early summer, branched stem produces 1–4 flowers, 5–10cm (2–4in) across. Standards are pale blue and falls speckled blue on a pale ground. Prefers moist soil.

I. spuria. Very variable, rhizomatous, beardless Spuria iris. H 50–90cm (20–36in), S indefinite. Strong, erect-branched stem produces 2–5 pale blue-purple, sky-blue, violet-blue, white or yellow flowers, 5–12cm (2–5in) across, in early summer. Prefers moist soil.

♀ ***I.* 'Stepping Out'** illus. p.236. Rhizomatous, bearded iris (Standard Tall). H 1m (3ft), S indefinite. Well-branched stem produces 8–11 white flowers, 14–15cm (5½–6in) wide, with deep blue-purple marks in early summer.

I. stylosa. See *I. unguicularis*.

♀ ***I.* 'Sun Miracle'** illus. p.235. Rhizomatous, bearded iris (Standard Tall). H 1m (3ft), S indefinite. Well-branched stem produces 7–10 pure yellow flowers, 15–18cm (6–7in) wide, in early summer.

***I.* 'Supreme Sultan'** illus. p.235. Vigorous, rhizomatous, bearded iris (Standard Tall). H 1m (3ft), S indefinite. In late spring and early summer bears large, ruffled flowers, with deep golden-yellow standards, rich dark red-brown falls that are paler at the margins, and deep yellow beards.

I. susiana (Mourning iris). Rhizomatous Oncocyclus iris. H 35–40cm (14–16in), S indefinite. In late spring produces a solitary, greyish-white flower, 8–15cm (3–6in) wide, heavily veined deep purple. Standards appear larger than incurved falls, which each carry a black blaze and a deep purple beard. Grows best in a frame or alpine house.

***I.* 'Sweet Musette'** illus. p.234. Vigorous, rhizomatous, bearded iris (Standard Tall). H 90–95cm (36–38in), S indefinite. In mid-and late spring produces large, ruffled, frilly flowers, with lavender-flushed, peach-pink standards, purplish-pink falls and orange beards.

I. tectorum (Japanese roof iris, Wall flag; illus. p.237). Evansia iris with stout rhizomes. H 25–35cm (10–14in), S indefinite. Frost hardy. Has fans of broadly lance-shaped, ribbed leaves. In early summer, sparsely branched stem produces 2–3 darker-veined, bright lilac flowers, 1–8cm (½–3in) across with a white crest on each fall, from each spathe. Prefers a sheltered, sunny site near a south- or west-facing wall.

I. tenax illus. p.237. Rhizomatous, beardless Pacific Coast iris. H 15–30cm (6–12in), S indefinite. From late spring to early summer produces 1 or 2 deep purple to lavender-blue flowers, 8–12cm (3–5in) across, often with yellow-and-white marking on falls. White, cream and yellow variants also occur. Narrow, dark green leaves are stained pink at base.

***I.* 'Theseus'.** Rhizomatous Regeliocyclus iris. H 45cm (18in), S indefinite. From late spring to early summer produces usually 2 flowers, 10–15cm (4–6in) across, with violet standards and violet-veined, cream falls. Is best in a frame or alpine house.

♀ ***I.* 'Thornbird'.** Rhizomatous, bearded iris (Standard Tall). H 90cm (3ft), S indefinite. In early summer, produces up to 7 flowers, with pale greenish-white standards and greenish-brown falls overlaid with deep violet lines. Long, horned beard is violet, tipped with mustard-yellow.

***I.* 'Titan's Glory'** illus. p.237. Robust, rhizomatous, well-branched, bearded iris (Standard Tall). H 90–100cm (36–38in), S indefinite. Produces very large, deep purple-blue flowers, with an almost silken texture, in mid-spring.

I. tolmeiana. See *I. missouriensis*.

***I.* 'Tropic Night'** illus. p.237. Strong-growing, rhizomatous, beardless Siberian iris. H 90cm (36in), S indefinite. In late spring and early summer produces deep violet-blue flowers; upright standards and rounded falls have strong, white feathering and veining near the bases and are touched yellow around the throats.

I. tuberosa. See *Hermodactylus tuberosus*.

♀ ***I. unguicularis***, syn. *I. stylosa* (Algerian iris, Algerian winter iris, Winter iris). Evergreen, rhizomatous, beardless iris. H to 20cm (8in), S indefinite. Has narrow, tough leaves. Almost stemless, primrose-scented, lilac flowers, 5–8cm (2–3in) across with yellow centres to the falls and with very long tubes, appear from late autumn to early spring. Buds are prone to slug attack. Is excellent for cutting. Prefers a sheltered site against a south- or west-facing wall. ♀ **'Mary Barnard'** has deep violet-blue flowers. subsp. ***cretensis*** (syn. *I. cretensis*; illus. p.236), H 10cm (4in), has violet or lavender-blue standards and white or yellow falls with violet veining at the bases and clear violet tips. Flowers of **'Walter Butt'** are pale silvery-lavender.

♀ ***I. variegata*** (Variegated iris; illus. p.235). Rhizomatous, bearded iris. H 30–50cm (12–20in), S indefinite. In early summer, branched stem produces 3–6 flowers, 5–8cm (2–3in) across, with bright yellow standards and white or pale yellow falls, heavily veined red-brown and appearing striped.

I. verna. Rhizomatous, beardless iris. H 5cm (2in), S indefinite. In mid-spring bears 1, occasionally 2, lilac-blue flowers, 2.5–5cm (1–2in) across, with a narrow, orange stripe in the centre of each fall. Prefers semi-shade and moist but well-drained soil.

♀ ***I. versicolor*** (Blue flag, Wild iris;

illus. p.237). Robust, rhizomatous, beardless iris. H 60cm (2ft), S indefinite. Branched stem produces 3–5 or more purple-blue, reddish-purple, lavender or slate-purple flowers, 5–10cm (2–4in) across, from early to mid-summer. Falls usually have a central white area veined purple. Prefers partial shade and thrives in moist soil or in shallow water. **'Kermesina'** (illus. p.236) has red-purple flowers, with dense, white feathering at the bases of the falls.
***I.* 'Violet Beauty'**, syn. *I. reticulata* 'Violet Beauty'. Bulbous Reticulata iris. H 10–15cm (4–6in), S 4–6cm (1½–2½in). In early spring bears a solitary, fragrant, long-tubed, deep violet-purple flower, 4–6cm (1½–2½in) wide, with an orange ridge down the centre of each fall. Narrow, squared leaves elongate after flowering time.
I. warleyensis. Bulbous Juno iris. H 20–45cm (8–18in), S 7–8cm (3in). In spring produces up to 5 pale lilac or violet-blue flowers, 5–7cm (2–3in) across, in leaf axils. Each fall has a darker blue apex and a yellow stain in the centre. Bears scattered, lance-shaped, channelled, mid-green leaves. Is best in an unheated greenhouse.
***I.* 'White Excelsior'.** Bulbous Xiphium iris (Dutch). H to 80cm (32in), S 15cm (6in). From spring to early summer bears 1 or 2 white flowers, 6–8cm (2½–3in) wide, with a yellow stripe down each fall centre. Narrowly lance-shaped, channelled, mid-green leaves are scattered on flower stem.
♡ ***I. winogradowii*** illus. p.235. Bulbous Reticulata iris. H 6–10cm (2½–4in), S 6–7cm (2½–3in). Solitary pale primrose-yellow flower, 6–7cm (2½–3in) wide, spotted green on falls, appears in early spring. Narrow, squared leaves are very short at flowering time but elongate later.
***I.* 'Wisley White'** illus. p.234. Rhizomatous, beardless Siberian iris. H to 1m (3ft), S indefinite. Each stem carries 2 or 3 white flowers, held well above the foliage, in early summer.
I. xiphioides. See *I. latifolia*.
I. xiphium. Bulbous Xiphium iris (Spanish). H to 80cm (32in), S 15cm (6in). Has 1 or 2 blue or violet, occasionally yellow or white, flowers, 6–8cm (2½–3in) across, with central orange or yellow marks on the falls, in spring and early summer. Narrowly lance-shaped, channelled, mid-green leaves are scattered on flower stem. **'Blue Angel'** produces bright mid-blue flowers with a yellow mark in the centre of each fall. Flowers of **'Lusitanica'** are pure yellow. **'Queen Wilhelmina'** produces white flowers in spring. **'Wedgwood'** (illus. p.236) has bright blue flowers.

Iris
Algerian. See *Iris unguicularis*.
Algerian winter. See *Iris unguicularis*.
Bristle-pointed. See *Iris setosa*, illus. p.237.
Dalmatian. See *Iris pallida*.
Dwarf bearded. See *Iris pumila*.
English. See *Iris latifolia*, illus. p.237.
Japanese roof. See *Iris tectorum*, illus. p.237.
Mourning. See *Iris susiana*.
Stinking. See *Iris foetidissima*.
Variegated. See *Iris variegata*, illus. p.235.
Widow. See *Hermodactylus tuberosus*, illus. p.430.
Wild. See *Iris versicolor*, illus. p.237.
Winter. See *Iris unguicularis*.
Irish ivy. See *Hedera hibernica*.
Iron cross begonia. See *Begonia masoniana*, illus. p.307.
Ironwood. See *Ostrya virginiana*, illus. p.73.
Catalina. See *Lyonothamnus floribundus*.
Persian. See *Parrotia persica*, illus. p.78.

ISATIS

CRUCIFERAE/BRASSICACEAE

Genus of summer-flowering annuals, biennials and perennials. Fully hardy. Needs sun and fertile, well-drained soil. Propagate by seed in autumn or spring.
I. tinctoria (Woad). Vigorous, upright biennial. H to 1.2m (4ft), S 45cm (1½ft). Has oblong to lance-shaped, glaucous leaves and, in summer, large, terminal panicles of 4-petalled, yellow flowers.

ISMELIA

COMPOSITAE/ASTERACEAE

Genus of one species of annuals, grown for its daisy-like flower heads. Half hardy. Needs full sun and well-drained soil. Propagate by seed in spring.
I. carinata, syn. *Chrysanthemum carinatum, C. tricolor.* **'Monarch Court Jesters'** (red with yellow centres) illus. p.341, (white with red centres) illus. p.332. **Tricolor Series** is a group of fast-growing, upright, branching annuals. H 30–60cm (12–24in), S 30cm (12in). Has feathery, light green leaves and, in summer, daisy-like, single or double flower heads, to 8cm (3in) wide, in many colour combinations. Tall cultivars, H 60cm (24in), S 30cm (12in), and dwarf, H and S 30cm (12in), are available.

Ismene calathina. See *Hymenocallis narcissiflora*.

ISOLEPIS

CYPERACEAE

See also GRASSES, BAMBOOS, RUSHES and SEDGES.
I. setaceus, syn. *Scirpus setaceus* (Bristle club-rush). Tuft-forming, annual or short-lived, perennial rush. H 10–15cm (4–6in), S 8cm (3in). Fully hardy. Has very slender, lax, basal leaves. Very slender, unbranched stems each bear 1–3 minute, egg-shaped, green spikelets in summer.

ISOPLEXIS

SCROPHULARIACEAE

Genus of evergreen, mainly summer-flowering shrubs, grown for their flowers. Is closely related to *Digitalis*. Frost tender, min. 7°C (45°F). Tolerates full light or partial shade and prefers well-drained soil. Water potted specimens freely when in full growth, moderately at other times. Remove spent flower spikes. Propagate by seed in spring or by semi-ripe cuttings in late summer.
I. canariensis, syn. *Digitalis canariensis*, illus. p.167.

ISOPYRUM

RANUNCULACEAE

Genus of spring-flowering perennials, grown for their small flowers and delicate foliage. Is suitable for peat beds, woodlands and rock gardens. Fully hardy. Requires shade and humus-rich, moist soil. Propagate by seed when fresh or by division in autumn. Self-seeds readily.
I. thalictroides. Dainty, clump-forming perennial. H and S 25cm (10in). Central stalk bears fern-like, 3-parted leaves, each leaflet being cut into 3. Has small, nodding, cup-shaped, white flowers in spring.

Isotrema griffithii. See *Aristolochia griffithii*.
Italian alder. See *Alnus cordata*, illus. p.62.
Italian buckthorn. See *Rhamnus alaternus*.
Italian ivy. See *Hedera helix* f. *poetarum*, illus. p.219.
Italian jasmine. See *Solanum seaforthianum*, illus. p.202.
Italian maple. See *Acer opalus*.
Italian millet. See *Setaria italica*.

ITEA

ESCALLONIACEAE

Genus of deciduous or evergreen trees and shrubs, grown for their foliage and flowers. Frost hardy, but in most areas protect by growing against a south- or west-facing wall. Needs sun or semi-shade and fertile, well-drained but not too dry soil. Propagate by softwood cuttings in summer.
♡ ***I. ilicifolia*** illus. p.142.

Ivy. See *Hedera*.
Bird's-foot. See *Hedera helix* 'Pedata'.
Boston. See *Parthenocissus tricuspidata*, illus. p.216.
Clustered. See *Hedera helix* 'Conglomerata'.
Common English. See *Hedera helix*.
Finger-leaved. See *Hedera hibernica* 'Digitata'.
Five-leaved. See *Parthenocissus quinquefolia*.
German. See *Senecio mikanioides*.
Grape. See *Cissus rhombifolia*, illus. p.218.
Ground. See *Glechoma hederacea*.
Irish. See *Hedera hibernica*.
Italian. See *Hedera helix* f. *poetarum*, illus. p.219.
Japanese. See *Hedera rhombea; Parthenocissus tricuspidata*, illus. p.216.
Kenilworth. See *Cymbalaria muralis*.
Miniature grape. See *Cissus striata*.
Natal. See *Senecio macroglossus*.
Nepalese. See *Hedera nepalensis*.
Persian. See *Hedera colchica*.
Poet's. See *Hedera helix* f. *poetarum*, illus. p.219.
Purple-leaved. See *Hedera helix* 'Atropurpurea', illus. p.219.
Shield. See *Hedera hibernica* 'Deltoidea', illus. p.219.
Swedish. See *Plectranthus oertendahlii; Plectranthus verticillatus*.
Sweetheart. See *Hedera hibernica* 'Deltoidea', illus. p.219.
Tree. See × *Fatshedera lizei*, illus. p.148.
Variegated ground. See *Glechoma hederacea* 'Variegata', illus. p.312.
Ivy of Uruguay. See *Cissus striata*.
Ivy peperomia. See *Peperomia griseoargentea*.
Ivy-leaved toadflax. See *Cymbalaria muralis*.
Ivy-leaved violet. See *Viola hederacea*.

IXIA

IRIDACEAE

Genus of spring- and summer-flowering corms with wiry stems and spikes of flattish flowers. Half hardy. Grow in an open, sunny situation and in well-drained soil. Plant in autumn for spring and early summer flowers; plant in spring for later summer display. Dry offafter flowering. Propagate in autumn by seed or by offsets at replanting time.
***I.* 'Mabel'.** Spring- to early summer-flowering corm. H 40cm (16in), S 2.5–5cm (1–2in). Has linear, basal, mid-green leaves and spikes of deep pink flowers.
I. maculata. Spring- to early summer-flowering corm. H 40cm (16in), S 2.5–5cm (1–2in). Leaves are linear, erect and mostly basal. Wiry stem bears a spike of flattish, orange or yellow flowers, 2.5–5cm (1–2in) across, with brown or black centres.
I. monadelpha. Spring- to early summer-flowering corm. H 30cm (12in), S 2.5–5cm (1–2in). Linear, erect leaves are mostly basal. Stem produces a dense spike of 5–10 flattish, white, pink, purple or blue flowers, 3–4cm (1¼–1½in) across, often with differently coloured eyes.
I. viridiflora illus. p.430.

IXIOLIRION

AMARYLLIDACEAE

Genus of bulbs, grown for their funnel-shaped flowers mainly in spring. Fully hardy. Needs a sheltered, sunny site and well-drained soil that becomes hot and dry in summer to ripen the bulb. Propagate, by seed or offsets, in autumn.
I. montanum. See *I. tataricum*.
I. tataricum, syn. *I. montanum*, illus. p.430.

IXORA

RUBIACEAE

Genus of evergreen, summer-flowering shrubs, grown primarily for their flowers, some also for their foliage. Frost tender, min. 13–16°C (55–61°F). Prefers full sun and humus-rich, well-drained soil. Water containerized specimens freely when in full growth, moderately at other times. Propagate by seed in spring or by semi-ripe cuttings in summer.
I. coccinea illus. p.161.

J

JACARANDA

BIGNONIACEAE

Genus of deciduous or evergreen trees, grown for their flowers in spring-summer and their foliage. Frost tender, min. 7–10°C (45–50°F). Grows in any fertile, well-drained soil and in full light. Water potted specimens freely when in full growth, sparingly at other times. Potted plants grown for their foliage only may be cut back hard in late winter. Propagate by seed in spring or by semi-ripe cuttings in summer.

J. acutifolia of gardens. See *J. mimosifolia*.

J. mimosifolia, syn. *J. acutifolia* of gardens, *J. ovalifolia*, illus. p.75.

J. ovalifolia. See *J. mimosifolia*.

Jack pine. See *Pinus banksiana*, illus. p.103.

Jack-in-the-pulpit. See *Arisaema triphyllum*, illus. p.430.

Jacobean lily. See *Sprekelia formosissima*, illus. p.429.

Jacobinia carnea. See *Justicia carnea*.

Jacobinia coccinea. See *Pachystachys coccinea*.

Jacobinia pohliana. See *Justicia carnea*.

Jacobinia spicigera. See *Justicia spicigera*.

Jacob's coat. See *Acalypha wilkesiana*, illus. p.139.

Jacob's ladder. See *Polemonium*.

JACQUEMONTIA

CONVOLVULACEAE

Genus of evergreen, twining climbers, grown for their flowers. Frost tender, min. 16–18°C (61–4°F). Any well-drained soil is suitable with full light. Water freely except in cold weather. Provide support and thin out by cutting old stems to ground level in spring. Propagate by seed in spring or by semi-ripe cuttings in summer. Red spider mite and whitefly may cause problems.

J. pentantha, syn. *J. violacea*. Fast-growing, evergreen, twining climber. H 2–3m (6–10ft). Has heart-shaped, pointed leaves and 2.5cm (1in) wide, funnel-shaped, rich violet-blue or pure blue flowers in long-stalked clusters in summer-autumn.

J. violacea. See *J. pentantha*.

Jade plant, Silver. See *Crassula arborescens*, illus. p.474.

Jade tree. See *Crassula ovata*, illus. p.473.

Jade vine. See *Strongylodon macrobotrys*, illus. p.202.

JAMESBRITTENIA

SCROPHULARIACEAE

Genus of annuals, perennials and evergreen shrubs. Frost hardy to frost tender. Needs a position in sun and in moist but well-drained soil. Propagate by seed or division in spring or by softwood cuttings in spring or summer.

J. grandiflora, syn. *Sutera grandiflora*. Much-branched, sub-shrubby perennial, used for summer bedding. H 1m (3ft), S 30–45cm (12–18in). Frost tender, min. 5°C (41°F). Has oval to oblong, round-toothed leaves. Tubular, 5-lobed, frilled, deep purple flowers are produced from mid-summer to autumn.

JAMESIA

HYDRANGEACEAE

Genus of one species of deciduous shrub, grown for its flowers. Fully hardy. Needs full sun and fertile, well-drained soil. Propagate by softwood cuttings in summer.

J. americana. Deciduous, bushy shrub. H 1.5m (5ft), S 2.5m (8ft). Rounded, grey-green leaves are grey-white beneath. Clusters of small, slightly fragrant, star-shaped, white flowers are produced during late spring.

JANCAEA, syn. JANKAEA

GESNERIACEAE

Genus of one species of evergreen, rosetted perennial, grown for its flowers and silver-green leaves. Makes a good alpine house plant. Frost hardy. Is difficult to grow, as needs shade from mid-day sun in high summer, a humus-rich, gritty, moist, alkaline soil and a gritty collar. Dislikes winter wet. Propagate by seed in spring or by leaf cuttings in mid-summer.

J. heldreichii illus. p.381.

Jankaea. See *Jancaea*.

Japan pepper. See *Zanthoxylum piperitum*, illus. p.141.

Japanese anemone. See *Anemone* × *hybrida*.

Japanese angelica tree. See *Aralia elata*.

Japanese apricot. See *Prunus mume*.

Japanese aralia. See *Fatsia japonica*.

Japanese arrowhead. See *Sagittaria sagittifolia* 'Flore Pleno'.

Japanese banana. See *Musa basjoo*, illus. p.233.

Japanese big-leaf magnolia. See *Magnolia obovata*, illus. p.71.

Japanese bitter orange. See *Poncirus trifoliata*.

Japanese black pine. See *Pinus thunbergii*, illus. p.102.

Japanese cedar. See *Cryptomeria japonica*.

Japanese climbing fern. See *Lygodium japonicum*.

Japanese flag. See *Iris ensata*.

Japanese hemlock. See *Tsuga diversifolia; Tsuga sieboldii*.

Japanese holly. See *Ilex crenata*.

Japanese honeysuckle. See *Lonicera japonica*.

Japanese horse-chestnut. See *Aesculus turbinata*.

Japanese hydrangea vine. See *Schizophragma hydrangeoides*.

Japanese ivy. See *Hedera rhombea; Parthenocissus tricuspidata*, illus. p.216.

Japanese larch. See *Larix kaempferi*.

Japanese maple. See *Acer japonicum; Acer palmatum*.

Japanese pittosporum. See *Pittosporum tobira*.

Japanese privet. See *Ligustrum japonicum*.

Japanese quince. See *Chaenomeles japonica*.

Japanese red pine. See *Pinus densiflora*.

Japanese roof iris. See *Iris tectorum*, illus. p.237.

Japanese rose. See *Rosa rugosa*, illus. p.183.

Japanese sago palm. See *Cycas revoluta*, illus. p.148.

Japanese shield fern. See *Dryopteris erythrosora*.

Japanese snowball tree. See *Viburnum plicatum*.

Japanese spindle. See *Euonymus japonicus*.

Japanese umbrella pine. See *Sciadopitys verticillata*, illus. p.102.

Japanese walnut. See *Juglans ailantifolia*.

Japanese white pine. See *Pinus parviflora*, illus. p.101.

Japanese wisteria. See *Wisteria floribunda*.

Japanese witch hazel. See *Hamamelis japonica*.

Japanese yew. See *Taxus cuspidata*, illus. p.105.

Japonica. See *Chaenomeles; C. japonica*.

JASIONE

CAMPANULACEAE

Genus of summer-flowering annuals, biennials and perennials, grown for their attractive flower heads. Fully hardy. Needs sun and sandy soil. Remove old stems in autumn. Propagate by seed in autumn or by division in spring.

J. laevis, syn. *J. perennis* (Sheep's bit). Tufted perennial. H 5–30cm (2–12in), S 10–20cm (4–8in). Has narrowly oblong, very hairy or glabrous, grey-green leaves and, in summer, spiky, spherical, blue flower heads borne on erect stems. Is good for a rock garden.

J. perennis. See *J. laevis*.

Jasmine. See *Jasminum*.
- **Cape.** See *Gardenia augusta*.
- **Carolina.** See *Gelsemium sempervirens*, illus. p.202.
- **Chilean.** See *Mandevilla laxa*.
- **Common.** See *Jasminum officinale*.
- **Confederate.** See *Trachelospermum jasminoides*, illus. p.203.
- **False.** See *Gelsemium sempervirens*, illus p.202.
- **Italian.** See *Solanum seaforthianum*, illus. p.202.
- **Madagascar.** See *Stephanotis floribunda*, illus. p.200.
- **Orange.** See *Murraya paniculata*.
- **Primrose.** See *Jasminum mesnyi*, illus. p.203.
- **Star.** See *Trachelospermum jasminoides*, illus. p.203.
- **West Indian.** See *Plumeria alba*.
- **Winter.** See *Jasminum nudiflorum*, illus. p.147.
- **Yellow.** See *Jasminum humile*, illus. p.142.

JASMINUM
Jasmine

OLEACEAE

Genus of deciduous or evergreen shrubs and woody-stemmed, scrambling or twining climbers, grown for their often fragrant flowers and their foliage. Fully hardy to frost tender, min. 7–18°C (45–64°F). Needs full sun and fertile, well-drained soil. *J. nudiflorum*, which needs supporting, benefits from having old shoots thinned out after flowering, when others may be pruned. Propagate by semi-ripe cuttings in summer.

♀ ***J. angulare***, syn. *J. capense*. Evergreen, woody-stemmed, scrambling climber. H 2m (6ft) or more. Frost tender, min. 7–10°C (45–50°F). Dark green leaves have 3 oval leaflets. Small clusters of fragrant, tubular, 5-lobed, white flowers are carried in late summer.

J. beesianum. Evergreen, woody-stemmed, scrambling climber, deciduous in cool areas. H to 5m (15ft). Frost hardy. Has lance-shaped leaves. Fragrant, tubular, usually 6-lobed, pinkish-red flowers, 1–3 together, borne in early summer; then shiny, black berries.

J. capense. See *J. angulare*.

J. grandiflorum of gardens. See *J. officinale* f. *affine*.

J. humile (Yellow jasmine) illus. p.142. ♀ **'Revolutum'** is an evergreen, bushy shrub. H 2.5m (8ft), S 3m (10ft). Fully hardy. Bears large, fragrant, tubular, upright, bright yellow flowers, with 5 spreading lobes, on long, slender, green shoots from early spring to late autumn. Glossy, bright green leaves each consist of 3–7 oval leaflets. f. ***wallichianum*** has semi-pendent flowers and 7–13 leaflets.

♀ ***J. mesnyi***, syn. *J. primulinum*, illus. p.203.

J. nobile subsp. ***rex,*** syn. *J. rex*. Evergreen, woody-stemmed, twining climber. H 3m (10ft). Frost tender, min. 18°C (64°F). Has broadly oval, leathery, deep green leaves, 10–20cm (4–8in) long. Scentless, tubular, 5-lobed, pure white flowers are pink-tinged in bud and appear intermittently all year if warm enough.

♀ ***J. nudiflorum*** illus. p.147.

♀ ***J. officinale*** (Common jasmine, Jessamine). Semi-evergreen or deciduous, woody-stemmed, twining climber. H to 12m (40ft). Leaves comprise 7 or 9 leaflets. Has clusters of fragrant, 4- or 5-lobed, white flowers in summer-autumn. f. ***affine*** (syn. *J. grandiflorum* of gardens) illus. p.204.

J. parkeri. Evergreen, domed shrub. H 15cm (6in), S 38cm (18in) or more. Frost hardy. Produces a tangled mass of fine stems and twigs bearing minute, oval leaves. Masses of tiny, tubular, 5-lobed, yellow flowers appear from leaf axils in early summer.

♀ ***J. polyanthum*** illus. p.217.

J. primulinum. See *J. mesnyi*.

J. rex. See *J. nobile* subsp. *rex*.

JEFFERSONIA

BERBERIDACEAE

Genus of spring-flowering perennials. Fully hardy. Needs shade or partial shade and humus-rich, moist soil. Extensive root systems resent disturbance. Top-dress crown in late autumn. Propagate by seed as soon as ripe.

J. diphylla illus. p.359.
J. dubia, syn. *Plagiorhegma dubia*, illus. p.381.

Jeffrey pine. See *Pinus jeffreyi*, illus. p.99.
Jelly palm. See *Butia capitata*, illus. p.96.
Jersey elm. See *Ulmus minor* 'Sarniensis'.
Jerusalem cherry. See *Solanum pseudocapsicum*.
Jerusalem cross. See *Lychnis chalcedonica*, illus. p.253.
Jerusalem sage. See *Phlomis fruticosa*, illus. p.166.
Jerusalem thorn. See *Paliurus spina-christi*, illus. p.118; *Parkinsonia aculeata*.
Jessamine. See *Jasminum officinale*.
Jesuit's nut. See *Trapa natans*, illus. p.465.
Jewel in the lotus. See *Paeonia suffruticosa* 'Tama-fuyo'.
Job's tears. See *Coix lacryma-jobi*, illus. p.320.
Joe Pye weed. See *Eupatorium purpureum*, illus. p.231.
Jonquil. See *Narcissus jonquilla*, illus. p.434.
Campernelle. See *Narcissus* × *odorus*.
Queen Anne's. See *Narcissus jonquilla* 'Flore Pleno'.
Wild. See *Narcissus jonquilla*, illus. p.434.
Josephine's lily. See *Brunsvigia josephinae*.

JOVIBARBA

CRASSULACEAE

Genus of evergreen perennials that spread by short stolons and are grown for their symmetrical rosettes of oval to strap-shaped, pointed, fleshy leaves. Makes ground-hugging mats, suitable for rock gardens, screes, walls, banks and alpine houses. Fully hardy. Needs sun and gritty soil. Takes several years to reach flowering size. Rosettes die after plants have flowered, but leave numerous offsets. Propagate by offsets in summer.

J. hirta, syn. *Sempervivum globiferum* subsp. *hirtum*, illus. p.400.
J. sobolifera, syn. *Sempervivum globiferum* subsp. *globiferum*. Vigorous, evergreen, mat-forming perennial. H 10cm (4in), S 20cm (8in). Rounded, greyish-green or olive-green rosettes are often red-tinged. Flower stems bear terminal clusters of small, cup-shaped, 6-petalled (rarely 5 or 7), pale yellow flowers in summer.

JUANULLOA

SOLANACEAE

Genus of evergreen, summer-flowering shrubs, grown for their flowers. Frost tender, min. 13–15°C (55–9°F). Low temperatures cause leaf drop. Prefers full light and fertile, freely draining soil. Water potted specimens moderately, less when not in full growth. To encourage a branching habit, tip prune young plants. Propagate by semi-ripe cuttings in summer. Whitefly, red spider mite and mealy bug may be troublesome.

J. aurantiaca. See *J. mexicana*.
J. mexicana, syn. *J. aurantiaca*, illus. p.167

JUBAEA

PALMAE/ARECACEAE

Genus of one species of evergreen palm, grown for its overall appearance. Frost hardy. Needs full light and fertile, well-drained soil. Water potted specimens moderately, less frequently in winter. Propagate by seed in spring at not less than 25°C (77°F). Red spider mite may be a nuisance.

J. chilensis, syn. *J. spectabilis*, illus. p.81.
J. spectabilis. See *J. chilensis*.

Judas tree. See *Cercis*.

JUGLANS

Walnut

JUGLANDACEAE

Genus of deciduous trees, with aromatic leaves, grown for their foliage, stately habit and, in some species, edible nuts (walnuts). Produces greenish-yellow catkins in spring and early summer. Fully hardy, but young plants are prone to frost damage. Requires full sun and deep, fertile, well-drained soil. Propagate by seed, when ripe, in autumn.

J. ailantifolia, syn. *J. sieboldiana* (Japanese walnut). Deciduous, spreading tree with stout shoots. H and S 15m (50ft). Very large leaves consist of 11–17 oblong, glossy, bright green leaflets. Bears edible walnuts in autumn. var. ***cordiformis*** (syn. *J. cordiformis*) illus. p.64.
J. cathayensis (Chinese walnut). Deciduous, spreading tree. H and S 20m (70ft). Has very large leaves, consisting of 11–17 oval to oblong, dark green leaflets. Bears edible walnuts in autumn.
J. cinerea (Butternut). Fast-growing, deciduous, spreading tree. H 25m (80ft), S 20m (70ft). Leaves are large and very aromatic, with 7–19 oval to oblong, pointed, bright green leaflets. Bears dense clusters of large, rounded nuts in autumn.
J. cordiformis. See *J. ailantifolia* var. *cordiformis*.
J. microcarpa, syn. *J. rupestris*, illus. p.88.
♀ ***J. nigra*** illus. p.63.
♀ ***J. regia*** illus. p.62.
J. rupestris. See *J. microcarpa*.
J. sieboldiana. See *J. ailantifolia*.

JUNCUS

JUNCACEAE

See also GRASSES, BAMBOOS, RUSHES AND SEDGES.

J. effusus f. ***spiralis***, syn. *J. effusus* 'Spiralis', *Scirpus lacustris* 'Spiralis', illus. p.320.

Juneberry. See *Amelanchier*.
Juniper. See *Juniperus*.
Bonin Isles. See *Juniperus procumbens*, illus. p.106.
Chinese. See *Juniperues chinensis*.
Coffin. See *Juniperus recurva* var. *coxii*.
Common. See *Juniperus communis*.
Creeping. See *Juniperus horizontalis*.
Drooping. See *Juniperus recurva*, illus. p.104.
Flaky. See *Juniperus squamata*.
Himalayan weeping. See *Juniperus recurva*, illus. p.104.
Rocky Mountain. See *Juniperus scopulorum*.
Shore. See *Juniperus conferta*.
Syrian. See *Juniperus drupacea*.
Temple. See *Juniperus rigida*.

JUNIPERUS

Juniper

CUPRESSACEAE

See also CONIFERS.

J. chinensis (Chinese juniper). Conical conifer, making a tree. H 15m (50ft), S 2–3m (6–10ft), or a spreading shrub H 1–5m (3–15ft), S 3–5m (10–15ft). Fully hardy. Has peeling bark. Both scale- and needle-like, aromatic, dark green leaves, paired or in 3s, are borne on same shoot. Globose, fleshy, berry-like fruits are glaucous white. Many cultivars commonly listed under *J. chinensis* are forms of *J.* × *pfitzeriana*. ♀ **'Aurea'**, H 10–15m (30–50ft), S 3–4m (10–12ft), is a slow-growing, oval or conical form with gold foliage and abundant yellow, male cones. ♀ **'Blaauw'** (syn. *J.* × *media* 'Blaauw'), H and S 2m (6ft), is a spreading shrub with blue-green foliage. **'Expansa Variegata'** (syn. *J. davurica* 'Expansa Variegata'; illus. p.107) is a conifer with trailing or ascending branchlets. H 75cm (30in), S 1.5–2m (5–6ft). Fully hardy. Bears scale- and needle-like, aromatic, yellow-variegated, bluish-green leaves. ♀ **'Kaizuka'**, H 5m (15ft), S 3–5m (10–15ft), forms a sprawling, irregular bush and has a profusion of cones. **'Keteleeri'** illus. p.101. ♀ **'Obelisk'** illus. p.104. ♀ **'Plumosa Aurea'** (syn. *J.* × *media* 'Plumosa Aurea'; illus. p.107) is more erect, with green-gold foliage, turning bronze in winter. ♀ **'Pyramidalis'**, H 10m (30ft), S 1–2m (3–6ft), is a columnar, dense form with ascending branches bearing needle-like, blue-green leaves. **'Robust Green'** syn. *J. virginiana* 'Robusta Green' illus. p.104. **'Stricta'** (illus. p.106), H to 5m (15ft), S to 1m (3ft), is conical, with soft, blue-green, young foliage.
J. communis (Common juniper). Conifer, ranging from a spreading shrub to a narrow, upright tree. H 30cm–8m (1–25ft), S 1–4m (3–12ft). Fully hardy. Has needle-like, aromatic, glossy, mid- or yellow-green leaves in 3s and bears globular to ovoid, fleshy, greenish berries that become glaucous blue, then ripen to black in their third year. ♀ **'Compressa'**, H 75cm (30in), S 15cm (6in), is a dwarf, erect form. ♀ **'Hibernica'** (illus. p.107), H 3–5m (10–15ft), S 30cm (12in), is columnar. ♀ **'Hornibrookii'**, H 50cm (20in), S 2m (6ft), and **'Prostrata'**, H 20–30cm (8–12in), S 1–2m (3–6ft), are carpeting plants.
J. conferta, syn. *J. rigida* subsp. *conferta* (Shore juniper). Prostrate, shrubby conifer. H 15cm (6in), S 1–2m (3–6ft). Fully hardy. Spreading branches bear dense, needle-like, aromatic, glossy, bright green leaves, glaucous beneath. Produces glaucous black berries. Tolerates salty, coastal air.
***J. davurica* 'Expansa Variegata'.** See *J. chinensis* 'Expansa Variegata'.
J. drupacea (Syrian juniper). Columnar conifer. H 10–15m (30–50ft), S 1–2m (3–6ft). Fully hardy. Has needle-like, aromatic, light green leaves, in 3s, and ovoid or almost globose, fleshy, brown berries.
J. horizontalis (Creeping juniper). Prostrate, wide-spreading, shrubby conifer, eventually forming mats up to 50cm (20in) thick. Fully hardy. Has scale- or needle-like, aromatic, blue-green or -grey leaves and pale blue-grey berries. Leaves of **'Andorra Compact'** (syn. *J.h.* 'Plumosa Compacta') turn bronze-purple in winter. **'Douglasii'** (illus. p.106) has glaucous blue foliage that turns plum-purple in winter. **'Plumosa'** is less dense than 'Andorra Compact' and has grey-green leaves, becoming purple during winter. **'Plumosa Compacta'** see *J.h.* 'Andorra Compact'.**'Prince of Wales'** has bright green foliage, tinged blue when young and turning purple-brown in winter. **'Turquoise Spreader'** (illus. p.106) has turquoise-green foliage. ♀ **'Wiltonii'** has bluish-grey leaves that retain their colour over winter.
***J.* × *media*.** See *J.* × *pfitzeriana*. **'Blaauw'** see *J. chinensis* 'Blaauw'.**'Blue and Gold'** see *J.* × *pfitzeriana* 'Blue and Gold'.**'Hetzii'** see *J. virginiana* 'Hetzii'.**'Pfitzeriana'** see *J.* × *pfitzeriana* 'William Pfitzer'. **'Pfitzeriana Aurea'** see *J.* × *pfitzeriana* 'Aurea'.**'Pfitzeriana Glauca'** see *J.* × *pfitzeriana* 'Glauca'.**'Plumosa'**, H 1m (3ft), S 2–3m (6–10ft), is a spreading shrub with drooping sprays of mid-green foliage. **'Plumosa Aurea'** see *J. chinensis* 'Plumosa Aurea'.
J.* × *pfitzeriana, syn. *J.* × *media*. Group of spreading to conical conifers. H 15m (50ft), S 2–3m (6–10ft). Fully hardy. Has peeling bark. Mainly scale-like, dark green leaves exude a fetid smell when crushed. Fruits are globose to rounded, white or blue-black. Cultivars are suitable as ground cover or as specimen plants in a small garden. Some forms are commonly listed under *J. chinensis*. **'Aurea'** (syn. *J.* × *media* 'Pfitzeriana Aurea'; illus. p.107) has golden foliage. **'Blue and Gold'** (syn. *J.* × *media* 'Blue and Gold'; illus. p.107), H to 1m (3ft), S 1m (3ft), is a spreading form with leaves variegated sky-blue and gold. **'Glauca'** (syn. *J.* × *media* 'Pfitzeriana Glauca'; illus. p.106) has grey-blue leaves. **'William Pfitzer'** (syn. *J.* × *media* 'Pfitzeriana'; illus. p.107), H 3m (10ft), S 3–5m (10–15ft), is a spreading, flat-topped shrub with grey-green leaves.
J. procumbens (Bonin Isles juniper; illus. p.106). Spreading, prostrate, shrubby conifer. H 75cm (30in), S 2m (6ft). Fully hardy. Has red-brown bark.

Thick branches carry needle-like, aromatic, light green or yellow-green leaves and globose, fleshy, brown or black berries. ♀ **'Nana'** (illus. p.106), H 15–20cm (6–8in), S 75cm (30in), is less vigorous and is mat-forming.
J. recurva (Drooping juniper, Himalayan weeping juniper) illus. p.104. var. ***coxii*** (Coffin juniper) is a slow-growing, conical conifer. H to 15m (50ft), S to 7m (22ft). Fully hardy. Smooth bark flakes in thin sheets. Weeping sprays of long, needle-like, aromatic, incurved leaves are bright green. Globose or ovoid, fleshy berries are black. **'Densa'** (syn. *J. recurva* 'Nana'; illus. p.106), H 30cm (1ft), S 1m (3ft), is a spreading shrub with sprays of green leaves that are erect at tips. **'Nana'** see *J.r.* 'Densa'.
J. rigida (Temple juniper). Sprawling, shrubby conifer. H and S 8m (25ft). Fully hardy. Grey or brown bark peels in strips. Very sharp, needle-like, aromatic, bright green leaves, in 3s, are borne in nodding sprays. Globose, fleshy fruits are purplish-black. subsp. ***conferta*** see *J. conferta*.
J. sabina (Savin). Spreading, shrubby conifer. H to 4m (12ft), S 3–5m (10–15ft). Fully hardy. Has flaking, red-brown bark. Slender shoots bear mainly scale-like, aromatic, dark green leaves that give off a fetid smell when crushed. Bears rounded, blue-black berries. **'Blaue Donau'** (syn. *J.s.* 'Blue Danube'), H 2m (6ft), S 2–4m (6–12ft), is a spreading form with branch tips curved upwards and grey-blue foliage. **'Blue Danube'** see *J.s.* 'Blaue Donau'.**'Cupressifolia'** (syn. *J.s.* Cupressifolia Group; illus. p.106), H 2m (6ft), S 4m (12ft), is a free-fruiting, female form with horizontal or ascending branches and blue-green leaves. **'Mas'** (illus. p.106), has ascending branches. Leaves are blue above, green below, purplish in winter. var. ***tamariscifolia*** (syn. *J.s.* 'Tamariscifolia'; illus. p.106), H 1m (3ft), S 2m (6ft), has tiered layers of mainly needle-like, bright green or blue-green leaves.
J. scopulorum (Rocky Mountain juniper). Slow-growing, round-crowned conifer. H 10m (30ft), S 4m (12ft). Fully hardy. Reddish-brown bark is furrowed into strips or squares and peels on branches. Scale-like, aromatic leaves are grey-green to dark green. Bears globose, fleshy, blue berries. **'Skyrocket'** (syn. *J. virginiana* 'Skyrocket'; illus. p.106), H 8m (25ft), S 75cm (2½ft), is very narrow in habit with glaucous blue foliage. **'Springbank'** (illus. p.106) is narrowly conical with drooping branch tips and intense silvery-blue foliage. **'Tabletop'**, H 2m (6ft), S 5m (15ft), has a flat-topped habit and silvery-blue leaves.
J. squamata (Flaky juniper). Prostrate to sprawling, shrubby conifer. H 30cm–4m (1–12ft), S 1–5m (3–15ft). Fully hardy. Bark is red-brown and flaking. Needle-like, aromatic, fresh green or bluish-green leaves spread at tips of shoots. Produces ovoid, fleshy, black berries. ♀ **'Blue Carpet'**, H 30cm (1ft), S 2–3m (6–10ft), is vigorous and prostrate, with glaucous blue foliage. ♀ **'Blue Star'** (illus. p.106), H 50cm (20in), S 60cm (24in), forms a dense, rounded bush and has blue foliage. **'Chinese Silver'** (illus. p.106), H and S 3–4m (10–12ft), has branches with nodding tips and bluish leaves with bright silver undersides. ♀ **'Holger'** (illus. p.106), H and S 2m (6ft), has sulphur-yellow young leaves that contrast with steel-blue old foliage. **'Meyeri'**, H and S 5m (15ft), sprawls and has steel-blue foliage.
J. virginiana (Pencil cedar). Slow-growing, conical or broadly columnar conifer. H 15–20m (50–70ft), S 6–8m (20–25ft). Fully hardy. Both scale- and needle-like, aromatic, grey-green leaves are borne on same shoot. Ovoid, fleshy berries are brownish-violet and very glaucous. ♀ **'Grey Owl'** (illus. p.106), H 3m (10ft), S 3–5m (10–15ft), is a low, spreading cultivar with ascending branches and silvery-grey foliage. **'Hetzii'** (syn. *J.* × *media* 'Hetzii'), H 3–4m (10–12ft), S 4m (12ft), has tiers of grey-green foliage. **'Robusta Green'** see *J. chinensis* 'Robust Green'.**'Skyrocket'** see *J. scopulorum* 'Skyrocket'.

JUSTICIA

ACANTHACEAE

Genus of evergreen perennials, sub-shrubs and shrubs, grown mainly for their flowers. Frost tender, min. 7–15°C (45–59°F). Requires full light or partial shade and fertile, well-drained soil. Water containerized specimens freely when in full growth, moderately at other times. Some species need regular pruning. Propagate by softwood or greenwood cuttings in spring or early summer. Whitefly may cause problems.
J. adhatoda, syn. *Adhatoda duvernoia, Duvernoia adhatodoides* (Snake bush). Evergreen, erect shrub. H 2–3m (6–10ft), S 1–2m (3–6ft). Min. 7°C (45°F). Has elliptic, dark green leaves. Fragrant, tubular, white or mauve flowers, with pink, red or purple marks, appear in summer-autumn.
♀ ***J. brandegeeana***, syn. *Beloperone guttata, Drejerella guttata*, illus. p.162. **'Chartreuse'** illus. p.164.
J. carnea, syn. *Jacobinia carnea, J. pohliana*, illus. p.159.
J. coccinea. See *Pachystachys coccinea*.
J. floribunda. See *J. rizzinii*.
J. ghiesbreghtiana of gardens. See *J. spicigera*.
J. pauciflora. See *J. rizzinii*.
♀ ***J. rizzinii***, syn. *J. floribunda, J. pauciflora, Libonia floribunda*. Evergreen, rounded, freely branching shrub. H and S 30–60cm (1–2ft). Min. 15°C (59°F) to flower well in winter. Leaves are oval, mid-green. Bears nodding clusters of tubular, yellow-tipped, scarlet flowers mainly autumn-spring; best repropagated every few years.
J. spicigera, syn. *J. ghiesbreghtiana* of gardens, *Jacobinia spicigera*, illus. p.168.

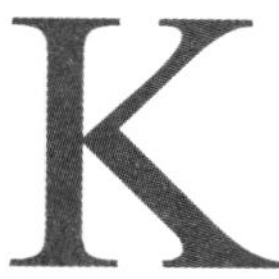

KADSURA

SCHISANDRACEAE

Genus of evergreen, twining climbers, grown for their foliage and fruits. Male and female flowers are borne on separate plants, so plants of both sexes must be grown to obtain fruits. Frost hardy. Grow in semi-shade and in any soil. Propagate by stem cuttings in late summer.
K. japonica. Evergreen, twining climber. H 3–4m (10–12ft). Has oval or lance-shaped, mid-green leaves. Solitary small, fragrant, cream flowers are produced in leaf axils in summer, followed by bright red berries.

KAEMPFERIA

ZINGIBERACEAE

Genus of tufted, rhizomatous perennials, grown for their aromatic leaves and their flowers. Frost tender, min. 18°C (64°F). Needs a moist atmosphere, partial shade and moist, humus-rich soil. Allow to dry out when plants become dormant. Propagate by division in late spring.
K. pulchra illus. p.293.
K. roscoeana. Rhizomatous perennial without an obvious stem. H 5–10cm (2–4in), S 20–25cm (8–10in). Usually has only 2 almost rounded, aromatic leaves, to 10cm (4in) long, dark green with pale green marks above, reddish-green below, that are held horizontally. Ashort spike of pure white flowers, each with a deeply lobed lip, appears from the centre of leaf tuft in autumn.

Kaffir fig. See *Carpobrotus edulis.*
Kaffir lily. See *Schizostylis.*
Kaki. See *Diospyros kaki.*

KALANCHOE, syn. BRYOPHYLLUM

CRASSULACEAE

Genus of perennial succulents or shrubs with very fleshy, mainly cylindrical, oval or linear leaves and bell-shaped to tubular flowers. Many species produce new plantlets from indented leaf margins. Frost tender, min. 7–15°C (45–59°F). Needs full sun or partial shade and well-drained soil. Keep moist from spring to autumn. Water lightly and only occasionally in winter. Propagate by seed, offsets or stem cuttings in spring or summer.
K. beharensis illus. p.476.
K. blossfeldiana (Flaming Katy). Bushy, perennial succulent. H and S 30cm (12in). Min. 10°C (50°F). Has oval to oblong, glossy, dark green leaves with toothed edges and clusters of tubular, scarlet flowers, 0.5cm (¼in) across, in spring. Prefers partial shade. Many hybrids are available in a range of colours (salmon pink, illus. p.480).
K. daigremontiana illus. p.478.
K. delagoensis, syn. *K. tubiflora*, illus. p.484.
K. fedtschenkoi. Bushy, perennial succulent. H and S 1m (3ft). Min. 10°C (50°F). Produces oval, indented, blue-grey leaves with new plantlets in each notch. Bell-shaped, brownish-pink flowers, 2cm (¾in) long, appear in late winter. Prefers a sunny position.
'Variegata' illus. p.478.
♀ ***K. pumila.*** Creeping, perennial succulent. H 10cm (4in), S indefinite. Min. 10°C (50°F). Has oval, powdery grey-white leaves with indented margins. Tubular, pink flowers, 1cm (½in) long, appear in spring. Suits a hanging basket in a sunny position.
♀ ***K.* 'Tessa'** illus. p.480.
♀ ***K. tomentosa*** illus. p.483.
K. tubiflora. See *K. delagoensis.*
K. uniflora, syn. *Kitchingia uniflora.* Creeping, perennial succulent. H 6cm (2½in), S indefinite. Min. 15°C (59°F). Produces rounded, mid-green leaves, 0.5–3cm (¼–1¼in) long, and bell-shaped, yellow-flushed, reddish-purple flowers, 1cm (½in) long, in late winter. Prefers partial shade.
♀ ***K.* 'Wendy'** illus. p.479.

Kale, Sea. See *Crambe maritima*, illus. p.286.

KALMIA

ERICACEAE

Genus of evergreen, summer-flowering shrubs, grown for their clusters of distinctive, usually cup-shaped flowers. Fully hardy. Needs sun or semi-shade and moist, peaty, acid soil. Propagate species by softwood cuttings in summer or by seed in autumn, selected forms by softwood cuttings in summer. All parts may cause severe discomfort if ingested.
K. angustifolia (Sheep laurel). f. ***rubra*** (syn. *K. angustifolia* 'Rubra') illus. p.161.
♀ ***K. latifolia*** (Calico bush) illus. p.137. ♀ **'Ostbo Red'** is an evergreen, bushy, dense shrub. H and S 3m (10ft). Has oval, glossy, rich green leaves. Large, showy clusters of deep pink flowers open in early summer from distinctively crimped, deep red buds. Prefers full sun.

KALMIOPSIS

ERICACEAE

Genus of one species of evergreen, spring-flowering shrub, grown for its flowers. Fully hardy. Requires semi-shade and moist, peaty, acid soil. Propagate by softwood or semi-ripe cuttings in summer.
***K. leachiana* 'La Piniec'**, syn. *K.l.* 'M le Piniec'. Evergreen, bushy shrub. H and S 30cm (12in). Terminal clusters of small, widely bell-shaped, purplish-pink flowers are produced from early to late spring. Has small, oval, glossy, dark green leaves.

KALOPANAX

ARALIACEAE

Genus of one species of deciduous, autumn-flowering tree, grown for its foliage and fruits. Fully hardy, but unripened wood on young plants is susceptible to frost damage. Does best in sun or semi-shade and in fertile, moist but well-drained soil. Propagate by softwood cuttings in summer.
K. pictus. See *K. septemlobus.*
K. ricinifolius. See *K. septemlobus.*
K. septemlobus, syn. *Acanthopanax ricinifolius, K. pictus, K. ricinifolius*, illus. p.76.

Kangaroo paw. See *Anigozanthos.*
Red-and-green. See *Anigozanthos manglesii*, illus. p.254.
Yellow. See *Anigozanthos flavidus*, illus. p.260.
Kangaroo vine. See *Cissus antarctica*, illus. p.218.
Kansas gay feather. See *Liatris pycnostachya.*
Kapok. See *Ceiba pentandra.*
Karo. See *Pittosporum crassifolium.*
Kashmir cypress. See *Cupressus cashmeriana*, illus. p.97.
Katsura. See *Cercidiphyllum japonicum*, illus. p.67.

KELSEYA

ROSACEAE

Genus of one species of extremely small, evergreen sub-shrub. Is difficult to grow and is best in an alpine house as foliage deeply resents both summer and winter wet. Fully hardy. Needs full sun and moist, alkaline soil. Propagate by soft-tip cuttings in late spring or by seed in autumn. Is susceptible to moulds, so remove any dead rosettes at once.
K. uniflora. Slow-growing, evergreen, rosetted sub-shrub. H 1cm (½in), S to 20cm (8in). Forms a hard mat of closely packed, small rosettes of tiny, oval, dark green leaves. In early spring carries stemless, star-shaped, occasionally pink-flushed, white flowers.

Kenilworth Ivy. See *Cymbalaria muralis.*

KENNEDIA, syn. KENNEDYA

LEGUMINOSAE/PAPILIONACEAE

Genus of evergreen, woody-stemmed, trailing and twining climbers, grown for their pea-like flowers. Frost tender, min. 5–7°C (41–5°F). Provide full light and moderately fertile, sandy soil. Water regularly when in full growth, sparingly in cold weather. Requires support. Thin out congested growth after flowering or in spring. Propagate by seed in spring or by semi-ripe cuttings in summer.
K. nigricans (Black bean). Vigorous, evergreen, woody-stemmed, twining climber. H to 2m (6ft). Leaves are divided into 3 leaflets with notched tips. Has small trusses of pea-like, velvety, black-purple flowers, with yellow blazes, in spring-summer.
K. rubicunda illus. p.201.

Kennedya. See *Kennedia.*
Kentia fosteriana. See *Howea fosteriana.*
Kentucky coffee tree. See *Gymnocladus dioica.*
Kermes oak. See *Quercus coccifera.*

KERRIA

ROSACEAE

Genus of one species of deciduous shrub, grown for its showy, yellow flowers. Fully hardy. Needs sun or semi-shade and fertile, well-drained soil. Thin out old shoots after flowering. Propagate by softwood cuttings in summer or by division in autumn.
♀ ***K. japonica* 'Pleniflora'** illus. p.127. var. ***simplex*** is a deciduous, arching, graceful shrub. H and S 2m (6ft). Has bright green foliage. Single, buttercup-like, golden yellow flowers are borne from mid- to late spring.

KIGELIA

BIGNONIACEAE

Genus of one species of evergreen tree, grown for its flowers, curious, sausage-like fruits and for shade. Frost tender, min. 16°C (61°F). Requires full light and humus-rich, well-drained soil. Water potted specimens moderately, very little when temperatures low. Propagate by seed in spring at not less than 23°C (73°F).
K. africana, syn. *K. pinnata* (Sausage tree). Evergreen, spreading, fairly bushy tree. H and S 8m (25ft) or more. Leaves have 7–11 oblong to oval leaflets. Scented, bell-shaped, purplish-red flowers open at night from autumn to spring. Bears inedible, cylindrical, hard-shelled, brown fruits, 30–45cm (12–18in) long.
K. pinnata. See *K. africana.*

Kilmarnock willow. See *Salix caprea* 'Kilmarnock'.
King of the bromeliads. See *Vriesea hieroglyphica.*
King palm. See *Archontophoenix.*
King protea. See *Protea cynaroides*, illus. p.157.
King William pine. See *Athrotaxis selaginoides.*
King's crown. See *Justicia carnea*, illus. p.159.
King's spear. See *Eremurus.*
Kingcup. See *Caltha palustris*, illus. p.467.
Kingfisher daisy. See *Felicia bergeriana*, illus. p.346.

KIRENGESHOMA

HYDRANGEACEAE

Genus of late summer- and autumn-flowering perennials. Fully hardy. Grow in light shade and in deep, moist, lime-free soil. Propagate by seed or division in autumn or spring.
♀ ***K. palmata*** illus. p.271.

KITAIBELA, syn. KITAIBELIA

MALVACEAE

Genus of one species of summer-flowering perennial. Fully hardy. Needs full sun and fertile, preferably dry soil. Propagate by seed in autumn or spring.
K. vitifolia. Bushy, upright perennial. H to 1.5m (5ft), S 60cm (2ft). In summer bears small clusters of open cup-shaped, white or rose-pink flowers. Has palmately lobed, coarsely toothed leaves.

Kitaibelia. See *Kitaibela*
Kitchingia uniflora. See *Kalanchoe uniflora.*
Kiwi fruit. See *Actinidia deliciosa.*
Kleinia articulata. See *Senecio articulatus.*
Kleinia rowleyana. See *Senecio rowleyanus.*
Knapweed. See *Centaurea.*

KNAUTIA

DIPSACACEAE

Genus of summer-flowering annuals and perennials. Fully hardy. Needs sun and well-drained soil. Requires staking. Propagate by basal cuttings in spring or by seed in autumn.
K. arvensis, syn. *Scabiosa arvensis* (Scabious). Erect perennial. H 1.2m (4ft), S 45cm (1½ft). Produces heads of pincushion-like, bluish-lilac flowers in summer. Stems are clothed in narrowly oval to lyre-shaped, deeply divided leaves.
K. macedonica, syn. *Scabiosa rumelica*, illus. p.253.

KNIGHTIA

PROTEACEAE

Genus of evergreen, summer-flowering trees, grown for their flowers, foliage and overall appearance. Half hardy, but is best at min. 3–5°C (37–41°F). Grows in any reasonably fertile, well-drained soil and in sun or partial shade. Water potted specimens moderately, less in winter. Propagate by seed in spring.
K. excelsa (New Zealand honeysuckle, Rewa rewa). Evergreen, upright tree. H 20m (70ft) or more, S 2–4m (6–12ft). Has oblong to lance-shaped, coarsely serrated, leathery leaves, glossy and deep green. Dense racemes of slender, tubular, deep red flowers are produced in summer.

KNIPHOFIA

Red-hot poker, Torch lily

LILIACEAE/ASPHODELACEAE

Genus of perennials, some of which are evergreen. Fully to half hardy. Needs full sun and well-drained conditions, with constantly moist soil in summer. Propagate species by seed or division in spring, cultivars by division only in spring.
***K.* 'Atlanta'.** Evergreen, upright perennial. H to 1m (3ft), S 45cm (1½ft). Fully hardy. In summer, stout stems bear dense, terminal racemes of tubular, bright orange-yellow flowers. Has thick, grass-like, channelled leaves. Does well in a coastal area.
***K.* 'Bee's Lemon'.** Upright perennial. H 1m (3ft), S 45cm (1½ft). Fully hardy. Has dense, terminal racemes of tubular, green-tinged, citron-yellow flowers on stout stems in late summer and autumn. Grass-like, deep green leaves have serrated edges.
♀ ***K. caulescens*** illus. p.271.
***K.* 'C.M. Prichard'** of gardens. See *K. rooperi.*
♀ ***K.* 'Little Maid'** illus. p.302.
***K.* 'Maid of Orleans'.** Upright perennial. H 1.2m (4ft), S 45cm (1½ft). Frost hardy. In summer, slender stems are each crowned with a dense raceme of yellow buds that open to tubular, creamy-white flowers. Leaves are fresh green, basal and strap-shaped.
***K.* 'Percy's Pride'** illus. p.271.
K. rooperi, syn. *K.* 'C.M. Prichard' of gardens, illus. p.271.
♀ ***K.* 'Royal Standard'** illus. p.266.
♀ ***K.* 'Samuel's Sensation'.** Upright perennial. H 1.5m (5ft), S 60cm (2ft). Fully hardy. In late summer, dense, terminal racemes of tubular, deep orange flowers are produced on stout stems. Has strap-shaped, basal, dark green leaves.
K. snowdenii of gardens. See *K. thomsonii* var. *snowdenii.*
K. thomsonii var. ***snowdenii***, syn. *K. snowdenii* of gardens, illus. p.266.
♀ ***K. uvaria*** (Red-hot poker). **'Nobilis'** is an upright perennial with erect, then spreading leaves. H 2m (6ft), S 1m (3ft). Fully hardy. In late summer and autumn, stout stems each bear a dense, terminal raceme of tubular, bright red flowers. Has strap-shaped, channelled, dark green leaves.

Knotweed. See *Persicaria.*
Kochia. See *Bassia.*

KOELREUTERIA

SAPINDACEAE

Genus of deciduous, summer-flowering trees, grown for their foliage, flowers and fruits. Fully hardy to frost tender, min. 10°C (50°F). Requires full sun, doing best in hot summers, and fertile, well-drained soil. Propagate by seed in autumn or by root cuttings in late winter.
♀ ***K. paniculata*** illus. p.88.

KOHLERIA

GESNERIACEAE

Genus of erect perennials with scaly rhizomes, grown for their showy, tubular flowers borne mainly in summer. Frost tender, min. 15°C (59°F). Grow in moist but well-drained soil and in full sun or semi-shade. Water sparingly in winter; over-watering will cause rhizomes to rot. Propagate in spring by division of rhizomes or by seed if available.
K. amabilis. Rhizomatous perennial. H 8–16cm (3–6in), S 60cm (2ft). Oval, hairy leaves, to 8cm (3in) long, are often marked with silver and brown above. Small, nodding, tubular, deep pink flowers, with red-marked lobes, appear in summer. Is useful for a hanging basket.
K. bogotensis. Erect, rhizomatous perennial. H and S 45cm (18in) or more. Oval, velvety, green leaves, to 8cm (3in) long, are sometimes marked with paler green above. In summer has small, tubular flowers, red with a yellow base outside, red-dotted, yellow within.
♀ ***K. digitaliflora*** illus. p.246.
♀ ***K. eriantha*** illus. p.254.
♀ ***K. warscewiczii.*** Erect, rhizomatous perennial. H 1m (3ft), S 60cm (2ft). Oval, dark green leaves have scalloped margins. In summer and autumn has tubular, hairy, yellow-based, scarlet flowers with red- or brown spotted, greenish-yellow or bright yellow lobes.

KOLKWITZIA

CAPRIFOLIACEAE

Genus of one species of deciduous shrub, grown for its abundant flowers. Fully hardy. Prefers full sun and fertile, well-drained soil. Cut out old shoots after flowering. Propagate by softwood cuttings in summer.
K. amabilis (Beauty bush). Deciduous, arching shrub. H and S 3m (10ft). Has peeling bark and oval, dark green leaves. Bell-shaped, yellow-throated, white or pink flowers are borne in late spring and early summer. ♀ **'Pink Cloud'** illus. p.117.

Korean fir. See *Abies koreana*, illus. p.105.
Korean mountain ash. See *Sorbus alnifolia.*
Korean thuja. See *Thuja koraiensis.*
Korolkowia sewerzowii. See *Fritillaria sewerzowii.*
Kowhai. See *Sophora.*
Kudzu vine. See *Pueraria lobata.*

KUNZEA

MYRTACEAE

Genus of evergreen shrubs and trees, grown for their flowers and overall appearance. Frost tender, min. 5–7°C (41–5°F). Prefers full light and sandy, well-drained, neutral to acid soil. Water potted specimens moderately, less when not in full growth. Propagate by semi-ripe cuttings in late summer or by seed in spring.
K. baxteri. Evergreen, rounded, wiry-stemmed shrub. H and S to 2m (6ft). Has narrow, cylindrical, pointed leaves and, in early summer, deep red flowers, each with a brush of stamens, in 5cm (2in) long spikes.

Kurrajong. See *Brachychiton populneus.*
Kusamaki. See *Podocarpus macrophyllus.*

L

LABLAB

LEGUMINOSAE/PAPILIONACEAE

Genus of one species of deciduous, woody-stemmed, twining climber, grown for its attractive, pea-like flowers (in tropics is grown for green manure and animal feed, and for its edible pods and seeds). Is often raised as an annual. Frost tender, min. 5–10°C (41–50°F). Grow in sun and in any well-drained soil. Propagate by seed in spring.

L. purpureus, syn. *Dolichos lablab, D. purpureus*, illus. p.207.

Lablab. See *Lablab purpureus*, illus. p.207.

Labrador tea. See *Ledum groenlandicum*, illus. p.150.

+ LABURNOCYTISUS

LEGUMINOSAE/PAPILIONACEAE

Deciduous tree, grown for its flowers. Is a graft hybrid between *Laburnum anagyroides* and *Cytisus purpureus*. Fully hardy. Needs full sun; grows in any but waterlogged soil. Propagate by grafting on laburnum in late summer.

+*L.* 'Adamii'. Deciduous, spreading tree. H 8m (25ft), S 6m (20ft). In late spring and early summer bears 3 types of blooms: yellow, laburnum flowers; purple, cytisus flowers; and laburnum-like, yellow and pinkish-purple flowers. Leaves, with 3 oval leaflets, are dark green.

LABURNUM

LEGUMINOSAE/PAPILIONACEAE

Genus of deciduous trees, grown for their profuse, pendent flower clusters in spring and summer. Fully hardy. Does best in full sun; grows in any but waterlogged soil. Seeds are very poisonous. Propagate species by seed in autumn, hybrids by budding in summer. All parts are highly toxic if ingested.

L. alpinum illus. p.89.

L. anagyroides, syn. *L. vulgare* (Common laburnum, Golden chain). Deciduous, spreading tree. H and S 7m (22ft). Leaves have 3 oval leaflets and are grey-green. Short, pendent, dense clusters of large, pea-like, yellow flowers appear in late spring and early summer.

L. vulgare. See *L. anagyroides*.

♀ ***L.* × *watereri* 'Vossii'** illus. p.88.

Laburnum
- **Common.** See *Laburnum anagyroides*.
- **Dalmatian.** See *Petteria ramentacea*.
- **Indian.** See *Cassia fistula*.
- **Scotch.** See *Laburnum alpinum*, illus. p.89.
- **Voss's.** See *Laburnum* × *watereri* 'Vossii', illus. p.88.

Lace aloe. See *Aloe aristata*, illus. p.496.

Lace aralia. See *Polyscias guilfoylei* 'Victoriae', illus. p.122.

Lace cactus. See *Mammillaria elongata*, illus. p.486.

Lace flower. See *Episcia dianthiflora*, illus. p.311.
- **Blue.** See *Trachymene coerulea*.

Lace-bark. See *Hoheria populnea*.

Lace-bark pine. See *Pinus bungeana*, illus. p.104.

LACHENALIA

LILIACEAE/HYACINTHACEAE

Genus of winter- and spring-flowering bulbs with tubular or bell-shaped flowers; some have attractively mottled leaves. Is useful as pot plants and in open borders. Half hardy. Requires light, well-drained soil and a sunny site. Plant in early autumn; dry off in summer when foliage has died down. Propagate in autumn by seed or freely produced offsets.

L. aloides, syn. *L. tricolor, L.* 'Tricolor'. Winter- and spring-flowering bulb. H 15–25cm (6–10in), S 5–8cm (2–3in). Produces 2 strap-shaped, semi-erect, basal, purple-spotted, green leaves. Has a spike of 10–20 pendent flowers, each 3cm (1¼in) long with a yellow tube shading to red at the apex and with flared, green tips. **'Nelsonii'** (syn. *L.* 'Nelsonii') illus. p.457.
♀ var. ***quadricolor*** illus. p.457.

L. angustifolia. See *L. contaminata*.

L. contaminata, syn. *L. angustifolia.* Winter- and spring-flowering bulb. H to 20cm (8in), S 5–8cm (2–3in). Has narrowly strap-shaped, semi-erect leaves in a basal cluster. Bears a spike of bell-shaped, white flowers, 0.5cm (¼in) long, suffused and tipped with red and green.

L. glaucina. See *L. orchioides* var. *glaucina*.

L. mutabilis. Winter- and spring-flowering bulb. H to 30cm (12in), S 5–8cm (2–3in). Has 2 strap-shaped, semi-erect, basal leaves. Stem bears a loose spike of up to 25 tubular, 1cm (½in) long flowers that are purple or lilac in bud and open to reddish-brown-tipped petals with a green tube base.

***L.* 'Nelsonii'.** See *L. aloides* 'Nelsonii'.

L. orchioides. Winter- and spring-flowering bulb. H 15–30cm (6–12in), S 5–8cm (2–3in). Has 2 strap-shaped, semi-erect, basal, green leaves, sometimes spotted blackish- or purple-brown. Stem produces a dense spike of fragrant, semi-erect, tubular, white flowers, 1cm (½in) long, blue-tinged and tipped with green. var. ***glaucina*** (syn. *L. glaucina*) illus. p.441.

L. rubida. Winter-flowering bulb. H to 25cm (10in), S 5–8cm (2–3in). Bears 2 strap-shaped, purple-spotted, green leaves, semi-erect and basal, and a loose spike of pendent, tubular, red flowers, 2–3cm (¾–1¼in) long, shading to yellow at tips.

L. tricolor. See *L. aloides*.

***L.* 'Tricolor'.** See *L. aloides*.

Lacquered wine-cup. See *Aechmea* Foster's Favorite Group, illus. p.273.

Lactuca alpina. See *Cicerbita alpina*.

Lactuca bourgaei. See *Cicerbita bourgaei*.

Lad's love. See *Artemisia abrotanum*, illus. p.172.

Ladder fern. See *Nephrolepis cordifolia*.

Lady fern. See *Athyrium filix-femina*.

Lady tulip. See *Tulipa clusiana*.

Lady's eardrops. See *Fuchsia magellanica*, illus. p.160.

Lady's mantle. See *Alchemilla*.
- **Alpine.** See *Alchemilla alpina*.

Lady's slipper orchid. See *Cypripedium calceolus*, illus. p.310.
- **Showy.** See *Cypripedium reginae*, illus. p.308.

Lady's smock. See *Cardamine pratensis*.

Lady-of-the-night. See *Brassavola nodosa*, illus. p.308.

LAELIA

ORCHIDACEAE

SEE ALSO ORCHIDS.

L. anceps illus. p.309. Evergreen, epiphytic orchid for a cool greenhouse. H 25cm (10in). Lilac-pink flowers, 6cm (2½in) wide, each with a deep mauve lip,are carried in tall spikes in autumn. Has oval, rigid leaves, 10–15cm (4–6in) long. Needs semi-shade in summer.

L. cinnabarina illus. p.311. Evergreen, epiphytic orchid for an intermediate greenhouse. H 15cm (6in). Produces sprays of slender, orange flowers, 5cm (2in) or more across, usually in winter. Has narrowly oval, rigid leaves, 8–10cm (3–4in) long. Needs good light in summer.

× LAELIOCATTLEYA

ORCHIDACEAE

SEE ALSO ORCHIDS.

×*L. Rojo* 'Mont Millais' illus. p.309. Evergreen, epiphytic orchid for an intermediate greenhouse. H 30cm (12in). In winter-spring bears arching heads of slender, reddish-orange flowers, 2cm (¾in) across. Oval leaves are up to 15cm (6in) long. Provide good light in summer.

LAGAROSIPHON

HYDROCHARITACEAE

Genus of semi-evergreen, perennial, spreading, submerged water plants grown for their decorative foliage. Oxygenates water. Fully hardy. Needs full sun. Thin regularly to keep under control. Propagate by stem cuttings in spring or summer.

L. major, syn. *Elodea crispa* of gardens, illus. p.465.

LAGERSTROEMIA

LYTHRACEAE

Genus of deciduous or evergreen, summer-flowering shrubs and trees, grown for their flowers. Frost hardy to frost tender, min. 3–5°C (37–41°F). Prefers fertile, well-drained soil and full light. Water potted specimens freely when in full growth, less at other times. To maintain as shrubs, cut back hard the previous season's stems each spring. Propagate by seed in spring or by semi-ripe cuttings in summer.

♀ ***L. indica*** illus. p.87.

L. speciosa (Pride of India, Queen's crape myrtle). Deciduous, rounded tree. H 15–20m (50–70ft), S 10–15m (30–50ft). Frost tender. Mid- to deep green leaves are narrowly oval, 8–18cm (3–7in) long. Has panicles of funnel-shaped, rose-pink to rose-purple flowers in summer-autumn, often when leafless.

LAGUNARIA

MALVACEAE

Genus of one species of evergreen tree, grown for its flowers in summer-autumn and its overall appearance. Frost tender, min. 3–5°C (37–41°F). Prefers fertile, well-drained soil and full light. Water potted plants freely when in full summer growth, moderately at other times. Pruning is tolerated if required. Propagate by seed in spring or by semi-ripe cuttings in summer. Under cover, red spider mite may be troublesome. Contact with the seeds may irritate skin.

L. patersonii (Norfolk Island hibiscus, Queensland pyramidal tree). Fast-growing, evergreen, upright tree, pyramidal when young. H 10–14m (30–46ft), S 5–7m (15–22ft). Oval, rough-textured leaves are matt-green above, whitish-green beneath. Bears hibiscus-like, rose-pink flowers, 5cm (2in) wide, in summer.

LAGURUS

GRAMINEAE/POACEAE

See also GRASSES, BAMBOOS, RUSHES and SEDGES.

♀ ***L. ovatus*** illus. p.318.

LAMARCKIA

GRAMINEAE/POACEAE

See also GRASSES, BAMBOOS, RUSHES and SEDGES.

L. aurea (Golden top). Tuft-forming, annual grass. H and S 20cm (8in). Fully hardy. Wiry stems bear scattered, pale green leaves and, in summer, erect, dense, one-sided, golden panicles. Needs sun.

Lamb's tongue. See *Stachys byzantina*, illus. p.316.

Lamb's-tail cactus. See *Echinocereus schmollii*, illus. p.478.

LAMIUM
Deadnettle

LABIATAE/LAMIACEAE

Genus of spring- or summer-flowering perennials, most of which are semi-evergreen, including a number of weeds; some species make useful ground cover. Fully hardy. Prefers full or partial shade and moist but well-drained soil. Resents excessive winter wet. Propagate by stem-tip cuttings of non-flowering shoots in mid-summer or by division in autumn or early spring.

L. galeobdolon subsp. ***montanum* 'Florentinum',** syn. *L.g.* 'Variegatum'. Semi-evergreen, carpeting perennial. H to 30cm (12in), S indefinite. Oval, mid-green leaves are marked with silver.Racemes of tubular, 2-lipped, lemon-yellow flowers appear in summer.

L. maculatum illus. p.277. **'Album'** illus. p.275. **'Aureum'** (syn. *L.m.* 'Gold Leaf') is a semi-evergreen, mat-forming perennial. H 20cm (8in), S 60cm (24in). Produces oval, yellow leaves with paler white centres. Whorls of hooded, pink flowers appear on short

stems in summer. **'Beacon Silver'** bears mauve-tinged, silver leaves, sometimes with narrow, green margins, and clear pale pink flowers. **'Gold Leaf'** see *L.m.* 'Aureum'. ♀ **'White Nancy'** illus. p.275.
L. orvala illus. p.279.

Lampranthus

AIZOACEAE

Genus of creeping, bushy, perennial succulents and sub-shrubs with daisy-like flowers. Becomes woody after several years, when is best replenished. Plants are good for summer bedding, particularly in arid conditions. Leaves redden in strong sun. Frost tender, min. 7°C (45°F) if dry. Requires full sun and very well-drained soil. Propagate by seed or stem cuttings in spring or autumn.
L. aurantiacus. See ***L. glaucoides***
L. deltoides. See *Oscularia deltoides*, illus. p.487.
L. glaucoides, syn. *L. aurantiacus*, illus. p.484.
L. haworthii. Erect to creeping, perennial succulent. H 50cm (20in), S indefinite. Blue-grey leaves are cylindrical and 5cm (2in) long. In spring bears masses of daisy-like, cerise flowers, 7cm (3in) across, that only open in sun.
L. roseus, syn. *Mesembryanthemum multiradiatum.* Creeping, perennial succulent. H 15cm (6in), S indefinite. Produces solid, 3-angled, mid- to glaucous green leaves, 5cm (2in) long. Daisy-like, dark rose-red flowers, 4cm (1½in) across, open only in sun from spring to autumn.
L. spectabilis illus. p.479.

Lampshade poppy. See *Meconopsis integrifolia*, illus. p.304.
Lancewood. See *Pseudopanax crassifolius*.

Lantana

VERBENACEAE

Genus of evergreen perennials and shrubs, grown for their flowers. Frost tender, min. 10–13°C (50–55°F). Needs full light and fertile, well-drained soil. Water containerized specimens freely when in full growth, moderately at other times. Tip prune young plants to promote a bushy habit. Propagate by seed in spring or by semi-ripe cuttings in summer. Red spider mite and whitefly may be troublesome. All parts may cause severe discomfort if ingested, and contact with foliage may irritate skin.
L. camara. Evergreen, rounded to spreading shrub. H and S 1–2m (3–6ft). Bears oval, finely wrinkled, deep green leaves. From spring to autumn, tiny, tubular, 5-lobed flowers, in dense, domed heads, open yellow, then turn red. Many colour forms have been selected.
L. delicatissima. See *L. montevidensis*.
L. montevidensis, syn. *L. delicatissima, L. sellowiana*, illus. p.163.
L. sellowiana. See *L. montevidensis*.
***L.* 'Spreading Sunset'** illus. p.167.

Lantern tree. See *Crinodendron hookerianum*, illus. p.138.
Lantern, Chinese. See *Physalis*.

Lapageria

PHILESIACEAE/LILIACEAE

Genus of one species of evergreen, woody-stemmed, twining climber, grown for its large, waxy blooms. Half hardy. Requires humus-rich, well-drained soil and partial shade. Water moderately, scarcely at all when not in full growth. Provide support. Thin out congested growth in spring. Propagate in spring by seed, soaked for 2 days before sowing, or in spring or autumn by layering.
♀ ***L. rosea*** illus. p.206. var. ***albiflora*** is an evergreen, woody-stemmed, twining climber. H to 5m (15ft). Has oblong to oval, leathery, dark green leaves. From summer to late autumn bears pendent, fleshy, narrowly bell-shaped, white flowers.

Lapeirousia cruenta. See *Anomatheca laxa*.
Lapeirousia laxa. See *Anomatheca laxa*.
Larch
European. See *Larix decidua*.
Golden. See *Pseudolarix amabilis*, illus. p.103.
Japanese. See *Larix kaempferi*.

Lardizabala

LARDIZABALACEAE

Genus of evergreen, woody-stemmed, twining climbers, grown for their foliage. Male and female flowers are produced on the same plant in late autumn to winter. Is useful for growing on trellises or pergolas. Frost to half hardy. Grow in any well-drained soil and sun or partial shade. Propagate by seed in spring or by stem cuttings in late summer or autumn.
L. biternata. See *L. funaria*
L. funaria, syn *L. biternata.* Evergreen, woody-stemmed, twining climber. H 3–4m (10–12ft). Half hardy. Rounded leaves have broadly oval, leathery, dark green leaflets. In winter produces brown flowers with tiny, whitish petals, the males in drooping spikes, the females solitary. In winter-spring bears many-seeded, berry-like, purple fruits, 5–8cm (2–3in) long.

Large self-heal. See *Prunella grandiflora*, illus. p.394.
Large yellow restharrow. See *Ononis natrix*, illus. p.371.
Large-leaved lime. See *Tilia platyphyllos*.

Larix

PINACEAE

See also CONIFERS.
♀ ***L. decidua***, syn. *L. europaea* (European larch). Fast-growing, deciduous conifer with a conical crown when young, broadening on maturity, and spaced branches. H 25–30m (80–100ft), S 5–15m (16–50ft). Fully hardy. Shoots are yellow-brown in winter. Has light green leaves and small, erect, conical cones.
L. europaea. See *L. decidua*.
♀ ***L. kaempferi***, syn. *L. leptolepis* (Japanese larch). Fast-growing, deciduous, columnar conifer with a conical tip. H 25–30m (80–100ft), S 5–8m (15–25ft). Fully hardy. Shoots are purplish-red and leaves are needle-like, flattened, greyish-green or bluish. Small cones have reflexed scales.
L. leptolepis. See *L. kaempferi*.

Larkspur. See *Consolida*.
Giant. See *Consolida ajacis Giant Imperial Series*, illus. p.344.
Late Dutch honeysuckle. See *Lonicera periclymenum* 'Serotina'.

Lathraea

SCROPHULARIACEAE

Genus of spreading perennials that grow as parasites on the roots of trees, in the case of *L. clandestina* on willow or poplar. True leaves are not produced. Fully hardy. Grows in dappled shade cast by host tree and prefers moist conditions. Roots resent being disturbed. Propagate by seed when fresh, in late summer.
L. clandestina illus. p.279.

Lathyrus

LEGUMINOSAE/PAPILIONACEAE

Genus of annuals and perennials, many of them tendril climbers, grown for their racemes of attractive flowers. Flowers are followed by long, thin seed pods. Fully to frost hardy. Grow in humus-rich, fertile, well-drained soil and in full light. Provide support and remove dead flowers regularly. Cut down perennials in late autumn. Propagate annuals by seed (soaked before sowing) in early spring or early autumn, perennials by seed in autumn or by division in spring. Botrytis and mildew may cause problems. Seeds may cause mild stomach upset if ingested.
L. grandiflorus illus. p.205.
♀ ***L. latifolius*** illus. p.207.
L. magellanicus of gardens. See *L. nervosus*.
L. nervosus, syn. *L. magellanicus* of gardens (Lord Anson's blue pea). Herbaceous, tendril climber. H to 5m (15ft). Frost hardy. Grey-green leaves each have a pair of leaflets, a 3-branched tendril and large stipules. Fragrant, purplish-blue flowers are borne in long-stalked racemes in summer.
♀ ***L. odoratus*** (Sweet pea). Moderately fast-growing, annual, tendril climber. H to 3m (10ft). Fully hardy. Has oval, mid-green leaves with tendrils. Scented flowers are produced in shades of pink, blue, purple or white, from summer to early autumn. Dwarf, non-climbing cultivars are available. **'Barry Dare'** illus. p.206. **'Bijou'** illus. p.336. **'Charles Unwin'** illus. p.205.
♀ **'Jayne Amanda'** bears racemes of usually 4, rarely 5, rose-pink flowers, and may be grown as a cordon or bush. **'Knee Hi'** illus. p.332. **'Lady Diana'** illus. p.212. **'Mrs Bernard Jones'** illus. p.204.
L. rotundifolius (Persian everlasting pea). Herbaceous, tendril climber with winged stems. H to 1m (3ft). Fully hardy. Leaves each have narrow stipules, a pair of leaflets and a 3-branched tendril. Has small racemes of 3–8 pink to purplish flowers in summer.
L. sylvestris (Everlasting pea, Perennial pea). Herbaceous, tendril climber with winged stems. H to 2m (6ft). Fully hardy. Leaves each have narrow stipules, a pair of leaflets and a terminal, branched tendril. In summer and early autumn bears racemes of 4–10 rose-pink flowers, marked with green and purple.
♀ ***L. vernus***, syn. *Orobus vernus*, illus. p.278. ♀ **'Alboroseus'** is a clump-forming perennial. H and S 30cm (12in). Fully hardy. In spring, slender stems each bear 3–5 white- and-deep-pink flowers. Has fern-like, much-divided, soft leaves.

Laurel. See *Laurus; Prunus laurocerasus; Prunus lusitanica*.
Alexandrian. See *Danäe racemosa*.
Bay. See *Laurus nobilis*.
Californian. See *Umbellularia californica*, illus. p.70.
Cherry. See *Prunus laurocerasus*.
Chilean. See *Laurelia sempervirens*.
Portugal. See *Prunus lusitanica*.
Sheep. See *Kalmia angustifolia*.
Spurge. See *Daphne laureola*.

Laurelia

MONIMIACEAE

Genus of evergreen trees and shrubs, grown for their aromatic foliage. Frost hardy, but needs shelter from cold winds. Requires sun or semi-shade; grows in any but very dry soil. Propagate by semi-ripe cuttings in summer.
L. sempervirens, syn. *L. serrata* of gardens (Chilean laurel). Evergreen, broadly conical tree or shrub. H and S to 15m (50ft). Oval, leathery leaves are glossy, dark green and very aromatic. In summer bears inconspicuous flowers.
L. serrata of gardens. See *L. sempervirens*.

Laurus

Bay tree, Laurel

LAURACEAE

Genus of evergreen trees, grown for their foliage. Frost hardy, but foliage may be scorched by extremely cold weather or strong, cold winds. Needs a sheltered position in sun or semi-shade and fertile, well-drained soil. In tubs may be grown well as standards, which should be trimmed during summer. Propagate by semi-ripe cuttings in summer or by seed in autumn.
♀ ***L. nobilis*** (Bay laurel, Sweet bay). Evergreen, broadly conical tree. H 12m (40ft), S 10m (30ft). Narrowly oval, leathery, glossy, dark green leaves are very aromatic and used in cooking. Has small, star-shaped, pale yellow flowers in spring, followed by globose to ovoid, green, then black fruits.

Laurustinus. See *Viburnum tinus*, illus. p.145.

Lavandula

Lavender

LABIATAE/LAMIACEAE

Genus of evergreen, mainly summer-flowering shrubs, with entire or divided, often grey-green leaves, rown for their aromatic foliage and flowers. Makes an effective, low hedge. Fully to

half hardy. Needs full sun and fertile, well-drained soil. Trim hedges lightly in spring to maintain a compact habit. Propagate by semi-ripe cuttings in summer.
***L. angustifolia* 'Hidcote'** see *L.* 'Hidcote'.**'Munstead'** is an evergreen, bushy, compact shrub. H and S 60cm (2ft.). Fully hardy. Narrowly oblong, narrow, aromatic leaves are grey-green. Produces dense spikes of tiny, fragrant, tubular, blue flowers from mid- to late summer.
L. dentata (French lavender). Evergreen, bushy shrub. H and S 1m (3ft). Frost hardy. Aromatic leaves are fern-like, toothed and grey-green. Dense spikes of small, slightly fragrant, tubular, lavender-blue flowers and purple bracts are borne from mid- to late summer.
***L.* 'Grappenhall'.** See *L.* × *intermedia* 'Grappenhall'.
♀ ***L.* 'Hidcote'**, syn. *L. angustifolia* 'Hidcote', illus. p.163.
L.* × *intermedia (English lavender). **'Grappenhall'**, syn. *L.* 'Grappenhall', is an evergreen, bushy shrub. H 1m (3ft), S 1.5m (5ft). Frost hardy. Produces narrowly oblong, aromatic, grey-green leaves. Produces long-stalked spikes of tiny, slightly fragrant, tubular, blue-purple flowers in mid- and late summer.
♀ ***L. stoechas*** illus. p.163.

LAVATERA
Tree mallow

MALVACEAE

Genus of mainly summer-flowering annuals, biennials, perennials and semi-evergreen sub-shrubs and shrubs. Fully to frost hardy. Needs sun and well-drained soil. Propagate perennials, sub-shrubs and shrubs by softwood cuttings in early spring or summer, annuals and biennials by seed in spring or early autumn.
L. assurgentiflora illus. p.137.
L. cachemiriana, syn. *L. cachemirica*, illus. p.225.
L. cachemirica. See *L. cachemiriana*.
♀ ***L.* × *clementii* 'Barnsley'.** Vigorous, semi-evergreen sub-shrub. H and S 2m (6ft). Fully hardy. Mid-green, palmate leaves have 3–5 lobes. Throughout summer bears profuse clusters of open funnel-shaped, red-eyed, white flowers, ageing to soft pink, with deeply notched petals. ♀ ***L.* × *c.* 'Rosea'**, syn. *L. olbia* 'Rosea', illus. p.137.
***L. olbia* 'Rosea'**, See *L.* × *clementii* 'Rosea'.
***L. trimestris* 'Mont Blanc'** illus. p.330. **'SilverCup'** illus. p.336.

Lavender. See *Lavandula*.
Cotton. See *Santolina chamaecyparissus*.
English. See *Lavandula* × *intermedia*.
French. See *Lavandula dentata; Lavandula stoechas*, illus. p.163.
Sea. See *Limonium*.
Lavender cotton. See *Santolina chamaecyparissus*.
Lawson cypress. See *Chamaecyparis lawsoniana*.

LAYIA

COMPOSITAE/ASTERACEAE

Genus of annuals, useful for hot, dry places. Fully hardy. Grow in sun and in poor to fertile, very well-drained soil. Propagate by seed sown outdoors in spring or early autumn.
L. elegans. See *L. platyglossa*.
L. platyglossa, syn. *L. elegans* (Tidy tips). Fast-growing, upright, bushy annual. H 45cm (18in), S 30cm (12in). Has lance-shaped, greyish-green leaves. Daisy-like flower heads, 5cm (2in) wide, with white-tipped, yellow ray petals and yellow centres, are produced from early summer to early autumn. Is suitable for cutting.

Lead plant. See *Amorpha canescens*.
Leadwort, Cape. See *Plumbago auriculata*, illus. p.213.
Least bur reed. See *Sparganium natans*.
Least duckweed. See *Wolffia arrhiza*.
Least snowbell. See *Soldanella minima*.
Least willow. See *Salix herbacea*.
Leatherleaf. See *Chamaedaphne calyculata*.
Leatherleaf sedge. See *Carex buchananii*.
Leatherwood. See *Cyrilla racemiflora*.
Lechenaultia. See *Leschenaultia*.

LEDEBOURIA

LILIACEAE/HYACINTHACEAE

Genus of bulbs, some of which are evergreen, with ornamental, narrowly lance-shaped leaves. Produces very small flowers with reflexed tips. Makes good pot plants in cool greenhouses. Half hardy. Needs full light, to allow leaf marks to develop well, and loose, open soil. Propagate by offsets in spring.
L. cooperi, syn. *Scilla adlamii, S. cooperi*. Summer-flowering bulb. H 5–10cm (2–4in), S 2.5–5cm (1–2in). Semi-erect, basal, green leaves, with brownish-purple stripes, die away in winter. Stem carries a short spike of small, bell-shaped, greenish-purple flowers.
L. socialis, syn. *Scilla socialis, S. violacea*, illus. p.450.

LEDUM

ERICACEAE

Genus of evergreen shrubs, grown for their aromatic foliage and small, white flowers. Fully hardy. Needs shade or semi-shade and moist, peaty, acid soil. Benefits from dead-heading. Propagate by semi-ripe cuttings in summer or by seed in autumn.
L. groenlandicum illus. p.150.

LEIOPHYLLUM

ERICACEAE

Genus of one species of evergreen shrub with an extensive, spreading root system. Fully hardy. Prefers semi-shade and well-drained, peaty, acid soil. Top-dress regularly with peaty soil. Propagate by seed in spring or by semi-ripe cuttings in summer.
♀ ***L. buxifolium.*** Evergreen, dome-shaped shrub. H 25cm (10in), S 45cm (18in). Stems are covered with tiny, oval, leathery, dark green leaves. In late spring, terminal clusters of deep pink buds develop into small, star-shaped, white flowers, with prominent stamens.

Lemaireocereus euphorbioides. See *Neobuxbaumia euphorbioides*.
Lemaireocereus marginatus. See *Pachycereus marginatus*.
Lemaireocereus thurberi. See *Stenocereus thurberi*.

LEMBOGLOSSUM

ORCHIDACEAE

See also ORCHIDS.
♀ ***L. bictoniense***, syn. *Odontoglossum bictoniense* illus. p.308. Evergreen, epiphytic orchid for a cool greenhouse. H 23cm (9in). Olive-green flowers, 4cm (1½in) across, barred with dark brown and each with a sometimes pink-flushed, white lip, are produced in spikes in late summer. Leaves are narrowly oval and 10–15cm (4–6in) long. Requires shade in summer.
L. cervantesii, syn. *Odontoglossum cervantesii* illus. p.308. Evergreen, epiphytic orchid for a cool greenhouse. H 8cm (3in). In winter produces sprays of papery, white flowers, 2.5cm (1in) across, with cobweb-like, light brown marks. Has narrowly oval leaves, 10–15cm (4–6in) long. Grow in shade in summer.
L. cordatum, syn. *Odontoglossum cordatum* illus. p.309. Evergreen, epiphytic orchid for a cool greenhouse. H 12cm (5in). Sprays of brown-marked, corn-yellow flowers, 2.5cm (1in) across, open in spring. Leaves are narrowly oval and 10–15cm (4–6in) long. Provide shade in summer and keep very dry in winter.
L. rossii, syn. *Odontoglossum rossii* illus. p.308. Evergreen, epiphytic orchid for a cool greenhouse. H 8cm (3in). In autumn-winter, white to mushroom-pink flowers, 2.5cm (1in) across and speckled with beige-brown, are borne in spikes. Narrowly oval leaves are 10–15cm (4–6in) long. Needs shade in summer.

Lembotropis nigricans. See *Cytisus nigricans*.
Lemon verbena. See *Aloysia triphylla*, illus. p.139.
Lemon vine. See *Pereskia aculeata*, illus. p.473.
Lent lily. See *Narcissus pseudonarcissus*, illus. p.434.
Lenten rose. See *Helleborus* × *hybridus*.

LEONOTIS

LABIATAE/LAMIACEAE

Genus of annuals, evergreen and semi-evergreen perennials, sub-shrubs and shrubs, grown for their flowers and overall appearance. Half hardy to frost tender, min. 5–7°C (41–5°F). Needs full sun and rich, well-drained soil. Water containerized specimens freely when in full growth, much less at other times. Cut back perennials, sub-shrubs and shrubs to within 15cm (6in) of ground in early spring. Propagate by seed in spring or by greenwood cuttings in early summer.
L. leonurus illus. p.145.

LEONTOPODIUM
Edelweiss

COMPOSITAE/ASTERACEAE

Genus of short-lived, spring-flowering, woolly perennials, grown for their flower heads. Is suitable for rock gardens. Fully hardy. Needs sun, gritty, well-drained soil and a deep collar of grit. Shelter from prevailing, rain-bearing winds, as crowns are very intolerant of winter wet. Propagate by division in spring or by seed when fresh. Many seeds are not viable.
L. alpinum illus. p.358.
L. stracheyi. Mound-forming, spreading, woolly perennial. H and S 10cm (4in). Star-shaped, glistening, white flower heads are produced among thick, oval, silver leaves in spring. Makes a good alpine house plant.

Leopard lily. See *Dieffenbachia; Lilium pardalinum*, illus. p.419.
Leopard plant. See *Farfugium japonicum* 'Aureomaculatum'.
Leopard's bane. See *Doronicum*.
Leopoldia comosa. See *Muscari comosum*.

LEPISMIUM

CACTACEAE

Genus of epiphytic and lithophytic (growing on rocks) perennial cacti often pendulous in habit with cylindrical, ribbed, angled or flat, usually segmented stems. Small, funnel- to disc-shaped flowers are followed by spherical, often purple or red berries. Frost tender, min. 6–10°C (43–50°F). Needs partial shade and rich, well-drained soil. Prefers 80% relative humidity – higher than for most cacti. Give only occasional, very light watering in winter. Propagate by seed or stem cuttings in spring or summer.
L. warmingianum, syn. *Rhipsalis warmingiana*, illus. p.477.

LEPTINELLA

COMPOSITAE/ASTERACEAE

Genus of annuals and creeping perennials that are effective as low ground cover. Fully hardy. Grow in full sun and moderately fertile, sharply drained soil. Propagate by seed as soon as ripe or by division in spring.
L. atrata, syn. *Cotula atrata*, illus. p.379. subsp. ***luteola*** illus. p.376.

LEPTOSPERMUM

MYRTACEAE

Genus of evergreen trees and shrubs, grown for their foliage and small, often profuse flowers. Grows well in coastal areas if not too exposed. Frost to half hardy, but in cold areas plant against a south- or west-facing wall. Needs full sun and fertile, well-drained soil. Propagate by semi-ripe cuttings in summer.
L. flavescens. See *L. polygalifolium*.
L. humifusum. See *L. rupestre*.

L. polygalifolium, syn. *L. flavescens*, illus. p.135.
♀ ***L. rupestre***, syn. *L. humifusum*, illus. p.156.
L. scoparium (Manuka, New Zealand tea-tree). ♀ **'Keatleyi'** is an evergreen, rounded shrub. H and S 3m (10ft). Half hardy. Narrowly lance-shaped, aromatic, grey-green leaves set off a profusion of large, star-shaped, pale pink flowers during late spring and summer. ♀ **'Nicholsii'** produces bronze-purple leaves and smaller, crimson flowers. ♀ **'Red Damask'** illus. p.127.

LESCHENAULTIA, syn. LECHENAULTIA

GOODENIACEAE

Genus of evergreen shrubs, grown for their flowers. Frost tender, min. 7–10°C (45–50°F). Needs full light and peaty, well-drained soil with few phosphates and nitrates. Water containerized plants moderately during growing season, sparingly at other times. Shorten over-long stems after flowering. Propagate by seed in spring or by semi-ripe cuttings in summer. Most species are not easy to grow under glass; good ventilation is essential.
L. floribunda. Evergreen, domed, wiry-stemmed shrub. H and S 30–60cm (12–24in). Has narrow, cylindrical, pointed leaves and, in spring-summer, short, tubular, pale blue flowers, each with 5 angular petals, in terminal clusters.

Lesser celandine. See *Ranunculus ficaria*.
Lesser periwinkle. See *Vinca minor*, illus. p.172.
Lettuce, Water. See *Pistia stratiotes*, illus. p.465.

LEUCADENDRON

PROTEACEAE

Genus of evergreen shrubs and trees, grown for their flower heads from autumn to spring and for their foliage. Frost tender, min. 5–7°C (41–5°F). Needs full light and sharply drained soil, mainly of sand and peat, ideally with very little nitrogen and phosphates. Water potted specimens moderately while in growth, sparingly at other times. Propagate by seed in spring.
L. argenteum illus. p.96.

LEUCANTHEMELLA

COMPOSITAE/ASTERACEAE

Genus of hairy perennials, grown for their daisy-like flower heads in autumn. Fully hardy. Grow in full sun or partial shade and reliably moist soil. Propagate by division or basal cuttings in spring.
♀ ***L. serotina***, syn. *Chrysanthemum serotinum, C. uliginosum.* Erect perennial. H 1.5m (5ft), S 90cm (3ft). Lance-shaped leaves are toothed and dark green. Leafy stems carry sprays of large, green-centred, white flower heads in late autumn.

LEUCANTHEMOPSIS

COMPOSITAE/ASTERACEAE

Genus of dwarf, tufted, clump- or mat-forming perennials, grown for their solitary, daisy-like flower heads in summer. Fully hardy. Grow in full sun and sharply drained soil. Propagate by seed as soon as ripe or by division or basal cuttings in spring.
L. alpina, syn. *Chrysanthemum alpinum.* Tuft-forming, short-lived perennial. H 10cm (4in), S 20cm (8in). Small tufts of deeply cut leaves are produced from short, rhizomatous stems. Has large, white flower heads, with yellow centres, in summer. Is good for a rock garden or scree.

LEUCANTHEMUM

COMPOSITAE/ASTERACEAE

Genus of annuals and perennials, grown for their attractive flowers. Fully hardy. Cultivars of L. × *superbum* are valued for their profusion of large daisy-like summer flowers. Some species are suitable for rock gardens. Needs full sun and well-drained soil. Propagate species by seed or division, cultivars by division only.
L. × superbum, syn. *Chrysanthemum maximum* of gardens, *C. × superbum* (Shasta daisy). ♀ **'Aglaia'** is a robust perennial. H 1m (3ft), S 60cm (2ft). Fully hardy. Large, daisy-like, semi-double, white flower heads are borne singly in summer. Has spoon-shaped, coarse, lobed, toothed leaves. Divide every 2 years. **'Elizabeth'** illus. p.242. **'Esther Read'** illus. p.285 **'Wirral Pride'** illus. p.243. ♀ **'Wirral Supreme'** is double with short, central florets.

LEUCHTENBERGIA

CACTACEAE

Genus of one species of perennial cactus. Looks like *Agave* in foliage, but its flowers, seed pods and seeds are similar to *Ferocactus*. Tubercles eventually form on short, rough, woody stems. Frost tender, min. 6°C (43°F). Needs full sun and very well-drained soil. Keep completely dry in winter; water sparingly from spring to autumn. Propagate by seed in spring or summer.
L. principis illus. p.482.

LEUCOCORYNE

LILIACEAE/ALLIACEAE

Genus of spring-flowering bulbs with loose heads of flattish flowers. Half hardy. Needs sun and well-drained soil. Plant in autumn, water when in growth, and keep almost dry when dormant in summer. Propagate by seed or offsets in autumn.
L. ixioides illus. p.429.

LEUCOGENES
New Zealand edelweiss

COMPOSITAE/ASTERACEAE

Genus of evergreen, woody-based perennials, grown mainly for their foliage. Is excellent for alpine houses in areas where summers are cool. Frost to half hardy. Needs sun and gritty, well-drained, peaty soil. Resents winter wet and may be difficult to grow. Propagate by seed when fresh or by softwood cuttings in late spring or early summer.
L. grandiceps illus. p.401.
L. leontopodium, syn. *Raoulia leontopodium (*North Island edelweiss). Evergreen, rosetted perennial. H and S 12cm (5in). Half hardy. Has oblong to oval, overlapping, silvery-white to yellowish leaves. In early summer has up to 15 small, star-shaped, woolly, silvery-white flower heads surrounded by thick, felted, white bracts.

LEUCOJUM
syn. ACIS
Snowflake

AMARYLLIDACEAE

Genus of bulbs, grown for their pendent, bell-shaped, white or pink flowers in autumn or spring. Fully to frost hardy. Some species prefer a moist, partially shaded site, others do best in sun and well-drained soil. Propagate by division in spring or early autumn or by seed in autumn.
L. aestivum illus. p.408.
♀ ***L. autumnale*** illus. p.453.
L. roseum. Early autumn-flowering bulb. H to 10cm (4in), S 2.5–5cm (1–2in). Frost hardy. Slender stems bear usually solitary, pale pink flowers, 1cm (½in) long. Thread-like, erect, basal leaves appear with, or just after, flowers. Prefers sun and well-drained soil.
♀ ***L. vernum*** illus. p.442.

LEUCOPHYTA
Cushion bush

COMPOSITAE/ASTERACEAE

Genus of annuals, evergreen perennials and small shrubs, often grown annually from cuttings and used as summer bedding. Frost tender, min. 7–10°C (45–50°F). Requires well-drained soil and full light. Water containerized plants moderately when in full growth, sparingly at other times. Remove stem tips of young plants to promote a bushy habit. Propagate by semi-ripe cuttings in late summer. Botrytis may be troublesome if plants are kept too cool and damp in winter.
L. brownii, syn. *Calocephalus brownii*, illus. p.171.

Leucopogon colensoi. See *Cyathodes colensoi.*

LEUCOSPERMUM

PROTEACEAE

Genus of evergreen shrubs, grown for their flower heads. Frost tender, min. 7–10°C (45–50°F). Requires full light and sandy, well-drained soil with few phosphates and nitrates. Water containerized specimens moderately when in growth, sparingly at other times. Propagate by seed in spring. Is not easy to cultivate long term under glass; good ventilation is essential.
L. cordifolium, syn. *L. nutans.* Evergreen, rounded to spreading, well-branched shrub. H and S 1.2m (4ft). Elongated, heart-shaped, blue-grey leaves each have a 3-toothed tip. In summer, very slender, tubular, brick-red to orange flowers, each with a long style, are borne in tight heads that resemble single blooms.
L. nutans. See *L. cordifolium*.
L. reflexum illus. p.127.

LEUCOTHÖE

ERICACEAE

Genus of evergreen, semi-evergreen or deciduous shrubs, grown for their white flowers and their foliage. Fully to frost hardy. Needs shade or semi-shade and moist, peaty, acid soil. Propagate by semi-ripe cuttings in summer.
L. catesbaei of gardens. See *L. fontanesiana*.
♀ ***L. fontanesiana***, syn. *L. catesbaei* of gardens, *L. walteri*. Evergreen, arching shrub. H 1.5m (5ft), S 3m (10ft). Fully hardy. Lance-shaped, leathery, glossy, dark green leaves have long points and sharp teeth. Short racemes of small, urn-shaped, white flowers are borne beneath shoots from mid- to late spring. **'Rainbow'** illus. p.173. **SCARLETTA ('Zeblid')** has dark red-purple young foliage, which turns dark green, then bronze in winter. **'Zeblid'** see *L.f.* SCARLETTA.
L. keiskei. Evergreen shrub with erect or semi-procumbent stems. H 15–60cm (6–24in), S 30–60cm (12–24in). Frost hardy. Oval, thin-textured, glossy, dark green leaves have a red flush when young and a leathery appearance. Bears pendent, urn-shaped, white flowers from leaf axils in summer. Is good for a rock garden, peat bed or alpine house. Prefers mild, damp climates.
L. walteri. See *L. fontanesiana*.

LEWISIA

PORTULACACEAE

Genus of perennials, some of which are evergreen, with rosettes of succulent leaves and deep tap roots. Most species are good in alpine houses, troughs and rock gardens. Fully to frost hardy. Evergreen species need semi-shaded, humus-rich, moist or well-drained, neutral to acid soil and resent water in their rosettes at all times. Herbaceous species shed their leaves in summer and require sun and well-drained, neutral to acid soil; dry off after flowering. Propagate herbaceous species by seed in spring or autumn, evergreen species by seed in spring or by offsets in summer. Seed of *L.* Cotyledon Hybrids may not come true.
L. columbiana. Evergreen, basal-rosetted perennial. H 15cm (6in) or more, S 10–15cm (4–6in). Fully hardy. Bears thick, narrowly oblong, flat, glossy, green leaves and, in early summer, terminal sprays of small, cup-shaped, deeply veined, white to deep pink flowers. Prefers moist soil.
***L.* Cotyledon Hybrids** illus. p.366.
***L.* 'George Henley'** illus. p.364.
L. nevadensis. Loose, basal-rosetted perennial. H 4–6cm (1½–2½in), S 8cm (3in). Fully hardy. In summer, large, almost stemless, cup-shaped, white flowers appear above small clusters of strap-shaped, dark green leaves.
L. rediviva [pink form] illus. p.391; [white form] illus. p.385.
♀ ***L. tweedyi*** illus. p.376.

Leycesteria

CAPRIFOLIACEAE

Genus of deciduous shrubs, grown for their showy flower clusters. Frost to half hardy. Needs full sun and fertile, well-drained soil. Propagate by softwood cuttings in summer or by seed or division in autumn.

L. formosa (Himalayan honeysuckle). Deciduous, upright shrub. H and S 2m (6ft). Frost hardy. Has blue-green shoots and slender, oval, dark green leaves. In summer and early autumn, small, funnel-shaped, white flowers are produced at tip of each pendent cluster of purplish-red bracts and are followed by spherical, reddish-purple fruits. Cut weak shoots to ground level in early spring.

Leymus

GRAMINEAE/POACEAE

See also GRASSES, BAMBOOS, RUSHES and SEDGES.

L. arenarius, syn. *Elymus arenarius* (Lyme grass). Vigorous, spreading, herbaceous, rhizomatous, perennial grass. H to 1.5m (5ft), S indefinite. Fully hardy. Has broad, glaucous leaves. Has stout, terminal spikes of greyish-green flowers on erect stems in late summer. Is useful for binding coastal dunes.

Liatris
Gay feathers

COMPOSITAE/ASTERACEAE

Genus of summer-flowering perennials with thickened, corm-like rootstocks. Fully hardy. Prefers sun and well-drained soil. Propagate by division in spring.

L. callilepis of gardens. See *L. spicata*.

L. pycnostachya (Kansas gay feather). Clump-forming perennial. H 1.2m (4ft), S 30cm (1ft). In summer bears tall spikes of clustered, feathery, mauve-pink flower heads. Grass-like, dark green leaves form basal tufts.

L. spicata, syn. *L. callilepis* of gardens, illus. p.289.

Libertia

IRIDACEAE

Genus of rhizomatous perennials, grown for their foliage, decorative seed pods and flowers. Frost to half hardy. Needs a sheltered, sunny or partially shaded site and well-drained soil. Propagate by division in spring or by seed in autumn or spring.

L. grandiflora illus. p.241.

L. ixioides. Clump-forming, rhizomatous perennial. H and S 60cm (24in). Frost hardy. Produces panicles of saucer-shaped, white flowers in summer. Grass-like, dark green leaves turn orange-brown during winter.

Libocedrus chilensis. See *Austrocedrus chilensis*.

Libocedrus decurrens. See *Calocedrus decurrens*.

Libonia floribunda. See *Justicia rizzinii*.

Ligularia

COMPOSITAE/ASTERACEAE

Genus of perennials, grown for their foliage and large, daisy-like flower heads. Fully to half hardy. Grow in sun or semi-shade and in moist but well-drained soil. Propagate by division in spring or by seed in autumn or spring. Is prone to damage by slugs and snails.

***L. clivorum* 'Desdemona'.** See *L. dentata* 'Desdemona'.

♀ ***L. dentata* 'Desdemona',** syn. *L. clivorum* 'Desdemona'. Compact, clump-forming perennial. H 1.2m (4ft), S 60cm (2ft). Fully hardy. Has heart-shaped, long-stalked, leathery, basal, dark brownish-green leaves, almost mahogany beneath, and bears terminal clusters of large, daisy-like, vivid orange flower heads on branching stems from mid- to late summer.

♀ ***L.* 'Gregynog Gold'.** Clump-forming perennial. H 2m (6ft), S 60cm (2ft). Fully hardy. Leaves are large, heart-shaped and deep green. Conical panicles of daisy-like, orange-yellow flower heads are borne from mid- to late summer.

L. przewalskii, syn. *Senecio przewalskii*, illus. p.227.

L. stenocephala illus. p.227.

L. tussilaginea. See *Farfugium japonicum*.

Ligustrum
Privet

OLEACEAE

Genus of deciduous, semi-evergreen or evergreen shrubs and trees, grown for their foliage and, in some species, flowers. Fully to frost hardy. Requires sun or semi-shade, the variegated forms doing best in full sun. Thrives on any well-drained soil, including chalky soil. All except *L. lucidum* occasionally need cutting back in mid-spring to restrict growth. Propagate by semi-ripe cuttings in summer. All parts may cause severe discomfort if ingested.

L. japonicum (Japanese privet). Evergreen, bushy, dense shrub. H 3m (10ft), S 2.5m (8ft). Frost hardy. Has oval, glossy, very dark green leaves and, from mid-summer to early autumn, large, conical panicles of small, tubular, white flowers with 4 lobes. **'Coriaceum'** see *L.j.* 'Rotundifolium'

'Rotundifolium', syn. *L.j.* 'Coriaceum', is slow-growing, with a dense mass of rounded, leathery leaves.

♀ ***L. lucidum*** (Chinese privet). Evergreen, upright shrub or tree. H 10m (30ft), S 8m (25ft). Frost hardy. Bears large, oval, glossy, dark green leaves. Produces large panicles of small, tubular, white flowers, with 4 lobes, in late summer and early autumn. ♀ **'Excelsum Superbum'** illus. p.123.

L. ovalifolium illus. p.122.

♀ **'Aureum'** is a vigorous, evergreen or semi-evergreen, upright, dense shrub. H 4m (12ft), S 3m (10ft). Fully hardy. Leaves are oval, glossy and mid-green, broadly edged with bright yellow. Dense panicles of small, rather unpleasantly scented, tubular, white flowers, with 4 lobes, appear in mid-summer and are succeeded by spherical, black fruits. Cut back hedges to 30cm (1ft) after planting and prune hard for first 2 years; then trim as necessary during the growing season.

L. sinense illus. p.114.

***L.* 'Vicaryi'**, syn. *L.* × *vicaryi*, illus. p.149.

***L.* × *vicaryi*.** See *L.* 'Vicaryi'.

L. vulgare. Deciduous or semi-evergreen, bushy shrub. H and S 3m (10ft). Fully hardy. Leaves are narrowly lance-shaped and dark green. Produces panicles of small, strongly scented, tubular, white flowers, with 4 lobes, from early to mid-summer, then spherical, black fruits. Cut back hedges to 30cm (1ft) after planting and prune hard for first 2 years; then trim as necessary during the growing season. **'Aureum'**, H and S 2m (6ft), has golden-yellow foliage.

Lijiang spruce. See *Picea likiangensis*.

Lilac. See *Syringa*.

Himalayan. See *Syringa emodi*.

Persian. See *Melia azedarach*, illus. p.72; *Syringa* × *persica*, illus. p.116.

Lilac (continued)

Rouen. See *Syringa* × *chinensis*.

St Vincent. See *Solanum seaforthianum*, illus. p.202.

Vine. See *Hardenbergia violacea*.

Lilium
Lily

LILIACEAE

Genus of mainly summer-flowering bulbs, grown for their often fragrant, brightly coloured flowers. Each fleshy-scaled bulb produces one unbranched, leafy stem, in some cases with annual roots in lower part. Mostly lance-shaped or linear leaves, to 22cm (9in) long, are scattered or in whorls, sometimes with bulbils in axils. Flowers, usually several per stem, are mainly trumpet- to bowl-shaped or with the 6 petals strongly reflexed to form a turkscap shape. (Petals of *Lilium* are known botanically as perianth segments.) Three categories of flower size – small, medium and large – are used in the descriptions below. For turkscap, bowl-, cup- and star-shaped flowers: small is up to 5cm (2in) across; medium is 5–7cm (2–3in) across; large is over 7cm (3in) across. For trumpet- and funnel-shaped flowers: small is up to 7cm (3in) long; medium is 7–10cm (3–4in) long; large is over 10cm (4in) long. Each plant has a spread of up to 30cm (12in). Frost hardy, unless otherwise stated. Needs sun and any well-drained soil, unless otherwise stated. Propagate by seed in autumn or spring, by bulb scales in summer or by stem bulbils (where present) in autumn. Virus and fungal diseases (such as botrytis) and lily beetle may cause problems. Lilies are classified into 9 divisions. See also feature panel pp.416–19.

Division 1 (Asiatic hybrids)
These lilies are derived from various Asiatic species, including *L. bulbiferum*, *L. cernuum*, *L. concolor*, *L. davidii*, *L. lancifolium* and *L. maculatum*. The flowers are borne in racemes or umbels, and are usually unscented. The leaves are narrowly ovate and arranged alternatively. There are 3 subdivisions: **1a)** upward-facing flowers; **1b)** outward-facing flowers; **1c)** pendent flowers.

Division 2 (Martagon hybrids)
Derived primarily from *L. hansonii* and *L. martagon*, these lilies produce racemes of turkscap, sometimes scented flowers, and have whorls of elliptic leaves.

Division 3 (Candidum hybrids)
Derived from *L. candicum* and other European species, except *L. martagon*, these lilies produce sometimes scented, mostly turkscap flowers, singly or in umbels or racemes. Leaves are elliptic, and spirally arranged or scattered.

Division 4 (American hybrids)
Derived from American species, these lilies bear racemes of sometimes scented, mostly turkscap, but occasionally funnel-shaped flowers, and have whorls of lance-shaped to elliptic leaves.

Division 5 (Longiflorum hybrids)
Derived from *L. formosanum* and *L. longiflorum*, these lilies bear racemes or umbels of large, often sweetly scented, trumpet- or funnel-shaped flowers, sometimes only 2 or 3 per stem. Leaves are linear to narrowly lance-shaped, and scattered.

Division 6 (Trumpet and Aurelian hybrids)
Derived from Asiatic species, including *L. regale*, *L. henryi* and *L. sargentiae*, these lilies bear racemes or umbels of usually scented flowers. Leaves are elliptic to linear, and alternate or spirally arranged. There are 4 subdivisions: **6a)** trumpet-shaped flowers; **6b)** bowl-shaped flowers; **6c)** very shallowly bowl-shaped flowers, some almost flat; **6d)** distinctly recurved flowers.

Division 7 (Oriental hybrids)
Derived from E. Asian species, such as *L. auratum*, *L. japonicum* and *L. speciosum*, as well as their hybrids with *L. henryi*, these lilies have flowers borne in racemes or panicles, and are often scented. Leaves are lance-shaped and alternate. There are 4 subdivisions: **7a)** trumpet-shaped flowers; **7b)** bowl-shaped flowers; **7c)** flat or very shallowly bowl-shaped flowers; **7d)** turkscap or various recurved flowers.

Division 8. Other hybrids

Division 9. All true species.

L. amabile. Summer-flowering Division 9 lily with stem roots. H 30cm–1m (1–3ft). Scattered leaves are lance-shaped. Has up to 10 unpleasant-smelling, nodding, turkscap, black-spotted, red flowers; each petal is 5–5.5cm (2–2¼in) long.

***L.* 'Amber Gold'** illus. p.418. Summer-flowering Division 1c lily. H 1.2–1.5m (4–5ft). Has medium-sized, nodding, turkscap, deep yellow flowers, each with maroon spots in throat.

***L.* 'Angela North'** illus. p.417. Mid-summer flowering Division 1c lily. H to 1m (3ft). Has medium-sized, slightly fragrant, dark red flowers, spotted darker red, that have strongly recurved petals.

♀ ***L.* 'Apollo'** illus. p.419. Summer-flowering Division 1a lily. H 1.2m (4ft). Has downward-facing, turkscap, pale orange flowers with strongly reflexed petals.

L. 'Arena' illus. p.416. Vigorous, summer-flowering Division 7b lily. H 1.25m (4ft). Has large, outward-facing, bowl-shaped to slightly trumpet-shaped, recurving, greenish- to yellowish-white flowers, with deep red central veining on the insides and yellow-green throats with deep red spots.
L. auratum (Golden-rayed lily of Japan). Summer- and autumn-flowering Division 9 lily with stem roots. H 60cm–1.5m (2–5ft). Has long, scattered, lance-shaped leaves. Produces up to 10, sometimes more, fragrant, outward-facing, widely bowl-shaped, white flowers; each petal is 12–18cm (5–7in) long with a central, red or yellow band and often red or yellow spots. Requires semi-shade and neutral to acid soil. var. ***platyphyllum*** (illus. p.416) has broader leaves; petals have a central, yellow band and fewer spots.
L. 'Black Beauty' illus. p.417. Summer-flowering Division 7d lily. H 1.5–2m (5–6ft). Has medium-sized, outward-facing, flattish, green-centred, very deep red flowers with recurved, white-margined petals.
L. 'Black Dragon'. Summer-flowering Division 6a lily. H 1.5m (5ft). Has large, outward-facing, trumpet-shaped flowers with dark purplish-red outsides and white insides.
L. 'Black Magic' illus. p.416. Summer-flowering Division 6a lily. H 1.2–2m (4–6ft). Scented, outward-facing, trumpet-shaped flowers are purplish-brown outside and white inside.
L. 'Bonfire'. Late summer-flowering Division 7b lily. H 1.2–1.5m (4–5ft). Produces outward-facing, bowl-shaped flowers with broad petals, white outside flushed with pink, and dark crimson inside spotted paler crimson.
L. 'Bright Star' illus. p.416. Summer-flowering Division 6b lily. H 1–1.5m (3–5ft). Has large, flattish, white flowers; petals have recurved tips and a central, orange streak inside.
L. 'Brocade' illus. p.418. Early summer-flowering Division 2 lily. H 1.5m (5ft). Has nodding, turkscap, orange-yellow flowers, suffused rosy-pink, with dark purple-red spots on the inner surfaces of the recurved petals.
L. 'Bronwen North' illus. p.417. Mid-summer-flowering Division 1c lily. H to 1m (3ft). Each stem carries 7 or more medium-sized, slightly fragrant flowers with strongly recurving, pale mauve-pink petals, paler at the tips, and pale pink throats with dark spots and lines; nectaries are reddish-black.
L. 'Brushmarks' illus. p.419. Early summer-flowering Division 1a lily. H 1.35m (4½ft). Large, upward-facing, cup-shaped, orange flowers are green-throated. Petals each have deep red blotches and sometimes spots.
L. bulbiferum (Fire lily, Orange lily). Summer-flowering Division 9 lily with stem roots. H 40cm–1.5m (16in–5ft). Stem bears scattered, lance-shaped leaves and, usually, bulbils in leaf axils. Bears 1–5 or more upward-facing, shallowly cup-shaped, orange-red flowers. Each petal is 6–8.5cm (2½–3¼in) long and spotted black or deep red. var. ***croceum*** (illus. p.419) has orange flowers and does not normally bear bulbils.
L. 'California Gold' illus. p.418. Vigorous, summer-flowering Division 6a lily. H 1–1.2m (3–4ft). Produces sprays of outward-facing, trumpet- to bowl-shaped, deep lemon-yellow flowers, with the reverses of the gently recurving petals bronze-green.
L. canadense (Canada lily, Meadow lily, Wild yellow lily; illus. p.418). Summer-flowering Division 9 lily with stem roots. H to 1.5m (5ft). Narrowly to broadly lance-shaped leaves are mainly in whorls. Bears about 10 nodding, bell-shaped, yellow or red flowers; each petal is 5–8cm (2–3in) long, with dark red or purple spots in lower part.
♀ ***L. candidum*** (Madonna lily; illus. p.416). Summer-flowering Division 9 lily. H 1–2m (3–6ft). Flower stem bears scattered, lance-shaped leaves and 5–20 fragrant, outward-facing, broadly funnel-shaped, white flowers. Each petal is 5–8cm (2–3in) long with a yellow base and a slightly recurved tip. In autumn bears basal leaves, which remain throughout winter but die off as flowering stems mature. Prefers lime-rich soil.
L. carniolicum. See *L. pyrenaicum* subsp. *carniolicum*.
♀ **L. 'Casa Blanca'** illus. p.416. Late summer-flowering Division 7b lily. H 90cm (3ft). Large, waxy, white flowers, have yellowish-white midribs and violet-red nectaries.
L. cernuum. Summer-flowering Division 9 lily with stem roots. H to 60cm (2ft). Long, linear leaves are scattered. Produces 7–15 fragrant, nodding, turkscap flowers, usually pinkish-purple with purple spots. Each petal is 3.5–5cm (1½–2in) long.
L. chalcedonicum, syn. *L. heldreichii* (Scarlet turkscap lily; illus. p.419). Summer-flowering Division 9 lily with stem roots. H 50cm–1.5m (20in–5ft). Leaves are scattered and mostly lance-shaped, lower ones spreading, upper ones smaller and closer to stem. Bears up to 12 slightly scented, nodding, turkscap flowers with red or reddish-orange petals, each 5–7cm (2–3in) long.
L. 'Connecticut King' illus. p.418. Early to mid-summer-flowering Division 1a lily. H 1m (3ft). Flowers are medium-sized, upward-facing, cup-shaped and bright yellow.
L. 'Corsage' illus. p.417. Summer-flowering Division 1b lily. H 1.2m (4ft). Bears outward-facing, bowl-shaped flowers with recurved petals, pink-flushed outside and pink inside with white centres and maroon spots.
L. 'Côte d'Azur' illus. p.417. Summer-flowering Division 1a lily. H 40cm (16in). Strong stems bear deep rose-pink flowers with darker-spotted throats.
L. 'Cover Girl' illus. p.417. Summer to early autumn-flowering Division 7c lily. H 1.5–1.9m (5–6ft). Has very large, outward- or slightly downward-facing, soft pink flowers, with white at the tips of the gently recurved petals which are centrally banded deep pink and strongly red-spotted.
L. 'Crimson Pixie' illus. p.419. Early summer-flowering Division 1a lily. H 40cm (16in). Has umbels of upright, open bowl-shaped, unspotted, deep warm red-orange flowers. Is good as a pot plant.
L. × dalhansonii illus. p.417. Variable, summer-flowering Division 9 lily. H 1.5–2m (5–6ft). Has unpleasant-smelling, turkscap flowers that are chestnut brown or dark maroon with gold spots. **'Marhan'** see *L.* 'Marhan'.
L. davidii. Summer-flowering Division 9 lily with stem roots. H 1–1.4m (3–4½ft). Linear leaves are scattered. Produces 5–20 nodding, turkscap, red or reddish-orange flowers; each petal is 5–8cm (2–3in) long with dark purple spots. var. ***willmottiae*** (illus. p.419) differs in its slender, arching stems to 2m (6ft) and pendent flower stalks.
L. 'Destiny' illus. p.418. Early summer-flowering Division 1a lily. H 1–1.2m (3–4ft). Flowers are medium-sized, upward-facing, cup-shaped and yellow with brown spots.
L. duchartrei illus. p.416. Summer-flowering Division 9 lily. H 60cm–1m (2–3ft). Lance-shaped leaves are scattered up stems. Has up to 12 fragrant, nodding, turkscap, white flowers that are flushed purple outside and spotted deep purple inside.
L. 'Ed', syn. *L.* 'Mr Ed' illus. p.416. Summer to early autumn-flowering Division 7 lily. H 40cm (16in). Has large, outward-facing, bowl-shaped, greenish-white flowers, with the petals centrally banded pale yellow and flushed pale red, and dark red spots on one-third of each petal.
L. 'Enchantment' illus. p.419. Early summer-flowering Division 1a lily. H 1m (3ft). Produces medium-sized, upward-facing, cup-shaped, orange-red flowers with black-spotted throats.
L. 'Eros' illus. p.417. Mid-summer-flowering Division 1c lily. H 90cm–1.1m (3–3½ft). Produces small, unscented, turkscap, buff flowers.
L. Golden Clarion Group illus. p.418. Late spring to early summer-flowering bulb. H 1–2m (3–6ft). Has outward-facing, trumpet-shaped, pale to deep yellow flowers that may be flushed with reddish-purple outside.
♀ **L. Golden Splendor Group** illus. p.418. Vigorous, mid-summer-flowering, variable Division 6a lily with stem roots. H 1.2–2m (4–6ft). Produces large, shallowly trumpet-shaped, almost bowl-shaped flowers in shades of yellow with dark burgundy-red bands outside.
♀ **L.'Gran Cru'** illus. p.418. Early summer-flowering Division 1a lily. H 1.2m (4ft). Has upright, open bowl-shaped, vivid-yellow flowers, strongly red-suffused in the throats for about half the petal lengths, and with a few red spots at the base internally. Is good as a pot plant.
L. 'Gran Paradiso' illus. p.419. Mid-summer-flowering Division 1a lily. H 1m (3ft). Produces medium-sized, unscented, bowl-shaped, red flowers with slightly recurved petals.
L. hansonii illus. p.419. Summer-flowering Division 9 lily with stem roots. H 1–1.5m (3–5ft). Long leaves in whorls are lance-shaped to oval. Has 3–12 scented, nodding, turkscap, orange-yellow flowers. Each thick petal is 3–4cm (1¼–1½in) long with brown-purple spots towards base.
L. 'Harmony' illus. p.419. Summer-flowering Division 1a lily. H 50cm–1m (1½–3ft). Orange flowers are upward-facing, cup-shaped and spotted with maroon.
L. heldreichii. See *L. chalcedonicum*.
♀ ***L. henryi.*** Late summer-flowering Division 9 lily with stem roots. H 1–3m (3–10ft). Has scattered, lance-shaped leaves. Produces 5–20, sometimes up to 70, nodding, turkscap, orange flowers; petals are 6–8cm (2½–3in) long with dark spots and prominent warts towards bases. Prefers lime-rich soil.
L. Imperial Crimson Group. Late summer-flowering Division 7c lily. H 1.5m (5ft). Large, fragrant, flattish, deep crimson flowers have white throats and white-margined petals.
L. Imperial Gold Group illus. p.416. Summer-flowering Division 7c lily. H 2m (6ft). Bears large, fragrant, flattish, white flowers, spotted maroon, and with a yellow stripe up each petal centre.
L. 'Journey's End' illus. p.417. Late summer-flowering Division 7d lily. H 2m (6ft). Large, outward-facing, bowl-shaped, maroon-spotted, deep pink flowers have recurved petals, white at tips and edges.
L. 'Karen North' illus. p.419. Summer-flowering Division 1c lily. H to 1.4m (4½ft). Turkscap flowers are medium-sized, downward-facing, with orange-pink petals sparsely spotted with deep pink.
L. 'Lady Bowes Lyon' illus. p.419. Summer-flowering Division 1c lily. H 1–1.2m (3–4ft). Downward-facing, black-spotted, rich red flowers have reflexed petals.
L. lancifolium, syn. *L. tigrinum* (Tiger lily). Summer- to early autumn-flowering Division 9 lily with stem roots. H 60cm–1.5m (2–5ft). Produces long, scattered, narrowly lance-shaped leaves. Produces 5–10, sometimes up to 40, nodding, turkscap, pink- to red-orange flowers; each petal is 7–10cm (3–4in) long and spotted with purple. var. ***flaviflorum*** has yellow flowers. Vigorous ♀ var. ***splendens*** (illus. p.419) bears larger, brighter red-orange flowers.
L. lankongense illus. p.417. Summer-flowering Division 9 lily with stem roots. H to 1.2m (4ft). Leaves are scattered and lance-shaped. Has up to 15 scented, nodding, turkscap, pink flowers. Petals, each 4–6.5cm (1½–2½in) long with a central, green stripe and red-purple spots mainly on edges, are often mauve-flushed. Needs partial shade in warm areas.
L. leichtlinii illus. p.418. Summer-flowering Division 9 lily with stem roots. H to 1.2m (4ft). Scattered leaves are linear to narrowly lance-shaped. Produces 1–6 nodding, turkscap, yellow flowers; each petal is 6–8.5cm (2½–3¼in) long with dark reddish-purple spots. Needs semi-shade.
L. 'Limelight' illus. p.418. Moderately robust, mid-summer-flowering Division 9 lily. H 1–2m (3–6ft). Large, fragrant, slightly pendent, trumpet-shaped, lime-yellow flowers are flushed with green, especially outside.
L. 'Lime Star' illus. p.416. Vigorous, summer-flowering Division 7a/b lily. H 1.2m (4ft). Has outward-facing, bowl-shaped to flat flowers, with recurving, white petals. Each petal is strongly banded bright greenish-yellow

and has slightly ruffled margins.

***L.* 'Lollypop'** illus. p.417. Early summer-flowering Division 1a lily. H 60cm (2ft). Has upright, open bowl-shaped, white flowers, with the upper parts of the gently recurving petals strongly suffused deep red.

♀ ***L. longiflorum*** (Bermuda lily, Easter lily, White trumpet lily; illus. p.416). Summer-flowering Division 9 lily with stem roots. H 30cm–1m (1–3ft). Leaves are scattered and lance-shaped. Produces 1–6 fragrant, outward-facing, funnel-shaped, white flowers. Each petal is 13–20cm (5–8in) long with slightly recurved tips.

***L.* 'Luxor'** illus. p.418. Vigorous, summer-flowering Division 1b lily. H 90cm–1.5m (3–5ft). Produces large, outward-facing, bowl-shaped, bright yellow flowers, slightly darker yellow and speckled with dark red spots on the lower half of each petal.

L. mackliniae (Manipur lily; illus. p.417). Late spring- to summer-flowering Division 9 lily with stem roots. H to 40cm (16in). Small, narrowly lance-shaped to narrowly oval leaves are scattered or whorled near top of stem. Has 1–6 usually nodding, broadly bell-shaped, purplish-pink flowers; each petal is 4.5–5cm (1¾–2in) long. Needs semi-shade.

L. maculatum, syn. *L. thunbergianum.* Summer-flowering Division 9 lily with stem roots. H to 60cm (2ft). Fully hardy. Scattered leaves are lance-shaped or oval. Has 1–6 upward-facing, cup-shaped, yellow, orange or red flowers with darker spots; each petal is 8–10cm (3–4in) long.

***L.* 'Magic Pink'** illus. p.417. Early summer-flowering Division 7b lily. H 1–1.2m (3–4ft). Large flowers are satin pink with darker pink spots.

***L.* 'Marhan'**, syn. *L.* × *dalhansonii* 'Marhan'. Early summer-flowering Division 2 lily. H 1.2–2m (4–6ft). Medium-sized, nodding, turkscap, deep orange flowers are spotted red-brown.

♀ ***L. martagon*** (Martagon lily; illus. p.417). Summer-flowering Division 9 lily with stem roots. H 1–2m (3–6ft). Fully hardy. Has lance-shaped to oval leaves in whorls and up to 50 scented, nodding, turkscap flowers. Petals are 3–4.5cm (1¼–1¾in) long and pink or purple, often with darker spots. ♀ var. ***album*** (illus. p.416) has pure white flowers.

L. medeoloides illus. p.418. Summer-flowering Division 9 lily. H to 75cm (2½ft). Has lance-shaped leaves and up to 10 turkscap, apricot to orange-red flowers, usually with darker spots.

L. monadelphum, syn. *L. szovitsianum* illus. p.418. Summer-flowering Division 9 lily with stem roots. H 50cm–2m (1½–6ft). Has scattered, lance-shaped to oval leaves. Produces usually 1–5, sometimes up to 30, scented, nodding, turkscap, yellow flowers, usually with deep red or purple spots inside. Each petal is 6–10cm (2½–4in) long.

***L.* 'Mona Lisa'** illus. p.416. Summer-flowering Division 7b/c lily. H 45cm (18in). Has large, shallowly bowl-shaped to flat, light reddish-purple flowers, with ivory-white margins suffused red, greenish petal tips, dark red spots on the lower half of each petal and light green throats.

***L.* 'Mont Blanc'** illus. p.416. Summer-flowering Division 1a lily. H 90cm (3ft). Has large, upward-facing, creamy-white flowers, spotted with brown.

***L.* 'Montreux'** illus. p.417. Mid-summer-flowering Division 1a lily. H 1m (3ft). Bears about 8 medium-sized, pink flowers with darker pink midribs; orange-pink throats are spotted with brown.

***L.* 'Mr Ed'.** See *L.* 'Ed'.

L. nanum, syn. *Nomocharis nana.* Late spring- or summer-flowering Division 9 lily. H 6–45cm (2½–18in). Scattered leaves are linear. Bears a usually nodding, broadly bell-shaped, purplish-pink flower, with 4.5–5cm (1¾–2in) long petals. Needs partial shade. var. ***flavidum*** has pale yellow flowers.

L. nepalense illus. p.417. Summer-flowering Division 9 lily with stem roots. H 70cm–1m (28–36in). Has scattered, lance-shaped leaves. Produces often unpleasant-smelling, nodding, funnel-shaped, greenish-white or greenish-yellow flowers, each with a dark reddish-purple base inside and petals to 15cm (6in) long.

***L.* 'Olivia'** illus. p.416. Late summer-flowering Division 7b lily. H 75cm–1m (2½–3ft). Has medium-sized, scented, slightly reflexed, bowl-shaped, pure white flowers.

***L.* Olympic Group** illus. p.416. Vigorous, summer-flowering Division 6a lily. H 1.2–2m (4–6ft). Produces racemes of up to 15 large, sweetly scented, trumpet-shaped flowers ranging from white, greenish-white, cream and yellow to pink and purple, often yellow in the throats. Petals are flushed pink or purplish-red on the outside.

***L.* 'Orange Pixie'** illus. p.419. Early summer-flowering Division 1a lily. H 25–30cm (10–12in). Has upright umbels of open bowl-shaped, deep golden-orange flowers. Is good as a pot plant.

♀ ***L. pardalinum*** (Leopard lily, Panther lily; illus. p.419). Summer-flowering Division 9 lily. H 2–3m (6–10ft). Long, narrowly elliptic leaves are mainly in whorls. Has up to 10 often scented, nodding, turkscap flowers. Each petal is 5–9cm (2–3½in) long with red, upper parts. Orange, lower parts have maroon spots, some of which are encircled with yellow.

♀ ***L.* Pink Perfection Group** illus. p.417. Summer-flowering Division 6a lily with stout stems. H 1.5–2m (5–6ft). Produces large, scented, slightly nodding, trumpet-shaed flowers, which are deep purplish-red or purple-pink, with bright orange anthers.

***L.* 'Pink Tiger'** illus. p.417. Vigorous, late summer-flowering Division 1b lily. H 1.2m (4ft). Produces medium-sized, unscented, turkscap, pink flowers.

L. pomponium illus. p.419. Slender, stem-rooting, summer-flowering Division 9 lily with green stems that are spotted purple on the lower halves. H1m (3ft). Has scattered, linear, mid-green leaves with silver-hairy margins. Produces racemes of up to 6 (rarely up to 10) pungently scented, pendent, turkscap, sealing-wax-red flowers, generally with black spots and streaks in the throats. Prefers alkaline soil in full sun or partial shade.

L. ponticum. See *L. pyrenaicum* subsp. *ponticum*.

♀ ***L. pumilum***, syn. *L. tenuifolium.* Summer-flowering Division 9 lily with stem roots. H 15cm–1m (6–36in). Small, scattered leaves are linear. Produces usually up to 7 but occasionally up to 30 slightly scented, nodding, turkscap flowers; each petal is 3–3.5cm (1¼–1½in) long and scarlet with or without basal, black spots.

L. pyrenaicum (Yellow turkscap lily; illus. p.418). Late spring to early summer-flowering Division 9 lily often with stem roots. H 30cm–1.35m (1–4½ft). Has scattered, linear to narrowly elliptic, hairless leaves. Produces up to 12 unpleasant-smelling, nodding, turkscap flowers. Each petal is 4–6.5cm (1½–2½in) long and yellow or green-yellow with deep purple spots and lines. subsp. ***carniolicum*** (syn. *L. carniolicum*) has red- or orange-spotted flowers. Leaves may be hairless or downy. subsp. ***ponticum*** (syn. *L. ponticum*) bears deep yellow flowers, densely lined and spotted with red-brown or purple; leaves are downy beneath. var. ***rubrum*** (illus. p.419) has orange-red or dark red flowers.

***L.* 'Red Carpet'** illus. p.419. Early summer-flowering Division 1a lily. H 30cm (1ft). Has upright umbels of open bowl-shaped, unspotted, deep red flowers. Is good as a pot plant.

♀ ***L. regale*** (Regal lily; illus. p.416). Summer-flowering Division 9 lily with stem roots. H 50cm–2m (20in–6ft). Linear leaves are scattered. Produces up to 25 fragrant, outward-facing, funnel-shaped flowers. Petals are each 12–15cm (5–6in) long, white inside with a yellow base and pinkish-purple outside. **'Royal Gold'** see *L.* 'Royal Gold'.

***L.* 'Roma'** illus. p.418. Early summer-flowering Division 1a lily. H 1.5m (5ft). Green buds open to cream flowers that sometimes age to pale greenish-yellow.

***L.* 'Rosemary North'** illus. p.418. Mid- to late summer-flowering Division 1c lily. H to 1m (3ft). Produces 12 or more medium-sized, slightly fragrant, rich orange flowers that sometimes have darker spots.

***L.* 'Rosita'** illus. p.417. Early summer-flowering Division 1a lily. H 75cm (2½ft).Has umbels of upright, open bowl-shaped, green-centred, blush-pink flowers, with slightly recurving petals.

L. rosthornii illus. p.418. Vigorous, stem-rooting, clump-forming, summer-flowering Division 9 lily. H 40–100cm (16–39in). Has long, scattered, lance-shaped leaves on the lower part of the stem, the upper stem leaves being much shorter and oval in shape. Produces up to 9 nodding, turkscap, orange or orange-yellow flowers. Strongly recurved, channelled petals have green central bands and purple-red basal spots.

***L.* 'Royal Gold'**, syn. *L. regale* 'Royal Gold' illus. p.416. Vigorous, summer-flowering Division 9 lily. H 1.2–1.5m (4–5ft). Has clusters of large, outward-facing, trumpet-shaped flowers, mid-yellow inside and purple-brown outside.

L. rubellum illus. p.417. Early summer-flowering Division 9 lily with stem roots. H 30–80cm (12–32in). Has scattered, narrowly oval leaves and up to 9 scented, outward-facing, broadly funnel-shaped, pink flowers with dark red spots at bases; each petal is 6–8cm (2½–3in) long.

***L.* 'Shuksan'.** Summer-flowering Division 4 lily. H 1.2–2m (4–6ft). Medium-sized, nodding, turkscap, yellowish-orange flowers are flushed red at petal tips and sparsely spotted with black.

L. speciosum. Late summer-flowering Division 9 lily with stem roots. H 1–1.7m (3–5½ft). Has long, scattered, broadly lance-shaped leaves. Produces up to 12 scented, nodding, turkscap, white or pink flowers; each petal is up to 10cm (4in) long, with pink or crimson spots. Requires neutral to acid soil. var. ***album*** has white flowers and purple stems. Flowers of var. ***rubrum*** (illus. p.417) are carmine, stems are purple.

***L.* 'Star Gazer'** illus. p.417. Late summer-flowering Division 7c lily. H 90cm (3ft). Large, fragrant, rich crimson flowers are spotted maroon.

***L.* 'Sterling Star'** illus. p.416. Summer-flowering Division 1a lily. H 1–1.2m (3–4ft). Has large, upward-facing, cup-shaped, white flowers with tiny, brown spots.

L. superbum (Swamp lily, Turkscap lily; illus. p.418). Late summer- to early autumn-flowering Division 9 lily with stem roots. H 1.5–3m (5–10ft). Lance-shaped to elliptic leaves are mainly in whorls. Bears up to 40 nodding, turkscap, orange flowers. Each petal is 6–10cm (2½–4in) long, with a green base inside and usually flushed red and spotted maroon. Requires neutral to acid soil.

L. szovitsianum. See *L. monadelphum*.

L. tenuifolium. See *L. pumilum*.

♀ ***L.* × *testaceum*** (Nankeen lily; illus, p.416). Summer-flowering Division 9 lily. H 1–1.5m (3–5ft). Has scattered, linear, often twisted leaves. Produces 6–12 fragrant, nodding, turkscap, light orange to brownish-yellow flowers; each petal is 8cm (3in) long, usually with reddish spots inside.

L. thunbergianum. See *L. maculatum*.

L. tigrinum. See *L. lancifolium*.

L. tsingtauense illus. p.419. Summer-flowering Division 9 lily with stem roots. H 1m (3ft). Lance-shaped leaves are mainly in whorls. Produces 1–5 upward-facing, cup-shaped, orange to orange-red flowers; petals are up to 5cm (2in) long and spotted with maroon.

L. wallichianum. Late summer- to autumn-flowering Division 9 lily with stem roots. H to 2m (6ft). Half hardy. Long, scattered leaves are linear or lance-shaped. Bears 1–4 fragrant, outward-facing, funnel-shaped, white or cream flowers that are green or yellow towards bases. Each petal is 15–30cm (6–12in) long.

L. wigginsii illus. p.418. Stem-rooting, mid-summer-flowering Division 9 lily with hairless stems. H 90cm–1.2m (3–4ft). Linear-lance-shaped, deep green leaves are scattered and in 2–4 whorls roughly halfway up the stems. Produces few-flowered racemes of unscented, pendent, turkscap, deep yellow flowers, with purple spots. Needs moist acid soil and partial shade.

Lily. See *Lilium.*
African. See *Agapanthus africanus.*
Arum. See *Zantedeschia aethiopica.*
Atamasco. See *Zephyranthes atamasco.*
August. See *Hosta plantaginea*, illus. p.299.
Aztec. See *Sprekelia formosissima*, illus. p.429.
Belladonna. See *Amaryllis belladonna*, illus. p.424.
Bermuda. See *Lilium longiflorum*, illus. p.416.
Blood. See *Haemanthus coccineus*, illus. p.451.
Boat. See *Tradescantia spathacea.*
Canada. See *Lilium canadense.*
Chinese-lantern. See *Sandersonia aurantiaca*, illus. p.439.
Dwarf white wood. See *Trillium nivale.*
Easter. See *Lilium longiflorum*, illus. p.416.
Fire. See *Lilium bulbiferum.*
Flax. See *Dianella.*
Foxtail. See *Eremurus.*
Giant. See *Cardiocrinum giganteum*, illus. p.410.
Giant pineapple. See *Eucomis pallidiflora*, illus. p.409.
Ginger. See *Hedychium.*
Globe. See *Calochortus albus*, illus. p.425.
Glory. See *Gloriosa superba.*
Golden arum. See *Zantedeschia elliottiana*, illus. p.414.
Golden spider. See *Lycoris aurea.*
Guernsey. See *Nerine sarniensis*, illus. p.440.
Jacobean. See *Sprekelia formosissima*, illus. p.429.
Josephine's. See *Brunsvigia josephinae.*
Kaffir. See *Schizostylis.*
Lent. See *Narcissus pseudonarcissus*, illus. p.434.
Leopard. See *Dieffenbachia; Lilium pardalinum*, illus. p.419.
Madonna. See *Lilium candidum*, illus. p.416.
Manipur. See *Lilium mackliniae*, illus. p.417.
Martagon. See *Lilium martagon*, illus. p.417.
May. See *Maianthemum.*
Meadow. See *Lilium canadense*, illus. p.418.
Nankeen. See *Lilium × testaceum*, illus. p.416.
Orange. See *Lilium bulbiferum.*
Painted wood. See *Trillium undulatum.*
Panther. See *Lilium pardalinum*, illus. p.419.
Peace. See *Spathiphyllum wallisii*, illus. p.312.
Plantain. See *Hosta.*
Rain. See *Zephyranthes.*
Red spider. See *Lycoris radiata*, illus. p.436.
Regal. See *Lilium regale*, illus. p.416.
Rienga. See *Arthropodium cirratum.*
Rock. See *Arthropodium cirratum.*
Scarlet turkscap. See *Lilium chalcedonicum*, illus. p.419.
Sea. See *Pancratium maritimum.*
St Bernard's. See *Anthericum liliago*, illus. p.286.
St Bruno's. See *Paradisea liliastrum.*
Swamp. See *Lilium superbum*, illus. p.418; *Saururus cernuus*, illus. p.463.
Tiger. See *Lilium lancifolium.*
Toad. See *Tricyrtis.*
Torch. See *Kniphofia.*
Turkscap. See *Lilium superbum*, illus. p.418.
Voodoo. See *Sauromatum venosum*, illus. p.429.
Water. See *Nymphaea.*
White ginger. See *Hedychium coronarium.*
White trumpet. See *Lilium longiflorum*, illus. p.416.
Wild yellow. See *Lilium canadense*, illus. p.418.
Wood. See *Trillium.*
Yellow pond. See *Nuphar advena.*
Yellow turkscap. See *Lilium pyrenaicum*, illus. p.418.

Lily of Japan, Golden-rayed. See *Lilium auratum.*
Lily tree. See *Magnolia denudata*, illus. p.71.
Lily-of-the-valley. See *Convallaria.*
Wild. See *Pyrola rotundifolia.*
Lily-of-the-valley tree. See *Clethra arborea.*
Lilyturf. See *Liriope.*
Lime. See *Tilia.*
American. See *Tilia americana.*
Broad-leaved. See *Tilia platyphyllos.*
Caucasian. See *Tilia × euchlora.*
Common. See *Tilia × europaea.*
Crimean. See *Tilia × euchlora.*
European white. See *Tilia tomentosa.*
Large-leaved. See *Tilia platyphyllos.*
Mongolian. See *Tilia mongolica.*
Pendent silver. See *Tilia* 'Petiolaris', illus. p.64.
Silver. See *Tilia tomentosa.*
Small-leaved. See *Tilia cordata.*
Limnanthemum nymphoides. See *Nymphoides peltata.*

LIMNANTHES

LIMNANTHACEAE

Genus of annuals, useful for rock gardens and for edging. Fully hardy. Prefers a sunny situation and fertile, well-drained soil. Propagate by seed sown outdoors in spring or early autumn. Self seeds freely.
♀ ***L. douglasii*** illus. p.348.

LIMONIUM
Sea lavender

PLUMBAGINACEAE

Genus of summer- and autumn-flowering perennials, sometimes grown as annuals, and sub-shrubs, some of which are evergreen. Fully hardy to frost tender, min. 7–10°C (45–50°F). Grows in full sun and in well-drained soil. Propagate by division in spring, by seed in autumn or early spring or by root cuttings in winter.
L. bellidifolium, syn. *L. reticulatum.* Evergreen, dome-shaped perennial with a woody base. H 15–20cm (6–8in), S 10cm (4in). Frost hardy. Has basal rosettes of rounded, dark green leaves. Much-branched flower stems produce masses of small, **'everlasting'**, trumpet-shaped blue flowers in summer-autumn. Is excellent for a rock garden.
L. latifolium **'Blue Cloud'** illus. p.296.

L. perezii. Evergreen, rounded sub-shrub. H and S 1m (3ft) or more. Frost tender, min. 7–10°C (45–50°F). Has long-stalked, oval to diamond-shaped, deep green leaves. Dense clusters, 20cm (8in) wide, of tiny, tubular, deep mauve-blue flowers are carried well above the leaves in autumn. Needs good ventilation if grown under glass.
L. reticulatum. See *L. bellidifolium.*
L. sinuatum illus. p.334. **Fortress Series** is a slow-growing, upright, bushy perennial, grown as an annual. H 45cm (18in), S 30cm (12in). Half hardy. Has lance-shaped, lobed and often wavy-margined, deep green leaves and, in summer and early autumn, clusters of small, tubular flowers in a mixture of shades such as pink, yellow or blue.
L. suworowii. See *Psylliostachys suworowii.*

LINARIA
Toadflax

SCROPHULARIACEAE

Genus of spring-, summer- or autumn-flowering annuals, biennials and perennials, useful for rock gardens and borders. Fully to frost hardy. Prefers sun or light shade; thrives in any well-drained soil. Propagate by seed in autumn or spring. Self seeds freely.
L. alpina (Alpine toadflax). Tuft-forming, compact, annual, biennial or short-lived perennial with a sparse root system. H 15cm (6in), S 10–15cm (4–6in). Fully hardy. Has whorls of linear to lance-shaped, fleshy, grey-green leaves. Asuccession of snapdragon-like, yellow-centred, purple-violet flowers is borne in loose racemes in summer.
L. dalmatica. See *L. genistifolia* var. *dalmatica.*
L. genistifolia. Upright perennial. H 60cm–1.2m (2–4ft), S 23cm (9in). Fully hardy. From mid-summer to autumn produces racemes of small, snapdragon-like, orange-marked, yellow flowers. Lance-shaped, glossy, mid-green leaves clasp the stems. var. ***dalmatica*** (syn. *L. dalmatica; Dalmatian toadflax*), H 1–1.2m (3–4ft), S 60cm (2ft), bears much larger, golden-yellow flowers, from mid- to late summer, and has broader, more glaucous leaves.
L. maroccana **'Fairy Lights'** illus. p.342.
L. purpurea (Purple toadflax). Upright perennial. H 60cm–1m (2–3ft), S 60cm (2ft). Fully hardy. From mid- to late summer, racemes of snapdragon-like, purplish-blue flowers, touched with white at throats, are produced above narrowly oval, grey-green leaves. **'Canon J. Went'** illus. p.245.
L. triornithophora illus. p.255.

Linden. See *Tilia.*

LINDERA

LAURACEAE

Genus of deciduous or evergreen shrubs and trees, grown for their foliage, which is often aromatic, and their autumn colour. Fruits are produced on female plants if male plants are also grown. Fully to frost hardy. Needs semi-shade and moist, acid soil. Propagate by softwood cuttings in summer or by seed in autumn.
L. benzoin illus. p.127.
♀ ***L. obtusiloba.*** Deciduous, bushy shrub. H and S 6m (20ft). Fully hardy. Bears 3-lobed, aromatic, glossy, dark green leaves, becoming butter-yellow in autumn. Clusters of small, star-shaped, deep yellow flowers, borne on bare shoots from early to mid-spring, are followed by small, spherical, black fruits.

LINDHEIMERA

COMPOSITAE/ASTERACEAE

Genus of late summer- and early autumn-flowering annuals. Fully hardy. Grow in sun and in fertile, well-drained soil. Propagate by seed sown under glass in early spring or outdoors in late spring.
L. texana illus. p.348.

Ling. See *Calluna vulgaris.*

LINNAEA
Twin flower

CAPRIFOLIACEAE

Genus of one species of evergreen, creeping, summer-flowering, sub-shrubby perennial that makes an extensive, twiggy mat. Is useful as ground cover on peat beds and rock gardens. Fully hardy. Requires partial shade and moist, peaty, acid soil. Propagate by rooted runners in spring, by softwood cuttings in summer or by seed in autumn.
L. borealis illus. p.387.

LINUM

LINACEAE

Genus of annuals, biennials, perennials, sub-shrubs and shrubs, some of which are evergreen or semi-evergreen, grown for their flowers. Is suitable for rock gardens. Fully to half hardy, but in cold areas some species need a sheltered position. Prefers sun and humus-rich, well-drained, peaty soil. Propagate sub-shrubs and shrubs by semi-ripe cuttings in summer or by seed in autumn, annuals, biennials and perennials by seed in autumn.
♀ ***L. arboreum*** illus. p.370.
L. flavum (Golden flax, Yellow flax). Bushy perennial with a woody rootstock. H 30cm (12in), S 15cm (6in). Fully hardy. Has narrowly oval, green leaves and, in summer, upward-facing, funnel-shaped, yellow flowers in terminal clusters. **'Compactum'** illus. p.397.
♀ ***L.* 'Gemmell's Hybrid'.** Semi-evergreen, domed perennial with a woody rootstock. H 15cm (6in), S 20cm (8in). Frost hardy. Leaves are oval and grey-green. In summer, short-stalked, broadly funnel-shaped, bright chrome-yellow flowers are produced in terminal clusters. Prefers alkaline soil.
L. grandiflorum **'Rubrum'** illus. p.339.
L. narbonense illus. p.297.
L. perenne illus. p.368.
L. salsoloides. See *L. suffruticosum* subsp. *salsoloides.*
L. suffruticosum subsp. ***salsoloides,*** syn. *L. salsoloides.* Perennial with spreading, sometimes woody-based, stems. H 5–20cm (2–8in), S 8cm (3in). Frost hardy. Slender stems produce

fine, heath-like, grey-green leaves and, in summer, a succession of short-lived, saucer-shaped, pearl-white flowers, flushed blue or pink, in terminal clusters.

Lion's ear. See *Leonotis leonurus*, illus. p.145.
Lippia citriodora. See *Aloysia triphylla*.
Lipstick plant. See *Aeschynanthus pulcher*.

Liquidambar

HAMAMELIDACEAE

Genus of deciduous trees, with inconspicuous flowers, grown for their maple-like foliage and autumn colour. Fully to frost hardy. Requires sun or semi-shade and fertile, moist but well-drained soil; grows poorly on shallow, chalky soil. Propagate by softwood cuttings in summer or by seed in autumn.
L. formosana, syn. *L. monticola*. Deciduous, broadly conical tree. H 12m (40ft), S 10m (30ft). Frost hardy. Has large, 3-lobed, toothed leaves, purple when young, dark green in summer and turning orange, red and purple in autumn.
L. monticola. See *L. formosana*.
L. orientalis (Oriental sweet gum). Slow-growing, deciduous, bushy tree. H 6m (20ft), S 4m (12ft). Frost hardy. Small, 5-lobed, mid-green leaves turn orange in autumn.
L. styraciflua (Sweet gum) illus. p.66. ♀ **'Lane Roberts'** is a deciduous, broadly conical to spreading tree. H 25m (80ft), S 12m (40ft). Fully hardy. Shoots usually have corky ridges. Glossy, green leaves, each with 5 lobes, turn deep reddish-purple in autumn.

Liquorice fern. See *Polypodium glycyrrhiza*, illus. p.322.
Liquorice. See *Glycyrrhiza*.

Liriodendron

MAGNOLIACEAE

Genus of deciduous trees, grown for their foliage and flowers in summer. Flowers are almost hidden by unusual leaves and are not produced on young trees. Fully hardy. Requires sun or semi-shade and deep, fertile, well-drained, preferably slightly acid, soil. Propagate species by seed in autumn, selected forms by budding in late summer.
L. chinense (Chinese tulip tree). Fast-growing, deciduous, spreading tree. H 25m (80ft), S 12m (40ft). Bears large, deep green leaves, cut off at the tips and with a deep lobe on each side; leaves become yellow in autumn. Cup-shaped, orange-based, greenish-white flowers appear in mid-summer.
♀ ***L. tulipifera*** illus. p.61.
♀ **'Aureomarginatum'** illus. p.65.

Liriope

Lilyturf

LILIACEAE/CONVALLARIACEAE

Genus of evergreen perennials with swollen, fleshy rhizomes. Some are grown as ground cover. Fully to frost hardy. Requires sun and well-drained soil. Propagate by division in spring or by seed in autumn.
L. graminifolia var. ***densiflora.*** See *L. muscari*.
♀ ***L. muscari***, syn. *L. graminifolia* var. *densiflora, L. platyphylla* illus. p.306. **'Majestic'** is an evergreen, spreading, rhizomatous perennial. H 30cm (12in), S 45cm (18in). Frost hardy. In late autumn produces spikes of thickly clustered, rounded-bell-shaped, violet flowers among linear, glossy, bright green leaves.
L. platyphylla. See *L. muscari*.
L. spicata. Evergreen, spreading, rhizomatous perennial. H 30cm (12in), S 30–40cm (12–16in). Fully hardy. Grass-like, glossy, dark green leaves make good ground cover. Produces spikes of rounded-bell-shaped, pale lavender flowers in late summer.

Lisianthus russellianus. See *Eustoma grandiflorum*.

Lithocarpus

FAGACEAE

Genus of evergreen trees, grown for their foliage. Frost hardy. Needs sun or semi-shade. Prefers well-drained, neutral to acid soil. Shelter from strong winds. Propagate by seed, when ripe, in autumn.
L. densiflorus (Tanbark oak). Evergreen, spreading tree. H and S 10m (30ft). Has sweet chestnut-like, leathery, glossy, dark green leaves and upright, pale yellow flower spikes borne in spring and often again in autumn.
L. henryi illus. p.96.

Lithodora

BORAGINACEAE

Genus of evergreen sub-shrubs and shrubs, grown for their flowers. Is excellent in rock gardens. Fully to frost hardy. Needs full sun and moist, well-drained soil; some species are limestone haters and need acid conditions. Resents root disturbance. Propagate by semi-ripe cuttings in mid-summer or by seed in autumn.
L. diffusa, syn. *Lithospermum diffusum*. ♀ **'Grace Ward'** is an evergreen, compact, semi-prostrate shrub. H 15–30cm (6–12in), S to 30cm (12in). Frost hardy. Trailing stems bear lance-shaped, hairy, dull green leaves. In early summer bears masses of funnel-shaped, deep blue flowers in terminal clusters. Needs acid soil. Plants should be trimmed back after flowering. ♀ **'Heavenly Blue'** illus. p.369.
♀ ***L. oleifolia***, syn. *Lithospermum oleifolium*, illus. p.368.
L. zahnii, syn. *Lithospermum zahnii*. Evergreen, much-branched, upright shrub. H and S 30cm (12in) or more. Frost hardy. Stems are covered in oval, hairy, dark green or greyish-green leaves. Funnel-shaped, azure-blue flowers, with spreading lobes, open in succession from early spring to mid-summer. Sets buds and flowers intermittently until mid-autumn. Prefers alkaline soil.

Lithophragma

SAXIFRAGACEAE

Genus of tuberous perennials, grown for their campion-like flowers. Is dormant in summer. Fully hardy. Tolerates all but deepest shade and prefers humus-rich, moist soil. Propagate by seed or division in spring or autumn.
L. parviflorum illus. p.358.

Lithops

Living stones, Stone plant

AIZOACEAE

Genus of prostrate, egg-shaped, perennial succulents, with almost united pairs of swollen, erect leaves that are separated on upper surface by a fissure from which a daisy-like flower emerges. Each pair of old leaves splits and dries away to papery skin in spring to reveal a pair of new leaves growing at right angles to old ones. Slowly forms clumps after 3–5 years. Frost tender, min. 5°C (41°F). Needs full sun and extremely well-drained soil or gritty compost. Water regularly in growing season (mid-summer to early autumn), not at all in winter. Propagate by seed in spring or summer.
L. aucampiae. Egg-shaped, perennial succulent. H 1cm (½in), S 3cm (1¼in). Pairs of brown leaves have flat, upper surfaces bearing darker marks. Produces a yellow flower in late summer or early autumn.
L. bella. See *L. karasmontana* subsp. *bella*.
L. bromfieldii. Egg-shaped, perennial succulent. H 2–3cm (¾–1¼in), S 2cm (¾in). Slightly convex, upper surfaces of paired, brown leaves have dark green windows and red dots and lines. Produces a yellow flower in late summer or early autumn.
L. dorotheae illus. p.494.
L. fulleri. Egg-shaped, perennial succulent. H and S 2cm (¾in). Pairs of leaves are dove-grey to brown-yellow. Convex, upper surfaces have sunken, darker marks. In late summer or early autumn bears a white flower.
L. hookeri. See *L. turbiniformis*.
L. julii. Egg-shaped, perennial succulent.H 2–3cm (¾–1¼in), S 5cm (2in). Has paired, pearl- to pink-grey leaves, each with a slightly convex, darker-marked, upper surface. In late summer or autumn produces a white flower.
L. karasmontana illus. p.485. subsp. ***bella***, syn. *L. bella*, is an egg-shaped, perennial succulent. H 2–3cm (¾–1¼in), S 1.5cm (⅝in). Has pairs of brown to brown-yellow leaves with darker marks on convex, upper surfaces. Produces a white flower in late summer or early autumn.
L. lesliei. Egg-shaped, perennial succulent. H 1cm (½in), S 2cm (¾in). Is similar to *L. aucampiae*, but upper leaf surfaces are convex. var. ***albinica*** illus. p.486.
L. marmorata illus. p.485.
L. olivacea. Egg-shaped, perennial succulent. H and S 2cm (¾in). Paired, dark olive-green leaves have darker windows on convex, upper surfaces. Yellow flower appears in late summer or early autumn.
L. otzeniana. Egg-shaped, perennial succulent. H 3cm (1¼in), S 2cm (¾in). Paired, grey-violet leaves each have a convex, upper surface with a distinctive, light border and large, semi-translucent windows. In late summer or early autumn bears a yellow flower.
L. pseudotruncatella. Egg-shaped, perennial succulent. H 3cm (1¼in), S 4cm (1½in). Bears pairs of pale grey or blue to lilac leaves with darker marks on convex, upper surfaces. Fissure reaches from side to side only on mature plants. Has a yellow flower in late summer or early autumn. subsp. ***dendritica*** illus. p.494.
L. schwantesii, illus. p.494.
L. turbiniformis. Egg-shaped, perennial succulent. H 4cm (1½in), S 2cm (¾in). Has a flattish, upper surface with, usually, sunken, dark brown marks on paired, brown leaves. Yellow flower appears in late summer or early autumn.

Lithospermum diffusum. See *Lithodora diffusa*.
Lithospermum oleifolium. See *Lithodora oleifolia*.
Lithospermum zahnii. See *Lithodora zahnii*.
Litsia glauca. See *Neolitsia sericea*.
Little walnut. See *Juglans microcarpa*, illus. p.88.

Littonia

LILIACEAE/COLCHICACEAE

Genus of deciduous, perennial, scandent, tuberous climbers, grown for their pendent, bell-shaped flowers in summer. Frost tender, min. 8–16°C (46–61°F). Requires full sun and rich, well-drained soil. Provide support. Dies down in winter; lift and dry off tubers and store in a frost-free place. Propagate by seed in spring; tubers sometimes will divide naturally.
L. modesta illus. p.415.

Living rock. See *Ariocarpus; Pleiospilos bolusii*, illus. p.495.
Living stones. See *Lithops*.
Livingstone daisy. See *Dorotheanthus bellidiformis*.

Livistona

PALMAE/ARECACEAE

Genus of evergreen palms, grown for their overall appearance. Has clusters of insignificant flowers in summer. Frost tender, min. 7°C (45°F). Needs full light or partial shade and fertile, well-drained soil, ideally neutral to acid. Water potted specimens moderately, less in winter. Propagate by seed in spring at not less than 23°C (73°F). Red spider mite may be a nuisance on containerized plants.
L. australis (Australian cabbage palm, Gippsland fountain palm). Slow-growing, evergreen palm with a fairly slender trunk. H 15–20m (50–70ft), S 3–6m (10–20ft). Has fan-shaped leaves, 1.2–2.5m (4–8ft) wide, divided into narrow, slender-pointed, glossy, green leaflets. Leaf stalks are spiny.
♀ ***L. chinensis*** illus. p.81.

Lizard's tail. See *Saururus cernuus*, illus. p.463.

Lloydia

LILIACEAE

Genus of summer-flowering bulbs, grown for their small, graceful, bell-shaped flowers. Fully to half hardy. Is not easy to grow. Requires partial shade and well-drained, peaty soil; provide plenty of moisture in summer but, preferably, keep fairly dry in winter. Propagate by seed in spring.
L. graeca. See *Gagea graeca*.
L. serotina illus. p.451.

Lobelia

CAMPANULACEAE

Genus of annuals, perennials and deciduous or evergreen shrubs, grown for their flowers. Some are suitable for wild gardens or by the waterside. Fully hardy to frost tender, min. 5°C (41°F). Prefers sun and moist but well-drained soil. Resents wet conditions in winter; in cold areas some perennials and shrubs are therefore best lifted in autumn and placed in well-drained compost in frames. Propagate annuals by seed in spring, perennial species by seed or division in spring, perennial cultivars by division only and shrubs by semi-ripe cuttings in summer. Contact with the milky sap of some species may irritate skin.
♀ ***L. cardinalis,*** syn. *L. fulgens, L. splendens* (Cardinal flower). Clump-forming perennial. H 1m (3ft), S 23cm (9in). Frost hardy. Bears racemes of 2-lipped, brilliant scarlet flowers from mid- to late summer. Lance-shaped leaves may be fresh green or red-bronze.
***L.* 'Cherry Ripe'** illus. p.253.
***L.* 'Dark Crusader'.** Clump-forming perennial. H 1m (3ft), S 23cm (9in). Half hardy. From mid- to late summer bears racemes of 2-lipped, dark red flowers above lance-shaped, fresh green or red-bronze leaves.
***L. erinus* 'Blue Cascade'.** Slow-growing, pendulous, spreading annual, occasionally perennial. H 10–20cm (4–8in), S 10–15cm (4–6in). Half hardy. Oval to lance-shaped leaves are pale green. Small, 2-lipped, pale blue flowers are produced continuously in summer and early autumn.
♀ **'Cambridge Blue'** is compact and has blue flowers. ♀ **'Colour Cascade'** has flowers in a mixture of colours, such as blue, red, pink, mauve or white. ♀ **'Crystal Palace'** illus. p.346. **'Red Cascade'** produces white-eyed, purple-red flowers. **'Sapphire'** illus. p.344.
L. fulgens. See *L. cardinalis*.
***L. × gerardii* 'Vedrariensis',** syn *L.* 'Vedrariensis'. Clump-forming perennial. H 1m (3ft), S 30cm (1ft). Frost hardy. In late summer produces racemes of 2-lipped, purple flowers. Has lance-shaped, dark green leaves.
♀ ***L.* 'Queen Victoria'** illus. p.253.
L. siphilitica. Clump-forming perennial. H 1m (3ft), S 23cm (9in). Fully hardy. Racemes of 2-lipped, blue flowers appear in late summer and autumn above narrowly oval, green leaves. Thrives in damp, heavy soil.
L. splendens. See *L. cardinalis*.
L. tupa. Clump-forming perennial. H 1.5–2m (5–6ft), S 1m (3ft). Half hardy. Bears large spikes of 2-lipped, brick-red flowers in late summer, above narrowly oval, hairy, light green leaves. Does best in a sheltered, sunny site.
***L.* 'Vedrariensis'.** See *L. × gerardii* 'Vedrariensis'.
***L.* 'Will Scarlet'.** Clump-forming perennial. H 1m (3ft), S 30cm (1ft). Frost hardy. Racemes of 2-lipped, bright red flowers are borne in summer. Lance-shaped leaves are coppery-green.

Lobel's maple. See *Acer cappadocicum* subsp. *lobelii*, illus. p.62.

Lobivia aurea. See *Echinopsis aurea*.
Lobivia backebergii. See *Echinopsis bachebergii*.
Lobivia cinnabarina. See *Echinopsis cinnabarina*.
Lobivia cylindrica. See *Echinopsis aurea*.
Lobivia haageana. See *Echinopsis marsoneri*.
Lobivia pentlandii. See *Echinopsis pentlandii*.
Lobivia pygmaea. See *Rebutia pygmaea*.
Lobivia shaferi. See *Echinopsis aurea*.
Lobivia silvestrii. See *Echinopsis chamaecereus*.
Loblolly bay. See *Gordonia lasianthus*.
Lobster cactus. See *Schlumbergera truncata*, illus. p.489.
Lobster claws. See *Heliconia*.

Lobularia

CRUCIFERAE/BRASSICACEAE

Genus of summer- and early autumn-flowering annuals. Fully hardy. Grow in sun and in fertile, well-drained soil. Dead-head to encourage continuous flowering. Propagate by seed sown under glass in spring, or outdoors in late spring.
L. maritima, syn. *Alyssum maritimum* (Sweet alyssum). Fast-growing, spreading annual. H 8–15cm (3–6in), S 20–30cm (8–12in). Has lance-shaped, greyish-green leaves. Rounded heads of tiny, scented, 4-petalled, white flowers are produced in summer and early autumn. **'Carpet of Snow'** illus. p.330. **'Rosie O' Day'** illus. p.334.

Locust. See *Robinia pseudoacacia*.
Caspian. See *Gleditsia caspica*.
Honey. See *Gleditsia triacanthos*.
Lodgepole pine. See *Pinus contorta* var. *latifolia*, illus. p.102.

Loiseleuria

ERICACEAE

Genus of one species of evergreen, creeping, prostrate shrub, grown for its flowers. Fully hardy. Requires full light and humus-rich, well-drained, acid soil. Is difficult to grow. Propagate by seed in spring or by softwood or semi-ripe cuttings in summer.
L. procumbens (Alpine azalea) illus. p.389.

Lollipop plant. See *Pachystachys lutea*, illus. p.153.

Lomatia

PROTEACEAE

Genus of evergreen shrubs and trees, grown for their foliage and flowers, which have 4 narrow, twisted petals. Frost hardy, but in cold areas needs shelter from strong winds. Requires sun or semi-shade and moist but well-drained, acid soil. Propagate by softwood or semi-ripe cuttings in summer.
L. ferruginea. Evergreen, upright shrub or tree. H 10m (30ft), S 5m (15ft). Stout, brown-felted shoots bear oblong to oval, dark green leaves, deeply cut into 6–15 oblong lobes. Racemes of yellow-and-red flowers are borne in mid-summer. Thrives outside only in mild, moist areas.
L. silaifolia illus. p.157.

Lombardy poplar. See *Populus nigra* 'Italica', illus. p.62.
London plane. See *Platanus × hispanica*, illus. p.63.
London pride. See *Saxifraga × urbium*.

Lonicera

Honeysuckle

CAPRIFOLIACEAE

Genus of deciduous, semi-evergreen or evergreen shrubs and woody-stemmed, twining climbers, grown mainly for their flowers, which are often fragrant. Flowers are tubular, with spreading, 2-lipped petal lobes. Climbers may be trained into large shrubs. Fully hardy to frost tender, min. 5°C (41°F). Grows in any fertile, well-drained soil in sun or semi-shade. Prune out flowered wood of climbers after flowering. Prune shrubs only to remove dead shoots or restrain growth. Propagate by seed in autumn or spring, by semi-ripe cuttings in summer or by hardwood cuttings in late autumn. Aphids may be a problem. The berries may cause mild stomach upset if ingested.
L. × americana, syn. *L. × italica of gardens*, illus. p.213.
L. × brownii (Scarlet trumpet honeysuckle). **'Dropmore Scarlet'** illus. p.206.
L. etrusca (Etruscan honeysuckle). Deciduous or semi-evergreen, woody-stemmed, twining climber. H to 4m (12ft). Half hardy. Oval, mid-green leaves are blue-green beneath, the upper ones united into cups. Fragrant, long-tubed, pale yellow flowers, borne in summer-autumn, turn deeper yellow and become red-flushed with age. Grow in sun.
L. fragrantissima. Deciduous or semi-evergreen, bushy, spreading shrub. H 2m (6ft), S 4m (12ft). Fully hardy. Bears oval, dark green leaves. Fragrant, short-tubed, creamy-white flowers open in winter and early spring.
***L.* 'Gold Flame'.** See *L. × heckrottii* 'Gold Flame'.
L. × heckrottii. Deciduous or semi-evergreen, twining climber. H 5m (15ft). Fully hardy. Oval, dark green leaves are blue-green beneath, the upper pairs united. Bears terminal whorls of fragrant, pink flowers, orange-yellow inside, in summer, sometimes followed by red berries. **'Gold Flame'** (syn. *L.* 'Gold Flame') illus. p.205.
L. henryi. Evergreen or semi-evergreen, woody-stemmed, twining climber. H to 10m (30ft). Frost hardy. Narrowly oval, dark green leaves are paler beneath. Terminal clusters of long-tubed, red-purple flowers appear in summer-autumn, followed by black berries.
L. hildebrandiana (Giant Burmese honeysuckle). Evergreen or semi-evergreen, woody-stemmed, twining climber. H to 20m (70ft). Frost tender. Oval or rounded, mid-green leaves are paler beneath. Long-tubed, white or cream flowers, ageing to creamy-orange or brownish-yellow, appear in pairs in leaf axils or at shoot tips in summer. Grow in sun.
L. × italica of gardens. See *L. × americana*.
L. japonica (Japanese honeysuckle). **'Aureoreticulata'** is an evergreen or semi-evergreen, twining climber with soft-haired, woody stems. H to 10m (30ft). Frost hardy. Oval, sometimes lobed, leaves are bright green with bright yellow veins. Fragrant, long-tubed, white flowers, becoming yellowish, are produced in summer-autumn. Is useful for hiding a tree stump or an unsightly wall or fence. ♀ **'Halliana'** illus. p.213.
L. ledebourii illus. p.138.
L. maackii. Vigorous, deciduous, bushy shrub. H and S 5m (15ft). Fully hardy. Leaves are oval and dark green. Fragrant, short-tubed, white, later yellow flowers, in early summer, are followed by spherical, bright red fruits.
L. morrowii. Deciduous, spreading shrub with arching branches. H 2m (6ft), S 3m (10ft). Fully hardy. Has oval, dark green leaves and, in late spring and early summer, small, short-tubed, creamy-white flowers that age to yellow.
L. nitida. Evergreen, bushy, dense shrub. H 2m (6ft), S 3m (10ft). Fully hardy. Leaves are small, oval, glossy and dark green. Tiny, fragrant, short-tubed, creamy-white flowers appear in late spring and are followed by small, spherical, purple fruits. Is good for hedging. ♀ **'Baggesen's Gold'** illus. p.173. **'Yunnan'** is more upright, has stouter shoots and larger leaves and flowers more freely.
L. periclymenum (Common honeysuckle, Woodbine). ♀ **'Graham Thomas'** illus. p.213. ♀ **'Serotina'** (Late Dutch honeysuckle) is a deciduous, woody-stemmed, twining climber. H to 7m (22ft). Fully hardy. Oval or oblong, mid-green leaves are grey-green beneath. Very fragrant, long-tubed, dark purple flowers, pinkish within, are borne in mid- and late summer. Grow in sun or shade.
L. pileata illus. p.172.
L. × purpusii illus. p.169. ♀ **'Winter Beauty'** has red-purple shoots and freely bears very fragrant, white flowers.
♀ ***L. sempervirens*** illus. p.206.
L. standishii. Evergreen, bushy shrub. H and S 2m (6ft). Fully hardy. Has peeling bark, oblong, bristly, dark green leaves and, in winter, fragrant, short-tubed, creamy-white flowers.
L. tatarica illus. p.136. **'Hack's Red'** is a deciduous, bushy shrub. H and

S 2.5m (8ft). Fully hardy. Produces short-tubed, deep pink flowers in late spring and early summer, followed by spherical, red fruits. Leaves are oval and dark green.
♀ ***L. × tellmanniana*** illus. p.215.
♀ ***L. tragophylla.*** Deciduous, woody-stemmed, twining climber. H 5–6m (15–20ft). Frost hardy. Oval leaves are bluish-green, the uppermost pair united into a cup. Produces clusters of up to 20 long-tubed, bright yellow flowers in early summer.
***L. × xylosteoides* 'Clavey's Dwarf'.** Deciduous, upright, dense shrub. H 2m (6ft), S 1m (3ft). Fully hardy. Leaves are oval and grey-green. Bears short-tubed, pink flowers in late spring, then spherical, red fruits.
L. xylosteum illus. p.136.

Loosestrife. See *Lysimachia*.
Garden. See *Lysimachia punctata*, illus. p.261.
Purple. See *Lythrum*.
Lophocereus schottii. See *Pachycereus schottii*.

LOPHOMYRTUS

MYRTACEAE

Genus of evergreen shrubs or small trees, grown for their flowers, foliage and fruit. Frost to half hardy. Needs partial shade and fertile, humus-rich, moist but well-drained soil. Propagate by seed sown as soon as ripe or by semi-ripe cuttings in summer.
L. bullata, syn. *Myrtus bullata*. Evergreen, upright shrub. H 5m (15ft), S 3m (10ft). Half hardy. Rounded, puckered leaves, bronze-purple when young, mature to gloss, dark green. Produces saucer-shaped, white flowers in late spring and early summer, then egg-shaped, black-red fruits.

LOPHOPHORA

Peyote

CACTACEAE

Genus of very slow-growing, perennial cacti that resemble small, blue dumplings, with up to 10 ribs, each separated by an indented line. Has long tap roots. Flowering areoles each produce tufts of short, white hairs. Frost tender, min. 5–10°C (41–50°F). Needs sun and well-drained soil. Is very prone to rotting, so water lightly from spring to autumn. Propagate by seed in spring or summer.
L. echinata. See *L. williamsii*.
L. lutea. See *L. williamsii*.
L. williamsii, syn. *L. echinata, L. lutea*, illus. p.487.

LOPHOSPERMUM

SCROPHULARIACEAE

Genus of deciduous and evergreen, perennial climbers and shrubs. Has triangular to rounded leaves and tubular to funnel-shaped flowers. Half hardy to frost tender, min. 5°C (41°F). Needs sun and moist but well-drained soil. Propagate by seed in spring or semi-ripe cuttings in late summer.
♀ ***L. erubescens***, syn. *Asarina erubescens, Maurandya erubescens*, illus. p.205.

LOPHOSTEMON

MYRTACEAE

Genus of evergreen trees and shrubs, grown for their overall appearance when mature and for shade. Is related to Tristania and Eucalyptus. Half hardy to frost tender, min. 3–5°C (37–41°F). Needs sun or partial shade and fertile, well-drained soil. Other than shaping plants in winter, pruning is seldom necessary. Propagate by seed in spring or by semi-ripe cuttings in summer.
L. confertus, syn. *Tristania conferta*. (Brisbane box, Brush-box tree). Fast-growing, evergreen, round-headed tree. H and S 15–40m (50–130ft). Frost tender. Produces lance-shaped, leathery, lustrous leaves. In spring bears white flowers with prominent, feathery stamen bundles. **'Perth Gold'** has bright green leaves strongly variegated yellow.

Loquat. See *Eriobotrya japonica*.
Lord Anson's blue pea. See *Lathyrus nervosus*.
Lords and ladies. See *Arum*.

LOROPETALUM

HAMAMELIDACEAE

Genus of evergreen shrubs, grown for their flowers. Half hardy, but needs min. 5°C (41°F) to flower well. Requires full light or semi-shade and rich, well-drained, neutral to acid soil. Water containerized plants freely when in full growth, moderately at other times. Propagate by layering or seed in spring or by semi-ripe cuttings in late summer.
L. chinense. Evergreen, rounded, well-branched shrub. H and S 1.2m (4ft). Asymmetrically oval leaves are deep green. White flowers, each with 4 strap-shaped petals, are borne in tufted, terminal clusters, mainly in winter-spring.

Lorraine begonia. See *Begonia* 'Gloire de Lorraine'.

LOTUS

LEGUMINOSAE/PAPILIONACEAE

Genus of summer-flowering perennials, some of which are semi-evergreen, and evergreen sub-shrubs, grown for their foliage and flowers. Fully hardy to frost tender, min. 5°C (41°F). Prefers sun and well-drained soil. Propagate by softwood cuttings from early to mid-summer or by seed in autumn or spring.
♀ ***L. berthelotii*** illus. p.293.
L. hirsutus, syn. *Dorycnium hirsutum*. Deciduous, upright sub-shrub. H and S 60cm (24in). Bears silver-grey leaves with 3 oval leaflets. Dense clusters of pea-like, pink-tinged, white flowers in summer and early autumn are followed by oblong to ovoid, reddish-brown seed pods.

Lotus
American. See *Nelumbo lutea*.
Sacred. See *Nelumbo nucifera*, illus. p.463.
Love-in-a-mist. See *Nigella damascena*.
Love-lies-bleeding. See *Amaranthus caudatus*, illus. p.338.
Low-bush blueberry. See *Vaccinium angustifolium* var. *laevifolium*, illus. p.168.
Lucombe oak. See *Quercus × hispanica* 'Lucombeana', illus. p.69.

LUCULIA

RUBIACEAE

Genus of evergreen shrubs, grown for their flowers and foliage. Frost tender, min. 5–10°C (41–50°F). Needs full light or partial shade and fertile, well-drained soil. Water potted specimens freely when in full growth, moderately at other times. Cut back flowered stems hard in spring, if container-grown. Propagate by seed in spring or by semi-ripe cuttings in summer.
L. grandifolia. Evergreen, rounded to upright, robust shrub. H and S 3–6m (10–20ft). min. 5°C (41°F). Oval, green leaves have red veins and stalks. Fragrant, tubular, white flowers, each 6cm (2½in) long, with 5 rounded, petal lobes, appear in terminal clusters in summer.

LUETKEA

ROSACEAE

Genus of one species of deciduous sub-shrub, grown for its fluffy flower heads. Is suitable for banks and rock gardens. Fully hardy. Requires shade and well-drained but not too dry soil. Propagate by division or seed in spring.
L. pectinata. Deciduous, spreading, decumbent sub-shrub. H to 30cm (12in), S 20cm (8in). Stems are clothed in finely dissected, very dark green leaves. In summer has terminal racemes of small, fluffy, off-white flower heads.

LUMA

MYRTACEAE

Genus of evergreen shrubs and small trees, grown for their aromatic leaves and cup-shaped, white flowers. Frost hardy. Grow in full sun or partial shade and fertile, ideally humus-rich, well-drained soil. Propagate by seed in spring or by semi-ripe cuttings in late summer.
♀ ***L. apiculata***, syn. *Amomyrtus luma, Myrceugenia apiculata, Myrtus apiculata, M. luma*, illus. p.115. **'Glanleam Gold'** is a strong-growing, evergreen, upright shrub. H and S 10m (30ft). Has stout stems, peeling, brown-and-white bark and oval, bright green leaves edged with creamy-yellow. Slightly fragrant flowers are borne from mid-summer to mid-autumn.
L. chequen, syn. *Myrtus chequen*. Strong growing upright-shrub or small tree. H 6m (20ft) S 5m (15ft). Frost hardy. Has broadly ovate, wavy-margined, aromatic, dark green leaves. In late summer and early-autumn bears cup-shaped white flowers singly or in small clusters followed by black berries.

LUNARIA

Honesty

CRUCIFERAE/BRASSIACEAE

Genus of biennials and perennials, grown for their flowers and silvery seed pods. Fully hardy. Will grow in sun or shade, but prefers partial shade and well-drained soil. Propagate perennials by seed in autumn or spring or by division in spring, biennials by seed only. Self seeds prolifically.
L. annua, syn. *L. biennis*, illus. p.337. **'Variegata'** illus. p.335.
L. biennis. See *L. annua*.
L. rediviva. Rosette-forming perennial. H 60–75cm (24–30in), S 30cm (12in). Produces racemes of 4-petalled, lilac or white flowers in spring, followed by elliptical, silvery seed pods that are useful for indoor decoration. Has oval, coarse, sometimes maroon-tinted, mid-green leaves.

Lungwort. See *Pulmonaria*.
Lupin. See *Lupinus*.
Tree. See *Lupinus arboreus*, illus. p.165.

LUPINUS

Lupin

LEGUMINOSAE/PAPILIONACEAE

Genus of annuals, perennials and semi-evergreen shrubs, grown for their large, imposing racemes of pea-like flowers. Fully to frost hardy. Prefers sun and well-drained soil. Remove seed heads of most varieties to prevent self seeding.Propagate species by seed when fresh, in autumn, selected forms by cuttings from non-flowering side-shoots in spring or early summer. The seeds may cause severe discomfort if ingested.
♀ ***L. arboreus*** illus. p.165.
♀ ***L.* Band of Nobles Series.** Clump-forming perennial. H to 1.5m (5ft), S 75cm (2½ft). Fully hardy. In early and mid-summer, racemes of flowers in white, yellow, pink, red, blue or bicolours (usually white or yellow in combination with another colour) arise above palmate, deeply divided, mid-green leaves.
***L.* 'My Castle'.** Clump-forming perennial. H 90cm (3ft), S 75cm (2½ ft). Fully hardy. Bears racemes of deep rose-pink flowers above palmate, deeply divided, mid-green leaves in early and mid-summer.
***L.* 'Noble Maiden'.** Clump-forming perennial. H 90m (3ft), S 75cm (2½ft). Fully hardy. In early and mid-summer, racemes of creamy-white flowers arise above palmate, deeply divided, mid-green leaves.
***L.* 'The Chatelaine'** illus. p.246.
***L.* 'The Page'** illus. p.247.

LURONIUM

ALISMATACEAE

Genus of deciduous, perennial, marginal water plants and marsh plants, grown for their foliage and flowers. Fully hardy. Requires shallow water and full sun. Thin plants when overcrowded. Propagate in spring by seed or division.
L. natans, syn. *Alisma natans* (Floating water plantain). Deciduous, perennial, marginal water plant. H 2.5–5cm (1–2in), S 30cm (12in). Produces small, elliptic to lance-shaped, mid-green leaves and, in summer, small, 3-lobed, yellow-spotted, white flowers.

Luzula
Woodrush

JUNCACEAE

See also GRASSES, BAMBOOS, RUSHES and SEDGES.
L. maxima. See *L. sylvatica.*
L. nivea illus. p.319.
L. sylvatica, syn. *L. maxima* (Greater woodrush). **'Marginata'** (syn. *L.s.* 'Aureomarginata') is a slow-growing, evergreen, spreading, rhizomatous, perennial grass. H to 30cm (12in), Sindefinite. Fully hardy. Produces thick tufts of broad, hairy-edged, mid-green leaves, with white margins. Leafy stems bear terminal, open, brown flower spikes in summer. Tolerates shade.

Lycaste

ORCHIDACEAE

See also ORCHIDS.
L. cruenta illus. p.311. Vigorous, deciduous, epiphytic orchid for a cool greenhouse. H 30cm (12in). Fragrant, triangular, green-and-yellow flowers, 5cm (2in) across, are produced singly in spring. Has broadly oval, ribbed, soft leaves, to 30cm (12in) long. Grow in semi-shade during summer and avoid spraying, which can mark leaves.

Lychnis

CARYOPHYLLACEAE

Genus of summer-flowering annuals, biennials and perennials. Fully hardy. Requires sun and well-drained soil. Propagate by division or seed in autumn or spring.
***L.* 'Abbotswood Rose'.** See *L. × walkeri* 'Abbotswood Rose'.
L. alpina, syn. *Viscaria alpina* (Alpine catchfly). Tuft-forming perennial. H 5–15cm (2–6in), S 10–15cm (4–6in). Has dense tufts of thick, linear, deep green leaves. In summer, sticky stems each bear a rounded head of pale to deep pink or, rarely, white flowers with spreading, frilled petals. Suits a rock garden.
♀ ***L. chalcedonica*** illus. p.253.
L. coeli-rosa. See *Silene coeli-rosa.*
L. coronaria illus. p.292.
L. flos-jovis illus. p.289.
L. × haageana, syn. *L. × haagena.* Short-lived, clump-forming perennial. H 45cm (18in), S 30cm (12in). Produces clusters of large, 5-petalled, white, orange or red flowers in summer. Oval leaves are mid-green. Is best raised regularly from seed.
L. × haagena. See *L. × haageana.*
***L. × walkeri* 'Abbotswood Rose',** syn. *L.* 'Abbotswood Rose'. Neat, clump-forming perennial. H 30–38cm (12–15in), S 23cm (9in). Has oval, grey leaves and grey, branching stems that, from mid- to late summer, bear sprays of rounded, 5-petalled, bright rose-pink flowers.
L. viscaria. Clump-forming perennial. H 30cm (12in), S 30–45cm (12–18in). From early to mid-summer, rather sticky, star-shaped, reddish-purple flowers are borne in dense clusters above narrowly oval to oblong, dark green leaves. Is suitable for the front of a border or a rock garden.
♀ **'Splendens Plena'** illus. p.292.

Lycianthes rantonnetii. See *Solanum rantonnetii.*

Lycium

SOLANACEAE

Genus of deciduous shrubs, sometimes with long, scandent branches, grown for their habit, flowers and fruits. Is useful for poor, dry soil and coastal gardens. May be grown as a hedge. Fully hardy. Prefers full sun and not too rich, well-drained soil. Remove dead wood in winter and cut back to restrict growth if necessary. Cut back hedges hard in spring. Propagate by softwood cuttings in summer, by seed in autumn or by hardwood cuttings in winter.
L. barbarum, syn. *L. halimifolium* (Chinese box thorn, Duke of Argyll's tea-tree). Deciduous, arching, often spiny shrub. H 2.5m (8ft), S 5m (15ft). Funnel-shaped, purple or pink flowers in late spring and summer are followed by spherical, orange-red berries. Leaves are lance-shaped, bright green or grey-green.
L. halimifolium. See *L. barbarum.*

Lycoris

AMARYLLIDACEAE

Genus of late summer- and early autumn-flowering bulbs with showy flower heads on leafless stems. Frost hardy; in cool areas is best grown in pots or planted in greenhouse borders. Needs sun, well-drained soil and a warm period in summer to ripen bulbs so they flower. Provide regular liquid feed while in growth. After summer dormancy, water from early autumn until following summer, when foliage dies away. Propagate by seed when ripe or in spring or summer or by offsets in late summer.
L. aurea (Golden spider lily). Late summer- and early autumn-flowering bulb. H 30–40cm (12–16in), S 10–15cm (4–6in). Produces a head of 5or 6 bright yellow flowers that have narrow, reflexed petals, with very wavy margins, and conspicuous stamens. Strap-shaped, semi-erect, basal leaves appear after flowering.
L. radiata illus. p.436.
L. squamigera. Late summer- or early autumn-flowering bulb. H 45–60cm (18–24in), S 10–15cm (4–6in). Carries a head of 6–8 fragrant, funnel-shaped, rose-pink flowers, 10cm (4in) long, with reflexed petal tips. Strap-shaped, semi-erect, basal leaves form after flowers.

Lygodium

SCHIZAEACEAE

Genus of deciduous or semi-evergreen, climbing ferns, usually with 2 kinds of fronds: vegetative and fertile. Half hardy to frost tender, min. 5°C (41°F). Needs shade or semi-shade and humus-rich, moist, peaty soil. Is best grown among shrubby plants that can provide support. Plants grown under glass in pots need strong, twiggy supports. Remove faded fronds regularly. Propagate by division in spring or by spores in summer.
L. japonicum (Japanese climbing fern). Deciduous, climbing fern. H 2m (6ft), S indefinite. Frost tender. Mid-green, vegetative fronds consist of delicate, finger-shaped pinnae; fertile fronds are broader and 3–5 lobed, with a longer, terminal lobe.

Lyme grass. See *Leymus arenarius.*

Lyonia

ERICACEAE

Genus of deciduous, semi-evergreen or evergreen shrubs and trees, grown for theirracemes of small, urn-shaped flowers. Fully hardy. Needs shade or semi-shade and moist, peaty, acid soil. Propagate by semi-ripe cuttings in summer.
L. ligustrina. Deciduous, bushy shrub. H and S 2m (6ft). Oval, dark green leaves set off dense racemes of globular urn-shaped, white flowers from mid- to late summer.
L. ovalifolia. Deciduous or semi-evergreen, bushy shrub. H and S 2m (6ft). Produces red shoots and oval, dark green leaves. Racemes of urn-shaped, white flowers appear in late spring and early summer.

Lyonothamnus

ROSACEAE

Genus of one species of evergreen tree, grown for its foliage and flowers. Frost hardy. Needs sun or semi-shade, a warm, sheltered position and fertile, well-drained soil. Propagate by softwood cuttings in summer or by seed in autumn.
L. floribundus (Catalina ironwood). Evergreen tree grown only in the form subsp. ***aspleniifolius.*** This slender tree, H 12m (40ft), S 6m (20ft), has rather stringy, reddish-brown bark and much divided, fern-like, dark green leaves. Large, flattened heads of 5-petalled, star-shaped white flowers are produced in early summer.

Lysichiton

ARACEAE

Genus of deciduous, perennial, marginal water plants and bog plants, grown for their handsome spathes and very large, glossy foliage. Fully hardy. Prefers full sun, but tolerates semi-shade. Tolerates both still and running water. Propagate by seed when fresh, in late summer.
L. americanum. See *L. americanus.*
♀ ***L. americanus***, syn. *L. americanum*, illus. p.467.
♀ ***L. camtschatcensis*** illus. p.462.

Lysimachia
Loosestrife

PRIMULACEAE

Genus of summer-flowering annuals and perennials, suitable for the border or rock garden. Fully to half hardy. Prefers sun or semi-shade and moist but well-drained soil. Propagate by division in spring or by seed in autumn.
♀ ***L. clethroides*** illus. p.243.
L. ephemerum. Neat, clump-forming perennial. H 1m (3ft), S 30cm (1ft). Fully hardy. Erect, terminal racemes of star-shaped, greyish-white flowers are borne on slender stems in summer, followed by light green seed heads. Lance-shaped leaves are leathery and glaucous.
L. nummularia (Moneywort).
♀ **'Aurea'** illus. p.398.
L. punctata illus. p.261.

Lythrum
Purple loosestrife

LYTHRACEAE

Genus of summer-flowering perennials that thrive by the waterside and in bog gardens. Fully hardy. Grows in full sun or semi-shade and in moist or wet soil. Propagate cultivars by division in spring, species by seed or division in spring or autumn. Some species have become noxious weeds in the USA.
♀ ***L. salicaria* 'Feuerkerze',** syn. *L.s.* 'Firecandle', illus. p.247.
'Firecandle' see *L.s.* 'Feuerkerze'.
'Robert' is a clump-forming perennial. H 75cm (30in), S 45cm (18in). Produces racemes of 4-petalled, clear pink flowers from mid- to late summer. Leaves are mid-green and lance-shaped.
***L. virgatum* 'Rose Queen'.** Clump-forming perennial. H 1m (3ft), S 60cm (2ft). Racemes of 4-petalled, star-shaped, light pink flowers are produced from mid- to late summer above lance-shaped, hairless, mid-green leaves.
'The Rocket' illus. p.247.

MAACKIA

LEGUMINOSAE/PAPILIONACEAE

Genus of deciduous, summer-flowering trees, grown for their foliage and flowers. Fully hardy. Requires full sun and fertile, well-drained soil. Propagate by seed in autumn.
M. amurensis illus. p.86.

MACADAMIA

PROTEACEAE

Genus of evergreen trees, grown for their foliage and fruits. Frost tender, min. 10–13°C (50–55°F). Prefers full light, though some shade is tolerated. Provide humus-rich, moisture-retentive but well-drained soil. Water freely while in full growth, moderately at other times. Pruning is not usually necessary, but is tolerated in autumn. Propagate by seed when ripe, in autumn, or in spring.
M. integrifolia illus. p.69.

Macadamia nut. See *Macadamia integrifolia*, illus. p.69.
Mace sedge. See *Carex grayi*.
Macedonian pine. See *Pinus euce*, illus. p.97.

MACFADYENA,
syn. DOXANTHA

BIGNONIACEAE

Genus of evergreen, woody-stemmed, tendril climbers, grown for their foxglove-like flowers. Frost tender, min. 5°C (41°F). Any fertile, well-drained soil is suitable with full light. Water regularly, less when not in full growth. Provide support for stems. Thin out crowded shoots after flowering or in spring. Propagate by semi-ripe cuttings in summer.
M. unguis-cati, syn. *Bignonia unguis-cati, Doxantha unguis-cati*, illus. p.214.

MACKAYA

ACANTHACEAE

Genus of one species of evergreen shrub, grown for its flowers and overall appearance. Frost tender, min. 7–10°C (45–50°F). Requires full light or partial shade and fertile, well-drained soil. Water potted plants freely when in full growth, moderately at other times. Pruning is tolerated in winter if necessary. Propagate by greenwood cuttings in spring or by semi-ripe cuttings in summer.
🏆 ***M. bella***, syn. *Asystasia bella*. Evergreen, erect, then spreading, well-branched shrub. H to 1.5m (5ft), S 1.2–1.5m (4–5ft). Leaves are oval, pointed, glossy and mid- to deep green. Has spikes of tubular, dark-veined, lavender flowers, each with 5 large, flared petal lobes, from spring to autumn. In warm conditions, above 13°C (55°F), will flower into winter.

Mackay's heath. See *Erica mackaiana*.

MACLEANIA

ERICACEAE

Genus of evergreen, spring- to summer-flowering shrubs and scrambling climbers, grown primarily for their flowers. Frost tender, min. 10°C (50°F). Needs partial shade and humus-rich, freely draining, neutral to acid soil. Water potted specimens moderately, less when not in full growth. Long shoots may be shortened in winter or after flowering. Propagate by seed in spring, by semi-ripe cuttings in summer or by layering in autumn.
M. insignis. Evergreen, scrambling climber with erect, sparingly branched, wand-like stems. H 3m (10ft), S 1–3m (3–10ft). Has oval, leathery, deep green leaves, red-flushed when young. Tubular, waxy, scarlet flowers, with white tips, hang in clusters in summer. Needs support.

MACLEAYA
Plume poppy

PAPAVERACEAE

Genus of summer-flowering perennials, grown for their overall appearance. Fully hardy. Grows in sun and in well-drained soil. May spread rapidly. Propagate by division in early spring or by root cuttings in winter.
🏆 ***M. cordata***, syn. *Bocconia cordata*. Spreading, clump-forming perennial. H 1.5m (5ft) or more, S 60cm (2ft) or more. Large, rounded, lobed, grey-green leaves, grey-white beneath, are produced at base of plant and up lower parts of stems. Large, feathery panicles of dainty, creamy-white flowers are produced in summer.
***M. microcarpa* 'Coral Plume'.** See *M.m.* 'Kelway's Coral Plume'.
🏆 **'Kelway's Coral Plume'** (syn. *M.m.* 'Coral Plume) illus. p.225.

MACLURA

MORACEAE

Genus of one species of deciduous tree, grown for its foliage and unusual fruits. Both male and female trees need to be planted to obtain fruits. Fully hardy, but young plants are susceptible to frost damage. Requires full sun and needs hot summers to thrive in cold areas. Grows in any but waterlogged soil. Propagate by softwood cuttings in summer, by seed in autumn or by root cuttings in late winter.
M. aurantiaca. See *M. pomifera*.
M. pomifera, syn. *M. aurantiaca* (Osage orange). Deciduous, rounded, spreading tree. H 15m (50ft), S 12m (40ft). Has spiny shoots and oval, dark green leaves that turn yellow in autumn. Tiny, cup-shaped, yellow flowers in summer are followed on female trees by large, rounded, wrinkled, pale green fruits.
M. tricuspidata, syn. *Cudrania tricuspidata*. Deciduous, spreading tree. H 7m (22ft), S 6m (20ft). Bears oval, dark green leaves that are sometimes 3-lobed. Produces small, rounded clusters of tiny, green flowers in mid-summer.

Macroplectrum sesquipedale. See *Angraecum sesquipedale*.
Macrotomia echioides. See *Arnebia pulchra*.

MACROZAMIA

ZAMIACEAE

Genus of slow-growing, evergreen shrubs and small trees, with or without trunks, grown for their palm-like appearance. Mature plants may produce conical, green flower spikes. Frost tender, min. 13–16°C (55–61°F). Needs full light or partial shade and well-drained soil. Water containerized plants moderately when in full growth, less at other times. Propagate by seed in spring.
M. corallipes. See *M. spiralis*.
M. spiralis, syn. *M. corallipes*. Evergreen, palm-like shrub with a very short, mainly underground trunk. H and S 60cm–1m (2–3ft). Has a rosette of deep green leaves, each with a spirally twisted mid-rib and very narrow, leathery leaflets.

Madagascar dragon tree. See *Dracaena marginata*.
Madagascar jasmine. See *Stephanotis floribunda*, illus. p.200.
Madeira vine. See *Anredera*.
Madonna lily. See *Lilium candidum*, illus. p.416.
Madroña See *Arbutus menziesii*.
Madroña See *Arbutus menziesii*.

MAGNOLIA

MAGNOLIACEAE

Genus of deciduous, semi-evergreen or evergreen trees and shrubs, grown for their showy, usually fragrant flowers. Leaves are mainly oval. Fully to frost hardy. Flowers and buds of early-flowering magnolias may be damaged by late frosts. Needs sun or semi-shade and shelter from strong winds. Does best in fertile, well-drained soil. *M. delavayi, M. kobus, M. sieboldii* and *M. wilsonii* grow on chalky soil. Other species prefer neutral to acid soil, but will grow in alkaline soil if deep and humus-rich. Dry, sandy soils should be generously enriched with manure and leaf mould before planting. Propagate species by semi-ripe cuttings in summer or by seed, when ripe, in autumn, selected forms by semi-ripe cuttings in summer or by grafting in winter. See also feature panel p.71.
M. acuminata (Cucumber tree). Vigorous, deciduous tree, conical when young, later spreading. H 20m (70ft), S 10m (30ft). Fully hardy. Fragrant, cup-shaped, bluish-green flowers appear from early to mid-summer amid large, oval, pale green leaves, followed by small, egg-shaped, green, later red fruits.
M. campbellii illus. p.71. Deciduous tree, upright when young, later spreading. H 15m (50ft), S 10m (30ft). Frost hardy. Large, slightly fragrant, pale to deep pink flowers are borne on leafless branches from late winter to mid-spring on trees 15–20 years old or more. **'Charles Raffill'** (illus. p.71) bears large, fragrant, cup-shaped, purplish-pink flowers from late winter to mid-spring on trees at least 15 years old. Leaves are large, oval and mid-green. **'Darjeeling'** (illus. p.71) has large, very deep pink flowers. **'Kew's Surprise'** produces deep purplish-pink flowers. subsp. ***mollicomata*** (illus. p.71) has lilac-pink flowers slightly earlier in the year.
***M.* 'Charles Coates'.** Deciduous, rounded, open, spreading tree. H 19m (70ft), S 8m (25ft). Fully hardy. Extremely fragrant, creamy-white flowers with conspicuous, red stamens are produced in late spring and early summer amid large, light green leaves.
M. cylindrica. Deciduous, spreading tree or large shrub. H and S 5m (15ft). Fully hardy. Fragrant, upright, creamy-white flowers are produced in mid-spring, after which the young leaves turn dark green.
M. cylindrica of gardens. See *M.* 'Pegasus'.
M. dawsoniana. Deciduous tree or shrub, with a broadly oval head. H 15m (50ft), S 10m (30ft). Frost hardy. In early spring, large, fragrant, pendent, open cup-shaped, pale lilac-pink flowers are carried profusely on older plants (20 years from seed, 10 years from grafting). Leaves are oval, leathery and deep green.
M. delavayi. Evergreen, rounded, dense shrub or tree. H and S 10m (30ft). Frost hardy. Large, slightly fragrant, bowl-shaped, parchment-white flowers are short-lived and open intermittently from mid-summer to early autumn. Large, oval leaves are deep blue-green above and bluish-white beneath.
🏆 ***M. denudata***, syn. *M. heptapeta* (Lily tree, Yulan; illus. p.71). Deciduous, rounded, bushy shrub or spreading tree. H and S 10m (30ft). Fully hardy. Produces masses of fragrant, cup-shaped, white flowers from mid- to late spring before oval, mid-green leaves appear.
M. fraseri illus. p.71. Deciduous, spreading, open tree. H 10m (30ft), S 8m (25). Fully hardy. Fragrant white or pale yellow flowers open in late spring and early summer amid large, pale green leaves.
M. globosa. Deciduous, bushy shrub. H and S 5m (15ft). Frost hardy. In early summer, large, oval, glossy, dark green leaves set off fragrant, cup-shaped, creamy-white flowers with red anthers.
M. grandiflora (Bull bay). Evergreen, broadly conical or rounded, dense tree. H and S 10m (30ft). Frost hardy. Bears large, very fragrant, bowl-shaped, white flowers intermittently from mid-summer to early autumn. Has oblong, glossy, mid- to dark green leaves.
🏆 **'Exmouth'** has creamy-white flowers and narrow, leathery leaves.
'Ferruginea' (illus. p.71) has dark green leaves, rust-brown beneath.
🏆 ***M.* 'Heaven Scent'** illus. p.71. Vigorous, deciduous shrub or tree. H and S 10m (30ft). Fully hardy. Fragrant, vase-shaped flowers, each with usually 9 petals that are pink outside, white within, are borne from mid-spring to early summer. Leaves are broadly elliptic and glossy green.
M. heptapeta. See *M. denudata*.
M. hypoleuca. See *M. obovata*.
M. insignis. See *Manglietia insignis*.
***M. × kewensis* 'Wada's Memory'.** See *M. salicifolia* 'Wada's Memory'.
M. kobus. Deciduous, broadly conical

tree. H 10m (30ft), S 8m (25ft). Fully hardy. Bears a profusion of fragrant, pure white flowers in mid-spring before small, slightly aromatic, dark green leaves appear.
M. liliiflora, syn. *M. quinquepeta.* Deciduous, bushy shrub. H 3m (10ft), S 4m (12ft). Fully hardy. Has fragrant, upright, vase-shaped, purplish-pink flowers that are borne amid oval, very dark green leaves from mid-spring to mid-summer. ♀ **'Nigra'** (illus. p.71) has large, deep purple flowers.
♀ ***M. × loebneri*** **'Leonard Messel'** illus. p.71. Deciduous, upright shrub or small tree. H 8m (25ft), S 6m (20ft). Fully hardy. In mid-spring, fragrant flowers with many pale lilac-pink petals appear before and after oval, deep green leaves emerge. ♀ **'Merrill'** has funnel-shaped, white flowers.
M. macrophylla. Deciduous, broadly upright tree, becoming rounded with age. H and S 10m (30ft). Frost hardy. Produces stout, blue-grey shoots and very large, oval, bright green leaves. Large, fragrant, bowl-shaped, parchment-white flowers are borne in early summer.
***M.* 'Manchu Fan'** illus. p.71. Vigorous, deciduous shrub or tree. H 6m (20ft), S 5m (15ft). Fully hardy. In late spring has large, goblet-shaped, creamy-white flowers with usually 9 petals, the inner ones flushed purple-pink at the base. Leaves are ovate.
***M.* 'Norman Gould'** illus. p.71. Deciduous, spreading tree or bushy shrub. H and S 5m (15ft). Fully hardy. Silky buds open into fragrant, star-shaped, white flowers in mid-spring. Leaves are oblong and dark green.
♀ ***M. obovata***, syn. *M. hypoleuca* (Japanese big-leaf magnolia; illus. p.71). Vigorous, deciduous, upright tree. H 15m (50ft), S 10m (30ft). Fully hardy. Large, fragrant, pink-flushed, white or pale cream flowers with crimson stamens appear in early summer.
***M.* 'Pegasus'**, syn. *M. cylindrica* of gardens illus. p.71. Deciduous shrub or multi-stemmed tree, initially vase-shaped, later spreading. H and S 6m (20ft). Fully hardy. Has elliptic, dark green leaves, pale green beneath. In spring, before and with the young leaves, produces cup-shaped, creamy-white or yellowish-white flowers, suffused purplish-pink at the bases.
M. quinquepeta. See *M. liliiflora.*
***M.* 'Ricki'** illus. p.71. Upright, deciduous shrub. H and S 4m (12ft). Fully hardy. Goblet-shaped flowers, each with 15 twisted petals that are pink to dark purple-pink at the bases, are produced from dark purple-pink buds in mid-spring. Leaves are broadly oval and mid-green.
♀ ***M. salicifolia*** (Willow-leaved magnolia; illus. p.71). Deciduous, conical tree. H 10m (30ft), S 5m (15ft). Fully hardy. Has aromatic, oval leaves, mid-green above, grey-white beneath. Fragrant, pure white flowers open in mid-spring before foliage appears.
♀ **'Wada's Memory'** (syn. *M. × kewensis* 'Wada's Memory') has dark green foliage and a profusion of large flowers borne from mid- to late spring.
M. sargentiana. Deciduous, broadly conical tree. H 15m (50ft), S 10m (30ft). Fully hardy. Large, fragrant, narrowly bowl-shaped, many-petalled flowers, white inside, purplish-pink outside, open from mid- to late spring, before oval, dark green leaves emerge.
♀ ***M. sieboldii.*** Deciduous, arching shrub or wide-spreading tree. H 8m (25ft), S 12m (40ft). Frost hardy. Fragrant, cup-shaped, white flowers, with crimson anthers, are carried above oval, dark green leaves from late spring to late summer. subsp. ***sinensis*** (syn. *M. sinensis*) has slightly larger, fully pendent flowers and morerounded, oval leaves.
M. sinensis. See. *M. sieboldii* subsp. *sinensis.*
M. × soulangeana **'Alba'** see *M. × s.* 'Alba Superba'.**'Alba Superba'** (syn. *M. × s.* 'Alba') is a deciduous, rounded, spreading shrub or small tree. H and S 6m (20ft). Fully hardy. Bears large, fragrant, tulip-like, white flowers, faintly flushed with pink at the bases, from mid- to early spring, the first before mid- to dark green leaves emerge. ♀ **'Brozzonii'**, H 8m (25ft), S 6m (20ft), is tree-like, with large, purple-flushed, white flowers.
♀ **'Etienne Soulange-Bodin'** (illus. p.71) bears purple-flushed, white blooms. Flowers of ♀ **'Lennei'** are large, goblet-shaped and deep rose-purple. ♀ **'Lennei Alba'** (illus. p.71) has ivory-white blooms. **'Picture'**, H 8m (25ft), S 6m (20ft), is vigorous, compact and upright, with large, erect, deep reddish- purple flowers.**'Rubra'** of gardens see *M. × s.* 'Rustica Rubra'.
♀ **'Rustica Rubra'** (syn. *M. × s.* 'Rubra' of gardens; illus. p.71) has purplish-red blooms suffused pink.
M. sprengeri illus. p.71. Deciduous, spreading tree. H 15m (50ft), S 10m (30ft). Frost hardy. In mid-spring has fragrant, bowl-shaped, white flowers sometimes fringed with red or pale pink, before oval, dark green leaves appear. **'Wakehurst'** (illus. p.71) has deep purplish-pink flowers.
♀ ***M. stellata*** (Star magnolia). Deciduous, bushy, dense shrub. H 3m (10ft), S 4m (12ft). Fully hardy. Fragrant, star-shaped flowers with many narrow petals open from silky buds during early to mid-spring. Leaves are narrow and deep green.
♀ **'Waterlily'** (illus. p.71) has large, white flowers with many petals.
M. tripetala. Deciduous, spreading, open tree, conical when young. H 10m (30ft), S 8m (25ft). Fully hardy. Has large, dark green leaves, clustered about shoot tips, and rather unpleasantly scented, creamy-white flowers with narrow petals in late spring and early summer.
M. × veitchii **'PeterVeitch'** illus. p.71. Fast-growing, deciduous, spreading tree. H 20m (60ft), S 15m (52ft). Frost hardy. Bears large, fragrant, pale pink and white flowers in mid-spring, before dark green leaves emerge. Usually flowers within 10 years of planting.
M. virginiana (Sweet bay). Deciduous or semi-evergreen, conical shrub or tree. H 9m (28ft), S 6m (20ft). Fully hardy. Has very fragrant, cup-shaped, creamy-white flowers from early summer to early autumn. Oblong, glossy, mid- to dark green leaves are bluish-white beneath.
M. × watsonii. See *M. × wieseneri.*
M. × wieseneri, syn. *M. × watsonii* illus. p.71. Deciduous, spreading, open tree or shrub. H 8m (25ft), S 5m (15ft). Fully hardy. Rounded, white buds open in late spring to early summer to fragrant, creamy-white flowers, flushed pink outside and with crimson stamens.
♀ ***M. wilsonii*** illus. p.71. Deciduous, spreading tree or shrub. H 8m (25ft), S 7m (22ft). Frost hardy. In late spring and early summer, fragrant, cup-shaped, white flowers with crimson stamens hang from arching branches amid narrow, dark green leaves.

Magnolia
Japanese big-leaf. See *Magnolia obovata*, illus. p.71.
Star. See *Magnolia stellata.*
Willow-leaved. See *Magnolia salicifolia*, illus. p.71.

× Mahoberberis

BERBERIDACEAE

Hybrid genus *(Berberis × Mahonia)* of evergreen shrubs, grown for their foliage, flowers and botanical interest. Fully hardy. Needs sun or semi-shade and fertile, well-drained soil. Propagate by semi-ripe cuttings in summer.
♀ **× *M. aquisargentii.*** Evergreen, upright, densely leaved shrub. H and S 2m (6ft). Leaves are bright green, often with 3 leaflets, some oblong and finely toothed, others holly-shaped. Terminal clusters of berberis-like, yellow flowers are sparsely produced in late spring.

Mahoe. See *Melicytus ramiflorus; Thespesia populnea.*

Mahonia

BERBERIDACEAE

Genus of evergreen shrubs, grown for their foliage, their usually short racemes of often fragrant, rounded, bell-shaped, yellow flowers and, with tall species and cultivars, for their deeply fissured bark. Large mahonias make good specimen plants; low-growing ones are excellent for ground cover. Fully to half hardy. Prefers shade or semi-shade and fertile, well-drained but not too dry soil. Propagate species by leaf-bud or semi-ripe cuttings in summer or by seed in autumn, selected forms by leaf-bud or semi-ripe cuttings only.
M. acanthifolia. See *M. napaulensis.*
M. aquifolium illus. p.153.
M. bealei. See *M. japonica* 'Bealei'.
***M.* 'Heterophylla'.** Evergreen, upright shrub. H 1m (3ft), S 1.5m (5ft). Frost hardy. Has reddish-purple shoots and glossy, bright green leaves, each composed of 5 or 7 narrowly lance-shaped, wavy-edged or curled leaflets, that turn reddish-purple in winter. Small clusters of yellow flowers appear in spring.
♀ ***M. japonica*** illus. p.147. **'Bealei'** (syn. *M. bealei*). Bears blue-green leaves divided into broad leaflets and pale yellow flowers in shorter, upright racemes.
♀ ***M. lomariifolia.*** Evergreen, very upright shrub. H 3m (10ft), S 2m (6ft). Frost hardy. Large, dark green leaves each have 19–37 narrow, holly-like, spiny leaflets. Fragrant, bright yellow flowers are produced in dense, upright racemes during late autumn and winter.
M. × media. ♀ **'Buckland'** and ♀ **'Charity'** illus. p.121.
M. napaulensis, syn. *M. acanthifolia.* Evergreen, upright, open shrub. H 2.5m (8ft), S 3m (10ft). Frost hardy. Leaves are composed of up to 15 holly-like, spiny, dark green leaflets. Produces long, slender racemes of yellow flowers in early and mid-spring.
M. repens. Evergreen, upright shrub that spreads by underground stems. H 30cm (1ft), S 2m (6ft). Fully hardy. Blue-green leaves each consist of 3–7 oval leaflets, with bristle-like teeth. Dense clusters of deep yellow flowers are borne from mid- to late spring.
♀ ***M. × wagneri*** **'Undulata'.** Evergreen, upright shrub. H and S 2m (6ft). Fully hardy. Glossy, dark green leaves each have 5–9 holly-like, wavy-edged leaflets that become bronzed in winter. Bears dense clusters of deep yellow flowers in mid- and late spring.

Maianthemum

May lily

LILIACEAE/CONVALLARIACEAE

Genus of perennials with extensive, spreading rhizomes. Is useful as ground cover in woodlands and wild areas. Fully hardy. Prefers shade and humus-rich, moist, sandy, neutral to acid soil. Propagate by seed in autumn or by division in any season.
M. bifolium. Spreading, rhizomatous perennial. H 10cm (4in), S indefinite. Pairs of large, oval, glossy, dark green leaves, with wavy edges, arise direct from rhizomes. Slender stems each produce a raceme of 4-petalled, white flowers in early summer, followed by small, spherical, red berries. May be invasive.
M. canadense illus. p.375.
M. racemosum. See *Smilacina racemosa.*

Maiden pink. See *Dianthus deltoides.*
Maidenhair
Delta. See *Adiantum raddianum.*
Tassel. See *Adiantum raddianum* 'Grandiceps'.
Maidenhairfern. See *Adiantum capillus-veneris.*
Maidenhair spleenwort. See *Asplenium trichomanes*, illus. p.323.
Maidenhair tree. See *Ginkgo biloba*, illus. p.99.

Maihuenia

CACTACEAE

Genus of slow-growing, summer-flowering, alpine cacti, clump-forming with age, with cylindrical stems. Fully to frost hardy. Requires sun and well-drained soil. Protect from winter rain. Propagate by seed or stem cuttings in spring or summer.
M. poeppigii illus. p.493.

Maiten. See *Maytenus boaria.*
Maize. See *Zea.*
Ornamental. See *Zea mays.*
Majorcan peony. See *Paeonia cambessedesii*, illus. p.238.
Malay ginger. See *Costus speciosus.*

MALCOLMIA

CRUCIFERAE/BRASSICACEAE

Genus of spring- to autumn-flowering annuals. Fully hardy. Grow in sun and in fertile, well-drained soil. Propagate by seed sown outdoors in spring, summer or early autumn. Self-seeds freely.
M. maritima illus. p.335.

Male fern. See *Dryopteris filix-mas*, illus. p.322.

MALEPHORA

AIZOACEAE

Genus of erect or spreading, perennial succulents with semi-cylindrical leaves. Frost tender, min. 5°C (41°F). Needs sun and very well-drained soil. Propagate by seed or stem cuttings in spring or summer.
M. crocea illus. p.496.

Mallow. See *Malva*.
Sleepy. See *Malvaviscus arboreus*, illus. p.117.
Tree. See *Lavatera*.

MALOPE

MALVACEAE

Genus of annuals, grown for their showy flowers that are ideal for cutting. Fully hardy. Grow in sun and in fertile, well-drained soil. Propagate by seed sown outdoors in spring. Self-seeds freely.
M. trifida illus. p.336.

Maltese cross. See *Lychnis chalcedonica*, illus. p.253.

MALUS

Crab apple

ROSACEAE

Genus of deciduous, mainly spring-flowering trees and shrubs, grown for their shallowly cup-shaped flowers, fruits, foliage or autumn colour. Crab apples may be used to make preserves. Fully hardy. Prefers full sun, but tolerates semi-shade; grows in any but waterlogged soil. In winter, cut out dead or diseased wood and prune to maintain a balanced branch system. Propagate by budding in late summer or by grafting in mid-winter. Trees are sometimes attacked by aphids, caterpillars and red spider mite, and are susceptible to fireblight and apple scab.

***M.* 'Almey'.** Deciduous, rounded tree. H and S 8m (25ft). Oval leaves are reddish-purple when young, maturing to dark green. Single, deep pink flowers, with paler pink, almost white centres, in late spring are followed by long-lasting, rounded, orange-red crab apples, which are subject to apple scab.
M.* × *arnoldiana illus. p.83.
***M.* × *atrosanguinea*.** Deciduous, spreading tree. H and S 6m (20ft). Produces oval, glossy, dark green leaves. Red flower buds open to single, rich pink blooms in late spring. Bears small, rounded, red-flushed, yellow crab apples.
M. baccata (Siberian crab). Deciduous, spreading tree. H and S 15m (50ft). Has oval, dark green leaves, a profusion of single, white flowers from mid- to late spring and tiny, rounded, red or yellow crab apples. var. ***mandschurica*** illus. p.70.
***M.* 'Chilko'.** Deciduous, spreading tree. H and S 8m (25ft). Oval, dark green leaves are reddish-purple when young. Has single, rose-pink flowers in mid-spring, followed by large, rounded, bright crimson crab apples.
***M. coronaria* 'Charlottae'.** Deciduous, spreading tree. H and S 9m (28ft). Broadly oval, lobed or deeply toothed leaves are dark green, turning red in autumn. Semi-double, pale pink flowers are borne in late spring and early summer.
***M.* 'Cowichan'** illus. p.90.
***M.* 'Dorothea'.** Deciduous, spreading tree. H and S 8m (25ft). Semi-double, silvery-pink flowers, red in bud, are borne in late spring, followed by rounded, yellow crab apples. Oval leaves are mid-green. Is subject to apple scab.
***M.* 'Eleyi'**, syn. *M.* × *purpurea* 'Eleyi'. Deciduous, spreading tree. H and S 8m (25ft). Oval leaves are dark reddish-purple when young, dark green when mature. Bears single, deep purplish-red flowers from mid- to late spring and rounded, purplish-red crab apples.
🏆 ***M. floribunda*** illus. p.84.
***M.* 'Frettingham's Victoria'.** Deciduous, upright tree. H 8m (25ft), S 4m (12ft). Single, white flowers, borne amid oval, dark green leaves in late spring, are followed by rounded, red-flushed, yellow crab apples.
🏆 ***M.* 'Golden Hornet'**, syn. *M.* × *zumi* 'Golden Hornet', illus. p.93.
***M.* × *hartwigii* 'Katherine'.** See *M.* 'Katherine'.
***M.* 'Hopa'.** Deciduous, spreading tree. H and S 10m (30ft). Oval, dark green leaves are reddish-purple when young. Single, deep pink flowers in mid-spring are succeeded by rounded, orange-and-red crab apples.
🏆 ***M. hupehensis*** illus. p.70.
***M.* 'John Downie'** illus. p.91.
🏆 ***M.* 'Katherine'**, syn. *M.* × *hartwigii* 'Katherine'. Deciduous, round-headed tree. H and S 6m (20ft). Has oval, mid-green leaves, large, double, pale pink flowers, fading to white, from mid- to late spring and tiny, rounded, yellow-flushed, red crab apples.
***M.* 'Lemoinei'**, syn. *M.* × *purpurea* 'Lemoinei', illus. p.85.
***M.* 'Magdeburgensis'** illus. p.84.
***M.* 'Marshall Oyama'** illus. p.92.
***M.* × *moerlandsii* 'Profusion'.** See *M.* 'Profusion'.
🏆 ***M.* 'Neville Copeman'**, syn. *M.* × *purpurea* 'Neville Copeman'. Deciduous, spreading tree. H and S 9m (28ft). Oval, dark green leaves are purplish-red when young. Single, dark purplish-pink flowers, borne from mid- to late spring, are followed by rounded, orange-red to carmine crab apples.
M. niedzwetskyana, syn. *M. pumila* var. *niedzwetskyana*. Deciduous, spreading tree. H 6m (20ft), S 8m (25ft). Oval leaves are red when young, later purple. Produces clusters of single, deep reddish-purple flowers in late spring, then very large, conical, reddish-purple crab apples.
***M. prattii*.** Deciduous tree, upright when young, later spreading. H and S 10m (30ft). Oval, red-stalked, glossy, mid-green leaves become orange and red in autumn. Single, white flowers in late spring are followed by small, rounded or egg-shaped, white-flecked, red crab apples.
***M.* 'Professor Sprenger'** illus. p.92.
***M.* 'Profusion'**, syn. *M.* × *moerlandsii* 'Profusion', illus. p.73.
M. prunifolia illus. p.91.
M. pumila var. ***niedzwetskyana*.** See *M. niedzwetskyana*.
M.* × *purpurea (Purple crab). Deciduous, spreading tree. H 8m (25ft), S 10m (30ft). Oval, young leaves are reddish, maturing to green. Single, deep ruby-red flowers, which become paler with age, are produced in late spring and are followed by rounded, reddish-purple crab apples. **'Eleyi'** see *M.* 'Eleyi'.**'Lemoinei'** see *M.* 'Lemoinei'.**'Neville Copeman'** see *M.* 'Neville Copeman'.
***M.* 'Red Jade'**, syn. *M.* × *scheideckeri* 'Red Jade'. Deciduous, weeping tree. H 4m (12ft), S 6m (20ft). In late spring has single, white flowers, sometimes pale pink-flushed, then long-lasting, rounded to egg-shaped, red crab apples. Leaves are dark green and oval.
***M.* × *robusta*.** Vigorous, deciduous, spreading tree. H 12m (40ft), S 10m (30ft). Bears masses of single, white or pink flowers above oval, dark green leaves in late spring. These are followed by long-lasting, rounded, yellow or red crab apples. 🏆 **'Yellow Siberian'** produces white flowers, which are sometimes pink-tinged, and yellow crab apples.
***M.* 'Royalty'** illus. p.85.
***M. sargentii*.** See *M. toringo* subsp. *sargentii*.
***M.* × *scheideckeri* 'Red Jade'.** See *M.* 'Red Jade'.
***M. sieboldii*.** See *M. toringo*.
***M. spectabilis*.** Deciduous, round-headed tree. H and S 10m (30ft). Has oval, dark green leaves, large, single, blush-pink flowers, rose-red in bud, from mid- to late spring and large, rounded, yellow crab apples.
***M. toringo*,** syn *M. sieboldii*, illus. p.126. subsp. ***sargentii*,** syn. *M. sargentii*, illus. p.112
***M. toringoides*.** Deciduous, spreading tree. H 8m (25ft), S 10m (30ft). Oval, deeply lobed, glossy, bright green leaves turn yellow in autumn. Bears single, white flowers in late spring and rounded or egg-shaped, red-flushed, yellow crab apples in autumn.
🏆 ***M. transitoria*.** Deciduous, spreading, elegant tree. H 8m (25ft), S 10m (30ft). Oval, deeply lobed, mid-green leaves turn yellow in autumn. Has masses of single, white flowers in late spring, followed by small, rounded, pale yellow crab apples.
***M. trilobata*.** Deciduous, conical tree. H 15m (50ft), S 7m (22ft). Has maple-like, lobed, glossy, bright green leaves that often become brightly coloured in autumn. Bears single, white flowers in early summer, followed by small, rounded or pear-shaped, red or yellow crab apples.
🏆 ***M. tschonoskii*.** Deciduous, conical tree. H 12m (40ft), S 7m (22ft). Broadly oval, glossy, mid-green leaves turn brilliant shades of orange, red and purple in autumn. Single, pink-tinged, white flowers, borne in late spring, are succeeded by rounded, red-flushed, yellowish-green crab apples.
***M.* 'Van Eseltine'.** Deciduous, upright tree. H 6m (20ft), S 4m (12ft). Bears double, pink flowers in late spring and rounded, yellow crab apples in autumn. Has oval, dark green leaves.
***M.* 'Veitch's Scarlet'** illus. p.90.
M. yunnanensis var. ***veitchii*** illus. p.87.
M.* × *zumi* 'Calocarpa',** syn. *M.* × *z.* var. *calocarpa*, illus. p.92. var. ***calocarpa see *M.* × *z.* 'Calocarpa'.**'Golden Hornet'** see *M.* 'Golden Hornet'.

MALVA

Mallow

MALVACEAE

Genus of annuals, biennials and free-flowering, short-lived perennials. Fully hardy. Requires sun and fertile, well-drained soil. Propagate species by seed in autumn, selected forms by cuttings from firm, basal shoots in late spring or summer. These shoots may be encouraged by cutting plant back after first flowers have faded.
M. moschata illus. p.245.

***Malvastrum capensis*.** See *Anisodontea capensis*.

MALVAVISCUS

MALVACEAE

Genus of evergreen shrubs and trees, grown for their flowers. Frost tender, min. 13–16°C (55–61°F). Requires a position in full light and in fertile, well-drained soil. Water containerized plants freely during growing season, moderately at other times. To maintain shape, flowered stems may be cut back hard in late winter. Propagate by seed in spring or by semi-ripe cuttings in summer. Whitefly and red spider mite may be troublesome.
M. arboreus illus. p.117.

Mamaku. See *Cyathea medullaris*.

MAMMILLARIA

Pincushion cactus

CACTACEAE

Genus of hemispherical, spherical or columnar cacti, grown for their rings of funnel-shaped flowers that develop near crowns. Flowers, offsets and long, slender to spherical seed pods grow between tubercles on a spiny, green stem with extended areoles. Frost tender, min. 5–10°C (41–50°F). Requires full sun and very well-drained soil. Keep completely dry in winter, otherwise plants rot easily. Propagate by seed in spring or summer.
🏆 ***M. bocasana*** illus. p.487.
🏆 ***M. candida*,** syn. *Mammilloydia candida* (Snowball pincushion). Slow-growing, clump-forming, perennial cactus. H and S 15cm (6in). Min. 5°C (41°F). Columnar, green stem is densely covered with short, stiff, white spines. Produces cream to rose flowers, 1–2cm (½–¾in) across, in spring. Water sparingly in summer.
***M. centricirrha*.** See *M. magnimamma*.
***M. conoidea*.** See *Neolloydia conoidea*.

M. crinita, syn *M. zeilmanniana,* illus. p.489.
M. densispina. Slow-growing, spherical, perennial cactus. H 10cm (4in), S 20cm (8in). min. 5°C (41°F). Has a green stem densely covered with stout, golden spines and, in spring, yellow flowers, 1–2cm (½–¾in) wide.
M. elegans of gardens. See *M. haageana*.
♀ ***M. elongata*** illus. p.486.
♀ ***M. geminispina*** illus. p.481.
M. gracilis. Clump-forming, perennial cactus. H 5cm (2in), S 20cm (8in). Min. 5°C (41°F). Produces a columnar, green stem densely covered with pure white spines. In early summer carries pale cream flowers, 1–2cm (½–¾in) across. Stem is shallow-rooted and reroots readily. var. ***fragilis***, H 4cm (1½in), is more fragile and has off-white spines.
M. haageana, syn. *M. elegans of gardens.* Spherical to columnar, perennial cactus. H 30cm (12in), S 20cm (8in). min. 5°C (41°F). Bears a green stem densely covered with short, bristly spines and bright red flowers, 1cm (½ in) across, in spring. Offsets occasionally.
♀ ***M. hahniana*** illus. p.481.
M. magnimamma, syn. *M. centricirrha.* Clump-forming, perennial cactus. H 30cm (1ft), S 60cm (2ft). Min. 5°C (41°F). Green stem has very pronounced, angular, dark green tubercles with white spines of variable length. Bears cream, pink or red flowers, 1–2cm (½–¾in) wide, in spring and possibly again in late summer.
M. microhelia illus. p.494.
♀ ***M. plumosa*** illus. p.485.
♀ ***M. prolifera*** (Strawberry cactus). Clump-forming, perennial cactus. H 10cm (4in), S 30cm (12in). Min 5°C (41°F). Green stem bears dense, golden to white spines. Produces masses of cream or yellow flowers, 1–2cm (½–¾in) wide, in summer, followed by red berries that taste like strawberries.
M. rhodantha. Spherical to columnar, perennial cactus. H and S 60cm (2ft). Min. 5°C (41°F). Green stem, branching from crown with age, is densely covered with brown to yellow spines, often curved. In late summer produces bright red flowers, 1–2cm (½–¾in) across.
M. schiedeana illus. p.486.
M. sempervivi illus. p.488.
M. zeilmanniana. See *M. crinita.*

Mandarin's hat plant. See *Holmskioldia sanguinea.*

MANDEVILLA, syn. DIPLADENIA

APOCYNACEAE

Genus of evergreen, semi-evergreen or deciduous, woody-stemmed, twining climbers, grown for their large, trumpet-shaped flowers. Half hardy to frost tender, min. 7–10°C (45–50°F). Grow in any well-drained soil, with light shade in summer. Water freely when in full growth, sparingly at other times. Provide support and thin out and spur back congested growth in early spring. Propagate by seed in spring or by semi-ripe cuttings in summer. Whitefly and red spider mite may cause problems. Contact with the sap may cause skin irritation, and all parts may cause mild stomach upset if ingested.
***M. × amabilis* 'Alice du Pont'.** See *M. × amoena* 'Alice du Pont'.
♀ ***M. × amoena* 'Alice du Pont',** syn. *M. × amabilis* 'Alice du Pont', illus. p.205.
M. boliviensis, syn. *Dipladenia boliviensis.* Vigorous, evergreen, woody-stemmed, twining climber. Frost tender. H to 4m (12ft). Oblong, pointed leaves are lustrous green. Large, trumpet-shaped, white flowers with gold eyes are produced in small clusters in summer.
M. laxa, syn. *M. suaveolens, M. tweediana* (Chilean jasmine). Fast-growing, deciduous or semi-evergreen, woody-stemmed, twining climber. H 5m (15ft) or more. Half hardy. Oval leaves have heart-shaped bases. Clusters of fragrant, white flowers are borne in summer.
M. splendens, syn. *Dipladenia splendens*, illus. p.200.
M. suaveolens. See *M. laxa.*
M. tweediana. See *M. laxa.*

MANDRAGORA
Mandrake

SOLANACEAE

Genus of rosetted perennials with large, deep, fleshy roots. Fully to frost hardy. Needs sun or partial shade and deep, humus-rich, well-drained soil. Resents being transplanted. Propagate by seed in autumn. Alkaloids in the plant may be harmful if ingested.
M. officinarum illus. p.383.

Mandrake. See *Mandragora.*

MANETTIA

RUBIACEAE

Genus of evergreen, soft- or semi-woody-stemmed, twining climbers, grown for their small but showy flowers. Frost tender, min. 5°C (41°F), but 7–10°C (45–50°F) is preferred. Grow in any humus-rich, well-drained soil, with partial shade in summer. Water regularly, sparingly when temperatures are low. Stems need support. Cut back if required in spring. Propagate by softwood or semi-ripe cuttings in summer. Whitefly is sometimes a problem.
M. bicolor. See *M. luteorubra.*
M. cordifolia (Firecracker vine). Fast-growing, evergreen, soft-stemmed, twining climber. H 2m (6ft) or more. Has narrowly heart-shaped, glossy leaves. Funnel-shaped, red flowers, sometimes yellow flushed on the lobes, appear in small clusters in summer.
M. inflata. See *M. luteorubra.*
M. luteorubra, syn. *M. bicolor, M. inflata*, illus. p.201.

MANGLIETIA

MAGNOLIACEAE

Genus of evergreen trees, grown for their foliage and flowers. Half hardy, but is best at min. 3–5°C (37–41°F). Provide humus-rich, moisture-retentive but well-drained, acid soil and full light or partial shade. Water potted plants freely when in full growth, less at other times. Pruning is tolerated if necessary. Propagate by seed in spring.
M. insignis, syn. *Magnolia insignis.* Evergreen, broadly conical tree. H 8–12m (25–40ft) or more, S 3–5m (10–15ft) or more. Leaves are narrowly oval, lustrous, dark green above, bluish-green beneath. In early summer produces solitary, magnolia-like, pink to carmine flowers that are cream-flushed.

Manipur lily. See *Lilium mackliniae*, illus. p.417.
Manna ash. See *Fraxinus ornus*, illus. p.72.
Manna gum. See *Eucalyptus viminalis.*
Manuka. See *Leptospermum scoparium.*
Manzanita. See *Arctostaphylos.*
Pine-mat. See *Arctostaphylos nevadensis.*
Stanford. See *Arctostaphylos stanfordiana.*
Maple. See *Acer.*
Amur. See *Acer tataricum* subsp. *ginnala*, illus. p.91.
Ash-leaved. See *Acer negundo.*
Cappadocian. See *Acer cappadocicum.*
Coral-bark. See *Acer palmatum* 'Sango-kaku', illus. p.120.
Full-moon. See *Acer japonicum.*
Hawthorn. See *Acer crataegifolium.*
Hers's. See *Acer davidii* subsp. *grosseri.*
Hornbeam. See *Acer carpinifolium*, illus. p.88.
Italian. See *Acer opalus.*
Japanese. See *Acer japonicum; Acer palmatum.*
Lobel's. See *Acer cappadocicum* subsp. *lobelii*, illus. p.62.
Montpelier. See *Acer monspessulanum.*
Nikko. See *Acer maximowiczianum.*
Norway. See *Acer platanoides.*
Oregon. See *Acer macrophyllum*, illus. p.60.
Paper-bark. See *Acer griseum*, illus. p.96.
Père David's. See *Acer davidii.*
Red. See *Acer rubrum*, illus. p.66.
Silver. See *Acer saccharinum.*
Snake-bark. See *Acer capillipes*, illus. p.78; *Acer davidii; Acer davidii* subsp. *grosseri; Acer pensylvanicum*, illus. p.80; *Acer rufinerve*, illus. p.78.
Sugar. See *Acer saccharum.*
Trident. See *Acer buergerianum.*
Van Volxem's. See *Acer velutinum* var. *van-volxemii.*
Vine. See *Acer circinatum.*
Mapleleaf begonia. See *Begonia dregei; Begonia* 'Weltoniensis', illus. p.307.

MARANTA

MARANTACEAE

Genus of evergreen perennials, grown for their distinctively patterned, coloured foliage. Frost tender, min. 10–15°C (50–59°F). Needs constant, high humidity and a shaded position away from draughts or wind. Grow in humus-rich, well-drained soil. Propagate by division in spring or summer or by stem cuttings in summer.
M. leuconeura (Prayer plant). **'Erythroneura'** (syn. *M.l.* 'Erythrophylla') illus. p.315. **'Erythrophylla'.** See *M.l.* 'Erythroneura'.
♀ **'Kerchoviana'** illus. p.316.
'Massangeana' is an evergreen, short-stemmed perennial, branching at the base. H and S 30cm (1ft). Each oblong, velvety, dark green leaf, 15cm (6in) long, has a wide, irregular, pale midrib, white, lateral veins and often purplish-green below, stand upright at night but lie flat during the day. Bears small, 3-petalled, white to mauve flowers in slender, upright spikes year-round.

Marguerite. See *Argyranthemum frutescens*, illus. p.242.
Blue. See *Felicia amelloides.*
Marginatocereus marginatus. See *Pachycereus marginatus.*

MARGYRICARPUS

ROSACEAE

Genus of evergreen shrubs, grown for their fruits. Is good for rock gardens. Frost hardy. Needs a sheltered, sunny position and well-drained soil. Propagate by softwood cuttings in early summer or by seed in autumn.
M. pinnatus, syn. *M. setosus* (Pearl berry). Evergreen, prostrate shrub. H 23–30cm (9–12in), S 1m (3ft). Has dark green leaves divided into linear, silky leaflets. Has tiny, inconspicuous, green flowers in early summer, then small, globose, glossy, white fruits.
M. setosus. See *M. pinnatus.*

Marigold. See *Calendula.*
African. See *Tagetes erecta.*
Aztec. See *Tagetes erecta.*
Cape. See *Dimorphotheca.*
French. See *Tagetes patula.*
Marsh. See *Caltha palustris*, illus. p.467.
Pot. See *Calendula officinalis.*
Mariposa tulip. See *Calochortus.*
Mariposa, Yellow. See *Calochortus luteus*, illus. p.431.
Maritime pine. See *Pinus pinaster*, illus. p.99.
Marjoram, Wild. See *Origanum vulgare.*
Marmalade bush. See *Streptosolen jamesonii*, illus. p.218.
Marsdenia erecta. See *Cionura erecta.*
Marsh bucklerfern. See *Thelypteris palustris*, illus. p.324.
Marsh fern. See *Thelypteris palustris*, illus. p.324.
Marsh marigold. See *Caltha palustris*, illus. p.467.
Martagon lily. See *Lilium martagon*, illus. p.417.

MARTYNIA

PEDALIACEAE

Genus of annuals, grown for their flowers and horned fruits. Half hardy. Needs a sunny, sheltered site and fertile, well-drained soil. Propagate by seed sown under glass in early spring.
M. annua illus. p.332.
M. louisianica. See *Proboscidea louisianica.*

Marvel of Peru. See *Mirabilis.*

Masdevallia

ORCHIDACEAE

See also ORCHIDS.

♀ ***M. coccinea*** illus. p.309. Evergreen, epiphytic orchid for a cool greenhouse. H 15cm (6in). Narrowly oval leaves are 10cm (4in) long. Bears rich cerise flowers, 8cm (3in) long, in summer. Needs shade in summer.

♀ ***M. infracta*** illus. p.308. Evergreen, epiphytic orchid for a cool greenhouse. H 15cm (6in). Narrowly oval leaves are 10cm (4in) long. Bears rounded, red-and-white flowers, 5cm (2in) long, with tail-like, greenish sepals, in summer. Needs shade in summer.

♀ ***M. tovarensis*** illus. p.308. Evergreen, epiphytic orchid for a cool greenhouse. H 15cm (6in). Has oval leaves, 10cm (4in) long, and in autumn milky-white flowers, 4cm (1½in) long, with short-tailed sepals, singly or up to 3 to a stem. Grow in shade in summer.

M. wageneriana illus. p.310. Evergreen, epiphytic orchid for a cool greenhouse. H 8cm (3in). Narrowly oval leaves are 10cm (4in) long. Bears pale yellow flowers, 4cm (1½in) long, with long, tail-like sepals, singly or in pairs in summer. Needs summer shade.

Mask flower. See *Alonsoa warscewiczii*, illus. p.341.
Masterwort. See *Astrantia.*
Mastic tree. See *Pistacia lentiscus.*
Peruvian. See *Schinus molle.*

Matteuccia

DRYOPTERIDACEAE/WOODSIACEAE

Genus of deciduous, rhizomatous ferns. Fully hardy. Prefers semi-shade and wet soil. Remove faded fronds regularly and divide plants when crowded. Propagate by division in autumn or winter.

M. orientalis. Deciduous, rhizomatous fern. H and S to 1m (3ft). Produces a **'shuttlecock'** of sterile, arching, broadly ovate, divided fronds, to 80cm (32in) long, light green when young, becoming darker. Fertile, erect, blackish-green fronds appear from the centre of the plant in summer.

♀ ***M. struthiopteris*** illus. p.324.

Matthiola
Stock

CRUCIFERAE/BRASSICACEAE

Genus of annuals, biennials, perennials and evergreen sub-shrubs. Flowers of most annual or biennial stocks are highly scented and excellent for cutting. Fully hardy to frost tender, min. 4°C (39°F). Grow in sun or semi-shade and in fertile, well-drained, ideally lime-rich soil. Tall cultivars may need support. If grown as biennials outdoors, provide cloche protection during winter. To produce flowers outdoors the same summer, sow seed of annuals under glass in early spring, or outdoors in mid-spring. Sow seed of perennials under glass in spring. Propagate sub-shrubs by semi-ripe cuttings in summer. Is prone to aphids, flea beetle, club root, downy mildew and botrytis.

***M.* Brompton Group** (mixed) illus. p.333, (pink) illus. p.335.

***M.* East Lothian Group.** Group of fast-growing, upright, bushy biennials and short-lived perennials, grown as annuals. H and S 30cm (1ft). Fully hardy. Has lance-shaped, greyish-green leaves and, in summer, spikes, 15cm (6in) or more long, of scented, 4-petalled, single or double flowers, in shades of pink, red, purple, yellow or white.

***M.* 'Giant Excelsior'** illus. p.333.

***M.* 'Giant Imperial'** illus. p.330.

M. incana (Brompton stock). Fast-growing, upright, bushy biennial or short-lived perennial, grown as an annual. H 30–60cm (1–2ft), S 30cm (1ft). Fully hardy. Has lance-shaped, greyish-green leaves and, in summer, scented, 4-petalled, light purple flowers borne in spikes, 7–15cm (3–6in) long.

***M.* 'Mammoth Column'.** Fast-growing, upright, bushy biennial or short-lived perennial, grown as an annual. H to 75cm (2½ft), S 30cm (1ft). Fully hardy. Has lance-shaped, greyish-green leaves and, in summer, 30–38cm (12–15in) long spikes, of scented, 4-petalled flowers, available in mixed or single colours. Flowers are excellent for cutting.

***M.* Park Series.** Group of fast-growing, upright, bushy biennials and short-lived perennials, grown as annuals. H and S to 30cm (1ft). Fully hardy. Lance-shaped leaves are greyish-green. In summer, spikes, at least 15cm (6in) long, of scented, 4-petalled flowers are borne in a wide range of colours.

***M.* Ten-week Group.** Group of fast-growing, upright, bushy biennials and short-lived perennials, grown as annuals. H and S to 30cm (1ft). Fully hardy. Has lance-shaped, greyish-green leaves. Has scented, 4-petalled flowers, in spikes at least 15cm (6in) long, in a wide range of colours in summer. Dwarf (illus. p.337) and **'selectable'** cultivars have double flowers.

***M.* 'Trysomic'.** Fast-growing, upright, bushy biennial or short-lived perennial, grown as an annual. H and S to 30cm (1ft). Fully hardy. Lance-shaped leaves are greyish-green. Spikes, at least 15cm (6in) long, of scented, mostly double flowers are produced in a wide range of colours in summer.

Matucana

CACTACEAE

Genus of low-growing, spherical to shortly cylindrical, solitary to clustering perennial cacti, with thick, ribbed stems, often with some spines, usually branching from the base. Solitary, narrowly funnel-shaped yellow, orange or red flowers are produced around the stem tips in summer. Frost tender, min. 10°C (50°F). Needs full sun and very well-drained, slightly alkaline soil. Propagate by seed in spring or summer.

Matucana aurantiaca, syn. *Oreocereus aurantiacus*, illus. p.496

Matucana haynei. Slow-growing, spherical to columnar, perennial cactus. H 60cm (24in), S 10cm (4in). Has a cylindrical, much-ribbed, grass-green stem densely covered with short, white or yellow spines. Red, orange-brown or purple-crimson flowers appear in summer on plants over 15cm (6in) high.

Maurandya

SCROPHULARIACEAE

Genus of twining, woody-based, perennial climbers, grown against a wall or to clothe a trellis. Half hardy. Needs full sun and moderately fertile, moist but well-drained soil. Propagate by seed in spring or softwood cuttings in late spring.

M. barclayana, syn. *Asarina barclayana.* Evergreen, soft-stemmed, scandent climber, herbaceous in cold climates. H to 2m (6ft). Has angular, heart-shaped, hairless leaves. Trumpet-shaped, white, pink or purple flowers, each with a green or whitish throat, 6–7cm (2½–3in) long, are produced in summer-autumn.

M. erubescens. See *Lophospermum erubescens.*

Maxillaria

ORCHIDACEAE

See also ORCHIDS.

M. picta. Evergreen, epiphytic orchid for a cool greenhouse. H 23cm (9in). Fragrant, deep yellow to white flowers, 2.5cm (1in) across, marked purple to dark reddish-brown outside, are produced singly beneath foliage in winter. Has narrowly oval leaves, 15–23cm (6–9in) long. Requires semi-shade in summer.

M. porphyrostele illus. p.311. Evergreen, epiphytic orchid for a cool greenhouse. H 8cm (3in). White- and red-lipped, yellow flowers, 1cm (½in) across, are borne singly in summer-autumn. Narrowly oval leaves are 8cm (3in) long. Grow in good light during summer.

♀ ***M. tenuifolia.*** Evergreen, epiphytic orchid for a cool greenhouse. H 15cm (6in). Fragrant, yellow flowers, 2.5cm (1in) across, heavily overlaid with red and with white lips, are borne singly throughout summer. Has narrowly oval leaves, 15cm (6in) long. Needs good light in summer.

May. See *Crataegus laevigata.*
May, Foam of. See *Spiraea* 'Arguta'.
May apple. See *Podophyllum peltatum.*
Himalayan. See *Podophyllum hexandrum*, illus. p.276.
May lily. See *Maianthemum.*
Mayflower. See *Epigaea repens.*

Maytenus

CELASTRACEAE

Genus of evergreen trees, grown for their neat foliage. Frost hardy, but needs shelter from strong, cold winds when young. Requires sun or semi-shade and fertile, well-drained soil. Propagate by semi-ripe cuttings in summer or by suckers in autumn or spring.

M. boaria, syn. *M. chilensis* (Maiten). Evergreen, bushy-headed, elegant tree. H 10m (30ft), S 8m (25ft). Bears narrowly oval, glossy, dark green leaves on slender shoots, and tiny, star-shaped, green flowers in late spring.

M. chilensis. See *M. boaria.*

Mazus

SCROPHULARIACEAE

Genus of creeping, spring-flowering perennials. Is useful for rock gardens and in paving. Frost hardy. Needs a sheltered, sunny site and moist soil. Propagate by division in spring or by seed in autumn.

M. reptans illus. p.380.

Meadow buttercup. See *Ranunculus acris.*
Meadow cranesbill. See *Geranium pratense.*
Meadow foam. See *Limnanthes douglasii*, illus. p.348.
Meadow lily. See *Lilium canadense.*
Meadow rue. See *Thalictrum.*
Meadow saffron. See *Colchicum autumnale*, illus. p.453.
Meadow saxifrage. See *Saxifraga granulata*, illus. p.358.
Meadowsweet. See *Filipendula.*

Meconopsis

PAPAVERACEAE

Genus of perennials, some short-lived, others monocarpic (die after flowering), grown for their flowers. Fully hardy. Needs shade and, in warm areas, a cool position. Most prefer humus-rich, moist, neutral to acid soil. May be propagated by seed when fresh, in late summer; *M. cambrica, M. grandis, M. quintuplinervia* and their cultivars may also be propagated by division after flowering.

♀ ***M. betonicifolia*** illus. p.259.

M. cambrica illus. p.285.

♀ ***M. grandis*** illus. p.259.

M. integrifolia illus. p.304.

***M.* 'Lingholm' (Fertile Blue Group).** Clump-forming perennial. H 1.2–1.5m (4–5ft), S 45–60cm (1½–2ft). In early summer bears clusters of cup-shaped, clear deep blue flowers. Has rosettes of oblong to oval, toothed, hairy, mid-green leaves. Divide every three years to maintain vigour.

M. paniculata. Short-lived, clump-forming perennial that dies after flowering. H 1.5m (5ft), S 60cm (2ft). Produces racemes of nodding, shallowly cup-shaped, yellow flowers in late spring or early summer. Bears large rosettes of oblong to lance-shaped, deeply lobed and cut, hairy, yellowish-green leaves.

♀ ***M. quintuplinervia*** illus. p.279.

Medicago

LEGUMINOSAE/PAPILIONACEAE

Genus of annuals, perennials and evergreen shrubs, grown for their flowers. Is good in mild, coastal areas as is very wind-resistant. Frost hardy, but in cold areas plant against a south- or west-facing wall. Requires sun and well-drained soil. Cut out dead wood in spring. Propagate shrubs by semi-ripe or softwood cuttings in summer or by seed in autumn or spring, annuals and perennials by seed in autumn or spring.

M. arborea (Moon trefoil, Tree medick). Evergreen, bushy, dense shrub. H and S 2m (6ft). Bears clusters of small, pea-like, yellow flowers from mid-spring to late autumn or winter, followed by curious, flattened, snail-like, green, then brown seed pods. Has dark green leaves, each composed of 3 narrowly triangular leaflets, which are silky-haired when young.

Medick, Tree. See *Medicago arborea.*

MEDINILLA

MELASTOMATACEAE

Genus of evergreen shrubs and scrambling climbers, grown for their flowers and foliage. Frost tender, min. 16–18°C (61–4°F). Needs partial shade and humus-rich, well-drained soil. Water potted plants freely when in full growth, moderately at other times. Propagate by greenwood cuttings in spring or summer.
M. magnifica illus. p.137.

Medlar. See *Mespilus.*
Bronvaux. See + *Crataegomespilus dardarii.*

MEEHANIA

LABIATAE/LAMIACEAE

Genus of perennials often with creeping stems, grown mainly as ground cover. Frost hardy. Prefers shade and well-drained but not dry, humus-rich soil. May be propagated by seed, division or stem cuttings in spring.
M. urticifolia. Trailing, hairy perennial with long, creeping, leafy stems and erect flowering stems. H to 30cm (1ft), S indefinite. Oval to triangular, toothed leaves are 10cm (4in) or more long on the creeping stems – smaller on flowering stems. Whorls of fragrant, 2-lipped, purplish-blue flowers, to 5cm (2in) long, are carried in erect spikes in late spring.

Megasea. Reclassified as *Bergenia.*

MELALEUCA

MYRTACEAE

Genus of evergreen, spring- and summer-flowering trees and shrubs, grown for their flowers and overall appearance. Half hardy to frost tender, min. 4–7°C (39–45°F). Needs full light and well-drained soil, preferably without much nitrogen. Some species tolerate waterlogged soils. Water containerized specimens moderately, less in low temperatures. Propagate by seed in spring or by semi-ripe cuttings in summer.
M. armillaris (Bracelet honey myrtle). Evergreen, rounded, wiry-stemmed shrub or tree. H 3–6m (10–20ft), S 1.2–3m (4–10ft). Frost tender. Has needle-like, deep green leaves and, in summer, dense, bottlebrush-like clusters, 3–6cm (1¼–2½in) long, each flower consisting of a small brush of white stamens.
M. elliptica illus. p.138.
M. hypericifolia. Evergreen, rounded shrub. H and S 2–5m (6–15ft). Frost tender. Leaves are oblong to elliptic and mid- to deep green above, paler beneath. Crimson flowers, each composed of a 2–2.5cm (¾–1in) long brush of stamens of the same colour, are borne in summer, mainly in bottlebrush-like spikes, 4–8cm (1½–3in) long.
M. nesophila, syn. *M. nesophylla*, illus. p.141.
M. nesophylla. See *M. nesophila.*
M. quinquenervia. See *M. viridiflora* var. *rubriflora.*
M. squarrosa (Scented paper-bark). Evergreen, erect, wiry-stemmed shrub or tree. H 3–6m (10–20ft), S 2–4m (6–12ft). Frost tender. Has tiny, oval, deep green leaves. Bears 4cm (1½in) long spikes of scented flowers, each comprising a tiny brush of cream stamens, in late spring and summer.
M. viridiflora var. ***rubriflora***, syn. *M. quinquenervia* (Paper-bark tree). Strong-growing, evergreen, rounded tree. H 6–12m (20–40ft), S 3–6m (10–20ft). Frost tender. Leaves are elliptic and lustrous. Has peeling, papery, tan-coloured bark and, in spring, small, white or creamy-pink flowers in bottlebrush-like clusters. Tolerates waterlogged soil.

MELASPHAERULA

IRIDACEAE

Genus of one species of spring-flowering corm, grown mainly for botanical interest. Half hardy. Needs sun and well-drained soil. Plant in autumn and keep watered until after flowering, then dry off. Propagate by seed or offsets in autumn.
M. graminea. See *M. ramosa.*
M. ramosa, syn. *M. graminea.* Spring-flowering corm. H to 60cm (24in), S 10–15cm (4–6in). Has narrowly sword-shaped, semi-erect leaves in a basal fan. Wiry, branched stem bears loose sprays of small, pendent, funnel-shaped, yellowish-green flowers with pointed petals.

MELASTOMA

MELASTOMATACEAE

Genus of evergreen, mainly summer-flowering shrubs and trees, grown for their flowers and foliage. Frost tender, min. 10–13°C (50–55°F). Requires full light or partial shade and fertile, well-drained soil. Water containerized specimens freely when in full growth, moderately at other times. Pruning is tolerated in late winter if necessary. Propagate by softwood or greenwood cuttings in spring or summer. Red spider mite and whitefly may cause problems.
M. candidum. Evergreen, rounded, bristly-stemmed shrub. H and S 1–2m (3–6ft). Bears oval, leathery, bristly leaves. Small, terminal clusters of fragrant, 5–7-petalled, white or pink flowers are produced profusely in summer.

MELIA

MELIACEAE

Genus of deciduous, spring-flowering trees, grown for their foliage, flowers and fruits. Is useful for very dry soil and does well in coastal gardens in mild areas. Frost hardy. Requires a position in full sun; grows in any well-drained soil. Propagate by seed in autumn.
M. azedarach illus. p.72.

MELIANTHUS

MELIANTHACEAE

Genus of evergreen perennials and shrubs, grown primarily for their foliage. Half hardy to frost tender, min. 5°C (41°F). Requires sun and fertile, well-drained soil. Water potted specimens freely in summer, moderately at other times. Long stems may be shortened in early spring. May be propagated by seed in spring or by greenwood cuttings in summer. Red spider mite may be troublesome.
♀ ***M. major*** (Honeybush). Evergreen, sprawling, sparingly branched shrub. H and S 2–3m (6–10ft). Half hardy, but best at min. 5°C (41°F). Leaves are 25–45cm (10–18in) long, with 7–13 oval, toothed, blue-grey leaflets. Has tubular, rich brownish-red flowers in terminal spikes, 30cm (12in) long, in spring-summer.

Melic
Siberian. See *Melica altissima.*
Tall. See *Melica altissima.*

MELICA

GRAMINEAE/POACEAE

See also GRASSES, BAMBOOS, RUSHES and SEDGES.
M. altissima (Siberian melic, Tall melic). Evergreen, tuft-forming, perennial grass. H 60cm (24in), S 20cm (8in). Fully hardy. Bears slender stems and broad, mid-green leaves, rough beneath. In summer produces pendent, tawny spikelets in narrow panicles.
'Atropurpurea' illus. p.319.

MELICYTUS,
syn. HYMENANTHERA

VIOLACEAE

Genus of evergreen shrubs and trees, grown for their overall appearance and ornamental fruits. Fully hardy to frost tender, min. 3–5°C (37–41°F). Requires a position in full light or partial shade and in well-drained soil. Water pot plants moderately, less in winter. Pruning is tolerated if required. Propagate by seed when ripe, in autumn, or in spring.
M. crassifolius, syn. *Hymenanthera crassifolia.* Evergreen, densely twiggy shrub of irregular outline. H and S to 1.2m (4ft). Frost hardy. Bears narrowly oval to oblong, leathery, mid-green leaves. Carries tiny, bell-shaped, 5-petalled, yellow flowers in spring-summer, followed by egg-shaped, purple fruits.
M. ramiflorus (Mahoe, Whiteywood). Evergreen, spreading shrub or tree. H and S 6–10m (20–30ft). Frost tender. Bark is grey-white. Bears lance-shaped, bluntly serrated, bright green leaves. Small, rounded, greenish flowers are produced in axillary clusters in summer, followed by tiny, violet to purple-blue berries.

MELINIS

GRAMINEAE/POACEAE

See also GRASSES, BAMBOOS, RUSHES and SEDGES.
M. repens, syn. *Rhynchelytrum repens, R. roseum* (Natal grass, Ruby grass). Tuft-forming, annual or short-lived, perennial grass. H 1.2–2m (4–6ft), S 60cm–1m (2–3ft). Frost tender, min. 5°C (41°F). Leaves are mid-green, flat and finely pointed. Produces loose panicles of awned, pink spikelets in summer.

MELIOSMA

MELIOSMACEAE

Genus of deciduous trees and shrubs, grown for their habit, foliage and flowers, which, however, do not appear reliably. Frost hardy. Prefers full sun and deep, fertile, well-drained soil. Propagate by seed in autumn.
M. oldhamii. See *M. pinnata* var. *oldhamii*
M. pinnata var. ***oldhamii***, syn. *M. oldhamii.* Deciduous, stout-branched tree, upright when young, spreading when mature. H 10m (30ft), S 6m (20ft). Has very large, dark green leaves divided into 5–13 oval leaflets. Bears large clusters of small, fragrant, star-shaped, white flowers in early summer.
M. veitchiorum illus. p.76.

MELITTIS
Bastard balm

LABIATAE/LAMIACEAE

Genus of one species of summer-flowering perennial. Fully hardy. Does best in light shade and requires fertile, well-drained soil. Propagate by seed in autumn or by division in spring or autumn.
M. melissophyllum illus. p.287.

MELOCACTUS
Turk's cap

CACTACEAE

Genus of spherical, ribbed, perennial cacti. On reaching flowering size, usually 15cm (6in) high, stems produce woolly crowns; then stems appear to stop growing while woolly crowns develop into columns. Has funnel-shaped flowers in summer, followed by elongated or rounded, red, pink or white seed pods. Frost tender, min. 11–15°C (52–9°F). Requires a position in full sun and extremely well-drained soil. Propagate by seed in spring or summer.
M. actinacanthus. See *M. matanzanus.*
M. bahiensis. Spherical, perennial cactus. H and S 15cm (6in). Min. 15°C (59°F). Dull green stem bears 10–15 ribs. Produces stout, slightly curved, dark brown spines that become paler with age. Crown bears brown bristles and pink flowers, 1–2cm (½–¾in) across, in summer.
M. communis. See *M. intortus.*
M. curvispinus, syn. *M. oaxacensis.* Spherical to columnar, perennial cactus. H 20cm (8in), S 15cm (6in). Min. 15°C (59°F). Green stem has 15 rounded ribs. Areoles each bear a straight central spine and curved radial spines. Flat, woolly crown bears deep

pink flowers, 1cm (½in) across, in summer.
M. intortus, syn. *M. communis*, illus. p.488.
M. matanzanus, syn. *M. actinacanthus*. Spherical, perennial cactus. H and S 10cm (4in). Min. 15°C (59°F). Dark green stem has neat, short spines and develops a woolly crown about 5 years from seed. In summer produces pink flowers, 1cm (½in) across.
M. oaxacensis. See *M. curvispinus*.

Melon cactus. See *Melocactus intortus*, illus. p.488.

Menispermum
Moonseed

MENISPERMACEAE

Genus of deciduous, woody or semi-woody, twining climbers, grown for their attractive fruits that each contain a crescent-shaped seed – hence the common name. Male and female flowers are carried on separate plants; to produce fruits, plants of both sexes must be grown. Frost hardy. Grow in sun and in any well-drained soil. Propagate by seed or suckers in spring. The fruits may cause severe discomfort if ingested.
M. canadense (Canada moonseed, Yellow parilla). Vigorous, deciduous, woody-stemmed, twining climber, producing a dense tangle of stems and spreading by underground suckers. H to 5m (15ft). Produces oval to heart-shaped, rounded leaves that are usually 3–7-lobed. Small, cup-shaped, greenish-yellow flowers are carried in summer, followed by clusters of poisonous, spherical, glossy, blackish fruits.

Mentha
Mint

LABIATAE/LAMIACEAE

Genus of perennials, some of which are semi-evergreen, grown for their aromatic foliage, which is both decorative and used as a culinary herb. Plants are invasive, however, and should be used with caution. Fully to frost hardy. Grow in a sunny or shady position and in well-drained soil. Propagate by division in spring or autumn.
M. corsica. See *M. requienii*.
***M. × gentilis* 'Variegata'.** See *M. × gracilis* 'Variegata'.
***M. × gracilis* 'Variegata'**, syn. *M. × gentilis* 'Variegata'. Spreading perennial. H 45cm (18in), S 60cm (24in). Fully hardy. Forms a mat of oval, dark green leaves that are speckled and striped with yellow, most conspicuously in full sun. Produces stems that carry whorls of small, 2-lipped, pale mauve flowers in summer.
M. × piperita* f. *citrata (Eau-de-Cologne mint) is a vigorous, spreading perennial. H 30–60cm (12–24in), S 60cm (24in). Fully hardy. Reddish-green stems, bearing terminal spikes of small, 2-lipped, purple flowers in summer, arise from a carpet of oval, slightly toothed, mid-green leaves that have a scent which is similar to eau de Cologne.
M. requienii, syn. *M. corsica* (Corsican mint). Semi-evergreen, mat-forming, creeping perennial. H to 1cm (½in), S indefinite. Frost hardy. When they are crushed, the rounded, bright apple-green leaves exude a strong peppermint fragrance. Carries tiny, stemless, lavender-purple flowers in summer. Is suitable for a rock garden or paved path. Needs shade and moist soil.
M. rotundifolia of gardens. See *M. suaveolens*.
M. suaveolens, syn. *M. rotundifolia* of gardens (Apple mint). **'Variegata'** illus. p.286.

Mentzelia

LOASACEAE

Genus of annuals, perennials and evergreen shrubs. Fully hardy to frost tender, min. 4°C (39°F). Requires a position in sun and in fertile, very well-drained soil; tender species are best grown in pots under glass. Propagate by seed in spring; shrubs may also be propagated by semi-ripe cuttings in summer.
M. lindleyi, syn. *Bartonia aurea*, illus. p.348.

Menyanthes

MENYANTHACEAE

Genus of deciduous, perennial, marginal water plants, grown for their foliage and flowers. Fully hardy. Prefers an open, sunny position. Remove fading flower heads and foliage, and divide overcrowded clumps in spring. Propagate by stem cuttings in spring.
M. trifoliata illus. p.462.

Menziesia

ERICACEAE

Genus of deciduous shrubs, grown for their small, urn-shaped flowers. Fully hardy. Needs semi-shade and fertile, moist, peaty, acid soil. Propagate by softwood cuttings in summer or by seed in autumn.
M. ciliicalyx* var. *lasiophylla*.** See *M.c.* var. *purpurea*. var. ***purpurea (syn. *M.c.* var. *lasiophylla*) illus. p.151.

Merendera

LILIACEAE/COLCHICACEAE

Genus of corms similar to *Colchicum* but with less showy flowers. Fully to frost hardy. Needs a sunny position and well-drained soil. In cool, damp areas grow in an unheated greenhouse or frame where corms can dry out in summer. Plant in autumn and keep watered through winter and spring. Propagate by seed or offsets in autumn.
M. bulbocodium. See *M. montana*.
M. montana, syn. *M. bulbocodium*, illus. p.455.
M. robusta. Spring-flowering corm. H 8cm (3in), S 5–8cm (2–3in). Frost hardy. Narrowly lance-shaped, semi-erect, basal leaves appear at the same time as upright, funnel-shaped flowers, 5–6cm (2–2½in) wide, with narrow, pale purplish-pink or white petals.

Merremia

CONVOLVULACEAE

Genus of evergreen, twining climbers, grown for their flowers and fruits. Frost tender, min. 7–10°C (45–50°F). Prefers fertile, well-drained soil and full light. Water moderately, much less when not in full growth. Provide support. Thin out congested stems during spring. Propagate by seed in spring. Red spider mite may be a problem.
M. tuberosa, syn. *Ipomoea tuberosa, Operculina tuberosa* (Wood rose, Yellow morning glory). Fast-growing, evergreen, twining climber. H 6m (20ft) or more. Leaves have 7 radiating lobes. In summer bears funnel-shaped, yellow flowers, followed by semi-woody, globose, ivory-brown fruits.

Merrybells. See *Uvularia grandiflora*, illus. p.284.

Mertensia

BORAGINACEAE

Genus of perennials, grown for their funnel-shaped flowers. Fully hardy. Requires sun or shade and deep, well-drained soil. Propagate by division in spring or by seed in autumn.
M. echioides illus. p.369.
M. maritima illus. p.381.
M. pulmonarioides. See *M. virginica*.
♀ ***M. virginica***, syn. *M. pulmonarioides*, illus. p.279.

Meryta

ARALIACEAE

Genus of evergreen trees, grown for their handsome foliage. Frost tender, min. 5°C (41°F). Requires full light or partial shade and humus-rich, moisture-retentive but moderately drained soil. Water freely containerized plants in full growth, less at other times. Propagate by semi-ripe cuttings in summer or by seed when ripe in late summer.
M. sinclairii illus. p.96.

Mescal button. See *Lophophora williamsii*, illus. p.487.
Mesembryanthemum cordifolium. See *Aptenia cordifolia*.
Mesembryanthemum criniflorum. See *Dorotheanthus bellidiformis*.
Mesembryanthemum multiradiatum. See *Lampranthus roseus*.

Mespilus
Medlar

ROSACEAE

Genus of one species of deciduous tree or shrub, grown for its habit, flowers, foliage and edible fruits. Fully hardy. Needs sun or semi-shade and fertile, well-drained soil. Propagate species by seed in autumn and named forms (for fruit) by budding in late summer.
M. germanica illus. p.81.

Metake. See *Pseudosasa japonica*, illus. p.320.
Metal-leaf begonia. See *Begonia metallica*.

Metasequoia

TAXODIACEAE

See also CONIFERS.
♀ ***M. glyptostroboides*** illus. p.98.

Metrosideros

MYRTACEAE

Genus of evergreen, winter-flowering shrubs, trees and scrambling climbers, grown for their flowers, the trees also for their overall appearance and for shade. Frost tender, min. 5°C (41°F). Grows in fertile, well-drained soil and in full light. Water freely containerized specimens in full growth, moderately at other times. Pruning is tolerated if necessary. Propagate by seed in spring or by semi-ripe cuttings in summer.
M. excelsa, syn. *M. tomentosa*, illus. p.79.
M. robustus (Rata). Robust, evergreen, rounded tree. H 20–25m (70–80ft) or more, S 10–15m (30–50ft). Oblong to elliptic, leathery leaves are dark green and lustrous. Produces large clusters of flowers, which are mostly composed of long, dark red stamens, during winter.
M. tomentosa. See *M. excelsa*.

Meum

UMBELLIFERAE/APIACEAE

Genus of summer-flowering perennials, grown for their aromatic leaves. Is useful on banks and in wild gardens. Fully hardy. Needs sun and well-drained soil. Propagate by seed when fresh, in autumn.
M. athamanticum (Baldmoney, Spignel). Upright, clump-forming perennial. H 15–45cm (6–18in), S 10–15cm (4–6in). Mainly basal and deeply dissected leaves have narrowly linear leaflets. In summer produces flattish flower heads consisting of clusters of tiny, white or purplish-white flowers.

Mexican blood flower. See *Distictis buccinatoria*, illus. p.200.
Mexican bush sage. See *Salvia leucantha*.
Mexican cypress. See *Cupressus lusitanica*.
Mexican firecracker. See *Echeveria setosa*.
Mexican flame vine. See *Senecio confusus*, illus. p.215.
Mexican foxglove. See *Tetranema roseum*, illus. p.315.
Mexican giant hyssop. See *Agastache*.
Mexican hat plant. See *Kalanchoe daigremontiana*, illus. p.478.
Mexican orange blossom. See *Choisya ternata*, illus. p.123.
Mexican palo verde. See *Parkinsonia aculeata*.
Mexican stone pine. See *Pinus cembroides*, illus. p.105.
Mexican sunflower. See *Tithonia rotundifolia*.
Mexican tulip poppy. See *Hunnemannia fumariifolia*.
Mexican violet. See *Tetranema roseum*, illus. p.315.
Mezereon. See *Daphne mezereum*, illus. p.170.
Michaelmas daisy. See *Aster*.

MICHELIA

MAGNOLIACEAE

Genus of evergreen, winter- to summer-flowering shrubs and trees, grown for their flowers and foliage. Half hardy to frost tender, min. 5°C (41°F). Provide humus-rich, well-drained, neutral to acid soil and full light or partial shade. Water potted specimens freely when in full growth, less in winter. Pruning is seldom necessary. Propagate by semi-ripe cuttings in summer or by seed when ripe, in autumn, or in spring.
M. doltsopa illus. p.79.
M. figo illus. p.85.

Mickey-mouse plant. See *Ochna serrulata.*

MICROBIOTA

CUPRESSACEAE

See also CONIFERS.
♀ ***M. decussata*** illus. p.106. Spreading, shrubby conifer. H 50cm (20in), S 2–3m (6–10ft). Fully hardy. Flat sprays of scale-like, yellow-green leave turn bronze in winter. Globose, yellow-brown cones had only one seed.

Microglossa albescens. See *Aster albescens.*

MICROLEPIA

DENNSTAEDTIACEAE

Genus of deciduous, semi-evergreen or evergreen ferns, best grown in pans and hanging baskets. Frost tender, min. 5°C (41°F). Requires shade or semi-shade and moist soil. Remove faded fronds regularly. Propagate by division in spring or by spores in summer.
M. speluncae illus. p.322.

MICROMERIA

LABIATAE/LAMIACEAE

Genus of evergreen or semi-evergreen shrubs, sub-shrubs and perennials, suitable for rock gardens and banks. Frost hardy. Needs sun and well-drained soil. Propagate by seed in spring or by softwood cuttings in early summer.
M. juliana. Evergreen or semi-evergreen, bushy shrub or sub-shrub. H and S 30cm (12in). Has small, oval, aromatic, green leaves pressed close to stems. In summer, minute, tubular, bright deep pink flowers are carried in whorls on upper parts of stems.

Mignonette. See *Reseda.*
Mignonette vine. See *Anredera.*

MIKANIA

COMPOSITAE/ASTERACEAE

Genus of evergreen or herbaceous, scrambling or twining climbers, shrubs and erect perennials, grown for their foliage and flower heads. Half hardy to frost tender, min. 7°C (45°F). Any fertile, well-drained soil is suitable, with partial shade in summer. Water regularly, less when not in full growth. Support for stems is needed and ties may be necessary. Thin out congested growth in spring. Propagate by semi-ripe or softwood cuttings in summer. Aphids may be a problem.
M. scandens. Herbaceous, twining climber. H 3–5m (10–15ft). Half hardy. Oval to triangular, mid-green leaves have 2 basal lobes. Tiny, groundsel-like, pink to purple flower heads appear in compact clusters in summer-autumn.

Mile-a-minute plant. See *Fallopia aubertii; Fallopia baldschuanica,* illus. p.215.
Milfoil, Whorled water. See *Myriophyllum verticillatum,* illus. p.465.

MILIUM

GRAMINEAE/POACEAE

See also GRASSES, BAMBOOS, RUSHES and SEDGES.
M. effusum (Wood millet). **'Aureum'** is an evergreen, tuft-forming, perennial grass. H 1m (3ft), S 30cm (1ft). Fully hardy. Has flat, golden-yellow leaves. Produces open, tiered panicles of greenish-yellow spikelets in summer. Self seeds readily in shade.

Milkweed. See *Euphorbia.*

MILLA

LILIACEAE/ALLIACEAE

Genus of summer-flowering bulbs, grown for their fragrant flowers, each comprising a slender tube with 6 spreading, star-shaped petals at the tip. Half hardy. Needs a sheltered, sunny position and well-drained soil. Plant in spring. After flowering lift bulbs and partially dry off for winter. Propagate by seed or offsets in spring.
M. biflora. Summer-flowering bulb. H 30–45cm (12–18in), S 8–10cm (3–4in). Has long, narrow, semi-erect, basal leaves. Stem bears a loose head of 2–6 erect, white flowers, 3–6cm (1¼–2½in) across, each on a slender stalk to 20cm (8in) long.

Millet
Foxtail. See *Setaria italica.*
Italian. See *Setaria italica.*
Wood. See *Milium effusum.*

MILTONIA

ORCHIDACEAE

See also ORCHIDS.
M. candida illus. p.310. Evergreen, epiphytic orchid for a cool or intermediate greenhouse. H 20cm (8in). Cream-lipped, green-patterned, brown flowers, 5cm (2in) across, are borne in spikes in autumn. Has narrowly oval leaves, 10–12cm (4–5in) long. Grow in semi-shade in summer.
M. clowesii illus. p.310. Evergreen, epiphytic orchid for an intermediate greenhouse. H 20cm (8in). In early summer produces large spikes of 4cm (1½in) wide, yellow flowers, barred with reddish-brown and each with a white-and-mauve lip. Has broadly oval leaves, 30cm (12in) long. Grow in semi-shade in summer.

MILTONIOPSIS

Pansy orchid

orchidaceae

See also ORCHIDS.
***M.* Anjou 'St Patrick'** illus. p.309. Evergreen, epiphytic orchid for a cool greenhouse. H 15cm (6in). Has sprays of deep crimson flowers, 10cm (4in) across, with red and yellow patterns on each lip, mainly in summer. Narrowly oval, soft leaves are 10–12cm (4–5in) long. Needs shade in summer.
***M.* Robert Strauss 'Ardingly'** illus. p.308. Evergreen, epiphytic orchid for a cool greenhouse. H 15cm (6in). Bears sprays of white flowers, 10cm (4in) across, marked reddish-brown and purple; flowering season varies. Narrowly oval, soft leaves are 10–12cm (4–5in) long. Requires shade in summer.

Mimicry plant. See *Pleiospilos bolusii,* illus. p.495.

MIMOSA

LEGUMINOSAE/MIMOSACEAE

Genus of annuals, evergreen perennials, shrubs, trees and scrambling climbers, cultivated for their flowers and foliage. M. pudica is usually grown as an annual. Frost tender, min. 13–16°C (55–61°F). Needs partial shade and fertile, well-drained soil. Water potted specimens freely when in full growth, moderately at other times. Propagate by seed in spring, shrubs also by semi-ripe cuttings in summer. Red spider mite may be a nuisance.
M. pudica illus. p.172.

Mimosa. See *Acacia.*

MIMULUS

Monkey musk

SCROPHULARIACEAE

Genus of annuals, perennials and evergreen shrubs. Small species suit damp pockets in rock gardens. Fully to half hardy. Most prefer full sun and wet or moist soil; some, such as *M. aurantiacus* need a dry site. Propagate perennials by division in spring, sub-shrubs by softwood cuttings in late summer; annuals and all species by seed in autumn or early spring.
***M.* 'Andean Nymph'.** See *M. naiandinus.*
♀ ***M. aurantiacus***, syn. *Diplacus glutinosus, M. glutinosus*, illus. p.167.
♀ ***M. cupreus* 'Whitecroft Scarlet'..** Short-lived, spreading perennial. H 20–30cm (8–12in), S 30cm (12in). Half hardy. Bears snapdragon-like, scarlet flowers freely from early to late summer. Has oval, toothed, mid-green leaves.
M. glutinosus. See *M. aurantiacus.*
M. guttatus, syn. *M. langsdorffii.* Spreading, mat-forming perennial. H and S 60cm (24in). Frost hardy. Snapdragon-like, bright yellow flowers, spotted with reddish-brown on lower lobes, are borne in succession in summer and early autumn. Oval leaves are coarsely or sometimes deeply toothed and mid-green.
M. langsdorffii. See *M. guttatus.*
♀ ***M. lewisii*** illus. p.289.
M. luteus illus. p.304.
***M.* Magic Series.** Early-flowering perennial. H 15–20cm (6–8in). Produces small flowers, ranging from bright orange, yellow, and red to more usual pastel shades and bicolours.
M. moschatus (Musk). Spreading, mat-forming perennial. H and S 15–30cm (6–12in). Fully hardy. Bears snapdragon-like, pale yellow flowers, lightly speckled with brown, in summer-autumn. Leaves are oval, hairy and pale green.
♀ ***M. naiandinus***, syn. **'Andean Nymph'** illus. p.288.
***M.* 'Royal Velvet'** illus. p.293.

Mina. Reclassified as *Ipomoea.*
Mind-your-own-business. See *Soleirolia.*
Miniature date palm. See *Phoenix roebelenii.*
Miniature grape ivy. See *Cissus striata.*
Mint. See *Mentha.*
Apple. See *Mentha suaveolens.*
Corsican. See *Mentha requienii.*
Eau-de-Cologne. See *Mentha × piperita* f. *citrata.*
Variegated apple. See *Mentha suaveolens* 'Variegata', illus. p.286.
Mint bush. See *Elsholtzia stauntonii,* illus. p.169; Prostanthera.
Mint-bush, Round-leaved. See *Prostanthera rotundifolia,* illus. p.141.
Mintleaf. See *Plectranthus madagascariensis.*

MIRABILIS

Four o'clock flower, Marvel of Peru

NYCTAGINACEAE

Genus of summer-flowering annuals and tuberous perennials. Half hardy. Is best grown in a sheltered position in fertile, well-drained soil and in full sun. Lift tubers and store over winter in frost-free conditions. Propagate by seed or division of tubers in early spring.
M. jalapa illus. p.247.

Mirbeck's oak. See *Quercus canariensis,* illus. p.62.

MISCANTHUS

GRAMINEAE/POACEAE

See also GRASSES, BAMBOOS, RUSHES and SEDGES.
♀ ***M. sacchariflorus*** (Amur silver grass). Vigorous, herbaceous, slow-spreading, rhizomatous, perennial grass. H 3m (10ft), S indefinite. Frost hardy. Hairless, mid-green leaves last into winter, often turning bronze. Has rare, open, branched panicles of hairy, purplish-brown spikelets in summer.
***M. sinensis* 'Gracillimus'** illus. p.321.
'Zebrinus' illus. p.318.

Missouri flag. See *Iris missouriensis,* illus. p.234.
Mist flower. See *Eupatorium rugosum,* illus. p.242.
Mistletoe cactus. See *Rhipsalis.*
Mistletoe fig. See *Ficus deltoidea,* illus. p.148.

Mitchella

RUBIACEAE

Genus of evergreen, trailing sub-shrubs, grown for their foliage and fruits. Makes excellent ground cover, especially in woodlands, although is sometimes difficult to establish. Fully hardy. Prefers shade and humus-rich, neutral to acid soil. Propagate by division of rooted runners in spring or by seed in autumn.
M. repens (Partridge berry). Evergreen, trailing, mat-forming sub-shrub. H 5cm (2in), S indefinite. Bears small, oval, white-striped, green leaves with heart-shaped bases. In early summer has pairs of tiny, fragrant, tubular, white flowers, sometimes purple-tinged, followed by spherical, bright red fruits. Suits a rock garden or peat bed.

Mitella

SAXIFRAGACEAE

Genus of clump-forming, summer-flowering, slender-stemmed, rhizomatous perennials. Fully hardy. Requires shade and humus-rich, moist soil. Propagate by division in spring or by seed in autumn.
M. breweri illus. p.396.

Mitraria

GESNERIACEAE

Genus of one species of evergreen, woody-stemmed, scrambling climber. Half hardy. Requires a position in semi-shade and in peaty, acid soil. Propagate by seed in spring or by stem cuttings in summer.
M. coccinea illus. p.201.

Moccasin flower. See *Cypripedium acaule*, illus. p.308.
Mock orange. See *Philadelphus coronarius; Pittosporum tobira.*

Molinia

GRAMINEAE/POACEAE

See also GRASSES, BAMBOOS, RUSHES and SEDGES.
M. altissima. See *M. caerulea* subsp. *arundinacea.*
M. caerulea subsp. ***arundinacea,*** syn. *M. altissima.* Tuft-forming, herbaceous, perennial grass. H 2.5m (8ft), S 60cm (2ft). Fully hardy. Has broad, flat, grey-green leaves and spreading panicles of purple spikelets on stiff, erect stems in summer. Needs a dry, sunny position and acid soil. ♀ **'Variegata'** (Variegated purple moor grass), H 60cm (2ft), has yellow-striped, mid-green leaves and, in late summer, panicles of purplish spikelets.

Moltkia

BORAGINACEAE

Genus of deciduous, semi-evergreen or evergreen sub-shrubs and perennials, grown for their funnel-shaped flowers in summer. Fully to frost hardy. Prefers sun and well-drained, neutral to acid soil. Propagate by semi-ripe cuttings in summer or by seed in autumn.
♀ ***M. × intermedia.*** Evergreen, open, dome-shaped sub-shrub. H 30cm (12in), S 50cm (20in). Fully hardy. Stems are clothed in narrowly linear, dark green leaves. Masses of loose spikes of small, open funnel-shaped, bright blue flowers appear in summer.
M. petraea. Semi-evergreen, bushy shrub. H 30cm (12in), S 60cm (24in). Fully hardy. Has long, narrow, hairy leaves and clusters of pinkish-purple buds open into funnel-shaped, violet-blue flowers in summer.
M. suffruticosa illus. p.369.

Moluccella

LABIATAE/LAMIACEAE

Genus of annuals and perennials, grown for their flowers that may be dried successfully. Half hardy. Grow in sun and in rich, very well-drained soil. May be propagated by seed sown under glass in spring, or outdoors in late spring.
M. laevis illus. p.347.

Monarch birch. See *Betula maximowicziana.*
Monarch-of-the-East. See *Sauromatum venosum*, illus. p.429.

Monarda

Bergamot

LABIATAE/LAMIACEAE

Genus of annuals and perennials, grown for their aromatic foliage as well as their flowers. Fully hardy. Requires sun and moist soil. Propagate species and cultivars by division in spring, species only by seed in spring.
***M.* 'Adam'.** Clump-forming perennial. H 75cm (30in), S 45cm (18in). Bears dense whorls of 2-lipped, cerise flowers throughout summer. Oval, usually toothed, mid-green leaves are aromatic and hairy.
M. didyma (Bee balm, Bergamot).
♀ **'Cambridge Scarlet'** illus. p.254.
♀ **'Croftway Pink'** illus. p.245.
M. fistulosa illus. p.255.
***M.* 'Prairie Night'.** See *M.* 'Prärienacht'.
***M.* 'Prärienacht',** syn. *M.* 'Prairie Night'. Clump-forming perennial. H 1.2m (4ft), S 45cm (1½ft). Produces dense whorls of 2-lipped, rich violet-purple flowers from mid- to late summer. Oval, toothed leaves are mid-green.

Money tree. See *Crassula ovata*, illus. p.473.
Moneywort. See *Lysimachia nummularia.*
Mongolian lime. See *Tilia mongolica.*
Monkey musk. See *Mimulus.*
Monkey puzzle. See *Araucaria araucana*, illus. p.99.
Monkshood. See *Aconitum.*

Monstera

ARACEAE

Genus of evergreen, woody-stemmed, root climbers, grown for their large, handsome leaves. Bears insignificant, creamy-white flowers with hooded spathes intermittently. Frost tender, min. 15–18°C (59–64°F). Provide humus-rich, well-drained soil and light shade in summer. Water moderately, less when temperatures are low. Provide support. If necessary, shorten long stems in spring. Propagate by leaf-bud or stem-tip cuttings in summer. All parts except the fruit may cause mild stomach upset when ingested, and contact with the fruit may irritate skin.
M. acuminata (Shingle plant). Evergreen, woody-stemmed, root climber with robust stems. H 3m (10ft) or more. Has lopsided, oval, pointed, rich green leaves with a heart-shaped base, sometimes cleft into a few large lobes, to 25cm (10in) long.
♀ ***M. deliciosa*** illus. p.218.

Montbretia. See *Crocosmia.*
Monterey ceanothus. See *Ceanothus rigidus.*
Monterey cypress. See *Cupressus macrocarpa.*
Monterey pine. See *Pinus radiata*, illus. p.100.
Montpelier maple. See *Acer monspessulanum.*
Moon flower. See *Ipomoea alba.*
Moon trefoil. See *Medicago arborea.*
Moonlight holly. See *Ilex aquifolium* 'Flavescens'.
Moonseed. See *Menispermum.*
Canada. See *Menispermum canadense.*
Moonstones. See *Pachyphytum oviferum*, illus. p.491.

Moraea

IRIDACEAE

Genus of corms with short-lived, iris-like flowers. Divides into 2 groups: winter- and summer-growing species. Winter-growing species are half hardy, need full sun and well-drained soil; keep dry in summer during dormancy and start into growth by watering in autumn. Summer-growers are frost hardy and dormant in winter; grow in a sheltered, sunny site and well-drained soil. Propagate winter growers by seed in autumn, spring for summer growers.
M. huttonii illus. p.415.
M. polystachya. Winter-growing corm. H to 30cm (12in), S 5–8cm (2–3in). Bears long, narrow, semi-erect, basal leaves. Stem has a succession of erect, flattish, blue or lilac flowers, 8cm (3in) wide, in winter-spring. Outer petals each have a central, yellow mark.
M. ramosissima illus. p.414.
M. spathacea. See *M. spathulata.*
M. spathulata, syn. *M. spathacea.* Summer-growing corm. H to 1m (3ft), S 10–15cm (4–6in). Has one long, narrow, semi-erect, basal leaf. Tough flower stem carries a succession of up to 5 upward-facing, yellow flowers, 5–7cm (2–3in) wide, with reflexed, outer petals, in summer.

Moreton Bay chestnut. See *Castanospermum.*
Moreton Bay fig. See *Ficus macrophylla.*

Morina

Whorl flower

MORINACEAE

Genus of evergreen perennials, only one species of which is in general cultivation: this is grown for its thistle-like foliage and its flowers. Frost hardy, but needs protection from drying spring winds. Needs full sun and well-drained, preferably sandy soil. Propagate by division directly after flowering orby seed when fresh, in late summer.
M. longifolia illus. p.243.

Morinda spruce. See *Picea smithiana.*

Morisia

CRUCIFERAE/BRASSICACEAE

Genus of one species of rosetted perennial with a long tap root. Is good for rock gardens and alpine houses. Fully hardy. Needs sun and gritty, well-drained soil. Propagate by seed in autumn or by root cuttings in winter.
M. hypogaea. See *M. monanthos.*
M. monanthos, syn. *M. hypogaea*, illus. p.384.

Morning glory. See *Ipomoea hederacea*, illus. p.212.
Common. See *Ipomoea purpurea.*
Red. See *Ipomoea coccinea.*
Woolly. See *Argyreia nervosa.*
Yellow. See *Merremia tuberosa.*
Moroccan broom. See *Cytisus battandieri*, illus. p.119.

Morus

Mulberry

MORACEAE

Genus of deciduous trees, grown for foliage and edible fruits. Tiny flowers appear in spring. Fully hardy. Requires full sun and fertile, well-drained soil. Propagate by softwood cuttings in summer or by seed in autumn.
M. alba (White mulberry). **'Laciniata'** illus. p.88. **'Pendula'** is a deciduous, weeping tree. H 3m (10ft), S 5m (15ft). Rounded, sometimes lobed, glossy, deep green leaves turn yellow in autumn. Edible, oval, fleshy, pink, red or purple fruits ripen in summer.
♀ ***M. nigra*** (Black mulberry). Deciduous, round-headed tree. H 12m (40ft), S 15m (50ft). Heart-shaped, dark green leaves turn yellow in autumn. Bears edible, oval, succulent, dark purplish-red fruits in late summer or early autumn.

Moses-in-the-cradle. See *Tradescantia spathacea.*
Mosquito grass. See *Bouteloua gracilis*, illus. p.319.
Moss
Fairy. See *Azolla filiculoides*, illus. p.464.
Spanish. See *Tillandsia usneoides*, illus. p.273.
Water. See *Fontinalis antipyretica.*
Willow. See *Fontinalis antipyretica.*
Moss campion. See *Silene acaulis*, illus. p.377.
Mother of thousands. See *Saxifraga stolonifera; Soleirolia.*
Mother spleenwort. See *Asplenium bulbiferum.*
Mother-in-law's seat. See *Echinocactus grusonii*, illus. p.476.
Mother-in-law's tongue. See *Sansevieria trifasciata.*
Mother-of-pearl plant. See *Graptopetalum paraguayense*, illus. p.494.
Mount Etna broom. See *Genista aetnensis*, illus. p.89.
Mount Morgan wattle. See *Acacia podalyriifolia*, illus. p.131.

Mountain ash. See *Sorbus aucuparia*, illus. p.77.
American. See *Sorbus americana*.
Korean. See *Sorbus alnifolia*.
Mountain avens. See *Dryas*.
Mountain buckler fern. See *Oreopteris limbosperma*.
Mountain dogwood. See *Cornus nuttallii*, illus. p.72.
Mountain fern. See *Oreopteris limbosperma*.
Mountain fetterbush. See *Pieris floribunda*, illus. p.123.
Mountain flax. See *Phormium cookianum*.
Mountain gum. See *Eucalyptus dalrympleana*, illus. p.68.
Mountain hemlock. See *Tsuga mertensiana*.
Mountain pansy. See *Viola lutea*.
Mountain pepper. See *Drimys lanceolata*.
Mountain pine. See *Pinus mugo*.
Mountain pride. See *Penstemon newberryi*.
Mountain sow thistle. See *Cicerbita alpina*.
Mountain spruce. See *Picea engelmannii*, illus. p.101.
Mountain tassel. See *Soldanella montana*.
Mountain willow. See *Salix arbuscula*.
Mountain wood fern. See *Oreopteris limbosperma*.
Mourning iris. See *Iris susiana*.
Mourning widow. See *Geranium phaeum*, illus. p.240.
Mouse plant. See *Arisarum proboscideum*.
Mouse-ear, Alpine. See *Cerastium alpinum*.
Moutan. See *Paeonia suffruticosa*.

MUCUNA

LEGUMINOSAE/PAPILIONACEAE

Genus of vigorous, evergreen, twining climbers, grown for their large, pea-like flowers. Frost tender, min. 18°C (64°F). Humus-rich, moist but well-drained soil is essential, with partial shade in summer. Water freely when in full growth, less at other times. Needs plenty of space to climb; provide support. Thin out crowded stems in spring. Propagate by seed in spring or by layering in late summer. Whitefly and red spider mite may cause problems.
M. bennettii. Strong- and fast-growing, evergreen, twining climber. H 15–25m (50–80ft). Leaves are divided into 3 oval leaflets. In summer has pendent clusters of pea-like, orange-scarlet flowers.
M. deeringiana. See *M. pruriens* var. *utilis*.
M. pruriens var. ***utilis***, syn. *M. deeringiana*. Vigorous, evergreen, twining climber. H 15m (50ft) or more. Has pea-like, both green- and red-purple flowers in long, pendent clusters in summer-autumn. Leaves, of 3 oval leaflets, are used for fodder and green manure. May be short-lived.

MUEHLENBECKIA

POLYGONACEAE

Genus of deciduous or evergreen, slender-stemmed, summer-flowering shrubs and woody-stemmed, scrambling climbers, grown for their foliage. Frost hardy. Grow in sun or shade and in well-drained soil. Propagate by semi-ripe cuttings in summer.
M. axillaris of gardens. See *M. complexa*.
M. complexa, syn. *M. axillaris* of gardens. Deciduous, mound-forming shrub or twining climber. H 60cm–1m (2–3ft), S 1m (3ft). Slender, wiry stems bear variably shaped (oval to fiddle-shaped), dark green leaves. Produces tiny, star-shaped, greenish-white flowers in mid-summer that are followed by small, spherical, waxy, white fruits.

Mugwort, White. See *Artemisia lactiflora*, illus. p.225.
Mulberry. See *Morus*.
Black. See *Morus nigra*.
Paper. See *Broussonetia papyrifera*, illus. p.75.
White. See *Morus alba*.
Mulgedium. Reclassified as *Cicerbita*.
Mullein. See *Verbascum*.
White. See *Verbascum lychnitis*.
Muriel bamboo. See *Fargesia murieliae*.
Murray red gum. See *Eucalyptus camaldulensis*.

MURRAYA

RUTACEAE

Genus of evergreen trees and shrubs, grown for their overall appearance. Frost tender, min. 13–15°C (55–9°F). Requires a position in full light or partial shade and in humus-rich, well-drained soil. Water containerized plants freely when in full growth, moderately at other times. Pruning is tolerated in late winter if necessary. Propagate by seed in spring or by semi-ripe cuttings in summer. Whitefly may be troublesome.
M. exotica. See *M. paniculata*.
M. paniculata, syn. *M. exotica* (Orange jasmine). Evergreen, rounded shrub or tree. H and S 2–4m (6–12ft). Pungently aromatic, edible, glossy, rich green leaves each have 9 or more oval leaflets. Carries fragrant, 5-petalled, white flowers in terminal clusters year-round, followed by tiny, egg-shaped, red fruits.

MUSA
Banana

MUSACEAE

Genus of evergreen, palm-like, suckering perennials, with false stems formed from overlapping leaf sheaths, grown for their foliage, flowers and fruits (bananas), not all of which are edible. Frost hardy to frost tender, min. 18°C (64°F). Grow in sun or partial shade and in humus-rich, well-drained soil. Propagate by division year-round, by offsets in summer or by suckers after flowering.
M. arnoldiana. See *Ensete ventricosum*.
M. basjoo, syn. *M. japonica*, illus. p.233.
♀ ***M. coccinea***, syn. *M. uranoscopus* of gardens (Scarlet banana). Evergreen, palm-like perennial. H to 1m (3ft), S 1.5m (5ft). Frost tender. Bears oblong to oval, dark green leaves, to 1m (3ft) long, that are paler below. In summer produces erect spirals of tubular, yellow flowers, enclosed in red bracts, followed by banana-like, orange-yellow fruits, 5cm (2in) long.
M. ensete. See *Ensete ventricosum*.
M. japonica. See *M. basjoo*.
♀ ***M. ornata*** illus. p.232.
M. uranoscopus of gardens. See *M. coccinea*.

MUSCARI
Grape hyacinth

LILIACEAE/HYACINTHACEAE

Genus of spring-flowering bulbs, each with a cluster of narrowly strap-shaped, basal leaves, usually appearing in spring just before flowers. Leafless flower stems bear dense spikes of small flowers, most of which have constricted mouths. Fully to half hardy. Needs sun and fairly well-drained soil. Plant in autumn. Propagate by division in late summer or by seed in autumn.
♀ ***M. armeniacum*** illus. p.449. **'Blue Spike'** is a spring-flowering bulb. H 15–20cm (6–8in), S 8–10cm (3–4in). Frost hardy. Produces 3–6 long, narrow, semi-erect, basal leaves. Bears dense spikes of fragrant, bell-shaped, deep blue flowers; constricted mouths have rims of paler blue or white 'teeth'.
♀ ***M. aucheri***, syn. *M. lingulatum*, illus. p.449.
♀ ***M. azureum***, syn. *Hyacinthus azureus, Pseudomuscari azureum*. Spring-flowering bulb. H 10–15cm (4–6in), S 5–8cm (2–3in). Frost hardy. Bears 2 or 3 narrow, semi-erect, basal, greyish-green leaves, slightly wider towards the tips. Produces a very dense spike of bell-shaped, pale clear blue flowers; mouths have small 'teeth' with central, dark blue stripes. May self-seed freely.
M. botryoides. Spring-flowering bulb. H 15–20cm (6–8in), S 5–8cm (2–3in). Frost hardy. Bears 2–4 narrow, semi-erect, basal leaves that widen slightly at the tips. Each minute, nearly spherical, bright blue flower has a constricted mouth and white-toothed rim.
M. comosum, syn. *Leopoldia comosa* (Tassel grape hyacinth). Late spring-flowering bulb. H 20–30cm (8–12in), S 10–12cm (4–5in). Frost hardy. Has up to 5 strap-shaped, semi-erect, basal, grey-green leaves. Bears a loose spike of bell-shaped, fertile, brownish-yellow flowers with a tuft of thread-like, sterile, purplish-blue flowers at the tip. **'Monstrosum'** see *M.c.* 'Plumosum'. **'Plumosum'** (syn. *M.c.* 'Monstrosum') illus. p.448.
M. latifolium illus. p.429.
M. lingulatum. See *M. aucheri*.
M. macrocarpum illus. p.450.
M. neglectum, syn. *M. racemosum*, illus. p.449.
M. paradoxum of gardens. See *Bellevalia pycnantha*.
M. pycnantha. See *Bellevalia pycnantha*.
M. racemosum. See *M. neglectum*.

Musk. See *Mimulus moschatus*.
Monkey. See *Mimulus*.
Yellow. See *Mimulus luteus*, illus. p.304.
Musk willow. See *Salix aegyptiaca*.

MUSSAENDA

RUBIACEAE

Genus of evergreen shrubs and scrambling climbers, grown for their flowers. Frost tender, min. 16–18°C (61–4°F). Requires a position in full light and fertile, well-drained soil. Water freely when in full growth, less at other times. Provide support and thin out crowded stems in spring. Propagate by seed in spring or by air-layering in summer. Whitefly and red spider mite may cause problems.
M. erythrophylla. Moderately vigorous, evergreen, scrambling climber. H 6–10m (20–30ft). Has broadly oval, bright green leaves and flowers in summer-autumn. Each flower has one greatly enlarged, oval, bract-like, red sepal, a red tube and yellow petal lobes.

MUTISIA

COMPOSITAE/ASTERACEAE

Genus of evergreen, tendril climbers, grown for their long-lasting flower heads. Frost to half hardy. Plant with roots in shade and leafy parts in sun, in well-drained soil. Propagate by seed in spring, by stem cuttings in summer or by layering in autumn.
M. decurrens illus. p.215.
M. oligodon. Evergreen, tendril climber. H to 1.5m (5ft). Frost hardy. Oblong, glossy, green leaves with sharply toothed margins are 2.5–3.5cm (1–1½in) long. In summer-autumn produces long-stalked, daisy-like, pink flower heads with yellow centres. Grow against a low wall or through a shrub.

MYOPORUM

MYOPORACEAE

Genus of evergreen shrubs and trees, grown for their overall appearance and as hedges and windbreaks. Frost tender, min. 2–5°C (36–41°F). Prefers full light and well-drained soil; will tolerate poor soil. Water potted specimens moderately. Propagate by seed when ripe or in spring or by semi-ripe cuttings in late summer.
M. laetum. Evergreen, rounded to upright shrub or tree. H 3–10m (10–30ft), S 2–5m (6–15ft). Has fleshy, oval, lustrous, bright green leaves and axillary clusters of small, bell-shaped, white flowers, dotted with purple, in spring-summer, then tiny, narrowly oblong, pale to deep red-purple fruits.
M. parvifolium illus. p.158.

MYOSOTIDIUM
Chatham Island forget-me-not

BORAGINACEAE

Genus of one species of evergreen perennial that is suitable for mild, coastal areas. Half hardy. Prefers semi-shade and moist soil. Seaweed is often recommended as a mulch. Is not easy to cultivate, and once established should not be disturbed. Propagate by division in spring or by seed when ripe, in summer or autumn.
M. hortensia, syn. *M. nobile*, illus. p.297. Bears oval to heart-shaped, glossy leaves. H and S 60cm (24in). In early summer produces bell-shaped, pale to dark blue flowers, sometimes with white-margined lobes.
M. nobile. See *M. hortensia*.

MYOSOTIS
Forget-me-not

BORAGINACEAE

Genus of annuals, biennials and perennials, grown for their flowers. Most species are good for rock gardens and screes; *M. scorpioides* is best grown as a marginal water plant. Fully hardy. Most prefer sun or semi-shade and fertile, well-drained soil. Propagate by seed in autumn.
M. alpestris, syn. *M. rupicola*, (Alpine forget-me-not), illus. p.382.
M. australis. Short-lived, tuft-forming perennial. H 12cm (5in), S 8cm (3in). Has oval, rough-textured leaves and, in summer, tight sprays of open funnel-shaped, yellow or white flowers. Is good for a scree.
M. caespitosa. See *M. laxa* subsp. *caespitosa*.
M. laxa subsp. ***caespitosa,*** syn. *M. caespitosa.* Clump-forming annual or short-lived perennial. H 12cm (5in), S 15cm (6in). Lance-shaped, leathery leaves are dark green. Bears rounded, bright blue flowers in summer.
M. palustris. See *M. scorpioides*.
M. rupicola. See *M. alpestris*.
M. scorpioides, syn. *M. palustris* (Water forget-me-not). **'Mermaid'** illus. p.464.
♀ ***M. sylvatica*** **'Blue Ball'** illus. p.346. **'White Ball'** is a slow-growing, short-lived, bushy, compact perennial, grown as a biennial. H to 20cm (8in), S 15cm (6in). Leaves are lance-shaped. Sprays of tiny, 5-lobed, pure white flowers are produced in early summer.

Myrceugenia apiculata. See *Luma apiculata*.

MYRIOPHYLLUM

HALORAGIDACEAE

Genus of deciduous, perennial, submerged water plants, grown for their foliage. Most species are ideal as depositories for fish spawn. Fully hardy to frost tender, min. 5°C (41°F). Requires full sun. Spreads widely: keep in check by removing excess growth as required. Propagate by stem cuttings in spring or summer.
M. aquaticum, syn. *M. proserpinacoides*, illus. p.464.
M. hippuroides. Deciduous, perennial, spreading, submerged water plant with thin stems. S indefinite. Half hardy. Produces a dense mass of small, feathery, pale green leaves. Inconspicuous, greenish-cream flowers are borne from the axils of the emergent leaves in summer. Is suitable for a cold-water aquarium.
M. proserpinacoides. See *M. aquaticum*.
M. verticillatum illus. p.465.

Myrobalan. See *Prunus cerasifera*.

MYRRHIS
Sweet Cicely

UMBELLIFERAE/APIACEAE

Genus of one species of summer-flowering perennial. Fully hardy. Requires a position in sun or shade and in well-drained soil. Propagate by seed in autumn or spring.
M. odorata illus. p.242.

MYRSINE

MYRSINACEAE

Genus of evergreen shrubs and trees, with inconspicuous flowers, grown mainly for their foliage. Also bears decorative fruits, to obtain which plants of both sexes must be grown. Is suitable for rock and peat gardens. Frost hardy, but in cold areas requires shelter. Requires a position in sun or shade and in any fertile, well-drained soil other than a shallow, chalky one. Propagate by semi-ripe cuttings in summer.
M. africana (Cape myrtle). Very slow-growing, evergreen, bushy, dense shrub. H and S 75cm (30in). Small, glossy, dark green leaves are aromatic and rounded. Tiny, yellowish-brown flowers in late spring are succeeded by spherical, pale blue fruits.

MYRTILLOCACTUS

CACTACEAE

Genus of branching, perennial cacti with ribbed, spiny, blue-green stems. Bears star-shaped flowers that open at night. Frost tender, min. 11–12°C (52–4°F). Needs a sunny, well-drained site. Propagate by seed or stem cuttings in spring or summer.
M. geometrizans illus. p.472.

Myrtle. See *Myrtus*.
Bracelet honey. See *Melaleuca armillaris*.
Cape. See *Myrsine africana*.
Common. See *Myrtus communis*, illus. p.126.
Crape. See *Lagerstroemia indica*, illus. p.87.
Flag. See *Acorus calamus*.
Queen's crape. See *Lagerstroemia speciosa*.
Willow. See *Agonis*.

MYRTUS
Myrtle

MYRTACEAE

Genus of evergreen shrubs, sometimes tree-like, grown for their flowers, fruits and aromatic foliage. Frost to half hardy; in cold areas plant against a south- or west-facing wall. Requires full sun and fertile, well-drained soil. May be pruned in spring. Propagate by semi-ripe cuttings in late summer.
M. apiculata. See *Luma apiculata*
M. bullata. See *Lophomyrtus bullata*.
M. chequen. See *Luma chequen*.
♀ ***M. communis*** (Common myrtle) illus. p.126. ♀ subsp. ***tarentina*** is an evergreen, bushy shrub. H and S 2m (6ft). Frost hardy. Bears small leaves that are narrowly oval, glossy and dark green. Produces fragrant, saucer-shaped, white flowers, each with a dense cluster of stamens, from mid-spring to early summer, followed by spherical, white fruits. Is very wind-resistant and good for hedging in mild areas.
M. luma. See *Luma apiculata*.**'Glanleam Gold'** see *Luma apiculata* 'Glanleam Gold'.
M. ugni. See *Ugni molinae*.**Naked coral tree.** See *Erythrina americana*.

NANDINA

BERBERIDACEAE

Genus of one species of evergreen or semi-evergreen, summer-flowering shrub, grown for its foliage and flowers. Frost hardy. Prefers a sheltered, sunny site and fertile, well-drained but not too dry soil. On established plants prune untidy, old stems to base in spring. Propagate by semi-ripe cuttings in summer.

♀ ***N. domestica*** (Heavenly bamboo, Sacred bamboo). Evergreen or semi-evergreen, upright, elegant shrub. H and S 2m (6ft). Leaves have narrowly lance-shaped, dark green leaflets, purplish-red when young and in autumn-winter. Large panicles of small, star-shaped, white flowers, with large yellow anthers, in mid-summer are followed in warm climates by spherical, red fruits. **'Fire Power'** illus. p.147.

Nankeen lily. See *Lilium* × *testaceum* illus. p.416.

NARCISSUS

Daffodil

AMARYLLIDACEAE

Genus of bulbs, grown for their ornamental flowers. Daffodils have usually linear, basal leaves and a spread of up to 20cm (8in). Each flower has a trumpet or cup (the corona) and petals (botanically known as perianth segments). Fully hardy, except where otherwise stated. Prefer sun or light shade and well-drained soil, but Div.8 cultivars (see below) prefer a sunny site and tolerate lighter soils. Dead-head flowers and remove faded foliage during mid-summer. Most cultivars increase naturally by offsets; dense clumps should be divided no sooner than 6 weeks after flowering every 3–5 years. Species may be propagated by fresh seed in late summer or autumn. Narcissus yellow stripe virus, basal rot, slugs, large narcissus fly and bulb and stem eelworm may cause problems. Contact with the sap of daffodils may irritate skin or aggravate skin allergies. Horticulturally, *Narcissus* is split into the following divisions. See also feature panel pp.432–4:

Div.1 Trumpet – usually solitary flowers each have a trumpet that is as long as, or longer than, the petals. Early to late spring-flowering.
Div.2 Large-cupped – solitary flowers each have a cup at least one-third the length of, but shorter than, the petals. Spring-flowering.
Div.3 Small-cupped – flowers are often borne singly; each has a cup not more than one-third the length of the petals. Spring- or early summer-flowering.
Div.4 Double – most have solitary, large, fully or semi-double flowers, sometimes scented, with both cup and petals or cup alone replaced by petaloid structures. Some have smaller flowers, produced in clusters of 4 or more, which are often sweetly fragrant. Spring- or early summer-flowering.
Div.5 Triandrus – nodding flowers, with short, sometimes straight-sided cups and narrow, reflexed petals, are borne 2–6 per stem. Spring-flowering.
Div.6 Cyclamineus – flowers are borne usually 1 or 2 per stem, each with a cup sometimes flanged and often longer than those of Div.5. Petals are narrow, pointed and reflexed. Early to mid-spring-flowering.
Div.7 Jonquil and Apodanthus – sweetly scented flowers are borne usually 2 or more per stem. Cup is short, sometimes flanged; petals are often flat, fairly broad and rounded. Spring-flowering.
Div.8 Tazetta – sweetly fragrant flowers of small-flowered cultivars are borne in clusters of 12 or more per stem; large-flowered cultivars have 3 or 4 flowers per stem. All have a small, often straight-sided cup and broad, mostly pointed petals. Late autumn- to mid-spring-flowering. Most are frost to half hardy. Autumn-flowering hybrids provide valuable cut flowers; 'prepared' bulbs may be grown in pots for mid-winter flowering.
Div.9 Poeticus – flowers, sometimes borne 2 per stem, may be sweetly fragrant. Each has a small, coloured cup and glistening white petals. Some *N. poeticus* hybrids are categorized as Div.3 or 8. Late spring- or early summer-flowering.
Div.10 Bulbocodium – flowers usually borne singly on very short stems, showing all the hallmarks of hoop-petticoat daffodils (*N. bulbocodium* subsp. *bulbocodium)*, with insignificant petals and a disproportionately large, widely flaring cup. Winter- to spring-flowering.
Div.11 Split-corona – usually solitary flowers that have cups split for more than half their length. In (**a**), Collar daffodils, the overlapping segments of the cup lie against the petals, but in (**b**), Papillon daffodils, the segments of the cup tend to be narrower, with their tips arranged at the margin of the petals. Most flowers fall into category (a). Spring-flowering.
Div.12 Miscellaneous – a miscellaneous category containing hybrids with varying, intermediate flower shapes that cannot be satisfactorily classified elsewhere. Autumn- to spring-flowering.
Div.13 Daffodils distinguished solely by botanical name – a wide variety of flowers showing the huge range of floral characteristics of wild daffodils: from the tiny *N. cyclamineus* and the sweetly scented, many-flowered *N. tazetta* to the stately trumpet species. Flower in early autumn to early summer.

***N.* 'Acropolis'** illus. p.433. Div.4. Mid- to late spring-flowering bulb. H 42cm (17in). Large, double flowers have white, outer petals and petaloids; white, inner petals are interspersed with shorter, orange-red petaloids. Is suitable for exhibition.
♀ ***N.* 'Actaea'** illus. p.433. Div.9. Late spring-flowering bulb. H 40cm (16in). Fragrant flowers have glistening white petals and shallow, flanged, rich lemon cups with narrow, orange-red rims.
***N.* 'Aircastle'** illus. p.432. Div.3. Mid-spring-flowering bulb. H 40cm (16in). Flowers have white petals that age greenish; shallow, flat, lemon-yellow cups deepen in colour at the rim.
***N.* 'Albus Plenus Odoratus'.** See *N. poeticus* 'Plenus'.
***N.* 'Altruist'** illus. p.434. Div.3. Mid-spring-flowering bulb. H 45cm (18in). Flowers have smooth, pale orange petals and a neat, ribbed, shallow, orange-red cup.
***N.* 'Ambergate'** illus. p.434. Div.2. Mid-spring-flowering bulb. H 45cm (18in). Flowers each have a shallow, widely expanded, fiery scarlet cup and soft tangerine petals.
♀ ***N.* 'Arctic Gold',** Div.1. Mid-spring-flowering bulb. H 40cm (16in). Rich golden-yellow flowers have broad petals and well-proportioned, flanged trumpets with neatly serrated rims. Is suitable for exhibition.
N. assoanus, syn. *N. juncifolius, N. requienii*, Div.13. Mid-spring-flowering bulb. H 15cm (6in). Is similar to *N. jonquilla*, but has thin, cylindrical leaves and rounded, bright clear yellow flowers with a sweet, slightly lemony fragrance. Thrives in sunny, gritty soil.
♀ ***N. asturiensis***, syn. *N. minimus* of gardens, Div.13. Late winter- or early spring-flowering bulb. H 8cm (3in). Small, pale yellow flowers have waisted trumpets and slender petals. Prefers full sun.
***N.* 'Avalon',** Div.2. Mid-spring-flowering bulb. H 35cm (14in). Fully hardy. Rounded, bright lemon-yellow flowers have wide, fluted cups that become white with age.
♀ ***N.* 'Avalanche'** illus. p.433. Div.8. Early spring-flowering bulb. H 35cm (14in). Half hardy. Produces 8 or more sweetly fragrant flowers, each with white petals and a primrose-yellow cup that scarcely fades. May be forced for mid-winter flowering.
***N.* 'Bartley'** illus. p.434. Div.6. Early spring-flowering bulb. H 35cm (14in). Long, slender, golden flowers have reflexed petals and narrow, angled trumpets. Flowers are long-lasting.
***N.* 'Belcanto'**, Div.11a. Late spring-flowering bulb. H 45cm (18in). Flowers, 8–12cm (3–5in) across, have rounded perianth segments, almost obscured by the flattened, pale yellow cups.
N.* × *biflorus. See *N.* × *medioluteus*.
***N.* 'Binkie'** illus. p.433. Div.2. Early spring-flowering bulb. H 30cm (12in). Flowers open clear pale lemon and cups turn sulphur-white with ruffled, lemon rims.
***N.* 'Birma',** Div.3. Mid-spring-flowering bulb. H 45cm (18in). Flowers have soft yellow petals and fiery orange cups with heavily ruffled rims.
♀ ***N.* 'Bravoure'** illus. p.433. Div.1. Early to mid-spring-flowering bulb. H 38cm (15in). Large flowers have overlapping, white petals and unusually slender, only slightly flared, lemon-yellow trumpets, with entire rims.
♀ ***N.* 'Bridal Crown'** illus. p.433. Div.4. Late spring-flowering bulb. H 40cm (16in). Long-lasting, small, sweetly scented flowers are semi-double, with rounded, milk-white petals and white petaloids interspersed with shorter, saffron-orange ones towards centre.
***N.* 'Broadway Star'** illus. p.433. Div.11b. Mid-spring-flowering bulb. H 40cm (16in). Has white flowers, 8cm (3in) across. The expanded segments of the split cups are flattened against the perianth segments; each has a narrow, orange mid-stripe running lengthways.
***N.* 'Brunswick',** Div.2. Early spring-flowering bulb. H 40cm (16in). Long-lasting flowers have white petals and long, flared, primrose cups, which fade to lemon, with darker rims. Foliage is a striking bluish-green. Is suitable for cutting.
♀ ***N. bulbocodium*** (Hoop-petticoat daffodil) illus p.434. Div.13. Vigorous, spring-flowering bulb. H 8–15cm (3–6in). Flowers are golden-yellow with conical cups and narrow, pointed petals. Thrives in moist turf in full sun. var. ***citrinus***, H 15cm (6in), has slender, dark green leaves and clear pale lemon flowers. Hybrids of this species are placed in Div.10.
N. campernelli. See *N.* × *odorus*.
***N.* 'Canaliculatus'** of gardens illus. p.433. Div.8. Mid-spring-flowering bulb. H 23cm (9in). Frost hardy. Produces a cluster of 4 or more small, fragrant flowers per stem, each with reflexed, white petals and a shallow, straight-sided, dark yellow cup.
***N.* 'Canisp'** illus. p.432. Div.2. Mid-spring-flowering bulb. H 40cm (16in). Arobust garden and exhibition daffodil with large, milk-white flowers, with broad, overlapping petals, lightly reflexed at the apex, and a slightly darker, flanged, trumpet-like cup, with a rolled, crenate mouth.
♀ ***N.* 'Cantabile'** illus. p.433. Div.9. Late spring-flowering bulb. H 25cm (10in). Stiff stems bear neat, well-rounded, glistening white flowers, with tiny, red-rimmed, yellow cups with a prominent green eye.
♀ ***N. cantabricus*** illus. p.432. Div.13. Spring- and sometimes winter-flowering bulb. H 10cm (4in). Is similar in form to *N. bulbocodium* subsp. *bulbocodium*, but is less robust. Flowers are milk- or ice-white. Thrives in an alpine house or greenhouse.
***N.* 'Cantatrice',** Div.1. Mid-spring-flowering bulb. H 40cm (16in). Flowers have pure white petals and slender, milk-white trumpets.
***N.* 'Capax Plenus'.** See *N.* 'Eystettensis'.
***N.* 'Cassata'** illus. p.433. Div.11a. Mid-spring-flowering bulb. H 40cm (16in). Cups are soft primrose and distinctly split into segments with ruffled margins, while petals are broad and milk-white.
♀ ***N.* 'Charity May'** illus. p.434. Div.6. Early to mid-spring-flowering bulb. H 30cm (12in). Small, pale lemon flowers each have broad, reflexed petals and slightly darker cups.
♀ ***N.* 'Cheerfulness'** illus. p.432. Div.4. Mid-spring-flowering bulb. H 40cm (16in). Long-lasting, small, sweetly scented, fully double flowers, 5.5cm (2¼in) across, are borne several to a stem, with milk-white petals and petaloids interspersed with shorter, orange-yellow ones at the centre. Is excellent for cutting.
***N.* 'Cool Crystal'** illus. p.433. Div.3.

Mid-spring-flowering bulb. H 50cm (20in). Has white flowers with bowl-shaped, green-eyed cups.
♀ ***N. cyclamineus*** illus. p.434. Div.13. Late winter- to early spring-flowering bulb. H 15cm (6in). Slender, nodding, clear gold flowers have narrow, reflexed petals and long, slender, flanged, waisted trumpets.
♀ ***N.* 'Dove Wings'** illus. p.433. Div.6. Mid-spring-flowering bulb. H 30cm (12in). Has small flowers with milk-white petals and fairly long, soft primrose cups.
♀ ***N.* 'Empress of Ireland'** illus. p.433. Div.1. Mid-spring-flowering bulb. H 40cm (16in). Large, robust, milk-white flowers have broad, overlapping petals, reflexed at the apex, and a slightly darker, flanged trumpet with a rolled, crenate mouth.
***N.* 'Eystettensis',** syn. *N.* 'Capax Plenus' (Queen Anne's double daffodil), Div.4. Mid-spring-flowering bulb. H 20cm (8in). Dainty, double flowers are composed of pointed, soft pale primrose petaloids neatly arranged in whorls.
♀ ***N.* 'February Gold'** illus. p.434. Div.6. Early spring-flowering bulb. H 32cm (13in). Solitary, long-lasting flowers have clear golden petals and long, flanged, slightly darker trumpets. Is useful for borders and naturalizing.
***N.* 'February Silver'** illus. p.433. Div.6. Robust, early spring-flowering bulb. H 32cm (13in). Has long-lasting flowers with milk-white petals and long, sturdy, nodding trumpets that open rich lemon and age to creamy-yellow.
***N.* 'Fortune'** illus. p.434. Div.2. Early to mid-spring-flowering bulb. H 40cm (16in). Flowers have ribbed, dark lemon petals and bold, flared, copper-orange cups; they are good for cutting.
***N.* 'Foxfire',** Div.2. Mid-spring-flowering bulb. H 35cm (14in). Has very rounded flowers with conspicuously white petals. Small, greenish-cream cups each have a small, green eye zone and a coral-orange rim.
***N.* 'Golden Ducat'** illus. p.434. Div.4. Mid-spring-flowering bulb. H 38cm (15in). Produces variable, sometimes poorly formed, double, rich golden flowers. Is suitable for cutting.
***N.* 'Grand Primo Citronière',** Div.8. Late autumn- to early spring-flowering bulb. H 32cm (13in). Half hardy. Bears 8 or more fragrant flowers, each with milk-white petals and a clear lemon cup, which fades to cream. 'Treated' bulbs may be forced for mid-winter flowering. Is good for cutting.
***N.* 'Grand Soleil d'Or'** illus. p.434. Div.8. Late autumn- to early spring-flowering bulb. H 35cm (14in). Half hardy. Flowers are sweetly scented with a dash of lemon. Each has rich golden petals and a clear tangerine cup. May be forced for mid-winter flowering, but staking is needed. Is excellent for cutting.
♀ ***N.* 'Hawera'** illus. p.434. Div.5. Mid-spring-flowering bulb. H 20cm (8in). Nodding flowers are a delicate lemon-yellow. Requires a sunny position. Makes a good pot plant.
***N.* 'Home Fires'** illus. p.434. Div.2. Early spring-flowering bulb. H 45cm (18in). Flowers each have pointed, rich lemon petals and an orange-scarlet cup with a lobed and frilled rim.
***N.* 'Honeybird'** illus. p.433. Div.1. Mid-spring-flowering bulb. H 50cm (20in). Well-proportioned flowers, 10.5cm (4½in) across, open greenish-yellow. The trumpets gradually fade almost to pure white.
♀ ***N.* 'Ice Follies'** illus. p.432. Div.2. Early spring-flowering bulb. H 40cm (16in). Flowers have milk-white petals and very wide, almost flat, primrose-yellow cups, fading to cream.
***N.* 'Irene Copeland'** illus. p.432. Div.4. Mid-spring-flowering bulb. H 35cm (14in). Bears large, fully double flowers of neatly arranged, milk-white petaloids interspersed with shorter, pale creamy-yellow ones. Is excellent for cutting.
♀ ***N.* 'Jack Snipe'** illus. p.433. Div.6. Sturdy, early to mid-spring-flowering bulb. H 23cm (9in). Long-lasting, milk-white flowers are similar to those of *N.* 'Dove Wings', but have narrower petals with incurved margins and medium-length cups of rich dark lemon-yellow.
♀ ***N.* 'Jenny',** Div.6. Early to mid-spring-flowering bulb. H 30cm (12in). Bears long-lasting flowers, each with milk-white petals and a medium-length, flanged, soft lemon trumpet that turns creamy-white.
♀ ***N.* 'Jetfire'** illus. p.434. Div.6. Floriferous, early spring-flowering bulb. H 23cm (9in). Flowers have overlapping, reflexed, clear golden-yellow petals and a cylindrical, ribbed, vibrant orange cup, slightly waisted before the crenate rim.
♀ ***N. jonquilla*** (Wild jonquil; illus. p.434), Div.13. Mid-spring-flowering bulb. H 30cm (12in). Richly fragrant flowers are borne in a cluster of 6 or more; each has tapering, yellow petals and a shallow, dark gold cup. Distinctive foliage is semi-cylindrical, dark, shining and grooved. **'Flore Pleno'** (Queen Anne's jonquil) has loosely double flowers; broad, incurved, yellow petals are interspersed with short, darker ones.
♀ ***N.* 'Jumblie'** illus. p.434. Div.12. Early spring-flowering bulb. H 20cm (8in). Bears 2 or 3 long-lasting flowers, each with broad, golden petals and a sturdy, flanged, orange-yellow cup. Is ideal as a pot plant.
N. juncifolius. See *N. assoanus.*
***N.* 'Kilworth'** illus. p.433. Div.2. Vigorous, late spring-flowering bulb. H 38cm (15in). Flowers have pointed, milk-white petals and dark reddish-orange cups with green eyes. Is effective in large groups.
♀ ***N.* 'Kingscourt'** illus. p.434. Div.1. Sturdy, mid-spring-flowering bulb. H 42cm (17in). Flowers have flanged, flared, rich gold trumpets with broad, rounded, paler gold petals.
***N.* 'Liberty Bells'** illus. p.434. Div.5. Sturdy, mid-spring-flowering bulb. H 32cm (13in). Flowers are slightly fragrant and clear lemon.
***N.* × *medioluteus*,** syn. *N.* × *biflorus* (Primrose peerless) illus. p.432. Div.13. Mid- to late-spring-flowering bulb. H 40cm (16in). Produces neat, medium-sized, sweetly scented flowers of rounded outline, with overlapping, almost pure white petals and a small, shallow, solid primrose-yellow, bowl-shaped cup. Is usually twin-headed.
♀ ***N.* 'Merlin'** illus. p.433. Div.3. Mid-spring-flowering bulb. H 35cm (14in). Flowers have broad, rounded, glistening white petals and relatively large, almost flat, rich gold cups, each with a small, green eye and a broad, lightly ruffled, orange-red rim. Is excellent for exhibition.
N. minimus of gardens. See *N. asturiensis.*
♀ ***N.* 'Minnow'** illus. p.433. Div.8. Robust, early to mid-spring-flowering bulb. H 18cm (7in). Has a cluster of 4 or more fragrant flowers per stem, each with rounded, creamy-yellow petals and a lemon cup. Increases freely. Is suitable for a container or rock garden.
♀ ***N. minor*,** syn. *N. nanus* of gardens illus. p.434. Div.13. Early spring-flowering bulb. H 20cm (8in). Flowers have slightly overlapping, soft yellow petals and almost straight, darker yellow trumpets with frilled rims. subsp. ***pumilus*** see *N. pumilus.*
N. minor of gardens. See *N. pumilus.*
***N. nanus*,** Div.13. Early spring-flowering bulb. H 12cm (5in). Flowers each have twisted, cream petals and a stout, straight, dull yellow trumpet with a frilled rim. Leaves are broad. Is suitable for naturalizing.
N. nanus of gardens. See *N. minor.*
♀ ***N. obvallaris*,** syn. *N. pseudonarcissus* subsp. *obvallaris* (Tenby daffodil), Div.13. Sturdy, early spring-flowering bulb. H 30cm (12in). Gold flowers have short petals and broad trumpets, borne on stiff stems.
***N.* × *odorus*,** syn. *N. campernelli* (Campernelle jonquil), Div.13. Robust, mid-spring-flowering bulb. H 20–30cm (8–12in). Has usually 2 richly fragrant, dark gold flowers. ♀ **'Rugulosus'** illus. p.434. Div.7, H 28cm (11in), is more vigorous and produces up to 4 small-cupped, rich gold flowers.
***N.* 'Panache'** illus. p.433. Div.1. Mid-spring-flowering bulb. H 40cm (16in). Produces very large, pure white flowers with well-balanced trumpets tinged green at the bases and broad overlapping petals.
***N.* 'Paper White Grandiflorus',** syn. *N. papyraceus* 'Grandiflorus', *N.* 'Paper White Snowflake', Div.8. Winter- to mid-spring-flowering bulb. H 35cm (14in). Half hardy. Has 10 or more long-lived, heavily fragrant, star-shaped, glistening white flowers, each with long, spreading petals and a small, flanged cup containing conspicuous, saffron-yellow stamens. Produces flowers continuously through winter indoors.
***N.* 'Paper White Snowflake'.** See *N.* 'Paper White Grandiflorus'.
***N. papyraceus* 'Grandiflorus'.** See *N.* 'Paper White Grandiflorus'.
♀ ***N.* 'Passionale'** illus. p.432. Div.2. Mid-spring-flowering bulb. H 40cm (16in). Each flower has milk-white petals and a long, flanged, apricot-tinged, pink cup.
***N.* 'Pencrebar'** illus. p.434. Div.4. Mid-spring-flowering bulb. H 18cm (7in). Fragrant flowers are small, rounded and fully double, often in pairs. Outer petaloids and large, inner ones are pale gold and are evenly interspersed with darker ones.
♀ ***N.* 'Pipit'** illus. p.434. Div.7. Mid-spring-flowering bulb. H 25cm (10in). Bears up to 3 scented flowers per stem, slightly greenish sulphur-yellow on opening. The ruffled, flared cup and the base of the overlapping petals become almost white at maturity.
N. poeticus (Poet's daffodil, Poet's narcissus), Div.13. Variable, late spring-flowering bulb. H 22–42cm (9–17in). Each fragrant flower comprises glistening white petals and a small, shallow, yellow or orange cup with a red rim. Is ideal for naturalizing in moist turf although slow to establish. **'Flore Pleno'** see *N.p.* 'Plenus'. **'Plenus'** (syn. *N.* 'Albus Plenus Odoratus', *N.p.* 'Flore Pleno'), H 40cm (16in), has loosely double, pure white flowers, with inconspicuous, greenish-yellow or orange centres, in late spring or early summer. Is good for cutting. ♀ var. ***recurvus*** (Pheasant's eye; illus. p.432 , p.433), H 42cm (17in), bears larger, long-lasting flowers with strongly swept-back petals and very shallow, greenish-yellow cups, with crimson rims, in early summer.
***N.* 'Portrush'** illus. p.432. Div.3. Late spring- to early summer-flowering bulb. H 35cm (14in). Produces small flowers, each with green-tinged, glistening milk-white petals and a small, shallow, flanged, creamy-white cup with a bright green eye.
***N.* 'Pride of Cornwall',** Div.8. Mid-spring-flowering bulb. H 38cm (15in). Bears several large, fragrant flowers, each with milk-white petals and a rich yellow cup shading to an orange-red rim outside. Is excellent for cutting. *N.*'Martha Washington' and *N.* 'Geranium' are similar.
♀ ***N. pseudonarcissus*** (Lent lily, Wild daffodil; illus. p.434), Div.13. Extremely variable, early spring-flowering bulb. H 15–30cm (6–12in). Nodding flowers have overlapping, straw-yellow petals and large, darker yellow trumpets. Is ideal for naturalizing. subsp. ***obvallaris*** see *N. obvallaris.*
***N. pumilus*,** syn. *N. minor* of gardens, *N. minor* subsp. *pumilus*, Div.13. Early spring-flowering bulb. H 15–22cm (6–9in). Bears bright gold flowers with separated, slightly paler petals and large trumpets with lobed and frilled rims. **'Plenus'** see *N.* 'Rip van Winkle'.
♀ ***N.* 'Rainbow'** illus. p.433. Div.2. Vigorous, mid-spring-flowering bulb. H 45cm (18in). White flowers have cups that are broadly banded with coppery-pink at the rim.
N. requienii. See *N. assoanus.*
***N.* 'Rip van Winkle',** syn. *N. pumilus* 'Plenus' illus. p.434. Div.4. Early spring-flowering bulb. H 15cm (6in). Shaggy, double flowers have densely arranged, flat, tapering, greenish-lemon petals with incurving tips.
***N.* 'Rockall'** illus. p.433. Div.3. Mid-spring-flowering bulb. H 50cm (20in). Produces neat flowers with overlapping, white petals and a shallow, ribbed, intense orange-red, bowl-shaped cup.
♀ ***N. romieuxii*** illus. p.433. Div.13. Early spring-flowering bulb. H 10cm (4in). Frost hardy, but is best grown in a frame or an alpine house. Is similar to *N. bulbocodium*, but each fragrant flower has a large, almost flat, flanged cup of glistening pale primrose.
N. rupicola illus. p.434. Div.13. Mid-spring-flowering bulb. H 8cm (3in). Is

similar to *N. assoanus*, but has more angled, bluish-green foliage and solitary, less scented, lemon flowers, each with a 6-lobed cup. subsp. ***watieri*** (illus. p.432), H 10cm (4in), produces relatively large, fragrant, crystalline-textured, white flowers with shallow, lobed cups.
♀ ***N.* 'Saint Keverne'** illus. p.434. Div.11b. Sturdy, early to mid-spring-flowering bulb. H 42cm (17in). Solitary flowers have clear rich golden petals and slightly darker cups of almost trumpet proportions.
***N.* 'Satin Pink'** illus. p.433. Div.2. Mid-spring-flowering bulb. H 42cm (17in). Each flower has broad, ribbed, milk-white petals and a long, barely flared, flanged, soft buff-pink cup of almost trumpet proportions.
***N.* 'Scarlet Gem'** illus. p.434. Div.8. Mid-spring-flowering bulb. H 35cm (14in). Frost hardy. Produces 7–8 scented flowers with golden petals and scarlet or deep orange-red cups.
***N.* 'Shining Light'** illus. p.434. Div.2. Mid-spring-flowering bulb. H 42cm (17in). Refined, well-balanced flowers have smooth, overlapping, clear, pale golden-yellow petals, and the slightly ribbed, cup-shaped cup is rich orange-red. The lightly dentate rim is slightly darker. Is good for exhibition.
***N.* 'Silver Chimes'** illus. p.433. Div.8. Sturdy, mid- to late spring-flowering bulb. H 32cm (13in). Has up to 10 fragrant flowers, each with broad, milk-white petals and a straight, shallow, creamy-primrose cup. Foliage is dark green. Thrives in a warm site.
♀ ***N.* 'Spellbinder'** illus. p.433. Div.1. Early spring-flowering bulb. H 42cm (17in). Long-lasting, bright sulphur-yellow flowers each have a slender, flanged trumpet, reversing to palest sulphur-white inside, except for the lobed, rolled-back rim, which is tinged with lemon.
♀ ***N.* 'Stratosphere'** illus. p.434. Div.7. Mid-spring-flowering bulb. H 40cm (16in). Bears usually 3 fragrant flowers, each with rich golden petals and a darker gold cup. Is excellent for exhibition.
♀ ***N.* 'Suzy'** illus. p.434. Div.7. Robust, mid-spring-flowering bulb. H 38cm (15in). Produces 3 or 4 long-lasting, large, fragrant flowers, each with clear golden petals and a large, flanged, rich tangerine cup.
♀ ***N.* 'Sweetness'** illus. p.434. Div.7. Early spring-flowering bulb. H 38cm (15in). Sweetly fragrant flowers, occasionally borne in pairs, have intense, golden-yellow petals and a darker, waved cup of strong substance.
♀ ***N.* 'Tahiti'** illus. p.434. Div.4. Robust, mid-spring-flowering bulb. H 38cm (15in). Solitary, loosely double flowers have golden petals and petaloids, interspersed with short, fiery orange, inner petaloids.
N. tazetta (Bunch-flowered daffodil, Polyanthus daffodil), Div.13. Extremely variable, late autumn- to mid-spring-flowering bulb. H 30–40cm (12–16in). Bears usually 12 or more fragrant flowers, generally with slender, white or yellow petals and shallow, white or yellow cups.
♀ ***N.* 'Tête-à-Tête'** illus. p.434. Div.12. Early spring-flowering bulb. H 15–30cm (6–12in). Produces long-lasting flowers, each with reflexed, rich golden petals and a square, flanged, warm yellowish-orange cup. Should be twin-flowered. Is very susceptible to viruses.
***N.* 'Thalia'** illus. p.432. Div.5. Vigorous, mid-spring-flowering bulb. H 38cm (15in). Has 3 or more long-lived, charming, milk-white flowers per stem, each with irregularly formed, often propeller-shaped petals and a flanged, bold cup.
***N.* 'Tresamble'**, Div.5. Sturdy, early spring-flowering bulb. H 40cm (16in). Bears up to 6 flowers per stem, each with milk-white petals and a flanged, creamy-white cup that is paler at the rim.
♀ ***N.* 'Trevithian'**, Div.7. Vigorous, early to mid-spring-flowering bulb. H 45cm (18in). Produces 2 or 3 large, fragrant flowers, rounded and soft primrose, each with broad petals and a short cup.
♀ ***N. triandrus*** (Angel's tears; illus. p.433, Div.13. Early spring-flowering bulb. H 12cm (5in). Bears nodding, milk-white flowers, each with narrow, reflexed petals and a fairly long, straight-sided cup. Makes a good container plant.
***N.* 'Trousseau'** illus. p.432. Div.1. Early spring-flowering bulb. H 42cm (17in). Flowers each have milk-white petals and a straight, flanged, soft lemon trumpet, with a flared, lobed rim turning rich creamy-buff tinged with pale pink.
***N.* 'Tudor Minstrel'**, Div.2. Mid-spring-flowering bulb. H 42cm (17in). Produces flowers with white, pointed petals. Chrome-yellow cups are slender and flanged.
***N.* 'Waterperry'**, Div.7. Mid-spring-flowering bulb. H 25cm (10in). Flowers have dull creamy-white petals; lightly flanged, spreading, primrose cups turn rich buff-yellow, shading to pinkish-apricot rims.
***N.* 'White Lady'**, Div.3. Vigorous, mid- to late-spring-flowering bulb. H 45cm (18in). Large, scented flowers have spreading, slightly overlapping, pure white petals. The small, shallow, heavily frilled cup is strong primrose-yellow on opening, becoming more creamy-yellow with maturity.
***N.* 'Woodland Star'** illus. p.433. Div.3. Mid-spring-flowering bulb. H 50cm (20in). Large flowers have white petals and small, bowl-shaped, deep red cups.
***N.* 'W.P. Milner'**, Div.1. Early spring-flowering bulb. H 23cm (9in). Nodding flowers each have slender, twisted, light creamy-yellow petals and a flared, pale lemon trumpet, which fades to palest sulphur.

Narcissus, Poet's. See *Narcissus poeticus*.
Narihira bamboo. See *Semiarundinaria fastuosa*, illus. p.320.
Narrow buckler fern. See *Dryopteris carthusiana*.
Narrow-leaved ash. See *Fraxinus angustifolia*.
Nasturtium. See *Tropaeolum*.
Flame. See *Tropaeolum speciosum*, illus. p.206.
Natal grass. See *Melinis repens*.
Natal ivy. See *Senecio macroglossus*.
Natal plum. See *Carissa macrocarpa*.
Native Australian frangipani. See *Hymenosporum flavum*.

NAUTILOCALYX

GESNERIACEAE

Genus of evergreen, erect, bushy perennials, grown for their flowers and foliage. Frost tender, min. 15°C (59°F). Requires high humidity, partial shade and well-drained soil; avoid waterlogging, especially in winter. Propagate by stem cuttings in summer or by seed, if available, in spring.
N. bullatus, syn. *N. tessellatus*. Evergreen, erect, bushy perennial. H and S 60cm (2ft). Narrowly oval, wrinkled leaves, to 23cm (9in) long, are dark green with a bronze sheen above, reddish-green beneath. Clusters of small, tubular, white-haired, pale yellow flowers are produced in the leaf axils mainly in summer.
N. lynchii illus. p.317.
N. tessellatus. See *N. bullatus*.

Navelwort, Venus's. See *Omphalodes linifolia*, illus. p.330
Neanthe bella. See *Chamaedorea elegans*.

NECTAROSCORDUM

LILIACEAE/ALLIACEAE

Genus of flowering bulbs, related to *Allium*, with long, linear, erect leaves. Exudes a very strong onion smell when bruised. Stems with erect, shuttlecock-like seed heads may be dried for winter decoration. Frost hardy. Needs partial shade. Grow in rough grass or borders in any soil that is neither too dry nor waterlogged. Propagate by freely produced offsets in late summer or by seed in autumn.
N. dioscoridis. See *N. siculum* subsp. *bulgaricum*.
N. siculum subsp. ***bulgaricum***, syn. *N. dioscoridis*, illus. p.410.

Needle spike-rush. See *Eleocharis acicularis*.

NEILLIA

ROSACEAE

Genus of deciduous shrubs, grown for their graceful habit and profuse clusters of small flowers. Fully hardy. Requires sun or semi-shade and fertile, well-drained soil. Established plants benefit from having some older shoots cut to base after flowering. Propagate by softwood cuttings in summer or by suckers in autumn.
N. longiracemosa. See *N. thibetica*.
N. sinensis. Deciduous, arching shrub. H and S 2m (6ft). Has peeling brown bark and oval, sharply toothed, mid-green leaves. Bears nodding racemes of small, tubular, pinkish-white flowers in late spring and early summer.
N. thibetica, syn. *N. longiracemosa*, illus. p.136.

NELUMBO

NYMPHAEACEAE

Genus of deciduous, perennial, marginal water plants, grown for their foliage and flowers. Half hardy to frost tender, min. 1–7°C (34–45°F). Needs an open, sunny position and 60cm (24in) depth of water. Remove fading foliage; flowers may be left to develop into decorative seed pods. Divide overgrown plants in spring. Propagate species by seed in spring, selected forms by division in spring.
N. lutea (American lotus). Vigorous, deciduous, perennial, marginal water plant. H and S 1m (3ft). Half hardy. Rounded, blue-green leaves, prominently veined beneath, develop on stout, 30–60cm (1–2ft) long stems. Large, chalice-shaped, yellow flowers open in summer.
N. nucifera illus. p.463. **'Alba Grandiflora'** is a vigorous, deciduous, perennial, marginal water plant. H 1.2–1.8m (4–6ft), S 1.2m (4ft). Frost tender, min. 1°C (34°F). Has very large, rounded, wavy-margined, dark green leaves, on sturdy stems, with large, fragrant, chalice-shaped, white flowers, 22–25cm (9–10in) across, in summer. **'Alba Striata'** bears white flowers, 15cm (6in) across, with jagged red margins. **'Rosea Plena'** has double, soft pink flowers to 30cm (12in) across.

NEMATANTHUS

GESNERIACEAE

Genus of perennials and soft-stemmed, evergreen shrubs, grown for their flowers and foliage. Frost tender, min. 13–15°C (55–9°F). Requires partial shade and humus-rich, moist but well-drained soil. Water potted specimens moderately, allowing soil almost to dry out between applications. Tip prune young plants to stimulate branching. Propagate by softwood or greenwood cuttings in summer.
N. gregarius, syn. *Hypocyrta radicans*, *N. radicans*, illus. p.153.
N. radicans. See *N. gregarius*.
N. strigillosus, syn. *Hypocyrta strigillosa*. Evergreen, prostrate shrub. H 15–30cm (6–12in), S 60cm–1m (2–3ft). Elliptic, slightly cupped leaves are clothed in dense down. Small, tubular, orange or orange-red flowers appear in leaf axils mainly from spring to autumn.

NEMESIA

SCROPHULARIACEAE

Genus of annuals, perennials and evergreen sub-shrubs, grown for summer bedding and as greenhouse plants. Half hardy. Prefers sun and fertile, well-drained soil. Cut back stems after flowering. Pinch out growing shoots of young plants to ensure a bushy habit. Propagate by seed sown under glass in early spring, or outdoors in late spring.
N. strumosa. Fast-growing, bushy annual. H 20–45cm (8–18in), S 15cm (6in). Has lance-shaped, serrated, pale green leaves and, in summer, trumpet-shaped, yellow, white or purple flowers, 2.5cm (1in) across, that are suitable for cutting. **Carnival Series** illus. p.340 and p.351.

Nemophila

HYDROPHYLLACEAE

Genus of annuals, useful for rock gardens and for edging. Fully hardy. Grow in sun or semi-shade and in fertile, well-drained soil. Propagate by seed sown outdoors in spring or early autumn. Is prone to aphids.
N. insignis. See *N. menziesii*.
N. maculata illus. p.331.
N. menziesii, syn. *N. insignis*, illus. p.345.

Neobuxbaumia

CACTACEAE

Genus of columnar or tree-like perennial cacti with cylindrical stems and usually low-set ribs. Nocturnal flowers, produced in summer, are followed by angular fruits, which open like stars when ripe. Frost tender, min. 15°C (59°F). Requires sun and poor to moderately fertile, sharply drained, gritty soil. Propagate by seed in spring.
N. euphorbioides, syn. *Lemaireocereus euphorbioides, Rooksbya euphorbioides*, illus. p.475.

Neochilenia mitis of gardens. See *Neoporteria napina*.

Neolitsea

LAURACEAE

Genus of evergreen trees and shrubs, grown for their foliage. Frost to half hardy. In cold areas needs shelter from strong winds; does best against a south- or west-facing wall. Requires sun or semi-shade and fertile, well-drained soil. Propagate by semi-ripe cuttings in late summer.
N. glauca. See *N. sericea*.
N. sericea, syn. *Litsea glauca, N. glauca*. Evergreen, broadly conical, dense tree or shrub. H and S 6m (20ft). Frost hardy. Narrowly oval, pointed leaves are glossy, mid-green above, white beneath and, when young, are densely covered with silky, brown hairs. Small, star-shaped, yellow flowers are borne in autumn.

Neolloydia

CACTACEAE

Genus of spherical to columnar, perennial cacti with dense spines and short tubercles in spirals. Most species are exceptionally difficult to cultivate unless grafted. Frost tender, min. 10°C (50°F). Needs full sun and well-drained soil. Water sparingly from spring to autumn; keep dry in winter. Propagate by seed in spring or summer.
N. conoidea, syn. *Mammillaria conoidea*, illus. p.491.
N. macdowellii. See *Thelocactus macdowellii*.

Neomarica

IRIDACEAE

Genus of evergreen, summer-flowering, iris-like, rhizomatous perennials with clusters of short-lived flowers. Frost tender, min. 10°C (50°F). Needs partial shade and fertile, moist, preferably humus-rich soil. Water freely in summer; reduce water in winter but do not allow plants to dry out. Propagate by seed in spring or by division in spring or summer.
N. caerulea illus. p.414.

Neopanax. See *Pseudopanax*.
Neoporteria. See *Eriosyce*.

Neoregelia

BROMELIACEAE

Genus of evergreen, rosette-forming, epiphytic perennials, grown for their overall appearance. Frost tender, min. 10°C (50°F). Requires semi-shade and a rooting medium of equal parts humus-rich soil and sphagnum moss or bark or plastic chips used for orchid culture. Using soft water, water moderately during growing season, sparingly at other times, and keep rosette centres filled with water from spring to autumn. Propagate by offsets in spring or summer.
N. carolinae, syn. *Aregelia carolinae, Nidularium carolinae* (Blushing bromeliad). Evergreen, spreading, basal-rosetted, epiphytic perennial. H 20–30cm (8–12in), S 40–60cm (16–24in). Strap-shaped, finely spine-toothed, lustrous, bright green leaves are produced in dense rosettes. A compact cluster of tubular, blue-purple flowers, surrounded by red bracts, is borne at the heart of each mature rosette, usually in summer. ♀ f. ***tricolor*** (syn. *N.c.* 'Tricolor'; illus. p.273) has leaves striped with ivory-white, that flushpink with age. ♀ **'Tricolor'.** See *N.c.* f. *tricolor*.
N. concentrica illus. p.273. Evergreen, spreading, basal-rosetted, epiphytic perennial. H 20–30cm (8–12in), S to 70cm (28in). Very broadly strap-shaped to oval, glossy, dark green leaves, with spiny, black teeth and usually with dark blotches, are borne in dense rosettes. In summer, a compact cluster of tubular, pale blue flowers, surrounded by pinkish-lilac bracts, is produced at the heart of each mature rosette. var. ***plutonis*** (syn. *N.c.* 'Plutonis') has bracts flushed with red. **'Plutonis'** see *N.c.* var. *plutonis*.

Nepalese ivy. See *Hedera nepalensis*.

Nepenthes
Pitcher plant

NEPENTHACEAE

Genus of evergreen, insectivorous, mostly epiphytic perennials, with leaves adapted to form pendulous, lidded, coloured pitchers that trap and digest insects. Is suitable for hanging baskets. Frost tender, min. 18°C (64°F). Requires a humid atmosphere, partial shade and moist, fertile soil with added peat and moss. Propagate by seed in spring or by stem cuttings in spring or summer.
N. × hookeriana illus. p.272.
N. rafflesiana. Evergreen, epiphytic, insectivorous perennial. H 3m (10ft), S 1–1.2m (3–4ft). Has lance-shaped, dark green leaves. Greenish-yellow pitchers, to 25cm (10in) long, are mottled purple and brown and have spurred lids. Inconspicuous, green flowers are borne in racemes and produced intermittently.

Nepeta
Catmint

LABIATAE/LAMIACEAE

Genus of summer-flowering perennials, useful for edging, particularly where they can tumble over paving. Fully hardy. Grows in sun or partial shade and any well-drained soil. Propagate by division in spring or by stem-tip or softwood cuttings in spring or summer, species only by seed in autumn.
***N.* 'Blue Beauty'.** See *N.* 'Souvenir d' André Chaudon'.
N. × faassenii illus. p.296.
N. grandiflora. Neat, erect perennial. H 40–80cm (16–32in), S 45–60cm (18–24in). Has slightly hairy stems, oval, round-toothed, light green leaves, with heart-shaped bases, and, in summer, racemes of small, hooded, blue flowers.
N. macrantha. See *N. sibirica*.
N. nervosa. Clump-forming perennial. H 35cm (14in), S 30cm (12in). Forms a mound of narrowly oblong to lance-shaped, pointed, prominently veined, mid-green leaves. Produces dense racemes of small, tubular, pale blue flowers from early to mid-summer.
N. sibirica, syn. *Dracocephalum sibiricum, N. macrantha*, illus. p.260.
'Souvenir d' André Chaudron' see *N.* 'Souvenir d' André Chaudron'.
***N.* 'Souvenir d' André Chaudron',** syn. *N.* 'Blue Beauty', *N. sibirica* 'Souvenir d' André Chaudon'. Spreading, clump-forming perennial. H and S 45cm (18in). Tubular, blue flowers are borne throughout summer above oval to lance-shaped, toothed, grey leaves.

Nephrolepis

NEPHROLEPIDACEAE/OLEANDRACEAE

Genus of evergreen or semi-evergreen ferns. Frost tender, min. 5°C (41°F). Needs a shady position. Prefers moist soil, but is extremely tolerant of both drought and waterlogging. Remove fading fronds and divide regularly. Propagate by division in summer or early autumn.
N. cordifolia (Ladder fern, Sword fern). Semi-evergreen fern. H 45cm (18in), S 30cm (12in). Has narrowly lance-shaped, arching, dark green fronds with rounded, finely serrated pinnae.
♀ ***N. exaltata*** illus. p.324.

Nephthytis

ARACEAE

Genus of evergreen, tufted perennials, with horizontal, creeping rhizomes, grown for their foliage. Frost tender, min. 18°C (64°F). Requires a humid atmosphere, moist, humus-rich soil and partial shade. Propagate by division in spring or summer.
N. afzelii. Evergreen, creeping, rhizomatous perennial. H to 75cm (30in), S indefinite. Has tufts of arrow-shaped, lobed, dark green leaves, to 25cm (10in) long. Intermittently bears a hooded, greenish spathe, enclosing a green spadix, followed by spherical, orange fruits.
N. triphylla of gardens. See *Syngonium podophyllum*.

Nerine

AMARYLLIDACEAE

Genus of bulbs, some of which are semi-evergreen, grown for their spherical heads of wavy-petalled, pink to red, occasionally white, flowers. Most flower in autumn before leaves appear. Frost to half hardy. Needs full sun and light, sandy soil. Plant in early autumn. Dislikes being disturbed. Water until leaves die down, then dry off. Propagate by seed when fresh or divide offsets in autumn or when leaves have died down. If ingested, all parts may cause mild stomach upset.
***N.* 'Baghdad'.** Autumn-flowering bulb. H 60cm (24in), S 15–20cm (6–8in). Half hardy. Leaves are strap-shaped, semi-erect and basal. Has crimson flowers, paler towards centres; long, narrow petals have recurved tips and crisped margins.
***N.* 'Blanchefleur'.** Autumn-flowering bulb. H 30–50cm (12–20in), S 15–20cm (6–8in). Half hardy. Produces strap-shaped, semi-erect, basal leaves and a tight head of 5–10 pure white flowers. Upper parts of petals are twisted.
♀ ***N. bowdenii*** illus. p.440. f. ***alba*** illus. p.440.
***N.* 'Brian Doe'** illus. p.440.
***N.* 'Corusca Major',** syn. *N. sarniensis* var. *corusca* 'Major'. Autumn-flowering bulb. H 60cm (24in), S 12–15cm (5–6in). Half hardy. Forms strap-shaped, semi-erect, basal leaves. Stout stem bears 10–15 scarlet-red flowers with narrow petals. Is useful for cutting.
N. crispa. See *N. undulata*.
N. filifolia. Autumn-flowering bulb. H to 25cm (10in), S 8–10cm (3–4in). Half hardy. Has thread-like, semi-erect leaves in a basal tuft. Slender stem has pale pink flowers with narrow petals.
N. flexuosa. Semi-evergreen, autumn-flowering bulb. H 40–50cm (16–20in), S 12–15cm (5–6in). Half hardy. Bears strap-shaped, semi-erect, basal leaves and 10–15 pink flowers; each petal has a deeper pink mid-vein and a recurved, wavy upper half. **'Alba'** has white flowers.
***N.* 'Fothergillii Major'.** Late summer- to early autumn-flowering bulb. H 45–60cm (18–24in), S 12–15cm (5–6in). Half hardy. Leaves are strap-shaped, semi-erect and basal. Very strong stem has about 10 bright scarlet-salmon flowers with recurved petals.
N. masoniorum. Autumn-flowering bulb. H 15–20cm (6–8in), S 8–10cm (3–4in). Half hardy. Produces thread-like, semi-erect leaves in a basal tuft. Stem bears pink flowers with very crisped petal margins.
***N.* 'Orion'** illus. p.440.
N. sarniensis illus. p.440. var. ***corusca*** **'Major'** see *N.* 'Corusca Major'.
N. undulata, syn. *N. crispa*, illus. p.440.

Nerium

APOCYNACEAE

Genus of evergreen shrubs, grown for their flowers. Frost tender, min. 10°C (50°F). Requires full sun and well-drained soil. Water containerized plants freely when in full growth, sparingly at other times. Tip prune young plants to

promote branching. Propagate by seed in spring or by semi-ripe cuttings in summer. All parts are highly toxic if ingested; contact with foliage may irritate skin.
N. oleander illus. p.117.

NERTERA

RUBIACEAE

Genus of creeping perennials, grown for their mass of spherical, bead-like fruits in autumn. Makes excellent alpine house plants. Half hardy. Requires a sheltered, semi-shaded position in gritty, moist but well-drained, sandy soil. Resents winter wet. Propagate in spring by seed, division or tip cuttings.
N. depressa. See *N. granadensis.*
N. granadensis, syn. *N. depressa*, illus. p.399.

Net bush, Common. See *Calothamnus quadrifidus.*
Net-leaf
Painted. See *Fittonia albivenis Verschaffeltii Group*, illus. p.314.
Silver. See *Fittoniaalbivenis Argyroneura Group*, illus. p.312.
Nettle tree. See *Celtis.*
Nettle-leaved bellflower. See *Campanula trachelium*, illus. p.258.
Net-veined willow. See *Salix reticulata*, illus. p.382.
New Zealand bluebell. See *Wahlenbergia albomarginata.*
New Zealand cabbage palm. See *Cordyline australis.*
New Zealand Christmas tree. See *Metrosideros excelsus*, illus. p.79.
New Zealand edelweiss. See *Leucogenes.*
New Zealand flax. See *Phormium.*
New Zealand honeysuckle. See *Knightia excelsa.*
New Zealand satin flower. See *Libertia grandiflora*, illus. p.241.
New Zealand tea-tree. See *Leptospermum scoparium.*

NICANDRA

SOLANACEAE

Genus of one species of annual with short-lived flowers. Fully hardy. Grow in sun and in rich, well-drained soil. Propagate by seed sown in spring.
N. physalodes (Apple of Peru, Shoo-fly). Fast-growing, upright, branching annual. H 1m (3ft), S 30cm (1ft) or more. Has oval, serrated, mid-green leaves. In summer to early autumn has bell-shaped, white-throated, light violet-blue flowers, over 2.5cm (1in) wide that last one day. Spherical, green fruits, 5cm (2in) wide, are surrounded by purple and green calyces. Is thought to repel flies, hence its name.

Nicodemia madagascariensis. See *Buddleja madagascariensis.*

NICOTIANA

SOLANACEAE

Genus of annuals, perennials, that are usually grown as annuals, and semi-evergreen shrubs. Frost hardy to frost tender, min. 1°C (34°F). Needs sun or partial shade and fertile, well-drained soil. Propagate annuals and perennials by seed in early spring, shrubs by seed in spring or by semi-ripe cuttings in summer. Contact with the foliage may irritate skin.
N. affinis. See *N. alata.*
N. alata, syn. *N. affinis*, illus. p.241.
N. glauca. Semi-evergreen, upright shrub. H and S 2.5–3m (8–10ft). Half hardy. Stout, blue-grey shoots bear narrowly oval, fleshy, blue-grey leaves. Showy, tubular, bright yellow flowers are produced in summer and early autumn.
♀ ***N. langsdorffii*** illus. p.346.
♀ ***N.* 'Lime Green'.** Upright annual. H 60cm (24in), S 25cm (10in). Half hardy. Mid-green leaves are spoon-shaped. In late summer and autumn produces racemes of open trumpet-shaped, greenish-yellow flowers that are fragrant at night.
***N. × sanderae* 'Crimson Rock'.** Fairly slow-growing, bushy annual. H 60cm (2ft), S 30cm (1ft). Half hardy. Oval leaves are mid-green. Evening-scented, trumpet-shaped, bright crimson flowers, to 8cm (3in) long, are produced throughout summer and early autumn. **Nicki Series**, H 38cm (15in), produces fragrant flowers in an extensive colour range that includes white, pink, red and purple. **Saratoga Series** (white) illus. p.331; (rose) illus p.338.
♀ ***N. sylvestris*** illus. p.224.

NIDULARIUM

BROMELIACEAE

Genus of evergreen, rosette-forming, epiphytic perennials, grown for their overall appearance. Frost tender, min. 10–15°C (50–59°F). Requires a position in semi-shade and a rooting medium of equal parts humus-rich soil and sphagnum moss or bark or plastic chips generally used for orchid culture. Using soft water, water moderately during the growing season, sparingly at other times, and keep centres of rosettes filled with water from spring to autumn. Propagate by offsets in spring or summer.
N. carolinae. See *Neoregelia carolinae.*
N. fulgens (Blushing bromeliad). Evergreen, spreading, basal-rosetted, epiphytic perennial. H 20cm (8in) or more, S 40–50cm (16–20in). Has dense rosettes of strap-shaped, spiny-toothed, arching, glossy, rich green leaves. Tubular, white-and-purple flowers, almost hidden in a rosette of bright scarlet bracts, are mainly produced in summer.
N. innocentii (Bird's-nest bromeliad). Evergreen, spreading, basal-rosetted, epiphytic perennial. H 20–30cm (8–12in), S 60cm (24in). Has dense rosettes of strap-shaped, prickle-toothed, arching, dark green, sometimes reddish-green leaves with reddish-purple undersides. Tubular, white flowers, partially hidden in a rosette of bright red bracts, appear mainly in summer.
N. procerum. Evergreen, spreading, basal-rosetted, epiphytic perennial. H 20–30cm (8–12in), S 50–75cm (20–30in). Strap-shaped, spiny-toothed, bright green leaves are produced in dense rosettes. Clusters of small, tubular, blue flowers are produced in summer.

NIEREMBERGIA

SOLANACEAE

Genus of summer-flowering perennials, sometimes grown as annuals, and deciduous or semi-evergreen sub-shrubs. Frost to half hardy. Prefers sun and moist but well-drained soil. Propagate by division in spring, by semi-ripe cuttings in summer or by seed in autumn.
N. caerulea, syn. *N. hippomanica.* **'Purple Robe'** illus. p.343.
N. hippomanica. See *N. caerulea.*
N. repens, syn. *N. rivularis*, illus. p.386.
N. rivularis. See *N. repens.*

NIGELLA

RANUNCULACEAE

Genus of annuals, grown for their attractive flowers, which are suitable for cutting, and their ornamental seed pods. Fully hardy. Grows best in sun and in fertile, well-drained soil. Dead-head plants to prolong flowering if seed heads are not required. Propagate by seed sown outdoors in spring or early autumn.
N. damascena (Love-in-a-mist). Fast-growing, upright annual. H 60cm (24in), S 20cm (8in). Has feathery, bright green leaves. Spurred, many-petalled, blue or white flowers appear in summer, followed by inflated, rounded, green, then brown seed pods that may be cut and dried. ♀ **'Miss Jekyll'** and **Persian Jewels Series** illus. p.345.

Night-blooming cereus. See *Hylocereus undatus.*
Nikko fir. See *Abies homolepis.*
Nikko maple. See *Acer maximowiczianum.*
Ninebark. See *Physocarpus opulifolius.*
Nirre. See *Nothofagus antarctica.*
Noble fir. See *Abies procera.*
Nodding catchfly. See *Silene pendula.*

NOLANA

SOLANACEAE

Genus of annuals, useful for growing in hot, dry sites and rock gardens and as edging. Frost hardy. Grow in sun and in fertile, well-drained soil. Propagate by seed sown outdoors in spring.
N. atriplicifolia. See *N. paradoxa.*
N. grandiflora. See *N. paradoxa.*
N. paradoxa, syn. *N. atriplicifolia, N. grandiflora.* Moderately fast-growing, prostrate annual. H 8cm (3in), S 15cm (6in). Has oval, mid-green leaves and, in summer, funnel-shaped, purplish-blue flowers, to 5cm (2in) wide, that have white-zoned, yellow throats.

Nolina recurvata. See *Beaucarnea recurvata.*
Nolina tuberculata. See *Beaucarnea recurvata.*

NOMOCHARIS

LILIACEAE

Genus of bulbs with a lily-like habit and, in summer, loose spikes of flattish flowers, often conspicuously spotted. Fully hardy. Requires partial shade and rich, well-drained soil with a high humus content. In summer needs moist but not waterlogged soil. Is dormant throughout winter. Propagate by seed in winter or spring.
N. mairei. See *N. pardanthina.*
N. nana. See *Lilium nanum.*
N. pardanthina, syn. *N. mairei*, illus. p.410.
N. saluenensis. Summer-flowering bulb. H 85cm (34in), S 12–15cm (5–6in). Leafy stems bear lance-shaped, scattered leaves. Has a loose spike of 2–6 saucer-shaped, white or pink flowers, with dark purple eyes and purple spots.

Nootka cypress. See *Chamaecyparis nootkatensis.*
Nopalxochia. See *Discocactus.*
Norfolk Island hibiscus. See *Lagunaria patersonii.*
Norfolk Island pine. See *Araucaria heterophylla.*
North Island edelweiss. See *Leucogenes leontopodium.*
Northern bungalow palm. See *Archontophoenix alexandrae*, illus. p.68.
Northern Japanese hemlock. See *Tsuga diversifolia.*
Northern maidenhair fern. See *Adiantum pedatum*, illus. p.324.
Northern pitch pine. See *Pinus rigida*, illus. p.102.
Norway maple. See *Acer platanoides.*
Norway spruce. See *Picea abies*, illus. p.100.

NOTHOFAGUS

Southern beech

FAGACEAE

Genus of deciduous or evergreen trees, grown for their habit, foliage and, in the case of deciduous species, autumn colour. Has inconspicuous flowers in late spring. Fully to frost hardy. Needs sun or semi-shade and, as it is not very resistant to strong winds, should have the shelter of other trees. Prefers deep, fertile, moist but well-drained soil; is not suitable for shallow, chalky soil. Propagate by seed in autumn.
N. × alpina, syn. *N. procera*, illus. p.63.
N. antarctica (Antarctic beech, Nirre). Deciduous, broadly conical tree, sometimes with several main stems. H 15m (50ft), S 10m (30ft). Fully hardy. Small, oval, crinkly-edged, glossy, dark green leaves turn yellow in autumn.
N. betuloides illus. p.70.
N. dombeyi illus. p.69.
N. menziesii (Silver beech). Evergreen, conical tree. H 20m (70ft), S 12m (40ft). Frost hardy. Has tiny, rounded, sharply toothed, glossy, dark green leaves.
N. obliqua illus. p.64.
N. procera. See *N. × alpina.*

NOTHOLIRION

LILIACEAE

Genus of summer-flowering bulbs, related to *Lilium*, grown for their funnel-shaped flowers. Frost hardy. Often produces early leaves, which may be damaged by spring frosts, so grow in a cool greenhouse in areas subject to alternating mild and cold periods in spring. Prefers partial shade or full sun and humus-rich, well-drained soil. Bulb dies after flowering. Propagate in spring or autumn by offsets, which take 2–3 years to reach flowering size. Alternatively propagate by seed in winter or spring.
N. campanulatum illus. p.412.

Nothopanax. Reclassified as *Pseudopanax*.
Nothoscordum neriniflorum. See *Caloscordum neriniflorum*.
Notocactus apricus. See *Parodia concinna*.
Notocactus graessneri. See *Parodia haselbergii* subsp. *graessneri*.
Notocactus haselbergii. See *Parodia haselbergii* subsp. *haselbergii*, illus p.491.
Notocactus leninghausii. See *Parodia leninghausii*.
Notocactus mammulosus. See *Parodia mammulosa*.
Notocactus ottonis. See *Parodia ottonis*.
Notocactus rutilans. See *Parodia rutilans*.
Notocactus scopa. See *Parodia scopa*.

NOTOSPARTIUM

LEGUMINOSAE/PAPILIONACEAE

Genus of leafless, summer-flowering shrubs, grown for their habit, green shoots and flowers. Frost hardy, but in cold areas does best against a south- or west-facing wall. Requires a sheltered, sunny position and well-drained soil. Older plants may need staking. Propagate by semi-ripe cuttings in summer or by seed in autumn.
N. carmichaeliae (Pink broom). Leafless, arching shrub. H 2m (6ft), S 1.5m (5ft). Short, dense spikes of pea-like, purple-blotched, pink flowers are produced in mid-summer on slender, drooping, green shoots.

NUPHAR

NYMPHAEACEAE

Genus of deciduous, perennial, deep-water plants, grown for their floating foliage and spherical flowers. Fully to frost hardy. Grows in shade or sun and in running or still water; is often grown for a water-lily effect in conditions where true water lilies would not thrive. Remove fading foliage and flowers, and periodically divide crowded plants. Propagate by division in spring.
N. advena (American spatterdock, Yellow pond lily). Deciduous, perennial, deep-water plant. S 1.2m (4ft). Fully hardy. Has broadly oval, floating, mid-green leaves; central ones are occasionally erect. Small, purple-tinged, yellow flowers in summer are followed by decorative seed heads.
N. lutea illus. p.467.

Nutallia. Reclassified as *Oemleria*.
Nutmeg, California. See *Torreya californica*, illus. p.103.

NYMANIA

AITONIACEAE/MELIACEAE

Genus of one species of evergreen, spring-flowering shrub, grown for its flowers and fruits. Frost tender, min. 7–10°C (45–50°F). Needs full light and fertile, well-drained soil. Water potted specimens moderately, less when not in full growth. Propagate by seed in spring or by semi-ripe cuttings in summer.
N. capensis illus. p.144.

NYMPHAEA

Water lily

NYMPHAEACEAE

Genus of deciduous, summer-flowering, perennial water plants, grown for their floating, usually rounded leaves and brightly coloured flowers. Fully hardy to frost tender, min. 10°C (50°F). Needs an open, sunny position and still water. Remove fading foliage to prevent it polluting water. Plants have tuber-like rhizomes and require dividing and replanting in spring or early summer every 3 or 4 years. Most frost tender plants may be treated as annuals. May also be propagated by seed or by separating plantlets in spring or early summer. See also feature panel p.466.
***N.* 'Amabilis'.** Deciduous, perennial water plant with floating leaves. S 1.5–2.2m (5–7ft). Fully hardy. Rounded leaves, reddish-purple when young, mature to dark green with red-margined, light green undersides. In summer, has star-shaped, pink flowers, 15–19cm (6–7in) across, with light pink tips and dark yellow stamens.
***N.* 'American Star'** illus. p.466. Deciduous, perennial water plant with floating leaves. S to 1.2m (4ft). Frost hardy. Young leaves are purplish-green or bronze, maturing to bright green. Star-shaped flowers, 10cm (4in) across, are deep pink and are held above water throughout summer.
***N.* 'Attraction'** illus. p.466. Deciduous, perennial water plant with floating leaves. S to 2m (6ft). Fully hardy. Has dark green leaves. In summer bears cup-shaped, garnet-red flowers, 15cm (6in) across and flecked with white.
***N.* 'Aurora'.** Deciduous, perennial water plant with floating leaves. S to 75cm (30in). Frost hardy. Olive-green leaves are mottled with purple. In summer has star-shaped flowers, 5cm (2in) across, cream in bud, opening to yellow, then passing through orange to blood-red. Suits a small- to medium-sized pool.
***N.* 'Blue Beauty'** illus. p.466. Deciduous, perennial water plant with floating leaves. S to 2.5m (8ft). Frost tender. Leaves are brown-freckled, dark green above, purplish-green beneath. Fragrant, rounded, deep blue flowers, to 30cm (12in) across, are produced in summer.
N. capensis (Cape blue water lily). Deciduous, perennial water plant with floating leaves. S to 2m (6ft). Frost tender. Large, mid-green leaves are often splashed with purple beneath. Star-shaped, bright blue flowers, 15–20cm (6–8in) across, appear in summer.
***N.* 'Emily Grant Hutchings'.** Deciduous, perennial water plant with floating leaves. S to 1.2m (4ft). Frost tender. Has small, green leaves overlaid with bronze-crimson. Cup-shaped, pinkish-red flowers, 15–20cm (6–8in) across, open at night in summer.
♀ ***N.* 'Escarboucle'** illus. p.466. Deciduous, perennial water plant with floating leaves. S to 3m (10ft). Fully hardy. Leaves are dark green. In summer has cup-shaped, deep crimson flowers, 10–15cm (4–6in) across, with golden centres.
***N.* 'Fabiola'.** Deciduous, perennial water plant with floating leaves. S to 1.5m (5ft). Fully hardy. In summer, produces fragrant, peony-shaped flowers, 15–18cm (6–7in) across, with strongly flecked pink petals, above mid-green leaves.
***N.* 'Firecrest'** illus. p.466. Deciduous, perennial water plant with floating leaves. S to 1.2m (4ft). Fully hardy. Dark green leaves are suffused with purple. In summer bears star-shaped, deep pink flowers, 15–20cm (6–8in) across, with red-tipped stamens.
***N.* 'Froebelii'** illus. p.466. Deciduous, perennial water plant with floating leaves. S 90cm (3ft). Fully hardy. Has rounded, pale green leaves, bronzed when young. In summer, produces cup-shaped, later star-shaped, burgundy-red flowers, 10–12cm (4–5in) across, with orange-red stamens.
***N.* 'General Pershing'** illus. p.466. Deciduous, perennial water plant with floating leaves. S 1.5–1.8m (5–6ft). Frost tender. Leaves are rounded, wavy-margined, olive-green and marked with purple. In summer, bears day-blooming, cup-shaped, later flat, highly fragrant, lavender-pink flowers, 20–27cm (8–11in) across, with yellow stamens.
♀ ***N.* 'Gladstoneana'** illus. p.466. Deciduous, perennial water plant with floating leaves. S to 3m (10ft). Frost hardy. Leaves are mid-green. Star-shaped, white flowers, 15–30cm (6–12in) across, appear in summer.
♀ ***N.* 'Gonnère'.** Deciduous, perennial water plant with floating leaves. S to 1.5m (5ft). Fully hardy. Has bright pea-green leaves and, in summer, rounded, white flowers, 15–20cm (6–8in) across.
***N.* 'Green Smoke'.** Deciduous, perennial water plant with floating leaves. S to 2m (6ft). Frost tender. Bronze-green leaves have bronze speckling. Star-shaped flowers, 10–20cm (4–8in) across, are chartreuse, shading to blue.
♀ ***N.* 'James Brydon'** illus. p.466. Deciduous, perennial water plant with floating leaves. S to 2.5m (8ft). Frost hardy. Fragrant, peony-shaped, orange-suffused, crimson flowers, 15–20cm (6–8in) across, are borne in summer above dark green leaves.
***N.* 'Laydekeri Fulgens'.** See *N.* Laydekeri Group 'Fulgens'.
***N.* Laydekeri Group 'Fulgens',** syn. *N.* 'Laydekeri Fulgens' illus. p.466. Deciduous, perennial water plant with floating leaves. S to 1m (3ft). Fully hardy. Dark green leaves have purplish-green undersides. Star-shaped, bright crimson flowers, 5–10cm (2–4in) across, appear in summer.
***N.* 'Lucida'** illus. p.466. Deciduous, perennial water plant with floating leaves. S 1.5–1.8m (5–6ft). Fully hardy. Has broadly ovate, mid-green leaves, and star-shaped flowers, 12–15cm (5–6in) across, with red inner petals, pink-veined, whitish-pink outer petals, and yellow stamens, in summer.
***N.* 'Madame Wilfon Gonnère'.** Deciduous, perennial water plant with floating leaves. S to 1.5m (5ft). Frost hardy. Has mid-green leaves and, in summer, cup-shaped, white flowers, 15cm (6in) across, spotted with deep rose-pink.
***N.* Marliacea Group 'Albida'** illus. p.466. Deciduous, perennial water plant with floating leaves. S to 2m (6ft). Fully hardy. Deep green leaves have red or purplish-green undersides. Bears fragrant, cup-shaped, pure white flowers, 15–20cm (6–8in) across, in summer. ♀ **'Chromatella'** (illus. p.466) has olive-green leaves, heavily mottled with maroon and bronze, and cup-shaped, canary-yellow flowers, 15–20cm (6–8in) across.
***N. odorata* 'Sulphurea Grandiflora',** syn *N.* 'Odorata Sulphurea Grandiflora'. Deciduous, perennial water plant with floating leaves. S to 1m (3ft). Fully hardy. Dark green leaves are heavily mottled with maroon. Bears fragrant, star-shaped, yellow flowers, 10–15cm (4–6in) across, throughout summer.
***N.* 'Odorata Sulphurea Grandiflora'.** See *N. odorata* 'Sulphurea Grandiflora'.
***N.* 'Pink Sensation'.** Deciduous, perennial water plant with floating leaves. S 1.2m (4ft). Fully hardy. In summer, bears cup-shaped, later star-shaped, pink flowers, 12–15cm (5–6in) across, with yellow inner stamens and pink outer stamens, above rounded, mid-green leaves, purple-green when young.
N. pygmaea. See *N. tetragona*.
***N.* 'Ray Davies'.** Deciduous, perennial water plant with floating leaves. S to 1.5m (5ft). Fully hardy. In summer, produces peony-shaped, light pink flowers, 15–18cm (6–7in) across, slightly yellow in the centre, above rounded, deep green leaves
***N.* 'Red Flare'.** Deciduous, perennial water plant with floating leaves. S 1.5–1.8m (5–6ft). Frost tender. Leaves are rounded, strongly toothed and reddish-green. In summer, bears night-blooming, flat, dark red flowers, 17–25cm (7–10in) across, with light pink or yellowish stamens.
***N.* 'Rose Arey'** illus. p.466. Deciduous, perennial water plant with floating leaves. S to 1.5m (5ft). Frost hardy. Leaves are reddish-green, purple when young. In summer produces star-shaped, deep rose-pink flowers, 10–15cm (4–6in) across, that pale with age and have a strong aniseed fragrance.
***N.* 'Saint Louis'.** Deciduous, perennial water plant with floating leaves. S to 2m (6ft). Frost tender. Bright green leaves are spotted with brown when young. Produces star-shaped, bright yellow flowers, 15–25cm (6–10in) across, in summer.
***N.* 'Sunrise'** illus. p.466. Deciduous, perennial water plant with floating

leaves. S to 2m (6ft). Frost hardy. Mid-green leaves have downy stalks and undersides. Bears star-shaped, yellow flowers, 10–15cm (4–6in) across, in summer.
N. tetragona, syn. *N. pygmaea.* **'Alba'** illus. p.466. Deciduous, perennial water plant with floating leaves. S to 30cm (12in). Fully hardy. Has small, dark green leaves, purplish-green beneath, and, in summer, star-shaped, white flowers, 2–3cm (¾–1¼in) across.
'Helvola' (illus. p.466), S to 45cm (18in), is frost hardy and has small, olive-green leaves with heavy purple or brown mottling. Produces star-shaped, yellow flowers, 2–4cm (¾–1½in) across, in summer.
***N.* 'Virginia'** illus. p.466. Deciduous, perennial water plant with floating leaves. S to 1.5m (5ft). Fully hardy. Has purplish-green leaves and, in summer, star-shaped, white flowers, 10–15cm (4–6in) across.
***N.* 'Wood's White Knight'.** Deciduous, perennial water plant with floating leaves. S to 2m (6ft). Frost tender. Leaves are mid-green, dappled with darker green beneath. In summer, produces star-shaped, creamy-white flowers, 10–20cm (4–8in) across and with prominent, gold stamens, that open at night.

NYMPHOIDES

MENYANTHACEAE

Genus of deciduous, perennial, deep-water plants, with floating foliage, grown for their flowers. Fully hardy to frost tender, min. 5°C (41°F). Requires an open, sunny position. Propagate by division in spring or summer.
N. peltata, syn. *Limnanthemum nymphoides, Villarsia nymphoides*, illus. p.467.

NYSSA

Tupelo

NYSSACEAE

Genus of deciduous trees grown for their foliage and brilliant autumn colour. Fully hardy. Needs sun or semi-shade; does best in hot summers. Requires moist, neutral to acid soil. Resents being transplanted. Propagate by softwood cuttings in summer or by seed in autumn.
♀ ***N sinensis*** illus. p.78.
♀ ***N. sylvatica*** illus. p.67.

Oak. See *Quercus.*
Algerian. See *Quercus canariensis*, illus. p.62.
American white. See *Quercus alba*, illus. p.67.
Armenian. See *Quercus pontica.*
Bartram's. See *Quercus × heterophylla*, illus. p.78.
Black. See *Quercus velutina.*
Black Jack. See *Quercus marilandica*, illus. p.76.
Bur. See *Quercus macrocarpa*, illus. p.76.
Californian live. See *Quercus agrifolia*, illus. p.81.
Caucasian. See *Quercus macranthera*, illus. p.62.
Common. See *Quercus robur.*
Cork. See *Quercus suber*, illus. p.69.
Daimio. See *Quercus dentata.*
Durmast. See *Quercus petraea.*
Holm. See *Quercus ilex.*
Hungarian. See *Quercus frainetto*, illus. p.65.
Kermes. See *Quercus coccifera.*
Lucombe. See *Quercus × hispanica* 'Lucombeana', illus. p.69.
Mirbeck's. See *Quercus canariensis*, illus. p.62.
Oregon. See *Quercus garryana*, illus. p.76.
Oriental white. See *Quercus aliena.*
Pedunculate. See *Quercus robur.*
Pin. See *Quercus palustris*, illus. p.65.
Pontine. See *Quercus pontica.*
Red. See *Quercus rubra*, illus. p.65.
Sawtooth. See *Quercus acutissima.*
Scarlet. See *Quercus coccinea*, illus. p.66.
Sessile. See *Quercus petraea.*
Shingle. See *Quercus imbricaria.*
Silky. See *Grevillea robusta.*
Tanbark. See *Lithocarpus densiflorus.*
Turkey. See *Quercus cerris.*
Water. See *Quercus nigra*, illus. p.64.
Willow. See *Quercus phellos*, illus. p.67.
Oak fern. See *Gymnocarpium dryopteris.*
Oak of Cyprus, Golden. See *Quercus alnifolia.*
Oak-leaved hydrangea. See *Hydrangea quercifolia*, illus. p.140.
Oats, Golden. See *Stipa gigantea*, illus. p.319.
Obedient plant. See *Physostegia.*

OCHNA

OCHNACEAE

Genus of mainly evergreen trees and shrubs, grown mostly for their flowers and fruits. Frost tender, min. 10°C (50°F). Prefers full light and well-drained soil. Water containerized specimens moderately, less when not in full growth. Prune, if necessary, in early spring. Propagate by seed in spring or by semi-ripe cuttings in summer.
O. multiflora. See *O. serrulata.*
O. serratifolia of gardens. See *O. serrulata.*
O. serrulata, syn. *O. multiflora*, *O. serratifolia* of gardens (Mickey-mouse plant). Evergreen, irregularly rounded, twiggy shrub that is semi-evergreen in low temperatures. H to 2m (6ft), S 1–2m (3–6ft) or more. Leaves are narrowly elliptic, toothed and glossy. Has 5-petalled, bright yellow flowers in spring-summer, then shuttlecock-shaped, red fruits, each with 1–5 berry-like seeds clustered on top.

Oconee bells. See *Shortia galacifolia*, illus. p.376.

× ODONTIODA

ORCHIDACEAE

See also ORCHIDS.
× *O.* (*O.* Chantos × *O.* Marzorka) × *Odontoglossum* Buttercrisp illus. p.311. Evergreen, epiphytic orchid for a cool greenhouse. H 23cm (9in). Produces arching spikes of intricately patterned, red, tan, orange and yellow flowers, 8cm (3in) across; flowering season varies. Has narrowly oval leaves, 10–15cm (4–6in) long. Needs shade in summer.
× *O.* Mount Bingham illus. p.309. Evergreen, epiphytic orchid for a cool greenhouse. H 23cm (9in). Bears pink-edged, red flowers, 9cm (3½in) across, in spikes; flowering season varies. Has narrowly oval leaves, 10–15cm (4–6in) long. Needs shade in summer.
× *O.* Pacific Gold × *Odontoglossum cordatum* illus. p.309. Evergreen, epiphytic orchid for a cool greenhouse. H 23cm (9in). Bears long spikes of yellow-striped and -marked, rich chocolate-brown flowers, 7cm (3in) across; flowering season varies. Leaves are narrowly oval and 10–15cm (4–6in) long. Grow in shade in summer.
× *O.* Petit Port. Evergreen, epiphytic orchid for a cool greenhouse. H 23cm (9in). Bears spikes of rich red flowers, 8cm (3in) across, each with a pink-and-yellow-marked lip; flowering season varies. Narrowly oval leaves are 10–15cm (4–6in) long. Needs shade in summer.

× ODONTOCIDIUM

ORCHIDACEAE

See also ORCHIDS.
× *O.* Artur Elle 'Colombian' illus. p.309. Evergreen, epiphytic orchid for a cool greenhouse. H 23cm (9in). Produces tall spikes of pale yellow flowers, 6cm (2½in) across and intricately patterned with brown; flowering season varies. Has narrowly oval leaves, 10–15cm (4–6in) long. Requires shade in summer.
× *O.* Tiger Butter × *Wilsonara* Wigg's 'Kay' illus. p.309. Evergreen, epiphytic orchid for a cool greenhouse. H 23cm (9in). Bears spikes of mottled, deep reddish-brown flowers, 5cm (2in) across, each with a rich golden-yellow lip; flowering season varies. Narrowly oval leaves are 10–15cm (4–6in) long. Grow in shade in summer.
× *O.* Tiger Hambuhren illus. p.311. Evergreen, epiphytic orchid for a cool greenhouse. H 23cm (9in). Deep yellow flowers, 8cm (3in) across and heavily patterned with chestnut-brown, are borne in tall spikes; flowering season varies. Has narrowly oval leaves, 10–15cm (4–6in) long. Needs shade in summer.
× *O.* Tigersun 'Orbec' illus. p.310. Evergreen, epiphytic orchid for a cool greenhouse. Is very similar to × *O.* Tiger Hambuhren, but flowers are slightly smaller and have lighter patterning.

ODONTOGLOSSUM

ORCHIDACEAE

See also ORCHIDS.
O. bictoniense. See *Lemboglossum bictoniense.*
O. cervantesii. See *Lemboglossum cervantesii.*
O. cordatum. See *Lemboglossum cordatum.*
O. crispum illus. p.308. Evergreen, epiphytic orchid for a cool greenhouse. H 15cm (6in). Bears long sprays of rounded flowers, 8cm (3in) across, white or spotted or flushed with pink, each with a red-and-yellow-marked lip; flowering season varies. Has narrowly oval leaves, 10–15cm (4–6in) long. Requires shade in summer.
***O.* Eric Young** illus. p.310. Evergreen, epiphytic orchid for a cool greenhouse. H 15cm (6in). Has spikes of white-lipped, pale yellow flowers, 8cm (3in) across, spotted with rich yellow; flowering season varies. Bears narrowly oval leaves, 10–15cm (4–6in) long. Grow in shade in summer.
O. grande. See *Rossioglossum grande.*
***O.* Le Nez Point** illus. p.309. Evergreen, epiphytic orchid for a cool greenhouse. H 15cm (6in). Crimson flowers, 6cm (2½in) across, are borne in spikes; flowering season varies. Has narrowly oval leaves, 10–15cm (4–6in) long. Needs shade in summer.
O. rossii. See *Lemboglossum rossii.*
***O.* Royal Occasion** illus. p.308. Evergreen, epiphytic orchid for a cool greenhouse. H 15cm (6in). Has spikes of white flowers, 8cm (3in) across, with deep yellow markings in the centres of the lips, in autumn-winter. Leaves are narrowly oval and 10–15cm (4–6in) long. Shade in summer.

× ODONTONIA

ORCHIDACEAE

See also ORCHIDS.
× *O.* Olga. Evergreen, epiphytic orchid for a cool greenhouse. H 15cm (6in). Pure white flowers, 10cm (4in) across, with large, reddish-brown-blotched lips, are borne in tall, arching racemes, mainly in autumn. Produces ovoid pseudobulbs and narrowly oval leaves, 12cm (5in) long. Is best grown in shade during the summer.

OEMLERIA,
syn. NUTTALLIA, OSMARONIA

ROSACEAE

Genus of one species of deciduous, early spring-flowering shrub, grown for its fragrant flowers and decorative fruits. Separate male and female plants are needed in order to obtain fruits. Fully hardy. Prefers sun or semi-shade and moist soil. To restrict growth remove suckers and cut old shoots back or down to base in late winter. Propagate by suckers in autumn.
O. cerasiformis. (Indian plum, Oso berry). Deciduous, upright, then arching shrub that forms dense thickets. H 2.5m (8ft), S 4m (12ft). Leaves are narrowly oval and dark blue-green. Has nodding clusters of small, fragrant, bell-shaped, white flowers in early spring, then small, plum-shaped, purple fruits.

OENOTHERA
Evening primrose

ONAGRACEAE

Genus of annuals, biennials and perennials, grown for their profuse but short-lived flowers in summer. Fully to frost hardy. Needs full sun and well-drained, sandy soil. Propagate by seed or division in autumn or spring or by softwood cuttings in late spring.
O. acaulis. Tuft-forming perennial. H 15cm (6in), S 20cm (8in). Fully hardy. Has oblong to oval, deeply toothed or lobed leaves. Cup-shaped, white flowers, turning pink, open at sunset in summer. Suits a rock garden.
O. caespitosa. Clump-forming, stemless perennial. H 12cm (5in), S 20cm (8in). Fully hardy. Has narrowly oval, entire or toothed, mid-green leaves. Flowers, opening at sunset in summer, are fragrant, cup-shaped and white, becoming pink with age. Suits a rock garden.
O. fraseri. See *O. fruticosa* subsp. *glauca.*
O. fruticosa* 'Fireworks'.** See *O.f.* 'Fyrverkeri'. ♀ **'Fyrverkeri'** (syn. *O.f.* 'Fireworks') illus. p.303. ♀ subsp. ***glauca (syn. *O. fraseri, O. glauca, O. tetragona*) is a clump-forming perennial. H 45–60cm (18–24in), S 45cm (18in). Fully hardy. Dense spikes of fragrant, cup-shaped, bright yellow flowers appear from mid- to late summer. Leaves, borne on reddish-green stems, are narrowly oval to lance-shaped and glossy, mid-green.
O. glauca. See *O. fruticosa* subsp. *glauca.*
♀ ***O. macrocarpa***, syn. *O. missouriensis*, illus. p.397.
O. missouriensis. See *O. macrocarpa.*
O. perennis, syn. *O. pumila.* Clump-forming perennial. H 15–60cm (6–4in), S 30cm (12in). Fully hardy. In summer, loose spikes of nodding buds open to fragrant, funnel-shaped, yellow flowers above narrowly spoon-shaped, mid-green leaves.
O. pumila. See *O. perennis.*
O. speciosa (White evening primrose). Often short-lived, clump-forming perennial with running rhizomes. H 45cm (18in), S 30cm (12in) or more. Frost hardy. In summer bears spikes of fragrant, saucer-shaped, green-centred, pure white flowers that age to pink and open flat. Leaves are narrowly spoon-shaped, deeply cut and mid-green.
O. tetragona. See *O. fruticosa* subsp. *glauca.*

Ohio buckeye. See *Aesculus glabra.*
Old blush china. See *Rosa × odorata* 'Pallida'.
Old man. See *Artemisia abrotanum*, illus. p.172.
Old man of the Andes. See *Oreocereus celsianus*, illus. p.478.
Old man's beard. See *Clematis.*
Old pink moss rose. See *Rosa × centifolia* 'Muscosa'.

Old-lady cactus. See *Mammillaria hahniana*, illus. p.481.
Old-man cactus. See *Cephalocereus senilis*, illus. p.476.
Peruvian. See *Espostoa lanata*, illus. p.473.
Old-witch grass. See *Panicum capillare*, illus. p.320.
Old-woman cactus. See *Mammillaria hahniana*, illus. p.481.

OLEA

OLEACEAE

Genus of evergreen trees, grown for their foliage and edible fruits. Frost to half hardy; in cold areas requires the protection of a sheltered, south- or west-facing wall. Needs full sun and deep, fertile, very well-drained soil. Propagate by semi-ripe cuttings in summer or by seed in autumn.
♀ ***O. europaea*** (Olive). Slow-growing, evergreen, spreading tree. H and S 10m (30ft). Frost hardy. Is very long-lived. Narrowly oblong leaves are grey-green above, silvery beneath. Tiny, fragrant, white flowers, borne in short racemes in late summer, are followed by edible, oval, green, later purple fruits.

Oleander. See *Nerium oleander*, illus. p.117.
Yellow. See *Thevetia peruviana*, illus. p.89.

OLEARIA

Daisy bush

COMPOSITAE/ASTERACEAE

Genus of evergreen shrubs and trees, grown for their foliage and daisy-like flower heads. In mild, coastal areas provides good, very wind-resistant shelter. Frost to half hardy. Needs full sun and well-drained soil. Cut out dead wood in spring. Propagate by semi-ripe cuttings in summer.
O. albida of gardens. See *O.* 'Talbot de Malahide'.
O. avicenniifolia. Evergreen, rounded, dense shrub. H 3m (10ft), S 5m (15ft). Frost hardy. Oval to lance-shaped, dark grey-green leaves are white beneath. Bears wide heads of fragrant, white flowers in late summer and early autumn.
O. × haastii illus. p.135.
♀ ***O. 'Henry Travers',*** syn. *O. semidentata* of gardens. Evergreen, rounded, compact shrub. H and S 3m (10ft). Half hardy. Has white shoots and narrowly lance-shaped, leathery, grey-green leaves. Large heads of purple-centred, lilac flowers appear from early to mid-summer.
O. ilicifolia. Evergreen, bushy, dense shrub. H and S 3m (10ft). Frost hardy. Narrowly oblong, rigid leaves are sharply toothed, grey-green and musk-scented. Fragrant, white flower heads are borne in clusters in early summer.
O. lacunosa. Evergreen, upright, dense shrub. H and S 3m (10ft). Frost hardy. Narrowly oblong, pointed, rigid leaves have rust-brown hairs when young and mature to glossy, dark green with central, white veins. Produces white flowerheads only rarely.
♀ ***O. macrodonta.*** Vigorous, evergreen, upright shrub, often tree-like. H 6m (20ft), S 5m (15ft). Frost hardy. Has holly-shaped, sharply toothed, grey-green leaves, silvery-white beneath. Large heads of fragrant, white flowers appear in early summer.
O. × mollis. Evergreen, rounded, dense shrub. H 1m (3ft), S 1.5m (5ft). Frost hardy. Has oval, wavy-edged, silvery-grey leaves. Large heads of small, white flowers are borne profusely in late spring. ♀ **'Zennorensis'**, H and S 2m (6ft), has narrowly oblong leaves.
O. nummulariifolia illus. p.132.
O. phlogopappa. Evergreen, upright, compact shrub. H and S 2m (6ft). Half hardy. Leaves are grey-green and oblong, with wavy edges. Massed, white flower heads are carried in late spring. var. ***subrepanda*** illus. p.154.
♀ ***O. × scilloniensis.*** Evergreen, upright, then rounded, dense shrub. H and S 2m (6ft). Frost hardy. Narrowly oblong, wavy-edged, dark grey-green leaves set off masses of white flower heads in late spring.
O. semidentata of gardens. See *O.* 'Henry Travers'.
O. 'Talbot de Malahide', syn. *O. albida* of gardens. Evergreen, bushy, dense shrub. H 3m (10ft), S 5m (15ft). Frost hardy. Oval, dark green leaves are silvery beneath. Bears broad heads of fragrant, white flowers in late summer. Excellent for exposed, coastal gardens.
O. virgata illus. p.114.

Oleaster. See *Elaeagnus angustifolia*, illus. p.118.
Olive. See *Olea europaea*.
Fragrant. See *Osmanthus fragrans*.
Oliveranthus elegans. See *Echeveria harmsii*.

OLSYNIUM

IRIDACEAE

Genus of fibrous-rooted, clump-forming perennials, grown for their nodding, trumpet- to bell-shaped flowers in spring. Fully hardy. Requires partial shade and moist, humus-rich, moderately fertile soil. Propagate by seed in autumn. Young plants take 2 or 3 years to flower.
O. biflorum, syn. *Phaiophleps biflora, Sisyrinchium odoratissimum.* Clump-forming, spring- to summer-flowering, rhizomatous perennial. H 25–35cm (10–14in), S 5–8cm (2–3in). Has cylindrical, rush-like, erect, basal leaves. Bears a small head of pendent, white flowers that are striped and veined red.
♀ ***O. douglasii***, syn. *Sisyrinchium douglasii, S. grandiflorum* (Grass widow, Spring bell). Stiff, upright, summer-deciduous perennial. H 25cm (10in), S 15cm (6in). Has grass-like leaves sheathing very short, thread-like flowering stems and, in early spring, a succession of pendent, bell-shaped, violet to red-purple, or sometimes white, flowers. Suits a rock garden oralpine house.

OMPHALODES

BORAGINACEAE

Genus of annuals and perennials, some of which are evergreen or semi-evergreen. Makes good ground cover, especially in rock gardens. Fully to half hardy. Needs shade or semi-shade and moist but well-drained soil, except for *O. linifolia* and *O. luciliae*, which prefer sun. Propagate by seed or division in spring.
♀ ***O. cappadocica*** illus. p.361.
♀ ***O. linifolia*** illus. p.330.
O. luciliae. Semi-evergreen, mound-forming perennial. H 7cm (3in), S 15cm (6in). Half hardy. Has oval, blue-grey leaves. In spring-summer, loose sprays of pink buds develop into flattish, sky-blue flowers. Resents winter wet, so plant in a sheltered site or alpine house. Prefers sun and very gritty soil.
O. verna illus. p.361.

OMPHALOGRAMMA

PRIMULACEAE

Genus of perennials, closely related to *Primula*, grown for their flowers. Makes good rock garden plants, but is difficult to grow, especially in hot, dry areas. Frost hardy. Needs shade and gritty, moist but well-drained, peaty soil. Propagate by seed in spring.
O. vinciflorum. Basal-rosetted perennial. H 15cm (6in), S 10cm (4in). Has oval, hairy leaves that are mid-green in colour. In spring produces nodding, funnel-shaped, violet flowers, each with a deeper violet throat and a flat, flared mouth.

ONCIDIUM

ORCHIDACEAE

See also ORCHIDS.
O. flexuosum (Dancing-doll orchid; illus. p.311). Evergreen, epiphytic orchid for a cool or intermediate greenhouse. H 23cm (9in). In autumn produces terminal sprays of many small, large-lipped, bright yellow flowers, 0.5cm (¼in) across, with red-brown markings on the sepals and petals. Bears narrowly oval leaves, 10cm (4in) long. Is best grown on a bark slab. Keep in semi-shade in summer.
♀ ***O. ornithorrhynchum*** illus. p.308. Evergreen, epiphytic orchid for a cool greenhouse. H 15cm (6in). Dense, arching sprays of very fragrant, rose-lilac flowers, 0.5cm (¼in) across, with a yellow highlight, are borne freely in autumn. Has narrowly oval leaves, 10cm (4in) long. Requires semi-shade in summer.
O. papilio. See *Psychopsis papilio*.
O. tigrinum illus. p.310. Evergreen, epiphytic orchid for a cool or intermediate greenhouse. H 23cm (9in). Branching spikes of fragrant, yellow-marked, brown flowers, 5cm (2in) across, each with a large, yellow lip, open in autumn. Has oval leaves, 15cm (6in) long. Requires semi-shade in summer.

Onion. See *Allium*.
Sea. See *Urginea maritima*.

ONIXOTIS,
syn. DIPIDAX

LILIACEAE/COLCHICACEAE

Genus of spring-flowering corms, cultivated mainly for botanical interest. Half hardy. Requires sun and well-drained soil. Plant corms in early autumn and keep them watered until after flowering. Dry off in summer. Propagate by seed in autumn.
O. triquetra, syn. *Dipidax triquetrum.* Spring-flowering corm. H 20–30cm (8–12in), S 5–8cm (2–3in). Long, narrow leaves are semi-erect and basal. Carries a spike of flattish, star-shaped, white flowers, each narrow petal having a basal, red mark.

ONOCLEA

WOODSIACEAE

Genus of one species of deciduous fern that rapidly colonizes wet areas. Fully hardy. Grows in sun or shade and in wet soil. Remove fronds as they fade. Propagate by division in autumn or winter.
♀ ***O. sensibilis*** illus. p.324.

ONONIS

LEGUMINOSAE/PAPILIONACEAE

Genus of summer-flowering annuals, perennials and deciduous or semi-evergreen shrubs and sub-shrubs, grown for their pea-like flowers. Is good for rock gardens, walls and banks. Fully hardy. Needs a sunny position in well-drained soil. Propagate by seed in autumn or spring, shrubs also by softwood cuttings in summer.
O. fruticosa illus. p.365.
O. natrix illus. p.371.
O. rotundifolia. Deciduous or semi-evergreen, glandular, upright sub-shrub. H 20–60cm (8–24in), S 20–30cm (8–12in) or more. Bears small, rounded, 3-parted, toothed, hairy, green leaves, with the terminal leaflet long-stalked. Flowers that are relatively large, red-streaked, and rose-pink appear in small clusters in summer.

Onopordon. See *Onopordum*.

ONOPORDUM,
syn. ONOPORDON

COMPOSITAE/ASTERACEAE

Genus of annuals, biennials and perennials, ranging from stemless to tall, branching plants. Fully hardy. Grow in sun or semi-shade and in rich, well-drained soil. To prevent self seeding remove dead flower heads. Propagate by seed sown outdoors in autumn or spring. Leaves are prone to slug and snail damage.
O. acanthium illus. p.334.

ONOSMA

BORAGINACEAE

Genus of summer-flowering annuals, semi-evergreen biennials, perennials and sub-shrubs, grown for their long, pendent, tubular flowers. Is suitable for rock gardens and banks. Fully to frost hardy. Requires full sun and well-drained soil. Dislikes wet summers. Propagate by softwood cuttings in summer or by seed in autumn.
O. alborosea illus. p.364.
O. stellulata. Semi-evergreen, upright sub-shrub. H and S 15cm (6in). Fully hardy. Leaves are oblong and covered in hairs which may irritate the skin. Clusters of yellow flowers open in late spring and summer.

OOPHYTUM

AIZOACEAE

Genus of clump-forming, egg-shaped, perennial succulents with 2 united, very fleshy leaves. These are covered in dry, papery sheaths, except in spring when sheaths split open, revealing a new pair of leaves. Flowers are produced from a slight central fissure on upper surface. Is difficult to grow. Frost tender, min. 5°C (41°F). Requires sun and well-drained soil. Propagate by seed or stem cuttings in spring or summer.
O. nanus illus. p.486.

Operculina tuberosa. See *Merremia tuberosa.*

OPHIOPOGON

LILIACEAE/CONVALLARIACEAE

Genus of evergreen perennials, grown mainly for their grass-like foliage. Fully to half hardy. Grows in sun or partial shade and in fertile, well-drained soil. Propagate by division in spring or by seed in autumn.
O. jaburan. Evergreen, clump-forming perennial. H 15cm (6in), S 30cm (12in). Frost hardy. Has dark green foliage. In early summer produces racemes of bell-shaped, white flowers, followed by deep blue berries.
'Variegatus' see *O.j.* 'Vittatus'.
'Vittatus' (syn. *O.j.* 'Variegatus') is half hardy, has white- or yellow-striped foliage and is much less robust.
O. japonicus illus. p.316.
♀ ***O. planiscapus* 'Nigrescens'** illus. p.315.

OPHRYS

ORCHIDACEAE

See also ORCHIDS.
O. aranifera. See *O. sphegodes.*
O. fuciflora. See *O. holoserica.*
O. fusca illus. p.310. Deciduous, terrestrial orchid. H 10–40cm (4–16in). Frost hardy. Spikes of greenish, yellow or brown flowers, 0.5cm (¼in) long, each with a yellow-edged, bluish, brown or purple lip, are produced in spring. Has oval or lance-shaped leaves, 8–12cm (3–5in) long. Grow in shade outdoors. Containerized plants require semi-shade in summer.
O. holoserica, syn. *O. fuciflora.* Deciduous, terrestrial orchid. H 15–55cm (6–22in). Frost hardy. Spikes of flowers, 1cm (½in) long, from white through pink to blue and green, appear in spring-summer. Leaves are oval to oblong, 5–10cm (2–4in) long. Cultivate as for *O. fusca.*
O. lutea illus. p.310. Deciduous, terrestrial orchid. H 8–30cm (3–12in). Frost hardy. In spring bears short spikes of flowers, 1cm (½in) long, with greenish sepals, yellow petals and brown-centred, bright yellow lips. Has oval, basal leaves, 5–10cm (2–4in) long. Cultivate as for *O. fusca.*
O. speculum. See *O. vernixia.*
O. sphegodes, syn. *O. aranifera* (Spider orchid). Deciduous, terrestrial orchid. H 10–45cm (4–18in). Frost hardy. In spring-summer carries spikes of flowers, 1cm (½in) long, that vary from green to yellow and have spider-like, blackish-brown marks on lips. Leaves are oval to lance-shaped and 4–8cm (1½–3in) long. Cultivate as for *O. fusca.*
O. tenthredinifera (Sawfly orchid; illus. p.309). Deciduous, terrestrial orchid. H 15–55cm (6–22in). Frost hardy. In spring has spikes of flowers, 1cm (½in) long, in colours of white to pink, or blue and green, each with a violet or bluish lip edged with pale green. Has a basal rosette of oval to oblong leaves, 5–9cm (2–3½in) long. Cultivate as for *O. fusca.*
O. vernixia, syn. *O. speculum.* Deciduous, terrestrial orchid. H 8–30cm (3–12in). Frost hardy. In spring produces dense spikes of flowers, 1cm (½in) long, with greenish or yellow sepals, purple petals and 3-centred, brown lips. Has oblong to lance-shaped leaves, 4–7cm (1½–3in) long. Cultivate as for *O. fusca.*

Ophthalmophyllum. See *Conophytum.*
Opium poppy. See *Papaver somniferum.*

OPLISMENUS

GRAMINEAE/POACEAE

See also GRASSES, BAMBOOS, RUSHES and SEDGES.
O. africanus, syn. *O. hirtellus* (Basket grass). ♀ **'Variegatus'** illus. p.313.
O. hirtellus. See *O. africanus.*

OPLOPANAX

ARALIACEAE

Genus of deciduous, summer-flowering shrubs, grown for their habit, fruits and spiny foliage. Fully hardy, but young growths may be damaged by late frosts. Does best in a cool, partially shaded position and in moist soil. Propagate by seed in autumn or by root cuttings in late winter.
O. horridus (Devil's club). Deciduous, spreading, open, sparsely branched shrub. H and S 2m (6ft). Prickly stems bear large, oval, 7–9-lobed, toothed, mid-green leaves. Bears dense umbels of small, star-shaped, greenish-white flowers from mid- to late summer, then spherical, red fruits.

OPUNTIA

Prickly pear

CACTACEAE

Genus of perennial cacti, ranging from small, alpine, ground-cover plants to large, evergreen, tropical trees, with at times insignificant glochids – short, soft, barbed spines produced on areoles. Mature plants carry masses of short-spined, pear-shaped, green, yellow, red or purple fruits (prickly pears), edible in some species. Fully hardy to frost tender, min. 5–10°C (41–50°F). Needs sun and well-drained soil. Water containerized specimens when in full growth. Propagate by seed or stem cuttings in spring or summer. Contact with the bristles causes intense irritation to skin, and they are difficult to remove.
O. brasiliensis, syn. *Brasiliopuntia brasiliensis.* Tree-like, perennial cactus. H 5.5m (18ft), S 3m (10ft). Frost tender, min. 10°C (50°F). Has a cylindrical, green stem bearing bright green branches of flattened, oval, spiny segments. Sheds 2–3-year-old side branches. Masses of shallowly saucer-shaped, yellow flowers, 4cm (1½in) across, appear in spring-summer, only on plants over 60cm (2ft) tall, and are followed by small, yellow fruits.
O. cylindrica, syn. *Austrocylindropuntia cylindrica.* Bushy, perennial cactus. H 4–6m (12–20ft). S 1m (3ft). Frost tender, min. 10°C (50°F). On cylindrical stems, 4–5cm (1½–2in) across, are borne short-lived, cylindrical, dark green leaves, to 2cm (¾in) long, on new growth. Areoles may lack spines or each produce 2 or 3 barbed ones. Shallowly saucer-shaped, pink-red flowers appear in spring-summer, only on plants over 2m (6ft) tall, and are followed by greenish-yellow fruits.
O. erinacea illus. p.481.
O. ficus-indica (Edible prickly pear, Indian fig). Bushy to tree-like, perennial cactus. H and S 5m (15ft). Frost tender, min. 10°C (50°F). Bears flattened, oblong, blue-green stem segments, 50cm (20in) long and spineless. In spring-summer has masses of shallowly saucer-shaped, yellow flowers, 10cm (4in) across, followed by edible, purple fruits.
O. humifusa illus. p.494.
O. microdasys (Bunny ears). Bushy, perennial cactus. H and S 60cm (2ft). Frost tender, min. 10°C (50°F). Has flattened, oval, green stem segments, 8–18cm (3–7in) long, that develop brown marks in low temperatures. Bears spineless areoles, with white, yellow, brown or red glochids, closely set in diagonal rows. Masses of funnel-shaped, yellow flowers, 5cm (2in) across, appear in summer on plants over 15cm (6in) tall, and are followed by small, dark red fruits. var. ***albispina*** illus. p.483.
O. robusta illus. p.476.
O. tunicata, syn. *Cylindropuntia tunicata*, illus. p.484.
O. verschaffeltii, syn. *Austrocylindropuntia verschaffeltii*, illus. p.490.

Orach, Red. See *Atriplex hortensis* var. *rubra.*
Orange
Japanese bitter. See *Poncirus trifoliata.*
Mock. See *Philadelphus coronarius; Pittosporum tobira.*
Osage. See *Maclura pomifera.*
Orange blossom, Mexican. See *Choisya ternata*, illus. p.123.
Orange jasmine. See *Murraya paniculata.*
Orange lily. See *Lilium bulbiferum.*

ORBEA

ASCLEPIADACEAE

Genus of clump-forming, perennial succulents with erect, 4-angled stems. Stem edges are often indented and may produce small leaves that drop after only a few weeks. Frost tender, min. 11°C (52°F). Needs sun or partial shade and well-drained soil. Propagate by seed or stem cuttings in spring or summer.
♀ ***O. variegata***, syn. *Stapelia variegata*, illus. p.492.

Orchard grass. See *Dactylis glomerata.*
Orchid
Butterfly. See *Psychopsis papilio*, illus. p.311.
Cradle. See *Anguloa clowesii.*
Dancing-doll. See *Oncidium flexuosum*, illus. p.311.
Green-veined. See *Orchis morio*, illus. p.310.
Lady's slipper. See *Cypripedium calceolus*, illus. p.310.
Pansy. See *Miltoniopsis.*
Poorman's. See *Schizanthus.*
Sawfly. See *Ophrys tenthredinifera*, illus. p.309.
Showy lady's slipper. See *Cypripedium reginae*, illus. p.308.
Slipper. See *Cypripedium; Paphiopedilum.*
Spider. See *Ophrys sphegodes.*
Star-of-Bethlehem. See *Angraecum sesquipedale*, illus. p.308.
Yellow lady's slipper. See *Cypripedium calceolus*, illus. p.310.
Orchid cactus. See *Epiphyllum.*

ORCHIDS

ORCHIDACEAE

Family of perennials, some of which are evergreen or semi-evergreen, grown for their beautiful, unusual flowers. These consist of 3 outer sepals and 3 inner petals, the lowest of which, known as the lip, is usually enlarged and different from the others in shape, markings and colour. There are about 750 genera and 17,500 species, together with an even greater number of hybrids, bred partly for their vigour and ease of care. They are divided into epiphytic and terrestrial plants. (The spread of an orchid is indefinite.)

Epiphytic orchids

Epiphytes have more flamboyant flowers than terrestrial orchids and are more commonly grown. In the wild, they grow on tree branches or rocks (lithophytes), obtaining nourishment through clinging roots and moisture through aerial roots. Most consist of a horizontal rhizome, from which arise vertical, water-storing, often swollen stems known as pseudobulbs. Flowers and foliage are produced from the newest pseudobulbs. Other epiphytes consist of a continuously growing upright rhizome; on these, flower spikes appear in the axils of leaves growing from the rhizome. In temperate climates, epiphytes need to be grown under glass.

Cultivation of epiphytes

For cultivation purposes, epiphytes, which are all frost tender, may be divided into 3 groups: cool-greenhouse types, which require min. 10°C (50°F) and max. 24°C (75°F); intermediate-greenhouse types, needing a range of 13–27°C (55–80°F); and warm-greenhouse types, requiring 18–27°C (65–80°F). In summer, temperatures need to be controlled by shading the glass and by ventilation. Cool-greenhouse orchids may be placed outdoors in summer; this improves flowering. Other types may also be grown outdoors if the air temperature remains within these ranges.

The amount of light required in summer is given in individual plant entries. All epiphytic orchids, however, need to be kept out of direct sun in summer to avoid scorching, and require full light in winter.

Epiphytic orchids, whether grown indoors or outside, require a special soil-free compost obtained from an orchid nursery or made by mixing 2 parts fibrous material (such as bark chippings and/or peat) with 1 part porous material (such as sphagnum moss and/or expanded clay pellets). Most epiphytes may be grown in pots, although some may be successfully cultivated in a hanging basket or on a slab of bark (with moss around their roots) suspended in the greenhouse.

In summer, water plants freely and spray regularly. Those suspended on bark slabs need a constantly moist atmosphere. In winter, water moderately and, if plants are in growth, spray occasionally. Some orchids rest in winter and require scarcely any water or none at all. Orchids benefit from weak foliar feeds; apply as for watering. Repot plants every other year, in spring; if they are about to flower, repot after flowering.

Terrestrial orchids
Terrestrial orchids, some of which also produce pseudobulbs, grow in soil or leaf mould, sustaining themselves in the normal way through roots or tubers. Some may be grown in borders, but many in temperate climates need to be cultivated in pots and protected under glass during winter.

Cultivation of terrestrial orchids
Terrestrial orchids are fully hardy to frost tender, min. 18°C (65°F). *Cypripedium* species may be grown outdoors in any area, preferably in neutral to acid soil, but cannot withstand severe frost, if frozen solid in pots or without snow cover, or tolerate very wet soil in winter. Other terrestrial orchids, except in very mild areas, are best grown in pots; use the same compost as for epiphytes but add 1 part grit to 2 parts compost. Place pots outdoors in a peat bed or in a glasshouse in the growing season. Keep dry when dormant. Under glass, light requirements, watering, feeding and repotting are as for epiphytes.

Orchid propagation
Orchids with pseudobulbs may be increased by removing and replanting old, leafless pseudobulbs when repotting in spring. Take care to retain at least 4 pseudobulbs on the parent plant. Some genera that may be propagated in this way are: *Ada*, × *Aliceara*, *Anguloa*, *Bletilla*, *Brassavola* (large plants only and retaining at least 6 pseudobulbs on the parent), × *Brassocattleya*, × *Brassolaeliocattleya*, *Bulbophyllum*, *Calanthe*, *Cattleya*, *Coelogyne*, *Cymbidium*, *Dendrobium*, *Dendrochilum*, *Encyclia*, *Gomesa*, *Gongora*, *Laelia*, × *Laeliocattleya*, *Lycaste*, *Maxillaria*, *Miltonia*, *Miltoniopsis*, × *Odontioda*, × *Odontocidium*, *Odontoglossum*, × *Odontonia*, *Oncidium*, *Phaius*, *Pleione*, × *Potinara*, × *Sophrolaeliocattleya*, *Stanhopea*, × *Vuylstekeara*, × *Wilsonara* and *Zygopetalum*.

Some orchids without pseudobulbs produce new growth from the base. When a plant has 6 new growths, divide it in spring into 2 and repot both portions. Propagate *Disa*, *Paphiopedilum* and *Phragmipedium* in this way. Large specimens of *Eria*, *Masdevallia* and *Pleurothallis* may be divided in spring, leaving 4–6 stems on each portion.

Propagation of *Phalaenopsis* is by stem cuttings taken soon after flowering. *Vanda* may be increased by removing the top half of the stem once it has produced aerial roots and leaves; new growths will develop from the leafless base. With both these methods achieving success is difficult and not recommended for the beginner.

Propagate terrestrial orchids with tubers by division of the tubers. Genera that may be increased in this way are: *Cypripedium* (in spring), *Dactylorhiza* (spring), *Ophrys* (autumn), *Orchis* (spring), *Serapias* (autumn) and *Spiranthes* (spring). *Calypso* is rarely propagated successfully in cultivation. *Angraecum* should not be propagated in cultivation, because the parent plant is easily endangered.

The most easily increased orchids are *Cymbidium*. Propagation of *Epidendrum* may be extremely difficult; see genus for specific details.

Orchids are illustrated on pp.308–11. See also *Ada*, × *Aliceara*, *Angraecum*, *Anguloa*, *Bletilla*, *Brassavola*, × *Brassocattleya*, × *Brassolaeliocattleya*, *Bulbophyllum*, *Calanthe*, *Calypso*, *Cattleya*, *Coelogyne*, *Cymbidium*, *Cypripedium*, *Dactylorhiza*, *Dendrobium*, *Dendrochilum*, *Encyclia*, *Epidendrum*, *Eria*, *Gomesa*, *Gongora*, *Laelia*, × *Laeliocattleya*, *Lemboglossum*, *Lycaste*, *Masdevallia*, *Maxillaria*, *Miltonia*, *Miltoniopsis*, × *Odontioda*, × *Odontocidium*, *Odontoglossum*, × *Odontonia*, *Oncidium*, *Ophrys*, *Orchis*, *Paphiopedilum*, *Phaius*, *Phalaenopsis*, *Phragmipedium*, *Pleione*, *Pleurothallis*, × *Potinara*, *Psychopsis*, *Rossioglossum*, *Serapias*, × *Sophrolaeliocattleya*, *Spiranthes*, *Stanhopea*, *Vanda*, × *Vuylstekeara*, × *Wilsonara* and *Zygopetalum*.

ORCHIS

ORCHIDACEAE

See also ORCHIDS.

O. elata. See *Dactylorhiza elata*.

O. morio (Gandergoose, Green-veined orchid; illus. p.310). Deciduous, terrestrial orchid. H 40cm (16in). Half hardy. Reddish-purple, mauve or rarely white flowers, 1cm (½in) long, with green veins on the cupped sepals, open along stems in spring. Has a basal cluster of lance-shaped or broadly oblong, pale to mid-green leaves, 10–16cm (4–6in) long. Requires sun or semi-shade.

Oregon grape. See *Mahonia aquifolium*, illus. p.153.
Oregon maple. See *Acer macrophyllum*, illus. p.60.
Oregon oak. See *Quercus garryana*, illus. p.76.

OREOCEREUS

CACTACEAE

Genus of mainly columnar, perennial cacti with thick, cylindrical, much-ribbed stems with spines, usually branching from the base, and, in some species, are covered in long hairs. Solitary, tubular-funnel-shaped flowers are produced near stem tips during the day in summer. Frost tender, min. 10°C (50°F). Requires a position in full sun and very well-drained, slightly alkaline soil. Propagate by seed in spring or summer.

O. aurantiacus. See *Matucana aurantiaca*.

O. celsianus, syn. *Cleistocactus celsianus*, illus. p.478.

O. trollii, syn. *Cleistocactus trollii* (Old man of the Andes). Slow-growing, columnar, perennial cactus. H 70cm (28in), S 10cm (4in). Cylindrical, green stem, 7–10cm (3–4in), with thick, golden spines is almost hidden by long, wispy, hair-like, white spines. Pink flowers, recurved at tips and 10cm (4in) long, appear in summer on fully mature plants.

OREOPTERIS

THELYPTERIDACEAE

Genus of deciduous ferns. Fully hardy. Tolerates sun or semi-shade. Grow in moist or very moist soil. Remove fading fronds regularly. Propagate by division in spring.

O. limbosperma, syn. *Thelypteris oreopteris* (Mountain buckler fern, Mountain fern, Mountain wood fern). Deciduous fern. H 60cm–1m (2–3ft), S 30cm (1ft). Has mainly lance-shaped, much-divided fronds, with oblong to lance-shaped, mid-green pinnae.

Organ-pipe cactus. See *Pachycereus marginatus*, illus. p.473.
Oriental beech. See *Fagus orientalis*.
Oriental bittersweet. See *Celastrus orbiculatus*.
Oriental plane. See *Platanus orientalis*.
Oriental poppy. See *Papaver orientale*.
Oriental spruce. See *Picea orientalis*.
Oriental sweet gum. See *Liquidambar orientalis*.
Oriental white oak. See *Quercus aliena*.

ORIGANUM

Dittany

LABIATAE/LAMIACEAE

Genus of deciduous sub-shrubs and perennials, sometimes with overwintering leaf rosettes. Some species are grown as culinary herbs, others for their clusters of tubular, usually pink flowers. Most species have arching, prostrate stems and are useful for trailing over rocks, banks and walls. Fully to frost hardy. Prefers sun and well-drained, alkaline soil. Propagate by division in spring, by cuttings of non-flowering shoots in early summer or by seed in autumn or spring.

♀ ***O. amanum.*** Deciduous, rounded, compact sub-shrub. H and S 15–20cm (6–8in). Frost hardy. Open funnel-shaped, pale pink or white flowers are borne all summer above small, heart-shaped, pale green leaves. Makes a good alpine house plant; dislikes a damp atmosphere.

O. dictamnus (Cretan dittany). Prostrate perennial. H 12–15cm (5–6in), S 40cm (16in). Frost hardy. Arching stems are clothed in rounded, aromatic, hairy, grey-white leaves. Has pendent heads of open funnel-shaped, purplish-pink flowers in summer.

***O.* 'Kent Beauty'** illus. p.365.

♀ ***O. laevigatum*** illus. p.366.

♀ ***O. rotundifolium.*** Deciduous, prostrate sub-shrub. H 23–30cm (9–12in), S 30cm (12in). Fully hardy. Throughout summer bears whorls of pendent, funnel-shaped, pale pink flowers, surrounded by yellow-green bracts. Has small, rounded, mid-green leaves.

O. vulgare (Wild marjoram). Mat-forming, woody-based perennial. H and S 45cm (18in). Fully hardy. Has oval, aromatic, dark green leaves, above which branched, wiry stems bear clusters of tiny, tubular, 2-lipped, mauve flowers in summer.

♀ **'Aureum'** illus. p.302.

Ornamental cabbage. See *Brassica oleracea forms*, illus. p.336.
Ornamental maize. See *Zea mays*.
Ornamental pepper. See *Capsicum annuum*.
Ornamental yam. See *Dioscorea discolor*, illus. p.217.

ORNITHOGALUM

Star-of-Bethlehem

LILIACEAE/HYACINTHACEAE

Genus of bulbs, grown for their mostly star-shaped, white flowers, usually backed with green. Fully hardy to frost tender, min. 7°C (45°F). Needs sun or partial shade and well-drained soil. Lift and dry tender species for winter, if grown outside in summer, and replant in spring. Propagate by seed or offsets, in autumn for spring-flowering bulbs, in spring for summer-flowering bulbs. All parts may cause severe discomfort if ingested; the sap may irritate skin.

O. arabicum illus. p.436.

O. balansae, syn. *O. oligophyllum* of gardens, illus. p.442.

O. lanceolatum illus. p.442.

O. montanum illus. p.442.

O. narbonense illus. p.435.

♀ ***O. nutans*** (Drooping star-of-Bethlehem). Spring-flowering bulb. H 15–35cm (6–14in), S 8–10cm (3–4in). Frost hardy. Has a cluster of linear, channelled, semi-erect, basal leaves. Stem bears a spike of pendent, bell-shaped, translucent, white flowers, 2–3cm (¾–1¼in) long with pale green outsides. Prefers partial shade.

O. oligophyllum of gardens. See *O. balansae*.

O. saundersiae. Summer-flowering bulb. H to 1m (3ft), S 15–20cm (6–8in). Half hardy. Produces a basal cluster of strap- or lance-shaped, semi-erect leaves. Stem bears a flat-topped head of erect, flattish, white or cream flowers, each with a blackish-green ovary forming a dark eye.

O. thyrsoides illus. p.436.

O. umbellatum. Spring-flowering bulb. H 10–30cm (4–12in), S 10–15cm (4–6in). Frost hardy. Linear, channelled, semi-erect, green leaves each have a white line on upper surface. Bears a loose, flat-topped head of star-shaped, white flowers, backed with green.

Orobus vernus. See *Lathyrus vernus*.

Orontium

ARACEAE

Genus of one species of deciduous, perennial, deep-water plant, grown for its floating foliage and flower spikes. Fully hardy. Needs full sun. Remove faded flower spikes. Propagate by seed when fresh, in mid-summer.
O. aquaticum illus. p.467.

Orostachys

CRASSULACEAE

Genus of short-lived, basal-rosetted, perennial succulents with very fleshy, sword-shaped leaves. Produces flowers 3 years from sowing seed, then dies. Frost tender, min. 8°C (46°F). Requires sun and well-drained soil. Propagate by seed or division in spring or summer.
O. chanetii. Basal-rosetted, perennial succulent. H 4cm (1½in), S 8cm (3in). Bears grey-green leaves that are shorter in rosette centre. Flower stem produces a dense, tapering spike of star-shaped, white or pink flowers, 1–2cm (½–¾in) across, in spring-summer.

Oroya

CACTACEAE

Genus of spherical, perennial cacti. Inner flower petals form a tube and outer ones open fully. Frost tender, min. 10°C (50°F). Needs a sunny, well-drained site. Propagate by seed in spring or summer.
O. neoperuviana. See *O. peruviana*.
O. peruviana, syn. *O. neoperuviana*, illus. p.480.

Orphanidesia gaultherioides. See *Epigaea gaultheriodes*.
Orris root. See *I. germanica* 'Florentina'.

Orthrosanthus

IRIDACEAE

Genus of perennials with short, woody rhizomes, grown for their flowers. Frost tender, min. 5°C (41°F). Prefers sun and well-drained soil. Propagate by division or seed in spring.
O. chimboracensis. Tufted, rhizomatous perennial. H 60cm (2ft) in flower, S 15cm (6in). Has very narrow, grass-like, ribbed, stiff leaves, to 45cm (18in) long, with finely toothed margins. In summer, produces clusters of short-lived, long-stalked, shallowly bowl-shaped, lavender-blue flowers, each enclosed in 2 leaf-like bracts.

Orychophragmus

CRUCIFERAE/BRASSICACEAE

Genus of late spring- to summer-flowering annuals. Half hardy. Grow in sun and in fertile, well-drained soil. Propagate by seed in spring.
O. violaceus illus. p.343.

Osage orange. See *Maclura pomifera*.

Osbeckia

MELASTOMATACEAE

Genus of evergreen, summer-flowering perennials, sub-shrubs and shrubs, grown for their flowers and foliage. Frost tender, min. 16°C (61°F). Needs full light or partial shade and humus-rich, well-drained soil. Water potted specimens freely when in full growth, moderately at other times. Cut back flowered stems by at least half in early spring to maintain vigour and to produce large flower trusses. Propagate by seed in spring or by greenwood cuttings in summer.
O. stellata. Evergreen, rounded, stiff-stemmed shrub. H and S 1–2m (3–6ft). Has narrowly oval, hairy, prominently veined leaves. Bears terminal clusters of 4-petalled, rose-purple flowers in late summer.

Oscularia

AIZOCEACE

Genus of spreading, sometimes erect, subshrubby perennial succulents with daisy-like, white to pink flowers, and usually angular, fleshy, greyish-green leaves. Frost tender, min 7°C (41°F), if dry. Use for summer bedding or as pot plants. Becomes woody with age. Requires full sun and very well-drained soil. Propagate by seed or stem cuttings in spring or autumn.
O. deltoides, syn. *Lampranthus deltoides*, illus. p.487.

Osier, Purple. See *Salix purpurea*.

Osmanthus

OLEACEAE

Genus of evergreen shrubs and trees, grown for their foliage and small, fragrant flowers. *O.* × *burkwoodii* and *O. heterophyllus* may be used for hedging. Fully to half hardy. Tolerates sun or shade and fertile, well-drained soil. Restrict growth by cutting back after flowering; trim hedges in mid-summer. Propagate by semi-ripe cuttings in summer.
O. armatus. Evergreen, bushy, dense shrub. H and S 4m (12ft). Frost hardy. Large, oblong, dark green leaves are rigid and sharply toothed. Has tubular, 4-lobed, white flowers in autumn, followed by egg-shaped, dark violet fruits.
♀ ***O. × burkwoodii***, syn. × *Osmarea burkwoodii*, illus. p.112.
O. decorus, syn. *Phillyrea decora*. Evergreen, upright, rounded, dense shrub. H 3m (10ft), S 5m (15ft). Fully hardy. Has large, oblong, glossy, dark green leaves. Bears tubular, 4-lobed, white flowers in mid-spring, then egg-shaped, blackish-purple fruits.
♀ ***O. delavayi***, syn. *Siphonosmanthus delavayi*, illus. p.112.
O. forrestii. See *O. yunnanensis*.
O. fragrans (Fragrant olive). Evergreen, upright shrub or tree. H and S 6m (20ft). Half hardy. Very fragrant, tubular, 4-lobed, white flowers are borne amid oblong, glossy, dark green leaves from early to late summer, followed by ovoid, blue-black fruits. Is suitable only for very mild areas. f. ***aurantiacus*** has orange flowers.
***O. heterophyllus* 'Aureomarginatus'** illus. p.123. ♀ **'Gulftide'** is an evergreen, bushy, dense shrub. H 2.5m (8ft), S 3m (10ft). Frost hardy. Holly-shaped, sharply toothed, glossy, dark green leaves set off tubular, 4-lobed, white flowers in autumn.
O. yunnanensis, syn. *O. forrestii*. Evergreen, tree-like, upright, then spreading shrub. H and S 10m (30ft). Frost hardy. Has large, oblong, glossy, bright green leaves, bronze when young. Produces tubular, 4-lobed, creamy-white flowers in clusters in late winter or early spring.

× *Osmarea burkwoodii.* See *Osmanthus* × *burkwoodii*.
Osmaronia. See *Oemleria*.

Osmunda

OSMUNDACEAE

Genus of deciduous ferns. Fully hardy. Requires shade, except for *O. regalis*, which also tolerates sun. *O. cinnamomea* and *O. claytoniana* need moist soil; *O. regalis* does best in very wet conditions. Remove fading fronds regularly. Propagate by division in autumn or winter or by spores as soon as ripe.
♀ ***O. cinnamomea*** (Cinnamon fern). Deciduous fern. H 1m (3ft), S 45cm (18in). Outer, lance-shaped, divided, pale green sterile fronds, with deeply cut pinnae, surround brown fertile fronds, all arising from a fibrous rootstock.
♀ ***O. claytoniana*** (Interrupted fern). Deciduous fern. H 60cm (2ft), S 30cm (1ft). Has lance-shaped, pale green fronds, divided into oblong, blunt pinnae; outer sterile fronds are larger than fertile ones at centre of plant.
♀ ***O. regalis*** illus. p.324.

Oso berry. See *Oemleria cerasiformis*.

Osteomeles

ROSACEAE

Genus of evergreen, summer-flowering shrubs, grown for their habit, foliage and flowers. Frost to half hardy. In most areas plant against a south- or west-facing wall. Requires a position in sun and fertile, well-drained soil. Propagate by semi-ripe cuttings in summer.
O. schweriniae illus. p.134.

Osteospermum

COMPOSITAE/ASTERACEAE

Genus of evergreen, semi-woody perennials. Frost to half hardy; does best in warm areas. Requires sun and well-drained soil. Propagate by cuttings of non-flowering shoots in mid-summer.
O. barberae of gardens. See *O. jucundum*.
***O.* 'Blue Streak'**, syn. *O. ecklonis* 'Blue Streak'. Evergreen, upright perennial. H and S 45cm (18in). Half hardy. In summer-autumn, daisy-like flower heads, with dark slate-blue centres and white ray florets, blue on the reverse, are borne above lance-shaped, grey-green leaves.
♀ ***O.* 'Buttermilk'** illus. p.302.
***O.* 'Cannington Roy'.** Evergreen, clump-forming, prostrate perennial. H 30cm (12in), S 45cm (18in). Half hardy. Large, daisy-like, pink flower heads, with darker eyes, are borne profusely in summer-autumn. Leaves are linear and grey.
O. ecklonis. Evergreen, upright or somewhat straggling perennial. H and S 45cm (18in). Half hardy. In summer-autumn, daisy-like, white flower heads, with dark blue centres, are borne singly above lance-shaped, grey-green leaves. **'Blue Streak'** see *O.* 'Blue Streak'.
♀ ***O. jucundum***, syn. *Dimorphotheca barberae* of gardens, *O. barberae* of gardens, illus. p.289.
***O.* 'Nairobi Purple'.** Evergreen, semi-prostrate perennial. H 30cm (12in), S 30–45cm (12–18in). Half hardy. Bears daisy-like, velvety, deep purple-red flower heads, with darker streaks on outside of ray petals, in summer. Has fresh green, lance-shaped leaves. Will not flower freely in rich soils.
***O.* 'Whirligig'.** See. *O.* 'Whirlygig'.
♀ ***O.* 'Whirlygig'**, syn. *O.* 'Whirligig', illus. p.287.

Ostrich fern. See *Matteuccia struthiopteris*, illus. p.324.
Ostrich-feather fern. See *Matteuccia struthiopteris*, illus. p.324.

Ostrowskia

CAMPANULACEAE

Genus of one species of summer-flowering perennial. Fully hardy. Prefers a warm, sunny situation and rich, moist but well-drained soil. May be difficult to grow as needs a resting period after flowering, so cover with a frame until late autumn to keep dry. Propagate by seed in autumn or spring.
O. magnifica. Erect perennial. H 1.5m (5ft), S 45cm (1½ft). From early to mid-summer produces very large, bell-shaped blooms of delicate light blue-purple, veined with darker purple. Produces whorls of oval, blue-grey leaves.

Ostrya

CORYLACEAE

Genus of deciduous trees, grown for their foliage, catkins and fruits. Fully hardy. Needs sun or semi-shade and fertile, well-drained soil. Propagate by seed in autumn.
O. carpinifolia (Hop hornbeam). Deciduous, rounded tree. H and S 15m (50ft). Has grey bark and oval, glossy, dark green leaves that turn yellow in autumn. Yellow catkins in mid-spring are followed by hop-like, greenish-white fruit clusters that become brown in autumn.
O. virginiana (American hop hornbeam) illus. p.73.

Othonna,
syn. OTHONNOPSIS

COMPOSITAE/ASTERACEAE

Genus of evergreen shrubs, grown for their daisy-like flower heads in summer. Half hardy. Needs sun and well-drained soil. Propagate by softwood cuttings in early summer.
O. cheirifolia illus. p.370.

Othonnopsis. See *Othonna.*

OURISIA

SCROPHULARIACEAE

Genus of evergreen perennials with creeping rootstocks. Excellent for peat beds and walls. Fully to frost hardy. Needs shade and moist, peaty soil. Propagate by division or seed in spring.
O. caespitosa illus. p.386.
***O.* 'Loch Ewe'.** Vigorous, evergreen, rosetted perennial. H and S 30cm (12in). Frost hardy. Prostrate stems have heart-shaped, leathery, green leaves. Produces dense spikes of outward-facing, tubular, salmon-pink flowers in late spring and early summer.
O. macrocarpa. Vigorous, evergreen, prostrate perennial. H 60cm (24in), S 20cm (8in). Frost hardy. Has rosettes of heart-shaped, leathery, dark green leaves. Produces spikes of open cup-shaped, yellow-centred, white flowers in late spring.
O. magellanica. See *O. ruellioides.*
O. microphylla illus. p.388.
O. ruellioides, syn. *O. magellanica.* Evergreen, straggling perennial. H 4cm (1½in), S to 15cm (6in). Frost hardy. In summer produces tubular, scarlet flowers above broadly heart-shaped leaves.

Ovens wattle. See *Acacia pravissima*, illus. p.93.
Owl-eyes. See *Huernia zebrina.*

OXALIS

OXALIDACEAE

Genus of tuberous, rhizomatous or fibrous-rooted perennials and semi-evergreen sub-shrubs, grown for their colourful flowers, which in bud are rolled like an umbrella, and their often attractive leaves. Leaves are mostly less than 2cm (¾in) across and are divided into 3 or more leaflets. Some species may be invasive; smaller species and cultivars suit a rock garden. Fully hardy to frost tender, min. 5°C (41°F). Needs full sun or semi-shade and well-drained soil. Propagate by division in autumn or early spring.
O. acetosella (Wood sorrel). Creeping, spring-flowering, rhizomatous perennial. H 5cm (2in), S 30–45cm (12–18in). Fully hardy. Forms mats of clover-like, 3-lobed leaves. Delicate stems bear cup-shaped, white flowers, each 1cm (½in) across with 5 purple-veined petals. Prefers semi-shade. var. ***purpurascens*** see *O.a.* var. *subpurpurascens*.var. ***subpurpurascens*** (syn. *O.a.* var. *purpurascens*) illus. p.377.
♀ ***O. adenophylla*** illus. p.378.
O. bowiei, syn. *O. purpurata* var. *bowiei.* Spring- to summer-flowering, tuberous perennial. H to 30cm (12in), S 15cm (6in). Half hardy. Has long-stalked, clover-like, 3-lobed leaves. Stems each produce a loose head of 3–10 widely funnel-shaped, pinkish-purple flowers, 3–4cm (1¼–1½in) across. Needs a sheltered, sunny site.
O. chrysantha. Creeping, fibrous-rooted perennial. H 4–5cm (1½–2in), S 15–30cm (6–12in). Half hardy. Forms mats of clover-like, 3-lobed leaves. Stems each produce a funnel-shaped, bright yellow flower, 2–3cm (¾–1¼in) across, in summer. Needs a sheltered site.
O. deppei. See *O. tetraphylla.*
O. depressa, syn. *O. inops*, illus. p.390.
♀ ***O. enneaphylla*** (Scurvy grass). Tuft-forming, rhizomatous perennial. H 5–7cm (2–3in), S 8–10cm (3–4in). Frost hardy. Grey-green leaves are divided into narrowly oblong to oval leaflets. In summer, stems bear widely funnel-shaped, 3–4cm (1¼–1½in) wide, lilac-pink or white flowers.
O. hedysaroides. Semi-evergreen, bushy sub-shrub. H 1m (3ft), S 30–45cm (1–1½ft). Half hardy. Stems have clover-like, 3-lobed, green leaves. Leaf axils bear clusters of widely funnel-shaped, yellow flowers, 2–3cm (¾–1¼in) across, in spring-summer.
O. hirta. Late summer-flowering, tuberous perennial. H 30cm (12in), S 10–15cm (4–6in). Half hardy. Stem produces scattered leaves, with 3 narrowly lance-shaped leaflets. Leaf axils each produce a widely funnel-shaped, rose-purple flower, 2–3cm (¾–1¼in) wide, with a yellow centre.
O. inops. See *O. depressa.*
♀ ***O.* 'Ione Hecker'.** Tuft-forming, rhizomatous perennial. H 5cm (2in), S 5–8cm (2–3in). Frost hardy. Grey leaves are composed of narrowly oblong, wavy leaflets. In summer bears funnel-shaped, pale purple-blue flowers, 4cm (1½in) across, with darker veins.
O. laciniata. Tuft-forming, rhizomatous perennial. H 5cm (2in), S 5–8cm (2–3in). Frost hardy. Has blue-grey leaves with narrowly oblong, crinkly-edged leaflets. In summer bears wide funnel-shaped, steel-blue flowers, 4cm (1½in) across, with darker veins.
O. lobata illus. p.399.
O. purpurata var. ***bowiei.*** See *O. bowiei.*
O. tetraphylla, syn. *O. deppei*, illus. p.365.

Ox-eye, Yellow. See *Buphthalmum salicifolium*, illus. p.304.
Oxlip. See *Primula elatior*, illus. p.282.

OXYDENDRUM

ERICACEAE

Genus of one species of deciduous tree, grown for its flowers and spectacular autumn colour. Fully hardy. For good colouring plant in an open position in sun or semi-shade. Needs moist, acid soil. Propagate by softwood cuttings in summer or by seed in autumn.
O. arboreum illus. p.74.

Oxypetalum caeruleum. See *Tweedia caerulea.*

OZOTHAMNUS

COMPOSITAE/ASTERACEAE

Genus of evergreen, summer-flowering shrubs, grown for their foliage and small, densely clustered flower heads. Fully to half hardy. Requires full sun and well-drained soil. Propagate by semi-ripe cuttings in summer.
♀ ***O. coralloides***, syn. *Helichrysum coralloides*, illus. p.373.
♀ ***O. ledifolius***, syn. *Helichrysum ledifolium*, illus. p.156.
O. rosmarinifolius, syn. *Helichrysum rosmarinifolium*, illus. p.134.
O. selago, syn. *Helichrysum selago*, illus. p.373.

P

PACHYCEREUS

CACTACEAE

Genus of slow-growing, columnar, perennial cacti, branching with age. The funnel-shaped flowers are unlikely to appear in cultivation as they are produced only on plants over 3m (10ft) high. Frost tender, min. 10°C (50°F). Requires sun and well-drained soil. Propagate by seed in spring or summer.
P. marginatus, syn. *Lemaireocereus marginatus, Marginatocereus marginatus, Stenocereus marginatus*, illus. p.473.
P. pecten-aboriginum. Columnar, perennial cactus. H 11m (35ft), S 3m (10ft). Dark green stems bear 9–11 deep ribs. Each areole has 8 radial spines, 1cm (½in) long, and longer central spines. All spines are dark brown with red bases and fade to grey.
P. pringlei illus. p.476.
P. schottii, syn. *Lophocereus schottii*, illus. p.474. **'Monstrosus'** is a columnar, perennial cactus. H 7m (22ft), S 2m (6ft). Irregular, olive- to dark green stems have 4–15 ribs and no spines. Has funnel-shaped, pink flowers, 3cm (1¼in) wide, at night in summer.

PACHYPHRAGMA

CRUCIFERAE/BRASSICACEAE

Genus of perennials with rosettes of basal leaves, often grown as ground cover under shrubs. Fully hardy. Needs sun or partial shade and moist soil. Propagate by division or stem cuttings in late spring or by seed in autumn.
P. macrophyllum, syn. *Thlaspi macrophyllum*, illus. p.275.

PACHYPHYTUM

CRASSULACEAE

Genus of rosetted, perennial succulents, closely related to *Echeveria*, with which it hybridizes. Frost tender, min. 5–10°C (41–50°F). Needs sun and well-drained soil. Propagate by seed, or leaf or stem cuttings in spring or summer.
P. compactum illus. p.496.
P. oviferum illus. p.491.

PACHYPODIUM

APOCYNACEAE

Genus of bushy or tree-like, perennial succulents, mostly with swollen stems, closely related to *Adenium*, except that most species have spines. Frost tender, min. 10–15°C (50–59°F). Requires full sun and very well-drained soil. May be very difficult to grow. Propagate by seed in spring or summer.
♀ ***P. lamerei*** illus. p.472.
P. succulentum. Tree-like, perennial succulent. H 60cm (2ft), S 30cm (1ft). Min. 10°C (50°F). Swollen trunk, 15cm (6in) across, has narrow, vertical, green to grey-brown stems. Has trumpet-shaped, pink-crimson flowers, 2cm (¾in) across, near stem tips in summer.

PACHYSANDRA

BUXACEAE

Genus of evergreen, creeping perennials and sub-shrubs, grown for their tufted foliage. Is useful for ground cover. Fully hardy. Tolerates dense shade and will grow well in any but very dry soil. Propagate by division in spring.
P. axillaris. Evergreen, mat-forming sub-shrub. H 20cm (8in), S 25cm (10in). Stems are each crowned by 3–6 oval, toothed, leathery leaves. Carries small, white flowers in erect spikes in late spring.
P. terminalis illus. p.400.
♀ **'Variegata'** is an evergreen, creeping perennial. H 10cm (4in), S 20cm (8in). Diamond-shaped, cream-variegated leaves are clustered at stem tips. In early summer bears spikes of tiny, white flowers, sometimes flushed purple.

PACHYSTACHYS

ACANTHACEAE

Genus of evergreen perennials and shrubs, grown for their flowers. Frost tender, min. 13–18°C (55–64°F). Needs partial shade and fertile, well-drained soil. Water potted plants freely when in full growth, moderately at other times. Cut back flowered stems in late winter to maintain a bushy habit. Propagate by greenwood cuttings in early summer. Whitefly and red spider mite may cause problems.
P. cardinalis. See *P. coccinea*.
P. coccinea, syn. *Jacobinia coccinea, Justicia coccinea, P. cardinalis* (Cardinal's guard). Evergreen, erect, robust shrub. H 1.2–2m (4–6ft), S 60cm–1m (2–3ft). Min. 15–18°C (59–64°F) to flower well. Leaves are oval and deep green. Has tubular, bright red flowers in tight, green-bracted spikes, 15cm (6in) long, in winter.
♀ ***P. lutea*** illus. p.153.

Pachystima. See *Paxistima*.

× PACHYVERIA

CRASSULACEAE

Hybrid genus *(Echeveria × Pachyphytum)* of clump-forming, rosetted, perennial succulents, sometimes almost stemless. Frost tender, min. 5–7°C (41–5°F). Requires a position in full sun or partial shade and very well-drained soil. Propagate by leaf or stem cuttings in spring or summer.
× ***P. glauca*** illus. p.482.

Pacific dogwood. See *Cornus nuttallii*, illus. p.72.
Pacific fir. See *Abies amabilis*.

PAEONIA

Peony

PAEONIACEAE

Genus of late spring-flowering perennials and deciduous shrubs ('tree peonies'), valued for their bold foliage, showy blooms and, in some species, colourful seed pods. Fully hardy, unless otherwise stated, although young growth (especially on tree peonies) may be damaged by late spring frosts. Prefers sun (but tolerates light shade) and rich, well-drained soil. Tall and very large-flowered cultivars need support. Propagate all species by seed in autumn (may take up to 3 years to germinate), tuberous species by root cuttings in winter, tree peonies by semi-ripe cuttings in late summer or by grafting in winter. Perennials may also be propagated by division in autumn or early spring. Is prone to peony wilt. All parts can cause mild stomach upset if ingested. See also feature panel pp.238–9.

Flower forms
Unless stated otherwise, peonies described below flower between late spring and early to mid-summer and have large, alternate leaves divided into oval to lance-shaped or linear leaflets. Flowers are single, semi-double, double or anemone-form.
Single – flowers are mostly cup-shaped, with 1 or 2 rows of large, often lightly ruffled, incurving petals and a conspicuous central boss of stamens.
Semi-double – flowers are similar to single ones, but have 2 or 3 rows of petals.
Double – flowers are rounded, usually composed of 1 or 2 outer rows of large, often lightly ruffled, incurving petals, the remaining petals being smaller, usually becoming more densely arranged and diminishing in size towards the centre. Stamens are few, inconspicuous, or absent.
Anemone-form (Imperial or Japanese) – flowers usually have 1 or 2 rows of broad, incurving, outer petals; the centre of the flower is often filled entirely with numerous densely arranged, sometimes deeply cut, narrow petaloids derived from stamens.

***P.* 'Alice Harding'** illus. p.238. Clump-forming perennial. H and S to 1m (3ft). Bears very large, fragrant, double, creamy-white flowers.
***P.* 'America'** illus. p.238. Clump-forming perennial. H and S to 1m (3ft). Has large, single flowers with very broad, crimson petals, lightly ruffled at edges.
***P.* 'Argosy'** illus. p.239. Deciduous, upright shrub (tree peony). H and S to 1.5m (5ft). Magnificent, large, single flowers are lemon-yellow, each with a crimson-purple blotch at base. Is hard to propagate.
P. arietina. See *P. mascula* subsp. *arietina*.
***P.* 'Auguste Dessert'**. Clump-forming perennial. H and S to 75cm (30in). Foliage provides rich autumn colour. Has masses of fragrant, semi-double flowers; carmine petals are tinged salmon-pink and have slightly ruffled, striking silvery-white margins.
***P.* 'Avant Garde'**. Clump-forming perennial. H and S to 1m (3ft). Has luxuriant foliage. Medium-sized to large, fragrant, single flowers are pale rose-pink with darker veins and bright golden anthers that have yellow-red filaments. Flowers are borne on stiff, straight stems in mid-spring and are ideal for cutting.
***P.* 'Ballerina'** illus. p.238. Clump-forming perennial. H and S 1m (3ft). Foliage provides autumn colour. Fragrant, double flowers are soft blush-pink, tinged lilac at first, later fading to white. Outer rows of petals are loosely arranged, very broad and incurving; inner petals are also incurving, but more densely arranged, narrower, more uneven in size and often have slightly ruffled margins.
***P.* 'Baroness Schroeder'**. Vigorous, clump-forming perennial. H and S to 1m (3ft). Is very free-flowering with large, fragrant, globe-shaped, double flowers, tinged with pale flesh-pink on opening but fading to almost pure white. Has several rows of nearly flat, outer petals; inner petals are incurving, ruffled and very tightly arranged. Is one of the best peonies for cutting.
***P.* 'Barrymore'**. Clump-forming perennial. H and S to 85cm (34in). Has very large, anemone-form flowers with broad, outer petals that are palest blush-pink on opening, later white. Clear pale golden-yellow petaloids are very narrow, relatively short and are neatly and densely arranged.
♀ ***P.* 'Bowl of Beauty'** illus. p.238. Clump-forming perennial. H and S to 1m (3ft). Has very large, striking, anemone-form flowers with pale carmine-pink, outer petals and numerous narrow, densely arranged, ivory-white petaloids.
♀ ***P. cambessedesii*** (Majorcan peony; illus. p.238). Clump-forming perennial. H and S 45cm (18in). Half hardy. Has especially attractive foliage, dark green above with veins, stalks and under-surfaces suffused purple-red. Single, deep rose-pink flowers are borne in mid-spring.
***P.* 'Cheddar Cheese'**. Clump-forming perennial. H and S to 1m (3ft). Produces well-formed, large, double flowers in mid-summer. Neatly and densely arranged, slightly ruffled, ivory-white petals, the inner ones incurving, are interspersed with shorter, yellow petals.
***P.* 'Chocolate Soldier'** illus. p.239. Clump-forming perennial. H and S to 1m (3ft). Has mid- to dark green leaves that are often tinged bronze-red when young. Semi-double, purple-red flowers, borne in early summer, have yellow-mottled centres.
***P.* 'Colonel Heneage'**. Clump-forming perennial of upright habit. H and S to 85cm (34in). Has masses of anemone-form flowers with both outer petals and inner petaloids of dark rose-crimson.
P. corallina. See *P. mascula* subsp. *mascula*.
***P.* 'Cornelia Shaylor'** . Erect, clump-forming perennial. H and S to 85cm (34in). Fragrant, double flowers, flushed rose-pink on opening and gradually fading to blush-white, are borne freely from early to mid-summer. Ruffled petals are neatly and densely arranged.
***P.* 'Dayspring'**. Clump-forming perennial. H and S to 70cm (28in). Has an abundance of fragrant, single, clear pink flowers borne in trusses.
P. decora. See *P. peregrina*.
***P.* 'Defender'** illus. p.239. Clump-forming, vigorous perennial. H and S to 1m (3ft). Single, satiny crimson flowers, to 15cm (6in) across, with a central boss of golden anthers, are carried on strong stems.

P. delavayi . Deciduous, upright, open, sometimes suckering shrub (tree peony). H to 2m (6ft), S to 1.2m (4ft). Leaves are divided into pointed-oval leaflets, often with reddish stalks. Produces small, bowl-shaped, rich dark red, orange, yellow or white flowers, 5–6cm (2–2½in) across, with conspicuous, leafy bracts beneath, in late spring. var. ***angustiloba***, H to 1m (3ft), is a suckering shrub or sub-shrub that produces flowers in red, red-purple, yellow, orange or white. var. ***angustiloba*** f. ***alba*** (syn. *P. potaninii* f. *alba*) has white flowers. var. ***angustiloba*** f. ***angustifolia*** (syn. *P. potaninii*) produces dark red, red or reddish-purple flowers. var. ***angustiloba*** f. ***trollioides*** (syn. *P. potaninii* var. *trollioides*, *P. trollioides*; illus. p.239) has yellow or orange flowers. ♀ var. ***delavayi*** f. ***delavayi*** has dark red to purplish flowers. var. ***delavayi*** f. ***lutea*** (syn. *P. lutea*) has orange, yellow or greenish-yellow flowers, sometimes red at the bases or on the petal margins. var. ***ludlowii*** see *P. ludlowii*.

***P.* 'Dresden'.** Robust, clump-forming perennial. H and S to 85cm (34in). Foliage provides autumn colour. Single flowers are ivory-white, tinged with soft blush-rose-pink.

♀ ***P.* 'Duchesse de Nemours',** syn. *P.* 'Mrs Gwyn Lewis' illus. p.238. Vigorous, clump-forming perennial. H and S to 70cm (28in). Produces masses of richly fragrant, double flowers with very large, incurving, outer petals, tinged palest green at first, soon fading to pure white; inner petals with irregular margins are densely arranged towards the centre and are creamy-yellow at their base.

P. emodi illus. p.238. Clump-forming perennial. H to 1.2m (4ft), Sto 1m (3ft). Glossy, green foliage is topped by tall stems bearing several large, fragrant, single, pure white flowers with golden-yellow anthers.

***P.* 'Evening World'**. Clump-forming perennial. H and S to 1m (3ft). Has abundant, large, anemone-form flowers with soft blush-pink, outer petals and very tightly arranged, pale flesh-pink petaloids.

♀ ***P.* 'Félix Crousse',** syn. *P.* 'Victor Hugo'. Vigorous, clump-forming perennial. H and S to 75cm (30in). Bears a profusion of fragrant, double, rich carmine-pink flowers with darker red centres. Petals are ruffled, very numerous and tightly arranged, with edges sometimes tipped silvery-white.

♀ ***P.* 'Festiva Maxima'.** Clump-forming perennial. H and S to 1m (3ft). Has dense, spreading foliage and huge, fragrant, double flowers borne on strong stems. Rather loosely arranged petals are large with irregular margins; outer petals are pure white, inner ones each have a basal, crimson blotch.

***P.* 'Flamingo'.** Clump-forming perennial. H and S to 85cm (34in). Foliage provides autumn colour. Double flowers are large and clear pale salmon-pink.

***P.* 'Globe of Light'** illus. p.238. Clump-forming perennial. H and S to 1m (3ft). Has large, fragrant, anemone-form flowers. Outer petals are pure rose-pink, petaloids clear golden-yellow.

***P.* 'Heirloom'.** Compact, clump-forming perennial. H and S to 70cm (28in). Bears masses of large, fragrant, double, pale lilac-pink flowers.

***P.* 'Instituteur Doriat'** illus. p.239. Clump-forming perennial. H and S to 1m (3ft). Foliage provides autumn colour. Has abundant, large, anemone-form flowers with reddish-carmine, outer petals and densely arranged, relatively broad petaloids, paler and more pink than outer petals, with ruffled, silvery-white margins.

***P.* 'Kelway's Gorgeous'** illus. p.239. Clump-forming perennial. H and S to 85cm (34in). Single, intense clear carmine flowers, with a hint of salmon-pink, are borne very freely.

***P.* 'Kelway's Majestic'.** Clump-forming perennial. H and S to 1m (3ft). Freely borne, large, fragrant, anemone-form flowers have bright cherry rose-pink, outer petals and lilac-pink petaloids flecked with silver or pale gold.

***P.* 'Kelway's Supreme'** illus. p.238. Clump-forming perennial. H and S to 1m (3ft). Foliage provides autumn colour. Has large, strongly fragrant, double flowers, produced over a long period, sometimes borne in clusters on well-established plants. Petals are broad, incurving, soft blush-pink, fading to milk-white. Single or semi-double axillary flowers are often produced.

***P.* 'Knighthood'** illus. p.239. Clump-forming perennial. H and S to 75cm (30in). Double flowers have densely arranged, rather narrow, ruffled petals of unusually rich burgundy-red.

***P.* 'Krinkled White'** illus. p.238. Robust, clump-forming perennial. H and S to 80cm (32in). Large, bowl-shaped, single, milk-white flowers are sometimes flushed palest pink. Petals are large with ruffled margins.

♀ ***P.* 'Laura Dessert'** illus. p.239. Clump-forming perennial. H and S to 75cm (30in). Produces fragrant, double flowers with creamy blush-white, outer petals. Densely arranged, incurving, inner petals are flushed rich lemon-yellow, and their margins are sometimes deeply cut.

***P.* 'L'Espérance',** syn. *P.* × *lemoinei* 'L'Espérance' illus. p.239. Has very large, single, primrose-yellow flowers with a carmine blotch at the base of each petal.

***P.* × *lemoinei* 'L'Espérance'.** See *P.* 'L'Espérance'.

P. lobata. See *P. peregrina.*

♀ ***P. ludlowii***, syn. *P. delavayi* var. *ludlowii*, *P. lutea* var. *ludlowii* illus. p.239. Deciduous, upright, slightly suckering shrub. H to 3.5m (11ft), S to 1.5m (5ft). Leaves are divided into sharply pointed, bright green leaflets. Produces large, bright yellow flowers, to 12cm (5in) across, in late spring.

P. lutea. See *P. delavayi* var. *delavayi* f. *lutea*. var. ***ludlowii*** see *P. ludlowii.*

***P.* 'Madame Louis Henri'** illus. p.239. Deciduous, upright shrub (tree peony). H and S to 1.5m (5ft). Has loosely semi-double, whitish-yellow flowers with large, incurving, outer petals very heavily suffused with rusty-red. Smaller, often darker, inner petals each have a basal, dull red blotch.

***P.* 'Magic Orb'** illus. p.238. Clump-forming perennial. H and S to 1m (3ft). Foliage provides autumn colour. Bears masses of large, strongly fragrant, double flowers, each with several outer whorls of fairly broad, ruffled, intense cherry-pink petals and a centre of densely arranged, smaller, incurving petals. Outermost rows of central petals are blush-white, heavily shaded with mid-rose-carmine; the innermost petals are mostly creamy-white.

P. mascula subsp. ***arietina,*** syn. *P. arietina.* Tuberous perennial. H and S to 75cm (30in). Foliage is hairy underneath and dark green; stems are dark red. Has single, reddish-pink flowers. Seed capsules with 2–5 boat-shaped sections split to reveal purplish-black seeds. subsp. ***mascula*** (syn. *P. corallina*; illus. p.238) is clump-forming, H and Sto 1m (3ft), with hairless leaflets. Produces purple-or carmine-red, occasionally pink or white, flowers with bosses of golden-yellow anthers borne on purple filaments.

♀ ***P. mlokosewitschii*** illus. p.239. Clump-forming perennial. H and S to 75cm (30in). Soft bluish-green foliage, sometimes edged reddish-purple, is topped by large, single, lemon-yellow flowers.

***P.* 'Mother of Pearl'** (illus p.238) Clump-forming perennial. H to 75cm (30in) and S to 60cm (24in). Greyish-green leaves provide an attractive foil for the single, dog rose-pink flowers.

***P.* 'Mrs Gwyn Lewis'.** See *P.* 'Duchesse de Nemours'.

♀ ***P. obovata*** var. ***alba*** illus. p.238. Clump-forming perennial. H and S 70–90cm (28–36in). Has erect stems and large, deep green leaves, each with 9 uneven, broadly elliptic leaflets, pale grey-green and slightly hairy beneath. Bears single, cup-shaped, white flowers with purple filaments.

P. officinalis. Clump-forming, tuberous perennial. H and S to 60cm (24in). This single, red apothecaries'peony has long been in cultivation, but is seldom seen today, having been superseded by larger, often double-flowered hybrids, such as the following. **'Alba Plena'** (illus. p.238), H and S to 75cm (30in), has double, white flowers that are sometimes tinged with pink. **'China Rose'** (illus. p.239), H and S to 45cm (18in), has handsome, dark green foliage and single flowers with incurving, clear dark salmon-rose petals contrasting with central bosses of orange-yellow anthers. **'Crimson Globe'** (illus. p.239), H and S 70–85cm (28–34in), produces single, garnet-red flowers with golden-yellow stamens. ♀ **'Rubra Plena'** (illus. p.239), H and S to 75cm (30in), is long-lived and has distinctive foliage, divided into broadly oval leaflets, and double, vivid pinkish-crimson flowers with ruffled petals.

P. peregrina, syn. *P. decora*, *P. lobata* illus. p.239. Clump-forming, tuberous perennial. H and S to 1m (3ft). Produces bowl-shaped, single, ruby-red flowers. ♀ **'Otto Froebel'** (syn. *P.p.* 'Sunshine'; illus. p.239) has glossy, bright green leaves and bears large, single, vermilion flowers, tinged with salmon-rose.

P. potaninii. See *P. delavayi* var. *angustiloba* f. *angustiloba*. f. ***alba*** see *P. delavayi* var. *angustiloba* f. *alba.* var. ***trollioides*** see *P. delavayi* var. *angustiloba* f. *trollioides.*

***P.* 'Président Poincaré'.** Clump-forming perennial. H and S to 1m (3ft). Foliage provides autumn colour. Fragrant, double, clear rich ruby-crimson flowers are borne very freely.

P. rockii, syn. *P. suffruticosa* subsp. *rockii* illus. p.238. Deciduous, upright shrub (tree peony). H and S to 2.2m (7ft). Produces large, spreading, semi-double, white flowers; inner petals each have a basal, dark maroon blotch. Is difficult to propagate. .

♀ ***P.* 'Sarah Bernhardt'** illus. p.238. Vigorous, erect, clump-forming perennial. H and S to 1m (3ft). Produces an abundance of huge, fragrant, fully double flowers with large, ruffled, slightly dull rose-pink petals, fading to silvery blush-white at margins.

***P.* 'Shirley Temple'** illus. p.238. Clump-forming perennial. H and S to 85cm (34in). Profuse, soft rose-pink flowers, fading to palest buff-white, are fully double, with broad petals arranged in whorls; innermost petals are smaller and more loosely packed.

***P.* 'Silver Flare'** illus. p.239. Clump-forming perennial. H and S to 1m (3ft). Foliage gives autumn colour. Stems are flushed dull reddish-brown. Produces masses of fragrant, single flowers with rather long, slender, rich carmine-pink petals, each feathering to a striking silvery-white margin.

***P.* 'Sir Edward Elgar'** illus. p.239. Clump-forming perennial. H and S to 75cm (30in). Foliage provides autumn colour. Has an abundance of single, chocolate-brown-tinged, rich crimson flowers with bosses of loosely arranged, clear lemon-yellow anthers.

P.* × *smouthii illus. p.239. Clump-forming perennial. H and S to 60cm (24in). Produces an abundance of fragrant, single, glistening, dark crimson flowers, to 10cm (4in) across, with conspicuous, yellow stamens, although both flowers and foliage may vary in colour.

***P.* 'Souvenir de Maxime Cornu'** illus. p.239. Deciduous, upright shrub (tree peony). H and S to 1.5m (5ft). Large, richly fragrant flowers are fully double with warm golden-yellow petals densely arranged towards centres; ruffled margins are dull reddish-orange.

P. suffruticosa (Moutan). Deciduous, upright shrub (tree peony). H and S to 2.2m (7ft). Bears variable, large, cup-shaped flowers, single or semi-double, with incurving, rose-pink or white petals, each sometimes with a basal, usually chocolate-maroon blotch. Has given rise to many cultivars with semi-double and double flowers. **'Cardinal Vaughan'** illus. p.239 has semi-double, ruby-purple flowers. **'Godaishu'** ('Large Globe'; illus. p.238) bears semi- or fully double, white flowers with yellow centres amid light green leaves that are fringed and twisted. **'Hana-daijin'** ('Magnificent Flower'; illus. p.239), H and S 2m (6ft) or more, is a vigorous cultivar that bears masses of double, purple flowers. **'Hana-kisoi'** ('Floral Rivalry'; illus. p.238) has double, pale cerise-pink flowers. **'Kamada-nishiki'** ('Kamada Brocade'; illus. p.238), H and S to 1.2m (4ft), produces large, double flowers, to 20cm (8in) across, that are lilac-pink

striped white at the edge of each petal. **'Reine Elizabeth'** (illus. p.238), H and S to 2m (6ft), has large, fully double flowers with broad, salmon-pink petals, flushed with bright copper-red and lightly ruffled at margins. **'Renkaku'** ('Flight of Cranes'), H and S to 1m (3ft), bears double flowers, each with broad, incurving, slightly ruffled, ivory-white petals, loosely arranged in 3 or more whorls, that surround a large boss of long, golden-yellow anthers. subsp. ***rockii*** see *P. rockii*. **'Tama-fuyo'** ('Jewel in the Lotus') is vigorous and freely produces double, pink flowers earlier than most other cultivars.
P. tenuifolia illus. p.239. Clump-forming perennial. H and S to 45cm (18in). Elegant leaves are finely divided into many linear segments. Has single, dark crimson flowers, with golden-yellow anthers.
P. trollioides. See *P. delavayi* var. *angustiloba* f. *trollioides*.
P. veitchii illus. p.238. Clump-forming perennial. H and S to 75cm (30in). Shiny, bright green leaves are divided into oblong to elliptic leaflets. In early summer produces nodding, cup-shaped, single, purple-pink flowers.
***P.* 'VictorHugo'.** See *P.* 'Félix Crousse'.
***P.* 'White Wings'** illus. p.238. Clump-forming perennial. H and S to 85cm (34in). Glossy, dark green foliage also provides autumn colour. In mid-summer produces masses of large, fragrant, single flowers with broad, white petals, sometimes tinged sulphur-yellow, that are each slightly ruffled at the apex.
♀ ***P.* 'Whitleyi Major'** illus. p.238. Clump-forming perennial. H to 1m (3ft), S to 60cm (2ft). Foliage and stems are flushed rich reddish-brown. Large, single, ivory-white flowers have a satin sheen and central bosses of clear yellow anthers.
P. wittmanniana illus. p.239. Clump-forming perennial. H and S to 1m (3ft). Has large, single, pale primrose-yellow flowers, each with a large, central boss of yellow anthers on purple-red filaments. Leaves are divided into broadly oval leaflets, shiny dark green above, paler beneath.

Pagoda tree. See *Sophora japonica*.
Paintbrush. See *Haemanthus albiflos*.
Royal. See *Scadoxus puniceus*.
Painted fern. See *Athyrium niponicum*, illus. p.325.
Painted net-leaf. See *Fittonia albivenis* Verschaffeltii Group, illus. p.314.
Painted trillium. See *Trillium undulatum*.
Painted wood lily. See *Trillium undulatum*.

PALIURUS

RHAMNACEAE

Genus of deciduous, spiny, summer-flowering shrubs and trees, grown for their foliage and flowers. *P. spinachristi* is also grown for its religious association, reputedly being the plant from which Christ's crown of thorns was made. Frost hardy. Requires full sun and well-drained soil. Propagate by softwood cuttings in summer or by seed in autumn.
P. spina-christi illus. p.118.

Palm
Alexandra. See *Archontophoenix alexandrae*, illus. p.68.
Australian cabbage. See *Livistona australis*.
Bamboo. See *Rhapis excelsa*, illus. p.148.
Canary Island date. See *Phoenix canariensis*.
Chilean wine. See *Jubaea chilensis*, illus. p.81.
Chinese fan. See *Livistona chinensis*, illus. p.81.
Chinese fountain. See *Livistona chinensis*, illus. p.81.
Chusan. See *Trachycarpus fortunei*, illus. p.80.
Cuban royal. See *Roystonea regia*.
Desert fan. See *Washingtonia filifera*.
Dwarf fan. See *Chamaerops humilis*, illus. p.172.
Dwarf mountain. See *Chamaedorea elegans*, illus. p.148.
European fan. See *Chamaerops humilis*, illus. p.172.
Gippsland fountain. See *Livistona australis*.
Golden-feather. See *Dypsis lutescens*, illus. p.96.
Illawarra. See *Archontophoenix cunninghamiana*.
Japanese sago. See *Cycas revoluta*, illus. p.148.
Jelly. See *Butia capitata*, illus. p.96.
King. See *Archontophoenix*.
Miniature date. See *Phoenix roebelenii*.
Northern bungalow. See *Archontophoenix alexandrae*, illus. p.68.
Paradise. See *Howea forsteriana*.
Parlour. See *Chamaedorea elegans*, illus. p.148.
Piccabeen. See *Archontophoenix cunninghamiana*.
Pygmy date. See *Phoenix roebelenii*.
Queen. See *Syagrus*.
Royal. See *Roystonea*.
Sentry. See *Howea forsteriana*.
Slender lady. See *Rhapis excelsa*, illus. p.148.
Thatch-leaf. See *Howea forsteriana*.
Thread. See *Washingtonia robusta*, illus. p.69.
Virgin's. See *Dioon edule*.
Windmill. See *Trachycarpus fortunei*, illus. p.80.
Yatay. See *Butia*.
Yellow. See *Dypsis lutescens*, illus. p.96.
Palmetto
Dwarf. See *Sabal minor*, illus. p.172.
Saw. See *Serenoa repens*.
Scrub. See *Serenoa repens*.
Palo verde, Mexican. See *Parkinsonia aculeata*.

PAMIANTHE

AMARYLLIDACEAE

Genus of one species of evergreen, spring-flowering bulb, grown for its large, strongly fragrant, showy flowers. Frost tender, min. 12°C (54°F). Needs partial shade and rich, well-drained soil. Feed with high-potash liquid fertilizer in summer. Reduce watering in winter but do not allow to dry out. Propagate by seed in spring or by offsets in late winter.
P. peruviana illus. p.425.

Pampas grass. See *Cortaderia selloana*.

PANCRATIUM

AMARYLLIDACEAE

Genus of bulbs with large, fragrant, daffodil-like flowers in summer. Frost to half hardy. Needs sun and well-drained soil that is warm and dry in summer when bulbs are dormant. Plant at least 15cm (6in) deep. Feed with a high-potash liquid fertilizer every 2 weeks from autumn to spring. Propagate by seed in autumn or by offsets detached in early autumn.
P. illyricum illus. p.435.
P. maritimum (Sea daffodil, Sea lily). Late summer-flowering bulb. H 45cm (18in), S 25–30cm (10–12in). Half hardy. Has strap-shaped, erect, basal, greyish-green leaves. Produces a head of 5–12 white flowers, each with a large, deep cup in the centre and 6 spreading petals. Is shy-flowering in cultivation.

Panda plant. See *Kalanchoe tomentosa*, illus. p.483.

PANDANUS

Screw pine

PANDANACEAE

Genus of evergreen trees, shrubs and scramblers, grown for their foliage and overall appearance. Flowers and fruits only appear on large, mature specimens. Frost tender, min. 13–16°C (55–61°F). Requires full light or partial shade and fertile, well-drained soil. Water containerized plants freely when in full growth, moderately at other times. Propagate by seed or suckers in spring or by cuttings of lateral shoots in summer. Red spider mite may be troublesome.
P. odoratissimus. See *P. tectorius*.
P. tectorius, syn. *P. odoratissimus*. Evergreen, rounded tree. H to 6m (20ft), S 3m (10ft) or more. Has rosettes of strap-shaped, deep green leaves, each 1–1.5m (3–5ft) long, with spiny margins and a spiny midrib beneath. Small flowers, the males in clusters, each with a lance-shaped, white bract, appear mainly in summer. Fruits are like round pineapples.
♀ **'Veitchii'** (syn. *P. veitchii*) illus. p.171.
P. veitchii. See *P. tectorius* 'Veitchii'.

PANDOREA

BIGNONIACEAE

Genus of evergreen, woody-stemmed, twining climbers, grown for their handsome flowers and attractive leaves. Frost tender, min. 5°C (41°F). Grow in sun and in any well-drained soil. Prune after flowering to restrain growth. Propagate by seed sown in spring or by stem cuttings or layering in summer.
P. jasminoides, syn. *Bignonia jasminoides*, illus. p.204.
P. lindleyana. See *Clytostoma callistegioides*.
P. pandorana, syn. *Bignonia pandorana, Tecoma australis* (Wonga-wonga vine). Fast-growing, evergreen, woody-stemmed, twining climber. H 6m (20ft) or more. Leaves have 3–9 scalloped leaflets. Small, funnel-shaped, cream flowers, which are streaked and often spotted with red, brown or purple, are borne in clusters in summer.
P. ricasoliana. See *Podranea ricasoliana*.

PANICUM

GRAMINEAE/POACEAE

See also GRASSES, BAMBOOS, RUSHES and SEDGES.
P. capillare illus. p.320.

Pansy. See *Viola × wittrockiana*.
Mountain. See *Viola lutea*.
Wild. See *Viola tricolor*, illus. p.381.
Pansy orchid. See *Miltoniopsis*.
Panther lily. See *Lilium pardalinum*, illus. p.417.

PAPAVER

Poppy

PAPAVERACEAE

Genus of annuals, biennials and perennials, some of which are semi-evergreen, grown for their cup-shaped flowers. Fully hardy. Needs sun or semi-shade and prefers moist but well-drained soil. Propagate by seed in autumn or spring. *P. orientale* and its cultivars are best propagated by root cuttings in winter. Self-seeds readily.
P. alpinum subsp. ***burseri.*** See *P. burseri*.
P. atlanticum. Clump-forming, short-lived perennial. H and S 10cm (4in). Has oval, toothed, hairy leaves and, in summer, single, dull orange flowers. Is good for a rock garden.
P. burseri, syn. *P. alpinum* subsp. *burseri* (Alpine poppy). Semi-evergreen, tuft-forming, short-lived perennial, best treated as an annual or biennial. H 15–20cm (6–8in), S 10cm (4in). Has finely cut, grey leaves. Carries single, white flowers throughout summer. Suits a rock garden, wall or bank.
♀ ***P. commutatum***, syn. *P.c.* 'Ladybird'. Fast-growing, erect, branching annual. H and S 45cm (18in). Has elliptic, deeply lobed, mid-green leaves and, insummer, single, red flowers, each with a black blotch in centre.
'Ladybird' see *P. commutatum*.
P. croceum, syn. *P. nudicaule* of gardens (Iceland poppy). Tuft-forming perennial. H to 30cm (12in), S 10cm (4in). Hairy stems each produce a fragrant, single, white-and-yellow flower, sometimes marked green outside, in summer. Many colour forms have been selected. Leaves are oval, toothed and soft green. Needs partial shade. Is good for a rock garden.
P. fauriei, syn *P. miyabeanum* of gardens, illus. p.396.
P. miyabeanum of gardens. See *P. fauriei*.
P. nudicaule of gardens. See *P. croceum*.
P. orientale (Oriental poppy). Rosetted perennial. H 1m (3ft), S 30cm–1m (1–3ft). Single, brilliant vermilion flowers, with dark blotches at bases of petals, are borne in early summer. Has broadly lance-shaped, toothed or cut, rough, mid-green leaves. Flowering stems need support. **'Allegro'** (syn. *P.o.* 'Allegro Viva') illus. p.254. **'Allegro**

'Viva' see *P.o.* 'Allegro'. **'Beauty of Livermere'** illus. p.254. **'Indian Chief'** has deep mahogany-red flowers. **'May Queen'** bears double, orange flowers. **'Mrs Perry'** has large, salmon-pink flowers. **'Perry's White'** illus. p.243.
P. rhoeas (Corn poppy, Field poppy). **Shirley Series** (double) illus. p.334; (single) illus. p.340.
P. somniferum (Opium poppy). Fast-growing, upright annual. H 75cm (30in), S 30cm (12in). Has oblong, lobed, light greyish-green leaves. Large, single flowers, to 10cm (4in) wide, in shades of red, pink, purple or white, are produced in summer. Several double-flowered forms are available, including **Carnation-flowered Series**, with fringed flowers in mixed colours; **'Peony Flowered'** illus. p.333; **'Pink Beauty'**, which has salmon-pink flowers; and **'White Cloud'**, which produces large, white flowers.

Paper mulberry. See *Broussonetia papyrifera*, illus. p.75.
Paper reed. See *Cyperus papyrus*, illus. p.319.
Paper-bark maple. See *Acer griseum*, illus. p.96.
Paper-bark tree. See *Melaleuca viridiflora* var. *rubriflora*.
Paper-bark, Scented. See *Melaleuca squarrosa*.

PAPHIOPEDILUM

Slipper orchid

ORCHIDACEAE

Contact with foliage may aggravate skin allergies. See also ORCHIDS.
P. appletonianum illus. p.308. Evergreen, terrestrial orchid. H 8cm (3in). Frost tender, min. 13°C (55°F). In spring, green flowers, 6cm (2½in) across and each with a pouched, brownish lip and pink-flushed petals, are borne singly on tall, slender stems. Has oval, mottled leaves, 10cm (4in) long. Needs shade in summer.
P. bellatulum illus. p.308. Evergreen, terrestrial orchid. H 5cm (2in). Frost tender, min. 18°C (64°F). Bears almost stemless, rounded, pouch-lipped, white flowers, 8cm (3in) across, spotted with dark maroon, singly in spring. Oval, marbled leaves are 8cm (3in) long. Grow in shade in summer.
***P.* Buckhurst 'Mont Millais'** illus. p.310. Evergreen, terrestrial orchid. H 10cm (4in). Frost tender, min. 13°C (55°F). Rounded, yellow-and-white flowers, to 12cm (5in) across and lined and spotted with red, are produced singly in winter. Has oval leaves, 10cm (4in) long. Requires shade in summer.
P. callosum illus. p.308. Evergreen, terrestrial orchid. H 8cm (3in). Frost tender, min. 13°C (55°F). Purple- and green-veined, white flowers, 8cm (3in) across, are borne on tall stems in spring-summer. Has oval, mottled leaves, 10cm (4in) long. Needs shade in summer.
P. fairrieanum illus. p.308. Evergreen, terrestrial orchid. H 8cm (3in). Frost tender, min. 10°C (50°F). Rich purple- and green-veined flowers, 5cm (2in) across, with curved petals and orange-brown pouches, are borne singly in autumn. Oval leaves are 8cm (3in) long. Grow in shade in summer.
***P.* Freckles** illus. p.308. Evergreen, terrestrial orchid. H 10cm (4in). Frost tender, min. 13°C (55°F). Rounded, reddish-brown-spotted and pouched, white flowers, 10cm (4in) across, are produced singly in winter. Has oval leaves, 10cm (4in) long. Grow in shade in summer.
P. haynaldianum illus. p.308. Evergreen, terrestrial orchid. H 12cm (5in). Frost tender, min. 13°C (55°F). In summer, long-petalled, brown-marked, green-, pink-and-white flowers, to 15cm (6in) across, are produced singly. Has oval leaves, 20–23cm (8–9in) long. Requires shade in summer.
***P.* Lyric 'Glendora'** illus. p.309. Evergreen, terrestrial orchid. H 10cm (4in). Frost tender, min. 13°C (55°F). Rounded, glossy, white-, red-and-green flowers, 10cm (4in) across, appear singly in winter. Has oval leaves, 15cm (6in) long. Needs shade in summer.
***P.* Maudiae** illus. p.309. Evergreen, terrestrial orchid. H 10cm (4in). Frost tender, min. 13°C (55°F). Clear apple-green or deep reddish-purple flowers, 10cm (4in) across, appear singly on long stems in spring or early summer. Has oval, mottled leaves, 10cm (4in) long. Requires shade in summer.
P. niveum illus. p.308. Evergreen, terrestrial orchid. H 5cm (2in). Frost tender, min. 13–18°C (55–64°F). White flowers, 4cm (1½in) across, are produced singly, mainly in spring. Oval, marbled leaves are 8cm (3in) long. Needs shade in summer.
P. sukhakulii illus. p.310. Evergreen, terrestrial orchid. H 8cm (3in). Frost tender, min. 13°C (55°F). In spring-summer, purple-pouched, black-spotted, green flowers, 8cm (3in) across, appear singly on tall stems. Has oval, mottled leaves, 10cm (4in) long. Grow in shade in summer.
P. venustum illus. p.311. Evergreen, terrestrial orchid. H 10cm (4in). Frost tender, min. 13°C (55°F). Variably coloured flowers, ranging from pink to orange with green veins and darker spots, are 6cm (2½in) across and borne singly in autumn. Has oval, mottled leaves, 10cm (4in) long. Needs shade in summer.

Papyrus. See *Cyperus papyrus*, illus. p.319.
Para para. See *Pisonia umbellifera*.
Parachute plant. See *Ceropegia sandersonii*.
Paradise palm. See *Howea forsteriana*.

PARADISEA

LILIACEAE/ASPHODELACEAE

Genus of perennials, grown for their flowers and foliage. Fully hardy. Requires a sunny site and fertile, well-drained soil. Propagate by division in spring or by seed in autumn. After division may not flower for a season.
♀ ***P. liliastrum*** (St Bruno's lily). Clump-forming, fleshy-rooted perennial. H 30–60cm (12–24in), S 30cm (12in). Slender stems, bearing racemes of saucer-shaped, white flowers in early summer, arise above broad, grass-like, greyish-green leaves.

PARAHEBE

SCROPHULARIACEAE

Genus of evergreen or semi-evergreen, summer-flowering perennials, sub-shrubs and shrubs, similar to *Hebe* and *Veronica*. Is suitable for rock gardens. Frost hardy. Needs sun and well-drained, peaty, sandy soil. Propagate by semi-ripe cuttings in early summer.
P. catarractae illus. p.368.
P. lyallii. Semi-evergreen, prostrate shrub. H 15cm (6in), S 20–25cm (8–10in). Has oval, toothed, leathery leaves and, in early summer, erect stems bearing loose sprays of flattish, pink-veined, white flowers.
♀ ***P. perfoliata***, syn. *Veronica perfoliata*, illus. p.296.

PARAQUILEGIA

RANUNCULACEAE

Genus of tufted perennials, grown for their cup-shaped flowers and fern-like foliage. Is difficult to cultivate and flower successfully. Prefers dry winters and cool climates. Is good in alpine houses and troughs. Fully hardy. Needs sun and gritty, well-drained, alkaline soil. Propagate by seed in autumn.
P. anemonoides, syn. *P. grandiflora*, illus. p.376.
P. grandiflora. See *P. anemonoides*.

PARASERIANTHES

LEGUMINOSAE/MIMOSACEAE

Genus of deciduous or semi-evergreen trees, grown for their feathery foliage and unusual flower heads, composed of numerous stamens and resembling bottlebrushes. Half hardy to frost tender, min. 4–5°C (39–41°F). In frost-prone areas grow half-hardy species against a south- or west-facing wall and tender species under glass; in cold areas do not plant out until late spring. Requires full sun and well-drained soil. Propagate by seed in spring.
♀ ***P. lophantha***, syn. *Albizia distachya*, *A. lophantha*, illus. p.89.

Parasol tree, Chinese. See *Firmiana simplex*, illus. p.64.
Parilla, Yellow. See *Menispermum canadense*.

PARIS

Herb Paris

LILIACEAE/TRILLIACEAE

Genus of summer-flowering, rhizomatous perennials. Fully hardy. Requires shade or semi-shade and humus-rich soil. Propagate by division in spring or by seed in autumn. The flowers are followed by fleshy fruits with black or red seeds; these may cause mild stomach upset if ingested.
P. polyphylla, syn. *Daiswa polyphylla*. Erect, rhizomatous perennial. H 60cm–1m (2–3ft), S to 30cm (1ft). In early summer, at tips of slender stems, produces unusual flowers consisting of a ruff of green sepals, with another ruff of greenish-yellow petals, marked with crimson above, crowned by a violet-purple stigma. Leaves, borne in whorls at stem tips, are lance-shaped to oval and mid-green.

PARKINSONIA

LEGUMINOSAE/CAESALPINIACEAE

Genus of evergreen, spring-flowering shrubs and trees, grown for their flowers and overall appearance. Frost tender, min. 15°C (59°F). Needs as much sunlight as possible to thrive, a dry atmosphere and fertile, free-draining soil. Water potted specimens moderately when in full growth, sparingly at other times. Pruning is tolerated, but spoils the natural habit. Propagate by seed in spring.
P. aculeata (Jerusalem thorn, Mexican palo verde). Evergreen, feathery shrub or tree with a spiny, green stem. H and S 3–6m (10–20ft) or more. Long, linear leaves have winged midribs bearing tiny, elliptic, short-lived leaflets. Produces fragrant, 5-petalled, yellow flowers in arching racemes in spring.

Parlour palm. See *Chamaedorea elegans*, illus. p.148.

PARNASSIA

PARNASSIACEAE

Genus of rosetted, mainly summer-flowering perennials, grown for their saucer-shaped flowers. Is good for rock gardens. Fully hardy. Needs sun and wet soil. Propagate by seed in autumn.
P. palustris illus. p.362.

PAROCHETUS

LEGUMINOSAE/PAPILIONACEAE

Genus of one species of evergreen perennial. Grows best in alpine houses. Half hardy. Needs semi-shade and gritty, moist soil. Propagate by division of rooted runners in any season.
P. communis illus. p.396.

PARODIA

CACTACEAE

Genus of rounded, perennial cacti with tubercles arranged in ribs that often spiral around green stems. Crown forms woolly buds, then funnel-shaped flowers. Frost tender, min. 5–10°C (41–50°F). Requires full sun or partial shade and very well-drained soil. Water very lightly in winter; tends to lose roots during a long period of drought. Propagate by seed in spring or summer.
P. chrysacanthion illus. p.484.
P. concinna, syn. *Notocactus apricus*. Flattened spherical, perennial cactus. H 7cm (3in), S 10cm (4in). Min. 10°C (50°F). Much-ribbed, pale green stem is densely covered with short, soft, golden-brown spines. In summer, crown produces flattish, glossy, bright yellow flowers, 8cm (3in) across, with purple stigmas. Prefers partial shade.
P. erinacea, syn. *Wigginsia vorwerkiana*, illus. p.495.
P. haselbergii subsp. ***haselbergii***, syn. *Notocactus haselbergii*, illus. p.491. subsp. ***graessneri*** (syn. *Notocactus graessneri*) is a slow-growing, flattened spherical, perennial cactus. H 10cm (4in), S 25cm (10in). Min 10°C (50°F). Bristle-like, golden spines completely cover much-ribbed, green stem. Slightly sunken crown bears funnel-shaped, glossy, greenish-yellow flowers, with yellow stigmas, in early

spring. Prefers partial shade.
P. leninghausii, syn. *Notocactus leninghausii*, illus. p.484.
P. mammulosa, syn. *Notocactus mammulosus*, illus. p.493.
P. microsperma, syn. *P. sanguiniflora*, illus. p.490.
P. nivosa illus. p.490.
P. ottonis, syn. *Notocactus ottonis*. Variable, spherical, perennial cactus. H and S 10cm (4in). Min. 5°C (41°F). Has pale to dark green stem with 8–12rounded ribs bearing stiff, golden radial spines and longer, soft, red central spines. In summer, crown bears flattish, glossy, golden flowers, 8cm (3in) across, with purple stigmas. Offsets freely from stolons. Prefers sun.
P. rutilans, syn. *Notocactus rutilans*, illus. p.487.
P. sanguiniflora. See *P. microsperma*.
P. scopa, syn. *Notocactus scopa* (Silver ball cactus). Spherical to columnar, perennial cactus. H 25cm (10in), S 15cm (6in). Min. 10°C (50°F). Stem, with 30–35 ribs, is densely covered with white radial spines and longer, red central spines, 3 or 4 per areole. Crown bears funnel-shaped, glossy, yellow flowers, 4cm (1½in) across, with purple stigmas, in summer. Prefers a sunny position.

PARONYCHIA

ILLECEBRACEAE

Genus of evergreen perennials making loose mats of prostrate stems. Is useful for rock gardens and walls. Fully to frost hardy. Needs sun and well-drained soil. Propagate by division in spring.
P. capitata. Vigorous, evergreen, mat-forming perennial. H 1cm (½in), S 40cm (16in). Fully hardy. Silvery leaves are small and oval. In summer produces inconspicuous flowers surrounded by papery bracts. Makes good ground cover.
P. kapela subsp. ***serpyllifolia*** illus. p.403.

Parrot feather. See *Myriophyllum aquaticum*, illus. p.464.
Parrot leaf. See *Alternanthera ficoidea*.
Parrot's bill. See *Clianthus puniceus*, illus. p.200.
Parrot's flower. See *Heliconia psittacorum*, illus. p.227.
Parrot's plantain. See *Heliconia psittacorum*, illus. p.227.

PARROTIA

HAMAMELIDACEAE

Genus of one species of deciduous tree, grown for its flowers and autumn colour. Fully hardy, but flower buds may be killed by hard frosts. Requires full sun and grows best in fertile, moist but well-drained soil. Is lime-tolerant, but usually colours best in acid soil. Propagate by softwood cuttings in summer or by seed in autumn.
♀ ***P. persica*** illus. p.78.

PARROTIOPSIS

HAMAMELIDACEAE

Genus of one species of deciduous tree or shrub, grown for its ornamental, dense flower heads surrounded by conspicuous bracts. Fully hardy. Needs sun or semi-shade. Grows in any fertile, well-drained soil except very shallow soil over chalk. Propagate by softwood cuttings in summer or by seed in autumn.
P. jacquemontiana. Deciduous, shrubby or upright tree. H 6m (20ft), S 4m (12ft). Has witch-hazel-like, dark green leaves that turn yellow in autumn. From mid- to late spring and in summer bears clusters of minute flowers, with tufts of yellow stamens, surrounded by white bracts.

Parsley fern. See *Cryptogramma crispa*, illus. p.325.
Parson's pink china. See *Rosa* × *odorata* 'Pallida', illus. p.183.

PARTHENOCISSUS

VITACEAE

Genus of deciduous, woody-stemmed, tendril climbers, grown for their leaves, which often turn beautiful colours in autumn. Broad tips of tendrils have sucker-like pads that cling to supports. Has insignificant, greenish flowers in summer. Will quickly cover north- or east-facing walls or fences and may be grown up large trees. Fully to half hardy. Grow in semi-shade or shade and in well-drained soil. Propagate by softwood or greenwood cuttings in summer or by hardwood cuttings in early spring. The berries may cause mild stomach upset if ingested.
♀ ***P. henryana***, syn. *Vitis henryana*. Deciduous, tendril climber with 4-angled, woody stems. H to 10m (30ft) or more. Frost hardy. Leaves have 3–5 toothed, oval leaflets, each 4–13cm (1½–5in) long, and are velvety, deep green or bronze with white or pinkish veins. Small, dark blue berries are produced in autumn. Leaf colour is best with a north or east aspect.
♀ ***P. quinquefolia***, syn. *Vitis quinquefolia* (Five-leaved ivy, Virginia creeper). Deciduous, woody-stemmed, tendril climber. H 15m (50ft) or more. Frost hardy. Leaves have 5 oval, toothed, dull green leaflets, paler beneath, that turn a beautiful crimson in autumn. Blue-black berries are produced in autumn. Is ideal for covering a high wall or building.
P. striata. See *Cissus striata*.
P. thomsonii. See *Cayratia thomsonii*.
♀ ***P. tricuspidata***, illus. p.216. **'Lowii'** and **'Veitchii'** (syn. *Ampelopsis veitchii*) illus. p.216.

Partridge berry. See *Mitchella repens*.
Partridge-breasted aloe. See *Aloe variegata*, illus. p.480.
Pasque flower. See *Pulsatilla vulgaris*, illus. p.360.

PASSIFLORA

Passion flower

PASSIFLORACEAE

Genus of evergreen or semi-evergreen, woody-stemmed, tendril climbers, grown for their unique flowers, each one with a central corona of filaments. Produces egg-shaped to rounded, fleshy, edible fruits that mature to orange or yellow in autumn. Half hardy to frost tender, min. 5–16°C (41–61°F). Grow in full sun or partial shade and in any fertile, well-drained soil. Water freely in full growth, less at other times. Stems need support. Thin out and spur back crowded growth in spring. Propagate by seed in spring or by semi-ripe cuttings in summer.
P.* × *allardii, syn. *P.* 'Allardii'. Strong-growing, evergreen, woody-stemmed, tendril climber. H 7–10m (22–30ft). Frost tender, min. 7°C (45°F). Has 3-lobed leaves. Flowers, 7–10cm (3–4in) wide, are white, tinted pink, with purple-banded crowns, and are carried in summer-autumn.
***P.* 'Allardii'.** See *P.* × *allardii*.
♀ ***P. antioquiensis***, syn. *Tacsonia van-volxemii* (Banana passion fruit). Fast-growing, evergreen, woody-stemmed, tendril climber. H 5m (15ft) or more. Frost tender, min. 7°C (45°F). Has downy leaves, with 3 deep lobes. Produces long-tubed, rose-red flowers, 10–12cm (4–5in) across, with purplish-blue centres, in summer-autumn.
♀ ***P. caerulea*** illus. p.212. **'Constance Elliot'** is a fast-growing, evergreen or semi-evergreen, woody-stemmed, tendril climber. H 10m (30ft) or more. Frost hardy. Has rich green leaves and, in summer-autumn, produces bowl-shaped, fragrant, white flowers with pale blue or white filaments.
P.* × *caeruleoracemosa. See *P.* × *violacea*.
***P.* × *caponii* 'John Innes'** illus. p.212.
P. coccinea illus. p.201.
♀ ***P.* × *exoniensis.*** Fast-growing, evergreen, woody-stemmed, tendril climber. H 8m (25ft) or more. Frost tender, min. 7°C (45°F). Leaves have 3 deep lobes and are softly downy. Rose-pink flowers, 8cm (3in) across, with purplish-blue crowns, are produced in summer-autumn.
P. manicata illus. p.215.
♀ ***P. mollissima***, syn. *Tacsonia mollissima*. Fast-growing, evergreen, woody-stemmed, tendril climber. H 5m (15ft) or more. Frost tender, min. 7°C (45°F). Softly downy leaves have 3 deep lobes. Long-tubed, pink flowers, to 8cm (3in) wide, each with a purplish-blue crown, appear in summer-autumn.
♀ ***P. quadrangularis*** illus. p.213.
♀ ***P. racemosa*** (Red passion flower). Fast-growing, evergreen, tendril climber with slender, woody stems. H 5m (15ft). Frost tender, min. 15°C (59°F). Has wavy, leathery leaves with 3 deep lobes. In summer-autumn bears terminal racemes of pendent, crimson flowers, 8–10cm (3–4in) across, with white- and purple-banded crowns.
P. sanguinea. See *P. vitifolia*.
♀ ***P.* × *violacea***, syn. *P.* × *caeruleoracemosa*. Vigorous, evergreen, woody-stemmed, tendril climber. H 10m (30ft). Frost tender, min. 7–10°C (45–50°F). Has 3-lobed leaves. Purple flowers, 8cm (3in) across, appear in summer-autumn.
P. vitifolia, syn. *P. sanguinea*. Evergreen, woody-stemmed, tendril climber; slender stems have fine, brown hairs. H to 5m (15ft). Frost tender, min. 16°C (61°F). Has 3-lobed, lustrous leaves. In summer-autumn bears bright scarlet flowers, 13cm (5in) wide, each with a short crown, banded red, yellow and white.

Passion flower. See *Passiflora*.
  Blue. See *Passiflora caerulea*, illus. p.212.
  Common. See *Passiflora caerulea*, illus. p.212.
  Red. See *Passiflora coccinea*, illus. p.201; *Passiflora racemosa*.
Passion fruit, Banana. See *Passiflora antioquiensis*.
Patagonian cypress. See *Fitzroya cupressoides*, illus. p.102.

PATERSONIA

IRIDACEAE

Genus of evergreen, clump-forming, spring- and early summer-flowering, rhizomatous perennials. Half hardy. Needs full sun and light, well-drained soil. Leave undisturbed once planted. Propagate by seed in autumn. soil. Leave undisturbed once planted. Propagate by seed in autumn.
P. umbrosa illus. p.437.

PATRINIA

VALERIANACEAE

Genus of perennials, with neat clumps, grown for their flowers. Is suitable for rock gardens and peat beds. Fully hardy. Needs a site in partial shade with moist soil. Propagate by division in spring or by seed in autumn. Self-seeds freely.
P. triloba. Clump-forming perennial. H 20–50cm (8–20in), S 15–30cm (6–12in). Neat heads of small, golden-yellow flowers are borne throughout summer. Rounded, 3- to 5-lobed, green leaves turn gold in autumn.

PAULOWNIA

SCROPHULARIACEAE

Genus of deciduous trees, grown for their large leaves and foxglove-like flowers, borne before the foliage emerges. Fully to frost hardy, but flower buds and young growth of small plants may be damaged by very hard frosts. Requires full sun and fertile, moist but well-drained soil. In cold areas may be grown for foliage only by cutting back young shoots hard in spring and cutting out all but one of the subsequent shoots; this results in very large leaves. Propagate by seed in autumn or spring or by root cuttings in winter.
P. fortunei. Deciduous, spreading tree. H and S 8m (25ft). Fully hardy. Has large, oval, mid-green leaves. In late spring bears large, fragrant flowers, purple-spotted and white inside, pale purple outside.
P. imperialis. See *P. tomentosa*.
♀ ***P. tomentosa***, syn. *P. imperialis*, illus. p.73.

PAVONIA

MALVACEAE

Genus of evergreen, mainly summer-flowering perennials and shrubs, grown usually for their flowers. Frost tender, min. 16–18°C (61–4°F). Needs full light or partial shade and humus-rich, well-drained soil. Water freely when in full growth, moderately at other times. Leggy stems may be cut back hard in spring. Propagate by seed in spring or by greenwood cuttings in summer. Whitefly and red spider mite may be troublesome.

P. hastata. Evergreen, erect shrub. H 2–3m (6–10ft), S 1–2m (3–6ft). Has lance-shaped to oval, mid-green leaves, each with 2 basal lobes. Funnel-shaped, pale red to white flowers, with darker basal spotting, appear in summer.

Pawpaw. See *Asimina triloba*.

PAXISTIMA, syn. PACHYSTIMA

CELASTRACEAE

Genus of evergreen, spreading shrubs and sub-shrubs, grown for their foliage. Is suitable for ground cover. Fully hardy. Prefers shade and humus-rich, moist soil. Propagate by division in spring or by semi-ripe cuttings in summer.

P. canbyi. Evergreen, spreading sub-shrub. H 15–30cm (6–12in), S 20cm (8in). Leaves are linear or oblong, and short, pendent spikes of tiny, greenish-white flowers are produced in summer.

Pea
- **Australian.** See *Lablab purpureus*, illus. p.207.
- **Coral.** See *Hardenbergia violacea*.
- **Darling.** See *Swainsona galegifolia*.
- **Dusky coral.** See *Kennedia rubicunda*, illus. p.201.
- **Everlasting.** See *Lathyrus grandiflorus*, illus. p.205; *Lathyrus latifolius*, illus. p.207; *Lathyrus sylvestris*.
- **Holly flame.** See *Chorizema ilicifolium*, illus. p.153.
- **Lord Anson's blue.** See *Lathyrus nervosus*.
- **Perennial.** See *Lathyrus latifolius*, illus. p.207; *Lathyrus sylvestris*.
- **Persian everlasting.** See *Lathyrus rotundifolius*.
- **Shamrock.** See *Parochetus communis*, illus. p.396.
- **Sweet.** See *Lathyrus odoratus*.

Peace lily. See *Spathiphyllum wallisii*, illus. p.312.

Peach. See *Prunus persica*.
- **David's.** See *Prunus davidiana*.

Peacock flower. See *Tigridia pavonia*, illus. p.439.

Peacock plant. See *Calathea makoyana*, illus. p.316.

Peanut cactus. See *Echinopsis chamaecereus*, illus. p.491.

Pear. See *Pyrus*.
- **Callery.** See *Pyrus calleryana*.
- **Common.** See *Pyrus communis*.
- **Prickly.** See *Opuntia*.

Pearl berry. See *Margyricarpus pinnatus*.

Pearl everlasting. See *Anaphalis*.

PEDILANTHUS

EUPHORBIACEAE

Genus of bushy, summer-flowering, perennial succulents. Produces small, yellowish-green, pink, red or brown bracts that are each shaped like a bird's head. Frost tender, min. 10–11°C (50–52°F). Needs sun or partial shade and well-drained soil. Propagate by seed or stem cuttings in spring or summer. The stems and leaves contain a milky sap that may cause stomach upset if ingested.

P. tithymaloides. Bushy, perennial succulent. H 3m (10ft), S 30cm (1ft). Min 10°C (50°F). Has thin, erect stems zigzagging at each node. Leaves are mid-green and boat-shaped, with prominent ribs beneath. Red to yellowish-green bracts are produced at each of the stem tips in summer. Prefers partial shade. ♀ **'Variegata'** illus. p.475.

Pedunculate oak. See *Quercus robur*.
Peepul. See *Ficus religiosa*.

PELARGONIUM
Geranium

GERANIACEAE

Genus of mainly summer-flowering perennials, most of which are evergreen, often cultivated as annuals. Is grown for its colourful flowers and is useful in pots or as bedding plants; in warm conditions flowers are borne almost continuously. Frost tender, min. 2°C (36°F), unless otherwise stated. A sunny site with 12 hours of daylight is required for good flowering. Prefers well-drained, neutral to alkaline soil. Dislikes very hot, humid conditions. Dead-head frequently and fertilize regularly if grown in pots; do not overwater. Plants may be kept through winter in the greenhouse by cutting back in autumn-winter to 12cm (5in) and repotting. Propagate by softwood cuttings from spring to autumn. Contact with the foliage may occasionally aggravate skin allergies.

Pelargoniums may be divided into 6 groups; all flower in summer-autumn unless stated otherwise. See also feature panel pp.248–9.

Angel – plants with rounded, sometimes scented, usually mid-green leaves, and clusters of small, single flowers of the regal type.
Ivy-leaved – trailing, evergreen plants, ideal for hanging baskets, with lobed, sometimes pointed, stiff, fleshy, usually mid-green leaves and flowers similar to those of zonal pelargoniums.
Regal – shrubby, evergreen plants with rounded, sometimes lobed or partially toothed, mid-green leaves and clusters of single, rarely double, broadly trumpet-shaped, exotic-coloured flowers that are prone to weather-damage in the open.
Scented-leaved and **species** – evergreen plants with small, single, often irregularly star-shaped flowers; scented-leaved forms are grown for their fragrance.
Unique – Tall-growing, evergreen sub-shrubs with rounded or lobed, sometimes incised, mid-green leaves, often with a pungent scent when crushed. Produces clusters of single, trumpet-shaped, brightly coloured flowers of the regal type, which are borne continuously through the season.
Zonal – succulent-stemmed, evergreen plants with rounded, leaves, distinctively marked with a darker 'zone', and single (5-petalled), semi-double or fully double flowers. Zonal pelargoniums can be separated into the following groups: cactus-flowered; double- and semi-double-flowered; fancy-leaved; Formosum hybrids; Rosebud; Single-flowered; and Stellar.

P. acetosum illus. p.248. Species pelargonium. H 50–60cm (20–24in), S 20–25cm (8–10in). Stems are succulent with fleshy, grey-green leaves that are often margined red. Bears single, salmon-pink flowers. Is good as a pot plant in a greenhouse.

***P.* 'Alberta'** illus. p.248. Evergreen, single-flowered zonal pelargonium. H 45cm (18in), S 30cm (12in). Bears clusters of small, crimson-and-white flowers. Is best grown as a bedding plant.

♀ ***P.* 'Amethyst'** illus. p.249. Evergreen, trailing ivy-leaved pelargonium. H and S to 1.5m (5ft). Leaves are fleshy with pointed lobes. Bears fully double, light mauve-purple flowers.

♀ ***P.* 'Apple Blossom Rosebud'** illus. p.248. Evergreen, rosebud zonal pelargonium. H 30cm (12in), S 23cm (9in). Fully double, pinkish-white flowers, margined with red, look like miniature rosebuds.

***P.* 'Autumn Festival'** illus. p.248. Evergreen, bushy regal pelargonium. H and S 30cm (12in). Salmon-pink flowers have pronounced, white throats.

♀ ***P.* 'Bird Dancer'** illus. p.248. Dwarf, stellar zonal pelargonium. H 15–20cm (6–8in), S 12–15cm (5–6in). Has clusters of single flowers, with pale pink lower petals and salmon-pink upper petals.

♀ ***P.* 'Bredon'** illus. p.249. Strong-growing, evergreen regal pelargonium. H 45cm (18in), S to 30cm (12in). Has large, maroon flowers.

***P.* 'Brookside Primrose'** illus. p.248. Dwarf, fancy-leaved zonal pelargonium. H 10–12cm (4–5in), S 7–10cm (3–4in). Bears double, pale pink flowers. Leaves have a butterfly mark in the centre of each leaf. Is good as a pot plant or for bedding.

***P.* 'Butterfly Lorelei'** illus. p.248. Fancy-leaved, zonal pelargonium. H 25–30cm (10–12in), S 15–20cm (6–8in). Has butterfly-shaped leaves and double, pale salmon-pink flowers. Is suitable as a pot plant in a greenhouse.

***P.* 'Caligula'** illus. p.249. Evergreen, miniature, semi-double-flowered zonal pelargonium. H 15–20cm (6–8in), S 10cm (4in). Has small, crimson flowers and tiny, dark green leaves. Suits a windowsill.

***P.* 'Capen'** illus. p.249. Bushy, semi-double-flowered zonal pelargonium. H 38–45cm (15–18in), S 15–20cm (6–8in). Bears coral-pink, semi-double flowers. Is good as a pot plant.

P. capitatum illus. p.249. Evergreen, scented-leaved pelargonium. H 30–60cm (12–24in), S 30cm (12in). Has mauve flowers and irregularly 3-lobed leaves that smell faintly of roses. Is mainly used to produce geranium oil for the perfume industry, but may be grown as a pot plant.

P. carnosum. Deciduous, shrubby pelargonium (unclassified), with thick, succulent stems and a woody, swollen, tuber-like rootstock. H and S 30cm (12in). Min. 10°C (50°F). Has long, grey-green leaves with triangular, deeply lobed leaflets. Produces branched, umbel-like flower heads with white or greenish-yellow flowers, the upper petals streaked red and shorter than the green sepals.

***P.* 'Cherry Blossom'** illus. p.248. Vigorous, evergreen, single-flowered zonal pelargonium. H and S to 45cm (18in). Mauve-pink flowers have white centres.

***P.* 'Chew Magna'.** Evergreen regal pelargonium. H 30–45cm (12–18in), S to 30cm (12in). Each petal of the pale pink flowers has a wine-red blaze.

***P.* 'Clorinda'** illus. p.248. Vigorous, scented-leaved pelargonium. H 45–50cm (18–20in), S 20–25cm (8–10in). Leaves smell of cedar and are 3-lobed. Bears large, single, rose-pink flowers and is excellent in a large pot. Is suitable for a greenhouse or patio.

***P.* 'Coddenham'** illus. p.249. Miniature, double-flowered zonal pelargonium. H 10–12cm (4–5in), S 7–10cm (3–4in). Produces clusters of orange-red flowers.

♀ ***P. crispum* 'Variegatum'** illus. p.249. Evergreen, upright scented-leaved pelargonium. H to 1m (3ft), S 30–45cm (1–1½ft). Has gold-variegated leaves and small, pale lilac flowers. Foliage tends to become creamy-white in winter.

***P.* 'Dale Queen'** illus. p.248. Evergreen, bushy, single-flowered zonal pelargonium. H 23–30cm (9–12in), S 23cm (9in). Flowers are delicate salmon-pink. Is particularly suitable for a pot.

♀ ***P.* 'Dolly Varden'** illus. p.249. Evergreen, fancy-leaved zonal pelargonium. H 30cm (12in), S 23cm (9in). Green leaves have handsome, purple-brown, white and crimson markings. Single, scarlet flowers are insignificant.

***P.* 'Emma Hössle'.** See *P.* 'Frau Emma Hössle'.

***P.* 'Fair Ellen'** illus. p.248. Compact scented-leaved pelargonium. H and S 30cm (12in). Has dark green leaves and pale pink flowers marked with red.

♀ ***P.* 'Flower of Spring'** (Silver-leaved geranium; illus. p.249). Vigorous, evergreen, fancy-leaved zonal pelargonium. H 60cm (24in), S 30cm (12in). Has green-and-white leaves and single, red flowers.

P. × fragrans. See *P.* 'Fragrans'.

***P.* 'Fragrans',** syn. *P. × fragrans, P. Fragrans Group* illus. p.248. Evergreen, very bushy scented-leaved pelargonium. H and S 30cm (12in). Rounded, shallowly lobed, grey-green leaves smell strongly of pine. Bears small, white flowers.

P. Fragrans Group. See *P.* 'Fragrans'.

***P.* 'Fraiche Beauté',** syn. *P.* 'Fraicher Beauty' illus. p.248. Evergreen, double-flowered zonal pelargonium. H 30cm (12in), S 23cm (9in). Flowers are perfectly formed with delicate

colouring: white with a thin, red edge to each petal. Is excellent as a pot plant.
P. 'Fraicher Beauty'. See *P.* 'Fraiche Beauté'.
♀ **P. 'Francis Parrett'** illus. p.248. Evergreen, short-jointed, double-flowered zonal pelargonium. H 15–20cm (6–8in), S 10cm (4in). Bears purplish-mauve flowers and small, green leaves. Is good for a windowsill.
P. 'Frau Emma Hössle, syn. *P.* 'Emma Hössle'. Evergreen, dwarf, double-flowered zonal pelargonium. H 20–25cm (8–10in), S 15cm (6in). Bears large, mauve-pink flowers. Is useful for a window box.
P. 'Friesdorf' illus. p.249. Evergreen, fancy-leaved zonal pelargonium. H 25cm (10in), S 15cm (6in). Has dark green foliage and narrow-petalled, single, orange-scarlet flowers. Is good for a window box or planted in a large group.
P. 'Golden Lilac Mist' illus. p.248. Bushy, fancy-leaved zonal pelargonium. H 25–30cm (10–12in), S 15–20cm (6–8in). Leaves are gold marked with bronze. Bears double, lavender-pink flowers. Is a good window-box plant.
P. 'Gustav Emich' illus. p.249. Vigorous, evergreen, semi-double-flowered zonal pelargonium. H and S to 60cm (24in). Semi-double flowers are vivid scarlet.
♀ **P. 'Happy Thought'** illus. p.249. Fancy-leaved zonal pelargonium. H 40–45cm (16–18in), S 20–25cm (8–10in). Rounded leaves each have a greenish-yellow butterfly marking in the centre. Bears single, light crimson flowers in clusters.
♀ **P. 'Irene'**. Evergreen, semi-double-flowered zonal pelargonium. H 45cm (18in), S 23–30cm (9–12in). Bears large, light crimson blooms.
P. 'Ivalo' illus. p.248. Evergreen, bushy, short-jointed, semi-double-flowered zonal pelargonium. H 23–30cm (9–12in), S 23cm (9in). Large, semi-double flowers are pale pink with crimson-dotted, white centres.
P. 'Lachsball' illus. p.248. Vigorous, semi-double-flowered zonal pelargonium. H 45–50cm (18–20in), S 15–20cm (6–8in). Bears salmon-pink flowers each with a scarlet eye. Is good for summer bedding.
P. 'Lachskönigin' illus. p.248. Evergreen, trailing, brittle-jointed pelargonium. H and S to 60cm (24in). Has fleshy leaves, with pointed lobes, and semi-double, deep rosy-pink flowers. Suits a hanging basket or window box.
♀ **P. 'Lady Plymouth'** illus. p.248. Scented-leaved pelargonium. H 30–40cm (11–16in), S 15–20cm (6–8in). Has eucalyptus-scented, silver-margined leaves and lavender-pink flowers borne in clusters.
♀ **P. 'L'Elégante'** illus. p.249. Evergreen, trailing ivy-leaved pelargonium. H and S to 60cm (24in). Foliage is variegated with creamy-white margins, sometimes turning pink at the edges; semi-double flowers are pale mauve. Is best grown in a hanging basket.
P. 'Leslie Judd' illus. p.248. Vigorous, evergreen, bushy regal pelargonium. H 30–45cm (12–18in), S to 30cm (12in). Flowers are soft salmon-pink with a central, red blotch. Pinch out growing tips before flowering to control shape.
♀ **P. 'Mabel Grey'** illus. p.249. Evergreen, scented-leaved pelargonium. H 45–60cm (18–24in), S 30–45cm (12–18in). Has diamond-shaped, rough-textured, toothed, strongly lemon-scented leaves, with 5–7 pointed lobes, and mauve flowers.
P. 'Madame Fournier' illus. p.249. Evergreen, short-jointed, single-flowered zonal pelargonium. H 15–20cm (6–8in), S 10cm (4in). Small, scarlet flowers contrast well with almost black leaves. Is useful for a pot or as a summer bedding plant.
P. 'Manx Maid' illus. p.249. Evergreen regal pelargonium. H 30–38cm (12–15in), S 25cm (10in). Flowers and leaves are small for regal type. Pink flowers are veined and blotched with burgundy.
P. 'Mauritania' illus. p.248. Evergreen, single-flowered zonal pelargonium. H 30cm (12in), S 23cm (9in). White flowers are ringed towards centres with pale salmon-pink.
P. 'Mini Cascade' illus. p.249. Evergreen, trailing, short-jointed, ivy-leaved pelargonium. H and S 30–45cm (12–18in). Bears many single, red flowers. Regular dead-heading is essential for continuous display.
P. 'Mr Everaarts' illus. p.248. Bushy, dwarf, double-flowered zonal pelargonium. H 15–20cm (6–8in), S 10–12cm (4–5in). Bears bright pink flowers. Is good in a window box.
♀ **P. 'Mr Henry Cox',** syn. *P.* 'Mrs Henry Cox' illus. p.248. Evergreen, fancy-leaved zonal pelargonium. H 30cm (12in), S 15cm (6in). Mid-green leaves are marked with red, yellow and purple-brown. Flowers are single and pink.
P. 'Mrs Henry Cox'. See *P.* 'Mr Henry Cox'.
P. 'Mrs Pollock' illus. p.249. Evergreen, single-flowered zonal pelargonium. H 30cm (12in), S 15cm (6in). Each golden leaf has a grey-green butterfly mark in centre, with a bronze zone running through it. Bears small, orange-red flowers.
♀ **P. 'Mrs Quilter'** illus. p.249. Evergreen, fancy-leaved zonal pelargonium. H 30cm (12in), S 23cm (9in). Has yellow leaves with wide, chestnut-brown zones and single, pink flowers.
♀ **P. Multibloom Series** illus. p.340. Seed-raised, single-flowered zonal pelargonium. H 25–30cm (10–12in) and S 30cm (12in). Abundant flowers in shades of white, pink and red, some with white eyes, are borne in clusters. Early flowering over a long period. Is tolerant of wet conditions.
P. 'Orange Ricard' illus. p.249. Vigorous, robust, evergreen, semi-double-flowered zonal pelargonium. H 45–60cm (18–24in), S 30cm (12in). Produces masses of large, orange blooms.
P. Orbit Series. Group of slow-growing, evergreen, bushy, single-flowered zonal pelargoniums, grown as annuals. H and S 30–60cm (12–24in). Has rounded, lobed, bronze- or red-zoned, mid-green leaves and large, domed, single flower heads in mixed or separate colours, including shades of white, pink, red and orange (salmon, illus. p.333).
♀ **P. 'Paton's Unique'** illus. p.249. Vigorous unique pelargonium with pungent-smelling leaves. H 38–45cm (15–18in), S 15–20cm (6–8in). Flowers are single, red or pale pink, each with a small, white eye.
P. peltatum. Evergreen, trailing, brittle-jointed pelargonium from which ivy-leaved cultivars have been derived. H and S to 1.5m (5ft). Has fleshy leaves, with pointed lobes, and produces single, mauve or white flowers. Cultivars suit hanging baskets and window boxes.
P. 'Polka' illus. p.249. Vigorous unique pelargonium. H 45–50cm (18–20in), S 20–25cm (8–10in). Flowers are semi-double. Upper petals are orange-red, blotched and feathered deep purple; lower ones are salmon-orange.
P. 'Prince of Orange' illus. p.249. Scented-leaved pelargonium. H 25–30cm (10–12in), S 15–20cm (6–8in). Small, rounded leaves smell of orange. Bears single, mauve flowers. Is good as a pot plant indoors.
P. 'Purple Emperor' illus. p.249. Evergreen regal pelargonium. H 45cm (18in), S 30cm (12in). Pink-mauve flowers have a deeper, central coloration. Flowers well into autumn.
P. 'Purple Unique' illus. p.249. Vigorous, evergreen, upright, shrubby unique pelargonium. H and S 1m (3ft) or more. Rounded, large-lobed leaves are very aromatic. Has single, open trumpet-shaped, light purple flowers. Does well when trained against a sunny wall.
P. 'Rica' illus. p.248. Bushy, single-flowered zonal pelargonium. H 30–38cm (12–15in), S 15–20cm (6–8in). Flowers are deep rose-pink, each with a large, white eye. Is good in a window box or as a greenhouse pot plant.
P. 'Robe'. Vigorous, semi-double-flowered zonal pelargonium. H 38–45cm (15–18in), S 15–20cm (6–8in). Bears cerise-crimson flowers. Is suitable as a pot plant in a greenhouse, or as a bedding plant, and is good for exhibition.
P. 'Rollisson's Unique' illus. p.249. Evergreen, shrubby pelargonium (unique). H 60cm (24in) or more, S 30cm (12in). Has oval, notched, pungent leaves and small, single, open trumpet-shaped, wine-red flowers with purple veins.
P. 'Rouletta' illus. p.249. Vigorous, evergreen, trailing ivy-leaved pelargonium. H and S 60cm–1m (2–3ft). Bears semi-double, red-and-white flowers. To control shape, growing tips should be pinched out regularly.
♀ **P. 'Royal Oak'** illus. p.249. Evergreen, bushy, compact scented-leaved pelargonium. H 38cm (15in), S 30cm (12in). Oak-like, slightly sticky leaves have a spicy fragrance and are dark green with central, brown markings. Flowers are small and mauve-pink.
P. 'Schöne Helena' illus. p.248. Evergreen, semi-double-flowered zonal pelargonium. H 30–45cm (12–18in), S 23cm (9in). Produces masses of large, salmon-pink blooms.
P. 'Splendide' illus. p.249. Slow-growing, short-branching pelargonium. H 25–30cm (10–12in), S 15–20cm (6–8in). Butterfly-shaped flowers are borne singly or in clusters. Dark red upper petals each have a black spot at the base; lower petals are white, sometimes stained red.
P. Sprinter Series. Group of slow-growing, evergreen, branching, bushy, single-flowered zonal pelargoniums, grown as annuals. H and S 30–60cm (12–24in). Has rounded, lobed, light to mid-green leaves. Bears large, domed flower heads in shades of red. Is very free-flowering.
P. 'Tavira' illus. p.249. Evergreen, trailing, brittle-jointed pelargonium. H and S 30–40cm (12–16in). Has fleshy leaves, with pointed lobes, and single, soft cerise-red flowers. Suits a hanging basket or window box.
♀ **P. 'The Boar'** illus. p.248. Evergreen, trailing pelargonium (species). H and S to 60cm (24in). Has unusual, 5-lobed, notched leaves, each with a central, dark brown blotch, and long-stemmed, single, salmon-pink flowers. Is useful for a hanging basket.
P. 'Timothy Clifford' illus. p.248. Evergreen, short-jointed, semi-double-flowered zonal pelargonium. H 15–20cm (6–8in), S 10cm (4in). Has dark green leaves and fully double, salmon-pink flowers. Suits a windowsill.
♀ **P. 'Tip Top Duet'** illus. p.249. Evergreen, bushy, free-branching regal pelargonium. H 30–38cm (12–15in), S 25cm (10in). Leaves and blooms are small for regal type. Bears pink-veined, white flowers; uppermost petals have dark burgundy blotches.
♀ ***P. tomentosum*** (Peppermint geranium; illus. p.249). Evergreen, bushy scented-leaved pelargonium. H 30–60cm (12–24in), S 1m (36in). Large, rounded, shallowly lobed, velvety, grey-green leaves have a strong peppermint aroma. Bears clusters of small, white flowers. Growing tips should be pinched out to control spread. Dislikes full sun.
♀ **P. Video Series.** Group of slow-growing, evergreen, branching, bushy, single-flowered zonal pelargoniums, grown as annuals. H and S 30–60cm (12–24in). Has rounded, lobed, bronze-zoned, deep green leaves and large, domed, single flower heads in white and shades of pink or red.
♀ **P. 'Voodoo'** illus. p.249. Unique pelargonium. H 50–60cm (20–24in), S 20–25cm (8–10in). Flowers are single and pale burgundy with a purple-black blaze on each petal. Is suitable as a greenhouse pot plant.

Pelican flower. See *Aristolochia grandiflora.*

PELLAEA

ADIANTACEAE

Genus of deciduous, semi-evergreen or evergreen ferns. Half hardy to frost tender, min. 5°C (41°F). Grow in semi-shade and gritty, moist but well-drained soil. Remove fading fronds regularly. Propagate by spores in summer.
P. atropurpurea (Purple rock brake, Purple-stemmed cliff brake). Semi-evergreen or evergreen fern. H and S

30cm (12in). Frost tender. Small, narrowly lance-shaped, divided fronds have oblong, blunt pinnae and are dark green with a purplish tinge.
♡ ***P. rotundifolia*** (Button fern). Evergreen fern. H and S 15cm (6in). Frost tender. Small, narrowly lance-shaped, divided fronds are dark green and have rounded pinnae.

Pellionia. See *Elatostema*.
Peltiphyllum. See *Darmera*.
Pencil cedar. See *Juniperus virginiana*.
Pendent silverlime. See *Tilia* 'Petiolaris', illus. p.64.
Pendulous sedge. See *Carex pendula*, illus. p.321.

PENNISETUM

GRAMINEAE/POACEAE

See also GRASSES, BAMBOOS, RUSHES and SEDGES.
P. alopecuroides, syn. *P. compressum* (Chinese fountain grass). Tuft-forming, herbaceous, perennial grass. H 1m (3ft), S 45cm (1½ft). Frost hardy. Has narrow, mid-green leaves; leaf sheaths each have a hairy tip. In late summer bears arching, cylindrical panicles with decorative, purple bristles that last well into winter.
P. compressum. See *P. alopecuroides*.
P. longistylum. See *P. villosum*.
P. rueppellii. See *P. setaceum*.
♡ ***P. setaceum***, syn. *P. rueppellii* (African fountain grass). Tuft-forming, herbaceous, perennial grass. H 1m (3ft), S 45cm (1½ft). Frost hardy. Has very rough, mid-green leaves and stems. In summer bears dense, cylindrical panicles of copper-red spikelets, with decorative, bearded bristles, that last well into winter.
♡ ***P. villosum***, syn. *P. longistylum*, illus. p.319.

Penny-cress, Alpine. See *Thlaspi alpinum*.

PENSTEMON

SCROPHULARIACEAE

Genus of annuals, perennials, sub-shrubs and shrubs, most of which are semi-evergreen or evergreen. Fully to half hardy. Prefers full sun and fertile, well-drained soil. Propagate species by seed in autumn or spring or by softwood or semi-ripe cuttings of non-flowering shoots in mid-summer, cultivars by cuttings only. See also feature panel pp.250–52.
♡ ***P.* 'Alice Hindley'** illus. p.250. Large-leaved, semi-evergreen perennial. H 90cm (36in), S 45cm (18in). Frost hardy. Bears tubular to bell-shaped, pale lilac-blue flowers, white inside, tinged mauve-pink outside, from mid-summer to early or mid-autumn. Leaves are linear to lance-shaped and mid-green.
♡ ***P.* 'Andenken an Friedrich Hahn'**, syn. *P.* 'Garnet' illus. p.252. H 60–75cm (2–2½ft), S 60cm (2ft). Vigorous, semi-evergreen, bushy perennial. Frost hardy. Bears sprays of tubular, deep wine-red flowers from mid-summer to autumn. Has narrow, fresh green leaves.
♡ ***P.* 'Apple Blossom'** illus. p.250. Semi-evergreen, bushy perennial. H and S 60cm (24in). Frost hardy. Carries sprays of small, tubular, pale pink flowers from mid-summer onwards above narrow, fresh green foliage.
P. barbatus, syn. *Chelone barbata* illus. p.252. Semi-evergreen, rosette-forming perennial. H 1m (3ft), S 30cm (1ft). Frost hardy. From mid-summer to early autumn bears racemes of slightly nodding, tubular, 2-lipped, rose-red flowers. Flower stems rise from rosettes of oblong to oval, mid-green leaves.
***P.* 'Barbara Barker'.** See *P.* 'Beech Park'.
♡ ***P.* 'Beech Park'**, syn. *P.* 'Barbara Barker' illus. p.250. Semi-evergreen perennial. H and S 60cm (24in). Frost hardy. Bears bright pink and white flowers. Leaves are linear and light green.
***P.* 'Blackbird'** illus. p.251. Vigorous, semi-evergreen perennial. H 1.2m (4ft), S 45cm (18in). Frost hardy. Produces willowy, purplish-red stems clothed in long, lance-shaped, dark green leaves and racemes of deep red-purple flowers, the throats densely streaked deep red, from mid-summer to autumn.
***P.* 'Burford Seedling'.** See *P.* 'Burgundy'.
***P.* 'Burford White'.** See *P.* 'White Bedder'.
***P.* 'Burgundy'**, syn. *P.* 'Burford Seedling' illus. p.251. Robust, semi-evergreen perennial. H 1.2m (4ft), S 60cm (2ft). Frost hardy. Produces purplish-red flowers with white throats streaked dark red. Leaves are linear and light green.
P. campanulatus, syn. *P. pulchellus*. Semi-evergreen, upright perennial. H 30–60cm (12–24in), S 30cm (12in). Frost hardy. Long racemes of bell-shaped, dark purple, violet or, occasionally, white flowers appear in early summer above lance-shaped, toothed, mid-green leaves.
***P.* 'Candy Pink'.** See *P.* 'Old Candy Pink'.
P. cardwellii illus. p.250. Spreading, sometimes stem-rooting, evergreen sub-shrub. H and S 30–50cm (12–20in). Fully hardy. In early summer, produces raceme-like panicles of slender, tubular to funnel-shaped, deep purple flowers. Leaves are elliptic, finely toothed and mid-green.
***P.* 'Cherry'** of gardens. See *P.* 'Cherry Ripe'.
♡ ***P.* 'Cherry Ripe'**, syn. *P.* 'Cherry' of gardens, illus. p.251. Semi-evergreen perennial. H 1.1m (3½ft), S 45–60cm (1½–2ft). Frost hardy. Has lance-shaped, mid-green leaves. From mid-summer to autumn produces an abundance of deep rose-red flowers, with a golden sheen and white throats, streaked deep red.
♡ ***P.* 'Chester Scarlet'** illus. p.252. Semi-evergreen perennial. H and S 90cm (36in). Frost hardy. Large, bright red flowers are borne above narrowly lance-shaped, light green leaves.
P. confertus. Semi-evergreen, neat, clump-forming perennial. H 45cm (18in), S 30cm (12in). Frost hardy. Bears spikes of tubular, creamy-yellow flowers above long, lance-shaped, mid-green leaves in early summer.
♡ ***P.* 'Connie's Pink'** illus. p.251. Erect, much-branched, semi-evergreen perennial. H 1.2m (4ft), S 60cm (2ft). Frost hardy. Has slender, bright rose-pink flowers, with deep pink corolla lobes and red-pencilled, white throats, from early summer to autumn. Pale green leaves are lance-shaped to oval.
***P.* 'Countess of Dalkeith'** illus. p.251. Erect, semi-evergreen perennial. H 1m (3ft), S 60cm (2ft). Frost hardy. Produces large, deep purple flowers, each with a pure white throat. Leaves are linear and light green.
P. davidsonii. Evergreen, prostrate shrub. H 8cm (3in), occasionally more, S 15cm (6in) or more. Frost hardy. In late spring and early summer, funnel-shaped, violet to ruby-red flowers, with protruding lips, develop from leaf axils. Leaves are small, oval to rounded and leathery. Trim after flowering. ♡ var. ***menziesii*** (syn. *P. menziesii*), H 5cm (2in), S 20cm (8in), produces lavender-blue flowers and rounded, toothed leaves.
P. diffusus. See *P. serrulatus*.
***P. digitalis* 'Husker Red'** illus. p.250. Vigorous, semi-evergreen or deciduous, basal-rosetted perennial. H50–75cm (20–30in), S 30cm (12in). Fully hardy. Has stems often marked reddish-purple bearing inversely lance-shaped, entire or sparsely toothed, mid-green leaves that are maroon-red when young. Produces panicles of tubular to bell-shaped, pink-tinted, white flowers, with purple lines inside, in summer.
♡ ***P.* 'Evelyn'** illus. p.251. Semi-evergreen, bushy perennial. H and S 45cm (18in). Frost hardy. Racemes of small, tubular, pink flowers open from mid-summer onwards. Has broadly lance-shaped, mid-green leaves.
***P.* 'Firebird'.** See *P.* 'Schoenholzeri'.
***P.* 'Flamingo'** illus. p.251. Open, much-branched, semi-evergreen perennial. H 90–95cm (36–38in), S 60cm (24in). Frost hardy. From summer to autumn produces white-throated, deep purplish-pink flowers, the white extending onto the corolla lobes, with a few darker, reddish-pink pencillings on the lower lobes. Leaves are mid-green, lance-shaped to oval.
P. fruticosus. Evergreen, upright, woody-based sub-shrub. H and S 15–30cm (6–12in). Frost hardy. Has lance-shaped to oval, toothed leaves and, in early summer, funnel-shaped, lipped, lavender-blue flowers. Is suitable for a rock garden. Trim back after flowering. ♡ var. ***scouleri*** (syn. *P. scouleri*) has pale to deep purple flowers. ♡ var. ***scouleri* f. *albus*** (syn. *P. scouleri* f. *albus*; illus. p.250) has white flowers.
***P.* 'Garnet'.** See *P.* 'Andenken an Friedrich Hahn'.
***P.* 'Geoff Hamilton'** illus. p.252. Vigorous, semi-evergreen perennial. H 75cm (30in), S 60cm (24in). Frost hardy. Has lance-shaped to oval, mid-green leaves. Produces large, open, purple flowers, with white throats and white-flecked lobes, from early summer to autumn.
♡ ***P.* 'George Home'** illus. p.252. Narrow-leaved perennial. H 75cm (30in), S 45cm (18in). Frost hardy. Produces small, tubular to bell-shaped, wine-red flowers, with white throats, the white extending over the lips, from mid-summer to early or mid-autumn.
P. glaber illus. p.251. Evergreen, variable sub-shrub. H and S 50–75cm (20–30in). Frost hardy. In summer produces clusters of snapdragon-like, sky-blue to indigo flowers, with maroon pencillings in the white or pale blue throats. Lance-shaped to inversely oval leaves are mid-green. Requires a sunny, dry site.
♡ ***P. hartwegii*** illus. p.252. Semi-evergreen, erect perennial. H 60cm (24in) or more, S 30cm (12in). Frost hardy. Bears sprays of slightly pendent, tubular to bell-shaped, scarlet flowers from mid- to late summer. Lance-shaped leaves are mid-green.
P. heterophyllus (Foothill penstemon) illus. p.251. Evergreen sub-shrub. H and S 30–50cm (12–20in). Fully hardy (borderline). In summer produces racemes of tubular to funnel-shaped, pinkish-blue flowers, with blue or lilac lobes. Leaves are linear to lance-shaped, entire and mid-green or bluish-green. **'True Blue'** has pale green leaves and pure blue flowers, borne on short side shoots. Trim back after flowering. Is suitable for a rock garden.
♡ ***P.* 'Hidcote Pink'** illus. p.251. Narrow-leaved perennial. H 60–75cm (24–30in), S 45cm (18in). Frost hardy. Produces small, tubular, pale pink flowers, with spreading lobes marked with crimson lines inside, from mid-summer to early or mid-autumn.
P. hirsutus. Short-lived, evergreen, open sub-shrub. H 60cm–1m (2–3ft), S 30–60cm (1–2ft). Frost hardy. In summer produces hairy, tubular, lipped, purple- or blue-flushed, white flowers. Leaves are oval and dark green. Is suitable for a rock garden. var. ***pygmaeus*** illus. p.392.
***P.* 'Hopley's Variegated'** illus. p.250. Large-leaved, semi-evergreen perennial. H 90cm (36in), S 45cm (18in). Frost hardy. Is a sport of *P.* 'Alice Hindley' with yellow-speckled leaves.
♡ ***P. isophyllus*** illus. p.159.
***P.* 'Kilimanjaro'** illus. p.250. Vigorous, semi-evergreen perennial. H 80cm (32in), S 60cm (24in). Frost hardy. Has long, lance-shaped, mid-green leaves. From summer to autumn produces long racemes of purplish-pink flowers, with white throats.
***P.* 'King George V'** illus. p.252. Narrow-leaved perennial. H 60cm (24in), S 45cm (18in). Frost hardy. Bears small, tubular to bell-shaped, bright, deep scarlet flowers, with white throats, from mid-summer to early to mid-autumn.
P. kunthii illus. p.252. Variable, woody-based, willowy perennial. H 90cm–1.2m (3–4ft), S 60cm (2ft). Frost hardy. Has lance-shaped, toothed, mid-green leaves. From mid-summer to late autumn produces many-flowered racemes of red to maroon-red flowers, with white streaks in the throats. Requires a sunny, dry site.
***P.* 'Madame Golding'** illus. p.250. Strong-growing, semi-evergreen perennial. H 75cm (30in), S 40–45cm (16–18in). Frost hardy. Is similar to *P.* 'Old Candy Pink' but has paler pink flowers.
♡ ***P.* 'Margery Fish'** illus. p.250. Almost mat-forming, woody-based perennial. H and S 50cm (20in). Frost

hardy. Has narrow, shiny, mid-green leaves. Produces dense spikes of pale blue to violet-mauve flowers, with white pencilling in the throats, in summer-autumn.

♀ ***P.* 'Maurice Gibbs'** illus. p.252. Semi-evergreen perennial. H 90cm (3ft), S 60cm (2ft). Bears claret-red flowers, with white throats. Has lance-shaped, light green leaves.

P. menziesii. See *P. davidsonii* var. *menziesii.*

***P.* 'Modesty'** illus. p.252. Strong-growing, erect, semi-evergreen perennial. H 90cm (3ft), S 45cm (1½ft). Frost hardy. Has lance-shaped, glossy, olive-green leaves. Produces bright red-pink flowers, with white throats sparsely pencilled purplish-red, in summer-autumn.

***P.* 'Mother of Pearl'** illus. p.250. Narrow-leaved perennial. H to 75cm (30in), S 45cm (18in). Frost hardy. Has small, tubular to bell-shaped, pearl-mauve flowers, tinted pink and white, with white throats and red lines, from mid-summer to early or mid-autumn.

♀ ***P. newberryi*** (Mountain pride). Evergreen, mat-forming shrub. H 15–20cm (6–8in), S 30cm (12in). Frost hardy. Branches are covered in small, oval, leathery, dark green leaves. Bears short sprays of tubular, lipped, deep rose-pink flowers in early summer. Trim back after flowering. Is good for a rock garden. f. ***humilior*** illus. p.366.

***P.* 'Old Candy Pink'**, syn. *P.* 'Candy Pink' illus. p.252. Strong-growing, semi-evergreen perennial. H 75cm (30in), S 40–45cm (16–18in). Frost hardy. Has lance-shaped, mid-green leaves. Produces bright crimson flowers, with darker crimson lines in the white throats and small, rounded, white patches at the bases of each lobe, from early summer to mid-autumn.

♀ ***P.* 'Osprey'** illus. p.251. Vigorous, open-branched, semi-evergreen perennial. H 1.1m (3½ft), S 60cm (2ft). Frost hardy. Has lance-shaped to oval, mid-green leaves. Produces creamy-white flowers, with spreading, purplish-pink lobes and white throats, in summer-autumn. As the flowers age the pink coloration deepens and extends into the flower tubes.

♀ ***P.* 'Pennington Gem'** illus. p.251. Vigorous, semi-evergreen perennial. H 1m (3ft), S 45cm (18in). Frost hardy. Bears sprays of tubular, pink flowers from mid-summer to autumn. Leaves are narrow and fresh green.

***P.* 'Pensham Just Jane'** illus. p.252. Robust, bushy, semi-evergreen perennial. H 90cm–1.2m (3–4ft), S 60cm (2ft). Frost hardy. Has lance-shaped to oval, deep green leaves. Produces rich, deep cerise-pink flowers, with faintly white-lined, magenta throats, from early summer to autumn.

♀ ***P. pinifolius*** illus. p.366. **'Mersea Yellow'** is an evergreen, bushy sub-shrub, H 10–20cm (4–8in), S 25cm (10in), with branched stems clothed in fine, dark green leaves. In summer, very narrow, tubular, bright deep yellow flowers are borne in loose, terminal spikes.

♀ ***P.* 'Port Wine'** illus. p.251. Vigorous, upright, semi-evergreen perennial. H 1m (3ft), S 60cm (2ft). Frost hardy. Has lance-shaped to oval, mid- to dark green leaves. Produces deep claret to deep purple flowers, with white throats heavily pencilled deep claret, from early summer to autumn.

P. procerus. Upright, semi-evergreen perennial. H 50cm (20in), S 20cm (8in). Frost hardy. Leaves are oblong to lance-shaped. Produces slim spikes of funnel-shaped, blue-purple flowers in summer. Is suitable for a rock garden.

P. pulchellus. See *P. campanulatus.*

♀ ***P.* 'Raven'** illus. p.251. Strong-growing, erect, semi-evergreen perennial. H 1.1m (3½ft), S 60cm (2ft). Frost hardy. Has lance-shaped to oval, mid- to dark green leaves. Dark purple-red flowers, with white throats pencilled faint, dark red in the tubes coalescing into patches of blackish-purple-red at the lobe bases, are produced freely in summer-autumn.

***P.* 'Red Emperor'** illus. p.252. Robust, erect, semi-evergreen perennial. H 90cm (3ft), S 45–50cm (18–20in) Frost hardy. Has lance-shaped to oval, mid-green leaves and vivid, bright scarlet flowers, with a golden sheen and white throats streaked and suffused red, in summer-autumn.

***P.* 'Rich Ruby'** illus. p.252. Strong-growing, erect, semi-evergreen perennial. H 80–100cm (32–39in), S 60cm (24in). Frost hardy. Red-purple stems bear lance-shaped to oval, dark green leaves. In summer-autumn produces large, rich, dark red-purple blooms, with white throats heavily streaked and suffused dark red, coalescing into a dark brown-purple patch at the mouth of each flower tube.

***P.* 'Royal White'.** See *P.* 'White Bedder'.

♀ ***P.* 'Rubicundus'** illus. p.251. Erect, semi-evergreen perennial. H 1.2m (4ft), S 60cm (2ft). Frost hardy. Bears very large, bright red flowers each with a white throat. Leaves are linear and light green.

♀ ***P. rupicola.*** Evergreen, prostrate shrub. H 5cm (2in), S 15cm (6in). Frost hardy. Has rounded to oval, fleshy, blue-grey leaves and, in summer, variable, funnel-shaped, pale to deep pink flowers. Is best grown in a rock garden.

♀ ***P.* 'Schoenholzeri'**, syn. *P.* 'Firebird' illus. p.251. Vigorous, semi-evergreen, upright perennial. H 1m (3ft), S 30–45cm (1–1½ft). Frost hardy. Produces racemes of trumpet-shaped, brilliant scarlet flowers from mid-summer to autumn. Lance-shaped to narrowly oval leaves are mid-green.

P. scouleri. See *P. fruticosus* var. *scouleri.*f. ***albus*** see *P. fruticosus* var. *scouleri* f. ***albus.***

P. serrulatus, syn. *P. diffusus*, illus. p.367.

***P.* 'Six Hills'.** Evergreen, prostrate shrub. H 5cm (2in), S 15cm (6in). Frost hardy. Has rounded, fleshy, grey-green leaves. In summer carries funnel-shaped, cool lilac flowers at stem tips. Is suitable for a rock garden.

***P.* 'Snow Storm'.** See *P.* 'White Bedder'.

♀ ***P.* 'Sour Grapes'** illus. p.251. Semi-evergreen perennial. H 90cm (36in), S 60cm (24in). Light green leaves are narrowly lance-shaped. Bears deep purple-blue flowers suffused violet.

***P.* 'Southgate Gem'** illus. p.252. Vigorous, semi-evergreen perennial. H 75cm (30in), S 45cm (18in). Frost hardy. Has lance-shaped, dark green leaves. Produces an abundance of bright rose-red flowers, with white throats sparsely pencilled crimson, in summer-autumn.

♀ ***P.* 'Stapleford Gem'** illus. p.250. Large-leaved, semi-evergreen perennial. H to 60cm (24in), S 45cm (18in). Fully hardy. Bears large, tubular to bell-shaped, lilac-purple flowers from mid-summer to early or mid-autumn; upper lips are pale pink-lilac; lower lips and throats are white with purple lines. Leaves are linear to lance-shaped and mid-green.

***P.* 'Stromboli'** illus. p.250. Vigorous, semi-evergreen perennial. H 60–90cm (2–3ft), S 45–60cm (1½–2ft). Frost hardy. Produces pale creamy-white flowers, with purplish-pink lobes and faintly purple-pink-streaked, white throats, in summer-autumn. Mid-green leaves are lance-shaped to oval.

***P.* 'Torquay Gem'** illus. p.252. Semi-evergreen, woody-based perennial. H 60cm (2ft), S 30–40cm (12–16in). Frost hardy. Has long, lance-shaped, light green leaves. Produces deep rose-red flowers, with a few carmine lines in the white throats, in summer-autumn.

♀ ***P.* 'White Bedder'**, syn. *P.* 'Burford White', *P.* 'Royal White', *P.* 'Snow Storm' (illus p.250). Semi-evergreen, free-flowering perennial. H 70cm (28in), S 60cm (24in). Frost hardy. Has white flowers with dark anthers, and linear, fresh green leaves.

PENTACHONDRA

EPACRIDACEAE

Genus of evergreen, spreading shrubs with heath-like leaves. Frost hardy. Needs full light and gritty, moist, peaty soil. Is difficult to grow, especially in hot, dry areas. Propagate by rooted offsets in spring, by semi-ripe cuttings in summer or by seed in autumn.

P. pumila. Evergreen, mat-forming, dense shrub. H 3–10cm (1¼–4in), S 20cm (8in) or more. Has oblong to narrowly oval, purplish-green leaves. Small, tubular, white flowers, with reflexed lobes, open in early summer, followed, though rarely in cultivation, by small, spherical, orange fruits.

Pentapterygium. See *Agapetes.*

PENTAS

RUBIACEAE

Genus of mainly evergreen perennials and shrubs, grown for their flowers. Frost tender, min. 10–15°C (50–59°F). Needs full light or partial shade and fertile, well-drained soil. Water freely when in full growth, moderately at other times. May be hard pruned in winter. Propagate by softwood cuttings in summer or by seed in spring. Is prone to whitefly.

P. carnea. See *P. lanceolata.*

P. lanceolata, syn. *P. carnea*, illus. p.159.

Peony. See *Paeonia.*
Majorcan. See *Paeonia cambessedesii*, illus. p.239.
Tree. See *Paeonia potaninii.*

PEPEROMIA

PIPERACEAE

Genus of annuals and evergreen perennials, grown for their foliage. Frost tender, min. 10°C (50°F). Grow in full light or partial shade, ideally in a peat-based compost. Do not overwater. Propagate by division, by seed or by leaf or stem cuttings in spring or summer.

♀ ***P. argyreia***, syn. *P. sandersii* (Watermelon plant). Evergreen, bushy, compact perennial. H and S 20cm (8in). Has red-stalked, oval, fleshy, dark green leaves, to 10cm (4in) or more long, striped with broad bands of silver. Flowers are insignificant.

P. caperata illus. p.312.

P. clusiifolia (Baby rubber plant). Evergreen perennial with branching, sometimes prostrate, reddish-green stems. H to 20cm (8in), S 25cm (10in). Narrowly oval, fleshy leaves, 8–15cm (3–6in) long, are dark green, edged with red. Flowers are insignificant. Leaves of **'Variegata'** have cream-and-red margins.

P. glabella illus. p.317.

♀ ***P. griseoargentea***, syn. *P. hederifolia* (Ivy peperomia, Silver-leaf peperomia). Evergreen, bushy perennial. H to 15cm (6in), S 20cm (8in). Oval, fleshy leaves, 5cm (2in) or more long, each have a heart-shaped base, a quilted green surface and a silvery sheen. Flowers are insignificant.

P. hederifolia. See *P. griseoargentea.*

P. magnoliifolia. See *P. obtusifolia.*

P. marmorata illus. p.316.

P. metallica. Evergreen perennial with erect, branching, reddish-green stems. H and S to 15cm (6in). Narrowly oval, dark green leaves, to 2.5cm (1in) long, have a metallic sheen, and wide, pale midribs above, reddish-green veins below. Flowers are insignificant.

P. nummulariifolia. See *P. rotundifolia.*

♀ ***P. obtusifolia***, syn. *P. magnoliifolia* (Pepper face) Evergreen perennial with leathery, dull green leaves. H and S 25cm (10in). Bears spikes of white flowers. **'Green and Gold'** has green leaves with golden-yellow margins. **'Variegata'** illus. p.317.

P. rotundifolia, syn. *P. nummulariifolia.* Evergreen, creeping perennial. H 5–8cm (2–3in), S 30cm (12in) or more. Very slender stems produce tiny, rounded, fleshy, bright green leaves, 1cm (½in) wide. Flowers are insignificant. Is useful for a hanging basket.

P. rubella. Evergreen perennial with erect, branching, red stems. H and S 15cm (6in). Leaves, in whorls of 4, are 1cm (½ in) long, narrowly oval, fleshy and dark green above, crimson below. Flowers are insignificant.

P. sandersii. See *P. argyreia.*

♀ ***P. scandens*** (Cupid peperomia). Evergreen, climbing or trailing perennial with pinkish-green stems. H and S to 1m (3ft). Oval, pointed, fleshy leaves, to 5cm (2in) or more long, are waxy and bright green. Flowers are insignificant.

Peperomia
Cupid. See *Peperomia scandens.*
Ivy. See *Peperomia griseoargentea.*
Silver-leaf. See *Peperomia griseoargentea.*

Pepper
Japan. See *Zanthoxylum piperitum*, illus. p.141.
Mountain. See *Drimys lanceolata*.
Ornamental. See *Capsicum annuum*.
Pepper-bush, Sweet. See *Clethra alnifolia*.
Pepper face. See *Peperomia obtusifolia*.
Peppermint geranium. See *Pelargonium tomentosum*, illus. p.249.
Peppermint tree. See *Agonis flexuosa*, illus. p.86.
Pepper-tree. See *Pseudowintera axillaris*.
Californian. See *Schinus molle*.
Peruvian. See *Schinus molle*.
Père David's maple. See *Acer davidii*.
Perennial pea. See *Lathyrus latifolius*, illus. p.207; *Lathyrus sylvestris*.

PERESKIA

CACTACEAE

Genus of deciduous cacti, some of which are climbing, with fleshy leaves and woody, green, then brown stems. Is considered the most primitive genus of the Cactaceae, producing true leaves unlike most members of the family. Frost tender, min. 5–10°C (41–50°F). Needs sun and well-drained soil. Water moderately in summer. Propagate by stem cuttings in spring or summer.
P. aculeata illus. p.473. **'Godseffiana'** (syn. *P.a.* var. *godseffiana*) is a fast-growing, deciduous, erect, then climbing cactus. H to 10m (30ft), S 5m (15ft). Min. 5°C (41°F). Broadly oval, slightly fleshy, orange-brown leaves, usually purplish beneath and 9cm (3½in) long, mature to glossy, green. Short flower stems, carrying rose-like, single, orange-centred, cream flowers, 5cm (2in) across, appear in autumn only on plants over 1m (3ft) high. Cut back hard to main stems in autumn.
P. grandifolia, syn. *Rhodocactus grandifolius*, illus. p.474.

PERICALLIS

COMPOSITAE/ASTERACEAE

Genus of perennials and sub-shrubs, sometimes grown as annuals, especially for their daisy-like flower heads. Frost tender, min. 5°C (41°F). Requires sun or partial shade and fertile, well-drained soil. Propagate by seed sown from spring to mid-summer.
P. × hybrida, syn. *Cineraria cruentus* of gardens, *C. × hybridus*, *Senecio × hybridus* (Cineraria). H 45–60cm (18–24in), S 25–60cm (10–24in). Slow-growing, evergreen, mound- or dome-shaped perennial. Cultivars are grown as biennials. Half hardy. All have oval, serrated, mid- to deep green leaves. Large, daisy-like, single, semi-double or double flower heads, in shades of blue, red, pink or white, sometimes bicoloured, are produced in winter or spring. **'Brilliant'** has large flower heads in a mixture of white, blue, deep red, copper and rose-pink, and bicolours. **'Royalty'** is late-flowering, with flower heads in sky-blue, cherry-red, lilac with a white eye, and bicolours. **'Spring Glory'** illus. p.344. **'Star Wars'**, H 15cm (6in), S 20cm (8in), is compact, with flower heads in a mixture of white, blue, rose-pink, carmine-red and purple; ideal for small containers.

PERILLA

LABIATAE/LAMIACEAE

Genus of annuals, grown for their foliage. Half hardy. Grow in sun and in fertile, well-drained soil. Pinch out growing tips of young plants to encourage a bushy habit. Propagate by seed sown under glass in early spring.
P. frutescens. Moderately fast-growing, upright, bushy annual. H 60cm (24in), S 30cm (12in). Has oval, serrated, aromatic, reddish-purple leaves. In summer produces spikes of very small, tubular, white flowers.

PERIPLOCA

ASCLEPIADACEAE

Genus of deciduous or evergreen, twining climbers, grown for their leaves. Stems exude milky juice if cut. Frost hardy. Grow in sun and in any well-drained soil. Propagate by seed in spring or by semi-ripe cuttings in summer. The fruits and sap may cause stomach upset if ingested.
P. graeca (Silk vine). Deciduous, twining climber. H to 9m (28ft). Oval, glossy leaves are 2.5–5cm (1–2in) long. In summer has clusters of 8–12 greenish-yellow flowers, purplish-brown inside, each with 5 lobes. Pairs of narrowly cylindrical seed pods, 12cm (5in) long, contain winged, tufted seeds. Scent of the flowers is thought by some to be unpleasant.

PERISTROPHE

ACANTHACEAE

Genus of mainly evergreen perennials and sub-shrubs, grown usually for their flowers. Frost tender, min. 15°C (59°F). Grow in sun or partial shade and in well-drained soil; do not overwater in winter. Propagate by stem cuttings in spring or summer.
P. angustifolia. See *P. hyssopifolia*.
P. hyssopifolia, syn. *P. angustifolia*. Evergreen, bushy perennial. H to 60cm (2ft), S 1–1.2m (3–4ft). Broadly lance-shaped leaves, with long-pointed tips, are 8cm (3in) long. Small clusters of tubular, deep rose-pink flowers are borne in winter. **'Aureovariegata'** illus. p.275.

Periwinkle. See *Vinca*.
Greater. See *Vinca major*.
Lesser. See *Vinca minor*, illus. p.172.
Rose. See *Catharanthus roseus*, illus. p.156.
Pernettya mucronata. See *Gaultheria mucronata*.
Pernettya prostrata. See *Gaultheria myrsinoides*.
Pernettya pumila. See *Gaultheria pumila*.
Pernettya tasmanica. See *Gaultheria tasmanica*.

PEROVSKIA

LABIATAE/LAMIACEAE

Genus of deciduous sub-shrubs, grown for their aromatic, grey-green foliage and blue flowers. Fully hardy. Needs full sun and very well-drained soil. Cut plants back hard, almost to base, in spring, as new growth starts. Propagate by softwood cuttings in late spring.
P. atriplicifolia. Deciduous, upright sub-shrub. H 1.2m (4ft), S 1m (3ft). Grey-white stems bear narrowly oval, coarsely toothed leaves. Bears 2-lipped, violet-blue flowers in long, slender spikes from late summer to mid-autumn.
♀ ***P.*** **'Blue Spire'** illus. p.164.
P. **'Hybrida'.** Deciduous, upright sub-shrub. H 1m (3ft), S 75cm (2½ft). Has oval, deeply lobed and toothed leaves and, from late summer to mid-autumn, tall spires of 2-lipped, deep lavender-blue flowers.

Perry's weeping silver holly. See *Ilex aquifolium* 'Argentea Marginata Pendula', illus. p.94.
Persian buttercup. See *Ranunculus asiaticus*, illus. pp.437 and 439.
Persian everlasting pea. See *Lathyrus rotundifolius*.
Persian ironwood. See *Parrotia persica*, illus. p.78.
Persian ivy. See *Hedera colchica*.
Persian lilac. See *Melia azedarach*, illus. p.72; *Syringa × persica*, illus. p.116.
Persian stone cress. See *Aethionema grandiflorum*, illus. p.364.
Persian violet. See *Exacum affine*, illus. p.343.

PERSICARIA

Knotweed

POLYGONACEAE

Genus of annuals, sometimes invasive perennials and rarely evergreen, semi-evergreen or deciduous sub-shrubs, grown for their autumn leaf colour. Has spikes or panicles of small, usually long-lasting, white, pink or red flowers. Fully to frost hardy. Needs sun or partial shade and moist soil. Propagate by seed in spring. Divide perennials in spring or autumn. Contact with all parts may irritate skin; the sap may cause mild stomach upset if ingested.
P. affinis, syn. *Polygonum affine*. Mat-forming, evergreen perennial. H 15–30cm (6–12in), S 30cm (12in) or more. Fully hardy. Stout stems bear small, lance-shaped, glossy, green leaves that turn red-bronze in winter. From midsummer to mid-autumn carries dense spikes of small, funnel-shaped, rose-red flowers, fading to pale pink. Is good on a bank or in a rock garden. ♀ **'Darjeeling Red'**, H 20–25cm (8–10in), has long spikes of deep red flowers. ♀ **'Donald Lowndes'** illus. p.388.
P. amplexicaulis, syn. *Polygonum amplexicaule*. Clump-forming, leafy perennial. H and S 1.2m (4ft). Fully hardy. Bears profuse spikes of small, rich red flowers in summer-autumn. Has oval to heart-shaped, mid-green leaves. ♀ **'Firetail'** illus. p.253.
P. bistorta, syn. *Polygonum bistorta* (Bistort). ♀ **'Superba'** illus. p.245.
P. campanulata, syn. *Polygonum campanulatum*, illus. p.267.
P. capitata, syn. *Polygonum capitatum*. Compact, spreading perennial. H 5cm (2in), S 15–20cm (6–8in). Frost hardy. Small, oval leaves are green with darker marks. Small, spherical heads of pink flowers are borne in summer. Is suitable for a rock garden or bank.
P. macrophylla, syn. *P. sphaerostachya*, *Polygonum macrophyllum*, *P. sphaerostachyum*, illus. p.289.
P. milletii, syn. *Polygonum milletii*. Compact perennial. H and S 60cm (24in). Fully hardy. Produces slender spikes of rich crimson flowers from mid-summer to early autumn. Narrow, lance-shaped leaves are mid-green.
P. sphaerostachya. See *P. macrophylla*.
♀ ***P. vacciniifolia***, syn. *Polygonum vacciniifolium*, illus. p.399.
P. virginiana **'Painter's Palette'**, syn. *Polygonum virginianum* 'Painter's Palette', *Tovara virginiana* 'Painter's Palette', illus. p.302.

Persimmon. See *Diospyros kaki*.
Chinese. See *Diospyros kaki*.
Peruvian daffodil. See *Hymenocallis narcissiflora*, illus. p.436.
Peruvian mastic tree. See *Schinus molle*.
Peruvian old-man cactus. See *Espostoa lanata*, illus. p.473.
Peruvian pepper-tree. See *Schinus molle*.

PETASITES

COMPOSITAE/ASTERACEAE

Genus of invasive perennials, grown for their usually large leaves and value as ground cover. Fully hardy. Tolerates sun or shade and prefers moist but well-drained soil. Propagate by division in spring or autumn.
P. fragrans (Winter heliotrope). Spreading, invasive perennial. H 23–30cm (9–12in), S 1.2m (4ft). Has rounded to heart-shaped, dark green leaves. Small, vanilla-scented, daisy-like, pinkish-white flower heads are produced in late winter before foliage.
P. japonicus illus. p.284.

PETREA

VERBENACEAE

Genus of evergreen shrubs and woody-stemmed, twining climbers, grown for their flowers. Frost tender, min. 13–15°C (55–9°F). Needs full light and fertile, well-drained soil. Water regularly, less when not in full growth. Provide support. Thin out and spur back crowded growth in spring. Propagate by semi-ripe cuttings in summer. Mealy bug and whitefly may cause problems.
P. volubilis illus. p.202.

PETROCOSMEA

GESNERIACEAE

Genus of evergreen, rhizomatous perennials. Frost tender, min. 2–5°C (36–41°F). Requires shade and well-drained, peaty soil. Propagate by seed in early spring or by leaf cuttings in early summer.
P. kerrii illus. p.386.

Petrophyton. See *Petrophytum*.

PETROPHYTUM, syn. PETROPHYTON

ROSACEAE

Genus of evergreen, summer-flowering shrubs, grown for their spikes of small, fluffy flowers. Is good for growing on tufa or in alpine houses. Fully hardy. Needs sun and gritty, well-drained, alkaline soil. May be difficult to grow. Propagate by softwood or semi-ripe cuttings in summer or by seed in autumn. Aphids and red spider mite may be troublesome in hot weather.

P. caespitosum. Evergreen, mat-forming shrub. H 5–8cm (2–3in), S 10–15cm (4–6in). Has clusters of small, spoon-shaped, silky-hairy, bluish-green leaves. Flower stems, 2cm (¾in) long, each carry a conical spike of small, fluffy, white flowers, with prominent stamens, in summer.

P. hendersonii. Evergreen, mound-forming shrub. H 5–10cm (2–4in), S 10–15cm (4–6in). Has branched stems covered in hairy, rounded, blue-green leaves. Conical spikes of small, cup-shaped, fluffy, white to creamy flowers are produced on 2.5cm (1in) stems in summer.

PETRORHAGIA

CARYOPHYLLACEAE

Genus of annuals and perennials, grown for their flowers. Is suitable for rock gardens and banks. Fully hardy. Prefers sun and well-drained, sandy soil. Propagate by seed in autumn. Self-seeds readily.

♀ ***P. saxifraga***, syn. *Tunica saxifraga* (Tunic flower), illus. p.387. **'Rosette'** is a mat-forming perennial. H 10cm (4in), S 15cm (6in). Has tufts of grass-like leaves. In summer, slender stems carry a profusion of cup-shaped, double, white to pale pink flowers, sometimes veined deeper pink.

PETTERIA

LEGUMINOSAE/PAPILIONACEAE

Genus of one species of deciduous shrub, grown for its flowers. Is related to *Laburnum*, differing in its erect racemes. Fully hardy. Requires full sun and fertile, well-drained soil. Propagate by softwood cuttings in summer or by seed in autumn. The seeds may cause stomach upset if ingested.

P. ramentacea (Dalmatian laburnum). Deciduous, upright shrub. H 2m (6ft), S 1m (3ft). Dense, upright spikes of fragrant, laburnum-like, yellow flowers appear in late spring and early summer. Mid-green leaves are each composed of 3 oval leaflets.

PETUNIA

SOLANACEAE

Genus of annuals and perennials, wholly grown as annuals, with showy, colourful flowers. Half hardy. Grow in a sunny position that is sheltered from wind and in fertile, well-drained soil. Dead-head regularly. Propagate by seed sown under glass in autumn or mid-spring. May suffer from viruses, including cucumber mosaic and tomato spotted wilt.

The many cultivars that have been produced are moderately fast-growing, branching, bushy plants, H 15–30cm (6–12in), S 30cm (12in), with oval, mid- to deep green leaves, usually 5–12cm (2–5in) long. In summer-autumn, they produce flared, trumpet-shaped, single or double flowers in a wide range of colours (available in mixtures or singly), including blue, violet, purple, red, pink and white. Some have dark veining, central white stars, halos (throats in contrasting colours), or picotee margins. The cultivars are divided into 2 groups, Grandiflora and Multiflora petunias.

Grandiflora petunias have very large flowers, 8–10cm (3–4in) wide, but they are easily damaged by rain and are best grown in sheltered hanging baskets and containers.

Multiflora petunias are bushier than the Grandiflora petunias, and produce smaller flowers, 5cm (2in) wide, in greater quantity. They tend to be more resistant to rain damage, and are excellent for summer bedding or for a mixed border.

P. **Aladdin Series.** Grandiflora petunias, illus. p.334.

P. **Carpet Series.** Multiflora petunias, illus. p.340.

P. **Cascade Series.** Grandiflora petunias. H 20–30cm (8–12in), S 30–90cm (12–36in). Trailing stems produce flowers in a wide range of colours.

P. **'Cherry Tart'.** Multiflora petunia. H 5–30cm (6–12in), S 30–60cm (12–24in). Bears double, deep pink-and-white flowers.

P. **'Colour Parade'.** Grandiflora petunia. H 20–30cm (8–12in), S 30–90cm (12–36in). Has a wide colour range of flowers with ruffled petals.

P. **Daddy Series.** Grandiflora petunias. H 35cm (14in), S 30–90cm (12–36in). Bear large, heavily veined flowers in pastel to deep pink, salmon-pink, purple or lavender-blue. **'Sugar Daddy'** illus p.343.

P. **Flash Series.** Compact, Grandiflora petunias. H 23–40cm (9–16in), S 30–90cm (12–36in). Produce flowers in a range of bright colours, including bicolours.

P. **'Gypsy'.** Multiflora petunia. H 5–30cm (6–12in), S 30–60cm (12–24in). Has salmon-red flowers.

P. **Jamboree Series.** Multiflora petunias. H 15–30cm (6–12in), S 30–90cm (12–36in). Produce pendulous stems bearing flowers in a range of colours.

P. **'Magic Cherry'.** Compact, Grandiflora petunia. H 20–30cm (8–12in), S 30–60cm (12–24in). Has cherry-red flowers.

P. **'Mirage Velvet'.** Multiflora petunia, illus. p.338.

P. **Pearl Series.** Dwarf, Multiflora petunias. H 15–20cm (6–8in), S 20–50cm (8–20in). Bear small flowers in a wide range of colours.

P. **Picotee Ruffled Series.** Multiflora petunias. H 15–30cm (6–12in), S 30–90cm (12–36in). Bear ruffled flowers, edged with white, in a range of colours.

P. **Picotee Series.** Grandiflora petunias, illus. p.340. **'Picotee Rose'** illus. p.338.

P. **Plum Crazy Series.** Multiflora petunias. H 15–20cm (6–8in), S 30–90cm (12–36in). Produce flowers that have contrasting veins and throats. Colours available include white, with yellow throat and veins, and shades of violet, pink and magenta, all with darker throats and veins.

P. **Primetime Series.** Multiflora petunias, illus. p.335.

P. **'Razzle Dazzle'.** Grandiflora petunia. H 20–30cm (8–12in), S 30–90cm (12–36in). Has flowers in various colours, striped with white.

P. **Recoverer Series.** Grandiflora petunias, illus. p.330.

P. **'Red Satin'.** Multiflora petunia. H 5–30cm (6–12in), S 30–60cm (12–24in). Has brilliant scarlet flowers.

P. **Resisto Series.** Multiflora petunias, [blue] illus. p.344; [rose-pink] illus. p.337.

♀ ***P.*** **Surfinia Series 'Surfinia Purple'.** Vigorous Grandiflora petunia. H 23–40cm (9–16in), S 30–90cm (12–36in). Bears masses of magenta flowers with purple veining. Has good wet-weather tolerance.

Peyote. See *Lophophora.*

PHACELIA

HYDROPHYLLACEAE

Genus of annuals, biennials and perennials. Fully hardy. Grow in sun and in fertile, well-drained soil. Tall species may need support. Propagate by seed sown outdoors in spring or early autumn. Contact with foliage may aggravate skin allergies.

P. campanularia illus. p.346.

P. tanacetifolia. Moderately fast-growing, upright annual. H 60cm (24in) or more, S 30cm (12in). Has feathery, deep green leaves. In summer, bears spikes of bell-shaped, lavender-blue flowers.

PHAEDRANASSA

AMARYLLIDACEAE

Genus of bulbs with tubular, often pendent flowers. Half hardy. Needs full sun or partial shade and fairly rich, well-drained soil. Feed with high-potash fertilizer in summer. Reduce watering in winter. Propagate by seed or offsets in spring.

P. carmiolii illus. p.412.

Phaedranthus buccinatorius. See *Distictis buccinatoria.*

Phaiophleps biflora. See *Olsynium biflorum.*

PHAIUS

ORCHIDACEAE

See also ORCHIDS.

P. tankervilleae illus. p.309. Semi-evergreen, terrestrial orchid. H 75cm (30in). Frost tender, min. 10°C (55°F). Tall spikes of flowers, 9cm (3½in) across, brown within, silvery-grey outside and each with a long, red-marked, pink lip, open in early summer. Leaves are broadly oval, ribbed and 60cm (24in) long. Provide semi-shade in summer.

PHALAENOPSIS

ORCHIDACEAE

See also ORCHIDS.

P. **Allegria** illus. p.308. Evergreen, epiphytic orchid for a warm greenhouse. H 15cm (6in). Carries sprays of white flowers, to 12cm (5in) across; flowering season varies. Broadly oval, fleshy leaves are 15cm (6in) long. Needs shade in summer.

P. cornu-cervi illus. p.310. Evergreen, epiphytic orchid for a warm greenhouse. H 15cm (6in). Yellowish-green flowers, 5cm (2in) across, with brown marks, are borne successively, either singly or in pairs, in summer. Has broadly oval leaves, 10cm (4in) long. Needs shade in summer.

P. **Lady Jersey × Lippeglut** illus. p.309. Evergreen, epiphytic orchid for a warm greenhouse. H 15cm (6in). Tall, pendent spikes of pink flowers, 9cm (3½in) across, appear at varying times of year. Broadly oval leaves are 10cm (4in) long. Requires shade in summer.

P. **Lundy** illus. p.310. Evergreen, epiphytic orchid for a warm greenhouse. H 15cm (6in). Has sprays of yellow flowers, 8cm (3in) across, with red-stripes; flowering season varies. Broadly oval leaves are 23cm (9in) long. Grow in shade in summer.

PHALARIS

GRAMINEAE/POACEAE

See also GRASSES, BAMBOOS, RUSHES and SEDGES.

♀ ***P. arundinacea*** var. ***picta***, syn. *P.a.* 'Picta', illus. p.318. **'Picta'** see *P.a.* var. *picta*.

Phanerophlebia fortunei. See *Cyrtomium fortunei.*

Pharbitis. See *Ipomoea.*

Phaseolus caracalla. See *Vigna caracalla.*

Pheasant grass. See *Stipa arundinacea.*

Pheasant's eye. See *Narcissus poeticus* var. *recurvus*, illus. p.433.

Phedimus aizoon. See *Sedum aizoon.*

Phedimus kamtschaticus. See *Sedum kamtschaticum.*

Phedimus spurius. See *Sedum spurium.*

PHEGOPTERIS

THELYPTERIDACEAE

Genus of deciduous ferns. Fully hardy. Grow in semi-shade and in humus-rich, moist but well-drained soil. Propagate by division in spring or by spores in summer.

P. connectilis, syn. *Thelypteris phegopteris* (Beech fern). Deciduous fern. H 23cm (9in), S 30cm (12in). Broadly lance-shaped, mid-green fronds, each consisting of tiny, triangular pinnae on wiry stalks, arise from a creeping rootstock. Is useful for ground cover.

PHELLODENDRON

RUTACEAE

Genus of deciduous trees, grown for their foliage, which colours well in autumn. Male and female flowers are produced on different plants. Fully hardy, but young growth is susceptible to damage by late frosts. Needs full sun and fertile, well-drained soil. Does best in hot summers. Propagate by softwood cuttings in summer, by seed in autumn or by root cuttings in late winter.
P. amurense (Amur cork tree). Deciduous, spreading tree. H 12m (40ft), S 15m (50ft). Has corky, dark bark when old. Aromatic leaves, each with 5to 11 oblong leaflets, are glossy, dark green, becoming yellow in autumn. Tiny, green flowers in early summer are followed by small, rounded, black fruits.
P. chinense illus. p.77.

PHILADELPHUS

HYDRANGEACEAE/PHILADELPHACEAE

Genus of deciduous, mainly summer-flowering shrubs, grown for their usually fragrant flowers. Fully to frost hardy. Needs sun and fertile, well-drained soil. After flowering, cut some older shoots back to young growths, leaving young shoots to flower the following year. Propagate by softwood cuttings in summer. May become infested with aphids.
♀ ***P.* 'Beauclerk'** illus. p.131.
♀ ***P.* 'Belle Etoile'** illus. p.132.
***P.* 'Boule d'Argent'** illus. p.133.
P. coronarius (Mock orange).
♀ **'Aureus'** is a deciduous, upright shrub. H 2.5m (8ft), S 1.5m (5ft). Fully hardy. Clusters of very fragrant, 4-petalled, creamy-white flowers are produced in late spring and early summer. Oval, golden-yellow, young leaves turn yellow-green in summer. Protect from full sun. ♀ **'Variegatus'** illus. p.135.
***P.* 'Dame Blanche'** illus. p.133.
P. delavayi. Deciduous, upright shrub. H 3m (10ft), S 2.5m (8ft). Frost hardy. Dense clusters of very fragrant, 4-petalled, white flowers, with sometimes purple-flushed, green sepals, open from early to mid-summer. Leaves are dark green, oval and toothed. f. ***melanocalyx*** (syn. *P. purpurascens*) illus. p.135.
P. × lemoinei. See *P.* 'Lemoinei'.
***P.* 'Lemoinei'**, syn. *P. × lemoinei*, illus. p.134.
P. magdalenae. Deciduous, bushy shrub. H and S 4m (12ft). Fully hardy. Bark peels on older shoots. Narrowly oval, dark green leaves set off fragrant, 4-petalled, white flowers in late spring and early summer.
♀ ***P.* 'Manteau d' Hermine'** illus. p.154.
P. purpurascens. See *P. delavayi* f. *melanocalyx*.
♀ ***P.* 'Sybille'.** Deciduous, arching shrub. H 1.2m (4ft), S 2m (6ft). Fully hardy. Bears fragrant, 4-petalled, white flowers, each with a central, pink stain, profusely in early and mid-summer. Leaves are mid-green and oval.
***P.* 'Virginal'.** Vigorous, deciduous, upright shrub. H 3m (10ft), S 2.5m (8ft). Fully hardy. Has oval, dark green leaves. Produces masses of large, very fragrant, double or semi-double, pure white flowers in loose racemes from early to mid-summer.

× PHILAGERIA

LILIACEAE/PHILESIACEAE

Hybrid genus (*Philesia × Lapageria*) of one evergreen, scrambling or twining shrub. Frost tender, min. 5°C (41°F). Grow in semi-shade and in well-drained, preferably acid soil. Propagate by layering in late summer or autumn.
× *P. veitchii.* Evergreen, scrambling or twining shrub. H 3–4m (10–12ft). Has oblong, slightly toothed leaves. Nodding, tubular, rose-pink flowers are produced in leaf axils in summer.

PHILESIA

LILIACEAE/PHILESIACEAE

Genus of one species of evergreen shrub, grown for its showy flowers. Frost hardy, but thrives only in mild, moist areas. Needs semi-shade and humus-rich, moist, acid soil. Benefits from an annual dressing of leaf mould. Propagate by semi-ripe cuttings in summer or by suckers in autumn.
P. magellanica. Evergreen, erect shrub. H m (3ft), S 2m (6ft). Bears trumpet-shaped, waxy, crimson-pink flowers, in leaf axils, from mid-summer to late autumn. Narrowly oblong, dark green leaves are bluish-white beneath.

Philippine violet. See *Barleria cristata.*

PHILLYREA

OLEACEAE

Genus of evergreen shrubs and trees, with inconspicuous flowers, grown for their foliage. Frost hardy, but in cold areas requires shelter. Does best in full sun and in fertile, well-drained soil. To restrict growth, cut back in spring. Propagate by semi-ripe cuttings in summer.
P. angustifolia. Evergreen, bushy, dense shrub. H and S 3m (10ft). Leaves are narrowly oblong and dark green. Small, fragrant, 4-lobed, greenish-white flowers in late spring and early summer are followed by spherical, blue-black fruits.
P. decora. See *Osmanthus decorus.*
P. latifolia. Evergreen, rounded shrub or tree. H and S 8m (25ft). Has oval, glossy, dark green leaves. Bears tiny, fragrant, 4-lobed, greenish-white flowers from late spring to early summer, then spherical, blue-black fruits.

PHILODENDRON

ARACEAE

Genus of evergreen shrubs and woody-based, root climbers, grown for their handsome leaves. Intermittently bears insignificant flowers. Frost tender, min. 15–18°C (59–64°F). Needs partial shade and humus-rich, well-drained soil. Water moderately, sparingly in cold weather. Provide support. Young stem tips may be removed to promote branching. Propagate by leaf-bud or stem-tip cuttings in summer. All parts may cause severe discomfort if ingested; contact with sap may irritate skin.
P. auritum of gardens. See *Syngonium auritum.*
♀ ***P. bipinnatifidum***, syn. *P. selloum* (Tree philodendron; illus. p.148). Tree-like shrub with a single, erect stem and very long-stalked leaves.
♀ ***P.* 'Burgundy'.** Slow-growing, evergreen, woody-based, root climber. H 2m (6ft) or more. Leaves are narrowly oblong, red-flushed, deep green above, wine-red beneath, and up to 30cm (12in) long.
P. cordatum. See *P. hederaceum.*
P. domesticum, syn. *P. hastatum* of gardens (Elephant's ear, Spade leaf). Fairly slow-growing, evergreen, woody-based, root climber. H 2–3m (6–10ft). Lustrous, bright green leaves, 30–40cm (12–16in) long, are arrow-shaped on young plants and later have prominent, basal lobes.
♀ ***P. erubescens*** (Blushing philodendron). Evergreen, erect, woody-based, root climber. H to 3m (10ft). Oval to triangular leaves, 15–25cm (6–10in) long, have long, red stalks and are dark green with a lustrous, coppery flush.
P. hastatum of gardens. See *P. domesticum.*
P. hederaceum, syn. *H. cordatum* (Heart leaf). Moderately vigorous, evergreen, woody-based, root climber. H 3m (10ft) or more. Has heart-shaped, lustrous, rich green leaves, to 45cm (18in) long.
P. laciniatum. See *P. pedatum.*
P. melanochrysum illus. p.218.
P. pedatum, syn. *P. laciniatum.* Slow-growing, evergreen, woody-based, root climber. H 2–3m (6–10ft). Has oval, lustrous, deep green leaves, 30–80cm (12–32in) long, cut into 5 or 7 prominent lobes.
P. sagittatum. See *P. sagittifolium.*
P. sagittifolium, syn. *P. sagittatum.* Slow-growing, evergreen, woody-based, root climber. H 2–3m (6–10ft). Oval leaves with basal lobes are up to 40–60cm (16–24in) long and glossy, bright green.
♀ ***P. scandens*** illus. p.218.
P. selloum. See *P. bipinnatifidum.*
P. trifoliatum. See *Syngonium auritum.*

Philodendron, Blushing. See *Philodendron erubescens.*

PHLEBODIUM

POLYPODIACEAE

Genus of evergreen or semi-evergreen ferns. Frost tender, min. 5°C (41°F). Needs full light or semi-shade and humus-rich, moist but well-drained soil. Remove fading fronds regularly. Propagate by division in spring or by spores in summer.
♀ ***P. aureum***, syn. *Polypodium aureum*, illus. p.323. **'Mandaianum'** illus. p.322.

PHLOMIS

LABIATAE/LAMIACEAE

Genus of evergreen, summer-flowering shrubs and perennials, grown for their conspicuous, hooded flowers, which are borne in dense whorls, and for their foliage. Fully to frost hardy. Prefers full sun and well-drained soil. Propagate by seed in autumn; increase shrubs from softwood cuttings in summer, perennials by division in spring.
P. cashmeriana. Evergreen, upright shrub. H 60cm (24in), S 45cm (18in). Frost hardy. Produces masses of 2-lipped, pale lilac flowers in summer. Narrowly oval, mid-green leaves have woolly, white undersides.
♀ ***P. chrysophylla.*** Evergreen, rounded, stiffly branched shrub. H and S 1m (3ft). Frost hardy. Bears 2-lipped, golden-yellow flowers in early summer. Oval leaves are grey-green when young, becoming golden-green.
♀ ***P. fruticosa*** illus. p.166.
P. italica illus. p.158.
P. longifolia var. ***bailanica.*** Evergreen, bushy shrub. H 1.2m (4ft), S 1m (3ft). Frost hardy. Leaves are oblong to heart-shaped, deeply veined and bright green. Has 2-lipped, deep yellow flowers from early to mid-summer.
♀ ***P. russeliana*** illus. p.261.

PHLOX

POLEMONIACEAE

Genus of mainly late spring- or summer-flowering annuals and perennials, some of which are semi-evergreen or evergreen, grown for their terminal panicles or profusion of brightly coloured flowers. Fully to half hardy. Does best in sun or semi-shade and in fertile, moist but well-drained soil; some species prefer acid soil; in light, dry soils is better grown in partial shade. Trim back rock garden species after flowering. Propagate rock garden species and hybrids by cuttings from non-flowering shoots in spring or summer; species by seed in autumn or spring; *P. maculata*, *P. paniculata* and their cultivars also by division in early spring or by root cuttings in winter; and annuals by seed in spring. *P. maculata*, *P. paniculata* and their cultivars are susceptible to eelworm. See also feature panel p.244.
♀ ***P. adsurgens.*** Evergreen, mat-forming, prostrate perennial. H 10cm (4in), S 30cm (12in). Fully hardy. Woody-based stems are clothed in oval, light to mid-green leaves. In summer produces terminal clusters of short-stemmed, saucer-shaped, purple, pink or white flowers with overlapping petals. Is good for a rock garden or peat bed. Prefers partial shade and gritty, peaty, acid soil. **'Wagon Wheel'** illus. p.388.
***P. amoena* 'Variegata'.** See *P. × procumbens* 'Variegata'.
P. bifida illus. p.393.
P. caespitosa. Evergreen, mound-forming, compact perennial. H 8cm (3in), S 12cm (5in). Fully hardy. Leaves are narrow and needle-like. Solitary almost stemless, saucer-shaped, lilac or white flowers are borne in summer. Suits a rock garden or trough. Needs sun and very well-drained soil.
***P.* 'Camla'** illus. p.391.
***P.* 'Chatahoochee'.** See *P. divaricata* subsp. *laphamii* 'Chatahoochee'.
♀ ***P. divaricata.*** Semi-evergreen, creeping perennial. H 30cm (12in) or more, S 20cm (8in). Fully hardy. In early summer, upright stems carry saucer-shaped, lavender-blue flowers in loose clusters. Leaves are oval. Suits a rock garden or peat bed. Prefers semi-

shade and moist but well-drained, peaty soil. subsp. ***laphamii*** illus. p.368. ♀ subsp. ***laphamii*** **'Chatahoochee'** (syn. *P.* 'Chatahoochee') illus. p.368.
♀ ***P. douglasii*** **'Boothman's Variety'** illus. p.392. ♀ **'Crackerjack'** illus. p.391. **'May Snow'** is an evergreen, mound-forming perennial. H 8cm (3in), S 20cm (8in). Fully hardy. Masses of saucer-shaped, white flowers are carried in early summer. Leaves are lance-shaped and mid-green. Is suitable for a rock garden, wall or bank. Vigorous, compact ♀ **'Red Admiral'**, H 5cm (6in), has crimson flowers.
P. drummondii (Annual phlox). **Beauty Series** is a group of moderately fast-growing, compact, upright annuals. H 5cm (6in), S 10cm (4in). Half hardy. Has lance-shaped, pale green leaves and, from summer to early autumn, heads of star-shaped flowers in many colours, including red, pink, blue, purple and white. **Buttons Series** illus. p.339.**'Carnival'** has larger flowers with contrasting centres. **'Chanal'** illus. p.338. **'Petticoat'** has bicoloured flowers. **'Sternenzauber'** (syn. *P.d.* 'Twinkle') illus. p.338. **'Twinkle'** see *P.d.* 'Sternenzauber'.
P. **'Emerald Cushion'** illus. p.393.
P. hoodii. Evergreen, compact, prostrate perennial. H 5cm (2in), S 10cm (4in). Fully hardy. Solitary, flat, white flowers open in early summer above fine, needle-like, hairy leaves. Suits a rock garden. Needs sun and very well-drained soil.
P. maculata. Erect perennial. H 1m (3ft), S 45cm (1½ft). Fully hardy. In summer produces cylindrical panicles of tubular, 5-lobed, mauve-pink flowers above oval, mid-green leaves.♀ **'Alpha'** (illus. p.244) has rose-pink flowers.♀ **'Omega'** (illus. p.244) has white flowers, each with a lilac eye.
P. paniculata. Upright perennial, seldom grown, as is replaced in gardens by its more colourful cultivars. H 1.2m (4ft), S 60cm (2ft). Fully hardy. Tubular, 5-lobed flowers are borne in conical heads above oval, mid-green leaves in late summer. **'Aida'** is purple-red, each flower with a purple eye. Flowers of **'Amethyst'** (illus. p.244) are pale lilac with paler-edged petals. **'Balmoral'** (illus. p.244) has large, rosy-mauve flowers. ♀ **'Brigadier'** (illus. p.244) has deep orange-red flowers. ♀ **'Bright Eyes'** has pale pink flowers, each with a red eye. **'Eva Cullum'** (illus. p.244) has clear pink flowers with magenta eyes.
♀ **'Eventide'** (illus. p.244) produces lavender-blue flowers. ♀ **'Fujiyama'** (illus. p.244) has star-shaped, white flowers. Flowers of **'Graf Zeppelin'** (illus. p.244) are white with red centres. **'Hampton Court'** (illus. p.244) is a mauve-blue cultivar, with dark green foliage. **'Harlequin'** (illus. p.244) has reddish-purple flowers. Leaves are variegated ivory-white. ♀ **'Le Mahdi'** (illus. p.244) has deep purple flowers. **'Mia Ruys'** (illus. p.244), H 45cm (18in), has large, white flowers, and is shorter than most other cultivars.
♀ **'Mother of Pearl'** (illus. p.244) has white flowers tinted pink. **'Norah Leigh'** (illus. p.244) has pale lilac flowers and ivory-variegated leaves.
♀ **'Prince of Orange'** (illus. p.244) is orange-red. **'Russian Violet'** is of open habit and has pale lilac-blue flowers. Flowers of **'Sandringham'** (illus. p.244) have widely spaced petals and are pink with darker centres. **'Sir John Falstaff'** has large, deep salmon flowers, each with a cherry-red eye.
♀ **'White Admiral'** (illus. p.244) bears pure white flowers. Those of
♀ **'Windsor'** (illus. p.244) are carmine-rose with red eyes.
♀ ***P.* × *procumbens*** **'Millstream'.** Evergreen, prostrate perennial. H to 15cm (6in), S 30cm (12in). Fully hardy. Has narrowly oval, glossy, green leaves. In early summer produces small, saucer-shaped, deep lavender-pink flowers with white eyes. Is suitable for a rock garden. **'Variegata'** (syn. *P. amoena* 'Variegata'), H 2.5cm (1in), S 25cm (10in), has white-margined leaves and bright cerise-pink flowers.
P. stolonifera (Creeping phlox). Evergreen, prostrate, spreading perennial. H 10–15cm (4–6in), S 30cm (12in) or more. Fully hardy. Has small, saucer-shaped, pale blue flowers in early summer. Leaves are oblong to oval. Prefers moist, peaty, acid soil; is good for a peat bed or rock garden. **'Ariane'** illus. p.385. ♀ **'Blue Ridge'** has masses of lavender-blue flowers.
P. subulata. Evergreen, mound-forming perennial. H 10cm (4in), S 20cm (8in). Fully hardy. Bears fine, needle-like leaves. Masses of star-shaped, white, pink or mauve flowers appear in early summer. Is good for a sunny rock garden. **'Marjorie'** illus. p.390.

Phlox
Annual. See *Phlox drummondii.*
Creeping. See *Phlox stolonifera.*
Sand. See *Phlox bifida*, illus. p.393.

PHOENIX

PALMAE/ARECACEAE

Genus of evergreen palms, grown for their overall appearance and their edible fruits. Frost tender, min. 10–15°C (50–59°F). Grows in full light, though tolerates partial shade, in any fertile, well-drained soil. Water potted specimens moderately, less during winter. Propagate by seed in spring at not less than 24°C (75°F). Red spider mite may be a nuisance.
♀ ***P. canariensis*** (Canary Island date palm). Evergreen, upright palm with a robust trunk. H 18m (60ft) or more, S 10m (30ft) or more. Min. 10°C (50°F). Feather-shaped, arching leaves, each to 5m (15ft) long, are divided into narrowly lance-shaped, leathery, bright green leaflets. Bears large, pendent clusters of tiny, yellowish-brown flowers that on mature specimens are followed by shortly oblong, yellow to red fruits in autumn-winter.
♀ ***P. roebelenii*** (Miniature date palm, Pygmy date palm). Evergreen palm with a slender trunk. H 2–4m (6–12ft), S 1–2m (3–6ft). Min. 15°C (59°F). Has feather-shaped, arching, glossy, dark green leaves, 1–1.2m (3–4ft) long, and, in summer, large panicles of tiny, yellow flowers. Egg-shaped, black fruits are borne in pendent clusters, 45cm (18in) long, in autumn.

PHORMIUM
New Zealand flax

AGAVACEAE/PHORMIACEAE

Genus of evergreen perennials, grown for their bold, sword-shaped leaves. Frost hardy. Requires sun and moist but well-drained soil. Propagate by division or seed in spring.
P. **'Bronze Baby'** illus. p.314.
P. colensoi. See *P. cookianum.*
P. cookianum, syn. *P. colensoi* (Mountain flax). Evergreen, upright perennial. H 1–2m (3–6ft), S 30cm (1ft). Has tufts of sword-shaped, dark green leaves. Panicles of tubular, pale yellowish-green flowers are borne in summer. ♀ subsp. ***hookeri*** **'Tricolor'** has leaves striped vertically with red, yellow and green. **'Variegatum'** has cream-striped leaves.
P. **'Dazzler'** illus. p.272.
♀ ***P. tenax.*** Evergreen, upright perennial. H 3m (10ft), S 1–2m (3–6ft). Has tufts of sword-shaped, stiff, dark green leaves. Panicles of tubular, dull red flowers are produced on short, slightly glaucous green stems in summer. Thrives by the sea. **'Aurora'** has leaves vertically striped with red, bronze, salmon-pink and yellow.
♀ **Purpureum Group** illus. p.232. **'Veitchianum'** (syn. *P.t.* 'Veitchii') bears broad, creamy-white-striped leaves. **'Veitchii'** see *P.t.* 'Veitchianum'.

PHOTINIA,
syn. STRANVAESIA

ROSACEAE

Genus of evergreen or deciduous shrubs and trees, with small, white flowers, grown for their foliage and, in the case of deciduous species, for their autumn colour and fruits. Fully to frost hardy, but protect evergreen species from strong, cold winds. Requires sun or semi-shade and fertile, well-drained soil; some species prefer acid soil. Propagate evergreen and deciduous species by semi-ripe cuttings in summer, deciduous species also by seed in autumn.
P. arbutifolia. See *Heteromeles salicifolia.*
P. davidiana illus. p.90.
P.* × *fraseri. Group of evergreen, hybrid shrubs. Frost hardy. Has good resistance to damage by late frosts. Leaves are bold and oblong. Young growths are attractive over a long period. **'Birmingham'** illus. p.113.
♀ **'Red Robin'** is upright and dense. H 6m (20ft), S 4m (12ft). Glossy, dark green leaves are brilliant red when young. Bears 5-petalled flowers in late spring.
P. nussia. Evergreen, spreading tree. H and S 6m (20ft). Frost hardy. Produces oblong, leathery, glossy, dark green leaves and saucer-shaped, 5-petalled, white flowers in mid-summer, followed by rounded, orange-red fruits.
P. serratifolia, syn. *P. serrulata.* Evergreen, upright shrub or bushy-headed tree. H 10m (30ft), S 8m (25ft). Frost hardy. Oblong, often sharply toothed leaves are red when young, maturing to glossy, dark green. Small, 5-petalled flowers from mid- to late spring are sometimes followed by spherical, red fruits. Young growth may be damaged by late frosts.
P. serrulata. See *P. serratifolia.*
♀ ***P. villosa.*** Deciduous, upright shrub or spreading tree. H and S 5m (15ft). Fully hardy. Oval, dark green leaves, bronze-margined when young, become brilliant orange-red in autumn. Clusters of 5-petalled flowers, produced in late spring, are followed by spherical, red fruits. Prefers acid soil.

PHRAGMIPEDIUM

ORCHIDACEAE

See also ORCHIDS.
P. caudatum. Evergreen, epiphytic orchid for an intermediate greenhouse. H 3cm (9in). In summer produces sprays of flowers with light green and tan sepals and pouches and drooping, ribbon-like, yellow and brownish-crimson petals, to 30cm (12in) long. Has narrowly oval leaves, 30cm (12in) long. Needs shade in summer.

PHUOPSIS

RUBIACEAE

Genus of one species of mat-forming, summer-flowering perennial, grown for its small, pungent, tubular flowers. Is good for ground cover, especially on banks and in rock gardens. Fully hardy. Needs sun and well-drained soil. Propagate by division in spring, by semi-ripe cuttings in summer or by seed in autumn.
P. stylosa, syn. *Crucianella stylosa*, illus. p.364.

PHYGELIUS

SCROPHULARIACEAE

Genus of evergreen or semi-evergreen shrubs and sub-shrubs, grown for their showy, tubular flowers. Frost hardy, but in most areas plant in a sheltered position; will attain a considerably greater height when grown against a south- or west-facing wall. Needs sun and fertile, well-drained but not too dry soil. Usually loses leaves or has shoots cut to ground by frosts. Cut back to just above ground level in spring, or, if plants have woody bases, prune to live wood. Propagate by softwood cuttings in summer.
P. aequalis illus. p.162. ♀ **'Yellow Trumpet'** illus. p.165.
♀ ***P. capensis***, syn. *P.c.* 'Coccineus'. Evergreen or semi-evergreen, upright sub-shrub. H 1.5m (5ft), S 2m (6ft). Tubular, curved, bright orange-red flowers, each with a red mouth and a yellow throat, are produced from mid-summer to early autumn in tall, slender spires amid triangular, dark green leaves.
P.* × *rectus **'Winchester Fanfare'.** Evergreen or semi-evergreen, upright sub-shrub. H 1.5m (5ft), S 2m (6ft). Has pendulous, tubular, dusky, reddish-pink flowers, each with scarlet lobes and a yellow throat, from mid-summer to early autumn, and triangular, dark green leaves.

Phyllanthus nivosus. See *Breynia disticha.*

× Phylliopsis

ERICACEAE

Hybrid genus *(Phyllodoce* × *Kalmiopsis)* of one species ofevergreen shrub, grown for its flowers.Is suitable for peat beds and rock gardens. Fully hardy. Needs partial shade and peaty, acid soil. Trim back after flowering to maintain a compact habit. Propagate by semi-ripe cuttings in late summer.
× *P. hillieri* 'Pinocchio'. Evergreen, upright shrub. H 20cm (8in), S 25cm (10in). Branched stems bear thin, oval leaves. Long, open clusters of bell-shaped, very deep pink flowers appear in spring and intermittently thereafter.

Phyllitis scolopendrium. See *Asplenium scolopendrium.*
***Phyllitis scolopendrium* 'Marginatum'.** See *Asplenium scolopendrium* Marginatum Group.

Phyllocladus

PHYLLOCLADACEAE

See also CONIFERS.
P. aspleniifolius (Tasman celery pine). Slow-growing, upright conifer. H 5–10m (15–30ft), S 3–5m (10–15ft). Half hardy. Instead of true leaves has flattened, leaf-like shoots known as phylloclades; these are dull dark green and resemble celery leaves in outline. Produces inedible, white-coated nuts with fleshy, red bases.
P. trichomanoides illus. p.102.

Phyllodoce

ERICACEAE

Genus of evergreen shrubs, grown for their heath-like leaves and attractive flowers. Fully to frost hardy. Needs semi-shade and moist, peaty, acid soil. Propagate by semi-ripe cuttings in late summer or by seed in spring.
♀ ***P. caerulea***, syn. *P. taxifolia*, illus. p.360.
P. empetriformis illus. p.360.
***P. × intermedia* 'Drummondii'** illus. p.359. **'Fred Stoker'** is an evergreen, upright shrub. H and S 23cm (9in). Fully hardy. Has narrow, glossy, green leaves. From late spring to early summer carries terminal clusters of pitcher-shaped, bright reddish-purple flowers on slender, red stalks.
♀ ***P. nipponica.*** Evergreen, upright shrub. H 10–20cm (4–8in), S 10–15cm (4–6in). Frost hardy. Freely branched stems bear fine, linear leaves and, in late spring and summer, stalked, bell-shaped, white flowers from their tips.
P. taxifolia. See *P. caerulea.*

Phyllostachys

GRAMINEAE/POACEAE

See also GRASSES, BAMBOOS, RUSHES and SEDGES.
♀ ***P. aurea*** (Fishpole bamboo, Golden bamboo). Evergreen, clump-forming bamboo. H 6–8m (20–25ft), S indefinite. Frost hardy. Erect, grooved stems have cup-shaped swellings beneath most nodes, which, towards the base, are often close together and distorted. Bears mid-green leaves. Flowers are unimportant as they are so rarely produced.
P. aureosulcata (Golden-groove bamboo). Evergreen, clump-forming bamboo. H 6–8m (20–25ft), S indefinite. Frost hardy. Bears striped sheaths and yellow grooves on rough, brownish-green stems. Mid-green leaves are up to 15cm (6in) long; flowers are unimportant as they are so rarely produced.
P. bambusoides illus. p.320.
P. flexuosa illus. p.320.
***P.* 'Henonis'.** See *P. nigra* f. *henonis.*
♀ ***P. nigra*** (Black bamboo). Evergreen, clump-forming bamboo. H 6–8m (20–25ft), S indefinite. Frost hardy. Grooved, greenish-brown stems turn black in second season. Almost unmarked culm sheaths bear bristled auricles and mid-green leaves. Flowers are unimportant as they are so rarely produced. ♀ f. ***henonis*** (syn. *P.* 'Henonis') illus. p.320.
P. viridiglaucescens illus. p.321.

× Phyllothamnus

ERICACEAE

Hybrid genus (*Phyllodoce* × *Rhodothamnus*) of one species of evergreen shrub, grown for its foliage and flowers. Is good for peat beds and rock gardens. Fully hardy. Needs a sheltered, semi-shaded site and moist, acid soil. Propagate by semi-ripe cuttings in late summer.
× *P. erectus.* Evergreen, upright shrub. H and S 15cm (6in). Has small, linear, glossy, deep green leaves. Clusters of slender-stalked, bell-shaped, soft rose-pink flowers are produced in late spring and early summer.

Physalis

Chinese lantern

SOLANACEAE

Genus of summer-flowering perennials and annuals, grown mainly for their decorative, lantern-like calyces and fruits, produced in autumn. Fully to half hardy. Grows in sun or shade and in well-drained soil. Propagate by division or softwood cuttings in spring, annuals by seed in spring or autumn. All parts of *P. alkekengi*, except the fully ripe fruit, may cause mild stomach upset if ingested; contact with foliage may irritate skin.
♀ ***P. alkekengi*** (Bladder cherry, Winter cherry). Spreading perennial, grown as an annual. H 45cm (18in), S 60cm (24in). Fully hardy. Inconspicuous, nodding, star-shaped, white flowers in summer are followed, in autumn, by rounded, bright orange-red fruits, surrounded by inflated, orange calyces. Leaves are mid-green and oval.

Physocarpus

ROSACEAE

Genus of deciduous, mainly summer-flowering shrubs, grown for their foliage and flowers. Fully hardy. Requires sun and fertile, not too dry soil. Prefers acid soil and does not grow well on shallow, chalky soil. Thin established plants occasionally by cutting some older shoots back to ground level after flowering. Propagate by softwood cuttings in summer.
P. opulifolius (Ninebark). Deciduous, arching, dense shrub. H 3m (10ft), S 5m (15ft). Has peeling bark and broadly oval, toothed and lobed, mid-green leaves. Clusters of tiny, sometimes pink-tinged, white flowers are borne in early summer. ♀ **'Dart's Gold'** illus. p.142.

Physoplexis

CAMPANULACEAE

Genus of one species of tufted perennial, grown for its flowers. Is good grown on tufa, in rock gardens, troughs and alpine houses. Fully hardy. Needs sun and very well-drained, alkaline soil, but should face away from midday sun. Keep fairly dry in winter. Propagate by seed in autumn or by softwood cuttings in early summer. Is susceptible to slug damage.
♀ ***P. comosa***, syn. *Phyteuma comosum*, illus. p.392.

Physostegia

Obedient plant

LABIATAE/LAMIACEAE

Genus of summer- to early autumn-flowering perennials. Fully hardy. Needs sun and fertile, moist but well-drained soil. Propagate by division in spring.
P. virginiana. Erect perennial. H 1m (3ft), S 60cm (2ft). In late summer produces spikes of hooded, 2-lipped, rose-purple flowers with hinged stalks that allow flowers to remain in position once moved. Has lance-shaped, toothed, mid-green leaves. subsp. ***speciosa* 'Variegata'** see *P.v.* 'Variegata'. ♀ **'Summer Snow'** has pure white flowers. **'Variegata'** (syn. *P.v.* subsp. *speciosa* 'Variegata') illus. p.246. ♀ **'Vivid'** illus. p.289.

Phyteuma

CAMPANULACEAE

Genus of early- to mid-summer-flowering perennials that are useful for rock gardens. Fully hardy. Needs sun and well-drained soil. Propagate by seed in autumn.
P. comosum. See *Physoplexis comosa.*
P. scheuchzeri illus. p.369.

Phytolacca

PHYTOLACCACEAE

Genus of perennials and evergreen shrubs and trees, grown for their overall appearance and decorative but poisonous fruits. Fully hardy to frost tender, min. 5°C (41°F). Tolerates sun or shade and requires fertile, moist soil. Propagate by seed in autumn or spring. All parts may cause severe discomfort if ingested; the fruit of *P. americana* may be lethal if eaten. Contact with the sap may irritate skin.
P. americana, syn. *P. decandra* (Red-ink plant, Virginian pokeweed). Upright, spreading perennial. H and S 1.2–1.5m (4–5ft). Fully hardy. Oval to lance-shaped, mid-green leaves are tinged purple in autumn. Shallowly cup-shaped, sometimes pink-flushed, white-and-green flowers, borne in terminal racemes in summer, are followed by poisonous, rounded, fleshy, blackish-purple berries.
P. clavigera. See *P. polyandra.*
P. decandra. See *P. americana.*
P. polyandra, syn. *P. clavigera.* Stout, upright perennial. H and S 1.2m (4ft). Fully hardy. Has brilliant crimson stems, oval to lance-shaped, mid-green leaves that turn yellow in autumn. In summer bears clusters of shallowly cup-shaped, pink flowers, followed by poisonous, blackish-purple berries.

Piccabeen palm. See *Archontophoenix cunninghamiana.*

Picea

Spruce

PINACEAE

Genus of conifers with needle-like leaves set on a pronounced peg on the shoots and arranged spirally. Cones are pendulous and ripen in their first autumn; scales are woody and flexible. See also CONIFERS.
P. abies (Common spruce, Norway spruce; illus. p.100). Fast-growing conifer, narrowly conical when young, broader with age. H 20–30m (70–100ft), S 5–7m (15–22ft). Fully hardy. Has needle-like, dark green leaves and bears pendulous cones. **'Clanbrassiliana'**, H 5m (15ft), S 3–5m (10–15ft), is slow-growing, rounded and spreading. **'Gregoryana'** (illus. p.107), H and S 60cm (2ft), is slow-growing, with a dense, globose form. **'Inversa'**, H 5–10m (15–30ft), S 2m (6ft), has an erect leader, but pendent side branches. ♀ **'Little Gem'**, H and S 30–50cm (12–20in), has a nest-shaped, central depression caused by spreading branches.
♀ **'Nidiformis'**, H 1m (3ft), S 1–2m (3–6ft), is larger and faster-growing.**'Ohlendorffii'** (illus. p.106), H andS 1m (3ft), is slow-growing, initiallyrounded, becoming conical with age.**'Reflexa'** (illus. p.106), H 30cm (1ft),S 5m (15ft), is prostrate and ground-hugging, but may be trained up a stake,to form a mound of weeping foliage.
♀ ***P. breweriana*** illus. p.101.
P. engelmannii illus. p.101.
P. glauca (White spruce). Narrowly conical conifer. H 10–15m (30–50ft), S 4–5m (12–15ft). Fully hardy. Glaucous shoots produce blue-green leaves. Ovoid, light brown cones fall after ripening. var. ***albertiana* 'Conica'** (syn. *P.g.* 'Albertiana Conica'; illus. p.107), H 2–5m (6–15ft), S 1–2m (3–6ft), is of neat, pyramidal habit and slow-growing, with longer leaves and smaller cones. **'Albertiana Conica'** see *P.g.* var. *albertiana* 'Conica'.**'Coerulea'** illus. p.101. ♀ **'Echiniformis'**, H 50cm (20in), S 90cm (36in), is a dwarf, flat-topped, rounded form.
P. likiangensis (Lijiang spruce). Upright conifer. H 15m (50ft), S 5–10m (15–30ft). Fully hardy. Bluish-white leaves are well-spaced. Cones, 8–15cm (3–6in) long, are cylindrical, females bright red when young, ripening to purple, males pink.
P. mariana (Black spruce). Conical conifer, whose lowest branches often layer naturally, forming a ring of stems around the parent plant. H 10–15m (30–50ft), S 3m (10ft). Fully hardy. Leaves are bluish-green or bluish-white. Oval cones are dark grey-brown.

'Doumetii' illus. p.104. 🏆 **'Nana'** (illus. p.106), H 50cm (20in), S 50–80cm (20–32in), is a neat shrub with blue-grey foliage.
***P.* × *mariorika* 'Gnom'**, syn. *P. omorika* 'Gnom' (illus. p.99), is a shrub-like conifer with pendent branches arching at tips. H to 1.5m (5ft), S 1–2m (3–6ft). Fully hardy. Dark green leaves are white beneath.
P. morrisonicola illus. p.103.
🏆 ***P. omorika*** illus. p.103. **'Gnom'** see *P.* × *mariorika* 'Gnom'. 🏆 **'Nana'**, H and S 1m (3ft), is a slow-growing, rounded or oval cultivar.
🏆 ***P. orientalis*** (Caucasian spruce, Oriental spruce). Columnar, dense conifer. H 20m (70ft), S 5m (15ft). Fully hardy. Has glossy, deep green leaves and ovoid to conical cones, 6–10cm (2½–4in) long, dark purple, ripening to brown, the males brick-red in spring. 🏆 **'Aurea'** has golden, young foliage in spring, later turning green. **'Skylands'** illus. p.100.
P. pungens (Colorado spruce). Columnar conifer. H 15m (50ft), S 5m (15ft). Fully hardy. Has scaly, grey bark and very sharp, stout, greyish-green or bright blue leaves. Cylindrical, light brown cones have papery scales. 🏆 **'Hoopsii'**, H 10–15m (30–50ft), hassilvery-blue foliage. 🏆 **'Koster'** illus. p.101. **'Montgomery'** (illus. p.106), H and S 1m (3ft), is dwarf, compact, spreading or conical, with grey-blueleaves.
P. sitchensis (Sitka spruce). Very vigorous, broadly conical conifer. H 30–50m (100–160ft) in damp locations, 15–20m (50–70ft) in dry situations, S 6–10m (20–30ft). Fully hardy. Bark scales on old trees. Has prickly, bright deep green leaves and cylindrical, papery, pale brown or whitish cones, 5–10cm (2–4in) long. Is good on an exposed or poor site.
P. smithiana (Morinda spruce, West Himalayan spruce). Slow-growing conifer, conical when young, columnar with horizontal branches and weeping shoots when mature. H 25–30m (80–100ft), S 6m (20ft). Fully hardy. Has dark green leaves and produces cylindrical, bright brown cones, 10–20cm (4–8in) long.

Pick-a-back plant. See *Tolmiea menziesii.*
Pickerel weed. See *Pontederia cordata*, illus. p.464.

PICRASMA

SIMAROUBACEAE

Genus of deciduous trees, grown for their brilliant autumn colour. Produces insignificant flowers in late spring. Fully hardy. Requires sun or semi-shade and fertile, well-drained soil. Propagate by seed in autumn.
P. ailanthoides. See *P. quassioides.*
P. quassioides, syn. *P. ailanthoides*, illus. p.93.

PIERIS

ERICACEAE

Genus of evergreen shrubs, grown for their foliage and small, profuse, urn-shaped flowers. Fully to frost hardy. Needs a sheltered site in semi-shade or shade and in moist, peaty, acid soil. *P. floribunda*, however, grows well in any acid soil. Young shoots are sometimes frost-killed in spring and should be cut back as soon as possible. Dead-heading after flowering improves growth. Propagate by soft tip or semi-ripe cuttings in summer. Leaves may cause severe discomfort if ingested.
***P.* 'Bert Chandler'.** Evergreen, bushy shrub. H 2m (6ft), S 1.5m (5ft). Frost hardy. Lance-shaped leaves are bright pink when young, becoming creamy-yellow, then white and finally dark green. Produces white flowers only very rarely. Likes an open position.
P. floribunda illus. p.123.
🏆 ***P.* 'Forest Flame'.** Evergreen, upright shrub. H 4m (12ft), S 2m (6ft). Frost hardy. Narrowly oval, glossy leaves are brilliant red when young, then turn pink, cream and finally dark green. White flowers are borne with the young leaves from mid- to late spring.
P. formosa. Evergreen, bushy, dense shrub. H and S 4m (12ft). Frost hardy. Large, oblong, glossy, dark green leaves are bronze when young. Bears large clusters of white flowers from mid- to late spring. 🏆 var. ***forrestii* 'Wakehurst'** illus. p.138. **'Henry Price'** has deep-veined leaves, which are bronze-red when young.
P. japonica illus. p.112. **'Daisen'** is an evergreen, rounded, dense shrub. H and S 3m (10ft). Fully hardy. Oval, bronze leaves mature to glossy, dark green. Bears drooping clusters of red-budded, deep pink flowers in spring. **'Dorothy Wyckoff'** has deep crimson buds, opening to pink blooms; foliage is bronze in winter. Young foliage of 🏆 **'Mountain Fire'** is brilliant red. **'Scarlett O'Hara'** illus. p.123. **Taiwanensis Group** (syn. *P. taiwanensis*), S 5m (15ft), has narrow leaves that are bronze-red when young. Bears clusters of white flowers in early and mid-spring. **'Variegata'** is slow-growing, with small leaves, edged with white.
P. nana, syn. *Arcterica nana.* Evergreen, prostrate, dwarf shrub. H 2.5–5cm (1–2in), S 10–15cm (4–6in). Fully hardy. Has tiny, oval, leathery, dark green leaves, usually in whorls of 3, on fine stems that root readily. In early spring bears small, terminal clusters of white flowers with green or red calyces. Is excellent for binding a peat wall or in a rock garden.
P. taiwanensis. See *P. japonica* Taiwanensis Group.

Pigeon berry. See *Duranta erecta*, illus. p.146.
Pignut. See *Carya glabra.*
Pignut hickory. See *Carya glabra.*

PILEA

URTICACEAE

Genus of bushy or trailing annuals and evergreen perennials, grown for their ornamental foliage. Frost tender, min. 10°C (50°F). Grow in any well-drained soil out of direct sunlight and draughts; do not overwater in winter. Pinch out tips in growing season to avoid straggly plants. Propagate perennials by stem cuttings in spring or summer, annuals by seed in spring or autumn. Red spider mite may be a problem.
🏆 ***P. cadierei*** (Aluminium plant) illus. p.312.
P. involucrata, syn. *P. mollis* (Friendship plant). Evergreen, bushy perennial. H 15cm (6in), S 30cm (12in). Oval to rounded leaves, to 5cm (2in) long, have corrugated surfaces and are bronze above, reddish-green below; leaves are green when grown in shade.
P. mollis. See *P. involucrata.*
P. nummulariifolia illus. p.317.

PILEOSTEGIA

HYDRANGEACEAE

Genus of evergreen, woody-stemmed, root climbers. Frost hardy. Grows in sun or shade and in any well-drained soil; is therefore useful for planting against a north wall. Prune in spring, if required. Propagate by semi-ripe cuttings in summer.
🏆 ***P. viburnoides***, syn. *Schizophragma viburnoides*, illus. p.204.

PILOSOCEREUS

CACTACEAE

Genus of columnar, summer-flowering, perennial cacti with wool-like spines in flowering zones at crowns. Some species are included in *Cephalocereus*. Frost tender, min. 11°C (52°F). Needs full sun and very well-drained soil. Propagate by seed or stem cuttings in spring or summer.
P. leucocephalus, syn. *P. palmeri*, illus. p.474.
P. palmeri. See *P. leucocephalus*.

PIMELEA

THYMELAEACEAE

Genus of evergreen shrubs, grown for their flowers and overall appearance. Frost hardy to frost tender, min. 5–7°C (41–5°F). Needs full sun and well-drained, neutral to acid soil. Water potted plants moderately, less when temperatures are low. Needs good winter light and ventilation in northern temperate greenhouses. Propagate by seed in spring or by semi-ripe cuttings in late summer.
P. ferruginea illus. p.158.

Pimpernel, Bog. See *Anagallis tenella.*

Pin cherry. See *Prunus pensylvanica.*

PINELLIA

ARACEAE

Genus of summer-flowering, tuberous perennials that produce slender, hood-like, green spathes, each enclosing and concealing a pencil-shaped spadix. Frost hardy. Needs partial shade or sun and humus-rich soil. Water well in spring-summer. Is dormant in winter. Propagate in early spring by offsets or in late summer by bulbils borne in leaf axils.
P. ternata. Summer-flowering, tuberous perennial. H 15–25cm (6–10in), S 10–15cm (4–6in). Has erect stems crowned by oval, flat, 3-parted leaves. Leafless stem bears a tubular, green spathe, 5–6cm (2–2½in) long, with a hood at the tip.

Pin oak. See *Quercus palustris*, illus. p.65.
Pincushion
  Rose. See *Mammillaria zeilmanniana*, illus. p.489.
  Snowball. See *Mammillaria candida.*
Pincushion cactus. See *Mammillaria.*
Pine. See *Pinus.*
  Aleppo. See *Pinus halepensis*, illus. p.103.
  Armand. See *Pinus armandii.*
  Arolla. See *Pinus cembra*, illus. p.102.
  Austrian. See *Pinus nigra* var. *nigra*, illus. p.100.
  Beach. See *Pinus contorta*, illus. p.103.
  Bhutan. See *Pinus wallichiana*, illus. p.99.
  Big-cone. See *Pinus coulteri*, illus. p.98.
  Bishop. See *Pinus muricata*, illus. p.99.
  Black. See *Pinus jeffreyi*, illus. p.99; *Pinus nigra.*
  Bosnian. See *Pinus heldreichii*, illus. p.100.
  Bristle-cone. See *Pinus aristata*, illus. p.104.
  Chile. See *Araucaria araucana*, illus. p.99.
  Cluster. See *Pinus pinaster*, illus. p.99.
  Corsican. See *Pinus nigra* subsp. *laricio.*
  Coulter. See *Pinus coulteri*, illus. p.98.
  Cow's-tail. See *Cephalotaxus harringtonii.*
  David's. See *Pinus armandii.*
  Dwarf. See *Pinus mugo.*
  Dwarf Siberian. See *Pinus pumila.*
  Eastern white. See *Pinus strobus*, illus. p.98.
  Himalayan. See *Pinus wallichiana*, illus. p.99.
  Holford. See *Pinus* × *holfordiana*, illus. p.97.
  Jack. See *Pinus banksiana*, illus. p.103.
  Japanese black. See *Pinus thunbergii*, illus. p.102.
  Japanese red. See *Pinus densiflora.*
  Japanese umbrella. See *Sciadopitys verticillata*, illus. p.102.
  Japanese white. See *Pinus parviflora*, illus. p.101.
  Jeffrey. See *Pinus jeffreyi*, illus. p.99.
  King William. See *Athrotaxis selaginoides.*
  Lace-bark. See *Pinus bungeana*, illus. p.104.
  Lodgepole. See *Pinus contorta var.* latifolia, illus. p.102.
  Macedonian. See *Pinus peuce*, illus. p.97.
  Maritime. See *Pinus pinaster*, illus. p.99.
  Mexican stone. See *Pinus cembroides*, illus. p.105.
  Monterey. See *Pinus radiata*, illus. p.100.
  Mountain. See *Pinus mugo.*
  Norfolk Island. See *Araucaria heterophylla.*
  Northern pitch. See *Pinus rigida*, illus. p.102.
  Scots. See *Pinus sylvestris.*
  Screw. See *Pandanus.*
  Scrub. See *Pinus virginiana*, illus. p.103.
  Shore. See *Pinus contorta*, illus. p.103.

Stone. See *Pinus pinea*, illus. p.105.
Swiss mountain. See *Pinus mugo.*
Tasman celery. See *Phyllocladus aspleniifolius.*
Umbrella. See *Pinus pinea*, illus. p.105.
Veitch's screw. See *Pandanus tectorius* 'Veitchii', illus. p.171.
Virginia. See *Pinus virginiana*, illus. p.103.
Western yellow. See *Pinus ponderosa*, illus. p.99.
Weymouth. See *Pinus strobus*, illus. p.98.
Pineapple
Red. See *Ananas bracteatus.*
Wild. See *Ananas bracteatus.*
Pineapple broom. See *Cytisus battandieri*, illus. p.119.
Pineapple flower. See *Eucomis.*
Giant. See *Eucomis pallidiflora*, illus. p.409.
Pineapple guava. See *Acca sellowiana*, illus. p.139.
Pineapple lily, Giant. See *Eucomis pallidiflora*, illus. p.409.
Pine-mat manzanita. See *Arctostaphylos nevadensis.*

PINGUICULA

LENTIBULARIACEAE

Genus of summer-flowering perennials with sticky leaves that trap insects and digest them for food. Is useful in pots under glass among plants at risk from aphids. Fully hardy to frost tender, min. 7°C (45°F). Needs sun and wet soil. Propagate by division in early spring or by seed in autumn.
P. caudata. See *P. moranensis* var. *caudata.*
P. grandiflora illus. p.394.
P. moranensis var. ***caudata,*** syn. *P. caudata.* Basal-rosetted perennial. H 12–15cm (5–6in), S 5cm (2in). Frost tender. Leaves are narrowly oval and dull green with inrolled, purplish margins. In summer, 5-petalled, deep carmine flowers are produced on long stems.

Pink. See *Dianthus.*
Alpine. See *Dianthus alpinus*, illus. p.390.
Cheddar. See *Dianthus gratianopolitanus*, illus. p.389.
Deptford. See *Dianthus armeria.*
Indian. See *Dianthus chinensis.*
Maiden. See *Dianthus deltoides.*
Sea. See *Armeria maritima.*
Swamp. See *Helonias bullata.*
Pink arum. See *Zantedeschia rehmannii.*
Pink broom. See *Notospartium carmichaeliae.*
Pink dandelion. See *Crepis incana.*
Pink snowball. See *Dombeya × cayeuxii*, illus. p.84.
Pink trumpet tree. See *Tabebuia rosea.*

PINUS
Pine

PINACEAE

Genus of small to large conifers with spirally arranged leaves in bundles, usually of 2, 3 or 5 needles. Cones ripen over 2 years and are small in the first year. See also CONIFERS.
P. aristata illus. p.104.
P. armandii (Armand pine, David's pine). Conical, open conifer. H 10–15m (30–50ft), S 5–8m (15–25ft). Fully hardy. Has pendent, glaucous blue leaves and conical, green cones, 8–25cm (3–10in) long, ripening to brown.
P. banksiana illus. p.103.
P. bungeana illus. p.104.
P. cembra illus. p.102.
P. cembroides illus. p.105.
P. chylla. See *P. wallichiana.*
P. contorta illus. p.103. var. ***latifolia*** illus. p.102. **'Spaan's Dwarf'** is a conical, open, dwarf conifer with short, stiffly erect shoots. H and S 75cm (30in). Fully hardy. Has bright green leaves in 2s.
♀ ***P. coulteri*** illus. p.98.
P. densiflora (Japanese red pine). Flat-topped conifer. H 15m (50ft), S 5–7m (15–22ft). Fully hardy. Has scaling, reddish-brown bark, bright green leaves and conical, yellow or pale brown cones. **'Alice Verkade'**, H and S 75cm (30in), is a diminutive, rounded form with fresh green leaves. **'Tagyosho'** see *P.d.* 'Umbraculifera'.**'Umbraculifera'** (syn. *P.d.* 'Tagyosho'), H 4m (12ft), S 6m (20ft), is a slow-growing, rounded or umbrella-shaped form.
P. excelsa. See *P. wallichiana.*
P. griffithii. See *P. wallichiana.*
P. halepensis illus. p.103.
♀ ***P. heldreichii***, syn. *P.h.* var. *leucodermis, P. leucodermis*, illus. p.100. **'Compact Gem'** (syn. *P.h.* var. *leucodermis* 'Compact Gem') is a broadly conical, dense, dwarf conifer. H and S 25–30cm (10–12in). Fully hardy. Has very dark green leaves in 2s. Grows only 2.5cm (1in) a year. var. ***leucodermis*** see *P. heldreichii.*
♀ **'Smidtii'** (syn *P.h.* var. *leucodermis* 'Schmidtii'; illus. p.107) is a dwarf form with an ovoid habit and sharp, dark green leaves.
P. × holfordiana illus. p.97.
P. insignis. See *P. radiata.*
♀ ***P. jeffreyi*** illus. p.99.
P. leucodermis. See *P. heldreichii.*
P. mugo (Dwarf pine, Mountain pine, Swiss mountain pine). Spreading, shrubby conifer. H 3–5m (10–15ft), S 5–8m (15–25ft). Fully hardy. Has bright to dark green leaves in 2s and ovoid, brown cones. **'Gnom'**, H and S to 2m (6ft), and ♀ **'Mops'**, H 1m (3ft), S 2m (6ft), are rounded cultivars.
♀ ***P. muricata*** illus. p.99.
♀ ***P. nigra*** (Black pine). Upright, later spreading conifer, generally grown in one of the following forms. **'Hornibrookiana'**, H 1.5–2m (5–6ft), S 2m (6ft), is fully hardy and shrubby with stout, spreading or erect branches and dark green leaves in 2s. ♀ subsp. ***laricio*** (syn. *P.n.* var. *maritima; Corsican pine*), H 25–30m (80–100ft), S 8m (25ft), is fast-growing and narrowly conical with an open crown; bears grey-green leaves, in 2s, and ovoid to conical, yellow- or pale grey-brown cones. var. ***maritima*** see *P.n.* subsp. *laricio*.subsp. ***nigra*** illus. p.100.
P. parviflora illus. p.101. ♀ **'Adcock's Dwarf'** is a slow-growing, rounded, dense, dwarf conifer. H 2–3m (6–10ft), S 1.5–2m (5–6ft). Fully hardy. Bears grey-greenleaves in 5s.
P. peuce illus. p.97.
♀ ***P. pinaster*** illus. p.99.
♀ ***P. pinea*** illus. p.105.
♀ ***P. ponderosa*** illus. p.99.
P. pumila (Dwarf Siberian pine). Spreading, shrubby conifer. H 2–3m (6–10ft), S 3–5m (10–15ft). Fully hardy. Has bright blue-green leaves in 5s. Ovoid cones are violet-purple, ripening to red-brown or yellow-brown, the males bright red-purple in spring. **'Globe'**, H and S 50cm–1m (1½–3ft), is a rounded cultivar with blue foliage.
♀ ***P. radiata***, syn. *P. insignis*, illus. p.100.
P. rigida illus. p.102.
P. strobus illus. p.98. ♀ **'Radiata'** is a rounded, dwarf conifer with an open, sparse, whorled crown. H 1–2m (3–6ft), S 2–3m (6–10ft). Fully hardy. Grey bark is smooth at first, later fissured. Bears grey-green leaves in 5s.
♀ ***P. sylvestris*** (Scots pine). Conifer, upright and with whorled branches when young, that develops a spreading, rounded crown with age. H 15–25m (50–80ft), S 8–10m (25–30ft). Fully hardy. Bark is flaking and red-brown on upper trunk, fissured and purple-grey at base. Has blue-green leaves in 2s and conical, green cones that ripen to pale grey- or red-brown. ♀ **'Aurea'** (illus. p.107), H 10m (30ft), S 4m (12ft), has golden-yellow leaves in winter-spring, otherwise blue-green.
♀ **'Beuvronensis'**, H and S 1m (3ft), is a rounded shrub. **'Doone Valley'** (illus. p.106), H and S 1m (3ft), is an upright, irregularly shaped shrub.f. ***fastigiata*** see *P.s.* 'Fastigiata'.**'Fastigiata'** (syn. *P.s.* f. *fastigiata*) illus. p.104. **'Gold Coin'** (illus. p.107), H and S 2m (6ft), is a dwarf version of *P.s.* 'Aurea'. **'Nana'** of gardens see *P.s.* 'Watereri'. **'Watereri'** (syn. *P.s.* 'Nana' of gardens; illus. p.106), H and S 50cm (20in), is a very dense cultivar with widely spaced leaves.
P. thunbergii illus. p.102.
P. virginiana illus. p.103.
♀ ***P. wallichiana***, syn. *P. chylla, P. excelsa, P. griffithii*, illus. p.99.

Pinwheel. See *Aeonium haworthii*, illus. p.482.
Pinyon. See *Pinus cembroides*, illus. p.105.

PIPTANTHUS

LEGUMINOSAE/PAPILIONACEAE

Genus of deciduous or semi-evergreen shrubs, grown for their foliage and flowers. Frost hardy. In cold areas needs the protection of a south- or west-facing wall. Requires sun and fertile, well-drained soil. In spring cut some older shoots back to ground level and prune any frost-damaged growths back to healthy wood. Propagate by seed in autumn.
P. laburnifolius. See *P. nepalensis.*
P. nepalensis, syn. *P. laburnifolius*, illus. p.142.

PISONIA

NYCTAGINACEAE

Genus of evergreen shrubs and trees, grown for their foliage and overall appearance. Frost tender, min. 10–15°C (50–59°F). Needs full light or partial shade and humus-rich, well-drained soil. Water containerized specimens freely when in full growth, moderately at other times. Pruning is tolerated if required. Propagate by seed in spring or by semi-ripe cuttings in summer.
P. brunoniana. See *P. umbellifera.*
P. umbellifera, syn. *Heimerliodendron brunonianum, P. brunoniana* (Bird-catcher tree, Para para). Evergreen, rounded large shrub or small tree. H and S 3–6m (10–20ft). Bears oval, leathery, lustrous leaves. In spring, produces clusters of tiny, green or pink flowers, followed by 5-winged, sticky, brownish fruits.

PISTACIA

ANACARDIACEAE

Genus of evergreen or deciduous trees, grown for their foliage and overall appearance. Frost tender, min. 10°C (50°F). Requires full light and free-draining, even dry soil. Water containerized plants moderately when in full growth, sparingly at other times. Pruning is tolerated if necessary. Propagate by seed in spring or by semi-ripe cuttings in summer.
P. lentiscus (Mastic tree). Evergreen, irregularly rounded shrub or tree. H 5m (15ft), S to 3m (10ft). Bears leaves that are divided into 2–5 pairs of oval, leathery, glossy leaflets. Produces auxillary clusters of insignificant flowers from spring to early summer that develop into globose, red, then black fruits in autumn.
P. terebinthus (Cyprus turpentine, Terebinth tree). Deciduous, rounded to ovoid tree. H 6–9m (20–28ft), S 3–6m (10–20ft). Leaves have 5–9 oval, usually lustrous, rich green leaflets. Axillary clusters of small flowers borne in spring and early summer develop into tiny, globular to ovoid, red, then purple-brown fruits in autumn.

PISTIA

ARACEAE

Genus of one species of deciduous, perennial, floating water plant, grown for its foliage. In water above 19–21°C (66–70°F) is evergreen. Is suitable for tropical aquariums and frost-free pools. Frost tender, min 10–15°C (50–59°F). Grows in sun or semi-shade. Remove fading foliage and thin plants out as necessary. Propagate by separating plantlets in summer.
P. stratiotes illus. p.465.

PITCAIRNIA

BROMELIACEAE

Genus of evergreen, rosette-forming perennials, grown for their overall appearance. Frost tender, min. 10°C (50°F). Needs semi-shade and well-drained soil. Water moderately during growing season, sparingly at other times. Propagate by offsets or division in spring.
P. andreana. Evergreen, clump-forming, basal-rosetted perennial. H 20cm (8in), S 30cm (12in) or more. Loose rosettes comprise narrowly lance-shaped, strongly arching, green leaves, grey-scaled beneath. Racemes of tubular, orange-and-red flowers are borne in summer.
P. heterophylla. Evergreen, basal-rosetted perennial with swollen, much-branched rhizomes. H 10cm (4in) or more, S to 30cm (12in). Forms loose rosettes; outer leaves resemble barbed spines, inner leaves are strap-shaped,

low-arching and green, with downy, white undersides. Produces almost stemless spikes of tubular, bright red, or rarely white flowers in summer.

Pitch apple. See *Clusia major.*
Pitcherplant. See *Nepenthes*; *Sarracenia.*
Common. See *Sarracenia purpurea.*
Yellow. See *Sarracenia flava*, illus. p.302.

PITTOSPORUM

PITTOSPORACEAE

Genus of evergreen trees and shrubs, grown for their ornamental foliage and fragrant flowers. Frost hardy to frost tender, min. 7°C (45°F). Does best in mild areas; in cold regions grow against a south- or west-facing wall. *P. crassifolium* and *P. ralphii* make wind-resistant hedges in mild, coastal areas; like forms with variegated or purple leaves, prefer sun. Others will grow in sun or semi-shade. All need well-drained soil. Propagate *P. dallii* by budding in summer, other species by seed in autumn or spring or by semi-ripe cuttings in summer; selected forms by semi-ripe cuttings only in summer.
P. crassifolium (Karo). Evergreen, bushy-headed, dense tree or shrub. H 5m (15ft), S 3m (10ft). Frost hardy. Has oblong, dark green leaves, grey-felted beneath. Clusters of small, fragrant, star-shaped, dark reddish-purple flowers are borne in spring. **'Variegatum'** illus. p.95.
P. dallii illus. p.96.
P. eugenioides. Evergreen, columnar tree. H 10m (30ft), S 5m (15ft). Frost hardy. Narrowly oval, wavy-edged leaves are glossy, dark green. Honey-scented, star-shaped, pale yellow flowers are produced in spring. ♀ **'Variegatum'** illus. p.95.
♀ ***P.* 'Garnettii'** illus. p.122.
P. ralphii. Evergreen, bushy-headed tree or shrub. H 4m (12ft), S 3m (10ft). Frost hardy. Large leaves are oblong, leathery and grey-green, very hairy beneath. Produces small, fragrant, star-shaped, dark red flowers in spring.
♀ ***P. tenuifolium*** illus. p.123. **'Margaret Turnbull'** is an evergreen, compact shrub. H 1.8m (6ft), S 1m (3ft). Frost hardy. Has dark green leaves, centrally splashed golden yellow. ♀ **'Tom Thumb'** illus. p.173.
♀ ***P. tobira*** (Japanese pittosporum, Mock orange). Evergreen, bushy-headed, dense tree or shrub. H 6m (20ft), S 4m (12ft). Frost hardy. Has oblong to oval, glossy, dark green leaves. Very fragrant, star-shaped, white flowers, opening in late spring, later become creamy-yellow.
P. undulatum (Victorian box). Evergreen, broadly conical tree. H 12m (40ft), S 8m (25ft). Half hardy. Has long, narrowly oval, pointed, wavy-edged, dark green leaves. Fragrant, star-shaped, white flowers are borne in late spring and early summer, followed by rounded, orange fruits.

Pittosporum, Japanese. See *Pittosporum tobira.*

PITYROGRAMMA

PTERIDACEAE/ADIANTACEAE

Genus of semi-evergreen or evergreen ferns, suitable for hanging baskets. Frost tender, min. 10°C (50°F). Needs semi-shade and humus-rich, moist but well-drained soil. Remove fading fronds regularly. Water carefully to avoid spoiling farina on fronds. Propagate by spores in late summer.
P. triangularis. Semi-evergreen or evergreen fern. H and S 45cm (18in). Has broadly triangular, delicately divided, mid-green fronds with orange or creamy-white farina.

Plagiorhegma dubia. See *Jeffersonia dubia.*
Plane. See *Platanus.*
London. See *Platanus × hispanica*, illus. p.63.
Oriental. See *Platanus orientalis.*

PLANTAGO

PLANTAGINACEAE

Genus of summer-flowering annuals, biennials and evergreen perennials and shrubs. Many species are weeds, but a few are grown for their foliage and architectural value. Fully hardy to frost tender, min. 7–10°C (45–50°F). Needs full sun and well-drained soil. Water potted plants moderately, sparingly in winter. Propagate by seed or division in spring.
P. nivalis (illus. p.403) has lance-shaped, silky-hairy, silver-green leaves and tiny, grey-brown flowers.

Plantain
Floating water. See *Luronium natans.*
Parrot's. See *Heliconia psittacorum*, illus. p.227.
Water. See *Alisma plantago-aquatica*, illus. p.462.
Plantain lily. See *Hosta.*

PLATANUS

Plane

PLATANACEAE

Genus of deciduous trees, grown for their habit, foliage and flaking bark. Flowers are inconspicuous. Spherical fruit clusters hang from shoots in autumn. Fully to half hardy. Needs full sun and deep, fertile, well-drained soil. Propagate species by seed in autumn, *P. × hispanica* by hardwood cuttings in early winter. All except *P. orientalis* are susceptible to the fungal disease plane anthracnose. Contact with the basal tufts of hair on the fruits may irritate the skin and respiratory system.
P. × acerifolia. See *P. × hispanica*.
♀ ***P. × hispanica***, syn. *P. × acerifolia*, illus. p.63. **'Suttneri'** is a vigorous, deciduous, spreading tree. H 20m (70ft), S 15m (50ft). Fully hardy. Has flaking bark and large, palmate, 5-lobed, sharply toothed, bright green leaves that are blotched with creamy-white.
♀ ***P. orientalis*** (Oriental plane). Deciduous, spreading tree. H and S 25m (80ft) or more. Fully hardy. Produces large, palmate, glossy, pale green leaves with 5 deep lobes.

PLATYCARYA

JUGLANDACEAE

Genus of one species of deciduous tree, grown for its foliage and catkins. Fully hardy. Requires full sun and fertile, well-drained soil. Propagate by seed in autumn.
P. strobilacea. Deciduous, spreading tree. H and S 10m (30ft). Has ash-like, bright green leaves with 5–15 leaflets. Upright, green catkins are borne from mid- to late summer; males are slender and cylindrical, often drooping at tips, females are cone-like, become brown and persist through winter.

PLATYCERIUM

Stag's-horn fern

POLYPODIACEAE

Genus of evergreen, epiphytic ferns, best grown in hanging baskets or fastened to and suspended from pieces of wood. Produces 2 kinds of fronds: permanent, broad, sterile 'nest leaves' forming the main part of the plant; and strap-shaped, usually partly bifurcated, arching fertile fronds. Frost tender, min. 5°C (41°F). Thrives in warm, humid conditions in semi-shade, and needs fibrous, peaty compost with hardly any soil. Propagate by detaching buds in spring or summer and planting in compost, or by spores in summer or early autumn.
P. alcicorne of gardens. See *P. bifurcatum.*
♀ ***P. bifurcatum***, syn. *P. alcicorne* of gardens, illus. p.322.

PLATYCLADUS

CUPRESSACEAE

Contact with the foliage may aggravate skin allergies. See also CONIFERS.
P. orientalis, syn. *Biota orientalis*, *Thuja orientalis* (Biota, Chinese arbor-vitae, Chinese thuja). Conifer withan irregularly rounded crown. H 10–15m (30–50ft), S 5m (15ft). Fully hardy. Has fibrous bark and flattened, vertical sprays of scale-like, scentless, dark green leaves. Egg-shaped cones are glaucous grey. ♀ **'Aurea Nana'** (illus. p.107), H and S 60cm (24in), is a dwarf cultivar with yellow-green foliage that turns bronze in winter. **'Semperaurea'** (illus. p.107), H 3m (10ft), S 2m (6ft), is compact, with golden leaves.

PLATYCODON

Balloon flower

CAMPANULACEAE

Genus of one species of perennial, grown for its flowers in summer. Fully hardy. Needs sun and light, sandy soil. Propagate by basal cuttings of non-flowering shoots in summer, preferably with a piece of root attached, or by seed in autumn.
♀ ***P. grandiflorus*** illus. p.294. ♀ var. ***mariesii*** (syn. *P.g.* 'Mariesii') is a neat, clump-forming perennial. H and S 30–45cm (12–18in). In mid-summer produces solitary terminal, large, balloon-like flower buds opening to bell-shaped, blue or purplish-blue flowers. Has oval, sharply toothed, bluish-green leaves. **'Mariesii'** see *P.g.* var. *mariesii.*

PLATYSTEMON

PAPAVERACEAE

Genus of one species of summer-flowering annual. Fully hardy. Grow in sun and in fertile, well-drained soil. Propagate by seed sown outdoors in spring or early autumn.
P. californicus illus. p.347.

PLECTRANTHUS

LABIATAE/LAMIACEAE

Genus of evergreen, trailing or bushy perennials, grown for their foliage. Frost tender, min. 4–10°C (39–50°F). Is easy to grow if kept moist in partial shade or bright light. Cut back stem tips in growing season if plants become too straggly. Propagate by stem cuttings or division in spring or summer.
P. australis of gardens. See *P. verticillatus.*
***P. coleoides* 'Variegatus'** of gardens. See *P. madagascariensis* 'Variegated Mintleaf'.
***P. forsteri* 'Marginatus'**, illus. p.272.
P. madagascarienis (Mintleaf) Creeping perennial. H 30cm (12in), S indefinite. Min. 10°C (50°F). Has rounded, scalloped, fleshy leaves. Bears 2-lipped, lavender-blue or white flowers, often dotted with red.
♀ **'Variegated Mintleaf'** (syn. *P. coleoides* 'Variegatus' of gardens) has variegated white leaves.
♀ ***P. oertendahlii*** (Prostrate coleus, Swedish ivy). Evergreen, prostrate perennial. H to 15cm (6in), S indefinite. Min. 10°C (50°F). Rounded, scalloped, dark green leaves are reddish-green below, with white veins above. Racemes of tubular, white or pale mauve flowers are produced at irregular intervals throughout the year.
P. thyrsoideus, syn. *Coleus thyrsoideus.* Fast-growing, bushy perennial, often grown as an annual. H to 1m (3ft), S 60cm (2ft). Min. 4°C (39°F). Has heart-shaped, serrated, mid-green leaves. Bears spikes of tubular, bright blue flowers at various times of year.
♀ ***P. verticillatus***, syn. *P. australis* of gardens (Swedish ivy). Evergreen, trailing perennial with square stems. H to 15cm (6in), S indefinite. Min.10°C (50°F). Has rounded, waxy, glossy, green leaves with scalloped edges. Racemes of tubular, white or pale mauve flowers are produced intermittently through the year.

PLEIOBLASTUS

GRAMINEAE/POACEAE

See also GRASSES, BAMBOOS, RUSHES and SEDGES.
P. auricomus, syn. *Arundinaria auricoma,* illus. p.321.
♀ ***P. variegatus***, syn. *Arundinaria fortunei, A. variegata*, illus. p.318.

PLEIONE

ORCHIDACEAE

See also ORCHIDS.
P. bulbocodioides illus. p.309. Deciduous, terrestrial orchid. H 20cm (8in). Frost hardy. In spring, usually before solitary leaf appears, bears pink, rose or magenta flowers, 5–12cm (2–5in) across, with darker purple marks

on lips. Leaf is narrowly lance-shaped, 14cm (5½in) long. Is often difficult to flower: regular feeding helps to increase pseudobulbs to flowering size.
P.* × *confusa. Deciduous, terrestrial orchid. H 15cm (6in). Frost hardy. Canary-yellow flowers, 5–8cm (2–3in) across, with brown or purple blotches on lips, appear singly in spring, before foliage. Has lance-shaped leaves, 10–18cm (4–7in) long. Does best in an alpine house. Needs semi-shade.
P. hookeriana. Deciduous, terrestrial orchid. H 8–15cm (3–6in). Frost hardy. Lilac-pink, rose or white flowers, 5–7cm (2–3in) across, each with a brown- or purplish-spotted lip, are borne singly in spring with lance-shaped leaves, 5–20cm (2–8in) long. Cultivate as for *P.* × *confusa.*
P. humilis. Deciduous, terrestrial orchid. H 5–8cm (2–3in). Frost hardy. In winter, before foliage appears, white flowers, 7–9cm (3–3½in) across, each with a crimson-spotted lip, are borne singly or in pairs. Lance-shaped leaves are 18–25cm (7–10in) long. Cultivate as for *P.* × *confusa.*
P. praecox. Deciduous, terrestrial orchid. H 8–13cm (3–5in). Frost hardy. Flowers, to 8cm (3in) across, appear in pairs in autumn, after foliage. They are white to pinkish-purple or lilac-purple, with violet marks. Leaves are oblong to lance-shaped and 15–25cm (6–10in) long. Cultivate as for *P.* × *confusa.*

PLEIOSPILOS

AIZOACEAE

Genus of clump-forming, perennial succulents with almost stemless rosettes bearing up to 4 pairs of fleshy, erect leaves, like pieces of granite, each with a flat upper surface and each pair united at the base. Flowers are daisy-like. Individual species are very similar, and many are difficult to identify. Frost tender, min. 5°C (41°F). Needs sun and well-drained soil. Propagate by seed or division in spring or summer.
♀ ***P. bolusii*** illus. p.495.
♀ ***P. compactus*** illus. p.494.

PLEUROTHALLIS

ORCHIDACEAE

See also ORCHIDS.
P. grobyi. Evergreen, epiphytic orchid for a cool greenhouse. H 2.5cm (1in). In summer produces sprays of minute, white flowers, 0.25cm (⅛in) long. Leaves are oval, fleshy and 0.5cm (¼in) long. Provide shade in summer.

Plum
Cherry. See *Prunus cerasifera.*
Date. See *Diospyros lotus.*
Indian. See *Oemleria cerasiformis.*
Natal. See *Carissa macrocarpa.*
Sugared-almond. See *Pachyphytum oviferum*, illus. p.491.
Plum yew. See *Cephalotaxus harringtonii; Prumnopitys andina.*

PLUMBAGO

PLUMBAGINACEAE

Genus of annuals, evergreen or semi-evergreen shrubs, perennials and woody-stemmed, scrambling climbers, grown for their primrose-shaped flowers. Frost hardy to frost tender, min. 7°C (45°F). Grow in full light or semi-shade and in fertile, well-drained soil. Water regularly, less when not in full growth. Tie stems to supports. Thin out or spur back all previous year's growth in early spring. Propagate by semi-ripe cuttings in summer. Whitefly may be a problem.
♀ ***P. auriculata***, syn. *P. capensis*, illus. p.213.
P. capensis. See *P. auriculata.*
♀ ***P. indica***, syn. *P. rosea.* Evergreen or semi-evergreen, spreading shrub or semi-climber. H 2m (6ft), S 1–2m (3–6ft). Frost tender. Leaves are oval to elliptic and mid-green. Has terminal racemes of primrose-shaped, red or pink flowers, 2.5cm (1in) long. These are produced in summer, if hard pruned annually in spring, or from late winter onwards, if left unpruned and trained as a climber.
P. rosea. See *P. indica.*

Plume poppy. See *Macleaya.*

PLUMERIA
Frangipani

APOCYNACEAE

Genus of mainly deciduous, fleshy-branched shrubs and trees, grown for their flowers in summer-autumn. Frost tender, min. 13°C (55°F). Requires full sun and freely draining soil. Water potted specimens moderately while in growth, keep dry in winter when leafless. Stem tips may be cut out to induce branching. Propagate by seed or leafless stem-tip cuttings in late spring. Red spider mite may be a nuisance. The milky sap may cause mild stomach upset if ingested.
P. acuminata. See *P. rubra* f. *acutifolia.*
P. acutifolia. See *P. rubra* f. *acutifolia.*
P. alba (West Indian jasmine). Deciduous, rounded, sparingly branched tree. H to 6m (20ft), S to 4m (12ft). Leaves are lance-shaped and slender-pointed, to 30cm (12in) long. Terminal clusters of fragrant, yellow-eyed, white flowers, each with 5 spreading petals and a tubular base, appear in summer.
♀ ***P. rubra*** illus. p.92. f. ***acutifolia*** (syn. *P. acuminata, P. acutifolia*) is a deciduous, spreading, sparsely branched tree or shrub. H and S 4m (12ft) or more. Produces fragrant, yellow-centred, white flowers, with 5 spreading petals, in summer-autumn. Leaves are lance-shaped to oval and 20–30cm (8–12in) long.

Plum-fruited yew. See *Prumnopitys andina.*
Plush plant. See *Echeveria pulvinata*, illus. p.480.
Poached-egg flower. See *Limnanthes douglasii*, illus. p.348.
Pocket handkerchief tree. See *Davidia involucrata*, illus. p.73.

PODALYRIA

LEGUMINOSAE/PAPILIONACEAE

Genus of evergreen, mainly summer-flowering shrubs, grown for their flowers and overall appearance. Frost tender, min. 7–10°C (45–50°F). Requires full light and fertile, well-drained soil. Water containerized plants moderately, less when not in full growth. Prune, if necessary, after flowering. Propagate by seed in spring or by semi-ripe cuttings in summer.
P. sericea. Vigorous, evergreen, rounded shrub. H and S 1.2–3m (4–10ft). Has oval, downy, mid-green leaves and sweet pea-like, pink flowers, 3–4cm (1¼–1½in) wide, in summer.

Podocarp, Tasmanian. See *Podocarpus alpinus.*

PODOCARPUS

PODOCARPACEAE

See also CONIFERS.
P. alpinus (Tasmanian podocarp). Rounded, spreading, shrubby conifer. H 2m (6ft), S 3–5m (10–15ft). Frost hardy. Has linear, dull green leaves and rounded, egg-shaped, fleshy, bright red fruits.
P. andinus. See *Prumnopitys andina.*
P. macrophyllus (Kusamaki). Erect conifer. H 10m (30ft), S 3–5m (10–15ft). Half hardy. Long, linear leaves are bright green above, glaucous beneath. May be grown as a shrub, H and S 1–2m (3–6ft), and planted in a tub in hot climates.
P. nivalis (Alpine totara; illus. p.106). Rounded, spreading, shrubby conifer. H 2m (6ft), S 3–5m (10–15ft). Frost hardy. Is very similar to *P. alpinus*, but bears longer, broader, more rigid leaves.
♀ ***P. salignus*** illus. p.102.

PODOPHYLLUM

BERBERIDACEAE

Genus of spring-flowering, rhizomatous perennials. Fully hardy, but young leaves may be damaged by frost. Does best in semi-shade and moist, peaty soil. Propagate by division in spring or by seed in autumn. All parts of the plants are highly toxic if ingested.
P. emodi. See *P. hexandrum.*
P. hexandrum, syn. *P. emodi*, illus. p.276.
P. peltatum (May apple). Vigorous, spreading, rhizomatous perennial. H 30–45cm (12–18in), S 30cm (12in). Palmate, sometimes brown-mottled, light green leaves, with 3–5 deep lobes, push up through soil, looking like closed umbrellas, and are followed, in spring, by nodding, cup-shaped, white flowers. Produces large, fleshy, plum-like, glossy, deep rose-pink fruits in autumn.

PODRANEA

BIGNONIACEAE

Genus of evergreen, twining climbers, grown for their foxglove-like flowers. Frost tender, min. 5–10°C (41–50°F). Grow in full light and any fertile, well-drained soil. Water regularly, less in cold weather. Provide support. Thin out crowded growth in winter or early spring. Propagate by seed in spring or by semi-ripe cuttings in summer.
P. ricasoliana, syn. *Pandorea ricasoliana, Tecoma ricasoliana.* Fast-growing, evergreen, twining climber. H 4m (12ft) or more. Has leaves of 7 or 9 lance-shaped to oval, wavy, deep green leaflets. Loose clusters of fragrant, pink flowers with darker veins appear from spring to autumn.

Poet's daffodil. See *Narcissus poeticus.*
Poet's ivy. See *Hedera helix* f. *poetarum*, illus. p.219.
Poet's narcissus. See *Narcissus poeticus.*
Poinciana gilliesii. See *Caesalpinia gilliesii.*
Poinciana pulcherrima. See *Caesalpinia pulcherrima.*
Poinsettia. See *Euphorbia pulcherrima*, illus. p.146.
Pokeweed, Virginian. See *Phytolacca americana.*

POLEMONIUM
Jacob's ladder

POLEMONIACEAE

Genus of late spring- or summer-flowering annuals and perennials, some perennials tending to be short-lived. Fully hardy. Prefers sun and fertile, well-drained soil. Propagate by division in spring or by seed in autumn.
P. caeruleum illus. p.295.
P. carneum illus. p.293.
♀ ***P. foliosissimum.*** Vigorous, clump-forming perennial. H 75cm (30in), S 60cm (24in). Terminal clusters of cup-shaped, lilac flowers, with yellow stamens, are borne in summer above oblong to lance-shaped, mid-green leaves, each composed of numerous, small leaflets.
P. pulcherrimum illus. p.294.

POLIANTHES

AGAVACEAE

Genus of tuberous perennials, grown for their fragrant flowers in summer. Half hardy to frost tender, min. 15–20°C (59–68°F). Needs a sheltered site in full sun and well-drained soil. Water well in spring-summer; feed liquid fertilizer every 2 weeks when in growth. Dry off after leaves die down in winter. Propagate by seed or offsets in spring.
P. geminiflora, syn. *Bravoa geminiflora*, illus. p.439.
♀ ***P. tuberosa*** (Tuberose). Summer-flowering, tuberous perennial. H 60–90cm (24–36in), S 10–15cm (4–6in). Half hardy. Has a basal cluster of strap-shaped, erect leaves; flower stem also bears leaves on lower part. Produces a spike of funnel-shaped, single, white flowers with 6 spreading petals. Adouble form is also available.

POLIOTHYRSIS

FLACOURTIACEAE

Genus of one species of deciduous tree, grown for its foliage and flowers. Fully hardy. Needs sun or semi-shade and fertile, well-drained soil. Propagate by softwood cuttings in summer.
♀ ***P. sinensis.*** Deciduous, spreading tree. H 10m (30ft), S 6m (20ft). Bears long, oval, sharply toothed leaves, glossy and dark green, with wine-red stalks. Fragrant, star-shaped, white, later yellow flowers are produced in late summer and early autumn.

Polka-dot plant. See *Hypoestes phyllostachya*, illus. p.272.
Polyanthus. See *Primula Pacific Series*, and (dwarf) illus. p.340.
Polyanthus daffodil. See *Narcissus tazetta.*

POLYGALA

POLYGALACEAE

Genus of annuals, evergreen perennials, shrubs and trees, grown mainly for their pea-like flowers. Fully hardy to frost tender, min. 7°C (45°F). Needs full light or partial shade and moist but sharply drained soil. Water potted specimens freely when in full growth, moderately at other times. Lanky stems may be cut back hard in late winter. Propagate by seed in spring or by semi-ripe cuttings in late summer. Is susceptible to whitefly.
P. calcarea illus. p.396. **'Bulley's Form'** illus. p.396.
🏆 ***P. chamaebuxus*** illus. p.397.
🏆 var. ***grandiflora*** (syn. *P.c.* var. *purpurea, P.c.* var. *rhodoptera*) illus. p.380. var. ***purpurea*** see *P.c.* var. *grandiflora.* var. ***rhodoptera*** see *P.c.* var. *grandiflora.*
🏆 ***P. × dalmaisiana***, syn. *P. myrtifolia* var. *grandiflora* of gardens, illus. p.163.
P. myrtifolia var. ***grandiflora*** of gardens. See *P. × dalmaisiana.*
P. vayredae. Evergreen, mat-forming shrub. H 5–10cm (2–4in), S 20–30cm (8–12in). Frost hardy. Slender, prostrate stems bear small, linear leaves. Pea-like, reddish-purple flowers, each with a yellow lip, are produced in late spring and early summer. Suits a rock garden or alpine house.

POLYGONATUM
Solomon's seal

LILIACEAE/CONVALLARIACEAE

Genus of spring- or early summer-flowering, rhizomatous perennials. Fully hardy to frost tender, min. 5°C (41°F). Requires a cool, shady situation and fertile, well-drained soil. Propagate by division in early spring or by seed in autumn. Sawfly caterpillar is a common pest. All parts may cause mild stomach upset if ingested.
P. biflorum, syn. *P. canaliculatum, P. commutatum, P. giganteum* (Great Solomon's seal). Arching, rhizomatous perennial. H 1.5m (5ft) or more, S 60cm (2ft). Fully hardy. Bears oval to oblong, mid-green leaves. Pendent clusters of bell-shaped, white flowers are borne in leaf axils during late spring.
P. canaliculatum. See *P. biflorum.*
P. commutatum. See *P. biflorum.*
P. giganteum. See *P. biflorum.*
P. hirtum, syn. *P. latifolium.* Upright, then arching, rhizomatous perennial. H 1m (3ft), S 30cm (1ft). Fully hardy. Clusters of 2–5 drooping, tubular, green-tipped, white flowers open in late spring. Undersides of stems, leaf stalks and oval to lance-shaped, mid-green leaves are hairy.
P. hookeri illus. p.379.
🏆 ***P. × hybridum*** illus. p.240.
P. latifolium. See *P. hirtum.*
P. multiflorum. Arching, leafy perennial with fleshy rhizomes. H 1m (3ft), S 30cm (1ft). Fully hardy. Bears clusters of 2–6 pendent, tubular, green-tipped, white flowers in late spring, then spherical, black fruit. Has oval to lance-shaped, mid-green leaves. **'Flore Pleno'** has double flowers that look like ballet dancers' skirts. **'Striatum'** (syn. *P.m.* 'Variegatum'), H 60cm (2ft), has leaves with creamy-white stripes. **'Variegatum'** see *P.m.* 'Striatum'.
🏆 ***P. odoratum*** (Angled Solomon's seal). Arching, rhizomatous perennial. H 60cm (24in), S 30cm (12in). Fully hardy. Produces pairs of fragrant, tubular to bell-shaped, green-tipped, white flowers in late spring. Oval to lance-shaped leaves are mid-green.
P. verticillatum (Whorled Solomon's seal). Upright, rhizomatous perennial. H 1.2m (4ft), S 45cm (1½ft). Fully hardy. Bears whorls of stalkless, lance-shaped, mid-green leaves. In early summer produces narrowly bell-shaped, greenish-white flowers.

Polygonum affine. See *Persicaria affinis.*
Polygonum amplexicaule. See *Persicaria amplexicaulis.*
Polygonum aubertii. See *Fallopia aubertii.*
Polygonum baldschuanicum. See *Fallopia baldschuanica.*
Polygonum bistorta. See *Persicaria bistorta.*
Polygonum campanulatum. See *Persicaria campanulata.*
Polygonum capitatum. See *Persicaria capitata.*
Polygonum macrophyllum. See *Persicaria macrophylla.*
Polygonum milletii. See *Persicaria milletii.*
Polygonum sphaerostachyum. See *Persicaria macrophylla.*
Polygonum vacciniifolium. See *Persicaria vacciniifolia.*
***Polygonum virginianum* 'Painter's Palette'.** See *Persicaria virginiana* 'Painter's Palette'.

POLYPODIUM

POLYPODIACEAE

Genus of deciduous, semi-evergreen or evergreen ferns, grown for their sculptural fronds. Fully hardy to frost tender, min. 10°C (50°F). Grow in semi-shade and fibrous, moist but well-drained soil. Propagate by division in spring or by spores in late summer.
P. aureum. See *Phlebodium aureum.*
P. australe. See *P. cambricum.*
P. cambricum, syn. *P. australe, P. vulgare* subsp. *serratum* (Southern polypody, Wintergreen fern). Deciduous, creeping fern. H 15–60cm (6–24in), Sindefinite. Fully hardy. Has broadly lance-shaped to broadly triangular-ovate, divided, mid-green fronds, to 60cm (24in) long, with linear or oblong pinnae that often have toothed margins. New fronds appear in late summer and die back by early summer. Sori are conspicuously yellow in winter.
P. glycyrrhiza illus. p.322.
P. scouleri illus. p.323.
P. vulgare illus. p.325. **'Cornubiense'** illus. p.324. **'Cristatum'** is an evergreen, creeping fern. H and S 25–30cm (10–12in). Fully hardy. Narrowly lance-shaped, divided, mid-green fronds, with semi-pendulous, terminal crests, grow from creeping rhizomes covered with copper-brown scales. subsp. ***serratum*** see *P. cambricum.*

Polypody. See *Polypodium vulgare*, illus. p.325.
Common. See *Polypodium vulgare*, illus. p.325.
Southern. See *Polypodium cambricum.*

POLYSCIAS

ARALIACEAE

Genus of evergreen trees and shrubs, grown for their foliage. Sometimes has insignificant flowers in summer, but only on large, mature specimens. Frost tender, 15–18°C (59–64°F). Needs partial shade and humus-rich, well-drained soil. Water containerized plants freely when in full growth, moderately at other times. Straggly stems may be cut out in spring. Propagate by seed in spring or by stem-tip or leafless stem-section cuttings in summer. Red spider mite may be troublesome.
P. filicifolia illus. p.148. **'Marginata'** is an evergreen, erect, sparsely branched shrub. H 2m (6ft) or more, S 1m (3ft) or more. Has 30cm (1ft) long leaves with many small, oval to lance-shaped, serrated, bright green leaflets with white edges.
🏆 ***P. guilfoylei*** (Wild coffee). Slow-growing, evergreen, rounded tree. H 3–8m (10–25ft), S to 2m (6ft) or more. Leaves are 25–40cm (10–16in) long and divided into oval to rounded, serrated, deep green leaflets.
🏆 **'Victoriae'** illus. p.122.

POLYSTICHUM

DRYOPTERIDACEAE

Genus of evergreen, semi-evergreen or deciduous ferns. Fully to frost hardy. Does best in semi-shade and moist but well-drained soil enriched with fibrous organic matter. Remove faded fronds regularly. Propagate species by division in spring or by spores in summer, selected forms by division in spring.
P. acrostichoides (Christmas fern). Evergreen fern. H 60cm (24in), S 45cm (18in). Fully hardy. Slender, lance-shaped, deep green fronds have small, holly-like pinnae. Is excellent for cutting.
🏆 ***P. aculeatum*** (Hard shield fern, Prickly shield fern). Semi-evergreen fern. H 60cm (24in), S 75cm (30in). Fully hardy. Broadly lance-shaped, yellowish-green, then deep green fronds, with oblong to oval, spiny-edged, glossy pinnae, are produced on stems often covered in brown scales. **'Pulcherrimum'** see *P. setiferum* 'Pulcherrimum Bevis'.
P. braunii. Evergreen or semi-evergreen fern. H and S 45–75cm (18–30in). Fully hardy. Produces a rosette of spreading to arching, lance-shaped, divided, dark green fronds, to 60cm (2ft) long. Young fronds are densely covered with orange-brown scales when unfurling in spring.
🏆 ***P. munitum*** illus. p.322.
🏆 ***P. polyblepharum.*** Evergreen fern. H 60–80cm (24–32in), S 90cm (36in). Fully hardy. Produces 'shuttlecocks' of spreading, lance-shaped, divided, shiny, dark green fronds, 30–80cm (12–32in) long, covered with golden hairs when they unfurl. Pinnae lobes are oblong-ovate and have spiny-toothed margins.
P. rigens. Evergreen fern. H 40cm (16in), S 60cm (24in). Fully hardy. Has 'shuttlecocks' of narrowly ovate-oblong, divided, leathery, harsh-textured, dull green fronds, 30–45cm (12–18in) long. Broad, lance-shaped pinnae are divided into ovate, spiny-toothed lobes. Fronds are yellowish-green in spring.
🏆 ***P. setiferum*** (Soft shield fern). **'Divisilobum'** see *P.s.* Divisilobum Group. **Divisilobum Group** (syn. *P.s.* 'Divisilobum') illus. p.323. **Plumosodivisilobum Group** illus. p.325. **'Pulcherrimum Bevis'** (syn. *P. aculeatum* 'Pulcherrimum') illus p.322.
🏆 ***P. tsussimense.*** Semi-evergreen fern. H 30cm (12in), S 23cm (9in). Frost hardy. Has broadly lance-shaped, dull green fronds divided into oblong, finely spiny-edged pinnae. Is suitable for a peat garden or alpine house.

Pomegranate. See *Punica.*
Dwarf. See *Punica granatum* var. *nana*, illus. p.367.

PONCIRUS

RUTACEAE

Genus of one species of very spiny, deciduous shrub or small tree, grown for its foliage, showy flowers and orange-like fruits. Is very effective as a protective hedge. Fully hardy. Needs sun and fertile, well-drained soil. Cut out dead wood in spring, and trim hedges in early summer. Propagate by semi-ripe cuttings in summer or by seed when ripe, in autumn.
P. trifoliata (Japanese bitter orange). Deciduous, bushy shrub or tree. H and S 5m (15ft). Stout, spiny, green shoots bear dark green leaves each composed of 3 oval leaflets. Fragrant, white flowers, with 4 or 5 large petals, borne in late spring and often again in autumn, are followed by rounded, 2–3cm (¾–1¼ in) wide fruits.

Pond lily, Yellow. See *Nuphar advena.*
Pondweed
Cape. See *Aponogeton distachyos*, illus. p.463.
Curled. See *Potamogeton crispus*, illus. p.464.
Fennel-leaved. See *Potamogeton pectinatus.*

PONTEDERIA

PONTEDERIACEAE

Genus of deciduous, perennial, marginal water plants, grown for their foliage and flower spikes. Fully to frost hardy. Needs full sun and up to 23cm (9in) depth of water. Remove fading flowers regularly. Propagate in spring by division or seed.
🏆 ***P. cordata*** illus. p.464.

Pontine oak. See *Quercus pontica.*
Pony-tail. See *Beaucarnea recurvata*, illus. p.96.
Poorman's orchid. See *Schizanthus.*

Poplar. See *Populus.*
Balsam. See *Populus balsamifera.*
Berlin. See *Populus* × *berolinensis.*
Black. See *Populus nigra.*
Canadian. See *Populus* × *canadensis.*
Chinese necklace. See *Populus lasiocarpa.*
Grey. See *Populus* × *canescens*, illus. p.61.
Lombardy. See *Populus nigra* 'Italica', illus. p.62.
Necklace. See *Populus deltoides.*
Western balsam. See *Populus trichocarpa.*
White. See *Populus alba*, illus. p.60.
Poppy. See *Papaver.*
Alpine. See *Papaver burseri.*
Blue. See *Meconopsis betonicifolia*, illus. p.259.
California. See *Eschscholzia.*
Corn. See *Papaver rhoeas.*
Field. See *Papaver rhoeas.*
Harebell. See *Meconopsis quintuplinervia*, illus. p.279.
Horned. See *Glaucium.*
Iceland. See *Papaver croceum.*
Lampshade. See *Meconopsis integrifolia*, illus. p.304.
Mexican tulip. See *Hunnemannia fumariifolia.*
Opium. See *Papaver somniferum.*
Oriental. See *Papaver orientale.*
Plume. See *Macleaya.*
Prickly. See *Argemone mexicana*, illus. p.347.
Snow. See *Eomecon chionantha.*
Tree. See *Romneya.*
Water. See *Hydrocleys nymphoides*, illus. p.465.
Welsh. See *Meconopsis cambrica*, illus. p.285.

POPULUS
Poplar

SALICACEAE

Genus of deciduous trees, grown for their habit, foliage and very quick growth. Has catkins in late winter or spring. Female trees produce copious amounts of fluffy, white seeds. Fully hardy. Prefers full sun and needs deep, fertile, moist but well-drained soil; resents dry soil, apart from *P. alba*, which thrives in coastal gardens. Extensive root systems can undermine foundations and so make poplars unsuitable for planting close to buildings, particularly on clay soil. Propagate by hardwood cuttings in winter. Is susceptible to bacterial canker and fungal diseases.

P. alba illus. p.60. Is much confused with the commoner *P. canescens*. f. ***pyramidalis*** (syn. *P.a.* 'Pyramidalis') is a vigorous, deciduous, upright tree. H 20m (70ft), S 5m (15ft). Broadly oval, wavy-margined or lobed, dark green leaves, white beneath, turn yellow in autumn. **'Pyramidalis'** see *P.a.* f. *pyramidalis*.**'Raket'** (syn. *P.a.*'Rocket') illus. p.65. **'Richardii'**, H 15m (50ft), S 12m (40ft), has leaves golden-yellow above.**'Rocket'** see *P.a.* 'Raket'.

P. balsamifera (Balsam poplar, Tacamahac). Fast-growing, deciduous, upright tree. H 30m (100ft), S 8m (25ft). Oval, glossy, dark green leaves, whitish beneath, have a strong fragrance of balsam when young.

P.* × *berolinensis (Berlin poplar). Deciduous, columnar tree. H 25m (80ft), S 8m (25ft). Has broadly oval, bright green leaves with white undersides.

P.* × *canadensis (Canadian poplar). **'Eugenei'** is a deciduous, columnar tree. H 30m (100ft), S 12m (40ft). Has broadly oval, bronze, young leaves, maturing to dark green, and red catkins in spring. **'Robusta'** illus. p.61. **'Serotina de Selys'** (syn. *P.* × *c.* 'Serotina Erecta') illus. p.62.

P.* × *candicans of gardens. See *P.* × *jackii.*

P.* × *canescens illus. p.61.

P. deltoides (Cottonwood, Eastern cottonwood, Necklace poplar). Very fast-growing, deciduous, spreading tree. H 30m (100ft), S 20m (70ft). Has lush growth of broadly oval, glossy, bright green leaves.

P. gileadensis. See *P.* × *jackii.*

P.* × *jackii, syn. *P.* × *candicans* of gardens, *P. gileadensis* (Balm of Gilead). Very fast-growing, deciduous, conical tree. H 25m (80ft), S 10m (30ft). Oval leaves are dark green and, when young, balsam-scented. Is very susceptible to canker. **'Aurora'**, H 15m (50ft) or more, S 6m (20ft), has leaves that are heavily but irregularly blotched with creamy-white.

♀ ***P. lasiocarpa*** (Chinese necklace poplar). Very fast-growing, deciduous, spreading tree. H 15m (50ft), S 12m (40ft). Has stout shoots and very large, heart-shaped, mid-green leaves with red veins, on long, red stalks. Bears stout, drooping, yellow catkins in spring.

P. maximowiczii illus. p.60.

P. nigra (Black poplar). Fast-growing, deciduous, spreading tree. H 25m (80ft), S 20m (70ft). Has dark bark. Diamond-shaped, bronze young leaves turn bright green, then yellow in autumn. Male trees bear red catkins in mid-spring. ♀ **'Italica'** illus. p.62.

P. szechuanica. Very fast-growing, deciduous, conical tree. H 25m (80ft), S 10m (30ft). Has flaking, pinkish-grey bark and large, heart-shaped, dark green leaves.

♀ ***P. tremula*** (Aspen). Vigorous, deciduous, spreading tree. H 15m (50ft), S 10m (30ft). Rounded leaves are bronze-red when young, grey-green when mature and yellow in autumn. Flattened stalks make foliage tremble and rattle in wind. **'Erecta'**, S 5m (15ft), has an upright habit. **'Pendula'** illus. p.75.

P. tremuloides (American aspen, Quaking aspen). Very fast-growing, deciduous, spreading tree. H 15m (50ft) or more, S 10m (30ft). Has rounded, finely toothed, glossy, dark green leaves that flutter in the wind and turn yellow in autumn.

P. trichocarpa (Black cottonwood, Western balsam poplar). Very fast-growing, deciduous, conical tree. H 30m (100ft) or more, S 10m (30ft). Bears dense growth of oval, glossy, dark green leaves with green-veined, white undersides, strongly balsam-scented when young. Foliage turns yellow in autumn.

PORANA

CONVOLVULACEAE

Genus of evergreen or deciduous, twining climbers, grown for their flowers. Frost tender, min. 5–7°C (41–45°F), 10–13°C (50–55°F) for good winter blooms. Provide full light and fertile, moisture-retentive, well-drained soil. Water freely in full growth, sparingly in cold weather. Stems require support. Thin out evergreen species and cut back deciduous ones to just above ground level in late winter or early spring. Propagate by basal, softwood cuttings in late spring or early summer or by seed in spring.

P. paniculata (Bridal bouquet, Snow creeper). Vigorous, evergreen, twining climber. H 6–10m (20–30ft). Large, loose panicles of small, elder-scented, trumpet-shaped, white flowers are produced from late summer to mid-winter. Leaves are heart-shaped.

Port Jackson fig. See *Ficus rubiginosa.*
Portia oil nut. See *Thespesia populnea.*
Portugal laurel. See *Prunus lusitanica.*
Portuguese heath. See *Erica lusitanica.*

PORTULACA

PORTULACACEAE

Genus of fleshy annuals and perennials with flowers that open in sun and close in shade. Half hardy. Needs full light and any well-drained soil. Propagate by seed sown under glass in early spring, or outdoors in late spring. Is prone to attack by aphids.

P. grandiflora (Sun plant). Slow-growing, partially prostrate annual. H 15–20cm (6–8in), S 15cm (6in). Has lance-shaped, succulent, bright green leaves. In summer and early autumn bears shallowly bowl-shaped flowers, 2.5cm (1in) wide and with conspicuous stamens, in shades of yellow, red, orange, pink or white. **Minilaca Hybrids** have a double-flowered cultivar. **Sundance Hybrids** illus. p.338. **Sundial Series** has double flowers in a broad colour range. Bred for longer flowering in poor conditions and cooler climates.

PORTULACARIA

PORTULACACEAE

Genus of one species of evergreen or semi-evergreen, succulent-leaved shrub, grown for its foliage and overall appearance. Frost tender, min. 7–10°C (45–50°F). Needs full sun and well-drained soil. Water potted plants moderately when in full growth, sparingly at other times. Propagate by semi-ripe cuttings in summer.

P. afra illus. p.149. **'Foliisvariegatus'** (syn. *P.a.* 'Variegatus') is an evergreen or semi-evergreen, erect shrub with more or less horizontal branches. H and S 2–3m (6–10ft). Has oval to rounded, fleshy, cream-edged, bright green leaves. From late spring to summer, bears tiny, star-shaped, pale pink flowers in small clusters. **'Variegatus'** see *P.a.* 'Foliisvariegatus'.

Pot marigold. See *Calendula officinalis.*

POTAMOGETON

POTAMOGETONACEAE

Genus of deciduous, perennial, submerged water plants, grown for their foliage. Is suitable for cold-water pools and aquariums. Fully hardy. Prefers sun. Remove fading foliage and thin plants as necessary. Propagate by stem cuttings in spring or summer.

P. crispus illus. p.464.

P. pectinatus (Fennel-leaved pondweed). Deciduous, perennial, submerged water plant. S 3m (10ft). Has very narrow, linear, green to brownish-green leaves, and produces inconspicuous flowers in summer. Is suitable for a medium to large pool.

Potato, Duck. See *Sagittaria latifolia*, illus. p.462.
Potato bush, Blue. See *Solanum rantonnetii.*
Potato creeper. See *Solanum seaforthianum*, illus. p.202.
Potato vine. See *Solanum jasminoides.*

POTENTILLA

ROSACEAE

Genus of perennials and deciduous shrubs, grown for their clusters of small, flattish to saucer-shaped flowers and for their foliage. Tall species – particularly the shrubs – are useful in borders. Dwarf potentillas are good for rock gardens. Fully hardy. Does best in full sun, but flower colour is better on orange-, red- and pink-flowered cultivars if they are shaded from hottest sun. Needs well-drained soil. Propagate perennial species by seed in autumn or by division in spring or autumn; selected forms by division only in spring or autumn. Shrubby species may be raised by seed in autumn or by softwood or greenwood cuttings in summer, selected forms by softwood or greenwood cuttings during summer.

***P.* 'Abbotswood'.** See *P. fruticosa* 'Abbotswood'.

P. alba illus. p.385.

P. arbuscula. See *P. fruticosa* var. *arbuscula.*

P. argyrophylla. See *P. atrosanguinea* var. *argyrophylla.*

P. atrosanguinea illus. p.293. var. ***argyrophylla*** (syn. *P. argyrophylla*) is a clump-forming perennial. H 45cm (18in), S 60cm (24in). Saucer-shaped, yellow or yellow-orange flowers are produced in profusion from early to late summer above strawberry-like, silvery leaves.

P. aurea illus. p.398.

***P.* 'Beesii'.** See *P. fruticosa* 'Beesii'.

P. crantzii (Alpine cinquefoil). Upright perennial with a thick, woody rootstock. H and S 10–20cm (4–8in). Produces wedge-shaped, 5-lobed leaves and, in spring, flattish, yellow flowers with orange centres. Is good in a rock garden.

P. davurica var. ***mandschurica*** of gardens. See *P. fruticosa* 'Manchu'.

***P.* 'Daydawn'.** See *P. fruticosa* 'Daydawn'.

***P.* 'Elizabeth'.** See *P. fruticosa* 'Elizabeth'.

P. eriocarpa illus. p.397.

***P.* 'Etna'.** Clump-forming perennial. H 75cm (30in), S 45cm (18in). In mid-

summer produces saucer-shaped, maroon flowers above strawberry-like, dark green leaves.
P. fruticosa. Deciduous, bushy, dense shrub. H 1m (3ft), S 1.5m (5ft). From late spring to late summer produces saucer-shaped, bright yellow flowers. Dark green leaves have 5 narrowly oblong leaflets. ♀ **'Abbotswood'** (syn. *P.* 'Abbotswood') illus. p.154. var. ***arbuscula*** (syn. *P. arbuscula*), S 1.2m (4ft), bears golden-yellow flowers amid grey-green to silver-grey leaves. **'Beesii'** (syn. *P.* 'Beesii', *P.* 'Nana Argentea'), H 75cm (30in), S 1m (3ft), is slow-growing and compact. Has golden-yellow flowers and silver leaves. **'Daydawn'** (syn. *P.* 'Daydawn') illus. p.157. **'Elizabeth'** (syn. *P.* 'Elizabeth') illus. p.165. **'Farrer's White'** illus. p.155. **'Friedrichsenii'** illus. p.165. **'Gold Drop'** (syn. *P. parvifolia* 'Gold Drop'), H and S 1.2m (4ft), bears a mass of golden-yellow flowers amid bright green leaves. ♀ **'Goldfinger'** (syn. *P.* 'Goldfinger') bears large, rich yellow flowers in profusion.
♀ **'Jackman's Variety'** (syn. *P.* 'Jackman's Variety'), H 1.2m (4ft), has large, bright yellow flowers. **'Manelys'** (syn. *P.* 'Maanelys', *P.* 'Manelys', *P.* 'Moonlight'), H 1.2m (4ft), S 2m (6ft), has soft yellow flowers and grey-green foliage. **'Manchu'** (syn. *P. davurica* var. *mandschurica* of gardens, *P.* 'Manchu') illus. p.154. **'Red Ace'** (syn. *P.* 'Red Ace') illus. p.162. **'Royal Flush'** (syn. *P.* 'Royal Flush'), H 45cm (18in), S 75cm (30in), produces mid-green leaves and sometimes semi-double, yellow-stamened, rich pink flowers, fading to white in full sun. **'Sunset'** (syn. *P.* 'Sunset') illus. p.167. **'Tangerine'** (syn. *P.* 'Tangerine'), H 1.2m (4ft), bears yellow flowers, flushed with pale orange-red, amid mid-green leaves. **'Vilmoriniana'** (syn. *P.* 'Vilmoriniana') illus. p.165.
♀ ***P.* 'Gibson's Scarlet'.** Clump-forming perennial. H and S 45cm (18in). Bears saucer-shaped, brilliant scarlet flowers from mid- to late summer. Dark green leaves are strawberry-like.
***P.* 'Gloire de Nancy',** syn. *P.* 'Glory of Nancy'. Clump-forming perennial. H and S 45cm (18in). Very large, saucer-shaped, semi-double, orange and coppery-red flowers appear throughout summer. Has strawberry-like, dark green leaves.
***P.* 'Glory of Nancy'.** See *P.* 'Gloire de Nancy'.
***P.* 'Goldfinger'.** See *P. fruticosa* 'Goldfinger'.
***P.* 'Jackman's Variety'.** See *P. fruticosa* 'Jackman's Variety'.
***P.* 'Maanelys'.** See *P. fruticosa* 'Maanelys'.
***P.* 'Manchu'.** See *P. fruticosa* 'Manchu'.
***P.* 'Manelys'.** See *P. fruticosa* 'Maanelys'.
♀ ***P. megalantha*** illus. p.304.
***P.* 'Monsieur Rouillard'.** Clump-forming perennial. H and S 45cm (18in). Bears saucer-shaped, double, blood-red flowers in summer above strawberry-like, dark green leaves.
***P.* 'Moonlight'.** See *P. fruticosa* 'Maanelys'.
***P.* 'Nana Argentea'.** See *P. fruticosa* 'Beesii'.
♀ ***P. nepalensis* 'Miss Willmott'** illus. p.292.
P. nitida. Dense, mat-forming perennial. H 2.5–5cm (1–2in), S 20cm (8in). Has rounded, 3-lobed, silver leaves. Flower stems each carry 1–2 rose-pink flowers with dark centres in early summer. Is often shy-flowering. Suits a rock garden or trough.
***P. parvifolia* 'Gold Drop'.** See *P. fruticosa* 'Gold Drop'.
P. recta. Clump-forming, hairy perennial. H 60cm (24in), S 45cm (18in). From early to late summer bears pale yellow flowers. **'Macrantha'** see *P.r.* 'Warrenii'.**'Warrenii'** (syn. *P.r.* 'Macrantha') illus. p.303.
***P.* 'Red Ace'.** See *P. fruticosa* 'Red Ace'.
***P.* 'Royal Flush'.** See *P. fruticosa* 'Royal Flush'.
***P.* 'Sunset'.** See *P. fruticosa* 'Sunset'.
***P.* 'Tangerine'.** See *P. fruticosa* 'Tangerine'.
♀ ***P. × tonguei.*** Mat-forming perennial. H 5cm (2in), S 25cm (10in). Has rounded, 3–5 lobed, green leaves. Prostrate branches bear flattish, orange-yellow flowers with red centres during summer. Is good for a rock garden.
***P.* 'Vilmoriniana'.** See *P. fruticosa* 'Vilmoriniana'.
♀ ***P.* 'William Rollison'.** Clump-forming perennial. H and S 45cm (18in). From mid- to late summer bears saucer-shaped, semi-double, scarlet-suffused, deep orange flowers with yellow centres. Has dark green leaves.
***P.* 'Yellow Queen'** illus. p.304

Pothos. See *Epipremnum*.

× POTINARA

ORCHIDACEAE

See also ORCHIDS.
× *P.* Cherub 'Spring Daffodil' illus. p.311. Evergreen, epiphytic orchid for an intermediate greenhouse. H 15cm (6in). Sprays of yellow flowers, 5cm (2in) across, open in spring. Broadly oval, rigid leaves are 10cm (4in) long. Provide good light in summer.

Powder-puff cactus. See *Mammillaria bocasana*, illus. p.487.

PRATIA

CAMPANULACEAE

Genus of evergreen, mat-forming perennials with small leaves, grown for their mass of star-shaped flowers; is suitable for rock gardens. Is sometimes included in *Lobelia*. Some species may be invasive. Fully to half hardy. Prefers shade and moist soil. Propagate by division or seed in autumn.
P. angulata. Evergreen, creeping perennial. H 1cm (½in), S indefinite. Frost hardy. Bears small, broadly oval, dark green leaves. Star-shaped, white flowers, with 5 unevenly spaced petals, are carried in leaf axils in late spring and are followed by globose, purplish-red fruits in autumn.
P. pedunculata illus. p.395. **'County Park'** is a vigorous, evergreen, creeping perennial. H 1cm (½in), S indefinite. Frost hardy. Has small, rounded to oval leaves and, in summer, a profusion of star-shaped, rich violet-blue flowers. Makes good ground cover.

Prayer plant. See *Maranta leuconeura*.
Prickly Moses. See *Acacia verticillata*.
Western. See *Acacia pulchella*, illus. p.153.
Prickly pear. See *Opuntia*.
Edible. See *Opuntia ficus-indica*.
Prickly poppy. See *Argemone mexicana*, illus. p.347.
Prickly shield fern. See *Polystichum aculeatum*.
Pride of Bolivia. See *Tipuana tipu*.
Pride of India. See *Koelreuteria paniculata*, illus. p.88; *Lagerstroemia speciosa*.
Primrose. See *Primula; P. vulgaris*, illus. p.281.
Bird's-eye. See *Primula farinosa*, illus. p.280.
Cape. See *Streptocarpus rexii*.
Evening. See *Oenothera*.
Primrose jasmine. See *Jasminum mesnyi*, illus. p.203.
Primrose peerless. See *Narcissus × medioluteus*.

PRIMULA
Primrose

PRIMULACEAE

Genus of mainly herbaceous perennials, some woody-based and evergreen. All have leaves in basal rosettes and tubular, bell- or primrose-shaped (flat) flowers. In some primulas, the flower stems, leaves, sepals and, occasionally, sections of the petals are covered with a waxy powder known as farina. There are primulas suitable for almost every type of site: the border, scree garden, rock garden, peat garden, bog garden, pool margin, greenhouse and alpine house. Some may be difficult to grow as they dislike winter damp or summer heat. Fully hardy to frost tender, min. 7–10°C (45–50°F). Repot pot-grown plants annually. Tidy up fading foliage and dead-head as flowering ceases. Propagate species by seed when fresh or in spring; increase selected forms when dormant, either by division in autumn-spring, or by root cuttings in winter. Auricula primulas should be propagated by offsets in early spring or early autumn. Border cultivars may be prone to slug damage in damp situations and to attack by root aphids when grown in very dry conditions or in pots.

Primulas are divided into many different horticultural groups, of which the following are in common use. See also feature panel pp.280–83.

Auricula primulas
These are evergreen primulas, derived from hybrids between *P. auricula* and *P. hirsuta*, producing flat, smooth flowers carried in an umbel on a stem above the foliage. There are 3 main sub-groups: alpine, border and show.
Alpine Auricula Group. In these, the colour of the flower centre is strikingly different from that of the petals. They may be either light-centred (white or pale in the centre) or gold-centred (yellow or gold in the centre). There is no meal or 'farina' on either leaves or flowers. Grow in an alpine house or rock garden.
Show Auricula Group has flowers with a distinct circle of white meal or 'paste' in the centre. Some are self-coloured, with one colour, which may be red, yellow, blue or violet, from the central paste to the petal margins; edged cultivars have a black ring surrounding the central paste, feathering out to an often green, grey or white margin; in fancy cultivars the paste is surrounded by a colour other than black, with a green, grey or white margin. Show Auriculas have white farina on their foliage (except those with green-edged flowers), on their flower eyes and, sometimes, on their petal margins. Grow under glass to protect the flowers from rain.
Border Auricula Group has generally robust, garden Auricula primulas, which are often very fragrant. Some have farina on flower stems and leaves. Grow in a mixed or herbaceous border.

Candelabra primulas
These are robust, herbaceous perennials with tubular, flat-faced flowers borne in tiered whorls up tall, sturdy stems. Some are deciduous, dying back to basal buds; others are semi-evergreen, dying back to reduced rosettes. Grow in moist shade or woodland, especially by streams.

Primrose-Polyanthus primulas
A diverse group of evergreen, semi-evergreen or deciduous perennial hybrids, derived from *P. vulgaris*, crossed with *P. veris, P. juliae* and other species. They are divided into two main groups.
Primrose Group Most produce solitary flowers among the leaves. Are mainly grown as herbaceous perennials, flowering in spring, or as biennial, greenhouse container plants flowering in winter-spring.
Polyanthus Group Produce flowers in long-stalked umbels. Usually grown as biennials for bedding, sown in summer to flower in winter and the following spring, or under glass as winter- and spring-flowering container plants.

Cultivation
Primulas have varying cultivation requirements. For ease of reference, these have been grouped as follows:
1 – Full sun or partial shade, in moist, but well-drained, humus-rich soil.
2 – Partial shade, in deep, humus-rich, moist, neutral to acid soil.
3 – Deep or partial shade, in peaty, gritty, moist but sharply drained, acid soil. Protect from excessive winter wet.
4 – Under glass in an alpine house or frame. Avoid wetting foliage of mealy species and hybrids.
5 – Full sun with some midday shade, or partial shade, in moist but sharply drained, gritty, humus-rich, slightly alkaline soil.
6 – In a cool or temperate greenhouse, or as a houseplant, in bright, filtered light.

***P.* 'Adrian'** illus. p.281. Alpine Auricula primula. H and S 10cm (4in). Fully hardy. Produces flat, light to dark blue flowers, with light centres and paler margins, in mid- to late spring. Leaves are oval to rounded and mid-green. Is useful for exhibition. Cultivation group 1 or 4.
♀ ***P. allionii*** illus. p.280. Rosette-forming, evergreen perennial.

H 7–10cm (3–4in), S 20cm (8in). Fully hardy, but better grown in an alpine house. Tubular, rose, mauve or white flowers cover a tight cushion of oval, mid-green leaves in spring. Cultivation group 4.

♀ ***P. alpicola.*** Compact, rosette-forming perennial. H 50cm (20in), S 30cm (12in). Fully hardy. Produces terminal clusters of pendent, bell-shaped, yellow to white or purple flowers on slender stems in early summer. Mid-green leaves are oval to lance-shaped. Cultivation group 2. var. ***alpicola*** (syn. *P.a.* var. *luna*; illus. p.282) has soft sulphur-yellow flowers. var. ***luna*** see *P.a.* var. *alpicola*.

P. aurantiaca. Small, rosette-forming Candelabra primula. H 30cm (12in), S 40cm (16in). Fully hardy. Tubular, reddish-orange flowers are borne in early summer. Has long, broadly oval to lance-shaped, coarse, mid-green leaves. Cultivation group 2.

P. aureata illus. p.282. Rosette-forming, evergreen perennial. H 15cm (6in), S 20cm (8in). Frost hardy. Produces small umbels of flat, cream to yellow flowers in spring. In summer, oval, toothed, mid-green leaves have striking purple-red midribs; in winter, leaves form tight buds covered with whitish farina. Cultivation group 3 or 4.

♀ ***P. auricula.*** Rosette-forming, evergreen, sometimes white-mealy perennial. H 20cm (8in), S 25cm (10in). Fully hardy. Bears fragrant, flat, yellow flowers in large umbels in spring. Oval, soft, pale green to grey-green leaves are densely covered with white farina. Cultivation group 1, 4 or 5.

P. beesiana, syn. *P. bulleyana* subsp. *beesiana* (illus p.281). Rosette-forming, deciduous or semi-evergreen Candelabra primula. H and S 60cm (2ft). Fully hardy. In summer, stout, white-mealy stems bear whorls of tubular, yellow-eyed, reddish-pink flowers. Has inversely lance-shaped to oval, toothed, mid-green leaves, with red midribs. Cultivation group 2.

***P. bhutanica* 'Sherriff's Variety'**, syn. *P. whitei* 'Sherriff's Variety' illus. p.281. Rosette-forming perennial. H 15cm (6in), S 20cm (8in). Fully hardy, but often short-lived. In spring produces neat umbels of tubular, pale ice-blue to sky-blue flowers, with strongly-toothed petals and a greenish-yellow eye surrounded by a broad white zone, close to oval to lance-shaped, crinkled, mid-green leaves. Cultivation group 3.

***P.* 'Blairside Yellow'** illus. p.282. Compact, border Auricula primula. H 10cm (4in), S 20cm (8in). Fully hardy. In early spring, bell-shaped, golden-yellow flowers nestle in a rosette of tiny, rounded to oval, pale green leaves. Cultivation group 2 or 5.

***P.* 'Blossom'** illus. p.283. Vigorous, alpine Auricula primula. H and S 10cm (4in). Fully hardy. Flat, deep crimson to bright red flowers with golden centres are borne profusely in spring. Has oval, dark green leaves. Is suitable for exhibition. Cultivation group 1 or 4.

♀ ***P. bulleyana*** illus. p.283. Rosette-forming, semi-evergreen, Candelabra primula. H and S 60cm (24in). Fully hardy. Tubular, deep orange flowers appear in early summer. Leaves are oval to lance-shaped, toothed and dark green. Cultivation group 2. subsp. ***beesiana*** see *P. beesiana*.

♀ ***P.* Charisma Series**. Rosette-forming, semi-evergreen or evergreen, Primrose Group primula. H and S 20cm (8in). Frost hardy. Has inversely oval, wrinkled, dark green leaves. In spring produces tubular flowers in a variety of different colours or self-coloured. Usually grown as a biennial. Cultivation group 1, 2 or 6. **'Charisma Blue'** (illus. p.281) has yellow-eyed, blue to purple-blue flowers. **'Charisma Red'** (illus. p.280) has pink to red flowers, with yellow centres.

P. chionantha subsp. ***melanops***, syn. *P. melanops* illus. p.280. Rosette-forming perennial. H 35cm (14in), S 50cm (20in). Fully hardy. In summer has umbels of pendent, narrowly funnel-shaped, deep violet-purple flowers, with black eyes, above long, strap-shaped, mid-green leaves. Cultivation group 2 or 4.

***P.* 'Chloë'** illus. p.282. Green-edged, show Auricula primula. H and S 10cm (4in). Fully hardy. In late spring produces flat, dark-green-edged flowers with a black body colour and brilliant white paste centres. Oval leaves are dark green and have no farina. Is good for exhibition. Cultivation group 4.

P. chungensis illus. p.282. Vigorous, rosette-forming Candelabra primula. H 80cm (32in), S 60cm (24in). Fully hardy. In summer bears tiered whorls of tubular, orange flowers among oval to lance-shaped, mid-green leaves. Cultivation group 2.

P. clarkei illus. p.281. Small, rosette-forming perennial. H 7cm (3in), S 15cm (6in). Fully hardy. In spring has flat, rose-pink flowers, with yellow eyes, just above a clump of rounded to oval, pale green leaves. Cultivation group 2 or 4. Divide in late winter.

P. clusiana illus. p.280. Small, rosette-forming, evergreen perennial. H 8cm (3in), S 15cm (6in). Fully hardy. In spring bears umbels of tubular, rose-pink flowers with white eyes. Leaves are oval, glossy and mid-green. Cultivation group 4 or 5.

***P.* 'Craddock White'** illus. p.280. Rosette-forming, deciduous or semi-evergreen, Primrose Group primula. H to 12cm (5in), S 25cm (10in). Fully hardy. Fragrant, upward-facing, flat, white flowers, with yellow eyes, are borne in spring just above long, oval, red-veined, dark green leaves. Cultivation group 1 or 2.

♀ ***P.* Crescendo Series** illus. p.283. Rosette-forming, semi-evergreen or evergreen, Polyanthus Group primula. H and S 20cm (8in). Fully hardy. Has inversely oval, wrinkled, dark green leaves. In spring produces umbels of tubular, yellow-centred flowers in a variety of different colours. Usually grown as a biennial. Cultivation group 1, 2 or 6.

***P.* 'David Green'.** Rosette-forming, Primrose Group primula. H 10cm (4in), S 15–20cm (6–8in). Fully hardy. In spring produces flat, bright crimson-purple flowers amid oval, coarse, mid-green leaves. Cultivation group 1 or 2.

♀ ***P. denticulata*** (Drumstick primula; illus. p.281). Robust, rosette-forming perennial. H and S 45cm (18in). Fully hardy. From early to mid-spring, dense, rounded heads of flat, lilac, purple or pink flowers are borne on tops of stout stems. Mid-green leaves are broadly lance-shaped and toothed. Cultivation group 1 or 2. var. ***alba*** (illus. p.280) has white flowers.

***P.* 'Dreamer'** illus. p.333; cultivation group 6.

P. edgeworthii. See *P. nana*.

♀ ***P. elatior*** (Oxlip; illus. p.282). Variable, rosette-forming, evergreen or semi-evergreen perennial. H 30cm (12in), S 25cm (10in). Fully hardy. Umbels of small, fragrant, tubular, yellow flowers appear in spring, above neat, oval to lance-shaped, toothed, mid-green leaves. Cultivation group 1 or 2.

***P.* 'E.R. Janes'.** Vigorous, rosette-forming, semi-evergreen, Primrose Group primula. H 10–15cm (4–6in), S 30–40cm (12–16in). Fully hardy. Flat, pale rose-pink flowers, flushed with orange, are borne in spring amid broadly oval, toothed, mid-green leaves. Cultivation group 1 or 2.

P. farinosa (Bird's-eye primrose; illus. p.280). Rosette-forming perennial. H and S 25cm (10in). Fully hardy. In spring, umbels of tubular, lilac-pink, occasionally white, flowers are borne on short, stout stems. Oval, toothed, mid-green leaves are densely covered with white farina. Cultivation group 2 or 4.

P. flaccida, syn. *P. nutans* of gardens. Lax, rosette-forming, short-lived perennial. H 50cm (20in), S 30cm (12in). Fully hardy. In early summer, each stout stem produces a conical head of pendent, bell-shaped, lavender or violet flowers above narrowly oval, pale to mid-green leaves. Cultivation group 3 or 4.

♀ ***P. florindae*** (Giant cowslip; illus. p.282). Bold, rosette-forming perennial. H 1.2m (4ft), S 1m (3ft). Fully hardy. In summer, large heads of pendent, bell-shaped, sulphur-yellow flowers appear above broadly lance-shaped, toothed, mid-green leaves. Cultivation group 1 or 2.

P. forrestii illus. p.282. Rosette-forming, evergreen perennial. H 60cm (24in), S 45cm (18in). Frost hardy. Dense umbels of flat, yellow flowers with orange eyes are borne in late spring or early summer. Has oval, toothed, dark green leaves. Cultivation group 4 or 5.

♀ ***P. frondosa*** illus. p.281. Compact, rosette-forming perennial. H 15cm (6in), S 25cm (10in). Fully hardy. In spring bears umbels of flat, yellow-eyed, lilac-rose to reddish-purple flowers on short stems above neat, oval, mid-green leaves, densely covered with white farina. Cultivation group 2 or 4.

***P.* 'Garryarde Guinevere'.** See *P.* 'Guinevere'.

***P.* Gold-laced Group** illus. p.282. Erect, semi-evergreen or evergreen, Polyanthus Group primulas. H 25cm (10in), S 30cm (12in). Fully hardy. Produces flat flowers, in a variety of colours, with gold-laced margins, from mid- to late spring. Leaves are oval and mid-green, sometimes tinged red. Raise annually by seed. Cultivation group 2 or 4.

P. gracilipes illus. p.281. Rosette-forming, evergreen or semi-evergreen perennial. H 1cm (4in), S 20cm (8in). Fully hardy. Tubular, purplish-pink flowers with greenish-yellow eyes are borne singly in spring or early summer among oval, wavy, toothed, mid-green leaves. Cultivation group 3 or 4.

***P.* Grand Burgundy Series** illus. p.283. Rosette-forming, semi-evergreen or evergreen, Polyanthus Group primula. H and S 15–20cm (6–8in). Frost hardy. Has inversely oval, wrinkled, mid- to dark green leaves. In spring produces umbels of tubular, yellow-eyed flowers in a variety of different colours. Cultivation group 1, 2 or 6.

♀ ***P.* 'Guinevere'**, syn. *P.* 'Garryarde Guinevere'. Vigorous, rosette-forming, evergreen Polyanthus Group primula. H 12cm (5in), S 25cm (10in). Fully hardy. Flat, purplish-pink flowers with yellow eyes are produced in spring among oval, toothed, bronze-green leaves. Cultivation group 2.

***P.* 'Harlow Car'.** Rosette-forming, Alpine Auricula primula. H 10–15cm (4–6in), S 15–20cm (6–8in). Fully hardy. In spring produces flat, white flowers on short stems above oval, soft, mid-green leaves. Cultivation group 1 or 4.

P. helodoxa. See *P. prolifera*.

P. hirsuta, syn. *P. rubra* illus. p.281. Rosette-forming, evergreen perennial. H 10cm (4in), S 25cm (10in). Fully hardy. Produces small umbels of flat, rose or lilac flowers in spring. Has small, rounded to oval, sticky, mid-green leaves. Cultivation group 1, 2 or 4.

♀ ***P.* 'Inverewe'** illus. p.283. Vigorous, rosette-forming, semi-evergreen, Candelabra primula. H 75cm (30in), S 60cm (24in). Fully hardy. Tubular, bright orange-red flowers are produced in summer on stems coated with white farina. Has oval to lance-shaped, toothed, coarse, mid-green leaves. Cultivation group 2.

P. ioessa. Rosette-forming perennial. H Clustered heads of funnel-shaped, pink or pinkish-mauve, or sometimes white, flowers are borne in spring or early summer above oval to lance-shaped, toothed, mid-green leaves. Cultivation group 2, 3 or 4.

***P.* 'Janet'** illus. p.281. Vigorous, rosette-forming, alpine Auricula. H 15–20cm (6–8in), S 15cm (6in). Fully hardy. In spring, clusters of outward-facing, flat, purplish-pink flowers are produced above a rosette of oval to rounded, soft, mid-green leaves. Cultivation group 1 or 4. Propagate by offsets after flowering.

***P.* 'Janie Hill'** illus. p.283. Rosette-forming, alpine Auricula. H 10cm (4in), S 15cm (6in). Fully hardy. Flat, dark to golden-brown flowers, with golden centres, open in mid- to late spring. Has oval, mid-green leaves. Is useful for exhibition. Cultivation group 4 or 5.

♀ ***P. japonica.*** Robust, rosette-forming, Candelabra primula. H and S 45cm (18in). Fully hardy. In early summer produces tubular, deep red flowers on stout stems above oval to lance-shaped, toothed, coarse, pale green leaves. Cultivation group 2. ♀ **'Miller's Crimson'** (illus. p.283) has intense crimson flowers. ♀ **'Postford White'** (illus. p.280) bears white flowers.

***P.* Joker Series.** Compact, rosette-forming, evergreen or semi-evergreen perennial. H 8–10cm (3–4in), S 25cm (10in). Half hardy. Has short-stemmed, inversely lance-shaped to oval, mid-green leaves. In spring produces tubular flowers, in a range of colours, including bicolours, with yellow or creamy-yellow eyes. Is also available in selected colour variants. **'Cherry'** (illus. p.281) has mid-pink petals with crimson bases. **'Red and Gold'** (illus. p.283) has golden-yellow flowers with wide, red margins.
♀ ***P. kewensis*** illus. p.282. Rosette-forming, evergreen perennial. H 45cm (18in), S 20cm (8in). Half hardy. Produces whorls of fragrant, tubular, bright yellow flowers in early spring. Oval to spoon-shaped, toothed, mid-green leaves are sparsely covered with white farina. Cultivation group 6.
***P.* 'Linda Pope'**, syn. *P. marginata* 'Linda Pope' illus. p.281. Vigorous, rosette-forming, evergreen or semi-evergreen perennial derived from *P. marginata*. H 15cm (6in), S 30cm (12in). Fully hardy. In spring bears flat, mauve-blue flowers on short stems above oval, toothed, mid-green leaves covered with white farina. Cultivation group 4 or 5.
P. malacoides (single pink, illus. p.280; double pink, illus. p.280). Erect, rosette-forming, evergreen perennial, usually grown as an annual. H 30–45cm (12–18in), S 20cm (8in). Half hardy. In winter-spring, small, flat, single or double, pale lilac-purple, reddish-pink and white flowers are borne in whorls of decreasing size up slender, softly hairy stems. Leaves are dainty, oval, slightly frilly-margined, softly downy and pale green. Cultivation group 6.
***P.* 'Margaret Martin'** illus. p.282. Rosette-forming, show Auricula primula. H 10cm (4in), S 15cm (6in). Fully hardy. Bears flat, grey-edged flowers, with a black body colour and white centres, in mid- to late spring. Has spoon-shaped, grey-green leaves covered with white farina. Is excellent for exhibition. Cultivation group 4.
♀ ***P. marginata*** illus. p.281. Rosette-forming, evergreen or semi-evergreen perennial. H 15cm (6in), S 30cm (12in). Fully hardy. In spring, clusters of funnel-shaped, blue-lilac flowers appear above oval, toothed, mid-green leaves densely covered with white farina. Cultivation group 4 or 5. **'Linda Pope'** see *P.* 'Linda Pope'. ♀ **'Prichard's Variety'** (illus. p.281) has lilac-purple flowers with white eyes.
***P.* 'Mark'** illus. p.283. Vigorous, alpine Auricula primula. H and S 10cm (4in). Fully hardy. Produces flat, pink flowers, with light yellow centres, in spring. Leaves are oval and vibrant green. Is good for exhibition. Cultivation group 4.
***P.* 'Matthew Yates'** illus. p.283. Vigorous, double auricula. H and S12cm (5in). Fully hardy. Produces fully double, very dark blackish-red flowers in tight trusses in spring. Leaves are inversely oval and mid-green with some farina. Is good for exhibition. Cultivation group 1 or 4.
P. melanops. See *P. chionantha* subsp. *melanops*.
***P.* 'Miss Indigo'**, syn. *P. vulgaris* 'Miss Indigo' illus. p.283. Vigorous, rosette-forming, evergreen or semi-evergreen perennial. H 20cm (8in), S 35cm (14in). Fully hardy. Has oval to lance-shaped, toothed, bright green leaves. In spring produces flat, double, deep rich purple flowers, with creamy-white tips. Cultivation group 2.
P. modesta. Rosette-forming perennial. H and S 20cm (8in). Fully hardy. Dense heads of small, tubular, pinkish-purple flowers appear on short stems in spring. Rounded to oval, mid-green leaves are covered with yellow farina. Cultivation group 1 or 4. var. ***fauriae*** (illus. p.281), H and S 5cm (2in), produces yellow-eyed, pinkish-purple flowers and leaves covered with white farina.
***P.* 'Moonstone'** illus. p.282. Rosette-forming, border Auricula primula. H 12cm (5in), S 15cm (6in). Fully hardy. Rounded, double, whitish- or greenish-yellow flowers are produced in profusion in spring. Leaves are oval and mid-green. Preferably, grow under glass. Cultivation group 4 or 5.
***P.* 'Mrs J.H. Wilson'**, syn. *P.* × *pubescens* 'Mrs J.H. Wilson' illus. p.281. Rosette-forming, alpine Auricula primula. H and S 10–15cm (4–6in). Fully hardy. Bears small umbels of flat, white-centred, purple flowers in spring. Oval leaves are greyish-green. Cultivation group 1 or 4.
P. nana, syn. *P. edgeworthii* illus. p.280. Rosette-forming perennial. H 10cm (4in), S 15cm (6in). Fully hardy. Flat, pale mauve flowers with white eyes appear singly among oval, toothed, pale green leaves in spring. Cultivation group 3 or 4.
P. nutans of gardens. See *P. flaccida*.
P. obconica. Erect, rosette-forming, evergreen perennial, usually grown as an annual. H 23–40cm (9–16in), S 25cm (10in). Frost tender to frost hardy. Flat, purple, lilac or white flowers, with yellow eyes, are borne in dense umbels during winter-spring. Leaves are oval, toothed, hairy and pale green. Cultivation group 6.
***P.* 'Orb'.** Neat, show Auricula primula. H and S 10cm (4in). Fully hardy. Flat, dark-green-edged flowers, each with a black body colour and a central zone of white paste, are produced from mid- to late spring. Has spoon-shaped, dark green leaves without farina. Is good for exhibition. Cultivation group 4.
***P.* Pacific Series** (Polyanthus). Polyanthus Group primula H and S 20–22cm (8–9in); dwarf, illus. p.340. Fully hardy. Rosette-forming perennial, normally grown as a biennial, with lance-shaped leaves. Has heads of large, fragrant, flat flowers in shades of blue, yellow, red, pink or white in spring. Cultivation group 1, 2, 4 or 6.
P. palinuri illus. p.282. Rosette-forming, evergreen perennial. H and S 30cm (12in). Fully to frost hardy. One-sided clusters of semi-pendent, narrowly funnel-shaped, yellow flowers appear on thick stems in early summer. Has rounded to oval, lightly toothed, thick-textured, powdered, green leaves. Cultivation group 1 or 4; requires full sun.
P. petiolaris illus. p.280. Rosette-forming, evergreen perennial. H 10cm (4in), S 20cm (8in). Fully hardy. Tubular, purplish-pink flowers, with toothed petals, are borne singly in spring. Has small, oval, toothed, mid-green leaves. Cultivation group 3 or 4.
P. poissonii illus. p.281. Rosette-forming, evergreen perennial. H 45–50cm (18–20in), S 20–25cm (8–10in). Fully hardy. Has long, inversely lance-shaped, dark green leaves. Produces 4–5 whorls of tubular, plum-purple flowers, with golden (rarely white) eyes, in early and mid-summer. Cultivation Group 3.
P. polyneura illus. p.281. Rosette-forming perennial. H and S 45cm (18in). Fully to frost hardy. Dense heads of tubular, pale rose, rich rose or purple-rose flowers are produced in late spring or early summer. Rounded to oval, shallowly lobed, downy, soft leaves are mid-green. Cultivation group 2.
♀ ***P. prolifera***, syn *P. helodoxa* illus. p.282. Rosette-forming, evergreen, Candelabra primula. H and S 60cm (24in). Fully hardy. Bell-shaped, yellow flowers are borne in summer. Leaves are oval, toothed and pale green. Cultivation group 2.
***P.* × *pubescens* 'Mrs J.H. Wilson'.** See *P.* 'Mrs J.H. Wilson'.
♀ ***P. pulverulenta*** illus. p.283. Rosette-forming, Candelabra primula. H 90cm (36in), S 60cm (24in). Fully hardy. In early summer bears tubular, deep red flowers with purple-red eyes on stems covered with white farina. Has broadly lance-shaped, toothed, coarse, mid-green leaves. Cultivation group 2. ♀ **'Bartley'** (illus. p.280) has pink flowers.
P. reidii. Robust, rosette-forming perennial. H 5–15cm (2–6in), S 10–15cm (4–6in). Fully to frost hardy. Produces dense clusters of bell-shaped, pure white flowers on slender stems in early summer. Has oval, hairy, pale green leaves. Cultivation group 3 or 4. var. ***williamsii*** (illus. p.281) is more robust and has purplish-blue to pale blue flowers.
♀ ***P. rosea*** illus. p.280. Rosette-forming perennial. H and S 20cm (8in). Fully hardy. In early spring bears small clusters of flat, glowing rose-pink flowers on short stems, among oval to lance-shaped, mid-green leaves, often bronze-flushed when young. Cultivation group 2.
***P.* 'Royal Velvet'.** Vigorous, rosette-forming, border Auricula primula. H and S 15–20cm (6–8in). Fully hardy. Flat, velvety, blue-tinged, maroon flowers, with frilled petals and large, creamy-yellow centres, are produced in spring. Has large, spoon-shaped, pale green leaves. Cultivation group 2 or 5.
P. rubra. See *P. hirsuta*.
P.* × *scapeosa illus. p.280. Vigorous, rosette-forming perennial. H 10cm (4in), S 25cm (10in). Fully hardy. Clusters of outward-facing, flat, mauve-pink flowers, in early spring, are initially hidden by broadly oval, sharply toothed, mid-green leaves covered at first with slight farina; later, flower stem elongates above leaves. Cultivation group 3 or 4.
P. secundiflora illus. p.281. Rosette-forming, evergreen or semi-evergreen perennial. H 60–90cm (24–36in), S 60cm (24in). Fully hardy. Has clusters of pendent, funnel-shaped, reddish-purple flowers in summer above lance-shaped, toothed leaves. Cultivation group 2.
♀ ***P. sieboldii*** illus. p.281. Rosette-forming perennial. H 30cm (12in), S 45cm (18in). Fully hardy. Umbels of flat, white, pink or purple flowers, with white eyes, open above oval, round-toothed, downy, soft, pale green leaves in early summer. Cultivation group 2. **'Sumina'** bears large, wisteria-blue flowers. **'Wine Lady'** (illus. p.280) has white flowers, strongly suffused with purplish-red.
♀ ***P. sikkimensis*** illus. p.282. Rosette-forming perennial. H 60–90cm (24–36in), S 60cm (24in). Fully hardy. Pendent clusters of funnel-shaped, yellow flowers are borne in summer. Has rounded to oval, toothed, pale green leaves. Cultivation group 2.
P. sinensis illus. p.280. Erect, rosette-forming, evergreen perennial. H and S 15–20cm (6–8in). Frost tender. Flat, purple, purple-rose, pink or white flowers, with yellow eyes, are produced in neat whorls in winter-spring. Leaves are oval, toothed, hairy and mid-green. Cultivation group 6.
P. sonchifolia illus. p.281. Rosette-forming, deciduous perennial. H 5cm (2in), S 30cm (12in). Fully hardy. Produces dense umbels of tubular, blue-purple flowers with white eyes and yellow margins in spring. Leaves are oval to lance-shaped, toothed and mid-green. Cultivation group 3 or 4.
***P.* Super Giants Series.** Rosette-forming Polyanthus Group primulas, usually grown as biennials. H and S 15–20cm (6–8in). Fully hardy. Produce large, fragrant, flat flowers in a wide range of colours in spring (blue, illus. p.344). Cultivation group 1 or 2.
***P.* 'Tawny Port'.** Very dwarf, rosette-forming, evergreen or semi-evergreen, Polyanthus Group primula. H 10–15cm (4–6in), S 15–20cm (6–8in). Fully hardy. Bears flat, port-wine-coloured flowers on short stems in spring. Rounded to oval, toothed leaves are reddish-green. Cultivation group 1, 2 or 4.
***P.* 'Trouble'** illus. p.283. Vigorous, double auricula. H and S 12cm (5in). Fully hardy. Leaves are broad, inversely oval, mid-green and irregularly toothed. Produces fully double flowers, a blend of yellow and pink, resulting in pale coffee-coloured blooms borne in tight trusses in spring. Cultivation group 1 or 4.
♀ ***P. veris*** (Cowslip; illus. p.282). Very variable, rosette-forming, evergreen or semi-evergreen perennial. H and S 25cm (10in). Fully hardy. Tight clusters of fragrant, tubular, yellow flowers are produced on stout stems in spring. Leaves are oval to lance-shaped, toothed and mid-green. Cultivation group 1 or 2.
P. verticillata illus. p.282. Rosette-forming perennial. H 20–25cm (8–10in), S 15–20cm (6–8in). Half hardy. Fragrant, bell-shaped, yellow flowers are borne in whorls in spring. Has oval, toothed, mid-green leaves. Cultivation group 4 or 6.
♀ ***P. vialii*** illus. p.283. Rosette-forming, often short-lived perennial. H 30–60cm (12–24in), S 30cm (12in). Fully to frost hardy. Dense, conical spikes of tubular, bluish-purple- and-

red flowers are produced in late spring. Has lance-shaped, toothed, soft, mid-green leaves. Cultivation group 1 or 2.
♀ ***P. vulgaris*** (Primrose; illus. p.282). Rosette-forming, evergreen or semi-evergreen perennial. H 20cm (8in), S 35cm (14in). Fully hardy. Flat, soft yellow flowers, with darker eyes, are borne singly among oval to lance-shaped, toothed, bright green leaves in spring. Cultivation group 2. **'Alba Plena'** (illus. p.280) has double, white flowers. **'Gigha White'** (illus. p.280) is very floriferous and has yellow-eyed, white flowers. **'Lilacina Plena'** (illus. p.281) is vigorous and free-flowering, with fully double, lilac-purple flowers. **'Miss Indigo'** see *P.* 'Miss Indigo'. ♀ subsp. ***sibthorpii*** (illus. p.280) has pink or purplish-pink flowers.
***P.* Wanda Supreme Series** illus. p.283. Evergreen or semi-evergreen perennial. H 8–10cm (3–4in), S 15cm (6in). Frost hardy. Has inversely lance-shaped to oval, bronze to dark green foliage. From winter to mid-spring produces flowers in a mixture of different shades of blue, yellow, purple, burgundy, red, rose and pink bicolours. Cultivation group 1 or 2.
P. warshenewskiana illus. p.280. Rosette-forming perennial. H 7cm (3in), S 15cm (6in). Fully hardy. Tiny, flat, white-eyed, bright pink flowers sit just above spoon-shaped, dark green leaves in early spring. Cultivation group 2 or 4. Divide clumps regularly in late winter before flowering.
***P. whitei* 'Sherriff's Variety'.** See *P. bhutanica* 'Sherriff's Variety'.
***P.* 'Yellow Dream'** illus p.351.

Primula, Drumstick. See *Primula denticulata*, illus. p.281.
Prince Albert's yew. See *Saxegothaea conspicua.*
Prince of Wales heath. See *Erica perspicua*, illus. p.174.
Prince's feather. See *Amaranthus hypochondriacus*, illus. p.342.
Princess tree. See *Paulownia tomentosa*, illus. p.73.

PRINSEPIA

ROSACEAE

Genus of deciduous, usually spiny, spring- and early summer-flowering shrubs, grown for their habit, flowers and fruits. Fully hardy. Needs sun and any not too dry soil. Does well against a south- or west-facing wall. Propagate by softwood cuttings in summer or by seed in autumn.
P. uniflora illus. p.133.

Privet. See *Ligustrum.*
Chinese. See *Ligustrum lucidum.*
Japanese. See *Ligustrum japonicum.*
Wax. See *Peperomia glabella*, illus. p.317.

PROBOSCIDEA

MARTYNIACEAE/PEDALIACEAE

Genus of annuals and perennials. Half hardy. Grow in a sunny, sheltered position and in fertile, well-drained soil. Propagate by seed sown under glass in early spring.
P. fragrans. Moderately fast-growing, upright annual. H 60cm (24in), S 30cm (12in). Has rounded, serrated or lobed leaves. Fragrant, bell-shaped, crimson-purple flowers, to 5cm (2in) long, appear in summer-autumn, followed by rounded, horned, brown fruits, 8–10cm (3–4in) long, which, if gathered young, may be pickled and eaten.
P. jussieui. See *P. louisianica.*
P. louisianica, syn. *Martynia louisianica, P. jussieui, P. proboscidea* (Common devil's claw, Common unicorn plant, Ram's horn) Erect to spreading annual. Has rounded to ovate, unlobed leaves. In summer, bears funnel-shaped, fragrant, reddish-purple to purple flowers, followed by narrow, crested fruit, to 6cm (2½in) long, with beak-like projections.
P. proboscidea. See *P. louisianica.*

Prometheum sempervivoides. See *Sedum sempervivoides.*
Prophet flower. See *Arnebia pulchra.*

PROSTANTHERA
Mint bush

LABIATAE/LAMIACEAE

Genus of evergreen shrubs, grown for their flowers and mint-scented foliage. Half hardy to frost tender, min. 5°C (41°F). Requires full light or partial shade and fertile, well-drained soil. Water containerized specimens freely when in full growth, moderately at other times. Leggy stems may be cut back after flowering. Propagate by seed in spring or by semi-ripe cuttings in late summer.
P. ovalifolia illus. p.141.
♀ ***P. rotundifolia*** illus. p.141.

Prostrate coleus. See *Plectranthus oertendahlii.*
Prostrate speedwell. See *Veronica prostrata*, illus. p.369.

PROTEA

PROTEACEAE

Genus of evergreen shrubs and trees, grown mainly for their colourfully bracted flower heads. Is difficult to grow. Frost tender, min. 5–7°C (41–5°F). Requires full light and well-drained, neutral to acid soil, low in phosphates and nitrates. Water containerized specimens moderately, less when not in full growth. Plants under glass must have plenty of ventilation throughout the year. Prune, if necessary, in early spring. Propagate by seed in spring or by semi-ripe cuttings in summer.
P. barbigera. See *P. magnifica.*
P. cynaroides illus. p.157.
P. magnifica, syn. *P. barbigera.* Evergreen, rounded to spreading shrub. H and S 1m (3ft). Has oblong to elliptic, leathery, mid- to greyish-green leaves. Spherical flower heads, 15–20cm (6–8in) wide, with petal-like, pink, red, yellow or white bracts, appear in spring-summer.
P. mellifera. See *P. repens.*
P. neriifolia illus. p.136.
P. repens, syn. *P. mellifera* (Sugar bush). Evergreen, ovoid to rounded shrub. H and S 2–3m (6–10ft). Mid-green leaves are narrowly oblong to elliptic and tinted blue-grey. In spring-summer produces cup-shaped, 13cm (5in) long flower heads, with petal-like, pink, red or white bracts.

Protea, King. See *Protea cynaroides*, illus. p.157.

PRUMNOPITYS

PODOCARPACEAE

See also CONIFERS.
P. andina, syn. *Podocarpus andinus* (Plum yew, Plum-fruited yew). Conifer with a domed crown on several stems. H 15m (50ft), S 8m (25ft). Frost hardy. Has smooth, grey-brown bark, needle-like, flattened, bluish-green leaves and edible, yellowish-white fruits like small plums.

PRUNELLA
Self-heal

LABIATAE/LAMIACEAE

Genus of semi-evergreen perennials with spreading mats of leaves from which arise short, stubby flower spikes in mid-summer. Suits rock gardens. Fully hardy. Grows well in sun or shade and in moist but well-drained soil. Propagate by division in spring.
P. grandiflora, syn. *P.* × *webbiana* (Large self-heal) illus. p.394.
♀ **'Loveliness'** Semi-evergreen, basal-rosetted, ground-cover perennial. H 10–15cm (4–6in), S 30cm (12in). Bears whorls of pale purple flowers in terminal spikes on leafy stems in summer. May be invasive; cut old flower stems before they seed.**'Pink Loveliness'** bears soft pink flowers in terminal spikes in summer. Makes good ground cover, but may be invasive. Cut off old flower stems before they produce seed. **'White Loveliness'** has white flowers.
P. × webbiana. See *P. grandiflora.*

PRUNUS
Cherry

ROSACEAE

Genus of deciduous or evergreen shrubs and trees. The trees are grown mainly for their single (5-petalled) to double flowers and autumn colour; the shrubs for their autumn colour, bark, flowers or fruits. All have oval to oblong leaves. Plants described here are fully hardy, unless otherwise stated. Evergreen species tolerate sun or shade; deciduous species prefer full sun. All may be grown in any but waterlogged soil. Trim deciduous hedges after flowering, evergreen ones in early or mid-spring. Propagate deciduous species by seed in autumn, deciduous hybrids and selected forms by softwood cuttings in summer. Increase evergreens by semi-ripe cuttings in summer. Bullfinches may eat flower buds and foliage may be attacked by aphids, caterpillars and the fungal disease silver leaf. Flowering cherries are prone to a fungus that causes 'witches' brooms' (abnormal, crowded shoots). Certain *Prunus* species and cultivars, notably cultivars of the almond (*P. dulcis*) and the peach (*P. persica*), are grown for their edible fruits. Leaves and fruits of most other species may cause severe discomfort if ingested.
♀ ***P.* 'Accolade'** illus. p.84.
♀ ***P.* 'Amanogawa'.** Deciduous, upright tree. H 10m (30ft), S 4m (12ft). Bears fragrant, semi-double, pale pink flowers in late spring. Oblong to oval, taper-pointed, dark green leaves turn orange and red in autumn.
***P. × amygdalopersica* 'Pollardii'.** See *P. × persicoides.*
♀ ***P. avium*** illus. p.67. ♀ **'Plena'** illus. p.72.
♀ ***P. × blireana.*** Deciduous, spreading shrub or small tree. H and S 4m (12ft). Bears double, pink flowers in mid-spring and has oval, purple leaves.
P. campanulata (Bell-flowered cherry, Taiwan cherry). Deciduous, spreading tree. H and S 8m (25ft). Frost hardy. Shallowly bell-shaped, deep rose-red flowers are produced from early to mid-spring, before or with oval, taper-pointed, dark green leaves. Fruits are small, rounded and reddish.
P. cerasifera (Cherry plum, Myrobalan). ♀ **'Nigra'** illus. p.87. **'Pissardii'** is a deciduous, round-headed tree. H and S 10m (30ft). Small, 5-petalled, pale pink flowers open from early to mid-spring and are often followed by edible, plum-like, red fruits. Has oval, red, young leaves turning deeper red, then purple. May be used for hedging.
***P.* 'Cheal's Weeping'.** See *P.* 'Kiku-shidare-zakura'.
♀ ***P. × cistena*** illus. p.150.
P. davidiana (David's peach). Deciduous, spreading tree. H and S 8m (25ft). Saucer-shaped, 5-petalled, white or pale pink flowers are carried on slender shoots in late winter and early spring, but are susceptible to late frosts. Leaves are narrowly oval and dark green. Fruits are rounded and reddish.
P. dulcis (Almond). **'Roseoplena'** is a deciduous, spreading tree. H and S 8m (25ft). Bears double, pink flowers in late winter and early spring, before oblong, pointed, toothed, dark green leaves.
***P. glandulosa* 'Alba Plena'** illus. p.149. **'Rosea Plena'** see *P.g.* 'Sinensis'. ♀ **'Sinensis'** (syn. *P.g.* 'Rosea Plena') is a deciduous, rounded, open shrub. H and S 1.5m (5ft). Produces double, bright rose-pink flowers in late spring and oval, mid-green leaves. Flowers best when grown against a south- or west-facing wall. Cut back young shoots to within a few buds of old wood after flowering.
***P.* 'Hally Jolivette'.** Deciduous, rounded, compact tree. H and S 5m (15ft). Double, white flowers open from pink buds in late spring. Leaves are oval and dark green.
***P. × hillieri* 'Spire'.** See *P.* 'Spire'.
***P.* 'Hokusai'**, syn. *P.* 'Uzuzakura', illus. p.83.
P. incisa (Fuji cherry) illus. p.82. **'February Pink'** is a deciduous, spreading tree. H and S 8m (25ft). Oval, sharply toothed, dark green leaves are reddish when young, orange-red in autumn. During mild, winter periods bears 5-petalled, pale pink flowers. Has tiny, rounded, reddish fruits.
P. jamasakura, syn. *P. serrulata* var. *spontanea*, illus. p.72.
♀ ***P.* 'Kanzan'** illus. p.73.
♀ ***P.* 'Kiku-shidare-zakura'**, syn. *P.* 'Cheal's Weeping', illus. p.84.
♀ ***P.* 'Kursar'.** Deciduous, spreading

tree. H and S 8m (25ft). Bears masses of small, 5-petalled, deep pink flowers in early spring. Oval, dark green leaves turn brilliant orange in autumn.
♀ ***P. laurocerasus*** (Cherry laurel, Laurel). Evergreen, dense, bushy shrub becoming spreading and open. H 6m (20ft), S 10m (30ft). Frost hardy. Has long spikes of small, single, white flowers from mid- to late spring, large, oblong, glossy, bright green leaves and cherry-shaped, red, then black fruits. Restrict growth by cutting back hard in spring. ♀ **'Otto Luyken'** illus. p.150. **'Schipkaensis'**, H 2m (6ft), S 3m (10ft), is fully hardy and of elegant, spreading habit, with narrow leaves and freely borne flowers in upright spikes. **'Zabeliana'** illus. p.150.
♀ ***P. lusitanica*** (Laurel, Portugal laurel). Evergreen, bushy, dense shrub or spreading tree. H and S 6–10m (20–30ft). Frost hardy. Reddish-purple shoots bear oval, glossy, dark green leaves. Slender spikes of small, fragrant, 5-petalled, white flowers appear in early summer, followed by egg-shaped, fleshy, deep purple fruits. Restrict growth by pruning hard in spring. subsp. ***azorica*** illus. p.122. **'Variegata'** illus. p.122.
P. maackii illus. p.80.
P. mahaleb illus. p.72.
***P.* 'Mount Fuji'.** See *P.* 'Shirotae'.
P. mume (Japanese apricot). **'Beni-chidori'** (syn. *P.m.* 'Beni-shidon', *P.m.* **'Beni-chidori'**) illus. p.126. **'Omoi-no-mama'** (syn. *P.m.* 'Omoi-no-wac') illus. p.126. **'Pendula'** is a deciduous, weeping tree with slender, arching branches. H and S 6m (20ft). Fragrant, 5-petalled, pink flowers appear in late winter or early spring, before broadly oval, bright green leaves, and are sometimes succeeded by edible, apricot-like, yellow fruits.
♀ ***P.* 'Okame'.** Deciduous, bushy-headed tree. H 10m (30ft), S 8m (25ft). Bears masses of 5-petalled, carmine-pink flowers in early spring. Oval, sharply toothed, dark green leaves turn orange-red in autumn.
P. padus (Bird cherry) illus. p.72.
♀ **'Colorata'** is a deciduous, spreading tree, conical when young. H 15m (50ft), S 10m (30ft). Produces pendent racemes of fragrant, cup-shaped, 5-petalled, pink flowers in late spring, followed by small, pea-shaped, black fruits. Oval, reddish-purple young leaves mature to dark green and then turn red or yellow in autumn. **'Grandiflora'** see *P.p.* 'Watereri'. **'Plena'** has long-lasting, double flowers and no fruits. ♀ **'Watereri'** (syn. *P.p.* 'Grandiflora') bears long racemes of flowers from mid- to late spring.
♀ ***P.* 'Pandora'** illus. p.83.
***P. pendula* 'Pendula Rubra'.** See *P.* × *subhirtella* 'Pendula Rubra'. **'Stellata'** (syn. *P.* 'Pink Star', *P.* × *subhirtella* 'Stellata') illus. p.83.
P. pensylvanica (Pin cherry). Deciduous, spreading tree. H 15m (50ft), S 10m (30ft). Has peeling, red-banded bark and oval, taper-pointed, bright green leaves. Produces clusters of small, star-shaped, 5-petalled, white flowers from mid- to late spring, followed by small, pea-shaped, red fruits.
P. persica (Peach). **'Clara Meyer'** is a deciduous, spreading tree. H 5m (15ft), S 6m (20ft). Bears double, bright pink flowers in mid-spring. Has slender, lance-shaped, bright green leaves. Is susceptible to the fungal disease peach leaf curl. **'Prince Charming'** illus. p.84.
P.* × *persicoides, syn. *P. amygdalopersica* 'Pollardii'. Deciduous, spreading tree. H and S 7m (22ft). Large, 5-petalled, bright pink flowers open from early to mid-spring, before oval, glossy, mid-green leaves emerge. Green, then brown fruits are like almonds in shape and taste.
♀ ***P.* 'Pink Perfection'** illus. p.83.
***P* 'Pink Star'.** See *P. pendula* 'Stellata'.
♀ ***P. sargentii*** illus. p.83.
P. serotina illus. p.61.
♀ ***P. serrula.*** Deciduous, round-headed tree. H and S 10m (30ft). Has gleaming, coppery-red bark that peels. In late spring bears small, 5-petalled, white flowers amid oval, tapering, toothed, dark green leaves that turn yellow in autumn. Fruits are tiny, rounded and reddish-brown.
P. serrulata* var. *spontanea. See *P. jamasakura.*
♀ ***P.* 'Shirofugen'** illus. p.83.
♀ ***P.* 'Shirotae',** syn. *P.* 'Mount Fuji', illus. p.82.
♀ ***P.* 'Shogetsu',** syn. *P.* 'Shimidsu', illus. p.82.
P. spinosa (Blackthorn, Sloe). **'Purpurea'** illus. p.118.
♀ ***P.* 'Spire',** syn. *P.* × *hillieri* 'Spire', illus. p.83.
P.* × *subhirtella (Higan cherry, Rosebud cherry). Deciduous, spreading tree. H and S 8m (25ft). From early to mid-spring, a profusion of small, 5-petalled, pale pink flowers appear before oval, taper-pointed, dark green leaves, which turn yellow in autumn. Has small, rounded, reddish-brown fruits.
♀ **'Autumnalis'** has semi-double,white flowers, pink in bud, in mild periods in winter. ♀ **'Pendula Rubra'** (syn. *P. pendula* 'Pendula Rubra') illus. p.84. **'Stellata'** see *P. pendula* 'Stellata'.
♀ ***P.* 'Taihaku'** illus. p.82.
P. tenella illus. p.151. ♀ **'Fire Hill'** is a deciduous, bushy shrub with upright, then spreading branches. H and S 2m (6ft). Narrowly oval, glossy, dark green leaves are a foil for small, almond-like, single, very deep pink flowers borne profusely from mid- to late spring, followed by small, almond-like fruits.
P. tomentosa (Downy cherry). Deciduous, bushy, dense shrub. H 1.5m (5ft), S 2m (6ft). Has small, 5-petalled, pale pink flowers from early to mid-spring before oval, downy, dark green leaves appear. Fruits are spherical and bright red. Thrives in hot summers.
***P.* 'Trailblazer'.** Deciduous, spreading tree. H and S 5m (15ft). Bears 5 petalled, white flowers from early to mid-spring, sometimes followed by edible, plum-like, red fruits. Oval, light green, young leaves mature to deep red-purple.
***P. triloba* 'Multiplex'.** Deciduous, bushy, spreading tree or shrub. H and S 4m (12ft). Double, pink flowers are borne in mid-spring. Has oval, dark green leaves, often 3-lobed, that turn yellow in autumn. Does best against a sunny wall. Cut back young shoots to within a few buds of old wood after flowering.
♀ ***P.* 'Ukon'** illus. p.82.
***P.* 'Uzuzakura'.** See *P.* 'Hokusai'.
P. virginiana (Virginian bird cherry). **'Shubert'** is a deciduous, conical tree. H 10m (30ft), S 8m (25ft). Produces dense spikes of small, star-shaped, white flowers from mid- to late spring, followed by dark purple-red fruits. Has oval, pale green, young leaves, turning deep reddish-purple in summer.
***P.* 'Yae-murasaki'** illus. p.84.
♀ ***P.* × *yedoensis*** illus. p.83.

PSEUDERANTHEMUM

ACANTHACEAE

Genus of evergreen perennials and shrubs, grown mainly for their foliage. Frost tender, min. 16°C (61°F). Requires partial shade and fertile, well-drained soil. Water potted plants freely when in full growth, moderately at other times. Tip prune young plants to promote a bushy habit. Cut leggy plants back hard in spring. Propagate annually or biennially as a pot plant by greenwood cuttings in spring or summer. Whitefly may sometimes be troublesome.
P. atropurpureum, syn. *Eranthemum atropurpureum.* Evergreen, erect shrub. H 1–1.2m (3–4ft), S 30–60cm (1–2ft). Has oval, strongly purple-flushed leaves and, mainly in summer, short spikes of tubular, purple-marked, white flowers.

PSEUDOCYDONIA

ROSACEAE

Genus of one species of deciduous or semi-evergreen, spring-flowering tree, grown for its bark, flowers and fruits. Frost hardy, but in cool areas grow against a south- or west-facing wall. Requires full sun and does well only in hot summers. Needs well-drained soil. Propagate by seed in autumn.
P. sinensis, syn. *Cydonia sinensis.* Deciduous or semi-evergreen, spreading tree. H and S 6m (20ft). Has decorative, flaking bark. Shallowly cup-shaped, pink flowers, borne from mid- to late spring, are followed after hot summers by large, egg-shaped, yellow fruits. Oval, finely toothed leaves are dark green.

Pseudofumaria lutea. See *Corydalis lutea.*
Pseudofumaria ochroleuca. See *Corydalis ochroleuca.*
Pseudogynoxys chenopodioides. See *Senecio confusus.*

PSEUDOLARIX

PINACEAE

See also CONIFERS.
♀ ***P. amabilis***, syn. *P. kaempferi*, illus. p.103.
P. kaempferi. See *P. amabilis.*

Pseudolobivia aurea. See *Echinopsis aurea.*
Pseudomuscari azureum. See *Muscari azureum.*

PSEUDOPANAX,
syn. NEOPANAX, NOTHOPANAX

ARALIACEAE

Genus of evergreen trees and shrubs, grown for their unusual foliage and fruits. Is excellent for landscaping and may also be grown in large containers. Insignificant flowers are produced in summer. Frost to half hardy. Grows in sun or semi-shade and in fertile, well-drained soil. Propagate by semi-ripe cuttings in summer or by seed in autumn or spring.
P. arboreus (Five fingers). Evergreen, round-headed, stout-branched tree. H 6m (20ft), S 4m (12ft). Frost hardy. Large, glossy, dark green leaves are divided into 5 or 7 oblong leaflets. Produces tiny, honey-scented, green flowers in summer, followed by rounded, purplish-black fruits on female plants.
P. crassifolius (Lancewood). Evergreen tree, unbranched for many years, then becoming round-headed. H 6m (20ft), S 2m (6ft). Frost hardy. Dark green leaves are extremely variable in shape on young trees, but eventually become long, narrow, rigid and downward-pointing on older specimens. Female plants produce small, rounded, black fruits.
P. ferox illus. p.88.
P. laetus. Evergreen, round-headed, stout-branched tree or shrub. H and S 3m (10ft). Half hardy. Has large, long-stalked, leathery leaves composed of 5 or 7 oblong, dark green leaflets, to 30cm (12in) long. Bears tiny, greenish-purple flowers, to 20cm (8in) across, in summer, followed by rounded, purplish-black fruits on female plants in autumn.

PSEUDOSASA

GRAMINEAE/POACEAE

See also GRASSES, BAMBOOS, RUSHES and SEDGES.
♀ ***P. japonica***, syn. *Arundinaria japonica*, illus. p.320.

PSEUDOTSUGA

PINACEAE

See also CONIFERS.
P. douglasii. See *P. menziesii.*
♀ ***P. menziesii***, syn. *P. douglasii, P. taxifolia* (Douglas fir). Fast-growing, conical conifer. H 25m (80ft), S 8–12m (25–40ft). Fully hardy. Has thick, corky, fissured, grey-brown bark. Spirally arranged, aromatic, needle-like, slightly flattened leaves, which develop from sharply pointed buds, are dark green with white bands beneath. Elliptic cones, 8–10cm (3–4in) long, with projecting bracts, are dull brown. **'Fletcheri'**, H 3m (10ft), S 2–3m (6–10ft), makes a flat-topped shrub. **'Fretsii'** (illus. p.106), H 6m (20ft) or more, S 3–4m (10–12ft), is slow-growing, with very short, dull green leaves. var. ***glauca*** illus. p.98. **'Oudemansii'** (illus. p.107) is very slow-growing, with ascending branches and short, glossy leaves, dark green all over.
P. taxifolia. See *P. menziesii.*

PSEUDOWINTERA

WINTERACEAE

Genus of evergreen shrubs and trees, grown for their foliage. Frost to half hardy. Needs full light or partial shade and humus-rich, well-drained but moisture-retentive soil, ideally neutral to acid. Water containerized plants freely when in full growth, only moderately at other times. Pruning is tolerated if needed. Propagate by semi-ripe cuttings taken in summer or by seed when ripe, in autumn, or in spring.

P. axillaris, syn. *Drimys axillaris* (Heropito, Pepper-tree).. Evergreen, rounded shrub or tree. H and S 3–8m (10–25ft). Half hardy. Has oval, lustrous, mid-green leaves, blue-grey beneath. Tiny, star-shaped, greenish-yellow flowers appear in spring-summer, followed by bright red fruits.
P. colorata, syn. *Drimys colorata.* Evergreen, bushy, spreading shrub. H 1m (3ft), S 1.5m (5ft). Half hardy. Has oval, leathery, pale yellow-green leaves, to 8cm (3in) long, blotched with pink and narrowly edged with deep red-purple; undersides are bluish-white. Clusters of 2–5 small, star-shaped, greenish-yellow flowers appear in mid-spring. Provide shelter in all but the mildest areas.

PSYCHOPSIS

ORCHIDACEAE

See also ORCHIDS.
P. papilio, syn. *Oncidium papilio* (Butterfly orchid; illus. p.311). Evergreen, epiphytic orchid for a warm greenhouse. H 15cm (6in). In summer, rich yellow-marked, orange-brown flowers, 8cm (3in) long, are borne singly and in succession on tops of stems. Has oval, semi-rigid, mottled leaves, 10–15cm (4–6in) long. Grow in good light in summer.

PSYLLIOSTACHYS
Statice

PLUMBAGINACEAE

Genus of annuals, perennials and evergreen sub-shrubs, grown for cut flowers and for drying. Is suitable for coastal areas. Fully to half hardy. Grow in sun and fertile, well-drained soil. If required for drying, cut flowers before they are fully open. Cut down dead stems of perennials in autumn. Propagate by seed sown under glass in early spring; perennials and sub-shrubs may also be increased by softwood cuttings in spring. Botrytis and powdery mildew may be troublesome.
P. suworowii, syn. *Limonium suworowii, Statice suworowii*, illus. p.342.

PTELEA

RUTACEAE

Genus of deciduous trees and shrubs, grown for their foliage and fruits. Fully hardy. Requires sun and fertile soil. Propagate species by softwood cuttings in summer or by seed in autumn, selected forms by softwood cuttings only in summer.
P. trifoliata (Hop tree). Deciduous, bushy, spreading tree or shrub. H and S 7m (22ft). Produces aromatic, dark green leaves with 3 narrowly oval leaflets. Clusters of small, star-shaped, green flowers from early to mid-summer are succeeded by clusters of winged, pale green fruits. 🏆 **'Aurea'** illus. p.141.

PTERIS

PTERIDACEAE/ADIANTACEAE

Genus of deciduous, semi-evergreen or evergreen ferns. Frost tender, min. 5°C (41°F). Tolerates sun or shade. Grow in moist, peaty soil. Remove faded fronds regularly. Propagate by division in spring or by spores in summer.
🏆 ***P. cretica*** (Cretan brake). Evergreen or semi-evergreen fern. H 45cm (18in), S 30cm (12in). Frost tender, min. 5°C (41°F). Produces triangular to broadly oval, divided, pale green fronds that have finger-like pinnae. var. ***albolineata*** see *P. c.* 'Albolineata'. 🏆 **'Albolineata'** (syn. *P.c.* var. *albolineata*) has pale green fronds centrally variegated with creamy-white. Variegated **'Mayi'**, H 30cm (12in), has crested frond tips. **'Wimsettii'** (illus. p.323) is compact, with the margins of the pinnae deeply and irregularly lobed.
P. ensiformis (Snow brake). Deciduous or semi-evergreen fern. H 30cm (12in), S 23cm (9in). Dark green fronds, often greyish-white around the midribs, are coarsely divided into finger-shaped pinnae. **'Arguta'**, H 45cm (18in), has deeper green fronds with central, silver-white marks.

PTEROCARYA
Wing nut

JUGLANDACEAE

Genus of deciduous trees, grown for their foliage and catkins. Fully hardy. Needs full sun and any deep, moist but well-drained soil. Suckers should be removed regularly. Propagate by softwood cuttings in summer or by suckers or seed, when ripe, in autumn.
🏆 ***P. fraxinifolia*** (Caucasian wing nut). Deciduous, spreading tree. H 25m (80ft), S 20m (70ft). Large, ash-like glossy, dark green leaves turn yellow in autumn. Long, green catkins are borne in summer, the females developing winged, green, then brown fruits.
P. × rehderiana illus. p.65.
P. stenoptera (Chinese wing nut). Deciduous, spreading tree. H 20m (70ft), S 15m (50ft). Ash-like, bright green leaves, each with a winged stalk, turn yellow in autumn. Produces long, green catkins in summer, the females developing winged, pink-tinged, green fruits.

PTEROCELTIS

ULMACEAE

Genus of one species of deciduous tree, with inconspicuous flowers in summer, grown for its foliage and fruits. Fully hardy. Needs full sun and does best in hot summers. Requires well-drained soil. Propagate by seed in autumn.
P. tatarinowii. Deciduous, spreading tree with arching branches. H 12m (40ft), S 10m (30ft). Has peeling, grey bark, and oval, dark green leaves, to 10cm (4in) long, with toothed margins. In autumn, bears small, spherical, green fruits, each with a broad, circular wing.

PTEROCEPHALUS

DIPSACACEAE

Genus of compact, summer-flowering annuals, perennials and semi-evergreen sub-shrubs, grown for their scabious-like flower heads and feathery seed heads. Is useful for rock gardens. Fully hardy. Requires sun and well-drained soil. Propagate by softwood or semi-ripe cuttings in summer or by seed in autumn. Self-seeds moderately.
P. parnassi. See *P. perennis.*
P. perennis, syn. *P. parnassi*, illus. p.392.

PTEROSTYRAX

STYRACACEAE

Genus of deciduous trees and shrubs, grown for their foliage and fragrant flowers. Fully hardy. Requires sun or semi-shade and deep, well-drained, neutral to acid soil. Propagate by softwood or semi-ripe cuttings in summer or by seed in autumn.
🏆 ***P. hispida*** (Epaulette tree). Deciduous, spreading tree or shrub with aromatic grey bark. H 15m (50ft), S 12m (40ft). Has oblong to oval, mid-green leaves, 20cm (8in) long. Bears large, drooping panicles of small, bell-shaped, white flowers from early to mid-summer.

Ptilotrichum spinosum. See *Alyssum spinosum.*
Pudding pipe-tree. See *Cassia fistula.*

PUERARIA

LEGUMINOSAE/PAPILIONACEAE

Genus of deciduous, woody-stemmed or herbaceous, twining climbers. Half hardy. Grow in full sun and in any well-drained soil. Propagate by seed in spring.
P. hirsuta. See *P. lobata.*
P. lobata, syn. *P. hirsuta, P. montana* var. *lobata, P. thunbergiana* (Kudzu vine). Deciduous, woody-stemmed, twining climber with hairy stems. H to 5m (15ft) or to 30m (100ft) in the wild. Leaves have 3 broadly oval leaflets. In summer produces racemes, to 30cm (12in) long, of small, scented, sweet pea-like, reddish-purple flowers, followed by long, slender, hairy pods, 6–8cm (2½–3in) long. In cold areas is best grown as an annual.
P. montana var. ***lobata.*** See *P. lobata.*
P. thunbergiana. See *P. lobata.*

Puka. See *Meryta sinclairii*, illus. p.96.
Pukanui. See *Meryta sinclairii*, illus. p.96.
Pukapuka. See *Brachyglottis repanda*, illus. p.123.

PULMONARIA
Lungwort

BORAGINACEAE

Genus of mainly spring-flowering perennials, some of which are semi-evergreen with small, overwintering rosettes of leaves. Fully hardy. Prefers shade; grows in any moist but well-drained soil. Propagate by division in spring or autumn.
🏆 ***P. angustifolia.*** Clump-forming, usually deciduous perennial. H 23cm (9in), S 20–30cm (8–12in) or more. Has lance-shaped, unspotted, mid-green leaves, 40cm (16in) long. In early spring produces heads of tubular, 5-lobed, borage-like, sometimes pink-tinged, deep blue flowers.
P. longifolia. Clump-forming, deciduous perennial. H 30cm (12in), S 45cm (18in). Bears very narrowly lance-shaped, dark green leaves, to 45cm (18in), spotted with silvery white. Heads of tubular, 5-lobed, borage-like, vivid blue flowers appear in late spring.
***P.* 'Mawson's Blue'** illus. p.279.
🏆 ***P. officinalis* 'Sissinghurst White'**, syn. *P. saccharata* 'Sissinghurst White', illus. p.275.
🏆 ***P. rubra.*** Semi-evergreen, clump-forming perennial. H 30cm (12in), S 60cm (24in). Has oval, velvety, mid-green leaves. Heads of tubular, 5-lobed, borage-like, brick-red flowers open from late winter to early spring.
P. saccharata illus. p.279.
'Sissinghurst White' see *P. officinalis* 'Sissinghurst White'.

PULSATILLA

RANUNCULACEAE

Genus of perennials, some of which are evergreen, grown for their large, feathery leaves, upright or pendent, bell- or cup-shaped flowers, covered in fine hairs, and feathery seed heads. Has fibrous, woody rootstocks. Leaves increase in size after flowering time. Is suitable for large rock gardens. Fully hardy. Needs full sun and humus-rich, well-drained soil. Resents disturbance to roots. Propagate by root cuttings in winter or by seed when fresh. All parts of the plant may cause mild stomach upset if ingested, and, in rare instances, contact with the sap may irritate skin.
P. alpina (Alpine anemone) illus. p.358. 🏆 subsp. ***apiifolia*** (syn. *P.a.* subsp. *sulphurea*) is a clump-forming perennial. H 15–30cm (6–12in), S to 10cm (4in). Has feathery, soft green leaves. Bears upright, bell-shaped, soft pale yellow flowers in spring, followed by feathery, silvery seed heads. subsp. ***sulphurea*** see *P.a.* subsp. *apiifolia*.
🏆 ***P. halleri*** illus. p.360. subsp. ***grandis*** (syn. *P. vulgaris* subsp. *grandis*) is a clump-forming perennial. H and S 15–23cm (6–9in). In spring, before feathery, light green leaves appear, bears large, upright, shallowly bell-shaped, lavender-blue flowers, 5cm (2in) wide, with bright yellow centres. Flower stems rapidly elongate as feathery, silvery seed heads mature.
P. occidentalis. Clump-forming perennial. H 20cm (8in), S 15cm (6in). In late spring to early summer, solitary nodding buds develop into erect, goblet-shaped, white flowers, stained blue-violet at base outside and sometimes flushed pink, followed by feathery, silvery seed heads. Bears feathery leaves. Is extremely difficult to grow and flower well at low altitudes.
🏆 ***P. vernalis*** illus. p.375.
🏆 ***P. vulgaris*** illus. p.360. subsp. ***grandis*** see *P. halleri* subsp. *grandis*.

PUNICA
pomegranate

LYTHRACEAE/PUNICACEAE

Genus of deciduous, summer-flowering shrubs and trees, grown for their bright red flowers and yellow to orange-red fruits, which ripen and become edible only in warm climates. Frost to half hardy. Needs a sheltered, sunny position and well-drained soil. Propagate by seed in spring or by semi-ripe cuttings in summer.
P. granatum. Deciduous, rounded shrub or tree. H and S 2–8m (6–25ft). Half hardy. Has narrowly oblong leaves and, in summer, funnel-shaped, bright red flowers, with crumpled petals. Fruits are spherical and deep yellow to orange. May be grown in a southern or eastern aspect, either free-standing or, in frost-prone climates, against a wall. ♀ var. ***nana*** illus. p.367.

Purple anise. See *Illicium floridanum.*
Purple beech. See *Fagus sylvatica* f. *atropunicea*, illus. p.61.
Purple broom. See *Chamaecytisus purpureus.*
Purple crab. See *Malus × purpurea.*
Purple loosestrife. See *Lythrum.*
Purple mountain saxifrage. See *Saxifraga oppositifolia*, illus. p.378.
Purple osier. See *Salix purpurea.*
Purple rock brake. See *Pellaea atropurpurea.*
Purple toadflax. See *Linaria purpurea.*

Purple-leaved ivy. See *Hedera helix* 'Atropurpurea', illus. p.219.
Purple-stemmed cliff brake. See *Pellaea atropurpurea.*
Purslane, Tree. See *Atriplex halimus.*

PUSCHKINIA

LILIACEAE/HYACINTHACEAE

Genus of dwarf, *Scilla*-like bulbs, grown for their early spring flowers. Fully hardy. Needs sun or partial shade and humus-rich soil that has grit or sand added to ensure good drainage. Plant in autumn. Dies down in summer. Propagate by offsets in late summer or by seed in autumn.
P. libanotica. See *P. scilloides* var. *libanotica.*
P. scilloides var. ***libanotica,*** syn. *P. libanotica*, illus. p.448. **'Alba'** illus. p.442.

Pussy ears. See *Cyanotis somaliensis*, illus. p.315; *Kalanchoe tomentosa*, illus. p.483.
Pussy willow. See *Salix caprea.*

PUYA

BROMELIACEAE

Genus of evergreen, rosette-forming perennials and shrubs, grown for their overall appearance. Half hardy to frost tender, min. 5–7°C (41–5°F). Requires full light and well-drained soil. Water moderately during the growing season, sparingly at other times. Propagate by seed or offsets in spring.
P. alpestris illus. p.273. Evergreen perennial with stout, branched, prostrate stems. H to 2m (6ft), S 3m (10ft). Half hardy. Linear, tapering, arching, bright green leaves are fleshy, with hooked, spiny teeth along the edges and dense, white scales beneath. Tubular, deep metallic-blue flowers, ageing to purple-red, are borne in stiff, erect panicles and are produced in early summer.
P. chilensis illus. p.273. Evergreen, upright perennial with a short, woody stem. H and S to 2m (6ft). Half hardy. Stem is crowned by a dense rosette of linear, tapering, arching, fleshy, grey-green leaves with margins of hooked, spiny teeth. Bears tubular, metallic- or greenish-yellow flowers in erect, branched panicles in summer.

PYCNOSTACHYS

LABIATAE/LAMIACEAE

Genus of bushy perennials, grown for their whorled clusters of flowers. Frost tender, min. 15°C (59°F). Grow in bright light and in fertile, well-drained soil. Propagate by stem cuttings in early summer.
P. dawei illus. p.233.
P. urticifolia. Strong-growing, erect perennial with square stems. H 1–2m (3–6ft), S 20–60cm (8–24in). Has oval, toothed, hairy, mid-green leaves. Bears whorls of small, tubular, bright blue flowers in racemes in winter.

Pygmy date palm. See *Phoenix roebelenii.*

PYRACANTHA
Firethorn

ROSACEAE

Genus of evergreen, spiny, summer-flowering shrubs, grown for their foliage, flowers and fruits. Fully to frost hardy. Requires a sheltered site in sun or semi-shade and fertile soil. To produce a compact habit on a plant grown against a wall, train and cut back long shoots after flowering. Propagate by semi-ripe cuttings in summer. Issusceptible to scab and fireblight. The seeds may cause mild stomach upset if ingested.
P. angustifolia. Evergreen, bushy, dense shrub. H and S 3m (10ft). Frost hardy. Has narrowly oblong leaves, dark green above, grey beneath. Bears clusters of small, 5-petalled, white flowers in early summer, followed by spherical, orange-yellow fruits, 8mm (3/8in) across, in autumn.
P. atalantioides. Vigorous, evergreen shrub, part upright, part arching. H 5m (15ft), S 4m (12ft). Frost hardy. Oblong leaves are glossy and dark green. Large clusters of small, 5-petalled, white flowers in early summer are followed by spherical, red fruits in early autumn. **'Aurea'** illus. p.120.
P. coccinea. Evergreen, dense, bushy shrub. H and S 4m (12ft). Fully hardy. Dense clusters of small, 5-petalled, white flowers open amid oval, dark green leaves in early summer and are succeeded by spherical, bright red fruits. **'Lalandei'** has larger leaves and larger, orange-red fruits.
♀ ***P.* 'Golden Charmer'** illus. p.145.
***P.* 'Golden Dome'** illus. p.145.
***P.* 'Mohave'.** Vigorous, evergreen, bushy shrub. H 4m (12ft), S 5m (15ft). Frost hardy. Produces clusters of small, 5-petalled, white flowers in early summer, then spherical, orange-red fruits. Leaves are broadly oval and dark green. Is disease-resistant.
♀ ***P.* 'Orange Glow'.** Evergreen, upright, dense shrub. H 5m (15ft), S 3m (10ft). Frost hardy. Has oblong, glossy, dark green leaves. Clusters of small, 5-petalled, white flowers, in early summer, are followed by spherical, orange fruits.
♀ ***P. rogersiana.*** Evergreen, upright, then arching shrub. H and S 3m (10ft). Frost hardy. Leaves are narrowly oblong, glossy and bright green. Produces clusters of small, 5-petalled, white flowers in early summer, followed by round, orange-red or yellow fruits.
P. × watereri, syn. *P.* 'Waterer's Orange', illus. p.132.
***P.* 'Waterer's Orange'.** See *P. × watereri.*

Pyramidal bugle. See *Ajuga pyramidalis.*
Pyrethropsis hosmariense. See *Rhodanthemum hosmariense.*
Pyrethrum. See *Tanacetum coccineum.*

***Pyrethrum* 'Brenda'.** See *Tanacetum coccineum* 'Brenda'.
Pyrethrum coccineum. See *Tanacetum coccineum.*
Pyrethrum parthenium. See *Tanacetum parthenium.*
Pyrethrum roseum. See *Tanacetum coccineum.*

PYROLA
Wintergreen

PYROLACEAE

Genus of evergreen, spreading, spring- and summer-flowering perennials. Fully hardy. Needs partial shade, cool conditions and well-drained, peaty, acid soil; is best suited to light woodlands. Resents disturbance. Propagate by seed in autumn or spring or by division in spring.
P. asarifolia. Evergreen, rosette-forming perennial. H 15–25cm (6–10in), S 15cm (6in) or more. Has kidney-shaped, leathery, glossy, light green leaves. Bears open tubular, pale to deep pink flowers in spring.
P. rotundifolia (Round-leaved wintergreen, Wild lily-of-the-valley). Creeping, evergreen, rosette-forming perennial. H 23cm (9in), S 30cm (12in). Produces rounded, leathery, glossy, mid-green leaves and, in late spring and early summer, sprays of fragrant, white flowers that resemble lily-of-the-valley.

PYROSTEGIA

BIGNONIACEAE

Genus of evergreen, woody-stemmed, tendril climbers, grown for their flowers. Frost tender, min. 13–15°C (55–9°F). Needs full light and fertile, well-drained soil. Water regularly, less in winter. Provide support. Thin stems after flowering. Propagate by semi-ripe cuttings or layering in summer.
P. ignea. See *P. venusta.*
P. venusta, syn. *P. ignea*, illus. p.216.

PYRUS
Pear

ROSACEAE

Genus of deciduous, spring-flowering trees, grown for their habit, foliage, flowers and edible fruits (pears). Fully hardy. Does best in full sun and needs well-drained soil. Propagate species by seed in autumn, cultivars by budding in summer or by grafting in winter. Many species are susceptible to fireblight and scab and, in North America, pear decline.
P. amygdaliformis. Deciduous, spreading tree. H 10m (30ft), S 8m (25ft). Lance-shaped leaves are grey when young, maturing to glossy, dark green. Clusters of 5-petalled, white flowers are produced in mid-spring, and are followed by small, brownish fruits.
P. calleryana (Callery pear). Deciduous, broadly conical tree. H and S to 15m (50ft). Oval, glossy, dark green leaves often turn red in autumn. Bears 5-petalled, white flowers from mid- to late spring and small, brownish fruits. **'Bradford'**, S 10m (30ft), is resistant to fireblight. ♀ **'Chanticleer'** illus. p.72.
P. communis (Common pear). **'Beech Hill'** is a deciduous, narrowly conical tree. H 10m (30ft), S 7m (22ft). Oval, glossy, dark green leaves often turn orange and red in autumn. From mid- to late spring produces 5-petalled, white flowers as the leaves emerge, followed by small, brownish fruits.
P. elaeagrifolia. Deciduous, spreading, thorny tree. H and S 8m (25ft). Has lance-shaped, grey-green leaves. Produces loose clusters of 5-petalled, creamy white flowers in mid-spring, followed by small, pear-shaped, brownish fruits.
P. salicifolia. Deciduous, mound-shaped tree with slightly drooping branches. H 5–8m (15–25ft), S 4m (12ft). White flowers, with 5 petals, open as lance-shaped, grey leaves emerge in mid-spring. Fruits are small and brownish. ♀ **'Pendula'** illus. p.87.

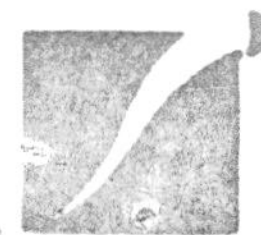
WARWICKSHIRE COLLEGE LIBRARY

Quaking aspen. See *Populus tremuloides*.
Quaking grass. See *Briza*.
Common. See *Briza media*.
Quamash. See *Camassia quamash*.
Quamoclit coccinea. See *Ipomoea coccinea*.
Quamoclit lobata. See *Ipomoea lobata*.
Quamoclit pennata. See *Ipomoea quamoclit*.
Quassia. See *Picrasma quassoides*, illus. p.93.
Quater. See *Vinca major*.
Queen Anne's double daffodil. See *Narcissus* 'Eystettensis'.
Queen Anne's jonquil. See *Narcissus jonquilla* 'Flore Pleno'.
Queen palm. See *Syagrus romanzoffiana*.
Queen's crape myrtle. See *Lagerstroemia speciosa*.
Queen's tears. See *Billbergia nutans*, illus. p.273.
Queencup. See *Clintonia uniflora*.
Queen-of-the-night. See *Hylocereus undatus; Selenicereus grandiflorus*, illus. p.472.
Queensland nut. See *Macadamia integrifolia*, illus. p.69.
Queensland pyramidal tree. See *Lagunaria patersonii*.
Queensland silver wattle. See *Acacia podalyriifolia*, illus. p.131.
Queensland umbrella tree. See *Schefflera actinophylla*, illus. p.80.

QUERCUS
Oak

FAGACEAE

Genus of deciduous or evergreen trees and shrubs, grown for their habit, foliage and, in some deciduous species, autumn colour. Produces insignificant flowers from late spring to early summer, followed by egg-shaped to rounded, brownish fruits (acorns). Fully to frost hardy. Does best in sun or semi-shade and in deep, well-drained soil. Except where stated otherwise, will tolerate limestone. Propagate species by seed in autumn, selected forms and hybrids by grafting in late winter. May be affected, though not usually seriously, by mildew and various galls, and, in North America, by oak wilt.

Q. acutissima (Sawtooth oak). Deciduous, round-headed tree. H and S 15m (50ft). Fully hardy. Has sweet-chestnut-like, glossy, dark green leaves, edged with bristle-tipped teeth, that last until late in the year.

Q. aegilops. See *Q. ithaburensis* subsp. *macrolepis*.

Q. agrifolia illus. p.81.

Q. alba (American white oak) illus. p.67.

Q. aliena (Oriental white oak). Deciduous, spreading tree. H 15m (50ft), S 12m (40ft). Fully hardy. Has large, oblong, prominently toothed, glossy, dark green leaves.

Q. alnifolia (Golden oak of Cyprus). Evergreen, spreading tree. H 6m (20ft), S 5m (15ft). Frost hardy. Rounded, leathery leaves are glossy, dark green above, with mustard-yellow or greenish-yellow felt beneath.

♀ ***Q. canariensis*** illus. p.62.

Q. castaneifolia illus. p.64.

♀ ***Q. cerris*** (Turkey oak). Fast-growing, deciduous, spreading tree of stately habit. H 30m (100ft), S 25m (80ft). Fully hardy. Oblong, glossy, dark green leaves are deeply lobed. Thrives on shallow, chalky soil. **'Argenteovariegata'** (syn. *Q.c.* 'Variegata') illus. p.74.

Q. coccifera (Kermes oak). Evergreen, bushy, compact tree or shrub. H and S 5m (15ft). Frost hardy. Holly-like leaves are glossy, dark green and rigid with spiny margins.

Q. coccinea illus. p.66. ♀ **'Splendens'** is a deciduous, round-headed tree. H 20m (70ft), S 15m (50ft). Fully hardy. Has oblong, glossy, mid-green leaves, with deep, tooth-like lobes, that turn deep scarlet in autumn. Prefers acid soil.

Q. dentata (Daimio oak). Deciduous, spreading, stout-branched tree of rugged habit. H 15m (50ft), S 10m (30ft). Fully hardy. Has oval, lobed, dark green leaves, 30cm (12in) or more long. Prefers acid soil.

Q. ellipsoidalis illus. p.66.

Q. frainetto illus. p.65.

Q. garryana illus. p.76.

Q.* × *heterophylla illus. p.78.

♀ ***Q.* × *hispanica* 'Lucombeana'**, syn. *Q.* × *lucombeana* 'William Lucombe', illus. p.69.

♀ ***Q. ilex*** (Holm oak). Evergreen, round-headed tree. H 25m (80ft), S 20m (70ft). Frost hardy. Glossy, dark green leaves are silvery-grey when young and very variably shaped, but are most often oval. Thrives on shallow chalk and is excellent for an exposed, coastal position.

Q. imbricaria (Shingle oak). Deciduous, spreading tree. H 20m (70ft), S 15m (50ft). Fully hardy. Bears long, narrow leaves that are yellowish when young, dark green in summer and yellowish-brown in autumn.

Q. ithaburensis subsp. ***macrolepis***, syn. *Q. aegilops, Q. macrolepis*, illus. p.76.

Q. laurifolia illus. p.65.

***Q.* × *lucombeana* 'William Lucombe'.** See *Q.* × *hispanica* 'Lucombeana'.

Q. macranthera illus. p.62.

Q. macrocarpa illus. p.76.

Q. macrolepis. See *Q. ithaburensis* subsp.*macrolepis*.

Q. marilandica illus. p.76.

Q. mongolica subsp. ***crispula*** var. ***grosseserrata.*** Deciduous, spreading tree. H 20m (70ft), S 15m (50ft). Fully hardy. Has large, oblong, lobed, dark green leaves with prominent, triangular teeth.

Q. muehlenbergii illus. p.63.

Q. myrsinifolia illus. p.80.

Q. nigra illus. p.64.

♀ ***Q. palustris*** illus. p.65.

♀ ***Q. petraea*** (Durmast oak, Sessile oak). Deciduous, spreading tree. H 30m (100ft), S 25m (80ft). Fully hardy. Has oblong, lobed, leathery, dark green leaves with yellow stalks. **'Columna'** illus. p.64.

Q. phellos illus. p.67.

Q. pontica (Armenian oak, Pontine oak). Deciduous, sometimes shrubby tree with upright, stout branches and broadly oval head. H 6m (20ft), S 5m (15ft). Fully hardy. Large, oval, toothed, glossy, bright green leaves turn yellow in autumn.

♀ ***Q. robur*** (Common oak, Pedunculate oak). Deciduous, spreading, rugged tree. H and S 25m (80ft). Fully hardy. Bears oblong, wavy, lobed, dark green leaves. **'Concordia'**, H 10m (30ft), is slow-growing and has golden-yellow, young foliage that becomes yellowish-green in mid-summer. f. ***fastigiata*** illus. p.62.

♀ ***Q. rubra*** illus. p.65. **'Aurea'** illus. p.76.

Q. suber illus. p.69.

Q.* × *turneri illus. p.69.

Q. velutina (Black oak). Fast-growing, deciduous, spreading tree. H 30m (100ft), S 25m (80ft). Fully hardy. Large, oblong, lobed, glossy, dark green leaves turn reddish-brown in autumn.

Quince. See *Cydonia oblonga*.
Flowering. See *Chaenomeles*.
Japanese. See *Chaenomeles japonica*.

QUISQUALIS

COMBRETACEAE

Genus of evergreen or deciduous, scandent shrubs and twining climbers, grown for their flowers. Frost tender, min. 10–18°C (50–64°F). Provide humus-rich, moist but well-drained soil and full light or semi-shade. Water freely when in full growth, less in cold weather. Stems need support. Thin out crowded growth in spring. Propagate by seed in spring or by semi-ripe cuttings in summer.

Q. indica illus. p.207.

Rabbit tracks. See *Maranta leuconeura* var. *kerchoviana*, illus. p.316.
Rain daisy. See *Dimorphotheca pluvialis*, illus. p.331.
Rain lily. See *Zephyranthes.*
Rainbow star. See *Cryptanthus bromelioides.*
Raisin-tree. See *Hovenia dulcis*, illus. p.75.

RAMONDA

GESNERIACEAE

Genus of evergreen perennials, grown for their rosettes of rounded, crinkled, hairy leaves and for their flowers. Is useful for rock gardens and peat walls. Fully hardy. Prefers shade and moist soil. Water plants well if they curl in a dry spell. Propagate by rooting offsets in early summer or by leaf cuttings or seed in early autumn.
🏆 ***R. myconi***, syn. *R. pyrenaica*, illus. p.394.
🏆 ***R. nathaliae.*** Evergreen, basal-rosetted perennial. H and S 10cm (4in). Has small, pale green leaves and, in late spring and early summer, bears umbels of small, outward-facing, flattish, white or lavender flowers, with yellow anthers.
R. pyrenaica. See *R. myconi.*
R. serbica. Evergreen, basal-rosetted perennial. H and S 10cm (4in). Is similar to *R. nathaliae*, but has cup-shaped, lilac-blue flowers and dark violet-blue anthers. May be difficult to grow.

Ram's horn. See *Proboscidea louisianica.*
Rangiora. See *Brachyglottis repanda*, illus. p.123.
Rangoon creeper. See *Quisqualis indica*, illus. p.207.

RANUNCULUS

Buttercup

RANUNCULACEAE

Genus of annuals, aquatics and perennials, some of which are evergreen or semi-evergreen, grown mainly for their flowers. Many species grow from a thickened rootstock or a cluster of tubers. Some are invasive. Aquatic species are seldom cultivated. Fully to half hardy. Grows in sun or shade and in moist but well-drained soil. Propagate by seed when fresh or by division in spring or autumn. Contact with the sap may irritate skin.
R. aconitifolius and 🏆 **'Flore Pleno'** illus. p.233.
R. acris (Meadow buttercup). 🏆 **'Flore Pleno'** illus. p.304.
R. alpestris (Alpine buttercup) illus. p.375.
R. amplexicaulis. Upright perennial. H 25cm (10in), S 10cm (4in). Fully hardy. Has narrowly oval, blue-grey leaves. In early summer produces clusters of shallowly cup-shaped, white flowers with yellow anthers. Needs humus-rich soil.
R. aquatilis (Water crowfoot). Aquatic annual or usually evergreen perennial. H 1cm (½in), S indefinite. Fully hardy. Submerged, branched, slender stems bear dark green leaves, these having many thread-like segments; the floating leaves are kidney-shaped to rounded, deeply divided into 3–7 lobes. In mid-summer, produces solitary, bowl- or saucer-shaped, white-based yellow flowers, 1cm (½in) across, on the surface.
R. asiaticus var. ***asiaticus*** illus. p.437. var. ***flavus*** illus. p.439.
***R. bulbosus* 'Speciosus Plenus' of gardens.** See *R. constantinopolitanus* 'Plenus'.
R. bullatus. Clump-forming perennial with thick, fibrous roots. H 5–8cm (2–3in), S 8–10cm (3–4in). Half hardy. Produces fragrant, shallowly cup-shaped, bright yellow flowers in autumn above neat mounds of foliage. Oblong to oval, green leaves have sharply toothed tips and are puckered. Suits an alpine house or rock garden.
🏆 ***R. calandrinioides*** illus. p.372.
***R. constantinopolitanus* 'Plenus'**,syn. *R. bulbosus* 'Speciosus Plenus' of gardens, *R. gouanii* 'Plenus', *R. speciosus* 'Plenus', illus. p.304.
R. crenatus. Semi-evergreen, rosetted perennial with thick, fibrous roots. H and S 10cm (4in). Fully hardy. Produces rounded, toothed, green leaves and, in summer, short stems bearing 1 or 2 shallowly cup-shaped, white flowers just above foliage. May also be propagated by removing a flower stem at its first joint in summer; rosettes will form and may then be rooted. Rarely sets seed in cultivation. Suits an alpine house or rock garden.
R. ficaria (Lesser celandine). var. ***albus*** (syn. *R.f.* 'Albus') illus. p.375. var. ***aurantiacus*** (syn. *R.f.* 'Aurantiacus') illus. p.385. **'Brazen Hussy'** is a mat-forming, tuberous perennial. H 5cm (2in), S to 20cm (8in). Fully hardy. Isgrown for its heart-shaped, purple-bronze leaves produced in spring. Shallowly cup-shaped, glossy, sulphur-yellow flowers, with bronze reverses, appear in early spring. All *R. ficaria* forms die down in late spring. May spread rapidly; is good for a wild garden. var. ***flore-pleno*** (syn. *R.f.* 'Flore Pleno') illus. p.384.
R. glacialis. Hummock-forming perennial with fibrous roots. H 5–25cm (2–10in), S 5cm (2in) or more. Fully hardy. Bears rounded, deeply lobed, glossy, dark green leaves and, in late spring and early summer, clusters of shallowly cup-shaped, white or pink flowers. Is very difficult to grow at low altitudes. Suits a scree or alpine house. Prefers humus-rich, moist, acid soil that is drier in winter. Slugs may be troublesome.
***R. gouanii* 'Plenus'.** See *R. constantinopolitanus* 'Plenus'.
🏆 ***R. gramineus*** illus. p.371.
R. lingua illus. p.467. **'Grandiflorus'** is a deciduous, perennial, marginal water plant. H 1m (3ft), S 30cm (1ft). Fully hardy. Has stout, pinkish-green stems, lance-shaped, glaucous leaves and, in late spring, racemes of large, saucer-shaped, yellow flowers.
R. lyallii (Giant buttercup). Evergreen, stout, upright, tufted perennial. H and S 30cm (12in) or more. Frost hardy. Has rounded, leathery, dark green leaves, each 15cm (6in) or more across, and, in summer, bears panicles of large, shallowly cup-shaped, white flowers. Is very difficult to flower in hot, dry climates. Is suitable for an alpine house. Rarely sets seed in cultivation.
🏆 ***R. montanus* 'Molten Gold'.** Clump-forming, compact perennial. H 15cm (6in), S 10cm (4in). Fully hardy. Leaves are rounded and 3-lobed. Flower stems each produce a shallowly cup-shaped, shiny, bright golden-yellow flower in early summer. Is useful for a sunny rock garden.
***R. speciosus* 'Plenus'.** See *R. constantinopolitanus* 'Plenus'.

RANZANIA

BERBERIDACEAE

Genus of one species of perennial, grown for its unusual appearance as well as its flowers. Is ideal for woodland gardens. Fully hardy. Prefers shade or semi-shade and humus-rich, moist soil. Propagate by division in spring or by seed in autumn.
R. japonica. Upright perennial. H 45cm (18in), S 30cm (12in). Produces 3-parted, fresh green leaves and, in early summer, small clusters of nodding, shallowly cup-shaped, pale mauve flowers.

RAOULIA

COMPOSITAE/ASTERACEAE

Genus of evergreen, mat-forming perennials, grown for their foliage. Some species are suitable for alpine houses, others for rock gardens. Fully to frost hardy. Needs sun or semi-shade and gritty, moist but well-drained, peaty soil. Propagate by seed when fresh or by division in spring.
R. australis illus. p.402.
R. eximia. Evergreen, cushion-formingperennial. H 2.5cm (1in), S 5cm (2in). Fully hardy. Has oblong to oval, overlapping, woolly, grey leaves and, in late spring-summer, small, rounded heads of yellowish-white flowers. Suits an alpine house. Prefers some shade.
R. haastii illus. p.403.
R. hookeri var. ***albosericea*** illus. p.401.
R. leontopodium. See *Leucogenes leontopodium.*

Raspberry, Flowering. See *Rubus odoratus.*
Rat's-tail cactus. See *Aporocactus flagelliformis*, illus. p.479.
Rata. See *Metrosideros robustus.*
Rauli. See *Nothofagus procera*, illus. p.63.

RAVENALA

STRELITZIACEAE

Genus of one species of evergreen, palm-like tree, grown for its foliage and overall appearance. Is related to *Strelitzia.* Frost tender, min. 16°C (61°F). Requires full light and humus-rich, well-drained soil. Water potted specimens freely in summer, less in winter or when temperatures are low. Propagate by seed in spring. Red spider mite may be troublesome.
R. madagascariensis (Traveller's tree). Evergreen, upright, fan-shaped tree. H and to 10m (30ft). Has banana-like, long-stalked leaves, each 3–6m (10–20ft) long, with expanded stalk bases. Groups of boat-shaped spathes with 6-parted, white flowers emerge from leaf axils in summer.

REBUTIA

CACTACEAE

Genus of mostly clump-forming, spherical to columnar, perennial cacti. Produces flowers in profusion from plant bases, usually 2–3 years after raising from seed. Much-ribbed, tuberculate, green stems have short spines. Afew species are sometimes included in *Aylostera.* Frost tender, min. 5–10°C (41–50°F). Requires a position in sun or partial shade and well-drained soil. Is easy to grow. Propagate by seed in spring or summer.
R. arenacea, syn. *Sulcorebutia arenacea*, illus. p.496.
🏆 ***R. aureiflora*** illus. p.496.
🏆 ***R. fiebrigii***, syn. *R. muscula*, illus. p.496.
R. krainziana. See *R. marsoneri.*
🏆 ***R. marsoneri***, syn. *R. krainziana*, illus. p.490.
🏆 ***R. minuscula***, syn. *R. senilis*, *R. violaciflora*, illus. p.488
R. muscula. See *R. fiebrigii.*
🏆 ***R. neocumingii***, syn. *Weingartia neocumingii.* Spherical, perennial cactus. H and S 10cm (4in). Stem is tuberculate and green. Areoles bear dense clusters of yellow spines, 1.5cm (⅝in) long, some thicker than others, and several cup-shaped, dark yellow flowers, 3cm (¼in) long, in spring.
R. pygmaea, syn. *Lobivia pygmaea.* Clump-forming, columnar, perennial cactus. H 5cm (2in), S 10cm (4in). Very short, comb-like spines are pressed against grey- to purple-green stem. Trumpet-shaped, pink to salmon or rose-purple flowers, to 2cm (¾in) across, appear in spring. Prefers a sunny position.
R. rauschii. See *Rebutia steinmannii.*
R. senilis. See *R. minuscula.*
R. spegazziniana illus. p.491.
R. steinmannii, syn. *R. rauschii*, *Sulcorebutia rauschii.* Flattened spherical, perennial cactus. H 5cm (2in), S 10cm (4in). Grey-green stem bears very short, comb-like, golden or black spines. Bears flattish, 3cm (1¼) wide, deep purple flowers in spring. Grows better when grafted.
R. steinbachii subsp. ***tiraquensis***, syn. *R. tiraquensis*, *Sulcorebutia tiraquensis*, illus. p.490.
R. tiraquensis. See *R. steinbachii* subsp. *tiraquensis.*
R. violaciflora. See *R. minuscula.*

Red ash. See *Fraxinus pennsylvanica.*
Red baneberry. See *Actaea rubra.*
Red chokeberry. See *Aronia arbutifolia*, illus. p.126.
Red horse-chestnut. See *Aesculus × carnea.*
Red maple. See *Acer rubrum*, illus. p.66.
Red morning glory. See *Ipomoea coccinea.*
Red mountain spinach. See *Atriplex hortensis* var. *rubra.*
Red oak. See *Quercus rubra*, illus. p.65.
Red orach. See *Atriplex hortensis* var.

rubra.
Red orchid cactus. See *Nopalxochia ackermannii.*
Red passion flower. See *Passiflora coccinea*, illus. p.201; *Passiflora racemosa.*
Red pineapple. See *Ananas bracteatus.*
Red rose of Lancaster. See *R. gallica* var. *officinalis.*
Red spider lily. See *Lycoris radiata*, illus. p.436.
Red spike. See *Cephalophyllum alstonii*, illus. p.490.
Red valerian. See *Centranthus ruber*, illus. p.247.
Red-and-green kangaroo paw. See *Anigozanthos manglesii*, illus. p.254.
Red-barked dogwood. See *Cornus alba.*
Red-berried elder. See *Sambucus racemosa.*
Redbird flower. See *Pedilanthus tithymaloides* 'Variegata', illus. p.475.
Redbud. See *Cercis.*
Eastern. See *Cercis canadensis.*
Red-hot cat's tail. See *Acalypha hispida.*
Red-hot poker. See *Kniphofia; K. uvaria.*
Red-ink plant. See *Phytolacca americana.*
Redwood. See *Sequoia sempervirens.*
Coast. See *Sequoia sempervirens.*
Dawn. See *Metasequoia glyptostroboides*, illus. p.98.
Giant. See *Sequoiadendron giganteum*, illus. p.98.
Reed
Branched bur. See *Sparganium erectum*, illus. p.465.
Bur. See *Sparganium.*
Giant. See *Arundo donax.*
Least bur. See *Sparganium natans.*
Paper. See *Cyperus papyrus*, illus. p.319.
Reflexed stonecrop. See *Sedum rupestre*, illus. p.371.
Regal lily. See *Lilium regale*, illus. p.416.

REHDERODENDRON

STYRACACEAE

Genus of deciduous, spring-flowering trees, grown for their flowers and fruits. Frost hardy. Needs sun or semi-shade, some shelter and fertile, moist, but well-drained, acid soil. Propagate by semi-ripe cuttings in summer or by seed in autumn.
R. macrocarpum. Deciduous, spreading tree. H 10m (30ft), S 7m (22ft). Young shoots are red. Pendent clusters of lemon-scented, cup-shaped, pink-tinged, white flowers are borne amid oblong, taper-pointed, red-stalked, glossy, dark green leaves in late spring. Bears cylindrical, woody, red, then brown fruits in autumn.

REHMANNIA

SCROPHULARIACEAE

Genus of spring- and summer-flowering perennials. Half hardy to frost tender, min. 1–5°C (34–41°F). Needs a warm, sunny position and light soil. Propagate by seed in autumn or spring or by root cuttings in winter.
R. angulata of gardens. See *R. elata.*
♀ ***R. elata***, syn. *R. angulata* of gardens, illus. p.246.
♀ ***R. glutinosa.*** Rosette-forming perennial. H 30cm (12in), S 25cm (10in). Frost tender, min. 1°C (34°F). Tubular, pink, red-brown or yellow flowers, with purple veins, are borne on leafy shoots in late spring and early summer. Leaves are oval to lance-shaped, toothed, hairy and light green.

REINWARDTIA

LINACEAE

Genus of evergreen sub-shrubs, grown for their flowers. Frost tender, min. 7–10°C (45–50°F). Needs full light or partial shade and fertile, well-drained soil. Water freely when growing, moderately at other times. Tip prune young plants to promote branching; cut back hard after flowering. Raise soft-wood cuttings annually in late spring. Red spider mite may cause problems.
R. indica, syn. *R. trigyna*, illus. p.166.
R. trigyna. See *R. indica.*

RESEDA
Mignonette

RESEDACEAE

Genus of annuals and biennials with flowers that attract bees and that are also suitable for cutting. Fully hardy. Grow in a sunny position and in any fertile, well-drained soil. Dead-heading regularly ensures a prolonged flowering period. Propagate by sowing seed outdoors in spring or early autumn.
R. odorata illus. p.331.

Restharrow
Large yellow. See *Ononis natrix*, illus. p.371.
Shrubby. See *Ononis fruticosa*, illus. p.365.
Resurrection plant. See *Selaginella lepidophylla.*

RETAMA

LEGUMINOSAE/PAPILIONACEAE

Genus of deciduous shrubs grown for their willowy, dark green or silky grey stems and pea-like, white or yellow flowers. Half hardy. Needs full sun and sharply drained soil and a sheltered position against a south- or west-facing wall. Propagate from seed in a cold frame or under glass or by semi-ripe cuttings in summer.
R. monosperma, syn. *Genista monosperma.* Deciduous, almost leafless, graceful, arching shrub. H to 4m (12ft), S 1.5m (5ft). Half hardy. Slender, silky-grey shoots bear clusters of small, very fragrant, white flowers in early spring. Has a few linear leaves, which soon fall. Grow against a south- or west-facing wall.

Rewa rewa. See *Knightia excelsa.*
Rex begonia vine. See *Cissus discolor.*
Reynoutria. See *Fallopia.*

RHAMNUS
Buckthorn

RHAMNACEAE

Genus of deciduous or evergreen shrubs and trees, with inconspicuous flowers, grown mainly for their foliage and fruits. Fully to frost hardy. Requires sun or semi-shade and fertile soil. Propagate deciduous species by seed in autumn, evergreen species by semi-ripe cuttings in summer. All parts may cause severe discomfort if ingested.
R. alaternus (Italian buckthorn). ♀ **'Argenteovariegata'** is an evergreen, bushy shrub. H and S 3m (10ft). Frost hardy. Has oval, leathery, glossy, grey-green leaves margined creamy-white. Tiny, yellowish-green flowers are produced from early to mid-summer and followed by spherical, red, then black fruits.
R. imeretina. Deciduous, spreading, open shrub. H 3m (10ft), S 5m (15ft). Fully hardy. Stout shoots bear large, broadly oblong, prominently veined, dark green leaves that turn bronze-purple in autumn. Small, green flowers are borne in summer.

RHAPHIOLEPIS

ROSACEAE

Genus of evergreen shrubs, grown for their flowers and foliage. Frost to half hardy. In most areas does best against a sheltered wall; *R. umbellata* is the most hardy. Needs sun and fertile, well-drained soil. Propagate by semi-ripe cuttings in late summer.
***R. × delacourii* 'Coates' Crimson'.** Evergreen, rounded shrub. H 2m (6ft), S 2. 5m (8ft). Frost hardy. Clusters of fragrant, star-shaped, deep pink flowers, produced in spring or summer, are set off by the oval, leathery, dark green leaves.
R. indica (Indian hawthorn). Evergreen, bushy shrub. H 1.5m (5ft), S 2m (6ft). Half hardy. Clusters of fragrant, star-shaped, white flowers, flushed with pink, are borne in spring or early summer amid narrowly lance-shaped, glossy, dark green leaves.
R. japonica. See *R. umbellata.*
R. ovata. See *R. umbellata.*
♀ ***R. umbellata***, syn. *R. japonica, R. ovata*, illus. p.156.

RHAPIS

PALMAE/ARECACEAE

Genus of evergreen fan palms, grown for their foliage and overall appearance. May have tiny, yellow flowers in summer. Frost tender, min.15°C (59°F). Needs partial shade and humus-rich, well-drained soil. Water containerized specimens freely when growing, moderately at other times. Propagate by seed, suckers or division in spring. Is susceptible to red spider mite.
♀ ***R. excelsa***, syn. *R. flabelliformis*,illus. p.148.
R. flabelliformis. See *R. excelsa.*

Rhazya orientalis. See *Amsonia orientalis.*

RHEUM
Rhubarb

POLYGONACEAE

Genus of perennials, grown for their foliage and striking overall appearance. Includes the edible rhubarb and various ornamental plants. Some species are extremely large and require plenty of space. Fully hardy. Prefers sun or semi-shade and deep, rich, well-drained soil. Propagate by division in spring or by seed in autumn. Leaves may cause severe discomfort if ingested.
R. nobile. Clump-forming perennial. H 15m (5ft), S 1m (3ft).. Leaves are oblong to oval, leathery, basal, mid-green, 60cm (2ft) long. In late summer produces long stems and conical spikes of large, overlapping, pale cream bracts that hide insignificant flowers.
R. palmatum. Clump-forming perennial. H and S 2m (6ft). Has 60–75cm (2–2½ft) long, rounded, 5-lobed, mid-green leaves. In early summer has broad panicles of small, creamy-white flowers. ♀ **'Atrosanguineum'** illus. p.225.

Rhipsalidopsis gaertneri. See *Hatiora gaertneri.*
Rhipsalidopsis rosea. See *Hatiora rosea.*

RHIPSALIS
Mistletoe cactus

CACTACEAE

Genus of epiphytic, perennial cacti with usually pendent, variously formed stems. Flowers are followed by spherical, translucent berries. Frost tender, min. 10–11°C (50–52°F). Needs partial shade and rich, well-drained soil. Prefers 80% relative humidity – higher than for most cacti. Give only occasional, very light watering in winter. Propagate by seed or stem cuttings in spring or summer.
R. capilliformis. See *R. teres.*
R. cereuscula illus. p.477.
R. clavata. See *R. gaertneri.*
R. crispata. Bushy, then pendent, perennial cactus. H 1m (3ft), Sindefinite. Min. 11°C (52°F). Has leaf-like, elliptic to oblong, pale green stem segments, to 12cm (5in) long, with undulating edges that produce short, funnel-shaped, cream or pale yellow flowers, to 1cm (½in) across, with recurved tips, in winter-spring, then white berries.
R. floccosa illus. p.477.
R. gaertneri, syn. *R. clavata, Hatiora clavata.* Pendent, perennial, epiphytic cactus. H 60cm (2ft), S 1m (3ft). min. 11°C (52°F). Multi-branched, cylindrical, dark green stems each widen towards tips. Masses of terminal, bell-shaped, white flowers, 1.5cm (⅝in) wide, appear in late winter and early spring on plants over 30cm (1ft) high.
R. paradoxa (Chain cactus). Bushy, then pendent, perennial cactus. H 1m (3ft), S indefinite. Min. 11°C (52°F). Triangular, green stems have segments alternately set at different angles. Short, funnel-shaped, white flowers, 2cm (¾in) across, with recurved tips, appear from stem edges in winter-spring and are followed by red berries.
R. salicornioides. See *Hatiora salicornioides.*
R. teres, syn. *R. capilliformis.* Pendent, perennial cactus. H 1m (3ft), S 50cm (20in). Min. 10°C (50°F). Has freely branching, cylindrical, green stems and, in winter-spring, short, funnel-shaped, white flowers, to 1cm (½in) wide, with recurved tips, then white berries.
R. warmingiana. See *Lepismium warmingianum.*

RHODANTHE,
syn. ACROCLINIUM
Strawflower

COMPOSITAE/ASTERACEAE

Genus of drought-tolerant annuals, perennials and sub-shrubs, grown for their daisy-like, papery flower heads, which are excellent for cutting and drying. Half hardy. Grow in sun and in poor, very well-drained soil. Propagate by seed sown outdoors in mid-spring. Aphids may cause problems.
R. chlorocephala subsp. ***rosea,***syn. *Acroclinium roseum, Helipterum roseum*, illus. p.333.
R. manglesii, syn. *Helipterum manglesii*, illus. p.333.

RHODANTHEMUM

COMPOSITAE/ASTERACEAE

Genus of mat-forming, often rhizomatous perennials and sub-shrubs, grown for their solitary, large, daisy-like, white flower heads, surrounded by prominent, usually green bracts. Fully to frost hardy. Needs full sun and moderately fertile, very well-drained soil. Propagate by seed in spring or by softwood cuttings in summer.
♀ ***R. hosmariense***, syn. *Chrysanthemum hosmariense, Pyrethropsis hosmariense*, illus. p.358.

RHODIOLA

CRASSULACEAE

Genus of perennials, some dioecious, with thick, fleshy rhizomes producing scaly, brown basal leaves and stiffly erect stems that bear triangular-oval to lance-shaped, fleshy, grey-green leaves. Star-shaped flowers have prominent stamens, and may be unisexual or bisexual. Fully hardy. Grow in full sun and moderately fertile soil. Propagate by seed in spring or autumn, divide rhizomes in spring or early summer or take leaf cuttings in summer.
R. heterodonta, syn. *Sedum heterodontum, S. rosea* var. *heterodontum*, illus. p.305.
R. rosea, syn. *Sedum rosea* (Roseroot). Clump-forming perennial. H and S 30cm (12in). Stems are clothed with oval to inversely lance-shaped, toothed, fleshy, glaucous leaves and, in late spring or early summer, bear dense, terminal heads of pink buds that open to small, star-shaped, greenish-, yellowish- or purplish-white flowers.

Rhodocactus grandifolius. See *Pereskia grandifolia.*

RHODOCHITON

SCROPHULARIACEAE

Genus of one species of evergreen, leaf-stalk climber, grown for its unusual flowers. Does best when grown as an annual. May be planted against fences and trellises or used as ground cover. Frost tender, min. 5°C (41°F). Grow in sun and in any well-drained soil. Propagate by seed in early spring.
♀ ***R. atrosanguineus***, syn. *R. volubilis*, illus. p.207.
R. volubilis. See *R. atrosanguineus*.

RHODODENDRON
Azalea, rhododendron

ERICACEAE

Genus of evergreen, semi-evergreen or deciduous shrubs, ranging from a dwarf habit to a tree-like stature, grown mainly for beauty of flower. Fully hardy to frost tender, min. 4–7°C (39–45°F). Most prefer dappled shade, but a considerable number tolerates full sun, especially in cool climates. Needs neutral to acid soil – ideally, humus-rich and well-drained. Shallow planting is essential, as plants are surface-rooting. Dead-head spent flowers, wherever practical, to encourage energy into growth rather than seed production. Propagate by layering or semi-ripe cuttings in late summer. Yellowing leaves are usually caused by poor drainage, excessively deep planting or lime in soil. Weevils and powdery mildew may also cause problems. The nectar of some rhododendron flowers may cause severe discomfort if ingested. See also feature panel pp.128–30.

Rhododendrons and **azaleas**
The genus *Rhododendron* includes not only evergreen, large-leaved and frequently large-flowered species and hybrids but also dwarf, smaller-leaved shrubs, both evergreen and deciduous, with few-flowered clusters of usually small blooms. 'Azalea' is the common name given to the deciduous species and hybrids as well as to a group of compact, evergreen shrubs derived mainly from Japanese species. They are valued for their mass of small colourful blooms produced in late spring. Many of the evergreen azaleas (sometimes known as Belgian azaleas) may also be grown as house plants. Botanically, however, all are classified as *Rhododendron*. The flowers are usually single, but may be semi-double or double, including hose-in-hose (one flower tube inside the other). Unless otherwise stated below, flowers are single and leaves are mid- to dark green and oval.

R. aberconwayi. Evergreen, distinctly erect rhododendron. H to 2.5m (8ft), S 1.2m (4ft). Frost hardy. Small, broadly lance-shaped leaves are rigid and deep green. Bears saucer-shaped, white flowers in late spring.
R. albrechtii. Deciduous, upright, bushy azalea. H to 3m (10ft), S 2m (6ft). Fully hardy. Has spoon-shaped leaves, clustered at branch tips, and, in spring, loose clusters of 3–5 bell-shaped, green-spotted, purple or pink flowers.
***R.* 'Alison Johnstone'.** Evergreen, bushy, compact rhododendron. H and S 2m (6ft). Frost hardy. Produces an abundance of exquisite, bell-shaped, peach-pink flowers in spring and bears waxy, grey-green leaves.
***R.* 'Angelo'.** Evergreen, bushy rhododendron. H and S to 4m (12ft). Frost hardy. Has bold foliage and large, fragrant, bell-shaped, white flowers in mid-summer. Is good in light woodland.
R. arboreum illus. p.129. Evergreen, tree-like rhododendron. H to 12m (40ft), S 3m (10ft). Frost hardy. Undersides of broadly lance-shaped leaves are silver, fawn or cinnamon. In spring has dense clusters of bell-shaped flowers in colours ranging from red (most tender form) through pink to white.
R. argyrophyllum illus. p.128. Evergreen, spreading rhododendron. H and S to 5m (15ft). Fully hardy. Oblong leaves are silvery-white on undersides. Loose bunches of bell-shaped, rich pink flowers, sometimes with deeper coloured spots, are borne in spring. Is ideal for a light woodland.
R. arizelum. See *R. rex* subsp. *arizelum.*
***R.* 'Ascot Brilliant'.** Evergreen, bushy rhododendron. H and S 3m (10ft). Frost hardy. Leaves are broadly oval. In spring produces loose bunches of funnel-shaped, waxy, rose-red blooms with darker margins.
R. augustinii illus. p.130. Evergreen, bushy rhododendron. H and S to 4m (12ft). Fully hardy. Has lance-shaped to oblong, light green leaves and, in spring, bears an abundance of multi-stemmed, widely funnel-shaped, pale to deep blue or lavender flowers.
R. auriculatum illus. p.128. Evergreen, bushy, widely branching rhododendron. H and S to 6m (20ft). Fully hardy. Has large, oblong, hairy leaves with distinct, ear-like lobes at their base. In late summer bears loose bunches of 7–15 large, heavily scented, tubular to funnel-shaped, white flowers. Is best in light woodland.
***R.* 'Azor'.** Evergreen, upright rhododendron. H and S to 4m (12ft). Frost hardy. Leaves are broadly oval. Especially valuable as it produces large, fragrant, funnel-shaped, salmon-pink flowers in mid-summer.
***R.* 'Azuma-kagami'** illus. p.129. Evergreen, compact azalea. H and S 1.2m (4ft). Frost hardy. Bears many small, hose-in-hose, deep pink flowers in mid-spring. Is best in semi-shade.
R. barbatum. Evergreen, upright rhododendron. H and S to 10m (30ft). Fully hardy. Bears lance-shaped, dark green leaves covered with bristles, on stems; bark is plum-coloured and peeling. Produces tight bunches of tubular to bell-shaped, bright scarlet flowers in early spring.
***R.* 'Beauty of Littleworth'** illus. p.128. Evergreen, open, shrubby rhododendron. H and S 4m (12ft). Frost hardy. Bears huge, conical bunches of scented, funnel-shaped, crimson-spotted, white flowers in late spring.
***R.* 'Beefeater'.** Evergreen, bushy rhododendron. H and S to 2.5m (8ft). Frost hardy. Leaves are broadly lance-shaped. Produces striking, flat-topped bunches of bell-shaped, scarlet flowers in late spring and early summer.
***R.* 'Blue Diamond'** (illus p.130). Evergreen, upright rhododendron. H and S to 1.5m (5ft). Fully hardy. Small, neat leaves contrast with funnel-shaped, bright blue flowers borne in mid- to late spring. Likes full sun.
♀ ***R.* 'Blue Peter'** illus. p.130. Evergreen, bushy rhododendron. H and S to 4m (12ft). Fully hardy. In early summer produces bold, open funnel-shaped, 2-tone lavender-purple flowers, with frilled petal margins.
R. calendulaceum (Flame azalea). Deciduous, bushy azalea. H and S 2–3m (6–10ft). Fully hardy. In early summer bears funnel-shaped, scarlet or orange flowers in bunches of 5–7.
♀ ***R. calophytum*** illus. p.128. Evergreen, widely-branched rhododendron. H and S to 6m (20ft). Frost hardy. Produces large, lance-shaped leaves and, in early spring, huge bunches of bell-shaped, white or pale pink flowers, with crimson spots.
R. calostrotum illus. p.129. Evergreen, compact rhododendron. H and to 1m (3ft). Fully hardy. Has blue-green leaves and, in late spring, saucer-shaped, purple or scarlet flowers in clusters of 2–5.
***R.* 'Catawbiense Album'.** Evergreen, rounded rhododendron. H and S to 3m (10ft). Fully hardy. Bears glossy leaves and, in early summer, dense, rounded bunches of bell-shaped, white flowers.
***R.* 'Catawbiense Boursault'.** Evergreen, rounded rhododendron. H and S to 3m (10ft). Fully hardy. Has glossy leaves. Dense, rounded bunches of bell-shaped, lilac-purple blooms are borne in early summer.
♀ ***R.* 'Cilpinense'**, syn. *R.* × *cilpinense.* Semi-evergreen, compact rhododendron. H and S to 1.5m (5ft). Frost hardy. Leaves are dark green and glossy. Bears masses of large, bell-shaped, blush-pink flowers, flushed deeper in bud, in early spring. Flowers are vulnerable to frost damage.
R. cinnabarinum illus. p.129. Evergreen, upright rhododendron. H and 1.5–4m (5–12ft). Frost hardy. Has blue-green leaves with small scales. Narrowly tubular, waxy, orange to red flowers are borne in loose, drooping bunches in late spring. subsp. ***xanthocodon*** (syn. *R. xanthocodon*; illus. p.130) is of open, upright habit and has aromatic, mid-green leaves, which are blue-green when young. Bears bell-shaped, yellow flowers in late spring.
♀ ***R.* 'Coccineum Speciosum'.** Deciduous, bushy azalea. H and S 1.5–2.5m (5–8ft). Fully hardy. Produces open funnel-shaped, brilliant rich orange-red blooms in early summer. Broadly lance-shaped leaves provide good autumn colour.
♀ ***R.* 'Corneille'** illus. p.129. Deciduous, bushy azalea. H and S 1.5–2.5m (5–8ft). Fully hardy. In early summer produces fragrant, honeysuckle-like, cream flowers, flushed pink outside. Has attractive autumn foliage.
♀ ***R.* 'Crest',** syn. *R.* 'Hawk Crest' illus. p.130. Evergreen rhododendron of open habit. H and S 1.5–4m (5–12ft). Frost hardy. Has broadly lance-shaped leaves. Bell-shaped flowers are borne in loose, flat-topped bunches, and are apricot in bud, opening to clear sulphur-yellow in late spring.
R. cubittii illus. p.128. Evergreen rhododendron now included in *R. veitchianum*. H 1.5m (5ft), S to 1m (3ft). Half hardy. Has purple-brown young shoots and oblong to elliptic, leathery, sparsely scaly, mid- to dark green leaves. In mid- and late spring bears funnel-shaped, white to pale pink flowers, with brownish or yellow-orange markings.
♀ ***R.* 'Curlew'** illus. p.130. Evergreen rhododendron of compact, spreading

habit. H and S 30cm (1ft). Fully hardy. Produces dull green leaves and, in late spring, relatively large, open funnel-shaped, yellow flowers.

♀ ***R.* 'Cynthia'.** Vigorous, evergreen, dome-shaped rhododendron. H and S to 6m (20ft). Fully hardy. Bears conical bunches of bell-shaped, magenta-purple flowers, marked blackish-red within, in late spring. Is excellent for sun or shade.

R. dauricum. Evergreen, upright rhododendron. H and S to 1.5m (5ft). Fully hardy. Produces funnel-shaped, vivid purple flowers in loose clusters throughout winter. Green leaves turn purple-brown in frosty conditions.

♀ ***R. davidsonianum.*** Deciduous, upright rhododendron. H 1.5–4m (5–12ft). Fully hardy. Aromatic leaves are lance-shaped to oblong. In late spring has clusters of funnel-shaped flowers, ranging from pale pink to mid-lilac-mauve.

♀ ***R. decorum.*** Evergreen, bushy rhododendron. H and S 4m (12ft). Frost hardy. Oblong to lance-shaped leaves are mid-green above, paler beneath. Has large, fragrant, funnel-shaped, white or shell-pink flowers, green- or pink-spotted within, in early summer.

R. degronianum var. ***heptamerum***, syn. *R. metternichii*. Evergreen, upright rhododendron. H and S 1.5–4m (5–12ft). Fully hardy. Has oblong leaves, glossy and green above, reddish-brown-felted beneath. Bell-shaped, rose-red flowers, borne in spring, are in rounded bunches of 10–15, often subtly spotted within.

R. discolor. See *R. fortunei* subsp. *discolor*.

***R.* 'Doncaster'.** Evergreen, compact rhododendron. H and S 2–2.5m (6–8ft). Frost hardy. Has leathery, glossy leaves and, in late spring, funnel-shaped, dark red flowers in dense bunches.

♀ ***R.* 'Dora Amateis'.** Evergreen, compact rhododendron. H and S 60cm (2ft). Fully hardy. Leaves are slender, glossy and pointed. Masses of broadly funnel-shaped, white flowers, tinged with pink and marked with green, appear in late spring. Is sun tolerant.

***R.* 'Elizabeth'.** Evergreen, dome-shaped rhododendron. H and S to 1.5m (5ft). Frost hardy. Leaves are oblong. Has large, trumpet-shaped, brilliant red flowers in late spring. Is good in sun or partial shade.

***R.* 'Elizabeth Lockhart'.** Evergreen, dome-shaped rhododendron. H and S 60cm (2ft). Frost hardy. Produces shiny, purple-green leaves that become darker in winter. Bell-shaped, deep pink flowers are carried in spring.

***R.* 'English Roseum'.** Evergreen, vigorous, bushy rhododendron. H and S to 2.5m (8ft). Fully hardy. Dark green leaves are paler beneath. Bears compact bunches of funnel-shaped, lilac-rose flowers in late spring.

♀ ***R.* 'Fabia'** illus. p.130. Evergreen, dome-shaped rhododendron. H and S 2m (6ft). Frost hardy. Leaves are lance-shaped. Loose, flat trusses of funnel-shaped, orange-tinted, scarlet flowers are produced in early summer.

♀ ***R.* 'Fastuosum Flore Pleno'.** Evergreen, dome-shaped rhododendron. H and S 1.5–4m (5–12ft). Fully hardy. In early summer bears loose bunches of funnel-shaped, double, rich mauve flowers, with red-brown marks and wavy margins.

R. falconeri (illus p.128). Multi-stemmed, evergreen rhododendron. H to 12m (40ft), S 5m (15ft). Fully hardy. Has flaking, red-brown bark and broadly elliptic to oval, dark green leaves, brown-felted beneath. In mid-spring produces widely bell-shaped, fleshy, creamy-white or yellow flowers, sometimes pink-tinged, often with purple marks inside.

R. fictolacteum. See *R. rex* subsp. *fictolacteum*

***R.* 'Firefly'.** See *R.* 'Hexe'.

♀ ***R. fortunei*** subsp. ***discolor***, syn. *R. discolor*. Evergreen, tree-like rhododendron. H and S to 8m (25ft). Frost hardy. Leaves are oblong to oval. Bears fragrant, funnel-shaped, pink flowers in mid-summer. Is ideal in a light woodland.

♀ ***R.* 'Fragrantissimum'** illus. p.128. Lax, evergreen rhododendron. H and S 2m (6ft). Half hardy. Nutmeg-scented, broadly funnel-shaped, sometimes pink-flushed, white flowers, with yellow throats, are borne in mid-spring. Leaves are hairy.

***R.* 'Freya'** illus. p.130. Deciduous azalea of compact, shrubby habit. H and S 1.5m (5ft). Fully hardy. Fragrant, funnel-shaped, pink-flushed, orange-salmon flowers appear from late spring to early summer.

***R.* 'Frome'** illus. p.130. Deciduous azalea of shrubby habit. H and S to 1.5m (5ft). Fully hardy. In spring bears trumpet-shaped, saffron-yellow flowers, overlaid red in throats; petals are frilled and wavy-margined.

♀ ***R. fulvum.*** Evergreen, bushy rhododendron. H and S 1.5–4m (5–12ft). Frost hardy. Oblong to oval, polished, deep green leaves are brown-felted beneath. In early spring has loose bunches of bell-shaped, red-blotched, pink flowers, which fade to white.

***R.* 'George Reynolds'** illus. p.130. Deciduous, bushy azalea. H and S to 2m (6ft). Fully hardy. Large, funnel-shaped, yellow flowers, flushed pink in bud, are borne with or before the leaves in spring.

***R.* 'Gloria Mundi'** illus. p.130. Deciduous, twiggy azalea. H and S to 2m (6ft). Fully hardy. Produces fragrant, honeysuckle-like, yellow-flared, orange flowers, with frilled margins, in early summer.

***R.* 'Glory of Littleworth'** illus. p.130. Evergreen or semi-evergreen, bushy hybrid between a rhododendron and an azalea. H and S 1.5m (5ft). Frost hardy. Compact bunches of fragrant, bell-shaped, orange-marked, creamy-white flowers are borne abundantly in late spring and early summer. Is not easy to cultivate.

***R.* 'Gold Crown'.** See *R.* 'Goldkrone'.

♀ ***R.* 'Goldkrone'**, syn. *R.* 'Gold Crown' illus. p.130. Compact, evergreen shrub. H and S 1.5m (5ft). Fully hardy. Funnel- to bell-shaped, bright golden-yellow flowers, delicately spotted ruby-red inside, are borne in succession in mid-spring.

♀ ***R.* 'Gomer Waterer'.** Evergreen, compact rhododendron. H and S 1.5–4m (5–12ft). Fully hardy. Leaves are curved back at margins. Bell-shaped flowers, borne in dense bunches in early summer, are white, flushed mauve, each with a basal, mustard blotch. Likes sun or partial shade.

***R.* 'Hatsugiri'** illus. p.129. Evergreen, compact azalea. H and S 60cm (2ft). Frost hardy. Has small, but very numerous, funnel-shaped, bright crimson-purple flowers in spring. Flowers very reliably.

***R.* 'Hawk Crest'.** See *R.* 'Crest'.

***R.* 'Hexe'**, syn. *R.* 'Firefly'. Evergreen azalea of neat habit. H and S 60cm (2ft). Frost hardy. Has numerous relatively large, hose-in-hose, glowing, crimson flowers in spring.

***R.* 'Hinode-giri'** illus. p.129. Evergreen, compact azalea. H and S 1.5m (5ft). Frost hardy. Funnel-shaped, bright crimson flowers are small, but produced in abundance in late spring. Likes sun or light shade.

♀ ***R.* 'Hinomayo'** illus. p.129. Evergreen, compact azalea. H and S 1.5m (5ft). Frost hardy. Small, funnel-shaped, clear pink flowers are produced in great abundance in spring. Likes sun or light shade.

R. hippophaeoides illus. p.130. Evergreen, erect rhododendron. H and S 1.5m (5ft). Fully hardy. Narrowly lance-shaped, aromatic leaves are grey-green. Has small, funnel-shaped, lavender or lilac flowers in spring. Tolerates wet, but not stagnant, soil.

♀ ***R.* 'Homebush'** illus. p.129. Deciduous, compact azalea. H and S 1.5m (5ft). Frost hardy. In late spring bears tight, rounded heads of trumpet-shaped, semi-double, rose-purple flowers with paler shading.

♀ ***R.* 'Hotei'.** Evergreen, rhododendron of neat, compact habit. H and S 1.5–2.5m (5–8ft). Fully hardy. Has excellent foliage. Large, funnel-shaped, deep yellow flowers are freely produced in late spring.

***R.* 'Humming Bird'.** Evergreen, dome-shaped rhododendron of neat, compact habit. H and S to 1.5m (5ft). Fully hardy. From mid- to late spring produces bell-shaped, rose-pink flowers in loose, nodding bunches, above rounded, glossy leaves.

♀ ***R.* 'Hydon Hunter'.** Evergreen rhododendron of neat habit. H and S to 1.5m (5ft). Fully hardy. In late spring or early summer has masses of large, narrowly bell-shaped, red-rimmed flowers, paler towards the centre and orange-spotted within.

R. impeditum. Slow-growing, evergreen rhododendron. H and S to 60cm (2ft). Fully hardy. Aromatic leaves are grey-green. Funnel-shaped, purplish-blue flowers appear in spring. Is ideal for a rock garden.

♀ ***R.* 'Irohayama'** illus. p.129. Evergreen, compact azalea. H and S to 1.5m (5ft). Frost hardy. Has abundant, small, funnel-shaped, white flowers, with pale lavender margins and faint brown eyes, in spring. Does well in light shade.

***R.* 'Jalisco'.** Deciduous, open, bushy rhododendron. H and S 1.5–4m (5–12ft). Frost hardy. Bears bunches of narrowly bell-shaped, straw-coloured flowers, tinted orange-rose at tips, in early summer.

***R.* 'Jeanette'.** Semi-evergreen, upright azalea. H and S 1.5–2m (5–6ft). Frost hardy. Has funnel-shaped, vivid phlox-pink, dark blotched flowers, in spring. Is good in light shade or full sun.

***R.* 'John Cairns'** illus. p.129. Evergreen, upright, compact azalea. H and 1.5–2m (5–6ft). Fully hardy. Bears abundant funnel-shaped, orange-red flowers in spring. Grows reliably and consistently in sun or semi-shade.

R. kaempferi illus. p.129. Semi-evergreen, erect, loosely branched azalea. H and S 1.5–2.5m (5–8ft). Fully hardy. Leaves are lance-shaped. Has an abundance of funnel-shaped flowers in various shades of orange or red in late spring and early summer.

***R.* 'Kilimanjaro'.** Evergreen, bushy rhododendron. H and S 1.5–4m (5–12ft). Frost hardy. Bears broadly lance-shaped leaves. Produces large, rounded bunches of funnel- to bell-shaped, wavy-edged, maroon-red flowers, spotted chocolate within, in late spring and early summer.

***R.* 'Kirin'** illus. p.129. Evergreen, compact azalea. H and S to 1.5m (5ft). Frost hardy. In spring has numerous hose-in-hose flowers that are deep rose, shaded a delicate silvery-rose. Looks best in light shade.

♀ ***R. kiusianum***. Semi-evergreen azalea of compact habit. H and S to 60cm (2ft). Fully hardy. Leaves are narrowly oval. Produces clusters of 2–5 funnel-shaped flowers, usually lilac-rose or mauve-purple, in late spring. Prefers full sun.

♀ ***R.* 'Lady Alice Fitzwilliam'.** Evergreen, bushy rhododendron. H and S 1.5–4m (5–12ft). Half hardy. Leaves are glossy, dark green. Loose bunches of heavily scented, broadly funnel-shaped, white flowers, flushed pale pink, are produced in mid- to late spring. Grow against a south- or west-facing wall.

♀ ***R.* 'Lady Clementine Mitford'.** Evergreen, rounded, dense rhododendron. H and S 4m (12ft). Fully hardy. Has broadly oval, glossy, dark green leaves that are silvery when young and, in late spring and early summer, bold bunches of tubular- to bell-shaped flowers, peach-pink fading to white in the centre, with V-shaped, pink, green and brown marks within.

***R.* 'Lady Rosebery'.** Evergreen, stiffly branched rhododendron. H and S 1.5–4m (5–12ft). Frost hardy. Bears clusters of drooping, narrowly bell-shaped, waxy, deep pink flowers, which are paler towards petal margins, in late spring. Is ideal for a woodland margin.

R. laetum illus. p.130. Erect, evergreen rhododendron. H and S 1.5m (5ft). Min. 5°C (41°F). Elliptic to broadly elliptic, glossy, dark green leaves have tiny, white scales beneath. In spring, red flower stalks bear funnel-shaped, golden-yellow flowers, later suffused orange-red.

♀ ***R.* 'Lem's Cameo'.** Evergreen, rounded, bushy rhododendron. H and S 1.5–2.5m (5–8ft). Frost hardy. Leaves are rounded. In spring has large-domed bunches of open funnel-shaped, pale peach flowers, deep pink in bud, shaded to pink at margins, with basal, deep rose-coloured blotches.

R. leucaspis (illus p.128). Densely branched, evergreen rhododendron. H 1m (3ft), S 1.5m (5ft). Frost hardy. Has broadly elliptic, dark green leaves, bristly above, scaly and yellowish-green beneath. In early spring produces

saucer-shaped, white flowers, with chocolate-brown anthers.
♀ ***R.* 'Loderi King George'** illus p.128. Large, evergreen rhododendron of open habit. H and 4m (12ft). Fully hardy. Has large leaves. In late spring and early summer, pale pink buds open to huge trusses of fragrant, funnel-shaped, pure white flowers, with subtle green marks in the throats.
R. lutescens illus. p.130. Semi-evergreen, upright rhododendron. H and 1.5–3m (5–10ft). Fully hardy. Has oval to lance-shaped leaves that are bronze-red when young. In early spring bears funnel-shaped, primrose-yellow flowers. Is effective in a light woodland.
♀ ***R. luteum*** illus. p.130. Open deciduous azalea. H and S 1.5–2.5m (5–8ft). Fully hardy. Leaves are oblong to lance-shaped. Has very fragrant, funnel-shaped, bold yellow blooms in spring. Autumn foliage is rich and colourful.
♀ ***R. macabeanum*** illus. p.130. Evergreen, tree-like rhododendron. H and up to 13.5m (45ft). Frost hardy. Has bold, broadly oval leaves, dark green above, grey-felted beneath, and, in early spring, large bunches of bell-shaped, yellow flowers, blotched purple within.
R. mallotum. Evergreen, upright, open rhododendron, occasionally tree-like. H and to 4m (12ft). Frost hardy. Oblong to oval leaves are deep green above, red-brown-felted beneath. Showy, tubular, crimson flowers in loose bunches are borne in early spring.
♀ ***R.* 'May Day'** illus. p.129. Evergreen, spreading rhododendron. H and to 1.5m (5ft). Frost hardy. Leaves are fresh green above, whitish-felted beneath. Has masses of loose bunches of long-lasting, funnel-shaped, scarlet flowers in late spring; petal-like calyces match the flower colour.
***R.* 'Medway'** illus. p.130. Deciduous, bushy, open azalea. H and S 1.5–2.5m (5–8ft). Fully hardy. In late spring has large, trumpet-shaped, pale pink flowers with darker margins and orange-flashed throats; petal margins are frilled.
R. metternichii. See *R. degronianum* var. *heptamerum*.
***R.* 'Moonshine Crescent'** illus. p.130. Evergreen, rounded to upright rhododendron. H 2–2.5m (6–8ft), S 2m (6ft). Frost hardy. In late spring produces compact trusses of bell-shaped, yellow flowers. Leaves are oblong to oval and dark green.
R. moupinense. Evergreen, rounded, compact rhododendron. H and S to 1.5m (5ft). Frost hardy. Produces funnel-shaped, pink blooms in loose bunches in late winter and early spring. Leaves are glossy, dark green above, paler beneath. Is best grown in a sheltered situation to reduce risk of frosted flowers.
***R.* 'Mrs G.W. Leak'** illus. p.129. Evergreen, upright, compact rhododendron. H and S 4m (12ft). Fully hardy. In late spring bears compact, conical bunches of funnel-shaped, pink flowers, with black-brown and crimson marks within,.
R. nakaharae. Evergreen, mound-forming azalea. H and S 60cm (2ft). Frost hardy. Shoots and oblong to oval leaves are densely hairy. Funnel-shaped, dark brick-red flowers are borne in small clusters. Is valuable for mid-summer flowering and is ideal for a rock garden.
♀ ***R.* 'Nancy Waterer'.** Deciduous, twiggy azalea. H and S 1.5–2.5m (5–8ft). Fully hardy. Has large, long-tubed and honeysuckle-like, brilliant golden-yellow flowers in early summer. Is ideal in a light woodland or full sun.
♀ ***R.* 'Narcissiflorum'** illus. p.130. Vigorous, deciduous, compact azalea. H and S 1.5–2.5m (5–8ft). Fully hardy. Sweetly scented, hose-in-hose, pale yellow flowers, darker outside and in centre, are borne in late spring or early summer. Autumn foliage is bronze.
***R.* Nobleanum Group** illus. p.129. Evergreen, upright shrub or tree-like rhododendron. H and S to 5m (15ft). Frost hardy. Bears large, compact bunches of broadly funnel-shaped, rose-red, pink or white flowers in winter or early spring. Will flower for long periods in mild weather; is best in a sheltered position.
♀ ***R.* 'Norma'.** Vigorous, deciduous, compact azalea. H and S to 1.5m (5ft). Fully hardy. Bears masses of hose-in-hose, rose-red flowers, with a salmon glow, in spring. Grows well in sun or light shade.
***R.* 'Nova Zembla'.** Vigorous, evergreen, upright rhododendron. H and 1.5–4m (5–12ft). Fully hardy. Has funnel-shaped, dark red flowers in closely set bunches from late spring to early summer.
♀ ***R. occidentale.*** Bushy, deciduous, azalea. H and S 1.5–2.5m (5–8ft). Fully hardy. Glossy leaves turn yellow or orange in autumn. Bears fragrant, funnel-shaped, white or pale pink flowers, each with a basal, yellow-orange blotch, in early to mid-summer.
***R.* 'Olive'** illus. p.128. Upright, evergreen rhododendron. H 1.2m (4ft), S 1m (3ft). Fully hardy. Small, oval to elliptic, mid-green leaves are paler green beneath. Has funnel-shaped, mauve-pink flowers, with darker spots inside, in early spring.
♀ ***R. orbiculare*** illus. p.129. Evergreen rhododendron of compact habit. H and S to 3m (10ft). Fully hardy. Has rounded, bright green leaves. Bell-shaped, rose-pink flowers are borne in loose bunches in late spring.
R. oreotrephes illus. p.129. Deciduous, upright shrub or tree-like rhododendron. H and S to 5m (15ft). Fully hardy. Has attractive, scaly, grey-green foliage. In spring bears loose bunches of 3–10 broadly funnel-shaped flowers, usually mauve or purple, but variable, often with crimson spots.
♀ ***R.* 'Palestrina'** illus. p.128. Evergreen or semi-evergreen, compact, free-flowering azalea. H and S to 1.2m (4ft). Frost hardy. Has large, open funnel-shaped, white flowers, with faint, green marks, in late spring. Grows well in light shade.
♀ ***R.* 'Percy Wiseman'** illus. p.128. Evergreen rhododendron with a domed, compact habit. H and S to 2m (6ft). Fully hardy. In late spring produces open funnel-shaped, peach-yellow flowers that fade to white.
♀ ***R.* 'Peter John Mezitt'**, syn. *R.* 'P.J. Mezitt'. Evergreen, compact rhododendron. H and S up to 1.5m (5ft). Fully hardy. Aromatic leaves are small, dark green in summer, bronze-purple in winter. Bears frost-resistant, funnel-shaped, lavender-pink flowers in early spring. Is good in full sun.
***R.* 'Pink Pearl'** illus. p.129. Vigorous, evergreen, upright, open rhododendron. H and S 4m (12ft) or more. Frost hardy. Bears tall bunches of open funnel-shaped, pink flowers in late spring.
***R.* 'P.J. Mezitt'.** See *R.* 'Peter John Mezitt'.
♀ ***R.* 'Polar Bear'** (illus p.128). Vigorous, multi-stemmed, evergreen rhododendron. H 5m (15ft), S 4m (12ft). Fully hardy. In late summer produces strongly scented, tubular to funnel-shaped, white flowers, with light brown-flecked, pale green throats.
♀ ***R.* 'Ptarmigan'** illus. p.128. Evergreen, spreading rhododendron that forms a compact mound. H to 30cm (1ft), S 75cm (2½ft) or more. Fully hardy. Funnel-shaped, pure white flowers are borne in early spring. Prefers full sun.
♀ ***R.* 'Purple Splendour'.** Evergreen, bushy rhododendron. H and S to 3m (10ft). Fully hardy. Has well-formed bunches of open funnel-shaped, rich royal-purple flowers, with prominent, black marks in throats, in late spring or early summer.
♀ ***R.* 'Queen Elizabeth II'** illus. p.130. Evergreen, bushy rhododendron. H and S 1.5–4m (5–12ft). Frost hardy. Bears funnel-shaped, greenish-yellow flowers in loose bunches in late spring. Leaves are narrowly oval or lance-shaped, glossy and mid-green above, paler beneath.
***R.* 'Queen of Hearts'.** Evergreen, open rhododendron. H and S 1.5–4m (5–12ft). Frost hardy. Has masses of domed bunches of funnel-shaped, deep crimson flowers, black-speckled within, in mid-spring.
R. racemosum illus. p.129. Evergreen, upright, stiffly branched rhododendron. H and S to 2.5m (8ft). Fully hardy. Has clusters of widely funnel-shaped, bright pink flowers carried along the stems in spring. Small, aromatic, broadly oval leaves are dull green above, grey-green below.
R. rex. Vigorous, evergreen, upright shrub or tree-like rhododendron. H and S 4m (12ft) or more. Frost hardy. Leaves are pale buff-felted beneath. Pink or white flowers each have a crimson blotch and a spotted throat. subsp. ***arizelum*** (syn. *R. arizelum*; illus p.130), H and S 8m (25ft), has inversely oval leaves and usually yellow, sometimes pink, rarely white flowers, with crimson marks in the throats. ♀ subsp. ***fictolacteum*** (syn. *R. fictolacteum*; illus. p.128), H to 13.5m (45ft), has large leaves, green above, brown-felted beneath. Bears bunches of bell-shaped, white flowers in spring, each with a maroon blotch and often a spotted throat.
***R.* 'Romany Chai'.** Vigorous, evergreen rhododendron, open when young, becoming denser with age. H and S 1.5–4m (5–12ft). Frost hardy. Has dark green, bronze-tinged foliage. In early summer, bears large, compact bunches of broadly funnel-shaped, rich brown-red flowers, each with a basal, maroon blotch. Suits a light woodland.
***R.* 'Roseum Elegans'.** Vigorous, evergreen, rounded rhododendron. H and S 2.5m (8ft) or more. Fully hardy. Foliage is bold and glossy, deep green. In early summer bears rounded bunches of broadly funnel-shaped, reddish-purple flowers, each marked with yellow-brown.
♀ ***R.* 'Roza Stevenson'.** Vigorous, evergreen, upright rhododendron of open habit. H and S 1.5–4m (5–12ft). Frost hardy. Produces masses of fine, loose bunches of saucer-shaped, lemon flowers in mid- to late spring. Is excellent in light shade.
R. rubiginosum. Vigorous, evergreen, upright, well-branched rhododendron. H 6m (20ft), S 2.5m (8ft). Frost hardy. Aromatic leaves are lance-shaped, dull green above, reddish-brown beneath. Has funnel-shaped, lilac-purple flowers in loose bunches in mid-spring.
R. schlippenbachii. Deciduous, rounded, open azalea. H and 2.5m (8ft). Fully hardy. Spoon-shaped leaves are in whorls at branch ends. Bears loose bunches of 3–6 saucer-shaped, pink flowers in mid-spring. Suits a light woodland.
***R.* 'Seta'** illus. p.129. Evergreen, erect rhododendron. H 1.5m (5ft), S 1–1.5m (3–5ft). Frost hardy. In early spring bears loose bunches of tubular, shiny, vivid pink-and-white-striped flowers, fading to white at bases.
***R.* 'Seven Stars'.** Vigorous, evergreen, upright, dense rhododendron. H and S 2–3m (6–10ft). Fully hardy. Has yellowish-green foliage and, in spring, masses of bunches of large, bell-shaped, wavy-margined, white flowers, flushed with apple-blossom pink, pink in bud.
♀ ***R. sinogrande*** illus. p.128. Evergreen, bushy rhododendron. H and S 10m (30ft). Fully hardy. Has very large, oblong to lance-shaped, glossy, dark green leaves, silver- to buff-felted beneath. In mid- and late spring bears widely bell-shaped, pale yellow to creamy-white flowers, marked crimson inside.
***R.* 'Snowdrift'.** Deciduous, bushy azalea. H and S to 2.5m (8ft). Fully hardy. Bears bunches of large, slender-tubed flowers in spring before the leaves appear. Flowers are white with yellow marks that deepen to orange.
R. souliei illus. p.128. Evergreen, open rhododendron. H and S 1.5–4m (5–12ft). Fully hardy. Has rounded leaves and, in late spring, saucer-shaped, soft pink flowers. Grows best in areas of low rainfall.
♀ ***R.* 'Spek's Orange'.** Deciduous, bushy azalea. H and S to 2.5m (8ft). Fully hardy. In late spring carries bold bunches of large, slender-tubed blooms that are bright reddish-orange with greenish marks within.
♀ ***R.* 'Strawberry Ice'** illus. p.129. Deciduous, bushy azalea. H and S 1.5–2.5m (5–8ft). Fully hardy. Bears trumpet-shaped flowers, deep pink in bud, opening flesh-pink, and mottled deeper pink at petal margins with deep yellow-marked throats, in late spring.
***R.* 'Surprise'.** Evergreen, dense azalea. H and S to 1.5m (5ft). Frost hardy. Has abundant, small, funnel-shaped, light orange-red flowers in mid-spring. Looks effective when mass planted and is ideal in light shade or full sun.

♀ ***R.* 'Susan'** illus. p.129. Close-growing, evergreen rhododendron. H and S 1.5–4m (5–12ft). Fully hardy. Foliage is glossy, dark green. In spring bears large bunches of open funnel-shaped flowers in 2 shades of blue-mauve, spotted purple within.
R. sutchuenense illus. p.128. Evergreen, spreading shrub or tree-like rhododendron. H and S to 5m (16ft). Frost hardy. Has large leaves and, in early spring, large bunches of broadly funnel-shaped, pink flowers, spotted deeper within. Is suitable for a light woodland.
♀ ***R.* 'Temple Belle'.** Evergreen rhododendron of neat, compact habit. H and S 1.5–2.5m (5–8ft). Fully hardy. Loose bunches of bell-shaped, clear pink flowers are produced in spring. Rounded leaves are dark green above, grey-green beneath.
R. thomsonii illus. p.129. Evergreen, rounded rhododendron of open habit. H and S to 5.5m (18ft). Frost hardy. Leaves are waxy, dark green above, whiter beneath. Peeling, fawn-coloured bark contrasts well with bell-shaped, waxy, red flowers in spring.
♀ ***R.* 'Vuyk's Scarlet'** illus. p.129. Evergreen, compact azalea. H and S to 60cm (2ft). Frost hardy. In spring bears an abundance of relatively large, open funnel-shaped, brilliant red flowers, with wavy petals, which completely cover the glossy foliage.
R. wardii illus. p.130. Evergreen, compact rhododendron. H and S 1.5–4m (5–12ft). Fully hardy. Leaves are rounded. In late spring bears loose bunches of saucer-shaped, clear yellow flowers, with crimson basal blotches.
♀ ***R. williamsianum*** illus. p.129. Evergreen rhododendron of compact, spreading habit. H and S 1.5m (5ft). Fully hardy. Young leaves are bronze, maturing to mid-green. Has loosely clustered, bell-shaped, pink flowers in spring. Is ideal for a small garden.
***R.* 'Woodcock'.** Evergreen, compact, spreading rhododendron. H and S 1.5–2.5m (5–8ft). Fully hardy. Has semi-glossy, dark green leaves and, in spring, masses of loose bunches of funnel-shaped, rose-red flowers.
R. xanthocodon. See *R. cinnabarinum* subsp. *xanthocodon*.
R. yakushimanum illus. p.128. Evergreen, dome-shaped rhododendron of neat, compact habit. H 1m (3ft), S 1.5m (5ft). Fully hardy. Leaves are broadly oval, silvery at first, maturing to deepest green, and brown-felted beneath. In late spring has open funnel-shaped, pink flowers that fade to near white and are flecked green within.
♀ ***R.* 'Yellow Hammer'** illus. p.130. Evergreen, erect, bushy rhododendron. H and S to 2m (6ft). Fully hardy. Bears abundant clusters of tubular, bright yellow flowers in spring; frequently flowers again in autumn.
R. yunnanense. Semi-evergreen, open rhododendron. H and S 1.5–4m (5–12ft). Fully hardy. Has aromatic, grey-green leaves and masses of butterfly-like, pale pink or white flowers, with blotched throats, in spring.

RHODOHYPOXIS

HYPOXIDACEAE

Genus of dwarf, spring- to summer-flowering, tuberous perennials, grown for their pink, red or white flowers, each comprising 6 petals that meet at the centre, so the flower has no eye. Frost hardy, if kept fairly dry while dormant. Needs full sun, sandy, peaty soil and plenty of moisture in summer. Propagate in spring by seed or offsets.
***R.* 'Albrighton'** illus. p.392.
♀ ***R. baurii.*** Spring- and early summer-flowering, tuberous perennial. H 5–10cm (2–4in), S 2.5–5cm (1–2in). Has an erect, basal tuft of narrowly lance-shaped, hairy leaves. Bears a succession of erect, flattish, white, pale pink or red flowers, 2cm (¾in) across, on slender stems. var. ***platypetala*** has 2.5cm (1in) wide, white or very pale pink flowers.
***R.* 'Douglas'** illus. p.392.
***R.* 'Margaret Rose'** illus. p.388.

RHODOLEIA

HAMAMELIDACEAE

Genus of evergreen, mainly spring-flowering trees, grown for their foliage and flowers. Frost tender, min. 7–10°C (45–50°F). Needs full light or partial shade and humus-rich, well-drained, neutral to acid soil. Water potted specimens freely; sparingly when not in full growth. Tolerates pruning if necessary. Propagate by semi-ripe cuttings in summer or by seed when ripe, in autumn or in spring.
R. championii. Evergreen, bushy tree. H and S 4–8m (12–25ft). Elliptic to oval, bright green leaves, each to 9cm (3½in) long, are borne near the shoot tips. Clusters of tiny flowers, surrounded by petal-like, pink bracts, appear in spring.

RHODOPHIALA

AMARYLLIDACEAE

Genus of bulbs, grown for their large, funnel-shaped flowers. Frost hardy to frost tender, min. 13–15°C (55–9°F). Needs full sun or partial shade and well-drained soil. Keep dormant bulbs dry in winter. Propagate by seed in spring or by offsets in spring (summer-flowering species).
R. advena, syn. *Hippeastrum advenum*, illus. p.437.

RHODOTHAMNUS

ERICACEAE

Genus of one species of evergreen, semi-prostrate, open shrub, grown for its flowers. Is suitable for rock gardens and peat beds. Fully hardy. Needs sun and humus-rich, well-drained, acid soil. Propagate by seed in spring or by semi-ripe cuttings in summer.
R. chamaecistus illus. p.364.

RHODOTYPOS

ROSACEAE

Genus of one species of deciduous shrub, grown for its flowers. Fully hardy. Needs sun or semi-shade and moist but well-drained, fertile soil. After flowering, on established plants, cut some older shoots back or to ground level. Propagate by softwood cuttings in summer or by seed in autumn.
R. kerrioides. See *R. scandens*.
R. scandens, syn. *R. kerrioides*, illus. p.154.

Rhoeo discolor. See *Tradescantia spathacea*.
Rhoeo spathacea. See *Tradescantia spathacea*.

RHOICISSUS

VITACEAE

Genus of evergreen, tendril climbers, grown for their handsome foliage. Bears inconspicuous flowers intermittently during the year. Frost tender, min. 7–10°C (45–50°F). Grow in any fertile, well-drained soil with light shade in summer. Water regularly, less in cold weather. Provide support. Remove crowded stems when necessary or in early spring. Propagate by seed in spring or by semi-ripe cuttings in summer.
♀ ***R. capensis*** (Cape grape). Vigorous, evergreen, tendril climber. H and S to 5m (15ft). Rounded, toothed, lustrous, mid- to deep green leaves, to 20cm (8in) wide, have deeply rounded, heart-shaped bases.
R. rhombifolia. See *Cissus rhombifolia*.
R. rhomboidea. See *Cissus rhombifolia*.

RHOMBOPHYLLUM

AIZOACEAE

Genus of mat-forming, perennial succulents with dense, basal rosettes of linear or semi-cylindrical leaves, each expanded towards middle or tip; leaf tip is reflexed or incurved. Frost tender, min. 5°C (41°F). Needs sun and very well-drained soil. Propagate by seed or stem cuttings in spring or summer.
♀ ***R. rhomboideum*** illus. p.494.

Rhubarb. See *Rheum*.

RHUS

Sumach

ANACARDIACEAE

Genus of deciduous trees, shrubs and scrambling climbers, grown for their divided, ash-like foliage, autumn colour and, in some species, showy fruit clusters. Fully to frost hardy. Requires sun and well-drained soil. Propagate by semi-ripe cuttings in summer, by seed in autumn or by root cuttings in winter. May be attacked by coral spot fungus. All parts of *R. verniciflua* are highly toxic if ingested; contact with its foliage, and that of a number of related species, including *R. succedanea*, may aggravate skin allergies.
R. aromatica. Deciduous, bushy shrub. H 1m (3ft), S 1.5m (5ft). Fully hardy. Deep green leaves, each composed of 3 oval leaflets, turn orange or reddish-purple in autumn. Tiny, yellow flowers are borne in mid-spring, before foliage, followed by spherical, red fruits.
R. copallina (Dwarf sumach). Deciduous, upright shrub. H and S 1–1.5m (3–5ft), or more. Fully hardy. Has glossy, dark green leaves, with numerous lance-shaped leaflets, that turn red-purple in autumn. Minute, greenish-yellow flowers, borne in dense clusters from mid- to late summer, develop into narrowly egg-shaped, bright red fruits.
R. cotinoides. See *Cotinus obovatus*.
R. cotinus. See *Cotinus coggygria*.
R. glabra illus. p.139.
R. hirta. See. *R. typhina* **'Laciniata'** see. *R. typhina* 'Dissecta'.
R. potaninii. Deciduous, round-headed tree. H 12m (40ft), S 8m (25ft). Fully hardy. Has large, dark green leaves, with usually 7–11 oval leaflets that turn red in autumn. In summer produces dense clusters of tiny, yellow-green flowers. Female flower clusters develop into tiny, spherical, black or brownish fruits.
R. succedanea, syn. *Toxicodendron succedaneum* (Wax tree). Deciduous, spreading tree. H and S 10m (30ft). Frost hardy. Large, glossy, dark green leaves, each made up of 9–15 oval leaflets, turn red in autumn. Has dense clusters of tiny, yellow-green flowers in summer. Female flowers develop into tiny, spherical, black or brownish fruits.
R. trichocarpa illus. p.91.
♀ ***R. typhina***, syn. *R. hirta* (Stag's horn sumach). Deciduous, spreading, suckering, open shrub or tree. H 5m (15ft), S 6m (20ft). Fully hardy. Velvety shoots are clothed in dark green leaves with oblong leaflets. Produces minute, greenish-white flowers from mid- to late summer. Leaves become brilliant orange-red in autumn, accompanying clusters of spherical, deep red fruits on female plants. ♀ **'Dissecta'** (syn. *R. hirta* 'Laciniata', *R.t.* 'Laciniata' of gardens), illus. p.120. **'Laciniata'** of gardens see *R.t.* 'Dissecta'.
R. verniciflua, syn. *Toxicodendron vernicifluum* (Varnish tree). Deciduous, spreading tree. H 15m (50ft), S 10m (30ft). Fully hardy. Large, glossy, bright green leaves, with 7–13 oval leaflets, redden in autumn. Bears dense clusters of tiny, yellow-green flowers in summer, followed by berry-like, brownish-yellow fruits. Contact with the sap may severely irritate the skin.

Rhynchelytrum repens. See *Melinis repens*.
Rhynchelytrum roseum. See *Melinis repens*.
Ribbon gum. See *Eucalyptus viminalis*.
Ribbon plant. See *Dracaena sanderiana*, illus. p.147.
Ribbonwood. See *Hoheria sexstylosa*.

RIBES

Currant

GROSSULARIACEAE

Genus of deciduous or evergreen, mainly spring-flowering shrubs, grown for their edible fruits (currants and gooseberries) or their flowers. Fully to frost hardy. Needs full sun and well-drained, fertile soil, but *R. laurifolium* tolerates shade. After flowering cut out some older shoots and, in winter or early spring, prune straggly, old plants hard. Propagate deciduous species by hardwood cuttings in winter,

evergreens by semi-ripe cuttings in summer. Aphids attack young foliage.
R. aureum of gardens. See *R. odoratum*.
R. laurifolium illus. p.171.
R. odoratum, syn. *R. aureum* of gardens (Buffalo currant). Deciduous, upright shrub. H and S 2m (6ft). Fully hardy. Clusters of fragrant, tubular, golden-yellow flowers are borne from mid- to late spring, followed by rounded, purple fruits. Rounded, 3-lobed, bright green leaves turn red and purple in autumn.
R. sanguineum (Flowering currant). **'Brocklebankii'** illus. p.151. **'King Edward VII'** is a deciduous, upright, compact shrub. H and S 2m (6ft). Fully hardy. Small, tubular, deep reddish-pink flowers are freely borne amid rounded, 3–5-lobed, aromatic, dark green leaves, from mid- to late spring, and are sometimes succeeded by spherical, black fruits with a white bloom. Is useful for hedging.
🏆 **'Pulborough Scarlet'** illus. p.126. **'Tydeman's White'**, H and S 2.5m (8ft), is less compact, with white flowers.
🏆 ***R. speciosum*** (Fuchsia-flowered currant). Deciduous, bushy, spiny shrub. H and S 2m (6ft). Frost hardy. Slender, drooping, tubular, red flowers, with long, red stamens, open mid-late spring. Fruits are spherical and red. Has red, young shoots and oval, 3–5-lobed, glossy, bright green leaves. Train against a south- or west-facing wall.

Rice, Canada wild. See *Zizania aquatica*.
Rice-paperplant. See *Tetrapanax papyrifer*, illus. p.122.

RICHEA

EPACRIDACEAE

Genus of evergreen, summer-flowering shrubs, grown for their foliage and densely clustered flowers. Frost to half hardy. Needs sun or semi-shade and moist, peaty, neutral to acid soil. Propagate by semi-ripe cuttings in summer or by seed in autumn.
R. scoparia. Evergreen, upright shrub. H and S 2m (6ft). Frost hardy. Shoots are covered with narrowly lance-shaped, sharp-pointed, dark green leaves. Bears dense, upright spikes of small, egg-shaped, pink, white, orange or maroon flowers in early summer.

RICINUS

EUPHORBIACEAE

Genus of one species of fast-growing, evergreen, tree-like shrub, grown for its foliage. In cool climates is grown as an annual. Half hardy. Needs sun and fertile to rich, well-drained soil. May require support in exposed areas. Propagate by seed sown under glass in early spring. All parts of *R. communis*, particularly the seeds, are highly toxic if ingested; contact with the foliage may aggravate skin allergies.
R. communis illus. p.347. **'Impala'** illus. p.342.

Rienga lily. See *Arthropodium cirratum*.
River red gum. See *Eucalyptus camaldulensis*.
Roast-beef plant. See *Iris foetidissima*.

ROBINIA

LEGUMINOSAE/PAPILIONACEAE

Genus of deciduous, mainly summer-flowering trees and shrubs, grown for their foliage and clusters of pea-like flowers. Is useful for poor, dry soil. Fully hardy. Needs a sunny position. Grows in any but waterlogged soil. Branches are brittle and may be damaged by strong winds. Propagate by seed or suckers in autumn or by root cuttings in winter. All parts may cause severe discomfort if ingested.
R. × ambigua **'Decaisneana'**. Deciduous, spreading tree. H 15m (50ft), S 10m (30ft). Dark green leaves have numerous oval leaflets. Long, hanging clusters of pea-like, pink flowers are borne in early summer.
R. hispida illus. p.137. var. ***kelseyi*** (syn. *R. kelseyi*) is a deciduous, spreading, open shrub. H 2.5m (8ft), S 4m (12ft). Clusters of pea-like, rose-pink flowers open in late spring or early summer, followed by pendent, red seed pods. Dark green leaves consist of 9 or 11 oval leaflets.
R. kelseyi. See *R. hispida* var. *kelseyi*.
R. pseudoacacia (False acacia, Locust). Fast-growing, deciduous, spreading tree. H 25m (80ft), S 15m (50ft). Dark green leaves consist of 11–23 oval leaflets. Dense, drooping clusters of fragrant, pea-like, white flowers are borne in late spring and early summer.
🏆 **'Frisia'** illus. p.77. **'Umbraculifera'** (Mop-head acacia), H and S 6m (20ft), rarely produces a rounded, dense flower head.

Roblé. See *Nothofagus obliqua*, illus. p.64.
Rochea coccinea. See *Crassula coccinea*.
Rock lily. See *Arthropodium cirratum*.
Rock rose. See *Cistus; Helianthemum*.
Rock speedwell. See *Veronica fruticans*.
Rocket
 Sweet. See *Hesperis matronalis*, illus. p.241.
 Yellow. See *Barbarea vulgaris*.
Rocky Mountain juniper. See *Juniperus scopulorum*.

RODGERSIA

SAXIFRAGACEAE

Genus of summer-flowering, rhizomatous perennials. Is ideal for pond sides. Fully to frost hardy. Grows in sun or semi-shade and in soil that is moist; requires shelter from strong winds, which may damage foliage. Propagate by division in spring or by seed in autumn.
🏆 ***R. aesculifolia*** illus. p.243.
🏆 ***R. pinnata*** **'Superba'**. Clump-forming, rhizomatous perennial. H 1–1.2m (3–4ft), S 75cm (2½ft). Frost hardy. Leaves are bronze-tinged, emerald-green, with 5–9 narrowly oval leaflets. Long, much-branched, dense panicles of star-shaped, bright pink flowers appear in mid-summer.
🏆 ***R. podophylla*** illus. p.242.
R. sambucifolia illus. p.242.

Roman wormwood. See *Artemisia pontica*, illus. p.302.

ROMNEYA

Tree poppy

PAPAVERACEAE

Genus of summer-flowering, woody-based perennials and deciduous sub-shrubs. Frost hardy. Requires a warm, sunny position and deep, well-drained soil. Is difficult to establish, resents being moved and, in very cold areas, roots may need protection in winter. Once established, may spread rapidly. Propagate by softwood cuttings of basal shoots in early spring, by seed in autumn (transplanting seedlings without disturbing rootballs) or by root cuttings in winter.
🏆 ***R. coulteri*** illus. p.224.
🏆 ***R.*** **'White Cloud'**. Vigorous, bushy, woody-based perennial. H and S 1m (3ft). Throughout summer produces large, slightly fragrant, shallowly cup-shaped, white flowers with prominent golden stamens. Leaves are oval, deeply lobed and grey.

ROMULEA

IRIDACEAE

Genus of crocus-like corms, grown for their funnel-shaped flowers. Frost to half hardy. Needs full light and well-drained, sandy soil. Water freely during the growing period. Most species die down in summer and then need warmth and dryness. *R. macowanii*, however, is dormant in winter. Propagate by seed in autumn, or in spring for *R. macowanii*.
R. bulbocodioides of gardens. See *R. flava*.
R. bulbocodium illus. p.447.
R. flava, syn. *R. bulbocodioides* of gardens. Early spring-flowering corm. H to 10cm (4in), S 2.5–5cm (1–2in). Half hardy. Has a thread-like, erect, basal leaf and 1–5 upright, widely funnel-shaped, usually yellow flowers, 2–4cm (¾–1½in) across, with deeper yellow centres.
R. longituba. See *R. macowanii* var. *alticola*.
R. macowanii var. ***alticola***, syn. *R. longituba*. Summer-flowering corm. H and S 1–2cm (½–¾in). Half hardy. Leaves are thread-like, erect and basal. Produces 1–3 upright, yellow flowers, each 3cm (1¼in) across with a long tube expanding to become a wide funnel shape.
R. sabulosa. Early spring-flowering corm. H 5–15cm (2–6in), S 2.5–5cm (1–2in). Half hardy. Forms thread-like, erect, basal leaves. Stems bear 1–4 upward-facing, funnel-shaped, black-centred, bright red flowers that open flattish, to 4–5cm (1½–2in) across, in the sun.

RONDELETIA

RAUBIACEAE

Genus of evergreen, mainly summer-flowering trees and shrubs, grown primarily for their flowers. Frost tender, min. 13–16°C (55–61°F). Requires full light or partial shade and fertile, well-drained soil. Water containerized specimens freely when in full growth, moderately at other times. Stems may be shortened in early spring if necessary. Propagate by seed in spring or by semi-ripe cuttings in summer.
R. amoena. Evergreen, rounded shrub. H and S 2–4m (6–12ft). Oval, dark green leaves have dense, brown down on undersides. Produces dense clusters of tubular, 4- or 5-lobed, pink flowers in summer.

Roof houseleek. See *Sempervivum tectorum*, illus. p.401.
Rooksbya euphorbioides. See *Neobuxbaumia euphorbioides*.

ROOF HOUSELEEK. SEE *SEMPERVIVUM TECTORUM*, ILLUS. P.401.
Rooksbya euphorbioides. See *Neobuxbaumia euphorbioides*.

ROSA

Rose

ROSACEAE

Genus of deciduous or semi-evergreen, open shrubs and scrambling climbers, grown for their profusion of flowers, often fragrant, and sometimes for their fruits (rose hips). Leaves are divided into usually 5 or 7 oval leaflets, with rounded or pointed tips, that are sometimes toothed. Stems usually bear thorns, or prickles. Fully hardy, unless otherwise stated below. Prefers an open, sunny site and requires fertile, moist but well-drained soil. Avoid planting in an area where roses have been grown in recent years, as problems due to harmful organisms may occur: either exchange the soil, which may be used satisfactorily elsewhere, or choose another site for the new rose. To obtain blooms of high quality, feed in late winter or early spring with a balanced fertilizer and apply a mulch. In spring and summer feed regularly at 3-weekly intervals. Remove spent flower heads from plants that are 'remontant' ('rising up again'; other terms used are repeat- or perpetual-flowering). May be trimmed for tidiness in early winter. To improve health, flower quality and shape of bush, prune in the dormant season or, preferably, in early spring, before young shoots develop from dormant growth buds: remove dead, damaged and dying wood; lightly trim Old Garden and Ground-cover roses (see below); remove two-thirds of previous summer's growth of Modern bush, including miniature, roses. Correct treatment of Modern shrub and climbing roses, ramblers and Species roses depends on the individual cultivar but in general they should be pruned only lightly. Propagate by budding in summer or by hardwood cuttings in autumn. All roses are prone to attack by various pests and diseases, including aphids, blackspot, powdery mildew, rust and sawfly.

Rose species and cultivars are often regarded as 2 separate groups. Cultivars are further divided into Old Garden and Modern roses. Each group comprises different types, based, it is claimed, on the functional qualities of each plant, such as whether it is remontant, rather than on any historical, botanical or genetical relationships. Flowers occur in a variety of forms (illustrated and described on p.180) and are single (4–7 petals), semi-double (8–20 petals), double (20–30 petals) or fully double (over 30 petals).

Many modern rose cultivars are sold under names other than the registered Plant Breeder's Rights (PBR) names; where this is the case, the plant is listed under its trade name, with the PBR name in brackets afterwards. Roses are illustrated on pp.176–95.

Species roses

Species, or wild, roses (including those interspecific hybrids that share most of the characteristics of their parent species) are either shrubs or climbers, mostly bearing single, 5-petalled, often fragrant flowers in summer, usually in one flush on short shoots from second-year wood: the flowers are followed by red or black hips in autumn.

Old Garden roses

This category is so large that it is divided into two groups. Roses in Group A are mostly of European origin, while those in Group B are hybrids between Oriental and European roses.

GROUP A

Alba – large, freely branching shrubs with only a few prickles on the stems. They bear clusters of 5–7 semi- to fully double, scented flowers in mid-summer, on shoots from second-year wood. Have abundant, greyish-green leaves. Are very hardy and most are good for borders and as hedges or as specimen plants.
Centifolia (or **Provence**) – lax, thorny shrubs that produce often scented, double to fully double flowers, borne singly or in 3s, in summer, on shoots from second-year wood. Leaves are matt, dark green. Are suitable for borders.
Damask – open shrubs with prickly stems and downy leaves. They produce often very fragrant, semi- to fully double flowers, borne singly or in loose clusters of 5–7 mainly in summer, on shoots from second-year wood; a few also flower on new wood in autumn. Are suitable for borders or training against a support.
Gallica – shrubs of fairly dense, free-branching habit, with usually thorny stems, and mostly dull, dark green leaves. Produce mostly scented, single to fully double, richly coloured flowers, often in clusters of 3, in summer on shoots from second-year wood. Are suitable for borders and as hedging.
Moss – often lax shrubs with a furry, moss-like growth on stems and calyces. Leaves are usually dark green. Usually fragrant, semi- to fully double flowers, often in clusters of 3 or more, are borne on very thorny shoots from second-year wood in summer. Are suitable for beds and borders.
Scots (or **Scotch**) – Suckering shrubs, selections or hybrids of *R. spinosissima*, of low, spreading, rarely upright habit, with prickly stems and dark green leaves. Occasionally scented, single to double flowers are solitary or borne in clusters of 3 or more, on short stems from second-year wood, usually in early summer. Are suitable for beds and borders.
Sweet Briar – Vigorous, free-branching shrubs with usually thorny stems and sweetly scented, dark green leaves. In summer, they bear usually scented, single to double flowers, singly or in clusters of up to 7, on short shoots from second-year wood. Use as hedges, as specimen plants and in large borders.

GROUP B

Bourbon – large, open, remontant shrubs and climbing roses, often with long, smooth or prickly stems, which may be trained to climb. They have often glossy leaves and numerous scented, double or fully double flowers, borne commonly in 3s, in flushes in summer and usually autumn. Flowers are borne on short shoots from second-year wood and on new wood. Are suitable for borders and for training over fences, walls and pillars.
Boursault – climbing roses with long, arching, usually smooth stems and dark green leaves. They bear slightly scented, semi-double or double flowers, singly or in clusters of 3, in early summer, on short shoots from second-year wood. Grow against a sheltered wall or fence.
China – spindly, remontant shrubs with mostly smooth stems, bearing only a few reddish-brown prickles, and glossy leaves. They produce sometimes scented, single to fully double flowers, borne singly or in clusters of 3–13, in flushes in summer-autumn. Flowers are borne on short shoots from second-year wood and on new wood. Need a sheltered position. Are suitable for borders and walls.
Hybrid Musk – Vigorous, remontant shrubs with prickly stems and abundant foliage. They produce mainly double blooms, often very fragrant, either singly or in clusters of 2–7 or more, in flushes from mid-summer to autumn. Are good for shrub borders, and can be trained on walls.
Hybrid Perpetual – free-branching, remontant shrubs with upright, prickly growth and dark green leaves. They bear often scented, fully double flowers, held singly or in 3s, in flushes in summer-autumn on shoots from second-year wood and on new wood. Are suitable for beds and borders.
Noisette – remontant climbing roses that bear clusters of 3–15 usually double to fully double flowers, with a slight spicy fragrance, in flushes in summer-autumn. Flowers are borne on shoots from second-year wood, occasionally on new wood. Have generally smooth stems and glossy leaves. Are suitable for sheltered, south- or west-facing walls.
Portland (or **Damask Portland**) – upright, compact, remontant shrubs with thorny stems and usually dark green leaves. They produce usually scented, semi- to fully double flowers, held singly or in 3s, in flushes in summer-autumn, mainly on shoots from second-year wood. Are suitable for beds and borders.
Sempervirens – vigorous, semi-evergreen climbing or rambler roses with shiny, light green leaves. Arching, thorny stems bear clusters of 3–15 unscented, semi- to fully double flowers in summer, on short stems from second-year wood. Are ideal for naturalizing or for growing on fences and pergolas.
Tea – remontant shrubs and climbing roses with smooth to thorny stems, sometimes bearing a few large, red prickles, and glossy, light or sometimes dark green leaves. They produce spicy-scented, slender-stemmed, semi- to fully double flowers, borne singly or in 3s, in flushes in summer-autumn, on shoots from second-year wood and on new wood. Need a sheltered position. Are suitable for beds and borders and trained against walls.

Modern roses

Climber – often vigorous climbing roses with thorny, arching, stiff stems and usually dense, glossy, mid- to dark green foliage. They bear generally scented flowers in a variety of forms, singly or in clusters of 3–7 or more. Some bloom in summer only, on short shoots from second-year wood; many are remontant and also flower on new wood. Train against walls, fences or use to cover garden structures.
Climbing Miniature – Remontant, climbing roses with restrained, sparsely thorny growth. Clusters of 3–9 tiny, rarely scented, single to fully double flowers are borne in flushes in summer-autumn, on shoots from second-year wood and on new wood. Grow against low walls, fences and pillars.
Floribunda (or **Cluster-flowered bush**) – remontant, free-branching shrubs of upright or bushy habit, usually with prickly stems and glossy, dark green leaves. Sometimes scented, single to double flowers are usually in clusters of 3–25, rarely solitary, and are borne continuously in summer-autumn on shoots from second-year wood and on new wood. Are excellent for borders and as hedges.
Ground-cover – trailing and spreading roses, mostly with prickly stems, producing often glossy leaves. They bear clusters of numerous, sometimes scented, single to fully double flowers; some flower in summer only, on short shoots from second-year wood; others are remontant, and also flower on new wood. Many bear flowers all along the stems. Are ideal for beds, banks and containers, and for trailing over walls.
Hybrid Tea (or **Large-flowered bush**) – remontant, free-branching shrubs of upright or bushy habit, with usually thorny stems and glossy or matt, mid- to dark green leaves. Large, often scented, usually double flowers are borne singly or in 3s in flushes in summer-autumn on shoots from second-year wood and on new wood. Use in formal borders, as hedges and for cut flowers.
Miniature – remontant shrubs with very compact, rarely spreading, sparsely thorny, short growth. Sprays of 3–11 tiny, rarely scented, single to fully double flowers are borne in flushes in summer-autumn on very short shoots from second-year wood and on new wood. Have tiny leaves. Are suitable for edging paths and driveways, and for rock gardens, raised beds and container growing.
Patio (or **Dwarf cluster-flowered bush**) – remontant shrubs with compact growth, sometimes prickly stems, and usually glossy leaves. They bear clusters of 3–11 usually unscented, single to double flowers in flushes in summer-autumn, on shoots from second-year wood and on new wood. Are ideal for beds, borders and as hedges and for growing in containers.
Polyantha – compact, remontant shrubs with sparsely thorny stems and glossy leaves. Sprays of many small, rarely scented, single to double flowers are borne in summer-autumn. on shoots from second-year wood and on new wood. Are suitable for beds and borders, as hedges and for containers.
Rambler – a diverse group of vigorous roses with long, arching, thorny stems and dense, usually glossy foliage. They have clusters of 3–21 sometimes scented, single to fully double flowers, mainly in summer, on short shoots from second-year wood and on new wood. Train over walls, fences, pergolas and into trees.
Rugosa – Hardy shrubs with tough, wrinkled, usually bright green leaves and prickly stems. Most bear scented, single or semi-double flowers, in clusters of 3–11, in summer-autumn, on short shoots from second-year wood. They are often followed by tomato-like, usually red hips. Use as hedges, for beds and borders and as specimen plants.
Shrub – Roses in this diverse group are usually larger than bush roses (a general term used to describe Floribundas, Hybrid Teas, Miniatures, Patio roses and occasionally Ground-cover roses). They often have thorny stems and bear usually scented, semi-double to double flowers in few- to many-flowered clusters, sometimes singly, in summer-autumn. Some bloom in summer only from second-year wood; most are remontant and also flower on new wood. Use as hedges, in beds and borders and as specimen plants.

***R.* 'Aimée Vibert'**, syn. *R.* 'Bouquet de la Mariée'. Noisette rose with long, smooth stems. H 5m (15ft), S 3m (10ft). Bears clusters of lightly scented, cupped, fully double, blush-pink to white flowers, 8cm (3in) across, in summer-autumn. Leaves are glossy, dark green. May be grown as a shrub.
♀ ***R.* 'Alba Semiplena'**, syn. *R.* × *alba* 'Semiplena'. Vigorous, bushy Alba rose. H 2m (6ft), S 1.5m (5ft). Bears sweetly scented, flat, semi-double, white flowers, 8cm (3in) across, in mid-summer. Has greyish-green leaves. Is suitable for a hedge.
♀ ***R.* 'Albéric Barbier'** illus. p.192.
♀ ***R.* 'Albertine'** illus. p.193.
***R.* ALEC'S RED ('Cored')** illus. p.188.
♀ ***R.* ALEXANDER ('Harlex')**, syn. *R.* 'Alexandra', illus. p.188.
***R.* 'Alfred de Dalmas'** of gardens. See *R.* 'Mousseline'.
♀ ***R.* 'Alister Stella Gray'**, syn. *R.* 'Golden Rambler'. Noisette rose with long, vigorous, upright stems. H 5m (15ft), S 3m (10ft). Bears clusters of musk-scented, quartered, fully double, yolk-yellow flowers, 6cm (2½in) across, in summer-autumn. Has glossy, mid-green leaves.
♀ ***R.* 'Aloha'** illus. p.194.

***R.* 'Alpine Sunset'** illus. p.186.

🏆 ***R.* AMBER QUEEN ('Harroony')** illus. p.189.

***R.* 'American Pillar'.** Vigorous Rambler of lax growth. H to 5m (15ft), S 4m (12ft). Large clusters of cupped, single, carmine-red flowers, with white eyes, are borne freely in mid-summer. Leathery foliage is glossy, mid-green.

***R.* 'Amruda'.** See *R.* RED ACE.

***R.* 'Andeli'.** See *R.* DOUBLE DELIGHT.

***R.* ANGELA RIPPON ('Ocaru')** illus. p.191.

***R.* 'Angelita'.** See *R.* 'Snowball'.

🏆 ***R.* ANISLEY DICKSON ('Dickimono')**, syn. *R.* 'Dicky', illus. p.187.

🏆 ***R.* ANNA FORD ('Harpiccolo')** illus. p.187.

***R.* 'ANNE HARKNESS' ('Harkaramel')** illus. p.190.

***R.* 'Apothecary's Rose'.** See *R. gallica* var. *officinalis*.

🏆 ***R.* 'Arthur Bell'.** Upright Floribunda rose. H 1m (3ft), S 60cm (2ft). Clusters of fragrant, cupped, double, yellow flowers, 8cm (3in) across, are borne in summer-autumn. Foliage is bright green.

***R.* 'Assemblage des Beautés'**, syn. *R.* 'Rouge Eblouissante'. Upright, dense Gallica rose. H 1.2m (4ft), S 1m (3ft). In summer bears faintly scented, rounded, fully double, green-eyed, cerise to crimson-purple flowers, 8cm (3in) across. Has rich green leaves.

***R.* 'Ausmary'.** See *R.* MARY ROSE.

***R.* 'Ausmas'.** See *R.* GRAHAM THOMAS.

***R.* 'Austance'.** See *R.* CONSTANCE SPRY.

***R.* 'Baby Carnival'.** See *R.* BABY MASQUERADE.

***R.* BABY MASQUERADE ('Tanba')**, syn. 'Baby Carnival', illus. p.191.

R. banksiae, syn. *R.b.* var. *normalis* (Banksian rose). Climbing Species rose. H and S 10m (30ft). Frost hardy. Dense clusters of fragrant, flat, single, white flowers, 2.5cm (1in) across, are borne on slender, thornless, light green stems in late spring. Leaves are small and pale green. Is uncommon in cultivation. 🏆 **'Lutea'** (syn. *R.b.* var. *lutea*) illus. p.195.

***R.* 'Beauty of Glazenwood'.** See *R.* × *odorata* 'Pseudindica'.

***R.* 'Belle Courtisanne'.** See *R.* 'Königin von Dänemark'.

🏆 ***R.* 'Belle de Crécy'** illus. p.184.

***R.* 'Belle de Londres'.** See *R.* 'Compassion'.

***R.* 'Bizarre Triomphant'.** See *R.* 'Charles de Mills'.

***R.* 'Blanche Moreau'.** Moss rose of rather lax growth. H 1.5m (5ft), S 1.2m (4ft). Fragrant, cupped, fully double, white flowers, 10cm (4in) across, with brownish 'mossing', appear in summer. Has dull green leaves.

🏆 ***R.* 'Blessings'** illus. p.186.

***R.* BLUE MOON ('Tannacht')**, syn. *R.* 'Mainzer Fastnacht', *R.* 'Sissi'. Hybrid Tea rose of open habit. H 1m (3ft), S 60cm (2ft). Sweetly scented, pointed, fully double, lilac flowers, 10cm (4in) across, are borne in summer-autumn. Leaves are large and dark green.

***R.* BLUE PETER ('Ruiblun')**, syn. *R.* 'Bluenette'. Miniature rose of neat habit. H 35cm (14in), S 30cm (12in). Slightly scented, cupped, double, purple flowers, 5cm (2in) across, are produced in summer-autumn. Leaves are small and plentiful.

***R.* 'Blue Rambler'.** See *R.* 'Veilchenblau'.

***R.* 'Bluenette'.** See *R.* BLUE PETER.

***R.* 'Blush Noisette'.** See *R.* 'Noisette Carnée'.

***R.* 'Blush Rambler'.** Vigorous Rambler. H 3m (10ft), S 4m (12ft). Clusters of delicately fragrant, cupped, semi-double, light pink flowers, 4cm (1½in) across, are borne in summer. Has an abundance of glossy leaves. Is a particularly good scrambler for an arch, pergola or tree.

🏆 ***R.* 'Bobbie James'.** Rampant Rambler. H to 10m (30ft), S 6m (20ft). Large clusters of cupped, semi-double, scented, creamy-white flowers, 5cm (2in) across, are produced in summer. Glossy leaves are reddish-green when young, mid-green when mature.

🏆 ***R.* BONICA ('Meidomonac')**, syn. *R.* 'Bonica '82', illus. p.182.

***R.* 'Boule de Neige'** illus. p.180.

***R.* 'Bouquet de la Mariée'.** See *R.* 'Aimée Vibert'.

***R.* 'Brass Ring'.** See *R.* PEEK-A-BOO.

***R.* BREATH OF LIFE ('Harquanne')** illus. p.193.

***R.* BRIGHT SMILE ('Dicdance')** illus. p.189.

🏆 ***R.* 'Buff Beauty'.** Rounded Hybrid Musk rose. H and S 1.2m (4ft). Slightly fragrant, cupped, fully double, apricot-buff flowers, 9cm (3½in) across, are borne freely in summer, sparsely in autumn. Has plentiful, glossy, dark green leaves.

R. californica. Shrubby Species rose. H 2.2m (7ft), S 2m (6ft). Fragrant, flat, single, lilac-pink flowers, 4cm (1½in) across, are borne freely in mid-summer, sparsely in autumn. Has small dull green leaves. **'Plena'** see. *R. nutkana* 'Plena'.

***R.* 'Canary Bird'.** See *R. xanthina* 'Canary Bird'.

***R.* 'Candide'.** See *R.* GOLDSTAR.

🏆 ***R.* 'Capitaine John Ingram'.** Vigorous, bushy Moss rose. H and S 1.2m (4ft). In summer bears fragrant, cupped, fully double, rich maroon-crimson flowers, 8cm (3in) across; petals are paler on reverses. Foliage is dark green.

🏆 ***R.* 'Cardinal de Richelieu'** illus. p.184.

***R.* CARDINAL HUME ('Harregale')** illus. p.184.

***R.* CASINO ('Macca')**, syn. *R.* 'Gerbe d'Or', illus. p.195.

🏆 ***R.* 'Cécile Brünner'**, syn. *R.* 'Mignon'. Upright, spindly China rose with fairly smooth stems. H 75cm (30in), S 60cm (24in). Produces slightly scented, urn-shaped, fully double, light pink flowers, 4cm (1½in) across, in summer-autumn. Small, dark green leaves are sparse.

🏆 ***R.* 'Céleste'**, syn. *R.* 'Celestial', illus. p.181.

***R.* 'Celestial'.** See *R.* 'Céleste'.

🏆 ***R.* × *centifolia* 'Cristata'**, syn. *R.* 'Chapeau de Napoléon', *R.* 'Cristata' (Crested moss). Bushy, lanky Centifolia rose. H 1.5m (5ft), S 1.2m (4ft). In summer, very fragrant, cupped, fully double, pink flowers, 9cm (3½in) across and with tufted sepals, are borne on nodding stems amid dull green foliage. May be grown on a support. **'Muscosa'** (Common moss, Old pink moss) is a vigorous, lax Moss rose. H 1.5m (5ft), S 1.2m (4ft). Bears fragrant, rounded to cupped, fully double, mossed, pink flowers, 8cm (3in) across, in summer. Leaves are matt, dull green. Is best with support.

🏆 ***R.* 'Cerise Bouquet'.** Very vigorous Shrub rose of arching habit. H and S to 3.5m (11ft). Produces a spectacular display of flat, semi-double, cherry-red flowers, 6cm (2½in) across, in summer. Leaves are small and greyish-green.

🏆 ***R.* CHAMPAGNE COCKTAIL ('Horflash')** illus. p.188.

***R.* 'Chapeau de Napoléon'.** See *R.* × *centifolia* 'Cristata'.

***R.* 'Chaplin's Pink Companion'** illus. p.193.

🏆 ***R.* 'Charles de Mills'**, syn. *R.* 'Bizarre Triomphant'. Upright, arching Gallica rose with fairly smooth stems. H 1.2m (4ft), S 1m (3ft). Very fragrant, quartered-rosette, fully double, crimson-purple flowers, 10cm (4in) across, appear in summer. Leaves are plentiful and mid-green. May be grown on a support.

***R.* 'Chewarvel'.** See *R.* LAURA FORD.

R. chinensis* var. *minima. See *R.* 'Rouletii'. **'Mutabilis'** see *R.* × *odorata* 'Mutabilis'.

***R.* CITY GIRL ('Harzorba')** illus. p.194.

***R.* CITY OF LONDON ('Harukfore').** Rounded Floribunda rose. H 1m (3ft), S 75cm (2½ft). In summer-autumn, bears dainty sprays of sweet-smelling, urn-shaped, double, blush-pink flowers, 8cm (3in) across, amid bright green foliage.

***R.* CLARISSA ('Harprocrustes').** Upright Floribunda rose. H 75cm (30in), S 45cm (18in). Dense sprays of slightly scented, urn-shaped, fully double, apricot flowers, 5cm (2in) across, appear in summer-autumn. Has many small, glossy leaves. Makes a good, narrow hedge.

🏆 ***R.* 'Climbing Lady Hillingdon'.** Stiff climbing Tea rose. H 4m (12ft), S 2m (6ft). Has dark green leaves on reddish-green stems. Bears spice-scented, pointed, double, apricot-yellow flowers, 10cm (4in) across, in summer-autumn. Is best in a sheltered site.

🏆 ***R.* 'Climbing Mrs Sam McGredy'.** Vigorous, stiff, branching Climber. H and S 3m (10ft). Leaves are glossy, rich reddish-green. Bears faintly fragrant, large, urn-shaped, fully double, coppery salmon-pink flowers, 11cm (4½in) across, in summer and again, sparsely, in autumn.

***R.* 'Cocabest'.** See *R.* WEE JOCK.

***R.* 'Cocdestin'.** See *R.* REMEMBER ME.

***R.* COLIBRE '79 ('Meidanover')** illus. p.192.

***R.* 'Commandant Beaurepaire'**, syn. *R.* 'Panachée d' Angers'. Vigorous, spreading Bourbon rose. H and S 1.2m (4ft). Fragrant, cupped, double flowers, 10cm (4in) across, are borne in summer-autumn. They are blush-pink, splashed with mauve, purple, crimson and scarlet. Light green leaflets have wavy margins.

🏆 ***R.* 'Compassion'**, syn. *R.* 'Belle de Londres', illus. p.194.

🏆 ***R.* 'Complicata'** illus. p.182.

***R.* 'Comte de Chambord'** of gardens. See *R.* 'Madame Knorr'.

***R.* CONGRATULATIONS ('Korlift')**, syn. *R.* 'Sylvia'. Upright, vigorous Hybrid Tea rose. H 1.2m (4ft), S 1m (3ft). Produces neat, urn-shaped, fully double, deep rose-pink flowers, 11cm (4½in) across, on long stems in summer-autumn. Leaves are large and dark green. Makes a tall hedge.

***R.* 'Conrad Ferdinand Meyer'** illus. p.181.

🏆 ***R.* CONSTANCE SPRY ('Austance')** illus. p.182.

***R.* 'Cored'.** See *R.* ALEC'S RED.

***R.* 'Cristata'.** See *R.* × *centifolia* 'Cristata'.

***R.* 'Cuisse de Nymphe'.** See *R.* 'Great Maiden's Blush'.

***R.* 'Danse du Feu'**, syn. *R.* 'Spectacular', illus. p.194.

***R.* DARLING FLAME ('Meilucca').** Well-branched Miniature rose. H 40cm (16in), S 30cm (12in). Leaves are glossy and dark green. Urn-shaped, double, orange-red flowers, 4cm (1½in) across, are borne freely from summer to autumn.

***R.* 'Dicdance'.** See *R.* BRIGHT SMILE.

***R.* 'Dicdivine'.** See *R.* POT O' GOLD.

***R.* 'Dicgrow'.** See *R.* PEEK-A-BOO.

***R.* 'Dicjana'.** See *R.* ELINA.

***R.* 'Dicjem'.** See *R.* FREEDOM.

***R.* 'Dicjubell'.** See *R.* LOVELY LADY.

***R.* 'Dickimono'.** See *R.* ANISLEY DICKSON.

***R.* 'Dicky'.** See *R.* ANISLEY DICKSON.

***R.* 'Diclittle'.** See *R.* LITTLE WOMAN.

***R.* 'Diclulu'.** See *R.* GENTLE TOUCH.

***R.* 'Dicmagic'.** See *R.* SWEET MAGIC.

***R.* 'Dicwitness'.** See *R.* IRISH EYES.

***R.* 'Doris Tysterman'** illus. p.190.

🏆 ***R.* 'Dortmund'** illus. p.194.

***R.* DOUBLE DELIGHT ('Andeli')** illus. p.187.

***R.* 'Double Velvet'.** See *R.* 'Tuscany Superb'.

***R.* 'Doux Parfum'.** See *R.* L'AIMANT.

***R.* DRUMMER BOY ('Harvacity').** Dwarf Floribunda rose of bushy, spreading habit. H and S 50cm (20in). Faintly scented, cupped, double, bright crimson flowers, 5cm (2in) across, appear in dense sprays amid a mass of small, dark green leaves in summer-autumn. Makes a good, low hedge.

🏆 ***R.* DUBLIN BAY ('Macdub')** illus. p.194.

***R.* 'Duchesse d'Istrie'.** See *R.* 'William Lobb'.

***R.* 'Duftzauber '84'.** See *R.* ROYAL WILLIAM.

***R.* 'Du Maître d'Ecole'.** Bushy, spreading Gallica rose. H 1.2m (4ft), S 1m (3ft). Bears fragrant, quartered-rosette, fully double, carmine to light pink flowers, 10cm (4in) across, in summer. Foliage is dull green.

***R.* 'Dupontii'**, syn. *R. moschata* var. *nivea*, illus. p.181.

🏆 ***R.* 'Easlea's Golden Rambler'.** Vigorous, arching Rambler. H 5m (15ft), S 3m (10ft). Pleasantly scented, cupped, fully double, yellow flowers, 10cm (4in) across and flecked with red, appear, usually in clusters, during summer. Has plentiful, leathery foliage.

***R.* 'Easter Morning'**, syn. *R.* 'Easter Morn'. Upright Miniature rose. H 40cm (16in), S 25cm (10in). In summer-autumn, faintly fragrant, urn-shaped, fully double, ivory-white flowers, 3cm (1¼in) across, are borne freely amid glossy, dark green leaves.

R. ecae illus. p.184.

R. eglanteria. See *R. rubiginosa*.

♡ ***R.*** **Elina ('Dicjana')**, syn. *R.* 'Peaudouce'. Vigorous, shrubby Hybrid Tea rose. H 1.1m (3½ft), S 75cm (2½ft). Lightly scented, rounded, fully double, ivory-white flowers, 15cm (6in) across, with lemon-yellow centres, are borne freely in summer-autumn. Has abundant, reddish foliage.
R. **'Elizabeth Harkness'** illus. p.185.
R. **'Emily Gray'** illus. p.195.
R. **'Empereur du Maroc'** illus. p.184.
♡ ***R.*** **Escapade ('Harpade')** illus. p.187.
♡ ***R.*** **'Fantin-Latour'** illus. p.181.
♡ ***R.*** **Fascination ('Poulmax')**, syn. *R.* 'Fredensborg'. Vigorous Floribunda rose. H 1m (3ft), S 60cm (2ft). In summer-autumn bears clusters of fragrant, rounded, double, shrimp-pink blooms amid dark green, glossy foliage. Is good for beds and hedges.
♡ ***R.*** **'Felicia'** illus. p.181.
♡ ***R.*** **'Félicité Parmentier'**. Vigorous, compact, upright Alba rose. H 1.2m (4ft), S 1m (3ft). Fragrant, cupped to flat, fully double, pale flesh-pink flowers, 6cm (2½in) across, are borne in mid-summer. Has abundant, greyish-green leaves. Makes a good hedge.
♡ ***R.*** **'Félicité Perpétue'** illus. p.192.
R. **Felicity Kendal ('Lanken')**. Sturdy, well-branched Hybrid Tea rose. H 1.1m (3½ft), S 75cm (2½ft). Lightly fragrant, rounded, fully double, bright red flowers, 11cm (4½in) across, appear among a mass of dark green foliage in summer-autumn.
R. **'Fellemberg'**, syn. *R.* 'Fellenberg'. Vigorous, shrubby Noisette rose. H 2.5m (8ft), S 1.2m (4ft). Leaves are purplish-green. Clusters of faintly scented, rounded to cupped, fully double flowers, 5cm (2in) across, in shades of light crimson, appear in summer-autumn. Prune to grow as a bedding rose or support as a climber.
♡ ***R. filipes*** **'Kiftsgate'** illus. p.192.
R. **'Fire Princess'** illus. p.191.
R. foetida **'Persiana'**, syn. *R.* 'Persian Yellow', illus. p.184.
R. **'Fortune's Double Yellow'**. See *R.* × *odorata* 'Pseudindica'.
R. **Fragrant Cloud ('Tanellis')**. Bushy, dense Hybrid Tea rose. H 75cm (30in), S 60cm (24in). Very fragrant, rounded, double, dusky-scarlet flowers, 12cm (5in) across, are borne freely in summer-autumn. Has plentiful, dark green foliage.
♡ ***R.*** **'Fragrant Delight'**. Bushy Floribunda rose of uneven habit. H 1m (3ft), S 75cm (2½ft). Produces an abundance of reddish-green foliage, amid which clusters of fragrant, urn-shaped, double, salmon-pink flowers, 8cm (3in) across, are borne freely in summer-autumn.
♡ ***R.*** **'François Juranville'**. Vigorous, arching Rambler. H 6m (20ft), S 5m (15ft). Bears clusters of apple-scented, rosette, fully double, rosy-salmon-pink flowers, 8cm (3in) across, in summer. Produces a mass of glossy leaves. Is prone to mildew in a dry site.
R. **'Fredensborg'**. See *R.* Fascination.
♡ ***R.*** **Freedom ('Dicjem')** illus. p.189.
R. **'Friesia'**. See *R.* 'Korresia'.
R. **'Frühlingsmorgen'**, syn. *R.* 'Spring Morning'. Open, free-branching Shrub rose. H 2m (6ft), S 1.5m (5ft). Foliage is greyish-green. In late spring produces hay-scented, cupped, single, pink flowers, 12cm (5in) across, with a primrose centre and reddish stamens.
R. **'Fryminicot'**. See *R.* Sweet Dream.
♡ ***R. gallica*** var. ***officinalis***, syn. *R.* 'Apothecary's Rose', *R. officinalis* (Red rose of Lancaster). Bushy Species rose of neat habit. H to 80cm (32in), S 1m (36in). In summer bears flat, semi-double, pinkish-red flowers, 8cm (3in) across, with a moderate scent.
♡ **'Versicolor'** illus. p.183.
R. **'Gaumo'**. See *R.* Rose Gaujard.
♡ ***R.*** **Gentle Touch ('Diclulu')**. Upright, dwarf Floribunda rose. H 50cm (20in), S 30cm (12in). Bears sprays of faintly scented, urn-shaped, semi-double, pale salmon-pink flowers, 5cm (2in) across, in summer-autumn. Leaves are small and dark green. Is good as a low hedge.
R. **'Geranium'**. See *R. moyesii* 'Geranium'.
R. **'Gerbe d'Or'**. See *R.* 'Casino'.
R. **'Gioia'**. See *R.* 'Peace'.
R. **'Gipsy Boy'**. See *R.* 'Zigeunerknabe'.
♡ ***R. glauca***, syn. *R. rubrifolia*, illus. p.182.
R. **'Glenfiddich'** illus. p.189.
R. **'Gloire de Dijon'** illus. p.192.
R. **'Gloire des Mousseux'**. Vigorous, bushy Moss rose. H 1.2m (4ft), S 1m (3ft). Has plentiful, light green foliage. In summer bears fragrant, cupped, fully double flowers, 15cm (6in) across. These are bright pink, paling to blush-pink, with light green 'mossing'.
R. **'Gloria Dei'**. See *R.* 'Peace'.
R. **'Gold of Ophir'**. See *R.* × *odorata* 'Pseudindica'.
R. **Golden Penny ('Rugul')**, syn. *R.* 'Guletta', *R.* 'Tapis Jaune', illus. p.188.
R. **'Golden Rambler'**. See *R.* 'Alister Stella Gray'.
♡ ***R.*** **'Golden Showers'** illus. p.195.
R. **'Golden Sunblaze'**. See *R.* 'Rise 'n' Shine'.
♡ ***R.*** **'Golden Wings'**. Bushy, spreading Shrub rose. H 1.1m (3½ft), S 1.35m (4½ft). Bears fragrant, cupped, single, pale yellow flowers, 12cm (5in) across, amid light green foliage, in summer-autumn. Is good for a hedge.
R. **'Goldfinch'**. Vigorous, arching Rambler. H 2.7m (9ft), S 2m (6ft). In summer produces lightly scented, rosette, double, yolk-yellow flowers, 4cm (1½in) across, that fade to white. Has plentiful, bright light green leaves.
R. **'Goldsmith'**. See *R.* Simba.
R. **Goldstar ('Candide')**. Neat, upright Hybrid Tea rose. H 1m (3ft), S 60cm (2ft). Amid glossy, dark green leaves, lightly scented, urn-shaped, fully double, yellow flowers, 8cm (3in) across, are borne in summer-autumn.
♡ ***R.*** **Graham Thomas ('Ausmas')** illus. p.185.
R. **'Grandpa Dickson'**, syn. *R.* 'Irish Gold', illus. p.189.
R. **'Great Maiden's Blush'**, syn. *R.* 'Cuisse de Nymphe', *R.* 'La Séduisante', illus. p.181.
♡ ***R.*** **Grouse ('Korimro')** illus. p.185.

R. **'Guinée'** illus. p.195.
R. **'Guletta'**. See *R.* Golden Penny.
♡ ***R.*** **Handel ('Macha')** illus. p.193.
R. **Hannah Gordon ('Korweiso')**. Bushy, open Floribunda rose. H 75cm (30in), S 60cm (2ft). Sprays of slightly fragrant, cupped, double, blush-pink flowers, 8cm (3in) across, margined with reddish-pink, appear in summer-autumn. Leaves are dark green.
R. **'Harbabble'**. See *R.* Sunset Boulevard.
R. **'Hardinkum'**. See *R.* Princess of Wales.
R. **'Hardwell'**. See *R.* Penny Lane.
R. **'Harkaramel'**. See *R.* Anne Harkness.
R. **'Harkuly'**. See *R.* Margaret Merril.
R. **'Harlex'**. See *R.* Alexander.
R. **'Harlightly'**. See *R.* Princess Michael of Kent.
R. **'Harmantelle'**. See *R.* Mountbatten.
R. **'Harpade'**. See *R.* Escapade.
R. **'Harpiccolo'**. See *R.* Anna Ford.
R. **'Harprocrustes'**. See *R.* Clarissa.
R. **'Harquanne'**. See *R.* Breath of Life.
R. **'Harqueterwife'**. See *R.* Paul Shirville.
R. **'Harregale'**. See *R.* Cardinal Hume.
R. **'Harroony'**. See *R.* Amber Queen.
R. **'Harrowbond'**. See *R.* Rosemary Harkness.
R. **'Harsherry'**. See *R.* Sheila's Perfume.
R. **'Harukfore'**. See *R.* City of London.
R. **'Harvacity'**. See *R.* Drummer Boy.
R. **'Harwanna'**. See *R.* Jacqueline du Pré.
R. **'Harwanted'**. See *R.* Many Happy Returns.
R. **'Haryup'**. See *R.* High Hopes.
R. **'Harzola'**. See *R.* L'Aimant.
R. **'Harzorba'**. See *R.* City Girl.
R. **'Heartthrob'**. See *R.* 'Paul Shirville'.
R. **'Heideröslein'**. See *R.* 'Nozomi'.
R. **'Henri Martin'**, syn. *R.* 'Red Moss', illus. p.183.
♡ ***R.*** **Hertfordshire ('Kortenay')**. Free-flowering Ground-cover rose of compact, uneven, spiky habit. H 45cm (18in), S 1m (3ft). Has dense, bright green leaves and flat, single, carmine-pink flowers, 4.5cm (1¾in) across, with paler pink centres, in large clusters on short stems, from summer to autumn.
♡ ***R.*** **High Hopes ('Haryup')** illus. p.194.
R. **'Honorine de Brabant'**. Vigorous, bushy, sprawling Bourbon rose. H and S 2m (6ft). Fragrant, quartered, double flowers, 10cm (4in) across, lilac-pink, marked with light purple and crimson, are produced in summer-autumn. Has plentiful, light green foliage.
R. **'Horflash'**. See *R.* Champagne Cocktail.
R. **'Hula Girl'** illus. p.191.
♡ ***R.*** **Iceberg ('Korbin')**, syn. *R.* 'Schneewittchen', illus. p.185.
R. **'Iced Ginger'** illus. p.186.
♡ ***R.*** **Ingrid Bergman ('Poulman')**. Upright, branching Hybrid Tea rose. H 75cm (30in), S 60cm (24in). Bears slightly scented, urn-shaped, double, dark red flowers, 11cm (4½in) across, in summer-autumn. Has leathery, semi-glossy, dark green foliage.
R. **'Interall'**. See *R.* Rosy Cushion.
R. **Invincible ('Runatru')**. Upright Floribunda rose. H 1m (3ft), S 60cm (2ft). Faintly scented, cupped, fully double, bright crimson flowers, 9cm (3½in) across, appear in open clusters in summer-autumn. Leaves are semi-glossy.
R. **Irish Eyes ('Dicwitness')**. Vigorous Floribunda rose. H 75cm (2½ft), S 1m (3ft). Well-filled sprays of scented, rounded, double, scarlet-flushed, yellow flowers, 7cm (3in) across, appear in summer-autumn. Makes a good low hedge.
R. **'Irish Gold'**. See *R.* 'Grandpa Dickson'.
♡ ***R.*** **'Ispahan'**, syn. *R.* 'Pompon des Princes', *R.* 'Rose d'Isfahan'. Vigorous, bushy, dense Damask rose. H 1.5m (5ft), S 1.2m (4ft). Produces fragrant, cupped, double, clear pink flowers, 8cm (3in) across, amid greyish-green foliage in summer-autumn.
♡ ***R.*** **Jacqueline du Pré ('Harwanna')**. Vigorous, arching Shrub rose. H 2m (6ft), S 1.5m (5ft). In summer-autumn bears musk-scented, cupped, double, ivory-white flowers, 10cm (4in) across, with scalloped petals and red stamens. Has abundant glossy leaves. Makes a large hedge.
R. **'John Cabot'**. Vigorous Shrub rose. H 1.5m (5ft), S 1.2m (4ft). Has yellow-green leaves and, in summer-autumn, clusters of fragrant, cupped, double, magenta flowers, 6cm (2½in) across. May be grown as a climber or hedge.
R. **'Julia's Rose'**. Spindly, branching Hybrid Tea rose. H 75cm (30in), S 45cm (18in). In summer-autumn produces faintly scented, urn-shaped, double, brownish-pink to buff flowers, 10cm (4in) across. Foliage is reddish-green. Is good for flower arrangements.
♡ ***R.*** **'Just Joey'** illus. p.190.
R. **'Kathleen Harrop'**. Arching, lax Bourbon rose. H 2.5m (8ft), S 2m (6ft). Fragrant, double, cupped, pale pink flowers, 8cm (3in) across, are borne in summer-autumn. Plentiful, dark green foliage is susceptible to mildew. May be grown as a climber or hedge.
R. **Keepsake ('Kormalda')** illus. p.187.
♡ ***R.*** **Kent ('Poulcov')**. Compact, spreading Ground-cover rose. H 45cm (18in), S 1m (3ft). Has cupped to flat, semi-double, white flowers, 4.5cm (1¾in) across, on short stems from summer to autumn. Leaves are shiny and dark green.
♡ ***R.*** **'Königin von Dänemark'**, syn. *R.* 'Belle Courtisanne', illus. p.182.
R. **'Königliche Hoheit'**. See *R.* 'Royal Highness'.
R. **'Korbelma'**. See *R.* Simba.
R. **'Korbin'**. See *R.* Iceberg.
R. **'Korblue'**. See *R.* Shocking Blue.
R. **'Korgund'**. See *R.* Loving Memory.
R. **'Korimro'**. See *R.* Grouse.
R. **'Korlift'**. See *R.* Congratulations.
R. **'Kormalda'**. See *R.* Keepsake.
R. **'Korpeahn'**. See *R.* The Times Rose.
R. **'Korresia'**, syn. *R.* 'Friesia', illus. p.189.
R. **'Kortenay'**. See *R.* Hertfordshire.
R. **'Korweiso'**. See *R.* Hannah Gordon.
R. **'Korzaun'**. See *R.* Royal William.
♡ ***R.*** **L'Aimant ('Harzola')**, syn. *R.* 'Doux Parfum'. Vigorous Floribunda rose. H 1m (3ft), S 75cm (2½ft).

Strongly fragrant, cupped, fully double, pink blooms, 9cm (3½in) across, appear in summer-autumn on dark-foliaged plants. Is good for bedding and cutting.

***R.* 'La Séduisante'.** See *R.* 'Great Maiden's Blush'.

***R.* La Sévillana ('Meigekanu').** Dense, bushy Ground-cover rose. H 75cm (2½ft), S 1m (3ft). Clusters of faintly scented, cupped, double, bright red flowers, 8cm (3in) across, are borne freely in summer-autumn. Produces an abundance of dark green leaves. Is suitable for growing as a hedge or ground cover.

***R.* 'Lady Waterlow'.** Stiff Climbing Hybrid Tea rose. H 4m (12ft), S 2m (6ft). Bears pleasantly scented, pointed to cupped, double, light pink shaded, salmon flowers, 12cm (5in) across, mainly in summer, but some may also appear in autumn. Leaves are mid-green.

***R.* 'Lanken'.** See *R.* Felicity Kendal.

♀ ***R.* Laura Ford ('Chewarvel')** illus. p.195.

***R.* 'Leggab'.** See *R.* Pearl Drift.

***R.* 'Legnews'.** See *R.* News.

***R.* 'Lenip'.** See *R.* Pascali.

***R.* Little Woman ('Diclittle').** Upright Patio rose. H 50cm (20in), S 40cm (16in). In summer-autumn bears sprays of faintly fragrant, urn-shaped, double, salmon-pink flowers, 5cm (2in) across. Has small, dark green leaves. Is suitable for a narrow hedge.

***R.* 'Louise Odier'**, syn. *R.* 'Madame de Stella'. Elegant, upright Bourbon rose. H 2m (6ft), S 1.2m (4ft). Has light greyish-green foliage and fragrant, cupped, fully double, warm rose-pink flowers, 12cm (5in) across, borne in summer-autumn.

♀ ***R.* Lovely Lady ('Dicjubell')** illus. p.186.

***R.* Loving Memory ('Korgund').** Upright, robust Hybrid Tea rose. H 1.1m (3½ft), S 75cm (2½ft). Bears slightly fragrant, pointed, fully double, deep red flowers, 12cm (5in) across, on stiff stems in summer-autumn. Foliage is dull green.

***R.* 'Macangeli'.** See *R.* Snowball.

***R.* 'Macar'.** See *R.* Piccadilly.

***R.* 'Macca'.** See *R.* Casino.

***R.* 'Maccarpe'.** See *R.* Snow Carpet.

***R.* 'Macdub'.** See *R.* Dublin Bay.

***R.* 'Macha'.** See *R.* Handel.

***R.* 'Macmi'.** See *R.* Mischief.

***R.* 'Macrexy'.** See *R.* Sexy Rexy.

R. macrophylla. Vigorous Species rose. H 4m (12ft), S 3m (10ft). Bears moderately fragrant, flat, single, red flowers, 5cm (2in) across, in summer, followed by flask-shaped, red hips. Has red stems and large, mid-green leaves.

***R.* 'Macspash'.** See *R.* Sue Lawley.

***R.* 'Mactru'.** See *R.* Trumpeter.

♀ ***R.* 'Madame Alfred Carrière'** illus. p.192.

***R.* 'Madame A. Meilland'.** See *R.* Peace.

***R.* 'Madame de Stella'.** See *R.* 'Louise Odier'.

***R.* 'Madame Ernest Calvat'.** Vigorous, arching Bourbon rose. H 2–3m (6–10ft), S 2m (6ft). Fragrant, cupped to quartered-rosette, fully double, rose-pink flowers, 15cm (6in) across, are borne freely in summer-autumn. Has plentiful, large leaves.

♀ ***R.* 'Madame Grégoire Staechelin'**, syn. *R.* 'Spanish Beauty', illus. p.193.

♀ ***R.* 'Madame Hardy'** illus. p.180.

***R.* 'Madame Hébert'.** See *R.* 'Président de Sèze'.

♀ ***R.* 'Madame Isaac Pereire'** illus. p.183.

♀ ***R.* 'Madame Knorr'**, syn. *R.* 'Comte de Chambord' of gardens. Vigorous, erect Portland rose. H 1.2m (4ft), S 1m (3ft). In summer-autumn, fragrant, quartered-rosette, fully double, lilac-tinted, pink flowers, 10cm (4in) across, appear amid plentiful, light green foliage. Is suitable for a hedge.

***R.* 'Madame Pierre Oger'.** Lax Bourbon rose. H 2m (6ft), S 1.2m (4ft). In summer-autumn, slender stems carry sweetly scented, cupped or bowl-shaped, double, pink flowers, 8cm (3in) across, with rose-lilac tints. Has light green leaves. Grows well on a pillar.

***R.* Magic Carousel ('Moorcar').** Bushy, Miniature rose. H 40cm (16in), S 30cm (12in). Slightly scented, rosette, fully double, yellow-and-red flowers, 4cm (1½in) across, with petals arranged in diminishing circles, appear in summer-autumn. Has small, glossy leaves.

♀ ***R.* 'Maigold'** illus. p.195.

***R.* 'Mainzer Fastnacht'.** See *R.* Blue Moon.

♀ ***R.* Many Happy Returns ('Harwanted')**, syn. *R.* 'Prima'. Bushy, spreading Floribunda rose. H 1m (3ft), S 1.2m (4ft). In summer-autumn bears lightly fragrant, cupped, double, blush-pink flowers, 10cm (4in) across, freely amid glossy, dark green leaves.

***R.* 'Maréchal Davoust'.** Vigorous, bushy Moss rose. H 1.5m (5ft), S 1.2m (4ft). In summer bears moderately fragrant, cupped, fully double, deep reddish-pink to purple flowers, 10cm (4in) across, with a green eye and brownish 'mossing'. Leaves are dull green and lance-shaped.

***R.* 'Maréchal Niel'.** Vigorous, spreading Noisette or Climbing Tea rose. H 3m (10ft), S 2m (6ft). Drooping stems carry rich green foliage and moderately scented, pointed, fully double, clear yellow flowers, 10cm (4in) across, in summer-autumn.

♀ ***R.* Margaret Merril ('Harkuly')** illus. p.185.

♀ ***R.* 'Marguerite Hilling'**, syn. *R.* 'Pink Nevada', illus. p.182.

♀ ***R.* Mary Rose ('Ausmary').** Bushy, spreading Shrub rose. H and S 1.2m (4ft). Produces moderately fragrant, cupped, fully double, rose-pink flowers, 9cm (3½in) across, in summer-autumn. Has plentiful leaves.

***R.* 'Meidanover'.** See *R.* Colibre '79.

***R.* 'Meidomonac'.** See *R.* Bonica.

***R.* 'Meigekanu'.** See *R.* La Sévillana.

***R.* 'Meijikitar'.** See *R.* Orange Sunblaze.

***R.* 'Meilucca'.** See *R.* Darling Flame.

♀ ***R.* 'Mermaid'** illus. p.195.

***R.* 'Mignon'.** See *R.* 'Cécile Brünner'.

***R.* Mischief ('Macmi').** Upright Hybrid Tea rose. H 1m (3ft), S 60cm (2ft). Moderately fragrant, urn-shaped, double, salmon-pink flowers, 10cm (4in) across, are borne freely in summer-autumn. Leaves are plentiful but prone to rust.

***R.* 'Moorcar'.** See *R.* Magic Carousel.

♀ ***R.* 'Morning Jewel'.** Free-branching Climber. H 2.5m (8ft), S 2.2m (7ft). Has plentiful, glossy foliage and cupped, double, bright pink flowers, 9cm (3½in) across, freely borne, usually in clusters, in summer-autumn. May be pruned to a shrub.

***R.* 'Morsherry.** See *R.* Sheri Anne.

R. moschata* var. *nivea. See *R.* 'Dupontii'.

♀ ***R.* Mountbatten ('Harmantelle')** illus. p.189.

***R.* 'Mousseline'**, syn. *R.* 'Alfred de Dalmas' of gardens. Bushy Moss rose with twiggy growth. H and S 1m (3ft). Mainly in summer bears scented, cupped, fully double, blush-pink flowers, 8cm (3in) across, with little 'mossing'. Has matt green leaves.

R. moyesii. Vigorous, arching Species rose. H 4m (12ft), S 3m (10ft). In summer, faintly scented, flat, single, dusky-scarlet flowers, 5cm (2in) across, with yellow stamens, are borne close to branches. Produces long, red hips in autumn. Sparse, small, dark green leaves are composed of 7–13 leaflets.

♀ **'Geranium'** (syn. *R.* 'Geranium') illus. p.183.

***R.* 'Mrs John Laing'** illus. p.183.

***R.* 'National Trust'.** Compact Hybrid Tea rose. H 75cm (30in), S 60cm (24in). Slightly scented, urn-shaped, fully double, scarlet-crimson flowers, 10cm (4in) across, are borne freely in summer-autumn. Produces plentiful, dark green foliage. Makes a good, low hedge.

♀ ***R.* 'Nevada'** illus. p.181.

♀ ***R.* 'New Dawn'** illus. p.193.

***R.* News ('Legnews').** Upright Floribunda rose. H 60cm (24in), S 50cm (20in). Has dark green leaves and, in summer-autumn, clusters of slightly fragrant, cupped, wide-opening, double, bright reddish-purple flowers, each 8cm (3in) across.

***R.* 'Niphetos'.** Branching, climbing Tea rose. H 3m (10ft), S 2m (6ft). Long, pointed buds on nodding stems open to rounded, double, white flowers, 12cm (5in) across, mainly in summer, a few later. Pale green leaves are pointed.

***R.* 'Noisette Carnée'**, syn. *R.* 'Blush Noisette'. Noisette rose of branching habit and lax growth. H 2–4m (6–12ft), S 2–2.5m (6–8ft). In summer-autumn, smooth stems bear clusters of spice-scented, cupped, double, blush-pink flowers, 4cm (1½in) across. Has matt foliage. May be grown as a shrub.

♀ ***R.* 'Nozomi'**, syn. *R.* 'Heideröslein', illus. p.185.

♀ ***R.* 'Nuits de Young'**, syn. *R.* 'Old Black'. Erect Moss rose with wiry stems. H 1.2m (4ft), S 1m (3ft). In summer has slightly scented, double, flat, dark maroon-purple flowers, 5cm (2in) across, with brownish 'mossing'. Leaves are small and dark green.

♀ ***R. nutkana* 'Plena'**, syn. *R. californica* 'Plena'. Robust Species rose. H to 3m (10ft), S 2m (6ft). Fragrant, cupped, semi-double, pink flowers, 4cm (1½in) across, are borne singly in summer. Has toothed, mid-green leaves.

***R.* 'Ocaru'.** See *R.* Angela Rippon.

♀ ***R.* × *odorata* 'Mutabilis'**, syn. *R. chinensis* 'Mutabilis', illus. p.183. **'Pallida'** illus. p.183. **'Pseudindica'** (syn. *R.* 'Beauty of Glazenwood', *R.* 'Fortune's Double Yellow', *R.* 'Gold of Ophir', *R.* 'San Rafael Rose') is a lax Climber of restrained growth. H 2.5m (8ft), S 1.5m (5ft). Frost hardy. In summer bears small clusters of scented, pointed to cupped, semi-double, copper-suffused, yellow flowers, 5cm (2in) across. Leaves are glossy, light green. Prune very lightly.

R. officinalis. See *R. gallica* var. *officinalis*.

***R.* 'Old Black'.** See *R.* 'Nuits de Young'.

***R.* 'Omar Khayyám'.** Dense, prickly Damask rose. H and S 1m (3ft). Fragrant, quartered-rosette, fully double, light pink flowers, 8cm (3in) across, are borne amid downy, greyish foliage in summer.

R. omeiensis* f. *pteracantha. See *R. sericea* subsp. *omeiensis* f. *pteracantha*.

***R.* 'Opa Potschke'.** See *R.* 'Precious Platinum'.

***R.* 'Ophelia'.** Upright, open Hybrid Tea rose. H 1m (3ft), S 60cm (2ft). In summer-autumn has sweetly fragrant, urn-shaped, double, creamy-blush-pink flowers, 10cm (4in) across, singly or in clusters. Dark green foliage is sparse.

***R.* Orange Sunblaze ('Meijikitar')**, syn. *R.* 'Sunblaze', illus. p.192.

***R.* 'Panachée d'Angers'.** See *R.* 'Commandant Beaurepaire'.

***R.* Pascali ('Lenip').** Upright Hybrid Tea rose. H 1m (3ft), S 60cm (2ft). Bears faintly scented, neat, urn-shaped, fully double, white flowers, 9cm (3½in) across, in summer-autumn. Has deep green leaves.

♀ ***R.* Paul Shirville ('Harqueterwife')**, syn. *R.* 'Heartthrob', illus. p.187.

♀ ***R.* 'Paul Transon'.** Vigorous, rather lax Rambler. H 4m (12ft), S 1.5m (5ft). In summer bears slightly fragrant, flat, double, faintly coppery, salmon-pink flowers, 8cm (3in) across, with pleated petals. Plentiful foliage is glossy, dark green.

♀ ***R.* 'Paul's Himalayan Musk'**, syn. *R.* 'Paul's Himalayan Musk Rambler'. Very vigorous Rambler. H and S 10m (30ft). Large clusters of slightly fragrant, rosette, double, blush-pink flowers, 4cm (1½in) across, are freely borne in late summer. Has thorny, trailing shoots and drooping leaves. Is suitable for growing up a tree or in a wild garden.

***R.* 'Paul's Himalayan Musk Rambler'.** See *R.* 'Paul's Himalayan Musk'.

***R.* 'Paul's Lemon Pillar'** illus. p.192.

♀ ***R.* Peace ('Madame A. Meilland')**, syn. *R.* 'Gioia', *R.* 'Gloria Dei', illus. p.188.

***R.* Pearl Drift ('Leggab')** illus. p.181.

***R.* 'Peaudouce'.** See *R.* Elina.

***R.* Peek-a-boo ('Dicgrow')**, syn. *R.* 'Brass Ring', illus. p.186.

♀ ***R.* 'Penelope'** illus. p.180.

♀ ***R.* Penny Lane ('Hardwell').** Vigorous Climber. H 3m (10ft), S 2.2m (7ft). Bears wide sprays of quartered, scented, fully double flowers of creamy, blush-tinted apricot, 12cm (4½in) across, in summer-autumn. Has dark green foliage on flexible stems. Is useful for pillars, fences and walls.

♀ ***R.* 'Perle d'Or'.** China rose that forms a twiggy, leafy, small shrub.

H 75cm (2½ft), S 60cm (2ft). Small, slightly scented, urn-shaped, fully double, honey-pink flowers, 4cm (1½in) across, are borne in summer-autumn. Leaves have pointed, glossy leaflets.
***R.* 'Persian Yellow'.** See *R. foetida* 'Persiana'.
***R.* Piccadilly ('Macar')** illus. p.190.
***R. pimpinellifolia*.** See *R. spinosissima*.
***R.* Pink Bells ('Poulbells')** illus. p.186.
🏆 ***R.* 'Pink Grootendorst'** illus. p.182.
***R.* 'Pink Nevada'.** See *R.* 'Marguerite Hilling'.
***R.* 'Pink Parfait'.** Bushy Floribunda rose. H 75cm (2½ft), S 60cm (2ft). In summer-autumn, slightly fragrant, urn-shaped, double flowers, 9cm (3½in) across, in shades of light pink, are produced freely. Has plentiful foliage.
***R.* 'Pink Perpétué'** illus. p.193.
***R.* 'Pompon de Paris'.** See *R.* 'Rouletii'.
***R.* 'Pompon des Princes'.** See *R.* 'Ispahan'.
***R.* Pot o' Gold** ('Dicdivine') illus. p.190.
***R.* 'Poulbells'.** See *R.* Pink Bells.
***R.* 'Poulcov'.** See *R.* Kent.
***R.* 'Poulman'.** See *R.* Ingrid Bergman.
***R.* 'Poulmax'.** See *R.* Fascination.
***R.* 'Poumidor'.** See *R.* Troika.
***R.* 'Precious Platinum'**, syn. *R.* 'Opa Potschke', illus. p.188.
🏆 ***R.* 'Président de Sèze'**, syn. *R.* 'Madame Hébert'. Vigorous, rather open Gallica rose. H and S 1.2m (4ft). Bears fragrant, quartered-rosette, fully double, magenta-pink to pale lilac-pink flowers, 10cm (4in) across, in summer.
***R.* 'Prima'.** See *R.* 'Many Happy Returns'.
🏆 ***R. primula*** illus. p.184.
***R.* Princess Michael of Kent ('Harlightly').** Neat, compact Floribunda rose. H 60cm (24in), S 50cm (20in). In summer-autumn has scented, rounded, fully double, yellow flowers, 9cm (3½in) across, singly or in clusters. Leaves are glossy, bright green and very healthy. Makes a good, low hedge.
🏆 ***R.* Princess of Wales ('Hardinkum').** Vigorous, compact Floribunda rose. H 80cm (30in), S 60cm (24in). Tight clusters of scented, rounded, fully double, paper-white blooms, 9cm (3½in) across, nestle among crisp dark leaves in summer-autumn. Is good for beds and hedges.
***R.* 'Queen Elizabeth'**, syn. *R.* 'The Queen Elizabeth', illus. p.186.
***R.* 'Queen of the Violets'.** See *R.* 'Reine des Violettes'.
🏆 ***R.* 'Rambling Rector'** illus. p.194.
***R.* 'Ramona'**, syn. *R.* 'Red Cherokee'. Rather stiff, open Climber. H 2.7m (9ft), S 3m (10ft). Fragrant, flat, single, carmine-red flowers, 10cm (4in) across, with a greyish-red reverse and gold stamens, appear mainly in summer, a few later. Has sparse foliage. Does best against a warm wall.
***R.* Red Ace ('Amruda')** illus. p.191.
***R.* 'Red Cherokee'.** See *R.* 'Ramona'.
***R.* 'Red Moss'.** See *R.* 'Henri Martin'.
***R.* 'Reine des Violettes'**, syn. *R.* 'Queen of the Violets'. Spreading, vigorous Hybrid Perpetual rose. H and S 2m (6ft). Has greyish-toned leaves and fragrant, quartered-rosette, fully double, violet to purple flowers, 8cm (3in) across, in summer-autumn. May be grown on a support.
***R.* 'Reine Victoria'** illus. p.182.
🏆 ***R.* Remember Me ('Cocdestin')** illus. p.190.
***R.* 'Rise 'n' Shine'**, syn. *R.* 'Golden Sunblaze', illus. p.192.
***R.* 'Robert le Diable'.** Lax, bushy Centifolia rose. H and S 1m (3ft). In summer bears slightly scented, pompon, double flowers, 8cm (3in) across, in mixed bright and dull purple. Has narrowly oval, dark green leaves. Is best trailing over a low support.
***R.* 'Rose d'Isfahan'.** See *R.* 'Ispahan'.
***R.* Rose Gaujard ('Gaumo').** Upright, strong Hybrid Tea rose. H 1.1m (3½ft), S 75cm (2½ft). Has plentiful glossy foliage. Bears slightly scented, urn-shaped, double, cherry-red and blush-pink flowers, 10cm (4in) across, freely in summer-autumn.
***R.* Rosemary Harkness ('Harrowbond')** illus. p.186.
🏆 ***R.* 'Roseraie de l'Haÿ'** illus. p.183.
🏆 ***R.* Rosy Cushion ('Interall')** illus. p.182.
***R.* 'Rosy Mantle'** illus. p.193.
***R.* 'Rouge Eblouissante'.** See *R.* 'Assemblage des Beautés'.
***R.* 'Rouletii'**, syn. *R. chinensis* var. *minima, R.* 'Pompon de Paris'. Compact Miniature rose with thin stems. H and S 20cm (8in). Has mid-green leaves comprising many lance-shaped leaflets, and freely produces cupped, double, deep pink flowers, 2cm (¾in) across, in summer-autumn.
***R.* 'Royal Dane'.** See *R.* Troika.
***R.* 'Royal Highness'**, syn. *R.* 'Königliche Hoheit'. Upright Hybrid Tea rose. H 1.1m (3½ft), S 60cm (2ft). In summer-autumn, firm stems bear leathery, dark green foliage and large, fragrant, pointed, fully double, pearl-pink flowers, 12cm (5in) across.
🏆 ***R.* Royal William ('Korzaun')**, syn. *R.* 'Duftzauber '84', illus. p.188.
R. rubiginosa, syn. *R. eglanteria*, illus. p.181.
***R. rubrifolia*.** See *R. glauca*.
R. rugosa illus. p.183. 🏆 var. ***alba*** is a dense, vigorous Species rose. H and S 1–2m (3–6ft). Bears a succession of fragrant, cupped, single, white flowers, 9cm (3½in) across, in summer-autumn. They are followed by large, tomato-shaped hips. Abundant foliage is leathery, wrinkled and glossy.
***R.* 'Rugul'.** See *R.* Golden Penny.
***R.* 'Ruiblun'.** See *R.* Blue Peter.
***R.* 'Runatru'.** See *R.* Invincible.
***R.* 'Saint Nicholas'.** Vigorous, erect Damask rose. H and S 1.2m (4ft). In summer bears lightly scented, cupped, semi-double, rose-pink flowers, 12cm (5in) across, with golden stamens, followed by red hips in autumn. Has plentiful, dark green foliage.
***R.* 'San Rafael Rose'.** See *R.* × *odorata* 'Pseudindica'.
🏆 ***R.* 'Sander's White Rambler'.** Vigorous Rambler of lax growth. H 3m (10ft), S 2.5m (8ft). Fragrant, rosette, fully double, white flowers, 5cm (2in) across, appear in clusters in late summer. Small, glossy leaves are plentiful.
***R.* 'Schneewittchen'.** See *R.* Iceberg.
***R.* 'Schoolgirl'.** Stiff, rather lanky, large-flowered Climber. H 2.7m (9ft), S 2.2m (7ft). Large, deep green leaves set off moderately fragrant, rounded, fully double, apricot-orange flowers, 10cm (4in) across, borne in summer-autumn.
R. sericea subsp. ***omeiensis*** f. ***pteracantha***, syn. *R. omeiensis* f. *pteracantha* (Winged thorn rose). Stiff, upright, vigorous Species rose. H 2.5m (8ft), S 2.2m (7ft). Has small, fern-like, light green leaves and large, red prickles on young stems. In summer, solitary, flat, white flowers, 2.5–6cm (1–2½in) across, are borne briefly along the stems.
🏆 ***R.* Sexy Rexy ('Macrexy')** illus. p.186.
***R.* Sheila's Perfume ('Harsherry').** Upright Floribunda rose. H 75cm (2½ft), S 60cm (2ft). Has glossy, reddish foliage. Fragrant, urn-shaped, double, red-and-yellow flowers, 9cm (3½in) across, are produced singly or in clusters in summer-autumn.
***R.* Sheri Anne ('Morsherry')** illus. p.191.
***R.* Shocking Blue ('Korblue').** Bushy Floribunda rose. H 75cm (2½ft), S 60cm (2ft). In summer-autumn bears fragrant, pointed, well-formed, fully double, purple flowers, 10cm (4in) across, singly or in clusters. Foliage is dark green.
🏆 ***R.* 'Silver Jubilee'** illus. p.187.
***R.* Simba ('Korbelma')**, syn. *R.* 'Goldsmith', illus. p.189.
***R.* 'Sissi'.** See *R.* Blue Moon.
***R.* Snow Carpet ('Maccarpe').** Prostrate, creeping Miniature rose. H 15cm (6in), S 50cm (20in). Has many small glossy leaves and pompon, fully double, white flowers, 3cm (1¼in) across, in summer, a few in autumn. Makes good, compact ground cover.
***R.* Snowball ('Macangeli')**, syn. *R.* 'Angelita', illus. p.191.
🏆 ***R.* 'Southampton'**, syn. *R.* 'Susan Ann', illus. p.190.
***R.* 'Souvenir d'Alphonse Lavallée'.** Vigorous, sprawling Hybrid Perpetual rose. H 2.2m (7ft), S 2m (6ft). Fragrant, cupped, double, burgundy-red to maroon-purple flowers, 10cm (4in) across, are borne in summer-autumn. Leaves are small and mid-green. Is best grown on a light support.
***R.* 'Souvenir de la Malmaison'.** Dense, spreading Bourbon rose. H and S 1.5m (5ft). Bears spice-scented, quartered-rosette, fully double, blush-pink to white flowers, 12cm (5in) across, in summer-autumn. Rain spoils flowers. Has large, dark green leaves.
***R.* 'Spanish Beauty'.** See *R.* 'Madame Grégoire Staechelin'.
***R.* 'Spectacular'.** See *R.* 'Danse du Feu'.
R. spinosissima, syn. *R. pimpinellifolia* (Burnet rose, Scotch rose). **'Plena'** illus. p.180.
***R.* 'Spring Morning'.** See *R.* 'Frühlingsmorgen'.
***R.* 'Stacey Sue'** illus. p.191.
***R.* Sue Lawley ('Macspash').** Open Floribunda rose. H 75cm (2½ft), S 60cm (2ft). Bears sprays of faintly fragrant, cupped, wide-opening, double, pink-and-white flowers, 9cm (3½in) across, in summer-autumn. Leaves are dark green.
***R.* 'Sunblaze'.** See *R.* Orange Sunblaze.
🏆 ***R.* Sunset Boulevard ('Harbabble').** Upright Floribunda rose. H 1m (3ft), S 60cm (2ft). Bears open sprays of lightly scented, pointed to cupped, double, salmon-pink flowers, 9cm (3½in) across, in summer-autumn on glossy-foliaged plants. Is excellent for beds and cutting.
***R.* 'Susan Ann'.** See *R.* 'Southampton'.
🏆 ***R.* Sweet Dream ('Fryminicot').** Compact Patio rose. H 40cm (16in), S 35cm (14in). Clusters of slightly scented, pompon, fully double, peach-apricot flowers, 6cm (2½in) across, appear in summer-autumn. Leaves are small.
🏆 ***R.* Sweet Magic ('Dicmagic')** illus. p.190.
***R.* 'Sylvia'.** See *R.* Congratulations.
***R.* 'Sympathie'** illus. p.194.
***R.* 'Tanba'.** See *R.* Baby Masquerade.
***R.* 'Tanellis'.** See *R.* Fragrant Cloud.
***R.* 'Tanky'.** See *R.* Whisky Mac.
***R.* 'Tannacht'.** See *R.* Blue Moon.
***R.* 'Tapis d'Orient'.** See *R.* 'Yesterday'.
***R.* 'Tapis Jaune'.** See *R.* Golden Penny.
🏆 ***R.* 'The Fairy'** illus. p.185.
***R.* 'The Queen Elizabeth'.** See *R.* 'Queen Elizabeth'.
🏆 ***R.* The Times Rose ('Korpeahn')** illus. p.188.
***R.* 'Tour de Malakoff'** illus. p.184.
***R.* 'Tricolore de Flandre'.** Vigorous, upright Gallica rose. H and S 1m (3ft). Fragrant, pompon, fully double, blush-pink flowers, 6cm (2½in) across, striped with pink and purple, open in summer. Has dull green leaves.
🏆 ***R.* Troika ('Poumidor')**, syn. *R.* 'Royal Dane', illus. p.190.
🏆 ***R.* Trumpeter ('Mactru')** illus. p.187.
🏆 ***R.* 'Tuscany Superb'**, syn. *R.* 'Double Velvet'. Vigorous, upright Gallica rose. H 1.1m (3½ft), S 1m (3ft). In summer produces, slightly scented, cupped to flat, double flowers, 5cm (2in) across, deep crimson-maroon, ageing to purple, with gold stamens. Leaves are dark green.
***R.* 'Variegata di Bologna'.** Upright, arching Bourbon rose. H 2m (6ft), S 1.4m (4½ft). Has small leaves and, in summer-autumn, fragrant, quartered-rosette, fully double flowers, 8cm (3in) across, blush-pink, striped with rose-purple. Needs fertile soil and is prone to blackspot.
🏆 ***R.* 'Veilchenblau'**, syn. *R.* 'Blue Rambler', illus. p.195.
***R.* 'Wedding Day'.** Rampant Rambler. H 8m (25ft), S 4m (12ft). Produces large clusters of fruity-scented, flat, single, creamy-white flowers, 2.5cm (1in) across, that mature to blush-pink, in late summer. Is suitable for growing up a tree or in a wild garden.
***R.* Wee Jock. ('Cocabest')** illus. p.188.
***R.* Whisky Mac ('Tanky').** Neat, upright Hybrid Tea rose. H 75cm (2½ft), S 60cm (2ft). Fragrant, rounded, fully double, amber flowers, 9cm (3½in) across, appear freely in summer-autumn. Reddish foliage is prone to mildew. May die back during a hard winter.
***R.* 'White Cockade'.** Slow-growing, bushy, upright Climber. H 2–3m (6–10ft), S 1.5m (5ft). Bears slightly

fragrant, rounded, well-formed, fully double, white flowers, 9cm (3½in) across, in summer-autumn. May be pruned and grown as a shrub.
♀ ***R.* 'William Lobb'**, syn. *R.* 'Duchesse d'Istrie', illus. p.184.
♀ ***R. xanthina* 'Canary Bird'**, syn. *R.* 'Canary Bird', illus. p.185.
♀ ***R.* 'Yesterday'**, syn. *R.* 'Tapis d'Orient'. Bushy, arching Polyantha rose. H and S 75cm (30in), or more if lightly pruned. Fragrant, rosette, semi-double, lilac-pink flowers, 2.5cm (1in) across, are borne, mainly in clusters, from summer through to early winter. Produces small, dark green leaves. Makes a good hedge.
♀ ***R.* 'Yvonne Rabier'.** Dense, bushy Polyantha rose. H 45cm (18in), S 40cm (16in). Plentiful leaves are bright green. Bears moderately scented, rounded, double, creamy-white flowers, 5cm (2in) across, in summer-autumn.
***R.* 'Zéphirine Drouhin'** illus. p.193.
***R.* 'Zigeunerknabe'**, syn. *R.* 'Gipsy Boy'. Vigorous, thorny Bourbon rose of lanky habit. H and S 2m (6ft). Faintly scented, cupped to flat, double, purplish-crimson flowers, 8cm (3in) across, are borne in summer. Leaves are dark green.
***R.* 'Zonta Rose'.** See *R.* PRINCESS ALICE.

Rosa mundi. See *Rosa gallica* 'Versicolor', illus. p.183.
Rosary vine. See *Ceropegia linearis* subsp. *woodii*, illus. p.478.

ROSCOEA

ZINGIBERACEAE

Genus of late summer- and early autumn-flowering, tuberous perennials, related to ginger, grown for their orchid-like flowers. Suits open borders, rock gardens and woodland gardens. Frost hardy. Grows in sun or partial shade and in cool, well-drained humus-rich soil that must be kept moist in summer. Dies down in winter, when a top dressing of leaf mould or well-rotted compost is beneficial. Propagate by division in spring or by seed, exposed to frost for best germination, in autumn or winter.
♀ ***R. cautleyoides*** illus. p.452.
♀ ***R. humeana*** illus. p.452.
R. procera. See *R. purpurea*.
R. purpurea, syn. *R. procera*. Summer-flowering, tuberous perennial. H 20–30cm (8–12in), S 15–20cm (6–8in). Lance-shaped, erect leaves are long-pointed and wrap around each other at base to form a false stem. Has long-tubed, purple flowers, each with a hooded, upper petal, wide-lobed, lower lip and 2 narrower petals.

Rose. See *Rosa*.
Banksian. See *Rosa banksiae*.
Burnet. See *Rosa* spinosissima.
Christmas. See *Helleborus*.
Common moss. *Rosa* × *centifolia* 'Muscosa'.
Confederate. See *Hibiscus mutabilis*.
Cotton. See *Hibiscus mutabilis*.
Crested moss. See *Rosa* × *centifolia* 'Cristata'.
Desert. See *Adenium*.
Guelder. See *Viburnum opulus*.
Hedgehog. See *Rosa rugosa*, illus. p.183.
Incense. See *Rosa primula*, illus. p.184.
Japanese. See *Rosa rugosa*, illus. p.183.
Lenten. See *Helleborus* × *hybridus*.
Old pink moss. See *Rosa* × *centifolia* 'Muscosa'.
Rock. See *Cistus; Helianthemum*.
Scotch. See *Rosa spinosissima*.
Snowbush. See *Rosa* 'Dupontii', illus. p.181.
Thornless. See *Rosa* 'Zéphirine Drouhin', illus. p.193.
Winged thorn. See *Rosa sericea* subsp. *omeiensis* f. *pteracantha*.
Wood. See *Merremia tuberosa*.
Rose acacia. See *Robinia hispida*, illus. p.137.
Rose cactus. See *Pereskia grandifolia*, illus. p.474.
Rose of Jericho. See *Selaginella lepidophylla*.
Rose of Lancaster, Red. See *Rosa gallica* var. *officinalis*.
Rose of Sharon. See *Hypericum calycinum*, illus. p.166.
Rose periwinkle. See *Catharanthus roseus*, illus. p.156.
Rose pincushion. See *Mammillaria zeilmanniana*, illus. p.489.
Rosebay, White. See *Epilobium angustifolium*f. *album*, illus. p.224.
Rosebud cherry. See *Prunus* × *subhirtella*.
Rosemary. See *Rosmarinus officinalis*, illus. p.163.
Australian. See *Westringia fruticosa*, illus. p.154.
Roseroot. See *Rhodiola rosea*.

ROSMARINUS

LABIATAE/LAMIACEAE

Genus of evergreen shrubs, grown for their flowers and aromatic foliage, which can be used as a culinary herb. Frost hardy, but in cold areas grow against a south- or west-facing wall. Requires sun and well-drained soil. Cut back frost-damaged plants to healthy wood in spring; straggly, old plants may be cut back hard at same time. Trim hedges after flowering. Propagate by semi-ripe cuttings in summer.
R. lavandulaceus of gardens**.** See *R. officinalis* 'Prostratus'.
R. officinalis (Rosemary) illus. p.163.
♀ **'Miss Jessopp's Upright'** is an evergreen, compact, upright shrub. H and S 2m (6ft). From mid- to late spring and sometimes again in autumn bears small, 2-lipped, blue flowers amid narrowly oblong, aromatic, dark green leaves. Is good when grown for hedging. **'Prostratus'** (syn. *R. lavandulaceus* of gardens), H 15cm (6in), is prostrate and the least hardy form. ♀ **'Severn Sea'**, H 1m (3ft), is arching, with bright blue flowers.

ROSSIOGLOSSUM

ORCHIDACEAE

See also ORCHIDS.
♀ ***R. grande***, syn. *Odontoglossum grande* illus. p.309. Evergreen, epiphytic orchid for a cool greenhouse. H 15cm (6in). Spikes of rich yellow flowers, to 15cm (6in) across and heavily marked chestnut-brown, are produced in autumn. Has broadly oval, stiff leaves, 15cm (6in) long. Provide shade in summer and keep very dry in winter.

ROTHMANNIA

RUBIACEAE

Genus of evergreen, summer-flowering shrubs and trees, grown for their flowers. Is related to *Gardenia*. Frost tender, min. 16°C (61°F). Needs a position in full light or partial shade and humus-rich, well-drained, neutral to acid soil. Water potted plants freely when in full growth, moderately at other times. Propagate by seed in spring or by semi-ripe cuttings in summer.
R. capensis, syn. *Gardenia capensis, G. rothmannia*. Evergreen, ovoid shrub or tree. H 6m (20ft) or more, S 3m (10ft) or more. Leaves are oval, lustrous and rich green. Has fragrant, tubular flowers, each with 5 arching, white to creamy-yellow petal lobes and a purple-dotted throat, in summer.

Rouen lilac. See *Syringa* × *chinensis*.
Round-headed club-rush. See *Scirpoides holoschoenus*.
Round-leaved mint-bush. See *Prostanthera rotundifolia*, illus. p.141.
Round-leaved wintergreen. See *Pyrola rotundifolia*.
Rowan. See *Sorbus aucuparia*, illus. p.77.
Hupeh. See *Sorbus hupehensis*.
Sargent's. See *Sorbus sargentiana*.
Royal agave. See *Agave victoriae-reginae*, illus. p.477.
Royal fern. See *Osmunda regalis*, illus. p.324.
Royal paintbrush. See *Scadoxus puniceus*.
Royal palm. See *Roystonea*.
Cuban. See *Roystonea regia*.
Royal red bugler. See *Aeschynanthus pulcher*.

ROYSTONEA

Royal palm

PALMAE/ARECACEAE

Genus of evergreen palms, grown for their majestic appearance. Produces racemes of insignificant flowers in summer. Frost tender, min. 16–18°C (61–64°F). Needs full light or partial shade and fertile, well-drained but moisture-retentive soil. Water potted plants freely when in full growth, less at other times, especially when temperatures are low. Propagate by seed in spring at not less than 27°C (81°F). Red spider mite may be a problem.
R. regia (Cuban royal palm). Evergreen palm with an upright stem, sometimes thickened about the middle. H 20m (70ft) or more, S to 6m (20ft). Leaves are feather-shaped, 3m (10ft) long, upright at first, then becoming arching and pendent, and are divided into narrowly oblong, leathery, bright green leaflets.

Rubber plant. See *Ficus elastica*.
Baby. See *Peperomia clusiifolia*.
Rubbervine. See *Cryptostegia grandiflora*.

RUBUS

Blackberry, Bramble

ROSACEAE

Genus of deciduous, semi-evergreen or evergreen shrubs and woody-stemmed, scrambling climbers. Some species are cultivated solely for their edible fruits, which include raspberries and blackberries. Those described here are grown mainly for their foliage, flowers or ornamental, often prickly stems, though some may also bear edible fruits. Fully to frost hardy. Deciduous species grown for their winter stems prefer full sun; other deciduous species need sun or semi-shade; evergreens and semi-evergreens tolerate sun or shade. All *Rubus* require fertile, well-drained soil. Cut old stems of *R. biflorus, R. cockburnianus* and *R. thibetanus* to ground after fruiting. Propagate by seed or cuttings (semi-ripe for evergreens, softwood or hardwood for deciduous species) in summer or winter. Or *R. odoratus* may be increased by division, and *R.* 'Benenden' and *R. ulmifolius* 'Bellidiflorus' by layering in spring.
♀ ***R.* 'Benenden'**,syn. *R.* 'Tridel', illus. p.132.
♀ ***R. biflorus*** illus. p.145.
R. cockburnianus. Deciduous, arching shrub. H and S 2.5m (8ft). Fully hardy. Prickly shoots are brilliant blue-white in winter. Dark green leaves, white beneath, each have usually 9 oval leaflets. Bears panicles of 5-petalled, purple flowers in early summer, followed by unpalatable, spherical, black fruits.
R. henryi var. ***bambusarum.*** Fast-growing, vigorous, evergreen, woody-stemmed, scrambling climber, grown mainly for its attractive foliage. H to 6m (20ft). Fully hardy. Leaves have 3 broadly oval leaflets, white-felted beneath. Tiny, pink flowers are borne in small clusters in summer.
R. odoratus (Flowering raspberry, Thimbleberry). Vigorous, deciduous, upright, thicket-forming shrub. H and S 2.5m (8ft). Fully hardy. Thornless, peeling shoots bear large, velvety, dark green leaves, each with 5 broadly triangular lobes. Large, fragrant, 5-petalled, rose-pink flowers appear from early summer to early autumn, and are sometimes followed by unpalatable, flattened, red fruits.
♀ ***R. thibetanus*** illus. p.145.
R. tricolor. Evergreen shrub with both prostrate and arching shoots covered in red bristles. H 60cm (2ft), S 2m (6ft). Fully hardy. Oval, toothed, glossy, dark green leaves set off cup-shaped, 5-petalled, white flowers borne in mid-summer. Has edible, raspberry-like, red fruits. Makes good ground cover.
***R.* 'Tridel'.** See *R.* 'Benenden'.
***R. ulmifolius* 'Bellidiflorus'.** Vigorous, deciduous or semi-evergreen, arching shrub. H 2.5m (8ft), S 4m (12ft). Fully hardy. Prickly stems bear dark green leaves, with 3 or 5 oval leaflets, and, in mid- to late summer, large panicles of daisy-like, double, pink flowers.

Ruby grass. See *Melinis repens*.

Rudbeckia

Coneflower

COMPOSITAE/ASTERACEAE

Genus of annuals, biennials and perennials grown for their flowers. Fully hardy. Thrives in sun or shade and well-drained or moist soil. Propagate by division in spring or by seed in autumn or spring.

R. fulgida (Black-eyed Susan). ♀ var. ***deamii*** is an erect perennial. H 1m (3ft), S 60cm (2ft) or more. In late summer and autumn produces daisy-like, yellow flower heads with central, black cones. Has narrowly lance-shaped, mid-green leaves. Prefers moist soil. ♀ var. ***sullivantii* 'Goldsturm'** illus. p.262.

***R.* 'Goldquelle'.** See *R. laciniata* 'Goldquelle'.

***R.* 'Herbstsonne'.** illus. p.232.

R. hirta. Moderately fast-growing, upright, branching, short-lived perennial, grown as an annual. H 30cm–1m (1–3ft), S 30–45cm (1–1½ft). Has lance-shaped, mid-green leaves and, in summer-autumn, large, daisy-like, deep yellow flower heads, with conical, purple centres. Needs sun and well-drained soil. **'Goldilocks'** illus. p.352. **'Irish Eyes'**, H to 75cm (2½ft), has yellow flower heads with olive-green centres. **'Marmalade'** illus. p.352. **'Rustic Dwarfs'**, H to 60cm (24in), bears yellow, mahogany, or bronze flower heads. **'Toto gold'.** illus. p.352.

***R. laciniata* 'Golden Glow'.** Erect perennial. H 2–2.2m (6–7ft), S 60cm–1m (2–3ft). Bears daisy-like, double, golden-yellow flower heads, with green centres, in late summer and autumn. Mid-green leaves are divided into lance-shaped leaflets, themselves further cut. Prefers well-drained soil. ♀ **'Goldquelle'** (syn. *R.* 'Goldquelle') illus. p.227.

R. purpurea. See *Echinacea purpurea.*

Rue. See *Ruta.*
 Common. See *Ruta graveolens.*
 Meadow. See *Thalictrum.*

Ruellia

ACANTHACEAE

Genus of perennials and evergreen sub-shrubs and shrubs with showy flowers. Frost tender, min. 15°C (59°F). Grow in a humid atmosphere, partial shade and in moist but well-drained soil. Propagate by stem cuttings or seed, if available, in spring.

R. amoena. See *R. graecizans.*

R. devosiana illus. p.287.

R. graecizans, syn. *R. amoena*, illus. p.253.

Ruschia

AIZOACEAE

Genus of mostly small, tufted, perennial succulents and evergreen shrubs with leaves united up to one-third of their lengths around stems or with very short sheaths. Frost tender, min. 5°C (41°F). Needs sun and well-drained soil. Propagate by seed or stem cuttings in spring or summer.

R. acuminata. Evergreen, erect, succulent shrub. H 20cm (8in), S 50cm (20in). Has woody stems as well as non-woody, bluish-green stems with darker dots. Produces solid, 3-angled, 3cm (1¼in) long leaves, each with a blunt keel and a short sheath. Daisy-like, white to pale pink flowers, 3cm (1¼ in) across, appear in summer.

R. crassa. Evergreen, erect, succulent shrub. H and S 50cm (20in). Bears solid, 3-angled, bluish-green leaves, 2cm (¾in) long, with short, white hairs; the undersides are keeled, each with a single tooth. Has 2.5cm (1in) wide, daisy-like, white flowers in summer.

R. macowanii. Erect, then spreading, perennial succulent. H 15cm (6in), S 1m (3ft). Has solid, slightly keeled, 3-angled, bluish-green leaves, to 3cm (1¼in) long. In summer carries masses of daisy-like, bright pink flowers, 3cm (1¼in) across, with darker stripes.

Ruscus

LILIACEAE/RUSCACEAE

Genus of evergreen, clump-forming, spring-flowering shrubs, grown for their foliage and fruits. The apparent leaves are actually flattened shoots, on which flowers and fruits are borne. Usually, separate male and female plants are required for fruiting. Is particularly useful for dry, shady sites. Fully to frost hardy. Tolerates sun or shade and any soil other than waterlogged. Cut back dead shoots to base in spring. Propagate by division in spring. The berries of *R. aculeatus* may cause mild stomach upset if ingested.

R. aculeatus (Butcher's broom). Evergreen, erect, thicket-forming shrub. H 75cm (2½ft), S 1m (3ft). Fully hardy. Spine-tipped 'leaves' are glossy and dark green. Tiny, star-shaped, green flowers in spring are succeeded by large, spherical, bright red fruits.

R. hypoglossum illus. p.172.

Rush
 Corkscrew. See *Juncus effusus* f. *spiralis*, illus. p.320.
 Flowering. See *Butomus umbellatus*, illus. p.464.

Rushes. See Grasses, Bamboos, Rushes and Sedges.

Russelia

SCROPHULARIACEAE

Genus of evergreen shrubs and sub-shrubs with showy flowers. Frost tender, min. 10–15°C (50–59°F). Needs sun or partial shade. Requires humus-rich, light, well-drained soil. Propagate by stem cuttings or division in spring.

♀ ***R. equisetiformis***, syn. *R. juncea*, illus. p.254.

R. juncea. See *R. equisetiformis.*

Russian comfrey. See *Symphytum* x *uplandicum.*

Russian vine. See *Fallopia aubertii* of gardens; *Fallopia baldschuanica*, illus. p.215.

Rusty-back fern. See *Asplenium ceterach*, illus. p.323.

Rusty-leaved fig. See *Ficus rubiginosa.*

Ruta

Rue

RUTACEAE

Genus of evergreen, summer-flowering sub-shrubs, with deeply divided, aromatic leaves, grown for their foliage and flowers and used as a medicinal herb. Fully hardy. Requires a sunny position and well-drained soil. Cut back to old wood in spring to keep compact. Propagate by semi-ripe cuttings in summer. All parts may cause severe discomfort if eaten; the foliage may cause photodermatitis on contact.

R. graveolens (Common rue). **'Jackman's Blue'** illus. p.173.

Sabal

PALMAE/ARECACEAE

Genus of evergreen fan palms, grown for their foliage and overall appearance. Half hardy to frost tender, min. 5–7°C (41–5°F). Prefers full sun and fertile, well-drained soil. Water moderately, less when not in full growth. Propagate by seed in spring. Red spider mite may be troublesome.
S. minor illus. p.172.

Sacred bamboo. See *Nandina domestica.*
Sacred fig tree. See *Ficus religiosa.*
Sacred lotus. See *Nelumbo nucifera*, illus. p.463.
Saffron crocus. See *Crocus sativus.*
Saffron, Meadow. See *Colchicum autumnale*, illus. p.453.
Sage. See *Salvia.*
Bog. See *Salvia uliginosa.*
Mexican bush. See *Salvia leucantha.*

Sagina

CARYOPHYLLACEAE

Genus of mat-forming annuals and ever-green perennials, grown for their foliage. Is suitable for banks and in paving. Some species may be very invasive. Fully hardy. Prefers sun and gritty, moist soil; dislikes hot, dry conditions. Propagate by division in spring, by seed in autumn or, for *S. boydii*, by tip cuttings in summer. Aphids and red spider mite may cause problems.
S. boydii illus. p.402.

Sagittaria
Arrowhead

ALISMATACEAE

Genus of deciduous, perennial, submerged and marginal water plants, grown for their foliage and flowers. Fully hardy to frost tender, min. 5°C (41°F). Some species are suitable for pools, others for aquariums. All require full sun. Remove fading foliage as necessary. Propagate by division in spring or summer or by breaking off turions (scaly, young shoots) in spring.
S. japonica. See *S. sagittifolia* 'Flore Pleno'.
S. latifolia (American arrowhead) illus. p.462.
S. sagittifolia (Common arrowhead). Deciduous, perennial, marginal water plant. H 45cm (18in), S 30cm (12in). Fully hardy. Upright, mid-green leaves are acutely arrow-shaped. In summer produces 3-petalled, white flowers with dark purple centres. May be grown in up to 23cm (9in) depth of water. **'Flore Pleno'** (syn. *S. japonica;* Japanese arrowhead) has double flowers.

Saguaro. See *Carnegiea gigantea*, illus. p.472.
St Augustine grass. See *Stenotaphrum secundatum.*
St Bernard's lily. See *Anthericum liliago*, illus. p.286.
St Bruno's lily. See *Paradisea liliastrum.*
St Catherine's lace. See *Eriogonum giganteum*, illus. p.135.
St Dabeoc's heath. See *Daboecia cantabrica.*
St Vincent lilac. See *Solanum seaforthianum.*

Saintpaulia
African violet

GESNERIACEAE

Genus of evergreen, rosette-forming perennials, grown for their showy flowers. Frost tender, min. 15°C (59°F). Needs a constant temperature, a humid atmosphere, partial shade and fertile soil. Propagate by leaf cuttings in summer. Whitefly and mealy bug may cause problems with indoor plants.

African violet cultivars
There are over 2,000 cultivars, mainly derived from *S. ionantha*, with star- or bell-shaped, white, pink, red, blue, violet, bi- or multi-coloured flowers, borne throughout the year. They may be single, semi-double or fully double. Petal edges may be ruffled, rounded, frilled or fringed. The broadly ovate to oval leaves are usually mid- or dark green, and may be feathered, flecked or variegated white, pink or cream. See also feature panel p.314.
Cultivars are divided into 5 groups, according to rosette size. The measurement given below is the diameter of the rosette; the spread of each cultivar is the same as this: Micro-miniature – less than 8cm (3in); Miniature – 8–16cm (3–6in); Semi-miniature – 16–21cm (6–8in); Standard – 21–40cm (8–16in); Large – over 40cm (16in).

🏆 ***S.* 'Bright Eyes'** illus. p.314. Standard Group. H to 15cm (6in). Has dark green leaves and single, deep violet-blue flowers with yellow centres.
***S.* 'Chantabent'.** Semi-miniature Group. H 10–15cm (4–6in). Has dark green leaves with deep red undersides, and bears large, single, violet-blue flowers.
🏆 ***S.* 'Colorado'** illus. p.314. Standard Group. H 15–20cm (6–8in). Bears dark green leaves and frilled, single, magenta flowers.
🏆 ***S.* 'Delft'** illus. p.314. Standard Group. H to 15cm (6in). Leaves are dark green, and flowers are semi-double and violet-blue.
***S.* 'Dorothy'.** Standard Group. H to 15cm (6in). Has long-stalked, light green leaves, and bears large, single, rich pink flowers with frilled, white margins.
🏆 ***S.* 'Garden News'** illus. p.314. Standard Group. H to 15cm (6in). Has bright green leaves and double, pure white flowers.
🏆 ***S.* 'Ice Maiden'** illus. p.314. Standard Group. H to 15cm (6in). Bears single, white flowers with purple-blue markings.
S. ionantha. Evergreen, stemless, rosette-forming perennial, often forming clumps. H to 10cm (4in), S 25cm (10in). Almost rounded, scalloped, long-stalked, fleshy, usually hairy leaves, to 8cm (3in) long, are mid-green above and often reddish-green below. Loose clusters of 2–8 tubular, 5-lobed, violet-blue flowers, to 2.5cm (1in) across, are produced on stems held above leaves and appear year-round.
***S.* 'Pip Squeek'** illus. p.314. Micro-miniature Group. H to 8cm (3in). Has oval, unscalloped, deep green leaves, 1–2cm (½–¾in) long, and bell-shaped, pale pink flowers, 1cm (½in) wide.
***S.* 'Porcelain'** illus. p.314. Standard Group. H to 15cm (6in). Bears semi-double, white flowers with purple-blue edges.
🏆 ***S.* 'Rococo Anna',** syn. *S.* 'Rococo Pink' illus. p.314. Standard Group. H to 15cm (6in). Bears double, iridescent pink flowers.
🏆 ***S.* 'Starry Trail'** illus. p.314. Standard Group. H to 15cm (6in). Has dark green leaves and narrow-petalled, semi-double to double, white flowers, sometimes flushed pale pink.
***S.* 'Zoja'** illus. p.314. Standard Group. H to 15cm (6in). Produces large, single to semi-double, purple-blue flowers with a bold white line at the margin of each petal.

Salix
Willow

SALICACEAE

Genus of deciduous trees and shrubs, grown for their habit, foliage, catkins and, in some cases, colourful winter shoots. Male catkins are more striking than female; each plant usually bears catkins of only one sex. Fully to frost hardy. Most prefer full sun. Most species grow well in any but very dry soil; *S. caprea, S. purpurea* and their variants also thrive in dry soil. Plants grown for their colourful winter shoots should be cut back hard in early spring, every 1–3 years. Propagate by semi-ripe cuttings in summer or by hardwood cuttings in winter. Fungal diseases may cause canker, particularly in *S. babylonica* and *S.* × *sepulcralis* var. *chrysocoma.* Willows may become infested with such pests as caterpillars, aphids and gall mites.
S. aegyptiaca (Musk willow). Vigorous, deciduous, bushy shrub or tree. H 4m (12ft), S 5m (15ft). Fully hardy. Grey catkins that turn to yellow appear on bare, stout shoots in late winter or early spring, before large, narrowly oval, deep green leaves.
S. alba (White willow). f. ***argentea*** see *S.a.* var. *sericea.* **'Britzensis'** see *S.a.* var. *vitellina* 'Britzensis'. var. ***caerulea*** (Cricket-bat willow) is a very fast-growing, deciduous, conical tree with upright branches. H 25m (80ft), S 10m (30ft). Fully hardy. Has long, narrowly lance-shaped, deep bluish-green leaves and, in early spring, small, pendent, yellowish-green catkins. **'Chermesina'** see *S.a.* var. *vitellina* 'Chermesina'. **'Sericea'** see *S.a.* var. *sericea.* 🏆 var. ***sericea*** (syn. *S.a.* f. *argentea, S.a.* 'Sericea'; Silver willow), H 15m (50ft), S 8m (25ft), is a spreading tree that is conical when young and has bright silver-grey leaves. **'Tristis'** (syn. *S. vitellina* 'Pendula') has a more weeping habit and only produces female catkins. **'Tristis'** of gardens see *S.* × *sepulcralis* var. *chrysocoma.* 🏆 var. ***vitellina*** illus. p.70. 🏆 var. ***vitellina* 'Britzensis'** (syn. *S.a.* 'Britzensis'), which has green leaves and bright orange-red, young shoots, is usually cut back to near ground level to provide winter colour. var. ***vitellina* 'Chermesina'** (syn. *S.a.* 'Chermesina') has carmine-red, young winter shoots.
S. apoda illus. p.375.
S. arbuscula (Mountain willow). Deciduous, spreading shrub. H and S 60cm (2ft) or more. Fully hardy. In spring, dark brown stems produce narrowly oval, toothed leaves and white-haired, sometimes red-tinged, yellow catkins. Suits a rock garden.
S. babylonica (Weeping willow). Deciduous, weeping tree with slender, pendent shoots that reach almost to the ground. H and S 12m (40ft). Fully hardy. Bears narrowly lance-shaped, long-pointed leaves. Has yellowish-green catkins in early spring. Is susceptible to canker and has been largely replaced in cultivation by *S.* × *sepulcralis* var. *chrysocoma.* 🏆 var. ***pekinensis* 'Tortuosa'** (syn. *S. matsudana* 'Tortuosa') illus. p.81.
S. bockii. Deciduous, bushy shrub. H and S 2.5m (8ft). Fully hardy. Has slender, upright, grey-hairy shoots and oblong, glossy, bright green leaves, with silky-hairy undersides. Usually female in cultivation; bears green catkins in early and mid-autumn.
🏆 ***S.* × *boydii*** (syn.'Boydii') illus. p.373.
S. caprea (Goat willow, Pussy willow). Deciduous, bushy shrub or tree. H 10m (30ft), S 8m (25ft). Fully hardy. Oval leaves are dark green above, grey beneath. Catkins are borne in spring before foliage emerges: females are silky and grey, males are grey with yellow anthers. 🏆 **'Kilmarnock'** (Kilmarnock willow), H 1.5–2m (5–6ft), S 2m (6ft), is dense-headed and weeping. From early to mid- spring produces grey catkins that later become yellow.
***S.* 'Chrysocoma'.** See *S.* × *sepulcralis* var. *chrysocoma.*
S. daphnoides illus. p.70.
🏆 ***S. elaeagnos*** (Hoary willow). Deciduous, upright, dense shrub. H 3m (10ft), S 5m (15ft). Fully hardy. In spring, long shoots bear slender, yellow catkins as leaves appear. These are narrowly oblong and dark green, with white undersides, and turn yellow in autumn.
S. fargesii, syn. *S. moupinensis* of gardens. Deciduous, upright, open shrub. H and S 3m (10ft). Fully hardy. Has purplish-red winter shoots and buds. Slender, erect, green catkins are carried in spring, at same time as bold, oblong, glossy, dark green leaves.
S. fragilis (Crack willow). Deciduous tree with a broad, bushy head. H 15m (50ft), S 12–15m (40–45ft). Fully hardy. Has long, narrow, pointed, glossy, bright green leaves. Catkins, borne in early spring, are yellow on male plants, green on females.
S. gracilistyla. Deciduous, bushy shrub. H 3m (10ft), S 4m (12ft). Fully hardy. Large, silky, grey catkins with red, then bright yellow anthers are produced from early to mid-spring, and are followed by lance-shaped, silky, grey, young leaves that mature to bright, glossy green.
🏆 **'Melanostachys'** (syn.

S. 'Melanostachys'; Black willow) bears almost black catkins, with red anthers, in early spring, before bright green leaves emerge.
♀ ***S. hastata* 'Wehrhahnii'** illus. p.149.
♀ ***S. helvetica*** illus. p.361.
S. herbacea (Dwarf willow, Least willow). Deciduous, creeping shrub. H 2.5cm (1in), S 20cm (8in) or more. Fully hardy. Has small, rounded to oval leaves and, in spring, small, yellow or yellowish-green catkins are produced. Is good for a rock garden. Needs moist soil.
S. irrorata. Deciduous, upright shrub. H 3m (10ft), S 5m (15ft). Fully hardy. Purple, young shoots are white-bloomed in winter. Catkins with red, then yellow anthers appear from early to mid-spring before narrowly oblong, glossy, bright green leaves emerge.
♀ ***S. lanata*** illus. p.152. **'Stuartii'** see *S.* 'Stuartii'.
S. lindleyana. Deciduous, creeping, mat-forming shrub with long, creeping stems. H 2–3cm (¾–1¼in), S 40cm (16in) or more. Frost hardy. Small, narrowly oval to linear, pale green leaves are densely set on short branchlets that produce brownish-pink catkins, 1cm (½in) long, in spring. Suits a rock garden or bank. Needs partial shade and damp soil. Is often confused with the very similar *S. furcata* (syn. *S. fruticulosa, S. hylematica*), which is more lax, with spreading, sometimes erect stems.
♀ ***S. magnifica.*** Deciduous, upright shrub. H 5m (15ft), S 3m (10ft). Fully hardy. Produces very long, slender, green catkins on stout, red shoots in spring, as large, magnolia-like, blue-green leaves emerge.
***S. matsudana* 'Tortuosa'.** See *S. babylonica* var. *pekinensis* 'Tortuosa'.
***S.* 'Melanostachys'.** See *S. gracilistyla* 'Melanostachys'.
S. moupinensis of gardens. See *S. fargesii.*
S. pentandra (Bay willow). Deciduous, large shrub, then small tree with broad, bushy head. H and S 10m (30ft). Fully hardy. Oval, glossy, green leaves are blue-white beneath. Catkins – males bright yellow, females grey-green – open in early summer when the tree is in full leaf.
S. purpurea (Purple osier). Deciduous, bushy, spreading shrub. H and S 5m (15ft). Fully hardy. Grey, male catkins, with yellow anthers, and insignificant, female catkins are both borne on slender, often purple shoots in spring, before narrowly oblong, deep green leaves emerge. **'Nana'** (syn. *S.p.* f. *gracilis, S.p.* 'Gracilis'), H and S 1.5m (5ft), is dense, with silver-grey leaves; is good as a hedge.
S. repens illus. p.152.
♀ ***S. reticulata*** illus. p.382.
***S. × rubens* 'Basfordiana'.** Deciduous, spreading tree. H 15m (50ft), S 10m (30ft). Fully hardy. Has bright orange-yellow, young shoots in winter and long, narrow leaves, grey-green when young, becoming glossy, bright green in summer. Yellowish-green catkins appear in early spring.
***S. sachalinensis* 'Sekka'.** See *S. udensis* 'Sekka'.
♀ ***S. × sepulcralis* var. *chrysocoma,*** syn. *S. alba* 'Tristis' of gardens, *S.* 'Chrysocoma', illus. p.70.
***S.* 'Stuartii',** syn. *S. lanata* 'Stuartii'. Slow-growing, deciduous, spreading shrub. H 1m (3ft), S 2m (6ft). Fully hardy. Has yellow winter shoots. Stout, grey-green catkins open from orange buds in spring, as oval, woolly, grey leaves emerge.
***S. udensis* 'Sekka',** syn. *S. sachalinensis* 'Sekka'. Deciduous, spreading shrub. H 5m (15ft), S 10m (30ft). Fully hardy. Has flattened shoots that are red in winter and lance-shaped, glossy, bright green leaves. Silver catkins are produced in early spring.
***S. vitellina* 'Pendula'.** See *S. alba* 'Tristis'.

SALPIGLOSSIS

SOLANACEAE

Genus of annuals and biennials. Usually only annuals are cultivated, either for colour in borders or as greenhouse plants. Half hardy. Grow in sun and in rich, well-drained soil. Stems need support. Dead-head regularly. Propagate by seed sown under glass in early spring, or in early autumn for winter flowering indoors. Aphids may be troublesome.
***S. sinuata* Bolero Hybrids.** Group of moderately fast-growing, branching, upright annuals. H 60cm (2ft), S 30cm (1ft). Has lance-shaped, pale green leaves. Outward-facing, widely flared, trumpet-shaped, conspicuously veined flowers, 5cm (2in) across, appear in summer and early autumn. Is available in a mixture of rich colours. ♀ **Casino Series** illus. p.341. **'Friendship'** has upward-facing flowers in a range of colours.

SALVIA

Sage

LABIATAE/LAMIACEAE

Genus of annuals, biennials, perennials and evergreen or semi-evergreen shrubs and sub-shrubs, grown for their tubular, 2-lipped, often brightly coloured flowers and aromatic foliage. Leaves of some species may be used for flavouring foods. Fully hardy to frost tender, min. 5°C (41°F). Needs sun and fertile, well-drained soil. Propagate perennials by division in spring, perennials, shrubs and sub-shrubs by softwood cuttings in mid-summer. Sow seed of half-hardy annuals under glass in early spring and of fully-hardy species outdoors in mid-spring.
S. blepharophylla. Spreading, rhizomatous perennial. H and S 45cm (18in). Frost tender. Has oval, glossy, dark green leaves and slender racemes of bright red flowers, with maroon calyces, in summer-autumn.
S. bulleyana. Rosette-forming perennial. H and S 60cm (24in). Fully hardy. Racemes of nettle-like, yellow flowers, with maroon lips, are borne in summer above a basal mass of broadly oval, coarse, prominently veined, dark green leaves.
S. farinacea* f. *alba. Moderately fast-growing, upright perennial, grown as an annual. H 1m (3ft), S 30cm (1ft). Half hardy. Has lance-shaped, mid-green leaves. Spikes of white flowers are produced in summer. **'Strata'** has blue and white flowers. ♀ **'Victoria'** illus. p.344. Dwarf forms are also available.
S. fulgens illus. p.162.
S. grahamii. See *S. microphylla* var. *microphylla.*
S. greggii. Evergreen, erect sub-shrub. H to 1m (3ft), S to 60cm (2ft). Frost tender. Leaves are narrowly oblong and matt, deep green. Has terminal racemes of bright red-purple flowers in autumn.
S. haematodes. See *S. pratensis* Haematodes Group.
S. horminum. See *S. viridis.*
♀ ***S. involucrata.*** Bushy, woody-based perennial. H 60–75cm (2–2½ft) or more, S 1m (3ft). Half hardy. Has oval, mid-green leaves and, in late summer and autumn, racemes of large, rose-crimson flowers. **'Bethellii'** illus. p.231.
S. jurisicii. Rosette-forming perennial. H 45cm (18in), S 30cm (12in). Fully hardy. Stems are clothed with mid-green leaves, divided into 4–6 pairs of linear leaflets. In early summer produces racemes of inverted, violet-blue flowers.
♀ ***S. leucantha*** (Mexican bush sage). Evergreen, erect, well-branched shrub. H and S to 60cm (2ft) or more. Frost tender. Narrowly lance-shaped, finely wrinkled leaves are deep green above, white-downy beneath. In summer-autumn produces terminal spikes of hairy, white flowers, each from a woolly, violet calyx.
S. microphylla* var. *microphylla, syn. *S. grahamii.* Evergreen, erect, well-branched shrub. H and S 1–1.2m (3–4ft). Half hardy, but best at 5°C (41°F). Has oval to elliptic, mid- to deep green leaves. Racemes of dark crimson flowers, ageing to purple and with purple-tinted calyces, appear in late summer and autumn. var. ***neurepia*** illus. p.162.
S. nemorosa, syn. *S. virgata* var. *nemorosa.* Neat, clump-forming perennial. H 1m (3ft), S 45cm (1½ft). Fully hardy. Has narrowly oval, rough, mid-green leaves and, in summer, branching racemes densely set with violet-blue flowers. **'East Friesland'** see *S.n.* 'Ostfriesland'. ♀ **'Lubecca'**, H 45cm (1½ft), is a dwarf form.
♀ **'Ostfriesland'** (syn. *S.n.* 'East Friesland'), H 75cm (2½ft), is smaller.
S. officinalis (Sage). ♀ **'Icterina'** illus. p.173. ♀ **'Purpurascens'** is an evergreen or semi-evergreen, bushy shrub. H 60cm (2ft), S 1m (3ft). Frost hardy. Oblong, grey-green leaves are used as a culinary herb and are purple-flushed when young. Racemes of blue-purple flowers are produced in summer.
♀ ***S. patens* 'Cambridge Blue'** illus. p.297.
♀ ***S. pratensis* Haematodes Group,** syn. *S. haematodes.* Short-lived, rosette-forming perennial. H 1m (3ft), S 45cm (1½ft). Fully hardy. In early summer produces panicles massed with lavender-blue flowers above large, broadly oval, wavy-edged, toothed, rough, dark green leaves.
S. sclarea* var. *turkestanica illus. p.342.
S. splendens. Slow-growing, bushy perennial or evergreen sub-shrub, grown as an annual. H to 30cm (12in), S 20–30cm (8–12in). Half hardy. Has oval, serrated, fresh green leaves, and dense racemes of scarlet flowers in summer and early autumn. **'Blaze of Fire'** has brilliant scarlet flowers. **Cleopatra Series** (salmon, illus. p.333; violet, illus. p.343) are available in mixed or single colours. **'Rambo'**, H to 60cm (24in), is very tall, vigorous, and bushy, with dark green leaves and scarlet flowers. ♀ **'Red Riches'** (syn. *S.s.* 'Ryco'), S 30–40cm (12–16in) has dark green leaves and scarlet flowers. **'Ryco'** see *S.s.* 'Red Riches'. ♀ **'Scarlet King'** illus. p.340. **Vista Series** (red), illus p.339.
♀ ***S. × superba.*** Clump-forming, erect, branched perennial. H 60–90cm (24–36in), S 45–60cm (18–24in). Fully hardy. Leaves are lance-shaped to oblong, scalloped and mid-green, slightly hairy beneath. Slender, terminal racemes of bright violet or purple flowers, to 1.5cm (½in) long, are produced from mid-summer to early autumn.
S. × sylvestris Clump-forming, erect, branched perennial. H 80cm (32in), S 30cm (12in). Fully hardy. Leaves are lance-shaped to oblong, scalloped and mid-green, softly hairy. Dense, terminal racemes of pinkish violet flowers, to 1cm (½in) long, are produced in early to mid-summer.
♀ **'Mainacht'** (syn. *S.* × *s.* MAY NIGHT) illus. p.258.
♀ ***S. uliginosa*** (Bog sage). Graceful, upright, branching perennial. H 2m (6ft), S 45cm (1½ft). Half hardy. Has oblong to lance-shaped, saw-edged, mid-green leaves and, in autumn, long racemes with whorls of bright blue flowers. Prefers moist soil.
S. virgata* var. *nemorosa. See *S. nemorosa.*
S. viridis, syn. *S. horminum*, illus. p.343. **'Bouquet'** (syn. *S.v.* 'Monarch Bouquet') is a moderately fast-growing, upright, branching annual with oval to oblong leaves. H 45–50cm (18–20in), S 23cm (9in). Fully hardy. Tubular, lipped flowers, with blue, rose-pink, white, deep carmine-pink, or purple bracts, are carried in spikes at tops of stems in summer and early autumn; also available as single colours. Bracts of **Claryssa Series** are in a wide range of brilliant colours, including white, pink, purple and blue. **'Monarch Bouquet'** see *S.v.* 'Bouquet'. **'Oxford Blue'**, H 30cm (12in), has violet-blue bracts.

SALVINIA

SALVINIACEAE

Genus of deciduous, perennial, floating water ferns, evergreen in tropical conditions and aquariums. Frost tender, min. 10–15°C (50–59°F). Does best in warm water, with plenty of light. Remove fading foliage, and thin plants when crowded. Propagate by dividing young plants in summer.
S. auriculata illus. p.465.
S. natans. Deciduous, perennial, floating water plant. S indefinite. Oval, elongated, mid-green leaves are borne on branching stems. Tolerates colder conditions than other species and is often used in a cold-water aquarium.

SAMBUCUS
Elder

CAPRIFOLIACEAE

Genus of perennials, deciduous shrubs and trees, grown for their foliage, flowers and fruits. Fully hardy. Needs sun and fertile, moist soil. For best foliage effect, either cut all shoots to ground in winter or prune out old shoots and reduce length of young shoots by half. Propagate species by softwood cuttings in summer, by seed in autumn or by hardwood cuttings in winter, some forms by cuttings only. All parts may cause severe discomfort if ingested, although fruits are safe when cooked; contact with the leaves may irritate skin.
S. canadensis, syn. *S. nigra* subsp. *canadensis* (American elder). **'Aurea'** is a deciduous, upright shrub. H and S 4m (12ft). Has large, golden-yellow leaves, each with usually 7 oblong leaflets. In mid-summer bears large, domed heads of small, star-shaped, creamy-white flowers, then spherical, red fruits.
S. nigra (Common elder). ♀ **'Aurea'** (Golden elder) is a deciduous, bushy shrub. H and S 6m (20ft). Has stout, corky shoots and golden-yellow leaves of usually 5 oval leaflets. Flattened heads of fragrant, star-shaped, creamy-white flowers in early summer are followed by spherical, black fruits. Dark green foliage of ♀ **'Guincho Purple'** matures to deep blackish-purple. Bears purple-stalked flowers, pink in bud and opening to white within, pink outside. subsp. ***canadensis***. See *S. canadensis*.
S. racemosa (Red-berried elder). Deciduous, bushy shrub. H and S 3m (10ft). Mid-green leaves each have usually 5 oval leaflets. Star-shaped, creamy-yellow flowers, borne in dense, conical clusters in mid-spring, are succeeded by spherical, red fruits. **'Plumosa'** has leaves with finely cut leaflets, as does **'Plumosa Aurea'**, but those of the latter are bronze when young, maturing to golden-yellow.

SANCHEZIA

ACANTHACEAE

Genus of evergreen, mainly summer-flowering perennials, shrubs and scrambling climbers, grown for their flowers and foliage. Frost tender, min. 15–18°C (59–64°F). Requires full light or partial shade and fertile, well-drained soil. Water potted plants freely when in full growth, less at other times. Tip prune young plants to promote a branching habit. Propagate by greenwood cuttings in spring or summer. Is prone to whitefly and soft scale.
S. nobilis of gardens. See *S. speciosa*.
S. speciosa, syn. *S. nobilis* of gardens, illus. p.173.

Sand phlox. See *Phlox bifida*, illus. p.393.

SANDERSONIA

LILIACEAE/COLCHICACEAE

Genus of one species of deciduous, tuberous climber with urn-shaped flowers in summer. Half hardy. Needs a sheltered, sunny site and well-drained soil. Support with sticks or canes. Lift tubers for winter. Propagate in spring by seed or by naturally divided tubers.
S. aurantiaca illus. p.439.

Sandwort. See *Arenaria*.

SANGUINARIA

PAPAVERACEAE

Genus of one species of spring-flowering, rhizomatous perennial. Fully hardy. Grow in sun or semi-shade and in humus-rich, moist but well-drained soil. Propagate by division of rhizomes in summer or by seed in autumn.
S. canadensis illus. p.375. ♀ **'Plena'** (syn. *S.c.* 'Flore Pleno') is a clump-forming, rhizomatous perennial with fleshy, underground stems that exude red sap when cut. H 15cm (6in), S 30–45cm (12–18in). Short-lived, rounded, fully double, white flowers emerge in spring followed by large, rounded to heart-shaped, scalloped, grey-green leaves with glaucous undersides.

SANGUISORBA
Burnet

ROSACEAE

Genus of perennials, grown for their bottlebrush-like flower spikes. Fully hardy. Requires sun and moist soil. Propagate by division in spring or by seed in autumn.
S. canadensis illus. p.224.
S. obtusa. Clump-forming perennial. H 1–1.2m (3–4ft), S 60cm (2ft). Arching stems bear spikes of rose-crimson flowers in mid-summer. Pairs of oval leaflets are pale green above, blue-green beneath.
S. officinalis (Great burnet). **'Rubra'** is a clump-forming perennial. H 1.2m (4ft), S 60cm (2ft). Produces small spikes of red-brown flowers in late summer above a mass of mid-green leaves, divided into oval leaflets.

SANSEVIERIA

AGAVACEAE/DRACAENACEAE

Genus of evergreen, rhizomatous perennials, grown for their rosettes of stiff, fleshy leaves. Frost tender, min. 10–15°C (50–59°F). Tolerates sun and shade and is easy to grow in most soil conditions if not overwatered. Propagate by leaf cuttings or division in summer.
S. cylindrica. Evergreen, stemless, rhizomatous perennial. H 45cm–1.2m (1½–4ft), S 10cm (4in). Has a rosette of 3–4 cylindrical, stiff, fleshy, erect leaves, to 1.2m (4ft) long, in dark green with paler horizontal bands. Racemes of small, tubular, 6-lobed, pink or white flowers are occasionally produced.
S. trifasciata (Mother-in-law's tongue). Evergreen, stemless, rhizomatous perennial. H 45cm–1.2m (1½–4ft), S 10cm (4in). Has a rosette of about 5lance-shaped, pointed, stiff, fleshy, erect leaves, to 1.2m (4ft) long, banded horizontally with pale green and yellow. Occasionally carries racemes of tubular, 6-lobed, green flowers.
♀ **'Golden Hahnii'** illus. p.317.
♀ **'Hahnii'** illus. p.315.
♀ **'Laurentii'** illus. p.275.

SANTOLINA

COMPOSITAE/ASTERACEAE

Genus of evergreen, summer-flowering shrubs, grown for their aromatic foliage and their button-like flower heads, each on a long stem. Frost hardy. Needs sun and not too rich, well-drained soil. Cut off old flower heads and reduce long shoots in autumn. Cut straggly, old plants back hard each spring. Propagate by semi-ripe cuttings in summer.
S. chamaecyparissus, syn. *S. incana* (Cotton lavender, Lavender cotton). Evergreen, rounded, dense shrub. H 75cm (2½ft), S 1m (3ft). Shoots are covered with woolly, white growth, and narrowly oblong, finely toothed leaves are also white. Bright yellow flower heads are borne in mid- and late summer.
S. incana. See *S. chamaecyparissus*.
S. neapolitana. See *S. pinnata* subsp. *neapolitana*.
S. pinnata. Evergreen shrub, mainly grown as ♀ subsp. ***neapolitana*** (syn. *S. neapolitana*), which is of rounded and bushy habit. H 75cm (2½ft), S 1m (3ft). Slender flower stems bear a head of lemon-yellow flowers in mid-summer, among feathery, deeply cut, grey-green foliage. subsp. ***neapolitana*** **'Sulphurea'** illus. p.165.
S. rosmarinifolia, syn. *S. virens* (Holy flax). Evergreen, bushy, dense shrub. H 60cm (2ft), S 1m (3ft). Has finely cut, bright green leaves. Each slender stem produces a head of bright yellow flowers in mid-summer. ♀ **'Primrose Gem'** has pale yellow flower heads.
S. virens. See *S. rosmarinifolia*.

SANVITALIA

COMPOSITAE/ASTERACEAE

Genus of perennials and annuals. Fully hardy. Grow in sun and in fertile, well-drained soil. Propagate by seed sown outdoors in spring or early autumn.
S. procumbens illus. p.348.
'Mandarin Orange' illus. p.353.

SAPIUM

EUPHORBIACEAE

Genus of evergreen trees, grown for their ornamental appearance. Has poisonous, milky sap. Frost tender, min. 5°C (41°F). Prefers fertile, well-drained soil and full light. Water containerized plants freely when in full growth, less at other times. Pruning is tolerated if necessary. Propagate by seed in spring or by semi-ripe cuttings in summer.
S. sebiferum (Chinese tallow tree). Fast-growing, evergreen, erect to spreading tree. H to 8m (25ft), S 4m (12ft) or more. Rhombic to oval, mid-green leaves turn red with age. Clusters of tiny, greenish-yellow flowers develop into rounded, black fruits covered by a layer of white wax.

SAPONARIA
Soapwort

CARYOPHYLLACEAE

Genus of summer-flowering annuals and perennials, grown for their flowers. Is good for rock gardens, screes and banks. Fully hardy. Needs sun and well-drained soil. Propagate by seed in spring or autumn or by softwood cuttings in early summer.
♀ ***S.*** **'Bressingham',** syn. *S.* 'Bressingham Hybrid'. Loose, mat-forming perennial. H 8cm (3in), S 10cm (4in). Has small, narrowly oval leaves. Flattish, deep vibrant pink flowers are produced in clustered heads in summer. Is good for a trough.
S. caespitosa illus. p.390.
♀ ***S. ocymoides*** illus. p.390.
S. officinalis **'Rubra Plena'** (Double soapwort). Upright perennial. H to 1m (3ft), S 30cm (1ft). Has oval, rough, mid-green leaves on erect stems. Clusters of ragged, double, red flowers are produced from leaf axils on upper part of flower stems in summer.
♀ ***S. × olivana*** illus. p.388.

Sapphire berry. See *Symplocos paniculata*, illus. p.134.
Sarana, Black. See *Fritillaria camschatcensis*, illus. p.429.

SARCOCAPNOS

PAPAVERACEAE

Genus of spring-flowering perennials. Is useful for rock gardens. Frost hardy. Prefers sun and well-drained, alkaline soil. Propagate by seed in spring.
S. enneaphylla. Loose, upright perennial. H and S 15cm (6in). Slender, much-branched stems bear small, much-divided, glaucous green leaves with oval to rounded segments. In spring, small, spurred, yellowish-white flowers, tipped with purple, are produced in short racemes. Protect from winter wet.

SARCOCOCCA
Christmas box, Sweet box

BUXACEAE

Genus of evergreen shrubs, grown for their foliage, fragrant, winter flowers and spherical fruits. Flowers are tiny – the only conspicuous part being the anthers. Is useful for cutting in winter. Fully to frost hardy. Grows in sun or shade and in fertile, not too dry soil. Propagate by semi-ripe cuttings in summer or by seed in autumn.
♀ ***S. confusa.*** Evergreen, bushy, dense shrub. H and S 1m (3ft). Fully hardy. Leaves are small, oval, taper-pointed, glossy and dark green. Has tiny, white flowers in winter, then black fruits.
♀ ***S. hookeriana.*** Evergreen, upright, dense, suckering shrub. H 1.5m (5ft), S 2m (6ft). Fully hardy. Forms clumps of narrowly oblong, pointed, dark green leaves and has tiny, white flowers in the leaf axils during winter. Fruits are black. ♀ var. ***digyna*** illus. p.170. var. ***humilis*** see *S. humilis*.
S. humilis, syn. *S. hookeriana* var. *humilis*, illus. p.170.
S. ruscifolia. Evergreen, upright, arching shrub. H and S 1m (3ft). Frost hardy. Has oval, glossy, dark green

leaves and, in winter, creamy-white flowers, then red fruits. ♀ var. ***chinensis*** has narrower leaves.

Sargent cherry. See *Prunus sargentii*, illus. p.83.
Sargent's rowan. See *Sorbus sargentiana*.

SARMIENTA

GESNERIACEAE

Genus of one species of evergreen, woody-stemmed, scrambling or trailing perennial. Suits hanging baskets. Half hardy. Likes semi-shade and humus-rich soil that does not dry out. Propagate by seed in spring or by stem cuttings in summer or autumn.
♀ ***S. repens***, syn. *S. scandens*. Evergreen, slender-stemmed, scrambling perennial. H and S 60cm (2ft) or more. Tips of oval leaves each have 3–5 teeth. In summer produces small, tubular, coral-pink flowers, each narrowed at the base and towards the mouth, which has 5 deeper pink lobes.
S. scandens. See *S. repens*.

SARRACENIA
Pitcher plant

SARRACENIACEAE

Genus of insectivorous perennials, some of which are evergreen, with pitchers formed from modified leaves with hooded tops. Frost tender, min. 5°C (41°F). Grow in sun or partial shade and in peat and moss. Keep very wet, except in winter, when drier conditions are needed. Propagate by seed in spring.
♀ ***S. flava*** illus. p.302.
S. purpurea (Common pitcher plant, Huntsman's cup). Evergreen, erect to semi-prostrate, rosette-forming perennial. H 30cm (12in), S 30–38cm (12–15in). Inflated, green pitchers, to 15cm (6in) long, are tinged and veined purplish-red. In spring, 5-petalled, purple flowers, 5cm (2in) or more wide, are carried well above pitchers.

Sarsparilla, Australian. See *Hardenbergia violacea*.

SASA

GRAMINEAE/POACEAE

See also GRASSES, BAMBOOS, RUSHES and SEDGES.
S. albomarginata. See *S. veitchii*.
♀ ***S. palmata.*** Evergreen, spreading bamboo. H 2m (6ft), S indefinite. Frost hardy. Afine foliage plant, it produces very broad, rich green leaves, to 40cm (16in) long. Hollow, purple-streaked stems have one branch at each node. Flower spikes are unimportant.
S. veitchii, syn. *S. albomarginata*, illus. p.318.

SASSAFRAS

LAURACEAE

Genus of deciduous trees, with inconspicuous flowers, grown for their aromatic foliage. Fully hardy. Needs sun or light shade and deep, fertile, well-drained, preferably acid soil. Propagate by seed or suckers in autumn or by root cuttings in winter.
S. albidum illus. p.64.

Sassafras
Australian. See *Atherosperma moschatum*.
Tasmanian. See *Atherosperma moschatum*.
Satin flower, New Zealand. See *Libertia grandiflora*, illus. p.241.

SATUREJA

LABIATAE/LAMIACEAE

Genus of summer-flowering annuals, semi-evergreen perennials and sub-shrubs, grown for their highly aromatic leaves and attractive flowers. Is useful for rock gardens and dry banks. Fully hardy. Needs sun and well-drained soil. Propagate by seed in winter or spring or by softwood cuttings in summer.
S. montana (Winter savory). Semi-evergreen, upright perennial or sub-shrub. H 30cm (12in), S 20cm (8in) or more. Leaves are linear to oval, aromatic and green or greyish-green. Carries loose whorls of tubular, 2-lipped, lavender flowers in summer. **'Prostrate White'**, H 7–15cm (3–6in), has a prostrate habit and produces white flowers.

SAUROMATUM

ARACEAE

Genus of spring-flowering, tuberous perennials with tubular spathes that expand into waved, twisted blades. Tubers will flower without soil or moisture, and before leaves appear. Frost tender, min. 5–7°C (41–5°F). Needs a sheltered, semi-shaded position and humus-rich, well-drained soil. Water well in summer. Dry off or lift when dormant in winter. Propagate by offsets in spring.
S. guttatum. See *S. venosum*.
S. venosum, syn. *S. guttatum*, illus. p.429.

SAURURUS

SAURURACEAE

Genus of deciduous, perennial, bog and marginal water plants, grown for their foliage. Fully hardy. Prefers full sun, but tolerates some shade. Remove faded leaves and divide plants as required to maintain vigour. Propagate by division in spring.
S. cernuus illus. p.463.

Sausage tree. See *Kigelia africana*.
Savin. See *Juniperus sabina*.
Savory, Winter. See *Satureja montana*.
Saw palmetto. See *Serenoa repens*.
Sawara cypress. See *Chamaecyparis pisifera*.
Sawfly orchid. See *Ophrys tenthredinifera*, illus. p.309.
Sawtooth oak. See *Quercus acutissima*.

SAXEGOTHAEA

PODOCARPACEAE

See also CONIFERS.
S. conspicua (Prince Albert's yew). Conifer that is conical in mild areas, more bushy in cold districts. H 5–15m (15–50ft), S 4–5m (12–15ft). Fully hardy. Needle-like, flattened, dark green leaves are produced in whorls at ends of shoots. Bears globose, fleshy, glaucous green cones.

SAXIFRAGA
Saxifrage

SAXIFRAGACEAE

Genus of often rosetted perennials, most of which are evergreen or semi-evergreen, grown for their flowers and attractive foliage. Is excellent in rock gardens, raised beds and alpine houses. Fully to half hardy. Propagate by seed in autumn or by rooted offsets in winter. For cultivation, saxifrages may be grouped as follows:

1 – Needs protection from midday sunand moist soil.
2 – Needs semi-shaded, well-drainedsoil. Is good among rocks and screes.
3 – Thrives in well-drained rockpockets, troughs, alpine-house pansetc, shaded from midday sun. Must never be dry at roots. Most form tight cushions and flower in early spring, flower stems being barely visible above leaves.
4 – Needs full sun and well-drained,alkaline soil. Suits rock pockets. Mosthave hard leaves encrusted in lime.

S. aizoides. Evergreen perennial forming a loose mat. H 15cm (6in), S 30cm (12in) or more. Fully hardy. Has small, narrowly oval, fleshy, shiny, green leaves and, in spring-summer, terminal racemes of star-shaped, bright yellow or orange flowers, often spotted red, on 8cm (3in) stems. Cultivation group 1.
S. aizoon. See *S. paniculata*.
♀ ***S. × anglica* 'Cranbourne'**, syn. *S.* 'Cranbourne'. Evergreen, cushion-forming perennial. H and S 12cm (5in). Fully hardy. In early spring produces solitary, cup-shaped, bright purplish-lilac flowers on short stems just above tight rosettes of linear, green leaves. Flower stems are longer if plant is grown in an alpine house. Cultivation group 3.
♀ ***S. × apiculata* 'GregorMendel',** syn. *S.* 'Gregor Mendel', illus. p.383; Cultivation group 2.
***S.* 'Arco'.** See. *S. × arco-valleyi* 'Arco'.
***S. × arco-valleyi* 'Arco',** syn. *S.* 'Arco'. Evergreen perennial forming a tight cushion. H and S 10cm (4in). Fully hardy. In early spring produces upturned, cup-shaped to flattish, pale lilac flowers almost resting on tight rosettes of oblong to linear leaves. Cultivation group 3.
***S.* 'Bob Hawkins'.** Evergreen perennial with a loose rosette of leaves. H 2.5–5cm (1–2in), S 15cm (6in). Fully hardy. Carries small, upturned, rounded, greenish-white flowers in summer on 5cm (2in) stems. Oval, green leaves are white-splashed. Cultivation group 1.
***S. × boydii* 'Hindhead Seedling'** illus. p.383; cultivation group 2.
***S.* 'Brookside'.** See *S. burseriana* 'Brookside'.
S. brunoniana. See *S. brunonis*.
S. brunonis, syn. *S. brunoniana*. Semi-evergreen, rosetted perennial. H 10cm (4in), S 20cm (8in). Frost hardy. Small, soft green rosettes of lance-shaped, rigid leaves produce masses of long, thread-like, red runners. Many of the rosettes die down to large terminal buds in winter. Short racemes of 5-petalled, spreading, pale yellow flowers are produced in late spring and summer on 5–8cm (2–3in) stems. Is difficult to grow; cultivation group 1.
S. burseriana illus. p.375. **'Brookside'** (syn. *S.* 'Brookside') is a slow-growing, evergreen perennial forming a hard cushion. H 2.5–5cm (1–2in), Sto 10cm (4in). Fully hardy. Has broadly linear, spiky, grey-green leaves. In early spring bears upturned, rounded, shallowly cup-shaped, bright yellow flowers on short, red stems. Flowers of **'Crenata'** (syn. *S.*'Crenata') have fringed, white petals and red sepals.
♀ **'Gloria'** (syn. *S.*'Gloria') has dark reddish-brown stems, each bearing 1 or 2 flowers, with red sepals and white petals, in late spring. Cultivation group 3.
♀ ***S. callosa***, syn. *S. lingulata*. Evergreen, tightly rosetted perennial. H 25cm (10in), S to 20cm (8in). Fully hardy. Bears long, linear, stiff, lime-encrusted leaves and, in early summer, upright, then arching panicles of star-shaped, white flowers with red-spotted petals. Rosettes die after flowering; new ones are produced annually from short stolons. Cultivation group 4.
S. cochlearis. Evergreen, rosetted perennial. H 20cm (8in), S 25cm (10in). Fully hardy. Has spoon-shaped, green leaves with white-encrusted edges. Produces loose panicles of rounded, white flowers, often with red-spotted petals, in early summer.
♀ **'Minor'**, H and S 12cm (5in), has smaller leaf rosettes and loose panicles of red-spotted, white flowers on red stems. Is ideal for a trough. Cultivation group 4.
S. cortusifolia var. ***fortunei.*** See *S. fortunei*.
S. cotyledon Evergreen perennial. H and S to 30cm (12in). Fully hardy. Has large, pale green rosettes of leaves, which die after flowering. In late spring and early summer produces arching, conical panicles of cup-shaped, white flowers sometimes strongly marked red internally. Cultivation group 2.
***S.* 'Cranbourne'.** See *S. × anglica* 'Cranbourne'.
***S.* 'Crenata'.** See *S. burseriana* 'Crenata'.
S. cuneifolia illus. p.363; cultivation group 1.
***S.* 'Elisabethae',** syn. *S. × elisabethae*, illus. p.383; cultivation group 2.
S. exarata subsp. ***moschata,*** syn. *S. moschata*. Evergreen perennial forming a loose to tight hummock. H and S 10cm (4in). Fully hardy. Rosettes comprise small, lance-shaped, sometimes 3-toothed, green leaves. Bears 2–5 star-shaped, creamy-white or dull yellow flowers on slender stems in summer. **'Cloth of Gold'** illus. p.403. Cultivation group 1.
♀ ***S. federici-augustii*** subsp. ***grisebachii* 'Wisley Variety',** syn. *S. grisebachii* 'Wisley Variety', illus. p.379; cultivation group 4.
♀ ***S. ferdinandi-coburgi.*** Evergreen, cushion-forming perennial. H and S 15cm (6in). Fully hardy. Forms rosettes of linear, spiny, glaucous green leaves and, in early spring, bears racemes of open cup-shaped, rich yellow flowers on stems 3–10cm (1–4in) long. Cultivation group 3.
♀ ***S. fortunei***, syn. *S. cortusifolia* var.

fortunei. Semi-evergreen or herbaceous, clump-forming perennial. H and S 30cm (12in). Frost hardy. Has rounded, 5- or 7-lobed, fleshy, green or brownish-green leaves, red beneath. In autumn produces panicles of tiny, moth-like, white flowers, with 4 equal-sized petals and one elongated petal, on upright stems. Propagate by division in spring. **'Rubrifolia'** has dark red flower stems and dark reddish-green leaves with beetroot-red undersides. Cultivation group 1.
S. × geum illus. p.359; cultivation group 1.
***S.* 'Gloria'.** See *S. burseriana* 'Gloria'.
S. granulata (Fair maids of France, Meadow saxifrage) illus. p.358. **'Plena'** is a clump-forming perennial. H 23–38cm (9–15in), S to 15cm (6in) or more. Fully hardy. Loses its kidney-shaped, glossy, pale to mid-green leaves soon after flowering. Has a loose panicle of large, rounded, double, white flowers in late spring or early summer. Bulbils or resting buds form at base of foliage. Cultivation group 1.
***S.* 'Gregor Mendel'.** See *S. × apiculata* 'Gregor Mendel'.
***S. grisebachii* 'Wisley Variety'.** See *S. frederici-augustii* subsp. *grisebachii* 'Wisley Variety'.
S. hirsuta illus. p.359; cultivation group 1.
***S.* 'Irvingii'.** See *S. × irvingii* 'Walter Irving'.
♡ ***S. × irvingii* 'Jenkinsiae',** syn. *S.* 'Jenkinsiae', illus. p.377; cultivation group 2. **'Walter Irving'** (syn. *S.* 'Irvingii') is a very slow-growing, evergreen, hard-domed perennial. H 2cm (¾in), S 8cm (3in). Fully hardy. Bears minute leaves in rosettes. Stemless, cup-shaped, lilac-pink flowers open in early spring. Cultivation group 3.
***S.* 'Jenkinsiae'.** See *S. × irvingii* 'Jenkinsiae'.
S. lingulata. See *S. callosa*.
S. longifolia. Rosetted perennial. H 60cm (24in), S 20–25cm (8–10in). Fully hardy. Has long, narrow, lime-encrusted leaves forming attractive rosettes that, after 3–4 years, develop long, arching, conical to cylindrical panicles bearing numerous rounded, 5-petalled, white flowers in late spring and summer. Rosettes die after flowering, and no daughter rosettes are formed, so propagate by seed in spring or autumn. In cultivation, hybridizes readily with other related species. Cultivation group 4.
S. moschata. See *S. exarata* subsp. *moschata*.
S. oppositifolia illus. p.378. **'Ruth Draper'** is an evergreen, loose mat-forming perennial. H 2.5–5cm (1–2in), S 15cm (6in). Fully hardy. Has small, opposite, oblong to oval, white-flecked, dark green leaves closely set along prostrate stems. Large, cup-shaped, deep purple-pink flowers appear in early spring just above foliage. Prefers peaty soil. Cultivation group 1.
S. paniculata, syn. *S. aizoon*. Evergreen, tightly rosetted perennial. H 15–30cm (6–12in), S 20cm (8in). Fully hardy. In summer produces loose panicles of rounded, usually white flowers, with or without purplish-red spots, on upright stems above rosettes of oblong to oval, lime-encrusted leaves. Is very variable in size. Pale yellow or pale pink forms also occur. Cultivation group 4.
S. × primulaize, syn. *S.* 'Primulaize'. Evergreen, loosely rosetted perennial. H and S 15cm (6in). Fully hardy. In summer, branched flower stems, 5–8cm (2–3in) long, produce star-shaped, salmon-pink flowers. Leaves are tiny, narrowly oval, slightly indented and fleshy. Cultivation group 1.
S. sancta illus. p.383; cultivation group 2.
S. sarmentosa. See *S. stolonifera*.
S. scardica illus. p.374; cultivation group 3.
S. sempervivum illus. p.379; cultivation group 3.
♡ ***S.* 'Southside Seedling'** illus. p.364; cultivation group 4.
♡ ***S. stolonifera***, syn. *S. sarmentosa* (Mother of thousands). Evergreen, prostrate perennial with runners. H 15cm (6in) or more, S 30cm (12in) or more. Frost hardy. Has large, rounded, shallowly lobed, hairy, silver-veined, olive-green leaves that are reddish-purple beneath. Loose panicles of tiny, moth-like, white flowers, each with 4 equal-sized petals and one elongated petal, appear in summer on slender, upright stems. Makes good ground cover. ♡ **'Tricolor'** (syn. *S.* 'Tricolor'; *Strawberry geranium*) has green-and-red leaves with silver marks and is half hardy. Cultivation group 1.
S. stribrnyi illus. p.380; cultivation group 3.
***S.* 'Tricolor'.** See *S. stolonifera* 'Tricolor'.
♡ ***S.* 'Tumbling Waters'** illus. p.359; cultivation group 4.
♡ ***S. × urbium*** (London pride). Evergreen, rosetted, spreading perennial. H 30cm (12in), S indefinite. Fully hardy. Has spoon-shaped, toothed, leathery, green leaves. Flower stems bear tiny, star-shaped, at times pink-flushed, white flowers, with red spots, in summer. Is useful as ground cover. Cultivation group 1.
***S.* 'Valerie Finnis'.** Evergreen, hard cushion-forming perennial. H and S 10cm (4in). Fully hardy. Short, red stems carry upturned, cup-shaped, sulphur-yellow flowers above tight rosettes of oval, green leaves in spring. Cultivation group 3.

Saxifrage. See *Saxifraga*.
Meadow. See *Saxifraga granulata*, illus. p.358.
Purple mountain. See *Saxifraga oppositifolia*, illus. p.378.

SCABIOSA
Scabious

DIPSACACEAE

Genus of annuals and perennials, some of which are evergreen, with flower heads that are good for cutting. Fully to frost hardy. Prefers sun and fertile, well-drained, alkaline soil. Propagate annuals by seed in spring and perennials by cuttings of young, basal growths in summer, by seed in autumn or by division in early spring.
S. arvensis. See *Knautia arvensis*.
S. atropurpurea (Sweet scabious). Moderately fast-growing, upright, bushy annual. H to 1m (3ft), S 20–30cm (8–12in). Fully hardy. Has lance-shaped, lobed, mid-green leaves. Domed heads of scented, pincushion-like, deep crimson flower heads, 5cm (2in) wide, are produced on wiry stems in summer and early autumn. Tall forms, H 1m (3ft), and dwarf, H 45cm (18in), are available with flower heads in shades of blue, purple, red, pink or white.
♡ ***S. caucasica.* 'Clive Greaves'** illus. p.295. **'Floral Queen'** is a clump-forming perennial. H and S 60cm (24in). Fully hardy. Large, frilled, violet-blue flower heads, with pincushion-like centres, are produced throughout summer. Light green leaves are lance-shaped at base of plant and segmented on stems. ♡ **'Miss Willmott'** has creamy-white flowers.
S. columbaria* var. *ochroleuca. See *S. ochroleuca*.
S. graminifolia. Evergreen, clump-forming perennial, often with a woody base. H and S 15–25cm (6–10in). Frost hardy. Has tufts of narrow, grass-like, pointed, silver-haired leaves. In summer produces stiff stems with spherical, bluish-violet to lilac flower heads like pincushions. Resents disturbance. Suits a rock garden.
S. lucida illus. p.367.
S. ochroleuca, syn. *S. columbaria* var. *ochroleuca*. Clump-forming perennial. H and S 1m (3ft). Fully hardy. In late summer, branching stems carry many heads of frilled, sulphur-yellow flower heads with pincushion-like centres. Has narrowly oval, toothed, grey-green leaves.
S. rumelica. See *Knautia macedonica*.

Scabious. See *Knautia arvensis; Scabiosa*.
Giant. See *Cephalaria gigantea*.
Sweet. See *Scabiosa atropurpurea*.
Yellow. See *Cephalaria gigantea*.

SCADOXUS

AMARYLLIDACEAE

Genus of bulbs with dense, mainly spherical, umbels of red flowers. Frost tender, min. 10–15°C (50–59°F). Requires partial shade and humus-rich, well-drained soil. Reduce watering in winter, when not in active growth. Propagate by seed or offsets in spring.
S. multiflorus, syn. *Haemanthus multiflorus*. Summer-flowering bulb. H to 70cm (28in), S 30–45cm (12–18in). Has broadly lance-shaped, semi-erect, basal leaves. Produces a spherical umbel, 10–15cm (4–6in) wide, of up to 200 narrow-petalled flowers. ♡ subsp. ***katherinae*** (syn. *Haemanthus katherinae*) illus. p.413.
S. puniceus, syn. *Haemanthus magnificus, H. natalensis, H. puniceus* (Royal paintbrush). Spring- and summer-flowering bulb. H 30–40cm (12–16in), S 30–45cm (12–18in). Has elliptic, semi-erect leaves in a basal cluster. Leaf bases are joined, forming a false stem. Flower stem bears up to 100 tubular, orange-red flowers in a conical umbel surrounded by a whorl of red bracts.

Scarlet ball cactus. See *Parodia haselbergii* subsp. *haselbergii*, illus p.491.
Scarlet banana. See *Musa coccinea*.
Scarlet fritillary. See *Fritillaria recurva*, illus. p.408.
Scarlet oak. See *Quercus coccinea*, illus. p.66.
Scarlet plume. See *Euphorbia fulgens*.
Scarlet trompetilla. See *Bouvardia ternifolia*, illus. p.169.
Scarlet trumpet honeysuckle. See *Lonicera × brownii*.
Scarlet turkscap lily. See *Lilium chalcedonicum*, illus. p.419.
Scented paper-bark. See *Melaleuca squarrosa*.

SCHEFFLERA,
syn. BRASSAIA, HEPTAPLEURUM

ARALIACEAE

Genus of evergreen shrubs and trees, grown mainly for their handsome foliage. Half hardy to frost tender, min. 3–16°C (37–61°F). Grows in any fertile, well-drained but moisture-retentive soil and in full light or partial shade. Water potted specimens freely when in full growth, moderately at other times. Pruning is tolerated if needed. Propagate by air-layering in spring, by semi-ripe cuttings in summer or by seed as soon as ripe, in late summer.
♡ ***S. actinophylla*** illus. p.80.
♡ ***S. arboricola.*** Evergreen, erect, well-branched shrub or tree. H 2–5m (6–15ft), S 1–3m (3–10ft). Frost tender, min. 15°C (59°F). Leaves each have 7–16 oval, stalked, glossy, deep green leaflets. Mature plants carry small, spherical heads of tiny, green flowers in spring-summer.
S. digitata. Evergreen, rounded to ovoid shrub or bushy tree. H and S 3–8m (10–25ft). Frost tender, min. 5°C (41°F). Leaves are hand-shaped, with 5–10 oval, glossy, rich green leaflets. Has tiny, greenish flowers in large, terminal panicles in spring and tiny, globular, dark violet fruits in autumn.
♡ ***S. elegantissima***, syn. *Aralia elegantissima, Dizygotheca elegantissima*, illus. p.123.

SCHIMA

THEACEAE

Genus of one species of very variable, evergreen tree or shrub, grown for its foliage and flowers. Is related to *Camellia*. Frost tender, min. 3–5°C (37–41°F). Prefers humus-rich, well-drained, neutral to acid soil and sun or partial shade. Water potted plants freely in full growth, moderately at other times. Pruning is tolerated if necessary. Propagate by seed as soon as ripe or by semi-ripe cuttings in summer.
S. wallichii. Robust, evergreen, ovoid tree or shrub. H 25–30m (80–100ft), S 12m (40ft) or more. Elliptic to oblong, red-veined, dark green leaves are 10–18cm (4–7in) long, red-flushed beneath. In late summer has solitary fragrant, cup-shaped, white flowers, 4cm (1½in) wide, red-flushed in bud.

SCHINUS

ANACARDIACEAE

Genus of evergreen shrubs and trees, grown mainly for their foliage and for shade. Frost tender, min. 5°C (41°F). Grows in any freely draining soil and in full light. Water potted specimens moderately, hardly at all in winter. Propagate by seed in spring or by semi-ripe cuttings in summer.
S. molle (Californian pepper-tree, Peruvian mastic tree, Peruvian pepper-tree). Fast-growing, evergreen, weeping tree. H and S to 8m (25ft). Fern-like leaves are divided into many narrowly lance-shaped, glossy, rich green leaflets. Has open clusters of tiny, yellow flowers from late winter to summer, followed by pea-sized, pink-red fruits.
S. terebinthifolius. Evergreen shrub or tree, usually of bushy, spreading habit. H 3m (10ft) or more, S 2–3m (6–10ft) or more. Leaves have 3–13 oval, mid- to deep green leaflets. Tiny, white flowers are borne in clusters in summer-autumn, followed by pea-sized, red fruits, but only if plants of both sexes are grown close together.

SCHISANDRA

SCHISANDRACEAE

Genus of deciduous, woody-stemmed, twining climbers. Male and female flowers are borne on separate plants, so grow plants of both sexes if fruits are required. Is useful for growing against shady walls and training up pillars and fences. Frost hardy. Grow in sun or partial shade and rich, well-drained soil. Propagate by greenwood or semi-ripe cuttings in summer.
S. grandiflora var. ***rubriflora.*** See *S. rubriflora.*
S. henryi. Deciduous, woody-stemmed, twining climber, with stems that are angled and winged when young. H 3–4m (10–12ft). Glossy, green leaves are oval or heart-shaped. Small, cup-shaped, white flowers appear in spring. Pendent spikes, 5–7cm (2–3in) long, of spherical, fleshy, red fruits are borne in late summer on female plants.
S. rubriflora, syn. *S. grandiflora* var. *rubriflora*, illus. p.207.

SCHIZANTHUS

Butterfly flower, Poor man's orchid

SOLANACEAE

Genus of annuals, grown for their showy flowers. Makes excellent pot plants. Half hardy to frost tender, min. 5°C (41°F). Grow in a sunny, sheltered position and in fertile, well-drained soil. Pinch out growing tips of young plants to ensure a bushy habit. Propagate by seed sown under glass in early spring for summer-autumn flowers and in late summer for plants to flower in pots in late winter or spring. Is prone to damage by aphids.
***S.* 'Dwarf Bouquet'** illus. p.334.
S. pinnatus illus. p.342.
***S.* 'Star Parade'.** Compact annual with a distinctive pyramidal habit. H 20–25cm (8–10in), S 23–30cm (9–12in). Frost tender, min. 5°C (41°F). Has almost fern-like, light green leaves. From spring to autumn, bears tubular, then flared, 2-lipped, white, yellow, pink, purple, or red flowers.

Schizocentron elegans. See *Heterocentron elegans.*

SCHIZOPETALON

CRUCIFERAE/BRASSICACEAE

Genus of annuals. Half hardy. Grow in sun and in well-drained, fertile soil. Propagate by seed sown under glass in spring.
S. walkeri. Moderately fast-growing, upright, slightly branching annual. H 45cm (18in), S 20cm (8in). Has deeply divided, mid-green leaves and, in summer, almond-scented, white flowers with deeply cut and fringed petals.

SCHIZOPHRAGMA

HYDRANGEACEAE

Genus of deciduous, woody-stemmed, root climbers, useful for training up large trees. Frost hardy. Flowers best in sun, but will grow against a north-facing wall. Needs well-drained soil. Tie young plants to supports. Propagate by seed in spring or by greenwood or semi-ripe cuttings in summer.
S. hydrangeoides (Japanese hydrangea vine). Deciduous, woody-stemmed, root climber. H to 12m (40ft). Broadly oval leaves are 10–15cm (4–6in) long. Small, white or creamy-white flowers, in flat heads 20–25cm (8–10in) across, are produced on pendent side-branches in summer; these are surrounded by marginal, sterile flowers, which each have an oval or heart-shaped, pale yellow sepal, 2–4cm (¾–1½in) long.
♀ ***S. integrifolium*** illus. p.204.
S. viburnoides. See *Pileostegia viburnoides.*

SCHIZOSTYLIS

Kaffir lily

IRIDACEAE

Genus of rhizomatous perennials with flowers that are excellent for cutting. Frost hardy. Requires sun and fertile, moist soil. Divide in spring every few years to avoid congestion.
♀ ***S. coccinea* 'Major'**, syn. *S.c* 'Grandiflora', illus. p.306. **'Mrs Hegarty'** is a vigorous, clump-forming, rhizomatous perennial. H 60cm (24in), S 23–30cm (9–12in). In mid-autumn produces spikes of shallowly cup-shaped, pale pink flowers above tufts of grass-like, mid-green leaves. ♀ **'Sunrise'** illus. p.306. **'Viscountess Byng'** has pink flowers that last until late autumn.

SCHLUMBERGERA

CACTACEAE

Genus of bushy, perennial cacti with erect, then pendent stems and flattened, oblong stem segments with indented notches at margins – like teeth in some species. Stem tips produce flowers with prominent stigmas and stamens and with petals of different lengths set in 2 rows. In the wild, often grows over mossy rocks, rooting at ends of stem segments. Frost tender, min. 10°C (50°F). Needs partial shade and rich, well-drained soil. Propagate by stem cuttings in spring or early summer.
***S.* 'Bristol Beauty'** illus. p.491.
♀ ***S.* × *buckleyi***, syn. (Christmas cactus). Erect, then pendent, perennial cactus. H 15cm (6in), S 1m (3ft). Has glossy, green stem segments and produces red-violet flowers in mid-winter.
***S.* 'Gold Charm'** illus. p.488.
S. truncata, syn. *Zygocactus truncatus* (Lobster cactus) illus. p.489.
***S.* 'Wintermärchen'.** Erect, then pendent, perennial cactus. H 15cm (6in), S 30cm (12in). Has glossy, green stem segments. In early autumn bears white flowers that become pink-and-white in winter.
***S.* 'Zara'.** Erect, then pendent, perennial cactus. H 15cm (6in), S 30cm (12in). Has glossy, green stem segments. Bears deep orange-red flowers in early autumn and winter.

SCHOENOPLECTUS

CYPERACEAE

See also GRASSES, BAMBOOS, RUSHES and SEDGES.
S. lacustris subsp. ***tabernaemontani* 'Zebrinus'**, syn. *Scirpus lacustris* var. *tabernaemontani* 'Zebrinus', *Scirpus tabernaemontani* 'Zebrinus', illus. p.318.

SCHWANTESIA

AIZOACEAE

Genus of cushion-forming, perennial succulents with stemless rosettes of unequal-sized pairs of keeled leaves and daisy-like, yellow flowers. Frost tender, min. 5°C (41°F). Needs full sun and well-drained soil. Propagate by seed or stem cuttings in spring or summer.
S. ruedebuschii illus. p.494.

SCIADOPITYS

SCIADOPITYACEAE

See also CONIFERS.
♀ ***S. verticillata*** illus. p.102.

SCILLA

LILIACEAE/HYACINTHACEAE

Genus of mainly spring- and summer-flowering bulbs with leaves in basal clusters and spikes of small, often blue flowers. Fully to half hardy. Needs an open site, sun or partial shade and well-drained soil. Propagate by division in late summer or by seed in autumn.
S. adlamii. See *Ledebouria cooperi.*
♀ ***S. bifolia.*** Early spring-flowering bulb. H 5–15cm (2–6in), S 2.5–5cm (1–2in). Fully hardy. Has 2 narrowly strap-shaped, semi-erect, basal leaves that widen towards tips. Stem produces one-sided spike of up to 20 star-shaped, purple-blue, pink or white flowers.
S. campanulata. See *Hyacinthoides hispanica.*
S. chinensis. See *S. scilloides.*
S. cooperi. See *Ledebouria cooperi.*
S. hispanica. See *Hyacinthoides* × *massartiana.*
S. italica. See *Hyacinthoides italica.*
S. japonica. See *S. scilloides.*
S. litardierei, syn. *S. pratensis.* Clump-forming, early summer-flowering bulb. H 10–25cm (4–10in), S 5–8cm (2–3in). Fully hardy. Bears up to 5narrowly strap-shaped, semi-erect, basal leaves. Stem has a dense spike of flat, star-shaped, violet flowers, 1–1.5cm (½–⅝in) across.
♀ ***S. mischtschenkoana***, syn. *S. tubergeniana, S.* 'Tubergeniana', illus. p.448.
S. natalensis. Clump-forming, summer-flowering bulb. H 30–45cm (12–18in), S 15–20cm (6–8in). Half hardy. Lance-shaped, semi-erect, basal leaves lengthen after flowering. Has a long spike of up to 100 flattish, blue flowers, each one around 1.5–2cm (⅝–¾in) across.
S. non-scripta. See *Hyacinthoides non-scripta.*
S. nutans. See *Hyacinthoides non-scripta.*
S. peruviana illus. p.452.
S. pratensis. See *S. litardierei.*
S. scilloides, syn. *S. chinensis, S. japonica*, illus. p.440.
S. siberica (Siberian squill). **'Atrocoerulea'** illus. p.448.
S. socialis. See *Ledebouria socialis.*
S. tubergeniana. See *S. mischtschenkoana.*
***S.* 'Tubergeniana'.** See *S. mischtschenkoana.*
S. violacea. See *Ledebouria socialis.*

SCINDAPSUS

ARACEAE

Genus of about 40 species of evergreen climbers, closley related to *Epipremnum*, which are grown for their attractive leaves with pointed tips. Frost tender, min. 15°C (59°F). In frost-prone regions grow under glass or as house plants and provide a moss pole for support. In warmer areas, grow against a wall, over a pergola, or through a tree. Outdoors requires fertile, moist, but well-drained soil and partial shade. Indoors, or under glass, needs bright, filtered light and plenty of water in the growing season; water sparingly during winter. Prune in early spring and propagate by stem-tip cuttings in summer with bottom heat, or by layering in spring and summer.
***S. aureus* 'Marble Queen'.** See *Epipremnum aureum* 'Marble Queen'.
***S. pictus* 'Argyraeus'**, syn. *Epipremnum pictum* 'Argyraeum', illus. p.217.

SCIRPOIDES

CYPERACEAE

See also GRASSES, BAMBOOS, RUSHES and SEDGES.
S. holoschoenus, syn. *Scirpus holoschoenus* (Round-headed club-rush). **'Variegatus'** is an evergreen, tuft-forming, perennial rush. H 1m (3ft), S 45cm (1½ft). Fully hardy. Rounded, leafless, green stems are striped horizontally with cream and bear long-stalked, dense, spherical heads of egg-shaped, awned, brown spikelets, produced from mid-summer to early autumn.

Scirpus holoschoenus. See *Scirpoides holoschoenus.*
***Scirpus lacustris* 'Spiralis'.** See *Juncus effusus* 'Spiralis'.
Scirpus lacustris subsp. ***tabernaemontani 'Zebrinus'.*** See *Schoenoplectus lacustris* subsp. *tabernaemontani* 'Zebrinus'.

Scirpus setaceus. See *Isolepsis setaceus*.
Scirpus tabernaemontani 'Zebrinus'. See *Schoenoplectus lacustris* subsp. *tabernaemontani* 'Zebrinus'.

SCLEROCACTUS

CACTACEAE

Genus of perennial cacti, grown for their depressed-spherical to club-shaped or columnar stems, each with a long, fleshy tap root and deeply notched or wartyribs. Frost tender, min. 7–10°C (45–50°F) if completely dry. Needs full sun with some midday shade and very well-drained soil. May rot if overwatered. Propagate by seed in spring.
S. scheeri, syn. *Ancistrocactus megarhizus, A. scheeri, Echinocactus scheeri*, illus. p.493.
S. uncinatus, syn. *Ancistrocactus uncinatus, Echinocactus uncinatus, Glandulicactus uncinatus, Hamatocactus uncinatus.* Globose to columnar, perennial cactus. H 20cm (8in), S 10cm (4in). Stem is blue-green. Areoles each produce 1–4 very long, hooked, reddish spines and 15–18 straight ones. Has cup-shaped, brown-green or reddish flowers, 2cm (¾in) across, in spring.

SCOLIOPUS

LILIACEAE/TRILLIACEAE

Genus of two species of spring-flowering perennial. Usually grown in alpine houses, where the neat habit and curious flowers, which arise directly from buds on the rootstock early in the season, may be better appreciated. Also suitable for rock gardens and peat beds. Frost hardy. Require sun or partial shade and moist but well-drained soil. Propagate by seed when fresh, in summer or autumn.
S. bigelowii, syn. *S. bigelovii*, illus. p.376.

Scolopendrium vulgare. See *Asplenium scolopendrium*.

SCOPOLIA

SOLANACEAE

Genus of spring-flowering perennials. Fully hardy. Prefers shade and fertile, very well-drained soil. Propagate by division in spring or by seed in autumn. All parts are highly toxic if ingested.
S. carniolica illus. p.279.

Scotch heather. See *Calluna vulgaris*.
Scotch laburnum. See *Laburnum alpinum*, illus. p.89.
Scotch rose. See *Rosa spinosissima*.
Scotch thistle. See *Onopordum acanthium*, illus. p.334.
Scots pine. See *Pinus sylvestris*.
Screw pine. See *Pandanus*.

SCROPHULARIA
Figwort

SCROPHULARIACEAE

Genus of perennials and sub-shrubs, some of which are semi-evergreen or evergreen. Most species are weeds, but some are grown for their variegated foliage. Fully hardy. Does best in semi-shade and moist soil. Propagate by division in spring or by softwood cuttings in summer.
***S. aquatica* 'Variegata'.** See *S. auriculata* 'Variegata'.
***S. auriculata* 'Variegata'**, syn. *S. aquatica* 'Variegata' (Water figwort). Evergreen, clump-forming perennial. H 60cm (24in), S 30cm (12in) or more. Has attractive, oval, toothed, dark green leaves with cream marks. Remove spikes of insignificant, maroon flowers, borne in summer.

Scrub palmetto. See *Serenoa repens*.
Scrub pine. See *Pinus virginiana*, illus. p.103.
Scurvy grass. See *Oxalis enneaphylla*.

SCUTELLARIA
Skullcap

LABIATAE/LAMIACEAE

Genus of rhizomatous perennials, grown for their summer flowers. Fully hardy to frost tender, min. 7–10°C (45–50°F). Needs sun and well-drained soil. Propagate by softwood cuttings in summer or by seed in autumn.
S. indica. Upright, rhizomatous perennial. H 15–30cm (6–12in), S 10cm (4in) or more. Frost hardy. Leaves are oval, toothed and hairy. Has dense racemes of long-tubed, 2-lipped, slate-blue, occasionally white flowers in summer. Suits a rock garden.
S. orientalis illus. p.397.
S. scordiifolia. Mat-forming, rhizomatous perennial. H and S 15cm (6in) or more. Fully hardy. Bears narrowly oval, wrinkled leaves. In summer-autumn has racemes of tubular, hooded, purple flowers, each with a white-streaked lip. Propagate by division in spring.

Sea buckthorn. See *Hippophäe rhamnoides*, illus. p.120.
Sea campion, Double. See *Silene uniflora* 'Robin Whitebreast'.
Sea daffodil. See *Pancratium maritimum*.
Sea holly. See *Eryngium*.
Sea kale. See *Crambe maritima*, illus. p.286.
Sea lavender. See *Limonium*.
Sea lily. See *Pancratium maritimum*.
Sea onion. See *Urginea maritima*.
Sea pink. See *Armeria maritima*.
Sea squill. See *Urginea maritima*.
Sea urchin. See *Astrophytum asterias*.
Sedge
Bowles' golden. See *Carex elata* 'Aurea', illus. p.321.
Greaterpond. See *Carex riparia*.
Leatherleaf. See *Carex buchananii*.
Mace. See *Carex grayi*.
Pendulous. See *Carex pendula*, illus. p.321.
Tufted. See *Carex elata*.
Sedges. See *Grasses, Bamboos, Rushes and Sedges*.

SEDUM
Stonecrop

CRASSULACEAE

Genus of often fleshy or succulent annuals, evergreen biennials, mostly evergreen or semi-evergreen perennials and evergreen shrubs and sub-shrubs, suitable for rock gardens and borders. Fully hardy to frost tender, min. 5°C (41°F). Needs sun. Does best in fertile, well-drained soil. Propagate perennials, sub-shrubs and shrubs by division or by softwood cuttings of non-flowering shoots from spring to mid-summer or by seed in autumn or spring. Propagate annuals and biennials by seed, sown under glass in early spring or outdoors in mid-spring. All parts may cause mild stomach upset if ingested; contact with the sap may irritate skin.
S. acre illus. p.396. **'Aureum'** illus. p.397.
S. aizoon syn. *Phedimus aizoon.* Evergreen, erect perennial. H and S 45cm (18in). Fully hardy. Mid-green leaves are oblong to lance-shaped, fleshy and toothed. In summer bears flat heads of star-shaped, yellow flowers. **'Aurantiacum'** illus. p.305.
S. anacampseros, syn. *Hylotelephium anacampseros.* Semi-evergreen, trailing perennial with overwintering foliage rosettes. H 10cm (4in), S 25cm (10in) or more. Frost hardy. Prostrate, loosely rosetted, brown stems bear oblong to oval, fleshy, glaucous green leaves. Dense, sub-globose, terminal heads of small, cup-shaped, purplish-pink flowers appear in summer.
S. caeruleum illus. p.345.
♀ ***S. cauticola***, syn. *Hylotelephium cauticola.* Trailing, shallow-rooted perennial with stolons. H 5cm (2in), S 20cm (8in). Fully hardy. Has oval to oblong, stalked, fleshy, blue-green leaves on procumbent, purplish-red stems. Bears leafy, branched, flattish heads of star-shaped, pale purplish-pink flowers in early autumn. Cut back old stems in winter.
S. ewersii, syn. *Hylotelephium ewersii.* Trailing perennial. H 5cm (2in), S 15cm (6in). Fully hardy. Is similar to *S. cauticola*, but has more rounded, stem-clasping leaves, often tinted red, and dense, rounded flower heads.
S. heterodontum. See *Rhodiola heterodonta*.
♀ ***S. kamtschaticum,*** syn. *Phedimus kamtschaticus.* Semi-evergreen, prostrate perennial with overwintering foliage rosettes. H 5–8cm (2–3in), S 20cm (8in). Fully hardy. Bears narrowly oval, toothed, fleshy, mid-green leaves. Spreading, terminal clusters of star-shaped, orange-flushed, yellow flowers appear in summer-autumn. ♀ **'Variegatum'** illus. p.403.
S. lydium illus. p.400.
♀ ***S. morganianum*** (Burro's tail, Donkey-tail). Evergreen, prostrate, succulent perennial. H 30cm (12in) or more, S indefinite. Frost tender. Stems are clothed in oblong to lance-shaped, almost cylindrical, fleshy, waxy, white leaves. Has terminal clusters of star-shaped, rose-pink flowers in summer.
S. obtusatum illus. p.400.
S. palmeri. Evergreen, clump-forming perennial. H 20cm (8in), S 30cm (12in). Half hardy. Bears sprays of star-shaped, yellow or orange flowers in early summer above oblong-oval to spoon-shaped, fleshy, grey-green leaves.
S. populifolium, syn. *Hylotelephium populifolium.* Semi-evergreen, bushy perennial. H 30–45cm (12–18in), S 30cm (12in). Fully hardy. Terminal clusters of hawthorn-scented, star-shaped, pale pink or white flowers are borne in late summer. Has broadly oval, irregularly toothed, fleshy, mid-green leaves.
S. reflexum. See *S. rupestre*.
S. rosea. See *Rhodiola rosea*. ***S. rosea*** var. ***heterodontum*** see *R. heterodonta*.
S. rupestre, syn. *S. reflexum*, illus. p.371.
S. sempervivoides syn. *Prometheum sempervivoides.* Evergreen, basal-rosetted biennial. H 8–10cm (3–4in), S 5cm (2in). Half hardy. Has rosettes that are similar to those of Sempervivum; oval to strap-shaped, leathery, glaucous green leaves are strongly marked red-purple. Produces domed heads of star-shaped, scarlet flowers in summer. Dislikes winter wet. Is good for an alpine house.
S. sieboldii syn. *Hylotelephium sieboldii.* **'Mediovariegatum',** *S.s.* 'Variegatum'. Evergreen, spreading, tuberous perennial with long, tapering tap roots. H 10cm (4in), S 20cm (8in) or more. Frost tender. Rounded, fleshy, blue-green leaves, splashed cream and occasionally red-edged, appear in whorls of 3. Bears open, terminal heads of star-shaped, pink flowers in late summer. Is good for an alpine house.
S. spathulifolium illus. p.401.
♀ **'Cape Blanco'** (syn. *S.s.* 'Cappa Blanca') illus. p.403.
♀ ***S. spectabile***, syn. *Hylotelephium spectabile* (Ice-plant). Clump-forming perennial. H and S 45cm (18in). Fully hardy. Has oval, indented, fleshy, grey-green leaves, above which flat heads of small, star-shaped, pink flowers that attract butterflies are borne in late summer. ♀ **'Brilliant'** illus. p.306.
S. spurium syn. *Phedimus spurius.* Semi-evergreen, mat-forming, creeping perennial. H 10cm (4in) or more, S indefinite. Frost hardy. Oblong to oval, toothed leaves are borne along hairy stems. Large, slightly rounded heads of small, star-shaped flowers are borne in summer. Flower colour varies from deep purple to white.
S. tatarinowii, syn. *Hylotelephium tatarinowii.* Arching, spreading, tuberous perennial. H 10cm (4in), S 20cm (8in). Fully hardy. Rounded, terminal heads of star-shaped, pink-flushed, white flowers appear in late summer above small, oval, toothed, green leaves borne along purplish stems. Suits an alpine house.

SELAGINELLA

SELAGINELLACEAE

Genus of evergreen, moss-like perennials, grown for their foliage. Frost tender, min. 5°C (41°F). Prefers semi-shade and needs moist but well-drained, peaty soil. Remove faded foliage regularly. Propagate from pieces with roots attached that have been broken off plant in any season.
♀ ***S. kraussiana*** illus. p.324. **'Aurea'** is an evergreen, moss-like perennial. H 1cm (½in), S indefinite. Spreading, filigreed, bright yellowish-green fronds are much-branched, denser towards the growing tips and easily root on soil surface. ♀ **'Variegata'** has foliage splashed with creamy-yellow.
S. lepidophylla (Resurrection plant, Rose of Jericho). Evergreen, moss-like perennial. H and S 10cm (4in). Bluntly

rounded, emerald-green fronds, ageing red-brown or grey-green, are produced in dense tufts. On drying, fronds curl inwards into a tight ball; they unfold when placed in water.
♀ ***S. martensii*** illus. p.323.

SELENICEREUS

CACTACEAE

Genus of summer-flowering, perennial cacti with climbing, 4–10-ribbed, green stems, to 2cm (¾in) across. Nocturnal, funnel-shaped flowers eventually open flat. Frost tender, min. 5°C (41°F). Needs sun or partial shade and rich, well-drained soil. Propagate by seed or stem cuttings in spring or summer.
S. grandiflorus illus. p.472.

Self-heal. See *Prunella*.
Large. See *Prunella grandiflora*, illus. p.394.

SELINUM

UMBELLIFERAE/APIACEAE

Genus of summer-flowering perennials, ideal for informal gardens and backs of borders. Fully hardy. Prefers sun, but will grow in semi-shade, and any well-drained soil. Once established, roots resent disturbance. Propagate by seed when fresh, in summer or autumn.
S. tenuifolium. See *S. wallichianum*.
S. wallichianum, syn *S. tenuifolium*. Upright, architectural perennial. H 1.5m (5ft), S 60cm (2ft). In summer produces small, star-shaped, white flowers, borne in large, flat heads, one above another. Has very finely divided, mid-green leaves.

SEMELE

LILIACEAE/RUSCACEAE

Genus of one species of evergreen, twining climber. Male and female flowers are produced on the same plant. Frost tender, min. 5°C (41°F). Needs partial shade and prefers rich, well-drained soil. Propagate by division or seed in spring.
S. androgyna (Climbing butcher's broom). Evergreen climber, twining in upper part, branched and bearing oval cladodes, 5–10cm (2–4in) long. H to 7m (22ft). Star-shaped, cream flowers appear in early summer, in notches on cladode margins, followed by orange-red berries.

SEMIAQUILEGIA

RANUNCULACEAE

Genus of perennials, grown for their flowers. These differ from those of *Aquilegia*, with which it is sometimes included, by having no spurs. Is good for rock gardens. Fully hardy. Requires sun and moist but well-drained soil. Propagate by seed in autumn.
S. ecalcarata illus. p.367.

SEMIARUNDINARIA

GRAMINEAE/POACEAE

See also GRASSES, BAMBOOS, RUSHES and SEDGES.
♀ ***S. fastuosa***, syn. *Arundinaria fastuosa*, illus. p.320.

SEMPERVIVUM
Houseleek

CRASSULACEAE

Genus of evergreen perennials that spread by short stolons and are grown for their symmetrical rosettes of oval to strap-shaped, pointed, fleshy leaves. Makes ground-hugging mats, suitable for rock gardens, screes, walls, banks and alpine houses. Flowers are star-shaped with 8–16 spreading petals. Fully hardy. Needs sun and gritty soil. Takes several years to reach flowering size. Rosettes die after flowering but leave numerous offsets. Propagate by offsets in summer.
♀ ***S. arachnoideum*** illus. p.401.
♀ ***S. ciliosum*** illus. p.401.
♀ ***S. 'Commander Hay'.*** Evergreen, basal-rosetted perennial. H 15cm (6in), S to 30cm (12in). Is mainly grown for its very large, dark red rosettes to 10cm (4in) across. Bears terminal clusters of dull greenish-red flowers in summer.
S. giuseppii illus. p.403.
S. grandiflorum. Evergreen, basal-rosetted perennial. H 10cm (4in), S to 20cm (8in). Variable, densely haired, red-tinted, dark green rosettes exude a goat-like smell when crushed. Produces loose, terminal clusters of yellow-green flowers, stained purple in centres, on long flower stems in summer. Prefers humus-rich, acid soil.
S. globiferum subsp. ***globiferum.*** See *Jovibarba sobolifera*. subsp. ***hirtum.*** See *Jovibarba hirta*.
S. montanum illus. p.402.
♀ ***S. tectorum*** illus. p.401.

SENECIO

COMPOSITAE/ASTERACEAE

Genus of annuals, succulent and non-succulent perennials and evergreen shrubs, sub-shrubs and twining climbers, grown for their foliage and usually daisy-like flower heads. Some shrubby species are now referred to the genus *Brachyglottis*. Shrubs are excellent for coastal gardens. Fully hardy to frost tender, min. 5–10°C (41–50°F). Most prefer full sun and well-drained soil (although *S. articulatus* and *S. rowleyanus* tolerate partial shade and need very well-drained soil). Propagate shrubs and climbers by semi-ripe cuttings in summer, annuals by seed in spring, perennials by division in spring (*S. articulatus* and *S. rowleyanus* by seed or stem cuttings in spring or summer). All parts may cause severe discomfort if ingested.
S. articulatus, syn. *Kleinia articulata* (Candle plant). Deciduous, spreading, perennial succulent. H 60cm (2ft), S indefinite. Frost tender, min. 10°C (50°F). Branching, grey-marked, blue stems have weak joints. Bears rounded to oval, 3–5-lobed, grey leaves and flattish heads of small, cup-shaped, yellow flowers from spring to autumn. Offsets freely from stolons.
'Variegatus' illus. p.478.
S. cineraria, syn. *S. maritimus*. Moderately fast-growing, evergreen, bushy sub-shrub, often grown as an annual. H and S 30cm (1ft). Half hardy. Has long, oval, very deeply lobed, hairy, silver-grey leaves. Rounded, yellow flower heads appear in summer, but are best removed. **'Cirrus'** has elliptic, finely toothed or lobed, silvery-green to white leaves.
♀ **'Silver Dust'** illus. p.346.
S. clivorum **'Desdemona'.** See *Ligularia dentata* 'Desdemona'.
S. compactus. See *Brachyglottis compacta*.
S. confusus, syn. *Pseudogynoxys chenopodioides*, illus. p.215.
S. Dunedin Hybrids. See *Brachyglottis* Dunedin Hybrids.
S. elegans. Moderately fast-growing, upright annual. H 45cm (18in), S 15cm (6in). Half hardy. Has oval, deeply lobed, deep green leaves. Daisy-like, purple flower heads appear on branching stems in summer.
S. grandifolius, syn. *Telanthophora grandiflora*. Evergreen, erect, robust-stemmed shrub. H 3–5m (10–15ft), S 2–3m (6–10ft). Frost tender, min. 10°C (50°F) to flower well. Has oval, toothed, boldly veined leaves, 20–45cm (8–18in) long, glossy, rich green above, red-brown-haired beneath. Carries terminal clusters, 30cm (12in) wide, of small, daisy-like, yellow flower heads in winter-spring.
S. greyi of gardens. See *Brachyglottis* Dunedin Hybrids.
S. × hybridus. See *Pericallis × hybrida*.
S. laxifolius. See *Brachyglottis laxifolia*.
S. laxifolius of gardens. See *Brachyglottis* Dunedin Hybrids.
S. macroglossus (Natal ivy, Wax vine). Evergreen, woody-stemmed, twining climber. H 3m (10ft). Frost tender, min. 7°C (45°F), best at 10°C (50°F). Leaves are sharply triangular, fleshy-textured and glossy. Loose clusters of daisy-like flower heads, each with a few white ray petals and a central, yellow disc, are borne mainly in winter.
♀ **'Variegatus'** illus. p.217.
S. maritimus. See *S. cineraria*.
S. mikanioides, syn. *Delairea odorata* (German ivy). Evergreen, semi-woody, twining climber. H 2–3m (6–10ft). Frost tender, min. 5°C (41°F), best at 7–10°C (45–50°F). Has fleshy leaves with 5–7 broad, pointed, radiating lobes. Mature plants carry large clusters of small, yellow flower heads in autumn-winter.
S. monroi. See *Brachyglottis monroi*.
S. przewalskii. See *Ligularia przewalskii*.
S. pulcher illus. p.306.
S. reinholdii. See *Brachyglottis rotundifolia*.
S. rotundifolius. See *Brachyglottis rotundifolia*.
S. rowleyanus, syn. *Kleinia rowleyana*. illus. p.478.
S. smithii. Bushy perennial. H 1–1.2m (3–4ft), S 75cm–1m (2½–3ft). Fully hardy. Woolly stems are clothed with long, oval, toothed, leathery, dark green leaves. Daisy-like, white flower heads, with yellow centres, are borne in terminal clusters, up to 15cm (6in) across, in early summer. Likes boggy conditions.
S. 'Spring Glory'. See *Pericallis × hybrida* 'Spring Glory'.
S. 'Sunshine'. See *Brachyglottis* Dunedin Hybrids 'Sunshine'.
S. tamoides. Evergreen, woody-stemmed, twining climber. H 5m (15ft) or more. Frost tender, min. 5–10°C (41–50°F). Has ivy-shaped, light green leaves. In autumn-winter bears yellow flower heads that are daisy-like, but with only a few ray petals.

SENNA

LEGUMINOSAE/CAESALPINIACEAE

Genus of evergreen trees, shrubs and perennials, grown for their pea-like flowers. Frost tender, min. 7–18°C (45–64°F). Requires full sun and moist but well-drained soil. Propagate by seed sown in spring, or by semi-ripe cuttings in summer. Divide perennials in spring.
♀ ***S. artemisioides***, syn. *Cassia artemisioides* (Silver cassia, Wormwood cassia). Evergreen, erect to spreading, wiry shrub. H and S 1–2m (3–6ft). Frost tender, min. 10–13°C (50–55°F). Leaves each have 6–8linear leaflets covered with silky, white down. Axillary spikes of cup-shaped, yellow flowers appear from winter to early summer.
S. corymbosa, syn. *Cassia corymbosa*, illus. p.143.
S. didymobotrya, syn. *Cassia didymobotrya*, illus. p.143.
♀ ***S. × floribunda***, syn. *Cassia corymbosa* var. *plurijuga* of gardens, *C. × floribunda*. Vigorous, evergreen or deciduous, rounded shrub with robust stems. H and S 1.5–2m (5–6ft). Frost tender, min. 7°C (45°F). Bright green leaves consist of 4–6 oval leaflets. Carries very large clusters of bowl-shaped, rich yellow flowers in late summer.
S. siamea, syn. *Cassia siamea*. Fast-growing, evergreen, rounded tree. H and S 8–10m (25–30ft) or more. Frost tender, min. 16–18°C (61–4°F). Leaves, 15–30cm (6–12in) long, have 7–12 pairs of elliptic leaflets. Large terminal panicles of small, cup-shaped, bright yellow flowers are borne in spring, followed by flat, dark brown pods, to 23cm (9in) long.

Senna, Bladder. See *Colutea arborescens*, illus. p.142.
Sensitive fern. See *Onoclea sensibilis*, illus. p.324.
Sensitive plant. See *Mimosa pudica*, illus. p.172.
Sentry palm. See *Howea forsteriana*.

SEQUOIA

TAXODIACEAE

See also CONIFERS.
♀ ***S. sempervirens*** (Coast redwood, Redwood). Very vigorous, columnar to conical conifer with horizontal branches. H 20–30m (70–100ft), S 5–8m (15–25ft), although one specimen – which is believed to be the tallest tree in the world – has reached 112m (375ft). Fully hardy. Has thick, soft, fibrous, red-brown bark and needle-like, flattened, pale green leaves, spirally arranged on shoots. Produces rounded to cylindrical cones, initially green, ripening to dark brown. Will regrow if cut back. Very cold winters kill foliage, but without affecting tree.

SEQUOIADENDRON

TAXODIACEAE

See also CONIFERS.
♀ ***S. giganteum*** illus. p.98.
'Pendulum' is a weeping conifer.

H 10m (30ft), S 2m (6ft) or more. Fully hardy. Bark is thick, soft, fibrous and red-brown. Has spiralled, needle-like, incurved, grey-green leaves that darken and become glossy.

SERAPIAS

ORCHIDACEAE

See also ORCHIDS.
S. cordigera. Deciduous, terrestrial orchid. H 40cm (16in). Half hardy. Spikes of reddish or dark purple flowers, 4cm (1½in) long, are borne in spring. Has lance-shaped, red-spotted leaves, 15cm (6in) long. Grow in semi-shade.

Serbian spruce. See *Picea omorika*, illus. p.99.

SERENOA

PALMAE/ARECACEAE

Genus of one species of evergreen fan palm, grown for its foliage. Frost tender, min. 10–13°C (50–55°F). Requires full light or partial shade and well-drained soil. Water potted plants moderately during growing season, less at other times. Propagate by seed or suckers in spring. Red spider mite may be troublesome.
S. repens (Saw palmetto, Scrub palmetto). Evergreen, rhizomatous fan palm, usually stemless. H 60cm–1m (2–3ft), S 2m (6ft) or more. Palmate leaves, 45–75cm (18–30in) wide, are grey to blue-green, and each divided into 6–20 strap-shaped lobes. Clusters of tiny, fragrant, cream flowers are hidden among leaves in summer, followed by egg-shaped, purple-black fruits.

SERISSA

RUBIACEAE

Genus of one species of evergreen shrub, grown for its overall appearance. Frost tender, min. 7–10°C (45–50°F). Needs sun or partial shade and fertile, well-drained soil. Water containerized specimens moderately, less when not in growth. May be trimmed after flowering. Propagate by semi-ripe cuttings in summer.
S. foetida. See *S. japonica*.
S. japonica, syn. *S. foetida*. Evergreen, spreading to rounded, freely branching shrub. H to 60cm (2ft), S 60cm–1m (2–3ft). Tiny, oval leaves are lustrous and deep green. Small, funnel-shaped, 4- or 5-lobed, white flowers are produced from spring to autumn.

SERRATULA

COMPOSITAE/ASTERACEAE

Genus of perennials, grown for their thistle-like flower heads. Fully hardy. Requires sun and well-drained soil. Propagate by seed or by division in spring.
S. seoanei, syn. *S. shawii*. Upright, compact perennial. H 23cm (9in), S 12–15cm (5–6in). Stems bear feathery, finely cut leaves and, in autumn, terminal panicles of small, thistle-like, purple flower heads. Is useful for a rock garden.
S. shawii. See *S. seoanei*.

Service tree of Fontainebleau. See *Sorbus latifolia*.
Serviceberry. See *Amelanchier*.

SESLERIA

GRAMINEAE/POACEAE

See also GRASSES, BAMBOOS, RUSHES and SEDGES.
S. heufleriana (Balkan blue grass). Evergreen, tuft-forming, perennial grass. H 50cm (20in), S 30–45cm (12–18in). Fully hardy. Bears rich green leaves, glaucous beneath, and, in spring, compact panicles of purple spikelets.

Sessile oak. See *Quercus petraea*.

SETARIA

GRAMINEAE/POACEAE

See also GRASSES, BAMBOOS, RUSHES and SEDGES.
S. italica (Foxtail millet, Italian millet). Moderately fast-growing, annual grass with stout stems. H 1.5m (5ft), S to 1m (3ft). Half hardy. Has lance-shaped, mid-green leaves, to 45cm (1½ft) long, and loose panicles of white, cream, yellow, red, brown or black flowers in summer-autumn.

Setcreasea purpurea. See *Tradescantia pallida* 'Purpurea'.
Shadbush. See *Amelanchier*.
Shag-bark hickory. See *Carya ovata*, illus. p.65.
Shallon. See *Gaultheria shallon*, illus. p.158.
Shamrock pea. See *Parochetus communis*, illus. p.396.
Shasta daisy. See *Leucanthemum* × *superbum*.
Sheep laurel. See *Kalmia angustifolia*.
Sheep's bit. See *Jasione laevis*.
Sheepberry. See *Viburnum lentago*.
Shell flower. See *Alpinia zerumbet*, illus. p.225; *Moluccella laevis*, illus. p.347.
Shell ginger. See *Alpinia zerumber*, illus. p.225.

SHEPHERDIA

ELAEAGNACEAE

Genus of deciduous or evergreen shrubs, grown for their foliage and fruits. Separate male and female plants are needed in order to obtain fruits. Fully hardy. Requires sun and well-drained soil. Propagate by softwood cuttings in summer or by seed in autumn.
S. argentea (Buffalo berry). Deciduous, bushy, often tree-like shrub. H and S 4m (12ft). Bears tiny, inconspicuous, yellow flowers amid oblong, silvery leaves in spring, followed by small, egg-shaped, bright red fruits.

SHIBATAEA

GRAMINEAE/POACEAE

See also GRASSES, BAMBOOS, RUSHES and SEDGES.
S. kumasasa illus. p.320.

Shield fern, Soft. See *Polystichum setiferum*.
Shield ivy. See *Hedera hibernica* 'Deltoidea', illus. p.219.
Shingle oak. See *Quercus imbricaria*.
Shingle plant. See *Monstera acuminata*.
Shoo-fly. See *Nicandra physalodes*.
Shooting stars. See *Dodecatheon*.
Shore juniper. See *Juniperus conferta*.
Shore pine. See *Pinus contorta*, illus. p.103.

SHORTIA

DIAPENSIACEAE

Genus of evergreen, spring-flowering perennials with leaves that often turn red in autumn-winter. Fully hardy, but buds may be frosted in areas without snow cover. Is difficult to grow in hot, dry climates. Needs shade or semi-shade and well-drained, peaty, sandy, acid soil. Propagate by runners in summer or by seed when available.
S. galacifolia illus. p.376.
S. soldanelloides illus. p.378. var. ***ilicifolia*** is an evergreen, mat-forming perennial. H 5–10cm (2–4in), S 10–15cm (4–6in). Has rounded, toothed leaves. In late spring each flower stem carries 4–6 small, pendent, bell-shaped flowers with fringed edges and rose-pink centres shading to white. Flowers of var. ***magna*** are rose-pink throughout.
***S. uniflora* 'Grandiflora'.** Vigorous, evergreen, mat-forming perennial with a few rooted runners. H 8cm (3in), S 20cm (8in). Leaves are rounded, toothed, leathery and glossy. Flower stems bear cup-shaped, 5cm (2in) wide, white-pink flowers, with serrated petals, in spring.

Showy lady's slipper orchid. See *Cypripedium reginae*, illus. p.308.
Shrimp plant. See *Justicia brandegeeana*, illus. p.162.
Shrubby germander. See *Teucrium fruticans*.
Shrubby hare's ear. See *Bupleurum fruticosum*, illus. p.142.
Shrubby restharrow. See *Ononis fruticosa*, illus. p.365.
Siberian bugloss. See *Brunnera macrophylla*.
Siberian crab. See *Malus baccata*.
Siberian elm. See *Ulmus pumila*.
Siberian flag. See *Iris sibirica*.
Siberian melic. See *Melica altissima*.
Siberian squill. See *Scilla siberica*.
Siberian wallflower. See *Erysimum* × *allionii*.

SIBIRAEA

ROSACEAE

Genus of deciduous shrubs, grown for their foliage and flowers. Fully hardy. Needs sunny, well-drained soil. Established plants benefit from having old or weak shoots cut to base after flowering. Propagate by softwood cuttings in summer.
S. altaiensis, syn. *S. laevigata*. Deciduous, spreading, open shrub. H 1m (3ft), S 1.5m (5ft). Has narrowly oblong, blue-green leaves and, in late spring and early summer, dense, terminal clusters of tiny, star-shaped, white flowers.
S. laevigata. See *S. altaiensis*.

SIDALCEA

MALVACEAE

Genus of summer-flowering perennials, grown for their hollyhock-like flowers. Fully hardy. Needs sun and well-drained soil. Propagate by division in spring.
***S.* 'Loveliness'.** Upright perennial. H 1m (3ft), S 45cm (1½ft). Has buttercup-like, divided leaves with narrowly oblong segments. In summer bears racemes of shallowly cup-shaped, shell-pink flowers.
***S.* 'Oberon'** illus. p.245.
***S.* 'Puck'.** Upright perennial. H 60cm (2ft), S 45cm (1½ft). Has buttercup-like, divided leaves with narrowly oblong segments. In summer bears racemes of shallowly cup-shaped, deep pink flowers.
***S.* 'Sussex Beauty'.** Upright perennial. H 1.2m (4ft), S 45cm (1½ft). Has buttercup-like, divided leaves, with narrowly oblong segments, and, in summer, shallowly cup-shaped, deep rose-pink flowers.

SIDERITIS

LABIATAE/LAMIACEAE

Genus of evergreen perennials, sub-shrubs and shrubs, grown mainly for their foliage. Half hardy to frost tender, min. 7–10°C (45–50°F). Needs full light and well-drained soil. Water containerized plants moderately, less when temperatures are low. Remove spent flower spikes after flowering. Propagate by seed in spring or by semi-ripe cuttings in summer.
S. candicans. Evergreen, erect, well-branched shrub. H to 75cm (2½ft), S to 60cm (2ft). Frost tender. Lance-shaped to narrowly oval or triangular leaves bear dense, white wool. Produces leafy, terminal spikes of tubular, pale yellow-and-light-brown or orange-red flowers in summer.

SILENE

Campion, Catchfly

CARYOPHYLLACEAE

Genus of annuals and perennials, some of which are evergreen, grown for their mass of 5-petalled flowers. Fully to half hardy. Needs sun and fertile, well-drained soil. Propagate by softwood cuttings in spring or by seed in spring or early autumn.
S. acaulis illus. p.377.
S. alpestris, syn. *Heliosperma alpestre*, illus. p.385.
***S. armeria* 'Electra'** illus. p.335.
S. coeli-rosa, syn. *Agrostemma coeli-rosa, Lychnis coeli-rosa, Viscaria elegans*, illus. p.332. **'Rose Angel'** illus. p.337.
S. elisabethae. Basal-rosetted perennial. H 10cm (4in), S 20cm (8in). Fully hardy. Has rosettes of strap-shaped, mid-green leaves. In summer, stems bear large, often solitary, deep rose-red flowers with green centres and long-clawed petals. Is suitable for a rock garden.
S. hookeri. Short-lived, trailing, prostrate, late summer-deciduous perennial with a long, slender tap root. H 5cm (2in), S 20cm (8in). Fully hardy. Slender stems bear oval, grey leaves and, in late summer, soft pink,

salmon or orange flowers, deeply cleft to base.
***S. maritima* 'Flore Pleno'.** See *S. uniflora* 'Robin Whitebreast'.
S. pendula (Nodding catchfly). Moderately fast-growing, bushy annual. H and S 15–20cm (6–8in). Half hardy. Has oval, hairy, mid-green leaves and, in summer and early autumn, clusters of light pink flowers.
♀ ***S. schafta*** illus. p.391.
***S. uniflora* 'Robin Whitebreast',** syn. *S. maritima* 'Flore Pleno', *S. u.* 'Flore Pleno', *S. vulgaris* subsp. *maritima* 'Flore Pleno' (Double sea campion). Lax perennial with deep, wandering roots. H and S 20cm (8in). Fully hardy. Leaves are lance-shaped and grey-green. Has pompon-like, double, white flowers on branched stems in summer.
***S. vulgaris* subsp. *maritima* 'Flore Pleno'.** See *S. uniflora* 'Robin Whitebreast'.

Silk cotton tree. See *Ceiba pentandra.*
Silk tree. See *Albizia julibrissin*, illus. p.86.
Floss. See *Chorisia speciosa*, illus. p.66.
Silk vine. See *Periploca graeca.*
Silk weed. See *Asclepias.*
Silk-tassel bush. See *Garrya elliptica*, illus. p.121.
Silky oak. See *Grevillea robusta.*
Silky wisteria. See *Wisteria brachybotrys* 'Shiro Kapitan'.

SILPHIUM

COMPOSITAE/ASTERACEAE

Genus of fairly coarse, summer-flowering perennials. Fully hardy. Does best in sun or semi-shade and in moist but well-drained soil. Propagate by division in spring or by seed when fresh, in autumn.
S. laciniatum (Compass plant). Clump-forming perennial. H 2m (6ft), S 60cm (2ft). Mid-green leaves, composed of opposite pairs of oblong to lance-shaped leaflets, face north and south wherever the plant is grown, hence the common name. Large clusters of slightly pendent, daisy-like, yellow flower heads are borne in late summer.

Silver ball cactus. See *Parodia scopa.*
Silver beech. See *Nothofagus menziesii.*
Silver bell. See *Halesia.*
Silver birch. See *Betula pendula.*
Silver cassia. See *Senna artemisioides.*
Silver chain. See *Dendrochilum glumaceum.*
Silver dollar cactus. See *Astrophytum asterias.*
Silver fir. See *Abies.*
Silver heart. See *Peperomia marmorata*, illus. p.316.
Silver hedgehog holly. See *Ilex aquifolium* 'Ferox Argentea', illus. p.95.
Silver inch plant. See *Tradescantia zebrina*, illus. p.313.
Silver jade plant. See *Crassula arborescens*, illus. p.474.
Silver lime. See *Tilia tomentosa.*
Pendent. See *Tilia* 'Petiolaris', illus. p.64.
Silver maple. See *Acer saccharinum.*
Silver net-leaf. See *Fittonia albivenis Argyroneura Group*, illus. p.312.
Silver torch. See *Cleistocactus strausii*, illus. p.475.
Silver tree. See *Leucadendron argenteum*, illus. p.96.
Silver vase plant. See *Aechmea fasciata*, illus. p.273.
Silver vine. See *Actinidia polygama; Scindapsus pictus* 'Argyraeus', illus p.217.
Silver wattle. See *Acacia dealbata*, illus. p.79.
Silver willow. See *Salix alba* var. *sericea.*
Silver-leaf peperomia. See *Peperomia griseoargentea.*
Silver-leaved geranium. See *Pelargonium* 'Flower of Spring', illus. p.249.
Silver-margined holly. See *Ilex aquifolium* 'Argentea Marginata', illus. p.94.

SILYBUM

COMPOSITAE/ASTERACEAE

Genus of thistle-like biennials, grown for their spectacular foliage. Fully hardy. Grow in sun and in any well-drained soil. Propagate by seed in late spring or early summer. Is prone to slug and snail damage.
S. marianum illus. p.334.

Sinarundinaria jaunsarensis. See *Yushania anceps.*
Sinarundinaria murieliae. See *Fargesia murieliae.*
Sinarundinaria nitida. See *Fargesia nitida.*

SINNINGIA

GESNERIACEAE

Genus of usually summer-flowering, tuberous perennials and deciduous sub-shrubs with showy flowers. Frost tender, min. 15°C (59°F). Grow in bright light but not direct sun. Prefers a humid atmosphere and moist but not waterlogged, peaty soil. When leaves die down after flowering, allow tubers to dry out; then store in a frost-free area. Propagate in spring by seed or in late spring or summer by stem cuttings or by dividing tubers into sections, each with a young shoot.
S. barbata. Bushy, tuberous perennial with square, red stems. H and S 60cm (2ft) or more. Broadly lance-shaped leaves, to 15cm (6in) long, are glossy, mid-green above, reddish-green beneath. In summer has 5-lobed, pouched, white flowers, 4cm (1½in) long.
S. concinna. Rosetted perennial with very small tubers. H and S to 15cm (6in). Oval to almost round, scalloped, velvety, red-veined, mid-green leaves, 2cm (¾in) long, are red below. Trumpet-shaped, bicoloured, purple and white or yellowish-white flowers, to 2cm (¾in) long, are produced in summer.
***S.* 'Etoile du Feu'.** Short-stemmed, rosetted, tuberous perennial. H 30cm (12in), S 40cm (16in) or more. Has oval, velvety leaves, 20–24cm (8–9½in) long. Upright, trumpet-shaped, carmine-red flowers appear in summer.
***S.* 'Mont Blanc'.** Short-stemmed, rosetted, tuberous perennial. H 30cm (12in), S 40cm (16in) or more. Oval, velvety, mid-green leaves are 20–24cm (8–9½in) long. In summer bears upright, trumpet-shaped, pure white flowers.
***S.* 'Red Flicker'** illus. p.292.
S. speciosa, syn. *Gloxinia speciosa* (Gloxinia). Short-stemmed, rosetted, tuberous perennial. H and S to 30cm (1ft). Oval, velvety, green leaves are 20cm (8in) long. Nodding, funnel-shaped, fleshy, violet, red or white flowers, to 5cm (2in) long and pouched on lower sides, are produced in summer. Is a parent of many named hybrids, of which a selection is included above and below.
***S.* 'Switzerland'** illus. p.292.
***S.* 'Waterloo'.** Short-stemmed, rosetted, tuberous perennial. H 30cm (12in), S 40cm (16in) or more. Has oval, velvety leaves, 20–24cm (8–9½in) long. Upright, trumpet-shaped, bright scarlet flowers open in summer.

SINOFRANCHETIA

LARDIZABALACEAE

Genus of one species of deciduous, twining climber, grown mainly for its handsome leaves. Is suitable for covering buildings and growing up large trees. Male and female flowers are produced on separate plants. Frost hardy. Grow in semi-shade and in any well-drained soil. Propagate by semi-ripe cuttings in summer.
S. chinensis. Deciduous, twining climber. H to 15m (50ft). Mid- to dark green leaves have 3 oblong to oval leaflets, each 5–15cm (2–6in) long. In late spring has small, dull white flowers in pendent racemes, to 10cm (4in) long. Pale purple berries, containing many seeds, follow in summer.

SINOJACKIA

STYRACACEAE

Genus of deciduous shrubs and trees, grown for their flowers. Fully hardy. Requires a sheltered position in sun or partial shade and fertile, humus-rich, moist, acid soil. Propagate by softwood cuttings in summer.
S. rehderiana. Deciduous, bushy shrub or spreading tree. H and S 6m (20ft). Nodding, saucer-shaped, white flowers, each with a central cluster of yellow anthers, appear in late spring and early summer. Oval leaves are dark green.

SINOWILSONIA

HAMAMELIDACEAE

Genus of one species of deciduous tree, grown for its foliage and catkins. Fully hardy. Requires sun or semi-shade and fertile, moist but well-drained soil. Propagate by seed in autumn.
S. henryi. Deciduous, spreading, sometimes shrubby tree. H and S 8m (25ft). Has oval, toothed, glossy, bright green leaves, and long, pendent, green catkins in late spring.

Siphonosmanthus delavayi. See *Osmanthus delavayi.*

SISYRINCHIUM

IRIDACEAE

Genus of annuals and perennials, some of which are semi-evergreen. Fully to half hardy. Prefers sun, but tolerates partial shade, and well-drained or moist soil. Propagate by division in early spring or by seed in spring or autumn.
S. angustifolium. See *S. graminoides.*
S. bellum of gardens. See *S. idahoense.*
S. bermudiana. See *S. graminoides.*
S. brachypus. See *S. californicum.*
S. californicum (Golden-eyed grass). Semi-evergreen, upright perennial. H 30–60cm (12–24in), S 30cm (12in). Frost hardy. Has grass-like tufts of basal, light green leaves. For a long period in spring-summer produces flattish, bright yellow flowers, with slightly darker veins, on winged stems. Outer leaves may die off and turn black in autumn. Dwarf forms are known as ***S. brachypus.*** Prefers moist soil.
S. douglasii. See *Olsynium douglasii.*
S. graminoides, syn. *S. angustifolium. **S. bermudiana***, illus. p.368.
S. grandiflorum. See *Olsynium douglasii.*
S. idahoense, syn. *S. bellum* of gardens, illus. p.395.
S. odoratissimum. See *Olsynium biflorum.*
S. striatum illus. p.302. **'Aunt May'** (syn. *S.s.* 'Variegatum') is a semi-evergreen, upright perennial. H 45–60cm (18–24in), S 30cm (12in). Fully hardy. Produces tufts of long, narrow, cream-striped, greyish-green leaves. Slender spikes of trumpet-shaped, purple-striped, straw-yellow flowers are borne in summer.

Sitka spruce. See *Picea sitchensis.*

SKIMMIA

RUTACEAE

Genus of evergreen shrubs and trees, grown for their spring flowers, aromatic foliage and their fruits. Except with *S. japonica* subsp. *reevesiana*, separate male and female plants are needed in order to obtain fruits. Fully to frost hardy. Needs shade or semi-shade and fertile, moist soil. Poor soil or too much sun may cause chlorosis. Propagate by semi-ripe cuttings in late summer or by seed in autumn. The fruits may cause mild stomach upset if ingested.
S. anquetilia. Evergreen, bushy, open shrub. H 1.2m (4ft), S 2m (6ft). Fully hardy. Produces small clusters of tiny, yellow flowers from mid- to late spring, then spherical, scarlet fruits. Leaves are oblong to oval, pointed, strongly aromatic and dark green.
S. × foremanii of gardens. See *S. japonica* 'Veitchii'.
S. japonica illus. p.171. **'Fructo Albo'** (female) illus. p.169. ♀ subsp. ***reevesiana* 'Robert Fortune'** (syn. *S. reevesiana; hermaphrodite*) and ♀ **'Rubella'** (male) illus. p.170. **'Veitchii'** (syn. *S. × foremanii* of gardens) is a vigorous, evergreen, upright, dense, female shrub. H and S 1.5m (5ft). Fully hardy. Broadly oval leaves are rich green. In mid- and late spring bears dense clusters of small, star-shaped, white flowers, followed by large, spherical, bright red fruits.
S. reevesiana. See *S. japonica* subsp. *reevesiana* 'Robert Fortune'.

Skullcap. See *Scutellaria.*
Sky plant. See *Tillandsia ionantha.*
Skyflower. See *Duranta erecta*, illus. p.146.
Sleepy mallow. See *Malvaviscus arboreus*, illus. p.117.
Slender lady palm. See *Rhapis excelsa*, illus. p.148.
Slipper orchid. See *Cypripedium; Paphiopedilum.*
Sloe. See *Prunus spinosa.*
Small-leaved box. See *Buxus microphylla.*
Small-leaved lime. See *Tilia cordata.*

SMILACINA

LILIACEAE/CONVALLARIACEAE

Genus of perennials, grown for their graceful appearance. Fully hardy. Prefers semi-shade and humus-rich, moist, neutral to acid soil. Propagate by division in spring or by seed in autumn.
♀ ***S. racemosa,*** syn. *Maianthemum racemosum,* illus. p.233.

SMILAX

LILIACEAE/SMILACACEAE

Genus of deciduous or evergreen, woody-stemmed or herbaceous, scrambling climbers with tubers or rhizomes. Male and female flowers are borne on separate plants. Frost hardy to frost tender, min. 5°C (41°F). Grow in any well-drained soil and in sun or semi-shade. Propagate by division or seed in spring or by semi-ripe cuttings in summer.
S. china. Deciduous, woody-based, scrambling climber with straggling, sometimes spiny stems. H to 5m (15ft). Frost hardy. Leaves are broadly oval to rounded. Umbels of yellow-green flowers are produced in spring; tiny, red berries appear in autumn.

SMITHIANTHA

GESNERIACEAE

Genus of bushy, erect perennials with tuber-like rhizomes, grown for their flowers and foliage. Frost tender, min. 15°C (59°F). Grow in humus-rich, well-drained soil and in bright light but out of direct sun. Reduce watering after flowering and water sparingly in winter. Propagate by division of rhizomes in early spring.
S. cinnabarina (Temple bells). Robust, erect, rhizomatous perennial. H and S to 60cm (2ft). Broadly oval to almost rounded, toothed leaves, to 15cm (6in) long, are dark green with dark red hairs. Bell-shaped, orange-red flowers, lined with pale yellow, are produced in summer-autumn.
***S.* 'Orange King'** illus. p.293.
S. zebrina. Bushy, rhizomatous perennial with velvety-haired stems. H and S to 1m (3ft). Oval, toothed, hairy leaves, to 18cm (7in) long, are deep green marked with reddish-brown. In summer produces tubular flowers, scarlet above, yellow below, spotted red inside and with orange-yellow lobes.

Smoke tree. See *Cotinus coggygria.*
Smooth cypress. See *Cupressus arizonica* var. *glabra.*
Smooth sumach. See *Rhus glabra*, illus. p.139.
Smooth-leaved elm. See *Ulmus minor.*

SMYRNIUM

UMBELLIFERAE/APIACEAE

Genus of biennials, grown for their flowers. Fully hardy. Grow in sun and in fertile, well-drained soil. Propagate by seed sown outdoors in autumn or spring.
S. perfoliatum illus. p.347.

Snail flower. See *Vigna caracalla.*
Snake bush. See *Justicia adhatoda.*
Snake gourd. See *Trichosanthes cucumerina* var. *anguina.*
Snake-bark maple. See *Acer capillipes*, illus. p.78; *Acer davidii; Acer davidii* subsp. *grosseri; Acer pensylvanicum*, illus. p.80; *Acer rufinerve*, illus. p.78.
Snake's-head fritillary. See *Fritillaria meleagris*, illus. p.429.
Snakeroot, White. See *Eupatorium rugosum*, illus. p.242.
Snapdragon. See *Antirrhinum.*
Sneezeweed. See *Helenium.*
Snow brake. See *Pteris ensiformis.*
Snow bush. See *Breynia disticha*, illus. p.171.
Snow creeper. See *Porana paniculata.*
Snow gum. See *Eucalyptus pauciflora* subsp. *niphophila*, illus. p.80.
Snow poppy. See *Eomecon chionantha.*
Snow trillium. See *Trillium nivale.*
Snowball pincushion. See *Mammillaria candida.*
Snowball, Pink. See *Dombeya × cayeuxii*, illus. p.84.
Snowball tree, Japanese. See *Viburnum plicatum.*
Snowbell. See *Soldanella.*
  Alpine. See *Soldanella alpina*, illus. p.380.
  Fragrant. See *Styrax obassia.*
  Least. See *Soldanella minima.*
Snowberry. See *Symphoricarpos albus.*
Snowbush rose. See *Rosa* 'Dupontii', illus. p.181.
Snowdrop. See *Galanthus.*
  Autumn. See *Galanthus reginae-olgae.*
  Common. See *Galanthus nivalis.*
  Double common. See *Galanthus nivalis* 'Flore Pleno', illus. p.455.
Snowdrop tree. See *Halesia.*
Snowdrop windflower. See *Anemone sylvestris*, illus. p.276.
Snowflake. See *Leucojum.*
  Autumn. See *Leucojum autumnale*, illus. p.453.
  Spring. See *Leucojum vernum*, illus. p.442.
  Summer. See *Leucojum aestivum*, illus. p.408.
Snow-in-summer. See *Cerastium tomentosum*, illus. p.373; *Euphorbia marginata*, illus. p.331.
Snow-on-the-mountain. See *Euphorbia marginata*, illus. p.331.
Snowy woodrush. See *Luzula nivea*, illus. p.319.
Soapwort. See *Saponaria.*
  Double. See *Saponaria officinalis* 'Rubra Plena'.
Soft shield fern. See *Polystichum setiferum.*

SOLANDRA

SOLANACEAE

Genus of evergreen, woody-stemmed, scrambling climbers, grown for their large, trumpet-shaped flowers. Frost tender, min. 10°C (50°F), but prefers 13–16°C (55–61°F). Needs full light and fertile, well-drained soil. Water freely when in full growth, sparingly in cold weather. Tie to supports. Thin out crowded stems after flowering. Propagate by semi-ripe cuttings in summer.
S. maxima, syn. *S. grandiflora* of gardens, illus. p.202.

SOLANUM

SOLANACEAE

Genus of annuals, perennials (some of which are evergreen) and evergreen, semi-evergreen or deciduous sub-shrubs, shrubs (occasionally scandent) and woody-stemmed, scrambling or leaf-stalk climbers, grown for their flowers and ornamental fruits. Frost hardy to frost tender, min. 5–10°C (41–50°F). Requires full sun and fertile, well-drained soil. Water regularly but sparingly in winter. Support scrambling climbers. Thin out and spur back crowded growth of climbers in spring. Propagate by seed in spring or by semi-ripe cuttings in summer. Red spider mite, whitefly and aphids may cause problems. All parts of most species, especially the fruits of *S. capsicastrum* and *S. pseudocapsicum*, can cause severe discomfort if ingested.
S. capsicastrum (Winter cherry). Fairly slow-growing, evergreen, bushy subshrub, grown as an annual. H and S 30–45cm (1–1½ft). Half hardy. Has lance-shaped, deep green leaves. In summer bears small, star-shaped, white flowers, followed by egg-shaped, pointed, orange-red or scarlet fruits, at least 1cm (½in) in diameter, which are at their best in winter.
♀ ***S. crispum* 'Glasnevin'** illus. p.212.
S. jasminoides. See *S. laxum.*
S. laxum, syn. *S. jasminoides* (Potato vine). Semi-evergreen, woody-stemmed, scrambling climber. H to 6m (20ft). Half hardy. Oval to lance-shaped leaves may be lobed or have leaflets at base. Small, 5-petalled, pale grey-blue flowers are produced in summer-autumn; tiny, purple berries appear in autumn. ♀ **'Album'** illus. p.203.
S. pseudocapsicum (Jerusalem cherry). Fairly slow-growing, evergreen, bushy shrub, usually grown as an annual. H and S to 1.2m (4ft). Half hardy. Has oval or lance-shaped, bright green leaves. Small, star-shaped, white flowers appear in summer and are followed by spherical, scarlet fruits. Has several smaller selections: **'Balloon'** illus. p.353; **'Fancy'**, H 30cm (1ft), with scarlet fruits; **'Red Giant'** illus. p.353; and **'Snowfire'**, H 30cm (1ft), with white fruits that later turn red.
S. rantonnetii, syn. *Lycianthes rantonnetii* (Blue potato bush). **'Royal Robe'** illus. p.141.
S. seaforthianum illus. p.202.
S. wendlandii illus. p.212.

SOLDANELLA

Snowbell

PRIMULACEAE

Genus of evergreen perennials, grown for their early spring flowers. Is good for rock gardens, troughs and alpine houses. Fully hardy, but flower buds are set in autumn and may be destroyed by frost if there is no snow cover. Requires partial shade and humus-rich, well-drained, peaty soil. Propagate by seed in spring or by division in late summer. Slugs may attack flower buds.

S. alpina (Alpine snowbell) illus. p.380.
S. minima (Least snowbell). Evergreen, prostrate perennial. H 2.5cm (1in), S 10cm (4in). Forms a mat of minute, rounded leaves on soil surface. In early spring produces solitary almost stemless, bell-shaped, pale lavender-blue or white flowers with fringed mouths.
S. montana (Mountain tassel). Evergreen, mound-forming perennial. H 10cm (4in), S 15cm (6in). In early spring produces tall flower stems carrying long, pendent, bell-shaped, lavender-blue flowers with fringed mouths. Leaves are rounded and leathery.
S. villosa illus. p.380.

SOLEIROLIA

Baby's tears, Mind-your-own-business, Mother of thousands

URTICACEAE

Genus of one species of, usually evergreen, prostrate perennial that forms a dense carpet of foliage. Frost hardy, although leaves are killed by winter frost. Recovers to grow vigorously again in spring. Tolerates sun or shade, and prefers moist soil. Propagate by division from spring to mid-summer.
S. soleirolii, syn. *Helxine soleirolii*, illus. p.316.

SOLENOSTEMON

LABIATAE/LAMIACEAE

Genus of evergreen, bushy, sub-shrubby perennials, grown for their colourful leaves amd flowers. Makes excellent pot plants. Frost tender, min. 4–10°C (39–50°F). Grow in sun or partial shade and in fertile, well-drained soil, choosing a sheltered position. Water freely in summer, much less at other times. Pinch out growing shoots of young plants to encourage a bushy habit. Propagate by seed sown under glass in spring or by softwood cuttings in spring or summer. Mealy bugs and whitefly may cause problems.
S. scutellarioides, syn. *Coleus blumei* var. *verschaffeltii*, illus. p.336. **'Brightness'** illus. p.341. **'Fashion Parade'** is a fast-growing, bushy perennial, grown as an annual. H to 45cm (18in), S 30cm (12in) or more. Min. 10°C (50°F). Has multicoloured, serrated leaves of various shapes, from oval and unlobed to deeply lobed. Spikes of tiny, blue flowers are produced in summer and are best removed. **'Scarlet Poncho'**, with a pendulous habit and oval, serrated,

bright red leaves, and **Wizard Series**, also with oval, serrated leaves, but in a very wide range of leaf colours, are both dwarf forms, H 30cm (12in).

SOLIDAGO
Golden rod

COMPOSITAE/ASTERACEAE

Genus of summer- and autumn-flowering perennials, some species of which are vigorous, coarse plants that tend to crowd out others in borders. Fully hardy. Most tolerate sun or shade and any well-drained soil. Propagate by division in spring. Occasionally self-seeds.
***S.* 'Golden Wings'.** Upright perennial. H 1.5m (5ft), S 1m (3ft). Bears large, feathery panicles of small, bright yellow flower heads in early autumn. Has lance-shaped, toothed, slightly hairy, mid-green leaves.
♀ ***S.* 'Goldenmosa'** illus. p.261.
***S.* 'Laurin'** illus. p.262.
S. virgaurea subsp. ***minuta,*** syn. *S.v.* subsp. *alpestris.* Mound-forming perennial. H and S 10cm (4in). Has small, lance-shaped, green leaves and, in autumn, neat spikes of small, yellow flower heads. Is suitable for a rock garden, trough or alpine house. Needs shade and moist soil.

× SOLIDASTER

COMPOSITAE/ASTERACEAE

Hybrid genus *(Solidago × Aster)* of one summer-flowering perennial. Fully hardy. Grows in sun or shade, and in any fertile soil. Propagate by division in spring.
× *S. hybridus.* See × *S. luteus.*
× *S. luteus*, syn. × *S. hybridus*, illus. p.303.

SOLLYA
Bluebell creeper

PITTOSPORACEAE

Genus of evergreen, woody-based, twining climbers, grown for their attractive flowers. Half hardy. Grow in sun and well-drained soil. Propagate by seed in spring or by softwood or greenwood cuttings in summer.
♀ ***S. heterophylla*** illus. p.202.

Solomon's seal. See *Polygonatum.*
Angled. See *Polygonatum odoratum.*
Great. See *Polygonatum biflorum.*
Whorled. See *Polygonatum verticillatum.*

SONERILA

MELASTOMATACEAE

Genus of evergreen, bushy perennials and shrubs, grown for their foliage and flowers. Frost tender, min. 15°C (59°F). Prefers a humid atmosphere in semi-shade and peaty soil. Propagate by tip cuttings in spring.
♀ ***S. margaritacea.*** Evergreen, bushy, semi-prostrate perennial. H and S 20–25cm (8–10in). Red stems produce oval, dark green leaves, 5–8cm (2–3in) long, reddish below, silver-patterned above. Has racemes of 3-petalled, rose-pink flowers in summer. **'Argentea'** has more silvery leaves with green veins; **'Hendersonii'** is more compact with white-spotted leaves.

Sop, Sweet. See *Annona.*

SOPHORA
Kowhai

LEGUMINOSAE/PAPILIONACEAE

Genus of deciduous or semi-evergreen trees and shrubs, grown for their habit, foliage and flowers. Fully to frost hardy. Requires full sun (*S. microphylla* and *S. tetraptera* usually need to be grown against a south- or west-facing wall) and fertile, well-drained soil. Propagate by seed in autumn; semi-evergreens may also be raised from softwood cuttings in summer.
***S. davidii*,** syn. *S. viciifolia*, illus. p.141.
♀ ***S. japonica*** (Pagoda tree). Deciduous, spreading tree. H and S 20m (70ft). Fully hardy. Dark green leaves consist of 9–15 oval leaflets. On mature trees, long clusters of pea-like, creamy-white flowers appear in late summer and early autumn. Does best in hot summers. **'Pendula'**, H and S 3m (10ft), has long, hanging shoots clothed with dark green foliage. **'Violacea'** illus. p.67.
***S. microphylla*,** syn. *Edwardsia microphylla.* Semi-evergreen, spreading tree. H and S 8m (25ft). Frost hardy. Dark green leaves are composed of numerous tiny, oblong leaflets. Produces clusters of pea-like, deep yellow flowers in late spring.
♀ ***S. tetraptera*** illus. p.85.
S. viciifolia. See *S. davidii.*

× SOPHROLAELIO-CATTLEYA

ORCHIDACEAE

See also ORCHIDS.
× *S. Hazel Boyd* 'Apricot Glow' illus. p.311. Evergreen, epiphytic orchid for an intermediate greenhouse. H 10cm (4in). In spring and early summer produces small heads of apricot-orange flowers, 9cm (3½in) across, with crimson marks on lips. Has oval, rigid leaves, 10cm (4in) long. Grow in good light in summer.
× *S. Trizac* 'Purple Emperor' illus. p.309. Evergreen, epiphytic orchid for an intermediate greenhouse. H 10cm (4in). In spring, has crimson-lipped, pinkish-purple flowers, 6cm (2½in) across, in small heads. Has oval, rigid leaves, 10cm (4in) long. Provide good light in summer.

SORBARIA

ROSACEAE

Genus of deciduous, summer-flowering shrubs, grown for their foliage and large panicles of small, white flowers. Fully hardy. Prefers sun and deep, fertile, moist soil. In winter cut out some older stems on mature plants and prune back remaining shoots to growing points. Remove suckers at base to prevent *Sorbaria* spreading too widely. Propagate by softwood cuttings in summer, by division in autumn or by root cuttings in late winter.
S. aitchisonii. See *S. tomentosa* var. *angustifolia.*
S. arborea. See *S. kirilowii.*
***S. kirilowii*,** syn. *S. arborea, Spiraea arborea.* Vigorous, deciduous, arching shrub. H and S 6m (20ft). Leaves are composed of 13–17 lance-shaped, taper-pointed, deep green leaflets. Nodding panicles of star-shaped, white flowers are produced in mid- and late summer.
***S. sorbifolia*,** syn. *Spiraea sorbifolia*, illus. p.133.
♀ ***S. tomentosa*** var. ***angustifolia,*** syn. *S. aitchisonii, Spiraea aitchisonii.* Deciduous, arching shrub. H and S 3m (10ft). Shoots are red when young. Leaves have 11–23 narrowly lance-shaped, taper-pointed, dark green leaflets. Upright panicles of star-shaped, white flowers are produced from mid- to late summer.

SORBUS

ROSACEAE

Genus of deciduous trees and shrubs, grown for their foliage, small, 5-petalled flowers, attractive fruits and, in some species, autumn colour. Leaves may be whole or divided into leaflets. Fully to frost hardy. Needs sun or semi-shade and fertile, well-drained but moist soil. Species with leaves composed of leaflets do not grow well in very dry soil. Propagate by softwood cuttings or budding in summer, by seed in autumn or by grafting in winter. Is susceptible to fireblight. Raw fruit may cause mild stomach upset if ingested.
S. alnifolia (Korean mountain ash). Deciduous, conical, then spreading tree. H 15m (50ft), S 8m (25ft). Fully hardy. Oval, toothed, bright green leaves turn orange and red in autumn. Has small, white flowers in late spring, then egg-shaped, orange-red fruits.
S. americana (American mountain ash). Deciduous, round-headed tree. H 10m (30ft), S 7m (22ft). Fully hardy. Light green leaves, divided into 11–17 narrowly oval leaflets, usually colour well in autumn. Bears small, white flowers in early summer, then rounded, bright red fruits, ripening in early autumn.
S. aria (Whitebeam). Deciduous, spreading tree. H 15m (50ft), S 10m (30ft). Fully hardy. Oval, toothed leaves are silver-grey when young, maturing to dark green above, white-felted beneath. Clusters of small, white flowers in late spring are followed by rounded, brown-speckled, deep red fruits. **'Chrysophylla'**, H 10m (30ft), S 7m (22ft), bears golden-yellow, young leaves. **'Decaisneana'** see *S.a.* 'Majestica'. ♀ **'Lutescens'** illus. p.74. ♀ **'Majestica'** (syn. *S.a.* 'Decaisneana') has larger leaves, white-haired when young, and larger fruits.
S. aucuparia (Mountain ash, Rowan) illus. p.77. **'Fastigiata'** (syn. *S. scopulina* of gardens) is a deciduous, dense, conical tree with upright branches. H 8m (25ft), S 5m (15ft). Fully hardy. Bears divided, dark green leaves, and clusters of small, white flowers in late spring or early summer followed by large, dark red fruits, 1cm (½in) across. ♀ **'Fructu Luteo'** is a spreading tree, H 15m (50ft), S 8m (25ft). Leaves consist of 13–15 narrowly oval, mid-green leaflets that turn yellow or red in autumn. Bears orange-yellow fruits. Fruits of **'Rossica Major'** (syn. *S.a.* 'Rossica') are large and deep red. ♀ **'Sheerwater Seedling'**, S 4m (12ft), has a narrow, upright habit.
♀ ***S. cashmiriana*** illus. p.89.
***S. commixta*,** syn. *S. discolor* of gardens, illus. p.77. ♀ **'Embley'** is a vigorous, deciduous, elegant tree with steeply ascending branches. H 12m (40ft), S 9m (28ft). Fully hardy. Glossy, deep green leaves, each with 13–17 slender, lance-shaped leaflets, turn orange and red in late autumn. Bears small, white flowers in late spring, and rounded, bright red fruits in autumn.
S. cuspidata. See *S. vestita.*
S. decora. Deciduous, spreading, sometimes shrubby tree. H 10m (30ft), S 8m (25ft). Fully hardy. Leaves are composed of oblong, blue-green leaflets. Small, white flowers in late spring are succeeded by rounded, orange-red fruits.
S. discolor of gardens. See *S. commixta.*
S. esserteauana. Deciduous, spreading tree. H and S 10m (30ft). Fully hardy. Dark green leaves, with broadly oblong leaflets, redden in autumn. Has small, white flowers in late spring, followed by large clusters of rounded, bright red, sometimes orange-yellow fruits.
♀ ***S. hupehensis*** (Hupeh rowan). Deciduous, spreading tree. H 12m (40ft), S 8m (25ft). Fully hardy. Leaves have 9–17 oblong, blue-green leaflets that turn orange-red in late autumn. Small, white flowers in late spring are followed by clusters of rounded, pink-tinged, white fruits. ♀ **'Rosea'** (syn. *S.h.* var. *obtusa*) illus. p.77.
S. insignis. Deciduous, spreading tree. H 8m (25ft), S 6m (20ft). Frost hardy. Leaves consist of usually 9–21 large, oblong, glossy, dark green leaflets. Large clusters of small, creamy-white flowers in late spring are followed by rounded, pink fruits that become white in winter.
S. intermedia (Swedish whitebeam). Deciduous, broad-headed, dense tree. H and S 12m (40ft). Fully hardy. Has broadly oval, deeply lobed, dark green leaves. Carries clusters of small, white flowers in late spring, succeeded by rounded, red fruits.
♀ ***S.* 'Joseph Rock'** illus. p.78.
♀ ***S.* × *kewensis*,** syn. *S. pohuashanensis* of gardens. Deciduous, spreading tree. H 10m (30ft), S 8m (25ft). Fully hardy. Dark green leaves are divided into 11–15 oblong leaflets. Has small, white flowers in late spring, followed by dense clusters of rounded, red fruits.
S. latifolia (Service tree of Fontainebleau). Deciduous, spreading tree. H 12m (40ft), S 10m (30ft). Fully hardy. Has peeling bark and broadly oval, sharply lobed, glossy, dark green leaves. Small, white flowers in late spring are succeeded by rounded, brownish-red fruits.
***S.* 'Mitchellii'.** See *S. thibetica* 'John Mitchell'.
S. pohuashanensis of gardens. See *S.* × *kewensis.*
S. prattii. Deciduous, spreading tree. H and S 6m (20ft). Fully hardy. Dark green leaves are divided into 21–9 oblong, sharply toothed leaflets. Produces small, white flowers in late spring, followed by rounded, white fruits.
♀ ***S. reducta*** illus. p.372.

♀ ***S. sargentiana*** (Sargent's rowan). Deciduous, sparsely branched, spreading tree. H and S 6m (20ft). Fully hardy. Has stout shoots and large, mid-green leaves, consisting of 7–11 oblong leaflets, that turn brilliant red in autumn. Small, white flowers in late spring are succeeded by rounded, red fruits.
♀ ***S. scalaris.*** Deciduous, spreading, graceful tree. H and S 10m (30ft). Fully hardy. Produces leaves with 21–33 narrowly oblong, glossy, deep green leaflets that become deep red and purple in autumn. Produces small, white flowers in late spring, followed by rounded, red fruits in large, dense clusters.
S. scopulina of gardens. See *S. aucuparia* 'Fastigiata'.
S. thibetica. Deciduous, conical tree. H 20m (70ft), S 15m (50ft). Fully hardy. Large, broadly oval, dark green leaves are silvery-white when young and remain so on undersides. Heads of small, white flowers in late spring are followed by rounded, brown fruits.
♀ **'John Mitchell'** (syn. *S.* 'Mitchellii') illus. p.75.
S. × thuringiaca. Deciduous, broadly conical, compact tree. H 12m (40ft), S 8m (25ft). Fully hardy. Oval, dark green leaves are deeply lobed and have basal leaflets. Small, white flowers appear in late spring, followed by rounded, bright red fruits. **'Fastigiata'** has upright branches and a broad, oval, dense crown.
S. vestita. syn. *S. cuspidata*, illus. p.74.
♀ ***S. vilmorinii*** illus. p.90.
***S.* 'Wilfred Fox'.** Deciduous tree, upright when young, later with a dense, oval head. H 15m (50ft), S 10m (30ft). Fully hardy. Has broadly oval, glossy, dark green leaves and small, white flowers in late spring, followed by rounded, orange-brown fruits.

Sorrel tree. See *Oxydendrum arboreum*, illus. p.74.
Sorrel, Wood. See *Oxalis acetosella.*
South Sea arrowroot. See *Tacca leontopetaloides.*
Southern beech. See *Nothofagus.*
Southern Japanese hemlock. See *Tsuga sieboldii.*
Southern polypody. See *Polypodium cambricum.*
Southernwood. See *Artemisia abrotanum*, illus. p.172.
Spade leaf. See *Philodendron domesticum.*
Spanish bayonet. See *Yucca aloifolia*, illus. p.149.
Spanish bluebell. See *Hyacinthoides × massartiana*, illus. p.430.
Spanish broom. See *Spartium junceum*, illus. p.143.
Spanish chestnut. See *Castanea sativa.*
Spanish dagger. See *Yucca gloriosa*, illus. p.133.
Spanish gorse. See *Genista hispanica*, illus. p.166.
Spanish heath. See *Erica australis.*
Spanish moss. See *Tillandsia usneoides*, illus. p.273.
Spanish tree heath. See *Erica australis.*

SPARAXIS
Harlequin flower

IRIDACEAE

Genus of spring- and early summer-flowering corms, grown for their very gaudy flowers. Half hardy. Needs a sunny, well-drained site. Plant in autumn. Dry off corms after flowering. Propagate by offsets in late summer or by seed in autumn.
S. elegans, syn. *Streptanthera cuprea, S. elegans.* Spring-flowering corm. H 10–25cm (4–10in), S 8–12cm (3–5in). Has lance-shaped leaves in an erect, basal fan. Stem produces a loose spike of 1–5 flattish, orange or white blooms, each 3–4cm (1¼–1½in) wide and with a yellow centre surrounded by a purple-black band.
S. fragrans subsp. ***grandiflora,*** syn. *S. grandiflora.* Spring-flowering corm. H 15–40cm (6–16in), S 8–12cm (3–5in). Has sword-shaped leaves in an erect, basal fan. Stem bears a loose spike of up to 5 flattish, yellow-tubed, deep purple flowers, each 4–5cm (1½–2in) across.
S. grandiflora. See *S. fragrans* subsp. *grandiflora.*
S. tricolor illus. p.446.

SPARGANIUM
Bur reed

SPARGANIACEAE/TYPHACEAE

Genus of deciduous or semi-evergreen, perennial, marginal water plants, grown for their foliage. Fully hardy. Tolerates deep shade and cold water. Remove faded foliage and cut plants back regularly to control growth. Propagate by seed or division in spring.
S. erectum, syn. *S. ramosum*, illus. p.465.
S. minimum. See *S. natans.*
S. natans, syn. *S. minimum* (Least bur reed). Vigorous, deciduous or semi-evergreen, perennial, marginal water plant. H 30cm–1m (1–3ft), S 30cm (1ft). Mid-green leaves are grass-like, some erect, some floating. In summer has insignificant, brownish-green flowers, in the form of burs.
S. ramosum. See *S. erectum.*

Sparmannia. See *Sparrmannia.*

SPARRMANNIA,
syn. SPARMANNIA
African hemp

TILIACEAE

Genus of evergreen trees and shrubs, grown for their flowers and foliage. Frost tender, min. 7°C (45°F). Prefers full light and fertile, well-drained soil. Water freely when in full growth, moderately at other times. Flowered stems may be cut back after flowering to promote a more compact habit. Propagate by greenwood cuttings in late spring. Is prone to whitefly.
♀ ***S. africana*** illus. p.114.

SPARTINA

GRAMINEAE/POACEAE

See also GRASSES, BAMBOOS, RUSHES and SEDGES.
***S. pectinata* 'Aureomarginata',** syn. *S.p.* 'Aureovariegata', illus. p.321.

SPARTIUM

LEGUMINOSAE/PAPILIONACEAE

Genus of one species of deciduous, almost leafless shrub, grown for its green shoots and showy flowers. Frost hardy. Needs sun and not too rich, well-drained soil. To maintain a compact habit, trim in early spring. Propagate by seed in autumn.
♀ ***S. junceum*** illus. p.143.

SPATHIPHYLLUM

ARACEAE

Genus of evergreen perennials, with rhizomes, grown for their foliage and flowers. Frost tender, min. 15°C (59°F). Prefers a humid atmosphere, humus-rich, moist soil and partial shade. Propagate by division in spring or summer. All parts of the plants may cause mild stomach upset if ingested, and contact with the sap may irritate skin.
***S.* 'Clevelandii'.** See *S. wallisii* 'Clevelandii'.
S. floribundum. Evergreen, tufted, short-stemmed perennial. H and S to 30cm (1ft). Has clusters of lance-shaped, long-pointed, long-stalked, glossy, dark green leaves, to 15cm (6in) long. Intermittently, bears narrowly oval, white spathes, to 8cm (3in) long, each enclosing a green-and-white spadix.
♀ ***S.* 'Mauna Loa'** illus. p.311.
S. wallisii illus. p.312. **'Clevelandii'** (syn. *S.* 'Clevelandii') is an evergreen, tufted perennial. H and S to 60cm (2ft). Has broadly lance-shaped, semi-erect, glossy, mid-green leaves, 30cm (1ft) or more long. Intermittently bears oval, white spathes, each 15cm (6in) long with a central, green line, that surround fragrant, white spadices.

SPATHODEA

BIGNONIACEAE

Genus of evergreen trees, grown for their flowers, mainly from autumn to spring, and for their overall appearance. Frost tender, min. 16–18°C (61–4°F). Needs full light and fertile, well-drained but moisture-retentive soil. Container-grown and immature plants seldom bear flowers. Propagate by seed in spring or by semi-ripe cuttings in summer.
S. campanulata (African tulip tree) illus. p.67.

Spatterdock, American. See *Nuphar advena.*
Speedwell
  Digger's. See *Parahebe perfoliata*, illus. p.296.
  Prostrate. See *Veronica prostrata*, illus. p.369.
  Rock. See *Veronica fruticans.*
  Spiked. See *Veronica spicata.*

SPHAERALCEA

MALVACEAE

Genus of perennials and deciduous sub-shrubs that are evergreen in warm climates. Half hardy. Requires a warm, sunny situation and fertile, well-drained soil. Propagate by seed or division in spring or by softwood cuttings in mid-summer.
S. ambigua illus. p.266.
S. munroana. Branching, woody-based perennial. H and S 45cm (18in). Broadly funnel-shaped, brilliant coral-pink flowers are borne singly in leaf axils from summer until first frosts. Has oval, round-toothed, hairy, mid-green leaves.

Sphaeropteris. Reclassified as *Cyathea.*
Spice bush. See *Lindera benzoin*, illus. p.127.
Spiceberry. See *Ardisia crenata*, illus. p.146.
Spider flower. See *Cleome.*
Spider orchid. See *Ophrys sphegodes.*
Spider plant. See *Anthericum; Chlorophytum comosum.*
Spiderwort. See *Tradescantia.*
Spignel. See *Meum athamanticum.*
Spike heath. See *Erica spiculifolia.*
Spiked speedwell. See *Veronica spicata.*
Spikenard, False. See *Smilacina racemosa*, illus. p.233.
Spike-rush, Needle. See *Eleocharis acicularis.*
Spiloxene capensis. See *Hypoxis capensis.*
Spinach, Red mountain. See *Atriplex hortensis* 'Rubra'.
Spindle
  Japanese. See *Euonymus japonicus.*
  Winged. See *Euonymus alatus*, illus. p.144.
Spindle tree. See *Euonymus europaeus.*
Spinning gum. See *Eucalyptus perriniana*, illus. p.96.

SPIRAEA

ROSACEAE

Genus of deciduous or semi-evergreen shrubs, grown for their mass of small flowers and, in some species, their foliage. Fully hardy. Requires sun and fertile, well-drained but not over-dry soil. On species and cultivars that flower on the current year's growth – *S. × billiardii*, *S. douglasii* and *S. japonica* and its cultivars – cut back young stems and remove very old ones in early spring. On species that flower on old wood, cut out older shoots in early spring, leaving young shoots to flower that year. Propagate *S. douglasii* by division between late autumn and early spring, other species and cultivars by softwood cuttings in summer.
S. aitchisonii. See *Sorbaria tomentosa* var. *angustifolia.*
S. arborea. See *Sorbaria kirilowii.*
***S.* 'Arguta'** (Bridal wreath, Foam of May). Deciduous, arching, dense shrub. H and S 2.5m (8ft). Produces clusters of 5-petalled, white flowers from mid- to late spring. Leaves are narrowly oblong and bright green.
S. aruncus. See *Aruncus dioicus.*
S. × billiardii. Deciduous, upright, dense shrub. H and S 2.5m (8ft). Has oval, finely toothed, dark green leaves and dense panicles of 5-petalled, pink flowers in summer. **'Triumphans'** has large, broadly conical panicles of bright purplish-pink flowers.
S. canescens illus. p.132.
S. douglasii. Vigorous, deciduous, upright shrub. H and S 2m (6ft). Dense, narrow panicles of 5-petalled, purplish-pink flowers are borne from early to

mid-summer among oblong, mid-green leaves with grey-white undersides. Leaves of subsp. ***menziesii***, H 1m (3ft), are green on both sides.
♀ ***S. japonica*** **'Anthony Waterer'**, ♀ **'Goldflame'** and **'Little Princess'** illus. p.159.
S. nipponica. Deciduous, arching shrub. H and S 2.5m (8ft). Bears dense clusters of 5-petalled, white flowers in early summer. Stout, red shoots carry small, rounded, dark green leaves. **'Halward's Silver'**, H and S 1m (3ft), is slow-growing, very dense and flowers profusely. ♀ **'Snowmound'** (syn. *S.n.* var. *tosaensis* of gardens) illus. p.135.
S. prunifolia. Deciduous, arching, graceful shrub. H and S 2m (6ft). In mid- and late spring has clusters of rosette-like, double, white flowers amid rounded to oblong, bright green leaves, colouring to bronze-yellow in autumn.
S. **'Snow White'**, syn. *S. trichocarpa* 'Snow White'. Deciduous, arching shrub. H and S 2m (6ft). Leaves are oblong and mid-green. Dense clusters of 5-petalled, white flowers are borne in late spring and early summer.
S. sorbifolia. See *Sorbaria sorbifolia*.
♀ ***S. thunbergii.*** Deciduous or semi-evergreen, arching, dense shrub. H 1.5m (5ft), S 2m (6ft). Small clusters of 5-petalled, white flowers are borne from early to mid-spring. Has narrowly oblong, pale green leaves.
S. trichocarpa **'Snow White'.** See *S.* 'Snow White'.
S. trilobata. Deciduous, arching, graceful shrub. H 1m (3ft), S 1.5m (5ft). In early summer bears 5-petalled, white flowers in clusters along slender shoots. Has rounded, shallowly lobed, toothed, blue-green leaves.
S. ulmaria. See *Filipendula ulmaria*.
♀ ***S.*** **x** ***vanhouttei*** illus. p.150.
S. veitchii. Vigorous, deciduous, upright shrub. H and S 3m (10ft). Has arching, red branches and oblong, dark green leaves. Produces heads of 5-petalled, white flowers from early to mid-summer.

SPIRANTHES

ORCHIDACEAE

See also ORCHIDS.
S. cernua illus. p.308. Deciduous, terrestrial orchid. H 50cm (20in). Frost hardy. Spikes of delicate, white flowers, 1cm (½in) long, with pale yellow centres, appear in autumn. Has narrowly lance-shaped leaves, 5–12cm (2–5in) long. Requires semi-shade in summer.

Spleenwort
Maidenhair. See *Asplenium trichomanes*, illus. p.323.
Mother. See *Asplenium bulbiferum*.

SPREKELIA

AMARYLLIDACEAE

Genus of one species of bulb, grown for its showy, red flowers in spring. Half hardy. Needs an open, sunny site and well-drained soil. Keep dry in winter; start into growth by watering in spring. Propagate by offsets in early autumn.
♀ ***S. formosissima*** illus. p.429.

Spring beauty. See *Claytonia virginica*.
Spring bell. See *Olsynium douglasii*.
Spring crocus. See *Crocus vernus*, illus. p.445.
Spring gentian. See *Gentiana verna*, illus. p.382.
Spring snowflake. See *Leucojum vernum*, illus. p.442.
Spruce. See *Picea*.
Black. See *Picea mariana*.
Brewer's. See *Picea breweriana*, illus. p.101.
Caucasian. See *Picea orientalis*.
Colorado. See *Picea pungens*.
Common. See *Picea abies*, illus. p.100.
Engelmann. See *Picea engelmannii*, illus. p.101.
Lijiang. See *Picea likiangensis*.
Morinda. See *Picea smithiana*.
Mountain. See *Picea engelmannii*, illus. p.101.
Norway. See *Picea abies*, illus. p.100.
Spruce (continued)
Oriental. See *Picea orientalis*.
Serbian. See *Picea omorika*, illus. p.99.
Sitka. See *Picea sitchensis*.
Taiwan. See *Picea morrisonicola*, illus. p.103.
West Himalayan. See *Picea smithiana*.
White. See *Picea glauca*.
Spurge. See *Euphorbia*.
Wood. See *Euphorbia amygdaloides*.
Spurge laurel. See *Daphne laureola*.
Squawroot. See *Trillium erectum*, illus. p.277.
Squill
Sea. See *Urginea maritima*.
Siberian. See *Scilla siberica*.
Striped. See *Puschkinia scilloides* var. *libanotica*, illus. p.448.
Squirrel tail grass. See *Hordeum jubatum*, illus. p.319.
Squirrel's-foot fern. See *Davallia mariesii*.

STACHYS

LABIATAE/LAMIACEAE

Genus of late spring- or summer-flowering perennials, shrubs and sub-shrubs, some of which are evergreen. Fully hardy to frost tender, min. 5°C (41°F). Grows in any well-drained soil, tolerating even poor soil. Species mentioned below prefer an open, sunny position; others are woodland plants and grow better in semi-shade. Propagate by division in spring.
S. byzantina, syn. *S. lanata, S. olympica*, illus. p.316. **'Primrose Heron'** illus. p.303. **'Silver Carpet'** is an evergreen, mat-forming perennial. H 15cm (6in), S 60cm (24in). Fully hardy. Has oval, woolly, grey leaves. Rarely produces flowers. Makes an excellent front-of-border or ground-cover plant.
S. coccinea. Clump-forming perennial. H 60cm (24in), S 45cm (18in). Frost tender. Has oval, mid-green leaves with a pronounced network of veins. From early to late summer, spikes of small, hooded, bright scarlet flowers, protruding from purple calyces, arise from leaf axils.
S. lanata. See *S. byzantina*.
S. macrantha. Clump-forming perennial. H and S 30cm (12in). Fully hardy. Has heart-shaped, crinkled, round-toothed, soft green leaves. Whorls of large, hooded, rose-purple flowers are produced in summer. **'Superba'** illus. p.295.
S. officinalis, syn. *Betonica officinalis* (Betony). Mat-forming perennial. H 45–60cm (18–24in), S 30–45cm (12–18in). Fully hardy. Bears whorls of hooded, tubular, purple, pink or white flowers on sturdy stems, arising, in summer, from mats of oval to oblong, round-toothed, mid-green leaves. **'Rosea'** has flowers of clearer pink.
S. olympica. See *S. byzantina*.

STACHYURUS

STACHYURACEAE

Genus of deciduous shrubs, grown for their flowers, which are borne before the leaves. Fully to half hardy; flower spikes, formed in autumn, are usually unharmed by hard frosts. Requires a position in sun or semi-shade, and fertile, moist but well-drained, not too heavy soil, preferably peaty and acid. Does well when trained against a south- or west-facing wall. Propagate by softwood cuttings in summer.
S. chinensis. Deciduous, spreading, open shrub. H 2m (6ft), S 4m (12ft). Fully hardy. Pendent spikes of small, bell-shaped, pale yellow flowers open in late winter and early spring. Leaves are oval and deep green.
♀ ***S. praecox*** illus. p.146. **'Magpie'** is a deciduous, spreading, open shrub, less vigorous than the species. H 1.5m (5ft), S 2m (6ft). Has arching, red-purple shoots and oval, tapered, grey-green leaves, edged with creamy-white. Bell-shaped, pale yellow flowers are borne in late winter and early spring.

Staff tree. See *Celastrus scandens*.
Staff vine. See *Celastrus orbiculatus*.
Stag's-horn fern. See *Platycerium*.
Stag's-horn sumach. See *Rhus typhina*.
Stanford manzanita. See *Arctostaphylos stanfordiana*.

STANHOPEA

ORCHIDACEAE

See also ORCHIDS.
♀ ***S. tigrina.*** Evergreen, epiphytic orchid for a cool greenhouse. H 23cm (9in). Pendent spikes of fragrant, waxy, rich yellow and maroon flowers, 15cm (6in) across, with red-spotted, white lips, are produced in summer. Has broadly oval, ribbed leaves, 30cm (12in) long. Is best grown in a hanging, slatted basket. Provide semi-shade in summer.

STAPELIA

ASCLEPIADACEAE

Genus of clump-forming, perennial succulents with erect, 4-angled stems. Stem edges are often indented and may bear small leaves that drop after only a few weeks. Flowers are often foul-smelling. Frost tender, min. 11°C (52°F). Needs a site in sun or partial shade, with well-drained soil. Propagate by seed or stem cuttings in spring or summer.
S. europaea. See *Caralluma europaea*.
S. flavirostris. See *S. grandiflora*.
♀ ***S. gigantea*** illus. p.492.
S. grandiflora, syn. *S. flavirostris*, illus. p.492.
S. variegata. See *Orbea variegata*.

STAPHYLEA

Bladder nut

STAPHYLEACEAE

Genus of deciduous, spring-flowering shrubs and trees, grown for their flowers and bladder-like fruits. Fully hardy. Requires sun or semi-shade and fertile, moist soil. Propagate species by softwood or greenwood cuttings in summer or by seed in autumn, selected forms by softwood or greenwood cuttings in summer.
♀ ***S. colchica.*** Deciduous, upright shrub. H and S 3.5m (11ft). Erect panicles of bell-shaped, white flowers are borne in late spring and are followed by inflated, greenish-white fruits. Bright green leaves each consist of 3–5 oval leaflets.
♀ ***S. holocarpa*** **'Rosea'** illus. p.113.
S. pinnata illus. p.112.

Star, Blue. See *Amsonia*.
Star daisy. See *Lindheimera texana*, illus. p.348.
Star flower. See *Orbea variegata*, illus. p.492.
Star ipomoea. See *Ipomoea coccinea*.
Star jasmine. See *Trachelospermum jasminoides*, illus. p.203.
Star magnolia. See *Magnolia stellata*.
Star-cluster. See *Pentas lanceolata*, illus. p.159.
Star-of-Bethlehem. See *Ornithogalum*.
Drooping. See *Ornithogalum nutans*.
Star-of-Bethlehem orchid. See *Angraecum sesquipedale*.
Statice. See *Limonium* except for:
S. suworowii for which see *Psylliostachys suworowii*.
Statice. See *Psylliostachys*.

STAUNTONIA

LARDIZABALACEAE

Genus of evergreen, woody-stemmed, twining climbers. Male and female flowers are produced on separate plants. Frost hardy. Grow in any well-drained soil and in sun or semi-shade. To keep under control, prune in early spring. Propagate by seed in spring or by stem cuttings in summer or autumn.
S. hexaphylla. Evergreen, woody-stemmed, twining climber. H to 10m (30ft) or more. Leaves have 3–7 oval leaflets, each 5–13cm (2–5in) long. In spring has racemes of small, fragrant, cup-shaped, pale violet flowers, followed by egg-shaped, edible, fleshy, purple fruits, 2.5–5cm (1–2in) long, if plants of both sexes are grown together.

Stemless gentian. See *Gentiana acaulis*, illus. p.382.

STENANTHIUM

LILIACEAE/MELANTHIACEAE

Genus of summer-flowering bulbs, attractive but seldom cultivated. Frost hardy. Needs an open, sunny position in any well-drained soil. In cool areas, plant in a warm, sheltered site in light soil that does not dry out excessively.

Propagate by seed in autumn or by division in spring.
S. gramineum. Summer-flowering bulb. H to 1.5m (5ft), S 45–60cm (1½–2ft). Has long, narrowly strap-shaped, semi-erect, basal leaves. Stem produces a dense, branched, often arching spike of fragrant, star-shaped, white or green flowers, each 1–1.5cm (½–⅝in) across.

STENOCACTUS, syn. ECHINOFOSSULOCACTUS

CACTACEAE

Genus of spherical, perennial cacti with spiny, green stems that have very narrow, wavy ribs. Frost tender, min. 7°C (45°F). Needs a sunny position and well-drained soil. Propagate by seed in spring or summer.
S. coptonogonus illus. p.492.
S. crispatus syn. *Echinofossulatus lamellosus, Stenocactus lamellosus.* Spherical, perennial cactus. H and S 8cm (3in). Green stem has 30–35 ribs. Funnel-shaped, flesh-coloured or red flowers, 1–3cm (½–1¼in) across, are produced from crown in spring. Has flattened upper radial spines, shorter, more rounded lower ones and longer, rounded central spines with darker tips.
S. lamellosus. See *S. crispatus.*
S. obvallatus, syn. *Echinofossulatus pentacanthus, E. violaciflorus*, illus. p.488.

STENOCARPUS

PROTEACEAE

Genus of evergreen, summer- and autumn-flowering trees, grown for their flowers and foliage. Frost tender, min. 5–7°C (41–5°F). Needs full light and fertile, well-drained soil. Water containerized plants moderately, less in winter. Pruning is rarely necessary. Propagate by seed in spring or by semi-ripe cuttings in summer.
S. sinuatus (Australian firewheel tree). Slow-growing, evergreen, upright tree. H 12m (40ft) or more, S 5m (15ft). Has lustrous, deep green leaves, each 12–25cm (5–10in) long, lance-shaped and entire or with pairs of oblong lobes. Bottle-shaped, bright scarlet flowers, clustered like the spokes of a wheel, are produced from late summer to autumn.

STENOCEREUS

CACTACEAE

Genus of tree-like or shrubby, perennial cacti with prominently ribbed stems often densely spined. Frost tender, min. 13°C (55°F), otherwise plants may become badly marked. Needs full sun and very well-drained soil. Propagate by seed in spring or stem cuttings in summer.
S. marginatus. See *Pachycereus marginatus.*
S. thurberi, syn. *Lemaireocereus thurberi.* Columnar, perennial cactus, branching from low down. H to 7m (22ft), S 1m (3ft). Has 5- or 6-ribbed, glossy, dark green stems with very short-spined areoles set in close rows down each rib. Produces funnel-shaped, purple or pink flowers with red sepals in summer.

Stenolobium stans. See *Tecoma stans.*

STENOMESSON

AMARYLLIDACEAE

Genus of bulbs, grown for their long, often pendent, tubular flowers. Frost tender, min. 5–10°C (41–50°F). Needs an open, sunny situation and well-drained soil. Propagate by offsets in autumn.
S. incarnatum. See *S. variegatum.*
S. miniatum, syn. *Urceolina peruviana*, illus. p.435.
S. variegatum, syn. *S. incarnatum*, illus. p.435.

STENOTAPHRUM

GRAMINEAE/POACEAE

See also GRASSES, BAMBOOS, RUSHES and SEDGES.
S. secundatum (St Augustine grass) ♀ **'Variegatum'** is an evergreen, spreading, rhizomatous, perennial grass. H 15cm (6in), S indefinite. Frost tender, min. 5°C (41°F). Leaves are mid-green with cream stripes and last well into winter. Has erect racemes of brownish-green spikelets in summer. In warm climates is used for lawns.

STEPHANANDRA

ROSACEAE

Genus of deciduous, summer-flowering shrubs, grown for their habit, foliage, autumn colour and winter shoots. Fully hardy. Needs sun or semi-shade and fertile, not too dry soil. On established plants cut out some older shoots after flowering. Propagate by softwood cuttings in summer or by division in autumn.
S. incisa. Deciduous, arching shrub. H 1.5m (5ft), S 3m (10ft). Oval, deeply lobed and toothed, bright green leaves turn orange-yellow in autumn and stems become rich brown in winter. Produces crowded panicles of tiny, star-shaped, greenish-white flowers in early summer. **'Crispa'**, H 60cm (2ft), has wavy-edged and more deeply lobed leaves.
S. tanakae illus. p.136.

STEPHANOTIS

ASCLEPIADACEAE

Genus of evergreen, woody-stemmed, twining climbers, grown for their scented, waxy flowers. Frost tender, min. 13–16°C (55–61°F). Provide a humus-rich, well-drained soil and partial shade in summer. Water moderately, less in cold weather. Provide stems with support. Shorten over-long or crowded stems in spring. Propagate by seed in spring or by semi-ripe cuttings in summer.
♀ ***S. floribunda*** illus. p.200.

Sterculia acerifolia. See *Brachychiton acerifolius.*
Sterculia diversifolia. See *Brachychiton populneus.*
Sterculia platanifolia. See *Firmiana simplex.*

STERNBERGIA

AMARYLLIDACEAE

Genus of spring- or autumn-flowering bulbs, grown for their large, crocus-like flowers. Frost hardy, but in cool areas grow against a sunny wall. Needs a hot, sunny site and any well-drained, heavy or light soil that dries out in summer, when bulbs die down and need warmth and dryness. Leave undisturbed to form clumps. Propagate by division in spring or autumn.
S. candida illus. p.442.
S. clusiana. Autumn-flowering bulb. H to 2cm (¾in), S 8–10cm (3–4in). Strap-shaped, semi-erect, basal, greyish-green leaves, often twisted lengthways, appear after flowering. Stems carry erect, goblet-shaped, yellow or greenish-yellow flowers, 4–8cm (1½–3in) long.
S. lutea illus. p.455.
S. sicula. Autumn-flowering bulb. H 2.5–7cm (1–3in), S 5–8cm (2–3in). Narrowly strap-shaped, semi-erect, basal, deep green leaves, each with a central, paler green stripe, appear with flowers. Each stem bears a funnel-shaped, bright yellow flower, 2–4cm (¾–1½in) long.

STETSONIA

CACTACEAE

Genus of one species of tree-like, perennial cactus with a stout trunk. Nocturnal, funnel-shaped flowers are 15cm (6in) long. Frost tender, min. 10°C (50°F). Needs a sunny, well-drained position. Propagate by seed in spring or summer.
S. coryne illus. p.473.

STEWARTIA, syn. STUARTIA

THEACEAE

Genus of deciduous trees and shrubs, grown for their flowers, autumn colour and usually peeling bark. Fully to frost hardy. Needs a sunny position, but preferably with roots in shade, and shelter from strong winds. Requires fertile, moist but well-drained, neutral to acid soil. Resents being transplanted. Propagate by softwood cuttings in summer or by seed in autumn.
S. malacodendron. Deciduous, spreading tree or shrub. H 4m (12ft), S 3m (10ft). Frost hardy. Rose-like, purple-stamened, white flowers, sometimes purple-streaked, are borne in mid-summer amid oval, dark green leaves.
S. monadelpha illus. p.78.
♀ ***S. pseudocamellia*** illus. p.74.
♀ ***S. sinensis.*** Deciduous, spreading tree. H 12m (40ft), S 7m (22ft). Fully hardy. Has peeling bark and oval, bright green leaves that turn brilliant red in autumn. Fragrant, rose-like, white flowers are produced in mid-summer.

STIGMAPHYLLON

MALPIGHIACEAE

Genus of evergreen, woody-stemmed, twining climbers, grown for their flowers. Frost tender, min. 15–18°C (59–64°F). Fertile, well-drained soil is needed with partial shade in summer. Water freely when in full growth, less in low temperatures. Provide stems with support. Thin out crowded stems in spring. Propagate by semi-ripe cuttings in summer.
S. ciliatum illus. p.214.

Stinking hellebore. See *Helleborus foetidus*, illus. p.317.
Stinking iris. See *Iris foetidissima.*

STIPA

GRAMINEAE/POACEAE

See also GRASSES, BAMBOOS, RUSHES and SEDGES.
S. arundinacea See *Anemanthele lessoniana.*
S. calamagrostis, syn. *Achnatherum calamagrostis.* Evergreen, tuft-forming, perennial grass. H 1m (3ft), S 45cm (1½ft). Fully hardy. Leaves are bluish-green and inrolled. In summer bears decorative, large, loose panicles of sand-brown spikelets that dry and last well into winter.
♀ ***S. gigantea*** illus. p.319.

Stock. See *Matthiola.*
Brompton. See *Matthiola incana.*
Virginian. See *Malcolmia maritima*, illus. p.335.

STOKESIA

COMPOSITAE/ASTERACEAE

Genus of one species of evergreen, summer-flowering perennial. Fully hardy. Requires sun or semi-shade and fertile, well-drained soil. Propagate by division in spring or by seed in autumn.

S. laevis illus. p.295. **'Blue Star'** is an evergreen, basal-rosetted perennial. H and S 30–45cm (12–18in). Bears cornflower-like, deep blue flower heads singly at stem tips in summer. Has rosettes of narrowly lance-shaped, dark green leaves.

STOMATIUM

AIZOACEAE

Genus of mat-forming, perennial succulents with short stems, each bearing 4–6 pairs of solid, 3-angled or semi-cylindrical leaves, often with toothed edges and incurved tips. Frost tender, min. 5°C (41°F). Needs sun and well-drained soil. Propagate by seed or stem cuttings in spring or summer.
S. agninum. Mat-forming, perennial succulent. H 5cm (2in), S 1m (3ft) or more. Has solid, 3-angled or semi-cylindrical, soft grey-green leaves, 4–5cm (1½–2in) long, often without teeth. In summer, fragrant, daisy-like, yellow flowers, 2–5cm (¾–2in) across, open in evening.
S. patulum. Mat-forming, perennial succulent. H 3cm (1¼in), S 1m (3ft). Has semi-cylindrical, grey-green leaves, each 2cm (¾in) long, with rough dots and 2–9 teeth-like tubercles on upper surface. Bears 2cm (¾in) wide, fragrant, daisy-like, pale yellow flowers in evening in summer.

Stone pine. See *Pinus pinea*, illus. p.105.
Mexican. See *Pinus cembroides*, illus. p.105.

Stone plant. See *Lithops.*
Stonecrop. See *Sedum.*
Biting. See *Sedum acre*, illus. p.396.
Common. See *Sedum acre*, illus. p.396.
Reflexed. See *Sedum rupestre*, illus. p.371.
Strangweja spicata. See *Bellevalia hyacinthoides.*
Stranvaesia. Reclassified as *Photinia.*
Strap cactus. See *Epiphyllum.*

STRATIOTES

HYDROCHARITACEAE

Genus of semi-evergreen, perennial, submerged, free-floating water plants, grown for their foliage. Fully hardy. Requires sun. Grows in any depth of cool water. Thin plants as required. Propagate by separating young plants from runners in summer.
S. aloides illus. p.463.

Strawberry cactus. See *Mammillaria prolifera.*
Strawberry geranium. See *Saxifraga stolonifera* 'Tricolor'.
Strawberry tree. See *Arbutus unedo*, illus. p.89.
Grecian. See *Arbutus andrachne.*
Strawflower. See *Bracteantha bracteata; Rhodanthe.*

STRELITZIA

Bird-of-paradise flower

MUSACEAE/STRELITZIACEAE

Genus of large, evergreen, tufted, clump-forming, palm-like perennials, grown for their showy flowers. Frost tender, min. 5–10°C (41–50°F). Grow in fertile, well-drained soil and in bright light shaded from direct sun in summer. Reduce watering in low temperatures. Propagate by seed or division of suckers in spring.
S. nicolai illus. p.232.
♀ ***S. reginae*** illus. p.275.

Streptanthera cuprea. See *Sparaxis elegans.*
Streptanthera elegans. See *Sparaxis elegans.*

STREPTOCARPUS

GESNERIACEAE

Genus of perennials, some of which are evergreen, with showy flowers. Frost tender, min. 10–15°C (50–59°F). Grow in a humid atmosphere in humus-rich, moist soil and in bright light away from direct sunlight. Avoid wetting leaves when watering; water less during cold periods. Propagate by seed, if available, in spring, by division after flowering or by tip cuttings from bushy species or leaf cuttings from stemless species in spring or summer.
S. caulescens illus. p.286.
S. 'Constant Nymph' illus. p.315.
S. 'Nicola' illus. p.313.
S. rexii (Cape primrose). Stemless perennial. H to 25cm (10in), S to 50cm (20in). Has a rosette of strap-shaped, wrinkled, green leaves. Stems, 15cm (6in) or more long, bear loose clusters of funnel-shaped, pale blue or mauve flowers, 5cm (2in) long and with darker lines, intermittently at any time of year.
♀ ***S. saxorum*** (False African Violet) illus. p.294.

STREPTOSOLEN

SOLANACEAE

Genus of one species of evergreen or semi-evergreen, loosely scrambling shrub, grown for its flowers. Frost tender, min. 7–10°C (45–50°F). Requires full sun and humus-rich, well-drained soil. Water freely when in full growth, less at other times. After flowering or in spring, remove flowered shoots and tie in new growths. Propagate by softwood or semi-ripe cuttings in summer.
♀ ***S. jamesonii*** illus. p.218.

String-of-beads. See *Senecio rowleyanus*, illus. p.478.
String-of-hearts. See *Ceropegia linearis* subsp. *woodii*, illus. p.478.
Striped squill. See *Puschkinia scilloides* var. *libanotica*, illus. p.448.
Striped torch. See *Guzmania monostachia*, illus p.273.

STROBILANTHES

ACANTHACEAE

Genus of perennials and evergreen sub-shrubs, grown for their flowers. Frost hardy to frost tender, min. 15°C (59°F). Grow in semi-shade in fertile, well-drained soil. Propagate by seed, basal stem cuttings or division in spring.
S. atropurpureas illus. p.271.

STROMANTHE

MARANTACEAE

Genus of evergreen, creeping perennials, grown mainly for their foliage. Frost tender, min. 15°C (59°F). Prefers high humidity and partial shade. Grow in open soil or compost, use soft water if possible and do not allow to dry out completely. Propagate by division in spring.
S. sanguinea. Strong-growing, evergreen, creeping perennial. H and S to 1.5m (5ft). Lance-shaped leaves, to 45cm (18in) long, are glossy, green above with paler midribs, reddish below. Bears panicles of small, 3 petalled, white flowers in axils of showy, bright red bracts, usually in spring but also in summer-autumn.

STROMBOCACTUS

CACTACEAE

Genus of extremely slow-growing, hemispherical to cylindrical, perennial cacti. Takes 5 years from seed to reach 1cm (½in) high. Funnel-shaped flowers are 4cm (1½in) across. Frost tender, min. 5°C (41°F). Needs sun and very well-drained soil. Is difficult to grow and very susceptible to overwatering. Propagate by seed or grafting in spring or summer.
S. disciformis illus. p.486.

STRONGYLODON

LEGUMINOSAE/PAPILIONACEAE

Genus of evergreen, woody-stemmed, twining climbers, grown for their large, claw-like flowers. Frost tender, min. 18°C (64°F). Needs humus-rich, moist but well-drained soil and partial shade in summer. Water freely when in full growth, less at other times. Provide support. If necessary, thin crowded stems in spring. Propagate by seed or stem cuttings in summer or by layering in spring.
S. macrobotrys illus. p.202.

Stuartia. See *Stewartia.*

STYLIDIUM

STYLIDIACEAE

Genus of perennials with grass-like leaves, grown for their unusual flowers that have fused, 'triggered' stamens adapted for pollination by insects. Frost tender, min. 10°C (50°F). Grow in fertile soil and in bright light. Propagate by division or seed in spring.
S. graminifolium (Trigger plant). Rosetted perennial. H and S to 15cm (6in) or more. Grass-like, stiff, dark green leaves, with toothed margins, rise from ground level. Bears tiny, pale pinkish-mauve flowers in narrow spikes, 30cm (12in) or more long, in summer.

STYLOPHORUM

PAPAVERACEAE

Genus of spring-flowering perennials with large, deeply lobed leaves, nearly all as basal rosettes. Fully hardy. Needs semi-shade and humus-rich, moist, peaty soil. Propagate by division in spring or by seed in autumn.
S. diphyllum. Perennial with basal rosettes of large, lobed, hairy leaves. H and S to 30cm (12in) or more. Bears open cup-shaped, golden-yellow flowers in spring on upright, branched stems. Prefers rich, woodland conditions.

STYRAX

STYRACACEAE

Genus of deciduous, summer-flowering trees and shrubs, grown for their foliage and flowers. Fully hardy to frost tender, min. 7–10°C (45–50°F). Prefers a sheltered position in sun or semi-shade and moist, neutral to acid soil. Propagate by softwood cuttings in summer or by seed in autumn.
♀ ***S. japonicus*** illus. p.73.
♀ ***S. obassia*** (Fragrant snowbell). Deciduous, spreading tree. H 12m (40ft), S 7m (22ft). Fully hardy. Bears long, spreading clusters of fragrant, bell- to funnel-shaped, white flowers in early summer. Has broad, rounded, deep green leaves.
S. officinalis illus. p.114.
S. wilsonii illus. p.134.

Subalpine fir. See *Abies lasiocarpa.*
Sugar bush. See *Protea repens.*
Sugar maple. See *Acer saccharum.*
Sugared-almond plum. See *Pachyphytum oviferum*, illus. p.491.
Sulcorebutia arenacea. See *Rebutia arenacea.*
Sulcorebutia rauschii. See *Rebutia steinmannii.*
Sulcorebutia tiraquensis. See *Rebutia steinmannii* subsp. *tiraquensis.*
Sultan, Sweet. See *Amberboa.*
Sumach. See *Rhus.*
Dwarf. See *Rhus copallina.*
Smooth. See *Rhus glabra*, illus. p.139.
Stag's-horn. See *Rhus typhina.*
Venetian. See *Cotinus coggygria.*
Summer cypress. See *Bassia scoparia* f. *trichophylla*, illus. p.347.
Summer holly. See *Arctostaphylos diversifolia.*
Summer hyacinth. See *Galtonia candicans*, illus. p.409.
Summer snowflake. See *Leucojum aestivum*, illus. p.408.
Sun plant. See *Portulaca grandiflora.*
Sundew. See *Drosera.*
Cape. See *Drosera capensis*, illus. p.317.
Sunflower. See *Helianthus.*
Mexican. See *Tithonia rotundifolia.*
Willow-leaved. See *Helianthus salicifolius.*
Sunrise horse-chestnut. See *Aesculus × neglecta.*
Sutera grandiflora. See *Jamesbrittenia grandiflora.*

SUTHERLANDIA

LEGUMINOSAE/PAPILIONACEAE

Genus of evergreen shrubs, grown for their flowers and fruits. Frost tender, min. 7–10°C (45–50°F). Requires full light and fertile, well-drained soil. Water containerized specimens freely when in full growth, moderately at other times. Remove old, twiggy stems at ground level in late winter. Propagate by seed in spring. Red spider mite may be troublesome.
S. frutescens illus. p.161.

SWAINSONA

LEGUMINOSAE/PAPILIONACEAE

Genus of annuals, evergreen perennials, sub-shrubs and shrubs, grown for their flowers. Frost tender, min. 5–7°C (41–5°F). Needs full light or partial shade and humus-rich, well-drained soil. Water freely when in active growth, moderately at other times. Propagate by seed in spring or by semi-ripe cuttings in summer.
S. galegifolia (Darling pea). Evergreen, sprawling sub-shrub. H 60cm–1.2m (2–4ft), S 30–60cm (1–2ft). Leaves have 11–25 narrowly oval, mid- to deep green leaflets. Bears pea-like, red, pink, purple, blue or yellow flowers in late spring and summer. Remove old, flowered shoots in late winter.

Swamp cypress. See *Taxodium distichum*, illus. p.100.
Swamp lily. See *Lilium superbum; Saururus cernuus*, illus. p.463.
Swamp pink. See *Helonias bullata.*
Swan flower. See *Aristolochia grandiflora.*
Swan River daisy. See *Brachycome iberidifolia*, illus. p.346.
Swedish ivy. See *Plectranthus oertendahlii; Plectranthus verticillatus.*
Swedish whitebeam. See *Sorbus intermedia.*
Sweet alyssum. See *Lobularia maritima.*
Sweet bay. See *Laurus nobilis; Magnolia virginiana.*
Sweet box. See *Sarcococca.*
Sweet briar. See *Rosa rubiginosa*, illus. p.181.
Sweet buckeye. See *Aesculus flava*, illus. p.78.
Sweet chestnut. See *Castanea sativa.*

Sweet Cicely. See *Myrrhis*.
Sweet corn. See *Zea mays*.
Sweet flag. See *Acorus calamus*.
Sweet gum. See *Liquidambar styraciflua*, illus. p.66.
Sweet pea. See *Lathyrus odoratus*.
Sweet pepper-bush. See *Clethra alnifolia*.
Sweet rocket. See *Hesperis matronalis*, illus. p.241.
Sweet scabious. See *Scabiosa atropurpurea*.
Sweet sop. See *Annona*.
Sweet sultan. See *Amberboa*.
Sweet viburnum. See *Viburnum odoratissimum*.
Sweet violet. See *Viola odorata*.
Sweet William. See *Dianthus barbatus*.
Sweetheart ivy. See *Hedera hibernica* 'Deltoidea', illus. p.219.
Swiss mountain pine. See *Pinus mugo*.
Swiss-cheese plant. See *Monstera deliciosa*, illus. p.218.
Sword fern. See *Nephrolepis cordifolia; Nephrolepis exaltata*, illus. p.324.

SYAGRUS
Queen palm

PALMAE/ARECACEAE

Genus of one species of evergreen palm, grown for its majestic appearance. Frost tender, min. 18°C (64°F). Requires full light or partial shade and humus-rich, well-drained soil. Water containerized specimens moderately, less when temperatures are low. Propagate by seed in spring at not less than 24°C (75°F). Red spider mite may be a nuisance.
S. romanzoffiana illus. p.69.

Sycamore. See *Acer pseudoplatanus*.

SYCOPSIS

HAMAMELIDACEAE

Genus of evergreen trees and shrubs, grown for their foliage and flowers. Frost hardy. Needs a sheltered position in sun or semi-shade and fertile, not too dry, peaty soil. Propagate by semi-ripe cuttings in summer.
S. sinensis. Evergreen, upright shrub. H 5m (15ft), S 4m (12ft). Leaves are oval, glossy and dark green. Flowers lack petals but have showy, dense clusters of red-tinged, yellow anthers in late winter or early spring.

Sydney golden wattle. See *Acacia longifolia*.

SYMPHORICARPOS

CAPRIFOLIACEAE

Genus of deciduous shrubs, with inconspicuous, bell-shaped flowers, grown mainly for their clusters of showy, long-persistent fruits. Fully hardy. Requires sun or semi-shade and fertile soil. Propagate by softwood cuttings in summer or by division in autumn. Fruits may cause mild stomach upset if ingested; contact with them may irritate skin.
S. albus (Snowberry). var. ***laevigatus*** is a vigorous, deciduous, dense shrub, part upright, part arching. H and S 2m (6ft). Large, marble-like, white fruits follow pink flowers borne in summer. Rounded leaves are dark green.
***S.* × *chenaultii* 'Hancock'.** Deciduous, procumbent, dense shrub. H 1m (3ft), S 3m (10ft). Has oval, bronze leaves maturing to bright green. White flowers appear from early to mid-summer. Small, spherical, deep lilac-pink fruits are sparsely borne. Makes excellent ground cover.
S. orbiculatus (Coralberry, Indian currant). Deciduous, bushy, dense shrub. H and S 2m (6ft). Has white or pink flowers in late summer and early autumn, then spherical, deep purplish-red fruits. Oval leaves are dark green. Does best after a hot summer. **'Foliis Variegatis'** (syn. *S.o.* 'Variegatus') illus. p.164.

SYMPHYANDRA

CAMPANULACEAE

Genus of short-lived, summer-flowering perennials, best grown as biennials. Suits large rock gardens and bases of banks. Fully hardy. Needs sun and well-drained soil. Propagate by seed in autumn. Self-seeds readily.
S. armena, syn. *Campanula armena.* Upright or spreading perennial. H 30–60cm (1–2ft), S 30cm (1ft). Produces panicles of upright, bell-shaped, blue or white flowers in summer. Leaves are oval, irregularly toothed, hairy and mid-green.
S. pendula, syn. *Campanula pendula.* Arching perennial. H 30–60cm (1–2ft), S 30cm (1ft). Produces panicles of pendent, bell-shaped, cream flowers in summer. Has oval, hairy, pale green leaves. Becomes woody at base with age.
S. wanneri, syn. *Campanula wanneri.* illus. p.369.

SYMPHYTUM
Comfrey

BORAGINACEAE

Genus of vigorous, coarse perennials, best suited to wild gardens. Fully hardy. Prefers sun or semi-shade and moist soil. Propagate by division in spring or by seed in autumn; usually self-seeds. Propagate named cultivars by division only. Roots and leaves may cause severe discomfort if ingested; contact with foliage may irritate skin.
S. caucasicum illus. p.240.
***S.* 'Goldsmith'**, syn. *S. ibericum* 'Jubilee', *S. ibericum* 'Variegatum', *S.* 'Jubilee'. Clump-forming perennial. H and S 30cm (12in). Has ovate, hairy, dark green leaves with gold and cream markings. Bears pale blue flowers, tinged cream or pink, in spring.
S. grandiflorum of gardens. See *S. ibericum*.
***S.* 'Hidcote Blue'.** Clump-forming perennial. H 50cm (20in), S 60cm (24in). Is similarto *S. ibericum*, but has pale blue flowers.
S. ibericum, syn. *S. grandiflorum* of gardens. Clump-forming perennial. H 25cm (10in), S 60cm (24in). Has lance-shaped, hairy, rich green leaves. Bears one-sided racemes of tubular, creamy flowers in spring. Makes good ground cover. **'Jubilee'** see *S.* 'Goldsm ith'.**'Variegatum'** see *S.* 'Goldsmith'.
***S.* 'Jubilee'.** See *S.* 'Goldsmith'.
S.* × *uplandicum (Russian comfrey). ♀ **'Variegatum'** illus. p.240.

SYMPLOCOS

SYMPLOCACEAE

Genus of evergreen or deciduous trees and shrubs, of which only the species described is in general cultivation. This is grown for its flowers and fruits. Fruits are most prolific when several plants are grown together. Fully hardy. Needs full sun and fertile, moist but well-drained soil. Propagate by seed in autumn.
S. paniculata illus. p.134.

SYNADENIUM

EUPHORBIACEAE

Genus of evergreen, semi-succulent shrubs, grown for their foliage. Frost tender, min. 7–10°C (45–50°F). Requires full light and fertile, freely draining soil. Water containerized plants moderately, less in winter. Prune in late winter if necessary. Propagate by seed in spring or by softwood cuttings in summer. All parts are highly toxic if ingested; sap may irritate skin.
S. compactum var. ***rubrum,*** syn. *S. grantii* 'Rubrum'. Evergreen, erect, robust-stemmed shrub. H 3–4m (10–12ft), S 2m (6ft) or more. Has very small, red flowers in autumn, largely concealed by lance-shaped to oval, glossy, purplish-green leaves, red-purple beneath.
***S. grantii* 'Rubrum'.** See *S. compactum* var. *rubrum*.

SYNGONIUM

ARACEAE

Genus of evergreen, woody-stemmed, root climbers, grown for their ornamental foliage. Flowers are seldom produced in cultivation. Frost tender, min. 16–18°C (61–4°F). Needs partial shade and humus-rich, well-drained soil. Water moderately, less in low temperatures. Provide support, ideally with moss poles. Remove young stem tips to promote branching. Propagate by leaf-bud or stem-tip cuttings in summer. All parts may cause mild stomach upset if ingested; contact with the sap may irritate skin.
S. auritum, syn. *Philodendron auritum* of gardens, *P. trifoliatum* (Five fingers). Fairly slow-growing, evergreen, woody-stemmed, root climber. H 1–2m (3–6ft). Has glossy, rich green leaves divided into 3, sometimes 5, oval leaflets, the central one the largest.
S. erythrophyllum. Slow-growing, evergreen, root climber with slender, woody stems. H 1m (3ft) or more. Young plants have arrowhead-shaped leaves, flushed purple beneath. Leaves on mature plants have 3 lobes or leaflets and thicker, longer stems.
S. hoffmannii. Moderately vigorous, evergreen, woody-stemmed, root climber. H 2–3m (6–10ft). Young plants have arrowhead-shaped leaves; mature ones have leaves divided into 3 grey-green leaflets with silvery-white veins.
♀ ***S. podophyllum***, syn. *Nephthytis triphylla* of gardens, illus. p.218. **'Trileaf Wonder'** illus. p.217.

SYNNOTIA

IRIDACEAE

Genus of spring-flowering corms, with fans of lance-shaped leaves, grown for their loose spikes of flowers, each with 6 unequal petals, hooded like a small gladiolus. Half hardy. Needs sun and well-drained soil. Plant in autumn. Dry off after flowering. Propagate by seed or offsets in autumn.
S. variegata. Spring-flowering corm. H 10–35cm (4–14in), S 8–10cm (3–4in). Produces erect leaves in a basal fan. Flowers are long-tubed with upright, purple, upper petals and narrower, pale yellowish-purple, lower ones curving downwards. var. metelerkampiae has smaller flowers.

SYNTHYRIS

SCROPHULARIACEAE

Genus of evergreen or deciduous, spring-flowering perennials with gently spreading, rhizomatous rootstocks. Is useful for rock gardens and peat beds. Fully hardy. Prefers partial shade and moist soil. Propagate in late spring by seed or division.
S. missurica var. stellata, See *S. stellata*.
S. reniformis. Evergreen, clump-forming perennial. H 8–10cm (3–4in), S 15cm (6in). Has kidney-shaped to rounded, toothed, dark green leaves and, in spring, short, dense racemes of small, bell-shaped, blue flowers.
S. stellata syn. *S. missurica* var. *stellata* illus. p.381.

Syrian juniper. See *Juniperus drupacea*.

SYRINGA
Lilac

OLEACEAE

Genus of deciduous shrubs and trees, grown for their dense panicles of small, tubular flowers, usually extremely fragrant. Fully hardy. Needs sun and deep, fertile, well-drained, preferably alkaline soil. Obtain plants on their own roots, since grafted plants usually sucker freely. Remove flower heads from newly planted lilacs, and dead-head for first few years. Cut out weak shoots in winter and, to maintain shape, prune after flowering. Straggly, old plants may be cut back hard in winter, but the next season's flowers will then be lost. Propagate by softwood cuttings in summer. Leaf miners, leaf spot and lilac blight may be troublesome. See also feature panel p.116
***S.* 'Belle de Nancy'.** See *S. vulgaris* 'Belle de Nancy'.
***S.* 'Bellicent'.** See *S.* × *josiflexa* 'Bellicent'.
***S.* 'Blue Hyacinth'.** See *S.* × *hyacinthiflora* 'Blue Hyacinth'.
***S.* 'Charles Joly'.** See *S. vulgaris* 'Charles Joly'.
S.* × *chinensis (Rouen lilac). Deciduous, arching shrub. H and S 4m (12ft). Bears large, arching panicles of fragrant, tubular, single, lilac-purple flowers in late spring. Oval leaves are dark green. **'Alba'** (illus. p.116) has white flowers.
***S.* 'Clarke's Giant'.** See *S.* × *hyacinthiflora* 'Clarke's Giant'.
***S.* 'Congo'.** See *S. vulgaris* 'Congo'.
***S.* 'Cora Brandt'.** See *S.* × *hyacinthiflora* 'Cora Brandt'.
***S.* 'Decaisne'.** See *S. vulgaris* 'Decaisne'.
S. emodi (Himalayan lilac). Vigorous,

deciduous, upright shrub. H 5m (15ft), S 4m (12ft). Bears unpleasantly scented, tubular, single, very pale lilac flowers in large, upright panicles in early summer. Has large, oval, dark green leaves.
***S.* 'Esther Staley'.** See *S.* × *hyacinthiflora* 'Esther Staley'.
***S.* 'Fountain'.** Vigorous, deciduous, arching, open shrub. H 4m (12ft), S 5m (15ft). Large, nodding panicles of fragrant, tubular, single, deep pink flowers open above large, oval, dark green leaves in early summer.
***S.* × *hyacinthiflora* 'Blue Hyacinth',** syn. *S.* 'Blue Hyacinth' illus. p.116. Deciduous, bushy shrub, upright when young, later spreading. H and S 3m (10ft). Bears large, loose panicles of fragrant, single, pale lilac-blue flowers from mid-spring to early summer and has broadly heart-shaped, mid-green leaves. Vigorous **'Clarke's Giant'** (syn. *S.* 'Clarke's Giant'; illus p.116), H and S 5m (15ft), has lavender flowers, mauve-pink within, opening from mauve-pink buds from mid- to late spring. Has dark green leaves. **'Cora Brandt'** (syn. *S.* 'Cora Brandt'; illus. p.116) produces double, white flowers in large open panicles. ♀ **'Esther Staley'** (syn. *S.* 'Esther Staley'; illus. p.116) is vigorous, with broadly conical panicles of red buds opening to lilac-pink flowers.
***S.* 'Isabella'.** See *S.* × *prestoniae* 'Isabella'.
***S.* 'Jan van Tol'.** See *S. vulgaris* 'Jan van Tol'.
♀ ***S.* × *josiflexa* 'Bellicent',** syn. *S.* 'Bellicent'. Deciduous, upright, then arching shrub. H 4m (12ft), S 5m (15ft). Large panicles of fragrant, tubular, single, clear pink flowers are borne above oval, dark green leaves in late spring and early summer.
***S.* 'Katherine Havemeyer'.** See *S. vulgaris* 'Katherine Havemeyer'.
***S.* 'Madame Antoine Buchner'.** See *S. vulgaris* 'Madame Antoine Buchner'.
***S.* 'Madame F. Morel'.** See *S. vulgaris* 'Madame F. Morel'.
***S.* 'Madame Florent Stepman'.** See *S. vulgaris* 'Madame Florent Stepman'.
***S.* 'Madame Lemoine'.** See *S. vulgaris* 'Madame Lemoine'.
***S.* 'Maréchal Foch'.** See *S. vulgaris* 'Maréchal Foch'.
***S.* 'Masséna'.** See *S. vulgaris* 'Masséna'.
***S.* 'Maud Notcutt'.** See *S. vulgaris* 'Maud Notcutt'.
♀ ***S. meyeri* 'Palibin',** syn. *S. palibianina* of gardens, *S. velutina* of gardens, illus. p.116. Slow-growing, deciduous, bushy, dense shrub. H and S 1.5m (5ft). Produces dense panicles of fragrant, tubular, single, lilac-pink flowers in late spring and early summer. Has small, oval deep green leaves.
***S.* 'Michel Buchner'.** See *S. vulgaris* 'Michel Buchner'.
S. microphylla. See *S. pubescens* subsp. *microphylla.*
***S.* 'Monge'.** See *S. vulgaris* 'Monge'.
***S.* 'Mrs Edward Harding'.** See *S. vulgaris* 'Mrs Edward Harding'.
S. palibiniana of gardens. See *S. meyeri* 'Palibin'.
***S.* 'Paul Thirion'.** See *S. vulgaris* 'Paul Thirion'.
♀ ***S.* × *persica*** (Persian lilac; illus. p.116). Deciduous, bushy, dense shrub. H and S 2m (6ft). Produces small, dense panicles of fragrant, purple flowers in late spring. Leaves are narrow, pointed and dark green.
***S.* 'Président Grévy'.** See *S. vulgaris* 'Président Grévy'.
***S.* × *prestoniae* 'Isabella',** syn. *S.* 'Isabella'. Vigorous, deciduous, upright shrub. H and S 4m (12ft). Has large, nodding panicles of fragrant, tubular, single, lilac-purple flowers, almost white within, in early summer, and large, oval, dark green leaves.
***S.* 'Primrose'.** See *S. vulgaris* 'Primrose'.
***S. pubescens* subsp. *microphylla*,** syn. *S. microphylla.* Deciduous, bushy shrub. H and S 2m (6ft). Small panicles of very fragrant, tubular, single, pink flowers appear in early summer, and often again in autumn, amid oval, mid-green leaves. ♀ **'Superba'** illus. p.116.
S. reticulata. Deciduous, broadly conical tree or shrub. H 10m (30ft), S 6m (20ft). Large panicles of fragrant, tubular, single, creamy-white flowers open above oval, taper-pointed, bright green leaves from early to mid-summer.
***S.* 'Souvenir de Louis Spaeth'.** See *S. vulgaris* 'Andenken an Ludwig Spaeth'.
S. velutina of gardens. See *S. meyeri* 'Palibin'.
S. vulgaris ♀ **'Andenken an Ludwig Spaeth'** (syn. *S.* 'Souvenir de Louis Spaeth'). Deciduous, upright, then spreading shrub. H and S 5m (15ft). Long, slender panicles of fragrant, tubular, single, deep purplish-red flowers are borne profusely above heart-shaped, dark green leaves in late spring. **'Belle de Nancy'** (syn. *S.*'Belle de Nancy') has large, dense panicles of double, mauve-pink flowers opening from purple-red buds. ♀ **'Charles Joly'** (syn. *S.* 'Charles Joly'; illus. p.116), H and S 3m (10ft), carries deep purple-red flowers from mid-spring to early summer. **'Congo'** (syn. *S.* 'Congo'; illus. p.116) bears large panicles of single, deep lilac-purple flowers, purplish-red in bud, in spring. **'Decaisne'** (syn. *S.* 'Decaisne'; illus. p.116) is compact, with masses of single, dark blue flowers that are shaded purple, and mid-green leaves. **'Jan van Tol'** (syn. *S.* 'Jan van Tol'; illus. p.116) bears long, semi-pendent panicles of single, narrow-petalled, pure white flowers. ♀ **'Katherine Havemeyer'** (syn. *S.* 'Katherine Havemeyer') has double, lavender-purple, then lavender-pink flowers in dense, conical panicles. ♀ **'Madame Antoine Buchner'** (syn. *S.* 'Madame Antoine Buchner'; illus. p.116) carries long, narrow panicles of deep purple-red buds, which open to double, pinkish-mauve flowers, fading with age. **'Madame F. Morel'** (syn. *S.* 'Madame F. Morel'; illus. p.116) produces large panicles of single, light violet-purple flowers that are purple in bud. **'Madame Florent Stepman'** (syn. *S.* 'Madame Florent Stepman'; illus. p.116) bears large panicles of single, white flowers. ♀ **'Madame Lemoine'** (syn. *S.* 'Madame Lemoine'; illus. p.116) bears compact panicles of large, double, white flowers. **'Maréchal Foch'** (syn. *S.*'Maréchal Foch'; illus. p.116) has broad, open panicles of very large, single, carmine-pink flowers. **'Masséna'** (syn. *S.* 'Masséna'; illus. p.116). bears loose panicles of large, deep red-purple flowers. **'Maud Notcutt'** (syn. *S.* 'Maud Notcutt') produces large panicles of single, pure white flowers. **'Michel Buchner'** (syn. *S.* 'Michel Buchner'; illus. p.116) has large panicles of double, pink-lilac flowers, each with a white eye. **'Monge'** (syn. *S.* 'Monge'; illus. p.116) produces masses of very large, single, deep purple-red flowers. ♀ **'Mrs Edward Harding'** (syn. *S.* 'Mrs Edward Harding'; illus. p.116) has large panicles of double or semi-double, purple-red flowers that fade to pink. **'Paul Thirion'** (syn. *S.* 'Paul Thirion'; illus. p.116) carries double lilac-pink flowers that open from deep purple-red buds. **'Président Grévy'** (syn. *S.* 'Président Grévy'; illus. p.116) bears very large panicles of double, lilac-blue flowers that open from red-violet buds. **'Primrose'** (syn. *S.* 'Primrose'; illus. p.116) produces small, dense panicles of pale yellow flowers.
S. yunnanensis illus. p.116. Deciduous, upright shrub. H 3m (10ft), S to 3m (10ft). In early summer, large, oval, pointed, dark green leaves set off slender panicles of 4-petalled, pale pink or white flowers.

SYZYGIUM

MYRTACEAE

Genus of evergreen shrubs and trees, grown for their overall appearance. Frost tender, min. 10–13°C (50–56°F). Prefers full light (but tolerates some shade) and fertile, well-drained soil. Water containerized plants freely when in full growth, moderately at other times. Is very tolerant of pruning, but is best grown naturally. Propagate by seed in spring or semi-ripe cuttings in summer.
***S. paniculatum*,** syn. *Eugenia australis* of gardens, *E. paniculata*, illus. p.77.

Szechuan birch. See *Betula szechuanica.*

T

TABEBUIA

BIGNONIACEAE

Genus of deciduous or evergreen, mainly spring-flowering trees, grown for their flowers and for shade. Frost tender, min. 16–18°C (61–4°F). Requires full light and fertile, well-drained but not dry soil. Pot-grown plants are unlikely to flower. Pruning, other than shaping while young in autumn, is not needed. Propagate by seed or air-layering in spring or by semi-ripe cuttings in summer.

T. chrysotricha illus. 97.

T. donnell-smithii. See *Cybistax donnell-smithii*.

T. pentaphylla of gardens. See *T. rosea*.

T. rosea, syn. *T. pentaphylla* of gardens (Pink trumpet tree). Fast-growing, evergreen, rounded tree, deciduous in cool climates. H and S 15m (50ft) or more. Leaves have 5 oval leaflets. Produces trumpet-shaped rose- to lavender-pink or white flowers, with yellow throats, in terminal clusters in spring.

Tacamahac. See *Populus balsamifera*.

TACCA

TACCACEAE

Genus of perennials with rhizomes, grown for their curious flowers. Frost tender, min. 18°C (64°F). Needs a fairly humid atmosphere, partial shade and peaty soil. Water sparingly during resting period in winter. Propagate by division or seed, if available, in spring.

T. chantrierei (Bat flower, Cat's whiskers). Clump-forming, rhizomatous perennial. H and S 30cm (1ft). Narrowly oblong, stalked, arching leaves are 45cm (1½ft) or more long. In summer produces flower umbels with green or purplish bracts on stems up to 60cm (2ft) long. Individual flowers are nodding, bell-shaped, 6-petalled and green, turning purple with long, pendent, maroon to purple threads.

T. leontopetaloides (East Indian arrowroot, South Sea arrowroot). Clump-forming, rhizomatous perennial. H and S 45cm (1½ft). Green leaves, to 1m (3ft) long, are deeply 3-lobed, each lobe also divided, on stalks to over 1m (3ft). In summer, on stems up to 1m (3ft) long, flower umbels are produced with 4–12 purple or brown bracts and 20–40 small, 6-petalled, yellow or purplish-green flowers, with long, purple to brown threads. Rhizomes yield edible starch.

Tacitus bellus. See *Graptopetalum bellum*.

Tacsonia mollissima. See *Passiflora mollissima*.

Tacsonia van-volxemii. See *Passiflora antioquiensis*.

TAGETES

COMPOSITAE/ASTERACEAE

Genus of annuals that flower continuously throughout summer and until the autumn frosts. Is useful as bedding plants and for edging. Half hardy. Grow in sun and in fertile, well-drained soil. Dead-head to ensure a long flowering period. Propagate by seed sown under glass in mid-spring. Is prone to slugs, snails and botrytis. The African marigolds are excellent for formal bedding, whereas the French, Afro-French, and Signet marigolds are more suitable for the edge of a mixed border. All are good in containers and provide long-lasting cut flowers. Contact with the foliage may aggravate skin allergies. Four main hybrid groups are in cultivation.

African marigolds (African Group) Compact annuals, derived from *T. erecta*, with angular, hairless stems and pinnate, sparsely glandular leaves, 5–10cm (2–4in) long, each with 11–17 narrowly lance-shaped, pointed, sharply toothed leaflets, to 5cm (2in) long. Large, densely double, pompon-like, terminal flower heads, usually to 12cm (5in) across, each with 5–8 or more ray-florets and numerous orange to yellow disc-florets, are produced from late spring to autumn. Sto 45cm (18in).

French marigolds (French Group) Compact annuals, derived from *T. patula*, with hairless, purple-tinged stems and pinnate leaves, to 10cm (4in) long, with lance-shaped to narrowly lance-shaped, toothed leaflets, to 3cm (1¼in) long. Solitary, usually double flower heads, typically to 5cm (2in) across, with few to many red-brown, yellow, orange, or parti-coloured ray-florets and usually several disc-florets, are borne singly or in cyme-like inflorescences from late spring to autumn. Sto 30cm (12in).

Afro-French marigolds (Afro-French Group) Bushy annuals, derived from crosses of *T. erecta* and *T. patula*, with angular to rounded stems, branched and sometimes stained purple, and pinnate leaves, 5–13cm (2–5in) long, with lance-shaped leaflets, to 5cm (2in) long. Numerous small, single or double, yellow or orange flower heads, usually 2.5–6cm (1–2½in) across, often marked red-brown, are borne singly or in cyme-like inflorescences from late spring to autumn. S 30–40cm (12–16in).

Signet marigolds (Signet Group) Upright annuals, derived from *T. tenuifolia*, with cylindrical, simple or many-branched stems and pinnate leaves, 5–13cm (2–5in) long, with narrowly lance-shaped, toothed leaflets, to 2cm (¾in) long. Many single flower heads, usually to 2.5cm (1in) across, with yellow or orange florets (few ray-florets and several disc-florets), are borne in cyme-like inflorescences from late spring to autumn. S to 40cm (16in).

***T.* Antigua Series.** illus. p.352. African marigolds. H to 30cm (12in). Bear orange, lemon-yellow, golden-yellow, or primrose-yellow flower heads from late spring to early autumn.

***T.* Beaux Series.** Afro-French marigolds. H 35cm (14in). Bear double flower heads of rich golden-yellow, orange with a red splash, or copper-red, from late spring to early autumn.

***T.* Bonanza Series.** French marigolds. H 30cm (12in). In summer, they have double flower heads in deep orange-mahogany with gold margins, golden orange-mahogany, or orange-yellow-mahogany.

***T.* Boy Series** illus. p.352.

***T.* Boy-o-boy** illus. p.350.

***T.* 'Cinnabar'** illus. p.341.

***T.* Disco Series.** French marigolds. H 20–25cm (8–10in). Single, weather-resistant flower heads in a range of colours, including yellow, golden-yellow with mahogany markings, golden-red and red-orange, are borne from late spring to early autumn.

T. erecta (African marigold, Aztec marigold). Fast-growing, upright, bushy annual. H 30cm–1m (1–3ft), S 30–45cm (1–1½ft). Has very deeply divided, aromatic, glossy, deep green leaves. Daisy-like, double flower heads, 5cm (2in) wide, are carried in summer and early autumn.

***T.* Gem Series.** Signet marigolds. H to 23cm (9in). Produce flower heads in lemon-yellow, deep orange, or bright orange with darker markings. **'Lemon Gem'** has lemon-yellow flower heads. **'Tangerine Gem'** illus. p.352.

♀ ***T.* 'Gold Coins'** illus. p.348.

♀ ***T.* 'Honeycomb'.** French marigold. H 25cm (10in). Produces crested, double, yellow- and reddish-orange flower heads.

***T.* Lady Series.** African marigolds. H 40–45cm (16–18in). Produce orange, primrose-yellow, yellow, or golden-yellow flower heads from late spring to early autumn.

***T.* Marvel Series.** Compact African marigolds. H 45cm (18in). Produce densely double flower heads in gold, orange, yellow, lemon-yellow, or in a formula mixture of colours, from late spring to early autumn.

***T.* Mischief Series.** French marigolds. H to 30cm (12in) or more. Have single flower heads in mahogany-red, yellow, or golden-yellow, with some bicolours, from late spring to early autumn.

***T.* 'Naughty Marietta'** illus. p.350.

T. patula (French marigold). Fast-growing, bushy annual. H and S to 30cm (1ft). Has deeply divided, aromatic, deep green leaves. Single or carnation-like, double flower heads, in shades of yellow, orange, red or mahogany, are borne in summer and early autumn.

♀ ***T.* Safari Series 'Safari Tangerine'.** French marigolds. H 20–25cm (8–10in). Has double, broad-petalled, rich tangerine-orange flower heads from late spring to early autumn.

***T.* 'Vanilla'.** African marigold. H to 35cm (14in). Has creamy-white flower heads from late spring to early autumn.

***T.* Voyager Series.** Compact African marigolds. H 30–35cm (12–14in). Large, yellow or orange flower heads, to 10cm (4in) across, are borne from late spring to early autumn.

***T.* Zenith Series.** Afro-French marigolds. H 30cm (12in). Have flower heads in yellow, golden-yellow, lemon-yellow, red, or orange, from late spring to early autumn.

Tail flower. See *Anthurium andraeanum*, illus. p.272.

Taiwan cherry. See *Prunus campanulata*.

Taiwan spruce. See *Picea morrisonicola*, illus. p.103.

Talbotia elegans. See *Vellozia elegans*.

TALINUM

PORTULACACEAE

Genus of summer-flowering perennials, some of which are evergreen, grown for their flowers and succulent foliage. Is useful for rock gardens, troughs and alpine houses and as pot plants. Fully hardy to frost tender, min. 7°C (45°F). Needs sun and gritty, not too dry, well-drained soil. Propagate by seed in autumn.

T. okanoganense. Cushion- or mat-forming, prostrate perennial. H to 4cm (1½in), S to 10cm (4in). Fully hardy. Succulent stems produce tufts of cylindrical, succulent, greyish-green leaves and, in summer, bear tiny, cup-shaped, white flowers. Is excellent for cultivating in a trough or alpine house.

Tall melic. See *Melica altissima*.

Tallow tree, Chinese. See *Sapium sebiferum*.

Tamarind. See *Tamarindus indica*.

TAMARINDUS

LEGUMINOSAE/CAESALPINIACEAE

Genus of one species of evergreen tree, grown for its edible fruits and overall appearance as well as for shade. Frost tender, min. 15–18°C (59–64°F). Needs full light and well-drained soil. Propagate by seed or air-layering in spring.

T. indica (Tamarind). Slow-growing, evergreen, rounded tree. H and S to 25m (80ft). Leaves have 10–15 pairs of oblong to elliptic, bright green leaflets. Produces profuse racemes of asymmetric, 5-petalled, pale yellow flowers, veined red, in summer, then long, brownish pods containing edible but acidic pulp.

Tamarisk. See *Tamarix*.

TAMARIX

Tamarisk

TAMARICACEAE

Genus of deciduous or evergreen shrubs and trees, grown for their foliage, habit and abundant racemes of small flowers. In mild areas is very wind-resistant and thrives in exposed, coastal positions, making excellent hedges. Fully to frost hardy. Requires sun and fertile, well-drained soil. Restrict growth by cutting back in spring; trim hedges at the same time. Propagate by semi-ripe cuttings in summer or by hardwood cuttings in winter.

T. gallica. Deciduous, spreading shrub or tree. H 4m (12ft), S 6m (20ft). Frost hardy. Purple, young shoots are clothed with tiny, scale-like, blue-grey leaves. Star-shaped, pink flowers are borne in slender racemes in summer.

T. pentandra. See *T. ramosissima*.

T. ramosissima, syn. *T. pentandra*, illus. p.117.

TANACETUM

COMPOSITAE/ASTERACEAE

Genus of perennials, some of which are evergreen, often with aromatic foliage, grown for their daisy-like flower heads. Fully to frost hardy. Grow in sun and in fertile, well-drained soil. Propagate by division in spring. Contact with the foliage may aggravate skin allergies.

T. argenteum, syn. *Achillea argentea*, illus. p.372.

T. coccineum, syn. *Chrysanthemum coccineum, Pyrethrum coccineum, Pyrethrum roseum* (Pyrethrum). **'Brenda'** (syn *Pyrethrum* 'Brenda') An erect perennial, H 60cm (24in), S 45cm (18in) or more. Fully hardy. Has somewhat aromatic, feathery leaves. Single, magenta-pink flower heads are borne in late spring and early summer. ♀ **'Eileen May Robinson'** (illus. p.240), is an upright perennial. H to 75cm (30in), S 45cm (18in). Fully hardy. Has slightly aromatic, feathery, recurved leaves, 5cm (2in) long. In summer bears strong-stemmed, pink flower heads, 5cm (2in) wide, with yellow centres. Is useful for cut flowers. ♀ **'James Kelway'** has deep crimson flower heads ageing to pink.

T. densum subsp. ***amani***, syn. *Chrysanthemum densum*, illus. p.373.

T. haradjanii, syn. *Chrysanthemum haradjanii.* Evergreen, mat-forming, woody-based perennial with a tap root. H and S 23–38cm (9–15in). Frost hardy. Has broadly lance-shaped, much-divided, silvery-grey leaves and, in summer terminal clusters of bright yellow flower heads. Is useful for a rock garden or alpine house.

T. parthenium, syn. *Chrysanthemum parthenium, Pyrethrum parthenium*, illus. p.331. **'Aureum'** is a short-lived, bushy perennial, grown as an annual. H and S 20–45cm (8–18in). Half hardy. Has oval, lobed, aromatic, green-gold leaves and, in summer and early autumn, daisy-like, white flower heads.

TANAKAEA

SAXIFRAGACEAE

Genus of one species of evergreen, spreading perennial, grown for its foliage and flowers. Is suitable for rock gardens and peat beds. Fully hardy. Needs partial shade and well-drained, peaty, sandy soil. Propagate by runners in spring.

T. radicans. Evergreen, dense, basal-rosetted perennial. H 6–8cm (2½–3in), S 20cm (8in). Leaves are narrowly oval to heart-shaped, leathery and mid- to dark green. Bears small panicles of tiny, outward-facing, star-shaped, white flowers in late spring.

Tanbark oak. See *Lithocarpus densiflorus*.
Tansy-leaved thorn. See *Crataegus tanacetifolia*.
Tape grass. See *Vallisneria spiralis*.

TAPEINOCHILOS

COSTACEAE/ZINGIBERACEAE

Genus of mostly evergreen perennials, grown for their colourful, leaf-like bracts. Frost tender, min. 18°C (64°F). Needs high humidity, partial shade and humus-rich soil. Is not easy to grow successfully in pots. Propagate by division in spring. Red spider mite may be a problem with pot-grown plants.

T. ananassae. Evergreen, tufted perennial. H to 2m (6ft), S 75cm (2½ft). Non-flowering stems are erect and unbranched, with narrowly oval, long-pointed leaves, to 15cm (6in) long. Flowering stems are leafless, to over 1m (3ft) long, and, in summer, bear ovoid, dense spikes, 15cm (6in) or more long, of small, tubular, yellow flowers. Showy, recurved, hard, scarlet bracts enclose and almost hide flowers.

Tarajo holly. See *Ilex latifolia*.
Taro. See *Alocasia macrorrhiza; Colocasia esculenta*, illus. p.464.
Tasman celery pine. See *Phyllocladus aspleniifolius*.
Tasmanian blue gum. See *Eucalyptus globulus*.
Tasmanian podocarp. See *Podocarpus alpinus*.
Tasmanian sassafras. See *Atherosperma moschatum*.
Tasmanian snow gum. See *Eucalyptus coccifera*, illus. p.68.
Tasmanian waratah. See *Telopea truncata*, illus. p.127.
Tassel flower. See *Amaranthus caudatus*, illus. p.338; *Emilia coccinea*, illus. p.353.
Tassel grape hyacinth. See *Muscari comosum*.
Tassel maidenhair. See *Adiantum raddianum* 'Grandiceps'.
Tassel, Mountain. See *Soldanella montana*.
Tawny daylily. See *Hemerocallis fulva*.

TAXODIUM

TAXODIACEAE

See also CONIFERS.
♀ ***T. distichum*** illus. p.100.

TAXUS

TAXACEAE

All parts (but not the seed coating) are highly toxic if ingested. See also CONIFERS.

♀ ***T. baccata*** (Yew). Slow-growing conifer with a broadly conical, later domed crown. H 10–15m (30–50ft), S 5–10m (15–30ft). Fully hardy. Needle-like, flattened leaves are dark green. Female plants bear cup-shaped, fleshy, bright red fruits; only the red part, not the seed, is edible. Will regrow if cut back. The following forms are H 6–10m (20–30ft), S 5–8m (15–25ft) unless otherwise stated. **'Adpressa'** is a shrubby, female form with short, broad leaves. **Aurea Group** (syn. *T.b.* 'Aurea'; illus. p.107) has golden-yellow foliage. ♀ **'Dovastoniana'** is spreading, with weeping branchlets. ♀ **'Dovastonii Aurea'** (illus. p.107) is similar to *T.b.* 'Dovastoniana', but has golden shoots and yellow-margined leaves. ♀ **'Fastigiata'**, H 10–15m (30–50ft), S 4–5m (12–15ft), has erect branches and dark green foliage that stands out all around shoots. **'Fastigiata Aurea'** is similar to *T.b.* 'Fastigiata', but has gold-variegated leaves. ♀ **'Repandens'**, H 60cm (2ft), S 5m (15ft), is a spreading form. ♀ **'Semperaurea'**, H 3m (10ft), S 5m (15ft), has ascending branches with dense, golden foliage.

T. cuspidata illus. p.105. **'Aurescens'** is a spreading, bushy, dwarf conifer. H 30cm (1ft), S 1m (3ft). Fully hardy. Is hardier than *T. baccata* forms. Needle-like, flattened leaves are deep golden-yellow in their first year and mature to dark green. **'Capitata'**, H 10m (30ft), S 2m (6ft), is upright in habit. **'Densa'**, H 1.2m (4ft), S 6m (20ft), is a female form with short, erect shoots.

T. × media. Dense conifer that is very variably shaped. H and S 3–6m (10–20ft). Fully hardy. Has needle-like, flattened leaves, spreading either side of olive-green shoots. Leaves are stiff, broad and widen abruptly at the base. Fruits are similar to those of *T. baccata*. **'Brownii'**, H 2.5m (8ft), S 3.5m (11ft), is a dense, globose form with dark green foliage. **'Densiformis'**, H 2–3m (6–10ft), is dense and rounded, with masses of shoots that have bright green leaves. ♀ **'Hicksii'**, H to 6m (20ft), is columnar and has ascending branches. Male and female forms exist. **'Hillii'**, H and S 3m (10ft), is a broadly conical to rounded, dense bush with glossy, green leaves. **'Wardii'**, H 2m (6ft), S 6m (20ft), is a flat, globose, female form.

Tea, Labrador. See *Ledum groenlandicum*, illus. p.150.
Tea-myrtle, Western. See *Melaleuca nesophila*, illus. p.141.
Tea-tree
Duke of Argyll's. See *Lycium barbarum*.
New Zealand. See *Leptospermum scoparium*.
Teasel. See *Dipsacus*.

TECOMA,
syn. TECOMARIA

BIGNONIACEAE

Genus of mainly evergreen shrubs and trees, grown for their flowers from spring to autumn. Frost tender, min. 5–13°C (41–55°F). Prefers moist but well-drained soil and full light. Water potted specimens moderately, hardly at all in winter. May be pruned annually after flowering to maintain as a shrub. Propagate by seed in spring or by semi-ripe cuttings in summer. Red spider mite may be troublesome.

T. australis. See *Pandorea pandorana*.

♀ ***T. capensis***, syn. *Bignonia capensis, Tecomaria capensis* (Cape honeysuckle). Evergreen, scrambling climber, shrub-like when young. H 2–3m (6–10ft). Leaves have 5–9 rounded, serrated, glossy, dark green leaflets. Tubular, orange-red flowers are carried in short spikes mainly in spring-summer. **'Aurea'** (syn. *Tecomaria capensis* 'Aurea') illus. p.202.

T. grandiflora. See *Campsis grandiflora*.

T. radicans. See *Campsis radicans*.

T. ricasoliana. See *Podranea ricasoliana*.

T. stans, syn. *Bignonia stans, Stenolobium stans*, illus. p.92.

TECOMANTHE

BIGNONIACEAE

Genus of evergreen, twining climbers, grown for their flowers. Frost tender, min. 16–18°C (61–4°F). Provide humus-rich, well-drained soil and light shade in summer. Water freely when in full growth, less at other times. Provide stems with support. If necessary, thin out crowded stems in spring. Propagate by seed in spring or by semi-ripe cuttings in summer.

T. speciosa. Strong-growing, evergreen, twining climber. H to 10m (30ft) or more. Has leaves of 3 or 5 oval leaflets. Bears dense clusters of foxglove-like, fleshy-textured, cream flowers, tinged with green, in autumn.

Tecomaria. See *Tecoma*.

TECOPHILAEA

LILIACEAE/TECOPHILAEACEAE

Genus of spring-flowering corms, rare in cultivation and extinct in the wild, grown for their beautiful flowers. Fully hardy, but because of rarity usually grown in a cold greenhouse or cold frame. Requires sun and well-drained soil. Water in winter and spring. Keep corms dry, but not sunbaked, from early summer to autumn, then replant. Propagate in autumn by seed or offsets.

♀ ***T. cyanocrocus*** illus. p.449. ♀ var. ***leichtlinii*** (syn. *T.c.* 'Leichtlinii') illus. p.448.

Teddy-bearvine. See *Cyanotis kewensis*.

TELEKIA

COMPOSITAE/ASTERACEAE

Genus of summer-flowering perennials, grown for their bold foliage and large flower heads. Fully hardy. Grows in sun or shade and in moist soil. Propagate by division in spring or by seed in autumn.

T. speciosa, syn. *Buphthalmum speciosum.* Upright, spreading perennial. H 1.2–1.5m (4–5ft), S 1–1.2m (3–4ft). Mid-green leaves are heart-shaped at base of plant, oval on stems. In late summer, branched stems bear large, daisy-like, rich gold flower heads. Is ideal for a pool side or woodland.

Telesonix jamesii. See *Boykinia jamesii*.

TELLIMA

SAXIFRAGACEAE

Genus of one species of semi-evergreen, late spring-flowering perennial. Makes good ground cover and is ideal for cool, semi-shaded woodland gardens and beneath shrubs in sunny borders. Fully hardy. Grows in any well-drained soil. Propagate by division in spring or by seed in autumn.

T. grandiflora (Fringecups). Semi-evergreen, clump-forming perennial. H and S 60cm (24in). Has heart-shaped, toothed, hairy, purple-tinted, bright green leaves. Bears racemes of small, bell-shaped, fringed, cream flowers, well above foliage, in late spring. **Rubra Group** (syn. *T.g.* 'Purpurea') illus. p.314.

TELOPEA

PROTEACEAE

Genus of evergreen trees and shrubs, grown mainly for their flower heads. Half hardy to frost tender, min. 5°C (41°F). Requires full sun or semi-shade and humus-rich, moist but well-drained, neutral to acid soil. Water containerized plants freely when in full growth, moderately at other times. Propagate by seed in spring or by layering in winter.
T. speciosissima illus. p.138.
T. truncata illus. p.127.

Temple bells. See *Smithiantha cinnabarina*.
Temple juniper. See *Juniperus rigida*.

TEMPLETONIA

LEGUMINOSAE/PAPILIONACEAE

Genus of evergreen shrubs, grown for their flowers. Frost tender, min. 7°C (45°F). Prefers full light and freely draining, alkaline soil. Water potted specimens moderately, less in winter. Propagate by seed in spring or by semi-ripe cuttings in summer.
T. retusa (Coral bush). Evergreen, erect, irregularly branched shrub. H 2m (6ft), S 1–1.5m (3–5ft). Has oval to elliptic, leathery, bluish-green leaves. Pea-like, red flowers, sometimes pink or cream, appear in spring-summer.

Tenby daffodil. See *Narcissus obvallaris*.
Terebinth tree. See *Pistacia terebinthus*.

TERMINALIA

COMBRETACEAE

Genus of evergreen trees and shrubs, grown for their overall appearance, edible seeds (nuts) and for shade. Frost tender, min. 16–18°C (61–4°F). Requires full light and well-drained soil. Water potted specimens moderately, scarcely at all when temperatures are low. Pruning is seldom necessary. Propagate by seed in spring.
T. catappa (Indian almond, Tropical almond). Evergreen, rounded tree. H and S 15m (50ft) or more. Has broadly oval, lustrous, green leaves at stem tips. Small, greenish-white flowers appear in spring, followed by flattened ovoid, keeled, green to red fruits, each with an edible seed.

TERNSTROEMIA

THEACEAE

Genus of evergreen trees and shrubs, grown for their overall appearance. Half hardy. Requires full sun or semi-shade and humus-rich, well-drained, neutral to acid soil. Water containerized specimens copiously when in full growth, moderately at other times. Prune in spring if necessary. Propagate by seed when ripe or in spring or by semi-ripe cuttings in late summer.

T. gymnanthera, syn. *T. japonica*. Evergreen, rounded, dense shrub. H and S 2m (6ft). Oval leaves are lustrous, mid- to deep green. In summer, pendent, 5-petalled, white flowers are borne singly from leaf axils. Pea-sized, berry-like, bright red fruits appear in autumn. Leaves of **'Variegata'** are white-bordered with a pink tinge.
T. japonica. See *T. gymnathera*.

Testudinaria elephantipes. See *Dioscorea elephantipes*.

TETRACENTRON

TETRACENTRACEAE

Genus of one species of deciduous tree, grown for its foliage and catkins. Fully hardy. Needs sun or partial shade and fertile, well-drained soil. Propagate by seed in autumn.
T. sinense. Deciduous, spreading tree of graceful habit. H and S 10m (30ft) or more. Bears oval, finely toothed, dark green leaves and long, slender, yellow catkins in early summer.

TETRADIUM, syn. EUODIA, EVODIA

RUTACEAE

Genus of deciduous trees, grown for their foliage, late flowers and fruits. Fully hardy. Needs full sun and fertile, well-drained soil. Propagate by softwood cuttings in summer, by seed in autumn or by root cuttings in late winter.
T. daniellii, syn. *Euodia hupehensis*. Deciduous, spreading tree. H and S 15m (50ft). Ash-like, dark green leaves, with 5–11 oval to oblong leaflets, turn yellow in autumn. Has small, fragrant, 5-petalled, white flower clusters in early autumn, then beaked, red fruits.

TETRANEMA

SCROPHULARIACEAE

Genus of perennials, grown for their flowers. Frost tender, min. 13°C (55°F). Grow in a light position, shaded from direct sunlight, and in well-drained soil; avoid waterlogging and a humid atmosphere. Propagate by division, or seed if available, in spring.
T. mexicanum. See *T. roseum*.
♀ ***T. roseum***, syn. *T. mexicanum*, illus. p.315.

TETRAPANAX

ARALIACEAE

Genus of one species of evergreen, summer- to autumn-flowering shrub, grown for its foliage. Half hardy. Requires full sun or partial shade and humus-rich, moist but well-drained soil. Water containerized specimens freely, less in winter. Leggy stems may be cut back to near ground level in winter. Propagate by suckers or seed in early spring.
♀ ***T. papyrifer***, syn. *Fatsia papyrifera*, illus. p.122.

TETRASTIGMA

VITACEAE

Genus of evergreen, woody-stemmed, tendril climbers, grown for their handsome leaves. Frost tender, min. 15–18°C (59–64°F). Grow in any fertile, well-drained soil, with shade in summer. Water freely while in active growth, less in low temperatures. Provide stems with support; cut out crowded stems in spring. Propagate by layering in spring or by semi-ripe cuttings in summer.
♀ ***T. voinierianum***, syn. *Cissus voinieriana*, illus. p.218.

TEUCRIUM

LABIATAE/LAMIACEAE

Genus of evergreen or deciduous shrubs, sub-shrubs and perennials, grown for their flowers, foliage (sometimes aromatic) or habit. Fully to half hardy. Needs full sun and well-drained soil. Propagate shrubs and sub-shrubs by softwood or semi-ripe cuttings in summer, perennials by seed or division in spring.
T. aroanium. Evergreen, procumbent, much-branched sub-shrub. H 2.5cm (1in), S 10–15cm (4–6in). Frost hardy. Has white-haired twigs and oblong to oval, slightly hairy leaves, which are densely hairy below, and, in summer, whorls of small, tubular, 2-lipped, purple flowers. Is good for a trough.
T. fruticans (Shrubby germander, Tree germander). ♀ **'Azureum'** is an evergreen, arching shrub. H 2m (6ft), S 4m (12ft). Half hardy. Has oval, aromatic, grey-green leaves, white beneath. Bears tubular, 2-lipped, deep blue flowers with prominent stamens in summer. Cut out dead wood in spring.
T. polium illus. p.391.

Texan walnut. See *Juglans microcarpa*, illus. p.88.

THALIA

MARANTACEAE

Genus of deciduous, perennial, marginal water plants, grown for their foliage and flowers. Frost tender, min. 7°C (45°F). Needs an open, sunny position in up to 45cm (18in) depth of water. Some species tolerate cool water. Remove fading foliage regularly. Propagate in spring by division or seed.
T. dealbata. Deciduous, perennial, marginal water plant. H 1.5m (5ft), S 60cm (2ft). Oval, long-stalked, blue-green leaves have a mealy, white covering. Spikes of narrowly tubular, violet flowers in summer are followed by decorative seed heads. Tolerates cool water.
T. geniculata. Deciduous, perennial, marginal water plant. H 2m (6ft), S 60cm (2ft). Has oval, long-stalked, blue-green leaves and, in summer, spikes of narrowly tubular, violet flowers. Needs a warm pool.

THALICTRUM

Meadow rue

RANUNCULACEAE

Genus of perennials, grown for their divided foliage and fluffy flower heads. Flowers lack petals, but each has prominent tufts of stamens and 4 or 5 sepals, which rapidly fall. Does well at edges of woodland gardens. Tall species and cultivars make excellent foils in borders for perennials with bolder leaves and flowers. Fully hardy. Requires sun or light shade. Grows in any well-drained soil, although some species prefer cool, moist conditions. Propagate by seed when fresh, in autumn, or by division in spring.
T. aquilegiifolium illus. p.255. **'White Cloud'** illus. p.242.
T. chelidonii. Clump-forming perennial. H 1–1.5m (3–5ft), S 60cm (2ft). Has finely divided, mid-green leaves and, in summer, produces panicles of fluffy, 4- or 5-sepalled, mauve flowers. Prefers cool soil that does not dry out.
♀ ***T. delavayi***, syn. *T. dipterocarpum* of gardens. Elegant, clump-forming perennial. H 1.5–2m (5–6ft), S 60cm (2ft). Has much-divided, mid-green leaves, above which large panicles of nodding, lilac flowers, with 4 or 5 sepals and prominent, yellow stamens, appear from mid- to late summer. ♀ **'Hewitt's Double'** has double flowers.
T. diffusiflorum. Clump-forming perennial. H 1m (3ft), S 30–60cm (1–2ft). Has much-divided, basal, mid-green leaves. Slender stems produce large sprays of delicate, drooping, mauve flowers in summer. Prefers cool, moist soil.
T. dipterocarpum of gardens. See *T. delavayi*.
T. flavum. Clump-forming perennial. H 1.2m–1.5m (4–5ft), S 60cm (2ft). Has much-divided, glaucous blue-green leaves and, from mid- to late summer, clusters of fluffy, pale yellow flowers on slender stems. **'Illuminator'** is a pale yellow cultivar with bright green foliage.
T. kiusianum. Mat-forming perennial with short runners. H 8cm (3in), S 15cm (6in). Has small, fern-like, 3-lobed leaves and, throughout summer, loose clusters of tiny, purple flowers. Is excellent in a peat bed, rock garden, trough or alpine house. Is difficult to grow in hot, dry areas. Prefers shade and moist, sandy, peaty soil.
T. lucidum illus. p.260.
T. orientale. Spreading perennial with short runners. H 15cm (6in), S 20cm (8in). Leaves are fern-like with oval to rounded, lobed leaflets. Bears small, saucer-shaped, blue-mauve to violet flowers, with yellow stamens and large sepals, in late spring.

Thamnocalamus falconeri. See *Himalayacalamus falconeri*.
Thamnocalamus murieliae. See *Fargesia murieliae*.
Thamnocalamus spathaceus of gardens. See *Fargesia murieliae*.
Thatch-leaf palm. See *Howea forsteriana*.

THELOCACTUS

CACTACEAE

Genus of spherical to columnar, perennial cacti with ribbed or tuberculate stems. Elongated areoles in crowns produce funnel-shaped flowers. Frost tender, min. 7°C (45°F). Requires sun and well-drained soil. Propagate by seed in spring or summer.
♀ ***T. bicolor*** illus. p.488.
T. leucacanthus. Clump-forming, perennial cactus. H 10cm (4in), S 30cm (12in). Spherical to columnar, dark green stem has 8–13 tuberculate ribs. Areoles each bear up to 20 short, golden spines and yellow flowers, 5cm (2in) across, in summer.
T. macdowellii, syn. *Echinomastus macdowellii.* Also sometimes included in *Neolloydia.* Spherical, perennial cactus. H and S 15cm (6in). Has a tuberculate, dark green stem densely covered with white spines, to 3cm (1¼in) long. Violet-red flowers, 4cm (1½in) across, appear in spring-summer.
♀ ***T. setispinus***, syn. *Ferocactus setispinus, Hamatocactus setispinus*, illus. p.483.

THELYPTERIS

THELYPTERIDACEAE

Genus of deciduous ferns. Fully hardy. Tolerates sun or semi-shade. Grow in moist or very moist soil. Remove fading fronds regularly. Propagate by division in spring.
T. oreopteris. See *Oreopteris limbosperma.*
T. palustris illus. p.324.
T. phegopteris. See *Phegopteris connectilis.*

THERMOPSIS

LEGUMINOSAE/PAPILIONACEAE

Genus of summer-flowering perennials. Fully hardy. Prefers sun and rich, light soil. Propagate by division in spring or by seed in autumn.
T. caroliniana. See *T. villosa.*
T. montana. See *T. rhombifolia.*
T. rhombifolia, syn. *T. montana*, illus. p.262.
T. villosa, syn. *T. caroliniana.* Straggling perennial. H 1m (3ft) or more, S 60cm (2ft). Bears racemes of pea-like, yellow flowers in late summer. Glaucous leaves are divided into 3 oval leaflets.

THESPESIA

MALVACEAE

Genus of evergreen perennials, shrubs and trees, grown for their flowers. Frost tender, min. 16–18°C (61–4°F). Needs full light and well-drained soil. Water containerized plants freely when in full growth, less at other times. Prune in early spring to maintain as a shrub. Propagate by seed in spring or by semi-ripe cuttings in summer. Whitefly and red spider mite may be a nuisance.
T. populnea (Mahoe, Portia oil nut). Evergreen tree, bushy when young, thinning with age. H 12m (40ft) or more, S 3–6m (10–20ft). Leaves are heart-shaped. Intermittently, or all year round if warm enough, produces cup-shaped, yellow flowers, each with a maroon eye, that age to purple. Grows well by the sea.

THEVETIA

APOCYNACEAE

Genus of evergreen shrubs and trees, grown for their flowers from winter to summer. Is related to *Frangipani*. Has poisonous, milky sap. Frost tender, min. 16–18°C (61–4°F). Needs full light and well-drained soil. Water containerized specimens moderately, less in winter. Young stems may be tip pruned in winter to promote branching. Propagate by seed in spring or by semi-ripe cuttings in summer. The seeds are highly toxic if ingested.
T. neriifolia. See *T. peruviana.*
T. peruviana, syn. *T. neriifolia*, illus. p.89.

Thimbleberry. See *Rubus odoratus.*
Thistle. See *Carlina.*
  Alpine. See *Carlina acaulis*, illus. p.387.
  Blessed Mary's. See *Silybum marianum*, illus. p.334
  Cotton. See *Onopordum acanthium*, illus. p.334.
  Globe. See *Echinops.*
  Mountain sow. See *Cicerbita alpina.*
  Scotch. See *Onopordum acanthium*, illus. p.334.

THLADIANTHA

CUCURBITACEAE

Genus of herbaceous or deciduous, tendril climbers, grown for their bell-shaped, yellow flowers and oval to heart-shaped, mid-green leaves. Frost hardy to frost tender, min. 4°C (39°F). Requires a sheltered position in full sun and fertile, well-drained soil. Propagate by seed sown under glass in spring or by division in early spring.
T. dubia illus. p.214.

THLASPI

CRUCIFERAE/BRASSICACEAE

Genus of annuals and perennials, some of which are evergreen, grown for their flowers. Small plants may flower themselves to death, so remove buds for 2 years, to encourage a large plant. Is difficult to grow at low altitudes and may require frequent renewal from seed. Is good for screes and troughs. Fully hardy. Needs sun and moist but well-drained soil. Propagate by seed in autumn.
T. alpestre of gardens. See *T. alpinium.*
T. alpinum, syn. *T. alpestre* of gardens (Alpine penny-cress). Evergreen, mat-forming perennial. H 5cm (2in), S 10cm (4in). Has small, oval, mid-green leaves. Produces racemes of small, 4-petalled, white flowers in spring.
T. bulbosum. Clump-forming, tuberous perennial. H 8cm (3in), S 15–20cm (6–8in). Bears broadly oval, glaucous leaves and, in summer, racemes of 4-petalled, dark violet flowers. Suits a rock garden.
T. cepaeifolium subsp. ***rotundifolium***, syn. *T. rotundifolium*, illus. p.377.
T. macrophyllum. See *Pachyphragma macrophyllum.*
T. rotundifolium. See *T. cepaeifolium* subsp. *rotundifolium.*

Thorn. See *Crataegus.*
  Chinese box. See *Lycium barbarum.*
  Christ's. See *Paliurus spina-christi*, illus. p.118.
  Cockspur. See *Crataegus crus-galli.*
  Glastonbury. See *Crataegus monogyna* 'Biflora'.
  Jerusalem. See *Paliurus spina-christi*, illus. p.118; *Parkinsonia aculeata.*
  Tansy-leaved. See *Crataegus tanacetifolia.*
  Washington thorn. See *Crataegus phaenopyrum.*
Thornless rose. See *Rosa* 'Zéphirine Drouhin', illus. p.193.
Thread agave. See *Agave filifera*, illus. p.481.
Thread palm. See *Washingtonia robusta*, illus. p.69.
Three birds toadflax. See *Linaria triornithophora*, illus. p.255.
Thrift. See *Armeria maritima.*
Throatwort. See *Trachelium caeruleum*, illus. p.342.

THUJA

CUPRESSACEAE

Contact with the foliage may aggravateskin allergies. See also CONIFERS.
T. koraiensis (Korean thuja). Upright conifer, sometimes sprawling and shrubby. H 3–10m (10–30ft), S 3–5m (10–15ft). Fully hardy. Scale-like foliage is bright green or yellow-green above, glaucous silver beneath, and smells of almonds when crushed. Contact with the foliage may aggravate skin allergies.
T. occidentalis (American arbor-vitae, Eastern white cedar, White cedar). Slow-growing conifer with a narrow crown. H 15m (50ft), S 3–5m (10–15ft). Fully hardy. Has orange-brown bark and flat sprays of scale-like, yellowish-green leaves, pale or greyish-green beneath, smelling of apples when crushed. Ovoid cones are yellow-green, ripening to brown. **'Caespitosa'** (illus. p.106). H 30cm (12in), S 40cm (16in), is a cushion-shaped, dwarf cultivar. **'Fastigiata'**, H to 15m (50ft), S to 5m (15ft), is broadly columnar, with erect, spreading branches and light green leaves. **'Filiformis'** (illus. p.107), H 1.5m (5ft), S 1.5–2m (5–6ft), forms a mound with pendent, whip-like shoots. **'Hetz Midget'**, H and S 50cm (20in), growing only 2.5cm (1in) each year, is a globose, dwarf form with blue-green foliage. ♀ **'Holmstrup'**, H 3–4m (10–12ft), S 1m (3ft), is slow-growing, dense and conical, with rich green foliage. **'Little Champion'**, H and S 50cm (20in) or more, is a globose, dwarf form, conical when young, with foliage turning brown in winter. ♀ **'Lutea Nana'**, H 2m (6ft), S 1–2m (3–6ft), is a dwarf form with golden-yellow foliage. ♀ **'Rheingold'**, H 3–4m (10–12ft), S 2–4m (6–12ft), is slow-growing, with golden-yellow foliage that becomes bronze in winter. ♀ **'Smaragd'**, H 2–2.5m (6–8ft), S 60–75cm (2–2½ft), is slow-growing and conical, with erect sprays of bright green leaves. **'Spiralis'**, H 10–15m (30–50ft), S 2–3m (6–10ft), produces foliage in twisted, fern-like sprays. **'Woodwardii'**, H 2.5m (8ft), S to 5m (15ft), is very slow-growing and globose, with mid-green foliage.
T. orientalis. See *Platycladus orientalis.*
T. plicata (Western red cedar). Fast-growing, conical conifer that has great, curving branches low down. H 20–30m (70–100ft), S 5–8m (15–25ft), greater if lower branches self-layer. Fully hardy. Has red-brown bark, scale-like, glossy, dark green leaves, which have a pineapple aroma when crushed, and erect, ovoid, green cones, ripening to brown. ♀ **'Atrovirens'** has darker green foliage. ♀ **'Aurea'** has golden-yellow foliage. **'Collyer's Gold'** (illus. p.107), H to 2m (6ft), S 1m (3ft), is a dwarf form with yellow, young foliage turning light green. **'Cuprea'**, H 1m (3ft), S 75cm–1m (2½–3ft), is a conical shrub with copper- to bronze-yellow leaves. **'Hillieri'** (illus. p.107), H and S to 1m (3ft), is a slow-growing, dense, rounded, dwarf shrub with moss-like, rich green foliage. ♀ **'Stoneham Gold'** (illus. p.107), H 1–2m (3–6ft), S 1m (3ft), is a conical, dwarf form with bright gold foliage. **'Zebrina'**, H 15m (50ft), has leaves banded with yellowish-white.

Thuja
  Chinese. See *Platycladus orientalis.*
  Korean. See *Thuja koraiensis.*

THUJOPSIS

CUPRESSACEAE

See also CONIFERS.
♀ ***T. dolabrata*** (Hiba). Conical or bushy conifer with a mass of stems. H 10–20m (30–70ft), S 8–10m (25–30ft). Fully hardy. Produces heavy, flat sprays of scale-like leaves, glossy, bright green above, silvery-white beneath. Small, rounded cones are blue-grey. **'Variegata'** illus. p.105.

THUNBERGIA

ACANTHACEAE

Genus of annual or mainly evergreen, perennial, twining climbers, perennials and shrubs, grown for their flowers. Half hardy to frost tender, min. 10–15°C (50–59°F). Any fertile, well-drained soil is suitable, with full sun or light shade in summer. Water freely when in full growth, less at other times. Requires support. Thin out crowded stems in early spring. Propagate by seed in spring or by softwood or semi-ripe cuttings in summer.
T. alata illus. p.214.
T. coccinea. Evergreen, woody-stemmed, perennial, twining climber with narrowly oval leaves. H 6m (20ft) or more. Frost tender, min. 15°C (59°F). Pendent racemes of tubular, scarlet flowers are produced in winter-spring.
T. gibsonii. See *T. gregorii.*
♀ ***T. grandiflora*** (Blue trumpet vine). Evergreen, woody-stemmed, perennial, twining climber. H 6–10m (20–30ft). Frost tender, min. 10°C (50°F). Oval leaves, 10–20cm (4–8in) long, have a few tooth-like lobes. In summer has trumpet-shaped, pale to deep violet-blue flowers.
♀ ***T. gregorii***, syn. *T. gibsonii*, illus. p.215.
♀ ***T. mysorensis*** illus. p.203.

Thyme. See *Thymus.*
Caraway. See *Thymus herba-barona*, illus. p.393.

THYMUS
Thyme

LABIATAE/LAMIACEAE

Genus of evergreen, mat-forming and dome-shaped shrubs, sub-shrubs and woody-based perennials with aromatic leaves. Is useful for growing on banks and in rock gardens, troughs and paving. Fully to half hardy. Requires sun and moist but well-drained soil. Propagate by softwood or semi-ripe cuttings in summer.
T. azoricus. See *T. caespititius.*
T. caespititius, syn. *T. azoricus*, *T. micans*. Evergreen, mat-forming, aromatic sub-shrub. H 2.5cm (1in) S 20cm (8in). Frost hardy. Has slender, wooden stems covered in minute, hairy, mid-green leaves. Bears tiny, pale lilac or lilac-pink flowers in small clusters in summer.
T. carnosus. Evergreen, spreading shrub. H and S 20cm (8in). Frost hardy. Has tiny, narrowly oval, aromatic leaves. Erect flowering stems bear whorls of small, 2-lipped, white flowers in summer. Needs a sheltered position.
T. cilicicus illus p.387.
♀ ***T. × citriodorus* 'Silver Queen'.** Evergreen, rounded shrub. H to 30cm (12in), S to 25cm (10in). Has narrow, oval-diamond-shaped to lance-shaped, more or less hairless, aromatic, silvery-green leaves, with creamy-white markings. In summer produces 2-lipped, pale lavender-pink flowers in terminal clusters.
T. herba-barona illus. p.393.
T. leucotrichus illus. p.393.
T. micans. See *T. caespititius.*
***T.* 'Porlock'.** Evergreen, dome-shaped perennial. H 8cm (3in), S 20cm (8in). Fully hardy. Thin stems are covered in small, rounded to oval, very aromatic, glossy, green leaves. In summer produces clusters of small, 2-lipped, pink flowers.
T. pseudolanuginosus. Evergreen, prostrate shrub. H 2.5–5cm (1–2in), S 20cm (8in) or more. Fully hardy. Has dense mats of very hairy stems bearing tiny, aromatic, grey leaves. Produces 2-lipped, pinkish-lilac flowers in leaf axils in summer.
♀ ***T. pulegioides* 'Aureus'.** Evergreen, spreading shrub. H 10cm (4in), S 10–25cm (4–10in). Frost hardy. Tiny, rounded to oval, golden-yellow leaves are very fragrant when crushed. Produces terminal clusters of small, 2-lipped, lilac flowers in summer. Cut back in spring.
T. serpyllum. Evergreen, mat-forming sub-shrub. H 25cm (10in), S 45cm (18in). Fully hardy. Finely hairy, trailing stems bear linear to elliptic to oval, mid-green leaves. Whorls of two-lipped, purple flowers are borne in summer. **'Annie Hall'**, H 5cm (2in), S 20cm (8in), has pale purple-pink flowers and light green leaves. **'Elfin'**, H 5cm (2in), S 10cm (4in), produces emerald-green leaves in dense hummocks; occasionally bears purple flowers.

Ti tree. See *Cordyline fruticosa.*

TIARELLA
Foamflower

SAXIFRAGACEAE

Genus of perennials, some of which are evergreen, that spread by runners. Is excellent as ground cover. Fully hardy. Tolerates deep shade and prefers moist but well-drained soil. Propagate by division in spring.
♀ ***T. cordifolia*** illus. p.359. var. ***collina*** see *T. wherryi.*
♀ ***T. wherryi***, syn. *T. cordifolia* var. *collina.* Slow-growing, clump-forming perennial. H 10cm (4in), S 15cm (6in). Triangular, lobed, hairy, basal, green leaves are stained dark red, with heart-shaped bases. Bears racemes of tiny, star-shaped, soft pink or white flowers from late spring to early summer.

TIBOUCHINA

MELASTOMATACEAE

Genus of evergreen perennials, sub-shrubs, shrubs and scandent climbers, grown for their flowers and leaves. Frost tender, min. 5–7°C (41–5°F). Prefers full sun and fertile, well-drained, neutral to acid soil. Water potted specimens freely when in full growth, moderately at other times. Cut back flowered stems, each to 2 pairs of buds, in spring. Tip prune young plants to promote branching. Propagate by greenwood or semi-ripe cuttings in late spring or summer.
T. semidecandra of gardens. See *T. urvilleana.*
♀ ***T. urvilleana***, syn. *T. semidecandra* of gardens, illus. p.118.

Tickseed. See *Coreopsis.*
Tidy tips. See *Layia platyglossa.*
Tiger flower. See *Tigridia pavonia*, illus. p.439.
Tiger lily. See *Lilium lancifolium.*
Tiger-jaws. See *Faucaria tigrina*, illus. p.495.

TIGRIDIA

IRIDACEAE

Genus of summer-flowering bulbs, grown for their highly colourful but short-lived flowers, rather iris-like in shape, with 3 large, outer petals. Half hardy. Needs sun and well-drained soil, with ample water in summer. Plant in spring. Lift in autumn; then partially dry bulbs and store in peat or sand at 8–12°C (46–54°F). Propagate by seed in spring.
T. pavonia illus. p.439.

TILIA
Lime, Linden

TILIACEAE

Genus of deciduous trees, grown for their small, fragrant, cup-shaped flowers and stately habit. Flowers attract bees, but are toxic to them in some cases. Fully hardy. Requires sun or semi-shade and fertile, well-drained soil. Propagate species by seed in autumn, selected forms and hybrids by grafting in late summer. Except for *T. × euchlora*, trees are usually attacked by aphids, which cover growth and ground beneath with sticky honeydew. The nectar of *T.* 'Petiolaris' and *T. tomentosa* and may be toxic, especially to bumblebees.
T. americana (American lime, Basswood). Deciduous, spreading tree. H 25m (80ft), S 12m (40ft). Has large, rounded, sharply toothed, glossy, dark green leaves. Small, yellowish-white flowers appear in summer.
♀ ***T. cordata*** (Small-leaved lime). Deciduous, spreading tree. H 30m (100ft), S 12m (40ft). In mid-summer has small, glossy, dark green leaves and small, yellowish-white flowers.
♀ **'Greenspire'**, S 8m (25ft), is very vigorous and pyramidal in habit, even when young. **'Rancho'** illus. p.76.
♀ ***T. × euchlora*** (Caucasian lime, Crimean lime). Deciduous, spreading tree with lower branches that droop with age. H 20m (70ft), S 10m (30ft). Rounded, very glossy, deep green leaves turn yellow in autumn. Bears small, yellowish-white flowers, toxic to bees, in summer. Is relatively pest-free.
T. × europaea, syn. *T. × vulgaris.* (Common lime). Vigorous, deciduous, spreading tree. H 35m (120ft), S 15m (50ft). Trunk develops many burs. Has rounded, dark green leaves. Small, yellowish-white flowers, toxic to bees, appear in summer. Periodically remove shoots from burs at base.
T. henryana. Deciduous, spreading tree. H and S 10m (30ft). Broadly heart-shaped, glossy, bright green leaves, fringed with long teeth, are often tinged red when young. Has masses of small, creamy-white flowers in autumn.
T. mongolica (Mongolian lime). Deciduous, spreading, graceful tree. H 15m (50ft), S 12m (40ft). Young shoots are red. Heart-shaped, coarsely toothed, glossy, dark green leaves turn yellow in autumn. Small, yellowish-white flowers appear in summer.
T. oliveri illus. p.63.
T. petiolaris. See *T.* 'Petiolaris'.
♀ ***T.* 'Petiolaris'**, syn. *T. petiolaris*, illus. p.64.
T. platyphyllos (Broad-leaved lime, Large-leaved lime). Deciduous, spreading tree. H 30m (100ft), S 20m (70ft). Has rounded, dark green leaves and small, dull yellowish-white flowers in mid-summer. **'Prince's Street'** is upright, with bright red shoots in winter.
T. tomentosa (European white lime, Silver lime). Deciduous, spreading tree. H 25m (80ft), S 20m (70ft). Leaves are large, rounded, sharply toothed, dark green above and white beneath. Very fragrant, small, dull white flowers, toxic to bees, are borne in late summer.
T. × vulgaris. See. *T. × europaea.*

TILLANDSIA

BROMELIACEAE

Genus of evergreen, epiphytic perennials, often rosette-forming, some with branching stems and spirally arranged leaves, all grown for their flowers or overall appearance. Frost tender, min. 7–10°C (45–50°F). Requires semi-shade. Provide a rooting medium of equal parts humus-rich soil and either sphagnum moss or bark or plastic chips used for orchid culture. May also be grown on slabs of bark or sections of trees. Using soft water, water moderately in summer, sparingly at other times; spray plants grown on bark or tree sections with water several times a week from mid-spring to mid-autumn. Propagate by offsets or division in spring.
♀ ***T. argentea*** illus. p.273. Evergreen, basal-rosetted, epiphytic perennial. H and S 10–15cm (4–6in). Very narrow, almost thread-like leaves, covered with white scales, are produced in dense, near-spherical rosettes, each with a fleshy, bulb-like base. In summer, small, loose racemes of tubular, red flowers are produced.
T. caput-medusae illus. p.273. Evergreen, basal-rosetted, epiphytic perennial. H and S 15cm (6in) or more. Linear, channelled, twisted and rolled, incurved leaves, covered in grey scales, develop in loose rosettes that have hollow, bulb-like bases. In summer, spikes of tubular, violet-blue flowers appear above foliage.
♀ ***T. cyanea*** illus. p.273. Evergreen, basal-rosetted, epiphytic perennial. H and S 25cm (10in). Forms dense rosettes of linear, pointed, channelled, arching, usually deep green leaves. In summer, broadly oval, blade-like spikes of pansy-shaped, deep purple-blue flowers, emerging from pink or red bracts, are produced among foliage.
T. fasciculata illus. p.273. Evergreen, basal-rosetted, epiphytic perennial. H and S 30cm (12in) or more. Has dense rosettes of narrowly triangular, tapering, arching, mid-green leaves. In summer, flat spikes of tubular, purple-blue flowers emerge from red or reddish-yellow bracts, just above leaf tips. Bracts require strong light to develop reddish tones.
T. ionantha (Sky plant). Evergreen, clump-forming, basal-rosetted, epiphytic perennial. H and S 12cm (5in). Linear, incurved, arching leaves, covered in grey scales, are produced in dense rosettes; the inner leaves turn red at flowering time. Spikes of tubular, violet-blue flowers, emerging in summer from narrow, white bracts, are borne just above foliage.
♀ ***T. lindenii*** (Blue-flowered torch; illus. p.273). Evergreen, basal-rosetted, epiphytic perennial. H and S 40cm (16in). Linear, pointed, channelled, arching, mid-green leaves, with red-brown lines, form dense rosettes. In summer, produces blade-like spikes of widely pansy-shaped, deep blue flowers, emerging from sometimes pink-tinted, green bracts, which are borne just above leaves.
T. recurvata. Evergreen, basal-rosetted, epiphytic perennial. H and S 10–20cm (4–8in). Has long, loose, stem-like rosettes of linear, arching to recurved leaves, densely covered in silvery-grey scales. In summer produces short, dense spikes of small, tubular, pale blue or pale green flowers, whichappear above the leaves.
T. stricta illus. p.273. Evergreen, clump-forming, basal-rosetted, epiphytic perennial. H and S 20–30cm (8–12in). Narrowly triangular, tapering, arching, mid-green leaves, usually with grey scales, are produced in dense rosettes. Large, tubular, blue flowers emerge from drooping, cone-like spikes of bright red bracts, usually in summer.
T. usneoides (Spanish moss; illus. p.273). Evergreen, pendent, epiphytic

perennial. H 1m (3ft) or more, S 10–20cm (4–8in). Slender, branched, drooping stems bear linear, incurved leaves densely covered in silvery-white scales. Inconspicuous, tubular, greenish-yellow or pale blue flowers, hidden among foliage, are produced in summer.

Timberbamboo. See *Phyllostachys bambusoides*, illus. p.320.
Tingiringi gum. See *Eucalyptus glaucescens*.
Tipa tree. See *Tipuana tipu*.
Tipu tree. See *Tipuana tipu*.

TIPUANA

LEGUMINOSAE/PAPILIONACEAE

Genus of one species of evergreen, spring-flowering tree, grown for its flowers and overall appearance when mature and for shade. In certain conditions, may be deciduous. Frost tender, min. 10–13°C (50–55°F). Requires full light and fertile, well-drained soil. Container-grown plants will not produce flowers. Young specimens may be pruned in winter. Propagate by seed in spring.
T. speciosa. See *T. tipu*.
T. tipu, syn. *T. speciosa* (Pride of Bolivia, Tipa tree, Tipu tree). Fast-growing, mainly evergreen, bushy tree. H 10m (30ft), S 8–10m (25–30ft). Bears leaves, 25cm (10in) long, with 11–25 oval leaflets. Produces pea-like, orange-yellow flowers, 3cm (1¼in) wide, in spring, followed by short, woody, winged, brownish pods in autumn-winter.

TITANOPSIS

AIZOACEAE

Genus of basal-rosetted, perennial succulents eventually forming small, dense clumps. Produces 6–8 opposite pairs of fleshy, triangular leaves, 2–3cm (¾–1¼in) long, narrow at stems and expanding to straight tips. Frost tender, min. 8°C (46°F). Requires a position in sun and well-drained soil. Propagate by seed in spring or summer.
♀ ***T. calcarea*** illus. p.495.
T. schwantesii. Clump-forming, perennial succulent. H 3cm (1¼in), S 10cm (4in). Has a basal rosette of triangular, grey-blue leaves, covered with small, wart-like, yellow-brown tubercles. Carries daisy-like, light yellow flowers, 2cm (¾in) wide, in summer-autumn.

TITHONIA

COMPOSITAE/ASTERACEAE

Genus of annuals. Half hardy. Grow in sun and in fertile, well-drained soil. Provide support and dead-head regularly. Propagate by seed sown under glass in late winter or early spring.
T. rotundifolia (Mexican sunflower). **'Torch'** illus. p.352.

Toad lily. See *Tricyrtis*.
Toadflax. See *Linaria*.
  Alpine. See *Linaria alpina*.
  Dalmatian. See *Linaria genistifolia* var. *dalmatica*.
  Ivy-leaved. See *Cymbalaria muralis*.
  Purple. See *Linaria purpurea*.
  Three birds. See *Linaria triornithophora*, illus. p.255.
Toadshade. See *Trillium sessile*, illus. p.277.
Tobacco, Flowering. See *Nicotiana sylvestris*, illus. p.224.

TOLMIEA

SAXIFRAGACEAE

Genus of one species of perennial that is sometimes semi-evergreen and is grown as ground cover. Is suitable for cool woodland gardens. Fully hardy. Prefers a position in shade and requires well-drained, neutral to acid soil. Propagate by division in spring or by seed in autumn.
T. menziesii (Pick-a-back-plant, Youth-on-age). Mat-forming perennial, sometimes semi-evergreen. H 45–60cm (18–24in), S 30cm (12in) or more. Young plantlets develop where ivy-shaped, mid-green leaves join stem. Produces spikes of tiny, nodding, tubular to bell-shaped, green and chocolate-brown flowers, which appear in spring.

TOLPIS

COMPOSITAE/ASTERACEAE

Genus of summer-flowering annuals and perennials. Fully hardy. Grow in sun and in fertile, well-drained soil. Propagate by seed sown outdoors in spring.
T. barbata. Moderately fast-growing, upright, branching annual. H 45–60cm (1½–2ft), S 30cm (1ft). Has lance-shaped, serrated, mid-green leaves. Daisy-like, bright yellow flower heads, 2.5cm (1in) or more wide, with maroon centres, are produced in summer.

Tomato, Tree. See *Cyphomandra betacea*, illus. p.121.

TOONA

MELIACEAE

Genus of deciduous trees, grown for their foliage, autumn colour and flowers. Fully hardy. Prefers full sun; requires fertile, well-drained soil. Propagate by seed in autumn, root cuttings in winter.
T. sinensis, syn. *Cedrela sinensis*, illus. p.75.

Toothwort. See *Lathraea clandestina*, illus. p.279.
Torch.
  Blue-flowered. See *Tillandsia lindenii*, illus. p.273.
  Striped. See *Guzmania monostachia*, illus p.273.
Torch cactus. See *Echinopsis spachiana*, illus. p.473.
Torch lily. See *Kniphofia*.
Torch plant. See *Aloe aristata*, illus. p.496.
Torch, Striped. See *Guzmania monostachya*, illus. p.273.

TORENIA

SCROPHULARIACEAE

Genus of annuals and perennials. Half hardy to frost tender, min. 5°C (41°F). Grow in semi-shade and in a sheltered position in fertile, well-drained soil. Pinch out growing shoots of young plants to encourage a busy habit. Propagate by seed sown under glass in early spring.
T. fournieri illus. p.345.

TORREYA

TAXACEAE

See also CONIFERS.
T. californica illus. p.103.

Totara, Alpine. See *Podocarpus nivalis*, illus. p.106.
Tovara virginiana 'Painter's Palette'. See *Persicaria virginiana* 'Painter's Palette'.

TOWNSENDIA

COMPOSITAE/ASTERACEAE

Genus of evergreen, short-lived perennials and biennials, grown for their daisy-like flower heads. Suits alpine houses as dislikes winter wet. Fully hardy. Needs sun and moist soil. Propagate by seed in autumn.
T. grandiflora illus. p.395.
T. parryi. Evergreen, basal-rosetted, short-lived perennial. H 7–15cm (3–6in), S 5cm (2in). In late spring produces daisy-like, lavender or violet-blue flower heads, with bright yellow centres, above spoon-shaped leaves.

Toxicodendron succedaneum. See *Rhus succedanea*.
Toxicodendron vernicifluum. See *Rhus verniciflua*.
Toyon. See *Heteromeles salicifolia*.

TRACHELIUM, syn. DIOSPHAERA

CAMPANULACEAE

Genus of small perennials, useful for rock gardens and mixed borders. Some are good in alpine houses. Flowers of half-hardy species are ideal for cutting. Fully to half hardy, but protect fully-hardy species under glass in winter as they resent damp conditions. Grow in a sunny, sheltered position and in fertile, very well-drained soil (*T. asperuloides* prefers lime-rich soil). Propagate by seed in early or mid-spring or by softwood cuttings in spring.
T. asperuloides, syn. *Diosphaera asperuloides*, illus. p.395.
♀ ***T. caeruleum*** illus. p.342.

TRACHELOSPERMUM

APOCYNACEAE

Genus of evergreen, woody-stemmed, twining climbers with stems that exude milky sap when cut. Frost hardy. Grow in any well-drained soil and in sun or semi-shade. Propagate by seed in spring, by layering in summer or by semi-ripe cuttings in late summer or autumn.
♀ ***T. asiaticum.*** Evergreen, woody-stemmed, much-branched, twining climber. H to 6m (20ft). Bears oval, glossy, dark green leaves that are 2.5cm (1in) long. Scented, tubular, cream flowers, with expanded mouths, that age to yellow, are produced in summer. Pairs of long, slender pods, 12–22cm (5–9in) long, contain silky seeds.
♀ ***T. jasminoides*** illus. p.203.

TRACHYCARPUS

PALMAE/ARECACEAE

Genus of evergreen, summer-flowering palms, grown for their habit, foliage and flowers. Frost hardy. Requires full sun and does best in a position sheltered from strong, cold winds, especially when young. Needs fertile, well-drainedsoil. Propagate by seed in autumn or spring.
♀ ***T. fortunei*** illus. p.80.

TRACHYMENE

UMBELLIFERAE/APIACEAE

Genus of summer-flowering annuals. Half hardy. Grow in a sunny, sheltered position and in fertile, well-drained soil. Support with sticks. Propagate by seed sown under glass in early spring.
T. coerulea, syn. *Didiscus coeruleus* (Blue lace flower). Moderately fast-growing, upright, branching annual. H 45cm (18in), S 20cm (8in). Has deeply divided, pale green leaves. Spherical heads, to 5cm (2in) wide, of tiny, blue flowers are produced in summer. Flowers are excellent for cutting.

TRADESCANTIA

Spiderwort

COMMELINACEAE

Genus of perennials, some of which are evergreen, grown for their flowers or ornamental foliage. Fully hardy to frost tender, min. 10–15°C (50–59°F). Grow in fertile, moist to dry soil and in sun or partial shade. Cut back or repropagate trailing species when they become straggly. Propagate hardy species by division, frost-tender species by tip cuttings in spring, summer or autumn. Contact with the foliage may irritate skin.
T. albiflora. See *T. fluminensis*.
♀ ***T.* Andersoniana Group 'J.C. Weguelin'**, syn. *T.* 'J.C. Weguelin'. Clump-forming perennial. H to 60cm (2ft), S 45cm (1½ft). Fully hardy. Has narrowly lance-shaped, fleshy, green leaves, 15–30cm (6–12in) long. In summer producess clusters of 3-petalled, lavender-blue flowers, 2.5cm (1in) or more wide, surrounded by 2 leaf-like bracts. ♀ **'Osprey'** (syn. *T.* 'Osprey') illus. p.286. **'Purple Dome'** (syn. *T.* 'Purple Dome') illus. p.294.
T. blossfeldiana. See *T. cerinthoides*.
T. cerinthoides, syn. *T. blossfeldiana*. Evergreen, creeping perennial. H 5cm (2in), S indefinite. Frost tender. Narrowly oval, fleshy, stem-clasping leaves, to 10cm (4in) long, are glossy, dark green above, purple with long, white hairs below. Intermittently produces clusters of tiny, pink flowers, with white centres, surrounded by 2 leaf-like bracts. Leaves of ♀ **'Variegata'** have longitudinal, cream stripes.
T. fluminensis, syn. *T. albiflora* (Wandering Jew). Evergreen perennial with trailing, rooting stems. H 5cm (2in), S to 60cm (24in) or more. Frost tender. Oval, fleshy leaves, 4cm (1½in) long, that clasp the stem, are glossy and green above, sometimes tinged purple below. Intermittently has clusters of tiny, white flowers enclosed in 2 leaf-like bracts. **'Albovittata'** and

'Variegata' illus. p.312.
***T.* 'J.C. Weguelin'.** See *T.* Andersoniana Group 'J.C. Weguelin'.
T. navicularis. See *Callisia navicularis.*
***T.* 'Osprey'.** See *T.* Andersoniana Group 'Osprey'.
♀ ***T. pallida* 'Purpurea',** syn. *T.p.* 'Purple Heart', *Setcreasea purpurea*, illus. p.315.
T. pexata. See *T. sillamontana.*
***T.* 'Purple Dome'.** See *T.* Andersoniana Group 'Purple Dome'.
T. purpusii. See *T. zebrina* 'Purpusii'.
♀ ***T. sillamontana***, syn. *T. pexata, T. velutina*, illus. p.315.
T. spathacea, syn. *Rhoeo discolor, R. spathacea* (Boat lily, Moses-in-the-cradle). Evergreen, clump-forming perennial. H 50cm (20in), S 25cm (10in). Frost tender. Rosette of lance-shaped, fleshy leaves, to 30cm (12in) long, is green above, purple below. Bears tiny, white flowers, enclosed in boat-shaped, leaf-like bracts, year-round. ♀ **'Vittata'** has leaves striped longitudinally with pale yellow.
T. velutina. See *T. sillamontana.*
♀ ***T. zebrina***, syn. *Zebrina pendula*, illus. p.313. ♀ **'Purpusii'** (syn. *T. purpusii*) is a strong-growing, evergreen, trailing or mat-forming perennial. H 10cm (4in), S indefinite. Frost tender. Has elliptic, purple-tinged, bluish-green leaves and tiny, shallowly cup-shaped, pink flowers.
♀ **'Quadricolor'** has leaves striped green, pink, red and white.

Trailing arbutus. See *Epigaea repens.*
Trailing azalea. See *Loiseleuria procumbens*, illus. p.389.

TRAPA

TRAPACEAE

Genus of deciduous, perennial and annual, floating water plants, grown for their foliage and flowers. Frost hardy to frost tender, min. 5°C (41°F). Requires sun. Propagate in spring from seed gathered in autumn and stored in water or damp moss.
T. natans illus. p.465.

Traveller's joy. See *Clematis.*
Traveller's tree. See *Ravenala madagascariensis.*
Tree cotoneaster. See *Cotoneaster frigidus.*
Tree fern
Australian. See *Cyathea australis*, illus. p.96; *Dicksonia antarctica*, illus. p.322.
Black. See *Cyathea medullaris.*
Tree fuchsia. See *Fuchsia arborescens*, illus. p.160.
Tree germander. See *Teucrium fruticans.*
Tree heath. See *Erica arborea.*
Spanish. See *Erica australis.*
Tree ivy. See × *Fatshedera lizei*, illus. p.148.
Tree lupin. See *Lupinus arboreus*, illus. p.165.
Tree mallow. See *Lavatera.*
Tree medick. See *Medicago arborea.*
Tree of heaven. See *Ailanthus altissima.*
Tree peony. See *Paeonia potaninii.*
Tree poppy. See *Romneya.*
Tree purslane. See *Atriplex halimus.*
Tree tomato. See *Cyphomandra betacea*, illus. p.121.
Trefoil, Moon. See *Medicago arborea.*
Trichocereus bridgesii. See *Echinopsis lageniformis.*
Trichocereus candicans. See *Echinopsis candicans.*
Trichocereus spachianus. See *Echinopsis spachiana.*

TRICHODIADEMA

AIZOACEAE

Genus of bushy, perennial succulents with woody or tuberous roots and cylindrical to semi-cylindrical leaves. Frost tender, min. 5°C (41°F). Needs sun and well-drained soil. Propagate by seed or stem cuttings in spring or summer.
♀ ***T. densum.*** Tufted, perennial succulent. H 10cm (4in), S 20cm (8in). Cylindrical, pale green leaves are each 1–2cm (½–¾in) long and tipped with clusters of white bristles. Roots and prostrate, green stem are both fleshy and form caudex. Stem tip has daisy-like, cerise flowers, 3cm (1¼in) across, in summer.
T. mirabile illus. p.485.

TRICHOSANTHES

CUCURBITACEAE

Genus of annual and evergreen, perennial, tendril climbers, grown for their fruits and overall appearance. Frost tender, min. 15–18°C (59–64°F). Needs full sun or partial shade and humus-rich soil. Water freely in growing season, less in cool weather. Provide support. Propagate by seed in spring at not less than 21°C (70°F).
T. anguina. See *T. cucumerina* var. *anguina.*
T. cucumerina* var. *anguina, syn. *T. anguina* (Snake gourd). Erect to spreading, annual, tendril climber. H 3–5m (10–15ft). Has broadly oval to almost triangular, sometimes shallowly 3- to 5-lobed, mid- to pale green leaves, to 20cm (8in) long. In summer produces 5-petalled, white flowers, 2.5–5cm (1–2in) across, with heavily fringed petals; females are solitary, the males in racemes. Cylindrical fruits, 60cm (2ft) or rarely to 2m (6ft) long, often twisted or coiled, are green-and-white striped and ripen to dull orange.

Trichosma suavis. See *Eria coronaria.*
Tricuspidaria lanceolata. See *Crinodendron hookerianum.*

TRICYRTIS

Toad lily

LILIACEAE/CONVALLARIACEAE

Genus of late summer- and autumn-flowering, rhizomatous perennials. Fully hardy. Grows in sun or, in warm areas, in partial shade. Needs humus-rich, moist soil. Propagate by division in spring or by seed in autumn.
♀ ***T. formosana***, syn. *T. stolonifera*, illus. p.267.
T. hirta. Upright, rhizomatous perennial. H 30cm–1m (1–3ft), S 45cm (1½ft). In late summer and early autumn, clusters of large, open bell-shaped, white-spotted, purple flowers appear from axils of uppermost leaves. Leaves are narrowly oval, hairy and dark green and clasp stems. var. ***alba*** illus. p.306.
T. macrantha. Upright, rhizomatous perennial. H and S 60cm (24in). In early autumn has loose sheaves of open bell-shaped, deep primrose-yellow flowers, spotted light chocolate, at tips of arching stems, and small, oval leaves are dark green.
T. stolonifera. See *T. formosana.*

Trident maple. See *Acer buergerianum.*

TRIFOLIUM

Clover

LEGUMINOSAE/PAPILIONACEAE

Genus of annuals, biennials and perennials, some of which are semi-evergreen, with round, usually 3-lobed leaves and heads of pea-like flowers. Some species are useful in rock gardens or on banks, others in agriculture. Many are invasive. Fully to frost hardy. Needs sun and well-drained soil. Propagate by division in spring or by seed in autumn. Self-seeds readily.
***T. repens* 'Purpurascens'** illus. p.400.

Trigger plant. See *Stylidium graminifolium.*

TRILLIUM

Trinity flower, Wood lily

LILIACEAE/TRILLIACEAE

Genus of perennials with petals, sepals and leaves that are all borne in whorls of 3. Is excellent for woodland gardens. Fully hardy. Enjoys partial shade and fertile, moist but well-drained, neutral to acid soil. Propagate by division after foliage has died down in summer or by seed in autumn.
T. cernuum illus. p.275.
T. chloropetalum illus. p.276.
♀ ***T. erectum*** illus. p.277.
♀ ***T. grandiflorum*** illus. p.276.
♀ **'Flore Pleno'** is a clump-forming perennial. H 38cm (15in), S 30cm (12in). Large, double, pure white flowers, are borne singly in spring, turning pink with age. Has large broadly oval, dark green leaves.
T. nivale (Dwarf white wood lily, Snow trillium). Early spring-flowering, rhizomatous perennial. H 7cm (3in), S 10cm (4in). Whorls of 3 oval leaves emerge at same time as outward-facing, slightly nodding, white flowers, each with 3 narrowly oval petals. Thrives in a trough or alpine house. Is difficult to grow.
T. ovatum illus. p.276.
♀ ***T. rivale*** illus. p.377.
T. sessile illus. p.277.
T. undulatum (Painted trillium, Painted wood lily). Clump-forming perennial. H 10–20cm (4–8in), S 15–20cm (6–8in). Open funnel-shaped flowers with red-bordered, green sepals and 3white or pink petals, each with a basal carmine stripe, are borne singly in spring, above broadly oval, basal, blue-green leaves.

Trillium
Painted. See *Trillium undulatum.*
Snow. See *Trillium nivale.*
Trinity flower. See *Trillium.*

TRIPETALEIA

ERICACEAE

Genus of one species of deciduous shrub, grown for its flowers; is now often included in *Elliottia.* Fully hardy. Needs semi-shade and moist, peaty, neutral to acid soil. Propagate by softwood cuttings in summer or by seed in autumn.
T. paniculata, syn. *Elliottia paniculata.* Deciduous, upright shrub. H and S 1.5m (5ft). Bears upright panicles of pink-tinged, white flowers, each with 3 (or 4 or 5) narrow petals, from mid-summer to early autumn. Lance-shaped, dark green leaves persist well into autumn.

TRIPTERYGIUM

CELASTRACEAE

Genus of deciduous, twining or scrambling climbers, grown for their foliage and fruits. Frost hardy. Grow in any fertile, well-drained soil and in full sun or light shade. Water freely while in full growth, less in low temperatures. Provide stems with support. Thin out crowded stems in winter or early spring. Propagate by seed when ripe or in spring or by semi-ripe cuttings in summer.
T. regelii. Deciduous, thin-stemmed, twining or scrambling climber. H 10m (30ft). Leaves are oval and usually rich green. In late summer produces clusters, 20–25cm (8–10in) long, of small, off-whiteflowers, followed by 3-winged, pale green fruits.

Tristania conferta. See *Lophostemon confertus.*

TRITELEIA

LILIACEAE/ALLIACEAE

Genus of late spring- and early summer-flowering corms with wiry stems carrying *Allium* -like umbels of funnel-shaped flowers. Long, narrow leaves usually die away by flowering time. Frost hardy. Needs an open but sheltered, sunny situation and well-drained soil that dries out to some extent in summer. Dies down in mid-to late summer until winter or spring; plant during dormancy in early autumn. Propagate by seed or offsets in autumn.
T. hyacinthina, syn. *Brodiaea hyacinthina, B. lactea*, illus. p.435.
T. ixioides, syn. *Brodiaea ixioides, B. lutea.* Early summer-flowering corm. H to 50cm (20in), S 8–10cm (3–4in). Bears semi-erect, basal leaves. Stem has a loose umbel, to 12cm (5in) across, of yellow flowers; petals each have a purple-stripe.
T. laxa, syn. *Brodiaea laxa*, illus. p.438.
T. peduncularis, syn. *Brodiaea peduncularis.* Early summer-flowering corm. H 10–40cm (4–16in), S 10–15cm (4–6in). Bears semi-erect, basal leaves. Stem has a loose umbel, to 35cm (14in) across, of white flowers, each 1.5–3cm (⅝–1¼in) long, faintly tinged blue.

TRITONIA

IRIDACEAE

Genus of corms, with flattish fans of sword-shaped, erect leaves, grown for their spikes of colourful flowers. Frost to half hardy. Needs a sunny, sheltered site and well-drained soil. Plant corms in autumn (*T. disticha* subsp. *rubrolucens* in spring). Dry off once leaves start dying back in summer (winter for *T. disticha* subsp. *rubrolucens*). Propagate by seed in autumn or by offsets at replanting time.

♀ ***T. crocata***, syn. *T. hyalina*. Spring-flowering corm. H 15–35cm (6–14in), S 5–8cm (2–3in). Half hardy. Has erect, basal leaves. Each wiry stem has a loose spike of up to 10 widely cup-shaped, orange or pink flowers, 4–5cm (1½–2in) across, with transparent margins.

T. disticha subsp. ***rubrolucens,*** syn. *T. rosea, T. rubrolucens*, illus. p.436.

T. hyalina. See *T. crocata*.

T. rosea. See *T. disticha* subsp. *rubrolucens*.

T. rubrolucens. See *T. disticha* subsp. *rubrolucens*.

TROCHOCARPA

EPACRIDACEAE

Genus of evergreen shrubs, grown for their nodding flower spikes. Frost hardy to frost tender, min. 7°C (45°F). Needs sun and moist but well-drained, peaty, sandy soil. Propagate by semi-ripe cuttings in summer.

T. thymifolia. Slow-growing, evergreen, erect shrub. H 30cm (12in), S to 20cm (8in). Frost hardy. Stems are covered in minute, thyme-like leaves. Carries 4cm (1½in) long spikes of tiny, bell-shaped, pink flowers in summer-autumn. Suits an alpine house.

TROCHODENDRON

TROCHODENDRACEAE

Genus of one species of evergreen tree, grown for its foliage and flowers. Frost hardy, but needs shelter from strong, cold winds. Tolerates a sunny or shady position and requires moist but well-drained soil; dislikes very dry or very shallow, chalky soil. Propagate by semi-ripe cuttings in summer or by seed in autumn.

T. aralioides illus. p.80.

TROLLIUS
Globeflower

RANUNCULACEAE

Genus of spring- or summer-flowering perennials that thrive beside pools and streams. Fully hardy. Tolerates sun or shade. Does best in moist soil. Propagate by division in early autumn or by seed in summer or autumn.

***T. × cultorum* 'Alabaster'** illus. p.284. **'Earliest of All'** is a clump-forming perennial. H 60cm (24in), S 45cm (18in). Globular, butter-yellow flowers are borne singly in spring, above rounded, deeply divided, mid-green leaves. ♀ **'Goldquelle'** has large, rich orange flowers. ♀ **'Orange Princess'**, H 75cm (30in), S 45cm (18in), bears orange-gold flowers.

T. europaeus illus. p.285. **'Canary Bird'** is a clump-forming perennial. H 60cm (24in), S 45cm (18in). In spring bears globular, canary-yellow flowers above rounded, deeply divided, mid-green leaves.

T. pumilus illus. p.385.

T. yunnanensis. Clump-forming perennial. H 60cm (2ft), S 30cm (1ft). Has broadly oval leaves with 3–5 deep lobes. Produces buttercup-like, bright yellow flowers in late spring or summer.

Trompetilla, Scarlet. See *Bouvardia ternifolia*, illus. p.169.

TROPAEOLUM
Nasturtium

TROPAEOLACEAE

Genus of annuals, perennials and herbaceous, twining climbers, grown for their brightly coloured flowers. Fully hardy to frost tender, min. 5°C (41°F). Most species prefer sun and well-drained soil. Propagate by seed, tubers or basal stem cuttings in spring. Aphids and caterpillars of cabbage white butterfly and its relatives may cause problems.

♀ ***T.* Alaska Series** illus. p.351.

T. azureum. Herbaceous, leaf-stalk climber with small tubers. H to 1.2m (4ft). Frost tender. Leaves, to 5cm (2in) across, have 5 narrow lobes. Small, purple-blue flowers, with notched petals, open in late summer.

T. canariense. See *T. peregrinum*.

***T.* 'Empress of India'.** Fast-growing, bushy annual. H 23cm (12in), S 45cm (18in). Fully hardy. Has rounded, purple-green leaves. Trumpet-shaped, spurred, semi-double, rich scarlet flowers, 5cm (2in) wide, are borne from early summer to early autumn.

***T.* Gleam Series.** Fast-growing, semi-trailing annual. H 40cm (16in), S 60cm (24in). Fully hardy. Have rounded, mid-green leaves. From early summer to early autumn, bears trumpet-shaped, spurred, semi-double flowers, 5cm (2in) wide, in single colours or in a mixture that includes scarlet, yellow and orange and pastel shades.

***T.* Jewel Series** illus. p.353.

T. majus. Fast-growing, bushy annual. H 1–3m (3–10ft), S 1.5–5m (5–15ft). Frost tender. Has rounded to kidney-shaped, wavy-margined, pale green leaves. From summer to autumn bears long-spurred, red, orange or yellow flowers, 5–6cm (2–2½in) wide. Many cultivars often attributed to *T. majus*, and with similar characteristics to the species, are of hybrid origin, and are described in this book under their cultivar names.

***T.* 'Peach Melba'.** Fast-growing, bushy annual. H to 45cm (18in), S 30cm (12in). Fully hardy. Bears rounded, mid-green leaves. Trumpet-shaped, spurred, pale yellow, flowers, 5cm (2in) wide, and blotched with scarlet are produced from early summer to early autumn.

T. peregrinum, syn. *T. canariense* (Canary creeper). Herbaceous, leaf-stalk climber. H to 2m (6ft). Frost tender. Grey-green leaves have 5 broad lobes. Small, bright yellow flowers, the 2 upper petals much larger and fringed, are borne from summer until first frosts. In cool areas is best grown as an annual.

T. polyphyllum illus. p.305.

♀ ***T. speciosum*** illus. p.206.

T. tricolor. See *T. tricolorum*.

♀ ***T. tricolorum***, syn. *T. tricolor*, illus. p.201.

T. tuberosum illus. p.216. ♀ var. ***lineamaculatum* 'Ken Aslet'** illus. p.214.

♀ ***T.* Whirlybird Series'.** Fast-growing, bushy annual. H 25cm (10in), S 35cm (14in). Fully hardy. Have rounded, mid-green leaves. Trumpet-shaped, spurred, single to semi-double flowers, 5cm (2in) wide, are borne in a mixture or in single colours from early summer to early autumn.

Tropical almond. See *Terminalia catappa*.

Trumpet creeper, Chinese. See *Campsis grandiflora*.

Trumpet creeper. See *Campsis radicans*.

Trumpet flower. See *Bignonia capreolata*.

Trumpet gentian. See *Gentiana clusii*.

Trumpet, Golden. See *Allamanda cathartica*.

Trumpet, Herald's. See *Beaumontia grandiflora*, illus. p.201.

Trumpet honeysuckle. See *Campsis radicans*.

Trumpet tree, Golden. See *Tabebuia chrysotricha*, illus. p.93.

Trumpet tree, Pink. See *Tabebuia rosea*.

Trumpet vine. See *Campsis radicans*.

Trumpets. See *Sarracenia flava*, illus. p.302.

TSUGA

PINACEAE

See also CONIFERS.

T. canadensis illus. p.103. **'Aurea'** (illus. p.107) is a broadly conical conifer, often with several stems. H 5m (15ft) or more, S 2–3m (6–10ft). Fully hardy. Shoots are grey with spirally arranged, needle-like, flattened leaves, golden-yellow when young, ageing to green in second year, those along top inverted to show silver bands. Has ovoid, light brown cones. **'Bennett'**, H 1–2m (3–6ft), S 2m (6ft), is a compact, dwarf form with arching branches and a nest-shaped, central depression. ♀ **'Pendula'** (syn. *T.c.* f. *pendula*) has weeping branches that may be trained to create a domed mound, H and S 3–5m (10–15ft), or left to spread at ground level, H 50cm (20in), S 2–5m (6–15ft).

T. caroliniana (Carolina hemlock). Conifer with a conical or ovoid crown. H 10–15m (30–50ft), S 5–8m (15–25ft). Fully hardy. Red-brown shoots produce spirally set, needle-like, flattened, glossy, dark green leaves. Bears ovoid, green cones, ripening to brown.

T. diversifolia (Japanese hemlock, Northern Japanese hemlock). Conifer with a broad, dense crown. H 10–15m (30–50ft), S 8–12m (25–40ft). Fully hardy. Has orange shoots and needle-like, flattened, glossy, deep green leaves, banded with white beneath, that are spirally set. Ovoid cones are dark brown.

♀ ***T. heterophylla*** (Western hemlock). Vigorous, conical conifer with drooping branchlets. H 20–30m (70–100ft), S 8–10m (25–30ft). Fully hardy. Grey shoots bear spirally set, needle-like, flattened, dark green leaves with silvery bands beneath. Bears ovoid, pale green cones that ripen to dark brown.

T. mertensiana (Mountain hemlock). Narrowly conical conifer with short, horizontal branches. H 8–15m (25–50ft), S 3–6m (10–20ft). Fully hardy. Red-brown shoots bear needle-like, flattened, glaucous blue-green or grey-green leaves, spirally arranged. Cones are cylindrical and yellow-green to purple, ripening to dark brown. **'Glauca'** illus. p.101.

T. sieboldii (Japanese hemlock, Southern Japanese hemlock). Broadly conical conifer. H 15m (50ft), S 8–10m (25–30ft). Fully hardy. Has glossy, buff shoots that bear needle-like, flattened, lustrous, dark green leaves, set spirally. Cones are ovoid and dark brown.

TSUSIOPHYLLUM

ERICACEAE

Genus of one species of semi-evergreen shrub, grown for its flowers. Is similar to *Rhododendron* and is suitable for rock gardens and peat beds. Frost hardy. Requires shade and well-drained, peaty, sandy soil. Propagate by softwood cuttings in spring or early summer or by seed in autumn or spring.

T. tanakae. Semi-evergreen, spreading shrub. H 15cm (6in) or more, S 25cm (10in). Twiggy, branched stems bear tiny, narrowly oval, hairy leaves. In early summer produces small, tubular, white or pinkish-white flowers at stem tips.

TUBERARIA

CISTACEAE

Genus of annuals. Fully hardy. Grow in sun and in any very well-drained soil. Propagate by seed in spring.

T. guttata, syn. *Helianthemum guttatum*. Moderately fast-growing, upright, branching annual. H and S 10–30cm (4–12in). Has lance-shaped, hairy, mid-green leaves and, in summer, yellow flowers, sometimes red-spotted at base of petals, that look like small, single roses.

Tuberose. See *Polianthes tuberosa*.

Tufted hairgrass. See *Deschampsia cespitosa*.

Tufted sedge. See *Carex elata*.

TULBAGHIA

LILIACEAE/ALLIACEAE

Genus of semi-evergreen perennials. Frost to half hardy. Needs full sun and well-drained soil. Propagate by division or seed in spring.

T. natalensis. Semi-evergreen, clump-forming perennial. H 12cm (5in), S 10cm (4in). Frost hardy. In mid-summer, umbels of delicately fragrant, tubular, yellow-centred, white flowers, with spreading petal lobes, open above fine, grass-like, mid-green foliage.

T. violacea illus. p.293.

Tulip. See *Tulipa*.
Golden globe. See *Calochortus amabilis*, illus. p.450.
Horned. See *Tulipa acuminata*, illus. p.427.
Lady. See *Tulipa clusiana*, illus. p.427.
Mariposa. See *Calochortus*.
Water lily. See *Tulipa kaufmanniana*, illus. p.428.
Tulip tree. See *Liriodendron tulipifera*, illus. p.61.
African. See *Spathodea campanulata*, illus. p.67.
Chinese. See *Liriodendron chinense*.

TULIPA
Tulip

LILIACEAE

Genus of mainly spring-flowering bulbs, grown for their bright, upward-facing flowers. Each bulb bears a few linear to lance-shaped, green or grey-green leaves on the stem. Flowers bear 6 usually pointed petals (botanically known as perianth segments) and 6 stamens, singly, unless otherwise stated below. Each plant has a spread of up to 20cm (8in). All are fully hardy unless otherwise stated. Requires a sunny position with well-drained soil and appreciates a summer baking; in cool, wet areas, bulbs may be lifted, when the leaves have died down, and stored in a dry place for replanting in autumn. Propagate by division of bulbs in autumn or for species by seed in spring or autumn. If ingested, all parts may cause mild stomach upset, and contact with any part may aggravate skin allergies.

Horticulturally, tulips are grouped into the following divisions. See also feature panel pp.426–8.

Single Early Group (Div.1) – has cup-shaped, single, white to dark purple flowers, to 7cm (3in) across, often margined, 'flamed' or flecked with a contrasting colour, from early to mid-spring. H 15–45cm (6–18in).
Double Early Group (Div.2) – has bowl-shaped, fully double, dark red to yellow or white flowers, to 8cm (3in) across, often margined or flecked with another colour, borne in mid-spring. H 30–40cm (12–16in).
Triumph Group (Div.3) – sturdy stems bear cup-shaped, single flowers, to 6cm (2½in) across, in a range of colour and often margined or flecked with a contrasting colour, in mid- and late spring. H 35–60cm (14–24in).
Darwin Hybrid Group (Div.4) – has egg-shaped, single flowers, to 7cm (3in) across, in a range of colours and usually flushed, 'flamed' or margined with a different colour and often with contrasting bases, from mid- to late spring. H 50–70cm (20–28in).
Single Late Group including Cottage and Darwin Hybrids (Div.5) – has cup- or goblet-shaped, single flowers, sometimes several to a stem, in white to yellow, pink, red or almost black, often with contrasting margins, in late spring. H 45–75cm (18–30in).
Lily-flowered Group (Div.6) – strong stems bear goblet-shaped, single flowers, to 8cm (3in) across, with reflexed, pointed petal tips and sometimes margined, 'flamed' or flushed with a contrasting colour, in late spring. H 45–65cm (18–26in).
Fringed Group (Div.7) – flowers are similar to those in Div.6, but have fringed petals. H 35–65cm (14–26in).
Viridiflora Group (Div.8) – has cup- or almost closed bowl-shaped, single flowers, to 8cm (3in) across, sometimes entirely green, margined with another colour, or white to yellow, red or purple, 'flamed' or striped green, with contrasting centres, borne in late spring. H 40–55cm (16–22in).
Rembrandt Group (Div.9) – comprises mostly very old cultivars, similar to Div.6, but has colours 'broken' into striped or feathered patterns owing to virus. Flowers in late spring. H 45–65cm (18–26in).
Parrot Group (Div.10) – has cup-shaped, single, white to pink or violet-blue flowers, to 10cm (4in) across, often unevenly striped with different colours, including green, borne in late spring. Petals are finely and irregularly cut. H 35–65cm (14–26in).
Double Late Group (peony-flowered) (Div.11) – has bowl-shaped, fully double flowers, to 12cm (5in) across, in white to purple, sometimes margined or 'flamed' in a different colour, borne in late spring. H 35–60cm (14–24in).
Kaufmanniana Group (Div.12) – comprises *T. kauffmanniana* and hybrids and has bowl-shaped, single flowers, 8–10cm (3–4in) across, frequently multicoloured and usually with distinctively coloured bases, in early or mid-spring. Leaves are sometimes marked bronze, red or purple. H 15–30cm (6–12in).
Fosteriana Group (Div.13) – comprises *T. fosteriana* and hybrids and has bowl-shaped, single flowers, to 12cm (5in) across, in white to yellow or dark red, sometimes margined or 'flamed' in another colour and with contrasting bases, borne in mid-spring. Leaves are sometimes marked red-purple. H 20–65cm (8–26in).
Greigii Group (Div.14) – comprises *T. greigii* and hybrids and has bowl-shaped, single, yellow to red flowers, to 10cm (4in) across, sometimes 'flamed' or margined in a different colour and with contrasting bases, usually borne in early or mid-spring. Blue-green leaves are generally wavy-margined and always marked dark bluish-maroon. H 15–30cm (6–12in).
Miscellaneous Group (Div.15) – comprises all species and hybrids not included in other divisions. Flowers appear from late winter to late spring.

T. acuminata (Horned tulip) illus. p.427. Div.15. Mid-spring-flowering bulb. H 30–45cm (12–18in). Flowers are 7–13cm (3–5in) long, with long-pointed, tapered, pale red or yellow petals, often tinged with red or green outside.
***T.* 'Ad Rem'** illus. p.427. Div.4. Mid- to late spring-flowering bulb. H 60cm (24in). Flowers are scarlet with black bases and yellow margins. Anthers are yellow.
T. aitchisonii. See *T. clusiana*.
♀ ***T.* 'Ancilla'**, Div.12. Early spring-flowering bulb. H 15cm (6in). Flowers are pink and reddish outside, white inside, each with a central, red ring.
***T.* 'Angélique'** illus. p.426. Div.11. Late spring-flowering bulb. H 40cm (16in). Delicately scented, double, pale pink flowers deepen with age. Each petal has paler streaks and a lighter margin. Is good for bedding.
♀ ***T.* 'Apeldoorn's Elite'** illus. p.427. Div.4. Mid- to late spring-flowering bulb. H 60cm (24in). Has buttercup-yellow flowers feathered with cherry-red and with yellowish-green bases.
♀ ***T.* 'Apricot Beauty'**, Div.1. Early spring-flowering bulb. H 40cm (16in). Flowers are salmon-pink faintly tinged with red.
♀ ***T.* 'Artist'** illus. p.428. Div.8. Late spring-flowering bulb. H 45cm (18in). Flowers are salmon-pink and purple outside, sometimes marked with green, and deep salmon-pink and green inside.
***T.* 'Attila'** illus. p.426. Div.3. Mid-spring-flowering bulb. H 40cm (16in). Strong stems carry long-lasting, pink flowers. Is good for bedding.
♀ ***T. aucheriana***, Div.15. Early spring-flowering bulb. H to 20cm (8in). Has grey-green leaves. Yellow-centred, pink flowers, 2–5cm (¾–2in) long, each tapered at the base, have oval petals.
T. australis. See *T. sylvestris*.
T. bakeri. See *T. saxatilis*.
***T.* 'Balalaika'** illus. p.427. Div.5. Late spring-flowering bulb. H 50cm (20in). Bright red flowers each have a yellow base and black stamens.
♀ ***T.* 'Ballade'** illus. p.426. Div.6. Late spring-flowering bulb. H 50cm (20in). Reddish-magenta flowers with a white-margined, yellow base have long petals that are margined white.
♀ ***T. batalinii*** illus. p.427). Div.15. Early spring-flowering bulb. H 10–30cm (4–12in). Is often included under *T. linifolia*. Leaves are grey-green. Flowers, 2–6cm (¾–2½in) long, have broadly oval petals and are bowl-shaped at the base. Pale yellow petals are darker yellow or brown at bases inside. Several cultivars are hybrids between *T. batalinii* and *T. linifolia*. These include **'Apricot Jewel'** with flowers that are orange-red outside, yellow inside; ♀ **'Bright Gem'**, which has yellow flowers flushed with orange; and **'Bronze Charm'**, which bears yellow flowers with bronze feathering.
***T.* 'Bellona'** illus. p.428. Div.1. Early spring-flowering bulb. H 30cm (12in). Fragrant flowers are deep golden-yellow. Is good for bedding and forcing.
T. biflora, syn. *T. polychroma* illus. p.426. Div.15. Early spring-flowering bulb. H 5–10cm (2–4in). Has grey-green leaves. Stem bears 1–5 fragrant, yellow-centred, white flowers, 1.5–3.5cm (⅝–1½in) long and tapered at the bases. Narrowly oval petals are flushed outside with greenish-grey or greenish-pink. Suits a rock garden.
***T.* 'Bing Crosby'** illus. p.427. Div.3. Mid- to late spring-flowering bulb. H 50cm (20in). Has glowing, scarlet flowers.
***T.* 'Bird of Paradise'** illus. p.426. Div.10. Late spring-flowering bulb. H 45cm (18in). Produces orange-margined, cardinal-red flowers with bright yellow bases. Anthers are purple.
***T.* 'Blue Parrot'** illus. p.428. Div.10. Late spring-flowering bulb. H 60cm (24in). Very large, bright violet flowers, sometimes bronze outside, are borne on strong stems.
***T.* 'Burgundy Lace'**, Div.7. Late spring-flowering bulb. H 60cm (24in). Flowers are wine-red, each petal with a fringed margin.
***T.* 'Candela'** illus. p.428. Div.13. Early to mid-spring-flowering bulb. H 30cm (12in). Large flowers are yellow, with black anthers, and long-lasting.
***T.* 'Cape Cod'** illus. p.427. Div.14. Mid- to late spring-flowering bulb. H 45cm (18in). Grey-green leaves have reddish stripes. Yellowish-bronze flowers each have a black-and-red base; petals are margined yellow outside.
♀ ***T.* 'Carnaval de Nice'** illus. p.426. Div.11. Late spring-flowering bulb. H 40cm (16in). Double flowers are white feathered with deep red.
♀ ***T.* 'China Pink'** illus. p.426. Div.6. Late spring-flowering bulb. H 55cm (22in). Flowers are pink, each with a white base, and have slightly reflexed petals.
***T.* 'Chopin'**, Div.12. Early spring-flowering bulb. H 20cm (8in). Has brown-mottled, grey-green leaves. Lemon-yellow flowers have black bases.
T. chrysantha. See *Tulipa clusiana* var. *chrysantha*.
***T.* 'Clara Butt'**, Div.5. Late spring-flowering bulb. H 60cm (24in). Flowers are salmon-pink. Is particularly good for bedding.
T. clusiana, syn. *T. aitchisonii* (Lady tulip; illus. p.427), Div.15. Mid-spring-flowering bulb. H to 30cm (12in). Has grey-green leaves. Each stem bears 1 or 2 flowers, 2–6.5cm (¾–2½in) long, that are bowl-shaped at the base. Narrowly oval, white petals are purple or crimson at base inside, striped deep pink outside. Stamens are purple. Flowers of ♀ var. ***chrysantha*** (syn. *T. chrysantha*; illus. p.428) are yellow, flushed red or brown outside, with yellow stamens, var. ***stellata*** has white flowers with yellow bases and yellow stamens.
***T.* 'Couleur Cardinal'.** Div.3. Mid-spring-flowering bulb. H 35cm (14in). Plum-purple flowers are dark crimson-scarlet inside.
T. dasystemon of gardens**.** See *T. tarda*.
***T.* 'Dawnglow'**, Div.4. Mid- to late-spring-flowering bulb. H 60cm (24in). Pale apricot flowers are flushed with deep pink outside and are deep yellow inside. Has purple anthers.
***T.* 'Diana'** illus. p.426. Div.1. Early spring-flowering bulb. H 28cm (11in). Large, pure white flowers are carried on strong stems.
***T.* 'Dillenburg'** illus. p.428. Div.5. Late spring-flowering bulb. H 65cm (26in). Flowers are brick-orange and are good for bedding.
♀ ***T.* 'Don Quichotte'** illus. p.426. Div.3. Mid-spring-flowering bulb. H 40cm (16in). Purple-pink flowers are long-lasting.
***T.* 'Dreamboat'** illus. p.428. Div.14. Mid- to late spring-flowering bulb. H 25cm (10in). Produces grey-green leaves with brown stripes. Urn-shaped, red-tinged, amber-yellow flowers have greenish-bronze bases with red blotches.
***T.* 'Dreaming Maid'** illus. p.428. Div.3. Mid- to late spring-flowering bulb. H 55cm (22in). Flowers have white-margined, violet petals.

♀ *T.* **'Dreamland'** illus. p.426. Div.5. Late spring-flowering bulb. H 60cm (24in). Flowers are red with white bases and yellow anthers.
T. eichleri. See *T. undulatifolia.*
T. **'Estella Rijnveld'** illus. p.427. Div.10. Late spring-flowering bulb. H 60cm (24in). Large flowers are red, streaked with white and green.
♀ *T.* **'Fancy Frills'** illus. p.426. Div.10. Late spring-flowering bulb. H 50cm (20in). Fringed, ivory-white petals are striped and margined pink outside; inside, base is rose-pink. Anthers are pale yellow.
T. **'Flaming Parrot'** illus. p.427. Div.10. Late-spring flowering bulb. H 55cm (22in). Deep yellow flowers, 'flamed' dark red, have primrose-yellow bases. Insides are primrose-yellow with glowing, blood-red 'flames'. Anthers are purple-black.
T. fosteriana, Div.15. Early spring-flowering bulb. H 20–45cm (8–18in). Has a downy stem and grey-green leaves, downy above. Flowers 4.5–10cm (1¾–4in) long, are bowl-shaped at the base with narrowly oval, bright red petals, and each has a purplish-black centre inside, ringed with yellow.
♀ *T.* **'Fringed Beauty'** illus. p.427. Div.7. Early to mid-spring-flowering bulb. H 32cm (13in). Fringed petals are bright red with yellow margins. Is excellent for forcing.
♀ *T.* **'Fringed Elegance'** illus. p.428. Div.7. Late spring-flowering bulb. H 50cm (20in). Has pale yellow flowers dotted with pink outside; inside, bases have bronze-green blotches. Each petal has a yellow fringe. Anthers are purple.
T. **'Gala Beauty'**, Div.9. Late spring-flowering bulb. H 60cm (24in). Yellow flowers are streaked with crimson.
♀ *T.* **'Garden Party'** illus. p.427. Div.3. Mid- to late spring-flowering bulb. H 40–45cm (16–18in). Produces white flowers; petals are margined deep pink outside and inside are streaked with deep pink.
T. **'Giuseppe Verdi'** illus. p.428. Div.12. Mid-spring-flowering bulb. H 20cm (8in). Produces yellow-margined, carmine-red flowers, which are golden-yellow with small, red marks inside. Leaves have purple marks.
♀ *T.* **'Glück'** illus. p.427. Div.12. Early spring-flowering bulb. H 15cm (6in). Has reddish-brown-mottled, grey-green leaves. Petals are red outside, margined yellow, and yellow inside, each with a darker base.
T. **'Golden Apeldoorn'** illus. p.428. Div.4. Mid- to late spring-flowering bulb. H 50–60cm (20–24in). Golden-yellow flowers each have a black base and black stamens.
T. **'Golden Artist'** illus. p.428. Div.8. Late spring-flowering bulb. H 45cm (18in). Flowers are bright golden-yellow.
T. **'Gordon Cooper'** illus. p.426. Div.4. Mid- to late spring-flowering bulb. H 60cm (24in). Petals are deep pink outside, margined red; inside they are red with blue-and-yellow bases. Has black anthers.
T. **'Greenland'.** See *T.* 'Groenland'.
T. greigii, Div.15. Early spring-flowering bulb. H 20–45cm (8–18in). Has downy stems. Leaves are streaked or mottled with red or purple. Cup-shaped flowers, 3–10cm (1¼–4in) long, with broadly oval, red or yellow petals, have yellow-ringed, black centres.
T. **'Greuze'** illus. p.428. Div.5. Late spring-flowering bulb. H 65cm (26in). Flowers are dark violet-purple and are good for bedding.
T. **'Groenland'**, syn. *T.* 'Greenland' illus. p.426. Div.8. Late spring-flowering bulb. H 50cm (20in). Bears flowers with green petals that are margined rose-pink. Is a good bedding tulip.
T. hageri illus. p.427. Div.15. Mid-spring-flowering bulb. H 10–30cm (4–12in). Frost hardy. Stem has 1–4 flowers, 3–6cm (1½–2½in) long, tapered at the base and with oval, dull red petals tinged with green outside.
T. **'Heart's Delight'**, Div.12. Early spring-flowering bulb. H 20–25cm (8–10in). Has green leaves striped red-brown. Bears deep pinkish-red flowers, margined pale pink, and pale pink inside with red-blotched, yellow bases.
T. **'Hollywood'**, Div.8. Late spring-flowering bulb. H 30cm (12in). Red flowers, tinged and streaked with green, have yellow bases. Is good for bedding.
T. humilis illus. p.428. Div.15. Early spring-flowering bulb. A variable species, often considered to include *T. aucheriana*, *T. pulchella* and *T. violacea*. H to 20cm (8in). Has grey-green leaves. Stem bears usually 1, sometimes 2 or 3, pinkish-magenta flowers, 2–5cm (¾–2in) long, tapered at the base and with a yellow centre inside. Petals are oval. Is suitable for a rock garden.
T. **'Jack Laan'**, Div.9. Late spring-flowering bulb. H 60cm (24in). Purple flowers are shaded with brown and feathered with white and yellow.
♀ *T.* **'Juan'** illus. p.427. Div.13. Early to mid-spring-flowering bulb. H 35cm (14in). Flowers are deep orange overlaid with scarlet. Leaves are marked with reddish-brown.
T. kaufmanniana (Water lily tulip; illus. p.428), Div.15. Early spring-flowering bulb. H 10–35cm (4–14in). Leaves are grey-green. Stem has 1–5 often scented flowers, 3–10cm (1½–4in) long and bowl-shaped at the base. Narrowly oval petals are usually either cream or yellow, flushed with pink or grey-green outside; centres are often a different colour. Pink, orange or red forms occasionally occur.
♀ *T.* **'Keizerskroon'** illus. p.427. Div.1. Early spring-flowering bulb. H 35cm (14in). Flowers have crimson-scarlet petals, with broad, bright yellow margins. Is a good, reliable bedding tulip.
♀ *T.* **'Kingsblood'** illus. p.427. Div.5. Late spring-flowering bulb. H 60cm (24in). Cherry-red flowers are margined scarlet.
♀ *T. linifolia* illus. p.427. Div.15. Early spring-flowering bulb. H 10–30cm (4–12in). A variable species, often considered to include *T. batalinii* and *T. maximowiczii.* Has grey-green leaves. Red flowers, 2–6cm (¾–2in) long, are bowl-shaped at the base and, inside, have blackish-purple centres that are usually ringed with cream or yellow. Petals are broadly oval.
T. **'Lustige Witwe'**, syn. *T.* 'Merry Widow' illus. p.427. Div.3. Mid- to late spring-flowering bulb. Flowers have deep glowing red petals margined white.
T. **'Madame Lefeber'**, syn. *T.* 'Red Emperor' illus. p.427. Div.13. Early to mid-spring-flowering bulb. H 35–40cm (14–16in). Produces very large, brilliant red flowers.
T. **'Maja'** illus. p.428. Div.7. Late spring-flowering bulb. H 50cm (20in). Produces egg-shaped, pale yellow flowers, with fringed petals, that are bronze-yellow at the base. Anthers are yellow.
T. **'Margot Fonteyn'** illus. p.427. Div.3. Mid- to late spring-flowering bulb. H 40–45cm (16–18in). Flowers have yellow-margined, bright red petals, each with a yellow base inside. Anthers are black.
T. marjolletii illus. p.427. Div.15. Mid-spring-flowering bulb. H 40–50cm (16–20in). Produces flowers, 4–6cm (1½–2½in) long and bowl-shaped at the base, with broadly oval, creamy-white petals, margined and marked deep pink.
T. maximowiczii, Div.15. Early spring-flowering bulb. H 10–30cm (4–12in). Has grey-green leaves. Bright red flowers, 2–6cm (¾–2½in) long, with broadly oval petals, have white-bordered, black centres and are bowl-shaped at the base.
T. **'Menton'** illus. p.426. Div.5. Late spring-flowering bulb. H 60cm (24in). Flowers have light orange-margined, rose-pink petals with bright yellow and white bases. Anthers are yellow.
T. **'Merry Widow'.** See *T.* 'Lustige Witwe'.
♀ *T.* **'Monte Carlo'**, Div.2. Early spring-flowering bulb. H 40cm (16in). Has double, yellow flowers with sparse, red streaks.
T. **'New Design'** illus. p.426. Div.3. Mid-spring-flowering bulb. H 40cm (16in). Flowers have yellow petals that fade to pinkish-white and are margined red outside and marked apricot inside. Leaves have pinkish-white margins.
♀ *T.* **'Orange Emperor'**, Div.13. Early to mid-spring-flowering bulb. H 40cm (16in). Flowers are bright orange, each with a yellow base inside and have black anthers.
T. **'Orange Triumph'**, Div.11. Late spring-flowering bulb. H 50cm (20in). Has double, soft orange-red flowers flushed with brown; each petal has a yellow margin.
♀ *T.* **'Oranje Nassau'**, Div.2. Early spring-flowering bulb. H 25–30cm (10–12in). Has double, blood-red flowers flushed fiery orange-red. Is good for forcing.
♀ *T.* **'Oratorio'**, Div.14. Mid- to late spring-flowering bulb. H 20cm (8in). Has reddish-brown-mottled, grey-green leaves. Broadly urn-shaped flowers are rose-pink outside, apricot-pink inside with black bases.
T. orphanidea illus. p.428. Div.15. Mid-spring-flowering bulb. H 10–30cm (4–12in). Frost hardy. Green leaves often have reddish margins. Stem has 1–4 flowers, 3–6cm (1¼–2½in) long and tapered at the base. Oval petals are orange-brown, tinged outside with green and often purple.
T. **'Page Polka'** illus. p.426. Div.3. Mid-spring-flowering bulb. Large, deep red flowers have white bases and are striped with white. Anthers are yellow.
T. **'Palestrina'**, Div.5. Late spring-flowering bulb. H 45cm (18in). Petals of large, salmon-pink flowers are green outside.
T. **'Peach Blossom'**, Div.2. Early spring-flowering bulb. H 25–30cm (10–12in). Produces double, silvery-pink flowers flushed with deep pink.
T. **'Peer Gynt'** illus. p.426. Div.3. Mid- to late spring-flowering bulb. H 50cm (20in). Purple-margined, fuchsia-red flowers have white bases spotted with yellow. Anthers are purplish-grey.
♀ *T.* **'Plaisir'** illus. p.427. Div.14. Mid- to late spring-flowering bulb. H 15–20cm (6–8in). Has grey-green leaves mottled with red-brown. Bears broadly urn-shaped, pale yellow-margined, deep pinkish-red flowers, with black-and-yellow bases.
T. polychroma. See *T. biflora*.
♀ *T. praestans* **'Fusilier'**, Div.15. Early spring-flowering bulb. H 10–45cm (4–18in). Has a minutely downy stem and downy, grey-green leaves. Stem bears 3–5 flowers that are 5.5–6.5cm (2¼–2½in) long and bowl-shaped at the base. Oval petals are orange-scarlet. **'Unicum'** (illus. p.427) has leaves that are margined pale yellow. Flowers have bright red petals with yellow bases and blue-black anthers. **'Van Tubergen's Variety'** (illus. p.428) produces 2–5 flowers per stem that are often yellow at the base; it increases very freely.
♀ *T.* **'Prinses Irene'** (illus. p.428), Div.1. Early spring-flowering bulb. H 30–35cm (12–14in). Produces orange flowers streaked with purple.
T. pulchella, Div.15. Early spring-flowering bulb. H to 20cm (8in). Has grey-green leaves. Flowers, 2–5cm (¾–2in) long and tapered at the base, have oval, purple petals and yellow or bluish-black centres inside. Is useful for a rock garden.
♀ *T.* **'Purissima'**, syn. *T.* 'White Emperor' illus. p.426. Div.13. Early to mid-spring-flowering bulb. H 35–40cm (14–16in). Flowers are pure white.
T. **'Queen of Night'** illus. p.428. Div.5. Late spring-flowering bulb. H 60cm (24in). The darkest of all tulips, has long-lasting, very dark maroon-black flowers on sturdy stems. Is useful for bedding.
T. **'Queen of Sheba'** illus. p.427. Div.6. Late-spring-flowering bulb. H 60cm (24in). Bears orange-margined, glowing, brownish-red flowers.
T. **'Red Emperor'.** See *T.* 'Madame Lefeber'.
T. **'Red Parrot'** illus. p.427. Div.10. Late spring-flowering bulb. H 60cm (24in). Large, raspberry-red flowers are carried on strong stems.
♀ *T.* **'Red Riding Hood'** illus. p.427. Div.14. Late spring-flowering bulb. H 20cm (8in). Produces vivid, black-based, scarlet flowers amid spreading, dark green leaves that are mottled brownish-purple.
T. saxatilis, syn. *T. bakeri* illus. p.426. Div.15. Early spring-flowering bulb. H 15–45cm (6–18in). Frost hardy. Has shiny, green leaves. Stem produces 1–4 scented flowers, 4–5.5cm (1½–2¼in) long and tapered at the base. Oval, pink to lilac petals are yellow at the base inside.
T. **'Shakespeare'** illus. p.428. Div.12. Early spring-flowering bulb. H 12–15cm (5–6in). Petals are deep red

outside, margined salmon, and salmon inside, flushed red with a yellow base.
♀ ***T. sprengeri*** illus. p.427. Div.15. Late spring- and early summer-flowering bulb. H 30–45cm (12–18in). Flowers are 4.5–6.5cm (1¼–2½in) long and tapered at the base. Bears narrowly oval, orange-red petals, the outer 3 with buff-yellow backs. Is the latest-flowering tulip. Increases very rapidly.
♀ ***T.* 'Spring Green'** illus. p.426. Div.8. Late spring-flowering bulb. H 35–38cm (14–15in). Has white flowers feathered with green. Anthers are pale green.
T. sylvestris, syn. *T. australis* illus. p.428. Div.15. Early spring-flowering bulb. H 10–45cm (4–18in). Yellow flowers, usually borne singly, are 3.5–6.5cm (1½–2½in) long and tapered at the base. Narrowly oval petals are often tinged with green outside.
♀ ***T. tarda***, syn. *T. dasystemon* of gardens, illus. p.428. Div.15. Early spring-flowering bulb. H to 15cm (6in). Has glossy, green leaves. Flowers, 4–6 per stem, are 3–4cm (1¼–1½in) long and tapered at the base. Oval, white petals have yellow lower halves inside and are tinged with green and sometimes red outside. Suits a rock garden or raised bed.
♀ ***T.* 'Toronto'**, Div.14. Mid- to late spring-flowering bulb. H 30cm (12in). Has mottled leaves and 2 or 3 long-lasting flowers per stem. Open, broadly cup-shaped flowers have pointed, bright red petals each with a brownish-green-yellow base inside. Anthers are bronze.
♀ ***T. turkestanica*** illus. p.426. Div.15. Early spring-flowering bulb. H 10–30cm (4–12in). Has a hairy stem and grey-green leaves. Unpleasant-smelling flowers, up to 12 per stem, are 1.5–3.5cm (⅝–1½in) long and tapered at the base. Oval, white petals are flushed green or pink outside; flowers have yellow or orange centres inside.
***T.* 'Uncle Tom'** illus. p.427. Div.11. Late spring-flowering bulb. H 50cm (20in). Double flowers are maroon-red.
T. undulatifolia, syn. *T. eichleri* illus. p.427. Div.15. Early to mid-spring-flowering bulb. H 15–50cm (6–20in). Has a downy stem and grey-green leaves. Flowers, 3–8cm (1¼–3in) long, are bowl-shaped at the base. Narrowly oval, red or orange-red petals each have a pale red or buff back and a yellow-bordered, dark green or black blotch at the base inside.
♀ ***T.* 'Union Jack'** illus. p.427. Div.5. Late spring-flowering bulb. H 60cm (24in). Ivory-white petals, marked with deep pinkish-red 'flames', have blue-margined, white bases.
♀ ***T. urumiensis*** illus. p.427. Div.15. Early spring-flowering bulb. H 10–20cm (4–8in). Stem is mostly below soil level. Leaves are green or greyish-green. Bears 1 or 2 flowers, each 4cm (1½in) long and tapered at the base. Narrowly oval, yellow petals are flushed mauve or red-brown outside. Is useful for a rock garden.
T. violacea illus. p.428. Div.15. Early spring-flowering bulb. H to 20cm (8in). Has grey-green leaves. Violet-pink flowers, 2–5cm (¾–2in) long, are tapered at the base and have yellow or bluish-black centres inside. Petals are oval. Suits a rock garden or raised bed.
♀ ***T.* 'West Point'** illus. p.427. Div.6. Late spring-flowering bulb. H 50cm (20in). Primrose-yellow flowers have long-pointed, recurved petals.
***T.* 'White Dream'** illus. p.426. Div.3. Mid- to late spring-flowering bulb. H 40–45cm (16–18in). Flowers are white with yellow anthers.
***T.* 'White Emperor'.** See *T.* 'Purissima'.
***T.* 'White Parrot'** illus. p.426. Div.10. Late spring-flowering bulb. H 55cm (22in). Large flowers have ruffled, white petals flecked green near the base. Is good for cutting.
♀ ***T.* 'White Triumphator'** illus. p.426. Div.6. Late spring-flowering bulb. H 65–70cm (26–28in). White flowers have elegantly reflexed petals.
T. whittallii illus. p.428. Div.15. Mid-spring-flowering bulb. H 30–35cm (12–14in). Frost hardy. Stem produces 1–4flowers, 3–6cm (1¼–2½in) long and tapered at the base. Oval petals are bright brownish-orange.
***T.* 'Yokohama'** illus. p.428. Div.1. Early to mid-spring-flowering bulb. H 35cm (14in). Pointed flowers are deep yellow.

Tumbling Ted. See *Saponaria ocymoides*, illus. p.390.
Tunic flower. See *Petrorhagia saxifraga*, illus. p.387.
Tunica saxifraga. See *Petrorhagia saxifraga*.
Tupelo. See *Nyssa*.
Turk's cap. See *Melocactus*.
Turkey oak. See *Quercus cerris*.
Turkish hazel. See *Corylus colurna*.
Turkscap lily. See *Lilium superbum*.
Turpentine, Cyprus. See *Pistacia terebinthus*.

TURRAEA

MELIACEAE

Genus of evergreen trees and shrubs, grown for their flowers and foliage. Frost tender, min. 12–15°C (54–9°F). Prefers full sun. Needs fertile, well-drained soil. Water freely in full growth, less at other times. Young plants may need growing point removed to promote branching. Prune after flowering if necessary. Propagate by seed in spring or by semi-ripe cuttings in summer.
T. obtusifolia illus. p.168.

Turtle-head. See *Chelone*.

TWEEDIA

ASCLEPIADACEAE

Genus of herbaceous, twining climbers; only one species is in general cultivation. Frost tender, min. 5°C (41°F). In cool climates may be grown as an annual. Grow in sun and in well-drained soil. Pinch out tips of shoots to encourage branching. Propagate by seed in spring.
♀ ***T. caerulea***, syn. *Oxypetalum caeruleum*, illus. p.213

Twin flower. See *Linnaea*.
Twin-flowered violet. See *Viola biflora*.

TYLECODON

CRASSULACEAE

Genus of deciduous, bushy, winter-growing, succulent shrubs with very swollen stems. Frost tender, min. 7°C (45°F). Likes sun and very well-drained soil. Propagate by seed or stem cuttings in summer. The leaves of *T. wallichii* are highly toxic if ingested.
T. paniculatus, syn. *Cotyledon paniculata* (Butter tree). Deciduous, bushy, succulent shrub. H and S 2m (6ft). Swollen stem and branches have papery, yellow coverings. Leaves are oblong to oval, fleshy and bright green. In summer produces clusters of tubular, green-striped, red flowers at stem tips.
T. papillaris subsp. ***wallichii.*** See *T. wallichii.*
T. reticulatus, syn. *Cotyledon reticulata*, illus. p.481.
T. wallichii, syn. *T. papillaris* subsp. *wallichii, Cotyledon wallichii.* Deciduous, bushy, succulent shrub. H and S 30cm (1ft). Has 3cm (1¼in) thick stems with cylindrical, grooved-topped, green leaves at tips. After leaf fall, stems are neatly covered in raised leaf bases. Bears tubular, yellow-green flowers, 2cm (½in) long, in autumn.

TYPHA

TYPHACEAE

Genus of deciduous, perennial, marginal water plants, grown for their decorative, cylindrical seed heads. Fully hardy. Grows in sun or shade. Propagate in spring by seed or division.
T. latifolia illus. p.464. **'Variegata'** is a deciduous, perennial marginal water plant. H 90cm–1.2m (3–4ft), S indefinite. Strap-shaped, mid-green leaves have longitudinal, cream stripes. Spikes of beige flowers in late summer are followed by decorative, cylindrical, dark brown seed heads.
T. minima illus. p.465.

UGNI

MYRTACEAE

Genus of densely leafy, evergreen shrubs or trees. *U. molinae*, the only species usually cultivated, is valued for its foliage, flowers and fruit. Frost hardy. Needs full sun or partial shade and moist but well-drained soil. Propagate by semi-ripe cuttings in late summer.

U. molinae, syn. *Eugenia ugni, Myrtus ugni.* Evergreen, upright, densely branched shrub. H 1.5m (5ft), S 1m (3ft). Glossy, dark green leaves are oval. Has fragrant, slightly nodding, cup-shaped, white-pink-tinted flowers in late spring, then aromatic, edible, spherical, dark red fruits. Is good for hedging in mild areas.

ULEX

LEGUMINOSAE/PAPILIONACEAE

Genus of leafless, or almost leafless, shrubs that appear evergreen as a result of their year-round, green shoots and spines. Is grown for its flowers in spring. Fully hardy. Needs full sun, and prefers poor, well-drained, acid soil. Trim each year after flowering to maintain compact habit. Straggly, old plants may be cut back hard in spring. Propagate by seed in autumn. The seeds may cause mild stomach upset if ingested.

U. europaeus illus. p.157.

♀ **'Flore Pleno'** is a leafless, or almost leafless, bushy shrub. H 1m (3ft), S 1.2m (4ft). In spring, bears masses of fragrant, pea-like, double, yellow flowers on leafless, dark green shoots.

Ulmo. See *Eucryphia cordifolia.*

ULMUS

Elm

ULMACEAE

Genus of deciduous or, rarely, semi-evergreen trees and shrubs, often large and stately, grown for their foliage and habit. Inconspicuous flowers appear in spring. Fully hardy. Requires full sun and fertile, well-drained soil. Propagate by softwood cuttings in summer or by seed or suckers in autumn. Is susceptible to Dutch elm disease, which is quickly fatal, although *U. parvifolia* and *U. pumila* appear more resistant than other species and hybrids.

U. americana (American white elm, White elm). Deciduous, spreading tree. H and S 30m (100ft). Has grey bark and drooping branchlets. Large, oval, dark green leaves are sharply toothed and rough-textured.

U. angustifolia. See *U. minor* subsp. *angustifolia*.var. ***cornubiensis*** see *U. minor* 'Cornubiensis'.

***U.* 'Camperdownii'.** See *U. glabra* 'Camperdownii'.

U. carpinifolia. See *U. minor.*

***U.* 'Dicksonii'.** See *U. minor* 'Dicksonii'.

U. glabra (Wych elm). Deciduous, spreading tree. H 30m (100ft), S 25m (80ft). Has broadly oval, toothed, very rough, dark green leaves, often slightly lobed at tips. From mid- to late spring bears clusters of winged, green fruits on bare branches. **'Camperdownii'** (syn. *U.* 'Camperdownii') illus. p.92. **'Exoniensis'** (Exeter elm), H 15m (50ft), S 5m (15ft), is narrow with upright branches when young, later becoming more spreading.

U. × hollandica (Dutch elm). Vigorous, deciduous tree with a short trunk and spreading to arching branches. H 30m (100ft), S 25m (80ft). Has oval, toothed, glossy, dark green leaves. Is very susceptible to Dutch elm disease. **'Jacqueline Hillier'**, H and S 2m (6ft), is slow-growing and suitable for hedging. Small leaves, rough-textured and sharply toothed, form 2 rows on each shoot; they persist into early winter. **'Vegeta'** (Huntingdon elm), H 35m (120ft), has upright, central branches and pendent, outer shoots. Broadly oval leaves turn yellow in autumn.

U. minor, syn. *U. carpinifolia* (Smooth-leaved elm). Deciduous, spreading tree with arching branches and pendent shoots. H 30m (100ft), S 20m (70ft). Small, oval, toothed, glossy, bright green leaves turn yellow in autumn. subsp. ***angustifolia*** (syn. *U. angustifolia;* Goodyer's elm) has a rounded canopy and elliptic to oval, double-toothed, mid- to dark green leaves, paler beneath. **'Cornubiensis'** (syn. *U. angustifolia* var. *cornubiensis;* Cornish elm), S 15m (50ft), is conical when young and with a vase-shaped head when mature. **'Dicksonii'** (syn. *U.m.* 'Sarniensis Aurea', *U.*'Dicksonii', *U.* 'Wheatleyi Aurea') illus. p.81. **'Sarniensis'** (Jersey elm, Wheatley elm), S 10m (30ft), is a conical, dense tree with upright branches. Small, broadly oval leaves are mid-green. **'Sarniensis Aurea'** see *U.m.* 'Dicksonii'.

U. parvifolia (Chinese elm). Deciduous or semi-evergreen, rounded tree. H and S 15m (50ft). Small, oval, glossy, dark green leaves last well into winter or, in mild areas, may persist until fresh growth appears.

U. procera (English elm). Vigorous, deciduous, spreading tree with a bushy, dense, dome-shaped head. H 35m (120ft), S 15m (50ft). Broadly oval, toothed, rough, dark green leaves turn yellow in autumn.

U. pumila (Siberian elm). Deciduous, spreading, sometimes shrubby tree. H 15m (50ft), S 12m (40ft). Has oval, toothed, dark green leaves. Has some resistance to Dutch elm disease, but seedlings may be susceptible in hot summers.

***U.* 'Wheatleyi Aurea'.** See *U. minor* 'Dicksonii'.

UMBELLULARIA

Headache tree

LAURACEAE

Genus of evergreen, spring-flowering trees, grown for their aromatic foliage, although the scent of the crushed leaves may induce headaches and nausea in some people. Frost hardy, but requires shelter from strong, cold winds when young. Needs sun and fertile, moist but well-drained soil. Propagate by seed in autumn.

U. californica illus. p.74.

Umbrella leaf. See *Diphylleia cymosa.*

Umbrella pine. See *Pinus pinea*, illus. p.109.

Japanese. See *Sciadopitys verticillata*, illus. p.106

Umbrella plant. See *Darmera.*

Umbrella tree, Queensland. See *Schefflera actinophylla*, illus. p.84.

Unicorn plant. See *Martynia annua*, illus. p.320.

Urceolina peruviana. See *Stenomesson miniatum.*

URGINEA

LILIACEAE/HYACINTHACEAE

Genus of late summer- or early autumn-flowering bulbs, growing on or near soil surface, with spear-shaped flower spikes up to 1.5m (5ft) high. Frost to half hardy. Needs sun and well-drained soil that dries out while bulbs are dormant in summer. Plant in mid- to late summer. Water until leaves die down. Propagate by seed in autumn or by offsets in late summer.

U. maritima (Crusaders' spears, Sea onion, Sea squill). Late summer- or early autumn-flowering bulb. H 1.5m (5ft), S 30–45cm (1–1½ft). Half hardy. Broadly sword-shaped, erect, basal leaves appear in autumn after a long spike of star-shaped, white flowers, each 1–1.5cm (½–⅝in) across, has developed.

Urn plant. See *Aechmea fasciata*, illus. p.265.

URSINIA

COMPOSITAE/ASTERACEAE

Genus of annuals, evergreen perennials and sub-shrubs, grown mainly for their flower heads usually in summer, a few species for their foliage. Half hardy to frost tender, min. 5–7°C (41–5°F). Needs full light and well-drained soil. Water potted plants moderately, less when not in full growth. Requires good ventilation if grown under glass. Propagate by seed or greenwood cuttings in spring. Aphids are sometimes troublesome.

U. anthemoides illus. p.338.

U. chrysanthemoides. Evergreen, bushy perennial. H and S 60cm (2ft) or more. Frost tender. Narrowly oval, feathery, strongly scented, green leaves are 5cm (2in) long. Has small, long-stalked, daisy-like, yellow flower heads, sometimes coppery below, in summer.

U. sericea. Evergreen, bushy sub-shrub. H and S 25–45cm (10–18in). Frost tender. Leaves are cut into an elegant filigree of very slender, silver-haired segments. Daisy-like, yellow flower heads, 4cm (1½in) across, in summer. Mainly grown for its foliage.

UTRICULARIA

LENTIBULARIACEAE

Genus of deciduous or evergreen, perennial, carnivorous water plants with bladder-like, modified leaves that trap and digest insects. Most species in cultivation are free-floating. Frost hardy to frost tender, min. 7°C (45°F). Some species are suitable only for tropical aquariums; those grown in outdoor pools require full sun. Thin out plants that are overcrowded or become laden with algae. Propagate by division of floating foliage in spring or summer.

U. exoleta. See *U. gibba.*

U. gibba, syn. *U. exoleta.* Deciduous, perennial, free-floating water plant. S 15cm (6in). Frost tender. Slender stems carry finely divided, mid-green leaves on which small bladders develop. Pouched, bright yellow flowers are borne in summer. Is evergreen in very warm water; suitable only for a tropical aquarium.

U. vulgaris. Deciduous, perennial, free-floating water plant. S 30cm (12in). Frost hardy. Much-divided, bronze-green leaves, studded with small bladders, are produced on slender stems. Bears pouched, bright yellow flowers in summer. May be grown in a pool or cold-water aquarium.

UVULARIA

LILIACEAE/CONVALLARIACEAE

Genus of spring-flowering perennials that thrive in moist woodlands. Fully hardy. Requires semi-shade and prefers moist but well-drained, peaty soil. Propagate in early spring, before flowering, by division.

♀ ***U. grandiflora*** illus. p.274.

U. perfoliata. Clump-forming perennial. H 45cm (18in), S 30cm (12in). In spring, clusters of pendent, bell-shaped, pale yellow flowers with twisted petals appear on numerous slender stems above stem-clasping, narrowly oval, mid-green leaves.

VACCINIUM

ERICACEAE

Genus of deciduous or evergreen sub-shrubs, shrubs and trees, grown for their foliage, their autumn colour (on deciduous species), their flowers and their fruits, which are often edible. Fully to frost hardy. Requires a position in sun or semi-shade and moist but well-drained, peaty or sandy, acid soil. Propagate by semi-ripe cuttings in summer or by seed in autumn.

V. angustifolium. var. ***laevifolium*** illus. p.168.

V. arctostaphylos (Caucasian whortleberry). Deciduous, upright shrub. H 3m (10ft), S 2m (6ft). Fully hardy. Has red-brown young shoots and oval, dark green leaves that mature to red and purple in autumn. Bell-shaped, white flowers, tinged with red, are produced in spreading racemes in early summer, followed by spherical, purplish-black fruits.

♀ ***V. corymbosum*** (Highbush blueberry) illus. p.156. **'Pioneer'** illus. p.169.

♀ ***V. glaucoalbum*** illus. p.172.

V. myrtillus (Bilberry, Whortleberry). Deciduous, usually prostrate shrub. H 15cm (6in) or more, S 30cm (12in) or more. Fully hardy. Bears small, heart-shaped, leathery, bright green leaves. Produces pendent, bell-shaped, pale pink flowers in early summer; these are followed by edible, round, blue-black fruits.

V. nummularia. Evergreen, prostrate shrub. H 10cm (4in), S 20cm (8in). Frost hardy. Slender stems, covered in red-brown bristles, bear oval, wrinkled, bright green leaves with red-brown bristles at their margins. Produces small racemes of bell-shaped, white to deep pink flowers at stem tips in early summer, followed by small, round, black fruits. Is suitable for growing in a rock garden or peat bed. Needs semi-shade. May also be propagated by division in spring.

V. parvifolium illus. p.169.

V. vitis-idaea. Vigorous, evergreen, prostrate shrub, spreading by underground runners. H 2–25cm (¾–10in), S indefinite. Fully hardy. Forms hummocks of oval, hard, leathery leaves. Bell-shaped, white to pink flowers are borne in nodding racemes from early summer to autumn, followed by bright red fruits in autumn-winter. May also be propagated by division in spring. subsp. ***minus*** (syn. *V.v.-i.* 'Minus') illus. p.378.

Valerian. See *Valeriana.*
Cat's. See *Valeriana officinalis*, illus. p.243.
Common. See *Valeriana officinalis*, illus. p.243.
Red. See *Centranthus ruber*, illus. p.247.

VALERIANA
Valerian

VALERIANACEAE

Genus of summer-flowering perennials that are suitable for growing in borders and rock gardens. Fully hardy. Requires a position in sun and well-drained soil. Propagate by division in autumn, but V. officinalis is best propagated by seed in spring.

V. officinalis illus. p.243.

V. phu **'Aurea'** illus. p.284.

VALLEA

ELAEOCARPACEAE

Genus of one species of evergreen shrub, grown for its overall appearance. Half hardy, but best at 3–5°C (37–41°F) to prevent foliage being damaged by cold. Prefers a position in full sun and humus-rich, well-drained soil. Containerized plants should be watered freely during the growing season, moderately at other times. Untidy growth may be cut out in early spring. Propagate by seed in spring or by semi-ripe cuttings in summer. Red spider mite may be a nuisance.

V. stipularis. Evergreen, erect, then loose and spreading shrub. H and S 2–5m (6–15ft). Leaves are lance-shaped to rounded and lobed, deep green above, grey beneath. Small, cup-shaped flowers, each with 5 deep pink petals that have 3 lobes, are borne in small, terminal and lateral clusters in spring-summer.

VALLISNERIA

HYDROCHARITACEAE

Genus of evergreen, perennial, submerged water plants, grown for their foliage. Is suitable for pools and aquariums. Frost tender, min. 5°C (41°F). Requires sun or semi-shade and deep, clear water. Remove fading foliage, and thin overcrowded plants as required. Propagate by division in spring or summer.

V. americana, syn. *V. gigantea.* Vigorous, evergreen, perennial, submerged water plant. Sindefinite. Quickly grows to form colonies of long, strap-shaped, mid-green leaves. Produces insignificant, greenish flowers all year-round.

V. gigantea. See *V. americana.*

V. spiralis (Eel grass, Tape grass). Vigorous, evergreen, perennial, submerged water plant. S indefinite. Forms a mass of long, strap-shaped, mid-green leaves, but on a smaller scale than V. americana. Insignificant, greenish flowers are borne year-round.

Vallota speciosa. See *Cyrtanthus elatus.*
Van Volxem's maple. See *Acer velutinum* var. *vanvolxemii.*

VANCOUVERIA

BERBERIDACEAE

Genus of perennials, some of which are evergreen, suitable for ground cover. Fully hardy. Prefers cool, partially shaded positions and moist, peaty soil. Propagate by division in spring.

V. chrysantha. Evergreen, sprawling perennial. H 30cm (12in), S indefinite. Oval, dark green leaves borne on flower stems are divided into rounded diamond-shaped leaflets with thickened, undulating margins. Loose sprays of small, bell-shaped, yellow flowers are borne in spring.

V. hexandra. Vigorous, spreading perennial. H 20cm (8in), S indefinite. Leathery leaves are divided into almost hexagonal leaflets. Bears open sprays of many tiny, white flowers in late spring and early summer. Makes good woodland ground cover.

VANDA

ORCHIDACEAE

See also ORCHIDS

♀ *V.* **Rothschildiana** illus. p.310. Evergreen, epiphytic orchid for a cool or intermediate greenhouse. H 60cm (24in). Sprays of dark-veined, violet-blue flowers, 10cm (4in) across, are borne twice a year in varying seasons. Has narrowly oval, rigid leaves, 10–12cm (4–5in) long. Grow in a hanging basket and provide good light in summer.

Variegated apple mint. See *Mentha suaveolens* 'Variegata', illus. p.286.
Variegated Bishop's weed. See *Aegopodium podagraria* 'Variegatum', illus. p.286.
Variegated creeping soft grass. See *Holcus mollis* 'Albovariegatus', illus. p.318.
Variegated gout weed. See *Aegopodium podagraria* 'Variegatum', illus. p.286.
Variegated ground ivy. See *Glechoma hederacea* 'Variegata', illus. p.312.
Variegated iris. See *Iris variegata*, illus. p.235.
Variegated Leyland cypress. See × *Cupressocyparis leylandii* 'Harlequin', illus. p.100.
Variegated purple moorgrass. See *Molinia caerulea* 'Variegata'.
Varnish tree. See *Rhus verniciflua.*
Veitch fir. See *Abies veitchii*, illus. p.98.
Veitch's screw pine. See *Pandanus tectorius* 'Veitchii', illus. p.171.

VELLOZIA

VELLOZIACEAE

Genus of evergreen perennials and shrubs, grown for their showy flowers. Frost tender, min. 10°C (50°F). Grow in full sun and moderately fertile, sharply drained soil. Propagate by seed or division in spring.

V. elegans, syn. *Barbacenia elegans, Talbotia elegans.* Evergreen, mat-forming perennial with slightly woody stems. H to 15cm (6in), S 15–30cm (6–12in). Lance-shaped, leathery, dark green leaves, to 20cm (8in) long, each has a V-shaped keel. In late spring bears solitary small, star-shaped, white flowers on slender stems above leaves.

VELTHEIMIA

LILIACEAE/HYACINTHACEAE

Genus of winter-flowering bulbs with dense spikes of pendent, tubular flowers and rosettes of basal leaves. Frost tender, min. 10°C (50°F). Requires good light, to keep foliage compact and to develop flower colours fully, and well-drained soil. Plant in autumn with tips above soil surface. Reduce watering in summer. Propagate by seed or offsets in autumn.

♀ ***V. bracteata***, syn. *V. capensis* of gardens, *V. undulata, V. viridifolia*, illus. p.441.

♀ ***V. capensis***, syn. *V. glauca, V. viridifolia* of gardens. Winter-flowering bulb. H 30–45cm (12–18in), S 20–30cm (8–12in). Has a basal rosette of lance-shaped leaves, usually with very wavy edges. Stem produces a dense spike of pink or red flowers, each 2–3cm (¾–1¼in) long.

V. capensis of gardens. See *V. bracteata.*

V. glauca. See *V. capensis.*

V. undulata. See *V. bracteata.*

V. viridifolia. See *V. bracteata.*

V. viridifolia of gardens. See *V. capensis.*

Velvet plant. See *Gynura aurantiaca*, illus. p.218.
Venetian sumach. See *Cotinus coggygria.*
× ***Venidioarctotis.*** Reclassified as *Arctotis*, also as *Arctotis* Harlequin Hybrids.
Venus flytrap. See *Dionaea muscipula*, illus. p.317.
Venus's navelwort. See *Omphalodes linifolia*, illus. p.330.

VERATRUM

LILIACEAE/MELANTHIACEAE

Genus of perennials, with poisonous black rhizomes, ideal for woodland gardens. Fully hardy. Requires semi-shade and fertile, moist soil. Propagate by division or seed in autumn. All parts are highly toxic if ingested. Contact with the foliage may irritate the skin.

V. album (White false hellebore). Clump-forming perennial. H 2m (6ft), S 60cm (2ft). Basal leaves are pleated, oval and dark green. Stems bear dense, terminal panicles of saucer-shaped, yellowish-white flowers in summer.

♀ ***V. nigrum*** illus. p.226.

VERBASCUM
Mullein

SCROPHULARIACEAE

Genus of mainly summer-flowering perennials, some of which are semi-evergreen or evergreen, and evergreen biennials and shrubs. Fully to frost hardy. Tolerates shade, but prefers an open, sunny site and well-drained soil. Propagate species by seed in spring or late summer or by root cuttings in winter, selected forms by root cuttings only. Some species self seed freely.

♀ ***V. bombyciferum.*** Evergreen, erect biennial. H 1.2–2m (4–6ft), S 60cm (2ft). Fully hardy. Oval leaves and stems are covered with silver hairs. Produces upright racemes densely set with 5-lobed, yellow flowers in summer.

V. chaixii. Erect perennial, covered with silvery hairs. H 1m (3ft), S 60cm (2ft). Fully hardy. Has oval, toothed, rough, nettle-like leaves. Produces slender spires of 5-lobed, yellow, sometimes white flowers, with purple stamens, in summer.

***V.* 'Cotswold Queen'.** Short-lived,

rosette-forming perennial. H 1–1.2m (3–4ft), S 30–60cm (1–2ft). Fully hardy. Throughout summer, branched racemes of 5-lobed, apricot-buff flowers are borne on stems that arise from oval, mid-green leaves.
V. densiflorum, syn. *V. thapsiforme.* Fairly slow-growing, semi-evergreen, upright perennial. H 1.2–1.5m (4–5ft), S 60cm (2ft). Fully hardy. Has a rosette of large, oval, crinkled, hairy, mid-green leaves. Hairy stems each produce a bold spike of flattish, 5-lobed, yellow flowers in summer.
🏆 ***V. dumulosum*** illus. p.371.
🏆 ***V.* 'Gainsborough'** illus. p.260.
🏆 ***V.* 'Letitia'** illus. p.370.
V. lychnitis (White mullein). Slow-growing, evergreen, upright, branching biennial. H 60cm–1m (2–3ft), S 60cm (2ft). Fully hardy. Has lance-shaped, dark grey-green leaves. Flattish, 5-lobed, white flowers are borne on branching stems in summer.
V. nigrum illus. p.262.
V. olympicum illus. p.227.
🏆 ***V.* 'Pink Domino'.** Short-lived, rosette-forming perennial. H 1.2m (4ft), S 30–60cm (1–2ft). Fully hardy. Produces branched racemes of 5-lobed, rose-pink flowers throughout summer above oval, mid-green leaves.
V. thapsiforme. See *V. densiflorum.*

VERBENA

VERBENACEAE

Genus of summer- and autumn-flowering biennials and perennials, some of which are semi-evergreen. Frost hardy to frost tender, min. 1°C (34°F). Prefers sun and well-drained soil. Propagate by stem cuttings in late summer or autumn or by seed in autumn or spring.
V. alpina of gardens. See *V.* × *maonettii.*
V. bonariensis, syn. *V. patagonica*, illus. p.226.
V. chamaedrifolia. See *V. peruviana.*
V. chamaedrioides. See *V. peruviana.*
***V.* × *hybrida* Derby Series.** Erect, bushy perennial, grown as an annual. H 25cm (10in), S 30cm (12in). Half hardy. Has oval, serrated, mid- to deep green leaves. Clusters of small, tubular, lobed flowers, in a wide colour range including red, pink, blue, mauve and white, appear in summer and early autumn. Cultivars of **Novalis Series** are erect and bushy, with flowers in rose-pink, deep blue, pinkish-red and scarlet, as well as single colours of bright scarlet, white or rose-pink. **'Peaches and Cream'** is spreading and branching, and produces pastel orange-pink flowers, maturing to apricot-yellow, and eventually creamy-yellow. **'Quartz Mix'** illus. p.340. **Romance Series** cultivars are erect and bushy, and has flowers in deep wine-red, intense scarlet, carmine-rose-red and blue-purple, as well as single colours of white, bright scarlet, dark rose or lavender-pink. **'Showtime'** illus. p.338.
V.* × *maonettii, syn. *V. alpina* of gardens, *V. tenera* var. *maonetti.* Spreading perennial with a slightly woody base. H 8cm (3in), S 15cm (6in). Half hardy. Has oblong to oval leaves, deeply cut into linear, toothed, mid-green segments, and, in summer, terminal clusters of small, tubular, reddish-violet flowers, with white-edged lobes.
V. patagonica. See *V. bonariensis.*
V. peruviana, syn. *V. chamaedrifolia, V. chamaedrioides.* Semi-evergreen, prostrate perennial. H to 8cm (3in), S 1m (3ft). Frost tender. Heads of small, tubular, brilliant scarlet flowers, with spreading petal lobes, are produced from early summer to early autumn. Oval, toothed leaves are mid-green. Prefers to grow in dry soil that is not too rich.
🏆 ***V. rigida***, syn. *V. venosa*, illus. p.294.
🏆 ***V.* 'Sissinghurst'** illus. p.292.
V. tenera var. ***maonettii.*** See *V.* × *maonettii.*
V. venosa. See *V. rigida.*

Verbena, Lemon. See *Aloysia triphylla*, illus. p.139.

VERONICA

SCROPHULARIACEAE

Genus of perennials and sub-shrubs, some of which are semi-evergreen or evergreen, grown for their usually blue flowers. Fully to frost hardy. Some need sun and well-drained soil, others prefer a moist site in sun or partial shade. Propagate by division in spring or autumn, by softwood or semi-ripe cuttings in summer or by seed in autumn.
V. austriaca. Mat-forming or upright perennial. H and S 25–50cm (10–20in). Fully hardy. Leayes are very variable: from broadly oval to narrowly oblong, and from entire to deeply cut and fern-like. Short, dense or lax racemes of small, saucer-shaped, bright blue flowers appear in early summer. Suits a rock garden or bank. subsp. ***teucrium*** (syn. *V. teucrium*) illus. p.370. 🏆 subsp. ***teucrium* 'Royal Blue'** hasdeep royal-blue flowers. Propagate bydivision in spring or by softwoodcuttings in summer.
🏆 ***V. cinerea.*** Spreading, much-branched, woody-based perennial. H 15cm (6in), S 30cm (12in). Fully hardy. Has small, linear, occasionally oval, hairy, silvery-white leaves. Trailing flower stems bear saucer-shaped, deep blue to purplish-blue flowers, with white eyes, in early summer. Is suitable for a sunny rock garden.
V. exaltata. See *V. longifolia.*
V. fruticans (Rock speedwell). Deciduous, upright to procumbent sub-shrub. H 15cm (6in), S 30cm (12in). Fully hardy. Leaves are oval and green. Spikes of saucer-shaped, bright blue flowers, each with a red eye, are borne in summer. Is suitable for a rock garden.
🏆 ***V. gentianoides*** illus. p.297.
V. incana. See *V. spicata* subsp. *incana.*
V. longifolia, syn. *V. exaltata.* Variable, upright perennial. H 1–1.2m (3–4ft), S 30cm (1ft) or more. Fully hardy. In late summer and early autumn, long, terminal racemes of star-shaped, lilac-blue flowers are borne on stems clothed with whorls of narrowly oval to lance-shaped, toothed, mid-green leaves.
V. pectinata. Dense, mat-forming perennial that is sometimes semi-erect. H and S 20cm (8in). Fully hardy. Has small, narrowly oval, hairy leaves and bears loose sprays of saucer-shaped, soft blue to blue-violet flowers in summer. Is good for a rock garden or bank. **'Rosea'**, H 8cm (3in), has rose-lilac flowers.
V. peduncularis illus. p.297.
V. perfoliata. See *Parahebe perfoliata.*
🏆 ***V. prostrata***, syn. *V. rupestris*, illus. p.369. **'Kapitan'** and **'Trehane'** illus. p.369. 🏆 **'Spode Blue'** is a dense, mat-forming perennial. H to 30cm (12in), S indefinite. Fully hardy. Up-right spikes of small, saucer-shaped, china-blue flowers appear in early sum-mer. Leaves are narrowly oval and toothed.
V. rupestris. See *V. prostrata.*
V. spicata (Spiked speedwell). Clump-forming perennial. H 30–60cm (12–24in), S 45cm (18in). Fully hardy. Spikes of small, star-shaped, bright blue flowers are borne in summer above narrowly oval, toothed, mid-green leaves. 🏆 subsp. ***incana*** (syn. *V. incana*) illus. p.297. **'Romiley Purple'** illus. p.255.
V. teucrium. See *V. austriaca* subsp. *teucrium.*
V. virginica. See *Veronicastrum virginicum*.f. ***alba*** see *Veronicastrum virginicum* f. *album.*

VERONICASTRUM

SCROPHULARIACEAE

Genus of evergreen perennials grown for their elegant, pale blue flowers. Fully hardy. Requires a position in sun and moist soil. Propagate by division in spring or autumn, by softwood or semi-ripe cuttings in summer or by seed in autumn.
V. virginicum, syn. *Veronica virginica.* Upright perennial. H 1.2m (4ft), S 45cm (1½ft). Fully hardy. In late summer, racemes of small, star-shaped, purple-blue or pink flowers crown stems clothed with whorls of narrowly lance-shaped, dark green leaves. f. ***album*** (syn. *Veronica virginica* f. *alba*) illus. p.243.

VESTIA

SOLANACEAE

Genus of one species of evergreen shrub, grown for its flowers and foliage. Frost hardy, but in cold areas is often cut to ground level and is best grown against a south-facing wall. Requires sun and fertile, well-drained soil. Propagate by semi-ripe cuttings in summer or by seed in autumn or spring.

🏆 ***V. foetida***, syn. *V. lycioides.* Evergreen, upright shrub. H 2m (6ft), S 1.5m (5ft). Oblong, glossy, dark green leaves have an unpleasant scent. Has pendent, tubular, pale yellow flowers from mid-spring to mid-summer.
V. lycioides. See *V. foetida.*

Vetch. See *Hippocrepis.*
Horseshoe. See *Hippocrepis comosa*, illus. p.398.

VIBURNUM

CAPRIFOLIACEAE

Genus of deciduous, semi-evergreen or evergreen shrubs and trees, grown for their foliage, autumn colour (in many deciduous species), flowers and, often, fruits. Fruiting is generally most prolific when several plants of different clones are planted together. Fully to frost hardy. Grow in sun or semi-shade and in deep, fertile, not too dry soil. To thin out overgrown plants cut out some older shoots after flowering. Propagate by cuttings (softwood for deciduous species, semi-ripe for evergreens) in summer or by seed in autumn. The fruits of viburnums may cause mild stomach upset if ingested.
V. acerifolium illus. p.157.
V. betulifolium illus. p.144.
V. bitchiuense. Deciduous, bushy shrub. H and S 2.5m (8ft). Fully hardy. Has oval, dark green leaves, rounded heads of fragrant, tubular, pale pink flowers, from mid- to late spring, and egg-shaped, flattened, black fruits.
🏆 ***V.* × *bodnantense* 'Dawn'** illus. p.146. 🏆 **'Deben'** is a deciduous, upright shrub. H 3m (10ft), S 2m (6ft). Fully hardy. Oval, toothed, dark green leaves are bronze when young. Clusters of fragrant, tubular, white flowers, tinted with pale pink, open during mild periods from late autumn through to early spring.
V.* × *burkwoodii. Semi-evergreen, bushy, open shrub. H and S 2.5m (8ft). Fully hardy. Rounded heads of fragrant, tubular, pink, then white flowers are borne amid oval, glossy, dark green leaves from mid- to late spring. 🏆 **'Anne Russell'**, H and S 1.5m (5ft), is deciduous and has very fragrant, white flowers. 🏆 **'Park Farm Hybrid'** bears very fragrant, white flowers that are slightly pink in bud, and older leaves turn bright red in autumn.
🏆 ***V.* × *carlcephalum*** illus. p.113.
V. carlesii illus. p.150. **'Diana'** is a deciduous, bushy, dense shrub. H and S 2m (6ft). Fully hardy. Broadly oval leaves are bronze when young and turn purple-red in autumn. From mid- to late spring bears rounded heads of red buds that open to very fragrant, tubular, pink flowers fading to white.
🏆 ***V. cinnamomifolium.*** Evergreen, bushy or tree-like shrub. H and S 5m (15ft). Frost hardy. Large, oval, mid-green leaves, each has 3 prominent veins. Bears broad clusters of small, star-shaped, white flowers in early summer, then egg-shaped, blue fruits.
🏆 ***V. davidii*** illus. p.171.
V. dilatatum. Deciduous, upright shrub. H 3m (10ft), S 2m (6ft). Fully hardy. Oval, sharply toothed, dark green leaves sometimes redden in autumn. Flat heads of small, star-shaped, white flowers in late spring and early summer are succeeded by showy, egg-shaped, bright red fruits. **'Catskill'** illus. p.135.
🏆 ***V. farreri***, syn. *V. fragrans*, illus. p.143. **'Candidissimum'** is a deciduous, upright shrub. H 3m (10ft), S 2m (6ft). Fully hardy. Oval, toothed, dark green leaves are pale green when young. Produces clusters of fragrant, tubular, pure white flowers in late autumn and during mild periods in winter and early spring.
V. foetens, syn. *V. grandiflorum* f. *foetens*, illus. p.145.
V. fragrans. See *V. farreri.*
V. grandiflorum. Deciduous, upright, open shrub. H and S 2m (6ft). Fully hardy. Stiff branches bear oblong, dark green leaves that become deep purple in autumn. Dense clusters of fragrant, tubular, white-and-pink flowers open

from deep pink buds from mid-winter to early spring. f. ***foetens*** see *V. foetens*.
♀ ***V. × juddii*** illus. p.150.
V. lantana (Wayfaring tree). Vigorous, deciduous, upright shrub. H 5m (15ft), S 4m (12ft). Fully hardy. Has broadly oval, grey-green leaves that redden in autumn, flattened heads of small, 5-lobed, white flowers in late spring and early summer, then egg-shaped, red fruits that ripen to black.
V. lentago (Sheepberry). Vigorous, deciduous, upright shrub. H 4m (12ft), S 3m (10ft). Fully hardy. Oval, glossy, dark green leaves turn red and purple in autumn. Bears flattened heads of small, fragrant, star-shaped, white flowers in late spring and early summer, then egg-shaped, blue-black fruits.
V. odoratissimum (Sweet viburnum). Evergreen, bushy shrub. H and S 5m (15ft). Frost hardy. Clusters of small, fragrant, star-shaped, white flowers, borne amid oval, leathery, glossy, dark green leaves in late spring, are followed by egg-shaped, red fruits that ripen to black.
V. opulus (Guelder rose). Vigorous, deciduous, bushy shrub. H and S 4m (12ft). Fully hardy. Bears broadly oval, lobed, deep green leaves that redden in autumn and, in late spring and early summer, flattened, lace-cap-like heads of white flowers. Produces large bunches of spherical, bright red fruits.
♀ **'Compactum'** illus. p.168.
♀ **'Xanthocarpum'** has yellow fruits and mid-green leaves that become yellow in autumn.
V. plicatum (Japanese snowball tree). Deciduous, bushy, spreading shrub. H 3m (10ft), S 4m (12ft). Fully hardy. Leaves are oval, toothed, deeply veined and dark green, turning reddish-purple in autumn. Dense, rounded heads of large, sterile, flattish, white flowers are borne along branches in late spring and early summer. ♀ **'Mariesii'** illus. p.112. **'Nanum Semperflorens'** (syn. *V.p.* 'Watanabe', *V.p.* 'Watanabei', *V. watanabei*), H 2m (6ft), S 1.5m (5ft), is slow-growing, conical and dense, and produces small flower heads from late spring until early autumn.
♀ **'Pink Beauty'** illus. p.126. f. ***tomentosum*** has tiered branches, flattish, lace-cap-like flower heads and red fruits, ripening to black.
'Watanabe' see *V. p.* 'Nanum Semperfl orens'.**'Watanabei'** see *V. p.* 'Nanum Semperflorens'.
V. × pragense. See *V.* 'Pragense'.
♀ ***V.* 'Pragense'**, syn. *V. × pragense*, illus. p.135.
V. rhytidophyllum illus. p.114.
V. sargentii. Deciduous, bushy shrub. H and S 3m (10ft). Fully hardy. Maple-like, mid-green foliage often changes to yellow or red in autumn. Broad, flattish, lace-cap-like heads of white flowers in late spring are followed by spherical, bright red fruits.
♀ **'Onondaga'**, S 2m (6ft), has bronze-red, young leaves, becoming deep green, then bronze-red again in autumn. Flower buds are pink.
V. sieboldii. Deciduous, rounded, dense shrub. H 4m (12ft), S 6m (20ft). Fully hardy. Has large, oblong to oval, glossy, bright green leaves. Rounded heads of tubular, creamy-white flowers are borne in late spring, followed by egg-shaped, red-stalked, red fruits that ripen to black.
V. tinus (Laurustinus) illus. p.145.
♀ **'Eve Price'** is an evergreen, bushy, very compact shrub. H and S 3m (10ft). Frost hardy. Flattened heads of small, star-shaped, white flowers are freely borne from deep pink buds amid oval, dark green leaves in winter-spring and are followed by ovoid, blue fruits.
♀ **'Gwenllian'** has pale pink flowers and fruits very freely.
V. watanabei. See *V. plicatum* 'Nanum Semperflorens'.

Viburnum, Sweet. See *Viburnum odoratissimum.*
Victorian box. See *Pittosporum undulatum.*

VIGNA

LEGUMINOSAE/PAPILIONACEAE

Genus of evergreen, annual and perennial, erect or scrambling and twining climbers, grown mainly as crop plants for their leaves, pods and seeds. Frost tender, min. 13–15°C (55–9°F). Provide full light and humus-rich, well-drained soil. Water freely when in full growth, sparingly at other times. Stems require support. Thin crowded stems or cut back hard in spring. Propagate by seed in autumn or spring.
V. caracalla, syn. *Phaseolus caracalla* (Snail flower). Evergreen, perennial, fast-growing, twining climber. H 3–5m (10–15ft). Leaves comprise 3oval leaflets. From summer to early autumn carries pea-like, purple-marked, cream flowers that turn orange-yellow.

Villarsia nymphoides. See *Nymphoides peltata.*

VINCA
Periwinkle

APOCYNACEAE

Genus of evergreen, trailing sub-shrubs and perennials, grown for their foliage and flowers. Flowers are tubular with 5 spreading lobes. Fully to frost hardy. Is useful for ground cover in shade, but flowers more freely given some sun. Grows in any soil that is not too dry. Propagate by semi-ripe cuttings in summer or by division from autumn to spring. All parts may cause mild stomach upset if ingested.
V. difformis. Evergreen, prostrate sub-shrub. H 30cm (12in), S indefinite. Frost hardy. Slender, trailing stems bear oval, glossy, dark green leaves. Erect flower stems produce pale blue flowers in late autumn and early winter.
V. major (Greater periwinkle, Quater). Evergreen, prostrate, arching sub-shrub. H 45cm (18in), S indefinite. Fully hardy. Leaves are broadly oval, glossy and dark green. Large, bright blue flowers are produced from late spring to early autumn. subsp. ***hirsuta*** see *V.m.* var. *oxyloba*.var. ***oxyloba*** (syn. *V.m.* subsp. *hirsuta*) has leaves, leaf stalks and calyces edged with long hairs. ♀ **'Variegata'** illus. p.171.
V. minor (Lesser periwinkle) illus. p.172. **'Alba Variegata'** is an evergreen, prostrate sub-shrub. H 15cm (6in), S indefinite. Fully hardy. Forms extensive mats of small, oval, glossy, dark green leaves, edged with pale yellow, above which white flowers are carried from mid-spring to early summer, then intermittently into autumn. **'Bowles' Blue'** see *V.m.* ' La Grave'.**'Bowles' White'** bears large, white flowers that are pinkish-white in bud. ♀ **'Gertrude Jekyll'** is of dense growth and produces a profusion of small, white flowers. Flowers of ♀ **'La Grave'** (syn. *V.m.* 'Bowles' Blue') are large and lavender-blue.
V. rosea. See *Catharanthus roseus.*

Vine. See *Vitis.*
Alleghany. See *Adlumia fungosa.*
Balloon. See *Cardiospermum halicacabum.*
Blue trumpet. See *Thunbergia grandiflora.*
Bower. See *Pandorea jasminoides*, illus. p.204.
Chestnut. See *Tetrastigma voinierianum*, illus. p.218.
Chinese trumpet. See *Campsis grandiflora.*
Chocolate. See *Akebia quinata*, illus. p.202.
Coral. See *Antigonon.*
Crimson glory. See *Vitis coignetiae*, illus. p.216.
Cross. See *Bignonia capreolata.*
Cup-and-saucer. See *Cobaea scandens*, illus. p.212.
Cypress. See *Ipomoea quamoclit*, illus. p.206.
Firecracker. See *Manettia cordifolia.*
Flame. See *Pyrostegia venusta*, illus. p.216.
Vine. (continued)
Glory. See *Eccremocarpus scaber*, illus. p.215.
Golden-chalice. See *Solandra maxima*, illus. p.202.
Grape. See *Vitis vinifera.*
Heart. See *Ceropegia linearis* **subsp.** *woodii*, illus. p.478.
Hearts-and-honey. See *Ipomoea × multifida.*
Jade. See *Strongylodon macrobotrys*, illus. p.202.
Japanese hydrangea. See *Schizophragma hydrangeoides.*
Kangaroo. See *Cissus antarctica*, illus. p.218.
Kudzu. See *Pueraria lobata.*
Lemon. See *Pereskia aculeata*, illus. p.473.
Madeira. See *Anredera.*
Mexican flame. See *Senecio confusus*, illus. p.215.
Mignonette. See *Anredera.*
Potato. See *Solanum jasminoides.*
Rex begonia. See *Cissus discolor.*
Rosary. See *Ceropegia linearis* subsp. *woodii*, illus. p.478.
Rubber. See *Cryptostegia grandiflora.*
Russian. See *Fallopia aubertii; Fallopia baldschuanica*, illus. p.215.
Silk. See *Periploca graeca.*
Silver. See *Actinidia polygama; Epipremnum pictum* 'Argyraeum', illus. p.217.
Staff. See *Celastrus orbiculatus.*
Teddy-bear. See *Cyanotis kewensis.*
Trumpet. See *Campsis radicans.*
Wax. See *Senecio macroglossus.*
Wonga-wonga. See *Pandorea pandorana.*
Vine lilac. See *Hardenbergia violacea.*
Vine maple. See *Acer circinatum.*

VIOLA
Violet

VIOLACEAE

Genus of annuals, perennials, some of which are semi-evergreen, and deciduous sub-shrubs, grown for their distinctive flowers. Annuals are suitable as summer bedding, perennials and sub-shrubs are good in rock gardens, screes and alpine houses. Fully to half hardy. Grow in sun or shade and well-drained but moisture-retentive soil unless otherwise stated; a few species prefer acid soil. Propagate annuals by seed sown according to flowering season, perennials and sub-shrubs by softwood cuttings in spring unless otherwise stated. Species may also be propagated by seed in spring or autumn.
V. aetolica illus. 371.
V. biflora (Twin-flowered violet). Creeping, rhizomatous perennial. H 5–15cm (2–6in), S 15cm (6in). Fully hardy. Flat-faced, deep lemon-yellow flowers, veined dark brown, are borne singly or in pairs on upright stems in summer. Leaves are kidney-shaped and mid-green. Needs shade. May also be propagated by division.
V. calcarata illus. p.380.
V. cazorlensis. Tufted, woody-based perennial. H to 5cm (2in), S to 8cm (3in). Frost hardy. Has small, linear to lance-shaped leaves and in late spring carries small, flat-faced, long-spurred, deep pink flowers, singly on short stems. Suits an alpine house. Is difficult to grow.
V. cenisia. Spreading perennial with runners. H 7cm (3in), S 10cm (4in). Fully hardy. Small, flat-faced, bright violet flowers, each with a deep purple line radiating from the centre, are produced on very short stems in summer. Has a deep tap root and tiny, heart-shaped or oblong, dark green leaves. Suits a scree. Propagate by division in spring.
♀ ***V. cornuta*** illus. p.361.
V. cucullata. See *V. obliqua.*
V. elatior. Upright, little-branched perennial. H 20–30cm (8–12in), S 15cm (6in). Fully hardy. Leaves are broadly lance-shaped and toothed. Produces flat-faced, pale blue flowers, with white centres, in early summer. Prefers semi-shade and moist soil. Propagate in spring by division.
V. glabella. Clump-forming perennial with a scaly, horizontal rootstock. H 10cm (4in), S 20cm (8in). Fully hardy. Produces flat-faced, bright yellow flowers, with purplish-veined lower petals, in late spring above toothed, heart-shaped, bright green leaves. Needs shade. Propagate by division in spring.
V. gracilis. Mat-forming perennial. H 12cm (5in), S 15cm (6in) or more. Fully hardy. Flat-faced, yellow-centred, violet-blue or sometimes yellow flowers are produced in summer. Has small, dissected leaves with linear or oblong segments. Needs sun.
***V.* 'Haslemere'.** See *V.* 'Nellie Britton'.
V. hederacea, syn. *Erpetion reniforme, V. reniforme* (Australian violet, Ivy-leaved violet). Evergreen, creeping, mat-forming perennial. H 2.5–5cm (1–2in), S indefinite. Half hardy. Has tiny, rounded leaves and bears purple or

white flowers, with a squashed appearance, on short stems in summer. Suits an alpine house. Prefers semi-shade. Propagate by division in spring.
♀ *V.* **'Huntercombe Purple'** illus. p.394.
V. **'Irish Molly'.** Evergreen, clump-forming, short-lived perennial. H 10cm (4in), S 15–20cm (6–8in). Fully hardy. Has broadly oval, dissected leaves and, in summer, a succession of flat-faced, old-gold flowers with brown centres. Flowers itself to death. Needs sun.
♀ *V.* **'Jackanapes'** illus. p.384.
V. labradorica **'Purpurea'.** See *V. riviniana* 'Purpurea'.
V. lutea (Mountain pansy). Mat-forming, rhizomatous perennial. H 10cm (4in), S 15cm (6in). Fully hardy. Has small, oval to lance-shaped leaves. Flat-faced, yellow, violet or bicoloured flowers are produced in spring and summer.
♀ *V.* **'Nellie Britton',** syn. *V.* 'Haslemere', illus. p.393.
♀ ***V. obliqua***, syn. *V. cucullata.* Variable, spreading perennial with fleshy rhizomes. H 5cm (2in), S 10–15cm (4–6in). Fully hardy. Has kidney-shaped, toothed, mid-green leaves. In late spring produces flat-faced, blue-violet, sometimes white or pale blue flowers. Propagate in spring
V. odorata (Sweet violet). Semi-evergreen, spreading, rhizomatous perennial. H 7cm (3in), S 15cm (6in) or more. Fully hardy. Leaves are heart-shaped and toothed. Long stems each carry a fragrant, flat-faced, violet or white flower from late winter to early spring. Is useful in a wild garden. Self seeds prolifically. May also be propagated by division.
V. palmata. Spreading perennial. H 10cm (4in), S 15cm (6in). Fully hardy. Has short-stemmed, flat-faced, pale violet flowers in late spring and deeply dissected leaves. Prefers dry, well-drained soil. Self seeds readily.
V. pedata illus. p.381. var. ***bicolor*** is a clump-forming perennial with a thick rootstock. H 5cm (2in), S 8cm (3in). Fully hardy. Flat-faced, velvety-purple or white flowers are borne singly on slender stems in late spring and early summer. Leaves are finely divided into 5–7 or more, narrow, toothed segments. Suits an alpine house. May be difficult to grow; needs peaty, sandy soil.
V. reniforme. See *V. hederacea.*
V. riviniana **'Purpurea',** syn. *V. labradorica* 'Purpurea', illus. p.381.
V. tricolor illus. p.381. **'Bowles' Black'** illus. p.382.
V. × wittrockiana (Pansy). Group of slow- to moderately fast-growing, mainly bushy perennials, usually grown as annuals or biennials. H 15–20cm (6–8in), S 20cm (8in). Fully hardy. Has oval, often serrated, mid-green leaves. Flattish, 5-petalled flowers, 2.5–10cm (1–4in) across, in a very wide colour range, appear throughout summer or in winter-spring. The following are among those available:
'Baby Lucia' (summer-flowering) has small, deep blue flowers.
Clear Crystals Series (summer-flowering) is in a wide range of clear colours.
'Clear Sky Primrose' (winter- to spring-flowering) illus p.348.
Crystal Bowl Series (summer-flowering) is in a range of colours (yellow, illus. p.349).
Floral Dance Series (winter-flowering) has a wide range of colours (mixed, illus. p.341; white, illus. p.331).
Forerunner Series (winter- to spring-flowering) illus. p.350.
Imperial Series 'Imperial Frosty Rose' (summer-flowering) illus. p.339.
Imperial Series 'Orange Prince' (summer-flowering) has orange flowerswith black blotches.
Imperial Series 'Sky Blue' (summer-flowering) has sky-blueflowers, each with a deeper-coloured blotch.
♀ **Joker Series** (summer-flowering) illus. p.344.
'Majestic Giants' (summer-flowering) has large flowers in a wide colour range.
Panola Series (yellow) illus. p.349.
♀ **Princess Series** (spring- to summer-flowering) are neat in habit,and produce small flowers in blue,cream, bicoloured purple and white,dark purple or yellow.
'Silver Princess' (summer-flowering) has white flowers, each with a deep pink blotch.
'Super Chalon Giants' (summer- to autumn-flowering) illus. p.348.
'True Blue' (winter- to summer-flowering) illus p.345.
♀ **Ultima Series** (winter- to spring-flowering) has medium-sized flowersin a very broad range of colours,including bicolours.
♀ **Universal Series** (winter- to spring-flowering) produces flowers inan extensive range of separate colours (apricot, illus. p.351) as well as in amixture of colours.

Violet. See *Viola.*
African. See *Saintpaulia.*
Australian. See *Viola hederacea.*
Bird's-foot. See *Viola pedata*, illus. p.381.
Bush. See *Browallia speciosa*, illus. p.274.
Dame's. See *Hesperis matronalis*, illus. p.241.
Dog's-tooth. See *Erythronium dens-canis*, illus. p.446.
Flame. See *Episcia cupreata*, illus. p.313.
Horned. See *Viola cornuta*, illus. p.361.
Ivy-leaved. See *Viola hederacea.*
Mexican. See *Tetranema roseum*, illus. p.315.
Persian. See *Exacum affine*, illus. p.343.
Philippine. See *Barleria cristata.*
Sweet. See *Viola odorata.*
Twin-flowered. See *Viola biflora.*
Water. See *Hottonia palustris*, illus. p.463.
Violet cress. See *Ionopsidium acaule.*
Violet willow. See *Salix daphnoides*, illus. p.70.

VIRGILIA

LEGUMINOSAE/PAPILIONACEAE

Genus of short-lived, evergreen shrubs and trees, grown for their flowers which are borne in spring and summer. Frost tender, min. 5°C (41°F). Prefers a position in full light and well-drained soil. Water pot-grown plants freely when in full growth, less at other times. Pruning is usually not required. Propagate in spring by seed, ideally soaked in warm water for 24 hours before sowing.
V. capensis. See *V. oroboides.*
V. oroboides, syn. *V. capensis.* Fast-growing, evergreen, rounded shrub or tree. H and S 6–10m (20–30ft). Has leaves of 11–21 oblong leaflets. Racemes of fragrant, pea-like, bright mauve-pink flowers, sometimes pink, crimson or white, are produced in late spring and summer, usually in great profusion.

Virgin's palm. See *Dioon edule.*
Virginia creeper. See *Parthenocissus quinquefolia.*
Virginia pine. See *Pinus virginiana*, illus. p.103.
Virginian bird cherry. See *Prunus virginiana.*
Virginian pokeweed. See *Phytolacca americana.*
Virginian stock. See *Malcolmia maritima*, illus. p.335.
Virginian witch hazel. See *Hamamelis virginiana*, illus. p.121.
Viscaria alpina. See *Lychnis alpina.*
Viscaria elegans. See *Silene coeli-rosa.*

VITALIANA

PRIMULACEAE

Genus of one species of evergreen, spring-flowering perennial, grown for its flowers. Is often included in *Douglasia* and is useful for rock gardens, screes and alpine houses. Fully hardy. Requires sun and moist but well-drained soil. Propagate by softwood cuttings in summer or by seed in autumn.
V. primuliflora, syn. *Douglasia vitaliana*, illus. p.384.

VITEX

VERBENACEAE

Genus of evergreen or deciduous trees and shrubs, grown for their flowers. Cultivated species are frost hardy, but in cold areas grow against a south- or west-facing wall. Needs full sun and well-drained soil. Propagate by semi-ripe cuttings in summer or by seed in autumn or spring.
V. agnus-castus (Chaste tree). Deciduous, spreading, open, aromatic shrub. H and S 2.5m (8ft). Upright panicles of fragrant, tubular, violet-blue flowers appear in early and mid-autumn. Dark green leaves are each divided into 5 or 7 long, narrowly lance-shaped leaflets.
V. negundo. Deciduous, bushy shrub. H and S 3m (10ft). Mid-green leaves are each composed of 3–7 narrowly oval, sharply toothed leaflets. Produces loose panicles of small, tubular, violet-blue flowers from late summer through to early autumn.

VITIS

Vine

VITACEAE

Genus of deciduous, woody-stemmed, tendril climbers, grown for their foliage and fruits (grapes), which are produced in bunches. Fully to half hardy. Prefers fertile, well-drained, chalky soil and sun or semi-shade. Produces the best fruits and autumn leaf-colour when planted in a warm situation. Propagate by hardwood cuttings in late autumn.
V. aconitifolia. See *Ampelopsis aconitifolia.*
V. amurensis (Amur grape). Vigorous, deciduous, woody-stemmed, tendril climber. H 6m (20ft). Fully hardy. Bears dark green, 3- or 5-lobed leaves, 12–30cm (5–12in) long, that mature to red and purple in autumn. Produces inconspicuous flowers throughout the summer, followed in late summer and autumn, by tiny, black fruits.
♀ *V.* **'Brant'.** Deciduous, woody-stemmed, tendril climber. H to 7m (22ft) or more. Fully hardy. Bears leaves that are lobed, toothed, 10–22cm (4–9in) long and bright green. In autumn they mature to brown-red, except for the veins. Produces inconspicuous flowers in summer, followed by green or purple fruits.
♀ ***V. coignetiae*** illus. p.216.
V. davidii. Deciduous, woody-stemmed, tendril climber; young stems are densely covered with short prickles. H to 8m (25ft) or more. Half hardy. Heart-shaped leaves, 10–25cm (4–10in) long, are blue- or grey-green beneath, turning scarlet in autumn. Insignificant, greenish flowers in summer are followed by small, black fruits.
V. henryana. See *Parthenocissus henryana.*
V. heterophylla. See *Ampelopsis brevipedunculata* var. *maximowiczii.*
V. quinquefolia. See *Parthenocissus quinquefolia.*
V. striata. See *Cissus striata.*
V thomsonii. See *Cayratia thomsonii.*
V. vinifera. (Grape vine)
♀ **'Purpurea'** illus. p.216.

Voodoo lily. See *Sauromatum venosum*, illus. p.429.
Voss's laburnum. See *Laburnum × watereri* 'Vossii'.

VRIESEA

BROMELIACEAE

Genus of evergreen, rosette-forming, epiphytic perennials, grown for their flowers and overall appearance. Frost tender, min. 15°C (59°F). Needs a position in semi-shade and a rooting medium of equal parts humus-rich soil and either sphagnum moss or bark or plastic chips used for orchid culture. Using soft water, water moderately when in growth, sparingly at other times, and from mid-spring to mid-autumn keep rosette centres filled with water. Propagate plants by offsets or seed in spring.
V. fenestralis. Evergreen, epiphytic perennial with dense, funnel-shaped rosettes. H and S 30–40cm (12–16in). Pale green leaves, with dark lines and cross-bands, are very broadly strap-shaped and arching or rolled under at tips. In summer, flat racemes of tubular, yellowish-green flowers, with green bracts, are carried above the foliage.
♀ ***V. fosteriana.*** Evergreen, epiphytic perennial with dense, funnel-shaped rosettes. H and S 60cm (24in) or more. Has broadly strap-shaped, arching, yellowish- to deep green leaves, cross-banded with reddish-brown, particularly beneath. In summer-

autumn, flat spikes of tubular, pale yellow or greenish-yellow flowers, with brownish-red tips, are produced well above the foliage.
V. hieroglyphica (King of the bromeliads). Evergreen, epiphytic perennial with dense, funnel-shaped rosettes. H and S 60cm–1m (2–3ft). Produces very broadly strap-shaped, arching, yellowish-green leaves, cross-banded and chequered with dark brownish-green. In summer bears panicles of tubular, yellow flowers well above the leaves.
V. platynema. Evergreen, basal-rosetted, epiphytic perennial. H and S 60cm (24in). Broadly strap-shaped, mid- to light green leaves, with purple tips, form dense rosettes. In summer flat racemes of tubular, green-and-yellow flowers, with red or yellow bracts, are produced.
♀ ***V. psittacina.*** Evergreen, spreading, basal-rosetted, epiphytic perennial. H and S 40–60cm (16–24in). Has dense rosettes of strap-shaped, arching, pale green leaves. Flat spikes of tubular, yellow flowers with green tips, emerging from red-and-yellow or red-and-green bracts, are borne above foliage in summer-autumn.
♀ ***V. splendens*** (Flaming sword; illus. p.273). Evergreen, basal-rosetted, epiphytic perennial. H and S 30cm (12in). Has dense rosettes of strap-shaped, arching, olive-green leaves, with purple to reddish-brown cross-bands. Bears flat, sword-shaped racemes of tubular, yellow flowers, between bright red bracts, in summer and autumn.

× VUYLSTEKEARA

ORCHIDACEAE

See also ORCHIDS.
♀ **× *V.* Cambria 'Lensing's Favorite'** illus. p.309. Evergreen, epiphytic orchid for a cool greenhouse. H 23cm (9in). Has narrowly oval leaves, 10–15cm (4–6in) long. Bears long sprays of wine-red flowers, 10cm (4in) across, heavily marked with white; flowering season varies. Needs shade in summer.

WACHENDORFIA

HAEMODORACEAE

Genus of summer-flowering perennials with deep roots, to guard against frost. Half hardy. Requires full sun and moist soil. Propagate by division in spring or by seed in autumn or spring.
W. thyrsiflora. Clump-forming perennial. H 1.5–2m (5–6ft), S 45cm (1½ft). Shallowly cup-shaped, yellow to orange flowers are produced in dense panicles in early summer. Mid-green leaves are narrowly sword-shaped, pleated and rather coarse.

WAHLENBERGIA

CAMPANULACEAE

Genus of summer-flowering annuals, biennials and short-lived perennials, grown for their bell-shaped flowers. Is useful for alpine houses. Frost hardy. Needs a sheltered site, partial shade and well-drained, peaty, sandy soil. Propagate by seed in autumn.
W. albomarginata (New Zealand bluebell). Basal-rosetted, rhizomatous perennial. H and S 15cm (6in) or more. Slender stems each carry a bell-shaped, clear blue flower that opens flat in summer. Has narrowly elliptic to oval, mid-green leaves in tufts. Is good in a rock garden.
W. congesta, syn. *W. saxicola* var. *congesta*. Mat-forming, creeping, rhizomatous perennial. H 7cm (3in), S 10cm (4in). Has small, rounded or spoon-shaped, mid-green leaves and, in summer, bell-shaped, lavender-blue or white flowers held singly on wiry stems.
***W. saxicola* var. *congesta*.** See *W. congesta*.
W. serpyllifolia. See *Edraianthus serpyllifolius*.

Wake-robin. See *Trillium grandiflorum*, illus. p.276; *Trillium sessile*, illus. p.277.

WALDSTEINIA

ROSACEAE

Genus of semi-evergreen, creeping perennials with runners. Makes good ground cover. Fully hardy. Needs sun and well-drained soil. Propagate by division in early spring.
W. ternata, syn. *W. trifolia*, illus. p.397.
W. trifolia. See *W. ternata*.

Wall flag. See *Iris tectorum*, illus. p.234.
Wallflower. See *Erysimum*.
 Siberian. See *Erysimum × allionii*.
Wallich's wood fern. See *Dryopteris wallichiana*.
Wall-spray. See *Cotoneaster horizontalis*, illus. p.168.
Walnut. See *Juglans*.
 Black. See *Juglans nigra*, illus. p.63.
Walnut (continued)
 Chinese. See *Juglans cathayensis*.
 Japanese. See *Juglans ailantifolia*.
 Little. See *Juglans microcarpa*, illus. p.88.
 Texan. See *Juglans microcarpa*, illus. p.88.
Wandering Jew. See *Tradescantia fluminensis*.
Wandflower. See *Dierama*.
Waratah. See *Telopea speciosissima*, illus. p.138.
 Tasmanian. See *Telopea truncata*, illus. p.127.
Warminster broom. See *Cytisus × praecox* 'Warminster', illus. p.152.
Washington. See *Crataegus phaenopyrum*.
Washington grass. See *Cabomba caroliniana*.
Washington thorn. See *Crataegus phaenopyrum*.

WASHINGTONIA

ARECACEAE/PALMAE

Genus of evergreen palms, grown for their stately appearance. Frost tender, min. 10°C (50°F). Grows in fertile, well-drained soil and in full sun. Water containerized specimens freely in summer, moderately at other times. Remove skirt of persistent, dead leaves regularly as they are a fire risk. Propagate by seed in spring at not less than 24°C (75°F). Red spider mite may be a nuisance.
♀ ***W. filifera*** (Desert fan palm). Fast-growing, evergreen palm. H and S to 25m (80ft). Has fan-shaped, long-stalked, grey-green leaves, each lobe with a filamentous tip. Long-stalked clusters of tiny, creamy-white flowers are borne in summer and berry-like, black fruits in winter.
W. robusta illus. p.69.

Water chestnut. See *Trapa natans*, illus. p.465.
Water crowfoot. See *Ranunculus aquatilis*.
Water dragon. See *Saururus cernuus*, illus. p.463.
Water fern. See *Azolla filiculoides*, illus. p.464; *Ceratopteris thalictroides*.
Water figwort. See *Scrophularia auriculata* 'Variegata'.
Water forget-me-not. See *Myosotis scorpioides*.
Water fringe. See *Nymphoides peltata*, illus. p.467.
Water hawthorn. See *Aponogeton distachyos*, illus. p.463.
Water hyacinth. See *Eichhornia crassipes*, illus. p.464.
Water lettuce. See *Pistia stratiotes*, illus. p.465.
Water lily. See *Nymphaea*.
 Cape blue. See *Nymphaea capensis*.
 Fringed. See *Nymphoides peltata*, illus. p.467.
Water lily (continued)
 Yellow. See *Nuphar lutea*, illus. p.467.
Water lily tulip. See *Tulipa kaufmanniana*, illus. p.428.
Water moss. See *Fontinalis*; *Fontinalis antipyretica*.
Water oak. See *Quercus nigra*, illus. p.64.
Water plantain. See *Alisma plantago-aquatica*, illus. p.462.
 Floating. See *Luronium natans*.
Water poppy. See *Hydrocleys nymphoides*, illus. p.465.
Water soldier. See *Stratiotes aloides*, illus. p.463.
Water violet. See *Hottonia palustris*, illus. p.463.
Watermelon begonia. See *Elatostema repens*, illus. p.315.
Watermelon plant. See *Peperomia argyreia*.

WATSONIA

IRIDACEAE

Genus of clump-forming corms, *Gladiolus* -like in overall appearance, although flowers are more tubular. Half hardy. Requires an open, sunny position and light, well-drained soil. Plant in autumn, 10–15cm (4–6in) deep; protect with bracken, loose peat or similar during first winter, if frost is expected. Feed with slow-acting fertilizer, such as bonemeal, in summer. Corms are best left undisturbed to form clumps. Propagate by seed in autumn.
W. beatricis. See *W. pillansii*.
W. borbonica, syn. *W. pyramidata*, illus. p.412.
W. fourcadei. Clump-forming, summer-flowering corm. H to 1.5m (5ft), S 30–45cm (1–1½ft). Sword-shaped, erect leaves are mostly basal. Has a dense spike of tubular, salmon-red flowers, each 8–9cm (3–3½in) long and with 6 lobes.
W. merianiae. Clump-forming, summer-flowering corm. H to 1m (3ft), S 30–45cm (1–1½ft). Has sword-shaped, erect leaves both on stem and at base. Stem carries a loose spike of tubular, pinkish-red flowers, each 5–6cm (2–2½in) long and with 6 spreading lobes.
W. pillansii, syn. *W. beatricis*, illus. p.412.
W. pyramidata. See *W. borbonica*.

Wattakaka sinensis. See *Dregea sinensis*.
Wattle
 Cootamundra. See *Acacia baileyana*, illus. p.93.
 Mount Morgan. See *Acacia podalyriifolia*, illus. p.131.
 Ovens. See *Acacia pravissima*, illus. p.93.
 Queensland silver. See *Acacia podalyriifolia*, illus. p.131.
Wattle (continued)
 Silver. See *Acacia dealbata*, illus. p.79.
 Sydney golden. See *Acacia longifolia*.
Wax flower. See *Stephanotis floribunda*, illus. p.200.
Wax plant. See *Hoya carnosa*, illus. p.204.
Wax privet. See *Peperomia glabella*, illus. p.317.
Wax tree. See *Rhus succedanea*.
Wax vine. See *Senecio macroglossus*.
Waxflower, Geraldton. See *Chamelaucium uncinatum*, illus. pp.145 and 146.
Wayfaring tree. See *Viburnum lantana*.
Wedding-cake tree. See *Cornus controversa* 'Variegata', illus. p.85.
Weeping aspen. See *Populus tremula* 'Pendula', illus. p.75.

Weeping beech. See *Fagus sylvatica* f. *pendula*, illus. p.62.
Weeping birch. See *Betula pendula* 'Tristis', illus. p.69.
Weeping fig. See *Ficus benjamina*.
Weeping silverholly, Perry's. See *Ilex aquifolium* 'Argentea Marginata Pendula', illus. p.94.
Weeping willow. See *Salix babylonica*.
Golden. See *Salix × sepulcralis* var. *chrysocoma*, illus. p.70.

WEIGELA

CAPRIFOLIACEAE

Genus of deciduous shrubs, grown for their showy, funnel-shaped flowers. Fully hardy. Prefers sunny, fertile soil. To maintain vigour, prune out a few older branches to ground level, after flowering each year. Straggly, old plants may be pruned hard in spring (though this will lose one season's flowers). Propagate by softwood cuttings in summer.
***W.* 'Bristol Ruby'.** Vigorous, deciduous, upright shrub. H 2.5m (8ft), S 2m (6ft). Deep red flowers open from darker buds amid oval, toothed, mid-green leaves in late spring and early summer.
***W.* 'Candida'.** Deciduous, bushy shrub. H and S 2.5m (8ft). Pure white flowers appear in late spring and early summer. Leaves are oval, toothed and bright green.
***W.* 'Eva Rathke'.** Deciduous, upright, dense shrub. H and S 1.5m (5ft). Has oval, toothed, dark green leaves. Broad-mouthed, crimson flowers open from darker buds from late spring to early summer.
W. florida. Deciduous, arching shrub. H and S 2.5m (8ft). Bears deep pink flowers, pale pink to white inside, in late spring and early summer. Oval, toothed leaves are mid-green.
♀ **'Foliis Purpureis'** illus. p.159.
♀ **'Variegata'** illus. p.156.
***W.* 'Looymansii Aurea'.** Weak-growing, deciduous, upright shrub. H 1.5m (5ft), S 1m (3ft). Produces, from late spring through to early summer, pale pink flowers amid oval, toothed, golden-yellow leaves with narrow red-rims. Needs protection from hot sun.
W. middendorffiana illus. p.164.
W. praecox. Deciduous, upright shrub. H 2.5m (8ft), S 2m (6ft). Fragrant, pink flowers, marked inside with yellow, are produced in late spring. Leaves are bright green, oval and toothed. ♀ **'Variegata'** has leaves with broad, creamy-white margins.

Weingartia neocumingii. See *Rebutia neocumingii*.

WEINMANNIA

CUNONIACEAE

Genus of evergreen trees and shrubs, grown for their foliage, flowers and overall appearance. Frost tender, min. 5–7°C (41–5°F). Requires a position in partial shade or full light and humus-rich, well-drained but not dry soil, ideally neutral to acid. Water containerized plants freely when in full growth, moderately at other times. Pruning is tolerated if needed. Propagate by seed in spring or by semi-ripe cuttings in summer.
W. trichosperma. Evergreen, ovoid to round-headed tree. H 12m (40ft) or more, S 8–10m (25–30ft). Glossy, rich green leaves have 9–19 oval, boldly toothed leaflets borne on a winged midrib. Spikes of tiny, fragrant, white flowers, with pink stamens, are produced in early summer.

WELDENIA

COMMELINACEAE

Genus of one species of summer-flower-ing, tuberous perennial, grown for its flowers. Half hardy. Needs sun and gritty, well-drained soil. Keep dry from autumn until growth restarts in late winter. Is suitable for growing in alpine houses. Propagate by root cuttings in winter or by division in early spring.
W. candida illus. p.374.

Wellingtonia. See *Sequoiadendron giganteum*, illus. p.98.
Welsh poppy. See *Meconopsis cambrica*, illus. p.285.

WELWITSCHIA

WELWITSCHIACEAE

Genus of one species of evergreen, desert-growing perennial with a deep tap root. Has only 2 leaves, which lie on the ground and grow continuously from the base for up to 100 years. Frost tender, min.10°C (50°F). Requires sun and sharply drained soil. Requires desert conditions: may succeed in a mixture of stone chippings and leaf mould, in a length of drainpipe to take its long tap root. Propagate by seed when ripe.
W. bainesii. See *W. mirabilis*.
W. mirabilis, syn. *W. bainesii*, illus. p.316.

West Himalayan birch. See *Betula utilis* var. *jacquemontii*, illus. p.79.
West Himalayan spruce. See *Picea smithiana*.
West Indian jasmine. See *Plumeria alba*
Western balsam poplar. See *Populus trichocarpa*.
Western hemlock. See *Tsuga heterophylla*.
Western prickly Moses. See *Acacia pulchella*, illus. p.153.
Western red cedar. See *Thuja plicata*
Western tea-myrtle. See *Melaleuca nesophila*, illus. p.141.
Western yellow pine. See *Pinus ponderosa*, illus. p.99.

WESTRINGIA

LABIATAE/LAMIACEAE

Genus of evergreen shrubs, grown for their flowers and overall appearance. Frost tender, min.5–7°C (41–5°F). Requires full light and well-drained soil. Water containerized specimens moderately, less when not in full growth. Propagate by seed in spring or by semi-ripe cuttings in late summer.
♀ ***W. fruticosa***, syn. *W. rosmariniformis*, illus. p.154.
W. rosmariniformis. See *W. fruticosa*.

Weymouth pine. See *Pinus strobus*, illus. p.98.
Wheatley elm. See *Ulmus minor* 'Sarniensis'.
White ash. See *Fraxinus americana*.
White asphodel. See *Asphodelus albus*, illus. p.241.
White baneberry. See *Actaea pachypoda*, illus. p.267.
White cedar. See *Thuja occidentalis*.
White Chinese birch. See *Betula albosinensis*, illus. p.70.
White cypress. See *Chamaecyparis thyoides*, illus. p.103.
White elm. See *Ulmus americana*.
White evening primrose. See *Oenothera speciosa*
White false hellebore. See *Veratrum album*.
White fir. See *Abies concolor*
White gingerlily. See *Hedychium coronarium*.
White mugwort. See *Artemisia lactiflora*, illus. p.225.
White mulberry. See *Morus alba*.
White mullein. See *Verbascum lychnitis*.
White poplar. See *Populus alba illus*. p.60.
White rosebay. See *Epilobium angustifolium* f. *album*, illus. p.224.
White sails. See *Spathiphyllum wallisii*, illus. p.312.
White Sally. See *Eucalyptus pauciflora*, illus. p.80.
White snakeroot. See *Eupatorium rugosum*, illus. p.242.
White spruce. See *Picea glauca*
White trumpet lily. See *Lilium longiflorum*, illus. p.416.
White willow. See *Salix alba*
White-backed hosta. See *Hosta hypoleuca*.
Whitebeam. See *Sorbus aria*
Swedish. See *Sorbus intermedia*.
Whiteywood. See *Melicytus ramiflorus*

Whorl flower. See *Morina*
Whorled Solomon's seal. See *Polygonatum verticillatum*
Whorled water milfoil. See *Myriophyllum verticillatum*, illus. p.465.
Whortleberry. See *Vaccinium myrtillus*.
Caucasian. See *Vaccinium arctostaphylos*.
Widow iris. See *Hermodactylus tuberosus*, illus. p.430.

WIGANDIA

HYDROPHYLLACEAE

Genus of evergreen perennials and shrubs, grown for their flowers and foliage. Frost tender, min.7–10°C (45–50°F). Needs full light and moist but well-drained soil. Water potted plants freely when in full growth, moderately at other times. Cut down flowered stems in spring to prevent plants becoming straggly. Propagate by seed or softwood cuttings in spring. Whitefly is sometimes troublesome. Contact with foliage may aggravate skin allergies.
W. caracasana. Evergreen, erect, sparsely branched shrub. H 2–3m (6–10ft), S 1–2m (3–6ft). Produces oval, wavy-edged, toothed, deep green leaves, 45cm (18in) long and covered with white-hairs beneath. Carries 5-petalled, violet-purple flowers in large, terminal clusters from spring through to autumn. Is often grown annually from seed purely for its handsome leaves.

Wigginsia vorwerkiana. See *Parodia erinacea*.
Wilcoxia albiflora. See *Echinocereus leucanthus*.
Wilcoxia schmollii. See *Echinocereus schmollii*.
Wild buckwheat. See *Eriogonum*.
Wild cherry. See *Prunus avium*, illus. p.67.
Wild coffee. See *Polyscias guilfoylei*.
Wild daffodil. See *Narcissus pseudonarcissus*, illus. p.433.
Wild ginger. See *Asarum*.
Wild iris. See *Iris versicolor*, illus. p.234.
Wild Irishman. See *Discaria toumatou*.
Wild jonquil. See *Narcissus jonquilla*, illus. p.434.
Wild lily-of-the-valley. See *Pyrola rotundifolia*.
Wild marjoram. See *Origanum vulgare*.
Wild pansy. See *Viola tricolor*, illus. p.381.
Wild pineapple. See *Ananas bracteatus*.
Wild rum cherry. See *Prunus serotina*, illus. p.61.
Wild yellow lily. See *Lilium canadense*.
Willow. See *Salix*.
Bay. See *Salix pentandra*.
Black. See *Salix gracilistyla* 'Melanostachys'.
Crack. See *Salix fragilis*.
Creeping. See *Salix repens*, illus. p.152.
Cricket-bat. See *Salix alba* var. *caerulea*.
Dragon's-claw. See *Salix babylonica* var. *pekinensis* 'Tortuosa', illus. p.81.
Dwarf. See *Salix herbacea*.
Goat. See *Salix caprea*.
Golden. See *Salix alba* var. *vitellina*, illus. p.70.
Willow (continued)
Golden weeping. See *Salix × sepulcralis* var. *chrysocoma* illus. p.70.
Hoary. See *Salix elaeagnos*.
Kilmarnock. See *Salix caprea* 'Kilmarnock'.
Least. See *Salix herbacea*.
Mountain. See *Salix arbuscula*.
Musk. See *Salix aegyptiaca*.
Net-veined. See *Salix reticulata*, illus. p.382.
Pussy. See *Salix caprea*.
Silver. See *Salix alba* var. *sericea*.
Violet. See *Salix daphnoides*, illus. p.70.
Weeping. See *Salix babylonica*.
White. See *Salix alba*.
Woolly. See *Salix lanata*, illus. p.152.
Willow gentian. See *Gentiana asclepiadea*, illus. p.271.
Willow herb. See *Epilobium*.
Willow moss. See *Fontinalis antipyretica*.
Willow myrtle. See *Agonis*.
Willow oak. See *Quercus phellos*, illus. p.67.
Willow-leaved magnolia. See *Magnolia salicifolia*, illus. p.71.
Willow-leaved sunflower. See *Helianthus salicifolius*.

× Wilsonara

ORCHIDACEAE

See also ORCHIDS.
× ***W. Hambuhren Stern* 'Cheam'** illus. p.309. Evergreen, epiphytic orchid for a cool greenhouse. H 23cm (9in). Narrowly oval leaves are 10cm (4in) long. Bears spikes of deep reddish-brown flowers, 9cm (3½in) across, each with a yellow lip; flowering season varies. Requires shade in summer.

Windflower. See *Anemone Zephyranthes.*
Snowdrop. See *Anemone sylvestris*, illus. p.276.
Windmill palm. See *Trachycarpus fortunei*, illus. p.80.
Wine-cup, Lacquered. See *Aechmea Foster's Favorite Group*, illus. p.273.
Winecups. See *Babiana rubrocyanea*, illus. p.447.
Wing nut. See *Pterocarya*.
Caucasian. See *Pterocarya fraxinifolia*.
Chinese. See *Pterocarya stenoptera*.
Winged spindle. See *Euonymus alatus*, illus. p.144.
Winged thorn rose. See *Rosa sericea* subsp. *omeiensis* f. *pteracantha*.
Winter aconite. See *Eranthis hyemalis*, illus. p.457.
Winter cherry. See *Cardiospermum halicacabum; Physalis alkekengi; Solanum capsicastrum*.
Winter cress. See *Barbarea vulgaris*.
Winter heath. See *Erica carnea*.
Winter heliotrope. See *Petasites fragrans*.
Winter iris. See *Iris unguicularis*.
Winter jasmine. See *Jasminum nudiflorum*, illus. p.147.
Winter savory. See *Satureja montana*.
Winter's bark. See *Drimys winteri*, illus. p.74.
Wintera aromatica. See *Drimys winteri*.
Winterberry. See *Ilex verticillata*, illus. p.94.
Wintergreen. See *Pyrola*.
Round-leaved. See *Pyrola rotundifolia*.
Wintergreen fern. See *Polypodium cambricum*.
Wintersweet. See *Acokanthera oblongifolia*, illus. p.146; *Chimonanthus praecox*.
Wire-netting bush. See *Corokia cotoneaster*, illus. p.148.
Wishbone flower. See *Torenia fournieri*, illus. p.345.

Wisteria

LEGUMINOSAE/PAPILIONACEAE

Genus of deciduous, woody-stemmed, twining climbers, grown for their spectacular flowers and suitable for walls and pergolas and for growing against buildings and trees. Fully to frost hardy. Grows in sun and in fertile, well-drained soil. Prune after flowering and again in late winter. Propagate by bench grafting in winter or by seed in autumn or spring. Plants produced from seed may not flower until some years old and often have poor flowers. All parts may cause severe discomfort if ingested.
W. brachybotrys (Silky Wisteria) is a deciduous, woody-stemmed, twining climber. H to 9m (28ft) or more. Fully hardy. Leaves are 20–35cm (8–14in) long, each with 9–13oval leaflets. Produces 10–15cm (4–6in) long racemes of scented, pea-like, violet to white flowers, each with a yellow blotch at base of upper petal, in early summer; sometimes flowers again sparsely in autumn. **'Alba'** see 'Shiro-kapitan'. **f. *alba*** see 'Shiro-kapitan'.**'Alba Plena'** see 'Shiro-kapitan'. **'Murasaki-kapitan'** syn. *W. venusta* 'Violacea', *W. venusta* f. violacea has deep blue-violet flowers with prominent white, slightly yellow-tinged markings on the standards. **f. *plena*** see 'Shiro-kapitan'**. 'Shiro-kapitan'** syn, 'Alba', f. *alba*, 'Alba Plena', f. *plena, W. venusta, W. venusta* 'Alba', *W. venusta f. alba, W. venusta* 'Alba Plena' produces white flowers witha yellow stain at the base of each standard. Double flowers are occasionally produced.
W. chinensis. See *W. sinensis*
W. floribunda (Japanese wisteria). vigorous twining climber with pinnate leaves, each composed of 11–19 ovate to lance-shaped leaflets. In early summer, pea-like, fragrant, blue to violet, pink, or white flowers, the standards marked with white and yellow, are produced in pendent racemes, to 30cm (12in) or more long, the flowers opening gradually from the bases to the tips; they are often followed by bean-like, velvety green seed pods, to 15cm (6in) long. H 9m (28ft) or more.
♀ **'Alba'** (syn.'Shiro Noda') illus. p.203 bears white flowers in racemes 60cm (24in) long. **'Black Dragon'** (syn *W* x *formosa* 'Yaekokuryu') has racemes 30–50cm (12–20in) long with violet-purple flowers.**'Multijuga'** (syn. *W.f.* 'Macrobotrys') has lilac-blue flowers in racemes 0.9–1.2m (3–4ft) long. *W.f* **'Macrobotrys'** see 'Multijuga'. **'Shiro Noda'** see *W.f.* 'Alba'.
W.* x *formosa .(*W. floribunda* x *W. sinensis)* illus. p.213. Vigorous twining climber with pinnate leaves, each composed of 9–15, broadly ovate to elliptic leaflets. Pea-like, fragrant, violet-blue flowers,with white and yellow markings, are borne in pendent racemes, to 25cm (10in) long, in late spring and early summer, often followed by bean-like velvety green seed pods to 15cm (6in) long. H9m (28ft) or more. **'Yaekokuryu'** (syn. *W. floribunda* 'Black Dragon'
♀ ***W. sinensis*** syn. *W. chinensis* (Chinese wisteria) illus. p.213. Vigorous twining climber with pinnate leaves, each composed of 7–13, elliptic or ovate leaflets. Pea-like, fragrant, lilac-blue towhite flowers, in dense, pendent racemes, to 30cm (12in) long, are borne in late spring and early summer, often followed by bean-like velvety green seed pods to 15cm (6in) long.
H 9m (28ft) or more. ♀ **'Alba'** illus p.203 has white flowers. **'Prolific'** bears many lilac-blue to pale violet-blue flowers.
W. venusta see *W. brachybrotrys* 'Shiro-kapitan'
***W. venusta* 'Alba'** see *W. brachybrotrys* 'Shiro-kapitan'
W. venusta* f. *alba see *W. brachybrotrys* 'Shiro-kapitan
***W. venusta* 'Alba Plena'** see *W. brachybrotrys* 'Shiro-kapitan
***W. venusta* 'Violacea'** see *W. brachybrotrys* 'Murasaki-kapitan
***W. venusta* f.** *violacea* see *W. brachybrotrys* 'Murasaki-kapitan

Wisteria
Chinese. See *Wisteria sinensis*, illus. p.213.
Japanese. See *Wisteria floribunda*.
Silky. See *Wisteria brachybotrys* 'Shiro-kapitan'.
Witch alder. See *Fothergilla gardenii*.
Witch hazel. See *Hamamelis*.
Chinese. See *Hamamelis mollis*.
Japanese. See *Hamamelis japonica*.
Virginian. See *Hamamelis virginiana*, illus. p.121.
Woad. See *Isatis tinctoria*.

Wolffia

Duckweed

LEMNACEAE

Genus of semi-evergreen, perennial, floating water plants, grown for their curiosity value as the smallest-known flowering plants. Is ideal for cold-water aquariums. Half hardy. Needs a sunny position. Remove excess plantlets as required. Propagate by redistribution of plantlets as required.
W. arrhiza (Least duckweed). Semi-evergreen, perennial, floating water plant. S 1mm (1/32in). Leaves are rounded and mid-green. Insignificant, greenish flowers appear year-round.

Wolf's bane. See *Aconitum*.
Wonga-wonga vine. See *Pandorea pandorana*.
Wood anemone. See *Anemone nemorosa*.
Wood lily. See *Trillium*.
Wood millet. See *Milium effusum*.
Wood rose. See *Merremia tuberosa*.
Wood sorrel. See *Oxalis acetosella*.
Wood spurge. See *Euphorbia amygdaloides*.
Woodbine. See *Lonicera periclymenum*.
Woodruff. See *Galium odoratum*, illus. p.285.
Woodrush. See *Luzula*.
Greater. See *Luzula sylvatica*.
Snowy. See *Luzula nivea*, illus. p.319.

Woodsia

DRYOPTERIDACEAE

Genus of deciduous ferns, suitable for rock gardens and alpine houses. Fully hardy. Tolerates sun or semi-shade. May be difficult to cultivate: soil must provide constant moisture and also be quick-draining, and crowns of plants must sit above soil to avoid rotting. Propagate by division in early spring.
♀ ***W. polystichoides*** (Holly-fern woodsia). Deciduous, tufted fern. H 10–30cm (4–12in), S 20–40cm (8–16in). In early spring, has lance-shaped, divided, pale green fronds, to 35cm (14in) long, softly hairy on both surfaces and scaly beneath; each is composed of 15–30 pairs of narrowly sickle-shaped or oblong pinnae, with slightly toothed margins. May be damaged by late frosts.

Woodsia, Holly-fern. See *Woodsia polystichoides*.

Woodwardia

BLECHNACEAE

Genus of evergreen or deciduous ferns. Fully to frost hardy. Prefers semi-shade and fibrous, moist, peaty soil. Remove faded fronds regularly. Propagate by division in spring.
♀ ***W. radicans*** (Chain fern). Vigorous, evergreen, spreading fern. Fully hardy H 1.2m (4ft), S 60cm (2ft). Large, broadly lance-shaped, coarsely divided, arching fronds, with narrowly oval pinnae, are mid-green.
W. unigemmata (Asian chain fern). Evergreen fern very similar to W. radicans. H 1m (3ft), S 3m (10ft). Frost hardy. New foliage emerges brilliant red and fades to brown and then green.

Woolly morning glory. See *Argyreia nervosa*.
Woolly willow. See *Salix lanata*, illus. p.152.
Wormwood. See *Artemisia*.
Wormwood cassia. See *Senna artemisioides*.
Roman. See *Artemisia pontica*, illus. p.302.

Worsleya

Blue amaryllis

AMARYLLIDACEAE

Genus of one species of evergreen, winter-flowering bulb, with a neck up to 75cm (2½ft) high crowned by a tuft of leaves and a 20–30cm (8–12in) leafless flower stem. Frost tender, min. 15°C (59°F). Needs full sun and well-drained soil, or compost mixed with osmunda fibre, perlite or bark chips and some leaf mould. Soil should never dry out. Propagate by seed in spring.
W. procera. See *W. rayneri*
W. rayneri, syn. *Hippeastrum procerum, W. procera*. Evergreen, winter-flowering bulb. H 1–1.2m (3–4ft), S 45–60cm (1½–2ft). Bears long, strap-shaped, strongly curved leaves and up to 14 funnel-shaped, lilac-blue flowers, 15cm (6in) long, with wavy-edged petals.

Wulfenia

SCROPHULARIACEAE

Genus of evergreen, summer-flowering perennials with rough-textured leaves. Is suitable for alpine houses as it dislikes winter wet. Fully hardy. It needs to have full sun and well-drained soil. Propagate by division in spring or by seed in autumn.
W. amherstiana illus. p.368.
W. carinthiaca. Evergreen, basal-rosetted perennial. H and S 25cm (10in). Has oblong to oval, toothed, dark green leaves, hairy beneath. The top quarter of each flower stem is covered in a dense spike of small, tubular, violet-blue flowers in summer.

Wych elm. See *Ulmus glabra*.

XANTHOCERAS

SAPINDACEAE

Genus of one species of deciduous, spring- to summer-flowering shrub or tree, grown for its foliage and flowers. Fully hardy. Requires sun and fertile, well-drained soil. Does best in areas with hot summers. Propagate by seed in autumn or by root cuttings or suckers in late winter. Is susceptible to coral spot fungus.
♀ ***X. sorbifolium*** illus. p.114.

XANTHOPHTHALMUM

COMPOSITAE/ASTERACEAE

Genus of annuals, grown for their daisy-like flower heads. Fully hardy. Prefers full sun and well-drained soil. Propagate by seed in spring.
X. coronarium, syn. *Chrysanthemum coronarium*. Fast-growing, upright, branching annual. H 30cm–90cm (1–3ft), S 38cm (15in). Has feathery, divided, light green leaves. In summer bears single or semi-double, daisy-like, yellow or yellow-and-white flower heads, to 5cm (2in) across.
X. segetum, syn. *Chrysanthemum segetum*, illus. p.349.

XANTHORHIZA

RANUNCULACEAE

Genus of one species of deciduous, spring-flowering shrub, grown for its foliage and flowers. Fully hardy. Prefers shade or semi-shade and moist soil. Propagate by division in autumn.
X. apiifolia. See *X. simplicissima*.
X. simplicissima, syn. *X. apiifolia* (Yellow-root). Deciduous, upright shrub that spreads by underground stems. H 60cm (2ft), S 1.5m (5ft). Bright green leaves, each consisting of usually 5 oval to lance-shaped, sharply toothed leaflets, turn bronze or purple in autumn. Bears nodding panicles of tiny, star-shaped, purple flowers from early to mid-spring as foliage emerges.

XANTHORRHOEA

Blackboy, Grass tree

XANTHORRHOEACEAE

Genus of evergreen, long-lived perennials, grown mainly as foliage plants. Frost tender, min. 10°C (50°F). Needs full sun, well-drained soil and a fairly dry atmosphere. Propagate by basal offsets or seed in spring.
X. australis. Evergreen perennial with a stout, dark trunk. H 60cm–1.2m (2–4ft), S 1.2–1.5m (4–5ft). Very narrow, arching, flattened, silvery-green leaves, 60cm (2ft) or more long, 2mm (1/10in) wide, spread from top of the trunk. In summer may produce small, fragrant, 6-petalled, white flowers, in dense, candle-like spikes, 60cm (2ft) or more long, on stems of similar length.

XANTHOSOMA

ARACEAE

Genus of perennials, with underground tubers or thick stems above ground, grown mainly for their attractive foliage. Many species are cultivated in the tropics for their edible, starchy tubers. Frost tender, min. 15°C (59°F). Requires a position in partial shade and rich, moist soil. The atmosphere should be kept moist at all times. Propagate by division; alternatively take stem cuttings in spring or summer.
X. nigrum, syn. *X. violaceum*. Stemless perennial with large, underground tubers and leaves rising from ground level. H and S 1.2m (4ft). Purplish leaf stalks, to over 60cm (2ft) long, carry broadly arrow-shaped leaf blades, 70cm (28in) long, dark green with purple midribs and veins. Intermittently bears greenish-purple spathes, yellower within, surrounding a brownish spadix.
X. sagittifolium illus. p.274.
X. violaceum. See *X. nigrum*

XERANTHEMUM

Immortelle

COMPOSITAE/ASTERACEAE

Genus of summer-flowering annuals. Half hardy. Grow in sun and in fertile, very well-drained soil. Propagate by seed sown outdoors in spring.
X. annuum. Fairly fast-growing, upright annual with branching flower heads. H 60cm (2ft), S 45cm (1½ft). Has lance-shaped, silvery leaves. Daisy-like, papery, purple flower heads are produced in summer. Double forms are available in shades of pink, mauve, purple or white (illus. p.337).

XEROCHRYSUM, syn. BRACHTEANTHA

COMPOSITAE/ASTERACEAE

Genus of herbaceous perennials and annuals, grown for their daisy-like flower heads with papery bracts. Stalkless, hairy leaves are borne on erect, branching stems. Frost to half hardy. Needs full sun and moderately fertile, moist but well-drained soil. Propagate by seed sown in spring. *X. bracteatum* is often grown for cutting and drying.
X. bracteatum (Everlasting flower, Immortelle, Strawflower). ♀ **'Bright Bikini'** is a moderately fast-growing, upright, branching annual. H and S 30cm (12in). Half hardy. Has lance-shaped, mid-green leaves. From summer to early autumn produces papery, daisy-like flower heads in many colours, including red, pink, orange, yellow and white.
Monstrosum Series illus. p.352.

XERONEMA

AGAVACEAE/PHORMIACEAE

Genus of evergreen, robust, tufted perennials, with short, creeping rootstocks, grown for their flowers. Frost tender, min. 10°C (50°F). Grow in sun or partial shade and in humus-rich, well-drained soil. Propagate by seed or division in spring.
X. callistemon. Evergreen, iris-like, clump-forming perennial. H 60cm–1m (2–3ft), S indefinite. Erect, folded leaves, 60cm–1m (2–3ft) long, are very narrow and hard-textured. In summer, short-stalked, 6-petalled, red flowers, to 3cm (1¼in) wide, are borne on one-sided racemes, 15–30cm (6–12in) long.

XEROPHYLLUM

LILIACEAE/MELANTHIACEAE

Genus of elegant, summer-flowering, rhizomatous perennials. Frost hardy. Prefers full sun and moist, peaty soil. May be difficult to cultivate. Propagate by seed in autumn.
X. tenax. Clump-forming perennial. H 1–1.2m (3–4ft), S 30–60cm (1–2ft). Star-shaped, white flowers, with violet anthers, are borne in dense, terminal racemes in summer. Basal leaves are linear and mid-green.

Yam, Ornamental. See *Dioscorea discolor*, illus. p.217.
Yarrow. See *Achillea millefolium*.
Yatay palm. See *Butia*.
Yellow asphodel. See *Asphodeline lutea*, illus. p.240.
Yellow banksia. See *Rosa banksiae* 'Lutea', illus. p.195.
Yellow bells. See *Tecoma stans*, illus. p.92.
Yellow birch. See *Betula alleghaniensis*.
Yellow buckeye. See *Aesculus flava*, illus. p.78.
Yellow elder. See *Tecoma stans*, illus. p.92.
Yellow flag. See *Iris pseudacorus*, illus. p.235.
Yellow flax. See *Linum flavum; Reinwardtia indica*, illus. p.166.
Yellow foxglove. See *Digitalis grandiflora*.
Yellow fritillary. See *Fritillaria pudica*, illus. p.450.
Yellow haw. See *Crataegus flava*, illus. p.86.
Yellow jasmine. See *Jasminum humile*, illus. p.142.
Yellow kangaroo paw. See *Anigozanthos flavidus*, illus. p.260.
Yellow lady's slipper orchid. See *Cypripedium calceolus*, illus. p.310.
Yellow mariposa. See *Calochortus luteus*, illus. p.431.
Yellow morning glory. See *Merremia tuberosa*.
Yellow musk. See *Mimulus luteus*, illus. illus. p.304.
Yellow oleander. See *Thevetia peruviana*, illus. p.89.
Yellow ox-eye. See *Buphthalmum salicifolium*,
Yellow palm. See *Dypsis lutescens*, illus. p.96.
Yellow parilla. See *Menispermum canadense*.
Yellow pitcher plant. See *Sarracenia flava*, illus. p.302.
Yellow pond lily. See *Nuphar advena*.
Yellow rocket. See *Barbarea vulgaris*.
Yellow scabious. See *Cephalaria gigantea*.
Yellow skunk cabbage. See *Lysichiton americanus*, illus. p.467.
Yellow turkscap lily. See *Lilium pyrenaicum*.
Yellow waterlily. See *Nuphar lutea*, illus. p.467.
Yellow whitlow grass. See *Draba aizoides*.
Yellow wood. See *Cladrastis kentukea*, illus. p.78.
Yellow-root. See *Xanthorhiza simplicissima*.
Yesterday-today-and-tomorrow. See *Brunfelsia pauciflora*.
Yew. See *Taxus baccata*.
  Japanese. See *Taxus cuspidata*, illus. p.105.
Yew (continued)
  Plum. See *Cephalotaxus harringtonii; Prumnopitys andina*.
  Plum-fruited. See *Prumnopitys andina*.

Prince Albert's. See *Saxegothaea conspicua.*
Yoshino cherry. See *Prunus × yedoensis*, illus. p.83.
Young's weeping birch. See *Betula pendula* 'Youngii', illus. p.88.
Youth-on-age. See *Tolmiea menziesii.*

YUCCA,
syn. HESPEROYUCCA

AGAVACEAE

Genus of evergreen shrubs and trees, grown for the architectural value of their bold, sword-shaped, clustered leaves and their showy panicles of usually white flowers. Makes excellent container-grown plants. Fully hardy to frost tender, min. 7°C (45°F). Requires a position in full sun and well-drained soil. Water containerized specimens moderately except when they are not in full growth and watering should then be reduced. Regularly remove spent flowering stems. Propagate in spring: frost-tender species by seed or suckers, hardier species by root cuttings or division.
Y. aloifolia illus. p.149.
***Y. elephantipes* 'Variegata'.** Evergreen, large, upright shrub or small tree. H to 10m (30ft), S 5–8m (15–25ft). Min. 10°C (50°F). Several to many sparsely branched trunks arise near ground level. Leaves are narrowly lance-shaped, stiffly leathery, light to mid-green and creamy-white at the margins. On mature plants, pendent, hemispherical, white to cream flowers are borne in dense, erect panicles from summer to autumn.
♡ ***Y. filamentosa*** (Adam's needle). Clump-forming, evergreen, basal-rosetted shrub. H 2m (6ft), S 1.5m (5ft). Fully hardy. From mid-through to late summer produces tall panicles of pendulous, tulip-shaped, white flowers, which rise up through low-growing tufts of sword-shaped, deep green leaves, each edged with white threads.
***Y. filifera* 'Ivory'.** See *Y. flaccida* 'Ivory'.
♡ ***Y. flaccida* 'Ivory'**, syn. *Y. filifera* 'Ivory', illus. p.156.
♡ ***Y. gloriosa*** (Spanish dagger) illus. p.133. **'Nobilis'** is an evergreen shrub. H and S 2m (6ft). Frost hardy. Stem is stout and usually unbranched, and crowned with a large tuft of long, sword-shaped, sharply pointed, blue-green leaves, the outer ones semi-pendent. Pendulous, tulip-shaped, red-backed, white flowers are borne in long, erect panicles from mid-summer to early autumn.
Y. parviflora. See *Hesperaloe parviflora.*
Y. whipplei illus. p.156.

Yulan. See *Magnolia denudata*, illus. p.71.

YUSHANIA

GRAMINEAE/POACEAE

See also GRASSES, BAMBOOS, RUSHES and SEDGES.
♡ ***Y. anceps***, syn. *Arundinaria anceps, A. jaunsarensis, Sinarundinaria jaunsarensis* (Anceps bamboo), illus. p.320.

Z

ZALUZIANSKYA

SCROPHULARIACEAE

Genus of sticky, low-growing annuals and evergreen perennials and sub-shrubs, grown for their spikes of very fragrant, tubular flowers with spreading petals. Frost hardy. Needs full sun and moist but sharply drained, humus-rich soil. Propagate by stem-tip cuttings regularly in summer as plants are short-lived.
Z. ovata. Clump-forming, evergreen perennial. H to 25cm (10in), S to 60cm (24in). Branching, brittle stems bear ovate, toothed, sticky, grey-green leaves. Produces crimson-backed, white flowers over a long period in summer.

ZANTEDESCHIA

ARACEAE

Genus of summer-flowering, tuberous perennials, usually remaining evergreen in a warm climate, grown for their erect, funnel-shaped spathes, each of which encloses a club-shaped spadix. Frost hardy to frost tender, min. 10°C (50°F). Requires a position in full sun or partial shade and well-drained soil. *Z. aethiopica*, however, will also grow in 15–30cm (6–12in) of water and therefore is suitable as a marginal water plant. Propagate by offsets in winter. All parts of the plant may cause mild stomach upset if ingested, and contact with the sap may irritate the skin.
♡ ***Z. aethiopica*** (Arum lily).
♡ **'Crowborough'** illus. p.409.
♡ **'Green Goddess'** illus. p.409.
Z. albomaculata, syn. *Z. melanoleuca.* Summer-flowering, tuberous perennial. H 30–40cm (12–16in), S 30cm (12in). Frost tender. Bears arrow-shaped, semi-erect, basal leaves with transparent spots. Produces a yellow spadix inside a white spathe, 12–20cm (5–8in) long, shading to green at the base and with a deep purple blotch inside.
***Z.* 'Black-eyed Beauty'.** Summer-flowering, tuberous perennial. H 30–40cm (12–16in), S 15cm (6in). Frost tender. Broadly heart-shaped, semi-erect, mid- to dark green, basal leaves are heavily white spotted. Each flower stem has a golden-yellow spadix, surrounded by a cream spathe, 15cm (6in) long, with a central black mark in the throat.
***Z.* 'Black Magic'.** Summer-flowering, tuberous perennial. H 75cm (30in), S 20cm (8in). Frost tender. Broadly heart-shaped, semi-erect, mid- to dark green, basal leaves are heavily mottled with white. Each flower stem produces a golden-yellow spadix, surrounded by a black-throated, yellow spathe, 15cm (6in) long.
♡ ***Z. elliottiana*** illus. p.414.
Z. melanoleuca. See *Z. albomaculata.*
♡ ***Z. rehmannii*** (Pink arum). Summer-flowering, tuberous perennial. H 40cm (16in), S 30cm (12in). Frost tender. Basal leaves are arrow-shaped, semi-erect, green and generally without marks. Each flower stem produces a yellow spadix, surrounded by a reddish-pink spathe, 7–8cm (3in) long and narrowly tubular at the base.

ZANTHOXYLUM

RUTACEAE

Genus of deciduous or evergreen, spiny shrubs and trees, grown for their aromatic foliage, fruits and habit. Fully to frost hardy. Requires a position in sun or semi-shade and in fertile soil. Propagate by seed in autumn or by root cuttings in late winter.
Z. piperitum illus. p.141.
Z. simulans illus. p.144.

ZAUSCHNERIA

ONAGRACEAE

Genus of sub-shrubby, evergreen or deciduous perennials, grown for their mass of flowers. Fully to frost hardy. Requires a sunny position and well-drained soil. Propagate by seed or division in spring or by taking side-shoot cuttings in summer.
Z. californica, syn. *Epilobium californicum.* Clump-forming, woody-based, evergreen or semi-evergreen perennial. H and S 45cm (18in). Frost hardy. Terminal clusters of tubular, bright scarlet flowers, borne on slender stems, are produced in late summer and early autumn. Bears lance-shaped, rich green leaves. subsp. ***cana*** (syn. *Epilobium canum, Z. cana*), H 30cm (12in) is deciduous and produces linear, grey leaves and fuchsia-like, brilliant scarlet flowers. ♡ subsp. ***cana* 'Dublin'** (syn. *Z.c.* 'Glasnevin') illus. p.367. **'Glasnevin'** see *Z.c.* subsp. *cana* 'Dublin'.
Z. cana. See *Z. californica* subsp. *cana.*
Z. septentrionalis, syn. *Epilobium septentrionale.* Mat-forming, non-woody, deciduous perennial. H 10–20cm (4–8in), S to 20cm (8in). Fully hardy. Terminal clusters of numerous, short-stalked, tubular, scarlet flowers are produced in late summer. Has oval to lance-shaped, grey to grey-green leaves.

ZEA
Indian corn, Maize

GRAMINEAE/POACEAE

See also GRASSES, BAMBOOS, RUSHES and SEDGES.
Z. mays (Ornamental maize, Sweet corn). **'Gracillima Variegata'** illus. p.332. **'Harlequin'** is a fairly fast-growing, upright annual. H 1–2m (3–6ft), S 60cm (2ft). Half hardy. Lance-shaped leaves are 60cm (2ft) long and striped with green, red and white. Feathery, silky flower heads, 15cm (6in) long, borne on long stems, are produced in mid-summer, followed by large, cylindrical, green-sheathed, yellow seed heads, known as cobs, with deep red grains. **'Strawberry Corn'**, H 1.2m (4ft), produces seed heads with small, yellow to burgundy-red grains, enclosed within yellow-green spathe-bracts.

Zebra plant. See *Aphelandra squarrosa; Calathea zebrina*, illus. p.274.
Zebrina pendula. See *Tradescantia zebrina.*

ZELKOVA

ULMACEAE

Genus of deciduous trees, grown mainly for their foliage and habit and are best when planted as isolated specimens. Produces insignificant flowers in spring. Fully hardy, but prefers some shelter. Does best in full sun and requires deep, fertile, moist but well-drained soil. Propagate by seed in autumn.
Z. abelicea, syn. *Z. cretica.* Deciduous, bushy-headed, spreading tree. H 5m (15ft), S 7m (22ft). Produces small leaves which are oval, prominently toothed and glossy, dark green.
Z. carpinifolia (Caucasian elm). Deciduous tree with a short, stout trunk from which many upright branches arise to make an oval, dense crown. H 30m (100ft), S 25m (80ft). Produces oval, sharply toothed, dark green leaves, turning to orange-brown in autumn.
Z. cretica. See *Z. abelicea.*
♡ ***Z. serrata*** illus. p.67.

ZENOBIA

ERICACEAE

Genus of one species of deciduous or semi-evergreen, summer-flowering shrub, grown for its flowers. Fully hardy. Requires semi-shade and moist, peaty, acid soil. Prune out older, weaker shoots after flowering to maintain vigour. Propagate by semi-ripe cuttings in summer.
Z. pulverulenta illus. p.134.

ZEPHYRANTHES
Rain lily, Windflower

AMARYLLIDACEAE

Genus of clump-forming bulbs with an erect, crocus-like flower on each stem. Frost to half hardy. Needs a sheltered, sunny site and open, well-drained but moist soil. Container-grown bulbs need a dryish, warm period after foliage dies down in summer, followed by copious amounts of water to stimulate flowering. Propagate by seed in autumn or in spring.
Z. atamasco (Atamasco lily). Clump-forming, early summer-flowering bulb. H 15–25cm (6–10in), S 8–10cm (3–4in). Half hardy. Basal leaves are very narrow, grass-like and semi-erect. Each stem produces a widely funnel-shaped, purple-tinged, white flower, opening to 10cm (4in) wide, in spring or summer.
Z. candida illus. p.453.
Z. carinata. See *Z. grandiflora.*
Z. citrina. Clump-forming, autumn-flowering bulb. H 10–15cm (4–6in), S 5–8cm (2–3in). Half hardy. Has rush-like, erect, basal, green leaves. Stems produce funnel-shaped, bright yellow flowers, opening to 4–5cm (1½ –2in) wide, in autumn.
Z. grandiflora, syn. *Z. carinata, Z. rosea* of gardens, illus. p.440.
Z. robusta. See *Habranthus robustus.*
Z. rosea. Clump-forming, autumn-

flowering bulb. H 15–20cm (6–8in), S 8–10cm (3–4in). Half hardy. Has semi-erect, grass-like, basal, green leaves. Stems produce short-tubed, funnel-shaped, pink flowers.
Z. rosea of gardens. See *Z. grandiflora.*

ZIGADENUS

LILIACEAE/MELANTHIACEAE

Genus of summer-flowering bulbs with spikes of star-shaped, 6-petalled flowers. Frost hardy. It requires a position in sun or partial shade and well-drained soil. Water copiously in spring and summer, when in growth; less at other times. Remains dormant in winter. Propagate by division in early spring or by seed in autumn or spring. All parts are highly toxic if ingested.
Z. elegans. Clump-forming, summer-flowering bulb. H 30–50cm (12–20in), S 10–15cm (4–6in). Bears long, narrowly strap-shaped, semi-erect, basal leaves. Every stem produces a spike of greenish-white flowers, each 1cm (½in) wide and with a yellowish-green nectary near the base of every petal.
Z. fremontii illus. p.436.
Z. nuttallii. Clump-forming, summer-flowering bulb. H 30–60cm (12–24in), S 8cm (3in). Narrowly strap-shaped, semi-erect, basal leaves are mid- to dark green. Produces dense spikes of numerous, tiny, creamy-yellow flowers, each 6–8mm (¼–⅜in) across.

Zigzag bamboo. See *Phyllostachys flexuosa*, illus. p.320.

ZINNIA

COMPOSITAE/ASTERACEAE

Genus of annuals with large, dahlia-like flower heads that are excellent for cutting. Half hardy. Requires a position in sun and in fertile, well-drained soil. Dead flower heads should be removed regularly to promote flowering. Propagate by seed sown under glass in early spring.
***Z. angustifolia* 'Orange Star'.** See *Z. haageana* 'Orange Star'.**'Persian Carpet'** see *Z. haageana* 'Persian Carpet'.
Z. elegans. Moderately fast-growing, upright, sturdy annual. H 60–75cm (2–2½ft), S 30cm (1ft). Bears oval to lance-shaped leaves that are pale or mid-green. Dahlia-like, purple flower heads, over 5cm (2in) wide, are produced in summer and early autumn. Hybrids of *Z. elegans* are available in shades of yellow, red, pink, purple, cream or white.
Cactus-flowered Group, H 60–90cm (24–36in), have large, semi-double flower heads, similar to those of cactus dahlias, with long, narrow, quilled petals, in a broad range of colours.
Dreamland Series (pink) illus. p.334; (♀ scarlet) illus. p.340; (♀ yellow) ilus. p.350.
'Envy' illus. p.347.
Hobgoblin Series, H to 45cm (18in), produce sturdy, bushy plants, with small, single, weather-resistant flower heads in a broad range of colours.
Peter Pan Series, H 20cm (8in), are very dwarf, with double flower heads in a wide range of colours.
'Red Sun' illus. p.341.
Short Stuff Series, H 25cm (10in), are dwarf, with double flower heads in a broad range of colours.
Small World Series, H to 45cm (18in), are dwarf and produce long-lasting, double flower heads in an extensive range of colours, including pale pink.
'State Fair', H to 75cm (30in), is vigorous, and produces large, double, lavender, rose-pink, orange, purple or scarlet flower heads.
***Z. haageana* 'Classic'.** See *Z.h.* 'Orange Star'.**'Orange Star'** (syn. *Z. angustifolia* 'Orange Star', *Z. haageana* 'Classic') illus p.353.
'Persian Carpet' (syn. *Z. angustifolia* 'Persian Carpet') is a moderately fast-growing, upright, dwarf annual. H 38cm (15in), S 30cm (12in). Pale-green leaves are lance-shaped and hairy. Small, weather-resistant, dahlia-like, double flower heads, opening to over 2.5cm (1in) wide, are produced through the summer, in a range of colours.

Zinnia, Creeping. See *Sanvitalia procumbens*, illus. p.348.

ZIZANIA

GRAMINEAE/POACEAE

See also GRASSES, BAMBOOS, RUSHES and SEDGES.
Z. aquatica (Canada wild rice). Annual, grass-like, marginal water plant. H 3m (10ft), S 45cm (18in). Half hardy. Has grass-like, mid-green leaves and, in summer, grass-like, pale green flowers, followed by rice-like seeds that attract waterfowl. Needs sun; suitable for up to 23cm (9in) deep water. Propagate from seed stored damp and sown in spring.

Zygocactus truncatus. See *Schlumbergera truncata.*

ZYGOPETALUM

ORCHIDACEAE

See also ORCHIDS.
Z. mackaii, syn. *Z. mackayi* illus. p.310. Evergreen, epiphytic orchid for growing in a cool or intermediate greenhouse. H 30cm (12in). In autumn produces long sprays of fragrant, brown-blotched, green flowers, 8cm (3in) across, with reddish-indigo veins, and white lips. Ribbed leaves are narrowly oval, and 30cm (12in) long. Requires semi-shade in summer.
Z. mackayi. See *Z. mackaii.*
***Z.* Perrenoudii** illus. p.310. Evergreen, epiphytic orchid for a cool or intermediate greenhouse. H 30cm (12in). Spikes of fragrant, violet-purple-lipped, dark brown flowers, 8cm (3in) across, are produced in winter. Has narrowly oval, ribbed leaves, 30cm (12in) long. Requires a position in semi-shade in summer.

Glossary of Terms

Terms printed in italics refer to other glossary entries.

Acid [of soil]. With a *pH* value of less than 7; see also *alkaline* and *neutral*.

Adventitious [of roots]. Arising directly from a stem or leaf.

Aerial root. See *root*.

Air-layering. A method of propagation by which a portion of stem is induced to root by enclosing it in a suitable medium such as damp moss and securing it with plastic sheeting; roots will form if the moss is kept moist.

Alkaline [of soil]. With a *pH* value of more than 7; some plants will not tolerate alkaline soils and must be grown in *neutral* or *acid* soil.

Alpine house. An unheated greenhouse, used for the cultivation of mainly alpine and bulbous plants, that provides greater ventilation and usually more light than a conventional greenhouse.

Alternate [of leaves]. Borne singly at each *node*, on either side of a stem.

Annual. A plant that completes its life cycle, from germination through to flowering and seeding and then death, in one growing season.

Anther. The part of a *stamen* that produces pollen; it is usually borne on a *filament*.

Apex. The tip or growing point of an organ such as a leaf or shoot.

Areole. A modified, cushion-like *tubercle*, peculiar to the family Cactaceae, that bears hairs, spines, leaves, side-branches or flowers.

Asclepiad. A member of the family Asclepiadaceae, e.g. *Asclepias*, *Hoya*, *Stephanotis*.

Auricle. An ear-like lobe such as is sometimes found at the base of a leaf.

Awn. A stiff, bristle-like projection commonly found on grass seeds and *spikelets*.

Axil. The angle between a leaf and stem where an axillary bud develops.

Bedding plant. A plant that is mass-planted to provide a temporary display.

Biennial. A plant that flowers, seeds and dies in the second season after germination, producing only stems, roots and leaves in the first season.

Blade. The flattened and often broad part of a leaf.

Bloom. 1. A flower or blossom. 2. A fine, waxy, whitish or bluish-white coating on stems, leaves or fruits.

Bog garden. An area where the soil is kept permanently damp but not waterlogged.

Bole. The trunk of a *tree* from ground level to the first major branch.

Bolt. To produce flowers and seed prematurely, particularly in the case of vegetables such as lettuce and beetroot.

Bonsai. A method of producing dwarf trees or shrubs by special techniques that include pruning roots, pinching out shoots, removing growth buds and training branches and stems.

Bract. A modified leaf at the base of a flower or flower cluster. Bracts may resemble normal leaves or be reduced and scale-like in appearance; they are often large and brightly coloured.

Bud. A rudimentary or condensed shoot containing embryonic leaves or flowers.

Bulb. A storage organ consisting mainly of fleshy scales and swollen, modified leaf-bases on a much reduced stem. Bulbs usually, but not always, grow underground.

Bulbil. A small, *bulb*-like organ, often borne in a leaf *axil*, occasionally in a *flower head*; it may be used for propagation.

Bulblet. A small *bulb* produced at the base of a mature one.

Bur. 1. A prickly or spiny *fruit*, or aggregate of fruits. 2. A woody outgrowth on the stems of certain trees.

Cactus (pl. cacti). A member of the family Cactaceae, often *succulent* and spiny.

Calyx (pl. calyces). The outer part of a flower, usually small and green but sometimes showy and brightly coloured, that encloses the petals in bud and is formed from the *sepals*.

Capsule. A dry *fruit* that splits open when ripe to release its seeds.

Carpel. The female portion of a flower, or part of it, consisting of an *ovary*, *stigma* and *style*.

Catkin. A flower cluster, normally pendulous. Flowers lack petals, are often stalkless, surrounded by scale-like *bracts*, and are usually unisexual.

Caudex (pl. caudices). The stem base of a woody plant such as a *palm* or tree fern.

Cladode. A stem, often flattened, with the function and appearance of a leaf.

Claw. The narrow, basal portion of petals in some genera, e.g. *Dianthus*.

Climber. A plant that climbs using other plants or objects as a support: a **leaf-stalk** climber by coiling its leaf stalks around supports; a **root** climber by producing aerial, supporting roots; a **self-clinging** climber by means of suckering pads; a **tendril** climber by coiling its tendrils; a **twining** climber by coiling stems. **Scandent**, **scrambling** and **trailing climbers** produce long stems that grow over plants or other supports; they attach themselves only loosely, if at all.

Clone. A group of genetically identical plants, propagated vegetatively.

Compound. Made up of several or many parts, e.g. a leaf divided into 2 or more *leaflets*.

Cone. The clustered flowers or woody, seed-bearing structures of a conifer.

Coppice. To cut back to near ground level each year in order to produce vigorous, ornamental shoots, as is usual with some *Cornus* and *Eucalyptus*.

Cordon. A trained plant restricted in growth to one main stem, occasionally 2–4 stems.

Corm. A *bulb*-like, underground storage organ consisting mainly of a swollen stem base and often surrounded by a papery tunic.

Cormlet. A small *corm* arising at the base of a mature one.

Corolla. The part of a flower formed by the petals.

Corona (crown). A petal-like outgrowth sometimes borne on the *corolla*, e.g. the trumpet or cup of a *Narcissus*.

Corymb. A racemose flower cluster in which the inner flower stalks are shorter than the outer, resulting in a rounded or flat-topped head.

Cotyledon. See *seed leaf*.

Creeper. A plant that grows close to the ground, usually rooting as it spreads.

Crisped. Minutely wavy-edged.

Crown. 1. The part of the plant at or just below the soil surface from which new shoots are produced and to which they die back in autumn. 2. The upper, branched part of a tree above the *bole*. 3. A *corona*.

Culm. The usually hollow stem of a grass or bamboo.

Cutting. A section of a plant that is removed and used for propagation. The various types of cutting are: **basal** – taken from the base of a plant (usually *herbaceous*) as it begins to produce growth in spring; **greenwood** – made from the tip of young growth; **hardwood** – mature wood taken at the end of the growing season; **leaf** – a detached leaf or part of a leaf; **root** – part of a semi-mature or mature root; **semi-ripe** – half-ripened wood taken during the growing season; **softwood** – young growth taken at the beginning of the growing season; **stem** – a greenwood, hardwood, semi-ripe or softwood cutting; **tip** – a greenwood cutting.

Cyme. A flower cluster in which each growing point terminates in a flower.

Dead-head. To remove spent flower heads so as to promote further growth or flowering, prevent seeding or improve appearance.

Deciduous. Losing its leaves annually at the end of the growing season; **semi-deciduous** plants lose only some leaves.

Decumbent. Growing close to the ground but ascending at the tips.

Dentate. With toothed margins.

Die-back. Death of the tips of shoots due to frost or disease.

Dioecious. Bearing male and female flowers on separate plants.

Disbud. To remove surplus buds to promote larger flowers or fruits.

Disc floret, disc flower. A small and often individually inconspicuous, usually tubular flower, one of many that comprise the central portion of a composite flower head such as a daisy.

Division. A method of propagation by which a clump is divided into several parts during dormancy.

Elliptic [of leaves]. Broadening in the centre and narrowing towards each end.

Entire [of leaves]. With untoothed margins.

Epiphyte. A plant that in nature grows on the surface of another without being parasitic.

Evergreen. Retaining its leaves at the end of the growing season although losing some older leaves regularly throughout the year; **semi-evergreen** plants retain only some leaves or lose older leaves only when the new growth is produced.

F1 hybrid. The first generation derived from crossing 2 distinct plants, usually when the parents are pure-bred lines and the offspring are vigorous. Seed from F1 hybrids does not come *true* to type.

Fall. An outer *perianth segment* of an iris, which projects outwards or downwards from the inner segments.

Fan palm. A *palm* with *palmate* rather than *pinnate* leaves.

Farina. A powdery, white, sometimes yellowish deposit naturally occurring on some leaves and flowers.

Fibrous root. A fine, young root, usually one of many.

Filament. The stalk of an *anther*.

Floret. A single flower in a head of many flowers.

Flower. The basic flower forms are: **single**, with one row of usually 4–6 *petals*; **semi-double**, with more petals, usually in 2 rows; **double**, with many petals in several rows and few or no *stamens*; **fully double**, usually rounded in shape, with densely packed petals and the stamens absent or obscured.

Flower head. A mass of small *flowers* or *florets* that together appear as one flower, e.g. a daisy.

Force. To induce artificially the early production of growth, flowers or *fruits*.

Frond. The leaf-like organ of a fern. Some ferns produce both barren and fertile fronds, the fertile fronds bearing *spores*.

Fruit. The structure in plants that bears one or more ripe seeds, e.g. a berry or nut.

Glabrous. Not hairy.

Glaucous. Bluish-white, bluish-green or bluish-grey.

Globose. Spherical.

Glochid. One of the barbed bristles or hairs, usually small, borne on a cactus *areole*.

Grafting. A method of propagation by which an artificial union is made between different parts of individual plants; usually the *shoot* (scion) of one is grafted onto the *rootstock* (stock) of another.

Heel. The small portion of old wood that is retained at the base of a cutting when it is removed from the stem.

Herbaceous. Dying down at the end of the growing season.

Hose-in-hose [of flowers]. With one *corolla* borne inside another, forming a double or semi-double *flower*.

Inflorescence. A cluster of flowers with a distinct arrangement, e.g. *corymb*, *cyme*, *panicle*, *raceme*, *spike*, *umbel*.

Insectivorous plant. A plant that traps and digests insects and other small animals to supplement its nutrient intake.

Key. A winged seed such as those produced by the sycamore (*Acer pseudoplatanus*).

Lateral. A side growth that arises from the side of a shoot or root.

Layering. A method of propagation by which a stem is induced to root by being pegged down into the soil while it is still attached to the parent plant. See also *air-layering*.

Leaflet. The subdivision of a compound leaf.

Lenticel. A small, usually corky area on a stem or other part of a plant, which acts as a breathing pore.

Lime. Compounds of calcium; the amount of lime in soil determines whether it is *alkaline*, *neutral* or *acid*.

Linear [of leaves]. Very narrow with parallel sides.

Lip. A lobe comprising 2 or more flat or sometimes pouched *perianth segments*.

Loam. Well-structured, fertile soil that is moisture-retentive but free-draining.

Marginal water plant. A plant that grows partially submerged in shallow water or in moist soil at the edge of a pond.

Midrib. The main, central vein of a leaf or the central stalk to which the *leaflets* of a *pinnate* leaf are attached.

Monocarpic. Flowering and fruiting only once before dying; such plants may take several years to reach flowering size.

Mulch. A layer of organic matter applied to the soil over or around a plant to conserve moisture, protect the roots from frost, reduce the growth of weeds and enrich the soil.

Naturalize. To establish and grow as if in the wild.

Nectar. A sweet, sugary liquid secreted by the **nectary** – glandular tissue usually found in the flower but sometimes found on the leaves or stems.

Neutral [of soil]. With a *pH* value of 7, the point at which soil is neither *acid* nor *alkaline*.

Node. The point on a stem from which a leaf or leaves arise.

Offset. A small plant that arises by natural vegetative reproduction, usually at the base of the mother plant.

Opposite [of leaves]. Borne 2 to each *node*, one opposite the other.

Ovary. The part of the female portion of the flower, containing embryonic seeds, that will eventually form the *fruit*.

Palm. An evergreen *tree* or *shrub*-like plant, normally single-stemmed, with *palmate* or *pinnate* leaves usually in terminal rosettes; strictly a member of the family Palmae.

Palmate. Lobed in the fashion of a hand, strictly with 5 lobes arising from the same point.

Pan. A shallow, free-draining pot in which alpine plants or bulbs are grown.

Panicle. A branched *raceme*.

Papilla (pl. papillae). A minute protuberance or gland-like structure.

Pea-like [of flowers]. Of the same structure as a pea flower.

Peat bed. A specially constructed area, edged with peat blocks and containing moisture-retentive, acidic, peaty soil.

Pedicel. The stalk of an individual flower.

Peduncle. The stalk of a flower cluster.

Peltate [of leaves]. Shield-shaped, with the stalk inserted towards or at the centre of the blade and not at the margin.

Perennial. Living for at least 3 seasons. In this book the term when used as a noun, and unless qualified, denotes an *herbaceous* perennial. A woody-based perennial dies down only partially, leaving a woody stem at the base.

Perianth. The outer parts of the flower comprising the *calyx* and the *corolla*. The term is often used when the calyx and the corolla are very similar in form.

Perianth segment. One portion of the *perianth*, resembling a *petal* and sometimes known as a tepal.

Petal. One portion of the often showy and coloured part of the *corolla*. In some families, e.g. Liliaceae, the *perianth segments* are petal-like and referred to horticulturally as petals.

Petaloid. Like a petal.

Petiole. The stalk of a *leaf*.

pH. The scale by which the acidity or alkalinity of soil is measured. See also *acid*, *alkaline*, *neutral*.

Phyllode. A flattened leaf stalk, which functions as and resembles a leaf.

Pinch out. To remove the growing tips of a plant to induce the production of side-shoots.

Pinna (pl. pinnae). The primary division of a *pinnate* leaf. The fertile pinnae of ferns produce *spores*, vegetative pinnae do not.

Pinnate [of leaves]. Compound, with *leaflets* arranged on opposite sides of a central stalk.

Pistil. The female part of a flower comprising the *ovary*, *stigma* and *style*.

Pollard [of a tree]. To cut back to its main branches in order to restrict growth.

Pollination. The transfer of pollen from the *anthers* to the *stigma* of the same or different flowers, resulting in the fertilization of the embryonic seeds in the *ovary*.

Procumbent. Prostrate, creeping along the ground.

Raceme. An unbranched flower cluster with several or many stalked flowers borne singly along a main axis, the youngest at the apex.

Ray floret, ray flower. One of the flowers, usually with strap-shaped petals, that together form the outer ring of flowers in a composite *flower head* such as a daisy.

Ray petal. The petal or fused petals, often showy, of a ray *floret*.

Recurved. Curved backwards.

Reflexed. Bent sharply backwards.

Revert. To return to its original state, as when a plain green leaf is produced on a variegated plant.

Rhizome. An underground, creeping stem that acts as a storage organ and bears leafy shoots.

Root. The part of a plant, normally underground, that functions as anchorage and through which water and nutrients are absorbed. An **aerial root** emerges from the stem at some distance above the soil level.

Rootball. The roots and accompanying soil or compost visible when a plant is lifted.

Rootstock. A well-rooted plant onto which a scion is grafted; see *grafting*.

Rosette. A group of leaves radiating from approximately the same point, often borne at ground level at the base of a very short stem.

Runner. A horizontally spreading, usually slender stem that forms roots at each node; often confused with *stolon*.

Scale. 1. A reduced or modified leaf. 2.-Part of a conifer *cone*.

Scandent. See *climber*.

Scarify. To scar the coat of a seed by abrasion in order to speed water intake and hence germination.

Scion. See *grafting*.

Scree. An area composed of a deep layer of stone chippings mixed with a small amount of loam. It provides extremely sharp drainage for plants that resent moisture at their base.

Seed head. Any usually dry *fruit* that contains ripe seeds.

Seed leaf (cotyledon). The first leaf, pair of leaves or occasionally group of leaves produced by a seed as it germinates. In some plants they remain below ground.

Self-seed. To produce seedlings around the parent plant.

Sepal. Part of a *calyx*, usually insignificant but sometimes showy.

Series. The name applied to a group of similar but not identical plants, usually annuals, linked by one or more common features.

Sessile. Without a stalk.

Sheath. A cylindrical structure that surrounds or encircles, partially or fully, another plant organ such as a stem.

Shoot. The aerial part of a plant which bears leaves. A **side-shoot** arises from the side of a main shoot.

Shrub. A plant with *woody stems*, usually well-branched from or near the base.

Shy-flowering. Reluctant to flower; producing few flowers.

Simple [of leaves]. Not divided into leaflets.

Soft-stemmed. The opposite of *woody-stemmed.*

Spadix (pl. spadices). A *spike*-like flower cluster that is usually fleshy and bears numerous small flowers. Spadices are characteristic of the family Araceae, e.g. *Arum*.

Spathe. A large *bract*, or sometimes 2, frequently coloured and showy, that surrounds a *spadix* (as in *Arum*) or an individual flower bud (as in *Narcissus*).

Sphagnum. Mosses common to bogs; their moisture-retentive character makes them ideal components of some growing media. They are used particularly for orchid cultivation.

Spike. A racemose flower cluster with several or many unstalked flowers borne along a common axis.
Spikelet. 1. The flowering unit of grasses comprising one or several flowers with basal *bracts*. 2. A small *spike*, part of a branched flower cluster.

Spore. The minute reproductive structure of flowerless plants, e.g. ferns, fungi and mosses.

Sporangium (pl. sporangia). A body that produces *spores*.

Sport. A mutation, caused by an accidental or induced change in the genetic make-up of a plant, which gives rise to a shoot with different characteristics to those of the parent plant.

Spur. 1. A hollow projection from a petal, often producing *nectar*. 2. A short stem bearing a group of flower buds such as is found on fruit trees.

Spur back. To cut back side-shoots to within 2 or 3 buds of the main shoot.

Stamen. The *anther* and *filament*.

Standard. 1. A *tree* or *shrub* with a clear length of bare stem below the first branches. Certain shrubs, e.g. roses and fuchsias, may be trained to form standards. 2. One of the 3 inner and often erect *perianth segments* of the iris flower. 3. The larger, usually upright back petal of a flower in the family Leguminosae, e.g. *Lathyrus*.

Stapeliad. A member of the genus *Stapelia* and closely related genera of the family Asclepiadaceae.

Stem segment. A portion of a jointed stem between 2 *nodes*, most frequently occurring in cacti.

Sterile. Infertile, not bearing *spores*, pollen, seeds etc.

Stigma. The part of the female portion of the flower, borne at the tip of the *style*, that receives pollen.

Stipule. A small scale, or leaf-like appendage, usually one of a pair, mostly borne at a *node* or below a leaf stalk.

Stock. See *rootstock*.

Stolon. A horizontally spreading or arching stem, usually above ground, which roots at its tip to produce a new plant.

Stop. To remove certain growing points of a plant so as to control growth or the size and number of flowers.

Stratify. To break the dormancy of some seeds by exposing them to a period of cold.

Style. The part of the flower on which the *stigma* is borne.

Sub-globose. Almost spherical.

Sub-shrub. A plant that is woody at the base although the terminal shoots die back in winter.

Succulent. A plant with thick, fleshy leaves and/or stems; in this book, it is evergreen unless otherwise stated.

Sucker. A shoot that arises from below ground level, directly from the *root* or *rootstock*.

Summer-deciduous. Losing its leaves naturally in summer.

Taproot. The main, downward-growing root of a plant; it is also applied generally to any strong, downward-growing root.

Tendril. A thread-like structure, used to provide support; see also *climber*.

Tooth. A small, marginal, often pointed lobe on a leaf, *calyx* or *corolla*.

Tepal. See *perianth segment*.

Tree. A woody plant usually having a well-defined trunk or stem with a head of branches above.

Trifoliate. With 3 leaves; loosely, with 3 *leaflets*; **trifoliolate,** with 3 *leaflets*.

True [of seedlings]. Retaining the distinctive characteristics of the parent when raised from seed.

Truss. A compact cluster of flowers, often large and showy, e.g. those of pelargoniums and rhododendrons.

Tuber. A thickened, usually underground, storage organ derived from a stem or root.

Tubercle. A small, rounded protuberance; see also *areole*.

Turion. 1. A bud on a *rhizome*. 2. A fleshy, overwintering bud found on certain water plants.

Umbel. A usually flat-topped or rounded flower cluster in which the individual flower stalks arise from a central point. In a compound umbel each primary stalk ends in an umbel.

Upright [of habit]. With vertical or semi-vertical main branches.

Water bud. See *turion*.

Whorl. The arrangement of 3 or more organs arising from the same point.

Winged [of seeds or fruits]. Having a marginal flange or membrane.

Woody-stemmed. With a stem composed of woody fibres and therefore persistent, as opposed to soft-stemmed and *herbaceous*. A **semi-woody stem** contains some softer tissue and may be only partially persistent.

× The sign used to denote a hybrid plant derived from the crossing of 2 or more botanically distinct plants.
+ The sign used to denote a graft hybrid; see *grafting*.

Acknowledgements

1	4	7	10
2	5	8	11
3	6	9	12

The publisher would like to thank the following for their kind permission to reproduce their photographs. Most of the photographs are found in the Plant Catalogue and are referenced by two numbers: the page number is given first, followed by the specific number or numbers of the photographs separated by hyphens. The photograph number is determined by the position of the photograph's caption according to one of two page grids. The twelve grid is shown alongside. The same numbering principle has been used for photographs in the feature panels, with numbers from 1 to 42; illustrations elsewhere in the book use the key: A=above; B=below; C=centre; L=left; R=right; T=top.

Every effort has been made to trace the copyright holders. Dorling Kindersley apologizes for any unintentional ommissions, and would be pleased, if any such case should arise, to add an appropriate acknowledgement in future editions.

Anne Green Armytage 3/C, 256/8, 257/5, 12
Alpine Garden Society Slide Library 298/41, 346/5, 360/4–9, 366/3, 368/11, 374/3, 376/10, 385/9, 387/12, 390/6, 391/5, 395/5, 400/3, 408/10, 412/3, 444/13, 445/2–26, 451/1, 452/9
Claire Austin 234/13-17, 19, 21–23; 235/7, 236/7, 9, 13, 16, 17, 21; 237/4, 7, 8, 10, 13, 17, 18
Jacques Amand Ltd/John Amand 238/5–26, 299/42, 447/24
Aylett Nurseries 420/7
A–Z Botanical Collection 140/26, 171/9, 192/6, 195/10, 216/11, 234/35, 244/35, 292/7, 359/6, 386/2, 416/31, 463/2–10, 464/6; Malcolm Richards 13/Row4/1; A. Young 13/Row5/2
Gillian Beckett 115/1, 119/2–3, 128/21, 136/5, 141/1, 146/5, 150/4, 151/7, 158/12, 164/12, 167/1, 170/11, 217/6, 254/4, 255/4, 260/12, 262/1, 272/1, 281/12, 302/5, 304/3, 323/4, 325/10, 332/1, 360/5, 366/11, 368/12, 372/2, 373/1, 375/1, 379/11, 380/12, 385/1, 386/8–9, 389/6, 390/1, 393/10, 395/2, 397/3, 401/1, 414/9, 417/5–33, 428/3–6, 429/3–6, 430/10, 431/3, 433/21–38, 437/3, 439/6, 447/37, 448/2–3, 449/8, 450/1, 451/7, 455/9–10, 456/3–7, 462/6, 464/7–9
Kenneth A. Beckett 73/4, 202/3, 378/2, 380/4
Biofotos/Heather Angel 201/8, 464/12
Bloom Pictures 16B, 17B, 264/13, 21
Patrick Booth/John Thirkell 230/26–37–38
Ann & Roger Bowden 298/35, 299/15
Christopher Brickell 89/4, 96/1, 127/2–4, 128/17, 129/4–25, 130/6, 131/1, 138/12, 143/4, 144/1–5, 160/22, 201/4; 244/19
Pat Brindley 132/4, 204/12, 213/4, 235/5, 239/20, 244/26, 252/30, 307/19, 325/4, 332/2, 333/8, 334/11, 336/8–12, 337/1, 338/10, 340/1–12, 341/1, 343/6, 344/3–4, 345/9, 348/4, 353/6, 411/5, 426/23, 427/8–41, 428/13–17–27–31, 445/7–29–37, 464/8
British Iris Society 235/2–14–20
Jonathan Buckley 125/2
Brinsley Burbridge 205/12
Ray Cobb 445/9
Eric Crichton 61/5, 66/4, 67/2, 89/1, 93/3, 95/10, 139/3, 153/9, 164/4, 173/11, 204/10, 213/1, 231/3, 234/7–15–29, 240/3, 245/1, 261/1–10, 292/10, 308/22, 309/10, 325/9, 332/10, 336/7, 350/7, 361/9, 364/1, 366/10, 367/1, 369/9, 370/3, 381/1, 387/3, 391/1, 394/9, 395/3, 399/3, 408/7, 421/9, 426/17, 435/11, 436/1, 445/31, 466/31
Philip Damp 420/33
DK Images: Jacqui Hurst 2; James Young 6, 36, 108-9/T, 251/16; Steven Wooster 31, 174/6, 71B, 393/8; Beth Chatto 33, 47; Dave Watts 40T; Clive Boursnell 40B, 219; Michael Booher 250/3; Andrew Butler 71T, 236/10; Neil Fletcher 95/6, 13, 128/1, 3, 7, 15, 18, 129/3, 130/22, 24, 234/1, 235/10, 268/1, 427/21, 24, 428/8, 12, 433/14, 18, 445/6; Deni Bown 95/14, 107/27, 248/5, 249/9, 19, 28, 269/4, 291/3; Juliet Wade 106/25, 128/4; John Glover 124/16; Jonathan Buckley 128/2, 219/19, 254/9, 281/1, 300/2, 4, 18 301/8, 10, 387/8; Howard Rice 128/7, 130/20 250/2, 283/2, 12, 13, 14, 299/16; Geoff Dann 301, Tom Woodham 238/11; Craig Knowles 248/1; Roger Smith 250/10, 12 251/1, 252/4, 9,13, 283/9, 299/14, 300/1, 301/17, 404-5/1, 432/6 Andrew Lawson 251/14, 252/12, 362/2; Bill Balham 128/9, 130/1; John Fielding 254/1, Colin Walton 298/14
Kate Donald 432/21–28
Alan M. Edwards 434/2, 444/17
Raymond J. Evison 208/3–5, 8–10, 27–31, 32–39; 209/1, 4–9, 11–15, 17–33, 35–41; 210/1, 4–9, 11–15; 211/1–6, 12, 13
John Fielding 33/BR, 36/BL, 44/TL, 46/TL, 47/TR, 49/TR
Valerie Finnis 366/7
Ron & Christine Foord 280/11
Maureen Foster 235/13
John Galbally 291/10
Garden Exposure 263/6, 8-10, 12-13
Garden Photo Library 264/16
Garden Picture Library Brian Carter 40/TR; Eric Crichton 442&443; Geoff Dann 44/CR; Ron Evans 112&113, 342&343; John Glover 180&181, 222&223, 252/37, 259/10, 265/5, 14, 329/BC, 356/TC; Neil Holmes 200/6, 202/4, 239/19; Mayer/Le Scanff 461/BR; Jerry Pavia 314&315, 351/5, 356&357/T, 452&453; Morley Read 39/TR; Howard Rice 343/12, 407/L; JS Sira 35/BR, 41/TL, 179/TL; Ron Sutherland 357/BL; Brigitte Thomas 36&37/T; Steven Wooster 178/CL, 200&201, 198/BL, 264/1, 20, 417/3
Garden World Images 256/4, 14, 257/2, 4, 6, 7, 10, 11, 13, 15; 340/8, 348/3 ,350/1, 351/4, 416/1, 418/17
John Glover 127/3, 130/27, 154/8, 244/42, 253/9, 256/2, 5-7, 13-15, 257/8, 13, 15, 17, 19, 296/1, 331/5,10, 338/3-4, 339/2, 416/8, 17, 418/18, 419/1, 459/3
Derek Gould 112/11, 120/11, 130/4, 131/4, 140/40, 146/6, 149/6, 153/10, 166/2, 201/10, 204/7, 216/6, 233/7, 238/21, 242/4, 243/3, 6, 8, 253/1, 259/12, 266/11, 276/12, 280/34, 287/6, 289/8, 302/3, 334/3 346/11, 359/2, 371/7, 398/7, 402/4, 409/7, 428/11, 421/8, 443/3, 463/7
Diana Grenfell 263/6, 10, 299/18
Christopher Grey–Wilson 10/BL
Peter Harkness 194/3, 4
Jerry Harpur 51/BL, 51/TR 263/2, 418/3,
Marcus Harpur 349/2, 416/2, 417/19, 20, Cherry Williams, 418/2, 9, 419/16, 19
The Heather Society Slide Library 13/Row5/3, 174/12
Terry Hewitt 472/9, 488/2, 490/2, 496/1
D. Hewlett 421/23
Muriel Hodgeman 365/11, 371/10, 395/12, 397/1
Hortico 434/15
International Flower Bulb Centre 311/7, 447/35
The Image Biz 257/1, 9
Mike Ireland 379/2, 386/3, 389/7, 445/4–38
Brita Johansson 175/22
Roy Lancaster 11/C–CR
Andrew Lawson 18/Hodges Barn, 19/T, 2, 32/Beth Chatto, 34, 35/Exbury Gardens, 37, 38, 39, 41, 42, 43, 44, 45, 48, 49, 50, 51, 52, 53, 54, 55/Spetchly Park,Worcs, 47/Beth Chatto, 60&61, 110/BR, 178&179/B, 201/9, 216/11–16, 256/9-11, 257/16, 16, 263/3, 265/15-16, 336/1, 338/2, 340/1, 392&393, 416/4, 13, 20, 417/2, 5, 418/6, 16, 419/4, 11
Sidney Linnegar 234/4 (G.E. Cassidy)–11 (R. Henley)–31 (R. Henley)–37 (G.E. Cassidy), 235/3–34 (G.E. Cassidy)– 40 (G.E. Cassidy)
Clive Nichols 16/1, 17/3
Brian Mathew 414/3, 430/11, 435/1–4, 437/9, 439/11, 440/3, 442/9, 450/11
S. & O. Mathews 151/7
Marianne Majerus 417/1
Dr E. Charles Nelson 13/Row2/2–Row3/1
Oxford Scientific Films/Fredrik Ehrenstrom 465/11
Photos Horticultural 101/3, 200/3, 231/12, 234/10, 239/1, 244/18–21, 287/3, 334/2, 341/1, 347/5, 348/10, 380/4, 413/8, 417/11, 440/2, 464/6
Plant Pictures Worldwide 351/2
Picturesmiths 230, 234/1, 3, 7, 11, 13, 235/9, 11, 14, 16, 20, 24-25, 27 236/18, 237/20, 23, 24, 31, 32; 257/18, 418/7, 15
Collection & Photo Riviere (**France, 26 Drôme**) 238/19, 239/23–36
Howard Rice 14 & 15, 34 & 35, 202/5, 460 & 461/B
Royal Botanic Gardens, Kew 11/TR
Royal Horticultural Society, Lindley Library 11BL Curtis's Botanical Magazine (CBM), cliv (1928), T.9241; 433 CBM, vii (1794), T.258
A.D. Schilling 79/10, 86/11, 128/4, 162/8, 165/9
Harry Smith Collection 13/Row1/1, 61/6, 65/3–12, 66/1, 67/4–10, 68/7–10, 71/7–22–36, 76/4–11(inset), 77/3, 78/6–8, 79/9, 85/6, 87/1–6, 88/3–12, 89/2–6–7–9, 91/8, 93/4–6, 98/1, 100/3–12, 102/9, 104/8–12, 105/6, 107/33, 112/7, 113/1–6, 114/11, 115/4, 117/11, 119/1, 120/1–7, 121/6, 122/9, 125/26–32, 126/12, 127/5–11, 128/20–22–27–32–35, 129/16, 130/16, 131/2, 137/4, 138/7, 139/5, 141/9,

142/7, 143/2–5–12, 144/10, 145/2, 146/1, 147/11, 150/7, 151/3–6, 154/12, 155/25, 156/6, 160/24–36, 161/12, 163/8–10, 166/10, 167/3, 168/6, 169/5–6–12, 173/7, 192/8, 195/1–2–3, 200/10, 202/7, 203/3, 204/1–9, 205/3–9, 206/1–5–6, 207/2–3–7, 212/2–3–4, 215/2–12, 216/8–10, 217/2–3, 218/12, 219/26, 224/3, 226/9, 230/19–35–40, 231/9, 232/1–5, 235/4–23, 238/15, 239/17–18–37, 240/10, 244/13–19–29, 246/11, 252/33–40, 260/6, 263/16, 266/9, 271/9–10, 274/1, 276/8, 277/7, 278/1–4, 279/8, 281/1–4–18, 285/12, 288/6, 292/1–9, 293/12, 296/4, 297/6, 298/26–38, 305/6–10, 307/19, 331/10–12, 332/4, 333/4–9, 339/1, 341/11, 342/4, 343/3–4–5–7, 344/12, 346/3–4–6–7, 350/10, 351/4–8–9, 352/9, 353/4–8–9, 359/1–5, 361/2–10, 363/9, 364/6, 368/9, 369/6, 372/1–4–7, 373/4, 376/5–12, 377/9, 378/11, 380/10, 381/9–11, 383/6–7–8–10, 385/2, 387/5–9, 392/12, 393/5, 395/1–7, 398/8–9, 399/8–12, 400/4, 403/6, 409/4, 410/2, 411/14–26–32–37, 412/1–2, 413/12, 414/5, 415/12, 416/12–15–17–18–19, 417/10–12–19–40, 424/1–6, 425/6, 427/32, 428/5–38, 429/12, 430/6, 431/6, 436/7, 437/6, 438/7–9, 439/1, 440/9, 441/1–11, 442/7, 443/12, 444/16–28–30–42, 445/8–16–34, 446/10, 448/1–4–11, 450/9, 451/3, 452/1–7–10, 453/11, 454/1–4, 455/4, 456/2–11, 457/4–7–10, 463/3–4–12, 465/7–10, 466/11, 483/7, 491/10

Suttons Seeds 339/4
Thompson & Morgan 256/12, 345/12, 347/6, 348/1
Unwin Seeds Ltd 334/12, 338/9, 340/9, 343/9, 344/1, 348/3, 352/3
Van Staaveren Aalsmeer BV 441/12
W.B. Wade 268/6–13–29–30–33–38, 269/6–13–16–18–21–22–27–28
Jack Wemyss–Cooke 281/13–14–35
John Wright 160/3, 165/10.

Picture research Andrew Brown, Susan Mennel
Picture research for the second edition Anna Lord
Picture research for the fourth edition Melanie Watson

The publishers would like to thank all those who generously assisted the photographers and provided plants for photography, in particular the curators, directors and staff of the following organizations and those private individuals listed below. Special thanks are due to those at the Royal Botanic Gardens, Kew, and the Royal Horticultural Society's Garden, Wisley, for their invaluable assistance and support.

African Violet Centre, Terrington St Clement, Norfolk; Ken Akers, Great Saling, Essex; Jacques Amand Ltd, Clamphill, Middx; Anmore Exotics, Havant, Hants; David Austin Roses, Albrighton, Shrops; Avon Bulbs, Bradford-on-Avon, Wilts; Ayletts Nurseries, St Albans, Herts; Steven Bailey Ltd, Sway, Hants; Bill Baker, Tidmarsh, Berks; Batsford Arboretum, Moreton-in-Marsh, Glos; Booker Seeds, Sleaford, Lincs; Rupert Bowlby, Reigate, Surrey; Bressingham Gardens, Diss, Norfolk; Roy Brooks, Newent, Glos; British Orchid Growers' Association; Broadleigh Gardens, Somerset; Burford House Gardens, Tenbury Wells, Shrops; Cambridge Bulbs, Newton, Cambs; Nola Carr, Sydney, Australia; Beth Chatto Gardens, Colchester, Essex; Chelsea Physic Garden, London; Colegrave Seeds, Banbury, Oxon; County Park Nurseries, Hornchurch, Essex; Jill Cowley, Chelmsford, Essex; Mrs Anne Dexter, Oxford; Edrom Nurseries, Coldingham, Berwicks; Dr Jack Elliott, Ashford, Kent; Joe Elliott, Broadwell, Glos; Erdigg (National Trust), Clwyd, Wales; Fibrex Nurseries, Pebworth, Warwicks; Fisk's Clematis Nursery, Westleton, Suffolk; Mr & Mrs Thomas Gibson, Westwell, Oxon; Glasgow Botanic Garden, Glasgow; 'Glazenwood', Braintree, Essex.

R. Harkness & Co. Ltd, Hitchin, Herts; Harry Hay, Lower Kingswood, Surrey; Hazeldene Nurseries, East Farleigh, Kent; Hidcote Manor (National Trust), Chipping Camden, Glos; Hillier Gardens and Arboretum, Romsey, Hants; Hillier Nurseries (Winchester) Ltd, Romsey, Hants; Holly Gate Cactus Nursery, Ashington, Sussex; Hopleys Plants, Much Hadham, Herts; Huntingdon Botanical Gardens, San Marino, California; W.E.Th. Ingwersen Ltd, East Grinstead, Sussex; the late Clive Innes; Kelways Nurseries, Langport, Somerset; Kiftsgate Court Gardens, Chipping Camden, Glos; Lechlade Fuchsia Centre, Lechlade, Glos; The Living Desert, Palm Desert, California; Robin Loder, Leonardslee, Sussex; Los Angeles State and County Arboreta and Botanical Gardens, Los Angeles, California; Lotusland Foundation, Santa Barbara, California; McBeans Orchids, Lewes, Sussex; Merrist Wood Agricultural College, Worplesdon, Surrey; Mrs J.F. Phillips, Westwell, Oxon; Mr & Mrs Richard Purdon, Ramsden, Oxon; Ramparts Nurseries, Colchester, Essex; Ratcliffe Orchids, Didcot, Oxon; Mrs Joyce Robinson, Denmans, Fontwell, Sussex; Peter Q. Rose, Castle Cary, Somerset; Royal Botanic Garden, Edinburgh; Royal Botanic Gardens, Kew, Surrey; Royal Botanic Gardens, Sydney, Australia; Royal National Rose Society, St Albans, Herts; Royal Horticultural Society's Garden, Wisley, Surrey.

Santa Barbara Botanic Garden, Santa Barbara, California; Savill Garden, Windsor, Berks; Mr & Mrs K. Schoenenberger, Shipton-under-Wychwood, Oxon; Mrs Martin Simmons, Burghclere, Berks; Dr James Smart, Barnstaple, Devon; Arthur Smith, Wigston, Leics; P.J. Smith, Ashington, Sussex; Springfields Gardens, Spalding, Lincs; Staite & Sons, Evesham, Worcs; Stapeley Water Gardens, Nantwich, Cheshire; Strybing Arboreta Society of Golden Gate Park, San Francisco, California; David Stuart, Dunbar, East Lothian; Suffolk Herbs, Sudbury, Suffolk; University Botanic Garden, Cambridge; University of British Columbia Botanical Garden, Vancouver; University of California Arboretum, Davis, California; University of California Arboretum, Santa Cruz, California; University of California Botanical Garden, Berkeley, California; University of California Botanical Gardens, Los Angeles, California; University of Reading Botanic Garden, Reading, Berks; Unwins Seeds Ltd, Histon, Cambridge; Jack Vass, Haywards Heath, Sussex; Rosemary Verey, Barnsley, Glos; Vesutor Air Plants, Ashington, Sussex; Wakehurst Place (Royal Botanic Gardens, Kew), Ardingly, Sussex; Primrose Warburg, Oxford; Waterperry Gardens, Wheatley, Oxon; Westonbirt Arboretum, Westonbirt, Glos; Woolman's Nurseries, Dorridge, West Midlands; Wyld Court Orchids, Newbury, Berks; Eric Young Orchid Foundation, Jersey, Channel Islands.

WARWICKSHIRE
COLLEGE
LIBRARY